MACM

Essential

DICTIONARY

FOR LEARNERS OF ENGLISH

Macmillan Education
Between Towns Road, Oxford OX4 3PP
A division of Macmillan Publishers Limited
Companies and representatives throughout the world

ISBN
0 333 99209 1 paperback edition
0 333 99210 5 paperback edition + CD-ROM
1 405 01429 6 UK paperback edition
1 405 01428 8 UK paperback edition + CD-ROM

First published 2003

The Macmillan Essential Dictionary was conceived, compiled and edited
by the Reference and Electronic Media Division of Bloomsbury Publishing
Plc.

This Dictionary includes words on the basis of their use in the English
language today. Some words are identified as being trademarks or service
marks. Neither the presence nor absence of such identification in this
Dictionary is to be regarded as affecting in any way, or expressing a
judgement on, the validity or legal status of any trademark, service mark,
or other proprietary rights anywhere in the world.

World English Corpus
The definitions in the Macmillan Essential Dictionary have been based on
information derived from 200,000,000 words of English which make up the
World English Corpus. This consists of the Bloomsbury Corpus of World
English® with additional material exclusively developed for this
Dictionary, including ELT materials and a corpus of common errors made
by learners of English.

Designed by Peter Burgess
Cover design by Boag Associates, London
Typeset by Selwood Systems, Midsomer Norton, Radstock, United Kingdom

Printed and bound in China

2007 2006 2005 2004 2003
10 9 8 7 6 5 4 3 2 1

CONTENTS

Editor-in-Chief
Michael Rundell

Associate Editor
Gwyneth Fox

EDITORIAL TEAM

Managing Editor
Michael Mayor

Editors
Robert Clevenger
Rosalind Combley
Korey Egge
Gloria George
Stephen Handorf
Dan Malt

Stella O'Shea
Elizabeth Potter
Glennis Pye
Howard Sargeant
Karen Stern
Penny Stock
Donald Watt

Phonetician
Dinah Jackson

Proofreaders
Sandra Anderson
Ruth Hillmore
Irene Lakhani

PROJECT TEAM

Project Manager
Katy McAdam

Database Manager
Edmund Wright

Production Editor
Nicky Thompson

Production Manager
Rowena Drewett

Production Director
Penny Edwards

Design
Peter Burgess
Helen Taylor

Dictionaries' Publisher
Faye Carney

Publishing Directors
Kathy Rooney
Sue Bale

Project Coordinators
Joel Adams
Katalin Süle

Database Administrator
James Orpin

Corpus Development
Gloria George

OTHER CONTRIBUTORS

Editorial and Keyboarding Assistance
Simon Arnold
Rebecca McKee
Lisa Milford
Ian M Spackman

Illustrations
Ian Foulis and Associates
Peter Harper
Illustrated Arts
Stuart Lafford
Alan Male
Oxford Illustrators
Peter Richardson
Martin Shovel

ADVISORY PANEL

Chief Adviser
Professor Michael Hoey
Baines Professor of English Language and Director of the Applied
English Language Studies Unit, University of Liverpool, UK

Professor Chen Lin
Professor of English, Foreign
Languages University,
Beijing, China

Simon Greenall
ELT author and trainer

Vaughan Jones
ELT author and teacher

Sue Kay
ELT author and teacher

Cindy Leaney
ELT author and trainer

Jane Magee
Course Director, English
Language Teaching,
University of St Andrews, UK

Amy Chi Man-lai
Instructor, Language Centre,
Hong Kong University of
Science and Technology,
Hong Kong

Professor Kevin Mark
Professor, School of Politics
and Economics, Meiji
University, Japan

Ron Martinez
ELT author and trainer

Dr Don R McCreary
Associate Professor,
Department of English,
University of Georgia, Athens,
Georgia, USA

Professor Rukmini Nair
Professor of Linguistics and
English, Department of
Humanities and Social
Sciences, Indian Institute of
Technology, Delhi, India

Dr Hilary Nesi
Senior Lecturer, Centre for
English Language Teacher
Education, University of
Warwick, UK

Philip Prowse
ELT author and trainer

Susan Stempleski
Coordinator of Faculty
Development, Hunter
College International English
Language Institute, City
University of New York, USA

Adrian Underhill
ELT consultant, trainer, and
author

Sara Walker
Coordinator of the English
Programme, Brazilian
Diplomatic Academy, Ministry
of Foreign Relations, Brasilia
DF, Brazil

ACKNOWLEDGMENTS

The publishers would like to thank the many people who have given valuable
advice and support and who have helped to pilot the dictionary, in particular:

Maria Birkenmajer
Jan Borsbey
Claudia Finkbeiner
Christopher Gallagher
Galia Komarova
Anne McCabe

Vera Muller
Roy Norris
Vincent Ooi
Anne Pakir
Péter Rádai
Kim Jeong Ryeol

Piotr Steinbrich
Jerome Su
H A Swan
Ruth Swan
Michael Vaughan-Rees
Michael Vince

Introduction

MICHAEL RUNDELL
Editor-in-Chief

The *Macmillan Essential Dictionary* has been especially designed to meet the needs of intermediate students of English. The word 'essential' has two meanings, and both meanings are relevant to this dictionary. First, because it provides the information that is *completely necessary* for your success as a learner of English. And secondly, because it focuses on the most *basic and important* features of the English language – the things that you need to know most thoroughly in order to make effective progress.

Dictionaries exist in order to answer questions. To help us to give the right answers to the right questions, we – as dictionary makers – need to know who will be using the dictionary and what kinds of information they really need. All of this means making a careful *selection* from the enormous amount of data available to us. So how do we decide what is really 'essential', and how can we be sure that we have made the *right* selection?

In creating the *Macmillan Essential Dictionary*, we have benefited from two valuable resources:

- high-quality linguistic data: our large language corpora and advanced software give us the tools to identify the essential facts about English

- expert advice: at every stage, experienced teachers, coursebook writers, and language students have contributed their suggestions and comments, telling us what learners really need to know

The *Macmillan Essential Dictionary* builds on the success of its sister dictionary, the *Macmillan English Dictionary*, adapting its unique features to the different needs of intermediate learners. These include:

- the 'red words': the most frequent and useful words in English are shown in red, so that you can easily recognize the vocabulary that – as an intermediate learner – you need to know especially well. For this dictionary, we have identified 3,500 red words. More information about these words is given on the inside front cover.

- maximum coverage: our goal is to include as many vocabulary items as possible, and this dictionary has more entries than any other intermediate learners' dictionary

- special attention to 'collocation' (the way words regularly combine with each other): over 130 new collocation boxes provide a unique bank of data on natural-sounding word combinations

- dozens of special notes: information on common errors and boxes that will help you to increase your vocabulary

- Study Pages: a 24-page central section, packed with ideas that will help you to become a better learner, including information on collocation, word formation, vocabulary development, and much more

We hope you will enjoy using the *Macmillan Essential Dictionary*, and we are confident that you will soon find that it is an essential part of your language-learning experience.

USING YOUR DICTIONARY

Finding a word

Words with more than one entry

Sometimes the same word belongs to
more than one word class: for
example, the word **jet** can be a noun
and a verb. Each word class is shown
as a separate entry. The small
number at the end of the headword
tells you that a word has more than
one entry.

Compound words

These are shown as separate entries
in the alphabetical list.

Derived words

Some words are shown at the end of
the entry for the word that they are
derived from. These words can be
understood by reading the definition
for the main entry.

Word classes (noun, verb etc)

There is a list of word classes on the
inside front cover.

Idioms and other fixed expressions

Some words are often used in idioms
or other fixed expressions. These are
shown at the end of the main entry,
following the small box that says
PHRASE . Look for fixed expressions
at the entry for the first main word
in the expression.

Phrasal verbs are shown after the
entry for the main verb, following
the small box that says
PHRASAL VERB .

Finding the meaning of a word

Words with more than one meaning

Many words have more than one
meaning, and each different
meaning is shown by a number.

Some words have many different
meanings, and so the entries can be
long. Entries with five or more
meanings have a 'menu' at the top
to make it easier to find the specific
meaning you are looking for.

jet[1] /dʒet/ noun ★
   1 [C] a plane that can fly very fast: *a jet
   fighter*
   2 [C] a stream of liquid that comes out of
   something very quickly and with a lot of
   force: *The firefighter sprayed **a jet of water**
   on the flames.*
   3 [U] a hard black shiny stone that is used
   for making jewellery

jet[2] /dʒet/ verb [I] to fly somewhere in a plane:
   *They will be jetting off to Spain this
   weekend.*

jet-'black adj very dark black in colour

jet 'engine noun [C] a type of engine that
   combines air and burning fuel to create
   power for a plane

'jet lag noun [U] the feeling of being very tired
   because you have travelled on a plane
   across parts of the world where the time is
   different —**jet-lagged** /'dʒet,lægd/ adj

dash[1] /dæʃ/ verb **1** [I] to go somewhere in a
   hurry: *I dashed out into the street, still in
   my pyjamas.* **2** [I/T] to hit something
   violently, or to throw something violently
   against a surface: *Huge waves dashed
   against the side of the boat.*
   PHRASE **dash sb's hopes** to make it
   impossible for someone to do what they
   had hoped to do: *Saturday's defeat has
   dashed their hopes of success in the FA Cup
   this year.*
   PHRASAL VERB **dash 'off** to leave in a hurry

bilingual /baɪ'lɪŋgwəl/ adj **1** able to speak two
   languages **2** written in two languages: *a
   bilingual dictionary*

bill[1] /bɪl/ noun [C] ★★★

1 amount that you owe	4 paper money
2 in a restaurant	5 bird's beak
3 proposal for law	

   1 a written statement that shows how much
   money you owe for goods or services that
   you have received: *a telephone bill* ♦ *I
   always **pay my bills** on time.* ♦ *I wonder
   what the **bill for** the repairs will be?*

Definitions

All the definitions are written using a carefully selected 'defining vocabulary' of under 2,300 words so that it is easier to understand the definitions.

Any word in a definition that is not part of the defining vocabulary, and that is not the entry immediately before or after the one you are looking at, is shown in CAPITAL letters. You can find its meaning by looking it up in the dictionary.

'salad ,dressing noun [C/U] a sauce that adds flavour to salads, usually made by mixing oil, VINEGAR, and HERBS or SPICES

salami /sə'lɑːmi/ noun [C/U] a type of SAUSAGE containing strong SPICES, cut into thin pieces and served cold

Finding out more about a word

Red words

Some words are printed in red with a 'star rating' to show their frequency. This helps you to identify the words that you are most likely to need to use. For more information about red words, see the inside front cover.

discover /dɪ'skʌvə/ verb [T] ★★★

friendly /'fren(d)li/ adj ★★

local¹ /'ləʊk(ə)l/ adj ★

Pronunciation

The International Phonetic Alphabet shows you how a word is pronounced. A list of the symbols used is given on the inside back cover.

When British and American pronunciations are very different, both are given.

You can find the pronunciations for compound entries at the main entry for each of the words in the compound.

Stress marks tell you which part of a compound to stress when you are saying it.

aroma /ə'rəʊmə/ noun [C] a smell that is strong but nice —**aromatic** /,ærə'mætɪk/ adj

laboratory /lə'bɒrət(ə)ri, American 'læbrə,tɔːri/ noun [C] ★ a building or large room where people do scientific research: *our new research laboratory* ♦ *laboratory tests/experiments/studies* → LANGUAGE LABORATORY

'baseball ,cap noun [C] a hat that fits close to your head, with a flat curved part that sticks out above your eyes —*picture* → HAT

Inflections

Irregular inflections are shown.

do¹ /duː/ (3rd person singular **does** /*weak* dəz, *strong* dʌz/; past tense **did** /dɪd/; past participle **done** /dʌn/) verb ★★★

Labels

Labels (in *italics*) show whether a word is used in only British or American English, or tell you whether it is used in informal contexts, specialized contexts etc. Lists of these labels are given on page 861.

precinct /'priːsɪŋkt/ noun [C] **1** *British* a part of a town that has a particular use, especially an area where no cars are allowed: *a shopping precinct* **2** *American* a district in a town or city, usually organized for voting, police, or government purposes

prognosis /prɒg'nəʊsɪs/ (plural **prognoses** /prɒg'nəʊsiːz/) noun [C] **1** *medical* a doctor's opinion about how a disease is likely to develop **2** *formal* a statement about what is likely to happen in a particular situation → DIAGNOSIS

Examples

Example sentences in *italics* show you how a word is used in context.

Information about collocation and syntax – how words combine and which structures they can be used with – is shown in **bold type**.

When a word has many collocations, these are shown in a box at the end of the entry.

promote /prəˈməʊt/ verb [T] ★★
1 to support something, or to help something to develop: *a campaign to promote recycling* ♦ *Young plants are exposed to bright light to **promote** growth.*
2 to attract people's attention to a product or event, for example by advertising: *They are going on tour to **promote** their new album.*
3 to move someone to a job at a higher level: **promote sb to sth** *Steve Burrows was recently promoted to senior manager.*

Words often used with **promote**

*Adverbs often used with **promote** (sense 1)*
■ **actively, heavily, strongly, vigorously** + PROMOTE: promote something in a determined way
*Nouns often used with **promote** (sense 1)*
■ PROMOTE + **awareness, competition, development, efficiency, growth, interest, understanding, use**: increase the level of something

Grammar boxes

Grammar boxes give extra information to help you to learn more about how a word is used.

The is not usually used before the names of streets, towns, countries, counties, states, or continents: *My parents live in Surrey.*

Notes are also given to help you to avoid common errors.

News looks like a plural, but it is never used with a plural verb and cannot be used with a: *I've got a wonderful **piece of news** (NOT a wonderful news) for you.* ♦ *Do you have **any news** about Laura's baby?* ♦ *Here's **some news** about the World Cup.*

Expanding your vocabulary

There are many ways that you can use this dictionary to expand your vocabulary.

Sometimes the opposite of a word is shown.

'left-hand adj on the left side ≠ RIGHT-HAND: *The plates are on the left-hand side of the cupboard.*

Some definitions give you synonyms.

lastly /ˈlɑːs(t)li/ adv used when you want to say one more thing before you finish speaking=FINALLY: *And lastly, remember that your essays are due tomorrow.*

Sometimes you are told to look at another word or page in the dictionary where you will find additional information, a related entry, or a picture.

hardback /ˈhɑːdˌbæk/ noun [C] a book that has a hard cover → PAPERBACK

'Word family' boxes bring together groups of words that are formed from the same 'base word'.

Word family: **compete**

*Words in the same family as **compete***
■ **competition** *n*   ■ **competitor** *n*
■ **competitive** *adj*   ■ **uncompetitive** *adj*

Vocabulary building boxes bring together words that are related to a particular subject, or suggest more specific alternatives for very common words.

Other ways of saying **famous**

■ **eminent** famous and respected for doing important work
■ **legendary** very famous and admired by many people
■ **notorious/infamous** famous for something bad
■ **well-known** fairly famous

NUMBERS THAT ARE ENTRIES

000 /ˌtrɪp(ə)lˈəʊ/ in Australia, the telephone number that you use in an emergency to call the police, the FIRE BRIGADE, or an AMBULANCE

0800 number /ˌəʊ eɪt ˈhʌndrəd ˌnʌmbə/ noun [C] in the UK, a telephone number beginning with 0800 that is free to use and is usually for calling business services

1 /wʌn/ abbrev used in emails and TEXT MESSAGES to replace '-one': *NE1* (=anyone)

1040 form /ˌten ˈfɔːti ˌfɔːm/ noun [C] a form used by people in the US when they are calculating how much tax they have to pay on the money that they have earned

1099 /ˌten naɪmti ˈnaɪn/ noun [C] in the US, a document you send to the IRS (=the US tax department) that gives details of money that you have earned in addition to your salary

12 /twelv/ in the UK, a number given to a video that should only be watched by children who are at least 12 years old

12A /ˌtwelv ˈeɪ/ in the UK, a number given to a film that should only be watched by children under the age of 12 if they are with an adult

1471 /ˌwʌn fɔː sevˈ(ə)n ˈwʌn/ in the UK, a telephone number that you can call to find out which was the last telephone number to call you

15 /fɪfˈtiːn/ in the UK, a number given to a film or video that should only be watched by children who are at least 15 years old

18 /ˌeɪˈtiːn/ in the UK, a number given to a film or video that should only be watched by people who are at least 18 years old

1800 number /ˌwʌn eɪt ˈhʌndrəd ˌnʌmbə/ in Australia, a telephone number beginning with 1800 that is free to use and is usually for calling business services

18-wheeler /ˌeɪtiːn ˈwiːlə/ noun [C] *American* a large truck that has 18 wheels

1922 Committee, the /ˌnaɪntiːn twenti ˈtuː kəˌmɪti/ the Conservative members of the British parliament who are BACKBENCHERS (=not ministers)

2 /tuː/ abbrev **1** to or too: used in emails and TEXT MESSAGES: *it's up 2 U* (=it's up to you) ♦ *me 2* (=me too) **2** used for replacing 'to-' in other words: *2day* (=today)

20/20 vision /ˌtwenti ˌtwenti ˈvɪʒ(ə)n/ noun [U] the ability to see normally without wearing glasses

2.1 /ˌtuːˈwʌn/ noun [C] in the UK and Australia, the second-highest mark for an UNDERGRADUATE degree from a university, lower than a **first** but higher than a **2.2**

2.2 /ˌtuːˈtuː/ noun [C] in the UK and Australia, the third-highest mark for an UNDERGRADUATE degree from a university, lower than a **2.1** but higher than a **third**

.22 /ˌpɔɪntuːˈtuː/ noun [C] a type of gun that shoots small bullets

24/7 /ˌtwenti fɔː ˈsevˈ(ə)n/ adv *informal* all the time: *He thinks about her 24/7.*

3-D /ˌθriːˈdiː/ adj a 3-D film, picture etc looks as if it has length, depth, and width

4 /fɔː/ abbrev **1** for: used in emails and TEXT MESSAGES: *4 U* (=for you) **2** used for replacing '-fore' in other words: *B4* (=before)

401(k) /ˌfɔː əʊ wʌn ˈkeɪ/ noun [C] in the US, a special account in which people can save some of the money that they earn for their RETIREMENT without paying taxes on it

4×4 /ˌfɔː baɪ ˈfɔː/ noun [C] a FOUR-WHEEL DRIVE vehicle

.45 /ˌfɔːtiˈfaɪv/ noun [C] a PISTOL (=small gun)

4-F /ˌfɔːr ˈef/ adj if someone is listed 4-F, they are not allowed to serve in the US armed forces

4WD abbrev a FOUR-WHEEL DRIVE vehicle

$64,000 question, the /ˌsɪksti fɔːˈθaʊz(ə)nd dɒlə ˈkwestʃ(ə)n/ noun [singular] a question that is the most important and most difficult to answer concerning a particular problem or situation

8 /eɪt/ abbrev used in emails and TEXT MESSAGES to replace '-ate' or '-eat': *C U L8R* (=see you later) ♦ *GR8* (=great)

800 number /ˌeɪt ˈhʌndrəd ˌnʌmbə/ noun [C] in the US, a telephone number that is free to use and is usually for calling business services

911 /ˌnaɪn wʌn ˈwʌn/ in the US, the telephone number that you use in an emergency to call the police, the FIRE BRIGADE, or an AMBULANCE

9/11 /ˌnaɪn ɪˈlev(ə)n/ 11 September, the date in 2001 when TERRORISTS attacked the US, flying planes into the World Trade Centre and killing thousands of people

999 /ˌnaɪn naɪn ˈnaɪn/ in the UK, the telephone number that you use in an emergency to call the police, the FIRE BRIGADE, or an AMBULANCE

Roman numerals

Roman numerals were used in ancient Rome to represent numbers. They are still sometimes used today, for example on clocks and watches and in official documents.

I	one	XVII	seventeen
II	two	XVIII	eighteen
III	three	XIX	nineteen
IV	four	XX	twenty
V	five	XXI	twenty-one
VI	six	XXX	thirty
VII	seven	XL	forty
VIII	eight	L	fifty
IX	nine	LX	sixty
X	ten	LXX	seventy
XI	eleven	LXXX	eighty
XII	twelve	XC	ninety
XIII	thirteen	C	one hundred
XIV	fourteen	CC	two hundred
XV	fifteen	D	five hundred
XVI	sixteen	M	one thousand

Aa

a¹ or **A** /eɪ/ noun **1** [C/U] the first letter of the English alphabet **2 A** [C/U] a mark that a teacher gives to a student's work to show that it is excellent **3 A** [U] a common BLOOD GROUP

PHRASES **from A to B** from one place to another

A to Z *British* a book of maps showing all the roads in a particular town

a² /weak ə, strong eɪ/ or **an** /weak ən, strong æn/ determiner ★★★

> **A and an are indefinite articles.**
> ■ **A** is used when the next word begins with a consonant.
> ■ **An** is used when the next word begins with a vowel sound.

1 used when you are mentioning a person or a thing for the first time: *I have an idea.* ♦ *There's a concert on Sunday night.*
2 one: *I have a sister and two brothers.* ♦ *a hundred/thousand/million*
3 used when you mean any person or thing of a particular type, but not a specific one: *Have you got a car?* ♦ *Children must be accompanied by an adult.*
4 used when you say what job someone does: *Ruth was a lawyer.* ♦ *I want to be an actor.*
5 used when you say what type someone or something belongs to: *Maria is a Catholic.* ♦ *Greece has been a republic since 1973.*
6 used before a singular noun that represents every person or thing of a particular type: *A dog needs regular exercise.* ♦ *A molecule consists of two or more atoms.*
7 used in phrases showing prices, rates, or speeds to mean 'each' or 'every': *Meetings are held four times a year* (=four times every year). ♦ *Tomatoes are £1.20 a kilo* (=each kilo costs £1.20). ♦ *90 miles an hour*
8 used in expressions of quantity such as 'a lot', 'a few', or 'a great deal': *a lot of money* ♦ *a bit of luck* ♦ *We all appreciate a little encouragement.*
9 used before a noun that is formed from a verb and means a single action of that verb: *Can I have a try?* ♦ *Let's take a walk round the garden.*

A&E /ˌeɪ ənd ˈiː/ noun [C/U] *British* accident and emergency: the part of a hospital where people go when they are injured or suddenly become ill = CASUALTY

aback /əˈbæk/ adv **be taken aback** to be very shocked or surprised

abacus /ˈæbəkəs/ noun [C] an object used for counting or doing simple calculations. An abacus consists of a frame with small balls in rows.

abandon /əˈbændən/ verb [T] ★
1 to leave someone or something and never come back: *His mother abandoned him when he was five days old.* ♦ *The stolen car was abandoned only five miles away.*
2 to stop doing something before it is finished, or before you have achieved your aims: *The game had to be abandoned because of rain.* ♦ *The climbers finally abandoned their attempt on the mountain.*
—**abandonment** noun [U]

abandoned /əˈbændənd/ adj **1** left empty or no longer used: *an abandoned farm* **2** left alone by someone who should stay with you and look after you: *a home for abandoned children*

abashed /əˈbæʃt/ adj embarrassed or ashamed about something that you have done

abate /əˈbeɪt/ verb [I] *formal* to gradually become less serious or extreme

abattoir /ˈæbəˌtwɑː/ noun [C] *British* a place where animals are killed for meat

abbey /ˈæbi/ noun [C] a large church with buildings connected to it for MONKS or NUNS to live in

abbreviated /əˈbriːviˌeɪtɪd/ adj shorter because some parts have been removed

abbreviation /əˌbriːviˈeɪʃ(ə)n/ noun [C] a short form of a word or phrase: *MIA is an abbreviation for 'Missing in Action'.*

abdicate /ˈæbdɪˌkeɪt/ verb **1** [I/T] if a king or queen abdicates, he or she formally gives up being king or queen **2** [T] *formal* to stop accepting responsibility for something
—**abdication** /ˌæbdɪˈkeɪʃ(ə)n/ noun [C/U]

abdomen /ˈæbdəmən/ noun [C] *formal* the front part of your body below your waist

abdominal /æbˈdɒmɪn(ə)l/ adj in the abdomen

abduct /æbˈdʌkt/ verb [T] to take someone away using force = KIDNAP —**abduction** /æbˈdʌkʃ(ə)n/ noun [C/U]

aberration /ˌæbəˈreɪʃ(ə)n/ noun [C] *formal* something that is not normal, or not what you would usually expect

abhorrent /əbˈhɒrənt/ adj *formal* if something is abhorrent, you hate it because it is immoral

abide /əˈbaɪd/ verb **can't abide sth** to hate something

PHRASAL VERB **aˈbide by sth** to follow a rule, decision, or instruction

abiding /əˈbaɪdɪŋ/ adj *formal* an abiding feeling or belief is one that you have had for a long time

ability /əˈbɪləti/ noun [C/U] ★★★ the skill that you need in order to do something ≠ INABILITY: *She has good organizational abilities.* ♦ **ability to do sth** *Tiredness can affect your ability to drive.*

PHRASE **to the best of your ability** as well as you can: *Just try to do the job to the best of your ability.*

abject /ˈæbdʒekt/ adj *formal* **1** used for emphasizing how bad something is: *abject poverty* **2** showing that you feel ashamed: *a look of abject embarrassment*

ablaze /əˈbleɪz/ adj burning with a lot of flames

able /ˈeɪb(ə)l/ adj ★★★ intelligent, or good at doing something

PHRASE **be able to do sth** used for saying

A

that it is possible for someone to do something: *I don't know if I'll be able to come. ♦ I'd love to be able to sing like you.*

Word family: able

Words in the same family as able
- **ability** *n*
- **unable** *adj*
- **inability** *n*
- **disability** *n*
- **disabled** *adj*
- **enable** *v*

---

able-bodied /ˌeɪb(ə)l ˈbɒdid/ adj not suffering from any disability

ably /ˈeɪbli/ adv very well, or very skilfully

abnormal /æbˈnɔːm(ə)l/ adj not normal, and therefore a sign that there is a problem: *abnormal behaviour ♦ abnormal eating habits* —**abnormality** /ˌæbnɔːˈmæləti/ noun [C/U], **abnormally** adv: *Her blood pressure was abnormally high.*

aboard /əˈbɔːd/ adv, preposition in or on a ship, train, or plane

abode /əˈbəʊd/ noun [C] *literary* the place where you live=RESIDENCE

  PHRASE **of no fixed abode** *British legal* without a permanent home

abolish /əˈbɒlɪʃ/ verb [T] to officially get rid of a law or system: *Britain abolished slavery in 1807.*

abolition /ˌæbəˈlɪʃ(ə)n/ noun [U] the official end to a law or system

abominable /əˈbɒmɪnəb(ə)l/ adj *formal* extremely bad —**abominably** adv

Aborigine /ˌæbəˈrɪdʒəni/ or **Aboriginal** /ˌæbəˈrɪdʒən(ə)l/ noun [C] an Australian who belongs to the race of people who were living in Australia before Europeans arrived

abort /əˈbɔːt/ verb [T] **1** to stop something before it is finished: *The mission had to be aborted because of a technical problem.* **2** to remove a developing baby from a woman's body, so that it is not born alive

abortion /əˈbɔːʃ(ə)n/ noun [C/U] a medical operation in which a developing baby is removed from a woman's body, so that it is not born alive

abortive /əˈbɔːtɪv/ adj not finished, and therefore not successful: *abortive peace negotiations*

abound /əˈbaʊnd/ verb [I] to be present in large numbers or amounts

about /əˈbaʊt/ grammar word ★★★

About can be:
- a **preposition**: *He told me about your problem.*
- an **adverb**: *Stop rushing about.*
- followed by an infinitive with 'to': *I was just about to explain.*

---

1 used for stating who or what is being considered or discussed: *a book about American history ♦ They were talking about their holiday. ♦ There's nothing to get excited about.*
2 used for giving an amount, number, or time that is not exact=APPROXIMATELY: *About 250 people were killed in the explosion. ♦ I woke up at about 3 am.*
3 almost: *Pam's about the only person that I can trust. ♦ I'm just about ready to go.*
4 *British* in or to many different parts or areas=AROUND: *The children were running about the room. ♦ Dirty clothes were scattered about.*

  PHRASE **be about to do sth** to be going to happen very soon, or to be going to do something very soon: *I was about to get undressed when someone knocked. ♦ The show was about to begin.*
→ HOW, WHAT

a·bout-'turn noun [C] *British* a change from one opinion or decision to the opposite opinion or decision

above /əˈbʌv/ grammar word ★★★

Above can be:
- a **preposition**: *The birds were flying high above the trees.*
- an **adverb**: *She stared up at the stars above.*
- an **adjective**: *Please reply to the above address.*

---

1 **in a higher position** at a higher level than something, or directly over it: *We lived in the room above the shop. ♦ Her leg was broken above the knee.*
2 **higher in amount or standard** more than a particular number, amount, or level: *The company's profits were 23% above the previous year's. ♦ In most subjects the students scored well above average.*
3 **louder or higher than another sound** louder or higher than the other sounds that you can hear: *I couldn't hear his voice above all the noise.*
4 **in an earlier part of writing** in an earlier part of a piece of writing, or higher up on the same page: *Many of the documents mentioned above are now available on the Internet.*
5 **with a higher rank** higher in rank, or more important than someone else: *As a major, Stuart was a rank above me.*

  PHRASE **above all** used for saying what is most important: *We hope you will learn new skills, meet new people, and above all enjoy yourself.*

- Use **above** when something is not directly over something else, but at a higher level: *on the hillside above the river.*
- Use **over** when something moves or stretches across the space above something else: *flying over London ♦ the bridge over the river.*
- Use **over** when something covers something else: *She put a scarf over her hair.*

---

a·bove 'board adj completely honest and legal

abrasive /əˈbreɪsɪv/ adj **1** someone who is abrasive behaves in a way that seems rude **2** an abrasive substance has a rough surface that is used for rubbing other surfaces

abreast /əˈbrest/ adv next to each other, facing or moving in the same direction

  PHRASE **keep abreast of sth** to make sure that you know the most recent information about something

abridged /əˈbrɪdʒd/ adj an abridged book or play is shorter than the original

abroad /əˈbrɔːd/ adv ★★ in or to a foreign country: *We try to go abroad at least once a year. ♦ special arrangements for voters living abroad*

abrupt /əˈbrʌpt/ adj **1** sudden and unexpected, often in an unpleasant way **2** someone who is abrupt speaks in an unfriendly way using very few words —**abruptly** adv

A

abscess /'æbses/ noun [C] a painful swollen area on your skin or inside your body

abscond /əb'skɒnd/ verb [I] formal **1** to escape from a place where you are being kept as a punishment **2** to suddenly leave a place and take something with you that does not belong to you

abseil /'æbseɪl/ verb [I] British to come down from a high place by sliding down a rope —**abseiling** noun [U]

absence /'æbs(ə)ns/ noun ★
1 [C/U] a time when someone is not where they should be or where they usually are: *We are concerned about your child's frequent absences from school.* ♦ *Mark will be in charge in my absence* (=while I am away). **2** [U] the fact that something does not exist or is not present: *a complete absence of humour*

absent /'æbs(ə)nt/ adj **1** not in the place where you should be ≠ PRESENT: *He's been absent from school for three days.* **2** formal missing from a place or situation: *The story has been absent from the news for weeks.*

absentee /ˌæbs(ə)n'tiː/ adj not able to do a job well because you are not in the place where you should be: *an absentee father*

absenteeism /ˌæbsən'tiːˌɪz(ə)m/ noun [U] the habit of not being at school or work when you should be

absent-minded adj likely to forget or not notice things because you are not paying attention —**absent-mindedly** adv

absolute /'æbsəluːt, ˌæbsə'luːt/ adj **1** used for emphasizing an opinion, feeling, or statement = TOTAL: *The way they've been treated is an absolute disgrace.* ♦ *You're talking absolute nonsense.* ♦ *I have absolute confidence in her.* **2** used for emphasizing that something is the most or least possible in a particular situation: *£9,000 is the absolute maximum we can spend.*

absolutely /'æbsəluːtli, ˌæbsə'luːtli/ adv ★
1 completely: *Are you absolutely certain you saw him?* ♦ *The food was absolutely fantastic.* ♦ *They have absolutely no idea how this happened.*
2 spoken used for emphasizing that you agree or mean 'yes': *'Are you sure it's OK?' 'Absolutely!'*
PHRASE **absolutely not** used for showing that you disagree strongly, or used as a strong way of saying 'no': *'Do you think I should forgive him?' 'Absolutely not!'*

absolve /əb'zɒlv/ verb [T] formal **1** to state officially that someone is not responsible for something bad **2** to forgive someone

absorb /əb'zɔːb/ verb [T] **1** to take in heat, light, liquid, or some other substance: *When wood gets wet, it absorbs water and expands.* ♦ *a device that produces energy by absorbing sunlight* ♦ *be absorbed into sth Caffeine is rapidly absorbed into the bloodstream.* **2** to make something become a part of something larger: *His music has absorbed influences from all over the world.* ♦ *be absorbed into sth After the war, the whole region was absorbed into the Roman Empire.* **3** to learn and understand new facts: *We had to absorb a lot of information.* **4** business to accept an increase in your costs, instead of

increasing the prices that you charge: *Oil companies say they will absorb these tax increases.*

absorbed /əb'zɔːbd/ adj completely interested or involved in something: *Richard was totally absorbed in his book.*

absorbent /əb'zɔːbənt/ adj an absorbent material can take in and hold liquids

absorbing /əb'zɔːbɪŋ/ adj taking all your attention: *an absorbing book*

absorption /əb'zɔːpʃ(ə)n/ noun [U] **1** the process by which something takes in heat, light, liquid, or some other substance **2** the process of becoming part of something larger

abstain /əb'steɪn/ verb [I] **1** to deliberately avoid doing something enjoyable **2** to decide not to vote

abstention /əb'stenʃ(ə)n/ noun [C] a decision not to vote

abstinence /'æbstɪnəns/ noun [U] the practice of avoiding something such as alcohol or sex

abstract /'æbstrækt/ adj **1** abstract ideas are not related to physical objects or real events **2** abstract art expresses ideas or feelings, rather than showing the exact appearance of people or things —**abstraction** /æb'strækʃ(ə)n/ noun [C/U]

abstract noun noun [C] a word that names a quality, idea, or feeling, such as 'happiness' or 'beauty'

absurd /əb'sɜːd/ adj silly, unreasonable, or impossible to believe = RIDICULOUS —**absurdity** noun [C/U], **absurdly** adv

abundance /ə'bʌndəns/ noun [U] formal a very large quantity of something ≠ SCARCITY

abundant /ə'bʌndənt/ adj formal existing or available in large quantities ≠ SCARCE

abundantly /ə'bʌndəntli/ adv formal in large quantities
PHRASE **abundantly clear** very obvious

abuse¹ /ə'bjuːs/ noun **1** [C/U] cruel, violent, or unfair treatment: *human rights abuses* ♦ *Many of the children were victims of sexual abuse.* **2** [C/U] the use of something in a bad, dishonest, or harmful way: *alcohol/drug/substance abuse* ♦ *This is clearly an abuse of executive power.* **3** [U] angry offensive comments: *racist abuse*

abuse² /ə'bjuːz/ verb [T] **1** to have sex with someone who is unable to refuse, especially a child: *She was abused as a child.* **2** to treat someone in a cruel or violent way **3** to use something in a bad, dishonest, or harmful way **4** to speak to someone in an angry, offensive way —**abuser** noun [C]

abusive /ə'bjuːsɪv/ adj **1** offensive or insulting = RUDE: *abusive language* ♦ *When we asked him to leave, he became abusive.* **2** treating someone in a cruel way, either by being violent or by forcing them to have sex: *an abusive parent* —**abusively** adv

abysmal /ə'bɪzm(ə)l/ adj extremely bad = APPALLING

abyss /ə'bɪs/ noun [C] **1** a very frightening or dangerous situation **2** literary a large deep hole

a/c abbrev account (at a bank)

academic¹ /ˌækə'demɪk/ adj ★
1 relating to education, especially in

colleges and universities: *We expect our students to meet high academic standards.* ◆ *We are approaching the end of **the academic year** (=time during the year when there is teaching).*

2 based on learning from study rather than practical skills and experience: *The college offers both academic and vocational qualifications.*

3 not relating to a real situation, and therefore not relevant: *Given the lack of funding, any discussion of future plans was somewhat academic.*

—**academically** /ˌækəˈdemɪkli/ adv

academic² /ˌækəˈdemɪk/ noun [C] a teacher at a college or university

academy /əˈkædəmi/ noun [C] **1** a school or college that teaches a particular subject or skill **2** an organization that was created to encourage interest and development in a particular subject

accelerate /əkˈseləreɪt/ verb **1** [I] if a vehicle accelerates, it moves faster **2** [I/T] to happen at a faster rate, or to make something do this: *Can we accelerate the development process?*

—**acceleration** /əkˌseləˈreɪʃ(ə)n/ noun [U]

accelerator /əkˈseləreɪtə/ noun [C] a PEDAL that you press with your foot to make a vehicle go faster —*picture* → C6

accent¹ /ˈæks(ə)nt/ noun ★

1 [C] a way of pronouncing words that shows what country, region, or social class you come from: *an upper-class British accent* ◆ *Tom hasn't lost his broad Irish accent.*

2 [C] a mark above a letter that shows how you pronounce it

3 [singular] the emphasis on a particular part of a word or phrase when you say it: *The accent is on the first syllable.*

PHRASE **the accent is on sth** used for saying that a particular thing is given importance: *At the hotel, the accent is on luxury.*

Words often used with accent

*Adjectives often used with **accent** (noun, sense 1)*
■ **broad, heavy, strong, thick** + ACCENT: used about accents that are easy to notice

accent² /ækˈsent/ verb [T] to emphasize a word, sound, or feature

accentuate /ækˈsentʃueɪt/ verb [T] to make something more noticeable

accept /əkˈsept/ verb ★★★

1 take sth offered	4 know sth bad is true
2 say yes to invitation	5 let sb be part of sth
3 recognize as true	

1 [T] to take something that someone gives you: *It gives me great pleasure to accept this award.* ◆ *Two police officers were accused of accepting bribes.*

2 [I/T] to say yes to an invitation, offer, or suggestion ≠ REJECT: *Our clients will never accept this proposal.* ◆ *They offered her a job, and she accepted without hesitation.*

3 [T] to recognize that something is true, fair, or right: *This argument is unlikely to be accepted by the court.* ◆ *We cannot accept responsibility for any damage.* ◆ +that *Most scientists accept that climate change is linked to pollution.*

4 [T] to recognize that a bad situation exists

and cannot be changed: *I know it's not fair, but you'll just have to accept it.* ◆ *They found it hard to accept defeat.* ◆ +that *For a long time, he simply could not accept that she was dead.*

5 [T] to allow someone to become part of an organization or group: *Under the new law, gay people will be accepted in the armed forces.* ◆ **accept sb into sth** *The children soon accepted her into the family.*

■ Use **accept** to mean that you take something that someone gives you, or you recognize that something is true, fair, or right: *We accepted her gifts.* ◆ *They accepted the court's decision.*
■ Use **agree** to mean that you are willing to do something: *She agreed to work at the weekend.*
■ You **accept** something, but you **agree to do** something.

acceptable /əkˈseptəb(ə)l/ adj ★

1 if something is acceptable, most people approve of it or accept it ≠ UNACCEPTABLE: *That kind of behaviour is not acceptable.* ◆ *an agreement that is **acceptable** to both sides*

2 good enough = REASONABLE ≠ UNACCEPTABLE: *A success rate of 65% is acceptable.*

—**acceptability** /əkˌseptəˈbɪləti/ noun [U]

acceptance /əkˈseptəns/ noun [U] **1** agreement that something is true, reasonable, or cannot be changed ≠ REJECTION: *There is widespread acceptance of these principles.* **2** agreement to a plan, offer, or suggestion ≠ REJECTION: *The union has recommended acceptance of the pay offer.* **3** an attitude of accepting a bad situation because it cannot be changed: *a religion that teaches acceptance of suffering* **4** the fact of being accepted into an organization or group: *my acceptance into Cambridge University*

accepted /əkˈseptɪd/ adj thought by most people to be reasonable, right, or normal

access¹ /ˈækses/ noun [U] ★★

1 the right or opportunity to have or to use something: *Only a small number of our students have **access** to the Internet.* ◆ *Some groups still have difficulty **gaining access** to health care.*

2 the means by which you get to a place: *A lift provides **access** to the upper floors.*

3 official permission to see someone: *All prisoners have **access** to a lawyer.*

access² /ˈækses/ verb [T] to get information, especially from a computer

access course noun [C] *British* a course of study in which you learn enough about a subject to allow you to go to a college or university to continue studying the subject

accessible /əkˈsesəb(ə)l/ adj **1** easy to obtain, use, or understand ≠ INACCESSIBLE: *information that should be accessible to the public* **2** easy to find or get to ≠ INACCESSIBLE: *The city is easily accessible by road, rail, or air.* —**accessibility** /əkˌsesəˈbɪləti/ noun [U]

accessory /əkˈsesəri/ noun [C] **1** an additional object or piece of equipment that makes something more attractive or useful **2** a small thing that you wear such as a piece of jewellery or a belt **3** *legal* someone who helps a criminal

accident /'æksɪd(ə)nt/ noun [C] ★★★
1 a crash involving a car, train, or other vehicle: *The accident was caused by ice on the road.*
2 an unexpected event that causes injury or damage: *He was killed in a climbing accident.* ♦ *I didn't mean to break the vase, it was an accident.*
3 something that happens without being planned: *To be honest, my second pregnancy was an accident.*
PHRASE **by accident** by chance, without being planned or intended: *I discovered the answer by accident.*

> **Words often used with accident**
>
> *Adjectives often used with accident (sense 1)*
> ■ **bad, horrific, nasty, serious, fatal, tragic** + ACCIDENT: used about accidents that cause serious injuries or death
> ■ **minor, slight** + ACCIDENT: used about accidents that are not serious
> *Verbs often used with accident (sense 1):*
> ■ **be involved in, have** + ACCIDENT: have an accident

accidental /ˌæksɪ'dent(ə)l/ adj not intended ≠ DELIBERATE: *accidental death* ♦ *an accidental release of dangerous chemicals* —**accidentally** adv

acclaim /ə'kleɪm/ noun [U] public praise

acclaimed /ə'kleɪmd/ adj publicly praised

acclimatize /ə'klaɪmə,taɪz/ verb [I/T] to become familiar with a new place or situation —**acclimatization** /əˌklaɪmətaɪ'zeɪʃ(ə)n/ noun [U]

accolade /'ækə,leɪd/ noun [C] an honour or praise that someone is given for their work

accommodate /ə'kɒmə,deɪt/ verb [T] **1** to provide a room or a place for someone to stay: *The hotel can accommodate 600 guests.* ♦ *The teams will be accommodated in luxury hotels.* **2** to provide enough space for something or someone: *The new office will easily accommodate 50 desks.* **3** *formal* to do what someone asks you to do: *We will do our best to accommodate your request.*

accommodating /ə'kɒmə,deɪtɪŋ/ adj helpful and easy to work with=OBLIGING: *The staff were very accommodating.*

accommodation /əˌkɒmə'deɪʃ(ə)n/ noun [U] ★★ a place for someone to stay, live, or work in: *The hotel provides accommodation for up to 100 people.* ♦ *We live in **rented accommodation**.*

accompaniment /ə'kʌmp(ə)nɪmənt/ noun **1** [C/U] music that supports someone who is singing or playing the main tune **2** [C] something that you provide as an addition, especially to a meal

accompany /ə'kʌmp(ə)ni/ verb [T] **1** *formal* to go with someone to a place or event: *Children must be accompanied by an adult.* **2** *formal* to happen or exist with something else: *A sore throat sometimes accompanies a fever.* ♦ *The book is accompanied by a CD-ROM.* **3** to play music while someone sings or plays the main tune

accomplice /ə'kʌmplɪs/ noun [C] someone who

helps another person to do something illegal

accomplish /ə'kʌmplɪʃ/ verb [T] to succeed in doing something difficult → MISSION

accomplished /ə'kʌmplɪʃt/ adj good at doing something that needs a lot of skill

accomplishment /ə'kʌmplɪʃmənt/ noun [C/U] something difficult that you succeed in doing

accord¹ /ə'kɔːd/ noun [C] a formal agreement between countries or groups
PHRASE **do sth of your own accord** to do something without being asked, forced, or helped to do it

accord² /ə'kɔːd/ verb [T] *formal* to give someone something such as power, respect, or status

accordance /ə'kɔːd(ə)ns/ noun **in accordance with** in a way that follows a rule, system, or someone's wishes

accordingly /ə'kɔːdɪŋli/ adv **1** as a result of something=CONSEQUENTLY: *No formal complaint was made; accordingly, the police took no action.* **2** in a way that is suitable: *They have broken the rules and will be punished accordingly.*

according to /ə'kɔːdɪŋ ˌtuː/ preposition ★★★
1 used for stating where information or ideas have come from: *According to newspaper reports, fighting has broken out in the northern provinces.*
2 in a way that agrees with or obeys a particular plan, system, or set of rules: *The game was played according to the rules.* ♦ *If everything goes according to plan, they should finish by Thursday.*
3 used for saying that something changes or is different depending on the situation: *The amount of tax people pay varies according to where they live.*

accordion /ə'kɔːdiən/ noun [C] a musical instrument that is played by moving the ends of a box in and out while pressing buttons

accost /ə'kɒst/ verb [T] *formal* to stop someone and speak to them, especially when this annoys them

account¹ /ə'kaʊnt/ noun ★★

1 agreement with bank	**5** regular customer
2 report/description	**6** for email
3 financial records	**+** PHRASES
4 agreement with shop	

1 [C] an arrangement in which a bank looks after your money: *There was only £50 in his bank account.* ♦ *How do I **open an account** (=start having an account)?* → CURRENT ACCOUNT
2 [C] a written or spoken report about something that has happened: *a brief account of the meeting* ♦ *He was too shocked to give a clear account of events.*
3 **accounts** [plural] a detailed record that a business keeps of the money it receives and spends: *The accounts showed a loss of £498 million.*
4 [C] an arrangement that you have with a shop or other business that allows you to pay for goods or services later: *I have an account with Marks and Spencer.*
5 [C] *business* a company that regularly buys goods or services from another company

A

6 [C] an arrangement with a company or Internet PROVIDER to use a service they provide: *an email account*

PHRASES **by/from all accounts** according to what people say

on sb's account if you do something on someone's account, you do it because you think they want you to: *Please don't stay home on my account.*

on account of because of someone or something: *She can't work much on account of the children.*

on no account used for emphasizing that something must not happen

take account of sth or **take sth into account** to consider something when you are trying to make a decision: *A good transport strategy must take account of the environmental issues.* ♦ *If you take inflation into account, the cost of computers has fallen in the last ten years.*

account² /əˈkaʊnt/ verb ★★★ PHRASAL VERB
ac'count for sth 1 to form a particular amount or part of something: *Electronic goods account for over 30% of our exports.* **2** to be the reason for something: *The increase in carbon dioxide emissions may account for changes in the climate.* **3** to give an explanation for something: *How do you account for this sudden improvement in his test scores?*

accountable /əˈkaʊntəb(ə)l/ adj in a position where people can criticize you or ask you why something happened
≠ UNACCOUNTABLE —**accountability** /əˌkaʊntəˈbɪləti/ noun [U]

accountancy /əˈkaʊntənsi/ noun [U] the work or profession of an accountant

accountant /əˈkaʊntənt/ noun [C] someone whose job is to prepare or check financial records

accounting /əˈkaʊntɪŋ/ noun [U] the work of accountants, or the methods they use

accredited /əˈkredɪtɪd/ adj having official approval

accumulate /əˈkjuːmjʊˌleɪt/ verb **1** [T] to get more and more of something over a period of time: *Over the years, I had accumulated hundreds of books.* **2** [I] to increase in quantity over a period of time: *The snow accumulated in the streets overnight.*
—**accumulation** /əˌkjuːmjʊˈleɪʃ(ə)n/ noun [U]

accuracy /ˈækjʊrəsi/ noun [U] the ability to do something in an accurate way, or the quality of being accurate ≠ INACCURACY: *The accuracy of the report is being checked.*

accurate /ˈækjʊrət/ adj ★ correct in every detail, and without any mistakes=PRECISE ≠ INACCURATE: *We need to get an accurate estimate of what the new building will cost.* ♦ *accurate measurements* ♦ *an accurate description of the events* —**accurately** adv

accusation /ˌækjʊˈzeɪʃ(ə)n/ noun [C] a claim that someone has done something illegal or wrong: *The Minister denied the accusation that she had lied.*

accuse /əˈkjuːz/ verb [T] ★★ to say that someone has done something wrong or illegal: **accuse sb of sth** *Her employers accused her of theft.* ♦ **accuse sb of doing sth** *Are you accusing me of lying?* —**accuser** noun [C]

accused, the /əˈkjuːzd/ (plural **the accused**) noun [C] someone who is accused of a crime in a court of law

accusing /əˈkjuːzɪŋ/ adj showing that you think someone has done something wrong: *an accusing stare* —**accusingly** adv

accustomed /əˈkʌstəmd/ adj **be/get accustomed to sth** to think that something is normal or natural because you have experienced it regularly over a period of time: *He had become accustomed to living without electricity.*

ace¹ /eɪs/ noun [C] in card games, a card with only one symbol and either the highest or lowest value —*picture* → C16

ace² /eɪs/ adj *informal* very good or skilful

ache¹ /eɪk/ verb [I] to feel a continuous but not very strong pain in part of your body

ache² /eɪk/ noun [C] a pain that is continuous but usually not very strong

achieve /əˈtʃiːv/ verb ★★★
1 [T] to succeed in doing or having something: *We have achieved what we set out to do.* ♦ *Most of the students achieved high test scores.*
2 [I] to be successful and do things that people admire: *Many managers are driven by a desire to achieve.*
—**achievable** adj

achievement /əˈtʃiːvmənt/ noun ★★
1 [C] a particular thing that someone has achieved: *Winning the gold medal was a remarkable achievement.*
2 [U] the fact of achieving something: *It was hard work, but the sense of achievement is huge.*

acid /ˈæsɪd/ noun [C/U] a strong chemical that can damage other substances

acidic /əˈsɪdɪk/ adj **1** containing acid **2** very sour

acid 'rain noun [U] rain that contains a high level of acid that can damage the environment

acid 'test noun [singular] a fact, event, or situation that proves whether something is true or effective

acknowledge /əkˈnɒlɪdʒ/ verb [T] **1** to accept that something exists, is true, or has a particular quality: *She won't acknowledge that there's a problem.* ♦ *He is acknowledged as one of our greatest medical experts.* **2** to thank someone for something that they have given you, or for helping you: *We gratefully acknowledge the efforts of everyone who helped us.*

acknowledgment or **acknowledgement** /əkˈnɒlɪdʒmənt/ noun **1** [singular/U] something that shows that you accept that something exists or is true **2** [C/U] something that you say or write to thank someone, or to tell them that you have received something that they sent you

acne /ˈækni/ noun [U] a medical condition in which your face is covered in spots

acorn /ˈeɪkɔːn/ noun [C] the nut of an OAK tree

acoustic /əˈkuːstɪk/ adj **1** relating to sound **2** an acoustic musical instrument does not use electricity to make sounds louder —**acoustically** adv

acoustics /əˈkuːstɪks/ noun [plural] the way that sound is heard in a room

A

acquaintance /əˈkweɪntəns/ noun [C] someone who you know but who is not a close friend

acquainted /əˈkweɪntɪd/ adj formal **1** if two people are acquainted, they know each other, but usually not very well **2** if you are acquainted with something, you know about it

acquire /əˈkwaɪə/ verb [T] **1** to get something: *She has acquired an impressive reputation as a negotiator.* **2** business to buy something, especially a company or a share in a company

acquisition /ˌækwɪˈzɪʃ(ə)n/ noun **1** [U] the process of getting something: *the acquisition of knowledge* **2** [C] business something that someone has bought

acquit /əˈkwɪt/ verb [T] to state officially that someone is not guilty of a crime: *He was eventually acquitted of the charges.*
PHRASE **acquit yourself well** to behave or perform in a way that other people admire

acquittal /əˈkwɪt(ə)l/ noun [C/U] an official judgment that someone is not guilty of a crime

acre /ˈeɪkə/ noun [C] a unit for measuring large areas of land, equal to 4,047 square metres

acrid /ˈækrɪd/ adj very strong, bitter, and unpleasant: *an acrid smell*

acrimonious /ˌækrɪˈməʊniəs/ adj unpleasant because people feel angry towards each other: *an acrimonious meeting*

acrobat /ˈækrəbæt/ noun [C] a performer who balances, jumps, and turns their body in skilful ways

acrobatics /ˌækrəˈbætɪks/ noun [plural] the skills or movements of an acrobat
—**acrobatic** adj

acronym /ˈækrənɪm/ noun [C] a word made from the first letters of a series of words: *NATO is an acronym for the North Atlantic Treaty Organization.*

across /əˈkrɒs/ grammar word ★★★

> **Across** can be:
> ■ a **preposition**: *I walked across the road.*
> ■ an **adverb**: *Our host hurried across to meet us.*

1 moving, looking, or reaching from one side of something to the other: *Over 70 airlines fly across the Atlantic between Europe and North America.* ♦ *Barbara looked across the room at her husband.* ♦ *There are four bridges across the River Danube.*
2 on the opposite side of a road, river, or line: *There's a bus stop just across the road.* ♦ *They had opened a new factory across the border in Mexico.* ♦ *I'm staying at a little hotel just across from the Libyan Embassy.*
3 in many parts of something, or covering all of an area or surface: *an insurance company with 120 offices across Europe* ♦ *There has been growth across all areas of the economy.*

a,cross-the-'board adj involving everyone or everything in a place or situation: *across-the-board budget cuts* —**a,cross the 'board** adv

acrylic /əˈkrɪlɪk/ adj made from a chemical substance that is used for making cloth and paint

act¹ /ækt/ noun ★★★

1 single thing sb does	**5** part of play
2 behaviour hiding truth	**6** law
3 performance	**+ PHRASES**
4 performer/performers	

1 [C] a single thing that someone does: *an act of violence against innocent people* ♦ *a simple act of kindness* ♦ *groups committing criminal acts*
2 [singular] a way of behaving that is not sincere: *She isn't really upset: it's all an act.*
3 [C] a short performance: *Her act includes singing and dancing.*
4 [C] a person or group who performs on stage: *They're one of rock music's most exciting live acts.*
5 [C] one of the major divisions of a play, opera, or BALLET
6 [C] a law: *the Data Protection Act* ♦ *an act of Parliament*
PHRASES **act of God** something bad such as a flood that people cannot control because it is produced by natural forces
be a hard/tough act to follow informal to do something so well that it is hard for other people to be as good as you
get in on the act informal to take part in an activity in order to gain the same advantages as other people
get your act together informal to organize your life or work in a better way

act² /ækt/ verb ★★★

1 do sth	**4** do a particular job
2 behave	**5** have an effect
3 perform in plays/films	**+ PHRASAL VERBS**

1 [I] to do something: *Now is the time to act.* ♦ *I'm acting on the advice of my doctor.* ♦ *She claims that she acted out of necessity* (=because she had to).
2 [I] to behave in a particular way: *He's been acting strangely all day.* ♦ *Despite her problems, she acted as if nothing was wrong.*
3 [I/T] to perform in plays or films: *I've always wanted to act.* ♦ *Philip Schofield acted the part of Joseph.*
4 [I] to do the job of a particular kind of person: *You speak Greek – will you act as our interpreter?*
5 [I] to have a particular effect: *Don't expect the medicine to act immediately.* ♦ *The measures are intended to act as a deterrent to criminals.*
PHRASAL VERBS **,act sth 'out** to copy events that happened by pretending to be the people involved
,act 'up informal **1** if children act up, they behave badly **2** if a part of your body or a piece of equipment acts up, it develops problems

acting¹ /ˈæktɪŋ/ adj doing someone else's job for a short time: *the acting manager*

acting² /ˈæktɪŋ/ noun [U] the job or skill of being an actor

action /ˈækʃ(ə)n/ noun ★★★

1 process of doing sth	**4** events in play/film
2 sth sb does	**5** movement of object
3 fighting in war	**+ PHRASE**

1 [U] the process of doing something: *Police*

A

say they will **take** tough **action** against drug dealers. ♦ *If a student complains of harassment, what is the most appropriate* **course of action** (=way of dealing with the problem)? ♦ *We aren't quite ready to* **put our plans into action** (=start doing something). ♦ *It's interesting to watch a good salesman* **in action** (=doing his job).
2 [C] something that you do: *How can you justify your actions?*
3 [U] fighting in a war: *a list of soldiers* **missing in action**
4 [singular] the events that form part of a play or film: *In Scene 1, the action takes place in an expensive restaurant.*
5 [singular/U] the movement of an object or machine: *This switch slows down* **the action of** *the pump.*

PHRASE **out of action 1** unable to do your usual activities because you are injured or ill **2** equipment that is out of action is unable to be used because it is broken or being repaired

'**action-packed** adj full of exciting events

,**action 'replay** noun [C] *British* on television, an important moment in a sports game that is shown a second time, just after it happens

activate /ˈæktɪˌveɪt/ verb [T] to make a piece of equipment or a process start working

active /ˈæktɪv/ adj ★★★
1 always doing things, especially with energy and enthusiasm: *Rose is still active at the age of 87.* ♦ *She continues to be* **active in** *politics.* ♦ *He is* **an active member** *of the American Cancer Society.*
2 an active VOLCANO is likely to ERUPT (=explode and pour out fire) at any time → EXTINCT
3 *linguistics* an active verb or sentence has the person or thing doing the action as the SUBJECT → PASSIVE
—**actively** adv

> **Word family: active**
> *Words in the same family as* **active**
> ■ **activate** *v* ■ **inactive** *adj*
> ■ **actively** *adv* ■ **interactive** *adj*
> ■ **activity** *n* ■ **proactive** *adj*

active, the /ˈæktɪv/ noun [singular] *linguistics* the active form of a verb → PASSIVE

activist /ˈæktɪvɪst/ noun [C] someone who is an active member of an organization that aims to achieve political or social change: *environmental activists*

activity /ækˈtɪvəti/ noun ★★★
1 [C/U] things that people do in order to achieve an aim: *an increase in criminal activity in the area* ♦ *We plan to expand our business activities in East Africa.*
2 [U] a situation in which a lot of things are happening: *On Saturdays, there's always lots of activity in the streets.* ♦ *a high level of electrical activity in the atmosphere*
3 [C] something enjoyable or interesting that people do: *Guests can enjoy activities like swimming and surfing.* ♦ *We have several activities in which students work in groups.*

actor /ˈæktə/ noun [C] ★★★ someone who performs in plays and films

actress /ˈæktrəs/ noun [C] a woman who performs in plays and films. Many women

performers prefer to be called actors rather than actresses.

actual /ˈæktʃuəl/ adj ★★ real, true, or exact: *The actual number of people killed is not yet known.* ♦ *The actual situation was quite different from the way she described it.* ♦ *The play is based on actual events.*

actually /ˈæktʃuəli/ adv ★★★
1 used for emphasizing what is really true or what really happened: *We've spoken on the phone but we've never actually met.*
2 used for emphasizing that something is surprising: *I think she actually agreed to go out with him.*
3 *spoken* used when correcting a statement: *It was yesterday, no actually it was Monday morning.*
4 *spoken* used for admitting something: *'Did you spend much money?' 'Well, yes. Quite a lot, actually.'*

acupuncture /ˈækjʊˌpʌŋktʃə/ noun [U] a medical treatment that involves putting needles into particular parts of someone's body —**acupuncturist** /ˈækjʊˌpʌŋktʃərɪst/ noun [C]

acute /əˈkjuːt/ adj **1** very serious or severe: *an acute pain in his chest* ♦ *acute food shortages* **2** able to notice things very quickly and easily: *an acute sense of smell* **3** an acute angle is less than 90 degrees —*picture →* C8 **4** an acute ACCENT is the mark ´ above a letter in some languages that shows it is pronounced in a particular way → GRAVE[3]

acutely /əˈkjuːtli/ adv used for emphasizing that a feeling is very strong: *He was acutely aware of his public image.*

ad /æd/ noun [C] *informal* ★ an ADVERTISEMENT → AD HOC

AD /ˌeɪ ˈdiː/ abbrev used after a date to show that it is later than the birth of Jesus Christ → BC

adage /ˈædɪdʒ/ noun [C] a well-known phrase about life and human experience

adamant /ˈædəmənt/ adj determined not to change a belief or decision: *He was adamant that he was right.* —**adamantly** adv

Adam's 'apple noun [C] the lump at the front of a man's throat

adapt /əˈdæpt/ verb **1** [I] to change your ideas or behaviour in order to deal with a new situation: *The children adapted quickly to the new school.* **2** [T] to make something more suitable for a new use or situation

adaptable /əˈdæptəb(ə)l/ adj able to change or be changed easily to deal with new situations

adaptation /ˌædæpˈteɪʃ(ə)n/ noun **1** [C] a film or TV programme made from a book or play **2** [U] the process of changing something so that it can be used for a different purpose

adapter or **adaptor** /əˈdæptə/ noun [C] **1** *British* an object for connecting several pieces of electrical equipment to one electricity supply **2** an object for connecting two pieces of equipment of different types

add /æd/ verb ★★★
1 [T] to put something with another thing: *When the sauce has thickened, add the cheese.* ♦ **add sth to sth** *They've added two major companies to their list of clients.*

A

2 [I/T] to calculate the total of two or more numbers: *What do you get if you add 75 and 63?*

3 [T] to say something more: *'Don't worry,' Jenny added hastily.* ♦ +(that) *I should add that I am not happy about this decision.*

4 [T] to give something an extra quality: **add sth to sth** *The Italian chairs add a touch of elegance to the room.*

PHRASAL VERBS ˌadd sth ˈon to include something extra: *If you add on legal fees, the total cost is over $1000.*

ˈadd to sth to make a quality more extreme: *The arrival of five more guests only added to the confusion.*

ˌadd (sth) ˈup **1** to calculate the total of several numbers or amounts **2 not add up** if information does not add up, it does not seem true because it does not match other information that you have

added /ˈædɪd/ adj extra or additional: *Baby food should contain no added sugar or salt.*

addict /ˈædɪkt/ noun [C] **1** someone who cannot stop taking illegal or harmful drugs: *a heroin addict* **2** someone who likes doing a particular activity very much: *a TV addict*

addicted /əˈdɪktɪd/ adj **1** unable to stop taking an illegal or harmful drug: *He was addicted to cocaine.* **2** doing a particular activity as much as you can: *I admit I'm addicted to that programme.*

addiction /əˈdɪkʃ(ə)n/ noun [C/U] a strong need to keep taking an illegal or harmful drug

addictive /əˈdɪktɪv/ adj **1** an addictive drug is difficult to stop taking **2** an addictive activity is difficult to stop doing

addition /əˈdɪʃ(ə)n/ noun ★★
1 [C] something that is added to something else: *The latest addition to her business empire is a chain of clothes shops.*
2 [U] the process of adding two or more numbers or amounts together to make a total
PHRASE in addition as well as something else: *About 30 people were killed in the explosion. In addition, 120 people were injured.* ♦ *In addition to the twins, Jason has another child by his first wife.*

additional /əˈdɪʃ(ə)nəl/ adj extra: *The new factory will create an additional 400 jobs.*
—**additionally** adv: *150 trucks were sent with supplies, and additionally, two cargo ships brought food and medicine.*

additive /ˈædətɪv/ noun [C] a chemical substance that is added to food to make it last longer or look or taste better

address¹ /əˈdres/ noun [C] ★★★
1 the exact name of the place where you live or work: *I'll need your name and address.* ♦ *My address is 125 Carter Street.*
2 a series of letters, numbers, and symbols that you use to find a particular WEBSITE on the Internet, or to send someone an email
3 a formal speech

address² /əˈdres/ verb [T] **1** to write a name and address on an envelope or parcel: *This letter is addressed to Alice McQueen.* **2** to speak to a person or group: *He stood up to address the meeting.* **3** to call someone a particular name or title when you are speaking to them: *The prince should be*

addressed as 'Sir' at all times. **4** to try to deal with a problem or question: *Governments have been slow to address the problem of global warming.*

adˈdress ˌbook noun [C] a book or a piece of software in which you write people's names, addresses, telephone numbers, and email addresses in alphabetical order

adept /əˈdept/ adj skilful at doing something: *He had quickly become adept at handling difficult customers.*

adequate /ˈædɪkwət/ adj ★
1 good enough or large enough = SUFFICIENT ≠ INADEQUATE: *The state has an adequate supply of trained teachers.* ♦ *It's a small office but it's adequate for our needs.*
2 satisfactory, but not extremely good ≠ INADEQUATE: *an adequate knowledge of the subject*
—**adequately** adv

adhere /ədˈhɪə/ verb [I] *formal* to stick to something
PHRASAL VERB adˈhere to sth to do the things that are stated in a rule, law, or agreement

adhesive /ədˈhiːsɪv/ noun [C] a substance that you use for making things stick together
—**adhesive** adj

ad hoc /ˌæd ˈhɒk/ adj done only when it is needed for a specific purpose: *Members of the committee are elected on an ad hoc basis.*

adj. abbrev adjective

adjacent /əˈdʒeɪs(ə)nt/ adj next to or near something else: *The fire spread to an adjacent office block.*

adjectival /ˌædʒɪkˈtaɪv(ə)l/ adj relating to or used as an adjective

adjective /ˈædʒɪktɪv/ noun [C] ★ a word used for describing a noun or pronoun

adjoining /əˈdʒɔɪnɪŋ/ adj next to and connected to another building, room, or area

adjourn /əˈdʒɜːn/ verb [I/T] to stop something such as a meeting or a trial for a short time and continue it later —**adjournment** noun [C/U]

adjudicate /əˈdʒuːdɪkeɪt/ verb [I/T] to make an official decision about a problem or legal disagreement —**adjudication** /əˌdʒuːdɪˈkeɪʃ(ə)n/ noun [U], **adjudicator** noun [C]

adjust /əˈdʒʌst/ verb **1** [T] to change or move something slightly so that it works or fits better: *She stopped to adjust the strap on her sandal.* ♦ *Use the thermostat to adjust the temperature.* **2** [I] to get used to a new situation by changing your ideas or the way you do things: *It took her two years to adjust to life in England.*

adjustable /əˈdʒʌstəb(ə)l/ adj something that is adjustable can be changed in order to make it work or fit better: *an adjustable strap/seat*

adjustment /əˈdʒʌs(t)mənt/ noun [C/U] a small change that you make to improve something: *I've made a few adjustments – I think it's working better now.*

ad-lib /ˌæd ˈlɪb/ verb [I/T] to say something in a speech or play without preparing or writing it: *I lost the notes for my talk and had to ad-lib.*

administer /ədˈmɪnɪstə/ verb [T] **1** to be

A

responsible for managing or organizing something **2** *formal* to give someone a drug or medical treatment

administration /əd,mını'streıʃ(ə)n/ noun ★
1 [U] the activities, processes, or people involved in managing a business, organization, or institution: *Too much money is spent on administration.*
2 **the administration** [C] the government of a country at a particular time, especially in the US: *the Reagan administration*
—**administrative** /əd'mınıstrətıv/ adj

administrator /əd'mını,streıtə/ noun [C] someone whose job is to manage a business, organization, or institution

admirable /'ædm(ə)rəb(ə)l/ adj an admirable quality, action, or person deserves to be admired and respected —**admirably** adv

admiral /'ædm(ə)rəl/ noun [C] an officer of high rank in the navy

admiration /,ædmə'reıʃ(ə)n/ noun [U] a feeling of respect and approval: *We're full of admiration for all your hard work.*

admire /əd'maıə/ verb [T] ★
1 to greatly respect and approve of someone or something: *I've always admired her dedication and commitment.* ♦ *Ferguson is widely* **admired** *for his team management skills.*
2 to look at someone or something that you think is attractive: *We stopped to admire the view.*
—**admirer** noun [C]

> **Word family: admire**
>
> *Words in the same family as admire*
> ■ **admirable** *adj*   ■ **admirer** *n*
> ■ **admiration** *n*

admiring /əd'maıərıŋ/ adj full of admiration for someone or something —**admiringly** adv

admissible /əd'mısəb(ə)l/ adj admissible evidence can be legally used in a trial

admission /əd'mıʃ(ə)n/ noun **1** [C] a statement accepting that something is true, or that you have done something bad or wrong: *an admission of guilt* **2** [U] the act of accepting someone into a place, organization, or institution: *Several people were refused admission* (=not allowed in). **3** [U] the amount that you pay to enter a place or event: *Admission to the game is free.*

admit /əd'mıt/ verb ★★★
1 [I/T] to agree that something bad is true, or to agree that you have done something wrong: *admit (to) doing sth Davis admitted causing death by careless driving.* ♦ *In court he admitted to lying about the accident.* ♦ *+(that) She freely admits that she made mistakes.*
2 [T] to allow someone to enter a place, join an organization, or be treated in a hospital: *Children will not be admitted.* ♦ *admit sb to sth The Baltic States were admitted to the United Nations in 1991.*
> **PHRASE** **admit defeat** to accept that you cannot succeed at something, and stop trying to do it

admittance /əd'mıt(ə)ns/ noun [U] *formal* permission to enter a place or to join an organization

admittedly /əd'mıtıdli/ adv used for saying that you accept that something is true even though it does not support the main point of what you are saying: *Admittedly, she's not very experienced, but she can do the job.*

adolescence /,ædə'les(ə)ns/ noun [U] the period of your life when you are changing from being a child to being an adult, especially when you are a young teenager: *He spent his adolescence in a children's home.*

adolescent /,ædə'les(ə)nt/ noun [C] a young teenager who is changing from being a child into being an adult —**adolescent** adj

adopt /ə'dɒpt/ verb ★
1 [I/T] to legally become the parent of another person's child: *The couple are hoping to adopt a baby girl.*
2 [T] to start using a new or different way of doing something: *He decided to adopt a more radical approach to the problem.*
3 [T] to formally accept a proposal, usually by voting

adopted /ə'dɒptıd/ adj an adopted child has been legally made the son or daughter of someone who is not their natural parent

adoption /ə'dɒpʃ(ə)n/ noun **1** [C/U] the process of making a child legally part of your family: *For many childless couples, adoption is the best solution.* **2** [U] the decision to start using a new or different way of doing something

adoptive /ə'dɒptıv/ adj adoptive parents have ADOPTED a child

adorable /ə'dɔːrəb(ə)l/ adj extremely attractive

adoration /,ædə'reıʃ(ə)n/ noun [U] a feeling of great love and respect for someone

adore /ə'dɔː/ verb [T] **1** to love someone very much **2** *informal* to like something very much

adoring /ə'dɔːrıŋ/ adj an adoring person or group of people has a great feeling of love and admiration for someone: *Adoring crowds lined the streets to wait for her.* —**adoringly** adv

adorn /ə'dɔːn/ verb [T] to decorate something —**adornment** noun [C/U]

adrenalin or **adrenaline** /ə'drenəlın/ noun [U] a chemical that your body produces when you are frightened, excited, or angry

adrift /ə'drıft/ adj floating on the water without being tied to anything or controlled by anyone

adroit /ə'drɔıt/ adj *formal* clever or skilful

ADSL /eı di: es 'el/ noun [U] *computing* asymmetric digital subscriber line: a method of connecting a computer to the Internet that allows very fast exchange of information, and allows you to be connected at all times without having to pay any extra money

adulation /,ædjʊ'leıʃ(ə)n/ noun [U] great praise or admiration, especially for someone who is famous

adult¹ /'ædʌlt, ə'dʌlt/ noun [C] ★★★
1 someone who is no longer a child and is legally responsible for their actions: *Tickets are £2.50 for adults and £1.50 for children.*
2 a fully grown animal or bird

adult² /'ædʌlt, ə'dʌlt/ adj **1** relating to or typical of adults: *About 59% of the adult population said they were suffering from stress.* **2** adult magazines, films, and books are about sex **3** an adult animal, bird etc is fully grown

adultery /əˈdʌlt(ə)ri/ noun [U] sex between a married person and someone who is not their husband or wife

adulthood /ˈædʌltˌhʊd, əˈdʌltˌhʊd/ noun [U] the period of your life when you are an adult

adv. abbrev adverb

advance¹ /ədˈvɑːns/ noun **1** [C] an instance of progress in science, technology, human knowledge etc: *major advances in computer technology* **2** [C] a payment for work that is given before the work is complete **3** [C] a forward movement towards someone or something, especially by an army **4 advances** [plural] an attempt to have a sexual relationship with someone, especially when the other person does not want this

PHRASE **in advance** done in preparation for a particular time or event in the future: *You have to make reservations six months in advance.*

advance² /ədˈvɑːns/ verb **1** [I/T] to progress and become better or more developed, or to help something to do this: *Technology has advanced dramatically since the 1960s.* ♦ *He will do anything to advance his career.* **2** [I] if an army advances, it moves forward and towards something —**advancement** noun [C/U]

advance³ /ədˈvɑːns/ adj **1** done before a particular time or event: *advance notice/warning* **2** sent to a place before a larger group that will arrive later: *an advance party/team/unit*

advanced /ədˈvɑːnst/ adj ★ **1** based on the most recent methods or ideas: *advanced technology* **2** having achieved a high standard or level: *She is very advanced for her age.* **3** at a high academic level: *a dictionary for advanced students*

advantage /ədˈvɑːntɪdʒ/ noun ★★ **1** [C/U] something that makes one person or thing more likely to succeed than others =BENEFIT: *the advantages of a good education* ♦ *Her teaching experience gives her an advantage when working with children.* ♦ *It would be to your advantage* (=make you more likely to succeed) *to prepare questions in advance.* ♦ *The home team always has an advantage over their opponents.* **2** [C] a good feature or quality that something has ≠ DISADVANTAGE: *Having children when you're older has both advantages and disadvantages.* ♦ *The equipment has the additional advantage of being easy to carry.*

PHRASES **take advantage of sb** to unfairly use the fact that someone is nice or trusts you in order to get what you want from them: *salesmen who take advantage of elderly customers*

take advantage of sth to use a situation or opportunity in a way that will help you or be good for you: *Many schools don't take full advantage of the Internet.*

advantageous /ˌædvənˈteɪdʒəs/ adj likely to make someone or something more successful

advent /ˈædvent/ noun **the advent of sth** the introduction of a new product, idea, custom etc: *the advent of the personal computer*

adventure /ədˈventʃə/ noun [C/U] ★ an exciting, unusual, and sometimes dangerous experience: *The trip was quite an adventure.* ♦ *The children were looking for adventure.*

adventurous /ədˈventʃ(ə)rəs/ adj **1** keen to try new or exciting things **2** new, exciting, and possibly dangerous: *an adventurous skiing trip*

adverb /ˈædvɜːb/ noun [C] ★ a word used for describing a verb, an adjective, another adverb, or a whole sentence. Adverbs in English often consist of an adjective with '-ly' added, for example 'quickly'. —**adverbial** /ədˈvɜːbiəl/ adj

adversary /ˈædvəs(ə)ri/ noun [C] formal an enemy or opponent

adverse /ˈædvɜːs/ adj not good, or likely to cause problems: *adverse weather conditions* ♦ *an adverse reaction from the public* —**adversely** adv

adversity /ədˈvɜːsəti/ noun [C/U] a time in your life during which you have a lot of bad things happening to you

advert /ˈædvɜːt/ noun [C] British an ADVERTISEMENT

advertise /ˈædvəˌtaɪz/ verb [I/T] ★ **1** to announce a product, service, or event on television, on the Internet, in newspapers etc so that people will buy it, use it, or go to it: *The perfume has been advertised in all the major women's magazines.* **2** to invite people to apply for a job by announcing it in a newspaper, on the Internet etc: *We need to advertise for a new chef.* —**advertiser** noun [C]

advertisement /ədˈvɜːtɪsmənt/ noun [C] an announcement in a newspaper, on television, on the Internet etc that is designed to persuade people to buy a product or service, go to an event, or apply for a job

advertising /ˈædvəˌtaɪzɪŋ/ noun [U] ★ the business of making advertisements, or advertisements in general: *We spend $5 million a year on advertising.* ♦ *an advertising agency*

Talking or writing about **advertising**

- **ad** (*informal*) an advertisement
- **advert** British (*informal*) an advertisement
- **advertisement** an announcement in a newspaper, or on the television or radio, that encourages people to buy something
- **billboard** a large outdoor sign used for advertising
- **campaign** a series of advertisements and events used for advertising something
- **the classified ads** small advertisements printed together in newspapers and magazines
- **commercial** an advertisement on the television or radio
- **flyer** a small piece of paper with a printed advertisement on it. Flyers are given to people in the street, or delivered to their homes

A

■ **poster** a large piece of paper with a printed advertisement on it
■ **slogan** a short sentence used for advertising something

advice /əd'vaɪs/ noun [U] ★★★ an opinion that someone gives you about the best thing to do in a particular situation: *Ask your father for advice.* ♦ *We are here to give people advice about health issues.* ♦ *I took his advice* (=did what he advised) *and left.* ♦ *She's acting on her lawyer's advice.*

Words often used with **advice**

Verbs often used with advice
■ **give, offer, provide** + ADVICE: give someone advice
■ **ask for, seek** + ADVICE: ask for advice
■ **accept, act on, follow, take** + ADVICE: do what someone advises
■ **disregard, ignore, reject** + ADVICE: not do what someone advises

Advice is never used in the plural and cannot be used with an: *She gave me a useful piece of advice* (NOT *a useful advice*). ♦ *Do you have any advice about the best places to eat?* ♦ *His son asked him for some advice.*

advisable /əd'vaɪzəb(ə)l/ adj if something is advisable, it is a good idea to do it, especially in order to avoid problems ≠ INADVISABLE: *It is advisable to keep your belongings with you at all times.*
advise /əd'vaɪz/ verb [I/T] ★★
1 to give your opinion to someone about the best thing to do in a particular situation: **advise sb to do sth** *Her doctor advised her to rest.* ♦ *I strongly advise you to reject the offer.* ♦ **advise sb against sth** *Police are advising the public against travelling in the fog.* ♦ **+that** *Experts advise that sunscreen should be reapplied on an hourly basis.*
2 *formal* to tell someone facts or information that they need to know: **advise sb of sth** *The committee will advise all applicants of its decision by 30th June.*

Word family: **advise**

Words in the same family as advise
■ advice *n*   ■ advisory *adj*
■ advisable *adj*   ■ inadvisable *adj*
■ adviser *n*

adviser or **advisor** /əd'vaɪzə/ noun [C] ★ someone whose job is to give advice on subjects that they know a lot about: *the Prime Minister's advisers* ♦ *a financial adviser*
advisory /əd'vaɪz(ə)ri/ adj existing in order to give advice about a particular subject: *an advisory board/committee/panel*
advocacy /'ædvəkəsi/ noun [U] strong public support for something
advocate¹ /'ædvəkeɪt/ verb [T] to publicly support a particular policy or way of doing something
advocate² /'ædvəkət/ noun [C] **1** someone who strongly and publicly supports someone or something: *an advocate of political reform* **2** a LAWYER → DEVIL'S ADVOCATE
aerial¹ /'eəriəl/ adj **1** from a plane: *an aerial view* **2** taking place in the air

aerial² /'eəriəl/ noun [C] *British* a piece of equipment made of wire or thin metal, used for receiving radio or television signals —*picture* → C1
aerobic /eə'rəʊbɪk/ adj aerobic exercise is a very active type of exercise that makes your heart and lungs stronger
aerobics /eə'rəʊbɪks/ noun [U] very active physical exercises done to music, often in a class
aerodynamic /,eərəʊdaɪ'næmɪk/ adj shaped in a way that makes it easier for something to move forward or through the air smoothly and quickly
aerodynamics /,eərəʊdaɪ'næmɪks/ noun [U] the science of how objects move through the air
aeroplane /'eərəpleɪn/ noun [C] *British* a PLANE
aerosol /'eərəsɒl/ noun [C] a container in which a liquid such as paint or PERFUME is kept under high pressure so that it can be SPRAYED (=forced out in very small drops): *an aerosol can/spray*
aerospace /'eərəʊspeɪs/ adj relating to the science or business of building and flying planes and space vehicles
aesthetic /iːs'θetɪk/ adj relating to beauty —**aesthetically** /iːs'θetɪkli/ adv
aesthetics /iːs'θetɪks/ noun [U] the study of beauty, especially in art
afar /ə'fɑː/ adv **from afar** *literary* from a distance
affable /'æfəb(ə)l/ adj friendly, relaxed, and easy to talk to —**affably** adv
affair /ə'feə/ noun ★★★
1 affairs [plural] events and activities relating to the government, politics, economy etc of a country or region: *The Senator is an expert on foreign affairs.* ♦ *a government spokesperson on consumer affairs*
→ CURRENT AFFAIRS
2 affairs [plural] things relating to your personal life, for example what is happening in your family or with your financial situation: *We are friends, but I don't know much about their private affairs.*
3 [C] something that happens, especially something shocking, in public or political life: *The president's popularity was unaffected by the whole affair.*
4 [C] a sexual relationship between two people, especially when one of them is married to someone else: *Her husband denied that he was having an affair.*
affect /ə'fekt/ verb [T] ★★★
1 to change or influence something, often in a negative way: *Did the newspapers really affect the outcome of the election?* ♦ *The disease affects many different organs of the body.*
2 to have a strong effect on someone's emotions: *She had been deeply affected by her parents' divorce.*
affectation /,æfek'teɪʃ(ə)n/ noun [C/U] something that is not part of your natural personality but that you do or say to impress people
affected /ə'fektɪd/ adj not natural, but done to impress other people
affection /ə'fekʃ(ə)n/ noun [U] a feeling of liking and caring about someone or

something: *He has great affection for the country.*

affectionate /əˈfekʃ(ə)nət/ adj showing that you love or care about someone or something —**affectionately** adv

affidavit /ˌæfɪˈdeɪvɪt/ noun [C] a legal document containing a written promise that something is true

affiliate /əˈfɪliˌeɪt/ verb **be affiliated with sth** to be officially connected with a larger organization or group —**affiliated** adj, **affiliation** /əˌfɪliˈeɪʃ(ə)n/ noun [C/U]

affinity /əˈfɪnəti/ noun [singular] a feeling that you understand and like someone or something because they are like you

affirm /əˈfɜːm/ verb [T] *formal* to state that something is true or that you agree with it —**affirmation** /ˌæfəˈmeɪʃ(ə)n/ noun [C]

affirmative /əˈfɜːmətɪv/ adj an affirmative statement or answer means 'yes'

affix /ˈæfɪks/ noun [C] *linguistics* a part added to the beginning or end of a word that changes its meaning → PREFIX, SUFFIX

afflict /əˈflɪkt/ verb [T] *formal* if you are afflicted by an illness or serious problem, you suffer from it

affliction /əˈflɪkʃ(ə)n/ noun [C/U] *formal* an illness or serious problem

affluent /ˈæfluːənt/ adj rich —**affluence** /ˈæfluːəns/ noun [U]

afford /əˈfɔːd/ verb [T] ★★★
1 can afford or **be able to afford** to have enough money to pay for something: *I'm not sure how they are able to afford such expensive holidays.* ♦ **can afford to do sth** *The company simply cannot afford to keep all its staff.*
2 can afford or **be able to afford** to be able to do something without having to worry about the problems that it might cause you: *We can't afford any more delays.* ♦ **can afford to do sth** *No politician can afford to ignore the power of television.*

affordable /əˈfɔːdəb(ə)l/ adj cheap enough for ordinary people to afford: *a shortage of affordable housing*

affront /əˈfrʌnt/ noun [C] something insulting that makes you shocked and angry

afield /əˈfiːld/ adv **far afield** far away

afloat /əˈfləʊt/ adj **1** floating on water **2** able to pay the money that you owe

afraid /əˈfreɪd/ adj ★★★
1 worried that something bad might happen: +**(that)** *I was afraid that you'd miss the flight.* ♦ **afraid to do sth** *The boy was afraid to say that he didn't know the answer.* ♦ **afraid of doing sth** *A lot of people are afraid of losing their jobs.*
2 frightened: *Don't be afraid – I won't hurt you.* ♦ *Everyone seems to be **afraid of** her.*
PHRASE **I'm afraid** *spoken* used for politely telling someone something that might make them sad, disappointed, or angry: *I can't help you, I'm afraid.* ♦ +**(that)** *I'm afraid I really don't agree.*

afresh /əˈfreʃ/ adv *formal* in a new or different way

African American /ˌæfrɪkən əˈmerɪkən/ noun [C] someone from the US who belongs to a race of people that has dark skin and whose

family originally came from Africa —**African American** adj

African Caribbean /ˌæfrɪkən kærəˈbiːən/ noun [C] someone from the Caribbean who belongs to a race of people that has dark skin and whose family originally came from Africa —**African Caribbean** adj

Afro-Caribbean noun [C] an AFRICAN CARIBBEAN —**Afro-Caribbean** adj

after /ˈɑːftə/ grammar word ★★★

> **After** can be:
> ■ a **preposition**: *I went for a swim after breakfast.*
> ■ an **adverb**: *He died on 3rd June and was buried the day after.*
> ■ a **conjunction**: *After you'd left, I got a phone call from Stuart.*

1 at a later time when a particular time has passed, or when an event or action has ended: *You can call us any time after 6.00 this evening.* ♦ *After the war, I went back to work on the farm.* ♦ *This message arrived after everyone had gone home.* ♦ *It seems noisy at first, but **after a while** you get used to it.* ♦ **after doing sth** *Wash your hands after touching raw meat.*
2 saying how much later used for saying how much later something is: *His birthday is two days after mine.* ♦ *I can start work tomorrow or **the day after**.* ♦ *You shouldn't go swimming **straight after** a big meal.*
3 at a later position in a list following someone or something else in order in a list or in a piece of writing: *N comes after M in the alphabet.* ♦ *The US is our largest export market after Germany.*
4 past a place further along a road, railway etc: *You turn right just after the pub.* ♦ *We get off at the station after Providence.*
5 trying to get sb/sth trying to catch, find, or get someone or something: *I ran after her to apologize.* ♦ *Watch out, he's only after your money.* ♦ *The police are after him for burglary.*
6 because of sth used for saying how someone is influenced by something that happened in the past: *After what happened last time, I was careful not to make the same mistakes.*
7 despite sth despite everything that was done in the past: *After everything that I'd done for her, she didn't even say thank you.*
8 time past the hour *American* used in telling the time, for giving the number of minutes past the hour
PHRASES **after all 1** despite what was said or planned before: *I'm sorry, but we've decided not to come after all.* ♦ *Maybe she was right after all.* **2** used when giving a reason to explain what you have just said: *She shouldn't be working so hard – she is 70, after all.*
after you *spoken* used for politely telling someone that they can do something before you or walk somewhere in front of you
day after day/year after year etc happening again and again every day/year etc for a long time: *Many families come back to our hotel year after year.*
one after another or **one after the other** used

for saying that each person or thing is immediately followed by the next: *One day I had three different exams one after the other.*

after-ef.fects noun [plural] the unpleasant effects that last for a long time after a situation or event

afterlife /ˈɑːftəˌlaɪf/ noun [singular] another life that some people believe begins after you die

aftermath, the /ˈɑːftəˌmæθ/ noun [singular] the effects and results of something bad or important: *In the aftermath of the shootings, there were calls for new gun laws.*

afternoon /ˌɑːftəˈnuːn/ noun [C/U] ★★★ the period of time between the middle of the day and the beginning of the evening: *What are you doing tomorrow afternoon?* ♦ *I might go shopping this afternoon.* ♦ *an afternoon nap/class*

aftershave /ˈɑːftəˌʃeɪv/ noun [C/U] a liquid with a nice smell that a man puts on his face after SHAVING

aftershock /ˈɑːftəˌʃɒk/ noun [C] a small EARTHQUAKE that happens after a bigger one

aftertaste /ˈɑːftəˌteɪst/ noun [C] a taste that remains in your mouth after you eat or drink something

afterthought /ˈɑːftəˌθɔːt/ noun [C] something that you say or do after something else because you did not think of it at first

afterward /ˈɑːftəwəd/ adv *American* AFTERWARDS

afterwards /ˈɑːftəwədz/ adv ★★ after something else that you have already mentioned: *Let's go and see a film and afterwards we could go for a meal.* ♦ *I didn't see her again until a few days afterwards.*

again /əˈgen/ adv ★★★
1 one more time: *If you fail the exam you will have to take it again.* ♦ *Oh no, now I'll have to start all over again* (=a second time from the beginning). ♦ *I read through her letter again and again* (=many times). ♦ *Once again* (=it has already happened more than once) *the troops moved forward, and once again they were driven back.* → ONCE
2 returning to the same condition as before: *I turned over and went back to sleep again.* ♦ *The streets of the city are quiet again.*
3 *spoken* used for asking someone to repeat something that they have already told you: *That friend of yours – what's her name again?*

PHRASES **half/twice etc as much again** used for comparing two amounts and saying how much more one amount is than the other: *A house in London costs half as much again as a house in Edinburgh.*
then/there again used for introducing a statement that makes what you have just said seem less true: *The hotel was awful. But there again, you can't expect much for £20 a night.*

against /əˈgenst/ preposition ★★★
1 in opposition to sth used for stating which plan, idea, or action someone opposes and thinks is wrong: *I'm against all forms of censorship.* ♦ *She argued against changing the design.* ♦ *the fight against drugs in our city's schools*

2 competing with sb/sth used for stating who or what you are trying to defeat in a game, race, or fight: *England's World Cup game against Argentina*
3 directed towards sb/sth in a negative way used for stating who or what a negative feeling or action is directed towards: *illegal discrimination against homosexuals* ♦ *There was growing resentment against the military government.* ♦ *Police are expected to bring criminal charges against Warren.*
4 touching or hitting sb/sth touching, hitting, or being supported by the surface of something: *I fell heavily against the bookshelves.* ♦ *Ron's bike was leaning against a tree.*
5 providing protection from sth used for stating what someone or something is being protected from: *All of the children have been vaccinated against diseases such as polio.*
6 not allowing sth if there is a law against doing something, it is illegal: *The state has a law against cruelty to animals.*
7 in the opposite direction in the opposite direction to the wind, the current etc: *We were sailing against a strong easterly wind.*
PHRASES **against the law/rules** not allowed by the law/rules: *It is against the law to park here overnight.*
against your will if someone makes you do something against your will, you do not want to do it: *No one will be forced to leave home against their will.*
against sb's wishes/advice even though someone does not want you to do something/advises you not to do it: *She took the two children away against her husband's wishes.*
have something against sb/sth to dislike or not approve of someone or something for a particular reason: *I think he's got something against artists.*

age¹ /eɪdʒ/ noun ★★★

1 how old sb is	5 period of history
2 how old sth is	6 long time
3 time of life for sth	+ PHRASE
4 being/becoming old	

1 [C/U] the number of years that someone has lived: *The average age of the delegates was over 60.* ♦ *At the age of 10, I went to live with my aunt.* ♦ *The film is designed to appeal to people of all ages.* ♦ *Darren's very tall for his age.*
2 [C/U] the number of years that something has existed: *The value of the furniture depends on its age and condition.* ♦ *It's hard to guess the age of the object.*
3 [C/U] the time of life when it is possible, legal, or typical for people to do something: *young people who have reached voting age*
4 [U] the state of being old or of becoming old: *His face is starting to show signs of age.* ♦ *Good wines improve with age.*
5 [C] a period of history: *We live in a materialistic age.* ♦ *It was an age of great scientific progress.*
6 ages [plural] *informal* a long time: *She's lived here for ages.* ♦ *He took ages to answer the*

phone. ♦ *We spent ages trying to print this out.* ♦ *For the first time in ages, we sat down and talked.* ♦ *After what seemed like ages, the doctor came back.*

PHRASE **come of age** to reach the age when you are legally an adult

---

Talking or writing about someone's age

asking about age
- **how old** used for asking someone their age
- **what age** used for talking about someone's age at a time in the past or future. Say 'How old are you?', not 'What age are you?', when you are asking someone their age

saying how old someone is
- **be 2/10/40 etc (years old)** the most usual way of saying how old someone is
- **be 2/9/18 months old** used for saying how old a baby or young child is
- **aged 2/10/40 etc** used in writing, for example in newspapers, for saying how old someone is
- **a 2-/10-/40-year-old** someone who is 2/10/40 years old
- **a 2-year-old child/a 10-year-old girl/a 40-year-old man** used for saying that someone is 2/10/40 years old

when you are not saying exactly how old someone is
- **in your teens/twenties/thirties etc** used for saying that someone is aged between 13–19, 20–29, 30–39 etc
- **twenty-something/thirty-something etc** used as an adjective or noun for talking about someone aged between 20–29, 30–39 etc
- **teenage** aged between 13 and 19
- **teenager** someone aged between 13 and 19
- **middle-aged** no longer young, but not yet old, usually used for someone aged between 40 and 60

---

age² /eɪdʒ/ verb [I/T] to become older or look older, or to make someone do this: *Her father had aged a lot since she had last seen him.*

aged¹ /eɪdʒd/ adj ★★ someone who is aged 18, 35, 70 etc is 18, 35, 70 etc years old

aged² /'eɪdʒɪd/ adj very old

age group noun [C] all the people between two particular ages, considered as a group: *a game for children in the 7–10 age group*

ageing¹ /'eɪdʒɪŋ/ adj becoming old: *a town with an ageing population*

ageing² /'eɪdʒɪŋ/ noun [U] the process of becoming old: *the ageing process*

age limit noun [C] the oldest or the youngest age at which you are allowed to do something

agency /'eɪdʒ(ə)nsi/ noun [C] ★★
1 a business that provides a service: *an employment/advertising agency*
2 a government department or organization that deals with a particular subject: *the official Chinese news agency* ♦ *law enforcement agencies*

agenda /ə'dʒendə/ noun [C] 1 all the things that need to be done or thought about: *Cutting the number of workers is not on the agenda.* 2 someone's plans or intentions for what they want to achieve: *Beth wanted to get married, but her boyfriend had his own agenda.* ♦ *Getting fit is at the top of my*

---

agenda. 3 a list of things that people will discuss at a meeting

agent /'eɪdʒ(ə)nt/ noun [C] ★
1 someone whose job is to help a person by finding work for them, or to help a person or company by dealing with their business for them: *a literary/shipping/travel agent*
2 someone who works for a government and collects secret information=SPY

age-old adj having existed for a long time: *the age-old problem of poverty*

aggravate /'æɡrə‚veɪt/ verb [T] 1 to make something bad become worse: *His headache was aggravated by all the noise.* 2 *spoken* to annoy someone —**aggravation** /‚æɡrə'veɪʃ(ə)n/ noun [C/U], **aggravating** /'æɡrə‚veɪtɪŋ/ adj

aggression /ə'ɡreʃ(ə)n/ noun [U] 1 an angry feeling that makes you want to behave violently or attack someone else 2 a situation in which a person or country attacks another person or country: *an act of aggression against a neighbouring country*

aggressive /ə'ɡresɪv/ adj 1 behaving in an angry or rude way that shows you want to fight, attack, or argue with someone: *The taxis have features that protect drivers from aggressive passengers.* ♦ *aggressive behaviour* 2 very determined to win or be successful: *an aggressive election strategy* —**aggressively** adv

aggressor /ə'ɡresə/ noun [C] a country that starts a war, or someone who starts a fight

aggrieved /ə'ɡriːvd/ adj feeling angry and unhappy because you think that you have been treated unfairly

aghast /ə'ɡɑːst/ adj shocked and upset

agile /'ædʒaɪl/ adj able to move your body quickly and easily —**agility** /ə'dʒɪləti/ noun [U]

agitate /'ædʒɪ‚teɪt/ verb [I] to try to cause social or political changes by arguing or protesting, or through other political activity: *students agitating for more freedom* —**agitator** noun [C]

agitated /'ædʒɪ‚teɪtɪd/ adj worried or upset ≠ CALM: *She became increasingly agitated as the interview proceeded.* —**agitation** /‚ædʒɪ'teɪʃ(ə)n/ noun [U]

AGM /‚eɪ dʒiː 'em/ noun [C] *British* Annual General Meeting: a meeting that a business or organization has every year to discuss issues and elect new officials

agnostic /æɡ'nɒstɪk/ noun [C] someone who believes that it is not possible to know whether God exists or not —**agnostic** adj, **agnosticism** /æɡ'nɒstɪ‚sɪz(ə)m/ noun [U]

ago /ə'ɡəʊ/ adv ★★★

> **Ago** follows a word or expression that refers to a period of time. It is usually used with a past tense, not with a perfect tense.

used for saying how much time has passed since something happened: *Your wife phoned a few minutes ago.* ♦ *How long ago did this happen?* ♦ ***Long ago*** *in a far-off land, there was a king called Midas.*

- Use **ago** to say how long before the present time something happened: *He died two years ago.*
- Use **before** to say how long before a time in the past something happened: *I remembered that I had met her ten years before.*
- Use **for** to say how long something in the past continued: *Their marriage lasted for fifteen years.*

agonize /'ægə,naɪz/ verb [I] to spend a long time worrying about something, especially when you have to make a decision: *For days I agonized over whether to accept his offer.*

agonizing /'ægə,naɪzɪŋ/ adj **1** making you feel very worried and upset for a long time **2** very painful

agony /'ægəni/ noun [C/U] **1** great pain **2** great worry or sadness: *She had to go through the agony of leaving her children.*

agony aunt noun [C] *British* a woman who gives advice about personal problems in a newspaper or magazine by answering readers' letters

agree /ə'griː/ verb ★★★
1 [I/T] to have the same opinion as someone else: *Doreen thought that the house was too small, and Jim agreed.* ♦ *I agree with my mother about most things.* ♦ *The committee members agreed on the need for more information.* ♦ **+(that)** *We all agree that we should celebrate this event.*
2 [I] to say that you will do something that someone else wants or suggests: *I asked her to marry me, and she agreed.* ♦ *We have agreed to their request for a full investigation.* ♦ **agree to do sth** *The school agreed to send the students on the course.*
3 [I/T] to decide together what will be done and how it will be done: *Management and unions have agreed a pay deal.* ♦ *We need to agree on a date for our next meeting.*
4 [I] if two pieces of information agree, they are the same or they suggest the same thing: *The observations agree with the predictions we made earlier.*
→ ACCEPT

PHRASAL VERBS a**gree with sb** if food or drink does not agree with you, it makes you feel ill
a**gree with sth** to think that something is the right thing to do: *I don't agree with corporal punishment in schools.*

Word family: agree

Words in the same family as agree
- agreeable *adj*   ■ disagreeable *adj*
- agreement *n*   ■ disagreement *n*
- disagree *v*

agreeable /ə'griːəb(ə)l/ adj **1** acceptable: *a compromise that is agreeable to both sides* **2** *formal* friendly or nice ≠ DISAGREEABLE **3** *formal* willing to do or accept something —**agreeably** adv

agreed /ə'griːd/ adj **1** an agreed price, limit, date etc is one that people have talked about and accepted **2** if people are agreed, they all agree about what to do

agreement /ə'griːmənt/ noun ★★★
1 [C] an arrangement or decision about what

to do, made by two or more people, groups, or organizations: *Our agreement was that you would pay by the first of the month.* ♦ *an agreement between political parties* ♦ *a licence agreement with the software company* ♦ *Management announced that it had reached an agreement with the unions.* ♦ *an agreement on military cooperation*
2 [U] a situation when people have the same opinion or make the same decision: *After a long discussion, there was still no agreement about what to do next.* ♦ *We are all in agreement that Mr Ross should resign.*

agriculture /'ægrɪ,kʌltʃə/ noun [U] the work or business of farming —**agricultural** /,ægrɪ'kʌltʃ(ə)rəl/ adj

aground /ə'graʊnd/ adv **run/go aground** if a ship runs aground, it becomes stuck on a piece of ground under the water

ah /ɑː/ interjection **1** used for showing that you see or understand something **2** used for showing that you are interested, surprised, pleased, or annoyed

aha /ɑː'hɑː/ interjection used for showing that you have suddenly realized or understood something

ahead /ə'hed/ adv ★★★
1 in front of sb in the direction in front of you: *There's a motel just a few miles ahead.* ♦ *She walked ahead of him along the corridor.* ♦ *Instead of turning left, he drove straight ahead towards the river.*
2 in the future used for saying what will happen in the future: *Where will the money come from in the years ahead?* ♦ *Looking ahead to next summer, where would you like to go?* ♦ *We have a busy day ahead of us.*
→ LIE[1]
3 before sb leaving or arriving before someone else: *You go on ahead and tell them we're coming.* ♦ *David finished ahead of me in last year's race.*
4 having made more progress achieving more success or making more progress than someone else: *The Russians were now ahead of the US in space research.* ♦ *If you want to get ahead in politics (=become more successful), you have to look confident.*
5 referring to the time in different places if one place is ahead of another, the clocks there show a later time: *Moscow is three hours ahead of London.*

PHRASES **ahead of your/its time** very advanced or modern: *As a writer, Sterne was ahead of his time.*
ahead of time/schedule at an earlier time than was planned
→ GO AHEAD

aid[1] /eɪd/ noun ★★
1 [U] money, food, or other help that a government or organization gives to people who need it: *financial aid* ♦ *overseas aid*
2 [U] help with doing something: *Chromosomes can be seen with the aid of a microscope.* ♦ *Several people heard her screams, but no one went to her aid.*
3 [C] something that makes it easier to do something: *Hypnosis can be an aid to giving up smoking.*

PHRASE **in aid of** *British* in order to make money to help an organization or group: *a*

A

concert in aid of victims of the war

aid² /eɪd/ verb [T] *formal* to help someone to do something, or to help to make something happen more easily: *Gentle exercise aids the circulation of blood around the body.*

PHRASE **aid and abet** *legal* to help someone to commit a crime

aide /eɪd/ noun [C] someone whose job is to help another person in their work

AIDS or **Aids** /eɪdz/ noun [U] acquired immune deficiency syndrome: a serious disease that destroys the body's ability to defend itself against infection

ailing /ˈeɪlɪŋ/ adj not strong, healthy, or successful: *an ailing business*

ailment /ˈeɪlmənt/ noun [C] a minor illness

aim¹ /eɪm/ noun ★★★

1 [C] the thing that you hope to achieve by doing something = GOAL: *We visit schools with the aim of getting young people interested in the theatre.* ♦ *My main aim on this course is to gain confidence.* ♦ *The aim of this project is to help patients to be more independent.*

2 [singular] your ability to hit something when you throw, kick, or shoot something at it: *My aim isn't very good.*

PHRASE **take aim (at)** to point a gun at something before you shoot

aim² /eɪm/ verb ★★★

1 [I] to intend or hope to achieve something: *Most of the students were aiming for jobs in television.* ♦ **aim to do sth** *The project aims to provide support for young musicians.*

2 [I/T] to point something such as a gun at a person or thing that you want to hit: *He was aiming at the tree but he missed.* ♦ **aim sth at sb/sth** *I looked up to see Betty aiming a gun at me.*

3 [T] **be aimed at sb** to be intended to be read, watched, or used by people of a particular type: *The book is aimed at people with no specialized knowledge.*

4 [T] **be aimed at doing sth** to have the goal of achieving a particular thing: *an energy programme that is aimed at reducing our dependence on fossil fuels*

aimless /ˈeɪmləs/ adj without any particular purpose or plan —**aimlessly** adv

ain't /eɪnt/ *spoken* a way of saying 'am not', 'is not', 'are not', 'has not', or 'have not'. Many people think that 'ain't' is not correct.

air¹ /eə/ noun ★★★

1 [U] the mixture of gases that we breathe: *She breathed in the cold air.* ♦ *I'd like to open the window – I need some air.*

2 the air [singular] the space around things and above the ground: *They threw their hats up into the air.* ♦ *birds flying through the air*

3 [singular] a feeling or attitude: *She spoke with her usual air of authority.*

4 airs [plural] the false behaviour of someone who is trying to impress other people: *My friends are people I trust, and I don't have to put on airs with them.*

PHRASES **by air** travelling in a plane

sth is in the air used for saying that people all have a similar feeling, especially a feeling that something exciting or new is happening: *Spring is in the air.*

off air or **off the air** no longer broadcasting on radio or television

on air or **on the air** on radio or television

up in the air if a plan is up in the air, you have not yet decided what will happen

→ CLEAR², FRESH AIR, OPEN AIR

air² /eə/ verb **1** [T] to publicly make a complaint or state your opinion: *In an interview, the singer aired his views on family life.* **2** [T] to broadcast something on radio or television **3** [I/T] if you air a place or piece of clothing, or if they air, you let fresh air pass through them until they smell clean and fresh

ˈair ˌbag noun [C] a piece of equipment in a car that protects people in a crash by immediately filling with air

airborne /ˈeəbɔːn/ adj moving or carried in the air

air conditioning /ˈeə kənˌdɪʃ(ə)nɪŋ/ noun [U] a system that makes the air inside a building, room, or vehicle colder —**ˈair-conˌditioned** adj: *air-conditioned rooms*

aircraft /ˈeəkrɑːft/ (plural **aircraft**) noun [C] ★★★ a plane, HELICOPTER, or other vehicle that flies

ˈaircraft ˌcarrier noun [C] a ship that carries military planes

airfare /ˈeəˌfeə/ noun [C] the money that you pay to go somewhere by plane

airfield /ˈeəfiːld/ noun [C] a small airport for military or private aircraft

ˈair ˌforce noun [C] the part of a country's military forces that fights using planes

ˈair ˌhostess noun [C] *British old-fashioned* a female FLIGHT ATTENDANT

ˈairing ˌcupboard noun [C] *British* a cupboard with shelves where clean clothes, sheets etc can be kept warm and dry

airlift /ˈeəˌlɪft/ noun [C] an action by which people or things are taken into or away from a dangerous place by aircraft —**airlift** verb [T]

airline /ˈeəˌlaɪn/ noun [C] ★ a company that owns aircraft and takes people or goods by plane from one place to another

airliner /ˈeəˌlaɪnə/ noun [C] a large plane for passengers

airmail /ˈeəˌmeɪl/ noun [U] the system for sending post by plane

airplane /ˈeəˌpleɪn/ noun [C] *American* a PLANE

airport /ˈeəpɔːt/ noun [C] ★★★ a place where planes arrive and leave

airspace /ˈeəˌspeɪs/ noun [U] the sky above a particular country

airtight /ˈeəˌtaɪt/ adj not allowing air to enter or leave: *an airtight container*

ˈair ˌtime noun [U] the amount of time that is given to someone or something in a radio or television broadcast

ˈair traffic conˌtroller noun [C] someone whose job is to organize the movement of planes in a particular area by giving instructions to pilots by radio

airwaves /ˈeəˌweɪvz/ noun [plural] radio waves that are used for sending signals for radio, television, and MOBILE PHONES

airy /ˈeəri/ adj with a lot of fresh air and space

aisle /aɪl/ noun [C] a passage between rows of

A

seats, for example in a theatre, church, or plane, or between the shelves of a supermarket

ajar /ə'dʒɑː/ adj a door that is ajar is slightly open —*picture* → OPEN¹

aka /ˌeɪ keɪ 'eɪ/ also known as: used when giving someone's real name followed by a different name that they also use

à la carte /ˌɑː lɑː 'kɑːt/ adj, adv priced separately on a menu rather than as part of a meal

alarm¹ /ə'lɑːm/ noun ★★
1 [U] the worried feeling that something unpleasant or dangerous might happen: *She is a little unwell but there is no cause for alarm* (=reason to worry). ♦ *There was a note of alarm in her voice.*
2 [C] a piece of electrical equipment that warns you of danger by making a loud noise: *a burglar/fire/smoke alarm* ♦ *My car alarm went off in the middle of the night.*
3 [C] an ALARM CLOCK: *I'll set the alarm for eight.*
PHRASE **raise/sound the alarm** to tell people about something dangerous that is happening: *The crash was seen by a farmer, who raised the alarm on his mobile phone.*
→ FALSE ALARM

alarm² /ə'lɑːm/ verb [T] to make someone worried that something unpleasant or dangerous might happen: *School officials were alarmed by the number of children with the disease.*

a'larm ,bells noun [plural] if something rings alarm bells, or sets alarm bells ringing, it makes you very careful because you think something bad is going to happen

a'larm ,clock noun [C] a clock that wakes you up at a particular time by making a noise

alarmed /ə'lɑːmd/ adj **1** worried that something unpleasant or dangerous might happen **2** protected by an ALARM

alarming /ə'lɑːmɪŋ/ adj frightening or worrying —**alarmingly** adv

alarmist /ə'lɑːmɪst/ adj causing unnecessary fear or worry

alas /ə'læs/ interjection *often humorous* an old word used for saying that you are sad about something

albeit /ɔːl'biːɪt/ conjunction *formal* although: *The United States finally agreed, albeit unwillingly, to support the UN action.*

album /'ælbəm/ noun [C] **1** a CD, record, or CASSETTE with several songs or pieces of music on it **2** a book in which you can collect things such as photographs or stamps

alcohol /'ælkəhɒl/ noun [U] ★
1 drinks such as wine and beer that can make people drunk: *a ban on the advertising of alcohol*
2 the substance in drinks such as wine and beer that makes you drunk

alcoholic¹ /ˌælkə'hɒlɪk/ adj **1** containing alcohol ≠ NON-ALCOHOLIC: *alcoholic drinks* **2** affected by ALCOHOLISM: *alcoholic patients*

alcoholic² /ˌælkə'hɒlɪk/ noun [C] someone who finds it difficult to control the amount of alcohol that they drink

alcoholism /'ælkəhɒlˌɪz(ə)m/ noun [U] a medical condition that makes it difficult to

control the amount of alcohol that you drink

alcove /'ælkəʊv/ noun [C] a small area in a room that has been created by building part of a wall further back than the rest of the wall

ale /eɪl/ noun [C/U] a type of dark-coloured beer

alert¹ /ə'lɜːt/ adj **1** able to think clearly: *She's remained physically fit and mentally alert.* **2** paying attention to what is happening and ready to react to it: *Parents must be alert to the symptoms of the disease.*

alert² /ə'lɜːt/ verb [T] to tell someone about a danger or problem

alert³ /ə'lɜːt/ noun [C] a warning about something dangerous
PHRASE **on the alert** or **on full alert** ready to deal with a dangerous situation

A level /'eɪ ˌlev(ə)l/ noun [C] an examination that students in England and Wales take before going to university

algae /'ældʒiː, 'ælgiː/ noun [plural] plants with no leaves that grow in water

algebra /'ældʒɪbrə/ noun [U] a type of mathematics that uses letters and symbols to represent numbers —**algebraic** /ˌældʒɪ'breɪɪk/ adj

alias¹ /'eɪliəs/ preposition used before a different name that someone uses instead of their real name: *Zeljko Raznatovic, alias Arkan*

alias² /'eɪliəs/ noun [C] a different name that someone uses instead of their real name

alibi /'æləbaɪ/ noun [C] evidence that someone was not in a particular place when a crime was committed there

alien¹ /'eɪliən/ adj **1** not familiar = STRANGE **2** from another planet

alien² /'eɪliən/ noun [C] **1** a creature from another planet **2** someone who is not a citizen of the country they are living in

alienate /'eɪliəneɪt/ verb [T] **1** to make someone dislike you or not want to help you: *Their campaign has alienated the public.* **2** to make someone feel that they do not belong in a place or group —**alienation** /ˌeɪliə'neɪʃ(ə)n/ noun [U]

alienated /'eɪliəneɪtɪd/ adj feeling that you do not belong in a place or group: *angry and alienated teenagers*

alight¹ /ə'laɪt/ adj burning

alight² /ə'laɪt/ verb [I] *formal* to get off a train, bus, or other vehicle

align /ə'laɪn/ verb [T] **1** to give your support to a group or country: *Many women do not want to align themselves with the movement.* **2** to organize things so that they are in the correct position in relation to other things —**alignment** noun [C/U]

alike¹ /ə'laɪk/ adj similar: *The sisters don't really look alike.*

alike² /ə'laɪk/ adv **1** in the same way or in a similar way: *Students of both sexes dressed alike.* **2** used for referring to two people or things equally: *It's a show that appeals to young and old alike.*

alive /ə'laɪv/ adj ★★★
1 living and not dead: *My father died last year but my mother is still alive.* ♦ *He is*

lucky to be alive after his fall. ♦ *The family was stealing food just to* **stay alive**.
2 still existing and not gone or forgotten: *Memories of the war are still very much alive.* ♦ *They struggled to* **keep** *their language and traditions* **alive**.
3 full of excitement or activity: *The village really* **comes alive** *at Christmas.* ♦ *The street was* **alive with** *the sound of children playing.*
PHRASE **alive and well/kicking 1** still living **2** still existing and not gone or forgotten

alkaline /'ælkə,laɪn/ adj not ACID

all /ɔːl/ grammar word ★★★

All can be:
■ a **determiner**: *All children deserve encouragement.*
■ a **pronoun**: *I want to invite all of you.* ♦ *We can all relax.*
■ an **adverb**: *Bernard was all alone in a strange city.*

1 the whole of an amount, thing, situation, or period of time: *Have you spent all your money?* ♦ *There's no cake left. They've eaten it all.* ♦ *I've been awake all night worrying.* ♦ *You can't blame it all on David.* ♦ *Oh, look, you spilt it all over the carpet.* ♦ *Make sure that* **all of** *the equipment has been checked.*
2 every person or thing: *We all enjoyed the party.* ♦ *No one can solve all these problems.* ♦ *All seven astronauts were killed in the explosion.* ♦ *I want* **all of** *you to listen carefully.* ♦ **Not all** *lawyers have large incomes.* ♦ *We play* **all kinds of** *music – rock, reggae, jazz, even classical.*
3 used for emphasizing something: *I'm* **all in favour** *of giving children more freedom.* ♦ *Now we're going to be late, and it's* **all because** *of you.* ♦ *The exam season is so stressful – I'll be glad when it's* **all over** (=completely finished).
4 used for saying that there is nothing more than what you are mentioning: *Just three pounds –* **that's all** *I've got left.* ♦ *All we can do is sit and wait.* ♦ *I wasn't interfering. I was just trying to help,* **that's all**.
PHRASES **all along** during the whole time that something is happening: *Mary knew all along what I was planning to do.*
all but almost: *The job is all but finished.*
all in all used for showing that you are considering every aspect of something: *All in all, I think it has been a very successful conference.*
all of a sudden or **all at once** very suddenly: *All of a sudden there was a knock at the door.*
first/best/most etc of all before anything else/better than anything else/more than anything else etc: *First of all, I want to welcome our guest speaker.* ♦ *His music was the thing he loved most of all.*
for all sth despite something: *For all its faults, she loved the city.*
for all I know/care *spoken* used for saying that even if something was true, you would not know/care about it: *He might be a murderer, for all we know.*
go all out to use all your energy, strength, and determination in order to achieve something
in all or **all told** when the whole of an amount

or number is included: *In all, there are over 120 languages spoken in London's schools.*
not all that good/bad/big etc used for saying that something is not very good/bad/big etc: *I didn't finish the book – it wasn't all that interesting.*
→ AT

Allah /'ælə/ the name of God in Islam

allay /ə'leɪ/ verb [T] *formal* if you allay feelings such as fears or worries, you make someone feel less afraid or worried

all-clear, the noun [singular] **1** a statement from a doctor that someone is well again **2** a signal or statement that a period of danger has ended

all-day adj continuing or available for the whole day: *an all-day meeting* ♦ *an all-day breakfast*

allegation /,ælə'geɪʃ(ə)n/ noun [C] a statement claiming that someone has done something wrong or illegal

allege /ə'ledʒ/ verb [T] to say that someone has done something wrong or illegal, even though this has not been proved

alleged /ə'ledʒd/ adj claimed to be true but not proved: *his alleged part in a terrorist plot* —**allegedly** /ə'ledʒɪdli/ adv

allegiance /ə'liːdʒ(ə)ns/ noun [C/U] loyalty to a person, group, idea, or country

allegory /'æləg(ə)ri/ noun [C/U] a story, poem, or picture in which events and characters are used as symbols to express a moral or political idea —**allegorical** /,ælə'gɒrɪk(ə)l/ adj

allergic /ə'lɜːdʒɪk/ adj **1** affected by an allergy: *I'm allergic to nuts.* **2** caused by an allergy: *an allergic reaction*

allergy /'ælədʒi/ noun [C/U] a medical condition in which you become ill as a reaction to something that you eat, breathe, or touch

alleviate /ə'liːvi,eɪt/ verb [T] to make something less painful, severe, or serious

alley /'æli/ or **alleyway** /'æli,weɪ/ noun [C] a narrow street or passage between buildings

alliance /ə'laɪəns/ noun [C] **1** an arrangement in which people, groups, or countries agree to work together: *The two companies have formed a strategic alliance.* ♦ *an alliance between the two parties* **2** an arrangement in which two or more countries join together to defend themselves against an enemy

allied /'ælaɪd/ adj **1** joined together in a military alliance: *the allied army* **2** /ə'laɪd, 'ælaɪd/ if something is allied to or with something else, it is connected with it

alligator /'ælɪ,geɪtə/ noun [C] a large REPTILE with a long pointed mouth and sharp teeth. Alligators look like CROCODILES.

all-important adj very important, or the most important of all

all-night adj continuing or available for the whole night: *an all-night party* ♦ *an all-night restaurant*

allocate /'ælə,keɪt/ verb [T] **1** to provide something for someone: *We allocate a personal tutor to each student.* **2** to decide to use something for a particular purpose: *Extra money has been allocated for equipment.* —**allocation** /,ælə'keɪʃ(ə)n/ noun [C/U]

A

allot /əˈlɒt/ verb [T] to give someone a share of something, such as time, money, or work

allotment /əˈlɒtmənt/ noun [C] British a small piece of land that you can rent and use for growing vegetables

all-out adj using everything available in order to succeed in something

allow /əˈlaʊ/ verb [T] ★★★
1 to give someone permission to do something or have something: *I'm sorry, sir, but smoking is not allowed.* ♦ **allow sb to do sth** *She only allows the children to watch television at weekends.* ♦ **allow sb sth** *Some prisoners are allowed visitors.*
2 to give someone or something the time or opportunity to do something: **allow sth to do sth** *Allow the cake to cool for five minutes before taking it out of the tin.* ♦ **allow sb to do sth** *a program that allows you to create web pages*
3 to make certain that you have enough of something such as time, food, or money for a particular purpose: *How much rice do you allow for each person?*
PHRASAL VERB **alˈlow for sth** to consider something when you are making a plan or calculation: *The cost will be about £17 million, allowing for inflation.*

allowable /əˈlaʊəb(ə)l/ adj allowed by a set of rules or by the law

allowance /əˈlaʊəns/ noun [C] 1 an amount of money that someone receives regularly to pay for things that they need: *a housing/clothing allowance* 2 an amount of something that you are officially allowed: *Your baggage allowance is 30 kilos.*
PHRASE **make allowances (for)** to accept behaviour that you would not normally accept because you know why someone has behaved that way: *We have to make allowances for his lack of experience.*

alloy /ˈælɔɪ/ noun [C/U] a metal made by combining two or more other metals

all-purpose adj able to be used in a lot of different ways

all right¹ adj, adv spoken ★★

1 fairly good	4 not hurt/ill
2 going well	5 for making sb calm
3 for permission	+ PHRASE

1 satisfactory or fairly nice, but not excellent: *Manchester's all right, but I'd rather live in London.*
2 going well or happening successfully: *Did the party go all right?* ♦ *My brother was unemployed for years but he's doing all right now* (=he's fairly successful).
3 used for asking for or giving permission to do something: **be all right if sb does sth** *Is it all right if I open the window?* ♦ **be all right to do sth** *It's all right to use that computer.*
4 not hurt or ill: *You look terrible, are you all right?*
5 used for making someone feel less worried or upset: *It's all right, I'm here.*
PHRASE **that's all right** used when someone has thanked you or said sorry to you: *'Thanks for the lift.' 'That's all right.'*

all right² interjection 1 used for agreeing to something: *'Can't we stay a bit longer?' 'Oh, all right, but just five minutes.'* 2 used for

checking that someone understands or agrees: *I'm playing football after school today, all right?* 3 used for showing that you have heard or understood that someone has said: *'We need to leave in ten minutes.' 'All right, I'll be ready.'* 4 British used for saying hello to someone: *'All right Andy?' 'All right.'*

all-round adj British good at doing a lot of different things, especially in sport — **allˈrounder** noun [C]

all-time adj used for comparing all the people or things of a particular type that have ever existed: *Interest rates are at an all-time high.* ♦ *the all-time worst player*

allude /əˈluːd/ **PHRASAL VERB** **alˈlude to sth** formal to mention someone or something in an indirect way

allure /əˈlʊə, əˈljʊə/ noun [U] an exciting and attractive quality

alluring /əˈlʊərɪŋ, əˈljʊərɪŋ/ adj attractive in an exciting way

allusion /əˈluːʒ(ə)n/ noun [C/U] a statement that refers to something in an indirect way

ally¹ /ˈælaɪ/ noun [C] 1 a country that makes an agreement to help another country, especially in a war: *the United States and its European allies* 2 someone who helps you, especially against people who are causing problems for you: *If you're going to succeed in this job you will need allies.*

ally² /əˈlaɪ, ˈælaɪ/ verb **ally yourself with** to support another country, group, or person

almighty /ɔːlˈmaɪti/ adj 1 informal used for emphasizing how great, loud, or serious something is 2 **Almighty** with power over everyone and everything: *Almighty God*

almond /ˈɑːmənd/ noun [C] a flat white nut that has a brown skin and can be eaten

almost /ˈɔːlməʊst/ adv ★★★ nearly but not completely: *'Are you ready?' 'Almost! I'm just putting my shoes on.'* ♦ *It's almost a year since she died.* ♦ *Almost all of the students here are from South America.* ♦ **almost as...as** *Sam's almost as tall as his mother.*

alone /əˈləʊn/ adj, adv ★★

Alone can be:
■ an **adjective**: *I was alone in the house.*
■ an **adverb**: *Kim prefers to travel alone.*

1 if you are alone, no one else is with you: *Shelley is divorced and lives alone.* ♦ *She was all alone in a dark forest.* ♦ *It was the first time he had been alone with Maria* (=just the two of them and nobody else).
2 without any help from other people: *Was the killer acting alone?*
3 without including numbers or amounts from anywhere else: *Last year, she earned over a million pounds from television advertisements alone.*
4 used for emphasizing that a particular person or thing is the only one that has something or can do something: *Time alone will show whether the voters made the right choice.* ♦ **alone in (doing) sth** *Am I alone in thinking that Biggs could be wrong?*
PHRASE **go it alone** to live, work, or make decisions on your own, without any help from other people

A

along /əˈlɒŋ/ grammar word ★★★

> **Along** can be:
> ■ a **preposition**: *Go along South Street and turn left.*
> ■ an **adverb**: *Can I bring the children along?*

1 moving forwards on a line, path, or near the edge of something: *Mrs Barnes was hurrying along the path towards us.* ♦ *We walked along in silence.* ♦ *They were sailing along the southern coast of Australia.*
2 placed in a line beside a road, river, wall etc: *a line of trees along the river bank*
3 used for saying that you go somewhere with someone, or you take someone or something with you: *Do you mind if I come along too?* ♦ *Be sure to take your notes along with you.*
4 coming to the place where someone is: *Finally a taxi came along, and we jumped in.* ♦ *Just wait here. The doctor should be along* (=should arrive) *in a few minutes.*
  PHRASES along with in addition to: *Ramos was arrested along with 11 other men.*
be getting/coming along used for saying how well someone is progressing or succeeding: *How is your garden coming along?* ♦ *How are you getting along with your Arabic?*

alongside /əˌlɒŋˈsaɪd/ grammar word

> **Alongside** can be:
> ■ a **preposition**: *A police car drove up alongside us.*
> ■ an **adverb**: *Peter was riding on a donkey with his father walking alongside.*

1 along the side of someone or something, or close to their side: *The railway runs alongside the road.* **2** working together with someone in the same place: *We worked alongside people from 71 other countries.* **3** existing at the same time as another system, process, or idea: *In Hong Kong, a communist government and a capitalist economy operate alongside each other.* **4** in comparison with another person or thing: *Our profits seem small alongside the amounts that the big companies make.*

aloof /əˈluːf/ adj **1** not friendly **2** not willing to be involved in something

aloud /əˈlaʊd/ adv loud enough for other people to hear

alphabet /ˈælfəˌbet/ noun [C] ★ a set of letters in a particular order that are used for writing a language

alphabetical /ˌælfəˈbetɪk(ə)l/ adj arranged according to the order of letters in the alphabet: *Here is a list of words in alphabetical order.* —**alphabetically** /ˌælfəˈbetɪkli/ adv

already /ɔːlˈredi/ adv ★★★
1 before now, or before another point in time: *He's only 24, but he's already achieved worldwide fame.* ♦ *The gang leader had already left the country.*
2 used for saying that a situation has started to exist and still continues: *By the time the doctor arrived, I was already feeling better.*
3 sooner than you expected: *Are you tired already? I don't believe it!* ♦ *Is it 12 o'clock already?*
→ YET

alright /ɔːlˈraɪt/ adj, adv ALL RIGHT. Many people think that this is incorrect.

Alsatian /ælˈseɪʃ(ə)n/ noun [C] *British* a large dog with thick brown or black hair

also /ˈɔːlsəʊ/ adv ★★★
1 used for adding another fact or idea to what you have already said: *Khaled is a keen photographer who also loves to paint.* ♦ *The electric drill can also be used as a screwdriver.* ♦ *Not only is it more expensive, it's also a horrible colour.*
2 used for showing that what you have just said about someone or something is true about another person or thing: *Jeremy is now at Dartmouth College, where his father also studied.* ♦ *The film was popular not only with children, but also with their parents.*

> **Also, as well**, and **too** all have a similar meaning.
> ■ **As well** and **too** come at the end of a clause: *My wife speaks French as well/too.* But **also** usually comes before the verb, or after an auxiliary or modal verb or the verb **to be**: *She also speaks French.* ♦ *She can also speak French.* ♦ *He was also a fine musician.*
> ■ **Also** is not normally used with negatives. **Not...either** is used instead: *I don't speak French, and I don't speak German either.*

altar /ˈɔːltə/ noun [C] a table where religious ceremonies are performed

alter /ˈɔːltə/ verb [I/T] to change, or to make changes to something=MODIFY: *He had altered all the information on the forms.* ♦ *After all these years, the town has hardly altered.*

alteration /ˌɔːltəˈreɪʃ(ə)n/ noun [C] a change in something or someone=MODIFICATION

alternate¹ /ˈɔːltəˌneɪt/ verb [I/T] to change from one thing, idea, or feeling to another, and keep repeating that pattern: *The government alternates between tough talk and silence.* ♦ *The course allows students to alternate work with education.*

alternate² /ɔːlˈtɜːnət/ adj **1** happening or coming one after another, in a regular pattern: *alternate periods of good and bad weather* **2** happening on one day, week etc, but not on the day, week etc that immediately follows: *I go and visit him on alternate weekends.* **3** *American* ALTERNATIVE: *You'll have to find an alternate route.* —**alternately** adv

alternative¹ /ɔːlˈtɜːnətɪv/ noun [C] ★★ something that you can choose to do instead of something else: *There was no alternative – we had to close the bridge.*

alternative² /ɔːlˈtɜːnətɪv/ adj ★★
1 able to be used or done instead of something else: *We are now looking for an alternative method.*
2 not traditional, or not done in the usual way: *an alternative lifestyle*

alternatively /ɔːlˈtɜːnətɪvli/ adv used for making another suggestion: *We could drive all the way. Alternatively, we could fly.*

alternative medicine noun [U] medical treatments that are based on traditional ideas, not on modern methods

although /ɔːlˈðəʊ/ conjunction ★★★
1 used for introducing a statement that

A

makes your main statement seem surprising=THOUGH: *She used to call me 'Tiny' although I was at least as tall as she was.*

2 used for introducing a statement that makes what you have just said seem less true or less likely: *The Lamberts liked their new home, although they missed their friends.*

altitude /ˈæltɪˌtjuːd/ noun [C] the height of a place or object above SEA LEVEL

altogether /ˌɔːltəˈɡeðə/ adv ★★
1 completely: *These rare animals may soon disappear altogether.* ♦ *I'm **not altogether** sure who he is.*
2 including everyone or everything: *How many guests will there be altogether?*

Do not confuse **altogether** with **all together**, which means 'everyone or everything together': *Write down the numbers and add them all together.*

altruistic /ˌæltruˈɪstɪk/ adj doing something for the benefit of other people ≠ SELFISH —**altruism** /ˈæltruˌɪz(ə)m/ noun [U]

aluminium /ˌæləˈmɪniəm/ noun [U] a light silver-coloured metal

aluminum /əˈluːmɪnəm/ the American spelling of **aluminium**

always /ˈɔːlweɪz/ adv ★★★
1 on every occasion: *I always get the eight o'clock train.* ♦ *Starting a new job is always a bit of a shock.*
2 all the time: *Is he always this silly?*
3 for all time in the past or future: *I'll always remember how kind she was.* ♦ *Jimmy was always a difficult boy.*
4 used for saying that something happens often, especially when this annoys you: *He's always forgetting my name.*
PHRASES as always as on every other occasion: *As always, her father was there to meet her.*
I/you/they etc could always... *spoken* used for making a suggestion: *You could always phone him yourself.*
there's always... used for making a suggestion: *There's always Sue if Jane isn't available.*

Alzheimer's disease /ˈæltshaɪməz dɪˌziːz/ noun [U] a serious illness that affects someone's brain and memory

am¹ /weak əm, strong æm/ see **be**

am² /ˌeɪˈem/ abbrev used for showing that a time is between midnight and noon → PM

amalgamate /əˈmælɡəˌmeɪt/ verb [I/T] to join two or more organizations, companies etc to make a single large one, or to be joined in this way —**amalgamation** /əˌmælɡəˈmeɪʃ(ə)n/ noun [C/U]

amass /əˈmæs/ verb [T] to collect a lot of money or information

amateur¹ /ˈæmətə, ˈæmətʃʊə/ adj **1** done for pleasure instead of as a job ≠ PROFESSIONAL: *amateur photography* **2** done or made badly: *a very amateur performance*

amateur² /ˈæmətə, ˈæmətʃʊə/ noun [C] **1** someone who does something because they enjoy it, instead of as a job ≠ PROFESSIONAL **2** someone who does not do something very well

amateurish /ˈæmətərɪʃ, ˌæmətʃʊərɪʃ/ adj done or made without much skill

amaze /əˈmeɪz/ verb [T] to surprise someone very much by being very impressive or unusual: *What amazes me is that they never get tired.*

amazed /əˈmeɪzd/ adj very surprised: *Frankly, I was amazed that he was interested.*

amazement /əˈmeɪzmənt/ noun [U] a feeling of being very surprised: *They were shaking their heads in amazement.*

amazing /əˈmeɪzɪŋ/ adj ★ very good, surprising, or impressive: *Her story was quite amazing.* ♦ *Their last CD sold an amazing 2 million copies.* —**amazingly** adv

ambassador /æmˈbæsədə/ noun [C] a senior official who lives in a foreign country and represents his or her own country there

amber /ˈæmbə/ noun [U] a hard yellow-brown substance used for making jewellery

ambidextrous /ˌæmbɪˈdekstrəs/ adj able to use both hands with equal skill

ambience /ˈæmbiəns/ noun [C/U] the character of a place, or the general feeling that you have in a place=ATMOSPHERE

ambiguity /ˌæmbɪˈɡjuːəti/ noun [C/U] something that is not clear because it has more than one possible meaning

ambiguous /æmˈbɪɡjuəs/ adj something that is ambiguous is not clear because it has more than one possible meaning or intention ≠ UNAMBIGUOUS: *The wording of his statement was highly ambiguous.* —**ambiguously** adv

ambition /æmˈbɪʃ(ə)n/ noun ★
1 [C] something that you very much want to achieve: *His ambition was to become a successful writer.* ♦ *I had no idea about Jesse's political ambitions.*
2 [U] determination to become successful, rich, or famous

ambitious /æmˈbɪʃəs/ adj **1** determined to become successful, rich, or famous: *an ambitious young lawyer* **2** an ambitious plan or attempt will need a lot of hard work and skill in order for it to be successful

ambivalent /æmˈbɪvələnt/ adj having two different opinions about something at the same time —**ambivalence** /æmˈbɪvələns/ noun [U]

amble /ˈæmb(ə)l/ verb [I] to walk in a slow relaxed way

ambulance /ˈæmbjʊləns/ noun [C] ★ a vehicle for taking people to hospital

ambush /ˈæmbʊʃ/ verb [T] to attack someone suddenly from a hidden position —**ambush** noun [C/U]

amen /ˌɑːˈmen, ˌeɪˈmen/ interjection said at the end of a Christian or Jewish prayer

amenable /əˈmiːnəb(ə)l/ adj willing to do something, or willing to agree with someone

amend /əˈmend/ verb [T] to make changes that improve a document, law, or agreement

amendment /əˈmen(d)mənt/ noun [C] a change to a document, law, or agreement

amends /əˈmendz/ noun **make amends** to try to make a situation better after you have done something wrong

amenities /əˈmiːnətiz/ noun [plural] things that make it comfortable or enjoyable to live or work somewhere: *Amenities include a gym and a pool.*

American Dream, the /əˌmerɪkən ˈdriːm/ noun [singular] the idea that anyone can be successful in the US if they work hard enough

American football /əˌmerɪkən ˈfʊtbɔːl/ noun [U] *British* a game in which two teams throw, carry, or kick an OVAL ball (=shaped like an egg) and try to cross their opponents' goal line

American Indian /əˌmerɪkən ˈɪndiən/ noun [C] a NATIVE AMERICAN —**American Indian** adj

Americanize /əˈmerɪkənaɪz/ verb [T] to make a language or culture more American —**Americanization** /əˌmerɪkənaɪˈzeɪʃ(ə)n/ noun [U]

amethyst /ˈæməθɪst/ noun [C/U] a purple stone that is used in jewellery

amiable /ˈeɪmiəb(ə)l/ adj friendly and easy to like

amicable /ˈæmɪkəb(ə)l/ adj friendly and without arguments: *an amicable divorce* —**amicably** adv

amid /əˈmɪd/ or **amidst** /əˈmɪdst/ preposition **1** while something is happening or changing: *Banks and shops closed yesterday amid growing fears of violence.* **2** surrounded by things or people

amino acid /əˌmiːnəʊ ˈæsɪd/ noun [C] one of the substances in the body that combine to make proteins

amiss /əˈmɪs/ adj if something is amiss, it is not as it should be

ammonia /əˈməʊniə/ noun [U] a poisonous gas or liquid with a strong unpleasant smell, used in cleaning products

ammunition /ˌæmjʊˈnɪʃ(ə)n/ noun [U] **1** bullets and bombs that can be fired from a weapon **2** facts that can be used against someone in an argument

amnesia /æmˈniːziə/ noun [U] a medical condition that makes you unable to remember things

amnesty /ˈæmnəsti/ noun [C] an official order not to punish people who have committed a particular crime

amoeba /əˈmiːbə/ noun [C] a very small ORGANISM (=living thing) that consists of a single cell —**amoebic** /əˈmiːbɪk/ adj

amok /əˈmɒk/ adv **run amok** to behave in an uncontrolled and often violent way

among /əˈmʌŋ/ or **amongst** /əˈmʌŋst/ preposition ★★★
1 included in a particular group of people or things: *Robert was the only one among them who had ever ridden a horse.* ♦ *They discussed, among other things, the future of the oil industry.* ♦ *The winner was selected from among 500 candidates.*
2 used for saying what happens within a particular group of people: *The suicide rate among young male prisoners is high.* ♦ *The team were fighting among themselves.*
3 used for saying that different people receive parts of something when it is divided up: *The money has to be shared out among several projects.*

4 with other people or things all around: *It was pleasant strolling among the olive trees.*

> **Between** and **among** are used in similar ways.
> ■ Use **between**, not **among**, when just two people are mentioned: *It was an agreement between Carl and me.*
> ■ When three or more people are mentioned, you can use either, but **among** is more formal: *The money was divided up among/between the four children.*
> ■ Use **between** for saying that there are people or things on two sides of someone or something: *I sat between my parents.*
> ■ Use **among** for saying that someone or something is in the middle of a group of people or things: *We strolled among the trees.*

amoral /ˌeɪˈmɒrəl/ adj someone who is amoral does not care if their behaviour is right or wrong

amorous /ˈæmərəs/ adj involving sexual love

amount¹ /əˈmaʊnt/ noun [C] ★★★ a quantity of something: *This amount (=quantity of money) should be paid within two weeks.* ♦ *A computer can store vast amounts of information.*
PHRASE **no amount of sth** used for saying that something will never be enough to have an effect: *No amount of training could have prepared him for this.*

> **Amount** and **number** are both used for talking about quantities, but they are used in different ways.
> ■ **Number** is used with plural nouns: *a small number of cars* ♦ *a certain number of people.*
> ■ **Amount** is used with uncountable nouns: *a small amount of milk* ♦ *a certain amount of confidence.*
> ■ Say a **large** or **small** number/amount and NOT a **big** or **little** number/amount.

amount² /əˈmaʊnt/ PHRASAL VERB **aˈmount to sth 1** to be the same as something else, or to have the same effect as something else: *Most people believe his statements amount to a declaration of war.* **2** to add up to a particular total: *His monthly earnings amount to about £2,000.*

amp /æmp/ or **ampere** /ˈæmpeə/ noun [C] *science* a unit for measuring an electric current

amphetamine /æmˈfetəmiːn/ noun [C/U] a drug that increases energy and excitement

amphibian /æmˈfɪbiən/ noun [C] an animal that can live both in water and on land

amphibious /æmˈfɪbiəs/ adj living, being used, or happening both in water and on land

amphitheatre /ˈæmfɪˌθɪətə/ noun [C] a large circular building with no roof that is used for sports competitions or plays

ample /ˈæmp(ə)l/ adj **1** enough, and often more than you need **2** used for referring to a part of someone's body that is large: *an ample bosom* —**amply** adv

amplifier /ˈæmplɪˌfaɪə/ noun [C] a piece of electronic equipment that makes sounds louder

amplify /ˈæmplɪˌfaɪ/ verb [T] to make sounds louder —**amplification** /ˌæmplɪfɪˈkeɪʃ(ə)n/ noun [C/U]

A

amputate /ˈæmpjʊˌteɪt/ verb [I/T] to cut off a part of someone's body in a medical operation —**amputation** /ˌæmpjʊˈteɪʃ(ə)n/ noun [C/U]

amuse /əˈmjuːz/ verb [T] **1** to do or say something that other people think is funny or entertaining **2** to keep someone interested or entertained, so that they do not get bored: *We need something that will amuse a 10-year-old for an afternoon.*

amused /əˈmjuːzd/ adj showing that you think that something is funny or entertaining: *an amused expression*

amusement /əˈmjuːzmənt/ noun **1** [U] a feeling of being amused **2** [C] an enjoyable activity

aˈmusement arˌcade noun [C] British a place where you can play games on machines by putting coins in them

aˈmusement ˌpark noun [C] a place where people pay money to go on RIDES (=large machines that you ride on for pleasure) =FUNFAIR

amusing /əˈmjuːzɪŋ/ adj funny or entertaining: *an amusing birthday card*

an /weak ən, strong æn/ determiner ★★★ used instead of 'a' when the next word begins with a vowel sound: *an accident ♦ an hour ♦ an X-ray*

anachronism /əˈnækrənɪz(ə)m/ noun [C] something that is no longer suitable for modern times —**anachronistic** /əˌnækrəˈnɪstɪk/ adj

anaemia /əˈniːmiə/ noun [U] a medical condition in which your blood contains too few red blood cells —**anaemic** /əˈniːmɪk/ adj

anaesthetic /ˌænəsˈθetɪk/ noun [C/U] a drug or gas that is given to someone before a medical operation to stop them feeling pain

anaesthetist /əˈniːsθətɪst/ noun [C] British a doctor who is trained to give people ANAESTHETICS

anaesthetize /əˈniːsθəˌtaɪz/ verb [T] to give someone an ANAESTHETIC so that they do not feel pain during a medical operation

anagram /ˈænəˌgræm/ noun [C] a word or phrase that you can form from another word or phrase by putting the letters in a different order

anal /ˈeɪn(ə)l/ adj relating to the ANUS

analogous /əˈnæləgəs/ adj formal similar to another situation, process etc

analogy /əˈnælədʒi/ noun [C/U] a comparison between two things that shows how they are similar: *He uses the analogy of the family to explain the role of the state.*

analyse /ˈænəˌlaɪz/ verb [T] to examine something in detail in order to understand or explain it: *Scientists analysed samples of leaves taken from the area.*

analysis /əˈnæləsɪs/ (plural **analyses** /əˈnæləsiːz/) noun ★
1 [C/U] the process of examining something in order to understand it, or to find out what it contains: *The blood samples have been sent away for analysis. ♦ The study included an analysis of accident statistics.*
2 [U] PSYCHOANALYSIS

PHRASE **in the final analysis** used for giving the facts that are most relevant in a

situation: *In the final analysis, it is up to the students to decide.*

analyst /ˈænəlɪst/ noun [C] **1** someone whose job is to carefully examine a situation, event etc in order to provide other people with information about it: *a stock market analyst* **2** a PSYCHOANALYST

analytical /ˌænəˈlɪtɪk(ə)l/ or **analytic** /ˌænəˈlɪtɪk/ adj examining a problem or issue by separating it into its different parts or aspects: *analytical skills* —**analytically** /ˌænəˈlɪtɪkli/ adv

analyze /ˈænəˌlaɪz/ the American spelling of analyse

anarchist /ˈænəkɪst/ noun [C] someone who believes that there should be no government or laws

anarchy /ˈænəki/ noun [U] a situation in which people ignore normal rules and laws, and are unable to be controlled

anathema /əˈnæθəmə/ noun [singular/U] formal something that you strongly dislike or strongly disagree with

anatomy /əˈnætəmi/ noun **1** [C] the body of a human or animal, or the structure of a plant **2** [U] the scientific study of the physical structure of an animal or plant —**anatomical** /ˌænəˈtɒmɪk(ə)l/ adj

ancestor /ˈænsestə/ noun [C] someone who lived a long time ago and is related to you —**ancestral** /ænˈsestrəl/ adj → DESCENDANT

ancestry /ˈænsestri/ noun [singular/U] your ancestors and family history: *His family was of Danish ancestry.*

anchor[1] /ˈæŋkə/ noun [C] **1** a heavy object that is dropped into the water to prevent a boat from moving **2** American a NEWSREADER

anchor[2] /ˈæŋkə/ verb **1** [I/T] to prevent a boat from moving by dropping its anchor into the water **2** [T] to fix something firmly somewhere

anchovy /ˈæntʃəvi/ noun [C/U] a type of small fish that tastes of salt and is often preserved in oil

ancient /ˈeɪnʃ(ə)nt/ adj ★★
1 very old: *an ancient city/book/tradition*
2 relating to a period of history a very long time ago: *the ancient Greeks/Britons/Egyptians*

and /weak ən, weak ənd, strong ænd/ grammar word ★★★

And can be:
■ a **conjunction**: *Rachel plays the piano and sings.*
■ a way of starting a new sentence and relating it to the previous sentence: *The telephone isn't working. And that's not the only problem.*

1 used for connecting words or phrases together: *the lakes and mountains of Scotland ♦ Everyone was singing and dancing. ♦ You cook the lunch, and I'll look after the children.*

When more than two words or phrases are joined in a list, **and** is used only between the last two: *She speaks German, French, Spanish, and English.*

2 used for showing that one thing happens after another: *He switched off the television and went to bed.*

3 used after verbs such as 'go', 'come', 'try', or 'wait', for showing what your purpose is: *I'll try and find out where we can buy tickets.* ♦ *Come and see our new kitchen.*
4 used for showing that one thing causes another: *He lied to us before, and now no one believes him.*
5 used for connecting words that are repeated for emphasis: *The situation is getting more and more complicated.* ♦ *I've tried and tried, but I can't understand it.*
6 *spoken* used in calculations for showing that numbers are added together: *Two and two is four.*
7 *spoken* used in numbers after the word 'hundred' or 'thousand', or between whole numbers and fractions: *a hundred and ten metres* ♦ *two and three quarters* (=2 ¾)

anecdotal /ˌænɪkˈdəʊt(ə)l/ adj based on someone's personal experience or on what they say rather than on facts that can be checked

anecdote /ˈænɪkˌdəʊt/ noun [C] a story that you tell people about something interesting or funny that has happened to you

anemia /əˈniːmiə/ an American spelling of **anaemia**

anesthetic /ˌænəsˈθetɪk/ an American spelling of **anaesthetic**

angel /ˈeɪndʒ(ə)l/ noun [C] **1** a spirit that in some religions is believed to live in heaven with God. In pictures, angels are shown as beautiful people with wings. **2** *spoken* a very kind person —**angelic** /ænˈdʒelɪk/ adj

anger¹ /ˈæŋgə/ noun [U] ★★ the strong feeling you get that makes you want to hurt someone or shout at them: *Some people express their anger through violence.*

anger² /ˈæŋgə/ verb [T] to make someone feel angry: *The school board's decision angered many students and parents alike.*

angle¹ /ˈæŋg(ə)l/ noun [C] ★★
1 the shape that is made where two lines or surfaces join each other: *An angle that measures 90 degrees is a right angle.*
2 the direction from which something comes, or the direction from which you look at something, especially when it is not directly in front of you: *Guns were firing at them from several different angles.*
3 a particular way of thinking about something: *We have considered the whole subject from many different angles.*
　PHRASE **at an angle** not straight, but leaning to one side: *Hold the knife at a slight angle.*

angle² /ˈæŋg(ə)l/ verb [T] to make something move or point in a direction that is not directly in front of you
　PHRASAL VERB **'angle for sth** *informal* to try to make someone give you something without asking for it directly: *She didn't want Ron thinking that she was angling for sympathy.*

Anglican /ˈæŋglɪkən/ noun [C] a Christian who is a member of the Church of England —**Anglican** adj

anglicize /ˈæŋglɪˌsaɪz/ verb [T] to make someone or something more English

angling /ˈæŋglɪŋ/ noun [U] the sport of catching fish —**angler** noun [C]

Anglo- /ˈæŋgləʊ/ prefix involving or related to England or the UK: *an Anglo-Russian trading agreement*

angry /ˈæŋgri/ adj ★★★ very annoyed: *There's no point in getting angry.* ♦ *His attitude makes me really angry.* ♦ *He is very angry about the way he's been treated.* ♦ *Are you angry with me?* ♦ +(that) *Anne was a little angry that no one told her about the party.* —**angrily** adv

angst /æŋst/ noun [U] a strong feeling of worry

anguish /ˈæŋgwɪʃ/ noun [U] *formal* a feeling of great physical or emotional pain: *The rejection filled him with anguish.* —**anguished** /ˈæŋgwɪʃt/ adj: *an anguished cry*

animal¹ /ˈænɪm(ə)l/ noun [C] ★★★
1 a living creature that is not a human, bird, fish, or insect: *lions, tigers, and other wild animals*
2 any living creature, including humans
3 *informal* someone who behaves in a very violent, cruel, or rude way

animal² /ˈænɪm(ə)l/ adj **1** relating to animals: *animal behaviour* **2** relating to people's basic physical needs such as food and sex: *animal instincts/urges/desires*

animated /ˈænɪˌmeɪtɪd/ adj **1** lively or active: *an animated conversation* **2** an animated film consists of a series of drawings that look as if they are moving

animation /ˌænɪˈmeɪʃ(ə)n/ noun [U]
1 ANIMATED films, or the process of making them **2** energy and excitement

animosity /ˌænɪˈmɒsəti/ noun [U] a strong feeling of disliking someone or something =HOSTILITY

ankle /ˈæŋk(ə)l/ noun [C] the part at the bottom of your leg where your foot joins your leg —*picture →* C14

annex¹ /əˈneks, ˈæneks/ verb [T] to take control of a country or region by force —**annexation** /ˌænekˈseɪʃ(ə)n/ noun [C/U]

annex² /ˈæneks/ noun [C] the American spelling of ANNEXE

annexe /ˈæneks/ noun [C] a building that is added to a larger building or is built next to it

annihilate /əˈnaɪəˌleɪt/ verb [T] to completely destroy or defeat a group of people or things —**annihilation** /əˌnaɪəˈleɪʃ(ə)n/ noun [U]

anniversary /ˌænɪˈvɜːs(ə)ri/ noun [C] a date when you celebrate something that happened in a previous year that is important to you: *a wedding anniversary* ♦ *the 10th anniversary of the end of the war*

announce /əˈnaʊns/ verb [T] ★
1 to make a public statement about a plan or decision: *There was a press release announcing the Senator's resignation.* ♦ +(that) *I am pleased to announce that the Board has agreed to our proposal.*
2 to tell people something clearly or loudly: +(that) *Bill suddenly announced he was taking the day off.*
3 to give information over a LOUDSPEAKER in a public place such as an airport: *When your flight is announced, make your way to the departure lounge.*

announcement /əˈnaʊnsmənt/ noun ★
1 [C] a public statement that gives people

information about something: *Observers expect the president to make an announcement about his plans tonight.* ♦ **+that** *Ms Baker stunned her fans with an announcement that she was quitting the music business.*
2 [U] the act of publicly stating something: *The announcement of Prince Charles' visit caused widespread media interest.*

annoy /əˈnɔɪ/ verb [T] to make someone feel slightly angry or impatient=IRRITATE: *I don't dislike her – she just annoys me sometimes.*

annoyance /əˈnɔɪəns/ noun **1** [U] a slightly angry or impatient feeling **2** [C] something that makes you feel slightly angry

annoyed /əˈnɔɪd/ adj ★★ feeling slightly angry or impatient: *We were all annoyed with him for forgetting.* ♦ **+(that)** *I was really annoyed that I hadn't been invited.*

annoying /əˈnɔɪɪŋ/ adj ★ making you feel slightly angry or impatient: *an annoying habit/problem* ♦ *What's really annoying is that we made the same mistake last time.*

annual /ˈænjuəl/ adj ★★
1 happening once a year=YEARLY: *an annual conference/festival/holiday*
2 calculated over a period of one year =YEARLY: *an annual salary*
—**annually** /ˈænjuəli/ adv

annul /əˈnʌl/ verb [T] to state officially that something such as a marriage or an agreement has no legal authority —**annulment** noun [C/U]

anomaly /əˈnɒməli/ noun [C] *formal* something unusual or unexpected

anonymity /ˌænəˈnɪməti/ noun [U] a situation in which the name of a person is not known or is kept secret

anonymous /əˈnɒnɪməs/ adj **1** if someone is anonymous, no one knows their name: *an anonymous caller* **2** done or written by someone whose name is not known: *an anonymous phone call/letter* —**anonymously** adv

anorak /ˈænəˌræk/ noun [C] *British* a short coat with a HOOD (=the part that covers your head)

anorexia /ˌænəˈreksiə/ noun [U] a serious illness that makes you want to stop eating. It mainly affects young women. → BULIMIA

anorexic /ˌænəˈreksɪk/ adj extremely thin and suffering from anorexia —**anorexic** noun [C]

another /əˈnʌðə/ grammar word ★★★

Another can be:
- a **determiner**: *Can I have another cup of tea, please?*
- a **pronoun**: *We're changing from one system to another.*

1 one more person or thing of the same type as before: *Peter's mum is expecting another baby in June.* ♦ *'These sandwiches are delicious.' 'Would you like another?'* ♦ *Another 2,000 nurses are needed in NHS hospitals.* ♦ *We're doing a big concert tomorrow night and another one on Saturday.* ♦ *They are having another of their parties.*
2 a different person or thing of the same type: *Isn't there another word that has the same meaning?* ♦ *Fatima's husband was working in another part of the country.* → ONE ANOTHER

answer¹ /ˈɑːnsə/ noun [C] ★★★
1 a spoken or written reply to something such as a question, a letter, or a telephone call: *I wrote to her in May but I never got an answer.* ♦ *I'll give you a definite answer tomorrow.* ♦ *The answer to your question is yes.*
2 a spoken or written reply to a question in a test or competition: *I'm sorry, but 'Paris' is the wrong answer.* ♦ *Do you know the answer to question 10?*
3 a way of dealing with a problem =SOLUTION: *There are no easy answers to this crisis.*

answer² /ˈɑːnsə/ verb [I/T] ★★★
1 to give a spoken or written reply to a question, letter etc: *Mark answered my letter right away.* ♦ *I'm still waiting for you to answer.* ♦ *What's the matter? Answer me!* ♦ *'I don't have it,' he answered truthfully.* ♦ **+that** *We asked him if he agreed with us, and he answered that he did.*
2 to come to the door when someone calls at your house, or to pick up the phone when it rings: *I knocked and a young man answered the door.*
3 to try to give the correct reply to a question in a test or competition: *Not everyone answered correctly.*

PHRASAL VERBS **answer for sth** to be responsible for explaining something that you have done: *You have to answer for any problems that happen during the show.*
answer to sb to have to explain to someone why you did something

answering machine /ˈɑːns(ə)rɪŋ məˌʃiːn/ noun [C] a machine that answers your telephone and records messages that people leave for you

answerphone /ˈɑːnsəfəʊn/ noun [C] *British* an ANSWERING MACHINE

ant /ænt/ noun [C] a small insect that lives under the ground in large organized groups —*picture* → C13

antagonism /ænˈtæɡəˌnɪz(ə)m/ noun [U] a strong feeling of disliking someone or of opposing something: *the growing antagonism between the two groups* —**antagonistic** /ænˌtæɡəˈnɪstɪk/ adj

antagonize /ænˈtæɡəˌnaɪz/ verb [T] to make someone feel angry with you and dislike you

Antarctic, the /ænˈtɑːktɪk/ the extremely cold region that is the most southern part of the world → ARCTIC

antelope /ˈæntɪˌləʊp/ noun [C] a brown animal with horns and long thin legs. It can run very fast.

antenatal /ˌæntiˈneɪt(ə)l/ adj *British* relating to the medical care of pregnant women, or to the time before a baby is born

antenna /ænˈtenə/ noun [C] **1** (plural **antennae** /ænˈteniː/) one of the two long thin parts on an insect's head that it uses to feel things with **2** *American* an AERIAL used for receiving radio and television signals

anthem /ˈænθəm/ noun [C] the official song of a particular country

A

anthology /ænˈθɒlədʒi/ noun [C] a book containing poems, stories, or songs that were written by different people

anthrax /ˈænθræks/ noun [U] a very serious illness that affects cows and sheep and sometimes people

anthropology /ˌænθrəˈpɒlədʒi/ noun [U] the study of human societies, customs, and beliefs —**anthropological** /ˌænθrəpəˈlɒdʒɪk(ə)l/ adj, **anthropologist** /ˌænθrəˈpɒlədʒɪst/ noun [C]

anti- /ænti/ prefix **1** opposing: *antiwar protesters* **2** with the opposite qualities: *an anti-hero* **3** preventing or curing: *antibacterial*

antibiotic /ˌæntibaɪˈɒtɪk/ noun [C] a drug that cures illnesses and infections caused by bacteria

antibody /ˈæntɪˌbɒdi/ noun [C] a substance in your blood that helps your body to fight illnesses and infections

anticipate /ænˈtɪsɪˌpeɪt/ verb [T] **1** to think that something will probably happen: *Organizers say they do not anticipate any difficulties.* ♦ *We anticipate that the river level will rise very slowly.* **2** to guess that something will happen, and be ready to deal with it: *The businesses that survive are those that anticipate changes in technology.*

anticipation /ænˌtɪsɪˈpeɪʃ(ə)n/ noun [U] a feeling of excitement about something enjoyable that is going to happen soon **PHRASE in anticipation of sth** if you do something in anticipation of an event, you do something to prepare for it

anticlimax /ˌæntiˈklaɪmæks/ noun [C] something that is not as exciting as you expected it to be

anticlockwise /ˌæntiˈklɒkwaɪz/ adj, adv British moving in the direction opposite to the direction of the hands of a clock

antics /ˈæntɪks/ noun [plural] behaviour that is funny or silly

antidepressant /ˌæntidɪˈpres(ə)nt/ noun [C] a drug that is used for treating someone who is DEPRESSED

antidote /ˈæntɪˌdəʊt/ noun [C] **1** a substance that prevents a poison from having bad effects **2** something that helps to improve the effects of something bad: *The game was a welcome antidote to the day's worries.*

antifreeze /ˈæntiˌfriːz/ noun [U] a chemical that you add to the water in a car engine to prevent it from freezing

antipathy /ænˈtɪpəθi/ noun [U] formal a strong feeling of not liking someone or something

Antipodes, the /ænˈtɪpədiːz/ British Australia and New Zealand —**Antipodean** /ænˌtɪpəˈdiən/ adj, noun [C]

antiquated /ˈæntɪˌkweɪtɪd/ adj too old or old-fashioned to be useful

antique /ænˈtiːk/ noun [C] an old valuable object such as a piece of furniture or jewellery

antiquity /ænˈtɪkwəti/ noun **1** [U] ancient times **2 antiquities** [plural] objects or buildings that existed in ancient times and still exist

anti-Semitic /ˌænti səˈmɪtɪk/ adj showing a feeling of hate towards Jewish people —**anti-Semitism** /ˌænti ˈseməˌtɪz(ə)m/ noun [U]

antiseptic /ˌæntiˈseptɪk/ noun [C/U] a substance that you use for cleaning injured skin and preventing infections —**antiseptic** adj

antisocial /ˌæntiˈsəʊʃ(ə)l/ adj **1** not interested in meeting other people or not enjoying friendly relationships with them **2** showing a lack of care for other people: *antisocial activities*

antithesis /ænˈtɪθəsɪs/ noun [singular] formal the exact opposite of something

antlers /ˈæntləz/ noun [plural] the horns on the head of a male DEER

antonym /ˈæntənɪm/ noun [C] a word that means the opposite of another word → SYNONYM

anus /ˈeɪnəs/ noun [C] the hole in your bottom through which you get rid of solid waste

anxiety /æŋˈzaɪəti/ noun **1** [U] a worried feeling that you have because you think that something bad might happen: *There was a lot of anxiety about the results of the talks.* **2** [C] something that you are worried about

anxious /ˈæŋkʃəs/ adj ★
1 worried because you think that something bad might happen: *His silence made me anxious.* ♦ *We had an anxious few moments while the results were announced.* ♦ *People are naturally anxious about these tests.*
2 wanting something very much and feeling nervous, excited, or impatient: *We were all anxious for peace.* ♦ **anxious to do sth** *We're anxious to hear from anyone who can help.* ♦ **+(that)** *They were anxious that everyone should enjoy themselves.*
—**anxiously** adv

any /ˈeni/ grammar word ★★★

Any can be:
■ a **determiner**: *Any intelligent child can use this software.*
■ a **pronoun**: *I needed milk, but there wasn't any.* ♦ *Have you read any of his books?*
■ an **adverb**: *Are you feeling any better?*

1 used instead of 'some' in negatives, questions, and conditional sentences: *Did you bring any warm clothes?* ♦ *He didn't do any work at all.* ♦ *I tried to get a ticket but there weren't any left.* ♦ *If you need any help, just let me know.* ♦ *Did any of her friends come?*

2 used when something is true for every person or thing in a group: *Pick any design you want – they're all the same price.* ♦ *It was the first time that any of us had been in a plane.*

3 in any way, or by any amount: *If your headache gets any worse, you should see a doctor.* ♦ *I was too tired to walk any further.*
PHRASES any day now or **any time now** or **any minute now** very soon: *He should be home any minute now.*

be any use/good used for saying or asking whether something is at all good or effective: *It isn't any use complaining – they never listen.*

not...any more/longer used for saying that a situation has ended: *The Campbells don't live here any more.*

A

anybody /'eni,bɒdi/ pronoun ★★★ anyone: *Would anybody like a cup of coffee? ♦ Is there anybody who doesn't understand?*

anyhow /'eni,haʊ/ adv ANYWAY

anymore /,eni'mɔː/ adv used when talking or asking about a situation that has ended: *Don't you love me anymore?*

anyone /'eni,wʌn/ pronoun ★★★
1 used instead of 'someone' in negatives, questions, and conditional sentences: *I don't know anyone here. ♦ Was there anyone at home? ♦ If anyone wants coffee, here it is. ♦ Is anyone else coming with us?*
2 used for referring to any person, when it does not matter which person, or when you do not know which person: *Anyone can make a mistake. ♦ You can invite anyone you like. ♦ Jackie knows more than anyone else about this.*

anything /'eni,θɪŋ/ pronoun ★★★
1 used instead of 'something' in negatives, questions, and conditional sentences: *Don't do anything stupid. ♦ He never does anything to help. ♦ Do you know anything about cricket? ♦ If anything happens, call me. ♦ Do you want anything else to eat?*
2 used when something is true for every thing in a group, or for every possible thing: *You can buy anything you want on the Internet. ♦ She would do anything for her children. ♦ Pigs will eat almost anything. ♦ Get me a sandwich – anything but cheese* (=anything except cheese).
PHRASES **anything like** used in questions or negatives to mean 'at all similar to': *Is Tom anything like his brother?*
...or anything *spoken* used for referring to a group of similar things without being specific: *I wasn't in any pain or anything.*

anytime /'eni,taɪm/ adv at any time: *You can come and see me anytime you like.*

anyway /'eni,weɪ/ adv *spoken* ★★★
1 used when you want to change the subject of a conversation, or end the conversation: *What are you doing here, anyway? ♦ Anyway, I have to go now.*
2 used for showing why something is not important, or is not a problem: *I don't understand politics, and anyway I'm not really interested. ♦ I'll get some bread – I was going to the shops anyway.*
3 despite something that you have previously mentioned: *It's illegal to park here, but people do it anyway.*
4 used for adding a statement that limits what you have just said: *It's something I can't tell you – not just now, anyway.*

anywhere /'eni,weə/ grammar word ★★

> **Anywhere** can be:
> ■ an adverb: *I'm not going anywhere today.*
> ■ a pronoun: *a village a long way from anywhere.*

1 used instead of 'somewhere' in negatives, questions, and conditional sentences: *He never travels anywhere without his camera. ♦ Have you seen Mike anywhere? ♦ If we go anywhere else, we'll let you know.*
2 used when something is true for every place, and it is not important which: *You can sit anywhere you like. ♦ A trained teacher can find work anywhere.*

3 used for saying that a number or amount is within a particular range: *The journey can take anywhere from 10 to 40 minutes.*
PHRASE **not be getting/going anywhere** to not be making any progress or achieving anything
→ NEAR[1]

apart /ə'pɑːt/ grammar word ★★★

> **Apart** can be:
> ■ an adverb: *We had to take the engine apart.*
> ■ used after the verb 'to be': *I'm never happy when we're apart.*
> ■ used in the preposition phrase **apart from**: *Everyone was there apart from Ann.*

1 at a distance away from each other, or away from someone or something else: *Stand with your feet apart. ♦ Their two farms are about a mile apart. ♦ Aitken and his wife are living apart. ♦ He doesn't like being apart from his family.*
2 broken or separated into different pieces: *The book came apart in my hands. ♦ I had to take the printer apart to fix it.*
3 used for saying how much time there is between events: *The two brothers were born six years apart.*
4 different from each other or from other people or things: *Our political views are not really very far apart. ♦ His style sets him apart from other writers.* → TELL SB/STH APART
PHRASE **apart from** not including someone or something: *Do you speak any languages apart from English?*

apartheid /ə'pɑːt,heɪt, ə'pɑːt,haɪt/ noun [U] the political system that existed in the past in South Africa, in which only white people had political rights and power

apartment /ə'pɑːtmənt/ noun [C] *American* ★ a FLAT for living in

apartment building or **apartment house** noun [C] *American* a BLOCK OF FLATS

apathetic /,æpə'θetɪk/ adj not interested in anything, or not enthusiastic about anything —**apathetically** /,æpə'θetɪkli/ adv

apathy /'æpəθi/ noun [U] a feeling of not being interested in anything or not enthusiastic about anything

ape /eɪp/ noun [C] a large monkey without a tail

aperitif /ə,perə'tiːf/ noun [C] an alcoholic drink that you have before a meal

aperture /'æpətʃə/ noun [C] *formal* a small hole or space

apex /'eɪpeks/ noun [C] the pointed top part of something

aphrodisiac /,æfrə'dɪziæk/ noun [C] a food, drink, or drug that makes people want to have sex

apiece /ə'piːs/ adv for each one: *Tickets were being sold for £20 apiece.*

apocalypse /ə'pɒkəlɪps/ noun [singular] **1** a time when the whole world will be destroyed **2** a situation in which many people die and many things are destroyed

apocalyptic /ə,pɒkə'lɪptɪk/ adj describing a time when very bad things will happen

apologetic /ə,pɒlə'dʒetɪk/ adj showing that you are sorry for doing something wrong —**apologetically** /ə,pɒlə'dʒetɪkli/ adv

A

apologise /əˈpɒləˌdʒaɪz/ a British spelling of apologize

apologize /əˈpɒləˌdʒaɪz/ verb [I] ★★ to tell someone that you are sorry for doing something wrong: *I apologize for taking so long to reply.* ♦ *You should apologize to your brother.*

apology /əˈpɒlədʒi/ noun [C] a statement that tells someone that you are sorry for doing something wrong: *They were kind enough to accept my apology.* ♦ *I think I owe you an apology.*

apostrophe /əˈpɒstrəfi/ noun [C] the symbol ' used in English to show the POSSESSIVE form of a noun, for example 'Bob's car', or to mark the place where a letter has been removed to make a word shorter, for example 'isn't'

appalled /əˈpɔːld/ adj offended or shocked: *I'm appalled that a doctor would behave like that.* —**appal** verb [T]

appalling /əˈpɔːlɪŋ/ adj extremely bad or shocking: *The conditions they live in are appalling.* ♦ *appalling weather*

apparatus /ˌæpəˈreɪtəs/ noun [U] equipment: *divers wearing underwater breathing apparatus*

apparent /əˈpærənt/ adj ★
1 easy to see or understand = OBVIOUS:
+(that) *It was apparent that the two women knew each other.* ♦ *It should be apparent to anyone that the letter was written by a child.*
2 an apparent quality, feeling, or situation seems to exist although it may not be real: *His apparent lack of interest in her work always annoyed her.*

apparently /əˈpærəntli/ adv ★
1 based only on what you have heard, not on what you are certain is true: *Apparently, she resigned because she had an argument with her boss.*
2 used for saying what seems to be true when people do not yet know all the facts of a situation: *Seven people were shot yesterday in two apparently unrelated incidents.*

apparition /ˌæpəˈrɪʃ(ə)n/ noun [C] *formal* a strange image or creature that someone sees

appeal¹ /əˈpiːl/ noun ★
1 [C] an urgent request for people to do something or give something: *There have been several appeals for an end to the fighting.* ♦ *The organization has launched an appeal to send food to the flood victims.*
2 [U] a quality that something has that makes people like it or want it: *How do you explain the appeal of horror films?* → SEX APPEAL
3 [C] a formal request for a court of law to change its decision

appeal² /əˈpiːl/ verb [I] ★
1 to make an urgent request for people to do something or give something: *appeal to sb to do sth She appealed to her former husband to return their baby son.* ♦ *appeal to sb for sth They're appealing to local businesses for money.*
2 if something appeals to you, you like it or want it: *The show's mixture of comedy and songs will appeal to children.*

3 to formally ask a court of law to change its decision: *Green's family say they will appeal against the verdict.*

appealing /əˈpiːlɪŋ/ adj attractive and interesting: *The building has an appealing old-fashioned charm.* ♦ *We've tried to make the design more appealing to young people.*

appear /əˈpɪə/ verb ★★★

1 seem	**4** be written/printed
2 begin to be seen	**5** be on TV etc
3 start to exist	

1 [linking verb] to make other people think that you are something, or that you feel something: *Matt appears unaffected by all the media attention.* ♦ *There appears to be very little we can do about the problem.* ♦ *It appears that she's changed her mind.* ♦ *appear to do sth No one appeared to notice me.*
2 [I] if someone or something appears somewhere, you see them suddenly or for the first time: *Cracks began to appear in the ceiling.*
3 [I] to start to exist, or to start to be available for the first time: *the latest Internet guide to appear on the market*
4 [I] to be written or printed somewhere: *Jane's name did not appear on the list.*
5 [I] to be on television or in a play, film, or concert: *She is currently appearing in a Broadway musical.*

appearance /əˈpɪərəns/ noun ★★★
1 [U] the way that someone or something looks: *The twins are almost identical in appearance.* ♦ *His thinning hair gave him the appearance of a much older man.* ♦ *He always gives the appearance of being very busy.*
2 [U] the time when something starts to exist, or starts to be seen: *the appearance of fast food restaurants on every high street*
3 [U] the fact that someone arrives somewhere: *She was startled by Julie's sudden appearance in the doorway.*
4 [C] an occasion when you are on television or in a play, film, or concert: *a public appearance* ♦ *She has made numerous appearances on TV game shows.*
PHRASE **put in/make an appearance** to go somewhere because you think that you should go there: *I think I ought to put in an appearance at the office before lunch.*

appease /əˈpiːz/ verb [T] to give someone what they want because you want to avoid arguing or fighting —**appeasement** noun [U]

appendicitis /əˌpendɪˈsaɪtɪs/ noun [U] an illness in which your appendix becomes infected and has to be removed

appendix /əˈpendɪks/ noun [C] **1** (plural **appendixes**) a small tube in your body near your stomach **2** (plural **appendices** /əˈpendɪsiːz/) an extra section at the end of a book

appetite /ˈæpətaɪt/ noun [C] ★
1 the natural feeling of wanting to eat: *a child with a healthy appetite* ♦ *Don't have any more chocolate – you'll spoil your appetite* (=make you want to eat less at the next meal).
2 a feeling of wanting something: *Young*

children have a natural **appetite for** stories.

appetizing /ˈæpəˌtaɪzɪŋ/ adj appetizing food smells or looks very good ≠ UNAPPETIZING

applaud /əˈplɔːd/ verb **1** [I/T] to show that you enjoyed someone's performance by hitting the palms of your hands together = CLAP **2** [T] to praise a decision or action

applause /əˈplɔːz/ noun [U] the sound made by people applauding: *Let's have a round of applause for all the organizers.*

apple /ˈæp(ə)l/ noun [C/U] ★★★ a hard round green or red fruit that is white inside and grows on trees —*picture* → C10

appliance /əˈplaɪəns/ noun [C] a piece of electrical equipment that you have in your home: *appliances such as washing machines and refrigerators*

applicable /əˈplɪkəb(ə)l/ adj relevant to a particular situation or group of people: *This section of the law is applicable only to businesses.*

applicant /ˈæplɪkənt/ noun [C] someone who applies for a job

application /ˌæplɪˈkeɪʃ(ə)n/ noun [C] ★★
1 a formal request to do something or have something, for example a job: *His application for membership was rejected.* ♦ **application to do sth** *her application to study at Columbia University*
2 a particular use that something has: *the practical applications of this technology*
3 *computing* a piece of computer software

appli'cation form noun [C] a printed list of questions that you answer as part of a formal request for something

apply /əˈplaɪ/ verb ★★★
1 [I] to make a formal request to do something or have something: *Students can **apply** for money to help with their living costs.* ♦ *You have to **apply to** the passport office for a visa.* ♦ **apply to do sth** *Bill is applying to join the fire service.*
2 [I] to be relevant to a particular person or thing: *The rule no longer **applies to** him, because he's over 18.*
3 [T] to use something: **apply sth to sth** *A similar technique can be applied to the treatment of cancer.*
4 [T] to put a layer of something such as paint onto a surface

appoint /əˈpɔɪnt/ verb [T] ★★ to choose someone to do a particular job: *We need to appoint a new school secretary.*

appointment /əˈpɔɪntmənt/ noun ★★★
1 [C/U] an arrangement to see someone, for example a doctor, at a particular time: *Why don't you **make an appointment with** one of our nurses?* ♦ **appointment to do sth** *I have an appointment to see my lawyer next Saturday.*
2 [C] a job: *academic appointments*
3 [U] the decision to give someone a job: *his appointment as governor of Hong Kong*

appreciable /əˈpriːʃəb(ə)l/ adj enough to be noticed: *an appreciable improvement in the student's test scores* —**appreciably** adv

appreciate /əˈpriːʃieɪt/ verb ★★
1 [T] to understand a situation and know why it is important or serious = REALIZE: **+how/why/where etc** *Doctors are beginning to appreciate how dangerous this drug can*

be. ♦ **+that** *We appreciate that you cannot make a decision immediately.*
2 [T] to be grateful for something: *I really appreciate all your help.*
3 [T] to realize that someone or something has good qualities: *She feels that her family doesn't really appreciate her.*
4 [I] to increase in value ≠ DEPRECIATE

PHRASE **I/we etc would appreciate it if...** *spoken* used for politely asking someone to do something: *We'd appreciate it if you didn't smoke in here.*

appreciation /əˌpriːʃiˈeɪʃ(ə)n/ noun **1** [U] the feeling of being grateful: *The award is given in appreciation of her huge contribution to the film industry.* **2** [U] the ability to understand a situation and know why it is important or serious: *Most people have no appreciation of the dangers involved in the process.* **3** [singular/U] pleasure that comes from understanding something good or beautiful: *We share an appreciation of music.*

appreciative /əˈpriːʃətɪv/ adj showing that you are grateful, or that you enjoyed something: *an appreciative audience* —**appreciatively** adv

apprehension /ˌæprɪˈhenʃ(ə)n/ noun [C/U] a feeling of worry that something bad might happen = ANXIETY

apprehensive /ˌæprɪˈhensɪv/ adj slightly worried or nervous —**apprehensively** adv

apprentice /əˈprentɪs/ noun [C] someone who is learning how to do a particular job

apprenticeship /əˈprentɪsʃɪp/ noun [C/U] the time when someone works as an apprentice

approach¹ /əˈprəʊtʃ/ noun ★★
1 [C] a way of dealing with something: *He has a relaxed **approach to** life.*
2 [singular] the fact that something is coming closer in time or in distance: *the approach of war*
3 [C] the action of asking for something, or of offering something formally: *The company has **made** some **approaches to** the government.*
4 [C] a path or road: *All approaches to the palace have been closed by the police.*

approach² /əˈprəʊtʃ/ verb ★★
1 [I/T] to move closer in distance or time: *She heard footsteps approaching from behind.* ♦ *A strange boat was approaching the shore.* ♦ *The day of the election approached.*
2 [T] to formally ask someone for something, or formally offer something: **approach sb about sth** *I have already approached my boss about a pay rise.*
3 [T] to almost reach a particular level or condition: *They played in temperatures approaching 40 degrees.*
4 [T] to deal with a situation in a particular way: *There are several ways of approaching this problem.*

approachable /əˈprəʊtʃəb(ə)l/ adj friendly and easy to talk to ≠ UNAPPROACHABLE

appropriate /əˈprəʊpriət/ adj ★★ suitable for a particular situation ≠ INAPPROPRIATE: *This isn't the appropriate time to discuss the problem.* —**appropriately** adv

approval /əˈpruːv(ə)l/ noun [U] ★
1 a positive opinion about someone or

A

something ≠ DISAPPROVAL: *Children are constantly looking for signs of approval from their parents.*
2 official permission: *The government has not yet given the scheme its approval.*

approve /əˈpruːv/ verb ★
1 [I] to think that someone or something is good ≠ DISAPPROVE: *You're leaving college! Do your parents approve? ♦ He seemed to approve of my choice. ♦* **approve of sb doing sth** *I don't really approve of children wearing make-up.*
2 [T] to give official permission for something: *The new stamps were personally approved by the Queen.*

Word family: **approve**

*Words in the same family as **approve***
- **approval** *n*
- **approving** *adj*
- **disapprove** *v*
- **disapproval** *n*
- **disapproving** *adj*

approving /əˈpruːvɪŋ/ adj showing that you like someone or something ≠ DISAPPROVING: *an approving smile* —**approvingly** adv
approximate /əˈprɒksɪmət/ adj not exact, but close to an exact amount or number: *the approximate cost of the repairs*
approximately /əˈprɒksɪmətli/ adv ★ used for showing that an amount or number is not exact=ROUGHLY: *Approximately 60,000 people filled the stadium. ♦ We have approximately 300 copies left.*
apricot /ˈeɪprɪˌkɒt/ noun [C] a fruit with an orange-yellow skin and a large hard seed inside —*picture →* C10
April /ˈeɪprəl/ noun [C/U] ★★★ the fourth month of the year, between March and May: *Her birthday is in April. ♦ My appointment is on 8th April.*
apron /ˈeɪprən/ noun [C] something that you wear to protect the front of your clothes when you are cooking
apt /æpt/ adj very suitable: *It seemed apt that the winning goal was scored by the captain.*
  PHRASE **be apt to do sth** to have a tendency to do something
  —**aptly** adv
aptitude /ˈæptɪˌtjuːd/ noun [C/U] natural ability that makes it easy for you to do something well: *an aptitude for maths*
aquarium /əˈkweəriəm/ noun [C] **1** a glass container for fish and other water animals **2** a building with aquariums in it
Aquarius /əˈkweəriəs/ noun [U] one of the 12 signs of the ZODIAC. An **Aquarius** or **Aquarian** is someone who is born between 20 January and 19 February.
aquatic /əˈkwætɪk/ adj living in or near water: *aquatic birds*
Arab /ˈærəb/ noun [C] someone from the Middle East or North Africa who speaks Arabic —**Arab** adj
Arabic /ˈærəbɪk/ noun [U] the language that most people speak in the Middle East and North Africa —**Arabic** adj
arbiter /ˈɑːbɪtə/ noun [C] **1** someone who has the official power to settle disagreements **2** someone whose opinions about art, fashion, food etc have a lot of influence
arbitrary /ˈɑːbɪtrəri/ adj not done for any

particular reason and therefore often unfair: *an arbitrary decision* —**arbitrarily** /ˈɑːbɪtrərəli, ˌɑːbɪˈtreərəli/ adv
arbitration /ˌɑːbɪˈtreɪʃ(ə)n/ noun [U] the official process of trying to settle a disagreement —**arbitrate** /ˈɑːbɪˌtreɪt/ verb [I], **arbitrator** /ˈɑːbɪˌtreɪtə/ noun [C]
arc /ɑːk/ noun [C] a curved shape, or a curved line
arcade /ɑːˈkeɪd/ noun [C] **1** an AMUSEMENT ARCADE **2** a covered area with shops on both sides
arch¹ /ɑːtʃ/ noun [C] **1** a shape or structure with straight sides and a curved top. The curved top part is also called an arch. **2** the curved bottom part of your foot
arch² /ɑːtʃ/ verb [T] to make something curve: *The cat arched its back.*
archaeologist /ˌɑːkiˈɒlədʒɪst/ noun [C] someone who studies archaeology
archaeology /ˌɑːkiˈɒlədʒi/ noun [U] the study of ancient societies, done by looking at old bones, buildings, and other objects —**archaeological** /ˌɑːkiəˈlɒdʒɪk(ə)l/ adj
archaic /ɑːˈkeɪɪk/ adj old and no longer used or useful
archbishop /ɑːtʃˈbɪʃəp/ noun [C] a priest of the highest rank in some Christian churches
archeologist /ˌɑːkiˈɒlədʒɪst/ an American spelling of **archaeologist**
archeology /ˌɑːkiˈɒlədʒi/ an American spelling of **archaeology**
archery /ˈɑːtʃəri/ noun [U] the sport of shooting ARROWS from a BOW —**archer** noun [C]
archetypal /ˌɑːkɪˈtaɪp(ə)l/ adj very typical of a particular type of person or thing
architect /ˈɑːkɪˌtekt/ noun [C] someone whose job is to design buildings
architecture /ˈɑːkɪˌtektʃə/ noun [U] **1** a particular style of building: *The church is a typical example of Gothic architecture.* **2** the study or practice of designing buildings —**architectural** /ˌɑːkɪˈtektʃ(ə)rəl/ adj
archive /ˈɑːkaɪv/ noun [C] **1** a collection of historical documents, or the place where it is kept **2** *computing* a collection of computer files that have been saved together in COMPRESSED form
archway /ˈɑːtʃweɪ/ noun [C] a curved roof over an entrance or passage
Arctic, the /ˈɑːktɪk/ the cold region that is the most northern part of the world —**Arctic** adj → ANTARCTIC
ardent /ˈɑːd(ə)nt/ adj feeling a particular emotion very strongly: *ardent supporters of the president* —**ardently** adv
arduous /ˈɑːdjuəs/ adj extremely difficult and involving a lot of effort
are /weak ə, strong ɑː/ *see* be
area /ˈeəriə/ noun ★★★
1 [C] a part of a place or building: *Bus services in rural areas are not very good. ♦ The hotel has a spacious and comfortable reception area. ♦ My family has lived in this area of England for years.*
2 [C] a particular subject or type of activity: *His area of expertise is engineering. ♦ What is your main area of concern?*
3 [C] a place on the surface of something,

A

for example on a part of your body: *sensitive areas of your skin*
4 [U] the amount of space that the surface of a place or shape covers: *The screen has a large surface area.*

area code noun [C] a series of numbers that you have to DIAL when you are making a telephone call to someone in a different area

arena /əˈriːnə/ noun [C] **1** a large area surrounded by seats, used for sports or entertainment **2** the people and activities that are involved with a particular subject: *Today, businesses must be able to compete in the international arena.*

aren't /ɑːnt/ short form **1** the usual way of saying 'are not': *We aren't going to Spain this year.* **2** the usual way of saying 'am not' in questions: *I'm looking thinner, aren't I?*

arguable /ˈɑːgjuəb(ə)l/ adj **1** *formal* if a fact or statement is arguable, there is evidence that it may be true: *It is arguable that we should have sold the company at that point.* **2** not clearly true or correct: *Whether good students make good teachers is arguable.*

arguably /ˈɑːgjuəbli/ adv used for stating your opinion or belief, especially when you think that other people may disagree: *Ali was arguably the best boxer of all time.*

No, it isn't!   Yes, it is!

argue

argue /ˈɑːgjuː/ verb ★★★
1 [I] to discuss something that you disagree about, usually in an angry way =QUARREL: *Those girls are always arguing!* ♦ *Don't argue with me – you know I'm right.* ♦ *We used to argue about who should drive.*
2 [I/T] to give reasons why you believe that something is right or true: *Woolf's report argued for* (=supported) *an improvement in prison conditions.* ♦ *Several people stood up to argue against* (=to oppose) *moving the students to the new school.* ♦ *+that Reuben opposed the new road, arguing that it wasn't worth $25 million.*

Words often used with argue

Adverbs often used with argue (sense 2)

■ ARGUE + **convincingly, forcefully, persuasively, plausibly**: used for saying that someone's arguments convince people

■ ARGUE + **passionately, strongly**: used for saying that someone's beliefs are strong

argument /ˈɑːgjəmənt/ noun ★★★
1 [C] an angry disagreement between people =QUARREL: *The decision led to a heated argument* (=extremely angry disagreement). ♦ *My girlfriend and I have*

had an argument. ♦ *Every time we visit my family, he gets into an argument with my sister.* ♦ *I try to avoid arguments about money.*
2 [C/U] a set of reasons that you use for persuading people to support your opinion: *There are powerful arguments against releasing them from prison.* ♦ *You could make an argument for working shorter hours.*

argumentative /ˌɑːgjʊˈmentətɪv/ adj often arguing or disagreeing with people

arid /ˈærɪd/ adj very dry with few plants

Aries /ˈeəriːz/ noun [C/U] one of the 12 signs of the ZODIAC. An **Aries** is someone who is born between 21 March and 20 April.

arise /əˈraɪz/ (past tense **arose** /əˈrəʊz/; past participle **arisen** /əˈrɪz(ə)n/) verb [I] to begin to exist or develop: *Problems arose over plans to build a new supermarket here.* ♦ *We can have another meeting if the need arises.*

aristocracy /ˌærɪˈstɒkrəsi/ noun [C] the people in the highest class of society, who usually have money, land, and power and who often have special titles

aristocrat /ˈærɪstəˌkræt/ noun [C] a member of the aristocracy —**aristocratic** /ˌærɪstəˈkrætɪk/ adj

arithmetic /əˈrɪθmətɪk/ noun [U] the part of mathematics that involves basic calculations such as adding or multiplying numbers

arm¹ /ɑːm/ noun [C] ★★★
1 one of the two long parts of your body with your hands at the end: *I put my arm around his shoulders.* ♦ *She was holding the baby in her arms.* ♦ *Jim was carrying a parcel under his arm.* ♦ *She folded her arms across her chest.* ♦ *Lovers were strolling by arm in arm.* —picture → C14
2 the part of a chair that you rest your arm on when you are sitting in it
3 a part of an organization that deals with a particular subject or activity: *the insurance arm of a major bank*
PHRASES **at arm's length 1** held away from your body with your arm stretched out straight: *He held the baby out at arm's length.* **2** in a situation where you avoid becoming involved with someone else: *She never gives interviews, and tends to keep the media at arm's length.*
up in arms angry and complaining about something: *Residents are up in arms about the closure of the local library.*
→ ARMS, OPEN¹

arm² /ɑːm/ verb [T] to provide someone with weapons

armaments /ˈɑːməmənts/ noun [plural] weapons and military equipment used by the armed forces

armband /ˈɑːmˌbænd/ noun [C] **1** *British* a plastic ring that is filled with air, worn around each arm by people learning to swim **2** a small piece of cloth that you wear around one arm

armchair /ˈɑːmˌtʃeə/ noun [C] a large comfortable chair with parts for you to rest your arms on —picture → CHAIR¹

armed /ɑːmd/ adj ★★
1 carrying a weapon, or involving the use

of weapons: *armed robbery* ♦ *a bank robber armed with a shotgun*

2 armed with sth having useful or impressive equipment, information etc: *a group of reporters armed with long-lens cameras*

armed 'forces, the noun [plural] a country's army, navy, and air force

armful /ˈɑːmfʊl/ noun [C] the amount of something that you can carry in your arms

armistice /ˈɑːmɪstɪs/ noun [C] a formal agreement to stop fighting a war
→ CEASEFIRE

armour /ˈɑːmə/ noun [U] metal clothing that soldiers wore in the past to protect their bodies

armoured /ˈɑːməd/ adj an armoured vehicle is covered with layers of hard metal to protect it from attack

armpit /ˈɑːm.pɪt/ noun [C] the part of your body that is under your arm, where your arm joins your shoulder

arms /ɑːmz/ noun [plural] weapons such as guns or bombs: *the international arms trade*

arms con'trol noun [U] agreements between countries to reduce or limit the number of weapons in the world

arms ,race noun [C] competition between countries to increase the number or power of their weapons

army /ˈɑːmi/ noun [C] ★★★
1 a large organization of soldiers who are trained to fight wars on land: *Both of her sons are in the army.* ♦ *an army officer/colonel*
2 a large group of people who are doing the same thing or are in the same situation: *Armies of rescue workers are sorting through the rubble.*

aroma /əˈrəʊmə/ noun [C] a smell that is strong but nice —**aromatic** /ˌærəˈmætɪk/ adj

aromatherapy /əˌrəʊməˈθerəpi/ noun [U] a health treatment in which oils with a nice smell are used to make you feel relaxed —**aromatherapist** /əˌrəʊməˈθerəpɪst/ noun [C]

arose the past tense of **arise**

around /əˈraʊnd/ grammar word ★★★

Around can be:
■ a preposition: *We walked around the old town.*
■ an adverb: *She turned around and smiled at me.*
■ used after the verb 'to be': *Don't discuss this when the children are around.*

1 in or to many places in or to many different parts or areas: *We drove around looking for a hotel.* ♦ *I glanced around the room, but I couldn't see him.* ♦ *The Games were watched by millions of people around the world.*
2 in the opposite direction moving so that you face in the opposite direction: *I turned around to see what the noise was.*
3 to the other side to the other side of something: *At that moment a truck came around the corner.*
4 in a place in or close to a place: *the quiet country roads around Chester* ♦ *There's a phone around here somewhere.* ♦ *Is your wife around? I'd like to talk to her.*
5 moving in circles moving in a circular

way: *The Earth goes around the Sun.* ♦ *The wheels spun around.*
6 surrounding sth surrounding or enclosing something: *Arrange the chairs around the table.* ♦ *a cottage with woods all around* ♦ *Sam had his arm around Mandy's waist.*
7 not exact used for giving a number, amount, or time that is not exact
=APPROXIMATELY: *There must have been around 500 people there.* ♦ *We got back at around 11.*
8 doing nothing useful spending time not doing anything important or useful: *We got tired of waiting around.*
9 existing now available or existing at this time: *There are some really good new video games around.* ♦ *It's one of the biggest shopping centres around.*

arouse /əˈraʊz/ verb [T] **1** to cause an emotion or attitude: *These rumours have aroused interest among investors.* **2** to make someone feel sexually excited

arrange /əˈreɪndʒ/ verb [T] ★★★
1 to make plans for something to happen, and to manage the details of it: *I'm trying to arrange a meeting with the sales director.* ♦ *Who's arranging the wedding?* ♦ **arrange to do sth** *They arranged to go swimming the following day.* ♦ **arrange for sb/sth to do sth** *Please arrange for a taxi to pick me up at six.*
2 to put things in a neat, attractive, or useful order: *Here is the list arranged chronologically.* ♦ *We'll need to arrange the chairs around the table.*

arrangement /əˈreɪndʒmənt/ noun ★★★
1 arrangements [plural] practical plans for organizing and managing the details of something: *sleeping/seating arrangements* ♦ *Her husband is away, so she'll have to make other childcare arrangements.*
2 [C] an agreement or plan that you make with someone else: *They have an arrangement with Pepsi-Cola to share distribution facilities.*
3 [C/U] a set of things that have been arranged to look attractive, or the way that they have been arranged: *a floral arrangement*

array /əˈreɪ/ noun [C] a large group of people or things that are related in some way: *a dazzling array of products*

arrears /əˈrɪəz/ noun **in arrears** late in making a regular payment: *We are writing to inform you that your mortgage payment is a month in arrears.*

arrest¹ /əˈrest/ verb [T] ★★
1 if the police arrest someone, they take that person to a police station because they think that he or she has committed a crime: *Police raided the building and arrested six men.* ♦ **arrest sb for sth** *He was arrested for possession of illegal drugs.*
2 *formal* to stop a process or bad situation from continuing or developing: *A cut in interest rates failed to arrest the decline in prices.*

arrest² /əˈrest/ noun [C/U] a situation in which the police arrest someone: *The information led to the arrest of three suspects.* ♦ *Six men*

A

are under arrest in connection with the drug smuggling operation. ♦ *We hope to make an arrest in the near future.* → CARDIAC ARREST, HOUSE ARREST

arrival /ə'raɪv(ə)l/ noun ★★
1 [singular/U] the time when someone or something arrives at a place from somewhere else: *Her arrival livened up the party.* ♦ *The arrival of BA 106 from Boston has been delayed.*
2 [U] the time when something begins: *the arrival of spring*
3 [C] someone who has arrived or who has joined a group

arrive /ə'raɪv/ verb [I] ★★★
1 to reach a place: *What time does your plane arrive?* ♦ *A letter arrived for you this morning.* ♦ *Four police officers suddenly arrived at their house.*
2 to happen, or to begin to exist: *Society changed forever when television arrived.* ♦ *The baby arrived* (=was born) *earlier than we expected.*

PHRASAL VERB ar'rive at sth to reach a result, decision, or solution to a problem: *The two studies arrive at very different conclusions.*

- You **arrive in** a town or country, and you **arrive at** a building or place: *What time will she arrive in New York?* ♦ *He arrived at the airport early.*
- You can also say that you **reach** or **get to** a town, country, or building. **Reach** is more formal than **get to**: *The ambulance took 30 minutes to reach the hospital.* ♦ *I'll call you when I get to my hotel.*

arrogant /'ærəgənt/ adj someone who is arrogant thinks that they are better or more important than other people —**arrogance** /'ærəgəns/ noun [U], **arrogantly** adv

arrow /'ærəʊ/ noun [C] **1** a weapon in the form of a thin straight stick with a sharp point at one end and feathers at the other. It is fired using a **bow. 2** a sign that looks like an arrow →, used for showing people where to go or look

arsenal /'ɑːsn(ə)l/ noun [C] a large collection of weapons

arsenic /'ɑːsnɪk/ noun [U] a strong poison

arson /'ɑːs(ə)n/ noun [U] the crime of deliberately burning a building —**arsonist** noun [C]

art /ɑːt/ noun ★★★

1 beautiful objects	**4** film, theatre etc
2 painting, drawing etc	**5** special skills
3 non-scientific subjects	

1 [U] paintings, drawings, and other objects that are created in order to be beautiful or interesting: *Do you like modern art?* ♦ *the art of ancient Mexico*
2 [U] the activity or study of creating paintings, drawings, and other objects that are beautiful or interesting → WORK²
3 arts [plural] subjects of study that are not scientific, such as history, literature, and languages: *the Faculty of Arts*
4 the arts [plural] activities such as art, music, film, theatre, and dance
5 [C] an activity that needs special skill: *the art of letter-writing*

artefact /'ɑːtɪˌfækt/ noun [C] an interesting object from the past

artery /'ɑːtəri/ noun [C] **1** one of the tubes in your body that carries blood from your heart to the rest of your body → VEIN **2** an important road, railway, or river —**arterial** /ɑː'tɪəriəl/ adj

arthritis /ɑː'θraɪtɪs/ noun [U] a serious medical condition that makes your JOINTS swollen and painful —**arthritic** /ɑː'θrɪtɪk/ adj

artichoke /'ɑːtɪˌtʃəʊk/ noun [C/U] a round green vegetable with layers of thick pointed leaves

article /'ɑːtɪk(ə)l/ noun [C] ★★★
1 a piece of writing in a newspaper or magazine: *He has written several articles for* The Times. ♦ *an article on/about women in politics*
2 an object: *The shop sells small household articles.* ♦ *an article of clothing*
3 linguistics a type of word that is used before a noun. The **indefinite article** in English is 'a' or 'an' and the **definite article** is 'the'.

articulate¹ /ɑː'tɪkjʊlət/ adj someone who is articulate speaks very well because they use words effectively ≠ INARTICULATE —**articulately** adv

articulate² /ɑː'tɪkjʊleɪt/ verb **1** [T] to use words effectively to express your ideas **2** [I/T] to say words clearly —**articulation** /ɑːˌtɪkjʊ'leɪʃ(ə)n/ noun [U]

articulated lorry /ɑː'tɪkjʊleɪtɪd ˌlɒri/ noun [C] British a large truck that consists of two separate parts joined together

artifact /'ɑːtɪˌfækt/ another spelling of artefact

artificial /ˌɑːtɪ'fɪʃ(ə)l/ adj ★
1 not natural or real, but made by people: *The growers use both natural and artificial light.* ♦ *artificial flowers/fur/snow* ♦ *The product contains no artificial colours or flavours.*
2 not sincere=FALSE: *an artificial laugh* —**artificially** /ˌɑːtɪ'fɪʃəli/ adv

artificial in'telligence noun [U] the use of computer technology to make computers and machines think like people

artillery /ɑː'tɪləri/ noun [U] large powerful guns that soldiers use

artisan /ˌɑːtɪ'zæn/ noun [C] someone who uses traditional skills and tools to make things

artist /'ɑːtɪst/ noun [C] ★★
1 someone who creates paintings or other objects that are beautiful or interesting
2 a professional performer in music, dance, or the theatre

artiste /ɑː'tiːst/ noun [C] a singer, dancer, or other professional entertainer

artistic /ɑː'tɪstɪk/ adj **1** good at drawing and painting: *You don't need to be very artistic to produce great designs.* **2** relating to painting, music, or other forms of art: *high artistic standards* —**artistically** /ɑː'tɪstɪkli/ adv

artistry /'ɑːtɪstri/ noun [U] great skill

artwork /'ɑːtˌwɜːk/ noun [U] **1** paintings, drawings, and other objects that artists create **2** the pictures or photographs in a book or magazine

arty /'ɑːti/ adj very enthusiastic about art, in a way that might not be sincere

A

as /*weak* əz, *strong* æz/ grammar word ★★★

As can be:
■ a **conjunction**: *As I was leaving, the phone rang.*
■ a **preposition**: *He works as a waiter.*
■ an **adverb**: *I'm as fast as you.*

1 used in comparisons used for comparing one person, thing, or situation with another: *Simon isn't as tall as his brother.* ♦ *I don't play football as much as I used to.* ♦ *There were twice as many visitors as last weekend.* ♦ *We need to collect as much information as possible.* ♦ *Barbara's hair looks exactly the same as mine.* ♦ *We all need exercise, but a healthy diet is just as* (=equally) *important.* → LESS
2 used for referring to what is known used for referring to something that has already been talked about: *As you know, Jack is leaving next month.*
3 in a particular way happening or done in a particular way: *Leave everything just as you found it.* ♦ *I invested the money as you suggested.* ♦ *Judith was late, as usual.*
4 saying what sb/sth is used when you are saying what someone or something is or does: *As a parent, you naturally want the best for your children.* ♦ *a portrait of the princess as a child* ♦ *An electric drill can also be used as a screwdriver.*
5 saying how sb/sth is considered considered or described in a particular way: *Van Dyck was regarded as the greatest painter of his time.* ♦ *Madeira is described as having the best climate in the world.*
6 when or while happening at the same time as something else: *As we were sitting down to dinner, the phone rang.* ♦ *We got to the check-in desk just as they were about to close.* ♦ *I'm ready to go out as soon as it stops raining.*
7 because used for giving a reason for something: *As it was getting late, we decided to go home.*

PHRASES as for used for introducing a subject that is related to what you have just been talking about: *As for me, I went home and left them to get on with it.*
as if or **as though 1** in such a way that something seems to be true: *It looks as if it's going to rain.* ♦ *Jack smiled as though he knew the answer.* **2** used when you imagine an explanation for something that you know is not the real one: *My car looked as if an elephant had sat on it.*
as it is already: *I've got enough problems as it is.*
as to *formal* concerning: *There is some doubt as to his true identity.*
→ YET

asap /ˌeɪ es eɪ ˈpiː, ˈeɪsæp/ as soon as possible: *I want those files on my desk asap.*
asbestos /æsˈbestəs/ noun [U] a substance that was used in buildings in the past. You get very ill if you breathe the dust from it.
ascend /əˈsend/ verb [I/T] *formal* to go upwards, or to climb something ≠ DESCEND
ascendancy /əˈsendənsi/ noun [U] the advantage, power, or influence that one person or group has over another: *the party's political ascendancy*

ascent /əˈsent/ noun **1** [C/U] the process of climbing or of going upwards ≠ DESCENT: *the plane's ascent to 35,000 feet* **2** [C] a path that goes up a hill **3** [C/U] the process of becoming more important or famous
ascertain /ˌæsəˈteɪn/ verb [T] *formal* to find out something: *Police are trying to ascertain the facts of the case.*
ascribe /əˈskraɪb/ **PHRASAL VERB** **a**ˈscribe sth to sth *formal* to believe that something is the cause of something else: *Their defeat was ascribed to a poor defence.*
asexual /eɪˈsekʃuəl/ adj **1** an asexual animal has no sex organs **2** not interested in sex
ash /æʃ/ noun **1** [U] the grey powder that remains after something has burned **2** [C] a tree with a smooth grey BARK **3 ashes** [plural] the substance that remains after a person's body has been CREMATED (=burned after death)
ashamed /əˈʃeɪmd/ adj feeling guilty or embarrassed about something that you have done: *He's extremely ashamed of his behaviour last night.*
PHRASE ashamed of sb disappointed and upset by someone else's behaviour: *I'm ashamed of you – lying to your teacher!*
ashore /əˈʃɔː/ adv onto land from the sea: *He quickly rowed ashore.*
ashtray /ˈæʃˌtreɪ/ noun [C] a small container for ASH and cigarettes that are smoked
Asian /ˈeɪʒ(ə)n, ˈeɪʃ(ə)n/ adj **1** of or from the countries in East and Southeast Asia, such as China, Japan, Thailand, or Korea **2** *British* of or from the countries of South Asia (India, Pakistan, Bangladesh, and Sri Lanka) —**Asian** noun [C]
aside¹ /əˈsaɪd/ adv ★
PHRASES aside from except for: *Aside from hanging about in the street, there's nothing for kids to do here.*
leave sth aside to deliberately not consider something: *Let's leave aside the issue of money.*
move/step aside to move away from someone or something: *Helen stepped aside to let him pass.*
set/put sth aside to keep something such as time or money for a particular purpose: *Try to set aside half an hour every day for something you really enjoy doing.*
aside² /əˈsaɪd/ noun [C] a remark about something that is not the main subject of your discussion
ask /ɑːsk/ verb ★★★
1 [I/T] to speak to someone in order to get information from them: *I wondered who had given her the ring but was afraid to ask.* ♦ *The police wanted to ask us a few questions.* ♦ **ask (sb) why/how/whether etc** *She asked me how I knew about it.* ♦ **ask (sb) about sth** *Did you ask about the money?*
2 [I/T] to speak to someone because you want them to give you something, or do something for you: *If you need any help, just ask.* ♦ *Can I ask you a favour?* ♦ **ask (sb) for sth** *The children were asking for drinks.* ♦ **ask sb to do sth** *He asked us to move over a little.* ♦ **ask to do sth** *I asked to see the manager.* ♦ **ask (sb) if/whether** *Ask if we can go backstage.*

3 [T] to invite someone to do something, or to go somewhere with you: *We waited for half an hour before he asked us in* (=invited us to come inside). ♦ **ask sb to do sth** *They asked me to stay the night.*

4 [T] to expect someone to do something, or to give you something: *It's a nice house, but they're asking over half a million pounds.*

PHRASES **be asking for it/trouble** to behave in a way that makes something bad likely to happen: *She's asking for trouble if she speaks to the boss like that.*

don't ask me *spoken* used for telling someone that you do not know the answer to their question, when you are annoyed or surprised that they have asked you

if you ask me *spoken* used before you give someone your opinion about something: *If you ask me, she doesn't really want the job.*

PHRASAL VERB **ask sb 'out** to invite someone to go somewhere with you because you want to start a romantic relationship with them

askew /əˈskjuː/ adj not as straight as it should be

asleep /əˈsliːp/ adj ★★ not awake: *The children are fast asleep* (=sleeping deeply). ♦ *She was so tired she fell asleep* (=began sleeping) *in her chair.*

asparagus /əˈspærəgəs/ noun [U] a long thin green vegetable with pointed ends —*picture* → C11

aspect /ˈæspekt/ noun [C] ★★ a particular part, feature, or quality of something: *This chapter covers several important aspects of the teaching process.* ♦ *The Internet affects every aspect of our business.*

aspersions /əˈspɜːʃ(ə)nz/ noun **cast aspersions (on)** to criticize someone or something

asphalt /ˈæsfælt/ noun [U] a black sticky substance that is used for making the surface of a road

asphyxiate /æsˈfɪksiˌeɪt/ verb [I/T] to kill someone by preventing them from breathing, or to die in this way =SUFFOCATE —**asphyxiation** /æsˌfɪksiˈeɪʃ(ə)n/ noun [U]

aspiration /ˌæspɪˈreɪʃ(ə)n/ noun [C] a strong wish to achieve something=AMBITION: *He has no political aspirations.*

aspire /əˈspaɪə/ PHRASAL VERB **a'spire to sth** to want to achieve something: *students who aspire to be professional actors*

aspirin /ˈæsprɪn/ noun [C/U] a drug that cures minor pain, or a pill that contains the drug

aspiring /əˈspaɪərɪŋ/ adj trying to be successful at something: *an aspiring actor*

ass /æs/ noun [C] *old-fashioned* an old word for a DONKEY

assailant /əˈseɪlənt/ noun [C] *formal* someone who violently attacks another person

assassin /əˈsæsɪn/ noun [C] someone who deliberately kills an important person

assassinate /əˈsæsɪˌneɪt/ verb [T] to kill an important person deliberately —**assassination** /əˌsæsɪˈneɪʃ(ə)n/ noun [C/U]

assault¹ /əˈsɔːlt/ noun [C/U] a violent attack, or the crime of physically attacking someone: *an assault on a young student*

assault² /əˈsɔːlt/ verb [T] to attack someone violently: *An elderly woman was assaulted and robbed.*

assemble /əˈsemb(ə)l/ verb **1** [I/T] to bring a group together, or to come together and form a group: *The children assembled outside the building.* **2** [T] to build something by putting all its parts together: *You have to assemble the shelves yourself.* ♦ *They are assembling a peace-keeping force to send to the region.*

assembly /əˈsembli/ noun **1** [C] a group of people who have been chosen to make laws or deal with particular issues: *the French National Assembly* **2** [C/U] a regular meeting of students and teachers in a school **3** [U] the process of building something by putting all its parts together

as'sembly ˌline noun [C] a system for making products in a factory. Each worker or machine does a single job as the product moves past them=PRODUCTION LINE

assent /əˈsent/ noun [U] formal agreement or approval

assert /əˈsɜːt/ verb [T] **1** to state firmly that something is true **2** to behave in a determined or confident way: *He quickly asserted his authority as a leader.* ♦ *It's hard for shy people to assert themselves in a group.*

assertion /əˈsɜːʃ(ə)n/ noun [C] a statement in which you say that something is definitely true

assertive /əˈsɜːtɪv/ adj expressing your opinions firmly and confidently =FORCEFUL —**assertiveness** noun [U]

assess /əˈses/ verb [T] to think about something carefully and make a judgment about it: *We tried to assess his suitability for the job.* ♦ *Our agent will assess the value of your property.* —**assessment** noun [C/U]: *a clear assessment of the investment's risks*

asset /ˈæset/ noun [C] **1** something such as money or property that a company owns **2** something that gives you benefits: *He is a definite asset to the team.* ♦ *Youth is a tremendous asset in this job.*

assiduous /əˈsɪdjʊəs/ adj *formal* someone who is assiduous works very hard and does things carefully

assign /əˈsaɪn/ verb [T] **1** to give someone a particular job: *We assigned her the job of maintaining our website.* **2** to put someone in a particular group, or send them to a particular place: *Tina has been assigned to the intermediate learners' group.* **3** to give someone money or equipment so that they can use it for a particular purpose

assignment /əˈsaɪnmənt/ noun [C] a piece of work that you must do: *a homework assignment* ♦ *His first assignment as a reporter was to cover the local election.*

assimilate /əˈsɪmɪˌleɪt/ verb **1** [I/T] to feel that you belong to the new community that you have started to live in, or to make someone feel like this **2** [T] to learn new ideas or information: *Picasso assimilated an amazing variety of techniques in his art.* —**assimilation** /əˌsɪmɪˈleɪʃ(ə)n/ noun [U]

assist /əˈsɪst/ verb [I/T] ★ to help someone or something: *Her job is to assist the head chef.* ♦ *Several designers assisted in the creation of the garden.*

assistance /əˈsɪst(ə)ns/ noun [U] ★ help: *financial/military assistance* ♦ *He's been running the company **with the assistance of** his son.* ♦ *Can I **be of assistance** (=can I help)?*

assistant¹ /əˈsɪst(ə)nt/ noun [C] ★★ someone whose job is to help another person in their work, for example by doing the easier parts of it: *a personal assistant*

assistant² /əˈsɪst(ə)nt/ adj an assistant manager, teacher etc is someone whose job is to help the main manager or teacher

associate¹ /əˈsəʊsieɪt/ verb [T] **1** to connect people or things in your mind: *Most people associate food with pleasure.* **2** if one thing is associated with another, they are connected: *The problem is often associated with heavy drinking.*
PHRASAL VERB as·so·ci·ate with sb *formal* to spend time with someone

associate² /əˈsəʊsiət/ noun [C] someone that you work with

associate³ /əˈsəʊsiət/ adj an associate position or job is not at the highest level: *an associate professor/director* ♦ *an associate producer/editor*

association /əˌsəʊsiˈeɪʃ(ə)n/ noun ★
1 [C] an organization for people who have similar interests or aims: *the Parent-Teacher Association*
2 [C] a connection between people or things: *Smoking has a close **association with** lung cancer.*
3 associations [plural] memories or feelings that are connected with a particular place or event: *The town has many happy childhood associations for me.*
PHRASE in association with with the help of a person or organization

assorted /əˈsɔːtɪd/ adj including various types

assortment /əˈsɔːtmənt/ noun [C] a group of things of various types

assume /əˈsjuːm/ verb [T] ★
1 to believe that something is true, even though you cannot be certain: **+(that)** *I'm assuming everyone here has an email address.*
2 *formal* to start to control something or take an important position: *His first priority was assuming control of the army.*
3 *formal* to pretend to have a particular feeling or attitude: *Fay assumed an air of innocence.*

assumed name /əˌsjuːmd ˈneɪm/ noun [C] a name that someone uses so that no one will know their real name

assuming /əˈsjuːmɪŋ/ conjunction if: sometimes used for emphasizing that something may not be true

assumption /əˈsʌmpʃ(ə)n/ noun **1** [C] something that you think is likely to be true, although you cannot be certain **2** [U] the process of starting to have power or responsibility

assurance /əˈʃɔːrəns/ noun **1** [U] the feeling of being certain or confident about something **2** [C] a statement in which you tell someone that something is definitely true or will definitely happen

assure /əˈʃɔː/ verb [T] **1** *formal* to tell someone that something is definitely true or will definitely happen: *There's no mistake, I can assure you.* **2** to make certain that something happens

assured /əˈʃɔːd/ adj confident and certain
→ SELF-ASSURED —**assuredly** /əˈʃɔːrɪdli/ adv

asterisk /ˈæst(ə)rɪsk/ noun [C] the symbol *, used for showing that more information is given in a FOOTNOTE

asteroid /ˈæstərɔɪd/ noun [C] a mass of rock that moves around in space

asthma /ˈæsmə/ noun [U] a medical condition that makes it difficult to breathe

asthmatic /æsˈmætɪk/ noun [C] someone who suffers from asthma —**asthmatic** adj

astonish /əˈstɒnɪʃ/ verb [T] to surprise someone very much

astonished /əˈstɒnɪʃt/ adj very surprised: *We were astonished to hear that she'd lost her job.*

astonishing /əˈstɒnɪʃɪŋ/ adj very surprising: *It's astonishing that so many people watch that programme.* —**astonishingly** adv

astonishment /əˈstɒnɪʃmənt/ noun [U] very great surprise

astound /əˈstaʊnd/ verb [T] to surprise or shock someone very much

astounded /əˈstaʊndɪd/ adj very surprised or shocked

astounding /əˈstaʊndɪŋ/ adj very surprising or shocking

astray /əˈstreɪ/ adv
PHRASES go astray to become lost: *The cheque I sent them seems to have gone astray.*
lead sb astray to make someone behave badly

astride /əˈstraɪd/ preposition with one leg on each side of something: *sitting astride a bicycle*

astrology /əˈstrɒlədʒi/ noun [U] the study of how the stars and planets influence people's lives —**astrologer** noun [C], **astrological** /ˌæstrəˈlɒdʒɪk(ə)l/ adj

astronaut /ˈæstrənɔːt/ noun [C] someone who travels in space

astronomical /ˌæstrəˈnɒmɪk(ə)l/ adj **1** *informal* an astronomical amount is extremely large: *astronomical prices* **2** relating to the scientific study of the stars and planets

astronomy /əˈstrɒnəmi/ noun [U] the scientific study of stars and planets —**astronomer** noun [C]

astute /əˈstjuːt/ adj good at making decisions that benefit you: *an astute judge of the stock market* —**astutely** adv

asylum /əˈsaɪləm/ noun **1** [U] the right to stay in a country that you have come to because you were in a dangerous situation in your own country **2** [C] *old-fashioned* a hospital for people with mental illnesses

asylum seeker /əˈsaɪləm ˌsiːkə/ noun [C] someone who wants permission to stay in another country because their own country is dangerous

asymmetrical /ˌeɪsɪˈmetrɪk(ə)l/ or **asymmetric** /ˌeɪsɪˈmetrɪk/ adj something that is asymmetrical does not have the same shape and size on both sides

at /weak ət, strong æt/ preposition ★★★
1 in a place in a particular place: *I'll meet you at the main entrance.* ♦ *Does this train*

A

stop at Newport? ♦ *We live at 23 Brookfield Avenue.* ♦ *He wants to spend more time at home with his family.* ♦ *Dad should be at work by now.* ♦ *Trevor's at the doctor's – he'll be back soon.* ♦ *I'm babysitting at Sally's (=at Sally's house) tomorrow night.*
2 near sth sitting or standing close to something: *She was standing at the window, staring out.* ♦ *Why isn't he at his desk?*
3 used for saying when sth happens used for saying what time something happens, or someone's age when something happens: *The match starts at three o'clock.* ♦ *What are you doing at the weekend?* ♦ *At night temperatures sometimes fall to 30 degrees below zero.* ♦ *Mozart was already composing music at the age of five.*
4 during a process in a particular part of a process or series of events: *He dies right at the start of the film.* ♦ *At some point things started to go wrong.*
5 doing sth taking part in an activity, or involved in a situation: *We were at a party last night when you called.* ♦ *Has Karen graduated, or is she still at college?*
6 used for talking about reactions used for stating what causes a particular reaction: *Audiences still laugh at his jokes.* ♦ *She was annoyed at being interrupted.*
7 used with levels and amounts used for showing the level of prices, temperatures, speeds etc: *His Ferrari crashed at 120 miles an hour.* ♦ *The plastic pipes will melt at high temperatures.*
8 in a particular direction used for saying where an action such as looking, pointing, or hitting is directed: *Why are you staring at me like that?* ♦ *She swung her bat at the ball, but missed.*
9 used for talking about abilities used for saying which skills or abilities someone has or does not have: *I've never been very good at sports.* ♦ *He is an expert at getting what he wants.*
　PHRASES **at all** used for emphasis when you are saying or asking whether something is even slightly true: *Has the situation improved at all?* ♦ *Don't you have any money at all?* ♦ *He knows nothing at all about computers.*
at sth's best/worst/strongest etc showing the best/worst etc qualities of something: *This is British cooking at its best.*
ate the past tense of **eat**
atheist /ˈeɪθiːɪst/ noun [C] someone who believes that God does not exist
→ AGNOSTIC —**atheism** /ˈeɪθiˌɪz(ə)m/ noun [U]
athlete /ˈæθliːt/ noun [C] someone who is good at sports and takes part in sports competitions
athletic /æθˈletɪk/ adj **1** physically strong and good at sports **2** relating to athletes or ATHLETICS
athletics /æθˈletɪks/ noun [U] British sports such as running and jumping
atlas /ˈætləs/ noun [C] a book of maps
atmosphere /ˈætməsˌfɪə/ noun [singular] ★★
1 the mood that exists in a place and affects the people there: *There is an atmosphere of tension in the city today.*
2 the air round the Earth or round another

planet: *The Earth's atmosphere is getting warmer.*
3 the air inside a room or other place
atmospheric /ˌætməsˈferɪk/ adj **1** existing in the atmosphere **2** creating a special mood or feeling
atom /ˈætəm/ noun [C] the smallest unit of a chemical element
atom bomb or **atomic bomb** noun [C] a bomb that causes a very large nuclear explosion
atomic /əˈtɒmɪk/ adj science **1** using the energy that is produced by SPLITTING atoms (=breaking them apart) **2** relating to the atoms in a substance
atone /əˈtəʊn/ verb [I] formal to do something that shows that you are sorry —**atonement** noun [U]
atrocious /əˈtrəʊʃəs/ adj extremely bad: *atrocious weather conditions* —**atrociously** adv
atrocity /əˈtrɒsəti/ noun [C/U] something very cruel and violent that someone does
attach /əˈtætʃ/ verb [T] ★
1 attach sth to sth to fasten one thing to another: *Attach the rope to the branch of a tree.*
2 to send another document with a letter or an email: *I attach a copy of his reply.*
3 be attached to if one thing is attached to another, it is part of it: *There is a riding school attached to the farm.*
4 be attached to to be sent to work temporarily in a different place: *She is now attached to the American Embassy in Beijing.*
　PHRASE **attach importance/significance/value/weight to sth** to think that something is important or true and that it should be considered seriously
attached /əˈtætʃt/ adj **1** joined or fixed to something **2 attached to sth/sb** if you are attached to something or someone, you like them very much: *Danny is very attached to his teddy bear.*
attachment /əˈtætʃmənt/ noun **1** [C] a special tool that you attach to something in order to do a particular job **2** [C/U] a feeling of liking a person or place very much **3** [C] a computer file that you send with an email
attack¹ /əˈtæk/ verb ★★★
1 [I/T] to use violence against a person or place: *It was shortly before midnight when the terrorists attacked.* ♦ **attack sb with sth** *Two prison officers were brutally attacked with a knife.*
2 [T] to strongly criticize someone or something: **attack sb/sth for (doing) sth** *Parliament has been attacked for failing to take action.*
3 [I/T] to cause damage or disease in something: *The virus attacks the body's red blood cells.*
4 [I/T] to try to score points in a game: *They attack well, but their defence is weak.*

Words often used with attack

Adverbs often used with attack (verb, sense 2)
■ ATTACK + **bitterly, fiercely, openly, strongly, vigorously**: used for saying that someone expresses strong criticism

A

attack² /əˈtæk/ noun ★★★
1 [C/U] a violent attempt to harm someone or something: *a vicious attack on an unarmed man ♦ The city was under attack throughout the night.*
2 [C] strong criticism: *McCann launched an attack on his own players.*
3 [C] an occasion when you are affected by an illness, or when you have a particular strong feeling: *an asthma attack ♦ an attack of nerves →* HEART ATTACK
4 [C] an attempt to score points in a game

Words often used with **attack**

*Adjectives often used with **attack** (noun, sense 2)*
■ **bitter, fierce, scathing, stinging** + ATTACK: used about attacks that show strong criticism
*Verbs often used with **attack** (noun, sense 2)*
■ **launch, mount** + ATTACK: make an attack

attacker /əˈtækə/ noun [C] someone who physically attacks someone else
attain /əˈteɪn/ verb [T] *formal* to succeed in achieving something that involves a lot of effort= ACHIEVE —**attainable** adj, **attainment** noun [C/U]
attempt¹ /əˈtempt/ noun [C] ★★
1 an effort to do something: **an attempt to do sth** *the president's final attempt to reach a settlement with the rebel forces ♦ an attempt on the world record ♦ It's his fourth attempt at flying a balloon around the world.*
2 an attack on someone that is intended to kill them but fails: *an assassination attempt*
attempt² /əˈtempt/ verb [T] ★★ to try to do something: *Few people knew that she had once attempted suicide. ♦ attempt to do sth The book attempts to explain the origins of the war.*
attempted /əˈtemptɪd/ adj used about crimes that someone tries to commit without success: *attempted murder*
attend /əˈtend/ verb [I/T] ★★
1 to be present at an event or activity: *Most of his colleagues attended the wedding.*
2 to go regularly to a place such as a school or a church: *Born in India, he attended high school in Madras.*
PHRASAL VERB **atˈtend to sth** to deal with something: *We still have a number of other matters to attend to.*
attendance /əˈtendəns/ noun **1** [C/U] the number of people who are present at an event or in a place such as a school or church: *Church attendance dropped sharply in the 1970s. ♦ Attendance at the first meeting was high* (=there were a lot of people). **2** [U] the fact that someone is present in a place, or goes there regularly
PHRASE **in attendance** *formal* present at an important event
attendant /əˈtendənt/ noun [C] someone whose job is to help customers or people who visit a public place: *a museum attendant*
attention /əˈtenʃ(ə)n/ noun [U] ★★★
1 the fact that you are listening to someone or something, or you are looking at them: *May I please have your attention – I have an important announcement. ♦ The man paid no attention to them.*
2 the fact that you know about something

or notice something: *I have been asked to draw your attention to the following matters. ♦ We should bring the problem to their attention.*
3 special care, help, or treatment: *She needs urgent medical attention.*
PHRASE **for the attention of sb** used on a business letter to show that you intend it for a particular person
atˈtention ˌspan noun [singular] the length of time that you can pay attention to one thing without becoming bored or thinking about something else
attentive /əˈtentɪv/ adj **1** listening to or watching something carefully **2** behaving in a way that shows that you care about someone —**attentively** adv
attic /ˈætɪk/ noun [C] a room in a house under the roof
attitude /ˈætɪˌtjuːd/ noun ★★★
1 [C/U] opinions or feelings that you show by your behaviour: *We can win if we keep a positive attitude. ♦ People here have a more relaxed attitude to their work. ♦ Attitudes towards the older members of the group will have to change.*
2 [U] *informal* a proud confident way of behaving that some people think is rude: *There's no denying the guy has attitude.*
attorney /əˈtɜːni/ noun [C] *American* a lawyer
atˌtorney ˈgeneral noun [C] the most senior lawyer in some countries or US states
attract /əˈtrækt/ verb [T] ★★
1 to make someone like something, or be interested in something: *The show attracts viewers from all walks of life. ♦ attract sb to sth What first attracted you to Buddhism?*
2 to cause people to behave in a particular way towards something: *His paintings have attracted considerable criticism. ♦ The trial attracted a lot of media interest.*
3 if you are attracted to someone, you are interested in them in a romantic or sexual way: *She's old enough now to be attracted to boys.*
4 to make something move near someone or something: *Insects are often attracted by smells that aren't obvious to us.*
PHRASE **attract (sb's) attention** to make someone notice someone or something
attraction /əˈtrækʃ(ə)n/ noun **1** [C] an interesting place or object that people come to see **2** [C/U] a reason for liking something or being interested in it **3** [singular/U] the feeling of liking someone in a romantic or sexual way
attractive /əˈtræktɪv/ adj ★★
1 nice to look at ≠ UNATTRACTIVE: *a stunningly attractive woman*
2 worth having, thinking about, or doing: *a company that will be increasingly attractive to investors*
attributable /əˈtrɪbjʊtəb(ə)l/ adj caused by a particular event, situation, or activity: *illnesses attributable to cigarette smoking*
attribute¹ /əˈtrɪbjuːt/ **PHRASAL VERB** **atˈtribute sth to sb/sth** to believe that something was caused by something else, or done by someone else: *a painting attributed to Picasso*
attribute² /ˈætrɪˌbjuːt/ noun [C] *formal* a quality or feature

A

aubergine /ˈəʊbəʒiːn/ noun [C/U] British a vegetable with a smooth purple skin —picture → C11

auburn /ˈɔːbən/ adj auburn hair is red-brown in colour

auction[1] /ˈɔːkʃ(ə)n/ noun [C] a public occasion when things are sold to the people who offer the most money for them

auction[2] /ˈɔːkʃ(ə)n/ verb [T] to sell something at an auction

auctioneer /ˌɔːkʃəˈnɪə/ noun [C] someone whose job is to sell things at an auction

audacious /ɔːˈdeɪʃəs/ adj done with extreme confidence, or behaving with extreme confidence

audacity /ɔːˈdæsəti/ noun [U] the confidence to say or do what you want, despite difficulties, risks, or the negative attitudes of other people

audible /ˈɔːdəb(ə)l/ adj loud enough for people to hear —**audibly** adv

audience /ˈɔːdiəns/ noun [C] ★★★
1 the people who watch or listen to a performance: *Chaplin's films were loved by audiences throughout the world.* ♦ *His jokes offended many people in the audience.*
2 all the people who watch a particular television programme, read a particular book etc: *The series has attracted an audience of more than 10 million.*
3 a formal meeting with a very important person: *an audience with the Pope*

> In British English, **audience** can be used with a singular or plural verb. You can say *The audience was cheering.* OR *The audience were cheering.*

audio /ˈɔːdiəʊ/ adj relating to sound that is recorded or broadcast

audiovisual /ˌɔːdiəʊˈvɪʒuəl/ adj using both recorded sounds and images

audit /ˈɔːdɪt/ noun [C] an official examination of a company's financial records —**audit** verb [T]

audition[1] /ɔːˈdɪʃ(ə)n/ noun [C] an occasion when you sing, dance, or act so that someone can decide if you are good enough to perform

audition[2] /ɔːˈdɪʃ(ə)n/ verb [I] to perform at an audition: *She auditioned for a part in Tarantino's next movie.*

auditor /ˈɔːdɪtə/ noun [C] someone whose job is to examine the financial records of a company

auditorium /ˌɔːdɪˈtɔːriəm/ noun [C] the part of a theatre or cinema where the audience sits

augment /ɔːgˈment/ verb [T] formal to increase the size, amount, or value of something

augur /ˈɔːgə/ verb [I/T] formal to be a sign of what may happen in the future: *The look on her face did not augur well.*

August /ˈɔːgəst/ noun [C/U] ★★★ the eighth month of the year, between July and September: *We'll be on holiday in August.* ♦ *It's my birthday on August 6th.*

aunt /ɑːnt/ noun [C] ★★ the sister of your mother or father, or the wife of your UNCLE: *I loved visiting my aunt and uncle.* ♦ *Hello, Aunt Betty.* —picture → FAMILY TREE

au pair /əʊ ˈpeə/ noun [C] a young woman who lives with a family in a foreign country and helps to look after their children

aura /ˈɔːrə/ noun [C] a quality that seems to come from a person or place: *an aura of innocence*

auspices /ˈɔːspɪsɪz/ noun **under the auspices of** formal with the help and support of a particular person or organization

auspicious /ɔːˈspɪʃəs/ adj formal showing signs that suggest that something will be successful

Aussie /ˈɒzi/ noun [C] informal someone from Australia

austere /ɔːˈstɪə/ adj **1** plain or simple in style **2** severe or strict in manner

austerity /ɔːˈsterəti/ noun [U] **1** a bad economic situation in which people do not have much money **2** the quality of being austere

Australasia /ˌɒstrəˈleɪʒə/ a region that includes Australia, New Zealand, New Guinea, and some South Pacific islands

authentic /ɔːˈθentɪk/ adj **1** real, not false or copied=GENUINE: *The letter is certainly authentic.* **2** based on facts: *an authentic account of life in rural China* —**authenticity** /ˌɔːθenˈtɪsəti/ noun [U]

author /ˈɔːθə/ noun [C] ★★
1 someone who writes books or articles as their job
2 the person who wrote a particular document or other piece of writing: *the author of the report*

authoritarian /ɔːˌθɒrɪˈteəriən/ adj controlling everything and forcing people to obey strict rules

authoritative /ɔːˈθɒrɪtətɪv/ adj based on careful research and the most reliable information: *an authoritative report on climate change*

authority /ɔːˈθɒrəti/ noun ★★

1 power	4 expert in subject
2 people with power	5 official permission
3 organization	

1 [U] the power to make decisions and make people do what you want: *The president's authority is being questioned in the press.* ♦ *Parents have legal authority over their children.* ♦ *I don't have the authority to hire staff.*
2 the authorities [plural] the police or other organizations with legal power to make people obey laws: *The French authorities have refused to issue him a visa.*
3 [C] an organization or institution that controls a public service: *She took her complaint to the local health authority.* → LOCAL AUTHORITY
4 [C] an expert on a particular subject: *Charles was an authority on antique musical instruments.*
5 [U] formal official permission to do something: *We do not release the names of our customers without their authority.*

authorize /ˈɔːθəraɪz/ verb [T] to give official permission for something: *The guard is authorized to carry a gun.* —**authorization** /ˌɔːθəraɪˈzeɪʃ(ə)n/ noun [U]

autism /ˈɔːtɪz(ə)m/ noun [U] a serious mental condition that makes it difficult to

A

communicate with other people —**autistic** /ɔːˈtɪstɪk/ adj

autobiography /ˌɔːtəʊbaɪˈɒɡrəfi/ noun [C] a book about your life that you write yourself —**autobiographical** /ˌɔːtəʊbaɪəˈɡræfɪk(ə)l/ adj

autocratic /ˌɔːtəˈkrætɪk/ adj ruling in a strict or cruel way —**autocrat** noun [C]

autograph /ˈɔːtəɡrɑːf/ noun [C] a famous person's name that they sign on something —**autograph** verb [T]

automated /ˈɔːtəmeɪtɪd/ adj using machines instead of people

automatic¹ /ˌɔːtəˈmætɪk/ adj ★
1 an automatic machine can work by itself without being operated by people: *an automatic door* → MANUAL²
2 an automatic action is something that you do without thinking, or without intending to do it: *an automatic response*
3 happening as part of an established process, without a special decision being made: *Taxpayers who do not send in their forms face an automatic fine.*
—**automatically** /ˌɔːtəˈmætɪkli/ adv: *He automatically assumed that the engineer would be a man.*

automatic² /ˌɔːtəˈmætɪk/ noun [C] **1** a car in which the GEARS change by themselves **2** a weapon that shoots bullets until you take your finger off the TRIGGER

automation /ˌɔːtəˈmeɪʃ(ə)n/ noun [U] a system that uses machines to do work instead of people, or the process of changing to such a system

automobile /ˈɔːtəməbiːl/ noun [C] a car

automotive /ˌɔːtəˈməʊtɪv/ adj relating to cars: *the automotive industry*

autonomy /ɔːˈtɒnəmi/ noun [U] **1** the right of a state, region, or organization to govern itself=INDEPENDENCE **2** the power to make your own decisions=INDEPENDENCE
—**autonomous** /ɔːˈtɒnəməs/ adj

autopsy /ˈɔːtɒpsi/ noun [C] a medical examination of a dead person's body that is done in order to find out why they died =POSTMORTEM

autumn /ˈɔːtəm/ noun [C/U] ★★★ the season of the year that comes between summer and winter: *We haven't heard from him since last autumn.* ♦ *They were married in the autumn of 1953.* ♦ *a cold autumn afternoon*
—**autumnal** /ɔːˈtʌmn(ə)l/ adj

auxiliary /ɔːɡˈzɪliəri/ adj **1** additional and available for use: *an auxiliary engine* **2** helping more senior or permanent workers: *auxiliary nurses*

auxiliary ˈverb noun [C] *linguistics* a verb that is used with another verb to form questions, tenses, and negative or passive phrases. The main auxiliary verbs in English are 'be', 'have', and 'do'.

avail¹ /əˈveɪl/ noun **to no avail** *formal* without getting the effect that you wanted

avail² /əˈveɪl/ verb **avail yourself of sth** *formal* to use something

available /əˈveɪləb(ə)l/ adj ★★
1 able to be obtained, taken, or used
≠ UNAVAILABLE: *We'll notify you as soon as tickets become available.* ♦ *Not all the facts are made available to us.* ♦ *There is no money available for this project.*
2 not too busy to do something
≠ UNAVAILABLE: *I'm available next Tuesday if you want to meet then.* ♦ **available to do sth** *My tutor is always available to talk to her students.*
—**availability** /əˌveɪləˈbɪləti/ noun [U]: *Parents are concerned about the availability of drugs in the school.*

avalanche /ˈævəlɑːntʃ/ noun [C] **1** a large amount of snow that suddenly falls down a mountain **2** a large quantity of things that arrive suddenly: *an avalanche of letters*

avant-garde /ˌævɒnˈɡɑːd/ adj very modern in style

Ave abbrev Avenue: used in addresses

avenge /əˈvendʒ/ verb [T] *formal* to react to something wrong by punishing the person who did it

avenue /ˈævənjuː/ noun [C] **1** a wide straight road in a town or city **2** a method of achieving something: *We tried every avenue, but couldn't borrow the money we needed.*

average¹ /ˈæv(ə)rɪdʒ/ noun ★
1 [C/U] the typical amount or level: *Unemployment here is twice the national average.* ♦ *Her performance in the test was below average.*
2 [C] an amount that is calculated by adding several numbers together and dividing the total by the number of things that you added together=MEAN
PHRASE **on average** used for talking about what is usually true, although it may not be true in every situation: *On average, women live longer than men.*

average² /ˈæv(ə)rɪdʒ/ adj ★★
1 usual or ordinary: *He's about average height.*
2 not very good=MEDIOCRE: *a very average performance*
3 calculated by adding several numbers together and dividing the total by the number of things that you added together: *winds with an average speed of 15 miles per hour*

average³ /ˈæv(ə)rɪdʒ/ verb [T] to usually do, have, or involve a particular level or amount: *The cost of developing a new drug now averages around £500 million.*

averse /əˈvɜːs/ adj **not averse to sth** if you are not averse to something, you like it or feel positive about it

aversion /əˈvɜːʃ(ə)n/ noun [C/U] *formal* a strong feeling that you dislike someone or something

avert /əˈvɜːt/ verb [T] to prevent something bad from happening: *We managed to avert disaster this time.*
PHRASE **avert your eyes** to look away from something that you do not want to see

aviation /ˌeɪviˈeɪʃ(ə)n/ noun [U] the activity of flying or making planes

avid /ˈævɪd/ adj very enthusiastic —**avidly** adv

avocado /ˌævəˈkɑːdəʊ/ noun [C/U] a fruit with green or black skin, a very large seed in the middle, and pale green flesh —*picture* → C10

avoid /əˈvɔɪd/ verb [T] ★★★
1 to try to prevent something from

A

happening: *Try to avoid confrontation.* ♦
avoid doing sth *I want to avoid being drawn
into the argument.*
2 to stay away from someone or something:
We went early to avoid the crowds.
3 to choose not to do something: *Her brother
will try to avoid work whenever he can.* ♦
avoid doing sth *Where possible, we have
avoided using technical terms.*
—**avoidance** /ə'vɔɪd(ə)ns/ noun [U]: *the
avoidance of confrontation*

avoidable /ə'vɔɪdəb(ə)l/ adj capable of being
prevented ≠ UNAVOIDABLE: *avoidable
costs/mistakes/errors*

await /ə'weɪt/ verb [T] *formal* **1** to wait for
something: *They were awaiting the birth of
their first child.* **2** if something awaits you,
it will happen to you: *Well, I wonder what
surprises await us today.*

awake¹ /ə'weɪk/ adj ★ not sleeping: *I've been
awake for hours.* ♦ *Do you **lie awake** at
night, worrying about things?* ♦ *I managed
to **stay awake** long enough to watch the
film.* ♦ *We've been **kept awake** all night by
the noise.* ♦ *When the alarm went off, I was
already **wide awake** (=completely awake).*

awake² /ə'weɪk/ (past tense **awoke** /ə'wəʊk/;
past participle **awoken** /ə'wəʊkən/) verb [I/T] to
wake up, or to wake someone up: *They
awoke to find that several inches of snow had
fallen.*

awaken /ə'weɪkən/ verb *formal* **1** [T] to make
someone have a particular feeling **2** [I/T] to
wake up, or to wake someone up

awakening /ə'weɪk(ə)nɪŋ/ noun [singular] the
moment when you first realize or
experience something

award¹ /ə'wɔːd/ noun [C] ★★
1 a prize that is given to someone who has
achieved something: *She won the Player of
the Year award.* ♦ *an **award for** outstanding
services to the industry*
2 an amount of money that is given by a
court of law or other authority: *an award
for compensation*

award² /ə'wɔːd/ verb [T] ★
1 to give someone a prize: *Students who
complete the course successfully will be
awarded a diploma.*
2 to officially give someone something such
as a contract or an amount of money: *He
has been awarded a scholarship to do
research.*

aware /ə'weə/ adj ★★★
1 knowing about a situation or fact
≠ UNAWARE: *As far as I'm aware, he didn't
tell her anything.* ♦ *+that I was not aware
that she had already spoken to you.* ♦ *They're
aware of the dangers.* ♦ *I was **well aware** of
this fact.*
2 interested and involved in something: *The
charity aims to create a new generation of
environmentally aware consumers.*
3 if you become aware of someone or
something, you notice them: *I became
aware of someone following me.* ♦ *+that He
suddenly became aware that the music had
stopped.*
—**awareness** noun [U]: *The aim of our
campaign is to **raise awareness about**
(=make people learn about) heart disease.*

awash /ə'wɒʃ/ adj **1** thoroughly covered with
a liquid **2** full of something or having a lot
of something: *The town is awash with
tourists this time of year.*

away¹ /ə'weɪ/ adv ★★★
1 in a different direction in a direction that
takes you further from a person, place, or
thing: *When Sykes saw the police, he ran
away.* ♦ *Bruce was staring at her, but she
looked away.* ♦ *Please move **away from** the
doors.*
2 not in your usual place not at home, or
not at the place where you work or study:
*My brother looks after the farm while I'm
away.* ♦ *Graham's **away on holiday** this
week.* ♦ *Amy has spent a lot of time **away
from** school.*
3 not near at a distance from someone or
something: *The nearest hospital is 30 miles
away.* ♦ *Keep **away from** the stove – it's very
hot.*
4 removing sth used for showing that
something is removed: *We need to have this
rubbish taken away.* ♦ *She wiped away her
tears.*
5 after a period of time used for saying how
much time will pass before something
happens: *The examinations are less than
three weeks away.*
6 gradually disappearing used for saying
that something gradually disappears: *The
sound of their voices faded away into the
distance.*
7 doing sth continuously doing something
continuously or for a long time: *Molly was
at her desk working away as usual.*
8 in a safe or usual place in a safe place,
or in the place where something is usually
kept: *Put your toys away before you go to
bed.*
9 at an opponents' ground going to an
opponents' ground to play a game

away² /ə'weɪ/ adj an away game is one in
which a team goes to their opponents'
ground to play

awe /ɔː/ noun [U] a feeling of great respect
and admiration: *He is totally in awe of his
father.*

awe-inspiring adj making you feel great
respect and admiration

awesome /'ɔːs(ə)m/ adj **1** very impressive
and sometimes a little frightening **2** *informal*
extremely good

awful /'ɔːf(ə)l/ adj ★★ extremely bad
=TERRIBLE: *This wine tastes awful.* ♦ *There
were these awful people sitting behind us
who talked all through the film.* ♦ *That's an
awful thing to say.*
PHRASES **an awful lot** *spoken* a very large
amount: *There were an awful lot of people
just standing around.*
look/feel awful to look or feel ill or sad

awfully /'ɔːf(ə)li/ adv *spoken* extremely: *I'm
awfully sorry I'm late.*

awkward /'ɔːkwəd/ adj **1** difficult and
embarrassing: *Luckily, nobody asked any
awkward questions.* **2** not comfortable,
relaxed, or confident: *He stood there looking
stiff and awkward in his uniform.* **3** an object
that is awkward is difficult to use or carry
because of its shape or position

awkwardly /ˈɔːkwədli/ adv **1** in a way that shows you are not comfortable, relaxed, or confident: *They smiled awkwardly at the camera.* **2** in a way that is not graceful: *He moved to get out of the way and fell awkwardly.*

awning /ˈɔːnɪŋ/ noun [C] a sheet of cloth above a window or door, used as protection against the rain or sun

awoke the past tense of **awake**[2]

awoken the past participle of **awake**[2]

awry /əˈraɪ/ adj **go awry** to not happen in the way that was planned

axe[1] /æks/ noun [C] a tool used for cutting wood, consisting of a long wooden handle and a heavy metal blade

axe[2] /æks/ verb [T] to end or reduce something: *Almost 1,000 jobs were axed.*

axis /ˈæksɪs/ (plural **axes** /ˈæksiːz/) noun [C] **1** an imaginary line through the middle of an object, around which the object spins **2** one of the two fixed lines that are used for showing measurements on a GRAPH

axle /ˈæks(ə)l/ noun [C] a metal bar that connects a pair of wheels on a car or other vehicle

aye /aɪ/ interjection *British* a word used for saying 'yes' in some parts of the UK

B b

b or **B** /biː/ noun **1** [C] the second letter of the English alphabet **2** B [C] a mark that is given in a school, college, or university for work that is better than average **3** B [U] a common BLOOD GROUP

B abbrev be: used in emails and TEXT MESSAGES

b. abbrev born: used before the date of someone's birth

B & B /ˌbiː ən ˈbiː/ noun [C] a BED AND BREAKFAST

BA /ˌbiː ˈeɪ/ noun [C] Bachelor of Arts: a first degree from a university in a subject such as languages or history

baa /bɑː/ verb [I] to make the sound that a sheep makes —**baa** noun [C]

babble[1] /ˈbæb(ə)l/ verb [I/T] to speak quickly in a way that is boring or difficult to understand

babble[2] /ˈbæb(ə)l/ noun [singular] the noise of a lot of voices all talking at the same time

babe /beɪb/ noun [C] **1** *literary* a baby **2** *informal* an attractive young woman or man. Many women think that this word is offensive.

baboon /bəˈbuːn/ noun [C] a type of large monkey from Africa or South Asia

baby /ˈbeɪbi/ noun [C] ★★★
1 a very young child who cannot yet talk or walk: *their new baby daughter* ♦ *Sally's going to have a baby* (=give birth) *in May.* —*picture* → CHILD
2 a very young animal: *a baby elephant*

3 someone who is behaving in a way that is weak, silly, or not brave: *Don't be such a big baby!*

4 *informal* a project or piece of work that you care about a lot, especially because it was your idea: *Steve has always seen the book as his baby.*

baby boomer noun [C] someone who was born during the period after the Second World War when many babies were born

baby carriage noun [C] *American* a PRAM

babyish /ˈbeɪbiɪʃ/ adj *showing disapproval* suitable only for a baby or young child

baby oil noun [C/U] a type of oil that you put on your skin to make it softer

babysit /ˈbeɪbiˌsɪt/ (past tense and past participle **babysat** /ˈbeɪbiˌsæt/) verb [I/T] to look after children while their parents are not at home —**babysitter** noun [U], **babysitting** noun [U]

bachelor /ˈbætʃələ/ noun [C] a man who has never been married

bachelor's degree noun [C] a first university degree

back[1] /bæk/ adv ★★★

1 returning to place	5 away from the front
2 to earlier state	6 in/into the past
3 as reply or reaction	7 in a different place
4 away from sb/sth	+ PHRASE

1 returning to a place or position: *Put those CDs back where you found them.* ♦ *Can we go back to what we were talking about earlier?*

2 returning to an earlier state or condition: *We're hoping things will be back to normal again soon.* ♦ *I couldn't get back to sleep.*

3 as a reply or reaction to what someone else has said or done: *Jane phoned, and I said you'd phone her back later.* ♦ *Just because he hit you doesn't mean you have to hit him back.*

4 away from a person, thing, or position: *Get back – he's got a gun!* ♦ *The band started playing as the curtain slowly went back.*

5 in the direction that is behind you: *Don't look back, but there's a man following us.*

6 in or to a time in the past: *Back in the '70s, disco music was very popular.* ♦ *Think back: don't you remember anything?*

7 used for talking about a place that you mentioned or were in before: *I have no idea what's going on back home.* ♦ *Back at the hospital, the baby had just been born.*

PHRASE **back and forth** moving first in one direction and then in the opposite direction many times

→ BACK-TO-BACK

back[2] /bæk/ adj ★★
1 furthest from the front ≠ FRONT: *There's a map on the back page.*
2 used for describing money that is owed from an earlier date and has not been paid yet: *back wages/taxes/rent*

PHRASE **back street/road** a street/road that is away from main streets/roads

back[3] /bæk/ noun [C] ★★★
1 the part of your body between your neck and your bottom, on the opposite side to your chest and stomach: *I have a pain in my back.* ♦ *She was lying flat on her back on the bed.* —*picture* → C14

B

2 the part or side of something that is furthest from the front ≠ FRONT: *Get in the back of the car.* ♦ *The sun burnt the back of my neck.* ♦ *I'll put my name on the back of the envelope.* —*picture* → C14

3 the part of a chair that you lean on when you are sitting on it: *What's that mark on the back of the sofa?*

4 an outside area behind a building: *The kids are playing out the back.*

PHRASES **at/in the back of your mind** if something is at the back of your mind, you are slightly conscious of it all the time
back to front with the back part at the front: *Your skirt is on back to front.*
behind sb's back if you do something bad or unkind behind someone's back, you do it without them knowing
have your back to the wall to be in a difficult situation with few choices, so that you have to work or fight very hard
on sb's back *informal* criticizing someone, or telling them to do things
on the back of sth because of something, or helped by something: *Share prices rose sharply on the back of a rise in profits.*
when sb's back is turned when someone is not there, or is not paying attention: *As soon as her back is turned, he's flirting with other women!*
→ TURN[1]

back[4] /bæk/ verb ★

1 [T] to support a person, organization, or plan, so that they are more likely to succeed: *Both main parties are backing these proposals.*

2 [I/T] to move backwards, or to make a person or a vehicle move backwards: *She backed out of the room carrying a tray.* ♦ **back sb into sth** *Steve backed me into a corner at the party.*

3 [T] to risk an amount of money by saying that a particular person or animal will win a race or competition: *I'm backing France to win the championship.*

PHRASAL VERBS ,back 'down to stop asking for something, or to stop saying that you will do something, because a lot of people oppose you: *Neither side is willing to back down.*
,back 'off to move backwards in order to get further away from something
,back 'out to refuse to do something that you agreed to do: *We're hoping that no one will back out of the deal.*
,back 'up to move backwards a short distance
,back (sth) 'up 1 to make a copy of information on your computer 2 to make a car go backwards = REVERSE
,back sb 'up to give support to someone by telling other people that you agree with them: *If I file a complaint, will you back me up?*
,back sth 'up to show that an explanation or belief is probably true: *All the evidence backs up her story.*

backache /'bækeɪk/ noun [C/U] pain in your back

backbencher /ˌbæk'bentʃə/ noun [C] *British* an ordinary member of the British Parliament who does not have a senior position

backbone /'bækbəʊn/ noun **1** [C] the row of small bones that goes down the middle of your back = SPINE **2** [U] the determination and strong personality that you need in order to deal with a difficult situation
PHRASE **the backbone of sth** the part of something that makes it successful or strong: *Our volunteers are the backbone of our organization.*

backdate /ˌbæk'deɪt/ verb [T] **1** to make a rule or law start to be effective from a date in the past **2** to write a date on a document or cheque that is earlier than the real date

backdrop /'bækdrɒp/ noun [C] the situation or place in which something happens: *Negotiations were carried out against a backdrop of continued fighting.*

backer /'bækə/ noun [C] someone who gives help or money to a plan or organization

backfire /ˌbæk'faɪə/ verb [I] **1** if a plan or idea backfires, it has the opposite effect to the one that you wanted **2** if a car backfires, its engine makes a loud noise like an explosion

backgammon /'bækgæmən/ noun [U] a game for two people that you play on a board using DICE and two sets of round pieces —*picture* → C16

background /'bækgraʊnd/ noun ★★

1 sb's experiences	4 extra sounds
2 information	5 general situation
3 position behind sb/sth	+ PHRASE

1 [C] the general experiences and influences that have formed someone's character, or the type of education and training they have had: *students from very different backgrounds* ♦ *We are looking for writers with a background in law.*

2 [singular/U] information and details that help you to understand a situation: *We need to know the background to the case.* ♦ *You'll need some background information on the local economy.*

3 [C] the part of a picture or pattern that is behind the main people or things in it ≠ FOREGROUND: *a picture of palm trees with mountains in the background*

4 [singular] the sounds that you can hear in addition to the main thing that you are listening to: *background noise/music* ♦ *I could hear a TV in the background.*

5 [singular/U] the general situation in which something happens: *The statement was made against a background of intense pressure from the government.*
PHRASE **in the background** in a place or situation in which people do not notice you: *Jo does the publicity work, while Ed stays very much in the background.*

Words often used with background

Adjectives often used with background (sense 1)
■ cultural, educational, ethnic, religious, social + BACKGROUND: used about a particular type of background

backhand /'bækhænd/ noun [C] in tennis and similar sports, a movement made to hit the ball in which the back of your hand moves towards the ball —*picture* → C15

backing /'bækɪŋ/ noun [U] support, help, or strong approval: *The new policy has the* *backing of several leading Democrats.*

backlash /'bæk.læʃ/ noun [C] a strong, negative, and often angry reaction to something that has happened

backlog /'bæk.lɒg/ noun [singular] an amount of work that you should already have finished

backpack /'bæk.pæk/ noun [C] a RUCKSACK —*picture* → BAG

backpacker /'bæk.pækə/ noun [C] someone, especially a young person without much money, who travels around an area on foot or public transport —**backpacking** noun [U]

backpedal /'bæk.ped(ə)l/ verb [I] to show that you are no longer certain about a previous opinion, intention, or promise: *Ministers are backpedalling on the proposed legislation.*

,**back 'seat** noun [C] a seat behind the driver of a car

PHRASE **take a back seat** to deliberately become less active, and give up trying to control things

,**back seat 'driver** noun [C] someone in a car who keeps telling the driver how to drive

backside /'bæk.saɪd/ noun [C] *informal* the part of your body that you sit on

backslash /'bæk.slæʃ/ noun [C] the symbol \ used for separating words or numbers, especially in the names of computer files

backstage /,bæk'steɪdʒ/ adv in the area behind the stage in a theatre, which includes the rooms where the actors get dressed

backswing /'bæk.swɪŋ/ noun [C] the first part of the movement you make when hitting a ball in golf, starting with the CLUB on the ground and moving it into the air above your head —*picture* → C15

,**back-to-'back** adj, adv **1** happening one after the other: *Bill won two golf tournaments back-to-back.* **2** with the back of someone or something against the back of someone or something else: *chairs placed back-to-back*

backtrack /'bæk.træk/ verb [I] **1** to show that you have become less likely to do something that you said you would do: *The government is backtracking on its commitment to increase spending.* **2** to go back in the direction from which you have come

backup /'bæk.ʌp/ noun **1** [C/U] people or equipment that can be used when extra help is needed: *The gang was armed, so the police called for backup.* ♦ *a backup generator/crew* **2** [C] *computing* a copy of information on your computer that you make in case you lose the original information

backward /'bæk.wəd/ adj **1** moving or looking in the direction that is behind you: *a backward glance* **2** not developing quickly, normally, or successfully: *a remote and backward region* **3** *old-fashioned* unable to make normal progress in learning. It is now more acceptable to say that someone has **learning difficulties**.

backwards /'bæk.wədz/ adv ★

1 in the direction that is behind you: *The car rolled backwards down the hill.*
2 in the opposite way or order from usual:

Count backwards from ten to one. ♦ *Your skirt is on backwards.*
3 towards a time in the past: *We should plan for the future, not look backwards.*

PHRASE **backwards and forwards** moving first in one direction and then in the opposite direction many times
→ BEND[1]

backwater /'bæk.wɔːtə/ noun [singular] a place far from main cities where nothing exciting or important happens

backyard /,bæk'jɑːd/ noun [C] **1** *British* an area with a hard surface that is behind a house **2** *American* a GARDEN behind a house

PHRASE **in your (own) backyard** *informal* close to where you live, or in a situation that you are directly involved in

bacon /'beɪkən/ noun [U] meat from a pig that is treated with smoke or salt, and is often cooked in RASHERS (=thin pieces)

bacteria /bæk'tɪəriə/ noun [plural] very small living things that consist of a single cell. Some types of bacteria cause diseases. —**bacterial** adj

bad[1] /bæd/ (comparative **worse** /wɜːs/; superlative **worst** /wɜːst/) adj ★★★

1 not nice or enjoyable	**5** painful/injured
2 causing problems	**6** evil/behaving badly
3 of low quality/skill	**7** no longer fresh/good
4 not suitable	**+** PHRASES

1 not nice or enjoyable: *The weather was really bad – it rained all week.* ♦ *I'm afraid I have some bad news for you.*
2 causing major problems, harm, or damage: *a bad accident/mistake/case of flu* ♦ *I tried to help, but I just made things worse.* ♦ *Too much salt can be **bad** for your heart.*
3 showing a lack of quality or skill: *one of this year's worst films* ♦ *a bad driver/teacher* ♦ *I'm really **bad** at remembering people's names.*
4 not suitable or convenient: *I can come back later if this is a bad time for you.*
5 painful or injured: *a bad back/leg/stomach*
6 cruel, evil, or morally wrong
7 no longer fresh or good to eat or drink: *It will **go bad** if you don't put it in the refrigerator.*

PHRASES **feel bad (about)** to feel guilty or unhappy about something: *Tim felt bad about leaving without saying goodbye.*
not bad *informal* fairly good, or better than you expected: *Those pictures aren't bad for a beginner.*
too bad *spoken* **1** used for showing that you are sorry or sympathetic about something: *That's too bad about your sister losing her job.* **2** used for showing that you are not sympathetic at all, or that you do not really care what someone else thinks: *If you don't like the truth, that's just too bad.*
→ BADLY

Words that you can use instead of bad

Bad is a very general word. Here are some words with more specific meanings that sound more natural and appropriate in particular situations.

meal/film/weather/ behaviour/book	appalling, atrocious, awful, terrible

person	horrible, nasty, unpleasant, wicked
illness/injury/problem	major, serious, severe
performance/ piece of work/ teacher/singer	not much good (*informal*), poor, terrible, useless (*informal*)
something that causes harm or bad effects	damaging, dangerous, harmful, poisonous, toxic, unhealthy

bad² /bæd/ adv *spoken* badly. Many people think that this use is incorrect.

,bad 'blood noun [U] angry feelings that people still have towards each other because of something that happened in the past

,bad 'debt noun [C] money that someone owes but will never pay

badge /bædʒ/ noun [C] **1** *British* a small round object with words or symbols on it. You fasten it onto your clothes with a pin, for example to show that you support an idea or a political party. **2** a special piece of metal, cloth, or plastic with words or symbols on it. You wear it or carry it to show your official position: *a police badge*

badger¹ /'bædʒə/ noun [C] a wild animal with dark fur and a white area on its head. It lives in a hole in the ground. —picture → C13

badger² /'bædʒə/ verb [T] to try to make someone do something by asking them many times: *They keep badgering me to take them to the show.*

,bad 'language noun [U] rude words

badly /'bædli/ (comparative **worse** /wɜːs/; superlative **worst** /wɜːst/) adv ★★
1 in a way that is not skilful, effective, or successful: *She spoke French so badly I couldn't understand her.* ♦ *a badly organized meeting*
2 in a serious or severe way: *One of the prisoners had been badly beaten by guards.*
3 in an unkind, unfair, or unreasonable way: *She feels as though she has been badly treated.*
4 if you need or want something badly, you need or want it very much

,badly 'off (comparative ,worse 'off; superlative ,worst 'off) adj **1** someone who is badly off does not have much money **2** without enough of something that you need

badminton /'bædmɪntən/ noun [U] a game in which two or four players use RACKETS to hit a SHUTTLECOCK (=a small light object with feathers on it) to each other across a net

badmouth /'bæd,maʊθ/ verb [T] *informal* to criticize someone or something

bad-tempered /,bæd 'tempəd/ adj made annoyed or angry very easily

baffle /'bæf(ə)l/ verb [T] to be confusing or difficult for someone to understand or solve: *Detectives remain baffled by these murders.* —**baffling** adj

bag /bæg/ noun [C] ★★★
1 a container made of paper, plastic, or cloth, used for carrying or storing things: *Put your dirty washing in the plastic bag.* ♦ *He was weighed down by shopping bags.*

2 a HANDBAG
3 a suitcase or similar container in which you carry clothes and other things that you need when you are travelling: *The customs officials may want to search your bags.*
4 the things in a bag, or the amount that it contains: *I've already used about half a bag of flour.*

PHRASES **bags of sth** *British spoken* a lot of something: *We've still got bags of time.*
bags under your eyes loose dark areas of skin below your eyes

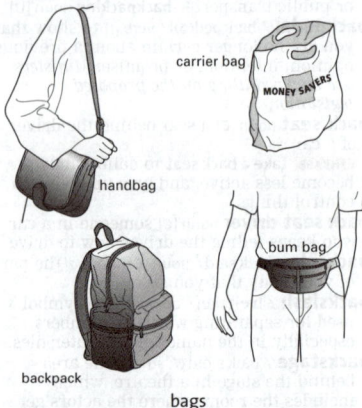

carrier bag

MONEY SAVERS

handbag

bum bag

backpack

bags

bagel /'beɪg(ə)l/ noun [C] a type of bread that is small and round with a hole in the middle

baggage /'bægɪdʒ/ noun [U] **1** the suitcases and bags that you take with you when you travel **2** *informal* problems that someone's past experiences sometimes cause in new situations: *emotional baggage*

baggy /'bægi/ adj baggy clothes are very loose and comfortable

bagpipes /'bæg,paɪps/ noun [plural] a Scottish musical instrument consisting of a bag with several pipes sticking out of it. You play bagpipes by blowing air through one of the pipes.

baguette /bæ'get/ noun [C] a long thin LOAF of bread that is soft inside and hard outside

bail¹ /beɪl/ noun [U] money that is given to a court so that someone is allowed to stay out of prison until their trial: *She was released on bail later that day.*

bail² /beɪl/
PHRASAL VERBS **bail sb 'out** to give money to a court so that someone is allowed to stay out of prison while they wait for their trial
bail sb/sth 'out to help a person or organization that is having financial problems

bailiff /'beɪlɪf/ noun [C] *British* an official whose job is to take away the possessions of someone who has not paid money that they owe

bait¹ /beɪt/ noun [C/U] **1** food that is used for attracting and catching fish, birds, or animals **2** something that is offered in order to persuade someone to do something

bait² /beɪt/ verb [T] **1** to deliberately try to

make someone angry **2** to put food on a hook or in a TRAP in order to catch fish, birds, or animals

bake /beɪk/ verb [I/T] ★ to cook food such as bread and cakes in an oven: *She baked me a cake for my birthday.* ♦ *a baked potato*

baked beans /ˌbeɪkt ˈbiːnz/ noun [plural] beans cooked in tomato sauce and sold in a can

baked potato /ˌbeɪkt pəˈteɪtəʊ/ noun [C] a potato that is baked and served with its skin on=JACKET POTATO

baker /ˈbeɪkə/ noun [C] someone whose job is to make bread, cakes etc

bakery /ˈbeɪkəri/ noun [C] a building where bread, cakes etc are made or sold

balance¹ /ˈbæləns/ noun ★★

1 ability to stay upright	**4** majority of sth
2 correct relationship	**5** emotional calm
3 amount of money	**+ PHRASES**

1 [U] the ability to remain steady in an upright position: *He lost his balance and tipped backwards in the chair.* ♦ *Ted kept pulling my arm, throwing me off balance.*
2 [C/U] a situation in which different aspects or features are treated equally or exist in the correct relationship to each other: *A healthy diet is about getting the correct balance of a variety of foods.* ♦ *We're trying to strike a balance between fun and learning.*
3 [C] the amount of money in a bank account or remaining to be paid for something
4 [singular] the majority of information, opinions, or facts: *The balance of public opinion was against the proposal.* → TIP²
5 [U] mental or emotional calm: *She quickly recovered her balance after the outburst.*
PHRASES balance of payments the difference between the amount of money that a country pays to foreign countries and the amount it receives from them
balance of power the way in which military or political power is divided between countries or groups
be/hang in the balance if something is in the balance, you do not know whether it will succeed or fail
on balance after thinking about all the relevant facts: *On balance, I think we made the right decision.*

balance² /ˈbæləns/ verb ★
1 [I] to keep your body steady without falling over, or to put something in a steady position so that it does not fall: *We had to balance our plates on our knees.*
2 [T] to create or preserve a good or correct balance between different features or aspects: *We have to balance the needs and tastes of all our customers.* ♦ **balance sth with/against sth** *There is a need to balance the demands of the workplace with those of family life.*
PHRASE balance the budget/books to make sure that you do not spend more money than you receive

balanced /ˈbælənst/ adj **1** thinking about all arguments, opinions, or aspects fairly and equally=UNBIASED: *We aim to provide balanced reporting of this difficult issue.*
2 with a sensible and reasonable attitude

towards life **3** with all parts combining well together or existing in the correct amounts: *a balanced diet*

balance ˌsheet noun [C] a written statement showing the value of a company at a particular time

balancing act /ˈbælənsɪŋ ˌækt/ noun [C] a difficult process in which you try to keep different groups satisfied, or try to do many different things at the same time

balcony /ˈbælkəni/ noun [C] **1** a place sticking out from the outside of a building where you can sit or stand **2** an upper floor in a theatre or cinema that sticks out over the main floor

bald /bɔːld/ adj **1** with little or no hair on your head **2** a bald tyre is no longer safe because its surface is worn smooth
—**baldness** noun [U]

balding /ˈbɔːldɪŋ/ adj beginning to lose your hair

baldly /ˈbɔːldli/ adv speaking in a direct way, without trying to be sensitive or polite

bale¹ /beɪl/ noun [C] a large quantity of something such as paper, cotton, or HAY that is tied tightly together

bale² /beɪl/ **PHRASAL VERB** ˌbale ˈout British to leave a project, situation, or relationship, especially when it becomes difficult

balk /bɔːk/ another spelling of **baulk**

ball /bɔːl/ noun [C] ★★★
1 a round object that you use in games and sports, or an object that is shaped like this: *a tennis/golf ball* ♦ *a ball of dough*
2 the part of your foot, hand, or thumb that is slightly round and sticks out
3 a formal social event at which there is dancing and usually a meal: *the college's summer ball*
PHRASES get/set/start the ball rolling to make something start happening
have a ball *informal* to enjoy yourself
on the ball *informal* quick to understand what is happening and what must be done

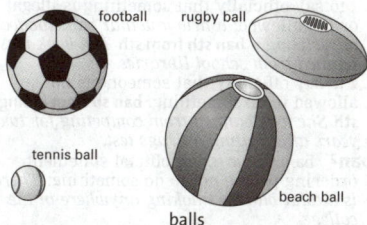

balls

ballad /ˈbæləd/ noun [C] a popular love song

ball ˌboy noun [C] a boy whose job is to pick up tennis balls at a tennis match and throw them back to the players —*picture* → C15

ballerina /ˌbæləˈriːnə/ noun [C] a woman who performs in ballets

ballet /ˈbæleɪ/ noun **1** [U] a type of complicated dancing that is used for telling a story and is performed in a theatre **2** [C] a performance of ballet

ball ˌgame noun [C] a game played with a ball, for example tennis or football
PHRASE a whole new ball game a situation that is completely different from what has happened before

B

'ball girl noun [C] a girl whose job is to pick up tennis balls at a tennis match and throw them back to the players —*picture* → C15

ballistic /bə'lıstık/ adj **go ballistic** *informal* to become extremely angry

bal,listic 'missile noun [C] a type of missile that travels long distances

balloon¹ /bə'lu:n/ noun [C] **1** a small coloured bag of thin rubber filled with air, used as a toy or decoration **2** a large strong bag filled with gas or hot air that can be used for travelling through the air

balloon² /bə'lu:n/ verb [I] to become larger and rounder in shape

ballot¹ /'bælət/ noun [C/U] a secret vote to decide about an issue or to decide who wins an election

ballot² /'bælət/ verb [T] to ask people to vote in a ballot

'ballot ,box noun **1** [C] a box in which you put a piece of paper with your vote on **2** [singular] the democratic system of voting

ballpark /'bɔ:lpɑ:k/ adj not calculated exactly: *a ballpark figure*

ballpoint /'bɔ:lpɔınt/ or **,ballpoint 'pen** noun [C] a pen with a very small ball at the end from which ink flows —*picture* → PEN

ballroom /'bɔ:lru:m/ noun [C] a very large room used for formal dances

,ballroom 'dancing noun [U] a type of formal dancing done by two people together, using a fixed series of movements

balm /bɑ:m/ noun [C/U] an oil with a nice smell for rubbing on sore skin

balmy /'bɑ:mi/ adj balmy weather is warm and pleasant

Baltic /'bɔ:ltık/ adj relating to the Baltic Sea in northern Europe and to the countries in this region

bamboo /,bæm'bu:/ noun [C/U] a tall tropical plant with thick light-brown stems, used for making things such as furniture

ban¹ /bæn/ verb [T] ★
1 to say officially that something is illegal or not allowed: *a new law that bans tobacco advertising* ♦ **ban sth from sth** *The book was banned from school libraries.*
2 to say officially that someone is not allowed to do something: **ban sb from (doing) sth** *She was banned from competing for two years after failing a drugs test.*

ban² /bæn/ noun [C] an official statement ordering people not to do something: *There is a total ban on smoking anywhere in the college.*

banal /bə'nɑ:l/ adj boring, with no new, interesting, or unusual qualities —**banality** /bə'næləti/ noun [C/U]

banana /bə'nɑ:nə/ noun [C/U] a long curved fruit with a yellow skin —*picture* → C10

band¹ /bænd/ noun [C] ★★★

1 group of musicians	**4** narrow circular object
2 group of same type	**5** line of colour/light
3 range of values/levels	

1 a group of musicians who play popular music: *He used to play in a band.*
2 a group of people who do something together or who share a particular feature: *a band of outlaws*
3 a range of values, prices etc in a system for measuring or organizing something: *students in the age band 11 to 14*
4 a flat narrow piece of something in the shape of a ring: *She wore a band around her hair.* ♦ *a rubber band*
5 a line of something such as colour or light: *The male bird has a brown band across its chest.*

In British English, a **band of musicians** can be used with a singular or plural verb. You can say *The band **was** playing.* OR *The band **were** playing.*

band² /bænd/ PHRASAL VERB **,band to'gether** to form a group in order to achieve an aim

bandage¹ /'bændıdʒ/ noun [C/U] a long thin piece of cloth that you wrap around an injured part of your body

bandage² /'bændıdʒ/ verb [T] to wrap a bandage around part of your body

'Band-Aid *American trademark* a type of PLASTER used for covering a cut on your skin

bandit /'bændıt/ noun [C] a member of a group of thieves who attack people while they are travelling

bandstand /'bæn(d),stænd/ noun [C] a building without walls in a park, used for musical performances

bandwagon /'bænd,wægən/ noun [C] an idea or activity that suddenly becomes very popular: *Every business was trying to jump on the 'dot-com' bandwagon.*

bandwidth /'bænd,wıdθ/ noun [C/U] *computing* the amount of information that can be sent each second through an Internet connection

bang¹ /bæn/ verb **1** [T] to hit or move something with a lot of force, making a loud noise: *We could hear them banging their drums.* ♦ *She banged her fist on the table.* **2** [I] to move with a lot of force, making a loud noise: *We heard a door bang.* ♦ *Who's banging around upstairs?* **3** [I/T] to knock against something when you are moving: *Be careful not to bang your head.*

bang² /bæn/ noun [C] **1** a short loud noise, for example the sound of a door closing with a lot of force **2** a knock or hit on a part of your body: *a bang on the head*
PHRASE **with a bang** in a very exciting or successful way

bang³ /bæn/ adv *British informal* used for emphasizing that something is exactly in a particular position or happens exactly at a particular time: *a small town, bang in the middle of Australia*

bang⁴ /bæn/ interjection **1** used by children for representing the sound made by a gun **2** used for showing that something happens very suddenly

banger /'bæŋə/ noun [C] *British* **1** *informal* a SAUSAGE **2** *informal* an old car in bad condition **3** a very loud FIREWORK

bangle /'bæŋg(ə)l/ noun [C] a stiff circular BRACELET (=jewellery worn around the wrist)

banish /'bænıʃ/ verb [T] **1** to officially order someone to leave a place as a punishment **2** to get rid of something such as a problem or worry

banister /'bænıstə/ noun [C] a structure like

a fence along the edge of stairs —*picture*
→ C1

banjo /ˈbændʒəʊ/ noun [C] a musical
instrument like a small round guitar

bank¹ /bæŋk/ noun [C] ★★★
1 a financial institution where people can
keep their money, or can borrow money: *I
need to go to the bank this morning.*
2 a raised sloping area of land, for example
along the side of a river: *We climbed a steep
bank.*
3 a large collection or store of something: *a
blood bank*
4 a large mass of cloud or FOG

bank² /bæŋk/ verb **1** [I] to have a bank account
with a particular bank: *Who do you bank
with?* **2** [T] to put money into a bank account:
Have you banked that cheque yet? **3** [I] if a
plane banks, it turns quickly in the air,
with one wing higher than the other
PHRASAL VERB **bank on sb/sth** to depend on
someone doing something or on something
happening

bank account noun [C] an arrangement with
a bank that allows you to keep your money
there: *We'll pay the money into your bank
account.*

bank balance noun [C] *British* the amount of
money in your bank account

bank card noun [C] a small plastic card for
making payments or for getting money
from the bank

banker /ˈbæŋkə/ noun [C] someone who has
an important position in a bank

bank holiday noun [C] *British* a public holiday
when shops and businesses may be closed

banking /ˈbæŋkɪŋ/ noun [U] the work done by
banks

banknote /ˈbæŋknəʊt/ noun [C] a piece of
paper money

bankrupt¹ /ˈbæŋkrʌpt/ adj a person or
business that is bankrupt has officially
admitted that they have no money and
cannot pay what they owe = INSOLVENT

bankrupt² /ˈbæŋkrʌpt/ noun [C] someone who
is officially bankrupt

bankrupt³ /ˈbæŋkrʌpt/ verb [T] to make a
person, business, or country BANKRUPT or
very poor

bankruptcy /ˈbæŋkrʌptsi/ noun [C/U] a
situation in which a person or business
becomes BANKRUPT

bank statement noun [C] a document
showing the money that went into or out
of a bank account during a particular period

banner /ˈbænə/ noun [C] **1** a wide piece of cloth
with a message on it **2** *computing* an
advertisement across a WEBSITE
PHRASE **under the banner of sth 1** because of
a particular principle or belief **2** controlled
or supported by a particular organization

banquet /ˈbæŋkwɪt/ noun [C] a formal meal
for a large number of people

banter /ˈbæntə/ noun [U] friendly
conversation in which people make jokes
about each other

bap /bæp/ noun [C] *British* a large soft BREAD
ROLL

baptism /ˈbæptɪz(ə)m/ noun [C/U] a ceremony
in which someone is covered or touched

with water in order to welcome them into
the Christian religion

Baptist /ˈbæptɪst/ noun [C] a member of a
Protestant religious group that believes
that only adults should be baptized
—**Baptist** adj

baptize /bæpˈtaɪz/ verb [T] **1** to welcome
someone into the Christian religion by
touching or covering them with water **2** to
name a child when it is baptized

bar¹ /bɑː/ noun ★★★

1 place serving alcohol	**6** in music
2 flat surface for drinks	**7** on computer screen
3 long piece of metal	**8** profession of a lawyer
4 block of sth solid	**+** PHRASE
5 sth that prevents sth	

1 [C] a place where you go to buy and drink
alcoholic drinks
2 [C] the COUNTER where alcoholic drinks
are served
3 [C] a long narrow piece of metal: *an old
house with iron bars on the windows*
4 [C] a solid block of a substance: *a bar of
soap ♦ a chocolate bar*
5 [C] something that prevents another thing
from happening: *The fact that you are a
woman should not be a bar to success.*
6 [C] one of the sections in a line of music
7 [C] a long narrow shape along one of the
sides of a WINDOW on a computer screen: *a
scroll/tool bar*
8 **the bar** [singular] the profession of being a
BARRISTER
PHRASE **behind bars** in prison

bar² /bɑː/ preposition *British* except: *I agreed
with all his arguments bar one.*

bar³ /bɑː/ verb [T] **1** to officially say that
something is not allowed: *The new rule
bars the export of live animals.* **2** to put
something across a door or window so that
no one can get through it **3** to prevent
someone from going somewhere by
standing in their way: *Three vicious-looking
dogs barred our way.*

barbarian /bɑːˈbeəriən/ noun [C] someone
who does not respect culture or who is
extremely violent and cruel

barbaric /bɑːˈbærɪk/ adj extremely violent
and cruel

barbarous /ˈbɑːbərəs/ adj extremely violent
and cruel

barbecue¹ /ˈbɑːbɪkjuː/ noun [C] **1** a meal at
which food is cooked and eaten outside **2** a
piece of equipment used for cooking food
outside

barbecue² /ˈbɑːbɪkjuː/ verb [T] to cook food
outside on a barbecue

barbed /bɑːbd/ adj barbed comments contain
cruel but clever criticisms

barbed wire noun [U] thick wire with a lot of
sharp points sticking out of it

barbell /ˈbɑːbel/ noun [C] a long metal bar
with weights at each end. You lift it in
order to make your muscles bigger.
—*picture* → C16

barber /ˈbɑːbə/ noun [C] someone whose job
is to cut men's hair

barbiturate /bɑːˈbɪtʃʊrət/ noun [C] a strong
drug that can make people calm or help
them to sleep

bar chart noun [C] a BAR GRAPH

bar code noun [C] a set of printed lines on a product that contains information such as its price

bare¹ /beə/ adj **1** not covered by any clothes **2** a bare surface has nothing on it **3** basic, with nothing extra: *the bare essentials like food and clothing*

   PHRASE **with your bare hands** without using any equipment or weapons

bare² /beə/ verb [T] to show something that was covered, for example a part of your body

barefoot /ˈbeəfʊt/ adj, adv without any shoes or socks on

barely /ˈbeəli/ adv **1** used for saying that something only just happens or exists, or is only just possible=HARDLY, SCARCELY: *He could barely stand.* ♦ *The roads were barely wide enough for two cars to pass.* **2** used for emphasizing that something happened a very short time before something else: *Roy had barely left the room before they started to laugh.* **3** used for emphasizing how small an amount is: *He's barely 12 years old.*

bargain¹ /ˈbɑːgɪn/ noun [C] **1** something you buy that costs much less than normal: *Her dress was a real bargain.* **2** an agreement in which each person or group promises something

   PHRASE **into the bargain** in addition to the things already mentioned

bargain² /ˈbɑːgɪn/ verb [I] to try to persuade someone to agree to a price or deal that is better for you

   PHRASE **more than you bargained for** something that is worse or more difficult than you expected

barge¹ /bɑːdʒ/ noun [C] a long flat boat that is used on rivers and CANALS

barge² /bɑːdʒ/ verb [I] to move in a fast careless way, often hitting people or things: *He barged past me without looking.*

   PHRASAL VERB **barge in** to enter a room suddenly in a rude way

bar graph noun [C] a GRAPH that represents amounts as thick lines of different lengths

baritone /ˈbærɪtəʊn/ noun [C] a man with a fairly deep singing voice, between a TENOR and a BASS

bark¹ /bɑːk/ verb [I] to make the short loud sound that a dog makes

   PHRASE **barking up the wrong tree** *informal* doing something that will not get the result that you want

bark² /bɑːk/ noun **1** [U] the hard substance that covers a tree —*picture* → TREE **2** [C] the short loud sound that a dog makes

barley /ˈbɑːli/ noun [U] a type of grain that is used for making food, beer, and WHISKY

barmaid /ˈbɑːmeɪd/ noun [C] a woman who serves drinks in a bar

barman /ˈbɑːmən/ (plural **barmen** /ˈbɑːmən/) noun [C] a man who serves drinks in a bar

bar mitzvah /bɑː ˈmɪtsvə/ noun [C] a Jewish ceremony held when a boy is 13, after which he is considered to be an adult in his religious life

barmy /ˈbɑːmi/ adj *British informal* crazy or silly

barn /bɑːn/ noun [C] a large building on a farm where animals, crops, or machines are kept

barometer /bəˈrɒmɪtə/ noun [C] **1** a piece of equipment that measures pressure in the air and tells you what kind of weather to expect **2** something that shows how a situation is changing or how people feel about something: *Investment levels are seen as a good barometer of business confidence.*

baron /ˈbærən/ noun [C] **1** a male member of the NOBILITY with low rank **2** a powerful person in a particular type of business: *the steel barons*

baroque /bəˈrɒk/ adj relating to the very detailed style of art, building, or music that was popular in Europe in the 17th and early 18th centuries

barracks /ˈbærəks/ noun [plural] a group of buildings where members of the armed forces live and work

barrage /ˈbærɑːʒ/ noun **1** [singular] a lot of criticisms, complaints, or questions that are directed at someone **2** [C] a long continuous attack of guns or bombs

barrel /ˈbærəl/ noun [C] **1** a large round container with a flat top and bottom, used for storing liquids **2** the part of a gun that a bullet is fired through

barren /ˈbærən/ adj **1** barren land is dry and plants cannot grow there **2** *old-fashioned* a woman who is barren cannot have babies

barricade¹ /ˌbærɪˈkeɪd/ noun [C] a temporary structure that is built across a road, gate, or door to prevent people from getting through

barricade² /ˌbærɪˈkeɪd/ verb [T] to block something with a barricade

barrier /ˈbæriə/ noun [C] ★
1 a structure that stops people or vehicles from entering a place: *Fans broke through the barriers and rushed onto the pitch.*
2 something that prevents progress or makes it difficult for people to communicate or achieve an aim
=OBSTACLE: *High levels of debt are a major barrier to economic development.*
3 something that separates one thing from another: *The river is the last barrier between the rebel army and the city.*

barring /ˈbɑːrɪŋ/ preposition unless the thing mentioned happens or exists: *Barring any further delays, we should be able to start tomorrow.*

barrister /ˈbærɪstə/ noun [C] a lawyer in England or Wales who is allowed to speak in the higher law courts

bartender /ˈbɑːtendə/ noun [C] *American* someone whose job is to serve drinks in a bar

barter /ˈbɑːtə/ verb [I/T] to exchange goods or services for other goods or services instead of using money —**barter** noun [U]

base¹ /beɪs/ noun [C] ★★★

1 lowest part of sth	**4** supporters/customers
2 place for soldiers	**5** ideas etc to start from
3 place for doing sth	**6** in baseball

1 the bottom part, edge, or surface of something: *The statue stands on a large round base.* ♦ *The pituitary gland is at the base of the brain.*

B

2 a place where members of the armed forces live and work: *a US naval base*

3 a place from which an activity can be planned, started, or carried out: *Hikers find this a convenient base for their mountain expeditions.*

4 a group of people or organizations that support someone or something: *They have built a loyal customer base.*

5 a set of ideas, facts, achievements etc from which something can develop: *The company lacks a strong financial base.* ♦ *a broad base of experience/knowledge/ expertise*

6 one of the four places on a baseball or ROUNDERS field that a player must touch in order to score points → FIRST BASE

base² /beɪs/ verb ★★★

PHRASE **be based in** to have somewhere as your main office or place of work, or the place where you live: *Our parent company is based in Osaka.* ♦ *Where are you based now?*

PHRASAL VERB 'base sth on sth **1** to use particular ideas or facts to make a decision, do a calculation, or develop a theory: *Her theories are based largely on personal experience.* **2** to use something as a model for a film, piece of writing, or work of art: *The film is based on a true story.*

base³ /beɪs/ adj *literary* not moral at all

baseball /'beɪsˌbɔːl/ noun **1** [U] a game played by two teams of nine players who score points by hitting a ball with a BAT and then running around four bases **2** [C] the small hard ball used in the game of baseball

baseball ,cap noun [C] a hat that fits close to your head, with a flat curved part that sticks out above your eyes —*picture* → HAT

baseless /'beɪsləs/ adj *formal* not based on facts or evidence

baseline /'beɪsˌlaɪn/ noun [C] the line that marks the back of the playing area in games such as tennis —*picture* → C15

basement /'beɪsmənt/ noun [C] the part of a building below the level of the ground —*picture* → C1

bases the plural of **basis**

bash¹ /bæʃ/ verb [I/T] *informal* to hit someone or something very hard, often causing injury or serious damage: *They had to bash the door down to get to the fire.*

bash² /bæʃ/ noun [C] *informal* a party or celebration

PHRASE **have a bash** *British* to try to do something

bashful /'bæʃf(ə)l/ adj easily embarrassed when you are with other people=SHY —*bashfully* adv

basic /'beɪsɪk/ adj ★★★

1 forming the main or most important part or aspect of something: *Rice is the basic ingredient of the dish.* ♦ *First you need to understand the basic principles of computers.*

2 simple, with nothing special or extra: *The state provides only basic health care.* ♦ *Sales reps receive a basic salary plus commission.* ♦ *It's an inexpensive hotel, and the accommodation is quite basic.*

basically /'beɪsɪkli/ adv ★

1 in the most important aspects, without

thinking about the specific details: *The book is basically a love story.*

2 *spoken* used for emphasizing the most important point or idea in what you are saying: *Basically, you should have asked me first.*

basics, the /'beɪsɪks/ noun [plural] the most important aspects or principles of something: *The basics of the game can be learned very quickly.*

basil /'bæz(ə)l, *American* 'beɪz(ə)l/ noun [U] a plant with sweet leaves that are used in salads and cooking

basilica /bə'zɪlɪkə/ noun [C] a large important Roman Catholic church

basin /'beɪs(ə)n/ noun **1** a round open container that is used for holding liquids or for storing or mixing food **2** a large bowl fixed to the wall in a bathroom for washing your face and hands in=WASHBASIN **3** a large area of land from which water flows into a particular river or lake: *the Colorado River Basin*

basis /'beɪsɪs/ (plural **bases** /'beɪsiːz/) noun [C] ★

1 a particular method or system that is used for doing or organizing something: *Salaries are paid on a weekly basis.* ♦ *Tickets will be sold on a first-come, first-served basis.*

2 the reason why something is done: *Don't make your decision on the basis of cost alone.*

3 the important ideas, facts, or actions from which something can develop =FOUNDATION: *Bernard's work forms the basis of all modern physiology.* ♦ *The agreement provides the basis for future negotiations.*

bask /bɑːsk/ verb [I] **1** to relax and enjoy yourself by lying in the sun **2** to enjoy people's attention and approval: *For now, she is content to bask in her newfound fame.*

basket /'bɑːskɪt/ noun [C] ★ a container for carrying or keeping things in, made from thin pieces of plastic, wire, or wood woven together: *a laundry basket* ♦ *a basket of food*

basketball /'bɑːskɪtˌbɔːl/ noun **1** [U] a game played by two teams of five players who score points by throwing a ball through a net **2** [C] the ball used in the game of basketball

bass¹ /beɪs/ noun **1** [C/U] the lowest male singing voice, or a man who sings with this type of voice **2** [U] the lower half of the full range of musical notes **3 bass** or **bass guitar** [C] an electric guitar that produces very low notes **4** [C] a DOUBLE BASS —**bass** adj: *a bass drum/voice*

bass² /bæs/ (plural **bass**) noun [C/U] a fish that lives in rivers and the sea

bassoon /bə'suːn/ noun [C] a musical instrument consisting of a long wooden tube that you hold upright and play by blowing into a thin metal pipe —*picture* → WOODWIND

bastard /'bɑːstəd/ noun [C] *offensive* **1** an insulting word for an unpleasant or annoying man **2** *old-fashioned* someone whose parents are not married to each other

baste /beɪst/ verb [I/T] to cover meat with hot fat or its own juices while it is cooking

bastion /ˈbæstiən/ noun [C] an organization, community, or system that supports and defends a particular way of life, tradition, or belief: *an all-male bastion of conservatism*

bat¹ /bæt/ noun [C] **1** a wooden object used for hitting the ball in games such as baseball, CRICKET, and TABLE TENNIS **2** a small animal that flies at night and looks like a mouse with large wings

bat² /bæt/ verb [I] to try to hit the ball with a bat in a game such as baseball or CRICKET

batch /bætʃ/ noun [C] a quantity of people or things that arrive, are made, or are dealt with at the same time: *a batch of cakes*

bated /ˈbeɪtɪd/ adj **with bated breath** worried or excited about what will happen

bath¹ /bɑːθ/ noun [C] ★★★
1 the process of washing yourself or someone else in a bath: *Have I got time to have a bath?*
2 *British* a long deep container that you fill with water and wash yourself in
3 the water in a bath: *Can you run a bath* (=fill a bath with water) *for me?*

bath² /bɑːθ/ verb [I/T] *British* to wash yourself or someone else in a bath

bathe /beɪð/ verb **1** [I/T] *American* to wash yourself or someone else in a bath **2** [T] to cover a part of your body with a liquid, especially in order to clean or treat a cut **3** [T] to fill an area with light: *The valley was bathed in warm light.*

bathrobe /ˈbɑːθrəʊb/ noun [C] a loose piece of clothing like a soft coat that you wear before or after taking a bath or shower

bathroom /ˈbɑːθruːm/ noun [C] ★★ a room containing a bath or shower, a WASHBASIN, and often a toilet
  PHRASE **go to the bathroom** *American* to use the toilet

bathtub /ˈbɑːθtʌb/ noun [C] *American* a BATH for washing yourself in

baton /ˈbætɒn, ˈbæt(ə)n/ noun [C] **1** a stick that the CONDUCTOR of an orchestra uses **2** a stick that a police officer can use as a weapon =TRUNCHEON

batsman /ˈbætsmən/ (plural **batsmen** /ˈbætsmən/) noun [C] a player who tries to hit the ball in CRICKET

battalion /bəˈtæljən/ noun [C] a large group of soldiers

batter¹ /ˈbætə/ verb [I/T] to hit someone or something many times: *Huge waves battered the little ship.*

batter² /ˈbætə/ noun [C/U] a liquid mixture of milk, flour, and eggs, used in cooking

battered /ˈbætəd/ adj **1** old and slightly damaged: *a battered old car* **2** having experienced a lot of problems: *his battered reputation* **3** *old-fashioned* treated violently by a member of your family

battery /ˈbæt(ə)ri/ noun [C] ★ an object that fits into something such as a radio, clock, or car and supplies it with electricity
  → RECHARGE

battle¹ /ˈbæt(ə)l/ noun ★★
1 [C/U] a fight between two armies in a war: *one of the bloodiest battles of the Second World War* ♦ *soldiers wounded in battle* ♦ *the Battle of Waterloo*

2 [C] a situation in which people or groups compete with each other: *The couple are locked in a bitter legal battle over custody of their children.* ♦ **the battle for** the leadership of the Labour Party

3 [C] a situation in which someone is trying very hard to deal with a difficult situation: *She has lost her battle against breast cancer.* ♦ **a battle to do sth** *It was a daily battle to get my son to go to school.*

battle² /ˈbæt(ə)l/ verb **1** [I/T] to try very hard to deal with a difficult situation: *Surgeons battled to save the man's life.* **2** [I] to compete with someone: *the three men battling for the world title*

battlefield /ˈbæt(ə)lˌfiːld/ or **battleground** /ˈbæt(ə)lˌɡraʊnd/ noun [C] a place where a battle takes place or where one took place in the past

battlements /ˈbæt(ə)lmənts/ noun [plural] a wall around the top of a castle, with spaces through which weapons could be fired

battleship /ˈbæt(ə)lˌʃɪp/ noun [C] the largest type of WARSHIP

bauble /ˈbɔːb(ə)l/ noun [C] a cheap decoration or piece of jewellery

baulk /bɔːk/ verb [I] to refuse to do something or let something happen: *He baulked at admitting he had done anything wrong.*

bawl /bɔːl/ verb **1** [I/T] to shout in a loud angry way **2** [I] to cry loudly

bay /beɪ/ noun [C] **1** an area of the coast where the land curves inwards **2** an area in a building or vehicle that is used for a particular purpose: *a loading/cargo bay*
  PHRASE **keep/hold sth at bay** to prevent something serious, dangerous, or unpleasant from affecting you

bay leaf noun [C] a leaf used in cooking for adding flavour

bayonet /ˈbeɪənɪt/ noun [C] a long sharp blade that is fixed onto the end of a RIFLE

bay window noun [C] a large window that sticks out from the main wall of a house —*picture* → C1

bazaar /bəˈzɑː/ noun [C] **1** a market, especially in the Middle East and South Asia **2** a sale to raise money for a particular project or organization

BBC, the /ˌbiː biː ˈsiː/ the British Broadcasting Corporation: an organization that broadcasts television and radio programmes and is owned by the British government

BBQ abbrev barbecue

BC abbrev before Christ: used after a date to show that it refers to a time before the birth of Jesus Christ → AD

be /biː/ verb ★★★

Be can have many different forms depending on its subject and on its tense:	
present tense	I am
	he/she/it **is**
	we/you/they **are**
past tense	I/he/she/it **was**
	we/you/they **were**
past participle	**been**
present participle	**being**

1 [auxiliary verb] used with a present participle for forming a PROGRESSIVE tense

of a verb: *I am studying English Literature.*
♦ *We were having breakfast when Terry phoned.*

2 [auxiliary verb] used with a past participle for forming the passive form of a verb: *Her husband was killed in a car accident.* ♦ *The orchestra will be conducted by David Norton.*

3 [linking verb] used for giving information about someone or something, for example their name, job, or position: *Our teacher is Miss Tiwana.* ♦ *He wants to be an actor.* ♦ *It was a cold frosty morning.* ♦ *Baltimore is not far from Washington.* ♦ *Nancy is tall and very thin.*

4 [linking verb] used for saying how someone behaves, or for telling them how to behave: *They are being very silly.* ♦ *Be quiet!*

PHRASES **have been to...** used for saying that someone has gone to a place and returned: *Have you ever been to Venice?*

there is/**are** used for saying that someone or something exists, happens, or can be found: *There is a problem with the car.* ♦ *How many people were there at the party?* ♦ *There have been six serious accidents on this road.*

Questions and negatives with 'be' are formed without 'do': *Are you busy?* ♦ *The book was not expensive.*

beach /biːtʃ/ noun [C] ★★ an area of sand or small stones beside the sea or a lake → SHORE

beachfront /ˈbiːtʃfrʌnt/ adj facing a beach or very close to a beach: *a large beachfront hotel*

beacon /ˈbiːkən/ noun [C] a bright light that is used as a signal to warn people or to show them the way somewhere

bead /biːd/ noun [C] **1** a small round piece of plastic, glass, metal etc that is used for making jewellery: *a string of beads* **2** a small drop of a liquid such as blood or SWEAT

beady /ˈbiːdi/ adj beady eyes are small, round, and bright

beagle /ˈbiːg(ə)l/ noun [C] a dog with short hair and long ears

beak /biːk/ noun [C] the hard curved or pointed part of a bird's mouth

beaker /ˈbiːkə/ noun [C] **1** British a plastic cup with straight sides **2** a glass or plastic container with straight sides, used in a laboratory

beam¹ /biːm/ noun [C] **1** a long thick piece of wood, metal, or CONCRETE that supports a roof **2** a line of light or energy: *a laser beam*

beam² /biːm/ verb **1** [I] to have a big smile on your face because you are very happy **2** [I/T] to send out light, heat, or radio or television signals: *Pictures of the famine were beamed to television audiences all over the world.*

bean /biːn/ noun [C] **1** a seed of various plants that is cooked and eaten, or a plant that produces these seeds **2** a dried bean that you GRIND and use to make drinks such as coffee and COCOA → FULL, SPILL¹

bear¹ /beə/ (past tense **bore** /bɔː/; past participle **borne** /bɔːn/) verb [T] ★

1 (not) like sb/sth	**6** have bad feeling
2 accept bad situation	**7** give birth to
3 have particular quality	+ PHRASES
4 have writing/design	+ PHRASAL VERBS
5 support weight	

1 if you cannot bear someone or something, you do not like them at all or cannot accept them: *Most of her friends can't bear her husband.* ♦ **can't bear the thought of** *moving again.* ♦ **can't bear doing sth/to do sth** *Sue can't bear to be parted from her baby daughter.*

2 to accept a difficult or unpleasant situation, especially without complaining: *She bore all her suffering with incredible patience.* ♦ *The pain was more than I could bear.*

3 to seem to be a particular kind of thing or to have particular qualities: *His description bore no relation to reality.*

4 formal if something bears writing or a design, it has writing or a design on it: *a blue banner bearing the words 'Civil Rights March'*

5 to support the weight of something: *The old floorboards could not bear the weight of the grand piano.*

6 to have a bad feeling towards someone: *I hope you don't still bear a grudge against me* (=continue to be angry about something I did in the past).

7 formal to give birth to a child

PHRASES **bear fruit** if a plan or effort bears fruit, it is eventually successful

bear sth in mind to remember to think about something when you are involved in doing something else: *When you speak to Lee, bear in mind he's still upset about what happened.*

bear left/**right** to turn left/right

bear the responsibility/**blame** to be responsible for something: *The Chancellor and his supporters bear the responsibility for starting this row.*

bear witness formal to show signs that prove that something happened or was true

PHRASAL VERBS ˌbear ˈdown on sb/sth to move quickly towards someone in a determined and threatening way: *I could see a police car bearing down on us.*

ˌbear sb/sth ˈout to show that someone is telling the truth or that something is true: +(that) *Scientific evidence bears out the claim that stress and disease are linked.*

ˌbear ˈup to behave in a brave way in a very sad or difficult situation: *Let's see how he bears up under the pressure.*

ˈbear ˌwith sb spoken used as a polite way of asking someone to be patient while you do something: *Bear with me – I won't be long.*

bear² /beə/ noun [C] **1** a large wild animal with thick fur **2** business someone who expects the price of company SHARES to fall, so they sell them → BULL 2

bearable /ˈbeərəb(ə)l/ adj something that is bearable is difficult or unpleasant, but you are able to accept or deal with it ≠ UNBEARABLE

beard /bɪəd/ noun [C] hair that grows on a man's chin and cheeks —**bearded** adj

bearer /ˈbeərə/ noun [C] someone who brings you a particular type of news or information: *I hate to be the bearer of bad news.*

bearing /ˈbeərɪŋ/ noun [singular] the particular way in which someone stands, moves, or behaves

B

PHRASES **get/find your bearings** to find out where you are and where other things are
have some/no bearing on sth to be relevant/not relevant to something: *His private life has no bearing on his competence as a manager.*
lose your bearings to become confused about where you are and where other things are

'**bear ,market** noun [C] *business* a situation in which the prices of SHARES are falling

beast /biːst/ noun [C] **1** an animal, especially a dangerous or strange one **2** *old-fashioned* a cruel or immoral person

beat¹ /biːt/ (past tense **beat**; past participle **beaten**) verb ★★★

1 defeat sb	6 of heart
2 hit sb several times	7 mix foods well
3 hit sth several times	+ PHRASES
4 arrive before sb	+ PHRASAL VERBS
5 be better than sth	

1 [T] to defeat someone in a game, competition, election, or BATTLE: *England needed to beat Germany to get to the final.*
2 [T] to hit someone violently several times: *They were arrested for beating their children.* ♦ *The two men had been **beaten to death**.*
3 [I/T] to hit something many times or for a long period of time: *The rain **was beating against** the windows.*
4 [T] to arrive before someone else: *See if you can beat me back to the house!*
5 [T] *informal* to be better than something else: *For me, surfing the Net beats watching TV any time.*
6 [I] if someone's heart beats, it makes regular sounds and movements: *The shock had made my heart beat faster.*
7 [T] to mix foods together using a fork or a special tool or machine

PHRASES **beat sb to it** to do something before someone else: *When I went to take the keys I found that someone had beaten me to it.*
it beats me *spoken* used for saying that you do not know or understand something: *'Why did he do such a stupid thing?' 'It beats me.'*
you can't beat sth used for saying that something is very good: *You can't beat a good book.*

PHRASAL VERBS ,beat 'down **1** if the sun beats down, it shines very brightly **2** if the rain beats down, it rains very hard
,beat sb 'off to succeed in winning or gaining something from an opponent: *Virgin Airlines must beat off stiff competition to win the contract.*
,beat sb 'up *informal* to hurt someone by hitting or kicking them many times: *They threatened to beat me up if I didn't give them my wallet.*

beat² /biːt/ noun **1** [C] the regular sound or movement of your heart: *I could feel the beat of his heart.* **2** [singular] the main pattern of regular strong sounds in a piece of music: *music with a slow bluesy beat* **3** [singular] a single regular sound, or a series of regular sounds, especially of two things hitting together: *the beat of the bird's wings* **4** [C] an area that a police officer has responsibility for and must walk around regularly

beaten /ˈbiːt(ə)n/ adj **off the beaten track** far away from the places that people usually visit

beating /ˈbiːtɪŋ/ noun [C] an act of hitting someone hard a number of times in a fight or as a punishment
PHRASE **take a beating** to be badly damaged or criticized

'**beat-up** adj *informal* old and in bad condition: *a beat-up old bicycle*

beautician /bjuːˈtɪʃ(ə)n/ noun [C] someone whose job is to give people beauty treatments

beautiful /ˈbjuːtəf(ə)l/ adj ★★★
1 a beautiful woman or child is extremely attractive ≠ UGLY: *What a beautiful baby!*
2 very nice to look at, hear, or experience =LOVELY: *The weather has been beautiful this week.* ♦ *a beautiful song/dress*
—**beautifully** adv: *They were all beautifully dressed.*

Other ways of saying **beautiful**

- **attractive** used for describing men and women whose looks make other people sexually interested in them
- **cute** used for describing children who are nice to look at and who behave in a nice way. It is also used for describing a man or woman who is sexually attractive
- **good-looking** used for describing adults and older children who are nice to look at.
- **gorgeous** very beautiful or handsome
- **handsome** used for describing men who are nice to look at
- **pretty** used for describing young women and girls who have nice faces

beautify /ˈbjuːtɪfaɪ/ verb [T] to make something look more beautiful

beauty¹ /ˈbjuːti/ noun ★★
1 [U] the quality of being beautiful: *He was impressed by her beauty and charm.* ♦ *the beauty of the landscape*
2 [C] *informal* something that you think is very good, or is a good example of its type: *I love old cars, and that one's a beauty.*
PHRASE **the beauty of sth** the advantage or good quality that something has: *The beauty of working at home is that you don't have to travel to work.*

beauty² /ˈbjuːti/ adj designed to make people look more beautiful: *beauty products/treatments*

'**beauty ,spot** noun [C] *British* a beautiful place in the countryside that attracts tourists

beaver /ˈbiːvə/ noun [C] a small North American animal that has a wide flat tail and thick fur

became the past tense of **become**

because /bɪˈkɒz/ grammar word ★★★

Because can be:
- a **conjunction**: *We went by bus because it was cheaper.*
- used in the preposition phrase **because of**: *The game was cancelled because of the snow.*

used for giving the reason for something: *I couldn't phone you because I hadn't got your number.* ♦ *It's a really useful book because it explains everything very clearly.* ♦ *Our profits fell because of the recession.* → JUST¹

beck /bek/ noun **at sb's beck and call** available to do things for another person whenever they want

beckon /'bekən/ verb [I/T] **1** to signal to someone to come towards you **2** to seem to be an attractive possibility to someone: *A bright future beckoned.*

become /bɪ'kʌm/ (past tense **became** /bɪ'keɪm/; past participle **become**) linking verb ★★★ to change and start to be something different: *The sky became dark.* ◆ *People were becoming increasingly angry about the delay.* ◆ *Christine decided to become a writer.* ◆ *São Paulo has become the largest city in South America.*

PHRASE **what has/will become of** used for asking what has happened to someone or something, or what will happen to them: *If she is sent to prison, what will become of her children?*

bed /bed/ noun ★★★
1 [C/U] a piece of furniture that you sleep on: *The room had two beds in it.* ◆ *It's midnight – why aren't you in bed?* ◆ *I never get out of bed before 10 am.* ◆ *I got home at 11 pm and went straight to bed.*
2 [C] the ground at the bottom of a sea or river: *fish that live close to the sea bed*
3 [C] an area of ground that has been prepared for growing plants in
→ FLOWERBED

PHRASES **bed and breakfast** a small hotel or private house that provides a room for the night and a meal the next morning
go to bed with sb *informal* to have sex with someone

bedclothes /'bed,kləʊðz/ noun [plural] sheets and covers that are used on beds

bedding /'bedɪŋ/ noun [U] sheets and covers that are used on beds

bedraggled /bɪ'dræg(ə)ld/ adj wet, dirty, and untidy

bedridden /'bed,rɪd(ə)n/ adj unable to get out of bed because you are too ill

bedrock /'bed,rɒk/ noun [singular] the principles on which a system is based

bedroom /'bedru:m/ noun [C] ★★ a room that you sleep in: *Your mum can stay in the spare bedroom.* ◆ *a two-bedroom flat* ◆ *the bedroom door*

bedside /'bedsaɪd/ noun [singular] the area near your bed: *a bedside table/lamp*

bedsit /'bedsɪt/ noun [C] *British* a room that you rent that is used for both living and sleeping in

bedspread /'bed,spred/ noun [C] a top cover for a bed

bedtime /'bed,taɪm/ noun [U] the time when you usually go to bed: *Come on, kids – it's bedtime!* ◆ *a bedtime story*

bee /bi:/ noun [C] a flying insect that has a black and yellow body, makes HONEY, and can sting you —*picture* → C13

beech /bi:tʃ/ noun [C/U] a large tree with smooth grey BARK and small nuts, or the wood of this tree

beef¹ /bi:f/ noun [U] ★ the meat from a cow: *a slice of roast beef*

beef² /bi:f/ PHRASAL VERB ,beef sth 'up *informal* to increase or improve something

double bed

camp bed ... bunk bed

four-poster bed

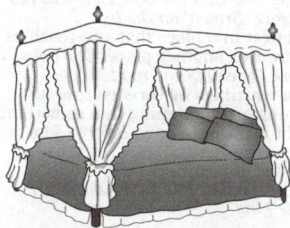
beds

beefburger /'bi:f,bɜ:gə/ noun [C] *British* a BURGER

beefy /'bi:fi/ adj *informal* a beefy person has a large heavy body

beehive /'bi:,haɪv/ noun [C] a large box that people keep BEES in when they want to get the HONEY that the bees produce

been the past participle of **be**

beep¹ /bi:p/ verb **1** [I] if a piece of electronic equipment beeps, it makes a short high sound **2** [I/T] if you beep the horn in your car, it makes a short loud noise

beep² /bi:p/ noun [C] **1** a short high sound made by a piece of electronic equipment **2** the short loud noise that a car horn makes

beeper /'bi:pə/ noun [C] a small piece of electronic equipment that you carry that makes a sound when someone sends you a message=PAGER

beer /bɪə/ noun ★
1 [U] a yellow or brown alcoholic drink made from grain: *a pint of beer*
2 [C] a glass or bottle of this drink: *Would you like another beer?*

beet /bi:t/ noun [C/U] *American* a BEETROOT

beetle /'bi:t(ə)l/ noun [C] an insect with a smooth hard back —*picture* → C13

beetroot /'bi:tru:t/ noun [C/U] *British* a round purple vegetable that is cooked and eaten cold —*picture* → C11

befall /bɪ'fɔ:l/ (past tense **befell** /bɪ'fel/; past participle **befallen** /bɪ'fɔ:lən/) verb [I/T] *literary* if something unpleasant befalls you, it happens to you

B

B

befit /bɪˈfɪt/ verb [T] *formal* to be suitable for someone or something: *She dressed as befitting the daughter of a millionaire.* —**befitting** adj

before /bɪˈfɔː/ grammar word ★★★

Before can be:
- a **conjunction**: *Think carefully before you choose.*
- a **preposition**: *We'll finish the project before Christmas.*
- an **adverb**: *I'd met him once before.*

1 earlier than something earlier than a particular time, event, or action: *I went for a run before breakfast.* ♦ *The others had got there before us.* ♦ *Won't you have another drink before you go?* ♦ *I joined the police in 1999. Before that I was in the army.* ♦ *Haven't we met somewhere before?* ♦ *Don was here the day before yesterday.* ♦ **before doing sth** *You should seek legal advice before signing anything.*
2 earlier in series placed earlier than something else in a list or series: *'Barnes' comes before 'Brown' on the list.*
3 passed first in a place that you reach as you go towards another place: *Our house is just before the end of the road.*
4 used in warnings or threats *spoken* used for warning or threatening that something bad could happen: *Get out, before I lose my temper.*
5 in front of sb/sth *formal* in front of someone or something: *Lawrence knelt before the king.*
→ AGO

beforehand /bɪˈfɔːhænd/ adv before a particular event: *If you do most of the cooking beforehand, you'll enjoy the evening more.*

befriend /bɪˈfrend/ verb [T] to become someone's friend and treat them in a kind way

beg /beg/ verb [I/T] **1** to ask for something in a way that shows you want it very much: *She had written a letter begging him to come back.* ♦ *We begged her for another chance.* ♦ *'Don't go!' he begged.* **2** to ask people for money or food: *homeless people begging on the streets*
▪ PHRASE **I beg your pardon** *spoken formal* **1** used for asking someone to repeat something **2** used for saying that you are sorry when you make a small mistake: *Oh, I beg your pardon, I didn't realize this was your chair.*

began the past tense of **begin**

beggar /ˈbegə/ noun [C] someone who lives by asking people for money or food

begin /bɪˈgɪn/ (past tense **began** /bɪˈgæn/; past participle **begun** /bɪˈgʌn/; present participle **beginning**) verb ★★★
1 [I] to start happening, or to be the first thing to happen: *The ceremony will begin at noon.* ♦ *We usually use 'an' before a word that begins with a vowel.*
2 [I/T] to start doing something: **begin doing sth** *He began shouting abuse at them.* ♦ **begin to do sth** *Now we were beginning to feel excited.* ♦ **begin (sth) as sth** *He began his working life as a waiter.* ♦ **begin (sth) with sth** *We began the meeting with a discussion about the budget.*

▪ PHRASE **to begin with 1** before or during the first part of an activity: *How did you get involved to begin with?* **2** *spoken* used for introducing the first thing in a list of things: *'Why were you annoyed?' 'Well, to begin with, I missed my train.'*

beginner /bɪˈgɪnə/ noun [C] someone who has just started to learn or do something =NOVICE

beginning /bɪˈgɪnɪŋ/ noun ★★★
1 [singular] the first part of something =START ≠ END: *I loved the beginning of the book but hated the rest.* ♦ *It was the beginning of a friendship that would last his whole life.* ♦ *In the beginning I found it hard to concentrate.*
2 beginnings [plural] the origin of something, for example where or how it started: *It was a decade that saw the beginnings of the space programme.*

begrudge /bɪˈgrʌdʒ/ verb [T] **1** to feel annoyed because someone has got something that you think they do not deserve **2** to feel annoyed because you have to do something =RESENT

begun the past participle of **begin**

behalf /bɪˈhɑːf/ noun ★
▪ PHRASE **on sb's behalf** or **on behalf of sb** **1** instead of someone, or as a representative of someone: *A lawyer read out a statement on behalf of the victim's family.* **2** in order to help someone: *I offered to speak to the manager on his behalf.*

behave /bɪˈheɪv/ verb ★★
1 [I] to do things in a particular way: *The children behaved very badly.* ♦ *a badly behaved dog* ♦ *You behaved like a complete idiot!* ♦ *He behaved as though he hadn't seen Ellie.*
2 [I/T] to be polite and not cause trouble: *Mum's always telling me to behave when we go out.* ♦ *I hope the children behave themselves.*

behavior /bɪˈheɪvjə/ the American spelling of **behaviour**

behaviour /bɪˈheɪvjə/ noun [U] ★★★
1 the way that someone behaves: *Anna was sick of her brother's behaviour.*
2 the way that a substance reacts in particular conditions: *Scientists are studying the behaviour of the new gas.*

behead /bɪˈhed/ verb [T] to cut off someone's head as a punishment

behind¹ /bɪˈhaɪnd/ grammar word ★★★

Behind can be:
- a **preposition**: *The car behind us was flashing its lights.*
- an **adverb**: *I stayed behind to look after the children.*

1 at the back of sb/sth at the back of someone or something, or following them: *The teacher was standing behind me.* ♦ *Some papers had fallen behind the cupboard.* ♦ *Shut the door behind you.* ♦ *You walk ahead and we'll follow along behind.* ♦ *Someone grabbed me from behind.*
2 late in doing sth late or too slow in doing things that you have to do: *The project is already a month behind schedule.* ♦ *I've been ill, and now I'm behind with my work.*

B

3 remaining after people leave remaining in a place after people have left: *A few people stayed behind to clear up.* ♦ *Some of the equipment got left behind.*

4 achieving less progress or success with less success or progress than others: *Technology in Eastern Europe was at least 20 years behind the West.* ♦ *At half time, our team was behind by 12 points.*

5 used for stating the real cause of sth used for stating what the true cause of something is, or what the true facts are in a situation: *Police believe that a racist group is behind the attacks.* ♦ *People want to know the truth behind these rumours.*

6 supporting sb/sth supporting a person, action, or idea: *I want you to know we're right behind you.*

7 in the past in the past, and no longer affecting you: *All those bad times are behind me now.*

PHRASE behind the times old-fashioned

behind² /bɪˈhaɪnd/ noun [C] *informal* the part of your body that you sit on

beige /beɪʒ/ adj very pale brown in colour —**beige** noun [U]

being /ˈbiːɪŋ/ noun [C] a person: *We are social beings as well as individuals.*

PHRASE come into being to start to exist

belated /bɪˈleɪtɪd/ adj happening or arriving late: *a belated apology* —**belatedly** adv

belch¹ /beltʃ/ verb **1** [I] to let air from your stomach come out through your mouth in a noisy way=BURP **2** [T] to produce a lot of smoke or steam

belch² /beltʃ/ noun [C] the action or sound of someone belching

beleaguered /bɪˈliːɡəd/ adj having a lot of problems or criticism to deal with

belie /bɪˈlaɪ/ verb [T] *formal* **1** to make something appear different from how it really is **2** to seem to show that something is not true

belief /bɪˈliːf/ noun ★★★

1 [C] a strong feeling that something is true, real, or good: *a belief in the possibility of a perfect society* ♦ *It is my firm belief that the government should act now.* ♦ **+that** *the mistaken belief that cocaine is not an addictive drug*

2 beliefs [plural] a set of ideas that you are certain are true: *Christian/Buddhist beliefs* ♦ *Everyone is entitled to express their own personal beliefs.* ♦ *our traditional beliefs about the origins of life*

PHRASE beyond belief used for emphasizing how bad or surprising something is: *The conditions they are living in are beyond belief.*

believable /bɪˈliːvəb(ə)l/ adj something that is believable seems possible or likely to be true=PLAUSIBLE

believe /bɪˈliːv/ verb ★★★

1 [T] to think that something is true: *Astronomers knew the Earth was round, but few people believed it.* ♦ *The police didn't believe her.* ♦ **+(that)** *I don't believe she's his sister at all.* ♦ *It is widely believed* (=believed by a lot of people) *that the disease originally came from monkeys.* ♦ *She found it hard to believe that he was a real businessman.*

2 [T] to have an opinion about what is true or what might happen, although there is no proof=THINK: **+(that)** *Scientists believe a cure for the disease will be discovered soon.* ♦ *We were led to believe* (=people told us) *we could make a large profit.*

3 [I] to have a religious belief

PHRASES believe it or not *spoken* used for emphasizing that something is very surprising but true: *Jason and Mel are finally getting married, believe it or not!*

I can't/don't believe it used for emphasizing that you are extremely surprised or shocked: *'He graduated from Oxford.' 'I don't believe it!'* **2** used when something annoys you: *I just don't believe it! I left my keys in the car again.*

PHRASAL VERB believe in sb/sth 1 to think that someone or something exists: *I don't believe in miracles.* **2** to think that someone or something is good: *She used to say she didn't believe in marriage.*

Word family: believe

Words in the same family as believe
- **belief** *n*
- **believable** *adj*
- **disbelieve** *adj*
- **disbelief** *n*
- **unbelievable** *v*

---

believer /bɪˈliːvə/ noun [C] someone who believes in God, a religion, or a set of principles

PHRASE be a great/firm believer in sth to believe that a particular idea or activity is good: *I'm a great believer in healthy eating and exercise.*

belittle /bɪˈlɪt(ə)l/ verb [T] to say that someone or something is not very good or important

bell /bel/ noun [C] ★★

1 a metal object that makes a noise when its sides are hit by a metal piece inside it: *the sound of church bells ringing*

2 a piece of equipment that makes a ringing sound, used for getting someone's attention: *There was no one at the counter, so I rang the bell.*

PHRASE give sb a bell *British informal* to phone someone

→ RING¹

belligerent /bəˈlɪdʒərənt/ adj very unfriendly and angry=AGGRESSIVE —**belligerence** noun [U]

bellow /ˈbeləʊ/ verb [I/T] to shout very loudly

belly /ˈbeli/ noun [C] *informal* your stomach, or the front part of your body between your chest and your legs

belly button noun [C] *informal* a person's NAVEL

belong /bɪˈlɒŋ/ verb [I] ★★★

1 to be in the right place: *That lamp belongs on the desk.* ♦ *When you've finished, put the cassettes back where they belong.*

2 to feel happy and comfortable in a particular place or group: *I just don't feel that I belong here.*

PHRASAL VERBS belong to sb to be owned by someone: *The car belongs to the woman next door.* ♦ *Who does this coat belong to?*

belong to sth to be a member of a group or organization: *She belongs to the school computer club.*

belongings /bɪˈlɒŋɪŋz/ noun [plural] the things that you own=POSSESSIONS

B

beloved /bɪˈlʌvɪd/ adj *literary* a beloved person, place, or thing is one that you love very much

below /bɪˈləʊ/ grammar word ★★★

Below can be:
- a **preposition**: *The lake is almost 900 feet below sea level.*
- an **adverb**: *I heard someone calling from the street below.*

1 in a lower place or position: *There was a party in the flat below.* ♦ *a gunshot wound below the left shoulder*

2 less than a particular number, amount, or level: *The temperature fell below zero.* ♦ *His score on the test was below average.*

3 lower in rank or less important than someone else: *officers below the rank of captain*

4 in a later part of a piece of writing: *For further information, see below.*

belt¹ /belt/ noun [C] ★

1 a narrow piece of leather or cloth that you wear around your waist

2 a circular band that turns or moves something in a machine

3 an area of land where there is a particular industry or activity: *the corn belt*

PHRASE **get/have sth under your belt** *informal* to achieve something that is important and useful: *You need to get a few more computer programming courses under your belt.*
→ TIGHTEN

belt² /belt/ verb [T] *informal* to hit someone or something very hard

PHRASAL VERBS ,**belt sth ˈout** *informal* to sing something loudly

,**belt ˈup** *British impolite* used for telling someone to be quiet

bemused /bɪˈmjuːzd/ adj confused

bench /bentʃ/ noun

1 long seat	4 in parliament
2 table for working on	5 job of being judge
3 in sports	

1 [C] a hard seat for two or more people to sit on outside: *a park bench —picture*
→ CHAIR **2** [C] a long table that you use when you are working with tools **3 the bench** [singular] a place where people in a sports team sit when they are not playing **4 benches** [plural] the seats in the British parliament where the politicians sit **5 the bench** [singular] the position of being a judge in a court of law, or the place where a judge sits

benchmark /ˈbentʃmɑːk/ noun [C] a level or standard that you can use for judging how good other things are

bend¹ /bend/ (past tense and past participle **bent** /bent/) verb [I/T] ★★

1 to lean forwards and downwards: *Helen bent down to pick up her pen.* ♦ *Bend over and touch your toes.*

2 to curve or fold something, or to be curved or folded: *Use thin wire than can be easily bent.* ♦ *His arm was so stiff he couldn't bend it at all.* ♦ *The slim branches were bending under the weight of their fruit.*

PHRASES **bend over backwards (to do sth)** *informal* to do everything that you can do in order to help

bend the rules (for sb) to allow something that is not usually allowed

bend² /bend/ noun [C] a curve in something such as a road or river: *We came to a sharp bend in the road.*

bendy /ˈbendi/ adj *informal* easy to bend

beneath /bɪˈniːθ/ grammar word ★★

1 directly under something, or at a lower level: *We sheltered beneath a tree.* ♦ *You can see through the clear water to the coral reefs beneath.*

2 if something is beneath you, you think that you are too good or important to have to do it

benefactor /ˈbenɪfæktə/ noun [C] someone who helps a person or organization by giving them money

beneficial /ˌbenɪˈfɪʃ(ə)l/ adj something that is beneficial has a good effect or influence ≠ DETRIMENTAL, HARMFUL

beneficiary /ˌbenɪˈfɪʃəri/ noun [C] someone who gets money or property from someone who has died

benefit¹ /ˈbenɪfɪt/ noun ★★

1 [C/U] an advantage that you get from a situation: *He has had the benefit of the best education money can buy.* ♦ *Consider the potential benefits of the deal for the company.* ♦ *Not all competition is of benefit to the consumer.* ♦ *We are working for the benefit of the whole community.*

2 [C/U] *British* money that the government gives people who need financial help, for example because they are unemployed: *housing/sickness/disability benefit* ♦ *There has been an increase in the number of people claiming benefit.* ♦ *She's been on unemployment benefit for six years.*

3 [C] something good that you get from your employer as part of your job: *The benefits include medical insurance and a company car.*

4 [C] an event that is organized in order to make money for a CHARITY: *a benefit concert/performance*

PHRASE **give sb the benefit of the doubt** to accept what someone says, although you know that they might be lying

benefit² /ˈbenɪfɪt/ (present participle **benefiting** or **benefitting**; past tense and past participle **benefited** or **benefitted**) verb [I/T] ★★ to get an advantage, or to give someone an advantage: *Thousands of households could benefit under the scheme.* ♦ *The system mainly benefited people in the cities.* ♦ *Some patients have benefited greatly from this treatment.*

Benelux /ˈbenɪlʌks/ Belgium, the Netherlands, and Luxembourg, considered as a group

benevolent /bəˈnev(ə)lənt/ adj kind and helpful —**benevolence** noun [U]

benign /bəˈnaɪn/ adj **1** a benign TUMOUR (=lump in your body) is not cancer and will not kill you ≠ MALIGNANT **2** *formal* kind and nice

bent¹ /bent/ adj **1** a bent object has a curved or twisted shape **2** *British informal* dishonest

bent² the past tense and past participle of **bend¹**

bequeath /bɪˈkwiːð/ verb [T] *formal* to give someone money or property after you die by making a legal document called a WILL

bequest /bɪˈkwest/ noun [C] *formal* money or property that you give to someone after you die by making a legal document called a WILL

bereaved /bɪˈriːvd/ adj a bereaved person is someone whose close friend or family member has recently died

bereavement /bɪˈriːvmənt/ noun [C/U] an occasion when a close friend or family member dies

bereft /bɪˈreft/ adj *literary* **bereft of sth** lacking something that you need

beret /ˈbereɪ/ noun [C] a round flat soft hat that fits tightly on the top of your head

berry /ˈberi/ noun [C] a small fruit that does not have a STONE inside it

berserk /bəˈzɜːk/ adj **go berserk 1** *informal* to become very excited **2** to become violent because you are very angry

berth /bɜːθ/ noun [C] **1** a bed on a train or ship **2** a place at a port where a ship stays for a period of time

beside /bɪˈsaɪd/ preposition ★★
1 at the side of someone or something: *Who's that standing beside Jeff?* ◆ *We found a picnic area down beside the river.*
2 used for comparing two people or things: *Their efforts were unimpressive beside Frederick's.*
　PHRASES **beside the point** not relevant to the subject that you are discussing
beside yourself unable to think clearly because you are very upset or excited

besides /bɪˈsaɪdz/ grammar word ★

Besides can be:
■ a **preposition**: *Did you talk to anyone besides Joan?*
■ an **adverb**: *I've read all the books on the list, and a few others besides.*

1 in addition to someone or something else: *A lot of them are studying other things besides Italian.* ◆ *Besides being a teammate, he's my friend.* ◆ *There are cakes and sandwiches, and lots more besides.*
2 used when you are adding another reason to support what you are saying: *It's too late to invite any more people. Besides, Tim hates parties.*

besiege /bɪˈsiːdʒ/ verb [T] **1** to make more requests or complaints than someone can deal with: *The department has been besieged with letters from angry students.* **2** if soldiers besiege a place, they surround it and prevent the people there from getting food and supplies

besotted /bɪˈsɒtɪd/ adj so much in love with someone that you are always thinking about them

best /best/ grammar word ★★★

Best can be:
■ an **adjective**: *Which apples are best for cooking?* ◆ *It was the best party I've ever been to.*
■ an **adverb**: *We'll choose the system that works best.*
■ a **noun**: *I'll do my best.*

1 the superlative form of 'good' and 'well', used for describing the person, thing, or

way that is the most satisfactory, suitable, skilful etc ≠ WORST: *the best hotel in town* ◆ *You need to find out which program works best on your computer.* ◆ *In the world of ballet she was quite simply the best.* ◆ *The new drug is safe and effective, and best of all, inexpensive.* ◆ *What kind of soil is best for growing roses?* ◆ *I'll try to deal with all these problems as best I can.*
2 liked or known more than anyone or anything else ≠ WORST: *What kind of music do you like best?* ◆ *The Mona Lisa is probably the world's best known painting.*
　PHRASES **at best** used for stating what is the best or biggest possible thing, when this is not very good: *You can hope for a 5% profit at best.*
at sb's/sth's best feeling or showing the most impressive or attractive qualities possible: *I'm not at my best early in the morning.*
at the best of times used for saying that something is fairly bad, difficult etc even in normal circumstances: *Persuading the bank to lend you money is a difficult task at the best of times.*
be for the best used for saying that something that seems bad will in fact make the situation better
sb's best friend the friend that someone likes best
the best of both worlds a situation where you have two different advantages at the same time
best wishes used as a polite and friendly greeting before you sign your name on a letter or card
do/try your best to try as hard as you can
make the best of it to try to deal with a bad or difficult situation as well as you can
→ BET², PART¹

best ˈman noun [singular] the friend who helps a BRIDEGROOM at his wedding

bestow /bɪˈstəʊ/ verb [T] *formal* to give someone something good or valuable

best-seller noun [C] a book that many people buy —**best-selling** adj: *a best-selling author/book*

bet¹ /bet/ (past tense and past participle **bet**) verb [I/T] ★ to risk an amount of money by saying what you think will happen in a race or game: *Thousands of people bet on the result of the match.* ◆ *bet sth on sth I bet £10 on each of the horses.* ◆ *bet (sb) that He bet me £20 that I couldn't keep quiet for ten minutes.*
　PHRASE **I bet/I'll bet (that)** *spoken* used for saying that you are sure about something: *I bet the train will be late again.*

bet² /bet/ noun [C] an agreement in which you bet money on what will happen, or the amount of money that you bet: *He likes to have a bet on his home team, even though they always lose.*
　PHRASES **the/sb's best bet** the thing that gives the best chance of a successful result: *Our best bet would be to take the train.*
a good/safe bet something that is likely to happen, or someone or something that is likely to be successful: *It's a safe bet that the others won't make the same mistake.*
→ BETTING

betray /bɪˈtreɪ/ verb [T] **1** if you betray your

B

country, your family, or your friends, you deliberately do something that harms them **2** if you betray a feeling that you want to hide, your words or face make the feeling clear to people: *The woman's face betrayed no emotion.* **3** if you betray your beliefs or principles, you do something that does not agree with them

betrayal /bɪ'treɪəl/ noun [C/U] an act of betraying someone or something

better /'betə/ grammar word ★★★

> **Better** can be:
> ■ an **adjective**: *a better method of teaching languages*
> ■ an **adverb**: *Our opponents played better than we did.*
> ■ a **noun**: *There has been a change for the better.*

1 the comparative form of 'good' and 'well', used for describing a person, thing, or way that is more satisfactory, suitable, skilful etc than another ≠ WORSE: *She's trying to find a better job.* ♦ *The machine works better if you change the oil regularly.* ♦ *The situation started to get better.* ♦ *It's a good book, but her first one was far better.* ♦ *The results were better than we had expected.* ♦ *Maggie's a better cook than me.* ♦ *It's not much, but it's better than nothing.*
2 healthy again, or no longer painful ≠ WORSE: *You shouldn't go back to school until you're better.* ♦ *Is your headache better?* ♦ *If you want to get better, you must take your medicine.*
3 liked or known more than someone or something else: *I've always liked Susan better than her sister.* ♦ *He is better known by the name 'Pele'.*
PHRASES better still/yet used when you are adding a new idea that you think is better: *Come for a weekend or, better still, come for a whole week.*
for the better if something changes for the better, it improves ≠ FOR THE WORSE
get the better of sb 1 if a feeling gets the better of you, it is too strong for you to control **2** to defeat someone in a game or argument
(had) better do sth *spoken* used for saying that someone should do something: *You'd better take an umbrella – it's going to rain.* ♦ *Do you think we'd better go now?*
the sooner/bigger/quicker etc the better used for saying that you want something to be as soon/big/quick etc as possible: *I want you to get rid of those people, and the sooner the better.*

better 'off adj someone who is better off is in a better situation, or has more money: *You'd be better off living on your own.*

betting /'betɪŋ/ noun [U] the activity of trying to win money by placing a BET (=guessing the result of a race or game)

between /bɪ'twiːn/ grammar word ★★★

> **Between** can be:
> ■ a **preposition**: *the distance between two places*
> ■ an **adverb**: *two classes with a short break between*

1 with sb/sth on each side or end in a

position with people or things on each side or end: *Hold the needle between your finger and thumb.* ♦ *Trains running between Liverpool and Manchester were delayed.* ♦ *A sandwich is two slices of bread with something in between.* ♦ *Charlotte sat in between her two sons.*
2 with times or events before and after in the period after one time or event and before the next: *The office will be closed between Christmas and New Year.* ♦ *I have two classes this morning, with a short break in between.*
3 within a range within a range of numbers or amounts: *children between the ages of 4 and 13*
4 involving two people or things used for showing which people or things are involved in something: *a conversation between the Prime Minister and the President* ♦ *Scientists believe there is a link between diet and cancer.* ♦ *a match between England and Germany* → AMONG
5 talking about differences used for showing which people or things are similar or different: *Does a five-year-old know the difference between right and wrong?* ♦ *There are parallels between computer systems and the human brain.*
6 shared or divided used for showing how something is shared or divided: *We agreed to split the profits equally between us.*
7 talking about choices used for showing that you can choose one of two or more things: *You can choose between pasta, pizza, or burgers.*
PHRASE between you and me used when you are telling someone something that you do not want anyone else to know

beverage /'bevərɪdʒ/ noun [C] *formal* a drink

beware /bɪ'weə/ verb [I/T] if someone tells you to beware of something, they are warning you that it might be dangerous: *Beware of the dog!*

bewildered /bɪ'wɪldəd/ adj confused and not certain what to do

bewildering /bɪ'wɪld(ə)rɪŋ/ adj making you feel confused and not certain what to do

bewilderment /bɪ'wɪldəmənt/ noun [U] a feeling of being confused

beyond /bɪ'jɒnd/ grammar word ★★★

> **Beyond** can be:
> ■ a **preposition**: *the world beyond the prison wall*
> ■ an **adverb**: *The empire extended to the River Danube and beyond.*

1 past a place further away than something else or outside a particular area: *I could see the sea beyond the fields.* ♦ *Dr Barnard's fame had spread far beyond South Africa.*
2 not within the limits of sth outside the range or limits of a subject, quality, or activity: *Their behaviour went far beyond what is acceptable.*
3 after a time or age, or above an amount continuing after a particular time or age, or moving past a particular level: *Some people will prefer to continue working beyond 65.* ♦ *Inflation has risen beyond 10%.*
4 not able to be done used for saying that

something cannot be done: *The situation is already **beyond** our **control**. ♦ I'm afraid the watch is damaged **beyond** repair. ♦ The centre of Manchester has changed **beyond** recognition.*

5 except used in negative sentences to mean 'except': *We know nothing about him beyond these few facts.*

PHRASE **be beyond sb** to be too difficult for someone to understand or deal with: *It's beyond me why anyone should want to marry him.*

bhangra /ˈbʌŋgrə/ noun [U] a type of dance music that combines traditional music from India and Pakistan with Western music

bias /ˈbaɪəs/ noun [singular/U] **1** an attitude that makes you treat someone in a way that is unfair or different from the way you treat other people: *Ideally we'd choose judges who are without political bias.* **2** emphasis on one thing more than others: *a French course with a bias towards the spoken language*

biased /ˈbaɪəst/ adj preferring one person, thing, or idea to another in a way that is unfair ≠ UNBIASED

bib /bɪb/ noun [C] a piece of cloth that is tied around a baby's neck to protect its clothes while it is eating

bible /ˈbaɪb(ə)l/ noun **1 the Bible** [singular] the holy book of the Christian and Jewish religions **2** [C] a copy of the Bible **3** [C] the most important book for a particular subject

biblical /ˈbɪblɪk(ə)l/ adj from the Bible, or described in the Bible

bibliography /ˌbɪbliˈɒgrəfi/ noun [C] a list of books and articles on a particular subject

biceps /ˈbaɪseps/ (plural **biceps**) noun [C] the muscle between your shoulder and elbow on the front of your arm

bicker /ˈbɪkə/ verb [I] to argue about things that are not important —**bickering** /ˈbɪkərɪŋ/ noun [U]

bicycle /ˈbaɪsɪk(ə)l/ noun [C] a vehicle with two wheels that you ride by pushing PEDALS with your feet —*picture* → C7

bid¹ /bɪd/ (past tense and past participle **bid**; present participle **bidding**) verb **1** [I/T] to offer a particular amount of money for something: *They bid £300 for the painting.* **2** [I] to offer to do work or provide a service for a particular amount of money: *Several firms are bidding for the job.* —**bidder** noun [C]: *The house will be sold to the highest bidder.*

bid² /bɪd/ noun [C] **1** an offer to pay a particular amount of money for something: *We received a bid of £5,000 for the table.* **2** an offer to do work or provide a service for a particular amount of money: *They've put in a bid for the catering contract.* **3** an attempt to do something: *a bid to win the championship*

bidding /ˈbɪdɪŋ/ noun [U] the process of making bids for things

PHRASE **do sb's bidding** to do what someone asks or tells you to do

bide /baɪd/ verb **bide your time** to wait in a patient way for an opportunity to do something

bidet /ˈbiːdeɪ/ noun [C] a large bowl in a

bathroom that you sit on to wash your bottom

biennial /baɪˈeniəl/ adj happening once every two years

big /bɪg/ adj ★★★

1 large	**4** older
2 important	**5** enthusiastic
3 successful	

1 large in size: *big brown eyes ♦ A big man stood in the doorway. ♦ At the end of the lane was a great big house.*

2 important or serious: *We have another big game next week.*

3 powerful or successful: *The place was full of big businessmen. ♦ It was her dream to **make it big** as a singer. ♦ Her mother is **big in** daytime television.*

4 *informal* your big sister or big brother is older than you ≠ LITTLE: *This is my big brother, Jake.*

5 enthusiastic: *They were big fans of the Beatles.*

Words that you can use instead of **big**

Big is a very general word. Here are some words with more specific meanings that sound more natural and appropriate in particular situations.

people	large, tall
animals/plants	enormous, gigantic, great big, huge, large, massive
objects	bulky, colossal, enormous, gigantic, immense, large, massive
buildings	high, huge, large, rambling, tall
places/areas/cities	huge, large, massive, vast
rooms	airy, spacious
groups/organizations/ systems	enormous, huge, large, massive
numbers/amounts	colossal, considerable, high, huge, immense, massive, significant, sizeable, substantial, tremendous
changes	drastic, major, radical, significant, sweeping
problems	considerable, important, major, serious

bigamy /ˈbɪgəmi/ noun [U] the crime of being married to more than one person at the same time —**bigamist** noun [C]

Big ˈApple, the an informal name for New York City

Big ˈBang, the an explosion that some scientists believe was the origin of the universe

Big ˈBrother noun [singular] a person or organization that watches people all the time and tries to control everything that they say or do

big ˈbusiness noun [U] important business activity that makes a lot of money

big ˈcheese noun [C] *informal* an important or powerful person

B

big 'money noun [U] *informal* a lot of money

big 'name noun [C] *informal* a famous person

bigot /ˈbɪgət/ noun [C] someone who has very strong and unreasonable opinions about politics, race, or religion —**bigoted** /ˈbɪgətɪd/ adj

bigotry /ˈbɪgətri/ noun [U] very strong and unreasonable opinions about politics, race, or religion

big 'screen, the noun [singular] the cinema

big 'shot noun [C] *informal* an important person in an organization

big 'time adv *spoken* used for emphasizing what you are saying: *'Did you have problems with it?' 'Yeah, big time.'*

big ,time, the noun [singular] the highest and most successful level in a profession

bigwig /ˈbɪgwɪg/ noun [C] *informal* an important and powerful person in an organization

bike¹ /baɪk/ noun [C] *informal* ★★★ a BICYCLE or a MOTORCYCLE

bike² /baɪk/ verb [I] *informal* to ride somewhere on a bicycle

biker /ˈbaɪkə/ noun [C] someone who rides a MOTORCYCLE

bikini /bɪˈkiːni/ noun [C] a swimming suit for women, with two separate parts that cover the breasts and the lower part of the body —*picture* → C5

bilateral /baɪˈlæt(ə)rəl/ adj involving two groups or countries: *bilateral negotiations/talks* —**bilaterally** adv

bile /baɪl/ noun [U] **1** a bitter liquid that your liver produces to help your body to DIGEST food **2** *literary* angry words or feelings

bilingual /baɪˈlɪŋgwəl/ adj **1** able to speak two languages **2** written in two languages: *a bilingual dictionary*

bill¹ /bɪl/ noun [C] ★★★

1 amount that you owe	4 paper money
2 in a restaurant	5 bird's beak
3 proposal for law	

1 a written statement that shows how much money you owe for goods or services that you have received: *a telephone bill* ♦ *I always pay my bills on time.* ♦ *I wonder what the bill for the repairs will be?*
2 a piece of paper that shows how much money you owe after you have eaten in a restaurant: *Could we have the bill, please?*
3 a written document that contains a proposal for a new law
4 *American* a BANKNOTE: *a $100 bill*
5 a bird's beak
→ FOOT¹

bill² /bɪl/ verb [T] to send or give someone a written statement that shows how much money they owe: *We were billed for three nights when we were only there for two.*
PHRASE **be billed as** to be advertised or described in a particular way: *It was billed as the wedding of the year.*

billboard /ˈbɪlbɔːd/ noun [C] a large board for advertisements = HOARDING

billiards /ˈbɪliədz/ noun [U] a game in which two people use long sticks called CUES to hit balls into POCKETS at the edges and corners of a table → POOL¹ 3, SNOOKER

billing /ˈbɪlɪŋ/ noun [U] **1** the process of sending bills for payment **2** the importance that is given to a performer or an event in advertising material: *I got top billing.*

billion /ˈbɪljən/ number the number 1,000,000,000

billow /ˈbɪləʊ/ verb [I] **1** to rise or move in clouds: *Black smoke billowed over the city.* **2** to be filled with air and swell out like a sail: *Their robes billowed in the wind.*

bimbo /ˈbɪmbəʊ/ noun [C] *informal* an insulting word for a young woman who is attractive but not very intelligent

bin /bɪn/ noun [C] **1** *British* a container for putting rubbish in: *He tore up the letter and put it in the bin.* **2** a container for storing something: *a recycling bin*

binary /ˈbaɪnəri/ adj **1** *computing* based on a system in which information is represented using combinations of the numbers 0 and 1 **2** *technical* consisting of two parts

bind /baɪnd/ (past tense and past participle **bound** /baʊnd/) verb [T] **1** to tie things together with rope or string: *Their hands were bound behind their backs.* **2** to make two people or groups feel closely connected to each other: *The troubles they had shared bound them much closer together.* **3** to limit what someone is allowed to do by making them obey a rule or agreement: *He is bound by a contract that prevents him from working for competitors.*

binder /ˈbaɪndə/ noun [C] a hard cover that holds loose papers together

binding¹ /ˈbaɪndɪŋ/ adj a binding agreement, contract, or decision must be obeyed

binding² /ˈbaɪndɪŋ/ noun [C] the cover of a book

binge /bɪndʒ/ noun [C] an occasion when someone does too much of something that they enjoy, such as eating —**binge** verb [I]

bingo /ˈbɪŋgəʊ/ noun [U] a game in which players try to match numbers on their cards with numbers that are called out

binoculars /bɪˈnɒkjʊləz/ noun [plural] a piece of equipment that you look through to see distant objects. It has a separate part for each eye.

biochemical /ˌbaɪəʊˈkemɪk(ə)l/ adj involving chemical substances and processes in living things

biochemistry /ˌbaɪəʊˈkemɪstri/ noun [U] the study of chemical processes in living things —**biochemist** noun [C]

biodegradable /ˌbaɪəʊdɪˈgreɪdəb(ə)l/ adj decaying naturally in a way that is not harmful to the environment

biodiversity /ˌbaɪəʊdaɪˈvɜːsəti/ noun [U] the variety of different types of plant and animal life in a particular region

biographer /baɪˈɒgrəfə/ noun [C] someone who writes a book about someone else's life

biographical /ˌbaɪəˈgræfɪk(ə)l/ adj relating to the facts of someone's life

biography /baɪˈɒgrəfi/ noun [C] a book that someone writes about someone else's life

biological /ˌbaɪəˈlɒdʒɪk(ə)l/ adj **1** relating to living things **2** using dangerous bacteria to

harm people: *biological weapons/warfare*
—**biologically** /ˌbaɪə lɒdʒɪkli/ adv

biologist /baɪ ɒlədʒɪst/ noun [C] a scientist
who studies living things

biology /baɪ ɒlədʒi/ noun [U] the scientific
study of living things

biopsy /ˈbaɪɒpsi/ noun [C] a medical test in
which cells are taken from your body and
are examined to find out if they are healthy

biotechnology /ˌbaɪəʊtekˈnɒlədʒi/ noun [U]
science the use of bacteria and cells from
plants and animals for industrial or
scientific purposes

bipartisan /ˌbaɪpɑːtɪˈzæn/ adj involving two
political parties

birch /bɜːtʃ/ noun [C/U] a tree with thin
branches and an outer layer that comes off
in thin strips

bird /bɜːd/ noun [C] ★★★ an animal with
feathers, two wings, and a BEAK (=a hard
pointed mouth)
  PHRASE **bird of prey** a bird that hunts and
eats other animals
  → EARLY BIRD

bird's-eye ˈview noun [singular] a good view
of something from a high position

Biro /ˈbaɪrəʊ/ (plural **Biros**) British trademark a
plastic pen with a metal ball at its point

birth /bɜːθ/ noun ★★
  1 [C/U] the occasion when a baby is born:
*We are happy to announce **the birth** of our
son Andrew. ♦ James has been blind **from
birth**. ♦ children who have medical problems
at birth ♦ Her **place of birth** was listed as
Oxford.* → DATE¹
  2 [U] your position in society according to
your family, or according to the place
where you were born: *She's French **by birth**.*
  3 [singular] the beginning of something: *the
birth of a new era in British politics*
  PHRASE **give birth (to sb)** to produce a baby
from inside your body: *She gave birth to a
baby boy.*

birth cerˌtificate noun [C] an official document
that shows your name, details of when and
where you were born, and who your parents
are

birth conˌtrol noun [U] the practice of avoiding
becoming pregnant, or the methods that
people use for this=CONTRACEPTION

birthday /ˈbɜːθdeɪ/ noun [C] ★★ the day each
year with the same date as the day when
you were born: *It's her seventeenth birthday
tomorrow. ♦ Her birthday is on 7th June. ♦
a birthday party/card/present ♦ Happy
birthday, Tessa!*

birthmark /ˈbɜːθmɑːk/ noun [C] a red or
brown mark on the skin that some people
are born with

birth ˌparent noun [C] one of the parents that
someone had when they were born, rather
than one of the parents who ADOPTED them

birthplace /ˈbɜːθpleɪs/ noun [C] **1** the place
where someone was born **2** the place where
something first started

birth ˌrate noun [C] the official number of
births in a particular year or place

biscuit /ˈbɪskɪt/ noun [C] British a small flat dry
cake that is usually sweet: *a packet of
chocolate biscuits*

bisexual /baɪˈsekʃuəl/ adj sexually attracted

to both men and women → HETEROSEXUAL,
HOMOSEXUAL —**bisexuality** /ˌbaɪsekʃuˈæləti/
noun [U]

bishop /ˈbɪʃəp/ noun [C] **1** a senior Christian
priest who is responsible for all the
churches in a particular area **2** a piece in
the game of CHESS, shaped like a bishop's
hat —*picture* → C16

bison /ˈbaɪs(ə)n/ (plural **bison**) noun [C] a large
wild animal like a cow with long hair and
a big head

bistro /ˈbiːstrəʊ/ noun [C] a small restaurant
or bar

bit¹ /bɪt/ grammar word ★★★

> **A bit** can be:
> ■ an **adverb**: *We waited a bit, and then decided
> to go. ♦ It's a bit cold in here, isn't it?*
> ■ a **pronoun**: *She only ate a little bit. ♦ I could
> use a bit of help.*

  PHRASES **a bit** *informal* **1** slightly, or a little:
*I'm feeling **a bit** tired. ♦ That was **a little
bit** stupid. ♦ The second interview was **a bit**
less formal.* **2** a short time: *You'll have to
wait **a bit**. ♦ Why don't you come and stay
with us **for a bit**?* **3** a small amount of
something: 'Would you like some more
sauce?' 'Just **a bit**.' ♦ I know **a bit of** German.*
4 to a limited degree: *I used to surf **a bit**
when I was younger.*
  a bit much *informal* unreasonable or unfair:
*It's **a bit much** to blame me for what
happened.*
  a bit of a... *informal* used for saying that
someone or something has a particular
quality or effect: *My letter has caused **a bit
of a** problem.*
  every bit as just as: *Her new book is **every bit**
as good as the first one.*
  a good/fair bit *British* a fairly large amount of
something: *We've still got **a fair bit** to do.*
  not a bit *British informal* not at all: *'Are you
disappointed?' 'Not **a bit**.'*
  quite a bit *informal* a lot: *You can fly there, but
it costs **quite a bit**.*

bit² /bɪt/ noun [C] ★★★
  1 a small piece or part of something: *There
were **bits** of broken glass everywhere. ♦ The
best **bit** in the film is the scene in the
restaurant.*
  2 *computing* the basic unit of computer
information → BYTE
  3 the part of a horse's BRIDLE that fits inside
the horse's mouth
  PHRASES **bit by bit** gradually, or in small
stages: *I'll move my things into the flat **bit
by bit**.*
  bits and pieces *informal* someone's
possessions or furniture
  do your bit *British informal* to do what you can
to help, or to do your part of what has to
be done
  to bits *informal* **1** into small pieces: *My shoes
are falling **to bits**.* **2** very much: *He's thrilled
to bits.*

bit³ the past tense of **bite¹**

bitch¹ /bɪtʃ/ noun [C] **1** *offensive* an insulting
word for a woman **2** a female dog

bitch² /bɪtʃ/ verb [I] *informal* to complain or say
unkind things about someone or something

bitchy /ˈbɪtʃi/ adj *informal* rude or cruel
towards someone

B

bite¹ /baɪt/ (past tense **bit** /bɪt/; past participle **bitten** /ˈbɪt(ə)n/) verb ★★
1 [I/T] to use your teeth to cut or break something, usually in order to eat it: *Stop biting your nails.* ♦ *I've just been bitten by a snake.* ♦ *Tom bit into his sandwich.*
2 [I] to have an unpleasant effect: *The economic slowdown is beginning to bite.*
PHRASES **bite the bullet** *informal* to force yourself to do something difficult or unpleasant
bite sb's head off *informal* to react angrily or rudely to someone, when this reaction seems too strong
bite your tongue to stop yourself from saying something that might upset or annoy someone
PHRASAL VERB **bite sth off** to separate something from the main part by biting: *I bit off a chunk of chocolate.*

bite

bite² /baɪt/ noun **1** [C] an act of cutting or breaking something with your teeth, usually in order to eat it: *Anthony ate half his burger in one bite.* **2** [C] a mark where an animal or insect has bitten you **3** **bite** or **bite to eat** [singular] a small meal, especially one that you eat in a hurry =SNACK

bite-sized /ˈbaɪt ˌsaɪzd/ or **bite-size** /ˈbaɪtˌsaɪz/ adj small enough to be put into your mouth whole

biting /ˈbaɪtɪŋ/ adj **1** a biting wind is extremely cold and unpleasant **2** a biting remark is cruel

bitten the past participle of **bite**¹

bitter¹ /ˈbɪtə/ adj ★

1 feeling angry	4 with a sharp taste
2 showing anger	5 extremely cold
3 making sb unhappy	**+ PHRASE**

1 angry or upset because you think that you have been treated unfairly: *I'm still bitter about the whole affair.*
2 involving very angry feelings: *a bitter dispute*
3 making you feel very unhappy or disappointed: *It was a bitter blow when he lost his job.*
4 something that is bitter has a strong sharp taste that is not sweet
5 extremely cold in an unpleasant way: *a bitter north wind*
PHRASE **to the bitter end** continuing until the end of a difficult or unpleasant situation or period
—**bitterness** noun [U]

bitter² /ˈbɪtə/ noun [C/U] a type of dark beer that tastes bitter, or a glass of this beer

bitterly /ˈbɪtəli/ adv **1** in an extremely angry, upset, or disappointed way: *He complained bitterly that no one had bothered to ask his opinion.* **2** in a determined and angry way: *Many people are bitterly opposed to the idea.*
PHRASE **bitterly cold** extremely cold

bitter-sweet adj **1** involving feelings of happiness and sadness at the same time: *a bitter-sweet love story* **2** tasting bitter and sweet at the same time

bitty /ˈbɪti/ adj *British informal* made up of many small parts that do not fit together well: *I found the novel too bitty.*

bizarre /bɪˈzɑː/ adj strange and difficult to explain: *a bizarre situation* —**bizarrely** adv

blab /blæb/ verb [I/T] *informal* to tell people about something that should be kept secret

black¹ /blæk/ adj ★★★

1 of darkest colour	5 angry or sad
2 of a race with dark skin	6 about unpleasant things
3 with no milk in it	**+ PHRASE**
4 involving sth bad/sad	

1 of the darkest colour, like the sky at night: *clouds of thick black smoke*
2 **black** or **Black** belonging to a race of people with dark skin, especially people whose families were originally from Africa: *a famous black actor*
3 tea or coffee that is black has no milk in it
4 making people lose hope or feel sad: *It's a black day for the car industry.*
5 showing angry or unhappy feelings: *a black mood/look*
6 involving sad or unpleasant things: *black humour*
PHRASE **black and blue** covered in BRUISES (=dark marks on your skin where you have been hit)
—**blackness** noun [U]

Words that avoid giving offence: black

Use the adjective **black** (sometimes spelt **Black**) to refer to people with dark skin whose families originally came from Africa. Do not use **black** as a noun because it is offensive. Black Americans usually prefer to be called **African American**. In Australian English, **black** refers to people whose families were living in Australia before Europeans arrived.

black² /blæk/ noun ★
1 [U] the darkest colour, like the colour of the sky at night: *You look good in black* (=wearing black clothes).
2 **black** or **Black** [C] *offensive* a black person
PHRASE **in the black** with money in your bank account ≠ IN THE RED: *We've managed to stay in the black for over a year now.*

black³ /blæk/ **PHRASAL VERB** **black out** to suddenly become unconscious =FAINT

black-and-white adj **1** using only black, white, and grey ≠ COLOUR: *a black-and-white photograph* **2** a black-and-white situation, description, or issue makes the difference between right and wrong seem very clear: *His version of the story sounds a little too black-and-white for me.*
PHRASE **in black and white** in a written or printed form: *We've got her confession right here in black and white.*

black belt noun [C] the highest level of skill

in JUDO or KARATE, or someone who has achieved this level of skill

blackberry /ˈblækbəri/ noun [C] a small soft dark fruit that grows on a bush

blackbird /ˈblækˌbɜːd/ noun [C] a bird that is common in Europe and North America. The male is black with an orange BEAK.

blackboard /ˈblækbɔːd/ noun [C] a large dark board that a teacher writes on with CHALK

black ˈbox noun [C] a piece of equipment in a plane that records details about the cause of a crash

blackcurrant /ˌblækˈkʌrənt/ noun [C/U] a small soft dark fruit that grows on bushes in Europe

blacken /ˈblækən/ verb [I/T] to become black, or to make something black

> **PHRASE** **blacken sb's reputation/name/ character** to say things in order to harm someone's reputation

black ˈeye noun [C] a dark mark on the skin around your eye that is caused by someone hitting you

blackhead /ˈblækˌhed/ noun [C] a small black spot on your skin, caused by dirt or oil blocking a PORE

black ˈhole noun [C] science an area in outer space that pulls everything around it into it

black ˈice noun [U] a dangerous layer of ice that is difficult to see on a road

blacklist¹ /ˈblækˌlɪst/ verb **be blacklisted** to be included on a list of people or things that are not approved of

blacklist² /ˈblækˌlɪst/ noun [C] a list of people or things that you do not approve of and want to prevent from being successful

black ˈmagic noun [U] magic that is used for evil purposes

blackmail /ˈblækˌmeɪl/ noun [U] the crime of forcing someone to do something for you by threatening to tell people embarrassing information about them —**blackmail** verb [T], **blackmailer** noun [C]

black ˈmark noun [C] something you have done that damages your reputation

black ˈmarket noun [singular] the illegal trade in goods that are difficult or expensive to obtain legally: *Rhino horns can fetch up to £4,000 on the black market.* —**black marketeer** /ˌblæk mɑːkɪˈtɪə/ noun [C]

blackout /ˈblækaʊt/ noun [C] **1** a short period when the electricity supply is stopped at night=POWER CUT **2** a period during a war when the lights are turned off so that an enemy cannot see them at night **3** a period when you suddenly become unconscious for a short time **4** a situation in which journalists are officially prevented from reporting news about something

black ˈpepper noun [U] pepper that is produced from dried crushed pepper seeds and their hard black cover

black ˈsheep noun [C] someone who is not approved of by the other members of their family or group

blacksmith /ˈblækˌsmɪθ/ noun [C] someone whose job is to make HORSESHOES and other objects out of metal

black ˈspot noun [C] British a place on a road where a lot of car accidents happen

black ˈtie noun [U] very formal men's clothes worn for a social event, usually including a black BOW TIE —**black-ˈtie** adj

bladder /ˈblædə/ noun [C] the part inside your body where URINE collects

blade /bleɪd/ noun [C] **1** the thin sharp part of a knife, tool, or weapon **2** a long thin leaf of grass **3** a flat wide part of a machine or piece of equipment → SHOULDER BLADE

blah /blɑː/ noun **blah, blah, blah** spoken used for completing a sentence when you do not have to be definite, or when the subject is boring: *They say they want to cut taxes, improve education, blah, blah, blah.*

blame¹ /bleɪm/ verb [T] ★★ to say or think that someone or something is responsible for an accident, problem, or bad situation: *If it all goes wrong, don't blame me.* ♦ *The hospital has launched an inquiry to find out who was to blame for the mistake.* ♦ **blame sth on sb/sth** *You can't blame all your problems on your family.* ♦ **blame sb/sth for sth** *Organizers blame the weather for the low turnout.*

> **PHRASE** **I don't blame you/him/her/them** spoken used for saying that you understand why someone did something, or why they feel the way they do: *'Then I told him to leave.' 'I don't blame you!'*

blame² /bleɪm/ noun [U] responsibility for an accident, problem, or bad situation: *Why do I always get the blame for everything?* ♦ *The management has to take the blame* (=accept they are responsible) *for recent failures.*

blameless /ˈbleɪmləs/ adj not responsible for anything bad

bland /blænd/ adj **1** not interesting or exciting: *The film is a bland adaptation of the novel.* **2** not having a strong taste and not very interesting to eat —**blandly** adv

blank¹ /blæŋk/ adj **1** containing no writing, pictures, or sound: *a blank sheet of paper* ♦ *a blank tape/disk* ♦ *rows of blank screens* ♦ *The last three boxes should be left blank.* **2** showing no emotion, or no sign of understanding something or recognizing someone: *a blank look/expression*

> **PHRASE** **go blank** if your mind goes blank, you are unable to remember something

blank² /blæŋk/ noun [C] an empty space on a piece of paper where you can write something: *Please put either a tick or an X in the blanks.*

blank ˈcheque noun [C] **1** a cheque that has been signed but does not have an amount of money written on it **2** freedom and authority to do whatever is necessary to deal with a problem

blanket¹ /ˈblæŋkɪt/ noun **1** [C] a thick cover made of wool or another material that you use to keep warm in bed **2** [singular] a thick layer of something that completely covers an area: *a blanket of snow*

blanket² /ˈblæŋkɪt/ adj affecting everyone or everything equally, even when this is not sensible or fair: *a blanket ban on tobacco advertising*

blanket³ /ˈblæŋkɪt/ verb [T] to cover something with a layer of something, for example snow

B

blankly /ˈblæŋkli/ adv without showing any emotion, reaction, or understanding: *She gazed at him blankly.*

blank ˈverse noun [U] poetry that does not have lines that RHYME

blare /bleə/ verb [I/T] to make a loud unpleasant noise —**blare** noun [singular]

blasphemy /ˈblæsfəmi/ noun [C/U] something that is considered to be offensive to God or to someone's religious beliefs
—**blasphemous** /ˈblæsfəməs/ adj

blast¹ /blɑːst/ noun [C] **1** an explosion: *Ten people were injured in the blast.* **2** a strong current of air, wind, or heat: *a blast of cold air* **3** a sudden short loud sound: *a sudden blast of music*
PHRASE (at) full blast as loudly or with as much power as possible: *The radio was on full blast.*

blast² /blɑːst/ verb **1** [T] to damage or destroy something with a bomb or gun: *A massive car bomb blasted the police headquarters.* **2** [I] to make a loud sound: *Music blasted from the open window.* **3** [T] to criticize someone very strongly: *Government officials have blasted the United Nations for its failure to take action.*
PHRASAL VERB blast ˈoff if a SPACECRAFT blasts off, it leaves the ground

blast-ˌoff noun [U] *informal* the moment when a SPACECRAFT leaves the ground=LIFT-OFF

blatant /ˈbleɪt(ə)nt/ adj done in an obvious way that shows you are not embarrassed or ashamed to be doing something bad or illegal: *a blatant lie* —**blatantly** adv

blaze¹ /bleɪz/ noun **1** [C] a large fire that causes a lot of damage: *Firefighters were called to a blaze at a warehouse yesterday.* **2** [singular] a strong bright light or area of colour
PHRASE a blaze of publicity/glory a lot of public excitement and attention from newspapers, radio, and television

blaze² /bleɪz/ verb [I] **1** to burn strongly and brightly: *A fire blazed in the grate.* **2** to shine very brightly: *A car roared towards them, its headlights blazing.*

blazer /ˈbleɪzə/ noun [C] a light jacket that is often worn as part of a uniform

blazing /ˈbleɪzɪŋ/ adj **1** burning very strongly: *a blazing building* **2** very hot: *the blazing sun* **3** showing a lot of anger or emotion: *a blazing row*

bleach¹ /bliːtʃ/ noun [U] a strong chemical that is used for killing bacteria or for making coloured things white

bleach² /bliːtʃ/ verb [T] to remove the colour from something

bleak /bliːk/ adj **1** with no reason to feel happy or hopeful: *Textile workers face a bleak future.* **2** cold and unpleasant: *bleak winter days* —**bleakly** adv

bleary /ˈblɪəri/ adj not able to see clearly because you are tired —**blearily** adv

bleat /bliːt/ verb [I] **1** to make the sound that a sheep or goat makes **2** to complain in a weak voice, or in an annoying way

bleed /bliːd/ (past tense and past participle **bled** /bled/) verb [I] to have blood flowing from your body, for example from a cut: *He was bleeding from a wound in his shoulder.*

—**bleeding** noun [U]: *They had to act quickly to stop the bleeding.*

bleep /bliːp/ noun [C] a short high sound made by a piece of electronic equipment
—**bleep** verb [I]

blemish /ˈblemɪʃ/ noun [C] **1** a mark or spot that spoils the appearance of something **2** a mistake or dishonest action that spoils someone's reputation

blend¹ /blend/ noun [C] **1** a combination of different tastes, styles, or qualities that produces an attractive or effective result: *a blend of modern and traditional Portuguese songs* **2** a mixture of different types of tea, coffee, alcoholic drinks, or tobacco

blend² /blend/ verb **1** [T] to mix things together: *Blend the flour with a little milk to make a smooth paste.* **2** [I] to combine with other things: *The pale blue of the curtains blends perfectly with the colour scheme.*
PHRASAL VERB blend ˈin to be similar to the other people or things in the same place or situation: *Security men were trying to blend in with the crowd.*

blender /ˈblendə/ noun [C] a piece of electrical equipment that mixes foods, or turns soft food into a liquid —*picture* → C2

bless /bles/ verb [T] **1** to say a prayer asking God to help and protect someone or something **2** to make something holy, so that it can be used in a religious ceremony
PHRASES be blessed with sth to have something very good or special
bless you *spoken* used when someone has SNEEZED

blessed /ˈblesɪd/ adj **1** holy, or loved by God **2** *literary* making you feel happy or grateful: *We found a patch of blessed shade under the trees.*

blessing /ˈblesɪŋ/ noun **1** [C] something good that you feel grateful or lucky to have: *It's a blessing that your children live so near.* **2** [singular] permission or support for something: *Mike finally gave up his stressful job with his wife's blessing.* **3** [U] protection and help from God
PHRASE a blessing in disguise something that seems to cause problems, but that you later realize is a good thing

blew the past tense of **blow¹**

blight /blaɪt/ noun [singular] something that damages or spoils something else —**blight** verb [T]

blind¹ /blaɪnd/ adj ★
1 unable to see. Some people think that this word is offensive and prefer to use the expression **visually impaired** ≠ SIGHTED: *Blind and sighted children attend the same school.* ♦ *The disease made her go blind.*
2 unable to realize or admit the truth about something: *He was blind to the importance of the occasion.*
3 a blind emotion or belief is so strong that you do not question it, even if it is unreasonable: *blind faith* ♦ *In a blind panic, I dropped the bag and ran.*
4 a blind corner is one where you cannot see what is coming towards you
PHRASE turn a blind eye (to sth) to pretend that you do not notice something bad or illegal
—**blindness** noun [U]

B

blind² /blaɪnd/ verb [T] **1** to damage someone's eyes so that they are unable to see: *Jimmy was temporarily blinded by the bright light.* **2** to prevent someone from realizing or admitting the truth about something: *Her hatred blinded her to the fact that Joe could have helped her.*

blind³ /blaɪnd/ noun [C] a window cover that you pull down from the top to the bottom

blind date noun [C] an arrangement in which two people who have never met before spend some time together, in order to find out whether they would like to start a relationship

blindfold¹ /ˈblaɪn(d)ˌfəʊld/ verb [T] to tie a cover over someone's eyes so that they cannot see

blindfold² /ˈblaɪn(d)ˌfəʊld/ noun [C] something that is tied over someone's eyes so that they cannot see

blinding /ˈblaɪndɪŋ/ adj **1** extremely bright: *a blinding light* **2** very great, or severe: *a blinding headache/rage/pain*

blindly /ˈblaɪn(d)li/ adv **1** without thinking or knowing enough about what you are doing: *This group is blindly loyal to the president.* **2** without being able to see: *She felt her way blindly towards the door.*

blind spot noun [C] **1** a subject that you do not understand well, often because you do not want to know or admit the truth about it **2** an area that you cannot see when you are driving

blink¹ /blɪŋk/ verb **1** [I/T] to close your eyes and quickly open them again **2** [I] if a light blinks, it goes on and off continuously

blink² /blɪŋk/ noun [C] the act of closing and opening your eyes quickly

blinkered /ˈblɪŋkəd/ adj blinkered opinions or attitudes are very limited and conservative=NARROW-MINDED

blinkers /ˈblɪŋkəz/ noun [plural] **1** *British* things that partly cover a horse's eyes so that it can only look straight ahead **2** *American* the INDICATORS on a car

blip /blɪp/ noun [C] **1** *informal* a minor problem **2** a small flashing light on the screen of a piece of equipment

bliss /blɪs/ noun [U] complete happiness

blissful /ˈblɪsf(ə)l/ adj giving you great pleasure —**blissfully** adv

blister /ˈblɪstə/ noun [C] a swollen area on your skin that contains liquid and is caused by being burned or rubbed —**blister** verb [I/T]

blistering /ˈblɪst(ə)rɪŋ/ adj **1** very fast: *a blistering shot to the baseline* **2** blistering criticism is very severe **3** blistering heat or temperatures are extremely hot

blithely /ˈblaɪðli/ adv without worrying about possible problems, or without realizing that anything is wrong: *He blithely ignores all our warnings.* —**blithe** adj

blitz /blɪts/ noun **1** [singular] a special effort to deal with something quickly and thoroughly: *It's time we had a blitz on the paperwork.* **2** [C] a sudden military attack —**blitz** verb [T]

blizzard /ˈblɪzəd/ noun [C] a storm with a lot of snow and strong winds

bloated /ˈbləʊtɪd/ adj **1** having an uncomfortable feeling in your stomach after eating or drinking too much **2** a bloated organization or system is not effective because it is too large or has too many workers

blob /blɒb/ noun [C] **1** a small amount of a thick liquid **2** something that seems to have no definite shape

bloc /blɒk/ noun [C] a group of countries or people with the same political aims

block¹ /blɒk/ noun [C] ★★

1 large building	**5** when you cannot think
2 solid piece of sth	**6** area in a town
3 amount of sth	**7** distance along street
4 sth stopping progress	

1 a large building with a lot of different levels: *an apartment/office block* ♦ *The whole block of flats was destroyed.* —*picture* → C1

2 a solid piece of wood, stone, ice etc with straight sides: *a block of marble*

3 an amount of something that you think of as a unit: *We need to find a two-hour block when we are all free for this seminar.* ♦ *You can move blocks of text using the mouse.*

4 something that stops you from doing something or making progress: *The issue of holiday pay was the major block in reaching an agreement.*

5 a short time when you are unable to think clearly or remember something: *a mental block*

6 an area of buildings in a town or city with streets on all four sides: *I was early, so I walked around the block a couple of times.*

7 *American* the distance along a street, from the place where one street crosses it to the place where the next street crosses it: *The school was only a few blocks from where she lived.*

→ STUMBLING BLOCK

block² /blɒk/ verb [T] ★

1 to stop something from moving along or passing through something: *A car was blocking the road.* ♦ *Something is blocking the flow of water through the pipe.*

2 to stop someone from going past you by standing in front of them: *A crowd of people blocked his way to the gate.*

3 to stop something from happening or succeeding: *She accused him of blocking her promotion.* ♦ *The plan to build a new school was blocked by local residents.*

4 to be in front of someone so that they cannot see something, or so that light cannot reach them: *Don't stand in the doorway, you're blocking the light.*

PHRASAL VERBS **block sth off** to cover or close something completely so that nothing can move through it: *Snow had blocked off several streets.*

block sth out 1 to stop light or sound from reaching something: *That tree in the neighbour's garden blocks out a lot of light.* **2** to stop yourself from thinking about or remembering something: *He had always managed to block out the incident.*

block sth up same as **block²** 1: *Falling leaves had blocked up the drains.*

blockade /blɒˈkeɪd/ noun [C] an official action

B

that is intended to prevent people or goods from moving from one place to another —**blockade** verb [T]

blockage /'blɒkɪdʒ/ noun [C] something that blocks a tube or pipe

blockbuster /'blɒkˌbʌstə/ noun [C] a very successful film, show, or novel

bloke /bləʊk/ noun [C] British informal a man

blonde¹ or **blond** /blɒnd/ adj **1** blonde hair is pale yellow in colour **2** with pale yellow hair

blonde² /blɒnd/ noun [C] a woman with pale yellow hair → BRUNETTE, REDHEAD

blood /blʌd/ noun [U] ★★★
1 the red liquid that flows around inside your body: Oxygen is carried in the blood. ♦ His face was covered in blood. ♦ a blood test
2 the family, nation, or group that you belong to through your parents and grandparents: Like many Canadians, she had some Scottish blood.
3 violence and death: The conflict continued for years, with a lot of **blood spilled** (=deaths caused) on both sides.
PHRASES **sth is in your blood** used for saying that it is natural for you to do something because your family has done it in the past
new/fresh blood people who join an organization with new ideas or new ways of doing things
→ BAD BLOOD, DRAW¹, FLESH¹

blood bank noun [C] a place where blood is stored so that it can be given to people during operations

bloodbath /'blʌdˌbɑːθ/ noun [singular] a period of fighting in which a lot of people are killed or injured

bloodcurdling /'blʌdˌkɜːdlɪŋ/ adj very frightening

blood donor noun [C] someone who gives some of their blood so that hospitals can use it to treat other people

blood group noun [C] British one of the groups that human blood can be divided into

bloodhound /'blʌdˌhaʊnd/ noun [C] a large dog that can smell very well

bloodless /'blʌdləs/ adj involving no violence or killing: a bloodless revolution

blood pressure noun [U] the pressure at which blood flows from your heart around your body. Blood pressure that is either very high or very low can be dangerous to your health.

bloodshed /'blʌdʃed/ noun [U] a situation in which people are killed or injured in fighting

bloodshot /'blʌdʃɒt/ adj bloodshot eyes are red in the part where they should be white

blood sports noun [plural] activities such as hunting that involve killing animals or birds

bloodstained /'blʌdˌsteɪnd/ adj marked with blood —**bloodstain** noun [C]

bloodstream /'blʌdˌstriːm/ noun [singular] the blood that moves around your body

bloodthirsty /'blʌdˌθɜːsti/ adj someone who is bloodthirsty enjoys being violent, or enjoys watching violence

blood transfusion noun [C] a medical

treatment in which blood from another person is put into someone's body

blood vessel noun [C] a tube that carries blood around your body

bloody¹ /'blʌdi/ adj, adv British impolite used for emphasizing what you are saying when you are angry or annoyed

bloody² /'blʌdi/ adj **1** covered in blood **2** a bloody fight or war is one in which a lot of people are killed or injured

bloody-minded /ˌblʌdi'maɪndɪd/ adj British informal someone who is bloody-minded refuses to change their opinion or attitude even when it is unreasonable —**bloody-mindedness** noun [U]

bloom¹ /bluːm/ noun [C] literary a flower: beautiful red blooms
PHRASE **in (full) bloom** if a tree or plant is in bloom, it is covered with flowers

bloom² /bluːm/ verb [I] **1** if a tree or plant blooms, flowers appear and open **2** to develop in a successful or healthy way

blossom¹ /'blɒs(ə)m/ noun [C/U] a flower on a tree, or all the flowers on a tree —picture → TREE

blossom² /'blɒs(ə)m/ verb [I] **1** to develop and become more successful: Their romance blossomed on a trip to Key West. **2** if a plant or tree blossoms, flowers appear and open

blot¹ /blɒt/ verb [T] to remove liquid from the surface of something using a piece of paper or cloth
PHRASAL VERB **blot sth out 1** to cover something so that you can no longer see it: Dark clouds overhead had blotted out the sun. **2** to forget something unpleasant: She tried hard to blot out the bitter memories of the divorce.

blot² /blɒt/ noun [C] a drop of ink or another liquid on the surface of something

blotch /blɒtʃ/ noun [C] a coloured mark on something

blotchy /'blɒtʃi/ adj covered with blotches

blouse /blaʊz/ noun [C] a shirt for women —picture → C5

blow¹ /bləʊ/ (past tense **blew** /bluː/; past participle **blown** /bləʊn/) verb ★★

1 when wind/air blows	6 waste an opportunity
2 move with the wind	7 waste money
3 push air from mouth	8 when sth electric stops
4 move/form sth	+ PHRASES
5 play an instrument	+ PHRASAL VERBS

1 [I] if wind or air blows, the air moves: A strong wind was blowing across the island.
2 [I/T] if something blows somewhere, or if it is blown somewhere, the wind moves it there: The wind was blowing snow along the street. ♦ Newspapers and plastic bags were blowing about in the wind.
3 [I] to push out air from your mouth: He bent towards the candle and blew gently.
4 [T] to move something or form something by pushing out air from your mouth: We were sitting on the steps, blowing bubbles. ♦ **blow sth off/away** She picked up a book and blew the dust off it.
5 [I/T] to make a musical sound by pushing air through something: The guard blew his whistle and the train started. ♦ Behind them they heard horns blowing.
6 [T] informal to destroy your own chance of

B

succeeding, or to waste a good opportunity: *I've completely blown my diet.* ♦ *We've been working very hard, and we don't intend to **blow it** now.*

7 [T] *informal* to spend a lot of money quickly on things that you do not need

8 [I/T] if something electrical blows, it stops working because of a fault

PHRASES **blow hot and cold** to keep changing your opinion about something or someone

blow (sb) a kiss to kiss your hand and pretend to blow the kiss to someone

blow your nose to clean your nose by forcing air through it

blow the whistle to tell the public or someone in authority that someone is doing something wrong or illegal: *People should be able to **blow the whistle on** corruption without losing their jobs.*

PHRASAL VERBS ,blow (sth) 'out if you blow out a flame, or if it blows out, it stops burning because you blow on it, or because of the wind: *He blew out all 60 candles on his birthday cake.*

,blow 'over if a dangerous or embarrassing situation blows over, people stop worrying about it and soon forget about it: *The scandal soon blew over.*

,blow (sth) 'up if something blows up, or if someone blows something up, it explodes and is destroyed: *Terrorists had threatened to blow up the embassy.*

,blow sth 'up to fill something with air or gas: *We blew up lots of balloons and hung them around the room.*

blow up

blow² /bləʊ/ noun [C] **1** an event that makes you feel very sad, disappointed, or shocked: *Her mother's death was a real blow to her.* **2** a hard hit from someone's hand or an object: *The victim was killed by a blow to the head.* **3** an act of blowing air from your mouth or nose

PHRASES **come to blows** if two people come to blows, they start hitting each other

soften the blow to make something that is unpleasant easier to deal with or accept

,blow-by-'blow adj including a lot of details: *a blow-by-blow account of her trip*

'blow-dry verb [T] to dry your hair with a HAIRDRYER

blown the past participle of **blow¹**

blowout /'bləʊaʊt/ noun [C] **1** an occasion when a tyre on a moving vehicle suddenly bursts = PUNCTURE **2** *informal* a celebration during which people eat and drink a lot

blubber¹ /'blʌbə/ noun [U] a layer of fat around the body of a sea animal such as a WHALE

blubber² /'blʌbə/ verb [I] *informal* to cry in a noisy and uncontrolled way

bludgeon /'blʌdʒ(ə)n/ verb [T] to hit someone hard with a heavy object

blue¹ /bluː/ adj ★★★

1 something that is blue is the same colour as the sky on a clear sunny day: *He looked at her with his pale blue eyes.*

2 *informal* feeling rather sad: *She usually calls her mother when she's feeling blue.*

3 *old-fashioned* dealing with sex in a way that some people find offensive: *a blue movie*

PHRASES **once in a blue moon** *informal* not very often at all

till you are blue in the face *informal* doing something continually and for a long time, but without success: *You can say 'don't do it' till you're blue in the face, but if kids want to do it, they will.*

blue² /bluː/ noun [C/U] ★ the colour of the sky on a clear sunny day: *The boy was dressed all in blue.* ♦ *bright blues and yellows*

PHRASE **out of the blue** happening in a way that is sudden and unexpected: *Out of the blue she said, 'Your name's John, isn't it?'*

→ BLUES

bluebell /'bluːbel/ noun [C] a wild plant with small blue flowers that are shaped like bells

blueberry /'bluːb(ə)ri/ noun [C/U] a small dark-blue fruit that grows on a bush —picture → C10

blue-blooded /ˌbluː 'blʌdɪd/ adj from a royal family, or from a family of a very high social class

,blue 'cheese noun [C/U] a strong-tasting cheese that is white or pale yellow and has blue lines in it

'blue 'chip noun [C] a company or INVESTMENT that is considered safe to invest in —'blue-chip adj

,blue-'collar adj blue-collar workers do physical work in places such as factories and mines → WHITE-COLLAR

blueprint /'bluːprɪnt/ noun [C] **1** a detailed plan for doing something **2** a drawing that shows how to build something such as a building or a machine

blues /bluːz/ noun **1** [U] a type of slow sad music that developed from the songs of black SLAVES in the southern US **2** the blues [plural] *informal* a feeling of sadness and loss

bluff¹ /blʌf/ verb [I/T] to try to trick someone by pretending that you know something or that you will do something: *They said they'd had another offer, but we knew they were just bluffing.*

bluff² /blʌf/ noun [C/U] an attempt to bluff someone

PHRASE **call sb's bluff** to ask someone to do what they are threatening to do, because you believe that they do not really intend to do it

bluish /'bluːɪʃ/ adj similar to blue

blunder¹ /'blʌndə/ noun [C] a careless or embarrassing mistake

blunder² /'blʌndə/ verb [I] **1** to make a careless or embarrassing mistake **2** to move around in a careless way

blunt /blʌnt/ adj **1** saying what is true or what you really think, even if this offends or upsets people **2** not pointed or sharp: *a* *blunt pencil/razor* —**bluntness** noun [U]

bluntly /ˈblʌntli/ adv speaking in a direct and honest way, even if this offends or upsets people

blur¹ /blɜː/ verb [I/T] **1** to become less clear, or to make something less clear: *The letters blurred together on the page.* **2** if the difference between two things blurs, or if something blurs it, they become more similar: *The law seems to blur the line between hard drugs and soft drugs.*

blur² /blɜː/ noun [C] **1** a shape that is difficult to see clearly, for example because it is moving very fast: *a blur of activity/ movement* **2** a thought or memory that is not very clear in your mind: *I remember a big house, but the rest of it is a blur.*

blurb /blɜːb/ noun [singular] information about a book that is printed on its back cover

blurred /blɜːd/ or **blurry** /ˈblɜːri/ adj **1** difficult to see clearly, or causing difficulty in seeing something clearly: *blurred photographs* ♦ *blurred vision* **2** difficult to remember clearly: *blurred memories*

blurt /blɜːt/ or **blurt sth ˈout** verb [T] to say something suddenly and without thinking about the effect that it will have

blush /blʌʃ/ verb [I] if you blush, your cheeks become red because you feel embarrassed or ashamed

blusher /ˈblʌʃə/ noun [U] British a pink powder or cream that women put on their cheeks —*picture* → MAKE-UP

bluster /ˈblʌstə/ verb [I/T] to speak in an angry or threatening way when you are frightened or nervous —**bluster** noun [U]

blustery /ˈblʌst(ə)ri/ adj with strong winds: *blustery weather*

BO /ˌbiː ˈəʊ/ noun [U] body odour: an unpleasant smell that comes from someone who has not washed or has been exercising

boa constrictor /ˌbəʊə kənˈstrɪktə/ noun [C] a large snake that kills animals by squeezing them

boar /bɔː/ noun [C] **1** a male pig **2** a wild pig

board¹ /bɔːd/ noun ★★★

1 long piece of wood	4 group of managers
2 thin flat surface	5 meals
3 for information	+ PHRASE

1 [C] a long thin flat piece of wood that is used for building: *There's a loose board in the bedroom floor.*
2 [C] a thin flat piece of wood or other material that is used for a particular purpose: *a chopping/ironing board* ♦ *We wanted to play chess, but I couldn't find the board.*
3 [C] a flat wide surface such as a NOTICEBOARD or BLACKBOARD that is used for showing information: *The exam results were pinned up on the board.*
4 [C] a group of people who control an organization or company: *an advisory/ editorial board* ♦ *The company's board of directors voted against the proposal.*
5 [U] meals provided for you when you stay at a hotel, live at another person's house etc → FULL BOARD, HALF BOARD

PHRASE **on board** **1** on a ship or plane: *The plane had 125 passengers and crew on board.* **2** involved in a project or organization, or working for a company: *Welcome to the team. It's great to have you on board.*
→ ACROSS-THE-BOARD

board² /bɔːd/ verb **1** [I/T] to get onto a ship, aircraft, train, or bus **2** [I] if a plane or ship is boarding, passengers are being allowed to get on it **3** [I] to live at another person's house in a room that you pay for

PHRASAL VERB **board sth ˈup** to cover a window or door with wooden boards: *a row of boarded up shops*

boarder /ˈbɔːdə/ noun [C] **1** someone who pays to live in someone else's house **2** a boy or girl who lives at a BOARDING SCHOOL

ˈboard ˌgame noun [C] any game in which you move objects around on a special board

ˈboarding ˌcard noun [C] a card that each passenger has to show before they are allowed to get on a plane or ship

ˈboarding ˌhouse noun [C] old-fashioned a house in which people pay to live as guests with the family who owns it

ˈboarding ˌpass noun [C] a BOARDING CARD

ˈboarding ˌschool noun [C] a school in which the students live during the part of the year that they go to lessons

boardroom /ˈbɔːdruːm/ noun [C] a room where the directors of a company have meetings

boast¹ /bəʊst/ verb **1** [I/T] to talk about your abilities, achievements, or possessions in a way that sounds too proud=BRAG: *The men sat at the bar boasting about their win.* ♦ *Mrs White liked to boast that she knew every person in the village.* **2** [T] formal to have something good that other people admire: *The island boasts the highest number of tourists in the area.*

boast² /bəʊst/ noun [C] a statement in which you talk about your abilities, achievements, or possessions in a way that sounds too proud

boastful /ˈbəʊstf(ə)l/ adj too eager to tell other people about your abilities, achievements, or possessions ≠ MODEST

boat /bəʊt/ noun [C] ★★★
1 a small vehicle for travelling on water: *The only way to get there was by boat.*
→ ROWING BOAT, SAILING BOAT
2 a ship that carries passengers
PHRASE **in the same boat** in the same difficult or unpleasant situation
→ BURN¹, ROCK²

boating /ˈbəʊtɪŋ/ noun [U] the activity of sailing in a boat for enjoyment

bob¹ /bɒb/ verb [I] to move up and down with short regular movements, especially in the water

bob² /bɒb/ noun [C] a woman's hairstyle in which her hair is cut to an even length at the level of her chin —*picture* → HAIRSTYLE

bode /bəʊd/ verb **bode well/ill** formal to be a sign that something good/bad will happen

bodily /ˈbɒdɪli/ adj relating to your body, or affecting your body: *bodily injury* ♦ *bodily fluids*

body /'bɒdi/ noun ★★★

1 of human/animal	5 of car/plane
2 not arms/legs	6 main part of sth
3 of a dead person	7 collection of work etc
4 group of people	8 appearance of hair

1 [C] the whole physical structure of a person or animal, including the head, arms, and legs: *My whole body ached.*
2 [C] the main part of a person's or animal's body, not including the head, arms, or legs
3 [C] the body of a dead person=CORPSE
4 [C] a group of people who have official responsibility for something: *the legislative body* (=group that makes laws) *of the government* ♦ *the school's governing body*
5 [C] the main outer part of a car or plane, not including the engine, wheels, or wings
6 [singular] the main part of something that has many parts: *You can find more details in **the body** of the report.*
7 [C] a large amount of knowledge, information, or work: *There is a growing **body of evidence** to support this theory.*
8 [U] the thick healthy appearance of your hair
→ FOREIGN BODY

body blow noun [C] a serious problem, or a great disappointment
body building noun [U] regular physical exercises with weights that make your muscles bigger —**body builder** noun [C]
bodyguard /'bɒdiɡɑːd/ noun [C] a person whose job is to protect an important person from being attacked
body language noun [U] the movements or positions of your body that show other people what you are thinking or feeling
bodywork /'bɒdiwɜːk/ noun [U] the painted metal outer part of a car or other vehicle
bog¹ /bɒɡ/ noun **1** [C/U] an area of ground that is always very wet and soft **2** [C] *British informal* a toilet
bog² /bɒɡ/ verb **be/get bogged down (in sth)** to be or become so involved with one particular thing that you cannot make any progress: *The trial got bogged down in legal complications.*
boggle /'bɒɡ(ə)l/ verb [I/T] if your mind boggles, or if something boggles your mind, you cannot imagine or understand it
boggy /'bɒɡi/ adj boggy ground is always very wet and soft
bog standard adj *British informal* ordinary and not special in any way
bogus /'bəʊɡəs/ adj not real, but pretending to be real: *bogus insurance claims*
bohemian /bəʊ'hiːmiən/ adj living or behaving in an informal way that is thought to be typical of artists and writers =UNCONVENTIONAL
boil¹ /bɔɪl/ verb ★
1 [I/T] if a liquid boils, or if you boil it, it becomes so hot that BUBBLES rise to the surface: *When the water boils, add the rice.*
2 [I/T] to cook something in boiling water, or to be cooked in this way: *How long does it take to boil an egg?*
3 [I] to feel something such as anger very strongly
PHRASAL VERBS **boil down to sth** to be the

main reason for something, or the most basic part of something: *Passing exams isn't difficult, it all **boils down to** good preparation.*
boil over 1 to flow over the top of a container while boiling **2** if a situation or feeling boils over, people cannot control their anger and start to fight or argue: *Racial tensions in the area were boiling over.*
boil² /bɔɪl/ noun [C] a painful lump on your skin that has become infected
PHRASES **bring sth to the boil** to heat something until it boils
come to the boil if a liquid comes to the boil, it starts to boil
boiler /'bɔɪlə/ noun [C] a machine that heats water and provides hot water for a heating system
boiling /'bɔɪlɪŋ/ or **boiling hot** adj extremely hot: *It was a boiling hot day.*
boiling point noun [C/U] the temperature at which a liquid boils
boisterous /'bɔɪst(ə)rəs/ adj lively and noisy
bold¹ /bəʊld/ adj **1** confident and not afraid of risks: *a bold plan to reduce crime* **2** clear, bright, and strong in colour: *a shirt with bold blue and yellow stripes* —**boldly** adv, **boldness** noun [U]
bold² /bəʊld/ noun [U] a way of printing letters that makes them thicker and darker than usual: *Try putting the title in bold.*
bollard /'bɒlɑːd/ noun [C] *British* a short post that is used for stopping cars from driving into an area
Bollywood /'bɒliwʊd/ *informal* the Indian film industry
bolster /'bəʊlstə/ or **bolster sth up** verb [T] to make something stronger or more effective: *The central bank cut interest rates in an attempt to bolster the economy.*
bolt¹ /bəʊlt/ noun [C] **1** a metal bar that you slide across a door or window in order to lock it **2** a type of screw without a point that is used for fastening things together
bolt² /bəʊlt/ verb **1** [T] to lock a door or window using a bolt **2** [T] to fasten two things together using a bolt: *The chairs were all bolted to the floor.* **3** [I] to run away suddenly, especially because you are frightened: *There was a gunshot and the horse bolted.* **4** bolt or **bolt sth down** [T] to eat food very quickly: *She bolted down her lunch and rushed back to work.*
bolt³ /bəʊlt/ adv **bolt upright** with your back very straight
bomb¹ /bɒm/ noun [C] ★ a weapon that is made to explode at a particular time or when it hits something: *The bomb had been planted in a busy street.* ♦ *Bombs fell on the city night for two weeks.*
bomb² /bɒm/ verb **1** [T] to attack a place with bombs: *NATO aircraft bombed the town again last night.* **2** [I] *British informal* to move somewhere very quickly, especially in a vehicle: *I saw you bombing along the street on your bike.* **3** [I] *informal* to be very unsuccessful: *His latest film bombed at the box office* (=not many people went to see it).
bombard /bɒm'bɑːd/ verb [T] to attack a place

B

by dropping a lot of bombs on it, or by firing guns at it for a long time

PHRASE bombard sb with questions/ messages/advice etc to ask someone so many questions or give them so much information that it is difficult for them to deal with it all

—**bombardment** noun [C/U]

bomber /ˈbɒmə/ noun [C] **1** a large military plane that drops bombs **2** someone who puts a bomb in a public place

bombshell /ˈbɒmˌʃel/ noun [C] *informal* an event or piece of news that is unexpected and shocking

bona fide /ˌbəʊnə ˈfaɪdi/ adj a bona fide person or thing is really what they seem or claim to be

bonanza /bəˈnænzə/ noun [C] a situation in which people quickly become very rich or successful

bond¹ /bɒnd/ noun [C] **1** a close special feeling of connection with other people or groups: *The experience formed a close bond between us.* **2** a document that a government or a company gives to someone who invests money in it. The government or company promises to pay back the money with interest. **3** the way that two surfaces stick together

bond² /bɒnd/ verb **1** [I] to develop a close special feeling towards other people: *He never felt like he bonded with any of the other students.* **2** [I/T] to fix two things firmly together, or to become fixed in this way

—**bonding** noun [U]

bondage /ˈbɒndɪdʒ/ noun [U] **1** the activity of tying someone up for sexual pleasure **2** *formal* a situation in which someone is a SLAVE or has no freedom

bone¹ /bəʊn/ noun ★★

1 [C] one of the hard parts that form the frame inside your body: *She fell and broke a bone in her foot.*

2 [U] the substance that bones are made of

PHRASES a bone of contention a subject that people disagree about: *The main bone of contention between us is money.*

chilled/frozen to the bone feeling very cold

cut sth to the bone to reduce something to the lowest possible level or amount: *We've had to cut our profit margins to the bone in order to survive.*

have a bone to pick with sb *informal* to be annoyed with someone and want to talk to them about it

make no bones about sth to talk about something without feeling ashamed or embarrassed: *He makes no bones about the fact that he wants my job.*

bone² /bəʊn/ verb [T] to remove the bones from meat or fish before cooking it

bone marrow noun [U] the soft substance inside bones

bonfire /ˈbɒnˌfaɪə/ noun [C] a large fire built outside for burning rubbish or for a celebration

Bonfire Night the night of 5th November, when British people have bonfires and light FIREWORKS

bonnet /ˈbɒnɪt/ noun [C] **1** *British* the front part of a car that covers the engine —*picture*

→ C6 **2** a hat that ties under the chin

bonny /ˈbɒni/ adj *Scottish* very attractive

bonus /ˈbəʊnəs/ noun [C] **1** something good that you get in addition to what you expect: *Customers will receive a free CD as a bonus.* **2** extra money that you are paid in addition to your usual salary: *a Christmas bonus*

bony /ˈbəʊni/ adj a bony part of the body is so thin that the shape of the bones can be seen: *bony fingers*

boo¹ /buː/ (3rd person singular **boos**; present participle **booing**; past tense and past participle **booed**) verb [I/T] to shout at a performer or sports team in order to show that you think they are not very good

boo² /buː/ interjection **1** you shout 'boo' suddenly to frighten someone as a joke **2** you shout 'boo' at a performer or sports team in order to show that you think they are not very good

boobs /buːbz/ noun [plural] *informal* a woman's breasts

booby prize /ˈbuːbi ˌpraɪz/ noun [C] a prize that is given as a joke to someone who comes last in a competition

booby trap /ˈbuːbi ˌtræp/ noun [C] a hidden bomb that explodes when someone touches something connected to it

boogie /ˈbuːgi/ verb [I] *informal* to dance to fast popular music —**boogie** noun [C]

book¹ /bʊk/ noun ★★★

1 [C] a written work that is printed on pages fastened together inside a cover: *Please open your books at page 25.* ♦ *Have you read any books by John Grisham?* ♦ *a book about American history* ♦ *She has written over 20 books on the subject.*

2 [C] something that you write in, consisting of pages fastened together inside a cover: *an exercise book* ♦ *an address book*

3 [C] a set of small objects, such as stamps, tickets, or matches, fastened together inside a paper cover

4 the books [plural] the financial records of an organization or business

PHRASES by the book correctly, following all the rules or systems for doing something

in sb's bad/good books *informal* used for saying that someone is annoyed with you/pleased with you

Talking or writing about **books**

- **autobiography** a book about your own life
- **biography** a book about someone's life
- **cookery book** a book of instructions for cooking
- **guidebook** a book for tourists
- **hardback** a book with a hard cover
- **manual** a book of instructions
- **notebook** a book with empty pages for writing in
- **novel** a book that tells a story
- **paperback** a book with a thick paper cover
- **textbook** a book that you use for studying at school, college, or university

book² /bʊk/ verb ★

1 [I/T] to arrange to have or use something at a particular time in the future: *Shall I book a room for you?* ♦ *'Can we have a table for two, please?' 'Have you booked, sir?'* ♦

book sb on sth *Could you book me on the 8.30 flight* (=get a ticket for me)?

2 [T] to arrange for someone to perform or speak at a public event: **book sb to do sth** *Several leading businessmen were booked to speak at the conference.*

3 [T] *British* if a sports player is booked, the REFEREE writes their name in an official book because they have broken the rules: *Adams was booked for dangerous play.*

4 [T] if the police book someone, they take them to the police station and make a record of their crime

PHRASAL VERBS .book 'in *British* to formally tell the staff in a hotel that you have arrived there: *I'd just arrived at the conference and hadn't had time to book in.*

.book sb 'in *British* to arrange for someone to stay at a hotel or similar place: **book sb in at sth** *He's booked himself in at a health spa.*

bookcase /'bʊkˌkeɪs/ noun [C] a piece of furniture with shelves in it for books

'book ˌclub noun [C] **1** an organization that sells books at low prices to its members, usually by MAIL ORDER **2** a group of people who meet regularly to discuss books that they have read

bookie /'bʊki/ noun [C] *informal* a BOOKMAKER

booking /'bʊkɪŋ/ noun [C] an arrangement to do something such as buy a travel ticket or stay in a hotel room in the future =RESERVATION: *Have you made a booking?*

'booking ˌoffice noun [C] *British* a place where you can buy travel tickets

bookkeeping /'bʊkˌkiːpɪŋ/ noun [U] the job of recording a business's financial accounts —**bookkeeper** noun [C]

booklet /'bʊklət/ noun [C] a small thin book that contains information: *a 12-page booklet called 'You and Your Child's Health'*

bookmaker /'bʊkˌmeɪkə/ noun [C] someone whose job is to take BETS from people and to pay them money if they win

bookmark /'bʊkˌmɑːk/ noun [C] **1** something that you put inside a book so that you can find the page you want again **2** a way of marking an Internet WEBSITE so that you can easily find it again —**bookmark** verb [T]

bookshelf /'bʊkˌʃelf/ (plural **bookshelves** /'bʊkˌʃelvz/) noun [C] a shelf that you put books on

bookshop /'bʊkˌʃɒp/ noun [C] a shop that sells books

bookstall /'bʊkˌstɔːl/ noun [C] *British* a small shop with an open front that sells books, newspapers, and magazines, for example at a railway station

'book ˌtoken noun [C] *British* a piece of paper that you can use for buying books in a BOOKSHOP. You give a book token to someone as a present.

bookworm /'bʊkˌwɜːm/ noun [C] *informal* someone who spends a lot of time reading books

boom¹ /buːm/ noun [C] **1** a sudden increase in economic activity or success: *the economic boom of the 1980s* ♦ *The island is experiencing a boom in tourism.* **2** a deep loud sound that continues for some time **3** a pole with a camera or MICROPHONE attached to it, used in making films

PHRASE **boom and bust** a situation in which a country's economy regularly goes through periods of success followed by periods of failure

boom² /buːm/ verb [I] **1** to make a deep loud sound that continues for some time **2** if a place or an industry is booming, it is experiencing a period of economic success: *The housing market is booming.* **3** if an activity is booming, it is becoming very popular

boomerang /'buːməˌræŋ/ noun [C] a curved stick that comes back to you when you throw it

boon /buːn/ noun [singular] something that brings you benefits or makes your life easier: *Falling PC prices are a boon for consumers.*

boorish /'bʊərɪʃ/ adj rude and not caring about other people's feelings

boost¹ /buːst/ verb [T] to help something to increase or improve: *The cold weather boosted demand for electricity.* ♦ *The new coach has boosted the team's confidence.*

boost² /buːst/ noun [singular] something that helps something to increase or improve: *The festival has been a major boost for the local economy.*

booster /'buːstə/ noun [C] **1** an extra amount of a medical drug that you are given so that a drug you had before will continue to be effective **2** something that makes you feel better: *a morale/confidence booster*

boot¹ /buːt/ noun [C] ★★

1 a type of shoe that covers all of your foot and part of your leg: *walking/riding/hiking boots* ♦ *a pair of black boots* —*picture* → SHOE **2** *British* the covered space at the back of a car, used for carrying things in —*picture* → C6

PHRASES **get the boot** or **be given the boot** *informal* to be forced to leave your job: *He was useless, and soon got the boot.*

to boot used for adding an extra thing to a list of comments: *The trains are slow, dirty, and very unreliable to boot.*

boot² /buːt/ verb [T] *informal* to kick something or someone hard: *He booted the ball over the line.*

PHRASAL VERBS .boot sb 'out *informal* to make someone leave a place or an organization: *They were booted out of the club for fighting.*

.boot 'up *computing* if a computer boots up, or if you boot it up, it starts working and becomes ready to use

booth /buːð/ noun [C] **1** a small enclosed space where you do something private, especially vote or make a phone call **2** a small enclosed space where you can buy things or use a service: *a ticket booth* **3** a private, enclosed table in a restaurant

bootleg /'buːtˌleg/ adj bootleg goods are products that are made and sold illegally —**bootlegger** noun [C]

booty /'buːti/ noun [U] *literary* valuable goods that someone takes illegally or by force, especially in a war

booze¹ /buːz/ noun [U] *informal* alcoholic drinks

booze² /buːz/ verb [I] *informal* to drink alcohol

B

border¹ /ˈbɔːdə/ noun [C] ★★
1 the official line that separates two countries or regions: *border guards* ♦ *the border between Hungary and Romania* ♦ *Iraq's northern border with Turkey* ♦ *Thousands of refugees were fleeing across the border.* ♦ *a town on the Canadian border* (=near it)
2 a narrow decorated area around the edge of something: *cotton sheets with a lace border*

border² /ˈbɔːdə/ verb [T] **1** to be next to another country or region: *Jordan holds a key position, bordering both Israel and Iraq.* **2** to form a line along the edge of something: *The canal is bordered by poplar trees.*
PHRASAL VERB **border on sth** to be nearly the same as a particular quality, feeling, or state: *a feeling of mistrust bordering on hatred*

borderline¹ /ˈbɔːdəlaɪn/ adj in a position between two standards or types, and therefore difficult to judge: *students with borderline test scores*

borderline² /ˈbɔːdəlaɪn/ noun [singular] an imaginary point that divides one feeling or condition from another: *the borderline between friendship and love*

bore¹ /bɔː/ verb [T] **1** to make someone feel bored: *I hope I'm not boring you.* **2** to make a deep hole in something hard

bore² /bɔː/ noun **1** [C] someone who talks too much about things that are not interesting **2** [singular] a boring or annoying activity or situation

bore³ the past tense of **bear¹**

bored /bɔːd/ adj ★★ feeling impatient and annoyed because nothing is interesting: *The waiter looked very bored.* ♦ *Steve was getting bored with the game.*

■ **Bored** describes how you feel: *I hated school, and I was always bored.*
■ **Boring** describes things or situations that make you feel bored: *I always found school very boring.*

boredom /ˈbɔːdəm/ noun [U] the feeling of being bored

boring /ˈbɔːrɪŋ/ adj ★★ not at all interesting: *a boring badly-paid job* ♦ *Our maths teacher is so boring!* → BORED

born /bɔːn/ adj ★★★
1 when a baby is born, it comes out of its mother's body and starts its life: *Her grandfather died before she was born.* ♦ *The twins were born on 29 August, 1962.* ♦ *a German-born tennis player* (=who was born in Germany) ♦ *He was born blind* (=he was blind when he was born).
2 used for saying that someone has a natural ability to do something well: *a born salesman/leader/optimist*
3 if something such as a new organization or idea is born, it begins to exist

born-again Christian noun [C] a Christian who wants to tell other people about their strong religious beliefs

borough /ˈbʌrə/ noun [C] a town, or a district in a big city

borrow /ˈbɒrəʊ/ verb ★★
1 [T] to receive and use something that

belongs to someone else, and promise to give it back: *Can I borrow your calculator?* ♦ **borrow sth from sb/sth** *I borrowed a camera from Alex.*
2 [I/T] to borrow money from a bank and pay it back gradually: *We borrowed £20,000 to start up the business.*
3 [I/T] to use something such as an idea or word that was first used by another person or used in another place: *A lot of English words were borrowed from other languages.*

■ If you **borrow** something from someone, they give it to you and you agree to give it back: *Can I borrow your umbrella?*
■ If you **lend** something to someone, you give it to them and they agree to give it back to you: *Could you lend me your umbrella?*

borrower /ˈbɒrəʊə/ noun [C] someone who borrows money from a bank

borrowings /ˈbɒrəʊɪŋz/ noun [plural] money that a business, country, or organization has borrowed

bosom /ˈbʊz(ə)m/ noun [singular] a woman's breasts
PHRASE **bosom friend/buddy/pal** a very close friend

boss¹ /bɒs/ noun [C] ★★
1 the person who is in charge of you at work: *I'll ask my boss for a day off next week.*
2 someone who has a powerful position in an organization
PHRASE **be your own boss** to work for yourself and not be employed by someone else

boss² /bɒs/ **PHRASAL VERB** **boss sb around** or **boss sb about** *informal* to keep telling other people what to do: *He's always bossing his little brother around.*

bossy /ˈbɒsi/ adj someone who is bossy is annoying because they keep telling other people what to do

botanist /ˈbɒtənɪst/ noun [C] someone who studies plants

botany /ˈbɒt(ə)ni/ noun [U] the scientific study of plants —**botanical** /bəˈtænɪk(ə)l/ adj

botch /bɒtʃ/ verb [T] *informal* to do something very badly or carelessly: *The police botched the entire investigation.* —**botched** /bɒtʃt/ adj

both /bəʊθ/ grammar word ★★★

Both can be:
■ a **determiner**: *Both children are at school.*
■ a **pronoun**: *They are both good singers.* ♦ *Both of them are learning English.*

1 used for showing that you are referring to two people or things, and that you are saying the same thing about the two of them: *You can write on both sides of the paper.* ♦ *Both my parents are doctors.* ♦ *I like them both.* ♦ *Both of my brothers play on the football team.*

Do not use **both** in negative sentences. Use **neither**: *Neither of my parents wanted me to leave school* (=my mother did not and my father did not).

PHRASE **both...and...** used for emphasizing that each of two things is true: *a plant that grows in both Chile and Argentina* ♦ *The* *results of the research are both impressive and alarming.*

bother¹ /ˈbɒðə/ verb ★★

1 [I] if you do not bother to do something, you do not do it because it is not sensible or because you feel lazy: **bother to do sth** *It was such a stupid question, I didn't even bother to reply.* ♦ **bother doing sth** *Don't bother inviting Janet.* ♦ *Don't bother about driving me home, I'll walk.*

2 [T] to annoy someone by interrupting them: *I hope the children aren't bothering you.*

3 [T] to make someone feel worried, frightened, or upset: *There was something about him that really bothered her.* ♦ *If he keeps bothering you, you should call the police.* ♦ **it bothers sb that/when** *Does it bother you that people think you're older than him?*

4 [T] to cause someone pain: *His knee was bothering him.*

 PHRASES **I can't be bothered** *British informal* used for saying that you will not do something because you feel lazy: *I said I'd go out with them tonight, but I can't be bothered.* ♦ *She couldn't even be bothered to say hello.*

I'm not bothered *spoken* used for saying that something is not important to you: *I'm not bothered whether we go out or stay in.*

sorry to bother you *spoken* used for politely asking someone to do something for you: *Sorry to bother you, but would you move your bag?*

bother² /ˈbɒðə/ noun [U] trouble or difficulty that is annoying but not very serious

botox /ˈbəʊtɒks/ noun [U] botulinum toxin: a substance that can be INJECTED into someone's face to make the muscles relax and the skin look smoother and younger

bottle¹ /ˈbɒt(ə)l/ noun ★★★

1 [C] a glass or plastic container for liquids: *an empty beer bottle* ♦ *a bottle of cooking oil*

2 [C] the amount of liquid that a bottle contains: *They drank the whole bottle.*

3 [U] *British informal* the confidence or COURAGE that you need to do something difficult or frightening

 PHRASE **bring a bottle** used for asking someone to bring a bottle of wine or other alcoholic drink to a party

bottle² /ˈbɒt(ə)l/ verb [T] to put a liquid into bottles in order to sell it —**bottled** /ˈbɒt(ə)ld/ adj: *bottled beer/water*

 PHRASAL VERB **bottle sth ˈup** to stop yourself from showing negative emotions: *You've been bottling up your anger for years.*

bottle ˌbank noun [C] *British* a large container in a public place where people can put empty bottles so that the glass can be RECYCLED (=used again)

bottleneck /ˈbɒt(ə)lˌnek/ noun [C] **1** a problem that causes delays **2** a place where traffic moves slowly because the road is narrow or blocked

bottom¹ /ˈbɒtəm/ noun ★★★

1 lowest part of sth	5 trousers
2 ground under sea	6 part furthest from you
3 lowest level in status	+ PHRASE
4 part of body you sit on	

1 [singular] the lowest part of sth: *The page had a line missing from the bottom.* ♦ *She ran down to **the bottom of** the hill.* ♦ *The date and time are shown **at the bottom of** your screen.* ♦ *Read what is says **on the bottom** of the box* (=on the surface at the bottom).

2 [singular] the ground under the sea or under a lake or river

3 [singular] the lowest level or position: *She started at the bottom and ended up running the company.*

4 [C] the part of your body that you sit on

5 bottoms [plural] the trousers that are part of a set of loose clothes or sports clothes: *pyjama bottoms*

6 [singular] the part of something that is furthest away from where you are: *There's an apple tree at **the bottom of** our garden.* ♦ *Go to the bottom of the street and turn left.*

 PHRASE **get to the bottom of sth** to find out the true cause or explanation of a bad situation

bottom² /ˈbɒtəm/ adj in the lowest part or position: *She sat on the bottom step.* ♦ *the bottom half of the page* ♦ *people in the bottom 25% of the earnings table*

bottomless /ˈbɒtəmləs/ adj **1** having no limits: *There isn't a bottomless pit* (=an unlimited supply) *of public money.* **2** extremely deep: *a bottomless lake*

bottom ˈline, the noun [singular] **1** the most important fact in a situation: *The bottom line is that he lied to Parliament.* **2** *business* the amount of money that a business makes or loses

bottom-ˈup adj *British* starting with details rather than with a general idea ≠ TOP-DOWN: *a bottom-up approach to problem solving*

bough /baʊ/ noun [C] *literary* a branch of a tree

bought the past tense and past participle of **buy¹**

boulder /ˈbəʊldə/ noun [C] a large rock

boulevard /ˈbuːləˌvɑːd/ noun [C] a wide road in a city

bounce¹ /baʊns/ verb

1 hit sth & move off	5 of email
2 move up and down	+ PHRASE
3 of cheque	+ PHRASAL VERB
4 move in lively way	

1 [I/T] if a ball or other object bounces, or if you bounce it, it hits a surface then immediately moves away: *The ball bounced twice before hitting the net.* ♦ *Hailstones were bouncing off the roof.* ♦ *Josh bounced the ball down the street.* **2** [I/T] to move up and down, or to move something up and down: *She was bouncing the baby on her knee.* ♦ *The kids love bouncing on the bed.* **3** [I] if a cheque bounces, the bank refuses to pay it because there is not enough money in the account of the person who wrote it **4** [I] to move quickly and with a lot of energy: *The band came bouncing onto the stage.* **5** [I] if an email message bounces, it is sent back to you without reaching the person you sent it to

 PHRASE **bounce ideas around** to discuss ideas with someone in order to get their opinion

B

PHRASAL VERB ,bounce 'back to become healthy, happy, or successful again after something bad has happened to you

bounce² /baʊns/ noun [C] the movement of a ball when it hits a surface and moves away again

bouncer /'baʊnsə/ noun [C] someone whose job is to stop violent behaviour in a bar or club

bouncy /'baʊnsi/ adj **1** a bouncy ball BOUNCES well when it hits a surface **2** a bouncy surface moves up and down when you walk or jump on it **3** a bouncy person is happy, lively, and enthusiastic

bound¹ /baʊnd/ adj ★
1 bound to do sth something that is bound to happen will almost certainly happen: *If you have problems at home, it's bound to affect your work.*
2 bound to do sth used for saying that you must do something or you should do something: *We felt bound to tell her that her son had been taking drugs.*
PHRASE bound for sth travelling towards a place: *a taxi bound for Heathrow airport*

bound² /baʊnd/ verb [I] to run or jump with large steps
PHRASE be bounded by sth *formal* if an area is bounded by something such as a fence, the fence goes around the edge of the area

bound³ /baʊnd/ noun **1 bounds** [plural] limits that affect and control what can happen or what people are able to do: *A win is not beyond the bounds of possibility.* **2** [C] *literary* a long or high jump
PHRASE out of bounds 1 if a place is out of bounds, you are not allowed to go there **2** if a subject is out of bounds, you are not allowed to talk about it or know about it
→ LEAP²

bound⁴ the past tense and past participle of bind

boundary /'baʊnd(ə)ri/ noun ★
1 [C] the edge of an area of land, or a line that marks the edge: *The lane once formed the boundary between the two villages.* ♦ *a boundary fence/wall* → BORDER¹
2 boundaries [plural] the limits of an activity or experience: *new research that pushes back the boundaries of genetic science*

boundless /'baʊndləs/ adj very great

bountiful /'baʊntɪf(ə)l/ adj *literary* available in large quantities=ABUNDANT

bounty /'baʊnti/ noun **1** [C] money that is offered as a reward for catching or killing a criminal **2** [singular] *literary* the good things that something provides

bouquet /buː'keɪ, bəʊ'keɪ/ noun [C] flowers that are tied together in an attractive way and given to someone as a present

bourbon /'bɜːbən/ noun [C/U] American WHISKY, or a glass of this drink

bourgeois /'bʊəʒwɑː/ adj *showing disapproval* typical of middle-class people and their attitudes

bourgeoisie, the /,bʊəʒwɑː'ziː/ noun [singular] the middle class

bout /baʊt/ noun [C] **1** a short period when you have a particular illness or you do a particular activity: *a bout of flu* **2** a BOXING match or WRESTLING match

boutique /buː'tiːk/ noun [C] a small fashionable shop, especially one that sells clothes

bovine /'bəʊvaɪn/ adj *technical* relating to cows

bow¹ /baʊ/ verb **1** [I] to bend your body forwards from the waist in order to show respect for someone **2** [I/T] to bend your head forwards so that you are looking down
PHRASAL VERBS ,bow 'out to give up a job or position
,bow to sth/sb to agree to do something in an unwilling way: *They finally bowed to political pressure and signed the agreement.*

bow² /baʊ/ noun [C] **1** a forward movement of the top part of your body that you make in order to show respect for someone **2** the front part of a ship

bow³ /bəʊ/ noun [C] **1** a weapon made from a curved piece of wood. It is used for shooting ARROWS. **2** a knot that has two circular parts and two loose ends: *The ribbon was tied in a bow.* **3** an object that you use for playing instruments such as the VIOLIN and the CELLO

bowels /'baʊəlz/ noun [plural] the organ near your stomach where solid waste is formed and pushed out of your body
PHRASE the bowels of sth the inner parts of something

bowl¹ /bəʊl/ noun [C] ★★
1 a round container that you use for eating, serving, or preparing food: *In a large bowl, mix together the eggs, sugar, and butter.* ♦ *a bowl of fruit/soup*
2 the food in a bowl, or the amount that a bowl contains: *I always eat a bowl of cereal for breakfast.*
3 a large container without a lid, used for holding liquids: *a washing-up bowl*
→ BOWLS

bowl² /bəʊl/ verb [I/T] **1** to throw the ball towards the BATSMAN in the sport of CRICKET **2** to play BOWLS
PHRASAL VERB ,bowl sb 'over to surprise someone by being very impressive or unexpected: *We were bowled over by the beauty of the landscape.*

bow-legged /,bəʊ 'legɪd/ adj with legs that curve out sideways at the knees

bowler /'bəʊlə/ noun [C] the person who throws the ball towards the BATSMAN in the sport of CRICKET

bowling /'bəʊlɪŋ/ noun [U] an indoor game in which players roll heavy balls along a track and try to knock down a group of PINS (=objects that look like bottles)=TEN-PIN BOWLING

bowls /bəʊlz/ noun [U] *British* a game in which players roll large balls across the ground towards a small ball

bow tie /,bəʊ 'taɪ/ noun [C] a man's formal TIE in the shape of a BOW —*picture* → C4

box¹ /bɒks/ noun ★★★

1 container	4 in theatre
2 things in a container	5 television
3 space for writing in	

1 [C] a container with straight sides and a flat base: *a cardboard box*
2 [C] the things in a box, or the amount that

box 77 **brake**

B

a box contains: *We ate the whole box of chocolates*.

3 [C] a space for writing information on a printed form, or a space on a computer screen with information in it: *a dialog box*

4 [C] a small private space with seats in a theatre or sports ground

5 the box [singular] *British informal* the television: *Is there anything on the box tonight?*

box² /bɒks/ verb **1** [I] to fight in the sport of BOXING **2** [T] to put something into a box

PHRASAL VERB box sb 'in to surround someone so that they cannot move

boxer /'bɒksə/ noun [C] **1** someone who takes part in the sport of BOXING **2** a large dog with smooth hair and a flat face

boxer ,shorts or **boxers** noun [plural] loose underwear for men

boxing /'bɒksɪŋ/ noun [U] a sport in which two people fight each other wearing large leather GLOVES

Boxing ,Day noun [C/U] *British* the day after Christmas Day

box ,office noun [C] **1** the place in a theatre where you buy tickets **2** the number of people who buy tickets for a film or play: *a box-office success/failure* ♦ *The play was a huge success at the box office* (=a lot of people went to see it).

boy¹ /bɔɪ/ noun ★★★

1 [C] a male child, or a young man: *a 10-year-old boy* ♦ *Mr and Mrs Wylie have three boys.* ♦ *How old is your little boy* (=your son)?

2 [C] a man of any age, especially used for talking about where he comes from: *The Minnesota farm boy became a national hero.*

3 the boys [plural] *informal* a group of men who are friends

boy² /bɔɪ/ interjection used for expressing a strong reaction: *Boy, was she angry!*

boy ,band noun [C] a POP group consisting of attractive young men who sing and dance

boycott /'bɔɪkɒt/ verb [T] to protest about something by not taking part in an event or not buying certain products: *Turkey threatened to boycott the conference.*—**boycott** noun [C]

boyfriend /'bɔɪfrend/ noun [C] ★ a man or boy that you are having a sexual or romantic relationship with: *She's got a new boyfriend.* → GIRLFRIEND 1

boyhood /'bɔɪhʊd/ noun [U] *literary* the time when someone is a boy

boyish /'bɔɪɪʃ/ adj *showing approval* like a boy, or typical of a boy: *boyish good looks*

Boy 'Scout noun [C] a boy who is a member of the **Boy Scouts**, an organization that encourages boys to learn practical skills and help other people

bra /brɑː/ noun [C] a piece of underwear that supports a woman's breasts

brace¹ /breɪs/ verb [I/T] to get ready for something unpleasant: *Smith braced himself to give her the bad news.* ♦ *The stock market is braced for another week of falling prices.*

brace² /breɪs/ noun **1** [C] *British* a set of wires that you wear on your teeth to push them into the correct position **2 braces** [plural]

British two long narrow pieces of cloth that go over a man's shoulders and are fastened to his trousers to hold them up —*picture* → C4 **3** [C] an object that is designed to support something or to hold it in the correct position: *a back/neck brace*

bracelet /'breɪslət/ noun [C] a piece of jewellery that you wear around your wrist → BANGLE —*picture* → JEWELLERY

bracing /'breɪsɪŋ/ adj cold in a way that makes you feel full of energy

bracket /'brækɪt/ noun **1 brackets** [plural] *British* a pair of symbols ( ), used for showing that the words or numbers between them can be considered separately **2** [C] one of the groups that people or things are divided into, according to a feature that they all share: *people in the £75,000–£100,000 income bracket* **3** [C] a piece of wood, metal, or plastic that is fixed to a wall to support something like a shelf —**bracket** verb [T]

brag /bræg/ verb [I] to talk about your achievements or possessions in a proud way that annoys other people=BOAST: *She's always bragging about her famous father.*

braid¹ /breɪd/ noun **1** [U] twisted coloured rope that is used for decorating clothes, curtains, or furniture **2** [C] *American* a piece of long hair divided into three sections that are twisted around each other=PLAIT

braid² /breɪd/ verb [T] *American* to put someone's hair into braids —**braided** adj

braille /breɪl/ noun [U] a reading system for blind people that uses small raised marks that they feel with their fingers

brain /breɪn/ noun [C] ★★

1 the organ inside your head that allows you to think and feel, and controls your body: *The illness had affected his brain.* ♦ *a brain tumour/scan/operation*

2 mental ability or intelligence: *He's good-looking, and he's got brains.*

3 an intelligent person: *The best brains in the company can't solve the problem.*

PHRASES the brains behind sth the person who is responsible for inventing, developing, or organizing something

pick sb's brains *informal* to talk to someone who knows more about something than you do, in order to learn more about it

rack your brain(s) to try very hard to remember something or to solve a problem

brainchild /'breɪntʃaɪld/ noun [singular] a clever system, organization, or plan that someone thinks of and develops

brainless /'breɪnləs/ adj *informal* extremely stupid

brainstorming /'breɪnstɔːmɪŋ/ noun [U] a way of developing new ideas, in which people suggest lots of ideas and the best ones are chosen —**brainstorm** verb [I/T]

brainwash /'breɪnwɒʃ/ verb [T] to force someone to accept an idea by repeating it many times —**brainwashing** noun [U]

brainwave /'breɪnweɪv/ noun [C] **1** an electrical signal sent by your brain that can be recorded and measured **2** *British* a sudden very good idea

brainy /'breɪni/ adj *informal* very clever

brake¹ /breɪk/ noun [C] ★

1 the equipment in a vehicle or bicycle that

B

you use for slowing down or stopping: *I saw the child run out, so I* **slammed on the brakes** (=stopped suddenly). —*picture* → C6
2 an action or a situation that prevents something from developing: *The high level of debt* **put a brake on** *economic recovery.*

brake² /breɪk/ verb [I] to use the brakes to stop or slow down a vehicle or bicycle

brake light noun [C] a light on the back of a vehicle that comes on when you use the brakes —*picture* → C6

bran /bræn/ noun [U] the outside parts of the grains of plants such as wheat or OATS

branch¹ /brɑːntʃ/ noun [C] ★★

1 part of tree	4 part of area of study
2 shop/office	5 part of family
3 part of organization	6 part of river

1 one of the parts of a tree that grows out of its TRUNK (=main stem) —*picture* → TREE
2 a shop or office representing a large company or organization in a particular area: *The store has branches in over 50 cities.*
3 one part of a government or large organization that has particular responsibilities: *the local branch of the teachers' union* ♦ *the legislative branch of the US government*
4 a part of a particular area of study or knowledge: *Mechanics is a branch of physics.*
5 a section of a family who are all related to one person who lived in the past
6 a part of a river that leads away from the main part

branch² /brɑːntʃ/ verb [I] to divide into two or more parts: *The road branched into four paths.*

PHRASAL VERB **branch out** to start doing something new or different

brand¹ /brænd/ noun [C] ★
1 a product or group of products that has its own name and is made by one particular company: *I tried using a new* **brand of soap.**
2 a particular type of something: *He has his own special* **brand of humour.**

brand² /brænd/ verb [T] **1** to describe someone or something as a bad person or thing =LABEL: *The men were branded liars by the judge.* **2** to burn a mark onto a farm animal, in order to show who owns it

branded /ˈbrændɪd/ adj branded goods are made by well-known companies, and have the company name on them

brandish /ˈbrændɪʃ/ verb [T] to wave a weapon or other object around in your hand so that other people can see it

brand name noun [C] the name that a company chooses for its particular BRAND of product =TRADE NAME → TRADEMARK

brand-new adj extremely new

brandy /ˈbrændi/ noun [U] a strong alcoholic drink made from wine

brash /bræʃ/ adj *showing disapproval* **1** a brash person talks and behaves in a loud confident way **2** big, bright, or colourful

brass /brɑːs/ noun [U] **1** a shiny yellow metal that is a mixture of COPPER and ZINC **2** musical instruments made of brass such as TRUMPETS

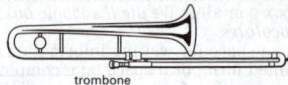
trombone
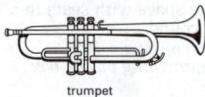
trumpet

French horn

tuba
brass instruments

brass band noun [C] a group of musicians who play brass instruments

brat /bræt/ noun [C] *informal* an annoying child who behaves badly

bravado /brəˈvɑːdəʊ/ noun [U] a brave, confident way of behaving, especially when you are in fact frightened

brave¹ /breɪv/ adj ★★ able to deal with danger, pain, or trouble without being frightened or worried =COURAGEOUS ≠ COWARDLY: *the brave soldiers who fought and died for their country* ♦ *his brave fight against corruption in the police force* —**bravely** adv

brave² /breɪv/ verb [T] to deal with a difficult situation in order to achieve something

bravery /ˈbreɪvəri/ noun [U] brave behaviour =COURAGE ≠ COWARDICE

bravo /ˌbrɑːˈvəʊ/ interjection used for showing that you admire what someone has done, or that you have enjoyed their performance

brawl /brɔːl/ noun [C] a noisy fight in a public place —**brawl** verb [I]

bray /breɪ/ verb [I] **1** to make the sound that a DONKEY makes **2** *showing disapproval* to talk or laugh very loudly

brazen /ˈbreɪz(ə)n/ adj *showing disapproval* behaving badly, and not caring if other people are shocked —**brazenly** adv

breach¹ /briːtʃ/ noun [C] **1** an action or situation in which a law, rule, or agreement is broken: *a clear breach of copyright* ♦ *The company was in breach of environmental regulations.* **2** *formal* a serious disagreement

breach² /briːtʃ/ verb [T] *formal* to break a law, rule, or agreement

bread /bred/ noun [U] ★★★ a common food made from flour, water, and usually YEAST: *a slice/loaf of bread* ♦ *white/brown bread* ♦ *a bread roll*

PHRASE **bread and butter** *informal* something that provides your main income: *Tourism is the island's bread and butter.*

bread bin noun [C] a container that you use for storing bread in —*picture* → C2

breadcrumbs /ˈbredkrʌmz/ noun [plural] very small pieces of bread, used in cooking

breadline /ˈbredlaɪn/ noun **on the breadline** *British* very poor

breadth /bredθ/ noun **1** [C/U] the distance

from one side of an object to the other =WIDTH: *5 metres in breadth* **2** [U] the wide range of different things or ideas that something includes: *The book demonstrates a remarkable breadth of knowledge.*
→ LENGTH

breadwinner /ˈbredˌwɪnə/ noun [C] the person who earns the money to support a family

break¹ /breɪk/ (past tense **broke** /brəʊk/; past participle **broken** /ˈbrəʊkən/) verb ★★★

1 separate into pieces	10 when waves fall
2 stop working	11 when the day starts
3 not obey rule/law	12 when a storm starts
4 not keep agreement	13 weather: change
5 make a hole/cut	14 when sb is upset
6 make sth end	15 of a boy's voice
7 when news is told	+ PHRASES
8 tell sb bad news	+ PHRASAL VERBS
9 destroy confidence	

1 [I/T] if something breaks, or if you break it, it separates into two or more pieces when it is hit, dropped etc: *I broke two dishes this morning.* ♦ *Joey broke three bones in his foot.* ♦ *Break the spaghetti in half* (=in the middle). ♦ *The glass broke into tiny pieces.*

2 [I/T] if a piece of equipment breaks, or if you break it, it stops working correctly: *Don't play with the camera – you'll break it.*

3 [T] to fail to obey a rule or law: *Students who break these rules will be punished.*

4 [T] to not do something that you promised or agreed to do: *Elliot claims that his business partner broke her contract.*

5 [T] to make a hole or cut in the surface of something: *The dog bit his leg, but didn't break the skin.*

6 [T] to make something end: *A bird's call broke the silence.* ♦ *I found it hard to break the habit of eating in the afternoons.*

7 [I/T] if important news breaks, or if a newspaper or television station breaks it, it becomes publicly known: *He was back in France when the news broke.*

8 [T] to tell someone bad news in a kind way: *I didn't know how to break it to her.*

9 [T] to destroy someone's confidence, determination, or happiness: *Twenty years in prison had not broken his spirit.*

10 [I] if waves break, they reach their highest point and start to fall

11 [I] when day breaks, it starts to get light in the morning=DAWN

12 [I] if a storm breaks, it starts

13 [I] if the weather breaks, it changes unexpectedly

14 [I] if someone's voice breaks, they cannot speak clearly, usually because they are upset

15 [I] when a boy's voice breaks, it starts to become deeper and sound like a man's

PHRASES **break even** if a person or business breaks even, they neither make a profit nor lose money

break sb's fall to stop someone who is falling from hitting the ground directly

break free 1 to escape from someone who is trying to hold you **2** to escape from an unpleasant situation that controls your life

break sb's heart to make someone feel extremely sad

break the ice to do or say something that makes people feel less shy or nervous when they first meet

break a record to do something better than anyone else has done before in a particular activity, especially a sport: *If she continues running at this pace, she'll break the world record.*

PHRASAL VERBS **break aˈway 1** to escape from a person, place, or situation: *Anna tried to break away, but he held her tight.* **2** to leave a political party or other group, especially in order to start another one **3** if a part of something breaks away from the rest, it becomes separated from it

break ˈdown 1 if a machine or vehicle breaks down, it stops working **2** if a relationship or discussion breaks down, it stops being successful: *At one point, the talks broke down completely.* **3** to start crying, especially in public: *People broke down and wept when they heard the news.*

break (sth) ˈdown if a substance breaks down, or if it is broken down, it separates into the parts that it is made up of: *The substance is easily broken down by bacteria.*

break sth ˈdown to hit something such as a door or wall very hard so that it falls down: *Firefighters had to break down the door.*

break ˈin 1 to enter a building by force, especially in order to steal things: *Someone had broken in through the bedroom window.* **2** to interrupt when someone is talking: *'Hilary,' he broke in gently, 'I'm just trying to help.'*

break ˈinto sth 1 to enter a building by force, especially in order to steal things: *A house in Brecon Place was broken into last night.* **2** to start doing something: *The children saw the sea and broke into a run.* **3** to start to have success in your career or an area of activity: *It's always been his ambition to break into broadcasting.*

break ˈoff to stop speaking: *Linda broke off, realizing that she was wrong.*

break (sth) ˈoff if a part of something breaks off, or if you break it off, it becomes separated from the main part: *Part of the chimney broke off and fell to the ground.*

break sth ˈoff to end a relationship or a discussion: *The two countries have broken off diplomatic relations.*

break ˈout 1 if something bad such as a war, fire, or disease breaks out, it starts **2** to start to appear on the skin: *An ugly rash broke out on my arm.* **3** to escape from a prison

break ˈthrough (sth) if something that was hidden breaks through, it appears: *The sun broke through the clouds.*

break ˈup 1 if two people break up, or if a relationship breaks up, the relationship ends: *He's just broken up with his girlfriend.* **2** if a meeting or event breaks up, it ends: *The talks didn't break up until after midnight.*

break (sth) ˈup to break into smaller pieces, or to make something do this: *Break the chocolate up into squares.*

break sth ˈup to stop a fight

break ˈwith sth 1 to leave a group that you have worked with, because of a

B

disagreement **2** if someone breaks with the past or with tradition, they start doing things in a new way

break² /breɪk/ noun [C] ★★

1 time for rest	5 where sth is broken
2 a short holiday	6 pause in programme
3 time of major change	7 a space in sth
4 chance to succeed	+ PHRASE

1 a period of time when you are not working and can rest or enjoy yourself: *OK, let's take a fifteen-minute break.* ♦ *The art class is the only time I get a break from the kids.*
2 a short holiday: *a weekend break for two in Florence*
3 a time at which one thing ends completely: *a break in relations with Uganda* ♦ *Lynn's decision helped her make the break with her past.*
4 an opportunity that helps you to be successful: *a lucky break* ♦ *Kiefer's big break came with the film* Stand By Me.
5 a place where something is broken: *a break in the gas pipeline*
6 a pause between television or radio programmes, especially when advertisements are broadcast: *We'll be back after the break.*
7 a space in something: *a break in the traffic/clouds*

PHRASE **give sb a break** to stop being unkind or making things difficult for someone: *Give the boy a break – he's just learning.* ♦ *Oh, give me a break* (=stop annoying me). *I was just joking.*

breakable /ˈbreɪkəb(ə)l/ adj a breakable object can break easily

breakaway /ˈbreɪkəweɪ/ adj consisting of people who have decided to separate from a larger group: *a breakaway republic*

breakdown /ˈbreɪkdaʊn/ noun [C] **1** a situation in which something has failed or is beginning to fail: *a breakdown in communication* **2** information that has been separated into different groups: *We'll need to see a breakdown of these figures.* **3** a NERVOUS BREAKDOWN **4** a situation in which a machine or vehicle stops working

breaker /ˈbreɪkə/ noun [C] a large wave that comes onto a beach

breakfast /ˈbrekfəst/ noun [C/U] ★★ the first meal that you have in the morning: *What did you have for breakfast this morning?* ♦ *breakfast cereal*

break-in noun [C] an occasion when someone enters a building illegally using force

breaking point /ˈbreɪkɪŋ ˌpɔɪnt/ noun [singular] a situation in which there are so many problems that it is impossible to deal with them

breakneck /ˈbreɪknek/ adj **at breakneck speed** very fast, in a way that is dangerous

breakout /ˈbreɪkaʊt/ noun [C] an occasion when prisoners escape from a prison

breakthrough /ˈbreɪkθruː/ noun [C] **1** a discovery or achievement that comes after a lot of hard work: *Scientists predict a major breakthrough within six months.* **2** a time when you begin to be successful: *The breakthrough came in the 20th minute with a header from Barnes.* ♦ *The breakthrough*

came when they discovered how to slow the virus down.

breakup /ˈbreɪkʌp/ noun [C] **1** the end of a marriage or serious relationship **2** the division of something such as an organization or country into smaller parts

breast /brest/ noun ★
1 [C] one of the two round soft parts on the front of a woman's body —*picture* → C14
2 [C] *literary* your chest and heart, thought of as the part of your body where you feel emotions
3 [C] the front part of a bird's body
4 [C/U] meat from the front part of a bird or some animals: *chicken breasts*

breastfeed /ˈbrestfiːd/ (past tense and past participle **breastfed** /ˈbrestfed/) verb [I/T] to feed a baby with milk from your breasts —**breastfeeding** noun [U]

breaststroke /ˈbreststrəʊk/ noun [U] a style of swimming in which you lie on your front and pull both arms back from your chest at the same time

breath /breθ/ noun [C/U] ★★ the air that goes in and out of your body when you breathe, or the action of getting air into your lungs: *His breath smelt of alcohol.* ♦ *She took a deep breath* (=filled her lungs with air). ♦ *Simon held his breath* (=breathed in and held the air inside) *and dived under the water.* ♦ *I was out of breath* (=breathing fast and with difficulty) *from running.*

PHRASES **a breath of fresh air 1** a short time outside a building when you have been inside **2** *informal* someone or something that is new, interesting, and exciting: *Young's singing style is a breath of fresh air for pop music.*

catch your breath or **get your breath back** to have a short rest after doing something tiring, so that you can start breathing normally again

don't hold your breath *spoken* used for telling someone not to expect something to happen because it probably will not: *Dan said he was coming, but don't hold your breath.*

in the same breath used for saying that someone has said two things that cannot both be true

take your breath away to be extremely impressive, beautiful, or shocking

under your breath said in a very quiet way, so that it is difficult for people to hear
→ CATCH¹

breathalyzer /ˈbreθəˌlaɪzə/ noun [C] a piece of equipment that the police use for checking how much alcohol a driver has drunk —**breathalyze** verb [T]

breathe /briːð/ verb ★★
1 [I/T] to take air into your lungs through your nose or mouth and let it out again: *Doctors said he was having difficulty breathing.* ♦ *We begin the exercise by breathing deeply* (=breathing large amounts of air). ♦ *She leant against the door, breathing heavily* (=with difficulty).
2 [T] to bring other substances than air into your body as you breathe: *I don't want to breathe other people's smoke.*

PHRASES **breathe down sb's neck** to watch closely what someone is doing, in a way that annoys them

not breathe a word to keep something a secret

PHRASAL VERBS ˌbreathe (sth) ˈin to take air or other substances into your lungs through your nose or mouth

ˌbreathe (sth) ˈout to send air or other substances out of your lungs through your nose or mouth

breather /ˈbriːðə/ noun [singular] *informal* a short rest from work or activity

breathing /ˈbriːðɪŋ/ noun [U] the process of taking air into your lungs and letting it out again

ˈbreathing ˌspace noun [singular/U] a period of rest from a difficult situation that allows you to get your energy back

breathless /ˈbreθləs/ adj **1** breathing very fast and hard, for example after running **2** experiencing a very strong emotion, especially excitement —**breathlessly** adv, **breathlessness** noun [U]

breathtaking /ˈbreθˌteɪkɪŋ/ adj extremely impressive or beautiful —**breathtakingly** adv

ˈbreath ˌtest noun [C] a test in which police officers check how much alcohol a driver has drunk

breed¹ /briːd/ (past tense and past participle **bred** /bred/) verb **1** [I] if animals breed, they become the parents of young animals **2** [T] to produce new plants or animals from existing ones **3** [T] to make bad feelings or situations develop: *Secrecy breeds distrust.*

breed² /briːd/ noun [C] **1** a particular type of animal that is different from others but not so different that it is another SPECIES: *different breeds of dog* **2** a particular type of person or thing: *the new breed of Internet millionaires*

breeder /ˈbriːdə/ noun [C] someone who breeds animals or plants

breeding /ˈbriːdɪŋ/ noun [U] **1** the process of MATING and producing young animals **2** the activity of keeping animals or plants in order to produce new animals or plants **3** *old-fashioned* polite behaviour that is thought to be connected with the type of family that you come from

breeze¹ /briːz/ noun [C] a light wind: *a gentle/light/slight breeze*

breeze² /briːz/ verb [I] to go somewhere in a very confident way: *He breezed into the meeting and took charge.*

PHRASAL VERB ˈbreeze through sth to do something very easily or confidently

breezy /ˈbriːzi/ adj **1** with a lot of light wind **2** lively, confident, and informal —**breezily** adv

brevity /ˈbrevəti/ noun [U] *formal* **1** the use of only a few words **2** the fact that something only lasts for a short time

brew /bruː/ verb **1** [I/T] to make beer **2** [I/T] if tea or coffee is brewing, or if you are brewing it, you have made it and left it to develop more flavour **3** [I] to begin to happen: *A storm was brewing.*

brewer /ˈbruːə/ noun [C] a company or person that makes beer

brewery /ˈbruːəri/ noun [C] **1** a company that makes beer **2** a place where beer is made

bribe¹ /braɪb/ verb [T] to give money or presents to someone so that they will help

you by doing something wrong or illegal: *They tried to bribe the judge to find their brother not guilty.*

bribe² /braɪb/ noun [C] money or a present that you give to someone so that they will help you by doing something wrong or illegal: *Some officials had accepted bribes from a major oil company.*

bribery /ˈbraɪb(ə)ri/ noun [U] the act of giving money or presents to someone so that they will help you by doing something wrong or illegal

bric-a-brac /ˈbrɪkəˌbræk/ noun [U] small objects for your home that are not very expensive

brick¹ /brɪk/ noun [C/U] ★★ a small block used as a building material to make walls, houses etc: *The church was built entirely of brick.* → WALL¹

brick² /brɪk/ **PHRASAL VERB** ˌbrick sth ˈup or ˌbrick sth ˈin to fill a space in a wall with bricks

bricklayer /ˈbrɪkˌleɪə/ noun [C] someone whose job is to build walls, houses etc using bricks —**bricklaying** noun [U]

bridal /ˈbraɪd(ə)l/ adj relating to a bride

bride /braɪd/ noun [C] a woman who is getting married, or one who has recently married

bridegroom /ˈbraɪdˌgruːm/ noun [C] a man who is getting married, or one who has recently married

bridesmaid /ˈbraɪdzˌmeɪd/ noun [C] a girl or young woman who helps a BRIDE at her wedding

bridge¹ /brɪdʒ/ noun ★★

1 for crossing river/road	4 card game
2 connection	5 upper part of nose
3 part of ship	

1 [C] a structure that supports a road, railway, or path going over a river, over another road etc: *Go over the bridge and then turn right.* ♦ *a railway bridge*

2 [C] something that forms a connection between two groups or situations: *Nursery school acts as a bridge between home and school.*

3 [C] the part of a ship from which it is controlled

4 [U] a card game for four players who make two teams

5 [C] the thin part of your nose between your eyes

bridge² /brɪdʒ/ verb [T] to reduce the differences that separate two things or groups: *ways to bridge the gap between income and spending*

bridle¹ /ˈbraɪd(ə)l/ noun [C] a set of leather bands that go over a horse's head

bridle² /ˈbraɪd(ə)l/ verb [I] to show that you are angry or offended

brief¹ /briːf/ adj ★★

1 lasting for only a short time: *a brief visit*

2 using only a few words: *I'll make my comments brief.*

PHRASE in brief using as few words as possible, and without many details → BRIEFLY

brief² /briːf/ noun [C] **1** *British* official instructions on how to do a job **2** a

document giving the facts of a legal case
→ BRIEFS

brief³ /briːf/ verb [T] to give someone official information about a situation: *The President's military advisors are briefing him on the situation.*

briefcase /'briːfkeɪs/ noun [C] a case for carrying documents —*picture* → C3

briefing /'briːfɪŋ/ noun [C] a meeting or document in which people receive official information

briefly /'briːfli/ adv **1** in a way that does not take much time or give many details: *Tell me briefly what your story is about.* **2** for a short time: *I saw her briefly yesterday before she left for the airport.*

briefs /briːfs/ noun [plural] men's short tight UNDERPANTS or women's KNICKERS

brigade /brɪ'geɪd/ noun [C] **1** a large group of soldiers **2** *showing disapproval* a group of people who have the same opinions: *the anti-hunting brigade*

brigadier /ˌbrɪgə'dɪə/ noun [C] an officer of high rank in the British Army

bright /braɪt/ adj ★★★
1 bright colours are strong but not dark: *She was wearing a bright red scarf.* ♦ *They have used warm bright colours all through the house.*
2 full of strong shining light: *It was a bright sunny day.* ♦ *I could see a bright light in the sky.*
3 intelligent: *one of the brightest students in the class*
4 happy and lively=CHEERFUL: *She gave him a bright smile.*

PHRASE **look on the bright side** to think about the good parts of a situation that is mainly bad
—**brightly** adv, **brightness** noun [U]

brighten /'braɪt(ə)n/ verb **1** [I/T] to start to have more colour or light, or to give something more colour or light **2** [I] to start looking or feeling happier

PHRASAL VERBS **brighten up** *same as* **brighten** 2: *Viola brightened up when she saw him.*
brighten (sth) up to start to have more colour or light, or to give something more colour or light: *It was beginning to brighten up* (=the weather was beginning to improve).

brilliance /'brɪljəns/ noun [U] **1** great skill or intelligence **2** great brightness

brilliant /'brɪljənt/ adj ★
1 very intelligent: *a brilliant scientist*
2 very skilful, impressive, or successful: *The goalkeeper made a brilliant save.*
3 *British informal* extremely good or enjoyable: *The kids had a brilliant time.*
4 extremely bright: *a brilliant light*
—**brilliantly** adv: *Their plan worked brilliantly.* ♦ *brilliantly coloured birds*

brim¹ /brɪm/ noun [C] **1** the part of a hat that sticks out from the base **2** the top edge of a cup or bowl

brim² /brɪm/ **PHRASAL VERB** **brim with sth 1** to be extremely full of something liquid: *Her eyes were brimming with tears.* **2** to be feeling a strong emotion

bring /brɪŋ/ (past tense and past participle **brought** /brɔːt/) verb [T] ★★★

1 take sb/sth with you	6 start a legal case
2 move sth somewhere	7 used to change subject
3 attract to a place	♦ PHRASES
4 cause sth	♦ PHRASAL VERBS
5 make sth reach a total	

1 to take someone or something with you from one place to another: *Bring a coat in case it turns cold.* ♦ **bring sth for sb** *I brought that book for you.* ♦ **bring sb sth** *Could you bring me a plate from the kitchen?* ♦ **bring sth to sb** *Don't get up – I'll bring your tea to you.*
2 to move something somewhere: **bring sth down/up** *She reached up to the shelf and brought down a box.*
3 to make someone or something come to a place: **bring sb/sth to sth** *Government investment has brought thousands of new jobs to the area.* ♦ *What brought you to Chicago in the first place?*
4 to be the cause of a state, situation, or feeling: *efforts to bring peace to the region* ♦ *My work **brings** me **into contact with** all kinds of people.* ♦ **bring sb sth** *The baby has brought them great joy.*
5 to make a number reach a particular total: *He scored 10 points, bringing the team's total to 85.*
6 to start a legal case against someone: *The authorities are expected to **bring charges**.*
7 to come to a particular point as you are talking or writing: *This brings us to the end of this part of the discussion.*

PHRASES **bring sth to an end/a close** to make something stop
can't bring yourself to do sth to be unable to do something because it is too unpleasant, embarrassing, or sad: *He can't even bring himself to talk to me.*
→ BOIL²

PHRASAL VERBS **bring sth a'bout** to cause changes in a situation
bring sb/sth a'long to take someone or something with you when you go somewhere
bring sth 'back 1 to cause ideas, feelings, or memories to be in your mind again: *Do these stories bring back any memories?* **2** to start using or doing things that were used or done in the past: *They'll never bring back the death penalty.* **3** to bring something with you when you come back from a place
bring sth 'down 1 to cause a government or politician to lose power **2** to reduce the rate, level, or amount of something: *policies designed to bring down inflation* **3** to make someone or something move or fall to the ground: *Strong winds brought down power lines across the region.*
bring sth 'forward to change the date or time of an event so that it happens earlier: *The match has been brought forward to 1.00 pm.*
bring sth 'in 1 to cause someone or something to get money or customers: *Renting out a spare room can bring in £250 a month.* **2** to introduce a new law or system: *She said the government would bring in the necessary legislation to deal with the problem.* **3** to use the skills of a particular group or person:

B

This is an opportunity to bring in new talent.

,bring sth 'on to be the cause of something bad: *Stress can bring on headaches.*

,bring sth 'out 1 to produce a new product and start to sell it =RELEASE: *They have recently brought out a new CD.* 2 to make a particular quality appear in someone or something: *Tragedies like this sometimes bring out the best* in people (=make them show their best qualities).

,bring sb 'round *British* to make someone who is unconscious become conscious

,bring sb/sth 'round *British* to take someone or something to someone's house: *He promised to bring the letter round in the morning.*

,bring sb 'up to look after a child until he or she becomes an adult =RAISE: *She brought up three sons on her own.* ♦ **bring sb up to be/do sth** *Our parents brought us up to believe in our own abilities.*

,bring sth 'up to start discussing a subject: *I hate to bring this up but you owe me £50.*

- If you **bring**, **take**, or **fetch** something, you hold it and go with it to another place. But which word you choose depends on the situation.
- **Bring** describes movement to another place when the speaker or listener is already there: *Bring the photos when you come to visit me.* ♦ *I'll bring the photos to your house tonight.*
- **Take** describes movement to another place when the speaker or listener is NOT already there: *Take the photos when you go to visit her tonight.* ♦ *I'll take the photos to her house.*
- **Fetch** describes movement to another place AND back again, bringing someone or something with you: *Fetch the photos from the kitchen, will you.*

---

brink /brɪŋk/ noun **the brink of sth** the point in time when something very bad or very good is about to happen: *The crisis brought the two nations to the brink of war.*

brisk /brɪsk/ adj 1 moving or acting quickly 2 if business is brisk, a lot of things are being sold quickly —**briskly** adv

bristle¹ /ˈbrɪs(ə)l/ noun [C] 1 a short stiff fibre in a brush 2 a short stiff hair

bristle² /ˈbrɪs(ə)l/ verb [I] to be angry or offended

Brit /brɪt/ noun [C] *informal* someone who comes from the UK

British /ˈbrɪtɪʃ/ adj 1 of the UK, or from the UK 2 **the British** the people of the UK

Briton /ˈbrɪt(ə)n/ noun [C] *mainly journalism* someone from the UK

brittle /ˈbrɪt(ə)l/ adj hard and easily broken

broach /brəʊtʃ/ verb [T] to begin discussing a subject that may make someone upset or embarrassed: *He decided it was time to broach the subject of a pay rise.*

broad /brɔːd/ adj ★★★
1 wide ≠ NARROW: *He had very broad shoulders.* ♦ *a broad shady path*
2 including many different things or people ≠ NARROW: *I meet a broad range of people in my job.*
3 expressed in a general way, without many details: *We need a broad strategy for the company's future development.* ♦ *This*

chapter can only give *a broad outline* of the subject.
4 a broad ACCENT (=way of speaking) is very noticeable and typical of the area you come from: *a broad northern accent*

PHRASE **in broad daylight** during the day, when people can easily see what is happening: *They robbed the bank in broad daylight.*
→ BROADLY

broadband /ˈbrɔːdˌbænd/ noun [U] a type of connection between a computer and the Internet that allows you to send or receive a large amount of information in a short time

broadcast¹ /ˈbrɔːdˌkɑːst/ (past tense and past participle **broadcast** or **broadcasted**) verb [I/T] to send out messages or programmes to be received by radios or televisions: *The BBC will be broadcasting the match live from Paris.*
—**broadcasting** noun [U]

broadcast² /ˈbrɔːdˌkɑːst/ noun [C] a programme that is broadcast: *Channel 5's main news broadcast*

broadcaster /ˈbrɔːdˌkɑːstə/ noun [C] someone whose job is to speak on radio or television programmes

broaden /ˈbrɔːd(ə)n/ verb [I/T] 1 to become wider, or to make something wider: *There are plans to broaden the road.* 2 to start to include more things or people, or to make something include more things or people: *We have broadened the scope of the investigation.*

broadly /ˈbrɔːdli/ adv 1 in a general way, although not in every detail: *The proposal was broadly welcomed by teachers.* 2 in a way that includes a large number of people or things: *a broadly-based committee*

broad-minded /ˌbrɔːdˈmaɪndɪd/ adj willing to accept different types of behaviour and not easily shocked ≠ NARROW-MINDED

broadsheet /ˈbrɔːdˌʃiːt/ noun [C] *British* a serious type of newspaper that is printed on large sheets of paper

broadside /ˈbrɔːdˌsaɪd/ noun [C] a strong written or spoken attack

Broadway /ˈbrɔːdˌweɪ/ a street in New York City that is famous for having many theatres

brocade /brəˈkeɪd/ noun [U] expensive thick cloth with a pattern woven into it

broccoli /ˈbrɒkəli/ noun [U] a vegetable consisting of green stems with many small green or purple parts on the ends —*picture* → C11

brochure /ˈbrəʊʃə/ noun [C] a small magazine containing details of goods or services that you can buy

broil /brɔɪl/ verb [I/T] *American* to GRILL food

broiler /ˈbrɔɪlə/ noun [C] *American* a GRILL for cooking

broke¹ /brəʊk/ adj *informal* without any money: *Can you lend me £5? I'm completely broke.*

broke² the past tense of **break¹**

broken¹ /ˈbrəʊkən/ adj ★★★

1 damaged and in pieces	4 extremely sad
2 not working	5 not as promised
3 injured and cracked	+ PHRASES

B

1 a broken object has been damaged with the result that it is in two or more pieces: *Nearly all the houses had broken windows.* ♦ *Be careful not to step on the broken glass.*
2 if a piece of equipment is broken, it is not working correctly: *You can't use the microwave – it's broken.*
3 a broken bone has a crack in it: *He had several broken ribs.* ♦ *a broken arm*
4 *literary* if your heart is broken, you feel extremely sad
5 a broken promise is one that someone has not kept

PHRASES **broken English** English with a lot of mistakes, spoken by someone who does not know it very well
a broken home a family in which the parents no longer live together

---

Words that you can use instead of broken

Broken is a very general word. Here are some words with more specific meanings that sound more natural and appropriate in particular situations.

cars/machines/equipment	faulty, not working
houses/buildings	falling down, in disrepair
systems/computers	down, not working
objects	chipped, cracked, dented, smashed
containers	burst, leaky, split
fabric	frayed, ripped, split, torn
paper	in shreds, ripped, torn

---

broken² the past participle of **break¹**
broken-down adj no longer working, or in very bad condition
broken-hearted /ˌbrəʊkən ˈhɑːtɪd/ adj extremely sad
broker¹ /ˈbrəʊkə/ noun [C] **1** someone who buys and sells things like property or insurance for other people **2** someone who arranges an agreement
broker² /ˈbrəʊkə/ verb [T] to arrange the details of a deal so that everyone can agree to it
brolly /ˈbrɒli/ noun [C] *British informal* an UMBRELLA
bronchitis /brɒŋˈkaɪtɪs/ noun [U] an illness that affects your breathing and makes you cough
bronze /brɒnz/ noun **1** [U] a hard brown metal made from COPPER and TIN **2** [C] a BRONZE MEDAL **3** [U] a red-brown colour
bronzed /brɒnzd/ adj with attractive brown skin because of spending time in the sun
bronze 'medal noun [C] a round flat piece of metal that you get as a prize for coming third in a competition
brooch /brəʊtʃ/ noun [C] a piece of jewellery that you fasten to your clothes —*picture* → JEWELLERY
brood¹ /bruːd/ verb [I] to think and worry about something a lot
brood² /bruːd/ noun [C] a group of young birds that are born at the same time to the same mother
brook /brʊk/ noun [C] a small river
broom /bruːm/ noun [C] a brush with a long handle, used for cleaning floors

broth /brɒθ/ noun [U] a thick soup with pieces of meat or vegetables in it
brothel /ˈbrɒθ(ə)l/ noun [C] a place where men pay to have sex
brother /ˈbrʌðə/ noun [C] ★★★
1 a boy or man who has the same parents as you: *his younger/older/little/big brother* —*picture* → FAMILY TREE
2 used by men for referring to a man that they feel loyalty and friendship towards
3 a man who is a member of a religious group, especially a MONK
4 *American* a black man. This word is mainly used by black people.
brotherhood /ˈbrʌðəhʊd/ noun **1** [U] the friendship and support that a group of people get from one another **2** [C] a group of people who have similar interests
brother-in-law (plural **brothers-in-law**) noun [C] **1** your sister's husband **2** the brother of your husband or wife —*picture* → FAMILY TREE
brotherly /ˈbrʌðəli/ adj typical of the feelings that a brother shows
brought the past tense and past participle of bring
brow /braʊ/ noun [C] **1** *literary* the part of your face above your eyes **2** an EYEBROW **3** the highest part of a hill
brown¹ /braʊn/ adj ★★★ having the same colour as wood or coffee: *brown eyes* —**brown** noun [C/U]: *The skirt is also available in brown.*
brown² /braʊn/ verb [I/T] to cook something until it turns brown, or to become brown in this way
brownfield /ˈbraʊnfiːld/ adj relating to land in a town that was previously used for industry and where new buildings can now be built: *brownfield sites*
brownie /ˈbraʊni/ noun [C/U] a type of flat chocolate cake that is served in squares
browse /braʊz/ verb **1** [I] to look at information or pictures in a book or magazine, without looking for anything in particular: *I sat in the waiting room and browsed through the magazines.* **2** [I/T] *computing* to look for information on a computer, especially on the Internet **3** [I] to look at things in a shop without being sure whether you want to buy anything
browser /ˈbraʊzə/ noun [C] *computing* a computer program that allows you to use the Internet
bruise¹ /bruːz/ verb [T] to cause a bruise on someone's skin or on a piece of fruit: *She bruised her leg quite badly when she fell.* —**bruising** noun [U]
bruise² /bruːz/ noun [C] a dark mark on your body or on a piece of fruit where it has been hit: *He had a large bruise over his eye.*
brunch /brʌntʃ/ noun [C/U] a meal that combines breakfast and lunch
brunette /bruːˈnet/ noun [C] a woman with dark-brown hair
brunt /brʌnt/ noun **bear/take the brunt of sth** to suffer the worst effects of sth
brush¹ /brʌʃ/ verb ★
1 [T] to make something clean or tidy using a brush: *She hadn't bothered to brush her hair.* ♦ *How often do you brush your teeth?*

B

2 [T] to remove something by moving your hands or a brush quickly over a surface: *Maggie **brushed away** her tears as she listened.* ♦ **brush sth from/off sth** *We had to brush the snow off the windscreen.*

3 [I/T] to touch someone or something for a very short time as you go past: *She **brushed past** him.*

PHRASAL VERBS **brush sth aside** to refuse to accept that something is important or true: *The minister brushed aside accusations that he had lied.*

brush sth up or **brush up on sth** to improve your skills or knowledge of something: *I took a class to brush up my German before the trip.*

brush² /brʌʃ/ noun ★★
1 [C] an object that you use for painting, cleaning things, or making your hair tidy, consisting of a handle with fibres fixed to it: *Remove any loose dirt using a soft brush.*
2 [singular] an act of making something clean or tidy using a brush: *I'll give my teeth a brush before we leave.*
3 [C] a short experience of a dangerous or unpleasant situation: *He'd had a few **brushes** with the law, but nothing serious.*
4 [singular] a very gentle movement against something

brusque /bruːsk, brʊsk/ adj speaking quickly in an unfriendly way using very few words =CURT —**brusquely** adv

Brussels /ˈbrʌs(ə)lz/ the capital city of Belgium, where the HEADQUARTERS of the European Union is. People often use 'Brussels' for referring to the government of the European Union.

Brussels sprout noun [C] a small round vegetable consisting of many green leaves —*picture* → C11

brutal /ˈbruːt(ə)l/ adj **1** extremely violent: *brutal attacks/atrocities* **2** extremely honest, in a way that seems unkind: *Let's be brutal here – he's not good enough.* —**brutality** /bruːˈtæləti/ noun [C/U], **brutally** adv

brute¹ /bruːt/ noun [C] a strong man who acts in a cruel or violent way

brute² /bruːt/ adj **brute force/strength** great physical force/strength

brutish /ˈbruːtɪʃ/ adj *literary* cruel and lacking intelligence

B.S. /ˌbiː ˈes/ noun [C] *American* a BSC

BSc /ˌbiː es ˈsiː/ noun [C] *British* Bachelor of Science: a first degree from a university in a subject such as physics or biology

BSE /ˌbiː es ˈiː/ noun [U] a disease in cows that affects their brains and kills them

BTW abbrev by the way: used in emails and TEXT MESSAGES for introducing additional information

bubble¹ /ˈbʌb(ə)l/ noun [C] a ball of air or gas in a liquid or other substance: *Heat the milk until bubbles form around the edge of the pan.*

bubble² /ˈbʌb(ə)l/ verb [I] if liquid bubbles, bubbles form and move in it: *When the sauce starts to bubble, remove it from the heat.*

PHRASAL VERB **bubble with sth** or **bubble**

over with sth to be full of a happy or excited feeling

bubble gum noun [C/U] a type of brightly coloured sweet that you blow into to form bubbles, but do not swallow

bubbly /ˈbʌbli/ adj **1** lively, happy, and friendly **2** full of BUBBLES

buck /bʌk/ noun [C] **1** *American informal* a dollar **2** a male deer → DOE
PHRASE **pass the buck** to make someone else deal with something that you should take responsibility for

bucket /ˈbʌkɪt/ noun [C] **1** a round open container with a handle, used for carrying liquid and other substances **2** the amount that a bucket contains: *a bucket of soapy water*

buckle¹ /ˈbʌk(ə)l/ verb [I/T] **1** to fasten a buckle, or to be fastened with a buckle: *The bag buckles at the side.* **2** to bend, or to make something bend under pressure: *The pillars began to buckle under the strain.*

buckle² /ˈbʌk(ə)l/ noun [C] a metal object used for fastening a belt, shoe, or bag

bud /bʌd/ noun [C] a part of a plant that opens to form a leaf or flower: *yellow rose buds* → NIP, TASTE BUDS

Buddha /ˈbʊdə/ the title used for referring to Siddhartha Gautama, the founder of Buddhism

Buddhism /ˈbʊdɪz(ə)m/ noun [U] the set of religious beliefs based on the teaching of Siddhartha Gautama, the Buddha —**Buddhist** adj, noun [C]

budding /ˈbʌdɪŋ/ adj just beginning or developing: *a budding musician*

buddy /ˈbʌdi/ noun [C] *American informal* a friend

budge /bʌdʒ/ verb [I/T] to move, or to make something move, especially something that is difficult to move: *I pulled again, but the wheel wouldn't budge.*
PHRASE **not budge** to refuse to change your opinion or decision → INCH¹

budgerigar /ˈbʌdʒəriɡɑː/ noun [C] a small bright blue, green, or yellow bird that is often kept as a pet

budget¹ /ˈbʌdʒɪt/ noun [C] ★ the amount of money a person, organization, or government has to spend, or their plan to spend it: *Two-thirds of their budget goes on labour costs.* ♦ *Try to work out a monthly budget and stick to it.* ♦ *The film is already over budget* (=it has cost more than was expected).

budget² /ˈbʌdʒɪt/ verb [I] to carefully plan the way you will spend your money: *As a student, you have to learn how to budget.*

budget³ /ˈbʌdʒɪt/ adj very cheap: *a budget hotel*

budgie /ˈbʌdʒi/ noun [C] *informal* a BUDGERIGAR

buff /bʌf/ noun [C] someone who is very interested in and knows a lot about a particular subject: *a film/computer/wine buff*

buffalo /ˈbʌfələʊ/ noun [C] a large animal similar to a cow with curved horns

buffer /ˈbʌfə/ noun [C] something that protects someone or something from harm: *The air bag acts as a buffer between the driver and the steering wheel.*

buffet¹ /ˈbʊfeɪ/ noun [C] a meal at which all the food is put on a table and people go and choose what they want

buffet² /ˈbʌfɪt/ verb [T] to keep hitting against something with force

bug¹ /bʌg/ noun [C] **1** informal a minor infectious illness: *a flu bug* **2** a minor fault in a computer system or in a computer program **3** a small piece of electronic equipment that is used for secretly listening to people **4** informal an insect

bug² /bʌg/ verb [T] **1** informal to annoy someone: *It really bugs me when people smoke in restaurants.* **2** to hide a piece of electronic equipment somewhere so that you can secretly listen to people

buggy /ˈbʌgi/ noun [C] a light folding chair with wheels, used for pushing small children in

bugle /ˈbjuːg(ə)l/ noun [C] a musical instrument, consisting of a curved metal tube that is wide at one end

build¹ /bɪld/ (past tense and past participle **built** /bɪlt/) verb ★★★
1 [I/T] to make a building or other large structure by putting its parts together: *Do you know when this house was built?* ♦ *They're building a new bridge over the river.* ♦ *The cabin was built of logs.*
2 [T] to develop something: *He set out to build a business empire and succeeded.*
3 [I/T] to increase, or to make something increase: *The company has worked hard to build sales.*

PHRASAL VERBS **build sth ˈin/ˈinto sth** to make something part of a plan, system, or calculation: *The cost of hiring equipment is built into the price.*
ˈbuild ˌon/uˌpon sth to do something in addition to what you have already achieved: *We need to build on the ideas we have had so far.*
ˌbuild (sth) ˈup same as **build¹** 3: *These exercises are good for building up leg strength.*
→ BUILD-UP
ˌbuild sth ˈup same as **build¹** 2: *Stevens played a key role in building up the company.*
ˌbuild ˈup to sth to prepare for something: *She'd been building up to telling them she was leaving.*

build² /bɪld/ noun [singular] the size and shape of someone's body: *He was of medium build and about my height.*

Words often used with **build**

*Adjectives often used with **build** (noun)*
- **muscular, solid, stocky, sturdy** + BUILD: used about someone with a big body
- **slender, slim, wiry** + BUILD: used about someone with a thin body

---

builder /ˈbɪldə/ noun [C] someone whose job is to build and repair houses

building /ˈbɪldɪŋ/ noun ★★★
1 [C] a structure such as a house that has a roof and walls: *The town hall was a large impressive building.*
2 [U] the process of building houses, factories, office buildings etc: *the building of a new hospital* ♦ *building materials/regulations*

building ˌblock noun [C] one of the basic parts from which something is made: *Proteins are the essential building blocks of the body's cells.*

ˈbuilding soˌciety noun [C] British a financial organization in which people invest money, and from which they can borrow money to buy a house or flat

ˈbuild-ˌup noun [C] **1** a gradual increase in the amount or level of something: *a build-up of carbon dioxide in the atmosphere* **2** the time before an event when people are preparing for it: *the build-up to the wedding*

built the past tense and past participle of **build¹**

ˌbuilt-ˈin adj forming part of something, and not separate from it

ˌbuilt-ˈup adj a built-up area has a lot of buildings in it

bulb /bʌlb/ noun [C] **1** a glass object with a very thin wire inside, that produces light when it is connected to an electricity supply **2** the part of a plant from which it grows. Bulbs are shaped like onions.

bulbous /ˈbʌlbəs/ adj big and round

bulge¹ /bʌldʒ/ noun [C] a shape that curves outwards on the surface of something

bulge² /bʌldʒ/ verb [I] to stick out in a curved shape

bulging /ˈbʌldʒɪŋ/ adj **1** completely full: *a bulging suitcase/briefcase* **2** sticking out

bulimia /bjuːˈlɪmiə/ noun [U] a serious illness in which you try to control your weight by VOMITING (=bringing food up from your stomach and out of your mouth) → ANOREXIA

bulk /bʌlk/ noun [U] the fact of being large
PHRASES **the bulk of sth** the majority or largest part of something: *Women still do the bulk of domestic work in the home.*
in bulk in large quantities: *large companies that buy and sell in bulk*

bulky /ˈbʌlki/ adj too big to be carried or stored easily

bull /bʊl/ noun [C] **1** a male cow —*picture* → C12 **2** business someone who expects the price of company SHARES to rise → BEAR² 2
PHRASE **take the bull by the horns** to deal with a problem in a direct confident way

bulldog /ˈbʊldɒg/ noun [C] a dog with short hair, a short neck and large head, and short thick legs

bulldoze /ˈbʊldəʊz/ verb [I/T] to clear an area with a bulldozer

bulldozer /ˈbʊldəʊzə/ noun [C] a heavy vehicle with a large curved open container at the front, used for moving earth and stones and destroying buildings

bullet /ˈbʊlɪt/ noun [C] ★ a small piece of metal that is shot from a gun: *a bullet wound/hole* → BITE¹

bulletin /ˈbʊlətɪn/ noun [C] **1** a short news broadcast **2** a newspaper that a club or organization produces regularly for its members

ˈbulletin ˌboard noun [C] **1** computing a place on a computer system or on the Internet where you can leave and read messages **2** American a NOTICEBOARD

ˈbullet ˌpoint noun [C] a printed circle, square etc before each item on a list in order to emphasize it

bulletproof /ˈbʊlɪtpruːf/ adj made from a

material that stops bullets from passing through

bullfight /ˈbʊlfaɪt/ noun [C] a traditional entertainment in Spain, Mexico, and Portugal in which someone fights a BULL (=male cow) —**bullfighter** noun [C], **bullfighting** noun [U]

bullion /ˈbʊliən/ noun [U] gold or silver in the form of solid bars

bullish /ˈbʊlɪʃ/ adj expecting a successful future=OPTIMISTIC

bull market noun [C] *business* a situation in which prices of SHARES are rising → BEAR MARKET

bull's-eye noun [C] the circle in the centre of a TARGET that you try to hit

bully¹ /ˈbʊli/ verb [T] to frighten or hurt someone who is smaller or weaker than you —**bullying** noun [U]

bully² /ˈbʊli/ noun [C] someone who uses their strength or status to threaten or frighten people

bum /bʌm/ noun [C] *informal* **1** *British* the part of your body that you sit on=BOTTOM **2** *American* someone without a job or place to live. This word is now considered offensive by some people. **3** *American* a lazy person

bum bag noun [C] *British* a small bag on a belt that you wear around your waist to keep small things in —*picture* → BAG

bumblebee /ˈbʌmblˌbiː/ noun [C] a large BEE (=flying insect)

bumbling /ˈbʌmblɪŋ/ adj confused or badly organized

bump¹ /bʌmp/ verb **1** [I/T] to hit against something solid, or to accidentally make something do this: *I bumped my knee on the corner of the desk.* **2** [I] to move over a surface that is not even: *The truck bumped slowly across the field.*

PHRASAL VERBS **bump into sb** to meet someone unexpectedly: *I bumped into your mother at the supermarket.*
bump sb off *informal* to murder someone
bump sth up *informal* to increase something

bump² /bʌmp/ noun [C] **1** a raised part on your skin where you have been injured: *Her body was covered in bumps and bruises.* **2** a raised part on a surface: *a bump in the road* **3** a hit or knock against something solid: *We felt a bump as the boat hit something.*

bumper¹ /ˈbʌmpə/ noun [C] a long thin bar on the front or back of a vehicle that protects the vehicle if it hits anything —*picture* → C6

bumper² /ˈbʌmpə/ adj bigger or more successful than usual: *a bumper crowd of 80,000*

bumpy /ˈbʌmpi/ adj **1** a bumpy surface is rough **2** a bumpy journey is uncomfortable because of bad weather or a bad road

bun /bʌn/ noun [C] **1** *British* a small round cake: *a currant bun* **2** a small round piece of bread: *a burger in a bun* **3** a hairstyle in which a woman's hair is tied in a tight round ball at the back of her head

bunch¹ /bʌntʃ/ noun **1** [C] a group or set of similar things that are fastened together: *a bunch of grapes/flowers/keys* **2** [singular] *informal* a group of people: *They're a lovely*

bunch who have made me feel welcome. **3 bunches** [plural] *British* a girl's or woman's hairstyle in which the hair is tied together in two parts on either side of her head —*picture* → HAIRSTYLE

bunch² /bʌntʃ/ or **bunch (sth) up** verb [I/T] to form a group or a tight round shape, or to make something do this

bundle¹ /ˈbʌnd(ə)l/ noun [C] **1** a group of things that have been tied together: *bundles of firewood* **2** a group of things that are sold or offered as a set

PHRASE **be a bundle of sth** *informal* used for emphasizing that someone has a lot of a particular quality: *Susan is a real bundle of energy.*

bundle² /ˈbʌnd(ə)l/ verb [T] **1** to make someone go to a particular place by pushing them in a rough way: *He was quickly bundled into a police car.* **2** to wrap or tie things together **3** to put things together so that they can be sold or offered as a single product

bung /bʌŋ/ verb [T] *British informal* to put something somewhere quickly and carelessly

bungalow /ˈbʌŋgələʊ/ noun [C] a house that is all on one level —*picture* → C1

bungee jumping /ˈbʌndʒi ˌdʒʌmpɪŋ/ noun [U] the sport of jumping from a very high place while attached to a long piece of rubber

bungle /ˈbʌŋg(ə)l/ verb [I/T] to spoil something by doing it very badly

bunk /bʌŋk/ noun [C] a narrow bed fixed to a wall

bunk beds noun [plural] two small beds that are joined together with one above the other —*picture* → BED

bunker /ˈbʌŋkə/ noun [C] **1** a room with very strong walls that is built underground as a shelter against bombs **2** in golf, a large hole full of sand —*picture* → C15

bunny /ˈbʌni/ noun [C] a RABBIT. This word is used by or to children.

buoy¹ /bɔɪ/ noun [C] an object that floats on water to show ships where there is danger

buoy² /bɔɪ/ or **buoy sb up** verb [T] to encourage someone and make them feel confident

buoyant /ˈbɔɪənt/ adj **1** happy and confident **2** capable of floating **3** successful and likely to remain successful: *The housing market remains buoyant.* —**buoyancy** /ˈbɔɪənsi/ noun [U]

burden¹ /ˈbɜːd(ə)n/ noun [C] **1** a serious or difficult responsibility that you have to deal with **2** *literary* something heavy that you have to carry

burden² /ˈbɜːd(ə)n/ verb [T] to create a problem or serious responsibility for someone

bureau /ˈbjʊərəʊ/ (plural **bureaux** /ˈbjʊərəʊz/) noun [C] **1** an organization that collects or provides information: *an advice bureau* **2** a government department, or part of a government department: *the Federal Bureau of Investigation* **3** *British* a piece of furniture with drawers and a top part that opens to make a writing table **4** *American* a CHEST OF DRAWERS

bureaucracy /bjʊəˈrɒkrəsi/ noun **1** [U] a complicated and annoying system of rules

B

and processes **2** [C/U] the people employed to run government organizations
—**bureaucratic** /ˌbjʊərəˈkrætɪk/ adj

bureaucrat /ˈbjʊərəkræt/ noun [C] showing disapproval someone who is employed to help to run an office or government department

burgeoning /ˈbɜːdʒ(ə)nɪŋ/ adj growing or developing quickly

burger /ˈbɜːɡə/ noun [C] a food made by pressing small pieces of meat into a flat round shape and cooking it. It is eaten between two parts of a bread roll.

burglar /ˈbɜːɡlə/ noun [C] someone who enters a building illegally in order to steal things

ˈburglar aˌlarm noun [C] a piece of equipment that makes a loud noise if someone enters a building

burglary /ˈbɜːɡləri/ noun [C/U] the crime of entering a building illegally in order to steal things

burgle /ˈbɜːɡ(ə)l/ verb [T] British to enter a building and steal things

burgundy /ˈbɜːɡəndi/ noun [U] a dark red colour —**burgundy** adj

burial /ˈberiəl/ noun [C/U] the process of burying a dead body

burly /ˈbɜːli/ adj a burly man is fat and strong

burn¹ /bɜːn/ (past tense and past participle **burned** or **burnt** /bɜːnt/) verb ★★★

1 damage with fire	7 feel strong emotion
2 be on fire	8 when cheeks are pink
3 produce light/heat	9 put information on CD
4 spoil food	+ PHRASE
5 cause injury	+ PHRASAL VERBS
6 of chemicals	

1 [T] to damage or destroy something with fire: *Demonstrators burned flags outside the embassy.* ♦ *The old part of the city was **burned to the ground** (=completely destroyed by fire).*

2 [I] if something is burning, it is being damaged or destroyed by fire: *Homes were burning all over the village.*

3 [I] if a fire or flame burns, it produces light and heat

4 [I/T] if food burns, or if you burn it, it gets spoiled by being cooked for too long or at too high a temperature: *Have you burnt the toast?*

5 [T] to injure someone or a part of your body with something hot: *The sand was so hot it burnt my feet.*

6 [I/T] if a chemical burns something, it causes damage or pain: *The acid had burnt a hole in my shirt.*

7 [I] to feel a very strong emotion or a great need for someone or something: *I was burning with curiosity.*

8 [I] if your cheeks are burning, they are red because you are embarrassed

9 [T] to put information onto a CD-ROM

PHRASE **burn your boats/bridges** to do something that makes it impossible for you to return to the situation you were in before: *She had burned her boats in Hollywood, and returned to London.*

PHRASAL VERBS **burn (sth) ˈdown** to destroy something large with fire, or to be destroyed in this way: *The entire house burnt down in 20 minutes.*

burn sth ˈoff to use up energy or get rid of fat from your body by doing physical activity: *Swimming can help you burn off calories.*

burn sth ˈup same as **burn sth off**: *Dancers burn up a lot of calories.*

burn² /bɜːn/ noun [C] an injury or mark caused by heat or fire

burned-out /ˌbɜːnd ˈaʊt/ adj BURNT-OUT

burning /ˈbɜːnɪŋ/ adj **1** being destroyed by fire **2** very hot **3** painful, and feeling as if a part of your body is touching something hot: *She felt a burning sensation in her mouth.* **4** felt extremely strongly: *burning ambition*

PHRASE **burning issue/question** something that people have strong opinions about and think is very important

burnt¹ /bɜːnt/ adj injured or damaged by burning

burnt² a past tense and past participle of **burn¹**

burnt-out adj **1** a burnt-out building or vehicle has had everything inside it destroyed by fire **2** someone who is burnt-out is very tired and has no energy, usually because of too much work or worry

burp /bɜːp/ verb [I] to make a noise when air from your stomach passes out through your mouth —**burp** noun [C]

burrow¹ /ˈbʌrəʊ/ verb [I] **1** to make a hole or tunnel in the ground **2** to search for something, especially using your hands: *She burrowed in her bag, and came up with a bunch of keys.*

burrow² /ˈbʌrəʊ/ noun [C] a hole or tunnel in the ground made by an animal

bursar /ˈbɜːsə/ noun [C] someone who is in charge of financial business in a school or college

bursary /ˈbɜːs(ə)ri/ noun [C] an amount of money that is given to someone to pay for their education

burst¹ /bɜːst/ (past tense and past participle **burst**) verb ★★

1 [I/T] if an object bursts, or if you burst it, it breaks suddenly: *Did a tyre burst?* ♦ *She burst the little boy's balloon.*

2 [I] to move quickly or suddenly: *A man burst into the room.* ♦ *The door burst open and in came Sam.*

PHRASAL VERBS **burst ˈin on sb/sth** to suddenly enter a room where someone is doing something

ˈburst ˌinto sth 1 to suddenly start doing something: *Terri keeps bursting into tears (=starting to cry) for no reason.* **2 burst into flames** to suddenly start burning

ˌburst ˈout 1 to suddenly say or shout something: *'I hate you!' Julia suddenly burst out.* **2 burst out laughing/crying** to suddenly start laughing or crying

burst² /bɜːst/ noun [C] a sudden short noise, activity, or feeling: *a burst of anger* ♦ *After an initial burst of enthusiasm, she lost interest in her job.*

bursting /ˈbɜːstɪŋ/ adj **1** if you are bursting with something such as love or energy, you feel a lot of it **2** very keen to do something: *She was bursting to tell us what had happened.* **3** if a place is bursting, it is very full

bury /ˈberi/ verb [T] ★

1 put body in ground	4 push sth into sth else
2 put sth under ground	5 avoid feeling/memory
3 cover sth	+ PHRASE

1 to put someone's dead body in the ground during a funeral ceremony: *All his family are buried in the same cemetery.*

2 to put something in the ground and cover it with earth: *There's supposed to be treasure buried around here.*

3 to cover something with a layer or pile of things: *My homework is buried somewhere under this pile of books.*

4 to push one thing into another very hard =SINK: *Diane screamed as the dog buried its teeth in her arm.*

5 to try to stop yourself from having a feeling or memory, by not allowing yourself to think about it: *feelings of anger that had been buried for years*

PHRASE bury your face/head in sth to hide your face or head with something: *She buried her face in her hands.*
→ HATCHET

bus¹ /bʌs/ noun [C] ★★★ a large road vehicle that people pay to travel on: *The children go to school by bus.* ♦ *If you hurry, you can catch the next bus.* —*picture* → C7

bus² /bʌs/ (past tense and past participle **bused** or **bussed**; present participle **busing** or **bussing**) verb [T] to take someone somewhere by bus

bush /bʊʃ/ noun ★★
1 [C] a plant that is smaller than a tree and has a lot of thin branches: *a holly/rose/currant bush*
2 the bush [singular] wild areas in hot places like Australia and Africa that are not used for growing crops

bushel /ˈbʊʃ(ə)l/ noun [C] a unit for measuring grain, vegetables etc equal to 36.4 litres in the UK or 35.24 litres in the US

bushy /ˈbʊʃi/ adj bushy hair or fur is very thick

busily /ˈbɪzɪli/ adv in a busy way

business /ˈbɪznəs/ noun ★★★

1 buying and selling	5 sth to deal with
2 business people	6 sth that is private
3 the work that you do	7 event
4 organization	+ PHRASES

1 [U] the work of buying or selling products or services: *the music/fashion business* ♦ *They're trying to attract new business* (=get more customers) *by cutting prices.* ♦ *We have been in business since 1983* (=buying or selling products or services). ♦ *It was a mistake to go into business with my brother.* ♦ *I found them very easy to do business with.*

2 [U] people who work in business: *The conference brought together representatives from business, the media, and politics.* ♦ *the business community*

3 [U] the work that you do as your job: *Jon was away on business.* ♦ *a business trip*

4 [C] an organization that buys or sells products or services: *a small family business* ♦ *Sheryl's parents run a small clothing business.* ♦ *After leaving school,*

Bob started his own computer business.

5 [singular/U] something that you have to deal with: *Disposing of chemicals can be a dangerous business.* ♦ *We've still got some unfinished business to settle* (=things that need to be dealt with).

6 [U] something that affects or involves a particular person and no one else: *It's my business who I go out with.*

7 [singular] something that has happened, especially something that has caused problems: *Ever since that business with her boyfriend, Becky's been really depressed.*

PHRASES get down to business to start doing something that you need to do
go out of business if a company goes out of business, it stops doing business permanently, usually because it has failed
have no business doing sth to do something you should not do, because it does not affect or involve you at all: *You had no business reading my private papers.*
mean business to be very serious about something you have to do: *This is not a game. We mean business.*
mind your own business *spoken* used for telling someone rudely that you are not going to tell them about something because it does not affect or involve them: *'Who were you with last night?' 'Mind your own business.'*
→ MONKEY BUSINESS

business ˌclass noun [U] part of a plane that is more comfortable and has better service than the part where most people sit

businesslike /ˈbɪznəsˌlaɪk/ adj serious and effective in the way that you deal with things =EFFICIENT

businessman /ˈbɪznəsmæn/ (plural **businessmen** /ˈbɪznəsmen/) noun [C] a man who works at a fairly high level in business

businessperson /ˈbɪznəsˌpɜːs(ə)n/ (plural **businesspeople** /ˈbɪznəsˌpiːp(ə)l/) noun [C] someone who works at a fairly high level in business

business ˌplan noun [C] a document giving details of a company's plans for the future

businesswoman /ˈbɪznəsˌwʊmən/ (plural **businesswomen** /ˈbɪznəsˌwɪmɪn/) noun [C] a woman who works at a fairly high level in business

busk /bʌsk/ verb [I] to perform music in the streets for money —**busker** noun [C]

bus ˌshelter noun [C] a structure that protects you from the weather while you are waiting for a bus

bus ˌstation noun [C] a building where buses start and finish their journeys

bus ˌstop noun [C] a place marked by a sign at the side of a road where buses stop to let passengers get on and off

bust¹ /bʌst/ noun [C] **1** a model of the head and shoulders of a person **2** a woman's breasts

bust² /bʌst/ (past tense and past participle **bust** or **busted**) verb [T] *informal* **1** to break or damage something **2** to arrest someone, especially for offences relating to drugs

bust³ /bʌst/ adj *informal* **1** a company or organization that has gone bust has lost all its money and can no longer continue to operate =BANKRUPT **2** *British* broken

bustle¹ /'bʌs(ə)l/ noun [U] a lot of noisy activity in a crowded place

bustle² /'bʌs(ə)l/ verb [I] to do something or go somewhere quickly because you are very busy

bustling /'bʌs(ə)lɪŋ/ adj full of noise and activity: *a bustling city/market/street*

bust-up noun [C] *British informal* **1** a serious argument **2** the end of a relationship

busy¹ /'bɪzi/ adj ★★★
1 having a lot of things to do: *He is an extremely busy man.* ♦ *It's been a very busy day.* ♦ *We have enough work here to keep us busy for weeks.* ♦ *Irina and Marcus were busy with preparations for their wedding.* ♦ **busy doing sth** *We're all busy preparing for Christmas.*
2 full of people or vehicles: *a busy main road* ♦ *Shops are always busier at weekends.*
3 if someone's telephone is busy, it is being used when you try to call = ENGAGED

busy² /'bɪzi/ verb **busy yourself** to make yourself busy by doing a particular job or activity

busybody /'bɪzi,bɒdi/ noun [C] *informal* someone who is too interested in other people's private lives

but / *weak* bət, *strong* bʌt/ grammar word ★★★

> **But** can be:
> - a **conjunction**: *She's 83 but she still goes swimming every day.*
> - a **preposition**: *There's been nothing but trouble since he came.*

1 used for introducing a different idea used for joining two ideas or statements when the second one is different from the first, or surprising after the first: *Anna's an intelligent girl, but she's lazy.* ♦ *a simple but effective way of filtering water* ♦ *I thought I had solved the problem. But I'd forgotten one thing.*
2 used for changing the subject *spoken* used when you are saying that you should not say any more about a particular subject: *It was really awful. But you don't want to hear about that.*
3 used in polite questions and statements *spoken* used after expressions such as 'I'm sorry' and 'excuse me' to introduce a polite question, request, or statement: *Excuse me, but is there a post office anywhere around here?* ♦ *I'm sorry, but all our operators are busy at the moment.*
4 except used especially after words such as 'nothing', 'everyone', or 'anything' to mean 'except': *She does nothing but grumble all day long.*
5 used for expressing surprise *spoken* used for showing that you are surprised or annoyed, or that you disagree: *'I've decided to resign.' 'But why?'* ♦ *But you promised not to do anything without asking me first.*
PHRASE **but for** except for something, or without something: *The work was now complete, but for a final coat of paint.*

butcher¹ /'bʊtʃə/ noun [C] someone whose job is to sell meat. The shop they work in is called a **butcher's** or a **butcher's shop**.

butcher² /'bʊtʃə/ verb [T] **1** to kill an animal and cut it up so that it can be eaten **2** to kill

someone, often a lot of people, in a cruel way

butler /'bʌtlə/ noun [C] the most important male servant in a rich person's house

butt¹ /bʌt/ noun [C] **1** the part of a cigarette or CIGAR that is left after you have finished smoking it **2** the end of the handle of a gun **3** *American informal* the part of your body that you sit on = BOTTOM
PHRASE **be the butt of sth** if you are the butt of jokes or criticism, people often make jokes about you or criticize you

butt² /bʌt/ verb [T] to hit someone or something with your head
PHRASAL VERB **butt in** *informal* to join a conversation or activity without being asked to

butter¹ /'bʌtə/ noun [U] ★★ a solid yellow food made from cream that you spread on bread or use in cooking —**buttery** adj
→ BREAD

butter² /'bʌtə/ verb [T] to spread butter on something
PHRASAL VERB **butter sb up** *informal* to be nice to someone so that they will help or support you

buttercup /'bʌtəkʌp/ noun [C] a plant with small bright yellow flowers —*picture* → C9

butterfly /'bʌtəflaɪ/ noun **1** [C] an insect with large colourful wings —*picture* → C13 **2** **the butterfly** [singular] a way of swimming in which you lie on your front and move both your arms together above your head
PHRASE **have butterflies (in your stomach)** to feel very nervous or excited about something important that you have to do

buttocks /'bʌtəks/ noun [plural] the two round parts of your body that you sit on —*picture* → C14

button¹ /'bʌt(ə)n/ noun [C] ★★
1 a small object that you press to make a machine do something: *Press this button to start the computer.* ♦ *a push-button phone*
2 a small round object that is used for fastening clothes by pushing it through a hole: *He had undone the top button of his shirt.*
3 *American* a round BADGE that you wear on your clothes

button² /'bʌt(ə)n/ or **button (sth) up** verb [I/T] to fasten something with buttons, or to be fastened with buttons ≠ UNBUTTON

buttonhole /'bʌt(ə)n,həʊl/ noun [C] **1** a small hole in a piece of clothing through which you push a button to fasten it **2** *British* a flower that you wear on your clothes, for example at a wedding

buxom /'bʌksəm/ adj a buxom woman is rather fat in an attractive way, with large breasts

buy¹ /baɪ/ (past tense and past participle **bought** /bɔːt/) verb ★★★
1 [I/T] to get something by paying money for it: *I need to buy some clothes.* ♦ **buy sb sth** *He's always buying me presents.* ♦ **buy sth for sb** *When I go away on business, I usually buy something for my daughter.* ♦ **buy sth for £50/£60 etc** *They offered to buy the car for £1,000.* ♦ **buy sth from sb** *Do you like my new carpet? I bought it from that Swedish shop.*
2 [T] *spoken* to believe or accept something

that is unlikely to be true: *'I told her I had to work late.' 'She'll never buy that!'*

3 [T] if you buy time, you delay something in order to get more time to do or finish something else: *That should buy us another week.*

PHRASE **buy sb (off)** *informal* to give someone something so that they will do something dishonest for you

PHRASAL VERBS **buy in** *British* to buy a large quantity of something: *Supermarkets have been buying in champagne for Christmas.*
,**buy 'into sth** *informal* to start to believe something that a lot of other people believe: *You don't buy into all this nonsense, do you?*
,**buy sth 'up** to buy large amounts of something or all of it that is available: *Developers bought up old theatres and converted them into cinemas.*

buy² /baɪ/ noun [C] something that you buy

buyer /'baɪə/ noun [C] **1** someone who buys something **2** someone whose job is to choose and buy goods for a large shop to sell

buyout /'baɪaʊt/ noun [C] *business* a situation in which a group of people buy the company that they work for

buzz¹ /bʌz/ verb [I] **1** to make a rough continuous noise like a fly or an electric tool **2** if a place is buzzing, there is a lot of noise or activity

PHRASAL VERB **buzz 'off** *informal* used for telling someone in a rude way to go away

buzz² /bʌz/ noun [singular] **1** a continuous noise like the sound of a fly **2** *informal* a strong feeling of pleasure or excitement

buzzer /'bʌzə/ noun [C] a small piece of equipment that makes a sound when you press it

buzzword /'bʌzwɜːd/ noun [C] a word relating to a particular activity or subject that has become very popular: *The buzzword of the moment is 'accountability'.*

by /baɪ/ grammar word ★★★

> **By can be:**
> ■ **a preposition**: *The building was destroyed by fire.*
> ■ **an adverb**: *As time went by, things improved.*

1 stating who or what does sth used for stating who or makes something, or what causes something: *She was helped by her friends.* ♦ *Children are fascinated by magic.* ♦ *damage caused by the storm* ♦ *a painting by Goya*

2 stating how sth is done using a particular method or in a particular way: *Reading is taught by traditional methods here.* ♦ *We decided to go by car.* ♦ *They exchanged New Year's greetings by email.* ♦ *Every bit of lace is made by hand* (=not using a machine). ♦ *We met completely by chance.* ♦ **by doing sth** *By using the Internet you can do your shopping from home.*

3 before not later than a particular time or date: *The meeting should have finished by 4.30.* ♦ *Application forms must be received by 31st March.* ♦ *By the time I arrived, everyone had left.*

4 past moving past someone or something: *She walked right by me without saying a word.* ♦ *A police car drove by.*

5 saying that time passes used for saying that time passes, or how it passes: *As time went by, people's attitudes changed.* ♦ *The days seem to fly by.*

6 stating changes or differences used for stating how large a change or difference is: *House prices rose by 23% last year.* ♦ *Owen broke the world record by 2.4 seconds.*

7 in calculations and measurements used for stating what numbers or units are involved in calculations and measurements: *I am paid by the hour.* ♦ *To convert gallons to litres multiply by 4.54.* ♦ *a 10 by 15 cm photograph*

8 beside beside or close to someone or something: *She was sitting over there by the window.*

9 according to rules according to rules, laws, or standards: *By law, the hospital must treat patients whether or not they can pay.* ♦ *You can't judge children and adults by the same standard.*

10 used for stating how you hold sb/sth used for saying which part you take in your hand when you hold someone or something: *She took me by the hand.* ♦ *Always pick up a CD by the outer edge.*

11 gradually used when saying that something happens gradually in small units: *Little by little Philip got more confident.* ♦ *His condition is improving day by day.* ♦ *One by one the men were given their medals.*

12 visiting a place used for saying that someone stops somewhere for a short time: *Why don't you stop by on your way home from work?*

PHRASES **(all) by yourself/itself/himself etc**
1 alone: *I want to be by myself for a while.*
2 without being helped by anyone else: *You can't carry that big table all by yourself.*
by and large used for saying that something is generally true: *By and large I think you're right.*
by night/day during the night/day: *We travelled by night to avoid the heat.*
by the way *spoken* used for adding a remark that is not relevant to the main subject of your conversation: *By the way, Jeff called this afternoon.*

bye /baɪ/ or **'bye-bye** interjection ★ goodbye: *Bye for now – see you later.*

by-e'lection noun [C] an election in one particular area of the UK to choose a new representative in parliament

bygone /'baɪgɒn/ adj happening or existing during a period of time in the past

bygones /'baɪgɒnz/ noun **let bygones be bygones** to decide to forget about a disagreement or something unpleasant that has happened in the past

bypass¹ /'baɪpɑːs/ noun [C] **1** a road that goes round a town or city so that you can avoid going through its centre **2** a medical operation to make someone's blood flow past a blocked or damaged part of their heart

bypass² /'baɪpɑːs/ verb [T] **1** to avoid dealing with someone or something because you think you can do something more quickly without using them **2** to avoid the centre of a town or city by using a road that goes round it

by-product noun [C] **1** a product that is made as a result of making something else **2** something that happens unexpectedly as a result of something else

bystander /ˈbaɪˌstændə/ noun [C] someone who sees an event happen, but who is not directly involved in it

byte /baɪt/ noun [C] *computing* a basic unit for storing computer information, used for measuring the size of a document

byway /ˈbaɪˌweɪ/ noun [C] a quiet minor road

byword /ˈbaɪˌwɜːd/ noun [singular] **a byword for sth** someone or something that has a strong reputation for a particular quality: *The company's name had become a byword for bad service and overpriced goods.*

Cc

c¹ or **C** /siː/ noun [C/U] **1** the third letter of the English alphabet **2 C** a mark that a teacher gives to a student's work to show that it is average

c² abbrev **1** cent(s) **2** century **3 c** or **ca** circa: used before a date that is not exact

C abbrev **1** Celsius **2** see: used in emails and TEXT MESSAGES

© a symbol meaning 'copyright'

cab /kæb/ noun [C] **1** a taxi **2** the front part of a bus, train, or LORRY where the driver sits

cabaret /ˈkæbəreɪ/ noun [C/U] entertainment in a restaurant or club that is performed while you eat or drink

cabbage /ˈkæbɪdʒ/ noun [C/U] a hard round vegetable with green or purple leaves —*picture* → C11

cabbie or **cabby** /ˈkæbi/ noun [C] *informal* a taxi driver

cabin /ˈkæbɪn/ noun [C] **1** a bedroom on a ship **2** the part of a plane where the passengers sit **3** a small simple wooden house in the mountains or in a forest

cabin crew noun [C] the people on a plane whose job is to look after the passengers

cabinet /ˈkæbɪnət/ noun [C] ★
1 a cupboard that you use for storing or showing things: *a medicine cabinet*
2 a group of advisers who are chosen by the leader of a government

cable /ˈkeɪb(ə)l/ noun **1** [C/U] thick wire used for carrying electricity or electronic signals=LEAD **2** [C/U] strong thick metal rope **3** [U] CABLE TELEVISION

cable car noun [C] a small vehicle that hangs from a cable. It is used for taking people up and down mountains.

cable television or **cable T V** noun [U] a system for broadcasting television programmes in which signals are sent through underground wires

cache /kæʃ/ noun [C] **1** a quantity of things that have been hidden, or the place where they have been hidden **2** *computing* an area of a computer's memory for storing information that is frequently needed

cackle /ˈkæk(ə)l/ verb [I/T] to laugh in a loud unpleasant way —**cackle** noun [C]

cacophony /kəˈkɒfəni/ noun [singular] an unpleasant mixture of loud sounds

cactus /ˈkæktəs/ (plural **cacti** /ˈkæktaɪ/) noun [C] a desert plant with thick stems and sharp points

CAD /kæd/ noun [U] computer-aided design: the use of computers to design things

caddy /ˈkædi/ noun [C] someone who carries the GOLF CLUBS for a golf player —*picture* → C15

cadet /kəˈdet/ noun [C] a young person who is training to be a police officer or military officer

caesarean /sɪˈzeərɪən/ or **caesarean section** noun [C/U] a medical operation in which a baby is born by being removed through a cut in its mother's ABDOMEN

café /ˈkæfeɪ/ noun [C] ★★ a small informal restaurant serving drinks and snacks

cafeteria /ˌkæfəˈtɪərɪə/ noun [C] a restaurant in which you take the food to the table yourself

cafetière /ˌkæfəˈtjeə/ noun [C] *British* a glass container for making and serving coffee

caffeine /ˈkæfiːn/ noun [U] a substance in coffee and tea that makes you feel awake

cage /keɪdʒ/ noun [C] a container that is made of wire or metal bars, used for keeping birds or animals in

caged /keɪdʒd/ adj kept in a cage

cagey /ˈkeɪdʒi/ adj *informal* not saying much about something, because you do not want people to know about it

cajole /kəˈdʒəʊl/ verb [I/T] to persuade someone to do something by being nice to them

cake /keɪk/ noun ★★
1 [C/U] a sweet food made by baking a mixture of sugar, eggs, flour, and butter or oil: *a chocolate cake* ♦ *She was **making a cake** for Peter's birthday.*
2 [C] a small amount of food formed into a flat round shape and cooked: *rice/potato cakes*
3 [C] a small hard block of something: *a cake of soap*
PHRASES have your cake and eat it to try to have all the benefits of a situation, when, in fact, you can only have some of them
a piece of cake *informal* something that is very easy: *The test was a piece of cake.*
→ ICING

caked /keɪkd/ adj covered with a thick layer of something

calamity /kəˈlæməti/ noun [C/U] an event that causes serious damage or makes a lot of people suffer=DISASTER

calcium /ˈkælsiəm/ noun [U] a white chemical element that is an important part of bones and teeth

calculate /ˈkælkjʊˌleɪt/ verb [T] ★★
1 to discover a number or amount by using mathematics: *Calculate the size of the angle.*

♦ +(that) *He calculates that the proposal would cost £4 million.*

2 to make a judgment about what is likely to happen or be true: *It's difficult to calculate the long-term effects of these changes.*

PHRASE **be calculated to do sth** to be deliberately intended to have a particular result

calculated /ˈkælkjʊˌleɪtɪd/ adj done deliberately in order to have a particular effect

calculating /ˈkælkjʊˌleɪtɪŋ/ adj using careful planning to get what you want, even if it hurts other people

calculation /ˌkælkjʊˈleɪʃ(ə)n/ noun ★★
1 [C/U] numbers or symbols that you write when you are calculating something, or the process of calculating something: *a piece of paper covered with calculations*
2 [C] a judgment about what is likely to happen, based on available information

calculator /ˈkælkjʊˌleɪtə/ noun [C] a small piece of electronic equipment that is used for doing calculations —*picture* → C3

calculus /ˈkælkjʊləs/ noun [U] a type of mathematics, used for calculating such things as the slopes of curves

calendar /ˈkælɪndə/ noun [C] **1** a set of pages showing the days, weeks, and months of a particular year **2** a system for measuring and dividing a year: *the Jewish/Roman calendar* **3** a list of important events and the dates on which they take place: *one of the major events of the sporting calendar*

calf /kɑːf/ (plural **calves** /kɑːvz/) noun [C] **1** a young cow **2** the thick back part of your leg between your knee and your ANKLE

caliber /ˈkælɪbə/ the American spelling of **calibre**

calibrate /ˈkæləˌbreɪt/ verb [T] to check or change a piece of equipment that is used for measuring things in order to make it accurate —**calibration** /ˌkæləˈbreɪʃ(ə)n/ noun [U]

calibre /ˈkælɪbə/ noun **1** [U] the high standard or quality of someone or something **2** [C] the width of a bullet, or of a gun BARREL (=the tube through which the bullet travels)

call¹ /kɔːl/ verb ★★★

1 use a name for sb/sth	6 organize sth
2 describe sb/sth	7 train, bus, or ship
3 telephone sb	8 visit sb
4 speak loudly	+ PHRASES
5 ask/tell sb to come	+ PHRASAL VERBS

1 [T] to use a particular name or title for someone or something: *They called the area the Gold Coast.* ♦ *The book was called* The Journey. ♦ **call sb/sth sth** *Her name's Elizabeth, but we call her Liz.*
2 [T] to describe or refer to someone or something in a particular way: **call sb/sth sth** *One candidate called it a scandal.* ♦ *The other children **called her names** (=said unkind things about her).*
3 [I/T] to telephone someone=PHONE, RING: *He called her from the station.*
4 [I/T] to say something loudly, or to shout to someone: *Did you call me?* ♦ *When I call your name, raise your hand.*

5 [T] to ask or tell someone by phone to come to a place: **call sb across/up/over/to etc** *She called me up to her office.*
6 [T] to organize something: *Harris wants to call a meeting.*
7 [I] if a train, bus, or ship calls somewhere, it stops there during its journey: *This train calls at Hagley and all stations to Birmingham.*
8 [I] to visit someone, usually for a short time: *James called to see you.*

PHRASES **call (sb's) attention to** to make someone notice and think about a person or thing
call it a day/night to decide that you have finished doing something
what do you call it/him/her/them? *spoken* used when you are trying to think of the correct name for someone or something: *Do you have a – what do you call it – lemon squeezer?*
(now) that's what I call sth *spoken* used for emphasizing that something is a very good example of what you are talking about: *Now that's what I call a real cup of tea!*
→ BLUFF²

PHRASAL VERBS **call (sb) back** to telephone someone again, or to telephone someone who telephoned you earlier: *Can you call me back later?*
call for sth 1 to say publicly that something must happen: *Several of the newspapers were calling for his resignation.* **2** to make something necessary or suitable: *I think that calls for a celebration!* → UNCALLED FOR
call for sb/sth to go and get someone or something in order to take them somewhere: *I'll call for you at eight.*
call in 1 *same as* **call¹** **8**: *She wondered whether to call in on Mark on the way home.*
2 to telephone the place where you work and tell them something: *Harry's called in sick again* (=telephoned to say he is ill).
call sb in to ask someone to come and deal with something: *The company have called in the police to investigate.*
call sth off 1 to decide that something will not happen=CANCEL: *She's called off the wedding.* **2** to decide to stop something that is already happening=ABANDON: *They've called off the search for survivors.*
call on sb 1 to visit someone, usually for a short time: *We could call on my parents if we have time.* **2** to officially ask someone to do something: *He called on both sides to stop fighting.*
call (sth) out to shout something when you are trying to get someone's attention: *'In here!' she called out.*
call (sb) up to telephone someone: *I called him up and told him the news.*
call sb up to force sb to join the armed forces
call sth up to make information appear on the screen: *Call up the menu and click on 'Documents'.*
call upon *formal same as* **call on sb 2**

call² /kɔːl/ noun ★★★

1 act of telephoning	6 animal sound
2 shout	7 announcement
3 formal request	8 decision
4 short visit	9 guess
5 sth needing attention	+ PHRASE

C

C

1 [C] an act of telephoning someone=PHONE CALL: *Can you wait while I make a call?* ♦ *He took the call in his study.* ♦ *Why don't you give me a call in the morning?*

2 [C] a loud shout to someone who is not near you: *A passer-by heard his calls for help.*

3 [C] a formal or public request that something should happen: *The government has rejected calls for tougher immigration laws.*

4 [C] a short visit to someone: *We decided to pay another call on the Browns.*

5 [C] something that needs your time, money, or attention: *Parents of young children have so many other calls on their time.*

6 [C/U] the sound that a bird or animal usually makes

7 [C] an announcement in an airport telling passengers to go to their plane because it is leaving soon: *This is the last call for flight BA6774 to Stuttgart.*

8 [C] a decision that is the responsibility of a particular person: *'Do we offer him the job?' 'It's your call.'*

9 [C] a guess about what will happen: *The election looks so close that it's anybody's call.*

PHRASE **on call** available in case you are needed at work: *Tim's on call this weekend.*

CALL /kɔːl/ noun [U] computer-assisted language learning: the use of computers for learning languages

'call ˌbox noun [C] **1** *British* a public telephone box=PHONE BOX **2** *American* a telephone at the side of a road that you use to call for help

'call ˌcentre noun [C] a place where a large number of people are employed to deal with customers by telephone

caller /'kɔːlə/ noun [C] **1** someone who makes a telephone call **2** someone who comes to your house

calligraphy /kə'lɪɡrəfi/ noun [U] beautiful writing that you do using special pens or brushes

'call-in noun [C] *American* a PHONE-IN

calling /'kɔːlɪŋ/ noun [C] a strong feeling that you must do a particular type of job

callous /'kæləs/ adj not caring about other people's trouble or pain=HEARTLESS

'call-out noun [C] *British* a visit to your home or office by someone who provides a service

'call-up noun [C] *British* a situation in which people are officially ordered to join the armed forces

'call ˌwaiting /ˌkɔːl 'weɪtɪŋ/ noun [U] a system that lets you answer a second telephone call without ending your first telephone call

calm¹ /kɑːm/ adj ★★

1 not affected by strong emotions: *a calm voice* ♦ *Try to stay calm.*

2 peaceful: *The city appears calm after last night's missile attack.*

3 if the weather is calm, there is very little wind

4 calm water does not move very much —**calmly** adv

calm² /kɑːm/ verb [T] to make someone feel more relaxed and less emotional

PHRASAL VERB **calm (sb) 'down** to begin to feel more relaxed and less emotional, or to make someone do this: *Calm down and tell us what's going on.*

calm³ /kɑːm/ noun [U] **1** a situation in which everything is peaceful: *the calm of the evening* **2** a state in which you are not affected by strong emotions

PHRASE **the calm before the storm** a quiet time just before problems or arguments start

calorie /'kæləri/ noun [C] a unit for measuring how much energy you get from food

calorific /ˌkælə'rɪfɪk/ adj containing a lot of calories and therefore likely to make you fat

calves the plural of **calf**

camcorder /'kæmˌkɔːdə/ noun [C] a small camera used for recording pictures and sound onto VIDEOTAPE

came the past tense of **come**

camel /'kæm(ə)l/ noun [C] a large animal with one or two HUMPS (=large round raised parts) on its back

cameo /'kæmiəʊ/ noun [C] **1** a small part that a well-known actor plays in a film or play **2** a piece of jewellery with a design of a woman's head on it in a different colour

camera /'kæm(ə)rə/ noun [C] ★★★

1 a piece of equipment for taking photographs

2 a piece of equipment for making television programmes, films, or videos

cameraman /'kæm(ə)rəˌmæn/ (plural **cameramen** /'kæm(ə)rəˌmen/) noun [C] someone who operates a camera for making films or television programmes

camouflage /'kæməˌflɑːʒ/ noun [singular/U] colours or clothes that hide people, objects, or animals by making them look like the natural background —**camouflage** verb [T]

camp¹ /kæmp/ noun ★★

1 [C] a place where soldiers or prisoners live during a war

2 [C/U] a place where people go for a holiday that often has tents or other temporary shelters: *music camp* ♦ *scout camp*

3 [C] a group of people who support a particular person or idea: *People in the Brown camp (=who support Brown) deny this rumour.*

PHRASE **set up camp** to put tents somewhere and stay there for a while

camp² /kæmp/ verb [I] **1** to stay somewhere for a short time in a tent or another temporary shelter: *They camped for two nights in the forest.* **2** to stay outside a place until you get what you want: *Journalists had camped in front of the house.*

PHRASAL VERB **camp 'out 1** to sleep outside, with or without a tent or another temporary shelter **2** *same as* **camp²** **2**

camp³ /kæmp/ adj a man who is camp behaves in a way that does not follow traditional ideas about male behaviour

campaign¹ /kæm'peɪn/ noun [C] ★

1 a series of actions that are intended to achieve something such as a social or political change: *an election/advertising campaign* ♦ *Local people have launched a campaign against the closure of the*

hospital. ♦ **campaign to do sth** *There's been a campaign by local fishermen to ban imported fish.*
2 a series of actions by an army trying to win a war: *a bombing campaign*

campaign² /kæmˈpeɪn/ verb [I] **1** to try to achieve a social or a political change by persuading other people or the government to do something **2** to try to win an election

camper /ˈkæmpə/ noun [C] **1** someone who is staying in a campsite **2** a CAMPER VAN

camper ˌvan noun [C] British a vehicle that can be used for living in when you are on holiday

camping /ˈkæmpɪŋ/ noun [U] the activity of living in a tent or other temporary shelter for fun: *We don't go camping as much as we used to.*

campsite /ˈkæmpˌsaɪt/ noun [C] British a place where people on holiday can stay in tents or other temporary shelters

campus /ˈkæmpəs/ noun [C/U] an area of land containing all the main buildings of a university

can¹ /weak kən, strong kæn/ modal verb ★★★

- **Can** is usually followed by an infinitive without 'to': *I can speak French.* Sometimes it is used without a following infinitive: *Come and help us, if you can.*
- **Can** has no participles and no infinitive form. It does not change its form, so the third person singular form does not end in '-s': *She can speak Japanese.*
- Questions and negatives are formed without 'do': *Can you swim?*
- The negative form **cannot** is often shortened in conversation or informal writing to **can't**: *I can't find my brown jacket.*
- **Could** is used as the past tense of **can** when it means that someone had the ability to do something, or that something was possible: *New York was a place where anyone could start a business.* But **was/were able to** is used for saying that someone actually succeeded in doing something: *By climbing on the table he was able to reach the window.*

1 able to do sth to have the ability to do something: *'Can you swim?' 'No I can't.'* ♦ *The machine can translate messages into 24 different languages.* ♦ *I will help as much as I can.* ♦ *I can hear someone crying.*
2 for saying what is possible used for saying that something is possible, or that it might happen: *Tickets can be bought from the Tourist Information Centre.* ♦ *Even minor head injuries can be serious.*
3 be allowed to do sth to be allowed to do something, or to have the right or power to do it: *You can borrow my calculator if you want.* ♦ *Anyone aged 18 or over can vote.* ♦ *You can't sit there. Those seats are reserved.*
4 in requests, offers etc spoken used in requests, or when offering or suggesting something: *Can you tell me where Mr Lawson's office is?* ♦ *Can I have another piece of cake?*
5 when you are fairly certain used for saying that you feel fairly sure about something: *The hotel can't be far from here.* ♦ *Can there be any doubt that he is lying?* ♦

I can't tell you how pleased I am to see you.
6 when sth should not happen used for emphasizing that something should not happen or should not continue: *We can't let them cheat and get away with it.*
7 for expressing surprise spoken used for showing how surprised or shocked you are: *He can't be here already!*
8 for emphasizing how you feel spoken used with verbs such as 'say', 'imagine', or 'believe' for emphasizing how strongly you feel: *I can imagine how upset you must be.*

can² /kæn/ noun [C] ★★
1 a metal container with round sides, used for holding food, or drink or other liquids: *empty beer cans* ♦ *There's a little paint left in the can.* ♦ *a can of beans*
2 the amount that a can holds: *Add two **cans** of tomatoes to the sauce and stir.*

can³ /kæn/ verb [T] to preserve food in metal containers by storing it without air

canal /kəˈnæl/ noun [C] an artificial river

canary /kəˈneəri/ noun [C] a small yellow bird that is kept as a pet

cancel /ˈkæns(ə)l/ (present participle **cancelling**; past tense and past participle **cancelled**) verb [T]
1 to say that something that has been arranged will not now happen =CALL STH OFF: *The 4.05 train has been cancelled.* **2** to say officially that you do not want to receive something: *Did you remember to cancel the taxi?*

PHRASAL VERB ˌcancel sth ˈout if two things cancel each other out, they stop each other from having any effect

cancellation /ˌkænsəˈleɪʃ(ə)n/ noun **1** [C/U] a decision to stop something that has been arranged from taking place **2** [C] a ticket or place that becomes available because someone else has said they do not want it

cancer /ˈkænsə/ noun [U] ★ a serious illness that is caused when cells in the body increase in an uncontrolled way: *He died of lung cancer.* —**cancerous** adj

Cancer /ˈkænsə/ noun [U] one of the 12 signs of the ZODIAC. A **Cancer** or a **Cancerian** is someone who is born between 22 June and 22 July.

candid /ˈkændɪd/ adj honest and direct, even when the truth is not pleasant —**candidly** adv

candidacy /ˈkændɪdəsi/ noun [U] the fact that someone is a candidate in an election

candidate /ˈkændɪˌdeɪt, ˈkændɪdət/ noun [C] ★ one of the people who is competing in an election or competing for a job: *the Labour/Liberal/Conservative candidate* ♦ *There were two **candidates for** the post.*

candidature /ˈkændɪdətʃə/ noun [U] CANDIDACY

candle /ˈkænd(ə)l/ noun [C] a stick of WAX with a string in it that you burn to give light

candlelight /ˈkænd(ə)lˌlaɪt/ noun [U] the light from a burning candle

candlelit /ˈkænd(ə)lˌlɪt/ adj lit only by CANDLES

candlestick /ˈkænd(ə)lˌstɪk/ noun [C] an object for holding a CANDLE

ˌcan-ˈdo adj always keen to try hard in order to succeed: *a can-do attitude*

C

C

candor /ˈkændə/ the American spelling of **candour**

candour /ˈkændə/ noun [U] honesty, even when the truth is not pleasant

candy /ˈkændi/ noun [C/U] *American* a sweet, or sweets

candyfloss /ˈkændiˌflɒs/ noun [U] *British* a sweet food consisting of very thin strings of sugar wrapped around a stick

cane /keɪn/ noun **1** [C/U] the hard light stem of some plants, often used for making furniture: *cane chairs* **2** [C] a long thin stick that a person uses to help them to walk

canine /ˈkeɪnaɪn/ adj relating to dogs

canister /ˈkænɪstə/ noun [C] a metal container for storing a gas or dry foods such as sugar and flour

cannabis /ˈkænəbɪs/ noun [U] a drug that is made from the HEMP plant, and usually smoked=MARIJUANA

canned /kænd/ adj canned food has been preserved in a metal container without air =TINNED

cannibal /ˈkænɪb(ə)l/ noun [C] someone who eats human flesh —**cannibalism** /ˈkænɪbəlɪz(ə)m/ noun [U]

cannon /ˈkænən/ noun [C] **1** a large gun used in the past to shoot heavy metal balls **2** a large gun on a ship or TANK

cannot /ˈkænɒt/ modal verb ★★★ the negative form of CAN: *You cannot escape the law.*

canoe¹ /kəˈnuː/ noun [C] a light narrow boat that you push through the water using a PADDLE

canoe² /kəˈnuː/ verb [I] to travel in a canoe —**canoeing** noun [U]

canon /ˈkænən/ noun [C] a Christian priest who works in a CATHEDRAL

ˈcan ˌopener noun [C] a TIN OPENER

canopy /ˈkænəpi/ noun [C] a cloth cover above something such as a bed or chair

can't /kɑːnt/ short form the usual way of saying or writing 'cannot'. This is not often used in formal writing: *I can't remember where my keys are.*

cantaloupe /ˈkæntəluːp/ noun [C] a grey-green MELON (=large round fruit) with sweet orange flesh

cantankerous /kænˈtæŋk(ə)rəs/ adj always complaining or arguing and easily annoyed

canteen /kænˈtiːn/ noun [C] a room in a factory, school, or hospital where meals are served

canter /ˈkæntə/ verb [I] if a horse canters, it runs fairly fast but not as fast as it can

canvas /ˈkænvəs/ noun **1** [U] strong heavy cotton cloth that is used for making tents, shoes, and sails **2** [C/U] cloth on which artists paint, or a painting done on this cloth

canvass /ˈkænvəs/ verb **1** [I/T] to encourage people to vote for someone or support something: *Party supporters were called on to help canvass for their candidate.* **2** [T] to ask people for their opinions about something: *We will be canvassing the views of teachers all over the country.*

canyon /ˈkænjən/ noun [C] a long valley with steep sides made of rock

cap¹ /kæp/ noun [C] ★★
1 a soft hat with a stiff part that comes out above your eyes: *a baseball cap*

2 a lid or part that fits over the top of something: *Meg screwed the cap back on the bottle.*

cap² /kæp/ verb [T] **1** to set a limit on the amount of money that someone can spend or charge **2** to say or do something that is better than something that someone else has just said or done

capability /ˌkeɪpəˈbɪləti/ noun [C/U] the ability to do something: *the company's manufacturing capability* ♦ *We have the capability to produce faster trains.*

capable /ˈkeɪpəb(ə)l/ adj ★★
1 capable of (doing) sth able to do something ≠ INCAPABLE: *The port is capable of handling 10 million tonnes of coal a year.* ♦ *I don't think I've achieved everything I'm capable of.*
2 very good at doing a job: *The staff all seem very capable.*

capacity /kəˈpæsəti/ noun ★
1 [C/U] the amount of something that can be put in a container, or the number of people that a place has room for: *a concert hall with **a** seating **capacity** of 800* ♦ *All the country's prisons are **filled to capacity** (=completely full).* ♦ *The games attract **capacity crowds** (=audiences that fill a place).*
2 [U] the amount of goods that a company can produce: *The factory is now operating **at full capacity** (=doing as much work as possible).*
3 [C/U] the ability to do something: **capacity to do sth** *They are worried about their capacity to invest for the future.* ♦ *Harry had a tremendous **capacity for** work.*
4 [singular] the job or position you have when you do something: *The Princess was there **in her capacity as** patron of the charity.*

cape /keɪp/ noun [C] **1** a type of coat that has no sleeves and hangs from your shoulders **2** a large area of land that continues further out into the sea than the land that it is part of

capillary /kəˈpɪləri/ noun [C] *science* a very small tube that carries blood around your body

capital¹ /ˈkæpɪt(ə)l/ noun ★★★
1 capital or **capital city** [C] the city where a country or region has its government: *Madrid is **the capital** of Spain.*
2 capital or **capital letter** [C] the large form of a letter that you use at the beginning of a sentence or name, for example 'A' or 'B': *He wrote the title **in capitals**.*
3 [C] the most important place for an activity or industry: *Houston is **the capital** of the American oil industry.*
4 [U] money or property that you use to start a business or that you invest

capital² /ˈkæpɪt(ə)l/ adj a capital letter is the large form of a letter that you use at the beginning of a sentence or name

ˌcapital-inˈtensive adj a capital-intensive business or activity needs to have a lot of money invested in it → LABOUR-INTENSIVE

capitalism /ˈkæpɪtəlɪz(ə)m/ noun [U] an economic system in which property and businesses are owned by individual people, not by the government

capitalist /ˈkæpɪt(ə)lɪst/ noun [C] someone who supports the system of capitalism —**capitalist** adj

capitalize /ˈkæpɪtəˌlaɪz/ verb [T] to write something using capital letters

PHRASAL VERB **capitalize on sth** to use an event or situation to help you to get an advantage: *The team needed to capitalize on their early successes.*

capital letter noun *see* **capital**[1] 2

capital offence noun [C] a crime for which the punishment is death

capital punishment noun [U] the punishment of legally killing someone who has committed a serious crime

Capitol Hill the US Congress, or the area in Washington D.C. where members of Congress work

capitulate /kəˈpɪtjʊˌleɪt/ verb [I] *formal* to stop opposing or fighting someone, and agree to what they want —**capitulation** /kəˌpɪtjʊˈleɪʃ(ə)n/ noun [U]

cappuccino /ˌkæpəˈtʃiːnəʊ/ noun [C/U] strong coffee made with hot FROTHY milk, or a cup of this coffee

capricious /kəˈprɪʃəs/ adj suddenly and unexpectedly changing your opinion or behaviour for no reason

Capricorn /ˈkæprɪˌkɔːn/ noun [C/U] one of the 12 signs of the ZODIAC. A **Capricorn** is someone who is born between 22 December and 19 January.

capsize /kæpˈsaɪz/ verb [I] if a boat capsizes, it turns over in the water

capsule /ˈkæpsjuːl/ noun [C] **1** a small round container filled with medicine that you swallow **2** the part of a space vehicle in which people travel

captain[1] /ˈkæptɪn/ noun [C] ★★
1 the person who is in charge of a ship or aircraft
2 an officer of middle rank in the armed forces
3 the person who is in charge of a team or organization: *She was captain of the Olympic swimming team.*

captain[2] /ˈkæptɪn/ verb [T] to be the captain of a team, organization, ship, or aircraft

captaincy /ˈkæptənsi/ noun [C/U] the job of being the captain of a sports team, or the time during which someone is captain

caption /ˈkæpʃ(ə)n/ noun [C] words printed near a picture that explain what the picture is about

captivate /ˈkæptɪˌveɪt/ verb [T] to attract or interest someone very much

captivating /ˈkæptɪˌveɪtɪŋ/ adj very interesting or attractive in a way that takes all your attention: *a captivating story*

captive[1] /ˈkæptɪv/ noun [C] someone who is being kept as a prisoner

captive[2] /ˈkæptɪv/ adj **1** kept as a prisoner: *She was kidnapped and held captive for over a week.* **2** a captive wild animal is kept in a park or ZOO

captive audience noun [C] a group of people who must listen to something because they cannot leave

captivity /kæpˈtɪvəti/ noun [U] **1** a situation in which wild animals are kept in a place

such as a park or ZOO: *crocodiles that were born in captivity* **2** a situation in which a person is being kept as a prisoner

captor /ˈkæptə/ noun [C] someone who is keeping someone else as a prisoner

capture[1] /ˈkæptʃə/ verb [T] ★★
1 to catch a person or animal and stop them from escaping: *Most of the men had been either killed or captured.*
2 to get control of something, for example in a war or in business: *Rebel forces have captured the village.*
3 to express what someone or something is really like in a way that people can clearly recognize: *The film succeeds in capturing the mood of the 1960s.*
4 to record an event in a film or photograph: *The whole incident was captured by a young American photographer.*

PHRASE **capture sb's interest/imagination/ attention** to make someone interested in something, or excited about something: *Her story captured the interest of the world's media.*

capture[2] /ˈkæptʃə/ noun [U] **1** the act of catching someone so that they become your prisoner: *He tried to avoid capture by leaving the country.* **2** the act of getting control of something, for example in a war or in business

car /kɑː/ noun [C] ★★★
1 a road vehicle for one driver and a few passengers: *a car accident/factory/manufacturer* ♦ *We usually go to work in my husband's car.* ♦ *She got into a black car and drove away.* ♦ *It's quicker to go by car.* ♦ *She's learning to drive a car.* —*picture* → C6, C7
2 *American* a CARRIAGE of a train

carafe /kəˈræf/ noun [C] a glass container with a wide top, used for serving wine

caramel /ˈkærəmel/ noun [C/U] a soft or hard sweet made from sugar, butter, and milk

carat /ˈkærət/ noun [C] **1** a unit for measuring how pure gold is **2** a unit for measuring the weight of DIAMONDS and other jewels

caravan /ˈkærəˌvæn/ noun [C] **1** *British* a vehicle that people can live and travel in on holiday **2** a group of people and animals who are travelling together in a desert

carbohydrate /ˌkɑːbəʊˈhaɪdreɪt/ noun [C/U] a substance in foods such as bread and potatoes that gives your body heat and energy

carbon /ˈkɑːbən/ noun [U] a chemical element that exists in all living things and in coal and DIAMONDS

carbonated /ˈkɑːbəˌneɪtɪd/ adj a carbonated drink has small BUBBLES in it

carbon copy noun [C] someone or something that is almost exactly like another person or thing

carbon dioxide /ˌkɑːbən daɪˈɒksaɪd/ noun [U] the gas that is produced when you breathe out

carbon emissions noun [plural] carbon dioxide and carbon monoxide that vehicles and factories produce and send into the atmosphere

carbon monoxide /ˌkɑːbən mɒˈnɒksaɪd/ noun

C

[U] the poisonous gas that is produced by the engines of vehicles

carbon tax noun [C/U] a tax on vehicles or factories that produce a lot of CARBON EMISSIONS

car boot sale noun [C] *British* a market where people sell things that they do not want from the back of their car

carburettor /ˌkɑːbəˈretə/ noun [C] the part of a car engine that mixes air and petrol

carcass /ˈkɑːkəs/ noun [C] the body of a dead animal

carcinogen /kɑːˈsɪnədʒ(ə)n/ noun [C] *medical* a substance that can cause cancer

carcinogenic /ˌkɑːsɪnəˈdʒenɪk/ adj *medical* likely to cause cancer

card /kɑːd/ noun ★★★

1 for sending greetings	**6** games
2 for money	**7** thick stiff paper
3 with information	**8** in a computer
4 postcard	**+ PHRASES**
5 for playing games	

1 [C] a folded piece of thick stiff paper with a picture and a message on it: *a birthday/ Christmas card*

2 [C] a small flat piece of plastic that you use for buying things, or for getting money from a bank: *I gave the waiter my card.*

3 [C] a small piece of thick stiff paper or plastic that shows who you are: *a library/membership card*

4 [C] a POSTCARD

5 [C] one of a set of 52 small pieces of thick stiff paper, used for various games=PLAYING CARD: *I'll teach you some new card games.* —*picture* → C16

6 cards [plural] the activity of playing games with a set of 52 cards: *Let's play cards this evening.* ♦ *Do you have time for a game of cards?*

7 [U] *British* thick stiff paper, thinner than CARDBOARD

8 [C] *computing* a part inside a computer that holds a CHIP

PHRASES have a card up your sleeve to have a secret advantage that you can use later
lay your cards on the table to tell people exactly what you are thinking or what you are intending to do
on the cards very likely to happen

cardboard /ˈkɑːdbɔːd/ noun [U] very thick stiff paper that is used for making boxes

cardiac /ˈkɑːdiæk/ adj *medical* relating to your heart

cardiac arrest noun [C] *medical* a HEART ATTACK

cardigan /ˈkɑːdɪɡən/ noun [C] a piece of woollen clothing that fastens at the front, worn on the top part of your body —*picture* → C5

cardinal¹ /ˈkɑːdɪn(ə)l/ noun [C] a senior priest in the Roman Catholic Church

cardinal² /ˈkɑːdɪn(ə)l/ adj *formal* very important: *The cardinal rule in this job is never to take any risks.*

cardinal number noun [C] an ordinary number such as 1, 2, or 3

cardiovascular /ˌkɑːdiəʊˈvæskjʊlə/ adj *medical* connected with the heart and the BLOOD VESSELS

care¹ /keə/ noun ★★★

1 avoiding mistakes	**4** place for children
2 looking after sb	**5** sth to worry about
3 looking after sth	**+ PHRASES**

1 [U] the effort that you make when you avoid making mistakes or causing harm: *The label on the box said 'Handle with care'.* ♦ *He was choosing his words with great care.*

2 [U] the activity of looking after someone who needs help or protection: *specialist medical care* ♦ *I left him in your care – you should have watched him!*

3 [U] the activity of keeping something in good condition: *skin care* ♦ *advice on the proper care of your new car*

4 [U] in the UK, the system in which local government looks after some children, for example because their parents are dead: *Her two children were taken into care.*

5 [C] something that makes you feel worried: *She acted like she didn't have a care in the world* (=was not worried about anything).

PHRASES take care 1 to be careful: *Take care on those steps!* ♦ **+(that)** *Take care that you don't fall.* ♦ **take care (not) to do sth** *Please take care not to tread on the cables.* **2** *spoken* used for saying goodbye to someone in a friendly way: *Bye now! Take care!*

take care of 1 to do the necessary things for someone who needs help or protection: *Who will take care of the children?* **2** to treat something carefully so that it stays in good condition: *All the neighbours take very good care of their gardens.* **3** to deal with a person or situation: *Can you take care of this customer, please?*

care² /keə/ verb [I/T] ★★★ to be interested in someone or something and think that they are important: *Her son didn't care enough to come and visit her.* ♦ *I don't think she cares about him at all.* ♦ **+what/why etc** *Of course I care what happens to the school!* ♦ *They cared deeply about the environment.*

PHRASES sb couldn't care less used for emphasizing that someone thinks that something is unimportant: *I couldn't care less how you do it – just do it.*

not care for to not like someone or something: *I don't really care for chocolate.*

who cares? *spoken* used for saying that you do not think that something is important and that you are not worried about it: *Who cares whether he lied or not?*

would you care for sth *spoken formal* used for asking someone politely whether they would like something: *Would you care for a coffee?*

would you care to do sth *spoken formal* used for asking someone politely whether they would like to do something: *Would you care to sit down?*

PHRASAL VERBS care for sb 1 to love someone: *He really cared for her.* **2** to do the necessary things for someone who needs help or protection=LOOK AFTER: *Teach your children how to care for their pets.*

care for sth to treat something carefully so that it stays in good condition=LOOK AFTER: *Your clothes won't last if you don't care for them properly.*

C

career¹ /kəˈrɪə/ noun [C] ★★
1 a job or profession that you work at for some time: *the problems of combining a career and a family* ♦ *Rosen had decided on an academic career.* ♦ *He felt like having a career change and went into teaching.* ♦ *a career in computer science* ♦ *He has just started out on a career as a photographer.*
2 the period of someone's life that they spend doing their job: *the most important game of her career* ♦ *the injury that ended his playing career*
→ CAREERS

Words often used with career

Adjectives often used with *career (noun, sense 2)*
- brilliant, distinguished, glittering, successful + CAREER: used about a career that is successful

career² /kəˈrɪə/ adj a career politician, soldier, teacher etc wants to stay in their profession for a long time and be successful
career³ /kəˈrɪə/ verb [I] to move very quickly in an uncontrolled way
careers /kəˈrɪəz/ adj British connected with the process of choosing a career: *She went to the university's careers service for advice.*
carefree /ˈkeəfriː/ adj happy and without any worries, problems, or responsibilities
careful /ˈkeəf(ə)l/ adj ★★★ thinking about what you do, so that you avoid problems, damage, or danger: *She took a few careful steps into the water.* ♦ *After careful consideration, we are giving the prize to a children's book.* ♦ *Please be very careful with those plates!* ♦ **be careful to do sth** *Marta was careful to keep her records up to date.*
—**carefully** adv: *He washed everything carefully.*
careless /ˈkeələs/ adj ★
1 not thinking about what you are doing, so that you cause problems or damage: *careless driving* ♦ *The letter was full of careless spelling mistakes.*
2 natural and relaxed: *a careless laugh*
—**carelessly** adv, **carelessness** noun [U]
carer /ˈkeərə/ noun [C] British someone who looks after a child or a person who is unable to look after themselves
caress /kəˈres/ verb [T] to move your hands gently over someone's face or body in a way that shows love —**caress** noun [C]
caretaker /ˈkeəˌteɪkə/ noun [C] someone whose job is to look after a large building such as a school
cargo /ˈkɑːɡəʊ/ (plural **cargoes**) noun [C/U] things that are being sent by ship, plane, train, or truck: *The ship and all its cargo sank.* ♦ *a cargo ship*
cargo pants noun [plural] loose trousers made of heavy cotton with pockets on the legs
caricature /ˈkærɪkətjʊə/ noun [C] a drawing or description of someone that emphasizes particular features in order to make them seem silly —**caricature** verb [T]

caring /ˈkeərɪŋ/ adj kind, helpful, and sympathetic towards other people
carjacking /ˈkɑːˌdʒækɪŋ/ noun [C/U] a crime in which someone attacks the driver of a car and steals the car —**carjacker** noun [C]
carnage /ˈkɑːnɪdʒ/ noun [U] a situation in which there is a lot of death and destruction
carnal /ˈkɑːn(ə)l/ adj literary involving sex
carnation /kɑːˈneɪʃ(ə)n/ noun [C] a flower that is often worn as a decoration on formal occasions —**picture** → C9
carnival /ˈkɑːnɪv(ə)l/ noun **1** [C/U] a festival in the streets in which people play music, dance, and wear colourful clothes **2** [C] American a FAIR where there are machines for riding on and games in which you can win prizes
carnivore /ˈkɑːnɪvɔː/ noun [C] an animal that eats other animals
carnivorous /kɑːˈnɪv(ə)rəs/ adj a carnivorous animal eats other animals
carol /ˈkærəl/ noun [C] a traditional song that people sing at Christmas
carousel /ˌkærəˈsel/ noun [C] **1** a moving surface in an airport from which you collect your bags **2** American a MERRY-GO-ROUND
car park noun [C] British an area or building where people can leave their cars for a short time
carpenter /ˈkɑːpɪntə/ noun [C] someone whose job is to make or repair wooden things
carpentry /ˈkɑːpɪntri/ noun [U] the activity of making and repairing wooden things
carpet¹ /ˈkɑːpɪt/ noun ★★
1 [C/U] a thick soft cover for a floor
2 [C] literary a layer of something soft covering the ground: *a carpet of leaves*
→ RED¹, SWEEP¹
carpet² /ˈkɑːpɪt/ verb [T] to cover a floor with a carpet
carpet-bomb verb [T] to drop a lot of bombs from planes, so that everything on the ground is destroyed
carpeted /ˈkɑːpɪtɪd/ adj a carpeted room has carpet on the floor
carriage /ˈkærɪdʒ/ noun [C] **1** a vehicle pulled by horses, used in the past for carrying passengers **2** British one of the vehicles that are joined together to make a train
carriageway /ˈkærɪdʒˌweɪ/ noun [C] British one side of a major road, used by vehicles travelling in the same direction → DUAL CARRIAGEWAY
carrier /ˈkæriə/ noun [C] **1** a company that moves goods or people from one place to another **2** a vehicle or ship used for moving goods or people → AIRCRAFT CARRIER
3 someone who can infect another person with a disease without getting it themselves
carrier bag noun [C] British a cheap bag that a shop gives you for carrying your shopping home —**picture** → BAG
carrot /ˈkærət/ noun **1** [C/U] a long hard orange vegetable that grows under the ground —**picture** → C11 **2** [C] informal something that someone promises you to encourage you to do something

carry /ˈkæri/ verb ★★★

1 take in your hands	**8** accept responsibility
2 in your pocket/bag	**9** lead to punishment
3 transport sb/sth	**10** have message
4 have goods for sale	**11** of smells/sounds
5 publish/broadcast sth	✦ PHRASES
6 spread disease	✦ PHRASAL VERBS
7 develop	

1 [T] to hold someone or something using your hands, arms, or body and take them somewhere: *Do you mind carrying this box for me?* ✦ *Sarah carried her cup of coffee back to her desk.* ✦ *Luke was carrying the boy on his shoulders.*

carry

lift

pick up

2 [T] to have something with you, usually in your pocket or bag: *I never carry much cash with me.* ✦ *British police officers don't normally carry guns.*

3 [T] to transport someone or something from one place to another: *a plane carrying 225 passengers* ✦ *They carried the message back to their villages.* ✦ *a cable carrying electricity*

4 [T] if a shop carries goods or products, it has them for sale: *We carry several models of microwaves.*

5 [T] to publish or broadcast a news story: *All the papers carried the story the next day.*

6 [T] to have a disease and be capable of infecting someone else with it

7 [T] to do or develop something to a particular level: *If this behaviour is carried to extremes, it can be destructive.*

8 [T] if you carry responsibility or blame for something, you accept it

9 [T] if a crime carries a particular punishment, that is the punishment that people will receive for committing it

10 [T] if something carries a message, the message is written on it: *Packets of cigarettes must carry a government health warning.*

11 [I] if a sound carries, it can be heard far away: *The child's cries carried down the quiet street.*

PHRASES **carry weight** to be respected and have influence: *Dr Watson's opinions carry a lot of weight in court.*

get carried away to become so excited or involved in something that you lose control of your feelings or behaviour

PHRASAL VERBS **carry sth 'off** to deal successfully with something difficult: *Both actors have the confidence needed to carry off these roles.*

carry 'on to continue going in the same direction: *Turn left at the traffic lights and carry on up the high street.*

carry (sth) 'on to continue doing something: *She moved to London to carry on her work.* ✦ *Just carry on with what you were doing.* ✦ **carry on doing sth** *If you carry on spending money like that, you'll end up in debt.*

carry sth 'out 1 to do a particular piece of work: *The building work was carried out by a local contractor.* **2** to do something that you have been told to do or that you have promised to do: *Maybe she ought to have carried out her threat to go to the police.* ✦ *Your orders have been carried out, sir.*

'carry-on adj carry-on bags or cases are ones that you can keep with you on a plane

carsick /ˈkɑːsɪk/ adj feeling ill from travelling in a car —**carsickness** noun [U]

cart¹ /kɑːt/ noun [C] an open vehicle with four wheels that is pulled by a horse

cart² /kɑːt/ verb [T] *informal* to carry something large or heavy somewhere

carte blanche /ˌkɑːt ˈblɑːntʃ/ noun [U] the freedom to do what you want in a particular situation

cartel /kɑːˈtel/ noun [C] a group of companies who agree to sell something at the same price so that they do not have to compete with one another

cartilage /ˈkɑːtəlɪdʒ/ noun [U] a substance that surrounds the JOINTS in your body

carton /ˈkɑːt(ə)n/ noun [C] a container for liquids made of stiff thick paper, or the amount of liquid that can be put into this container

cartoon /kɑːˈtuːn/ noun [C] **1** a film or TV programme made by photographing a series of drawings so that things in them seem to move **2** a humorous drawing or series of drawings in a newspaper or magazine

cartridge /ˈkɑːtrɪdʒ/ noun [C] **1** a small container with ink inside that you put into a printer or pen **2** a metal tube that you put into a gun, containing a bullet and a substance that will explode

cartwheel /ˈkɑːtwiːl/ noun [C] a movement in which you throw yourself sideways onto your hands, swing your legs over your head, and land on your feet

carve /kɑːv/ verb [I/T] **1** to make an object by cutting it from stone or wood, or to make a pattern by cutting into stone or wood **2** to cut a large piece of meat into pieces before you serve it

PHRASAL VERBS **carve 'out sth (for yourself)** to develop a career or position for yourself by working hard

carve sth 'up to divide something such as land between different people or countries, usually unfairly

carving /ˈkɑːvɪŋ/ noun [C] an object or pattern made by cutting stone or wood

'car wash noun [C] a place with special equipment for washing cars

cascade /kæˈskeɪd/ verb [I] to flow or hang down in large amounts —**cascade** noun [C]

case /keɪs/ noun [C] ★★★

1 situation affecting sth	**6** situation/person
2 legal matter for court	**7** container/cover
3 set of reasons	**8** suitcase
4 crime	**+ PHRASES**
5 instance of disease	

1 a situation that involves a particular person or thing: *In the majority of cases, it's easy to keep costs down.* ♦ *If that's the case, I'm not surprised she was angry.* ♦ *It was a case of love at first sight.* ♦ 'I don't need it tonight.' 'In that case, I'll keep it until tomorrow.'

2 a legal matter that will be decided in a court: *He was confident that the case against him would be dropped.* ♦ *a murder/rape/ libel case*

3 a set of facts used to support one side of an argument or legal matter: *The lawyers told me I had a strong case* (=had a good chance of winning in court).

4 a crime that the police are trying to solve: *a murder case*

5 an instance of a disease: *a bad case of food poisoning*

6 a situation or person that an official is dealing with: *Each social worker was assigned 30 cases.*

7 a container or cover for something: *Have you seen my glasses' case anywhere?* ♦ *a case of wine*

8 a SUITCASE

PHRASES **a case in point** used for giving an example of the situation or behaviour that you are talking about

in any case whatever the situation is, was, or will be: *Traffic may be bad, but in any case we'll be there in time for dinner.*

in case 1 in order to be prepared for something that may happen: *Take an umbrella in case it rains.* ♦ *I'll make some sandwiches, just in case we get hungry later on.* ♦ *In case of* (=if there is) *bad weather, the wedding will be held indoors.* **2** *American* if: *In case you can't come, give me a call.*

case study noun [C] a piece of research that records details of how a situation develops over a period of time

cash¹ /kæʃ/ noun [U] ★★★ money in the form of notes and coins: *Do you want to pay in cash or by credit card?*

cash² /kæʃ/ verb [T] to exchange a cheque for its value in notes and coins

PHRASAL VERB **cash in** to use an opportunity to make a profit or gain an advantage

cashback /ˈkæʃbæk/ noun [U] *British* money from your bank account that you can get from a shop when you pay for goods with a **debit card**

cash card noun [C] a BANK CARD

cash desk noun [C] *British* the place in a shop where you pay for your goods

cash dispenser noun [C] *British* a CASHPOINT

cashew /ˈkæʃuː, kæˈʃuː/ or **cashew nut** noun [C] a curved nut that you can eat

cash flow noun [U] *business* the process of money coming into and going out of a company

cashier /kæˈʃɪə/ noun [C] someone whose job is to receive or give money to customers in a shop, bank etc

cash machine noun [C] a CASHPOINT

cashmere /ˈkæʃmɪə/ noun [U] very soft wool that comes from a type of goat

cashpoint /ˈkæʃpɔɪnt/ noun [C] *British* a machine that gives you money from your bank account when you put in a **bank card** into it

cash register noun [C] a TILL

casing /ˈkeɪsɪŋ/ noun [C] a layer of a substance covering the outside of something to protect it

casino /kəˈsiːnəʊ/ noun [C] a place where people GAMBLE (=risk money in the hope of winning more)

casket /ˈkɑːskɪt/ noun [C] **1** a small decorated box for keeping jewellery and valuable objects in **2** *American* a COFFIN

casserole /ˈkæsərəʊl/ noun [C/U] a deep dish with a lid, used for cooking in the oven, or the mixture of food that is cooked —*picture* → C2

cassette /kəˈset/ noun [C] a flat plastic case that contains TAPE for playing and recording sound or pictures

cassette player noun [C] a machine that plays music cassettes

cast¹ /kɑːst/ (past tense and past participle **cast**) verb ★

1 [T] to choose an actor for a particular part, or to choose all the actors for a particular play, film etc: **cast sb as sth** *She was always cast as a mother.*

2 [T] to make light or a shadow appear in a particular place

3 [I/T] to throw a FISHING LINE or net into the water

4 [T] to form an object by pouring liquid metal or liquid plastic into a MOULD

PHRASES **cast doubt on sth** to make something seem less certain, good, or real: *The latest information casts doubt on his story.*

cast your eyes over/cast a glance at to look at someone or something: *Harry cast his eyes around the room.*

cast (new/fresh) light on sth to provide information that helps people to understand something more clearly

cast a shadow over sth to make a situation seem less hopeful or more likely to end badly

cast a spell on/over sb to use magic to make something happen to someone, or to seem to do this

cast a vote to vote in an election

PHRASAL VERBS **cast sb/sth aside** to get rid of someone or something because they are no longer interesting or valuable

cast off to remove the rope that is fastening your boat to the land, so that you can sail away

cast sb/sth off to get rid of someone or something: *It took many years for Chicago to cast off its violent reputation.*

cast² /kɑːst/ noun [C] **1** all the performers in a film, play etc **2** *medical* a hard cover for protecting a broken part of your body while it is getting better **3** an object made by pouring a liquid into a MOULD that is removed when the liquid is hard

castaway /ˈkɑːstəˌweɪ/ noun [C] someone whose ship has sunk and who is left alone on an island

caste /kɑːst/ noun [C] one of the social classes that people are born into in Hindu society

castigate /ˈkæstɪˌɡeɪt/ verb [T] formal to criticize someone or something severely

,casting 'vote noun [C] the vote that gives one group a majority when the other votes are equally divided

,cast 'iron noun [U] very hard iron used for making objects such as cooking pans and fences

,cast-'iron adj **1** made of cast iron **2** very definite, and certain to be effective: *a cast-iron alibi*

castle /ˈkɑːs(ə)l/ noun [C] ★★
1 a large strong building with thick walls that was built in the past to protect the people inside from being attacked
2 one of the pieces used in the game of CHESS —*picture* → C16

'cast-off noun [C] British something that you give to someone else because you no longer want it

castrate /kæˈstreɪt/ verb [T] to remove the TESTICLES (=pair of sexual organs) of a male animal or a man —**castration** /kæˈstreɪʃ(ə)n/ noun [U]

casual /ˈkæʒuəl/ adj

1 relaxed/informal	4 not planned
2 comfortable to wear	5 temporary
3 without strong feeling	

1 relaxed and informal: *The bar has a casual atmosphere.* **2** casual clothes are comfortable and suitable for wearing in informal situations **3** not involving strong feelings or emotions: *casual relationships/ friendships* **4** happening without being planned or thought about: *a casual meeting/remark* **5** used for describing temporary employment, and the people involved in it —**casually** adv

casualty /ˈkæʒuəlti/ noun **1** [C] someone who is injured or killed in an accident or war: *There were reports of heavy casualties* (=many people injured or killed). **2** [C] someone or something that is damaged or harmed as a result of something: *Education has again been a casualty of government spending cuts.* **3** [U] British the part of a hospital where people go when they are injured, or when they suddenly become ill

cat /kæt/ noun [C] ★★★
1 an animal with soft fur, a long thin tail, and WHISKERS. It is kept as a pet or for catching mice.
2 a wild animal that looks like a big cat, for example a lion
PHRASES **cat and mouse** a situation in which two people use skill or tricks to try to defeat each other: *Hammond played cat and mouse with the police for weeks.*
let the cat out of the bag to tell someone something that was intended to be secret → FAT CAT

cataclysm /ˈkætəˌklɪz(ə)m/ noun [C] literary a sudden violent change or event

cataclysmic /ˌkætəˈklɪzmɪk/ adj changing a situation in a sudden, violent, and unpleasant way

catalog /ˈkætəˌlɒg/ the American spelling of catalogue

catalogue¹ /ˈkætəˌlɒg/ noun [C] **1** a book that contains pictures of things that you can buy: *a mail order catalogue* **2** a list of all the things in an exhibition, sale, or library **3** a series of bad things that happen: *a catalogue of disasters*

catalogue² /ˈkætəˌlɒg/ verb [T] to make a list of all the things in a collection

catalyst /ˈkætəlɪst/ noun [C] **1** someone or something that causes something to happen or change **2** science a substance that causes a chemical reaction to happen more quickly

catapult¹ /ˈkætəˌpʌlt/ noun [C] British an object that children use for firing stones. It consists of a stick in the shape of a 'Y' with a thin band of rubber across the top.

catapult² /ˈkætəˌpʌlt/ verb [T] **1** to suddenly put someone into an important position: *The song catapulted the band to fame in the 1960s.* **2** to fire something through the air very quickly

cataract /ˈkætəˌrækt/ noun [C] a white area that grows on your eye as a result of disease. It makes you gradually lose your sight.

catastrophe /kəˈtæstrəfi/ noun [C] an event that causes a lot of damage, or makes a lot of people suffer=DISASTER: *an economic/ natural catastrophe*

catastrophic /ˌkætəˈstrɒfɪk/ adj causing a lot of damage, or making a lot of people suffer: *catastrophic floods* —**catastrophically** /ˌkætəˈstrɒfɪkli/ adv

catch¹ /kætʃ/ (past tense and past participle caught /kɔːt/) verb ★★★

1 stop a falling object	10 hear sth that sb says
2 stop an escape	11 talk to/telephone sb
3 find and arrest	12 discover a problem
4 get on public vehicle	13 get sb's attention etc
5 discover sb doing sth	14 of light
6 find sb not prepared	15 hit part of body
7 get into bad situation	+ PHRASES
8 get stuck on sth	+ PHRASAL VERBS
9 get disease/illness	

1 [I/T] to stop something that is falling or moving through the air, and hold it: *Stewart caught the ball with one hand.* ♦ *A bucket stood under the hole to catch the rain.*
2 [T] to get hold of and stop a person or animal so that they cannot escape: *She raced to catch the child before he got to the edge.* ♦ *Wolves hunt and catch their prey in packs.* ♦ *Laura shouted, "Wait!" and caught hold of his arm.* ♦ *Did you catch any fish* (=using a fishing rod or net)?
3 [T] if the police catch someone, they find them and arrest them
4 [I/T] to get on a train, bus, plane, or boat that is travelling somewhere: *I caught the next train to London.* ♦ *I have a flight to catch at 4.40.*
5 [T] to find someone doing something that they do not expect or want you to see: *catch sb doing sth Several times she'd caught him staring at her.* ♦ *Diana was caught red-*

handed (=caught while doing something wrong).

6 [T] to surprise someone in an unpleasant way, by doing something that they are not prepared for: *The question **caught** their spokesperson **by surprise**.* ♦ *Harry looked up suddenly, **catching** Emily **off her guard*** (=when she was not ready).

7 [T] to become unexpectedly involved in an unpleasant situation: *We were **caught in** a heavy storm.* ♦ *She **got caught up in** a clash between protesters and police.*

8 [I/T] to become stuck on something, or to make something get stuck: *I must have **caught** my shirt **on** a nail.*

9 [T] to get a disease or illness: **catch sth from sb/sth** *Brian caught chickenpox from his nephew.*

10 [T] to hear something that someone says: *I'm sorry, I didn't catch what you said.*

11 [T] *informal* to find someone available to talk by going to them or telephoning them: *Margaret caught me just as I was leaving.*

12 [T] to discover a problem or medical condition and stop it from becoming worse: *Doctors assured her that they had caught the cancer in time.*

13 [T] to have a sudden effect on someone's attention or imagination: *It was Myra's red hair that first caught my attention.*

14 [T] if light catches something, or if something catches the light, the light makes it look bright and shiny

15 [T] to hit someone on a part of their body, or to hit a part of your body on something by accident

PHRASES **catch your breath 1** to stop breathing suddenly for a short time because you are surprised or impressed **2** to take time to start to breathe normally again after physical exercise

catch sb's eye 1 if something catches your eye, you suddenly notice it: *There was one painting that caught my eye.* **2** to get someone's attention by looking at them

catch sight of/a glimpse of to see someone or something for a very short time

PHRASAL VERBS **ˌcatch ˈon 1** to become popular or fashionable: *We were surprised at how quickly the idea caught on.* **2** to understand: *He didn't catch on at first.*

ˌcatch sb ˈout *British* **1** to show that someone has made a mistake, or is not telling the truth: *He asked her casual questions to see if he could catch her out.* **2** to put someone into a situation that they are not prepared for: *The climbers are hoping that they won't be caught out by bad weather again.*

ˌcatch (sb/sth) ˈup 1 to go faster so that you reach the person or vehicle in front of you **2** to improve in order to reach the same standard or rate as someone or something: *He's missed so much school that he's going to find it hard to catch up.* ♦ *Recently, salaries have **caught up with** inflation.*

ˌcatch ˈup on sth to do something that you have not done enough of before: *I just want to go home and catch up on some sleep.*

ˌcatch ˈup with sb 1 to begin to have an effect on someone: *The lack of sleep caught up with her, and she began to doze off.* **2** to talk to someone who you have not seen for some time and find out what they have been doing: *Come over tomorrow and we can catch up.*

catch² /kætʃ/ noun ★★

1 [C] an act of stopping and holding a ball that is moving through the air: *Well done! Good catch!*

2 [C] an object used for fastening something such as a window, door, or container

3 [C] a hidden problem or difficulty in something that seems extremely good: *It sounds so cheap – is there a catch?*

4 [U] a game in which children throw a ball to each other

catch

catch-22 /ˌkætʃ twentiˈtuː/ noun [C] a difficult situation that is impossible to escape from because each part of the problem must be solved first

ˈcatch-ˌall noun [C] a word, phrase, or group that includes a lot of different things

catchment area /ˈkætʃmənt ˌeəriə/ noun [C] *British* the area for which a school or hospital provides a service

catchphrase /ˈkætʃˌfreɪz/ noun [C] a short phrase that many people know from television, movies etc

catchy /ˈkætʃi/ adj a tune or phrase that is catchy gets your attention and is easy to remember

categorically /ˌkætəˈɡɒrɪkli/ adv in a very clear and definite way —**categorical** adj

categorize /ˈkætɪɡəˌraɪz/ verb [T] to put people or things into groups according to their qualities ═ CLASSIFY —**categorization** /ˌkætɪɡəraɪˈzeɪʃ(ə)n/ noun [U]

category /ˈkætəɡ(ə)ri/ noun [C] a group of people or things that have similar qualities: *There will be two winners in each category.* ♦ *The proposal would ban some categories of weapons.*

cater /ˈkeɪtə/ verb [I/T] to provide food and drinks at an event such as a party or meeting —**caterer** noun [C]

PHRASAL VERBS **ˈcater for sb** *British* to provide people with everything that they want or need: *The school aims to cater for children of all abilities.*

ˈcater to sb to provide a particular group of people with something that they want or need: *TV shows catering to young male audiences*

catering /ˈkeɪtərɪŋ/ noun [U] the job of organizing the food and drinks for an event such as a party or meeting

caterpillar /ˈkætəpɪlə/ noun [C] an insect with many legs that develops into a BUTTERFLY or MOTH —*picture* → C13

catfish /ˈkætˌfɪʃ/ noun [C] a fish with long hard hairs near its mouth. It lives in lakes and rivers.

catharsis /kəˈθɑːsɪs/ noun [U] the process of expressing strong feelings that have been affecting you so that they do not upset you any longer —**cathartic** adj

cathedral /kəˈθiːdrəl/ noun [C] the most important church in the area that a BISHOP controls

Catholic /ˈkæθ(ə)lɪk/ noun [C] a member of the Roman Catholic Church —**Catholic** adj, **Catholicism** /kəˈθɒlɪˌsɪz(ə)m/ noun [U]

cattle /ˈkæt(ə)l/ noun [plural] cows and BULLS that are kept by farmers for their milk or meat

catty /ˈkæti/ adj saying cruel or unpleasant things about other people

catwalk /ˈkætˌwɔːk/ noun [C] **1** the raised area at a FASHION SHOW that the MODELS walk along **2** a structure for people to walk on, built high on a building or above a stage

Caucasian /kɔːˈkeɪziən/ adj formal used for describing a white person, for example someone from North America, Europe, or Australia —**Caucasian** noun [C]

caught the past tense and past participle of **catch**[1]

cauldron /ˈkɔːldrən/ noun [C] a large round metal container that you use for cooking over a fire

cauliflower /ˈkɒliˌflaʊə/ noun [C/U] a vegetable with a hard round white central part surrounded by green leaves —picture → C11

'cause /kɒz/ conjunction informal because

cause[1] /kɔːz/ noun ★★★

1 [C] an event, thing, or person that makes something happen: *The cause of death was found to be a heart attack.* ♦ *an essay on the* **causes** *of the First World War*

2 [C/U] a reason for behaving in a particular way, or for feeling a particular emotion: *He wouldn't have done it without* **good cause** (=a good reason). ♦ *His departure was* **cause** *for celebration in the village.* ♦ *The doctor's report states that there is* **no cause for** *concern.*

3 [C] an aim, idea, or organization that you support or work for: *Campaigners hope that people will be sympathetic to their cause.* ♦ *Please give as much as you can: it's for a* **good cause**.

→ LOST CAUSE

cause[2] /kɔːz/ verb [T] ★★★ to make something happen, usually something bad: *Police confirmed that the explosion was* **caused by** *a bomb.* ♦ *Indigestion is* **caused by** *excess acid in the stomach.* ♦ *Bad weather continues to* **cause problems** *for travellers.* ♦ **cause sb/sth to do sth** *A small sound caused him to turn his head.* ♦ **cause sb sth** *He apologizes for causing you any embarrassment.*

Words often used with cause

Nouns often used with cause

■ CAUSE + **alarm, concern, confusion, damage, distress, embarrassment, harm, problems, suffering, trouble:** cause a bad situation

causeway /ˈkɔːzˌweɪ/ noun [C] a raised road or path across ground that is wet or covered by water

caustic /ˈkɔːstɪk/ adj expressing severe criticism, often in a funny or clever way

caution[1] /ˈkɔːʃ(ə)n/ noun **1** [U] careful thought and lack of hurry in order to try to avoid risks or danger: *He was instructed to act with extreme caution.* ♦ *Politicians should exercise greater caution with taxpayers' money.* **2** [U] advice that you should be careful: *A word of caution: the roads are very icy.* **3** [C] British an official warning that the police give someone who has broken the law

caution[2] /ˈkɔːʃ(ə)n/ verb [T] **1** formal to warn someone about a possible danger or problem: *Researchers cautioned that the drug is only partly effective.* **2** British if the police caution someone who has broken the law, they warn them officially

cautionary /ˈkɔːʃ(ə)nəri/ adj warning someone that they should be careful: *cautionary remarks*

cautious /ˈkɔːʃəs/ adj careful to avoid problems or danger —**cautiously** adv

cavalier /ˌkævəˈlɪə/ adj not caring enough about other people's feelings or about a serious situation: *a cavalier attitude*

cavalry /ˈkævəlri/ noun [U] the part of an army that consists of soldiers who ride horses

cave[1] /keɪv/ noun [C] a large hole in the side of a hill or under the ground

cave[2] /keɪv/ PHRASAL VERB **cave in 1** if a roof or wall caves in, it falls down or inwards **2** to suddenly stop opposing something because someone has persuaded you

caveat /ˈkæviˌæt/ noun [C] formal a warning of the limits of a particular agreement or statement

caveman /ˈkeɪvˌmæn/ (plural **cavemen** /ˈkeɪvˌmen/) noun [C] someone who lived thousands of years ago when people lived in CAVES

cavern /ˈkævən/ noun [C] a large CAVE

cavernous /ˈkævənəs/ adj a cavernous room or building is very large and dark

caviar /ˈkæviˌɑː/ noun [U] fish eggs that are eaten as a special and expensive food

cavity /ˈkævəti/ noun [C] **1** a hole or space inside a solid object or your body **2** a hole in a tooth, caused by decay

CBI, the /ˌsiː biː ˈaɪ/ the Confederation of British Industry: an organization in the UK that represents large businesses

cc /ˌsiː ˈsiː/ abbrev **1** used on a business letter or email for saying that a copy is being sent to the person mentioned: *To Jack Brown, cc: Paul Davis.* **2** cubic centimetre: used for measuring the amount of a liquid or the size of an engine: *a 750cc motorbike*

CCTV noun [U] closed-circuit television: a system of cameras and television screens that allows someone to see what is happening in different parts of a building or town

CD /ˌsiː ˈdiː/ noun [C] ★ compact disc: a small round piece of hard plastic with sound recorded on it or computer information stored on it

CD burner noun [C] a CD WRITER

CD player noun [C] a piece of equipment used

for playing CDs with music on them

CD-ROM /ˌsi: di: 'rɒm/ noun [C/U] compact disc read-only memory: a CD that stores large amounts of information for use by a computer

CD-RW /ˌsi: di: ɑ: 'dʌb(ə)lju:/ abbrev compact disc rewritable: a CD that you can use for recording music or information from a computer

CD ˌwriter noun [C] a piece of equipment used for recording information onto CDs

cease /si:s/ verb [I/T] formal to stop happening or continuing, or to stop something happening or continuing: *Conversation ceased when she entered the room.* ♦ *The government has ceased all contact with the rebels.* ♦ *He had ceased caring what she did.*

ceasefire /'si:sˌfaɪə/ noun [C] an agreement to stop fighting for a period of time

ceaseless /'si:sləs/ adj formal continuing without stopping —**ceaselessly** adv

cedar /'si:də/ noun [C/U] a tall EVERGREEN tree, or the wood from this tree

cede /si:d/ verb [T] formal to allow someone to take something such as power or land away from you

ceiling /'si:lɪŋ/ noun [C] ★
1 the surface that is above you in a room: *There were cracks in the walls and the ceiling.*
2 an upper limit set on the number or amount of something: *A ceiling of £100 was put on all donations.*
→ GLASS CEILING

celeb /sə'leb/ noun [C] informal a CELEBRITY

celebrate /'seləˌbreɪt/ verb ★★
1 [I/T] to do something enjoyable in order to show that an occasion or event is special: *Let's have a party to celebrate.* ♦ *They're celebrating the end of their exams.*
2 [T] formal to show admiration for someone or something in a piece of writing, music, or art, or in a ceremony: *The bravery of warriors was celebrated in song.*

celebrated /'seləˌbreɪtɪd/ adj famous and praised by many people: *a celebrated artist*

celebration /ˌseləˈbreɪʃ(ə)n/ noun ★★★
1 [C] a party or special event at which you celebrate something: *The whole family showed up for our anniversary celebration.*
2 [U] the activity of celebrating something: *It was a night of dancing and celebration.* ♦ *He's having a party in celebration of his 84th birthday.*

celebrity /sə'lebrəti/ noun [C] ★ a famous entertainer or sports personality: *TV/sports celebrities*

celery /'seləri/ noun [U] a pale green vegetable with long stems that are eaten raw or cooked —*picture* → C11

ceˌlestial ˈbody noun [C] technical a star or planet

celibate /'seləbət/ adj someone who is celibate does not have sex —**celibacy** /'seləbəsi/ noun [U]

cell /sel/ noun [C] ★★
1 the smallest part of a living human being, animal, or plant that can operate as an independent unit: *nerve/blood/brain/cancer cells*

2 a small room where a prisoner is kept: *a police/prison cell*

cellar /'selə/ noun [C] a room under a building, below the ground → SALT CELLAR

cello /'tʃeləʊ/ noun [C] a large musical instrument with strings. You hold it between your legs and play it with a BOW. —*picture* → STRINGED INSTRUMENT —**cellist** /'tʃelɪst/ noun [C]

cellophane /'seləˌfeɪn/ noun [U] a very thin clear material that you use for wrapping things

cellphone /'selˌfəʊn/ noun [C] American a MOBILE PHONE

cellular /'seljʊlə/ adj **1** relating to human, animal, or plant cells **2** relating to mobile phones

cellular ˈphone noun [C] formal a MOBILE PHONE

cellulite /'seljʊˌlaɪt/ noun [U] small lumps of fat just below the skin

celluloid /'seljʊˌlɔɪd/ noun [U] a thin clear plastic material that was used in the past for making FILM

Celsius /'selsiəs/ noun [U] a system for measuring temperature in the METRIC SYSTEM → FAHRENHEIT

Celt /kelt/ noun [C] a member of an ancient group of people who lived in parts of Western Europe

Celtic /'keltɪk/ adj of the Celts

cement¹ /sə'ment/ noun [U] a grey powder used in building. It becomes very hard when it is mixed with sand and water.

cement² /sə'ment/ verb [T] **1** to make a relationship or idea stronger or more certain **2** to cover a surface with cement

cemetery /'semət(ə)ri/ noun [C] an area of ground where dead people are buried → GRAVEYARD

censor /'sensə/ verb [T] to remove parts of a book, film, or letter for moral, religious, or political reasons —**censor** noun [C]

censorship /'sensəʃɪp/ noun [U] the process of removing parts of books, films, or letters that are considered unsuitable for moral, religious, or political reasons

censure /'senʃə/ verb [T] formal to criticize someone severely —**censure** noun [U]

census /'sensəs/ noun [C] an occasion when government officials count all the people in a country and record information about them

cent /sent/ noun [C] a small unit of money used in many countries, for example the US, Canada, and Australia. There are 100 cents in a dollar.

centenary /sen'ti:nəri, sen'tenəri/ noun [C] a day or year that people celebrate exactly 100 years after an important event

centennial /sen'teniəl/ noun [C] American a CENTENARY

center /'sentə/ the American spelling of centre

centigrade /'sentiˌgreɪd/ noun [U] old-fashioned CELSIUS

centilitre /'sentiˌli:tə/ noun [C] a unit for measuring an amount of liquid or gas in the METRIC SYSTEM. There are 100 centilitres in one litre.

centimeter /'sentiˌmi:tə/ the American spelling of centimetre

centimetre /'sentɪˌmiːtə/ noun [C] a unit for measuring length in the METRIC SYSTEM. There are 100 centimetres in one metre.

centipede /'sentɪˌpiːd/ noun [C] a small insect with a narrow body and many pairs of legs

central /'sentrəl/ adj ★★★
1 in the middle of a space or area: *central London* ♦ *The hotel is built around a central courtyard.*
2 main or major: *He played a central role in the development of US economic policy.* ♦ *skills that are* **central to** (=very important for) *a child's development*
3 belonging to the main organization that controls other smaller organizations: *the Communist Party's central committee*
—**centrally** /'sentrəli/ adv

central 'government noun [C/U] the government of a whole country: *a new partnership between local and central government*

central 'heating noun [U] a system that heats a whole building by sending hot air or water through pipes to all the rooms

centralize /'sentrəˌlaɪz/ verb [T] to give control of a country, organization, or industry to one central group of people

central 'nervous ˌsystem noun [C] the part of your NERVOUS SYSTEM that consists of your brain and your SPINAL CORD

centre¹ /'sentə/ noun ★★★

1 middle	**5** main subject/cause
2 part of town	**6** not left- or right-wing
3 a building for sth	**+** PHRASE
4 important place for sth	

1 [C] the middle of a space or area: *chocolates with soft centres* ♦ **in the centre of** *the room*
2 [C] *British* the part of a town or city that contains most of the shops, restaurants, and places of entertainment: *We caught a bus into the centre.*
3 [C] a building or group of buildings that is used for a particular activity or for providing a particular service: *a health/job centre* ♦ *a sports/shopping centre*
4 [C] a place where a particular thing is important, or where a particular thing exists in large amounts or numbers: *one of the world's most important financial centres* ♦ *people who live in the* **centres of** *population*
5 [singular] **the centre of sth** the main subject or cause of something: *He hates being the* **centre of attention**.
6 **the centre** [singular] a political party, group of parties, or position that is not extreme because it is neither left-wing nor right-wing
PHRASE **centre of gravity** the point in any object around which its weight balances

centre² /'sentə/ verb [T] to put something in the centre of an area
PHRASAL VERB **centre aˌround sb/sth** or **'centre ˌon sb/sth** if something centres around someone or something, they are its main subject of attention or interest: *The debate centred around the issue of finance.*

centrepiece /'sentəˌpiːs/ noun [C] **1** the most important feature of something: *The president's speech was the centrepiece of the event.* **2** a decoration or arrangement of flowers that you put in the middle of a table

centre 'stage noun [U] *mainly journalism* a position in which someone or something is attracting a lot of attention

century /'sentʃəri/ noun [C] ★★★
1 a period of 100 years, usually counted from a year ending in –00: *16th century paintings* ♦ *His family has ruled Morocco since the 17th century.*
2 any period of 100 years: *the worst storm in nearly a century* ♦ *The tribe had died out* *centuries* (=hundreds of years) *before.*

CEO /ˌsiː iː 'əʊ/ noun [C] Chief Executive Officer: the most senior manager in a company

ceramic /sə'ræmɪk/ adj made from baked clay

ceramics /sə'ræmɪks/ noun **1** [U] the art or process of making ceramic objects **2** [plural] ceramic objects

cereal /'sɪəriəl/ noun **1** [C/U] a food made from grain. You eat it with milk for breakfast.
2 [C] any grain that can be made into flour, or a plant that produces grain

cerebral /'serəbrəl, sə'riːbrəl/ adj *medical* relating to your brain, or affecting your brain

cerebral palsy /ˌserəbrəl 'pɔːlzi/ noun [U] a medical condition that affects someone's ability to control their movement and speech

ceremonial /ˌserə'məʊniəl/ adj connected with a ceremony

ceremony /'serəməni/ noun ★
1 [C] a formal public event with special traditions, actions, or words: *a ceremony to honour those who died in the war* ♦ *an awards ceremony*
2 [U] the formal traditions, actions, and words used for celebrating a public or religious event: *They celebrated Easter with lavish ceremony.*

certain¹ /'sɜːt(ə)n/ adj ★★★
1 having no doubts that something is true =SURE ≠ UNCERTAIN: *I'm not absolutely certain, but I think I'm right.* ♦ **+(that)** *You can be pretty certain she's not going to like it.* ♦ **+who/how/why etc** *We still can't be certain who is going to win.* ♦ *I've never been more* **certain of** *anything in my entire life.*
2 definitely going to happen, or definitely known: *One thing was certain: someone had been in his room.* ♦ **be certain to do sth** *Interest rates seem certain to rise next month.* ♦ **+(that)** *It's not certain that this method would work.* ♦ *Mexico is now* **certain of** *a place in the finals.*
PHRASE **make certain** to take action in order to be sure that something happens or be sure that something is true =MAKE SURE: **+(that)** *Call the office to make certain everything is OK.*

certain² /'sɜːt(ə)n/ determiner ★★ used for referring to someone or something without being specific about who or what they are: *There are certain things we need to discuss.*
PHRASE **a certain** some, but not very much: *A* **certain amount** *of fat in your diet is good for you.*

certainly /'sɜːt(ə)nli/ adv ★★★
1 used for emphasizing that something is definitely true or will definitely happen:

There certainly wasn't any point in going now.

2 *spoken* used for expressing agreement or for giving permission: *'We'd like you to explain your proposal to us in greater detail.' 'Certainly.' ♦ 'Can I borrow your car?' 'Certainly not!'*

certainty /ˈsɜːt(ə)nti/ noun **1** [C] something that will definitely happen, or that you feel very sure about: *Victory looked like a certainty.* **2** [U] the feeling of being completely sure about something = CONVICTION ≠ UNCERTAINTY: *I can say with certainty that there will be no more information today.*

certificate /səˈtɪfɪkət/ noun [C] ★★
1 an official document that states that particular facts are true: *a birth/marriage certificate*
2 an official document that proves that you have passed an examination or have successfully completed a course

certify /ˈsɜːtɪˌfaɪ/ verb [T] **1** to state officially that something is true, accurate, or satisfactory **2** to give someone an official document that proves that they have passed an examination or have successfully completed a training course

cervical /ˈsɜːvɪk(ə)l, səˈvaɪk(ə)l/ adj *medical* relating to a woman's CERVIX

cervix /ˈsɜːvɪks/ noun [C] the entrance to the WOMB (=the part of a woman's body where a baby grows)

cesarean /sɪˈzeəriən/ the American spelling of **caesarean**

cessation /seˈseɪʃ(ə)n/ noun [C/U] *formal* an end to something: *a cessation of hostilities*

CFC /ˌsiː ef ˈsiː/ noun [C] chlorofluorocarbon: a gas used in REFRIGERATORS and in some AEROSOLS

chafe /tʃeɪf/ verb [I/T] to rub the skin on a part of your body and make it sore

chain¹ /tʃeɪn/ noun ★★
1 [C/U] a series of metal rings that are connected to each other: *The crate was attached to the deck with a chain.* ♦ *a gold chain* ♦ *Women prisoners were kept in chains.*
2 [C] a series of people or things that are connected: *a chain of events that eventually led to murder* ♦ *a chain of small islands*
3 [C] a group of businesses that all belong to the same company: *Japan's leading hotel chain* ♦ *a chain of electrical goods shops*

chain

chain² /tʃeɪn/ verb [T] to use a chain to fasten something so that it cannot be stolen, or to fasten a prisoner with a chain so that they cannot escape

chain reʹaction noun [C] a series of events or chemical reactions that happens very fast,

with each one causing the next one

ˈchain ˌsaw noun [C] a tool with a motor, used for cutting down trees or cutting up wood

ˈchain ˌstore noun [C] one of a group of shops that all belong to the same company

chair¹ /tʃeə/ noun [C] ★★★
1 a piece of furniture for one person to sit on, with a back, legs, and sometimes two arms
2 the person who is in charge of a meeting, committee, company, or organization: *All questions must be addressed to the chair.* ♦ *He is the former chair of the Atomic Energy Commission.* → CHAIRMAN, CHAIRPERSON, CHAIRWOMAN
3 *British* the position of being a PROFESSOR in a university

sofa

bench

wheelchair

armchair

stool

chairs

chair² /tʃeə/ verb [T] to be the person in charge of a meeting, committee, company, or organization

chairman /ˈtʃeəmən/ (plural **chairmen** /ˈtʃeəmən/) noun [C] ★ the person who is in charge of a meeting, committee, company, or organization

chairmanship /ˈtʃeəmənʃɪp/ noun [C/U] the position of being a chairman, or the time during which someone is a chairman

chairperson /ˈtʃeəˌpɜːs(ə)n/ (plural

C

chairpersons /ˈtʃeəˌpɜːs(ə)ns/ noun [C] the person who is in charge of a meeting, committee, company, or organization

chairwoman /ˈtʃeəˌwʊmən/ (plural **chairwomen** /ˈtʃeəˌwɪmɪn/) noun [C] the woman who is in charge of a meeting, committee, company, or organization

chalet /ˈʃæleɪ/ noun [C] a wooden house in a mountain or holiday area

chalk¹ /tʃɔːk/ noun **1** [U] a type of soft white stone **2** [C/U] a stick of chalk used for writing or drawing → LONG¹

chalk² /tʃɔːk/ PHRASAL VERB ˌchalk sth ˈup achieve or win something

chalky /ˈtʃɔːki/ adj similar to chalk, or containing chalk

challenge¹ /ˈtʃælɪndʒ/ noun ★★
1 [C/U] something that needs a lot of skill, energy, and determination to deal with or achieve: *I felt I needed a new challenge at work.* ♦ *Are western nations ready to meet the environmental challenges that lie ahead?* ♦ *The new government faces the challenge of completing the building on time.*
2 [C] an action or idea that questions whether something is true, fair, accurate, legal etc: *Recent discoveries present a serious challenge to accepted views on the age of the universe.* ♦ *The strike was a direct challenge to the authority of the government.*
3 [C] an occasion when someone tries to win a game or competition

Words often used with challenge

*Adjectives often used with **challenge** (noun, sense 1)*
- **daunting, formidable, major, serious** + CHALLENGE: used about a challenge that worries or frightens you
*Verbs often used with **challenge** (noun, sense 1)*
- **accept, rise to** + CHALLENGE: deal with a challenge in a brave way
- **pose, present** + CHALLENGE: create a challenge that you must deal with
- **enjoy, relish** + CHALLENGE: enjoy being challenged

challenge² /ˈtʃælɪndʒ/ verb [T] **1** to question whether something is true, fair, accurate, legal etc: *This decision is likely to be challenged by the oil companies.* ♦ *The president has accused the governor of challenging his leadership.* **2** to invite someone to compete or fight: *The girls challenged the boys to a cricket match.*

challenging /ˈtʃælɪndʒɪŋ/ adj difficult to deal with or achieve, but interesting and enjoyable ≠ UNCHALLENGING

chamber /ˈtʃeɪmbə/ noun **1** [C] a room used for a particular purpose: *a torture chamber* ♦ *the debating chamber* **2** [C] one of the sections of a parliament: *the upper/lower chamber* **3** [C] an enclosed space, especially one inside a machine or someone's body: *the chambers of the heart* **4 chambers** [plural] *British* the offices used by judges or BARRISTERS

PHRASE **chamber of commerce** an organization of business owners whose aim is to improve conditions for business in their town

chambermaid /ˈtʃeɪmbəˌmeɪd/ noun [C] a

woman whose job is to clean the bedrooms in a hotel

ˈchamber ˌmusic noun [U] a type of classical music that is played by a small group of musicians

champ /tʃæmp/ noun [C] *informal* a CHAMPION

champagne /ʃæmˈpeɪn/ noun [U] a type of French SPARKLING wine that people drink on special occasions

champion¹ /ˈtʃæmpiən/ noun [C] ★
1 someone who has won an important competition, especially in sport: *the world heavyweight boxing champion*
2 someone who publicly supports or defends something: *a champion of the rights of developing nations*

champion² /ˈtʃæmpiən/ verb [T] to publicly support or defend something

championship /ˈtʃæmpiənʃɪp/ noun ★
1 [C] a competition to find the best player or team in a sport or game: *the World Chess Championships*
2 [singular] the position of being a champion: *Two more points and the championship will be his!*

chance¹ /tʃɑːns/ noun ★★★
1 [C] an opportunity to do something, especially something that you want to do = OPPORTUNITY: **the chance to do sth** *Students are given the chance to learn another language.* ♦ *We work together whenever we get a chance.* ♦ *I warned her that this was her last chance.*
2 [C/U] the possibility that something will happen: **a chance of (doing) sth** *I think she has a good chance of getting the job.* ♦ *(that) Is there any chance they will reverse their decision?* ♦ *He doesn't stand a chance of winning the tournament (=it is not at all likely that he will win).*
3 [U] the way that things happen without being planned or expected = LUCK: *The results may simply be due to chance.* ♦ *It was simply by chance that Nicholson was cast in the film.*

PHRASES **by any chance** *spoken* used when you are asking questions to find out whether something is true: *Do you remember his name, by any chance?*
sb's chances how likely someone is to achieve something: **sb's chances of (doing) sth** *What are their chances of survival?*
(the) chances are *spoken* used for saying that something is likely to happen but is not certain
take a chance (on) or **take chances** to do something even though it involves risk

chance² /tʃɑːns/ verb [T] to do something even though you know it involves a risk: *It looked like rain so I decided not to chance it and brought my umbrella.*

chance³ /tʃɑːns/ adj not planned or expected: *a chance meeting/discovery*

chancellor /ˈtʃɑːnsələ/ noun [C] **1** the leader of the government in some countries **2** *British* the CHANCELLOR OF THE EXCHEQUER **3** someone who is the official leader of a university

Chancellor of the Exˈchequer noun [C] the member of the British government who is responsible for taxes and for deciding how the government spends its money

chandelier /ˌʃændəˈlɪə/ noun [C] a light that hangs from a ceiling and has a lot of branches for holding lights or CANDLES

change¹ /tʃeɪndʒ/ verb ★★★

1 become different	**5** get on different vehicle
2 start sth new	**6** exchange money
3 replace sth	**+** PHRASES
4 of clothes	**+** PHRASAL VERBS

1 [I/T] to become different, or to make someone or something different: *After a few days the weather changed.* ♦ *The law was changed in 1989.* ♦ *The leaves are already starting to change colour* (=become a different colour). ♦ **change (sth) from sth to sth** *The town has changed from a small fishing village to a modern tourist centre.*

2 [I/T] to stop doing one thing and start doing something different: *Dave said he might be changing jobs.* ♦ **change (sth) to sth** *Consumers are increasingly changing to low-fat milk.*

3 [T] to replace something with a new or different thing: *Can you help me change a tyre?*

4 [I/T] to take off the clothes that you are wearing and put on different ones: *Hang on, I'll just go and change.* ♦ *I had a bath and changed my clothes.* ♦ *Have I got time to get changed before we go?* ♦ *You should change into some dry socks.*

5 [I/T] to leave one plane, train, bus etc to get on another: *We changed planes in Paris.*

6 [T] to exchange one type of money for another: *Can anyone change a ten-pound note?* ♦ *I need to change some dollars into pesos.*

PHRASES change hands to be given or sold by one person to another

change your mind to change a decision you have made or an opinion you have about something: *I've changed my mind about Steve.*

change the subject to stop talking about one thing and start talking about another
→ CHOP¹

PHRASAL VERBS ˈchange (sth) into sth to stop being in one condition or form and start being in another, or to make something do this: *At what point does boiling water change into steam?*

ˌchange ˈover to stop doing or using one thing and start doing or using something else: *When did the UK change over to the metric system?*

Other ways of saying change

- **adapt** to change something in order to make it suitable for a specific situation
- **adjust** to change something slightly so that it is exactly the way you want it
- **alter** a more formal word for 'change'
- **convert** to change something so that it can be used for a different purpose
- **modify** to make small changes to a machine or system in order to make it suitable for a different situation
- **transform** to change something completely so that it looks or works much better than before

change² /tʃeɪndʒ/ noun ★★★

1 [C/U] a situation or process in which something becomes different or is replaced, or the result of this process: *A number of changes have taken place since the 1960s.* ♦ *Older people sometimes find it hard to accept change.* ♦ *We made a few changes to the team.* ♦ *a change in the law* ♦ *a change from military to civilian rule*

2 [U] the money that someone gives back to you when you give more money than it costs to buy something: *Here's your change.*

3 [U] coins rather than notes: *I'm sorry I haven't got any change.* ♦ *Have you got change for a five-pound note* (=notes or coins of lower value that you can exchange for it)?

PHRASES a change of clothes/socks/ underwear etc another set of clothes, socks etc that you take with you so that you can wear them later

a change of heart an occasion when you change your opinion or plan

for a change instead of what usually happens: *It's nice to hear some good news for a change.*
→ SEA CHANGE

Words often used with change

Adjectives often used with change (noun, sense 1)
■ **dramatic, fundamental, major, radical** + CHANGE: used about big changes

changeable /ˈtʃeɪndʒəb(ə)l/ adj tending to change suddenly and often
=UNPREDICTABLE

changed /tʃeɪndʒd/ adj different from before
≠ UNCHANGED

changeover /ˈtʃeɪndʒˌəʊvə/ noun [C] a change from one method, system, or activity to another

changing room /ˈtʃeɪndʒɪŋ ˌruːm/ noun [C] **1** a room in which people change their clothes before and after they play a sport **2** *British* a room in a shop in which people can try on clothes before they buy them=FITTING ROOM

channel¹ /ˈtʃæn(ə)l/ noun [C] ★★

1 a television station and the programmes that it broadcasts: *What's on the other channel?*

2 a way of communicating or expressing something: *It is important to keep channels of communication open.* ♦ *a channel for her creative energies*

3 a narrow passage made in the ground so that water can go along it

4 a narrow area of water that joins two seas

channel² /ˈtʃæn(ə)l/ verb [T] **1** to use money or supplies for a particular purpose: *The company has channelled £1.2 million into developing new products.* **2** to use your energy, ability, feelings, or ideas for a particular purpose

Channel, the /ˈtʃæn(ə)l/ the narrow area of sea between England and France

channeled /ˈtʃæn(ə)ld/ an American past tense and past participle of **channel**

channeling /ˈtʃæn(ə)lɪŋ/ an American present participle of **channel**

ˌ**Channel Tunnel, the** a train tunnel under

C

the English Channel between England and France

chant /tʃɑːnt/ verb [I/T] to shout or sing a word or phrase many times —**chant** noun [C]

Chanukah /ˈhɑːnəkə/ another spelling of **Hanukkah**

chaos /ˈkeɪɒs/ noun [U] a situation in which everything is confused and not organized

chaotic /keɪˈɒtɪk/ adj happening in a confused way and without any order or organization —**chaotically** /keɪˈɒtɪkli/ adv

chap /tʃæp/ noun [C] *British informal old-fashioned* a man

chapel /ˈtʃæp(ə)l/ noun [C] a small church, or a special room used as a church

chaplain /ˈtʃæplɪn/ noun [C] a priest who works in an institution such as a school or hospital, or in the army

chapped /tʃæpt/ adj chapped skin is dry and painful because of cold weather

chapter /ˈtʃæptə/ noun [C] ★★★
1 one of the sections of a book: *See Chapter Three for more details.*
2 a period of someone's life, or a period in history: *The war was now entering its final chapter.*

character /ˈkærɪktə/ noun ★★★

1 personality	**5** unusual person
2 qualities of sth	**6** letter/number/symbol
3 sb in book, film etc	**7** determination
4 attractive qualities	

1 [C] the qualities that make up someone's personality: *This selfishness was one aspect of Steve's character that I didn't like.* ♦ *Why did Simon refuse? It seems so out of character* (=not typical of his usual behaviour).
2 [C/U] the qualities that make something clearly different from anything else: *The two villages are similar in size but very different in character.*
3 [C] a person in a book, play, film etc: *The film's main character is played by George Clooney.*
4 [U] qualities that make someone or something good, interesting, or attractive: *a traditional hotel with a lot of character and charm*
5 [C] a person of a particular type: *a shady/suspicious character*
6 [C] a letter, number, or symbol that is written or printed: *Your computer password may be up to 12 characters long.*
7 [U] the qualities of being brave and determined: *She showed real character in standing up to her parents.*

characterise /ˈkærɪktəˌraɪz/ a British spelling of **characterize**

characteristic¹ /ˌkærɪktəˈrɪstɪk/ noun [C] a typical quality or feature: *the main characteristics of 20th-century culture*

characteristic² /ˌkærɪktəˈrɪstɪk/ adj typical of someone or something ≠ UNCHARACTERISTIC: *Sue answered with her characteristic truthfulness.* —**characteristically** /ˌkærɪktəˈrɪstɪkli/ adv

characterization /ˌkærɪktəraɪˈzeɪʃ(ə)n/ noun [U] the way in which a writer creates CHARACTERS

characterize /ˈkærɪktəˌraɪz/ verb [T] **1** be

characterized by to have something as a typical quality or feature: *The 1980s were characterized by high inflation and high unemployment.* **2 be characterized as** to be described as a particular type of person or thing: *The military is usually characterized as being conservative.*

charade /ʃəˈrɑːd/ noun [C] an attempt to pretend that a situation is good when it is not

charades /ʃəˈrɑːdz/ noun [U] a game in which you can use only actions to help the other players to guess a word or phrase

charcoal /ˈtʃɑːkəʊl/ noun [U] a black substance made from burnt wood. It is used as a fuel and for drawing.

charge¹ /tʃɑːdʒ/ noun ★★★

1 amount of money	**4** an attack running fast
2 when sb is accused	**5** amount of electricity
3 a claim sb/sth is bad	**+ PHRASES**

1 [C/U] an amount of money that you have to pay when you visit a place, or when someone does something for you: *There is no **charge for** using the library.* ♦ *The organization provides a range of services free of charge* (=with no charge). ♦ *There's a small **admission charge**.*
2 [C] an official statement that accuses someone of committing a crime: *murder/corruption/fraud charges* ♦ *In the end we decided not to **press charges*** (=officially accuse someone of a crime). ♦ *They faced **charges of** conspiracy and murder.* ♦ *The investigation resulted in criminal **charges against** three police officers.*
3 [C] a claim that someone or something is bad, or that they have done something bad: *charges of racism* ♦ *+(that) The leadership rejected charges that its policies were not effective.*
4 [C] an attack by people or animals running very fast towards someone or something
5 [singular/U] the amount of electricity that something holds or carries
PHRASES in charge (of) if you are in charge, you have control over someone or something and are responsible for them: *Who's in charge here?* ♦ *He was **put in charge of** the whole investigation.*
take charge (of) to take control and become responsible for someone or something: *Heather arrived and took charge of the project.*

charge² /tʃɑːdʒ/ verb ★★★

1 ask sb to pay money	**4** run to attack
2 arrange for sb to pay	**5** move quickly
3 accuse sb of crime	**6** put electricity into

1 [I/T] to ask someone to pay an amount of money for something: *How much do you charge for delivery?* ♦ *charge sb sth (for sth) They charged us £20 for three drinks.* ♦ *be charged at sth Phone calls are charged at 36p per minute.*
2 [T] to arrange to pay for something later: *charge sth to sb/sth The flights were charged to his personal account.*
3 [T] to accuse someone of committing a crime: *Two men have been charged in*

connection with the fire. ♦ **charge sb with sth** *The police have charged him with murder.*

4 [I/T] to attack someone or something by running very fast towards them

5 [I] to move somewhere quickly and carelessly: *You can't just go charging into the meeting.*

6 [I/T] to put electricity into a BATTERY: *The phone won't work if it isn't charged.*

'charge ,card noun [C] a CREDIT CARD that you can use only in a particular shop

charisma /kə'rızmə/ noun [U] a strong personal quality that makes other people like you and feel attracted to you=CHARM —**charismatic** /,kærız'mætık/ adj

charitable /'tʃærɪtəb(ə)l/ adj **1** intended to give money and help to people who need it **2** kind to other people and not judging them too severely ≠ UNCHARITABLE

charity /'tʃærəti/ noun ★★
1 [C/U] an organization that gives money and help to people who need it: *a registered charity*
2 [U] money or food that is given to people who need it: *The event raised £59,000 for charity.*
3 [U] kind behaviour

'charity ,shop noun [C] *British* a shop that sells used things. The money that it receives is given to organizations that help people.

charm¹ /tʃɑːm/ noun **1** [C/U] an attractive quality: *President Roosevelt's charm and humour* ♦ *The building has kept its traditional charm.* **2** [C] an object that brings luck or has magic powers

charm² /tʃɑːm/ verb [T] to make someone like you, or make them want to do something for you: *He charmed my mother into giving him money.*

charmed /tʃɑːmd/ adj extremely lucky: *a charmed life*

charming /'tʃɑːmɪŋ/ adj attractive and pleasant: *a charming man/smile* ♦ *a charming little restaurant*

chart¹ /tʃɑːt/ noun **1** [C] a list, drawing, or GRAPH that shows information **2** [C] a map used for planning a journey by ship or aircraft **3 the charts** [plural] a list of the CDs that people have bought the most copies of in the previous week

chart² /tʃɑːt/ verb [T] **1** to record how something develops and changes: *A team visits every week to chart their progress.* **2** to make a map of an area

charter¹ /'tʃɑːtə/ noun **1** [C] a document that describes the aims of an organization or the rights of a group of people **2** [C/U] the process of hiring a boat, plane, or bus, or the vehicle that is hired

charter² /'tʃɑːtə/ verb [T] to hire a boat, plane, or bus

chartered accountant /,tʃɑːtəd ə'kaʊntənt/ noun [C] *British* an ACCOUNTANT who has passed a professional examination

'charter ,flight noun [C] a plane journey that is arranged by a travel company

chase¹ /tʃeɪs/ verb ★
1 [I/T] to follow someone or something quickly in order to catch them=PURSUE: *The band have often been chased down the street by enthusiastic fans.* ♦ *I chased after*

the robbers for more than a mile.
2 [T] to follow someone or something quickly in order to make them go away: *We chased the cat out of the house.* ♦ *Suddenly a man came out and **chased** the kids **away**.*
3 [T] to try hard to get something such as a job, prize, or money: *Tiger Woods was chasing another European title.*

PHRASAL VERB ,chase sb/sth 'up to ask someone who should have done something why they have not done it: *Why don't you chase up those software people today?*

chase

chase² /tʃeɪs/ noun **1** [C] the action of following someone or something quickly because you want to catch them: *a high-speed car chase* **2** [singular] the act of trying to get something that you want

chasm /'kæz(ə)m/ noun [C] **1** a very big difference that separates one person or group from another=GULF **2** a very deep crack in rock or ice

chassis /'ʃæsi/ (plural **chassis** /'ʃæsiz/) noun [C] the frame and wheels of a vehicle

chat¹ /tʃæt/ verb [I] ★
1 to talk in a friendly way: *They sat waiting, chatting about their families.* ♦ *She laughed and chatted happily with the other women.*
2 *computing* to exchange messages with someone using computers, in a way that lets you see each other's messages immediately

PHRASAL VERB ,chat sb 'up *British informal* to start a conversation with someone because you want to have a sexual relationship with them

chat² /tʃæt/ noun [C/U] a friendly conversation: *I had an interesting chat with his sister.*

'chat ,room noun [C] a WEBSITE that people can use for exchanging messages → NEWSGROUP

'chat ,show noun [C] *British* a television or radio programme in which famous people talk about themselves and their work

chatter /'tʃætə/ verb [I] **1** to talk in a fast informal way about unimportant subjects **2** if your teeth chatter, they knock together from fear or cold —**chatter** noun [U]

chatty /'tʃæti/ adj **1** someone who is chatty enjoys talking a lot **2** a chatty writing style is friendly and informal

chauffeur /'ʃəʊfə, ʃəʊ'fɜː/ noun [C] someone whose job is to drive a rich or important person around in their car —**chauffeured** /'ʃəʊfəd/ adj: *a chauffeured limousine*

chauvinist /'ʃəʊvɪnɪst/ noun [C] someone who believes that their own country, race, sex, or group is better than any other —**chauvinism** noun [U], **chauvinistic** adj

C

cheap¹ /tʃiːp/ adj ★★★

1 not expensive	**4** without value
2 not of good quality	**5** against spending money
3 unkind/unfair	

1 not expensive: *People should have access to cheap, fresh food.*
2 not expensive and not of good quality: *cheap wine*
3 a cheap action or remark is unfair or unkind
4 not considered important or valuable: *It happened during the war when life was cheap.*
5 not willing to spend money: *She's so cheap she wouldn't even buy her own mother a birthday card.*
—**cheaply** adv

cheap² /tʃiːp/ adv at a low price: *I can't believe I managed to get it so cheap.*

cheat¹ /tʃiːt/ verb ★
1 [I] to behave dishonestly, or to not obey rules: *Kids have always found ways of cheating in school exams.*
2 [T] to treat someone dishonestly: *He trusted these people and they cheated him.* ♦ **cheat sb (out) of sth** *He was accused of cheating investors out of their life savings.*
3 [I] to do something that is not correct but makes it easier to succeed: *You can cheat by adding a little flour.*

PHRASAL VERB **cheat on sb** to secretly have sex with someone other than your husband, wife, or partner: *He discovered she'd been cheating on him.*

cheat² /tʃiːt/ noun [C] someone who cheats

check¹ /tʃek/ verb ★★★
1 [I/T] to examine something in order to get information, or to find out whether it is good or correct: *Always check your spelling.* ♦ *You should have your sight checked regularly.* ♦ *The doctor checked for a pulse.* ♦ **check sth for sth** *Check our website for details of our special offers.*
2 [I/T] to make certain of something, for example by looking at the information again or by asking someone: *I think he's gone home – I'll just check.* ♦ *I'll check the dates.* ♦ **+that** *First, check that you have everything you need.* ♦ **+if/whether** *Could you please check whether a package has arrived for me?* ♦ *For further information, check with your local tax office.* ♦ *He checked to see if Gail was still there.*
3 [T] to give your bags and cases to an official at an airport so that they can be put on a plane: *How many bags do you have to check?*
4 [T] to stop something bad from happening or getting worse: *They are taking measures to check the spread of the disease.*

PHRASAL VERBS **check sth against sth** to find out whether information is accurate or useful by comparing it with other information

check in 1 to arrive at a hotel and give your personal details to the person at the RECEPTION desk: *Have you checked in yet?* **2** to arrive at an airport and show your ticket to an official

check sth in same as **check¹** 3: *When you check in your luggage you will be given a receipt for each bag.*

check into sth to arrive at a hotel and give your personal details to the person at the RECEPTION desk: *We won't be able to check into the hotel until 3 o'clock.*

check on sb/sth to look at someone or something so that you are certain they are safe, satisfactory etc: *I sent Michael to check on the kids.*

check out to leave a hotel after you have paid the bill: *Joan had already checked out of the hotel.*

check sb/sth out to examine someone or something in order to be certain that everything is correct, true, or satisfactory: *I've been taking loads of photographs, just to check out the camera.*

check sth over to look at something in order to make certain that it is good or correct: *Check over your writing for spelling mistakes.*

check up on sb to find out information about someone, especially secretly

check² /tʃek/ noun ★★

1 examination of sb/sth	**4** amount you owe
2 sth controlling sth else	**5** cheque
3 pattern of squares	**+** PHRASE

1 [C] an examination of something that is intended to find out whether it is good or correct: *a check for errors* ♦ *routine checks on the condition of the planes* ♦ *They'll be doing a sound check before the concert.*
→ SPOT CHECK
2 [C] something that controls another thing and stops it from becoming worse or more extreme: *Economic forces act as a check on political power.*
3 [C/U] a pattern of squares: *a sheet with red and white checks*
4 [C] American the BILL in a restaurant: *Could we get the check, please?*
5 the American spelling of **cheque**

PHRASE **keep sb/sth in check** to control someone or something that might cause damage or harm: *attempts to keep global warming in check*

checked /tʃekt/ adj printed or woven in a pattern of squares: *a red and blue checked shirt*

checkers /ˈtʃekəz/ noun [U] American the game of DRAUGHTS

check-in noun [singular/U] the place that you go to when you arrive at an airport or hotel, or the process that you go through before you go to your flight or room

checking account noun [C] American a CURRENT ACCOUNT

checklist /ˈtʃeklɪst/ noun [C] a list of all the things that you need to do or consider

checkout /ˈtʃekaʊt/ noun **1** [C] the place where you pay in a supermarket or other large shop **2** [C/U] the time when you have to leave a hotel room

checkpoint /ˈtʃekpɔɪnt/ noun [C] a place where traffic can be stopped by soldiers or police

check-up noun [C] an examination that a doctor or DENTIST does in order to make sure that you are healthy: *You should have regular dental check-ups.*

cheddar /ˈtʃedə/ noun [U] a type of hard yellow cheese

cheek /tʃiːk/ noun ★★
1 [C] the soft part on each side of your face below your eyes: *Sarah kissed her on the cheek.* —*picture* → C14
2 [singular/U] behaviour that is rude or does not show respect: *He had the cheek to suggest that I should be the one to apologize!*

cheekbone /'tʃiːkbəʊn/ noun [C] the bone in your cheek

cheeky /'tʃiːki/ adj behaving in a way that does not show respect, especially towards someone who is older or more important —**cheekily** adv

cheer¹ /tʃɪə/ verb [I/T] to give a loud shout of happiness or approval: *The crowd cheered and threw flowers.*
PHRASAL VERBS **cheer sb on** to shout loudly in order to encourage someone
cheer (sb) up to become less sad, or to make someone feel less sad: *I tried to cheer him up, but he just kept staring out of the window.*

cheer² /tʃɪə/ noun [C] a loud shout of happiness or approval → CHEERS

cheerful /'tʃɪəf(ə)l/ adj 1 behaving in a happy friendly way: *Stephen was a cheerful, affectionate child.* 2 pleasant or enjoyable, and making you feel happy: *bright cheerful colours* —**cheerfully** adv, **cheerfulness** noun [U]

cheerleader /'tʃɪəˌliːdə/ noun [C] one of a group of young women who sing and dance together at a sports event

cheers /tʃɪəz/ interjection 1 used for expressing good wishes before you drink something 2 *British spoken* thank you

cheery /'tʃɪəri/ adj feeling or showing happiness

cheese /tʃiːz/ noun [C/U] ★★ a solid food made from milk: *a slice of cheese* → BIG CHEESE

cheeseburger /'tʃiːzˌbɜːgə/ noun [C] a BURGER with a piece of cheese on top of the meat

cheesecake /'tʃiːzˌkeɪk/ noun [C/U] a type of sweet cake made with soft cheese

cheesy /'tʃiːzi/ adj *informal* lacking style or good quality and slightly silly: *cheesy songs*

cheetah /'tʃiːtə/ noun [C] a large African wild cat that can run extremely fast —*picture* → C12

chef /ʃef/ noun [C] someone whose job is to cook food in a restaurant

chemical¹ /'kemɪk(ə)l/ noun [C] ★★★ a substance used in chemistry, or one produced by a process that involves chemistry: *toxic chemicals* ♦ *the chemical industry*

chemical² /'kemɪk(ə)l/ adj involving chemistry, or produced by a method used in chemistry: *chemical processes*

chemist /'kemɪst/ noun [C] 1 **chemist** or **chemist's** *British* a shop that sells medicines, beauty products, and TOILETRIES =PHARMACY 2 *British* someone whose job is preparing and selling medicines in a chemist's shop=PHARMACIST 3 a scientist who studies chemistry

chemistry /'kemɪstri/ noun [U] 1 the scientific study of the structure of substances and the way they react with other substances 2 the chemical structure of something and the reactions that take place in it 3 the emotional relationship between people

chemotherapy /ˌkiːməʊ'θerəpi/ noun [U] the treatment of cancer using drugs

cheque /tʃek/ noun [C] ★ a piece of printed paper that you can use instead of money: *a cheque for £50* ♦ *Can I pay by cheque?*

chequebook /'tʃekbʊk/ noun [C] a book of CHEQUES

cheque card noun [C] a card from your bank that you show in a shop when you write a cheque

chequered /'tʃekəd/ adj a chequered pattern consists of squares

cherish /'tʃerɪʃ/ verb [T] 1 to think that something is very important and to want to keep it: *I cherished my independence.* 2 to look after someone or something because you love them very much

cherry /'tʃeri/ noun [C] 1 a small round red or black fruit —*picture* → C10 2 a tree that produces cherries, or the wood from this tree

chess /tʃes/ noun [U] a game that two people play on a board with black and white squares. The pieces that you use have different shapes and move in different ways. —*picture* → C16

chessman /'tʃesˌmæn/ (plural **chessmen** /'tʃesˌmen/) or **chesspiece** /'tʃesˌpiːs/ noun [C] one of the pieces used for playing CHESS —*picture* → C16

chest /tʃest/ noun [C] ★★★
1 the upper front part of your body between your neck and your stomach: *a broad/hairy chest* ♦ *chest pains* —*picture* → C14
2 a large strong box, used for moving or storing things
PHRASES **chest of drawers** a piece of wooden furniture with several drawers for storing clothes
get something off your chest to talk to someone about something that has been worrying you, so that you feel better about it

chestnut /'tʃesˌnʌt/ noun [C] 1 a large smooth red-brown nut that you can eat 2 **chestnut** or **chestnut tree** a tall tree that produces chestnuts —*picture* → C9

chew /tʃuː/ verb [I/T] ★
1 to use your teeth to bite food in your mouth into small pieces: *She chewed her food slowly.*
2 to bite something continuously but not swallow it: *We're not allowed to chew gum in class.* ♦ *The dog was chewing on an old bone.*

chewing gum /'tʃuːɪŋ ˌgʌm/ noun [U] a type of sweet that you chew for a long time but do not swallow

chewy /'tʃuːi/ adj chewy food needs to be CHEWED a lot before you can swallow it

chic /ʃiːk/ adj fashionable and attractive in style

chick /tʃɪk/ noun [C] a baby bird

chicken¹ /'tʃɪkɪn/ noun ★★
1 [C] a bird that is kept for its eggs and meat —*picture* → C12
2 [U] the meat of a chicken: *fried/roast/grilled chicken* → COUNT¹

chicken² /'tʃɪkɪn/ adj *informal* not brave

enough to do something: *I didn't want the others to think I was chicken.*

chicken³ /ˈtʃɪkɪn/ PHRASAL VERB ˌchicken ˈout *informal* to not do something because you are too frightened

chickenpox /ˈtʃɪkɪnˌpɒks/ noun [U] an infectious disease that most children get once, in which the skin is covered with red spots

chickpea /ˈtʃɪkˌpiː/ noun [C/U] a round yellow-brown seed that can be cooked and eaten

chief¹ /tʃiːf/ adj ★★
1 main, or most important: *Unemployment was the chief cause of poverty during the 1930s.* ♦ *the company's chief competitor*
2 highest in authority, position, or rank: *the government's Chief Medical Officer*

chief² /tʃiːf/ noun [C] **1** the person who is in charge of an organization or department, or who has the main responsibility for something: *the chief of the Red Cross mission in the war zone* **2** the leader of a TRIBE = CHIEFTAIN

ˌchief exˈecutive noun [C] the most senior person in a company or organization who is responsible for running it = CEO

chiefly /ˈtʃiːfli/ adv mainly or mostly, but not completely: *He will be remembered chiefly for his years of dedicated service to the school.*

chieftain /ˈtʃiːftən/ noun [C] the leader of a TRIBE

chiffon /ˈʃɪfɒn/ noun [U] very thin transparent cloth made from silk or NYLON

child /tʃaɪld/ (plural **children** /ˈtʃɪldrən/) noun [C] ★★★
1 a young person from the time when they are born until they are about 14 years old: *The nursery has places for 30 children.* ♦ *He can't understand – he's just a child.*
2 someone's son or daughter of any age: *All of our children are grown and married.* ♦ *They're expecting their second child in May.* ♦ *I was an only child* (=with no brothers or sisters).

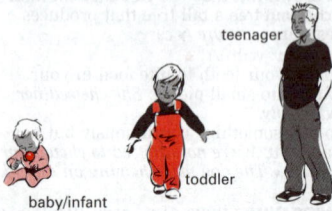

teenager

toddler

baby/infant

ˈchild aˌbuse noun [U] bad treatment of a child by an adult

childbirth /ˈtʃaɪldˌbɜːθ/ noun [U] the process of giving birth to a baby

childcare /ˈtʃaɪldˌkeə/ noun [U] the job of looking after children, especially while their parents are working: *the high cost of childcare*

childhood /ˈtʃaɪldhʊd/ noun [C/U] the time of your life when you are a child: *We spent our childhood in a small town in the mountains.*

childish /ˈtʃaɪldɪʃ/ adj **1** behaving in a silly and

annoying way, like a small child **2** typical of a child —**childishly** adv, **childishness** noun [U]

childlike /ˈtʃaɪldlaɪk/ adj similar to the way that a child looks, behaves, or thinks: *childlike excitement*

childminder /ˈtʃaɪldˌmaɪndə/ noun [C] *British* someone whose job is to look after children while their parents are at work, usually in his or her own home

childproof /ˈtʃaɪldpruːf/ adj something that is childproof is designed so that children cannot use it, open it, or hurt themselves on it: *a bottle of pills with a childproof lid*

children the plural of **child**

ˈchild supˌport noun [U] money that a parent pays to support a child who does not live with him or her

chill¹ /tʃɪl/ verb [I/T] if you chill food or drink, or if it chills, it becomes cold enough to eat or drink **2** [I] *informal* to relax and stop being angry or nervous, or to spend time relaxing: *I'm just going to chill this weekend.*
PHRASAL VERB **chill out** *informal* same as **chill¹** 2

chill² /tʃɪl/ noun **1** [singular] a feeling of being cold: *a chill in the air* **2** [C] a minor illness like a COLD **3** [C] a feeling of fear: *The cry sent a chill down her spine.*

chilli /ˈtʃɪli/ (plural **chillies**) noun **1** chilli or **chilli pepper** [C] a red or green vegetable with a very hot taste **2** [U] a Mexican meal made from meat, beans, and chillies cooked together

chilling /ˈtʃɪlɪŋ/ adj making you feel suddenly very frightened or worried: *The chilling truth is that the killers are still out there.* —**chillingly** adv

chilly /ˈtʃɪli/ adj **1** cold enough to be unpleasant: *The evenings are getting chilly.* **2** unfriendly

chime /tʃaɪm/ verb [I/T] to make a high ringing sound like a bell: *Somewhere a clock chimed midnight.* —**chime** noun [C]
PHRASAL VERB **chime in** to join a conversation by saying something

chimney /ˈtʃɪmni/ noun [C] a passage that takes smoke from a fire up through a building and out through the roof —*picture* → C1

chimpanzee /ˌtʃɪmpænˈziː/ noun [C] an African APE (=animal like a monkey)

chin /tʃɪn/ noun [C] ★★ the centre of the bottom part of your face, below your mouth and above your neck —*picture* → C14

china /ˈtʃaɪnə/ noun [U] plates and cups of good quality

chink /tʃɪŋk/ noun [C] **1** a very small space in a wall or between two things **2** the sound that is made when two glass or metal objects hit each other = CLINK

chinos /ˈtʃiːnəʊz/ noun [plural] trousers made from thick strong cotton cloth

chip¹ /tʃɪp/ noun [C] ★★

1 potato cooked in oil	5 crisp
2 in computers	6 in games for money
3 small piece	+ PHRASES
4 missing bit of cup etc	

1 *British* a long thin piece of potato cooked in hot oil: *fish and chips*

2 a very small piece of SILICON that is marked with electronic connections. It is used in computers and other machines =MICROCHIP, SILICON CHIP

3 a small piece of something such as wood or glass that has broken off something: *wood chips*

4 a place on a plate, cup etc where a small piece of it has broken off: *The cup had a tiny chip in it.*

5 *American* a CRISP

6 a small piece of plastic that people use instead of money when they are GAMBLING (=playing games for money)

PHRASES **have a chip on your shoulder** to feel offended and angry whenever people mention a particular subject

when the chips are down *spoken* used for saying what happens when a situation becomes difficult

→ BLUE CHIP

chip² /tʃɪp/ verb [I/T] if something hard chips, or if you chip it, a small piece of it breaks off: *These cups chip easily.*

PHRASAL VERBS **chip sth away 1** to gradually make something weaker, smaller, or less effective: *Her comments were beginning to chip away at his self-confidence.* **2** to remove small pieces from something hard by hitting it with a tool: *She was chipping away at the ice with a shovel.*

chip in *informal* to add something to someone else's conversation

chip in (sth) *informal* if people chip in, they each give some money to help to pay for something: *The three of us chipped in and bought the boat for Dad.*

chipmunk /'tʃɪpmʌŋk/ noun [C] a small furry Asian and North American animal with bands of darker colour on its back

chiropodist /kɪ'rɒpədɪst/ noun [C] someone whose job is to treat problems with people's feet —**chiropody** /kɪ'rɒpədi/ noun [U]

chirp /tʃɜːp/ verb [I] when a bird or an insect chirps, it makes a short high sound —**chirp** noun [C]

chirpy /'tʃɜːpi/ adj happy and lively

chisel /'tʃɪz(ə)l/ noun [C] a tool with a flat metal blade used for cutting wood or stone

chit-chat noun [U] *informal* friendly conversation about things that are not very important

chivalry /'ʃɪvəlri/ noun [U] polite and kind behaviour by men towards women —**chivalrous** /'ʃɪvəlrəs/ adj

chives /tʃaɪvz/ noun [plural] a plant with long thin leaves that taste like onion

chlorinated /'klɔːrɪneɪtɪd/ adj chlorinated water has had chlorine added to it in order to kill bacteria

chlorine /'klɔːriːn/ noun [U] a gas that is used for killing bacteria in water

chocolate /'tʃɒklət/ noun ★★
1 [U] a sweet brown food that is eaten as a sweet or used for flavouring other food: *a bar of chocolate ♦ chocolate cake*
2 [C] a small sweet made from chocolate: *a box of chocolates*
→ HOT CHOCOLATE

choice¹ /tʃɔɪs/ noun ★★★
1 [singular/U] the opportunity or right to choose between different things: *We try to provide greater choice for our customers. ♦ Students have a choice between studying French or German. ♦ These people have the choice of whether to buy a house or rent one. ♦ If you were given the choice, would you prefer a cat or a dog? ♦ I had no choice – I had to believe what he said.*
2 [C] a decision to choose someone or something: *He was facing a difficult choice between staying with his family or working abroad. ♦ Our childhood experiences can influence our choice of career. ♦ He wants people to make their own choices.*
3 [C] a range of things that you can choose from: *The restaurant offers a good choice of dishes. ♦ London has a wide choice of cinemas and theatres.*
4 [C] someone or something that you choose: *Greece is a popular choice for a family holiday. ♦ I think Edinburgh University would be my first choice.*
PHRASE **by choice** if you do something by choice, you do it because you want to and not because you have to

choice² /tʃɔɪs/ adj *formal* of very high quality: *the choicest ingredients*

choir /kwaɪə/ noun [C] a group of singers who perform together, for example in a church or school: *the church/cathedral/school choir*

choke¹ /tʃəʊk/ verb **1** [I/T] if you choke, or if something chokes you, you cannot breathe because there is not enough air, or because something is blocking your throat: *Joe took a bite of the steak and started to choke. ♦ Ruth almost choked on a mouthful of cake.* **2** [T] to squeeze someone's neck so that they cannot breathe

PHRASAL VERBS **choke sth back** to stop yourself from showing a feeling or emotion: *Ms Ross choked back tears as she described what had happened.*

choke (sb) up if someone chokes up, or if something chokes them up, they cannot speak because they are starting to cry

choke² /tʃəʊk/ noun [C] the part of a vehicle that helps it to start by reducing the amount of air going into the engine —*picture* → C6

choked /tʃəʊkt/ or **choked up** adj *informal* **1** feeling so sad, angry, or excited that you find it difficult to speak **2** full of something: *streets choked with traffic*

cholera /'kɒlərə/ noun [U] a serious disease that affects your stomach and INTESTINES

cholesterol /kə'lestərɒl/ noun [U] a substance in your blood that can cause heart disease if you have too much of it

choose /tʃuːz/ (past tense **chose** /tʃəʊz/; past participle **chosen** /'tʃəʊz(ə)n/) verb [I/T] ★★★
1 to decide which person or thing you want from a number of people or things: *Do you feel that you chose the wrong career? ♦ There is a huge range of holidays to choose from. ♦ She is forced to choose between her husband and her parents. ♦ +which/where/whether etc How do you choose which car you are going to buy? ♦ choose sb/sth out of sb/sth The winner was chosen out of thousands who sent in photos.*
2 to decide to do something: **choose to do sth**

C

More and more people are choosing to live alone.

PHRASE **choose your words (carefully)** to think carefully about what you are saying

choosy /ˈtʃuːzi/ adj someone who is choosy has definite ideas about what they like and is not willing to accept other things

chop¹ /tʃɒp/ verb [T] to cut something such as food or wood into pieces: *Chop the meat into small cubes.* —picture → c2

PHRASE **chop and change** British informal to keep changing from one thing to another

PHRASAL VERBS **chop sth down** to make a tree or tall plant fall down by cutting through it

chop sth off to remove something by cutting

chop sth up same as **chop¹**: *Sarah was busy chopping up onions.*

chop² /tʃɒp/ noun [C] **1** a small piece of meat with a bone in it: *lamb/pork chops* **2** an act of hitting someone or something hard with the side of your hand or a sharp tool

chopper /ˈtʃɒpə/ noun [C] informal a helicopter

choppy /ˈtʃɒpi/ adj choppy water has a lot of waves because the wind is blowing across it

chopsticks /ˈtʃɒpˌstɪks/ noun [plural] a pair of thin sticks used in East Asian cultures for eating food

choral /ˈkɔːrəl/ adj sung by a CHOIR: *choral music/singing*

chord /kɔːd/ noun [C] two or more musical notes played together

PHRASE **strike/touch a chord (with sb)** to produce an emotion such as sympathy in someone

chore /tʃɔː/ noun [C] an ordinary, boring, or unpleasant job that must be done: *You can go and play after you've done your chores.*

choreography /ˌkɒriˈɒɡrəfi/ noun [U] the art of planning the movements of dancers, or the steps that the dancers perform —**choreographer** noun [C], **choreograph** /ˈkɒriəˌɡrɑːf/ verb [T]

chorus /ˈkɔːrəs/ noun [C] **1** the part of a song that is repeated several times **2** an opinion that several people express at the same time: *a chorus of disapproval* **3** a piece of music that is sung by a large group of people: *the Prisoners' Chorus from* Fidelio **4** a large group of people who sing together

chose the past tense of **choose**

chosen the past participle of **choose**

Christ /kraɪst/ Jesus Christ, whose ideas the Christian religion is based on

christen /ˈkrɪs(ə)n/ verb [T] **1** to perform a religious ceremony in which a baby is made a member of the Christian religion and is given a name=BAPTIZE **2** to give a name to someone or something

christening /ˈkrɪs(ə)nɪŋ/ noun [C] a religious ceremony during which a baby is made a member of the Christian religion and is given a name=BAPTISM

Christian /ˈkrɪstʃən/ noun [C] someone whose religion is Christianity —**Christian** adj

Christianity /ˌkrɪstiˈænɪti/ noun [U] the religion that is based on the ideas of Jesus Christ

Christian name noun [C] someone's first name, or the name that is not someone's family name

Christmas /ˈkrɪsməs/ noun [C/U] ★★★
1 25 December, celebrated by Christians as the day that Jesus Christ was born: *Did you get some nice Christmas presents this year?*
2 the period before and after 25 December: *We spent Christmas abroad last year.*

Christmas card noun [C] a card that you send to your friends and family at Christmas

Christmas carol noun [C] a song that people sing at Christmas

Christmas Day noun [C/U] 25 December, celebrated by Christians as the day that Jesus Christ was born

Christmas Eve noun [C/U] the day or evening before Christmas Day

Christmas tree noun [C] a tree that people cover with lights and other decorations at Christmas

chrome /krəʊm/ noun [U] a hard metal substance used for covering other metals to make them shiny

chromosome /ˈkrəʊməˌsəʊm/ noun [C] one of the parts of all living cells that contains genes

chronic /ˈkrɒnɪk/ adj **1** a chronic illness or pain is serious and lasts for a long time **2** a chronic problem is always happening and is very difficult to solve: *chronic energy shortages*

chronicle /ˈkrɒnɪk(ə)l/ noun [C] a record of events that happened in the past, in the order in which they happened —**chronicle** verb [T]

chronological /ˌkrɒnəˈlɒdʒɪk(ə)l/ adj arranged or described in the order in which events happened —**chronologically** /ˌkrɒnəˈlɒdʒɪkli/ adv

chrysanthemum /krɪˈsænθɪməm/ noun [C] a plant with large round brightly coloured flowers —picture → c9

chubby /ˈtʃʌbi/ adj informal slightly fat

chuck /tʃʌk/ verb [T] informal **1** to throw something **2** to get rid of something that you do not want **3** British to end a relationship with someone

PHRASAL VERBS **chuck sth away** informal same as **chuck** 2

chuck sth in British informal to leave something, or to stop doing something

chuck sth out informal **1** to force someone to leave a place or a job **2** same as **chuck** 2

chuckle /ˈtʃʌk(ə)l/ verb [I] to laugh quietly —**chuckle** noun [C]

chuffed /tʃʌft/ adj British informal very pleased about something

chug /tʃʌɡ/ verb [I] if a vehicle chugs, it moves slowly making a series of low sounds

chunk /tʃʌŋk/ noun [C] **1** a large thick piece of something: *chunks of meat* **2** a large amount or part of something

chunky /ˈtʃʌŋki/ adj thick and square in shape

church /tʃɜːtʃ/ noun ★★★
1 [C/U] a building that Christians go to in order to worship: *the church choir* ♦ *She doesn't go to church very often these days.*
2 [C] a group of Christian churches with its

own particular beliefs and structures: *the Roman Catholic Church*

PHRASES **the Church of England** the official Christian Church in England
the Church of Scotland the official Christian Church in Scotland

churchgoer /ˈtʃɜːtʃˌɡəʊə/ noun [C] someone who goes to church regularly

churchyard /ˈtʃɜːtʃˌjɑːd/ noun [C] the area of land around a church where dead people are buried

churlish /ˈtʃɜːlɪʃ/ adj rude and unfriendly

churn¹ /tʃɜːn/ verb **1** [I/T] if a liquid churns, or if something churns it, it moves around violently **2** [I] if your stomach churns, you feel sick **3** [T] to mix milk or cream in a special container in order to make butter
PHRASAL VERBS **churn sth out** to produce something in large quantities quickly and often carelessly
churn sth up *same as* **churn¹** 1

churn² /tʃɜːn/ noun [C] a container in which butter is made

chute /ʃuːt/ noun [C] a tube or narrow open structure that people or things slide down

chutney /ˈtʃʌtni/ noun [C/U] a cold food made from fruit, SPICES, and VINEGAR. You eat it with meat or cheese.

CIA, the /ˌsiː aɪ ˈeɪ/ the Central Intelligence Agency: a US government organization that collects secret information about other countries and protects secret information about the US → FBI

CID, the /ˌsiː aɪ ˈdiː/ the Criminal Investigation Department: the department of the police in the UK that is responsible for solving serious crimes

cider /ˈsaɪdə/ noun [U] **1** an alcoholic drink made from apples **2** *American* a drink made from apples

cigar /sɪˈɡɑː/ noun [C] a thick tube of dried tobacco leaves that people smoke

cigarette /ˌsɪɡəˈret/ noun [C] ★★ a narrow paper tube containing tobacco that people smoke: *a packet of cigarettes*

cinder /ˈsɪndə/ noun [C] a small piece of something that has been burnt almost completely

Cinderella story /ˌsɪndəˈrelə ˌstɔːri/ noun [C] a situation in which someone or something with good qualities is treated badly or ignored

cinema /ˈsɪnəmə/ noun ★★
1 [C] a building where you go to watch films: *We went to the cinema last night.* ♦ *a 10-screen cinema*
2 [U] the business of making films, or films in general

cinematic /ˌsɪnəˈmætɪk/ adj relating to films

cinnamon /ˈsɪnəmən/ noun [U] a brown powder or small stick used for giving a special taste to food

circa /ˈsɜːkə/ preposition *formal* used before a date or number for showing that it is not exact

circle¹ /ˈsɜːk(ə)l/ noun [C] ★★★
1 a curved line that creates a round enclosed space and is the same distance from the centre at every point —*picture* → C8
2 a group of people or things arranged in a circle: *a circle of stones*

3 a group of people who know one another or are interested in the same things: *international financial circles* ♦ *They have a large **circle** of friends.*
PHRASES **come/go/turn full circle** if a situation comes, goes, or turns full circle, it becomes the same again as it was at the beginning
go around/round in circles to do something for a long time without achieving any results because you always return to the same problem

circle² /ˈsɜːk(ə)l/ verb **1** [I/T] to move in a circle, or to move something in a circle **2** [T] to draw a circle around something

circuit /ˈsɜːkɪt/ noun [C] **1** a series of places that someone regularly goes to: *He is a performer on the New York comedy club circuit.* **2** a track that cars, bicycles etc race around **3** the complete path that an electric current flows around → SHORT CIRCUIT

circuit board noun [C] a board with electrical connections or computer chips on it, fitted inside a piece of electronic equipment

circuit breaker noun [C] a piece of equipment that is designed to stop an electric current automatically if it becomes dangerous

circular¹ /ˈsɜːkjʊlə/ adj **1** in the shape of a circle, or moving in a circle **2** a circular argument or theory does not mean anything because it consists of a series of causes and effects that lead you back to the original cause

circular² /ˈsɜːkjʊlə/ noun [C] a document or advertisement that is sent to a lot of people at the same time

circulate /ˈsɜːkjʊˌleɪt/ verb **1** [I] if information or ideas circulate, more and more people start to know about them **2** [T] to send something to all the people in a group **3** [I/T] to move around continuously inside a system or area, or to make something do this: *a machine designed to circulate warm air* **4** [I] to move around at a party, talking to different people

circulation /ˌsɜːkjʊˈleɪʃ(ə)n/ noun **1** [U] the movement of blood around your body **2** [U] the continuous movement of liquid, air etc inside a system or area **3** [singular] the number of copies of a newspaper or magazine that are sold each day, week etc **4** [U] the process by which something such as information passes from one person to another

circumcise /ˈsɜːkəmˌsaɪz/ verb [T] to remove the skin at the end of a boy's PENIS, or to remove part of a girl's sex organs
—**circumcision** /ˌsɜːkəmˈsɪʒ(ə)n/ noun [C/U]

circumference /səˈkʌmf(ə)rəns/ noun [C/U] the distance measured around the edge of a circle or a round object —*picture* → C8

circumflex /ˈsɜːkəmˌfleks/ noun [C] the symbol ^ that is written above a vowel in some languages → ACUTE⁴, GRAVE³

circumstance /ˈsɜːkəmstəns/ noun ★★
1 [C] the facts or conditions that affect a situation: *The circumstances of this case are unusual.* ♦ *It's amazing that they did so well **under the circumstances** (=because the situation was difficult or unusual).*
2 [plural] the conditions in which you live,

especially how much money you have: *It is very important to make a will, whatever your circumstances.*
3 [U] *formal* events and situations that cannot be controlled

PHRASE **under no circumstances** used for emphasizing that you mean 'never': *Under no circumstances will I give you any more money.*

circumstantial /ˌsɜːkəmˈstænʃ(ə)l/ adj *legal* circumstantial evidence makes it seem likely that something is true but does not prove it

circumvent /ˌsɜːkəmˈvent/ verb [T] *formal* to find a clever way of avoiding a rule or law

circus /ˈsɜːkəs/ noun **1** [C] a group of people who travel from place to place and entertain people by performing tricks **2** [singular] a situation in which there is too much excitement and uncontrolled activity

cistern /ˈsɪstən/ noun [C] **1** a large container for holding water **2** the part of a toilet that holds the water used for FLUSHING it (=making water go through it)

cite /saɪt/ verb [T] **1** to mention something as an example, explanation, or proof **2** to officially mention someone in a legal case **3** to officially praise someone for something that they have done

citizen /ˈsɪtɪz(ə)n/ noun [C] ★★
1 someone who has the right to live permanently in a particular country: *She married an American and became a US citizen.*
2 someone who lives in a particular town or city: *the citizens of Edinburgh*

citizenship /ˈsɪtɪz(ə)nʃɪp/ noun [U] the legal right to be a citizen of a particular country

citrus fruit /ˈsɪtrəs ˌfruːt/ noun [C/U] a fruit such as a lemon or orange

city /ˈsɪti/ noun [C] ★★★
1 a large important town: *an industrial city* ♦ *Tokyo is Japan's capital city* (=most important city).
2 the institutions of a city: *The city has agreed to pay for the rebuilding.* ♦ *the city hospital*

- A **city** is a larger than a **town**, and has important buildings such as a university, a cathedral, and a large hospital.
- A **village** is smaller than a town and may have only a few houses and one or two shops.

city centre noun [C] *British* the part of a city where the main shops and businesses are

civic /ˈsɪvɪk/ adj relating to a town or city

civil /ˈsɪv(ə)l/ adj ★★★

1 polite	**4** of state not religion
2 private not criminal	**5** not military
3 involving citizens	

1 polite, but not friendly: *He could barely force himself to be civil to them.*
2 relating to private legal disagreements between people, rather than to criminal law: *civil court*
3 involving protests or fighting by the people of a country: *civil disturbances*
4 done by the state, rather than by religious authorities: *We were married in a civil ceremony.*

5 involving ordinary people, not the armed forces: *civil employees*

civil engineering noun [U] the job of designing and building roads, bridges etc —**civil engineer** noun [C]

civilian /səˈvɪliən/ noun [C] someone who does not belong to the armed forces or the police —**civilian** adj

civilisation /ˌsɪvəlaɪˈzeɪʃ(ə)n/ a British spelling of civilization

civilization /ˌsɪvəlaɪˈzeɪʃ(ə)n/ noun **1** [C/U] a society that has developed its own culture and institutions **2** [U] *often humorous* a place such as a large city where modern things make life easy

civilize /ˈsɪvəˌlaɪz/ verb [T] **1** to make someone behave in a more polite and reasonable way **2** *old-fashioned* to help a society to develop its culture and institutions

civilized /ˈsɪvəˌlaɪzd/ adj **1** a civilized country or society has developed an advanced culture and advanced institutions **2** polite and reasonable: *Let's discuss this in a civilized way.* **3** pleasant and comfortable

civil law noun [U] the part of law that deals with disagreements between people, rather than with crime

civil liberties noun [plural] the basic freedom that all citizens have to do or say what they want

civil rights noun [plural] the basic rights that all people in a society have, for example the right to be treated fairly by the law

civil servant noun [C] someone who works for a government department

civil service, the noun [singular] a country's government departments and the people who work in them

civil war noun [C/U] a war that is fought between different groups of people within the same country

CJD /ˌsiː dʒeɪ ˈdiː/ noun [U] Creutzfeldt-Jakob Disease: a serious disease that gradually destroys your brain

cl abbrev centilitre

clad /klæd/ adj wearing a particular type of clothing

claim[1] /kleɪm/ verb ★★★
1 [T] to say that something is true, even though there is no definite proof: **+(that)** *He claims he is innocent.* ♦ **claim to do sth** *The organization claims to represent more than 20,000 firms.*
2 [I/T] to ask for something that belongs to you, or to ask for something that you have a right to: *The back of the form tells you how to claim your refund.* ♦ *Has anyone claimed the wallet I handed in yesterday?* ♦ *She claimed political asylum in 1986.*
3 [T] if war, disease, or an accident claims someone's life, they die as a result of it: *The flood has now claimed over 500 lives.*
4 [T] to need something such as your attention or time: *Several more urgent matters were claiming her attention.*

PHRASE **claim credit/responsibility/victory etc** to say that you have achieved or done something: *I can't claim all the credit for our success.*

claim[2] /kleɪm/ noun [C] ★★★
1 a statement that something is true but

with no definite proof: *claims of bullying* ♦ +**that** *I don't believe his claim that he fought in Vietnam.*
2 an official request for something that you believe you have a right to: *an insurance claim* ♦ *a claim for asylum*
3 a legal or moral right to something: *She has no* **claim on** *her husband's estate.*
4 claim on sth a right to someone's attention, love etc: *There are so many competing claims on our attention these days.*
PHRASE **claim to fame** *often humorous* the thing that makes a person or place famous or interesting

claimant /ˈkleɪmənt/ noun [C] **1** someone who makes an official request for money **2** someone who says that they have a right to something

clairvoyant /kleəˈvɔɪənt/ noun [C] someone who claims to know what will happen in the future —**clairvoyant** adj

clam /klæm/ noun [C] a small sea animal with a hard shell. It can be eaten.

clamber /ˈklæmbə/ verb [I] to climb something with difficulty, using your hands and feet =SCRAMBLE

clammy /ˈklæmi/ adj cold and wet in an unpleasant way

clamour¹ /ˈklæmə/ noun [singular/U] **1** an urgent request for something by a lot of people **2** a very loud noise made by a lot of people or things

clamour² /ˈklæmə/ verb [I] to say loudly that you must have something: *children clamouring for attention*

clamp¹ /klæmp/ verb [T] **1** to put or hold something firmly in position **2** to hold two things together using a clamp **3** *British* to put a piece of equipment on a wheel of a car to stop it being moved because it is illegally parked
PHRASAL VERB **,clamp ˈdown** to make a determined attempt to stop people doing something bad or illegal: *Police are clamping down on local drug dealers.*

clamp² /klæmp/ noun [C] **1** a tool used for holding two things together firmly **2** *British* a piece of equipment put on a wheel of an illegally parked car to stop it being moved

clampdown /ˈklæmpdaʊn/ noun [C] a determined attempt by someone in authority to stop people doing something bad or illegal

clan /klæn/ noun [C] a large group of families that are related to each other, especially in Scotland

clandestine /klænˈdestɪn, ˈklændeˌstaɪn/ adj secret and often illegal

clang /klæŋ/ verb [I/T] if something made of metal clangs, it makes a loud sound —**clang** noun [C]

clank /klæŋk/ verb [I/T] if a heavy metal object clanks, it makes a short loud sound —**clank** noun [C]

clap¹ /klæp/ verb **1** [I/T] to hit your hands together many times as a way of showing that you liked something, or in order to get attention: *At the end of the speech everyone clapped.* **2** [T] to suddenly put something somewhere: *The boy clapped his hands over his ears.* —**clapping** noun [U] → EYE¹

clap² /klæp/ noun **1** [singular] an action of hitting your hands together, to show enjoyment or to get attention **2** [C] a sudden loud sound: *a clap of thunder*

clarification /ˌklærəfɪˈkeɪʃ(ə)n/ noun [U] *formal* an explanation that makes something easier to understand

clarify /ˈklærəfaɪ/ verb [T] *formal* to explain something more clearly so that it is easier to understand

clarinet /ˌklærəˈnet/ noun [C] a musical instrument consisting of a long black tube that you play by blowing into it —*picture* → WOODWIND —**clarinettist** noun [C]

clarity /ˈklærəti/ noun [U] **1** the ability to think clearly or understand things clearly **2** the quality of being easy to see, hear, or understand

clash¹ /klæʃ/ noun [C] **1** a very angry argument or fight between two people or groups: *violent clashes between police and protesters* **2** a situation in which two people or things are so different that they cannot exist or work together: *a personality clash between a pupil and a teacher* **3** a loud sound that is made when two metal objects hit each other **4** an annoying situation in which two events happen at the same time

clash² /klæʃ/ verb [I] **1** to argue angrily, or to fight with someone **2** if two events clash, they happen at the same time **3** if colours or patterns clash, they do not look good together

clasp¹ /klɑːsp/ verb [T] to hold someone or something tightly

clasp² /klɑːsp/ noun [C] a metal object used for fastening something such as a bag or a piece of jewellery

class¹ /klɑːs/ noun ★★★

1 group of students	**5** type of thing/person
2 teaching period	**6** standard of service
3 series of lessons	**7** style/ability/skill
4 group in society	**8** university degree level

1 [C] a group of students who are taught together: *What class is Sophie in now?*

In British English, **class** can be used with a singular or plural verb. You can say *Her class has a new teacher.* OR *Her class have a new teacher.*

2 [C/U] a period of time during which a group of students is taught together =LESSON: *I've got classes all afternoon.* ♦ *We had to write an essay in class.*
3 [C] a course of lessons in a particular subject: *I* **go to** *my art* **class** *on Mondays.*
4 [C/U] one of the groups into which people in a society are divided according to education, income etc: *tax cuts for the middle class* ♦ *the relationship between social class and your level of education*
5 [C] a group of things, animals, or people with similar features or qualities: *The race has competitions for ten classes of boat.*
6 [C] one of the standards of service that are available to someone travelling by train, plane etc
7 [U] *informal* impressive natural style, social ability, or skill: *Hilary has too much class to say something like that.*
8 [C] *British* one of the levels of university degree

C

class² /klɑːs/ verb [T] to include someone or something in a particular group: *She is now classed as a professional athlete.*

class 'act noun [C] *informal* a person or group with great style and skill

Class A 'drug noun [C] *British* a strong and dangerous illegal drug such as HEROIN or COCAINE

classic¹ /ˈklæsɪk/ adj 1 completely typical: *a classic example of poor management* 2 a classic song, book, play etc is very good and has been popular for a long time 3 a classic style of clothes, furniture etc is beautiful in a very simple way

classic² /ˈklæsɪk/ noun [C] a song, book, play etc that is very good and has been popular for a long time → CLASSICS

classical /ˈklæsɪk(ə)l/ adj 1 following the original or traditional standard for something: *classical economics* 2 relating to Ancient Greece and Rome: *classical mythology* 3 relating to CLASSICAL MUSIC: *classical composers* —**classically** /ˈklæsɪkli/ adv

classical 'music noun [U] serious music that is played on instruments such as the piano and the VIOLIN

classics /ˈklæsɪks/ noun [U] the study of the language, literature, and culture of Ancient Greece and Rome

classification /ˌklæsɪfɪˈkeɪʃ(ə)n/ noun [C/U] the process of putting people or things into particular groups according to the features that they have, or one of these groups

classified /ˈklæsɪˌfaɪd/ adj classified information is officially secret and can only be known by a few government officials or military officials

classified 'ad or **classified ad'vertisement** noun [C] a short advertisement that you put in a newspaper, for example so that you can sell something=SMALL AD

classify /ˈklæsɪˌfaɪ/ verb [T] to put people or things into groups according to the features that they have=CATEGORIZE: *Families were classified according to their incomes.*

classless /ˈklɑːsləs/ adj not divided into social classes

classmate /ˈklɑːsˌmeɪt/ noun [C] someone who is in your class at school

classroom /ˈklɑːsˌruːm/ noun [C] ★★ a room where you have classes in a school

classy /ˈklɑːsi/ adj *informal* expensive, fashionable, and very good: *a classy hotel*

clatter /ˈklætə/ verb [I] if a hard object clatters, it makes a lot of loud short noises as it hits something hard —**clatter** noun [singular]

clause /klɔːz/ noun [C] ★
1 a part of a legal document or law
2 *linguistics* a group of words that includes a verb and a SUBJECT

claustrophobia /ˌklɔːstrəˈfəʊbiə/ noun [U] fear of being in a small space

claustrophobic /ˌklɔːstrəˈfəʊbɪk/ adj 1 feeling afraid because you are in a small space 2 a claustrophobic place makes you uncomfortable because it is small or crowded

claw¹ /klɔː/ noun [C] one of the sharp curved nails that some birds and animals have on their feet

claw² /klɔː/ verb [I/T] to attack someone or damage something using claws

PHRASAL VERB **claw sth 'back** *British* to gradually get back something that you used to have but lost

clay /kleɪ/ noun [U] a type of heavy wet soil used for making cups, plates, and other objects

clean¹ /kliːn/ adj ★★★
1 not dirty or polluted: *Go and put on a clean shirt.* ♦ *the clean country air* ♦ *Tom had scrubbed the floor clean.* ♦ *I like to keep the place clean and tidy.* ♦ *Everything in the house was spotlessly clean* (=extremely clean).
2 a clean piece of paper does not have anything written on it
3 not illegal or unfair, or not involved in anything illegal or unfair: *It was a good clean fight.* ♦ *I've got a clean driving licence* (=I have not committed any driving offences).
4 clean language or humour does not offend people because it does not involve sex or swearing

PHRASES **a clean slate/sheet** a situation in which everything bad that you have done in the past has been forgiven or forgotten: *We have the chance to start over, with a clean slate.*
come clean to tell the truth about something that you have kept secret
→ SQUEAKY CLEAN

clean² /kliːn/ verb ★★★
1 [T] to remove the dirt from something: *Paul is cleaning his car.* ♦ *You should clean your teeth twice a day.*
2 [I/T] to remove the dirt and dust in a house: *We've cleaned the house from top to bottom.* ♦ *I was cleaning all morning.*

PHRASAL VERBS **clean sth 'out** to make a place clean or tidy by removing things that are not wanted and by getting rid of dirt: *They spent the day cleaning out the garage.*
clean (sth) 'up to make a place completely clean and tidy: *Let's start getting this place cleaned up.*
clean sth 'up 1 to remove pollution from a place or an industrial process **2** to stop bad or criminal behaviour in a place or activity: *Does the government have plans to clean up the banking system?*
clean 'up after sb to clean a place after someone has made it dirty or untidy: *Residents have been told to clean up after their dogs.*

Other ways of saying clean

- **brush** to clean something by rubbing it with a brush
- **cleanse** to clean your skin thoroughly using a special liquid or cream
- **dust** to remove dust from furniture and other surfaces using a soft cloth
- **scrub** to clean something by rubbing it hard with a brush and soap and water
- **sweep** to clean a floor using a brush with a long handle
- **wash** to clean something using water and soap
- **wipe** to clean a surface such as a table using a cloth that is slightly wet

clean³ /kli:n/ adv *informal* used for emphasizing that something happens completely: *The blast blew the windows clean out of the building.*

clean⁴ /kli:n/ noun [singular] *British* an occasion when you clean something

clean-cut adj a clean-cut man looks clean and tidy

cleaner /'kli:nə/ noun **1** [C] someone whose job is to clean the rooms in a building **2** [C] a chemical substance used for cleaning things **3 the cleaner's** [singular] a place where you can get clothes DRY-CLEANED (=cleaned with chemicals) = DRY CLEANER'S

cleaning /'kli:nɪŋ/ noun [U] the activity or job of making rooms in a building clean

cleanliness /'klenlinəs/ noun [U] the process of keeping yourself and your possessions clean

cleanly /'kli:nli/ adv **1** with one smooth movement **2** without creating a lot of mess or pollution

cleanse /klenz/ verb [T] to clean your skin thoroughly → ETHNIC CLEANSING

cleanser /'klenzə/ noun [C/U] a special substance that you use for cleaning your face

clean-shaven adj a clean-shaven man does not have a BEARD or MOUSTACHE

clean-up noun [C] **1** an occasion when you clean a place thoroughly **2** an attempt to stop bad or criminal behaviour

clear¹ /klɪə/ adj ★★★

1 obvious	**5** not confused
2 easy to understand	**6** not blocked
3 easy to see/hear	**7** without clouds
4 transparent	**8** without guilty feelings

1 obvious and certain to be true: *It appears to be a clear case of discrimination.* ♦ +(that) *It was very clear that something was worrying him.* ♦ **it is not clear whether** *It is not clear whether the firemen are still alive.*
2 easy to understand: *Clear instructions are provided.* ♦ *Let me **make** this **clear** – I will not help you again!*
3 easy to see or hear: *'I did it,' she said in a clear voice.* ♦ *The picture was clear and sharp.*
4 transparent: *a clear glass bottle*
5 not confused: *Are you **clear about** the purpose of the meeting?*
6 if a surface, road, or passage is clear, there is nothing that blocks it: *a clear view of the mountains* ♦ *All the main roads are **clear of** snow.*
7 if the sky is clear, there are no clouds
8 not affected by guilty feelings: *She had done her duty, and her **conscience was clear**.*
→ COAST¹, CRYSTAL CLEAR

Word family: clear

Words in the same family as clear
- **clarity** *n*
- **unclear** *adj*
- **clearly** *adv*

---

clear² /klɪə/ verb ★★★

1 empty a place	**6** pass without touching
2 remove sth	**7** start to disappear
3 prove sb not guilty	**8** accept cheque
4 weather: improve	**+** PHRASES
5 give/get permission	**+** PHRASAL VERBS

1 [T] to remove people or things from a place, or to become empty when people leave or things are removed: *Millions of acres of tropical forest have been cleared.* ♦ *The room cleared quickly after the speech.* ♦ *To start with, you should **clear** the ground of weeds.*
2 [T] to remove something that is blocking a place: *The police cleared a path through to the front of the building.*
3 [T] to prove officially that someone did not do something wrong: *The two men **were cleared** of murder yesterday.*
4 [I] if the sky or the weather clears, it becomes brighter with no clouds or rain
5 [T] to give or obtain permission for something to happen: *You'll have to **clear** this project **with** head office.*
6 [T] to go over, under, or past an object without touching it: *The horse cleared the fence.*
7 [I] if something such as smoke clears, it starts to disappear
8 [I/T] if a cheque clears, or if a bank clears it, the bank allows the money to be used
PHRASES clear the air to discuss a problem or difficult situation with someone in order to make it better
clear your throat to make a noise in your throat before you speak, so that you can speak without any difficulty
PHRASAL VERBS clear sth away to remove something in order to make a place tidy: *A young woman cleared away their empty cups.*
clear off *British informal* to leave a place quickly: *They've all cleared off and left me to clean this mess up.*
clear sth out to make a place tidy by removing things: *I'm going to clear out the cupboards tomorrow.*
clear up if the weather clears up, the clouds or rain go away
clear (sth) up to make a place tidy by removing things: *I'll clear up if you want to go to bed.*
clear sth up to solve a problem or a mystery

clear³ /klɪə/ noun
PHRASE in the clear 1 no longer believed to be guilty of something bad or illegal **2** no longer in a difficult or dangerous situation

clear⁴ /klɪə/ adv completely away from something: *Stand clear of the closing doors.*
PHRASE keep/stay/steer clear of to avoid someone or something unpleasant or dangerous: *No one mentioned the divorce, so Lisa decided to steer clear of that subject.*

clearance /'klɪərəns/ noun [U] **1** official permission to do something: *clearance to do sth The pilot has just received clearance to land.* **2** an amount of space between two things that keeps them from touching each other

clear-cut adj definite and easy to understand or make a decision about

clearing /'klɪərɪŋ/ noun [C] an area in a forest where there are no trees or bushes

clearly /'klɪəli/ adv ★★★
1 used for emphasizing that what you are saying is true = OBVIOUSLY: *Both companies clearly like to do things their own way.* ♦ *Clearly we wouldn't want to upset anyone.*
2 in a way that people can easily see, hear,

or understand: *His contract clearly states that he cannot leave before next year.* ♦ *The road signs were clearly visible.*

3 in a way that is sensible and not confused: *You can't think clearly on four hours' sleep.*

cleavage /'kli:vɪdʒ/ noun [C] the space between a woman's breasts

clef /klef/ noun [C] a symbol written at the beginning of a line of music to show the PITCH of the notes

clemency /'klemənsi/ noun [U] *formal* a decision not to punish someone severely, made by someone in a position of authority

clench /klentʃ/ verb **clench your teeth/jaw/fist** to press your teeth or fingers together tightly because you are angry or upset

clergy /'klɜːdʒi/ noun [plural] priests and other people who lead religious services

cleric /'klerɪk/ noun [C] *formal* a member of the clergy

clerical /'klerɪk(ə)l/ adj **1** connected with the ordinary work that people do in offices **2** relating to priests

clerk /klɑːk, *American* klɜːk/ noun [C] **1** someone whose job is to look after the documents in an office **2** *American* a SHOP ASSISTANT **3** *American* a RECEPTIONIST in a hotel

clever /'klevə/ adj ★★
1 *British* good at learning or understanding things=INTELLIGENT: *I'd like to be a doctor but I'm not clever enough.*
2 good at achieving what you want, especially by using unusual or slightly dishonest methods: *She had a clever lawyer.*
3 a clever tool or idea is effective because it was designed in an intelligent way
—**cleverly** adv

cliché /'kli:ʃeɪ/ noun [C] a phrase or idea that is boring because people use it a lot and it is no longer original —**clichéd** adj

click¹ /klɪk/ verb **1** [I/T] to make a short high sound like the sound of a switch, or to make an object make this sound: *The cameras continued clicking as they drove away.* ♦ *The young soldier clicked his heels and saluted.* ♦ *You get the waiter's attention by clicking your fingers.* **2** [I/T] *computing* to make a computer do something by pressing a button on the mouse: *To send the message, click on the 'send' button.* **3** [I] *informal* if something clicks, you suddenly understand or realize it **4** [I] *informal* if two people click, they realize immediately that they like each other and understand each other

click² /klɪk/ noun [C] **1** a short sound like the sound of a switch **2** *computing* the action of making a computer do something by pressing a button on the mouse

client /'klaɪənt/ noun [C] someone who uses the services of a professional person such as a lawyer, or of a business or organization that provides help or advice: *Our clients are not all wealthy people.*

clientele /ˌkliːɒnˈtel/ noun [singular] the customers of a shop, hotel, or restaurant

cliff /klɪf/ noun [C] the steep side of an area of high land

cliffhanger /'klɪfˌhæŋə/ noun [C] *informal* an exciting end to a part of a book or television programme

climactic /klaɪˈmæktɪk/ adj a climactic event

or moment is the most exciting or important one in a series

climate /'klaɪmət/ noun ★★
1 [C/U] the climate of a country or region is the type of weather it has: *Mexico is renowned for its hot climate and spicy food.*
2 [C] the general situation or attitudes that people have at a particular time: *We are unable to increase wages in the current economic climate.* ♦ *a climate of fear and mistrust*

climatic /klaɪˈmætɪk/ adj relating to the type of weather that a place has

climax¹ /'klaɪmæks/ noun [C] the most exciting or important moment in a story, event, or situation, usually near the end: *the climax to this season's Champions' Cup*

climax² /'klaɪmæks/ verb [I/T] if a story, event, or situation climaxes, it reaches the most exciting or important moment

climb¹ /klaɪm/ verb ★★★
1 [I/T] to use your hands and feet to move up, over, down, or across something: *He climbed onto the roof.* ♦ *We escaped by climbing through a window.* ♦ *I didn't think he could climb the wall.*
2 [T] to walk up a slope or up some steps: *We left the road and climbed the hill.* ♦ *They had to climb ten flights of stairs.*
3 [I] to get into or out of something, especially by stepping to a higher or lower position: *Sara climbed wearily into bed.*
4 [I] if something such as a temperature, price, or level climbs, it becomes higher: *Their profits climbed from £20 million to £5 million last year.*

PHRASAL VERB **climb down** *British* to admit that you were wrong

climb

climb² /klaɪm/ noun [singular] an occasion when you go up a slope or up some steps

climb-down noun [C] *British* a change of attitude in which someone admits that they were wrong

climber /'klaɪmə/ noun [C] someone who takes part in the activity of climbing

climbing /'klaɪmɪŋ/ noun [U] the activity of climbing mountains and rocks for enjoyment and exercise

climbing frame noun [C] *British* a large structure designed for children to climb on

clinch /klɪntʃ/ verb [T] to manage to win or achieve something by doing one final thing that makes it certain

cling /klɪŋ/ (past tense and past participle **clung** /klʌŋ/) verb [I] **1** to hold onto something or someone tightly, for example because you are afraid: *Some children were crying and clinging to their mothers.* **2** to stick to something, or to fit very tightly on something: *Gareth's wet clothes clung to his body.*

PHRASAL VERB 'cling to sth **1** to keep believing that something is right or real, even though other people do not: *Older people cling to the religion they had as children.* **2** cling to sth to try very hard to keep something: *The Prime Minister is still clinging to power.*

clingfilm /ˈklɪŋfɪlm/ noun [U] *British* a transparent plastic substance used for wrapping food to keep it fresh

clingy /ˈklɪŋi/ or **clinging** /ˈklɪŋɪŋ/ adj *informal* a clingy child or person wants to be with another person all the time

clinic /ˈklɪnɪk/ noun [C] a place where people go to receive a particular type of medical treatment or advice

clinical /ˈklɪnɪk(ə)l/ adj **1** involving working with people who are ill, rather than in a laboratory: *a clinical study of the drug* **2** not showing any excitement or emotion: *a cold and clinical manner* **3** very skilful and effective —**clinically** /ˈklɪnɪkli/ adv

clink /klɪŋk/ verb [I/T] to make a short high sound like glass or metal objects hitting each other —**clink** noun [singular]

clip¹ /klɪp/ verb **1** [I/T] *formal* to fasten something somewhere using a small object, or to be fastened somewhere in this way: *Clip the microphone to your shirt.* **2** [T] to cut off small parts of something in order to make it tidy: *I clipped my nails.* **3** [T] to hit something accidentally while passing it

clip² /klɪp/ noun [C] **1** a small object that holds something in position: *hair clips* **2** a short part of a film or television programme that is shown separately

clipboard /ˈklɪpbɔːd/ noun [C] **1** a small board that you carry and attach papers to so that you can write while you are moving around **2** *computing* the part of a computer program where you store information that you are going to copy to another document

clipped /klɪpt/ adj if someone speaks in a clipped voice, they speak clearly and quickly but they seem unfriendly

clippers /ˈklɪpəz/ noun [plural] an object used for cutting things to make them tidy, consisting of two blades that you press or push together: *nail clippers*

clipping /ˈklɪpɪŋ/ noun [C] **1** an article that you have cut from a newspaper or magazine =CUTTING **2** a small piece that you remove when you cut something to make it tidy

clique /kliːk/ noun [C] a small group of people who seem unfriendly to other people

clitoris /ˈklɪtərɪs/ noun [C] a woman's sexual organ above her VAGINA

cloak¹ /kləʊk/ noun **1** [C] a long coat without sleeves that fastens around your neck **2** [singular] something that covers or hides something else: *a cloak of secrecy*

cloak² /kləʊk/ verb [T] to cover or hide something: *The whole investigation has been cloaked in secrecy.*

cloakroom /ˈkləʊkˌruːm/ noun [C] a room in a theatre or restaurant where people can leave their coats

clobber /ˈklɒbə/ verb [T] *informal* **1** to hit someone very hard **2** to have a very bad effect on someone or something

clock¹ /klɒk/ noun [C] ★★★ an object that shows the time. The similar object that you wear on your wrist is called a **watch**: *The only sound was the clock ticking.* ♦ *I glanced at the kitchen clock.*

PHRASES **against the clock** as fast as possible in order to finish something before a particular time: *Staff are working against the clock to meet the deadline.*
around/round the clock all day and all night: *Rescuers worked around the clock to free people trapped in the wreckage.*
put/turn/set the clock back 1 to change the time on a clock to an earlier time **2** to return to a time in the past: *If we could turn the clock back, would you actually change anything?*

clock² /klɒk/ verb [T] to measure the speed that something is travelling at

PHRASAL VERB ,clock sth ˈup *informal* to reach a particular number or amount: *Dawson has clocked up 34 years' service as a police officer.*

clockwise /ˈklɒkˌwaɪz/ adj, adv moving in a circle in the same direction as the HANDS on a clock ≠ ANTICLOCKWISE

clockwork /ˈklɒkˌwɜːk/ noun

PHRASES **like clockwork** happening or working correctly, with no problems
(as) regular as clockwork very regularly

clog /klɒg/ verb [I/T] to block something such as a pipe, or to become blocked

clogs /klɒgz/ noun [plural] shoes with wooden SOLES (=bottom part)

cloistered /ˈklɔɪstəd/ adj kept away from the unpleasant responsibilities of ordinary life

clone¹ /kləʊn/ noun [C] **1** *science* an exact copy of an animal or plant that has been created in a laboratory **2** *informal* something that is exactly like something else

clone² /kləʊn/ verb [T] *science* to create an exact copy of an animal or plant in a laboratory

close¹ /kləʊz/ verb ★★★

1 shut	**5** stop people entering
2 stop doing business	**6** of computer program
3 stop operating	**+ PHRASAL VERBS**
4 end/finish	

1 [I/T] if you close something, or if it closes, it moves to cover an open area: *I was just closing my eyes to go to sleep when the phone rang.* ♦ *Did the fridge door close completely?*
2 [I/T] to stop doing business for a short time: *We close the office at noon on Fridays.* ♦ *Snow forced both airports to close.*
3 [I/T] to stop existing as a business, or to stop something operating as a business: *The government plans to close 10 coal mines.* ♦ *Small shops are closing because of competition from the large chains.*
4 [I/T] if an activity or event closes, or if you close it, it ends: *Her latest show closed after only three performances.* ♦ **close sth by doing sth** *He closed the meeting by thanking everyone for coming.*
5 [T] to stop people from entering a place or using a road: *The bridge will have to be closed for repairs.*

C

close

lock

fasten

6 [I/T] *computing* if a computer program closes, or if you close it, it stops operating and disappears from your computer screen

PHRASAL VERBS ,close (sth) 'down **1** *same as* **close**[1] 3: *We had to close down the factory.* **2** *same as* **close**[1] 6

,close 'in **1** to move nearer to someone, especially in order to surround them: *Armed police began closing in on the house.* **2** *literary* if night or darkness closes in, it becomes night or it gets darker

,close sth 'off to prevent people from entering a place or using a road

,close (sth) 'up to lock the doors of a building

close² /kləʊs/ adj ★★★

1 short distance away	**7** related to you directly
2 short time away	**8** involved with sb a lot
3 likely to happen soon	**9** almost equal to sth
4 careful	**10** won by small amount
5 similar but different	**11** dangerous
6 connected by feelings	**12** warm

1 only a short distance away: *We can walk to the swimming pool – it's quite close.* ♦ *The hotel is close to the centre of town.*
2 only a short time away: *Sam's birthday is close to Christmas.*
3 likely to happen soon: *Everyone believes that a peace deal is close.* ♦ *close to doing sth We're closer to signing a contract after today's meeting.* ♦ *She was close to tears (=almost crying) as she said goodbye to her sister.*
4 giving careful attention to every detail: *I'll take a closer look at it tomorrow.* ♦ *The local police kept a close eye on his activities.*
5 similar to something but not exactly the same: *That's not exactly the shade of blue, but it's close.* ♦ *The sensation is close to the feeling of floating.*
6 connected by shared feelings such as love and respect: *My brother and I are very close.* ♦ *close friends* ♦ *She's close to both her parents.*
7 related to you directly, for example by being your parent, child, brother, or sister: *my close relatives*
8 directly involved with someone and communicating with them a lot: *a close business associate* ♦ *We worked in close cooperation with local people.*
9 almost the same as a particular amount or number: *Unemployment on the island is close to 12 per cent.*
10 if a game, competition, or election is close, the scores of the players, teams etc are nearly equal: *The game was close, but Real Madrid eventually won.*
11 *spoken* very dangerous or unpleasant: *That was close! He almost hit us.* ♦ *We had a close shave (=were in a dangerous situation) on our bikes today.*
12 warm and uncomfortable because there is not enough fresh air
—**closeness** noun [U]

close³ /kləʊs/ adv ★★★
1 only a short distance away: *She moved closer, trying to hear what Jack was saying.* ♦ *He clutched his bag close to his chest.*
2 only a short time away: *As the summer grew closer, we started to think about a holiday.*
3 close on/to sth almost a particular amount or number: *Close on 500 people attended the meeting.*

PHRASES close up or up close from only a short distance away: *I didn't see his face close up.*
come close to (doing) sth to nearly do something: *I came close to giving up several times.*

close⁴ /kləʊz/ noun [singular] the end of something such as a period of time or an event: *towards the close of the 18th century*

closed /kləʊzd/ adj ★★
1 if something such as a door or window is closed, it is not open: *All the doors are closed and locked.*
2 not operating or doing business ≠ OPEN: *All the shops were closed.* ♦ *This part of the museum is closed to the public.*
PHRASE behind closed doors in a place where other people cannot see or know what is happening

closed-circuit television noun [U] CCTV

close-knit /ˌkləʊsˈnɪt/ adj consisting of people who like and support each other: *a close-knit family*

closely /ˈkləʊsli/ adv ★★
1 in a way that involves careful attention to every detail: *Inspectors will examine the accounts very closely.*
2 in a way that involves sharing ideas, thoughts, or feelings: *We are all working closely with each other.*
3 in a way that is very similar to something, or that has a strong connection with it: *The Northern Ireland economy is closely linked to that of the rest of the United Kingdom.*
4 with very little time or distance between one thing and another

closet¹ /ˈklɒzɪt/ noun [C] *American* a small room or space built into a wall for storing things
PHRASE **come out of the closet** *informal* to say publicly that you are gay
→ SKELETON

closet² /ˈklɒzɪt/ adj keeping your beliefs or activities secret: *I've always been a closet fan of science-fiction books.*

close-up /ˈkləʊs ʌp/ noun [C] a photograph of someone or something that is taken from a position very near them

closing /ˈkləʊzɪŋ/ adj happening at the end of something: *the closing moments of the game*

closing date noun [C] the date by which you must do something

closure /ˈkləʊʒə/ noun [C/U] an occasion when a business or institution stops operating permanently, or the process of stopping it: *an increase in hospital closures*

clot¹ /klɒt/ noun [C] a lump consisting of thick blood or another liquid

clot² /klɒt/ verb [I] if blood or another liquid clots, it becomes thick and stops flowing

cloth /klɒθ/ noun ★★★
1 [C/U] material used for making things such as clothes and curtains: *linen/cotton cloth*
2 [C] a piece of cloth that is used for a particular purpose such as cleaning or covering a table

clothe /kləʊð/ verb [T] to provide someone with clothes

clothed /kləʊðd/ adj dressed in a particular way

clothes /kləʊðz/ noun [plural] ★★★ shirts, dresses, trousers, and other things that you wear: *a pile of dirty clothes* ♦ *a clothes shop* ♦ *I'm going to **put on** some clean **clothes**.* ♦ *Why don't you **take** those wet **clothes** off?*

> ■ **Clothes** is a general word meaning 'things that you wear'. It is always plural: *His clothes were dirty.* ♦ *I bought some new clothes.* If you want to talk about 'one thing that you wear' use **a piece/an item of clothing**.
> ■ **Dress** is a less common word and refers to special clothes that are typical of a particular country or time: *men in national dress*
> ■ **A dress** is a single piece of clothing worn by a woman.

clothing /ˈkləʊðɪŋ/ noun [U] ★ clothes: *a piece/item/article of clothing* ♦ *waterproof clothing* ♦ *the clothing industry*

cloud¹ /klaʊd/ noun [C] ★★★
1 a white or grey mass of drops of water in the sky: *a few white clouds in the sky* ♦ *There's more cloud than yesterday.*
2 a large amount of something such as smoke or dust in the air: *a huge cloud of black smoke*
3 something unpleasant that spoils a situation: *Violent protests cast a cloud over the president's visit.*
PHRASE **under a cloud** with your reputation damaged

cloud² /klaʊd/ verb **1** [T] to affect your ability to think in a sensible way: *Make sure that your feelings do not cloud your judgment.*
2 [T] to make something more complicated or confusing: *Unanswered questions have further clouded the issue.* **3** [T] to spoil an event **4** [I/T] if something such as glass clouds, or if something clouds it, it becomes difficult to see through
PHRASAL VERB **cloud over** to become darker because grey clouds are forming in the sky

cloudless /ˈklaʊdləs/ adj a cloudless sky has no clouds in it

cloudy /ˈklaʊdi/ adj **1** full of clouds **2** a cloudy liquid is not clear

clout /klaʊt/ noun *informal* **1** [U] the authority to make decisions, or the power to influence events: *political/financial/economic clout* **2** [C] a hard hit with your hand

clove /kləʊv/ noun [C] **1** a brown dried flower BUD used for flavouring food **2** a section of a BULB of GARLIC

clover /ˈkləʊvə/ noun [U] a small plant with leaves that have three round parts

clown¹ /klaʊn/ noun [C] **1** a performer in a CIRCUS who wears funny clothes and does silly things **2** someone who is stupid or annoying

clown² /klaʊn/ or **clown around** verb [I] to do funny or annoying things

club¹ /klʌb/ noun ★★★

1 society for activity	**4** for hitting ball in golf
2 sports team & staff	**5** suit of playing cards
3 place for dancing	**6** stick used as weapon

1 [C] an organization for people who take part in a particular activity, or the building that they use: *a sailing club* ♦ *Why don't you **join** a chess club?* ♦ *Are you a **member** of the club?*
2 [C] a team of sports players and the staff who work with them: *Manchester United football club*
3 [C] a place where you go in the evening to dance and drink = NIGHTCLUB
4 [C] an object used for hitting the ball in golf = GOLF CLUB
5 **clubs** [plural] the suit (=group) of playing cards that has a pattern of three black balls on a black stem: *the king of clubs* —picture → C16
6 [C] a thick heavy stick used as a weapon

club² /klʌb/ verb [T] to hit someone with a heavy object
PHRASAL VERB **club together** if people club together, each of them gives some money so that someone can buy something

clubbing /ˈklʌbɪŋ/ noun [U] the activity of going out in the evenings to dance and drink in CLUBS

C

clubhouse /ˈklʌbˌhaʊs/ noun [C] the building used by members of a sports club

club ˈsoda noun [U] *American* SODA WATER

cluck /klʌk/ verb [I] if a chicken clucks, it makes its usual short low sound —**cluck** noun [C]

clue /kluː/ noun [C] ★
1 an object or fact that helps someone to solve a crime or mystery: *Detectives were brought in to help search for clues.* ♦ *Police still have no clues as to the identity of the killer.*
2 a piece of information that helps you to understand something: *His face gave her no clue as to what he was thinking.*
3 a word or phrase provided to help you to guess the answer in a CROSSWORD
PHRASE **not have a clue** *informal* to not know or understand something: *'What's wrong with him?' 'I don't have a clue.'*

clued up /ˌkluːd ˈʌp/ adj *informal* someone who is clued-up knows about a particular subject or situation

clueless /ˈkluːləs/ adj *informal* someone who is clueless knows nothing or is stupid

clump /klʌmp/ noun [C] a group of trees or plants growing very close together

clumsy /ˈklʌmzi/ adj **1** a clumsy person often has accidents because they are not careful **2** a clumsy object is too large and heavy to be useful **3** showing a lack of skill in judging people or situations —**clumsily** adv, **clumsiness** noun [U]

clung the past tense and past participle of **cling**

cluster¹ /ˈklʌstə/ noun [C] a small group of things that are very close to each other

cluster² /ˈklʌstə/ verb [I] to form a small close group

clutch¹ /klʌtʃ/ verb [T] to hold someone or something firmly

clutch² /klʌtʃ/ noun **1** [C] a piece of equipment in a vehicle that you press with your foot when you change GEAR —*picture* ➔ C6
2 clutches [plural] power or control over someone: *They left the country to escape the clutches of the secret police.*

clutter¹ /ˈklʌtə/ or ˌ**clutter sth ˈup** verb [T] to put too many things in a place so that it looks untidy

clutter² /ˈklʌtə/ noun [U] the mess created when there are too many things in a place

cm abbrev centimetre

Co. /kəʊ/ abbrev **1** Company **2** County

c/o abbrev care of: used in an address on a letter that you are sending to someone at another person's house

coach¹ /kəʊtʃ/ noun [C] ★
1 someone who trains a sports player or team: *a baseball coach*
2 *British* a comfortable bus for long journeys —*picture* ➔ C7
3 a vehicle pulled by horses, used in the past

coach² /kəʊtʃ/ verb [T] **1** to train a sports player or team **2** to teach someone a particular skill —**coaching** noun [U]

coagulate /kəʊˈægjʊˌleɪt/ verb [I] if a liquid coagulates, it becomes thick and hard

coal /kəʊl/ noun ★
1 [U] a hard black substance that is dug from the ground and burned as fuel: *a piece/lump of coal* ♦ *the coal industry*
2 coals [plural] pieces of burning coal

coalition /ˌkəʊəˈlɪʃ(ə)n/ noun [C] a government formed by different political parties that are working together for a short time

ˈcoal ˌmine noun [C] a place where coal is dug up from under the ground

coarse /kɔːs/ adj **1** not smooth or soft, or consisting of rough or thick pieces: *She had short, coarse hair.* **2** rude and offensive —**coarsely** adv

coast¹ /kəʊst/ noun [C] ★★ an area of land along the edge of a sea: *the east coast of England* ♦ *a little town on the coast* ➔ SHORE
PHRASE **the coast is clear** used for saying that it is safe to do something because there is no one to catch you

coast² /kəʊst/ verb [I] **1** to be successful without making much effort **2** to continue to move in a car or on a bicycle after you have switched off the engine or stopped PEDALLING

coastal /ˈkəʊst(ə)l/ adj relating to a coast, or existing on or near a coast: *coastal areas/roads*

coaster /ˈkəʊstə/ noun [C] a small flat object that you put under a cup to protect the table

coastguard /ˈkəʊs(t)ˌɡɑːd/ noun [C/U] a person or organization that helps people who are in trouble at sea, and tries to prevent illegal activities on or near the COAST

coastline /ˈkəʊstˌlaɪn/ noun [C] the land along a coast, or the shape that it makes

coat¹ /kəʊt/ noun [C] ★★★
1 a piece of clothing with long sleeves that you wear over your other clothes when you go outside: *a fur coat* ♦ *Put your coat on – we're going out.*
2 the fur or hair on an animal's skin
3 a layer of something such as paint that you put onto a surface
PHRASE **coat of arms** a special design that is used as the symbol of a family, institution, city etc

coat² /kəʊt/ verb [T] to cover something with a layer of a substance

ˈcoat ˌhanger noun [C] a frame used for hanging clothes on

coating /ˈkəʊtɪŋ/ noun [C] a thin layer that covers a surface

coax /kəʊks/ verb [T] to gently persuade someone to do something

cobalt /ˈkəʊˌbɔːlt/ noun [U] a blue-green colour

cobble /ˈkɒbl/ **PHRASAL VERB** ˌ**cobble sth toˈgether** to make something quickly, using whatever is available

cobbled /ˈkɒb(ə)ld/ adj a cobbled street or road surface is made from many small round stones fixed closely together

cobbler /ˈkɒblə/ noun [C] *old-fashioned* someone who repairs shoes as a job

cobblestones /ˈkɒb(ə)lstəʊnz/ noun [plural] small stones with round tops used in the past to make the surface of a road

cobra /ˈkəʊbrə/ noun [C] a poisonous African or Asian snake

cobweb /ˈkɒbˌweb/ noun [C] a net that a SPIDER

makes out of thin sticky strings to catch insects in

cocaine /kəʊˈkeɪn/ noun [U] a strong illegal drug, usually sold in the form of a white powder

cock¹ /kɒk/ noun [C] a male bird, especially a male chicken

> **PHRASE** **cock and bull story** a story that is silly and difficult to believe

cock² /kɒk/ verb [T] to raise a part of your body, or to move it to one side

> **PHRASAL VERB** **cock sth up** British impolite to spoil something by doing it wrongly

cockerel /ˈkɒk(ə)rəl/ noun [C] a young male chicken

cockney or **Cockney** /ˈkɒkni/ noun **1** [U] a type of informal English spoken in London **2** [C] someone who speaks cockney —**cockney** adj

cockpit /ˈkɒkpɪt/ noun [C] the place where the pilot sits in a plane or where the driver sits in a racing car

cockroach /ˈkɒkrəʊtʃ/ noun [C] an insect similar to a BEETLE that lives in places where food is kept —picture → C13

cocktail /ˈkɒkteɪl/ noun [C] **1** an alcoholic drink made by mixing different drinks together **2** a combination of substances, for example drugs

cocktail party noun [C] a small formal party in the early evening

cock-up noun [C] British impolite a bad mistake, or something that has been done very badly

cocky /ˈkɒki/ adj informal very confident in an annoying way

cocoa /ˈkəʊkəʊ/ noun **1** [U] a brown powder made from a type of bean. It is used for making chocolate and chocolate-flavoured food and drink. **2** [C/U] a hot drink made from this powder

coconut /ˈkəʊkənʌt/ noun **1** [C] a large nut that has a hard brown shell and white flesh —picture → C10 **2** [U] the white flesh of a coconut, that can be eaten

cocoon¹ /kəˈkuːn/ noun [C] a cover that some young insects make to protect themselves while they change into their adult form

cocoon² /kəˈkuːn/ verb [T] to keep someone safe and protected

cod /kɒd/ (plural cod) noun [C/U] a large sea fish that can be eaten

code /kəʊd/ noun ★★

1 [C/U] a system of words, numbers, or signs used for sending secret messages: *The message was written in code.* ♦ *They never cracked the enemy's code* (=discovered how it worked).

2 [C] a set of rules about how something should be done or how people should behave: *the company's code of conduct*

3 [C] a set of numbers, letters, or symbols used for a particular purpose, for example to give information about a product or as part of a phone number

coded /ˈkəʊdɪd/ adj written using a secret system of words or signs

code name noun [C] a name for someone or something that you use when you want to keep their real name secret

coed /ˈkəʊed/ adj including students of both sexes

coerce /kəʊˈɜːs/ verb [T] to make someone do something by using force or threats

coercion /kəʊˈɜːʃ(ə)n/ noun [U] the use of force or threats to make someone do something

coexist /ˌkəʊɪgˈzɪst/ verb [I] formal to live or exist at the same time or in the same place —**coexistence** /ˌkəʊɪgˈzɪstəns/ noun [U]

coffee /ˈkɒfi/ noun ★★★

1 [U] a hot brown drink made by pouring hot water over crushed beans: *Would you like a cup of coffee? ♦ Do you take sugar in your coffee?*

2 [C] a cup of this drink: *We stopped for a coffee on the way. ♦ Can we have three coffees please?*

3 [U] a light brown colour

coffee machine noun [C] **1** a machine that you put money into in order to get a hot drink **2** a machine for making coffee —picture → C2

coffee shop noun [C] a small café where tea, coffee, sandwiches, cakes etc are served

coffee table noun [C] a small low table in a LIVING ROOM

coffers /ˈkɒfəz/ noun [plural] the supply of money that an organization has available to spend

coffin /ˈkɒfɪn/ noun [C] a box in which a dead person is buried

cog /kɒg/ noun [C] a wheel in a machine that fits into the edge of another wheel and makes it turn

cognac /ˈkɒnjæk/ noun [U] a type of French BRANDY

cognitive /ˈkɒgnətɪv/ adj technical connected with the way the brain recognizes or understands things: *cognitive changes/skills*

cohabit /kəʊˈhæbɪt/ verb [I] formal to live with someone in a sexual relationship without being married —**cohabitation** /kəʊˌhæbɪˈteɪʃ(ə)n/ noun [U]

coherent /kəʊˈhɪərənt/ adj clear and sensible, or capable of being understood ≠ INCOHERENT —**coherently** adv

cohesion /kəʊˈhiːʒ(ə)n/ noun [U] a situation in which people or things combine well to form a unit

cohesive /kəʊˈhiːsɪv/ adj combining to form a strong well-organized unit

coil¹ /kɔɪl/ noun [C] a long piece of rope, hair, or wire, that forms several circles, each on top of the other

coil² /kɔɪl/ verb [I/T] to make something into a coil —**coiled** /kɔɪld/ adj

coin¹ /kɔɪn/ noun [C] ★★★ a flat round piece of metal used as money: *Put a coin into the slot.*

> **PHRASES** **flip/toss a coin** to throw a coin in the air to make a decision. Your decision depends on which side of the coin is on top when it lands.
> **two sides of the same coin** two different aspects of the same situation

coin² /kɔɪn/ verb [T] to use a word or phrase that no one has used before

> **PHRASE** **to coin a phrase** spoken used when you realize that something that you have said is a very well-known phrase or expression

coincide /ˌkəʊɪnˈsaɪd/ verb [I] to happen at the same time as something else

C

coincidence /kəʊˈɪnsɪd(ə)ns/ noun [C/U] an unusual situation in which two things happen by chance at the same time or in the same way

coincidental /kəʊˌɪnsɪˈdent(ə)l/ adj happening or existing by chance and not because of being planned or intended —**coincidentally** adv

Col abbrev Colonel

cola /ˈkəʊlə/ noun [U] a sweet brown FIZZY drink (=with gas in it)

colander /ˈkʌləndə/ noun [C] a bowl with small holes in it. You put food into it to remove any liquid.

cold¹ /kəʊld/ adj ★★★
1 with a low temperature, or a temperature that is lower than normal ≠ HOT: *The water was too cold for a shower.* ♦ *a cold winter morning* ♦ *I was cold and hungry.* ♦ *Their house is always freezing cold.*
2 not seeming friendly or sympathetic: *Her father was a cold and distant man.*
3 cold food has been cooked but is not eaten hot: *cold chicken*

PHRASES **get/be given the cold shoulder** *informal* to be treated in an unfriendly way by someone you know
get cold feet to suddenly feel nervous about something that you have planned or agreed to do: *Two days before the wedding he got cold feet.*
in cold blood in a cruel way without showing any sympathy

> Other ways of saying that the weather is cold
> - **chilly** cold enough to make you feel uncomfortable
> - **cool** slightly cold in a nice, comfortable way
> - **freezing cold/freezing** extremely cold

cold² /kəʊld/ noun ★★
1 [U] cold air or temperatures: *Plants need protection against extreme cold.* ♦ *Heavy curtains help to keep the cold out.*
2 [C] a minor illness that blocks your nose and makes you cough: *I didn't go to the game because I had a cold.* ♦ *I must have caught a cold on my holiday.*

cold³ /kəʊld/ adv if you do something cold, you do it without preparing for it
PHRASE **out cold** completely unconscious

cold-blooded /ˌkəʊld ˈblʌdɪd/ adj
1 deliberately cruel and showing no emotion **2** cold-blooded animals have a body temperature that changes to suit their environment

cold-hearted /ˌkəʊld ˈhɑːtɪd/ adj with no sympathy for other people ≠ WARM-HEARTED

coldly /ˈkəʊldli/ adv in a way that is unfriendly or not sympathetic

cold-shoulder verb [T] to be unfriendly towards someone you know

coleslaw /ˈkəʊlˌslɔː/ noun [U] a type of salad made from raw CABBAGE and CARROTS mixed with MAYONNAISE

colic /ˈkɒlɪk/ noun [U] pain that a baby has in its stomach

collaborate /kəˈlæbəreɪt/ verb [I] **1** to work with someone in order to produce something **2** to work secretly to help an enemy or opponent —**collaborator** noun [C]

collaboration /kəˌlæbəˈreɪʃ(ə)n/ noun [U] **1** the process of working with someone to produce something **2** help that someone secretly gives to an enemy or opponent

collaborative /kəˈlæb(ə)rətɪv/ adj involving people working together: *collaborative efforts*

collage /ˈkɒlɑːʒ/ noun [C] a picture made by sticking pieces of different materials together on a surface

collapse¹ /kəˈlæps/ verb [I] ★
1 if a building or other structure collapses, it suddenly falls down: *There were fears that the roof would collapse.*
2 to suddenly fall down and become very ill or unconscious: *A man had collapsed on the hospital steps.*
3 to suddenly fail or stop existing: *The country's economy is collapsing.*
4 an object that collapses can be folded or separated into parts, so that it takes up less space

collapse² /kəˈlæps/ noun **1** [U] a situation in which something fails or stops existing: *the collapse of the military government* **2** [U] an occasion when a building or other structure falls down **3** [C/U] an occasion when someone falls down and becomes very ill or unconscious

collapsible /kəˈlæpsəb(ə)l/ adj able to be folded into a smaller size: *a collapsible bicycle*

collar¹ /ˈkɒlə/ noun [C] ★ a thin piece of leather or plastic that a dog or cat wears around its neck

collar² /ˈkɒlə/ verb [T] to find someone so that you can talk to them

collarbone /ˈkɒləbəʊn/ noun [C] the bone along the front of your shoulder

collateral /kəˈlæt(ə)rəl/ noun [U] property that you agree to give to a bank if you fail to pay back money that you have borrowed

colleague /ˈkɒliːg/ noun [C] ★★ someone who works in the same organization or department as you: *Friends and colleagues will remember him with affection.*

collect /kəˈlekt/ verb ★★★

1 get and keep things	**4** get money
2 keep valuable things	**5** come together
3 go and get sb/sth	**+ PHRASE**

1 [T] to get things and keep them together for a particular reason: *A lot of families collect newspapers for recycling.*
2 [T] to get and keep objects because they are interesting or valuable: *I didn't know she collected modern art.*
3 [T] to go and get a person or thing = PICK UP: *What time do you collect the kids from school?*
4 [T] to get money from someone for a particular purpose: *She is collecting money for charity.* ♦ *He's old enough to collect his pension.*
5 [I] to gradually come together, or to become present = GATHER: *Rain often collects in the corners of flat roofs.*
PHRASE **collect your thoughts** to spend a short time thinking about a decision or forming an opinion

collected /kəˈlektɪd/ adj able to control your

nervous or confused feelings: *She tried to stay calm and collected.*

PHRASE **sb's collected works/poems/letters etc** all of someone's work, poetry etc published together

collection /kəˈlekʃ(ə)n/ noun ★★★

1 [C] a group of similar things that are kept together: *a book borrowed from Jon's huge collection* ♦ *The gallery has one of the finest collections of Impressionist art.* ♦ *a collection of baseball caps*

2 [C/U] the process of collecting things for a particular purpose, or an instance of this: *the collection of household waste* ♦ *Your new glasses are awaiting collection.* ♦ *the collection and analysis of information*

3 [C/U] the activity of collecting money for a particular purpose, or the money that is collected: *The house-to-house collection raised £255.41.*

4 [C] a group of people: *a motley collection of protesters and student groups*

collective¹ /kəˈlektɪv/ adj involving all the members of a group ≠ INDIVIDUAL: *collective responsibility* —**collectively** adv

collective² /kəˈlektɪv/ noun [C] a business run by a group of workers

collector /kəˈlektə/ noun [C] **1** someone who collects things for fun: *a stamp collector* **2** someone whose job is to collect something from people: *the ticket collector*

college /ˈkɒlɪdʒ/ noun ★★★

1 [C/U] a place that gives students qualifications below the level of a university degree, often in the skills that they need to do a particular job: *He teaches cookery at the local college.* ♦ *She's at secretarial college.*

2 [C] one of the parts that some universities are divided into: *King's College, Cambridge*

3 [C] *American* in the US, a university, often a smaller one: *Boston College* ♦ *Colleges all over the country are receiving government money.*

4 [U] *American* the situation or time when you are studying at a college or university: *Kaitlin's going to college next year.*

collide /kəˈlaɪd/ verb [I] if people or things collide, they crash into each other: *The truck collided with a row of parked cars.*

colliery /ˈkɒljəri/ noun [C] *British* a coal mine and the buildings around it

collision /kəˈlɪʒ(ə)n/ noun [C/U] an accident in which a person or vehicle that is moving crashes into something: *The stolen car was involved in a head-on collision with a truck* (=the front of the vehicles hit each other).

colloquial /kəˈləʊkwiəl/ adj used in informal conversation rather than in writing or formal language —**colloquially** adv

colloquialism /kəˈləʊkwiəlɪz(ə)m/ noun [C] a colloquial word or expression

collusion /kəˈluːʒ(ə)n/ noun [U] *formal* the secret activities of people who work together to do something dishonest

cologne /kəˈləʊn/ noun [C/U] a liquid with a nice smell that you put on your skin

colon /ˈkəʊlɒn/ noun [C] **1** the symbol : used in writing, for example before an explanation or a list **2** *medical* the lower part of your BOWELS

colonel /ˈkɜːn(ə)l/ noun [C] an officer of high rank in the army, the MARINES, or the US Air Force

colonial /kəˈləʊniəl/ adj relating to a system or period in which one country rules another: *years of colonial rule*

colonialism /kəˈləʊniəlɪz(ə)m/ noun [U] a situation in which one country rules another —**colonialist** adj

colonist /ˈkɒlənɪst/ noun [C] one of the people who establish a COLONY or go to live in it

colonize /ˈkɒlənaɪz/ verb [T] to take control of another country by going to live there or by sending people to live there —**colonization** /ˌkɒlənaɪˈzeɪʃ(ə)n/ noun [U]

colony /ˈkɒləni/ noun [C] **1** a country that is controlled by another country **2** a group of people or animals of a particular type who live together: *a colony of artists* ♦ *an ant colony*

color /ˈkʌlə/ the American spelling of **colour**

colored /ˈkʌləd/ the American spelling of **coloured**

colorful /ˈkʌləf(ə)l/ the American spelling of **colourful**

coloring /ˈkʌlərɪŋ/ the American spelling of **colouring**

colorless /ˈkʌlələs/ the American spelling of **colourless**

colossal /kəˈlɒs(ə)l/ adj extremely great or large: *It was a colossal waste of money.*

colour¹ /ˈkʌlə/ noun ★★★

1 red, blue etc	4 of sb's face
2 quality of colour	5 interest
3 of sb's skin	

1 [C/U] red, blue, green, yellow etc: *Pink is my favourite colour.* ♦ *a light brown colour* ♦ *Many fruits change colour as they become ripe.* ♦ *His hair is reddish in colour.*

2 [U] the quality of having colour: *Pot plants add colour to a room.* ♦ *Are the pictures in colour or black and white?*

3 [C/U] the colour of someone's skin as a sign of their race: *people of all creeds and colours*

4 [U] the colour of someone's face when it shows how they are feeling: *Suddenly, the colour drained from his cheeks.*

5 [U] interest or excitement: *The examples chosen add colour to the writing.*

→ FLYING¹, OFF-COLOUR

Talking or writing about **colours**

general
- **shade** one of the light or dark types of a particular colour
- **tone** one of the different types of a particular colour

dark colours
- **dark** used for describing colours that look more like black than like white
- **deep** used for describing dark colours that look attractive
- **rich** used for describing dark colours that look beautiful and expensive

bright colours
- **bright** strong and noticeable
- **colourful** brightly coloured, or having a lot of bright colours

C

- **loud** bright in a way that you think looks silly or ugly

pale colours
- **pale** like white with a small amount of a colour mixed in
- **light** pale

colour² /ˈkʌlə/ verb **1** [T] to add colour to something, or to make it a different colour: *I think I'll colour my hair.* **2** [T] to affect someone's decision or opinion about something: *Don't allow your friends' opinions to colour your judgment.* **3** [I/T] to use pens, pencils, or CRAYONS to add colour to a picture

PHRASAL VERB ˌcolour (sth) ˈin same as colour² 3

Word family: colour

Words in the same family as colour
- **coloured** *adj*
- **colourful** *adj*
- **colouring** *n*
- **discoloured** *adj*
- **colourless** *adj*
- **multicoloured** *adj*

colour³ /ˈkʌlə/ adj **1** a colour photograph, magazine etc is in colour, not black and white **2** a colour television, MONITOR etc shows colour pictures or images

colour-blind adj unable to see the difference between some colours, especially red and green —**colour-blindness** noun [U]

coloured /ˈkʌləd/ adj **1** red, green, orange etc rather than black and white or transparent: *pieces of coloured paper* **2** *offensive* a coloured person has dark skin

colourful /ˈkʌləf(ə)l/ adj **1** with bright colours, or a lot of different colours: *colourful Mexican rugs* **2** interesting, exciting, and sometimes funny or shocking: *a family of eccentric and colourful characters* ♦ *a colourful past* —**colourfully** adv

colouring /ˈkʌlərɪŋ/ noun **1** [U] the colour of something, especially someone's hair, skin, and eyes **2** [C/U] a substance that you add to change the colour of food: *food colouring*

colourless /ˈkʌlələs/ adj **1** without any colour: *Carbon monoxide is a colourless, poisonous gas.* **2** not interesting, exciting, or original: *a rather colourless individual*

colt /kəʊlt/ noun [C] a young male horse

column /ˈkɒləm/ noun [C] ★★

1 tall thick post	**4** in newspaper
2 line of people/vehicles	**5** sth rising into the air
3 of writing/numbers	

1 a tall thick post that is used for supporting a roof, decorating a building, or reminding people of an important event or person: *marble columns*
2 a long line of people or vehicles moving together: *a column of soldiers*
3 a series of short lines of writing or numbers arranged one below the other on a page
4 a regular newspaper or magazine article on a particular subject or by a particular journalist
5 something that rises up into the air in a straight line: *a column of smoke and ash*

column

columnist /ˈkɒləmnɪst/ noun [C] a journalist who writes a regular series of articles for a particular newspaper or magazine

com abbrev *computing* commercial organization: used in Internet addresses

coma /ˈkəʊmə/ noun [C] a state in which someone is unconscious for a long time: *She was in a coma for a week.*

comb¹ /kəʊm/ noun [C] an object with one row of thin pointed parts that you use to make your hair tidy

comb² /kəʊm/ verb [T] **1** to make your hair tidy with a comb **2** to search a place thoroughly: *Dozens of officers combed the area with search dogs.*

combat¹ /ˈkɒmˌbæt/ noun [U] fighting during a war: *servicemen killed in combat* ♦ *combat forces/troops/aircraft*

combat² /ˈkɒmˌbæt/ verb [T] to try to stop something bad from happening or a bad situation from becoming worse: *the need for effective action to combat global warming* ♦ *measures to combat crime*

combatant /ˈkɒmbətənt/ noun [C] *formal* a person, group, or country that takes part in a war

combative /ˈkɒmbətɪv/ adj ready to fight, argue, or oppose someone: *He has a reputation as a combative player.*

combination /ˌkɒmbɪˈneɪʃ(ə)n/ noun [C] ★ **1** something that combines several things: *a striking colour combination* ♦ *a combination of text, illustration, and graphics*
2 a series of numbers or letters used for opening a lock: *I've forgotten the combination.*

combine /kəmˈbaɪn/ verb [I/T] ★★ if you combine things, or if they combine, they are used, done, or put together: *an attempt to combine the advantages of two systems* ♦ **combine sth with sth** *Combine the excitement of a week in Bangkok with a week on the unspoilt beaches of Phuket.* ♦ **combined with sth** *High tides combined with strong winds caused severe flooding.* ♦ **combine to do sth** *One oxygen and two hydrogen atoms combine to form a molecule of water.*

combined /kəmˈbaɪnd/ adj **1** done by people or groups working together=JOINT: *a combined effort* **2** formed by adding things together: *What is your combined family income?*

combustible /kəmˈbʌstəb(ə)l/ adj *formal* able to burn easily

combustion /kəmˈbʌstʃ(ə)n/ noun [U] *formal* the process of burning

come /kʌm/ (past tense **came** /keɪm/; past participle **come**) verb [I] ★★★

1 move/travel (to here)	**6** happen
2 reach particular state	**7** be produced/sold
3 start doing sth	**8** be somewhere in order
4 reach particular point	**+ PHRASES**
5 be received	**+ PHRASAL VERBS**

1 to move to the place where the person who is speaking is, or to the place that they are going, or to the place that they are talking about: *Billy, I want you to come here at once!* ♦ *A tall woman in black was **coming across** the lawn.* ♦ *All the glasses came **crashing** onto the floor.* ♦ **come to do sth** *She's got someone coming this morning to fix the computer.* ♦ **come and do sth** *Come and tell me all about it.*

2 to reach a particular state: *We **came to the conclusion that** she must be telling the truth.* ♦ *All good things must **come to an end**.* ♦ *When the Conservatives **came to power** they continued these policies.*

3 to start being a different state or condition: *The new changes will **come into effect** next month.* ♦ *As we turned the corner, the Eiffel Tower **came into view*** (=started to be seen).

4 to reach a particular point or level: *The road comes as far as the post office and then ends.* ♦ *The water **came up to** my shoulders.*

5 if something such as a letter or message comes, you receive it: *The news came at the perfect time.*

6 to happen: *Gorbachev's resignation came after seven tough years in office.* ♦ *It came as no surprise that she left the company.*

7 to be produced or sold: *The dress comes in yellow or blue.* ♦ *All new cars come with one year's free insurance.*

8 to be in a particular position in a series or list or at the end of a race: *July comes before August.* ♦ *She came first in a national poetry competition.*

PHRASES **come naturally/easily/easy (to sb)** to be easy for someone to do: *Fame and fortune have come easily to Carmen.*
come undone/untied/unstuck etc to become UNDONE/UNTIED/UNSTUCK etc: *Be careful! Your shoelaces have come undone.*
here comes sb used for telling another person that someone is moving towards you: *Here comes Dad, and he doesn't look very happy.*
to come in the future: *We were to remain enemies for years to come.*

PHRASAL VERBS **,come a'bout** to happen, especially by chance: *The company's growth has come about through the use of advanced technology.*
,come a'cross to make someone have a particular opinion of you when they meet you: *She comes across as very self-confident.*
,come a'cross sb/sth to meet someone or find something by chance: *I came across a word I'd never seen before.*
,come 'after sb to try to find or catch someone, in order to punish or harm them
,come a'long 1 to arrive, or to become available: *He decided to give the money to the first stranger who came along.* **2** to go somewhere with someone: *I've never seen a baseball game – do you mind if I come along?* **3** to make progress, or to get better in

quality, skill, or health: *The building work was coming along nicely.*
,come a'part to separate easily into pieces
,come a'round *same as* **come round**
'come at sb to move towards someone in order to threaten them or attack them physically: *A stranger came at him with a knife.*
'come at sth to examine or deal with something such as a problem in a particular way: *Try coming at it from a different angle.*
,come 'back 1 to return to a place: *We decided to come back to Scotland for another holiday.* **2** to be remembered again: *I can't think of her name right now, but I'm sure it'll come back to me.* **3** to become fashionable again
,come be'tween sb to cause a disagreement or argument between people: *He didn't want this to come between them.*
,come 'by (sth) to go to the place where someone is for a short visit: *I'll come by this afternoon and we can talk about what happened.*
'come by sth to get something, especially something that is hard to get: *At that time, teaching jobs were hard to come by.*
,come 'down to become less in amount, level, price etc: *Interest rates have come down a lot lately.*
,come 'down on sb to criticize or punish someone severely: *She came down on us pretty hard for making a mess.*
,come 'down to sth to be the most important aspect of a situation or problem: *In the end, it all comes down to who wants the job the most.*
,come 'down with sth to become ill with a particular disease, usually one that is not serious
,come 'forward to offer help or information: *Police said that several people had come forward with information about the attack.*
'come from sth 1 to have been born or lived in a particular place: *My parents came from Italy.* **2** to be produced by a particular place or thing, or to start from there: *The word comes from an African language.* ♦ *I can't tell where the noise is coming from, can you?*
,come 'in 1 to enter a room, building, or other place: *Come in and sit down.* **2** to arrive somewhere: *What time does his train come in?* **3** to finish a race in a particular position: *My horse came in third.* **4** if something such as a message comes in, it is received by someone: *Reports are coming in of a major air accident.* **5** when the TIDE comes in, the sea moves higher up the beach ≠ GO OUT **6 come in useful/handy** to be useful for a particular situation: *A big sheet of plastic always comes in handy when you're camping.*
,come 'in for sth to receive something such as criticism: *Fast food has come in for further criticism in a report published today.*
,come 'into sth to be an aspect of a situation: *The argument was over artistic freedom – money never came into it.*
'come of sth to be the result of something: *I looked for work for months, but nothing came of my efforts.*

C

C

,come 'off to succeed: *The party didn't quite come off as we had hoped.*

,come 'off (sth) 1 be removed from something: *I pulled at the drawer, and the handle came off.* ♦ *The grease won't come off your skin with ordinary washing.* **2 come off it** *spoken* used for telling someone to stop saying something because you do not believe them, or they are annoying you

,come 'on 1 to start working by being switched on: *I saw a light come on in an upstairs window.* **2** to develop, improve, or make progress: *She's coming on fine with her music.* **3** *spoken* used for telling someone to hurry or for encouraging them to do something: *Come on! We're going to be late.* **4** *spoken* used for telling someone that you do not believe what they are saying

,come 'out 1 if something such as a book or a film comes out, it becomes available to buy or see: *Our new album is coming out in the spring.* **2** to become known: *It eventually came out that she was already married.* **3** to be spoken, heard, or understood in a particular way: *She had tried to say 'sorry', but it had come out all wrong.* **4** to be removed from something by washing or rubbing: *The stains still haven't come out.* **5** to tell people that you are gay **6** if the sun, moon, or stars come out, they start to be able to be seen in the sky

,come 'out in sth *British* to become covered in spots because you are ill: *She can't eat shellfish without coming out in spots.*

,come 'out with sth to say something suddenly, usually something that surprises or shocks people: *You never know what the children are going to come out with.*

,come 'over to visit someone in the place where they are, especially their house: *Why don't you come over for dinner?*

,come 'over sb if a feeling comes over you, it suddenly affects you in a strong way

,come 'round *British* **1** if a regular event comes round, it happens again **2** to go to a place where someone is, especially their house, in order to visit them: *Why don't you come round after work?* **3** to become conscious again

,come 'through 1 if something such as a signal or a message comes through, you receive it **2** if a document that you are expecting comes through, it is sent to you: *The job offer still hasn't come through.*

,come 'through sth to be still alive, working, or making progress after a difficult or dangerous experience: *It's been a very upsetting time but we've come through it together.*

,come 'to *same as* **come round** 3

'come to sb if something comes to you, you think of it or remember it: *The idea came to me when we were on holiday.*

'come to sth to reach a particular total when everything is added together: *The total came to £752,000.*

,come 'under sth to be forced to experience something unpleasant: *President Bush has come under pressure to step up the sanctions.*

,come 'up 1 if a problem comes up, it happens and needs to be dealt with immediately:

I'm going to have to cancel our lunch – something's come up. **2** to be mentioned and need to be considered: *A number of interesting points came up at today's meeting.* **3** to move towards someone, usually because you want to talk to them: *Strangers come up to him in the street and say how much they enjoy his books.* **4** to be about to happen soon: *We've got a busy period coming up in a couple of weeks.* **5** if something such as a job comes up, it becomes available **6** if the sun or the moon comes up, it starts to appear in the sky

,come 'up against sth to have to deal with something difficult or unpleasant: *In the first week, we came up against a problem.*

,come 'up to sth to be as good as you want, need, or expect something to be: *The food didn't come up to her standards.*

,come 'up with sth to think of something such as an idea or a plan: *Is that the best you can come up with?*

'come u,pon sb/sth *literary* to meet someone or find something by chance

'come with sth to exist or develop as a result of something: *He has the kind of skill that comes with years of practice.*

comeback /ˈkʌmbæk/ noun [C] **1** a period when someone or something becomes successful or popular again: *Seventies styles have been making a comeback.* **2** a quick clever reply to a comment or criticism

comedian /kəˈmiːdiən/ noun [C] someone whose job is to entertain people by making them laugh = COMIC

comedown /ˈkʌmdaʊn/ noun [C] a situation in which you suddenly have less status or fewer advantages than you had previously

comedy /ˈkɒmədi/ noun ★
1 [C] a funny film, play, or television programme
2 [U] entertainment intended to make people laugh

comet /ˈkɒmɪt/ noun [C] a bright object in space that has a tail of gas and dust

comfort¹ /ˈkʌmfət/ noun ★
1 [U] a physically relaxed state, without any pain or other unpleasant feelings: *The airline is keen to improve passenger comfort.* ♦ *There is plenty of room to lie down and sleep in comfort.*
2 [U] a feeling of being less sad or worried about something than you were previously: *My mother was always there to offer comfort.* ♦ *I take comfort from the fact that his friends are there to help him.*
3 [C] someone or something that makes you feel better when you are sad or worried: *Her children have been a great comfort to her.*
4 [U] a pleasant way of life in which you have everything you need: *Now he can live in comfort for the rest of his life.*
5 **comforts** [plural] things that make your life easier and more pleasant: *the comforts of home*

Word family: **comfort**	
Words in the same family as comfort	
■ comfortable *adj*	■ uncomfortable *adj*
■ comforting *adj*	■ discomfort *n*

comfort² /ˈkʌmfət/ verb [T] to make someone feel less sad, worried, or disappointed
—**comforting** adj

comfortable /ˈkʌmftəb(ə)l/ adj ★★
1 feeling physically relaxed, without any pain or other unpleasant feelings
≠ UNCOMFORTABLE: *If you're not comfortable, try changing positions.* ♦ *Make yourself comfortable and I'll be back in a minute.*
2 making you have a pleasant satisfied feeling in your body: *loose comfortable clothes* ♦ *The bed looked warm and comfortable.*
3 rich enough to pay for everything that you need
4 not worried about something and willing to accept it: *Is everyone comfortable with the arrangement?*
—**comfortably** /ˈkʌmftəbli/ adv

comfy /ˈkʌmfi/ adj *informal* comfortable

comic¹ /ˈkɒmɪk/ adj funny

comic² /ˈkɒmɪk/ noun [C] **1** a magazine that contains stories told in a series of drawings **2** someone whose job is to entertain people by telling jokes and stories to make them laugh=COMEDIAN

comical /ˈkɒmɪk(ə)l/ adj funny in a strange or silly way —**comically** /ˈkɒmɪkli/ adv

comic strip noun [C] a series of drawings that tell a story, especially a funny story

coming¹ /ˈkʌmɪŋ/ adj happening soon, or happening next: *the coming elections*

coming² /ˈkʌmɪŋ/ noun
PHRASES **the coming of** the time when someone or something arrives or happens: *the coming of spring*
comings and goings activity that consists of people arriving and leaving many times

comma /ˈkɒmə/ noun [C] the symbol , used in writing and printing between parts of a sentence or things in a list

command¹ /kəˈmɑːnd/ noun ★
1 [C] an official order to do something: *He refuses to obey my commands.*
2 [U] control of a group of people or of a situation: *Franco was in command of the military.* ♦ *United soon took command of the game.*
3 [C] an instruction that you give to a computer to make it do something: *the log-on command*
PHRASE **command of sth** knowledge of a particular subject, especially the ability to speak a foreign language

command² /kəˈmɑːnd/ verb **1** [T] to be in charge of an activity that involves a group of people: *Lovell commanded the Apollo 13 mission to the moon.* **2** [I/T] to officially order someone to do something: *He commanded his men to retreat.* **3** [T] to have something such as people's respect or attention: *He commands the respect of everyone who works for him.*

commandant /ˈkɒmənˌdænt/ noun [C] a military officer of high rank who controls a particular institution or group of people

commandeer /ˌkɒmənˈdɪə/ verb [T] to officially take someone's property for military use

commander /kəˈmɑːndə/ noun [C] **1** an officer who is in charge of a military group or operation **2** an officer of middle rank in the British navy

commanding /kəˈmɑːndɪŋ/ adj powerful and impressive: *his commanding voice/presence*

commandment /kəˈmɑːn(d)mənt/ noun [C] according to the Bible, one of the ten rules of behaviour that God gave people to obey

commando /kəˈmɑːndəʊ/ noun [C] a soldier who is trained to attack in areas controlled by an enemy

commemorate /kəˈmeməreɪt/ verb [T] to show that you remember an important person or event: *A huge bronze statue commemorating the poet stands in the main square.* —**commemoration** /kəˌmeməˈreɪʃ(ə)n/ noun [C/U]

commemorative /kəˈmem(ə)rətɪv/ adj produced for an important event in order to help you to remember it: *a commemorative stamp*

commence /kəˈmens/ verb [I/T] *formal* to begin, or to begin something: *The trial will commence in 30 days.*

commencement /kəˈmensmənt/ noun [singular/U] *formal* the beginning of something

commend /kəˈmend/ verb [T] *formal* to praise someone or something formally or publicly: *They were commended for the way they handled the job.* —**commendation** /ˌkɒmenˈdeɪʃ(ə)n/ noun [C/U]

commendable /kəˈmendəb(ə)l/ adj *formal* deserving praise or admiration
—**commendably** adv

commensurate /kəˈmenʃərət/ adj *formal* intended to be suitable for the quality, status, or value of something or someone: *a pay increase commensurate with job performance*

comment¹ /ˈkɒment/ noun [C/U] ★★★ a written or spoken remark giving an opinion: *I've had enough of your sarcastic comments.* ♦ *Did she make any comment about Eddie?* ♦ *We would welcome your comments on our work.*
PHRASE **no comment** *spoken* used for saying that you are not willing to answer a question that a journalist asks

comment² /ˈkɒment/ verb [I/T] ★★ to make a written or spoken remark about someone or something: *I'm afraid I can't comment on the matter.* ♦ *+that Researchers who read the report commented that it had many errors.*

commentary /ˈkɒmənt(ə)ri/ noun **1** [C] a spoken description of an event that is given as the event is happening, especially on radio or television **2** [C/U] a discussion of something such as an event or theory: *a commentary on seventh-century English life*

commentator /ˈkɒmənˌteɪtə/ noun [C]
1 someone whose job is to give a description of an event on television or radio as it happens **2** someone whose job is to write about or discuss a particular subject

commerce /ˈkɒmɜːs/ noun [U] the activity of buying and selling goods and services

commercial¹ /kəˈmɜːʃ(ə)l/ adj ★
1 relating to the business of buying and selling goods and services: *One of their first*

C

commercial products was an electronic typewriter.
2 relating to making a profit: *The film's commercial success made her a star.*
3 making money by broadcasting advertisements instead of being given money by the government: *commercial radio stations*
—**commercially** adv

commercial² /kə'mɜːʃ(ə)l/ noun [C] an advertisement on television or radio

commercialism /kə'mɜːʃ(ə)lɪz(ə)m/ noun [U] the activities or attitudes of people who think that making a profit is more important than anything else

commercialized /kə'mɜːʃəlaɪzd/ adj done or changed in order to make a profit: *the increasingly commercialized world of football*

commiserate /kə'mɪzəreɪt/ verb [I] to express sympathy to someone who is unhappy about something=SYMPATHIZE —**commiseration** /kəˌmɪzə'reɪʃ(ə)n/ noun [U]

commission¹ /kə'mɪʃ(ə)n/ noun ★
1 [C] a group of people that is officially put in charge of something or asked to find out about something: *a special parliamentary commission*
2 [C] a request for an artist, writer, or musician to produce a piece of work for someone in exchange for payment
3 [C/U] an extra amount of money that someone earns when they sell a product or get a new customer: *All our salespeople* **work on commission** (=are paid according to how much they sell).
PHRASE **out of commission** not being used, or not able to be used: *Five of their rescue vehicles were out of commission.*

commission² /kə'mɪʃ(ə)n/ verb [T] to officially ask someone to do some work or to produce something for you: *We have commissioned a full survey of the property.* ♦ *She's been commissioned to write a symphony.*

commissioner /kə'mɪʃ(ə)nə/ noun [C] an official who is in charge of something: *the Metropolitan Police Commissioner*

commit /kə'mɪt/ verb ★★★

1 do sth illegal/wrong	**4** in relationships
2 (make sb) agree to sth	**5** send sb to prison
3 say sb/sth will be used	**+ PHRASES**

1 [T] to do something that is illegal or morally wrong: *The study aims to find out what makes people* **commit crimes**. ♦ *He had admitted to* **committing adultery**. ♦ *Reports suggest that the singer* **committed suicide** (=killed himself).
2 [I/T] to agree to do something, or to make someone agree to do something: **commit sb to (doing) sth** *The agreement commits them to a minimum of three years in the programme.* ♦ **commit to (doing) sth** *I do not want to commit to any particular date.*
3 [T] to say that you will use available people or things for a particular purpose: **commit sth to sth** *They'll have to commit more money to the project if it's to succeed.*
4 [I] to decide to have a permanent relationship with someone: *He's not ready to commit.*

5 [T] to say officially that someone must go to prison or go to court to be judged for a crime
PHRASES **commit sth to memory** to study something carefully so that you can remember it exactly
commit yourself 1 to agree to do something: *Take a little time to think before committing yourself.* **2** to give a definite opinion, or to make a definite decision: *She won't commit herself either way.*

commitment /kə'mɪtmənt/ noun ★★
1 [C/U] a promise to do something: *The Government will continue to honour its* **commitment to pensioners**. ♦ **make a commitment (to do sth)** *We've made a commitment to help, and we will.*
2 [U] enthusiasm for something and a determination to work hard at it: *There is a high* **level of commitment** amongst employees.
3 [C] a duty or responsibility that you have accepted: *I couldn't make it because of* **work commitments**. ♦ *He has huge* **financial commitments**.

committed /kə'mɪtɪd/ adj loyal to a belief, organization, or group, and willing to work hard for it

committee /kə'mɪti/ noun [C] ★★★ a group of people who represent a larger group or organization and are chosen to do a particular job: *a management committee* ♦ *committee meetings* ♦ *He's* **on the** golf club **committee**.

> In British English, **committee** can be used with a singular or plural verb. You can say *The committee* **is** *meeting tomorrow.* OR *The committee* **are** *meeting tomorrow.*

commodity /kə'mɒdəti/ noun [C] a product that can be bought and sold

common¹ /'kɒmən/ adj ★★★
1 happening frequently, or existing in large amounts or numbers: *Today smog is* **a common occurrence** *in many major cities.* ♦ *It's* **common practice** *in most companies these days.* ♦ **it is common for sb/sth to do sth** *It was common for children to play in the street.*
2 used, done, or shared by two or more people: *Members also agreed to pursue a common trade policy.* ♦ *These issues are common to all our clients.*
3 ordinary, with no special status or rank: *a common soldier/criminal*
4 old-fashioned an insulting way of describing someone from a low social class
PHRASE **the common good** the benefit of everyone

common² /'kɒmən/ noun [C] a large piece of open land in a village or town where anyone can walk or play games
PHRASES **have sth in common (with sb)** to have the same interests or opinions as someone else: *We've got such a lot in common.*
have sth in common (with sth) to have the same features as something else
in common with in the same way as someone or something else
→ HOUSE OF COMMONS

common 'cold, the noun [singular] a minor illness that makes you SNEEZE and cough

common 'ground noun [U] something that people can agree about when they disagree about other things

common 'knowledge noun [U] something that everyone knows

common 'law¹ noun [U] the system of law that has developed from customs and judges' decisions instead of from laws made by politicians

common 'law² adj involved in a relationship that has continued long enough to be considered a marriage, even though it is not official: *a common law husband/wife*

commonly /ˈkɒmənli/ adv usually, or frequently

commonplace /ˈkɒmənpleɪs/ adj completely normal: *It is now commonplace for people to use the Internet at home.*

common ,room noun [C] a room in a school or college where students go to relax

Commons, the /ˈkɒmənz/ the HOUSE OF COMMONS

common 'sense noun [U] the ability to use good judgment and make sensible decisions

Commonwealth, the /ˈkɒmənwelθ/ an organization of countries that used to be under the political control of the UK

commotion /kəˈməʊʃ(ə)n/ noun [C/U] noise and confused activity

communal /ˈkɒmjʊn(ə)l, kəˈmjuːn(ə)l/ adj owned or used by everyone in a group: *a communal kitchen/garden*

commune¹ /ˈkɒmjuːn/ noun [C] a group of people who live together and share work, food, income, and possessions

commune² /kəˈmjuːn/ verb [I] *literary* to communicate with someone or something without using words

communicate /kəˈmjuːnɪkeɪt/ verb ★
1 [I/T] to express thoughts, feelings, or information to someone else: *How do whales communicate?* ♦ *We communicate with each other via email.* ♦ **communicate sth to sb** *The information was communicated to officials in July 1981.*
2 [I/T] to make someone understand an emotion or idea without expressing it in words: *She has an amazing ability to communicate enthusiasm.*
3 [I] to let someone know what you are feeling or thinking, so that you have a good relationship: *She says that they no longer seem to communicate.*

communication /kəˌmjuːnɪˈkeɪʃ(ə)n/ noun ★★★
1 [U] the process of giving or exchanging information or of making emotions or ideas known to someone: *efforts to improve communication among the staff* ♦ *There was a breakdown in communication.* ♦ *The two groups are in regular communication.* ♦ *She has no communication with her family.* ♦ *a workshop to improve teachers' communication skills*
2 **communications** [plural] a system for sending information: *satellite communications*
3 [C] *formal* a message such as a letter, phone call, or email

communicative /kəˈmjuːnɪkətɪv/ adj willing to tell things to other people

communion /kəˈmjuːniən/ noun [U]
1 Communion or **Holy Communion** a Christian ceremony in which people eat bread and drink wine in order to remember Jesus Christ **2** *formal* communication with someone or something without using words

communiqué /kəˈmjuːnɪkeɪ/ noun [C] an official statement

communism /ˈkɒmjʊˌnɪz(ə)m/ noun [U] a political and economic system in which individual people do not own property or industries and in which people of all social classes are treated equally

communist /ˈkɒmjʊnɪst/ noun [C] someone who believes in communism —**communist** adj

community /kəˈmjuːnəti/ noun ★★★
1 [C] the people who live in an area: *small rural communities* ♦ *I wanted to work somewhere where I could serve the community.*
2 [C] a group of people in a larger society who are the same in some way: *areas where there are large Jewish communities*
3 [U] the feeling that you belong to a group and that this is a good thing: *One of the major goals is to develop **a sense of community**.*

> In British English, a **community** of people can be used with a singular or plural verb. You can say: *The community is opposed to the plan.* OR: *The community are opposed to the plan.*

com'munity ,service noun [U] **1** work that someone does as a punishment, instead of going to prison **2** work without payment that someone does to help their local community

commute¹ /kəˈmjuːt/ verb **1** [I] to travel regularly to and from work **2** [T] *legal* to change a punishment to one that is less severe

commute² /kəˈmjuːt/ noun [singular] the journey to and from work every day

commuter /kəˈmjuːtə/ noun [C] someone who travels regularly to and from work

compact¹ /ˈkɒmpækt, kəmˈpækt/ adj smaller than most things of the same kind: *a compact car/camera*

compact² /kəmˈpækt/ verb [T] to make something smaller or firmer by pressing it

compact³ /ˈkɒmpækt/ noun [C] a small flat container for FACE POWDER, with a mirror inside

compact 'disc noun [C] a CD

companion /kəmˈpænjən/ noun [C] someone who is with you or who you spend a lot of time with

companionship /kəmˈpænjənʃɪp/ noun [U] the relationship that you have with a good friend who spends a lot of time with you

company /ˈkʌmp(ə)ni/ noun ★★★
1 [C] an organization that sells services or goods: *Max works for a large oil company.*
2 [U] the activity of being with other people: *I thought you might want some company tonight.* ♦ *We always enjoy his company.* ♦ *She's not coming – she's got company* (=a guest or guests).

C

C

3 [C] a group of actors, singers, or dancers who perform together: *the Royal Shakespeare Company*

PHRASES **be good company** to be someone who people enjoy spending time with

keep sb company to spend time with someone so that they will not feel lonely

Talking or writing about **companies**

- **business** a company that makes or sells goods, or provides a service
- **cooperative** a company that is owned and run by all the people who work in it
- **corporation** a large company that employs a lot of people
- **firm** a company, especially one that provides professional or financial services
- **multinational** a large company that operates in many different countries
- **subsidiary** a company that is owned by a larger company

comparable /ˈkɒmp(ə)rəb(ə)l/ adj fairly similar to another thing, so that it is reasonable to compare them
≠ INCOMPARABLE: *The salary is comparable with that of a junior doctor.*

comparative[1] /kəmˈpærətɪv/ adj **1** judged in comparison with something such as a previous situation or state=RELATIVE: *We expected to win with comparative ease.*
2 involving the comparison of two or more things: *a comparative analysis* **3** linguistics the comparative form of an adjective or adverb is the form that shows that something has more of a quality than it previously had or more of a quality than something else has. For example, 'newer' is the comparative form of 'new'.
→ SUPERLATIVE[1] 1

comparative[2] /kəmˈpærətɪv/ noun [C] linguistics a comparative form of an adjective or adverb: *The comparative of 'good' is 'better'.*

comparatively /kəmˈpærətɪvli/ adv as compared with something else or with a previous situation or state=RELATIVELY: *The technology is still comparatively new.*

compare /kəmˈpeə/ verb ★★★
1 [T] to consider the ways in which people or things are similar or different: *The research compares and contrasts the two policies* (=shows how they are similar and how they are different). ♦ **compare sth with/to sth** *Compare the one that has been cleaned with the others.*
2 [I] to be as good or bad as someone or something else: *How does the UK's performance compare with performance in other European countries?*
3 [T] to say that one person or thing is similar to another: **compare sth to sth** *The band has been compared to the Beatles.*
PHRASE **compare notes** to discuss something with someone who has also experienced it or thought about it

Word family: **compare**
Words in the same family as **compare**
- **comparative** *adj*   ■ **comparatively** *adv*
- **comparable** *adj*   ■ **incomparable** *adj*
- **comparison** *n*

compared /kəmˈpeəd/ adj **compared with/to** used for talking about the ways in which two people or things are different, or about the ways in which someone or something has changed: *Profits were good compared with last year.*

comparison /kəmˈpærɪs(ə)n/ noun [C/U] ★★ the process of considering the ways in which people or things are similar or different: *It is very difficult to make comparisons with other schools.* ♦ *We cannot make a comparison between the two languages.* ♦ *There was some comparison of the techniques used by the different players.*
PHRASES **in/by comparison (with)** used for talking about the ways in which two people or things are different: *Our lives seem so dull in comparison with theirs.*
there's no comparison used for saying that one person or thing is much better than another

compartment /kəmˈpɑːtmənt/ noun [C] **1** one of the separate parts of a container or place where things are stored **2** one of the separate spaces into which a railway CARRIAGE is divided

compass /ˈkʌmpəs/ noun [C] a piece of equipment used for finding your way, with a needle that always points to the north

compasses /ˈkʌmpəsɪz/ noun [plural] a piece of equipment in the shape of the letter V, used for drawing circles

compassion /kəmˈpæʃ(ə)n/ noun [U] sympathy for someone who is in a bad situation

compassionate /kəmˈpæʃ(ə)nət/ adj caring about someone who is in a bad situation

compatible /kəmˈpætəb(ə)l/ adj **1** able to exist together with another idea or system: *The scheme is not compatible with environmental principles.* **2** computing able to be used together with another piece of computer equipment or software **3** likely to have a good relationship because of being similar
≠ INCOMPATIBLE: *We're just not compatible.* —**compatibility** /kəmˌpætəˈbɪləti/ noun [U]

compatriot /kəmˈpætriət/ noun [C] someone who is from the same country as you

compel /kəmˈpel/ verb [T] to force someone to do something

compelling /kəmˈpelɪŋ/ adj **1** interesting or exciting enough to keep your attention completely: *a compelling story* **2** able to persuade someone to do or believe something: *compelling evidence*

compensate /ˈkɒmpənˌseɪt/ verb **1** [I] to change or remove the bad effect of something: *Their enthusiasm compensates for their lack of skill.* **2** [I/T] to pay someone money because they have suffered an injury or loss: *They were compensated for the damage to the house.*

compensation /ˌkɒmpənˈseɪʃ(ə)n/ noun **1** [U] money that someone receives because something bad has happened to them: *She was awarded £200,000 compensation for her injuries.* **2** [C/U] something that changes or removes the bad effect of something: *He uses speed as compensation for his lack of strength.*

compère /ˈkɒmpeə/ noun [C] British someone

whose job is to introduce the performers in a show

compete /kəm'pi:t/ verb [I] ★★
1 to try to be more successful than other companies or people in business: *We're too small to* **compete with** *a company like that.*
2 to try to win a competition: *Her dream was to* **compete in** *the Olympics.* ♦ *You will be* **competing against** *the best athletes in the world.* ♦ *Ten teams will* **compete for** *the trophy.*

> **Word family: compete**
>
> *Words in the same family as* **compete**
> ■ **competition** *n*   ■ **competitor** *n*
> ■ **competitive** *adj*   ■ **uncompetitive** *adj*

competence /'kɒmpɪtəns/ noun [U] the ability to do something well ≠ INCOMPETENCE: *I am not questioning your competence.*

competent /'kɒmpɪtənt/ adj **1** capable of doing something well **2** good enough, but not extremely good ≠ INCOMPETENT
—**competently** adv

competing /kəm'pi:tɪŋ/ adj competing arguments, claims, or theories cannot all be true

competition /ˌkɒmpə'tɪʃ(ə)n/ noun ★★★
1 [U] the activities of companies that are trying to be more successful than others: *intense* **competition between** *the two computer giants*
2 [U] the activities of people who are trying to get something that other people also want: *There is a lot of* **competition for** *jobs.* ♦ *We must emphasize that we are not* **in competition with** (=competing with) *you.*
3 [C] an organized event in which people try to win prizes by being better than other people: *He'd* **entered a competition** *in the local newspaper.*
4 the competition the person, company, or thing that someone is competing with: *Let's look at what the competition is doing and do it better.*

> In British English, **the competition** can be used with a singular or plural verb. You can say *Let's look at what the competition* **is** *doing and do it better.* OR *Let's look at what the competition* **are** *doing and do it better.*

competitive /kəm'petətɪv/ adj ★★
1 a competitive activity is one in which companies or teams are competing against each other: *the struggle to survive in a* **highly competitive** *marketplace*
2 cheaper than others: *a wide range of goods at very competitive prices*
3 always trying to be more successful than other people: *a* **highly competitive** *player*
—**competitively** adv, **competitiveness** noun [U]

competitor /kəm'petɪtə/ noun [C] **1** a company that sells the same goods or services as another **2** someone who takes part in a sports competition

compilation /ˌkɒmpə'leɪʃ(ə)n/ noun [C] a set of things such as songs or stories that are brought together from different places

compile /kəm'paɪl/ verb [T] to make a list or book using information from many different places

complacent /kəm'pleɪs(ə)nt/ adj too confident

and relaxed because you think you can deal with something easily, even though this may not be true —**complacency** /kəm'pleɪs(ə)nsi/ noun [U], **complacently** adv

complain /kəm'pleɪn/ verb [I/T] ★★★ to say that you are not satisfied with something: *What are you* **complaining about?** ♦ *He threatened to* **complain to** *the boss.* ♦ **+(that)** *She complained that it was too hot.*
PHRASAL VERB **com'plain of sth** to say that you have a pain or an illness

complaint /kəm'pleɪnt/ noun ★★
1 [C/U] a statement that you are not satisfied with something: *I intend to* **make a complaint.** ♦ *There's been a* **complaint about** *your work.* ♦ *Several complaints have been* **made against** *him.* ♦ **+that** *complaints that the building is not safe*
2 [C] something that someone complains about: *The main complaint was the noise.*
3 [C] an illness or other medical problem

complement¹ /'kɒmplɪment/ verb [T] to combine well with something: *a simple sweater that was complemented by elegant jewellery*

complement² /'kɒmplɪmənt/ noun [C]
1 something that combines well with something else: *Our sauces are the perfect complement to any meal.* **2** the number of people or things that something has: *We already have our full complement of workers.* **3** *linguistics* a word or phrase after a verb such as 'be' that tells you about the SUBJECT. For example, in 'He was a nice man', the complement is 'a nice man'.

complementary /ˌkɒmplɪ'ment(ə)ri/ adj combining well together, or looking attractive together

complete¹ /kəm'pli:t/ adj ★★★
1 used for emphasizing that someone or something has a particular quality: *He's a complete idiot!*
2 including everything ≠ INCOMPLETE: *a complete set of her novels*
3 finished: *When the chart is complete, stick it on the wall.*
PHRASE **complete with** including something: *All our machines come complete with a three-year service warranty.*

complete² /kəm'pli:t/ verb [T] ★★★
1 to finish something: *The work was completed in March.*
2 to add the missing parts of something in order to finish it: *Complete the following sentence by writing in the correct form of the present tense.* ♦ *Please complete this form* (=write in the blank spaces).

completely /kəm'pli:tli/ adv ★★★ used for emphasis: *Ellen's suggestion took us completely by surprise.*

completion /kəm'pli:ʃ(ə)n/ noun [U] ★ the process of finishing an activity or job: *Nothing must delay the* **completion of** *the project.* ♦ *You will get a certificate* **on completion of** *the course.*

complex¹ /'kɒmpleks, kəm'pleks/ adj ★★ containing a lot of details or small parts and therefore difficult to understand or deal with: *These rules are highly complex.*

complex² /'kɒmpleks/ noun [C] **1** a group of buildings, or a building with several parts

C

2 an emotional problem caused by unreasonable fears or worries: *I used to have a complex about being so tall.*

complexion /kəmˈplekʃ(ə)n/ noun **1** [C] the appearance and colour of the skin on your face **2** [singular] the typical features of something

complexity /kəmˈpleksəti/ noun **1** [U] the complicated nature of something **2 complexities** [plural] the features of something that make it confusing or difficult to deal with

compliance /kəmˈplaɪəns/ noun [U] *formal* the practice of obeying a law, rule, or request: *All building work must be carried out in compliance with safety regulations.*

compliant /kəmˈplaɪənt/ adj extremely willing to do what people tell you to do

complicate /ˈkɒmplɪˌkeɪt/ verb [T] to make something more difficult to deal with or understand

complicated /ˈkɒmplɪˌkeɪtɪd/ adj ★★ difficult to do, deal with, or understand ≠ SIMPLE

complication /ˌkɒmplɪˈkeɪʃ(ə)n/ noun **1** [C/U] something that makes a process or activity more difficult to deal with **2** [C] a new medical problem that makes a medical condition more serious

complicity /kəmˈplɪsəti/ noun [U] the fact that someone is involved in or knows about something bad

compliment¹ /ˈkɒmplɪmənt/ noun [C] something nice that you say to praise someone ≠ INSULT: *He kept paying me compliments on my cooking.*

> **PHRASE with the compliments of sb** used for saying that you do not have to pay for something

compliment² /ˈkɒmplɪˌment/ verb [T] to say something nice to or about someone: *Everybody complimented her on the way she handled the emergency.*

complimentary /ˌkɒmplɪˈment(ə)ri/ adj **1** free: *complimentary tickets* **2** saying nice things about someone or something: *She was most complimentary about your work.*

comply /kəmˈplaɪ/ verb [I] to obey a rule or law, or to do what someone asks you to do: *You are legally obliged to comply with any investigations.*

Words often used with comply

Nouns often used with comply
- COMPLY WITH + **demand, order, request, requirement**: do something that someone says
- COMPLY WITH + **legislation, regulation, rule**: obey a law or rule

---

component /kəmˈpəʊnənt/ noun [C] ★
1 a part of a machine or piece of equipment
2 an individual quality or feature of something

Words often used with component

Adjectives often used with component (sense 2)
- **essential, key, major, principal, vital** + COMPONENT: used about a feature that is important or necessary

---

compose /kəmˈpəʊz/ verb ★
1 [I/T] to write a piece of music: *The song was composed for their wedding.*

2 [T] *formal* to write something after thinking carefully about it: *He sat down and composed a letter of resignation.*

> **PHRASES be composed of sth** to consist of something: *Muscle is composed of two different types of protein.*
> **compose yourself** to make yourself calm after being very angry, upset, or nervous

composed /kəmˈpəʊzd/ adj calm and relaxed

composer /kəmˈpəʊzə/ noun [C] someone who writes music

composite /ˈkɒmpəzɪt/ adj made up of separate parts —**composite** noun [C]

composition /ˌkɒmpəˈzɪʃ(ə)n/ noun ★
1 [U] the way in which something is formed from separate parts or people: *Households differ widely in their size and composition.*
2 [C] a piece of music, a piece of writing, or a painting
3 [U] the skill or process of producing music, writing, or paintings

compost /ˈkɒmpɒst/ noun [U] a mixture of decaying plants and vegetables that is added to soil to improve it

composure /kəmˈpəʊʒə/ noun [U] the feeling of being calm and relaxed

compound¹ /ˈkɒmpaʊnd/ noun [C] **1** *science* a chemical substance that consists of two or more elements **2** an enclosed area where a particular group of people live or exercise **3** *linguistics* a combination of two or more words used as a single word

compound² /kəmˈpaʊnd/ verb [T] to make a problem or difficult situation worse

comprehend /ˌkɒmprɪˈhend/ verb [I/T] *formal* to understand something

comprehensible /ˌkɒmprɪˈhensəb(ə)l/ adj able to be understood ≠ INCOMPREHENSIBLE

comprehension /ˌkɒmprɪˈhenʃ(ə)n/ noun [U] the ability to understand something: *These acts of cruelty are beyond my comprehension* (=impossible for me to understand).

comprehensive¹ /ˌkɒmprɪˈhensɪv/ adj including everything: *a comprehensive guide to university courses*

comprehensive² /ˌkɒmprɪˈhensɪv/ or **comprehensive school** noun [C] in the UK, a school for students of different levels of ability between the ages of 11 and 18

compress /kəmˈpres/ verb [T] **1** to press something so that it fits into a smaller space **2** to make something last for less time than usual —**compression** /kəmˈpreʃ(ə)n/ noun [U]

comprise /kəmˈpraɪz/ verb [T] *formal* to form something: *People aged 65 and over comprise 20% of the population.*

> **PHRASE be comprised of** to consist of two or more things: *The force is comprised of US and British troops.*

compromise¹ /ˈkɒmprəˌmaɪz/ noun [C/U] a way of solving a disagreement in which both people accept that they cannot have everything that they want: *Neither of them is willing to make compromises.* ♦ *Both sides have agreed to try to reach a compromise.*

compromise² /ˈkɒmprəˌmaɪz/ verb **1** [I] to solve a disagreement by accepting that you cannot have everything that you want: *Can we compromise on the schedule if not on pay?* **2** [T] to risk harming or losing something important: *We cannot compromise the safety of our workers.* **3** [T] to do things that do not agree with your beliefs or principles: *The party is obviously compromising its principles.*

compromising /'kɒmprəˌmaɪzɪŋ/ adj likely to damage your reputation

compulsion /kəm'pʌlʃ(ə)n/ noun **1** [C] an extremely strong feeling of wanting to do something **2** [U] an obligation to do something

compulsive /kəm'pʌlsɪv/ adj **1** impossible to control: *a compulsive need to succeed* **2** unable to control a habit: *a compulsive liar* —**compulsively** adv

compulsory /kəm'pʌlsəri/ adj ★ something that is compulsory must be done or used because of a rule or law ≠ OPTIONAL: *compulsory exams*

computer /kəm'pjuːtə/ noun [C] ★★★ an electronic machine that has programs on it for storing, writing, and calculating information. It also allows you to communicate on the Internet: *a computer program/game* —**picture →** C3

computer-aided design /kəmˌpjuːtər ˌeɪdɪd dɪ'zaɪn/ noun [U] CAD

computerize /kəm'pjuːtəraɪz/ verb [T] to use computers to do a particular job —**computerization** /kəmˌpjuːtəraɪ'zeɪʃ(ə)n/ noun [U]

computer-literate adj able to use a computer

computing /kəm'pjuːtɪŋ/ noun [U] the activity or skill of using or PROGRAMMING computers

comrade /'kɒmreɪd/ noun [C] *formal* a friend who you work with or who is in the same army as you —**comradeship** noun [U]

con[1] /kɒn/ noun [C] *informal* a trick for making someone believe something that is not true in order to get money from them

con[2] /kɒn/ verb [T] *informal* to make someone believe something that is not true in order to get money from them

concave /'kɒnkeɪv, kɒn'keɪv/ adj curved inwards ≠ CONVEX

conceal /kən'siːl/ verb [T] *formal* to hide something, or to keep something secret: *She could not conceal her annoyance.*

concede /kən'siːd/ verb **1** [T] to admit that something is true: *Myers was forced to concede that competition had badly affected profits.* **2** [I/T] to stop trying to win something because you realize that you cannot: *He finally had to concede defeat.* **3** [T] to give something that you own or control to someone, although you do not want to: *Some territory has been conceded to the rebels.*

conceit /kən'siːt/ noun [U] a conceited attitude or way of behaving

conceited /kən'siːtɪd/ adj *showing disapproval* behaving in a way that shows that you think you are very intelligent, skilful, or attractive

conceivable /kən'siːvəb(ə)l/ adj possible, or possible to imagine ≠ INCONCEIVABLE —**conceivably** adv

conceive /kən'siːv/ verb **1** [T] to think of a new idea, plan, or design: *The facilities had been*

conceived with families in mind. **2** [I/T] to imagine something, or to think of doing something: *How can they even conceive of doing such an appalling thing?* **3** [I/T] to become pregnant

concentrate /'kɒns(ə)nˌtreɪt/ verb ★★★ **1** [I/T] to give all your attention to the thing that you are doing: *Shh! I'm trying to concentrate.* ♦ *Just concentrate on your work.*
2 [T] **be concentrated** to exist mainly in a particular area: *The violence was concentrated mostly in the north.*

concentrated /'kɒns(ə)nˌtreɪtɪd/ adj **1** concentrated liquids or substances have been made stronger by having water removed **2** directed completely at one thing, person, or place: *The presidential palace has been hit again by concentrated artillery fire.*

concentration /ˌkɒns(ə)n'treɪʃ(ə)n/ noun ★★★ **1** [U] the process of giving all your attention to something: *It took all his concentration to stay awake.*
2 [C/U] a large number of people or things in one area: *The largest concentrations of ancient sites are around Cairo and Luxor.*

concen'tration ˌcamp noun [C] a prison where ordinary people are kept during a war in very unpleasant conditions

concentric /kən'sentrɪk/ adj concentric circles all have the same centre

concept /'kɒnsept/ noun [C] ★★★ an idea: *It's important that children learn to understand the concept of sharing.* —**conceptual** /kən'septʃuəl/ adj

conception /kən'sepʃ(ə)n/ noun **1** [C] a belief about what something is like: *His conception of the world is a very strange one.* **2** [U] the moment when a woman becomes pregnant

concern[1] /kən'sɜːn/ noun ★★★
1 [C/U] a feeling of worry, or something that worries you: *There's a lot of public concern about modern farming methods.* ♦ *The trip was cancelled because of concerns about safety.* ♦ *It's a matter of major concern to employers* (=it worries them). ♦ *Doctors said her condition was causing concern.*
2 [C/U] something that you think is important: *My only concern is to find my daughter.*
3 [singular] a responsibility: *If children are not attending school, then that is the parents' concern.*
4 [C] a business: *a large concern employing 60 people*

Words often used with **concern**
*Adjectives often used with **concern** (noun, sense 2)*
■ **central, chief, main, major, overriding, primary, principal** + CONCERN: used about something that is very important
*Verbs often used with **concern** (noun, sense 1)*
■ **express, raise, voice** + CONCERN: tell people that you are worried
■ **be a cause for, be a matter of, cause** + CONCERN: make someone worried

concern[2] /kən'sɜːn/ verb [T] ★★★
1 to worry someone: *It concerns me that these people are not getting the support they need.*
2 to be about a particular subject: *The story concerns a friend of mine.*

3 to involve or affect someone: *My past doesn't concern you.*

PHRASE concern yourself to think about or worry about something: *I'm too busy to concern myself with your affairs.*

concerned /kən'sɜːnd/ adj ★★★
1 *formal* worried about something ≠ UNCONCERNED: *Police said they were very concerned about the boy's safety.*
2 involved in something, or affected by something: *I suggest you speak to the person concerned.*
3 caring about what happens to someone: *I think she's genuinely concerned about you.*
4 giving your attention to something that you think is important: *Don't be so concerned with what other people think of you.*

PHRASES as far as I'm concerned used for giving your opinion about something: *As far as I'm concerned, the issue is over and done with.*

as far as sb/sth is concerned used for saying which person or thing you are talking about: *I make the decisions as far as finance is concerned.*

concerning /kən'sɜːnɪŋ/ preposition *formal* ★★ about a particular subject: *a newspaper article concerning pollution*

concert /'kɒnsət/ noun [C] ★★ an event at which an orchestra, band, or musician plays or sings in front of an audience

concerted /kən'sɜːtɪd/ adj involving a lot of people working together in a determined way: *a concerted effort*

concerto /kən'tʃeətəʊ/ noun [C] a piece of music for a musical instrument and an orchestra: *Beethoven's Violin Concerto*

concession /kən'seʃ(ə)n/ noun [C] **1** something that you agree to in order to reach an agreement: *He said they would not make concessions to the union.* **2** a reduction in the price or rate of something for a particular group of people: *concessions for pensioners* **3** a right that is given to a person or group to sell something or perform a particular activity: *timber concessions to Korean companies*

concessionary /kən'seʃ(ə)nəri/ adj cheaper than the usual price or rate, and offered to a particular group of people: *concessionary fares/travel*

conciliation /kən,sɪli'eɪʃ(ə)n/ noun [U] the process of trying to end an argument between two people or groups

conciliatory /kən'sɪliət(ə)ri/ adj trying to end an argument and make people feel less angry

concise /kən'saɪs/ adj expressed clearly using only a few words —**concisely** adv

conclude /kən'kluːd/ verb ★★
1 [T] to decide that something is true after looking at all the evidence: **+that** *The report concluded that a recession was unlikely.*
2 [I/T] *formal* to end, or to end something: *The article concludes with the names and addresses of organizations that can help.* ♦ *The president will conclude his visit with a trip to Munich.*
3 [T] *formal* to officially arrange something: *We hope to conclude an agreement by the end of the day.*

concluding /kən'kluːdɪŋ/ adj happening or done at the end of something: *concluding remarks*

conclusion /kən'kluːʒ(ə)n/ noun ★★★
1 [C] something that you decide is true after looking at all the evidence: *I finally came to the conclusion that Lenny wasn't interested in me.* ♦ *Hubble reached the conclusion that the universe was expanding.*
2 [singular] *formal* the end of something: *a successful conclusion to the season*
PHRASES in conclusion finally: *In conclusion, I would like to thank my wife and children.*
jump to conclusions to make a decision about something before you know all the facts

conclusive /kən'kluːsɪv/ adj conclusive evidence, proof, or information proves that something is true ≠ INCONCLUSIVE —**conclusively** adv

concoct /kən'kɒkt/ verb [T] **1** to invent a false explanation or false information **2** to produce something unusual by mixing things in a new way —**concoction** /kən'kɒkʃ(ə)n/ noun [C/U]

concourse /'kɒŋkɔːs/ noun [C] a large open area in an airport or railway station, or in front of a public building

concrete[1] /'kɒŋkriːt/ adj ★
1 made of concrete
2 based on facts: *concrete evidence*

concrete[2] /'kɒŋkriːt/ noun [U] a hard substance used in building that is made by mixing CEMENT, sand, small stones, and water

concrete[3] /'kɒŋkriːt/ or **concrete over sth** verb [T] to cover something with concrete

concrete noun noun [C] *linguistics* a noun that refers to an object that you can see or touch rather than to an idea or feeling

concur /kən'kɜː/ verb [I] *formal* to agree

concussion /kən'kʌʃ(ə)n/ noun [C/U] a head injury that makes someone feel ill or become unconscious for a short time

condemn /kən'dem/ verb [T] ★
1 to say publicly that you think someone or something is bad or wrong: *Politicians have condemned the attacks.* ♦ **condemn sb/sth as sth** *The minister condemned the proposal as 'very damaging'.*
2 to give a punishment to someone who has committed a crime: *Fifty rebels were condemned to death.*
3 to order something such as a building or machine to be destroyed because it is not safe

condemnation /,kɒndem'neɪʃ(ə)n/ noun [C/U] a public statement in which you criticize someone or something severely

condensation /,kɒnden'seɪʃ(ə)n/ noun [U] water that forms when steam or warm air changes into liquid

condense /kən'dens/ verb **1** [T] to make something shorter or smaller **2** [I/T] if gas or steam condenses, or if something condenses it, it changes into a liquid

condescending /,kɒndɪ'sendɪŋ/ adj showing that you think you are more important or intelligent than someone else —**condescend** /,kɒndɪ'send/ verb [I], **condescension** /,kɒndɪ'senʃ(ə)n/ noun [U]

condition[1] /kənˈdɪʃ(ə)n/ noun ★★★
1 [singular/U] the physical state of something or someone: *Engineers will examine the condition of the damaged buildings.* ♦ *The five people who were rescued were all in good condition.*
2 conditions [plural] the situation or environment in which something happens or someone lives: *Their role is to create the conditions for peace in the region.* ♦ *The project aims to provide better living conditions for elderly people.*
3 [C] something that must be true or must be done before another thing can happen: *Read the terms and conditions of the contract carefully.* ♦ *You will have to meet strict financial conditions to get the loan.*
4 [C] an illness or health problem that lasts a long time and affects the way you live: *a heart condition* ♦ *Both children suffer from the same medical condition.*
PHRASES **in no condition to do sth** too ill, upset, or drunk to do something
on condition (that) used for saying that one thing will happen only if another thing also happens: *They agreed to speak on condition that their names would not be used in the article.*

condition[2] /kənˈdɪʃ(ə)n/ verb [T] **1** to influence someone over a long period so that they think or behave in a particular way **2** to make your hair feel softer by putting a special liquid on it after you have washed it —**conditioning** /kənˈdɪʃ(ə)nɪŋ/ noun [U]

conditional /kənˈdɪʃ(ə)nəl/ adj ★
1 something that is conditional will only happen if something else happens: *The job offer is conditional on passing a medical examination.*
2 *linguistics* a conditional CLAUSE usually begins with 'if' or 'unless' and says what must happen or exist in order for the information in the main part of the sentence to be true

conditioner /kənˈdɪʃ(ə)nə/ noun [C/U] a liquid that you put on your hair after you have washed it in order to make it feel softer

condolences /kənˈdəʊlənsɪz/ noun [plural] the things that you say in order to show sympathy when someone has just died

condom /ˈkɒndɒm/ noun [C] a thin rubber tube that a man covers his PENIS with during sex in order to prevent a woman from becoming pregnant and to protect against diseases

condominium /ˌkɒndəˈmɪniəm/ noun [C] *American* a building containing flats that are owned by the people who live there, or one of these flats

condone /kənˈdəʊn/ verb [T] to approve of behaviour that most people think is wrong

conducive /kənˈdjuːsɪv/ adj **conducive to sth** creating a situation that helps something to happen

conduct[1] /kənˈdʌkt/ verb ★★
1 [T] to do something in an organized way: *The interview was conducted by telephone.*
2 [I/T] to stand in front of an orchestra or group of singers and direct the way they play or sing
3 [T] if something conducts heat or electricity, heat or electricity can move through it
PHRASE **conduct yourself** *formal* to behave in a particular way

conduct[2] /ˈkɒndʌkt/ noun [U] *formal* ★
1 the way someone behaves: *The coach criticized his team for their conduct.*
2 the way in which a process or activity is managed

conductor /kənˈdʌktə/ noun [C] **1** someone who directs the musicians in an orchestra or a group of singers **2** someone on a bus who checks tickets and collects money **3** a substance that allows heat or electricity to move through it

cone /kəʊn/ noun [C] **1** an object with a circular base that rises to a point —*picture* → C8 **2** an object shaped like a cone that you put ICE CREAM in. You can also eat the cone. **3** the fruit of a PINE tree

confectionery /kənˈfekʃ(ə)nəri/ noun [U] sweets and chocolate

confederation /kənˌfedəˈreɪʃ(ə)n/ noun [C] a group of people or organizations that are united

confer /kənˈfɜː/ verb **1** [I] to take part in a discussion about a particular subject **2** [T] *formal* to give something such as a legal right or an honour to someone

conference /ˈkɒnf(ə)rəns/ noun [C] ★★
1 a large meeting where people who are interested in a particular subject discuss ideas: *a conference hall/room/centre* ♦ *an international conference on the control of illegal drugs*
2 a meeting where a small number of people have formal discussions

conference call noun [C] a telephone call involving three or more people

confess /kənˈfes/ verb [I/T] **1** to admit that you have done something illegal or wrong: *Simpson has confessed to taking the money.* ♦ *He confessed that he had been seeing another woman.* **2** to admit something that you are embarrassed about: *He confessed he did not understand financial matters at all.* **3** to tell a priest about the bad things that you have done and ask to be forgiven

confession /kənˈfeʃ(ə)n/ noun [C/U] **1** a statement in which you admit that you have done something illegal or wrong **2** a statement that you make to a priest about the bad things that you have done

confetti /kənˈfeti/ noun [U] small pieces of coloured paper that people throw in the air to celebrate a wedding

confidant /ˈkɒnfɪˌdænt/ noun [C] someone who you trust and discuss your private feelings with

confidante /ˈkɒnfɪˌdænt/ noun [C] a woman who you trust and discuss your private feelings with

confide /kənˈfaɪd/ verb [I/T] to tell someone about something that is private or secret: *She confided to friends that she was scared of her mother.*

confidence /ˈkɒnfɪd(ə)ns/ noun [U] ★★★
1 the belief that you are able to do things well: *You should have more confidence in yourself.* ♦ *I'm doing this course mainly to gain a little confidence.* ♦ *The more he*

fails, the more he loses confidence.

2 the belief that someone or something is good and that you can trust them: *Public confidence in the police is very low.* ✦ *I have complete confidence in our chairman.* ✦ *Many businesses have lost confidence in the government's economic policies.* ✦ *It took me a while to gain her confidence* (=make her feel that she could trust me).

3 the belief that something is true: *I can say with confidence that all our targets have now been met.* ✦ *+that He expressed his confidence that the project would be a success.*

PHRASE **in confidence** if you tell someone something in confidence, you trust them not to tell anyone else: *Any information you give us will be treated in the strictest confidence.*

confident /ˈkɒnfɪd(ə)nt/ adj ★★★
1 certain about your abilities and not nervous or frightened: *a confident mood/smile/manner* ✦ *I was starting to feel more confident about the exam.*
2 certain that something will happen or be successful: *We were confident of victory.* ✦ *+that They are confident that the show will open on Thursday.*

confidential /ˌkɒnfɪˈdenʃ(ə)l/ adj **1** secret: *confidential information* **2** keeping information secret: *a confidential service*
—**confidentially** /ˌkɒnfɪˈdenʃ(ə)li/ adv

configuration /kənˌfɪɡjəˈreɪʃ(ə)n/ noun [C/U] *technical* the way in which the different parts of something are arranged —**configure** /kənˈfɪɡə/ verb [T]

confine /kənˈfaɪn/ verb [T] **1** to keep someone or something in a particular place: *Chris was ill, and confined to bed.* **2** *formal* to keep an activity within particular limits: *Try to confine the discussion to general principles.*

PHRASE **be confined to** to happen only in a particular area, or to affect a particular group of people: *The risk of infection is confined to a few small groups.*

confined /kənˈfaɪnd/ adj a confined space is small and difficult to move around in

confinement /kənˈfaɪnmənt/ noun [U] a situation in which someone is forced to stay in a place

confines /ˈkɒnfaɪnz/ noun [plural] the borders of a place, or the limits of an activity

confirm /kənˈfɜːm/ verb ★★★
1 [T] to show or say that something is true: *The study confirms the findings of earlier research.* ✦ *+(that) The doctor may do a test to confirm that you are pregnant.*
2 [I/T] to tell someone that something will definitely happen at the time or in the way that has been arranged: *You can make an appointment now, and then call nearer the time to confirm.*
—**confirmation** /ˌkɒnfəˈmeɪʃ(ə)n/ noun [U]: *The hotel will send you written confirmation of your booking.*

confirmed /kənˈfɜːmd/ adj always living or behaving in a particular way, or having a particular belief

confiscate /ˈkɒnfɪskeɪt/ verb [T] to officially remove someone's possessions
—**confiscation** /ˌkɒnfɪˈskeɪʃ(ə)n/ noun [C/U]

conflict¹ /ˈkɒnflɪkt/ noun [C/U] ★★
1 angry disagreement between people or

groups: *a conflict between the press and the police* ✦ *The management team is keen to resolve the conflict over wages.*
2 fighting between countries or groups: *a bloody border conflict*
3 a situation in which two things cannot easily exist together, or cannot both be true: *The two recommendations seem to be in conflict with each other.*

PHRASE **conflict of interest** a situation in which someone cannot make fair decisions because they will be affected by the results

conflict² /kənˈflɪkt/ verb [I] if different statements or suggestions conflict, they cannot all be right or they cannot all happen: *His story conflicted with reports from other journalists.*

conform /kənˈfɔːm/ verb [I] **1** to obey a rule, or to follow an accepted pattern: *Products are tested to make sure that they conform to safety standards.* **2** to behave in the way that people expect you to behave: *There is great pressure on women to conform.*
—**conformity** /kənˈfɔːməti/ noun [U]

conformist /kənˈfɔːmɪst/ adj behaving in a way that most people think is correct or suitable —**conformist** noun [C]

confound /kənˈfaʊnd/ verb [T] to make someone feel surprised or confused by not behaving in the way they expect

confront /kənˈfrʌnt/ verb [T] **1** to go close to someone in a threatening way: *The guard was confronted by an armed man.* **2** to deal with a difficult situation: *It takes courage to confront your fears.*

PHRASE **be confronted by/with sth** to be forced to deal with a difficult situation: *She was confronted with the biggest crisis of her political life.*

confrontation /ˌkɒnfrʌnˈteɪʃ(ə)n/ noun [C/U] a situation in which people are fighting or arguing angrily: *violent confrontations with the police*

confrontational /ˌkɒnfrʌnˈteɪʃ(ə)nəl/ adj behaving in a way that shows that you want to fight or have an argument

confuse /kənˈfjuːz/ verb [T] ★
1 to make someone feel that they do not understand something: *Don't confuse the reader with too much extra detail.*
2 to make something more complicated: *This latest piece of information just confuses the issue.*
3 to make the mistake of thinking that one thing is another thing: *It's easy to confuse the two containers because they're so similar.*

confused /kənˈfjuːzd/ adj ★
1 unable to understand something or think clearly about it: *She was completely confused.* ✦ *I'm still a little confused about what happened.*
2 complicated and not well organized or explained: *Their ideas were a bit confused.* ✦ *The situation is still fairly confused.*

confusing /kənˈfjuːzɪŋ/ adj ★ not easy to understand: *She left a very confusing message.*

confusion /kənˈfjuːʒ(ə)n/ noun ★
1 [U] a feeling that you do not understand something or cannot decide what to do: *There seems to be some confusion about who*

actually won. ♦ *These changes have just* **caused** *more* **confusion.**
2 [U] a situation in which things are untidy, badly organized, or not clear: *Inside the building was a scene of total confusion.* ♦ *In the confusion, I lost my bag.*
3 [singular/U] a situation in which you make the mistake of thinking that one person or thing is another: *I've put them in different coloured folders to avoid confusion.*

congeal /kənˈdʒiːl/ verb [I] if a liquid congeals, it becomes thick and almost solid —**congealed** /kənˈdʒiːld/ adj

congenial /kənˈdʒiːniəl/ adj *formal* making you feel welcome or comfortable

congenital /kənˈdʒenɪt(ə)l/ adj a congenital medical condition is one that someone has had since they were born

congested /kənˈdʒestɪd/ adj **1** so full of vehicles or people that it is difficult to move about: *Many of Europe's major airports are heavily congested.* **2** blocked with a liquid: *His nose was congested.*

congestion /kənˈdʒestʃ(ə)n/ noun [U] a situation or condition in which something is blocked

conglomerate /kənˈglɒmərət/ noun [C] a large business that was formed by joining together several businesses

conglomeration /kənˌglɒməˈreɪʃ(ə)n/ noun [C] a collection of many different types of things

congratulate /kənˈgrætʃʊˌleɪt/ verb [T] ★ to tell someone that you are pleased about their success, good luck, or happiness on a special occasion: **congratulate sb on sth** *I congratulated him on his recent promotion.*

congratulations /kənˌgrætʃʊˈleɪʃ(ə)nz/ noun [plural] *spoken* used for telling someone that you are pleased about their success, good luck, or happiness on a special occasion: *Congratulations on passing your exam!*

congregate /ˈkɒŋgrɪˌgeɪt/ verb [I] to come together in a group

congregation /ˌkɒŋgrɪˈgeɪʃ(ə)n/ noun [C] a group of people who go to a religious service

congress /ˈkɒŋgres/ noun [C] **1** a large formal meeting **2 Congress** a group of people who are elected to make laws in some countries, for example the US

congressman /ˈkɒŋgresmən/ (plural **congressmen** /ˈkɒŋgresmən/) noun [C] a man who is a member of the US Congress

congresswoman /ˈkɒŋgresˌwʊmən/ (plural **congresswomen** /ˈkɒŋgresˌwɪmɪn/) noun [C] a woman who is a member of the US Congress

conical /ˈkɒnɪk(ə)l/ adj with a circular base that rises to a point

conifer /ˈkɒnɪfə/ noun [C] a type of tree that produces CONES (=hard brown fruit) and stays green all year —**coniferous** /kəˈnɪf(ə)rəs/ adj

conjecture /kənˈdʒektʃə/ noun [C/U] a theory based on information that is not complete

conjugal /ˈkɒndʒʊg(ə)l/ adj *formal* relating to marriage

conjugate /ˈkɒndʒʊˌgeɪt/ verb [T] *linguistics* to state the different forms that a verb can have —**conjugation** /ˌkɒndʒʊˈgeɪʃ(ə)n/ noun [C/U]

conjunction /kənˈdʒʌŋkʃ(ə)n/ noun [C] *linguistics* a word that is used to join other words, phrases, and sentences, for example 'and', 'because', and 'although'
PHRASE in conjunction with combined with

conjure /ˈkʌndʒə/ verb [I/T] to perform magic tricks using quick hand movements
PHRASAL VERB ,**conjure sth ˈup 1** to bring something such as a feeling or memory to your mind **2** to create or achieve something as if by magic

conjurer or **conjuror** /ˈkʌndʒərə/ noun [C] someone who performs magic tricks using quick hand movements

connect /kəˈnekt/ verb ★★★

1 join things	**4** show a relationship
2 join to energy supply	**5** in changing vehicles
3 with phone/computer	**+ PHRASAL VERB**

1 [I/T] to join two things together: *She carefully connected the two wires.* ♦ *This cable connects to the back of the TV.* ♦ **connect sth to/with sth** *one of the bridges connecting Manhattan to the rest of New York*
2 [T] to join something to a supply of electricity, water, or gas: *Check that your printer is connected and that the power is turned on.*
3 [I/T] to make it possible for someone to communicate using a telephone or computer system: *Please wait, we are trying to connect you.* ♦ *Your modem enables you to connect to the Internet.*
4 [T] to show a relationship between one person or thing and another: *There was no evidence then to connect smoking and lung cancer.* ♦ **connect sb to/with sth** *Police found nothing that connected him with the murder.*
5 [I] to arrive in time for you to continue your journey on another plane, train, bus etc: *a connecting flight*
PHRASAL VERB con,**nect sth ˈup** *same as* **connect** 2: *The plumber came and connected up the dishwasher.*

connected /kəˈnektɪd/ adj **1** related to each other ≠ UNCONNECTED: *Were the two deaths connected?* **2** joined to each other or to something else: *connected underground tunnels* **3** able to communicate using a telephone or computer system

connection /kəˈnekʃ(ə)n/ noun ★★★

1 relationship	**5** of energy supply
2 in transport	**6** people you know
3 for phone/computer	**+ PHRASE**
4 where things join	

1 [C] a relationship between things or people: *I don't see a connection between the two cases.* ♦ *She was alleged to have connections with the secret police.*
2 [C] a train, bus, or plane that allows you to continue a journey: *My train was late and I missed my connection.*
3 [C] a means of communicating using a telephone or computer system: *high-speed Internet connections*
4 [C] a place where two things join: *The light keeps flickering – there must be a loose connection.*
5 [U] the process of joining something to a

C

supply of electricity, water, or gas: *a connection charge*

6 connections [plural] people you know who are able to use their influence to help you: *He used his connections to get a government job.*

PHRASE **in connection with sth** *formal* relating to something: *Police want to talk to him in connection with the murder.*

connector /kə'nektə/ noun [C] an object that is fixed to the end of a wire, used for connecting two pieces of equipment

connoisseur /ˌkɒnə'sɜː/ noun [C] someone who knows a lot about a particular thing and enjoys it very much

connotation /ˌkɒnə'teɪʃ(ə)n/ noun [C] an additional idea that a word suggests to you, that is not part of its usual meaning

conquer /'kɒŋkə/ verb **1** [I/T] to take control of land or people using force **2** [T] to gain control of a situation or emotion by making a great effort

conqueror /'kɒŋkərə/ noun [C] someone who has taken control of land or people by force

conquest /'kɒŋkwest/ noun [C/U] the process of taking control of something, or the thing or place that you take control of

conscience /'kɒnʃ(ə)ns/ noun [C/U] the ideas and feelings you have that tell you whether something that you are doing is right or wrong: *The decision must be a matter of individual conscience.* ♦ *Maybe he has a guilty conscience* (=a bad feeling because he knows he has done something wrong). ♦ *We want to leave with a clear conscience* (=the knowledge that we have done nothing wrong).

PHRASE **on your conscience** causing you to feel guilty

conscientious /ˌkɒnʃi'enʃəs/ adj working hard, and careful to do things well —**conscientiously** adv

conscious /'kɒnʃəs/ adj ★ **1** noticing that something exists or is happening and realizing that it is important=AWARE: *He was conscious of the fact that everyone was waiting for him.* ♦ **+(that)** *We are conscious that some people may not wish to work at night.* **2** awake and able to see, hear, and think ≠ UNCONSCIOUS: *The patient was fully conscious throughout the operation.* **3** done deliberately by someone who knows what the effect will be: *a conscious effort*

consciously /'kɒnʃəsli/ adv in a deliberate way

consciousness /'kɒnʃəsnəs/ noun **1** [U] the state of being awake and able to see, hear, and think: *The pain was so bad that I lost consciousness.* **2** [singular/U] the knowledge or understanding that something exists or is important: *We want to increase students' consciousness of health issues.*

conscript¹ /kən'skrɪpt/ verb [T] to make someone join the armed forces —**conscription** /kən'skrɪpʃ(ə)n/ noun [U]

conscript² /'kɒnskrɪpt/ noun [C] someone who has been forced to join the armed forces

consecrate /'kɒnsɪˌkreɪt/ verb [T] to perform a religious ceremony in order to make a

place or a thing holy —**consecration** /ˌkɒnsɪ'kreɪʃ(ə)n/ noun [C/U]

consecutive /kən'sekjʊtɪv/ adj following one after another: *her fifth consecutive defeat* —**consecutively** adv

consensual /kən'sensjʊəl/ adj *formal* agreed to by all the people involved

consensus /kən'sensəs/ noun [singular/U] agreement among all the people involved: *We have finally reached a consensus on this issue.*

consent¹ /kən'sent/ noun [U] permission to do something: *He entered the building without the owner's consent.*

consent² /kən'sent/ verb [I] to give someone permission to do something, or to agree to do something: *The child's parents would not consent to the treatment.*

consequence /'kɒnsɪkwəns/ noun [C] ★★★ a result or effect of something: *Climate change could have disastrous consequences.* ♦ *the economic consequences of government policies* ♦ *Demand for oil increased and, as a consequence, the price went up.*

PHRASE **of no consequence** *formal* not important in any way

> **Words often used with consequence**
>
> *Adjectives often used with consequence*
> ■ **dire, disastrous, fatal, serious, tragic, unfortunate** + CONSEQUENCES: used about consequences that are very bad
> *Verbs often used with consequence:*
> ■ **accept, face, suffer, take** + CONSEQUENCES: accept the bad results of something

consequent /'kɒnsɪkwənt/ adj *formal* happening as a result of something

consequently /'kɒnsɪkwəntli/ adv ★ as a result: *They've employed more staff and consequently the service is better.*

conservation /ˌkɒnsə'veɪʃ(ə)n/ noun [U] ★ **1** the management of land and water in ways that prevent it from being damaged or destroyed: *a wildlife conservation project* ♦ *groups calling for the conservation of the countryside* **2** the careful use of supplies of things such as electricity or water, so that they are not wasted: *energy conservation measures* **3** *British* the protection of buildings or objects of historical importance

conservationist /ˌkɒnsə'veɪʃ(ə)nɪst/ noun [C] someone who works to protect the environment from damage or destruction

conservatism /kən'sɜːvəˌtɪz(ə)m/ noun [U] **1** a tendency to dislike change **2** a political belief that it is better for society to change only gradually

conservative¹ /kən'sɜːvətɪv/ adj ★ **1** not willing to accept much change: *The small farming communities tend to be very conservative.* **2** conservative clothing or styles are traditional **3** a conservative guess about a price or a number is usually less than the actual amount —**conservatively** adv: *She dresses very conservatively.*

conservative² /kən'sɜːvətɪv/ noun [C]

someone who is not willing to accept much change

Conservative /kənˈsɜːvətɪv/ noun [C] someone who belongs to or supports the beliefs of the Conservative Party

Conˈservative ˌParty, the one of the three main political parties in the UK. It supports right-wing policies.

conservatory /kənˈsɜːvət(ə)ri/ noun [C] a room that is attached to a house and has glass walls and a glass roof —*picture* → C1

conserve /kənˈsɜːv/ verb [T] to use very little of something such as electricity or water so that it is not wasted

consider /kənˈsɪdə/ verb ★★★
1 [I/T] to think about something carefully before you make a decision: *The jury went out to consider its verdict.* ♦ *He is considering whether to accept another job offer.* ♦ **consider doing sth** *At one time I seriously considered leaving.*
2 [T] to have a particular opinion about someone or something: **consider sb/sth (to be) sth** *We all considered him a hero.*
3 [I/T] to think that something may exist or be true: *Have you considered the possibility that he just doesn't like you?*
4 [T] to think about someone's feelings or reactions: *I'm not the only one involved – there's my daughter to consider as well.*

considerable /kənˈsɪd(ə)rəb(ə)l/ adj ★ large in size, amount, or degree: *a considerable amount of money* ♦ *a matter of considerable importance*

considerably /kənˈsɪd(ə)rəbli/ adv a lot: *It was considerably colder in the mountains.*

considerate /kənˈsɪd(ə)rət/ adj thinking about the feelings and needs of other people ≠ INCONSIDERATE

consideration /kənˌsɪdəˈreɪʃ(ə)n/ noun ★
1 [U] careful thought before you make a decision about something: *We have given careful consideration to your request.* ♦ *Several possibilities are under consideration* (=being thought about). ♦ *We will take your good driving record into consideration* (=think about it before deciding something).
2 [C] something that you must think about carefully before you make a decision: *practical/ethical/political considerations*
3 [U] a kind way of behaving that shows that you care about other people's feelings and needs: *She treats all her patients with consideration and respect.*

considering /kənˈsɪdərɪŋ/ grammar word ★ used for showing that your opinion about something is affected by a particular fact: *They've made remarkable progress, considering they only started last week.*

consign /kənˈsaɪn/ verb [T] *formal* to put someone or something somewhere because you do not want to deal with them

consignment /kənˈsaɪnmənt/ noun [C] goods that are being delivered somewhere

consist /kənˈsɪst/ verb ★★★ **PHRASAL VERB**
conˈsist of sth to be made of particular parts or things: *Breakfast consisted of dry bread and a cup of tea.* ♦ **consist of doing sth** *My job seemed to consist of standing and smiling at people.*

consistency /kənˈsɪstənsi/ noun **1** [U] the ability to remain the same in behaviour, attitudes, or qualities ≠ INCONSISTENCY
2 [C/U] the degree to which a substance is thick, smooth, or firm

consistent /kənˈsɪstənt/ adj ★
1 not changing in behaviour, attitudes, or qualities ≠ INCONSISTENT: *A good manager is flexible but consistent.*
2 continuing or developing steadily in the same way: *a consistent improvement*
3 containing statements or ideas that are similar or have the same aim: *the need for a unified and consistent policy* ♦ *These results are consistent with the findings of the previous study.*
—**consistently** adv: *He has consistently denied the charges.*

consolation /ˌkɒnsəˈleɪʃ(ə)n/ noun [C/U] something that makes you feel less unhappy or disappointed

console[1] /kənˈsəʊl/ verb [T] to try to make someone feel better when they are unhappy or disappointed

console[2] /ˈkɒnsəʊl/ noun [C] **1** a board with switches that controls a machine or piece of equipment **2** a small piece of electronic equipment used for playing video games

consolidate /kənˈsɒlɪdeɪt/ verb **1** [T] to make something stronger or more effective **2** [I/T] to combine several small things into one large unit, or to become one large unit
—**consolidation** /kənˌsɒlɪˈdeɪʃ(ə)n/ noun [C/U]

consonant /ˈkɒnsənənt/ noun [C] *linguistics* ★ any letter of the English alphabet except for 'a', 'e', 'i', 'o', and 'u'

consortium /kənˈsɔːtiəm/ noun [C] a group of companies or people who have agreed to work together

conspicuous /kənˈspɪkjʊəs/ adj very noticeable, or easy to see ≠ INCONSPICUOUS —**conspicuously** adv

conspiracy /kənˈspɪrəsi/ noun [C/U] a secret plan by a group of people to do something that is bad or illegal

conspirator /kənˈspɪrətə/ noun [C] someone who is involved in making a secret plan to do something that is bad or illegal

conspiratorial /kənˌspɪrəˈtɔːriəl/ adj showing that you share knowledge of a secret with someone —**conspiratorially** adv

conspire /kənˈspaɪə/ verb [I] **1** to secretly plan with someone to do something that is bad or illegal **2 conspire to do sth** to produce a bad situation

constable /ˈkʌnstəb(ə)l/ noun [C] in the UK, a police officer of the lowest rank = POLICE CONSTABLE

constabulary /kənˈstæbjʊləri/ noun [C] *British* the police force of a particular place

constant /ˈkɒnstənt/ adj ★★
1 continuous or regular over a long period of time: *the constant noise of traffic* ♦ *His health has been a constant source of concern.*
2 continuing at the same rate, level, or amount over a particular period of time: *Maintain a constant speed.*

constantly /ˈkɒnstəntli/ adv always or regularly

constellation /ˌkɒnstəˈleɪʃ(ə)n/ noun [C] a

C

group of stars that are named after the pattern they form

consternation /ˌkɒnstəˈneɪʃ(ə)n/ noun [U] *formal* a shocked or worried feeling

constipation /ˌkɒnstɪˈpeɪʃ(ə)n/ noun [U] a condition in which you cannot easily move solid waste out of your body —**constipated** /ˈkɒnstɪˌpeɪtɪd/ adj

constituency /kənˈstɪtjuənsi/ noun [C] an area of a country that elects a representative to a parliament, or all the people who live in that area

constituent /kənˈstɪtjuənt/ noun [C] **1** someone who votes in a particular constituency **2** one of the parts of something

constitute /ˈkɒnstɪˌtjuːt/ linking verb *formal* **1** to be one of the parts of something **2** to be a particular thing: *This letter does not constitute an offer of employment.*

constitution /ˌkɒnstɪˈtjuːʃ(ə)n/ noun **1** [C] a set of basic laws or rules that control how a country is governed or how an organization operates **2** [singular] your general physical condition

constitutional /ˌkɒnstɪˈtjuːʃ(ə)nəl/ adj **1** allowed by the constitution of a country or organization ≠ UNCONSTITUTIONAL **2** relating to the constitution of a country or organization: *constitutional reform*

constrain /kənˈstreɪn/ verb [T] *formal* to limit someone's freedom to do what they want

constraint /kənˈstreɪnt/ noun [C] a limit on something = LIMITATION: *The time constraints on the project are quite strict.*

constrict /kənˈstrɪkt/ verb *formal* **1** [T] to limit what someone is able or allowed to do **2** [I/T] to become smaller or narrower, or to make something do this —**constriction** /kənˈstrɪkʃ(ə)n/ noun [C/U]

construct /kənˈstrʌkt/ verb [T] ★★ to build or make something: *The tunnel was constructed in 1996. ♦ She is able to construct simple sentences in Spanish.*

construction /kənˈstrʌkʃ(ə)n/ noun ★★★ **1** [U] the process of building something: *The company will finance the construction of a new sports centre. ♦ This website is under construction* (=being built). **2** [C/U] the way in which words are put together to form a sentence or phrase: *difficult grammatical constructions*

constructive /kənˈstrʌktɪv/ adj intended to be useful or helpful —**constructively** adv

construe /kənˈstruː/ verb [T] *formal* to understand the meaning of something in a particular way

consul /ˈkɒns(ə)l/ noun [C] a government official who lives in another country and whose job is to help the citizens of their own country who go there —**consular** /ˈkɒnsjʊlə/ adj

consulate /ˈkɒnsjʊlət/ noun [C] the government building in which a consul works

consult /kənˈsʌlt/ verb ★ **1** [T] to ask for advice from someone who has professional knowledge: *Consult your doctor before going on a diet. ♦ consult sb about sth I consulted my solicitor about the matter.* **2** [I/T] to discuss something with someone

before you make a decision: **consult sb about sth** *Why wasn't I consulted about this?* **3** [T] to look in a book or at a document in order to find information = REFER TO STH

consultancy /kənˈsʌltənsi/ noun [C] a company that has expert knowledge about something and provides professional help and advice to other companies

consultant /kənˈsʌltənt/ noun [C] **1** an expert whose job is to give help and advice on a particular subject **2** *British* a senior doctor in a hospital

consultation /ˌkɒns(ə)lˈteɪʃ(ə)n/ noun [C/U] **1** a process in which people give their opinions before an important decision is made **2** a meeting with a professional person in order to get advice or discuss a problem

consume /kənˈsjuːm/ verb [T] **1** to use a supply of something such as time, energy, or fuel **2** *formal* to eat or drink something

consumer /kənˈsjuːmə/ noun [C] ★★ someone who buys and uses goods and services: *The technology means better service for consumers. ♦ consumer protection groups*

consuming /kənˈsjuːmɪŋ/ adj extremely important or interesting to you

consumption /kənˈsʌmpʃ(ə)n/ noun [U] *formal* the use of something such as energy or fuel, or the amount of something that people use or buy: *We've reduced our energy consumption by 10%.*

contact¹ /ˈkɒntækt/ noun ★★★ **1** [C/U] communication between people, countries, or organizations: *Do you and Jo still keep in contact? ♦ I still haven't managed to make contact with Joe. ♦ There was no direct contact between the two sides in the dispute. ♦ I have lost contact with most of my university friends* (=no longer talk or write to them). **2** [U] a situation in which people or things touch each other: *The disease is spread through sexual contact. ♦ Are you likely to come into contact with any dangerous chemicals?* **3** [C] someone you know who can help you, for example by giving you information

contact² /ˈkɒntækt/ verb [T] ★★★ to communicate with someone by phone, email, letter etc: *Please contact us if you have any information.*

contact³ /ˈkɒntækt/ adj a contact address or phone number is one that people can use to write or talk to you

contact lens noun [C] a small piece of plastic that you wear in your eye to help you to see more clearly

contagious /kənˈteɪdʒəs/ adj **1** a contagious disease spreads easily from one person to another **2** a contagious feeling spreads quickly from one person to another

contain /kənˈteɪn/ verb [T] ★★★ **1** to have something inside: *boxes containing toys and books ♦ The envelope contained a few old photographs.* **2** to have or include something as a part: *Milk contains many important vitamins and minerals. ♦ I disagreed with some of the points contained in the report.* **3** to control something: *I couldn't contain my excitement any longer. ♦ Firefighters are* *still battling to contain the blaze.*

container /kənˈteɪnə/ noun [C] ★★
  1 something used for storing or keeping things in, for example a box, bottle, or bowl
  2 a very large metal or wooden box that has been designed to be loaded easily onto ships and trucks

containment /kənˈteɪnmənt/ noun [U] the process of controlling something that could become harmful or dangerous

contaminate /kənˈtæmɪˌneɪt/ verb [T] **1** to make something dirty, polluted, or poisonous by adding a harmful substance: *Industrial sewage continues to contaminate our beaches.* **2** to affect something or someone in a negative way —**contamination** /kənˌtæmɪˈneɪʃ(ə)n/ noun [U]

contemplate /ˈkɒntəmˌpleɪt/ verb **1** [T] to think about something that might be possible: *Have you ever contemplated working abroad?* **2** [I/T] to think about or look at something very carefully for a long time —**contemplation** /ˌkɒntemˈpleɪʃ(ə)n/ noun [U]

contemporary¹ /kənˈtemp(ə)rəri/ adj ★
  1 modern, or relating to the present time: *contemporary art/music/literature/dance*
  2 alive, or existing at the same time as a particular event or person: *contemporary evidence/documents/sources*

contemporary² /kənˈtemp(ə)rəri/ noun [C] someone who is or was alive at the same time as someone else: *He was a contemporary of Charles Dickens.*

contempt /kənˈtempt/ noun [U] a feeling that someone or something is stupid, unimportant, or deserves no respect: *I have nothing but contempt for their ridiculous opinions.*

contemptuous /kənˈtemptjʊəs/ adj showing that you do not respect someone or something at all —**contemptuously** adv

contend /kənˈtend/ verb [T] *formal* to claim that something is true
  PHRASAL VERB con**ˈtend with sth** to have to deal with problems or difficulties: *They had to contend with winds of over 40 miles an hour.*

contender /kənˈtendə/ noun [C] someone who competes with other people for a prize or job

content¹ /ˈkɒntent/ noun ★★★
  1 contents [plural] the things that are inside something such as a box, bottle, building, or room: *The entire contents of the house will be sold.* ♦ *He emptied out the contents of his pockets.*
  2 contents [plural] the things that are contained in a book, letter, document etc, or a list of these: *The contents of the report remain secret.*
  3 [U] the subject, ideas, or story that a piece of writing, television programme etc deals with: *the design and content of your website*
  4 [singular] the amount of a substance that something contains: *a breakfast cereal with a high sugar content*

content² /kənˈtent/ adj happy and satisfied with your life or with a particular situation: *When I last saw her, she seemed content.* ♦ *I'm content with the relationship the way it is.*

content³ /kənˈtent/ verb **content yourself with sth** to accept what you have, although you would prefer to have something else

contented /kənˈtentɪd/ adj happy and satisfied —**contentedly** adv

contention /kənˈtenʃ(ə)n/ noun *formal* **1** [U] disagreement: *The subject is a source of contention in the family.* **2** [C] an opinion or statement that something is true

contentious /kənˈtenʃəs/ adj likely to cause arguments = CONTROVERSIAL

contentment /kənˈtentmənt/ noun [U] a feeling of happiness and satisfaction

contest¹ /ˈkɒntest/ noun [C] **1** a competition: *a writing contest* **2** a situation in which two or more people or groups are competing to gain power or an advantage

contest² /kənˈtest/ verb [T] **1** to state formally that you disagree with something = DISPUTE **2** to compete for a job or for success in a competition

contestant /kənˈtestənt/ noun [C] someone who takes part in a competition

context /ˈkɒntekst/ noun [C/U] ★★
  1 the general situation in which something happens, that helps to explain it: *the historical context of the events* ♦ *This fall in prices has to be seen **in context**.*
  2 the words surrounding a particular word, that help to give it its meaning: *In this context, 'development' means economic growth.*
  PHRASE **take sth out of context** to use only part of something that someone said, so that the original meaning is changed

continent /ˈkɒntɪnənt/ noun [C] ★★ one of the very large areas of land on the Earth, for example Asia or Africa

Continent, the /ˈkɒntɪnənt/ noun *informal* the part of Western Europe that is on one continuous area of land. It does not include the UK or Ireland.

continental /ˌkɒntɪˈnent(ə)l/ adj relating to or belonging to a continent: *the wildlife of continental North America*

contingency /kənˈtɪndʒ(ə)nsi/ noun [C] something bad that might happen in the future

contingent /kənˈtɪndʒ(ə)nt/ noun [C] **1** a group of people who represent a particular place or organization **2** a group of soldiers or police officers that forms part of a larger group

continual /kənˈtɪnjʊəl/ adj **1** continuing without stopping **2** happening again and again, often in an annoying way —**continually** adv

continuation /kənˌtɪnjʊˈeɪʃ(ə)n/ noun **1** [C/U] a situation in which something continues without stopping **2** [C] a situation in which something begins again after a pause

continue /kənˈtɪnju/ verb ★★★
  1 [I/T] to keep doing something, or to keep happening without stopping: *Doctors advised him to continue the treatment for another six weeks.* ♦ *She decided to **continue with** her studies for another two years.* ♦ **continue doing sth** *He continued typing while he spoke.*
  2 [T] to start doing something again after

stopping: *She looked up briefly, and then* **continued** *reading.*

3 [I] to go further in the same direction: *The path continued for another fifty yards.* ♦ *The woman pushed past me and* **continued down** *the road.*

Word family: continue

Words in the same family as **continue**
- **continual** *adj*
- **continuous** *adj*
- **continuation** *n*
- **continuity** *n*
- **discontinue** *v*
- **discontinued** *adj*

continued /kən'tɪnjuːd/ adj provided, happening, or done regularly or for a long period: *We thank our customers for their* **continued** *support.*

con,tinuing edu'cation noun [U] lessons for adults in a wide variety of subjects

continuity /ˌkɒntɪ'njuːəti/ noun [U] a situation in which something happens or exists for a long time without stopping or changing

continuous /kən'tɪnjʊəs/ adj ★★
1 continuing without stopping: *a continuous flow of water*
2 *linguistics* the continuous form of a verb includes 'be' and the PRESENT PARTICIPLE of a verb to show that an activity is in progress. For example in 'He is running to catch the bus', 'is running' is the continuous form of 'run' = PROGRESSIVE
—**continuously** adv: *It rained continuously for five days.*

contort /kən'tɔːt/ verb [I/T] if your face or body contorts, or if you contort it, it twists into an unusual shape —**contortion** /kən'tɔːʃ(ə)n/ noun [C]

contorted /kən'tɔːtɪd/ adj twisted into an unusual shape or position

contour /'kɒntʊə/ noun [C] **1** the shape of the outside edge of something **2 contour** or **contour line** a line on a map joining points that are the same height above or below sea level

contraception /ˌkɒntrə'sepʃ(ə)n/ noun [U] the methods that are used for preventing a woman from becoming pregnant, or the use of these methods

contraceptive¹ /ˌkɒntrə'septɪv/ noun [C] a drug, method, or object that is used for preventing a woman from becoming pregnant

contraceptive² /ˌkɒntrə'septɪv/ adj designed to prevent a woman from becoming pregnant

contract¹ /'kɒntrækt/ noun [C] ★★★ a written legal agreement between two people or organizations: *After six months she was offered a contract of employment.* ♦ *He has* **signed** *a six-year* **contract with** *Manchester United.* —**contractual** /kən'træktʃuəl/ adj

Words often used with contract

Verbs often used with **contract** *(noun)*
- **enter into, negotiate, renew, secure, sign, win**
  + CONTRACT: **start or get a contract**

contract² /kən'trækt/ verb **1** [I/T] to make a formal agreement that work will be done or that something will happen: *They had contracted to supply the machinery by June.*
2 [I] to get smaller: *The steel contracts as it*

cools. **3** [T] *medical* to get a serious disease

contraction /kən'trækʃ(ə)n/ noun **1** [C] *medical* a strong painful movement of a muscle that helps to push a baby out during birth **2** [U] the process of becoming smaller **3** [C] *linguistics* a short form of a word that is made by leaving out a letter or letters. For example 'can't' is a contraction of the word 'cannot'.

contractor /kən'træktə/ noun [C] a person or company that provides goods or does work for someone else

contradict /ˌkɒntrə'dɪkt/ verb [T] **1** to say the opposite of what someone else has said **2** if one statement, piece of evidence, story etc contradicts another, they are different and cannot both be true

contradiction /ˌkɒntrə'dɪkʃ(ə)n/ noun [C/U] a difference between two statements, ideas, stories etc that makes it impossible for both of them to be true

contradictory /ˌkɒntrə'dɪkt(ə)ri/ adj contradictory statements, information, stories etc are different from each other and cannot both be true

contraption /kən'træpʃ(ə)n/ noun [C] a machine or piece of equipment that looks strange or complicated

contrary /'kɒntrəri/ adj completely different, or opposed to something else: *a contrary view/opinion*

contrary, the /'kɒntrəri/ noun
PHRASES **on the contrary** used for emphasizing that the opposite of what has been said is true: *The situation hasn't improved – on the contrary, it's getting worse.*
to the contrary making you think that the opposite may be true: *Despite all evidence to the contrary, he believed his plan would succeed.*

contrast¹ /'kɒntrɑːst/ noun ★★
1 [C/U] a noticeable difference between people or things: *There is a striking* **contrast between** *these two attitudes.* ♦ *In* **contrast to** *deserts in the south, the northern part of the state is very green.*
2 [C] something that is different from something else in a very noticeable way: *The little village was a total* **contrast to** *Athens.*
3 [U] the differences in light or colour that you can see in a painting or photograph, or on a television screen

contrast² /kən'trɑːst/ verb **1** [I] if one thing contrasts with another, the two things are very different from each other **2** [T] to compare two things in order to show the ways in which they are different

contrasting /kən'trɑːstɪŋ/ adj different from each other in a noticeable or interesting way: *contrasting styles/opinions/colours*

contravene /ˌkɒntrə'viːn/ verb [T] *formal* to do something that is not allowed by a rule, law, or agreement —**contravention** /ˌkɒntrə'venʃ(ə)n/ noun [C/U]

contribute /kən'trɪbjuːt/ verb ★★★
1 [I/T] to give money, goods, or your time and effort in order to help someone to achieve something: *Many local businesses offered to* **contribute to** *the fund.* ♦ **contribute**

C

sth **to/towards** sth *He promised to contribute £5,000 towards the cost of the lawsuit.*
2 [I/T] to be a part of a group or an activity and help it to be successful: **contribute sth to** sth *Davis didn't really contribute much to the game in the second half.*
3 [I] to be one of the causes of something: *The scandal contributed to the party's defeat at the last election.*
4 [I/T] to write stories or articles for a newspaper or magazine

contribution /ˌkɒntrɪˈbjuːʃ(ə)n/ noun [C] ★★★
1 something that you give or do that helps someone to achieve something or helps to make something successful: *We are asking all parents for a **contribution towards** the cost of the trip.*
2 a story or article that is written for a newspaper or magazine

> **Words often used with contribution**
>
> *Adjectives often used with **contribution** (sense 1)*
> ■ **great, huge, important, major, outstanding, significant, valuable** + CONTRIBUTION: used about contributions that are important and useful

contributor /kənˈtrɪbjʊtə/ noun [C] **1** someone who gives or does something in order to help someone to achieve something
2 someone who writes a story or article for a newspaper or magazine

contributory /kənˈtrɪbjʊt(ə)ri/ adj partly responsible for a situation or event

contrite /ˈkɒntraɪt, kənˈtraɪt/ adj very sorry or ashamed because you have done something bad —**contrition** /kənˈtrɪʃ(ə)n/ noun [U]

contrive /kənˈtraɪv/ verb [T] *formal* **1** to succeed in doing something difficult by using clever or dishonest methods **2** to invent or make something in a clever or unusual way

contrived /kənˈtraɪvd/ adj artificial, or not natural

control¹ /kənˈtrəʊl/ noun ★★★
1 [U] the power to make decisions about what happens in a situation: *The island is now **under** French **control**. ♦ When Marie's father died, **control** of the business passed to her. ♦ When we **took control** of the company, it was losing money. ♦ Democrats are hoping to **gain control** of the House of Representatives. ♦ I **lost control** of the car, and it skidded off the road.*
2 [C/U] a law, agreement, or method that limits something: *new **controls on** the importing of live animals ♦ an international agreement on **arms control***
3 [C] a part of a machine that you use to make it do something: *There was an experienced pilot **at the controls** (=operating the controls of a plane).*
4 [U] the process of checking something, or the place where it is checked: *She is responsible for quality **control** of all our products.*
> PHRASES **in control** with the power to decide what happens or what someone or something does: *Dr Marion is in control of all medical decisions at the hospital.*
> **out of control** impossible to stop or deal with successfully: *Forest fires can easily get out of control.*

under control being managed or dealt with successfully: *He sometimes has difficulty keeping his temper under control.*

control² /kənˈtrəʊl/ verb [T] ★★★
1 to have the power to make decisions about what happens in a situation: *The rebel army now controls the northern half of the country. ♦ New teachers often find it difficult to control their classes.*
2 to make something operate in the way that you want: *I hit a patch of ice and couldn't control the car. ♦ The temperature in the museum is carefully controlled.*
3 to prevent something harmful from spreading or becoming more dangerous: *We must do more to control the spread of the virus.*
4 to remain calm and not show that you are angry or upset: *Carol struggled to control her anger.*

control freak noun [C] *informal* someone who wants to control every aspect of a situation and will not allow other people to share in making decisions

controller or **comptroller** /kənˈtrəʊlə/ noun [C] someone whose job is to manage an organization's money

control tower noun [C] a tall building at an airport from which planes are given permission to take off and land

controversial /ˌkɒntrəˈvɜːʃ(ə)l/ adj ★ causing strong feelings of disagreement ≠ UNCONTROVERSIAL: *controversial plans to build a new motorway*

controversy /ˈkɒntrəvɜːsi, kənˈtrɒvəsi/ noun [C/U] a disagreement that a lot of people have strong feelings about: *the recent controversy over the school's new teaching methods ♦ The decision is sure to cause controversy in Europe.*

conurbation /ˌkɒnɜːˈbeɪʃ(ə)n/ noun [C] a large city area

convalesce /ˌkɒnvəˈles/ verb [I] to spend time resting after an illness in order to get better —**convalescent** /ˌkɒnvəˈles(ə)nt/ adj

convene /kənˈviːn/ verb [I/T] to arrange a formal meeting, or to gather for a meeting

convenience /kənˈviːniəns/ noun **1** [U] a condition that helps you to avoid wasting time or effort: *Her hair was cut short for convenience rather than fashion.* **2** [C] a piece of equipment that makes things easier for you: *The kitchen was equipped with a range of modern conveniences.* **3** [C] *British old-fashioned* a public toilet

convenience food noun [C/U] food that is quick and easy to prepare such as food that has already been cooked and only needs to be heated. **Fast food** is food that you can get quickly in a restaurant

convenient /kənˈviːniənt/ adj ★★
1 easy for you to do, or suitable for your needs ≠ INCONVENIENT: *If it's convenient, call me tomorrow. ♦ Travelling underground is fast and convenient.*
2 near to the place where you want to go: *a house that is convenient for the centre of town*
—**conveniently** adv

convent /ˈkɒnvənt/ noun [C] a building where NUNS (=women members of a religious organization) live and work

C

convention /kən'venʃ(ə)n/ noun ★★
1 [C/U] a way of behaving that is generally accepted as normal and right: *social conventions* ♦ *She rebelled against convention and refused to marry.*
2 [C] a formal agreement between governments: *the European Convention on Human Rights*
3 [C] a large meeting of people from a particular profession or organization

conventional /kən'venʃ(ə)nəl/ adj ★★
1 someone who is conventional follows traditional ways of thinking and behaving in their society ≠ UNCONVENTIONAL: *Her boyfriend is nice, but he's very conventional.*
2 using ordinary or traditional methods, not new ideas or new technology: *a conventional oven* ♦ *conventional weapons* (=not nuclear or chemical weapons)
3 conventional medical treatments are those that are based on drugs and operations → ALTERNATIVE
—**conventionally** adv: *a conventionally dressed young man*

converge /kən'vɜːdʒ/ verb [I] to come to the same place from different places or directions: *Top diplomats were converging on Washington from all over the world.*

conversant /kən'vɜːs(ə)nt/ adj formal if you are conversant with something, you know about it and understand it

conversation /ˌkɒnvə'seɪʃ(ə)n/ noun [C/U] ★★★ an informal talk between two or more people: *He's so boring – his only topic of conversation is football.* ♦ *conversations between friends* ♦ *a conversation with my neighbour* ♦ *She had a long telephone conversation with her mother.*
PHRASE **make conversation** informal to talk to someone that you do not know well in order to be polite
—**conversational** adj: *conversational skills*

converse /kən'vɜːs/ verb [I] formal to have a conversation

converse, the /'kɒnvɜːs/ noun [singular] formal the opposite of a statement or situation

conversely /'kɒnvɜːsli/ adv used for introducing one part of a sentence that says the opposite of an earlier part: *Some wrong answers were marked right and, conversely, some right answers had been rejected.*

conversion /kən'vɜːʃ(ə)n/ noun **1** [U] the process of changing from one system or use to another **2** [C] a change in someone's religious or political beliefs

convert[1] /kən'vɜːt/ verb [I/T] ★
1 to change from one system or use to another, or to make something change in this way: *Farmers are converting to new production methods.* ♦ *convert sth into sth They converted the old school into luxury flats.*
2 to change your religious or political beliefs, or to persuade someone to change their beliefs

convert[2] /'kɒnvɜːt/ noun [C] someone who has changed their religious or political beliefs

convertible[1] /kən'vɜːtəb(ə)l/ noun [C] a car with a roof that can be folded back or removed

convertible[2] /kən'vɜːtəb(ə)l/ adj something

that is convertible can be changed from one form or use to another

convex /'kɒnveks/ adj a convex surface curves outwards ≠ CONCAVE

convey /kən'veɪ/ verb [T] ★
1 to communicate ideas, feelings, or information: *A good photograph can convey far more than words.* ♦ *Please convey our thanks to the organizers.*
2 formal to move something from one place to another=TRANSPORT

conveyor belt /kən'veɪə ˌbelt/ noun [C] a machine that has a flat surface that moves and carries objects from one part of a factory to another

convict[1] /kən'vɪkt/ verb [T] ★ to prove in a court of law that someone is guilty of a crime: *There wasn't enough evidence to convict her.* ♦ *convict sb of sth Robinson was convicted of the murder of his brother.*
—**convicted** adj: *a convicted thief*

convict[2] /'kɒnvɪkt/ noun [C] someone who is in prison because they have committed a crime

conviction /kən'vɪkʃ(ə)n/ noun ★★
1 [C] a decision by a court of law that someone is guilty of a crime: *He had two previous convictions for dangerous driving.*
2 [C] a strong belief or opinion: *deep religious convictions*
3 [U] the feeling or appearance of being confident: *'Everything is fine,' she said with as much conviction as she could.*

convince /kən'vɪns/ verb [T] ★★
1 to make someone believe that something is true=PERSUADE: *convince sb of sth He failed to convince the court of his innocence.* ♦ *convince sb (that) Maria had convinced herself that James didn't love her.*
2 to persuade someone to do something: *convince sb to do sth They tried to convince him to buy a cheaper car.*

convinced /kən'vɪnst/ adj certain that something is true

convincing /kən'vɪnsɪŋ/ adj **1** something that is convincing makes you believe that it is true or good ≠ UNCONVINCING **2** if a player or team has a convincing win, they beat another player or team easily —**convincingly** adv

convoy /'kɒnvɔɪ/ noun [C] a group of vehicles or ships that are travelling together

convulsions /kən'vʌlʃ(ə)nz/ noun [plural] sudden violent movements of your body that you cannot control, caused by illness

cook[1] /kʊk/ verb ★★★
1 [I/T] to prepare and heat food so that it is ready to eat: *What's the best way to cook fish?* ♦ *When did you learn to cook?* ♦ *cook sth for sb Joe's cooking dinner for me tonight.* ♦ *cook sb sth He offered to cook me lunch.*
2 [I] when food cooks, it is heated until it is ready to eat: *The potatoes need to cook for about 20 minutes.*
—**cooked** /kʊkt/ adj

Word family: **cook**

*Words in the same family as **cook***
- **cooked** *adj*
- **overcooked** *adj*
- **cookery** *n*
- **cooker** *n*
- **under-cooked** *adj*
- **cooking** *n*

Other ways of saying cook

- **bake** to cook food such as bread or cakes in an oven
- **boil** to cook food in very hot water
- **fry** to cook food in hot oil
- **grill** *British* to cook food under or over a very strong heat. The American word is **broil**.
- **roast** to cook meat or vegetables in an oven with fat or oil
- **simmer** to boil something very gently

cook² /kʊk/ noun [C] someone who cooks food, either as their job or for pleasure

cookbook /ˈkʊkˌbʊk/ noun [C] a COOKERY BOOK

cooker /ˈkʊkə/ noun [C] *British* a large piece of kitchen equipment that you use for cooking food. It usually includes an oven and a HOB. —*picture* → C2

cookery /ˈkʊk(ə)ri/ noun [U] *British* the skill or activity of preparing or cooking food

cookery book noun [C] *British* a book that contains RECIPES (=instructions for preparing and cooking food)

cookie /ˈkʊki/ noun [C] **1** *American* a BISCUIT **2** *computing* a file that is sent by an Internet WEBSITE to a computer that visits it. If the computer visits the same website again, the file collects information about the computer user.
    PHRASE **tough/smart cookie** *informal* someone who has a strong character or is intelligent, and deals well with problems and disappointments

cooking /ˈkʊkɪŋ/ noun [U] the activity of preparing food, or a particular way of preparing it

cool¹ /kuːl/ adj ★★★

1 fairly cold	5 good
2 calm and relaxed	6 likeable
3 fashionable	+ PHRASE
4 not friendly	

1 fairly cold ≠ WARM: *The water was wonderfully cool and refreshing.* ♦ *the cool evening air*
2 calm and relaxed: *her cool way of handling the situation*
3 fashionable and attractive ≠ UNCOOL: *one of Britain's coolest young designers*
4 not friendly or enthusiastic: *Relations between the two countries were becoming increasingly cool.*
5 *spoken* good or enjoyable: *The restaurant was really cool.* ♦ *'We could go to see a film.' 'Cool.'*
6 *spoken* a cool person is one that you like or admire
    PHRASE **play it cool** *informal* to behave calmly and not show your emotions
    → COOLLY

cool² /kuːl/ verb **1** [I/T] to become cooler, or to make something cooler: *Allow the cake to cool completely.* **2** [I] if an emotion such as love or anger cools, it becomes less strong
    PHRASAL VERBS **cool down** *informal* to become less angry
    cool (sth) down same as **cool²** 1
    cool off 1 to become cooler after being very hot **2** *informal* to become less angry or excited

cool³ /kuːl/ noun [U] a fashionable quality that someone or something has
    =SOPHISTICATION
    PHRASES **keep your cool** to remain calm in a difficult situation
    lose your cool to become angry or excited in a difficult situation

coolbox /ˈkuːlˌbɒks/ noun [C] *British* a container for carrying food and drink in to keep it cool

coolly /ˈkuːlli/ adv **1** calmly, without getting excited or angry **2** in an unfriendly way

cooped up /ˌkuːpt ˈʌp/ adj in a place that you cannot leave or cannot move around in

cooperate /kəʊˈɒpəreɪt/ verb [I] **1** to work with other people in order to achieve something: *Residents are refusing to cooperate with the authorities.* **2** to do what someone asks you to do: *They threatened to harm him if he didn't cooperate.*

cooperation /kəʊˌɒpəˈreɪʃ(ə)n/ noun [U] a situation in which people help each other or work together to achieve something

cooperative¹ /kəʊˈɒp(ə)rətɪv/ adj **1** someone who is cooperative is willing to do what you ask them ≠ UNCOOPERATIVE: *One of the prisoners was very cooperative.* **2** done by different groups working together: *a cooperative research project*

cooperative² /kəʊˈɒp(ə)rətɪv/ noun [C] a business that is owned by all the people who work in it

coordinate /kəʊˈɔːdɪneɪt/ verb [T] to organize an activity so that all the people who are involved in it work together effectively: *Jean is coordinating the project.*

coordinated /kəʊˈɔːdɪneɪtɪd/ adj able to control the movements of your body well: *She's very coordinated for a two-year-old.*

coordinates /kəʊˈɔːdɪnəts/ noun [plural] a set of two numbers that give the exact position of something on a map or GRAPH

coordination /kəʊˌɔːdɪˈneɪʃ(ə)n/ noun [U] **1** the ability to control the parts of your body so that they move well together **2** the process of organizing people or things so that they work together effectively: *He asked for better coordination between NATO and the United Nations.*

coordinator /kəʊˈɔːdɪneɪtə/ noun [C] someone whose job is to organize an activity and to make sure that the people who are involved in it work well together

cop /kɒp/ noun [C] *informal* a police officer

cope /kəʊp/ verb [I] ★★ to deal successfully with a difficult situation: *Considering how bad her injuries are, she's coping very well.* ♦ *The safety system is designed to cope with engine failure.*

co-pilot noun [C] a pilot who helps the main pilot to fly an aircraft —**co-pilot** verb [T]

copious /ˈkəʊpiəs/ adj *formal* in large amounts

cop-out noun [C] *showing disapproval* something that you say or do in order to avoid doing what you should do

copper /ˈkɒpə/ noun **1** [U] a red-brown metal, that is used especially for making wire or pipes **2** [C] *British old-fashioned* a coin of low value

copulate /ˈkɒpjʊleɪt/ verb [I] *technical* to have sex —**copulation** /ˌkɒpjʊˈleɪʃ(ə)n/ noun [U]

C

copy¹ /ˈkɒpi/ noun [C] ★★★
1 something that is exactly like something else: *This is not the original painting – it's a copy.* ♦ *Please send **a copy of** your birth certificate.* ♦ *I made **copies of** the report.*
2 a single newspaper, book, CD etc that is one of many that are all exactly the same: *Her first album sold 100,000 copies.* ♦ *Have you got **a copy of** yesterday's newspaper?*
→ HARD COPY

copy² /ˈkɒpi/ verb ★★★
1 [T] to make a copy that is the same as the original thing: *They were illegally copying videotapes and selling them.* ♦ *You can use the mouse to copy text from one part of the document to another.* —picture → DRAW
2 [I/T] to do something in the same way as someone else=IMITATE: *Children learn by copying their parents.*
3 [T] to use someone else's ideas or methods: *Their style of music was copied by a lot of other bands.*
4 [I/T] to look at someone else's work and dishonestly write the same as they have written, especially in an examination
  PHRASAL VERBS **copy sb 'in** to send someone a copy of an email or letter that you are sending to another person: *I'll email her about it, and copy you in.*
'**copy sth ,to sb** to send a copy of a message or letter to someone: *I accidentally copied the email to everyone in the company.*

> **Other ways of saying copy**
> - **make a copy** to copy something, especially using a machine
> - **photocopy** to copy a document using a special machine
> - **reproduce** to copy a picture, sound, or piece of writing, especially using modern technology
> - **trace** to copy a picture by placing transparent paper on top of it and following the lines with a pencil
> - **plagiarize** to copy someone else's words or ideas and pretend that they are your own
> - **pirate** to make an illegal copy of something such as a book, software, or a video

copycat /ˈkɒpiˌkæt/ adj similar to something else: *a copycat murder/shooting*
copyright /ˈkɒpiˌraɪt/ noun [C/U] the legal right to decide who can make and sell copies of a book, show a film, perform a piece of music etc
coral /ˈkɒrəl/ noun [U] a hard pink, white, or red substance that grows in the sea: *a coral necklace* ♦ *a coral reef* (=large area of coral under the sea)
cord /kɔːd/ noun **1** [C/U] strong thick string **2** [C] an electrical wire that connects a machine to the main supply of electricity → CORDS
cordial /ˈkɔːdiəl/ adj formal friendly —**cordially** adv
cordless /ˈkɔːdləs/ adj a cordless piece of equipment works without being connected to the electricity supply
cordon¹ /ˈkɔːd(ə)n/ noun [C] a line of police officers or soldiers who stop other people from going somewhere
cordon² /ˈkɔːd(ə)n/ PHRASAL VERB ,cordon

sth 'off to prevent people from entering a place, by putting a rope around it or by surrounding it with police officers or soldiers
cords /kɔːdz/ noun [plural] trousers made of corduroy
corduroy /ˈkɔːdərɔɪ/ noun **1** [U] thick cotton cloth with a RIDGED surface (=covered with raised lines) **2** corduroys [plural] trousers made of corduroy
core¹ /kɔː/ noun [C] ★
1 the most important or most basic part of something: **the core of** the problem ♦ *The club has **a small core of** active members.*
2 the centre of something: *the seeds in an apple core* ♦ *the Earth's core* ♦ *These six countries are the geographical **core of** Western Europe.*
  PHRASE **to the core 1** used for emphasizing that an aspect of someone's character is very strong and will not change: *She's a feminist **to the core**.* **2 shaken/shocked to the core** very surprised or upset by something
core² /kɔː/ adj most important, or most basic: *Selling insurance is still our core business.*
coriander /ˌkɒriˈændə/ noun [U] British a plant whose leaves and seeds are used to give flavour to food
cork /kɔːk/ noun **1** [U] a soft light substance from the BARK (=outside part) of a special type of tree **2** [C] an object made from cork, used for closing the top of a bottle of wine
corkscrew /ˈkɔːkˌskruː/ noun [C] a tool used for pulling the corks out of wine bottles

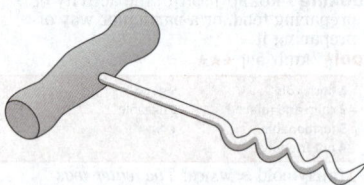

corkscrew

corn /kɔːn/ noun **1** [U] British wheat, or any similar crop of grain **2** [U] American MAIZE plants, or their seeds when they are cooked and eaten → SWEETCORN **3** [C] a small piece of painful hard skin on your foot
  PHRASE **corn on the cob** the top part of a MAIZE plant, cooked and eaten as a vegetable —picture → C11
corner¹ /ˈkɔːnə/ noun [C] ★★★

1 where two sides meet	**5** difficult situation
2 where roads meet	**6** in football/hockey etc
3 end of mouth/eye	✦ PHRASES
4 small (quiet) area	

1 the part of an object, space, or room where two edges or sides meet: *The baby banged his head on **the corner of** the table.* ♦ *The 'Start' button is in the left-hand **corner of** the screen.* ♦ *She sat **in the corner** reading.*
2 a place where two roads meet, or where there is a sharp bend in the road: *I get my newspaper from the shop **on the corner**.* ♦ *As she **turned the corner** (=went around it), she saw us.* ♦ *people begging on **street corners***

3 the end of your mouth or eye: *A tear fell from the corner of her eye.*

4 a particular area, especially one that is quiet, peaceful, or private: *Plant it in a sunny corner of your garden.*

5 a difficult situation that you cannot easily escape from=PREDICAMENT: *The government is in a tight corner on the issue of taxes.*

6 in football and other team games, an occasion when you are allowed to kick or hit the ball from a corner of the field near your opponent's GOAL.

PHRASES **around/round the corner** not far away in distance or time: *The kids go to school just around the corner.* ♦ *Spring is just around the corner.*

out of the corner of your eye without looking at something directly

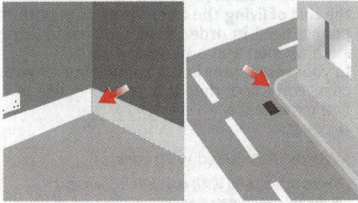

corner

corner² /'kɔːnə/ verb [T] to put someone in a situation where they must talk to you, fight you, or do what you want: *Carl cornered me by the coffee machine.*

PHRASE **corner the market** to get complete control of an area of business

'corner ,shop noun [C] *British* a small shop that sells food and other products

cornerstone, the /'kɔːnəstəʊn/ noun [singular] something important that everything else depends on: *Elections are the cornerstone of our democratic system.*

cornflakes /'kɔːnfleɪks/ noun [plural] a breakfast food made of small flat dried pieces of MAIZE. You eat them with milk.

cornflour /'kɔːnflaʊə/ noun [U] *British* white flour made from MAIZE, used in cooking to make liquids thicker

corny /'kɔːni/ adj corny stories or jokes have been told so often that they seem silly

coronary¹ /'kɒrən(ə)ri/ adj relating to your heart

coronary² /'kɒrən(ə)ri/ noun [C] a HEART ATTACK

coronation /ˌkɒrə'neɪʃ(ə)n/ noun [C] a ceremony at which someone officially becomes a king or queen

coroner /'kɒrənə/ noun [C] a public official whose job is to decide how someone died

corporal /'kɔːp(ə)rəl/ noun [C] an OFFICER of low rank in the army

,corporal 'punishment noun [U] punishment that consists of hitting someone

corporate /'kɔːp(ə)rət/ adj relating to a corporation: *corporate culture*

corporation /ˌkɔːpə'reɪʃ(ə)n/ noun [C] a large business company: *American tobacco corporations*

corps /kɔː/ (plural **corps** /kɔːz/) noun [C] **1** a

part of an army that has particular responsibilities **2** a group of people who all do the same type of job: *the press/diplomatic corps*

corpse /kɔːps/ noun [C] the body of a dead person

corpus /'kɔːpəs/ noun [C] *linguistics* a collection of written and spoken language that is stored on computer and used for language research and writing dictionaries

correct¹ /kə'rekt/ adj ★★★

1 right according to the facts or rules ≠ INCORRECT: *The first person to give the correct answer wins the contest.* ♦ *If my calculations are correct, we should be there soon.* ♦ *a grammatically correct sentence*

2 behaving in a way that is considered socially acceptable or morally right: *My father was always very formal and correct.* —**correctly** adv: *She guessed my age correctly.* ♦ *They refused, quite correctly, to give this information to the police.* —**correctness** noun [U]

> **Word family: correct**
>
> *Words in the same family as correct*
> - **correction** n
> - **correctly** adv
> - **corrective** adj
> - **incorrect** adj
> - **incorrectly** adv

correct² /kə'rekt/ verb [T] **1** to show that something is wrong, and make it right: *I want to correct this false impression that people have of me.* **2** to look at a piece of writing and make marks to show where the mistakes are: *She sat correcting the students' homework.* **3** to make something work in the way that it should: *She had surgery to correct a defect in her left eye.* **4** to tell someone that something they have said is not right: *I must correct you on one point.*

PHRASE **correct me if I'm wrong** *spoken* used for politely disagreeing with someone

correction /kə'rekʃ(ə)n/ noun ★

1 [C] a change that makes something correct or solves a problem: *I read the report and made a few small corrections.* ♦ *minor corrections to the car's steering mechanism* **2** [U] the process of changing something in order to make it correct: *some factual errors that need correction* ♦ *the correction of sight problems by surgery*

corrective /kə'rektɪv/ adj *formal* designed to solve a problem or improve a bad situation

correlate /'kɒrəleɪt/ verb [I/T] *formal* if two or more things correlate, or if one thing correlates with another, they are connected

correlation /ˌkɒrə'leɪʃ(ə)n/ noun [C/U] *formal* a connection or relationship between things

correspond /ˌkɒrɪ'spɒnd/ verb [I] **1** to be the same as something else, or very similar to something else: *Unfortunately, their statements did not correspond.* **2** *formal* if two people correspond with each other, they regularly write letters to each other

correspondence /ˌkɒrɪ'spɒndəns/ noun [U] the process of sending and receiving letters, or the letters that someone sends and receives

,corre'spondence ,course noun [C] an educational course that you take at home.

C

You send and receive work by post or by email.

correspondent /ˌkɒrɪˈspɒndənt/ noun [C] a journalist who deals with a particular subject: *an education/arts correspondent*

corresponding /ˌkɒrɪˈspɒndɪŋ/ adj related to something or similar to something —**correspondingly** adv

corridor /ˈkɒrɪˌdɔː/ noun [C] ★★
1 a long passage inside a building with doors on each side: *a hotel/hospital corridor*
2 a long narrow area of land
  PHRASE **the corridors of power** *mainly journalism* the places where major political decisions are made

corroborate /kəˈrɒbəˌreɪt/ verb [T] *formal* to support what someone says by giving information or evidence

corrode /kəˈrəʊd/ verb [I/T] if metal or another substance corrodes, or if something corrodes it, it is gradually destroyed by a chemical reaction

corrosion /kəˈrəʊʒ(ə)n/ noun [U] damage that is caused to metal or stone when it is corroded

corrosive /kəˈrəʊsɪv/ adj a corrosive substance contains chemicals that gradually cause damage

corrugated /ˈkɒrəˌgeɪtɪd/ adj corrugated metal, paper, or CARDBOARD has a surface of curved parallel folds

corrupt¹ /kəˈrʌpt/ adj **1** doing dishonest or illegal things in order to get money or power: *corrupt politicians/officials* **2** corrupt computer files are damaged and do not operate correctly —**corruptly** adv

corrupt² /kəˈrʌpt/ verb [T] **1** to encourage someone to do dishonest, illegal, or immoral things **2** to damage a computer file

corruption /kəˈrʌpʃ(ə)n/ noun [U] ★
1 dishonest or illegal behaviour by powerful people: *The men were arrested on charges of corruption.*
2 the process of corrupting someone or something: *corruption of the database*

cortisone /ˈkɔːtɪˌzəʊn/ noun [U] a drug that is used to improve medical conditions such as ARTHRITIS and ALLERGIES

cos /kəz/ conjunction *British informal* because

cosmetic /kɒzˈmetɪk/ adj **1** *showing disapproval* cosmetic changes affect only the appearance of something =SUPERFICIAL **2** relating to the improvement of someone's appearance: *cosmetic products* —**cosmetically** /kɒzˈmetɪkli/ adv

cosmetics /kɒzˈmetɪks/ noun [plural] substances that you use on your hair or skin to make yourself look more attractive

cosmetic surgery noun [U] medical operations that improve someone's appearance

cosmic /ˈkɒzmɪk/ adj relating to the planets and space

cosmopolitan /ˌkɒzməˈpɒlɪt(ə)n/ adj showing the influence of many different countries and cultures

cosmos, the /ˈkɒzmɒs/ noun [singular] the universe

cost¹ /kɒst/ noun ★★★
1 [C/U] the amount of money that you need in order to buy something or to do

something: *The cost of basic foods has risen dramatically.* ♦ *We need money to **cover the cost** of heating* (=to have enough to pay for it). ♦ *We're organizing a trip to London, **at a cost** of £15 per person.*
2 [C/U] damage or loss: *A new road is needed, but the **costs to** the environment would be too high.* ♦ *the **social costs** of unemployment*
3 **costs** [plural] money that you have to spend regularly in order to live somewhere or to run a business: *Housing costs are very high in Tokyo.* ♦ *manufacturing/running/operating costs* ♦ *New technology has helped us to **cut costs** (=reduce them).*
4 **costs** [plural] *legal* money that someone who is involved in a legal case must give to pay for the lawyers and the court
  PHRASES **at all costs** or **at any cost** used for saying that something must be done, even if it causes damage or harm
  the cost of living the amount of money that people need in order to pay for basic things such as food and a place to live
  to your cost if you know something to your cost, you know that it is true because of a bad experience
  → COUNT¹

cost² /kɒst/ (past tense and past participle **cost**) verb [T] ★★★
1 if something costs an amount of money, you need that amount to pay for it or to do it: *A new computer costs around £1,000.* ♦ **cost sb sth** *Unemployment costs the taxpayer billions of pounds each year.* ♦ **cost sth to do sth** *How much does it cost to hire a bike?*
2 to cause someone to lose something good or valuable: *The merger of the two companies will cost jobs.* ♦ **cost sb sth** *His decision to take the car cost him his life.*
3 (past tense and past participle **costed**) to calculate how much something will cost: *We have costed our proposals and sent them to the committee.*
  PHRASE **cost a fortune** or **cost the earth** or **cost an arm and a leg** *informal* to cost a lot of money

co-star noun [C] one of the main actors in a film, play, or television programme —**co-star** verb [I/T]

cost-cutting noun [U] actions taken to reduce the costs of a business or organization

cost-effective adj a cost-effective way of doing something brings the most profit or advantage for the money that is spent —**cost-effectively** adv

costing /ˈkɒstɪŋ/ noun [C/U] calculation of the expected cost of something

costly /ˈkɒs(t)li/ adj *formal* **1** causing problems and wasting money **2** expensive

costume /ˈkɒstjuːm/ noun [C/U] **1** clothes that

the actors wear in a play or film **2** clothes that are typical of a particular place or period in history

'costume ˌdrama noun [C] a play or film about a particular historical period in which the actors wear clothes that are typical of that period

'costume ˌjewellery noun [U] jewellery that is not valuable but looks expensive

cosy /'kəʊzi/ adj warm and comfortable, relaxing, or friendly —**cosily** adv

cot /kɒt/ noun [C] British a bed for a baby. It has high sides to stop the baby falling out.

'cot ˌdeath noun [C/U] British the sudden death of a young baby while he or she is sleeping

cottage /'kɒtɪdʒ/ noun [C] ★ a small house in a village or in the countryside —picture → C1

ˌcottage 'cheese noun [U] a soft white cheese that does not contain much fat

ˌcottage 'industry noun [C] a small business that involves people producing things at home

cotton¹ /'kɒt(ə)n/ noun [U] ★★
1 cloth made from the white fibres of a plant called a **cotton plant**: *a cotton dress*
2 British THREAD used for sewing: *a needle and cotton*

cotton² /'kɒt(ə)n/ **PHRASAL VERB** ˌcotton 'on *informal* to begin to realize or understand something

ˌcotton 'wool noun [U] British soft fibres of cotton that you use for cleaning your skin or for removing MAKE-UP

couch¹ /kaʊtʃ/ noun [C] a long seat that you can sit or lie on=SETTEE, SOFA

couch² /kaʊtʃ/ verb **be couched in sth** *formal* to be expressed in a particular way

'couch poˌtato noun [C] *showing disapproval* someone who spends a lot of time watching television

cough¹ /kɒf/ verb ★
1 [I] to force air up through your throat with a sudden noise, especially when you have a cold or when you want to get someone's attention: *My chest felt painful, and I was coughing uncontrollably.*
2 [T] to force something such as blood out of your lungs by coughing
—**coughing** noun [U]
PHRASAL VERB ˌcough sth 'up *same as* cough¹ 2

cough² /kɒf/ noun [C] **1** an illness in which you cough a lot and your throat hurts **2** the action of coughing, or the sound that you make when you cough

could /weak kəd, strong kʊd/ modal verb ★★★

- **Could** is used as the past tense of **can** when it means that someone had the ability to do something, or that something was possible: *The Roman army could march 30 miles in a day.*
- **Could** is usually followed by an infinitive without 'to': *I'm glad you could come.* Sometimes it is used without a following infinitive: *I came as quickly as I could.*
- **Could** has no tenses, no participles, and no infinitive form. It does not change its form, so the third person singular form does not end in '-s': *She could play the violin when she was six.*

- Questions and negatives are formed without 'do': *Could he help you?* ♦ *I could not breathe.*
- The negative form **could not** is often shortened in conversation or informal writing to **couldn't**: *I couldn't find her phone number.*

1 past tense of **'can'** used for saying that someone was able to do something: *Renee could read when she was four.* ♦ *In the distance I could see a cloud of smoke.*
2 for saying what is possible used for saying that something is possible or that it may happen: *We could still win.* ♦ *In a situation like this, anything could happen.*
3 in requests *spoken* used for asking something politely: *Could I have a glass of water?* ♦ *Could you post this letter for me?* ♦ *I wonder if we could borrow your car?* → CAN¹
4 for making a suggestion *spoken* used for suggesting to someone what they might do: *You could come and stay with us.* ♦ *You could always sell the car if you need extra money.*
5 for emphasis *spoken* used for emphasizing how strong your feelings are: *How could you be so stupid!*
PHRASES **could have** *spoken* **1** used for saying that something was possible in the past, even though it did not happen: *You could have been killed.* ♦ *She could have married Gerald if she'd wanted to.* **2** used for saying that perhaps something was true, although you are not sure: *The explosion could have been caused by a gas leak.*
couldn't be better/worse/nicer etc *spoken* used for emphasizing that someone or something is extremely good/bad/nice etc: *I was so nervous, but she couldn't have been nicer to me.*

couldn't /'kʊd(ə)nt/ short form the usual way of saying or writing 'could not'. This is not often used in formal writing: *I couldn't go to her party.*

council /'kaʊns(ə)l/ noun [C] ★★
1 the elected politicians who govern a city or local area, or the organization they work for: *The council has rejected their suggestion.* ♦ *a change in council policy*
2 a group of people who are chosen to make official decisions or give advice

In British English, **council** can be used with a singular or plural verb. You can say *The council has rejected their suggestion.* OR *The council have rejected their suggestion.*

'council esˌtate noun [C] British an area of a town consisting of council houses

'council ˌhouse noun [C] British a house that is owned by a local council. The people who live in it pay a low rent.

councillor /'kaʊns(ə)lə/ noun [C] an elected member of the council that governs a local area

'council ˌtax noun [U] a tax that people in the UK pay to their local council for services such as schools, roads, police, and libraries

counsel¹ /'kaʊns(ə)l/ (present participle **counselling**; past tense and past participle **counselled**) verb [T] to give someone advice about their problems, especially as your job

counsel² /ˈkaʊns(ə)l/ noun **1** [C] a lawyer who represents someone in a court of law **2** [C/U] *formal* advice and help

counselling /ˈkaʊns(ə)lɪŋ/ noun [U] professional advice that is given to someone who has problems

counsellor /ˈkaʊns(ə)lə/ noun [C] someone whose job is to give advice to people with problems

count¹ /kaʊnt/ verb ★★★

1 say how many	**5** be important
2 say numbers	+ PHRASES
3 include in calculation	+ PHRASAL VERBS
4 consider as sth	

1 [I/T] to calculate how many people or things there are in a group: *All the votes have been counted.* ♦ *At least 60 people were injured, but we're still counting.*

2 [I] to say numbers one after another in order: *I can count up to ten in German.*

3 [I/T] to include something or someone in a calculation, or to be included in a calculation: *Points scored after the bell do not count.* ♦ *Marks for this project count towards your final exam result.* ♦ *Do national holidays count as part of annual leave?*

4 [I/T] to consider someone or something in a particular way, or to be considered in a particular way: *We can count ourselves lucky that none of us got hurt.* ♦ **count sth as sth** *Is geography counted as a science subject?*

5 [I] to be important: *You're late, but you're here; and that's what counts.* ♦ *They made me feel that my views counted for nothing.*

PHRASES **count the cost** *British* to realize what has been lost or damaged as a result of something

count the days/hours/minutes etc to be impatient for something good to happen

don't count your chickens (before they're hatched) used for telling someone not to make plans that depend on the success of something that has not happened yet

make sth count to make something have as useful and positive an effect as possible

PHRASAL VERBS **count aˈgainst sb** to be a disadvantage for someone

count sb ˈin to include someone

count on sb to be sure that someone will do what you want or expect them to do: **count on sb for sth** *You can always count on him for good advice.* ♦ **count on sb to do sth** *I knew I could count on you to be on time.*

count on sth to expect that something will happen: *Tournament directors are counting on good weather.*

count sb ˈout to not include someone

count sth ˈup to count all the things or people in a group

count² /kaʊnt/ noun [C] ★★

1 counting process	**4** each crime
2 saying numbers	**5** person of high status
3 amount of sth in sth	+ PHRASES

1 the process of counting the people or things in a group, or the number of people or things that are counted: *After the count, Ellison had 25% of the votes.* ♦ *At the last*

count, 400 people had agreed to join.

2 the process of saying numbers in order: *Hold your breath for a count of ten.*

3 the amount of a substance that is present in another substance: *the pollen count* ♦ *a low sperm count*

4 *legal* each crime that someone is charged with: *Brown was jailed on three counts of corruption.*

5 Count a NOBLEMAN in some European countries

PHRASES **keep count (of sth)** to remember or record a number as it changes over a period of time: *It seemed like a long time, but I didn't keep count of the days.*

lose count (of sth) used for emphasizing that something has happened many times

on both/all/several/many counts in both/all/several/many ways

countable /ˈkaʊntəb(ə)l/ adj *linguistics* a countable noun is a noun that has a plural and can be used after 'a' when it is singular. Countable nouns are marked '[C]' in this dictionary ≠ UNCOUNTABLE

countdown /ˈkaʊntˌdaʊn/ noun [C] **1** the action of counting numbers backwards before something important happens **2** the period of time just before an important event

counter¹ /ˈkaʊntə/ noun [C] **1** a long flat surface where customers are served, for example in a shop or a bank **2** a small round coloured object that you use in a BOARD GAME —*picture* → C16

PHRASES **over the counter** drugs and medicines that are available over the counter can be bought without a doctor's PRESCRIPTION

under the counter bought or sold secretly and illegally

counter² /ˈkaʊntə/ verb **1** [I/T] to reply to a criticism or statement that you disagree with **2** [T] to oppose or stop something

counter³ /ˈkaʊntə/ adj, adv opposite, or with an opposite purpose: *a counter argument*

counter- /ˈkaʊntə/ prefix opposing something: *a counter-proposal*

counteract /ˌkaʊntərˈækt/ verb [T] to reduce the negative effect of something by doing something that has an opposite effect

counterattack /ˈkaʊntərəˌtæk/ noun [C] an attack that you make against someone who has just attacked you in a war, game, or argument —**counterattack** verb [I]

counterclockwise /ˌkaʊntəˈklɒkwaɪz/ adv *American* ANTICLOCKWISE

counterfeit /ˈkaʊntəfɪt/ adj counterfeit bank notes, documents, or products are illegal copies

counterfoil /ˈkaʊntəˌfɔɪl/ noun [C] the part of a cheque that you keep as a record

counterpart /ˈkaʊntəˌpɑːt/ noun [C] a person or thing that is similar to another in a different country or organization

counterproductive /ˌkaʊntəprəˈdʌktɪv/ adj having the opposite result to the one that you intended

countess /ˈkaʊntɪs/ noun [C] a woman who is the wife of an EARL or COUNT

countless /ˈkaʊntləs/ adj very many: *The temple attracts countless visitors.*

'count noun noun [C] a COUNTABLE noun

country /'kʌntri/ noun ★★★

1 area of land	4 area of particular type
2 areas away from cities	5 country music
3 people of a country	+ PHRASE

1 [C] an area of land that has its own government and official borders: *We have offices in 15 European countries.* ♦ *soldiers who fight for their country*
2 the country [singular] areas away from towns and cities, consisting of fields, farms, villages etc=COUNTRYSIDE: *We went for a picnic in the country.*
3 the country [singular] all the people who live in a country: *a crime that has shocked the whole country*
4 [U] an area that is known for a particular product, activity, person etc: *East of here is mostly farming country.*
5 [U] COUNTRY MUSIC

PHRASE country and western COUNTRY MUSIC

'country ,club noun [C] an expensive private club where the members hold social events and play sports such as golf and tennis
,country 'house noun [C] a large house in the countryside
countryman /'kʌntrimən/ (plural **countrymen** /'kʌntrimən/) noun [C] someone who is from the same country as you
'country ,music noun [U] a type of popular music from the southern US=COUNTRY, COUNTRY AND WESTERN
countryside /'kʌntri,said/ noun [U] ★★ areas away from towns and cities, with farms, fields, and trees
county /'kaʊnti/ noun [C] a region that has its own local government
,county 'fair noun [C] an event that happens every summer in US counties, with RIDES, games, and competitions for the best farm animals, best PIES etc
coup /ku:/ noun [C] **1 coup** or **coup d'état** an occasion when a group of people take control of a country using military force **2** an impressive and surprising success
couple¹ /'kʌp(ə)l/ noun ★★★
1 [singular] *informal* two things or people of the same type: *'Has he had any serious girlfriends?' 'A couple.'* ♦ *Take a couple of aspirin – you'll soon feel better.*
2 [singular] a small number of things or people: *There are a couple of things I want to discuss.*
3 [C] two people who are married to each other, or who have a romantic relationship with each other
4 [C] two people who are doing something together: *The room was full of dancing couples.*
couple² /'kʌp(ə)l/ verb [T] **1** if one thing is coupled with another, they are combined **2** to join vehicles or pieces of equipment so that they work together
coupon /'ku:pɒn/ noun [C] **1** a piece of paper that allows you to buy something at a reduced price **2** a piece of paper that you write your name and address on and send to someone, for example in order to enter a competition
courage /'kʌrɪdʒ/ noun [U] ★ the ability to do

things that are dangerous, frightening, or very difficult: *I didn't have the courage to admit that I was wrong.* ♦ *Eventually I plucked up the courage* (=tried to make myself feel brave enough) *to ask her to dance.*
courageous /kəˈreɪdʒəs/ adj very brave and determined —**courageously** adv
courgette /kɔːˈʒet/ noun [C/U] *British* a long vegetable with dark green skin —*picture* → C11
courier /'kʊriə/ noun [C] **1** someone whose job is to deliver documents or parcels **2** *British* someone whose job is to help tourists on an organized holiday
course¹ /kɔːs/ noun [C] ★★★

1 series of lessons	5 part of meal
2 direction sth follows	6 medical treatment
3 action sb chooses	7 area for sport
4 way things develop	+ PHRASES

1 a series of lessons or lectures in an academic subject or a practical skill: *a drama/secretarial/Spanish course* ♦ *You could do a language course abroad.* ♦ *The school runs courses for beginners.* ♦ *She's on a management course this week.* ♦ *an introductory course in economics*
2 the direction that a ship or plane is travelling in: *The captain had to change course quickly.*
3 the things that you choose to do in a particular situation: *What course of action do you recommend?*
4 the way that things develop over a period of time: *In the normal course of events, he would have left on time.* ♦ *a speech that changed the course of history*
5 one of the parts of a meal: *We both chose fish as our main course.*
6 *British* a medical treatment that someone is given over a period of time: *a course of antibiotics*
7 an area where a race or sport takes place: *a golf/race course*

PHRASES in/during/over the course of sth while something is happening or continuing: *In the course of the morning I learned a lot about the project.*
on course for sth or **on course to do sth** very likely to achieve something or to have a particular result
run/take its course to develop in the usual way and stop naturally: *We have to let the illness run its course.*

→ DUE¹, OF COURSE

course² /kɔːs/ adv *spoken* OF COURSE
coursebook /'kɔːs,bʊk/ noun [C] *British* a book that is used by students in class=TEXTBOOK
coursework /'kɔːs,wɜːk/ noun [U] school work that a student must do as part of a course of study
court¹ /kɔːt/ noun ★★★
1 [C/U] a place where trials take place and legal cases are decided=LAW COURT: *a court case* ♦ *The man will appear in court on Monday.* ♦ *She threatened to go to court* (=begin a court case) *if he did not pay.* ♦ *Lynn took her employers to court* (=began a court case against them).
2 the court [singular] the people in a court,

C

especially the judge and JURY: *A police officer told the court that he had seen Brown leaving the house.*
3 [C] an area marked with lines where some sports are played, including tennis and basketball: *a tennis/squash court —picture* → C15
4 [C/U] the place where a king or queen lives and works
PHRASE **court of law** a court where legal trials take place

court² /kɔːt/ verb [T] to try to impress someone because you want them to help you
PHRASES **court disaster/danger** to behave in a way that is likely to cause serious trouble
court popularity/publicity to try very hard to make yourself popular or well-known

courteous /ˈkɜːtiəs/ adj polite in a formal way ≠ DISCOURTEOUS —**courteously** adv

courtesy¹ /ˈkɜːtəsi/ noun [U] polite behaviour: *You might have had the courtesy to return my calls.*
PHRASE **courtesy of 1** used for saying who has provided something, and for thanking them for it **2** as a result of

courtesy² /ˈkɜːtəsi/ adj provided free: *a courtesy bus to the airport for guests of the hotel*

court-martial noun [C] a military trial of a member of the armed forces who has broken military laws —**court-martial** verb [T]

court order noun [C] an order from a court of law that tells someone that they must do something

courtroom /ˈkɔːtruːm/ noun [C] a room where legal cases are judged

courtship /ˈkɔːtʃɪp/ noun [C/U] *old-fashioned* the romantic relationship that a man and a woman have before they get married

courtyard /ˈkɔːtjɑːd/ noun [C] a square area outside that is surrounded by buildings or walls

couscous /ˈkuːskuːs/ noun [U] crushed wheat that is used in North African cooking

cousin /ˈkʌz(ə)n/ noun [C] ★★ a child of your UNCLE or AUNT —*picture* → FAMILY TREE

cove /kəʊv/ noun [C] a small area of sea that is partly surrounded by land

covenant /ˈkʌvənənt/ noun [C] a legal agreement, often an agreement to give money

cover¹ /ˈkʌvə/ verb [T] ★★★

1 put sth over sth else	6 provide insurance
2 be all over sth	7 travel a distance
3 include and deal with	+ PHRASES
4 report/describe	+ PHRASAL VERBS
5 pay for	

1 to put one thing over another in order to protect or hide it: *Cover the food until you are ready to eat it.* ♦ *The noise was so loud I had to cover my ears.* ♦ **cover sb/sth with sth** *They covered the baby with a blanket.*
2 to be all over a surface or object: *Bruises covered his entire body.* ♦ **be covered with/in sth** *His clothes were covered in mud.*
3 to deal with a particular situation or subject: *The programme covers all aspects of health and safety at work.*
4 to give a report of an event on television

or radio, or in a newspaper: *We will be covering the game on Saturday afternoon.*
5 to have enough money to pay for something: *We need £1,000 a month to cover the rent.*
6 if an insurance agreement covers a situation or person, it provides protection against loss or damage
7 to travel a particular distance: *We had to cover the last three miles on foot.*
PHRASES **cover your tracks** to try to hide evidence of something bad that you have done
cover yourself or **cover your back** to take action to protect yourself against criticism, blame, or legal problems
PHRASAL VERBS **cover for sb 1** to do someone's work while they are away **2** to protect someone from punishment, for example by telling a lie for them
cover up to put more clothes on
cover sth up 1 *same as* **cover¹ 1 2** to hide the truth about something: *The school tried to cover the whole thing up.*

cover² /ˈkʌvə/ noun ★★★

1 for putting over sth	6 false story
2 sheets/blankets	7 doing sb else's work
3 outside of book/CD	8 piece of music
4 insurance agreement	+ PHRASES
5 place for shelter	

1 [C] something that you put over something else in order to hide it, protect it, or close it: *She put plastic covers on all the furniture.* ♦ *cushion covers*
2 the covers [plural] sheets and BLANKETS that you lie under in bed
3 [C] the outside page on the front or back of a book or magazine: *Her face was once on the cover of* Vogue *magazine.* ♦ *On the train I* read *the newspaper from cover to cover* (=read it all).
4 [U] *British* an agreement by an insurance company to pay money in a particular situation
5 [U] places such as buildings or trees where people or animals can hide or shelter from the weather: *Everybody ran for cover as the rain started to fall.*
6 [singular] a false story that is used for hiding who someone really is
7 [U] *British* an arrangement in which a person does the work of someone who is away or ill
8 cover or **cover version** [C] a song that is recorded by someone who is not the original performer
PHRASES **under cover** pretending to be someone else in order to find out secret information
under cover of night/darkness hidden by darkness

coverage /ˈkʌv(ə)rɪdʒ/ noun [U] **1** news about something on television or radio or in the newspapers: *live coverage of England's game against France* **2** the amount of attention that television, radio, and newspapers give to something, or the way in which something is reported

cover girl noun [C] an attractive young woman whose photograph is on the front of a magazine

covering /ˈkʌv(ə)rɪŋ/ noun [singular]
something that covers something else

ˈcovering ˌletter noun [C] *British* a letter that
you send with something, to explain what
you are sending

covert /ˈkʌvət, ˈkəʊvɜːt/ adj secret ≠ OVERT
—**covertly** adv

ˈcover-up noun [C] an attempt to stop people
from discovering the truth about something
bad

ˈcover ˌversion noun [C] a COVER of a popular
song

covet /ˈkʌvət/ verb [T] *formal* to want
something that someone else has

coveted /ˈkʌvətid/ adj a coveted thing is
something that a lot of people want to have

cow¹ /kaʊ/ noun [C] ★★
1 an animal that is kept by farmers for its
milk or meat —*picture* → C12
2 the female of some types of animal such
as an elephant or a WHALE
3 *British offensive* an insulting word for a
woman

cow² /kaʊ/ verb [T] to make someone do what
you want by frightening them=INTIMIDATE:
They refused to be cowed.

coward /ˈkaʊəd/ noun [C] someone who is not
brave enough to do something that they
should do

cowardice /ˈkaʊədis/ noun [U] behaviour that
shows that you are not brave enough to do
something that you should do

cowardly /ˈkaʊədli/ adj **1** a cowardly person
is not brave enough to do something that
they should do **2** cruel towards someone
who is weaker than you: *a cowardly attack*

cowboy /ˈkaʊˌbɔɪ/ noun [C] **1** a man whose job
is to look after cows on a RANCH in the US
2 *British* someone who does very bad work
for you: *cowboy builders*

ˈcowboy ˌhat noun [C] a high hat with a wide
BRIM (=the flat part that surrounds a hat)
—*picture* → HAT

cower /ˈkaʊə/ verb [I] to move your body down
and away from someone because you are
frightened=CRINGE

ˈco-ˌworker noun [C] someone who works with
you

coy /kɔɪ/ adj pretending to be shy in order
to seem more attractive —**coyly** adv

coyote /kɔɪˈəʊti/ noun [C] a small wild North
American dog

cozy /ˈkəʊzi/ the American spelling of **cosy**

crab /kræb/ noun [C/U] a SHELLFISH with two
large CLAWS that walks sideways, or the
meat from this fish

crabby /ˈkræbi/ adj easily annoyed
=IRRITABLE

crabmeat /ˈkræbˌmiːt/ noun [U] the meat from
a CRAB

crack¹ /kræk/ verb ★

1 break so line appears	**6** when voice shakes
2 break sth open	**7** solve problem
3 make short loud noise	+ PHRASES
4 hit part of body hard	+ PHRASAL VERBS
5 lose control of yourself	

1 [I/T] if something cracks, or if you crack
it, a line or long narrow hole appears on
its surface, but it does not break into pieces:

The ice was starting to crack at the edges. ♦
I dropped a plate and cracked it.
2 [T] to break something open in order to
get what is inside: *Crack the egg open with
a knife.*
3 [I] to make a short loud noise like a small
explosion: *Thunder cracked overhead.*
4 [T] to accidentally hit a part of your body
against something with a lot of force: *Dad
fell and cracked his head against the door.*
5 [I] to say or do things that you would not
normally say or do, because you are very
tired or because someone is threatening
you: *She won because her opponent **cracked
under the pressure**.*
6 [I] if your voice cracks, it goes higher and
lower in a way that you cannot control
7 [T] to solve a complicated problem, or to
find the answer to a mystery: *Detectives
believe they can crack the case.*

PHRASES **crack a joke** *informal* to tell a joke
get cracking *informal* to start doing something
or going somewhere immediately
sth is not all it's cracked up to be *informal* used
for saying that something is not as good as
people say it is

PHRASAL VERBS **ˌcrack ˈdown** to start dealing
with someone or something much more
strictly than before: *The school is **cracking
down** on smoking.*
ˌcrack ˈup *informal* to become mentally ill
ˌcrack (sb) ˈup to suddenly laugh a lot at
something, or to make someone laugh a lot:
*Little kids crack me up with the things they
say.*

crack² /kræk/ noun ★

1 line where sth breaks	**5** attempt
2 narrow opening	**6** rude/insulting joke
3 sign sth is weak	**7** illegal drug
4 short loud noise	+ PHRASES

1 [C] a line on a surface where something is
beginning to break apart: *cracks in the
walls*
2 [C] a narrow opening between two things:
She looked through the crack in the curtains.
3 [C] a sign that an organization,
relationship, or plan is becoming weak:
*Cracks had started to appear in their
marriage.*
4 [C] a short loud noise
5 [C] *informal* an attempt to do something: *We
thought we'd **have a crack at** running our
own business.*
6 [C] *informal* a rude or insulting joke about
someone or something
7 [U] a pure form of the illegal drug COCAINE
PHRASES **at the crack of dawn** extremely
early in the morning
slip/fall through the cracks to not be helped
by a system that is designed to help you

crack³ /kræk/ adj very skilful as a result of
being trained well

crackdown /ˈkrækˌdaʊn/ noun [C] strong
action that someone in authority takes to
stop a particular activity=CLAMPDOWN: *a
new crackdown on drug dealing*

cracker /ˈkrækə/ noun [C] **1** a type of thin dry
BISCUIT that is often eaten with cheese
2 *British* a decorated paper tube that makes
a noise when you pull it apart. It usually
has a small toy inside.

C

crackle /ˈkræk(ə)l/ verb [I] **1** to continually make short sounds like the sound of wood burning **2** to be full of something such as nervousness or excitement: *The atmosphere crackled with expectation.*

crackling /ˈkræk(ə)lɪŋ/ noun [singular/U] the sound that something makes when it crackles

crackpot /ˈkrækpɒt/ adj *informal* slightly crazy —**crackpot** noun [C]

cradle¹ /ˈkreɪd(ə)l/ noun [C] **1** a small bed for a baby that can swing from side to side **2** the part of a telephone where you put the RECEIVER **3** the place where something began=BIRTHPLACE: *a region that is regarded as the cradle of African culture*

cradle² /ˈkreɪd(ə)l/ verb [T] to hold something gently in your hands or arms

craft¹ /krɑːft/ noun **1** [C] a traditional skill of making things by hand, or something such as furniture or jewellery that is made by hand: *traditional Egyptian arts and crafts* **2** [C] a boat or ship **3** [C/U] the skill needed for a particular profession

craft² /krɑːft/ verb [T] to make or produce something skilfully

craftsman /ˈkrɑːftsmən/ noun [C] a man who makes beautiful or practical objects

craftsmanship /ˈkrɑːftsmənʃɪp/ noun [U] the skill involved in making something beautiful or practical, or the beauty of something that has been made with skill

craftswoman /ˈkrɑːftsˌwʊmən/ noun [C] a woman who makes beautiful or practical objects

crafty /ˈkrɑːfti/ adj good at getting what you want, especially dishonestly —**craftily** adv

crag /kræg/ noun [C] a very steep rough part of a cliff or mountain

craggy /ˈkrægi/ adj **1** a craggy face looks strong and has deep lines in it=RUGGED **2** steep with a lot of rough rocks

cram /kræm/ verb **1** [T] to put people or things into a space that is too small: *The sacks of rice were crammed under a table.* ♦ *The hall was crammed with children.* **2** [I] *informal* to study hard in order to learn a lot in a short time

cramp /kræmp/ noun [C/U] sudden severe pain in a tired muscle that becomes very tight

cramped /kræmpt/ adj small and crowded: *cramped offices*

cranberry /ˈkrænb(ə)ri/ noun [C] a small sour red fruit: *a glass of cranberry juice*

crane¹ /kreɪn/ noun [C] **1** a very tall machine that is used for moving heavy objects and for building tall buildings **2** a large water bird with long legs and a long neck

crane² /kreɪn/ verb [I/T] to stretch your neck out to try to see something

cranium /ˈkreɪniəm/ noun [C] *medical* your SKULL

crank¹ /kræŋk/ noun [C] **1** *British informal* someone whose ideas or behaviour are very strange **2** a piece of equipment that turns to make something move or start

crank² /kræŋk/ PHRASAL VERB ,crank sth 'up *informal* to increase the level or amount of something

crash¹ /kræʃ/ verb ★

1 hit sth noisily	4 make sudden noise
2 when vehicle hits sth	5 of stock market
3 when plane falls	6 when computer fails

1 [I/T] to hit something hard and make a loud noise: *A ball came crashing through the window.* ♦ *The waves crashed against the rocks.*
2 [I/T] if a vehicle crashes, or if someone crashes it, it hits something: *Three people were killed when their car crashed into a tree.*
3 [I/T] if a plane crashes, or if someone crashes it, it falls from the sky
4 [I] to make a sudden loud noise, as if something is being hit
5 [I] if the STOCK MARKET crashes, its value falls suddenly
6 [I] if a computer or a computer program crashes, it suddenly stops working

crash² /kræʃ/ noun [C] ★
1 an accident that happens when a vehicle hits something: *He was seriously injured in a car crash.* ♦ *It was the worst train crash in thirty years.*
2 a loud noise like the sound of things hitting each other and breaking
3 a sudden fall in prices or in the value of the STOCK MARKET
4 an occasion when a computer or a computer program suddenly stops working

crash ,barrier noun [C] *British* a low metal fence at the side of a road or along the middle of a motorway

crash ,course noun [C] a course of study in which you are taught a lot about a subject in a short time

crash ,helmet noun [C] a hard round hat that you wear to protect your head while driving a MOTORCYCLE or RACING CAR —*picture* → HAT

crash ,landing noun [C] an occasion when an aircraft has to land in a sudden and dangerous way

crass /kræs/ adj offensive and not sensitive to other people's feelings —**crassly** adv

crate /kreɪt/ noun [C] a container for storing or moving things

crater /ˈkreɪtə/ noun [C] **1** the round hole at the top of a VOLCANO **2** a large round hole in the ground that is caused by an explosion

crave /kreɪv/ verb [I/T] to feel a very strong need that is hard to control: *As a child he craved attention.*

craving /ˈkreɪvɪŋ/ noun [C] a very strong feeling of wanting something: *a craving for chocolate*

crawl¹ /krɔːl/ verb [I]

1 used about people	4 used about time
2 used about vehicles	5 try to please sb
3 used about insects	+ PHRASE

1 to move along the ground on your hands and knees: *We crawled through the bushes.*
2 to move forwards very slowly: *Traffic crawled along the main road.* **3** if an insect crawls, it moves forwards using its legs **4** if time crawls by, it seems to pass very slowly
5 to try extremely hard to please someone in a way that makes people not respect you

PHRASE **be crawling with 1** to be too full of people: *The town was crawling with police.* **2** to be full of unpleasant insects or animals

crawl

crawl² /krɔːl/ noun [singular] **1** a very slow speed **2** a style of swimming in which you move one arm over your head and then the other while you are kicking your legs

crayon /ˈkreɪɒn/ noun [C] a stick of coloured WAX that is used for drawing

craze /kreɪz/ noun [C] something that suddenly becomes very popular for a short time

crazed /kreɪzd/ adj completely crazy and uncontrolled

crazy /ˈkreɪzi/ adj *informal* ★★ not at all sensible or practical: *It's crazy. Who would do a thing like that?* ♦ **be crazy to do sth** *She knew she would be completely crazy to refuse.*
PHRASES **crazy about sb** very much in love with someone
crazy about sth very enthusiastic about something
drive sb crazy to make someone very annoyed
go crazy 1 to become very angry about something **2** to become very bored and upset **3** to become very excited
like crazy to a very great degree=MAD: *The games are selling like crazy.*
—**crazily** adv

> Words that may cause offence: **crazy**
> Avoid using words like **crazy**, **mad**, and **insane** about people who have mental illnesses or mental health problems. Instead, use an expression such as **mentally ill**.

creak /kriːk/ verb [I] if something creaks, it makes a high noise when it moves, or when you put weight on it —**creak** noun [C], **creaky** adj

cream¹ /kriːm/ noun ★★
1 [U] a thick yellowish-white liquid that is taken from the top of milk
2 [C/U] a thick smooth substance that you put on your skin, for example when it is dry. Some medicines are in the form of a cream.
3 [U] a yellowish-white colour
PHRASE **the cream of the crop** the best people or things of a particular type
—**creamy** adj

cream² /kriːm/ adj yellowish-white in colour

cream cheese noun [U] a soft smooth white cheese that you spread on bread and similar foods

crease¹ /kriːs/ noun [C] **1** a line made on cloth or paper when it is folded or crushed **2** a line on someone's skin=WRINKLE

crease² /kriːs/ verb [I/T] to make lines on cloth or paper by folding or crushing it, or to become covered in these lines

creased /kriːst/ adj creased cloth or paper is marked with a crease

create /kriˈeɪt/ verb [T] ★★★ to make something new exist or happen: *His comments have created a lot of confusion.* ♦ *How do I create a new file?* ♦ *In the last week, 170 new jobs have been created.* ♦ *He was only 22 when he created this masterpiece.*

creation /kriˈeɪʃ(ə)n/ noun ★★
1 [U] the act of creating something: *The government is to provide more money for job creation.* ♦ *the creation of new industries*
2 [C] something that has been created using skill or imagination: *Have you seen my latest creation?*

creative /kriˈeɪtɪv/ adj ★
1 involving a lot of imagination and new ideas: *Painting is a creative process.* ♦ *the creative use of technology in everyday life*
2 having a lot of imagination and new ideas: *The programme offers children the chance to be creative.*
—**creatively** adv

creative writing noun [U] the activity of writing stories and poems

creativity /ˌkriːeɪˈtɪvəti/ noun [U] the ability to create new ideas or things using your imagination: *We want to encourage creativity in our employees.*

creator /kriˈeɪtə/ noun **1** [C] someone who has created something **2 the Creator** God

creature /ˈkriːtʃə/ noun [C] ★★
1 anything that lives except plants: *a small furry creature*
2 an imaginary living thing that is strange or frightening: *The Gorgon was a mythical creature.*

crèche /kreʃ/ noun [C] *British* a place where babies and small children are looked after while their parents are busy

credence /ˈkriːd(ə)ns/ noun **give/lend/add credence to sth** *formal* to make people think that something is likely to be true

credentials /krɪˈdenʃ(ə)lz/ noun [plural]
1 personal qualities, achievements, or experiences that make someone suitable for something: *His credentials as a football manager are impressive.* **2** documents that prove who you are, or that show your qualifications

credibility /ˌkredəˈbɪləti/ noun [U] qualities that someone or something has that make people believe them or trust them: *The government is losing credibility by its failure to act quickly.*

credible /ˈkredəb(ə)l/ adj **1** able to be believed or trusted: *credible evidence* **2** considered likely to happen or likely to be successful: *a credible opponent/candidate* —**credibly** adv

credit¹ /ˈkredɪt/ noun ★★

1 when you pay later	**5** at college/university
2 praise for sth you did	**6** list of who made film
3 money you pay in	**+** PHRASES
4 money you can use	

1 [U] an arrangement to receive money from a bank, or receive goods from a shop, and to pay for them later ≠ DEBIT: *I don't like*

C

buying things **on credit**. ♦ Some suppliers will not **offer credit** to their customers.

2 [U] praise for something that you have done: You deserve **credit for** all the help you gave us. ♦ He always **takes the credit** for my ideas.

3 [C] an amount of money that you add to an account

4 [C] an amount of money that you have a right to use: tax credits

5 [C] a part of a college or university course that you have completed successfully

6 the credits [plural] a list at the beginning or end of a film or television programme that shows the people who were involved in making it

PHRASES **be a credit to sb** if you are a credit to someone, they should be proud of you

give sb credit for sth to believe that someone is good at something, or that they have a particular good quality

to sb's credit used for saying that someone deserves praise: Jane, to her credit, helped the woman without knowing the situation.

credit² /ˈkredɪt/ verb [T] to add an amount of money to an account ≠ DEBIT: The money will be credited to your account.

PHRASE **credit sb with sth** to believe that someone has achieved something, or that they have particular good qualities

creditable /ˈkredɪtəb(ə)l/ adj good enough to deserve some praise or admiration

ˈcredit ˌcard noun [C] a small plastic card that you use to buy things now and pay for them later

ˈcredit ˌlimit noun [C] the maximum amount of money that a customer can borrow using a particular credit card

creditor /ˈkredɪtə/ noun [C] a person or company that is owed money by another person or company ≠ DEBTOR

creed /kriːd/ noun [C] formal a set of beliefs

creek /kriːk/ noun [C] **1** a long narrow area of sea that stretches into the land **2** American a narrow stream

creep¹ /kriːp/ (past tense and past participle **crept** /krept/) verb [I] **1** to move slowly and quietly: Sue crept up the stairs. ♦ The fog was creeping across the bay. **2** to gradually happen or start: A smile crept over her face.

PHRASAL VERB ˌcreep ˈup on sb **1** to move towards someone quietly and slowly, so that they do not hear you **2** if something creeps up on you, it happens so gradually that you do not notice it

creep² /kriːp/ noun [C] informal an unpleasant person, especially someone who tries to impress people in authority

PHRASE **give sb the creeps** to make someone feel nervous or frightened

creepy /ˈkriːpi/ adj informal unpleasant in a way that makes you feel frightened

cremate /krɪˈmeɪt/ verb [T] to burn the body of a dead person —**cremation** /krɪˈmeɪʃ(ə)n/ noun [C/U]

crematorium /ˌkreməˈtɔːriəm/ noun [C] a building where the bodies of dead people are cremated

crepe /kreɪp/ noun **1** [U] a light type of rubber **2** [C] a light thin PANCAKE **3** [U] a soft thin cloth with small folds in its surface

ˌcrepe ˈpaper noun [U] thin paper that stretches easily and is often used for making decorations

crept the past tense and past participle of **creep¹**

crescendo /krəˈʃendəʊ/ noun [C] a gradual increase in sound in a piece of music

crescent /ˈkrez(ə)nt/ noun [C] **1** a curved shape that is wide in the middle and pointed at the ends —picture → C8 **2** a curved street: used especially in street names

cress /kres/ noun [U] a small plant with round green leaves that have a strong flavour. The leaves are eaten raw in salads or used for decorating food.

crest /krest/ noun [C] **1** the top of a hill, mountain, or wave **2** a set of feathers on the top of the heads of some birds

crestfallen /ˈkrestˌfɔːlən/ adj sad and disappointed

crevasse /krəˈvæs/ noun [C] a very deep crack in rock or ice

crevice /ˈkrevɪs/ noun [C] a narrow crack in rock or in a wall

crew /kruː/ noun [C] ★★

1 the people who work on a ship, aircraft etc: can be followed by a singular or plural verb: All the passengers and crew on board the jet were killed.

2 the people on a military ship or aircraft who are not officers: can be followed by a singular or plural verb

3 a group of people with a particular skill who work together: can be followed by a singular or plural verb: a film crew ♦ an ambulance crew

> In British English, **crew** can be used with a singular or plural verb. You can say The crew is very experienced. OR The crew are very experienced.

crewman /ˈkruːmən/ (plural **crewmen** /ˈkruːmən/) noun [C] a man who is a member of the CREW of a ship, aircraft etc

ˈcrew ˌneck noun [C] a SWEATER with a round neck

crib /krɪb/ noun [C] American a baby's COT

crick /krɪk/ noun [C] a sudden pain in your neck or back that you get when the muscles become stiff

cricket /ˈkrɪkɪt/ noun **1** [U] a game in which teams get points by hitting a ball with a **bat** and running between two sets of sticks **2** [C] a brown insect that makes a loud noise at night

cricketer /ˈkrɪkɪtə/ noun [C] someone who plays cricket

cried the past tense and past participle of **cry¹**

crime /kraɪm/ noun ★★★

1 [C] an illegal activity or action: She was unaware that she had **committed a crime**. ♦ It took police eight years to **solve the crime** (=find out who did it).

2 [U] illegal activities in general: new laws to help **fight crime** ♦ The crime rate (=the number of crimes) in the city has risen sharply. ♦ **Rising crime** (=crime that is increasing) is a key election issue.

3 [singular] something that is bad, wrong, or unfair: It's not a crime to be curious.

ˈcrime ˌwave noun [C] a sudden increase in the

number of crimes in a particular area

criminal¹ /ˈkrɪmɪn(ə)l/ noun [C] ★★ someone who has committed a crime: *The scheme is designed to help former criminals find jobs.*

> **Words often used with criminal**
>
> *Adjectives often used with criminal (noun)*
> ■ **habitual, hardened, known, notorious** +
> CRIMINAL: used about someone who has committed many crimes

criminal² /ˈkrɪmɪn(ə)l/ adj ★★
1 relating to illegal acts, or to the parts of the legal system that deal with crime: *criminal behaviour* ♦ *a criminal investigation* (=one that is dealing with a crime) ♦ *the criminal justice system* ♦ *a criminal offence*
2 bad, wrong, or unfair in a way that makes you angry: *That's a criminal waste of resources.*

criminalize /ˈkrɪmɪnəˌlaɪz/ verb [T] to make an activity illegal by making a new law

criminal ˈlaw noun [U] the system of laws that deals with crimes and the punishment of criminals

criminally /ˈkrɪmɪnəli/ adv according to criminal law: *criminally insane*

criminal ˈrecord noun [C] an official list of crimes that someone has committed

crimson /ˈkrɪmz(ə)n/ adj dark purple-red in colour

cringe /krɪndʒ/ verb [I] **1** to move back slightly from something that is unpleasant or frightening **2** to feel embarrassed or ashamed about something

crinkle /ˈkrɪŋk(ə)l/ verb [I/T] if skin or cloth crinkles, or if you crinkle it, a lot of small folds appear in it —**crinkled** /ˈkrɪŋk(ə)ld/ adj, **crinkly** /ˈkrɪŋkli/ adj

cripple¹ /ˈkrɪp(ə)l/ verb [T] **1** to destroy something or damage it severely **2** to make someone physically disabled

cripple² /ˈkrɪp(ə)l/ noun [C] *offensive* an offensive word for someone who is physically disabled

crippling /ˈkrɪplɪŋ/ adj **1** causing severe damage or problems: *crippling taxes* **2** making someone physically disabled, or causing them to have severe health problems: *a crippling disease*

crisis /ˈkraɪsɪs/ (plural **crises** /ˈkraɪsiːz/) noun [C/U] ★★ an urgent and difficult or dangerous situation: *political crisis* ♦ *The nursing profession is in crisis.* ♦ *the current crisis in the farming industry*

crisp¹ /krɪsp/ adj **1** crisp food is firm in a pleasant way: *a crisp apple/carrot* **2** crisp cloth or paper is smooth, clean, and fresh: *crisp sheets* **3** crisp weather is pleasant because it is cold and dry: *crisp night air*

crisp² /krɪsp/ noun [C] *British* a thin flat round piece of potato that has been cooked in fat and is eaten cold

crispy /ˈkrɪspi/ adj food that is crispy is firm in a pleasant way

criss-cross /ˈkrɪsˌkrɒs/ verb **1** [I/T] to form a pattern of straight lines that cross each other **2** [T] to go across a place and back again many times, taking a different path each time

criteria /kraɪˈtɪəriə/ (singular **criterion** /kraɪˈtɪəriən/) noun [plural] ★ standards that are used for judging something or for making a decision about something: *Everyone whose qualifications meet our criteria will be considered.* ♦ *What criteria do you have for selecting patients for treatment?*

critic /ˈkrɪtɪk/ noun [C] ★
1 someone who does not like something and states their opinion about it: *a critic of the government's tax proposals*
2 someone whose job is to give their opinions about things such as books, films, or plays

critical /ˈkrɪtɪk(ə)l/ adj ★★

> | **1** saying sth is wrong | **4** considering carefully |
> |---|---|
> | **2** very important | **5** according to critics |
> | **3** seriously ill/injured | |

1 expressing your opinion when you think something is wrong or bad: *Her father was a very critical man.* ♦ *Warren was critical of the way she handled the affair.*
2 an event, time, or issue that is critical is very important, often because it affects the future: *a critical moment* ♦ *Winning the award is critical to our success.*
3 very seriously ill or injured: *Six of the patients were in a critical condition.*
4 considering something carefully and deciding what is good or bad about it: *a critical look at modern life*
5 according to the book, film, or theatre CRITICS: *The show has won much critical acclaim.*

critically /ˈkrɪtɪkli/ adv **1** extremely and seriously: *critically ill* **2** carefully judging something: *We teach children to think critically.* **3** in a way that shows that you do not like something: *Nobody spoke critically of the government.* **4** if a book, film, or play is critically acclaimed, it is said to be good by people whose job is to give their opinion

critical ˈmass noun [singular/U] the smallest number of people or things that are needed for something to happen

criticise /ˈkrɪtɪˌsaɪz/ a British spelling of criticize

criticism /ˈkrɪtɪˌsɪz(ə)m/ noun ★★
1 [C/U] a comment or comments that show that you think something is wrong or bad: *a valid/fair criticism* ♦ *criticism of the team's performance* ♦ *The new plans drew fierce criticism from local people.*
2 [U] the activity of giving your professional opinion about things such as new books, films, or plays

> **Words often used with criticism**
>
> *Adjectives often used with criticism (sense 1)*
> ■ **fierce, outspoken, severe, strong** +
> CRITICISM: showing that you think that something is very bad

criticize /ˈkrɪtɪˌsaɪz/ verb [I/T] ★★ to say what you think is wrong or bad about something: *We were told not to criticize the policy publicly.* ♦ **criticize sb/sth for (doing) sth** *The new proposals have been criticized for not going far enough to change the system.*

C

Word family: criticize

Words in the same family as criticize
- **critic** n
- **critical** adj
- **critically** adv
- **criticism** n
- **uncritical** adj

---

critique /krɪˈtiːk/ noun [C] a careful written examination of a subject that includes the writer's opinions

croak /krəʊk/ verb **1** [I/T] to speak or say something in a low rough voice **2** [I] when a FROG croaks, it makes a low loud rough sound **3** [I] *very informal* to die —**croak** noun [C]

crochet /ˈkrəʊʃeɪ/ verb [I/T] to make something with wool or cotton THREAD using a large needle with a hook on the end

crockery /ˈkrɒkəri/ noun [U] plates, cups, bowls etc that you use for serving food

crocodile /ˈkrɒkədaɪl/ noun [C] a large REPTILE with many sharp teeth that lives in water in hot countries —*picture* → C13

crocus /ˈkrəʊkəs/ noun [C] a small yellow, white, or purple flower that appears early in spring

croissant /ˈkwæsɒ̃/ noun [C] a type of light bread with a curved shape

crony /ˈkrəʊni/ noun [C] *showing disapproval* a friend or supporter of someone who is powerful

cronyism /ˈkrəʊniˌɪz(ə)m/ noun [U] *showing disapproval* the practice of giving jobs and other advantages to friends

crook /krʊk/ noun [C] **1** *informal* someone who is dishonest or is a thief **2** the place where something bends inwards: *the crook of your arm*

crooked /ˈkrʊkɪd/ adj **1** not straight **2** *informal* dishonest = CORRUPT —**crookedly** adv

croon /kruːn/ verb [I/T] to sing slowly in a soft voice —**crooner** noun [C]

crop¹ /krɒp/ noun ★
1 [C] a plant that is grown for food: *They're all out planting the crops today.* ♦ *Japan bought large amounts of rice overseas because of a crop failure* (=the crops did not grow).
2 [C] the amount of crops that are grown in a particular year: *a good crop of potatoes* ♦ *Last year we had a bumper crop of strawberries* (=a very large crop).
3 [singular] several things that happen or exist at the same time: *this summer's crop of Hollywood films* ♦ *the current crop of young players*

crop² /krɒp/ verb [T] to make something shorter or smaller by cutting it
  PHRASAL VERB **crop up** *informal* to appear or happen suddenly or unexpectedly = COME UP

croquet /ˈkrəʊkeɪ/ noun [U] a game in which players hit balls through curved pieces of metal using long wooden hammers

cross¹ /krɒs/ verb ★★★
1 [I/T] to go from one side of something to the other: *She watched the children cross the road.* ♦ *It was dark when we crossed the French border.*
2 [I] if things such as roads or lines cross, they go across each other = INTERSECT: *the point where the two paths cross*
3 [T] to combine one type of animal or plant

with another to produce a genetic mix
4 [T] if an expression crosses someone's face or lips, it appears there for a short time
  PHRASES **cross your arms** to put one arm over the other in front of your body, so that each hand is on the opposite elbow

cross your fingers to put your middle finger over your first finger as a wish for good luck
cross your legs to sit with one leg placed over the other at the knee
cross the line to go beyond accepted limits or standards of behaviour
cross sb's mind if something crosses your mind, you think of it, but not for very long: *It suddenly crossed his mind that maybe Stephanie had been right.*
  PHRASAL VERBS **cross sth off** to draw a line through something on a list to show that you have dealt with it
cross sth out to draw an X or a line through writing because it is wrong, or because you want to write something else

cross

cross² /krɒs/ noun ★★
1 [C] the symbol X, used for showing your choice on a written list, or for showing that an answer is wrong: *Put a cross next to the name of the person you are voting for.*
2 [C] a shape or an object with one long straight upright part and another shorter one across it, used as a symbol of Christianity → CRUCIFIXION
3 the Cross [singular] the structure on which Jesus Christ died according to the Bible
4 [C] a mixture of two different types of animals, plants, or things: *Most of their music is a cross between jazz and rock.*

cross³ /krɒs/ adj angry

crossbar /ˈkrɒsˌbɑː/ noun [C] **1** the bar that joins the two upright posts of a goal —*picture* → C15 **2** the metal bar between the seat and the front of a bicycle

crossbow /ˈkrɒsˌbəʊ/ noun [C] a weapon used for firing short heavy pointed sticks

cross-country adj **1** going across the countryside, not using tracks or roads **2** from one side of a country to the other —**cross-country** adv

crossed cheque /ˌkrɒst ˈtʃek/ noun [C] *British* a cheque that has two lines drawn across it to show that it can only be paid into the bank account of the person whose name is on it

cross-examination noun [C] an occasion when someone is asked a lot of questions by a lawyer during a trial —**cross-examine** verb [I/T]

cross-eyed /ˌkrɒs ˈaɪd/ adj someone who is cross-eyed has eyes that look towards each other slightly

crossfire /ˈkrɒsˌfaɪə/ noun [U] **1** bullets that come from two directions **2** arguments or violence that might affect people who are not directly involved

crossing /ˈkrɒsɪŋ/ noun [C] **1** a place where you are allowed to cross something such as a road or border: *a pedestrian crossing* **2** a journey across a river or sea: *a transatlantic crossing*

cross-legged /ˌkrɒs ˈleg(ɪ)d/ adj, adv in a sitting position on the floor, with your knees bent and your lower legs crossing each other —*picture* → POSTURE

crossover /ˈkrɒsˌəʊvə/ noun [C] a change from one situation or style to another

cross 'reference noun [C] a note in a book that tells you to look at another page for more information

crossroads /ˈkrɒsˌrəʊdz/ (plural **crossroads**) noun [C] **1** a place where one road crosses another **2** a point in time when you have to make an important decision about what to do next

cross 'section noun **1** [C] a group that contains an example of most types of people or things: *a cross section of the city's population* **2** [C/U] the inside of an object that you can see by cutting through the middle of it, or a picture of this

cross-trainer noun [C] a piece of exercise equipment that you stand on and move your legs and arms backwards and forwards —*picture* → C16

cross-training noun [U] the activity of training in more than one sport —**cross-train** verb [I]

crosswalk /ˈkrɒsˌwɔːk/ noun [C] *American* a PEDESTRIAN CROSSING

crossword /ˈkrɒsˌwɜːd/ or **crossword puzzle** noun [C] a word game in which the answers to questions are written in rows of squares that cross each other

crotch /krɒtʃ/ noun [C] the area between your legs where they join your body, or the part of a piece of clothing that covers this area

crotchety /ˈkrɒtʃəti/ adj *informal* easily annoyed

crouch /kraʊtʃ/ verb [I] **1** to move your body close to the ground by bending your knees and leaning forwards slightly: *She crouched down and spoke to the little boy.* —*picture* → POSTURE **2** to lean forwards with your head and shoulders bent: *Five or six men were crouched over the desk.*

crouton /ˈkruːtɒn/ noun [C] a small piece of bread that is served on soup and in salads

crow¹ /krəʊ/ noun [C] a large black bird that makes a loud sound

crow² /krəʊ/ verb [I] **1** if a COCK (=male chicken) crows, it makes a loud high noise **2** to talk very proudly about something that you have done=BOAST

crowbar /ˈkrəʊˌbɑː/ noun [C] a metal bar with a curved end, used for forcing things open

crowd¹ /kraʊd/ noun ★★★
1 [C] a large number of people in the same place: *The boys disappeared into the crowd.* ♦ *Crowds of people began making their way to the station.*
2 [C] the audience at an event: *He takes off his shirt and the crowd goes wild.*

3 [singular] *informal* a group of friends: *I spent an evening out with the usual crowd.*

crowd² /kraʊd/ verb **1** [I] to move to a place at the same time as a lot of other people: *We crowded into the kitchen.* **2** [T] to fill a place: *Hundreds of people crowded the streets.*
PHRASAL VERB **crowd sth 'out** to become more successful than another group so that they can no longer compete

crowded /ˈkraʊdɪd/ adj ★ containing a lot of people or things: *a crowded street/train/restaurant* ♦ *Was the pool crowded?* ♦ *a crowded schedule*

crown¹ /kraʊn/ noun ★

1 on king's/queen's head	5 top part of head/hat
2 position of winner	6 top part of hill
3 government	7 unit of money
4 cover for tooth	

1 [C] a circular decoration that a king or queen wears on their head
2 [C] the position of being the winner of an important sports competition: *France lost their World Cup crown.*
3 **the Crown** [singular] *formal* the government of a country that has a king or queen: *a minister of the Crown*
4 [C] a cover that is used to repair a tooth
5 [C] the top part of your head or of a hat
6 [C] the round top part of a hill
7 [C] a unit of money used in some European countries

crown² /kraʊn/ verb [T] **1** to make someone a king or queen: *James III was crowned at Kelso Abbey.* **2** to give someone a title for winning an important sports competition: *Schumacher went on to be crowned world champion.* **3** to put a cover on a tooth in order to repair it **4** to be the greatest in a series of achievements: *Iwan Roberts crowned his performance by scoring a second goal.*

crown 'court noun [C] a court of law in England and Wales in which a judge and JURY deal with serious crimes

crowning /ˈkraʊnɪŋ/ adj better or greater than anything else: *The garden is the hotel's crowning glory.*

crucial /ˈkruːʃ(ə)l/ adj ★ extremely important: *Your involvement is crucial to the success of the project.* ♦ *The talks are considered crucial for ending the violence.* ♦ **it is crucial that** *It is crucial that all students develop these basic skills.* —**crucially** adv

crucifix /ˈkruːsɪˌfɪks/ noun [C] a model of Jesus Christ dying on a CROSS

crucifixion /ˌkruːsɪˈfɪkʃ(ə)n/ noun [C/U] a method of killing someone by crucifying them

crucify /ˈkruːsɪˌfaɪ/ verb [T] **1** to kill someone by fastening them to a CROSS with nails or rope **2** *informal* to criticize someone in a very cruel way

crude¹ /kruːd/ adj **1** done or made using very simple methods=BASIC: *a crude home-made bomb* **2** referring to sex in a way that offends people: *crude language*

crude² /kruːd/ or **crude 'oil** noun [U] oil that is still in its natural state

cruel /ˈkruːəl/ adj ★★
1 causing pain to people or animals: *I can't bear to see people being **cruel to** animals.*
2 making someone unhappy or upset:

*Closing the school would be **a cruel blow to this community**.*
—**cruelly** adv

cruelty /ˈkruːəlti/ noun [C/U] cruel behaviour: *cruelty to children/animals ◆ the cruelties he witnessed during the war*

cruise¹ /kruːz/ noun [C] a journey on a ship for pleasure, often visiting a series of places

cruise² /kruːz/ verb [I] **1** to travel at a steady speed in a car or plane **2** to sail in a ship for pleasure **3** to achieve success easily in a race, game, or competition: *Liverpool cruised to victory this afternoon.*

cruise missile noun [C] a missile that is controlled by a computer and can travel very long distances

cruiser /ˈkruːzə/ noun [C] **1** a fast military ship **2** a large boat with a motor that is used for sailing in for pleasure

crumb /krʌm/ noun [C] **1** a very small piece that falls off a dry food such as bread or cake **2** a very small amount of something

crumble /ˈkrʌmb(ə)l/ verb **1** [I/T] to break into very small pieces, or to make something do this: *The soft earth crumbled under his feet.* **2** [I] to stop existing or being effective: *My determination crumbled as soon as I saw her.*

crumple /ˈkrʌmp(ə)l/ verb **1** [I/T] to crush something so that it forms untidy folds, or to be crushed in this way: *I quickly crumpled up the letter and put it in my pocket.* **2** [I] to fall to the ground suddenly, with your body, legs, and arms bent, because you are injured, ill, or upset

PHRASAL VERB **crumple (sth) up** *same as* **crumple 1**

crunch¹ /krʌntʃ/ verb **1** [I/T] to bite hard food, causing it to make a loud noise **2** [I] to make a noise like something being crushed

crunch² /krʌntʃ/ noun [singular] the noise that something makes when you crunch it

PHRASE **if it comes to the crunch** *informal* if something important or difficult happens

crunchy /ˈkrʌntʃi/ adj crunchy foods make a loud noise when you bite them

crusade /kruːˈseɪd/ noun [C] an effort over a long time to achieve something that you strongly believe is right=CAMPAIGN
—**crusader** /kruːˈseɪdə/ noun [C]

crush¹ /krʌʃ/ verb [T] **1** to press something so hard that you damage it or break it into small pieces —*picture* → C2 **2** to injure or kill someone by pressing on them very hard **3** to completely defeat an opponent

crush² /krʌʃ/ noun **1** [singular] a crowd of people in an area that is too small for them **2** [C] *informal* a strong feeling of love for someone

crushing /ˈkrʌʃɪŋ/ adj **1** complete and achieved very easily: *a crushing defeat/victory* **2** very severe: *It's a crushing blow for the president's foreign policy.*

crust /krʌst/ noun [C/U] **1** the hard brown edges of a piece of bread, or the outer part of a PIE **2** a hard layer on the surface of something

crusty /ˈkrʌsti/ adj covered with a hard CRUST

crutch /krʌtʃ/ noun **1** [C] a stick that fits under your arm and that helps you to walk when your leg or foot is injured **2** [singular] *showing*

disapproval something that you depend on for support or help

crux /krʌks/ noun **the crux (of sth)** the most important aspect of something

cry¹ /kraɪ/ (past tense and past participle **cried** /kraɪd/) verb [I/T] ★★★
1 to have tears coming from your eyes because you are sad or hurt: *I'm sorry – please don't cry. ◆ She was **crying for** her mother. ◆ I'm not going to waste time **crying over** him.*
2 to shout something: *'That's not what I meant,' Polly cried. ◆ Ted could hear a woman crying for help.*

PHRASAL VERBS **cry out 1** to make a loud noise because you are in pain or because you are afraid or shocked: *The girl cried out in alarm.* **2** *same as* **cry¹ 2**: *'Be careful!' Miss Lee cried out.*

cry out for sth to need something a lot in a way that is obvious: *This room is crying out for some new furniture.*

cry² /kraɪ/ noun **1** [C] a loud expression of emotion: *a cry of pain* **2** [C] something that someone shouts: *There was a cry of 'Fire!'* **3** [C] the noise that an animal or bird makes **4** [singular] a period of time when you have tears coming from your eyes because you are sad or hurt: *She had a good cry.*

PHRASE **be a far cry from** *informal* to be very different from someone or something

crypt /krɪpt/ noun [C] a room where dead people are buried, usually under a church

cryptic /ˈkrɪptɪk/ adj expressing something in a mysterious or indirect way

crystal /ˈkrɪst(ə)l/ noun **1** [C] a regular shape with many sides that is formed when a substance becomes solid: *ice/salt/sugar crystals* **2** [U] very good quality glass **3** [C/U] a clear rock that looks like glass

crystal ball noun [C] a glass ball that some people believe can show the future

crystal clear adj **1** completely transparent and very bright **2** extremely obvious or easy to understand

crystallize /ˈkrɪstəlaɪz/ verb [I/T] **1** to change into CRYSTALS, or to make something change into CRYSTALS **2** to become definite or easily understood, or to make something definite or easily understood

cub /kʌb/ noun [C] **1** a young bear, lion, or other wild animal **2 Cub** *British* a member of the Cubs

cube¹ /kjuːb/ noun [C] **1** an object like a box with six square sides that are all the same size —*picture* → C8 **2 the cube of sth** *technical* the result of multiplying a number by itself twice: *The cube of 2 is 8.*

cube² /kjuːb/ verb [T] **1** *technical* to multiply a number by itself twice **2** to cut something into cubes=DICE

cubic /ˈkjuːbɪk/ adj cubic units are used for measuring VOLUME (=the amount of space in an object)

cubicle /ˈkjuːbɪk(ə)l/ noun [C] a small enclosed area in a room

Cubs, the /kʌbz/ noun [plural] *British* the division of the SCOUTS for younger boys

cuckoo /ˈkʊkuː/ noun [C] a bird that leaves its eggs in other birds' NESTS and makes a call that sounds like its name

cucumber /ˈkjuːˌkʌmbə/ noun [C/U] a long, dark green vegetable that is usually eaten raw in salads —picture → C11

cuddle¹ /ˈkʌd(ə)l/ verb [I/T] to put your arms round someone and hold them close to show that you like or love them

PHRASAL VERB **cuddle up** to sit or lie with your body against someone else's because you want to feel warm or loved

cuddle² /ˈkʌd(ə)l/ noun [C] an act of cuddling someone

cuddly /ˈkʌd(ə)li/ adj soft and pleasant to cuddle

cue /kjuː/ noun [C] **1** an event, action, or statement that shows someone what they should do: Greg's arrival seemed to be the cue for everyone to get up and start dancing. **2** something that an actor does or says as a signal to another actor to do or say something **3** a long thin stick that you use for hitting the ball in games such as SNOOKER

PHRASES **(right) on cue** often humorous at exactly the right moment, or exactly when you expect

take your cue from sb to behave in the same way as someone else

cuff¹ /kʌf/ noun [C] the part of a sleeve that fits around your wrist → OFF-THE-CUFF

cuff² /kʌf/ verb [T] **1** informal to HANDCUFF someone **2** British to hit someone with your open hand

cuisine /kwɪˈziːn/ noun [C/U] a particular style of cooking: Thai/Italian cuisine

cul-de-sac /ˈkʌl də ˌsæk/ noun [C] a short street that is closed at one end

culinary /ˈkʌlɪn(ə)ri/ adj relating to food and how to cook it

cull¹ /kʌl/ verb [T] **1** to collect something such as information from different places **2** to kill animals in order to stop the population from becoming too large

cull² /kʌl/ noun [C] an act of culling animals

culminate /ˈkʌlmɪˌneɪt/ PHRASAL VERB **culminate in sth** to have or lead to an important result: A series of financial disasters culminated in the collapse of the country's largest bank.

culmination /ˌkʌlmɪˈneɪʃ(ə)n/ noun [singular] the final result of a process or situation

culpable /ˈkʌlpəb(ə)l/ adj formal responsible for doing something bad or illegal

culprit /ˈkʌlprɪt/ noun [C] **1** someone who is responsible for doing something bad or illegal **2** the cause of something bad that happens

cult¹ /kʌlt/ noun [C] **1** a religious group with beliefs that most people consider strange or dangerous **2** extreme admiration for someone or something: the cult of beauty

cult² /kʌlt/ adj very popular with a particular group of people: a cult figure/hero/film

cultivate /ˈkʌltɪˌveɪt/ verb [T] **1** to prepare land for growing crops or plants **2** to grow crops or plants: Rice is cultivated throughout the coastal regions. **3** to develop something: He's trying to cultivate a more caring image.
—**cultivation** /ˌkʌltɪˈveɪʃ(ə)n/ noun [U]

cultivated /ˈkʌltɪˌveɪtɪd/ adj **1** a cultivated person is well educated and knows how to behave politely **2** cultivated land is used for growing crops or plants **3** cultivated plants

are developed from wild plants and grown on farms or in gardens

cultural /ˈkʌltʃ(ə)rəl/ adj ★★
1 relating to the culture of a particular group, country, or society: cultural diversity ♦ the cultural traditions of our society
2 relating to music, literature, and other arts: The country enjoys a rich cultural life. ♦ During the summer New York offers a variety of cultural events.
—**culturally** adv

culture /ˈkʌltʃə/ noun ★★★
1 [U] activities involving music, literature, and other arts: If you're looking for culture, then Paris is the place for you. ♦ Britain's literary culture
2 [C/U] a set of ideas, beliefs, and ways of behaving: societies that share the same language and culture ♦ The two firms have very different corporate cultures. ♦ Some organizations encourage **a culture of** secrecy.
3 [C] a society that has its own set of ideas, beliefs, and ways of behaving: people from different cultures ♦ ancient cultures
4 [C/U] science a group of bacteria or cells that have been grown in a scientific experiment, or the process by which they are grown

cultured /ˈkʌltʃəd/ adj well educated and polite = REFINED

cumbersome /ˈkʌmbəs(ə)m/ adj
1 complicated, slow, and difficult to use
2 large, heavy, and difficult to move or carry

cumulative /ˈkjuːmjʊlətɪv/ adj developing or increasing gradually as a result of more and more additions: We studied the cumulative effect of long periods of stress on the body.

cunning¹ /ˈkʌnɪŋ/ adj good at tricking or cheating people —**cunningly** adv

cunning² /ˈkʌnɪŋ/ noun [U] the use of clever methods for tricking or cheating people

cup¹ /kʌp/ noun [C] ★★★
1 a small round container for a drink, usually with a handle: She filled my cup with hot tea.
2 the drink contained in a cup: I've already had two cups. ♦ Would you like **a cup of** coffee?
3 a large round metal container with two handles given as a prize to the winner of a competition, or the competition for which this prize is given: the winners of the World Cup

coffee cup

mug

teacup

cups

cup² /kʌp/ verb [T] to hold something in your hands, with your hands in a curved shape

cupboard /ˈkʌbəd/ noun [C] ★ a piece of furniture that is used for storing things, with shelves inside and one or two doors at the front: *a kitchen cupboard* ♦ *the cupboard door* → SKELETON —*picture* → C2

cupful /'kʌpfʊl/ noun [C] the amount of something that a cup contains

curable /'kjʊərəb(ə)l/ adj possible to cure ≠ INCURABLE

curate /'kjʊərət/ noun [C] an Anglican priest who helps a more senior priest

curator /kjʊ'reɪtə/ noun [C] someone whose job is to look after the objects in a museum

curb¹ /kɜːb/ verb [T] to control or limit something that is harmful or may cause problems: *efforts to curb inflation*

curb² /kɜːb/ noun [C] **1** a rule or control that stops or limits something **2** *American* a KERB at the edge of a road

curd /kɜːd/ noun [C/U] the solid substance that forms in milk when it becomes sour

curdle /'kɜːd(ə)l/ verb [I/T] if milk or another liquid curdles, or if something makes it curdle, lumps begin to form in it

cure¹ /kjʊə/ noun [C] ★
1 a medicine or treatment that makes someone who is ill become healthy: *Doctors say there are several possible cures.* ♦ *There's no cure for the disease.*
2 a solution to a problem: *It's the only possible cure for high unemployment.*

cure² /kjʊə/ verb [T] **1** to stop someone from being affected by an illness: *Only an operation will cure her.* ♦ *The disease is easy to prevent but almost impossible to cure.* **2** to solve a problem **3** to preserve meat, fish, or other foods by drying them, or by using smoke or salt

curfew /'kɜːfjuː/ noun [C] a period of time during which people must not go outside according to an order from the government

curiosity /ˌkjʊəri'ɒsəti/ noun **1** [U] a strong feeling of wanting to find out about something **2** [C] something that is unusual and interesting

curious /'kjʊəriəs/ adj ★
1 wanting to find out about something: *People were curious to know why the accident happened.* ♦ *Children are curious about animals and how they live.*
2 unusual and interesting: *He felt a curious mixture of happiness and fear.* ♦ *It is curious that you've never mentioned this before.*
—**curiously** /'kjʊəriəsli/ adv

curl¹ /kɜːl/ verb **1** [I/T] to form a curved or round shape, or to give something this shape: *As she talked, she curled a strand of hair on one finger.* **2** [I] to move in a curving or twisting way: *Smoke curled from tall chimneys.* **3** [I] to curve upwards or downwards at the edges: *The pages had begun to yellow and curl.*
PHRASAL VERB **curl up** to sit or lie in a comfortable position, with your legs bent and close to your body

curl² /kɜːl/ noun [C] **1** a section of hair that forms a curved shape **2** something long and thin that has a curved shape: *a curl of smoke*

curler /'kɜːlə/ noun [C] a plastic or metal tube that you wrap your hair round in order to curl it = ROLLER

curly /'kɜːli/ adj forming curves: *curly hair*

currant /'kʌrənt/ noun [C] **1** a small dark dried

fruit that is often used in cakes **2** a small round fruit that may be red, black, or white

currency /'kʌrənsi/ noun ★★
1 [C/U] the money that is used in a particular country: *Russian currency*
2 [U] the state of being accepted or used by many people: *The idea of withdrawing from the war has gained wide currency.*

current¹ /'kʌrənt/ adj ★★★
1 happening or existing now: *Production is likely to remain at current levels.* ♦ *There are several reasons for the current political situation.*
2 believed or used by many people now: *current thinking on prison reform* ♦ *current methods of funding research*
3 correct or legal now: *Is this your current address?* ♦ *a current licence*

current² /'kʌrənt/ noun **1** [C] a strong movement of water or air in one direction **2** [C/U] a flow of electricity

current account noun [C] *British* a bank account that you can take money out of whenever you want

current affairs noun [plural] political, social, and economic events that are happening now

currently /'kʌrəntli/ adv ★★★ at the present time: *Davis is currently appearing in a play at the National Theatre.* ♦ *the largest memory chips currently available*

curriculum /kə'rɪkjʊləm/ noun [C] ★★ the subjects that students study at a particular school or college: *the science curriculum* ♦ *curriculum planning/development*

curriculum vitae /kəˌrɪkjʊləm 'viːtaɪ/ noun [C] *British* a CV

curry /'kʌri/ noun [C/U] an Indian food consisting of meat, fish, or vegetables cooked in a sauce with a hot flavour

curse¹ /kɜːs/ verb **1** [I] to use offensive or impolite language: *She looked at her watch, cursed, and ran for a taxi.* **2** [T] to say or think offensive or impolite words about someone or something: *She cursed herself for being such a fool.* **3** [T] to use magic powers to make bad things happen to someone

curse² /kɜːs/ noun [C] **1** an offensive or impolite word or phrase **2** the words that are used for causing bad luck **3** an unpleasant situation or influence

cursor /'kɜːsə/ noun [singular] a small flashing line on a computer screen that you move to mark the point where you are going to type or do something

cursory /'kɜːsəri/ adj formal quick and not thorough = SUPERFICIAL: *a cursory examination/search*

curt /kɜːt/ adj using few words in a way that shows that you are impatient or angry = BRUSQUE —**curtly** adv

curtail /kɜː'teɪl/ verb [T] formal to reduce or limit something

curtain /'kɜːt(ə)n/ noun ★★★
1 [C] a long piece of cloth that hangs down to cover a window: *She closed the curtains.* ♦ *Open the curtains and let some light in.*
2 [C] a large piece of cloth that hangs in front of the stage in a theatre, or that divides one part of a room from another:

The audience cheered wildly as the curtain rose.

3 [singular/U] a large amount of a substance that is too thick to see through: *A dark curtain of cloud hung over the valley.*

curtsy or **curtsey** /ˈkɜːtsi/ noun [C] a formal greeting in which a woman bends her knees with one leg behind the other —**curtsy** verb [I]

curve¹ /kɜːv/ noun [C] a shape or line with a gradual smooth bend

curve² /kɜːv/ verb [I/T] to form a curve, or to make something form a curve

curved /kɜːvd/ adj forming a curve

cushion¹ /ˈkʊʃ(ə)n/ noun [C] **1** a cloth bag filled with something soft, used for making a seat more comfortable **2** something that gives protection against the effects of something bad

cushion² /ˈkʊʃ(ə)n/ verb [T] to protect a person or thing from the harmful effects of something

custard /ˈkʌstəd/ noun [U] a sweet yellow sauce made from milk, eggs, and sugar

custodial sentence /kʌˌstəʊdiəl ˈsent(ə)ns/ noun [C] *legal* a punishment that involves sending someone to prison

custodian /kʌˈstəʊdiən/ noun [C] someone who is responsible for something valuable

custody /ˈkʌstədi/ noun [U] **1** the protection or care of someone or something, especially given by a court: *The father was given custody of the children.* **2** a situation in which someone is kept in prison

custom /ˈkʌstəm/ noun ★★
1 [C/U] something that people do that is traditional or usual: *local customs and traditions* → HABIT
2 [U] *British* the practice of buying goods or services from a particular shop or company =BUSINESS: *Several restaurants compete for tourists' custom.*
→ CUSTOMS

customary /ˈkʌstəməri/ adj usual
—**customarily** /ˈkʌstəˌmerəli/ adv

custom-built adj designed and built for one particular person

customer /ˈkʌstəmə/ noun [C] ★★★
1 a person or company that buys goods or services: *Supermarkets use a variety of tactics to attract customers.* ♦ *customer services/relations/support* ♦ *Discounts are available for our regular customers.*
2 *informal* a particular type of person: *a cool customer* ♦ *a tricky/awkward/tough customer*

customize /ˈkʌstəˌmaɪz/ verb [T] to change the way that something looks or works so that it is exactly what you want or need

custom-made adj designed and made for one particular person

customs /ˈkʌstəmz/ noun [plural] **1** the place at a port, airport, or border where officials check that people are not bringing anything into a country illegally **2** a government department that collects taxes on goods that people bring into a country

cut¹ /kʌt/ (past tense and past participle **cut**) verb [T] ★★★

1 use knife/sharp tool	**5** stop sth working
2 injure part of body	**+ PHRASES**
3 remove parts of sth	**+ PHRASAL VERBS**
4 reduce sth	

1 to use a knife or other sharp tool to divide something into pieces, or to remove a piece of something: *I need a sharp knife to cut the bread with.* ♦ *The telephone wires had been cut.* ♦ *I'm going to **have my hair cut** tomorrow.* ♦ **cut sth in half/two** *The apples had been cut in half.* ♦ **cut sth into pieces/quarters/three etc** *Cut the cake into small pieces.* ♦ **cut sb sth** *Will you cut me a slice of pizza?* ♦ **cut sth in/through sth** *Firefighters had to cut a hole in the car roof to get him out.*

2 to injure a part of your body with something sharp that cuts the skin: *Be careful not to cut your finger.* ♦ *He cut himself shaving.*

3 to remove parts of something such as a piece of writing or a computer document: ***Cut and paste** the file* (=cut and move a computer file) *into your 'documents' folder.* ♦ **cut sth from sth** *They have cut some sex scenes from the film.* ♦ **cut sth by sth** *You need to cut your speech by about ten minutes.*

4 to reduce an amount or level: *Supermarkets are drastically cutting prices.* ♦ *We have cut our spending by 33%.* ♦ *Manufacturing companies have already cut thousands of jobs.*

5 to stop the supply of something or stop something working: *The injury had cut the oxygen to her brain.*

PHRASES **cut and dried** already clearly decided or settled: *It's a fairly cut and dried case.*

cut corners to do something quickly and carelessly because you want to save time or money

cut your losses to get out of a bad situation before it gets worse

cut sb short to interrupt someone who is talking

cut sth short to make something last for less time than it was planned to last for: *I'm sorry we had to cut our visit short.*

PHRASAL VERBS **cut across sth 1** to go across an area of land instead of going around it: *We cut across the field to save time.* **2** to affect two or more different groups: *These problems cut across class boundaries.*

cut (sth) back to reduce something, or do less of something: *plans to cut back investment in education* ♦ *If you **cut back on** fat and sugar, you'll lose weight.*

cut (sth) down to reduce something or do less of something: *These improvements will cut traffic noise down.* ♦ *I'm trying to **cut down on** salt.*

cut sth down to cut through a tree and make it fall to the ground

cut in if a piece of equipment cuts in, it starts operating automatically when it is needed =KICK IN: *The cooling system cuts in when the temperature gets too high.*

cut sb off if you are cut off when you are

talking on the telephone, something makes the telephone line stop working

cut sth 'off 1 to remove something by cutting it: *Cut the tops off the carrots.* ✦ *Why did you cut off all your hair?* **2** same as **cut**¹ 4: *They cut off the electricity last week.* **3** to make a place impossible to enter, leave, or communicate with: *The floods completely cut off the town.* ✦ **cut sth off from sth** *Our house was cut off from the rest of the village.*

cut 'out if an engine or machine cuts out, it suddenly stops working

cut sth 'out 1 to remove something from a larger piece by cutting: **cut sth out of sth** *I cut this article out of a magazine for you.* **2** to stop eating something or doing something because it is bad for your health: *I've cut out chocolate completely.* **3 cut it/that out** *spoken* used for telling someone to stop doing something that you do not like **4 not be cut out for sth/to do sth** to lack the right qualities or character for doing something: *Bill was never cut out to be a parent.* → WORK²

cut 'through sth to go through an area instead of going around it: *He decided to cut through the forest.*

cut sth 'up to cut something into several pieces: *You have to cut food up for young children.*

cut² /kʌt/ noun [C] ★★★

1 injury from sth sharp	**5** sb's part of money
2 reduction in sth	**6** piece of meat
3 mark/hole	+ PHRASE
4 part removed from sth	

1 an injury on your skin where something sharp has cut it: *My son's face was covered in cuts and bruises.*

2 a reduction in something: *job/tax/pay/defence cuts* ✦ *a cut in education spending*

3 a mark or hole in a surface where something sharp has cut it: *Make a series of small cuts in the meat.*

4 a part that has been removed from something such as a speech or a piece of writing

5 *informal* someone's part of a total amount of money: *Don't forget your agent takes a 10% cut.*

6 a piece of meat: *a lean cut of beef*

PHRASE **be a cut above** to be much better than someone or something else

→ POWER CUT

cutback /'kʌtbæk/ noun [C] a reduction in something such as the amount of money that is available to spend: *Many hospitals face cutbacks in services.*

cute /kjuːt/ adj **1** attractive: *a cute little house* **2** *informal* sexually attractive

cutlery /'kʌtləri/ noun [U] the knives, forks, and spoons that you use for eating food

cutlet /'kʌtlət/ noun [C] a flat piece of meat with a bone in it

cutoff /'kʌtɒf/ noun [C] a level or limit at which something stops: *the cutoff date by which all applications must be received*

cut-'price adj *British* cheaper than the normal price

cutter /'kʌtə/ noun [C] a tool that is used for cutting something

cutthroat /'kʌtθrəʊt/ adj a cutthroat activity or situation is one in which people behave in an unfair or immoral way in order to get an advantage

cutting¹ /'kʌtɪŋ/ noun [C] *British* an article that you have cut from a newspaper or magazine = CLIPPING

cutting² /'kʌtɪŋ/ adj a cutting remark is cruel and intended to upset someone

cutting 'edge noun [singular] **1** the most modern and advanced point in the development of something: *These models are at the cutting edge of computer design.* **2** a feature that gives someone or something an advantage

cutting-'edge adj extremely modern and advanced: *cutting-edge technology*

CV /ˌsiː ˈviː/ noun [C] *British* curriculum vitae: a document that gives details of your qualifications and the jobs you have had

cyanide /'saɪənaɪd/ noun [U] a very poisonous chemical

cybercafé /'saɪbəˌkæfeɪ/ noun [C] a café with computers for using the Internet

cyberspace /'saɪbəˌspeɪs/ noun [U] the imaginary place that emails pass through when they are going from one computer to another

cycle¹ /'saɪk(ə)l/ noun [C] ★★
1 a series of events that happen again and again in the same order or at the same times: *the cycle of hate and violence in the world*
2 a bicycle

cycle² /'saɪk(ə)l/ verb [I] to go somewhere on a bicycle

cyclical /'sɪklɪk(ə)l/ adj cyclical events happen again and again in the same order or at the same times

cyclist /'saɪklɪst/ noun [C] someone who rides a bicycle

cyclone /'saɪkləʊn/ noun [C] a severe storm in which the wind spins in a circle

cygnet /'sɪgnət/ noun [C] a young SWAN

cylinder /'sɪlɪndə/ noun [C] **1** an object shaped like a wide tube —*picture* → C8 **2** a metal container for gas or liquid **3** the tube in an engine that a PISTON moves up and down in

cylindrical /sɪ'lɪndrɪk(ə)l/ adj shaped like a cylinder

cymbal /'sɪmb(ə)l/ noun [C] a musical instrument that is a thin circular piece of metal. You hit it with a stick or hit two of them together. —*picture* → PERCUSSION

cynic /'sɪnɪk/ noun [C] someone who believes that people care only about themselves and are not sincere or honest

cynical /'sɪnɪk(ə)l/ adj **1** someone who is cynical believes that people care only about themselves and are not sincere or honest **2** willing to harm other people in order to get an advantage: *a cynical attempt to damage the government's reputation* —**cynically** /-ɪkli/ adv

cynicism /'sɪnɪˌsɪz(ə)m/ noun [U] **1** the belief that people care only about themselves and are not sincere or honest **2** the attitude of someone who is willing to harm other people in order to get an advantage

cyst /sɪst/ noun [C] a lump containing liquid

that grows under your skin or inside your body

czar /zɑː/ noun [C] **1** a senior official who is chosen by the government to make decisions about a particular subject: *the drugs czar* **2** another spelling of **tsar**

czarina /zɑːˈriːnə/ another spelling of **tsarina**

Dd

d or **D** /diː/ noun [C/U] **1** the fourth letter of the English alphabet **2 D** a mark that a teacher gives to a student's work to show that it is below average

-'d short form a way of writing 'had' or 'would'. This is not often used in formal writing: *He realized she'd asked him something.* ♦ *I'd like a glass of milk, please.*

DA /diː ˈeɪ/ noun [C] district attorney: a lawyer in the US who represents a state against a person or organization accused of committing a crime

dab¹ /dæb/ verb [I/T] to touch a surface gently several times with something such as a cloth, for example in order to dry it: *Marge dabbed at her eyes with a handkerchief.*

dab² /dæb/ noun [C] a small amount of a substance that is put on a surface

dabble /ˈdæb(ə)l/ verb [I] to be involved in an activity for a short time in a way that is not very serious: *When he was younger he dabbled in astrology.*

dachshund /ˈdæks(ə)nd/ noun [C] a small dog with very short legs and a long body

dad /dæd/ noun [C] *informal* ★★ your father: *His dad works in my office.* ♦ *Can I borrow some money, Dad?*

daddy /ˈdædi/ noun [C] *informal* your father. This word is usually used by and to young children.

daffodil /ˈdæfədɪl/ noun [C] a tall yellow flower that grows in spring —*picture* → C9

daft /dɑːft/ adj *British informal* not sensible or reasonable: *I think it's a daft idea.*

dagger /ˈdægə/ noun [C] a weapon like a very small sword

daily¹ /ˈdeɪli/ adj ★★
1 done or happening every day: *The information is updated on a daily basis.*
2 a daily newspaper is published every day, except Sunday
3 a daily amount is the amount for one day: *Workers stood waiting to receive their daily wages.*

daily² /ˈdeɪli/ adv every day: *Fresh bread is delivered daily.*

daily³ /ˈdeɪli/ noun [C] a newspaper that is published every day, except Sunday

daily 'life noun [C/U] all the things that happen or that you do regularly

dainty /ˈdeɪnti/ adj small and attractive in a delicate way —**daintily** adv

dairy¹ /ˈdeəri/ noun [C] **1** a company that sells milk and makes foods such as butter and cheese **2** a building on a farm where milk is kept and where foods such as butter and cheese are made

dairy² /ˈdeəri/ adj dairy products include milk and foods such as butter and cheese

daisy /ˈdeɪzi/ noun [C] a small white flower with a yellow centre —*picture* → C9

Dalmatian /dælˈmeɪʃ(ə)n/ noun [C] a large dog with smooth white hair and black spots

dam¹ /dæm/ noun [C] a wall built across a river to create a lake or to help to produce electricity

dam² /dæm/ verb [T] to stop a river or stream from flowing by building a dam across it

damage¹ /ˈdæmɪdʒ/ noun ★★★
1 [U] physical harm: *a new drug to treat nerve damage* ♦ *Luckily, no serious damage had been done.* ♦ *The house suffered only superficial damage in the fire.* ♦ *Damage to the building could take six months to repair.*
2 [U] negative effects on someone or something: *The damage to the bank's image is extremely serious.*
3 damages [plural] money that a court orders you to pay someone because you have harmed them or their property

damage² /ˈdæmɪdʒ/ verb [T] ★★★
1 to harm something physically: *Many buildings had been damaged in the blast.* ♦ *The house had been severely damaged by fire.*
2 to have a negative effect on someone or something: *His political reputation has been seriously damaged by the scandal.*

damaging /ˈdæmɪdʒɪŋ/ adj causing physical harm, or having a bad or negative effect: *The chemicals have a damaging effect on the environment.*

Dame /deɪm/ noun [C] used in front of the name of a woman who has been given a special honour by the British government

damn¹ /dæm/ interjection *impolite* used when you are annoyed about something: *Damn! I've broken one of my nails.*

damn² /dæm/ or **damned** /dæmd/ adj, adv *impolite* used for emphasizing what you are saying: *I can't open the damn window.* ♦ *She works damn hard.*

damn³ /dæm/ noun **not give a damn (about)** *impolite* to not care at all about someone or something

damn⁴ /dæm/ verb [T] to criticize someone or something extremely severely
PHRASE **damn it/you/him etc** *impolite* used when you are annoyed about something

damning /ˈdæmɪŋ/ adj showing that something is wrong or bad: *a damning report into the way the case was handled*

damp¹ /dæmp/ adj ★ something that is damp is slightly wet, often in an unpleasant way or when it should be dry: *The wood won't burn if it's damp.* —**dampness** noun [U]

damp² /dæmp/ noun [U] slightly wet areas in the walls of a building

dampen /ˈdæmpən/ verb [T] **1** to make something such as a feeling or hope less strong: *Not even defeat could dampen the enthusiasm of his supporters.* **2** to make something slightly wet

D

damper /'dæmpə/ noun **put a damper on sth** *informal* to make people feel less enthusiastic or hopeful about something

dance¹ /dɑːns/ verb [I/T] ★★★ to move your body in movements that follow the sound of music: *I was too shy to ask you to dance.* ♦ *They danced to the music of a Latin band.* ♦ *Who were you dancing with?* —**dancer** noun [C], **dancing** noun [U]

dance² /dɑːns/ noun ★★★
1 [C] a pattern of movements that you make with your feet and your body, following the sound of music: *They did a traditional Scottish dance.*
2 [C] a piece of music that is played for people to dance to: *dance tunes*
3 [C] a social event with music for people to dance to: *the school Christmas dance*
4 [U] the activity of dancing in order to entertain people: *She teaches drama and dance.* ♦ *a dance teacher/school/class*

dance music noun [U] a type of music with a strong beat for dancing to in clubs

dandelion /'dændɪˌlaɪən/ noun [C] a wild plant with a yellow flower —*picture* → C9

dandruff /'dændrəf/ noun [U] small white pieces of dry skin in your hair

danger /'deɪndʒə/ noun ★★★
1 [U] a situation in which serious harm, death, or damage is possible: *The notice said 'Danger! Keep Out!'* ♦ *All three children are now reported to be out of danger.* ♦ *There is danger from exposure to radiation.* ♦ *His actions put the child's life in danger.*
2 [C/U] a situation in which something unpleasant might happen: **+(that)** *There is a danger that the money will simply be wasted.* ♦ **in danger of (doing) sth** *The peace talks are now in danger of collapse.*
3 [C] a person or thing that might cause serious harm or damage: *Falling rocks pose a serious danger to tourists.* ♦ *a campaign to warn children of the dangers of electricity*

dangerous /'deɪndʒərəs/ adj ★★★ likely to cause serious harm, or to have a bad effect: *a dangerous dog* ♦ *an example of dangerous driving* ♦ *an exciting but highly dangerous sport* ♦ *We don't know whether these chemicals are dangerous to humans.* ♦ **it is dangerous (for sb) to do sth** *It's dangerous to walk around here at night.* —**dangerously** adv: *Fuel levels were dangerously low.*

dangle /'dæŋg(ə)l/ verb [I/T] if you dangle something, or if it dangles, it hangs or swings without anything stopping it: *A single light bulb dangled from the ceiling.*

dank /dæŋk/ adj a dank place is unpleasant because it is cold and slightly wet

dappled /'dæp(ə)ld/ adj with areas of lighter and darker colour or light and shadow

dare¹ /deə/ verb ★★
1 [I] to not be afraid to do something, even though it may be dangerous or may cause trouble: *I drove as fast as I dared.* ♦ **dare to do sth** *Sakharov was one of the few people who dared to protest.* ♦ **dare do sth** *Nobody dared argue with him.* ♦ **dare not do sth** *I daren't risk offending Audrey's parents.*
2 [T] to try to persuade someone to prove that they are not afraid to do something =CHALLENGE: *Go on, pick it up – I dare you!*

♦ **dare sb to do sth** *The older boys dared Jennings to go up on the roof.*

PHRASES **don't you dare** *spoken* used for telling someone not to do something, when you are warning them that you will be very angry if they do it: *Don't you dare come near me!*
how dare you *spoken* used for telling someone that you are shocked and angry about something that they have done or said

dare² /deə/ noun [C] an attempt to persuade someone to do something dangerous in order to prove that they are brave =CHALLENGE

daredevil /'deəˌdev(ə)l/ noun [C] someone who does dangerous things without worrying about the risk —**daredevil** adj

daring¹ /'deərɪŋ/ adj **1** involving brave behaviour **2** new and different in a way that might offend or upset some people: *a daring and highly original film* —**daringly** adv

daring² /'deərɪŋ/ noun [U] the brave attitude of someone who does new or dangerous things

dark¹ /dɑːk/ adj ★★★
1 with very little or no light: *a dark and stormy night* ♦ *When Maggie woke up, it was still dark.* ♦ *It was very dark in the bedroom.* ♦ *When they left, it was already starting to get dark* (=become dark at the end of a day).
2 close to black in colour: *He was dressed in a dark suit.* ♦ *She glanced up at the dark clouds above the cliffs.* ♦ *a dark blue shirt*
3 involving unpleasant or frightening things: *the darkest days of the war*

dark² /dɑːk/ noun [singular] ★★ **the dark** a situation or place in which there is very little or no light: *Tim is afraid of the dark.* ♦ *Why are you sitting here in the dark?*

PHRASES **after dark** after it has become night: *Do not go out on your own after dark.*
before dark before it becomes night: *We were hoping to get home before dark.*
in the dark (about sth) not knowing much about something because other people have not given you information: *We are still completely in the dark about how the money was lost.*

darken /'dɑːkən/ verb [I/T] to become darker, or to make something darker: *The sky darkened and heavy rain began to fall.*

dark horse noun [singular] **1** someone with a secret ability or achievement that surprises you when you discover it **2** someone who wins a race or competition unexpectedly

darkly /'dɑːkli/ adv in an angry and threatening way

darkness /'dɑːknəs/ noun [U] the lack of light: *The front rooms were all in darkness.* ♦ *The search had to be abandoned when darkness fell* (=it got dark).

darling¹ /'dɑːlɪŋ/ noun [C] **1** *spoken* used for talking to someone you love: *Are you sleepy, darling?* **2** someone who is very kind: *She's such a darling, isn't she?* **3** someone who is liked or admired very much by a particular group of people: *He quickly became the darling of the middle classes.*

darling² /'dɑːlɪŋ/ adj loved very much by someone: *my darling wife*

darn /dɑːn/ verb [I/T] to repair a piece of clothing by sewing stitches across the hole

dart¹ /dɑːt/ verb [I] to make a sudden quick movement somewhere: *A child darted out in front of our car.*

dart² /dɑːt/ noun **1** [C] a small pointed object that you throw or fire from a gun **2** [singular] a sudden short movement

darts /dɑːts/ noun [U] a game in which you throw darts at a round board

Darwinian /dɑːˈwɪniən/ adj relating to Darwinism

Darwinism /ˈdɑːwɪnɪz(ə)m/ noun [U] a theory of EVOLUTION

dash¹ /dæʃ/ verb **1** [I] to go somewhere in a hurry: *I dashed out into the street, still in my pyjamas.* **2** [I/T] to hit something violently, or to throw something violently against a surface: *Huge waves dashed against the side of the boat.*

> **PHRASE** **dash sb's hopes** to make it impossible for someone to do what they had hoped to do: *Saturday's defeat has dashed their hopes of success in the FA Cup this year.*

> **PHRASAL VERB** **dash off** to leave in a hurry

dash² /dæʃ/ noun **1** [singular] an act of going somewhere quickly: *We had a mad dash around town in search of a present for Dad.* ♦ *She made a dash for the door.* **2** [C] a small amount of something: *a dash of soy sauce* **3** [C] the symbol – used in writing to separate different parts of a sentence **4** [C] *informal* the DASHBOARD of a car

dashboard /ˈdæʃbɔːd/ noun [C] the part inside a car where the SPEEDOMETER and other instruments are —*picture* → C6

DAT /dæt/ noun [C] digital audio tape: a type of TAPE that is used for recording sound or information

data /ˈdeɪtə, ˈdɑːtə/ noun [U] ★★★
1 information in a form that a computer can use: *data storage/processing*
2 information that is used for making calculations or decisions: *The document contained data from tests of biological weapons.*

database /ˈdeɪtəˌbeɪs/ noun [C] *computing* a large amount of information that is stored in a computer in an organized way

data processing /ˌdeɪtə ˈprəʊsesɪŋ/ noun [U] *computing* the operations that are performed by a computer in order to store, organize, or find information

date¹ /deɪt/ noun [C] ★★★
1 a particular day, month, or year, or its name or number: *What was **the date of** the last meeting we had?* ♦ *'What's **today's date**?' 'The 25th.'* ♦ *Should we **set a date** for the next meeting* (=decide when it will happen)? ♦ *The exact details of the scheme will be worked out **at a later date*** (=at some time in the future).
2 an arrangement to meet someone who you are having a romantic relationship with: *I've got a date with one of the boys on my course tonight.*
3 a brown fruit that grows on PALM trees

> **PHRASES** **date of birth** the day, month, and year when you were born

> **make a date (with sb)** to arrange to meet someone on a particular day

to date *formal* until now: *There have been no reports of car theft to date.*
→ OUT-OF-DATE, UP-TO-DATE

date² /deɪt/ verb ★★
1 [T] to write the date on something: *The letter was dated 23 February.*
2 [T] to discover exactly how old something is or when it was made: *The paintings have not yet been accurately dated by the museum's experts.*
3 [I] to seem to be no longer modern or fashionable: *This style has hardly dated at all.*
4 [I/T] *American* to have a sexual or romantic relationship with someone: *They've been dating for over six months now.*

> **PHRASAL VERB** **date from sth** or **date back to sth** to have been made at a particular time in the past: *Some of the objects date from the middle of the 7th century.*

dated /ˈdeɪtɪd/ adj no longer modern or fashionable

date rape noun [C/U] a crime in which one person RAPES another (=forces them to have sex) while on a DATE with them —**date-rape** verb [T]

daub /dɔːb/ verb [T] to spread a wet substance such as paint on a surface in a careless way

daughter /ˈdɔːtə/ noun [C] ★★★ your female child —*picture* → FAMILY TREE

daughter-in-law noun [C] the wife of your son —*picture* → FAMILY TREE

daunting /ˈdɔːntɪŋ/ adj something that is daunting makes you worried because you think that it will be very difficult or dangerous to do

dawdle /ˈdɔːd(ə)l/ verb [I] to go somewhere or do something so slowly that people become annoyed with you

dawn¹ /dɔːn/ noun [C/U] the beginning of the day, when it begins to get light=DAYBREAK: *We had to get up at the crack of dawn* (=very early in the morning).

> **PHRASE** **the dawn of sth** *literary* the time when something such as a new period in history begins

dawn² /dɔːn/ verb [I] if a day or period dawns, it begins

> **PHRASAL VERB** **dawn on sb** if something dawns on you, you realize it for the first time: *It suddenly dawned on me that she hadn't told me the truth.*

day /deɪ/ noun ★★★

1 24 hours	**4** time in past/future
2 when it is light	**5** period of time
3 when you are available	**+** PHRASES

1 [C] one of the 7 periods of time that a week is divided into. It is equal to 24 hours: *We're going away for five days.* ♦ *The animals are kept inside for 14 hours a day.* ♦ *The shop is open **24 hours a day*** (=during the whole of the day and night).
2 [C/U] the period of time when it is light outside ≠ NIGHT: *There was not enough of the day left to finish the game.* ♦ *The restaurant is only open **during the day**.* ♦ *By day* (=during the day) *he is a banker, but by night he sings in a club.*
3 [C] the period of time when you are awake and doing things: *She came home exhausted*

D

after a hard day at the office (=a difficult or unpleasant day). ♦ *What do you do at home all day?* ♦ *Next week, I've got a day off* (=a day when you do not work). ♦ *All children enjoy a day out* (=a day when you go out somewhere for fun).

4 [singular] a time in the past or future: *We look forward to the day when nuclear weapons will no longer exist.* ♦ *The day may come when our air becomes too polluted to breathe.*

5 days [plural] a period of time when something is happening or is successful: *I think my days as a footballer are coming to an end.* ♦ *That was back in the days of the horse and cart.* ♦ *She became famous in the early days of television.*

PHRASES sb's day the period of time when someone was young: *The place has changed completely since my day.*

day after day every day for a long time, often in a way that is boring or unpleasant

the day after tomorrow two days from now: *We're going on holiday the day after tomorrow.*

the day before yesterday two days ago: *I got back home the day before yesterday.*

day by day in small slow stages as each day passes: *She's getting stronger day by day.*

day in, day out used for emphasizing that something is boring because it is the same every day

from day one ever since the very beginning of something

from day to day 1 in a way that changes quickly or often: *He seems to change his opinion from day to day.* **2** without thinking about what is going to happen in the future: *They lived from day to day.*

have had your/its day to have stopped being successful or fashionable: *I think the programme has had its day. Our viewers want something more fun.*

make sb's day to make someone feel very happy

one day 1 at some time in the future: *She hopes to own her own business one day.* **2** on a day in the past: *One day he just walked out and never came back.*

one of these days *spoken* at some time in the future: *One of these days I'm finally going to read that book.*

the other day *informal* recently: *I saw Kim the other day.*

some day at some time in the future: *I'll go back there some day.*

these days *spoken* used for talking about things that are happening or are true now: *Children grow up much more quickly these days.*

daybreak /ˈdeɪˌbreɪk/ noun [U] the time when light first appears in the morning=DAWN

day care noun [U] **1** *British* care that is given during the day to people who are very old or disabled **2** *American* CHILDCARE

daydream /ˈdeɪˌdriːm/ verb [I] to spend time thinking about something pleasant when you should be doing something more serious —**daydream** noun [C], **daydreamer** noun [C]

daylight /ˈdeɪˌlaɪt/ noun [U] the light

outside that you see during the day

daylight robbery noun [U] *British spoken* used for saying that you think something is much too expensive

daytime /ˈdeɪˌtaɪm/ noun [U] the period of time during the day when it is light

day-to-day adj happening every day as part of your normal life

day trip noun [C] a journey that you make for pleasure in which you go to a place and come back on the same day

daze /deɪz/ noun **in a daze** unable to think clearly or to understand what is happening

dazed /deɪzd/ adj unable to think clearly or to understand what is happening

dazzle /ˈdæz(ə)l/ verb [T] **1** if a bright light dazzles you, you cannot see for a short time **2** to impress someone a lot

dazzling /ˈdæzlɪŋ/ adj **1** a dazzling light is so bright that it makes you unable to see for a short time **2** extremely impressive: *a dazzling display of flowers*

deactivate /diːˈæktɪˌveɪt/ verb [T] to prevent something such as a bomb or an ALARM from being able to work

dead¹ /ded/ adj ★★★

1 not alive	**5** having no feeling
2 not working	**6** complete
3 not interesting	**+** PHRASE
4 no longer important	

1 no longer alive: *The shootings left 14 people dead.* ♦ *I raked up the dead leaves.* ♦ *The police don't know whether she's alive or dead.* ♦ *Rescue workers are still pulling dead bodies out of the rubble.* ♦ *Several children are among the dead* (=people who have died).

2 a piece of equipment that is dead is not working: *The battery was completely dead.* ♦ *The phone suddenly went dead.*

3 boring because there is no activity or noise: *The street seems dead without all the children.*

4 no longer important or likely to be successful: *It seems that the peace process is now dead.*

5 if a part of your body is dead, you cannot feel it: *My legs had gone completely dead.*

6 complete: *dead silence* ♦ *The bullet hit the target dead centre* (=exactly in the centre). ♦ *The truck suddenly came to a dead stop.*

PHRASE sb wouldn't be seen dead *spoken* used for saying that someone would never do something because they hate it or because it is not fashionable: *I wouldn't be seen dead in a jacket like that!*

dead² /ded/ adv *informal* **1** completely: *You're dead right!* ♦ *The package arrived dead on time.* ♦ *The editor is dead set on finishing the book by Christmas* (=determined to finish it). **2** very: *Using computers is dead easy.*

dead³ /ded/ noun **in the dead of night/winter** *literary* in the middle of the night or in the middle of the winter, when everything is quiet

deaden /ˈded(ə)n/ verb [T] **1** to make a feeling less strong **2** to make a sound less loud

dead end noun [C] **1** a road that has no way

out at one end **2** a situation in which no more progress is possible

dead-end job noun [C] a job that provides you with no chance of getting a better job

dead 'heat noun [C] a situation in which two people finish a race at exactly the same time, so that they both win

deadline /'dedlaɪn/ noun [C] a time or date by which you have to do something: *The deadline for applications was last Friday.* ♦ *If we can't meet the deadline* (=finish something in time), *they won't give us another contract.*

deadlock /'dedlɒk/ noun [singular/U] a disagreement between people who are not willing to change their opinions or decisions: *Hopes of breaking the deadlock* (=ending it) *are fading.* —**deadlocked** /'dedlɒkt/ adj

deadly¹ /'dedli/ adj **1** capable of killing people: *This is a potentially deadly disease.* ♦ *a deadly weapon* **2** complete: *Tom hit the target with deadly accuracy.*

deadly² /'dedli/ adv extremely: *Politics is a deadly serious business.*

deadpan /'dedpæn/ adj pretending to be serious when you are really joking: *deadpan humour*

dead 'wood noun [U] useless people or things

deaf /def/ adj ★★ not able to hear anything, or not able to hear very well. Some people think that this word is offensive and prefer to use the expression **hearing impaired**: *I'm a little deaf in one ear.*
> **PHRASE** **deaf to sth** not willing to listen to something
—**deafness** noun [U]

deafen /'def(ə)n/ verb [T] **1** if a noise deafens you, you cannot hear anything else because it is so loud **2** to make someone unable to hear, either for a short time or for ever

deafening /'def(ə)nɪŋ/ adj so loud that you can hear nothing else

deal¹ /di:l/ (past tense and past participle **dealt** /delt/) verb [I/T] ★★★
1 to give cards to the people who are playing a game of cards: *Each player is dealt three cards.*
2 to buy and sell illegal drugs: *Many drug addicts often deal as well.*
> **PHRASE** **deal a blow to** to harm or shock someone or something
> **PHRASAL VERBS** **'deal in sth** to buy and sell something: *a small company that deals in rare books*
,deal (sth) 'out same as **deal¹** 1: *He dealt all the cards out.*
'deal with sth 1 to take action to solve a problem: *The government must now deal with the problem of high unemployment.* **2** to be about a subject: *Chapter 5 deals with employment law.*
'deal with sb to buy goods or services from someone, or to sell them to someone: *We have dealt with the company for years.*

deal² /di:l/ noun ★★★
1 [C] a formal agreement: *a deal with a Japanese TV company* ♦ *I got a really good deal on my new computer* (=I got it for a low price). ♦ *We think there was a deal between the CIA and the FBI.* ♦ *We've cut a*

deal with Germany (=made an agreement with them) *on wine imports.* → DEALING
2 [singular] the way in which you are treated by other people: *Disabled people have got a raw deal* (=they are treated unfairly) *under the current government.* ♦ *Unions are demanding a fair deal for nurses.*
3 [singular] the act of giving cards to the people who are playing a game of cards: *Whose deal is it next?*
4 the deal [singular] *spoken* what is happening or going to happen: *So, what's the deal? Is she coming or not?*
> **PHRASES** **a big deal** *spoken* something that is very important: *Unemployment is a big deal in the region.*
big deal *spoken* used for showing that you do not think that something is very good or impressive: *So she's got a part in the school play? Big deal!*
a good/great deal of sth a large amount of something: *A great deal of research has been done already.*

dealer /'di:lə/ noun [C] **1** a person or company that buys and sells a particular product **2** someone who sells illegal drugs **3** the person who gives cards to the people who are playing a game of cards

dealership /'di:ləʃɪp/ noun [C] a business that sells the products of a particular company: *a Fiat dealership*

dealing /'di:lɪŋ/ noun **1** [U] the business of buying and selling: *property/drug dealing* **2 dealings** [plural] the business relationship that you have with another person or organization

dealt the past tense and past participle of **deal¹**

dean /di:n/ noun [C] **1** a senior Anglican priest **2** a senior official at a college or university

dear¹ /dɪə/ adj ★★★
1 Dear used in front of someone's name or title at the beginning of a letter to them: *Dear Diana, I hope you're feeling better now.* ♦ *Dear Sir or Madam*
2 loved, or liked very much: *a dear friend*
3 expensive: *Their products are good quality, but a bit dear.*

dear² /dɪə/ noun [C] **1** *spoken* used for talking to someone that you love or are friendly with: *Have you had a nice day, dear?* **2** someone who is nice, generous, and helpful to others: *She's an absolute dear.*

dear³ /dɪə/ interjection used when you are upset, disappointed, annoyed, or worried about something: *Oh dear, I spilt the coffee.*

dearest /'dɪərəst/ adj **1** most expensive **2** used about something that you want or hope for more than anything else: *her dearest wish* **3 Dearest** *old-fashioned* used in front of the name of someone you love at the beginning of a letter to them

dearly /'dɪəli/ adv very much: *I love him dearly in spite of all his faults.*

dearth /dɜːθ/ noun [singular] *formal* a situation in which there is not enough of something =LACK: *a dearth of talented students*

death /deθ/ noun ★★★
1 [C/U] the end of someone's life: *Sandra was very close to death.* ♦ *the rising number of deaths on the roads every year* ♦ *These people will starve to death unless they receive help*

D

soon. ♦ *The cause of death has not yet been discovered.*

2 [singular] the end of something: *the death of apartheid in South Africa*

PHRASE **to death** *informal* very, or very much: *bored/scared/worried to death*
→ MATTER[1]

deathbed /'deθ,bed/ noun [singular] a bed in which someone has died or is about to die
PHRASE **on your deathbed** *often humorous* going to die very soon

'**death cer,tificate** noun [C] an official document signed by a doctor that provides details of how and when someone died

deathly /'deθli/ adj making you think of death or a dead person: *a deathly silence/hush* —**deathly** adv: *deathly pale/white*

'**death penalty, the** noun [singular] legal punishment by death, usually for a serious crime such as murder

'**death ,rate** noun [C] the number of deaths in a particular area in one year

death row /,deθ 'rəʊ/ noun [U] *American* the part of a prison for criminals who are going to be EXECUTED (=legally killed)

'**death ,sentence** noun [C] a judge's official statement that orders someone to be punished by death

'**death ,squad** noun [C] a group of people who illegally kill their political opponents

'**death ,toll** noun [C] the number of people who are killed on a particular occasion

'**death ,trap** noun [C] *informal* a building or vehicle that is in such bad condition that it could be dangerous to people

'**death ,wish** noun [C] a feeling that you want to die

debacle /deɪ'bɑːk(ə)l/ noun [C] something that fails completely in an embarrassing way

debar /dɪ'bɑː/ verb [T] to officially prevent someone from doing something

debase /dɪ'beɪs/ verb [T] *formal* to reduce the value, quality, or status of something

debatable /dɪ'beɪtəb(ə)l/ adj something that is debatable is not certain because it is possible for people to have different opinions about it

debate[1] /dɪ'beɪt/ noun ★★★
1 [C/U] a discussion in which people or groups state different opinions about a subject: *The proposals provoked a fierce debate.* ♦ *There has been intense debate over the treatment of illegal immigrants.*
2 [C] a formal discussion that ends with a decision made by voting

debate[2] /dɪ'beɪt/ verb [I/T] **1** to discuss a subject formally before making a decision, usually by voting: *Parliament is still debating the bill.* **2** to consider an action or situation carefully before you decide what to do: *I debated whether or not to call her parents.*

debauchery /dɪ'bɔːtʃəri/ noun [U] immoral behaviour that involves a lot of sex, alcohol, or illegal drugs —**debauched** /dɪ'bɔːtʃt/ adj

debilitating /dɪ'bɪlɪ,teɪtɪŋ/ adj *formal* making someone physically or mentally weak: *a debilitating illness/condition*

debit[1] /'debɪt/ noun [C] an amount of money

that is taken from a bank account ≠ CREDIT

debit[2] /'debɪt/ verb [T] if a bank debits your account, it takes money out of it ≠ CREDIT

'**debit ,card** noun [C] a plastic card that you use to pay for things. It automatically takes the money you pay out of your bank account. → CASH CARD, CHEQUE CARD, CREDIT CARD

debrief /diː'briːf/ verb [T] to get information from someone who has just finished an important job for the armed forces or the government

debriefing /diː'briːfɪŋ/ noun [C/U] a meeting where someone gives a report about an important job that they have just finished for the armed forces or the government

debris /'debriː, 'deɪbriː/ noun [U] the broken pieces that are left when something large has been destroyed

debt /det/ noun ★★★
1 [C] an amount of money that you owe: *By this time we had debts of over £15,000.* ♦ *Many people experience difficulty in paying off their debts.*
2 [U] a situation in which you owe money to other people: *I don't like being in debt.* ♦ *She was terrified of getting into debt.*
3 [singular] an obligation to be grateful to someone because they have done something for you: *I'm forever in your debt.*

debtor /'detə/ noun [C] a person, organization, or country that owes money ≠ CREDITOR

'**debt re,lief** noun [U] the practice of allowing poor countries not to pay back what they owe to rich countries

debug /diː'bʌg/ verb [T] *computing* to look for and remove mistakes from a computer program

debunk /diː'bʌŋk/ verb [T] to prove that something such as an idea or belief is false and silly

debut[1] /'deɪbjuː/ noun [C] the first time a performer or sports player appears in public: *Easton made his debut in 2002.*

debut[2] /'deɪbjuː/ adj a debut CD, performance, novel etc is the first that a performer, sports player, writer etc makes

debut[3] /'deɪbjuː/ verb [I] to perform, or to be performed, in public for the first time

decade /'dekeɪd/ noun [C] ★★★ a period of ten years: *Prices have risen sharply in the last decade.*

decadent /'dekəd(ə)nt/ adj involving a lot of immoral pleasure —**decadence** /'dekəd(ə)ns/ noun [U]

decaf /'diːkæf/ noun [C/U] *informal* decaffeinated coffee, or a cup of this drink

decaffeinated /diː'kæfɪ,neɪtɪd/ adj decaffeinated coffee or tea has had the CAFFEINE (=a chemical substance that keeps you awake) removed

decapitate /dɪ'kæpɪ,teɪt/ verb [T] *formal* to cut off someone's head

decathlon /dɪ'kæθlɒn/ noun [C] a sports event that consists of ten different sports

decay /dɪ'keɪ/ verb **1** [I/T] to be gradually destroyed as a result of a natural process, or to destroy something in this way: *As dead trees decay, they feed the soil.* ♦ *Too much sugar will decay your teeth.* **2** [I] if a building or an area decays, its condition gradually gets worse because it has not been looked after —**decay** noun [U]: *tooth decay* ♦ *urban decay*

deceased /dɪˈsiːst/ adj *formal* **1** dead **2 the deceased** a dead person or dead people

deceit /dɪˈsiːt/ noun [C/U] dishonest behaviour that is intended to trick someone

deceitful /dɪˈsiːtf(ə)l/ adj behaving dishonestly in order to trick people → DECEPTIVE 2

deceive /dɪˈsiːv/ verb [T] **1** to trick someone by behaving in a dishonest way: *He was deceived into giving them all his money.* **2** to make someone believe something that is not true

December /dɪˈsembə/ noun [C/U] ★★★ the twelfth month of the year, between November and January: *House prices fell slightly in December.* ♦ *I received a letter from them on December 15th.*

decency /ˈdiːs(ə)nsi/ noun [U] behaviour that is moral, good, or reasonable: *You should at least have the decency to say you're sorry!*

decent /ˈdiːs(ə)nt/ adj **1** good, or good enough: *Are there any decent restaurants around here?* **2** if you behave in a decent way towards other people, you are honest, fair, and nice **3** *informal old-fashioned* wearing enough clothes to not be embarrassed to let other people see you —**decently** adv

decentralize /diːˈsentrəlaɪz/ verb [T] to take power from a central government or organization and give it to several smaller and more local ones —**decentralization** /ˌdiːsentrəlaɪˈzeɪʃ(ə)n/ noun [U]

deception /dɪˈsepʃ(ə)n/ noun [C/U] the act of tricking someone by telling them something that is not true

deceptive /dɪˈseptɪv/ adj **1** if something is deceptive, it seems very different from the way it really is: *a deceptive calmness in his voice* **2** if someone is being deceptive, they trick other people by telling them something that is not true: *deceptive advertising* —**deceptively** adv

decibel /ˈdesɪbel/ noun [C] a unit for measuring how loud a sound is

decide /dɪˈsaɪd/ verb ★★★
1 [I/T] to make a choice about what you are going to do: **decide to do sth** *He decided to stay and see what would happen.* ♦ **+(that)** *I decided that it would be best to tell George everything.* ♦ **+what/whether/how/when etc** *I can't decide where to go.* ♦ *She needs to decide whether or not she wants to keep the car.*
2 [T] to produce a particular result: *Today's match will decide the championship.*
PHRASAL VERBS de,cide a'gainst sb/sth to not choose someone or something: *We decided against the house because it was too small.* de'cide on sb/sth to choose someone or something from a number of possible choices: *We finally decided on the red curtains.*

Word family: decide

Words in the same family as decide
- **decided** *adj*   - **undecided** *adj*
- **decision** *n*   - **indecision** *n*
- **decisive** *adj*   - **indecisive** *adj*

---

decided /dɪˈsaɪdɪd/ adj impossible to doubt and easy to see: *a decided improvement on last year* —**decidedly** adv

deciduous /dɪˈsɪdjuəs/ adj deciduous trees lose all their leaves each autumn

decimal[1] /ˈdesɪm(ə)l/ noun [C] a number that consists of numbers on either side of a DECIMAL POINT. 0.5, 25.75, and 873.4 are all decimals

decimal[2] /ˈdesɪm(ə)l/ adj based on the number ten

decimal 'point noun [C] the symbol . in a DECIMAL

decimate /ˈdesɪˌmeɪt/ verb [T] to damage or destroy a large number of people or things

decipher /dɪˈsaɪfə/ verb [T] to discover the meaning of something that is difficult to read or understand

decision /dɪˈsɪʒ(ə)n/ noun ★★★
1 [C] a choice that you make after you have thought carefully about something: *The committee will **make a decision** by the end of the week.* ♦ *Sometimes managers need to **take decisions** quickly.* ♦ *Have you **come to a decision** yet?* ♦ **a decision to do sth** *Mrs Osman has announced her decision to retire.*
2 [U] the ability to make choices quickly, confidently, and effectively: *He acted with decision.*

de'cision-,making noun [U] the process of deciding what to do about something

decisive /dɪˈsaɪsɪv/ adj **1** if something is decisive, it makes the final result of a situation certain: *The UK has played a decisive role in these negotiations.* **2** a decisive victory or defeat is one in which the winner does much better than the LOSER **3** a decisive person can decide what to do quickly and confidently ≠ INDECISIVE —**decisively** adv

deck[1] /dek/ noun [C] **1** the outside top part of a ship that you can walk on **2** one of the levels on a ship or bus **3** a set of cards used for playing card games

deck[2] /dek/ verb [T] **1** *informal* to hit someone so hard that they fall to the ground **2** *same as* **deck sb/sth out**
PHRASAL VERB deck sb/sth 'out to decorate a person or object with something, usually for a special occasion

decking /ˈdekɪŋ/ noun [U] *British* wood used for making a floor outside

declaration /ˌdekləˈreɪʃ(ə)n/ noun [C/U] an important or official statement about something: *a declaration of war* ♦ *his declaration of love*

declare /dɪˈkleə/ verb [T] ★★
1 to announce officially that something is true or is happening: *I was in Germany when war was declared.* ♦ **+that** *Mrs Armitage declared that she would fight to clear her name.* ♦ **declare sb/sth (to be) sth** *Sarah was declared the winner.*
2 to state officially the value of the things that you have earned or bought, so that you can pay the correct amount of tax: *All income from investments must also be declared.*

declassified /diːˈklæsɪˌfaɪd/ adj declassified information is officially no longer secret —**declassify** verb [T]

D

decline¹ /dɪˈklaɪn/ verb ★★
1 [I] to become less or worse: *The number of people buying their own homes has declined.* ♦ *Share prices declined sharply last week.*
2 [I/T] to say politely that you will not accept something or do something: *They offered to fly him to Brussels, but he declined.* ♦ *We asked her to the reception, but she declined the invitation.* ♦ **decline to do sth** *The minister declined to comment on the rumours.*

decline² /dɪˈklaɪn/ noun [C/U] ★★ a reduction in the amount or quality of something: *a sharp/steep/dramatic decline* ♦ *There has been a steady decline in public services over recent years.*

decode /diːˈkəʊd/ verb [T] to succeed in understanding the meaning of a message that is written in CODE =DECIPHER ≠ DECODE

decolonization /ˌdiːkɒlənaɪˈzeɪʃ(ə)n/ noun [U] the process by which a COLONY becomes independent from the country that used to control it —**decolonize** verb [T]

decommission /ˌdiːkəˈmɪʃ(ə)n/ verb [T] to stop using something such as a weapon, ship, or nuclear power station

decompose /ˌdiːkəmˈpəʊz/ verb [I] to be destroyed by a slow natural process

decompress /ˌdiːkəmˈpres/ verb [T] to reduce the pressure on something —**decompression** /ˌdiːkəmˈpreʃ(ə)n/ noun [U]

decor or **décor** /ˈdeɪkɔː, ˈdekɔː/ noun [C/U] the style of decoration and furniture in a building

decorate /ˈdekəreɪt/ verb ★
1 [T] to make something more attractive by putting nice things on it or in it: *The room had been decorated with balloons.*
2 [I/T] *British* to put new paint or paper on the walls of a room: *We decorated the kitchen last weekend.*
3 [T] to give someone a MEDAL because they have done something brave

decoration /ˌdekəˈreɪʃ(ə)n/ noun **1** [C/U] something nice that you use to make something else look more attractive **2** [C] a MEDAL given to someone who has done something brave

decorative /ˈdek(ə)rətɪv/ adj attractive rather than useful: *decorative objects*

decorator /ˈdekəreɪtə/ noun [C] *British* someone whose job is to decorate houses

decorum /dɪˈkɔːrəm/ noun [U] *formal* polite behaviour

decoy /ˈdiːkɔɪ/ noun [C] a person or thing that you use to trick someone into going somewhere or doing something

decrease¹ /diːˈkriːs/ verb **1** [I] to become less ≠ INCREASE: *The number of visitors has decreased significantly.* **2** [T] to reduce something

---

Other ways of saying decrease

- **be/go/come down** to become less in number, value, or price
- **drop/fall** to decrease in number or quality by a large amount
- **dwindle** to decrease slowly and steadily until there is almost nothing left
- **plummet/plunge** to decrease suddenly and very quickly
- **slump** to decrease to a very low level or value, when this is seen as a bad thing

---

decrease² /ˈdiːkriːs/ noun [C/U] the process of becoming less, or the amount by which something is less ≠ INCREASE

decree /dɪˈkriː/ noun [C] **1** an official decision or order that is made by a leader or government **2** a judgment that is made by a court of law —**decree** verb [T]

decrepit /dɪˈkrepɪt/ adj old and no longer in good condition

decriminalize /diːˈkrɪmɪnəlaɪz/ verb [T] to change the law so that something that was illegal becomes legal —**decriminalization** /diːˌkrɪmɪnəlaɪˈzeɪʃ(ə)n/ noun [U]

dedicate /ˈdedɪkeɪt/
PHRASAL VERBS **dedicate sth to sth** to spend your time and effort doing something =DEVOTE: **dedicate sth to doing sth** *This woman has dedicated her life to helping others.*
dedicate sth to sb to say that a book or song that you have written was written for a person that you love or admire

dedicated /ˈdedɪkeɪtɪd/ adj **1** believing something is important and spending a lot of time and effort on it: *a dedicated teacher* **2** made or used for just one purpose: *a dedicated sports channel*

dedication /ˌdedɪˈkeɪʃ(ə)n/ noun **1** [U] the belief that something is good or right that makes you spend a lot of time and effort doing or supporting it: *his dedication to the fight against AIDS* **2** [C] a statement that dedicates a song or book to someone

deduce /dɪˈdjuːs/ verb [T] *formal* to decide that something is true by considering the information that you have

deduct /dɪˈdʌkt/ verb [T] to take an amount or number from a total

deductible /dɪˈdʌktəb(ə)l/ adj if money is deductible, it can be taken away from the total amount of money on which you pay tax

deduction /dɪˈdʌkʃ(ə)n/ noun [C/U] **1** an amount or number taken from a total, or the process of taking an amount or number away from a total **2** something that you know from the information you have, or the process of finding something out from the information you have

deed /diːd/ noun [C] **1** *literary* something that someone does: *a good deed* **2** an official document that gives the details about who owns a building or piece of land

deem /diːm/ verb [T] *formal* to decide that someone or something has a particular quality

deep¹ /diːp/ adj ★★★

1 a long way down	**6** colour: dark and strong
2 measuring a distance	**7** breathing a lot of air
3 going a long way in	**8** sleep: hard to wake up
4 feeling: strong	**9** serious
5 sound: low	**+ PHRASES**

1 going a long way down from the top or surface of something ≠ SHALLOW: *The river is quite deep here.*
2 used for talking about the distance from the surface to the bottom of something: *The pond needs to be about four feet deep.* ♦ *How deep is the snow?*
3 going a long way in from the front, edge,

or surface: *a deep cut on my arm* ♦ *We were deep inside the national park.*

4 a deep feeling is very strong: *I told him my deepest fears.*

5 a deep sound is low: *a deep voice*

6 a deep colour is dark and strong: *a beautiful deep red*

7 a deep breath or deep breathing brings a lot of air into and out of your body

8 a deep sleep is one that you do not wake up easily from

9 involving very serious thoughts, ideas, or feelings

PHRASES deep in thought/conversation so involved in thinking or talking to someone that you do not notice anything else

thrown in at the deep end having to deal with something difficult without being prepared for it

deep² /diːp/ adv ★★★

1 a long way down from the top or the surface, or a long way into something: *men who work deep under the ground* ♦ *They continued deep into the forest.*

2 if people or things are two deep, three deep etc, there are two, three etc rows of them

PHRASE deep down used for saying that you know something is true, although you do not like to admit it: *Deep down, I knew that Caroline was right.*

deepen /ˈdiːpən/ verb [I/T] to become, or to make something become, worse, stronger, deeper etc: *Both sides are deepening their commitment to peace.* ♦ *a deepening crisis*

deep-fried adj cooked in a lot of hot oil

deeply /ˈdiːpli/ adv ★★

1 very, or very much: *Your mother is deeply concerned.*

2 a long way into something: *The needle had penetrated deeply into his skin.*

3 if you breathe or SIGH deeply, you breathe a lot of air into or out of your body

deep-rooted /ˌdiːp ˈruːtɪd/ adj DEEP-SEATED

deep-sea adj in the deep areas of the sea

deep-seated /ˌdiːp ˈsiːtɪd/ adj a deep-seated feeling or belief is strong and difficult to change

deep-set adj deep-set eyes seem to be a long way back into your face

Deep South, the the states of Alabama, Georgia, Louisiana, Mississippi, and South Carolina in the southern part of the US

deer /dɪə/ noun [C] a large brown animal with long thin legs —picture → C12

deerstalker /ˈdɪəˌstɔːkə/ noun [C] a hat with pieces that cover your ears

deface /dɪˈfeɪs/ verb [T] to deliberately damage something, usually by writing on it

defamation /ˌdefəˈmeɪʃ(ə)n/ noun [U] *legal* the offence of writing or saying something bad about someone that is not true —**defamatory** /dɪˈfæmət(ə)ri/ adj

default¹ /dɪˈfɔːlt/ noun [C] the way that something will automatically appear or be done on a computer if you do not change it **PHRASES by default 1** if something happens by default, it happens only because you do not do something else **2** if you win something by default, you win because the

other person does not play or does not finish the game

in default *formal* not having done something that you were officially told to do

default² /dɪˈfɔːlt/ verb [I] **1** to fail to pay money that you owe: *They defaulted on the loan.* **2** to fail to appear in a court of law when you have been ordered to do so

defeat¹ /dɪˈfiːt/ noun [C/U] ★★ failure to win a competition or to succeed in doing something ≠ VICTORY: *England suffered a 2–0 defeat.*

defeat² /dɪˈfiːt/ verb [T] ★★

1 to win against someone=BEAT: *France defeated Italy 3–1.*

2 to prevent something from happening or being successful: *The proposal was defeated by 16 votes to 5.*

defect¹ /ˈdiːfekt/ noun [C] a fault in someone or something

defect² /dɪˈfekt/ verb [I] to leave one country or political party and go to another one —**defection** /dɪˈfekʃ(ə)n/ noun [C/U], **defector** noun [C]

defective /dɪˈfektɪv/ adj not made correctly, or not working correctly=FAULTY

defence /dɪˈfens/ noun ★★★

1 protecting a place	4 attempt to win again
2 protection for sb/sth	5 in sport
3 proof sb/sth is right	6 in court case

1 [C/U] the weapons, equipment, and people that are used to protect a country or place: *The government spends huge amounts of money on defence.*

2 [C/U] protection for someone or something that is being attacked: *Two of his friends came to his defence.*

3 [C/U] something that you say to support someone or something that is being criticized: *Several people spoke in my defence.* ♦ *a strong defence of government policy*

4 [singular] an attempt by someone to win a competition that they won last time

5 [C/U] the players in a team game who try to prevent the other team from scoring

6 the defence [singular] the people in a court case who try to prove that someone is not guilty

→ SELF-DEFENCE

defenceless /dɪˈfensləs/ adj weak and unable to protect yourself

defend /dɪˈfend/ verb ★★

1 protect from attack	4 try to win again
2 support sb/sth	5 in law
3 in sport	

1 [T] to protect someone or something from attack: *Can the military defend the city against attack?*

2 [T] to say things to support someone or something: *We will defend their right to free speech.*

3 [I] to try to prevent your team's opponents from scoring

4 [T] to attempt to win a competition that you won last time: *Baxter will defend his heavyweight championship.*

5 [I/T] to be the lawyer in a court case who tries to prove that someone is not guilty

D

Word family: defend

Words in the same family as defend
- **defence** n
- **defenceless** adj
- **defendant** n
- **defender** adj
- **defensive** adv
- **indefensible** adj

defendant /dɪˈfendənt/ noun [C] *legal* someone who has been accused of a crime and is on trial

defender /dɪˈfendə/ noun [C] **1** a player who tries to stop the other team from scoring in a game **2** someone who works to prevent something from being lost or taken away

defense /dɪˈfens/ the American spelling of defence

defensive¹ /dɪˈfensɪv/ adj **1** intended or used for protecting a place during an attack **2** becoming angry or offended when you think that someone is criticizing you: *Don't get so defensive!* **3** a defensive player tries to stop the other team from scoring points —**defensively** adv

defensive² /dɪˈfensɪv/ noun **on the defensive** trying to defend something from attacks or criticism

defer /dɪˈfɜː/ verb [T] to arrange for something to happen later than you had planned =POSTPONE

deference /ˈdefərəns/ noun [U] behaviour that shows that you respect someone —**deferential** /ˌdefəˈrenʃ(ə)l/ adj

defiance /dɪˈfaɪəns/ noun [U] refusal to obey a person or rule: *Goods were exported in defiance of the treaty.*

defiant /dɪˈfaɪənt/ adj refusing to obey a person or rule —**defiantly** adv

deficiency /dɪˈfɪʃ(ə)nsi/ noun [C/U] a lack of something, or a fault in someone or something

deficient /dɪˈfɪʃ(ə)nt/ adj lacking something, or not good enough: *a diet deficient in vitamin C ♦ a deficient education system*

deficit /ˈdefəsɪt/ noun [C] the amount by which something is less than you need or should have: *the budget deficit*

define /dɪˈfaɪn/ verb [T] ★★
1 to describe clearly and exactly what something is, or what something means: *No one has defined the aims of the project. ♦ How would you define the word 'love'?*
2 to show clearly the shape or edges of something
—**defined** /dɪˈfaɪnd/ adj: *a sharply defined image*

definite /ˈdefənət/ adj ★★
1 clearly decided and specific: *We haven't arranged a definite date for our visit yet.*
2 certain: *This book will be a definite bestseller.*

definite article noun [C] *linguistics* the word 'the' in English, or a similar type of word in another language

definitely /ˈdefənətli/ adv ★★
1 without any doubt: *I'm definitely going to Ben's party.*
2 used for emphasizing that you mean 'yes': *'So we'll see you on Sunday at 7 o'clock?' 'Definitely!'*

definition /ˌdefəˈnɪʃ(ə)n/ noun ★★
1 [C] a statement of what a word or expression means: *The definition of*

'family' has changed over the years.
2 [U] the quality of being clear: *Some of the photographs lack definition.*
PHRASE **by definition** as a part of the basic nature of something: *Being a soldier, by definition, involves risks.*

definitive /dɪˈfɪnətɪv/ adj **1** better than all others **2** certain and unlikely to change —**definitively** adv

deflate /diːˈfleɪt/ verb **1** [I/T] if a tyre or BALLOON deflates, or if you deflate it, air comes out of it ≠ INFLATE **2** [T] to make someone feel less confident or important

deflated /diːˈfleɪtɪd/ adj feeling less confident and happy

deflect /dɪˈflekt/ verb **1** [T] to direct criticism, attention, or blame away from yourself and towards someone else **2** [I/T] if something deflects, or if it is deflected, it hits something and starts to move in a different direction —**deflection** /dɪˈflekʃ(ə)n/ noun [C/U]

deforestation /diːˌfɒrɪˈsteɪʃ(ə)n/ noun [U] the process of removing the trees from an area of land

deformed /dɪˈfɔːmd/ adj something that is deformed is not attractive because it has a different shape from what is usual or natural

deformity /dɪˈfɔːməti/ noun [C/U] a part of someone's body that is not the normal shape

defragment /diːˈfrægment/ verb [T] *computing* to make a computer do an operation that brings together all free space and all similar files, in order to increase the speed at which it operates

defraud /dɪˈfrɔːd/ verb [I/T] to get money from a person or organization in a dishonest way

defrost /diːˈfrɒst/ verb [I/T] **1** if frozen food defrosts, or if you defrost it, it becomes warmer until it is no longer frozen **2** if a FREEZER defrosts, or if you defrost it, you switch it off so that the ice inside it MELTS

deft /deft/ adj done quickly and with skill —**deftly** adv

defunct /dɪˈfʌŋkt/ adj no longer existing or working

defuse /diːˈfjuːz/ verb [T] **1** to make a situation more relaxed by making people less angry or worried **2** to stop a bomb from exploding by removing its FUSE

defy /dɪˈfaɪ/ verb [T] to refuse to obey someone or something =DISOBEY
PHRASE **defy belief/explanation etc** to be almost impossible to believe, explain etc

degenerate¹ /dɪˈdʒenəreɪt/ verb [I] to become worse

degenerate² /dɪˈdʒen(ə)rət/ adj immoral

degrade /dɪˈgreɪd/ verb **1** [T] to treat someone very badly so that they lose the respect of other people **2** [I] *science* if a substance degrades, it separates into the different substances that it consists of —**degradation** /ˌdegrəˈdeɪʃ(ə)n/ noun [U]

degrading /dɪˈgreɪdɪŋ/ adj something that is degrading causes you to have less respect for yourself or for someone else

degree /dɪˈgriː/ noun ★★★
1 [C] a unit for measuring temperature, that is often shown as a number followed by the

symbol °: *It will probably be a few degrees colder by the weekend.*
2 [C] a unit for measuring angles, that is often shown as a number followed by the symbol °: *The two lines meet at a 90 degree angle.*
3 [C/U] an amount of something such as a feeling or a quality: *The job requires a high degree of skill.* ♦ *What you say is true to some degree* (=partly true).
4 [C] a course of study at a university, or the qualification that you get after completing the course: *a biology degree* ♦ *a master's degree in English literature* ♦ *She's doing a degree at Exeter University.*

dehydrate /diːˈhaɪdreɪt/ verb **1** [I] to lose so much water from your body that you feel weak or ill **2** [T] *science* to remove the water from something —**dehydration** /ˌdiːhaɪˈdreɪʃ(ə)n/ noun [U]

dehydrated /diːˈhaɪdreɪtɪd/ adj **1** feeling weak or ill because you have lost a lot of water from your body **2** dehydrated food has been preserved by having all of its water removed

deity /ˈdeɪəti, ˈdiːəti/ noun [C] a god

déjà vu /ˌdeɪʒɑː ˈvuː/ noun [U] the feeling that you are having exactly the same experience as one that you have had before

dejected /dɪˈdʒektɪd/ adj someone who is dejected has lost all of their hope or enthusiasm —**dejection** /dɪˈdʒekʃ(ə)n/ noun [U]

delay¹ /dɪˈleɪ/ noun [C/U] ★★ a situation in which something happens later or more slowly than you expected: *After a long delay, the plane finally took off.* ♦ **delay in doing sth** *Who is responsible for the delay in reaching an agreement?*

delay² /dɪˈleɪ/ verb ★
1 [I/T] to do something later than is planned or expected: *They delayed the decision for as long as possible.*
2 [T] to make someone or something late, or to slow them down: *His plane was delayed for five hours.*

delegate¹ /ˈdeləgət/ noun [C] someone who is chosen to represent a group of other people at a meeting

delegate² /ˈdeləgeɪt/ verb **1** [I/T] to give part of your work or responsibilities to someone else **2** [T] to choose someone to do a job for you or to represent you

delegation /ˌdeləˈgeɪʃ(ə)n/ noun **1** [C] a group of people who represent a country, government, or organization **2** [U] the process of giving some of your work or responsibilities to someone else

delete /dɪˈliːt/ verb [T] to remove something that has been written, recorded, or stored in a computer: *I deleted the file by mistake.*

deletion /dɪˈliːʃ(ə)n/ noun [C/U] the process of deleting something, or something that has been deleted

deli /ˈdeli/ noun [C] *informal* a DELICATESSEN

deliberate¹ /dɪˈlɪb(ə)rət/ adj ★
1 intended, and not done by chance or by accident =INTENTIONAL ≠ ACCIDENTAL: *This was a deliberate attack on unarmed civilians.*
2 slow and careful: *deliberate steps*

deliberate² /dɪˈlɪbəreɪt/ verb [I/T] to think

about or discuss something very carefully

deliberately /dɪˈlɪb(ə)rət(ə)li/ adv ★
1 with a definite intention, and not by chance or by accident =INTENTIONALLY ≠ ACCIDENTALLY: *Police believe the fire was started deliberately.*
2 in a slow careful way: *He spoke deliberately.*

deliberation /dɪˌlɪbəˈreɪʃ(ə)n/ noun **1** [C/U] long and careful thought or discussion **2** [U] a slow and careful way of speaking or moving

delicacy /ˈdelɪkəsi/ noun **1** a rare or expensive type of food **2** [U] a sensitive and careful way of doing something **3** [U] the quality of being delicate

delicate /ˈdelɪkət/ adj **1** easily damaged, broken, or hurt: *Delicate skin must be protected from the sun.* ♦ *delicate fabrics*
2 small and attractive: *delicate pink flowers*
3 needing care and skill: *The negotiations are at a very delicate stage.* **4** a delicate taste, smell, or colour is pleasant and not too strong —**delicately** adv

delicatessen /ˌdelɪkəˈtes(ə)n/ noun [C] a shop that sells food such as cooked meat and cheese

delicious /dɪˈlɪʃəs/ adj ★ with a very pleasant taste or smell: *This sauce is delicious with fish or vegetables.* —**deliciously** adv: *a deliciously creamy dessert*

delight¹ /dɪˈlaɪt/ noun **1** [U] a feeling of great happiness: *To my great delight, she said yes.* **2** [C] something that gives you pleasure

delight² /dɪˈlaɪt/ verb [T] to give someone a lot of enjoyment or pleasure
PHRASAL VERB de**light** ˌin doing sth to get a lot of pleasure from something

delighted /dɪˈlaɪtɪd/ adj **1** very happy about something: *We're delighted with our new grandson.* ♦ *The company is delighted at the response to its advertisement.* ♦ *I'm delighted that you got the job.* ♦ **delighted to do sth** *I was delighted to see my old friends again.*
2 used for saying politely that you are pleased about something: *'Will you come?' 'I'd be delighted.'* —**delightedly** adv

delightful /dɪˈlaɪtf(ə)l/ adj very nice —**delightfully** adv

delinquent¹ /dɪˈlɪŋkwənt/ adj **1** behaving in a criminal or immoral way **2** failing to pay money that you owe —**delinquency** noun [U]

delinquent² /dɪˈlɪŋkwənt/ noun [C] a young person whose behaviour is criminal or very bad

delirious /dɪˈlɪriəs/ adj **1** talking in a confused way because you are ill **2** extremely happy =ECSTATIC —**deliriously** adv

delirium /dɪˈlɪriəm, dɪˈlɪəriəm/ noun [U] a confused state caused by illness

deliver /dɪˈlɪvə/ verb ★★★

1 take sth to a place	4 give a statement
2 do what you promised	5 help at a birth
3 give a formal talk	

1 [T] to take something such as goods or letters to a place and give it to someone: *I can deliver the letter this afternoon.* ♦ *You can have groceries delivered to your door.*
2 [I/T] to do something that you have promised to do or are expected to do: *We're looking for a supplier who can deliver a*

D

reliable service. ♦ *How will the government* **deliver** *on its election promises?*

3 [T] *formal* to give a formal talk: *He delivered a speech lasting 40 minutes.*

4 [T] to officially give your decision or a message: *The jury has delivered its verdict.*

5 [T] to help a baby to be born: *Paramedics delivered the baby.*

delivery /dɪ'lɪv(ə)ri/ noun ★★
1 [C/U] the process of bringing goods or letters to a place: *Please allow ten days for delivery.* ♦ *When do you* **make deliveries***?*
2 [U] the process of providing a service: *We need to improve* **delivery** *of health care.*
3 [C/U] the process of giving birth to a baby

delta /'deltə/ noun [C] an area where a river divides into smaller rivers that flow into the sea

delude /dɪ'luːd/ verb [T] to make someone think something that is not true —**deluded** adj

deluge¹ /'deljuːdʒ/ noun [singular] **1** a lot of things all happening or arriving at the same time=FLOOD **2** a very heavy fall of rain=DOWNPOUR

deluge² /'deljuːdʒ/ verb **be deluged with sth** to have a lot of things to deal with

delusion /dɪ'luːʒ(ə)n/ noun [C/U] a belief that is not true

deluxe /də'lʌks/ adj better in quality and more expensive than other things of the same type=LUXURY: *the deluxe model/version*

delve /delv/ verb [I] **1** to try hard to find out information **2** to search for something in a bag or pocket

demand¹ /dɪ'mɑːnd/ noun ★★★
1 [C] a firm statement that you want something: *They* **made demands** *that our government could never accept.* ♦ **demands** *for a pay increase*
2 demands [plural] the things or qualities that are needed in a particular situation: *the* **demands** *of his new job* ♦ *She has a lot of* **demands on** *her time.*
3 [U] the amount of a product or service that people want, or the fact that they want it: *18,400 new houses will be needed to cope with the demand.* ♦ **Demand for** *organic food is increasing.*

> PHRASES **be in demand** to be wanted by a lot of people: *The software is in demand all over the world.*
> **by popular demand** because a lot of people have asked for it
> **on demand** whenever people want it

demand² /dɪ'mɑːnd/ verb [T] ★★★
1 to say firmly that you want something: *The demonstrators demanded the release of all prisoners.* ♦ **demand to do sth** *She demanded to know what was happening.* ♦ **+(that)** *The panel demanded that the report be made public.*
2 to expect something, or to make something necessary: *I demand absolute loyalty from my staff.* ♦ *a situation that demands careful handling*

demanding /dɪ'mɑːndɪŋ/ adj needing a lot of attention, time, or energy ≠ UNDEMANDING: *a demanding child/job*

demeaning /dɪ'miːnɪŋ/ adj making people

have less respect for someone=DEGRADING

demeanour /dɪ'miːnə/ noun [U] *formal* the way that you look and behave

demented /dɪ'mentɪd/ adj *informal* crazy

dementia /dɪ'menʃə/ noun [C/U] *medical* a serious illness affecting your brain and memory

demise /dɪ'maɪz/ noun [singular] *very formal* the time when something or someone stops existing

demo /'deməʊ/ noun [C] *informal* **1** *British* a protest DEMONSTRATION **2** something such as a piece of recorded music or software that is made to show what a product is like

democracy /dɪ'mɒkrəsi/ noun ★★
1 [U] a system of government in which people choose their political representatives in elections
2 [C] a country that has democracy
3 [U] a way of running an organization in which everyone can share in making decisions

democrat /'deməkræt/ noun [C] someone who supports democracy

Democrat /'deməkræt/ noun [C] a member of the Democratic Party in the US

democratic /ˌdemə'krætɪk/ adj ★★
1 involving elections in which people vote for their political representatives: *the democratic system*
2 based on the principle that all people should share in making decisions ≠ UNDEMOCRATIC: *a democratic organization* —**democratically** /ˌdemə'krætɪkli/ adv

Democratic Party, the one of the two main political parties in the US

demographic /ˌdemə'græfɪk/ adj relating to populations

demographics /ˌdemə'græfɪks/ noun [plural] the particular features of a population

demolish /dɪ'mɒlɪʃ/ verb [T] **1** to destroy a building **2** to completely defeat someone, or to destroy their hopes or their confidence

demolition /ˌdemə'lɪʃ(ə)n/ noun [C/U] the deliberate destruction of a building

demon /'diːmən/ noun [C] an evil spirit

demonic /dɪ'mɒnɪk/ adj like a demon

demonstrable /dɪ'mɒnstrəb(ə)l, 'demənstrəb(ə)l/ adj *formal* clear or obvious —**demonstrably** adv

demonstrate /'demən,streɪt/ verb ★★
1 [T] to show someone how to do something or how something works: *We will demonstrate various techniques.* ♦ *Let me demonstrate how we achieve this effect.*
2 [T] to show that something is true or exists: *Her story demonstrates the importance of keeping fit.* ♦ **+that** *The study demonstrates that children are affected by advertising.*
3 [I] to protest about something in a public place: *the right to demonstrate peacefully* ♦ *Students were* **demonstrating against** *the war.*

demonstration /ˌdemən'streɪʃ(ə)n/ noun ★★
1 [C] an occasion when people protest about something in public: *Angry students* **held demonstrations***.* ♦ **demonstrations against** *the new tax*
2 [C/U] an occasion when someone shows how something works or how to do something: *cookery demonstrations*

3 [C] an event or action that proves a fact: *This is **a demonstration** of the president's popularity*.

demonstrative /dɪˈmɒnstrətɪv/ adj showing love in the way that you behave towards someone

demonstrator /ˈdemənˌstreɪtə/ noun [C] **1** someone who takes part in a public protest **2** someone whose job is to show how something works or how to do something

demoralized /dɪˈmɒrəˌlaɪzd/ adj feeling unhappy and without any confidence

demoralizing /dɪˈmɒrəˌlaɪzɪŋ/ adj making you feel unhappy and without any confidence

demote /diːˈməʊt/ verb [T] to give someone or something lower status or a less important position —**demotion** /diːˈməʊʃ(ə)n/ noun [C/U]

demure /dɪˈmjʊə/ adj a demure woman is quiet, shy, and polite —**demurely** adv

den /den/ noun [C] **1** a place where a wild animal such as a lion lives **2** a place where people take part in secret or illegal activities: *a gambling den* **3** *American* a room in a house where someone can go to relax

denial /dɪˈnaɪəl/ noun **1** [C/U] a statement that something is not true: *the company's denial of the charges against it* **2** [U] the refusal to let someone have or do something: *the denial of health care to poor patients* **3** [U] *technical* the refusal to accept the unpleasant truth about something

denigrate /ˈdenɪˌgreɪt/ verb [T] to criticize something in a way that shows that you think it has no value at all

denim /ˈdenɪm/ noun [U] thick cotton cloth that is usually blue and is used for making JEANS

denomination /dɪˌnɒmɪˈneɪʃ(ə)n/ noun [C] **1** a religious group within one of the main religions **2** the value of a particular coin or BANKNOTE

denounce /dɪˈnaʊns/ verb [T] to criticize someone or something severely in public

dense /dens/ adj **1** consisting of a lot of things, people, trees etc that are all very close together: *a dense crowd/forest* **2** thick and difficult to see through: *dense smoke/cloud/fog* **3** *science* a dense substance is very heavy in relation to its size —**densely** adv

density /ˈdensəti/ noun [U] **1** the number of people or things in a particular area **2** *science* the relationship between the weight and the size of an object

dent[1] /dent/ noun [C] a place where a surface has been pushed or knocked inwards

dent[2] /dent/ verb [T] to make a dent in a surface

dental /ˈdent(ə)l/ adj relating to teeth: *dental health*

dental floss noun [U] a substance like very thin string that you use to clean between your teeth

dentist /ˈdentɪst/ noun [C] someone whose job is to examine and treat people's teeth

dentistry /ˈdentɪstri/ noun [U] **1** the job of examining and treating people's teeth **2** the medical study of the teeth and mouth

dentures /ˈdentʃəz/ noun [plural] artificial teeth

denunciation /dɪˌnʌnsiˈeɪʃ(ə)n/ noun [C/U] strong public criticism of someone or something

deny /dɪˈnaɪ/ verb [T] ★★★
1 to say that something is not true: +**(that)** *A spokesman denied that the company had acted irresponsibly.* ♦ **deny doing sth** *He still denies murdering his wife.*
2 to refuse to admit that you have a particular feeling, illness, or problem: *I had been denying this anger for years.*
3 to not allow someone to do or have something: *Doctors were accused of **denying** treatment **to** older patients.*

deodorant /diˈəʊd(ə)rənt/ noun [C/U] a substance that you put on your skin to prevent your body from having an unpleasant smell

depart /dɪˈpɑːt/ verb [I] *formal* to leave a place and start a journey
PHRASAL VERB **deˈpart from sth** to not do something in the usual or traditional way

department /dɪˈpɑːtmənt/ noun [C] ★★★
1 a section in a government, organization, or business that deals with a particular type of work: *the Department of Health* ♦ *the sales department*
2 an area in a large shop that sells a particular type of goods: *the menswear department*

deˈpartment ˌstore noun [C] a large shop that is divided into separate sections, with each section selling a different type of thing

departure /dɪˈpɑːtʃə/ noun [C/U] **1** an act of leaving a place, job, or organization **2** a plane, train, ship etc that leaves to start a journey **3** a way of doing something that is different from the usual or traditional way

depend /dɪˈpend/ verb ★★★
PHRASE **it/that depends** *spoken* used for saying that you cannot give a definite answer until certain details of the situation are described: *'How much will I have to pay for a car?' 'It **depends what** sort of car you want.'*
PHRASAL VERBS **deˈpend on sth** if one thing depends on another, it is changed or affected by the other thing: *Their future depends on how well they do in these exams.*
deˈpend on sb/sth to need someone or something in order to continue to exist or to be successful=RELY ON SB/STH: *The project's success depends on the support of everyone concerned.*
deˈpend on sb if you can depend on someone to do something, you can trust them to do it=RELY ON SB: *I knew I could depend on you.*

dependable /dɪˈpendəb(ə)l/ adj always behaving or working in the way that you expect=RELIABLE: *a dependable friend/worker/machine*

dependant /dɪˈpendənt/ noun [C] *British* a child or other relative that you are legally responsible for supporting

dependence /dɪˈpendəns/ or **dependency** /dɪˈpendənsi/ noun [U] **1** a situation in which you need someone or something in order to live or succeed=RELIANCE: *the industry's dependence on coal* **2** the fact that someone is ADDICTED to a drug or to alcohol

D

dependent /dɪˈpendənt/ adj ★★
1 if you are dependent on someone or something, you need them in order to live or succeed: *a married couple with dependent children* ♦ *They hate being* **dependent on** *their parents.*
2 if one thing is dependent on another, it is affected by the other thing and changes if the other thing changes: *Your pay is* **dependent on** *your work experience.*

depict /dɪˈpɪkt/ verb [T] to describe someone or something using words or pictures

deplete /dɪˈpliːt/ verb [T] to reduce the amount of something or the number of things —**depletion** /dɪˈpliːʃ(ə)n/ noun [U]

depleted /dɪˈpliːtɪd/ adj with a smaller amount of something or a smaller number of things than you want or need

deplorable /dɪˈplɔːrəb(ə)l/ adj *formal* extremely bad and shocking —**deplorably** adv

deplore /dɪˈplɔː/ verb [T] *formal* to think that something is bad and immoral

deploy /dɪˈplɔɪ/ verb [T] if a government or army deploys soldiers or weapons, it uses them —**deployment** noun [U]

deport /dɪˈpɔːt/ verb [T] to send someone back to the country that they came from —**deportation** /ˌdiːpɔːˈteɪʃ(ə)n/ noun [C/U]

depose /dɪˈpəʊz/ verb [T] to force someone out of their position of power

deposit[1] /dɪˈpɒzɪt/ noun [C] ★
1 a payment that you make as the first part of a total amount that you will have to pay later: *We've* **put down a deposit on** (=paid a deposit on) *a new house.*
2 an amount of money that you pay when you rent something. You get the money back if the thing is not damaged when you return it.
3 a payment that you make into a bank account
4 a layer of something that is formed by natural or chemical processes: *rich mineral deposits*

deposit[2] /dɪˈpɒzɪt/ verb [T] **1** to pay money into a bank account **2** *formal* to put something somewhere

deˈposit acˌcount noun [C] a bank account for saving money in

depot /ˈdepəʊ/ noun [C] **1** a large building where things are stored until they are needed **2** *British* a place where buses or trains are kept when they are not being used

depraved /dɪˈpreɪvd/ adj immoral or evil —**depravity** /dɪˈprævəti/ noun [U]

depreciate /dɪˈpriːʃieɪt/ verb [I] to become less valuable —**depreciation** /dɪˌpriːʃiˈeɪʃ(ə)n/ noun [U]

depress /dɪˈpres/ verb [T] **1** to make someone feel unhappy and without any enthusiasm or hope: *It depresses me to see all that money being wasted.* **2** *formal* to make something such as a price or value go down

depressed /dɪˈprest/ adj ★
1 very unhappy and without any feelings of hope or enthusiasm: *She got very depressed after her husband left her.*
2 a depressed area, industry, or economy is not successful

depressing /dɪˈpresɪŋ/ adj making you feel very unhappy and without any feelings of hope or enthusiasm —**depressingly** adv

depression /dɪˈpreʃ(ə)n/ noun ★
1 [U] a feeling of great sadness that is sometimes so extreme that it is considered to be a mental illness: *Some children show signs of anxiety and depression at exam time.*
2 [C/U] a period of time when there is a lot of unemployment and POVERTY because there is very little economic activity: *the world depression of the 1930s*
3 [C] *formal* an area on a surface that is lower than the parts around it

deprivation /ˌdeprɪˈveɪʃ(ə)n/ noun [U] a situation in which people are very poor and do not have the basic things that they need

deprive /dɪˈpraɪv/ verb [T] to prevent someone from having something that they need or want: *people who are deprived of their freedom*

deprived /dɪˈpraɪvd/ adj not having enough of the basic things that you need, for example food or money: *deprived children in the inner cities*

depth /depθ/ noun ★★★
1 [C/U] a distance relating to how deep something is, for example the sea, a river, or a hole: *What's* **the depth of** *the water here?*
2 [U] the distance from the front to the back of something: *the depth of the shelf*
3 [C/U] interesting qualities or ideas that are not obvious at first: *His first album had more depth than this one.*
4 [U] a high level of something such as a feeling or the amount of information that is given: *The newspaper is proud of* **the depth of** *its coverage.*
PHRASES **the depths of sth 1** a place that is very far inside an area: *the depths of the forest* **2** the worst part of an unpleasant time, feeling, or situation: *She was* **in the depths of** *despair.*
in depth in a very detailed way and giving a lot of information: *This subject will be covered in depth next term.*
out of your depth in a situation that you cannot deal with because it is too difficult or dangerous

deputy /ˈdepjʊti/ noun [C] ★★
1 someone whose job is the second most important in a department or organization. A deputy does the job of the most important person in some situations.
2 a police officer who works for the SHERIFF in some parts of the US

derail /diːˈreɪl/ verb [I] if a train derails, or if something derails it, it comes off its tracks —**derailment** noun [C/U]

deranged /dɪˈreɪndʒd/ adj behaving in an uncontrolled or dangerous way because of a mental illness

derby /ˈdɑːbi/ noun [C] *informal* a race or competition

deregulation /diːˌregjʊˈleɪʃ(ə)n/ noun [U] the process of removing the rules that control something such as an industry —**deregulate** /diːˈregjʊˌleɪt/ verb [T]

derelict /ˈderəlɪkt/ adj a derelict building or area is empty, not used, and in bad condition

deride /dɪˈraɪd/ verb [T] *formal* to say that someone or something is stupid or useless

derision /dɪˈrɪʒ(ə)n/ noun [U] the attitude that someone or something is stupid or useless

derisive /dɪˈraɪsɪv/ adj showing that you think that someone or something is stupid or useless —**derisively** adv

derisory /dɪˈraɪsəri/ adj if money that you are offered or given is derisory, you feel insulted because it is not very much

derivation /ˌderɪˈveɪʃ(ə)n/ noun [C/U] *linguistics* the original form from which something such as a word developed

derive /dɪˈraɪv/ verb [T] to get something from something else

dermatologist /ˌdɜːməˈtɒlədʒɪst/ noun [C] a doctor who treats diseases of the skin —**dermatology** noun [U]

derogatory /dɪˈrɒɡət(ə)ri/ adj intended to criticize or insult

descend /dɪˈsend/ verb **1** [I/T] *formal* to go down something such as a mountain, a slope, or stairs ≠ ASCEND **2** [I] to move closer to the ground from the air or from a high point **3 be descended from** to be related to a person or animal that lived long ago

PHRASAL VERBS des'cend into sth to develop into a very bad state: *Filming descended into chaos after further arguments.*
des'cend on sb/sth if people descend on a person or a place, a lot of them arrive together

descendant /dɪˈsendənt/ noun [C] a relative of a person who lived in the past

descent /dɪˈsent/ noun **1** [C/U] the act of moving down to a lower place or position ≠ ASCENT: *The plane began its descent.* **2** [U] the origin of your parents or other older members of your family: *They're all of Irish descent.* **3** [singular] the process of gradually changing to a worse condition: *her gradual descent into alcoholism*

describe /dɪˈskraɪb/ verb [T] ★★★ to give details about someone or something in order to explain to another person what they are like: *It's hard to describe my feelings.* ♦ **describe sb/sth as sth** *The attacker is described as tall, with dark hair.* ♦ **describe sb/sth to sb** *Could you describe her to me?*

Word family: describe

*Words in the same family as **describe***
- **description** *n*
- **descriptive** *adj*
- **indescribable** *adj*
- **nondescript** *adj*

---

description /dɪˈskrɪpʃ(ə)n/ noun [C] ★★★ a statement about what someone or something is like: *a brief description of the area* ♦ *Barry was unable to give the police a description of his attacker.*

descriptive /dɪˈskrɪptɪv/ adj describing something: *descriptive writing*

desecrate /ˈdesɪˌkreɪt/ verb [T] to deliberately spoil something that is special or holy —**desecration** /ˌdesɪˈkreɪʃ(ə)n/ noun [U]

desegregation /ˌdiːsegrɪˈɡeɪʃ(ə)n/ noun [U] the process of ending a system in which people of different races are separated —**desegregate** /diːˈsegrɪˌɡeɪt/ verb [T]

desert¹ /ˈdezət/ noun [C/U] ★★ a large area of

land with few plants and dry weather

desert² /dɪˈzɜːt/ verb **1** [T] to leave a person or place and not come back **2** [I] if soldiers desert, they leave the army without permission —**desertion** /dɪˈzɜːʃ(ə)n/ noun [C/U]

deserted /dɪˈzɜːtɪd/ adj a deserted place has no people in it

deserter /dɪˈzɜːtə/ noun [C] someone who leaves the armed forces without permission

desert island /ˌdezət ˈaɪlənd/ noun [C] a small tropical island with no people living on it

deserve /dɪˈzɜːv/ verb [T] ★★
1 if you deserve something, it is right that you get it, because of the way that you are or the way that you have behaved: *After five hours on your feet you deserve a break.* ♦ *Chambers got what he deserved* (=was punished correctly for something he did). ♦ **deserve to do sth** *I think I deserve to be well paid.*
2 to be worth spending time on or giving thought to: *an issue that deserves careful thought*

deserving /dɪˈzɜːvɪŋ/ adj worth supporting or helping

design¹ /dɪˈzaɪn/ noun ★★★
1 [C/U] the way that something is made so that it works and looks a certain way, or a drawing that shows what it will look like: *The car has a new design.* ♦ *designs for the new bridge*
2 [U] the process of deciding how something will be made, how it will work, and what it will look like, or the study of this process: *software design* ♦ *the design and construction of new buildings* ♦ *I studied design at college.*
3 [C] a pattern that decorates something: *simple geometric designs*
PHRASE by design *formal* deliberately

design² /dɪˈzaɪn/ verb [T] ★★★ to decide how something will be made, how it will work, or what it will look like, and often to make drawings of it: *The bride wore a dress that she designed herself.* ♦ *She has a job designing websites.*

designate /ˈdezɪɡˌneɪt/ verb [T] **1** to formally choose someone or something for a particular purpose **2** *formal* to give someone or something a particular name —**designation** /ˌdezɪɡˈneɪʃ(ə)n/ noun [C/U]

designer¹ /dɪˈzaɪnə/ noun [C] ★ someone whose job is to decide how to make things, how they will work, and what they will look like: *a fashion designer*

designer² /dɪˈzaɪnə/ adj designer clothes and products are expensive and fashionable

desirable /dɪˈzaɪrəb(ə)l/ adj **1** something that is desirable has qualities that make you want it **2** sexually attractive

desire¹ /dɪˈzaɪə/ noun ★★
1 [C/U] a strong feeling of wanting to have or do something: *a desire for peace* ♦ **a desire to do sth** *his desire to travel*
2 [U] *literary* a strong feeling that you want to have sex with someone

desire² /dɪˈzaɪə/ verb [T] **1** *formal* to want something **2** *literary* to want someone as a sexual partner
PHRASE leave a lot to be desired used for

D

saying that something is of a very low
standard

desired /dɪˈzaɪəd/ adj making you want to
have or achieve something

desk /desk/ noun ★★★
1 [C] a table that you sit at to write or work,
often with drawers in it
2 [singular] a place that provides information
or a service, for example in a hotel: *the
information desk*
3 [singular] a particular department of an
organization such as a television company
or a newspaper: *the sports desk*

desk tidy noun [C] *British* a container that you
keep on top of a desk and use for holding
pens and other small pieces of office
equipment —*picture* → C3

desktop /ˈdeskˌtɒp/ noun [C] the main screen
on a computer that shows the programs
that are available

desktop publishing noun [U] the use of small
computers to produce newspapers,
magazines, or professional documents

desolate /ˈdesələt/ adj **1** a desolate place is
completely empty with no pleasant features
2 feeling very sad and alone —**desolation**
/ˌdesəˈleɪʃ(ə)n/ noun [U]

despair[1] /dɪˈspeə/ noun [U] the feeling that a
situation is so bad that nothing can change
it —**despairing** adj

despair[2] /dɪˈspeə/ verb [I] to feel that a
situation is so bad that nothing can change
it

despatch /dɪˈspætʃ/ another spelling of
dispatch[1]

desperate /ˈdesp(ə)rət/ adj ★
1 very upset and willing to do anything
because you are in a bad situation: *The
missing man's family are getting
increasingly desperate.* ♦ *In a desperate
attempt to escape, he killed a guard.*
2 needing or wanting something very much:
*be desperate to do sth She was desperate to
see him again.*
3 extremely severe or serious: *Parts of this
school are in desperate need of repair.*
—**desperately** adv, **desperation**
/ˌdespəˈreɪʃ(ə)n/ noun [U]

despicable /dɪˈspɪkəb(ə)l/ adj extremely
unpleasant: *despicable crimes*

despise /dɪˈspaɪz/ verb [T] to hate someone or
something and have no respect for them

despite /dɪˈspaɪt/ preposition ★★★ used for
saying that something happens or is true
even though something else makes it seem
unlikely = IN SPITE OF: *He still loves her,
despite the fact that she left him.*
PHRASE **despite yourself** even though you
did not intend or expect to do something: *I
began to enjoy the party despite myself.*

despondent /dɪˈspɒndənt/ adj very unhappy
because you do not believe that an
unpleasant situation will improve
—**despondency** noun [U]

dessert /dɪˈzɜːt/ noun [C/U] ★ sweet food that
you eat after the main part of a meal
= PUDDING

destabilize /diːˈsteɪbəˌlaɪz/ verb [T] to cause
problems for a country, government, or
person in authority so that they become

less effective —**destabilization**
/ˌdiːsteɪbəlaɪˈzeɪʃ(ə)n/ noun [U]

destination /ˌdestɪˈneɪʃ(ə)n/ noun [C] ★ the
place where someone or something is going

destined /ˈdestɪnd/ adj **1** certain to do
something, or certain to happen: *We felt
that we were destined to meet.* **2** travelling,
or being sent, to a particular place

destiny /ˈdestəni/ noun **1** [C] the things that
you will do or the type of person that you
will become **2** [U] a power that some people
believe controls everything that happens

destitute /ˈdestɪtjuːt/ adj with no money or
possessions

destroy /dɪˈstrɔɪ/ verb [T] ★★★ to damage or
harm something so severely that it cannot
exist as it was before: *An earthquake
destroyed the town.* ♦ *This action destroyed
any hope of reaching an agreement.*

> **Words family: destroy**
>
> *Words in the same family as destroy*
> - **destroyer** *n*
> - **destruction** *n*
> - **destructive** *adj*
> - **indestructible** *adj*
> - **self-destruct** *v*

destroyer /dɪˈstrɔɪə/ noun [C] a small fast ship
that is used for fighting enemy ships

destruction /dɪˈstrʌkʃ(ə)n/ noun [U] ★ damage
that is so severe that something cannot
exist as it was before: *the destruction of the
environment*

destructive /dɪˈstrʌktɪv/ adj causing severe
damage or harm

detach /dɪˈtætʃ/ verb [I/T] to remove a part
from something, or to become removed
from something = SEPARATE
PHRASE **detach yourself (from)** to stop being
involved in something in an emotional way

detachable /dɪˈtætʃəb(ə)l/ adj able to be
removed and put back on again

detached /dɪˈtætʃt/ adj **1** not feeling involved
in something in an emotional way **2** a
detached house is not joined to another
house —*picture* → C1

detachment /dɪˈtætʃmənt/ noun **1** [U] a feeling
of not being involved with someone or
something in a close or emotional way **2** [C]
a small group of soldiers who are sent to
do a particular job

detail[1] /ˈdiːteɪl, *American* dɪˈteɪl/ noun ★★★
1 [C/U] one of many small facts or pieces of
information relating to a situation: *No
details of the offer were revealed.* ♦ *Please
enter your details* (=personal information
such as your name and address) *below.* ♦
She talked in detail (=including many
smaller facts) *about her plans.* ♦ *Mr Shaw
refused to go into detail* (=talk about more
than general facts) *about the discussions.*
2 [U] all the small aspects or features that
something has, especially those that are
difficult to notice: *Attention to detail is
important in this job.*

detail[2] /ˈdiːteɪl/ verb [T] to list all the facts or
aspects of a situation

detailed /ˈdiːteɪld/ adj ★★ including many
small facts or aspects: *a detailed
description/report*

detain /dɪˈteɪn/ verb [T] **1** to not allow someone
to leave a POLICE STATION or prison **2** *formal*

to delay someone who has to go somewhere

detect /dɪˈtekt/ verb [T] **1** to prove that something is present by using scientific methods **2** to notice something when it is not obvious: *I thought I detected a hint of irony in her words.* —**detection** /dɪˈtekʃ(ə)n/ noun [U]

detective /dɪˈtektɪv/ noun [C] ★
1 a police officer whose job is to try to discover information about a crime
2 someone who is paid by other people to find out information

detector /dɪˈtektə/ noun [C] a piece of equipment that is used for checking whether something is present

detention /dɪˈtenʃ(ə)n/ noun **1** [U] the state of being kept in a POLICE STATION or prison and not being allowed to leave **2** [C/U] a punishment in which a child has to stay at school after other children have left

deter /dɪˈtɜː/ verb [T] to make someone decide not to do something

detergent /dɪˈtɜːdʒ(ə)nt/ noun [C/U] a liquid or powder that you use for washing clothes or dishes

deteriorate /dɪˈtɪəriəˌreɪt/ verb [I] to become worse —**deterioration** /dɪˌtɪəriəˈreɪʃ(ə)n/ noun [U]

determination /dɪˌtɜːmɪˈneɪʃ(ə)n/ noun [U] ★ the refusal to let anything stop you from doing what you want to do: **determination to do sth** *The president's determination to pursue the rebels was clear* .

Words often used with determination

Adjectives often used with determination
■ dogged, fierce, grim, sheer, steely + DETERMINATION: used for saying that someone is very determined

Verbs often used with determination
■ demonstrate, show, signal, underline + DETERMINATION: show people that you are determined

---

determine /dɪˈtɜːmɪn/ verb **1** [T] to control what something will be: *Our prices are determined by the market.* **2** [I/T] to officially decide something: *The court must determine whether she is guilty.* **3** [I/T] to calculate something, or to discover it by examining evidence = FIND OUT: *Technicians were trying to determine why the missile didn't fire.*

determined /dɪˈtɜːmɪnd/ adj ★ not willing to let anything stop you from doing what you want to do: *a strong, determined woman* ♦ **determined to do sth** *I was determined to be a jazz musician.*

determiner /dɪˈtɜːmɪnə/ noun [C] *linguistics* a word such as 'a', 'the', 'this', or 'some' that is used before a noun for showing which thing or things you are talking about

deterrent /dɪˈterənt/ noun [C] **1** something that stops people from doing something by making them afraid of what will happen if they do it **2** a weapon whose purpose is to make other countries afraid to attack the country that owns it

detest /dɪˈtest/ verb [T] to hate someone or something

detonate /ˈdetəˌneɪt/ verb [I/T] to explode, or to make something such as a bomb

explode —**detonation** /ˌdet(ə)ˈneɪʃ(ə)n/ noun [C/U]

detonator /ˈdetəˌneɪtə/ noun [C] a piece of equipment on a bomb that makes it explode

detour /ˈdiːtʊə/ noun [C] a way of going from one place to another that is not the shortest or usual way

detox /ˈdiːtɒks/ noun [U] *informal* treatment to help someone to stop taking drugs or drinking alcohol

detract /dɪˈtrækt/ PHRASAL VERB **deˈtract from sth** to make something seem less good, attractive, or important: *The ugly high-rise buildings detract from the view.*

detriment /ˈdetrɪmənt/ noun [U] *formal* harm that is caused to something as a result of something else

detrimental /ˌdetrɪˈment(ə)l/ adj harmful or damaging ≠ BENEFICIAL

devalue /diːˈvæljuː/ verb **1** [T] to treat someone or something as if they are not important **2** [I/T] *business* to officially reduce the value of a country's money —**devaluation** /ˌdiːvæljuˈeɪʃ(ə)n/ noun [C/U]

devastate /ˈdevəˌsteɪt/ verb [T] **1** to destroy or seriously damage something **2** to make someone feel very shocked and upset: *Mary's death devastated the family.* —**devastation** /ˌdevəˈsteɪʃ(ə)n/ noun [U]

devastated /ˈdevəˌsteɪtɪd/ adj feeling very shocked and upset

devastating /ˈdevəˌsteɪtɪŋ/ adj **1** causing a lot of harm or damage: *a devastating fire/storm/flood* **2** very shocking or upsetting: *a devastating loss* **3** very impressive or attractive: *devastating good looks*

develop /dɪˈveləp/ verb ★★★

1 grow/change	**5** create new product
2 start to exist	**6** use land for sth
3 be affected by	**7** become complete
4 change	**8** prepare photograph

1 [I/T] to change, grow, or improve, or to make something grow, change, or improve: *All children develop at different rates.* ♦ *The area is working to develop its tourist industry.* ♦ *As the economy developed, social change took place.* ♦ *The cell **develops into** an embryo.*

2 [I] to start to exist, or to start to be noticeable: *Their friendship developed at college.* ♦ *A rash developed on my arm.*

3 [T] to start to have something or be affected by something: *Rob died two years after developing the illness.* ♦ *The engine developed a problem soon after takeoff.*

4 [I] if a situation develops, it changes as events happen or conditions change: *We're waiting to see how things develop before we make a decision.*

5 [T] to create a new product or method: *We've recently developed new communications software.*

6 [T] to use land for a particular purpose that increases its value

7 [I/T] if an idea or story develops, or if you develop it, it becomes clear and complete as you add details to it

8 [T] to treat a film with chemicals in order to make photographs

developed /dɪˈveləpt/ adj **1** a developed country, region, or economy has a lot of industries **2** a developed skill, idea, or quality has reached a high level: *a well-developed sense of smell*

developer /dɪˈveləpə/ noun [C] someone who buys land or buildings in order to put new or better buildings there

developing /dɪˈveləpɪŋ/ adj a developing country is poor and does not have many industries

development /dɪˈveləpmənt/ noun ★★★
1 [U] change, growth, or improvement over a period of time: *a child's physical development ♦ the development of the region's economy*
2 [C] a new event that changes a situation: *Were there any further developments in the case?*
3 [U] the process of creating a new product or method, or the product or method that is created: *software development ♦ developments in medical research*
4 [C/U] the process of putting new buildings on land, or a group of new buildings

deviant /ˈdiːviənt/ adj deviant behaviour is not considered normal or morally correct

deviate /ˈdiːvi.eɪt/ verb [I] to start doing something different from what is expected

deviation /ˌdiːviˈeɪʃ(ə)n/ noun [C/U] a difference in the usual or expected way of doing something

device /dɪˈvaɪs/ noun [C] ★★
1 a machine or piece of equipment that does a particular job: *a device for measuring humidity in the air ♦ a listening device*
2 a bomb
PHRASE **leave sb to their own devices** to leave someone alone to do whatever they want

devil /ˈdev(ə)l/ noun **1 the Devil** [singular] the most powerful evil spirit in many religions **2** [C] an evil spirit
PHRASES **poor/lucky devil** *informal* used for saying how you feel about someone, especially someone that you like
talk/speak of the devil *spoken* used when someone that you have just been talking about arrives unexpectedly

devil's advocate noun play/be devil's advocate to pretend to disagree with someone in order to start an argument or discussion

devious /ˈdiːviəs/ adj dishonest and clever =CUNNING

devise /dɪˈvaɪz/ verb [T] ★ to invent a method of doing something

devoid /dɪˈvɔɪd/ adj devoid of sth lacking something, especially a good quality

devolution /ˌdiːvəˈluːʃ(ə)n/ noun [U] the process of taking power from a central authority and giving it to smaller groups or regions

devote /dɪˈvəʊt/
PHRASAL VERBS **deˈvote sth to sth 1** to spend a lot of time or effort doing something =DEDICATE: *He's devoted most of his time to his painting.* **2** to use a particular amount of time, space, or money for dealing with something
deˈvote yourself to sth to spend a lot of your time or effort doing something: *Few people*

are able to devote themselves fully to their career.

devoted /dɪˈvəʊtɪd/ adj **1** loving someone very much: *a devoted family man* **2 devoted to sth** containing or dealing with one particular thing=DEDICATED: *an exhibition devoted to Rembrandt's etchings* **3** very enthusiastic about something

devotion /dɪˈvəʊʃ(ə)n/ noun [U] **1** great love, admiration, or loyalty **2** the process of spending a lot of time or energy on an activity **3** strong religious feeling

devour /dɪˈvaʊə/ verb [T] **1** to eat something very fast because you are hungry **2** to read, watch, or listen to something with a lot of interest **3** if you are devoured by a feeling, you feel it very strongly and cannot get rid of it

devout /dɪˈvaʊt/ adj **1** very religious **2** very enthusiastic about something —**devoutly** adv

dew /djuː/ noun [U] small drops of water that form on the ground at night

dexterity /dekˈsterəti/ noun [U] great skill in using your hands or your mind

dexterous /ˈdekst(ə)rəs/ adj able to use your hands skilfully

diabetes /ˌdaɪəˈbiːtiːz/ noun [U] *medical* a serious medical condition in which your body cannot reduce the amount of sugar in your blood

diabetic /ˌdaɪəˈbetɪk/ noun [C] *medical* someone who has diabetes —**diabetic** adj

diabolical /ˌdaɪəˈbɒlɪk(ə)l/ adj **1** *informal* very bad **2** evil or cruel

diagnose /ˈdaɪəɡnəʊz/ verb [T] to find out what physical or mental problem someone has by examining them: *Eva's been diagnosed with cancer.*

diagnosis /ˌdaɪəɡˈnəʊsɪs/ (plural **diagnoses** /ˌdaɪəɡˈnəʊsiːz/) noun [C/U] a statement about what disease someone has, based on examining them

diagnostic /ˌdaɪəɡˈnɒstɪk/ adj used for making a diagnosis

diagonal /daɪˈæɡən(ə)l/ adj a diagonal line is straight and sloping —*picture* → C8 —**diagonally** adv

diagram /ˈdaɪəɡræm/ noun [C] ★ a drawing that explains something: *a diagram of the manufacturing process*

dial¹ /ˈdaɪəl/ (present participle **dialling**; past tense and past participle **dialled**) verb [I/T] to press the buttons or turn the dial on a telephone in order to call someone

dial² /ˈdaɪəl/ noun [C] **1** the round part of a clock, watch, or machine that has numbers on it **2** a round control on a piece of equipment that you turn to change something

dialect /ˈdaɪəˌlekt/ noun [C/U] a way of speaking a language that is used only in a particular area or by a particular group

dialling code /ˈdaɪəlɪŋ ˌkəʊd/ noun [C] *British* a group of numbers at the beginning of a telephone number that represents a particular town, area, or country

dialling tone /ˈdaɪəlɪŋ ˌtəʊn/ noun [C] *British* the sound that a telephone makes when you pick it up

dialog /ˈdaɪəlɒg/ an American spelling of
dialogue

dialog box noun [C] *computing* a small area
that appears on a computer screen for you
to type messages, instructions, or choices

dialogue /ˈdaɪəlɒg/ noun ★★
1 [C/U] a process in which two people or
groups have discussions in order to solve
problems: *They are trying to start a
dialogue with the opposing party.*
2 [U] all the words that characters speak in
a book, play, or film, or a particular
conversation in a book, play, or film

dial-up adj *computing* a dial-up service or
system is one that connects with your
computer using a telephone line

diameter /daɪˈæmɪtə/ noun [C/U] a straight
line that crosses a circle through the
centre, or the length of this line —*picture*
→ C8

diamond /ˈdaɪəmənd/ noun **1** [C/U] a very hard
clear COLOURLESS stone that is used in
expensive jewellery: *a diamond
ring/necklace/bracelet* **2** [C] a shape with four
straight equal sides that stands on one of
its corners —*picture* → C8 **3** [C] a playing
card with a red diamond shape on it
—*picture* → C16

diaper /ˈdaɪəpə/ noun [C] *American* a baby's
NAPPY

diaphragm /ˈdaɪəfræm/ noun [C] **1** a large
muscle that helps you to breathe **2** a round
rubber object that a woman uses as a
CONTRACEPTIVE (=to avoid having a baby)

diarrhoea /ˌdaɪəˈriːə/ noun [U] *medical* an
illness in which the solid waste from your
body is like liquid

diary /ˈdaɪəri/ noun [C] ★★
1 a book in which you write your
experiences each day=JOURNAL: *She's kept
a diary since she was twelve.*
2 *British* a book that has spaces for each day
of the year, where you can write down
things that you have to do

dice¹ /daɪs/ (plural **dice**) noun [C] a small block
with a number of spots on each side, that
you use for playing games —*picture* → C16

dice² /daɪs/ verb [T] to cut food into small
square pieces —*picture* → C2

dicey /ˈdaɪsi/ adj *informal* involving danger
or risk

dichotomy /daɪˈkɒtəmi/ noun [C] *formal* a
difference between two opposite things or
ideas

dictate /dɪkˈteɪt/ verb **1** [I/T] to say something
that someone else will write down for you
2 [I/T] to tell someone exactly what to do and
how to behave **3** [T] to influence or control
how something is done: *The situation
dictates that we act cautiously.*

dictation /dɪkˈteɪʃ(ə)n/ noun **1** [U] the act of
saying something that someone else then
writes down **2** [C/U] an activity in which a
teacher reads sentences to students that
they write down so that the teacher can see
how well they understand and write a
language

dictator /dɪkˈteɪtə/ noun [C] someone who uses
force to take and keep power in a country
—**dictatorial** /ˌdɪktəˈtɔːriəl/ adj

dictatorship /dɪkˈteɪtəʃɪp/ noun [C/U]

government by someone who takes power
by force and does not allow elections

diction /ˈdɪkʃ(ə)n/ noun [U] the way that you
pronounce words

dictionary /ˈdɪkʃən(ə)ri/ noun [C] a book that
gives an alphabetical list of words with
their meanings or their translations

did the past tense of **do¹**

didn't /ˈdɪd(ə)nt/ short form the usual way of
saying or writing 'did not'. This is not often
used in formal writing: *I didn't hear the
phone ringing.*

die /daɪ/ (past tense and past participle **died**;
present participle **dying**) verb ★★★
1 [I/T] to stop being alive: *My grandfather
died at the age of 86.* ♦ *Several people in the
village have died violent deaths.* ♦ *She is
dying of cancer.* ♦ *Tragically, Keats died
young.*
2 [I] to disappear, or to stop existing: *Our
memory of her will never die.*

> **PHRASES** **be dying for sth/to do sth** *spoken* to
> want something very much, or to want to
> do something very much: *I'm dying for a
> cup of coffee.*
> **I nearly died** or **I could have died** *spoken* used
> for saying that you were very embarrassed
> or shocked by something

> **PHRASAL VERBS** **die down** if something dies
> down, it becomes much less noisy,
> powerful, or active: *I waited for the laughter
> to die down before I spoke.*
> **die off** if a group dies off, the members die
> one by one until none exist
> **die out** to gradually disappear or stop
> existing: *The tribe's traditional way of life
> is dying out.*

> **Words that may cause offence: die**
>
> When someone has died, people usually avoid
> mentioning death directly when they speak to
> the family and friends of the person who has
> died. They often say **pass away** or **pass on**
> instead of **die**, or they use indirect expressions
> such as 'I am sorry for your loss' or 'I was sorry
> to hear about your father/mother'.

diehard /ˈdaɪhɑːd/ noun [C] someone who
refuses to accept change or new ideas
—**diehard** adj

diesel /ˈdiːz(ə)l/ noun [U] heavy oil that is used
as fuel instead of petrol in some engines

diet¹ /ˈdaɪət/ noun ★★
1 [C/U] the food that a person or animal
usually eats: *Try to eat a balanced diet.* ♦
The bird has a diet of nuts and berries.
2 [C] a limited range or amount of food that
someone chooses to eat in order to be
healthy or to become thinner: *I can't fasten
my jeans – I'll have to go on a diet.*

> **Words often used with diet**
>
> *Adjectives often used with diet (noun, sense 1)*
> ■ **balanced, healthy, varied** + DIET: used about
> foods that are healthy

diet² /ˈdaɪət/ verb [I] to control your eating in
order to become thinner —**dieting** noun [U]

diet³ /ˈdaɪət/ adj containing less sugar or fat
than other similar foods: *diet cola*

dietary /ˈdaɪət(ə)ri/ adj relating to the foods
you eat

differ /ˈdɪfə/ verb [I] **1** to be different from something else: *Our approach differs from theirs in several ways.* **2** to disagree with someone about a subject: *Experts differ on the causes of the disease.*

difference /ˈdɪfrəns/ noun ★★★
1 [C/U] something that makes one person or thing not the same as another person or thing ≠ SIMILARITY: *cultural/social/political differences ♦ What's **the difference between** these two computers? ♦ There's **a big difference in** the attitudes of town and country people.*
2 [C] the amount by which one thing is different from another thing: *The same car costs £500 less here which is quite a difference! ♦ Despite this **age difference**, they fell in love.*
3 differences [plural] disagreements about something: *Joe and I have **had our differences**, but we work well together.*
PHRASES **a difference of opinion** a disagreement about something
make a difference to have an important effect on something, especially a good effect: *The extra space **makes a big difference**. ♦ This scheme will certainly **make a difference to** the way I do my job.*
make no/little difference to not be important, or to not have any effect: *Anybody can enjoy yoga, and your age makes absolutely no difference.*
tell the difference to notice what is different between similar people or things: *How do you **tell the difference between** the kittens?*

> **Word family: difference**
>
> *Words in the same family as **difference***
> - **differ** *v*
> - **different** *adj*
> - **differentiate** *v*
> - **indifference** *n*
> - **indifferent** *adj*

different /ˈdɪfrənt/ adj ★★★
1 not the same as another person or thing, or not the same as before ≠ SIMILAR: *Her new glasses make her look **completely different**. ♦ What makes him **different from** the rest of the students? ♦ American English is slightly **different to** British English. ♦ The two cars are **different in** shape.*
2 separate, but of the same type: *Six different boys asked me to dance. ♦ Her money is in different bank accounts.*
3 unusual and not like other things of the same kind: *I wanted something a bit different, so I painted the room green.*
—**differently** adv: *My sister and I look at life very differently. ♦ six differently shaped chairs*

differential /ˌdɪfəˈrenʃ(ə)l/ noun [C] the difference between two amounts, values, or rates

differentiate /ˌdɪfəˈrenʃieɪt/ verb **1** [I/T] to see or show a difference between things = DISTINGUISH: *Neil is colour-blind and cannot differentiate between red and green.* **2** [T] to be the quality or fact that makes one thing different from another: *The ability to speak differentiates humans from other animals.* —**differentiation** /ˌdɪfərenʃiˈeɪʃ(ə)n/ noun [U]

difficult /ˈdɪfɪk(ə)lt/ adj ★★★
1 not easy to do, deal with, or understand

= HARD ≠ EASY: *Choosing the winner was a difficult task. ♦ The exam questions were too difficult. ♦ Talking to teenagers can be **difficult for** parents. ♦ **it is difficult to do sth** It's difficult to say what time I will get home.*
2 causing a lot of problems and making it hard for you to succeed: *She had a difficult childhood.*
3 never seeming happy or satisfied: *Martin was a difficult baby.*

difficulty /ˈdɪfɪk(ə)lti/ noun ★★★
1 [C] a problem: *Many students have serious financial difficulties.*
2 [U] the state of not being able to do something easily ≠ EASE: *Seb was speaking **with difficulty**. ♦ **have difficulty with sth** She's having difficulty with her schoolwork this year. ♦ **have difficulty (in) doing sth** She still has difficulty walking.*
3 [U] the degree to which something is difficult: *The courses vary in content and difficulty.*

diffident /ˈdɪfɪdənt/ adj not confident —**diffidence** noun [U]

diffuse¹ /dɪˈfjuːz/ verb **1** [T] *formal* to spread something such as information, ideas, or power among a large group of people **2** [I/T] if light diffuses, or if something diffuses it, it shines over a large area but not very brightly —**diffusion** /dɪˈfjuːʒ(ə)n/ noun [U]

diffuse² /dɪˈfjuːs/ adj *formal* existing over a large area or in many areas

dig¹ /dɪg/ (past tense and past participle **dug** /dʌg/; present participle **digging**) verb [I/T] ★★
to make a hole in earth using your hands, a machine, or a tool: *The children like to dig in the sand. ♦ We dug a hole and planted the tree. ♦ The boys were **digging for** worms.*
PHRASE **dig your heels in** to refuse to do something even though other people are trying to persuade you
PHRASAL VERBS **ˈdig into sth** to press hard into something: *The seat belt was digging into my shoulder.*
ˌdig sth ˈout to find something that you have not used or seen for a long time: *I'll dig out my old college notes later.*
ˌdig sth ˈup 1 to remove something from under the ground by digging: *They dug up a body in his garden.* **2** to find information by searching carefully: *When we investigated, we dug up some interesting facts.*

dig² /dɪg/ noun [C] **1** an attempt to find ancient objects by digging in the ground **2** *informal* a remark that criticizes someone or makes a joke about them → DIGS

digest /daɪˈdʒest/ verb [T] **1** to change food in your stomach into the substances that your body needs **2** to try to understand information when it is difficult or unexpected = ABSORB, TAKE STH IN —**digestible** adj

digestion /daɪˈdʒestʃ(ə)n/ noun [U] the process of digesting food

digestive /daɪˈdʒestɪv/ adj relating to digestion: *the digestive process*

digit /ˈdɪdʒɪt/ noun [C] **1** *formal* one of the written numbers from 0 to 9 **2** *technical* one of your fingers or toes

digital /ˈdɪdʒɪt(ə)l/ adj ★
  1 storing information such as sound or pictures as numbers or electronic signals: *a digital recording*
  2 a digital clock or instrument shows information as a row of numbers

digital ˈcamera noun [C] a camera that takes and stores pictures in the form of electronic signals

dignified /ˈdɪɡnɪfaɪd/ adj behaving in a calm way that people respect ≠ UNDIGNIFIED: *a dignified manner*

dignitary /ˈdɪɡnɪt(ə)ri/ noun [C] someone who has an important official position

dignity /ˈdɪɡnəti/ noun [U] calm behaviour that makes people respect you: *She faced her death with dignity.*

digress /daɪˈɡres/ verb [I] to start to talk or write about something different from the subject that you were discussing —**digression** /daɪˈɡreʃ(ə)n/ noun [C/U]

digs /dɪɡz/ noun [plural] *informal old-fashioned* a room or flat that you rent and live in

dike /daɪk/ another spelling of **dyke**

dilapidated /dɪˈlæpɪdeɪtɪd/ adj old and in bad condition: *a dilapidated farm* —**dilapidation** /dɪˌlæpɪˈdeɪʃ(ə)n/ noun [U]

dilate /daɪˈleɪt/ verb [I] if part of your body dilates, it becomes bigger and wider —**dilation** /daɪˈleɪʃ(ə)n/ noun [U]

dilemma /dɪˈlemə/ noun [C] a situation in which you have to make a difficult decision =PREDICAMENT, QUANDARY

diligent /ˈdɪlɪdʒ(ə)nt/ adj *formal* working very hard and very carefully =HARD-WORKING —**diligence** noun [U], **diligently** adv

dilute¹ /daɪˈluːt/ verb [T] to make a liquid less strong by adding water or another liquid

dilute² /ˈdaɪluːt/ adj a dilute liquid has been mixed with another liquid to make it less strong

dim¹ /dɪm/ adj **1** not bright or clear: *a dim light/room* **2** a dim memory is something from long ago that you cannot remember very well ≠ CLEAR **3** *British informal* not clever ≠ BRAINY —**dimly** adv

dim² /dɪm/ verb [I/T] if a light dims, or if you dim it, it becomes less bright

dime /daɪm/ noun [C] a coin worth ten CENTS in the US and Canada

dimension /daɪˈmenʃ(ə)n/ noun **1** [C] an aspect of a situation that influences the way that you think about the situation: *Doing voluntary work has added a whole new dimension to my life.* **2** [C] length, height, or width **3 dimensions** [plural] the size of something: *Can you mark the dimensions of the room on the diagram?*

diminish /dɪˈmɪnɪʃ/ verb [I/T] to become less, or to make something become less: *The intensity of the sound diminished gradually.*

diminutive /dɪˈmɪnjʊtɪv/ adj *formal* very small =TINY

dimple /ˈdɪmp(ə)l/ noun [C] a small area on your cheek, chin etc that goes inwards

din /dɪn/ noun [singular] a very loud unpleasant noise that lasts for a long time

dine /daɪn/ verb [I] *formal* to eat DINNER (=your evening meal)
  PHRASAL VERB **ˌdine ˈout** *formal* to eat DINNER

(=an evening meal) in a restaurant =EAT OUT

diner /ˈdaɪnə/ noun [C] someone who is eating a meal at a restaurant

ding-dong /ˈdɪŋ ˌdɒŋ/ noun [U] the sound that a bell makes

dinghy /ˈdɪŋi, ˈdɪŋɡi/ noun [C] a small boat

dingy /ˈdɪndʒi/ adj dirty and dark: *a dingy room*

dining room /ˈdaɪnɪŋ ˌruːm/ noun [C] the room in a house or hotel where you eat meals

dinner /ˈdɪnə/ noun [C/U] ★★★ the main meal of the day, usually eaten in the evening: *I haven't had dinner yet.* ♦ *We had chicken again for dinner.*

ˈdinner ˌjacket noun [C] a man's black or white jacket that he wears on formal occasions

dinosaur /ˈdaɪnəsɔː/ noun [C] a large animal that lived a very long time ago but is now EXTINCT (=all of them have died)

diocese /ˈdaɪəsɪs/ noun [C] an area that a BISHOP (=a senior Christian priest) is in charge of

dip¹ /dɪp/ verb **1** [T] to lower something into a liquid for a moment and then take it out again **2** [I] to become less: *Our profits dipped 30%.*
  PHRASAL VERB **ˌdip ˈinto sth 1** to take some money from an amount that you have saved **2** to read different parts of a book, but not the whole book

dip² /dɪp/ noun **1** [C/U] a thick cold sauce for dipping pieces of food into before eating them **2** [C] a reduction in the amount or level of something: *a dip in the price of new homes* **3** [C] a place in a surface that is lower than the surrounding area: *a dip in the road* **4** [C] *informal* a quick swim: *Let's take a dip in the pool.*

diphtheria /dɪfˈθɪəriə, dɪpˈθɪəriə/ noun [U] a serious disease affecting your throat that makes it difficult for you to breathe

diploma /dɪˈpləʊmə/ noun [C] **1** *British* a course of study at a college or university in a subject that prepares you for a particular job **2** the qualification that you get when you have completed a diploma course → CERTIFICATE, DEGREE

diplomacy /dɪˈpləʊməsi/ noun [U] **1** the profession or skill of creating friendly relationships between countries **2** the ability to deal with people well, so that they are not upset or offended

diplomat /ˈdɪpləmæt/ noun [C] an official whose job is to represent their government in a foreign country

diplomatic /ˌdɪpləˈmætɪk/ adj **1** relating to the profession or skill of DIPLOMACY: *a diplomatic mission* **2** able to deal with people well, so that they are not upset or offended ≠ UNDIPLOMATIC: *a diplomatic answer* —**diplomatically** /ˌdɪpləˈmætɪkli/ adv

dire /ˈdaɪə/ adj very severe, serious, or bad: *dire warnings*

direct¹ /dɪˈrekt, daɪˈrekt/ adj ★★★
  1 going straight to a place without stopping or changing direction: *direct flights from Scotland to North America*
  2 involving only the two people or things that are mentioned and with no one or nothing else between ≠ INDIRECT: *Employees*

D

have little direct contact with management.
♦ *Their study found a direct link between poverty and crime.*
3 exact: *That's a direct quote from the man himself.*
4 saying what you really think in a very clear honest way: *I love New Yorkers – they're so funny and direct.*

direct² /dɪˈrekt, daɪˈrekt/ verb [T] ★★

1 aim sth	4 tell/show way
2 tell actors what to do	5 order sb to do sth
3 control/organize sth	

1 to aim something at a particular person or thing: **direct sth to/at etc sb/sth** *The incident directed public attention to pollution in the North Sea.* ♦ *At the time, all the criticism was directed at her rather than me.*
2 to be in charge of telling all the actors and technical staff who are involved in a film, play or programme what to do → PRODUCE
3 to control or organize how a person or group of people does something: *The manager's job is mainly to direct the activities of others.*
4 to tell or show someone the way to go: **direct sb to sth** *Could you direct me to the bus station?*
5 *formal* to order someone to do something: *The jury was directed to disregard everything Robinson had said.*

direct³ /dɪˈrekt, daɪˈrekt/ adv **1** going straight to a place and not stopping or changing direction: *All the major airlines fly direct to Los Angeles.* **2** in a way that involves only the two people or things that are mentioned, with no one or nothing else between: *You can buy direct from the manufacturer.*

direct ˈdebit noun [C/U] an order to a bank to regularly pay money from your account to a person or organization → STANDING ORDER

direction /dɪˈrekʃ(ə)n, daɪˈrekʃ(ə)n/ noun ★★★

1 of movement/look	4 purpose
2 instructions	5 control/management
3 way sb/sth changes	6 of film/play

1 [C] the place that someone or something moves, faces, or points towards: *Are you sure we're going in the right direction?* ♦ *The wind has changed direction.* ♦ *We drove off in the direction of the mountains.* ♦ *I'd give you a lift, but I'm going in the opposite direction.* ♦ *Michelle's always getting lost because of her terrible sense of direction.*
2 **directions** [plural] instructions for doing something or for getting to a place: *Follow the directions on the label.* ♦ *She gave the driver directions to her house.*
3 [C/U] the general development or progress of someone or something: *He was determined to change the direction of the business.*
4 [U] the feeling of having a definite purpose: *Your life seems to lack direction.*
5 [U] LEADERSHIP or management: *The project was under the direction of Henry Richardson.*
6 [U] the work of directing a film, programme, or play

directive /dɪˈrektɪv, daɪˈrektɪv/ noun [C] an official order

directly /dɪˈrek(t)li, daɪˈrek(t)li/ adv ★★★
1 in a way that involves only the two people or things that are mentioned, with no one or nothing else between ≠ INDIRECTLY: *I prefer to deal directly with the manager.* ♦ *You are directly responsible for this.* ♦ *Price is directly related to size.*
2 going straight to a place without stopping or changing direction: *We landed at the airport and went directly to the hotel.*
3 exactly: *The post office is directly opposite the town hall.* ♦ *There was no light on in the room directly above.*
4 in a very clear and honest way ≠ INDIRECTLY: *Jackson avoided saying directly that he disapproved.*

direct ˈobject noun [C] *linguistics* the noun or pronoun in a sentence that is affected by the action of a TRANSITIVE verb. In the sentence 'Harry was reading a book', 'a book' is the direct object of the verb 'was reading'.

director /dəˈrektə, daɪˈrektə/ noun [C] ★★★
1 someone whose job is to tell the actors and technical staff who are involved in a film, play, or programme what to do
2 someone whose job is to manage all or part of a company, organization, or institution: *the finance/marketing/ personnel director*

directory /dəˈrekt(ə)ri, daɪˈrekt(ə)ri/ noun [C] ★
1 a book or list of people's names, addresses, telephone numbers, or other information
2 a computer file that contains other files, documents, or programs

direct ˈtax noun [C/U] *technical* a tax that is collected directly from a person or organization rather than as part of the price of a product or service —**direct taxˈation** noun [U]

dirt /dɜːt/ noun [U] **1** a substance that makes something dirty: *Angelo brushed the dirt off his coat.* **2** soil or MUD: *children playing in the dirt* ♦ *a dirt road/track* **3** *informal* information about someone that could damage their reputation if people knew about it

dirt ˈcheap adj, adv *informal* very cheap

dirty¹ /ˈdɜːti/ adj ★★★
1 not clean: *piles of dirty washing* ♦ *dirty fingernails*
2 dealing with sex in a way that offends some people: *dirty jokes/films*
3 dishonest or unfair: *dirty tricks*
PHRASES **do sb's dirty work** to do an unpleasant job for someone so that they do not have to do it themselves
give sb a dirty look *informal* to look at someone in a way that shows that you are angry with them or do not like them

dirty² /ˈdɜːti/ verb [T] to make something dirty

disability /ˌdɪsəˈbɪləti/ noun [C/U] a condition in which someone is not able to use a part of their body or brain normally: *children with learning disabilities*

disabled /dɪsˈeɪb(ə)ld/ adj ★
1 unable to use part of your body or brain normally
2 **the disabled** people who are disabled. Many people think this word is offensive and prefer to use the expression **people with disabilities**.

Words that avoid giving offence: disabled

You can use the adjective **disabled** to describe people who have a permanent physical condition that makes them unable to do something, but you should avoid referring to these people as **the disabled**. Similarly, you can use **blind** to refer to someone who cannot see, and **deaf** to refer to someone who cannot hear, but you should avoid referring to these people as **the blind** and **the deaf**. Many people now prefer the expressions **the visually impaired** and **the hearing impaired**.

disadvantage /ˌdɪsədˈvɑːntɪdʒ/ noun [C] ★ something that makes someone or something less effective, successful, or attractive: *One of the disadvantages of the job is the long hours I work.* ♦ *Anyone not familiar with the Internet is at a serious disadvantage.* —**disadvantageous** /ˌdɪsædvənˈteɪdʒəs/ adj

disadvantaged /ˌdɪsədˈvɑːntɪdʒd/ adj not having the same advantages of money or education as other people

disaffected /ˌdɪsəˈfektɪd/ adj no longer feeling any loyalty towards a group or leader

disagree /ˌdɪsəˈɡriː/ verb [I] ★
1 to have a different opinion from someone else: *Teenagers and their parents often disagree.* ♦ *I disagree with you – I think she's done a very good job.* ♦ *Dole and Evans disagree about many aspects of the new policy.*
2 to contain different information, or to produce different results: *Two pathologists examined the body, but their findings disagreed.*
PHRASAL VERB disa**'**gree with sb if something that you eat or drink disagrees with you, it makes you feel ill

disagreeable /ˌdɪsəˈɡriːəb(ə)l/ adj formal **1** not nice or enjoyable **2** not friendly or polite —**disagreeably** adv

disagreement /ˌdɪsəˈɡriːmənt/ noun ★
1 [C/U] a situation in which people do not agree: *Bowen resigned from the club following a disagreement with the head coach.* ♦ *There has been considerable disagreement about how best to deal with the crisis.*
2 [U] a difference between things that should be the same: *There was some disagreement between the two statements he had given.*

disallow /ˌdɪsəˈlaʊ/ verb [T] to say officially that something cannot be accepted or allowed: *The referee disallowed the goal.*

disappear /ˌdɪsəˈpɪə/ verb [I] ★★★
1 to no longer happen or exist: *The symptoms should disappear within a few days.*
2 to become impossible to see or find: *The letter I had left on my desk had disappeared.* ♦ *The train disappeared from view.* ♦ *The couple disappeared without trace while on holiday in France.*
—**disappearance** noun [C/U]

disappoint /ˌdɪsəˈpɔɪnt/ verb [I/T] to make someone feel unhappy or not satisfied: *I hate to disappoint you, but the cake's all gone.*

disappointed /ˌdɪsəˈpɔɪntɪd/ adj ★ unhappy because something did not happen or because someone or something was not as good as you expected: **+(that)** *She was disappointed that he never replied to her letter.* ♦ *I am very disappointed at not getting the job.* ♦ *I'm really disappointed in you, Ruth.*

disappointing /ˌdɪsəˈpɔɪntɪŋ/ adj not as good as you had hoped or expected: *This year's sales figures were very disappointing.*

disappointment /ˌdɪsəˈpɔɪntmənt/ noun ★
1 [U] the feeling of being unhappy because something did not happen or because someone or something was not as good as you expected: *Diplomats expressed disappointment at the lack of progress.* ♦ *Jackson cancelled the concert, to the disappointment of his fans.*
2 [C] someone or something that is not as good as you thought they would be: *Newcombe has described the defeat as the biggest disappointment of his career.* ♦ *I'm such a disappointment to her.*

disapproval /ˌdɪsəˈpruːv(ə)l/ noun [U] a feeling of not approving of someone or something: *He made no secret of his disapproval of the way the affair was handled.*

disapprove /ˌdɪsəˈpruːv/ verb [I] ★ to not approve of someone or something: *Why do you always have to disapprove of everything I do?*

disapproving /ˌdɪsəˈpruːvɪŋ/ adj a disapproving expression or reaction shows that someone does not approve of something —**disapprovingly** adv

disarm /dɪsˈɑːm/ verb **1** [I] if a country or organization disarms, it reduces or gets rid of its weapons or armed forces **2** [T] to take someone's weapons so that they can no longer use them **3** [T] to make someone feel less angry or unfriendly: *Interviewers are disarmed by her straightforward approach.*

disarmament /dɪsˈɑːməmənt/ noun [U] the process by which a country reduces or gets rid of its weapons or armed forces

disarming /dɪsˈɑːmɪŋ/ adj making someone feel less angry or unfriendly: *her disarming honesty*

disarray /ˌdɪsəˈreɪ/ noun [U] a situation in which people are very confused or things are not organized: *The committee was in complete disarray.*

disaster /dɪˈzɑːstə/ noun ★
1 [C/U] something very bad that happens and causes a lot of damage or kills a lot of people: *A series of disasters forced the company to close down.* ♦ *natural disasters* (=floods, earthquakes etc)
2 [C] a very bad or annoying situation, or a complete failure: *Our party was a complete disaster.*

di'saster ˌarea noun **1** [C] a place or region that has been badly affected by a disaster **2** [singular] humorous a person, place, or system that is very untidy

disastrous /dɪˈzɑːstrəs/ adj very bad, harmful, or unsuccessful: *The spending cuts would be disastrous for schools.* ♦ *a disastrous start to the meeting*

D

disband /dɪsˈbænd/ verb [I/T] if a group of people disbands, or if it is disbanded, its members stop working together

disbelief /ˌdɪsbɪˈliːf/ noun [U] the feeling of not believing someone or something: *Liz stared at us in disbelief as we told her what had happened.*

disbelieve /ˌdɪsbɪˈliːv/ verb [T] to not believe someone or something

disc /dɪsk/ noun [C] **1** a flat circular object or shape **2** a computer DISK **3** a round flat piece of CARTILAGE between the bones in your back **4** a CD

discard /dɪsˈkɑːd/ verb [T] to get rid of something that you no longer want or need

discern /dɪˈsɜːn/ verb [T] *formal* to notice, see, or understand something: *It's hard to discern exactly what his motives are.* —**discernible** adj

discerning /dɪˈsɜːnɪŋ/ adj showing good judgment about things such as art, music, or fashion —**discernment** noun [U]

discharge¹ /dɪsˈtʃɑːdʒ/ verb **1** [T] to allow or force someone to leave a hospital, a prison, or the army **2** [T] *formal* to perform a duty or responsibility **3** [I/T] to allow liquid or gas to leave a place

discharge² /ˈdɪstʃɑːdʒ/ noun [C/U] **1** official permission to leave a hospital, a prison, or the army **2** a liquid, gas, or other substance that comes out of something else

disciple /dɪˈsaɪp(ə)l/ noun [C] someone who admires and is influenced by a political or religious leader

disciplinarian /ˌdɪsəplɪˈneəriən/ noun [C] someone who forces people to obey rules

disciplinary /ˈdɪsəplɪnəri/ adj connected with the punishment of people who do not obey rules

discipline¹ /ˈdɪsəplɪn/ noun ★★
1 [U] the practice of making people obey rules and punishing them if they do not: *He believes in strict discipline.*
2 [C] a subject that people study, especially at a university: *academic disciplines*
3 [U] the ability to control your own behaviour: *Many of the students lacked the discipline to learn.*

discipline² /ˈdɪsəplɪn/ verb [T] to punish someone for something wrong that they have done

disciplined /ˈdɪsəplɪnd/ adj well organized and following rules or standards
≠ UNDISCIPLINED: *the team's disciplined approach*

disc jockey noun [C] a DJ

disclaimer /dɪsˈkleɪmə/ noun [C] a statement in which someone says that they do not take responsibility for something

disclose /dɪsˈkləʊz/ verb [T] to give people information that was secret: *They failed to disclose that profits had fallen.*

disclosure /dɪsˈkləʊʒə/ noun [C/U] the act of telling people information that was secret, or the information that is told: *a series of disclosures that almost wrecked his career*

disco /ˈdɪskəʊ/ noun **1** [C] *British* a place where people dance to popular music **2** [U] a type of popular dance music from the 1970s

discolored /dɪsˈkʌləd/ the American spelling of **discoloured**

discoloured /dɪsˈkʌləd/ adj changed in colour and no longer looking new, clean, or healthy: *discoloured wallpaper* —**discolour** verb [T], **discoloration** /dɪsˌkʌləˈreɪʃ(ə)n/ noun [C/U]

discomfort /dɪsˈkʌmfət/ noun **1** [U] a feeling of slight pain: *discomfort in my lower back* **2** [C] something that makes you feel slightly ill or uncomfortable: *the discomforts of life in the desert*

disconcerted /ˌdɪskənˈsɜːtɪd/ adj feeling worried, confused, or surprised

disconcerting /ˌdɪskənˈsɜːtɪŋ/ adj making you feel worried, confused, or surprised: *a disconcerting habit/tendency* —**disconcert** verb [T]

disconnect /ˌdɪskəˈnekt/ verb [T] **1** to separate two things that were connected to each other: *A bomb disposal expert was called in to disconnect the timer.* **2** to stop someone's telephone service or supply of gas, water, or electricity: *His telephone has been disconnected.*

discontent /ˌdɪskənˈtent/ noun [U] the unhappy feeling that you have when you are not satisfied with something: *Public discontent with the government is growing.* —**discontented** adj

discontinue /ˌdɪskənˈtɪnjuː/ verb [T] **1** to stop doing something that you were doing regularly **2** to stop providing a product or service

discord /ˈdɪskɔːd/ noun [U] *formal* disagreement between people —**discordant** adj

discount¹ /ˈdɪskaʊnt/ noun [C] a reduction in the price of something: *Air Canada is currently offering a 10% discount on selected airfares.*

discount² /dɪsˈkaʊnt/ verb [T] **1** to reduce the price of something **2** to decide that something is not important, possible, or likely: *Police have discounted the possibility that this was a terrorist attack.*

discourage /dɪsˈkʌrɪdʒ/ verb [T] **1** to try to prevent something from happening
≠ ENCOURAGE: *We hope the bad weather won't discourage people from coming along.* **2** to make someone feel less confident or hopeful: *What she said didn't discourage me.* —**discouragement** noun [C/U]

discouraged /dɪsˈkʌrɪdʒd/ adj feeling less confident or hopeful: *Don't get discouraged – just keep trying.*

discouraging /dɪsˈkʌrɪdʒɪŋ/ adj making you feel less confident or hopeful
≠ ENCOURAGING

discourse /ˈdɪskɔːs/ noun [C] *formal* a long serious speech or piece of writing on a particular subject

discourteous /dɪsˈkɜːtiəs/ adj *formal* rude and lacking respect

discover /dɪsˈkʌvə/ verb [T] ★★★
1 to find something that was hidden or that no one knew about before: *William Herschel discovered Uranus in 1781.* ♦ *New antimalarial drugs have been discovered.*
2 to find out something that you did not know before: **+(that)** *He became very friendly when he discovered that she was my sister.*

3 to recognize the ability of someone and help to make them famous

discovery /dɪsˈkʌv(ə)ri/ noun ★★
1 [C/U] the act of finding or learning about someone or something that was hidden or not known: *Police announced the discovery of the body late last night.* ♦ *We made some interesting discoveries about our new neighbours.* ♦ **+that** *Mr Andrews told of his family's joy following the discovery that his son was alive.*
2 [C] something that is found, or something new that is learned: *This is one of the most important archaeological discoveries of the century.*

discredit /dɪsˈkredɪt/ verb [T] to make people stop believing or respecting someone or something: *She claims there was a conspiracy to discredit her.* —**discredit** noun [U]

discreet /dɪsˈkriːt/ adj careful not to say anything that is secret or that could upset someone ≠ INDISCREET —**discreetly** adv

discrepancy /dɪsˈkrepənsi/ noun [C/U] a difference between things that should be the same: *a discrepancy between estimated and actual spending*

discretion /dɪsˈkreʃ(ə)n/ noun [U] **1** the right or ability to make a judgment or decision: *The funds may be spent at the manager's discretion* (=according to decisions made by the manager). **2** careful and sensitive behaviour that does not upset or offend people ≠ INDISCRETION

discretionary /dɪsˈkreʃ(ə)n(ə)ri/ adj based on someone's judgment of a particular situation rather than on a set of rules: *a discretionary payment/budget*

discriminate /dɪsˈkrɪmɪneɪt/ verb **1** [I] to treat someone unfairly because of their religion, race, or other personal features: *laws that discriminate against women* **2** [I/T] to recognize the difference between things

discriminating /dɪsˈkrɪmɪˌneɪtɪŋ/ adj able to judge whether or not something is good or suitable ≠ UNDISCRIMINATING

discrimination /dɪsˌkrɪmɪˈneɪʃ(ə)n/ noun [U] ★
1 unfair treatment of someone because of their religion, race, or other personal features: *sex/racial/age discrimination* ♦ *discrimination against women*
2 the ability to judge whether something is good or suitable

discriminatory /dɪsˈkrɪmɪnət(ə)ri/ adj formal treating a particular group of people unfairly because of their religion, race, or other personal features: *discriminatory policies/practices*

discus, the /ˈdɪskəs/ noun [singular] a sports event in which a heavy circular flat object is thrown

discuss /dɪsˈkʌs/ verb [T] ★★★
1 to talk about something with someone: *We're meeting to discuss the matter next week.* ♦ **discuss sth with sb** *You should discuss this problem with your doctor.*
2 to write or talk about a subject in detail: *The causes of stress have already been discussed in Chapter 3.*

discussion /dɪsˈkʌʃ(ə)n/ noun [C/U] ★★★ a conversation about something important:

We need to have a discussion about your school work. ♦ *an interesting discussion on Internet censorship* ♦ *Discussions with management have broken down.* ♦ *Proposals for changing the system are under discussion* (=being discussed).

disdain /dɪsˈdeɪn/ noun [U] the feeling that someone or something is not important and does not deserve any respect —**disdainful** adj

disease /dɪˈziːz/ noun [C/U] ★★★ an illness that affects people, animals, or plants: *liver/heart/lung disease* ♦ *Studies have revealed that vegetarians suffer less from heart disease.* ♦ *Smoking can cause fatal diseases.* —**diseased** /dɪˈziːzd/ adj

disembark /ˌdɪsɪmˈbɑːk/ verb [I] formal to get off a ship or plane

disembodied /ˌdɪsɪmˈbɒdid/ adj a disembodied voice comes from someone who you cannot see

disenchanted /ˌdɪsɪnˈtʃɑːntɪd/ adj disappointed and no longer enthusiastic about someone or something —**disenchantment** noun [U]

disengage /ˌdɪsɪnˈgeɪdʒ/ verb [T] if you disengage part of a machine, it is no longer connected to the main part of the machine

disentangle /ˌdɪsɪnˈtæŋg(ə)l/ verb [T] to separate something from the thing that is holding it or that is twisted around it
PHRASE **disentangle yourself (from)** to get yourself out of a situation that you no longer want to be involved in

disfigure /dɪsˈfɪgə/ verb [T] to spoil the appearance of someone or something

disgrace¹ /dɪsˈgreɪs/ noun **1** [U] the loss of other people's respect because of something bad that you have done **2** [singular] someone or something that makes you angry because they are very bad: *The way he treats his dogs is a disgrace.*

disgrace² /dɪsˈgreɪs/ verb [T] formal to harm the reputation of a person or group by doing something bad or immoral

disgraceful /dɪsˈgreɪsf(ə)l/ adj extremely bad or shocking —**disgracefully** adv

disgruntled /dɪsˈgrʌnt(ə)ld/ adj disappointed and annoyed

disguise¹ /dɪsˈgaɪz/ verb [T] **1** to hide something such as your feelings or intentions: *He didn't try to disguise his bitterness.* **2** to change the way that someone looks so that other people will not recognize them **3** to make something look, sound, or seem like something else

disguise² /dɪsˈgaɪz/ noun [C/U] something that you wear in order to change the way that you look so that other people will not recognize you: *He often went out in disguise to avoid being recognized.*

disgust¹ /dɪsˈgʌst/ noun [U] **1** a very strong feeling of not liking something **2** the feeling that you are going to be physically ill when you see, smell, or taste something very unpleasant **3** a strong feeling of anger about something bad or immoral

disgust² /dɪsˈgʌst/ verb [T] **1** to be so bad or immoral that you feel angry and upset: *You attitude disgusts me.* **2** to make you feel physically ill

disgusted /dɪsˈgʌstɪd/ adj **1** feeling very angry

and upset about something that you do not approve of: *I was disgusted by the way he treated those women.* **2** feeling physically ill because something is extremely unpleasant to see, smell, or taste

disgusting /dɪsˈɡʌstɪŋ/ adj **1** extremely unpleasant=REVOLTING **2** very bad or shocking —**disgustingly** adv

D

dish¹ /dɪʃ/ noun ★★
1 [C] a container similar to a plate or bowl that is used for serving or cooking food: *Place the fruit in a large shallow dish.*
2 [C] food that has been prepared and cooked in a particular way: *Do you have any vegetarian dishes?*
3 dishes [plural] the plates, pans etc that have to be washed after a meal: *Who's going to do the dishes?*
4 [C] a round piece of equipment that sends or receives radio or television messages: *a satellite dish*

dish² /dɪʃ/
PHRASAL VERBS ˌdish sth ˈout *informal* to give things to a number of people
ˌdish (sth) ˈup to put food into on plates so that people can eat it

disheartened /dɪsˈhɑːt(ə)nd/ adj no longer confident or enthusiastic about something

disheartening /dɪsˈhɑːt(ə)nɪŋ/ adj making you less confident or enthusiastic

dishevelled /dɪˈʃevld/ adj with hair and clothes that do not look tidy

dishonest /dɪsˈɒnɪst/ adj willing to do things that are not honest ≠ HONEST —**dishonestly** adv

dishonesty /dɪsˈɒnəsti/ noun [U] behaviour that is not honest

dishwasher /ˈdɪʃˌwɒʃə/ noun [C] a machine that washes dishes —*picture* → C2

disillusion /ˌdɪsɪˈluːʒ(ə)n/ verb [T] to make someone disappointed by showing them that something is not as good as they thought it was —**disillusionment** noun [U]

disillusioned /ˌdɪsɪˈluːʒ(ə)nd/ adj disappointed because you realize that something is not as good as you thought it was

disinfect /ˌdɪsɪnˈfekt/ verb [T] to clean something by putting a substance on it that kills bacteria

disinfectant /ˌdɪsɪnˈfektənt/ noun [C/U] a chemical substance that kills bacteria. It is used for cleaning things.

disintegrate /dɪsˈɪntɪɡreɪt/ verb [I] **1** to be completely destroyed by breaking into lots of very small pieces **2** to become less effective and stop working —**disintegration** /dɪsˌɪntɪˈɡreɪʃ(ə)n/ noun [U]

disinterested /dɪsˈɪntrəstɪd/ adj not involved in something and therefore able to judge it fairly → UNINTERESTED

disjointed /dɪsˈdʒɔɪntɪd/ adj consisting of different parts that are not clearly connected: *a strange disjointed dream*

disk /dɪsk/ noun [C] **1** a small flat circular object that is used for storing information from a computer **2** an American spelling of **disc**

ˈdisk ˌdrive noun [C] the part of a computer that reads information from a disk or records information onto a disk

diskette /dɪˈsket/ noun [C] a FLOPPY DISK for storing computer information

dislike¹ /dɪsˈlaɪk/ verb [T] ★ to not like someone or something ≠ LIKE: *She knew Philip disliked her.* ♦ **dislike doing sth** *Cats dislike getting their fur wet.*

Other ways of saying dislike

- **not like** to have negative feelings about someone or something
- **not be crazy about/not be keen on** (*informal*) used for saying that you do not like something, in situations where you do not want to sound rude
- **hate** to dislike someone or something very much
- **can't stand/can't bear** to dislike someone or something so strongly that it makes you feel angry or upset
- **detest/loathe** used for emphasizing that you strongly dislike someone or something

dislike² /dɪsˈlaɪk/ noun **1** [singular/U] a feeling of not liking someone or something: *her dislike of small children* **2** [C] something that you do not like: *We were asked to list our likes and dislikes.*

dislocate /ˈdɪsləkeɪt/ verb [T] to do something that forces a bone out of its normal position —**dislocation** /ˌdɪsləˈkeɪʃ(ə)n/ noun [C/U]

dislodge /dɪsˈlɒdʒ/ verb [T] to force something out of a position where it is fixed

disloyal /dɪsˈlɔɪəl/ adj not loyal to someone who you have a close relationship with or to an organization that you belong to ≠ LOYAL —**disloyalty** noun [U]

dismal /ˈdɪzm(ə)l/ adj **1** making you feel unhappy and without hope or enthusiasm: *dismal living conditions* **2** very bad —**dismally** adv

dismantle /dɪsˈmænt(ə)l/ verb [T] **1** to separate the parts of something so that they no longer form a single unit **2** to end a political or economic system, or to get rid of an institution

dismay /dɪsˈmeɪ/ noun [U] the feeling of being very worried, disappointed, or sad about something that is surprising or shocking —**dismayed** /dɪsˈmeɪd/ adj

dismember /dɪsˈmembə/ verb [T] to cut someone's body into pieces

dismiss /dɪsˈmɪs/ verb [T] ★★
1 to refuse to accept that something could be true or important: *The minister dismissed the allegations.* ♦ **dismiss sth as sth** *Their evidence was dismissed as completely worthless.*
2 to force someone to leave their job=FIRE, SACK: *Edwards claimed that he had been unfairly dismissed.* ♦ **dismiss sb from sth** *Jackson was dismissed from her post.*
3 to give someone permission to leave a place: *The class is dismissed.*
4 to officially decide that a court case should not continue

dismissal /dɪsˈmɪs(ə)l/ noun **1** [C/U] an act of making someone leave their job: *The investigation led to five dismissals.* **2** [U] a refusal to accept that something could be true or important: *the committee's dismissal of their complaints* **3** [C/U] a decision to allow someone to leave a place **4** [C/U] a decision that a court case should not continue

dismissive /dɪsˈmɪsɪv/ adj showing that you do not think that something is worth paying attention to —**dismissively** adv

dismount /dɪsˈmaʊnt/ verb [I] formal to get off a horse or bicycle

disobedience /ˌdɪsəˈbiːdiəns/ noun [U] behaviour in which you refuse to obey orders or rules ≠ OBEDIENCE

disobedient /ˌdɪsəˈbiːdiənt/ adj refusing to do what someone in authority has told you to do or to obey orders or rules ≠ OBEDIENT

disobey /ˌdɪsəˈbeɪ/ verb [I/T] to deliberately not pay attention to a rule or an order from someone in authority = DEFY ≠ OBEY

disorder /dɪsˈɔːdə/ noun **1** [C/U] medical an illness, or a medical condition **2** [U] a situation in which people behave in a noisy or violent way **3** [U] a situation in which things are not tidy

disordered /dɪsˈɔːdəd/ adj not tidy, or not well organized

disorderly /dɪsˈɔːdəli/ adj **1** behaving in a noisy or violent way **2** not tidy

disorganized /dɪsˈɔːɡənaɪzd/ adj **1** not arranged according to a clear plan or system **2** not good at dealing with things in a clear or sensible way

disorientate /dɪsˈɔːriənteɪt/ or **disorient** /dɪsˈɔːriənt/ verb [T] to make someone confused about where they are or what direction they are moving in —**disorientation** /dɪsˌɔːriənˈteɪʃ(ə)n/ noun [U]

disown /dɪsˈəʊn/ verb [T] to say that you no longer want to be connected with someone or something: *I think my parents would disown me if I ever got a tattoo.*

disparaging /dɪˈspærɪdʒɪŋ/ adj showing that you have no respect for someone or something: *disparaging comments*

disparate /ˈdɪsp(ə)rət/ adj formal belonging to very different groups or classes

disparity /dɪˈspærəti/ noun [singular/U] formal a difference between things

dispatch¹ /dɪˈspætʃ/ verb [T] formal to send someone or something somewhere

dispatch² /dɪˈspætʃ/ noun [C] a report that someone sends from a foreign country

dispel /dɪˈspel/ verb [T] to get rid of unpleasant feelings or false beliefs

dispensary /dɪˈspensəri/ noun [C] a place in a hospital where you can get medicines and drugs

dispensation /ˌdɪspənˈseɪʃ(ə)n/ noun [C/U] formal official permission to do something that people are not normally allowed to do

dispense /dɪˈspens/ verb [T] to provide people with something

PHRASAL VERB **dispense with sb/sth** formal to stop using someone or something because you no longer want or need them

dispenser /dɪˈspensə/ noun [C] a machine or container from which you can get something such as drinks or money

dispersal /dɪˈspɜːs(ə)l/ noun [U] the process of spreading people or things in different directions over a wide area

disperse /dɪˈspɜːs/ verb [I/T] **1** if a crowd of people disperses, or if someone disperses

it, the people separate and go in different directions: *Soldiers fired tear gas to disperse the crowds.* **2** to spread in different directions over a wide area, or to make things do this

dispirited /dɪˈspɪrɪtɪd/ adj no longer feeling any hope, enthusiasm, or interest

displace /dɪsˈpleɪs/ verb [T] **1** to force someone to leave their own country and live somewhere else **2** to take the place of someone or something —**displacement** /dɪsˈpleɪsmənt/ noun [U]

display¹ /dɪˈspleɪ/ verb [T] ★★
1 to put something in a particular place so that people can see it easily: *She displayed some of her paintings at the local arts festival.*
2 to show a feeling, quality, or attitude by the way that you behave: *From an early age he displayed a talent for singing.*
3 to show information on a computer screen

display² /dɪˈspleɪ/ noun [C] ★★
1 an arrangement of things for people to look at: *a window display* ♦ *a display of exotic plants*
2 a performance for people to look at: *a firework display* ♦ *a display of circus skills*
3 an occasion when someone shows a particular feeling, quality, or attitude: *Displays of emotion disgusted her.* ♦ *a very public display of Anglo-American unity*
4 a computer screen, or a similar piece of equipment that shows information
PHRASE **on display** if something is on display, it is in a place where it can be seen by many people: *Her work is on display at the gallery.*

displeased /dɪsˈpliːzd/ adj formal annoyed or angry

displeasure /dɪsˈpleʒə/ noun [U] formal the feeling of being annoyed or angry

disposable /dɪˈspəʊzəb(ə)l/ adj designed to be thrown away after being used once or a few times

disposable income noun [U] money that you have left to spend after you have paid your bills

disposal /dɪˈspəʊz(ə)l/ noun [U] the process of getting rid of something: *the disposal of nuclear waste*
PHRASE **at sb's disposal** available for someone to use at any time

dispose /dɪˈspəʊz/ PHRASAL VERB **dispose of sth** to get rid of something that you no longer need or want: *Please dispose of litter in the containers provided.*

disposed /dɪˈspəʊzd/ adj formal **1** be disposed to sth likely to behave or think in a particular way **2** be disposed to do sth to be willing to do something

disposition /ˌdɪspəˈzɪʃ(ə)n/ noun [singular] the way that someone normally thinks and behaves: *a warm and friendly disposition*

disproportionate /ˌdɪsprəˈpɔːʃ(ə)nət/ adj too big or too small in comparison with something else —**disproportionately** adv

disprove /dɪsˈpruːv/ verb [T] to prove that something is not correct or true

dispute¹ /dɪˈspjuːt, ˈdɪspjuːt/ noun [C/U] ★★ a serious disagreement, especially one that involves groups of people and lasts for a

long time: *The two companies are still in
dispute.* ♦ *a territorial dispute between rival
gangs* ♦ *a dispute over pay* ♦ *We got involved
in a dispute with the neighbours.*

dispute² /dɪsˈpjuːt/ verb **1** [T] to say that
something is not true or correct **2** [I/T] to
argue about something

disqualification /dɪsˌkwɒlɪfɪˈkeɪʃ(ə)n/ noun
[C/U] a situation in which someone is not
allowed to take part in something, usually
because they have done something wrong

disqualify /dɪsˈkwɒlɪfaɪ/ verb [T] to not allow
someone to take part in something, usually
because they have done something wrong

disquiet /dɪsˈkwaɪət/ noun [U] *formal* a feeling
of being very worried or nervous

disregard¹ /ˌdɪsrɪˈɡɑːd/ noun [singular/U] the
attitude of someone who does not respect
something or does not think that it is
important

disregard² /ˌdɪsrɪˈɡɑːd/ verb [T] to not think
that something is important, or to not pay
any attention to it

disrepair /ˌdɪsrɪˈpeə/ noun [U] *formal* a broken
or damaged state

disreputable /dɪsˈrepjʊtəb(ə)l/ adj not
respected, and thought to be dishonest or
illegal

disrepute /ˌdɪsrɪˈpjuːt/ noun **bring sb/sth into
disrepute** *formal* to cause people to stop
respecting someone or something

disrespect /ˌdɪsrɪˈspekt/ noun [U] a lack of
respect for someone or something
—**disrespectful** adj

disrupt /dɪsˈrʌpt/ verb [T] to interrupt
something and prevent it from continuing:
Protesters tried to disrupt the meeting.
—**disruption** /dɪsˈrʌpʃ(ə)n/ noun [C/U]

disruptive /dɪsˈrʌptɪv/ adj causing difficulties
that interrupt something and prevent it
from continuing —**disruptively** adv

dissatisfaction /dɪsˌsætɪsˈfækʃ(ə)n/ noun [U]
the annoyed feeling that you get when
something is not as good as you expected it
to be

dissatisfied /dɪsˈsætɪsfaɪd/ adj annoyed
because something is not as good as you
expected it to be: *a dissatisfied customer*

dissect /dɪˈsekt/ verb [T] *technical* to cut the
body of a dead person or animal into pieces
in order to examine it —**dissection**
/dɪˈsekʃ(ə)n/ noun [C/U]

disseminate /dɪˈsemɪneɪt/ verb [T] *formal* to
make something such as information
available to a lot of people —**dissemination**
/dɪˌsemɪˈneɪʃ(ə)n/ noun [U]

dissent /dɪˈsent/ noun [U] strong
disagreement, especially with what people
in authority think or with what the
majority of people think —**dissent** verb [I]

dissenting /dɪˈsentɪŋ/ adj expressing strong
disagreement, especially with what people
in authority think or with what the
majority of people think

dissertation /ˌdɪsəˈteɪʃ(ə)n/ noun [C] a long
piece of writing on a particular subject that
you do as part of a university degree

disservice /dɪˈsɜːvɪs/ noun **do a disservice to
sb/sth** *formal* to have a bad effect on someone
or something

dissident /ˈdɪsɪdənt/ noun [C] someone who
disagrees publicly with a government
—**dissident** adj

dissimilar /dɪˈsɪmɪlə/ adj different from
someone or something else

dissipate /ˈdɪsɪˌpeɪt/ verb [I/T] *formal* to
gradually disappear by becoming less
strong, or to make something do this

dissociate /dɪˈsəʊsɪeɪt/ or **disassociate**
/ˌdɪsəˈsəʊsɪeɪt/ verb **dissociate yourself from** to
show clearly that you are not connected
with someone or something —**dissociation**
/dɪˌsəʊsɪˈeɪʃ(ə)n/ noun [U]

dissolution /ˌdɪsəˈluːʃ(ə)n/ noun [U] the
process of officially ending the existence of
an organization, institution, or agreement

dissolve /dɪˈzɒlv/ verb **1** [I/T] if a solid
substance dissolves in a liquid, or if you
dissolve it, it mixes into the liquid and
becomes included in it **2** [T] to officially end
the existence of an organization,
institution, or agreement

dissuade /dɪˈsweɪd/ verb [T] *formal* to persuade
someone not to do something

distance¹ /ˈdɪstəns/ noun [C/U] ★★★ the
amount of space between two people or
things: *the distance from the Earth to the
sun* ♦ *They started to walk the short
distance to the camp.* ♦ *The house is within
walking distance of the university.* ♦ *We
watched the fighting from a safe distance.*
PHRASES at/from a distance at/from a place
that is not close: *I've only ever seen him
from a distance.*
in/into the distance at/to a place that is very
far from where you are, although you can
still see or hear things that are there: *The
peaks of the Pyrenees could be seen in the
distance.* ♦ *He stared into the distance.*
keep your distance to avoid going near
someone or something
→ STRIKE¹

distance² /ˈdɪstəns/ verb **distance yourself from**
to act in a way that shows that you are not
connected with someone or something

distance learning noun [U] a system in which
students work at home and send work to
their teachers by post or email

distant /ˈdɪstənt/ adj ★
1 far away from the place where you are:
the distant sound of traffic ♦ *stories from
distant countries*
2 far away in time: *our ancestors from the
distant past*
3 related, but not in a close way: *a distant
relative/cousin*
4 unfriendly or not showing strong feelings:
Laura was cold and distant.
—**distantly** /ˈdɪstəntli/ adv: *distantly related
cousins* ♦ *Ivan smiled distantly.*

distaste /dɪsˈteɪst/ noun [U] a feeling of dislike
for someone or something that you do not
approve of

distasteful /dɪsˈteɪstf(ə)l/ adj unpleasant in a
way that upsets or offends you

distil /dɪsˈtɪl/ verb [T] to make a liquid stronger
or purer by heating it until it becomes a
gas and then making it a liquid again
—**distillation** /ˌdɪstɪˈleɪʃ(ə)n/ noun [C/U]

distillery /dɪsˈtɪləri/ noun [C] a place where

strong alcoholic drinks such as WHISKY are made

distinct /dɪˈstɪŋkt/ adj **1** separate and different in a way that is clear: *The animals were put into two distinct groups.* **2** able to be clearly seen, heard, smelled, or tasted ≠ INDISTINCT: *As dawn broke, the outline of a building became distinct against the sky.* ♦ *a distinct smell of burning* **3** definite and obvious: *a distinct disadvantage*

distinction /dɪˈstɪŋkʃ(ə)n/ noun ★
1 [C] a difference between two things: *the clear distinction between rich and poor* ♦ *The school does not make a distinction between education for girls and boys.*
2 [U] *formal* the excellent skills or features that someone or something has, or the high status that comes from these skills or features: *a writer of great distinction* ♦ *She held the distinction of being the first woman to edit a national newspaper.*
3 [C/U] *British* a very high mark in an examination

distinctive /dɪˈstɪŋktɪv/ adj easy to recognize because of being different from other people or things of the same type —**distinctively** adv

distinctly /dɪˈstɪŋk(t)li/ adv **1** clearly: *I distinctly remember seeing him.* **2** extremely: *Lucy felt distinctly uncomfortable.*

distinguish /dɪˈstɪŋgwɪʃ/ verb ★
1 [I/T] to recognize the differences between things=DIFFERENTIATE: *He learned to distinguish the songs of different birds.* ♦ *information on how to distinguish between the different diseases* ♦ *distinguish sth from sth the ability to distinguish right from wrong*
2 [T] to be a feature that makes someone or something clearly different from other similar people or things=DIFFERENTIATE: **distinguish sb/sth from sb/sth** *What distinguished Alex from the rest of us was his exceptional ability as a writer.*
3 [T] *formal* to be able to hear, see, smell, or taste something clearly
PHRASE **distinguish yourself** to do something very well so that people notice and respect you

distinguishable /dɪˈstɪŋgwɪʃəb(ə)l/ adj
1 clearly different from other people or things of the same type ≠ INDISTINGUISHABLE
2 easy to see, hear, smell, or taste

distinguished /dɪˈstɪŋgwɪʃt/ adj successful and respected by many people

distort /dɪˈstɔːt/ verb [T] **1** to change something so that it is no longer true or accurate: *The paper was accused of distorting the truth.*
2 to change the way that something looks, sounds, or behaves so that it becomes strange or difficult to recognize: *Her face was distorted with pain.* —**distortion** /dɪˈstɔːʃ(ə)n/ noun [C/U]: *a distortion of the facts*

distract /dɪˈstrækt/ verb [T] to get someone's attention and prevent them from concentrating on something: *The noise was distracting me.*

distracted /dɪˈstræktɪd/ adj not able to concentrate on something —**distractedly** adv

distraction /dɪˈstrækʃ(ə)n/ noun [C/U] something that gets your attention and

prevents you from concentrating on something else
PHRASE **drive sb to distraction** to annoy someone so much that they become angry or upset

distraught /dɪˈstrɔːt/ adj extremely worried, upset, or confused

distress¹ /dɪˈstres/ noun [U] **1** a feeling that you have when you are very unhappy, worried, or upset: *It was obvious that Gina was in great distress.* **2** a situation in which a ship or aircraft is in great danger and likely to sink or crash: *a message from a ship in distress* —**distressed** /dɪˈstrest/ adj

distress² /dɪˈstres/ verb [T] to make someone feel very unhappy, worried, or upset

distressing /dɪˈstresɪŋ/ adj making you feel extremely unhappy, worried, or upset: *distressing news*

distribute /dɪˈstrɪbjuːt/ verb [T] ★
1 to give something such as food, clothes, or money to a group of people, especially so that each person gets an equal share: *The two men were distributing anti-government leaflets.* ♦ **distribute sth to sb** *We distributed beans and maize to the refugees.*
2 to supply goods from one central place: *Hollywood movies are distributed worldwide.*
3 to spread something over an area: *Water beds distribute body pressure much more evenly than conventional beds.*

distribution /ˌdɪstrɪˈbjuːʃ(ə)n/ noun ★
1 [U] the process of giving something such as food, clothes, or money to a group of people: *the distribution of food and clothing in the disaster area*
2 [C/U] the way in which something is shared among people or spread over an area: *Brazil has a very unequal distribution of income and wealth.*
3 [U] the process of supplying goods from one central place: *the marketing and distribution of the software*

distributor /dɪˈstrɪbjʊtə/ noun [C] a company that supplies goods to shops and businesses

district /ˈdɪstrɪkt/ noun [C] ★★★
1 an area of a town or country: *They live in one of the most exclusive districts of Paris.* ♦ *the new financial district*
2 one of the areas into which a town or country is divided for official purposes: *Schools in the district continue to perform badly.* ♦ *a district judge*

district atˈtorney noun [C] a lawyer who works for a state or COUNTY government in the US

district ˈcouncil noun [C] a group of people who are elected to manage public services in a particular area of the UK

district ˈnurse noun [C] a nurse in the UK whose job is to give people medical treatment in their own homes

distrust /dɪsˈtrʌst/ noun [U] a feeling that you cannot trust someone or something → MISTRUST —**distrust** verb [T]

disturb /dɪˈstɜːb/ verb [T] ★★
1 to interrupt someone and stop them from continuing what they were doing: *Sorry to disturb you, but do you know where Miss Springer is?*

D

2 to upset and worry someone a lot: *We were disturbed by her resignation.*

3 to make something move: *A soft breeze gently disturbed the surface of the pool.*

disturbance /dɪˈstɜːbəns/ noun [C] **1** an occasion on which people behave in a noisy or violent way in a public place: *There were serious disturbances in the city last summer.* **2** something that interrupts you and stops you from continuing what you were doing: *We have a lot to do today, so we don't want any disturbances.*

disturbed /dɪˈstɜːbd/ adj **1** affected by mental or emotional problems **2** extremely worried or upset

disturbing /dɪˈstɜːbɪŋ/ adj making you feel extremely worried or upset

disused /dɪsˈjuːzd/ adj no longer used

ditch¹ /dɪtʃ/ noun [C] a long narrow hole that is dug along the side of a road or field

ditch² /dɪtʃ/ verb [T] *informal* to get rid of someone or something because you no longer like or need them

dither /ˈdɪðə/ verb [I] *showing disapproval* to be unable to make a decision about something

diva /ˈdiːvə/ noun [C] a famous female singer, especially of opera

divan /dɪˈvæn/ noun [C] a bed that consists of a MATTRESS on a solid base

dive¹ /daɪv/ verb [I] **1** to jump into water with your head first and with your arms stretched out in front of you: *I watched Paul dive into the pool.* **2** to swim UNDERWATER using special equipment so that you can breathe: *We went diving when we were on holiday .* **3** to move quickly and suddenly towards the ground, or in a particular direction: *The plane dived suddenly.* ♦ *She dived for the gun.*

dive² /daɪv/ noun [C] **1** a jump into water with your head first and your arms stretched out in front of you **2** a quick sudden movement towards the ground, or in a particular direction: *The plane lost control and went into a dive.* **3** *informal* a bar or club that is dirty, cheap, and unpleasant

diver /ˈdaɪvə/ noun [C] someone who swims deep under water

diverge /daɪˈvɜːdʒ/ verb [I] **1** to go in separate directions: *The two roads diverge at the entrance to the woods.* **2** to develop and become different after being the same: *He was prepared to diverge from established policies.*

divergence /daɪˈvɜːdʒ(ə)ns/ noun [C/U] a difference in the way that two or more things develop from the same thing

diverse /daɪˈvɜːs/ adj very different from each other: *a diverse range of issues*

diversify /daɪˈvɜːsɪfaɪ/ verb [I/T] *business* to develop additional products or activities —**diversification** /daɪˌvɜːsɪfɪˈkeɪʃ(ə)n/ noun [U]

diversion /daɪˈvɜːʃ(ə)n/ noun **1** [C] something that is intended to take your attention away from something else: *One man created a diversion while the other ran for the door.* **2** [C/U] a change in the use or purpose of something: *a diversion of funds* **3** [C/U] *British* a change in the road or path that you take to get somewhere because the usual road or path is closed **4** [C] *formal* an activity that you do for fun

diversity /daɪˈvɜːsəti/ noun [singular/U] the fact that very different people or things exist within a group or place: *ethnic and cultural diversity*

divert /daɪˈvɜːt/ verb [T] **1** to make something move or travel in a different direction **2** to take someone's attention away from something: *The government claimed that Cooper was trying to divert attention from his financial problems.* **3** to use something for a purpose that is different from its original or main purpose

divest /daɪˈvest/ PHRASAL VERB **di'vest sb of sth** *formal* to take something from someone

divide¹ /dɪˈvaɪd/ verb ★★★

1 separate/be separated	4 cause disagreement
2 separate and share	5 in mathematics
3 be in between	+ PHRASAL VERB

1 [I/T] to separate into groups or parts, or to make people or things separate into groups or parts: **divide sth into sth** *Divide the class into three groups.* ♦ *The problem is divided into four parts.*

2 [T] to separate something into smaller parts and share the parts between people or things: *Decide how you would like to divide the money.* ♦ **divide sth between/among sb** *After his death his property was divided among his children.* ♦ **divide sth between sth and sth** *She divides her time between teaching and research.*

3 [T] to keep two or more areas or parts separate: **divide sth from sth** *A busy road divides the hotel from the beach.*

4 [T] to be the cause of disagreement between people: *This is a subject that divides the nation.*

5 [I/T] to do a calculation to find out how many times a number contains a smaller number. This is usually shown by the symbol ÷: **divide sth by sth** *Divide 9 by 3.* ♦ *10 divided by 2 is 5.*

PHRASAL VERB **di,vide sth 'up 1** same as **divide¹** 1: *Divide the children up into groups of four.* **2** same as **divide¹** 2: *The money will be divided up between five different charities.*

divide² /dɪˈvaɪd/ noun [C] an important difference or disagreement between people: *a cultural/political divide*

dividend /ˈdɪvɪˌdend/ noun [C] a part of the profits of a company that is paid to the people who own shares in the company
PHRASE **pay dividends** *informal* to give you advantages

dividing line /dɪˈvaɪdɪŋ ˌlaɪn/ noun [singular] something that clearly shows the difference between one thing and another

divine /dɪˈvaɪn/ adj relating to a god, or sent by a god

diving /ˈdaɪvɪŋ/ noun [U] **1** the activity or sport of swimming deep under water **2** the activity or sport of jumping into water with your head first and your arms stretched out in front of you

division /dɪˈvɪʒ(ə)n/ noun ★★★

1 separation into groups	4 a difference
2 separation & sharing	5 a disagreement
3 part of organization	6 in mathematics

D

1 [C/U] the process of separating people or things into groups or parts: *The civil war led to a permanent division of the country.* ♦ **division of sth into sth** *the division of the land into small fields*
2 [C/U] the process of separating something into parts and sharing it between people: **division of sth between sb** *the division of responsibilities between members of the committee*
3 [C] one of the parts into which a large organization is divided: *the company's electronics division*
4 [C] a difference between people: *the growing division between rich and poor*
5 [C/U] a disagreement between people: *deep divisions within the Party*
6 [C/U] a calculation in mathematics of how many times a number is contained in a larger number

divisional /dɪˈvɪʒ(ə)nəl/ adj relating to a division of an organization

divisive /dɪˈvaɪsɪv/ adj likely to cause arguments between people

divorce¹ /dɪˈvɔːs/ noun [C/U] ★ a legal way of ending a marriage: *I want a divorce.* ♦ *Is it true Tom's getting a divorce?* ♦ *Both of her marriages ended in divorce.*

divorce² /dɪˈvɔːs/ verb **1** [I/T] to take legal action to end your marriage to someone
2 [T] to completely separate one thing from another: *Politics should not be divorced from the lives of ordinary people.*

divorced /dɪˈvɔːst/ adj ★ no longer married because your marriage has been legally ended: *a divorced mother of three* ♦ *After they got divorced, she never remarried.*

divorcée /dɪˌvɔːˈsiː/ noun [C] a woman who is divorced

divulge /daɪˈvʌldʒ/ verb [T] *formal* to give information about something that should be kept secret

Diwali /dɪˈwɑːli/ noun [C/U] an important festival in the Hindu religion that takes place in October or November

DIY /ˌdiː aɪ ˈwaɪ/ noun [U] *British* do-it-yourself: the activity of making or repairing things for your own home

dizzy /ˈdɪzi/ adj **1** feeling that the things around you are spinning and that you are going to fall **2** feeling excited or confused, or making you feel like this: *We were dizzy with excitement.* —**dizziness** noun [U]

DJ /ˈdiːˌdʒeɪ/ noun [C] disc jockey: someone who plays CDs and records in a club or on the radio

DNA /ˌdiː en ˈeɪ/ noun [U] a chemical substance in cells that contains genetic information

do¹ /duː/ (3rd person singular **does** /weak dəz, strong dʌz/; past tense **did** /dɪd/; past participle **done** /dʌn/) verb ★★★
1 for forming questions and negatives [auxiliary verb] used before another verb for forming a question or a negative: *Do you like cheese?* ♦ *What did the doctor say?* ♦ *Didn't they tell you I was coming?* ♦ *I did not know the answer.* ♦ *Max doesn't live here any more.*

In conversation and informal written English the negative forms of the auxiliary verb 'do', **does**

not, do not, did not are shortened to **doesn't, don't,** and **didn't.**

2 for referring back to a previous verb [I] used instead of repeating the same verb that was used earlier: *'You promised to come with me.' 'No I didn't.'* ♦ *She doesn't travel around as much as I do.* ♦ *I like Chinese food, but George doesn't.* ♦ *'I enjoyed our trip to Brighton.' 'So did I.'*
3 for emphasis [auxiliary verb] used for emphasizing the meaning of a positive statement: *I've forgotten her name, but I do remember her face.* ♦ *I did lock the door. I'm absolutely sure.*
4 perform an action, activity, or job [T] to perform an action or job, take part in an activity, or complete a piece of work: *I've done something awful.* ♦ *Have you done that essay yet?* ♦ *I just need to do my hair* (=brush and arrange it). ♦ *I do the cooking, and Peggy washes the dishes.* ♦ *There's nothing to do around here.* ♦ *I'm not sure what she does for a living* (=what her job is).
5 have an effect [T] to have a particular effect on someone or something: *Frost can do a lot of damage.* ♦ *The fresh air will do you good.* ♦ **do sth to sth** *What have you done to your hair?* ♦ **do sth to sb** *I'll never forgive him for what he did to me.*
6 for talking about health or success [I] used for talking about someone's health, progress, or their general situation: *Hi Sam! How are you doing?* ♦ *He did well in the exams.*
7 study [T] *British* to study a subject: *I'm doing English and History.*
PHRASES **what is sb/sth doing...?** *spoken* used for asking why someone or something is in a particular place: *What's my diary doing on your desk?*
will do used for saying that something is enough or is suitable for a particular purpose: *If you haven't got a bandage, a piece of clean cloth will do.* ♦ *I've only got 50 pence – will that do?*
PHRASAL VERBS **do away with sth** to get rid of something: *They discussed whether to do away with the agency completely.*
do sth up *British* **1** to fasten something ≠ UNDO: *Do up your shoelaces.* **2** to repair and decorate an old building
do with sth 1 could do with sth *spoken* used for saying that you want or need something: *I'm sure James could do with some help.* **2** **have something/anything to do with sth** to be connected with something: *The problem had something to do with his mother.* ♦ *Is this anything to do with school?* **3** **have nothing to do with sth** to not be connected with sth: *Her resignation had nothing to do with her health.* **4** **what is sb doing with sth?** *spoken* used for asking why someone has something: *What are you doing with my CD player?*
do without (sb/sth) to succeed in living or working without someone or something: *I couldn't do without my washing machine.*

do² /duː/ noun [C] *informal* a social event such as a party
PHRASE **do's and don'ts** instructions and warnings about what you should and

D

should not do in a particular situation

docile /ˈdəʊsaɪl, *American* ˈdɑːs(ə)l/ adj well-behaved and easy to control

dock¹ /dɒk/ noun **1** [C] an area in a port where ships stay while goods are taken on or off or while repairs are done **2 the dock** [singular] the part of a court of law where the person who is accused of a crime stands or sits

dock² /dɒk/ verb **1** [I/T] if a ship docks, it arrives at a dock **2** [I/T] if a SPACECRAFT docks, it joins to another spacecraft while they are still in space **3** [T] to take money out of someone's salary as a punishment

docker /ˈdɒkə/ noun [C] *British* someone whose job is to take goods on and off ships at a dock

docking station /ˈdɒkɪŋ ˌsteɪʃ(ə)n/ noun [C] *computing* a piece of equipment to which you can connect a PORTABLE computer for a short time, so that you can use it like a PC

dockyard /ˈdɒkjɑːd/ noun [C] a place where ships are built or repaired.

doctor¹ /ˈdɒktə/ noun [C] ★★★
1 someone whose job is to treat people who are ill or injured: *Have you seen a doctor yet?* ♦ *Consult your doctor before trying these exercises.* ♦ *Doctor Jones specializes in heart problems.*
2 someone who has the highest degree that a college or university gives: *a doctor of theology* ♦ *The research team is led by Doctor Beth Levinson.*

doctor² /ˈdɒktə/ verb [T] to change something in order to get an unfair advantage

doctorate /ˈdɒkt(ə)rət/ noun [C] the highest degree that a college or university gives —**doctoral** adj

doctrine /ˈdɒktrɪn/ noun [C/U] a set of religious or political beliefs

document¹ /ˈdɒkjʊmənt/ noun [C] ★★★
1 a piece of paper or a set of papers containing official information: *He refused to sign the documents.* ♦ *A secret policy document was leaked to the newspapers.*
2 *computing* a computer file that you can write in: *The program will automatically save any documents you have open.*

document² /ˈdɒkjʊˌment/ verb [T] **1** to record something in writing or on film: *Her report documents the effects of climate change.* **2** to support something with evidence: *Their allegations are fully documented.*

documentary¹ /ˌdɒkjʊˈment(ə)ri/ noun [C] a film or television programme that deals with real people and events

documentary² /ˌdɒkjʊˈment(ə)ri/ adj **1** dealing with real people and events: *a documentary film* **2** in the form of documents: *documentary evidence*

documentation /ˌdɒkjʊmenˈteɪʃ(ə)n/ noun [U] **1** documents that can be used for proving that something is true **2** written instructions about how to use a computer or computer program

doddle /ˈdɒd(ə)l/ noun **be a doddle** *British informal* to be very easy to do

dodge /dɒdʒ/ verb **1** [I/T] to avoid someone or something by moving quickly **2** [T] to avoid doing something in a clever or dishonest way: *He tried to dodge the question.* —**dodge** noun [C]

dodgy /ˈdɒdʒi/ adj *British informal* not honest or reliable: *Don't get involved in anything dodgy.*

doe /dəʊ/ noun [C] a female DEER or RABBIT

does 3rd person singular of the present tense of do¹

doesn't /ˈdʌz(ə)nt/ short form the usual way of saying or writing 'does not'. This is not often used in formal writing: *Sara doesn't live here any more.*

dog¹ /dɒg/ noun [C] ★★★ an animal kept as a pet, for guarding buildings, or for hunting

dog² /dɒg/ verb [T] **1** to cause trouble for someone over a long period of time: *These rumours had dogged the president for years.* **2** to follow someone closely in a way that annoys them

dog collar noun [C] **1** a white round collar that is worn by priests in the Christian church **2** a collar around a dog's neck that you can fasten to a LEAD (=a long piece of rope, leather etc)

dog-eared /ˈdɒg ˌɪəd/ adj a dog-eared page or book has been used so much that the corners or edges have become damaged or torn

dogged /ˈdɒgɪd/ adj determined to achieve something despite difficulties =TENACIOUS —**doggedly** adv

doghouse /ˈdɒghaʊs/ noun **in the doghouse** *informal* if you are in the doghouse, someone is angry with you because you have done something wrong

dogma /ˈdɒgmə/ noun [C/U] a belief or set of beliefs that people are expected to accept without asking questions about them

dogmatic /dɒgˈmætɪk/ adj so sure that your beliefs and ideas are right that you expect other people to accept them

do-gooder /ˌduːˈgʊdə/ noun [C] someone who always tries to help people in a way that is unnecessary or unsuitable

dogsbody /ˈdɒgzˌbɒdi/ noun [C] *British informal* someone who is forced to do all the jobs that no one else wants to do

doing¹ the present participle of do

doing² /ˈduːɪŋ/ noun
PHRASES **be sb's doing** to be someone's fault
take some doing to be very difficult to do

do-it-yourself noun [U] DIY

doldrums, the /ˈdɒldrəmz, ˈdəʊldrəmz/ noun [plural] a situation in which there is a lack of success, activity, or improvement

dole /dəʊl/ **PHRASAL VERB** **dole sth out** *informal* to give something such as food or money to a group of people

dole, the /dəʊl/ noun [singular] *British* money that people who do not have a job get from the government: *She's been on the dole* (=getting government money) *for over a year.*

doleful /ˈdəʊlf(ə)l/ adj looking sad —**dolefully** adv

doll /dɒl/ noun [C] a children's toy in the shape of a small person

dollar /ˈdɒlə/ noun ★★
1 [C] the unit of money used in the US and in several other countries such as Canada, Australia, and Singapore. Its symbol is $: *a coat costing one hundred dollars* ♦ *Payment must be in US dollars.*

2 [C] a BANKNOTE or coin that is worth a dollar: *a dollar bill*

3 the dollar [singular] used for talking about the value of US money, especially in comparison with that of other countries

dollop /ˈdɒləp/ noun [C] *informal* a large lump of a soft substance, especially food

dolphin /ˈdɒlfɪn/ noun [C] a large sea animal, similar to a fish, with a long nose

domain /dəʊˈmeɪn/ noun [C] **1** a particular area of activity or life **2** *computing* a DOMAIN NAME

doˈmain ˌname noun [C] an address on the Internet

dome /dəʊm/ noun [C] a roof shaped like the top half of a ball —**domed** /dəʊmd/ adj: *a domed roof/building*

domestic /dəˈmestɪk/ adj ★★
1 relating to a particular country: *domestic politics* ♦ *domestic and international flights*
2 relating to people's homes and family life: *domestic chores* ♦ *domestic appliances*
3 enjoying activities relating to your home, such as cooking and looking after children
4 kept as a pet or on a farm ≠ WILD: *the domestic cat*

domesticated /dəˈmestɪˌkeɪtɪd/ adj **1** a domesticated animal has been trained to live with or work for humans **2** enjoying activities such as cooking and cleaning, or good at them

domesticity /ˌdəʊmeˈstɪsəti/ noun [U] the activities relating to your home and family life

dominance /ˈdɒmɪnəns/ noun [U] a situation in which one person or thing has more influence or power than any other: *the growing dominance of the Green Party in the north of the country* ♦ *Japanese dominance of the electronics market*

dominant /ˈdɒmɪnənt/ adj more important, powerful, or successful than the other people or things of the same type: *The company cannot preserve its dominant position in the market.*

dominate /ˈdɒmɪˌneɪt/ verb ★★
1 [I/T] to control someone or something by having more power or influence: *She tends to dominate the conversation.*
2 [I/T] to be the most important aspect or feature of a particular situation: *The earthquake once again dominated the news.*
3 [T] if an object dominates a place, it is so big or high that it is easy to notice: *a little room dominated by a huge fireplace*

domination /ˌdɒmɪˈneɪʃ(ə)n/ noun [U] control or power over other people or things: *the team's domination of English football in the 1990s*

domineering /ˌdɒmɪˈnɪərɪŋ/ adj trying to control other people and make them obey you

dominion /dəˈmɪnjən/ noun *formal* **1** [U] control, or the right to rule over something **2** [C] an area that is ruled by one person or government

domino /ˈdɒmɪnəʊ/ noun **1 dominoes** [plural] a game in which players take turns to try to place each domino next to another one with the same number of spots on it **2** [C] a small

flat piece of wood with spots on it, used in the game of dominoes

don¹ /dɒn/ noun [C] *British* someone who teaches at a university, especially at Oxford or Cambridge

don² /dɒn/ verb [T] *literary* to put on a piece of clothing

donate /dəʊˈneɪt/ verb **1** [I/T] to give something such as money or goods to an organization: *Many big corporations donate to political parties.* **2** [T] to give something such as blood, SPERM, or a part of your body to help someone else

donation /dəʊˈneɪʃ(ə)n/ noun **1** [C] money or goods that you give to an organization: *a generous donation* **2** [C/U] the process of giving something such as blood, SPERM, or a part of your body to help someone else

done¹ /dʌn/ adj **1** finished doing something or using something: *I'm nearly done.* **2** if a job is done, it has been finished: *Is the painting done?* **3** cooked long enough to be eaten: *That chicken must be done by now.*
PHRASE **all done** *spoken* used for saying that you have finished doing something

done² /dʌn/ interjection used for saying that you will accept a price or offer

done³ the past participle of **do**

donkey /ˈdɒŋki/ noun [C] a grey or brown animal like a small horse with long ears —*picture* → C12
PHRASE **donkey's years** *British informal* an extremely long time

ˈdonkey ˌwork noun [U] *informal* the boring part of a job that needs a lot of effort

donor /ˈdəʊnə/ noun [C] **1** someone who gives something such as blood, SPERM, or a part of their body to help someone else **2** someone who gives something such as money or goods to an organization

don't /dəʊnt/ short form the usual way of saying or writing 'do not'. This is not often used in formal writing: *I don't believe you!*

donut /ˈdəʊnʌt/an American spelling of doughnut

doodle /ˈduːd(ə)l/ verb [I] to draw patterns or pictures because you are bored or thinking about other things —**doodle** noun [C]

doom /duːm/ noun [U] a bad event that cannot be avoided such as death, destruction, or complete failure
PHRASE **doom and gloom** a feeling that a situation is very bad and without hope

doomed /duːmd/ adj certain to end in death, destruction, or complete failure

door /dɔː/ noun [C] ★★★
1 a large flat object that you open when you want to enter or leave a building, room, or vehicle: *open/close/shut the door* ♦ *the bedroom/car door* ♦ *the back/front/side door* ♦ *I knocked on the door and a voice said 'Come in.'* ♦ *Go and answer the door* (=go to see who is there)*!* ♦ *There's someone at the door* (=outside the door to your house)*.* ♦ *We'll deliver the goods to your door* (=directly to your house) *within 24 hours.* —*picture* → C1, C6
2 the space created when you open a door =DOORWAY
PHRASES **(from) door to door 1** used for talking about the total length of a journey

from the place where you start to the place where you arrive: *It takes two hours door to door.* **2** going to all the houses in an area, trying to sell things or asking for information or votes

out of doors outside: *He spends a lot of time out of doors.*

→ CLOSED

D

doorbell /'dɔːbel/ noun [C] a button near the front door of a house that you press to make a sound to tell the person in the house that you are there —*picture* → C1

doorknob /'dɔːnɒb/ noun [C] a round handle on a door that you turn in order to open it

doorman /'dɔːmən/ noun [C] someone whose job is to be in charge of the main entrance of a building and help people when they go in or come out

doormat /'dɔːmæt/ noun [C] a piece of material that you clean the SOLES (=bottoms) of your shoes on before you go into a building

doorstep /'dɔːstep/ noun [C] a small step outside the main door to a building —*picture* → C1

PHRASE on your doorstep very close to where you live

door-to-door adj **1** going to all the houses in a particular area in order to sell something or ask for information or votes **2** taking someone or something directly from one place to the place they need to go to

doorway /'dɔːweɪ/ noun [C] the space that is created when you open a door

dope¹ /dəʊp/ noun *informal* **1** [C] a stupid person **2** [U] an illegal drug, especially CANNABIS

dope² /dəʊp/ verb [T] *informal* **1** to give someone a drug in order to take away their pain or make them sleep **2** to give a person or animal a drug so that they run faster in a race

dork /dɔːk/ noun [C] *informal* an insulting word for someone that you think is stupid and not fashionable

dormant /'dɔːmənt/ adj not active or developing now, but possibly becoming active in the future

dormitory /'dɔːmɪtri/ noun [C] **1** a large room in a school or army camp where a lot of people sleep **2** *American* a HALL OF RESIDENCE

dosage /'dəʊsɪdʒ/ noun [C/U] the amount of a medicine or drug that you take at one time

dose¹ /dəʊs/ noun [C] **1** a particular amount of a drug or medicine that has been measured so that you can take it: *a low dose of painkiller* **2** an amount of something, especially something bad: *I've just had a nasty dose of flu.* ♦ *I can only put up with Dave in small doses* (=for short periods of time).

dose² /dəʊs/ or **'dose sb ,up** verb [T] to give someone an amount of a drug or medicine that has been measured for them to take

dosh /dɒʃ/ noun [U] *British informal* money

doss /dɒs/ verb [I] **1 doss** or **doss about/around** to spend time doing nothing **2 doss** or **doss down** *British informal* to spend the night somewhere where you do not normally sleep and where you do not have a bed

dossier /'dɒsieɪ, 'dɒsiə/ noun [C] a set of documents about a person or situation

dot¹ /dɒt/ noun [C] **1** a very small spot of ink or colour **2** the way you say the symbol . in an Internet or email address **3** something that looks very small because it is far away: *The house was a tiny dot in the valley below.*

PHRASE on the dot at exactly the time that you mention: *He arrived at 8 o'clock on the dot.*

dot² /dɒt/ verb [T] **1** to put people or things in many parts of a place: *The company has more than thirty branches dotted around Spain.* **2** to put something, such as paint, on a surface in small amounts with spaces between **3** to put a dot over a letter of the alphabet

dot.com /ˌdɒt'kɒm/ noun [C] a company that uses the Internet to sell its products and services —**dot.com** adj

dote /dəʊt/ —**PHRASAL VERB** 'dote on sb to love someone so much that you do not notice their faults

doting /'dəʊtɪŋ/ adj a doting relative or friend loves you so much that they do not notice your faults

dotted line /ˌdɒtɪd 'laɪn/ noun [C] a line of small spots of ink that are very close together

PHRASE sign on the dotted line to sign a contract or other legal agreement

dotty /'dɒti/ adj *informal old-fashioned* slightly crazy

double¹ /'dʌb(ə)l/ adj ★★
1 consisting of two things or parts: *He went through the double doors.* ♦ *a double murder* ♦ *She suspected his words might have a double meaning* (=two different meanings).
2 containing or consisting of twice as much as normal: *Sometimes I would work a double shift.* ♦ *a double helping* of chips
3 large enough for two people or things: *a double room/bed/garage*

double² /'dʌb(ə)l/ verb ★
1 [I/T] to become twice as big, twice as much, or twice as many, or to make something do this: *The number of people without work has doubled in the last five years.* ♦ *The government doubled the tax on alcohol.* ♦ *Their house has **doubled in value** since they bought it.*
2 [T] to fold something so that it has two layers of equal size

PHRASAL VERBS 'double as sth to have another use or job as something: *an old sofa that doubled as Simon's bed*
,double 'back to turn and go back in the direction that you have come from
,double sth 'over *same as* **double²** 2: *The map on his desk was doubled over so I couldn't see it.*
,double (sb) 'over to bend forwards because you are in pain or because you are laughing a lot: **be doubled over with sth** *She was doubled over with pain.*
,double (sb) 'up *same as* **double (sb) over**
,double 'up as sth *same as* **double as sth**

double³ /'dʌb(ə)l/ determiner twice as much, or twice as many: *He now earns double the amount he used to.*

double⁴ /'dʌb(ə)l/ noun

1 sb looking like sb else	**4** a drink twice usual size
2 another actor	**5** room for two people
3 twice as much money	**6** game played in pairs

1 [C] someone who looks very similar to another person: *He's his father's double.* **2** [C] an actor who takes the place of another actor when making difficult or dangerous parts of a film **3** [U] twice as much money: *I get double for working evenings.* **4** [C] an amount of a strong alcoholic drink that is twice the usual amount **5** [C] a room or bed for two people to sleep in **6 doubles** [U] a game such as tennis that is played by pairs of players

double-barrelled /ˌdʌbl ˈbærəld/ adj **1** a double-barrelled gun has a pair of tubes that bullets come out from **2** *British* a double-barrelled name is a family name with two parts, usually joined by a HYPHEN, for example 'Lloyd-Webber'

double bass noun [C] a large musical instrument shaped like a VIOLIN that you rest on the floor and play standing up
—*picture* → STRINGED INSTRUMENT

double bed noun [C] a bed for two people
—*picture* → BED

double-breasted /ˌdʌb(ə)l ˈbrestɪd/ adj a double-breasted jacket or coat has two parallel lines of buttons down the front when it is fastened

double-check verb [I/T] to check something for a second time

double-click verb [I/T] *computing* to give an instruction to a computer by quickly pressing the MOUSE twice with your finger
—**double click** noun [C]

double-cross verb [T] to cheat someone who is helping you to do something dishonest or illegal

double-decker /ˌdʌb(ə)l ˈdekə/ or **double-decker bus** noun [C] a bus that has both an upper and a lower level where people can sit

double figures noun [plural] *British* the numbers 10 to 99

double glazing noun [U] *British* windows or doors that have two layers of glass, so that the building will be warmer and quieter —**double-glazed** adj

double life noun [C] a completely separate way of life that you have some of the time and keep secret from other people

double-sided /ˌdʌb(ə)l ˈsaɪdɪd/ adj able to be used on both sides: *double-sided disks*

double standard noun [C] a rule or principle that is applied to some people but not to others, in a way that is unfair

double take noun **do a double take** to react after a slight pause, because you are surprised by what you have just seen or heard

doubly /ˈdʌbli/ adv **1** by a much greater amount, or to a much greater degree than usual **2** for two reasons or in two ways

doubt¹ /daʊt/ noun [C] ★★★ a feeling of not being certain about something: *I have serious doubts about whether this system will work.* ♦ *I have no doubt that he will succeed.* ♦ *There's no doubt about it – we are in trouble.* ♦ *The accident raises doubts about* (=makes people have doubts about) *the safety of the aircraft.* ♦ *She is without a doubt one of our most talented students.*
PHRASES **be in doubt 1** if something is in doubt, it is not certain whether it will

succeed or continue: *The future of the company is still in doubt.* **2** if you are in doubt about something, you do not know what to do about it
beyond (any) doubt if something is beyond doubt, it is completely certain
if in doubt if you are not certain: used when giving advice: *If in doubt, get someone to help you.*
→ BENEFIT¹

doubt² /daʊt/ verb [T] ★★
1 to think that something is probably not true, probably does not exist, or probably will not happen: *'Do you think they'll win?' 'I doubt it.'* ♦ *I know a few people doubted my story.* ♦ **+(that)** *I doubt it will work, but we can try.*
2 to feel that you cannot trust or believe someone

doubtful /ˈdaʊtf(ə)l/ adj **1** not certain or likely to happen or to be true: *It is doubtful whether he will survive.* **2** not feeling certain about something: *Eddie looked doubtful, but agreed.* —**doubtfully** adv

doubtless /ˈdaʊtləs/ adv used for saying that you are certain that something is true or will happen, although you have no definite proof

dough /dəʊ/ noun [C/U] a mixture of flour, water, fat etc that is baked to make bread or PASTRY

doughnut /ˈdəʊˌnʌt/ noun [C] a sweet food, often in the shape of a ring, that is made by cooking dough in oil

dour /dʊə, ˈdaʊə/ adj very serious, and not smiling or friendly

douse /daʊs/ verb [T] **1** to cover someone or something with a liquid **2** to make a fire stop burning by pouring water over it

dove /dʌv/ noun [C] a white bird. Doves are often used as a sign of peace.

dowdy /ˈdaʊdi/ adj not attractive or fashionable

down¹ /daʊn/ grammar word ★★★

> **Down can be:**
> ■ a **preposition**: *She was walking down the street.*
> ■ an **adverb**: *She lay down and fell asleep.*
> ■ used after the verb 'to be': *Oil prices are down.*
> ■ an **adjective**: *I've been feeling rather down lately.*

1 to or towards a lower place to or towards a lower place, position, or surface: *He slipped on the ice and fell down.* ♦ *Tears were rolling down his cheeks.* ♦ *Get down off that roof!* ♦ *Put the box down on the table.* ♦ *the down escalator*
2 in a lower place in a lower place, or at a lower level: *It was dark and cold down in the cellar.* ♦ *Your name's further down the list.* ♦ *We could hear noises coming from down below.*
3 in or into a sitting or lying position with your body in or moving into a sitting, bending, or lying position: *Why don't you lie down and rest?* ♦ *exercises you can do while you are sitting down*
4 in a direction away from you in or towards a place that is in a direction away from you: *I was walking down the street with a couple of friends.*

D

D

5 when sth is reduced at or to a smaller amount or a lower or weaker level than before: *Turn down the radio.* ♦ *Profits are 15% down on* (=less than) *last year.*

6 when you write sth used for saying that you write something on a piece of paper: *Let me write that down before I forget it.*

7 south in or towards the south: *Thousands of Scottish fans travelled down to London for the match.*

8 when you eat or drink sth if food or drink goes down, it goes from your mouth to your stomach

9 sad *informal* unhappy: *He's been feeling very down.*

10 losing a game with a lower score than your opponent: *At half-time our team were two goals down.*

11 not working if a computer system is down, it is not working

12 already done used for saying how many things you have dealt with and how many more still need to be dealt with: *That's two classes down and four to go.*

PHRASES **be down to sb** *British* to be someone's responsibility

down to 1 used for emphasizing that everyone or everything is included: *Everything had been carefully planned, right down to the last detail.* **2** *British* because of something: *These delays are down to a lack of planning.*

down² /daʊn/ noun [U] the small soft feathers of a bird

down³ /daʊn/ verb [T] to drink all of something quickly

down-and-out noun [C] someone who has nowhere to live and has no job or money —**down-and-out** adj

downcast /ˈdaʊnkɑːst/ adj **1** sad or upset **2** downcast eyes are looking downwards

downer /ˈdaʊnə/ noun [singular] *informal* something that makes you feel sad or disappointed

downfall /ˈdaʊnfɔːl/ noun [singular] a sudden loss of power, status, or success, or something that causes this loss: *bad investments that led to the company's downfall* ♦ *His greed was his downfall.*

downgrade /ˈdaʊnɡreɪd/ verb [T] **1** to treat something in a way that makes it seem less important than before **2** to move someone to a job that is less important

downhearted /ˌdaʊnˈhɑːtɪd/ adj sad and feeling that things will not get better

downhill /ˌdaʊnˈhɪl/ adv towards the bottom of a hill or slope

PHRASE **go downhill** to get worse —**downhill** adj

Downing Street /ˈdaʊnɪŋ ˌstriːt/ noun [U] the prime minister or the government of the UK

download¹ /ˌdaʊnˈləʊd/ verb [I/T] *computing* to move information to your computer from a computer system or from the Internet

download² /ˈdaʊnləʊd/ noun [C/U] *computing* the process of downloading information to your computer, or a file that you have downloaded

downmarket /ˌdaʊnˈmɑːkɪt/ adj cheap, or of low quality —**downmarket** adv

down payment noun [C] a first payment that you make when you buy something and will pay the rest later

downplay /ˌdaʊnˈpleɪ/ verb [T] to deliberately make a situation seem less serious or important than it is =PLAY STH DOWN

downpour /ˈdaʊnpɔː/ noun [C] a large amount of rain that falls quickly =DELUGE

downright /ˈdaʊnraɪt/ adv *informal* completely or extremely: *She was downright rude!* —**downright** adj

downside /ˈdaʊnsaɪd/ noun [singular] the disadvantage or negative aspect of something ≠ UPSIDE

downsize /ˈdaʊnsaɪz/ verb [I/T] *business* to reduce the number of workers in a company or organization

Down's syndrome /ˈdaʊnz ˌsɪndrəʊm/ noun [U] a medical condition that makes someone develop in a different way from most people, mentally and physically

downstairs¹ /ˌdaʊnˈsteəz/ adv ★ to or on a lower floor of a building, especially the floor at ground level ≠ UPSTAIRS: *I ran downstairs.* —**downstairs** /ˈdaʊnsteəz/ adj: *a downstairs window*

downstairs² /ˌdaʊnˈsteəz/ noun [singular] the floor of a building that is at ground level ≠ UPSTAIRS

downstream /ˌdaʊnˈstriːm/ adv in the direction that a river or stream is flowing ≠ UPSTREAM

down time noun [U] **1** time when a computer or other machine is not working **2** time when you can relax and not work

down-to-earth adj practical and sensible

downtown /ˌdaʊnˈtaʊn/ adj, adv *American* in or near the business or shopping centre of a city ≠ UPTOWN

downtrodden /ˈdaʊnˌtrɒd(ə)n/ adj treated in a cruel or unfair way by someone with power

downturn /ˈdaʊntɜːn/ noun [C] a reduction in economic or business activity

downward¹ /ˈdaʊnwəd/ adv *American* DOWNWARDS

downward² /ˈdaʊnwəd/ adj going towards a lower place or level ≠ UPWARD: *a downward slope/movement*

downwards /ˈdaʊnwədz/ adv towards a lower place or level ≠ UPWARDS

PHRASE **face downwards 1** lying on the front of your body **2** lying on the side that normally faces up

downwind /ˌdaʊnˈwɪnd/ adj, adv in the same direction that the wind is moving

downy /ˈdaʊni/ adj covered in very soft small hairs or feathers

dowry /ˈdaʊri/ noun [C] money and property that, in some cultures, a woman's family gives to her husband when they get married

doze /dəʊz/ verb [I] to sleep for a short time, especially during the day

PHRASAL VERB **doze off** to start to sleep without intending to

dozen /ˈdʌz(ə)n/ (plural **dozen**) determiner **1** a set of 12 things or people: *a dozen red roses* ♦ *We need half a dozen eggs for the cake.* **2 dozens** [plural] lots of things or people: *Dozens of people were injured.*

Dr abbrev **1** doctor **2** drive

drab /dræb/ adj not colourful or interesting

draft¹ /drɑːft/ noun [C] **1** a piece of writing or a drawing that may have changes made to it before it is finished: *a first draft of the letter* **2** the American spelling of **draught**¹

draft² /drɑːft/ verb [T] to write a document, speech, or letter that may have changes made to it before it is finished

draft³ /drɑːft/ the American spelling of **draught**²

drag¹ /dræg/ verb ★

1 pull sth	5 when time seems slow
2 pull sb	6 in computing
3 make sb leave	+ PHRASE
4 touch ground	+ PHRASAL VERBS

1 [T] to pull something along with difficulty, especially something heavy: **drag sth down/along/through sth** *She dragged her suitcase down the path.*

2 [T] to pull someone strongly or violently when they do not want to go with you: *I grabbed his arm and dragged him over to the window.*

3 [T] to make someone leave or go to a place when they do not want to: *You dragged me away from my meeting just to tell me this!*

4 [I] if something drags on or along the ground, it touches the ground as you move along, because it is too long or too heavy: *I heard a chain **dragging along** the ground.*

5 [I] if time drags, it seems to pass very slowly

6 [T] *computing* to move something across a computer screen using the MOUSE

PHRASE **drag your feet** to do something very slowly because you do not really want to do it

PHRASAL VERBS **,drag sb 'into sth** to make someone become involved in a situation when they do not want to: *The US was afraid of being dragged into the war.*

,drag 'on to continue for longer than you want or think is necessary: *Some cases drag on for years.*

,drag sth 'out to make something continue for longer than necessary: *Let's not drag this meeting out any more than we have already.*

drag² /dræg/ noun **1** [singular] *informal* something that is boring or annoying **2** [U] women's clothes worn by a man, or men's clothes worn by a woman **3** [C] an act of breathing in smoke from a cigarette

dragon /'drægən/ noun [C] in stories, an imaginary large animal that breathes out fire

dragonfly /'drægən,flaɪ/ noun [C] an insect with a long narrow brightly coloured body and transparent wings

drain¹ /dreɪn/ verb **1** [I/T] if liquid drains, or if you drain it, it flows away from something: *Put the meat aside to let the fat drain off.* ♦ **drain sth from sth** *Drain the water from the tank.* —*picture* → C2 **2** [T] to get rid of the water in an area of land so that it can be used for other purposes **3** [T] to use so much of someone's energy or strength that they feel very tired

drain² /dreɪn/ noun **1** [C] a pipe or passage through which water or waste liquid flows away **2** [singular] something that uses a lot of something such as money or supplies

PHRASE **down the drain** *informal* completely lost or wasted: *That's three years' work down the drain!*

drainage /'dreɪnɪdʒ/ noun [U] a system of pipes and passages that take away water or waste liquid from an area, or the process of taking this waste away

drained /dreɪnd/ adj feeling as though you have no mental or physical energy left

draining board /'dreɪnɪŋ ,bɔːd/ noun [C] *British* the place next to the SINK in a kitchen where you leave wet dishes to dry —*picture* → C2

drainpipe /'dreɪn,paɪp/ noun [C] a pipe on the side of a building that carries RAINWATER from the roof to the ground —*picture* → C1

drama /'drɑːmə/ noun ★
1 [C] a play for the theatre, television, or radio
2 [U] plays in general or as a subject that you study: *He teaches drama.* ♦ *a drama course*
3 [C/U] something unusual or exciting that happens: *a game full of drama*

dramatic /drə'mætɪk/ adj ★
1 sudden and surprising, or easy to notice: *a dramatic increase in sales*
2 exciting and impressive: *a dramatic game*
3 dramatic behaviour is done to impress other people
4 relating to the theatre or plays
—**dramatically** /drə'mætɪkli/ adv

dramatics /drə'mætɪks/ noun [U] the activity of performing plays

dramatize /'dræmə,taɪz/ verb **1** [T] to make a book or story into a play **2** [I/T] to treat a situation as more serious or exciting than it really is —**dramatization** /,dræmətaɪ'zeɪʃ(ə)n/ noun [C/U]

drank the past tense of **drink**

drape /dreɪp/ verb [T] to put something made of cloth over or around something

drapes /dreɪps/ noun [plural] *American* curtains made of heavy cloth

drastic /'dræstɪk/ adj a drastic action or change has a very big effect —**drastically** /'dræstɪkli/ adv

draught¹ /drɑːft/ noun [C] cold air that blows into a room and makes you feel uncomfortable

draught² /drɑːft/ adj draught beer is served directly from a BARREL

draughts /drɑːfts/ noun [U] *British* a game for two people, played on a board with black and white squares, using 24 round pieces —*picture* → C16

draughtsman /'drɑːftsmən/ noun [C] someone whose job is to draw the plans for something that will be built or made

draughty /'drɑːfti/ adj a draughty place is uncomfortable because cold air blows into it

draw¹ /drɔː/ (past tense **drew** /druː/; past participle **drawn** /drɔːn/) verb ★★★

1 create picture	7 compare two things
2 move slowly/smoothly	8 make sb notice sth
3 pull sth	9 get particular reaction
4 take money	10 when neither side wins
5 choose sb/sth	+ PHRASES
6 get information from	+ PHRASAL VERBS

D

D

1 [I/T] to create a picture by making lines with a pen or pencil: *I can't draw faces very well.* ♦ *The kids drew on the pavement with chalk.*

2 [I] to move somewhere slowly or smoothly: *As we drew nearer, I noticed that the front door was open.*

3 [T] to pull something somewhere: *He drew a handkerchief out of his pocket.* ♦ *The curtains were still drawn at noon.*

4 [T] to take money from a bank account: *Customers can draw up to £250 a day from most accounts.*

5 [T] to choose someone or something from a group of similar things: *Elliot's name was drawn from over 200 entries.* ♦ *I drew two cards from the pack.*

6 [T] to get ideas, information, or knowledge from somewhere: **draw sth from sth** *She drew inspiration for her stories from her childhood.*

7 [T] to consider the ways in which two things are different or similar: *The writer drew comparisons between the two societies.*

8 [T] to make someone notice something: *My eyes were drawn to a painting over the fireplace.* ♦ *We tried to get in without drawing attention to ourselves.*

9 [T] to get a particular reaction from people: *The new exhibition has been drawing a lot of criticism.*

10 [I/T] *British* if two teams or opponents draw, or if they draw a match, they both have the same score, so that neither wins: *They drew 1–1 with Manchester United last week.*

PHRASES **draw a blank** to fail to find something, or to be unable to remember something

draw blood to make someone BLEED

draw a conclusion to decide what you believe about something after you have thought about all the facts

draw the line *informal* to say that you will definitely not allow or accept something: *I draw the line at breaking the law.*

draw to a close/an end to end

PHRASAL VERBS **draw on sth** to use something that you have gained or saved: *As an actor, you often draw on your own life experiences.*

draw sth out to make something continue for longer than usual

draw sth up to prepare and write something such as a document or plan: *Guidelines have been drawn up for dealing with emergencies.*

draw upon sth *same as* **draw on sth**

draw² /drɔː/ noun [C] ★

1 *British* a game in which both teams or players have the same number of points at the end, so that neither wins =TIE: *A last-minute goal earned Switzerland a 1–1 draw with Italy.*

2 a way of choosing something such as a name or number by chance

drawback /'drɔːˌbæk/ noun [C] a feature of something that makes it less useful than it could be: *The main drawback of the plan is its expense.*

drawer /'drɔːə/ noun [C] ★ a part of a piece

draw

sketch

trace

copy

of furniture that slides in and out and is used for keeping things in —*picture* → C2

drawing /'drɔːɪŋ/ noun ★★

1 [C] a picture that someone has drawn: *The children did drawings of themselves.*

2 [U] the activity or skill of making pictures with a pen or pencil: *I'm not very good at drawing.*

drawing board noun **go back to the drawing board** to try to think of a completely new idea because the one that you tried before was not successful

drawing pin noun [C] *British* a short pin with a flat top, used for fastening paper to a wall

drawing room noun [C] *old-fashioned* a LIVING ROOM

drawl /drɔːl/ noun [singular] a slow way of speaking, with long vowel sounds —**drawl** verb [I/T]

drawn¹ /drɔːn/ adj looking very tired, ill, or worried

drawn² /drɔːn/ the past participle of **draw**

drawn-out adj continuing for a long time so that you become bored: *a long-drawn out explanation*

dread¹ /dred/ verb [T] to feel very worried about something that could or will happen: *She started to dread seeing him.*

PHRASE I dread to think *spoken* used for saying that you are worried about a situation: *I dread to think what it will cost.*

dread² /dred/ noun [singular/U] fear of something bad that will or could happen: *The thought of making a speech fills me with dread.*

dreaded /ˈdredɪd/ adj *often humorous* a dreaded event, person, or thing is one that you do not want to happen or to see

dreadful /ˈdredf(ə)l/ adj **1** very unpleasant **2** used for emphasizing how bad something is

dreadfully /ˈdredf(ə)li/ adv **1** extremely **2** very severely

dreadlocks /ˈdred.lɒks/ noun [plural] twisted pieces of long hair, worn especially by RASTAFARIANS

dream¹ /driːm/ noun [C] ★★★
1 something that you experience in your mind while you are sleeping: *I had a strange dream last night.* ♦ *The idea came to him in a dream.*
2 something good that you hope that you will have or will achieve in the future: *a dream job/holiday/home* ♦ *She watched her dreams of success fade away.* ♦ *Finding my father again was a dream come true* (=something that you really wanted to happen).
PHRASES beyond your (wildest) dreams much better than you imagined or hoped
go/work like a dream to happen in the best way possible

dream² /driːm/ (past tense and past participle **dreamed** or **dreamt** /dremt/) verb [I/T] ★★
1 to experience things in your mind while you are sleeping: *I was dreaming about a black cat.* ♦ *+(that) He dreamt that he saw Rosa.*
2 to think about something that you hope to do: *dream of doing sth She had always dreamed of going to Africa.*
PHRASE would not dream of doing sth used for emphasizing that you would definitely not do something: *I wouldn't dream of asking him for money.*
PHRASAL VERB dream sth up to think of a new idea

dreamer /ˈdriːmə/ noun [C] someone who has a lot of ideas, but not very sensible ones

dreamt a past tense and past participle of **dream**

dreamy /ˈdriːmi/ adj showing that you are thinking about something pleasant rather than paying attention: *a dreamy look*

dreary /ˈdrɪəri/ adj making you feel bored or unhappy: *dreary weather*

dredge /dredʒ/ verb [T] to remove dirt from the bottom of a river or lake, often in order to look for something
PHRASAL VERB dredge sth up to tell people a secret from someone's past that they do not want other people to know about

dregs /dregz/ noun [plural] **1** the small solid pieces that are left in the bottom of a container of liquid: *dregs of coffee* **2** *informal* the least important or valuable part of something: *the dregs of society*

drench /drentʃ/ verb [T] to make someone or

something very wet —**drenched** /drentʃt/ adj

dress¹ /dres/ verb ★★★
1 [I] to put clothes on yourself or on someone else: *It only took her ten minutes to shower and dress.*
2 [I] to wear clothes of a particular type: *He tends to dress in dark colours.* ♦ *The nurses dressed as clowns for Halloween.*
3 [T] to clean an injury and cover it with a piece of soft cloth
PHRASAL VERBS dress up 1 to put on clothes that make you look like someone else, for fun: *They had dressed up as princes and princesses.* **2** to put on clothes that are more formal than the clothes that you usually wear: *Do I have to dress up for dinner?*
dress down to put on clothes that are more informal than the clothes that you usually wear

get dressed

be dressed in/
be wearing

put on

dress² /dres/ noun ★★
1 [C] a piece of clothing that covers a woman's body and part of her legs: *a blue cotton dress* —*picture* → C4
2 [U] the type of clothes that are typical of a particular place, time in history, or occasion: *traditional Norwegian dress* → CLOTHES

dressed /drest/ adj **1** wearing clothes of a particular type: *She was dressed in a black suit.* ♦ *a well-dressed man* **2** someone who is dressed is wearing clothes ≠ UNDRESSED: *Just a minute, I'm not dressed yet.*
PHRASE get dressed to put your clothes on: *I got dressed and went downstairs.*

dresser /ˈdresə/ noun [C] *British* a large piece of furniture with drawers and cupboards at the bottom and shelves on top

dressing /ˈdresɪŋ/ noun **1** [C/U] a mixture of liquids that you pour over salad **2** [C] a piece of material that is used for protecting a skin injury

dressing gown noun [C] *British* a piece of clothing like a long loose coat that you wear in your house —*picture* → C5

dressing room noun [C] a room that is used by a performer or sports players for preparing for a performance or game

dressing table noun [C] a piece of bedroom

furniture consisting of a table or set of drawers and a mirror

'dress re,hearsal noun [C] the last occasion when performers practise before a concert, play etc

dressy /'dresi/ adj dressy clothes are worn on formal occasions

drew the past tense of **draw**[1]

dribble /'drɪb(ə)l/ verb **1** [I/T] if a liquid dribbles, or if you dribble it, it flows slowly in small drops **2** [I/T] to move forwards with a ball by kicking or BOUNCING it —*picture* → C15 **3** [I] *British* if you dribble, SALIVA (=the liquid in your mouth) comes out onto your chin —**dribble** noun [C/U]

dried /draɪd/ adj dried food, milk, or flowers have had the water removed from them

drier /'draɪə/ another spelling of **dryer**

drift[1] /drɪft/ verb [I] **1** to be pushed along slowly by the movement of air or water: *The boat started to drift out to sea.* **2** to do something or happen in a way that is not planned: *I just drifted into nursing really.* **3** to move somewhere slowly as though you do not know where you are going: *For three months, Paul drifted from town to town.* **4** if snow or sand drifts, the wind blows it into a large pile

PHRASAL VERBS **drift a'part** if two or more people drift apart, their relationship gradually ends

drift 'off to start to sleep

drift[2] /drɪft/ noun **1** [C] a large pile of snow or sand that has been formed by the wind **2** [singular] a slow gradual change or movement **3** [singular] *informal* the meaning that someone is trying to express: *Do you get my drift?*

drill[1] /drɪl/ noun **1** [C] a tool that is used for making a hole in something —*picture* → TOOL **2** [C/U] a way of teaching people something by making them repeat it several times

drill[2] /drɪl/ verb **1** [I/T] to make a hole using a drill: *Drill two holes in the wall.* **2** [T] to teach someone by making them repeat something many times

drily /'draɪli/ adv in a way that expresses humour while appearing to be serious

drink[1] /drɪŋk/ (past tense **drank** /dræŋk/; past participle **drunk** /drʌŋk/) verb ★★★
1 [I/T] to take liquid into your body through your mouth: *Drink your juice, Thomas.* ♦ *Rosie drank thirstily from the mug.* → TAKE **2** [I] to drink alcohol, especially regularly or too often: *Dan had been out drinking with his friends.* ♦ *My parents don't drink.*
PHRASAL VERBS **drink to sb/sth** to express a wish for health, happiness, or success, then lift your glass and drink from it: *We will now drink a toast to the bride and groom.*

drink (sth) 'up to drink all of your drink

drink[2] /drɪŋk/ noun [C/U] ★★★
1 an amount of liquid that someone drinks, or drinks in general: *They had had no food or drink all day.* ♦ *I need a drink of water.*
2 an alcoholic drink, or alcohol in general: *We went for a drink after work.*

,**drink-'driving** noun [U] *British* driving after you have drunk too much alcohol

drinker /'drɪŋkə/ noun [C] **1** someone who

often drinks alcohol: *a heavy drinker* (=someone who drinks a lot of alcohol) **2** someone who often drinks a particular drink: *tea/beer/wine drinker*

drinking /'drɪŋkɪŋ/ noun [U] the activity of drinking alcohol

'**drinking ,water** noun [U] water that is safe to drink

drip[1] /drɪp/ verb **1** [I/T] if a liquid drips, or if you drip it somewhere, it falls in very small drops: *Red paint had dripped on the floor.*
2 [I] to produce small drops of liquid: *The tap was dripping.*

drip   gush

drip[2] /drɪp/ noun [C] **1** a small drop of liquid that falls from something, or the sound or action of it falling **2** a piece of equipment that is used for putting a liquid such as medicine directly into your body

dripping /'drɪpɪŋ/ adj very wet

drive[1] /draɪv/ (past tense **drove** /drəʊv/; past participle **driven** /'drɪv(ə)n/) verb ★★★

1 control vehicle	6 make sb work/try hard
2 take sb in vehicle	7 make sb determined
3 force into bad state	8 push sth strongly
4 force sb to leave	+ PHRASES
5 provide power to move	+ PHRASAL VERBS

1 [I/T] to control a vehicle so that it moves somewhere, or to go somewhere by doing this: *Usually, my sister drives and I read the map.* ♦ *You will drive carefully, won't you?* ♦ *He drove along for several miles before he saw anyone.* ♦ *We're driving to Italy this year.*

2 [T] to take someone somewhere in a vehicle that you drive: **drive sb to/from sth** *Lee drove me to the airport.*

3 [T] to force someone or something into a bad situation or state: *Supermarkets are driving small shops out of business.* ♦ *Would you be quiet – you're driving me mad!*

4 [T] to force someone to leave the place where they live: **drive sb from/out of sth** *Thousands of people have been driven from their homes by the fighting.*

5 [T] to provide the power that makes something move: *The pump is driven by an electric motor.*

6 [T] to make someone work or try very hard: *The coach really drives his team.*

7 [T] to make someone determined to do something: *What drives her to succeed?*

8 [T] to push, hit or kick something using a lot of force: *He drove the nail into the wall.*

PHRASES **drive a hard bargain** to be very firm when you are making an agreement or a deal

what sb is driving at what someone is really trying to say

PHRASAL VERBS **drive sb a'way** to make someone stop wanting something: *Increasing your prices will only drive customers away.*

drive 'off 1 if a vehicle or driver drives off, the vehicle starts moving and leaves **2** to force someone to go away, especially when they are attacking or threatening you

- **Drive** means to move and control a vehicle such as a car or truck: *Do you walk or drive to work?* ♦ *He drives a bus.*
- **Ride** means to move and control a bicycle or horse. You can also **ride** in a vehicle that is controlled by someone else: *She rides her bike to school.* ♦ *We rode all over town on the bus.*

drive² /draɪv/ noun ★★

1 journey in car	6 feeling causing action
2 wide path for car	7 effort to achieve sth
3 used in street names	8 hard hit/kick of ball
4 part of computer	9 power from engine
5 determination	

1 [C] a journey in a car: *The hotel is only 10 minutes' drive from the airport.* ♦ *We went for a drive in Jack's new car.*
2 [C] *British* a wide path for a car that joins someone's house to a street: *There was a strange car parked in the drive.* —picture → C1
3 Drive used in the names of streets: *25 Oakwood Drive*
4 [C] *computing* a part of a computer that reads and stores information: *a floppy/hard/CD-ROM drive*
5 [U] the energy and determination that makes you try hard to achieve something: *I admire her drive and ambition.*
6 [C] a feeling that makes you act in a particular way: *the human sex drive*
7 [C] a big effort to achieve something, especially by a company or government: *The company is launching a major recruitment drive.*
8 [C] a hard hit or kick of a ball
9 [U] the power from an engine that turns the wheels of a vehicle: *front-wheel drive*
'drive-by noun [C] an act of shooting someone from a moving car —**'drive-by** adj
'drive-in noun [C] *American* a cinema or restaurant where you sit in your car to watch a film or eat a meal —**'drive-in** adj
drivel /'drɪv(ə)l/ noun [U] stupid and unimportant things that someone says or writes
driven the past participle of **drive¹**
driver /'draɪvə/ noun [C] ★★★ someone who drives a vehicle, especially as their job: *a taxi driver*
'drive-through noun [C] a restaurant, bank etc that serves you through a special window, so that you do not have to leave your car —**'drive-through** adj
driveway /'draɪvˌweɪ/ noun [C] a DRIVE in front of someone's house
driving /'draɪvɪŋ/ adj **1** driving snow or rain falls very fast **2** having a strong influence, or making something happen: *Williams was the driving force behind the business.*

driving 'licence noun [C] *British* an official document that you need in order to drive
drizzle /'drɪz(ə)l/ noun [singular/U] very light rain —**drizzle** verb [I]
drone¹ /drəʊn/ verb [I] to make a low continuous noise
PHRASAL VERB **drone 'on** to talk about something for a long time in a very boring way
drone² /drəʊn/ noun [singular] a low continuous sound
drool /druːl/ verb [I] **1** to look at someone or something with great pleasure **2** to let SALIVA (=the liquid in your mouth) come out of your mouth
droop /druːp/ verb [I] **1** to hang downwards: *The leaves were drooping in the heat.* **2** to become tired, weak, or unhappy
drop¹ /drɒp/ verb ★★★

1 let sth fall	6 not continue with sth
2 fall	7 not include sth/sb
3 reduce/get less	8 speak less loudly
4 take sb somewhere	+ PHRASES
5 take sth somewhere	+ PHRASAL VERBS

1 [T] to let something fall: *The box was so heavy I almost dropped it.* ♦ **drop sth off sth** *The children were dropping stones off the bridge.* ♦ **drop sth into sth** *He dropped a few coins into my hand.*
2 [I] to fall: *She took off her jacket and let it drop to the floor.* ♦ *Everyone cheered as the ball dropped into the hole.* ♦ *Teresa dropped into the chair, exhausted.*
3 [I/T] to reduce the amount or rate of something, or to fall to a lower amount or rate: *We had to drop the price of our house to sell it.* ♦ *Be sure to drop your speed in wet weather.* ♦ *In winter the temperature often drops below freezing.*
4 [T] to take someone to a place in a car: *I'm driving into town – can I drop you somewhere?* ♦ **drop sb at/in** *Can you drop me at the corner of the street?*
5 [T] to take something to a place and not stay there very long: *Can you drop these magazines at Nora's house?*
6 [T] to stop doing something: *In Year 10 you can drop geography or history.* ♦ *He told me to drop everything and come over straight away.* ♦ *To her relief, Julius dropped the subject* (=stopped talking about it).
7 [T] to not include something or someone: *Rogers has been dropped from the team because of a knee injury.*
8 [I/T] if you drop your voice, or if your voice drops, you speak less loudly
PHRASES **drop dead** *informal* to die suddenly and unexpectedly: *He dropped dead of a heart attack.*
drop a hint/hints to say something in an indirect way
drop sb a line/note to write a short letter to someone
→ FLY²
PHRASAL VERBS **drop 'back 1** to fall to a lower amount or rate: *Economic growth will drop back to 3% this year.* **2** to start walking, running, driving etc behind other people in a group or race
drop be'hind *same as* **drop back 2**

D

,drop 'by or **,drop 'in** *informal* to make a short
visit somewhere: *Why don't you drop by for
coffee some time?*

,drop 'off to become weaker or smaller in
amount: *Her popularity has dropped off
recently.*

,drop sb 'off *same as* **drop**[1] 4: *Can you drop
the kids off at school this morning?*

,drop sth 'off 1 *same as* **drop**[1] 5

,drop 'out to leave something before you have
finished what you intended to do: *Too many
students drop out of college after only one
year.*

drop² /drɒp/ noun [C] ★

1 a very small amount of liquid with a
round shape: *a tear drop* ♦ *There were drops
of blood on his arm.*

2 a fall in the amount or value of something:
*The company announced a 15% drop in
profits.* ♦ *There was a sharp drop in
temperature during the night.*

3 a distance down to the ground from a high
place: *At the edge of the cliff is a 100-metre
drop.*

PHRASES **at the drop of a hat** immediately
a drop in the ocean a very small amount that
will not have much effect

'drop-down ,menu noun [C] *computing* a list of
choices on your computer screen that goes
away when you choose one

'drop-in ,centre noun [C] a place where people
can go to get information or help without
having to make an arrangement first

droplet /'drɒplət/ noun [C] a very small drop
of liquid

droppings /'drɒpɪŋz/ noun [plural] the FAECES
(=solid waste) of animals or birds

drought /draʊt/ noun [C/U] a long period of
time when there is little or no rain

drove the past tense of **drive**[1]

drown /draʊn/ verb ★

1 [I] to sink under water and die: *Thirty
people drowned when the boat sank in a
storm.*

2 [T] to kill someone by pushing them under
water

3 [T] to cover something completely with a
liquid: *shellfish drowned in a spicy sauce*

4 [T] *same as* **drown sth out**

PHRASAL VERB **,drown sth 'out** to prevent a
sound from being heard by making a louder
noise: *The music almost drowned out the
sound of his voice.*

drowsy /'draʊzi/ adj feeling that you want to
sleep —**drowsily** adv

drudgery /'drʌdʒəri/ noun [U] boring and
unpleasant work

drug¹ /drʌg/ noun [C] ★★★

1 an illegal substance that affects someone
physically or mentally when they put it
into their body: *drug smuggling* ♦ *a drug
addict* (=someone who cannot stop using
illegal drugs) ♦ *She had never taken drugs
in her life.* ♦ *He acted as if he was on drugs*
(=had taken drugs).

2 a substance that a doctor gives you in
order to treat a disease or medical problem:
*Your doctor may prescribe drugs for this
condition.* ♦ *a new anti-cancer drug*

drug² /drʌg/ verb [T] to give a drug to someone
so that they will go to sleep or become
unconscious

drugstore /'drʌgstɔː/ noun [C] *American* a
CHEMIST'S

drum¹ /drʌm/ noun [C] ★

1 a musical instrument that consists of a
tight skin stretched over a round frame.
You hit it with your hands or a stick.
—*picture* → PERCUSSION

2 a large round container for liquids: *an oil
drum*

drum² /drʌm/ verb **1** [I/T] to make a
continuous sound by hitting a surface **2** [I]
to play a drum —**drumming** noun [U]

PHRASAL VERBS **,drum sth into sb** to make
someone learn or understand something by
repeating it many times

,drum sth 'up to try to make people support
you or buy something from you: *They've
been in London trying to drum up business.*

drummer /'drʌmə/ noun [C] someone who
plays the drums

drunk¹ /drʌŋk/ adj ★ unable to control your
actions or behaviour because you have
drunk too much alcohol ≠ SOBER: *Everyone
else was getting drunk and enjoying
themselves.* ♦ *Andrew came home blind
drunk* (=very drunk).

drunk² /drʌŋk/ noun [C] *showing disapproval*
someone who has drunk too much alcohol
or who regularly drinks too much alcohol

drunk³ the past participle of **drink**[1]

drunkard /'drʌŋkəd/ noun [C] *showing
disapproval* a DRUNK

drunken /'drʌŋkən/ adj *showing disapproval* **1** a
drunken person is drunk **2** involving or
affecting someone who is drunk —**drunkenly**
adv, **drunkenness** noun [U]

dry¹ /draɪ/ adj ★★★

1 with no water in/on it	**5** food: with little liquid
2 without rain	**6** joking in serious way
3 no longer liquid	**7** boring/serious
4 hair/skin: rough	

1 something that is dry has little or no water
or other liquid inside or on it ≠ WET: *Are
your hands dry?* ♦ *Vegetables should be
stored in a cool dry place.*

2 with no rain ≠ WET: *warm dry places like
southern Spain* ♦ *Tomorrow will be mostly
dry.* ♦ *The weather is usually dry and sunny
at this time of year.*

3 when a liquid such as paint is dry, it has
become hard or solid ≠ WET: *Someone
walked on the concrete before it was dry.*

4 dry hair or skin feels rough ≠ GREASY

5 dry food contains little or no liquid: *The
chicken was overcooked and dry.* ♦ *dry bread*

6 dry humour involves saying funny things
in a serious way

7 very serious and boring: *The style was a
little too dry for a children's book.*
—**dryness** noun [U]

dry² /draɪ/ verb ★★

1 [T] to remove the water from something
by wiping it, heating it, or blowing air onto
it: *We washed and dried all the sheets.* ♦ *Dry
your hands on this towel.*

2 [I] to become dry: *I usually let my hair dry
naturally.*

3 [T] to remove the water from food or plants
as a way of preserving them: *dried
fruit/herbs/flowers*

4 [I] when a liquid such as paint dries, it becomes hard or solid: *Leave the varnish to dry overnight.*

→ CUT¹

PHRASAL VERBS ,dry (yourself/sth) 'off if something dries off, or if you dry it off, all the water comes out of it or is wiped from its surface: *My boots dried off in the sun.* ✦ *He got out of the shower and dried himself off.*

,dry (sth) 'out if something dries out, or if it is dried out, some or all the water comes out of it: *Water the plant regularly to stop the soil from drying out.*

,dry 'up to stop being available: *What will happen when the money dries up?*

,dry (sth) 'up if something dries up, or if it is dried up, all the water comes out of it: *The land had dried up and no crops would grow.*

dry-'clean verb [T] to clean clothes using chemicals rather than water

dry 'cleaner's noun [singular] a shop where you take your clothes to be dry-cleaned

dryer /'draɪə/ noun [C] a machine that dries things such as clothes or hair

dry 'land noun [U] land, rather than the sea

dryly /'draɪli/ another spelling of **drily**

DSL noun [U] *computing* digital subscriber line: a way of connecting to the Internet that allows a very fast exchange of information using ordinary phone connections

dual /'dju:əl/ adj with two aspects, parts, or uses: *a dual role*

dual 'carriageway noun [C] *British* a road with two or more lines of traffic going in each direction

dub¹ /dʌb/ verb [T] **1** *mainly journalism* to give someone or something a particular name: *The press have dubbed her 'the Quiet Princess'.* **2** to change the sound in a film by replacing the original speech with words spoken in a different language

dub² /dʌb/ noun [U] an electronic type of music based on REGGAE music

dubious /'dju:biəs/ adj **1** not completely good, safe, or honest: *a dubious reputation* **2** not sure about something: *I'm dubious about his ability to do the job.* **3** used for saying that something is the opposite of the good thing that you are describing it as: *a dubious honour/pleasure/distinction*
—**dubiously** adv

duchess /'dʌtʃɪs/ noun [C] a woman who has the same position as a DUKE, or the wife of a duke

duck¹ /dʌk/ noun **1** [C] a water bird with short legs and a large flat beak —*picture* → C12 **2** [U] the meat of a duck

duck² /dʌk/ verb **1** [I/T] to lower your head and body quickly, in order to move under something or to avoid being hit: *He ducked to avoid the blow.* **2** [I] to move quickly into or behind something to avoid being seen: *She ducked behind the wall.* **3** [T] to avoid something that is difficult: *Stop trying to duck the issue – who paid you for this?*

PHRASAL VERB ,duck 'out of sth to avoid doing something that you were intending to do or promised to do

duckling /'dʌklɪŋ/ noun [C] a young duck

duct /dʌkt/ noun [C] **1** a narrow tube inside

your body that carries liquid: *tear ducts* **2** a tube in a building that carries air or protects wires: *air-conditioning ducts*

dud /dʌd/ adj *British* broken, useless, or not working correctly —**dud** noun [C]

dude /du:d/ noun [C] *American informal* a man

due¹ /dju:/ adj ★★★

1 expected to happen or to be somewhere: *Her baby is due in May* (=expected to be born). ✦ *I'm due at a meeting in ten minutes.* ✦ **due to do sth** *The case is due to go to court next month.* ✦ *The prisoners are not due for release until next year.*

2 if money is due, it is time for it to be paid: *The rent is due on the first day of each month.*

3 according to the usual standards or rules: *A driver has to have due regard for the safety of other road users.*

4 if something is due to someone, they should receive it: *Some credit is due to the government for this improvement.*

PHRASES **in due course** *formal* later, when it is the right time, and not before

with (all) due respect used when you are going to disagree with someone or criticize someone, in order to sound more polite

→ DUE TO

due² /dju:/ noun **1** [singular] something that someone has a right to receive: *At last she has the justice that is her due.* **2 dues** [plural] money that someone pays regularly to be a member of a club or union

PHRASE **to give sb their due** used when you are going to say something good about someone, after you have been criticizing them

due³ /dju:/ adv **due north/south/east/west** directly towards the north, south, east, or west

duel /'dju:əl/ noun [C] **1** *mainly journalism* a competition or fight between two people or teams **2** a fight between two men with guns or swords —**duel** verb [I]

duet /dju:'et/ noun [C] a piece of music that is sung or played by two people

due to /'dju: tu:/ preposition ★★★ because of something: *We had problems due to poor management.* ✦ *These fears are usually due to ignorance.*

dug the past tense and past participle of **dig¹**

dugout /'dʌgaʊt/ noun [C] **1** a hole or tunnel in the ground, used as a shelter by soldiers during a battle **2** a small shelter by the side of a sports field

duke /dju:k/ noun [C] a man with a very high social position, just below that of a PRINCE

dull¹ /dʌl/ adj ★

1 boring	**4** low and not clear
2 not bright/shiny	**5** not sharp
3 weak and continuous	

1 boring, or not interesting: *Life in a small village can be very dull.* ✦ *a dull lecture*
2 not bright or shiny: *hair that looks dull and lifeless* ✦ *a dull colour*
3 a dull pain is not very strong but continues for a long time
4 a dull sound is low and not very clear
5 a dull blade is not sharp

dull² /dʌl/ verb [T] to make something slower

or weaker: *The drug is used to dull the pain.*

duly /'djuːli/ adv *formal* in a way that is correct or suitable

dumb¹ /dʌm/ adj **1** *informal* stupid **2** *old-fashioned* unable to speak. People now think that this word is offensive and prefer to use the expression **speech impaired**.

dumb² /dʌm/ PHRASAL VERB dumb (sth) 'down to spoil something by trying to make it easier to understand or more popular

dumbfounded /dʌm'faʊndɪd/ adj so surprised that you do not know what to do or say

dummy¹ /'dʌmi/ noun [C] **1** something that is made to look like a real object **2** a model of a person's body **3** *British* a small plastic or rubber object that a baby sucks **4** *informal* someone who is not very intelligent

dummy² /'dʌmi/ adj designed to look real but in fact not real: *a dummy company*

dump¹ /dʌmp/ verb [T] **1** to get rid of something that you no longer want or need: *Waste chemicals were being dumped into the sea.* **2** *informal* to put something somewhere in a careless way: *She dumped her bags on the floor.* **3** *informal* to end a sexual or romantic relationship with someone in an unkind way

dump² /dʌmp/ noun [C] **1** a place where large amounts of rubbish are taken **2** *informal* a place that is dirty or unpleasant
PHRASE (down) in the dumps *informal* feeling unhappy

dumpling /'dʌmplɪŋ/ noun [C] a small solid lump of cooked food made from flour and water

dune /djuːn/ noun [C] a hill of sand that has been formed by the wind or sea = SAND DUNE

dung /dʌŋ/ noun [U] waste from the body of a large animal

dungarees /ˌdʌŋɡə'riːz/ noun [plural] *British* a piece of clothing consisting of trousers and a square piece of cloth that covers the chest —*picture* → C4

dungeon /'dʌndʒ(ə)n/ noun [C] a dark underground room in a castle that was used as a prison in the past

dunk /dʌŋk/ verb [T] to put something into liquid for a short time before taking it out again

dunno /də'nəʊ/ short form a way of writing 'don't know' that shows how it sounds in informal conversation

duo /'djuːəʊ/ noun [C] two people who perform together or do something else together

dupe¹ /djuːp/ verb [T] to trick someone into believing or doing something stupid or illegal

dupe² /djuːp/ noun [C] someone who is tricked into believing or doing something stupid or illegal

duplicate¹ /'djuːplɪˌkeɪt/ verb [T] **1** to make an exact copy of something such as a document **2** to create a situation that is exactly like another one

duplicate² /'djuːplɪkət/ adj made as an exact copy of something else —**duplicate** noun [C]

duplication /ˌdjuːplɪ'keɪʃ(ə)n/ noun [U] **1** a situation in which one thing has the same

purpose or effect as another **2** the process of making an exact copy of something

durable /'djʊərəb(ə)l/ adj **1** able to stay in good condition for a long time, even after being used a lot **2** continuing to exist or be effective for a long time —**durability** /ˌdjʊərə'bɪləti/ noun [U]

duration /djʊ'reɪʃ(ə)n/ noun [C/U] the period of time during which something continues to happen or exist

duress /djʊ'res/ noun **under duress** *formal* if you do something under duress, you do it because someone has forced or threatened you

during /'djʊərɪŋ/ preposition ★★★
1 at one point within a period of time: *During his visit to South Africa, the president met Archbishop Tutu.*
2 through the whole of a period of time: *Many creatures stay underground during daylight hours.*

dusk /dʌsk/ noun [U] the period of time at the end of the day just before it gets dark

dusky /'dʌski/ adj *literary* fairly dark

dust¹ /dʌst/ noun [U] ★ very small pieces of dirt or another substance that form a layer on a surface or a cloud in the air: *The books were old and covered in dust.* ♦ *He drove off, leaving us in a cloud of dust.*
PHRASE **let the dust settle** to wait for a situation to become calm or normal again after something exciting or unusual has happened

dust² /dʌst/ verb **1** [I/T] to wipe the dust off the surface of something such as furniture **2** [T] to put a thin layer of powder on something
PHRASAL VERB dust sth 'off to wipe dust or dirt off the surface of something

dustbin /'dʌs(t)bɪn/ noun [C] *British* a container that you keep outside and use for putting rubbish in

duster /'dʌstə/ noun [C] a cloth for removing dust from furniture

'dust ˌjacket or **'dust ˌcover** noun [C] a loose paper cover for a book

dustman /'dʌs(t)mən/ (plural **dustmen** /'dʌs(t)mən/) noun [C] *British* a man whose job is to collect the rubbish from outside people's houses

dustpan /'dʌs(t)pæn/ noun [C] a small flat container that you put on the floor and brush dirt into

dusty /'dʌsti/ adj **1** covered with dust **2** covered with dry soil or sand

dutiful /'djuːtɪf(ə)l/ adj *formal* careful to do things that other people ask or expect you to do —**dutifully** adv

duty /'djuːti/ noun [C/U] ★★★
1 something that you should do as a legal or moral obligation: **sb's duty to do sth** *It is your duty as a parent to protect your children.* ♦ *The company **has a duty** to its shareholders.* ♦ *I was simply **doing my duty** as a good citizen.*
2 a tax that you must pay on something that you buy, or on something that you bring into one country from another
PHRASES **off duty** not working at that moment: *I was off duty when they called me in.*

on duty working at that moment: *The nurse on duty called for a doctor.*

duty-free[1] adj duty-free goods are cheaper than the usual price because you do not pay any tax on them —**duty-free** adv

duty-free[2] noun [U] goods such as cigarettes and alcohol that you buy without paying tax on them

duvet /'du:veɪ/ noun [C] *British* a warm cover for your bed, consisting of a large cloth bag that is filled with feathers or a soft material

DVD /,di: vi: 'di:/ noun [C] an object like a CD that has a film or television programme recorded on it

dwarf[1] /dwɔːf/ (plural **dwarves** /dwɔːvz/ or **dwarfs**) noun [C] an imaginary creature in children's stories that looks like a very small old man

dwarf[2] /dwɔːf/ adj a dwarf tree, plant, or animal is much shorter or smaller than others of the same type

dwarf[3] /dwɔːf/ verb [T] to make someone or something seem small or unimportant

dwell /dwel/ (past tense and past participle **dwelled** or **dwelt** /dwelt/) verb [I] *literary* to live somewhere

PHRASAL VERB **'dwell on sth** to spend a lot of time thinking or talking about something unpleasant

dweller /'dwelə/ noun [C] someone who lives in a particular type of place: *a city/country/cave dweller*

dwelling /'dwelɪŋ/ noun [C] *formal* a building that someone lives in

dwindle /'dwɪnd(ə)l/ verb [I] to get gradually less or smaller over a period of time until almost nothing remains

dye[1] /daɪ/ noun [C/U] a substance that is used for changing the colour of something such as cloth or hair

dye[2] /daɪ/ (present participle **dyeing**; past tense and past participle **dyed**) verb [T] to change the colour of something such as cloth or hair using dye

dying[1] /'daɪɪŋ/ adj not likely to exist or exist for much longer: *a dying man*

dying[2] the present participle of **die**

dyke /daɪk/ noun [C] a wall that prevents a river, a lake, or the sea from flooding the land

dynamic /daɪ'næmɪk/ adj **1** very lively and enthusiastic, with a lot of energy and determination: *dynamic leadership* **2** continuously changing, growing, or developing: *a dynamic process/situation/business* —**dynamically** /daɪ'næmɪkli/ adv

dynamite /'daɪnə,maɪt/ noun [U] **1** a substance that is used for causing explosions **2** *informal* someone or something that is very impressive or exciting

dynamo /'daɪnə,məʊ/ noun [C] **1** a piece of equipment that changes the movement of a machine into electricity **2** *informal* someone with a lot of energy and determination

dynasty /'dɪnəsti/ noun [C] **1** a family whose members rule a country or region for a long time **2** a family whose members are very successful in business or politics for a long time —**dynastic** /dɪ'næstɪk/ adj

dysentery /'dɪs(ə)ntri/ noun [U] a serious disease that causes severe DIARRHOEA

dysfunctional /dɪs'fʌŋkʃ(ə)nəl/ adj dysfunctional relationships do not work well and are not happy or successful

dyslexia /dɪs'leksiə/ noun [U] a medical condition that makes it difficult for someone to read, write, and spell words correctly —**dyslexic** /dɪs'leksɪk/ adj

Ee

e or **E** /iː/ noun **1** [C/U] the fifth letter of the English alphabet **2** E [C/U] *informal* the illegal drug ECSTASY **3** E [C] *British* a mark that shows that a student's work is very bad

E /iː/ abbrev **1** East **2** Eastern

e- /iː/ prefix on or using the Internet: *e-learning ♦ e-business*

each /iːtʃ/ grammar word ★★★

> **Each** can be:
> ■ a **determiner**: *in each corner of the room*
> ■ a **pronoun**: *three windows, with a different view from each ♦ I want each of you to fill out an application.*

used for referring to all the people or things in a group, when you are thinking about every one separately: *Each child will read a poem to the group. ♦ The United States, Russia, and Germany each won two gold medals. ♦ New batteries cost £3.50 each. ♦ I locked all the doors and then checked each one again. ♦ Each of us has a job to do.*

each 'other pronoun ★★★

1 used for saying that each person or thing does something to the other or others: *The women looked at each other.*
2 used for saying that each person or thing is related in the same way to the other or others: *Suitcases were piled on top of each other.*

> You can use **one another** with the same meaning as **each other**.

eager /'iːgə/ adj very keen to do something, or excited about something that is going to happen: *The girls were eager for new experiences. ♦* **eager to do sth** *He's so eager to learn that he stays late every evening.* —**eagerly** adv: *the most eagerly awaited film of the year* —**eagerness** noun [U]

eagle /'iːg(ə)l/ noun [C] a large bird that eats other animals

eagle-eyed /,iːg(ə)l 'aɪd/ adj able to see things that are very difficult to see

ear /ɪə/ noun ★★★

1 [C] one of the two parts at the sides of your head that you hear with —*picture* → C14
2 [singular] the ability to hear and judge sounds: *She has a very good ear for music.*
3 [C] the part at the top of a plant such as wheat that contains the grain: *ears of corn*

PHRASES **be all ears** *informal* to be ready to pay attention to what someone has to say

play it by ear to deal with a situation without having a plan, by reacting to things as they happen

earache /'ɪəreɪk/ noun [C/U] pain in your ear

eardrum /'ɪədrʌm/ noun [C] the part inside your ear that VIBRATES when sound reaches it

earl /ɜːl/ noun [C] a man with a very high social position in the UK

earlier /'ɜːliə/ adv used for referring to a time before the present or before the time that you are talking about: *A few days earlier, he had been in London.* —**earlier** adj: *an earlier period in history*

earliest, the /'ɜːliəst/ noun [singular] the earliest time that something can happen or be done: *The earliest we could be there is 7.30.*

earlobe /'ɪələʊb/ noun [C] the soft part at the bottom of your ear

early¹ /'ɜːli/ adj ★★★
1 near the beginning of a period of time ≠ LATE: *the early 19th century* ♦ *Julia is in her early thirties.* ♦ *It's too early to say what will happen.*
2 before the time that something usually happens or is expected to happen ≠ LATE: *Spring was early that year.* ♦ *My train was ten minutes early.* ♦ *I think I'll have an* **early night** (=go to bed earlier than usual).
3 used about the first people or things of a particular type: *The early settlers used to heat their cabins with coal.*
PHRASES **the early hours** the period of time between midnight and the very early morning
it's early days *spoken* used for saying that it is too soon to know whether someone or something will be successful
→ EARLIEST

early² /'ɜːli/ adv ★★★
1 before the usual or expected time ≠ LATE: *I don't get up very early.* ♦ *The flight arrived ten minutes early.*
2 near the beginning of a period of time ≠ LATE: *Let's meet again early next week.* ♦ *He showed great musical talent very* **early** *in life.*
3 near the beginning of a piece of writing ≠ LATE: *This point was discussed earlier in the chapter.*
4 soon enough to avoid problems: *If we begin treatment early, we have a better chance of success.*

early bird noun [C] *informal* someone who gets up early in the morning, or who does something before other people do

earmark /'ɪəmɑːk/ verb [T] to decide to use an amount of money for a particular purpose: *Part of the housing budget is earmarked for regenerating urban areas.*

earn /ɜːn/ verb ★★
1 [I/T] to receive money for work that you do: *Most people here earn about £30,000 a year.* ♦ *She* **earns a good living** *as a financial adviser* (=she gets a good salary).
2 [T] to make a profit from business or from money that you have in the bank: *The company earned profits of £14.9 million last year.*

3 [T] to get something as a result of your efforts or your behaviour: *Have a good rest now – you've earned it.* ♦ *You have to* **earn** *your employees' respect.*

earner /'ɜːnə/ noun [C] **1** someone who earns money by working: *a wage earner*
2 something that earns money: *Tourism is a major earner of foreign currency.*

earnest /'ɜːnɪst/ adj serious, determined, and sincere
PHRASE **in earnest 1** with more energy or determination than before: *After the rainy season, building work can begin in earnest.*
2 serious, and meaning what you say
—**earnestly** adv

earnings /'ɜːnɪŋz/ noun [plural] **1** the amount of money that you earn **2** the profit made by a company

earphones /'ɪəfəʊnz/ noun [plural] a piece of equipment that you wear over your ears to listen to recorded sound = HEADPHONES

earplug /'ɪəplʌg/ noun [C] a small object that you put in your ear to keep noise or water out

earring /'ɪərɪŋ/ noun [C] a piece of jewellery that you wear on your ear —*picture*
→ JEWELLERY

earshot /'ɪəʃɒt/ noun
PHRASES **out of earshot** too far away for you to hear
within/in earshot close enough for you to hear

ear-splitting adj extremely loud

earth /ɜːθ/ noun ★★★
1 **Earth** or **earth** [singular/U] the planet on which we live: *the planet Earth* ♦ *the Earth's surface* ♦ *the origins of life* **on Earth**
2 **the earth** [singular] the land on which we live: *They felt the earth shake.*
3 [U] the substance in which plants grow, that covers most of the land: *Cover the seeds with earth, then water them.*
4 [singular] *British* the wire in a piece of electrical equipment that makes it safe by connecting it to the ground
PHRASES **come/be brought back down to earth** to start normal life again after a time of great excitement or happiness
cost/pay the earth *British informal* to cost/pay a very large amount of money
on earth used for emphasizing that someone or something is the best, worst, biggest etc in the world: *the largest man-made structure on earth*
on/from the face of the earth on/from the whole of the earth
what/why/how/where on earth *spoken* used for adding emphasis to questions: *Why on earth would I want to work for you?*

earthenware /'ɜːθənweə/ noun [U] bowls, cups etc that are made of baked clay

earthly /'ɜːθli/ adj used for giving emphasis to negative statements or to questions: *There's no earthly reason why we should pay.*

earthquake /'ɜːθkweɪk/ noun [C] a sudden shaking movement of the ground

earth science noun [C/U] a science that involves studying the Earth

earthworm /'ɜːθwɜːm/ noun [C] a type of WORM that lives in soil

earthy /ˈɜːθi/ adj **1** looking or smelling like earth **2** showing an attitude to sex and the human body that is honest and direct

ease¹ /iːz/ noun [U] the ability to do something easily, or the fact that something is easy ≠ DIFFICULTY: *Children usually master computer games with ease.*

> **PHRASES** **at ease** confident and relaxed
> **ill at ease** not confident or relaxed

ease² /iːz/ verb **1** [I/T] to make something that is bad become less severe, or to become less severe: *Sometimes a mild painkiller is enough to ease the pain.* ♦ *The city's traffic problems are beginning to ease a little.* **2** [I/T] to move somewhere slowly and carefully, or to make something move in this way: *Joseph eased himself off the bed.* **3** [T] to make a rule or punishment less severe: *Sanctions against the country should be eased.*

> **PHRASAL VERB** ˌease ˈoff or ˌease ˈup if something unpleasant eases off, it becomes weaker: *The pain should ease off after a couple of hours.* ♦ *They waited for the storm to ease up.*

easel /ˈiːz(ə)l/ noun [C] a frame that you rest a painting on while you are painting it

easily /ˈiːzɪli/ adv ★★★
1 without difficulty or effort: *You could easily get there in a day.*
2 used for saying that something is likely to happen or be true: *The situation could easily get worse.*
3 definitely: *This is easily his best album in years.*
4 in a confident and relaxed way: *Sam and Luke had met before and chatted easily.*

east¹ /iːst/ noun ★★★
1 [U] the direction that is in front of you when you are facing the rising sun: *driving from east to west*
2 **the east** [singular] the part of a place that is in the east: *They live in the east of the city.* ♦ *Most of the region's forests are in the east.*
3 **the East** [singular] the eastern part of the world, especially China and Japan

east² /iːst/ adv towards the east: *Drive east until you come to the river.* ♦ *She lives 40 miles east of Rome.*

east³ /iːst/ adj **1** in the east, or facing towards the east **2** an east wind blows from the east

eastbound /ˈiːs(t)ˌbaʊnd/ adj going towards the east

ˌEast ˈCoast, the the eastern part of the US, along the Atlantic Ocean

Easter /ˈiːstə/ noun [C/U] a day when Christians celebrate the time when Jesus Christ died and then returned to life

ˈEaster ˌegg noun [C] a chocolate egg that you eat in celebration of Easter

easterly /ˈiːstəli/ adj **1** towards or in the east **2** an easterly wind blows from the east

eastern /ˈiːst(ə)n/ adj ★★ in the east of a place: *eastern France* ♦ *the eastern shore of the Mediterranean*

easterner /ˈiːstənə/ noun [C] someone who lives in or was born in the eastern part of a country

easternmost /ˈiːst(ə)nˌməʊst/ adj furthest towards the east

eastward /ˈiːstwəd/ adj towards or in the east

eastwards /ˈiːstwədz/ adv towards the east

easy¹ /ˈiːzi/ adj ★★★
1 not difficult, or not needing much work: *The test was easy.* ♦ *The easiest way to get to Hertford is on the train.* ♦ *It is easy to see why she likes him.* ♦ **easy to do** *This cake is very easy to make.*
2 happy, confident, and not worried about anything: *Doug had an easy charm.*

> **PHRASES** **the easy way out** an easy way of doing something, but not the right or best way
> **I'm easy** *spoken* used for saying that you will accept any choice or decision that someone else makes

easy² /ˈiːzi/ adv ★★
> **PHRASES** **easier said than done** *informal* used for saying that something is a good idea but will be difficult to achieve
> **go easy on sb** *spoken* to not be very angry or severe with someone
> **go easy on/with sth** *spoken* to not use, eat, or drink too much of something
> **take it easy 1** *informal* to rest and not do things that will make you tired **2** *spoken* used for telling someone to be calm

ˌeasy ˈchair noun [C] a large comfortable chair

easygoing /ˌiːziˈɡəʊɪŋ/ adj relaxed, calm, and not easy to upset

ˌeasy ˈlistening /ˌiːzi ˈlɪs(ə)nɪŋ/ noun [U] music that is relaxing and does not have complicated tunes or beats

eat /iːt/ (past tense **ate** /et, eɪt/; past participle **eaten** /ˈiːt(ə)n/) verb ★★★
1 [I/T] to put food into your mouth and swallow it: *Did you eat your sandwich?* ♦ *My sister doesn't eat meat, but she eats fish.* ♦ *Don't talk while you're eating.* ♦ *Where can we get **something to eat** (=food)?* → TAKE
2 [I] to have a meal: *What time shall we eat?* ♦ *We ate at a small Chinese restaurant.*

> **PHRASE** **eat sb out of house and home** to eat too much of someone's food when you are a guest in their house

> **PHRASAL VERBS** ˌeat ˈinto sth to use up more of your time and money than you intended: *The cost of new computer systems is eating into our profits.*
> ˌeat ˈout to have a meal in a restaurant instead of at home
> ˌeat sth ˈup to use large amounts of your available time or money: *Having children eats up a lot of a family's income.*

> Other ways of saying **eat**
> ■ **chew** to use your teeth to break up the food in your mouth
> ■ **eat up** to finish all the food that you have been given
> ■ **have breakfast/lunch/dinner** to eat a particular meal
> ■ **have something to eat** to eat something, or to have a meal
> ■ **munch** to eat something noisily
> ■ **nibble** to take very small bites from your food
> ■ **have a snack** to eat something small between your main meals

eater /ˈiːtə/ noun [C] **1** someone who eats in a particular way: *a messy/noisy eater* **2** a person or animal that eats a particular type of food: *a meat eater*

E

eating disorder /ˈiːtɪŋ dɪsˌɔːdə/ noun [C] a medical condition in which someone does not eat normally, and wrongly believes that they are too fat

eaves /iːvz/ noun [plural] the bottom edge of a roof that continues out over the walls

eavesdrop /ˈiːvzˌdrɒp/ verb [I] to listen to other people's conversation when they do not know that you are listening

eavesdrop

ebb¹ /eb/ noun [singular] the process in which the sea level at the coast becomes lower twice each day

   PHRASES **be at/reach (a) low ebb** to be in a very weak state

the ebb and flow a situation in which something keeps getting larger or stronger, then smaller or weaker

ebb² /eb/ verb [I] *literary* **1** to gradually become smaller or less: *He felt his confidence ebbing away.* **2** if the TIDE ebbs, the sea's level at the coast gradually becomes lower twice a day

ebony /ˈebəni/ noun [C/U] a tree with hard black wood, or the wood of this tree

e-business noun [C/U] *business* business done on the Internet, or an Internet company

eccentric /ɪkˈsentrɪk/ adj **1** an eccentric person often behaves in slightly strange or unusual ways **2** an eccentric action or decision is strange or unusual —**eccentric** noun [C]

eccentricity /ˌeksenˈtrɪsəti/ noun [C/U] strange or unusual behaviour

ecclesiastical /ɪˌkliːziˈæstɪk(ə)l/ adj relating to the Christian Church

echelon /ˈeʃəlɒn/ noun [C] one of the levels of status in an organization, or the people at that level: *the upper/lower echelons of society*

echo¹ /ˈekəʊ/ verb **1** [I] if a sound echoes, it is repeated because the sound hits a surface and returns: *Gunfire echoed across the streets.* **2** [I] if a place echoes, noises echo easily there **3** [T] to express the same words, ideas, or feelings that someone else has expressed: *Blake echoed the views of many players.*

echo² /ˈekəʊ/ (plural **echoes**) noun [C] **1** a sound that is repeated because the sound hits a surface and returns: *the echo of footsteps in the alley* **2** an idea or phrase that is like one that has been expressed before: *echoes of the past*

eclectic /ɪˈklektɪk/ adj *formal* consisting of many different types

eclipse¹ /ɪˈklɪps/ noun [C] a short period when

all or part of the Sun or Moon becomes dark: *a total eclipse of the Sun* (=when all of the Sun is dark)

eclipse² /ɪˈklɪps/ verb [T] to make someone or something seem less successful or important, by becoming more important than they are: *His performance was eclipsed by Francisco's winning goal.*

eco-friendly adj designed to cause as little harm as possible to the environment

ecological /ˌiːkəˈlɒdʒɪk(ə)l/ adj relating to the environment and the way living things affect each other: *an ecological disaster* —**ecologically** /ˌiːkəˈlɒdʒɪkli/ adv

ecology /ɪˈkɒlədʒi/ noun [U] the study of the environment and the way living things affect each other —**ecologist** noun [C]

e-commerce noun [U] buying and selling goods on the Internet

economic /ˌiːkəˈnɒmɪk, ˌekəˈnɒmɪk/ adj ★★★
1 relating to the economy, business, and trade: *economic development/growth* ♦ *the government's economic policies* ♦ *The project will bring great social and economic benefits to the region.*
2 providing a satisfactory profit from business activities ≠ UNECONOMIC: *It is no longer economic to mine coal here.*

economical /ˌiːkəˈnɒmɪk(ə)l, ˌekəˈnɒmɪk(ə)l/ adj not spending or costing much money: *The material is an economical substitute for plastic or steel.* ♦ *It's more economical to run the machines at night.*

economically /ˌiːkəˈnɒmɪkli, ˌekəˈnɒmɪkli/ adv **1** relating to the economy or to money: *Politically and economically, the country is going through enormous changes.* **2** done so that not much is wasted or little money is spent: *We aim to do the job as economically as possible.*

economic migrant noun [C] someone who goes to live in a new country because living conditions or opportunities for jobs are not good in their own country

economics /ˌiːkəˈnɒmɪks, ˌekəˈnɒmɪks/ noun [U] the study of the way that goods and services are produced and sold and the way that money is managed: *a degree in economics*

economist /ɪˈkɒnəmɪst/ noun [C] an expert in ECONOMICS

economize /ɪˈkɒnəˌmaɪz/ verb [I] to try to waste as little as possible of something such as money or fuel

economy¹ /ɪˈkɒnəmi/ noun ★★★
1 [C] the system by which a country's trade, industry, and money are organized, and all the business, industry, and trade in that system: *a modern industrial economy* ♦ *The economy grew at an average of about 3 per cent per year.* ♦ *The tax cuts are designed to boost the economy* (=make it stronger).
2 [C/U] the careful use of something so that very little is wasted, or an example of using something carefully: *In those days, fuel economy was a central factor in car design.* ♦ *If we make a few economies* (=spend money more carefully), *we can afford it.*
3 [U] the cheapest seats on a plane

economy² /ɪˈkɒnəmi/ adj **1** economy travel is the cheapest type of air travel available

2 economy goods are sold in large quantities so that they are cheaper

e'conomy ,class noun [U] the cheapest seats on a plane —**e'conomy ,class** adj, adv

ecosystem /'iːkəʊˌsɪstəm/ noun [C] science all the plants and animals in an area, considered as a system with parts that depend on each other

ecotourism /'iːkəʊˌtʊərɪz(ə)m/ noun [U] the business of creating and selling holidays that cause as little damage to the environment as possible —**ecotourist** noun [C]

ecstasy /'ekstəsi/ noun **1** [C/U] a feeling of great happiness and pleasure **2** [U] an illegal drug that young people take, especially in NIGHTCLUBS

ecstatic /ɪk'stætɪk/ adj extremely happy or pleased —**ecstatically** /ɪk'stætɪkli/ adv

eczema /'eksɪmə, American ɪgˈziːmə/ noun [U] a medical condition that makes your skin dry, sore, and ITCHY

ed. abbrev **1** edition **2** editor **3** education

eddy /'edi/ noun [C] a current of water or air that moves in a circular pattern

edge¹ /edʒ/ noun ★★★

1 [C] the part of something that is furthest from its centre: *Victoria was sitting on **the edge of the bed.*** ♦ *Many railway stations are built on **the edge of** town.*

2 [C] the sharp side of a blade or tool that is used for cutting things

3 [singular] an advantage over other people or things: *Training can **give** you **the edge** over your competitors.*

4 [singular] a quality in the way that someone speaks that shows they are becoming angry or upset: *Had she imagined the slight edge to his voice?*

PHRASES on edge nervous and unable to relax because you are worried

on the edge of your seat very excited and interested, because you want to know what happens next

edge² /edʒ/ verb **1** [I/T] to move slowly and carefully, or to make something do this: *Michael was edging towards the door.* **2** [I] to gradually increase or become less: *Food prices edged up by 0.2 per cent in November.* **3** [T] to put something round the edge of another thing: *white plates edged with gold*

PHRASAL VERB ,edge sb 'out to beat someone in a competition by a small amount

edgeways /'edʒweɪz/ adv sideways

PHRASE not get a word in edgeways to not manage to say something because someone else is talking a lot

edgy /'edʒi/ adj **1** in a bad mood because you are worried or nervous=IRRITABLE **2** edgy music, films, books etc have an unusual quality that is interesting or exciting

edible /'edɪb(ə)l/ adj safe to eat, or good enough to eat ≠ INEDIBLE: *edible mushrooms* ♦ *The food in the cafeteria is barely edible* (=it tastes very bad).

edict /'iːdɪkt/ noun [C] formal an official order that is given by a government or someone in authority

edifice /'edɪfɪs/ noun [C] formal a large impressive building

edit¹ /'edɪt/ verb [T] **1** to make changes to a book or document so that it is ready to be published **2** to be the EDITOR in charge of a book, newspaper, or magazine **3** to make changes to a film or to a television or radio programme before it is shown or broadcast

edit² /'edɪt/ noun [U] a menu in some computer programs that allows you to cut, copy, or move parts of a document, or look for particular words in it

edition /ɪ'dɪʃ(ə)n/ noun [C] a set of copies of a book, newspaper, or magazine that are published at the same time: *the Sunday edition of the local newspaper* ♦ *the 1993 edition of the* Guinness Book of Records

editor /'edɪtə/ noun [C] ★

1 someone who is in charge of a newspaper or magazine, or in charge of one of its sections

2 someone whose job is to EDIT books, documents, or films

3 a computer program that is used for writing or EDITING documents, files, or programs

editorial¹ /ˌedɪ'tɔːriəl/ adj relating to the EDITING of books, magazines, newspapers etc

editorial² /ˌedɪ'tɔːriəl/ noun [C] a newspaper article in which the editor gives their opinion on an issue in the news=LEADER

edu abbrev educational institution: used in Internet addresses

educate /'edjʊˌkeɪt/ verb ★

1 [T] to teach someone, especially at a school, college, or university: *More and more parents are choosing to educate their children at home.* ♦ **educate sb at sth** *He was educated at Eton and Trinity College, Cambridge.*

2 [I/T] to give someone necessary or useful knowledge: **educate sb about sth** *The mining museum was built to educate people about their local history.*

educated /'edjʊˌkeɪtɪd/ adj an educated person has received a good education and has a lot of knowledge ≠ UNEDUCATED: *The people who work here are well educated and open-minded.*

PHRASE an educated guess a guess that is based on knowledge of the situation

education /ˌedjʊ'keɪʃ(ə)n/ noun ★★★

1 [U] the activity of educating people in schools, colleges, and universities, and all the policies and arrangements concerning this: *Education is a major concern for voters.* ♦ *the Minister of Education*

2 [singular] someone's experience of learning or being taught: *Did you have a university education?* ♦ *He wants his children to **get an education**.*

3 [U] the process of providing people with information about an important issue: *a health education campaign*

Word family: education

*Words in the same family as **education***
- **educate** v
- **educated** adj
- **educational** adj
- **uneducated** adj

---

educational /ˌedjʊ'keɪʃ(ə)nəl/ adj ★★

1 relating to education: *educational opportunities for women*

2 giving people useful knowledge: *The*

programme was educational and
entertaining too.

educator /ˈedjʊˌkeɪtə/ noun [C] someone who
teaches, or someone who is an expert on
education

edutainment /ˌedjuˈteɪnmənt/ noun [U]
television programmes, videos, software
etc that entertain you while teaching you
something

Edwardian /edˈwɔːdiən/ adj in the styles that
were popular in the late 19th and early 20th
centuries in the UK

eel /iːl/ noun [C] a long thin fish that looks
like a snake

eerie /ˈɪəri/ adj strange and mysterious, and
sometimes frightening —**eerily** adv

effect¹ /ɪˈfekt/ noun ★★★
1 [C/U] a change that is produced in one
person or thing by another: *Scientists are
studying the chemical's **effect on** the
environment.* ♦ *Any change in lifestyle will
have an effect on your health.* ♦ *The new tax
rates will **have little effect on** most ordinary
people.*
2 [C] an appearance or reaction that is
deliberately produced, for example by a
writer or artist: *Students should learn how
they can **achieve** different **effects** in their
writing.*
3 effects [plural] special artificial images and
sounds that are created for a film = SPECIAL
EFFECTS
4 effects or **personal effects** [plural] *formal* the
things that belong to you
PHRASES **come into effect** if a rule or law
comes into effect, it starts to be used
for effect if you do something for effect, you
do it in order to impress people
in effect 1 used for giving a summary of what
you think the situation really is: *In effect,
this means we'll have to work more hours
for the same pay.* **2** if a law or rule is in
effect, it is operating
put sth into effect to start to use a plan or
idea
take effect 1 to start to produce the results
that were intended: *The tax cuts are
beginning to take effect.* **2** if a rule or law
takes effect, it starts to be used
to the effect that used for showing that you
are giving a general idea of what someone
said, but not their actual words: *Harry said
something to the effect that they would all
meet Margaret very soon.*
→ SIDE EFFECT

effect² /ɪˈfekt/ verb [T] *formal* to make
something happen = BRING STH ABOUT: *Swift
action was necessary if real change was to
be effected.*

effective /ɪˈfektɪv/ adj ★★★
1 working well and producing the result
that was intended ≠ INEFFECTIVE: *You need
more effective communication within the
organization.* ♦ *This is a very effective way
of controlling pests and weeds.* ♦ *The new
vaccine is highly **effective against** all
strains of the disease.*
2 *formal* when a law or agreement becomes
effective, it officially starts to be used:
*Government ministers reached a 30-month
agreement, **effective from** 1 July.*
—**effectiveness** noun [U]

effectively /ɪˈfektɪv(ə)li/ adv ★★
1 used for saying what the situation really
is, although it might seem to be different:
*With Australia 24 points ahead at half-time,
the game was effectively over.*
2 in a way that works well and produces
the result that you intended: *The system
could deliver services to local communities
more effectively.*

effeminate /ɪˈfemɪnət/ adj *showing disapproval*
an effeminate man looks, behaves, or speaks
like a woman

effervescent /ˌefəˈves(ə)nt/ adj **1** producing a
lot of small BUBBLES = FIZZY **2** lively and
enthusiastic

efficiency /ɪˈfɪʃ(ə)nsi/ noun [U] ★ the ability to
work well and produce good results, using
the available time, money, supplies etc in
the most effective way ≠ INEFFICIENCY: *new
technology aimed at improving efficiency and
customer service*

efficient /ɪˈfɪʃ(ə)nt/ adj ★★ working well and
producing good results by using the
available time, money, supplies etc in the
most effective way ≠ INEFFICIENT: *The new
machine is far more efficient than the old
one.* ♦ *The most efficient way to plan your
work is to put your tasks in order of
importance.* ♦ *The hotel's staff are friendly
and efficient.* —**efficiently** adv

effigy /ˈefɪdʒi/ noun [C] a model of someone,
especially one that is destroyed in a protest
against them

effluent /ˈefluənt/ noun [C/U] liquid waste

effort /ˈefət/ noun ★★★
1 [C/U] an attempt to do something that is
difficult or involves hard work: *Detectives
are talking to other witnesses **in an effort to**
find out more about the girl.* ♦ *I've **made an
effort** to drink less tea and coffee.* ♦ **an effort
to do sth** *The changes were part of an effort
to push profits up.*
2 [singular/U] physical or mental energy
needed to do something: *Writing a book
takes a lot of time and **effort**.* ♦ *Mary **put** a
lot of **effort into** this project.*
3 [C] the activities of people who are working
together to achieve a particular aim:
international relief efforts

EFFORT: used when someone tries very hard to
do something
■ **combined, concerted, joint, team** + EFFORT:
used about an effort that is made by a lot of
people together

effortless /ˈefətləs/ adj done well or
successfully and without any effort
—**effortlessly** adv

effusive /ɪˈfjuːsɪv/ adj expressing happiness,
praise etc in an extremely enthusiastic way

EFL /ˌiː ef ˈel/ noun [U] English as a Foreign
Language: English taught to people who do
not live in an English-speaking country

e.g. or **eg** /ˌiː ˈdʒiː/ abbrev for example: used
for giving an example of what you mean

egalitarian /ɪˌɡælɪˈteəriən/ adj supporting a
social system in which everyone has the
same status, money, and opportunities

egg¹ /eg/ noun ★★★
1 [C] the round object with a shell that a
baby bird develops in: *The chicken had **laid
an egg**.*
2 [C/U] a HEN's egg used as food: *We had
boiled eggs for breakfast.* ♦ *an egg sandwich*
3 [C] a small object produced by a female
insect, FROG, snake etc, that a young animal
comes out of
4 [C] a cell produced inside a woman or
female animal that can develop into a baby
PHRASE have/get egg on your face *informal* to
be embarrassed or appear stupid because
something you tried to do has gone wrong

fried egg / scrambled eggs / omelette / boiled egg

eggs

egg² /eg/ **PHRASAL VERB egg sb on** to
encourage someone to do something that
they should not do

eggshell /ˈegʃel/ noun [C] the hard outside
layer of an egg

egg white noun [C/U] the clear part of an egg
that becomes white when you cook it

ego /ˈiːgəʊ/ noun [C] the opinion that you
have of yourself and your own importance:
a guy with a huge ego ♦ *Being asked to speak
was a real boost to her ego.*

egotistical /ˌiːgəʊˈtɪstɪk(ə)l/ adj thinking that
you are more important than other people
and need not care about them —**egotist**
/ˈiːgəʊtɪst/ noun [C]

eh /eɪ/ interjection **1** *informal* used for asking
someone to repeat what they said: *Eh?
What's that again?* **2** used for asking
someone to agree with you: *Pretty good, eh?*

Eid /iːd/ noun [U] a festival in the Muslim
religion

eight /eɪt/ number the number 8

eighteen /ˌeɪˈtiːn/ number the number 18
—**eighteenth** /ˌeɪˈtiːnθ/ number

eighth /eɪtθ/ number **1** in the place or position
counted as number 8 **2** one of 8 equal parts
of something

eighty /ˈeɪti/ number the number 80
—**eightieth** /ˈeɪtiəθ/ number

either /ˈaɪðə/ grammar word ★★★

Either can be:
■ a **conjunction**: *Students could choose either
French or Spanish.* ♦ *You can either come by
bus or take a taxi.*
■ a **pronoun**: *You could have fish or chicken, but
I don't like either.* ♦ *Does either of you speak
Chinese?*
■ an **adverb**: *Jerry wasn't there either.*
■ a **determiner**: *a long room with a door at either
end*

1 one or the other of two people or things,
especially when it does not matter which:
Cheque or credit card – you can use either. ♦
*Applications are welcomed from people of
either sex and any age.* ♦ *It was a long time
before **either of** them spoke.*
2 used instead of 'also' in negative
statements: *We tried another method, but
that didn't work either.* ♦ *I can't come
tonight, and nobody else can either.*
3 used instead of 'both' in negative
statements: *Jackie could play the piano and
sing, but I couldn't do either.* ♦ *I didn't like
either of the candidates.* → ALSO
PHRASES either...or used for showing two
or more possibilities or choices: *You must
answer either yes or no.* ♦ *You can contact
us either by phone, by email, or by letter.*
either side/end/hand etc each of two sides/
ends/hands etc: *Her parents were sitting on
either side of her.*

When **either** is the subject of a sentence, it is
usually used with a singular verb: *Is either of
them at home?* But in spoken English a plural
verb is sometimes used: *Are either of them at
home?*

ejaculate /ɪˈdʒækjʊˌleɪt/ verb [I/T] if a man
ejaculates, SEMEN comes out of his PENIS
—**ejaculation** /ɪˌdʒækjʊˈleɪʃ(ə)n/ noun [C/U]

eject /ɪˈdʒekt/ verb **1** [T] to make something
such as a TAPE or CD come out from a
machine **2** [T] to make someone leave a place,
especially using physical force: *A group of
noisy protesters were ejected from the
meeting.* **3** [I] to jump out of a plane before
it crashes —**ejection** /ɪˈdʒekʃ(ə)n/ noun [U]

eke /iːk/ verb **eke out a living** to get just enough
money to be able to live

elaborate¹ /ɪˈlæb(ə)rət/ adj very detailed and
complicated: *elaborate geometrical patterns*
♦ *an elaborate system of inspections and
reports*

elaborate² /ɪˈlæbəˌreɪt/ verb [I] to give more
details or information about something:
*The police refused to elaborate on the
circumstances of the arrest.* —**elaboration**
/ɪˌlæbəˈreɪʃ(ə)n/ noun [U]

elapse /ɪˈlæps/ verb [I] *formal* if time elapses,
it passes

elastic¹ /ɪˈlæstɪk/ noun [U] a material that
stretches or bends easily and can return to
its original shape

elastic² /ɪˈlæstɪk/ adj **1** made of elastic **2** able
to stretch or bend and then return to its
original shape

elated /ɪˈleɪtɪd/ adj extremely happy and

excited —**elation** /ɪˈleɪʃ(ə)n/ noun [U]

elbow¹ /ˈelbəʊ/ noun [C] ★★ the part in the middle of your arm, where it bends: *She sat with her elbows on the table.* —*picture* → C14

elbow² /ˈelbəʊ/ verb [T] to push or hit someone with your elbow

elder¹ /ˈeldə/ adj older than someone, especially someone in your family: *advice from my elder brother*

elder² /ˈeldə/ noun [C] **1** someone in your family or community who is older than you **2** an older member of an organization or community who is given respect and authority

elderly /ˈeldəli/ adj ★★
1 old: *Not all elderly people can live with their relatives.*
2 the elderly old people

eldest /ˈeldəst/ adj oldest of the people in a group, especially the children in a family: *He was the eldest of three sons.*

elect¹ /ɪˈlekt/ verb [T] ★★ to choose someone to represent you or to hold an official position, by voting for them: *Every nation should have a right to elect its own government.* ♦ **elect sb to sth** *He was elected to parliament by a large majority.* ♦ **elect sb as sth** *Lee Yuan-tzu was elected the next day as Vice President.* ♦ **elect sb sth** *She was elected president of the association.*
> **PHRASE** **elect to do sth** *formal* to choose to do something: *They had elected to remain at home.*

elect² /ɪˈlekt/ adj elected to an important position, but not yet officially holding it: *the president elect*

election /ɪˈlekʃ(ə)n/ noun ★★★
1 [C] an occasion when people vote for someone to represent them, especially in a government: *an election victory/defeat* ♦ *The new regime is promising to **hold free elections** as soon as possible.* ♦ *She is standing in **elections for** the National Assembly.*
2 [U] the process of electing a person or government: *the **election of** a new leader* ♦ *a candidate for **election to** the Council* ♦ *His **election as** President will mean changes in foreign policy.*

elective /ɪˈlektɪv/ adj **1** an elective position is one that you hold because people have voted for you **2** done because someone chooses it, not because they have to do it: *elective surgery*

elector /ɪˈlektə/ noun [C] someone who has the right to vote in an election

electoral /ɪˈlekt(ə)rəl/ adj relating to elections: *a new electoral system*

electorate /ɪˈlekt(ə)rət/ noun [C] all the people who are allowed to vote in an election

electric /ɪˈlektrɪk/ adj ★
1 using or relating to electricity: *an electric kettle/drill/toothbrush* ♦ *an electric socket/plug/cable* ♦ *an electric current*
2 extremely exciting: *The atmosphere was electric.*

> ■ **Electric** describes things that use electricity to make them work: *an electric iron/shaver/guitar*

> ■ **Electrical** is used in more technical contexts, when you are talking about how electricity is made or used: *an electrical fault* ♦ *an electrical engineer*

electrical /ɪˈlektrɪk(ə)l/ adj ★ working by or relating to electricity: *electrical equipment/appliances* ♦ *an electrical fault*

e.lectric ˈchair, the noun [singular] a chair used in parts of the US for legally killing someone as a punishment, using a strong electrical current

electrician /ˌɪlekˈtrɪʃ(ə)n/ noun [C] someone whose job is to repair or fit electrical equipment

electricity /ˌɪlekˈtrɪsəti/ noun [U] ★★ a form of energy that can produce light, heat, and power for computers, televisions etc: *The machines run on electricity.* ♦ *an electricity supply*

electrics /ɪˈlektrɪks/ noun [plural] *British* the electrical system in a building or machine

e.lectric ˈshock noun [C] a sudden strong pain that is caused by electricity passing through your body

electrify /ɪˈlektrɪfaɪ/ verb [T] **1** to make someone feel extremely excited **2** to provide something with a supply of electricity —**electrification** /ˌɪlektrɪfɪˈkeɪʃ(ə)n/ noun [U]

electrocute /ɪˈlektrəkjuːt/ verb [T] to kill or injure someone with electricity —**electrocution** /ˌɪlektrəˈkjuːʃ(ə)n/ noun [U]

electrode /ɪˈlektrəʊd/ noun [C] a small metal object that allows electricity to flow through it

electron /ɪˈlektrɒn/ noun [C] a part of an atom that has a negative electrical CHARGE
→ NEUTRON

electronic /ˌelekˈtrɒnɪk/ adj ★★
1 using electricity and extremely small electrical parts such as MICROCHIPS: *an electronic calculator* ♦ *The information is held **in electronic form** (=on computer disks).*
2 involving the use of electronic equipment, especially computers: *an electronic voting system*
—**electronically** /ˌelekˈtrɒnɪkli/ adv

electronics /ˌelekˈtrɒnɪks/ noun [U] the science and technology of electronic equipment

elegant /ˈelɪgənt/ adj beautiful in a graceful simple way: *She always looks so elegant.* ♦ *an elegant room/restaurant* —**elegance** noun [U], **elegantly** adv

elegy /ˈelədʒi/ noun [C] a poem or other piece of writing that expresses sadness

element /ˈelɪmənt/ noun ★★★

1 basic part of sth	**4** for heating
2 in science	**5** weather
3 small amount	♦ PHRASES

1 [C] an important basic part of something, for example a system or plan: *Fieldwork is a key **element** of this course.* ♦ *Advertising is not the only **element** in the marketing process.*
2 [C] *science* a substance that consists of only one type of atom: *hydrogen, oxygen, and other elements*
3 [singular] a small but important amount of a quality or feeling: *There is **an element of** truth in what she said.*

E

4 [C] the part of a piece of electrical equipment that produces heat

5 the elements [plural] the weather, especially wind and rain

PHRASES **be in your element** to feel very happy and comfortable in a situation **be out of your element** to feel unhappy and uncomfortable in a situation

elementary /ˌelɪˈment(ə)ri/ adj **1** relating to the most basic and important part of something=BASIC: *He made a few elementary errors.* **2** easy: *elementary tasks* **3** relating to the first years of school

eleˈmentary ˈschool noun [C] in the US, a school for children between the ages of five and about eleven

elephant /ˈelɪfənt/ noun [C] a very large wild animal that lives in Africa and Asia. It has thick grey skin and a very long nose called a **trunk**. —*picture* → C12

elevate /ˈeləˌveɪt/ verb [T] *formal* **1** to improve someone or something, or to make them more important: *We need to work together to elevate the position of women in society.* **2** to raise something to a higher physical position=RAISE —**elevated** /ˈeləˌveɪtɪd/ adj, **elevation** /ˌeləˈveɪʃ(ə)n/ noun [C/U]

elevator /ˈeləˌveɪtə/ noun [C] *American* a LIFT in a building

eleven /ɪˈlev(ə)n/ number the number 11

eleventh /ɪˈlev(ə)nθ/ number **1** in the place or position counted as number 11 **2** one of 11 equal parts of something

PHRASE **the eleventh hour** the last possible moment when you can do something

elf /elf/ (plural **elves** /elvz/) noun [C] a small imaginary person with magic powers

elicit /ɪˈlɪsɪt/ verb [T] *formal* to get something such as a reaction or information from someone: *The question elicited a positive response.*

eligible /ˈelɪdʒəb(ə)l/ adj **1** allowed by rules or laws to do something ≠ INELIGIBLE: *She will be eligible to compete in the next Winter Games.* **2** considered to be a good marriage partner —**eligibility** /ˌelɪdʒəˈbɪləti/ noun [U]

eliminate /ɪˈlɪmɪˌneɪt/ verb [T] **1** to get rid of something that is not wanted or needed: *Many infectious diseases have been virtually eliminated.* ♦ **eliminate sth from sth** *He had to eliminate dairy products from his diet.* **2** to decide that someone or something is not responsible for something: *We've eliminated the possibility that the fire was started deliberately.* **3** to remove someone from a competition: *Five candidates were eliminated after the first interview.*

elimination /ɪˌlɪmɪˈneɪʃ(ə)n/ noun **1** [U] the process of getting rid of something that is not wanted **2** [C] defeat in a competition

PHRASE **a process of elimination** a way of solving a problem by getting rid of wrong solutions first

elision /ɪˈlɪʒ(ə)n/ noun [U] *linguistics* the practice of leaving a sound out when you say a word or group of words quickly in ordinary conversation

elite /ɪˈliːt/ noun [C] **1** a small group of people who have a lot of power or advantages: *the political elite* **2** the best or most skilful people in a group: *This book puts him among the*

elite of British novelists. ♦ *an elite group of athletes*

elitism /ɪˈliːˌtɪz(ə)m/ noun [U] the belief that a small group of people should keep the most power and influence —**elitist** adj

Elizabethan /ɪˌlɪzəˈbiːθ(ə)n/ adj relating to the time when Elizabeth I was the queen of England, 1558–1603 —**Elizabethan** noun [C]

elliptical /ɪˈlɪptɪk(ə)l/ adj in the shape of a circle that is longer than it is wide

elm /elm/ noun [C] a large tree with round leaves that fall off in winter

elongated /ˈiːlɒŋˌgeɪtɪd/ adj longer and narrower than is normal

elope /ɪˈləʊp/ verb [I] to go away secretly in order to get married

eloquent /ˈeləkwənt/ adj expressing something clearly and effectively: *an eloquent speech/speaker* —**eloquence** noun [U], **eloquently** adv

else /els/ adv ★★★ used after question words, or words such as 'anyone', 'something', 'everywhere', and 'nobody', to mean 'in addition' or 'other': *No one else was willing to help.* ♦ *Would you like to go somewhere else?* ♦ *What else have you been doing wrong, Kelly?* ♦ *The police had already interviewed everyone else.*

PHRASE **or else 1** used for stating the second of two possibilities: *You could drive across France, or else fly to Geneva and hire a car.* **2** used for saying that there will be a bad result if something does not happen: *We must leave now or else we'll miss our train.* → NOTHING

elsewhere /elsˈweə/ adv ★★ in or to another place or other places: *Car prices in the UK are higher than elsewhere in Europe.* ♦ *people who come here to work from elsewhere*

ELT /ˌiː el ˈtiː/ noun [U] English Language Teaching: the teaching of English to students whose first language is not English

elucidate /ɪˈluːsɪˌdeɪt/ verb [I/T] *formal* to make something easier to understand by giving more information

elude /ɪˈluːd/ verb [T] *formal* **1** if something eludes you, you cannot achieve it, understand it, or remember it: *Financial success eluded him.* **2** to manage to escape or hide from someone or something=EVADE

elusive /ɪˈluːsɪv/ adj **1** difficult or impossible to find or catch **2** difficult or impossible to achieve or understand

elves the plural of **elf**

'em /əm/ short form a way of writing 'them' that shows how it sounds in informal conversation

emaciated /ɪˈmeɪʃieɪtɪd/ adj extremely thin

email /ˈiːmeɪl/ or **e-mail** noun ★★★
1 [U] a system for sending messages from one computer to another: *We communicate by email.* ♦ *Do you know her email address?* **2** [C] a written message sent by email: *Send me an email with the details.* —**email** verb [T]

emanate /ˈeməˌneɪt/ **PHRASAL VERB** **ˈemanate from sth** *formal* to come from a particular place: *Wonderful smells emanated from the kitchen.*

emancipation /ɪˌmænsɪˈpeɪʃ(ə)n/ noun [U] *formal* the process of giving freedom and

rights to someone=LIBERATION
—**emancipate** /ɪˈmænsɪˌpeɪt/ verb [T],
emancipated /ɪˈmænsɪˌpeɪtɪd/ adj

embalm /ɪmˈbɑːm/ verb [T] to preserve a dead body using chemicals

embankment /ɪmˈbæŋkmənt/ noun [C] a sloping wall of earth or stone beside a road, railway, or river

embargo /ɪmˈbɑːgəʊ/ (plural **embargoes**) noun [C] a government order preventing trade with another country: *an arms/oil/trade embargo*

embark /ɪmˈbɑːk/ verb [I] to get on a ship ≠ DISEMBARK —**embarkation** /ˌembɑːˈkeɪʃ(ə)n/ noun [C/U]

PHRASAL VERB em**bark** ,on sth or em**bark** u,pon sth to start a new project or activity

embarrass /ɪmˈbærəs/ verb [T] to make someone feel nervous, ashamed, or stupid: *It embarrassed me to have to give my opinion in public.*

embarrassed /ɪmˈbærəst/ adj ★ feeling slightly ashamed, and worried about what other people will think of you: *She looked embarrassed when we asked her about her boyfriend.* ♦ **embarrassed to do sth** *I was too embarrassed to tell anyone about my illness.*

embarrassing /ɪmˈbærəsɪŋ/ adj ★ making you feel nervous, ashamed, or stupid: *an embarrassing situation* —**embarrassingly** adv

embarrassment /ɪmˈbærəsmənt/ noun **1** [U] a feeling of being embarrassed: *I felt my face burning with embarrassment.* **2** [C] someone or something that makes you feel embarrassed: *He is such an embarrassment to his family.*

embassy /ˈembəsi/ noun [C] a group of officials who represent their government in a foreign country, or the building where they work: *the Canadian Embassy in Paris*

embattled /ɪmˈbæt(ə)ld/ adj *mainly journalism* experiencing a lot of problems and likely to be defeated or destroyed

embedded /ɪmˈbedɪd/ adj fixed firmly in something: *A piece of metal had become embedded in her leg.*

embellish /ɪmˈbelɪʃ/ verb [I/T] to make something more interesting or beautiful by adding things to it

embers /ˈembərz/ noun [plural] pieces of wood or coal that are still hot and red after a fire has stopped burning

embezzle /ɪmˈbez(ə)l/ verb [I/T] to steal money that you are trusted to look after as part of your work —**embezzlement** noun [U]

embittered /ɪmˈbɪtəd/ adj angry and unhappy about things that have happened to you in the past

emblazoned /ɪmˈbleɪz(ə)nd/ adj printed, drawn, or decorated in a way that is very easy to notice

emblem /ˈembləm/ noun [C] a design or object that is a symbol of something such as a country, organization, or idea

embodiment /ɪmˈbɒdɪmənt/ noun **the embodiment of sth** the best possible example of a particular idea, quality, or principle

embody /ɪmˈbɒdi/ verb [T] to be the best possible example of a particular idea, quality, or principle

embrace /ɪmˈbreɪs/ verb **1** [T] *formal* to accept something new with enthusiasm: *Many older people have embraced new technology.* **2** [I/T] to put your arms around someone in order to show love or friendship —**embrace** noun [C]

embroider /ɪmˈbrɔɪdə/ verb [I/T] **1** to decorate cloth with a design of coloured stitches **2** to make a story more interesting by adding details that you have invented

embroidery /ɪmˈbrɔɪdəri/ noun [C/U] a design of coloured stitches on cloth, or the activity of decorating cloth in this way

embroiled /ɪmˈbrɔɪld/ adj involved in a difficult situation: *The mayor is embroiled in another scandal.*

embryo /ˈembriəʊ/ noun [C] an animal or human before it is born, when it is beginning to develop and grow

embryonic /ˌembriˈɒnɪk/ adj **1** just beginning to develop and grow: *an embryonic industry* **2** relating to an animal or human embryo

emerald /ˈem(ə)rəld/ noun [C] a bright green stone used in expensive jewellery

emerge /ɪˈmɜːdʒ/ verb [I] ★★
1 to come out of something, or out from behind something: *After a few weeks, the caterpillar emerges from its cocoon.* ♦ *The doors opened and people began to* **emerge** *into the street.*
2 to stop being involved in a difficult situation or period of time: *The country is slowly emerging from a recession.*
3 to become known or recognized: *Leeds is emerging as an important financial centre.* ♦ **+that** *It has emerged that Britons were among those injured.*

emergence /ɪˈmɜːdʒ(ə)ns/ noun [U] the process of appearing or becoming recognized: *the emergence of the modern French state*

emergency /ɪˈmɜːdʒ(ə)nsi/ noun [C] ★★ an unexpected situation in which immediate action is necessary, often because there is danger: *The club is now facing a financial emergency.* ♦ *We always carry a medical kit for emergencies.* ♦ *emergency surgery* ♦ *In an emergency, call this number.*

e**mergency ,room** noun [C] *American* the part of a hospital where you take someone who needs immediate care=A&E

e**mergency ,services** noun [plural] the organizations that deal with fire, crime, accidents, and injuries

emerging /ɪˈmɜːdʒɪŋ/ adj just beginning to exist or be noticed: *emerging businesses/technologies*

emigrant /ˈemɪgrənt/ noun [C] someone who leaves their country in order to live in another country

emigrate /ˈemɪgreɪt/ verb [I] to leave your country in order to live in another country —**emigration** /ˌemɪˈgreɪʃ(ə)n/ noun [U]

eminent /ˈemɪnənt/ adj important, respected, and admired

eminently /ˈemɪnəntli/ adv *formal* very: *eminently qualified*

emission /ɪˈmɪʃ(ə)n/ noun **1** [C] a substance, especially a gas, that goes into the air: *a proposal to reduce carbon dioxide emissions*

2 [U] the process of sending gas, light, or heat into the air

emit /ɪ'mɪt/ verb [T] to send out gas, light, heat, or sound

emoticon /ɪ'məʊtɪˌkɒn/ noun [C] a symbol that you type in an email or TEXT MESSAGE to show how you feel

emotion /ɪ'məʊʃ(ə)n/ noun [C/U] ★★ a feeling that you experience, for example love, fear, or anger: *Jealousy is an uncomfortable emotion.*

emotional /ɪ'məʊʃ(ə)nəl/ adj ★★
1 relating to feelings and the way in which they affect your life: *He is in need of emotional support.*
2 affected by and expressing strong emotion: *It was an emotional reunion.*
3 causing strong emotions: *This is such an emotional issue.*
—**emotionally** adv

emotive /ɪ'məʊtɪv/ adj causing strong feelings

empathize /'empəθaɪz/ verb [I] to understand how someone else feels

empathy /'empəθi/ noun [U] the ability to understand how someone else feels

emperor /'emp(ə)rə/ noun [C] a man who rules an EMPIRE

emphasis /'emfəsɪs/ (plural **emphases** /'emfəsiːz/) noun [C/U] ★★
1 special importance or attention that is given to one thing in particular: *We place great emphasis on staff development.*
2 the extra loudness with which you say a particular phrase, word, or part of a word =STRESS: *The emphasis is on the first syllable.*

emphasize /'emfəsaɪz/ verb [T] ★
1 to give particular importance or attention to something: *The report emphasizes the need for better health education.* ♦ **+that** *He emphasized that no one should be above the law.*
2 to say a phrase, word, or part of a word more loudly
3 to make something more noticeable: *Naomi's white dress emphasized her suntan.*

emphatic /ɪm'fætɪk/ adj **1** said or shown in a very strong clear way: *an emphatic shake of the head* **2** with a very clear result: *an emphatic victory/defeat* —**emphatically** /ɪm'fætɪkli/ adv

emphysema /ˌemfɪ'siːmə/ noun [U] a very serious illness that affects your lungs

empire /'empaɪə/ noun [C] ★
1 a number of countries that are ruled by one person or government: *the Roman empire*
2 a large powerful group of companies that are controlled by one person or company: *an international media empire*

empirical /ɪm'pɪrɪk(ə)l/ adj based on real experience or scientific experiments rather than on theory —**empirically** /ɪm'pɪrɪk(ə)li/ adv

employ /ɪm'plɔɪ/ verb [T] ★★
1 to pay someone regularly to work for you: *a large car factory that employs over 8,000 people* ♦ **employ sb as sth** *Jean was employed as a computer programmer.*
2 *formal* to use something for a particular

purpose: *They employed an imaginative marketing strategy.*

> **Word family: employ**
>
> *Words in the same family as* **employ**
> - **employed** *adj*
> - **unemployed** *adj*
> - **employment** *n*
> - **unemployment** *n*
> - **employer** *n*
> - **employee** *n*

employee /ɪm'plɔɪiː, ˌemplɔɪ'iː/ noun [C] ★★ someone who is paid regularly to work for a person or organization: *part-time employees*

employer /ɪm'plɔɪə/ noun [C] ★★ a person or organization that pays workers to work for them: *The factory is the largest single employer in the area.*

employment /ɪm'plɔɪmənt/ noun [U] ★★★
1 work that you are paid regularly to do: *Many qualified nurses are unable to find employment.*
2 a situation in which people have regular paid work ≠ UNEMPLOYMENT: *Employment has risen among people over 55.*

empower /ɪm'paʊə/ verb [T] **1** to make someone feel that they have control over their life and their work: *Our goal is to empower everyone on our staff.* **2** *formal* to give a person or organization the legal authority to do something —**empowerment** noun [U]

empress /'emprəs/ noun [C] a woman who rules an EMPIRE or who is married to an EMPEROR

empty¹ /'empti/ adj ★★★
1 containing no things or people ≠ FULL: *an empty jar* ♦ *The room was empty.* ♦ *empty streets*
2 lacking emotion, interest, or purpose: *Her life felt empty and meaningless.*
3 not true or serious: *an empty promise/threat/gesture*
—**emptiness** noun [U]

empty² /'empti/ verb **1** [T] to make something empty ≠ FILL **2** [I] if a place empties, all the people in it leave
PHRASAL VERB **empty sth 'out** *same as* **empty²** 1

empty-handed /ˌempti 'hændɪd/ adj without getting anything for your effort: *They returned empty-handed from the peace negotiations.*

emulate /'emjʊˌleɪt/ verb [T] *formal* to try to be like someone or something else

emulsion /ɪ'mʌlʃ(ə)n/ noun [C/U] **1** a type of paint that produces a surface that is not shiny **2** a smooth mixture of two or more liquids

enable /ɪn'eɪb(ə)l/ verb [T] ★★★ to give someone the ability or opportunity to do something: **enable sb to do sth** *This will enable users to conduct live video conversations.*

enact /ɪn'ækt/ verb [T] to make a proposal into a law —**enactment** noun [C/U]

enamel /ɪ'næm(ə)l/ noun [C/U] **1** a hard shiny substance that is used for protecting or decorating glass, metal, or clay **2** the hard white outer layer of teeth

enamoured /ɪ'næməd/ adj *formal* **1** impressed with or enthusiastic about something **2** in love with someone

E

E

encampment /ɪnˈkæmpmənt/ noun [C] a large group of tents or temporary shelters

encapsulate /ɪnˈkæpsjʊˌleɪt/ verb [T] to express something in a short clear form that gives the most clear facts or ideas about it

encase /ɪnˈkeɪs/ verb [T] to completely cover or enclose something

enchanted /ɪnˈtʃɑːntɪd/ adj **1** very attracted by something, or getting great pleasure from it: *She performed a Beethoven sonata, and we were all enchanted by her playing.* **2** affected by magic

enchanting /ɪnˈtʃɑːntɪŋ/ adj very attractive, or giving great pleasure

encircle /ɪnˈsɜːk(ə)l/ verb [T] to completely surround something

enclave /ˈenkleɪv/ noun [C] an area of a country or city where a particular group of people lives

enclose /ɪnˈkləʊz/ verb [T] **1** to surround someone or something: *The swimming pool was enclosed by a high fence.* **2** to send something such as a document in a letter: *Please enclose a copy of your birth certificate with your application.* —**enclosed** /ɪnˈkləʊzd/ adj

enclosure /ɪnˈkləʊʒə/ noun [C] an area that is surrounded by a fence or wall

encompass /ɪnˈkʌmpəs/ verb [T] *formal* to include a lot of people or things: *The term 'world music' encompasses a wide range of musical styles.*

encore /ˈɒŋkɔː/ noun [C] a short performance given after the main performance, because the audience asks for more

encounter¹ /ɪnˈkaʊntə/ noun [C] **1** a meeting, especially one that was not planned **2** an experience or DISCOVERY of a particular kind: *my earliest encounter with the theatre*

encounter² /ɪnˈkaʊntə/ verb [T] **1** to experience or deal with something, especially a problem: *We encountered one small problem during the first test.* **2** *formal* to meet someone or see something for the first time

encourage /ɪnˈkʌrɪdʒ/ verb [T] ★★★ **1** to try to persuade someone to do something that you believe would be good ≠ DISCOURAGE: *We encourage student participation in our classes.* ◆ **encourage sb to do sth** *Mum always encouraged us to discuss our problems.* **2** to provide conditions that make it easier for something to happen ≠ DISCOURAGE: *Bad hygiene encourages the spread of disease.* **3** to give someone confidence or hope ≠ DISCOURAGE: *His optimism encouraged me.* —**encouragement** noun [C/U]

Word family: **encourage**

Words in the same family as encourage
- **encouraging** *adj*
- **encouragement** *n*
- **discourage** *v*
- **discouraging** *adj*
- **discouragement** *n*
- **discouraged** *adj*

---

encouraging /ɪnˈkʌrɪdʒɪŋ/ adj giving you confidence or hope ≠ DISCOURAGING: *They are testing a new Aids drug, and the first results are encouraging.* —**encouragingly** adv

encroach /ɪnˈkrəʊtʃ/ | PHRASAL VERB

en·croach on sth or **en·croach u·pon sth 1** to gradually take something such as power or authority from someone else: *The federal government is encroaching on states' rights.* **2** to gradually cover more land

encrusted /ɪnˈkrʌstɪd/ adj covered with a hard layer of something

encyclopaedia /ɪnˌsaɪkləˈpiːdiə/ a British spelling of **encyclopedia**

encyclopedia /ɪnˌsaɪkləˈpiːdiə/ noun [C] a book or set of books that gives information about a lot of different subjects or one particular subject

end¹ /end/ noun [C] ★★★

1 final part	4 part in activity
2 when sth stops	5 purpose
3 part furthest out	+ PHRASES

1 the final part of a period of time: *We're going on holiday at the end of this month.* ◆ *They'll make their decision at the very end of the week.* ◆ *The work should be completed by the end of the year.*
2 the time when a situation or an event stops: *Are you going to stay till the end of the game?* ◆ *After the end of the war many promises were made.* ◆ *We both knew that the partnership had come to an end.* ◆ *We want to put an end to* (=stop) *discrimination.* ◆ *the final battle that brought the war to an end* (=made it end)
3 the part of something that is furthest away from the centre: *Hold both ends of the rope.* ◆ *The only door was at the far end of the corridor.*
4 *spoken* the part that you have in an activity or situation: *Kate is more involved in the research end of things.* ◆ *I've kept my end of the bargain* (=done what I promised)*, but he hasn't kept his.*
5 *formal* something that you want to achieve: *Governments make policies that suit their own political ends.* ◆ *She used people for her own ends.*

PHRASES **at the end of the day** *spoken* used for saying that something is the most important aspect of a situation: *There were problems, but at the end of the day, everyone got what they wanted.*
hours/days/weeks etc on end used for emphasizing how long something continues: *He talks for hours on end about absolutely nothing.*
in the end *spoken* finally: *In the end, I decided not to buy the shoes.*
make ends meet to have just enough money to buy the things that you need
no end *spoken* a lot: *Her English has improved no end.* ◆ *We've had no end of trouble with this car.*

→ DEEP¹, HAIR, MEANS, TETHER²

end² /end/ verb ★★★
1 [T] to be in a particular place or state at the end of a period: *We ended the day in a more hopeful mood.* ◆ *The team looks likely to end the season as champions.*
2 [I/T] to stop existing, or to make something stop existing: *The marriage ended after only 11 months.* ◆ *The injury ended his career.*
3 [I/T] if you end by doing or saying something, it is the last thing that you do

or say: *I'd like to end by thanking everyone for their help.* ♦ *Let's end the meeting with a short prayer.*

PHRASAL VERB **'end in sth** to have something as a final result: *All of our attempts ended in failure.*

,end 'up *spoken* to be in a place or state after doing something, or because of doing something: *Somehow they all ended up at my house.* ♦ *Keep on doing that and you'll end up in serious trouble.* ♦ **end up doing sth** *I ended up spending the night in the airport.*

endanger /ɪnˈdeɪndʒə/ verb [T] to put someone or something into a situation where they might be harmed

endangered species /ɪnˌdeɪndʒəd ˈspiːʃiːz/ noun [C] a type of animal or plant that may soon stop existing because not many of them are left in the world

endear /ɪnˈdɪə/ **PHRASAL VERB** **en'dear yourself to sb** to make someone like you

endearing /ɪnˈdɪərɪŋ/ adj making people like you

endeavor /ɪnˈdevə/ the American spelling of endeavour

endeavour /ɪnˈdevə/ verb [T] *formal* to try very hard to do something

endemic /enˈdemɪk/ adj very common in a place or situation

ending /ˈendɪŋ/ noun ★
1 [C] the way in which a story, film, or play ends: *Children usually prefer books with a happy ending.*
2 [singular] a time when something stops permanently: *Officials have announced the ending of price controls.*
3 [C] the last group of letters in a word: *a plural ending*

endless /ˈendləs/ adj lasting or continuing for a very long time: *endless questions* ♦ *There seemed to be an endless supply of food at the meeting.* —**endlessly** adv

endorse /ɪnˈdɔːs/ verb [T] to say publicly that you support someone or something —**endorsement** noun [C/U]

endow /ɪnˈdaʊ/ verb **be endowed with sth** to have a good ability or quality

,end 'product noun [C] the thing that is produced at the end of a process

endurance /ɪnˈdjʊərəns/ noun [U] the ability to continue doing something that is difficult or tiring

endure /ɪnˈdjʊə/ verb **1** [T] to suffer something unpleasant without becoming upset **2** [I] to last for a long time

enduring /ɪnˈdjʊərɪŋ/ adj lasting for a long time

enemy /ˈenəmi/ noun [C] ★★
1 someone who is opposed to someone else and tries to harm them ≠ FRIEND: *They searched for information on political enemies.* ♦ *Terrorists are described as enemies of the state.* ♦ *It's easy to make enemies in a job like this.*
2 a country that is fighting another country in a war ≠ ALLY: *enemy aircraft/soldiers/tanks* ♦ *They had to prevent the enemy from attacking.*

In British English, **enemy** can be used with a singular or plural verb. You can say *The enemy was advancing.* OR *The enemy were advancing.*

energetic /ˌenəˈdʒetɪk/ adj an energetic person has a lot of energy and is very active —**energetically** /ˌenəˈdʒetɪkli/ adv

energy /ˈenədʒi/ noun [U] ★★★
1 the power that your body needs in order to do physical things: *She didn't even have the energy to get out of bed.*
2 electricity and other forms of power used for making things work: *energy sources/supplies.* ♦ *Switching off lights is a good way to save energy.*

enforce /ɪnˈfɔːs/ verb [T] to make people obey a law, rule etc: *Troops were sent in to enforce the treaty.* ♦ —**enforcement** noun [U]

Eng. abbrev England or English

engage /ɪnˈɡeɪdʒ/ verb **1** [I/T] if a part of a machine engages, or if you engage it, it fits into another part and they start to move together ≠ DISENGAGE **2** [T] *formal* to attract someone's interest or attention and keep it **3** [T] *formal* to employ someone
PHRASAL VERB **en'gage in sth** *formal* to take part in something

engaged /ɪnˈɡeɪdʒd/ adj ★
1 if two people are engaged, they have formally agreed to get married: *She's engaged to someone she met at work.* ♦ *We got engaged about this time last year.*
2 if something is engaged, you cannot use it now because someone else is using it

engagement /ɪnˈɡeɪdʒmənt/ noun [C] **1** a formal agreement to get married: *an engagement ring* **2** an arrangement to meet someone or do something

engaging /ɪnˈɡeɪdʒɪŋ/ adj attractive and pleasant

engender /ɪnˈdʒendə/ verb [T] *formal* to make people have a particular feeling

engine /ˈendʒɪn/ noun [C] ★★★
1 the part of a vehicle that makes it move: *the ship's engine* ♦ *a jet/diesel/steam engine*
2 a vehicle that pulls a train = LOCOMOTIVE

engineer¹ /ˌendʒɪˈnɪə/ noun [C] ★
1 someone who designs things such as roads, railways, or machines
2 *British* someone who repairs machines or electrical equipment

engineer² /ˌendʒɪˈnɪə/ verb [T] to arrange something in a clever or secret way

engineering /ˌendʒɪˈnɪərɪŋ/ noun [U] ★ the activity of designing things such as roads, railways, or machines

,English 'breakfast noun [C] in the UK, a large breakfast of hot food that includes eggs and BACON

engrave /ɪnˈɡreɪv/ verb [T] to cut words or pictures into a hard surface such as stone, metal, or glass —**engraver** noun [C]

engraving /ɪnˈɡreɪvɪŋ/ noun [C] a picture that is printed using a piece of metal that has the picture cut into its surface

engrossed /ɪnˈɡrəʊst/ adj so interested or involved in something that you do not think about anything else

engulf /ɪnˈɡʌlf/ verb [T] **1** to cover something in a way that destroys it: *Within minutes, the car was engulfed in flames.* **2** to have a very strong effect on someone or something: *Feelings of panic engulfed them.*

enhance /ɪnˈhɑːns/ verb [T] to improve something, or to make something more attractive: *We've enhanced the quality of the picture.* —**enhancement** noun [U]

enigma /ɪˈnɪgmə/ noun [C] someone or something that is mysterious and difficult to understand

enigmatic /ˌenɪgˈmætɪk/ adj mysterious and difficult to understand

E

enjoy /ɪnˈdʒɔɪ/ verb [T] ★★★
1 to get pleasure from something: *Did you enjoy your meal?* ♦ **enjoy doing sth** *I don't enjoy going to the cinema as much as I used to.*
2 *formal* to have a particular good feature: *The hotel enjoys a magnificent view of the harbour.*
PHRASE enjoy yourself to get pleasure from something that you do: *I haven't enjoyed myself so much for a long time.*

enjoyable /ɪnˈdʒɔɪəb(ə)l/ adj something that is enjoyable gives you pleasure: *an enjoyable evening* ♦ *Most students find the course very enjoyable.*

enjoyment /ɪnˈdʒɔɪmənt/ noun [U] pleasure that you get from an activity or experience: *their enjoyment of life*

enlarge /ɪnˈlɑːdʒ/ verb [T] to make something bigger: *I sent the photos back to be enlarged.*
PHRASAL VERB en'large on sth or **en'large u,pon sth** to give more information about something

enlargement /ɪnˈlɑːdʒmənt/ noun [C/U] the process of making something bigger, or something that has been made bigger

enlighten /ɪnˈlaɪt(ə)n/ verb [T] to give someone information about something so that they understand more about it —**enlightening** adj

enlightened /ɪnˈlaɪt(ə)nd/ adj with sensible modern attitudes

enlightenment /ɪnˈlaɪt(ə)nmənt/ noun [U] the process of understanding something clearly: *spiritual enlightenment*

enlist /ɪnˈlɪst/ verb **1** [I] to join the armed forces **2** [T] if you enlist someone or enlist their help, you ask them to help or support you

enliven /ɪnˈlaɪv(ə)n/ verb [T] *formal* to make something more interesting or lively

en masse /ˌɒn ˈmæs/ adv all together as a group

enmity /ˈenməti/ noun [C/U] *formal* a feeling of hate

enormity /ɪˈnɔːməti/ noun [U] the fact that something is very big, important, or wrong: *the enormity of the problem*

enormous /ɪˈnɔːməs/ adj ★★ very large in size or quantity: *an enormous birthday cake* ♦ *The stress they're under is enormous.* ♦ *an enormous amount of money*

enormously /ɪˈnɔːməsli/ adv extremely, or very much: *an enormously valuable experience*

enough /ɪˈnʌf/ grammar word ★★★

Enough can be:
■ a **determiner**: *There isn't enough time.* ♦ *Have I made enough sandwiches?*
■ a **pronoun**: *I've only got £12 – will that be enough?*
■ an **adverb**: *The rope isn't long enough.* ♦ *She didn't move quickly enough.*

1 as much or as many as is necessary: *He doesn't have enough experience as a classroom teacher.* ♦ *'Would you like something more to eat?' 'No thanks, I've had enough.'* ♦ *Do we have **enough** knives and forks **for** everyone?* ♦ *There aren't **enough** of us to make up a team.* ♦ *You've had **more than enough** time to finish the job.* ♦ **enough to do sth** *Some of the workers don't earn enough to live on.*
2 with as much of a particular quality as is necessary: *Ken wants to join the army when he's old enough.* ♦ *He told me I wasn't working hard enough.* ♦ **be good/stupid/lucky etc enough to do sth** *I was lucky enough to meet her once.* ♦ *She's intelligent enough to understand that!*
3 *spoken* used for saying that you do not want to experience any more of something because it is annoying or boring: *I've only been to one of her lectures, and that was enough!* ♦ *I'm leaving. I've **had enough of** work for today.* ♦ ***That's enough!** Stop that noise!*
4 used after an adjective or adverb for emphasis: *It's natural enough to be upset, after what happened.*
PHRASES it's bad/difficult/hard enough used for saying that a situation is already bad and something else would make it even worse: *It's bad enough that you were late, without lying about the reason.*
strangely/oddly/funnily enough used for showing that you think a particular fact is strange or surprising: *Funnily enough, Robert was saying exactly the same thing yesterday.*

enquire /ɪnˈkwaɪə/ another spelling of **inquire**

enquiry /ɪnˈkwaɪri/ another spelling of **inquiry**

enrage /ɪnˈreɪdʒ/ verb [T] to make someone extremely angry —**enraged** /ɪnˈreɪdʒd/ adj

enrich /ɪnˈrɪtʃ/ verb [T] to make something better or more enjoyable: *Doing volunteer work has enriched my life.* —**enrichment** noun [U]

enrol /ɪnˈrəʊl/ (present participle **enrolling**; past tense and past participle **enrolled**) verb [I/T] to officially become a member of a school, course, or group, or to make someone else a member —**enrolment** noun [C/U]

enroll /ɪnˈrəʊl/ the American spelling of **enrol**

en route /ˌɒn ˈruːt/ adv on the way: *We went through London en route to Germany.*

ensconce /ɪnˈskɒns/ verb **be ensconced** *formal* to be in a comfortable or safe place

ensemble /ˌɒnˈsɒmb(ə)l/ noun [C] **1** a group of musicians, dancers, or actors who perform together **2** a group of things that look good together

enshrine /ɪnˈʃraɪn/ verb **be enshrined in** *formal* to be officially accepted by being included in a document

enslave /ɪnˈsleɪv/ verb [T] **1** to keep someone in a bad situation from which they cannot escape **2** to make someone a SLAVE

ensue /ɪnˈsjuː/ verb [I] to happen after something else, often as a result of it: *A fight quickly ensued.* —**ensuing** adj

en suite /ɒn ˈswiːt/ adj *British* an en suite bathroom is one that is joined to a bedroom

ensure /ɪnˈʃɔː/ verb [T] ★★ to make certain that something happens or is done: **+(that)** *Our new system ensures that everyone gets paid on time.*

entail /ɪnˈteɪl/ verb [T] *formal* to involve something, or to make something necessary: *These cuts will entail some job losses.*

entangled /ɪnˈtæŋ(ə)ld/ adj **1** so involved in a complicated situation that it is difficult to get out **2** stuck in something such as ropes or wires —**entanglement** noun [U]

enter /ˈentə/ verb ★★★

1 go or come in	4 take part in sth
2 start to do sth	5 start a period of time
3 write sth	+ PHRASAL VERB

1 [I/T] to go or come into a place: *The man had entered through the back door.* ♦ *They were imprisoned for illegally entering the country.*

2 [T] to start to do something: *There are dozens of new companies entering the software market.* ♦ *She had hoped to enter the legal profession.*

3 [T] to write something somewhere, for example in a book, on a form, or on a computer: *Enter your user name and password.*

4 [I/T] to arrange to be in a race or competition, or to arrange for someone else to do this: *The competition is free, and anyone over the age of 18 can enter.*

5 [T] to start or reach a period of time: *The war had already entered its third week.*

PHRASAL VERB ˌenter ˈinto sth **1** to start to take part in something: *Adams agreed to enter into talks with the British government.* **2** to be an important aspect of a situation: *When companies are trying to save money, loyalty to workers doesn't enter into it.*

enterprise /ˈentəpraɪz/ noun **1** [C] a large or important project, especially a new one: *an exciting scientific enterprise* **2** [C] a business: *Euro Disney is a much smaller enterprise than the American Disney parks.* **3** [U] the ability to create new businesses or projects: *The success of the band is mainly due to Jim's initiative and enterprise.*

enterprising /ˈentəpraɪzɪŋ/ adj willing to try or think of new ideas or methods

entertain /ˌentəˈteɪn/ verb ★

1 [T] to give a performance that people enjoy: *The children sang and danced to entertain the crowd.*

2 [I/T] to receive someone as a guest and give them food and drink: *The front room is used for entertaining visitors.*

3 [T] *formal* to consider an idea or feeling and allow it to develop in your mind: *Edberg entertained hopes of winning the championship.*

entertainer /ˌentəˈteɪnə/ noun [C] someone whose job is to entertain people

entertaining /ˌentəˈteɪnɪŋ/ adj enjoyable or interesting: *an entertaining talk/evening/programme*

entertainment /ˌentəˈteɪnmənt/ noun [C/U] ★★ performances that people enjoy: *A jazz band provided entertainment for the evening.* ♦ *He is organizing entertainments for the children.*

enthral /ɪnˈθrɔːl/ verb [I/T] to make you so interested in something that you give it all your attention —**enthralling** adj

enthusiasm /ɪnˈθjuːziˌæzəm/ noun [U] ★ the feeling of being very interested in something or excited by it: *His enthusiasm for music has stayed strong.*

enthusiast /ɪnˈθjuːziæst/ noun [C] someone who is very interested in something and spends time doing it or learning about it

enthusiastic /ɪnˌθjuːziˈæstɪk/ adj ★ very interested in something, or excited by it ≠ UNENTHUSIASTIC: *Business leaders gave an enthusiastic welcome to the proposal.* ♦ *For a while, we were enthusiastic about the idea.* —**enthusiastically** /ɪnˌθjuːziˈæstɪkli/ adv

entice /ɪnˈtaɪs/ verb [T] to persuade someone to do something by offering them an advantage or reward —**enticing** adj: *an enticing offer*

entire /ɪnˈtaɪə/ adj ★★ whole or complete: *She has spent her entire life in London.*

entirely /ɪnˈtaɪəli/ adv ★★★ completely, or in every way: *We have entirely different tastes in music.* ♦ *I'm not entirely sure I believe him.*

entirety /ɪnˈtaɪərəti/ noun **in its/their entirety** with all or everything included: *The film was shown in its entirety.*

entitle /ɪnˈtaɪt(ə)l/ verb [T] **1** to give someone the right to do something: **entitle sb to sth** *Membership entitles you to cheaper tickets.* ♦ **entitle sb to do sth** *Some children are entitled to claim free school meals.* **2** to give a title to a book, poem, or piece of music: *Her first novel was entitled* More Innocent Times.

entitlement /ɪnˈtaɪt(ə)lmənt/ noun [C/U] the right to receive something or to do something

entity /ˈentəti/ noun [C] *formal* something that exists separately from other things and has its own character

entourage /ˈɒntʊˌrɑːʒ/ noun [C] a group of people who go somewhere with an important person

entrance /ˈentrəns/ noun ★★★

1 [C] the place where you can enter a room, building, or area ≠ EXIT: *I'll meet you at the main entrance at six o'clock.* ♦ *The statue stands at the entrance to the harbour.*

2 [U] The right or ability to enter a place, or to join an organization: *Entrance to the museum is free.* ♦ *There is a £5 entrance fee.*

3 [C] the act of going into a place: *Crowds cheered as she made her entrance.*

entranced /ɪnˈtrɑːnst/ adj so impressed by someone or something that you cannot look at or think about anything else

entrant /ˈentrənt/ noun [C] someone who enters a competition or examination

entrenched /ɪnˈtrentʃt/ adj entrenched attitudes have existed for a long time and are difficult to change

entrepreneur /ˌɒntrəprəˈnɜː/ noun [C] someone who uses money to start

businesses and make business deals
—**entrepreneurial** adj

entrust /ɪnˈtrʌst/ verb [T] to give someone responsibility for an important job or activity

entry /ˈentri/ noun ★★★

1 into a place	**4** for a competition
2 right to be a member	**5** entrance
3 information	

1 [U] the right or ability to go into a place: *Entry to the exhibition costs £5.50.* ♦ *They were charged with illegal entry into the US.* ♦ *We had to remove the lock on the door to gain entry* (=get in).
2 [U] the right to become a member of an organization, profession, or other group: *Older students are being denied entry into full-time education.*
3 [C] a set of information that is written in a book, on a list, or on a computer: *the dictionary entry for the word 'play'*
4 [C] a piece of work that you do to try to win a competition: *The contest attracted entries from all over the country.*
5 [C] an entrance to a building

entwine /ɪnˈtwaɪn/ verb [T] to curl or twist one thing around another
   PHRASE **be entwined** to be closely connected

envelop /ɪnˈveləp/ verb [T] to surround someone or something completely

envelope /ˈenvələʊp/ noun [C] ★★★ a flat paper case that you put a letter in before you send it

enviable /ˈenviəb(ə)l/ adj an enviable quality or situation is one that someone has and that other people would like to have
   ≠ UNENVIABLE

envious /ˈenviəs/ adj unhappy because you want something that someone else has
   → JEALOUS

environment /ɪnˈvaɪrənmənt/ noun ★★★
1 [C] the place in which people live and work, including all the physical conditions that affect them: *Parents are responsible for providing the right environment for their children to learn in.* ♦ *He grew up in a harsh urban environment.*
2 **the environment** [singular] the natural world, including the land, water, air, plants, and animals: *Industrial development is causing widespread damage to the environment.*

Words often used with **environment**

*Adjectives often used with **environment** (sense 1)*
- **safe, stable** + ENVIRONMENT: used about environments that people like
- **classroom, rural, school, urban** + ENVIRONMENT: used about particular types of environment

*Verbs often used with **environment** (sense 2)*
- **damage, destroy, pollute** + THE ENVIRONMENT: have a bad effect on the environment
- **preserve, protect** + THE ENVIRONMENT: not allow the environment to be damaged

---

environmental /ɪnˌvaɪrənˈment(ə)l/ adj ★★★
1 relating to the natural world and the effect

that human activity has on it: *The Minister discussed environmental issues.*
2 intended to help or protect the environment: *Some environmental groups are opposed to tourism on the island.*
—**environmentally** adv

environmentalist /ɪnˌvaɪrənˈment(ə)lɪst/ noun [C] someone who wants to protect the environment

environmentally friendly adj not harming the natural environment

envisage /ɪnˈvɪzɪdʒ/ verb [T] to imagine that something will happen in the future

envision /ɪnˈvɪʒ(ə)n/ verb [T] *American* to ENVISAGE

envoy /ˈenvɔɪ/ noun [C] an official who represents their government in another country

envy¹ /ˈenvi/ noun [U] the unhappy feeling that you have when you want something that someone else has
   PHRASE **be the envy of** to have good qualities that people admire and would like to have themselves

envy² /ˈenvi/ verb [T] to have the unhappy feeling of wanting what someone else has
   PHRASE **I don't envy you/him etc** *spoken* used for saying that you would not like to do what someone else has to do

enzyme /ˈenzaɪm/ noun [C] a natural substance that is produced by animal and plant cells and that causes chemical reactions

ephemeral /ɪˈfemərəl/ adj lasting for only a short time

epic¹ /ˈepɪk/ noun [C] a long book, poem, or film that contains a lot of exciting events

epic² /ˈepɪk/ adj very long and exciting: *an epic journey*

epidemic¹ /ˌepɪˈdemɪk/ noun [C] **1** a situation in which a disease spreads very quickly and infects many people **2** a sudden increase in something bad or unpleasant that affects many people

epidemic² /ˌepɪˈdemɪk/ adj happening a lot and affecting many people: *In some cities, drug use has reached epidemic proportions.*

epilepsy /ˈepɪˌlepsi/ noun [U] a brain disease that makes you suddenly shake in an uncontrolled way or become unconscious

epileptic /ˌepɪˈleptɪk/ noun [C] someone who has epilepsy —**epileptic** adj

epilogue /ˈepɪˌlɒg/ noun [C] an extra comment or piece of information at the end of a book or play

Episcopal Church, the /ɪˌpɪskəp(ə)l ˈtʃɜːtʃ/ noun a Protestant Christian Church that developed from the Anglican Church

episode /ˈepɪsəʊd/ noun [C] **1** one part of a series in a television or radio story **2** an important event in a story, in someone's life, or during a particular period of time

epitaph /ˈepɪˌtɑːf/ noun [C] a piece of writing that honours a dead person, especially one written on their GRAVE (=place where they are buried)

epitome /ɪˈpɪtəmi/ noun **the epitome of** the best possible example of a particular type of person or thing

epitomize /ɪˈpɪtəˌmaɪz/ verb [T] to be the best

possible example of a particular type of person or thing

epoch /ˈiːpɒk/ noun [C] a long period of time in history

equal¹ /ˈiːkwəl/ adj ★★★
1 the same in value, amount, or size: *All the workers have an equal share in the profits.* ♦ *One unit of alcohol is equal to one small glass of wine.* ♦ *The two companies are equal in size.* ♦ *Every game is of equal importance to us.*
2 having or deserving the same rights, status, and opportunities as other people: *He believed that men and women were equal.* ♦ *They are equal partners in every aspect of their lives.*
PHRASE **on an equal footing** or **on equal terms** with the same rights and conditions as someone else: *In the early part of the century women got the vote, on equal terms with men.*

equal² /ˈiːkwəl/ (present participle **equalling**; past tense and past participle **equalled**) verb [T]
1 to be the same in value or amount as something else: *Five plus three equals eight.*
2 to be as good as someone or something else: *She equalled the record with a time of 27.69 seconds.*

equal³ /ˈiːkwəl/ noun [C] someone or something that has the same value, rights, or importance as another person or thing

equality /ɪˈkwɒləti/ noun [U] ★ the state of being equal, especially in having the same rights, status, and opportunities as other people ≠ INEQUALITY

equalize /ˈiːkwəlaɪz/ verb **1** [I] *British* to score a goal or point in a game that gives you the same score as your opponent **2** [T] to make something the same in size, amount, or importance

equally /ˈiːkwəli/ adv ★★
1 in equal amounts or quantities: *The money raised will be divided equally among the charities.*
2 to the same degree: *This recipe works equally well with soft fruit.*
3 used for adding another comment that has the same importance as one that you have already made: *The views of parents are important, but equally we must listen to teachers.*
4 in a way that is fair and the same for everyone: *We will treat all the cases equally.*

equal opportunity noun [C/U] a situation in which people have the same opportunities in life as other people, without being treated in an unfair way because of their race, sex, religion, or age

equals sign noun [C] the sign = used in mathematics to show that two sets of numbers are the same in quantity or amount

equate /ɪˈkweɪt/ verb [T] to consider something to be the same as something else: *These people seem to equate honesty with weakness.*

equation /ɪˈkweɪʒ(ə)n/ noun [C] a statement in mathematics that two sets of numbers or expressions are equal: *Solve the equation $5x − 3 = 27$.*

equator, the /ɪˈkweɪtə/ noun [singular] an imaginary line that goes around the centre of the Earth and divides it into northern and southern parts —**equatorial** /ˌekwəˈtɔːriəl/ adj

equestrian /ɪˈkwestriən/ adj connected with riding horses

equilibrium /ˌiːkwɪˈlɪbriəm/ noun [C/U] a situation in which there is a balance between different forces or aspects

equip /ɪˈkwɪp/ verb [T] **1** to provide a person or place with the things that they need for a particular purpose: *They received a grant to build and equip a new clinic.* **2** to provide someone with the skills or qualities that they need in order to deal with a situation successfully: *The training had equipped her to deal with emergency situations.*

equipment /ɪˈkwɪpmənt/ noun [U] ★★★ the tools, machines, or other things that you need for a particular job or activity: *camping equipment* ♦ *A computer is the most important piece of equipment you will buy.*

equitable /ˈekwɪtəb(ə)l/ adj *formal* fair and reasonable because everyone is treated in the same way: *an equitable distribution of funds*

equity /ˈekwəti/ noun [U] *formal* a fair and reasonable way of behaving towards people, so that everyone is treated equally

equivalent¹ /ɪˈkwɪvələnt/ adj ★ of the same size, value, importance, or meaning as something else: *The price is £30,000, or the equivalent amount in Euros.* ♦ *a distance equivalent to a return flight from Moscow to Beijing*

equivalent² /ɪˈkwɪvələnt/ noun [C] someone or something that has the same size, value, importance, or meaning as someone or something else

er /ɜː/ interjection *British* used for writing the sound that people make when they are thinking about what to say next

ER /ˌiː ˈɑː/ noun [C] *American* an EMERGENCY ROOM in a hospital

era /ˈɪərə/ noun [C] a historical period of time that has a particular quality or character: *The president promised to bring about a new era of peace.*

eradicate /ɪˈrædɪkeɪt/ verb [T] to get rid of something bad completely —**eradication** /ɪˌrædɪˈkeɪʃ(ə)n/ noun [U]

erase /ɪˈreɪz/ verb [T] to remove all the writing, sound, or pictures from something: *The virus erases all the files on your hard drive.*

eraser /ɪˈreɪzə/ noun [C] **1** a piece of rubber for removing marks on paper made by a pencil —*picture* → C3 **2** an object that you use for removing marks from a BLACKBOARD or WHITEBOARD

erect¹ /ɪˈrekt/ verb [T] *formal* to build something, or to put something in an upright position: *Police erected barriers to control the crowds.*

erect² /ɪˈrekt/ adj in a straight upright position: *the erect posture of a professional soldier*

erection /ɪˈrekʃ(ə)n/ noun **1** [C] a stiff PENIS **2** [U] *formal* the process of erecting something such as a building or fence

ergonomics /ˌɜːgəˈnɒmɪks/ noun [U] the study of the way in which furniture and

E

equipment can be designed so that the user is comfortable and can work effectively —**ergonomic** /ˌɜːɡəˈnɒmɪk/ adj

erode /ɪˈrəʊd/ verb [I/T] **1** to gradually damage the surface of rock or land so that it begins to disappear, or to be gradually damaged in this way **2** to gradually reduce the strength, importance, or value of something, or to be gradually reduced in this way —**erosion** /ɪˈrəʊʒ(ə)n/ noun [U]

erotic /ɪˈrɒtɪk/ adj containing scenes or descriptions that make you sexually excited: *erotic films*

err /ɜː/ verb [I] *formal* to make a mistake
PHRASE **err on the side of sth** to do more than is really necessary in order to avoid a particular situation: *We are erring on the side of caution and have closed the school.*

errand /ˈerənd/ noun [C] a small job that involves going to collect or deliver something

errant /ˈerənt/ adj *formal* behaving in a way that is bad or wrong

erratic /ɪˈrætɪk/ adj changing often, or not following a regular pattern =UNPREDICTABLE: *erratic behaviour* —**erratically** /ɪˈrætɪkli/ adv

erroneous /ɪˈrəʊniəs/ adj *formal* not correct: *reports based on erroneous information* —**erroneously** adv

error /ˈerə/ noun ★★★
1 [C/U] a mistake, for example in a calculation or a decision: *an error in our calculations* ♦ *He admitted that he'd made an error in rejecting their offer.* ♦ *I was guilty of an error of judgment in allowing myself to be placed in this situation.* ♦ *The computer had been switched off in error.*
2 [C] a failure in a computer process: *an error message* (=telling you that something is wrong)
→ TRIAL

erupt /ɪˈrʌpt/ verb [I] **1** if a VOLCANO erupts, it explodes inside and flames, rocks, and LAVA come out of the top **2** to start suddenly with a lot of violence or noise: *Heavy fighting erupted in the city on Sunday.* **3** to suddenly become very angry, excited, or noisy: *The crowd erupted into wild cheers.* —**eruption** /ɪˈrʌpʃ(ə)n/ noun [C/U]

escalate /ˈeskəleɪt/ verb **1** [I/T] to become much worse or more serious, or to make something much worse or more serious **2** [I] to increase at an uncontrolled rate: *escalating costs* —**escalation** /ˌeskəˈleɪʃ(ə)n/ noun [C/U]

escalator /ˈeskəleɪtə/ noun [C] a set of moving stairs that take people from one level of a building to another

escapade /ˈeskəpeɪd/ noun [C] something exciting or dangerous that someone is involved in

escape¹ /ɪˈskeɪp/ verb ★★
1 [I] to get away from a dangerous or unpleasant place: *Three people died in the fire, but John escaped through the bedroom window.* ♦ *She was shot while trying to escape from prison.*
2 [I/T] to avoid a dangerous or unpleasant experience: *Two security guards escaped injury in the attack.* ♦ *Durham narrowly*

escaped defeat in their first match of the season.
3 [T] if something escapes you, you cannot remember it or you do not notice it: *His name escapes me right now.*
4 [I] to come out of a container by accident: *How will we know if there's any gas escaping?* —**escaped** /ɪˈskeɪpt/ adj: *an escaped prisoner*

escape² /ɪˈskeɪp/ noun ★
1 [C/U] an act of avoiding or getting away from a person, place, or bad situation: *She was relieved to make her escape from the meeting.* ♦ *A couple had a narrow escape* (=were almost killed) *when a tree fell just in front of their car.*
2 [C/U] a way of helping yourself to stop thinking about an unpleasant situation you are in: *He used alcohol as a means of escape.*
3 [U] *computing* the ESCAPE KEY on a computer

esˈcape ˌkey noun [C] *computing* a key on a computer keyboard that allows you to stop an action or leave a program

escapism /ɪˈskeɪpɪzəm/ noun [U] a pleasant or exciting activity or entertainment that helps you to forget about real life —**escapist** adj

escort¹ /ˈeskɔːt/ noun [C] **1** a person or a group of people or vehicles that go somewhere with someone in order to protect them or prevent them from escaping: *He arrived in court under police escort.* **2** someone, especially a man, who goes with another person to a social event as their partner

escort² /ɪˈskɔːt/ verb [T] **1** to go somewhere with a person or vehicle, to protect them or prevent them from escaping **2** to go with another person to a social event as their partner

Eskimo /ˈeskɪməʊ/ noun [C] *old-fashioned* a member of the Inuit people. Some people think that this word is offensive and prefer to use the word **Inuit**.

ESL /ˌiː es ˈel/ noun [U] English as a Second Language: the activity of teaching English to people whose first language is not English, but who live in an English-speaking country

ESOL /ˈiːsɒl/ noun [U] English for Speakers of Other Languages: the activity of teaching English to people whose first language is not English

esoteric /ˌesəʊˈterɪk/ adj known about or understood by very few people

ESP /ˌiː es ˈpiː/ noun [U] English for Specific or Special Purposes: the activity of teaching English to people whose first language is not English, but who need to speak English for their job or for another purpose

esp. abbrev especially

especially /ɪˈspeʃ(ə)li/ adv ★★★
1 used when mentioning conditions that make something more relevant, important, or true =PARTICULARLY: *It was a very cold house, especially in winter.*
2 very, or very much =PARTICULARLY: *I'm not especially interested in football.*
3 used for showing that what you are saying affects one person or thing more than others =PARTICULARLY: *Don't talk to anyone about this – especially not my mother.*
4 for a particular purpose, or for a

particular person: *a service **especially for** local people*

espionage /ˈespiənɑːʒ/ noun [U] attempts to discover the secrets of a country that is your enemy

espouse /ɪˈspaʊz/ verb [T] *formal* to support an idea, principle, or belief

espresso /eˈspresəʊ/ noun [C/U] a small cup of very strong coffee, or this type of coffee

essay /ˈeseɪ/ noun [C] ★ a short piece of writing on a particular subject, especially by a student: *We have to write **an essay about** Romantic poetry.*

essence /ˈes(ə)ns/ noun **1** [singular/U] the most important and typical part of something: *images that captured the essence of life in our country before the war* **2** [C/U] a liquid that contains the strong taste or smell of the plant that it is taken from

PHRASE **in essence** *formal* used for emphasizing what is the most important feature of something

essential /ɪˈsenʃ(ə)l/ adj ★★★
1 completely necessary: *It is absolutely essential that all these issues are discussed.* ♦ *A good dictionary is **essential for** learning English.* ♦ *It is essential to involve your staff in the decision.*
2 basic and important: *food, fuel, and other essential supplies*

essentially /ɪˈsenʃ(ə)li/ adv ★★
1 used for emphasizing the most important aspect of something: *That, essentially, is the difference between them.*
2 used for saying that something is mostly true, but not completely true: *The list is essentially complete.*

essentials /ɪˈsenʃ(ə)lz/ noun [plural] things that are completely necessary or basic

establish /ɪˈstæblɪʃ/ verb [T] ★★
1 to make something start to exist or start to happen: *Mandela was eager to establish good relations with the business community.* ♦ *A proper procedure for complaints should be established.*
2 to start an organization or company: *The company was established in 1860.*
3 to discover, prove, or decide that something is true: *The cause of death has not yet been established.* ♦ *+(that) We have established that you were present that afternoon.*
4 to achieve success, so that people recognize your skill, qualities, or power: **establish yourself/sb (as sth)** *Reagan quickly established himself as a promising film actor.*

established /ɪˈstæblɪʃt/ adj having existed or done something for a long time, and therefore recognized as good or successful: *an old established family firm*

establishment /ɪˈstæblɪʃmənt/ noun ★★
1 [C] *formal* an institution, organization, or business: *a research/training establishment*
2 **the establishment** [singular] the most important and powerful people in a country or section of society
3 [U] the process of starting or creating something: *Davis proposed the establishment of the committee.*

estate /ɪˈsteɪt/ noun [C] ★★
1 *British* an area containing many houses or buildings of the same type=HOUSING ESTATE: *He grew up on an estate.*
2 a large area of countryside that belongs to one person with a big house on it
3 *British* a long car with an extra door at the back and a lot of space behind the back seats

estate agent noun [C] *British* someone whose job is to help people to buy, sell, or rent property

esteem /ɪˈstiːm/ noun [U] *formal* a feeling of admiration and respect for someone =REGARD

esteemed /ɪˈstiːmd/ adj *very formal* admired and respected

esthetic /iːsˈθetɪk/ an American spelling of aesthetic

esthetics /iːsˈθetɪks/ an American spelling of aesthetics

estimate¹ /ˈestɪˌmeɪt/ verb [T] ★★ to guess or calculate an amount or value by using available information: *It is impossible to estimate how many of the residents were affected.* ♦ **estimate sth at sth** *The total cost was estimated at £600,000.* ♦ **+(that)** *We estimate that 20 per cent of the harvest has been lost.*

estimate² /ˈestɪmət/ noun [C] ★
1 an amount that you guess or calculate by using the information that is available: *The figure mentioned is just **a rough estimate**.*
2 a statement that tells a customer how much money you will charge if they employ you to do a particular piece of work: *Can you give us an estimate for the repairs to the stonework?*

Words often used with **estimate**

*Adjectives often used with **estimate** (noun, sense 1)*

- **accurate, realistic, reliable** + ESTIMATE: used about an estimate that is likely to be correct
- **approximate, rough, unofficial** + ESTIMATE: used about an estimate that might not be correct

---

estimation /ˌestɪˈmeɪʃ(ə)n/ noun [singular] *formal* someone's opinion

estranged /ɪˈstreɪndʒd/ adj *mainly journalism*
1 no longer living with your husband or wife **2** no longer seeing friends or relatives because of a disagreement

estrogen /ˈiːstrədʒən/ the American spelling of oestrogen

estuary /ˈestjuəri/ noun [C] the part of a large river where it becomes wide and flows into the sea

etc /et ˈset(ə)rə/ abbrev ★★ et cetera: used after a list of things to mean 'and others of the same type', when you do not want to mention everything

etch /etʃ/ verb [I/T] to make marks on a hard surface by cutting into it

eternal /ɪˈtɜːn(ə)l/ adj continuing and never ending —**eternally** /ɪˈtɜːn(ə)li/ adv

eternity /ɪˈtɜːnəti/ noun **1** [U] the whole of time, with no beginning and no end **2** [singular] an extremely long time: *After what seemed like an eternity, he gave his answer.*

Ethernet /ˈiːθəˌnet/ *trademark* a system in

which several computers in an area are directly connected to each other by wires

ethic /ˈeθɪk/ noun **1 ethics** [plural] a set of principles that people use to decide what is right and what is wrong: *business/ medical/professional ethics* **2** [singular] a general principle or belief that affects the way that people behave: *a strong team ethic*

ethical /ˈeθɪk(ə)l/ adj **1** involving the principles that people use for deciding what is right and what is wrong: *ethical issues/ standards/objections* **2** morally right ≠ UNETHICAL: *Is it really ethical to keep animals in zoos?* —**ethically** /ˈeθɪkli/ adv

ethnic /ˈeθnɪk/ adj ★
1 relating to a group of people who have the same culture and traditions: *The country's population consists of three main ethnic groups.*
2 belonging a particular ethnic group that lives in a place where most people are from a different ethnic group: *ethnic Albanians living in Kosovo*
3 involving people from different ethnic groups: *ethnic conflict/violence*
4 ethnic clothing, food, or music comes from countries outside Western Europe and North America
—**ethnically** /ˈeθnɪkli/ adv

ethnic cleansing /ˌeθnɪk ˈklenzɪŋ/ noun [U] the use of violence to force people who belong to a particular ethnic group to leave an area

ethnicity /eθˈnɪsəti/ noun [C/U] the fact that someone belongs to a particular ETHNIC group

ethnic minority /ˌeθnɪk maɪˈnɒrəti/ noun [C] a group of people with the same culture and traditions who live in a place where most people have a different culture and different traditions

ethos /ˈiːθɒs/ noun [singular] *formal* the set of attitudes and beliefs that are typical of an organization or a group of people

etiquette /ˈetɪket/ noun [U] a set of rules for behaving correctly in social situations

etymology /ˌetɪˈmɒlədʒi/ noun **1** [U] the study of the origins and development of words **2** [C] the origin and development of a particular word —**etymological** /ˌetɪməˈlɒdʒɪk(ə)l/ adj

EU, the /ˌiː ˈjuː/ the European Union

eulogy /ˈjuːlədʒi/ noun [C] a speech at a funeral about the person who has died

euphemism /ˈjuːfəmɪzəm/ noun [C] a word or expression that people use when they want to talk about something unpleasant or embarrassing without mentioning the thing itself: *'Social exclusion' seems to be the latest euphemism for poverty.*

euphoria /juːˈfɔːriə/ noun [U] a feeling of great happiness that lasts for a short time only —**euphoric** /juːˈfɒrɪk/ adj

euro /ˈjʊərəʊ/ noun [C] ★ the unit of money that is used in most countries in the European Union. Its symbol is €.

Europe /ˈjʊərəp/ noun **1** the large area of land between Asia and the Atlantic Ocean **2** the European Union **3** *British* the whole of Europe apart from the UK

European¹ /ˌjʊərəˈpiːən/ adj **1** of Europe, or from Europe **2** relating to the European Union

European² /ˌjʊərəˈpiːən/ noun [C] someone from Europe

European Union, the noun an organization of European countries whose aim is to improve trade among its members and encourage closer political connections

euthanasia /ˌjuːθəˈneɪziə/ noun [U] the practice of killing a very old or very ill person in order to stop them from suffering

evacuate /ɪˈvækjueɪt/ verb [I/T] to leave a place because it is not safe, or to make people leave a place because it is not safe: *The building was immediately evacuated.* —**evacuation** /ɪˌvækjuˈeɪʃ(ə)n/ noun [U]

evacuee /ɪˌvækjuːˈiː/ noun [C] someone who is evacuated from their home because of a dangerous situation such as a war

evade /ɪˈveɪd/ verb [T] **1** to avoid dealing with someone or something that you should deal with: *He had become an expert at evading responsibility.* **2** to avoid being caught: *The armed robbers managed to evade the police.*

evaluate /ɪˈvæljueɪt/ verb [T] *formal* to think carefully about something before you make a judgment about its value, importance, or quality —**evaluation** /ɪˌvæljuˈeɪʃ(ə)n/ noun [C/U]

evangelical /ˌiːvænˈdʒelɪk(ə)l/ adj relating to a form of Christianity in which people express their religious beliefs in an enthusiastic way

evangelism /ɪˈvændʒəlɪzəm/ noun [U] the practice of teaching people about Christianity

evangelist /ɪˈvændʒəlɪst/ noun [C] someone who travels around trying to persuade people to become Christians

evaporate /ɪˈvæpəreɪt/ verb [I] **1** if liquid evaporates, it changes into gas or steam **2** if something such as a feeling or quality evaporates, it suddenly disappears —**evaporation** /ɪˌvæpəˈreɪʃ(ə)n/ noun [U]

evasion /ɪˈveɪʒ(ə)n/ noun **1** [U] the practice of avoiding doing something that you should do **2** [C/U] something that you say in order to avoid telling the truth about something

evasive /ɪˈveɪsɪv/ adj not talking or answering questions in an honest way
PHRASE **take evasive action** to do something to avoid a dangerous situation
—**evasively** adv

eve /iːv/ noun **on the eve of sth** on the day before an important event, or during the period of time just before it
→ CHRISTMAS EVE, NEW YEAR'S EVE

even¹ /ˈiːv(ə)n/ adv ★★★
1 used when you are saying something that is surprising: *It always feels cold in this room, even in summer.* ♦ *Even the dog refused to eat it.* ♦ *They didn't even offer me a cup of tea.* ♦ *Even now, after all these years, he still misses her.*

When emphasizing verbs, **even** comes before an ordinary verb: *They even served champagne at breakfast.* But **even** comes after an auxiliary verb, a modal verb, or the verb 'to be': *She doesn't even know his name.* ♦ *Some computers can even talk to you.*

2 used for emphasizing that something is bigger, better etc than something else that is also big, good etc: *Things are bad, but they were even worse before you came.* ♦ *She works even more quickly than I do.*

PHRASES **even if** used for emphasizing that although something may happen, another situation remains the same: *She won't apologize, even if she's proved wrong.*
even so used for introducing a statement that seems surprising after what you said before: *Crashes are rare, but, even so, there should be stricter safety regulations.*
even though used for introducing a fact that makes the main statement in your sentence very surprising: *Most of us ignore this good advice, even though we know it to be true.* ♦ *Even though I have a master's degree in business administration, I can't fill out my tax form.*

even² /ˈiːv(ə)n/ adj **1** flat and level ≠ UNEVEN: *The table kept wobbling because the floor wasn't quite even.* **2** not changing much in rate, level, or amount ≠ UNEVEN: *an even temperature* **3** an even number can be divided exactly by two ≠ ODD **4** with both teams or people having an equal chance of winning: *an even match*

PHRASES **be even** *informal* if two people are even, neither of them owes the other anything
get even (with sb) *informal* to punish someone by causing them as much trouble or harm as they have caused you
→ BREAK¹, KEEL

even³ /ˈiːv(ə)n/ **PHRASAL VERB** **,even (sth) ˈout** if things even out, or if you even them out, they show fewer changes or differences

evening¹ /ˈiːvnɪŋ/ noun [C/U] ★★★ the part of the day between the end of the afternoon and night: *We spend most evenings reading or listening to music.* ♦ *I'll see you on Monday evening, OK?* ♦ *We usually go to the cinema on Thursday evenings* (=every Thursday evening). ♦ *an evening meal/performance/newspaper* ♦ *I'm so tired in the evenings, all I want to do is sit and watch television.* ♦ *The incident took place at around 9 o'clock yesterday evening.*

evening² /ˈiːvnɪŋ/ interjection used for greeting someone in the evening

'evening ˌclass noun [C] a series of classes in a particular subject that adults go to in the evening

'evening ˌdress noun **1** [U] formal clothes that people wear when they go to important social events in the evening **2 evening dress** or **evening gown** [C] a long dress that a woman wears when she goes to an important social event in the evening

evenly /ˈiːv(ə)nli/ adv **1** in an equal or regular way: *Sprinkle the sugar evenly over the cake.* **2** with each person having an equal chance to win: *The two teams are fairly evenly matched.*

event /ɪˈvent/ noun [C] ★★★
1 something that happens: *the most important event of my life* ♦ *a series of events*
2 an organized occasion such as a party or sports competition: *The concert is an annual event.* ♦ *Staff at the hospital helped to organize the event.*
3 one of the planned activities that take

place during an occasion such as a sports competition: *the winner of the first event*

PHRASES **in any event** whatever happens or has happened: *In any event, the project would never have succeeded.*
in the event *British* used for saying what happened, especially when it was different from what was expected: *In the event, it wasn't cold and I didn't need my coat.*
in the event of sth used for saying what will happen in a particular situation: *the procedures to be followed in the event of fire*

eventful /ɪˈventf(ə)l/ adj with a lot of exciting or unusual things happening ≠ UNEVENTFUL

eventual /ɪˈventʃuəl/ adj happening or existing at the end of a long process or period of time=ULTIMATE: *This mistake led to his eventual capture and imprisonment.*

eventually /ɪˈventʃuəli/ adv ★★★ at the end of a long process or period of time: *Eventually, we became good friends.* ♦ *the scientific research that we hope will eventually produce a cure*

ever /ˈevə/ adv ★★★ used for meaning 'at any time in the past, present, or future', especially in questions, negatives, and CONDITIONAL sentences: *Have you ever been to Las Vegas?* ♦ *Don't ever do that again.* ♦ *If you ever need any help, just let me know.* ♦ *It hardly ever* (=almost never) *rains here in the summer.* ♦ *Isabel's looking lovelier than ever.* ♦ *It was her first time ever on a plane.*

PHRASES **all sb ever does/wants/gets etc** *spoken* used for emphasizing that the same thing happens all the time: *All he ever does is complain.*
ever since during the whole period of time since something happened: *I met Harry at school and we've been friends ever since.* ♦ *Ever since his wife left him, he's been depressed.*
ever so/ever such (a) *British spoken* very: *It was ever so kind of you to invite us.* ♦ *They're ever such nice people.*
for ever continuing always into the future: *He promised to stay with me for ever.*
→ FOREVER

evergreen /ˈevəɡriːn/ noun [C] a tree or plant that does not lose its leaves in winter
—**evergreen** adj

everlasting /ˌevəˈlɑːstɪŋ/ adj continuing for ever

every /ˈevri/ determiner ★★★
1 used for referring to all the people or things of a particular type: *Every bedroom has its own private bathroom.* ♦ *She wrote to every member of the committee.* ♦ *This is a decision that affects every single one of us.*
2 used for showing how often something happens or how far apart things are: *Take one tablet every four hours.* ♦ *There are army checkpoints every few miles along the road.* ♦ *I have to work every other weekend* (=on the first, third, fifth etc). ♦ *Every now and then* (=not too frequently) *an event occurs that changes public attitudes.*
3 used for showing how common something is by giving a number as a part of a larger number: *Almost one in every five computers was found to be faulty.*

E

4 used before some words for emphasis: *You have every reason to feel proud of your performance.*

PHRASE **every time** whenever something happens: *We can't keep calling the doctor every time you get a headache.*
→ BIT¹

■ A noun subject that follows **every** is used with a singular verb.
■ In formal writing, pronouns or possessive adjectives that refer back to a subject with **every** are usually singular: *Every employee has his or her own key to the building.* But in speech and informal writing, plural pronouns and possessive adjectives are more usual: *Every employee has their own key to the building.*

everybody /ˈevrɪˌbɒdi/ pronoun ★★★
everyone: *Has everybody remembered to bring a pen?* ♦ *Bill had the courage to say what **everybody else** was thinking.*

everyday /ˈevrɪdeɪ/ adj very common or completely normal: *everyday life*

everyone /ˈevriwʌn/ pronoun ★★★
1 every person in a group: *Happy New Year, everyone!* ♦ *Everyone is thrilled about Jean's baby.* ♦ *James made a point of shaking everyone's hand.* ♦ *Everyone else had finished eating.*
2 used for talking about people in general: *Everyone needs a friend.* ♦ *Maybe private healthcare is better, but not everyone can afford it.*

■ When **everyone** is a subject, it is used with a singular verb.
■ In formal writing, pronouns or possessive adjectives that refer back to **everyone** are usually singular: *Everyone should bring his or her own lunch.* But in speech and informal writing, plural pronouns and possessive adjectives are more usual: *Everyone should bring their own lunch.*

everything /ˈevriθɪŋ/ pronoun ★★★
1 all the things, activities etc that are involved in a situation: *The earthquake destroyed everything within 25 miles.* ♦ *Everything's done by computer nowadays.* ♦ *If you put the books back on the shelves, I'll put everything else away.*
2 life in general, or a particular situation: *You look upset – is everything all right?*
PHRASES **and everything** spoken used for referring to other similar things without saying exactly which: *Have you said goodbye and everything?*
be/mean everything to be more valuable or important than anyone or anything else: *Beauty isn't everything, you know!*

everywhere /ˈevriweə/ adv in or to every place: *Everywhere in the world people know his name.* ♦ *Rosie travels everywhere with me.* ♦ *My keys must be in the desk, I've searched everywhere else.*

evict /ɪˈvɪkt/ verb [T] to legally force someone to leave the house that they are living in —**eviction** /ɪˈvɪkʃ(ə)n/ noun [C/U]

evidence /ˈevɪd(ə)ns/ noun [U] ★★★
1 facts or physical signs that help to prove something: *the historical evidence for his theories* ♦ *We are seeing more evidence of*

economic growth. ♦ **+that** *The study found no evidence that fish feel pain.*
2 facts, statements, or objects that help to prove whether someone has committed a crime: *The police didn't have enough evidence to convict him.* ♦ *The evidence against them is overwhelming.* ♦ *He went to court to give evidence against his attacker.*

evident /ˈevɪd(ə)nt/ adj formal easy to see, notice, or understand

evidently /ˈevɪd(ə)ntli/ adv **1** used for saying that something is obvious: *Evidently annoyed, he left the room.* **2** used for showing that a statement is based on known facts: *Evidently, these plants don't do well in a cold climate.*

evil¹ /ˈiːv(ə)l/ adj **1** very bad or cruel: *a dangerous and evil dictator* **2** very unpleasant: *an evil-smelling chemical*

evil² /ˈiːv(ə)l/ noun [U] a power that makes people do very bad and cruel things ≠ GOOD
PHRASE **the evils of sth** the bad effects that something can have
→ LESSER¹, NECESSARY

evocative /ɪˈvɒkətɪv/ adj formal bringing a particular emotion, idea, or memory into your mind

evoke /ɪˈvəʊk/ verb [T] formal to bring a particular emotion, idea, or memory into your mind

evolution /ˌiːvəˈluːʃ(ə)n/ noun [U] **1** the theory that plants and animals change over long periods of time to become more suitable for their environment **2** the way in which something gradually changes and develops —**evolutionary** /ˌiːvəˈluːʃ(ə)n(ə)ri/ adj

evolve /ɪˈvɒlv/ verb **1** [I] to gradually change and develop over a period of time: *Computer software will continue to evolve in response to users' needs.* ♦ *a debate as to whether birds evolved from dinosaurs* **2** [T] to develop something gradually: *Teachers are evolving new ways of working.*

ewe /juː/ noun [C] a female sheep

ex /eks/ noun [C] informal the person that someone used to be married to or used to have a romantic relationship with

ex- /eks/ prefix used with nouns that describe someone's job, rank, or relationship to someone, showing that they no longer have that job, rank, or relationship: *an ex-boyfriend*

exacerbate /ɪɡˈzæsəˌbeɪt/ verb [T] formal to make a problem worse

exact¹ /ɪɡˈzækt/ adj ★ done, made, or described in a very thorough way, with all the details correct: *the exact sequence of events leading up to the accident* ♦ *The exact number of wounded people is unknown.*
PHRASE **the exact opposite** used for emphasizing that two things or people are completely different: *She's very friendly, the exact opposite of her sister.*

exact² /ɪɡˈzækt/ verb [T] formal to get something from someone by threatening or forcing them

exacting /ɪɡˈzæktɪŋ/ adj needing a lot of skill and effort

exactly /ɪɡˈzæk(t)li/ adv ★★★
1 no more and no less than a particular

amount or time=PRECISELY: *It's exactly three o'clock.* ♦ *The wood should measure five centimetres exactly.*

2 in every way, or in every detail=JUST: *She sounds exactly like her mother.* ♦ *The house is exactly the same as it was 20 years ago.*

3 used for emphasizing that you are referring to one particular thing and no other=JUST: *She was standing exactly where you are now.*

4 *spoken* used as a reply for saying that you completely agree with someone: *'If he does that again, he could lose his job.' 'Exactly!'*

PHRASES **not exactly** *spoken* **1** *often humorous* used for emphasizing that someone or something does not have a particular quality: *She's not exactly the world's greatest singer.* **2** used for saying that something that someone says is not completely right: *'You're leaving, aren't you?' 'Not exactly, I'm just going on holiday.'*
what/where/when etc exactly used for asking someone for more details about something: *What exactly did he say?*

exaggerate /ɪgˈzædʒəˌreɪt/ verb [I/T] ★ to describe something in a way that makes it seem better, worse, larger, more important etc than it really is: *Don't exaggerate! It wasn't that bad!* ♦ *We should not exaggerate the importance of this agreement.*

exaggerated /ɪgˈzædʒəˌreɪtɪd/ adj **1** describing something in a way that makes it seem better, worse, larger, more important etc than it really is: *exaggerated claims* **2** done in a way that does not seem sincere or natural: *a tone of exaggerated politeness*

exaggeration /ɪgˌzædʒəˈreɪʃ(ə)n/ noun **1** [C] a comment or description that makes something seem better, worse, larger, more important etc than it really is **2** [U] the act of making a comment or description of this type

exalted /ɪgˈzɔːltɪd/ adj *formal* very important

exam /ɪgˈzæm/ noun [C] ★★ an important test of your knowledge, especially one that you take at school or university: *I'm taking the exam in June.* ♦ *She really needs to pass this exam.*

examination /ɪgˌzæmɪˈneɪʃ(ə)n/ noun ★★★
1 [C] *formal* an exam: *Students will take an examination at the end of the year.*
2 [C/U] a careful look at something or someone: *The doctor will give you a full examination.* ♦ *Engineers made a thorough examination of the wreckage.*
3 [C/U] a careful study of something: *a close examination of the language of a text*
4 [C/U] an occasion when a lawyer asks someone questions in court

examine /ɪgˈzæmɪn/ verb [T] ★★★
1 to look at something or someone carefully: *She opened the suitcase and examined the contents.* ♦ *Dr Greene has come to examine the patient.*
2 to study or consider something carefully: *The committee will examine four proposals.*
3 to ask someone questions in a legal trial
4 *formal* to give students an examination to test their knowledge

examiner /ɪgˈzæmɪnə/ noun [C] someone whose job is to test people's knowledge or ability

example /ɪgˈzɑːmp(ə)l/ noun [C] ★★★
1 something that you mention in order to show the type of thing that you are talking about and to help to explain what you mean: *Many sports are still dominated by men – football is an obvious example.* ♦ *He gave several examples of how we could change things.* ♦ *The Mini is a classic example* (=a typical example) *of a great British car.*
2 a person or way of behaving that is considered as a model for other people to copy: *You should be setting an example for your little brother.*

PHRASE **for example** used when mentioning something that shows the type of thing that you are talking about and helps to explain what you mean: *There are good deals available – people under 25, for example, can get discounts of up to 50%.*

exasperated /ɪgˈzɑːspəˌreɪtɪd/ adj extremely annoyed —**exasperate** verb [T]

exasperating /ɪgˈzɑːspəˌreɪtɪŋ/ adj making you feel extremely annoyed

exasperation /ɪgˌzɑːspəˈreɪʃ(ə)n/ noun [U] the feeling of being extremely annoyed

excavate /ˈekskəˌveɪt/ verb [I/T] to dig in the ground in order to find things from the past —**excavation** /ˌekskəˈveɪʃ(ə)n/ noun [C/U]

exceed /ɪkˈsiːd/ verb [T] *formal* **1** to be greater than a number or amount: *a claim exceeding £500* **2** to go above an official limit: *drivers who exceed the speed limit*

exceedingly /ɪkˈsiːdɪŋli/ adv *formal* extremely

excel /ɪkˈsel/ verb [I] to do something extremely well

PHRASE **excel yourself** to do something much better than you usually do

excellence /ˈeksələns/ noun [U] the quality of being extremely good: *academic excellence*

excellent /ˈeksələnt/ adj ★★★ extremely good: *The food was absolutely excellent.* ♦ *It's quite an old bike, but it's in excellent condition.* —**excellently** adv

except /ɪkˈsept/ grammar word ★★★

Except can be:
- a **preposition**: *We haven't told anyone except Leslie's dad.*
- a **conjunction**: *I'd go and see him myself, except I don't know where he lives.*
- used before a **conjunction**: *I don't know much about the man, except that he's a fool.*
- used in the prepositional phrase **except for**: *Everything was perfect except for the weather.*

1 used for introducing the only thing, person, or fact that is not included in your main statement: *All the team were there except Eddie.* ♦ *The shop is open every day, except on Sundays.* ♦ *She was dressed all in black except for a white scarf.* ♦ *I never get a chance to study, except when the children have gone to bed.* ♦ **+(that)** *I don't know anything except that the flight is delayed.* ♦ **except do sth** *He's done nothing all day except watch television.*
2 *spoken* used for introducing a statement that makes what you have just said seem less true or less possible: *I'd be glad to help, except that I'm going away this weekend.*

E

E

exception /ɪkˈsepʃ(ə)n/ noun [C/U] ★★
someone or something that is different and cannot be included in a general statement: *There are some **exceptions to** every grammatical rule.* ♦ *The boat race always attracts a large crowd and this year **is no exception**.* ♦ ***With the exception of** the Metropole, all the hotels have their own restaurants.*

> **PHRASE** **make an exception** to deal with something differently on one particular occasion only: *I don't usually lend people money, but in your case I'll make an exception.*

exceptional /ɪkˈsepʃ(ə)nəl/ adj **1** extremely good or impressive in a way that is unusual ≠ UNEXCEPTIONAL: *Her scores were quite exceptional.* **2** much more or greater than usual: *the exceptional difficulty of this task* **3** unusual and not likely to happen or exist very often=EXTREME: *exceptional circumstances* —**exceptionally** adv

excerpt /ˈeksɜːpt/ noun [C] a short piece of writing or music that is taken from a longer piece=PASSAGE

excess¹ /ɪkˈses/ noun **1** [singular/U] a larger amount of something than is usual or necessary: *Tests revealed an excess of alcohol in the driver's blood.* **2 excesses** [plural] behaviour that is thought to be wrong because it is too extreme: *the worst excesses of the regime*

> **PHRASES** **in excess of sth** more than a particular amount
> **to excess** if you do something to excess, you do it so much that it harms you or causes problems

excess² /ˈekses/ adj more than is usual or necessary: *Drain off any excess liquid.*

excessive /ɪkˈsesɪv/ adj much more than is reasonable or necessary

exchange¹ /ɪksˈtʃeɪndʒ/ noun ★★
1 [C/U] a situation in which one person gives, does, or says something and another person gives, does, or says something in return: *a frank exchange of views* ♦ ***an exchange of** prisoners of war* ♦ *Russia supplied crude oil to Cuba **in exchange for** raw sugar.*
2 [U] the process of changing the money of one country for the money of another country: *a foreign exchange dealer* ♦ *What is **the rate of exchange** for US dollars?*
3 [C] an arrangement in which people or groups from different countries visit each other: *a cultural/educational exchange* ♦ *an exchange student from Spain*
→ STOCK EXCHANGE, TELEPHONE EXCHANGE

exchange² /ɪksˈtʃeɪndʒ/ verb [T] ★★
1 to give someone something in return for something that they give you: *We exchanged addresses and promised to write to one another.* ♦ ***exchange sth for sth** The tokens can be exchanged for goods in any of our shops.*
2 to change the money of one country for the money of another country
3 to say or do something to someone who says or does something to you: *We exchanged greetings.*

exˈchange ˌrate noun [C] the value of the money of one country when you change it for the money of another country

excise /ˈeksaɪz/ noun [U] *technical* a government tax on services used and goods sold within a country

excitable /ɪkˈsaɪtəb(ə)l/ adj easily excited or upset

excite /ɪkˈsaɪt/ verb [T] **1** to make someone feel very happy and enthusiastic about something good that is going to happen: *The idea of working in Australia really excites me.* **2** to make someone feel lively, nervous, or upset: *We were warned by the doctors not to excite him.* **3** to make someone feel that they want to have sex

excited /ɪkˈsaɪtɪd/ adj ★★
1 very happy and enthusiastic because something good is going to happen: *I was so excited I couldn't sleep.* ♦ *I'm so **excited about** the trip!* ♦ *He's **excited at** the prospect of showing his work in New York.*
2 upset, worried, or angry about something: *Look, Dad, stop getting so excited – I'm sure she'll be home soon.*
3 feeling that you want to have sex
—**excitedly** adv: *He talked excitedly about his plans.*

> ■ **Excited** describes how you feel: *I'm excited about my holiday.* ♦ *She didn't seem very excited.*
> ■ **Exciting** describes things or situations that make you feel excited: *I find circuses very exciting.* ♦ *It was such an exciting adventure.*

excitement /ɪkˈsaɪtmənt/ noun [U] ★★ the feeling of being excited: *The long wait only added to our excitement.* ♦ *the excitement of winning a major championship*

exciting /ɪkˈsaɪtɪŋ/ adj ★★
1 making you feel excited and enthusiastic ≠ UNEXCITING: *an exciting opportunity*
2 interesting and full of action ≠ BORING: *an exciting story of adventure*

exclaim /ɪkˈskleɪm/ verb [I/T] to say something suddenly and loudly because you are surprised or angry

exclamation /ˌekskləˈmeɪʃ(ə)n/ noun [C] something that you say because you are surprised or angry

exclaˈmation ˌmark noun [C] the mark ! used in writing to show that someone says something suddenly and loudly because they are surprised or angry

exclude /ɪkˈskluːd/ verb [T] ★★
1 to deliberately not include something ≠ INCLUDE: *These figures exclude administration costs.*
2 to deliberately prevent someone or something from being part of something or from entering a place ≠ INCLUDE: *I felt as though the other women were excluding me.* ♦ ***exclude sb from sth** The committee has decided to exclude him from the competition.*
3 to decide that something is not possible or not worth considering: *We cannot **exclude the possibility** that the patient has cancer.*
4 *British* to officially tell a child to leave a school because their behaviour is very bad

excluding /ɪkˈskluːdɪŋ/ preposition not including: *The cost of hiring equipment, excluding insurance, is around £600 a year.*

exclusion /ɪkˈskluːʒ(ə)n/ noun [U] a situation in which someone or something is deliberately prevented from being part of something or from entering a place ≠ INCLUSION: *the team's exclusion from the competition*

PHRASE **to the exclusion of sth** when you do something to the exclusion of other things, you only do that one thing and not the other things

exclusive¹ /ɪkˈskluːsɪv/ adj **1** very expensive and available only to people who have a lot of money: *an exclusive shop/restaurant/ neighbourhood* **2** limited to a particular person or group and not shared with others: *The road is for the exclusive use of residents.* **3** published or reported by only one newspaper, magazine, or television station: *an exclusive interview*

PHRASE **exclusive of sth** not including something: *The cost is £20 exclusive of delivery charges.*

exclusive² /ɪkˈskluːsɪv/ noun [C] a piece of news that is published or reported by only one newspaper, magazine, or television station

exclusively /ɪkˈskluːsɪvli/ adv only: *a club exclusively for women*

excrement /ˈekskrɪmənt/ noun [U] *formal* the solid waste that your body gets rid of

excrete /ɪkˈskriːt/ verb [I/T] *formal* to get rid of waste from your body

excruciating /ɪkˈskruːʃieɪtɪŋ/ adj causing extreme physical pain —**excruciatingly** adv

excursion /ɪkˈskɜːʃ(ə)n/ noun [C] a short journey that you make for pleasure

excuse¹ /ɪkˈskjuːs/ noun [C] ★★
1 a reason that you give to explain why you have done something bad, or why you should have not done something that you should have done: *a reasonable/valid/legitimate excuse* ♦ *He **made** some **excuse** about having a lot of work to do.* ♦ *What **excuse** did they **give** for the delay?*
2 a reason for doing something that you want to do: *Birthdays are always **a good excuse** for a party.* ♦ **an excuse to do sth** *Emily was glad of an excuse to change the subject.*
PHRASE **there is no excuse for sth 1** used for emphasizing that you think that someone's behaviour is very bad: *There's no excuse for treating a child that way.* **2** used for saying that someone should definitely do something: *She only lives five minutes away, so there's really no excuse for not visiting her.*

excuse² /ɪkˈskjuːz/ verb [T] ★★
1 to forgive someone for something: *Please excuse my untidy handwriting.* ♦ **excuse sb for (doing) sth** *I hope you'll excuse us for leaving so early.*
2 to provide a reason or explanation for something bad that someone has done, in order to make it seem less bad: *I know he's over 70, but that doesn't excuse his sexist attitudes.*
3 to give someone permission not to do something that they usually have to do: **excuse sb from (doing) sth** *You're excused from doing the washing up tonight.*
4 to give someone permission to leave: *Now*

if you'll excuse us, we have to get going.
PHRASES **excuse me** *spoken* **1** used for politely getting someone's attention, or for showing that you are sorry for interrupting or touching them: *Excuse me, do you know what time it is?* **2** used for politely asking someone to move so that you can get past them **3** used for politely telling someone that you are leaving: *Excuse me for a moment – I have to make a phone call.*
excuse yourself to politely say that you are going to leave a place

execute /ˈeksɪˌkjuːt/ verb [T] **1** to kill someone as a punishment for a crime: *The prisoner is due to be executed next week.* **2** *formal* to complete something that you have agreed or planned to do: *They were able to execute their task successfully.*

execution /ˌeksɪˈkjuːʃ(ə)n/ noun **1** [C/U] the act of killing someone as a punishment for a crime **2** [U] *formal* the act of completing something that you have agreed or planned to do

executioner /ˌeksɪˈkjuːʃ(ə)nə/ noun [C] someone whose job is to EXECUTE criminals

executive¹ /ɪɡˈzekjʊtɪv/ noun [C] ★
1 a senior manager in a business or other organization: *a meeting with some of the company's top executives*
2 a group of people who are responsible for making important decisions in an organization: *This matter will be decided by the party's national executive.*

executive² /ɪɡˈzekjʊtɪv/ adj **1** involved in making important decisions in an organization or government: *the executive director of the museum* ♦ *executive powers* **2** designed for rich or important people: *an executive jet*

exemplary /ɪɡˈzempləri/ adj *formal* excellent, or done in a way that other people should try to copy

exemplify /ɪɡˈzemplɪˌfaɪ/ verb [T] to be a typical example of something

exempt¹ /ɪɡˈzempt/ adj allowed to ignore something such as a rule, obligation, or payment

exempt² /ɪɡˈzempt/ verb [T] to allow someone to ignore something such as a rule, obligation, or payment —**exemption** /ɪɡˈzempʃ(ə)n/ noun [C/U]

exercise¹ /ˈeksəˌsaɪz/ noun ★★★

1 physical activity	4 written questions
2 physical action	5 for particular purpose
3 learning activity	6 use of power etc

1 [U] physical activity that you do in order to stay healthy and make your body stronger: *I **get** plenty of **exercise** being an aerobics instructor.* ♦ *You should **take** more exercise.*
2 [C] a physical action that you repeat several times in order to make a part of your body stronger or more healthy: *Roll over and repeat the exercise on the other leg.* ♦ *breathing exercises*
3 [C] an activity or set of activities that you do in order to learn or practise a skill: *military training exercises* ♦ *When did you **do** your piano **exercises**?*
4 [C] a set of written questions that you

answer in order to help you to learn something: *Next I'd like you to do the exercises on page 10.*

5 [singular] *formal* an action that has a particular plan, purpose, or result: *a cost-cutting exercise* ♦ *Good management is often an exercise in compromise.*

6 [U] *formal* the use of your power, rights, or skills: *General de Gaulle's military training influenced his exercise of power.*

exercise² /'eksəˌsaɪz/ verb ★★★

1 [I/T] to do a physical activity in order to stay healthy and to make your body stronger: *Do you eat properly and exercise regularly?* ♦ *The doctor said I should exercise my knee every morning.*

2 [T] *formal* to use power, skill, or a personal quality: *For centuries, the Church exercised authority over people's lives.*

exercise ˌbike noun [C] a bicycle that stays in one place, used for physical exercise —*picture* → C16

exert /ɪgˈzɜːt/ verb [T] *formal* to use influence, authority, or strength in order to affect or achieve something

PHRASE **exert yourself** to use a lot of physical or mental effort

exertion /ɪgˈzɜːʃ(ə)n/ noun [C/U] great physical or mental effort

exhale /eksˈheɪl/ verb [I/T] to breathe air out through your mouth or nose ≠ INHALE

exhaust¹ /ɪgˈzɔːst/ verb [T] **1** to make someone feel extremely tired and without energy: *Caring for young children can exhaust you physically and mentally.* **2** to use all that you have of something: *The expedition was forced to turn back when it exhausted its food supply.*

exhaust² /ɪgˈzɔːst/ noun **1** [C] an EXHAUST PIPE **2** [U] gases or steam that are produced by an engine as it works

exhausted /ɪgˈzɔːstɪd/ adj extremely tired and without enough energy to do anything else: *After two days of travel the children were completely exhausted.*

exhausting /ɪgˈzɔːstɪŋ/ adj extremely tiring

exhaustion /ɪgˈzɔːstʃ(ə)n/ noun [U] a feeling of being extremely tired and without energy

exhaustive /ɪgˈzɔːstɪv/ adj thorough, or complete: *The list is by no means exhaustive.*

exˈhaust ˌpipe noun [C] a pipe that carries the gases or steam out of an engine —*picture* → C6

exhibit¹ /ɪgˈzɪbɪt/ verb **1** [I/T] to put something interesting in a public place so that people can go and look at it: *His work will be exhibited in Moscow later this year.* **2** [T] *formal* to show a particular feeling, quality, ability, or form of behaviour: *She was exhibiting symptoms of stress.*

exhibit² /ɪgˈzɪbɪt/ noun [C] **1** an object that is part of an exhibition **2** an object or document that is used as evidence in a court of law **3** *American* an EXHIBITION

exhibition /ˌeksɪˈbɪʃ(ə)n/ noun [C] ★★

1 a public show where art or other interesting things are put so that people can go and look at them: *an exhibition hall/centre/space* ♦ *an exhibition of paintings by Henri Matisse*

2 a particular way of behaving or performing=DISPLAY: *a fine exhibition of skilful and exciting football*

exhibitor /ɪgˈzɪbɪtə/ noun [C] a person, company, or organization that shows their work or products in a public place

exhilarated /ɪgˈzɪləˌreɪtɪd/ adj extremely happy, excited, and full of energy —**exhilaration** /ɪgˌzɪləˈreɪʃ(ə)n/ noun [U]

exhilarating /ɪgˈzɪləˌreɪtɪŋ/ adj making you feel extremely happy, excited, and full of energy

exile¹ /ˈeksaɪl/ noun **1** [U] a situation in which someone is forced to live in a foreign country, usually for political reasons: *He died in exile in 1986.* **2** [C] someone who has been forced to live in a foreign country

exile² /ˈeksaɪl/ verb [T] to force someone to live in a foreign country, usually for political reasons

exist /ɪgˈzɪst/ verb [I] ★★★

1 to be present in a particular place, time, or situation: *Several exciting career opportunities exist in our company.* ♦ *The company officially ceased to exist at midnight on March 31st.*

2 to be real, not imaginary: *Dragons don't exist.*

3 to manage to live, especially when conditions are difficult=SURVIVE: *You can't exist for long without water.*

existence /ɪgˈzɪst(ə)ns/ noun ★★★

1 [U] the state of being a real or living thing, or of being present in a particular place, time, or situation: *The tests confirm the existence of a brain tumour.* ♦ *the only copy of the book that is still in existence* ♦ *The company came into existence at the end of the 1980s.*

2 [C] the way that someone lives their life: *Jones led a miserable existence in an isolated village.*

existing /ɪgˈzɪstɪŋ/ adj ★★★ used for describing something that exists now, especially when it might soon be changed or replaced: *The existing system needs to be changed.*

exit¹ /ˈeksɪt/ noun [C] ★

1 a door that leads out of a public place such as a room or building ≠ ENTRANCE: *Passengers should leave the plane by the nearest emergency exit.*

2 a minor road that you use to drive off a motorway: *Take the next exit going north.*

3 the act of leaving a place: *They made a hasty exit through the back door.*

exit² /ˈeksɪt/ verb [I/T] **1** *formal* to leave a place **2** to make a computer program stop running

exodus /ˈeksədəs/ noun [singular] a situation in which a lot of people leave a place at the same time

exonerate /ɪgˈzɒnəˌreɪt/ verb [T] *formal* to officially say that someone is not to blame for something

exorbitant /ɪgˈzɔːbɪt(ə)nt/ adj an exorbitant price or amount of money is much more than is reasonable

exorcize /ˈeksɔːˌsaɪz/ verb [T] to get rid of an evil spirit using a special religious ceremony or prayers —**exorcism** noun [C/U], **exorcist** noun [C]

exotic /ɪgˈzɒtɪk/ adj interesting or exciting because of being unusual or not familiar

expand /ɪkˈspænd/ verb [I/T] ★★
1 to become larger, or to make something larger: *The population is expanding rapidly.* ♦ *There are plans to expand the national park.*
2 if a business or service expands, or if you expand it, it grows by including more people and moving into new areas: *We are expanding the programme to provide more student places.*
PHRASAL VERB **ex'pand on sth** to talk or write more about something, adding more details or information

expanse /ɪkˈspæns/ noun [C] a large area of land, water, or sky

expansion /ɪkˈspænʃ(ə)n/ noun [U] 1 an increase in size 2 the process of developing to include more people, places, or things

expansionist /ɪkˈspænʃ(ə)nˌɪst/ adj an expansionist government or nation tries to get control over other regions and countries

expansive /ɪkˈspænsɪv/ adj friendly, generous, or willing to talk

expatriate /eksˈpætriət/ noun [C] someone who lives in a foreign country —**expatriate** adj

expect /ɪkˈspekt/ verb [T] ★★★
1 to think that something will happen: *We're expecting good weather at the weekend.* ♦ *As expected, the party was a great success.* ♦ **expect sb/sth to do sth** *I didn't really expect you to understand.* ♦ +(that) *Investors expect that interest rates will rise.* → WAIT
2 to be waiting for someone or something to arrive: *Are you expecting a parcel?* ♦ *What time do you expect Sara home?*
3 to think that it is right or reasonable that something should happen: *Our customers expect good service.* ♦ **expect to do sth** *I expect to get paid on time.* ♦ **expect sb/sth to do sth** *It's not fair to expect me to do all the housework.*
PHRASES **be expecting (a baby)** to be pregnant
I expect *spoken* used for saying that you think that something is probably true: *'Will David be coming to the party?' 'I expect so.'* ♦ +(that) *I expect you're hungry.*

Word family: expect

Words in the same family as expect
- **expected** *adj*
- **expectation** *n*
- **expectant** *adj*
- **unexpected** *adj*
- **expectancy** *n*

---

expectant /ɪkˈspektənt/ adj 1 feeling excited about something that you think is going to happen 2 an expectant mother or father will soon be a parent of a new baby —**expectancy** noun [U], **expectantly** adv

expectation /ˌekspekˈteɪʃ(ə)n/ noun ★★
1 [C] a belief or hope that something will be good, or that someone will do well: *We have high expectations of our students* (=expect them to succeed). ♦ *We had heard so much about the restaurant, but it did not live up to our expectations* (=was not as good as we expected).

2 [C/U] the belief that something will happen: *The team set off without any expectation of success.*

expected /ɪkˈspektɪd/ adj likely to happen or be true: *Events did not follow their expected course.*

expediency /ɪkˈspiːdiənsi/ noun [C/U] *formal* a way of dealing with something that produces the result that you want in a particular situation, especially when this is not the best or most honest thing to do

expedient /ɪkˈspiːdiənt/ adj an expedient action produces the result that you want in a particular situation, especially when this is not the best or most honest thing to do

expedition /ˌekspəˈdɪʃ(ə)n/ noun [C] 1 a long journey to a dangerous or distant place 2 a short journey for pleasure

expel /ɪkˈspel/ verb [T] 1 to officially force someone to leave a place, organization, or school, for example because of their bad behaviour 2 *technical* to force something out of a container or out of someone's body

expend /ɪkˈspend/ verb [T] *formal* to spend time, energy, or money on something

expendable /ɪkˈspendəb(ə)l/ adj someone or something that is expendable is no longer useful or necessary to you

expenditure /ɪkˈspendɪtʃə/ noun 1 [C/U] the amount of money that is spent by a government, organization, or person =SPENDING 2 [U] *formal* the use of time, money, or energy to do something

expense /ɪkˈspens/ noun ★★
1 [C] an amount of money that you spend in order to buy or do something: *travelling/ medical/legal expenses* ♦ *Rent is our biggest expense.*
2 [U] the high cost of something: *A powerful computer is worth the expense if you use it regularly.* ♦ *Previously, the chemical had to be imported at great expense.*
3 **expenses** [plural] money that you spend as part of your job that your employer gives back to you later: *Your salary will be £50,000 a year, plus expenses.*
PHRASES **at sb's expense** 1 used for saying who pays for something: *He did a six-month training course at his own expense.* 2 if someone has a joke at your expense, you are the person that the joke is about
at the expense of sth if one thing exists or happens at the expense of another, the second thing suffers because of the first

expensive /ɪkˈspensɪv/ adj ★★★ something that is expensive costs a lot of money ≠ INEXPENSIVE: *He always wears expensive clothes.* ♦ *It can be very expensive to train new personnel.* —**expensively** adv

experience¹ /ɪkˈspɪəriəns/ noun ★★★
1 [U] knowledge and skill that you get by doing a particular job or activity: *You don't need any experience to work here.* ♦ *business/teaching experience* ♦ *Do you have any previous experience with children?* ♦ *She has years of experience in the computer industry.*
2 [U] the knowledge that you get from life and from being in different situations: *I can say from personal experience that it's*

E

hard not having a job. ♦ Helen knew *from past experience* that there was no point in arguing with him.

3 [C] something that happens to you, or a situation that you are involved in: *our childhood experiences* ♦ *I had a bad experience in the last place I worked.*

experience² /ɪkˈspɪərɪəns/ verb [T] ★★★
1 if you experience a problem or situation, you have that problem or are in that situation: *Almost every country of the industrial world is experiencing economic problems.* ♦ *How can we end the discrimination experienced by older people?*
2 to feel an emotion or a physical feeling: *Are you experiencing any pain?*

experienced /ɪkˈspɪərɪənst/ adj ★ someone who is experienced has skill at something because they have done it a lot
≠ INEXPERIENCED: *I'm a lot more experienced than him.* ♦ *an experienced sailor* ♦ *She's experienced in dealing with difficult customers.*

experiment¹ /ɪkˈsperɪmənt/ noun [C] ★★
1 a scientific test to find out what happens to someone or something in particular conditions: *laboratory experiments* ♦ *a series of experiments on animals* ♦ *Researchers now need to conduct further experiments.*
2 an occasion when you test a new idea, method, or activity in order to find out what the result will be: *an experiment in tax reform*

experiment² /ɪkˈsperɪment/ verb [I] **1** to try new ideas, methods, or activities in order to find out what results they will have: *a designer who is not afraid to experiment* **2** to perform scientific tests in order to find out what happens to someone or something in particular conditions: *This lab does not experiment on animals.*

experimental /ɪkˌsperɪˈment(ə)l/ adj **1** using new ideas or methods that you have not tried before **2** relating to scientific experiments —**experimentally** adv

experimentation /ɪkˌsperɪmenˈteɪʃ(ə)n/ noun [U] the process of testing ideas, methods, or activities to see what effect they have

expert¹ /ˈekspɜːt/ noun [C] ★★ someone who has a particular skill or knows a lot about a particular subject: *a safety/health/computer expert* ♦ *an expert in radio communications*

expert² /ˈekspɜːt/ adj having special skills or knowledge about something —**expertly** adv

expertise /ˌekspɜːˈtiːz/ noun [U] special skill or knowledge that you get from experience, training, or study

expire /ɪkˈspaɪə/ verb [I] if an agreement, offer, or official document expires, the period of time during which it can be used comes to an end = RUN OUT

expiry /ɪkˈspaɪəri/ noun [U] British the end of a period of time during which an agreement, offer, or official document can be used

ex'piry ˌdate noun [C] the date after which something can no longer be used, or after which it is no longer safe to eat

explain /ɪkˈspleɪn/ verb ★★★
1 [T] to tell someone something in a way that helps them to understand it better:

explain sth to sb *The doctor explained the risks to me before the operation.* ♦ **+how/when/what etc** *I will try to explain how a car engine works.* ♦ **+(that)** *He explained that he would be moving to another city.*
2 [I/T] to give a reason for something that happens: *Science cannot explain everything.* ♦ *'Tom is in hospital.' 'That explains why he wasn't in school today.'* ♦ *Wait! Let me explain!*

PHRASAL VERB **ex,plain sth a'way** to tell someone about something in a way that makes it seem unimportant, so that they do not ask questions about it: *She made up stories to explain away the missing money.*

> **Word family: explain**
>
> *Words in the same family as explain*
> ■ explanation *n*   ■ inexplicable *adj*
> ■ explanatory *adj*   ■ unexplained *adj*

explanation /ˌekspləˈneɪʃ(ə)n/ noun [C/U] ★★★
1 a reason that you give for something that has happened or something that you have done: *I expected an explanation and an apology.* ♦ *The explanation for this is simple.* ♦ *He gave a detailed explanation of the events leading up to the accident.*
2 a description of how something works or of how to do something: *This book provides a clear explanation of how to use the Internet.*

explanatory /ɪkˈsplænət(ə)ri/ adj intended to help you to understand something

expletive /ɪkˈspliːtɪv/ noun [C] *formal* a swearword

explicit /ɪkˈsplɪsɪt/ adj **1** extremely clear **2** showing or describing sex or violence in a lot of detail —**explicitly** adv

explode /ɪkˈspləʊd/ verb ★
1 [I/T] to burst with a lot of force and a loud noise, or to make something do this, usually in a way that causes a lot of damage: *Bombs were exploding all over the city.* ♦ *France first exploded a nuclear device in 1960.*
2 [I] to suddenly express a strong emotion, especially anger: *She suddenly exploded with rage, and stormed off.*
3 [I] to increase a lot over a very short period of time: *The increased availability of food has caused the deer population to explode.*

exploit¹ /ɪkˈsplɔɪt/ verb [T] ★
1 to treat someone unfairly in order to get some benefit for yourself: *Children are being exploited in many of these factories.*
2 to use a situation so that you get an advantage from it, even if it is wrong or unfair to do this: *A lot of advertisements just exploit our insecurities.*
3 to make the best use of something so that you get from it as much as possible: *They're just beginning to exploit the country's natural resources.*
—**exploitation** /ˌeksplɔɪˈteɪʃ(ə)n/ noun [U]

exploit² /ˈeksplɔɪt/ noun [C] something unusual that someone does that you think is brave, exciting, or entertaining

exploration /ˌekspləˈreɪʃ(ə)n/ noun [C/U] **1** a journey around an area in order to learn about it or in order to search for something valuable such as oil **2** a thorough examination or discussion of something

exploratory /ɪkˈsplɒrət(ə)ri/ adj done in order to learn more about something

explore /ɪkˈsplɔː/ verb ★★
1 [I/T] to travel around an area in order to learn about it, or in order to search for something valuable such as oil: *The town is a good base from which to explore this part of Italy.*
2 [T] to examine or discuss something in order to see if it is possible or is worth doing: *We are **exploring the possibility of** taking legal action against the company.*

explorer /ɪkˈsplɔːrə/ noun [C] someone who travels around a place that other people do not know much about in order to find out what is there

explosion /ɪkˈspləʊʒ(ə)n/ noun [C] ★
1 an occasion when something such as a bomb explodes: *a gas/nuclear explosion* ♦ *The explosion could be heard for miles around.*
2 a very large increase in something over a very short period of time: *a **population explosion***
3 a sudden expression of a strong emotion, especially anger

explosive¹ /ɪkˈspləʊsɪv/ adj **1** something that is explosive is used for causing an explosion, or is capable of exploding: *This gas is highly explosive.* **2** likely to become violent or very difficult: *an explosive situation/issue* **3** increasing quickly: *the explosive growth in street crime*

explosive² /ɪkˈspləʊsɪv/ noun [C/U] a substance or object that can cause an explosion

exponent /ɪkˈspəʊnənt/ noun [C] *formal* someone who tries to persuade other people to support an idea, theory, policy etc: *a leading exponent of free trade*

export¹ /ˈekspɔːt/ noun ★★
1 [C] a product that is sold to another country ≠ IMPORT: *Agricultural produce is the country's largest export.* ♦ *There has been a rapid increase in oil **exports to** the West.*
2 [U] the business or process of selling goods to other countries ≠ IMPORT: *They are now manufacturing more goods for export.*

export² /ɪkˈspɔːt/ verb ★
1 [I/T] to send a product to another country so that it can be sold there ≠ IMPORT: *Their flowers are exported around the world.* ♦ *Weapons are being illegally **exported to** other countries.*
2 [T] to introduce an idea, tradition, or activity into another country ≠ IMPORT: *Blues music was exported throughout the Western world.*
3 [T] *computing* to copy information from one part of a computer to another part, or to copy it to a place where it can be stored ≠ IMPORT

exporter /ɪkˈspɔːtə/ noun [C] a person, business, or country that sells goods to another country ≠ IMPORTER: *Saudi Arabia is the world's largest oil exporter.*

expose /ɪkˈspəʊz/ verb [T]

1 let sth be seen	4 give sb experience
2 put in danger	5 let light reach film
3 make sth known	

1 to remove something that is covering something else so that it is no longer hidden or protected: *The snow had melted and exposed the rock underneath.* **2** to put someone or something into a situation that involves danger or risk: *Many of the soldiers had been exposed to radiation.* **3** to tell the public about something shocking or illegal that was previously not known **4** to give someone a particular experience: *These children are exposed to art at a very early age.* **5** to allow light to reach the FILM in a camera so that you can take a photograph

exposé /ɪkˈspəʊzeɪ/ noun [C] a story in a newspaper or on television that tells the truth about something shocking

exposed /ɪkˈspəʊzd/ adj **1** not covered or hidden **2** not protected from attack or from the bad effects of something

exposure /ɪkˈspəʊʒə/ noun

1 being in danger	4 experience of sth
2 telling public sth	5 being out in cold
3 public attention	6 single photograph

1 [C/U] the state of not being protected from something harmful: *exposure to the sun* **2** [C/U] the act of making something publicly known because you believe that it is wrong or illegal: *the exposure of corruption within the government* **3** [U] the fact that something is mentioned in newspapers and on television and is well known **4** [C/U] the act of giving someone a particular experience: *Children who have exposure to books in their early years are likely to read earlier.* **5** [U] the harmful effect of very cold weather on your body: *Two of the climbers died of exposure.* **6** [C] *technical* the amount of FILM that is used for taking one photograph

expound /ɪkˈspaʊnd/ verb [I/T] *formal* to explain something, or to express your opinion about it in detail

express¹ /ɪkˈspres/ verb [T] ★★★
1 to say or write about what your opinion is or what your feelings are about something: *His teachers expressed concern about his progress at school.* ♦ *The government has expressed an interest in the scheme.*
2 to show your feelings in the way that you look or behave: *Her eyes expressed total shock.*
PHRASE **express yourself 1** to talk in a way that other people can understand: *She finds it difficult to express herself in English.* **2** to show your feelings in a particular way

express² /ɪkˈspres/ adj much faster than the usual service: *an express train* ♦ *express delivery*

express³ /ɪkˈspres/ noun [C] a fast train or bus

expression /ɪkˈspreʃ(ə)n/ noun ★★★
1 [C] a look on someone's face that shows what their thoughts or feelings are: *She had a puzzled expression on her face.* ♦ *I noticed his **expression of** disgust.*
2 [C] a word or phrase: *He uses childish expressions like 'easy-peasy'.*
3 [C/U] the act of showing what your thoughts or feelings are

expressionless /ɪkˈspreʃ(ə)nləs/ adj not

E

showing your feelings in your face or voice

expressive /ɪkˈspresɪv/ adj clearly showing your thoughts or feelings: *She has wonderfully expressive features.*

expressly /ɪkˈspresli/ adv *formal* in a way that is clear and definite: *Smoking is expressly forbidden.*

expresso /ekˈspresəʊ/ noun [C] an ESPRESSO

expressway /ɪkˈspresˌweɪ/ noun [C] *American* a MOTORWAY

expulsion /ɪkˈspʌlʃ(ə)n/ noun [C/U] an occasion when someone is officially forced to leave an organization, institution, or country

exquisite /ɪkˈskwɪzɪt/ adj extremely beautiful and delicate: *an exquisite hand-painted vase*

extend /ɪkˈstend/ verb ★★★

1 increase size/length	**4** stretch arm/leg out
2 of distance/time	**5** offer greeting
3 include sb/sth	

1 [T] to increase the size, time, or range of something: *The ground floor could be extended to allow for an extra bedroom.* ♦ *The course has been extended to include the history of art.* ♦ *I asked if I could extend my holiday.*

2 [I] to continue for a particular distance or time: *an area extending from the Baltic coast to the Alps*

3 [I] to include someone or something: *This law extends to children under the age of 14 only.*

4 [T] to stretch out an arm or a leg

5 [T] *formal* to offer something such as thanks or a welcome: *We extend our sympathy to all the families of the victims.*

ex,tended 'family noun [C] the family that you belong to, including people such as your grandparents, COUSINS etc → NUCLEAR FAMILY

extension /ɪkˈstenʃ(ə)n/ noun [C] ★★

1 extra part added	**4** sth that develops
2 extra time allowed	**5** computer file name
3 telephone line	

1 an extra part that is added to a building: *We are building an extension on the back of our house.*

2 an extra period of time that is added to the original period: *Brady wants a two-year extension to his contract.* ♦ *Will the bank give you an extension on the loan?*

3 a telephone line that is one of two or more lines in the same building: *I'm on extension 334.*

4 something that develops from something else: *He sees local history as an extension of family history.*

5 *computing* the last part of the name of a computer file. For example 'exe' and 'doc' are extensions.

extensive /ɪkˈstensɪv/ adj ★

1 very large in amount or degree: *The accident caused extensive damage to both cars.*

2 involving a lot of details and information: *extensive knowledge/research*

3 spreading over a large area: *The hotel has extensive grounds, including a private lake.* —**extensively** adv: *The building was extensively damaged by fire.*

extent /ɪkˈstent/ noun ★★★

1 [singular/U] the degree to which something happens, or the degree to which something is affected: *They were shocked at the extent of the damage.* ♦ *Languages vary in the extent to which they rely on word order.*

2 [U] the size or area of something: *Open the table to its fullest extent.*

PHRASES to a large/great extent mainly: *The complaints were to a large extent valid.*

to some/a certain/a limited extent partly, but not completely: *To a certain extent, I was relieved.*

exterior¹ /ɪkˈstɪəriə/ noun [C] **1** the outside part of a building ≠ INTERIOR **2** the way that someone seems to be: *Beneath that gruff exterior is a very kind person.*

exterior² /ɪkˈstɪəriə/ adj on the outside of something ≠ INTERIOR: *exterior walls*

exterminate /ɪkˈstɜːmɪˌneɪt/ verb [T] to kill all the insects, animals, or people in a particular area —**extermination** /ɪkˌstɜːmɪˈneɪʃ(ə)n/ noun [C/U]

external /ɪkˈstɜːn(ə)l/ adj ★★

1 on, or relating to, the outside of something ≠ INTERNAL: *external doors/walls* ♦ *Her external appearance was calm and cool.*

2 from outside an organization or country ≠ INTERNAL: *We will need to find external sources of finance.* —**externally** adv

extinct /ɪkˈstɪŋkt/ adj **1** if something such as a type of animal or plant is extinct, it no longer exists **2** an extinct VOLCANO no longer ERUPTS

extinction /ɪkˈstɪŋkʃ(ə)n/ noun [U] a situation in which something such as a type of animal or plant stops existing: *Several species of monkey are in danger of extinction.*

extinguish /ɪkˈstɪŋgwɪʃ/ verb [T] *formal* to make a fire or cigarette stop burning

extinguisher /ɪkˈstɪŋgwɪʃə/ noun [C] a FIRE EXTINGUISHER

extol /ɪkˈstəʊl/ verb [T] *formal* to praise something in a very enthusiastic way

extort /ɪkˈstɔːt/ verb [T] to illegally get money or information from someone by using force or threats

extortion /ɪkˈstɔːʃ(ə)n/ noun [U] a crime of getting money or information from someone by using force or threats —**extortionist** noun [C]

extortionate /ɪkˈstɔːʃ(ə)nət/ adj an extortionate price is much higher than it should be

extra¹ /ˈekstrə/ adj ★★★ in addition to the usual amount: *There's no extra money for emergencies.* ♦ *We need extra space for guests.*

PHRASE be extra to cost an additional amount of money: *It's £20 for dinner, and drinks are extra.*

extra² /ˈekstrə/ noun [C] **1** something that is added to a basic service, product etc: *A virus checker is available as an optional extra for your computer.* **2** someone who has a very small part in a film

extra³ /ˈekstrə/ adv **1** more than a particular amount of money: *You have to pay extra for insurance.* **2** very: *Be extra careful when you go out alone at night.*

extract¹ /ɪkˈstrækt/ verb [T] **1** to remove

something from something else=OBTAIN: *a method of extracting sulphur from copper ore* **2** to get information from someone using force

extract² /'ekstrækt/ noun **1** [C] a short piece of writing that is taken from something such as a book or letter=EXCERPT **2** [C/U] a substance that has been taken from a plant or from another substance

extraction /ik'strækʃ(ə)n/ noun [C/U] the process of taking something from somewhere

PHRASE **of Chinese/German/British etc extraction** belonging to a family that was originally from China, Germany, Britain etc

extracurricular /,ekstrəkə'rikjʊlə/ adj extracurricular activities are things that you do at school or college that are not part of your usual classes

extradite /'ekstrədaɪt/ verb [T] to send someone who is wanted for a crime back to the country where the crime was committed, so that they can be judged in a law court there —**extradition** /,ekstrə'dɪʃ(ə)n/ noun [C/U]

extraordinary /ik'strɔ:d(ə)n(ə)ri/ adj ★
1 very unusual and surprising: *It's an extraordinary story.* ♦ *It's extraordinary that no one disagreed with him.*
2 much better or worse than is usual: *The picture does not capture her extraordinary beauty.*
—**extraordinarily** /ik,strɔ:d(ə)n'erəli/ adv

extrapolate /ik'stræpəleɪt/ verb [I/T] formal to say what is likely to happen or be true by using information that you already have —**extrapolation** /ik,stræpə'leɪʃ(ə)n/ noun [C/U]

extraterrestrial /,ekstrətə'restriəl/ adj existing on planets other than Earth

extravagance /ik'strævəgəns/ noun **1** [U] the act of spending a lot of money, especially spending it on something that is not really necessary **2** [C] something that you spend a lot of money on

extravagant /ik'strævəgənt/ adj **1** spending or costing a lot of money: *an extravagant present/lifestyle* **2** extreme or unreasonable: *an extravagant claim* —**extravagantly** adv

extravaganza /ik,strævə'gænzə/ noun [C] a large and impressive event

extreme¹ /ik'stri:m/ adj ★★
1 very great in degree: *extreme poverty/hardship/cold*
2 extreme actions or opinions are considered unreasonable by most people: *It seemed a bit extreme to call the police.* ♦ *extreme right-wing views*
3 very unusual=EXCEPTIONAL: *In extreme cases, your membership may be cancelled.*
4 furthest away from the centre of something: *My friend is on the extreme left of the picture.*

extreme² /ik'stri:m/ noun [C] a very large or very small degree of something: *extremes of temperature*

PHRASE **go to extremes** or **take/carry sth to extremes** to do something much more than is usual or reasonable: *This is political correctness taken to extremes.*

extremely /ik'stri:mli/ adv ★★★ very: *He*

knows the area extremely well. ♦ *It is extremely important to record everything that happens.*

ex'treme ,sport noun [C] a sport or activity that is exciting and dangerous

extremist /ik'stri:mist/ noun [C] someone who has beliefs that most people think are extremely unreasonable —**extremism** noun [U], **extremist** adj

extremity /ik'streməti/ noun formal **1** [C] a part of something that is furthest from the main part: *the southern extremity of the island* **2** extremities [plural] your fingers or toes

extricate /'ekstrikeɪt/ verb [T] formal to get someone or yourself out of a difficult situation or a dangerous place

extrovert /'ekstrəvɜ:t/ noun [C] someone who is very confident, lively, and likes social situations ≠ INTROVERT —**extroverted** adj

exuberant /ig'zju:bərənt/ adj happy, excited, and full of energy —**exuberance** noun [U]

exude /ig'zju:d/ verb [T] formal if you exude a particular quality, you obviously have a lot of it

eye¹ /aɪ/ noun [C] ★★★
1 one of the two parts of your face that you use for seeing: *Close your eyes and go to sleep.* ♦ *He gazed into her eyes as she spoke.* ♦ *He has blond hair and blue eyes.* —picture → C14
2 used for talking about the expression on someone's face: *He spoke to her with slight amusement in his eyes.*
3 used for saying what someone is looking at: *I fixed my eye on the clock.*
4 the hole at the top of a needle

PHRASES **can't take your eyes off** to be unable to stop looking at someone or something that is attractive, surprising, or interesting
an eye for an eye the idea that someone who has harmed another person should be punished by having the same thing done to them
have an eye for to have a natural ability for seeing or noticing something: *Proofreaders need to have a good eye for detail.*
have/keep your eye on sb to watch someone carefully because you think they are going to do something wrong
have/keep your eye on sth to keep looking at something, especially to avoid making a mistake: *It's important to keep your eye on the ball at all times.*
have your eye on sth to want to have or buy something: *I've got my eye on a new DVD player.*
have one eye on sth to be giving some attention to something at the same time that you are doing something else: *I had one eye on the clock the whole time.*
in sb's eyes according to what someone thinks or feels: *In his mother's eyes, the boy can do no wrong.*
keep an eye on to look after someone or something: *Will you keep an eye on things here until I get back?*
keep an eye out for to try to notice someone or something: *He asked me to keep an eye out for any houses to rent.*
keep your eyes open/peeled to keep looking for something that you hope to find: *Keep*

your eyes open for a petrol station.

look sb in the eye to look directly at someone, especially as a way to show that you are being honest: *Look me in the eye and tell me you didn't do it.*

see eye to eye (with sb) to have the same opinion as someone: *I don't see eye to eye with my father on many things.*

set/lay/clap eyes on to see someone or something, especially for the first time **with your eyes (wide) open** if you do something with your eyes wide open, you know all about any problems that there are likely to be
→ BLIND¹

eye² /aɪ/ verb [T] to look at someone or something carefully

PHRASAL VERB **eye sb up** *British informal* to look at someone in a way that shows that you are sexually attracted to them

eyeball /ˈaɪbɔːl/ noun [C] the round ball that forms your eye

eyebrow /ˈaɪbraʊ/ noun [C] the line of hair above an eye

PHRASE **raise your eyebrows** to make your eyebrows go higher as a way of showing surprise, or as a way of showing you are asking a question

eye-catching adj something that is eye-catching is attractive, impressive, or unusual, so that you notice it very easily

eye contact noun [U] a situation in which two people look at each other's eyes

eyelashes /ˈaɪlæʃɪz/ noun [plural] the hairs along the edges of your eyelids

eyelid /ˈaɪlɪd/ noun [C] one of the two pieces of skin that cover your eye when it is closed

eyeliner /ˈaɪlaɪnə/ noun [U] a type of MAKE-UP used for drawing a line around the edges of your eyes —*picture* → MAKE-UP

eye-opener noun [C] a situation that makes you realize surprising or shocking things that you did not know before: *Visiting people in prison was a real eye-opener for me.*

eye shadow noun [U] a type of coloured MAKE-UP that you put on your EYELIDS —*picture* → MAKE-UP

eyesight /ˈaɪsaɪt/ noun [U] the ability to see =SIGHT: *Reading in poor light can damage your eyesight.*

eyesore /ˈaɪsɔː/ noun [C] something that is ugly or unpleasant to look at, especially a building

eyewitness /ˈaɪwɪtnəs/ noun [C] someone who has seen a crime or an accident happen: *Eyewitnesses describe the man as tall with brown hair.*

e-zine /ˈiː ziːn/ noun [C] a magazine that you can read on the Internet

F f

f or **F** /ef/ noun [C/U] **1** the sixth letter of the English alphabet **2** F a mark that a teacher gives to a student's work to show that they have failed

F abbrev **1** Fahrenheit **2** false **3** female

FA, the /ˌef ˈeɪ/ the Football Association: the organization that controls professional football in England and Wales

fable /ˈfeɪb(ə)l/ noun [C] a traditional story about animals that teaches a moral lesson

fabled /ˈfeɪb(ə)ld/ adj very famous =LEGENDARY

fabric /ˈfæbrɪk/ noun ★
1 [C/U] cloth that is used for making things such as clothes or curtains =MATERIAL: *plain/patterned/floral fabric* ♦ *a wide range of fabrics*
2 [singular] the basic structure of something: *Drug abuse poses a major threat to the fabric of society.*
3 [singular] the roof and walls of a building

fabricate /ˈfæbrɪkeɪt/ verb [T] to make up a story or piece of information in order to trick someone —**fabrication** /ˌfæbrɪˈkeɪʃ(ə)n/ noun [C/U]

fabulous /ˈfæbjʊləs/ adj **1** *informal* extremely good =WONDERFUL: *You look fabulous.* ♦ *a fabulous opportunity* **2** very large or great: *fabulous wealth* —**fabulously** /ˈfæbjʊləsli/ adv

facade or **façade** /fəˈsɑːd/ noun **1** [C] the front of a large building **2** [singular] a way of behaving that hides your real feelings or character

face¹ /feɪs/ noun [C] ★★★
1 the front part of your head, where your eyes, nose, and mouth are: *She wiped her face.* ♦ *He had a big smile on his face.* ♦ *The ball hit me in the face.*
2 a side of something: *the mountain's north face* ♦ *the faces of a coin/cube*
3 a person: *There were a lot of famous faces at the party.* ♦ *Look out for a couple of new faces in the team.*
4 the way that something appears to people: *players who changed the face of tennis* ♦ *This is the new face of banking in America.*

PHRASES **face down** with the front or face towards the ground
face to face 1 in a situation where you are talking to another person directly: *It would be better if we talked face to face.* ♦ *I came face to face with his mother.* **2** in a situation where you are forced to deal directly with a problem: *Her work brings her face to face with human suffering.*
face up with the front or face upwards
in the face of in an unpleasant or difficult situation: *They won in the face of stiff competition from all over the country.*

lose face to lose people's respect

make/pull a face to put a silly or rude expression on your face, or an expression that shows that you dislike someone or something

on the face of it used for saying that something appears to be true, although it may not be true: *He didn't have to pay any rent, so on the face of it he didn't need much money.*

save face to avoid being embarrassed or losing people's respect

to sb's face if you say something to someone's face, you say it to them directly

→ BLUE¹, EGG¹, FACE-TO-FACE, FLY¹, IN-YOUR-FACE, PRETTY², STRAIGHT¹

face² /feɪs/ verb ★★★

1 be turned to	5 compete against sb
2 deal with problem	+ PHRASES
3 accept	+ PHRASAL VERB
4 talk to sb	

1 [I/T] to have your face or front towards someone or something: *The two men faced each other across the table.* ♦ *I turned to face the sun.* ♦ *My room faces north.*

2 [T] if you face a problem, or if it faces you, you have to deal with it: **be faced with/by sth** *The country is now faced with the prospect of war.* ♦ **face doing sth** *Many of the shipyard workers face losing their jobs.*

3 [T] to accept that a bad situation exists and try to deal with it: *She had to **face the fact that** she still missed him.*

4 [T] to talk to someone when this is difficult or embarrassing: *I'll never be able to face her again after what happened.*

5 [T] to compete against someone: *Williams will face Capriati for the title.*

PHRASES **can't face sth** *spoken* to not want to do something because it is too difficult or unpleasant: *He couldn't face the washing-up, so he left it until the morning.* ♦ **can't face doing sth** *I just can't face attending another conference.*

let's face it *spoken* used before saying something that people might not want to accept, although it is true: *Let's face it, we played badly today.*

PHRASAL VERB **face up to sth** *same as* **face²** 3: *He was the only one who faced up to the situation.*

faceless /ˈfeɪsləs/ adj a faceless person does not seem to be an individual because they represent a large organization

facelift /ˈfeɪslɪft/ noun [C] **1** a medical operation to make someone's face look younger **2** work that is done to make something look more attractive

face-saving adj done in order to stop people from losing respect for you

facet /ˈfæsɪt/ noun [C] an aspect of something

facetious /fəˈsiːʃəs/ adj trying to be funny in a way that is not suitable —**facetiously** adv

face-to-face adj involving two people who are together in the same place: *a face-to-face meeting*

face value noun **take sb/sth at face value** to accept someone or something without thinking about whether they really are what they claim to be: *These threats should not be taken at face value.*

facial¹ /ˈfeɪʃ(ə)l/ adj on your face: *facial expressions/features/injuries*

facial² /ˈfeɪʃ(ə)l/ noun [C] a beauty treatment in which someone rubs your face and puts creams on it

facile /ˈfæsaɪl/ adj too simple to deal with the difficulties of a real situation: *facile conclusions*

facilitate /fəˈsɪləteɪt/ verb [T] *formal* to make it possible or easier for something to happen

facility /fəˈsɪləti/ noun ★★★
1 [C] a feature of a machine or system that allows you to do something: *the text messaging facility on your phone* ♦ *Do you have an overdraft facility at your bank?*
2 **facilities** [plural] places, services, or pieces of equipment that are provided for people: *There are plans to improve toilet facilities at the station.* ♦ *Does the company offer any facilities for employees with young children?*

facsimile /fækˈsɪməli/ noun [C] **1** an exact copy of a book or document **2** *formal* a FAX

fact /fækt/ noun ★★★
1 [C] a piece of true information: *The classes are designed to help children discover basic scientific facts.* ♦ **The fact is**, he lost because he didn't try very hard. ♦ *He has never hidden **the fact that** he doesn't like me.* ♦ **The fact remains that** (=it is still true that) *women are paid less than men.* ♦ *I **know for a fact that** he was lying.*
2 [U] things that are true or that really happened, rather than things that are imaginary or not true: *The story is based on historical fact.* ♦ *Children soon learn the difference between fact and fiction.*

PHRASES **the facts of life** the facts about sex and how babies are made

in (actual) fact 1 used for saying what is really true, when this is surprising or different from what people think: *He was paid money for a job that did not in fact exist.* ♦ *In actual fact, she was quite right.* **2** used when you are adding something to what you have just said, especially something surprising: *She's a friend of mine, a very close friend in fact.*

→ MATTER¹

faction /ˈfækʃ(ə)n/ noun [C] a small group within a larger group, consisting of people with different opinions from the rest

factor /ˈfæktə/ noun [C] ★★★
1 one of the things that influence whether an event happens or the way that it happens: *Several factors have contributed to the increase in the number of road accidents.* ♦ *Public pressure was a **factor in** the government's decision.*
2 *technical* a number that you can divide a larger number by exactly: *2 and 3 are factors of 6.*

PHRASE **by a factor of sth** used for saying how many times bigger something is now than it was before: *The volume of traffic has grown by a factor of four.*

Words often used with **factor**

*Adjectives often used with **factor***
■ **crucial, deciding, decisive, determining, important, key** + FACTOR: used about factors that are very important

F

factory /ˈfæktri/ noun [C] ★★★ a building where large quantities of goods are produced using machines: *She works in a factory.* ♦ *a car factory* ♦ *factory workers/bosses*

ˈfactory ˌfarm noun [U] a system in which animals or birds are kept inside in small spaces and are made to grow or produce eggs very quickly —**ˈfactory ˌfarming** noun [U]

factual /ˈfæktʃuəl/ adj based on facts, rather than on theories or opinions: *factual information* —**factually** adv: *factually correct*

faculty /ˈfæk(ə)lti/ noun [C] **1** a department or group of departments in a university: *the Faculty of Medicine* **2** a natural ability that most people have: *the faculty of speech*

fad /fæd/ noun [C] something that is popular or fashionable for a short time only

fade /feɪd/ verb [I] **1** to gradually become less clear, bright, loud, or strong: *It was late afternoon and the light was fading.* ♦ *Hopes that he will be found alive are fading.* ♦ *They heard footsteps go past the room, then fade into the distance.* **2** to become less famous or less important: *After one hit record he faded into obscurity.* —**faded** /ˈfeɪdɪd/ adj

PHRASAL VERB **fade aˈway** same as **fade** 2: *Most of these fashions just fade away and are forgotten.*

faeces /ˈfiːsiːz/ noun [plural] *formal* solid waste from your body

fag /fæg/ noun [C] *British informal* a cigarette

Fahrenheit /ˈfærənhaɪt/ noun [U] a system for measuring temperature in which water freezes at 32° and boils at 212°

fail¹ /feɪl/ verb ★★★

1 be unsuccessful	4 stop working
2 not do sth expected	5 lose quality/ability
3 not do well enough	+ PHRASE

1 [I] to be unsuccessful ≠ SUCCEED: *It looks as if the negotiations are going to fail.* ♦ *He failed in his attempt to get compensation.* ♦ **fail to do sth** *They have failed to think of any practical solutions.*

2 [I] to not do something that people expect you to do: **fail to do sth** *He failed to come home at the usual time.*

3 [I/T] to not achieve a satisfactory standard in a test, or to decide that someone or something has not achieved a satisfactory standard ≠ PASS: *The new plane failed a safety test.* ♦ *Examiners failed nearly 30% of the candidates.*

4 [I] to stop working, developing, or existing: *The brakes failed and the van crashed into a tree.* ♦ *He is old now and his health is starting to fail.* ♦ *If interest rates go up, more small businesses will fail.*

5 [T] if a quality or ability fails you, you suddenly lose it when you need it: *At the last minute, her courage failed her.*

PHRASE **if all else fails** used for saying that, if other methods do not succeed, there is one last thing that you can try to do

fail² /feɪl/ noun [C] *British* a result that shows that someone or something has not achieved a satisfactory standard ≠ PASS

PHRASE **without fail** used for emphasizing that something always happens in the same way or at the same time

failed /feɪld/ adj unsuccessful: *a failed attempt*

failing¹ /ˈfeɪlɪŋ/ noun [C] a fault that makes someone or something less effective: *the failings of the educational system*

failing² /ˈfeɪlɪŋ/ preposition used for saying that there is something else you can try: *We could try the bank, or, failing that, ask my parents for the money.*

failure /ˈfeɪljə/ noun ★★★

1 [U] a lack of success ≠ SUCCESS: *Their first attempt to climb Everest ended in failure.* ♦ *The failure of the talks has made the situation worse.* ♦ **failure to do sth** *She is depressed by her continued failure to find a job.*

2 [U] a situation in which you do not do something that someone expects you to do: *the failure of teachers to inform parents about the problem* ♦ **failure to do sth** *Failure to follow safety procedures could put people in danger.*

3 [U] a situation in which a machine or a part of your body stops working correctly: *The crash seems to have been caused by engine failure.* ♦ *He died from liver failure.*

4 [C] someone or something that has not been successful ≠ SUCCESS: *I feel such a failure.* ♦ *The party was a total failure.*

faint¹ /feɪnt/ adj **1** not strong or clear: *the faint glow of a light through the fog* ♦ *a faint memory* ♦ *a faint hope/possibility* **2** feeling that you are going to become unconscious —**faintly** /ˈfeɪntli/ adv

faint² /feɪnt/ verb [I] to suddenly become unconscious for a short time

faintest /ˈfeɪntɪst/ adj **not have the faintest idea** used for emphasizing that you do not know or understand something=SLIGHTEST

fair¹ /feə/ adj ★★★

1 treating all equally	4 light in colour
2 reasonable	5 not very good
3 quite large in amount	+ PHRASES

1 if a situation is fair, everyone is treated equally and in a reasonable way ≠ UNFAIR: *free and fair elections* ♦ **it is not fair to sb** *It wouldn't be fair to the others if she is paid more.*

2 reasonable and morally right: *a fair wage/deal/price* ♦ **it is (not) fair to do sth** *It is not fair to blame him for our mistakes.*

3 used for emphasizing that an amount, size, or number is large: *We walked 3 miles to school, which is a fair distance.*

4 fair hair is BLONDE (=light yellow) or very light brown in colour ≠ DARK

5 not bad, but not very good=AVERAGE

PHRASES **fair enough** *spoken* used for saying that you understand and accept what someone says

have your fair share of sth to have a lot of something, especially something bad

to be fair used for making your criticism of someone or something seem less strong: *I don't like their music but, to be fair, millions of people disagree with me.*

fair² /feə/ noun [C] **1** an event where companies bring their products for you to look at or buy **2** an event where people ride on special machines and play games to win prizes

fair³ /feə/ adv

PHRASES **fair and square** in a way that is clear and fair, so that no one can complain or disagree

play fair to behave in a fair and honest way

fair 'game noun [U] someone or something that it is fair to criticize: *The media see politicians as fair game.*

fairground /'feəgraʊnd/ noun [C] an area of land that is used for FAIRS

fairly /'feəli/ adv ★★★
1 [U] to some degree, but not completely or extremely=RATHER, REASONABLY: *We went to the theatre fairly often.* ♦ *He enjoys fairly good health.*
2 in a fair way: *I do my best to treat all my children fairly.*

fairness /'feənəs/ noun [U] behaviour that is fair and reasonable
PHRASE **in (all) fairness** used for making your criticism of someone or something seem less strong=TO BE FAIR

fairway /'feəweɪ/ noun [C] the long part of a GOLF COURSE that you hit the ball along to get to the hole —*picture* → C15

fairy /'feəri/ noun [C] an imaginary creature with magic powers that looks like a small person with wings

'fairy tale or **'fairy story** noun [C] a traditional children's story in which magic things happen

fairytale /'feəriteɪl/ adj extremely good, beautiful, or happy: *a fairytale romance*

faith /feɪθ/ noun ★★
1 [U] a strong belief that someone or something is good: *I'm delighted to know you have such faith in me.* ♦ *The public have lost faith in what the government is doing.* ♦ *Maybe we put too much faith in doctors and medicine.*
2 [C/U] a religion, or religious belief: *people of many different faiths* ♦ *Faith in God helped him through his illness.*
PHRASE **in good faith** if you do something in good faith, you honestly believe that it is right or fair

faithful /'feɪθf(ə)l/ adj **1** continuing to support someone or something, even in difficult situations=LOYAL: *a faithful friend/servant/follower* ♦ *He remained faithful to his beliefs.* **2** showing or describing something in a way that is exactly correct: *a faithful reproduction of the original painting* **3** not having sex with anyone other than your partner ≠ UNFAITHFUL: *Ken has always been faithful to his wife.* —**faithfulness** noun [U]

faithfully /'feɪθf(ə)li/ adv **1** in a loyal and honest way **2** accurately
PHRASE **Yours faithfully** British used at the end of a formal letter when you begin it with 'Dear Sir' or 'Dear Madam'

fake¹ /feɪk/ adj **1** made to look like something real in order to trick people: *a fake passport/visa/document* **2** made to look like something expensive: *fake fur/pearls/leather*

fake² /feɪk/ noun [C] **1** a copy of something such as a painting that is intended to trick people **2** someone who pretends to have skills that they do not really have

fake³ /feɪk/ verb [T] **1** to pretend to do or feel something: *He left the country after faking his own death.* **2** to make an exact copy of something in order to trick people

falcon /'fɔːlkən/ noun [C] a bird that is often trained to hunt small animals

fall¹ /fɔːl/ (past tense **fell** /fel/; past participle **fallen** /'fɔːlən/) verb [I] ★★★

1 move quickly down	7 happen
2 hit ground by accident	8 lose power
3 come from sky	9 hang down
4 get lower in amount	+ PHRASES
5 belong to group	+ PHRASAL VERBS
6 start to be/do sth	

1 to move quickly downwards from a higher position by accident: *I keep falling off my bike.* ♦ *It's not unusual for small children to fall out of bed.*
2 to go quickly down onto the ground from an upright position by accident: *I slipped and almost fell.* ♦ *We heard the crash of falling trees.* ♦ *He collapsed and fell to the ground.*
3 to come down to the ground from the sky: *Snow began to quietly fall.* ♦ *Bombs fell on the city throughout the night.*
4 to become lower in level or amount ≠ RISE: *The temperature has been falling all day.* ♦ *Inflation has fallen to 3%.*
5 to belong to a particular group or area of activity: *Those items fall into the category of luxury goods.*
6 to change into another state or condition: *Shortly before Christmas she fell ill.* ♦ *I climbed into bed and fell into a deep sleep.*
7 to happen on a particular day or date: *Christmas falls on a Saturday this year.*
8 to lose a position of power
9 *literary* to hang down
PHRASES **fall in love** to start to love someone
fall into place 1 if something falls into place, you suddenly understand how the different pieces of it are connected **2** if things fall into place, events happen in a way that is satisfactory for you

fall short to not reach a particular level
fall to bits/pieces to be in a very bad condition because of being old or badly made

→ FOOT¹

PHRASAL VERBS **fall a'part 1** to break because of being old or badly made **2** if something such as an organization or system falls apart, it stops existing, or stops being effective
fall 'back to move so that you are behind someone or something
fall 'back on sth to do something else after other things have failed: *She always has her teaching experience to fall back on.*
fall be'hind sb 1 to make less progress than other people **2** to be behind other people because you have moved more slowly
fall 'down 1 same as **fall¹** 2: *I fell down and hurt my knee.* **2** if a building is falling down, it is in very bad condition
'fall for sb to fall in love with someone
'fall for sth to believe that a trick or a joke is true
fall 'off if the amount, level, or value of

something falls off, it gets smaller: *Sales always fall off in the winter months.*

fall out *informal* to stop being friendly with someone because you have had a disagreement with them: *Have you two fallen out?* ♦ *I'd fallen out with my parents.*

fall over 1 if something falls over, it falls so that its side is on the ground **2** if you fall over, you fall to the ground

fall through if something such as a plan or arrangement falls through, it fails to happen

Words often used with **fall**

Adverbs often used with fall (verb, sense 3)
■ FALL + **dramatically, rapidly, sharply, steeply**: used when a level becomes much lower very quickly

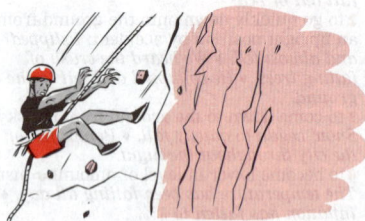

fall

fall² /fɔːl/ noun ★★★

1 when sb/sth falls	4 defeat or loss of power
2 amount that falls	5 waterfall
3 when amount etc falls	6 autumn

1 [C] an occasion when someone or something falls to the ground: *Her brother was killed in a fall from a horse.*
2 [C] an amount of something that falls to the ground: *a heavy fall of snow*
3 [C] an occasion when an amount or level falls ≠ RISE: *There has been a sharp fall in unemployment.* ♦ *We have seen a fall of 5% in sales this month.*
4 [singular] someone's defeat or loss of power
5 **falls** [plural] a WATERFALL
6 [singular] *American* autumn

fallacy /ˈfæləsi/ noun [C] an idea or belief that is false but that many people think is true

fallen the past participle of **fall¹**

fallible /ˈfæləb(ə)l/ adj not perfect, and likely to be wrong or to make mistakes

falling-out /ˌfɔːlɪŋ ˈaʊt/ noun [C] *informal* an angry disagreement

fallout /ˈfɔːlaʊt/ noun **1** [U] the dangerous dust produced by a nuclear explosion **2** [singular/U] the unpleasant effects of something

false /fɔːls/ adj ★★

1 not true	4 tricking people
2 not accurate	5 not sincere
3 like sth real	+ PHRASE

1 not true ≠ TRUE: *The report was dismissed as totally false.* ♦ *a false statement/claim/accusation*
2 based on a mistake or on wrong information: *a false impression/belief/hope*
3 made to look like something real =ARTIFICIAL: *false eyelashes*

4 not real and intended to trick people: *a false passport*
5 not showing what you really feel or intend =INSINCERE: *a false smile*

PHRASE **under false pretences** by tricking people

—**falsely** adv

Other ways of saying **false**

■ **artificial** made to have the same qualities as something else that exists naturally
■ **counterfeit** made to look exactly like real money and used illegally to trick people
■ **fake** made to look like something valuable or important, often in order to trick people
■ **forged** made to look exactly like something valuable or important and used illegally to trick people
■ **pirate** used for describing copies of things such as books or videos that have been made and sold illegally

false alarm noun [C] a situation in which you think that something bad is going to happen, but it does not

false start noun [C] an unsuccessful attempt to start something or to do something

falsify /ˈfɔːlsɪfaɪ/ verb [T] to change something deliberately in order to trick other people

falter /ˈfɔːltə/ verb [I] **1** to stop being effective **2** to do something in a way that shows that you are weak or are not confident

fame /feɪm/ noun [U] the state of being famous: *Albert Finney rose to fame in the British cinema of the early Sixties.* → CLAIM²

famed /feɪmd/ adj famous: *a restaurant famed for its seafood*

familiar /fəˈmɪliə/ adj ★★
1 well known to you, or easily recognized by you ≠ UNFAMILIAR: *People are more relaxed in familiar surroundings.* ♦ *His face looked vaguely familiar but I couldn't think why.* ♦ *I'm pleased to see so many familiar faces here tonight.* ♦ *The name Harry Potter will be familiar to many readers.*
2 something that is familiar happens a lot or exists in most places: *Horses used to be a familiar sight in our streets.* ♦ *an all-too familiar problem*
3 behaving in an informal way that shows a lack of respect for someone: *Don't be too familiar with the customers.*

PHRASE **familiar with sth** if you are familiar with something, you know about it: *Are you familiar with Windows software?*

familiarity /fəˌmɪliˈærəti/ noun **1** [U] knowledge that you have of something because you have dealt with it before: *a familiarity with international law* **2** [C/U] informal behaviour that shows a lack of respect for someone

familiarize /fəˈmɪliəraɪz/ verb [T] to show or teach someone something: *It's my job to familiarize new employees with office procedures.*

family¹ /ˈfæm(ə)li/ noun ★★★
1 [C] a group consisting of parents and children: *Is the Watson family going to be there?* ♦ *The tent is big enough for a family of six.*
2 [C/U] all the people who are related to you, including people who are now dead: *Does*

F

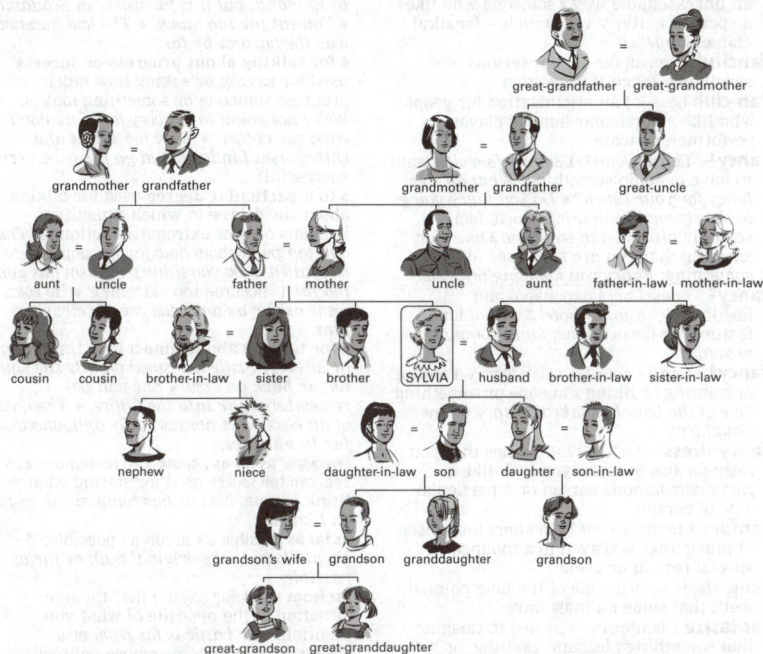

family tree

your family have any history of heart disease? ♦ *She did not want the property to go to anyone outside the family.* ♦ *The business had been in his family* (=belonged to his family) *for four generations.*

> In British English, **family** can be used with a singular or plural verb. You can say *His family was not at the wedding.* OR *His family were not at the wedding.*

3 [C] children: *It's difficult to bring up a family on one salary.* ♦ *They want to get married and start a family* (=have children).
4 [C] a group of things such as animals or plants that are related: *Kidney beans belong to the bean family.*

family² /ˈfæm(ə)li/ adj **1** relating to families, or typical of families: *Quarrels are a normal part of family life.* **2** suitable for a family with children: *family entertainment*

ˈfamily ˈname noun [C] the part of your name that all the people in your family have =LAST NAME, SURNAME

ˈfamily ˈplanning noun [U] the practice of controlling the number of children that you have by using CONTRACEPTIVES (=drugs or objects that stop a woman from becoming pregnant)

ˈfamily ˈtree noun [C] a drawing that shows the names of everyone in a family and shows the relationship between them

famine /ˈfæmɪn/ noun [C/U] a serious lack of food that causes many people to become ill or to die

famished /ˈfæmɪʃt/ adj informal very hungry
famous /ˈfeɪməs/ adj ★★★ if someone or something is famous, a lot of people know their name or have heard about them: *He dreamed of becoming a famous footballer.* ♦ *The town of Gouda is famous for its cheese.* ♦ *She became famous as a teacher and a writer.* → INFAMOUS —**famously** /ˈfeɪməsli/ adv

> **Other ways of saying famous**
> - **eminent** famous and respected for doing important work
> - **legendary** very famous and admired by many people
> - **notorious/infamous** famous for something bad
> - **well-known** fairly famous

fan¹ /fæn/ noun [C] ★★
1 someone who likes someone or something very much: *a crowd of football fans* ♦ *I'm a big fan of Madonna.*
2 a machine that makes the air in a room move so that it feels less hot
3 a flat object that you wave in front of your face in order to make yourself feel less hot
fan² /fæn/ verb [T] **1** to wave a flat object in front of someone's face in order to make them feel less hot **2** to make a fire burn more strongly by moving air onto it
PHRASAL VERB ˌfan ˈout if a group of people fan out, they spread out while moving forwards

fanatic /fəˈnætɪk/ noun [C] **1** someone who has strong beliefs that make them behave in

F

an unreasonable way **2** someone who likes a sport or activity very much —**fanatical** /fəˈnætɪk(ə)l/ adj

fanciful /ˈfænsɪf(ə)l/ adj not serious or sensible: *a fanciful suggestion*

fan ,club noun [C] an organization for people who like a particular famous player, performer, or team

fancy¹ /ˈfænsi/ verb [T] **1** *British informal* to want to have or to do something: *What do you fancy for your lunch?* ♦ *Do you fancy going to the cinema?* **2** *British informal* to feel sexually attracted to someone **3** used for showing that you are surprised about something: *Fancy you knowing my sister!*

fancy² /ˈfænsi/ adj **1** expensive and fashionable: *a fancy hotel* **2** with a lot of features or decorations: *fancy computer graphics*

fancy³ /ˈfænsi/ noun [singular] *literary* a feeling of wanting or liking someone or something: *One of the boys has taken a fancy to my daughter.*

,fancy 'dress noun [U] *British* clothes that you wear for fun to make you look like a particular famous person or a particular type of person

fanfare /ˈfænfeə/ noun [C] a short loud piece of music that is played to announce a special person or event

fang /fæŋ/ noun [C] one of the long pointed teeth that some animals have

fantasize /ˈfæntəˌsaɪz/ verb [I/T] to imagine that something pleasant, exciting, or unusual is happening to you

fantastic /fænˈtæstɪk/ adj **1** *informal* extremely good or pleasant: *You've done a fantastic job.* ♦ *He looked absolutely fantastic.* **2** *informal* extremely large: *You've all put in a fantastic amount of work.* **3** strange, or imaginary: *fantastic creatures/stories* —**fantastically** /fænˈtæstɪkli/ adv

fantasy /ˈfæntəsi/ noun [C] a pleasant, exciting, or unusual experience that you imagine is happening to you

FAQ /ˌef eɪ ˈkjuː/ noun [C] *computing* frequently asked questions: a list of typical questions that people ask and their answers

far /fɑː/ (comparative **farther** /ˈfɑːðə/ or **further** /ˈfɜːðə/; superlative **farthest** /ˈfɑːðɪst/ or **furthest** /ˈfɜːðɪst/) adj, adv ★★★
1 a long distance used for talking about a long distance, or for asking or stating how great a distance is: *You can go outside and play, but don't go far.* ♦ *How far* (=what distance) *is it to the next town?* ♦ *The main post office is not far from the library.* ♦ *We can't walk to the cinema, it's too far.* ♦ *I wish you didn't live so far away.*

> Far is used mainly in questions and negatives when talking about distance. In positive statements we usually say **a long way**: *It's a long way to the nearest hospital.*

2 most distant most distant from someone or from the centre: *He saw Lynn standing at the far end of the bar.* ♦ *I'm the one on the far left.*
3 for emphasis in comparisons used for emphasizing a difference when you are making a comparison: *The situation is bad*

in England, but it is far worse in Scotland. ♦ *You eat far too much.* ♦ *The last question was the hardest by far.*
4 for talking about progress or success used for saying or asking how much progress someone or something makes: *We're not going to get very far if we don't trust each other.* ♦ *With her talent and enthusiasm Linda should go far* (=be very successful).
5 to a particular degree used for talking about the degree to which something happens or how extreme an action is: *The opinion polls show how far his popularity has fallen.* ♦ *Do you think feminism has gone too far* (=become too extreme)? ♦ *He even went as far as to accuse me of betraying him.*
6 for talking about time a long time before or after: *A castle has stood on this site since as far back as 1230.* ♦ *She will be remembered far into the future.* ♦ *The date of an election is not normally announced so far in advance.*

PHRASES as far as I know/can remember/can see/can tell *spoken* used for stating what you think is true: *No one has complained, as far as I know.*

as far as possible as much as possible: *We should keep to the original plan as far as possible.*

far from used for saying that the real situation is the opposite of what you mention: *The battle is far from over.*

the far right/left people whose political views are extremely right-wing/extremely left-wing

so far 1 until now: *So far we have considered only the local area.* **2** up to a particular point or degree: *You can only get so far on good looks alone.*

so far, so good used for saying that something has been successful up to this point

→ CONCERNED, CRY², FARTHER, FARTHEST

> ■ **Further, farther, furthest,** and **farthest** can all be used for talking about distance: *Stand further/farther away from me.* ♦ *Who can jump furthest/farthest?*
> ■ **Further** is often used for talking about the degree to which something happens: *I expect prices to rise further* (=rise more). But **farther, farthest,** and **furthest** are not often used in this way.
> ■ **Further** is also used as an **adjective** to mean 'additional': *There has been no further news.* But **farther** cannot be used in this way.

faraway /ˌfɑːrəˈweɪ/ adj **1** a long way from you or from a particular place **2** showing that you are not concentrating on what is happening: *a faraway look in her eyes*

farce /fɑːs/ noun **1** [singular/U] a situation that is silly because it is very badly organized or unsuccessful **2** [C] a funny play or film that involves silly situations

farcical /ˈfɑːsɪk(ə)l/ adj something that is farcical is so badly organized or unsuccessful that it seems silly

fare¹ /feə/ noun **1** [C] the money that you pay for a journey **2** [U] *formal* the type of food that is available somewhere

fare² /feə/ verb **fare well/badly etc** used for saying how well or how badly someone does something

Far 'East, the the countries of the eastern part of Asia, including China, Malaysia, and Japan

farewell¹ /ˌfeəˈwel/ noun [C/U] *old-fashioned* an occasion when you say goodbye to someone

farewell² /ˌfeəˈwel/ adj done in order to celebrate the fact that someone is leaving a place or job: *a farewell dinner/party/speech*

far-fetched /ˌfɑː ˈfetʃt/ adj very unlikely to be true and therefore difficult to believe

farm¹ /fɑːm/ noun [C] an area of land that is used for growing crops or keeping animals

farm² /fɑːm/ verb [I/T] to use land for growing crops or keeping animals

farmer /ˈfɑːmə/ noun [C] someone who owns or manages a farm

farmhouse /ˈfɑːmˌhaʊs/ (plural **farmhouses** /ˈfɑːmˌhaʊzɪz/) noun [C] the main house on a farm

farming /ˈfɑːmɪŋ/ noun [U] the business of being a farmer

farmland /ˈfɑːmlænd/ noun [U] land that is used for farming

farmyard /ˈfɑːmjɑːd/ noun [C] an area that is surrounded by the buildings on a farm

far-'off adj far away in distance or in time

far-reaching /ˌfɑː ˈriːtʃɪŋ/ adj affecting a lot of people or things in an important way

far-'sighted adj good at judging what will happen in the future

fart /fɑːt/ verb [I] *impolite* to allow gases from your stomach to come out through your ANUS —**fart** noun [C]

farther /ˈfɑːðə/ adj, adv in or to a place that is more distant: *I live farther up the road. ♦ The children were too tired to walk any farther.*

farthest /ˈfɑːðɪst/ adj, adv in or to a place that is most distant: *Sam had chosen to sit farthest away from the door.*

fascinate /ˈfæsɪneɪt/ verb [T] to attract and interest you very much

fascinated /ˈfæsɪneɪtɪd/ adj very interested in, or attracted by, someone or something

fascinating /ˈfæsɪneɪtɪŋ/ adj ★ extremely interesting: *a fascinating story/person/place ♦* **it is fascinating to do sth** *It will be fascinating to see who they appoint. ♦* **find sb/sth fascinating** *I find him absolutely fascinating.*

fascination /ˌfæsɪˈneɪʃ(ə)n/ noun [singular/U] **1** the power to interest or attract people very strongly **2** the state of being very interested in something or very attracted by something

fascism /ˈfæʃɪz(ə)m/ noun [U] a very right-wing political system in which the government completely controls society and the economy

fascist /ˈfæʃɪst/ noun [C] **1** someone who supports or believes in fascism **2** an insulting word for someone who has very right-wing opinions —**fascist** adj

fashion¹ /ˈfæʃ(ə)n/ noun ★★ **1** [U] the activity or business that involves styles of clothes and people's appearance: *the world of fashion ♦ an Italian fashion designer*

2 [U] the state of being popular at a particular time: *High heels are back in fashion. ♦ His ideas have gone right out of fashion.*

3 [C] a style of dress or an activity that is popular at a particular time: *She was always dressed in the latest fashions. ♦ the fashion for naming children after pop stars*

4 [singular] a particular way of doing something: *The elections took place in a peaceful and orderly fashion.*

fashion² /ˈfæʃ(ə)n/ verb [T] *formal* to make something using a lot of skill or care

fashionable /ˈfæʃ(ə)nəb(ə)l/ adj ★★ **1** popular at a particular time ≠ UNFASHIONABLE: *fashionable clothes ♦* **it is fashionable to do sth** *It is now fashionable to buy organic food.*

2 popular with rich and successful people, and often expensive: *London's most fashionable shopping district*
—**fashionably** adv: *a fashionably dressed young woman*

fast¹ /fɑːst/ adj ★★★ **1** moving, happening, or doing something quickly: *Simon loves fast cars. ♦ The government has promised a fast response to the crisis. ♦ We were expected to work at a fast pace.*

2 if a clock is fast, it shows a time that is later than the correct time: *My watch is a few minutes fast.*

fast² /fɑːst/ adv ★★★ **1** quickly: *I can't run very fast. ♦ You need to get help fast!*

2 firmly and strongly or tightly: *She held fast to the railings and refused to move. ♦ The van was stuck fast in the mud.*

PHRASE **fast asleep** sleeping in a way that makes it difficult to wake you

fast³ /fɑːst/ verb [I] to eat no food or very little food for a period of time, usually for religious reasons —**fast** noun [C]

fasten /ˈfɑːs(ə)n/ verb ★★★ **1** [I/T] to close something such as a piece of clothing or a bag by fixing together the two parts of it, or to be closed in this way ≠ UNFASTEN: *Please keep your seat belts fastened.* —*picture →* CLOSE

2 [T] to fix one thing to another using something such as string or nails so that it is held firmly in position: **fasten sth to sth** *We fastened our boat to a post in the river.*

3 [T] to use something such as a lock in order to close a door, gate, or window: *I checked that all the windows were properly fastened.* —*picture →* CLOSE

fastening /ˈfɑːsnɪŋ/ or **fastener** /ˈfɑːsnə/ noun [C] **1** something such as a lock that you use to keep a door, gate, or window closed **2** something that you use to fix together the two parts of something such as a piece of clothing or a bag

fast 'food noun [U] food that is made and served very quickly, and that you can take away with you

fast-'forward verb [I/T] if you fast-forward a TAPE, or if it fast-forwards, it goes forwards quickly —**fast 'forward** noun [U]

F

fastidious /fæˈstɪdɪəs/ adj caring a lot about small details and wanting everything to be correct and tidy

ˈfast ˌtrack noun [singular] a way of achieving something more quickly than usual: *on the fast track to success*

fat¹ /fæt/ adj ★★

1 a person or animal that is fat has too much flesh on their body and weighs too much: *She can eat whatever she likes and she never gets fat*.

2 a fat object is thicker than other objects of the same type: *a big fat cigar*

3 *informal* used about an amount of money that is very large: *I bet he gets a nice fat salary!*

PHRASES **fat chance** *spoken* used for emphasizing that you think that something is extremely unlikely: *'Maybe Mike will help us.' 'Fat chance!'*

a fat lot *spoken* nothing, or not very much at all: *A fat lot of help she'll be!*

Other ways of saying fat

- **big/large** tall and fairly fat
- **chubby** used especially for describing babies and children who look fat in a healthy attractive way
- **obese** very fat in a way that is dangerous to your health
- **overweight** heavier than you should be
- **plump** slightly fat in a way that looks nice

fat² /fæt/ noun ★

1 [U] a soft white substance that you store in a layer under your skin

2 [C/U] a food substance like oil that is used by your body to create energy: *Reduce the amount of fat in your diet*.

3 [C/U] oil in a solid or liquid form that is obtained from plants or animals and is used in cooking: *Fry the meat in a small amount of fat*.

fatal /ˈfeɪt(ə)l/ adj ★

1 causing someone to die: *a fatal accident/injury/disease* ♦ *The condition can prove fatal* (=cause death).

2 with very bad effects: *I made the fatal mistake of falling in love with him*. —**fatally** /ˈfeɪt(ə)li/ adv

fatalism /ˈfeɪt(ə)lɪz(ə)m/ noun [U] the belief that you cannot prevent bad things from happening —**fatalistic** /ˌfeɪt(ə)lˈɪstɪk/ adj

fatality /fəˈtæləti/ noun [C] *formal* a death that is caused by an accident, war, violence, or disease

ˈfat ˌcat noun [C] *informal showing disapproval* a very rich and powerful person, usually in business or politics

fate /feɪt/ noun ★

1 [C] the things that happen to someone: *a meeting that would decide the fate of thousands of employees*

2 [U] a power that some people believe controls everything that happens in their lives: *Fate has dealt these people a cruel blow*.

fateful /ˈfeɪtf(ə)l/ adj affecting what happens in the future in an important and usually bad way

father¹ /ˈfɑːðə/ noun ★★★

1 [C] your male parent: *My father taught me to drive.* —*picture* → FAMILY TREE

2 **Father** used for talking to or about a Roman Catholic priest

father² /ˈfɑːðə/ verb [T] to make a woman pregnant and become the father of a child

ˌFather ˈChristmas *British* an imaginary old man with a long white BEARD and red clothes who brings children their Christmas presents=SANTA CLAUS

ˈfather ˌfigure noun [C] an older man who you go to for help and advice

fatherhood /ˈfɑːðəhʊd/ noun [U] the state of being a father

ˌfather-in-ˈlaw noun [C] the father of your husband or wife —*picture* → FAMILY TREE

fatherly /ˈfɑːðəli/ adj typical of a good, kind father

fathom /ˈfæðəm/ verb [T] to understand something that is complicated or mysterious: *For some reason she couldn't fathom, he seemed angry*.

fatigue /fəˈtiːɡ/ noun [U] **1** a feeling of being extremely tired: *He was suffering from fatigue and acute headaches*. **2** a tendency for metal or wood to break as a result of too much pressure —**fatigued** /fəˈtiːɡd/ adj

fatigues /fəˈtiːɡz/ noun [plural] simple loose clothes worn by soldiers

fatten /ˈfæt(ə)n/ verb [T] to make an animal fat so that it will be more suitable for eating

PHRASAL VERB **ˌfatten sb/sth ˈup** to make a person or animal fatter

fattening /ˈfæt(ə)nɪŋ/ adj likely to make you fat: *Avoid fattening foods and take more exercise*.

fatty /ˈfæti/ adj containing a lot of fat: *fatty foods*

fatuous /ˈfætjuəs/ adj *formal* stupid

faucet /ˈfɔːsɪt/ noun [C] *American* a TAP that controls the flow of water

fault¹ /fɔːlt/ noun ★★

1 [C/U] the fact of being responsible for a bad or unpleasant situation: *The teacher was at fault for not telling the child's parents.* ♦ **be sb's fault** *It's my fault – I forgot to give him the message.* ♦ **be sb's own fault** *If you didn't get enough sleep, it's your own fault*.

2 [C] a feature that makes someone or something less good: *She has her faults, but on the whole she's very nice.* ♦ *The book's main fault is that it is too long*.

3 [C] a problem with a machine or piece of equipment that stops it from working correctly: *The fire was caused by an electrical fault*.

4 [C] a crack in or below the Earth's surface: *the San Andreas Fault*

PHRASE **find fault with** to criticize someone or something after deliberately looking for mistakes

fault² /fɔːlt/ verb [T] to find something bad or wrong in a person or thing

faultless /ˈfɔːltləs/ adj containing no mistakes at all

faulty /ˈfɔːlti/ adj not working correctly, or not made correctly: *faulty brakes*

fauna /ˈfɔːnə/ noun [U] *formal* all the animals that live in a particular area

faux pas /ˌfəʊ ˈpɑː/ noun [C] *formal* an embarrassing mistake in a social situation

favor /ˈfeɪvə/ the American spelling of **favour**

favorable /ˈfeɪv(ə)rəb(ə)l/ the American spelling of **favourable**

favorite /ˈfeɪv(ə)rət/ the American spelling of **favourite**

favoritism /ˈfeɪv(ə)rətɪzəm/ the American spelling of **favouritism**

favour¹ /ˈfeɪvə/ noun ★★
  1 [C] something that you do for someone in order to help them: **do sb a favour** *Could you do me a favour?* ♦ *He wouldn't take any money for his work: he insisted he was doing it as a favour.*
  2 [U] support or admiration from people: *Nuclear power stations have lost favour in recent years.*
  PHRASES **be in favour/out of favour** to be popular/no longer popular at a particular time: *Stephenson is currently out of favour with the England team selectors.*
  in sb's favour helping you, or giving you an advantage: *The delay might actually work in our favour.*
  in favour of 1 supporting a person, idea, or proposal: *Those in favour of the proposal, please raise your hands.* **2** preferring to choose someone or something that you believe is better: *Manchester was rejected in favour of Liverpool as the site for the new stadium.*

favour² /ˈfeɪvə/ verb [T] ★
  1 to prefer to choose someone or something that you believe is better: *The report strongly favours reform of the electoral system.*
  2 to give someone an unfair advantage: *These tax cuts will favour the rich.*

favourable /ˈfeɪv(ə)rəb(ə)l/ adj **1** showing that you like or approve of someone or something=POSITIVE ≠ UNFAVOURABLE: *Reaction to the plan has been generally favourable.* **2** showing that something good is likely to happen: *a favourable weather forecast* —**favourably** /ˈfeɪv(ə)rəbli/ adv

favourite¹ /ˈfeɪv(ə)rət/ adj ★★ your favourite person or thing of a particular type is the one that you like the best: *What's your favourite food?*

favourite² /ˈfeɪv(ə)rət/ noun [C] ★
  1 the person or thing that you like the best: *The bacon sandwich is still a national favourite.*
  2 someone who is treated better than others because someone such as a teacher or parent prefers them: *Colin's always been mum's favourite.*
  3 the person, team, or animal that is expected to win a race or competition: *Chelsea are favourites to win the Premiership.*

favouritism /ˈfeɪv(ə)rətɪzəm/ noun [U] the unfair practice of giving someone help or advantages that you do not give to others

fawn¹ /fɔːn/ noun [C] a young DEER

fawn² /fɔːn/ PHRASAL VERB ˈfawn over sb or ˈfawn on sb to be extremely nice to someone because you want them to like you or to give you something

fawn³ /fɔːn/ adj light brown in colour

fax¹ /fæks/ noun **1** fax or **fax machine** [C] a piece of equipment that is used for sending

and receiving copies of documents in electronic form: *What's your fax number?* —*picture* → c3 **2** [C] a document that has been sent by a fax machine **3** [U] the system of sending documents using a fax machine: *Send me the details by fax.*

fax² /fæks/ verb [T] to send a message to someone using a fax machine: *Could you fax me the application form?*

faze /feɪz/ verb [T] *informal* to make someone feel confused, shocked, or upset

FBI, the /ˌef biː ˈaɪ/ the Federal Bureau of Investigation: a US government department that deals with serious crimes that affect more than one state

FDA, the /ˌef diː ˈeɪ/ the Food and Drug Administration: a US government department that controls the food and drugs that are allowed to be sold

fear¹ /fɪə/ noun ★★★
  1 [U] the feeling that you have when you are frightened: *She eventually managed to overcome her fear of the dark.* ♦ *Martin screamed in fear.* ♦ *She was shaking with fear.* ♦ *Many of these people live in fear* (=are afraid all the time).
  2 [C] something bad or unpleasant that you are afraid might happen: *He expressed fears for his missing wife's safety.* ♦ *This latest case has raised fears of an epidemic.* ♦ *There are fears about the safety of the nuclear plant.* ♦ +(that) *There are fears that the building might collapse.*
  PHRASES **for fear of (doing) sth** or **for fear (that)** in case you make something bad happen: *I didn't tell Susan about our meeting for fear of upsetting her.*
  no fear *British informal* used for saying that you definitely do not intend to do something

fear² /fɪə/ verb [T] ★★
  1 to feel worried and afraid that something bad will happen: *The refugees fear persecution if they return to their own country.* ♦ *One person is still missing, feared dead.* ♦ +(that) *Health experts fear that a flu epidemic will hit Britain this winter.*
  2 to feel afraid of someone or something because they might harm you: *He was hated and feared by his colleagues.*
  PHRASAL VERB ˈfear for sb/sth to feel worried about someone or something because you think that something bad may happen: *I fear greatly for their safety.*

fearful /ˈfɪəf(ə)l/ adj **1** frightened **2** *informal old-fashioned* very bad: *a fearful mess/muddle* —**fearfully** /ˈfɪəf(ə)li/ adv

fearless /ˈfɪələs/ adj *showing approval* not afraid of anyone or anything —**fearlessly** adv

fearsome /ˈfɪəs(ə)m/ adj very frightening

feasible /ˈfiːzəb(ə)l/ adj possible, or likely to succeed: *There seems to be only one feasible solution.* —**feasibility** /ˌfiːzəˈbɪləti/ noun [U]

feast¹ /fiːst/ noun [C] a large meal, usually for a special occasion

feast² /fiːst/ PHRASAL VERB ˈfeast on sth to eat a lot of a particular food with enjoyment: *We feasted on strawberries and cream.*

feat /fiːt/ noun [C] something that is impressive that someone does

F

feather /ˈfeðə/ noun [C] one of the narrow tubes with thin soft hairs on each side that cover a bird's body

feathery /ˈfeðəri/ adj like a feather

feature¹ /ˈfiːtʃə/ noun [C] ★★★
1 an important part or aspect of something: *The latest model has a lot of new safety features.* ♦ *the natural features of the landscape*
2 a part of your face such as your eyes, nose, or mouth: *Her large blue eyes were her best feature.*
3 a newspaper or magazine article, or a part of a television or radio programme that concentrates on a particular subject: *a special feature on new children's books*

> **Words often used with feature**
>
> Adjectives often used with feature (noun, sense 1)
> - **important, key, main** + FEATURE: used about aspects of something that are important
> - **distinctive, striking, unusual** + FEATURE: used about impressive or unusual features

feature² /ˈfiːtʃə/ verb ★★
1 [T] if something features a particular person or thing, they are an important part of it: *a concert featuring music by Haydn and Mozart* ♦ **feature sb/sth as** *The film features Diane Ashmann as a young French student.*
2 [I] to be an important part or aspect of something: *She has already featured in two award-winning films this year.*

feature ˌfilm noun [C] a long film that is made for the cinema

Feb. abbrev February

February /ˈfebruəri/ noun [C/U] ★★★ the second month of the year, between January and March: *I'm starting my new job in February.* ♦ *They fly to Spain on February 16th.*

feces /ˈfiːsiːz/ the American spelling of **faeces**

feckless /ˈfekləs/ adj a feckless person is not reliable and does not care about achieving anything

fed the past tense and past participle of **feed¹**

federal /ˈfed(ə)rəl/ adj ★
1 a federal country or system is one in which individual states make their own laws, but with a national government that is responsible for areas such as defence and foreign policy
2 connected with the national government of a country rather than with the government of one of its member states

federalism /ˈfed(ə)rəlɪz(ə)m/ noun [U] a FEDERAL political system —**federalist** noun [C], adj

federation /ˌfedəˈreɪʃ(ə)n/ noun [C] 1 a country that is made up of individual states with the power to make their own decisions, but with a national government that is responsible for areas such as defence and foreign policy 2 a large organization that is made up of several smaller organizations that share similar aims

fed ˈup adj informal annoyed or bored with something that you feel you have accepted for too long: *I'm fed up with this job.*

fee /fiː/ noun [C] ★★
1 money that you pay to a professional person or institution for their work: *tuition fees* ♦ *He will have to pay legal fees of £2,000.*
2 an amount of money that you pay to be allowed to do something such as join an organization: *The gallery charges a small entrance fee.*

feeble /ˈfiːb(ə)l/ adj 1 physically weak 2 not good enough to achieve the intended result: *a feeble attempt* ♦ *a feeble excuse* 3 not strong enough to be seen or heard clearly: *a feeble light/voice* —**feebly** adv

feed¹ /fiːd/ (past tense and past participle **fed** /fed/) verb ★★★
1 [T] to give food to a person or an animal: *We've been feeding the ducks on the river.* ♦ *All the children will be properly fed and cared for.* ♦ **feed sb/sth on sth** *The dogs were fed on raw meat.* ♦ **feed sth to sb/sth** *The leftover food is fed to the pigs.*
2 [I] if an animal or baby feeds, it eats: *Young babies need to feed every three to four hours.*
3 [T] to provide a supply of something for a person or a machine: **feed sth into sth** *Information is fed into the computer and stored in a database.* ♦ **feed sb with sth** *He's been feeding the police with information about terrorist activities.*
4 [T] to push something into a machine: **feed sth into sth** *She saw him feeding documents into the shredder.*

> PHRASAL VERB **feed on sth** if an animal feeds on something, it eats it as its usual food

feed² /fiːd/ noun 1 [C] British an occasion on which you give milk to a baby: *She had her last feed at two o'clock.* 2 [C/U] food that is given to animals: *Hay is used as winter feed for the cows.*

feedback /ˈfiːdbæk/ noun [U] comments about how well or how badly someone is doing something, which are intended to help them do it better: *Initial feedback from parents has been very positive.*

feel¹ /fiːl/ (past tense and past participle **felt** /felt/) verb ★★★

1 be in state mentioned	7 think particular way
2 have emotion/feeling	8 be affected by sth
3 give sb a feeling	9 try to find with hands
4 touch to discover sth	+ PHRASES
5 seem when touched	+ PHRASAL VERBS
6 notice sth	

1 [linking verb] to be in a particular state as a result of an emotion or a physical feeling: *I was feeling quite cheerful when we set out.* ♦ *Are you feeling ill?* ♦ *I feel such a fool for believing him.* ♦ *How do you feel now?* ♦ *I felt as though someone had just punched me in the stomach.* ♦ *When I came back to England, I felt like a stranger.*
2 [T] to experience a particular emotion or physical feeling: *He felt a sudden pain in his chest.* ♦ *Richard felt no guilt at all for what he had done.* ♦ *Cara felt the need to talk to someone.* ♦ *Children don't seem to feel the cold as much as adults do.*
3 [linking verb] if something feels nice, good, strange etc, it gives you this feeling: *It certainly felt good to be back home.* ♦ *The clock said it was only eight o'clock but it felt like midnight.*

4 [T] to touch something with your hand so that you can discover what it is like: *She felt the child's forehead to see if he was hot.*
5 [linking verb] if something feels soft, hard etc, that is what it is like when you touch it: *Your hair feels so soft.*
6 [T] to notice something that is touching you or something that is happening to you or near you: *Can you feel the draught coming from under the door?* ♦ +(that) *I felt I was being watched.*
7 [I/T] to have a particular way of thinking about something: +(that) *I feel that more should be done to help young people.* ♦ *I know that Sally feels strongly about this issue.*
8 [T] to be affected by something: *People should feel the benefits of the tax cuts by next summer.*
9 [I] to try to find something with your hands: *I felt around on the ground but couldn't find the torch.*

PHRASES **feel your age** to realize that you are becoming older and less able or willing to do things that younger people do
feel free *spoken* used for telling someone that they can do something if they want to: *Feel free to contact us at any time.*
feel like *spoken* to want something: *I feel like a cup of coffee.* ♦ **feel like doing sth** *Do you feel like going for a swim?*
feel your way 1 to move slowly and carefully, touching things with your hands because you cannot see **2** to make decisions and changes slowly, because you are not certain about what you are doing
→ HOME¹

PHRASAL VERBS ˈfeel for sb to feel sympathy for someone
ˌfeel ˈup to sth to feel that you are strong or healthy enough to do something: *I don't feel up to eating anything.*

feel² /fiːl/ noun [singular] **1** the way that something seems when you touch it or when it touches you: *Ben was enjoying the feel of the breeze in his hair.* **2** the way that something such as a place generally seems to you: *The village has a lovely friendly feel.* **3** an act of touching someone or something
PHRASES **get a feel for sth** or **get the feel of sth** *informal* to develop a good knowledge or understanding of something
have a feel for sth *informal* to have a natural ability to do or understand something

feelers /ˈfiːləz/ noun [plural] the two long thin parts on an insect's head that it uses for feeling things

ˈfeel-good adj intended to make you happy and satisfied: *a feel-good film*

feeling /ˈfiːlɪŋ/ noun ★★★
1 [C] an emotional state, for example anger or happiness: *He found it difficult to express his feelings.* ♦ *I didn't want to hurt his feelings* (=upset him). ♦ *Stephen had a sudden feeling of panic.*
2 [C] an opinion that you have about something, which is based on general thoughts: *My feeling is that we should wait a week or two.* ♦ *Sarah has very strong feelings about environmental issues.*
3 [C] something that you feel physically in your body: *a feeling of nausea*

4 [U] the ability to feel something such as pain or heat in your body: *She had lost all feeling in her right arm.*
PHRASES **bad/ill feeling** angry feelings that remain between people after a disagreement
have/get the feeling (that) or **have/get a feeling (that)** to be conscious of something but not certain about it: *I have a feeling we've met before.*
I know the feeling *spoken* used for showing sympathy
→ HARD¹

feet the plural of **foot**¹

feign /feɪn/ verb [T] *formal* to pretend to have a particular feeling

feisty /ˈfaɪsti/ adj full of energy and determination

feline /ˈfiːlaɪn/ adj connected with cats
—**feline** noun [C]

fell¹ /fel/ verb [T] to cut down a tree

fell² the past tense of **fall**¹

fellow¹ /ˈfeləʊ/ noun [C] **1** *old-fashioned* a man **2** a member of a professional society or educational institution

fellow² /ˈfeləʊ/ adj used for talking about people who are similar to you or are in the same situation as you: *his fellow students/ workers/citizens*

fellowship /ˈfeləʊʃɪp/ noun **1** [U] a feeling of friendship and support between people who do the same work or have the same interests **2** [C] an amount of money that is given to an advanced student for teaching and doing research

felt¹ /felt/ noun [U] a thick soft cloth made from wool, hair, or fur fibres that have been rolled and pressed flat

felt² the past tense and past participle of **feel**¹

ˌfelt-ˈtip or **ˌfelt-tip ˈpen** noun [C] a pen that has a piece of felt as its writing point

female¹ /ˈfiːmeɪl/ adj ★★★
1 a female person or animal belongs to the sex that can produce babies or eggs ≠ MALE
2 a female plant is one that produces fruit

female² /ˈfiːmeɪl/ noun [C] a female person or animal ≠ MALE

feminine /ˈfemənɪn/ adj **1** having qualities that are traditionally considered to be typical of women ≠ MASCULINE: *The look this year is soft and feminine.* ♦ *conventional notions of feminine beauty* **2** *linguistics* in some languages, feminine nouns, pronouns, and adjectives have different forms from MASCULINE or NEUTER words

femininity /ˌfeməˈnɪnəti/ noun [U] qualities that are considered to be typical of women ≠ MASCULINITY

feminism /ˈfemənɪz(ə)m/ noun [U] the belief that women should have the same rights and opportunities as men —**feminist** /ˈfemənɪst/ adj, noun [C]

fence¹ /fens/ noun [C] ★
1 a flat upright structure made of wood or wire that surrounds an area of land
—*picture* → C1
2 a structure that horses jump over in a competition or race

fence² /fens/ verb **1** [I] to fight with a light thin sword as a sport **2** [T] to put a fence around something

PHRASAL VERBS ,fence sth 'in *same as* fence² 2
,fence sth 'off to separate an area by
surrounding it with a fence

fencing /'fensɪŋ/ noun [U] **1** the sport of
fighting with a light thin sword **2** fences, or
the materials that are used for making them

fend /fend/

PHRASAL VERB ,fend for your'self to look after
yourself without help from anyone else:
*The kittens have been fending for themselves
since they were six weeks old.*

,fend sb/sth 'off to defend yourself against
criticism or an attack: *He tried to fend off
accusations of corruption.*

fender /'fendə/ noun [C] **1** a low frame round
a FIREPLACE that prevents burning coal or
wood from falling out **2** *American* a part of a
vehicle that covers or protects the area
round a wheel

feng shui /,fʌŋ 'ʃweɪ/ noun [U] a Chinese
system of designing buildings according to
special rules about the flow of energy that
is thought to influence people's lives

fennel /'fen(ə)l/ noun [U] a pale green
vegetable with seeds and leaves that are
used for adding flavour to food —*picture*
→ C11

ferment¹ /fə'ment/ verb [I/T] if a food or drink
ferments, or if it is fermented, a chemical
change happens to it and the sugar in it
produces alcohol —**fermentation**
/,fɜ:men'teɪʃ(ə)n/ noun [U]

ferment² /'fɜ:ment/ noun [U] a time of great
excitement or activity that usually leads to
change or violence: *a period of intense
political ferment*

fern /fɜ:n/ noun [C] a plant with no flowers
and leaves that are shaped like feathers

ferocious /fə'rəʊʃəs/ adj violent and able to
cause serious damage or injury: *a ferocious
attack* —**ferociously** adv

ferocity /fə'rɒsəti/ noun [U] violence, or
extreme force

ferret¹ /'ferɪt/ noun [C] a small thin furry
animal with a long tail that people
sometimes use for hunting

ferret² /'ferɪt/ **PHRASAL VERB** ,ferret sth 'out
to find something by searching in a
determined way

ferrous /'ferəs/ adj *science* containing or
connected with iron

ferry¹ /'feri/ or **ferryboat** /'feri,bəʊt/ noun
[C] a boat that makes short regular journeys
between two or more places: *They took the
ferry to Dover.* —*picture* → C7

ferry² /'feri/ verb [T] to carry people or goods
between two or more places: *Passengers
were ferried to the island in a small plane.*

fertile /'fɜ:taɪl/ adj **1** fertile land is able to
produce good crops or plants **2** a fertile
person, animal, or plant is able to produce
babies, young animals, or new plants
≠ INFERTILE **3** a fertile mind or situation is
able to produce good ideas or results: *a
child's fertile imagination*

fertility /fɜ:'tɪləti/ noun [U] **1** the ability of the
soil to produce a lot of good crops or plants
2 a woman's ability to have babies
≠ INFERTILITY: *fertility treatment*

fertilize /'fɜ:təlaɪz/ verb [T] **1** to make an egg,
a woman, or an animal start to produce a

baby **2** to add a substance to soil in order to
help plants to grow —**fertilization**
/,fɜ:təlaɪ'zeɪʃ(ə)n/ noun [U]

fertilizer /'fɜ:tə,laɪzə/ noun [C/U] a substance
that is added to soil in order to help plants
to grow

fervent /'fɜ:v(ə)nt/ adj very enthusiastic and
sincere about something that you believe
in or support —**fervently** adv

fervor /'fɜ:və/ the American spelling of
fervour

fervour /'fɜ:və/ noun [U] excitement caused
by strong feelings or beliefs

fester /'festə/ verb [I] **1** if an injury festers, it
becomes infected **2** if a problem or
unpleasant feeling festers, it becomes worse
because no one has dealt with it: *This
festering hatred could tear the community
apart.*

festival /'festɪv(ə)l/ noun [C] **1** a series of
performances of films, plays, music, or
dancing that is usually organized in the
same place at the same time each year **2** a
day or period when there is a public
holiday, often to celebrate a religious event:
the Hindu festival of Holi

festive /'festɪv/ adj connected with a festival
or celebration: *the festive season*
(=Christmas)

festivities /fe'stɪvətiz/ noun [plural] lively and
enjoyable activities in which people
celebrate something

festoon /fe'stu:n/ verb [T] to decorate
something with bright colourful objects

fetal /'fi:t(ə)l/ the American spelling of **foetal**

fetch /fetʃ/ verb [T] **1** to go and get someone or
something: *He went to fetch his coat.* ♦ *Peter
was sent to fetch the doctor.* → BRING **2** to be
sold for a particular amount of money: *The
painting is expected to fetch up to £220,000.*

fête¹ or **fete** /feɪt/ noun [C] *British* an outdoor
event with goods for sale and competitions,
usually organized by a school or church in
order to make money

fête² or **fete** /feɪt/ verb [T] to honour or
entertain someone at a public celebration

fetish /'fetɪʃ/ noun [C] **1** an unusual sexual
interest in a particular object or material
2 something that someone enjoys a lot, in a
way that is unusual or unreasonable: *an
exercise fetish*

fetus /'fi:təs/ the American spelling of **foetus**

feud /fju:d/ noun [C] an angry disagreement
between two people or groups that
continues for a long time: *a bitter feud
between rival gangs* —**feud** verb [I]

feudal /'fju:d(ə)l/ adj relating to the social
system that existed in Europe in the Middle
Ages, in which most people worked and
fought for the more powerful people who
owned their land —**feudalism** noun [U]

fever /'fi:və/ noun **1** [C/U] a medical condition
in which the temperature of your body is
very high =TEMPERATURE **2** [U] strong
excitement and enthusiasm: *The country
was gripped by World Cup fever.* —**fevered**
/'fi:vəd/ adj

feverish /'fi:vərɪʃ/ adj **1** affected by fever
2 extremely excited: *There was a lot of
feverish activity backstage.* —**feverishly** adv

F

few /fjuː/ (comparative **fewer**; superlative **fewest**) grammar word ★★★

> **Few** or **a few** can be:
> - a **determiner**: *Few people live there now.* ♦ *There were a few animals in the barn.*
> - a **pronoun**: *Many have tried, but few have succeeded.* ♦ *A few of the visitors left early.*
> **Few** can be:
> - an **adjective**: *Her few decent clothes were now dirty.*

1 some, but not many: *I spoke with a few colleagues about it.* ♦ *I'm not sure how many I'll need, so give me a few more.* ♦ *Everything is expected to change in the next few years.* ♦ *Clean the cage every few days.* ♦ *A few of the plates were chipped.*

2 very small in number: *Few managers attend the meetings.* ♦ *Why were there so few women in Parliament?* ♦ *We get very few complaints of racial discrimination.* ♦ *Few of the companies offer a home delivery service.* ♦ *Poe is among the few to have tackled this question.*

> - **A few** usually has a positive meaning and refers to a number of people or things that is not very large: *I've got a few questions for you.*
> - **Few** usually has a negative meaning and refers to a number that is smaller than you would like or expect: *Very few people came to her party.* **Few** is rather formal when used in this negative way and in spoken English it is more usual to say **not many**.

PHRASES **few and far between** not happening very often, or not existing in many places: *Opportunities for promotion are few and far between.*
quite a few a fairly large number of people or things: *The letter arrived quite a few days ago.*
→ LESS

> Both **fewer** and **less** can be used to refer to an amount that is smaller than another amount.
> - Use **fewer** before plural nouns: *Fewer people came than we expected.* ♦ *There are fewer restaurants in the area these days.*
> - Use **less** before uncountable nouns: *It took less time than I thought.* ♦ *You should use less paint.*

fiancé /fiˈɒnseɪ/ noun [C] the man that a woman is going to marry

fiancée /fiˈɒnseɪ/ noun [C] the woman that a man is going to marry

fiasco /fiˈæskəʊ/ noun [C] a complete and embarrassing failure

fib /fɪb/ verb [I] *informal* to tell a lie about something that is not important —**fib** noun [C]

fiber /ˈfaɪbə/ the American spelling of **fibre**

fibre /ˈfaɪbə/ noun **1** [U] the parts of fruit, vegetables, and grains that help food to pass through your body but that your body does not use: *foods that are high in fibre* **2** [C] a type of cloth, or one of the very thin natural or artificial pieces that cloth is made from: *natural fibres such as linen and cotton* **3** [C/U] one of the thin pieces that form the nerves and muscles in your body

fibreglass /ˈfaɪbəɡlɑːs/ noun [U] a light hard

substance made from very thin pieces of glass

fickle /ˈfɪk(ə)l/ adj always changing your mind about who or what you like

fiction /ˈfɪkʃ(ə)n/ noun ★★
1 [U] books and stories about imaginary events and people ≠ NON-FICTION: *Hardy wrote poetry as well as fiction.*
2 [C/U] a report, story, or explanation that is not true: *His account of what happened was pure fiction.*
→ SCIENCE FICTION

fictional /ˈfɪkʃ(ə)nəl/ adj invented for a book, play, or film: *a fictional character/place/event*

fictitious /fɪkˈtɪʃəs/ adj invented and not real or true

fiddle¹ /ˈfɪd(ə)l/ verb **1** [I] to keep touching or moving something: *Mary fiddled with her keys.* **2** [T] *informal* to produce false results or records, in order to get money or other benefits: *He fiddled the figures to make his business look profitable.*
PHRASAL VERB **fiddle around** or **fiddle about** *British* **1** *same as* **fiddle¹ 1 2** to waste time doing things that are not important or useful

fiddle² /ˈfɪd(ə)l/ noun [C] *informal* **1** a dishonest method of getting money or other benefits **2** a VIOLIN

fiddly /ˈfɪd(ə)li/ adj *British informal* complicated or detailed and needing attention or care

fidelity /fɪˈdeləti/ noun [U] **1** the attitude or behaviour of someone who is willing to have sex only with their partner ≠ INFIDELITY **2** *formal* loyalty to someone or something

fidget /ˈfɪdʒɪt/ verb [I] to keep making small quick movements because you are bored, nervous, or impatient —**fidgety** adj

field¹ /fiːld/ noun [C] ★★★

1 area for farming	**5** where force has effect
2 subject or type of work	**6** area with gas, coal etc
3 area for sport	**7** area that can be seen
4 space for information	**+** PHRASE

1 an area of land that is used for keeping animals or growing food: *a field of wheat*
2 a subject that you study, or a type of work that you do: *Professor Edwards is one of the main experts in his field.* ♦ *the field of organic chemistry*
3 an area of land that is covered in grass and used for sport: *a football field*
4 a space where you can type information in a computer program: *Type your name in the User field.*
5 an area where a particular force has an effect: *a magnetic field*
6 an area where gas, coal, oil, or other useful substances are found
7 an area that a person or piece of equipment can see at one time: *A man walked into my field of vision.* ♦ *a telescope's field of view*
PHRASE **in the field** in conditions that you find in the real world, not in a laboratory or classroom: *The new drugs have not yet been tested in the field.*

field² /fiːld/ verb [T] **1** to catch or pick up the ball in a sport such as CRICKET when a

F

player from the other team hits it **2** to use a person or group of people as your team or representative: *The Labour Party will be fielding over 400 candidates in the election.* **3** to deal with something such as a difficult question or a telephone call

'field ,day noun **have a field day** to have the chance to do something that you really enjoy

fielder /'fiːldə/ noun [C] a player in a sport such as CRICKET whose job is to catch or pick up the ball when a player from the other team hits it

'field ,event noun [C] a sports event that is not a race, for example throwing something or jumping

,field 'marshal noun [C] an officer of the highest rank in the British army

'field ,test noun [C] a test of something that involves using it in real conditions, rather than in a laboratory —**field-,test** verb [T]

'field ,trip noun [C] a visit to a place that gives students the chance to study something in a real environment, rather than in a classroom or laboratory

fieldwork /'fiːldwɜːk/ noun [U] work that involves going outside your classroom or laboratory to study something in a real environment

fiend /fiːnd/ noun [C] **1** a very evil person =MONSTER **2** *informal* someone who is extremely enthusiastic about something: *a football fiend*

fiendish /'fiːndɪʃ/ adj **1** a fiendish plan or idea is very clever but cruel **2** a fiendish problem or question is very difficult to solve or deal with —**fiendishly** adv

fierce /fɪəs/ adj ★
1 very angry, or ready to attack: *a fierce dog*
2 involving very strong feelings such as determination, anger, or hate: *a fierce debate*
3 very strong, or severe: *a fierce storm* ♦ *fierce competition*
—**fiercely** adv

fiery /'faɪəri/ adj **1** expressing strong feelings, especially anger: *a fiery speech* **2** very bright in colour

FIFA /'fiːfə/ the international organization that makes rules and decisions relating to the sport of football

fifteen /ˌfɪf'tiːn/ number the number 15

fifteenth /ˌfɪf'tiːnθ/ number **1** in the place or position counted as number 15 **2** one of 15 equal parts of something

fifth /fɪfθ/ number **1** in the place or position counted as number five **2** one of five equal parts of something

fifties /'fɪftiz/ noun [plural] the years from 1950 to 1959
PHRASE in your fifties aged between 50 and 59

fiftieth /'fɪftiəθ/ number **1** in the place or position counted as number 50 **2** one of 50 equal parts of something

fifty /'fɪfti/ number the number 50

,fifty-'fifty adj, adv equal, or into two equal parts: *a fifty-fifty chance of winning* ♦ *Expenses were shared fifty-fifty.*

fig /fɪg/ noun [C] a fruit with purple or green skin and many small seeds —*picture* → C10

fig. abbrev figure: a picture in a book

fight¹ /faɪt/ (past tense and past participle **fought** /fɔːt/) verb ★★★

1 use weapons	5 try not to show/do sth
2 hit/kick/bite	**+ PHRASES**
3 disagree/argue	**+ PHRASAL VERBS**
4 try hard to do sth	

1 [I/T] if people fight, they use guns or other weapons against each other: *Dan fought in the Gulf War.* ♦ *We were fighting for freedom.*
2 [I/T] if people or animals fight, they hit, kick, or bite each other: *Protesters fought with the police outside.* ♦ *Children fought over scraps of food.*
3 [I] to disagree or argue about something: *I don't want to fight over this.* ♦ *What are you two fighting about now?*
4 [I/T] to try very hard to achieve something, or to stop something bad from happening: *She spent her life fighting racism.* ♦ *We fought hard for our rights.* ♦ *fight to do sth Local campaigners are fighting to save the building.*
5 [T] to try very hard not to show a feeling, or not to do something that you want to do: *She fought the urge to run after him.*
PHRASES fight a fire/blaze to try to stop a large fire from burning
fight it out to fight or argue until something is decided
have a fighting chance to have a good chance of being successful
PHRASAL VERBS fight 'back to hit or kick someone who is attacking you, or to argue when someone criticizes you
fight sth 'back to try very hard not to show an emotion =HOLD BACK: *Mary fought back her tears.*
fight sb 'off to stop someone who is trying to attack you
fight sth 'off if your body fights off an illness, it prevents the illness from making you ill

Words often used with **fight**

Nouns often used with fight (verb, sense 4)
■ FIGHT + **corruption, crime, discrimination, prejudice, racism, terrorism: stop something bad**

fight² /faɪt/ noun [C] ★★★
1 a situation in which people hit each other: *He had a fight with a man in the pub.* ♦ *fights between rival fans*
2 a situation in which people disagree or argue with each other =DISAGREEMENT: *All teenagers have fights with their parents.*
3 a determined attempt to achieve something, or to stop something bad from happening =STRUGGLE: *the fight against terrorism* ♦ *a fight to do sth the fight to protect our children.*
4 an occasion when people fight in a BOXING match
PHRASE put up a good fight to try hard to achieve something even though you do not succeed

fighter /'faɪtə/ noun [C] **1** a military aircraft that is designed for battles with other aircraft **2** someone who refuses to be defeated even in the most difficult situations **3** someone who takes part in the sport of BOXING

figment /ˈfɪgmənt/ noun **a figment of your imagination** something that you have imagined, which therefore does not really exist

figurative /ˈfɪgərətɪv/ adj a figurative meaning is not the usual LITERAL meaning of a word or phrase, but makes a description more interesting: '*My love is like a red, red rose' is an example of the figurative use of language.* —**figuratively** adv

figure¹ /ˈfɪgə/ noun [C] ★★★

1 number	5 drawing in a book
2 amount of money	6 mathematical shape
3 person	+ PHRASE
4 woman's shape	

1 a number that has been counted or calculated: *This year's sales figures were excellent.*

2 a price, cost, or other amount of money: *It's difficult to* **put an** *exact* **figure on** *the rebuilding work.*

3 a person: *A small figure appeared in the doorway.* ♦ *She was the dominant figure in British politics in the 1980s.*

4 the shape of a woman's body: *She has a beautiful figure.*

5 a drawing in a book that gives information =DIAGRAM, ILLUSTRATION

6 *technical* a shape in mathematics: *a five-sided figure*

PHRASE **figure of speech** an expression in which the words are used in a figurative way

figure² /ˈfɪgə/ verb **1** [I] to be an important part of something **2** [I/T] *informal* to think that something is true, although you do not know for certain

PHRASE **it/that figures** *spoken* used for saying that you are not surprised about something that happens

PHRASAL VERBS **figure sb out** to understand what someone is like and why they behave in the way that they do

figure sth out to be able to understand something, or to solve a problem

figurehead /ˈfɪgəhed/ noun [C] a leader who has no power or influence

file¹ /faɪl/ noun [C] ★★★

1 a set of documents or records that you keep because they contain information: *medical files* ♦ *We have all your details on file* (=kept in a file). ♦ *The police file on the case has now been closed.*

2 a set of information that is stored on a computer and that is given a particular name

3 a metal tool that is used for making wood or metal smooth

4 a box or container in which papers are kept together —*picture* → C3

file² /faɪl/ verb ★★

1 [T] to put a document into a container with other documents: *File the forms in alphabetical order.*

2 [T] to make an official statement or complaint by giving it to people in authority: *The family has filed a lawsuit against the company.* ♦ *The couple filed for*

divorce (=told the court that they wanted to be divorced) *last month.*

3 [I] if people file somewhere, they walk there in a line: *Students filed into the lecture hall.*

4 [T] to rub something with a metal tool in order to make it smooth, or in order to cut it

PHRASE **file a report** to send an official news report to a newspaper or television station

file extension noun [C] *computing* the second part of the name of a computer file, that tells you what kind of file it is

filet /ˈfɪlɪt/ another spelling of **fillet¹**

filing cabinet noun [C] a tall piece of furniture with drawers in which you keep documents —*picture* → C3

filings /ˈfaɪlɪŋz/ noun [plural] very small pieces of metal that have been FILED off a larger piece

fill¹ /fɪl/ verb ★★★

1 make sth full	6 feel emotion strongly
2 become full of sth	7 spend time doing sth
3 put sth in hole/gap	+ PHRASE
4 of sound/smell/light	+ PHRASAL VERBS
5 be given job/position	

1 [T] to make something full: *Let me fill your glass.* ♦ *The room was* **filled with** *thick smoke.* ♦ **fill sth with sth** *She filled the bowl with warm water.*

2 [I] to become full of something: *The bar was slowly* **filling with** *people.*

3 [T] to put something into a hole or GAP so that the hole or GAP no longer exists: *We used cement to fill the cracks.*

4 [T] if sound, smell, or light fills a place, it is very strong or noticeable: *Brilliant sunlight filled the whole room.*

5 [T] if someone fills a job or position, they are given that job or position: *All the vacancies have now been filled.*

6 [T] if something fills you with a particular emotion, you feel that emotion very strongly: **fill sb with sth** *The sound of his voice filled me with dread.*

7 [T] if you fill a period of time, you spend it doing something

PHRASE **fill a need/gap/void/vacuum** to provide something that is missing or needed

PHRASAL VERBS **fill in** to do someone's job for them while they are away =STAND IN: *I'm filling in for the receptionist today.*

fill sb in *informal* to give someone details about something: *Carol will fill you in on what happened in the meeting.*

fill sth in to add information in the empty spaces on an official document =FILL STH OUT: *Please fill in the application form.*

fill out *informal* if someone fills out, their body becomes less thin

fill sth out to add information in the empty spaces on an official document =FILL STH IN: *Have you filled out the form?*

fill up *same as* **fill¹** **2**: *The room was beginning to fill up.*

fill sth up *same as* **fill¹** **1**: *Would you fill up that jug for me?*

fill² /fɪl/ noun **have your fill of sth** to experience so much of something that you do not want any more

fillet¹ /ˈfɪlɪt/ noun [C/U] a piece of meat or fish with no bones in it

fillet² /ˈfɪlɪt/ verb [T] to prepare fish or meat for cooking by removing the bones

filling¹ /ˈfɪlɪŋ/ noun **1** [C/U] the cream, fruit etc that forms the inside part of a cake or PIE **2** [C] a small amount of metal or plastic that is used for filling a hole in a tooth

filling² /ˈfɪlɪŋ/ adj food that is filling makes you feel full

film¹ /fɪlm/ noun ★★★

1 [C] moving pictures that tell a story =MOVIE: *Have you seen the new James Bond film?* ♦ *We watched a **film about** prison life.*
2 [U] the job or business of making films: *the film industry*
3 [C/U] the material that is used for taking photographs or for recording moving pictures: *I need a new film for my camera.*
4 [C] a very thin layer of something that forms on a surface: *a **film** of oil on the water*

film² /fɪlm/ verb [I/T] to use a camera to record moving pictures: *The programme was filmed in South Africa.*

filming /ˈfɪlmɪŋ/ noun [U] the activity of making a film

film-maker noun [C] a film director

film star noun [C] *British* a very famous film actor

filter¹ /ˈfɪltə/ noun [C] a piece of equipment that removes substances that are not wanted from a liquid or gas: *a water filter*

filter² /ˈfɪltə/ verb **1** [I] if light or sound filters into a place, a little of it enters that place: *The August sunlight filtered in through the blinds.* **2** [I] if information filters out or through to people, they receive it after a period of time: *News of the decision filtered out to reporters.* **3** [T] to pass something through a filter in order to remove particular things that are contained in it

PHRASAL VERB **filter sth out** to use a filter to remove something that is not wanted

filth /fɪlθ/ noun [U] **1** *informal* words or pictures that are very offensive, usually dealing with sex **2** dirt that is especially unpleasant

filthy /ˈfɪlθi/ adj **1** very dirty **2** *informal* very offensive and usually dealing with sex

fin /fɪn/ noun [C] a thin flat part that sticks out of the body of a fish

final¹ /ˈfaɪn(ə)l/ adj ★★★

1 existing at the end of a process: *These issues will be discussed in the final report.* ♦ *The **final score** was 2–2.*
2 last in a series: *The final payment is due next month.*
3 if something is final, it cannot be changed: *The editor's decision is final.*
4 showing that something has finished: *the final whistle of the match*

final² /ˈfaɪn(ə)l/ noun **1** [C] the last game, race etc in a competition, that decides who wins the whole competition **2 finals** [plural] the last set of examinations that students take before they finish at a college or university **3** [C] *American* the last examination that students take before they finish a class at a school or university

finale /fɪˈnɑːli/ noun [C] the last part of a performance with the most exciting music and dancing

finalist /ˈfaɪnəlɪst/ noun [C] a player or team that takes part in the final game in a competition

finalize /ˈfaɪnəlaɪz/ verb [T] to make the final decisions or arrangements for something

finally /ˈfaɪn(ə)li/ adv ★★★

1 after a long time, process, or series of events: *We finally arrived home at midnight.*
2 *spoken* as the last thing that you want to say: *Finally, I'd like to say thank you.*
3 *formal* decided or agreed in a way that cannot be changed: *The exact amount has not been finally decided.*

finance¹ /ˈfaɪnæns, faɪˈnæns/ noun ★

1 [U] decisions on how money is spent or invested: *the company's finance committee*
2 [U] money that is used to pay for something such as a large project: *Where will the finance for this project come from?*
3 finances [plural] the money that you have, and how well you spend it or save it: *My finances are in a terrible mess at the moment.*

finance² /ˈfaɪnæns, faɪˈnæns/ verb [T] to pay for something such as a large project: *The scheme is being financed by the Arts Council.*

financial /faɪˈnænʃ(ə)l/ adj ★★★ involving money: *banks and other financial institutions* ♦ *We offer a range of **financial services**.* —**financially** adv: *The decision does not affect us financially.*

financial year noun [C] *British* a period of 12 months that is used for calculating how much profit a company has made and how much it owes

financier /faɪˈnænsiə/ noun [C] a person or organization that manages or lends large amounts of money

finch /fɪntʃ/ noun [C] a small bird with a short thick beak

find¹ /faɪnd/ (past tense and past participle **found** /faʊnd/) verb [T] ★★★

1 discover (by searching)	**5** make formal decision
2 get sth	**6** have enough of sth
3 experience sth	**+** PHRASES
4 have as opinion	**+** PHRASAL VERB

1 to discover or to notice something, often after searching: *Have you found your shoes?* ♦ *We hope to find the answers to these questions.* ♦ **find sb doing sth** *I found her wandering in the streets.*
2 to get something: *Have you found accommodation yet?* ♦ *It is very difficult for young people in this area to **find work**.*
3 to experience something in a particular way: *William now finds walking very difficult.*
4 to have something as an opinion because of things that you have experienced: **+(that)** *I find that children need a lot of encouragement.*
5 to make a formal decision about something after listening to all the facts: *He was **found guilty** and sentenced to three years in prison.* ♦ **+(that)** *The court found that the company had broken the law.*
6 if you find the time or money to do something, you have enough time or money to do it

PHRASES **be found** if something is found in a particular place, it lives, grows, or exists there: *The flower is found only in the French Alps.*

find your way to manage to arrive in a place that you were not sure how to get to

find yourself doing sth to realize that you are doing something that you had not intended to do: *I found myself agreeing with everything she said.*

PHRASAL VERB **find out** to discover a fact or piece of information: *I don't want Jerry to find out about this.* ♦ *I want to find out what happened.* ♦ +(that) *Her parents found out that she had a boyfriend.*

find² /faɪnd/ noun [C] something good that you find by chance

findings /ˈfaɪndɪŋz/ noun [plural] information or opinions that come from doing research

fine¹ /faɪn/ adj ★★★

1 good enough	4 difficult to notice
2 healthy	5 thin and narrow
3 of high quality	+ PHRASE

1 good enough, or acceptable: *'Is your room all right?' 'Yes, fine, thanks.'* ♦ *Your blood pressure is absolutely fine.*
2 healthy and happy: *'How are you?' 'Fine, thanks.'*
3 of very good quality: *fine clothes/food/wine*
4 fine details are small and difficult to notice: *He spent hours explaining the finer points of the scheme.*
5 very thin and narrow, not thick or heavy: *fine hair* ♦ *a fine layer of dust*
PHRASE **a fine line between** if there is a fine line between two things, they are almost the same as each other

fine² /faɪn/ adv *informal* in a way that is acceptable and good enough: *My car's working fine now.*

fine³ /faɪn/ noun [C] an amount of money that you must pay because you have broken the law: *I had to pay a $40 fine for parking on the street overnight.* ♦ *The court has the right to impose heavy fines* (=large fines).

> **Words often used with fine**
>
> *Adjectives often used with fine (noun)*
> ■ **heavy, hefty, large, stiff, substantial** + FINE: used when you have to pay a lot of money

fine⁴ /faɪn/ verb [T] to make someone pay an amount of money as a punishment for breaking the law: *She was fined £250 for speeding.*

fine art noun [U] objects such as paintings that are created to be beautiful or interesting

finely /ˈfaɪnli/ adv **1** into very small pieces: *Add one onion, finely chopped.* **2** exactly, or with great care: *a finely crafted machine*

finesse /fɪˈnes/ noun [U] a skilful quality in the way that you move or deal with difficult situations

fine-tune verb [T] to make small changes to something in order to make it as good as possible

finger¹ /ˈfɪŋɡə/ noun [C] ★★★
1 the long thin parts on the end of your hands

2 a long thin piece of something: *Serve with fingers of toast.*
PHRASE **(keep your) fingers crossed** used for saying that you hope things will happen in the way that you want them to
→ LAY¹, POINT², PULSE¹, SLIP¹

finger² /ˈfɪŋɡə/ verb [T] to touch something with your fingers

fingernail /ˈfɪŋɡəneɪl/ noun [C] any of the hard smooth parts at the ends of your fingers

fingerprint /ˈfɪŋɡəprɪnt/ noun [C] a mark on something that you have touched that shows the pattern of lines on your fingers

fingertip /ˈfɪŋɡətɪp/ noun [C] the end of your finger
PHRASE **at your fingertips** available for you to use immediately: *He has all the information at his fingertips.*

finicky /ˈfɪnɪki/ adj someone who is finicky wants things to be correct in every detail

finish¹ /ˈfɪnɪʃ/ verb ★★★
1 [I/T] to do the last part of something so that it is complete: *I've nearly finished my work.* ♦ **finish doing sth** *I haven't finished eating yet.*
2 [I] to stop happening: *Lessons finish at midday.* ♦ *The game finished with the score at 1–1.*
3 [T] to eat, drink, or use all of something so that there is none left: *We finished the bottle of wine.*
4 [I/T] to be in a particular position at the end of a race or competition: *She finished fifth.*
PHRASE **the finishing touch/touches** the last small details that make something complete

PHRASAL VERBS **finish sth off 1** *same as* **finish¹** 1: *They hired a smaller company to finish off the job.* **2** *same as* **finish¹** 3: *Do you want to finish off these sandwiches?*
finish up to be in a particular place or situation at the end of a long series of events: *She eventually finished up in London.*
finish sth up *same as* **finish¹** 3: *Finish up your drinks, please.*
finish with sb *informal* to end a relationship with someone so that they are no longer your boyfriend or girlfriend
finish with sth if you have finished with something, you have stopped using it and no longer need it: *Have you finished with the scissors yet?*

finish² /ˈfɪnɪʃ/ noun [C] **1** the end of something **2** the appearance of a surface, for example whether it is smooth or rough

finished /ˈfɪnɪʃt/ adj **1** something that is finished has been completed: *We can move in as soon as building work is finished.* **2** if you are finished, you have completed the job that you were doing

finite /ˈfaɪnaɪt/ adj *formal* existing only in limited numbers or amounts, or continuing only for a limited time or distance
≠ INFINITE: *The world's finite resources must be used wisely.*

fir /fɜː/ noun [C] a tree with thin sharp leaves that do not fall off in winter —*picture* → C9

fire¹ /faɪə/ noun ★★★
1 [C/U] flames and heat from something that

is burning in an uncontrolled way: *Lightning may have **started the fire**. ♦ A tree in the middle of the field was **on fire*** (=burning). *♦ Suddenly the curtains **caught fire*** (=began to burn). *♦ That night a **fire broke out** in the nightclub. ♦ The boys **set fire to*** (=started a fire on) *an old couch.*
2 [C] a small pile of burning wood, coal etc that you make in order to produce heat: *a coal fire ♦ Bill started to **build a fire**.*
3 [C] *British* a piece of equipment that uses electricity or gas to heat a room: *an old gas fire*
4 [U] shots from a gun: *machine gun fire ♦ One of the men **opened fire on*** (=started shooting at) *the police.*
→ PLAY¹

fire² /faɪə/ *verb* ★★
1 [I/T] if a weapon fires, or if someone fires it, someone uses it to shoot something: *The rebels **fired** their machine guns into the air. ♦ Jed lifted his rifle and **fired at** the target.*
2 [T] to make someone leave their job as a punishment=SACK: *She was **fired** for refusing to include the information in her report.*

ˈfire aˌlarm *noun* [C] a piece of equipment that makes a loud noise to warn people that there is a fire

firearm /ˈfaɪərˌɑːm/ *noun* [C] *formal* a gun

ˈfire briˌgade *noun* [C] *British* the organization whose job is dealing with fires in a particular area

firecracker /ˈfaɪəˌkrækə/ *noun* [C] a FIREWORK that makes a loud noise when it explodes

ˈfire deˌpartment *noun* [C] *American* the fire brigade

ˈfire ˌdrill *noun* [C] an occasion when all the people in a building pretend that there is a fire inside and practise getting out safely

fired-up /ˌfaɪəd ˈʌp/ *adj informal* very excited and enthusiastic about something

ˈfire ˌengine *noun* [C] a large vehicle that takes FIREFIGHTERS and their equipment to a fire

ˈfire eˌscape *noun* [C] a metal STAIRCASE on the outside of a building that people use in order to escape when there is a fire

ˈfire exˌtinguisher *noun* [C] a metal container that is filled with water or with a chemical that stops fires

firefighter /ˈfaɪəˌfaɪtə/ *noun* [C] someone whose job is to put out fires and help people to escape from other dangerous situations

firefly /ˈfaɪəflaɪ/ *noun* [C] an insect that produces a flashing light when it flies

ˈfire ˌhydrant *noun* [C] a water pipe in a street from which water is taken to stop a fire

firelight /ˈfaɪəˌlaɪt/ *noun* [U] the light that a fire in a FIREPLACE produces

fireman /ˈfaɪəmən/ (plural **firemen** /ˈfaɪəmən/) *noun* [C] a male FIREFIGHTER

fireplace /ˈfaɪəˌpleɪs/ *noun* [C] a place in a room where a fire burns

fireproof /ˈfaɪəˌpruːf/ *adj* a fireproof object cannot be damaged by fire

ˈfire ˌservice *noun* [C] *British* the FIRE BRIGADE

fireside /ˈfaɪəˌsaɪd/ *noun* [C] the part of a room that is near a fire

ˈfire ˌstation *noun* [C] the building where FIREFIGHTERS have their office and keep their equipment

firewall /ˈfaɪəˌwɔːl/ *noun* [C] *computing* a computer program that prevents people from entering a computer system illegally

firewood /ˈfaɪəwʊd/ *noun* [U] wood that is used as fuel for a fire

fireworks /ˈfaɪəwɜːks/ *noun* [plural] objects that make loud noises and coloured lights in the sky when they explode

ˈfiring ˌsquad *noun* [C] a group of soldiers who shoot and kill someone as a punishment

firm¹ /fɜːm/ *noun* [C] ★★★ a business, or a company: *a building/engineering/law firm ♦ **a firm of** accountants/architects/solicitors*

firm² /fɜːm/ *adj* ★★
1 solid but not hard ≠ SOFT: *a firm mattress*
2 definite and not changing: *Have you set a firm date for the meeting? ♦ The institution has the firm support of the local people. ♦ Mark's **a firm believer in** discipline for children.*
3 showing that you are in control of a situation: *What the party needs now is firm leadership. ♦ You sometimes have to **be firm with** young children.*
4 physically or mentally strong: *She took a firm hold of the stick and pulled.*
—**firmly** *adv*: *I firmly believe that we must act at once.* —**firmness** *noun* [U]

firm³ /fɜːm/ **PHRASAL VERB** **firm sth ˈup** to make something more definite

first /fɜːst/ *grammar word* ★★★

First can be:
- **a number:** *This is the first car I've ever owned.*
- **a pronoun:** *Her second husband was much older than her first.*
- **an adverb:** *First, I want to explain the purpose of this meeting.*
- **a noun:** *That visit was a first for me.*

1 before any others coming, happening, or starting before any others: *What was your first job? ♦ This will be Kenny's first trip overseas. ♦ Julia got there first. ♦ He's had a lot of girlfriends, but Lucy was **the first**. ♦ Take the first turning on the right. ♦ He cooked me a meal, which was **a first** (=he had never done it before).*
2 before doing other things before you do something else: *First, let's go around the room and introduce ourselves. ♦ Can't I just finish reading this article first?*
3 at the beginning at the beginning of a period of time, a situation, an activity etc: *When I first started running, I could do a mile in nine minutes. ♦ The first few days of our holiday were wonderful.*
4 most important used for referring to the main or most important thing: *His first love was music. ♦ Our first consideration must be the safety of the passengers. ♦ My children will always **come first**.*
5 best in a competition better than anyone or anything else in a game, competition etc: *Phil Gray **came first** in the under-12 section. ♦ His painting won **first prize** in a competition.*
6 university degree in the UK and Australia, the highest mark for an UNDERGRADUATE degree from a college or university: *He got a first in maths from Imperial College.*

PHRASES **at first** in the beginning, before something changes: *At first he wouldn't even talk about it.*

at first sight/glance when you first see something or find out about something, before you know more details: *At first glance, the theory seems to make a lot of sense.*

sb's first choice the thing or person that someone likes more than all the others

first come, first served used for saying that if you arrive before other people you will be served or dealt with before them

first of all *spoken* **1** used for introducing the first of several things that you are going to say: *First of all, I'd like to give you a little background information.* **2** before doing anything else: *First of all, clean the surface that you are going to paint.*

first thing (in the morning) at the very beginning of the day

first things first used for saying that the most important things should be dealt with before anything else

in the first place 1 used for stating the most basic reason for something: *I'm not going because, in the first place, I can't afford it.* **2** at the beginning of a situation: *If you don't like her, why invite her in the first place?*

make the first move to take action before anyone else

first 'aid noun [U] basic medical treatment that is given as soon as someone is injured or ill

first 'aid ,kit noun [C] a small box or bag with the equipment that you need to give first aid

first 'base noun [singular] the first successful step in an attempt to achieve something

first 'class¹ noun [U] **1** the most expensive and most comfortable way to travel on a plane, train, or ship **2** the class of post that is the quickest and most expensive

first 'class² adj **1** of the best quality, or of the highest standard: *first class service* **2** providing the most expensive and most comfortable way to travel on a plane, train, or ship: *a first class ticket* **3** used for first class post

first 'class³ adv using the most expensive form of transport or post: *She always travels first class.*

first 'cousin noun [C] a child of your AUNT or UNCLE

first-de'gree adj **1** a first-degree burn is the least serious type **2** *American* a first-degree murder is the most serious type, in which someone deliberately plans to kill someone

first e'dition noun [C] one of the first printed copies of a book, newspaper, or magazine

first 'floor, the noun [singular] **1** *British* the floor of a building that is just above the GROUND FLOOR **2** *American* the floor of a building that is at the same level as the ground

first 'gear noun [U] the lowest GEAR in a vehicle, used for starting or moving slowly

first gene'ration noun [singular] **1** the GENERATION of people in a family who were the first from their country to go and live in another country **2** the first type of a

particular machine or piece of equipment to be produced —**first-gene'ration** adj

first 'half noun [C] the first part of a sports match

first-'hand adj obtained by experiencing something yourself, not by learning about it from other people: *first-hand knowledge/ information/experience* ♦ *a first-hand account of the situation* —**first-'hand** adv

First 'Lady, the the wife of the president of the US or of a GOVERNOR of a US state

first 'language noun [C] **1** the first language that you learn to speak **2** the main language that people speak in a region or country

firstly /'fɜːstli/ adv used for beginning a list of things that are in a particular order

first ,name noun [C] the name that comes before your family name

first 'person, the noun [singular] **1** *linguistics* the pronouns 'I' and 'we' and the verbs and object pronouns that are used with them **2** a way of writing a story as if it had happened to you

first-'rate adj of the highest quality

First World 'War, the a war that was fought mainly in Europe between 1914 and 1918

fiscal /'fɪsk(ə)l/ adj relating to money and financial matters —**fiscally** adv

fish¹ /fɪʃ/ (plural **fish** or **fishes**) noun [C/U] ★★★ an animal that lives in water and swims, or the meat of this animal

PHRASE **fish and chips** a meal of fish and long thin pieces of potato, cooked in hot oil

fish² /fɪʃ/ verb [I] **1** to try to catch fish **2** to try to find something by feeling inside a bag, a box etc: *She fished around in her bag for the keys.* **3** to try to make someone tell you something without asking directly: *'Having trouble?' he asked casually, fishing for information.*

PHRASAL VERB **,fish sth 'out** to pull something out from inside something else: *She reached into her bag and fished out a pen.*

fisherman /'fɪʃəmən/ (plural **fishermen** /'fɪʃəmən/) noun [C] a man who catches fish for fun, or as his job

fishing /'fɪʃɪŋ/ noun [U] the activity, sport, or business of catching fish: *We're going fishing tomorrow.*

fishing ,rod noun [C] a long thin pole that you use for catching fish

fishmonger /'fɪʃ,mʌŋɡə/ noun [C] someone whose job is to sell fish

fish ,slice noun [C] *British* an object used for turning food over while it is cooking

fishy /'fɪʃi/ adj **1** tasting or smelling like fish **2** not completely right, honest, or legal

fissure /'fɪʃə/ noun [C] a long deep crack in something

fist /fɪst/ noun [C] your hand when your fingers are closed tightly: *She was holding something tightly in her fist.*

fistful /'fɪstfʊl/ noun [C] the amount of something that you can hold in your fist

fit¹ /fɪt/ (past tense and past participle **fitted**) verb ★★★

1 be right size/shape	4 be the same as sth
2 about clothes	5 add sth to sth
3 be suitable for sth	✦ PHRASAL VERBS

F

1 [I/T] to be small enough or the right size and shape to go somewhere, or to manage to put someone or something in a space: *I don't think that box will fit.* ♦ *The book is small enough to fit in your pocket.* ♦ *The cover fits neatly over the chair.* ♦ **fit sth into/onto/over sth** *She can fit two more people into her car.*
2 [I/T] if clothes fit, they are the right size for you: *It is important that children's shoes fit correctly.* ♦ *I like the suit, but the jacket doesn't fit me.* ♦ *The dress **fitted** her **like a glove** (=fitted extremely well).*
3 [I/T] to be suitable or right for something: *We need a name that fits our image.* ♦ *A dark wooden table wouldn't **fit with** the decor in here.*
4 [I/T] to be the truth, or to be the same as something that someone describes or asks for: *He fits the description of a man seen running away from the scene.* ♦ *Something in her story did not fit.*
5 [T] to add a piece of equipment to something else: **fit sth with sth** *Some cars are fitted with hand controls for people with physical disabilities.* ♦ **fit sth to/onto sth** *You can fit a bike rack to the rear of your car.*

PHRASAL VERBS **fit 'in 1** to be a part of a group, plan, or situation: *He explained the project to me and how my job fits in.* **2** to be accepted by a group of people because you are similar to them: *I tried to fit in but they were all much younger than I was.*
fit sb 'in to have enough time to deal with someone or something: *Dr Halden can fit you in this morning at 10.*
fit sth 'out to put equipment into a room or building so that it can be used for a particular purpose: *The kitchen has been fitted out with pine cupboards.*
fit 'together if things such as ideas or facts fit together, they make a sensible story or explanation when you put them together: *We have all the evidence but we don't know yet how it fits together.*

fit² /fɪt/ adj ★
1 healthy, strong, and able to do physical exercise ≠ UNFIT: *Running around after the kids keeps me fit.* ♦ *I need to **get fit** before the football season starts.*
2 of a good enough standard for something ≠ UNFIT: *The house was not fit for human habitation.* ♦ **fit to do sth** *I don't think he's fit to be a teacher.*
PHRASE **see/think fit** to decide that something is the best thing to do: *The court will deal with the matter as it thinks fit.*

fit³ /fɪt/ noun **1** [C] a strong sudden physical reaction or emotion that you cannot control: *a coughing/sneezing fit* ♦ *a fit of rage* **2** [C] *informal* an occasion when someone becomes unconscious for a short time and their body shakes **3** [singular] used for saying whether something is the right size and shape for someone or something: *When buying shoes, it is important to get a good fit.*
PHRASE **have/throw a fit** *informal* to get very angry and shout or become violent

fitful /ˈfɪtf(ə)l/ adj starting and stopping often: *fitful sleep* —**fitfully** adv

fitness /ˈfɪtnəs/ noun [U] **1** the state of being physically healthy and strong: *a high level of physical fitness* **2** how suitable someone or something is: *There are questions as to his fitness for office.*

fitted /ˈfɪtɪd/ adj **1** made to fit the shape of something closely: *a fitted shirt* **2** *British* built or made to fit a particular space: *fitted cupboards/carpets*

fitting /ˈfɪtɪŋ/ adj suitable for a particular situation: *The dinner was a fitting end to Carter's 25 years with the company.*

'fitting ,room noun [C] a room in a clothes shop where you can put on clothes before you buy them = CHANGING ROOM

fittings /ˈfɪtɪŋz/ noun [plural] small parts that you connect to something: *pipe fittings*

five /faɪv/ number [C] the number 5

fiver /ˈfaɪvə/ noun [C] *British informal* a five pound note

'five-star adj a five-star hotel or restaurant is of excellent quality

fix¹ /fɪks/ verb [T] ★★

1 fasten so cannot move	**5** prepare food/drink
2 set price/amount/date	**6** arrange hair/clothing
3 cheat	♦ PHRASAL VERBS
4 make sth work again	

1 to fasten something somewhere so that it cannot move: **fix sth to/onto/on sth** *Smoke detectors should be fixed to the ceiling.*
2 to decide what a price, amount, or date will be: *Interest rates have been fixed at 5%.* ♦ *A delivery date has not yet been fixed.*
3 to dishonestly arrange the result of something such as a game or election
4 to repair something: *Jessica fixed my watch.* ♦ *I have to **get** my car **fixed**.*
5 *American* to prepare food or drink: *I'll fix dinner.* ♦ **fix sb sth** *Jackie fixed me a drink.*
6 *American* to arrange your hair or clothing so that you look nicer: *How should I fix my hair?*

PHRASAL VERBS **'fix sth on sb/sth** if you fix your eyes or your attention on someone or something, you look straight at them and at nothing else
fix sb 'up *informal* to arrange for two people to meet so that they might begin a romantic relationship: **fix sb up with sb** *Jimmy wants to fix Joe up with his sister.*
fix sth 'up to clean, repair, or decorate something: *I'm going to fix up the house before my mother-in-law arrives.*

fix² /fɪks/ noun **1** [C] something that solves a problem or corrects a mistake: *We need a long-term solution, not just a quick fix* (=a fast solution but one that is usually only temporary). **2** [singular] an amount of a drug that someone feels that they need to take regularly

fixation /fɪkˈseɪʃ(ə)n/ noun [C] a very strong interest in something that prevents you from paying attention to anything else: *Doug has a fixation with sports cars.* —**fixated** /fɪkˈseɪtɪd/ adj

fixed /fɪkst/ adj ★
1 not changing, or not able to be changed: *a fixed price* ♦ *a fixed smile* ♦ *My mother has fixed ideas about how to bring up children.*

2 fastened in one position and not able to be moved: *Make sure bookcases are securely fixed to the wall.*

fixed 'income noun [C] an income that does not change or get bigger over time

fixture /ˈfɪkstʃə/ noun [C] **1** a piece of furniture or equipment that is built into a building so that you do not take it with you when you move: *light fixtures* **2** British a sports event that happens at a regular time and place

fizz /fɪz/ noun [U] the small gas BUBBLES that are in some drinks —**fizz** verb [I]

fizzle /ˈfɪz(ə)l/ or ˌ**fizzle 'out** verb [I] to gradually fail, become less enthusiastic, or disappear: *The group's efforts at reform fizzled out after their leader left.*

fizzy /ˈfɪzi/ adj British a fizzy drink is a sweet drink without alcohol that has BUBBLES

fjord /ˈfiːɔːd, fjɔːd/ noun [C] a narrow section of sea that is between high rocks

flab /flæb/ noun [U] informal loose fat flesh

flabbergasted /ˈflæbəɡɑːstɪd/ adj very surprised or shocked

flabby /ˈflæbi/ adj with a lot of loose fat: *a flabby stomach*

flack /flæk/ another spelling of **flak**

flag¹ /flæɡ/ noun [C] a piece of cloth with colours or a pattern on it, used as a signal or for representing a country or organization

flag² /flæɡ/ verb **1** [I] to become tired or weak, or to begin to lack enthusiasm: *After a long day, his energy flagged.* **2** [T] to mark something so that you will be able to find it again

⎯ **PHRASAL VERB** ˌflag sb/sth 'down to wave at the driver of a car so that they stop: *tourists trying to flag down a cab*

flagpole /ˈflæɡpəʊl/ noun [C] a tall thin pole, used for hanging a flag on

flagrant /ˈfleɪɡrənt/ adj done in an obvious way that shows that you do not care what people think: *a flagrant disregard for the law* —**flagrantly** adv

flagship /ˈflæɡʃɪp/ noun [C] the biggest, most important, or best thing in a group

flail /fleɪl/ verb [I/T] to move your arms and legs about in an uncontrolled way

flair /fleə/ noun [U] an attractive, skilful, or interesting way of doing something: *She always dresses with flair.*

⎯ **PHRASE** **have a flair for sth** to be very skilful at something

flak /flæk/ noun [U] informal criticism and argument: *The policy is getting a lot of flak.*

flake¹ /fleɪk/ noun [C] a small flat piece of something

flake² /fleɪk/ or ˌ**flake 'off** verb [I] to come off a surface in small flat pieces: *Her skin was itchy and beginning to flake.*

flaky /ˈfleɪki/ adj **1** breaking off easily into small flat pieces: *flaky chocolate* **2** American informal crazy

flamboyant /flæmˈbɔɪənt/ adj behaving or dressing in a way that deliberately attracts attention —**flamboyantly** adv

flame /fleɪm/ noun [C] ★ the brightly burning gas that you see coming from a fire: *He sat by the fire staring at the flames.* ♦ *The whole*

building was soon in flames. ♦ *A car had overturned and burst into flames.* → OLD FLAME

flamenco /fləˈmeŋkəʊ/ noun [C/U] a traditional lively dance from Spain, or the music for this dance

flaming /ˈfleɪmɪŋ/ adj **1** burning brightly: *flaming torches* **2** British involving a lot of angry emotion=BLAZING: *a flaming row* **3** brightly coloured red, orange, or yellow: *a flaming orange sunset*

flamingo /fləˈmɪŋɡəʊ/ noun [C] a large pink tropical water bird with a long neck and long legs

flammable /ˈflæməb(ə)l/ adj likely to burn very quickly and easily=INFLAMMABLE ≠ NON-FLAMMABLE

> **Flammable** and **inflammable** both describe something that burns easily and quickly, but most people use **flammable** because **inflammable** looks as if it means 'not flammable'.

flan /flæn/ noun [C] British a cake or PIE without a top that has a filling of cheese, fruit, or vegetables

flank¹ /flæŋk/ verb [T] to be at the side of something or someone: *The Prime Minister entered the room, flanked by his advisers.*

flank² /flæŋk/ noun [C] **1** the side of an animal's body **2** a position on the right or left side of a team or army, or the people in that position

flannel /ˈflæn(ə)l/ noun **1** [U] soft cloth that is used for making clothes and sheets **2** [C] British a small piece of cloth that you use for washing yourself

flap¹ /flæp/ noun **1** [C] a thin flat piece of something that is fixed to something else along one edge **2** [singular] informal a situation in which people are confused, excited, or angry=FUSS: *They were in a real flap over the lost passport.*

flap² /flæp/ verb **1** [I/T] if a bird's wings flap, or if the bird flaps them, they move quickly up and down **2** [I] to be blown noisily by the wind: *I was running fast, my coat flapping in the wind.* **3** [I] British informal to be very worried, nervous, or excited about something: *Just keep calm and don't flap.*

flare¹ /fleə/ noun [C] **1** a bright light or flame that is used as a signal in the dark **2** a bright flame that burns for a short time

flare² /fleə/ verb [I] **1** to suddenly burn or shine brightly **2** to suddenly become worse or more violent **3** to become wider at one end: *The horse's nostrils flared.*

⎯ **PHRASAL VERB** ˌflare 'up **1** *same as* **flare²** 1: *The fire could flare up again at any time.* **2** *same as* **flare²** 2: *It looked as if the fighting might flare up again.* **3** if an illness flares up, it becomes worse

flared /fleəd/ adj much wider at the bottom than at the top: *flared trousers/skirts*

'flare-up noun [C] **1** an occasion when people suddenly start behaving in an angry or violent way **2** an occasion when a disease suddenly returns

flash¹ /flæʃ/ verb ★
1 [I/T] to shine on and off very quickly, or to make a light do this: *A truck behind me*

F

was flashing its headlights. ♦ His watch
flashed in the sunlight.
2 [I/T] to appear, or to make something
appear, for a very short time before
disappearing: Tom flashed me a smile from
across the room. ♦ The headlines flashed
across the screen.
3 [I] to pass very quickly: The thought that
I might die flashed through my mind.
—**flashing** adj

flash² /flæʃ/ noun [C] **1** a bright light that
appears for a very short time: a flash of
lightning **2** a bright light on a camera that
flashes as you take a photograph **3** a
moment when you suddenly understand or
feel something: a flash of anger/genius
PHRASES a flash in the pan spoken someone
or something that is popular or successful
for only a very short time
in/like a flash very quickly

flashback /ˈflæʃbæk/ noun **1** [C] a sudden clear
memory of something that happened in the
past **2** [C/U] a part of a book, film, or play
that tells you what happened earlier

flashcard /ˈflæʃkɑːd/ noun [C] a small card
printed with words, pictures, or numbers
that helps someone to learn something

flash flood noun [C] a sudden unexpected
flood

flashlight /ˈflæʃlaɪt/ noun [C] American a TORCH

flashpoint /ˈflæʃpɔɪnt/ noun [C] a situation or
place in which serious problems or
violence will probably develop: The site has
become a flashpoint of religious tensions.

flashy /ˈflæʃi/ adj very bright, fashionable, or
expensive in a way that is intended to
impress people: a flashy car

flask /flɑːsk/ noun [C] **1** British a VACUUM FLASK
2 a small flat bottle that fits in your pocket,
used especially for carrying alcohol

flat¹ /flæt/ adj ★★★

1 level/smooth	6 spoken directly
2 object: not thick	7 tyre: no air
3 lying on surface	8 battery: no power
4 rate/amount: fixed	9 drink: no bubbles
5 lacking emotion	10 musical note: lower

1 smooth and level on the surface, with no
lumps or slopes: The farmland is very flat.
♦ a firm flat stomach ♦ You need a flat surface
to work on.
2 not curving inwards or outwards, and not
very thick: a monitor with a flat screen
3 stretched out, or lying on a surface: She
was flat on her back asleep.
4 a flat rate or amount is the same in all
situations: The bank charges a flat fee of £5
for money transfers.
5 lacking emotion, interest, or excitement:
The celebrations seemed rather flat.
6 said directly and definitely: a flat refusal
7 a flat tyre does not have enough air in it
8 British a flat BATTERY does not have enough
power left in it
9 a drink that is flat has lost its gas BUBBLES
10 slightly lower than the musical note that
should be played or sung

flat² /flæt/ noun [C] ★★
1 British a set of rooms for living in, usually
on one floor of a large building: The family
live in a fourth-floor flat. ♦ a block of flats

(=a building with a lot of flats in it)
2 informal a PUNCTURE
PHRASE the flat of sth a flat surface or part
of something: She hit the table with the flat
of her hand.

flat³ /flæt/ adv **1** stretched out, or lying on a
surface: He laid the map out flat on the
table. ♦ Carole was lying flat on her back.
2 informal in exactly the very short period
of time that you mention: I fell asleep in five
seconds flat!
PHRASE fall flat to not succeed in
entertaining someone or making them
laugh

flatly /ˈflætli/ adv **1** in a firm, definite way:
He flatly denied being near the scene of the
crime. **2** without showing any emotion or
interest: 'How can I help you?' the clerk
asked flatly.

flatmate /ˈflætmeɪt/ noun [C] British someone
you share a flat with

flat-pack noun [C] a piece of furniture that
you buy in parts. You fit the parts together
yourself.

flat share noun [C] British a situation in which
two or more people share a flat

flatten /ˈflæt(ə)n/ verb [I/T] to become flat, or
to make something flat: This exercise helps
to flatten a flabby stomach.
PHRASAL VERB flatten (sth) out **1** same as
flatten: The mountainous region flattens out
to a vast plateau. **2** business to become lower
in price or amount, or to make a price or
amount lower: The price of crude oil is
expected to flatten out this summer.

flatter /ˈflætə/ verb [T] **1** to praise someone in
order to make them feel special, often in a
way that is not sincere: She flattered him
and told him what he wanted to hear. **2** if
something flatters you, it makes you look
good when you use it or wear it
PHRASE flatter yourself to persuade yourself
that you are better, more attractive, more
important etc than you are
—**flatterer** noun [C], **flattering** adj

flattered /ˈflætəd/ adj feeling pleased that
someone notices and admires you: I'm
flattered that you asked me to speak at the
convention.

flattery /ˈflætəri/ noun [U] praise that is not
sincere: She decided that a bit of flattery
might bring results.

flaunt /flɔːnt/ verb [T] to deliberately try to
make people notice something that you have
so that they admire you: Lawrence didn't
flaunt his wealth.

flautist /ˈflɔːtɪst/ noun [C] British someone who
plays the FLUTE

flavor /ˈfleɪvə/ the American spelling of
flavour

flavored /ˈfleɪvəd/ the American spelling of
flavoured

flavoring /ˈfleɪvərɪŋ/ the American spelling of
flavouring

flavour¹ /ˈfleɪvə/ noun ★
1 [C] the particular taste that food or drink
has: The drink has a very strong citrus
flavour. ♦ What flavour is the ice cream?
2 [U] the quality of having a pleasant or
strong taste: This beer has no flavour. ♦

Add flavour to your meal by using more herbs and garlic.

3 [singular/U] a particular quality that is typical of something: *The foreign visitors added an international flavour to the occasion.*

flavour² /ˈfleɪvə/ verb [T] to add something to food or drink that changes its taste or gives it a particular taste

flavoured /ˈfleɪvəd/ adj with a particular taste: *chocolate-flavoured milk*

flavouring /ˈfleɪvərɪŋ/ noun [C/U] a substance that is added to food or drink to give it a particular flavour

flaw /flɔː/ noun [C] a mark, mistake, or fault that makes someone or something less than perfect: *There was a tiny flaw in the diamond.* ♦ *My father definitely had his flaws and failings.*

flawed /flɔːd/ adj spoiled by something such as a mark, fault, or mistake: *The current healthcare system is seriously flawed.*

flawless /ˈflɔːləs/ adj with no mistakes, marks, or bad features=PERFECT: *a flawless performance* —**flawlessly** adv

flea /fliː/ noun [C] a small jumping insect that lives on animals and bites them

flea market noun [C] a market where old things are sold at low prices

fleck /flek/ noun [C] a small mark, piece, or amount of something: *flecks of grey in his hair*

flecked /flekt/ adj with small spots of colour: *green eyes flecked with brown*

fled the past tense and past participle of **flee**

fledgeling or **fledgeling** /ˈfledʒlɪŋ/ adj recently formed and still developing, without very much experience: *fledgling democracies*

flee /fliː/ (past tense and past participle **fled** /fled/) verb [I/T] to escape from a dangerous situation or place

fleece /fliːs/ noun **1** [C/U] the wool on a sheep **2** [U] a type of soft artificial cloth that is used for making clothes **3** [C] *British* a short jacket or PULLOVER made of soft artificial material —*picture* → C4

fleet /fliːt/ noun [C] **1** a group of vehicles that are owned by one organization or person **2** a group of ships, or all the ships in a nation's navy: *the French/US/Greek fleet* ♦ *Europe's largest fishing fleet*

fleeting /ˈfliːtɪŋ/ adj continuing for only a very short time —**fleetingly** adv

flesh¹ /fleʃ/ noun [U] ★
1 the soft substance under your skin that consists mostly of muscle and fat: *The dog's teeth sank into my flesh.*
2 the soft part of a fruit or vegetable that is under the skin: *Cut the avocado in half and scoop out the flesh.*

PHRASES flesh and blood used for saying that someone has the same weak qualities that all people share
in the flesh present here and now, instead of on a screen or in a picture=IN PERSON: *He was finally going to see her in the flesh.*
sb's (own) flesh and blood someone's relative → THORN

flesh² /fleʃ/ **PHRASAL VERB flesh sth out** to add more details to something

fleshy /ˈfleʃi/ adj with a lot of flesh

flew the past tense of **fly¹**

flex¹ /fleks/ verb [T] to bend a part of your body in order to stretch it or exercise it
PHRASE flex your muscles to show how powerful or strong you are as a warning to someone: *The country's military is just flexing its muscles.*

flex² /fleks/ noun [C] *British* a plastic covered wire that is used for carrying electricity

flexibility /ˌfleksəˈbɪləti/ noun [U] **1** the ability to make changes or to deal with a situation that is changing **2** the ability to bend or move easily

flexible /ˈfleksəb(ə)l/ adj ★
1 able to make changes or deal with a situation that is changing: *A more flexible approach is needed.* ♦ *The job offers flexible working hours.*
2 able to bend or move easily ≠ RIGID: *a flexible rubber strip*

flick¹ /flɪk/ verb **1** [I/T] to move quickly and suddenly, or to make something move quickly and suddenly: *She flicked back her long dark hair.* **2** [T] to move a switch in order to turn something on or off: *He flicked on the light.*
PHRASAL VERB flick through sth to look quickly at the pages of a magazine or book

flick² /flɪk/ noun [C] **1** a sudden quick movement **2** *informal* a film

flicker¹ /ˈflɪkə/ verb [I] **1** if a flame or light flickers, it does not burn evenly, or it goes on and off **2** to last for only a moment and then disappear

flicker² /ˈflɪkə/ noun [C] **1** a light that goes quickly on and off **2** a feeling that lasts for a very short time

flier /ˈflaɪə/ another spelling of **flyer**

flies /flaɪz/ noun [plural] *British* the opening at the front of a pair of trousers

flight /flaɪt/ noun ★★★
1 [C] a journey in a plane: *My flight has been delayed.* ♦ *The flight from New York to Heathrow took about 5 hours.*
2 [U] the process of moving through the air, or the ability to move through the air: *a flock of geese in flight*
3 [C/U] the act of running away, or of trying to escape from someone or something: *the refugees' desperate flight from their city*
4 [C] a set of stairs that go from one level to another: *The toilets are two flights up.* ♦ *A flight of stairs leads down to the courtyard.*

flight attendant noun [C] someone whose job is to look after passengers on a plane

flimsy /ˈflɪmzi/ adj **1** made of a thin or light substance: *a flimsy cotton blouse* **2** badly made and likely to break easily: *a flimsy wooden fence* **3** not very reliable, or not easy to believe: *a flimsy excuse*

flinch /flɪntʃ/ verb [I] to make a sudden small movement because you are afraid, surprised, or in pain
PHRASE not flinch from (doing) something to deal with a situation or responsibility even though it is difficult

fling¹ /flɪŋ/ (past tense and past participle **flung** /flʌŋ/) verb [T] **1** to throw something carelessly or with a lot of force: *She pulled off her coat and flung it on the chair.* **2** to

F

move something quickly and with a lot of force: *He flung open the window.*

fling² /flɪŋ/ noun [C] **1** a sexual relationship that does not last long and is not serious **2** a short time during which you have a lot of fun

flint /flɪnt/ noun [U] a hard grey stone that was used in the past for making tools

flip¹ /flɪp/ verb **1** [I/T] to turn over quickly, or to make something turn over: *His car flipped over and crashed.* ♦ *Flip a coin to decide who goes first.* **2** [I] *informal* to become very angry or excited
PHRASAL VERB **flip through sth** to quickly look at the pages of a magazine or book

flip² /flɪp/ noun [C] an action of jumping up and completely turning over in the air

flip chart noun [C] large sheets of paper that are connected at the top. You use them to show pictures or to write things on when you are talking to a group of people.

flip-flop noun [C] a rubber shoe without a top or back, held to your foot by a STRAP in the shape of a 'V' that goes between your toes —*picture* → SHOE

flippant /ˈflɪpənt/ adj treating a serious subject or situation in a way that is not serious enough

flipper /ˈflɪpə/ noun [C] **1** a wide flat part like an arm on the bodies of some sea animals **2** a wide flat rubber shoe that you wear when you swim under water

flip side, the noun [singular] the negative aspects of something

flirt¹ /flɜːt/ verb [I] to behave towards someone in a way that shows that you are sexually attracted to them
PHRASAL VERB **flirt with sth** to consider an idea or plan, but not very seriously

flirt² /flɜːt/ noun [C] someone who flirts a lot

flirtation /flɜːˈteɪʃ(ə)n/ noun **1** [U] behaviour that shows someone that you are sexually attracted to them **2** [C] a short period of time when someone is interested in a new idea or activity

flit /flɪt/ verb [I] to move quickly from one place to another without stopping long

float¹ /fləʊt/ verb ★
1 [I] to rest or move slowly on the surface of a liquid and not sink ≠ SINK: *Leaves and twigs floated on the water.*
2 [I] to move slowly through the air: *A cloud floated across the moon.*
3 [T] to suggest an idea for people to consider: *Various explanations for his resignation are being floated.*
4 [T] *business* to start to sell a company's SHARES

float² /fləʊt/ noun [C] **1** a large vehicle that is decorated and driven through the streets as part of a PARADE **2** an object that floats and supports your body when you are learning to swim

floating /ˈfləʊtɪŋ/ adj not fixed or permanent, and therefore likely to change: *a floating exchange rate*

flock¹ /flɒk/ noun [C] **1** a group of birds, sheep, or goats **2** a large group of people

flock² /flɒk/ verb [I] to gather together in a large group

flog /flɒg/ verb [T] **1** to hit someone very hard

with a stick or WHIP as a punishment **2** *British informal* to sell something

flogging /ˈflɒgɪŋ/ noun [C/U] a punishment in which someone is hit many times with a stick or WHIP

flood¹ /flʌd/ verb ★
1 [I/T] to cover a place with water, or to become covered with water: *Water burst through the dam and flooded local villages.* ♦ *The ground floor of the house was flooded.*
2 [I] if a river floods, water rises up over its BANKS and covers the land around it
3 [I/T] if people or things flood somewhere, they go there or arrive there in large numbers: *Two million visitors flood into our city each year.* ♦ **be flooded with sth** *The TV station was flooded with complaints.*
4 [I/T] to fill a place with light, or to become filled with light: *I opened the curtains and light flooded into the room.*
PHRASE **flood the market** to make such a large number of goods available for sale that they cannot all be sold and the price falls
PHRASAL VERB **flood back** if memories or feelings flood back, you suddenly remember them very clearly: *When he told me his name, it all came flooding back.*

flood² /flʌd/ noun ★
1 [C/U] a large amount of water that covers an area that was dry before: *The southwest of England has been badly hit by floods.* ♦ *After three weeks the flood waters finally receded.*
2 [C] a large number of people or things that move somewhere or arrive somewhere at the same time: *We received a flood of letters protesting against the change.*

floodgates /ˈflʌdˌgeɪts/ noun **open the floodgates** to suddenly make it possible for a lot of things to happen

flooding /ˈflʌdɪŋ/ noun [U] a situation in which water from a river or from heavy rain covers large areas of land

floodlight /ˈflʌdˌlaɪt/ noun [C] a very strong light that is used for lighting a public building or sports event at night

floodlit /ˈflʌdˌlɪt/ adj lit at night using floodlights

floor¹ /flɔː/ noun ★★★

1 flat area you walk on	4 audience at debate
2 level in building	5 lowest level allowed
3 of ocean/valley etc	

1 [C] the flat area that you walk on inside a building or room: *The house has polished wooden floors.* ♦ *We were sitting on the floor watching TV.*
2 [C] one of the levels in a building: *a first-floor flat* ♦ *The toy department is on the second floor.*
3 [C] the ground at the bottom of something: *a map of the ocean floor*
4 [singular] the audience at a public discussion or debate: *The speaker will now take questions from the floor.*
5 [singular] *business* the lowest level that an amount is allowed to reach
→ SHOP FLOOR

floor² /flɔː/ verb [T] **1** to make someone feel so surprised and confused that they cannot react **2** to hit someone so hard that they fall to the ground

floorboard /ˈflɔːˌbɔːd/ noun [C] a long wooden board that is part of a floor

flooring /ˈflɔːrɪŋ/ noun [U] materials that are used for making or covering a floor

flop¹ /flɒp/ verb [I] **1** to sit or lie down in a heavy way by letting your body fall: *He got home and flopped into a chair.* **2** to move or hang in a loose way: *Her long hair flopped down over her eyes.* **3** *informal* if a play, film, or new product flops, it is completely unsuccessful

flop² /flɒp/ noun [C] *informal* a complete failure

floppy /ˈflɒpi/ adj soft and hanging down in a loose or heavy way

floppy ˈdisk or **floppy** /ˈflɒpi/ noun [C] *computing* a small square plastic object that you use for storing information from a computer

floral /ˈflɔːrəl/ adj made of flowers, or decorated with pictures of flowers

florist /ˈflɒrɪst/ noun [C] **1** someone whose job is to arrange and sell flowers **2 florist** or **florist's** a shop that sells flowers

floss /flɒs/ verb [I/T] to clean between your teeth with DENTAL FLOSS

flotation /fləʊˈteɪʃ(ə)n/ noun [C/U] *business* the sale of SHARES in a company for the first time

flounce /flaʊns/ verb [I] to walk in an impatient angry way

flounder /ˈflaʊndə/ verb [I] **1** to experience difficulties and be likely to fail **2** to feel confused and not know what to say or do next **3** to move with great difficulty and in an uncontrolled way

flour /flaʊə/ noun [U] a white or brown powder made from grain. It is used for making bread, cakes, and pasta.

flourish¹ /ˈflʌrɪʃ/ verb **1** [I] to grow well and be healthy: *Most plants flourish in this rich soil.* **2** [I] to be very successful =THRIVE: *His new business is flourishing.* **3** [T] to wave something in the air so that people notice it: *She came in flourishing a photograph.*

flourish² /ˈflʌrɪʃ/ noun [C] a confident movement that you make so that other people notice it

flout /flaʊt/ verb [T] to deliberately refuse to obey a rule or custom

flow¹ /fləʊ/ noun [C/U] ★★
1 the continuous movement of something: *the flow of blood to the heart*
2 a supply of something that continues without stopping: *the agency's work flow* ♦ *The television provided a steady flow of information about the war.*
3 a way of talking or thinking in an easy natural way, without any pauses or difficulties: *The phone rang, interrupting the flow of his thoughts.*
PHRASE go with the flow *spoken* to do what seems to be the easiest thing in a particular situation

flow² /fləʊ/ verb [I] ★★
1 to move continuously: *Hot water flows through the pipes.* ♦ *A constant stream of people flowed past.* ♦ *Blood flowed from the wound on her face.*
2 if a supply of something flows, it continues

without stopping: *Millions of pounds of new investment are flowing into the region.*
3 if words or ideas flow, they follow each other in an easy, natural, continuous way: *The conversation did not flow smoothly.*
4 if hair or clothing flows, it falls or moves in a smooth graceful way around someone's body

ˈflow ˌchart noun [C] a drawing that represents a complicated process by a series of lines that show the different possibilities

flower¹ /ˈflaʊə/ noun [C] ★★★
1 the coloured part of a plant from which the plant's seeds develop: *The plant has small white flowers.* —picture → C9
2 a plant that is grown because its flowers are attractive: *I'm going to plant more flowers in the front garden this year.*

flower² /ˈflaʊə/ verb [I] to produce flowers

flowerbed /ˈflaʊəˌbed/ noun [C] an area of ground where flowers are grown —picture → C1

flowery /ˈflaʊəri/ adj **1** decorated with a pattern of flowers **2** flowery language uses many complicated words that are intended to make it more attractive

flown the past participle of **fly¹**

fl. oz. abbrev FLUID OUNCE

flu /fluː/ noun [U] a very common infectious disease that lasts for a short time and makes you feel weak and tired

fluctuate /ˈflʌktʃueɪt/ verb [I] to change frequently —**fluctuation** /ˌflʌktʃuˈeɪʃ(ə)n/ noun [C/U]

fluent /ˈfluːənt/ adj able to speak a foreign language very well: *I'm fluent in three languages.* ♦ *Steve speaks fluent Japanese.* —**fluency** noun [U], **fluently** adv

fluff¹ /flʌf/ noun [U] very small pieces of hair, dust, or cloth that stick together

fluff² /flʌf/ verb [T] **1** to shake something so that more air goes into it and it becomes larger and softer: *Fluff the pillows after you use them.* **2** *informal* to do something badly
PHRASAL VERB fluff sth ˈout or **fluff sth ˈup** same as **fluff²** 1

fluffy /ˈflʌfi/ adj **1** covered with very soft hair or feathers **2** made of something that is very soft

fluid¹ /ˈfluːɪd/ noun [C/U] *formal* a liquid: *Drink lots of fluids during exercise.* ♦ *cleaning fluid*

fluid² /ˈfluːɪd/ adj **1** graceful and continuous: *a fluid movement* **2** likely to change: *The situation remains fluid.*

fluid ˈounce noun [C] a unit for measuring an amount of a liquid, equal to 0.02841 litres

fluke /fluːk/ noun [C] *informal* something good that happens unexpectedly because of good luck

flung the past tense and past participle of **fling¹**

flunk /flʌŋk/ verb [I/T] *informal* to fail a test or a course

fluorescent /flɔːˈres(ə)nt/ adj **1** a fluorescent colour is very bright and seems to reflect light **2** a fluorescent substance produces light when you pass electricity through it

fluoˈrescent ˌlight noun [C] a very bright light that consists of a long glass tube containing fluorescent gas

fluoride /ˈflʊəraɪd/ noun [U] a chemical that protects your teeth

F

flurry /ˈflʌri/ noun [C] **1** a short period of activity or emotion **2** a small amount of snow or rain

flush¹ /flʌʃ/ verb **1** [I] if someone flushes, their face becomes red because they feel hot, angry, embarrassed, or excited: *Mark flushed with annoyance, but said nothing.* **2** [I/T] if you flush a toilet, or if it flushes, water passes through it **3** [T] to get rid of something by putting it into a toilet and flushing it

PHRASAL VERB **flush sb/sth out** to force a person or animal to leave a place where they have been hiding

flush² /flʌʃ/ noun [singular] **1** a red colour that appears on someone's face because they feel hot, angry, embarrassed, or excited **2** a sudden strong feeling: *a flush of irritation/anger*

flush³ /flʌʃ/ adj, adv fitted so that two surfaces or edges are exactly level

flushed /flʌʃt/ adj with a red face

flustered /ˈflʌstəd/ adj feeling confused, embarrassed, or nervous

flute /fluːt/ noun [C] a musical instrument that you hold sideways to your mouth and play by blowing over a hole at one end —*picture* → WOODWIND

flutter /ˈflʌtə/ verb **1** [I/T] to move with quick light movements, or to make something move in this way: *The bird fluttered from branch to branch.* **2** [I] if your heart or stomach flutters, you feel excited or nervous —**flutter** noun [singular]

flux /flʌks/ noun [U] a condition of continuous change: *The climate appears to be in a state of flux.*

fly¹ /flaɪ/ (past tense **flew** /fluː/; past participle **flown** /fləʊn/) verb ★★★

1 move with wings	6 move quickly
2 travel on plane	7 about time
3 take sb/sth on plane	8 when flag is on pole
4 control plane	+ PHRASES
5 move fast through air	

1 [I] to use wings to move through the air: *Not all insects can fly.*

2 [I] to travel on a plane: *Sometimes it's cheaper to fly.* ♦ *I flew from London to Amsterdam.* ♦ *We flew into Heathrow on Monday evening.*

3 [T] to take people or goods somewhere on a plane: *They flew her home for urgent medical treatment.* ♦ **fly sb/sth in/out** *Helicopters are being used to fly in supplies.*

4 [I/T] to control a plane when it is in the air: *He had always wanted to learn to fly.* ♦ *The pilots refused to fly the planes in icy conditions.*

5 [I] to move very fast through the air: *A bullet flew past his head.*

6 [I] to move suddenly or quickly: *The door flew open and the head teacher marched in.*

7 [I] if time flies, it seems to pass very quickly

8 [I/T] if you fly a flag, or if it is flying, it is on the top of a pole or building

PHRASES **fly in the face of sth** to be completely opposite to something that most people believe or accept: *This behaviour flies in the face of all the ideals we've worked towards.*

fly into a rage to suddenly become extremely angry

go flying *informal* to move quickly through the air and fall to the ground: *I tripped over a tree root and went flying.*

fly² /flaɪ/ (plural **flies**) noun [C] a common small insect with wings —*picture* → C13

PHRASES **dropping like flies** *informal* getting ill or dying in large numbers very quickly

on the fly in a very quick and informal way

sb wouldn't hurt a fly *spoken* used for saying that someone is very gentle and kind

flyer /ˈflaɪə/ noun [C] **1** an announcement or advertisement that is printed on paper and given to people = LEAFLET **2** an aircraft pilot or passenger

flying¹ /ˈflaɪɪŋ/ adj **1** able to fly: *a flying insect* **2** moving fast through the air: *About 20 people were injured by flying glass.*

PHRASE **with flying colours** very successfully

flying² /ˈflaɪɪŋ/ noun [U] **1** the activity of travelling in an aircraft: *I'm afraid of flying.* **2** the activity of operating or controlling an aircraft: *flying lessons*

flying 'saucer noun [C] a round flat vehicle from another planet

flying 'start noun [C] a very good beginning

flying 'visit noun [C] a very short visit

fly-on-the-'wall adj *British* showing real people doing what they normally do every day

flyover /ˈflaɪəʊvə/ noun [C] *British* a road that crosses above another road like a bridge

FM /ˌef ˈem/ noun [U] frequency modulation: a system that is used for broadcasting radio signals of high quality

foal /fəʊl/ noun [C] a young horse

foam /fəʊm/ noun [U] **1** a lot of BUBBLES that stick together on the surface of a liquid **2** a soft thick substance that contains a lot of BUBBLES. It is used for cleaning, washing, or stopping fires. **3** a soft light rubber or plastic substance that contains a lot of small holes: *foam mattresses/pillows/cushions*

fob /fɒb/ **PHRASAL VERB** **fob sb 'off 1** to give someone an answer or explanation that is not true in order to stop them from asking questions or complaining **2** to give someone something that is not what they want

focal point /ˈfəʊk(ə)l ˌpɔɪnt/ noun [C] the most important, interesting, or attractive part of something

focus¹ /ˈfəʊkəs/ (present participle **focusing** or **focussing**; past tense and past participle **focused** or **focussed**) verb [I/T] ★ if your eyes focus, or if you focus your eyes, you look at something carefully until you start to see it clearly: *It took a while for my eyes to focus in the dim light of the cave.*

PHRASAL VERBS **focus on sth** to concentrate on something and pay particular attention to it: *The course focuses on three main topics.* **focus sth on sth** to turn a camera towards something: *The cameras seemed to be focused on the crowd.*

focus² /ˈfəʊkəs/ noun ★ **1** [singular] the thing that people are concentrating on or paying particular attention to: *The oil crisis became the focus of Western concern in the early 1970s.* ♦ *We have chosen six communities as the focus for our study.*

2 [singular/U] particular attention that people pay to something: *The report calls for greater focus on the needs of the poor.*

3 [singular/U] the act of concentrating on a particular aim: *All the lessons have a very clear focus.* ♦ *I think this campaign has lost its focus.*

PHRASES **in focus** able to be seen clearly **out of focus** unable to be seen clearly: *Some of these photographs are out of focus.*

focused /'fəʊkəst/ adj *showing approval* concentrating on a particular aim and not wasting time or energy on other things

'focus group noun [C] a group of people who are asked to give their opinions about particular subjects

fodder /'fɒdə/ noun [U] food for animals such as cows and horses

foe /fəʊ/ noun [C] *literary* an enemy

foetal /'fiːtl/ adj *medical* relating to a foetus

foetus /'fiːtəs/ noun [C] a baby that is developing inside its mother's body

fog¹ /fɒg/ noun [U] thick clouds that form close to the ground and are difficult to see through

fog² /fɒg/ **PHRASAL VERB** **fog up** to become covered with steam and difficult to see through: *All the windows had fogged up.*

foggy /'fɒgi/ adj full of fog, or covered with fog

PHRASE **not have the foggiest (idea)** *spoken* used for emphasizing that you do not know anything at all about something

'fog light noun [C] a bright light on a car that helps drivers to see in the FOG —*picture* → C6

foible /'fɔɪb(ə)l/ noun [C] a way of thinking or behaving that is strange or annoying

foil¹ /fɔɪl/ noun **1** [U] very light thin sheets of metal that are used for wrapping food **2** [C] something that makes another thing seem better because it is different from it: *The plain stone floor is a perfect foil to the highly decorated walls.*

foil² /fɔɪl/ verb [T] to prevent someone from doing something that they want to do

foist /fɔɪst/ **PHRASAL VERB** **foist sth on sb** or **foist sth upon sb** to force someone to accept or deal with something that they do not want

fold¹ /fəʊld/ verb ★★★

1 [T] to bend a piece of paper or cloth and press one part of it over another part: *Carrie folded the letter and slid it into a drawer.* ♦ *Fold the paper in half.*

2 [I/T] if something folds, or if you fold it, you bend part of it so that it becomes smaller and easier to carry or store: *Jed folded the penknife and slipped it into his pocket.* ♦ *The bed folds away conveniently for storage.*

3 [I] if a business folds, it closes because it is not able to make enough money

PHRASE **fold your arms** to cross one arm over the other

PHRASAL VERB **fold sth up** to make something smaller by bending it over on

itself more than once: *His clothes were neatly folded up on a chair.*

fold² /fəʊld/ noun [C] **1** a line that you make on a piece of paper or cloth when you press one part of it over another **2** a curved piece of cloth that hangs in a loose way

-fold /fəʊld/ suffix used with numbers to make adjectives and adverbs describing how much something increases

folder /'fəʊldə/ noun [C] **1** a thin flat container for sheets of paper **2** a group of programs or documents that are stored in a computer

foliage /'fəʊliɪdʒ/ noun [U] the leaves of a plant or tree

folk¹ /fəʊk/ noun **1 folks** [plural] *informal* someone's parents **2** [plural] *informal* people: *city folk* **3** [U] FOLK MUSIC

folk² /fəʊk/ adj **1** traditional in a particular region: *folk art* **2** based on the beliefs and methods of ordinary people: *folk medicine/wisdom*

folklore /'fəʊklɔː/ noun [U] traditional stories, sayings, and beliefs from a particular region or community

'folk music noun [U] traditional music from a particular country, region, or community, or music played in a traditional style

follow /'fɒləʊ/ verb ★★★

1 walk/drive behind sb	7 understand sth
2 happen after sth else	8 do same as sb else
3 watch/listen carefully	9 happen in a pattern
4 obey order/advice	10 to have to be true
5 go along road/river	+ PHRASE
6 watch progress	+ PHRASAL VERBS

1 [I/T] to walk, drive etc behind someone who is going in the same direction as you: *Ralph set off down the hill, and I followed.* ♦ *I was convinced there was someone following me.* ♦ *Jim opened the door and followed me down the corridor.*

2 [I/T] to happen or come after something else: *The weather report follows shortly.* ♦ *In the weeks that followed the situation was very tense.*

3 [T] to pay close attention to what someone or something is doing or saying: *He followed every word of the trial.*

4 [T] to obey an order, or to do what someone has advised you to do: *She refused to follow our advice.* ♦ *The soldiers claimed they were only following orders.* ♦ *Follow the instructions carefully.*

5 [T] to go along a road, river etc in the same direction as it does: *Follow the road down the hill into the village.*

6 [T] to be interested in the progress of someone or something: *My father's followed the same football team for 40 years.*

7 [T] to understand something that is long or complicated: *I couldn't follow what Professor Hope was saying.*

8 [I/T] to do the same thing that someone else has done: *Canada may follow the EU's example by banning these products.* ♦ *Other students followed her lead and boycotted lectures.* ♦ *They began to offer takeaway food, and other restaurants followed suit (=did the same).*

9 [T] to happen according to a particular pattern or order: *All the murders have*

F

F

followed the same horrible pattern.

10 [I] if something follows, it must be true because of something else that is true: **+that** *If the two groups have the same goal, then it should follow that they work together.*

PHRASE **as follows** used when you are going to give more details about something: *The first line of the poem goes as follows:* I wandered lonely as a cloud...

→ FOOTSTEP

PHRASAL VERBS ,**follow sb a'round** or ,**follow sb a'bout** to follow someone wherever they go: *Henry's been following me around like a puppy!*

,**follow (sth) 'through** to continue doing something until it is finished: *Jack hasn't followed through on one project this year.*

,**follow sth 'up** to do something in addition to what you have already done: *Follow up the phone call with a written confirmation.*

follower /'fɒləʊə/ noun [C] **1** someone who believes in a religion or system of ideas, or who supports the person who established it **2** someone who is interested in the progress of something=SUPPORTER

following¹ /'fɒləʊɪŋ/ grammar word ★★★

Following can be:
- a **preposition**: *Following the lecture, there will be the opportunity to ask questions.*
- an **adjective**: *She arrived the following day.*
- a **pronoun**: *Please read the following carefully.*

1 after something happens, or as a result of something that happens: *Following his military service, Wilkins returned to his home town.*

2 the following day, month, page etc is the next one: *The problem will be discussed in the following chapter.*

3 used for referring to something that you are going to say or mention next: *Combine the following ingredients: brown sugar, flour, and butter.* ♦ *Make sure you bring the following: sunglasses, sunscreen, and a swimsuit.*

following² /'fɒləʊɪŋ/ noun [C] a group of people who support or admire another person or group

'**follow-up** noun **1** [C/U] something that is done in order to complete something or to check that an earlier action was effective **2** [C] a book, film, or article that is based on or develops from an earlier one=SEQUEL —'**follow-up** adj

folly /'fɒli/ noun [C/U] *formal* stupid or careless behaviour

fond /fɒnd/ adj ★

1 fond of sb/sth liking and caring about someone or something very much: *I was very fond of my Uncle Jim.* ♦ *I'm not fond of children.*

2 fond of (doing) sth getting enjoyment and satisfaction from something that you do

PHRASES **fond hope/wish etc** something that you very much want to happen

fond memory something that you remember with pleasure: *Jane has fond memories of a happy childhood.*

—**fondness** noun [U]

fondle /'fɒnd(ə)l/ verb [T] to squeeze or touch someone or something gently, often for sexual pleasure

fondly /'fɒndli/ adv in a way that shows that you like and care about someone or something: *She smiled fondly at her brother.*

font /fɒnt/ noun [C] a set of letters and numbers in a particular size and style

food /fuːd/ noun ★★★

1 [U] the things that people or animals eat: *Prices of food and clothing have risen recently.* ♦ *All the food is cooked and served by volunteer helpers.* ♦ *good fresh food*

2 [C/U] a particular type of food: *I can't eat spicy food.* ♦ *Italian/Chinese/French food*

PHRASE **food for thought** something that makes you think a lot about a particular subject

'**food chain** noun [singular] the natural process in which one living thing is eaten by another, which is then eaten by another, etc

'**food poisoning** noun [U] an illness caused by eating food that contains harmful bacteria

'**food processor** noun [C] a piece of electrical equipment, used for cutting food into very small pieces or for mixing foods together —*picture* → C2

fool¹ /fuːl/ noun [C] someone who does not behave in an intelligent or sensible way

PHRASES **make a fool of yourself** to make yourself seem stupid by behaving in a silly or embarrassing way

make a fool (out) of sb to deliberately make someone seem stupid

fool² /fuːl/ verb [T] to trick someone by making them believe something that is not true

PHRASE **you could have fooled me** *spoken* used for saying that you do not believe something that someone is telling you

PHRASAL VERBS ,**fool a'round** or ,**fool a'bout** to behave in a silly way for fun

,**fool a'round with sth** or ,**fool ,with sth** to handle or use something in a stupid or careless way: *The kids were fooling around with the rake, and one of them got hurt.*

foolhardy /'fuːlˌhɑːdi/ adj *formal* ignoring obvious dangers in a stupid way=RECKLESS

foolish /'fuːlɪʃ/ adj **1** behaving in a way that is stupid and likely to have bad results **2** embarrassed because of something stupid that you have done —**foolishly** adv, **foolishness** noun [U]

foolproof /'fuːlˌpruːf/ adj a foolproof method, plan, or system is so well designed that it cannot go wrong or fail

foot¹ /fʊt/ (plural **feet** /fiːt/) noun ★★★

1 [C] the part of your body at the end of your leg, on which you stand: *He wiped his feet on the mat.* ♦ *She injured her right foot playing basketball.* → SHOOT¹, STAND¹ —*picture* → C14

2 (plural **feet** or **foot**) [C] a unit used for measuring length that is equal to 12 INCHES or about 30 CENTIMETRES: *We had over two feet of snow last night.* ♦ *He's over six foot tall.*

3 [singular] **the foot of sth** the bottom or far end of something: *She paused at the foot of the stairs.* ♦ *Look at the notes at the foot of the page.*

PHRASES **back on your feet** well or successful again after being ill or having problems: *Jim's hoping he'll be back on his feet by next week.*

get/leap/rise etc to your feet to stand up in a particular way: *Steve jumped to his feet.*

have/keep your feet on the ground to have a sensible practical attitude to life

land on your feet to be lucky and get into a good situation after being in a difficult one: *Tim always manages to land on his feet.*

on your feet standing: *I'm exhausted – I've been on my feet all afternoon.*

on foot walking: *We set off on foot.*

put your feet up to sit down and relax with your feet raised off the ground

put your foot down to refuse very firmly to do or accept something: *Things can't carry on like this; you'll have to put your foot down.*

put your foot in it *British* to accidentally say something that is embarrassing or that upsets or annoys someone

set foot to go to a place: *It was the first time I had set foot on French soil.*

under sb's feet if someone is under your feet, they are annoying you by stopping you from doing what you need to do

foot² /fʊt/ verb **foot the bill (for sth)** *informal* to pay for something: *Are we expected to foot the bill for this?*

footage /ˈfʊtɪdʒ/ noun [U] film of a particular event

football /ˈfʊtbɔːl/ noun ★★
1 [U] *British* a game in which two teams of 11 players kick a ball and try to score goals =SOCCER
2 [C] a ball used for playing football —*picture* → BALL
3 [U] *American* AMERICAN FOOTBALL

footballer /ˈfʊtbɔːlə/ noun [C] *British* someone who plays football

footbridge /ˈfʊtˌbrɪdʒ/ noun [C] a narrow bridge for people to walk across

foothills /ˈfʊtˌhɪlz/ noun [plural] the low hills next to high mountains

foothold /ˈfʊtˌhəʊld/ noun [C] **1** a place on a surface where you can put your foot to support yourself when climbing **2** a position from which you can improve your status or become more successful

footing /ˈfʊtɪŋ/ noun [singular] **1** a firm position for your feet on a surface **2** the basic conditions in which something operates or develops: *a firm financial footing*

footlights /ˈfʊtˌlaɪts/ noun [plural] a row of very bright lights at the front edge of a theatre stage

footnote /ˈfʊtnəʊt/ noun [C] a note at the bottom of a page that gives more detailed information about something on the page

footpath /ˈfʊtpɑːθ/ noun [C] a path that is used only for walking along, usually in the countryside

footprint /ˈfʊtˌprɪnt/ noun [C] a mark made by a human or animal foot in a soft surface such as earth, snow, or sand

footstep /ˈfʊtstep/ noun [C] the sound of a foot touching the ground as someone walks
PHRASE **follow in sb's footsteps** to do the same work, or to achieve the same success, as someone else has done before you: *She followed in her mother's footsteps and became a doctor.*

footstool /ˈfʊtstuːl/ noun [C] a small low piece of furniture for resting your feet on

footwear /ˈfʊtweə/ noun [U] things that you wear on your feet, such as shoes or boots

footwork /ˈfʊtwɜːk/ noun [U] the way that you move your feet when you are dancing or playing sports

for /weak fə, strong fɔː/ preposition ★★★
1 intended to benefit sb/sth used for saying who or what is intended to receive something or get the benefit of it: *Claudia, this present is for you.* ♦ *The academy provides training for young musicians.* ♦ *They'll have to buy furniture for the new house.* ♦ *Betty will take care of things for us while we're away.*
2 stating a purpose used for stating the purpose of an object or action: *We use the basement for storage.* ♦ *The red button is for turning the machine off.*
3 stating a length of time used for saying how long something continues: *I've been waiting for 20 minutes.* ♦ *We haven't seen Kim for a while.* → SINCE
4 stating a distance used for saying how far something reaches, or how far someone goes: *They must have walked for at least three miles.* ♦ *The desert stretched for as far as we could see.*
5 employed by sb/sth used for stating the person or organization that employs someone: *She works for a firm of accountants.*
6 stating the cost of sth used for stating the cost of a product or a service: *I sold my car for £900.*
7 saying who experiences sth used for saying who is affected by a situation or feeling: *For me, it was a complete disaster.* ♦ *Living conditions for most people have improved.*
8 saying who or what your feelings are related to used for showing that your feelings are directed towards a particular person or thing: *I'm so happy for you!* ♦ *She felt sorry for his wife.*
9 enough to make sth possible used for saying what is possible with a particular amount of time, money, space etc: *We haven't got the money for a new car.* ♦ *Is there enough time for a drink?*
10 saying who or what does sth used after some adjectives, nouns, and verbs for saying who or what does an action: *It's time for us to go.* ♦ *All I want is for you to be happy.*
11 saying who or what you support used for saying which person or thing you support or agree with: *There is a lot of support for the reforms.* ♦ *Of course, I'm all for* (=I completely support) *freedom of speech.*
12 representing sb used for saying who you represent when you say or do something: *I'm speaking for all of us when I say how sorry we are.*
13 going to a place used for saying where you are going when you leave a place: *What time are you leaving for home?* ♦ *He got on the next plane for San Francisco.*
14 intended to happen at a particular time

F

used for saying the time or date when something is planned to happen: *The meeting was planned for 10 o'clock.*

15 in order to celebrate in order to celebrate a holiday or special occasion: *We haven't decided what to do for her birthday.*

16 considering what sb/sth is used for saying that something is surprising when you consider who or what someone is: *She sings amazingly well for a child.*

17 showing what sth means used for saying what something means or represents: *What's the Italian word for 'Goodbye'?*

PHRASES **for all 1** despite: *For all his complaining, I think he actually enjoyed the day.* **2** considering how large or small an amount is: *I might as well have said nothing, for all the difference it made.*

for the first/last etc time used for saying how often something has happened: *He was late this morning for the third time this week.*

for now or **for the moment** or **for the time being** for a short time, until a situation changes: *You'll have to stay here for now.*

it is for sb to do sth it is someone's right, responsibility, or duty to do something: *It's not for me to decide whether you should leave your job.*

forage /'forɪdʒ/ verb [I] to search in a wide area for food

foray /'foreɪ/ noun [C] **1** an attempt at doing something new or something that you do not usually do **2** a sudden quick attack on an enemy

forbade the past tense of **forbid**

forbid /fə'bɪd/ (past tense **forbade** or **forbad** /fə'bæd/; past participle **forbidden** /fə'bɪd(ə)n/) verb [T] to say that something is not allowed =PROHIBIT: *The army forbids soldiers from talking to the news media.* ♦ *She was forbidden to see him again.*

forbidden /fə'bɪd(ə)n/ adj ★ not allowed according to a rule or law: *Smoking is forbidden in all parts of the building.* ♦ *The use of mobile phones in the library is **strictly forbidden**.*

forbidding /fə'bɪdɪŋ/ adj someone who is forbidding seems unfriendly or threatening

force¹ /fɔːs/ noun ★★★

1 [U] physical strength, violence, or energy: *The force of the bomb blast shattered windows in 15 buildings.* ♦ *They accused the police of **using** excessive **force** during the arrest.* ♦ *The army took control of the region **by force**.* ♦ *You can achieve more by talking than by **brute force** (=physical force alone).*

2 [U] the power that something or someone has to influence people or events: *We have convinced people by **the force of** our argument.*

3 [C] someone or something that has a lot of influence on what happens: *the political forces that shape people's lives* ♦ *The UN should be a major force for stability in the area.*

4 [C] a group of people doing military or police work: *Both countries have now withdrawn their forces from the area.* ♦ *a UN peacekeeping force*

PHRASES **in force 1** if a law or rule is in force, it is being applied and people must

obey it: *The ban on arms exports remains in force.* **2** if people do something in force, a lot of people are involved

join/combine forces to work with someone else in order to achieve something together: *Aid workers have joined forces with police to get supplies to the town.*

through/from force of habit without thinking, because you always do a particular thing: *I locked the door from force of habit.*

force² /fɔːs/ verb [T] ★★★

1 to make someone do something that they do not want to do =COMPEL: **force sb to do sth** *The judge was forced to resign.* ♦ **force yourself to do sth** *Despite the pain, she forced herself to get out of bed.*

2 to use physical force to move something or to move somewhere: *She forced the package through the slot.* ♦ *We had to force the windows open.*

3 to make something happen: *Opposition to the plans forced a rapid change of policy.*

PHRASES **force sb's hand** to make someone do something that they did not want to do, or to make them do something before they are ready to

force a smile/laugh to smile or laugh when you do not really want to

PHRASAL VERBS **force sth back** if you force back tears, you try very hard not to cry

force sth down to eat or drink something even though you do not want to

force sth on sb or **force sth upon sb** to make someone accept something that they do not want: *She took over the meeting and forced her views on everyone.*

forced /fɔːst/ adj **1** not sincere or natural: *a forced smile* **2** done or happening because the situation makes it necessary or because someone makes you do it

forceful /'fɔːsf(ə)l/ adj **1** confident and good at influencing people =ASSERTIVE **2** likely to persuade people: *a forceful argument* —**forcefully** adv

forceps /'fɔːseps/ noun [plural] a medical tool that is used for holding or pulling things

forcible /'fɔːsəb(ə)l/ adj involving the use of force —**forcibly** adv

forearm /'fɔːrɑːm/ noun [C] the lower part of your arm, between your elbow and your wrist

forebears /'fɔːbeəz/ noun [plural] the people in your family who lived before you =ANCESTORS

foreboding /fɔː'bəʊdɪŋ/ noun [U] a strong feeling that something very bad is going to happen

forecast¹ /'fɔːkɑːst/ noun [C] a statement about what is likely to happen, usually relating to the weather, business, or the economy

forecast² /'fɔːkɑːst/ (past tense and past participle **forecast** or **forecasted**) verb [T] to make a statement about what is likely to happen, usually relating to the weather, business, or the economy

forecaster /'fɔːkɑːstə/ noun [C] someone whose job is to say what is likely to happen, for example what the weather will be like or what will happen in the economy

foreclose /fɔː'kləʊz/ verb [I] *legal* to take

someone's property because they failed to pay back the money they borrowed to buy it —**foreclosure** /fɔːˈkləʊʒə/ noun [C/U]

forecourt /ˈfɔːkɔːt/ noun [C] an open area in front of a large building or a petrol station

forefathers /ˈfɔːfɑːðəz/ noun [plural] formal people belonging to your family or nation who lived a long time ago=ANCESTOR

forefinger /ˈfɔːfɪŋɡə/ noun [C] the finger that is next to your thumb=INDEX FINGER

forefoot /ˈfɔːfʊt/ noun [C] one of the two front feet of an animal that has four feet

forefront, the /ˈfɔːfrʌnt/ noun [singular] a leading or important position

foregone conclusion /ˌfɔːɡɒn kənˈkluːʒ(ə)n/ noun [singular] a result that you can be certain about before it happens

foreground, the /ˈfɔːɡraʊnd/ noun [singular] the front part of a scene or picture ≠ BACKGROUND

forehand /ˈfɔːhænd/ noun [C] a way of hitting the ball in tennis with the palm of your hand towards your opponent —*picture* → C15

forehead /ˈfɒrɪd, ˈfɔːhed/ noun [C] the upper part of your face, between your eyes and your hair —*picture* → C14

foreign /ˈfɒrɪn/ adj ★★★
1 from another country, or in another country: *Working in **a foreign country** takes some getting used to.* ♦ *Do you speak any foreign languages?*
2 dealing with, or relating to, other countries: *foreign policy*
3 not typical of something or someone and therefore not expected or familiar=ALIEN: *emotions that were totally **foreign to** her nature*

foreign 'body noun [C] formal something that has entered a place where it should not be: *a foreign body in her eye*

foreigner /ˈfɒrɪnə/ noun [C] someone who comes from another country

foreign ex'change noun [C/U] a system for changing the money of one country for the money of another, or the money used in this system

Foreign 'Office, the the British government department that deals with Britain's relations with foreign countries

Foreign 'Secretary noun [C] the British government minister who is responsible for Britain's relationships with foreign countries

foreleg /ˈfɔːleɡ/ noun [C] one of the two front legs of an animal that has four legs

foreman /ˈfɔːmən/ (plural **foremen** /ˈfɔːmən/) noun [C] **1** a man who is in charge of a team of workers **2** the person who is chosen to be the leader of a JURY

foremost /ˈfɔːməʊst/ adj most important, or most well known

forensic /fəˈrensɪk/ adj relating to the use of scientific methods to solve crimes

forensics /fəˈrenzɪks/ noun [U] scientific methods that are used to solve crimes

forerunner /ˈfɔːrʌnə/ noun [C] an institution, custom, or thing that existed before a newer but similar thing=PRECURSOR

foresee /fɔːˈsiː/ (past tense **foresaw** /fɔːˈsɔː/; past participle **foreseen** /fɔːˈsiːn/) verb [T] to

see or know something that will happen in the future=PREDICT

foreseeable /fɔːˈsiːəb(ə)l/ adj a foreseeable event or time is one that can easily be imagined or known about before it happens =PREDICTABLE ≠ UNFORESEEABLE
PHRASE **the foreseeable future** the time in the near future in which you can guess what might happen

foreshadow /fɔːˈʃædəʊ/ verb [T] if something foreshadows a future event, it shows or gives a warning that it will happen

foresight /ˈfɔːsaɪt/ noun [U] the ability to think about and plan for what might happen

foreskin /ˈfɔːskɪn/ noun [C] the loose skin that covers the front part of a man's PENIS

forest /ˈfɒrɪst/ noun [C/U] ★★★ a large area of land that is covered by trees and other plants growing close together

forestall /fɔːˈstɔːl/ verb [T] to do something to prevent something from happening

forested /ˈfɒrɪstɪd/ adj covered with trees

forestry /ˈfɒrɪstri/ noun [U] the science or activity of caring for forests

foretell /fɔːˈtel/ (past tense and past participle **foretold** /fɔːˈtəʊld/) verb [T] literary to say what will happen in the future=PREDICT

forethought /ˈfɔːθɔːt/ noun [U] careful thought and planning that prepares you well for a future event

foretold the past tense and past participle of foretell

forever /fərˈevə/ or **for 'ever** adv ★
1 for all time in the future, or for as long as you can imagine: *They promised to love each other forever.*
2 informal for a long time, usually longer than you would like: *The film seemed to go on forever.*

forewarn /fɔːˈwɔːn/ verb [T] to warn someone about a problem or dangerous situation that is likely to happen

foreword /ˈfɔːwɜːd/ noun [C] a short introduction to a book

forfeit¹ /ˈfɔːfɪt/ verb [T] to be forced to give up something, usually because you have broken a rule or law

forfeit² /ˈfɔːfɪt/ noun [C] something that you must give, pay, or do because you have done something wrong=PENALTY

forgave the past tense of forgive

forge¹ /fɔːdʒ/ verb [T] **1** to develop or achieve something: *During the 1970s, the US forged trade links with China.* **2** to make an illegal copy of something in order to cheat people: *Someone forged my signature.*
PHRASAL VERB **forge a'head** to make strong steady progress

forge² /fɔːdʒ/ noun [C] a place where metal objects are made

forger /ˈfɔːdʒə/ noun [C] a criminal who makes illegal copies of documents or works of art

forgery /ˈfɔːdʒəri/ noun **1** [U] the crime of making illegal copies of documents or works of art **2** [C] an illegal copy of a document or a work of art

forget /fəˈɡet/ (present participle **forgetting**; past tense **forgot** /fəˈɡɒt/; past participle **forgotten** /fəˈɡɒt(ə)n/) verb [I/T] ★★★
1 to be unable to remember something: *I've*

F

forgotten her phone number. ♦ *Did you* **forget about** *our agreement?* ♦ *She always* **forgets where** *her car is parked.* ♦ **+(that)** *I'd forgotten that you'd already given me the money.*

2 to not remember to do something that you intended to do: *She had* **forgotten** *all* **about** *posting the letter.* ♦ **forget to do sth** *Don't forget to lock the door when you leave.*

3 to not take something with you when you should have taken it: *She forgot her sunglasses.* ♦ *I remembered everything else but I* **forgot about** *the beach towels.* → LEAVE

4 to stop thinking or worrying about something: *Try to* **forget about** *him.* ♦ **+(that)** *People forget that women didn't always have the right to vote.*

PHRASES **forget it** *spoken* used for telling someone not to worry about something because it is not important

forget yourself to behave in a way that is silly or embarrassing

Word family: **forget**

Words in the same family as **forget**
■ **forgetful** *adj*   ■ **unforgettable** *adj*
■ **forgetfulness** *n*

forgetful /fəˈgetf(ə)l/ adj often unable to remember things —**forgetfulness** noun [U]

forgive /fəˈgɪv/ (past tense **forgave** /fəˈgeɪv/; past participle **forgiven** /fəˈgɪv(ə)n/) verb [T] ★ to decide to stop being angry with someone who has done something that is bad: *John has never* **forgiven** *himself for the accident.* ♦ **forgive sb for doing sth** *She eventually forgave him for forgetting her birthday.* ♦ **forgive sb sth** *They're nice boys, so we tend to forgive them their occasional bad behaviour.*

forgiveness /fəˈgɪvnəs/ noun [U] the action of forgiving someone

forgiving /fəˈgɪvɪŋ/ adj willing to forget your anger towards someone

forgo /fɔːˈgəʊ/ (past tense **forwent** /fɔːˈwent/; past participle **forgone** /fɔːˈgɒn/) verb [T] *formal* to decide not to do or have something

forgot the past tense of **forget**

forgotten¹ /fəˈgɒt(ə)n/ adj a forgotten thing is something that most people no longer remember

forgotten² the past participle of **forget**

fork¹ /fɔːk/ noun [C] ★
1 an object that you use for eating, with a handle and three or four points on the end —*picture* → C2
2 a garden tool that you use for breaking up soil, with a long handle and metal points on the end
3 a place where a road divides into two parts to form a shape like a 'Y'

fork² /fɔːk/ verb [I] if a road forks, it divides into two separate parts

PHRASAL VERB **ˌfork (sth) ˈout** *informal* to spend money on something: *I'm not forking out £400 on ski clothes!*

forked /fɔːkt/ adj divided into two separate parts in a 'Y' shape

forlorn /fəˈlɔːn/ adj someone who is forlorn looks lonely and sad

form¹ /fɔːm/ noun ★★★

1 type of sth	**4** level of ability
2 way sth appears/exists	**5** shape of sb/sth
3 official document	

1 [C] a type of something: *He developed a rare* **form of** *cancer.* ♦ *Everyone agrees that the kids must receive* **some form of** *punishment.*
2 [C/U] the particular way in which something appears or exists: *The information is also available in electronic form.* ♦ *Help arrived* **in the form of** *six heavily armed police officers.* ♦ *The aid might* **take the form of** *food or medical supplies.*
3 [C] an official document with spaces where you write information: *Use the order form to get new office supplies.* ♦ *Make sure you* **fill in** *the application form.*
4 [C] the level of someone's ability at a particular time, especially in a sport: *Williams blames a foot injury for her recent loss of form.* ♦ *The band's new CD marks a welcome* **return to form** (=to a previous high standard). ♦ *She is hoping to* **be on top form** *in time for the Olympics.*
5 [C] the body of a person, or the shape of an object: *Three forms gradually emerged out of the darkness.*

form² /fɔːm/ verb ★★★
1 [I/T] to start to exist, or to make something develop: *The club was formed in 1972.* ♦ *A change in temperature causes moisture to form on the windows.* ♦ *A plan began to form in her mind.* ♦ *The interview will give you a chance to* **form an impression of** *the company.*
2 [linking verb] to be something, or to be the parts that something consists of: *Research forms an important part of the course.* ♦ *Mountains form a natural barrier that keeps invaders out.*
3 [T] to influence the development of something: *His political views were formed by years of service in the army.*
4 [T] to make or shape something: *Use your hands to form the damp clay into a small ball.* ♦ *The children formed a line behind their teacher.*

formal /ˈfɔːm(ə)l/ adj ★★★
1 following the correct official methods ≠ INFORMAL: *The government is promising a* **formal investigation.** ♦ *We intend to make a* **formal written complaint.**
2 suitable for serious situations or occasions ≠ INFORMAL: *'Ameliorate' is a more formal way of saying 'improve'.*
3 you get a formal education or formal training from studying rather than from working at a job
—**formally** adv

formality /fɔːˈmæləti/ noun **1** [C] something that you must do as part of an official process, even though it may not seem necessary or sensible: *We went through the usual formalities at customs and passport control.* **2** [U] a formal style of writing, speaking, behaving, or dressing

formalize /ˈfɔːməlaɪz/ verb [T] to make something such as a plan or agreement official

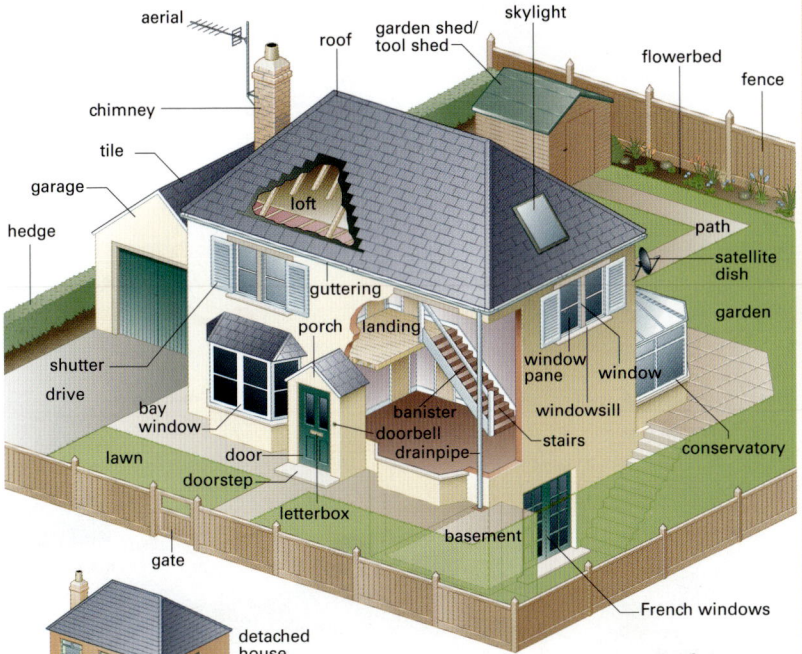

aerial
roof
garden shed/ tool shed
skylight
flowerbed
fence
chimney
tile
garage
hedge
loft
path
satellite dish
garden
guttering
shutter
drive
porch landing
window pane
window
windowsill
bay window
door
banister
doorbell
drainpipe
stairs
conservatory
lawn
doorstep
letterbox
gate
basement
French windows

detached house

semi-detached houses

bungalow

terraced houses

cottage

block of flats

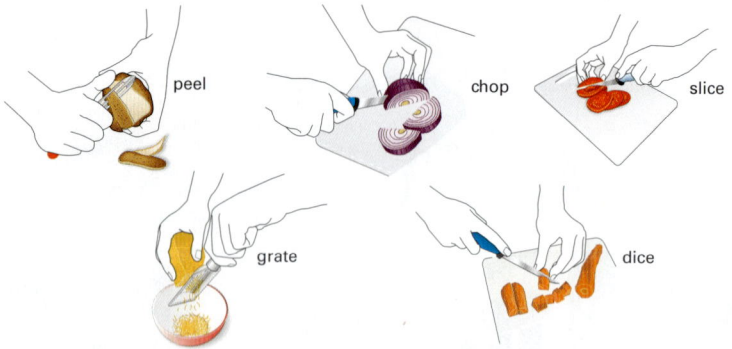

peel

chop

slice

grate

dice

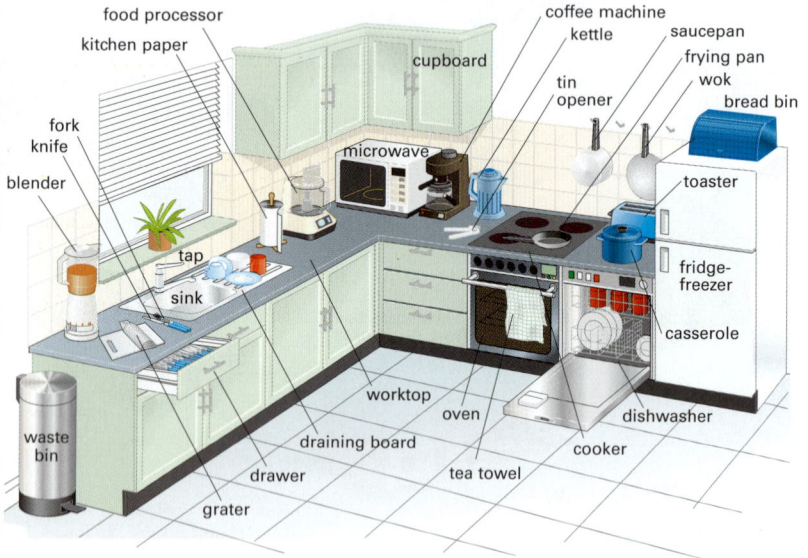

food processor

kitchen paper

coffee machine

kettle

saucepan

cupboard

frying pan

tin opener

wok

bread bin

fork

knife

blender

microwave

toaster

tap

sink

fridge-freezer

casserole

worktop

oven

dishwasher

waste bin

draining board

cooker

drawer

tea towel

grater

crush

drain

mix

whisk

paperclip

rubber

Post-it

2 p.m.

hole punch

calculator

desk tidy

in tray/out tray

keyboard monitor

desk lamp

filing cabinet

notepad

photocopier

telephone

fax

printer

briefcase

file

wastepaper computer
basket

stapler

mouse

mouse mat

mobile phone

CLOTHES

jeans

dungarees

leggings

sweatpants

kilt

shorts

suit
jacket
trousers

dress

tie

bow tie

braces

scarf

gloves
mittens

waistcoat
trousers

fleece

parka

raincoat

jacket

overcoat

 T-shirt

 blouse

 shirt

 vest

 sweatshirt

 cardigan

 sweater/jumper

socks

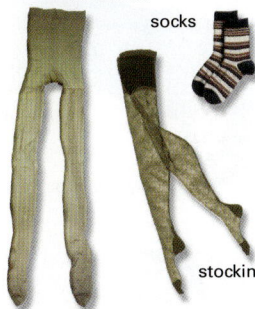 tights

stockings

 trunks

bikini

 swimsuit

 nightdress

 pyjamas

 dressing gown

CAR

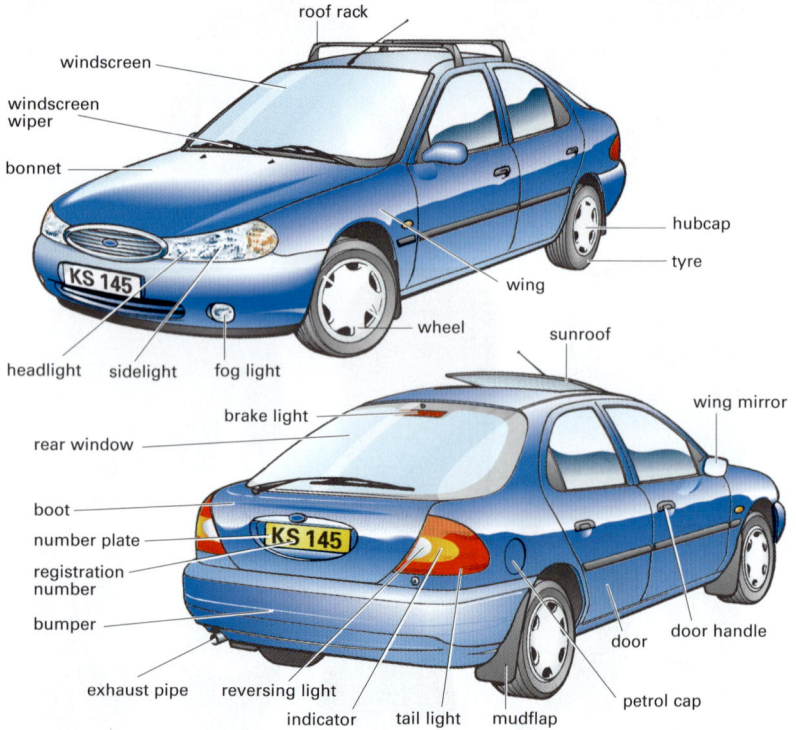

roof rack

windscreen

windscreen wiper

bonnet

headlight sidelight fog light

KS 145

hubcap

tyre

wing

wheel

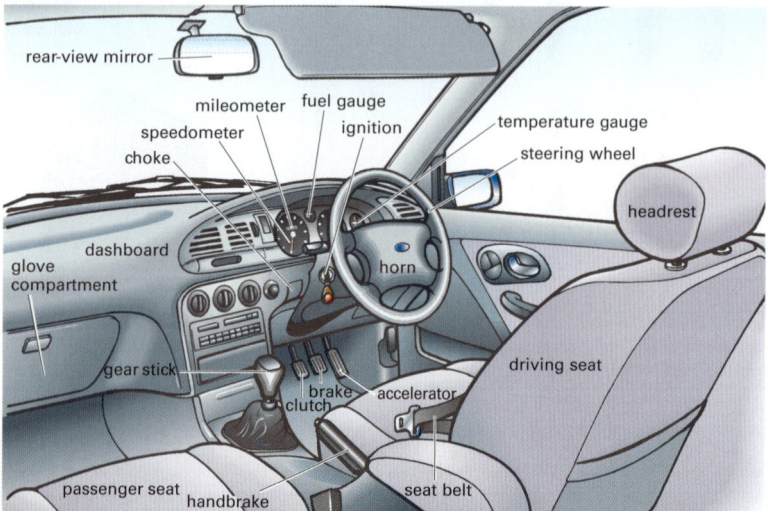

sunroof

wing mirror

brake light

rear window

boot

number plate

registration number

bumper

exhaust pipe reversing light

indicator tail light mudflap

door door handle

petrol cap

KS 145

rear-view mirror

mileometer fuel gauge

speedometer ignition

choke

temperature gauge

steering wheel

headrest

glove compartment

dashboard

horn

driving seat

gear stick

brake clutch accelerator

passenger seat handbrake

seat belt

plane

helicopter

train
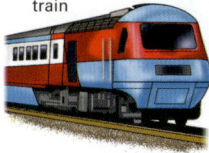

coach

car

moped

bicycle

bus

tram

minibus

taxi

ferry

hovercraft

hydrofoil

the Underground

SHAPES

circle

square

triangle

rectangle

diamond

star

crescent

heart

oval

parallelogram

trapezium

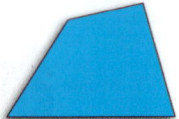
trapezoid

rhombus

pentagon

hexagon

octagon

sphere

cone

pyramid

cylinder

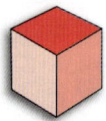
cube

acute angle

right angle

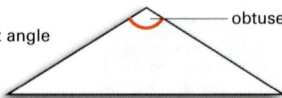
obtuse angle

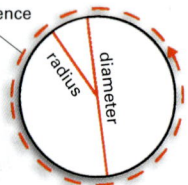
circumference

radius

diameter

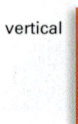
vertical

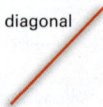
diagonal

horizontal

parallel

format¹ /ˈfɔːmæt/ noun [C/U] ★ the arrangement, size, or shape of something: *Changes have been proposed to the format of the competition.*

format² /ˈfɔːmæt/ verb [T] *computing* **1** to prepare a computer DISK so that information can be stored on it **2** to change the size, shape, or arrangement of the words in a computer file

formation /fɔːˈmeɪʃ(ə)n/ noun ★
1 [U] the process of starting or developing something: *factors that affect the formation of children's personalities*
2 [C/U] a pattern that people or things are arranged into: *planes flying in formation*

formative /ˈfɔːmətɪv/ adj strongly influencing the development of someone's character and beliefs

former /ˈfɔːmə/ grammar word ★★★

> **Former** can be:
> ■ an **adjective**: *She still visits her former husband.*
> ■ a **pronoun**: *He could resign or be dismissed, and he chose the former.*

1 used for stating the job, title, status etc that someone or something had in the past: *former president Bill Clinton ♦ the former Soviet Union*
2 *formal* used for referring to times in the past: *memories of former times*
3 the **former** *formal* used for referring to the first of two people or things that you have mentioned: *He attended with his wife and daughter, the former wearing a black dress.*
→ LATTER

formerly /ˈfɔːməli/ adv in the past

formidable /ˈfɔːmɪdəb(ə)l, fəˈmɪdəb(ə)l/ adj very impressive in size, power, or skill and therefore deserving respect

formula /ˈfɔːmjələ/ (plural **formulas** or **formulae** /ˈfɔːmjəliː/) noun [C] **1** a way of achieving something, or of dealing with a problem: *There is no magic formula for economic success.* **2** a group of letters or numbers that represents a rule in science **3** a list of the substances that you mix in order to make something

formulaic /ˌfɔːmjʊˈleɪɪk/ adj using a standard method that is effective but boring

formulate /ˈfɔːmjʊˌleɪt/ verb [T] **1** to develop something by thinking carefully about its details: *He formulated a plan to improve the team's performance.* **2** to express an idea in words that you choose carefully
—**formulation** /ˌfɔːmjʊˈleɪʃ(ə)n/ noun [C/U]

forsake /fəˈseɪk/ (past tense **forsook** /fəˈsʊk/; past participle **forsaken** /fəˈseɪkən/) verb [T] **1** *literary* to leave someone when they still need you=ABANDON **2** *formal* to stop doing something

fort /fɔːt/ noun [C] a strong building that is used by soldiers for defending a place

forte /ˈfɔːteɪ/ noun [singular] something that someone is very good at

forth /fɔːθ/ adv *literary* **1** away from a place **2** forwards, or out → SO

forthcoming /fɔːθˈkʌmɪŋ/ adj **1** happening or coming soon: *the forthcoming general election* **2** helpful and willing to tell you things ≠ UNFORTHCOMING: *James was more forthcoming than I expected.* **3** *formal* provided when someone asks for it

forthright /ˈfɔːθraɪt/ adj saying exactly what you think without being afraid of other people's reactions

forthwith /fɔːθˈwɪθ, fɔːθˈwɪð/ adv *formal* immediately

fortieth /ˈfɔːtiəθ/ number **1** in the place or position counted as number 40 **2** one of 40 equal parts of something

fortifications /ˌfɔːtɪfɪˈkeɪʃ(ə)nz/ noun [plural] strong buildings and walls that have been built to defend a place

fortify /ˈfɔːtɪfaɪ/ verb [T] **1** to protect a place against attack by building strong walls, towers, or other structures around it **2** to give someone energy or confidence

fortitude /ˈfɔːtɪtjuːd/ noun [U] *formal* a brave and determined attitude

fortnight /ˈfɔːtnaɪt/ noun [C] *British* a period of two weeks

fortnightly /ˈfɔːtnaɪtli/ adj, adv *British* happening every two weeks

fortress /ˈfɔːtrəs/ noun [C] a strong building that is used by soldiers for defending a place

fortuitous /fɔːˈtjuːɪtəs/ adj *formal* happening by chance in a way that is good for you
—**fortuitously** adv

fortunate /ˈfɔːtʃənət/ adj lucky
≠ UNFORTUNATE: *Not everyone is as fortunate as we are.* ♦ **fortunate to do sth** *She was extremely fortunate to escape without injury.* ♦ **fortunate enough to do sth** *I was fortunate enough to have a very supportive family.* ♦ **it is fortunate that** *It is very fortunate that the doctor was here today.*

fortunately /ˈfɔːtʃənətli/ adv ★ used for emphasizing that something good has happened by chance=LUCKILY
≠ UNFORTUNATELY: *I arrived at the station late, but fortunately the train was delayed.*

fortune /ˈfɔːtʃən/ noun ★
1 [C] a large amount of money: *They must have spent a fortune on flowers.* ♦ *He had made a fortune from mining.*
2 **fortunes** [plural] the good or bad things that happen to someone: *a career that illustrates the changing fortunes of the Labour Party*
3 [U] good luck: *I had the good fortune to know the manager of the company.*
PHRASE **tell sb's fortune** to use magic powers to find out what will happen to someone in the future

fortune-teller noun [C] someone who tells you what will happen to you in the future, for example by looking at the lines on your hand

forty /ˈfɔːti/ number the number 40

forum /ˈfɔːrəm/ noun [C] **1** a large meeting where people discuss something **2** a WEBSITE, newspaper, television programme etc where people can express their ideas and opinions

forward¹ /ˈfɔːwəd/ grammar word ★★★

> **Forward** can be:
> ■ an **adverb**: *I stepped forward to greet him.*
> ■ an **adjective**: *the forward section of the aircraft*

1 in the direction in front moving or

looking in the direction in front of you:
The car started to roll forward. ♦ *She made
a sudden forward movement.*
2 nearer the front in a position that is
towards the front of a room or vehicle: *Let's
sit further forward so that we can see the
stage better.* ♦ *the forward part of the train*
3 towards the future or a better state
thinking about the future or moving
toward a better state in the future: *We are
looking forward to new possibilities.* ♦ *a
giant leap forward in computer technology*
4 confident saying what you think in a
confident and direct way that is not socially
suitable
5 to a later time on a clock if you put a
clock or watch forward, you change the
time it shows to a later time

Forward and **forwards** have similar meanings
and uses, but speakers of American English
usually use the form **forward**. Speakers of British
English often use the form **forwards** for senses 1,
2, and 5.

forward² /ˈfɔːwəd/ verb [T] to send a letter,
parcel, email etc that has been sent to your
address to someone else at another address
forward³ /ˈfɔːwəd/ noun [C] a player in a game
such as basketball, football, or HOCKEY
whose job is to attack the other team and
score —*picture* → C15
forwarding address /ˈfɔːwədɪŋ əˌdres/ noun
[C] an address that someone can send your
letters to after you leave a place
forward-looking /ˈfɔːwəd ˌlʊkɪŋ/ adj
planning for the future in a positive way
by considering new ideas=PROGRESSIVE
forwards /ˈfɔːwədz/ adv FORWARD
forward slash noun [C] the symbol / used in
Internet addresses and computer
instructions
forwent the past tense of **forgo**
fossil /ˈfɒs(ə)l/ noun [C] an animal or plant
from the past that has been preserved in
rock
fossil fuel noun [C/U] coal or oil used as fuel
fossilized /ˈfɒsəlaɪzd/ adj preserved in rock
foster¹ /ˈfɒstə/ verb **1** [T] to help something to
develop over a period of time=PROMOTE
2 [I/T] to look after someone else's child as
part of your family for a period of time
→ ADOPT
foster² /ˈfɒstə/ adj a foster child is a child
who is being temporarily looked after in
someone else's family
fought the past tense and past participle of
fight¹
foul¹ /faʊl/ adj **1** very dirty, or very
unpleasant: *a foul smell* **2** if someone has a
foul TEMPER or is in a foul mood, they are
very angry
　　PHRASE **fall foul of** to do something that
annoys someone or breaks a rule
foul² /faʊl/ verb **1** [I/T] to break the rules of a
game **2** [T] to make something very dirty
　　PHRASAL VERB **foul (sth) up** to do something
wrong, or to spoil something
foul³ /faʊl/ noun [C] something that you do
in a game that is not allowed by the rules
foul play noun [U] dishonest or illegal
behaviour

foul-up noun [C] *informal* a mistake that causes
problems in a process or system
found¹ /faʊnd/ verb [T] ★ to start an
organization or institution: *The newspaper
was founded in 1909.*
　　PHRASE **be founded on sth** to be based on a
particular idea or principle: *a society
founded on the belief that all people are equal*
found² the past tense and past participle of
find¹
foundation /faʊnˈdeɪʃ(ə)n/ noun ★★

1 basic part of sth	4 creating an organization
2 base of building	5 face cream/powder
3 an organization	+ PHRASE

1 [C] the most basic part of something from
which the rest of it develops=BASIS: *The
first two years of study provide a solid
foundation in computing.* ♦ *a business
partnership that lays the foundation for
future success* ♦ *He believes that religion is
the foundation of a civilized society.*
2 [C] the part of a building that is below the
ground and that supports the rest of the
building
3 [C] an organization that provides money
for things such as medical research or for
a CHARITY: *the British Heart Foundation*
4 [U] the process of starting an organization
or institution: *the foundation of the first
grammar schools*
5 [C/U] a cream the same colour as your skin
that you put on your face before the rest of
your MAKE-UP —*picture* → MAKE-UP
　　PHRASE **be without foundation** or **have no
foundation** to not be based on fact and
therefore not possible to prove
foundation course noun [C] in the UK, a
course at university or college that covers
a range of subjects at a basic level and
prepares students for a longer, more
advanced course
founder /ˈfaʊndə/ noun [C] someone who
starts an organization or institution
foundry /ˈfaʊndri/ noun [C] a factory where
metal is MELTED and made into different
objects
fountain /ˈfaʊntɪn/ noun [C] a decoration for
gardens and streets in which a stream of
water is sent up into the air
fountain pen noun [C] a type of pen that you
fill with ink —*picture* → PEN
four¹ /fɔː/ number the number 4
four² /fɔː/ noun **on all fours** with your hands,
knees, and feet on the ground —*picture*
→ POSTURE
four-by-four noun [C] a FOUR-WHEEL DRIVE
four-poster noun [C] an old-fashioned bed
with four tall posts at the corners —*picture*
→ BED
foursome /ˈfɔːsəm/ noun [C] a group of four
people
fourteen /fɔːˈtiːn/ number the number 14
fourteenth /fɔːˈtiːnθ/ number **1** in the place
or position counted as number 14 **2** one of
14 equal parts of something
fourth /fɔːθ/ number **1** in the place or position
counted as number four **2** *American* one of
four equal parts of something=QUARTER
Fourth of July a US holiday that celebrates

the time when the United States became an independent country

four-wheel drive noun [C] a car with big wheels that is designed for driving on rough ground

fowl /faʊl/ (plural **fowl** or **fowls**) noun [C] a chicken or other bird that is kept on a farm for its eggs and meat

fox¹ /fɒks/ noun [C] a wild animal similar to a small dog, with red-brown fur and a thick tail —*picture* → C13

fox² /fɒks/ verb [T] British to be impossible for you to understand or solve

foyer /ˈfɔɪeɪ/ noun [C] a large open space just inside the entrance to a hotel or theatre =LOBBY

fracas /ˈfrækɑː/ noun [singular] a noisy fight or argument

fraction /ˈfrækʃ(ə)n/ noun [C] **1** a small part or amount of something: *His investment is now worth only a fraction of its original value.* **2** a part of a whole number, for example ½ or ¾ —**fractional** adj

fractionally /ˈfrækʃ(ə)nəli/ adv by a very small amount

fracture¹ /ˈfræktʃə/ noun [C] a break or crack in a bone or piece of rock

fracture² /ˈfræktʃə/ verb [I/T] if something hard such as a bone fractures, or if it is fractured, it breaks or cracks —**fractured** /ˈfræktʃəd/ adj

fragile /ˈfrædʒaɪl/ adj **1** easy to break or damage **2** not very strong or healthy: *His health has always been fragile.* —**fragility** /frəˈdʒɪləti/ noun [U]

fragment¹ /ˈfrægmənt/ noun [C] **1** a small piece of a larger object that has broken into a lot of pieces: *Police found fragments of glass on his clothing.* **2** a small part of something: *fragments of conversation*

fragment² /frægˈment/ verb [I/T] if something fragments, or if it is fragmented, it breaks into a lot of separate pieces or parts —**fragmented** adj

fragrance /ˈfreɪɡrəns/ noun [C/U] **1** a nice smell **2** PERFUME

fragrant /ˈfreɪɡrənt/ adj with a nice smell

frail /freɪl/ adj **1** physically weak and not very healthy **2** not strong and therefore likely to be damaged or destroyed

frailty /ˈfreɪlti/ noun [C/U] the condition of being physically or morally weak

frame¹ /freɪm/ noun ★★

1 border of picture etc	5 box on Internet page
2 basic structure	6 of pair of glasses
3 one photograph	+ PHRASE
4 shape of sb's body	

1 [C] a structure that forms the border of something: *a silver picture frame* ♦ *The window frames need painting.*

2 [C] the part of an object that forms its basic structure: *the frame of a bed/bike*

3 [C] one of the single photographs that form a film

4 [C] the particular shape or size of someone's body: *A shiver shook her small frame.*

5 [C] computing a box on an Internet page that contains information that you can SCROLL through (=go up and down by using the mouse)

6 frames [plural] the part of a pair of GLASSES that holds the LENSES (=parts that you see through) and that has pieces that go over your ears

PHRASE **frame of mind** the mood that someone is in

frame² /freɪm/ verb [T] **1** to put a picture or photograph in a frame **2** literary to form a border around something **3** informal to make someone seem to be guilty of a crime when they are not, for example by lying to the police **4** to express something in a particular way: *He was thinking about how to frame the question.*

framework /ˈfreɪmwɜːk/ noun [C] ★
1 a set of principles or rules: *a framework for the study of television's effect on society* **2** a structure that supports something and makes it a particular shape: *the wooden framework of the roof*

franchise /ˈfræntʃaɪz/ noun **1** [C] an arrangement in which someone operates a business using the name and the products of a big company **2** [C] a business that operates under a franchise system **3** [singular/U] the right to vote in elections

frank /fræŋk/ adj honest about a situation or your opinions, even if this offends people: *He was completely frank about the problems we face.*

PHRASE **to be frank** spoken used when you are going to say something that other people might not like to hear —**frankness** noun [U]

frankfurter /ˈfræŋkfɜːtə/ noun [C] a long thin SAUSAGE (=meat that is cut into very small pieces and put inside a thin skin). It is often eaten inside a long bread roll.

frankly /ˈfræŋkli/ adv **1** used for emphasizing that you are speaking honestly: *Frankly, I don't care what you think.* **2** in an honest and direct manner: *She talks frankly about her unhappy childhood.*

frantic /ˈfræntɪk/ adj **1** done in a very urgent way: *frantic attempts to rescue people from the fire* **2** very worried —**frantically** /ˈfræntɪkli/ adv

fraternal /frəˈtɜːn(ə)l/ adj of a brother, or like a brother

fraternity /frəˈtɜːnəti/ noun **1** [U] feelings of friendship, trust, and support between people **2** [C/U] people who have similar jobs or interests: *members of the legal fraternity* **3** [C] American a private club for male students at a university or college in the US

fraternize /ˈfrætənaɪz/ verb [I] formal to spend time with someone as a friend

fraud /frɔːd/ noun **1** [C/U] the crime of obtaining money from someone by tricking them: *tax/insurance fraud* **2** [C] someone who pretends to be an official or professional person in order to trick people

fraudulent /ˈfrɔːdjʊlənt/ adj done dishonestly or illegally with the intention of tricking someone —**fraudulently** adv

fraught /frɔːt/ adj very worried, or involving people who are very worried

PHRASE **fraught with sth** full of problems or dangers

F

fray /freɪ/ verb **1** [I/T] if cloth frays, or if something frays it, its fibres come apart at the edge **2** [I] if someone's nerves fray, they get nervous, and if someone's TEMPER frays, they get angry

fray, the /freɪ/ noun [singular] **1** an exciting situation in which people compete with each other **2** a fight, or an argument

frayed /freɪd/ adj **1** with fibres that are coming apart at the edge **2** if your nerves are frayed, you are nervous, and if your TEMPER is frayed, you are angry

freak¹ /friːk/ noun [C] **1** a very strange person or thing **2** informal someone who is extremely interested in a particular subject: *a fitness/health freak*

freak² /friːk/ adj extremely unusual and unexpected: *He was killed in a freak accident.*

freak³ /friːk/ or **freak (sb) out** verb [I/T] informal to suddenly become very angry, excited, or frightened, or to make someone very angry, excited, or frightened

freckles /ˈfrek(ə)lz/ noun [plural] small brown spots that are on someone's skin

free¹ /friː/ adj ★★★

1 not costing anything	5 not busy
2 not tied/fixed	6 not being used
3 not prisoner	+ PHRASES
4 not limited by rules	

1 something that is free does not cost anything: *There is plenty of free parking.* ♦ *The swimming pool is free for hotel guests.* **2** not held, tied, or fixed somewhere: *Hand me the free end of the rope.* ♦ *Sally struggled to get free from the branches.* **3** not a prisoner or a SLAVE: *He'll soon be a free man.* **4** not limited or controlled by rules: *We like to believe we live in a free society.* ♦ **free to do sth** *You are free to choose your own lawyer.* **5** available to see someone or do something: *I'm busy at the moment, but I'll be free this afternoon.* ♦ *Are you free for lunch?* **6** available for someone to use: *Is this seat free?* ♦ *I'll keep a day free next week for our meeting.* ♦ *I don't have much free time in this job.*

PHRASES **be free from/of sth** to be not containing or involving something that is unpleasant: *a world free from violence* ♦ *Doctors try to keep their patients free of pain.*
feel free spoken used for giving someone permission in a friendly way: *'Can I use the phone?' 'Feel free.'* ♦ *Feel free to help yourself to coffee.*
a free hand the right to make your own decisions without asking someone's permission: *The board gave me a free hand to reorganize the company.*

free² /friː/ verb [T] ★
1 to let someone leave a prison or similar place = RELEASE: *The organization works to free political prisoners.*
2 to help someone to get out of a place: **free sb/sth from sth** *They helped to free the injured driver from the wreckage.*
3 to remove something unpleasant that affects someone: **free sb/sth from sth** *The new president will take action to free the*
media from government control. ♦ **free sb/sth of sth** *He has been freed of direct responsibility for his staff.*
4 to make someone or something available to be used: **free sb/sth for sth** *We need to free more police officers for street duties.* ♦ **free sb/sth to do sth** *A classroom assistant frees teachers to concentrate on teaching.*

PHRASAL VERB **free sb/sth up** same as free²4: *We can probably free up £20,000 for new computer equipment.*

free³ /friː/ adv **1** without paying any money: *We got in free.* ♦ *Children can stay free of charge.* **2** out of a place where you are being kept: *The prisoner suddenly broke free and ran towards the car.* **3** without being controlled or stopped: *dogs running free*

free agent noun [C] someone who is free to do what they want

freebie /ˈfriːbi/ noun [C] informal something that someone gives you that you do not have to pay for

freedom /ˈfriːdəm/ noun ★★★
1 [U] the right or opportunity to do what you want: *a law that restricts religious freedom* ♦ *The school gives students freedom of choice about what to wear.* ♦ *Police road blocks were seen as an attempt to restrict freedom of movement.* ♦ **freedom to do sth** *My parents gave me total freedom to do whatever I liked.*
2 [plural] different types of freedom: *basic/fundamental/political freedoms*
PHRASES **freedom from sth** a situation in which you are not affected by something that is unpleasant: *freedom from hunger/ disease/poverty*
freedom of speech the legal right to express your opinions without being prevented or punished

freedom fighter noun [C] someone who fights against a cruel or unfair government

free enterprise noun [U] an economic system in which businesses can compete with each other without being controlled by government

free-for-all noun [C] informal **1** a situation in which people compete with each other using unfair or cruel methods **2** a noisy fight or argument that involves a lot of people = BRAWL

free kick noun [C] in football, an occasion when a player in one team is allowed to kick the ball without any opposition because a player in the other team has broken a rule

freelance¹ /ˈfriːlɑːns/ adj working for different companies rather than being permanently employed by a particular company

freelance² /ˈfriːlɑːns/ verb [I] to sell your work or services to many different companies

freelancer /ˈfriːlɑːnsə/ or **freelance** /ˈfriːlɑːns/ noun [C] a SELF-EMPLOYED person who works for different companies

freely /ˈfriːli/ adv

1 without limits	4 not exactly
2 without pauses	5 in an honest way
3 generously	6 in many places

1 without being controlled by rules: *Players can move freely between clubs.* **2** without being stopped or interrupted: *The traffic is moving quite freely this morning.* **3** generously, or in a willing way: *They give their time freely to support our cause.* **4** not in an exact way, but giving a general idea of the meaning of something: *Poems have to be translated quite freely.* **5** without trying to hide anything=OPENLY: *I freely admit I've made mistakes.* **6** something that is freely available is easy to obtain or buy

free 'market noun [C] an economic system in which the government does not control trade and prices

Freemason /ˈfriːˌmeɪs(ə)n/ noun [C] a member of an international secret society of men who agree to help each other

free-range adj free-range farm animals live outside in a lot of space

free 'speech noun [U] the legal or natural right to say what you believe is true, without being prevented or punished

free 'trade noun [U] a system in which companies do not pay high taxes on goods that are bought from other countries or are sold in other countries

freeware /ˈfriːweə/ noun [U] *computing* computer software that is available free on CD-ROM or from the Internet

freeway /ˈfriːweɪ/ noun [C] *American* a wide fast road in a US city that you do not pay to use

free 'will noun [U] people's ability to control their own lives, based on their own decisions

PHRASE of your own free will if you do something of your own free will, you do it because you want to do it, not because you are forced to

freeze¹ /friːz/ (past tense **froze** /frəʊz/; past participle **frozen** /ˈfrəʊz(ə)n/) verb ★

1 become hard with cold	**4** not increase a level
2 preserve food	**5** stop moving
3 feel extremely cold	

1 [I/T] to become solid or hard because of extreme cold, or to make something solid or hard: *The lake freezes in winter.* ♦ *The water had frozen solid.*
2 [T] to preserve food or drink by making it extremely cold in a freezer: *You should freeze meat on the day that you buy it.*
3 [I] to feel extremely cold: *You'll freeze if you go out in that thin coat.* ♦ *The lambs looked as if they had frozen to death in the snow.*
4 [T] to decide officially that the level of something will not increase: *Wages were frozen until the end of December.*
5 [I] to stop moving and keep completely still: *Kate froze in horror when she saw all the blood.*

freeze² /friːz/ noun [C] **1** an official decision to prevent any increase in something: *a pay/wage/price freeze* **2** a period of extremely cold weather

freezer /ˈfriːzə/ noun [C] a large piece of electrical equipment that is used for freezing food

freezing¹ /ˈfriːzɪŋ/ adj *informal* very cold: *It's absolutely freezing in here.*

freezing² /ˈfriːzɪŋ/ noun [U] the temperature at which water freezes and becomes ice: *five degrees below freezing*

freezing ,point noun [C] the temperature at which a particular liquid freezes

freight /freɪt/ noun [U] goods that are carried by vehicles

freighter /ˈfreɪtə/ noun [C] a large ship or plane that carries goods

French 'fries noun [plural] CHIPS (=long thin pieces of potato that have been fried)

French 'horn noun [C] a musical instrument consisting of a long curved metal tube that is very wide at one end —*picture* → BRASS

French 'windows noun [plural] a pair of glass doors that lead to a garden —*picture* → C1

frenetic /frəˈnetɪk/ adj done very fast and with a lot of energy, often by someone who is in a hurry —**frenetically** /frəˈnetɪkli/ adv

frenzied /ˈfrenzid/ adj done in an extremely uncontrolled way, often by someone who is crazy

frenzy /ˈfrenzi/ noun [singular] **1** the feeling of being unable to control your feelings or behaviour: *She was in a frenzy of rage.* **2** a period when there is a lot of activity

frequency /ˈfriːkwənsi/ noun **1** [U] the number of times that something happens during a period of time: *We hope this treatment will reduce the frequency of heart disease.* **2** [C] the WAVELENGTH on which a radio programme is broadcast

frequent¹ /ˈfriːkwənt/ adj ★ happening often ≠ INFREQUENT: *Their arguments were becoming more and more frequent.* ♦ *He was a frequent visitor to our house.* ♦ *Inspections must be carried out at frequent intervals* (=regularly).

frequent² /frɪˈkwent/ verb [T] *formal* if you frequent a place, you go there regularly

frequently /ˈfriːkwəntli/ adv ★★ often ≠ RARELY, SELDOM: *He has frequently been compared to Michael Jackson.* ♦ *The ten most frequently asked questions are listed below.*

fresh /freʃ/ adj ★★★

1 new	**6** with feeling of energy
2 food: not preserved	**7** of flowers
3 food: still good to eat	**8** water: with no salt
4 replacing sth	**+ PHRASE**
5 recently done/made	

1 clearly new and different: *We need a completely fresh approach to the problem.* ♦ *The programme takes a fresh look at this difficult issue.* ♦ *She regarded the birth of her children as a fresh start* (=a chance to start living in a better way).
2 fresh food has not been preserved in any way: *You can use fresh or tinned tomatoes for this recipe.*
3 food that is fresh is still good to eat because it was prepared or produced recently: *Cooked meat will keep fresh for several days in the fridge.*
4 replacing or adding to a previous thing: *The police made a fresh appeal for witnesses.* ♦ *I've put fresh towels in your room.*
5 recently made or experienced: *fresh footprints in the snow* ♦ *The details are still fresh in my mind.*

F

6 if you feel fresh, you have a lot of energy
=REFRESHED

7 fresh flowers have been recently PICKED (=taken from the place that they were growing in)

8 fresh water is water in lakes and rivers that does not contain any salt

PHRASE **fresh from/out of sth** if someone is fresh from a particular place or situation, they have recently come from there: *He was just a kid, fresh out of law school.*
—**freshness** noun [U]

fresh air noun [U] the air outside that is nice to breathe → BREATH

freshen /ˈfreʃ(ə)n/ verb [T] to make something fresher, cleaner, or more attractive: *She quickly freshened her make-up.*

PHRASAL VERBS **freshen up** to wash your hands and face and make yourself cleaner and tidier

freshen sth up *same as* **freshen**: *Freshen up your room with a coat of paint.*

fresher /ˈfreʃə/ noun [C] *British* a student in their first year at university

freshly /ˈfreʃli/ adv recently

freshman /ˈfreʃmən/ (plural **freshmen** /ˈfreʃmən/) noun [C] *American* a FRESHER

freshwater /ˈfreʃˌwɔːtə/ adj living in water that does not contain salt

fret /fret/ verb [I] to worry about something continuously

fretful /ˈfretf(ə)l/ adj someone who is fretful is worried and unhappy

Fri. abbrev Friday

friar /ˈfraɪə/ noun [C] a man who is a type of MONK (=a member of a Christian religious community)

friction /ˈfrɪkʃ(ə)n/ noun [U] **1** disagreement: *There is some friction between the various departments in the organization.* **2** the fact that one surface rubs against another

Friday /ˈfraɪdeɪ/ noun [C/U] ★★★ the day after Thursday and before Saturday: *Let's go swimming on Friday.* ♦ *We usually meet on Fridays* (=every Friday). ♦ *My birthday is on a Friday this year.*

fridge /frɪdʒ/ noun [C] ★ a piece of equipment that is used for storing food at low temperatures=REFRIGERATOR

fridge-freezer noun [C] *British* a machine that consists of a FRIDGE and a FREEZER —*picture* → C2

fried /fraɪd/ adj cooked in hot oil

friend /frend/ noun [C] ★★★ someone who you know well and like who is not a member of your family: *She's visiting friends in Scotland.* ♦ *Helga is **a close friend** of mine.* ♦ *I'm having lunch with **an old friend** (=someone who has been a friend for a long time).* ♦ *May I introduce Peter Flint, a very old **friend of the family**.* ♦ *She has a wide **circle of friends** (=group of friends).* ♦ *They used to **be friends** (=with each other).* ♦ *They **made friends with** the children next door (=started to be their friends).*

Words often used with friend

Adjectives often used with friend

■ **best, close, dear, good, great, lifelong, old, trusted** + FRIEND: someone who you know very well

friendly /ˈfren(d)li/ adj ★★
1 someone who is friendly is always pleasant and helpful towards other people ≠ UNFRIENDLY: *He will be remembered as a kind, friendly person.* ♦ *The local people were very **friendly towards** us.*
→ SYMPATHETIC
2 if you are friendly with someone, you are their friend: *Janet and I used to **be very friendly**.* ♦ *Doctors shouldn't get too **friendly with** their patients.*

-friendly /fren(d)li/ suffix **1** used for showing that something does not harm someone else: *wildlife-friendly farming methods* ♦ *environmentally-friendly cleaning materials* **2** suitable for a particular type of person: *child-friendly restaurants*

friendship /ˈfren(d)ʃɪp/ noun [C/U] ★ a relationship between people who are friends: *Whatever happened, I did not want to lose Sarah's friendship.* ♦ *his **friendship** with a local businessman* ♦ *She formed a **close friendship** with Vera Brittain.*

fries /fraɪz/ noun [plural] FRENCH FRIES

frieze /friːz/ noun [C] a line of decoration around the walls of a room or building

frigate /ˈfrɪɡət/ noun [C] a small fast ship that is used by a navy

fright /fraɪt/ noun [singular/U] a sudden strong feeling of being afraid: *He was shaking with fright.* ♦ *Kelly cried out in fright.*

frighten /ˈfraɪt(ə)n/ verb [T] ★ to make someone feel afraid=SCARE: *The thought of war frightens me.* ♦ *It frightens me how quickly children grow up these days.* ♦ **frighten sb into doing sth** *adverts that frighten people into buying expensive security equipment*

PHRASAL VERB **frighten sb/sth away** or **frighten sb/sth off** to make a person or animal so afraid that they run away

frightened /ˈfraɪt(ə)nd/ adj ★ feeling or showing fear=SCARED: *The puppy looked cold and frightened.* ♦ *Bruckner was watching him with wide, frightened eyes.* ♦ *There's nothing to be **frightened about**.* ♦ *I've always been **frightened of** snakes.* ♦ +(that) *I was frightened that he might see us.* ♦ **frightened to do sth** *Now he is frightened to go out at night.*

■ **Frightened** describes how you feel: *I am frightened of spiders.* ♦ *She looked very frightened.*
■ **Frightening** describes things or situations that make you feel frightened: *The look on his face was frightening.* ♦ *It was a very frightening experience.*

frightening /ˈfraɪt(ə)nɪŋ/ adj ★ making you feel afraid, nervous, or worried: *a frightening noise/thought/experience* ♦ *It was supposed to be a horror film but it wasn't very frightening.* ♦ *It's frightening that people like him get elected.*
—**frighteningly** adv

frightful /ˈfraɪtf(ə)l/ adj *informal old-fashioned* extremely serious or unpleasant: *a frightful headache*

frightfully /ˈfraɪtf(ə)li/ adv *informal old-fashioned* extremely: *I really am frightfully sorry.*

frigid /ˈfrɪdʒɪd/ adj **1** extremely formal and unfriendly=ICY **2** a frigid woman does not enjoy having sex

frill /frɪl/ noun [C] a decoration that consists of a long narrow piece of cloth with many small folds in it

PHRASE no frills used for referring to something that is good enough but that has no unnecessary extra features

frilly /ˈfrɪli/ adj decorated with a lot of frills

fringe¹ /frɪndʒ/ noun [C] **1** British short hair that hangs down over your forehead —*picture* → HAIRSTYLE **2** the outer edge of something: *factories on the northern fringe of the city* **3** people or activities that are considered strange: *He has been forced to live on the fringes of society.* **4** a decoration that consists of a row of fibres or thin pieces of cloth that hang down

fringe² /frɪndʒ/ verb [T] to form a line around the edge of something=BORDER

fringe³ /frɪndʒ/ adj involving people who do not form the main part of a group and are sometimes thought to be strange: *fringe meetings/issues/politics*

ˈfringe ˌbenefit noun [C] something that you get from your employer in addition to your salary, for example a car=PERK

frisk /frɪsk/ verb [T] to search someone with your hands in order to see if they are carrying anything illegal such as a gun or drugs

frisky /ˈfrɪski/ adj feeling lively and full of fun

fritter /ˈfrɪtə/ **PHRASAL VERB** ˌfritter sth aˈway to waste time or money on things that are not important: *He frittered away all his winnings.*

frivolity /frɪˈvɒləti/ noun [U] silly behaviour or attitudes

frivolous /ˈfrɪvələs/ adj **1** behaving in a silly way in situations in which you should be serious or sensible **2** lacking any real purpose or importance: *frivolous complaints*

frizzy /ˈfrɪzi/ adj frizzy hair has small tight stiff curls

fro /frəʊ/ *see* to

frog /frɒg/ noun [C] a small animal with smooth skin and long back legs that lives near water → TOAD

frogman /ˈfrɒgmən/ (plural **frogmen** /ˈfrɒgmən/) noun [C] someone who does police or military work under water. Frogmen wear special clothes and use special equipment.

frolic /ˈfrɒlɪk/ verb [I] to play in a happy way with a lot of energy

from /*weak* frəm, *strong* frɒm/ preposition ★★★ **1 given, sent, or provided by sb** used for saying who gives, sends, or provides something: *The watch was a present from his daughter.* ♦ *She got a letter from Tom.* ♦ *I borrowed the money from my parents.* **2 stating sb's origin** used for saying where someone was born, where they live or work, or the type of family they were born with: *I'm originally from Northern Ireland.* ♦ *Rosie Miller from Stratford, East London, received the award.* ♦ *a team of experts from the bank* ♦ *Those from poor families should not have to pay.*

3 saying where sb/sth started used for saying where someone or something started a journey, or where they were before moving: *the 3 o'clock flight from Chicago* ♦ *imports from Japan* ♦ *He took a hammer from his toolbox.* ♦ *What time does he come home from school?* ♦ *We drove from London to Glasgow.*

4 giving distances used for saying how far away something is in relation to something else: *We live a few miles from the city.*

5 giving a range used for giving a range of things, times, prices etc: *music ranging from classical to punk*

6 starting at a particular time starting at a point in time and continuing: *She will be working here full-time from tomorrow.* ♦ *He wanted to be an actor from the age of 10.* ♦ *From now on, things are going to be different.*

7 giving a reason used for saying what has caused something or why you have a particular opinion: *Her hair was wet from the rain.* ♦ *She's been suffering from stress.* ♦ *I could see from his expression that he was upset.*

8 saying where sb does sth used for saying where someone is when they hear, or do something: *He works from home.* ♦ *Let's watch the fireworks from the roof.*

9 made of sth used for saying what substance has been used for making something: *The toys are made from a very durable plastic.*

10 describing a change used for saying what someone or something was before changing to something else: *Colesville changed from a sleepy little town to a busy city.*

11 saying what is prevented used for saying what has been prevented or protected against: *Protect delicate plants from frost.* ♦ *His restlessness kept him from sleeping.*

12 showing differences used for talking about differences between two or more people or things: *This recipe is different from the one I usually use.* ♦ *He should know right from wrong by now.*

frond /frɒnd/ noun [C] a large long leaf that is divided into many narrow sections

front¹ /frʌnt/ noun ★★★

1 part facing forwards	**5** not sincere behaviour
2 part furthest forwards	**6** in war
3 aspect of situation	**7** in weather
4 activity to hide secret	**+** PHRASES

1 the front [singular] the surface of something that faces forwards ≠ BACK: *Go round to the front* (=of the building) *and I'll let you in.* ♦ *Attach a recent photograph to the front of your application.* ♦ *a book with a picture of a tiger on the front*

2 the front [singular] the part of something that is nearest the direction it faces ≠ BACK:

If you can't see the blackboard, come and sit at the front. ♦ *Tom was sitting at the front of the bus.* ♦ *He had signed his name in the front of the book.*

3 [C] a particular aspect of a situation: *There's bad news on the job front – two factories are going to close.* ♦ *His main problems were in maths and science, but he has made progress on both fronts.*

4 [C] an organization or activity that exists in order to hide something that is secret or illegal: *They kept a shop as a front for dealing in stolen goods.*

5 [singular] behaviour that is not sincere because you want to hide your real feelings: *He always pretended he didn't care but we knew it was just a front.* ♦ *She's putting on a brave front, but she's really very worried.*

6 [C] a FRONT LINE in a war

7 [C] *technical* a line where a large area of cold air meets a large area of warm air

PHRASES **front of house 1** the parts of a theatre, cinema, or CONCERT HALL that the audience uses **2** the activities in a theatre, cinema, or CONCERT HALL that involve dealing with members of the public

in front 1 a little further forwards than someone or something else: *I overtook the car in front.* **2** winning a competition, game, or election that is not yet finished: *Owen scored to put his team in front.*

in front of sb 1 if something is in front of you, it is in a position where you can see it if you look forwards: *In front of her, the motorway stretched for miles.* **2** in a situation where someone is there with you: *I would never say this in front of my mother.* **3** in a situation where someone is watching you do something: *The match took place in front of a crowd of 60,000 people.*

in front of sth 1 into a place where a moving vehicle might hit you: *He stepped into the road in front of a bus.* **2** in a position where you can see a particular thing when you look forwards: *She just sits in front of the television all day long.*

up front if you pay money up front, you pay it before you have received the goods that you are buying, or before someone starts to do work for you: *I'll need £500 up front for the cost of materials.*
→ BACK³

front² /frʌnt/ adj ★★★ at, in, or on the front of something: *You can go and play in the front garden.* ♦ *the front seat of the car* ♦ *front legs/paws*

frontal /ˈfrʌnt(ə)l/ adj *formal* at, in, or on the front part of something

front door noun [C] the main door at the front of a house

frontier /frʌnˈtɪə, ˈfrʌntɪə/ noun **1** [C] a border between two countries: *the frontier between Israel and Lebanon* **2** the frontiers [plural] the most advanced or recent ideas about something: *Their work was on the frontiers of science.*

front line noun [C] the area where two armies face each other and fight during a war —**front-line** adj

front-page adj important enough to be printed on the first page of a newspaper:

front-page news/stories/headlines

front runner noun [C] the person or thing that is thought to be the most likely to win a competition, game, or election

frost¹ /frɒst/ noun **1** [U] a thin white layer of ice that looks like powder and that forms on things outside when the weather is very cold: *bushes covered with frost* **2** [C/U] a period of weather that is cold enough to form frost

frost² /frɒst/ verb [T] *American* to put ICING on a cake

frostbite /ˈfrɒs(t)baɪt/ noun [U] a medical condition in which cold weather seriously damages your fingers, toes, ears, or nose

frostbitten /ˈfrɒs(t)bɪt(ə)n/ adj affected by frostbite

frosted glass noun [U] glass that has a rough surface so that you cannot see clearly through it

frosting /ˈfrɒstɪŋ/ noun [U] *American* ICING for a cake

frosty /ˈfrɒsti/ adj **1** cold enough to produce FROST, or covered with FROST: *a frosty morning* **2** unfriendly: *a frosty look*

froth¹ /frɒθ/ noun [singular/U] a mass of small air BUBBLES that form on the surface of a liquid

froth² /frɒθ/ verb [I] to produce froth

frothy /ˈfrɒθi/ adj covered with or consisting of froth

frown¹ /fraʊn/ verb [I] to move your EYEBROWS down and closer together because you are annoyed, worried, or thinking hard

PHRASAL VERB **frown on sb/sth** to not approve of something: *Personal phone calls are frowned on at work.*

frown² /fraʊn/ noun [C] an expression on your face that is made by moving your EYEBROWS down and closer together. It shows that you are annoyed, worried, or thinking hard.

froze the past tense of **freeze¹**

frozen¹ /ˈfrəʊz(ə)n/ adj ★
1 preserved by being made extremely cold and stored at a very low temperature: *frozen food/meals* ♦ *frozen vegetables/fish/yoghurt*
2 covered with a layer of ice, or made very hard because the weather is very cold: *a frozen pond* ♦ *the frozen ground*
3 *spoken* feeling very cold: *I'm frozen – can't we go inside?* ♦ *We were frozen stiff* (=extremely cold) *waiting for the bus.*

frozen² the past participle of **freeze¹**

frugal /ˈfruːg(ə)l/ adj **1** spending very little money and only on things that are really necessary **2** a frugal meal is simple, cheap, and not very big —**frugally** adv

fruit /fruːt/ noun [C/U] ★★★ (plural **fruit** or **fruits**) a type of food that grows on trees or plants, for example apples and oranges: *Eat plenty of fresh fruit and vegetables.* ♦ *She always has a piece of fruit for dessert.*
PHRASES **bear fruit** to have a successful result: *Our policies must be given time to bear fruit.*
the fruit/fruits of sth the good results that you get from something such as hard work:

The book is the fruit of a collaboration between several groups.

fruitful /ˈfruːtf(ə)l/ adj producing good results ≠ FRUITLESS: *a fruitful meeting/discussion*

fruition /fruːˈɪʃ(ə)n/ noun [U] *formal* the result that you wanted to achieve from a plan or idea: *Nobody was sure whether the deal would ever come to fruition.*

fruitless /ˈfruːtləs/ adj producing no good results ≠ FRUITFUL: *a fruitless search*

fruit ˈsalad noun [C/U] a food consisting of small pieces of different types of fresh fruit, usually eaten as a DESSERT

fruity /ˈfruːti/ adj tasting or smelling like fruit

frustrate /frʌˈstreɪt/ verb [T] **1** to make someone feel annoyed and impatient by preventing them from doing or getting something **2** to prevent someone or something from succeeding: *The bad weather frustrated their plans for a picnic.*

frustrated /frʌˈstreɪtɪd/ adj feeling annoyed and impatient because you are prevented from achieving something: *Parents are increasingly frustrated with the local school system.*

frustrating /frʌˈstreɪtɪŋ/ adj making you feel annoyed and impatient because you are prevented from achieving something: *It's frustrating to wait all day for a repairman who doesn't show up.*

frustration /frʌˈstreɪʃ(ə)n/ noun [C/U] an annoyed or impatient feeling that you get when you are prevented from doing what you want: *There is a growing sense of frustration among hospital staff.*

fry /fraɪ/ verb [I/T] ★ to cook food in hot oil or fat, or to be cooked in this way: *the smell of chicken frying in the kitchen* ♦ *Heat the oil in a large pan and fry the onion and garlic for 5 minutes.* → STIR-FRY

frying pan /ˈfraɪɪŋ ˌpæn/ noun [C] a flat metal pan with a long handle that is used for cooking food in hot oil or fat —*picture* → C2

ft abbrev foot or feet: *a 3 ft deep pond*

fuchsia /ˈfjuːʃə/ noun [C/U] a small bush with pink, red, or white flowers that hang down —*picture* → C9

fudge[1] /fʌdʒ/ noun [U] a soft brown sweet food made from sugar, butter, milk or cream, and usually chocolate

fudge[2] /fʌdʒ/ verb **1** [I/T] to avoid giving a clear decision or answer about something: *People have accused us of fudging the issue.* **2** [T] to change the details of something: *Journalists have always tended to fudge the facts.*

fuel[1] /ˈfjuːəl/ noun ★★
1 [C/U] a substance such as oil, gas, coal, or wood that produces heat or power when it is burned: *a shortage of food and fuel*
2 [U] petrol or DIESEL used in vehicles: *The stolen car was abandoned when it ran out of fuel.*

fuel[2] /ˈfjuːəl/ (present participle **fuelling**; past tense and past participle **fuelled**) verb [T] to make something increase or become worse: *People's fear of crime is fuelled by sensationalist reports.*

ˈfuel ˌcell noun [C] *technical* the piece of equipment that produces the power in an electric vehicle

fugitive /ˈfjuːdʒətɪv/ noun [C] someone who has done something that is illegal and is trying to avoid being caught by the police

fulfil /fʊlˈfɪl/ verb [T]

1 have purpose	**4** do sth promised
2 reach standard	**5** satisfy sb
3 achieve sth wanted	

1 to do a particular job, or to have a particular purpose: *The bus really fulfils a need for this community.* ♦ *The sports centre fulfils a necessary role in this town.* **2** to reach a particular standard or have the qualities that are necessary for something: *Do you fulfil the entry requirements for the course?* **3** to achieve something that you wanted to do, or to get something that you hoped for: *The journey fulfilled a lifelong dream.* ♦ *He never really fulfilled his potential* (=achieved as much as he could) *as a player.* **4** to do what you must do or what you have said you will do: *Landlords who refuse to fulfil their obligations may be liable to fines.* ♦ *The government has failed to fulfil its election promises.* **5** to make you happy and satisfied because you are using your skills and abilities: *This job doesn't really fulfil me.*

fulfill /fʊlˈfɪl/ the American spelling of **fulfil**

fulfilled /fʊlˈfɪld/ adj happy and satisfied because you are doing something important or are using your skills and abilities ≠ UNFULFILLED

fulfilling /fʊlˈfɪlɪŋ/ adj making you feel fulfilled: *a fulfilling career*

fulfillment /fʊlˈfɪlmənt/ the American spelling of **fulfilment**

fulfilment /fʊlˈfɪlmənt/ noun **1** [U] a feeling of happiness and satisfaction because you are doing something important or are using your skills and abilities: *Being a doctor gives me a real sense of fulfilment.* **2** [U] the act of doing or achieving something that is promised or expected: *Is there anything that might interfere with the fulfilment of your duties?* **3** [C/U] the act of something happening or being made to happen: *the fulfilment of a prediction*

full /fʊl/ adj ★★★

1 containing all that fits	**5** busy
2 unable to eat more	**6** body: large
3 complete	**+ PHRASES**
4 as much as possible	

1 containing the largest amount that will fit in a particular place ≠ EMPTY: *The petrol tank is almost full.* ♦ *a full car park* ♦ *This crisp packet is only half full.* ♦ *bins full of rubbish*
2 full or **full up** not wanting to eat any more because you have eaten a lot
3 complete: *full details/instructions* ♦ *She is expected to make a full recovery.* ♦ *Please give your full name and address.*
4 used for emphasizing that something is as loud, powerful, fast etc as possible: *He turned the radio on full volume.* ♦ *He drove at full speed along the road.*
5 busy: *a full day at the office* ♦ *She leads a*

F

very full life (=she takes part in many different activities).

6 if part of someone's body is full, it is large, wide, or has a round shape: *full lips*

PHRASES **be full of sth** to have or contain a lot of something: *Your trousers are full of holes!*

be full of yourself *informal* to be always talking about yourself or your achievements in a way that annoys other people

full of beans *old-fashioned* very lively and full of energy

in full completely, including the whole of something: *Fines must be paid in full within 30 days.*

to the full as much as possible: *My aim is to enjoy life to the full.*

,**full-'blown** adj in the most complete and developed form: *full-blown AIDS*

,**full 'board** noun [U] *British* a system in which you stay at a hotel and eat all your meals there

,**full-'fledged** adj *American* FULLY-FLEDGED

,**full-'grown** adj FULLY-GROWN

,**full 'house** noun [singular] a situation in which every seat is in a cinema, theatre, or sports STADIUM has someone sitting in it

,**full-'length** adj **1** a full-length coat, dress, or skirt goes down to your feet **2** a full-length mirror or picture shows someone's whole body including their feet **3** a full-length book, film etc is the normal length

,**full 'marks** noun [plural] *British* the highest score that a student can get in an examination: *She got full marks in French.*

,**full 'moon** noun [C] the moon when it looks like a complete circle

,**full-'on** adj *British* used for emphasizing that someone or something has a lot of a particular quality: *Things were developing into a full-on catastrophe.*

,**full-'page** adj printed on a whole page of a newspaper or magazine

'**full-scale** adj **1** complete, or not limited in any way: *a full-scale investigation into the murder* **2** a full-scale model or drawing of something is as big as the real thing

,**full 'stop** noun [C] *British* the mark . used in writing at the end of sentences and abbreviations

'**full-time** adj done or doing something for the number of hours that people normally work or study in a complete week: *a full-time student* ♦ *a full-time job* —**full-time** adv

fully /'fʊli/ adv ★★★ completely: *He was lying on the bed, fully dressed.* ♦ *I did not fully appreciate the seriousness of the situation.* ♦ *She still hasn't fully recovered from her shoulder injury.*

,**fully-'fledged** adj completely developed or trained

,**fully-'grown** adj a fully-grown person or animal has reached its biggest size and will not grow any more

fumble /'fʌmb(ə)l/ verb [I] to try to hold, move, or find something using your hands in a way that is not skilful or graceful

fume /fjuːm/ verb [I] **1** to be very angry **2** to send out smoke or gas

fumes /fjuːmz/ noun [plural] smoke or gas that

has an unpleasant smell and that may be harmful: *traffic/petrol fumes*

fumigate /'fjuːmɪˌgeɪt/ verb [T] to treat a place with smoke or with gas in order to kill bacteria or insects —**fumigation** /ˌfjuːmɪ'geɪʃ(ə)n/ noun [U]

fun¹ /fʌn/ noun [U] ★★ enjoyment from an activity that is not important or serious: *I hate to spoil your fun but it's time to go home now.* ♦ *We haven't had such fun for years.* ♦ *The kids had a lot of fun with that old tent.* ♦ *Do come – it'll be good fun.*

PHRASES **be no fun** or **not be any fun** to not be enjoyable: *It's no fun living on your own.*

for fun or **for the fun of it** because something is enjoyable or funny, not for any important or serious reason: *I swim every day for fun.*

in fun said or done as a joke, and not intended to annoy anyone: *The teasing was all in fun.*

make fun of to make jokes about someone or something in an unkind way: *The other children made fun of her because she was always so serious.*

fun² /fʌn/ adj enjoyable: *a fun day at a theme park*

■ **Funny** is used for talking about something or someone that makes you laugh: *He told a funny joke.* ♦ *She's one of the funniest people I know.* ♦ *Don't laugh; it isn't funny.*

■ **Fun** is used for talking about something that is enjoyable or someone that you enjoy being with: *Barcelona is a fun city.* ♦ *Our day at the beach was really fun.* ♦ *My sister is a fun person.*

function¹ /'fʌŋkʃ(ə)n/ noun ★★★

1 [C/U] a job that something is designed to do, or the duties or responsibilities that someone has in their job: *The function of advertising is to create a unique image for your company.*

2 [C] a social event such as a party: *an official function*

function² /'fʌŋkʃ(ə)n/ verb [I] to work or operate in a particular way: *We need to get this department functioning efficiently.*

PHRASAL VERB '**function as sth** to be used or work as something: *a phrase that functions as an adverb*

functional /'fʌŋkʃ(ə)nəl/ adj **1** designed to be effective, practical, and simple, with no unnecessary features or decorations **2** operating in the correct way

'**function ,key** noun [C] *computing* a special button on a computer keyboard that is used for a particular operation in a program

fund¹ /fʌnd/ noun ★★

1 [C] an amount of money that you collect, save, or invest: *an investment/pension fund*

2 funds [plural] money: *I'm a little low on funds just now.* ♦ *I'm not sure I can raise the funds for the holiday.*

→ FUNDING, TRUST FUND

fund² /fʌnd/ verb [T] to provide the money for something: *publicly funded legal services*

fundamental /ˌfʌndə'ment(ə)l/ adj ★★ relating to the basic nature or character of something: *a fundamental principle/difference* ♦ *There is a fundamental flaw in his argument.* ♦ *We* *shall have to make some **fundamental changes** in the way we do business.*

fundamentalism /ˌfʌndəˈment(ə)lɪz(ə)m/ noun [U] the belief that religious or political laws should be followed very strictly and should not be changed

fundamentalist /ˌfʌndəˈment(ə)lɪst/ noun [C] someone who believes that religious or political laws should be followed very strictly and should not be changed —**fundamentalist** adj

fundamentally /ˌfʌndəˈment(ə)li/ adv **1** in a very important or basic way: *His entire approach to the problem is fundamentally flawed.* **2** used for emphasizing the basic nature or character of something: *Fundamentally, she is a political writer.*

fundamentals, the /ˌfʌndəˈment(ə)lz/ noun [plural] the most basic and important aspects of something: *the fundamentals of classic French cookery*

funding /ˈfʌndɪŋ/ noun [U] money that a government or organization provides for a specific purpose

fundraiser /ˈfʌndreɪzə/ noun [C] a social event that is organized to make money for a CHARITY or political party

fundraising /ˈfʌndreɪzɪŋ/ noun [U] the activity of trying to persuade people or organizations to give money to a CHARITY or political party

funeral /ˈfjuːn(ə)rəl/ noun [C] ★ a ceremony that takes place after someone dies, and the formal process of taking the body to the place where it is buried or CREMATED: *He flew home to arrange for his father's funeral.* ♦ *a funeral service/procession*

funeral diˌrector noun [C] someone whose job is to organize funerals=UNDERTAKER

ˈfuneral ˌhome or **ˈfuneral ˌparlour** noun [C] a place where the body of a dead person is prepared and kept before a funeral

funfair /ˈfʌnˌfeə/ noun [C] *British* an event that is held outside at which people go on RIDES (=large machines that you ride on for pleasure) and play games to win prizes

fungus /ˈfʌŋɡəs/ (plural **fungi** /ˈfʌŋɡiː/ or **funguses**) noun [C/U] a type of plant without leaves, flowers, or green colour that grows in wet conditions or on decaying substances

funk /fʌŋk/ noun [U] a type of lively music with a strong beat that developed from SOUL and ROCK

funky /ˈfʌŋki/ adj **1** fashionable in a way that is unusual and that shows a lot of imagination **2** funky music has a strong simple beat that is good for dancing

funnel /ˈfʌn(ə)l/ noun [C] **1** a tube that is wide at the top and narrow at the bottom. It is used for pouring a liquid or powder into a container. **2** a tube that lets out smoke and steam from the engine of a boat or an old-fashioned train

funnily /ˈfʌnɪli/ adv in a strange or unusual way

PHRASE **funnily enough** *spoken* used for saying that you think that something is surprising or unusual: *Funnily enough, I heard someone say exactly the same thing this morning.*

funny /ˈfʌni/ adj ★★★
1 someone or something that is funny makes you laugh: *a funny story* ♦ *one of Britain's funniest comedians* ♦ *I don't think that's at all funny.* ♦ *Wouldn't it be funny if we played a trick on him?* → FUN
2 strange or unusual: *This tea tastes funny.* ♦ *You're in a funny mood today.* ♦ *That's funny – she was here a minute ago.*
PHRASE **feel funny** *informal* to feel slightly ill

Other ways of saying **funny**

- **amusing** funny in a way that makes you smile
- **comical/comic** funny and silly or strange
- **hilarious/hysterical** very funny
- **humorous** used for describing stories or remarks that are meant to be funny
- **light-hearted** dealing with a serious subject in a funny way that is meant to entertain people
- **witty** used for describing remarks that are funny and clever, or for describing people who often make remarks like this

fur /fɜː/ noun **1** [U] the soft hair that covers the body of some animals **2** [C/U] an animal skin that is covered with soft hair, used for making clothes: *a fur coat*

furious /ˈfjʊəriəs/ adj **1** extremely angry: *Rosie was absolutely furious that I'd borrowed her car without asking.* **2** done with a lot of speed, energy, or determination: *The game was played at a furious pace.* —**furiously** adv

furl /fɜːl/ verb [T] to fold or roll a piece of cloth or paper

furlong /ˈfɜːlɒŋ/ noun [C] a unit for measuring distance in horse races

furnace /ˈfɜːnɪs/ noun [C] a large enclosed container in which you burn fuel. It is used for heating a building or for an industrial process.

furnish /ˈfɜːnɪʃ/ verb [T] **1** to provide furniture for a room or house **2** to provide someone with something that they need, especially information: *Lyall's evidence may have furnished police with a vital clue.*

furnished /ˈfɜːnɪʃt/ adj a furnished house, flat, or room is one that you rent with furniture already in it ≠ UNFURNISHED

furnishings /ˈfɜːnɪʃɪŋz/ noun [plural] the things in a room such as furniture, carpets, and curtains

furniture /ˈfɜːnɪtʃə/ noun [U] ★★ the chairs, tables, beds, cupboards etc that you put in a room or house so that you can live in it: *modern/antique furniture*

Furniture is never used in the plural and cannot be used with a: *That's a lovely piece of furniture* (NOT *a lovely furniture*). ♦ *We don't need any more furniture for this room.* ♦ *I helped her to move some furniture.*

furore /fjʊˈrɔːri/ noun [singular] a lot of anger, excitement, or activity

furrow¹ /ˈfʌrəʊ/ noun [C] **1** a line that a farmer digs in the soil with a PLOUGH in order to grow plants **2** a deep line in the skin of someone's face

furrow² /ˈfʌrəʊ/ verb [I/T] if your BROW furrows, or if you furrow it, deep lines appear on your forehead

F

F

furry /'fɜːri/ adj covered with fur or with something like fur

further[1] /'fɜːðə/ grammar word ★★★

Further can be:
- an **adverb**: *She walked further up the hill.*
- used after the verb 'to be': *By road it's only six miles, but it's further if you follow the river.*
- an **adjective**: *Further details are available from the office.*

1 to or at a greater distance from a place: *I don't want to drive any further today.* ♦ *A little further ahead, you'll come to a crossroads.* ♦ *I would like to live further from the main road.* ♦ *Paul threw the ball further than Steve.*
2 additional: *I have nothing further to say on the subject.* ♦ *We need a further £10,000 to complete the work.*
3 more, or to a greater degree: *The situation was further complicated by Stuart's arrival.*
4 some time before or after a particular point: *His problems started a lot further back than his divorce.* ♦ *Six years further on and still there's been no decision.*
PHRASE **go further 1** to say or do something more extreme: *By sending Lister to prison, the judge went further than the law normally allows.* **2** to continue talking about something: *Before we go any further, shall we break for lunch?*
→ FAR, NOTICE[2]

further[2] /'fɜːðə/ verb [T] to help something to progress or to succeed: *efforts to further the peace process*

further edu`cation noun [U] *British* courses of study or training that some people do after they have left school when they do not go to university

furthermore /'fɜːðəˌmɔː/ adv *formal* used before adding another statement to what you have just said: *What you did was extremely irresponsible. Furthermore, it achieved nothing.*

furthest /'fɜːðɪst/ adj, adv **1** at the greatest distance from something: *My car is parked in the space furthest away from the building.* **2** most distant: *Merlin's fame had spread to the furthest corners of the land.* **3** the longest distance: *Trevor travelled furthest to get here.* → FAR

furtive /'fɜːtɪv/ adj done quickly and secretly in order to avoid being noticed: *a furtive glance* —**furtively** adv

fury /'fjʊəri/ noun [singular/U] **1** a feeling of very strong anger: *She was speechless with fury.* **2** the noise and force of a strong wind, storm, or flood

fuse[1] /fjuːz/ noun [C] **1** an object in electrical equipment that makes it stop working when there is too much electricity flowing through it **2** an object like string, or a piece of electrical equipment, that is used for making a bomb explode

fuse[2] /fjuːz/ verb [I/T] **1** *British* if a piece of electrical equipment fuses, or if you fuse it, it stops working because of a sudden increase in the electric current: *All the lights downstairs have fused.* **2** to join two substances together to form one thing, or to become joined together in this way

fuselage /'fjuːzəˌlɑːʒ/ noun [C] the main part of an aircraft that the wings are fixed to

fusion /'fjuːʒ(ə)n/ noun [C/U] a process in which different things combine to form something new

fuss[1] /fʌs/ noun [singular/U] unnecessary worry or excitement about something: *What is all the fuss about?*
PHRASE **make a fuss of** to give a person or animal a lot of attention in order to show that you love them

fuss[2] /fʌs/ verb [I] to behave in a way that shows that you are nervous or worried, especially about unimportant things
PHRASAL VERB **fuss over sb/sth** to give a person or animal a lot of attention in order to show that you love them

fussy /'fʌsi/ adj **1** only satisfied if things are exactly as you want them to be **2** containing too many small parts or details

futile /'fjuːtaɪl/ adj certain to fail or be unsuccessful: *a futile attempt* —**futility** /fjuː'tɪləti/ noun [U]

futon /'fuːtɒn/ noun [C] a type of firm MATTRESS, used as a bed or SOFA

future[1] /'fjuːtʃə/ noun ★★★
1 the future [singular] the time that follows the present time: *It's important to plan for the future.* ♦ *Check if the computer can be upgraded in the future.* ♦ *I have no plans to go abroad in the near future.*
2 [C] the things that will happen to someone or something after the present time: *Jack went on holiday to think about his future.* ♦ *The people of this village face an uncertain future.*
3 [C] the chance that something will continue to exist or be successful: *We see no future in continuing the negotiations.*
4 the future [singular] *linguistics* the FUTURE TENSE of a verb
PHRASE **in future** from the present time continuing forwards in time: *In future, please ask before you borrow my clothes.*
→ FORESEEABLE

future[2] /'fjuːtʃə/ adj ★★★
1 expected to exist or happen during the time following the present time: *at some future date* ♦ *future developments* ♦ *We need to protect the countryside for future generations.* ♦ *his future wife* (=the woman he is going to marry)
2 *linguistics* relating to the FUTURE TENSE of a verb
PHRASE **for future reference 1** so that you can find some information in the future: *Keep this document for future reference.* **2** used for telling someone something that you feel they should know, often when you are slightly annoyed with them: *For future reference, I expect all employees to be on time.*

future `perfect, the noun [singular] *linguistics* the verb tense that is used for showing that an action will be finished at a particular time in the future, as in 'He will have finished the work by Friday.'

future `tense, the noun [singular] *linguistics* the verb tense that is used for talking about future time

futuristic /ˌfjuːtʃə'rɪstɪk/ adj very modern in a way that seems to belong to the future

fuzz /fʌz/ noun [U] a lot of short soft hairs or fibres like hairs

fuzzy /ˈfʌzi/ adj **1** a fuzzy picture or image is not clear so that you cannot see all its details **2** covered with short soft hairs or fibres like hair

FYI abbrev for your information: used in emails and TEXT MESSAGES as a way of introducing a useful piece of information

G g

g¹ or **G** /dʒiː/ noun [C/U] the seventh letter of the English alphabet

g² abbrev gram

G /dʒiː/ noun [C] science gravity: a measurement of the force of GRAVITY

gabble /ˈɡæb(ə)l/ verb [I/T] informal to talk very quickly in a way that is difficult for people to understand

gable /ˈɡeɪb(ə)l/ noun [C] the top part of a wall of a building just below the roof. A gable is shaped like a TRIANGLE.

gadget /ˈɡædʒɪt/ noun [C] a small tool or piece of equipment that does something that is useful or impressive

Gaelic /ˈɡeɪlɪk, ˈɡælɪk/ noun [U] a Celtic language that people speak in parts of Scotland and Ireland —**Gaelic** adj

gag¹ /ɡæɡ/ verb **1** [T] to tie a piece of cloth over someone's mouth so that they cannot speak or make a noise **2** [T] to officially prevent someone from talking about or publishing something **3** [I] informal to be unable to swallow because you feel as if you are going to VOMIT (=bring food back up from your stomach)

gag² /ɡæɡ/ noun [C] **1** informal a joke, trick, or story that makes people laugh **2** a piece of cloth that you tie over someone's mouth in order to stop them from speaking or making a noise

gaggle /ˈɡæɡ(ə)l/ noun [C] **1** informal a noisy and uncontrolled group of people **2** a group of GEESE

gaily /ˈɡeɪli/ adv in a happy and lively way

gain¹ /ɡeɪn/ verb ★★★
1 [T] to get or achieve something, usually as a result of a lot of effort: Bolivia gained independence from Spain in 1825. ♦ Her theories have only recently gained acceptance. ♦ He gained entry to the building by showing a fake pass.
2 [T] to get more of something, usually as a result of a gradual process: I've gained a lot of weight this winter. ♦ The property has gained steadily in value since they bought it. ♦ gain sth from/by (doing) sth She hopes to gain experience by working abroad for a year.
3 [I/T] to get a benefit or advantage for yourself: Even if you fail, you are sure to gain from the experience. ♦ When the business is sold, all the brothers stand to gain (=are likely to benefit).

PHRASE **gain ground** to become more successful, popular, or accepted
PHRASAL VERB **gain on sb/sth** to gradually get closer to someone or something that you are trying to catch

gain² /ɡeɪn/ noun **1** [C/U] an improvement or increase in something: We have seen impressive gains in productivity over the last 12 months. **2** [C] a benefit or advantage: It is a policy that will bring significant gains to all sections of the community. **3** [U] the money or other benefits that you can get from something: He entered politics only for personal gain. → ILL-GOTTEN GAINS

gait /ɡeɪt/ noun [singular] the way that someone walks

gala /ˈɡɑːlə/ noun [C] **1** a special performance or event that celebrates something **2** British a sports competition

galaxy /ˈɡæləksi/ noun [C] an extremely large group of stars and planets —**galactic** /ɡəˈlæktɪk/ adj

gale /ɡeɪl/ noun [C] a very strong wind

gall /ɡɔːl/ noun [U] an attitude towards other people that shows a lack of respect: He had the gall to call me a bad parent!

gallant /ˈɡælənt/ adj **1** literary brave **2** a gallant effort, attempt, or fight is one in which you try very hard, but do not succeed **3** /ˈɡælənt, ɡəˈlænt/ old-fashioned a man who is gallant treats women in an extremely polite and helpful way —**gallantly** adv

gall bladder noun [C] the organ in your body that stores BILE

gallery /ˈɡæləri/ noun [C] **1** a public building where you can look at paintings and other works of art **2** an upper level in a building such as a church or court

galley /ˈɡæli/ noun [C] **1** the kitchen on a boat or plane **2** a long ancient Greek or Roman ship that used sails and SLAVES with OARS to move it

gallon /ˈɡælən/ noun [C] a unit for measuring an amount of liquid, equal to 4.55 litres

gallop /ˈɡæləp/ verb [I] if a horse gallops, it runs at its fastest speed —**gallop** noun [singular]

gallows /ˈɡæləʊz/ (plural **gallows**) noun [C] a wooden frame that is used for hanging criminals as a way of killing them

galore /ɡəˈlɔː/ adj used for emphasizing how large an amount or quantity is: There will be competitions galore, with terrific holidays to be won.

galvanize /ˈɡælvənaɪz/ verb [T] to shock or affect someone enough to produce a strong and immediate reaction

gambit /ˈɡæmbɪt/ noun [C] something that you say or do in an attempt to gain an advantage

gamble¹ /ˈɡæmb(ə)l/ verb [I/T] **1** to risk money in the hope of winning more if you are lucky: We used to gamble at the casino in Monte Carlo. **2** to do something that involves risks but may result in benefits if things happen as you hope they will: Some foreign investors are gambling on an *economic recovery.* —**gambler** noun [C], **gambling** noun [U]

gamble² /ˈgæmb(ə)l/ noun [singular] an action or plan that involves risks but will bring benefits if it is successful

game¹ /geɪm/ noun ★★★

1 activity you do for fun	**5** sports played at school
2 type of sport	**6** hunted animals etc
3 particular competition	**7** sth not important
4 major sports event	**+ PHRASES**

1 [C] an activity that you take part in for fun, usually one that has rules: *Monopoly is a game for all the family.* ♦ *The children were **playing** noisy **games** in the garden.* ♦ *computer/video games*
2 [C] a type of sport: *They take **the game** of cricket very seriously here.*
3 [C] a particular event in which people take part in a competition: *He won the money in a poker game.* ♦ *Let's **have a game** of volleyball.*
4 games [plural] an event where people from different countries compete in sports such as running, jumping, and swimming: *the Olympic Games*
5 games [singular] *British* sports that children play at school: *Miss Plumtree takes us for games.*
6 [U] wild animals, birds, and fish that people hunt, usually for food
7 [C] an activity or situation that someone seems to be treating less seriously than it should be treated: *Marriage is just a game to them.* ♦ *They are **playing** political **games** with people's safety.*
PHRASES give the game away to let people know a secret when you did not intend to let them know: *The expression on her face gave the game away.*
what's your/his/her game? *spoken* used for asking someone what their true intentions are when you think that they are not being honest
→ BALL GAME, BOARD GAME, FAIR GAME, NAME¹

game² /geɪm/ adj prepared to try a new, difficult, or dangerous activity: *'Do you want to try it?' 'I'm game if you are.'*

gamekeeper /ˈgeɪmˌkiːpə/ noun [C] someone whose job is to look after the wild animals, birds, and fish on a piece of private land

game show noun [C] a television programme in which people play games or answer questions in order to win prizes

gammon /ˈgæmən/ noun [U] *British* a type of HAM (=cooked meat from a pig's leg) that you eat hot

gamut /ˈgæmət/ noun [singular] the complete range of things of a particular type

gander /ˈgændə/ noun [C] a male GOOSE

gang¹ /gæŋ/ noun [C] **1** a group of young people who spend time together and often cause trouble: *a study of Chicago street gangs* **2** a group of criminals working together: *a gang of thieves* **3** *informal* a group of friends

gang² /gæŋ/ **PHRASAL VERB gang up on sb** to join together in a group in order to hurt, frighten, or fight someone

gangland /ˈgæŋlænd/ adj relating to organized criminal activities, or to the people who are involved in them

gangling /ˈgæŋglɪŋ/ or **gangly** /ˈgæŋgli/ adj very tall and thin, and not graceful

gangster /ˈgæŋstə/ noun [C] a member of an organized group of criminals

gangway /ˈgæŋweɪ/ noun [C] a space between two sets of seats

gaol /dʒeɪl/ a British spelling of **jail¹**

gap /gæp/ noun [C] ★★
1 a space or opening in the middle of something or between things: *He has **a gap** between his teeth.* ♦ *We waited for **a gap** in the busy traffic and crossed the road.*
2 something missing from a situation or a system that prevents it from being complete or perfect: *There are still some **gaps** in our knowledge.*
3 a large difference between things or groups: *the **gap** between rich and poor*
4 a period of time in which something does not happen: *The second book in the series came out after **a gap** of seven years.*
PHRASE a gap in the market an opportunity to produce something that is not yet available but that people would like to have

gape /geɪp/ verb [I] **1** to look at someone or something with your mouth open because you are very surprised **2** to open wide, or to be wide open: *The mouth of the bag gaped open.*

gaping /ˈgeɪpɪŋ/ adj a gaping hole is very large

garage /ˈgærɑːʒ, ˈgærɪdʒ/ noun ★
1 [C] a building for keeping a car in —*picture* → C1
2 [C] a place that repairs or sells cars
3 [C] a place where you go to buy petrol =PETROL STATION
4 [U] a type of US dance music that developed in the 1980s

garb /gɑːb/ noun [U] *formal* clothes: *military/formal/work garb*

garbage /ˈgɑːbɪdʒ/ noun [U] **1** *informal* something that someone says or writes that is completely false, silly, or wrong **2** waste material that you are throwing away, for example food that you do not want or empty containers

garbled /ˈgɑːb(ə)ld/ adj not correctly organized or explained, and difficult to understand: *a garbled explanation/message*

garden¹ /ˈgɑːd(ə)n/ noun ★★★
1 [C] *British* an area of land next to a house that belongs to the house, usually with grass and plants growing in it: *The children were playing in the back garden.* ♦ *a garden path/gate/shed* —*picture* → C1
2 gardens [plural] a large area of grass, flowers, and trees that is open to the public for their enjoyment: *They spent the afternoon wandering around the Botanical Gardens.*

garden² /ˈgɑːd(ə)n/ verb [I] to look after a garden and its plants —**gardener** noun [C]

garden centre noun [C] a place that sells plants and the tools and equipment that you need for looking after a garden

gardening /ˈgɑːd(ə)nɪŋ/ noun [U] the activity of looking after a garden

garden party noun [C] a formal party in a large garden

G

garden 'shed noun [C] a small building for storing garden tools, bicycles, and other equipment —*picture* → C1

gargle /'gɑːg(ə)l/ verb [I] to move liquid around in the back of your mouth, in order to clean your mouth and throat

garish /'geərɪʃ/ adj very bright and colourful in an ugly way

garland /'gɑːlənd/ noun [C] a ring of flowers or leaves that you decorate something with

garlic /'gɑːlɪk/ noun [U] a round white vegetable that is made up of sections. You use the sections in cooking in order to give it a strong flavour. —*picture* → C11

garment /'gɑːmənt/ noun [C] *formal* a piece of clothing

garnish /'gɑːnɪʃ/ noun [C] something that you add to a dish of food to make it look more attractive —**garnish** verb [T]

garrison /'gærɪs(ə)n/ noun [C] a group of soldiers who live in a particular place and defend it

gas¹ /gæs/ noun ★★★
  1 [C/U] a substance such as air that is neither a solid nor a liquid: *gases such as carbon dioxide*
  2 [U] a gas that is burned as fuel, for example to heat your house or cook food: *Can you smell gas?* ♦ *a gas cooker/heater/boiler* ♦ *She couldn't pay her gas bill.*
  3 [U] *American* PETROL

gas² /gæs/ verb [T] to attack or kill someone by making them breathe a poisonous gas

gas 'chamber noun [C] a room that is used for killing prisoners by filling the air with a poisonous gas

gash /gæʃ/ noun [C] a long deep cut in your skin or in the surface of something —**gash** verb [T]

gas ˌmask noun [C] a special covering for your face that protects you from a poisonous gas

gasoline /'gæsəˌliːn/ noun [C/U] *American* PETROL

gasp /gɑːsp/ verb [I] **1** to breathe in suddenly because you are surprised, shocked, or in pain: *He gasped as the freezing water hit his body.* **2** to make a violent effort to breathe because you need more air: *Laura coughed and spluttered as she gasped for air.* —**gasp** noun [C]: *a gasp of pain/surprise/relief*

gas ˌstation noun [C] *American* a PETROL STATION

gastric /'gæstrɪk/ adj *medical* relating to your stomach

gastronomic /ˌgæstrə'nɒmɪk/ adj *formal* relating to skilful methods of cooking food, or to the enjoyment of good food

gate /geɪt/ noun [C] ★★
  1 a door in a fence or wall that you go through in order to enter or leave a place: *Be sure to close the gate when you leave.* —*picture* → C1
  2 the place at an airport where people get on a plane: *Delta Airlines Flight 17 to New York is now boarding at Gate 21.*

gateau /'gætəʊ/ (plural **gateaux** /'gætəʊz/) noun [C/U] *British* a large cake that is decorated or filled with sweet foods such as fruit, cream, and chocolate

gatecrash /'geɪtˌkræʃ/ verb [I/T] *British* to go to

a party or other social event although you have not been invited —**gatecrasher** noun [C]

gateway /'geɪtweɪ/ noun [C] **1** an entrance that is opened and closed with a gate **2 a gateway to sth** a way of going somewhere or doing something: *Stranraer is the gateway to the whole of Ireland.* **3** *computing* a way of connecting two computer NETWORKS so that information can pass between them

gather /'gæðə/ verb ★★

1 come together	4 increase
2 find information	5 bring things together
3 find things you need	6 believe sth

  1 [I/T] if people gather, or if someone gathers them, they come together in one place in order to do something: *She gathered her children and ran for shelter.* ♦ *A crowd gathered outside the hotel.*
  2 [T] to look for and find information or documents in different places: *The information has been gathered from all parts of the country.* ♦ *The police have been gathering evidence against him.*
  3 [T] to search for and find similar things that you need or want: *Bees were gathering pollen.*
  4 [T] if something gathers force, speed, or strength, its force, speed, or strength increases: *The train pulled away slowly, then gathered speed.*
  5 [T] to bring things closer together, for example in order to protect something or make it tidy: *She gathered her hair into a knot at the back of her head.*
  6 [I/T] to believe that something is true, although no one has directly told you about it: *From what I can gather she's madly in love with him.* ♦ *I gather that the storm caused a power failure.*

gathering /'gæðərɪŋ/ noun [C] a group of people meeting together: *a large social/family gathering*

gaudy /'gɔːdi/ adj brightly coloured and ugly or of bad quality

gauge¹ /geɪdʒ/ noun [C] **1** a piece of equipment that measures the amount of something: *the fuel/pressure gauge* **2** a measurement of how thick or wide something is, or of how far apart two things are: *heavy-gauge plastic* **3** a fact or event that can be used for judging someone or something: *New orders are a gauge of how well manufacturers are doing.*

gauge² /geɪdʒ/ verb [T] **1** to make a judgment or guess about something using the information that you have: *He looked at her, trying to gauge her response.* **2** to measure the amount, strength, or speed of something

gaunt /gɔːnt/ adj looking very thin, tired, and not healthy

gauntlet /'gɔːntlət/ noun [C] a thick heavy GLOVE that you wear to protect your hand and lower arm
  PHRASES **run the gauntlet** to experience a difficult situation, for example a lot of questions, criticism, or attacks
  throw down the gauntlet to make it clear that you want to argue or fight with someone about something

gauze /gɔːz/ noun [U] white cotton cloth that

G

is very thin and has been woven in a loose way. It is often used for covering a cut or an injury.

gave the past tense of **give**

gawp /gɔːp/ verb [I] *British informal* to look at someone or something for a long time in a rude or stupid way

gay¹ /geɪ/ adj **1** sexually attracted to people of the same sex **2** *old-fashioned* brightly-coloured, or attractive **3** *old-fashioned* happy and excited

> **Words that avoid giving offence: gay**
>
> Use **gay** to describe men who are sexually attracted to other men. Avoid using **gay** as a noun, especially in the singular. **Gay** can also be used about women who are sexually attracted to other women, but the more usual word is **lesbian**.

gay² /geɪ/ noun [C] someone who is sexually attracted to people of the same sex

gaze¹ /geɪz/ verb [I] to look at someone or something for a long time: *They gazed into each other's eyes.*

gaze² /geɪz/ noun [singular] a look at someone or something that lasts for a long time: *His gaze remained fixed on her face.*

GB abbrev **1** gigabyte **2** Great Britain

GCSE /ˌdʒiː siː es ˈiː/ noun [C] General Certificate of Secondary Education: an examination that is taken by students in England and Wales, usually at the age of 15 or 16

GDP /ˌdʒiː diː ˈpiː/ noun [C] gross domestic product: the total value of the goods and services that a country produces in a year. It does not include income that is received from money that is invested in other countries. → GNP

gear¹ /gɪə/ noun ★
1 [C/U] the part of an engine that changes engine power into movement: *in first/second/third gear* ♦ *Helen changed gear as she approached the junction.*
2 [U] the special clothes and equipment that you use for a particular activity: *We took down the tent and packed all the gear away.* ♦ *The police were dressed in riot gear.* ♦ *Don't forget to bring walking gear.*
3 [U] a machine, or a part of a machine, that does a particular job: *heavy lifting gear*

gear² /gɪə/ verb [I/T] **be geared to/towards/for** to be organized in a way that is suitable for a particular person or thing: *The museum is geared towards children.*
> PHRASAL VERB **gear (yourself) up** to prepare for an activity or event: *The town is gearing up for the carnival this weekend.*

gearbox /ˈgɪəbɒks/ noun [C] a metal box that contains the gears of a vehicle, or the system of gears itself

gear ˌstick or **gear ˌlever** noun [C] *British* the part in a car that a driver uses to change GEAR —*picture* → C6

geek /giːk/ noun [C] *informal* someone who is boring, strange, or seems to be interested only in computers —**geeky** adj

geese the plural of **goose**

gel¹ /dʒel/ noun [C/U] a sticky substance that is used in products for your hair and skin

gel² /dʒel/ verb [I] **1** if a group gels, the people in it form a successful or friendly relationship **2** if a thought or idea gels, it becomes clearer **3** if a substance gels it becomes thicker

gelatine /ˈdʒelətɪn/ noun [U] a clear substance that is used in cooking for making liquids thick and firm

gem /dʒem/ noun [C] **1** a valuable stone that is used to make jewellery **2** someone or something that is special in some way: *a gem of an idea*

Gemini /ˈdʒemɪnaɪ/ noun [C/U] one of the 12 signs of the ZODIAC. A **Gemini** is someone who was born between May 22 and June 21.

gender /ˈdʒendə/ noun **1** [C/U] *formal* the fact of being either male or female =SEX: *The job is open to all applicants regardless of age, race, or gender.* **2** [C] all male people, or all female people =SEX: *the entire male gender* **3** [C/U] *linguistics* the gender of a word is whether it is MASCULINE, FEMININE, or NEUTER

gene /dʒiːn/ noun [C] *science* a pattern of chemicals within a cell. The chemicals carry information about the qualities that are passed from parent animals, plants, or organisms to their children.

general¹ /ˈdʒen(ə)rəl/ adj ★★★
1 not specific, exact, or detailed: *Could you just give us a general description of the work you do?* ♦ *I'm probably not making myself very clear, but you get the general idea.*
2 involving or true for most people, things, or situations: *There was general agreement at the meeting that the plan was too expensive.* ♦ *The fighting could escalate into a more general war.* ♦ *As a general rule, shorter sentences are easier to understand.*
3 used for describing the whole of something, without considering the details: *Your general health seems very good.*
4 dealing with all areas of a subject or activity, rather than concentrating on a particular area: *a good general introduction to the subject* ♦ *general knowledge*
> PHRASE **in general 1** in most situations or for most people: *I don't think people in general give much thought to the environment.* **2** as a whole, without giving details: *In general, the standard of your work is very high.*

general² /ˈdʒen(ə)rəl/ noun [C] an officer of high rank in the army or air force

general anaesˈthetic noun [C/U] a substance that a doctor puts into your body so that you will sleep and not feel any pain during an operation

general eˈlection noun [C] an election in which every adult in the country can vote for the people who will represent them

generalization /ˌdʒen(ə)rəlaɪˈzeɪʃ(ə)n/ noun [C/U] a statement that seems to be true in most situations but that may not be true in all situations

generalize /ˈdʒen(ə)rəlaɪz/ verb [I] **1** to make a statement or remark about a group of people or things without giving details: *We can generalize and say that most of our students are middle-class.* **2** to give an opinion about a group of people or things that is often unfair, because it makes them all seem the same when they are not

generally /ˈdʒen(ə)rəli/ adv ★★★
1 used for saying what is usually true or typical: *The food is generally pretty good in this restaurant.*
2 by most people, or in most instances: *Scientists generally agree that the new disease is caused by a virus.* ♦ *The church is generally accepted as one of the world's greatest buildings.*
3 used for describing or considering something as a whole, without details: *His attitude to me was generally unfriendly.*
→ SPEAK

,general prac'titioner noun [C] a doctor who is a GP

,general 'public, the noun ★ ordinary people in society, rather than a particular group

> In British English, **the general public** can be used with a singular or plural verb. You can say *The general public **has** shown a lot of interest.* OR *The general public **have** shown a lot of interest.*

,general 'strike noun [C] a situation in which most or all workers stop working in order to try to get better working conditions or higher pay

generate /ˈdʒenəˌreɪt/ verb [T] ★★
1 to produce something, or to cause something to exist: *The food processing industry generates billions of dollars a year.* ♦ *These new policies will generate jobs.*
2 to make people express feelings or opinions about something: *The advertising campaign generated a lot of interest in our work.*
3 to produce power or heat: *75% of France's electricity is generated by nuclear reactors.*

generation /ˌdʒenəˈreɪʃ(ə)n/ noun ★★★
1 [C] all the people, a group of people, or the members of a family who are born and live around the same time: *The site was preserved as a monument for future generations.* ♦ *Many people from her generation still remember the war.* ♦ *a candidate that appeals mainly to the **older/younger generation** (=the people in society at a particular time who are old or young) ♦ **Generations of** schoolchildren have sat at these desks.*
2 [C] the number of years that usually pass between someone's birth and the birth of their children: *Within a generation, the family had lost all its wealth.*
3 [C] a group of products that were made at about the same time: *a new generation of mobile phones*
4 [U] the process of producing something: *cheap electricity generation*

gene'ration ,gap, the noun [singular] the difference in opinions or behaviour between older and younger people

generator /ˈdʒenəˌreɪtə/ noun [C] a machine that produces electricity

generic /dʒəˈnerɪk/ adj *formal* relating to, or suitable for, a particular group of similar things —**generically** /dʒəˈnerɪkli/ adv

generosity /ˌdʒenəˈrɒsəti/ noun [U] kindness in giving things to people

generous /ˈdʒenərəs/ adj ★
1 giving people more of your time or money

than is usual or expected: *She is a warm and generous human being.* ♦ **generous of sb (to do sth)** *That's very generous of you.*
2 larger than is usual or necessary: *a generous helping of chips*
—**generously** adv

genetic /dʒəˈnetɪk/ adj ★ relating to genes or to the study of them: *a genetic disease* ♦ *We inherit **genetic characteristics** from our parents.* —**genetically** /dʒəˈnetɪkli/ adv

genetically modified /dʒəˌnetɪkli ˈmɒdɪˌfaɪd/ adj *see* **GM**

ge,netic engin'eering noun [U] the practice or science of changing the genes of a living thing

geneticist /dʒəˈnetɪsɪst/ noun [C] a scientist who studies or works in genetics

genetics /dʒəˈnetɪks/ noun [U] the study of how features of living things are passed through their genes to their children

genial /ˈdʒiːniəl/ adj friendly and kind

genitals /ˈdʒenɪt(ə)lz/ noun [plural] the outer sex organs of a person or animal —**genital** adj

genius /ˈdʒiːniəs/ noun **1** [C] someone who is much more intelligent or skilful than other people **2** [U] a very high level of intelligence or skill: *At the time, his appointment seemed like a **stroke of genius** (=a very intelligent act or idea).*

genocide /ˈdʒenəˌsaɪd/ noun [U] the murder of large numbers of people belonging to a particular race

genome /ˈdʒiːˌnəʊm/ noun [C] *science* the complete set of genes in a living thing

genre /ˈʒɒnrə/ noun [C] a particular type of film, writing, or art, that can be recognized by specific features

genteel /dʒenˈtiːl/ adj polite and typical of people belonging to a high social class

gentle /ˈdʒent(ə)l/ adj ★
1 kind and calm: *Joe is such a gentle, loving boy.*
2 not using or needing a lot of force or effort: *gentle exercise*
3 not strong or unpleasant: *a gentle breeze* ♦ *a gentle voice*
4 a gentle slope or curve is gradual, with no sudden changes
—**gently** adj

gentleman /ˈdʒent(ə)lmən/ (plural **gentlemen** /ˈdʒent(ə)lmən/) noun [C] ★
1 a polite honest man who thinks about what other people want or need
2 used for referring politely to a man whose name you do not know: *Please could you call a taxi for this gentleman?*

gentrification /ˌdʒentrɪfɪˈkeɪʃ(ə)n/ noun [U] the process by which an area where poor people lived becomes an area where middle-class people live, as they buy the houses and repair them —**gentrify** /ˈdʒentrɪˌfaɪ/ verb [T]

gentry, the /ˈdʒentri/ noun [plural] people from a high social class

gents, the /ˈdʒents/ noun [singular] *British* the men's toilet in a public place

genuine /ˈdʒenjuɪn/ adj ★
1 real, and not pretended or false ≠ FAKE: *Morley looked at her with genuine concern.* ♦ *a genuine 18th century desk*

2 honest, friendly, and sincere: *Greg was a humble, genuine person.*
—**genuinely** adv

genus /ˈdʒiːnəs, ˈdʒenəs/ noun [C] *science* a group that includes all living things that have similar features → SPECIES

geographical /ˌdʒiːəˈgræfɪk(ə)l/ or **geographic** /ˌdʒiːəˈgræfɪk/ adj relating to an area or place, or to geography
—**geographically** /ˌdʒiːəˈgræfɪkli/ adv

geography /dʒiˈɒgrəfi/ noun [U] the study of the Earth's physical features and the people, plants, and animals that live in different regions of the world —**geographer** noun [C]

G

geology /dʒiˈɒlədʒi/ noun [U] the scientific study of the structure of the Earth
—**geological** /ˌdʒiːəˈlɒdʒɪk(ə)l/ adj, **geologist** noun [C]

geometric /ˌdʒiːəˈmetrɪk/ or **geometrical** /ˌdʒiːəˈmetrɪk(ə)l/ adj **1** relating to geometry **2** relating to simple or regular shapes

geometry /dʒiˈɒmətri/ noun [U] the part of mathematics that deals with the relationships between lines, angles, and surfaces

geranium /dʒəˈreɪniəm/ noun [C] a plant with soft round leaves and bright pink, red, or white flowers —*picture* → C9

geriatric /ˌdʒeriˈætrɪk/ adj *medical* relating to old age, or to the process of getting older

geriatrics /ˌdʒeriˈætrɪks/ noun [U] the medical study, treatment, and care of old people and their diseases

germ /dʒɜːm/ noun **1** [C] a form of bacteria that spreads disease **2** [singular] something that could develop into a greater idea or plan: *the germ of an idea*

German ˈmeasles noun [U] an infectious disease that causes red spots on the skin
=RUBELLA

germinate /ˈdʒɜːmɪˌneɪt/ verb [I/T] to develop from a seed and begin to grow into a plant, or to make a seed begin to grow
—**germination** /ˌdʒɜːmɪˈneɪʃ(ə)n/ noun [U]

gerund /ˈdʒerənd/ noun [C] *linguistics* a noun that is formed from a verb by adding '-ing'. A gerund describes an action, for example 'running' or 'believing'. =VERBAL NOUN

gestation /dʒeˈsteɪʃ(ə)n/ noun [U] the time and process during which a baby develops inside its mother

gesticulate /dʒeˈstɪkjʊˌleɪt/ verb [I] to make movements with your hands and arms when you are talking

gesture¹ /ˈdʒestʃə/ noun [C] ★
1 a movement that communicates a feeling or instruction: *an impatient gesture* ♦ *Joan raised her arms in a gesture of triumph.*
2 something that you do to communicate your intentions: *Offering to drive us there was a very nice gesture.* ♦ *a gesture of support*

gesture² /ˈdʒestʃə/ verb [I] to make a movement in order to communicate something to someone

get /get/ (past tense **got** /gɒt/; past participle **got**) verb ★★★

1 obtain/receive	**13** send sth
2 buy sth	**14** make progress
3 bring sth	**15** fit/put sth in a place
4 think/feel sth	**16** understand
5 start to be ill	**17** be able to do sth
6 start to be	**18** catch/punish sb
7 be/become	**19** answer door/phone
8 cause to be	**20** use particular vehicle
9 do sth/have sth done	**21** talk to sb by phone
10 make sb do sth	**22** prepare meal
11 move to/from	+ PHRASAL VERBS
12 arrive	

1 [T] to obtain, receive, or be given something: *Ross's father got a new job.* ♦ *Did you get tickets for the game?* ♦ *You get ten points for each correct answer.* ♦ *Young players will* **get the chance** *to meet one of their heroes.* ♦ **get sth from sb** *She got a ring from her grandmother.* ♦ **get sb sth** *The social worker got the family a new flat.*
2 [T] to buy something: *They had to stop and get some petrol.* ♦ **get sb sth/get sth for sb** *I got my dad a sweater for his birthday.*
3 [T] to go and bring something back from somewhere else: *She went and got a photograph from the desk.* ♦ **get sb sth/get sth for sb** *Will you get me a glass of water?*
4 [T] to start to have an idea or feeling: *I got a strange feeling as we walked towards the house.* ♦ *I* **got the impression** *they were finding the work difficult.*
5 [T] to start to have an illness or a medical condition: *I hope I don't get the flu this winter.*
6 [linking verb] to start to be in a particular state, or to start to have a particular quality =BECOME: *It's getting late – I have to go.* ♦ *It was raining and we all got wet.* ♦ *Things are starting to get a bit difficult at home.*
7 [linking verb] to be or become: used with past participles to form PASSIVES: *I'm sick of getting shouted at for things that aren't my fault.* ♦ *Somehow the paper got ripped.* ♦ *You should wash that cut – it might get infected.*
8 [T] to cause someone or something to be in a particular state: *I'll get the children dressed.* ♦ *It took them three hours to get the fire under control.* ♦ *He got his suit all dirty.*
9 [T] to do something, or to have it done for you: **get sth done** *You need to get your hair cut.* ♦ *I should be able to get the first chapter finished by tonight.* ♦ **get sth doing sth** *Hal managed to get my email working again.*
10 [T] to make someone do something, or to persuade them to do it: **get sb to do sth** *I'll get Andrew to give you a call.* ♦ *She couldn't get them to understand what she was saying.*
11 [I/T] to move to or from a position or place, or to make someone or something do this: *Dad stopped the car and told me to get in.* ♦ *A car stopped and two men got out.* ♦ *Half the audience got up and walked out.* ♦ **get sb/sth in/into sth** *Let's get you into the house where it's warm.* ♦ **get sb/sth out (of sth)** *Get that dog out of my kitchen.*
12 [I] to arrive at a place: *What time did you get home last night?* ♦ *When will we get there?* ♦ *How long does it take to get from*

London to Leeds? ♦ *I usually get to work at about 8.30.* → ARRIVE

13 [T] to send something to a person or place: **get sth to sb/sth** *We'll get the timetable to you as soon as we have it.*

14 [I] to make progress: *How far did you get with your homework?* ♦ *I'm not getting anywhere with this essay* (=not making any progress). ♦ *At last she is starting to get somewhere in her career* (=make some progress). ♦ *Everyone finds driving difficult at first, but you're getting there* (=making progress).

15 [T] **get sth into/in/onto sth** to fit or put something in a place: *You can get a lot of things into this bag.*

16 [T] *informal* to understand someone or something: *Everyone laughed, but Harold didn't seem to get the joke.* ♦ *I don't get it – what's happening?*

17 [I/T] to have the opportunity or be able to do something: **get to do sth** *Did you get to visit the Louvre when you were in Paris?*

18 [T] to catch or punish someone: *The police need to get the person who did this.*

19 [T] *spoken* to answer the door or phone: *It's OK, I'll get it.*

20 [T] to use a particular means to travel somewhere: *It's easiest if you get a taxi from the station.*

21 [T] to succeed in talking to someone by phone: *Is there a number where I can get you this evening?*

22 [T] to prepare a meal: *It's time to start getting dinner.*

→ HOLD², KNOW¹

PHRASAL VERBS ,get sth a'cross to make people understand something: **get sth across to sb** *What message are you trying to get across to the consumer?*

,get a'head to become more successful or progress more quickly than other people: *The best way to get ahead is through hard work.* ♦ *Sometimes you have to be ruthless to get ahead in business.*

,get a'long 1 if people get along, they like each other and are friendly to each other: *Richard and his sister don't get along.* ♦ *I get along well with most of my colleagues.* 2 to manage to continue doing something, or to manage to make progress in a situation: *I got along much better in my new job.* ♦ *How are you getting along with your schoolwork?*

,get a'round if news gets around, a lot of people hear it

,get a'round sb to persuade someone to do something, especially by being nice to them

,get a'round sth to solve a problem, or to avoid a difficulty that something is causing: *There are ways of getting around the tax rules.* ♦ *You can't get around the fact she lied.*

,get a'round to sth to do something after you have intended to do it for some time: *I meant to call you, but somehow I never got around to it.* ♦ **get around to doing sth** *We must get around to cleaning those windows.*

'get at sb *British informal* to criticize someone unfairly: *Why are you always getting at me?*

'get at sth 1 to manage to reach or touch something: *I keep the sweets up here where*

the children can't get at them. 2 to try to suggest something without saying it directly: *What are you getting at?*

,get a'way 1 to escape from a person or place: *A police officer grabbed him, but he got away.* ♦ *The dog got away from me in the park.* 2 to manage to leave a place: *He said he'd meet me for lunch if he could get away.* 3 to go somewhere different from where you live in order to have a rest or a holiday: *On days like today, I just want to get away from it all.*

,get a'way with sth to manage to do something bad without being punished or criticized for it: *They have repeatedly broken the law and got away with it.* ♦ **get away with doing sth** *How can he get away with speaking to her like that?*

,get 'back 1 to return to a place: *It's late, I ought to get back.* ♦ *What time does Sara get back from work?* 2 to begin doing something again after not doing it for a period of time: *She was eager to get back to work after she had her baby.* 3 to return to the state or condition that you were in before: *I woke early and couldn't get back to sleep.*

,get sb 'back to hurt or upset someone because they have hurt or upset you

,get sth 'back to receive or have something again after a time when it was taken away from you or lost: *She left her briefcase on the train and she doesn't know how to get it back.*

,get 'back at sb to hurt or upset someone because they have hurt or upset you: *She was trying to get back at him for embarrassing her.*

,get 'back to sb *spoken* to phone, write, or speak to someone at a later time because you were busy or could not answer their question earlier: *Can you get back to me on those figures by the end of the day?*

,get be'hind if you get behind with work or payments, you have not done as much work or made as many payments as you should have done

,get 'by to have just enough of something such as money or knowledge so that you can do what you need to do: *My arithmetic isn't very good, but I get by.* ♦ *I couldn't possibly get by on £500 a month.* ♦ *You could probably get by with that computer, but a more powerful one would be better.*

,get sb 'down *informal* to make someone feel sad or lose hope: *Doing the same thing every day can get you down.*

,get 'down to sth to start doing something seriously or with a lot of effort: *After lunch we got down to discussing the issue of pay.*

,get 'in 1 to arrive at home or at work: *You got in very late last night!* 2 if a train, plane etc gets in, it arrives: *The London train gets in at 10.05.* 3 to be accepted to study at a school, or to be chosen to play for a team

,get 'in on sth *informal* to become involved in something

,get 'into sth 1 *informal* to start enjoying something, or to become enthusiastic about it: *You feel shy when you start your speech, but then you get into it.* 2 to become involved in a bad situation: *Those kids are always getting into trouble.* **3** to be accepted to study at a school, or to be chosen to play for a team

get 'off to not be punished severely, or to not be punished at all, for something that you have been accused of in court: *He was charged with manslaughter, but got off.* ♦ *At best you can hope to get off with a £100 fine.*

get 'off (sth) to leave the place you work at the end of the day: *What time do you get off work?*

get 'off (sb/sth) used for telling someone to stop touching someone or something: *Get off – you're hurting my back.* ♦ *Get off the grass right now!*

get sth 'off to have a particular period of time as a holiday: *Do you get much time off at Christmas?*

get 'off on sth *informal* to enjoy something and become very excited about it

get 'off with sb *British informal* to start a new sexual relationship with someone

get 'on *British* **1** to continue doing something with more effort or more quickly than before: *Can we please get on, because there are a lot of things still to discuss.* **2** *same as* **get along** 1: *My parents and I don't get on.* ♦ *She seems to get on with everybody.* **3** used for asking about or talking about how well someone has done a particular activity: *How did you get on in your exams?* **4** to be successful in life or at work: *He is prepared to do anything in order to get on.*

get 'onto sb *British* to write or speak to someone in order to ask them to do something for you: *You need to get onto your landlord about that leaky roof.*

get 'onto sth to start talking about a subject: *How did we get onto this subject?*

get 'on with sth to give your time to something and make progress with it: *Let's finish the speeches, so we can get on with the celebration.* ♦ **get on with doing sth** *I want to get on with preparing lunch.*

get 'out **1** used for telling someone to leave: *The teacher screamed at him to get out.* ♦ *Get out of my house!* **2** if something secret gets out, a lot of people find out about it: *There was a huge public outcry when the news got out.* ♦ *It quickly got out that Marie was leaving Danny.*

get sth 'out to manage to say something: *He tried to protest, but couldn't get the words out.*

get 'out of sth to avoid doing something that you should do, or that you said that you would do: *I said I'd meet him, but now I want to get out of it.* ♦ **get out of doing sth** *Ruth always tries to get out of doing the washing up.*

get sth 'out of sb to persuade someone to give you information or money

get sth 'out of sth to get pleasure or a benefit from something: *He gets a lot of satisfaction out of being a teacher.*

get 'over sth **1** to start to feel happy or well again after something bad has happened to you: *It can take weeks to get over an illness like that.* ♦ *Don's pretty upset, but he'll get over it.* **2 can't get over sth** used for saying that you are very surprised by something:

I just can't get over how well we played!

get sth 'over *British same as* **get sth across**: *We are trying to get this information over as clearly as possible.*

get sth 'over with to do something, or to allow something to happen, because you want it to be finished: *I wanted to get the interview over with as quickly as possible.*

get 'round *British same as* **get around**: *The news soon got round that people were going to lose their jobs.*

get 'round sb *same as* **get around sb**: *She gets round her dad easily, but her mother is more strict.*

get 'round sth *same as* **get around sth**: *We had to get round the problem that we didn't speak the same language.*

get 'round to sth *British same as* **get around to sth**: *I finally got round to reading that book you gave me.*

get 'through to succeed in talking to someone by phone: *I couldn't get through – the line was engaged.* ♦ *I finally got through to Warren on his mobile.*

get 'through sth **1** to manage to deal with a difficult situation, or to stay alive until it is over: *The refugees will need help to get through the winter.* **2** *British* to use or finish something: *How do we get through so much milk?*

get 'through to sb to make someone understand what you are trying to say: *I feel I'm not getting through to some of the kids in my class.*

get to sb *informal* to annoy or upset someone: *After a while his teasing started to get to me.*

get to'gether if people get together, they meet in order to do something or in order to spend time together: *The whole family usually gets together at Christmas.* ♦ *He got together with some friends to plan a party for her.*

get 'up to get out of bed after sleeping: *He never gets up before nine.*

get sb 'up to wake someone and tell them to get out of bed: *Will you get me up at six tomorrow?*

get 'up to sth *spoken* to do something, especially something that you should not do: *The children get up to all sorts of mischief when I'm not here.*

get 'with *spoken* **get with it** to pay attention to what is happening and start doing what you should be doing

getaway /'getəweɪ/ noun **make a getaway 1** to escape after committing a crime **2** to get away from a boring social situation

get-to'gether noun [C] an informal social occasion

geyser /'giːzə, 'gaɪzə/ noun [C] a place where hot water and steam move very quickly and suddenly up out of the earth

ghastly /'gɑːs(t)li/ adj very bad or unpleasant

ghetto /'getəʊ/ noun [C] an area in a city or town where people live in poor conditions

ghost /gəʊst/ noun [C] the spirit of a dead person that someone believes that they can see or hear

ghostly /'gəʊs(t)li/ adj reminding you of a ghost

ghost town noun [C] a town that most people have left

ghoul /guːl/ noun [C] an imaginary creature that eats dead people

GI /ˌdʒiː ˈaɪ/ noun [C] a US soldier

giant[1] /ˈdʒaɪənt/ noun [C] **1** a person in stories who is much bigger than a normal human **2** a very large successful company, or a successful important person: *the Dutch electronics giant Phillips*

giant[2] /ˈdʒaɪənt/ adj extremely large: *a giant bronze statue*

gibberish /ˈdʒɪbərɪʃ/ noun [U] *informal* nonsense

gibe /dʒaɪb/ noun [C] a remark that is intended to hurt someone or to make them feel stupid

giddy /ˈɡɪdi/ adj feeling that you might become unconscious and fall=DIZZY

gift /ɡɪft/ noun [C] ★★
1 something that you give to someone as a present: *a gift from a friend* ♦ *He bought gifts for everyone.*
2 a natural ability to do something well: *She has a gift for languages.*
3 something good that you are grateful that you have: *the gift of sight*

gifted /ˈɡɪftɪd/ adj a gifted person has an impressive natural ability

gift ˌtoken or **ˈgift ˌvoucher** noun [C] *British* a document that you buy in a shop as a present for someone, so that they can exchange it for something that they want to buy

ˈgift ˌwrap noun [U] attractive coloured paper that you use for wrapping presents

gift-wrapped /ˈɡɪft ˌræpt/ adj an object that is gift-wrapped is covered in attractive paper so that it can be given as a present —**gift-wrap** verb [T]

gig /ɡɪɡ/ noun [C] a public performance of popular music or jazz

gigabyte /ˈɡɪɡəˌbaɪt/ noun [C] *computing* a unit for measuring computer information, equal to 1,024 MEGABYTES

gigantic /dʒaɪˈɡæntɪk/ adj extremely large

giggle /ˈɡɪɡ(ə)l/ verb [I] to laugh in a nervous, excited, or silly way —**giggle** noun [C]

gild /ɡɪld/ verb [T] to cover a surface with a very thin layer of gold

gill /ɡɪl/ noun [C] one of the organs behind the head of a fish that allows it to breathe

gilt /ɡɪlt/ noun [U] a thin layer of gold or gold paint —**gilt** adj

gimme /ˈɡɪmi/ short form *informal* a way of writing 'give me' that shows how it sounds in informal conversation

gimmick /ˈɡɪmɪk/ noun [C] something that is intended to impress you or get your attention but is not necessary or useful: *a sales gimmick* ♦ *a gimmick to win votes* —**gimmicky** adj

gin /dʒɪn/ noun [C/U] a strong clear alcoholic drink, or a glass of this drink

ginger[1] /ˈdʒɪndʒə/ noun [U] a light brown root with a strong flavour that is used in cooking —*picture* ➔ C11

ginger[2] /ˈdʒɪndʒə/ adj **1** ginger hair or fur is orange-brown **2** containing or tasting of ginger

gingerly /ˈdʒɪndʒəli/ adv in a very slow and careful way

gipsy /ˈdʒɪpsi/ a British spelling of **gypsy**

giraffe /dʒəˈrɑːf/ noun [C] a tall African animal that has a very long neck and very long legs —*picture* ➔ C12

girder /ˈɡɜːdə/ noun [C] a large metal bar that is used for making the frame of a building or a bridge

girdle /ˈɡɜːd(ə)l/ noun [C] a piece of tight underwear that some women wear to make them look thinner

girl /ɡɜːl/ noun ★★★
1 [C] a female child: *There are 15 girls in my son's class.* ♦ *What a pretty little girl!*
2 [C] a daughter: *Mary's two girls still live at home.*
3 [C] a young adult woman. Many people think that this use is offensive: *Who was that beautiful girl I saw you with last night?*
4 the girls [plural] a woman's female friends. Some people think that this use is offensive when it is used by men.

girlfriend /ˈɡɜːlfrend/ noun [C] ★
1 a woman that you are having a romantic or sexual relationship with: *Have you got a girlfriend?*
2 a woman's female friend

ˌGirl ˈGuide noun [C] a girl who is a member of the Guides Association

girlish /ˈɡɜːlɪʃ/ adj looking or behaving like a young girl

girth /ɡɜːθ/ noun [C/U] the distance round something, for example a tree

gist, the /dʒɪst/ noun [singular] the main idea, or the general meaning of something

git /ɡɪt/ noun [C] *British informal* an insulting word for a stupid or annoying person

give[1] /ɡɪv/ (past tense **gave** /ɡeɪv/; past participle **given** /ˈɡɪv(ə)n/) verb ★★★

1 provide sb with sth	8 allow sb to do sth
2 make sb owner of sth	9 pass illness to sb else
3 have an effect	10 pay money
4 communicate	11 make sb believe sth
5 perform action	12 stretch/bend/break
6 put medicine in sb	+ PHRASE
7 help sb	+ PHRASAL VERBS

1 [T] to provide someone with something: **give sb sth** *Could you give me that pen?* ♦ *We don't know what to give our Dad for Christmas.* ♦ **give sth to sb** *I gave the keys to John.*
2 [T] to make someone the owner of something that you owned: **give sb sth** *Ken gave me his old tennis racket.* ♦ **give sth to sb** *He gave the house to his children.*
3 [T] to cause a general result or effect: **give sb/sth sth** *The results gave us quite a shock.* ♦ *Some washing powders give cotton a softer feel.*
4 [T] to show or communicate information: *The answers are given on page 78.* ♦ *Someone from the university will **give a talk** on the future of education.* ♦ **give sb sth/ give sth to sb** *Will you give him a message from me?*
5 [T] to perform an action: *I'd never ridden a horse before, but I was prepared to **give it a go** (=try to do it).* ♦ **give sb/sth sth** *I gave him a hug before he left.* ♦ *I'll **give you a ring** (=phone you) on Sunday.*
6 [T] to put medicine into someone's body using a particular method: *The drug is normally given by injection.*

G

7 [I/T] to do something good or helpful for someone: *a relationship where one partner gives more than the other* ♦ **give sth to sb/sth** *Aid will be given to areas where the flooding is worst.*

8 [T] to allow someone to do something: *We asked to go out, and the teacher **gave her permission**.* ♦ **give sb sth** *They should have given us more time to finish the test.*

9 [T] to pass an illness or disease to another person: **give sb sth** *She gave the whole office the flu.* ♦ **give sth to sb** *You could easily give the disease to your partner.*

10 [T] *spoken* to pay money for something: **give sb sth** *Martin gave me £300 for my computer.*

11 [T] to make someone think or believe something: *We don't want to **give the impression** that every child is at risk.* ♦ *The hotel isn't as comfortable as we were **given to understand*** (=as we were told).

12 [I] to stretch, bend, or break: *The bridge has to be able to give a little in the wind.*

PHRASE **give or take** used for saying that a number or quantity may be a little more or less than the number or quantity mentioned: *Each talk lasts half an hour, give or take five minutes.*

→ WAY¹

PHRASAL VERBS **give sth away 1** to let someone know a secret, often by accident: *If captured, they might give away vital military secrets.* ♦ *Her expression gave nothing away.* **2** to provide someone with something that you no longer want or need: *I gave my plants away to the neighbours.*

give sth back to give someone something that they had or owned before: *The company had to give back all the money.* ♦ **give sb back sth** *We just want them to give us back our home.*

give in to stop competing or arguing and accept that you cannot win: *The government has said that it will never give in to terrorist threats.*

give sth in *British* to give a piece of work to someone such as a teacher who is expecting it: *I have to give this essay in tomorrow.*

give off sth to produce something such as heat or a smell: *When they die, plants give off gases.*

give out to stop working correctly: *His heart finally gave out under the strain.*

give sth out to give something to several people: *The office gives out financial advice to students.*

give up (sth) to stop trying to do something because it is too difficult: *I give up. Tell me the answer.* ♦ **give up doing sth** *We've given up trying to persuade them to change.*

give sth up 1 to stop doing something that you do regularly: *I'm trying to give up smoking.* **2** to allow someone to have something that was yours: *The new arrangement would mean giving up some of their political independence.*

give yourself up if you give yourself up, you allow yourself to be arrested by the police

give up on sb to stop hoping that someone will improve, and stop trying to help them or to change them: *Most of the teachers gave up on her years ago.*

give² /gɪv/ noun [U] the tendency to bend or stretch

PHRASE **give and take** *informal* if there is give and take between people, each person allows the other to get something that they want

giveaway¹ /ˈgɪvəˌweɪ/ noun **1** [singular] a movement, action, or expression on someone's face that shows the truth about something: *I knew she'd passed. Her face was a dead giveaway* (=an obvious giveaway). **2** [C] a present that a company gives you to try to persuade you to buy things from them

giveaway² /ˈgɪvəˌweɪ/ adj very cheap, or free: *designer clothes at giveaway prices*

given¹ /ˈgɪv(ə)n/ adj **1** used for referring to a particular thing=PARTICULAR: *In a given situation, more than one method may be used.* **2** a given period has previously been decided on: *Many people pay off the money owed within a given time.*

given² /ˈgɪv(ə)n/ preposition because of a particular fact=CONSIDERING: *Given that conflict happens, we need to learn how to manage it.*

given³ the past participle of **give¹**

glacial /ˈgleɪʃ(ə)l/ adj relating to, or created by, glaciers

glacier /ˈglæsiə/ noun [C] a very large mass of ice that moves very slowly

glad /glæd/ adj ★★ happy and pleased about something: *'We're having a great time.' 'I'm so glad.'* ♦ **+(that)** *I'm glad he finally called you.* ♦ **glad to do sth** *Maggie was glad to be home.* → GLADLY

PHRASES **glad of sth** grateful for something: *I'd be glad of some help with the cooking.*

glad to do sth willing or ready to do something: *I'd be glad to watch the kids for you this afternoon.*

glade /gleɪd/ noun [C] *literary* an area in a forest where there are no trees or bushes =CLEARING

gladiator /ˈglædiˌeɪtə/ noun [C] in ancient Rome, someone who fought people or wild animals as a form of public entertainment

gladly /ˈglædli/ adv in a willing or happy way

glamor /ˈglæmə/ an American spelling of glamour

glamorize /ˈglæməˌraɪz/ verb [T] to make someone or something seem to be more attractive or exciting than they really are

glamorous /ˈglæmərəs/ adj **1** attractive or exciting in an unusual way: *a glamorous lifestyle* **2** a glamorous person is attractive, rich, and famous

glamour /ˈglæmə/ noun [U] a special quality that makes someone or something seem to be very attractive or exciting

glance¹ /glɑːns/ verb [I] ★

1 to look somewhere quickly and then look away: *'I must go,' Claudia said, glancing at her watch.* ♦ *Robin glanced around the room.*

2 to read something quickly and not very carefully: *I hadn't even glanced at the report.*

PHRASAL VERB **glance off sth** to hit something at an angle and then move away in a different direction

glance² /glɑːns/ noun [C] a quick look at someone or something: *She had a quick glance at the newspaper as she gulped down her coffee.*

PHRASE at a glance if you know something at a glance, you know it as soon as you see someone or something
→ FIRST

gland /glænd/ noun [C] a part of your body that produces a substance that your body needs —**glandular** /ˈglændjʊlə/ adj

glandular ˈfever noun [U] *British* a disease that mainly affects young people and makes them feel very tired and weak

glare¹ /gleə/ verb [I] 1 to look at someone or something in a very angry way: *Dan glared at me and immediately left the room.* 2 to shine with a very bright light that makes you feel uncomfortable

glare² /gleə/ noun 1 [C] an angry look 2 [singular/U] a very bright light that makes you feel uncomfortable

glaring /ˈgleərɪŋ/ adj 1 a glaring mistake is very obvious 2 a glaring light shines very brightly in a way that makes you feel uncomfortable —**glaringly** adv: *glaringly obvious*

glass /glɑːs/ noun ★★★
1 [U] a hard clear substance that is used for making objects such as windows or bottles: *the sound of breaking glass* ♦ *a glass bowl*
2 [C] a small container made of glass that you use for drinking from, or the drink in it: *a wine/brandy/beer glass* ♦ *She drank three glasses of milk.*
3 [U] attractive objects made of glass: *a beautiful collection of Italian glass*

glass ˈceiling noun [C] an unfair system that prevents some people from reaching the most senior positions in a company or organization

glasses /ˈglɑːsɪz/ noun [plural] an object that you wear in front of your eyes in order to help you to see better

glasshouse /ˈglɑːsˌhaʊs/ noun [C] *British* a large glass building that is used for growing plants in

glassware /ˈglɑːsˌweə/ noun [U] objects made of glass

glassy /ˈglɑːsi/ adj 1 glassy eyes show no interest or emotion, for example because of illness or drugs 2 smooth and shiny like glass

glaze /gleɪz/ noun [C/U] 1 a thin layer of milk, sugar, or egg that you put on foods to make them look shiny 2 a clear liquid that you put on paintings or clay objects to protect them and make them shiny —**glaze** verb [T]

glazed /gleɪzd/ adj 1 made of glass, or decorated with glass: *glazed doors* 2 decorated or protected by a smooth shiny surface: *glazed pastries* 3 a glazed look or expression shows that you are not at all interested in something

gleam¹ /gliːm/ verb [I] 1 to shine brightly 2 if your eyes gleam, you look excited or happy =SHINE

gleam² /gliːm/ noun [C] 1 a bright light that is reflected from something 2 a look of emotion or excitement in someone's eyes

glean /gliːn/ verb [T] to gradually get small

pieces of information about something

glee /gliː/ noun [U] a feeling of excitement and happiness, usually because of your own good luck or someone else's bad luck —**gleeful** adj, **gleefully** adv

glen /glen/ noun [C] *British* a valley in Scotland

glib /glɪb/ adj 1 a glib person speaks easily and confidently, but is not sincere 2 a glib remark is made without careful thought —**glibly** adv

glide /glaɪd/ verb [I] 1 to move in a smooth easy way with no noise 2 to fly without using power, carried by the wind

glider /ˈglaɪdə/ noun [C] a light plane with no engine

gliding /ˈglaɪdɪŋ/ noun [U] the activity of flying in a glider

glimmer¹ /ˈglɪmə/ noun [C] a soft weak light that is not steady

PHRASE a glimmer of hope a very small sign that something might improve or succeed

glimmer² /ˈglɪmə/ verb [I] to shine with a soft weak light that is not steady

glimpse¹ /glɪmps/ noun [C] 1 an occasion when you see someone or something for a very short time: *I only caught a glimpse of it, but I think it was a fox.* 2 an experience that gives you an idea of what something is like: *a glimpse of what the future might be like*

glimpse² /glɪmps/ verb [T] to see someone or something for a moment or not completely =CATCH SIGHT OF

glint /glɪnt/ verb [I] 1 to shine with quick flashes of light 2 if your eyes glint, they show a strong emotion such as anger —**glint** noun [C]

glisten /ˈglɪs(ə)n/ verb [I] if something glistens, it shines because it is wet or covered with oil

glitch /glɪtʃ/ noun [C] *informal* a small problem that prevents something from operating correctly =HITCH

glitter¹ /ˈglɪtə/ verb [I] 1 to shine with a lot of small flashes of light =SPARKLE 2 if your eyes glitter, they show a strong emotion such as anger

glitter² /ˈglɪtə/ noun [U] 1 small shiny pieces of metal or plastic that you stick on things to make them shine and look attractive 2 an attractive exciting quality: *the glitter and glare of Las Vegas* 3 a lot of small flashes of light

glittering /ˈglɪtərɪŋ/ adj 1 bright and shining with a lot of flashes of light 2 exciting and successful

glitz /glɪts/ noun [U] *informal* a special quality that makes something seem very exciting and attractive although it has no real value —**glitzy** adj

gloat /gləʊt/ verb [I] *showing disapproval* to show that you are happy about your own success or someone else's failure =CROW

global /ˈgləʊb(ə)l/ adj ★★
1 including or affecting the whole world: *The global economy has become increasingly unstable.*
2 *formal* complete, including all parts of something: *global changes*
—**globally** adv

G

globalization /ˌgləʊbəlaɪˈzeɪʃ(ə)n/ noun [U] the idea that the world is developing a single economy and culture as a result of improved communications and the influence of very large companies

globalize /ˈgləʊbəlaɪz/ verb [T] **1** to make something become generally accepted all over the world **2** to make a business begin operating all over the world

global warming noun [U] the increase in the temperature of the Earth that is caused partly by increasing amounts of CARBON DIOXIDE in the atmosphere

globe /gləʊb/ noun **1** [C] a round object that has a map of the world on it **2** [C] a round object **3** [singular] the world

globule /ˈglɒbjuːl/ noun [C] a small round drop of a thick liquid —**globular** adj

gloom /gluːm/ noun [U] **1** a feeling of sadness and a lack of hope **2** darkness in which it is difficult to see clearly → DOOM

gloomy /ˈgluːmi/ adj **1** feeling sad and without hope **2** showing that things are not going well and will probably not get better quickly: *The economic news is gloomy.* **3** dark in a way that makes you feel sad or a little afraid: *gloomy weather* —**gloomily** adv

glorified /ˈglɔːrɪˌfaɪd/ adj used for saying what something is really like when other people have described it as more impressive than it really is: *The 'yacht' we rented was just a glorified rowing boat.*

glorify /ˈglɔːrɪˌfaɪ/ verb [T] **1** to make someone or something seem to be more impressive than they really are **2** literary to praise someone —**glorification** /ˌglɔːrɪfɪˈkeɪʃ(ə)n/ noun [U]

glorious /ˈglɔːriəs/ adj **1** very beautiful in a way that makes you feel happy: *What glorious weather!* **2** extremely successful and likely to be remembered for a long time: *reminders of the country's glorious past* —**gloriously** adv

glory¹ /ˈglɔːri/ noun **1** [U] admiration and praise that you get because you have done something impressive: *I did the hard work and someone else got all the glory.* **2** [C] an impressive example, feature, or quality that makes you admire someone or something: *one of the glories of Italian architecture* **3** [U] great beauty: *It will cost millions of pounds to restore the mansion to its former glory.*

glory² /ˈglɔːri/ PHRASAL VERB **glory in sth** to get a lot of pleasure from something =REVEL

gloss¹ /glɒs/ noun **1** [singular/U] the shiny surface of something **2** [U] GLOSS PAINT **3** [C] a short explanation of what something means

gloss² /glɒs/ verb [T] to give an explanation of a word or a piece of writing
PHRASAL VERB **gloss over sth** to ignore or avoid unpleasant facts

glossary /ˈglɒsəri/ noun [C] a list of difficult words with explanations of their meaning

gloss paint noun [U] paint that is shiny when it is dry

glossy /ˈglɒsi/ adj **1** shiny in an attractive way **2** printed on shiny paper with a lot of bright pictures: *a glossy magazine*

glove /glʌv/ noun [C] a piece of clothing that covers your fingers and hand: *a pair of gloves* —*picture* → C4

glove compartment noun [C] the small cupboard or shelf in front of the passenger seat of a car —*picture* → C6

glow¹ /gləʊ/ verb [I] **1** to shine with a soft warm light: *The tip of a cigarette glowed in the darkness.* **2** to show that you are happy: *She glowed with satisfaction.* **3** if your face or body is glowing, it looks pink or red, for example because you are healthy or embarrassed

glow² /gləʊ/ noun [singular] **1** a soft warm light **2** the pink or red colour that your skin has when you are healthy, hot, embarrassed, or emotional **3** a pleasant feeling: *Anne felt a glow of pride at Sarah's words.*

glower /ˈglaʊə/ verb [I] to look angrily at someone =GLARE

glowing /ˈgləʊɪŋ/ adj full of praise: *a glowing reference from her former employer*

glucose /ˈgluːkəʊz/ noun [U] a natural sugar that exists in some foods

glue¹ /gluː/ noun [C/U] a sticky substance that you use for fixing things to each other

glue² /gluː/ verb [T] to stick things to each other with glue
PHRASE **be glued to sth** to be looking at something and not paying attention to anything else

glum /glʌm/ adj unhappy —**glumly** adv

glut /glʌt/ noun [singular] an amount of something that is more than people want or need

glutinous /ˈgluːtɪnəs/ adj thick and sticky, often in an unpleasant way

glutton /ˈglʌt(ə)n/ noun [C] someone who eats too much
PHRASE **a glutton for punishment** someone who seems to enjoy doing something that is difficult or unpleasant

gluttony /ˈglʌt(ə)ni/ noun [U] literary the bad habit of eating or drinking too much

GM /ˌdʒiː ˈem/ adj genetically modified: used for describing crops whose genes have been changed, or for describing foods made from these crops

GMO /ˌdʒiː em ˈəʊ/ noun [C] genetically modified organism: a plant or animal whose genes have been changed

GMT /ˌdʒiː em ˈtiː/ noun [U] Greenwich Mean Time: the time at Greenwich in England, used as an international standard

gnarled /nɑːld/ adj old and twisted and covered in lines: *gnarled hands*

gnat /næt/ noun [C] a very small flying insect that bites but is not dangerous

gnaw /nɔː/ verb [I/T] to keep biting something
PHRASAL VERB **gnaw at sb** or **gnaw away at sb** if something gnaws at you, you keep worrying about it or feeling upset about it

gnawing /ˈnɔːɪŋ/ adj continuously causing you pain or worrying you: *a gnawing fear that something would happen to her father*

gnome /nəʊm/ noun [C] an imaginary little man in children's stories who wears a pointed hat

GNP /ˌdʒiː en ˈpiː/ noun [U] Gross National

Product: the total value of all the goods and services that a country produces in a year

go¹ /gəʊ/ (past tense **went** /went/; past participle **gone** /gɒn/) verb ★★★

1 move to place	**14** when time passes
2 leave a place	**15** spend time doing sth
3 move to do sth	**16** to be spent/used
4 travel to activity	**17** disappear
5 continue to place	**18** leave a job
6 happen	**19** move/make a sound
7 change condition	**20** about story/music
8 be in state	**21** begin doing sth
9 stop working	**22** operate correctly
10 fit somewhere	**23** say
11 be kept somewhere	**+ PHRASES**
12 be right/attractive	**+ PHRASAL VERBS**
13 be sent	

1 [I] to move or travel to a place that is away from where you are now: *Where did Sue go?* ♦ *We're planning to go to Spain this winter.* ♦ *She went into the bathroom and rinsed her face in cold water.* ♦ *Are you going by train or are you flying?*

2 [I] to leave a place: *What time are you going tomorrow?* ♦ *I'm tired; let's go.*

3 [I] to move or travel to a place, or to leave a place, in order to do a particular thing: *They've gone to a concert in town tonight.* ♦ *He went into hospital for an operation last Tuesday.* ♦ *They went for a walk.* ♦ *On hot days the kids would go swimming in the river.* ♦ **go to do sth** *Jim went to buy some ice cream about ten minutes ago.* ♦ **go and do sth** *I have to go and pick up my friends at the airport.*

4 [I] to travel to a particular place regularly in order to take part in an activity: *None of her brothers went to college.* ♦ *When I was young, we went to church every Sunday.*

5 [I] to continue from one place or time to another: *The highway going from Georgetown to Brazil was built with World Bank funds.*

6 [I] to happen in a particular way: *How are things going at work?* ♦ *I think the interview went very well.* ♦ *The way things are going* (=things are not happening in the best way)*, we won't finish until next year!*

7 [linking verb] to change to another condition, usually a worse one: *Louise had gone completely blind before she died.* ♦ *The milk smells like it's going bad.*

8 [linking verb] to be in a particular state or situation, especially one in which you do not have something or in which something is not done: *We went barefoot all summer.* ♦ *Her comment went unnoticed.* ♦ *Thousands of people are being allowed to go hungry.*

9 [I] to start being in a worse state, or to stop working correctly, as a result of becoming old or damaged: *Her hearing is really starting to go.* ♦ *The battery in this watch is going.*

10 [I] if something goes in a particular place, it fits there because it is the right size or shape: *There's no way all this stuff will go in the box.*

11 [I] to be usually kept or put in a particular place: *The spoons go in the other drawer.*

12 [I] to be suitable, right, or attractive in a

particular place or in a particular combination: *It's the kind of furniture that would go well in any room.*

13 [I] to be sent: *The memo should go to all employees.* ♦ *I'd like this letter to go first class.*

14 [I] if time goes in a particular way, it passes in that way: *This week's gone so fast – I can't believe it's Friday already.*

15 [I/T] to continue or last for a particular amount of time while doing something: *He went several days without eating a single thing.*

16 [I] to be spent or used: *We were worried because the food was going fast.* ♦ *Half of the money went on new shoes for the kids.*

17 [I] to disappear: *I put my book on the table, and now it's gone.*

18 [I] to leave a job or organization, usually because you are forced to: *They can fire me, but I won't go quietly.*

19 [T] to make a particular sound or movement: *Cows go 'moo'.* ♦ *He kept going like this with his head.*

20 [I/T] to consist of a particular series of words, facts, or musical notes: *That's not the way the song goes.*

21 [I] to begin doing something: *Nobody starts until I say 'Go'.* ♦ *We've planned every detail and are ready to go.* ♦ *It won't take me long once I get going.*

22 [I] if a machine or piece of equipment goes, it operates correctly=WORK: *My old watch is still going.*

23 [T] *spoken* used when you are telling a story for saying what someone has said: *So he goes, 'I know what I'm doing,' and she goes, 'I don't think so.'*

PHRASES **be going to do sth 1** to intend to do something: *I'm going to watch TV tonight.* **2** to be about to do something: *You're going to fall if you're not careful.*

don't go there *spoken* used for saying that you do not want to hear about, discuss, or consider a particular subject

go all out (to do sth/for sth) to try as hard as you can to achieve something: *We're going all out for a big win in Saturday's game.*

go and do sth *spoken* **1** to do something that is silly or annoying: *She'll probably go and tell everyone our secret.* **2** used for telling someone to do something, especially when you are annoyed

to go 1 remaining: *There are just three weeks to go before the end of the term.* **2** if you order food to go from a restaurant, you take it and eat it somewhere else: *Do you want this pizza to go?*

PHRASAL VERBS **go a'bout sth 1** to start dealing with a problem, situation, or job in a particular way: *I think I'd go about it quite differently.* ♦ **go about doing sth** *How did you go about finding a job?* **2** to do something that you normally do in your usual way: *I watched the market traders as they went about their business.*

go after sb to try to catch or stop someone: *You'd better go after her and tell her you're sorry.*

go after sth to try to get something that other people are also competing for: *Graduates are going after jobs that they* *would not have considered before.*

go a'gainst sb if something such as a decision or judgment goes against you, you do not get the decision or judgment that you wanted to get

go a'gainst sb/sth to oppose someone or something: *Building a road here would go against the wishes of the local community.*

go a'head 1 to start, or continue to do something, especially after waiting for permission to do it: *'Go ahead,' he insisted. 'I won't interrupt again.'* ◆ *The club will be going ahead with its plans for a new stadium.* ◆ **go ahead and do sth** *Go ahead and eat before everything gets cold.* **2** to happen or take place: *The party went ahead as planned.* **3** to go to a place before someone else that you are with: *You go ahead and we'll wait here for Sally.* ◆ *Don went ahead of the others to try to find help.*

go a'long to continue doing something: *You'll learn a lot as you go along.*

go a'long with sb/sth to agree with someone or something: *I think I would tend to go along with what Tim was saying.*

go a'round 1 to behave or be dressed in a particular way: *Why do you always go around without any shoes on?* ◆ **go around doing sth** *You can't go around saying things like that!* **2** if something such as an illness or a piece of news is going around, people are giving it or telling it to each other: *He caught a nasty flu virus that's been going around.* **3** to be enough so that everyone can have one or some: *In some classes, there aren't even enough books to go around.* **4** to visit a person or a place: *I went around last night, but no one was in.* ◆ *Are you going around to Tom's after work?*

go at sb to attack someone violently

go at sth to do something with a lot of enthusiasm or energy

go a'way 1 to move away from, or to travel away from, a person or place: *If he's bothering you, tell him to go away.* **2** to leave your home for a period of time, especially for a holiday: *We've decided to go away for the weekend.* **3** to stop existing or being noticeable: *The pain should go away in a couple of hours.*

go 'back 1 to return to a person, place, subject, or activity: *It started to rain, so we decided to go back.* ◆ *I'd left my keys in the office and had to go back for them.* ◆ *She should be well enough to go back to work on Wednesday.* ◆ **go back to doing sth** *The computer breaks down and you go back to writing things down on pieces of paper.* **2** to have existed since or for a particular time: *My interest in the subject goes back many years.*

go 'back on sth to not do something that you have promised or agreed to do: *I don't think that the president would go back on his word.*

go 'by if time goes by, it passes: *Last month went by so fast.*

go 'by sth 1 to base an opinion on something: *It's never very wise to go by appearances.* **2** to move past a place: *I went by the post office on the way home.*

go 'down 1 to become less: *No one expects house prices to go down in the near future.*

◆ *How long will it take for the swelling to go down?* ◆ *The crime rate shows no signs of going down.* **2** when the sun goes down, it moves below the HORIZON so that you cannot see it any longer=SET **3** if something such as a computer or an electrical system goes down, it stops working for a period of time **4** to sink below the surface of the water: *The ship went down off the coast of Africa.* **5** to fall to the ground: *The plane went down during a thunderstorm.* **6** to be remembered or recorded in a particular place or way: *Hansen will go down as one of the best teachers this school has ever had.* ◆ *The efforts they made will go down in history.* **7** to produce a particular reaction: *The plan to put rents up has not gone down well with tenants.*

go 'down with sth *British informal* to become ill with a particular illness: *Three people in my office have gone down with the flu.*

go for sb *informal* to attack someone physically

go for sth 1 *informal* to try to get something that you have to compete for: *There were 200 people going for just three jobs.* **2** *informal* to choose a particular thing: *I think I'll go for the steak. What are you having?* **3** to be sold for a particular amount of money: *We expect the house to go for about £200,000.*

4 go for it *spoken* used for encouraging someone to do something or to try very hard

go for sb/sth 1 to be true or relevant for someone or something: *We expect you boys to behave yourselves, and the same goes for the girls.* **2** *informal* to like a particular type of person or thing: *So what type of men do you go for?*

go 'in when the sun or moon goes in, clouds move in front of it

go 'in for sth 1 to enjoy a particular thing or activity **2** *British* to take part in a competition, or to take an examination

go 'into sth 1 to start working in a particular type of job or business: *Alex has decided to go into nursing.* **2** to deal with something in detail: *That's a good question, but I don't want to go into it now.* ◆ *The company is refusing to go into detail about its offer.* **3** to be used or spent in order to do something: *Over 50% of the budget went into the design of the equipment.* ◆ **go into doing sth** *Months of hard work have gone into making tonight's ceremony a success.* **4** to crash into something: *The truck swerved violently and went into a wall.*

go 'off 1 to explode or be fired: *The gun went off while he was cleaning it.* **2** to start making a noise as a signal or warning: *I was lying in bed waiting for the alarm to go off.* **3** if something such as a light or an electricity supply goes off, it stops working or being available **4** to leave a place, especially for a particular purpose: *Dave's gone off to the south of France for the summer.* ◆ **go off to do sth** *He went off to have lunch in the canteen.* **5** *British* if food or drink goes off, it is no longer fresh **6** to happen in a particular way: *The whole conference went off just as we had planned.* **7** *British informal* to become worse in quality: *His work has really gone off recently.*

go 'off sb/sth *British* to stop liking someone or something: *I went off the idea of buying a sports car.*

go 'off with sth to leave with something that belongs to someone else: *Someone's gone off with my coffee cup.*

go 'on 1 to continue happening or doing something in the same way as before: *The meeting went on a lot longer than I expected.* ♦ *Burton smiled and went on with his work.* ♦ **go on doing sth** *She can't go on pretending that everything is fine when it clearly isn't.* **2** to happen: *I wonder what's going on next door – they're making a lot of noise.* **3** to talk so much that people become bored or annoyed: *She tends to go on about how clever her children are.* **4** to start talking again after a pause or interruption: *Please go on – I didn't mean to interrupt you.* **5** *spoken* used for encouraging someone to do something: *Go on, try it – it's really good.* **6** if time goes on, it passes **7** if something such as a light or an electricity supply goes on, it starts working or becomes available: *I heard the TV go on in the next room.*

go on sth to base an opinion or decision on something: *Since there were no witnesses, the police had little to go on.*

go 'on at sb *informal* to criticize someone regularly or for a long time: *My mum keeps going on at me about the way I dress.* ♦ **go on at sb to do sth** *Everyone's been going on at me to get a haircut.*

go 'out 1 to leave your house and go somewhere, especially to do something enjoyable: *I wanted the evenings free for going out with friends.* ♦ **go out doing sth** *We haven't gone out dancing for a long time.* ♦ **go out to do sth** *Let's go out to eat tonight.* **2** to have a romantic or sexual relationship with someone and spend a lot of time with them: *How long have Rob and Sue been going out?* ♦ *Greg used to go out with Katy.* ♦ *We've been going out together for three months now.* **3** to stop burning or shining: *The fire must have gone out during the night.* **4** to stop being fashionable: *That hairstyle went out about ten years ago.* ♦ *Classic jewellery like this will never go out of fashion.* **5** when the TIDE goes out, the water in the sea flows away from the land

go 'over sth 1 to check something carefully: *Could you go over this report and correct any mistakes?* **2** to repeat a series of things or think about them again in order to remember or understand them completely

go 'over to sth to change to a new system or way of behaving

go 'round *British same as* **go around**

go 'through if a request or proposal goes through, it is officially accepted or approved

go 'through sth 1 to examine or search something very carefully: *Someone had broken into the office and gone through all the drawers.* **2** to experience something difficult or unpleasant: *We can't really imagine what they're going through.* **3** to use, spend, or eat all of something: *He'd gone through all his money by the end of the first week of his holiday.*

go 'through with sth to do something that

you have planned or agreed to do: *I can't believe he went through with the divorce.*

go to'gether 1 if two or more things go together, they frequently exist together: *Too often greed and politics seem to go together.* **2** if two things go together, they seem good, natural, or attractive in combination with each other: *I don't think the colours go together very well.*

go to'wards sth to be used to help to pay for something: *The proceeds from the sale of the grounds will go towards a new stadium.* ♦ **go towards doing sth** *The money raised will go towards rebuilding the children's hospital.*

go 'under 1 if a business goes under, it fails completely and stops operating **2** to sink below the surface of the water: *The crowd watched as the ship went slowly under.*

go 'up 1 to increase: *The price of oil has gone up by over 50 per cent in less than a year.* **2** to be built: *A new office block is going up on Oxford Street.* **3** if something such as a notice or sign goes up somewhere, it is put in a place where people can see it: *Posters for the show are going up all over town.* **4** to explode, or to start burning quickly: *The whole building went up in just a few minutes.* ♦ *From the air, it looked as if the entire city was going up in flames.*

go 'with sb *informal* to have a romantic or sexual relationship with someone: *I heard that Carol is going with the guy who works downstairs.*

go 'with sth 1 to be provided or offered together with something: *the book that goes with the CD-ROM* ♦ *Does a car go with the job?* **2** to seem good, natural, or attractive in combination with something: *Which shoes go best with this dress?* **3** to choose or accept something: *I think we should go with yellow for the walls.*

go with'out sth to live without something that you need or would like to have: *Three villages have gone without water for days.* ♦ **go without doing sth** *He went without sleeping for two days.*

go² /ɡəʊ/ (plural **goes** /ɡəʊz/) noun [C] ★
1 an attempt to do something: *I'd thought about skiing for some time and finally decided to give it a go* (=try it) *this winter.* ♦ **have a go at (doing) sth** *She once had a go at writing a novel but quickly gave up.* **2** *British* your chance to play in a game or take part in an activity: *Whose go is it?*

PHRASES **be on the go** *informal* to be very busy or active

have a go at sb *British informal* to criticize someone strongly

have sth on the go *British informal* to be involved in doing something, especially something that needs a lot of your time and attention

make a go of sth *informal* to do something successfully

goad /ɡəʊd/ verb [T] to deliberately make someone feel very angry or upset so that they react in a particular way

go-a'head¹ noun **give/get the go-ahead** to give/get permission to do something

go-a'head² adj with a lot of energy and new

ideas: *an exciting, go-ahead company*

goal /gəʊl/ noun [C] ★★★
1 in games such as football, the net or structure that you try to get the ball into in order to score points —*picture* → C15
2 the action of putting a ball into a goal: *Nielsen scored two goals in the last ten minutes.*
3 something that you hope to achieve: *His goal is to win a medal at the Olympics.*

goalie /ˈgəʊli/ noun [C] *informal* a GOALKEEPER

goalkeeper /ˈgəʊlkiːpə/ noun [C] the player whose job is to stop the ball going into the goal in games such as football —*picture* → C15

goalpost /ˈgəʊlpəʊst/ noun [C] one of the two posts that the ball must go between to score a goal in games such as football —*picture* → C15

goat /gəʊt/ noun [C] an animal similar to a sheep but with longer legs and a thinner coat —*picture* → C12

goatee /ˌgəʊˈtiː/ noun [C] a small pointed BEARD

gobble /ˈgɒb(ə)l/ verb [T] to eat something quickly

gobbledegook or **gobbledygook** /ˈgɒb(ə)ldiˌguːk/ noun [U] *informal* 1 very complicated or technical language
2 nonsense

go-between noun [C] someone who takes messages between people who cannot meet or do not want to meet

goblet /ˈgɒblət/ noun [C] a metal or glass cup with no handles that was used in the past

goblin /ˈgɒblɪn/ noun [C] a small ugly creature in children's stories that enjoys causing trouble

god /gɒd/ noun [C] ★
1 one of the male spirits with special powers that some people believe in and worship: *Poseidon was the Greek god of the sea.*
2 a man who many people admire or find attractive

God[1] /gɒd/ the spirit or force that some people believe created and controls the universe
[PHRASE] **God (only) knows** *spoken* used for emphasizing that you do not know something

God[2] /gɒd/ interjection used for expressing strong feelings such as anger, surprise, or worry. Some people think that this expression is offensive.

godchild /ˈgɒdtʃaɪld/ (plural **godchildren** /ˈgɒdtʃɪldrən/) noun [C] a child that a GODPARENT promises to look after, especially by making certain that he or she gets a religious education

goddess /ˈgɒdes/ noun [C] 1 one of the female spirits with special powers that some people believe in and worship 2 a woman who many people admire or find attractive

godfather /ˈgɒdfɑːðə/ noun [C] a male GODPARENT

godforsaken /ˈgɒdfəˌseɪkən/ adj a godforsaken place is not at all interesting or attractive

godless /ˈgɒdləs/ adj *showing disapproval* not believing in God, or not living according to religious rules

godlike /ˈgɒdlaɪk/ adj better or more impressive than an ordinary human

godly /ˈgɒdli/ adj showing respect for God and living according to religious rules

godmother /ˈgɒdˌmʌðə/ noun [C] a female godparent

godparent /ˈgɒdˌpeərənt/ noun [C] an adult who promises during the Christian ceremony of BAPTISM to look after a child, especially by making certain that he or she gets a religious education

godsend /ˈgɒdˌsend/ noun [singular] something that you are very grateful for because it helps you in a difficult situation

go-getter /ˌgəʊ ˈgetə/ noun [C] *informal* someone who is determined to succeed and works hard to achieve this —**go-getting** adj

goggle-eyed /ˌgɒg(ə)l ˈaɪd/ adj *informal* looking at someone or something in a way that shows that you are very surprised or impressed by them

goggles /ˈgɒg(ə)lz/ noun [plural] special GLASSES that protect your eyes

going[1] /ˈgəʊɪŋ/ noun [U] 1 used for talking about how fast or easily you make progress: *We'd reached London by six o'clock, which was good going.* ♦ *The first half of the film is pretty slow going* (=is rather boring). 2 an occasion when someone leaves a place or job permanently: *None of us knew the reasons for his going.* → COMING[2] 3 the condition of the ground for a horse race
[PHRASE] **do sth while the going is good** *informal* to do something before any problems happen that will prevent you from doing it

going[2] /ˈgəʊɪŋ/ adj available: *It's one of the best jobs going in television.* → RATE[1]

going con'cern noun [C] a business that seems likely to continue to make a profit

going-'over noun [singular] *informal* a careful check of something
[PHRASE] **give sb a going-over** *British informal* to hit someone a lot

goings-on noun [plural] *informal* events or activities that are strange, dishonest, or illegal

go-kart noun [C] a small low vehicle with no roof, used for racing or for fun

gold[1] /gəʊld/ noun ★★
1 [U] a valuable yellow metal that is used for making jewellery: *The picture frames were made of solid gold.*
2 [C/U] a MEDAL made of gold that is given to the winner of a race: *We always thought Sally was going to win gold.* ♦ *So Australia gets the gold and Britain the silver.*
3 [C/U] the colour of gold: *The boat was painted in black and gold.*

gold[2] /gəʊld/ adj 1 something that is gold is the colour of gold: *blue fabric decorated with gold stars* 2 made of gold: *a gold ring/chain/watch*

golden /ˈgəʊld(ə)n/ adj ★
1 bright yellow in colour: *golden hair* ♦ *Fry the chicken in the oil until golden brown.*
2 very happy or successful: *The seventies were the golden years of Australian tennis.*
3 *literary* made of gold: *The queen wore a golden crown.*

golden ,age noun [singular] a period of time in the past when something was the most successful that it has ever been: *the golden age of radio*

golden oppor'tunity noun [C] a very good chance to do something

golden 'rule noun [C] an important basic principle that you should always obey when doing a particular activity

golden 'wedding noun [C] *British* the day when two people celebrate the fact that they have been married for 50 years

goldfish /'gəʊldfɪʃ/ (plural **goldfish**) noun [C] a small orange fish that is often kept as a pet

gold 'medal noun [C] a MEDAL that is given to the winner of a race or competition

gold 'medallist noun [C] someone who wins a gold medal

goldmine /'gəʊldˌmaɪn/ noun [C] **1** *informal* a business or an activity that makes large amounts of money very easily **2** a place under the ground where there are rocks containing gold

golf /gɒlf/ noun [U] ★ a game in which you use GOLF CLUBS to hit a small white ball into a hole in the ground: *I usually play a round of golf (=a game of golf) on Saturday.* —**golfer** noun [C]

golf ,ball noun [C] a small white ball that you use for playing golf

golf ,club noun [C] **1** a long stick that you use for hitting the ball in golf **2** a place with a golf course and a CLUBHOUSE where people go to play golf and meet their friends

golf ,course noun [C] a large area of land that is designed for playing golf

gone¹ /gɒn/ adj **1** someone who is gone is no longer present in a place **2** something that is gone no longer exists or has all been used

gone² /gɒn/ preposition *British informal* after a particular time = PAST: *It was gone ten o'clock by the time they arrived.*

gone³ the past participle of **go¹**

gonna /'gʌnə/ short form a way of writing 'going to' that shows how it sounds in informal conversation

goo /guː/ noun [U] *informal* a thick sticky unpleasant substance

good¹ /gʊd/ (comparative **better** /'betə/; superlative **best** /best/) adj ★★★

1 of high quality	8 kind/helpful
2 able to do sth well	9 giving benefits
3 suitable	10 fairly large
4 giving pleasant feeling	11 able to be used
5 showing pleasure	12 thorough and complete
6 morally correct	13 more than amount etc
7 behaving well	+ PHRASES

1 of a high quality or standard: *We saw a really good film last night.* ♦ *They were all dressed in their best clothes.* ♦ *How good is his English?*

2 able to do something well: *Francine was a very good cook.* ♦ *Bob is pretty good at fixing things.* ♦ *Gina has always been good with animals.*

3 suitable and likely to produce the results or conditions that you want: *What's the best way to get to the motorway from here?* ♦ *Now would be a good time to ask for a pay rise.*

♦ *Thursday is good for me – can you make it then?*

4 giving you a happy or pleasant feeling: *We had such a good time in Madrid.* ♦ *One more piece of good news: Beth had a baby girl!* ♦ **it is/feels good to do sth** *It's good to finally meet you.*

5 *spoken* used for saying that you are pleased with someone or pleased about something: *'They should be here in half an hour.' 'Good.'* ♦ *Oh, good, you remembered to buy the milk.*

6 honest and morally correct: *George had always tried to lead a good life.*

7 willing to obey and behave in a socially correct way: *Ruth's children are always so good.* ♦ *Be a good boy and play quietly.*

8 kind, generous, and willing to help: *Helen's parents were always good to us.* ♦ *Sheryl's brother has been good about helping out with the new baby.* ♦ **it is good of sb to do sth** *It was so good of you to come.*

9 producing benefits for someone or something: *Exercise is good for you.* ♦ *The recent tax cuts will be good for business.* ♦ **it is good (for sb) to do sth** *It's not good to eat so much junk food.*

10 fairly large in amount, size, range etc: *He earns a good salary as a consultant.* ♦ *They've known each other for a good many years.*

11 still able to be used: *Do you think the eggs are still good?* ♦ *Make sure your passport is good before you book your flight.* ♦ *I think these trousers are good for another few months.*

12 thorough and complete: *The witness said she got a good look at his face.*

13 *informal* more than a particular distance, amount, age etc: *We've been waiting for a good half hour.*

PHRASES **as good as** almost: *They've as good as admitted it was their fault.*

as good as new something that is as good as new is in almost the same good condition as it was before it was damaged or injured: *After the operation your back should be as good as new.*

good for sb used for saying that you are happy about something good that someone has done

a good friend someone that you know very well and like a lot

good Heavens/Lord/God/grief used for showing that you are very surprised, angry, or upset

it's a good thing/job that *British* used for saying that you are pleased that something has happened because it prevents something bad from happening: *It's a good thing you called – Mum was starting to get worried.*

too good to be true/to last so good that you cannot believe that such a situation is possible or can continue: *If you think the deal they are offering is too good to be true, it probably is.*

Words that you can use instead of **good**

Good is a very general word. Here are some words with more specific meanings that sound more natural and appropriate in particular situations.

G

films/books/events	brilliant, excellent, fabulous, fantastic, great, terrific
food/meals	delicious, tasty, wonderful
performance/ piece of work	brilliant, excellent, outstanding
people	decent, kind, moral, nice, respectable
ideas/ suggestions	appealing, brilliant, excellent, great, interesting

G

good² /gʊd/ noun [U] ★★★
1 advantage, or benefit: *I think a trip to the beach would do us all a lot of good.* ♦ *I'm only punishing you for your own good.* ♦ *Hartman should resign for the good of the party.*
2 morally correct behaviour ≠ EVIL: *the battle between good and evil*
 PHRASES **do no good** or **not do any good** to not have any effect or success: *I'll talk to her, but it won't do any good.*
for good permanently, without the possibility of change in the future: *It looks like Jamie has left for good this time.*
no good or **not any good** or **not much good 1** of a low quality or standard: *Most of the pictures I took weren't any good.* **2** not able to do something well: *I'm no good at chemistry.* ♦ *Ken's not much good with kids.* **3** not useful or effective: *My shoes are no good for hiking.* ♦ **it's no good doing sth** *It's no good trying to persuade her to come with us.* **4** not suitable or convenient: *Tomorrow's no good – I'm busy.*
up to no good *informal* doing or planning something bad, illegal, or immoral
→ GOODS

good after'noon interjection *formal* used for saying hello or goodbye to someone in the afternoon

goodbye¹ /ˌgʊdˈbaɪ/ interjection ★★★ used when you are leaving someone or when someone is leaving you, or when you are finishing a telephone call: *'Goodbye, Mr Taylor.' 'Goodbye, John.'*

goodbye² /ˌgʊdˈbaɪ/ noun [C] a word or phrase that you say when you leave someone or when someone leaves you: *Emma left without even a goodbye.* ♦ *I said goodbye to everyone and left.* ♦ *It was heartbreaking saying our goodbyes at the airport.*

good 'evening interjection *formal* used for saying hello to someone in the evening

good-for-nothing noun [C] someone who is lazy and never does anything useful

Good 'Friday noun [C/U] the Friday before Easter, when Christians believe that Jesus Christ died

good-humoured /ˌgʊd ˈhjuːməd/ adj friendly, happy, and not easily annoyed or upset

goodies /ˈgʊdiz/ noun [plural] *informal* things that are nice to eat

good-looking /ˌgʊd ˈlʊkɪŋ/ adj physically attractive

good 'looks noun [plural] the physically attractive appearance of someone

good 'morning interjection *formal* used for saying hello or goodbye to someone in the morning

good-natured /ˌgʊd ˈneɪtʃəd/ adj kind and friendly, and not easily annoyed —**good-'naturedly** adv

goodness¹ /ˈgʊdnəs/ interjection used for showing that you are surprised: *Goodness, is it that time already?* ♦ *My goodness, you're so tall!*
 PHRASE **for goodness sake** used for showing that you are annoyed, impatient, worried, or surprised: *Sit down and be quiet, for goodness sake!*
→ THANK

goodness² /ˈgʊdnəs/ noun [U] **1** the quality of being morally good **2** substances such as VITAMINS and proteins that are contained in some foods and help you to stay healthy

good 'night interjection used for saying goodbye to someone in the evening or at night, or before they go to bed at night

goods /gʊdz/ noun [plural] ★★★
1 objects that are produced for sale: *leather/electrical goods* ♦ *Wilkins was found in possession of £8,000 worth of stolen goods.* ♦ *The cost of household goods and services fell.*
2 *British* objects that are carried in large quantities from one place to another by road or railway: *a goods train/lorry*
 PHRASE **come up with/deliver the goods** *informal* to do what you have said you will do or what people expect

goodwill /ˌgʊdˈwɪl/ noun [U] a feeling of wanting to be friendly and helpful to someone ≠ ILL WILL: *As a gesture of goodwill, we agreed to do the work free of charge.*

goody /ˈgʊdi/ interjection *informal* used by children for saying that they are happy or excited about something

goody-goody or **goody-two-shoes** *informal* noun [C] *showing disapproval* someone who always tries to please people in authority

gooey /ˈguːi/ adj *informal* sticky and soft

goofy /ˈguːfi/ adj *informal* silly, but in a funny or pleasant way

goose /guːs/ (plural **geese** /giːs/) noun **1** [C/U] a large white or grey bird with a long beak —*picture* → C12 **2** [U] the meat of a goose

gooseberry /ˈgʊzb(ə)ri/ noun [C] a small green fruit with a sour taste that grows on a bush
 PHRASE **be a gooseberry** or **play gooseberry** *British informal* to be with two people who have a sexual or romantic relationship and want to be alone together

goose pimples or **goose bumps** noun [plural] very small lumps that appear on your skin because you are cold, frightened, or excited

gore¹ /gɔː/ noun [U] thick blood from an injured person

gore² /gɔː/ verb [T] if an animal such as a BULL gores someone, it injures them with its horns

gorge¹ /gɔːdʒ/ noun [C] a deep valley with high straight sides

gorge² /gɔːdʒ/ verb **gorge yourself (on sth)** to eat or drink so much of something that you cannot eat or drink any more

gorgeous /ˈgɔːdʒəs/ adj very beautiful or pleasant

gorilla /gəˈrɪlə/ noun [C] a large strong African wild animal that is similar to a monkey but much larger. Gorillas live in forests. —*picture* → C12

gorse /gɔːs/ noun [U] a small bush with yellow flowers and THORNS that grows wild in the countryside in Europe

gory /'gɔːri/ adj involving a lot of blood, killing, or injuries

gosh /gɒʃ/ interjection *old-fashioned* used for showing that you are surprised or a little annoyed

gosling /'gɒzlɪŋ/ noun [C] a young GOOSE

gospel /'gɒsp(ə)l/ noun **1 gospel** or **gospel music** [U] a type of Christian music that was developed by African Americans **2** [C] one of the four books in the Bible that tell about the life of Jesus Christ **3 the gospel** [singular] the things that Jesus Christ said and taught according to the Bible
  PHRASE **the gospel truth** the complete truth

gossip¹ /'gɒsɪp/ noun **1** [C/U] talk or a conversation about things that are not important or about people's private lives: *an interesting piece of gossip* **2** [C] someone who enjoys talking about other people

gossip² /'gɒsɪp/ verb [I] to talk about other people or about things that are not important

got¹ /gɒt/ verb **have got** *spoken* used especially in speech to mean 'have': *I've got an extra apple if you want one.*

got² the past tense and past participle of **get**

gotta /'gɒtə/ *short form* a way of writing 'got to' that shows how it sounds in informal conversation

gotten the American past participle of **get**

gouge /ɡaʊdʒ/ verb [T] to cut long deep holes in something —**gouge** noun [C]
  PHRASAL VERB **gouge sth out** to remove something from a surface by cutting or digging with a sharp object

gourd /ɡʊəd/ noun [C] a type of fruit with a hard thick skin

gourmet¹ /'ɡʊəmeɪ/ noun [C] someone who knows a lot about good food and wine

gourmet² /'ɡʊəmeɪ/ adj **1** gourmet food and wine is of a very high quality **2** a gourmet cook is someone who can make very good food

govern /'ɡʌv(ə)n/ verb ★
  1 [I/T] to officially control and manage a country or area and its people=RULE: *The region is now governed by Morocco.* ♦ *The party will not be able to govern alone.*
  2 [T] to control or influence the way that things happen or develop: *the laws that govern the movements of the stars* ♦ *Fear governed their lives.*

governess /'ɡʌv(ə)nəs/ noun [C] a woman whose job is to look after and teach her employer's children in their home

government /'ɡʌv(ə)nmənt/ noun ★★★
  1 [C/U] the people who control a country or area and make decisions about its laws and taxes: *The government has announced plans to raise the minimum wage next year.* ♦ *a democratically elected government* ♦ *government policy/ministers*

> In British English, **government** can be used with a singular or plural verb. You can say *the government is unpopular* OR *the government are unpopular.*

2 [U] the process, method, or effects of governing a country or area: *I'm not sure these reforms will necessarily lead to more effective government.*
  —**governmental** /ˌɡʌv(ə)n'ment(ə)l/ adj

governor /'ɡʌv(ə)nə/ noun [C] **1** someone who is in charge of an area such as a US state: *the governor of California* **2** *British* the person, or one of the people, in charge of an institution such as a bank, prison, or school —**governorship** noun [C/U]

gown /ɡaʊn/ noun [C] **1** a long dress that a woman wears for a special occasion **2** a long loose piece of clothing that a doctor or patient wears during an operation in a hospital

GP /ˌdʒiː 'piː/ noun [C] General Practitioner: a doctor who deals with general medical problems and treats the people in a particular area

grab¹ /ɡræb/ verb [T] ★
  1 to take hold of something in a rough or rude way: *He grabbed the knife before I could get to it.* ♦ *I grabbed hold of his hair.* ♦ **grab sb by sth** *Ben grabbed Marco by the arm.*
  2 to succeed in getting something, especially by being quick or by being the best at something: *We got there early and grabbed seats at the front.* ♦ *It's often the bad characters in a story who grab our attention.* ♦ *I grabbed the chance to escape for a few minutes.*
  3 *informal* if you grab food or sleep, you eat quickly or sleep for a short time: *I'll grab a sandwich back at the hotel.*
  PHRASAL VERB **grab at sth** to try to take hold of something in a rough or rude way: *Suddenly he was on his feet, grabbing at her sleeve.*

grab² /ɡræb/ noun [singular] an attempt to take hold of something: *Rose rushed at David and made a grab at his wrist.*
  PHRASE **up for grabs** *informal* if something is up for grabs, it is available and many people are trying to get it or win it

grace¹ /ɡreɪs/ noun **1** [U] a smooth and beautiful way of moving: *She moved with natural grace.* **2** [U] kind, polite, and fair behaviour: *He should have the grace to admit he was wrong.* ♦ *Davis accepted the defeat with good grace* (=in a pleasant way). **3** [U] extra time that you are given to do something such as pay money that you owe: *Could you give me a couple of days' grace to pay the rent?* **4** [singular/U] a short prayer that some people say before they eat in order to thank God for the food

grace² /ɡreɪs/ verb [T] **1** to make something more attractive, pleasing, or interesting: *Her photograph graced many a magazine cover.* **2** *humorous* if someone important graces a group or an event, they go to it: *How kind of you to grace us with your presence.*

graceful /'ɡreɪsf(ə)l/ adj **1** a graceful shape or object is attractive **2** a graceful movement is smooth and beautiful **3** showing good manners and respect for other people: *She was extremely graceful in defeat.* —**gracefully** adv

G

G

graceless /ˈgreɪsləs/ adj **1** not attractive **2** not polite

gracious¹ /ˈgreɪʃəs/ adj **1** showing kindness and good manners ≠ UNGRACIOUS **2** relating to a style of life that is enjoyed by people who have enough money to buy beautiful things —**graciously** adv

gracious² /ˈgreɪʃəs/ interjection old-fashioned used for expressing surprise

gradation /grəˈdeɪʃ(ə)n/ noun [C] one of the steps in a series that shows how one thing slowly becomes something else

grade¹ /greɪd/ noun [C] ★
1 a level of quality or importance: *Their wool is suitable for finer grades of cloth.* ♦ *He demanded to be put on a higher salary grade.*
2 a letter or number that shows the quality of a student's work: *You need to improve your grades.* ♦ *I got a Grade 2 for art.*
3 one of the levels of school in the US that lasts for one year: *The topic is covered in the seventh grade.* ♦ *eighth grade students*
PHRASE **make the grade** to succeed in doing something because you are good enough

grade² /greɪd/ verb [T] **1** to separate things into different groups according to quality, size, importance etc **2** to judge the quality of a student's work by giving it a letter or number

gradient /ˈgreɪdiənt/ noun [C] a measure of how steep a slope is

gradual /ˈgrædʒuəl/ adj happening slowly and by small amounts: *a gradual change in the climate*

gradually /ˈgrædʒuəli/ adv ★★ slowly and in small stages or amounts: *She gradually built up a reputation as a successful lawyer.* ♦ *Gradually add the flour.*

graduate¹ /ˈgrædʒuət/ noun [C] ★
1 someone who has a degree from a university: *careers for history graduates* ♦ *an Oxford graduate* ♦ *a graduate of Aston University* ♦ *Candidates should be graduates in science or engineering.*
2 American someone who has finished their studies at a HIGH SCHOOL, college, or university: *a high school graduate*

graduate² /ˈgrædʒueɪt/ verb [I] ★
1 to complete your studies at a university or college and get a degree: *He graduated from Yale University in 1936.* ♦ *one of the first women to graduate in history and languages at the Sorbonne*
2 American to finish your studies at a HIGH SCHOOL
3 graduate (from sth) to sth to make progress, or to reach a higher position: *Some children had graduated to reading books without pictures.* ♦ *He eventually graduated from clerical work to his present role.*

graduate³ /ˈgrædʒuət/ adj POSTGRADUATE

graduated /ˈgrædʒueɪtɪd/ adj **1** organized according to a series of levels **2** increasing by regular amounts

graduation /ˌgrædʒuˈeɪʃ(ə)n/ noun **1** [U] the act of receiving a degree or other qualification after finishing your studies at a college or university **2** [C/U] a ceremony at which you are given a degree or other qualification

graffiti /grəˈfiːti/ noun [U] words or pictures that are drawn on walls in public places

graft¹ /grɑːft/ noun **1** [C] a piece of skin or bone from one part of your body that is used to replace or repair a damaged part of your body **2** [C] a piece that is taken from a plant and joined to a cut that has been made in another plant, so that it can grow there **3** [U] British informal effort that is needed for doing hard work: *hard graft*

graft² /grɑːft/ verb **1** [T] to take a piece of skin or bone from one part of someone's body and use it to replace or repair a damaged part of their body **2** [T] to take a piece from a plant and join it to a cut that has been made in another plant, so that it can grow there **3** [I] British informal to work very hard

grain /greɪn/ noun

1 seed	**4** small amount of quality
2 plants used for food	**5** pattern of fibres
3 very small piece of sth	**+** PHRASE

1 [C/U] a seed, or the seeds from plants such as wheat, rice, or BARLEY that are used for food **2** [U] plants that are used for food such as wheat, rice, or BARLEY **3** [C] a very small individual piece of a substance such as sand, salt, or sugar **4** [singular] a very small amount of a quality or feeling: *There was more than a grain of truth in what he'd said.* **5** [U] the pattern or direction of the fibres in substances such as wood, stone, cloth, or paper
PHRASE **go against the grain** to be completely different from what you feel is right, natural, or normal for you
→ SALT¹

gram /græm/ noun [C] a unit for measuring weight in the METRIC SYSTEM

grammar /ˈgræmə/ noun ★★
1 [U] the set of rules that describe the structure of a language and control the way that sentences are formed: *errors in spelling and grammar* ♦ *The book covers all the essential points of English grammar.*
2 [C] a book explaining the rules of a language: *an Italian grammar*

grammar school noun [C] **1** a school in the UK for children between the ages of 11 and 18 who have passed a special examination in order to be allowed to go there **2** American a PRIMARY SCHOOL

grammatical /grəˈmætɪk(ə)l/ adj **1** relating to grammar: *grammatical errors* **2** a grammatical sentence correctly follows the rules of grammar ≠ UNGRAMMATICAL —**grammatically** adv

gramme /græm/ another spelling of **gram**

gran /græn/ noun [C] British informal a GRANDMOTHER

granary /ˈgrænəri/ noun [C] a building where grain is kept

grand¹ /grænd/ adj ★
1 very impressive: *The house was spacious and grand.* ♦ *The ball was a very grand affair.* ♦ *a grand plan to reform US health care*
2 a grand person behaves as if they are very important: *I could have given you some hints, but I suppose you thought yourself too grand.*
3 most important: *the grand prize* ♦ *Robert*

was the grand marshal of the Saint Patrick's Day parade.

4 *informal old-fashioned* very good, or enjoyable=GREAT: *It would be grand if she could come.* ♦ *We've been having a grand time.*

grand² /grænd/ *noun* [C] *informal* (plural **grand**) a thousand pounds, or a thousand dollars

grandad /'græn(d),dæd/ *noun* [C] *informal* a GRANDFATHER

grandchild /'græn(d),tʃaɪld/ (plural **grandchildren** /'græn(d),tʃɪldrən/) *noun* [C] the son or daughter of one of your children

granddad /'græn(d),dæd/ the American spelling of **grandad**

granddaughter /'græn(d),dɔːtə/ *noun* [C] the daughter of one of your children —*picture* → FAMILY TREE

grandeur /'grændʒə/ *noun* [U] an impressive quality

grandfather /'græn(d),fɑːðə/ *noun* [C] ★ the father of one of your parents —*picture* → FAMILY TREE

grandfather 'clock *noun* [C] an old-fashioned clock in a tall wooden box that stands on the floor

grandiose /'grændi,əʊs/ *adj* intended to achieve something that is important or difficult, but unlikely to be successful because of not being sensible

grandly /'grændli/ *adv* in a way that tries to impress you but often does not

grandma /'græn(d),mɑː/ *noun* [C] *informal* a GRANDMOTHER

grandmother /'græn(d),mʌðə/ *noun* [C] ★ the mother of one of your parents —*picture* → FAMILY TREE

grandpa /'græn(d),pɑː/ *noun* [C] *informal* a GRANDFATHER

grandparent /'græn(d),peərənt/ *noun* [C] ★ the mother or father of your mother or father

grand pi'ano *noun* [C] a type of large piano

Grand Prix /,grɒn 'priː/ *noun* [C] an international competition for RACING CARS or MOTORCYCLES

grand 'slam *noun* [C] a situation in which you win all of a set of important competitions in a particular sport in the same year

grandson /'græn(d),sʌn/ *noun* [C] the son of one of your children —*picture* → FAMILY TREE

grandstand /'græn(d),stænd/ *noun* [C] a large structure with rows of seats from which people watch sports events

grand 'total *noun* [C] a final total of all the amounts or totals that must be added together

granite /'grænɪt/ *noun* [U] a type of very hard stone

granny /'græni/ *noun* [C] *informal* a GRANDMOTHER

grant¹ /grɑːnt/ *verb* [T] *formal* ★★ to allow someone to have or to do what they want: *The Board has refused to **grant** your **request**.* ♦ *His wish was finally granted.*

PHRASES I grant you used for admitting that something is true: *You're thorough, I grant you that, but we don't need all this detail.*
take sb for granted to expect someone to always do things for you even when you do not show that you are grateful

take sth for granted to expect something always to happen or exist in a particular way and not think about any possible problems or difficulties: *Losing my job taught me never to take anything for granted.*

grant² /grɑːnt/ *noun* [C] ★★ an amount of money that the government or an organization gives you for a specific purpose and does not ask you to pay back: *a research grant*

granule /'grænjuːl/ *noun* [C] a small hard round piece of something: *coffee/gravy granules*

grape /greɪp/ *noun* [C] a small green or purple fruit that grows in BUNCHES on a VINE and that is often used for making wine —*picture* → C10

grapefruit /'greɪp,fruːt/ *noun* [C/U] a fruit like a large orange that is yellow on the outside, yellow or red inside, and has sour juice —*picture* → C10

grapevine /'greɪp,vaɪn/ *noun* [singular] *informal* the way in which information spreads quickly from one person to another through conversation: *I heard on the grapevine that you left your job.*

graph /grɑːf, græf/ *noun* [C] a picture that uses lines or curves to show the relationship between numbers or measurements that change

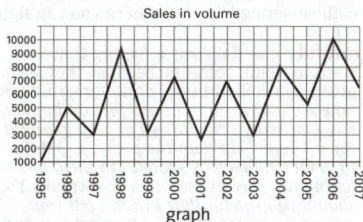

Sales in volume

graph

graphic /'græfɪk/ *adj* **1** containing a lot of detail so that you have a clear idea of something: *a graphic description* **2** relating to drawing —**graphically** /'græfɪkli/ *adv*

graphic de'sign *noun* [U] the art of designing pictures and TEXT for magazines, advertisements etc —**graphic de'signer** *noun* [C]

graphics /'græfɪks/ *noun* [plural] pictures that are produced by a computer, or that are included in a document, magazine etc

graphite /'græfaɪt/ *noun* [U] a soft black substance that is used in pencils

grapple /'græp(ə)l/ **PHRASAL VERB 'grapple with sth** to try hard to understand a difficult idea or solve a difficult problem

grasp¹ /grɑːsp/ *verb* [T] **1** to take and hold someone or something very tightly: *He grasped her firmly by the shoulders.* **2** to understand something: *Charlie grasped the point at once.* → NETTLE
PHRASAL VERB 'grasp at sth to try to take hold of something

grasp² /grɑːsp/ *noun* [singular] **1** the ability to understand something: *a good grasp of English* **2** the ability to achieve something: *Victory was now within their grasp.* **3** a very tight hold of someone or something:

Suddenly he broke free from her grasp.

grass /grɑːs/ noun ★★★

1 [U] a very common plant with thin green leaves that covers the ground: *We should cut the grass before it starts raining.* ♦ *Stephen was lying on the grass.*

2 [C] a particular type of grass: *tall flowering grasses*

3 [U] *informal* CANNABIS

4 [C] *British informal* someone, usually a criminal, who tells the police what other criminals have done

grasshopper /'grɑːsˌhɒpə/ noun [C] a large insect with long back legs that moves by jumping and that makes short high sounds —*picture* → C13

G

grassland /'grɑːsˌlænd/ noun [U] a large area of land where wild grass grows

grass 'roots, the noun [plural] the ordinary people in a community, country, or organization rather than its leaders

grassy /'grɑːsi/ adj covered in grass

grate¹ /greɪt/ verb **1** [T] to rub food against a GRATER in order to cut it into small pieces —*picture* → C2 **2** [I] to rub against something and make an unpleasant annoying sound: *Her nails grated against the wall.* **3** [I] to have an annoying effect on someone: *His intense stare began to grate on her nerves.*

grate² /greɪt/ noun [C] a frame of metal bars used for holding coal or wood in a FIREPLACE (=the opening in a wall where you can light a fire)

grateful /'greɪtf(ə)l/ adj ★ feeling that you want to thank someone because they have given you something or done something for you ≠ UNGRATEFUL: *Thanks for coming with me. I'm really grateful.* ♦ *I'm very grateful for all your help with the party.* ♦ **grateful to sb for sth** *She was grateful to them for letting her stay at their house.* ♦ **+(that)** *You should be grateful that I didn't tell your parents.* —**gratefully** adv: *All comments and suggestions will be gratefully received.*

grater /'greɪtə/ noun [C] a tool with a rough sharp surface that you rub foods such as cheese and vegetables against in order to cut them into very small pieces —*picture* → C2

gratify /'grætɪˌfaɪ/ verb [T] *formal* to make someone feel pleased or satisfied —**gratification** /ˌgrætɪfɪ'keɪʃ(ə)n/ noun [U]

grating¹ /'greɪtɪŋ/ noun [C] a metal frame with bars across it that is used for covering a hole or window

grating² /'greɪtɪŋ/ adj a grating voice, laugh, or sound is unpleasant and annoying

gratitude /'grætɪˌtjuːd/ noun [U] the feeling of being grateful ≠ INGRATITUDE

gratuitous /grə'tjuːɪtəs/ adj done or shown without any good reason: *There's too much gratuitous violence in the film.*

grave¹ /greɪv/ noun ★

1 [C] the place where a dead body is buried in a deep hole in the ground: *He's never even visited his mother's grave.*

2 the grave [singular] *literary* death: *His secret will go with me to the grave* (=I will die without telling anyone).

grave² /greɪv/ adj **1** so serious that you feel worried: *You're in grave danger.* **2** looking

serious and worried: *a grave expression/face* —**gravely** adv

grave³ /grɑːv/ or **grave 'accent** noun [C] the mark ˋ above a letter in French and some other languages that is used in order to show how it is pronounced → ACUTE 4, CIRCUMFLEX

gravel /'græv(ə)l/ noun [U] small pieces of stone that are used for making paths and roads

gravelly /'græv(ə)li/ adj a gravelly voice sounds low and rough

gravestone /'greɪvˌstəʊn/ noun [C] a stone by a GRAVE that shows the name of the person who is buried there and the dates when he or she was born and died

graveyard /'greɪvˌjɑːd/ noun [C] an area of land where dead people are buried, usually around a church

gravitate /'grævɪˌteɪt/ verb [I] *formal* to be attracted to someone or something and tend to move towards them

gravitational /ˌgrævɪ'teɪʃ(ə)nəl/ adj *science* relating to the force of gravity

gravity /'grævəti/ noun [U] **1** the force that makes something fall to the ground: *the laws of gravity* **2** the serious or important quality of something: *I'm sure you can appreciate the gravity of the situation.*

gravy /'greɪvi/ noun [U] a sauce made from the juices of cooked meat mixed with flour

gray /greɪ/ the American spelling of **grey**

graze¹ /greɪz/ verb **1** [I] to eat grass that is growing somewhere: *Goats grazed on the hillside.* **2** [T] to break the surface of your skin: *He fell off the swing and grazed his knee.* **3** [I/T] to touch something slightly when you pass it: *She let her fingers graze lightly against his skin.*

graze² /greɪz/ noun [C] a break in the surface of your skin: *a graze on my elbow*

grease¹ /griːs/ noun [U] **1** a thick substance similar to oil that is used on machine parts for making them work smoothly **2** fat that comes out of meat when you cook it

grease² /griːs/ verb [T] to put grease, fat, or oil on something

greasy /'griːsi/ adj **1** prepared with a lot of oil or fat: *greasy chips* **2** covered in GREASE or oil: *greasy hands/jeans* **3** producing a lot of natural oil ≠ DRY: *greasy hair/skin*

great¹ /greɪt/ adj ★★★

1 more than usual	**5** for emphasis
2 important/powerful	**6** able to do sth well
3 good/enjoyable	**7** enthusiastic
4 for showing pleasure	

1 bigger or more than is usual: *They could be in great danger.* ♦ *He was in a great hurry.* ♦ *It gives me great pleasure to welcome our next guest.* → DEAL²

2 important or powerful: *a great military power* ♦ *the greatest environmental disaster in decades* ♦ *one of the greatest writers of the modern age*

3 *informal* very good, enjoyable, or nice: *You looked great in that outfit.* ♦ *We had a great day.* ♦ *He's a great guy.*

4 *spoken* used for expressing pleasure or agreement: *It's great to be here.* ♦ *Great! I'll pick you up at eight, then.*

5 *spoken* used for emphasizing the large size or amount of something: *a **great big** piece of chocolate*
6 *informal* able to do something very well: *Paul's **great at** entertaining the kids.*
7 *informal* enthusiastic about someone or something: *I'm your greatest admirer.* ♦ *She's a great reader of biographies.*

great² /greɪt/ adv *informal* very well. Some people think that this use is not correct: *You're doing great.*

great³ /greɪt/ noun [C] someone or something that is well known and admired by a lot of people: *Fred Perry is one of the all-time greats of tennis.*

Great 'Britain the island that consists of England, Scotland, and Wales

great-'grandchild noun [C] the GRANDCHILD of your son or daughter

greatly /'greɪtli/ adv very much: *Your support is greatly appreciated.* ♦ *greatly reduced costs*

greatness /'greɪtnəs/ noun [U] a position of power, success, or respect: *a woman destined for greatness*

greed /griːd/ noun [U] **1** a strong wish to have more money, possessions, or power than you need **2** a strong wish to have more food than you need

greedy /'griːdi/ adj **1** *British* wanting to eat or drink more food than you need **2** wanting more money, possessions, or power than you need —**greedily** adv

green¹ /griːn/ adj ★★★

1 like grass in colour	4 not ready to be eaten
2 with lots of plants	5 not experienced
3 caring for nature	6 of Green Party

1 something that is green is the same colour as grass: *green eyes* ♦ *The first **bright green** leaves were showing.*
2 a green area has a lot of grass, plants, or trees: *a campaign to protect the city's green spaces*
3 concerned with protecting the environment: *wind farms and other green energy schemes* ♦ *green campaigners*
4 not yet ready to be eaten: *green tomatoes*
5 someone who is green is young and has no experience of life
6 Green relating to the GREEN PARTY

green² /griːn/ noun ★★

1 colour of grass	4 green vegetables
2 area of grass	5 Green Party member
3 area in golf	

1 [C/U] the colour of grass: *She was dressed in green.*
2 [C] a large area of grass where people can walk, sit, or play games: *They moved to a house overlooking the green.*
3 [C] in golf, the area of short grass around a hole —*picture* → C15
4 greens [plural] *spoken* vegetables that have green leaves
5 Green [C] a member of the GREEN PARTY

green 'bean noun [C] a long thin green vegetable that grows on a tall climbing plant —*picture* → C11

green 'belt noun [C/U] *British* an area of land around large cities where no buildings are allowed

green 'card noun [C] *American* an official document that allows someone who is not a US citizen to live and work in the US

greenery /'griːnəri/ noun [U] plants or leaves

greenfield site /ˌgriːnfiːld 'saɪt/ noun [C] *British* a piece of land that has not previously been built on

greengrocer /'griːnˌgrəʊsə/ noun [C] *British* **1 greengrocer's** a shop that sells fruit and vegetables **2** someone whose job is to sell fruit and vegetables in a shop

greenhouse /'griːnˌhaʊs/ noun [C] a building made of glass that is used for growing plants that need protection from the weather

greenhouse ef,fect, the noun [singular] the situation in which heat is unable to escape from the atmosphere, which causes the temperature of the Earth to rise

greenhouse 'gas noun [C] a gas that stops heat from escaping from the atmosphere and causes the greenhouse effect

greenish /'griːnɪʃ/ adj similar to green

green 'light noun [singular] official approval for something to be done

Green 'Party, the a political organization whose main aim is to protect the environment

Greenpeace /'griːnˌpiːs/ an international organization whose aim is to protect the environment

greet /griːt/ verb [T] **1** to behave in a polite or friendly way towards someone when you meet them: *Natalie rushed to open the door and greet the guests.* **2** to react to an action or news in a particular way: *The decision was greeted by violent demonstrations.* **3** if you are greeted by a sight, sound, or smell, it is the first thing that you notice

greeting /'griːtɪŋ/ noun **1** [C/U] something polite or friendly that you say or do when you meet someone: *They exchanged greetings and sat down.* **2** [C] a friendly message that you send to someone on a special occasion such as their birthday

gregarious /grɪ'geəriəs/ adj **1** a gregarious person enjoys being with other people **2** gregarious animals or birds live in groups

grenade /grɪ'neɪd/ noun [C] a small bomb that someone throws or fires from a gun

grew the past tense of **grow**

grey¹ /greɪ/ adj ★

1 shade of black	4 with a lot of clouds
2 when hair goes whiter	5 boring
3 when face looks pale	

1 between black and white in colour: *He wore a **dark grey** suit.*
2 if someone goes or turns grey, their hair starts to become white: *She seems to have **gone grey** very quickly.*
3 if someone's face is grey, they look pale because they are ill or shocked: *His face was **grey with** pain.*
4 used for describing the weather or the light when it is not very bright because there are a lot of clouds: *The rain stopped and the grey skies began to clear.* ♦ *In London it was **a grey November day.***
5 boring: *the drab grey tedium of his life*

grey² /greɪ/ noun [C/U] a colour that is between black and white

grey³ /greɪ/ verb [I] **1** to become grey in colour **2** if a person or their hair is greying, their hair is becoming white

grey area noun [C] a situation in which the rules are not clear, or in which you are not sure what is right or wrong

greyhound /ˈgreɪhaʊnd/ noun [C] a tall thin dog that can run very fast. It is used in races.

grid /grɪd/ noun [C] **1** a pattern of straight lines that cross each other to form squares: *streets laid out in a grid* **2** a pattern of straight lines that form squares on a map, that you use to find a particular place: *a grid reference* **3** a set of wires that carry the electricity supply: *the national grid* **4** a set of metal bars that are arranged in a pattern of straight lines

gridlock /ˈgrɪdlɒk/ noun [U] **1** a situation in which there are so many cars on the roads that traffic cannot move **2** a situation in which it is impossible to make progress

grief /griːf/ noun [U] a strong feeling of sadness, usually because someone has died

PHRASE **come to grief 1** to be unsuccessful **2** to have an accident
→ GOOD¹

grievance /ˈgriːvəns/ noun [C] a feeling or complaint that you have been treated unfairly

grieve /griːv/ verb [I/T] to feel extremely sad because someone has died

grievous /ˈgriːvəs/ adj formal extremely serious or severe: *He has made a grievous error.*

grievous bodily harm noun [U] legal very serious injuries caused by a violent attack

grill¹ /grɪl/ noun [C] **1** British the part of a COOKER where food is cooked under great heat **2** a flat frame of metal bars on which food can be placed and cooked over a fire

grill² /grɪl/ verb **1** [I/T] British to cook something by putting it close to great heat above or below it **2** [T] to ask someone a lot of difficult questions for a long period of time

grille or **grill** /grɪl/ noun [C] a metal frame with bars or wire across it that is used for protecting a door or window

grim /grɪm/ adj **1** grim news, situations, and events are unpleasant and make you feel upset and worried: *the grim reality of unemployment* **2** very serious and unfriendly: *a grim expression* **3** a grim place is ugly and unpleasant —**grimly** adv

grimace /ˈgrɪməs/ verb [I] to make an ugly expression by twisting your face, for example because you are in pain or because you do not like something —**grimace** noun [C]

grime /graɪm/ noun [U] thick dirt on a surface

grimy /ˈgraɪmi/ adj very dirty

grin /grɪn/ verb [I] to smile showing your teeth —**grin** noun [C]

grind¹ /graɪnd/ (past tense and past participle **ground** /graʊnd/) verb [T] **1** to break something into very small pieces or powder, either by using a machine or by crushing it between two hard surfaces: *The mill was used for grinding corn.* **2** to press something

down onto a surface using a lot of force: *She ground a half-smoked cigarette into the ashtray.* **3** to make something such as a knife smooth or sharp by rubbing it against a hard surface

PHRASES **grind to a halt 1** if a vehicle grinds to a halt, it moves more and more slowly until it finally stops **2** if a process or a country grinds to a halt, things gradually get worse until they finally stop

grind your teeth to rub your top and bottom teeth together in a way that makes a noise

grind² /graɪnd/ noun [singular] informal something that is hard work, boring, and tiring

grinding /ˈgraɪndɪŋ/ adj extreme: used for emphasizing how bad a situation is: *grinding poverty*

PHRASE **a grinding halt** a situation in which something stops operating completely

grip¹ /grɪp/ noun **1** [singular] a firm strong hold: *Pete tightened his grip on her arm.* **2** [singular] power and control over someone or something: *The President struggled to regain his grip on power.* **3** [singular/U] if shoes or tyres have grip, they hold a surface firmly and do not slip

PHRASES **be in the grip of sth** to be in a difficult or unpleasant situation

get a grip (on yourself) spoken to make an effort to control your emotions or your behaviour

get/come to grips with sth to start to deal with a problem, situation, or job that you have to do

grip² /grɪp/ verb **1** [T] to hold something tightly: *She gripped Frank's hand firmly.* **2** [T] to have a strong effect on someone: *A feeling of fear gripped the crowd.* **3** [T] to keep someone very interested in something: *The case has gripped the public because of the celebrities involved.* **4** [I/T] if shoes or tyres grip, they hold a surface firmly and therefore do not slip

gripe /graɪp/ noun [C] informal a complaint about something that is annoying but not very important —**gripe** verb [I]

gripping /ˈgrɪpɪŋ/ adj very exciting and interesting

grisly /ˈgrɪzli/ adj involving death or violence in a shocking way＝GRUESOME

grit¹ /grɪt/ noun [U] very small pieces of stone or sand

grit² /grɪt/ verb [T] British to spread grit on roads that have ice on them

PHRASE **grit your teeth 1** to press your teeth together tightly, for example because you are angry or in pain **2** to show determination in a difficult situation

gritty /ˈgrɪti/ adj **1** showing life as it really is, even when it is not nice or attractive: *a gritty television drama* **2** firm in your intentions: *a gritty determination to succeed* **3** containing grit, or covered with grit

grizzled /ˈgrɪz(ə)ld/ adj with grey hair

groan /grəʊn/ verb **1** [I] to make a long low sound because you are unhappy or in pain: *The Milan fans groaned at the news that the star was not fit to play.* **2** [I/T] to speak about something in a way that shows that you are unhappy —**groan** noun [C]

grocer /ˈɡrəʊsə/ noun [C] **1 grocer's** a small shop that sells food and other goods for the home **2** someone who owns or works in a grocer's shop

groceries /ˈɡrəʊsəriz/ noun [plural] food and other goods for the home that you buy regularly

grocery /ˈɡrəʊsəri/ adj relating to groceries or grocer's shops

groggy /ˈɡrɒɡi/ adj feeling tired, weak, or confused because you are ill or because you have not had enough sleep

groin /ɡrɔɪn/ noun [C] the area where your legs join the front of your body

groom¹ /ɡruːm/ verb [T] **1** to clean and brush an animal **2** to prepare someone for a particular job or activity

groom² /ɡruːm/ noun [C] **1** a BRIDEGROOM **2** someone who looks after horses

groove /ɡruːv/ noun [C] a line that has been cut into a surface

grope /ɡrəʊp/ verb **1** [I] to try to find something by feeling with your hands: *She was groping around in her bag for her keys.* ♦ *I groped my way to the door.* **2** [I] to search for an idea or a way to say something without being certain of what you are doing: *She hesitated, seeming to grope for words.* **3** [T] to touch someone sexually, especially someone who does not want to be touched

gross¹ /ɡrəʊs/ adj **1** a gross amount of money is the total amount before taxes or costs have been taken out **2** extreme and unreasonable: *a gross distortion of the truth* **3** *legal* gross actions are extremely bad and are considered immoral by most people: *gross misconduct* **4** *informal* extremely unpleasant

gross² /ɡrəʊs/ verb [T] to earn a particular amount of money before taxes or other costs have been taken out

gross do,mestic 'product noun [U] GDP

grossly /ˈɡrəʊsli/ adv extremely: *grossly unfair*

gross ,national 'product noun [U] GNP

gross 'profit noun [C] *business* the difference between the price that someone sells goods for and what it costs to produce them

grotesque /ɡrəʊˈtesk/ adj **1** extremely ugly and strange **2** unreasonable or offensive —**grotesquely** adv

ground¹ /ɡraʊnd/ noun ★★★

1 surface of Earth	6 reason for sth
2 layer of soil/rock	7 subject/idea
3 area of land	8 level of progress
4 area used for sth	9 wire
5 land around house	+ PHRASES

1 [singular/U] the top part of the Earth's surface that people walk on: *People were sitting on the ground in small groups.* ♦ *They were working 250 metres below ground.*

2 [singular] the layer of soil and rock that forms the Earth's surface: *the destruction caused by getting coal out of the ground* ♦ *Prepare the ground for planting.*

3 [U] an area of land: *an acre of ground*

4 [C] an area of land or sea that is used for a particular purpose: *soldiers on the parade ground* ♦ *a regular fishing ground*

5 grounds [plural] the land and gardens that surround a large house or public building: *She found him wandering around the grounds.*

6 grounds [plural] a reason for what you say or do: *The army turned him down on medical grounds.* ♦ *The Act prohibits discrimination on the grounds of sex or marital status.* ♦ *There do seem to be some grounds for their complaints.*

7 [singular/U] the subject, idea, or information that people are talking about or writing about: *We'll be covering a lot of new ground in today's lecture.* ♦ *Henry seems anxious to return to more familiar ground.*

8 [U] the level of success or progress that someone or something has achieved: *Most stock markets lost ground after their recent gains.*

9 [C] *American* an electrical EARTH

PHRASES get (sth) off the ground to start successfully, or to get something started successfully

on the ground 1 on the surface of the earth, rather than in the air **2** *mainly journalism* in the place or situation that is being discussed

stand your ground 1 to not move when someone attacks you or is going to attack you **2** to refuse to change your opinions, beliefs, or decisions despite pressure to change them

ground² /ɡraʊnd/ verb [T] **1** to stop a plane from leaving the ground: *All of their planes have been grounded.* **2** to base an idea or decision on a particular thing: *Kim's theory is grounded in practical experience.* **3** *American* to EARTH a piece of electrical equipment **4** to punish a child or young person by stopping them from going to places that they enjoy: *His parents grounded him for two weeks.*

ground³ the past tense and past participle of **grind**¹

groundbreaking /ˈɡraʊn(d)ˌbreɪkɪŋ/ adj using new methods or achieving new results

ground 'floor noun [singular] *British* the floor of a building that is at or near the level of the ground

grounding /ˈɡraʊndɪŋ/ noun [singular] a basic knowledge of a subject

groundless /ˈɡraʊn(d)ləs/ adj not based on evidence or good reasons

'ground ,rules noun [plural] the basic rules or principles that govern the way that something is done

groundswell /ˈɡraʊn(d)swel/ noun [singular] a sudden increase in people's feelings about something

groundwork /ˈɡraʊn(d)ˌwɜːk/ noun [U] work that you do in order to prepare for something: *The agreement will lay the groundwork (=do the work that is necessary) for peaceful relations between the two countries.*

ground 'zero noun [U] **1** a place where a lot of people have been killed, or a lot of damage has been done, especially because of a nuclear explosion **2** a place where changes are happening quickly or violently

group¹ /gru:p/ noun [C] ★★★

1 several people or things that are together or that are related to each other in some way: *Why don't you join the local drama group?* ♦ *Firms should employ more people in the over-55 age group.* ♦ *a group decision/activity* (=involving all the people in a group) ♦ *There was a* **group of** *girls following him.*

2 a small set of musicians who play POP MUSIC =BAND: *members of a pop group*

G

> In British English, **group** can be used with a singular or plural verb. You can say *The local drama group* **meets** *every week.* OR *The local drama group* **meet** *every week.*

group² /gru:p/ verb [T] to put people or things into groups: *The students are grouped according to ability.* ♦ *The new offices will be grouped around a central garden.*

groupie /'gru:pi/ noun [C] *informal* someone who admires a particular famous person and tries to meet them or make friends with them

grouping /'gru:pɪŋ/ noun [C] a set of people or things that are considered as a group

grouse¹ /graʊs/ noun [C] a large brown bird that lives on the ground and is hunted for its meat

grouse² /graʊs/ verb [I] *informal* to complain about something that is unimportant

grove /grəʊv/ noun [C] a group of trees that are arranged in lines

grovel /'grɒv(ə)l/ (present participle **grovelling**; past tense and past participle **grovelled**) verb [I] to show too much respect for someone, or to be too willing to obey someone

grow /grəʊ/ (past tense **grew** /gru:/; past participle **grown** /grəʊn/) verb ★★★

1 become taller	**4** look after plants
2 about hair/nails	**5** start to have quality
3 get bigger/stronger	**+ PHRASAL VERBS**

1 [I] if children, animals, or plants grow, they become taller: *She must have grown at least four inches since I saw her last.* ♦ *a fully grown lion* ♦ *Some of these creatures* **grew to a length of** *over 12 feet.*

2 [I/T] if your hair or nails grow, or if you grow them, they become longer: *My nails grow really quickly.* ♦ *Her husband is growing a beard.*

3 [I] to increase in size, strength, or importance: *The world's population is growing faster than anyone thought it would.* ♦ *The problem continues to grow.* ♦ *She could feel the anger growing inside her.* ♦ *The sound* **grew to** *a deafening roar.* ♦ *The economy has* **grown by** *7% over the past year.* ♦ *She was* **growing in** *confidence every day.*

4 [T] if you grow plants, you look after them and help them to develop =CULTIVATE, PRODUCE: *They grew all their own vegetables.* ♦ *Various crops are grown here.* ♦ *the country's largest rice-growing area*

5 [linking verb] *literary* used for saying that a feeling or quality gradually starts to exist: *The nights were growing darker.* ♦ *Nina was growing bored.* ♦ *She had* **grown used to** *the old man's habits.* ♦ **grow to do/be sth** *They had grown to love the place and the people.*

PHRASAL VERBS **grow a'part** if people grow apart, their relationship gradually changes and they become less close

grow 'into sth 1 to develop and become a particular thing or person: *She had grown into a beautiful woman.* **2** if children grow into clothes, they become the right size to wear clothes that were too big

grow on sb if something or someone grows on you, you start to like them more: *The new house slowly began to grow on her.*

grow 'out of sth 1 if children grow out of clothes, they grow bigger and the clothes become too small for them **2** if someone grows out of a habit, they stop doing it because they have become older or wiser **3** to develop from something: *The idea grew out of a wish to improve the lives of the children in the region.*

grow 'up 1 to change from being a child to being an adult: *She's really starting to grow up now.* ♦ *He rarely saw his father while he was growing up.* **2** to stop behaving like a child and become more sensible: *It wasn't until my marriage ended that I really started to grow up.*

> ### Word family: grow
> *Words in the same family as* **grow**
> - **grown** *adj*
> - **growing** *adj*
> - **growth** *n*
> - **outgrow** *v*
> - **overgrown** *adj*
> - **undergrowth** *n*

growing /'grəʊɪŋ/ adj ★★

1 becoming more severe or extreme: *There is* **growing public concern** *over the effects of this policy.*

2 becoming greater in size or amount: *the growing popularity of the Internet* ♦ *A* **growing number of** *people are choosing to eat less meat.* ♦ *Europe's* **fastest growing** *international airport*

growl /graʊl/ verb **1** [I] if an animal growls, it makes a frightening low noise **2** [I/T] to say something in an unfriendly and angry way —**growl** noun [C]

grown¹ /grəʊn/ adj adult: *a grown man/woman*

grown² the past participle of **grow**

grown-up¹ noun [C] an ADULT: used when talking to children

grown-up² adj adult, or intended for adults: *She has two grown-up sons.* ♦ *grown-up entertainment*

growth /grəʊθ/ noun ★★★

1 [singular/U] an increase in the number, size, or importance of something: *We are entering a* **period of** *rapid population growth.* ♦ *The annual* **rate of growth** *was 12 per cent.* ♦ *the international* **growth of** *capitalism* ♦ *a substantial* **growth in** *the number of available jobs*

2 [singular/U] an increase in the size or development of a living thing: *There is no evidence that the drug increases hair growth.*

3 [C] a lump on someone's body that is caused by a disease: *a cancerous growth*

> **Words often used with growth**
>
> *Verbs often used with* **growth** *(sense 1)*
> - **encourage, foster, increase, promote, stimulate** + GROWTH: make something increase
> - **inhibit, stunt** + GROWTH: prevent something from increasing

growth ,industry noun [C] an industry that is growing quickly

grub /grʌb/ noun [U] *very informal* food

grubby /'grʌbi/ adj dirty

grudge[1] /grʌdʒ/ noun [C] a feeling of anger towards someone because they have done something unfair to you: *There's a whole list of people who might bear a grudge against him.*

grudge[2] /grʌdʒ/ verb [T] to give something in an unwilling way=BEGRUDGE, RESENT: *I grudge every minute that I have to stay away from my writing.*

grudging /'grʌdʒɪŋ/ adj done in an unwilling way —**grudgingly** adv

gruelling /'gruːəlɪŋ/ adj involving a lot of continuous effort=PUNISHING

gruesome /'gruːs(ə)m/ adj something that is gruesome is very unpleasant because it involves violent injury or death=GRISLY

gruff /grʌf/ adj **1** rude and unfriendly **2** a gruff voice has a rough low sound —**gruffly** adv

grumble /'grʌmb(ə)l/ verb [I] to complain about something that is unimportant =MOAN —**grumble** noun [C]

grumpy /'grʌmpi/ adj someone who is grumpy complains a lot or is often unhappy —**grumpily** adv

grungy /'grʌndʒi/ adj *very informal* dirty and untidy

grunt /grʌnt/ verb [I] **1** to make a short low sound in your throat and nose **2** if a pig grunts, it makes its usual low sound —**grunt** noun [C]

guarantee[1] /ˌɡærən'tiː/ verb [T] ★
1 to make it certain that something will happen or will exist=ASSURE: *The government provides help for small businesses, but it cannot* **guarantee** *their success.* ♦ **+(that)** *We can't guarantee that you will get the cheapest fare possible.* ♦ **guarantee sb sth** *This win guarantees them a place in the final.*
2 if a company guarantees something that you buy, they promise to repair it if it stops working: *All our products are guaranteed for three years.*
3 to promise that something will happen: **+(that)** *He guaranteed they would be paid on time.*

guarantee[2] /ˌɡærən'tiː/ noun [C] ★
1 something that makes something else certain to happen: *Massive investment is no* **guarantee** *of success.* ♦ **+(that)** *There's no guarantee you will get in without a ticket.*
2 a promise that something will definitely happen: **give (sb) a guarantee** *I can't give you any guarantees at the moment.* ♦ **+(that)** *The company has given a guarantee that there will be no job losses.* ♦ *We need a cast-iron*

guarantee (=one that is completely reliable) *that you will stop killing these animals.*
3 a written promise that a company will repair something that you buy from them if it stops working=WARRANTY: *Many companies offer a 30-day* **money-back guarantee**. ♦ *My watch is still under* **guarantee** (=protected by a company's guarantee).

guaranteed /ˌɡærən'tiːd/ adj if something is guaranteed, you will definitely get it

guard[1] /ɡɑːd/ noun [C] ★★
1 someone whose job is to protect a place or person: *a prison guard* ♦ *There was an* **armed guard** *on duty outside his door.*
2 *British* an official on a train whose job is to check tickets
3 an object that covers something and protects it: *All boxers wear a mouth guard.*
PHRASES **let your guard down** or **drop your guard 1** to relax and trust people, even though this might be dangerous **2** to stop being careful while you are being attacked
off (your) guard not concentrating on something and therefore likely to do something that you did not intend to do
on your guard being careful not to do something that you did not intend to do
under guard protected by a guard, or prevented from escaping by a guard: *He was taken to prison under police guard.*

guard[2] /ɡɑːd/ verb [T] **1** to protect someone or something from danger or harm: **guard sth/sb from sth** *the trees that guarded the farm from the wind* **2** to prevent someone from escaping from a place: *There were two soldiers guarding the main gate.* **3** to try very hard to keep something that is important to you: *The company is fiercely guarding its independence.*
PHRASAL VERB **guard a,gainst sth** to try to prevent something from happening: *We need to guard against the possibility of failure.*

guarded /'ɡɑːdɪd/ adj careful not to give much information or show your real feelings

guardian /'ɡɑːdiən/ noun [C] **1** a person or organization that protects something **2** someone who is legally responsible for someone else's child

guardian 'angel noun [C] **1** a helpful spirit who some people believe looks after a particular person **2** someone who continuously supports someone else

guerrilla /ɡə'rɪlə/ noun [C] a member of a military group that fights to change a political situation: *guerrilla groups/ fighters/leaders*

guess[1] /ɡes/ verb [I/T] ★★
1 to say or decide what you think is true, without being certain about it: *a competition to guess the weight of the pig* ♦ *Whoever* **guesses** *correctly will win two tickets to the show.* ♦ *Would anyone like to* **guess what** *this object is?* ♦ *I could only* **guess at** *her age.* ♦ **+(that)** *She guessed that it was about noon from the position of the sun.*
2 to be correct about something that you guess: *He had already* **guessed** *the* **answer**. ♦ *Surely she would* **guess** *the* **truth**. ♦ **+(that)** *Tim guessed she was awake.*

G

PHRASES **guess what** *spoken* used before you tell someone something that you are pleased or excited about: *Guess what! I won a trip to the Caribbean!*
I guess *informal* used when you are saying something that you think is probably true or correct: *'So you won't be going there again?' 'I guess not* (=no).*'* ♦ *'Were you happy with the result?' 'Well, I guess so* (=yes, but not very happy).*'* ♦ **+(that)** *I guess I'll never be able to explain.*

guess² /ges/ *noun* [C] ★ an occasion when you say what you think is true without being certain: *We can only hazard a guess at what happened* (=make a guess that will probably not be accurate). ♦ *Have a guess and then check it on your calculator.* ♦ *I could probably make an educated guess* (=one that is based on some knowledge).
PHRASE **sth is anyone's guess** used for saying that no one knows a particular thing: *What this all means is anybody's guess.* ♦ *It's anyone's guess who'll win the election.*

Words often used with guess

*Adjectives often used with **guess** (noun)*
■ **educated, good, informed** + GUESS: used about a guess that is likely to be accurate
■ **rough, wild** + GUESS: used about a guess that is not likely to be accurate

guessing game /ˈgesɪŋ ˌgeɪm/ *noun* [C] a situation in which people have to guess what is going to happen

guesstimate /ˈgestɪmət/ *noun* [C] *informal* a calculation that you make when you do not have all the facts about something

guesswork /ˈgeswɜːk/ *noun* [U] the guesses that you make when you try to find the answer to something

guest¹ /gest/ *noun* [C] ★★
1 someone who you have invited to your home or your party: *We've got guests staying this weekend.* ♦ *advice about getting rid of unwanted guests* ♦ *He was a guest at our wedding.*
2 someone who is paying to stay at a hotel or eat in a restaurant: *There is live music to entertain guests.* ♦ *The pool is free to hotel guests.*
3 someone who appears on a television or radio programme that they do not regularly appear on: *My first guest tonight is famous for both her singing and acting talent.*
PHRASES **be my guest** *spoken* used for saying yes as a polite reply to a request: *'Do you mind if I sit down?' 'Be my guest.'*
guest of honour an important guest at a meeting, party, or other event

guest² /gest/ *adj* **1** provided for guests to use: *a set of guest towels* **2** appearing by invitation to perform at an event: *Tonight's guest speaker is Peter Bell.*

guest house *noun* [C] a small hotel or private home where people can pay to stay the night

guidance /ˈgaɪd(ə)ns/ *noun* [U] advice: *I need some guidance on which university I should choose.* ♦ *marriage guidance* (=help given to people who have problems in their marriage)

guide¹ /gaɪd/ *noun* ★★

1 book	4 Girl Guide
2 for making judgment	5 Guides Association
3 for visitors	

1 [C] a book that gives information: *It is worth buying a good travel guide.* ♦ *I bought a copy of* A Beginner's Guide to Building Your Own Home.
2 [C] something or someone that helps you to make a judgment about something: *The doctor will give you a guide as to how much you should weigh.* ♦ *The colour of a plant's leaves is a good guide to its health.* ♦ *Opinion polls only serve as a rough guide to how people vote.*
3 [C] someone whose job is to give information to people who are visiting a place: *a tour guide*
4 Guide [C] a GIRL GUIDE
5 the Guides [plural] the GUIDES ASSOCIATION

guide² /gaɪd/ *verb* [T] ★
1 to show someone where to go by going with them: **guide sb through/to/along etc sth** *He guided them through the forest.*
2 to help someone to do something or make a decision: *There was no research to guide them.* ♦ *His entire life was guided by his religious beliefs.*
3 to try to make a situation develop in a particular way: **guide sth towards sth** *Harry tried to guide the conversation towards the subject of money.*

guidebook /ˈgaɪdbʊk/ *noun* [C] a book for tourists that provides information about a place

guide dog *noun* [C] *British* a dog that is trained to lead a person who cannot see

guidelines /ˈgaɪdˌlaɪnz/ *noun* [plural] official instructions or advice about how to do something: *strict guidelines on the training of police officers*

Guides Association, the an international organization for girls that teaches them moral values and practical skills

guild /gɪld/ *noun* [C] an organization of people who all have the same job or interests

guile /gaɪl/ *noun* [U] *formal* clever ways of tricking people = CUNNING

guillotine /ˈgɪləˌtiːn/ *noun* [C] a machine that was used in the past for cutting off someone's head — **guillotine** *verb* [T]

guilt /gɪlt/ *noun* [U] **1** a feeling of being ashamed and sorry because you have done something wrong: *The failure of the company left her with an overwhelming sense of guilt.* **2** the fact that someone has committed a crime: *The court will decide on his guilt or innocence.*

guilty /ˈgɪlti/ *adj* ★★
1 ashamed and sorry because you have done something wrong: *a guilty look/expression* ♦ *It was a clear sign that he had a guilty conscience* (=a feeling that he had done something wrong). ♦ *You shouldn't feel guilty all the time – you've done nothing to be ashamed of.* ♦ *I still feel guilty about things I said to my mother when I was a teenager.*
2 someone who is guilty has committed a crime or has done something wrong:

*Patrick knew that he was **guilty** of lying.* ♦ **find sb guilty/not guilty of sth** (=officially decide that they are guilty/not guilty) *He was found guilty of murder.*
—**guiltily** adv

guinea pig /ˈgɪni ˌpɪg/ noun [C] **1** a small furry animal with short ears and no tail. It is often kept as a pet. **2** someone who is used in an experiment

guise /gaɪz/ noun [C] *formal* the way that someone or something appears to people: *Revolutions come in many guises.* ♦ *Arms dealers have been operating under the guise of* (=pretending to be) *import agents.*

guitar /gɪˈtɑː/ noun [C] ★★ a musical instrument with six strings that can be ACOUSTIC or electric: *Her son plays the guitar in a rock band.* —*picture* → STRINGED INSTRUMENT —**guitarist** noun [C]

gulf /gʌlf/ noun [C] **1** a large and important difference between people or groups =CHASM: *trying to close the widening gulf between the rich and the poor* **2** a large area of sea that is almost surrounded by land: *the Persian Gulf*

gull /gʌl/ noun [C] a large white bird that lives near the sea =SEAGULL

gullibility /ˌgʌləˈbɪləti/ noun [U] the tendency to be gullible

gullible /ˈgʌləb(ə)l/ adj a gullible person is easy to trick because they always trust people ≠ CYNICAL

gully /ˈgʌli/ noun [C] a long narrow valley with steep sides

gulp /gʌlp/ verb **1** [T] to swallow food or drink quickly **2** [I] to make the movement of swallowing because you are surprised, excited, or afraid —**gulp** noun [C]

> **PHRASAL VERB** ˌgulp sth ˈdown *same as* gulp 1: *I gulped down a coffee and left.*

gum /gʌm/ noun **1** [C] the firm pink flesh in your mouth that your teeth are fixed to **2** [U] CHEWING GUM **3** [C/U] *British* a type of glue used for paper **4** [U] a sticky substance that comes from some trees

gumption /ˈgʌmpʃ(ə)n/ noun [U] the ability to be sensible and brave enough to do the right thing in a difficult situation

gun¹ /gʌn/ noun [C] ★★★
1 a weapon that shoots bullets or large SHELLS: *Enemy guns fired a shell every two or three minutes.* ♦ *a gang armed with machine guns* ♦ *Their police officers all carry guns.* ♦ *He pointed the gun directly at me.* ♦ *She was learning how to fire a gun.* ♦ *A police gun went off* (=was fired) *accidentally.* ♦ *Suddenly the officer pulled a gun on them* (=took it out and pointed it at them).
2 a tool that forces something out of its container using pressure: *a paint/glue/staple gun*

> → JUMP¹, STICK TO STH 3

gun² /gʌn/ **PHRASAL VERB** ˌgun sb ˈdown *mainly journalism* to shoot someone and kill them

gunboat /ˈgʌnˌbəʊt/ noun [C] a small navy ship with large guns

ˈgun conˌtrol noun [U] laws that prevent people from keeping and using guns

gunfire /ˈgʌnˌfaɪə/ noun [U] shots from guns, or the sound of shots

gunge /gʌndʒ/ noun [U] *British informal* any soft, sticky, dirty, and unpleasant substance

gunman /ˈgʌnmən/ (plural **gunmen** /ˈgʌnmən/) noun [C] *mainly journalism* someone who uses a gun when they are fighting or committing a crime

gunpoint /ˈgʌnˌpɔɪnt/ noun **at gunpoint** in the position of threatening someone with a gun, or being threatened with a gun

gunshot /ˈgʌnˌʃɒt/ noun **1** [C] the sound that is made when someone fires a gun **2** [U] the bullets that are shot from a gun: *a gunshot wound*

gurgle /ˈgɜːg(ə)l/ verb [I] **1** to make the low sound that water makes when it is poured quickly from a bottle **2** if a person gurgles, they make a low sound in their throat —**gurgle** noun [C]

guru /ˈguːruː/ noun [C] **1** someone who other people respect and ask for advice about a particular subject: *a style/fitness guru* **2** a spiritual leader in some religions

gush¹ /gʌʃ/ verb [I] **1** if a liquid gushes, it flows quickly and in large quantities —*picture* → DRIP **2** to express a lot of admiration or pleasure in a way that does not seem to be sincere

gush² /gʌʃ/ noun [C] **1** a large quantity of liquid or gas that quickly flows out of something **2** a strong sudden feeling

gushing /ˈgʌʃɪŋ/ adj *informal* expressing admiration or pleasure in a way that does not seem to be sincere

gust¹ /gʌst/ noun [C] a sudden strong wind —**gusty** adj

gust² /gʌst/ verb [I] if a wind gusts, it blows very strongly for short periods of time

gusto /ˈgʌstəʊ/ noun **with gusto** with a lot of enthusiasm

gut¹ /gʌt/ noun [C] the tube in your body that carries food away from your stomach

> **PHRASE** gut feeling/instinct a feeling that you are certain is right, although you can give no good reason why

> → GUTS

gut² /gʌt/ verb [T] to destroy the inside of a building or vehicle: *The entire building was gutted by the fire.*

ˌgut reˈaction noun [C] something that you feel or believe strongly without stopping to think about it

guts /gʌts/ noun [plural] *informal* **1** the quality of being brave and determined: ♦ *It takes a lot of guts and hard work to get where he is.* **2** your stomach and the organs near it **3** the most important parts of a system, plan, or machine

gutsy /ˈgʌtsi/ adj *informal* brave and determined

gutted /ˈgʌtɪd/ adj **1** *British spoken* extremely disappointed **2** if a building is gutted, it is completely destroyed

gutter /ˈgʌtə/ noun **1** [C] the edge of a road, where water flows away **2** [C] a piece of GUTTERING **3** the gutter [singular] the bad social conditions of the poorest people in society

guttering /ˈgʌtərɪŋ/ noun [U] *British* open pipes

along the edge of a roof that carry rain water away —*picture* → c1

gutter press, the noun [singular] *British showing disapproval* newspapers that contain a lot of shocking stories about crime, sex, and famous people

guttural /ˈgʌt(ə)rəl/ adj a guttural sound is deep and made at the back of your throat

guy /gaɪ/ noun ★★
  1 [C] *informal* a man: *Bob's a really nice guy.*
  2 guys [plural] *spoken* used for talking to a group of people: *Okay, guys. What will we do now?*

guzzle /ˈgʌz(ə)l/ verb [T] *informal* to eat or drink a lot quickly

gym /dʒɪm/ noun **1** [C] a room or club with equipment for doing physical exercises **2** [U] the activity of doing indoor physical exercises at school

gymnasium /dʒɪmˈneɪziəm/ noun [C] *formal* a GYM

gymnast /ˈdʒɪmnæst/ noun [C] someone who does gymnastics

gymnastics /dʒɪmˈnæstɪks/ noun [U] a sport in which you perform physical exercises that involve bending and balancing —**gymnastic** adj

gynaecology /ˌgaɪnɪkəˈlɒdʒi/ noun [U] the treatment of medical conditions that affect women's REPRODUCTIVE organs —**gynaecological** /ˌgaɪnɪkəˈlɒdʒɪk(ə)l/ adj, **gynaecologist** /ˌgaɪnɪˈkɒlədʒɪst/ noun [C]

gynecology /ˌgaɪnɪˈkɒlədʒi/ the American spelling of **gynaecology**

gypsy /ˈdʒɪpsi/ noun [C] **1** someone who does not live in one place but travels around **2** *offensive* a ROMANY

gyrate /dʒaɪˈreɪt/ verb [I] **1** to move around quickly in circles **2** *humorous* to dance in a sexual way

Hh

h or **H** /eɪtʃ/ noun [C/U] the eighth letter of the English alphabet

ha /hɑː/ interjection **1** used for showing that you are pleased because you have discovered or achieved something **2** used for showing that you disagree with someone

habit /ˈhæbɪt/ noun ★★
  1 [C/U] something that you do often: *healthy eating habits* ♦ **be in the habit of doing sth** *They were in the habit of going for long walks.* ♦ **get in/into the habit of doing sth** *George has got into the habit of going to bed late.*
  2 [C] something that is bad that you often do without realizing it, or without being able to stop: *Over 10 million smokers have succeeded in kicking the habit* (=stopping it). ♦ **have the habit of doing sth** *He had the annoying habit of tapping the table when he was nervous.*

3 [C] a simple dress that is worn by NUNS and other members of religious communities

---

Words often used with habit

Adjectives often used with habit (sense 2)
  ■ **annoying, dirty, disgusting, filthy** + HABIT: used about a habit that is very unpleasant

---

  ■ A **habit** is something that someone does often or regularly, as a normal part of their life: *Eating sweets is a bad habit.* ♦ *I soon got into the habit of getting up early.*
  ■ A **custom** is something that a particular group of people do because it is traditional and usual: *the custom of shaking hands*

---

habitable /ˈhæbɪtəb(ə)l/ adj a building that is habitable is good enough to live in
  ≠ UNINHABITABLE

habitat /ˈhæbɪtæt/ noun [C] the type of place that an animal normally lives in or that a plant normally grows in

habitation /ˌhæbɪˈteɪʃ(ə)n/ noun [U] *formal* the fact that people are living in a place

habitual /həˈbɪtʃuəl/ adj **1** usual, or typical: *He spoke to the workers with his habitual honesty.* **2** used for describing a person who has a particular bad habit: *an habitual smoker/drinker/liar/criminal* —**habitually** adv

hack¹ /hæk/ verb [I/T] to cut something in a rough way or with a lot of energy: *The boys were hacking at the bushes with heavy sticks.*
  PHRASE **can't hack it** to be unable to deal with something because it is too difficult or boring
  PHRASAL VERB **hack into sth** to use a computer in order to connect secretly and illegally to someone else's computer: *They hack into banks and transfer huge amounts of cash.*

hack² /hæk/ noun [C] *informal* a journalist, artist, or writer who does boring work or work that is not very good

hacker /ˈhækə/ noun [C] someone who uses a computer in order to connect secretly and illegally to other people's computers

hackles /ˈhæk(ə)lz/ noun [plural] if your hackles rise, you begin to feel very angry

hackneyed /ˈhæknid/ adj hackneyed words or ideas have been used so often that they no longer interesting or original

had the past tense and past participle of **have**

haddock /ˈhædək/ (plural **haddock**) noun [C/U] a large fish that lives in the North Atlantic Ocean and that is eaten as food

hadn't /ˈhæd(ə)nt/ short form the usual way of saying or writing 'had not'. This is not often used in formal writing: *I wish I hadn't sent that email.*

haemophilia /ˌhiːməˈfɪliə/ noun [U] a serious illness that prevents your blood from CLOTTING (=becoming thick) when it should

haemophiliac /ˌhiːməˈfɪliæk/ noun [C] someone who has haemophilia

haemorrhage /ˈhem(ə)rɪdʒ/ noun [C/U] an occasion when someone loses a lot of blood because of an injury inside their body

haemorrhoids /ˈhemərɔɪdz/ noun [plural] painful swollen areas around your ANUS

(=the hole where solid waste comes out of your body)

haggard /ˈhæɡəd/ adj looking very tired, worried, or ill

haggis /ˈhæɡɪs/ noun [C/U] a Scottish food made from the organs of a sheep mixed with grain

haggle /ˈhæɡ(ə)l/ verb [I] to argue in order to agree on the price of something

hah /hɑ/ another spelling of **ha**

ha ha interjection used for representing the sound of laughter, or for showing that you think something is not funny

hail¹ /heɪl/ verb **1** [T] *formal* to shout to someone as a way of attracting their attention: *I stepped out into the street and hailed a taxi.* **2** [I] if it hails, small balls of ice fall from the sky

    PHRASE **be hailed as sth** to be publicly praised for being very good: *The ruling was hailed as one of the most important legal decisions of the last 20 years.*

hail² /heɪl/ noun [U] rain that falls as small balls of ice

    PHRASE **a hail of bullets/arrows/bottles** a lot of things such as bullets that come at you very quickly

hailstones /ˈheɪlˌstəʊnz/ noun [plural] small balls of ice that form from hail

hair /heə/ noun ★★★
   1 [U] the thing that grows on your head in a mass of thin fibres: *long black hair* ♦ *brush/comb your hair* —picture → C14
   2 [C] a single fibre of hair: *a few grey hairs* ♦ *dog hairs on the furniture*
   PHRASES **let your hair down** *informal* to relax and enjoy yourself
   make sb's hair stand on end *humorous* to make someone feel very frightened
   → SPLIT¹

> **Words often used with hair**
>
> *Adjectives often used with hair (sense 1)*
> ■ **curly, fine, long, short, straight, thick, wavy** + HAIR: used about a particular type of hair

> When **hair** is used to refer to the thing that grows on your head as a mass, it has no plural and cannot be used with *a*: *She has beautiful hair* (NOT *a beautiful hair*). ♦ *All the children have curly hair.* ♦ *I found some hair in the bath.*

haircut /ˈheəˌkʌt/ noun [C] **1** an act of cutting someone's hair: *He was badly dressed and needed a haircut.* **2** the style that your hair has been cut in: *a short stylish haircut*

hairdo /ˈheəˌduː/ noun [C] *informal* a woman's hairstyle

hairdresser /ˈheəˌdresə/ noun [C] someone whose job is to cut people's hair

hairdryer or **hairdrier** /ˈheəˌdraɪə/ noun [C] a piece of electrical equipment that you use for drying your hair after you have washed it

hair grip noun [C] *British* a small metal or plastic object that is used for holding a woman's hair in position

hairline¹ /ˈheəˌlaɪn/ noun [C] the line at the top of your forehead where your hair begins

hairline² /ˈheəˌlaɪn/ adj a hairline crack is very narrow

hairpin /ˈheəˌpɪn/ noun [C] a metal object that is used for holding a woman's hair in position

hairpin 'bend noun [C] *British* a very sharp bend in a road, where the road forms a 'U' shape

hair-raising /ˈheə ˌreɪzɪŋ/ adj very frightening but exciting at the same time

hair's breadth noun [singular] the smallest possible distance, amount, or degree

hairstyle /ˈheəˌstaɪl/ noun [C] the shape that your hair has been cut or arranged in

bob

bunches

plait

ponytail

fringe

hairstyles

hairy /ˈheəri/ adj **1** with a lot of hair: *a hairy chest* **2** *informal* frightening, or dangerous

hajj or **haj** /hædʒ/ noun [C] a journey to the holy city of Mecca that Muslims make as a religious duty

hajji /ˈhædʒi/ noun [C] a Muslim who has made a hajj

halal /həˈlɑːl, ˈhælæl/ adj halal meat has been prepared according to the religious laws of Islam

half /hɑːf/ (plural **halves** /hɑːvz/) grammar word ★★★

> **Half** can be:
> ■ a **determiner**: *We live half a mile up the road.*
> ■ a **pronoun**: *Let's share the prize money. You can have half.* ♦ *Half of us are still unemployed.*

- an **adjective**: *We ordered a half bottle of red wine.*
- an **adverb**: *I was only half awake.* ♦ *A nurse only earns half as much as a doctor.*
- a **noun**: *The group was divided into two halves.*
- a **number**: *Emma could talk well by the age of two and a half.*

1 one of two equal parts of a number, amount, group, or object: *Only half the population voted in the election.* ♦ *The students spend half their time on practical work.* ♦ *The fabric is half nylon, half cotton.* ♦ *Jasmine started school when she was four and a half.* ♦ *We had to wait half an hour for a bus.* ♦ *Peel the potatoes and cut them in half.* ♦ *The risk of developing lung cancer has been reduced by half.* ♦ *half a dozen* (=6) *eggs* ♦ *Prices rose by over 15% during the second half of 1988.*

2 partly but not completely: *The door was half open.* ♦ *I only half understood the instructions.* ♦ *a half-empty milk bottle*

3 one of the two equal periods of time into which a game of football, basketball etc is divided

PHRASES **half the fun/problem/trouble etc** a large part of the fun/problem/trouble etc that is involved in something: *Putting up the decorations is half the fun of Christmas.* **half one/two/three etc** *British spoken* thirty minutes after one o'clock/two o'clock etc **half past one/two etc** thirty minutes after one o'clock/two o'clock etc: *The shops close at half past five.*

not half as good/bad/much etc as used for emphasizing that one person or thing is not nearly as good/bad etc as another: *It wasn't half as difficult as I expected.*

half-baked /ˌhɑːf ˈbeɪkt/ *adj informal* a half-baked idea is not practical because it has not been thought about carefully

half board noun [U] *British* an arrangement in which you stay in a hotel and have breakfast and an evening meal there, but not lunch → FULL BOARD

half brother noun [C] a brother who has either the same mother or the same father as you have

half-hearted /ˌhɑːf ˈhɑːtɪd/ *adj* done with no real interest or enthusiasm —**half-heartedly** *adv*

half-hour¹ *adj* lasting for 30 minutes: *a half-hour meeting*

half-hour² or **half an hour** noun [C] a period of 30 minutes: *Shannon waited another half-hour and then left.*

half-hourly *adj* happening every 30 minutes: *half-hourly news programmes*

half-mast noun **at half-mast** a flag that is at half-mast has been lowered to the middle of a pole in order to show respect for someone who has died

half measures noun [plural] methods that are not effective enough

half sister noun [C] a sister who has either the same mother or the same father as you have

half term noun [C/U] *British* a short holiday from school or university in the middle of a TERM

half time noun [U] in football and some other

team sports, a period of rest between the two halves of a match

halfway /hɑːfˈweɪ/ *adj, adv* in the middle of a space or period of time: *at the halfway stage of the competition* ♦ *Their house is about halfway up the street.*

halibut /ˈhælɪbət/ (plural **halibut**) noun [C/U] a large flat sea fish, or this fish eaten as food

hall /hɔːl/ noun [C] ★★★
1 a building or large room that is used for public events: *Hundreds of students had packed into the dining hall.* ♦ *a concert at the Albert Hall*
2 an area or passage inside the front door of a building that leads to other rooms: *Leave your shoes in the hall.* ♦ *The house has a large entrance hall.*
3 **hall** or **hall of residence** *British* a large building in a university where students live
→ TOWN HALL

hallmark /ˈhɔːlmɑːk/ noun [C] **1** a typical feature **2** an official mark on an object made of gold or silver that shows its quality

hallo /həˈləʊ/ *interjection British* HELLO

Halloween /ˌhæləʊˈiːn/ noun [C/U] the night of 31st October, when children dress as WITCHES and GHOSTS

hallucinate /həˈluːsɪneɪt/ *verb* [I] to see or hear something that is not really there because you are ill or because you have taken drugs —**hallucination** /həˌluːsɪˈneɪʃ(ə)n/ noun [C/U]

hallway /ˈhɔːlˌweɪ/ noun [C] an area or passage inside the front door of a building that leads to other rooms = HALL

halo /ˈheɪləʊ/ noun [C] a circle of light that is shown around the head of a holy person in religious paintings

halt¹ /hɔːlt/ noun [singular] the fact that something stops moving or stops happening: *The taxi came to a halt outside his front door.* ♦ *Traffic was brought to a halt* (=stopped) *by the demonstration.* ♦ *He has appealed for a halt to the fighting.*
PHRASE **call a halt to sth** to end something formally
→ GRIND¹

halt² /hɔːlt/ *verb* [I/T] if you halt something, or if it halts, it stops moving or happening: *Building work had been halted by the bad weather.* ♦ *She halted at the door and turned towards him.*

halting /ˈhɔːltɪŋ/ *adj* with a lot of pauses between words or movements because you are nervous or not confident —**haltingly** *adv*

halve /hɑːv/ *verb* **1** [I/T] to reduce something to half its original size or amount, or to become half the original size or amount: *Many shops have halved their prices.* ♦ *The number of hospitals in the country has halved over the last five years.* **2** [T] to cut something into two pieces of equal size

halves the plural of **half**

ham /hæm/ noun [U] the meat from a pig's leg: *a slice of ham* ♦ *a ham sandwich*

hamburger /ˈhæmˌbɜːɡə/ noun [C] a BURGER

hamlet /ˈhæmlət/ noun [C] a small village

hammer¹ /ˈhæmə/ noun [C] a tool used for hitting nails into wood. It consists of a handle and a heavy metal top. —*picture* → TOOL

hammer² /ˈhæmə/ verb [I/T] **1** to hit something with a hammer **2** to hit something hard, or to hit it many times

`PHRASAL VERB` **hammer sth ˈout** to reach an agreement after a long discussion

hammock /ˈhæmək/ noun [C] a bed consisting of a long piece of cloth or net that is tied at each end to a post or tree

hamper¹ /ˈhæmpə/ verb [T] to prevent something from happening normally, or to prevent someone from moving normally

hamper² /ˈhæmpə/ noun [C] a large basket with a lid, especially one that contains food

hamster /ˈhæmstə/ noun [C] a very small furry animal with a short tail. It is often kept as a pet.

hamstring /ˈhæmˌstrɪŋ/ noun [C] a TENDON that is behind your knee

hamstrung /ˈhæmˌstrʌŋ/ adj prevented from doing what you want to do

hand¹ /hænd/ noun ★★★

1 body part	**5** set of cards
2 help	**6** clapping
3 advantages	**+** PHRASES
4 part of clock	

1 [C] the part of your body at the end of each arm that you use for holding things: *Mrs Bennet put her hands over her ears to shut out the noise.* ♦ *The park was full of young couples **holding hands** (=holding each other's hands).* ♦ *The two men introduced themselves and **shook hands**.* ♦ *He was **holding** a mug of coffee **in his left hand**.* —picture → C14

2 [singular] help: *Would you like **a hand** with the cleaning up?* ♦ *Lydia **lent a hand** (=helped) with the costumes.* ♦ *Can you **give me a hand** (=help me) with these boxes?*

3 [singular] informal the advantages that you have in a situation: *Everything depends on how the company **plays its hand** (=uses its advantages).* ♦ *The trick is not to **show your hand** too early (=let an opponent know what your advantages are).*

4 [C] the hands on a clock are the long parts that move round and show the time

5 [C] the cards that have been given to you in a game of cards —picture → C16

6 [singular] if people give someone a hand, they CLAP their hands to show that they have enjoyed a performance

`PHRASES` **at hand** quite close to you and easy to reach: *Help is always at hand if you need it.* ♦ *I always keep my calculator **close at hand**.*

by hand 1 using your hands rather than a machine **2** if a letter is delivered by hand, it is not delivered by the post service

first/second/third hand if you experience something first hand, you experience it yourself. If you experience something second hand or third hand, someone else tells you about it.

get/lay your hands on sth to manage to obtain something: *I couldn't lay my hands on a copy of the book.*

go hand in hand to happen or exist together

hands off spoken used for telling someone not to touch or take something

hands up spoken **1** used for asking people to tell you if they know the answer to a question **2** used for asking people to tell you if they want something

have a hand in sth to help to make something happen

have your hands full to be extremely busy

in hand if something is in hand, you are dealing with it

in sb's hands if something is in someone's hands, they are responsible for it: *I knew that the dog was **in safe hands** with my parents.*

keep your hands off informal to not touch someone or something

off your hands if something is off your hands, you are no longer responsible for it

on hand 1 if someone is on hand, they are available to help you if you need them **2** if something is on hand, it is available to be used

on the one hand ... on the other hand used for giving two different opinions about something

out of hand not well controlled: *We decided to leave before things **got out of hand**.*

out of your hands if something is out of your hands, someone else is now responsible for it

take/get your hands off informal to stop touching someone or something

to hand British near where you are and therefore available to use

→ FORCE²

hand² /hænd/ verb [T] ★★ to give something to someone by holding it in your hand and offering it to them: **hand sth to sb** *Talbot handed the paper to the man.* ♦ **hand sb sth** *Sarah handed me an envelope.*

`PHRASAL VERBS` **hand sth ˈback** to give something back to someone: **hand sth back to sb** *Jean handed the letter back to Doug.* ♦ **hand sb sth back** *The officer handed me my passport back.*

hand sth ˈdown to give something to a younger person who will use it after you have died: *These skills have been handed down from generation to generation.*

hand sth ˈin to give something to a person in authority: *Please hand in your keys when you leave the hotel.*

hand sth ˈout to give things to different people in a group: *Would you hand these papers out for me?*

hand sb ˈover to give someone to the police or another authority: **hand sb over to sb** *The suspects have now been handed over to the French authorities.*

hand sth ˈover 1 to give something to someone by holding it in your hand and offering it to them: *Albert bowed and handed over the letter.* ♦ **hand sth over to sb** *He handed the car keys over to Stella.* **2** to give power or control to someone else: **hand sth over to sb** *They formally hand power over to the new government next week.*

handbag /ˈhæn(d)ˌbæg/ noun [C] a small bag that women use for carrying personal things such as money and keys —picture → BAG

handbook /ˈhæn(d)ˌbʊk/ noun [C] a small book that gives information or instructions

handbrake /ˈhæn(d)ˌbreɪk/ noun [C] British the piece of equipment in a car that you pull with your hand in order to prevent the car from moving after you have stopped it —picture → C6

handcuff /ˈhæn(d)ˌkʌf/ verb [T] to put handcuffs on someone

handcuffs /ˈhæn(d)ˌkʌfs/ noun [plural] metal rings that a police officer puts round a prisoner's wrists to stop them from using their hands

handful /ˈhæn(d)fʊl/ noun **1** [singular] a very small number of people or things: *Only a handful of people attended the meeting.* **2** [C] the quantity of something that you can hold in your hand: *a handful of coins* **3** [singular] informal someone who is difficult to control: *Their children are a real handful at school.*

hand greˌnade noun [C] a small bomb that explodes after a soldier throws it

handgun /ˈhæn(d)ˌgʌn/ noun [C] any small gun that is used with one hand

hand-held /ˈhænd ˌheld/ adj small enough to hold in your hands: *a hand-held computer*

handicap /ˈhændiˌkæp/ noun [C] a disadvantage that prevents you from doing something well

handicapped /ˈhændiˌkæpt/ adj old-fashioned someone who is handicapped has a permanent injury, illness, or other problem that makes them unable to use their body or mind normally. People now think that this word is offensive and prefer to say that someone is **disabled**.

handily /ˈhændɪli/ adv in a position that is convenient: *The house is handily located near the park.*

handiwork /ˈhændiˌwɜːk/ noun [U] something that someone has done or created

handkerchief /ˈhæŋkətʃɪf/ noun [C] a small piece of cloth or paper that you use for wiping your nose or eyes

handle¹ /ˈhænd(ə)l/ verb [T] ★★★
1 to deal with someone or something: *The government was criticized for the way it handled the crisis.* ♦ *The newer computers can handle massive amounts of data.* ♦ *Flight attendants are trained to handle difficult passengers.* ♦ *I left the job because I couldn't handle the pressure.*
2 to touch or hold something: *All chemicals must be handled with care.*
3 to control an animal or a vehicle using your hands: *She handled the horse very confidently.*
4 to buy and sell goods, especially illegally: *He denied burglary but admitted handling stolen goods.*

handle² /ˈhænd(ə)l/ noun [C] ★ the part of something that you use for holding it: *knives with plastic handles* ♦ *a door handle*

handlebars /ˈhænd(ə)lˌbɑːz/ noun [plural] the part of a bicycle that you hold with your hands and use for controlling it

handling /ˈhændlɪŋ/ noun [U] the way that someone deals with a particular situation

hand ˌluggage noun [U] small bags that passengers are allowed to carry with them on a plane

handmade /ˌhæn(d)ˈmeɪd/ adj made by a person, not by a machine

handout /ˈhændaʊt/ noun [C] **1** a piece of paper with information on it that a teacher gives to everyone in a class **2** showing disapproval money or goods that are given to people who need them

handover /ˈhændˌəʊvə/ noun [C] the process of formally giving something to someone else

handpicked /ˌhæn(d)ˈpɪkt/ adj chosen very carefully for a particular purpose

handset /ˈhæn(d)ˌset/ noun [C] **1** the part of a telephone that you hold next to your ear **2** a small piece of electronic equipment that you hold and use for controlling another piece of equipment from a distance

ˈhands-free adj hands-free equipment can be operated without using your hands, for example by using a HEADSET or a REMOTE CONTROL

handshake /ˈhæn(d)ʃeɪk/ noun [C] the act of shaking someone's hand, for example as a greeting

handsome /ˈhæns(ə)m/ adj ★★
1 a handsome man or boy has a very attractive face =GOOD-LOOKING
2 a handsome amount of money is large: *a handsome profit/donation*

ˌhands-ˈon adj **1** hands-on experience involves you doing something, not just reading about it **2** someone who is hands-on is involved in something and does not make other people do the work

ˌhand-to-ˈmouth adj, adv with just enough money or food to live on

handwriting /ˈhændˌraɪtɪŋ/ noun [U] the particular way that someone writes when they use a pen or pencil

handwritten /ˌhændˈrɪt(ə)n/ adj written using a pen or pencil, not printed or TYPED

handy /ˈhændi/ adj **1** useful: *a handy tool* **2** close to you and therefore easy to reach or easy to get to: *Keep your pills handy just in case you feel seasick.* **3** good at doing things with your hands: *He's very handy with a paintbrush* (=good at painting).
PHRASE come in handy to be useful: *A spare set of keys might come in handy.*

handyman /ˈhændiˌmæn/ (plural **handymen** /ˈhændiˌmen/) noun [C] someone who is good at making and repairing things

hang¹ /hæŋ/ (past tense and past participle **hung** /hʌŋ/) verb ★★★
1 [I/T] to put something somewhere with its top part fixed and its bottom part free to move, or to be in this position: *Hang your jacket there.* ♦ **hang sth on/over sth** *Philip hung his hat on a hook behind the door.* ♦ *The children's coats were hanging on pegs behind the door.* ♦ *Her dark hair hung down over her shoulders.*
2 (past tense and past participle **hanged**) [T] to kill someone by putting a rope around their neck and making them fall: *He was hanged for murder in 1942.* ♦ *After his wife left, he tried to hang himself.*
3 [I] if something such as smoke or a smell hangs in the air, it remains there: *A thick mist hung over the fields.*
PHRASAL VERBS hang aˈround or hang aˈbout informal to spend time in a place waiting or doing nothing: *I hung around outside, waiting for the others.*

,hang a'round with sb *informal* to spend time with someone

hang 'back to not do something immediately because you are not confident or certain about it=HESITATE

,hang 'on **1** to hold tightly to something **2** *spoken* to wait, or to be patient: *I think we should hang on and see the end of the game.*

hang 'onto sth *informal* to keep something: *She still hung onto her wedding ring, even after the divorce.*

hang 'out *informal* to spend time in a particular place or with particular people: *She knew all the clubs where he usually hung out.*

,hang ,over sb if something is hanging over you, you are worrying about it

,hang 'round *same as* **hang around**

,hang to'gether *informal* if something hangs together, the different parts of it combine well so that it seems well planned and organized: *The speech doesn't really hang together.*

,hang 'up to put the telephone down at the end of a conversation: *Greg hung up and sat back in his chair.* ♦ *'Get lost!' she shouted, and* **hung up on** *me.*

,hang sth 'up to hang a piece of clothing on something: *The women hung up their coats and sat down.*

hang² /hæŋ/ noun **get the hang of sth** *informal* to learn to do something

hangar /ˈhæŋə/ noun [C] a very large building where planes are kept

hanger /ˈhæŋə/ noun [C] a small frame for hanging clothes such as jackets or shirts on=COAT HANGER

,hangers-'on noun [plural] *showing disapproval* people who spend time with a rich or important person so that they can get an advantage for themselves

'hang-glider noun [C] a simple aircraft with no engine that you hang under and control by moving your body —**hang-gliding** noun [U]

hanging /ˈhæŋɪŋ/ noun [C/U] a punishment in which someone is killed by hanging their body from a rope around their neck

hangout /ˈhæŋaʊt/ noun [C] *informal* a place where a particular person likes to spend time

hangover /ˈhæŋəʊvə/ noun [C] the feeling of being tired and ill because you have drunk too much alcohol

'hang-,up noun [C] *informal* something that you are worried or embarrassed about

hanker /ˈhæŋkə/ verb [I] *informal* to have a strong feeling of wanting something —**hankering** noun [singular]

hankie or **hanky** /ˈhæŋki/ noun [C] *informal* a HANDKERCHIEF

hanky-panky /ˌhæŋki ˈpæŋki/ noun [U] *informal* sexual activity

Hanukkah /ˈhɑːnəkə/ noun [C/U] an important Jewish religious festival that takes place in November or December

haphazard /hæpˈhæzəd/ adj done in a way that is not carefully planned or organized —**haphazardly** adv

hapless /ˈhæpləs/ adj a hapless person is someone that you feel sorry for because bad things have happened to them

happen /ˈhæpən/ verb [I] ★★★ to take place, usually without being planned=OCCUR: *The accident happened at 4.30 pm yesterday.* ♦ *He seemed to be unaware of what was happening around him.* ♦ *What happens if I press this button?* ♦ *Let's just wait and* **see what happens**.

PHRASES **as it happens** *spoken* used for saying that something is true, although it is surprising: *As it happens, I've got a bike I can lend you.*

happen to do sth to do something by chance: *I happened to meet an old friend in town.*

whatever happens used for saying that nothing will change a situation: *Whatever happens tomorrow, this experience has been very valuable.*

PHRASAL VERB 'happen to sb/sth to be affected by something: *This is the best thing that's ever happened to me.* ♦ *We don't understand what is happening to the economy.*

happening /ˈhæp(ə)nɪŋ/ noun [C] an unusual or important event

happily /ˈhæpɪli/ adv **1** used when you are pleased about something: *Happily, nobody was injured.* **2** in a happy way: *He and his wife are happily settled in their new home.* **3** in a willing way: *I'll happily cook the dinner if you want me to.*

happiness /ˈhæpɪnəs/ noun [U] the feeling of being happy

happy /ˈhæpi/ adj ★★★
1 feeling pleased and relaxed, with no worries ≠ UNHAPPY: *The children seem very happy at school.* ♦ *Sarah felt happy for the first time in her life.* ♦ *Money alone will never make you happy.* ♦ *You deserve all this success. We're very* **happy for you**. *♦ Anna was excited and* **happy about** *the baby.* ♦ **happy doing sth** *So you're happy living in London?*
2 satisfied that something is good or right: *Rising profits keep the bosses happy.* ♦ *Are you* **happy with** *this arrangement?* ♦ *I'm not very* **happy about** *the children being out so late.* ♦ **+that** *We were happy that a decision has finally been made.* ♦ **happy to do sth** *Her parents were happy to know she'd got a good job.*
3 making you feel happy, or showing that you feel happy: *a happy marriage/childhood/life* ♦ *a happy smile/expression*

PHRASES **be happy to do sth** if you are happy to do something, you are very willing to do it

Happy Birthday/Christmas/Easter/Anniversary used as a greeting on a particular occasion

,happy-go-'lucky adj a happy-go-lucky person does not usually worry about the future

'happy ,hour noun [C/U] a short period of time when drinks in a bar cost less than usual, usually in the early evening

,happy 'medium noun [singular] a way of doing something that is between two extreme positions or that is satisfactory to everyone

harangue /həˈræŋ/ verb [T] to criticize someone angrily —**harangue** noun [C]

harass /ˈhærəs, həˈræs/ verb [T] to annoy or upset someone, for example by regularly criticizing them or treating them in a way that is offensive

harassed /ˈhærəst, həˈræst/ adj tired and upset because you do not have enough time or energy

harassment /ˈhærəsmənt, həˈræsmənt/ noun [U] annoying or unpleasant behaviour towards someone that takes place regularly: *the victims of racial/sexual harassment*

harbor /ˈhɑːbə/ the American spelling of **harbour**

harbour¹ /ˈhɑːbə/ noun [C] an area of water next to the land where boats can stop

harbour² /ˈhɑːbə/ verb [T] **1** to keep a particular thought or feeling in your mind for a long time **2** to hide someone who has done something wrong so that the police will not find them

hard¹ /hɑːd/ adj ★★★

1 not easy to break	**5** not frightened
2 difficult to do	**6** unkind/angry
3 involving effort	**+** PHRASES
4 full of problems	

1 stiff, firm, and not easy to bend or break: *hard wooden benches* ♦ *The ice on the lake was so hard we could walk on it.*
2 difficult to do: *Some of the questions were very hard.* ♦ **find sth hard** *I found the English exam quite hard.* ♦ **hard for sb to do sth** *It is hard for young people to get jobs in this area.* ♦ **hard to do sth** *It's hard to explain why I love this place so much.*
3 involving a lot of effort: *Lifting stones this size is pretty hard work.* ♦ *I need to relax at the end of a hard day.*
4 unpleasant and full of problems: *My grandmother had a very hard life.* ♦ *The family has had a hard time recently.* ♦ *It's very hard on parents when their children are being bullied at school.*
5 strong and not easily frightened: *He likes to pretend he's hard, but he's really soft underneath.*
6 unkind, or angry: *Don't be too hard on her – she was only trying to help.*

PHRASES **be hard on sth** *informal* to cause damage to something: *These exercises are quite hard on the knees.*
give sb a hard time *informal* to be unpleasant to someone, or to criticize them a lot
hard and fast fixed and not able to be changed
hard of hearing unable to hear well
hard to come by *informal* difficult to find or get: *Good teachers are hard to come by.*
learn the hard way to learn how to do something by trying to do it and making a lot of mistakes
no hard feelings *spoken* used for telling someone that you are not angry with them after an argument or disagreement, and that you hope that they are not angry with you

hard² /hɑːd/ adv ★★★
1 using a lot of effort or force: *The whole team has worked very hard.* ♦ *I was trying very hard to remember her name.* ♦ *I didn't mean to hit him so hard.*
2 if it is raining or snowing hard, a lot of rain or snow is falling

PHRASE **take sth hard** to be very upset by something

hardback /ˈhɑːdbæk/ noun [C] a book that has a hard cover → PAPERBACK

hardboard /ˈhɑːdbɔːd/ noun [U] a type of thin wooden board

hard-boiled /ˌhɑːd ˈbɔɪld/ adj a hard-boiled egg has been cooked in boiling water until it is solid inside

hard copy noun [U] *computing* a printed copy of information that is held on a computer → SOFT COPY

hard core noun [singular] the most determined or enthusiastic people in a group

hardcore /ˈhɑːdkɔː/ noun [U] a type of very fast DANCE MUSIC

hard-core adj **1** hard-core PORNOGRAPHY shows sex in a very detailed way **2** very determined and completely unwilling to change your opinions or behaviour: *hard-core opposition* ♦ *hard-core criminals*

hard currency noun [U] money from a country with a strong economy

hard disk or **hard drive** noun [C] the part inside a computer that stores information → FLOPPY DISK

hard drugs noun [plural] illegal drugs that are ADDICTIVE, for example HEROIN

harden /ˈhɑːd(ə)n/ verb [I/T] **1** to become hard or firm, or to make something hard or firm ≠ SOFTEN: *The bread will harden if you don't cover it.* **2** to become less sympathetic or emotional, or to make someone less sympathetic or emotional ≠ SOFTEN: *His eyes hardened when he saw her.* **3** to become strong, or to make someone or something strong ≠ SOFTEN: *The soldiers have been hardened by months in the field.*

hardened /ˈhɑːd(ə)nd/ adj someone who is hardened has had a lot of unpleasant experiences and is no longer upset by unpleasant things: *hardened criminals/convicts* ♦ *The children became hardened to the violence.*

hard hat noun [C] a hat made of metal or hard plastic worn by workers to protect their heads —*picture* → HAT

hard-headed adj able to make decisions without being influenced by your emotions

hard-hearted /ˌhɑːd ˈhɑːtɪd/ adj someone who is hard-hearted has no sympathy for other people

hard-hitting /ˌhɑːd ˈhɪtɪŋ/ adj making criticisms in a very honest and direct way

hardline /ˈhɑːdlaɪn/ adj strict or extreme in your beliefs or opinions, and not willing to change them —**hardliner** noun [C]: *He's a right-wing hardliner.*

hardly /ˈhɑːdli/ adv ★★★
1 used for saying that something is almost not true, or almost does not happen at all: *He hardly spoke except to say hello.* ♦ *Alice was so busy she hardly noticed the days pass by.* ♦ *He had hardly changed at all.* ♦ *Hardly anyone believed the man's story.* ♦ *It hardly ever rains here in the summer.* ♦ *We could hardly afford to pay the rent.*
2 used for saying that something had only just happened when something else happened: *She had hardly arrived when she started talking about leaving again.*
3 used when you think it is obvious that something is not true, not possible, not surprising etc: *This is hardly the time to start discussing finances.* ♦ *It's hardly*

surprising that people complained.

> **Hardly** is a negative word and is often used with words like 'any' and 'ever', but it should not be used with other negative words such as 'not' or 'never'.

hard-nosed /ˌhɑːd ˈnəʊzd/ adj determined to succeed and not influenced by your emotions

hard-ˈpressed adj not having enough money for the things that you need
> PHRASE **be hard-pressed to do sth** to find it very difficult to do something

hard ˈsell noun [singular] any method of selling in which someone tries very hard to persuade customers to buy something

hardship /ˈhɑːdʃɪp/ noun [C/U] the state of having a difficult life, or something that makes life very difficult: *financial hardship*

hard ˈshoulder noun [C] *British* an area at the side of a motorway where drivers can stop if they have problems

hard ˈup adj *informal* not having much money

hardware /ˈhɑːdˌweə/ noun [U] **1** computer equipment **2** the equipment and vehicles that are used in an activity, especially in the armed forces **3** equipment such as tools, pans, and other things that you use in your home and garden

hard-ˈwired adj a machine that is hard-wired works in a particular way because of the way it was built, and it cannot be changed by the person using it

hard-ˈwon adj achieved only after a lot of effort: *hard-won success*

hardwood /ˈhɑːdˌwʊd/ noun [C/U] hard strong wood from trees such as OAK or MAHOGANY

hard-ˈworking adj putting a lot of effort into your work

hardy /ˈhɑːdi/ adj strong and able to deal with unpleasant or extreme conditions

hare /heə/ noun [C] an animal that is similar to a RABBIT but bigger

hare-brained /ˈheəˌbreɪnd/ adj silly, or very unlikely to succeed

harem /ˈhɑːriːm/ noun [C] **1** the wives of a rich man in some Muslim societies in the past **2** a part of a Muslim home in which only women live

hark /hɑːk/ PHRASAL VERB **hark ˈback to sth** to remember something from the past, or to be similar to something from the past

harlot /ˈhɑːlət/ noun [C] an old word meaning PROSTITUTE

harm¹ /hɑːm/ noun [U] ★ injury, damage, or problems caused by something that you do: *Eating sweets occasionally doesn't do children any harm.* ♦ *Changes to the law may do more harm than good* (=make things worse not better).
> PHRASES **not mean any harm** to not intend to hurt, damage, or upset someone or something
> **out of harm's way** in a safe place
> **there's no harm in (doing) sth** used for saying that something may be helpful: *There's no harm in trying.*

harm² /hɑːm/ verb [T] to injure, damage, or have a bad effect on someone or something: *chemicals that harm the environment* ♦ *Does watching violence on TV really harm children?*

harmful /ˈhɑːmf(ə)l/ adj causing harm: *the harmful effects of cigarette smoke* ♦ *The fungus is not harmful to humans.*

harmless /ˈhɑːmləs/ adj not causing any harm —**harmlessly** adv

harmonica /hɑːˈmɒnɪkə/ noun [C] a musical instrument that you play by blowing and sucking as you move it from side to side between your lips = MOUTH ORGAN

harmonious /hɑːˈməʊniəs/ adj **1** friendly and peaceful: *a harmonious environment/relationship/society* **2** looking, sounding, or combining well with each other —**harmoniously** adv

harmonize /ˈhɑːmənaɪz/ verb **1** [T] to make laws or policies that work with those of a different country, organization etc **2** [I] to sing or play different notes at the same time, producing a pleasant sound **3** [I/T] to combine with other things in a pleasant way, or to make things combine in this way

harmony /ˈhɑːməni/ noun **1** [U] a situation in which people live and work in a happy, peaceful way with others: *racial/social/domestic harmony* **2** [C/U] musical notes that are sung or played at the same time, making a pleasant sound

harness¹ /ˈhɑːnɪs/ noun [C] **1** strong leather bands that are used for fastening an animal to a vehicle that it pulls **2** strong bands of leather, cloth, or rope that are used for fastening someone in a particular place, or for fastening something to their body

harness² /ˈhɑːnɪs/ verb [T] **1** to get control of something in order to use it for a particular purpose: *Humans first harnessed the power of electricity over 200 years ago.* **2** to put a harness on a person or animal

harp /hɑːp/ noun [C] a musical instrument that consists of a row of strings stretched over a large upright frame —*picture*
→ STRINGED INSTRUMENT

harpoon /hɑːˈpuːn/ noun [C] a pole with a blade that is fixed to a rope, used for hunting WHALES —**harpoon** verb [T]

harried /ˈhærɪd/ adj tired and annoyed

harrowing /ˈhærəʊɪŋ/ adj extremely upsetting or frightening

harsh /hɑːʃ/ adj **1** harsh conditions, places, or weather are unpleasant and difficult to live in **2** strict, unkind, and often unfair = SEVERE: *harsh words/punishment* **3** unpleasantly loud or bright: *the harsh glare of the sun* —**harshly** adv

harvest¹ /ˈhɑːvɪst/ noun [C] **1** the activity of collecting a crop, or the time when crops are collected: *the corn/potato/grape harvest* **2** the amount of a crop that is collected

harvest² /ˈhɑːvɪst/ verb [I/T] to collect a crop from the fields

has 3rd person singular of the present tense of **have**

has-been /ˈhæz biːn/ noun [C] an insulting word for someone who was important in the past but that is not important now

hash /hæʃ/ noun [C] *British* the symbol #
> PHRASE **make a hash of sth** *informal* to do something very badly

hasn't /ˈhæz(ə)nt/ short form the usual way of saying or writing 'has not' when 'has' is an AUXILIARY VERB. This is not often used in formal writing: *He hasn't arrived yet.*

hassle¹ /'hæs(ə)l/ noun [C/U] *informal* a situation that causes annoying problems for you: *If it's too much hassle, we can do it another time.*

hassle² /'hæs(ə)l/ verb [T] to annoy someone, or to cause problems for them

haste /heɪst/ noun [U] *formal* great speed in doing something because you do not have much time

  PHRASE **in haste** too quickly, without careful planning or thought

hasten /'heɪs(ə)n/ verb [T] to make something happen sooner or more quickly

  PHRASES **hasten to add** used when you add something to what you have just said, in order to make your meaning clear: *I hasten to add that I am not accusing you of lying.*

  hasten to do sth to do or say something very quickly without waiting

hasty /'heɪsti/ adj done in a hurry, without thinking carefully, or doing something too quickly: *a hasty marriage* ♦ *Don't be hasty about making this decision.* —**hastily** adv

hat /hæt/ noun [C] ★★ a piece of clothing that you wear on your head: *a brown fur hat*
→ DROP²

top hat

cowboy hat

crash helmet

baseball cap

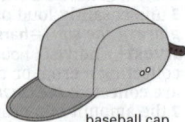

hard hat

hats

hatch¹ /hætʃ/ verb [I/T] if a baby bird, fish, or insect hatches, or if it is hatched, it comes out of its egg and is born

hatch² /hætʃ/ noun [C] a small door in a floor or ceiling, or above the ground in a wall

hatchback /'hætʃ,bæk/ noun [C] a type of car that has a door on the back that opens from the bottom

hatchet /'hætʃɪt/ noun [C] a tool like a small AXE

  PHRASE **bury the hatchet** to become friendly with someone again after a disagreement

hate¹ /heɪt/ verb [T] ★★★
1 to dislike someone or something very much ≠ LOVE: *I hate the smell of cigarettes.*
♦ *I really hate his guts* (=hate him very much).
2 if you hate a particular situation or activity, you think that it is unpleasant or upsetting: *I hate it when my parents argue.*
♦ **hate to do sth** *Glen hates to lose.*

  PHRASES **I hate to bother/interrupt you** *spoken* a polite way of saying that you are sorry for bothering or interrupting someone

  I hate to say/admit used for showing that it is unpleasant for you to say something: *I hate to say this, but I think you've probably lost your money.*

  I hate to think *spoken* used for emphasizing that what you are going to talk about is upsetting: *I hate to think how much money I have spent.*

hate² /heɪt/ noun [U] the feeling of hating someone or something ≠ LOVE

hateful /'heɪtf(ə)l/ adj extremely bad, unpleasant, or cruel

hate mail noun [U] letters that contain threats or offensive remarks

hatred /'heɪtrɪd/ noun [U] *formal* a feeling of hate

hat trick noun [C] three goals that are scored by the same person in one game

haughty /'hɔːti/ adj proud and unfriendly

haul¹ /hɔːl/ verb [T] **1** to pull or carry something that is heavy from one place to another with a lot of effort = DRAG: *I hauled my luggage to the nearest hotel.* **2** to move someone by pulling them = DRAG: *He grasped Judy's arm and hauled her to her feet.*

  PHRASAL VERB **haul sb off** to take someone away to a place that they do not want to go to

haul² /hɔːl/ noun [C] **1** a large amount of something illegal such as drugs that is found by the police **2** the amount of fish that is caught in a net → LONG-HAUL

haulage /'hɔːlɪdʒ/ noun [U] *British* the business of carrying goods by road or railway, or the cost of doing this

haunches /'hɔːnʃɪz/ noun [plural] the top parts of your legs and your BUTTOCKS

haunt¹ /hɔːnt/ verb [T] **1** if a place is haunted by the spirit of a dead person, people believe that it appears there **2** to make someone feel worried and upset for a long time: *Images from the war still haunt him.*
♦ *Our past mistakes are returning to haunt us.*

haunt² /hɔːnt/ noun [C] a place that someone visits often because they enjoy going there

haunted /ˈhɔːntɪd/ adj **1** lived in or visited by the spirit of a dead person **2** looking frightened or worried

haunting /ˈhɔːntɪŋ/ adj beautiful and sad in a way that stays in your memory: *haunting melodies*

have /weak əv, həv, strong hæv/ (3rd person singular **has** /weak əz, həz, strong hæz/; past tense and past participle **had** /weak əd, həd, strong hæd/) verb ★★★

1 used for forming perfect tenses [auxiliary verb] used for forming the PERFECT TENSES of verbs. The perfect tenses are used for talking about what happened or began before now, or before another point in time: *Has anybody seen Dave this afternoon?* ♦ *I've been looking for you everywhere.* ♦ *'Have you washed your hands?' 'Of course I have.'* ♦ *We didn't get a chance to talk to her, but I wish we had.*

2 have or **have got: used for describing sb/sth** [T] used for saying what the features or qualities of someone or something are: *Dr Morel had dark piercing eyes.* ♦ *The house didn't have electricity.* ♦ *She's got a lot of talent.* ♦ *The museum has a large section devoted to modern art.*

3 have or **have got: own or hold sth** [T] to own something, or to be carrying something: *They have a house in Hanover Square.* ♦ *If you had a computer, I could email you.* ♦ *What's that you've got in your hand?* ♦ *Do you have a pen I could borrow?* ♦ **have sth on you** *I haven't got any money on me.*

4 do sth [T] to do or experience something: *Can I have a look at your photos?* ♦ *You should have a rest.* ♦ *We almost had an accident on the motorway.* ♦ *I had a feeling I was being watched.* ♦ *Have a nice weekend!*

5 have or **have got: stating a relationship** [T] used for stating someone's relationship with another person or other people: *Stephen has a sister in Minneapolis.* ♦ *I've got a friend who works at the BBC.* ♦ *Gary knew he had some dangerous enemies.*

6 eat or drink sth [T] to eat or drink something: *Can I have another piece of cake?* ♦ *Why don't you stay and have lunch with us?* ♦ *I'll have the roast beef, please.*

7 have or **have got: saying what is available** [T] used for saying what is available: *Have you got a double room available?* ♦ *She hadn't got space for me in her car.* ♦ *I didn't have time to cook anything.* ♦ *We've got time for a quick swim before breakfast.*

8 arrange for sth to be done [T] to arrange for someone to do something: **have sth done** *They've had the house redecorated.* ♦ *I'm having my hair cut today.* ♦ **have sb do sth** *I'll have the porter bring your luggage up.*

9 have or **have got: place or arrange sth** [T] used for saying that you have put something in a particular position, or you have arranged it in a particular way: *Ralph had his back to the door, so he didn't see me come in.* ♦ *She'd got the book open in front of her.*

10 have or **have got: suffer from sth** [T] to suffer from an illness, disease, injury, or pain: *I've got a terrible headache.* ♦ *James had malaria while he was working in West Africa.* ♦ *The X-rays show that he has a broken ankle.*

11 have or **have got: receive sth** [T] to receive a message, advice, criticism etc: *We've not had any news from home.* ♦ *I've had a lot of phone calls today.* ♦ *Did you have any help from your friends?* ♦ *The airline has had thousands of complaints.*

12 have or **have got: be employed** [T] to be employed to do a particular job: *He can't pay the rent because he hasn't got a job.*

13 have or **have got: referring to arrangements** [T] used for saying that you have arranged or planned to do something: *I've got an appointment tomorrow afternoon.* ♦ *We have friends coming to dinner.* ♦ **have sth to do** *She has a lot of work to do today.*

14 have or **have got: hold sb** [T] to be holding someone by a particular part of their body so that they cannot get away: **have sb by sth** *The guard had her by the arm.*

15 give birth [T] to give birth to a baby: *Linda's having a baby in June.*

PHRASES **sb had better do sth** used for saying what someone should do: *You'd better be careful.*

have (got) it in for sb *informal* to want to cause trouble for someone because you dislike them

have had it *spoken* **1** if something has had it, it cannot be used any longer because it is in such bad condition **2** if someone has had it, they are in serious trouble, or they are going to fail

have to do sth or **have got to do sth** if you have to do something, you must do it because it is necessary: *I have to get up early tomorrow.* ♦ *You have to ask Jane if you want any drinks.* ♦ *You don't have to come* (=it is not necessary to come) *if you don't want to.*

- Questions and negatives using the auxiliary verb **have** are formed without **do**: *Has the meeting finished?* ♦ *You haven't eaten anything.*
- For many transitive senses of **have**, **have got** can also be used. Questions and negatives with these senses can be formed using **have got**, **have** alone, or **do**: *Has he got red hair?* ♦ *Have you any money?* ♦ *Does the car have four doors?* ♦ *I haven't got the courage to tell her.* ♦ *I'm afraid I haven't the time.* ♦ *Carol doesn't have much hair left.*
- Questions and negatives with other transitive senses of **have** are formed with **do**: *Did you have a nice walk?* ♦ *I didn't have breakfast this morning.*
- In conversation or informal writing the auxiliary use of **have** is often shortened. **Have** can be shortened to **'ve**, **has** can be shortened to **'s**, and **had** can be shortened to **'d**: *They've already left.* ♦ *John's lost his ticket.* ♦ *I'd forgotten to tell you.* These short forms can be followed by 'not' to make negative sentences: *I've not seen anyone.* ♦ *She'd not arrived.*
- The ordinary transitive uses of **have** are not usually shortened, though **'ve** and **'d** forms are sometimes possible: *I've a sister who lives in York.*

H

- Short forms are usually used before 'got': *I've got an idea.* ♦ *Jack's got the tickets.*
- Negative forms can also be shortened: **have not** can be shortened to **haven't**, **has not** can be shortened to **hasn't**, and **had not** can be shortened to **hadn't**.

PHRASAL VERBS ˈhave sth aˈgainst sb or have ˈgot sth aˈgainst sb to dislike someone for a particular reason: *I don't know what he's got against me.* ♦ *We've nothing against him personally, it's just that we don't trust politicians.*

ˈhave sth aˈgainst sth or have ˈgot sth aˈgainst sth to be opposed to a plan or suggestion for a particular reason: *I've got nothing against intelligence tests, as long as they're done properly.*

ˈhave sth ˈon or have ˌgot sth ˈon 1 to be wearing particular clothes, shoes etc: *Melissa had her new dress on.* 2 if you have the radio, television, heating etc on, you have switched it on and it is working 3 to have arranged to do something at a particular time

ˈhave sth ˈout 1 to have a tooth removed from your mouth or an organ removed from your body 2 **have it out** to talk to someone honestly about a disagreement between you: *He decided to have it out with Rose there and then.*

ˈhave sb ˈover if you have someone over, they come to your house to visit you or to stay with you

ˈhave sb ˈround *British* if you have someone round, they come to your house to visit you

haven /ˈheɪv(ə)n/ noun [C] a place where people or animals can feel safe and happy

haven't /ˈhæv(ə)nt/ short form the usual way of saying or writing 'have not' when 'have' is an AUXILIARY VERB. This is not often used in formal writing: *I haven't seen her all day.*

havoc /ˈhævək/ noun [U] a situation in which there is so much damage or trouble that something cannot continue normally: *Floods have wreaked havoc* (=caused havoc) *on the town.*

hawk /hɔːk/ noun [C] 1 a large bird that kills other birds and animals for food 2 a politician who prefers using military force to more peaceful methods ≠ DOVE

hay /heɪ/ noun [U] long grass that has been cut and dried so that it can be used for feeding animals

ˈhay ˌfever noun [U] a medical condition that affects your nose and eyes. It is caused by POLLEN (=powder produced by flowers).

haywire /ˈheɪˌwaɪə/ adj **go haywire** *informal* to stop working or behaving correctly

hazard¹ /ˈhæzəd/ noun [C] something that could be dangerous or could cause damage: *a fire/radiation/traffic hazard* ♦ *Pollution is a major health hazard* (=something that is dangerous to your health).

hazard² /ˈhæzəd/ verb [T] to make a guess or suggestion when you are not sure if it is true

ˈhazard ˌlights noun [plural] the lights on a car that flash on and off to warn other drivers of danger

hazardous /ˈhæzədəs/ adj dangerous to people's health or safety: *hazardous driving conditions*

haze /heɪz/ noun [C/U] smoke, dust, or water in the air that makes it difficult to see clearly

hazel /ˈheɪz(ə)l/ adj light brown and slightly green in colour

hazy /ˈheɪzi/ adj 1 not clear because there is smoke, dust, or water in the air 2 not exact or sure: *hazy memories from childhood*

he /weak i, hi, *strong* hiː/ pronoun ★★★
1 used for referring to a man, boy, or male animal, when they have already been mentioned, or when it is obvious which one you are referring to: *I told William, but he didn't believe me.* ♦ *Like all dogs, he'll chase a rabbit if he sees one.*
2 *old-fashioned* used in a general way for referring to any person whether they are male or female: *Everyone has a right to say what he thinks.*

Words that may cause offence

He, **him**, **his**, and **himself** are sometimes used for referring to a person of either sex, but many people avoid this use because it suggests that women are not included, or that men are more important than women. To avoid causing offence, you can use expressions such as **he or she**, **he/she**, **s/he**, **him/her**, or **him/herself** in writing. In conversation, many people say **they**, **them**, **their**, and **themselves** to avoid mentioning whether the person is male or female.

head¹ /hed/ noun [C] ★★★

1 top part of body	4 main teacher
2 your mind & thoughts	5 top/front part of sth
3 leader of group	**+ PHRASES**

1 the top part of your body that has your brain, eyes, mouth etc in it: *Lynn had a bruise on the side of her head.* ♦ *She shook her head* (=moved it from side to side). ♦ *Ron nodded his head* (=moved it up and down) *but said nothing.* —picture → C14
2 your mind and thoughts: *A thought suddenly came into my head.* ♦ *He did the sums quickly in his head.* ♦ *I can't get that song out of my head* (=cannot stop thinking about it).
3 the leader or most important person in a group: *the head waiter* ♦ *I'm meeting the head of the department tomorrow.*
4 *British* the teacher who is in charge of a school = HEADTEACHER
5 the top or front part of something: *We walked straight to the head of the queue.*
PHRASES **a/per head** for each person: *The meal cost £20 per head.*
come to a head *informal* if a situation comes to a head, it suddenly becomes worse
get it into your head to do sth *informal* to decide to do something, and be determined to do it even if other people do not like it
go over sb's head 1 if an idea, joke, or remark goes over someone's head, they cannot understand it **2** if you go over someone else's head, you speak directly to a person who is more important than the person who you should speak to

go to your head *informal* if success goes to your head, it makes you think that you are better or more important than you really are

head over heels completely in love with someone or something

keep your head above water *informal* to manage to live or keep a business working even though you are not earning much money

keep your head down *British informal* to try not to be noticed by anyone, when there is trouble happening around you

laugh/scream your head off *informal* to laugh or scream very loudly
→ BITE¹, BURY, TOP¹

head² /hed/ verb ★★★

1 [I] to go in a particular direction: *They headed north, across the desert.* ♦ *We decided to head for home.*

2 [T] to be in control of a group or an organization: *Lord Justice Scott will head the inquiry.*

3 [T] to be first on a list, or first in a line of people: *Williams heads the police's list of suspects.*

4 [T] to hit the ball with your head in football —*picture* → C15

PHRASES **be heading/headed for sth** if you are heading or headed for a situation, you are likely to be in that situation soon: *It appears that the current champions are heading for victory again.*

head of state the leader of a country, for example a king, queen, or president

PHRASAL VERBS **head off** *informal* to leave: *We should be heading off soon.*

head sth off to prevent something from taking place: *The report claims that the security officials could have headed off the terrorist attack.*

head sth up *same as* **head²** 2: *Judy Leighton was chosen to head up the department.*

headache /ˈhedeɪk/ noun [C] ★

1 a pain in your head: *I had a bad headache yesterday.*

2 *informal* something that causes you a lot of problems

headcount /ˈhedˌkaʊnt/ noun [C] an occasion when you count all the people in a place or organization, or the number of people that are counted

headed /ˈhedɪd/ adj with a particular title: *a document headed 'The Future of Farming'*

header /ˈhedə/ noun [C] something that is printed at the top of a page or a computer document

head first or **headfirst** /ˌhedˈfɜːst/ adv with your head in such a position that it hits something before the rest of your body

headgear /ˈhedˌɡɪə/ noun [U] hats and other things that you wear on your head

headhunt /ˈhedˌhʌnt/ verb [T] to try to persuade someone to leave their job in order to work for another company

headhunter /ˈhedˌhʌntə/ noun [C] a person or company who searches for good staff and tries to persuade them to leave their jobs in order to work for another company

heading /ˈhedɪŋ/ noun [C] the title at the top of a page or piece of writing

headlight /ˈhedˌlaɪt/ noun [C] one of the two lights on the front of a vehicle —*picture* → C6

headline¹ /ˈhedˌlaɪn/ noun **1** [C] the title of a newspaper story, printed in large letters **2 the headlines** [plural] the most important stories in the news: *The fuel crisis continues to dominate the headlines.* ♦ *Did the story make the headlines* (=appear as one of the main reports)?

headline² /ˈhedˌlaɪn/ verb **1** [T] to give a headline to a story in a newspaper **2** [I/T] to be the most famous performer at a concert or show where many other people are also performing

headlong /ˈhedˌlɒŋ/ adj, adv **1** moving with your head going first **2** very quickly and without thinking about what you are doing

headmaster /ˌhedˈmɑːstə/ noun [C] *British* a male teacher who is in charge of a school

headmistress /ˌhedˈmɪstrəs/ noun [C] *British* a female teacher who is in charge of a school

head office noun [C] the main office of an organization or company

head-on adv **1** if two vehicles crash head-on, the front of one hits the front of the other **2** if you deal with a problem head-on, you deal with it in a very direct way —**head-on** adj: *a head-on crash*

headphones /ˈhedˌfəʊnz/ noun [plural] a piece of equipment that you wear over your ears in order to listen to the radio or recorded sound

headquarters /ˈhedˌkwɔːtez/ noun [plural] the place where a company, organization, or military unit has its main offices or its main centre of control

headrest /ˈhedˌrest/ noun [C] the part of a chair or car seat that you lean your head against —*picture* → C6

headroom /ˈhedˌruːm/ noun [U] **1** the amount of space between your head and a ceiling, especially in a car **2** the amount of space between the top of a vehicle and a bridge

headset /ˈhedˌset/ noun [C] a piece of radio or telephone equipment that you wear over your ears with a part that you can speak into

head start noun [C] **1** an advantage over other people who are in the same situation as you: *The reading course gives young children a head start.* **2** a situation in which you start a race before or in front of your opponent

headstone /ˈhedˌstəʊn/ noun [C] a piece of stone that marks a GRAVE (=place where a dead person is buried)

headstrong /ˈhedˌstrɒŋ/ adj determined to do what you want even if other people warn you not to do it

headteacher /ˌhedˈtiːtʃə/ noun [C] *British* a teacher who is in charge of a school

head-to-head adj, adv competing or meeting directly with someone or something else

headway /ˈhedˌweɪ/ noun **make headway** to make progress with something that you are trying to achieve

headwind /ˈhedˌwɪnd/ noun [C] a wind that blows in the opposite direction to the one in which you are moving

heady /ˈhedi/ adj giving you a strong feeling of pleasure or excitement

H

H

heal /hiːl/ verb **1** [I/T] if an injury heals, or if someone heals it, the skin or bone grows back together and becomes healthy again: *The wound took a long time to heal.* **2** [T] to make people stop fighting and become friendly again

PHRASAL VERB **heal** ˈup if an injury heals up, the skin or bone grows back together and becomes healthy again

healing¹ /ˈhiːlɪŋ/ noun [U] the process of becoming healthy again

healing² /ˈhiːlɪŋ/ adj making someone feel better after they have been ill or unhappy: *a plant with healing properties*

health /helθ/ noun [U] ★★★
1 the condition of your body, especially whether or not you are ill: *His health improved once he stopped working.* ♦ *She's had serious health problems.* ♦ *Lola is 85 and still in very good health.* ♦ *My father has been in poor health for some time.*
2 how successful something is: *Officials are worried about the health of the local technology industry.*

PHRASE **health and safety** *British* the part of the government and legal system that deals with people's health and safety at work

health ˌcare noun [U] the services that look after people's health: *Homeless people need better access to health care.* —**healthcare** /ˈhelθˌkeə/ adj

health ˌcentre noun [C] *British* a building where people can go to see a doctor or nurse

health ˌclub noun [C] a club where members can go to do physical exercises

health ˌfood noun [C/U] food that is good for you because it does not contain artificial substances

health inˌsurance noun [U] a type of insurance that pays for your medical treatment when you are ill or injured

health ˌservice noun [C] a public service that is responsible for providing medical care

healthy /ˈhelθi/ adj ★★
1 physically strong and not ill ≠ UNHEALTHY: *a healthy baby* ♦ *I feel very healthy at the moment.*
2 making you strong and not ill ≠ UNHEALTHY: *healthy food* ♦ *a healthy diet/lifestyle*
3 working well and likely to continue to be successful ≠ UNHEALTHY: *The country still has a healthy economy.*
4 a healthy attitude is good and sensible ≠ UNHEALTHY
—**healthily** adv

heap¹ /hiːp/ noun [C] a large untidy pile of something: *a heap of old car parts* ♦ *Dirty rags lay in a heap on the floor.*

PHRASE **heaps of sth** a lot of something

heap² /hiːp/ verb [T] **1** to make a big untidy pile of things: *Clothing was heaped on the floor.* **2** if you heap praise or blame on someone, you praise or blame them a lot

heaped /hiːpt/ adj *British* **1** a heaped spoon is completely full **2** filled or covered with a lot of something in a high pile: *a plate heaped with spaghetti*

hear /hɪə/ (past tense and past participle **heard** /hɜːd/) verb ★★★
1 [I/T] to realize that someone or something is making a sound: *Mary heard the sound of voices.* ♦ *Shh — I can't hear.* ♦ *No one could hear what she said.* ♦ **hear sb/sth do sth** *He heard the door slam shut.* ♦ **hear sb/sth doing sth** *She heard the dog barking outside.*
2 [I/T] to receive information about something: *Did you hear about Jim's party?* ♦ *I came home as soon as I heard what happened.* ♦ *We didn't hear of his death until many years later.* ♦ **+(that)** *I heard he'd got a new job.*
3 [T] to listen to something such as a speech, performance, or programme: *I want to hear the news on the radio before I go.* ♦ **hear sb do sth** *He's got a great voice – you should hear him sing.*
4 [T] to listen to and judge a legal case in a court of law

PHRASE **have heard it (all) before** *spoken* to not believe what someone is saying, or to not be impressed by it

PHRASAL VERBS ˈ**hear from sb 1** if you hear from someone, they write to you or call you on the telephone: *It's ages since I heard from Jill.* **2** to listen to someone who is speaking about a particular thing: *The Commission heard from over thirty witnesses.*
ˈ**hear of sb/sth** if you have heard of someone or something, you know about their existence: *Have you heard of the author James Bomford?*
ˌ**hear sb ˈout** to let someone finish what they are saying without interrupting them: *I'm serious about this; hear me out, please.*

■ When you **hear** a sound, you become conscious of it: *Did you hear the thunder last night?* ♦ *I didn't hear the door open.*
■ When you **listen**, you deliberately pay attention to a sound in order to hear it: *I listened carefully but I couldn't hear what she was saying.* ♦ *I always listen to the radio in my car.*
■ You **hear** something, but you **listen to** something.

hearing /ˈhɪərɪŋ/ noun **1** [U] your ability to hear sounds: *My hearing is getting worse as I get older.* **2** [C] a meeting of a court of law or official organization in order to find out the facts about something

ˈ**hearing ˌaid** noun [C] a small piece of equipment that someone wears in their ear in order to help them to hear

ˈ**hearing-imˌpaired** adj unable to hear as well as most people can

hearsay /ˈhɪəˌseɪ/ noun [U] information that you have heard without having any proof that it is true

hearse /hɜːs/ noun [C] a large car that is used for carrying a dead person in a COFFIN

heart /hɑːt/ noun ★★★

1 organ in your chest	**4** shape
2 your feelings	**5** suit of playing cards
3 inner central part	**+ PHRASES**

1 [C] the organ in your chest that pumps blood around your body: *I could hear his heart beating.* ♦ *Did you know he had a weak heart?*
2 [C] your feelings when they are considered

as part of your character: *You have to do
what your heart tells you is right.*
3 [C] the central part of something: *a
beautiful house deep in the heart of an
English countryside*
4 [C] a shape that represents love —*picture*
→ C8
5 hearts [plural] the SUIT of playing cards that
have red heart shapes on them —*picture*
→ C16

PHRASES **at heart** used for saying what
someone's basic character is: *I'm really a
country person at heart.*
break sb's heart to upset someone very much,
especially by showing them that you do not
love them
have your heart set on (doing) sth to decide
that you want something very much
sb's heart goes out to sb used for saying that
someone feels sorry for someone else
sb's heart is in the right place used for saying
that someone tries to do good things even
though it does not always seem like this
sb's heart is not in sth used for saying that
someone does not really care about
something that they are doing
lose heart to feel disappointed and try less
hard because of this
not have the heart to do sth to not want to do
something because it seems cruel
(off) by heart if you know something by
heart, you can remember all the words or
music in it
(straight) from the heart being completely
honest about your feelings
take sth to heart to think about something
seriously, often so that it upsets you
to your heart's content as much or as often
as you like

heartache /ˈhɑːteɪk/ noun [U] great sadness
or worry
heart at.tack noun [C] an occasion when
someone suddenly has a lot of pain because
their heart stops working normally
heartbeat /ˈhɑːtbiːt/ noun [C] the movement
or sound of your heart as it pumps blood
around your body
heartbreak /ˈhɑːtbreɪk/ noun [U] a feeling of
great sadness
heartbreaking /ˈhɑːtbreɪkɪŋ/ adj making you
feel very sad or upset
heartbroken /ˈhɑːtbrəʊkən/ adj extremely
sad and upset
heartburn /ˈhɑːtbɜːn/ noun [U] a pain that
feels like burning in your chest and is a
type of INDIGESTION
heart dis.ease noun [U] a serious medical
condition that affects your heart
heartened /ˈhɑːt(ə)nd/ adj feeling happier
and more hopeful than before
heart failure noun [U] a serious medical
condition in which your heart stops
working normally
heartfelt /ˈhɑːtfelt/ adj *formal* a heartfelt
emotion, remark, or action is very sincere
hearth /hɑːθ/ noun [C] the floor around a
FIREPLACE
heartily /ˈhɑːtɪli/ adv **1** in a loud or
enthusiastic way: *Jones laughed heartily at
his little joke.* **2** completely, or extremely:
They are heartily sorry for the trouble

they've caused. **3** if you eat heartily, you eat
everything on your plate with enthusiasm
heartland /ˈhɑːtlænd/ noun [C] *mainly
journalism* a part of a country where a
particular activity or belief is especially
common
heartless /ˈhɑːtləs/ adj feeling or showing no
sympathy or kindness=CALLOUS
heart-rending /ˈhɑːtrendɪŋ/ adj making you
feel very sad and sympathetic because
someone is unhappy or very ill
heart-stopping /ˈhɑːt ˌstɒpɪŋ/ adj very
frightening or exciting: *For one heart-
stopping moment, I thought she was going
to kiss me.*
heartstrings /ˈhɑːtstrɪŋz/ noun **tug/pull at sb's
heartstrings** to make someone feel a lot of
love or sympathy
heart-to-heart noun [C] a private
conversation between two people about
their personal feelings
heartwarming /ˈhɑːtwɔːmɪŋ/ adj making
you feel happy because people are being
kind
hearty /ˈhɑːti/ adj **1** friendly and enthusiastic
2 a hearty meal is large
heat¹ /hiːt/ noun ★★★
1 [singular/U] the quality of being hot, or how
hot something is: *We felt the intense heat
from the fire.* ♦ *He could feel the heat of the
sun on his back.*
2 the heat [singular] very hot weather: *The
local people get out of the city to escape the
heat.*
3 the heat [singular] the flame or hot area on
a HOB that you cook on: *I turned the heat
down a little.*
4 [C] a game or race at the start of a
competition
PHRASES **in the heat of the moment** at a time
when you are too angry or excited to think
carefully
on heat a female animal that is on heat is
ready to MATE with a male
heat² /hiːt/ verb [I/T] ★ to make something
hot, or to become hot: *Heat the oil gently in
a large frying pan.*
PHRASAL VERBS **heat up** if a situation heats
up, it becomes more exciting, dangerous,
or serious: *The dispute was already heating
up.*
heat sth up same as **heat²**: *I was just heating
up some soup.*
heated /ˈhiːtɪd/ adj **1** made warm enough for
people to use: *a heated swimming pool*
2 angry and excited: *a heated discussion/
argument/debate* —**heatedly** adv
heater /ˈhiːtə/ noun [C] a piece of equipment
that is used for making a place warm, or
for heating water
heath /hiːθ/ noun [C] a wide area of wild land
where only rough grass and bushes grow
heather /ˈheðə/ noun [C/U] a plant with small
purple or white flowers that grows on hills
heating /ˈhiːtɪŋ/ noun [U] *British* equipment
that produces the heat used for heating a
building
heatwave /ˈhiːtweɪv/ noun [C] a continuous
period of very hot weather
heave¹ /hiːv/ verb **1** [I/T] to push, pull, throw,
or lift an object using a lot of effort: *Paul*

H

H

heaved the last box into the truck. **2** [I] to
move up and down with large regular
movements: *Her chest heaved as she
struggled to control her breathing.*
PHRASE **heave a sigh** to let out a deep
breath, for example because you are
pleased about something

heave² /hi:v/ noun [C] a strong pulling,
pushing, throwing, or lifting movement

heaven /ˈhev(ə)n/ noun **1 heaven** or **Heaven** [U]
the place where God is believed to live **2 the
heavens** [plural] *literary* the sky
PHRASE **for heaven's sake/sakes** *spoken* used
for emphasizing that you are annoyed or
impatient with someone

heavenly /ˈhev(ə)nli/ adj **1** in or from heaven
2 *informal* extremely nice, enjoyable, or
beautiful

heavily /ˈhevɪli/ adv **1** very, or to a large
degree: *heavily populated areas* ♦ *Her work
was heavily influenced by her father's.* ♦ *The
men were heavily armed* (=carrying a lot of
weapons). **2** in large amounts: *She had been
smoking heavily since her teens.* ♦ *They had
borrowed heavily to buy the boat.* **3** with a
lot of force or effort: *She leaned heavily on
the table.* ♦ *The older man was now
breathing heavily.* **4** slowly, in a way that
shows that you feel sad or tired: *She
grabbed the chair and pulled herself up
heavily.*

heavy /ˈhevi/ adj ★★★

1 with a lot of weight	4 serious/difficult
2 many things	5 of food
3 with physical effort	6 big or powerful

1 a heavy object weighs a lot ≠ LIGHT: *She
was struggling with a heavy suitcase.* ♦ *He
was too heavy for the nurses to lift.*
2 used for saying that there is a lot of
something, or that something is done a lot:
Traffic is very heavy on the M5 tonight. ♦
*The school places a heavy emphasis on
music.* ♦ *heavy rain and strong winds* ♦
*There was heavy fighting in the capital
yesterday.* ♦ *Sandra is a heavy smoker* (=she
smokes a lot).
3 involving a lot of physical effort or force
≠ LIGHT: *a heavy blow to the head* ♦ *They
did most of the heavy work in the morning.*
4 too serious, difficult, or frightening to be
good or enjoyable: *She felt their relationship
was getting too heavy.* ♦ *His new book is a
bit heavy.* ♦ *a heavy responsibility*
5 food that is heavy is rather solid and not
enjoyable ≠ LIGHT
6 large, thick, or powerful: *The men wore
heavy coats and gloves.* ♦ *a small fishing
boat struggling in heavy seas* ♦ *Do not
operate any heavy machinery while taking
this medication.*

heavy-duty adj strong and not easily
damaged: *heavy-duty plastic*

heavy-handed /ˌhevi ˈhændɪd/ adj using too
much force, or not considering people's
feelings enough when you are dealing with
a situation

heavy industry noun [U] industry that
produces materials such as coal or steel or
large objects such as cars or ships

heavy metal noun [U] a type of loud ROCK

music that developed in the 1970s =METAL

heavyweight /ˈheviˌweɪt/ noun [C] **1 a** BOXER
or WRESTLER in the heaviest weight group
2 someone or something that has a lot of
influence, status, or knowledge: *political
heavyweights*

Hebrew¹ /ˈhi:bru:/ noun **1** [U] one of the
official languages of Israel **2** [C] a Jewish
person in ancient times

Hebrew² /ˈhi:bru:/ adj **1** relating to the
Hebrew language **2** of Jewish people

heckle /ˈhek(ə)l/ verb [I/T] to interrupt a
speaker or performer by shouting at
them —**heckler** noun [C], **heckling** noun [U]

hectare /ˈhekteə/ noun [C] a unit for
measuring an area of land, equal to 10,000
square metres

hectic /ˈhektɪk/ adj full of busy activity

he'd /weak i:d, strong hi:d/ short form **1** the
usual way of saying or writing 'he had'
when 'had' is an AUXILIARY VERB. This is not
often used in formal writing: *He knew he'd
seen her before.* **2** the usual way of saying or
writing 'he would'. This is not often used in
formal writing: *He'd come if you asked him.*

hedge¹ /hedʒ/ noun [C] a line of bushes or
small trees that are growing close together
around a garden or a field —*picture* → C1
PHRASE **a hedge against sth** a way of trying
to protect yourself against a problem or risk:
a hedge against inflation

hedge² /hedʒ/ verb [I] to avoid answering a
question directly, or to avoid making a
definite decision
PHRASE **hedge your bets** to organize a
situation so that you have several choices
available to you, in order to increase your
chances of success

hedgehog /ˈhedʒˌhɒg/ noun [C] a small wild
animal with a round body that is covered
with sharp SPIKES

hedgerow /ˈhedʒˌrəʊ/ noun [C] a line of
bushes and small trees along the edge of a
field or road

hedonist /ˈhi:d(ə)nɪst/ noun [C] someone who
believes that pleasure is the most important
thing in life —**hedonism** noun [U], **hedonistic**
/ˌhi:dəˈnɪstɪk/ adj

heed¹ /hi:d/ verb [T] *formal* to listen carefully
to someone's advice or warning, and do
what they suggest

heed² /hi:d/ noun **pay heed to** or **take heed of**
formal to give careful attention to someone's
advice or warning

heel /hi:l/ noun [C] **1** the back part of your
foot, below your ANKLE —*picture* → C14 **2** the
part underneath the back of a shoe
PHRASE **(hard/hot/close) on the heels of**
1 following close behind someone or
something **2** happening soon after another
event
→ DIG¹, HEAD¹

hefty /ˈhefti/ adj **1** large and heavy **2** a hefty
amount of money is very large

heifer /ˈhefə/ noun [C] a young cow

height /haɪt/ noun ★★★
1 [C/U] how high something is, or how tall
someone is: *He was about the same height
as his wife.* ♦ *What height do you want the
picture at?*
2 [singular] the time or level of greatest

activity: *The excitement was at its height.*
♦ *Jeans were once again the height of
fashion.*

3 heights [plural] a high place or position:
*Dave was trying to overcome his fear of
heights.*

4 heights [plural] a high level of activity or
success: *His popularity has reached new
heights.*

heighten /ˈhaɪt(ə)n/ verb [I/T] if something
heightens a feeling or emotion, or if a
feeling or emotion heightens, it becomes
stronger

heinous /ˈheɪnəs/ adj *very formal* a heinous act
or crime is extremely evil

heir /eə/ noun [C] someone who will receive
money, property, or a title when another
person dies

heiress /ˈeəres/ noun [C] a woman or girl who
will receive money or property when
another person dies

heirloom /ˈeəˌluːm/ noun [C] a valuable or
special possession that has belonged to one
family for many years

held the past tense and past participle of **hold**[1]

helicopter /ˈhelɪˌkɒptə/ noun [C] an aircraft
with large metal blades on top that spin
round and lift it into the air —*picture* → C7

helium /ˈhiːliəm/ noun [U] a gas that is lighter
than air

he'll /*weak* iːl, *strong* hiːl/ short form the usual
way of saying or writing 'he will'. This is
not often used in formal writing: *He'll be here
around noon.*

hell /hel/ noun [U] **1** hell or Hell in some
religions, the place where bad people are
sent to suffer when they die **2** a situation
that is extremely unpleasant

> **PHRASES** **all hell breaks loose** *informal* used
> for saying that people start fighting or
> arguing because they are angry or upset
> **for the hell of it** *informal* just for fun, and not
> for any serious reason
> **the sth from hell** *informal* an especially
> unpleasant example of a person or thing:
> *the holiday from hell*
> **like hell** *spoken* with a lot of speed or effort: *I
> got out of the truck and ran like hell.*
> **a/one hell of a** *spoken* **1** used for emphasizing
> what you are saying: *It must be a hell of a
> job trying to organize all this information.*
> **2** used for emphasizing how good something
> is

hell-'bent adj determined to do or achieve
something

hellish /ˈhelɪʃ/ adj *informal* very difficult or
unpleasant

hello /həˈləʊ/ interjection ★★★
1 used as a greeting when you meet someone
or begin to talk to someone on the
telephone: *Hello, my name is Anna.*
2 used for calling to someone to get their
attention: *Hello! We're over here!*
3 *very informal* used for saying that you think
someone is being stupid: *Hello! There's no
way anyone will give you a job with that
haircut.*

helm /helm/ noun [C] a wheel or handle used
for making a boat go in the direction that
you want it to go in

> **PHRASE** **at the helm** in charge, or in the
> position of a leader

helmet /ˈhelmɪt/ noun [C] a hard hat that you
wear to protect your head

help[1] /help/ verb ★★★
1 [I/T] to give someone support or
information so that they can do something
more easily: **help sb (to) do sth** *Can you help
me find my glasses?* ♦ **help sb with sth** *Her
brother offered to help her with her
homework.* ♦ *Her work involves helping
people to find jobs.*
2 [I/T] to make something better or easier:
*Organic farming methods help the
environment.* ♦ **help (to) do sth** *We hope this
helps to clarify the situation.*
3 [T] to give someone food or drink: **help
yourself to sth** (=take some of it) *Help
yourselves to more wine.*

> **PHRASES** **cannot/can't help sth** used for
> saying that someone cannot stop
> themselves doing something: *She couldn't
> help laughing when she saw it.*
> **sb cannot/can't help it** if used for saying that
> someone cannot be blamed for a situation:
> *I can't help it if you're upset.*
> **help yourself** *spoken* used for giving someone
> permission to do or use something: *'Do you
> mind if I use the phone?' 'Help yourself.'*

> **PHRASAL VERB** ,**help (sb) 'out** to help someone
> by doing a particular job, or by giving them
> money: *My family has always helped me out.*
> ♦ *He always helped out with the housework.*

Word family: help

*Words in the same family as **help***
- **helpful** *adj*
- **helping** *n*
- **unhelpful** *adj*
- **helpless** *adj*

---

help[2] /help/ noun ★★★
1 [U] the process of helping someone, or
something that you do to help someone: *Do
you want some **help** with that?*
2 [singular/U] a person or thing that helps:
You've been a real help to me, Carrie.
3 [U] the part of a computer program that
gives you information: *Try the help menu.*

help[3] /help/ interjection used for asking for
urgent help: *Help! I'm going to fall.*

help ,desk noun [C] a service that is provided
by a company to give information and
support to its customers

helper /ˈhelpə/ noun [C] someone who helps a
person or organization

helpful /ˈhelpf(ə)l/ adj ★
1 a helpful person helps you by doing
something, or by giving you useful advice
or information ≠ UNHELPFUL: *a traditional
hotel with very helpful staff*
2 useful, or providing help: **it's helpful to do
sth** *It's helpful to have a calculator for this
exam.* ♦ **helpful for/in doing sth** *Exercise is
helpful for controlling high blood pressure.*
—**helpfully** adv

helping /ˈhelpɪŋ/ noun [C] an amount of food
that is served to one person at a meal
=SERVING

helpless /ˈhelpləs/ adj not able to do anything
without help —**helplessly** adv

helpline /ˈhelpˌlaɪn/ noun [C] *British* a telephone
service that is provided by an organization

in order to give people information and support=HOTLINE

hem¹ /hem/ noun [C] the bottom edge of something made of cloth that is folded and sewn in place

hem² /hem/ **PHRASAL VERB** **hem sb 'in** if someone is hemmed in, they are prevented from leaving or doing what they want

hemisphere /'hemɪˌsfɪə/ noun [C] **1** one half of the Earth **2** one half of the brain

hemophilia /ˌhiːməˈfɪliə/ the American spelling of **haemophilia**

hemophiliac /ˌhiːməˈfɪliæk/ the American spelling of **haemophiliac**

hemorrhage /'hem(ə)rɪdʒ/ the American spelling of **haemorrhage**

hemorrhoids /'heməˌrɔɪdz/ the American spelling of **haemorrhoids**

hemp /hemp/ noun [U] a plant that is used for making rope. It is also used for making the drug CANNABIS.

hen /hen/ noun [C] a female chicken

hence /hens/ adv *formal* therefore: *Alcohol can cause liver failure and hence death.*

henchman /'hentʃmən/ (plural **henchmen** /'hentʃmən/) noun [C] someone who helps a powerful person by doing immoral or violent things

'hen ˌnight or **'hen ˌparty** noun [C] *British* a celebration for a woman who is about to be married. Only her women friends go to it.
→ STAG NIGHT

hepatitis /ˌhepəˈtaɪtɪs/ noun [U] an infectious disease of the liver

her /weak ə, hə, strong hɜː/ grammar word ★★★

> **Her** can be:
> ■ a **pronoun**: *If you see Mary, give her my love.*
> ■ a **determiner**: *She was holding her baby.*

1 the object form of 'she', used for referring to a woman, girl, or female animal when they have already been mentioned or when it is obvious which one you are referring to: *Where's Susan? Has anyone seen her?* ♦ *Mary asked me to write to her.*
2 belonging to a woman, girl, or female animal that has already been mentioned: *She parked her car across the road.* ♦ *Emma's invited us to her party.* ♦ *She makes her own clothes.*

herald /'herəld/ verb [T] **1** to announce something, or to be a sign that something is going to happen soon **2** to praise something loudly or in a public way

herb /hɜːb/ noun [C] a plant that you use for adding flavour to food or as a medicine

herbal /'hɜːb(ə)l/ adj containing herbs, or made from herbs

herbicide /'hɜːbɪˌsaɪd/ noun [C/U] a chemical that you use for killing WEEDS (=plants that you do not want in your garden)

herbivore /'hɜːbɪˌvɔː/ noun [C] an animal that eats only plants

herd¹ /hɜːd/ noun [C] a large group of animals of the same type that live and move about together

herd² /hɜːd/ verb [T] to make a group of animals or people move somewhere together

here /hɪə/ grammar word ★★★

> **Here** can be:
> ■ an **adverb**: *Wait here. I'll be back in a minute.*
> ■ an **interjection**: *Here, have a drink of water.*

1 in or to this place in or to the place where you are, or where you are pointing: *We've lived here for over 20 years.* ♦ *Come here.* ♦ *Just sign your name here, at the bottom of the page.* ♦ *You can see the lighthouse from here.* ♦ *There aren't many good restaurants around here.* ♦ *It's freezing cold out here.* ♦ *She wrote her novels right here in this room.*
2 when offering or giving sth *spoken* used when you are offering or giving something to someone: *Here, use my handkerchief.* ♦ *Here's £20 – go and buy yourself something nice.* ♦ *Here you go, two cups of coffee.*
3 at this point at this point in a process, discussion, or series of events: *Let's stop here and consider what we've said so far.* ♦ *The question is, where does the peace process go from here?*
4 when sb/sth arrives or is found *spoken* used for saying that someone or something has just arrived, or has just been found: *I'm waiting for Linda. Oh, here she is.* ♦ *Here are my glasses. I thought I'd lost them.* ♦ *Here comes the bus.*
5 happening now happening at the present time, or in the present situation: *Summer is here at last.*
6 for stating a purpose used for saying what purpose someone is working for: *I'm here for an interview.* ♦ **here to do sth** *Our staff are here to help.*

PHRASES **here and there** in or to several different places: *Papers were scattered here and there.*
here goes or **here we go** *spoken* used when you are going to try to do something and you are not sure whether you will be successful: *I'm not much good at making speeches, but anyway here goes.*
here to stay if something is here to stay, it will continue to exist for a long time
→ NEITHER

hereby /ˌhɪəˈbaɪ/ adv *legal* used for stating that something that has been said or written is now official

hereditary /həˈredət(ə)ri/ adj **1** a hereditary disease or quality is passed from a parent to a child in their genes **2** a hereditary title or right is officially passed from a parent to their child

heredity /həˈredəti/ noun [U] the genetic process by which a parent's qualities or diseases are passed to their child

heresy /'herəsi/ noun [C/U] a belief that is considered wrong because it is very different from what most people believe, or because it opposes the official principles of a religion

heretic /'herətɪk/ noun [C] someone who believes things that are considered wrong because they are very different from what most people believe or because they oppose the official principles of a religion
—**heretical** /həˈretɪk(ə)l/ adj

heritage /'herɪtɪdʒ/ noun [C/U] the art, buildings, traditions, and beliefs that a society considers to be important parts of its history and culture

hermit /ˈhɜːmɪt/ noun [C] someone who chooses to live alone, or someone who spends most of their time alone

hernia /ˈhɜːniə/ noun [C] a medical condition in which an organ pushes itself through the muscles around it

hero /ˈhɪərəʊ/ (plural **heroes**) noun [C]
1 someone who has done something very brave **2** someone who you admire a lot **3** the main male character of a book, film, or play ≠ VILLAIN

heroic /hɪˈrəʊɪk/ adj **1** very brave =COURAGEOUS **2** showing great determination to achieve something: *their heroic effort to protect the future of the local hospital* —**heroically** /hɪˈrəʊɪkli/ adv

heroics /həˈrəʊɪks/ noun [plural] actions that are very brave but that are also dangerous and unnecessary

heroin /ˈherəʊɪn/ noun [U] a powerful illegal drug

heroine /ˈherəʊɪn/ noun [C] **1** the main female character of a book, film, or play **2** a woman who you admire a lot =HERO

heroism /ˈherəʊˌɪz(ə)m/ noun [U] actions that prove that someone is very brave

heron /ˈherən/ noun [C] a large bird with a long neck that lives near water

herpes /ˈhɜːpiːz/ noun [U] an infectious disease that can make sore red spots appear on someone's sex organs or near their mouth

herring /ˈherɪŋ/ noun [C/U] a long thin silver sea fish, or this fish eaten as food → RED HERRING

hers /hɜːz/ pronoun ★★ a POSSESSIVE form of 'she', used for referring to something that belongs to a woman, girl, or female animal that has already been mentioned: *Mrs Lansbury claims the money is all hers.* ♦ *His hand reached out and touched hers.* ♦ *My Japanese isn't as good as hers.* ♦ *She introduced us to some friends of hers.*

herself /weak əˈself, strong hɜːˈself/ pronoun ★★★
1 the REFLEXIVE form of 'she', used for showing that the woman, girl, or female animal that does something is also affected by what she does: *Lizzie had locked herself in the bathroom.* ♦ *She's going to buy herself a new jacket.* ♦ *Pam was looking at herself in the mirror.*
2 used for emphasizing that you are referring to a particular woman, girl, or female animal and not to anyone else: *It was Christina herself who told me that she was unhappy.* ♦ *The queen herself will attend the meeting.* ♦ *She has enough money to pay for it herself.*
PHRASES **(all) by herself 1** alone: *Annie's too young to travel by herself.* **2** without help from anyone else: *Sally had organized the whole party by herself.*
(all) to herself not sharing something with anyone else: *Everyone had gone away, and she had the apartment to herself.*
be/feel/seem herself to be in a normal mental or physical state: *Beth wasn't quite herself that evening.*

hertz /hɜːts/ (plural **hertz**) noun [C] a unit for measuring sound and radio waves

he's /weak iːz, strong hiːz/ short form **1** the usual way of saying or writing 'he is'. This is not often used in formal writing: *He's in Seattle this weekend.* **2** the usual way of saying or writing 'he has' when 'has' is an AUXILIARY VERB. This is not often used in formal writing: *He's decided to move.*

hesitant /ˈhezɪtənt/ adj doing something slowly because you are nervous or not certain about it —**hesitantly** adv

hesitate /ˈhezɪteɪt/ verb [I] ★ to pause before doing something because you are nervous or not certain about it: *He hesitated a moment, and then knocked on the door.*
PHRASE **don't hesitate to do sth** spoken used for encouraging someone to do something: *Don't hesitate to call me if you need any help.*

hesitation /ˌhezɪˈteɪʃ(ə)n/ noun [C/U] a pause before doing something, or a feeling that you should not do it, because you are nervous or not certain about it

heterosexual /ˌhetərəʊˈsekʃuəl/ adj sexually attracted to people of the opposite sex —**heterosexual** noun [C]

hexagon /ˈheksəgən/ noun [C] a GEOMETRIC shape that has six straight sides —*picture* → C8 —**hexagonal** /heksˈægən(ə)l/ adj

hey /heɪ/ interjection ★ used for getting someone's attention, or for showing that you are surprised or annoyed

heyday /ˈheɪdeɪ/ noun [C] the time when a person, idea, or object was most successful

HGV /ˌeɪtʃ dʒiː ˈviː/ noun [C] British heavy goods vehicle: a large truck

hi /haɪ/ interjection informal ★ hello: *Hi, I'm Tom.*

hiatus /haɪˈeɪtəs/ noun [C] formal a period of time when something does not happen

hibernate /ˈhaɪbəneɪt/ verb [I] if an animal hibernates, it sleeps through the winter —**hibernation** /ˌhaɪbəˈneɪʃ(ə)n/ noun [U]

hiccup¹ /ˈhɪkʌp/ noun [C] **1** a short repeated sound that you make in your throat because you have been eating or drinking too quickly **2** informal a small problem, or a problem that causes a short delay

hiccup² /ˈhɪkʌp/ (present participle **hiccupping**; past tense and past participle **hiccupped**) verb [I] to make a hiccup sound

hid the past tense of **hide¹**

hidden¹ /ˈhɪd(ə)n/ adj ★
1 if something is hidden, most people do not know about it or understand it: *the hidden costs of being in hospital*
2 a hidden object or place is not easy to find: *a hidden camera* ♦ *hidden valleys*

hidden² the past participle of **hide¹**

hidden agenda noun [C] a secret plan to do something because you will get an advantage from it

hide¹ /haɪd/ (past tense **hid** /hɪd/; past participle **hidden** /ˈhɪd(ə)n/) verb ★★★

1 put in secret place	5 try to avoid sth
2 go to secret place	+ PHRASE
3 not allow to be seen	+ PHRASAL VERB
4 not show feelings	

1 [T] to put something in a place so that no one can find it or see it: **hide sth in/at/under**

etc sth *She hid the key in the drawer.* ♦ **hide sth from sb** *I wanted to hide his present from him until his birthday.*

2 [I] to go somewhere or be somewhere where no one can find you or see you: *He ran and* **hid behind** *a bush.* ♦ *Robert is* **hiding from** *us.*

3 [T] to make something difficult or impossible to see clearly: *Dark clouds hid the sun.*

4 [T] to prevent people from knowing your thoughts or feelings, or the truth: *He could not hide his disappointment.*

5 [I] to try not to accept something, or to try not to be affected by something: *You can't* **hide from** *your feelings forever.*

> **PHRASE** **have nothing to hide** to not be afraid of what people may discover, because you have done nothing wrong

> **PHRASAL VERB** **,hide 'out** to go somewhere where no one can find you: *We used to hide out from our parents here.*

hide² /haɪd/ noun [C/U] the skin of an animal such as a cow that is used for making leather

hide-and-'seek noun [U] a children's game in which one player lets the other players hide, and then tries to find them

hideaway /'haɪdəˌweɪ/ noun [C] a private place where someone goes to relax or to be alone

hideous /'hɪdiəs/ adj very ugly, frightening, or unpleasant —**hideously** adv

hideout /'haɪdaʊt/ noun [C] a place where someone can hide

hiding /'haɪdɪŋ/ noun [U] a situation in which someone hides: *Davies, fearing arrest, went into hiding.*

hierarchical /ˌhaɪəˈrɑːkɪk(ə)l/ adj a hierarchical society or organization is one in which differences in status are considered to be very important

hierarchy /'haɪəˌrɑːki/ noun **1** [C/U] a system for organizing people according to their status **2** [C] the group of people who control an organization

hi-fi /'haɪˌfaɪ/ noun [C] a piece of electronic equipment that is used for playing recorded music = **STEREO**

high¹ /haɪ/ adj ★★★

1 large in size	**7** affected by drugs
2 a long way up	**8** happy/excited
3 measuring things	**9** about sounds
4 large in amount	**10** winds: very strong
5 very good	**11** best/most extreme
6 important	**+ PHRASE**

1 large in size from the top to the ground ≠ LOW: *Kilimanjaro is the highest mountain in Africa.* ♦ *The fence is too high to climb over.*

2 in a position that is a long way above the ground ≠ LOW: *high clouds* ♦ *the highest shelf*

3 used in measurements of how big or how far above the ground an object is: *Some of the waves are fifteen feet high.* ♦ *How high is that ceiling?*

4 large in amount ≠ LOW: *high prices/ temperatures/wages* ♦ *This is an area of* **high unemployment**. ♦ *Ice cream is very* **high in calories** (=contains a lot of calories).

5 very good or excellent ≠ LOW: *high quality products* ♦ *She has a very* **high opinion** of *herself.*

6 important compared to other people or things ≠ LOW: *What is the highest rank in the army?* ♦ *Both parties are giving* **high priority** to education.

7 *informal* affected by an illegal drug: *He was* **high on** *cocaine.*

8 *informal* very happy or excited: *The children have been* **in high spirits** all day.

9 a high sound is near the upper end of a range of sounds ≠ LOW: *Women's voices are usually higher than men's.* → HIGH-PITCHED

10 high winds are very strong

11 used in some expressions for referring to the greatest or most extreme example or part of something: *In the 1980s this was* **high fashion.**

> **PHRASE** **high hopes/expectations** if you have high hopes or EXPECTATIONS, you hope or expect that something very good will happen

> ■ **High** is used for talking about things that are a long way from the ground. It is also used to talk about mountains: *a high shelf* ♦ *a high window* ♦ *the world's highest mountain*
>
> ■ **Tall** is used about people or things that measure more than is usual from their bottom to their top: *a tall thin bottle* ♦ *a tall tree* ♦ *the tallest boy in the class*

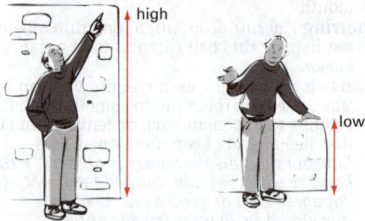

high

low

high² /haɪ/ adv ★★★

1 a long distance above the ground, or above a particular position ≠ LOW: *a first-class hotel built high on the hillside* ♦ *the sound of war planes flying* **high above** *the city*

2 reaching up a long way: *She stretched her arms up high.*

3 to or at an important position ≠ LOW: *She rose high in the company.* ♦ *A colonel ranks higher than a major.*

4 near the upper end of a range of sounds ≠ LOW: *I can't sing that high.*

high³ /haɪ/ noun [C] **1** a period or situation in which something reaches its highest level ≠ LOW: *Temperatures today are expected to reach a high of 87 degrees.* **2** a feeling of great happiness or excitement ≠ LOW

highbrow /'haɪˌbraʊ/ adj likely to interest people who are interested in learning, culture, and art ≠ LOWBROW

high ,chair noun [C] a tall chair that very young children sit in to have their meals

high-'class adj very good in quality or ability

high 'court noun [C] a court of law in the UK

that can change previous court decisions

'high-'end adj high-end goods and services are more expensive and more advanced than other similar goods and services

higher¹ /'haɪə/ adj at a more advanced level, or involving a greater degree of knowledge: *higher mathematics*

higher² /'haɪə/ the COMPARATIVE of **high**

higher edu'cation noun [U] education at a university, or at a similar level

high 'five noun [C] the action of holding your hand up and hitting your palm flat against that of another person

high 'flyer noun [C] someone who has achieved a lot and is determined to continue being successful —**high-'flying** adj

high-'grade adj very good in quality

high 'ground, the noun [singular] an advantage that you have in a situation or competition, especially because you have behaved more fairly or more honestly than your opponent

high-handed /ˌhaɪ 'hændɪd/ adj speaking or acting without considering other people's opinions=ARROGANT

high 'heels or **high-heeled shoes** /ˌhaɪ hi:ld 'ju:z/ noun [plural] women's shoes that have high heels —*picture* → SHOE

'high 'jump, the noun [singular] a sports event in which people try to jump over a bar that can be raised higher after each jump

highlands /'haɪləndz/ noun [plural] an area of land that consists of hills and mountains ≠ LOWLANDS —**highland** adj

high-'level adj 1 involving people in important or powerful positions: *a high-level meeting* 2 at a more extreme or advanced level than usual: *high-level radiation*

highlight¹ /'haɪˌlaɪt/ verb [T] ★
1 to report or describe something in a way that makes people notice it and think about it: *The case highlights the need for adequate controls on such experiments.*
2 to make something easier to see or notice: *Using contrasting colours will highlight the shape and dimensions of your room.*
3 to mark a word, picture, computer file etc so that you can see it more easily

highlight² /'haɪˌlaɪt/ noun [C] the most exciting, impressive, or interesting part of something: *The highlight of the trip was visiting the Great Wall of China.*

highlighter /'haɪˌlaɪtə/ noun [C] a brightly coloured pen that you use for marking particular words on a document

highlights /'haɪˌlaɪts/ noun [plural] parts of your hair that have been made a lighter colour using chemicals

highly /'haɪli/ adv ★★★
1 used before some adjectives to mean 'very', or 'very well': *It now seems **highly unlikely** that the project will be finished on time.* ♦ *She's a **highly educated** young woman.*
2 used for saying that someone or something is very good or very important: *a **highly valued** member of staff* ♦ *Everyone we talked to **spoke very highly of** him.*

Highness /'haɪnəs/ noun **Your/His/Her**

Highness used for talking to or about a king, queen, PRINCE, or PRINCESS

high-'pitched adj a high-pitched voice or sound is very high

'high 'point noun [C] the best part of something =HIGHLIGHT

high-powered /ˌhaɪ 'paʊəd/ adj 1 important and powerful: *a high-powered job* 2 very powerful and effective: *a high-powered rifle*

high-'profile adj often seen or mentioned in newspapers or on television: *a high-profile campaign/company/politician*

'high-'rise adj very tall with many floors: *high-rise apartment blocks* —**'high-'rise** noun [C]

'high 'school noun [C/U] **1** in the UK, a school for children between the ages of 11 and 18 =SECONDARY SCHOOL **2** in the US, a school for children between the ages of 14 and 18

high 'seas, the noun [plural] the parts of the sea that are far away from land and that are not owned by any country

high 'season noun [singular/U] the part of the year when many tourists visit a place ≠ LOW SEASON

'high 'street noun [C] British **1** [C] the main street in a town or city, with a lot of businesses along it **2** [singular] shops and the business that they do: *Sales in the high street continue to fall.*

high-tech /ˌhaɪ 'tek/ adj using the most advanced technology

high tech'nology noun [U] technology that involves the most advanced methods

high 'tide noun [C/U] the time when the sea reaches the highest level ≠ LOW TIDE

highway /'haɪˌweɪ/ noun [C] *American* a wide road that has been built for fast travel between towns and cities

hijack /'haɪˌdʒæk/ verb [T] **1** to illegally take control of a plane by using violence or threats **2** *showing disapproval* to take control of an organization or activity for your own purposes —**hijacker** /'haɪˌdʒækə/ noun [C], **hijacking** noun [C/U]

hike¹ /haɪk/ noun [C] **1** a long walk in the countryside **2** *informal* a sudden large increase, for example in prices or taxes

hike² /haɪk/ verb **1** [I/T] to go for a long walk in the countryside **2** [T] to suddenly increase the amount or level of something, for example a price or tax
PHRASAL VERB **hike sth 'up** *informal same as* **hike²** 2

hiking /'haɪkɪŋ/ noun [U] the activity of walking for long distances in the countryside —**hiker** noun [C]

hilarious /hɪ'leəriəs/ adj extremely funny —**hilariously** adv

hill /hɪl/ noun [C] ★★★ an area of land that is higher than the land surrounding it but that is smaller and lower than a mountain: *They climbed slowly to the top of the hill.* ♦ *The village is built on a steep hill.*
PHRASE **over the hill** *informal* no longer young and therefore unable to do things that you could do in the past=PAST IT

hillside /'hɪlˌsaɪd/ noun [C] the land on a hill below the top

hilltop /'hɪlˌtɒp/ noun [C] the top of a hill

hilly /'hɪli/ adj with a lot of hills: *a hilly landscape*

H

hilt /hɪlt/ noun **to the hilt** *informal* as much as possible, or to the highest level possible: *Mike's friends were prepared to defend him to the hilt.*

him /*weak* ɪm, *strong* hɪm/ pronoun ★★★
1 the object form of 'he', used for referring to a man, boy, or male animal when they have already been mentioned or when it is obvious which one you are referring to: *Luke wants me to marry him.* ♦ *I'm expecting a call from Jake. That must be him now.*
2 *old-fashioned* used in a general way for referring to any person: *Each patient should receive the treatment that suits him best.* → HE

himself /*weak* ɪm'self, *strong* hɪm'self/ pronoun ★★★
1 the REFLEXIVE form of 'he', used for showing that the man, boy, or male animal that does something is also affected by what he does: *William slipped once, but he didn't hurt himself.* ♦ *That man ought to be ashamed of himself.*
2 used for emphasizing that you are referring to a particular man, boy, or male animal and not to anyone else: *It is said that Shakespeare himself once acted in this play.* ♦ *You mean to tell me Jack built the whole cabin himself?*
3 *old-fashioned* used in a general way for referring back to the subject of a sentence when they may be either male or female: *Everyone has to look after himself.* → HE
PHRASES **(all) by himself 1** *I noticed Ben sitting all by himself.* **2** without help from anyone else: *There's too much work for one man to do all by himself.*
(all) to himself not sharing something with anyone else: *It was the first time he'd had a room to himself.*
be/feel/seem himself to be in a normal mental or physical state: *Joe felt more himself after a good night's sleep.*

hind /haɪnd/ adj the hind legs or feet of an animal are its back legs or feet

hinder /'hɪndə/ verb [T] to stop someone or something from making progress ≠ HELP

hindrance /'hɪndrəns/ noun [C] something that delays or prevents progress

hindsight /'haɪn(d)saɪt/ noun [U] the opportunity to judge or understand past events using knowledge that you have gained since then

Hindu /ˌhɪn'duː, 'hɪnduː/ noun [C] someone whose religion is Hinduism —**Hindu** adj

Hinduism /'hɪnduɪz(ə)m/ noun [U] the main religion of India

hinge¹ /hɪndʒ/ noun [C] an object that fastens a door to a wall, or a lid to a container, and allows it to open and shut

hinge² /hɪndʒ/ **PHRASAL VERB** **hinge on sth** to depend on something: *The result of the trial hinges on her evidence.*

hint¹ /hɪnt/ noun ★
1 [C] something that you say in order to show what you are thinking or feeling, without saying it directly: *She hoped he would take the hint and leave her alone.* ♦ *Sam keeps dropping hints about what he wants for his birthday.*
2 [C] a small piece of information that helps

someone guess something: *'You'll never guess who I saw today.' 'Give me a hint.'*
3 [singular] a small amount of something: *There was a hint of impatience in his voice.*
4 [C] a useful suggestion or piece of advice =TIP: *hints on how to improve your computer skills*

Words often used with hint
Adjectives often used with hint (noun, sense 1)
■ **broad, heavy, strong** + HINT: used when you say what you mean directly
■ **gentle, slight, subtle, vague, veiled** + HINT: used when you say what you mean indirectly

hint² /hɪnt/ verb [I/T] to say what you are thinking or feeling in an indirect way: *Officials are hinting at the possibility of signing an agreement this week.*

hinterland /'hɪntəˌlænd/ noun [C] an area that is far away from towns and cities and is not on the coast

hip¹ /hɪp/ noun [C] one of the two parts at either side of your body between your waist and the top of your legs: *She stood with her hands on her hips, waiting.* ♦ *He fell downstairs and broke his hip.* —picture → C14

hip² /hɪp/ adj *informal* modern and fashionable

hip hop noun [U] a type of music that uses RAP and SAMPLES (=short pieces of recorded music or sound)

hippie /'hɪpi/ noun [C] someone in the 1960s who was opposed to war and traditional attitudes, and who showed this by their long hair and informal clothes

hippo /'hɪpəʊ/ noun [C] *informal* a hippopotamus

hippopotamus /ˌhɪpə'pɒtəməs/ noun [C] a large African animal with a wide head and mouth and thick grey skin —*picture* → C12

hippy /'hɪpi/ another spelling of **hippie**

hire¹ /'haɪə/ verb ★
1 [T] *British* to pay to use something such as a car or a piece of equipment for a short time: *You can hire a car at the airport.*
2 [I/T] to pay someone to work for you =EMPLOY: *I hired someone to paint the house.*
PHRASAL VERB **hire sth out** *British* to let someone use something temporarily in return for money: *This room is often hired out for private parties.*

hire² /'haɪə/ noun [U] *British* the activity of paying money in order to use something for a short time: *We paid £50 for the hire of the hall.* ♦ *Bikes are available for hire.* ♦ *a hire car*

his /*weak* ɪz, *strong* hɪz/ grammar word ★★★

His is the possessive form of 'he', which can be:
■ a **determiner**: *He gave me his address.*
■ a **pronoun**: *My computer didn't cost as much as his.*

1 used for showing that something belongs to or is connected with a man, boy, or male animal that has already been mentioned: *She was attracted by his smile.* ♦ *Bader lost both his legs in a flying accident.* ♦ *The house isn't his, it's mine.* ♦ *I saw her parents at the wedding, but I didn't see his.* ♦ *Soon he* *had enough money to set up **his own** business.*

2 *old-fashioned* used in a general way for showing that something belongs to or is connected with any person, whether they are male or female: *Each child can choose his favourite story.* → HE

Hispanic /hɪˈspænɪk/ adj **1** used for describing someone whose family originally came from a country where Spanish is spoken **2** relating to countries where Spanish is spoken, or to the culture of these countries —**Hispanic** noun [C]

hiss /hɪs/ verb **1** [I/T] to say something in a quiet but angry way **2** [I] to make a long 's' sound like the sound that a snake makes —**hiss** noun [C]

historian /hɪˈstɔːriən/ noun [C] someone who studies history

historic /hɪˈstɒrɪk/ adj important enough to be remembered as a part of history: *historic events* ♦ *London's historic buildings*

historical /hɪˈstɒrɪk(ə)l/ adj ★★
1 connected with history or with the past: *The painting depicts an actual historical event.* ♦ *historical research/evidence*
2 based on people or events that existed in the past: *a historical novel*
—**historically** /hɪˈstɒrɪkli/ adv

history /ˈhɪst(ə)ri/ noun ★★★
1 [singular/U] the whole of time before now or since something began to exist, and everything that happened in that time: *Attitudes to gender roles have changed throughout history.* ♦ *The University has a distinguished history.* ♦ *the history of Spain*
2 [U] the study of the events of the past: *He teaches history at the local school.* ♦ *history books*
3 [C] an account of the events that happened during a particular period of the past: *He's writing a history of the Romans.*
  PHRASES **have a history of sth 1** to be well known for doing something because you have often done it in the past: *The country has a long history of political kidnappings.* **2** if you have a history of a medical condition or other problem, you have had it before: *He has a history of heart disease.*
make history to do something that many people will remember because it is very important

hit¹ /hɪt/ (past tense and past participle **hit**) verb ★★★

1 touch sth with force	5 press switch etc
2 hurt sb	+ PHRASES
3 have bad effect on	+ PHRASAL VERBS
4 realize sth	

1 [I/T] to move quickly against something, or to move an object quickly against something, touching it with force: *The glass smashed as it hit the ground.* ♦ **hit sth with sth** *The child was hitting the table with a toy hammer.*
2 [I/T] to move your hand or an object hard against someone's body, so that you hurt them: *Stop hitting your brother!* ♦ **hit sb on sth** *He hit me on the shoulder.* ♦ **hit sb in sth** *They hit me in the stomach.*
3 [I/T] to have a sudden or bad effect on

someone or something: ♦ *They were halfway down the mountain when the storm hit. The recession has* **hit** *small businesses hard.*
4 [T] if an idea hits you, you suddenly realize it=STRIKE: *It suddenly hit her that she would never see him again.*
5 [T] *spoken* to press something such as a switch on a machine, vehicle, or computer: *Just hit the Save button every few minutes.*
  PHRASES **hit it off** *spoken* if two people hit it off, they like each other when they first meet=GET ON
hit the nail on the head to say something that is exactly right
hit the road *informal* to leave, or to start a journey
hit the roof *spoken* to become very angry
  PHRASAL VERBS **ˌhit ˈback** to criticize someone who has criticized you
ˈhit on sb *informal* to try to start a conversation with someone because you are sexually attracted to them
ˈhit on sth or **ˈhit uˌpon sth** to suddenly have an idea=COME UP WITH STH: *They hit on a brilliant solution.*
ˌhit ˈout to criticize someone or something very strongly=ATTACK: *Ms Wallis hit out at the court's decision.*

hit² /hɪt/ noun [C] ★

1 successful record	4 when player hits ball
2 sth successful/popular	5 use of Internet
3 when sb/sth is hit	6 computer result

1 a song that sells a very large number of copies: *They played a lot of old hits from the 70s and 80s.* ♦ *an album of Madonna's greatest hits*
2 something or someone that is very successful and popular: *The film was a massive hit at the box-office.* ♦ *His magic act was **a hit with** the children.*
3 an occasion when someone or something touches another person or thing with a lot of force
4 an occasion when a player hits the ball in a game
5 *computing* an occasion when someone looks at a particular document on the Internet: *Their website gets a couple of hundred hits a day.*
6 *computing* a piece of information that a computer program finds for you

ˌhit-and-ˈrun adj a hit-and-run accident is one in which a driver does not stop after their vehicle has hit a person or another car

hitch¹ /hɪtʃ/ verb **1** [I/T] *informal* to hitchhike **2** [T] to fasten something to something else: *We hitched a trailer to the back of our car.*
  PHRASAL VERB **ˌhitch sth ˈup** to pull up something that you are wearing: *She hitched up her skirt and ran.*

hitch² /hɪtʃ/ noun [C] a problem that is not very serious: *The plane was delayed due to a last-minute hitch.*

hitchhike /ˈhɪtʃhaɪk/ verb [I] to travel by asking other people to take you in their car. You do this by standing at the side of a road and holding out your thumb or a sign. —**hitchhiker** noun [C]

hitherto /ˌhɪðəˈtuː/ adv *very formal* until the present time=PREVIOUSLY

H

HIV /ˌeɪtʃ aɪ ˈviː/ noun [U] human immunodeficiency virus: a VIRUS that can cause AIDS

hive /haɪv/ noun [C] a place in which BEES live and make HONEY

PHRASE **a hive of activity** a place where everyone is very busy

HIV 'positive adj infected with HIV

hiya /ˈhaɪə/ interjection informal used for saying 'hello' to someone who you know well

hm or **hmm** /m, hm/ interjection **1** used for representing a sound that you make when you pause to think before saying something else **2** used for representing a sound that you make to show you do not believe something

hoard¹ /hɔːd/ noun [C] a large amount of something that someone has hidden somewhere

hoard² /hɔːd/ verb [I/T] to get and keep a large amount of something because it might be valuable later

hoarding /ˈhɔːdɪŋ/ noun [C] British a large board used for advertising outside

hoarse /hɔːs/ adj speaking in a low rough voice —**hoarsely** adv

hoax /həʊks/ noun [C] a trick in which someone tells people that something bad is going to happen or that something is true when it is not

hob /hɒb/ noun [C] British the top part of a COOKER that you put pans on

hobble /ˈhɒb(ə)l/ verb [I] to walk slowly and with difficulty because your feet are sore or injured

hobby /ˈhɒbi/ noun [C] something that you enjoy doing when you are not working: *Mike's hobbies include reading and chess.*

hockey /ˈhɒki/ noun [U] **1** British a game that is played on grass by two teams of 11 players. They try to score goals by hitting a ball with a stick that has a curved end. **2** American ICE HOCKEY

hoe /həʊ/ noun [C] a tool with a long handle that you use for turning over the soil in a garden —**hoe** verb [I/T]

hog¹ /hɒg/ noun [C] American a PIG

PHRASE **go the whole hog** informal to do something in a very thorough or enthusiastic way

hog² /hɒg/ verb [T] informal to take or use a lot of something in a way that prevents other people from having it

hoist¹ /hɔɪst/ verb [T] to lift something or someone, often using special equipment

hoist² /hɔɪst/ noun [C] a piece of equipment that is used for lifting heavy objects

hold¹ /həʊld/ (past tense and past participle **held** /held/) verb ★★★

1 carry	**10** believe
2 stop sb/sth moving	**11** keep having feeling
3 put arms around sb	**12** not lose to opponent
4 be able to contain	**13** wait on telephone
5 organize event	**14** support weight
6 have a job/position	**15** have quality/feeling
7 keep prisoner	**16** own sth
8 store information	**+** PHRASES
9 continue in same state	**+** PHRASAL VERBS

1 [T] to carry something or someone using your hands or arms: *Can you hold my bag for a moment?* ♦ **hold sth in/under/between sth** *Barry was holding a coin between his finger and thumb.* ♦ *She was holding a baby in her arms.*

2 [T] to keep someone or something in a particular position so that they do not move: *Can you hold this parcel for me so I can tape it up?* ♦ *His silk tie was **held in place** with a small diamond pin.* ♦ **hold sb down** *Four people held him down* (=held him on the floor so that he could not move).

3 [T] to put your arms around someone for a long time because you love them or because they are unhappy: *He sat beside her and held her.* ♦ *She kissed him and held him tight.*

4 [T] to be able to fit an amount of something inside: *The stadium holds 80,000 people.* ♦ *How much does this jug hold?*

5 [T] to organize something such as a meeting or event: *The government agreed to hold a referendum.*

6 [T] to have a job or position: *She is the first woman to hold this post.* ♦ *President Mitterrand **held office** for 14 years.*

7 [T] to keep someone as a prisoner: *The four men had been **held captive** for over two years.*

8 [T] to keep information, for example on a computer: *His data was held on disk.*

9 [I] to stay in the same state or at the same level: *The fine weather should hold until Tuesday.* ♦ *The coffee market has **held steady** for a few months.*

10 [T] to have a particular belief or opinion: *She holds some pretty unpleasant views.* ♦ *Most people **hold** the president **responsible** for the riots.* ♦ **+(that)** *Baxter holds that significant changes in the population can occur within a decade.*

11 [T] to continue to have a particular feeling: *I no longer hold any resentment towards him.*

12 [T] to keep control of something: *Rebel fighters have held the territory for five years.*

13 [I/T] to wait to speak to someone on the telephone: *'Do you want to call back later?' 'No, I'll hold.'*

14 [T] to support the weight of someone or something: *Do you think this branch will hold us?*

15 [T] formal to have a particular quality: *The project holds a great deal of promise.* ♦ *He holds no authority over us.*

16 [T] formal to own something or have the right to use something: *Three per cent of our shares are now held by US investors.* ♦ *He holds a US passport.*

PHRASES **hold it** spoken **1** used for telling someone not to move: *Just hold it right there! Where do you think you're going with that?* **2** used for telling someone to wait: *Hold it, you two, wait for us!*

hold true to be true, or to remain true

hold your own to be as good as other more experienced or stronger people

PHRASAL VERBS **hold sth against sb** to feel angry with someone because of something that they have done in the past: *He knows it was an accident – I don't think he'll hold it against her.*

,hold 'back to decide not to do or say something: *He held back, remembering the mistake he had made before.*

,hold sb/sth 'back 1 to stop someone or something from moving forwards: *Ollie had to hold Tom back to prevent him fighting.* ♦ *Her hair was held back by two clips.* **2** to stop someone or something from being as successful as they should be: *Her parents worried that her classmates were holding her back.*

,hold sth 'down 1 to stop prices or numbers from rising: *a deal to hold down wages and prices* **2 hold down a job** to succeed in keeping a job: *Half of them have never held down a proper job.*

,hold 'off to delay doing something: *He may decide to hold off for a few days.* ♦ **hold off doing sth** *She held off calling him until the last possible moment.*

,hold sb 'off to stop someone who is trying to attack you from coming close

,hold 'on 1 to wait: *We'll hold on another minute, then we'll have to go.* ♦ *Hold on! You forgot your card!* **2** to hold something tightly or carefully so that you do not drop it or do not fall: *Hold on tight everyone – the driver's getting ready to go.*

,hold 'on to sth or **,hold 'onto sth 1** to hold something tightly or carefully so that you do not drop it or do not fall: *Hold on to the seat in front when we go round the corner.* **2** to not lose something or not let someone else have it=KEEP: *Hold on to the instructions in case you have any problems.* **3** to continue feeling or believing something

,hold 'out 1 to continue to be enough, or to continue to exist: *How long will your money hold out?* **2** to continue to defend a place that is being attacked

,hold sth 'out 1 to hold something where other people can reach it: *She held out her hand to him.* **2 hold out hope** to think that something is likely to happen or succeed

,hold 'out for sth to not accept an offer because you hope to get a better one

'hold sb to sth to make someone do what they have promised or decided

,hold sb/sth 'up 1 to cause a delay, or to make someone late: *Sorry, I'm late, but my train was held up.* ♦ *She got held up at work.* **2** to steal from a business, from a vehicle, or from people by threatening violence: *An armed raider held up the village store last week.*

hold² /həʊld/ noun ★
1 [singular] the fact that you are holding something: *His hold on her arm tightened.* ♦ *Bobby grabbed hold of the railing* (=suddenly started holding it). ♦ *She took hold of his hand* (=started holding it). **2** [singular] power or control over someone or something: *The rebels have a firm hold over the northern area.* ♦ *Does he have some sort of hold on you?* **3** [C] the area in a plane or ship that is used for goods, vehicles, or bags

PHRASES **get hold of sb** to manage to talk to someone: *Can you get hold of Mike and tell him the meeting's postponed?*
get hold of sth 1 to get something that you need or want: *I've managed to get hold of*

some rather good wine. **2** to start holding something with your hands: *Just get hold of the aerial and move it round to see if you can get a better picture.*

keep hold of sth 1 to not take your hands away from something that you are holding: *She kept hold of his arm.* **2** to not lose something or not let someone else get it: *They managed to keep hold of the ball in the second half.*

on hold 1 if something is on hold, you have stopped it from happening now, but it may happen later: *After the accident her career had to be put on hold.* **2** waiting to speak to someone on the telephone, after your call has been answered: *They've put me on hold.*

take hold to become stronger and difficult to stop: *They were fortunate to escape before the fire took hold.* ♦ *A sense of dread took hold of him.*

holdall /ˈhəʊldɔːl/ noun [C] British a large soft bag with handles

holder /ˈhəʊldə/ noun [C] **1** someone who owns something or who has been given something **2** something that is designed to hold or support another object

holding /ˈhəʊldɪŋ/ noun [C] a part of a company that someone owns

'holding ,company noun [C] a company that owns the majority of the SHARES in another company

'hold-up noun [C] **1** a delay **2** a situation in which someone with a gun steals money from a bank or shop

hole¹ /həʊl/ noun [C] ★★★
1 a space that has been dug in the surface of the ground: *Workers dug a 30-foot hole in the ground.* ♦ *rabbit holes*
2 a space in the surface of something that goes partly or completely through it: *All my socks have holes in them.* ♦ *Rain poured through a gaping hole in the roof* (=a very large hole).
3 a part of something such as an idea or explanation where important details are missing: *His argument was full of holes.*
4 in golf, a small space in the ground that you have to hit the ball into —picture ➝ C15

hole² /həʊl/ PHRASAL VERB **,hole (sb) 'up** if you hole up somewhere, or if you are holed up somewhere, you stay there, especially because you are hiding

,hole-in-the-'wall noun [C] British informal a CASHPOINT

'hole ,punch noun [C] a piece of equipment used for putting small holes in paper —picture ➝ C3

holiday¹ /ˈhɒlɪdeɪ/ noun ★★★
1 [C/U] British a period of time when you do not work or study and do things for pleasure instead: *Employees are entitled to four weeks' annual holiday.* ♦ *I am away on holiday for the next two weeks.* ♦ *The kids get bored by the end of the summer holidays.*
2 [C] British an occasion when you go and stay in another place for pleasure: *a golfing/ skiing/seaside holiday* ♦ *a holiday resort* ♦ *I'm going on holiday with some friends.*
3 [C] a day that is a celebration of something special, on which you do not have to work or go to school: *1st May is a holiday in many*

H

European countries. → BANK HOLIDAY

holiday² /ˈhɒlɪdeɪ/ verb [I] British to be on holiday in a particular place

holidaymaker /ˈhɒlɪdeɪˌmeɪkə/ noun [C] British a person who is visiting a place for their holiday

holistic /həʊˈlɪstɪk/ adj **1** treating the whole body, and not just the part of it that is ill: holistic medicine/healthcare **2** thinking about the whole of something, and not just dealing with particular aspects: a holistic approach to the region's development

hollow¹ /ˈhɒləʊ/ adj **1** empty inside: hollow chocolate eggs **2** not sincere or with any real meaning: a hollow display of friendship ♦ a hollow victory **3** a hollow sound is a low sound like something empty being hit **4** hollow eyes or cheeks seem to have sunk into your head

hollow² /ˈhɒləʊ/ noun [C] a small area in the ground that is lower than the ground around it

hollow³ /ˈhɒləʊ/ PHRASAL VERB ˌhollow sth ˈout to make a hole in something by removing what is inside

holly /ˈhɒli/ noun [C/U] a tree with dark green leaves with sharp points and small bright red BERRIES —picture → C9

Hollywood /ˈhɒliˌwʊd/ noun [U] the part of the US film industry that has a reputation for making very successful films that cost a lot of money to produce

holocaust /ˈhɒləkɔːst/ noun [C] a war in which very many people are killed

hologram /ˈhɒləɡræm/ noun [C] a kind of picture that is THREE-DIMENSIONAL (=does not look flat)

holster /ˈhəʊlstə/ noun [C] a leather container for a small gun, that is fixed to a belt

holy /ˈhəʊli/ adj ★★
1 important in a religion, or used in worship =SACRED: the holy book of the Sikhs ♦ the holy city of Jerusalem
2 respected for living a very religious life: a holy man and his followers
—**holiness** noun [U]

homage /ˈhɒmɪdʒ/ noun [singular/U] something that someone does or says in order to show respect or admiration

home¹ /həʊm/ noun ★★★

1 place where you live	**5** where people get care
2 where parents live	**6** base for sports team
3 your country/city etc	**7** where sth started
4 place to buy/rent	**+** PHRASES

1 [C/U] the place where you live: We go to a school close to our home. ♦ a child in need of a loving home ♦ Peter isn't at home today. ♦ I hate being away from home. → HOUSE
2 [U] the place where your parents live and where you grew up: He is 43 and still living at home. ♦ I left home when I was 18 (=stopped living there).
3 [U] the country or city where you live: a great opportunity in markets both at home and abroad ♦ Back home, the weather is much better.
4 [C] a building for people to buy or rent: One thousand new homes are being built in the area. ♦ There is a shortage of homes for rent.

5 [C] a building where people who need special care can live and be looked after: They didn't want to put their mother in a home. ♦ a home for orphans
6 [U] the place where a sports team is based and plays most of its games: United are playing at home tonight.
7 [singular] the place where something first started or was first made: Scotland is the home of golf.
PHRASES **be/feel at home** to be/feel relaxed and comfortable in a particular place or situation: They did everything they could to make me feel at home.
make yourself at home to feel relaxed and behave in the same way as you do in your own home: Make yourself at home while I go and find those photographs.

home² /həʊm/ adv ★★★
1 to the place where you live: I decided to walk home. ♦ What time are you coming home? ♦ I went home to France. ♦ On the way home from school, I met my friend Sue.
2 at the place where you live: Is Kathryn home? ♦ I'll be home all day Tuesday.

home³ /həʊm/ adj **1** relating to your home rather than your work: Write your home address at the top of the page. **2** done, made, or experienced at home: home cooking/shopping/banking **3** relating to things that happen within a country, rather than between different countries: These cameras sell well in the home market.
4 relating to the place where a sports team is based: a home win ♦ the team's home ground (=where they usually play)

home⁴ /həʊm/ PHRASAL VERB ˌhome ˈin on sth to aim at something and move quickly and directly to it: a missile homing in on its target

homecoming /ˈhəʊmˌkʌmɪŋ/ noun [C] an occasion when someone returns to a place where they used to live

home-ˈgrown adj **1** grown in someone's garden, not on a large farm **2** from a particular local area or small place: home-grown bands

home imˈprovement noun [C/U] work that you do to your house to make it better

homeland /ˈhəʊmˌlænd/ noun [C] the country where someone comes from

home ˈlanguage noun [C] American someone's native language

homeless /ˈhəʊmləs/ adj **1** without a place to live **2** the homeless people who are homeless

homely /ˈhəʊmli/ adj **1** British simple and pleasant in a way that makes you feel comfortable at home **2** American ugly

home-ˈmade adj made in someone's home rather than in a factory

Home ˈOffice, the in the UK, the government department that is responsible for JUSTICE and the police, and for deciding who is allowed into the country

homeopathic /ˌhəʊmiəˈpæθɪk/ adj homeopathic medicines or doctors use a way of treating an illness in which people are given very small amounts of natural substances that, in large amounts, would cause the illness —**homeopathy** /ˌhəʊmiˈɒpəθi/ noun [U]

home page noun [C] *computing* **1** a place on the Internet where a person or an organization gives information about themselves or their business **2** a place on the Internet that you choose to appear first on your computer screen each time you look at the Internet

home rule noun [U] a form of government in which people have control in their own country, rather than being controlled by another country

Home Secretary noun [C] in the UK, the person who is in charge of the HOME OFFICE

homesick /ˈhəʊmˌsɪk/ adj feeling sad and alone because you are far from home

homestead /ˈhəʊmˌsted/ noun [C] *American* a farm, including any buildings that are on the land

home town noun [C] the city or town where you lived as a child

home truths /ˌhəʊm ˈtruːðz/ noun [plural] unpleasant facts or opinions about you that someone tells you

homework /ˈhəʊmˌwɜːk/ noun [U] ★ work that a teacher gives a student to do at home: *Have the kids done their homework?*
> PHRASE **do your homework** to prepare for something by learning as much as you can about it: *You could tell that the interviewer hadn't really done his homework.*

homicidal /ˌhɒmɪˈsaɪd(ə)l/ adj likely to kill someone, or wanting to kill someone

homicide /ˈhɒmɪˌsaɪd/ noun [C/U] *American legal* the crime of killing someone

homogeneous /ˌhəʊməʊˈdʒiːniəs/ adj consisting of things that are similar or all of the same type

homonym /ˈhɒmənɪm/ noun [C] *linguistics* a word that is spelled the same as another word but that has a different meaning

homophobia /ˌhəʊməˈfəʊbiə/ noun [U] hate of gay people —**homophobic** adj

homophone /ˈhɒməfəʊn/ noun [C] *linguistics* a word that sounds the same as another word but that has a different spelling and meaning

homosexual¹ /ˌhəʊməʊˈsekʃuəl/ adj attracted sexually to people of the same sex —**homosexuality** /ˌhəʊməʊsekʃuˈæləti/ noun [U]

homosexual² /ˌhəʊməʊˈsekʃuəl/ noun [C] a person who is attracted sexually to people of the same sex

hone /həʊn/ verb [T] to improve a skill or TALENT that is already well developed

honest /ˈɒnɪst/ adj ★
  1 a person who is honest does not tell lies or cheat people, and obeys the law
  ≠ DISHONEST: *an honest man*
  2 telling the truth, or not cheating people: *I want you to give me an honest answer.* ♦ *I gave her the wrong amount of money, but it was an honest mistake* (=not intended).
  3 honest work is a job that you work fairly hard at: *When is the last time Charlie did any honest work?* ♦ *I'm just trying to earn an honest living* (=earn money by working hard).
> PHRASE **to be honest** *spoken* used when telling someone what you really think: *To be honest, the meal was terrible.*

Word family: honest

Words in the same family as honest
- honesty *n*
- honestly *adv*
- dishonest *adj*
- dishonesty *n*

honestly /ˈɒnɪs(t)li/ adv **1** *spoken* used for emphasizing that what you are saying is true: *I honestly can't remember.* **2** in a way that is honest: *She was trying to do her job honestly and fairly.* **3** *spoken* used for expressing slight anger at someone: *Oh honestly, now look what he's done!*

honesty /ˈɒnɪsti/ noun [U] an honest way of behaving, speaking, or thinking: *She is a woman of honesty and integrity.*
> PHRASE **in all honesty** *spoken* used when telling someone what you really think: *I can't, in all honesty, say that I enjoyed it.*

honey /ˈhʌni/ noun **1** [U] a sweet sticky yellow or brown food made by BEES **2** [C] *spoken* used for talking to someone who you like very much: *Hi, honey, I'm home!*

honeymoon /ˈhʌniˌmuːn/ noun [C] a holiday that two people take after they get married

honk /hɒŋk/ verb [I/T] to make a loud noise using the horn of a car —**honk** noun [C]

honor /ˈɒnə/ the American spelling of **honour**

honorable /ˈɒn(ə)rəb(ə)l/ the American spelling of **honourable**

honorary /ˈɒnərəri/ adj **1** an honorary university degree or title is given to honour someone, although they have not earned it in the usual way **2** an honorary member of a group is someone who is allowed to join without applying or without having the usual qualifications

honored /ˈɒnəd/ the American spelling of **honoured**

honour¹ /ˈɒnə/ noun **1** [U] the respect that people have for someone who achieves something great, is very powerful, or behaves in a way that is morally right: *They were prepared to die for the honour of their country.* **2** [U] the behaviour of someone who has high moral standards = INTEGRITY: *a man of honour* (=someone who always behaves in a morally correct way) ♦ *It's no longer just a legal issue, it's a matter of honour.* **3** [C] something that you do that you are proud of: *Being asked to perform at La Scala is an honour for any singer.* ♦ **be an honour to do sth** *It's a great honour to be here with you tonight.* **4** [C] a prize that someone is given because they have done something important: *Twenty children received honours for bravery.*
> PHRASE **in honour of** in order to show respect and admiration for someone or something: *St Petersburg was renamed Leningrad in honour of Lenin.*
→ HONOURS

honour² /ˈɒnə/ verb [T] **1** to show your respect or admiration for someone by giving them a prize or a title, or by praising them publicly: *We are here today to honour the men and women who gave their lives for their country.* **2** to do what you promised to do or what it is your duty to do: *Once a contract is signed, it has to be honoured.*

honourable /ˈɒn(ə)rəb(ə)l/ adj morally good and deserving respect: *Your father was an* *honourable man.* ♦ *the honourable thing to do* —**honourably** adv

honoured /ˈɒnəd/ adj **1** proud that you have been given special respect or a special opportunity: *I feel deeply honoured to have been invited here today.* **2** deserving special respect: *an honoured guest*

honours /ˈɒnəz/ noun [plural] a level of university degree that is higher than an ordinary degree

Hons /hɒns/ abbrev *British* Honours

hood /hʊd/ noun [C] **1** the part of a coat or jacket that covers your head **2** *American* a car BONNET

hooded /ˈhʊdɪd/ adj with a hood

hoof /huːf/ (plural **hoofs or hooves** /huːvz/) noun [C] the hard part of a horse's foot

hook¹ /hʊk/ noun [C] **1** a curved piece of metal or plastic, used for hanging things on or for catching fish: *He hung his coat on a hook on the back of the door.* **2** a way of hitting someone with your arm bent: *a left hook to the jaw*

PHRASE **off the hook 1** if a telephone is off the hook, the part that you speak into has not been put into its place, so that you cannot receive any calls **2** *informal* having avoided a duty, an unpleasant situation, or a punishment: *I can't believe his boss has let him off the hook again.*

hook² /hʊk/ verb **1** [I/T] to hang something on something else, or to be fastened to something else with a hook: *He hooked the umbrella over his arm and went outside.* **2** [T] to put your arm, finger, leg etc round something to hold it or bring it closer to you: *Lucy hooked her arm through Peter's.* **3** [T] to catch a fish with a hook

PHRASAL VERB **hook sth ˈup** to connect two pieces of electronic equipment, or to connect a piece of equipment to a computer or power supply

hooked /hʊkt/ adj **1** attracted by or interested in something so much that you want to do it as much as possible **2** if you are hooked on drugs, you cannot stop taking them **3** shaped like a hook

hooker /ˈhʊkə/ noun [C] *informal* a PROSTITUTE

hooligan /ˈhuːlɪɡən/ noun [C] someone who is noisy or violent in public places

hoop /huːp/ noun [C] an object in the shape of a circle, usually made of metal, plastic, or wood

hooray /hʊˈreɪ/ interjection *old-fashioned* a word that you shout to show that you are excited and happy about something

hoot¹ /huːt/ noun [C] **1** a short loud sound made by people who are laughing or criticizing something **2** *British* a short loud sound made by the horn of a car **3** the deep sound that an OWL makes

hoot² /huːt/ verb [I/T] **1** to make a short loud sound when you laugh or criticize something **2** *British* to use the horn of a car to make a short loud sound as a warning **3** to make the deep sound that an OWL makes

hoover /ˈhuːvə/ verb [I/T] *British* to clean a carpet or floor with a VACUUM CLEANER

Hoover /ˈhuːvə/ *trademark* a VACUUM CLEANER

hooves a plural of **hoof**

hop¹ /hɒp/ verb [I] **1** to move forward by jumping on one foot **2** if a bird or animal hops, it uses both or all four feet to jump forward **3** *informal* to get into, onto, or out of a vehicle quickly: *Hop in. I'll give you a lift into town.*

hop² /hɒp/ noun [C] **1** a quick jump on one foot **2** a short quick jump by a small animal or a bird

PHRASE **a short hop** a short journey

hope¹ /həʊp/ verb [I/T] ★★★ to want and expect something to happen or be true: *It wouldn't be sensible to hope for immediate success.* ♦ +(that) *I hope that you'll enjoy your stay with us.* ♦ **hope to do sth** *The university is hoping to raise £3,000,000.*

PHRASE **I hope not** *spoken* used in replies to questions for saying that you do not want something to happen or to be true: *'Do you have to work late tonight?' 'I hope not.'*
I hope so *spoken* used in replies to questions for saying that you would like something to happen: *'Do you think France will win the match?' 'I hope so.'*
I hope (that) used for showing that you do not like what someone is doing or is thinking of doing: *I hope you're not going to use all the milk.*

hope² /həʊp/ noun [C/U] ★★★
1 the feeling or belief that something that you want to happen is likely to happen: *She arrived in London, young and full of hope.* ♦ *These young people have no hope for the future.* ♦ *The team's hopes of a championship are fading fast.* ♦ *The research raises hopes of a significant improvement in the treatment of cancer.* ♦ **hope of doing sth** *Rescuers refused to give up hope of finding more survivors.* ♦ *He had lost hope of seeing his children again.*
2 someone or something that offers a chance of improvement: *Our only hope was to get her to a hospital fast.* ♦ *Many people saw the new president as their last hope for political change.*

PHRASES **have high hopes for sb** to hope and expect that someone will be very successful
in the hope that/of wanting something to happen: *Police are carrying out a search in the hope of finding the missing girl.*

hopeful¹ /ˈhəʊpf(ə)l/ adj **1** believing that something will happen in the way that you want it to: *In spite of our differences, we remain hopeful that a solution can be found.* ♦ *a hopeful look* **2** making you believe that something will happen in the way that you want it to: *a hopeful sign*

hopeful² /ˈhəʊpf(ə)l/ noun [C] someone who wants to succeed or who seems likely to win

hopefully /ˈhəʊpf(ə)li/ adv **1** used for saying that you hope that something will happen: *Hopefully, we'll get more news next week.* **2** feeling or showing hope: *He looked at her hopefully.*

hopeless /ˈhəʊpləs/ adj **1** if a situation is hopeless, it seems very unlikely to succeed or improve **2** *informal* not skilful at all: *I am hopeless at tennis.* —**hopelessly** adv, **hopelessness** noun [U]

horde /hɔːd/ noun [C] a large number of people

line in the distance where the sky seems to meet the Earth

PHRASE **on the horizon** likely to happen soon

horizons /hə'raɪz(ə)nz/ noun [plural] the limits of your experience

horizontal /ˌhɒrɪ'zɒnt(ə)l/ adj straight and parallel to the ground ≠ VERTICAL —*picture* → C8

hormone /'hɔːməʊn/ noun [C] a substance that is produced by your body that helps it to develop and grow —**hormonal** /hɔː'məʊn(ə)l/ adj

horn /hɔːn/ noun [C] **1** the object in a vehicle that makes a loud warning noise when you press it —*picture* → C6 **2** one of the two hard pointed parts that grow on the heads of some animals, for example cows or goats **3** a metal musical instrument that is wide at one end, and that you play by blowing → BULL

horoscope /'hɒrəˌskəʊp/ noun [C] a description of someone's character and the likely events in their life that is based on ASTROLOGY (=the position of the stars and the date they were born)

horrendous /hɒ'rendəs/ adj extremely bad or shocking —**horrendously** adv

horrible /'hɒrəb(ə)l/ adj ★ very unpleasant or unkind: *I've had a horrible day at work.* ♦ *The medicine tasted horrible.* ♦ *Stop being so horrible to me.* —**horribly** /'hɒrəbli/ adv

horrid /'hɒrɪd/ adj very unpleasant, or very unkind

horrific /hɒ'rɪfɪk/ adj shocking and upsetting —**horrifically** /hɒ'rɪfɪkli/ adv

horrify /'hɒrɪfaɪ/ verb [T] to shock someone very much —**horrifying** adj

horror /'hɒrə/ noun **1** [C/U] a strong feeling of shock or fear, or the thing that makes you feel shocked or afraid: *Millions watched in horror as the disaster unfolded on TV.* ♦ *the horrors of war* **2** [U] a type of book or film that is intended to frighten people: *a horror story/film*

hors d'oeuvre /ˌɔː 'dɜːv/ noun [C] a small amount of food that is served before the main part of a meal

horse /hɔːs/ noun [C] ★★★ a large animal that people ride

horseback /'hɔːsˌbæk/ noun **on horseback** riding on a horse

horse 'chestnut noun [C] a large tree that produces shiny hard brown seeds, or a seed from this tree

'horse-ˌdrawn adj pulled by one horse or by several horses

horsepower /'hɔːsˌpaʊə/ (plural **horsepower**) noun [C] *technical* a unit for measuring the power of a vehicle's engine

'horse-ˌriding noun [U] the activity of riding a horse

horseshoe /'hɔːsˌʃuː/ noun [C] a curved piece of iron that is fastened to the bottom of a horse's HOOF (=foot)

horticulture /'hɔːtɪˌkʌltʃə/ noun [U] the activity of growing and studying plants —**horticultural** /ˌhɔːtɪ'kʌltʃərəl/ adj

hose /həʊz/ or **hosepipe** /'həʊzpaɪp/ *British* noun [C] a very long tube that water can flow through

hosiery /'həʊziəri/ noun [U] socks, STOCKINGS, and TIGHTS

hospice /'hɒspɪs/ noun [C] a hospital that looks after people who are dying

hospitable /hɒ'spɪtəb(ə)l/ adj friendly and generous towards visitors

hospital /'hɒspɪt(ə)l/ noun [C] ★★★ a place where ill or injured people receive medical treatment: *He spent a week in hospital with food poisoning.* ♦ *He went into hospital last week for a heart operation.*

hospitality /ˌhɒspɪ'tæləti/ noun [U] friendly and generous behaviour towards visitors

hospitalize /'hɒspɪt(ə)laɪz/ verb **be hospitalized** to be kept in hospital for medical treatment

host¹ /həʊst/ noun [C] ★

1 sb who invites	4 a lot of people/things
2 on television/radio	5 main computer
3 sth arranging event	

1 someone who invites people to a meal or a party, or to stay for a short time in their home: *They had brought a present for their hosts.*
2 someone who introduces and talks to the people taking part in a television or radio programme: *a game show/chat show host*
3 a place or organization that arranges a special event and provides the area, equipment, or services needed for it: *Korea and Japan played host to the 2002 World Cup.*
4 a lot of people or things: *a host of possibilities*
5 *computing* the main computer in a system, which controls particular processes or files

host² /həʊst/ verb [T] **1** to arrange a special event and provide the area, equipment, or services needed for it **2** to introduce and talk to the people taking part in a television or radio programme **3** *computing* to organize WEBSITES by providing the equipment and software that is needed

hostage /'hɒstɪdʒ/ noun [C] a person who is the prisoner of someone who threatens to kill them if they do not get what they want: *Six visiting businessmen were taken hostage by rebel groups.*

hostel /'hɒst(ə)l/ noun [C] **1** *British* a building where people can live if they are away from home or if they have no home **2** a YOUTH HOSTEL

hostess /'həʊstɪs/ noun [C] **1** a woman who invites someone to a meal or a party, or to stay for a short time in her home **2** a woman who introduces and talks to the people taking part in a television or radio programme

hostile /'hɒstaɪl/ adj **1** behaving in a very unfriendly or threatening way **2** opposing something: *The local community was hostile to plans for a new motorway.* **3** a hostile place or situation is difficult or dangerous to be in

hostility /hɒ'stɪləti/ noun **1** [U] unfriendly or threatening behaviour: *She said she had experienced hostility from her male colleagues.* **2** [U] opposition to something: *There is always some hostility to new technology.* **3** **hostilities** [plural] *formal* fighting between enemies in a war

hot¹ /hɒt/ adj ★★★

1 high in temperature	5 clever/skilful
2 food: with spices	6 difficult/dangerous
3 exciting	7 involving sex
4 with strong feelings	

1 very high in temperature ≠ COLD: *Cook the fish under a hot grill for 5 minutes.* ♦ *Take your jacket off if you're hot.* ♦ *It's going to be hot again today.* ♦ *hot countries such as India*
2 hot food contains a lot of SPICES and create a burning feeling in your mouth =SPICY
3 *informal* exciting and interesting: *the hot new look in women's fashions* ♦ *one of Hollywood's hottest young directors*
4 involving strong feelings: *Tax cuts have become **a hot topic** in this election campaign.* ♦ *Our coach has **a really hot temper** (=gets angry easily).*
5 *informal* clever or skilful: *a hot tip (=a useful piece of advice)* ♦ *Kyle's pretty **hot at** tennis.*
6 difficult or dangerous: *When things got too **hot for** her at home, she'd stay with a friend.*
7 *informal* involving sexual feelings or images: *love scenes that are too hot for TV*

Other ways of saying **hot**

- **baking** very hot and dry
- **boiling (hot)** very hot in a way that is unpleasant or uncomfortable. Also used for referring to the temperature of a liquid when it starts to bubble
- **lukewarm** used for describing water that is only slightly hot
- **roasting** used for describing a room or building that is extremely hot
- **scalding (hot)** used for describing a liquid that is hot enough to burn your skin
- **sweltering** used for describing weather that is so hot that you feel uncomfortable
- **tepid** used for describing drinks that are not hot enough
- **warm** hot in a pleasant way

hot² /hɒt/ **PHRASAL VERB**   **hot up** *British informal* to become more lively or exciting
hot-air balloon noun [C] an extremely large bag full of hot air, with a basket attached that people can ride through the air in
hotbed /ˈhɒt.bed/ noun [C] a place where there are a lot of people involved in a particular activity: *a hotbed of invention/crime*
hot chocolate noun [C/U] a drink made with chocolate powder and hot milk or water
hot dog noun [C] a hot SAUSAGE inside a long piece of bread
hotel /həʊˈtel/ noun [C] ★★★ a building where you pay to stay in a room: *He always **stays in** the best hotels.* ♦ *We **booked into** a luxury hotel.*
hotelier /həʊˈteliər/ noun [C] the owner or manager of a hotel
hot key noun [C] *computing* a key on a computer keyboard that provides a quick way of performing a set of actions
hotline /ˈhɒt.laɪn/ noun [C] a telephone number that people can call for information =HELPLINE
hotly /ˈhɒtli/ adv **1** in a way that shows that you have very strong feelings about

something: *Rumours of a split have been hotly denied by the band's manager.*
2 involving people who are competing very hard with one another: *a hotly contested election*
hotplate /ˈhɒt.pleɪt/ noun [C] a flat hot surface on a COOKER
hot potato noun [C] *informal* a difficult issue that people try to avoid dealing with
hot spot noun [C] *informal* **1** a place where there is often a lot of violence or fighting **2** a place that is fashionable, popular, and lively **3** *computing* a small area on a computer screen that you CLICK on in order to make the computer do something
hot-water bottle noun [C] a rubber container that you fill with hot water, used for keeping a bed or a part of your body warm
hound¹ /haʊnd/ verb [T] **1** to follow someone in a determined way in order to get something from them: *She was sick of being hounded by the press.* **2** to force someone to leave a place or job by always being unpleasant to them: *His political opponents hounded him out of office.*
hound² /haʊnd/ noun [C] a dog that is used for hunting or racing
hour /aʊə/ noun ★★★

1 60 minutes of time	4 particular time of day
2 a long time	5 point in history/life
3 time when you do sth	+ PHRASE

1 [C] a period of time that consists of 60 minutes: *He left about **an hour ago**.* ♦ *Brighton is only **an hour away** (=it takes an hour to get there).* ♦ *I earn £12 **an hour** (=for each hour spent working).*
2 hours [plural] a long time: *I'm hungry and it's hours until dinner.*
3 hours [plural] the time during which you do something such as work or study: *My job is very flexible – I can fit my hours around my children.* ♦ *Jo has to work very **long hours**.*
4 [C] a particular time in the day or night: *You can call me at any hour of the day or night.* ♦ *You get cars coming down here **at all hours** (=at any time, even at night).*
5 [singular] a particular point in history or in someone's life or career: *His **finest hour** came in 1982 when his film* Gandhi *won eight Oscars.*

PHRASE   **after hours** after the time when a place such as an office or bar usually closes
hourly /ˈaʊəli/ adj **1** happening once every hour: *hourly news bulletins* **2** relating to one hour of work: *His hourly fee is £50.* —**hourly** adv: *Buses run hourly.*
house¹ /haʊs/ (plural **houses** /ˈhaʊzɪz/) noun ★★★

1 building for living in	5 area for audience
2 people in a house	6 type of music
3 company	7 old important family
4 restaurant/hotel etc	

1 [C] a building for living in, usually where only one family lives: *a three-bedroom house* ♦ *We're **moving house** (=going to live in a different house) **at the end of the month**.*
2 [singular] the people who are in a house or

who live there: *The noise woke the entire house.*

3 [C] a company or organization that is involved in a particular activity: *a publishing house*

4 the house [singular] a restaurant, hotel, PUB, or club: *Seafood is the speciality of the house.*
♦ *Your first drink is on the house* (=free).

5 [C] the part of a theatre, cinema etc that contains the audience: *Her new show has been playing to packed houses.*

6 [U] a type of modern dance music

7 [C] an old important or royal family: *the House of Hapsburg*

■ A **house** is a building for living in: *She lives in that big house.* ♦ *They're building some new houses on our street.*
■ Someone's **home** is the place where they live: *This little cottage is the home of a family of eight.*
■ Do not use **to** before **home**: *They all went to Dan's house, but I went home.*

house² /haʊz/ verb [T] ★
1 to give someone a place to live: *A large number of families are still waiting to be housed.*
2 to contain or provide a place for something: *The club is housed in a magnificent 16th century building.*

House, the /haʊs/ the House of Commons or the House of Lords in the UK, or the House of Representatives in the US

house arrest noun **be under house arrest** to be officially prevented from leaving your home because you have been accused of a political crime

houseboat /ˈhaʊsˌbəʊt/ noun [C] a boat that someone lives in

housebound /ˈhaʊsˌbaʊnd/ adj unable to leave your house because you are ill or disabled

household¹ /ˈhaʊsˌhəʊld/ noun [C] the people who live in a house or a flat

household² /ˈhaʊsˌhəʊld/ adj used in homes, or relating to homes: *household goods/ appliances*

PHRASE be a household name to be very well known

householder /ˈhaʊsˌhəʊldə/ noun [C] a person who owns or rents a house or a flat

house husband noun [C] a man who does not work outside the home and whose main job is looking after his children, cooking, cleaning etc

housekeeper /ˈhaʊsˌkiːpə/ noun [C] someone whose job is to clean or cook in a large house or a hotel

housekeeping /ˈhaʊsˌkiːpɪŋ/ noun [U] **1** the jobs that need to be done in a house, for example cleaning and cooking **2** the money that you use to pay for the things that you need at home, for example food and electricity

housemate /ˈhaʊsˌmeɪt/ noun [C] someone who lives in the same house as you but is not a member of your family

House of Commons, the part of the parliament in the UK or Canada that consists of politicians who have been elected by the people

House of Lords, the the part of the parliament in the UK that consists of politicians who are not elected by the people

House of Representatives, the the larger and less powerful part of the US CONGRESS (=the organization that makes laws in the US)

houseplant /ˈhaʊsˌplɑːnt/ noun [C] a plant that you keep inside your house for decoration

houseproud /ˈhaʊsˌpraʊd/ adj British always keeping your house clean and tidy

house-to-house adj, adv involving visits to every house in an area

house-trained adj British a pet that is house-trained knows that it must go outside or use a special container inside when it needs to go to the toilet

housewarming /ˈhaʊsˌwɔːmɪŋ/ noun [C] a party that you give in a house that you have just moved into

housewife /ˈhaʊsˌwaɪf/ (plural **housewives** /ˈhaʊsˌwaɪvz/) noun [C] a woman who does not work outside the home and whose main job is looking after her children, cooking, cleaning etc

housework /ˈhaʊsˌwɜːk/ noun [U] the work that you do in order to keep your house clean and tidy

housing /ˈhaʊzɪŋ/ noun [U] ★ buildings for people to live in: *Land had to be found for new housing.* ♦ *a housing shortage*

housing association noun [C] British an organization that owns houses for people with low incomes to live in

housing estate noun [C] British a large group of houses that were built at the same time and in the same style

hover /ˈhɒvə/ verb [I] **1** if a bird, insect, or aircraft hovers, it keeps itself in the same position in the air **2** to stay somewhere because you are waiting to do something or because you cannot decide what to do: *The waiter was hovering by their table.*

hovercraft /ˈhɒvəˌkrɑːft/ noun [C] a vehicle that can move over both land and water, raising itself above the surface by blowing air downwards —*picture* → C7

how /haʊ/ adv, conjunction ★★★
1 used for asking or talking about the way that something happens or is done: *How can I get from here to Oxford Street?* ♦ *Louis is the only person who understands how the camera works.* ♦ *How did she react when you mentioned my name?* ♦ *Cut her hair short if that's how she wants it.* ♦ **how to do sth** *Would you show me how to send an email?*
2 used for asking or talking about the quantity or degree of something: *How difficult will it be to change the system?* ♦ *I wonder how far we've walked today.* ♦ *I've forgotten how old she is.* ♦ *How many grandchildren do you have now?*
3 used for asking what someone thinks about an experience: *How was school today?* ♦ *How's life in the army?* ♦ *How did your driving test go?*
4 used for emphasizing a particular fact or quality: *How wonderful! This means we can all travel together.* ♦ *You know how much I*

H

love you. ♦ *I was amazed at just **how easy** it is to shop on the Internet.*

PHRASES **how about...?** *spoken* **1** used for suggesting a possible choice: *How about dinner tonight?* ♦ *How about Friday evening? Would that be convenient?* ♦ **how about doing sth?** *How about joining us for a game of cards?* **2** used for asking about another person or thing: *How about Philip? Is he coming too?* ♦ *I'm having coffee. How about you?*

how are things or **how's it going?** or **how are you doing?** *spoken* used for asking someone about their progress or their general situation

how are you? *spoken* used for asking in a polite way about someone's health

how come? *spoken* why: *How come you're not at work today?*

how do you do? *spoken formal* used as a polite greeting when you are introduced to someone for the first time

how much is/are...? used for asking the price of something: *How much was that CD player of yours?*

however /haʊˈevə/ adv, conjunction ★★★
1 used for adding a statement that seems surprising or that makes a previous statement seem less true: *He seemed to be working hard. His results, however, did not improve.*
2 used when you are changing the subject: *I'm delighted I could be here today. However, I didn't come here to talk about myself.*
3 used for saying that it makes no difference how good, bad, difficult etc something is or how much there is of something: *She would still love him however badly he behaved.* ♦ *We're determined to have a wonderful holiday, **however much** it costs.* ♦ *I'm going to solve this problem, **however long** it takes.*
4 in whatever way someone chooses: *We let the kids decorate their rooms however they want to.*

howl /haʊl/ verb [I] **1** if a dog or other animal howls, it makes a long loud sound **2** to cry very loudly in pain, anger, or sadness **3** if the wind howls, it blows with a long loud sound **4** to laugh very loudly —**howl** noun [C]

HQ /ˌeɪtʃ ˈkjuː/ noun [plural] headquarters

hr abbrev hour

HTML /ˌeɪtʃ tiː em ˈel/ noun [U] *computing* hypertext markup language: the computer language that is used for writing pages on the Internet

http /ˌeɪtʃ tiː tiː ˈpiː/ noun [U] *computing* hypertext transfer (or transport) protocol: the system that is used on the Internet to exchange documents in HTML

hub /hʌb/ noun [C] **1** the most important place where a particular activity takes place: *Bombay is the financial hub of India.* **2** the part at the centre of a wheel **3** a central airport that passengers can fly to from smaller local airports

hubbub /ˈhʌbʌb/ noun [singular/U] the noise of a lot of people talking at the same time

hubcap /ˈhʌbˌkæp/ noun [C] a metal cover for the central part of a wheel on a car —*picture* → C6

huddle¹ /ˈhʌd(ə)l/ verb [I] to move close

together in order to stay warm, feel safe, or talk

PHRASAL VERBS **huddle to·gether** *same as* **huddle**
huddle up *same as* **huddle**

huddle² /ˈhʌd(ə)l/ noun [C] a group of people who are close together

hue /hjuː/ noun [C] *literary* a colour

huff¹ /hʌf/ noun **in a huff** feeling annoyed and upset because someone has offended you

huff² /hʌf/ verb **huff and puff** to breathe loudly and with difficulty

hug¹ /hʌɡ/ verb **1** [I/T] to put your arms round someone in order to show your love or friendship: *Mike picked up his daughter and hugged her tight.* **2** [T] to hold something close to your chest: *Emma was sitting on the floor hugging her knees.* **3** [T] to stay close to something: *They kept to the back of the crowd, hugging the wall.*

hug² /hʌɡ/ noun [C] the action of putting your arms round someone in order to show your love or friendship

huge /hjuːdʒ/ adj ★★★
1 extremely large = ENORMOUS: *She arrived carrying two huge suitcases.* ♦ *Many top players earn huge amounts of money.* ♦ *The concert turned out to be **a huge success**.*
2 extremely successful and well known: *The band is huge in both Britain and the US.*
—**hugely** adv: *a hugely popular TV show*

huh /hʌ/ interjection *informal* **1** used after you have said something in order to show that you are asking for agreement: *Great shot, huh?* **2** used for asking someone to repeat something because you did not hear what they said: *'Did you enjoy it?' 'Huh?' 'Did you enjoy the film?'* **3** used as a way of showing that you do not like, believe, or agree with something: *What's wrong with you, huh?*

hulk /hʌlk/ noun [C] **1** the shape of something such as a large ship or building after the inside of it has been destroyed **2** someone who is very tall and heavy

hull /hʌl/ noun [C] the main part of a ship

hullo /həˈləʊ/ a British spelling of **hello**

hum¹ /hʌm/ verb **1** [I/T] to make musical sounds with your lips closed: *If you don't know the words, just hum the tune.* **2** [I] to make a low continuous sound: *The fridge hummed in the kitchen.* **3** [I] if a place hums, it is full of noise and activity: *The whole stadium was humming with excitement.*

hum² /hʌm/ noun [singular] a low continuous noise made by a machine or by a lot of people talking

human¹ /ˈhjuːmən/ adj ★★★
1 relating to people: *the human brain* ♦ *the study of **human behaviour*** ♦ *Tests show that the meat is **unfit for human consumption*** (=not safe for people to eat).
2 showing normal human feelings: *It is **only human** to want revenge when someone hurts you.*

PHRASE **sb is only human** used for saying that someone has been weak in the ways that most people are weak and should not be blamed for their behaviour

human² /ˈhjuːmən/ or **human being** noun [C] ★★ a person: *The disease can be fatal in humans.*

humane /hjuˈmeɪn/ adj caring about the quality of people's or animals' lives and trying to be kind to them ≠ CRUEL, INHUMANE —**humanely** adv

human ˈerror noun [U] a mistake made by a person who is controlling a machine or process, rather than something wrong with the machine or process itself

human ˈinterest noun [U] the part of a true story that interests people because it is about someone's life or experiences

humanitarian /hjuːˌmænɪˈteəriən/ adj relating to people who live in very bad conditions and to other people's efforts to help them

humanities, the /hjuːˈmænətiz/ noun [plural] subjects that you study such as history and literature, rather than science or mathematics

humanity /hjuːˈmænəti/ noun [U] **1** all people, thought of as a group: *Weapons of this type are a threat to the survival of humanity.* **2** a kind and sympathetic attitude towards other people ≠ INHUMANITY: *He was a man of great humanity who was deeply affected by the suffering of others.* **3** the state of being human

humankind /ˌhjuːmənˈkaɪnd/ noun [U] all people, thought of as a group

humanly /ˈhjuːmənli/ adv **humanly possible** possible for a person to do: *We will deal with the matter as soon as is humanly possible.*

human ˈnature noun [U] the attitudes, feelings, and reactions that are typical of most people

human ˈrace, the noun [singular] all people, thought of as a group

human reˈsources noun [U] the department within a company that is responsible for employing and training people, and for looking after workers who have problems =PERSONNEL

human ˈrights noun [plural] the rights that everyone should have in a society, including the right to express opinions or to have protection from harm

humble¹ /ˈhʌmb(ə)l/ adj **1** not proud, and not thinking that you are better than other people **2** from a low social class, or with low social status —**humbly** adv

humble² /ˈhʌmb(ə)l/ verb [T] to make someone realize that they are not as important, good, or clever as they thought they were

humdrum /ˈhʌmdrʌm/ adj boring because nothing new or interesting ever happens

humid /ˈhjuːmɪd/ adj hot and wet in a way that makes you feel uncomfortable: *a humid climate*

humidity /hjuːˈmɪdəti/ noun [U] the amount of water that is in the air

humiliate /hjuːˈmɪlieɪt/ verb [T] to make someone feel very embarrassed and ashamed —**humiliation** /hjuːˌmɪliˈeɪʃ(ə)n/ noun [C/U]

humiliating /hjuːˈmɪlieɪtɪŋ/ adj making you feel very embarrassed and ashamed

humility /hjuːˈmɪləti/ noun [U] a way of behaving that shows that you do not think that you are better or more important than other people

humor /ˈhjuːmə/ the American spelling of **humour**

humorous /ˈhjuːmərəs/ adj funny: *a humorous story* —**humorously** adv

humour¹ /ˈhjuːmə/ noun ★
1 [U] the quality that makes something funny: *a novel that is full of humour*
2 [U] the ability to know when something is funny and to laugh at funny situations: *Sally is a friendly person with a great **sense of humour**.*
3 [singular] *formal* someone's mood: *He laughed again, obviously **in a good humour**.*

humour² /ˈhjuːmə/ verb [T] to do what someone wants, or to pretend to agree with them, so that they do not become angry or upset

humourless /ˈhjuːmələs/ adj unable to see when something is funny, or showing that you do not think that something is funny

hump /hʌmp/ noun [C] **1** a large round shape that rises above a surface or above the ground **2** a large round part on the back of an animal or person

hunch¹ /hʌntʃ/ noun [C] a feeling that something is true or will happen, although you do not know any definite facts about it

hunch² /hʌntʃ/ verb [I/T] to sit or stand with your back and shoulders curved forwards

hunchback /ˈhʌntʃˌbæk/ noun [C] *offensive* an offensive word for someone who has a large round part on their back

hundred /ˈhʌndrəd/ number ★★
1 the number 100
2 **hundreds** a very large number or amount of people or things: *We received **hundreds of applications** for the job.*

hundredth /ˈhʌndrədθ/ number **1** in the place or position that is counted as number 100 **2** one of 100 equal parts of something

hundredweight /ˈhʌndrədˌweɪt/ noun [C] *British* a unit for measuring weight that is equal to 112 pounds or 50.8 kilograms

hung the past tense and past participle of **hang**

hunger /ˈhʌngə/ noun **1** [U] the feeling that you have when you need to eat: *a nutritious snack that will satisfy your hunger* **2** [U] a lack of food that can cause illness or death =STARVATION: *a new chance to fight world hunger and poverty* **3** [C/U] the feeling that you have when you want something very much: *his hunger for success/power*

ˈhunger ˌstrike noun [C] a refusal to eat for a long time by someone who is protesting against something

hungover /hʌŋˈəʊvə/ adj tired and ill in the morning because you drank too much alcohol the night before

hungry /ˈhʌngri/ adj ★
1 feeling that you want to eat: *We were cold, tired, and hungry.* ♦ *She was beginning to feel hungry again.*
2 wanting something very much: *a hungry young actor* ♦ *People are **hungry for news**.*
PHRASE **go hungry** to not have enough food —**hungrily** adv

H

H

Other ways of saying hungry

- **peckish** (*informal*) feeling hungry when it is not a mealtime
- **ravenous** or **famished** or **starving** (*informal*) very hungry

hunk /hʌŋk/ noun [C] **1** a large piece of a solid substance: *a hunk of meat/bread* **2** *informal* a strong and sexually attractive man

hunt¹ /hʌnt/ verb [I/T] **1** to catch and kill animals: *Crocodiles were hunted and killed for their teeth.* ♦ *Wild dogs usually hunt in packs.* ♦ *We hunted for rabbits in the hills.* **2** to try to find someone or something=LOOK FOR SB/STH: *Police are still hunting the killer.* ♦ *Detectives have been hunting for clues to the murderer's identity.*

PHRASAL VERB **hunt sb/sth ˈdown** to try very hard to find someone or something: *They'll actually hunt down old books for you.*

hunt² /hʌnt/ noun [C] **1** a search for someone or something: *the hunt for the missing child* **2** an attempt to catch and kill animals

hunter /ˈhʌntə/ noun [C] a person or animal that catches and kills wild animals

hunting /ˈhʌntɪŋ/ noun [U] **1** the activity of catching and killing wild animals **2** the activity of looking for a particular thing that you want or need: *bargain hunting* ♦ *flat-hunting*

hurdle /ˈhɜːd(ə)l/ noun **1** [C] an upright frame that a person or horse jumps over during a race **2** [C] one of several problems that you must solve before you can do something successfully: *Finding investors is the biggest hurdle we face.* **3 hurdles** [plural] a race in which people or horses jump over a series of upright frames

hurl /hɜːl/ verb [T] **1** to throw something using a lot of force **2** to direct angry remarks or criticism at someone: *The fans began hurling abuse at each other.*

hurray /hʊˈreɪ/ or **hurrah** /hʊˈrɑː/ interjection a word that you shout to show that you are excited and happy about something

hurricane /ˈhʌrɪkən, ˈhʌrɪkeɪn/ noun [C] a violent storm with extremely strong winds and heavy rain

hurried /ˈhʌrɪd/ adj done quickly, because you do not have enough time=RUSHED ≠ UNHURRIED —**hurriedly** adv

hurry¹ /ˈhʌri/ verb [I/T] ★ to do something or to move somewhere very quickly, or to make someone do this: *We must hurry or we'll be late.* ♦ *Alex had to hurry home, but I decided to stay.* ♦ *She hurried along the corridor towards his office.* ♦ *hurry sb away/in/out etc Liz took Anna's arm and hurried her away.* ♦ *hurry sb into doing sth Don't let them hurry you into signing anything.*

PHRASAL VERB **hurry ˈup 1** *spoken* used for telling someone to do something more quickly: *Hurry up and finish your soup.* **2** to do something or to move somewhere more quickly, or to make someone do this: *She wished George would hurry up with her cup of tea.*

hurry² /ˈhʌri/ noun ★

PHRASES **in a hurry** doing something or going somewhere quickly, because you do not have much time: *Donna's letter looked as though she had written it in a great hurry.*

in no hurry or **not in any hurry 1** able to wait to do something, because you have plenty of time: *I'm not in any hurry to get there.* **2** unwilling to do something, or not wanting to do it until a future time: *Lou's in no hurry to get married.*

(there's) no hurry *spoken* used for telling someone that they do not need to do something soon or quickly: *I'm ready whenever you are – there's no hurry.*

hurt¹ /hɜːt/ (past tense and past participle **hurt**) verb ★★★
1 [I] to feel pain somewhere in your body: *Fred's knees hurt after skiing all day.*
2 [I/T] to cause someone physical pain or injury: *You're hurting my arm!* ♦ *These new boots hurt.* ♦ *hurt yourself doing sth Don't hurt yourself exercising.*
3 [I/T] to cause someone emotional pain: *His comments hurt her deeply.* ♦ *I never meant to hurt your feelings.*
4 [T] to cause damage or problems, or to harm someone's chance to succeed at something: *The weakness of the dollar has hurt car sales.*

PHRASE **sth won't/doesn't/can't hurt** *spoken* used for saying that something helps or cannot harm a situation: *One more drink won't hurt.*

hurt² /hɜːt/ adj **1** injured, or feeling physical pain ≠ UNHURT: *Two young men were badly hurt in the accident.* **2** feeling emotional pain, usually because of someone's behaviour: *She left feeling angry and deeply hurt.*

Words often used with hurt

*Adverbs often used with **hurt** (adjective, sense 1)*
- **badly, seriously** + HURT: used when someone is injured severely

*Adverbs often used with **hurt** (adjective, sense 2)*
- **deeply, dreadfully, terribly** + HURT: used when someone is very upset

hurt³ /hɜːt/ noun [C/U] a feeling of emotional pain that is caused by someone's behaviour

hurtful /ˈhɜːtf(ə)l/ adj causing emotional pain

hurtle /ˈhɜːt(ə)l/ verb [I] to move very quickly in an uncontrolled way

husband /ˈhʌzbənd/ noun [C] ★★★ the man that a woman is married to —*picture* → FAMILY TREE

hush¹ /hʌʃ/ verb **1** [I] *spoken* used for telling someone to be quiet: *Hush! You'll wake the baby!* **2** [I] *spoken* used for trying to calm someone who is upset: *Hush, sweetheart, it's OK now.* **3** [I/T] to stop talking, crying, or making noise, or to make someone do this

PHRASAL VERB **hush sth ˈup** if someone in authority hushes something up, they try to keep it secret

hush² /hʌʃ/ noun [singular/U] a silence

hushed /hʌʃt/ adj very quiet: *People were talking in hushed voices.*

hush-ˈhush adj used for talking about official activities that very few people should know about

husky¹ /ˈhʌski/ noun [C] a large dog that is used for pulling SLEDGES over snow

husky² /ˈhʌski/ adj a husky voice is deep and sounds HOARSE (=as if you have a sore throat), often in an attractive way

hustle¹ /ˈhʌs(ə)l/ verb **1** [T] to make someone go quickly to the place where you want them to go: *As soon as he arrived in the country, he was hustled off to prison.* **2** [I/T] American to move or to do something in a quick effective way **3** [I/T] American to get or sell things in a dishonest way

hustle² /ˈhʌs(ə)l/ noun **1** [U] a lot of noisy activity: *the hustle and bustle of the city* **2** [C] American a dishonest way of making money

hut /hʌt/ noun [C] a small simple shelter

hutch /hʌtʃ/ noun [C] a box for keeping RABBITS in

hyacinth /ˈhaɪəsɪnθ/ noun [C] a plant with small blue, pink, or white sweet-smelling flowers that grow close together along the stem —*picture* → C9

hybrid /ˈhaɪbrɪd/ noun [C] **1** an animal or plant that has been produced from two different types of animal or plant **2** a mixture of different things or styles —**hybrid** adj

hydrant /ˈhaɪdrənt/ noun [C] an upright water pipe in the street that the FIRE SERVICE gets water from

hydraulic /haɪˈdrɔːlɪk/ adj using the pressure of water or oil to make a machine work

hydroelectric /ˌhaɪdrəʊˈlektrɪk/ adj using water power to produce electricity

hydrofoil /ˈhaɪdrəʊfɔɪl/ noun [C] a boat with wing-shaped pieces fixed to the bottom that lift the boat onto the surface of the water as it starts to travel quickly —*picture* → C7

hydrogen /ˈhaɪdrədʒən/ noun [U] a gas that has no colour or smell and that is lighter than air

hygiene /ˈhaɪdʒiːn/ noun [U] the practice of keeping yourself and the things around you clean in order to prevent illness and disease

hygienic /haɪˈdʒiːnɪk/ adj clean and not likely to cause illness or disease

hymn /hɪm/ noun [C] a religious song that Christians sing in churches

hype¹ /haɪp/ noun [U] *informal* the use of a lot of advertisements and information to interest people

hype² /haɪp/ verb [T] *informal* to publish and broadcast a lot of advertisements and information in order to interest people

PHRASAL VERB **hype sth 'up** *informal* to make something sound more interesting or impressive than it really is

hyper /ˈhaɪpə/ adj *informal* behaving in an excited and nervous way

hyperactive /ˌhaɪpərˈæktɪv/ adj very lively and finding it difficult to concentrate or relax —**hyperactivity** /ˌhaɪpəræˈktɪvəti/ noun [U]

hyperbole /haɪˈpɜːbəli/ noun [C/U] *formal* a way of emphasizing something by describing it as far more extreme than it really is

hyperlink /ˈhaɪpəlɪŋk/ noun [C] *computing* a word or image in a computer document that you can CLICK on in order to move to a related document, word, or image —**hyperlink** verb [T]

hypermarket /ˈhaɪpəmɑːkɪt/ noun [C] a very large supermarket that is built outside a town

hypersensitive /ˌhaɪpəˈsensətɪv/ adj **1** very easily upset or offended **2** *medical* extremely sensitive to certain substances

hypertension /ˌhaɪpəˈtenʃ(ə)n/ noun [U] *medical* a condition in which your blood pressure is extremely high

hypertext /ˈhaɪpətekst/ noun [U] *computing* a computer system in which you can CLICK on a word or image in order to move to a related document, word, or image

hyperventilate /ˌhaɪpəˈventɪleɪt/ verb [I] to breathe very fast because you are frightened or nervous

hyphen /ˈhaɪf(ə)n/ noun [C] the short line -, used for joining two words or parts of words, or for dividing a word at the end of a line of writing

hyphenated adj written with a hyphen

hypnosis /hɪpˈnəʊsɪs/ noun [U] a very relaxed state in which you seem to be sleeping but can still react to someone else's suggestions, or the practice of putting people into this state

hypnotic /hɪpˈnɒtɪk/ adj **1** something that is hypnotic makes you feel like sleeping, because it is repeated in a regular way: *the hypnotic rhythm of the drums* **2** relating to hypnosis, or caused by hypnosis: *a hypnotic trance*

hypnotist /ˈhɪpnətɪst/ noun [C] someone who hypnotizes people for medical reasons or for entertainment —**hypnotism** /ˈhɪpnətɪz(ə)m/ noun [U]

hypnotize /ˈhɪpnətaɪz/ verb [T] to put someone into a state that is similar to sleep, but in which they can still hear and react to suggestions

hypoallergenic /ˌhaɪpəʊæləˈdʒenɪk/ adj unlikely to cause an ALLERGIC reaction (=an illness or skin reaction produced in some people by certain substances)

hypochondriac /ˌhaɪpəʊˈkɒndriæk/ noun [C] someone who worries a lot about their health and thinks that they are ill when they are not

hypocrisy /hɪˈpɒkrəsi/ noun [C/U] behaviour in which someone pretends to be morally good or to believe something but does things that show that they are not sincere

hypocrite /ˈhɪpəkrɪt/ noun [C] someone who pretends to be morally good or to believe something but who behaves in a way that shows that they are not sincere

hypocritical /ˌhɪpəˈkrɪtɪk(ə)l/ adj someone who is hypocritical pretends to be morally good or to believe something but behaves in a way that shows that they are not sincere —**hypocritically** /ˌhɪpəˈkrɪtɪkli/ adv

hypothermia /ˌhaɪpəʊˈθɜːmiə/ noun [U] a serious medical condition in which your body temperature is very low

hypothesis /haɪˈpɒθəsɪs/ (plural **hypotheses** /haɪˈpɒθəsiːz/) noun [C] an idea that attempts to explain something, but that has not yet been tested or been proved to be correct =THEORY

hypothetical /ˌhaɪpəˈθetɪk(ə)l/ adj based on situations or events that seem possible rather than on actual ones =THEORETICAL —**hypothetically** /ˌhaɪpəˈθetɪkli/ adv

hysterectomy /ˌhɪstəˈrektəmi/ noun [C] a

H

medical operation to remove a woman's WOMB (=the part of her body where a baby can grow)

hysteria /hɪˈstɪəriə/ noun [U] a state of uncontrolled excitement or extreme fear

hysterical /hɪˈsterɪk(ə)l/ adj **1** behaving in an uncontrolled way because you are extremely excited, afraid, or upset **2** spoken extremely funny —**hysterically** /hɪˈsterɪkli/ adv

hysterics /hɪˈsterɪks/ noun [plural] an uncontrolled emotional state in which you are extremely excited, afraid, or upset

PHRASE **in hysterics** informal laughing in an excited and uncontrolled way

Hz abbrev hertz

i or **I** /aɪ/ noun [C/U] the ninth letter of the English alphabet

I /aɪ/ pronoun ★★★ used as the subject of a verb for referring to yourself, when you are the person speaking or writing: I don't like cats. ♦ I didn't hurt you, did I? ♦ Peter and I will do the cooking.

Iberia /aɪˈbɪəriə/ the part of Europe that includes Spain and Portugal —**Iberian** /aɪˈbɪəriən/ adj

ice¹ /aɪs/ noun [U] ★★ water that has frozen and become solid: a block/lump of ice ♦ Ice was forming on the windscreen. ♦ a drink with plenty of ice

PHRASES **break the ice** to make people feel more relaxed and ready to talk, for example at the beginning of a party: Joe told a few jokes, which helped to break the ice.

cut no ice (with sb) informal to fail to impress someone, or to fail to make them change their opinion: His excuses cut no ice with me.

put sth on ice informal to delay doing anything about something such as a plan or idea: The whole deal was put on ice when the stock market fell sharply.

ice² /aɪs/ verb [T] British to cover a cake with ICING

PHRASAL VERB **ice over** or **ice up** to become covered with ice

iceberg /ˈaɪsbɜːɡ/ noun [C] a very large piece of ice floating in the sea with only a small amount of it above the surface of the water

icebox /ˈaɪsbɒks/ noun [C] American old-fashioned a REFRIGERATOR

ice cap noun [C] a large area of ice that covers the land and sea around the North or South Pole

ice-cold adj very cold

ice cream noun **1** [U] a frozen sweet food made from cream or milk and sugar, often with

fruit or chocolate added to flavour it **2** [C] British an amount of ice cream for one person

ice cube noun [C] a small piece of ice that you put in a drink to make it cold

iced /aɪst/ adj **1** British an iced cake or BISCUIT is covered with ICING **2** an iced drink is very cold and contains pieces of ice

ice hockey noun [U] a game that is played on ice by two teams of six players. The players use long sticks to try to hit a small round flat object called a **puck** into the other team's goal.

ice lolly noun [C] British a piece of sweet flavoured ice or ICE CREAM on a stick

ice pack noun [C] **1** a bag full of ice that you hold against an injured or painful part of your body to stop it swelling or to make it less painful **2** an area of small pieces of ice floating in the sea

ice rink noun [C] a large flat area of ice inside a building, where people can go to ICE-SKATE

ice skate noun [C] a special boot with a metal blade on the bottom that you wear to move smoothly across ice

ice-skate verb [I] to move around on ice wearing ice skates —**ice-skater** noun [C]

ice-skating noun [U] the activity or sport of moving around on ice wearing ICE SKATES

icicle /ˈaɪsɪk(ə)l/ noun [C] a long thin piece of ice that hangs down from somewhere such as a roof

icing /ˈaɪsɪŋ/ noun [U] a mixture of sugar and water or butter that is used for covering cakes

PHRASE **the icing on the cake** something that makes a good situation even better

icon /ˈaɪkɒn/ noun [C] **1** a small picture on a computer screen that you choose by pressing a button with your MOUSE in order to open a particular program **2** someone who is very famous and who people think represents a particular idea **3** a picture or model of a holy person that is used in religious worship in the Russian or Greek Orthodox Church

icy /ˈaɪsi/ adj **1** very cold, in an unpleasant way **2** covered with ice **3** showing that you do not like someone and do not want to be friendly with them: an icy stare

I'd /aɪd/ short form **1** the usual way of saying or writing 'I had'. This is not often used in formal writing: I'd never seen so much money in my life. **2** the usual way of saying or writing 'I would'. This is not often used in formal writing: I'd love to go to Brazil.

ID /ˌaɪ ˈdiː/ noun [C/U] a document that gives the details of your name, address, and date of birth, sometimes with a photograph

ID card noun [C] an IDENTITY CARD

idea /aɪˈdɪə/ noun ★★★
1 [C] a thought that you have about how to do something or how to deal with something: What a brilliant idea! ♦ Then I **had an idea**: we could stay with Mark. ♦ Then she **got the idea** of sending the poems to a publisher. ♦ an idea for a new TV show

2 [C] an opinion, or a belief: *I don't agree with his **ideas on** education.* ♦ *She **has** some pretty strange **ideas about** how to bring up children.* ♦ *We didn't have a clear **idea of** what to expect from the training course.*
3 [singular/U] information or knowledge that you have about something: *They **had no idea** what time they were supposed to arrive.* ♦ *I had only a basic **idea of** how the machine worked.*
4 [C/U] a purpose, or an intention: *My parents wanted me to be a doctor, but I had other ideas.*
> PHRASES **get the idea** *informal* to understand something, often something that is not expressed directly: *Okay, I get the idea: you two want to be alone.* ♦ *+(that) I got the idea that he didn't want to answer the question.*
get the wrong idea *informal* to believe something that is not true: *I'll explain everything to George. I wouldn't want him to get the wrong idea.*
it's a good idea to do sth used for giving someone advice about what they should do: *It's a good idea to get someone else's opinion about it first.*
put ideas into sb's head *informal* to make someone think that they can or should do something: *Don't talk to Ralph about joining the army: I don't want you putting ideas into his head.*

ideal¹ /aɪˈdɪəl/ adj ★
1 of the best or most suitable type: *Upgrading your computer seems **the ideal solution.*** ♦ *Conditions were **ideal for** racing.*
2 as good as you can imagine, and probably too good to be real=PERFECT: *In an ideal world there would be no poverty.*

ideal² /aɪˈdɪəl/ noun [C] ★
1 an idea that you try to follow about what is good and right=PRINCIPLE: *the socialist ideal of equality for all members of society*
2 the best example of something that you can think of: *Sophie represented his **ideal of** beauty.*

idealism /aɪˈdɪəˌlɪz(ə)m/ noun [U] a very strong belief in something that is good but probably impossible to achieve

idealist /aɪˈdɪəlɪst/ noun [C] someone who is idealistic

idealistic /aɪˌdɪəˈlɪstɪk/ adj an idealistic person believes very firmly in something that is good but probably impossible to achieve

idealize /aɪˈdɪəˌlaɪz/ verb [T] to believe or suggest that someone or something is perfect or better than they really are —**idealization** /aɪˌdɪəˌlaɪˈzeɪʃ(ə)n/ noun [C/U]

ideally /aɪˈdɪəli/ adv **1** used for saying what you would like to happen or how things should be: *Ideally, we should finish everything by this afternoon.* **2** in the best possible way: *The lake is ideally suited to sailing.*

identical /aɪˈdentɪk(ə)l/ adj ★ exactly the same: *This house is almost **identical to** the one where I lived as a child.* —**identically** /aɪˈdentɪkli/ adv

identical twin noun [C] identical twins are TWINS of the same sex who look exactly like each other

identifiable /aɪˌdentɪˈfaɪəb(ə)l/ adj able to be recognized, or easy to recognize

identification /aɪˌdentɪfɪˈkeɪʃ(ə)n/ noun [U]
1 something that proves who you are, especially a document with your name and a photograph=ID: *Can you show me some identification?* **2** the action of recognizing someone or something: *the identification and arrest of two suspects* ♦ *The identification of a problem is the first step towards solving it.* **3** a feeling that you understand someone else and know how they feel

identify /aɪˈdentɪˌfaɪ/ verb [T] ★★★
1 to recognize someone and be able to say who they are: *One of the thieves has been identified by witnesses.*
2 to recognize something and to understand exactly what it is: *Several key problems have already been identified.*
> PHRASAL VERBS **i`dentify with sb/sth** to feel that you can understand and share someone else's feelings: *He didn't seem to be able to identify with ordinary people and their hopes.*
i`dentify sb/sth with sth to think that someone or something is connected with a particular group or opinion
i`dentify sth with sth *formal* to think that something is the same as something else or is closely related to it

identity /aɪˈdentɪti/ noun [C/U] ★★
1 the fact of who you are or what your name is: *Do you have any **proof of identity?*** ♦ *It was just a case of **mistaken identity** (=when you wrongly think that someone is someone else).*
2 the qualities that make someone or something what they are and different from other people: *The countries have kept their own political and cultural identities.* ♦ *Lorna went through a bit of **an identity crisis** (=was not certain about her identity) after her divorce.*

identity card noun [C] an official document that shows who you are

ideological /ˌaɪdɪəˈlɒdʒɪk(ə)l/ adj based on or relating to an IDEOLOGY: *ideological differences/disputes* —**ideologically** /ˌaɪdɪəˈlɒdʒɪkli/ adv

ideology /ˌaɪdɪˈɒlədʒi/ noun [C/U] a system of ideas and principles on which a political or economic theory is based: *Marxist/socialist/revolutionary ideology*

idiocy /ˈɪdiəsi/ noun **1** [U] very stupid ideas or behaviour **2** [C] a very stupid thing to say or do

idiom /ˈɪdiəm/ noun [C] an expression whose meaning is different from the meaning of the individual words. For example, 'to have your feet on the ground' is an idiom meaning 'to be sensible'.

idiomatic /ˌɪdiəˈmætɪk/ adj **1** expressing things in a way that sounds natural: *an*

idiomatic translation 2 containing idioms, or consisting of an idiom: *idiomatic expressions* —**idiomatically** /ˌɪdiəˈmætɪkli/ adv

idiosyncrasy /ˌɪdiəʊˈsɪŋkrəsi/ noun [C/U] an idiosyncratic feature or way of behaving

idiosyncratic /ˌɪdiəʊsɪŋˈkrætɪk/ adj unusual or strange, and not typical of anyone or anything else: *her own idiosyncratic style of painting*

idiot /ˈɪdiət/ noun [C] *informal* someone who behaves in an extremely stupid way: *Diana suddenly realized what an absolute idiot she had been.*

idiotic /ˌɪdiˈɒtɪk/ adj done or behaving in an extremely stupid way —**idiotically** /ˌɪdiˈɒtɪkli/ adv

idle¹ /ˈaɪd(ə)l/ adj **1** not working or being used: *Valuable machinery is left to lie idle for long periods.* **2** lazy **3** lacking a good reason or real purpose: *idle talk/gossip* —**idleness** noun [U], **idly** /ˈaɪd(ə)li/ adv

idle² /ˈaɪd(ə)l/ verb [I/T] if an engine idles, it runs slowly and does not produce any movement

idol /ˈaɪd(ə)l/ noun [C] **1** someone that you admire very much **2** a picture or STATUE that is worshipped as a god

idolize /ˈaɪdəˌlaɪz/ verb [T] to think that someone is perfect

idyllic /ɪˈdɪlɪk/ adj extremely beautiful and peaceful: *an idyllic scene* —**idyllically** /ɪˈdɪlɪkli/ adv

i.e. abbrev used when you are explaining the exact meaning of something that you have mentioned: *Senior officers – i.e. anyone with the rank of colonel or above – get their own administrative staff.*

if /ɪf/ conjunction ★★★
1 in a possible or imagined situation used for introducing a situation when you are talking about its likely or imaginary results: *If we miss the last bus, we'll have to walk home.* ♦ *If Luke paid more attention at school, he would get better results.* ♦ *If I had known who he was, I wouldn't have spoken to him like that.* ♦ *I'd like to be back here by 10.30 if possible.* ♦ *What if the boss walked in here now and saw us?*
2 when sth is always true used for introducing a situation that always has the same effect or meaning: *I get a headache if I watch too much television.* ♦ *If you drive without insurance, you're breaking the law.*
3 whether used when you are asking or talking about something that is not certain: *She asked me if I was fond of music.* ♦ *Can you tell me if they're planning to come?* ♦ *I haven't decided if I want to play.*
4 saying why sb may need information used for introducing the reason that you think someone may want to know something: *There are plenty of taxis if you're in a hurry.* ♦ *If anyone asks you where I am, I'll be in the library.*
5 saying how you feel about a possibility used for saying how you feel about the possibility that something may be true: *I'm*

sorry if I've upset you. ♦ *I don't care if I never see her again.*
6 in requests *spoken* used when you are politely asking someone to do something, or when you are asking for permission: *I would be grateful if you would send me further details.* ♦ *If you don't mind, I'd like to sit at the back.*

PHRASES if I were you *spoken* used when you are giving someone advice: *If I were you, I'd stay away from that man.*
if only *spoken* used for saying that you would like a situation to be different: *If only we could afford to buy a place of our own.*
→ AS

iffy /ˈɪfi/ adj *spoken* **1** not very good = DODGY: *That engine sounds a bit iffy to me.* **2** not certain = DOUBTFUL: *It's still iffy whether she'll be able to come to the party.*

igloo /ˈɪɡluː/ noun [C] a building made from snow or ice

ignite /ɪɡˈnaɪt/ verb **1** [I/T] *formal* to start to burn, or to make something start to burn **2** [T] to start a fight or argument = SPARK

ignition /ɪɡˈnɪʃ(ə)n/ noun **1** [singular] the place where you put in the key to make a car's engine start —*picture* → C6 **2** [U] *formal* the process of making something start to burn

ignominious /ˌɪɡnəˈmɪniəs/ adj *formal* very embarrassing = HUMILIATING: *an ignominious defeat* —**ignominiously** adv

ignorance /ˈɪɡnərəns/ noun [U] lack of knowledge about something

ignorant /ˈɪɡnərənt/ adj **1** not knowing something that you should know or that you need to know **2** *British spoken* not knowing the right way to behave or treat people —**ignorantly** adv

ignore /ɪɡˈnɔː/ verb [T] ★★
1 to not consider something, or to not let it influence you: *We had ignored the fact that it was getting darker.* ♦ *The government has ignored the advice it was given.*
2 to pretend that you have not noticed someone or something: *He completely ignored her and kept on walking.*

iguana /ɪˈɡwɑːnə/ noun [C] a large LIZARD with sharp points on its back that lives in tropical parts of North and South America —*picture* → C13

ikon /ˈaɪkɒn/ *see* icon 3

ill¹ /ɪl/ adj ★★★
1 not healthy because of a medical condition or an injury: *She was too ill to travel.* ♦ *She was unlucky enough to fall ill* (=become ill) *on holiday.* ♦ *Her husband is seriously ill in hospital.*
2 bad or harmful: *The fish didn't taste fresh, but we suffered no ill effects.*

Words often used with ill

Adverbs often used with ill (adj, sense 1)
■ critically, dangerously, gravely, seriously, severely + ILL: used for saying that someone is very ill

---

ill² /ɪl/ adv *formal* badly: *He was ill prepared for the demands of being a father.*

PHRASE can ill afford (to do) sth used for saying that someone should definitely not do something because it will cause problems: *These are issues that the government can ill afford to ignore.*
→ BODE

ill³ /ɪl/ noun [C] *formal* a problem, or a difficulty: *a cure for all the nation's ills*

I'll /aɪl/ short form the usual way of saying or writing 'I will' or 'I shall'. This is not often used in formal writing: *I'll see you at about six o'clock.*

ill-advised /ˌɪl ədˈvaɪzd/ adj likely to have a bad effect

ill-conceived /ˌɪl kənˈsiːvd/ adj an ill-conceived idea or plan is not sensible

illegal /ɪˈliːg(ə)l/ adj ★★ not allowed by the law: *illegal drugs* ♦ **it is illegal (for sb) to do sth** *It is illegal for employers to discriminate on the grounds of race.* —**illegality** /ˌɪliːˈɡæləti/ noun [U], **illegally** adv

illegal immigrant noun [C] someone who enters a country illegally, or who stays for a longer time than they are legally allowed

illegible /ɪˈledʒəb(ə)l/ adj difficult or impossible to read —**illegible** /ɪˈledʒəbli/ adv

illegitimate /ˌɪləˈdʒɪtəmət/ adj an illegitimate child is born to parents who are not legally married

ill-equipped /ˌɪl ɪˈkwɪpt/ adj *formal* lacking the necessary equipment, skills, or abilities to do something

ill-fated /ˌɪl ˈfeɪtɪd/ adj likely to end in failure or death

ill-fitting adj *formal* ill-fitting clothes are the wrong size for the person wearing them

ill-gotten gains /ˌɪl ɡɒt(ə)n ˈɡeɪnz/ noun [plural] *often humorous* money or property that someone has obtained in an illegal or dishonest way

illicit /ɪˈlɪsɪt/ adj **1** an illicit relationship, activity, or situation is one that people do not approve of **2** not allowed by the law =ILLEGAL: *illicit drugs* —**illicitly** adv

ill-informed adj lacking knowledge of a particular subject

illiterate /ɪˈlɪt(ə)rət/ adj **1** not able to read or write **2** containing a lot of mistakes in grammar and spelling **3** lacking knowledge in a particular subject: *politically illiterate* —**illiteracy** /ɪˈlɪt(ə)rəsi/ noun [U]

ill-mannered adj *formal* not polite =RUDE ≠ WELL-MANNERED

illness /ˈɪlnəs/ noun ★★★
1 [U] the state of feeling ill or having a disease: *He missed five days of school because of illness.*
2 [C] a particular disease, or a period of being ill: *a serious illness*

Other ways of saying illness
- **bug** (*informal*) a minor illness that is caused by a virus or bacteria and lasts a short time only
- **condition** a medical problem that affects someone for a long time

- **disease** a serious illness that usually lasts a long time
- **infection** an illness that is caused by bacteria and that usually lasts a short time only
- **virus** an illness that is caused by a very small germ

illogical /ɪˈlɒdʒɪk(ə)l/ adj not sensible, or not based on clear facts or reasons: *an illogical argument* —**illogically** /ɪˈlɒdʒɪkli/ adv

ill-treat verb [T] *formal* to treat someone in a cruel or unkind way =MALTREAT —**ill-treatment** noun [U]

illuminate /ɪˈluːmɪˌneɪt/ verb [T] *formal* **1** to make something bright with light or lights, or to shine a light on something =LIGHT **2** to make something clear and easier to understand

illuminating /ɪˈluːmɪˌneɪtɪŋ/ adj *formal* making something clearer and easier to understand

illumination /ɪˌluːmɪˈneɪʃ(ə)n/ noun **1** [U] light that is provided by something in a place **2** [C/U] an explanation that makes something easier to understand **3** **illuminations** [plural] *British* coloured lights that are used for decorating a town

illusion /ɪˈluːʒ(ə)n/ noun [C] **1** a false or wrong belief or idea **2** an appearance or effect that is different from the way that things really are

illusory /ɪˈluːsəri/ adj *formal* not real, but seeming real: *the illusory benefits of the scheme*

illustrate /ˈɪləˌstreɪt/ verb [T] ★★
1 to show or explain something by using examples, pictures, lists of numbers etc: *The process is illustrated in Figure 4.* ♦ *Miriam quoted three case studies to illustrate her point.*
2 to draw the pictures in a book, or to put pictures in a book: *The cookbook is beautifully illustrated with colour photographs.*

illustration /ˌɪləˈstreɪʃ(ə)n/ noun ★
1 [C] a picture, drawing, or photograph that is used for decorating a book or for explaining something: *a children's book with beautiful illustrations*
2 [U] the art of illustrating books
3 [C/U] an example, event, or fact that explains something or shows that something is true: *The project provides a good illustration of how people can work together.*

illustrator /ˈɪləˌstreɪtə/ noun [C] someone whose job is to draw pictures for books or magazines

illustrious /ɪˈlʌstriəs/ adj *formal* famous and respected because of what you have achieved =DISTINGUISHED

ill will noun [U] a strong feeling of disliking someone and wanting something bad to happen to them =ANIMOSITY ≠ GOODWILL

I'm /aɪm/ short form the usual way of saying or writing 'I am'. This is not often used in formal writing.

image /ˈɪmɪdʒ/ noun ★★★
1 [C/U] an opinion that people have about

someone or something: *The company needs to shake off its outdated image.* ♦ *We have **an image of** the US as a very rich country.* **2** [C] a picture, especially one in a mirror or on a computer, television, or cinema screen: *the flickering black-and-white images on the first cinema screens* ♦ *software for manipulating images after you have scanned them* ♦ *She stared at her image in the bathroom mirror.* ♦ *Images of Germany appeared on the screen.* **3** [C] a picture or idea of someone or something in your mind: *I had a sudden **mental image** of Robert waiting for me with flowers.* **4** [C] a description of something that uses language or combines ideas in an interesting way

imagery /ˈɪmɪdʒəri/ noun [U] **1** pictures, photographs, or objects that represent an idea **2** the use of words and phrases in literature to create an image of something

imaginable /ɪˈmædʒɪnəb(ə)l/ adj possible to imagine: *a situation that would have been hardly imaginable ten years ago*

imaginary /ɪˈmædʒɪnəri/ adj not real, but only created in your mind: *A lonely child sometimes creates an imaginary friend to play with.*

imagination /ɪˌmædʒɪˈneɪʃ(ə)n/ noun [C/U] ★ the ability to form pictures or original ideas in your mind: *Was he scared, or was it just my imagination?* ♦ *a child with a **vivid imagination*** ♦ *Try to **use your imagination** when planning main meals.* ♦ *Her essay showed a remarkable **lack of imagination**.* ♦ *They didn't have the **imagination** to deal with such complex problems.* → FIGMENT, STRETCH²

Word family: imagination

Words in the same family as imagination
- imagine *v*
- imaginable *adj*
- imaginative *adj*
- imaginary *adj*
- unimaginable *adj*
- unimaginative *adj*

imaginative /ɪˈmædʒɪnətɪv/ adj **1** involving new, different, or exciting ideas = CREATIVE ≠ UNIMAGINATIVE: *the imaginative use of computers in the classroom* **2** able to produce new, different, or exciting ideas ≠ UNIMAGINATIVE —**imaginatively** adv

imagine /ɪˈmædʒɪn/ verb [T] ★★★
1 to form a picture of someone or something in your mind: *She tried to imagine the scene.* ♦ *Imagine my surprise when they announced I had won!* ♦ **+(that)** *He had never imagined that digging would be such hard work.* ♦ *You can **imagine what** the newspapers would do if they ever found out about this.*
2 to have an idea that something exists or is happening, when in fact it does not exist or is not happening: *There's nothing there – you're just **imagining things**!*
3 to think that something is probably true = SUPPOSE: *It's difficult, **I imagine**, to keep your interest alive after doing the job for 30 years.* ♦ **+(that)** *I imagine they've left already.*

imaging /ˈɪmɪdʒɪŋ/ noun [U] the process of producing an image by using a machine that passes an electronic BEAM over something

imbalance /ɪmˈbæləns/ noun [C/U] a situation in which the balance between two things is not equal or fair

imbecile /ˈɪmbəsiːl/ noun [C] an insulting word for someone who behaves in a very stupid way = IDIOT

imbue /ɪmˈbjuː/ **PHRASAL VERB** im'bue sb/sth **with sth** *formal* to fill someone or something with a particular quality or emotion

IMF, the /ˌaɪ em ˈef/ the International Monetary Fund: an international organization that works to manage the world's economy

imitate /ˈɪmɪteɪt/ verb [T] **1** to copy something: *Italian ice cream is imitated all over the world.* **2** to copy what someone does or says, often in order to make people laugh = MIMIC —**imitator** /ˈɪmɪteɪtə/ noun [C]

imitation¹ /ˌɪmɪˈteɪʃ(ə)n/ noun **1** [C/U] the act of copying someone's actions, words, or behaviour, often in order to make people laugh **2** [C/U] the act of copying something **3** [C] something that is a copy of something else, and not as good as the original thing: *a crude imitation of Hitchcock's earlier work*

imitation² /ˌɪmɪˈteɪʃ(ə)n/ adj made to look like something that is more valuable or expensive: *imitation fur/leather/marble*

immaculate /ɪˈmækjʊlət/ adj **1** completely clean and tidy = SPOTLESS **2** correct or perfect in every way = IMPECCABLE —**immaculately** adv

immaterial /ˌɪməˈtɪəriəl/ adj not important or relevant

immature /ˌɪməˈtjʊə/ adj **1** behaving in a silly way, as though you are much younger than you really are ≠ MATURE **2** not fully grown or developed ≠ MATURE —**immaturity** /ˌɪməˈtjʊərəti/ noun [U]

immeasurable /ɪˈmeʒərəb(ə)l/ adj *formal* impossible to measure because of being so large or extreme —**immeasurably** /ɪˈmeʒərəbli/ adv

immediate /ɪˈmiːdiət/ adj ★★★

1 without delay	4 next to sb/sth
2 urgent	5 closely connected
3 directly before/after	

1 happening or done now, without delay: *Our government must take immediate action.* ♦ *The rebels demanded the immediate release of the prisoners.* ♦ *My immediate response was to say yes.*
2 existing now and needing urgent action: *There doesn't seem to be any immediate danger.*
3 existing in the period of time directly before or after an event: *plans for the **immediate future***
4 next to a person or place: *There are several pleasant walks in the **immediate vicinity*** (=very near).
5 closely connected to you: *She is my*

immediate superior (=the person directly in charge of me). ♦ *Only immediate family* (=parents, children, brothers, and sisters) *will be allowed to attend the ceremony.*

immediately /ɪˈmiːdiətli/ adv, conjunction
★★★
1 very quickly and without delay: *She decided to leave immediately.* ♦ *I immediately realized how serious the situation was.* ♦ *Immediately he saw her, he fell in love with her.*
2 just before or just after an event: *She was with Roosevelt immediately before his death.*
3 with no one or nothing between =DIRECTLY: *We could hear noises coming from the room immediately below us.*

immense /ɪˈmens/ adj extremely large =HUGE: *an immense amount of money*

immensely /ɪˈmensli/ adv very, or very much: *an immensely talented singer*

immensity /ɪˈmensəti/ noun [U] the very large size of something

immerse /ɪˈmɜːs/ verb [T] *formal* to put someone or something in a liquid so that they are covered completely
PHRASE **immerse yourself in sth** to spend most of your time doing something or thinking about it: *Sandra immersed herself in work to try and forget her problems at home.*
—**immersion** /ɪˈmɜːʃ(ə)n/ noun [U]

immigrant /ˈɪmɪɡrənt/ noun [C] someone who comes to live in a country from another country → EMIGRANT

immigrate /ˈɪmɪˌɡreɪt/ verb [I] to come into a country because you want to live there

immigration /ˌɪmɪˈɡreɪʃ(ə)n/ noun [U] **1** the process in which people enter a country in order to live there permanently **2** the place where you show your passport and are officially allowed into a country

imminent /ˈɪmɪnənt/ adj likely to happen very soon, or certain to do so —**imminence** noun [U], **imminently** adv

immobile /ɪˈməʊbaɪl/ adj **1** not moving =MOTIONLESS **2** not able to move —**immobility** /ˌɪməʊˈbɪləti/ noun [U]

immobilize /ɪˈməʊbɪˌlaɪz/ verb [T] **1** to stop something from working: *a device that immobilizes the car if anyone tries to steal it* **2** to make someone unable to move —**immobilization** /ɪˌməʊbɪlaɪˈzeɪʃ(ə)n/ noun [U]

immobilizer /ɪˈməʊbɪˌlaɪzə/ noun [C] a piece of equipment that prevents a car from moving if someone tries to steal it

immoral /ɪˈmɒrəl/ adj morally wrong: *immoral behaviour* —**immorality** /ˌɪməˈræləti/ noun [U], **immorally** adv

immortal /ɪˈmɔːt(ə)l/ adj **1** very well known and likely to be remembered for a long time **2** living or existing for all time —**immortality** /ˌɪmɔːˈtæləti/ noun [U]

immortalize /ɪˈmɔːt(ə)lˌaɪz/ verb [T] to make someone or something famous for a very long time

immovable /ɪˈmuːvəb(ə)l/ adj **1** with opinions or feelings that you refuse to change

2 impossible to move —**immovably** adv

immune /ɪˈmjuːn/ adj **1** safe from a disease, because you cannot be infected by it **2** relating to the body's IMMUNE SYSTEM **3** not influenced or affected by something: *Guy seemed totally immune to criticism.* **4** not affected by something such as a law, because of a special arrangement: *Diplomats are immune from prosecution.*

imˈmune ˌsystem noun [C] the system in your body that protects you against diseases

immunity /ɪˈmjuːnəti/ noun [C/U] a situation in which someone is not affected by something such as a law because they have a special job or position

immunize /ˈɪmjʊˌnaɪz/ verb [T] to prevent someone from getting a particular illness by putting a substance into their body —**immunization** /ˌɪmjʊnaɪˈzeɪʃ(ə)n/ noun [C/U]

imp /ɪmp/ noun [C] an imaginary creature that looks like a small child and likes to have fun by behaving badly

impact¹ /ˈɪmpækt/ noun ★★★
1 [C] an effect or influence: *Her paper discusses **the likely impact of** global warming.* ♦ *Internet shopping has begun to have a serious **impact on** traditional bookshops.*
2 [C/U] the force or act of one object hitting another: *the point of impact* ♦ *I was thrown to the ground **by the impact** of the blast.* ♦ *The missile exploded **on impact**.*

Words often used with **impact**

*Adjectives often used with **impact** (noun, sense 1)*
■ **adverse, devastating, negative, serious** + IMPACT: used about a bad effect
■ **dramatic, major, profound, significant** + IMPACT: used about a big effect
*Verbs often used with **impact** (noun, sense 1)*
■ **absorb, cushion, lessen, minimize, soften** + IMPACT: reduce the effect of something

impact² /ɪmˈpækt/ verb [I/T] to have an effect or influence on someone or something

impair /ɪmˈpeə/ verb [T] *formal* to make something less good or effective by damaging it

impaired /ɪmˈpeəd/ adj not fully able to do something: *methods of correcting impaired vision*

impairment /ɪmˈpeəmənt/ noun [C/U] the fact that a part of your body is unable to do something fully

impale /ɪmˈpeɪl/ verb [T] to push a pointed object through someone or something

impart /ɪmˈpɑːt/ verb [T] *formal* **1** to give something such as information, knowledge, or beliefs to someone **2** to give something a particular quality

impartial /ɪmˈpɑːʃ(ə)l/ adj not influenced by, or not preferring, one particular person or group —**impartiality** /ˌɪmpɑːʃiˈæləti/ noun [U], **impartially** adv

impassable /ɪmˈpɑːsəb(ə)l/ adj an impassable road or path is impossible to travel along

impasse /æmˈpɑːs/ noun [singular] a situation in which progress is not possible because none of the people involved is willing to change their opinion or decision =DEADLOCK

impassioned /ɪmˈpæʃ(ə)nd/ adj expressing a lot of emotion

impassive /ɪmˈpæsɪv/ adj not showing any emotion —**impassively** adv

impatient /ɪmˈpeɪʃ(ə)nt/ adj ★
1 annoyed because something is not happening as quickly as you want or in the way that you want: *'Come on!' said Maggie, becoming impatient.* ◆ *He gets **impatient with** people who don't agree with him.*
2 wanting something to happen as soon as possible: *They were **impatient for** news of their father.* ◆ **impatient to do sth** *After a couple of days, she was impatient to get back to work.*
—**impatience** /ɪmˈpeɪʃ(ə)ns/ noun [U], **impatiently** adv

impeccable /ɪmˈpekəb(ə)l/ adj perfect in every way=FAULTLESS —**impeccably** adv

impede /ɪmˈpiːd/ verb [T] *formal* to make it more difficult for someone to do something or for something to happen

impediment /ɪmˈpedɪmənt/ noun [C] **1** *formal* something that makes it more difficult for someone to do something or for something to happen **2** a physical or PSYCHOLOGICAL problem that affects how well someone can do something

impel /ɪmˈpel/ verb [T] *formal* if a feeling or idea impels you to do something, it forces you to do it

impending /ɪmˈpendɪŋ/ adj going to happen very soon: *He was unaware of the impending disaster.*

impenetrable /ɪmˈpenɪtrəb(ə)l/ adj **1** impossible to get into, get through, or see through **2** impossible to understand: *impenetrable writing*

imperative¹ /ɪmˈperətɪv/ adj **1** *formal* extremely important and urgent **2** *linguistics* the imperative form of a verb expresses an order to do something, for example 'Go!'

imperative² /ɪmˈperətɪv/ noun **1** the **imperative** [singular] *linguistics* the form of a verb that expresses an order **2** [C] *formal* something that is very important and urgent

imperceptible /ˌɪmpəˈseptəb(ə)l/ adj something that is imperceptible is so slight or small that it is very difficult to notice —**imperceptibly** adv

imperfect /ɪmˈpɜːfɪkt/ adj **1** something that is imperfect has some faults or other bad qualities **2** *linguistics* an imperfect form of a verb describes an action in the past that is continuous, repeated, or not finished —**imperfection** /ˌɪmpəˈfekʃ(ə)n/ noun [C/U], **imperfectly** adv

imperfect, the /ɪmˈpɜːfɪkt/ noun [singular] *linguistics* the form of a verb that describes an action in the past that is continuous, repeated, or not finished

imperial /ɪmˈpɪəriəl/ adj **1** relating to an EMPIRE (=a group of several countries that are ruled by one country) or the person

who rules it **2** belonging to a system of measurement in which weight is measured in pounds, length is measured in FEET, and VOLUME is measured in PINTS → METRIC

imperialism /ɪmˈpɪəriəˌlɪz(ə)m/ noun [U] the actions of a powerful country that tries to gain control of other countries —**imperialist** adj, noun

imperil /ɪmˈperəl/ verb [T] *formal* to put someone or something in danger =ENDANGER

impersonal /ɪmˈpɜːs(ə)nəl/ adj not showing your personal feelings or ideas: *His manner was cold and impersonal.* —**impersonally** adv

impersonate /ɪmˈpɜːsəˌneɪt/ verb [T] **1** to copy the way that someone speaks and behaves in order to pretend to be that person or to make people laugh=IMITATE **2** to pretend to be someone else by copying the way that they look, speak, or behave in order to trick people —**impersonation** /ɪmˌpɜːs(ə)nˈeɪʃ(ə)n/ noun [C/U], **impersonator** noun [C]

impertinent /ɪmˈpɜːtɪnənt/ adj *formal* rude and not showing respect for someone —**impertinence** noun [U], **impertinently** adv

impervious /ɪmˈpɜːviəs/ adj **1 impervious to sth** not affected by something: *He continued talking, impervious to the effect his words were having.* **2** something that is impervious to a substance does not let the substance pass through it

impetuous /ɪmˈpetʃuəs/ adj doing things quickly, without thinking about the results =RASH —**impetuously** adv

impetus /ˈɪmpɪtəs/ noun [singular/U] something that makes a process happen or develop more quickly

impinge /ɪmˈpɪndʒ/ **PHRASAL VERB** im**'pinge on sth** or im**'pinge u,pon sth** *formal* to have an effect on something

impish /ˈɪmpɪʃ/ adj behaving in a way that is slightly bad but that makes people smile =MISCHIEVOUS —**impishly** adv

implacable /ɪmˈplækəb(ə)l/ adj having or expressing very angry or determined feelings that will not change —**implacably** adv

implant¹ /ˈɪmplɑːnt/ noun [C] an object that is put into someone's body in a medical operation

implant² /ɪmˈplɑːnt/ verb [T] **1** to put something into someone's body in a medical operation **2** to put an idea or attitude into someone's mind

implausible /ɪmˈplɔːzəb(ə)l/ adj difficult to accept as true=UNCONVINCING —**implausibly** adv

implement¹ /ˈɪmplɪˌment/ verb [T] to make something such as an idea, plan, system, or law start to work and be used =CARRY STH OUT —**implementation** /ˌɪmplɪmənˈteɪʃ(ə)n/ noun [U]

implement² /ˈɪmplɪmənt/ noun [C] a tool, or a simple piece of equipment

implicate /ˈɪmplɪˌkeɪt/ verb [T] to show or claim that someone or something is involved in an activity that is illegal or morally wrong

implication /ˌɪmplɪˈkeɪʃ(ə)n/ noun ★
1 [C] a possible future effect or result: *What are the implications of this new technology?* ♦ *Improving your diet has important implications for your future health.*
2 [C/U] something that you suggest is true, although you do not say it directly: **+that** *I resent the implication that my work is not thorough.*
3 [U] the fact of suggesting or showing that someone is involved in something illegal or morally wrong

implicit /ɪmˈplɪsɪt/ adj **1** not stated directly, but expressed or suggested indirectly ≠ EXPLICIT: *an implicit criticism* **2** without any doubts or questions: *an implicit belief in the goodness of people* **3** implicit in sth forming a necessary part of something —**implicitly** adv

implode /ɪmˈpləʊd/ verb [I] to break up violently and fall inwards

implore /ɪmˈplɔː/ verb [T] *formal* to ask someone in an emotional way to do something, because you want it very much = BEG

imply /ɪmˈplaɪ/ verb [T] ★ to show or suggest that something exists or is true: **+(that)** *I didn't mean to imply that you were interfering.*

impolite /ˌɪmpəˈlaɪt/ adj not polite = RUDE —**impolitely** adv

import¹ /ɪmˈpɔːt/ verb [T] ★
1 to buy a product from another country and bring it to your country ≠ EXPORT: *We import most of our coal from other countries.* ♦ *imported luxury goods*
2 *computing* to move information into a file or program ≠ EXPORT
—**importation** /ˌɪmpɔːˈteɪʃ(ə)n/ noun [U], **importer** noun [C]

import² /ˈɪmpɔːt/ noun [C/U] ★ a product that is imported, or the process of importing products ≠ EXPORT: *oil/food/coal imports* ♦ *cheap imports from Eastern Europe* ♦ *We need controls on the import of meat.*

importance /ɪmˈpɔːt(ə)ns/ noun [U] ★★★ the fact of being important, or the degree to which something or someone is important: *The company recognizes the importance of training its employees.* ♦ *The issue has special importance for people in rural areas.* ♦ *I pretended the incident was of no importance.*

important /ɪmˈpɔːt(ə)nt/ adj ★★★
1 something that is important has a major effect on someone or something: *Music was an important part of the life of the community.* ♦ *Winning the game yesterday was important for us.* ♦ *Your interest and support are important to your child.* ♦ **it is important to do sth** *It is important to stress that the study only involved a small number of people.*
2 important people have a lot of influence or power: *We can't afford to lose such an important customer.*

importantly /ɪmˈpɔːt(ə)ntli/ adv **1** used for emphasizing that something is important: *How did Jamie know? And, more importantly, what did he know?* **2** in a way that shows that you think you are important

impose /ɪmˈpəʊz/ verb ★
1 [T] to force people to accept something: *If she lied under oath, the court will impose a severe penalty.* ♦ **impose sth on sb** *I wouldn't want to impose my views on anyone.*
2 [I] to cause extra work for someone: *They invited me to dinner, but I didn't like to impose.* ♦ *Please come and stay. You wouldn't be imposing on us at all.*

imposing /ɪmˈpəʊzɪŋ/ adj large and impressive

imposition /ˌɪmpəˈzɪʃ(ə)n/ noun **1** [U] the introduction of something that people are forced to accept **2** [C] an unfair or unreasonable situation that you are expected to accept

impossible /ɪmˈpɒsəb(ə)l/ adj ★★★
1 if something is impossible, no one can do it or it cannot happen: *We were faced with an impossible task.* ♦ **it is impossible to do sth** *It would be impossible to gather this information without using computers.*
2 extremely difficult to do or to deal with: *Dealing with her illness makes life pretty*

impossible for the rest of the family. ♦ *Young children are impossible at times.*
—**impossibility** /ɪmˌpɒsəˈbɪləti/ noun [C/U]

impossibly /ɪmˈpɒsəbli/ adv extremely: *impossibly high heels*

impostor or **imposter** /ɪmˈpɒstə/ noun [C] someone who pretends to be someone else

impotent /ˈɪmpətənt/ adj **1** unable to do anything that is effective because of a lack of power **2** a man who is impotent cannot have sex because his PENIS does not stay hard —**impotence** noun [U]

impound /ɪmˈpaʊnd/ verb [T] if the police or other officials impound something, they take it away from someone who has done something that is illegal =CONFISCATE

impoverished /ɪmˈpɒvərɪʃt/ adj very poor

impractical /ɪmˈpræktɪk(ə)l/ adj **1** not sensible, or not likely to be effective or successful **2** not good at doing practical things —**impracticality** /ɪmˌpræktɪˈkæləti/ noun [C/U]

imprecise /ˌɪmprɪˈsaɪs/ adj not exact, accurate, or clear —**imprecisely** adv

impregnable /ɪmˈpregnəb(ə)l/ adj a place that is impregnable is very well protected and difficult to attack

impregnate /ˈɪmpregneɪt/ verb [T] **1** to make a substance such as a liquid spread all the way through something **2** *formal* to make a woman or female animal pregnant —**impregnation** /ˌɪmpregˈneɪʃ(ə)n/ noun [U]

impress /ɪmˈpres/ verb [T] ★★ if someone or something impresses you, you admire them: *Her ability to deal with problems impresses me.* ♦ *I was extremely impressed by the novel.*
PHRASAL VERB im'press sth on sb to try to make someone understand how important something is: *They impressed on us the need to keep the project completely secret.*

impression /ɪmˈpreʃ(ə)n/ noun [C] ★★
1 an opinion, feeling, or idea about someone or something that is not based on much information, or that is only based on the way that they look, sound, or behave: *It is important to **make a good impression** at the interview.* ♦ *He gave me the impression that he really didn't care.* ♦ *I have the impression that she's very good at her job.* ♦ *Her first impression was that he was dead.* ♦ *I was under the impression* (=thought) *that we had met before.*
2 a performance in which someone copies the way another person speaks or behaves in order to make people laugh =IMITATION: *Jill does impressions of famous singers.*
3 *formal* a mark that is made when an object is pressed onto a surface

impressionable /ɪmˈpreʃ(ə)nəb(ə)l/ adj easily impressed and influenced by other people

impressionistic /ɪmˌpreʃəˈnɪstɪk/ adj based on reactions or opinions, rather than on specific facts or details

impressive /ɪmˈpresɪv/ adj ★ if someone or something is impressive, you admire them ≠ UNIMPRESSIVE: *an impressive performance*

♦ *The list of their achievements is pretty impressive.* —**impressively** adv

imprint¹ /ˈɪmprɪnt/ noun [C] **1** a mark that an object leaves on a surface when it is pressed into it **2** a strong permanent influence on someone or something

imprint² /ɪmˈprɪnt/ verb [T] **1** to leave a mark on a surface by pressing an object into it **2** to make something have a strong permanent influence on someone or something

imprison /ɪmˈprɪz(ə)n/ verb [T] to put someone in a prison, or to keep them in a place that they cannot escape from —**imprisonment** noun [U]

improbable /ɪmˈprɒbəb(ə)l/ adj **1** not likely to happen or be true =UNLIKELY **2** strange and unexpected —**improbably** adv

impromptu /ɪmˈprɒmptjuː/ adj not planned or prepared —**impromptu** adv

improper /ɪmˈprɒpə/ adj **1** not suitable or right according to accepted standards of behaviour =INAPPROPRIATE **2** not legal or honest =UNLAWFUL —**improperly** adv

impropriety /ˌɪmprəˈpraɪəti/ noun [C/U] *formal* behaviour that is not honest, professional, or socially acceptable

improve /ɪmˈpruːv/ verb [I/T] ★★★ to become better, or to make something better: *Your English will improve with practice.* ♦ *More money is needed to improve airline security.*
PHRASAL VERB im'prove on sth or **im'prove u,pon sth** to make something better than it was before, or to do something better than you did before: *We hope to improve on last year's performance.*

> **Words often used with improve**
>
> *Adverbs often used with improve*
> ■ IMPROVE + **considerably, dramatically, greatly, markedly, significantly, vastly**: used for saying that something improves a lot

improvement /ɪmˈpruːvmənt/ noun ★★★
1 [C/U] the state of being better than before, or the process of making something better than it was before: *The school is performing well, but we recognize the need for further improvement.* ♦ *There has been an improvement in relations between the two countries.*
2 [C] a change that you make to something in order to make it better: *home improvements*

improvise /ˈɪmprəvaɪz/ verb **1** [I/T] to do something or to make something without any previous preparation or using only what is available at the time: *I don't have a recipe, but we can improvise.* **2** [I] to perform something that has not been written down or practised earlier =AD-LIB —**improvisation** /ˌɪmprəvaɪˈzeɪʃ(ə)n/ noun [C/U]

impudent /ˈɪmpjʊd(ə)nt/ adj behaving in a rude way that shows no respect —**impudence** noun [U], **impudently** adv

impulse /ˈɪmpʌls/ noun **1** [C/U] a sudden strong feeling that you must do something **2** [C] *science* an electrical signal

impulsive /ɪmˈpʌlsɪv/ adj tending to do things without thinking about what will happen as a result —**impulsively** adv

impunity /ɪmˈpjuːnəti/ noun [U] *formal* freedom from any risk of being punished

impure /ˌɪmˈpjʊə/ adj containing another substance that should not be there

impurity /ɪmˈpjʊərəti/ noun **1** [C] a substance that is wrongly present in another substance **2** [U] the quality of not being pure

in¹ /ɪn/ grammar word ★★★

In can be:
- a **preposition**: *The children are in the garden.*
- an **adverb**: *Come in and sit down.*
- used after the verb 'to be': *'Is Philip in?'*

1 contained within sth inside or within a container, place, or substance: *His passport was in his coat pocket.* ♦ *Have you seen a bag with some tools in?* ♦ *a picnic in the park* ♦ *There wasn't a cloud in the sky.* ♦ *The books are printed in Hong Kong.*

2 into sth moving, falling, or looking into a place or substance: *The door was open so I just walked in.* ♦ *The guards fired a few shots in the air.* ♦ *I invited her in for a drink.* ♦ *The roof of the cave fell in.* ♦ *Look in the top drawer of my desk.*

3 inside a building at home or at work: *We usually stay in and watch television.* ♦ *I asked to speak to the manager but she wasn't in.*

4 arriving somewhere arriving somewhere, especially your home or place of work: *The ferry won't be in for another hour.* ♦ *What time did you get in last night?*

5 during a particular time during a particular period, month, season, or year, or during a part of the day: *Mel Gibson was born in 1956.* ♦ *In winter the lake freezes over.* ♦ *Let's meet again in the morning, at around 9.30.* ♦ *Our anniversary is in April.* ♦ *Unemployment has risen by over 15% in the past year.*

6 at the end of a period of time at the end of a period of time in the future: *The exams are in six weeks' time.* ♦ *I'll be ready in a few minutes.*

7 involved with an activity involved with or relating to a particular type of activity: *Bailey was in the long-distance cycle race.* ♦ *Her husband works in publishing.* ♦ *There have been amazing advances in medical science.* ♦ *a university degree in economics*

8 for describing a situation or relationship used for describing the state, situation, or relationship that exists for someone or something: *She's 85 and still in good health.* ♦ *Their lives were in danger.* ♦ *Are we all in agreement?*

9 wearing sth used for stating what someone is wearing: *She looked so beautiful in her wedding dress.* ♦ *a man in a tall hat* ♦ *a woman in black* (=wearing black clothes)

10 for saying what changes used for saying what changes, increases, improves etc: *There's going to be a change in the weather.* ♦ *the recent rise in oil prices*

11 for talking about the way sth is done using a particular method, style, or language: *We are trying to teach mathematics in a more interesting way.* ♦ *The houses are all built in the traditional style.* ♦ *You have to pay in cash.* ♦ *a drawing done in ink* ♦ *Go on, say something in French.*

12 included as part of sth used for saying which group, book, film etc someone or something is part of: *Beckham is back in the England team.* ♦ *Who's in the new film with Brad Pitt?*

13 for describing how things are arranged arranged in a particular order, shape, or pattern: *We all sat round in a circle.* ♦ *The vines are planted in rows.* ♦ *The names are listed in alphabetical order.*

14 affected by weather affected by a particular type of weather: *Have you been waiting outside in the rain?* ♦ *Flags were fluttering in the breeze.*

15 referring to an aspect of sth used for saying what aspect of something you are referring to: *She's so selfish in her attitude to other people.* ♦ *The words are similar but there is a difference in meaning.*

16 written or drawn to complete sth written or drawn where something is needed: *Fill in your name and address at the top of the form.* ♦ *I typed in my password and my email address.*

17 given or received given or sent to someone, or received by someone: *Homework must be handed in tomorrow morning.* ♦ *Have you sent in your application form?* ♦ *Tax forms must be in by the end of September.*

18 available to buy used for saying that something is available to buy: *They have fresh fish in on Fridays.*

19 elected elected to form the government: *We hoped things would get better when Labour got in.*

20 fashionable fashionable: *Pale colours are definitely in this summer.*

21 when the sea is high if the TIDE is in, the sea has reached its highest level on the land

> PHRASES **be in for sth** *informal* to be going to experience something: *It looks as if we're in for some stormy weather.*
> **be in on sth** to be involved in something that is being planned: *I don't know what they agreed to because I wasn't in on the deal.*

in² noun **the ins and outs (of sth)** all the details or facts that you need to know in order to deal with a complicated situation or process

inability /ˌɪnəˈbɪləti/ noun [U] **inability to do sth** the fact of not being able to do something

inaccessible /ˌɪnəkˈsesəb(ə)l/ adj difficult or impossible to reach=REMOTE —**inaccessibility** /ˌɪnəkˌsesəˈbɪləti/ noun [U]

inaccuracy /ɪnˈækjʊrəsi/ noun [C/U] something that is not accurate, or the failure to be accurate

inaccurate /ɪnˈækjʊrət/ adj not accurate or correct —**inaccurately** adv

inaction /ɪnˈækʃ(ə)n/ noun [U] lack of action

inactive /ɪnˈæktɪv/ adj **1** not taking part in physical activity or exercise **2** not working or operating —**inactivity** /ˌɪnækˈtɪvəti/ noun [U]

inadequacy /ɪnˈædɪkwəsi/ noun **1** [C/U] the failure to be good enough **2** [U] a lack of confidence that makes someone feel that they are not good enough

inadequate /ɪnˈædɪkwət/ adj ★ not enough, or not good enough: *Some people feel inadequate when they are faced with new responsibilities.* ◆ *The heating system is totally inadequate.* ◆ *The machinery is inadequate for the job.* ◆ **inadequate to do sth** *The roads are inadequate to deal with this amount of traffic.* —**inadequately** adv

inadmissible /ˌɪnədˈmɪsəb(ə)l/ adj *legal* inadmissible evidence cannot be used in a court of law

inadvertently /ˌɪnədˈvɜːt(ə)ntli/ adv *formal* without intending to do something =ACCIDENTALLY —**inadvertent** adj

inadvisable /ˌɪnədˈvaɪzəb(ə)l/ adj not sensible and likely to have bad results

inalienable /ɪnˈeɪliənəb(ə)l/ adj *formal* an inalienable right cannot be taken away from you

inane /ɪˈneɪn/ adj completely stupid =IDIOTIC —**inanely** adv

inanimate /ɪnˈænɪmət/ adj not alive

inappropriate /ˌɪnəˈprəʊpriət/ adj not suitable in a particular situation: *inappropriate behaviour* ◆ *The reading material is inappropriate for our students.* ◆ **it is inappropriate to do sth** *It would be inappropriate to publish the story.* —**inappropriately** adv

inarticulate /ˌɪnɑːˈtɪkjʊlət/ adj not able to express clearly what you want to say —**inarticulately** adv

inasmuch as /ˌɪnəzˈmætʃ æz/ conjunction *formal* used for adding a comment that explains or makes clearer what you have just said =IN THAT

inaudible /ɪnˈɔːdəb(ə)l/ adj difficult or impossible to hear —**inaudibly** adv

inaugural /ɪˈnɔːgjʊrəl/ adj made or happening at the beginning of something new: *the president's inaugural address*

inaugurate /ɪˈnɔːgjʊˌreɪt/ verb [T] **1** to have an official ceremony to celebrate the beginning of something =OPEN **2** *formal* to start or introduce something that is new and important —**inauguration** /ɪˌnɔːgjʊˈreɪʃ(ə)n/ noun [C/U]

inborn /ɪnˈbɔːn/ adj something that is inborn has existed in you since you were born =INNATE

inbox /ˈɪnbɒks/ noun [C] *computing* the place on a computer program where emails arrive for you

Inc. abbrev Incorporated: used in the US after the name of a large company

incandescent /ˌɪnkænˈdes(ə)nt/ adj **1** producing light as a result of being made very hot **2** *formal* extremely angry —**incandescence** noun [U]

incapable /ɪnˈkeɪpəb(ə)l/ adj **incapable of sth** unable to do something

incapacitate /ˌɪnkəˈpæsɪˌteɪt/ verb [T] *formal* to make someone or something unable to live or work normally

incapacity /ˌɪnkəˈpæsəti/ noun [U] **1** the condition of being unable to live normally because you are ill or weak **2** *formal* a lack of ability

incarcerate /ɪnˈkɑːsəˌreɪt/ verb [T] *formal* to put someone in prison =IMPRISON —**incarceration** /ɪnˌkɑːsəˈreɪʃ(ə)n/ noun [U]

incarnation /ˌɪnkɑːˈneɪʃ(ə)n/ noun **1** [singular] a person or thing that is an extremely strong example of a particular quality **2** [C] according to some religions, one in a series of lives that a person may have

incendiary /ɪnˈsendiəri/ adj **1** designed to cause a fire **2** likely to cause anger or violence =INFLAMMATORY

incense /ˈɪnsens/ noun [U] a substance that creates a strong but pleasant smell when it is burned

incensed /ɪnˈsenst/ adj extremely angry

incentive /ɪnˈsentɪv/ noun [C/U] ★ something that makes you want to do something or to work harder, because you know that you will benefit by doing this: *The high rate of pay is a great incentive.* ◆ **incentive to do sth** *Many farmers have little incentive to work for the environment.*

inception /ɪnˈsepʃ(ə)n/ noun [U] *formal* the beginning of something

incessant /ɪnˈses(ə)nt/ adj continuing for a long time without stopping =CONSTANT —**incessantly** adv

incest /ˈɪnsest/ noun [U] sexual activity between people who are closely related —**incestuous** /ɪnˈsestjuəs/ adj

inch¹ /ɪntʃ/ noun [C] ★★ a unit for measuring length that is equal to 2.54 CENTIMETRES: *The insect was about an inch long.*
PHRASES every inch (of sth) the whole of an area or place
not give/budge an inch to completely refuse to change your opinion or decision

inch² /ɪntʃ/ verb [I/T] to move somewhere very slowly and gradually, or to make something do this

incidence /ˈɪnsɪd(ə)ns/ noun [singular] the number of times that something happens

incident /ˈɪnsɪd(ə)nt/ noun [C] ★★ something that happens that is unusual, violent, or dangerous: *an embarrassing incident* ◆ *Police are appealing for witnesses to the incident.*

incidental /ˌɪnsɪˈdent(ə)l/ adj related to something, but thought to be less important than it

incidentally /ˌɪnsɪˈdent(ə)li/ adv used for adding related but less important information to what has just been said, or for suddenly introducing a new subject

incinerate /ɪnˈsɪnəˌreɪt/ verb [T] to burn something completely —**incineration** /ɪnˌsɪnəˈreɪʃ(ə)n/ noun [U]

incinerator /ɪnˈsɪnəˌreɪtə/ noun [C] a machine

that destroys rubbish or other material by burning it

incipient /ɪnˈsɪpiənt/ adj *formal* just beginning to appear or develop

incision /ɪnˈsɪʒ(ə)n/ noun [C/U] a cut made into your body during a medical operation

incisive /ɪnˈsaɪsɪv/ adj expressed in a clear and direct manner —**incisively** adv

incite /ɪnˈsaɪt/ verb [T] to encourage people to be violent or to commit crimes by making them angry or excited

inclination /ˌɪŋklɪˈneɪʃ(ə)n/ noun [C/U] **1** a feeling that you want to do something **2** a tendency to behave in a particular way or to have a particular interest

incline¹ /ɪnˈklaɪn/ verb [I/T] *formal* to slope in a particular direction, or to make something do this

incline² /ˈɪnklaɪn/ noun [C] a slope

inclined /ɪnˈklaɪnd/ adj **1** feeling that you want to do something: *Karen didn't feel inclined to help.* **2** tending to behave in a particular way, or to be interested in a particular thing: *Joe is inclined to be moody.*

PHRASE **inclined to think/believe/agree etc** having an opinion, but not completely sure about it: *I'm inclined to agree with you.*

include /ɪnˈkluːd/ verb [T] ★★★
1 to contain, or to have someone or something as a part: *The book includes activities, stories, and practical advice.*
2 to make someone or something be part of a group, set, or collection of things ≠ EXCLUDE: *Please include a photograph of yourself with your application.* ♦ **include sth in sth** *His work was recently included in an exhibition of young painters.*

included /ɪnˈkluːdɪd/ adj **1** contained in something as part of the whole **2** forming part of a group, set, or collection of things

including /ɪnˈkluːdɪŋ/ preposition ★★★ used for mentioning that someone or something is part of a particular group or amount: *Four more countries applied to join the EU, including Sweden and Austria.* ♦ *The news delighted everyone, including me.*

inclusion /ɪnˈkluːʒ(ə)n/ noun **1** [U] the action of including someone or something ≠ EXCLUSION **2** [C] someone or something that is added or included

inclusive /ɪnˈkluːsɪv/ adj **1** including all costs **2** *British* including the specific limits that have been mentioned and everything in between **3** deliberately aiming to involve all types of people

incoherent /ˌɪnkəʊˈhɪərənt/ adj **1** badly organized or expressed and therefore difficult to understand **2** unable to express yourself clearly —**incoherence** noun [U], **incoherently** adv

income /ˈɪŋkʌm/ noun [C/U] ★★★ money that someone gets from working or from investing money: *What is your approximate annual income?* ♦ *an average household income of £27,000*

income tax noun [C/U] a tax that is based on your income

incoming /ˈɪnˌkʌmɪŋ/ adj **1** coming in, or arriving ≠ OUTGOING **2** recently elected, or recently chosen for a job or position ≠ OUTGOING

incomparable /ɪnˈkɒmp(ə)rəb(ə)l/ adj so good that nothing else can be as good —**incomparably** adv

incompatible /ˌɪnkəmˈpætəb(ə)l/ adj not able to work or exist together —**incompatibility** /ˌɪnkəmˌpætəˈbɪləti/ noun [U]

incompetent /ɪnˈkɒmpɪt(ə)nt/ adj lacking the ability or skills to do something —**incompetence** noun [U], **incompetently** adv

incomplete /ˌɪnkəmˈpliːt/ adj not finished, not completely developed, or lacking one or more parts

incomprehensible /ɪnˌkɒmprɪˈhensəb(ə)l/ adj impossible to understand —**incomprehensibly** adv

inconceivable /ˌɪnkənˈsiːvəb(ə)l/ adj impossible to believe or imagine: *It is inconceivable that he would lose his job.* —**inconceivably** adv

inconclusive /ˌɪnkənˈkluːsɪv/ adj not producing a definite result or complete proof of something: *inconclusive evidence* —**inconclusively** adv

incongruous /ɪnˈkɒŋgruəs/ adj strange because of being very different from other things that happen or exist in the same situation —**incongruity** /ˌɪnkənˈgruːəti/ noun [U], **incongruously** adv

inconsequential /ɪnˌkɒnsɪˈkwenʃ(ə)l/ adj not important = UNIMPORTANT

inconsiderate /ˌɪnkənˈsɪdərət/ adj not thinking about other people and their feelings = THOUGHTLESS —**inconsiderately** adv

inconsistent /ˌɪnkənˈsɪstənt/ adj **1** containing parts that do not match each other: *an inconsistent account of what happened* **2** not always behaving in the same way or producing the same results —**inconsistency** /ˌɪnkənˈsɪstənsi/ noun [C/U]

inconspicuous /ˌɪnkənˈspɪkjuəs/ adj not easily seen or noticed ≠ NOTICEABLE —**inconspicuously** adv

incontinent /ɪnˈkɒntɪnənt/ adj unable to control your BLADDER or BOWELS —**incontinence** noun [U]

inconvenience¹ /ˌɪnkənˈviːniəns/ noun [C/U] a problem or situation that causes difficulties or needs extra effort

inconvenience² /ˌɪnkənˈviːniəns/ verb [T] to cause difficulties for someone

inconvenient /ˌɪnkənˈviːniənt/ adj causing difficulties or extra effort —**inconveniently** adv

incorporate /ɪnˈkɔːpəˌreɪt/ verb [T] to add or include something as a part of something else = INCLUDE: *We'll incorporate some of these ideas in the final report.* —**incorporation** /ɪnˌkɔːpəˈreɪʃ(ə)n/ noun [U]

incorporated /ɪnˈkɔːpəˌreɪtɪd/ adj *business* an incorporated company has the legal status of a CORPORATION

incorrect /ˌɪnkəˈrekt/ adj wrong, or not accurate or true ≠ RIGHT —**incorrectly** adv

incorrigible /ɪnˈkɒrɪdʒəb(ə)l/ adj *often humorous* someone who is incorrigible does bad things or has bad habits and will not change

increase¹ /ɪnˈkriːs/ verb [I/T] ★★★ to become larger in number or amount, or to make something do this: *We have managed to increase the number of patients treated.* ♦ *The population has **increased by** 15 per cent.* ♦ *The club has been **increasing in** popularity.* ♦ *The chances of having twins **increase with** a mother's age.*

Other ways of saying **increase**

- **be on the increase** to be increasing steadily
- **go up** to increase in price or level
- **double** to increase to twice the original amount or level
- **push sth up** to increase the price or level of something
- **mount** to increase steadily
- **rise** to increase
- **rocket** (*informal*) to increase quickly and suddenly
- **soar** to increase quickly to a very high level
- **treble** to increase to three times the original amount or level

---

increase² /ˈɪŋkriːs/ noun [C/U] ★★★ a rise in the number, amount, or degree of something: *price increases* ♦ *There has been a significant **increase in** the number of young people who smoke.* ♦ *Workplace stress is **on the increase** (=increasing).*

Words often used with **increase**

*Adjectives often used with **increase** (noun)*
- **dramatic, huge, large, marked, massive, sharp, significant, substantial** + INCREASE: used about increases that are big

---

increased /ɪnˈkriːst/ adj ★★ greater in size, amount, or degree: *an increased demand for qualified doctors* ♦ *The factory was unable to cope with the increased demand for new models.* ♦ *These conditions can lead to **an increased risk** of lung cancer.*

increasingly /ɪnˈkriːsɪŋli/ adv ★★ more and more over a period of time: *Her job has become increasingly difficult.*

incredible /ɪnˈkredəb(ə)l/ adj **1** surprising or difficult to believe: *They all have incredible stories to tell.* **2** great, extreme, or extremely good: *an incredible amount of money*

incredibly /ɪnˈkredəbli/ adv **1** extremely: *That's an incredibly important issue.* **2** used for saying that something is difficult to believe: *Incredibly, his wife did not know the truth.*

incredulous /ɪnˈkredjʊləs/ adj not believing something, or showing that you do not believe something —**incredulity** /ˌɪnkrəˈdjuːləti/ noun [U], **incredulously** adv

increment /ˈɪŋkrɪmənt/ noun [C] one in a series of increases in amount or value, for example a regular increase in pay

incremental /ˌɪŋkrɪˈment(ə)l/ adj increasing gradually

incriminate /ɪnˈkrɪmɪˌneɪt/ verb [T] to show that someone is guilty of a crime, or to make someone seem guilty of it

incumbent¹ /ɪnˈkʌmbənt/ noun [C] *formal* someone who has an elected job at the present time

incumbent² /ɪnˈkʌmbənt/ adj *formal* holding an elected job at the present time
   PHRASE **it is incumbent on sb to do sth** *formal* it is someone's duty or responsibility to do something

incur /ɪnˈkɜː/ verb [T] to experience something that is unpleasant as a result of something that you have done

incurable /ɪnˈkjʊərəb(ə)l/ adj **1** not able to be cured **2** not able to be changed: *an incurable romantic* —**incurably** adv

incursion /ɪnˈkɜːʃ(ə)n/ noun [C] a sudden attack on, or move into, an area that is controlled by other people

indebted /ɪnˈdetɪd/ adj **1** grateful to someone for their help **2** owing money

indecent /ɪnˈdiːs(ə)nt/ adj offensive or shocking —**indecency** /ɪnˈdiːs(ə)nsi/ noun [U], **indecently** adv

indecision /ˌɪndɪˈsɪʒ(ə)n/ noun [U] the feeling that you are unable to make a decision

indecisive /ˌɪndɪˈsaɪsɪv/ adj **1** unable to make decisions **2** not producing a clear result or winner: *an indecisive election* —**indecisively** adv

indeed /ɪnˈdiːd/ adv ★★
1 *British* used for emphasis with 'very': *Thank you very much indeed.* ♦ *The food was very good indeed.*
2 *formal* used for adding a statement that supports and increases the effect of what you have just said: *The service will benefit students, and, indeed, all young people.*
3 *formal* used for emphasis in statements, questions, and short answers: *'Do you remember Miss Hawkings?' 'I do indeed.'*
4 *formal* used for emphasizing that something is true when there is some doubt about it: *Three of the pictures were indeed genuine Rembrandts.*

indefensible /ˌɪndɪˈfensəb(ə)l/ adj impossible to defend from criticism —**indefensibly** adv

indefinable /ˌɪndɪˈfaɪnəb(ə)l/ adj impossible to describe or explain clearly —**indefinably** adv

indefinite /ɪnˈdef(ə)nət/ adj **1** continuing into the future with no fixed end **2** not clear —**indefinitely** adv

in,definite 'article noun [C] *linguistics* the word 'a' or 'an' in the English language, or a word in another language that is used in a similar way → DEFINITE ARTICLE

indelible /ɪnˈdeləb(ə)l/ adj impossible to remove or forget —**indelibly** adv

indelicate /ɪnˈdelɪkət/ adj rude and likely to offend people —**indelicately** adv

indemnity /ɪnˈdemnəti/ noun *legal* **1** [U] insurance or protection against an injury or loss **2** [C] a payment that is made to someone who has suffered an injury or loss

indent /ɪnˈdent/ verb [T] to start a line of writing or printing further from the edge of the page than the other lines —**indented** /ɪnˈdentɪd/ adj

indentation /ˌɪndenˈteɪʃ(ə)n/ noun **1** [C] a mark or hole in the surface of something **2** [C/U] the action of indenting lines of writing, or the space that is made by indenting a line

independence /ˌɪndɪˈpendəns/ noun [U] ★★
1 freedom from control by another country or organization: *Lithuania was the first of the Soviet republics to declare its independence.*
2 the ability to make decisions and live your life free from the control or influence of other people: *Employment gave young women a measure of independence.*

independent¹ /ˌɪndɪˈpendənt/ adj ★★★
1 not controlled by another country or organization: *an independent nation*
2 not influenced by anyone else, and therefore fair: *an independent inquiry* ♦ *Seek independent legal advice before entering into an agreement.*
3 not depending on other people ≠ DEPENDENT: *Michelle is young, independent, and confident.*
4 not connected with or joined to anything else: *The equipment has its own independent power supply.*
—**independently** adv

> **Words often used with independent**
>
> *Adverbs often used with independent (adj, sense 2)*
> ■ completely, entirely, genuinely, totally, truly
> + INDEPENDENT: used for saying that someone or something is very independent

independent² /ˌɪndɪˈpendənt/ noun [C] a politician who does not belong to any political party

in-depth adj thorough and detailed: *an in-depth study*

indescribable /ˌɪndɪˈskraɪbəb(ə)l/ adj something that is indescribable is impossible to describe because it is so extreme —**indescribably** adv

indestructible /ˌɪndɪˈstrʌktəb(ə)l/ adj impossible, or very difficult, to destroy

indeterminate /ˌɪndɪˈtɜːmɪnət/ adj not known, or not clearly established

index¹ /ˈɪndeks/ (plural **indexes** or **indices** /ˈɪndɪsiːz/) noun [C] ★★
1 an alphabetical list of subjects or names at the back of a book that shows on which page they are mentioned: *Look up the term you want in the index.*
2 *business* a number that shows the price, value, or level of something that is compared with something else: *the Dow Jones index* ♦ *a wage/price index*
3 index of sth a measure of how something is changing: *The test provides parents with a reliable index of their child's progress.*

index² /ˈɪndeks/ verb [T] to arrange information in an alphabetical list

index card noun [C] one of a set of small cards on which you write information

index finger noun [C] the finger next to your thumb —*picture* → C14

Indian /ˈɪndiən/ adj relating to NATIVE AMERICANS or their culture. Some people think that this word is offensive and prefer to use the word Native American. —**Indian** noun [C]

indicate /ˈɪndɪˌkeɪt/ verb ★★★
1 [T] to express an intention, opinion, or wish in an indirect way: *Both sides indicated a willingness to solve the problem.* ♦ **+(that)** *She indicated that she would like the job.*
2 [T] to show that something will happen, is true, or exists: **+(that)** *A survey indicated that 89 per cent of people recycle paper.* ♦ *Test results will indicate whether the treatment was successful.*
3 [T] to point towards someone or something: *'Here it is,' she said, indicating the house.*
4 [I/T] *British* to SIGNAL a left or right turn in a vehicle by using an INDICATOR

indication /ˌɪndɪˈkeɪʃ(ə)n/ noun [C/U] a sign that something will happen, is true, or exists

indicative /ɪnˈdɪkətɪv/ adj *formal* showing that something will happen, is true, or exists: *These latest figures are indicative of a slowing economy.*

indicative, the /ɪnˈdɪkətɪv/ noun [singular] *linguistics* a form of a verb that is used for making statements or asking questions

indicator /ˈɪndɪˌkeɪtə/ noun [C] **1** something that shows you what condition something is in: *economic indicators* **2** one of the lights on a car that shows in which direction it is turning —*picture* → C6

indices a plural of **index**¹

indict /ɪnˈdaɪt/ verb [T] *legal* to officially accuse someone of committing a serious crime =CHARGE

indictment /ɪnˈdaɪtmənt/ noun **1** [C] **indictment of sth** something that shows how bad or wrong something is **2** [C/U] *legal* an official statement accusing someone of committing a serious crime =CHARGE

indifferent /ɪnˈdɪfrənt/ adj lacking interest or sympathy —**indifference** /ɪnˈdɪfrəns/ noun [U], **indifferently** adv

indigenous /ɪnˈdɪdʒənəs/ adj **1** indigenous people lived in a place for a very long time before other people came to live there **2** indigenous plants and animals belong to a region because they developed there

indigestion /ˌɪndɪˈdʒestʃ(ə)n/ noun [U] pain that you get in your stomach when your body has difficulty in DIGESTING the food that you have eaten

indignant /ɪnˈdɪɡnənt/ adj angry, because a situation is unfair —**indignantly** adv

indignation /ˌɪndɪɡˈneɪʃ(ə)n/ noun [U] anger about an unfair situation

indignity /ɪnˈdɪɡnəti/ noun [C/U] a situation that makes you feel embarrassed or ashamed

indirect /ˌɪndəˈrekt, ˌɪndaɪˈrekt/ adj ★
1 not using the shortest or simplest way: *We took an indirect route through the mountains.* ♦ *an indirect approach to the problem*

2 not directly connected with something but done or obtained in some other way: *an indirect criticism of the president* ◆ *indirect evidence of ancient building methods*
3 not communicated in a direct way: *He made only indirect references to his opponent.*
—**indirectly** adv

indirect object noun [C] *linguistics* in a sentence with two objects, the person or thing that receives something through the action of the verb. For example 'me' is the indirect object in 'He gave me the book'.

indirect question noun [C] *linguistics* the words that you use to report a question that someone else has asked, for example 'She asked me where I was going'

indirect speech noun [U] *linguistics* the words that you use for reporting what someone else has said, for example 'She said that we must leave' =REPORTED SPEECH

indiscreet /ˌɪndɪˈskriːt/ adj telling or showing something that should be private
—**indiscreetly** adv

indiscretion /ˌɪndɪˈskreʃ(ə)n/ noun [U] the behaviour of someone who fails to keep something private

indiscriminate /ˌɪndɪˈskrɪmɪnət/ adj done in a careless way that causes extra harm or damage —**indiscriminately** adv

indispensable /ˌɪndɪˈspensəb(ə)l/ adj something that is indispensable is so useful or important that you must have it =ESSENTIAL

indisputable /ˌɪndɪˈspjuːtəb(ə)l/ adj a fact that is indisputable is so certain that nobody can say that it is not true=UNDENIABLE
—**indisputably** adv

indistinct /ˌɪndɪˈstɪŋkt/ adj difficult to see or hear clearly=UNCLEAR ≠ CLEAR
—**indistinctly** adv

indistinguishable /ˌɪndɪˈstɪŋgwɪʃəb(ə)l/ adj people or things that are indistinguishable are so similar that you cannot see any difference between them

individual¹ /ˌɪndɪˈvɪdʒuəl/ adj ★★★
1 considered separately from other people or things: *individual pieces of furniture*
2 intended for one person only or for a particular person ≠ COLLECTIVE: *individual rights/freedom/liberty* ◆ *Choose a holiday to match your individual needs.*
3 unusual or different in an interesting way: *a very individual style*

individual² /ˌɪndɪˈvɪdʒuəl/ noun [C] ★★★ a person: *We believe in the freedom of the individual.* ◆ *The colleges were usually built with money from private individuals* (=people who represent only themselves, not organizations).

individualism /ˌɪndɪˈvɪdʒuəlɪz(ə)m/ noun [U] the behaviour of someone who does things in their own way and is not afraid to be different from others —**individualist** noun [C], **individualistic** /ˌɪndɪvɪdʒuəˈlɪstɪk/ adj

individuality /ˌɪndɪvɪdʒuˈæləti/ noun [U] the qualities that make someone or something different from all others

individually /ˌɪndɪˈvɪdʒuəli/ adv as a separate person or thing, not as part of a group

indoctrinate /ɪnˈdɒktrɪneɪt/ verb [T] to teach someone a set of beliefs so thoroughly that they do not accept any other ideas
=BRAINWASH —**indoctrination** /ɪnˌdɒktrɪˈneɪʃ(ə)n/ noun [U]

indoor /ˈɪndɔː/ adj done or used inside a building ≠ OUTDOOR: *an indoor swimming pool* ◆ *indoor plants*

indoors /ɪnˈdɔːz/ adv in or into a building ≠ OUTDOORS: *I stayed indoors all day.*

induce /ɪnˈdjuːs/ verb [T] to cause a mental or physical condition
PHRASE **induce sb to do sth** to make someone decide to do something stupid: *I can't think what induced her to marry him.*

inducement /ɪnˈdjuːsmənt/ noun [C/U] something that someone offers you in order to persuade you to do something

induction /ɪnˈdʌkʃ(ə)n/ noun [C/U] the process of formally making someone part of a group or organization

induction course noun [C] a period of training that introduces people into an organization or institution

indulge /ɪnˈdʌldʒ/ verb **1** [I/T] to allow yourself to have something enjoyable: *The new job gave him the chance to indulge his passion for music.* **2** [I] **indulge in sth** to do something that people do not approve of: *He had indulged in affairs with several women.* **3** [T] to allow someone to do what they want when you should be more strict

indulgence /ɪnˈdʌldʒ(ə)ns/ noun **1** [U] the act of doing something that is not good for you: *indulgence in alcohol* **2** [C] something enjoyable that you do for pleasure **3** [U] kind behaviour in a situation where strict behaviour is needed

indulgent /ɪnˈdʌldʒ(ə)nt/ adj allowing someone to have what they want when you should be more strict: *indulgent parents*
—**indulgently** adv

industrial /ɪnˈdʌstriəl/ adj ★★★
1 relating to industries or to the people who work in industries: *industrial development/ production*
2 an industrial region or country has a lot of industries in it
—**industrially** adv

industrial action noun [U] *British* protests in which workers deliberately work slowly or STRIKE (=refuse to work)

industrial estate noun [C] *British* an area where there are a lot of factories

industrialist /ɪnˈdʌstriəlɪst/ noun [C] someone who owns a large industrial company

industrialized /ɪnˈdʌstriəlaɪzd/ adj an industrialized country or society has a lot of industries

industrial park noun [C] an INDUSTRIAL ESTATE

industrial relations noun [plural] the relationship between the workers and managers in an industry or company

industrial tribunal noun [C] *legal* a court in

the UK that makes a decision about a disagreement between a worker and their employer

industrious /ɪnˈdʌstriəs/ adj formal someone who is industrious works very hard

industry /ˈɪndəstri/ noun ★★★
1 [U] the production of goods in factories: *The town was severely hit by the decline in industry.* ♦ *industry experts/leaders/officials*
2 [C] all the businesses involved in producing a particular type of goods or services: *the oil/fishing/electronics industry*
3 [C] an activity that has become very popular or successful and earns money for businesses: *the fitness industry*
→ COTTAGE INDUSTRY, GROWTH INDUSTRY

inebriated /ɪˈniːbrieɪtɪd/ adj formal drunk

inedible /ɪnˈedɪb(ə)l/ adj too unpleasant or poisonous to eat

ineffective /ˌɪnɪˈfektɪv/ adj something that is ineffective does not work correctly or does not do what you want it to do

ineffectual /ˌɪnɪˈfektʃuəl/ adj someone who is ineffectual does not have the ability or confidence to do something well

inefficient /ˌɪnɪˈfɪʃ(ə)nt/ adj people or methods that are inefficient do not work well because they waste time, energy, materials, or money —**inefficiency** /ˌɪnɪˈfɪʃ(ə)nsi/ noun [C/U], **inefficiently** adv

ineligible /ɪnˈelɪdʒəb(ə)l/ adj not officially allowed to do something

inept /ɪˈnept/ adj someone who is inept does something badly ≠ CAPABLE —**ineptitude** /ɪˈneptɪˌtjuːd/ noun [U], **ineptly** adv

inequality /ˌɪnɪˈkwɒləti/ noun [C/U] an unfair situation in which some people have more opportunities, power, or money than other people ≠ EQUALITY

inert /ɪˈnɜːt/ adj **1** not moving **2** science an inert substance does not produce a chemical reaction when it is mixed with other substances

inertia /ɪˈnɜːʃə/ noun [U] **1** a feeling of not wanting to do anything **2** a situation in which no progress is made **3** science the force that makes an object stay in the same position

inescapable /ˌɪnɪˈskeɪpəb(ə)l/ adj impossible to avoid or ignore

inevitable /ɪnˈevɪtəb(ə)l/ adj ★
1 impossible to avoid or prevent: *War now seems almost inevitable.* ♦ **it is inevitable that** *It is perhaps inevitable that new technology will create unemployment.*
2 the inevitable something that is certain to happen: *You must face the inevitable and try to deal with it.*
—**inevitability** /ɪnˌevɪtəˈbɪləti/ noun [U], **inevitably** adv

inexcusable /ˌɪnɪkˈskjuːzəb(ə)l/ adj inexcusable behaviour is so bad that you cannot forgive the person who behaved like that = UNFORGIVABLE

inexhaustible /ˌɪnɪɡˈzɔːstəb(ə)l/ adj never completely used up, and therefore always available

inexpensive /ˌɪnɪkˈspensɪv/ adj something that is inexpensive does not cost much money = CHEAP —**inexpensively** adv

inexperienced /ˌɪnɪkˈspɪəriənst/ adj lacking experience —**inexperience** noun [U]

inexplicable /ˌɪnɪkˈsplɪkəb(ə)l/ adj impossible to explain —**inexplicably** adv

inextricably /ˌɪnɪkˈstrɪkəbli/ adv formal used for emphasizing that you cannot separate two things

infamous /ˈɪnfəməs/ adj well known for something bad = NOTORIOUS: *an infamous criminal*

infancy /ˈɪnfənsi/ noun [U] the time when you are a very young child
PHRASE **in its infancy** something that is in its infancy has only just started to exist

infant /ˈɪnfənt/ noun [C] a very young child —picture → CHILD

infantile /ˈɪnfənˌtaɪl/ adj infantile behaviour annoys you because it is very silly

infantry /ˈɪnfəntri/ noun [U] soldiers who fight on foot, not on horses or in TANKS or other vehicles

infatuated /ɪnˈfætjuˌeɪtɪd/ adj in love with someone in a way that seems silly

infatuation /ɪnˌfætjuˈeɪʃ(ə)n/ noun [C/U] a strong feeling of love that seems silly

infect /ɪnˈfekt/ verb [T] **1** to make someone get a disease: *Thousands of people have been infected with the disease.* **2** if a computer VIRUS infects a computer, it enters the computer and causes problems

infected /ɪnˈfektɪd/ adj **1** someone who is infected has a disease **2** containing bacteria or other substances that cause disease

infection /ɪnˈfekʃ(ə)n/ noun ★★
1 [U] the process of becoming infected with a disease: *There are ways to reduce your risk of infection.*
2 [C] a disease that is caused by bacteria or by a VIRUS: *a throat infection*

infectious /ɪnˈfekʃəs/ adj **1** an infectious disease can spread from one person to another: *The condition is highly infectious.* **2** behaviour that is infectious makes other people behave in the same way: *His enthusiasm was infectious.* ♦ *an infectious laugh*

infer /ɪnˈfɜː/ verb [T] formal to form an opinion about something that is based on information that you already have → IMPLY

inference /ˈɪnf(ə)rəns/ noun [C] an opinion about something that is based on information that you already have: *It's impossible to make inferences from such a small sample.*

inferior¹ /ɪnˈfɪəriə/ adj not good, or not as good as someone or something else ≠ SUPERIOR: *This design is inferior to the one the German company proposed.* —**inferiority** /ɪnˌfɪəriˈɒrəti/ noun [U]

inferior² /ɪnˈfɪəriə/ noun [C] someone who has a lower status than someone else

inferiority complex noun [C] a strong feeling that you are not as good or important as other people

inferno /ɪnˈfɜːnəʊ/ noun [C] a large and dangerous fire

infertile /ɪnˈfɜːtaɪl/ adj not physically able to have children —**infertility** /ˌɪnfəˈtɪləti/ noun [U]

infest /ɪnˈfest/ verb [T] if a place is infested with animals or insects, there are so many of them that they might cause damage or disease

infidelity /ˌɪnfɪˈdeləti/ noun [C/U] a situation in which someone has sex with someone other than their husband, wife, or partner

infighting /ˈɪnˌfaɪtɪŋ/ noun [U] disagreements about power among the members of a group

infiltrate /ˈɪnfɪlˌtreɪt/ verb [I/T] to join an organization in order to secretly get information for its enemies —**infiltration** /ˌɪnfɪlˈtreɪʃ(ə)n/ noun [U]

infinite /ˈɪnfɪnət/ adj **1** very great, and seeming to have no limit: *a teacher with infinite patience* ♦ *The possibilities are infinite.* **2** with no physical end or limit: *Space is infinite.*

infinitely /ˈɪnfɪnətli/ adv very, or very much: *It tastes infinitely better than the last coffee we had.* ♦ *I'm infinitely grateful for your help.*

infinitive /ɪnˈfɪnətɪv/ noun [C] *linguistics* the basic form of a verb. In English, it often has the word 'to' in front of it.

infinity /ɪnˈfɪnəti/ noun [U] **1** a space, time, or distance that has no limit **2** *technical* a number that is larger than any that exists

infirmary /ɪnˈfɜːməri/ noun [C] a hospital

inflame /ɪnˈfleɪm/ verb [T] to make a situation worse by making people more angry or excited

inflamed /ɪnˈfleɪmd/ adj swollen and painful because of an infection or injury

inflammable /ɪnˈflæməb(ə)l/ adj something that is inflammable burns easily ≠ NON-FLAMMABLE → FLAMMABLE

inflammation /ˌɪnfləˈmeɪʃ(ə)n/ noun [C/U] an area on your body that is swollen and painful because of an infection or injury

inflammatory /ɪnˈflæmət(ə)ri/ adj likely to make people feel angry: *inflammatory remarks*

inflatable /ɪnˈfleɪtəb(ə)l/ adj an inflatable object must be filled with air or gas before you can use it

inflate /ɪnˈfleɪt/ verb **1** [I/T] to fill something with air or gas, or to become full of air or gas = BLOW STH UP ≠ DEFLATE **2** [T] to make a number or price higher than it should be —**inflated** adj

inflation /ɪnˈfleɪʃ(ə)n/ noun [U] ★★ **1** an economic process in which prices increase so that money becomes less valuable: *Inflation has risen again this month.* ♦ *countries with high inflation* ♦ *The rate of inflation is 3.2%.* **2** the process of filling something with air or gas

inflationary /ɪnˈfleɪʃ(ə)n(ə)ri/ adj likely to cause an increase in prices

inflection /ɪnˈflekʃ(ə)n/ noun **1** [U] the way in which the sound of your voice becomes higher and lower when you speak **2** [C/U] *linguistics* a change in the basic form of a word that gives information about the tense, number etc

inflexible /ɪnˈfleksəb(ə)l/ adj **1** not willing to change your ideas or decisions: *an inflexible attitude/system* **2** stiff and not able to bend ≠ FLEXIBLE

inflict /ɪnˈflɪkt/ verb [T] to cause something unpleasant to happen: *the environmental damage we are inflicting on the Earth*

influence¹ /ˈɪnfluəns/ noun ★★★
1 [C/U] the effect that a person or thing has on someone or something: *He couldn't hope to exert any real influence in the new department.* ♦ *Teachers have considerable influence over what is taught in the classroom.*
2 [C] a person or thing that has an effect on someone or something
PHRASE under the influence *humorous* drunk

influence² /ˈɪnfluəns/ verb [T] ★★★ to affect someone or something: *What factors influenced your decision to take the job?* ♦ *Research has shown that the weather can influence people's behaviour.*

> ### Words often used with **influence**
>
> *Adverbs often used with **influence** (verb)*
> ■ INFLUENCE + **greatly, heavily, profoundly, significantly, strongly**: used when the influence is great
>
> *Nouns often used with **influence** (verb)*
> ■ INFLUENCE + **behaviour, choice, decision, outcome, policy**: influence something that someone does

influential /ˌɪnfluˈenʃ(ə)l/ adj able to influence the way that other people think or behave: *He is one of the most influential figures in the government.*

influx /ˈɪnflʌks/ noun [C] a large number of people or things coming to a place

info /ˈɪnfəʊ/ noun [U] *informal* INFORMATION

inform /ɪnˈfɔːm/ verb [T] ★★★ to officially tell someone about something: *The President has been fully informed of developments.* ♦ *I've been reliably informed that the delivery will arrive tomorrow.* ♦ **inform sb of/about sth** *Please inform us of any changes in your circumstances.* ♦ **inform sb (that)** *Parents were informed that the school was closing.*
PHRASAL VERB inform on sb to secretly give information about someone to the police

informal /ɪnˈfɔːm(ə)l/ adj ★
1 relaxed, friendly, and not official: *The hotel has an informal atmosphere.* ♦ *They cooperate with other groups on an informal basis.*
2 suitable for relaxed friendly situations: *informal clothes/language*
—**informality** /ˌɪnfɔːˈmæləti/ noun [U], **informally** adv

informant /ɪnˈfɔːmənt/ noun [C] someone who secretly gives information about someone to the police

information /ˌɪnfəˈmeɪʃ(ə)n/ noun [U] ★★★
knowledge or facts about someone or
something: *We're not allowed to give you
any information about our client's medical
records.* ♦ *We were able to get the
information we needed from the Internet.* ♦
*He gave us a very interesting piece of
information.* ♦ *If you require any further
information, do not hesitate to call us again.*

Information is never used in the plural and
cannot be used with **an**: *I've just discovered an
interesting piece of information (*NOT an
interesting information*) about the company.* ♦
*Do you have any information about local
attractions?* ♦ *I found some information on the
Net about cheap flights to Egypt.*

infor,mation tech'nology noun [U] the use of
computers and electronic systems for
storing information

informative /ɪnˈfɔːmətɪv/ adj giving a lot of
useful information ≠ UNINFORMATIVE

informed /ɪnˈfɔːmd/ adj **1** based on good
knowledge ≠ UNINFORMED: *an informed
choice/decision* **2** someone who is informed
has a lot of knowledge about something
≠ UNINFORMED

informer /ɪnˈfɔːmə/ noun [C] an INFORMANT

infraction /ɪnˈfrækʃ(ə)n/ noun [C/U] *formal* a
situation in which someone breaks a law
or a rule

infrared /ˌɪnfrəˈred/ adj using a type of light
that cannot be seen: *infrared sensors*

infrastructure /ˈɪnfrəˌstrʌktʃə/ noun [C] the set
of systems in a country or organization
that affect how well it operates, for example
telephone and transport systems

infrequent /ɪnˈfriːkwənt/ adj something that
is infrequent does not happen very often
= RARE —**infrequently** adv

infringe /ɪnˈfrɪndʒ/ verb **1** [T] to break a law
or a rule **2** [I/T] to limit someone's legal
rights or freedom —**infringement** noun [C]

infuriate /ɪnˈfjʊəriˌeɪt/ verb [T] to make
someone extremely angry

infuriating /ɪnˈfjʊəriˌeɪtɪŋ/ adj extremely
annoying

infuse /ɪnˈfjuːz/ verb [T] to give someone or
something a particular quality: *Her
paintings are infused with a natural
strength.*

infusion /ɪnˈfjuːʒ(ə)n/ noun [C/U] **1** a drink,
medicine, or beauty treatment made by
putting something such as leaves in hot
water **2** the addition of something such as
money or a particular quality

ingenious /ɪnˈdʒiːniəs/ adj **1** using new and
clever ideas **2** good at inventing things or
solving problems —**ingeniously** adv

ingenuity /ˌɪndʒəˈnjuːəti/ noun [U] the ability
to solve problems in new and clever ways

ingest /ɪnˈdʒest/ verb [T] *technical* to eat or
drink something

ingrained /ɪnˈɡreɪnd/ adj **1** an ingrained
attitude or habit has existed for a long time
and cannot easily be changed **2** ingrained
dirt is under the surface and is difficult to
remove

ingratiate /ɪnˈɡreɪʃiˌeɪt/ verb **ingratiate
yourself
with sb** *showing disapproval* to try to get
someone's approval by doing things that
will please them

ingratiating /ɪnˈɡreɪʃiˌeɪtɪŋ/ adj *showing
disapproval* done in an attempt to get
someone's approval

ingratitude /ɪnˈɡrætɪˌtjuːd/ noun [U] the fact
that someone is not grateful for something
when you think they should be grateful

ingredient /ɪnˈɡriːdiənt/ noun [C] **1** one of the
foods or liquids that you use in making a
particular meal: *Mix all the ingredients
together carefully.* ♦ *Our products contain
only natural ingredients.* **2** one of the things
that give something its character or make
it effective: *Good communication is an
essential ingredient of good management.*

inhabit /ɪnˈhæbɪt/ verb [T] to live in a
particular place

inhabitant /ɪnˈhæbɪtənt/ noun [C] a person or
animal that lives in a particular place

inhabited /ɪnˈhæbɪtɪd/ adj a place that is
inhabited has people living in it
≠ UNINHABITED

inhale /ɪnˈheɪl/ verb [I/T] to breathe air, smoke,
or other substances into your lungs
= BREATHE (STH) IN ≠ EXHALE —**inhalation**
/ˌɪnhəˈleɪʃ(ə)n/ noun [C/U]

inherent /ɪnˈherənt, ɪnˈhɪərənt/ adj an
inherent quality is a basic feature that
gives something its character —**inherently**
adv

inherit /ɪnˈherɪt/ verb [T] **1** to receive property
or money from someone when they die: *He
inherited the business from his father.* **2** to
be born with the same appearance or
character as one of your parents: *The boys
inherited Derek's good looks.* **3** to have
something because it was left by someone
who was in your situation before you:
*These are problems we inherited from the
previous government.*

inheritance /ɪnˈherɪt(ə)ns/ noun [C] property
or money that you receive from someone
when they die

inhibit /ɪnˈhɪbɪt/ verb [T] **1** to prevent
something from developing in a normal
way **2** to make someone feel too
embarrassed to behave in a normal way

inhibited /ɪnˈhɪbɪtɪd/ adj too embarrassed to
do something ≠ UNINHIBITED

inhibition /ˌɪnhɪˈbɪʃ(ə)n/ noun [C/U] a feeling
of being too embarrassed to do what you
want to do

inhospitable /ˌɪnhɒˈspɪtəb(ə)l/ adj **1** an
inhospitable place is unpleasant to live in
2 unfriendly to guests

inhuman /ɪnˈhjuːmən/ adj someone who is
inhuman does not care when other people
are suffering

inhumane /ˌɪnhjuːˈmeɪn/ adj inhumane
treatment is very cruel ≠ HUMANE
—**inhumanely** adv

inhumanity /ˌɪnhjuːˈmænəti/ noun [C/U]
extremely cruel behaviour

initial¹ /ɪˈnɪʃ(ə)l/ adj ★★ happening at the beginning of a process, or when you first see or hear about something: *the initial stages* of the project ♦ *My initial reaction was to panic.*

initial² /ɪˈnɪʃ(ə)l/ noun [C] the first letter of a name

initial³ /ɪˈnɪʃ(ə)l/ (present participle **initialling**; past tense and past participle **initialled**) verb [T] to write your initials on something

initially /ɪˈnɪʃ(ə)li/ adv ★★ at the beginning =ORIGINALLY: *Initially she worked for us as a secretary.* ♦ *I had initially thought I wanted to write novels.*

initiate /ɪˈnɪʃiˌeɪt/ verb [T] **1** *formal* to make something start **2** to teach someone about an activity that they have never done before **3** to make someone a member of a group, often with a special ceremony —**initiation** /ɪˌnɪʃiˈeɪʃ(ə)n/ noun [singular/U]

initiative /ɪˈnɪʃətɪv/ noun ★★
1 [U] the ability to take action in an independent way: *Employees are encouraged to use their initiative if faced with a problem.* ♦ *He developed the plan on his own initiative.*
2 [C] an important action that is intended to solve a problem: *a number of initiatives designed to address the problem of child poverty*
3 the initiative [singular] the opportunity to take action before other people do: *She would have to take the initiative in order to improve their relationship.*

inject /ɪnˈdʒekt/ verb [T] **1** to put a drug into your body through your skin using a SYRINGE **2** to add something new to a situation: *Young designers are injecting new life into the fashion industry.*

inject

injection /ɪnˈdʒekʃ(ə)n/ noun [C/U] ★
1 a drug that is injected into your body, or the process of injecting it into your body: *vaccines that are given by injection* ♦ *give sb an injection Did the doctor give you a measles injection?*
2 the act of providing more money for something: *an injection of cash*

injunction /ɪnˈdʒʌŋkʃ(ə)n/ noun [C] *legal* an official order from a court that prevents someone from doing something

injure /ˈɪndʒə/ verb [T] ★ to hurt someone: *Nine people died and 54 were injured in the accident.* ♦ *No one was seriously injured.*

injured /ˈɪndʒəd/ adj hurt in an accident or attack: *The injured man was taken to hospital.*

injury /ˈɪndʒəri/ noun [C/U] ★★★ physical harm: *an eye/leg injury* ♦ *All the passengers in the vehicle escaped injury.* ♦ *Both drivers sustained (=received) multiple injuries.*

Words often used with injury

Adjectives often used with injury
■ **serious, severe** + INJURY: used when someone is injured a lot
■ **minor, slight** + INJURY: used when the injury is not very bad

injustice /ɪnˈdʒʌstɪs/ noun [C/U] an unfair way of treating someone
PHRASE do sb an injustice to treat someone in an unfair way, for example by saying something bad about them that is not true

ink /ɪŋk/ noun [U] a black or coloured liquid that is used for writing, drawing, or printing

ink-jet ˌprinter noun [C] a type of printer for computers that prints using very small drops of ink

inkling /ˈɪŋklɪŋ/ noun **have an inkling** to think that something might be happening because of a small piece of information that you have

inland¹ /ˈɪnlənd/ adj not near a coast

inland² /ɪnˈlænd/ adv in a direction away from the coast

ˌInland ˈRevenue, the the government organization that is responsible for collecting taxes in the UK

ˈin-laws noun [plural] the parents or other relatives of your husband or wife

inlet /ˈɪnlət/ noun [C] **1** a long narrow area of water that continues into the land from a lake or sea **2** a tube through which a liquid or gas goes into a machine ≠ OUTLET

ˌin-line ˈskating noun [U] the activity of moving on boots called **in-line skates** that each have a single row of narrow wheels on them

in-line skates

inmate /ˈɪnˌmeɪt/ noun [C] someone who is kept in a prison or similar institution

inn /ɪn/ noun [C] a small hotel or PUB

innate /ɪˈneɪt/ adj an innate quality or ability is one that you have always had =INHERENT —**innately** adv

inner /ˈɪnə/ adj ★
1 inside or further towards the centre of

something ≠ OUTER: *the inner ear*
2 close to the centre of a city: *inner London*
3 private, or personal: *inner feelings*

,inner 'circle noun [C] a small group of people who have a lot of power within a larger group

,inner 'city noun [C] an area near the centre of a large city where a lot of social problems exist —**,inner-'city** adj

innermost /'ɪnəməʊst/ adj **1** your innermost thoughts and feelings are very personal and private **2** closest to the centre of something ≠ OUTERMOST

innings /'ɪnɪŋz/ (plural **innings**) noun [C] a period in a CRICKET match during which one player or one team tries to score RUNS

innocence /'ɪnəs(ə)ns/ noun [U] **1** the state of not being guilty of a crime or anything bad: *This new evidence would hopefully prove his innocence.* **2** lack of experience of life that makes you trust people too much

innocent /'ɪnəs(ə)nt/ adj ★
1 not guilty of a crime or anything bad ≠ GUILTY: *Under the law, everyone is considered innocent until proved guilty.* ♦ *the innocent victims of terrorism* ♦ *She was completely innocent of any crime.*
2 not intended to harm or upset anyone: *an innocent remark/mistake*
3 someone who is innocent does not have much experience of life and tends to trust people too much
—**innocently** adv

innocuous /ɪ'nɒkjuəs/ adj not likely to offend or upset anyone

innovation /,ɪnəʊ'veɪʃ(ə)n/ noun [C/U] a new idea or piece of equipment, or the use of new ideas or equipment

innovative /'ɪnəveɪtɪv, 'ɪnəvətɪv/ adj new and advanced

innuendo /,ɪnju'endəʊ/ (plural **innuendoes** or **innuendos**) noun [C/U] a remark that deliberately suggests something about sex but does not say it directly, or the use of remarks like this

innumerable /ɪ'nju:mərəb(ə)l/ adj *formal* too many to be counted: *There are innumerable examples of his generous nature.*

inoffensive /,ɪnə'fensɪv/ adj unlikely to offend anyone

inordinate /ɪn'ɔ:dɪnət/ adj *formal* much more than you expect or want —**inordinately** adv

inpatient /'ɪn,peɪʃ(ə)nt/ noun [C] someone who stays and sleeps in hospital while they are getting treatment → OUTPATIENT

input¹ /'ɪnpʊt/ noun [U] **1** comments and suggestions that you make as part of a discussion **2** information that you put into a computer ≠ OUTPUT **3** electrical power that is put into a machine

input² /'ɪnpʊt/ (present participle **inputting**; past tense and past participle **input**) verb [T] to put information into a computer

inquest /'ɪŋkwest/ noun [C] an official attempt by a court to find the cause of someone's death

inquire /ɪn'kwaɪə/ verb [I/T] to ask someone

for information about something: *I am writing to inquire whether you have any positions available.* —**inquirer** noun [C]
PHRASAL VERB in'quire ,into sth to try to find out the truth about something: *The committee inquired into complaints made by several prisoners.*

inquiring /ɪn'kwaɪərɪŋ/ adj **1** keen to learn about new things: *an inquiring mind* **2** showing that you want more information about something: *an inquiring look/ expression*

inquiry /ɪn'kwaɪri/ noun ★★
1 [C] a question that is intended to get information about someone or something: *There have already been over 300 inquiries from people interested.* ♦ *Police are making inquiries in the neighbourhood.*
2 [C/U] a process of trying to find out more information about something: *The public is demanding an official inquiry into the incident.*

inquisitive /ɪn'kwɪzətɪv/ adj keen to learn about a lot of different things, and asking a lot of questions = CURIOUS: *an inquisitive journalist* —**inquisitively** adv

inroads /'ɪn,rəʊdz/ noun **make inroads into/in/ on sth** to take or use a large part of something: *European cars have started to make inroads into the Japanese market.*

insane /ɪn'seɪn/ adj **1** *informal* very stupid or crazy: *You'd be totally insane to see him again.* **2** suffering from very severe mental illness —**insanely** adv

insanity /ɪn'sænəti/ noun [U] **1** very severe mental illness **2** *informal* very stupid or crazy behaviour

insatiable /ɪn'seɪʃəb(ə)l/ adj always wanting more and never feeling satisfied —**insatiably** adv

inscribe /ɪn'skraɪb/ verb [T] to write or cut words on or in something: *a gold watch inscribed with her initials*

inscription /ɪn'skrɪpʃ(ə)n/ noun [C] a piece of writing that is written on or cut into something

inscrutable /ɪn'skru:təb(ə)l/ adj making it impossible for other people to understand what you are thinking or feeling: *His face remained inscrutable and unsmiling.*

insect /'ɪnsekt/ noun [C] ★ a small animal that has six legs and often has wings

insecticide /ɪn'sekti,saɪd/ noun [C] a chemical for killing insects

insecure /,ɪnsɪ'kjʊə/ adj **1** not confident about yourself: *She's always been very insecure about the way she looks.* **2** not safe or protected: *In this economy, all our jobs are insecure.* —**insecurity** /,ɪnsɪ'kjʊərəti/ noun [C/U]

insemination /ɪn,semɪ'neɪʃ(ə)n/ noun [U] the process of putting SPERM into a woman or female animal to make her pregnant

insensitive /ɪn'sensətɪv/ adj not noticing or caring about other people's feelings and not worrying that the things you say or do may upset them —**insensitively** adv,

insensitivity /ˌɪnˌsensəˈtɪvəti/ noun [U]

inseparable /ɪnˈsep(ə)rəb(ə)l/ adj **1** people who are inseparable spend all their time together **2** things that are inseparable cannot exist or be considered separately: *His personal morality was inseparable from his religious beliefs.* —**inseparably** adv

insert

insert¹ /ɪnˈsɜːt/ verb [T] to put something into something else: **insert sth into/in sth** *Insert the plug into the earphone socket.* —**insertion** /ɪnˈsɜːʃ(ə)n/ noun [C/U]

insert² /ˈɪnsɜːt/ noun [C] something that is put into something else: *advertising inserts in the Sunday newspaper*

inset /ˈɪnset/ noun [C] **1** a small picture or map inside a larger one **2** something that is put in something else: *a gold ring with diamond insets*

inside¹ /ɪnˈsaɪd/ grammar word ★★★

> **Inside** can be:
> ■ a **preposition**: *What's inside the envelope?*
> ■ an **adverb**: *I opened the box and looked inside.*
> ■ an **adjective**: *the inside pages of a newspaper*

1 within a container or place, or in the inner part of something ≠ OUTSIDE: *I always keep important papers locked inside my desk.* ♦ *There were lights on inside and I could hear voices.* ♦ *houses without running water or an inside toilet* ♦ *She was standing just inside the door.* ♦ *The melon was still green inside.*
2 into a place or container ≠ OUTSIDE: *As I walked past the door, I glanced inside.* ♦ *You're not allowed to go inside the museum without paying.* ♦ *She reached inside her handbag and pulled out an envelope.*
3 within an organization or group ≠ OUTSIDE: *There is a battle being fought inside the Conservative Party.* ♦ *The rumours are coming from inside the company.*
4 only known by people who belong to a particular organization or group: *The thieves clearly had inside information.*

inside² /ˈɪnsaɪd/ noun [C] the inner part of something: *I had never seen the inside of a prison before.*

inside ˈleg noun [C] *British* the length of your leg measured on the inside from the top to the foot

inside ˈout adv with the inside part facing out: *Your jumper is on inside out.*
> **PHRASE** **know sb/sth inside out** to know someone or something very well

insider /ˌɪnˈsaɪdə/ noun [C] someone within an organization or group who knows about all the things happening in it

inˌsider ˈdealing or **inˌsider ˈtrading** noun [U] the crime of buying or selling shares in a company using information that is available only to people working within that company

insidious /ɪnˈsɪdiəs/ adj something that is insidious is dangerous because it seems to be harmless or not important but in fact causes harm or damage: *the insidious effects of gossip* —**insidiously** adv

insight /ˈɪnsaɪt/ noun [C/U] the ability to notice and understand a lot about people or situations, or a chance to do this: *Children can sometimes show quite remarkable insight.*

insignia /ɪnˈsɪɡniə/ (plural **insignia**) noun [C] a mark or sign that shows someone's rank or status, or shows what organization they belong to

insignificant /ˌɪnsɪɡˈnɪfɪkənt/ adj not large or important enough to be worth considering: *insignificant details* —**insignificance** /ˌɪnsɪɡˈnɪfɪkəns/ noun [U], **insignificantly** adv

insincere /ˌɪnsɪnˈsɪə/ adj not expressing your feelings or opinions honestly: *an insincere smile* —**insincerely** adv, **insincerity** /ˌɪnsɪnˈserəti/ noun [U]

insinuate /ɪnˈsɪnjuˌeɪt/ verb [T] to say something unpleasant in an indirect way: *He even went as far as insinuating that Roger was a liar.* —**insinuation** /ɪnˌsɪnjuˈeɪʃ(ə)n/ noun [C/U]

insipid /ɪnˈsɪpɪd/ adj *formal* boring, dull, or pale, with no interesting features

insist /ɪnˈsɪst/ verb [I/T] ★★
1 to say very firmly that something must happen or be done: *You must see a doctor immediately – I insist.* ♦ *Some companies insist on staff undergoing regular medical checks.* ♦ **+(that)** *She insisted that we stay at her house instead of a hotel.*
2 to keep saying very firmly that something is true: *He has insisted on his innocence from the beginning.* ♦ **+(that)** *The school insists that it is doing everything it can to cooperate.*
> **PHRASAL VERB** **inˈsist ˌon sth** or **inˈsist uˌpon sth 1** to say that you must have something: *She insists upon fresh fruit every morning.* **2 insist on/upon doing sth** to keep doing something that annoys people: *Why do you insist on leaving your dirty clothes all over the floor?*

insistence /ɪnˈsɪstəns/ noun [U] a very firm statement that something must happen or that something is true: *Despite his insistence that he wasn't involved, most people think he's dishonest.*

insistent /ɪnˈsɪstənt/ adj saying very firmly that something must happen or that something is true: *John was insistent that we shouldn't tell anyone else about our plans.* —**insistently** adv

insofar as /ˌɪnsəʊˈfɑːr æz/ conjunction *formal* to the degree that something happens or is true: *She cites other scholars' work only insofar as it supports her own theories.*

insolent /ˈɪnsələnt/ adj rude, especially when you should be showing respect ≠ POLITE —**insolence** /ˈɪnsələns/ noun [U], **insolently** adv

insoluble /ɪnˈsɒljʊb(ə)l/ adj **1** an insoluble substance does not DISSOLVE in liquid **2** impossible to solve

insolvent /ɪnˈsɒlvənt/ adj formal not having enough money to pay what you owe =BANKRUPT —**insolvency** /ɪnˈsɒlvənsi/ noun [U]

insomnia /ɪnˈsɒmniə/ noun [U] a medical condition in which you have difficulty sleeping —**insomniac** /ɪnˈsɒmniˌæk/ noun [C]

inspect /ɪnˈspekt/ verb [T] **1** to check something by looking at it carefully =EXAMINE: *Engineers will inspect the site later today.* ♦ *Make sure you inspect the goods carefully as soon as you receive them.* ♦ **inspect sth for sth** *The young plants are regularly inspected for disease and insects.* **2** to officially visit a place and check to see that everything is as it should be: *Restaurants are inspected regularly by the health department.*

inspection /ɪnˈspekʃ(ə)n/ noun [C/U] ★ **1** an official process of checking that things are as they should be: *All countries must allow international inspection of their nuclear weapons sites.* **2** an action of looking at something carefully to check it: *The documents are available for public inspection.*

inspector /ɪnˈspektə/ noun [C] **1** an official whose job is to check that things are in the correct condition, or that people are doing what they should: *health inspectors* **2** a senior police officer **3** British someone whose job is to check people's tickets on buses and trains

inspiration /ˌɪnspəˈreɪʃ(ə)n/ noun [C/U] someone or something that gives you the enthusiasm and new ideas to create something, or a feeling of enthusiasm like this: *Her short story was the original inspiration for the film.*
   PHRASE **be an inspiration to sb** to be so successful, or to deal with a difficult situation so well, that other people admire you and want to be like you: *She has been an inspiration to other young athletes from a similar background.* —**inspirational** adj

inspire /ɪnˈspaɪə/ verb [T] **1** to give someone the enthusiasm or idea to do or create something: *The sea inspired many of the artist's later paintings.* **2** to give people a particular feeling: *His athletic ability inspires awe in everyone who sees him in action.* ♦ *Her resignation will do little to inspire confidence in a company that is already struggling.* —**inspiring** adj

inspired /ɪnˈspaɪəd/ adj very special, or very impressive ≠ UNINSPIRED: *an inspired performance*

instability /ˌɪnstəˈbɪləti/ noun [U] a situation

or someone's mental state that keeps changing, so that you do not know what might happen: *This policy would lead to greater instability in the region.*

install /ɪnˈstɔːl/ verb [T] ★ to put a piece of equipment somewhere or a piece of software into a computer and make it ready for use: *Have you installed a smoke alarm in your office?* ♦ *It's important to install a virus checker.* —**installation** /ˌɪnstəˈleɪʃ(ə)n/ noun [C/U]

instalment /ɪnˈstɔːlmənt/ noun [C] **1** one of several payments that an amount you owe is divided into: *We paid for the television in 12 monthly instalments.* **2** one of several parts of a story or article that are published at different times in a magazine or newspaper

instance /ˈɪnstəns/ noun [C] ★★★ an example of something happening: *I have not found a single instance where someone was actually denied their right to vote.* ♦ *The study discusses instances of water pollution in this neighbourhood.*
   PHRASE **for instance** for example: *They intend to provide information, via the Internet for instance.*

instant¹ /ˈɪnstənt/ adj **1** immediate: *We can't promise instant solutions, but we can promise to listen.* ♦ *They took an instant liking to each other.* **2** instant food or drink can be prepared very quickly, usually by adding hot water: *instant coffee/soup* —**instantly** adv

instant² /ˈɪnstənt/ noun [C] a moment: *It took only an instant for him to react.*

instantaneous /ˌɪnstənˈteɪniəs/ adj immediate —**instantaneously** adv

instant messaging noun [U] computing the activity of communicating with someone directly over the Internet and replying to their messages as soon as they arrive

instead /ɪnˈsted/ adv ★★★ used for saying that one person, thing, or action replaces another: *If you don't have olive oil, you can use sunflower oil instead.* ♦ *Tickets will cost only £5, instead of the usual £6.50.* ♦ **instead of doing sth** *Can't we deal with this now instead of waiting until tomorrow?*

instep /ˈɪnˌstep/ noun [C] the raised part in the middle of your foot —*picture* → C14

instigate /ˈɪnstɪˌɡeɪt/ verb [T] formal to make something start —**instigation** /ˌɪnstɪˈɡeɪʃ(ə)n/ noun [U], **instigator** noun [C]

instil /ɪnˈstɪl/ (present participle **instilling**; past tense and past participle **instilled**) verb [T] to make someone have a particular feeling or belief: *His parents had instilled a lasting love of music in him.*

instinct /ˈɪnstɪŋkt/ noun [C/U] ★ **1** a natural tendency to behave in a particular way: *the instinct of ducklings to follow their mother* ♦ *the basic instinct for survival* **2** a natural ability to know what to do in a particular situation: *Instinct told me that it would be unwise to return home.* ♦ *My first* *instinct was to turn and run.* ♦ *It's always best to **trust your instincts**.*

instinctive /ɪnˈstɪŋktɪv/ adj done without thinking, because of a natural tendency or ability: *His reaction was purely instinctive.* —**instinctively** adv

institute¹ /ˈɪnstɪˌtjuːt/ noun [C] an organization that does a particular type of research or educational work

institute² /ˈɪnstɪˌtjuːt/ verb [T] *formal* to start something such as a system or an official process: *The company has instituted new security measures for its staff.*

institution /ˌɪnstɪˈtjuːʃ(ə)n/ noun [C] ★★★
1 a large organization such as a bank, hospital, university, or prison: *a financial/educational/charitable institution* ♦ *an institution of higher education*
2 a hospital or other building where people are looked after for a long time, for example if they are disabled or mentally ill
3 an important tradition on which society is based: *the institution of marriage* —**institutional** adj

instruct /ɪnˈstrʌkt/ verb [T] *formal* **1** to tell someone to do something, especially officially: *He instructed his men to collect information about troop movements.* **2** to teach someone a particular subject or skill: *All children are instructed in the use of the library.*

instruction /ɪnˈstrʌkʃ(ə)n/ noun ★★★
1 [C] a statement of something that must be done, or an explanation of how to do or use something: *Step-by-step instructions for assembling the workbench are included.* ♦ *I tried to **follow her instructions**, but I got confused.* ♦ **instructions to do sth** *The players were given strict instructions not to leave the hotel.*
2 [U] the teaching of a particular subject or skill: *golf/ski/maths instruction*

Words often used with **instruction**

*Verbs often used with **instruction** (sense 1)*
- **disobey, disregard, ignore** + INSTRUCTION: not do what someone tells you to do
- **carry out, follow, obey** + INSTRUCTION: do what someone tells you to do
- **give, issue, provide** + INSTRUCTION: tell someone what to do

---

instructive /ɪnˈstrʌktɪv/ adj giving useful information

instructor /ɪnˈstrʌktə/ noun [C] someone whose job is to teach a skill or a sport

instrument /ˈɪnstrʊmənt/ noun [C] ★★★
1 a tool that is used in science, medicine, or technology: *scientific instruments such as microscopes*
2 a MUSICAL INSTRUMENT, for example a piano or a guitar: *Do you **play an instrument**?*
3 a piece of equipment that measures something such as position, speed, or temperature: *Your compass and clock are the most essential instruments in sailing.*

instrumental /ˌɪnstrʊˈment(ə)l/ adj **1** involved

in an important way in making something happen: *The general was instrumental in helping both sides to reach a compromise.*
2 instrumental music is played by instruments only rather than being sung

insubordinate /ˌɪnsəˈbɔːdɪnət/ adj *formal* not obeying or not showing respect to someone who has authority over you —**insubordination** /ˌɪnsəbɔːdɪˈneɪʃ(ə)n/ noun [U]

insubstantial /ˌɪnsəbˈstænʃ(ə)l/ adj *formal* not very large or strong: *insubstantial evidence*

insufficient /ˌɪnsəˈfɪʃ(ə)nt/ adj not enough: *There are insufficient funds in your account.* —**insufficiently** adv

insular /ˈɪnsjʊlə/ adj not interested in meeting new people or learning new things —**insularity** /ˌɪnsjʊˈlærəti/ noun [U]

insulate /ˈɪnsjʊˌleɪt/ verb [T] **1** to cover something in order to prevent heat, cold, noise, or electricity from passing through it **2** to protect someone from unpleasant knowledge or harmful experiences

insulation /ˌɪnsjʊˈleɪʃ(ə)n/ noun [U] material that is used for preventing heat, cold, noise, or electricity from passing through something

insulin /ˈɪnsjʊlɪn/ noun [U] a substance that is produced in your body that controls the level of sugar in your blood

insult¹ /ˈɪnsʌlt/ noun [C] **1** an offensive remark **2** something that seems to show a lack of respect for someone or something: *This exam is an insult to my students' intelligence.*
PHRASE add insult to injury to do something that makes a bad situation even worse

insult² /ɪnˈsʌlt/ verb [T] ★ to say or do something that is offensive: *She has no right to insult us like that.* ♦ *You'll insult the cook if you don't at least taste the meal.* —**insulting** adj

insurance /ɪnˈʃʊərəns/ noun ★★★
1 [U] an arrangement in which you regularly pay a company an amount of money so that they will give you money if something that you own is damaged, lost, or stolen, or if you die or are ill or injured: *health/life/car insurance* ♦ *an insurance company/policy* ♦ *Do you **have insurance** for the house yet?*
2 [singular/U] a situation or action that is intended to prevent something bad from happening or affecting you: *The hostages were being held as **insurance against** further bombing raids.*
→ NATIONAL INSURANCE

insure /ɪnˈʃʊə/ verb [T] to buy or provide insurance for someone or something: *They've insured the painting for over half a million pounds.*

insurmountable /ˌɪnsəˈmaʊntəb(ə)l/ adj *formal* impossible to deal with successfully

insurrection /ˌɪnsəˈrekʃ(ə)n/ noun [C/U] an attempt by a large group of people to take control of their country by force

intact /ɪnˈtækt/ adj not harmed, damaged, or lacking any parts

intake /ˈɪnteɪk/ noun **1** [singular/U] the number

of people who are accepted by an institution such as a school, university, or company at one time **2** [singular] the amount of something that you eat or drink: *You should reduce your intake of salt.*

intangible /ɪnˈtændʒəb(ə)l/ adj not able to be touched or measured, and difficult to describe or explain: *She has that intangible quality that a player must possess to be a champion.*

integral /ˈɪntɪɡrəl, ɪnˈteɡrəl/ adj **1** forming an essential part of something and needed to make it complete: *Home visits by our trained technicians are an integral part of the service.* **2** *British* built to form part of something larger and not separate from it: *a house with an integral garage* —**integrally** adv

integrate /ˈɪntɪˌɡreɪt/ verb **1** [I/T] to become a full member of a society or group and be involved completely in its activities, or to help someone to do this **2** [T] to connect or combine two or more things so that together they form an effective unit or system: *We provide resources that can be integrated into the national teaching programme.* —**integration** /ˌɪntɪˈɡreɪʃ(ə)n/ noun [U]

integrity /ɪnˈteɡrəti/ noun [U] the quality of always behaving honestly and according to moral principles

intellect /ˈɪntəlekt/ noun [U] the ability to think in an intelligent way and to understand difficult or complicated ideas and subjects: *a lawyer of great intellect*

intellectual¹ /ˌɪntəˈlektʃuəl/ adj **1** relating to the ability to think in an intelligent way and to understand things **2** well educated and interested in serious subjects at an advanced level —**intellectually** adv

intellectual² /ˌɪntəˈlektʃuəl/ noun [C] someone who is well educated and interested in serious subjects at an advanced level

intellectual property noun [U] *legal* something that someone has created or invented and that no one else is legally allowed to make, copy, or sell

intelligence /ɪnˈtelɪdʒ(ə)ns/ noun [U] ★★
1 the ability to understand and think about things, and to gain and use knowledge: *Maria had spirit and intelligence as well as beauty.* ♦ *a person of **average intelligence*** **2** information that is collected about the secret plans and activities of a foreign government, enemy etc: *military intelligence*

intelligent /ɪnˈtelɪdʒ(ə)nt/ adj ★★ good at thinking, understanding, and learning =CLEVER ≠ UNINTELLIGENT: *He was **highly intelligent**, but disliked studying.* —**intelligently** adv

> Other ways of saying **intelligent**
> - **bright** intelligent and quick to understand things
> - **brilliant** extremely intelligent

- **clever** able to understand and learn things quickly: used especially in British English. In American English, **clever** often means intelligent and slightly dishonest
- **quick** able to understand things quickly and react to them quickly
- **sharp** quick to notice and understand things
- **smart** able to understand and learn things quickly
- **wise** able to use your knowledge and experience to judge what is right or true

intelligible /ɪnˈtelɪdʒəb(ə)l/ adj clear or simple enough to understand
≠ UNINTELLIGIBLE

intend /ɪnˈtend/ verb [T] ★★★
1 to have a plan in your mind to do something: **intend to do sth** *What do you intend to do about this?* ♦ **intend doing sth** *I intend using the report as evidence to support my case.* ♦ **intend sb/sth to do sth** *I never intended it to turn out like that.* ♦ **intend sb sth** *She felt certain that he intended her no harm.*
2 to want something to have a particular meaning: *I'm sorry – no offence was intended.* ♦ **intend sth as sth** *Perhaps it was intended as a joke.* ♦ **intend sth by sth** *She wondered what he intended by that statement.*
> **PHRASE** **be intended for** to be made, done, or said for a particular purpose or person: *The book is intended for use in the classroom.* ♦ *The meat was never intended for human consumption.*

> Word family: **intend**
>
> *Words in the same family as **intend***
> - **intended** *adj*
> - **intentional** *adj*
> - **intention** *n*
> - **unintended** *adj*
> - **unintentional** *adj*
> - **intent** *n*

intense /ɪnˈtens/ adj ★
1 very great, or extreme: *The pain was intense.* ♦ *the intense heat of the midday sun* ♦ *He's been under **intense pressure**.*
2 involving or done with a lot of effort, energy, attention etc: *This type of work requires intense concentration.*
3 feeling and showing emotions in a very strong way: *an intense person/personality/nature* —**intensely** adv, **intensity** noun [U]

intensify /ɪnˈtensɪˌfaɪ/ verb [I/T] if something intensifies, or if you intensify it, it becomes greater, stronger, or more extreme —**intensification** /ɪnˌtensɪfɪˈkeɪʃ(ə)n/ noun [U]

intensive /ɪnˈtensɪv/ adj involving a lot of effort, energy, learning, or attention in a short period of time: *three weeks of intensive negotiations* —**intensively** adv

intensive care noun [U] the department of a hospital for people who are very ill or badly injured and must be watched closely by doctors and nurses

intent¹ /ɪnˈtent/ noun [singular/U] *formal* the intention to do something

intent² /ɪnˈtent/ adj **1** concentrating hard on

something **2** determined to do something: *The people of the area are intent on keeping their club open.* —**intently** adv

intention /ɪnˈtenʃ(ə)n/ noun [C/U] ★★★ a plan in your mind to do something: *We **have no intention of** giving up.* ♦ *I **had every intention of** phoning* (=I really intended to phone) *her this morning, but I didn't get a chance.* ♦ *No one goes to college **with the intention of** failing.* ♦ ***intention to do sth** It wasn't my intention to upset you.*

intentional /ɪnˈtenʃ(ə)nəl/ adj deliberate ≠ UNINTENTIONAL: *I'm sorry I hurt you, but it wasn't intentional.* —**intentionally** adv

interact /ˌɪntərˈækt/ verb [I] **1** if people interact, they communicate with and react to each other: *In large classes, children feel that they cannot interact with the teacher properly.* **2** if things interact, they affect or change each other in some way —**interaction** /ˌɪntərˈækʃ(ə)n/ noun [C/U]

interactive /ˌɪntərˈæktɪv/ adj **1** an interactive computer program, video etc reacts to the information and instructions that you give it **2** involving people communicating with each other and reacting to each other —**interactively** adv

intercept /ˌɪntəˈsept/ verb [T] to stop, catch, or take control of someone or something before they can get to the place they are going to —**interception** /ˌɪntəˈsepʃ(ə)n/ noun [U]

interchangeable /ˌɪntəˈtʃeɪndʒəb(ə)l/ adj things that are interchangeable can be put or used in place of each other with the same effect —**interchangeably** adv

intercom /ˈɪntəˌkɒm/ noun [C] a system that allows people in different parts of a building, aircraft, or ship to speak to each other

intercontinental /ˌɪntəˌkɒntɪˈnent(ə)l/ adj between CONTINENTS: *intercontinental flights*

intercourse /ˈɪntəkɔːs/ noun [U] SEXUAL INTERCOURSE

interdependent /ˌɪntədɪˈpendənt/ adj things that are interdependent are related to each other in such a close way that each one needs the others in order to exist —**interdependence** noun [U]

interest¹ /ˈɪntrəst/ noun ★★★

1 a need to know	**5** advantage/benefit
2 quality attracting you	**6** right to own part of sth
3 activity you enjoy	**+ PHRASE**
4 money paid/received	

1 [singular/U] a feeling of wanting to know about or take part in something: *an **interest in** politics* ♦ *Apparently several buyers have expressed an interest in the deal.* ♦ *People are losing interest in the election.*
2 [U] the quality that something has that makes you notice it and want to know about it or take part in it: *The city has lots of museums and **places of interest**.* ♦ *publications that may **be of interest** to the self-employed* → HUMAN INTEREST

3 [C] an activity that you enjoy doing when you are not working: *Tell us about your interests and hobbies.*
4 [U] the money that a bank charges or pays you when you borrow or save money: *an increase on the interest charged on personal loans* ♦ *low **interest rates*** ♦ *We were required to repay the loan **with interest**.*
5 [C/U] an advantage or benefit to someone or something: *Publication of the documents is not **in the public interest**.* ♦ *It's **in their own interest** to cooperate.* ♦ *The council doesn't believe the scheme is **in the best interests of** pupils.*
6 [C] business a legal right to own part of a business or property

> **PHRASE** **in the interest(s) of** sth in order to preserve, develop, or achieve something: *It is vital that we reform the system in the interests of fairness to everyone.*

interest² /ˈɪntrəst/ verb [T] to make someone want to know about or take part in something: *Oceanography has always interested me.*

interested /ˈɪntrəstɪd/ adj ★★★
1 wanting to know about or take part in something ≠ UNINTERESTED: *Joe's always been **interested in** politics.*
2 willing or keen to do something: *We're going to the cinema. Are you interested* (=would you like to come too)*?* ♦ *Is anyone **interested in** a quick walk before lunch?*

> **Words often used with interested**
>
> *Adverbs often used with **interested** (sense 1)*
> ■ **deeply, extremely, genuinely, seriously +** INTERESTED: used for saying that someone is very interested

> ■ **Interested** describes how you feel: *I am interested in art.* ♦ *She didn't look very interested.*
> ■ **Interesting** describes things or situations that make you feel interested: *I find history very interesting.* ♦ *It was a really interesting lecture.*

interesting /ˈɪntrəstɪŋ/ adj ★★★ making you want to pay attention or know more: *an interesting topic* ♦ *She's a very interesting speaker.* ♦ *It would be interesting to hear their views on this problem.* ♦ ***it is interesting that/how** It's interesting that she suddenly changed her attitude.* —**interestingly** adv

ˈinterest ˌrate noun [C] the percentage that a bank charges or pays you in interest when you borrow money from it or keep money in an account

interface /ˈɪntəfeɪs/ noun [C] computing a point in a computer system where information passes from one part of the system to another, or from the computer to the person using it

interfere /ˌɪntəˈfɪə/ verb [I] to deliberately become involved in a situation, although you have no right to do this: *I don't want to interfere, but maybe you'd better listen to me.* ♦ *I don't want your mother interfering in our affairs.*

PHRASAL VERB **inter·fere with sth** to prevent something from happening or developing in the correct way: *Mum says I can get a job if it doesn't interfere with my homework.*

interference /ˌɪntəˈfɪərəns/ noun [U] **1** the process of deliberately becoming involved in a situation, although you have no right to do this: *They expressed resentment at outside interference in their domestic affairs.* **2** radio signals that make the sound or picture of a radio or television programme difficult to hear or see clearly, or the noise caused by this

interim¹ /ˈɪntərɪm/ adj intended to last or to perform an activity only until someone or something permanent or final is available: *an interim government/president/report*

interim² /ˈɪntərɪm/ noun **in the interim** during the time between one thing happening and another

interior /ɪnˈtɪəriə/ noun **1** [C] the inside part of something ≠ EXTERIOR: *The car has a surprisingly spacious interior.* **2 the interior** [singular] the inner part of a country or region

in·terior de·signer noun [C] someone whose job is to choose the colours of the walls and carpets and the style of the furniture for the inside of a room or building —**in·terior de·sign** noun [U]

interject /ˌɪntəˈdʒekt/ verb [I/T] *formal* to say something suddenly that interrupts the person who is speaking

interjection /ˌɪntəˈdʒekʃ(ə)n/ noun [C] *linguistics* a word or phrase that you use in speech for expressing a strong emotion such as surprise or anger. 'Oh' and 'ouch' are interjections =EXCLAMATION

interlude /ˈɪntəluːd/ noun [C] a short period of time between two longer periods

intermediary /ˌɪntəˈmiːdiəri/ noun [C] someone who talks to each of the people or groups that are involved in something in order to help them to agree about it

intermediate /ˌɪntəˈmiːdiət/ adj **1** in between two stages, places, levels, times etc: *The cells have a series of intermediate stages before they develop fully.* **2** at an academic level below advanced: *an intermediate English course* —**intermediately** adv

interminable /ɪnˈtɜːmɪnəb(ə)l/ adj continuing for a long time in a boring or annoying way: *an interminable journey/speech/meeting* —**interminably** adv

intermission /ˌɪntəˈmɪʃ(ə)n/ noun [C] a short break in the middle of a play, film, concert etc =INTERVAL

intermittent /ˌɪntəˈmɪt(ə)nt/ adj happening sometimes but not regularly or often: *a dull day with intermittent rain* —**intermittently** adv

intern¹ /ɪnˈtɜːn/ verb [T] to put someone in a prison without officially accusing them of a crime, especially for political reasons —**internment** noun [U]

intern² /ˈɪntɜːn/ noun [C] *American* a student who works in a job in order to get experience

internal /ɪnˈtɜːn(ə)l/ adj ★★ **1** existing or happening within a country, organization, or system ≠ EXTERNAL: *an internal memo ♦ They were opposed to foreign involvement in their internal affairs.* **2** existing or happening inside your body or your mind: *internal bleeding/injuries/organs ♦ an internal struggle* **3** existing or happening inside an object or building ≠ EXTERNAL: *internal walls* —**internally** adv

international /ˌɪntəˈnæʃ(ə)nəl/ adj ★★★ involving several countries, or existing between countries: *international trade/relations/diplomacy ♦ an international flight ♦ International aid organizations are appealing for donations from western governments.* —**internationally** adv

inter·national com·munity, the noun [singular] political leaders and important organizations from all parts of the world

Internet, the /ˈɪntənet/ noun [singular] ★★★ a computer system that allows people in different parts of the world to exchange information: *Do you have access to the Internet? ♦ The group posted the names of the men on the Internet.* → WORLD WIDE WEB

interpersonal /ˌɪntəˈpɜːs(ə)nəl/ adj involving relationships between people

interplay /ˈɪntəpleɪ/ noun [U] the way that people or things affect each other or react when they are put together: *the interplay of emotions*

interpret /ɪnˈtɜːprɪt/ verb ★★ **1** [I/T] to translate what someone is saying into another language: *I speak Spanish. Would you like me to interpret for you?* **2** [T] to understand an action, situation etc in a particular way: *This move was interpreted in two ways. ♦ Low voter turnout can be interpreted as a sign of satisfaction with the current government.* **3** [T] to explain the meaning of something: *We'll need some help to interpret all this data.*

interpretation /ɪnˌtɜːprɪˈteɪʃ(ə)n/ noun [C/U] ★★ **1** an explanation of the meaning or importance of something: *The Catholic interpretation of the Bible is slightly different.* **2** a way of performing a piece of music, a part in a play etc that shows how you understand it and feel about it: *He was best known for his interpretation of English folk music.*

interpreter /ɪnˈtɜːprɪtə/ noun [C] someone whose job is to translate what someone is saying into another language → TRANSLATOR

interrelated /ˌɪntərɪˈleɪtɪd/ adj things that are interrelated affect each other because they are connected in some way

interrogate /ɪnˈterəgeɪt/ verb [T] to ask someone a lot of questions in order to get information: *The suspects were interrogated*

by local police. —**interrogation**
/ɪnˌterəˈɡeɪʃ(ə)n/ noun [C/U], **interrogator** noun
[C]

interrogative /ˌɪntəˈrɒɡətɪv/ noun [C] *linguistics*
a word or phrase that you use for asking a
question, for example 'what?' or 'how?'
—**interrogative** adj

interrupt /ˌɪntəˈrʌpt/ verb ★
1 [I/T] to say or do something that stops
someone when they are speaking or
concentrating on something: *Please don't
interrupt her while she's working.* ♦ *She tried
to explain, but he interrupted her as soon as
she started talking.*
2 [T] to make something stop for a period of
time: *Rain interrupted the tournament for
an hour this afternoon.*
—**interruption** /ˌɪntəˈrʌpʃ(ə)n/ noun [C/U]

intersect /ˌɪntəˈsekt/ verb [I/T] if roads or lines
intersect, they cross each other, or they
join

intersection /ˈɪntəˌsekʃ(ə)n/ noun [C] a place
where roads, lines etc join or cross each
other: *The school is at the intersection of two
main roads.*

intersperse /ˌɪntəˈspɜːs/ verb [T] to put
something in various places in or among
something else: *The text can be interspersed
with full-page illustrations.*

interstate /ˌɪntəˈsteɪt/ adj existing or taking
place between states, especially between
the states in the US or Australia

interval /ˈɪntəv(ə)l/ noun [C] ★
1 a period of time between two events: *The
normal interval between our meetings is six
weeks.* ♦ *Payments are to be resumed after
an interval of several months.* ♦ *Progress is
reviewed at monthly intervals.* ♦ *Planes pass
overhead at regular intervals.* ♦ *It may be
necessary to stop at intervals* (=sometimes)
and go back over key points in the lesson.
2 *British* a short break between the parts of
something such as a play or concert
=INTERMISSION: *How long is the interval?*
3 a space or distance between two things:
*There are pillars at three-foot intervals for
reinforcement.*

intervene /ˌɪntəˈviːn/ verb [I] **1** to become
involved in a situation in order to try to
stop or change it: *The police had to intervene
when protesters blocked traffic.* **2** to happen
between two events, often in a way that
delays the second event: *Several months
intervened before we met again.*

intervening /ˌɪntəˈviːnɪŋ/ adj happening
between two events or times: *Not much has
changed during the intervening six years.*

intervention /ˌɪntəˈvenʃ(ə)n/ noun [C/U] a
situation in which someone becomes
involved in a particular issue, problem etc
in order to influence what happens

interview¹ /ˈɪntəvjuː/ noun ★★
1 [C] a meeting in which someone asks
another person, especially a famous person,
questions about themselves, their work, or
their ideas: *This is her first interview since
becoming Olympic champion.* ♦ *He doesn't*

give interviews to the press. ♦ *The magazine
has an exclusive interview with the couple.*
2 [C/U] a formal meeting in which someone
asks you questions in order to find out if
you are suitable for a job, course of study
etc: *I have an interview tomorrow for a job
as an interpreter.*
3 [C/U] *British* an official meeting in which the
police ask someone questions about a crime:
*The interview was terminated after two
hours.*

interview² /ˈɪntəvjuː/ verb ★
1 [T] to ask someone, especially someone
famous, questions about themselves, their
work, or their ideas: *He was interviewed on
the radio this morning.*
2 [I/T] to meet someone and ask them
questions in order to find out if they are
suitable for a job, course of study etc:
*Applicants will be interviewed early next
month.*
3 [I/T] *British* if the police interview someone
about a crime, they ask them questions
about it =QUESTION
—**interviewer** noun [C]

intestine /ɪnˈtestɪn/ noun [C] the long tube in
your body that processes food and carries
waste out of your body —**intestinal**
/ɪnˈtestɪn(ə)l/ adj

intimacy /ˈɪntɪməsi/ noun [singular/U] a close
personal relationship

intimate¹ /ˈɪntɪmət/ adj **1** an intimate friend
is someone who you know very well and
like very much =CLOSE **2** relating to very
private or personal things: *The magazine
published intimate details of their affair.*
3 private and friendly and making you feel
relaxed and comfortable: *It's a small hotel
with an intimate atmosphere.* **4** an intimate
relationship is a very close personal
relationship, especially a sexual one
PHRASE intimate knowledge of sth detailed
knowledge of something
—**intimately** adv

intimate² /ˈɪntɪmeɪt/ verb [T] *formal* to tell
people something in an indirect way
—**intimation** /ˌɪntɪˈmeɪʃ(ə)n/ noun [C/U]

intimidate /ɪnˈtɪmɪdeɪt/ verb [T] to make
someone feel frightened so that they will
do what you want —**intimidation**
/ɪnˌtɪmɪˈdeɪʃ(ə)n/ noun [U]

intimidated /ɪnˈtɪmɪˌdeɪtɪd/ adj feeling
nervous or frightened of someone or
something: *Children cannot learn if they feel
intimidated.*

intimidating /ɪnˈtɪmɪˌdeɪtɪŋ/ adj making you
feel nervous, frightened, or less confident:
*Working with such talented people can be
intimidating.*

into /ˈɪntə, ˈɪntʊ, strong ˈɪntuː/ preposition ★★★
1 **moving to the inside** moving from the
outside to the inside of a place or container:
She got into her car and drove away. ♦
*Hundreds of athletes marched into the
stadium for the opening ceremony.* ♦ *He put
his hands into his pockets.*
2 **towards sth** used for stating the direction

in which someone or something looks, faces, or points: *She was gazing into the mirror.* ♦ *Please speak into the microphone.*

3 hitting sth moving towards something and hitting it: *Their car had crashed into a tree.* ♦ *He was so angry he slammed his fist into the wall.*

4 changing to sth used for stating the result of a change from one thing to another: *Jemma had grown into a beautiful woman.* ♦ *The dispute turned into a major battle.* ♦ *Roll the dough into a ball.* ♦ *She fell into a deep sleep.* ♦ *Her stories have been translated into more than 30 languages.*

5 starting to be involved in sth used for saying that someone becomes involved in an activity or situation, or becomes part of a group: *Ted is trying to get into the financial industry* (=get a job in it). ♦ *She always manages to get into trouble.* ♦ *He went into the army when he left school.*

6 finding out about sth used for saying what you are trying to find out about: *I promise to look into the matter.*

7 interested in sth *informal* used for saying what activity or subject someone is interested in and enjoys: *I'm into yoga and things like that.*

intolerable /ɪnˈtɒlərəb(ə)l/ adj impossible to bear or deal with —**intolerably** adv

intolerance /ɪnˈtɒlərəns/ noun [U] someone's refusal to accept behaviour, beliefs, or opinions that are different from their own: *political/racial/religious intolerance*

intolerant /ɪnˈtɒlərənt/ adj not willing to accept behaviour, beliefs, or opinions that are different from your own

intonation /ˌɪntəˈneɪʃ(ə)n/ noun [C/U] the way in which your voice rises and falls when you speak

intoxicated /ɪnˈtɒksɪˌkeɪtɪd/ adj **1** *formal* drunk **2** *literary* extremely excited or happy —**intoxication** /ɪnˌtɒksɪˈkeɪʃ(ə)n/ noun [U]

intractable /ɪnˈtræktəb(ə)l/ adj *formal* very difficult or impossible to deal with

intranet /ˈɪntrəˌnet/ noun [C] *computing* a NETWORK (=system connecting computers) that only members of a particular organization can use → INTERNET

intransigent /ɪnˈtrænsɪdʒ(ə)nt/ adj *formal* refusing to change your ideas or behaviour with no good reason = STUBBORN —**intransigence** noun [U]

intransitive /ɪnˈtrænsətɪv/ adj *linguistics* an intransitive verb has no direct object. In the sentence 'The children played.' the verb 'play' is intransitive. Intransitive verbs are marked ' [I] ' in this dictionary.

intravenous /ˌɪntrəˈviːnəs/ adj put directly into a VEIN —**intravenously** adv

'in ˌtray noun [C] *British* a container on your desk where you keep documents that you have not dealt with yet —*picture* → C3

intrepid /ɪnˈtrepɪd/ adj not afraid to do dangerous things = DARING

intricacy /ˈɪntrɪkəsi/ noun **1 intricacies** [plural] the complicated parts or details of

something such as a system or problem: *the intricacies of international law* **2** [U] the quality of being intricate

intricate /ˈɪntrɪkət/ adj very detailed in design or structure: *an intricate tunnel system* —**intricately** adv

intrigue[1] /ɪnˈtriːg/ verb [T] to make someone very interested in knowing more about something: *That old house has always intrigued me.*

intrigue[2] /ˈɪntriːg/ noun [C/U] a secret plan to harm or cheat someone, or the process of making such a plan

intriguing /ɪnˈtriːgɪŋ/ adj very interesting and making you want to know more: *an intriguing subject for researchers* —**intriguingly** /ɪnˈtriːgɪŋli/ adv

intrinsic /ɪnˈtrɪnsɪk/ adj *formal* relating to the essential qualities or features of something or someone: *Providing good service is intrinsic to a successful business.* —**intrinsically** /ɪnˈtrɪnsɪkli/ adv

intro /ˈɪntrəʊ/ noun [C] *informal* the introduction to something

introduce /ˌɪntrəˈdjuːs/ verb [T] ★★★
1 to tell someone another person's name when they meet for the first time: *He introduced himself as* (=said his name was) *Major Desmond Morton.* ♦ **introduce sb to sb** *I would like to introduce you to my friend Martin.*

2 to bring something into existence or use for the first time: *City schools have introduced stricter rules for dealing with drug users.*

3 to provide someone with a new experience: **introduce sb to sth** *My father first introduced me to jazz when I was about five.*

4 to tell an audience about a programme, performer, performance etc that they are going to see or hear: *It is my pleasure to introduce tonight's speaker.*

introduction /ˌɪntrəˈdʌkʃ(ə)n/ noun ★★
1 [U] the process of bringing something into existence or use for the first time: *Opposition to the tax has decreased since its introduction last year.* ♦ *the introduction of new cancer-fighting drugs*

2 [C] the part at the beginning of a book, report etc that gives a general idea of what it is about

3 [C] something that provides an opportunity to learn or experience something for the first time: *My introduction to sailing happened on a trip to Switzerland.*

4 [C] the process of telling someone another person's name when they meet for the first time: *Donna quickly made the introductions* (=told people each other's names).

introductory /ˌɪntrəˈdʌkt(ə)ri/ adj **1** providing basic information about a subject, especially for people who know nothing about it: *introductory lessons* **2** an introductory offer or price is a low price that is intended to encourage people to buy a new product

introspective /ˌɪntrəˈspektɪv/ adj tending to examine your own thoughts, feelings, or ideas rather than communicating with other people

introvert /ˈɪntrəvɜːt/ noun [C] someone who tends to concentrate on their own thoughts and feelings rather than communicating with other people ≠ EXTROVERT —**introverted** adj

intrude /ɪnˈtruːd/ verb [I] to become involved in a situation in which you are not wanted, or to enter a place where you are not allowed to go: *I was very concerned about her, but I didn't want to intrude.*

intruder /ɪnˈtruːdə/ noun [C] someone who enters a place where they are not allowed to go

intrusion /ɪnˈtruːʒ(ə)n/ noun [C/U] something that interrupts a peaceful situation or a private event

intrusive /ɪnˈtruːsɪv/ adj becoming involved in something in a way that is not welcome

intuition /ˌɪntjuˈɪʃ(ə)n/ noun [C/U] an ability to know or understand something through your feelings, rather than by considering facts or evidence

intuitive /ɪnˈtjuːətɪv/ adj based on your feelings rather than on facts or evidence: *an intuitive judgment* —**intuitively** adv

Inuit /ˈɪnuɪt, ˈɪnjuɪt/ (plural **Inuit**) noun [C/U] a member of a group of people who live in northern Siberia, Canada, Alaska, and Greenland, or the language that they speak —**Inuit** adj

inundate /ˈɪnʌndeɪt/ verb [T] to send or provide much more of something than someone can easily deal with: *We've been inundated with calls.*

invade /ɪnˈveɪd/ verb **1** [I/T] to take or send an army into another country in order to get control of it: *The island was invaded during the war.* **2** [T] to enter a place, especially in large numbers or in a way that causes problems: *The town is invaded by tourists every summer.* —**invader** noun [C]

invalid¹ /ɪnˈvælɪd/ adj not legally effective ≠ VALID: *Your ticket is invalid.*

invalid² /ˈɪnvəlɪd/ noun [C] someone who is ill or injured and cannot look after themselves

invaluable /ɪnˈvæljuəb(ə)l/ adj extremely useful

invariably /ɪnˈveəriəbli/ adv always, or almost always

invasion /ɪnˈveɪʒ(ə)n/ noun [C/U] **1** an occasion when one country's army goes into another country in order to take control of it **2** a situation in which a very large number of people come to a place
PHRASE **invasion of privacy** an occasion when someone finds out or uses information about your private life, especially illegally

invent /ɪnˈvent/ verb [T] ★★
1 to design or create something that did not exist before: *Alfred Nobel invented dynamite.* ♦ *The mountain bike was invented in California.*
2 to make up a story, excuse etc that is not true

invention /ɪnˈvenʃ(ə)n/ noun [C/U] ★
1 something that someone has made, designed, or thought of for the first time, or the act of inventing something: *Inventions like the electric light bulb changed the way people lived.* ♦ *the invention of the Internet*
2 a story, excuse etc that is not true

inventive /ɪnˈventɪv/ adj **1** good at thinking of new ideas or methods **2** used when new and original ideas, methods etc: *an inventive strategy*

inventor /ɪnˈventə/ noun [C] someone who has invented something, or whose job is to invent things

inventory /ˈɪnvəntəri/ noun [C] a list that gives the details of all the things in a place

invert /ɪnˈvɜːt/ verb [T] *formal* to turn something upside down, or to put it in the opposite position —**inversion** /ɪnˈvɜːʃ(ə)n/ noun [C/U]

inverted commas /ˌɪnvɜːtɪd ˈkɒməz/ noun [plural] *British* one of a pair of marks " " or ' ', used in written English for showing the words that someone said, or the title of a book, film etc = QUOTATION MARKS

invest /ɪnˈvest/ verb [I/T] ★ to use your money with the aim of making a profit from it, for example by buying SHARES in a company: *Banks invested £20 million in the scheme.* ♦ *We've invested heavily* (=invested a lot of money) *in foreign markets.* —**investor** noun [C]
PHRASAL VERB **inˈvest in sth 1** to buy something that you will use a lot: *I finally invested in a new computer.* **2** to spend money on something in order to improve it or to make it more successful: *This government believes in investing in education.*

investigate /ɪnˈvestɪgeɪt/ verb [I/T] ★★ to try to find out all the facts about something in order to learn the truth about it: *We sent a reporter to investigate the rumour.* ♦ *Customer 'complaints' are investigated quickly and efficiently.* ♦ +*what/why/whether etc The research aims to investigate why schools are not doing better.* —**investigator** noun [C]

investigation /ɪnˌvestɪˈgeɪʃ(ə)n/ noun [C/U] ★★★ the process of trying to find out all the facts about something in order to discover who or what caused it or how it happened: *The murder investigation is continuing.* ♦ *She is still under investigation* (=being investigated) *by the Spanish police.* ♦ *the investigation into the crash of Flight 803*

investigative /ɪnˈvestɪgətɪv/ adj intended to discover new details and facts about something: *investigative journalism/techniques*

investment /ɪnˈves(t)mənt/ noun ★★★
1 [C/U] money that is used in a way that may earn you more money, for example money used for buying SHARES in a company: *Her investments were mainly in technology stocks.* ♦ *The new laws will attract foreign investment.*

2 [U] the process of spending money in order to improve something or make it more successful: *Investment in new technology is critical to our success.*

3 [C] something that you are willing to spend money on because it will give you benefits in the future: *Computer courses are a good investment for your career.*

inveterate /ɪnˈvetərət/ adj always doing a particular thing and unlikely to change: *an inveterate liar/gambler/critic*

invigorate /ɪnˈvɪɡəˌreɪt/ verb [T] to give someone more energy = REFRESH

invincible /ɪnˈvɪnsəb(ə)l/ adj too strong to be defeated

invisible /ɪnˈvɪzəb(ə)l/ adj something that is invisible cannot be seen —**invisibility** /ɪnˌvɪzəˈbɪləti/ noun [U], **invisibly** adv

invitation /ˌɪnvɪˈteɪʃ(ə)n/ noun [C] ★★ a request for someone to come to an event or to do something: *a wedding invitation* ♦ *The senator refused our invitation to speak.* ♦ *an invitation to the party*

invite¹ /ɪnˈvaɪt/ verb [T] ★★★

1 to ask someone to come to see you or to spend time with you socially: *How many people did you invite?* ♦ *We've invited all the neighbours to the party.* ♦ *Why don't you invite them for a drink?* ♦ **invite sb to do sth** *They've invited me to eat at their house tonight.*

2 to formally ask someone to do something or go somewhere: *Leaders of the two countries were invited to attend peace talks in Geneva.*

3 to do something that makes something bad or unpleasant more likely to happen: *His policies invited widespread criticism.*

PHRASAL VERBS **inˌvite sb ˈin** to ask someone to come into your house: *Did she invite you in for coffee?*

inˌvite sb ˈover or **inˌvite sb ˈround** *British* to invite someone to your house: *They had invited some friends over for dinner.*

invite² /ˈɪnvaɪt/ noun [C] *informal* an invitation to a social event

inviting /ɪnˈvaɪtɪŋ/ adj attractive in a way that makes you want to do something ≠ UNINVITING: *an inviting outdoor pool* —**invitingly** adv

invoice¹ /ˈɪnvɔɪs/ noun [C] a document giving details of goods or services that someone has bought and must pay for

invoice² /ˈɪnvɔɪs/ verb [T] to send someone an invoice for goods or services

invoke /ɪnˈvəʊk/ verb [T] *formal* to use a law or rule in order to achieve something

involuntary /ɪnˈvɒləntəri/ adj an involuntary movement, sound, or reaction is a sudden one that you cannot control —**involuntarily** adv

involve /ɪnˈvɒlv/ verb [T] ★★★

1 to include something as a necessary part of an activity, event, or situation: *The course involves a lot of hard work.* ♦ **involve doing sth** *The job involved working with a software development team.*

2 to include or affect someone or something in an important way: *Forty-six vehicles were involved in the accident.*

3 to encourage or allow someone to take part in something: **involve sb in sth** *The goal is to involve workers in the decision-making process.*

involved /ɪnˈvɒlvd/ adj **1** affected by or included in an activity, event, or situation: *They became involved in a lengthy dispute.* **2** someone who is involved in something takes part in it: *We want all departments to be involved.* ♦ *He denied that he was involved with organized crime.* ♦ *We were involved in the talks until today.* **3** complicated and difficult to understand: *a long involved explanation* **4** if you are involved with someone, you have a sexual or emotional relationship with them

involvement /ɪnˈvɒlvmənt/ noun [C/U] ★★ the act of taking part in an activity, event, or situation: *Our involvement with this project started in 1989.* ♦ *There is no evidence of his direct involvement in the bombing.* ♦ *the involvement of the local government*

inward¹ /ˈɪnwəd/ adj **1** felt in your own mind but not obvious to other people **2** going towards the inside or centre of something ≠ OUTWARD

inward² /ˈɪnwəd/ an American spelling of **inwards**

inwardly /ˈɪnwədli/ adv in a hidden way that is not obvious to other people ≠ OUTWARDLY

inwards /ˈɪnwədz/ adv towards the inside of something ≠ OUTWARDS

in-your-face adj *informal* extremely direct, in a way that is deliberately intended to shock or annoy people

IOU /ˌaɪ əʊ ˈjuː/ noun [C] *informal* a piece of paper that you sign to say that you owe someone an amount of money

IPA /ˌaɪ piː ˈeɪ/ noun [U] International Phonetic Alphabet: a system of symbols that are used to represent speech sounds

IQ /ˌaɪ ˈkjuː/ noun [C] intelligence quotient: a number that represents someone's intelligence

irate /aɪˈreɪt/ adj very angry

iris /ˈaɪrɪs/ noun [C] **1** a tall, usually purple, flower —*picture* → C9 **2** the coloured part of your eye

iron¹ /ˈaɪən/ noun ★★

1 [U] a hard heavy metal that is used for making steel

2 [C] a heated object that you push across clothes in order to make them smooth

iron² /ˈaɪən/ verb [I/T] to push an iron across clothes in order to make them smooth: *She ironed her skirt.* —*picture* → NEXT PAGE

PHRASAL VERB **ˌiron sth ˈout** to remove the last difficulties in order to solve a problem: *We have to iron out the final details of the contract.*

iron

iron³ /ˈaɪən/ adj **1** made of iron **2** very strong, strict, or severe: *an iron will*

ironic /aɪˈrɒnɪk/ adj **1** expressing the opposite of what you really think, especially in order to be humorous: *an ironic comment* **2** an ironic event or situation is interesting, because it is the opposite of what you expect

ironically /aɪˈrɒnɪkli/ adv **1** used for saying that a situation has developed in an unexpected or humorous way **2** in an ironic way

ironing /ˈaɪənɪŋ/ noun [U] the job of making clothes smooth with an iron, or the clothes that must be made smooth with an iron: *I'll do the ironing.*

ironing board noun [C] a tall narrow table that you use to do the ironing

irony /ˈaɪrəni/ noun **1** [U] a form of humour in which you use words to express the opposite of what the words really mean **2** [C/U] a strange, funny, or sad situation in which things happen in the opposite way to what you expect

irrational /ɪˈræʃ(ə)nəl/ adj without clear or sensible reasons, or not thinking in a sensible way: *irrational violence/fear/panic* —**irrationally** adv

irreconcilable /ˌɪrekənˈsaɪləb(ə)l/ adj irreconcilable opinions, aims, or disagreements are so opposed to each other that it is impossible to reach an agreement

irregular /ɪˈreɡjʊlə/ adj **1** not happening regularly: *His breathing had become irregular.* **2** not even, smooth, or straight in shape or appearance: *an irregular surface* **3** not following the rules, laws, or usual ways of doing things **4** *linguistics* not following the usual rules of grammar. For example, 'eat' is an irregular verb because its past tense is 'ate' and its past participle is 'eaten'. —**irregularly** adv

irregularity /ɪˌreɡjʊˈlærəti/ noun **1** [C] a situation in which the rules, laws, or usual ways of doing things have not been followed: *irregularities in the election process* **2** [C/U] a situation in which events do not happen at regular times **3** [C] a shape or appearance that is not even, smooth, or straight: *irregularities in the surface*

irrelevant /ɪˈreləvənt/ adj not important, or not relevant to what you are doing: *an irrelevant remark* —**irrelevance** /ɪˈreləvəns/ noun [C/U]

irreparable /ɪˈrep(ə)rəb(ə)l/ adj *formal* irreparable harm or damage is extremely bad and cannot be repaired

irreplaceable /ˌɪrɪˈpleɪsəb(ə)l/ adj valuable and impossible to replace if used, lost, or destroyed

irrepressible /ˌɪrɪˈpresəb(ə)l/ adj lively, confident, and impossible to control

irresistible /ˌɪrɪˈzɪstəb(ə)l/ adj **1** strong or powerful and impossible to control: *an irresistible urge to laugh* **2** impossible to refuse, not want, or not like: *an irresistible smile* —**irresistibly** adv

irrespective /ˌɪrɪˈspektɪv/ adv **irrespective of sth** despite a particular fact, situation, or quality

irresponsible /ˌɪrɪˈspɒnsəb(ə)l/ adj **1** done or said without thinking about the possible results: *It was irresponsible of you to leave her alone.* **2** not sensible, or not able to be trusted to be reasonable: *an irresponsible driver* —**irresponsibly** adv

irreverent /ɪˈrevərənt/ adj showing no respect for traditions, rules, or religious beliefs

irreversible /ˌɪrɪˈvɜːsəb(ə)l/ adj impossible to change or bring back to a previous condition or situation: *irreversible damage to the environment*

irrevocable /ɪˈrevəkəb(ə)l/ adj *formal* impossible to change or stop —**irrevocably** adv

irrigate /ˈɪrɪɡeɪt/ verb [T] to bring water to land through a system of pipes, DITCHES etc in order to make plants grow —**irrigation** /ˌɪrɪˈɡeɪʃ(ə)n/ noun [U]

irritable /ˈɪrɪtəb(ə)l/ adj likely to become easily annoyed or made angry —**irritability** /ˌɪrɪtəˈbɪləti/ noun [U], **irritably** adv

irritant /ˈɪrɪt(ə)nt/ noun [C] **1** something that annoys you **2** *medical* something that makes part of your body become painful or swollen

irritate /ˈɪrɪteɪt/ verb [T] **1** to make you feel annoyed or angry: *That little noise he makes really irritates me.* **2** to make part of your body painful or swollen —**irritation** /ˌɪrɪˈteɪʃ(ə)n/ noun [U]

irritated /ˈɪrɪteɪtɪd/ adj **1** annoyed or angry about something: *I was beginning to get irritated.* **2** painful or swollen

irritating /ˈɪrɪteɪtɪŋ/ adj making you feel annoyed or angry: *He had an irritating habit of cracking his knuckles.* —**irritatingly** adv

is 3rd person singular of the present tense of **be**

-ish /ɪʃ/ suffix 'slightly' or 'fairly': *a bluish tint*

Islam /ˈɪzlɑːm/ noun [U] the religion that is based on the ideas of Muhammad, or the people and countries who follow this religion —**Islamic** /ɪzˈlæmɪk/ adj

island /ˈaɪlənd/ noun [C] ★★★ a piece of land that is completely surrounded by water: *the best hotel on the island* ♦ *islands off the west coast of Canada*

islander /ˈaɪləndə/ noun [C] someone who lives on a small island

isle /aɪl/ noun [C] *literary* an island

isn't /ˈɪz(ə)nt/ short form the usual way of saying or writing 'is not'. This is not often used in formal writing: *Isn't she here yet?*

isolate /ˈaɪsəˌleɪt/ verb [T] **1** to keep someone in a place that is away from other people **2** to prevent a country or group from communicating with, doing business with, or getting support from other countries or groups **3** to separate something from other similar things so that you can consider it by itself

isolated /ˈaɪsəˌleɪtɪd/ adj **1** an isolated place is a long way from other places and is often difficult to get to=REMOTE: *isolated mountain villages* **2** happening only once, or existing only in one place: *an isolated incident* **3** feeling alone and unhappy, with no friends: *Many victims feel isolated and unable to talk about their experiences.* **4** an isolated country or organization is one that others refuse to deal with

isolation /ˌaɪsəˈleɪʃ(ə)n/ noun [U] **1** the state of being separated from other people, or a situation in which you do not have support from other people: *Isolation from family and friends can lead to feelings of anxiety.* **2** a situation in which a country or group is alone and without support because other countries or groups stop dealing with it
    PHRASE **in isolation 1** if something is considered in isolation, it is considered separately from other similar things **2** in a place that is away from other people, animals, or things: *The prisoners were kept in isolation.*

isolationism /ˌaɪsəˈleɪʃ(ə)nˌɪz(ə)m/ noun [U] a country's policy of not having political or economic relationships with other countries —**isolationist** adj

ISP /ˌaɪ es ˈpiː/ noun [C] Internet service provider: a company that provides a connection to the Internet

issue¹ /ˈɪʃuː, ˈɪsjuː/ noun [C] ★★★
1 a subject or problem that people discuss or argue about: *environmental issues* ♦ *Education was one of the biggest issues in the campaign.* ♦ *The chairman raised the issue* (=started discussing the issue) *of funding.*
2 a magazine that is published at a particular time: *The article appeared in the November issue.*
    PHRASES **make an issue of sth** to treat something as an important problem when it is not **take issue with sb/sth** to disagree with someone, or to disagree about something

---

Words often used with issue

Verbs often used with issue (noun, sense 1)
■ **address, confront, tackle, take up** + ISSUE: deal with an issue
■ **dodge, duck, evade** + ISSUE: avoid dealing with an issue
■ **cloud, complicate, confuse, fudge** + ISSUE: make an issue more difficult to understand, or more difficult to deal with
■ **consider, examine, explore** + ISSUE: think about an issue

---

issue² /ˈɪʃuː, ˈɪsjuː/ verb [T] ★★
1 to announce something officially: *The banks issued a warning that charges will rise.*
2 if you issue someone with something, you officially give it to them: *All visitors to the factory must be issued with protective goggles.*
3 to officially make things available for people to buy or use: *The post office is issuing a new range of stamps.*

it /ɪt/ pronoun ★★★
1 **referring to sth that has been mentioned** used for referring to something that has already been mentioned, or when it is obvious which thing you mean: *I can't find my ticket. I think I must have lost it.* ♦ *You should come to Rome – it's a wonderful city.* ♦ *The dog was howling, so she fed it.* ♦ *I can't move the baby without waking it.*
2 **used as the subject/object of a sentence** used instead of the subject or object of a sentence, when the real subject or object is a phrase or CLAUSE at the end of the sentence: *It's nice to be home again.* ♦ *It's strange that she never mentioned the wedding.* ♦ *The new law made it easier to get a divorce.* ♦ *I hate it when people talk about me behind my back.*
3 **referring to sb's life or situation** used for referring to someone's life, work, or general situation: *What's it like in the army these days?*
4 **talking about weather conditions** used for talking about the weather, the temperature, or the light: *It rained in the night.* ♦ *It's a glorious day.* ♦ *It's cooler indoors.* ♦ *It gets dark at around five.*
5 **talking about times and dates** used for saying or asking what the time, day, or date is: *'What time is it?' 'It's four o'clock.'* ♦ *Thank goodness it's Saturday tomorrow.*
6 **talking about distance** used for saying how large a distance is: *It's about ten miles from here to Plymouth.*
7 **emphasizing who or what you mean** used with the verb 'to be' for emphasizing that you are referring to a particular person or thing: *It's your brother I want to speak to.*
8 **saying or asking who sb is** *spoken* used for telling someone who you are, or asking who someone else is, especially on the telephone: *Hello, it's me, Geoffrey.* ♦ *'There's someone here to see you.' 'Who is it?'*
    PHRASE **it seems/looks/appears** used for saying what seems to be true: *It seems that no one is willing to accept responsibility for what happened.* ♦ *It looks as if we're going to lose our jobs.*

IT /ˌaɪ ˈtiː/ noun [U] information technology: the use of computers and other electronic equipment to store, process, and send information

italics /ɪˈtælɪks/ noun [plural] italics are letters that slope to the right, like the letters in examples in this dictionary

itch¹ /ɪtʃ/ verb [I] if your skin itches, you want to SCRATCH it (=rub it with your nails)
    PHRASE **be itching to do sth** *informal* to feel very impatient because you want to do something immediately

itch² /ɪtʃ/ noun [singular] a feeling on your skin that makes you want to SCRATCH it (=rub it with your nails)

itchy /ˈɪtʃi/ adj if you feel itchy, you want to SCRATCH your skin (=rub it with your nails)

it'd /ˈɪtəd/ short form **1** a way of saying or writing 'it would'. This is not often used in formal writing: *It'd be better to wait until later.* **2** a way of saying or writing 'it had' when 'had' is an AUXILIARY VERB. This is not often used in formal writing: *It'd been a difficult night.*

item /ˈaɪtəm/ noun [C] ★★★
1 one of several things in a group or on a list: *The first item to be discussed was the new computer system.* ♦ *Several items of equipment needed to be repaired.*
2 an article in a newspaper or magazine, or one part of a news programme on the television or radio

itemize /ˈaɪtəˌmaɪz/ verb [T] to make a detailed list of a number of things —**itemized** /ˈaɪtəˌmaɪzd/ adj

itinerant /aɪˈtɪnərənt/ adj travelling around frequently: *itinerant workers*

itinerary /aɪˈtɪnərəri/ noun [C] a written plan that shows the details of a journey

it'll /ˈɪt(ə)l/ short form the usual way of saying or writing 'it will'. This is not often used in formal writing: *It'll be fun!*

it's /ɪts/ short form **1** the usual way of saying or writing 'it is'. This is not often used in formal writing: *It's cold outside.* **2** the usual way of saying or writing 'it has' when 'has' is an AUXILIARY VERB. This is not often used in formal writing: *It's been raining for hours.*

its /ɪts/ determiner ★★★

> **Its** is the possessive form of **it**.

belonging or relating to something, when it has already been mentioned or when it is obvious which thing you are referring to: *The chair lay on its side.* ♦ *Europe and its many great cities* ♦ *The bull had a ring through its nose.*

> **Its** should not be confused with **it's**, which is the short form of 'it is' or 'it has'.

itself /ɪtˈself/ pronoun ★★★
1 the REFLEXIVE form of 'it', used for showing that an action affects the thing that does the action: *The young bird cannot feed itself.* ♦ *The government needs to defend itself against these attacks.*
2 used for emphasizing that you are referring to a particular thing and not to anything else: *The problem is not with the software, but with the computer itself.*
PHRASES **(all) by itself 1** not near or with any other thing: *His house stood by itself on the edge of the village.* **2** without help: *The door opened by itself.* ♦ *Can the baby stand up all by itself?*
in itself used for stating what is true about one particular thing, without considering anything else: *The fact that he lied to the police does not in itself prove that he is guilty.*

IV /ˌaɪ ˈviː/ noun [C] *American* a DRIP for putting liquid into your body

I've /aɪv/ short form the usual way of saying or writing 'I have'. This is not often used in formal writing: *I've just been to the supermarket.*

IVF /ˌaɪ viː ˈef/ noun [U] in vitro fertilization: the medical process in which a woman's egg is FERTILIZED outside her body and then put back inside so that it can grow into a baby

ivory¹ /ˈaɪvəri/ noun [U] the bone that an elephant's TUSKS are made of

ivory² /ˈaɪvəri/ adj pale yellow-white in colour

ivy /ˈaɪvi/ noun [U] a dark green plant that spreads and grows up walls —*picture* → C9

J j

j or **J** /dʒeɪ/ noun [C/U] the tenth letter of the English alphabet

jab¹ /dʒæb/ verb [I/T] to push something narrow or pointed into or toward something else with a sudden movement

jab² /dʒæb/ noun [C] **1** a hard straight push with something narrow or pointed **2** *British informal* an INJECTION (=amount of medicine given through a needle)

jack¹ /dʒæk/ noun [C] **1** a piece of equipment for lifting and supporting a heavy object, for example a car **2** a PLAYING CARD that has a picture of a young man on it —*picture* → C16

jack² /dʒæk/
PHRASAL VERBS **jack sth 'in** *British informal* to stop doing something: *Did you know that Jenna's jacked in her college course?*
jack sth 'up *informal* to increase the price, rate, or number of something by a large amount

jackal /ˈdʒækɔːl/ noun [C] a wild African or Asian animal like a dog

jacket /ˈdʒækɪt/ noun [C] ★★
1 a short coat: *a linen/denim/leather jacket* ♦ *a suit jacket* —*picture* → C4
2 a cover for a book

jacket po'tato noun [C] *British* a potato that is cooked in an oven with its skin on=BAKED POTATO

jack-in-the-box noun [C] a toy that consists of a box with a model of a man inside that jumps up when the box opens

jackknife /ˈdʒæknaɪf/ verb [I] if a truck or train jackknifes in an accident, it bends in the middle and its parts fold towards each other

jackpot /ˈdʒækpɒt/ noun [C] the largest amount of money that someone can win in a game
PHRASE **hit the jackpot** to be very successful at something

Jacuzzi /dʒəˈkuːzi/ *trademark* a type of hot bath with BUBBLY water in which people sit to relax

jade /dʒeɪd/ noun [U] a hard green stone that is used for making jewellery

jaded /ˈdʒeɪdɪd/ adj bored and no longer enthusiastic about something

jagged /ˈdʒægɪd/ adj a jagged surface or edge has a lot of rough pointed parts

jaguar /ˈdʒægjuə/ noun [C] a large wild cat with black spots from Central and South America

jail¹ /dʒeɪl/ noun [C/U] ★ a place where people are put as punishment for a crime=PRISON: *Adam spent 3 years in jail for drug possession.* ♦ *They put her in jail for murder.*

jail² /dʒeɪl/ verb [T] to put someone in jail: *He was jailed for drink-driving.*

Jain /dʒaɪn/ noun [C] a member of a religious group in India that believes that people should not be violent towards any living creature —**Jain** adj, **Jainism** noun [U]

jam¹ /dʒæm/ noun **1** [C/U] a sweet sticky food made from boiled fruit and sugar, that is usually spread onto bread: *strawberry jam* **2** [C] an occasion when a machine does not work because something prevents its parts from moving: *a paper jam in the printer* **PHRASE** **be in a jam** *informal* to be in a difficult situation
→ TRAFFIC JAM

jam² /dʒæm/ verb **1** [T] to use force to put something into a small space: *I tried to jam some paper into the cracks.* **2** [T] if people or things jam a place, there are so many of them that it is difficult to move: *The streets were jammed with cars.* **3** [I/T] if a machine, lock, window etc jams, or if something jams it, it does not work because something stops it from moving: *He fired one shot before his gun jammed.* **4** [T] to block a radio, television, or other electronic signal

jamboree /ˌdʒæmbəˈriː/ noun [C] a large celebration with a lot of music and entertainment

jam-packed adj completely full

Jan. abbrev January

jangle /ˈdʒæŋɡ(ə)l/ verb [I/T] if small metal objects jangle, they make a noise when they hit against each other

janitor /ˈdʒænɪtə/ noun [C] someone whose job is to clean and look after a public building =CARETAKER

January /ˈdʒænjuəri/ noun [C] ★★★ the first month of the year: *My class begins in January.* ♦ *The new year begins on January 1st .*

jar¹ /dʒɑː/ noun [C] a glass container for food, with a lid and a wide opening: *a jar of marmalade*

jar² /dʒɑː/ verb **1** [I/T] to accidentally push something hard against something else, in a way that causes pain or damage: *The shock of the fall jarred every bone in his body.* **2** [I] to be unpleasant or not suitable in a particular situation

jargon /ˈdʒɑːɡən/ noun [U] *showing disapproval* special words and phrases that are only understood by people who do the same kind of work: *medical/computer jargon*

jaundice /ˈdʒɔːndɪs/ noun [U] an illness that makes your skin and the white part of your eyes become yellow

jaundiced /ˈdʒɔːndɪst/ adj showing dislike of something, or criticizing it

jaunt /dʒɔːnt/ noun [C] a short journey that you make for fun

jaunty /ˈdʒɔːnti/ adj lively and confident

javelin /ˈdʒævəlɪn/ noun [C/U] a long pointed stick that is thrown in a sports competition, or the sport of throwing this stick

jaw /dʒɔː/ noun [C] **1** the part of your mouth where your teeth grow **2** the lower part of your face that includes your chin and stretches back almost to your ear —*picture* → C14
PHRASE **sb's jaw dropped** used for saying that someone was very surprised or shocked

jazz¹ /dʒæz/ noun [U] a type of music with a strong lively beat which players often IMPROVISE (=make up the music as they play)

jazz² /dʒæz/ **PHRASAL VERB** **jazz sth ˈup** *informal* to make something more lively or interesting

jealous /ˈdʒeləs/ adj ★
1 upset because someone has something that you would like to have, or can do something that you would like to do: *I expect some of your colleagues will be jealous.*
2 angry and upset because someone who you love is giving attention to another person: *He would dance with other women to make her jealous.*
—**jealously** adv

jealousy /ˈdʒeləsi/ noun [U] **1** a feeling of anger and sadness because someone has something that you would like to have: *Professional jealousy can cause problems at work.* **2** a strong feeling of anger and sadness because someone who you love is giving their attention to someone else: *sexual jealousy*

jeans /dʒiːnz/ noun [plural] ★★ informal trousers made of DENIM (=heavy cotton cloth): *a pair of faded blue jeans* —*picture* → C4

Jeep /dʒiːp/ *trademark* a car with no roof that can drive over all types of land

jeer /dʒɪə/ verb [I/T] to shout or laugh at someone in an unkind way —**jeer** noun [C]

jelly /ˈdʒeli/ noun [C/U] **1** *British* a soft sweet food, made from fruit juice, sugar, and GELATINE, that shakes when you touch it **2** a sweet sticky food made from boiled fruit juice and sugar, often spread on bread

jellyfish /ˈdʒeliˌfɪʃ/ noun [C] a soft transparent sea animal that can sting you

jeopardize /ˈdʒepəˌdaɪz/ verb [T] to risk damaging or destroying something important: *Cuts in funding could jeopardize our research.*

jeopardy /ˈdʒepədi/ noun **in jeopardy** likely to be damaged or destroyed

jerk¹ /dʒɜːk/ verb [I/T] to move suddenly, or to make something move suddenly: *The train jerked forwards.*

jerk² /dʒɜːk/ noun [C] **1** a quick sudden movement **2** *impolite* someone who does stupid or annoying things

jerky /ˈdʒɜːki/ adj a jerky movement consists of several separate short movements —**jerkily** adv

jersey /ˈdʒɜːzi/ noun **1** [C] a warm piece of clothing that covers your upper body and arms **2** [U] a soft cloth made from wool or cotton

Jesus Christ /ˌdʒiːzəs ˈkraɪst/ or **Jesus** the man on whose ideas Christianity is based

jet¹ /dʒet/ noun ★
 1 [C] a plane that can fly very fast: *a jet fighter*
 2 [C] a stream of liquid that comes out of something very quickly and with a lot of force: *The firefighter sprayed a jet of water on the flames.*
 3 [U] a hard black shiny stone that is used for making jewellery

jet² /dʒet/ verb [I] to fly somewhere in a plane: *They will be jetting off to Spain this weekend.*

jet-'black adj very dark black in colour

jet 'engine noun [C] a type of engine that combines air and burning fuel to create power for a plane

jet lag noun [U] the feeling of being very tired because you have travelled on a plane across parts of the world where the time is different —**jet-lagged** /ˈdʒet ˌlægd/ adj

Jet Ski *trademark* a very small fast boat for one or two people that you drive standing up

jettison /ˈdʒetɪs(ə)n/ verb [T] **1** to get rid of something that is not useful or successful: *We may have to jettison some parts of the business.* **2** to throw goods, equipment, or fuel from a ship or plane in order to make it less likely to sink or crash

jetty /ˈdʒeti/ noun [C] a long narrow structure that goes from the land out into a lake, sea, or river to provide a place for boats to stop

Jew /dʒuː/ noun [C] someone who believes in Judaism or who belongs to a family that believed in Judaism in the past

jewel /ˈdʒuːəl/ noun [C] a hard valuable stone that has been cut and made shiny

jeweller /ˈdʒuːələ/ noun [C] someone who makes, repairs, or sells jewellery

jewellery /ˈdʒuːəlri/ noun [U] ★★ objects such as rings that you wear as decoration: *She's got some lovely pieces of jewellery.* ♦ *I don't wear very much jewellery.* → COSTUME JEWELLERY

jewelry /ˈdʒuːəlri/ the American spelling of jewellery

Jewish /ˈdʒuːɪʃ/ adj **1** someone who is Jewish was born in the Jewish culture, and may practise Judaism **2** relating to Jews, their culture, or their religion

earring
necklace
bracelet
brooch
ring

jewellery

jibe /dʒaɪb/ noun [C] a comment that is intended to annoy or offend someone

jig /dʒɪg/ noun [C] a fast traditional dance, or the music for this dance

jiggle /ˈdʒɪg(ə)l/ verb [I/T] to move quickly up and down or from side to side, or to make something move in this way: *If the toilet won't flush, just jiggle the handle a little.*

jigsaw /ˈdʒɪgsɔː/ or **jigsaw puzzle** noun [C] a picture made of a lot of small pieces that you have to fit together

jingle¹ /ˈdʒɪŋg(ə)l/ noun [C] **1** a short phrase, usually with music, that is easy to remember. Jingles are used in advertising. **2** the sound that small metal objects make when they hit each other

jingle² /ˈdʒɪŋg(ə)l/ verb [I/T] if small metal objects jingle, or if you jingle them, they hit each other to make a noise

jinx /dʒɪŋks/ noun [C] *informal* someone or something that causes bad luck: *There seems to be a jinx on that family.* —**jinx** verb [T], **jinxed** /dʒɪŋkst/ adj

jitters /ˈdʒɪtəz/ noun [plural] *informal* a nervous feeling that you get when you do not know what will happen

jittery /ˈdʒɪtəri/ adj feeling nervous, often so that you cannot keep still

job /dʒɒb/ noun ★★★
 1 [C] work that you do regularly to earn money: *a part-time/full-time job* ♦ *Andy got a holiday job at a factory in Bristol.* ♦ *Emma finally found a job* (=got a job after looking). ♦ *My son has been offered a job in Tokyo.* ♦ *Dan left his job.* ♦ *Many steelworkers are worried that they'll lose their jobs.*
 2 [C] something that you have to do or deal with: *Our architects have done a great job.* ♦ *the job of doing sth No one wanted the job of telling Mum the bad news.*
 3 [singular] your duty in a particular situation or organization: *it is sb's job to do sth It's my job to welcome new members to the club.*

 PHRASES **have a job doing sth** *British informal* to have difficulties doing something: *We*

had quite a job finding your house.
(it's a) good job *British* used for saying that it is lucky that you did something or that something happened: *It's a good job I remembered to bring an umbrella.*
make a good/bad job of (doing) sth *British* to do something well or badly

---

Words often used with **job**

Adjectives often used with job (sense 1)
■ **dead-end, low-paid, menial, unskilled** + JOB: used about jobs that are not very good
■ **good, proper, semi-skilled, skilled, well-paid** + JOB: used about jobs that are good
■ **full-time, part-time, permanent, temporary** + JOB: used about a job that you do for a particular period of time

---

Talking or writing about **jobs**

general
■ **job** what you do regularly to earn money
■ **work** something that you do to earn money, or the place where you go to do it
■ **career** the jobs that someone does over a period of time that involve a particular type of work
■ **profession** a type of job that you need a lot of education or special training to do
■ **post** a particular job within a company or organization, especially a job with some responsibility
■ **position** a particular job: used especially in advertisements for jobs
getting a job
■ **apply** to officially say, usually in a letter or on a special form, that you would like to be considered for a particular job
■ **CV** a list of your qualifications and work experience
■ **applicant** someone who applies for a particular job
■ **candidate** someone who is competing with other people for a particular job
■ **interview** a meeting with the people you are hoping to work for where they ask you questions and find out more about you
■ **interviewee** an applicant who is asked to come for an interview
not having a job
■ **unemployed** *or* **jobless** *or* **out of work** used for describing someone who does not have a job
■ **retired** used for describing someone who is not working because they are old

---

job de,scription noun [C] a list of all the things that someone must do in their job
jobless /'dʒɒbləs/ adj *mainly journalism* without a job, or relating to people without a job =UNEMPLOYED: *a jobless steelworker ♦ Canada's jobless rate was 10.3 per cent.*
job se,curity noun [U] the knowledge that you will not be forced to leave your job
job-share verb [I] to share a single job with another person, so that each of you works for part of the day or week —**job-,share** noun [C]
jockey¹ /'dʒɒki/ noun [C] someone whose job

is to ride horses in races → DISC JOCKEY
jockey² /'dʒɒki/ verb **jockey for position** to try to get into the best situation possible when you are competing for something
jocular /'dʒɒkjʊlə/ adj *formal* humorous
jog¹ /dʒɒg/ verb **1** [I] to run at a slow steady speed, usually for exercise: *Let's jog around the lake.* **2** [T] to knock something so that it moves a little
PHRASE **jog sb's memory** to make someone remember something
jog² /dʒɒg/ noun [C] a run for exercise at a slow steady speed: *We went for a jog around the park.* —**jogger** noun [C]
jogging /'dʒɒgɪŋ/ noun [U] the activity of running at a slow steady speed: *I go jogging every morning.*
join¹ /dʒɔɪn/ verb ★★★
1 [T] to become a member of an organization, club, or group, or to start working for an organization ≠ LEAVE: *I'm thinking of joining a choir. ♦ Martin joined the firm in 1999. ♦ He wants to join the army.*
2 [T] to come together with other people or things: *Wendy went off to join her friends in the bar. ♦ The police car was soon joined by two ambulances. ♦* **join sb for sth** *Why don't you join us for dinner tonight?*
3 [I/T] to connect two things, or to become connected at a particular point ≠ DISCONNECT, SEPARATE: *The two roads join about five miles south of the city. ♦* **join sth together** *First, join the two pipes together.*
PHRASE **join forces (with sb)** to work together with someone else in order to achieve something
PHRASAL VERBS **,join 'in (sth)** to do an activity with people who are already doing it: *She laughed and Tom joined in. ♦ Pat didn't feel like joining in the celebrations.*
,join 'up to become a member of the armed forces
,join (sth) 'up *same as* **join¹** 3: *You need to join up these two lines.*
join² /dʒɔɪn/ noun [C] the place where two objects have been connected together
joined-up /,dʒɔɪnd 'ʌp/ adj organized in a way that allows all the separate parts of something to work well together: *joined-up government/thinking*
joiner /'dʒɔɪnə/ noun [C] someone who makes the wooden parts of buildings → CARPENTER
joint¹ /dʒɔɪnt/ adj ★★ involving two or more people, or done by two or more people together: *a joint decision ♦ The two presidents issued a joint statement.* —**jointly** adv: *a jointly owned property*
joint² /dʒɔɪnt/ noun [C]

1 part of your body	4 cannabis cigarette
2 connection	5 restaurant, bar etc
3 piece of meat	

1 a part of your body that can bend where two bones meet: *a knee joint* **2** a place where two parts of something are connected: *Make sure you seal the joints of the pipes with tape.* **3** a large piece of meat that is cooked in an oven: *a joint of beef* **4** *informal* a cigarette that contains CANNABIS **5** *informal* a restaurant, bar, or club

joint venture noun [C] *business* an agreement between two companies to work together on a particular job

joke¹ /dʒəʊk/ noun [C] ★ something that you say or do that is intended to make people laugh: *Do you want to hear a good joke?* ♦ *Greg sprayed her with water as a joke.* ♦ *The kids were telling jokes* (=short stories with funny endings). ♦ *Stephen decided to play a joke on* (=trick) *his teacher.*

PHRASES **be a joke** *informal* to be bad or silly in a way that is annoying: *That price is just a joke!*

be no joke to be very difficult or unpleasant: *It's no joke bringing up two kids on your own.*

sb can take a joke if you can take a joke, you are able to laugh when someone makes a joke about you or does something to trick you

joke² /dʒəʊk/ verb [I] to say things that are intended to make people laugh: *You shouldn't joke about such serious things.*

PHRASES **be joking** to say something but not mean it to be true: *I thought he was joking when he said he'd resigned.*

you're joking or **you must be joking** *spoken* used for saying that you cannot believe that someone really means what they have just said

—**jokingly** adv

joker /dʒəʊkə/ noun [C] **1** someone who likes to make people laugh **2** a type of PLAYING CARD that is used only in some card games —*picture* → C16

jolly /dʒɒli/ adj friendly and happy

jolt¹ /dʒəʊlt/ noun [C] **1** a sudden violent movement: *The bus stopped with a jolt and we were all flung forward.* **2** a sudden strong feeling of surprise or shock: *I realized with a jolt that she was staring at me.*

jolt² /dʒəʊlt/ verb **1** [I/T] to move with a sudden violent movement, or to make something move like this **2** [T] to give someone a sudden shock

Joneses /dʒəʊnzɪz/ noun **keep up with the Joneses** *informal* to try to be as rich, successful etc as your neighbours

jostle /dʒɒs(ə)l/ verb **1** [I] to compete for something: *The two parties are jostling for control of the parliament.* **2** [I/T] to push against someone in order to move past them in a crowd: *We managed to jostle our way to the front.*

jot /dʒɒt/ PHRASAL VERB **jot sth down** to write something in a quick informal way on a piece of paper so that you remember it

journal /dʒɜː(ə)l/ noun [C] **1** a newspaper or magazine that contains articles relating to a particular profession or subject: *a scientific journal* ♦ *the British Medical Journal* **2** a book in which you write about what happens to you every day = DIARY

journalism /dʒɜːnə(ə)lɪz(ə)m/ noun [U] the activity of reporting the news for a newspaper, magazine, radio programme, or television programme

journalist /dʒɜːnəlɪst/ noun [C] ★★ someone whose job is to report the news for a newspaper, magazine, radio programme, or television programme = REPORTER

journey /dʒɜːni/ noun [C] ★★★ an occasion when you travel from one place to another, especially over a long distance: *a train journey* ♦ *We had a long journey ahead of us.* ♦ *It's a seven-hour journey to Boston from here.* ♦ *He makes the journey to Moscow three times a year.*

Words often used with **journey**

■ **arduous, epic, gruelling** + JOURNEY: used about journeys that are difficult, long, and tiring

jovial /dʒəʊviəl/ adj happy and friendly

joy /dʒɔɪ/ noun **1** [U] a feeling of great happiness: *Penny could have shouted with joy.* **2** [C] something that makes you feel very happy or pleased: *the joys of skiing* **3** [U] *British spoken* success in doing something: *I tried to call her earlier, but no joy.* → PRIDE¹

joyful /dʒɔɪf(ə)l/ adj very happy, or causing happiness —**joyfully** adv

joyous /dʒɔɪəs/ adj *literary* causing happy feelings —**joyously** adv

joypad /dʒɔɪpæd/ noun [C] a small piece of equipment with buttons that you press in order to control the movement of the images in a computer game

joyriding /dʒɔɪˌraɪdɪŋ/ noun [U] *informal* the crime of stealing a car and driving it for pleasure —**joyrider** noun [C]

joystick /dʒɔɪˌstɪk/ noun [C] an upright handle that you use to control an aircraft or the movement of the images in a computer game

jubilant /dʒuːbɪlənt/ adj extremely happy because something good has happened —**jubilantly** adv, **jubilation** /ˌdʒuːbɪˈleɪʃ(ə)n/ noun [U]

jubilee /dʒuːbɪliː/ noun [C] a celebration on a date on which something important happened in an earlier year

Judaism /dʒuːdeɪˌɪz(ə)m/ noun [U] the religion of Jewish people, based on the writings of the Torah and the Talmud

judge¹ /dʒʌdʒ/ noun [C] ★★

1 someone whose job is to make decisions in a court of law: *The judge sentenced her to ninety days in prison.* → MAGISTRATE

2 someone who decides who the winner of a competition will be: *All entries will be examined by a panel of judges.*

PHRASE **be a good/bad/shrewd etc judge of sth** to be someone whose opinions about something are usually right, wrong, intelligent etc

judge² /dʒʌdʒ/ verb ★★

1 [I/T] to form an opinion about something after considering all the details or facts: +*that He left the room when he judged that* she was asleep. ♦ **judge sb/sth on sth** *Schools are judged on their exam results.* ♦ **judge sth (to be) sth** *The water was judged to be of good quality.*

2 [I/T] to decide who or what is the winner of a competition: **judge sth (to be) sth** *In the end, Debbie's cake was judged the winner.* ♦ **judge sb/sth on sth** *The paintings will be judged on imagination and technique.*

3 [I/T] to criticize someone because you think their moral behaviour is not very good: *It's difficult not to judge people sometimes.*

4 [T] to decide in a court of law whether or not someone is guilty

PHRASE **judging by/from sth** used for giving the reason why you think something is true: *Judging by his face, he was angry.*

judgment or **judgement** /ˈdʒʌdʒmənt/ noun ★★

1 [C/U] an opinion that you have after thinking carefully about something: *It is still too soon to form a judgment about this.* ♦ *He's too quick to make judgments about other people.* ♦ *She is not someone who passes judgment without knowing all the facts.* ♦ *In my judgment, he was not very good at his job.*

2 [U] your ability to understand a situation and make good decisions: *I trust your judgment.* ♦ *Her decision shows good judgment.*

3 [C/U] a decision that is made by a judge in a court of law = VERDICT

Words often used with **judgment**

Verbs often used with judgment (sense 2)
- **affect, cloud** + JUDGMENT: cause someone to make an unreasonable judgment
- **exercise, use** + JUDGMENT: be sensible when you are making a judgment

---

judgmental or **judgemental** /dʒʌdʒˈment(ə)l/ adj too willing to criticize other people

judicial /dʒuːˈdɪʃ(ə)l/ adj relating to judges or to courts of law

judiciary, the /dʒuːˈdɪʃəri/ noun [singular] the part of government that consists of all the judges and courts of law in a country

judicious /dʒuːˈdɪʃəs/ adj *formal* showing intelligence and good judgment

judo /ˈdʒuːdəʊ/ noun [U] a sport in which you fight using balance and the weight of your body to throw your opponent to the ground

jug /dʒʌg/ noun [C] a container from which you pour liquids

juggle /ˈdʒʌg(ə)l/ verb **1** [I/T] to keep objects moving through the air by catching them and throwing them back into the air **2** [T] to try to do several important things at the same time: *the pressures of juggling a career and children*

juggler /ˈdʒʌg(ə)lə/ noun [C] someone who juggles objects in order to entertain people

juice /dʒuːs/ noun [C/U] ★★

1 the liquid that comes out of fruit or vegetables, often used as a drink: *orange/apple/carrot juice* ♦ *a selection of fruit juices*

juggle

2 the liquid that comes out of meat when you cook it

juicy /ˈdʒuːsi/ adj **1** containing a lot of juice: *a sweet juicy apple* **2** *informal* slightly shocking but interesting or fun to listen to: *a juicy bit of gossip*

jukebox /ˈdʒuːkbɒks/ noun [C] a machine that plays music when you put money in it

Jul. abbrev July

July /dʒʊˈlaɪ/ noun [C/U] ★★★ the seventh month of the year, between June and August: *We're moving into our new house in July.* ♦ *The wedding is on July 19th.*

jumble¹ /ˈdʒʌmb(ə)l/ noun **1** [singular] a collection of different things that are mixed together: *a delightful jumble of pretty painted houses* **2** [U] *British* old things that are sold to raise money

jumble² /ˈdʒʌmb(ə)l/ or **jumble sth ˈup** verb [T] to mix things in a confusing or untidy way

ˈjumble ˌsale noun [C] *British* an event where people raise money by selling old things

jumbo /ˈdʒʌmbəʊ/ adj larger than other things of the same type: *jumbo sausages*

ˈjumbo ˌjet noun [C] a large plane for a lot of passengers

jump¹ /dʒʌmp/ verb ★★★

1 move off the ground	**5** move over sth
2 move because of shock	**6** move between ideas
3 increase very quickly	**+ PHRASES**
4 move suddenly	**+ PHRASAL VERB**

1 [I] to push your body off the ground using your legs: *The cat jumped up onto my lap.* ♦ *The children were all jumping up and down and cheering.*

2 [I] to get a shock and suddenly move your body slightly because of this: *The noise made her jump.*

3 [I] to increase or improve very quickly = SHOOT UP: *Profits jumped by 15% last year.* ♦ *Williams jumped from 39th to 5th in the world rankings.*

4 [I] to move somewhere quickly and suddenly: *He jumped in the car and drove off.* ♦ *Maggie jumped out of bed.*

5 [T] to move over something by pushing yourself off the ground using your legs: *Terry jumped the fence and walked across the field.*

J

6 [I] to move quickly from one idea to another: *The conversation suddenly jumped back to what had happened yesterday.*

PHRASES **jump down sb's throat** to criticize someone immediately, in an unfair way
jump the gun to do or say something too soon
jump the queue *British* to move in front of people who have been waiting for longer than you have
PHRASAL VERB **'jump at sth** to take an opportunity that is offered to you in a very enthusiastic way: *I jumped at the chance to go with him.*

jump² /dʒʌmp/ noun [C] **1** a movement in which you jump off the ground **2** a movement in which you jump from a high place: *a parachute/bungee jump* **3** a sudden increase =LEAP: *There has been another sharp jump in property prices.* **4** a structure that a horse or runner jumps over

jumper /ˈdʒʌmpə/ noun [C] *British* a piece of clothing that you pull over your head and that covers your upper body and arms =SWEATER —*picture* → C5

jumpy /ˈdʒʌmpi/ adj *informal* nervous

Jun. abbrev June

junction /ˈdʒʌŋkʃ(ə)n/ noun [C] *British* a place where one road or railway line crosses or joins another

juncture /ˈdʒʌŋktʃə/ noun [C] *formal* a point in a process or period of time

June /dʒuːn/ noun [C/U] ★★★ the sixth month of the year, between May and July: *The museum opens to the public in June.* ♦ *Our last class is on June 5th.*

jungle /ˈdʒʌŋɡ(ə)l/ noun **1** [C/U] a thick tropical forest **2** [U] *British* a type of dance music

junior¹ /ˈdʒuːniə/ adj ★
1 a junior person does not have a lot of responsibility or power in their job ≠ SENIOR: *junior doctors*
2 intended for young people, or involving them: *the world junior swimming championship*

junior² /ˈdʒuːniə/ noun [C] **1** a child in the UK who goes to a JUNIOR SCHOOL **2** a student in the US who is in the year before their last year at university or HIGH SCHOOL
PHRASE **be two years/ten years etc sb's junior** to be younger than someone else by a particular amount

junior³ /ˈdʒuːniə/ used after the name of a man who has the same name as his father

junior 'high school noun [C/U] a school in the US for children between the ages of 12 and 15

junior ,school noun [C/U] a school in the UK for children between the ages of 7 and 11

junk /dʒʌŋk/ noun [U] old things that are not valuable or not wanted =RUBBISH

junk ,food noun [C/U] food that is not healthy because it contains a lot of fat, salt, or sugar

junkie /ˈdʒʌŋki/ noun [C] *informal* **1** someone who is unable to stop taking illegal drugs **2** *often humorous* a person who likes doing

something very much and does it a lot: *a computer games junkie*

'junk ,mail noun [U] advertising and other information that is sent to you, but that you did not ask for

junta /ˈdʒʌntə/ noun [C] a group of military officers that governs a country

jurisdiction /ˌdʒʊərɪsˈdɪkʃ(ə)n/ noun [U] the right or power to make legal decisions

juror /ˈdʒʊərə/ noun [C] a member of a jury

jury /ˈdʒʊəri/ noun [C] ★★
1 a group of members of the public who decide whether someone is guilty in a court case: *The jury found him guilty.*
2 a group of people who judge a competition
PHRASE **the jury is (still) out (on sth)** used for saying that people have not yet decided what they think about something

just¹ /dʒʌst/ adv ★★★
1 a moment ago a short time ago, or a short time before something that happened in the past: *Mum's just gone down to the shops.* ♦ *Agassi had just arrived in Australia the day before.* ♦ *Just last week it was freezing, and now it's too hot.* ♦ *I've **only** just started, so I can't tell you anything yet.* ♦ *What were you saying to Lisa **just now** (=a moment ago)?*
2 at this time at the same time as something else: *I can't come now. I'm just putting the children to bed.* ♦ *Just then a knock at the door interrupted our conversation.* ♦ *Mahmud was **just about** to leave when someone called his name.* ♦ *I was **just going to** ask you the same question.*
3 only not more, bigger, more important etc than what you are mentioning: *The medicine costs just a few pence to produce.* ♦ *It was just a silly mistake.* ♦ *We just wanted to make sure everyone was safe.* ♦ *No, I don't want to buy anything. I'm just looking.* ♦ *It's **not** just me. Other people are complaining too.*
4 exactly exactly: *He's just like his father.* ♦ *Thank you so much, it was just what I wanted.* ♦ *Cameron's plan failed, **just as** I expected it would.*
5 slightly before, after, nearer, or further: *I spoke with him just after he won the award.* ♦ *Her parents were seated just behind her.*
6 used for emphasis *spoken* used for emphasizing what you are saying: *It was just awful seeing her so miserable.* ♦ *Just be quiet, will you?*
7 when sth almost does not happen used for saying that although something happens, it almost does not happen: *We should just get there in time if we hurry.*
8 used in requests *spoken* used for making a request more polite: *Could I just borrow your pen for a second?*
PHRASES **just about** very nearly: *I think we've just about finished.* ♦ *Another scandal would be just about the worst thing that could happen.*
just a minute/moment/second *spoken* **1** used

for asking someone to wait for a short time: *Just a moment. We're not ready for you yet.* **2** used when interrupting someone, especially when you disagree with what they are saying: *Just a minute. You can't make accusations like that.*

just as...(as) used for emphasizing that something is equally large, good, bad etc: *Less expensive machines are just as good or even better.* ♦ *Animals feel pain just as much as we do.*

just because... *spoken* used for saying that even if one thing is true, this is not a reason for thinking that something else is true: *Just because he's rich, it doesn't mean he's better than us.*

it/that is just as well *spoken* used for saying that a situation is good, even though it is not what you planned: *We cancelled the trip, which was just as well, because it rained.*
→ LIKE

just² /dʒʌst/ adj *formal* fair and morally right =FAIR ≠ UNJUST: *a just society*

justice /ˈdʒʌstɪs/ noun [U] ★★
1 treatment of people that is fair and morally right ≠ INJUSTICE: *The people want peace and justice.* ♦ *Victims are calling for justice.*
2 the legal process of judging and punishing people: *the criminal justice system* ♦ *Whoever committed these crimes must be brought to justice* (=judged in a court of law).
PHRASE **do sb/sth justice** to show or emphasize all the good qualities of someone or something

Justice of the Peace noun [C] an official similar to a judge who works in the lower courts =MAGISTRATE

justifiable /ˈdʒʌstɪˌfaɪəb(ə)l/ adj if something is justifiable, there is a good reason for it —**justifiably** adv

justification /ˌdʒʌstɪfɪˈkeɪʃ(ə)n/ noun [C/U] a reason why something is correct and morally right: *There can be no justification for such rude behaviour.*

justified /ˈdʒʌstɪˌfaɪd/ adj if something is justified, there is a good reason for it

justify /ˈdʒʌstɪˌfaɪ/ verb [T] ★★ to show that there is a good reason for something: *The results justify all our hard work.* ♦ *justify doing sth How can you justify spending all that money?*

jut /dʒʌt/ PHRASAL VERB ˌjut ˈout to be further forward than other things, or further forward than normal

juvenile¹ /ˈdʒuːvəˌnaɪl/ adj **1** relating to young people **2** silly and not suitable for an adult

juvenile² /ˈdʒuːvəˌnaɪl/ noun [C] a young person

juvenile deˈlinquent noun [C] a young person who has committed a crime

juxtapose /ˌdʒʌkstəˈpəʊz/ verb [T] *formal* to put different things together so that people can see how they are different —**juxtaposition** /ˌdʒʌkstəpəˈzɪʃ(ə)n/ noun [C/U]

K k

k or **K** /keɪ/ noun [C/U] the eleventh letter of the English alphabet

K¹ /keɪ/ abbrev **1** kilometre **2** kilobyte

K² /keɪ/ (plural **K**) noun [C] *informal* one thousand pounds, or one thousand dollars

kaleidoscope /kəˈlaɪdəˌskəʊp/ noun [C] **1** a scene, situation, or experience that keeps changing and has many different aspects **2** a toy that shows changing patterns. It consists of a tube with coloured pieces inside.

kangaroo /ˌkæŋɡəˈruː/ noun [C] a large Australian animal that moves by jumping and carries its baby in a POUCH (=pocket on the front of its body) —*picture* → C13

karaoke /ˌkæriˈəʊki/ noun [U] a type of entertainment in which people sing popular songs while recorded music is played

karate /kəˈrɑːti/ noun [U] a way of fighting from Japan, in which people hit each other using their hands, feet, arms, and legs

karma /ˈkɑːmə/ noun [U] in Hinduism and Buddhism, a belief that the way you behaved in past lives affects your present life, and the way you behave in future lives will affect your future lives

kayak /ˈkaɪæk/ noun [C] a small covered CANOE (=narrow boat with a point at each end)

kebab /kɪˈbæb/ noun [C] *British* a food that consists of small pieces of meat and vegetables cooked on a stick

keel /kiːl/ noun [C] a long thin piece of wood or metal along the bottom of a boat that helps it to balance in the water
PHRASE **on an even keel** operating or happening without problems

keen /kiːn/ adj ★★

1 wanting (sb) to do sth	4 very strong
2 wanting to do well	5 about sense/ability
3 very interested in	

1 wanting to do something or wanting other people to do something: **be keen to do sth** *The government is keen to avoid further conflict with the unions.* ♦ **be keen on doing sth** *The captain wasn't keen on having him in the team.* ♦ *I was quite keen on the idea of going to live in a bigger city.*
2 wanting to do something well =ENTHUSIASTIC: *Many of our players are very young and keen.*
3 very interested in an activity that you do often because you enjoy it: *a keen cyclist/ gardener* ♦ *Luke's keen on swimming.*
4 very strong: *a keen sense of duty* ♦ *Mr*

Lindsay always took a keen interest in his pupils' achievements.
5 keen sight, hearing etc makes you very good at seeing, hearing etc
—**keenly** /ˈkiːnli/ adv, **keenness** noun [U]

keep¹ /kiːp/ (past tense and past participle **kept** /kept/) verb ★★★

1 stay in state/position	**9** provide money for
2 continue/repeat	**10** look after animals
3 make sb/sth continue	**11** of food etc
4 continue to have	**12** for asking if sb is well
5 stay within limit	**13** delay sb
6 store sth somewhere	✦ PHRASES
7 store information	✦ PHRASAL VERBS
8 do what you said	

1 [I/T] to stay in a state, position, or place without changing or moving, or to make someone or something do this: *Keep still while I brush your hair.* ♦ *People kept quiet because they were afraid.* ♦ *Keep her warm and give her plenty to drink.*
2 [T] to do something many times, or to continue doing something: *Keep taking the tablets.* ♦ *I keep forgetting to put the answering machine on.* ♦ *Keep going straight until you reach the river.*
3 [T] to make someone or something continue doing something: *Sorry to keep you waiting.*
4 [T] to continue to have or own something: *We should keep this car and sell the other one.* ♦ *I've got two copies, you can keep that one.*
5 [T] to control something so that it stays within a limit: *Costs must be kept within reasonable limits.*
6 [T] to store something in a particular place so that you know where it is: *Where do you keep the washing powder?* ♦ *Read this letter carefully, and keep it in a safe place.*
7 [T] to store information by writing it or putting it into a computer: *Some companies do not keep detailed records.* ♦ *Every member of the group has to keep a diary.*
8 [T] to do what you said you would do: *If you cannot keep your appointment, please let us know.* ♦ *I have tried to keep my promise.*
9 [T] to provide money for yourself or someone else, in order to pay for the food, clothes, and other things that you or they need: *She keeps the family on two hundred pounds a week.*
10 [T] to own animals and look after them: *A few cows are kept to provide milk, cheese, and cream.*
11 [I] if food or other substances keep for a particular period of time, they stay in good condition for that period of time: *The sauce will keep for two weeks in the fridge.*
12 [I] *British spoken* used for asking if someone is well: *How are you keeping?* ♦ *Are you keeping well?*
13 [T] *spoken* to delay someone: *What kept you?* ♦ *I won't keep you long.*
PHRASES keep going 1 to continue to do something although it is difficult: *They*

forced themselves to keep going even though they felt exhausted.* **2** to continue to move without stopping: *The truck kept going and disappeared from view.*
keep sth to yourself to not tell anyone else about something
→ EYE¹

PHRASAL VERBS ,keep ˈat sth to continue doing something even if you want to stop: *The secret of dieting is to keep at it.*
,keep aˈway to avoid someone or something, or to not go near someone or something: *I've told him to keep away, but he won't listen.* ♦ *You should keep away from fried foods.*
,keep sth ˈback to not tell someone something, or to not show how you feel: *He said he was fine, but I knew he was keeping something back.*
,keep sth ˈdown to control something and prevent it from increasing in size or number: *We have to try and keep costs down.*
ˈkeep sb from sth to prevent someone from doing something, or to prevent something from happening: *These worries kept her from sleeping properly.*
ˈkeep sth from sb to not tell someone something: *I kept the news from him for a while.*
,keep sth ˈoff (sth) to not touch something, or to prevent something from touching something: *Keep the flies off the food.* ♦ *Keep your hands off, it's mine.*
keep (sb/sth) off sth to not go onto a particular area of land: *Dogs must be kept off the beach.* ♦ *Keep off the grass.*
,keep sb/sth ˈout 1 to prevent someone or something from entering a place: *Cars should be kept out of the city centre.* **2 keep out** used on signs to tell people not to go into a place
,keep ˈout of sth to not become involved with something: *You keep out of this. It's none of your concern.*
keep to sth to follow an agreement or a rule, by doing what you should do or what you said you would do: *Try to keep to a regular timetable of waking and sleeping.* ♦ *Always keep to the speed limit.*
ˈkeep sth to sth to prevent an amount or number from passing a limit: *You should keep your intake of alcohol to a minimum.*
,keep ˈup to move or develop at the same speed as someone or something: *By studying hard, she managed to keep up.* ♦ *He had to hurry to keep up with her.*
,keep sb ˈup to prevent someone from going to bed: *It's late, I'd better not keep you up any longer.*
,keep sth ˈup to continue to do something: *Keep up the good work.* ♦ *The trade unions continued to keep up pressure for higher wages.*
,keep ˈon doing sth to continue to do something: *My sister kept on asking me question after question.*
,keep ˈon *informal* to continue to talk about something in a way that annoys people: *I*

don't know why you **keep on** *about this.*

keep² /kiːp/ noun [U] the cost of the food and the other things such as clothes that you need to live

keeper /ˈkiːpə/ noun [C] someone who is responsible for looking after a place, a group of animals, or a collection of objects → SHOPKEEPER

keeping /ˈkiːpɪŋ/ noun **in/out of keeping with sth** in or not in the same manner or style as something else

keg /keg/ noun [C] a small BARREL (=round container with a flat top and bottom) that is used for storing beer or other drinks

kennel /ˈken(ə)l/ noun [C] **1** a small building where a dog sleeps and is protected from bad weather **2** a place where dogs stay while their owners are away

kept the past tense and past participle of **keep¹**

kerb /kɜːb/ noun [C] the edge of a PAVEMENT that is closest to the road

kernel /ˈkɜːn(ə)l/ noun [C] **1** the soft part inside a nut or a seed **2** the central or most important part of something

kerosene /ˈkerəsiːn/ noun [U] *American* PARAFFIN

ketchup /ˈketʃəp/ noun [U] a thick red sauce made from tomatoes

kettle /ˈket(ə)l/ noun [C] a container that is used for boiling water —*picture* → c2

key¹ /kiː/ noun [C] ★★★

1 for opening/locking	**5** in music
2 for achieving sth	**6** list of symbols
3 on keyboard	**7** list of answers
4 on instrument	

1 a small piece of metal that is used for opening or locking a door or a container, or for starting the engine of a vehicle: *a bunch of keys* ♦ *house/car keys* ♦ *I could hear someone* **turning the key** *in the lock.* ♦ *Where's the* **key to** *the back door?*
2 the thing that will do most to help you to achieve something: *Proper planning is the* **key to** *success.* ♦ *Tourism* **holds the key to** *the region's economic recovery.*
3 one of the parts that you press on a keyboard to make it produce letters, numbers, and symbols: *Highlight the file you want and* **press the** *RETURN* **key.**
4 one of the parts that you press on a musical instrument to make it produce sounds: *piano keys*
5 a set of musical notes that are based on one particular note: *a major/minor key* ♦ **in the key of** *D sharp*
6 a list of the symbols that are used on a map or a drawing
7 a list of answers to the questions in a test or in a book
→ LOCK²

key² /kiː/ adj ★★★ very important: *Foreign policy had been a* **key issue** *in the campaign.* ♦ *Women farmers are* **key to** *China's economic development.*

key³ /kiː/ or **key sth in** verb [T] to put information into a computer or other

electronic machine using a keyboard

keyboard /ˈkiːbɔːd/ noun [C] **1** a piece of computer equipment with keys on it, used for putting information into a computer —*picture* → c3 **2** the part of a musical instrument such as a piano that has the keys that you touch to make sounds **3** a musical instrument that has a keyboard, especially an electric piano

keyboard

computer keyboard

keyhole /ˈkiːhəʊl/ noun [C] the hole in a lock where you put the key

keynote /ˈkiːnəʊt/ adj a keynote speech is the most important speech at a formal meeting or event

keypad /ˈkiːpæd/ noun [C] a part of a piece of equipment that has keys that you press

key ring noun [C] a metal ring that you use for keeping your keys together

keyword /ˈkiːwɜːd/ noun [C] **1** a word that represents the main feature or idea of something: *The office was extremely tidy; efficiency was the keyword.* **2** a word that you type into a computer in order to find information about a particular subject

kg abbrev kilogram

khaki /ˈkɑːki/ adj green-brown or brown-yellow in colour —**khaki** noun [U]

kick¹ /kɪk/ verb ★★★

1 [I/T] to hit someone or something with your foot: *Mum! Jimmy kicked me!* ♦ **kick sth around** *A couple of children were kicking a ball around.* ♦ **kick sth open/closed/shut** *Southgate kicked the door open.* ♦ **kick sb in the stomach/face/head etc** *She felt as if she had been kicked in the stomach.*
2 [I/T] to move your legs as if you were kicking something: *A beetle lay on its back kicking its legs in the air.*
3 [T] *informal* to stop doing something that is bad for you: *Do you smoke and want to* **kick the habit?**

PHRASE **kick yourself** to be annoyed with yourself because you have made a mistake, or have missed an opportunity to do something
→ ALIVE

PHRASAL VERBS **kick in** *informal* to start to have an effect: *The medicine took some time to kick in.*

kick (sth) off *informal* to begin, or to begin something: *The game kicks off at noon.* ♦ *I'd like to* **kick off with** *a quick look at last month's sales figures.*

kick sb out *informal* to force someone to leave a place or organization: **kick sb out of sth**

K

Sonia's been kicked out of her house.

kick

kick² /kɪk/ *noun* **1** [C] a hit with your foot: *Bobby gave the door a good kick.* **2** [singular] *informal* a feeling of excitement or pleasure: *I get a real kick out of seeing my children do well in school.* ♦ *I just play the banjo for kicks – I'm not very good at it.*

kickoff /'kɪk,ɒf/ *noun* [C] the beginning of a game of football, when one player kicks the ball down the field

kick-'start *verb* [T] to make something start again after it has stopped or slowed down —**kick-,start** *noun* [C]

kid¹ /kɪd/ *noun* ★★
1 [C] *informal* a child or young adult: *There was a group of kids playing football in the street.* ♦ *a bunch of middle-class college kids* ♦ *When I was a kid, I was very shy.*
2 [C] a young goat
3 [U] leather made from a young goat's skin

kid² /kɪd/ *verb* [I/T] to say something that is not true, especially as a joke: *He said that? You're kidding me.* ♦ *Just kidding. Don't worry.*

kiddie or **kiddy** /'kɪdi/ *noun* [C] *informal* a young child

kidnap¹ /'kɪdnæp/ *verb* [T] to illegally take someone away and make them a prisoner, especially in order to make their family or a government give you money —**kidnapper** *noun* [C]

kidnap² or **kidnapping** /'kɪdnæp/ *noun* [C/U] the act of kidnapping someone

kidney /'kɪdni/ *noun* [C] one of the two organs in your body that clean your blood by removing waste liquids

'kidney ,bean *noun* [C] a red bean eaten as a vegetable —*picture* → C11

kill¹ /kɪl/ *verb* ★★★
1 [I/T] to make a person or other living thing die: *Each year thousands of people are killed and injured on the roads.* ♦ *Many people believe that killing animals for sport is morally wrong.* ♦ *Speed kills.*
2 [T] *informal* if part of your body is killing you, it is causing you a lot of pain: *My back's killing me.*
3 [T] to spend time doing a particular activity while you are waiting for something: *We killed a few hours watching videos.* ♦ *Shopping can be a good way to kill time at the airport.*
4 [T] to stop something from continuing: *The nurse will give you something to kill the pain.*

PHRASE **sb will kill sb** *spoken* used for saying that someone will be very angry with another person

PHRASAL VERB ,**kill sb/sth 'off 1** to destroy living things so that most or all of them are dead: *Antibiotics may kill off beneficial bacteria.* **2** to make something stop or fail completely: *The BBC has decided to kill off some of its best-loved programmes.*

Other ways of saying kill

- **assassinate** to kill an important or famous person for political reasons or for money
- **commit suicide** to deliberately kill yourself
- **execute** to kill someone legally as a punishment for a serious crime
- **massacre** to kill a very large number of people in a violent or cruel way
- **murder** to deliberately kill someone
- **put sth down** or **put sth to sleep** to kill an animal because it is ill or in pain

---

kill² /kɪl/ *noun* [singular] an act in which a hunted animal is killed

killer /'kɪlə/ *noun* [C] **1** someone who kills another person: *The young woman's killer has not yet been found.* **2** something that kills people: *Cancer is the second largest killer in the US.* **3** something that kills or destroys something else: *weed killer*

killing /'kɪlɪŋ/ *noun* [C] an act in which someone is deliberately killed

kiln /kɪln/ *noun* [C] a type of oven that is used for baking clay and bricks to make them hard

kilo /'kiːləʊ/ *noun* [C] a KILOGRAM

kilobyte /'kɪləʊ,baɪt/ *noun* [C] *computing* a unit for measuring computer information, containing 1024 BYTES

kilogram /'kɪlə,græm/ *noun* [C] a unit for measuring weight in the METRIC system, containing 1000 grams

kilometer /'kɪlə,miːtə, kɪ'lɒmɪtə/ the American spelling of **kilometre**

kilometre /'kɪlə,miːtə, kɪ'lɒmɪtə/ *noun* [C] a unit for measuring distance in the METRIC system, containing 1000 metres

kilowatt /'kɪlə,wɒt/ *noun* [C] a unit for measuring electrical power, containing 1000 WATTS

kilt /kɪlt/ *noun* [C] a type of traditional Scottish clothing, similar to a skirt, worn by men —*picture* → C4

kin /kɪn/ *noun* [U] *formal* all the people in your family → NEXT

kind¹ /kaɪnd/ *noun* [C] ★★★ a type of person or thing=SORT: *I guess I'm not the marrying kind.* ♦ *The bridge is the largest of its kind in the world.* ♦ *We've all had disappointments of some kind.* ♦ *There was no financial link between us of any kind.* ♦ *What kind of person is she?* ♦ *Francis taught me all kinds of stuff.* ♦ *Many people like to try lots of different kinds of food.*

PHRASES **in kind** payments or benefits in kind are in the form of goods or services rather than money

kind of *spoken* used when you are talking

about someone or something in a general way without being very exact or definite: *He was kind of strange, but I liked him.*

kind² /kaɪnd/ adj ★ behaving in a way that shows you care about other people and want to help them ≠ UNKIND: *Thank you, Mark, you've been very kind.* ♦ *We are grateful for your kind offer.* ♦ *She was very kind to me when the children were ill.* ♦ It is kind of sb to do sth *It was kind of you to help them.*

kinda /ˈkaɪndə/ adv a way of writing 'kind of' that shows how it sounds in informal conversation

kindergarten /ˈkɪndəˌɡɑːt(ə)n/ noun [C/U] **1** *British* a NURSERY SCHOOL **2** *American* the first year of formal education in the US, for children aged 5 or 6

kindle /ˈkɪnd(ə)l/ verb [T] **1** to start a strong interest or emotion in someone: *His interest in history was kindled by visits to the museum.* **2** to start a fire by lighting small pieces of wood or paper that will burn easily

kindling /ˈkɪndlɪŋ/ noun [U] small pieces of wood that you use for starting a fire

kindly¹ /ˈkaɪndli/ adv **1** in a kind way: *'Don't worry about it,' she said kindly.* **2** *spoken formal* used for making a polite request: *Would you kindly stop making that noise?* ♦ *Kindly return one copy of the letter to me.*
PHRASE **not take kindly to sth** to be annoyed by something

kindly² /ˈkaɪndli/ adj *old-fashioned* a kindly person behaves in a kind way towards other people

kindness /ˈkaɪn(d)nəs/ noun [U] kind behaviour, or kind feelings

king /kɪŋ/ noun [C] ★★★
1 a man who rules a country and is the senior male member of the royal family: *King George VI* ♦ *Oswald became king in 634.*
2 a man who is the best at doing a particular thing: *Elvis, the king of rock and roll*
3 a PLAYING CARD with the picture of a king on it: *the king of spades —picture →* C16
4 one of the two most important pieces in the game of CHESS *—picture →* C16

kingdom /ˈkɪŋdəm/ noun [C] a country or area that is ruled by a king or queen
PHRASE **the animal/plant kingdom** all the animals or plants that exist in the world

kingpin /ˈkɪŋpɪn/ noun [C] the most important person in a group or organization

king-size /ˈkɪŋ ˌsaɪz/ or **king-sized** /ˈkɪŋ ˌsaɪzd/ adj bigger than usual

kink /kɪŋk/ noun [C] **1** a bend or twist in something that is usually straight **2** something that is a problem or that seems strange: *We need time to iron out any kinks in the new system.*

kinship /ˈkɪnʃɪp/ noun [singular/U] *formal* the fact of being related to someone

kiosk /ˈkiːɒsk/ noun [C] a very small shop that sells newspapers, drinks etc

kipper /ˈkɪpə/ noun [C] a type of fish that has been preserved in salt and smoke

kiss¹ /kɪs/ verb [I/T] ★ to touch someone with your lips to show love or as a greeting: *They kissed again, and then he was gone.* ♦ *We all hugged and kissed each other.* ♦ *He went upstairs to kiss his son goodnight.*

kiss² /kɪs/ noun [C] an act of kissing someone: *Julius gave her another kiss.*

kit /kɪt/ noun **1** [C] a set of tools or equipment for a particular activity: *Cyclists should carry a repair kit.* ♦ *a sewing/shaving kit* **2** [U] *British* special clothes that you wear for a sport: *football/gym kit* **3** [C] all the pieces that you need to build something such as a vehicle or a computer

kitchen /ˈkɪtʃən/ noun [C] ★★★ a room where you prepare and cook food, and wash dishes: *We sometimes eat in the kitchen.* ♦ *kitchen utensils/appliances —picture →* C2

kite /kaɪt/ noun [C] a toy that flies in the air while you hold it by a long string

kitten /ˈkɪt(ə)n/ noun [C] a young cat

kitty /ˈkɪti/ noun [C] an amount of money collected by a group, to be spent by the group

kiwi fruit /ˈkiːwiː ˌfruːt/ noun [C/U] a fruit with green flesh, small black seeds, and a brown skin *—picture →* C10

km abbrev kilometre

knack /næk/ noun [singular] *informal* a particular skill or way of doing something: *She had a knack of making people feel really special.*

knackered /ˈnækəd/ adj *British informal* **1** very tired **2** damaged or destroyed

knead /niːd/ verb [T] to prepare DOUGH (=a mixture for making bread) or clay by pressing it continuously

knee /niː/ noun [C] ★★★
1 the part in the middle of your leg, where it bends: *a serious knee injury* ♦ *Bend your knees when you pick up heavy objects.* ♦ *We were up to our knees in mud.* ♦ *He got down on his knees for a closer look. —picture →* C14
2 the upper part of your legs when you are sitting down, where you can hold a child or object = LAP: *He was sitting in the armchair with the cat curled up on his knees.*
PHRASE **bring sb/sth to their knees** to almost defeat someone or something

kneecap /ˈniːkæp/ noun [C] the bone at the front of your knee

knee-jerk adj a knee-jerk reaction is immediate and not carefully considered

kneel /niːl/ (past tense and past participle **knelt** /nelt/) or **kneel down** verb [I] to put or have your knee or both knees on the ground: *She knelt in front of the fire to warm herself.* ♦ *He was kneeling at her feet. —picture →* POSTURE

knew the past tense of **know**

knickers /ˈnɪkəz/ noun [plural] *British* a piece of underwear for a woman's lower body

knife¹ /naɪf/ (plural **knives** /naɪvz/) noun [C] ★★★ an object with a blade, used for cutting food or as a weapon: *knives and*

K

forks ♦ *a kitchen/bread/carving knife* ♦ *The girls were threatened with a knife.* —picture → C2

knife² /naɪf/ verb [T] to injure or kill someone with a knife

knight¹ /naɪt/ noun [C] **1** in the past, a European soldier from a high social class who wore a suit of ARMOUR (=a metal suit) and rode a horse **2** a man in the UK who has been given a knighthood **3** a piece in the game of CHESS that is shaped like a horse's head —picture → C16

knight² /naɪt/ verb **be knighted** to be given a knighthood

knighthood /'naɪthʊd/ noun [C] an honour given by a British king or queen that allows a man to use the title 'Sir' before his name

knit /nɪt/ (past tense and past participle **knitted** or **knit**) verb [I/T] to make something such as a piece of clothing using wool and KNITTING NEEDLES (=sticks) → CLOSE-KNIT

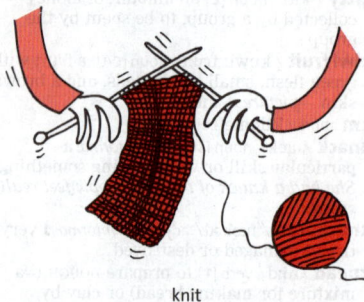

knit

knitting /'nɪtɪŋ/ noun [U] **1** the activity or process of knitting things **2** something that is being knitted

knitwear /'nɪt,weə/ noun [U] clothes that have been KNITTED

knives the plural of **knife¹**

knob /nɒb/ noun [C] **1** a round handle on a door or drawer **2** a round switch on a piece of equipment

knock¹ /nɒk/ verb ★★★

1 hit a door	4 hit sth hard
2 move sth by hitting	5 criticize sb/sth
3 hit sb hard	+ PHRASAL VERBS

1 [I] to hit a door with your hand or with a knocker: *They walked up to the door and knocked loudly.* ♦ *I knocked on his door but got no reply.*
2 [T] to hit something so that it moves somewhere: **knock sth off sth** *I knocked a picture off the wall.* ♦ **knock sth into sth** *He knocked a couple of nails into the door.*
3 [T] to hit someone very hard, so that they fall or become unconscious: *They knocked him to the ground.* ♦ *The driver had been knocked unconscious by the impact.*
4 [T] to hit something hard against an object: *Mike had knocked his leg against a table.*
5 [T] *informal* to criticize someone or something

PHRASAL VERBS **knock sb 'down** *British* to hit someone with a vehicle
,**knock sth 'down** to destroy a building or wall
,**knock 'off** to stop working
,**knock sth 'off (sth)** *informal* to reduce a price or an amount: *Kelly knocked two seconds off her previous time.*
,**knock sb 'out 1** to make someone unconscious **2** to make someone leave a competition by defeating them **3** *informal* to impress or surprise someone very much
,**knock sb 'over** *British same as* **knock sb down**: *Over 100 people are knocked over on Britain's roads every day.*

knock

knock² /nɒk/ noun [C] **1** the sound of someone knocking on a door: *There was a loud knock at the door.* **2** damage or an injury that is caused by being knocked: *a nasty knock on the head* **3** something bad that happens to someone: *Life is full of hard knocks.*

knocker /'nɒkə/ noun [C] a piece of metal on a door that you use for knocking

'**knock-on** adj *British* a knock-on effect is the indirect result of something

knockout /'nɒkaʊt/ noun [C] **1** a hit that knocks a BOXER down, so that they cannot get up **2** *British* a competition in which a player or team that loses a game leaves the competition

knot /nɒt/ noun [C] **1** a point where string, rope, or cloth is tied or twisted together and pulled tight: *Can you tie a knot in the end of this thread?* **2** a unit for measuring the speed of ships, aircraft, and wind, equal to one NAUTICAL MILE per hour

knotted /'nɒtɪd/ adj with knots: *a scarf with knotted corners*

know¹ /nəʊ/ (past tense **knew** /njuː/; past participle **known** /nəʊn/) verb ★★★

1 have information	6 experience
2 be familiar with	7 have learned sth
3 feel certain about	+ PHRASES
4 use particular name	+ PHRASAL VERB
5 remember sb for sth	

1 [I/T] to have information about something, or to understand something: *How do you know my name?* ♦ *'Have they arrived yet?' 'I don't know.'* ♦ *If you don't know the answer, just guess.* ♦ **+(that)** *I knew she wasn't really happy.* ♦ **+what/why/who etc** *None of us really knew what had gone wrong.* ♦ *I don't know if she's made a decision yet.* ♦ **know sth about sth** *Do you know anything about computers?* ♦ **be known to be/do sth** *Some* *drugs are known to cause damage to unborn children.*

2 [T] to be familiar with someone or something, for example because you have met someone before or been to a place before: *Do you know Terry Davis?* ♦ *Jane and I have* **known each other** *for years.* ♦ *Do you* **know** *Rome well?*

3 [I/T] to feel certain about something: +(that) *She knew it was Steven before she'd picked up the phone.*

4 [T] to use a particular name for someone or something: *They know all their tutors by their first names.* ♦ **be known as sth** *The village was known as Garden Mill.*

5 [T] to remember someone because of a particular skill or quality: *We know her mostly for her love poetry.* ♦ *He was* **best known as** *a painter.*

6 [T] to experience something: *It was the only comfort and warmth she had ever known.* ♦ **have never known sb (to) do sth** *I've never known her to make a joke.*

7 [T] to have learned a poem, story, or song, so that you can say it or sing it

PHRASES **for all I know** used for emphasizing that you do not know something: *He could be a murderer for all I know.*

get to know to start to be familiar with someone or something: *It took a while to get to know the city properly.*

how should I know? *spoken* used for saying in an annoyed way that you do not know something

I don't know 1 used for politely disagreeing or giving your opinion: *'It'll be boring.' 'Oh I don't know, it might be fun.'* ♦ **+that** *I don't know that we need to discuss this.* **2** used for criticizing someone: **+what/how/why etc** *I don't know how he could do that.*

I know 1 used for agreeing with what someone says: *'He's a complete idiot.' 'Yeah, I know.'* **2** used for showing that you understand that there is a problem, but you do not think it is important: *I know the plan is pretty rough, but you get the idea.* **3** used for showing that you understand someone and feel sympathy for them: *I know how hard this is for you.* **4** used when you have a sudden idea: *I know, let's go to the cinema instead.*

know best to be in the best position to decide something

know better 1 to understand that you should not do something, because you are sensible or experienced: *She should know better than to try to fool him.* **2** to know that what someone else says or thinks is wrong: *Everyone thought it was an innocent mistake, but I knew better.*

let sb know to tell someone something: *Let me know when he arrives.*

not want to know *informal* to refuse to listen to someone or get involved in something

you know *spoken* **1** used for emphasis: *Things are different now, you know.* **2** *informal* used while you think about what to say next: *My whole leg was, you know, soaked in blood.*

3 used when you are giving extra information about something: *Have you seen that bowl, you know, the blue one?* **4** used before you start to talk about a particular person or thing: *You know the woman next door, well, she's expecting a baby.*

you never know *spoken* used for saying that something good might happen

PHRASAL VERB **ˈknow of sb/sth 1** to know about someone or something: *I only know of one case in which this has happened.* ♦ *Do you know of anyone who's looking for a new car?* **2** **not that I know of** *spoken* used for answering that you think that something is not true, although you are not completely certain

Word family: know

Words in the same family as **know**
- **knowing** *adj*
- **knowingly** *adv*
- **knowledge** *n*
- **knowledgeable** *adj*
- **known** *adj*
- **unknowingly** *adv*
- **unknown** *adj*

know² /nəʊ/ noun **in the know** having more information about something than other people

ˈknow-all noun [C] *British informal* someone who is annoying because they always think that they know everything

ˈknow-how noun [U] *informal* the knowledge that is needed to do something

knowing /ˈnəʊɪŋ/ adj showing that you know about something: *Tom gave me a knowing look.*

knowingly /ˈnəʊɪŋli/ adv **1** deliberately, knowing that something is wrong or illegal: *Had her grandmother knowingly taken the money?* **2** in a way that shows that you know something: *She smiled knowingly.*

knowledge /ˈnɒlɪdʒ/ noun [U] ★★★
1 what you know, or what is known about a particular subject: *She had a lot of knowledge and experience.* ♦ *the pursuit of knowledge* ♦ *Candidates should have a good* **knowledge of** *Russian.*
2 the fact that you know that something is happening: *This was done without my knowledge.* ♦ *Daniels has denied all* **knowledge of** *the events.* ♦ **+that** *The staff had no knowledge that the company was in trouble.*

PHRASE **to (the best of) my knowledge** used for saying that you think that something is true, but you are not completely certain
→ COMMON KNOWLEDGE

Knowledge is never used in the plural and cannot be used with a: *a very important piece of knowledge* (NOT *a very important knowledge*) ♦ *They claim not to have* **any knowledge** *about what happened.* ♦ *Most of the students have* **some knowledge** *of computers.*

knowledgeable /ˈnɒlɪdʒəb(ə)l/ adj knowing a lot about one subject or many subjects

known¹ /nəʊn/ adj **1** discovered or known about by people: *a disease with no known cure* **2** famous: *internationally known TV personalities*

K

known² the past participle of **known¹**

knuckle /ˈnʌk(ə)l/ noun [C] one of the parts where your fingers can bend, or where they join your hand

koala /kəʊˈɑːlə/ or **koˈala ˌbear** noun [C] an Australian animal with grey fur, large ears, and no tail. It lives in trees. —*picture* → C12

Koran, the /kɔːˈrɑːn/ the holy book of Islam

kosher /ˈkəʊʃə/ adj approved or allowed by Jewish laws concerning food

Kremlin, the /ˈkremlɪn/ the government of Russia or, in the past, of the Soviet Union

kudos /ˈkjuːdɒs/ noun [U] praise and respect because of something that you have achieved

kung fu /ˌkʌŋ ˈfuː/ noun [U] a Chinese sport in which people fight using their hands and feet

kW abbrev kilowatts

I¹ or **L** /el/ noun [C/U] the 12th letter of the English alphabet

I² abbrev litre

L abbrev **1** large: used on clothes labels **2** *British* learner: fixed to a car in the UK to show that the driver is still learning to drive

lab /læb/ noun [C] *informal* a LABORATORY

label¹ /ˈleɪb(ə)l/ noun [C] ★★
1 a piece of paper or material fastened to an object that gives information about the object: *Always read the label on medical products.*
2 a company that produces records: *Their album was released on the Digital Experience label.*
3 a company that designs and makes expensive clothes: *After working with Armani, he launched his own label.*
4 a word or phrase that is used for describing someone or something: *a group of writers who were given the label 'Angry Young Men'*

label² /ˈleɪb(ə)l/ (past tense and past participle **labelled**; present participle **labelling**) verb [T] **1** to use a word or phrase in order to describe someone or something, especially in a way that is not fair or true=BRAND: *We shouldn't label these boys as criminals so early in their lives.* **2** to put a label on an object —**labelling** noun [U]

labor /ˈleɪbə/ the American spelling of **labour**

laboratory /ləˈbɒrət(ə)ri, *American* ˈlæbrətɔːri/ noun [C] ★ a building or large room where people do scientific research: *our new research laboratory ♦ laboratory tests/experiments/studies* → LANGUAGE LABORATORY

labored /ˈleɪbəd/ the American spelling of **laboured**

laborer /ˈleɪbərə/ the American spelling of **labourer**

laborious /ləˈbɔːriəs/ adj long, difficult, and boring: *a laborious task* —**laboriously** adv

ˈlabor ˌunion noun [C] *American* a TRADE UNION

labour¹ /ˈleɪbə/ noun ★★
1 [U] the workers in a country, industry, or company when they are thought of as a group: *labour costs ♦ a plentiful supply of cheap labour ♦ the demand for skilled labour*
2 [U] workers' organizations and their leaders when they are thought of as a group: *a meeting between management and labour ♦ a labour dispute*
3 [C/U] work, especially physical work: *The price includes the cost of labour.*
4 [singular/U] the process by which a baby is pushed from its mother's body when it is being born: *labour pains ♦ She went into labour early this morning. ♦ His wife was in labour for six hours.*

labour² /ˈleɪbə/ verb [I] **1** to work hard, or to put a lot of effort into something **2** to move very slowly and with difficulty

Labour¹ /ˈleɪbə/ the British LABOUR PARTY

Labour² /ˈleɪbə/ adj relating to or supporting the British LABOUR PARTY

laboured /ˈleɪbəd/ adj **1** if someone's breathing is laboured, they are breathing with difficulty **2** not natural because of being done with too much effort: *laboured jokes*

labourer /ˈleɪbərə/ noun [C] someone whose job involves hard physical work

ˈlabour ˌforce noun [C] all the people who work in an industry or country

ˌlabour-inˈtensive adj needing a lot of workers rather than machines

ˈlabour ˌmarket noun [C] the number of people who are available to work

ˈlabour ˌmovement, the noun [singular] political parties and other organizations whose aim is to improve conditions for workers

ˈLabour ˌParty, the one of the three main political parties in the UK. Its original aim was to try to improve conditions for workers.

Labrador /ˈlæbrədɔː/ noun [C] a large dog with short fur

labyrinth /ˈlæbərɪnθ/ noun [C] a place with a lot of paths or streets where you can easily become lost=MAZE

lace¹ /leɪs/ noun **1** [U] light delicate cloth with patterns of small holes in it **2** [C] a thick piece of string that is used for tying shoes or clothing

lace² /leɪs/ verb **1** [I/T] to fasten something with a lace, or to be fastened with a lace **2** [T] to put strong alcohol, a drug, or poison into a drink or food

PHRASAL VERB **ˌlace (sth) ˈup** same as **lace²** 1

laceration /ˌlæsəˈreɪʃ(ə)n/ noun [C/U] a deep cut in your skin

lack¹ /læk/ noun [singular/U] ★★ a situation in which you do not have something, or do not have enough of something: *The match was cancelled because of lack of support.* ♦ *a lack of confidence* ♦ *The court case was dismissed for lack of evidence.*

lack² /læk/ verb [T] ★ to not have something, or to not have enough of something: *He lacked the skills required for the job.* ♦ *Many people lack confidence in their own abilities.*

lacking /'lækɪŋ/ adj if something is lacking, there is none of it, or not enough of it: *Concern for passenger safety has been sadly lacking.* ♦ *She seems to be lacking in common sense.*

lacklustre /'læk،lʌstə/ adj not lively, exciting, or impressive

lacquer /'lækə/ noun [C/U] a liquid that you put on wood or metal in order to make it shiny —**lacquer** verb [T]

lactose /'læk،təʊs/ noun [U] a type of sugar that is in milk

lacy /'leɪsi/ adj made of LACE, or looking like LACE

lad /læd/ noun [C] *British informal* a boy, or a young man

ladder /'lædə/ noun [C] ★
1 a piece of equipment for reaching high places that consists of two long pieces of wood or metal joined by smaller pieces called **rungs**: *A fireman climbed the ladder.*
2 a system that has different levels through which you can progress: *She rose to a high position on the corporate ladder.*
3 *British* a long thin hole in STOCKINGS or TIGHTS

ladder

laden /'leɪd(ə)n/ adj carrying or supporting something heavy: *Passengers got off the train laden with boxes and suitcases.*

Ladies, the /'leɪdiz/ noun [plural] *British informal* a room with a toilet for women in a restaurant, hotel etc

ladle /'leɪd(ə)l/ noun [C] a large deep spoon with a long handle that is used for serving liquid food such as soup —**ladle** verb [T]

lady /'leɪdi/ noun [C] ★★★
1 a woman. Some people think that this use is polite, but other people think that it is old-fashioned and prefer to use 'woman': *Go and ask that lady over there.*
2 a woman who behaves politely and in a way that was traditionally considered suitable for a woman: *She doesn't talk like a lady.*
  PHRASE **ladies and gentlemen** *formal* used for

addressing an audience of men and women → FIRST LADY

Lady /'leɪdi/ in the UK, used as a title for some women who have important social or official positions

ladybird /'leɪdi،bɜːd/ noun [C] *British* a small insect that has a round red or yellow body with small black spots —*picture* → C13

ladylike /'leɪdi،laɪk/ adj behaving in a quiet polite way that was traditionally thought to be suitable for a woman

lag¹ /læg/ verb [I] **1** to not be as successful or advanced as other people or organizations =TRAIL: *Their software tends to lag behind other producers.* **2** to walk more slowly than the people you are with

lag² /læg/ noun [singular] a period of time or delay between one event and another → JET LAG

lager /'lɑːgə/ noun [C/U] a type of light-coloured beer, or a glass of this beer

lagoon /lə'guːn/ noun [C] an area of sea water that is separated from the sea by sand or rocks

laid the past tense and past participle of **lay¹**

laid-back adj *informal* calm and relaxed

lain the past participle of **lie¹**

lair /leə/ noun [C] a place where a wild animal lives

laissez-faire /،leɪseɪ 'feə/ adj allowing someone to do what they want to do, and to do it in any way that they want to

lake /leɪk/ noun [C] ★★ a large area of water surrounded by land: *There were some boys swimming in the lake.*

lamb /læm/ noun [C/U] a young sheep, or its meat

lambast /læm'bæst/ verb [T] *mainly journalism* to criticize someone angrily, especially in public

lame /leɪm/ adj **1** not at all impressive or likely to persuade someone: *a lame excuse* **2** a lame animal cannot walk very well because its leg or foot is damaged —**lamely** adv

lame 'duck noun [C] a person or organization that is not successful and needs a lot of help

lament /lə'ment/ verb [I/T] to show publicly that you feel sad or disappointed about something: *Some older people lament the loss of close local communities.* —**lament** noun [C]

lamentable /'læməntəb(ə)l/ adj extremely bad, and deserving criticism

laminate¹ /'læmɪnət/ noun [C/U] a substance that consists of several thin layers of wood, plastic, glass etc

laminate² /'læmɪ،neɪt/ verb [T] to cover something with a thin layer of plastic that protects it

lamp /læmp/ noun [C] ★★
1 an electric light that stands on a floor or table —*picture* → C3
2 an oil or gas light
3 a piece of equipment that produces light and heat: *an ultra-violet lamp*

lampoon /læm'puːn/ verb [T] to publicly

L

criticize someone or something by making jokes about them —**lampoon** noun [C]

lamppost /ˈlæmp.pəʊst/ noun [C] a tall post at the side of a road with a light on top

lampshade /ˈlæmpʃeɪd/ noun [C] a cover for a light that makes it less bright

LAN /læn, ˌel eɪ ˈen/ noun [C] *computing* local area network: a system that allows computers in the same building or area to exchange information

lance /lɑːns/ noun [C] a very long pointed weapon that was used in the past by soldiers on horses

land¹ /lænd/ noun ★★★
1 [U] an area of ground, especially one used for a particular purpose such as farming or building: *Some of his land had been flooded.* ♦ *The land around here is very fertile.*
♦ *acres of agricultural land*
2 [U] the part of the Earth's surface that is not water: *The vehicle can travel on land or in water.*
3 [C] *literary* a real or imaginary country: *a land of abundant wildlife and great beauty*
→ COUNTRY
→ NO-MAN'S-LAND

land² /lænd/ verb ★★

1 of plane	**4** be in bad situation
2 arrive by boat	**5** get sth you wanted
3 fall or fly to the ground	

1 [I/T] if an aircraft lands, or if you land it, it comes down to the ground ≠ TAKE OFF: *The plane landed a couple of hours before dawn.* ♦ *The pilot was able to land the aircraft safely.*
2 [I] to arrive at a place by boat: *The refugees landed on the east side of the island.*
3 [I] to come down to a surface after falling or flying: *She fell from the window, and landed in the bushes.*
4 [I/T] to put someone in an unexpected or unpleasant situation, or to be in this kind of situation: **land sb in sth** *His attitude could land him in trouble.*
5 [T] to get something that you wanted: *At the age of 19 she landed a part in a West End play.*
→ FOOT¹

landed /ˈlændɪd/ adj owning a lot of land: *a member of the landed gentry*

landfill /ˈlæn(d)fɪl/ or **ˈlandfill ˌsite** noun [C] a large hole in the ground where rubbish from people's homes or from industry is buried

landing /ˈlændɪŋ/ noun **1** [C/U] the process of moving a plane down from the air onto the ground: *The pilot was forced to make an emergency landing.* **2** [C] the area at the top of a set of stairs —*picture* → C1

landlady /ˈlæn(d)leɪdi/ noun [C] **1** a woman who owns a house, flat, or room that people can rent **2** *British* a woman who owns or manages a PUB or a small hotel → LANDLORD

landline /ˈlæn(d)laɪn/ noun [C] a telephone that is not a mobile phone

landlocked /ˈlæn(d)lɒkt/ adj a landlocked country is surrounded by land

landlord /ˈlæn(d)lɔːd/ noun [C] **1** a man who owns a house, flat, or room that people can rent **2** *British* a man who owns or manages a PUB or a small hotel → LANDLADY

landmark /ˈlæn(d)mɑːk/ noun [C] **1** a famous building or object that you can easily recognize **2** something that marks an important stage in a process, and influences how it will develop: *This book has become a landmark in art criticism.*

ˈland ˌmass noun [C] a CONTINENT or a large area of land that is surrounded by sea

landmine /ˈlæn(d)maɪn/ noun [C] a bomb hidden under the ground that explodes when someone moves over it

landowner /ˈlændˌəʊnə/ noun [C] someone who owns a large amount of land

landscape¹ /ˈlæn(d)skeɪp/ noun **1** [C] an area of land that has particular features: *a green, rural landscape* **2** [C] a painting of an area of land **3** [U] a way of arranging a page so that its long sides are at the top and bottom → PORTRAIT

landscape² /ˈlæn(d)skeɪp/ verb [T] to add features such as plants and paths to a piece of land —**landscaping** noun [U]

landslide /ˈlæn(d)slaɪd/ noun [C] **1** a heavy fall of earth and rocks down the side of a mountain **2** a victory by a very big majority in an election

lane /leɪn/ noun [C] ★★
1 *British* a narrow road, especially in the countryside: *They live down a little country lane.*
2 one of the parts that a wide road or motorway is divided into. A lane is intended for one line of traffic: *the fast/slow lane* ♦ *Are taxis allowed to drive in the bus lane?*
3 the part of a RACING TRACK or SWIMMING POOL that is used by one person in a competition
4 a course that a ship or aircraft follows

language /ˈlæŋɡwɪdʒ/ noun ★★★
1 [U] the method of human communication using spoken or written words: *language skills* ♦ *a new study of how a child learns language* ♦ *a comparison between spoken and written language*
2 [C] the particular form of words and speech that is used by the people of a country, area, or social group: *African languages* ♦ *English and French are the official languages of Canada.* ♦ *Do you speak any other languages?*
3 [C/U] signs, symbols, sounds, and other methods of communicating information or ideas: *computer languages* ♦ *the language of dance*
PHRASE **speak/talk the same language** to have the same ideas and attitudes as someone else
→ BODY LANGUAGE, FIRST LANGUAGE, SECOND LANGUAGE

'language la'boratory noun [C] a room with special equipment such as computers, CASSETTE RECORDERS and VIDEO RECORDERS for students who are learning a foreign language

languid /'læŋgwɪd/ adj very slow and relaxed

languish /'læŋgwɪʃ/ verb [I] to remain in a difficult or unpleasant situation

lanky /'læŋki/ adj tall, thin, and not very graceful: *a lanky teenager*

lantern /'læntən/ noun [C] a light inside a transparent container that has a handle for carrying it

lap¹ /læp/ noun [C] **1** the top half of your legs above your knees when you sit down: *The cat settled on Christine's lap.* **2** one complete journey around a course in a race

lap² /læp/ verb **1** [T] if an animal laps water, it drinks it with its tongue **2** [I/T] if water laps against something, it moves against it gently with a soft sound **3** [T] to pass someone else in a race when you are ahead of them by a whole lap

PHRASAL VERB **'lap sth 'up** to enjoy something very much: *There are photographers following her wherever she goes, but she's lapping it up.*

lapel /lə'pel/ noun [C] one of the two parts on each side of the front of a coat or jacket that are folded back

lapse¹ /læps/ noun [C] **1** a short period when you fail to do something, or fail to show a quality: *He suffers from memory lapses.* ♦ *lapses in concentration* **2** a period of time between two events: *There was a lapse of ten years between his visits.*

lapse² /læps/ verb [I] **1** to stop gradually or for a short time: *At this point conversation lapsed.* **2** if an official document, decision, or right lapses, it is no longer effective

PHRASAL VERB **'lapse into sth** to change to a different way of speaking or behaving: *She often lapses into French* (=starts speaking French).

laptop /'læp,tɒp/ noun [C] a small computer that you can carry with you=NOTEBOOK

lard /lɑːd/ noun [U] white fat that is used in cooking

larder /'lɑːdə/ noun [C] a cupboard or small room where food is stored

large /lɑːdʒ/ adj ★★★ bigger than usual in size, number, or amount: *a house with a very large garden* ♦ *a large software company* ♦ *large sums of money* ♦ *A large crowd had gathered outside the American Embassy.* ♦ *She's a rather large woman with red hair.*

PHRASES **at large** not yet caught and put into prison or into a cage: *The murderer is still at large.*

the public/population etc at large most people in a particular group: *the opinions of American society at large*

→ BY

largely /'lɑːdʒli/ adv ★★ mainly: *Our success is largely due to your efforts.* ♦ *Her poetry has largely been forgotten.*

'large-,scale adj **1** involving a large number of people or things, or happening over a large area **2** a large-scale map is one that shows a lot of details

lark /lɑːk/ noun [C] a small brown bird that is known for its singing

larva /'lɑːvə/ (plural **larvae** /'lɑːviː/) noun [C] an insect that looks like a small WORM, before it changes into an insect with wings

lasagne /lə'zænjə/ noun [C/U] an Italian meal made with layers of flat pasta with a sauce, cheese, and meat or vegetables

laser /'leɪzə/ noun [C] a piece of equipment that produces a powerful line of light that can be used as a tool, or the line of light that is produced: *laser surgery*

'laser ,printer noun [C] a type of computer printer that uses a laser to produce clear letters and images

lash¹ /læʃ/ verb **1** [T] to tie something firmly to something else **2** [I/T] to hit against something with a very strong force: *Waves lashed the shore.* **3** [T] to hit someone or something with a WHIP or a thin stick

PHRASAL VERB **,lash 'out 1** to try to hit or attack someone suddenly and violently **2** to speak angrily to or about someone

lash² /læʃ/ noun [C] **1** an EYELASH **2** a hit with a WHIP or a thin stick

lass /læs/ noun [C] British informal a girl, or a young woman

lasso /lə'suː/ noun [C] a long rope with one end tied in a circle that is used for controlling horses, cows etc, especially in North America —**lasso** verb [T]

last¹ /lɑːst/ grammar word ★★★

> **Last** can be:
> ■ a **determiner**: *I wasn't here last time.*
> ■ an **adjective**: *I ate the last piece of cake.* ♦ *I was last in the race.*
> ■ a **pronoun**: *Their new CD is even better than the last.*
> ■ an **adverb**: *I put my shoes on last.*
> ■ a **noun**: *I drank up the last of the wine.*

1 happening, coming, or ending most recently: *I don't agree with that last comment.* ♦ *During the last hour the storms have been getting worse.* ♦ *I last saw her three years ago.* ♦ **The last time** *we met, you were moving to Greenwich.* ♦ *How did you boys sleep* **last night**? ♦ **Last year** *the company made a profit of £350 million.* ♦ *We went to the play* **the night before last** (=two nights ago).

2 happening or coming at the end, after all the others: *Fry the onions until crisp, and add them last.* ♦ *That's* **the last time** *I'm ever going out with him.* ♦ **The last of the** *guests had arrived.* ♦ *Baker finished* **next to last** (=one before the last) *in the 1500 metres.* ♦ *Janice was* **the last to** *leave.*

3 remaining after all the rest have gone: *the last book left on the shelf* ♦ *Who wants the* **last** *of the ice cream?* ♦ *He is* **the last** *great writer of his generation.*

4 used for emphasizing that someone or something is not at all likely, suitable, or

L

wanted: *Hurting you is* **the last thing** *I'd want to do.* ♦ *I'm* **the last person** *you should be asking for advice.*

PHRASES **at the last moment/minute** when it is almost too late: *At the last minute she decided not to come after all.*

at (long) last used for saying that something that you have been waiting for finally happens: *I'm so glad to meet you at last.*

have the last word 1 to win an argument by making the last statement **2** to make the final decision about something: *The president has the last word.*

→ LAST-MINUTE, RESORT[1]

last² /lɑːst/ verb ★★★
1 [I] to continue happening for a particular period, or until a particular time: *The game lasts 80 minutes.* ♦ *The conference will last for two weeks.* ♦ *The party lasted until the early morning.*
2 [I/T] to continue to be available, or to be enough for what people need: *The water won't last long.* ♦ *Thirty pounds usually lasted him a week.*
3 [I] to continue in a good state without changing or failing: *I hope the good weather will last.* ♦ *These cars are built to last.*

last-ditch adj a last-ditch attempt, effort etc is a final try at achieving something difficult, when other attempts have already failed

lasting /ˈlɑːstɪŋ/ adj continuing to exist or to have an effect for a long time: *We have an opportunity here for a lasting peace.*

lastly /ˈlɑːs(t)li/ adv used when you want to say one more thing before you finish speaking=FINALLY: *And lastly, remember that your essays are due tomorrow.*

last-minute adj happening or done at the latest possible time: *You can do any last-minute shopping at the airport.*

last name noun [C] the name that you share with the other members of your family. In English, it comes at the end of your full name=FAMILY NAME, SURNAME

last orders noun [plural] *British* a request for people in a bar or PUB to order their last drinks before it closes

last word, the noun [singular] the newest and best type of something: *a five-star hotel that is the last word in luxury*

latch¹ /lætʃ/ noun [C] **1** an object for keeping a door, gate etc shut **2** a lock for a door that needs a key to open it from the outside, although it can be opened from the inside without one

latch² /lætʃ/ **PHRASAL VERB** **latch on** *informal* to suddenly understand or realize something

late /leɪt/ adj, adv ★★★
1 arriving somewhere or doing something after the expected or usual time ≠ EARLY: *The trains are all running about 15 minutes late.* ♦ *She phoned to say she'd be late.* ♦ *Sheila was late for work again this morning.*
2 near the end of an evening or night: *Late one night I heard a knock on the door.* ♦ *It*

was getting late and all the kids were sleepy. ♦ *We had a late night last night* (=went to bed when it was late).
3 near the end of a period of time ≠ EARLY: *the late 18th century* ♦ *These bulbs bloom in late spring.* ♦ *a girl in her late teens*
4 used for talking about someone who has died, especially recently: *my late aunt*

PHRASES **better late than never** used for saying that it is good that something has happened, but that it would have been better if it had been earlier

too late if you are too late, you have missed the best or only time for doing something: *The ambulance arrived, but it was too late.*

latecomer /ˈleɪtˌkʌmə/ noun [C] someone who arrives late

lately /ˈleɪtli/ adv recently: *Have you seen either of them lately?*

late-night adj happening late at night: *a late-night film*

latent /ˈleɪt(ə)nt/ adj something that is latent exists, but it is not obvious and has not developed yet: *latent aggression*

later¹ /ˈleɪtə/ adv ★★★ at some time in the future, or after the time that you have been talking about: *She'll be home later.* ♦ *We can make an appointment for later in the week.*

PHRASES **later on** at a time in the future, or after the time that you have been talking about: *I'll come and see you later on.*

see you later *informal* used for saying goodbye: *Okay, I'm leaving now. See you later.*

later² /ˈleɪtə/ adj **1** happening at some time in the future, or after the time that you have been talking about: *We can settle on the price at a later date.* **2** near the end of a period of time, or near the end of someone's life or career: *Her views changed in her later years.*

lateral /ˈlæt(ə)rəl/ adj *technical* on the side of something, or moving sideways

latest /ˈleɪtɪst/ adj ★★★ most recent or newest: *The latest figures show steady growth.*

latest, the /ˈleɪtɪst/ noun [singular] the most recent event, thing, piece of news etc: *Have you heard the latest? He's getting a divorce.*

PHRASE **at the latest** no later than a particular time

latex /ˈleɪteks/ noun [U] a substance that is used for making rubber, paint, and glue

lather /ˈlɑːðə, ˈlæðə/ noun [singular] the white mass of BUBBLES that is produced when you mix soap and water

Latin¹ /ˈlætɪn/ noun [U] the language that people spoke in ancient Rome. Modern European languages such as Italian, Spanish, and French developed from it.

Latin² /ˈlætɪn/ adj **1** written in Latin **2** relating to people who speak languages that developed from Latin, or to their culture

Latin American adj from or relating to Mexico, Central America, or South America —**Latin American** noun [C]

Latino /læˈtiːnəʊ/ noun [C] someone whose family is Latin American —**Latino** adj

latitude /ˈlætɪˌtjuːd/ noun [C/U] technical the distance of a point on the Earth from the EQUATOR (=the imaginary line around the centre of the Earth), measured in degrees north or south → LONGITUDE

latte /ˈlæteɪ, ˈlɑːteɪ/ noun [C/U] a drink made by mixing ESPRESSO (=strong coffee) with hot milk

latter /ˈlætə/ grammar word

> **Latter** can be:
> ■ an **adjective**: He considered his students either geniuses or idiots, and I fell into the latter category.
> ■ a **pronoun**: Given a choice between Tahiti and Hawaii, I prefer the latter.

1 formal used for referring to the second of two people, things, or groups that have just been mentioned: He did well in both schoolwork and sport and won a number of medals in the latter (=in sport). → FORMER
2 used for describing the later part of a period of time: the latter half of 1998

laugh¹ /lɑːf/ verb [I] ★★★
1 to make the noise with your voice that shows that you think that something is funny: We talked and laughed late into the night. ◆ The audience didn't **laugh** at his jokes. ◆ They were still **laughing about** the experience years later. ◆ She **burst out laughing** when she saw what he was wearing.
2 to show that you think that someone or something is stupid or deserves no respect: When I told them my idea, they just laughed. ◆ Are you **laughing at** me?
PHRASAL VERB **laugh sth off** to joke about something in order to show that you think that it is not important or serious

> **Other ways of saying laugh**
> ■ **chuckle** to laugh quietly in a private or secret way
> ■ **giggle** to laugh in a nervous or excited way at something silly
> ■ **snigger** to laugh secretly and quietly in an unkind way, or to laugh at something that is rude
> ■ **be in hysterics/stitches** to laugh in an excited and uncontrolled way

laugh² /lɑːf/ noun [C] ★ the sound that you make when you laugh: a hearty laugh
PHRASES **for a laugh** informal for enjoyment, rather than for any serious purpose: He decided to go along with them for a laugh. **a (good) laugh 1** British an activity, experience, or situation that is fun **2** British someone who is fun to be with
have the last laugh to finally be more successful than someone who was unpleasant to you
have a laugh to have fun

laughable /ˈlɑːfəb(ə)l/ adj stupid, or unreasonable —**laughably** adv

laughing stock /ˈlɑːfɪŋ ˌstɒk/ noun [C] someone or something that everyone thinks is stupid or silly

laughter /ˈlɑːftə/ noun [U] ★ the sound or action of someone laughing: The children's laughter drifted down the street. ◆ The men were **roaring with laughter** (=laughing a lot) at the boy's embarrassment.

launch¹ /lɔːntʃ/ verb [T] ★★
1 to send a space vehicle, missile, or other object into space or into the air: The agency will launch a new weather satellite next month.
2 to start a major activity such as a military attack, a public project, or a new career: The armies launched their attack at dawn.
3 to make a new product available for the public to buy for the first time: The company will launch a new version of the software in July.
4 to put a boat or ship into water, especially for the first time
PHRASAL VERB **launch into sth** to enthusiastically start something such as an explanation, criticism, or description: He launched into a detailed account of his trip.

launch² /lɔːntʃ/ noun [C] **1** the act of sending a space vehicle, missile, or other object into the air or into space: the launch of the space shuttle **2** the start of a major activity such as a military attack, a public project, or a new career **3** an occasion on which a company makes a new product available for the public to buy

launderette /ˌlɔːndəˈret/ noun [C] a place where people go to wash clothes in machines that they pay to use

laundry /ˈlɔːndri/ noun **1** [U] dirty clothes, sheets etc that you are washing, or clean clothes, sheets etc that have just been washed: My husband does (=washes) the laundry. ◆ a laundry basket **2** [C] a business that you pay for washing your clothes

laurel /ˈlɒrəl/ noun [C/U] a small tree with shiny dark green leaves
PHRASE **rest on your laurels** to be satisfied with your achievements so that you do nothing to achieve more

lava /ˈlɑːvə/ noun [U] rock in the form of extremely hot liquid that flows from a VOLCANO

lavatory /ˈlævətri/ noun [C] a toilet

lavender¹ /ˈlævəndə/ noun [C] a plant with small light purple flowers that have a pleasant smell

lavender² /ˈlævəndə/ adj light purple in colour

lavish¹ /ˈlævɪʃ/ adj given very generously, or very expensive —**lavishly** adv

lavish² /ˈlævɪʃ/ PHRASAL VERB **lavish sth on sb** or **lavish sth upon sb** to give someone a lot of something such as praise, attention, or presents

law /lɔː/ noun ★★★
1 the law [singular] the system of rules that must be obeyed in society: Failing to declare any extra income is **against the law**. ◆ How

can I bring my boyfriend into the country without **breaking the law** (=doing something that is not allowed by the law)?

2 [C/U] an official rule that people must obey, or a set of these rules: *The new law will be passed by Parliament in the spring.* ♦ *Several traffic laws had been broken.* ♦ *a law against shoplifting*

3 [U] the academic study of laws, or the profession of working as a judge, lawyer etc: *a degree in law* ♦ *My son is at law school.* ♦ *Anne's been practising law (=working as a lawyer) for 20 years.*

4 [C] an explanation of a natural or scientific process: *the laws of physics/gravity*

PHRASES **law and order** safe and peaceful conditions in society that result when people obey the law

take the law into your own hands to punish someone in your own way without involving the police or the courts, often by doing something illegal → LAY STH DOWN

law-a,biding adj obeying the law

law ,court noun [C] a place where trials take place and are officially judged

law ,firm noun [C] a company consisting of a group of lawyers who provide legal advice and services

lawful /ˈlɔːf(ə)l/ adj allowed by law ≠ UNLAWFUL —**lawfully** adv

lawless /ˈlɔːləs/ adj ignoring the laws of society —**lawlessness** noun [U]

lawn /lɔːn/ noun [C/U] an area of grass that is cut short, especially in a garden —*picture* → C1

lawnmower /ˈlɔːnˌməʊə/ noun [C] a machine for cutting grass = MOWER

lawsuit /ˈlɔːsuːt/ noun [C] a situation in which a disagreement between people or groups is formally judged in a law court

lawyer /ˈlɔːjə/ noun [C] ★★ someone whose profession is to provide people with legal advice and services: *Mayer's lawyer spoke to the press today.*

lax /læks/ adj not paying enough attention to rules, or not caring enough about quality or safety

laxative /ˈlæksətɪv/ noun [C] a medicine, food, or drink that helps solid waste to leave the body —**laxative** adj

lay¹ /leɪ/ (past tense and past participle **laid** /leɪd/) verb [T] ★★★

1 to put someone or something down in a careful way, especially so that they are lying flat: **lay sb/sth on sth** *Lay the baby on her back.* ♦ **lay sb/sth across sth** *He laid his coat across the arm of the chair.*

2 if a female animal such as a bird or fish lays an egg, it produces the egg by pushing it from its body

3 if you lay the table, you prepare a table for a meal by putting forks, knives, spoons, dishes etc on it = SET

4 to carefully plan and prepare something: *an agreement that laid the foundations for a lasting peace* ♦ *The gunman realized the*

police had **laid a trap** and surrendered.

PHRASES **be laid up (in bed) with sth** to have to stay in bed as a result of being ill or injured: *He's still laid up with a bad back.*

lay the blame/responsibility (for sth) on to say that someone or something is responsible for something that has happened: *Don't try to lay the blame on me.*

not lay a finger on sb to not hit or harm someone in any way
→ REST¹

PHRASAL VERBS **,lay sth 'down 1** to state officially what someone must do, or how they must do it: *The EU has laid down tough standards for water quality.* **2 lay down the law** to tell someone what to do and expect them to obey you completely: *With kids like that you have to lay down the law .*

,lay 'into sb *informal* to attack someone physically, or to criticize them angrily: *My parents really laid into me for being so late.*

,lay sb 'off to stop employing someone because there is not enough work for them

,lay 'off (sb/sth) *informal* to stop doing something that is annoying someone: *Lay off! I'm trying to study.*

,lay sth 'on *British* to provide something such as food, entertainment, or a service: *Extra buses are being laid on for late-night shoppers.*

,lay sth 'out 1 to spread something out or arrange things so that you can see them easily: *I had my dress all ready and laid out on the bed.* **2** to explain something carefully and clearly: *The documents lay out the principles clearly enough.* **3** to arrange something according to a plan: *The city was laid out with the town hall on a hill in its centre.*

- **Lay** means to put something in a particular place or position: *I always lay my clothes carefully on the chair when I undress.* ♦ *He laid the book on the desk.*
- **Lie** means to be in a particular place or position: *I found the cat lying in front of the fire.* ♦ *He loves to lie on the beach all day.* ♦ *Papers were lying all over the desk.*
- **Lay** is also the past form of the verb **lie**: *The book lay on the floor where I'd left it.*

lay² /leɪ/ adj lacking professional or advanced knowledge of a particular subject: *a book intended for a lay audience*

lay³ the past tense of **lie¹**

lay-by noun [C] *British* an area provided by the side of a road where vehicles can stop for a short period of time

layer /ˈleɪə/ noun [C] ★★
1 an amount or sheet of a substance that covers a surface or lies between two things: *Glue the layers together and let them dry.* ♦ *Put a layer of grated cheese on top.*

2 a level or rank within an organization or system: *another layer of bureaucracy*

layman /ˈleɪmən/ noun [C] someone who does not have professional or advanced knowledge of a particular subject

layout /ˈleɪaʊt/ noun [C] the way in which the different parts of something are arranged: *the layout of the keyboard*

laze /leɪz/ or **laze aˈround** verb [I] to relax and enjoy yourself, doing no work: *We found some time to swim and laze in the sun.*

lazy /ˈleɪzi/ adj ★
1 not willing to work or do anything that involves effort: *Get out of bed, you lazy slob!*
2 a lazy period of time is spent resting and relaxing: *a lazy afternoon in the sun*
—**lazily** adv, **laziness** noun [U]

lb (plural **lbs** or **lb**) abbrev pound: a unit for measuring weight that is equal to 0.454 kilograms

lead¹ /liːd/ (past tense and past participle **led** /led/) verb ★★★

1 take sb somewhere	**6** make sb do sth
2 go somewhere	**7** live life particular way
3 be winning	**+** PHRASE
4 be best	**+** PHRASAL VERBS
5 be in charge of sb/sth	

1 [T] to take someone to a place by going there with them, usually in front of them: **lead sb into/across/to etc** *The estate agent led us into the kitchen.* ♦ *She took the boy by the hand and led him from the room.*
2 [I/T] if something such as a road, river, or door leads somewhere, or if it leads you there, it goes there: *The road leads west for three miles then turns south.* ♦ *This door leads you to a large entrance hall.*
3 [I/T] to be winning at a particular time during a race or competition: *The polls show Labour leading with only 10 days left until the election.* ♦ **lead sb by sth** *France was leading England at half time by 3 goals to 2.*
4 [I/T] to be the most successful, popular, or advanced of all the people or groups that are involved in a particular activity: *They lead the world in oil production.*
5 [T] to be in charge of an organization, group of people, or an activity: *She led the team for over twelve years.*
6 [T] to influence someone to do or think something: *I had been led to believe that the job was mine if I wanted it.*
7 [T] to live your life in a particular way: *He had always led a quiet life until he met Emma.*
PHRASE **lead the way 1** to show other people the way to a place: *Sheila turned and led the way downstairs.* **2** to be the first person to do something and to show other people how to do it: *It is a country that has always led the way in its conservation policies.*
PHRASAL VERBS **ˈlead sb ˈon** to encourage someone to believe that you are attracted to them when you are not
ˈlead to sth to begin a process that causes something to happen: *There is no doubt that stress can lead to physical illness.*
ˌlead ˈup to sth to happen in the period of time before something else happens: *the events that led up to the war*

lead² /liːd/ noun ★★★

1 first position	**6** first piece of news
2 winning amount	**7** for controlling dog
3 main part or actor	**8** electrical wire
4 useful information	**+** PHRASE
5 sth that others copy	

1 [singular] the first position at any particular time during a race or competition: *He regained his lead in the final lap.* ♦ *The latest polls show the Labour candidate in the lead (=winning).*
2 [singular] the distance, amount of time, number of points etc by which someone is winning a race or competition: *They've now increased their lead to three points.*
3 [C] the main person or part in a play, film, or television programme: *She's playing the lead in her school play.*
4 [C] a piece of information that may help to solve a crime or help to find out the truth about something
5 [C] an action that is an example for someone to copy: *North Korea is to follow China's lead in attracting foreign investment.*
6 [C] the most important story on the front page of a newspaper, or the first piece of news on a news broadcast
7 [C] a chain or long narrow piece of leather that you fasten to a collar around a dog's neck in order to control the dog: *All dogs must be kept on a lead in the park.*
8 [C] *British* an electrical wire that connects a piece of equipment to a power supply =CABLE
PHRASE **take the lead 1** to start winning a race or competition: *She took the lead ten miles into the marathon.* **2** to do something first, especially as an example for other people to follow: *British farmers took the lead by sending tons of grain to the disaster area.*

Words often used with **lead**
Verbs often used with lead (noun, sense 1)
■ **establish, have, hold, keep, maintain** + LEAD: be or stay in the first position

lead³ /led/ noun **1** [U] a soft heavy grey metal **2** [C/U] the part of a pencil that you make marks with

leader /ˈliːdə/ noun [C] ★★★
1 someone who is in charge of a group, organization, or country: *a political/military/religious leader* ♦ *the leader of the French delegation*
2 someone or something that is winning at a particular time during a race or competition: *She remains the leader after the 17th hole.*
3 someone or something that is the most successful, most popular, most advanced etc: *He is a world leader in his field.*

leadership /ˈliːdəʃɪp/ noun ★★
1 [U] the position of being a leader: *The war was fought under the emperor's leadership.*
2 [U] the qualities and skills of a good leader

3 [C] the people who are in charge of an organization or country

leading /ˈliːdɪŋ/ adj ★★ main, most important, or most successful: *He became a leading figure in the London art world.* ♦ *a leading brand of toothpaste* ♦ *She played a leading role in the country's independence movement.*

leading-edge adj of the most modern or advanced type: *leading-edge technology*

leading question noun [C] a question that you ask in a way that tricks someone, or that forces them to give the answer that you want

leaf¹ /liːf/ (plural **leaves** /liːvz/) noun [C] ★★★
1 a flat, thin, usually green part of a tree or plant that grows on a branch or stem: *The autumn leaves were beginning to fall.* —*picture* → TREE
2 a page of a book
PHRASES **take a leaf out of/from sb's book** to copy what someone else does because they are successful at doing it
turn over a new leaf to change your life by starting to be a better person or by stopping a bad habit

leaf² /liːf/ **PHRASAL VERB** **leaf through sth** to turn pages quickly and without looking at them carefully

leaflet /ˈliːflət/ noun [C] a printed sheet of paper that is provided free and gives information about something = FLYER

leafy /ˈliːfi/ adj **1** covered with a lot of leaves: *leafy green vegetables* **2** a leafy town or area has a lot of trees: *a leafy neighbourhood*

league /liːg/ noun [C] ★★★
1 an organized group of teams or players who regularly compete against each other: *They were the league champions twice during the 1990s.* ♦ *Aston Villa are top of the league again.*
2 a group of people, organizations, or countries that have joined together because they have the same interests or aims: *the League of Nations*
PHRASES **be in league with sb** to be secretly working together with someone in order to do something bad
in a different league or **not in the same league** not nearly as good as someone or something else

leak¹ /liːk/ verb **1** [I/T] if a pipe, container, roof etc leaks, or if it leaks something, liquid or gas comes out of it through a hole: *The roof is still leaking.* **2** [I] if a liquid or gas leaks, it comes out of a pipe, container, roof etc through a hole: *Oil was leaking from the pipeline.* **3** [T] to give secret information about the organization you work for to a journalist or to the public: *The story was leaked to the press.*
PHRASAL VERB **leak out** to become known by the public

leak² /liːk/ noun [C] **1** a hole or crack in something that a liquid or gas comes out of, or the liquid or gas that comes out **2** an occasion when secret information about an

organization is told to a journalist or to the public

leakage /ˈliːkɪdʒ/ noun [C/U] an amount of gas or liquid that leaks out of something

leaky /ˈliːki/ adj a leaky object or container has a hole or crack in it so that liquid or gas comes out of it

lean¹ /liːn/ (past tense and past participle **leant** /lent/ or **leaned** /liːnd/) verb ★★
1 [I] to move your body by bending at the waist, bringing yourself closer to or further from someone or something: *The other girl leaned forward to hear what was going on.* ♦ *I leaned over her shoulder to study the maps.*
2 [I] to stand or be placed at an angle against something for support, instead of being upright: *There was a small ladder leaning against the wall.* ♦ *He walked in, leaning heavily on a cane.* —*picture* → POSTURE
3 [T] to put something at an angle against an object for support: **lean sth against sth** *John leaned his rake against the side of the barn.*
PHRASAL VERB **lean on sb 1** to depend on someone: *Everybody needs someone to lean on in times of trouble.* **2** *informal* to try hard to make someone do something that they do not want to do: *The Prime Minister's been leaning pretty heavily on her to resign.*

lean² /liːn/ adj **1** someone who is lean does not have any fat on their body and looks physically fit and healthy **2** lean meat contains very little fat

leaning /ˈliːnɪŋ/ noun [C] a tendency to prefer, support, or be interested in a particular idea or activity

leant a past tense and past participle of **lean¹**

leap¹ /liːp/ (past tense and past participle **leaped** /liːpt/ or **leapt** /lept/) verb [I] **1** to move somewhere suddenly and quickly: *He leapt out of bed.* ♦ *She leapt to her feet* (=suddenly stood up) *when she saw me.* **2** to jump into the air or over a long distance: *People leapt from the burning building.*
PHRASE **leap at the chance/opportunity/offer** to accept something quickly and enthusiastically: *Klein leapt at the chance to appear in the show.*

leap² /liːp/ noun [C] **1** a jump, especially one that is long or high **2** a sudden increase or improvement = JUMP: *a huge leap in the price of fuel*
PHRASE **by/in leaps and bounds** used for saying that something improves quickly or increases a lot: *Building work on the library is moving ahead in leaps and bounds.*

leapfrog /ˈliːpˌfrɒg/ noun [U] a children's game in which one child bends down so that another child can jump over them

leapt a past tense and past participle of **leap¹**

leap year noun [C] a year that has 366 days instead of 365. This happens once every four years.

learn /lɜːn/ (past tense and past participle **learnt** /lɜːnt/ or **learned** /lɜːnd/) verb ★★★
1 [I/T] to gain knowledge or experience of

something, for example by being taught: *What did you **learn at school** today?* ♦ **learn to do sth** *The children are learning to swim this summer.* ♦ **learn how to do sth** *I want to learn how to ride a motorbike.*

2 [T] to study something so that you remember it exactly = MEMORIZE: *I've got a list of German verbs to learn tonight.*

3 [I/T] to gain new information about a situation, event, or person = FIND OUT: *We didn't **learn about** the situation until it was too late.* ♦ **+(that)** *We were distressed to learn that American troops were the targets of the attack.*

4 [I] to improve your behaviour as a result of gaining greater experience or knowledge of something: *His girlfriend's left him again. Some people never learn, do they?*

PHRASE **learn your lesson** to be unlikely to do something stupid or wrong again, because the last time you did it something unpleasant happened

---

■ When you **learn**, you gain knowledge or skills through experience or as a result of practising, reading, or being taught: *I am learning to play the guitar.* ♦ *He wanted to learn about life in ancient Rome.*

■ When you **study**, you make an effort to learn a particular subject, usually by going to classes or reading and doing research: *He studied geography at university.* ♦ *If you want to learn English you must study hard.*

---

learned /ˈlɜːnɪd/ adj having or showing a lot of knowledge about academic subjects: *a learned man*

learner /ˈlɜːnə/ noun [C] someone who is learning something: *a learner driver*

learning /ˈlɜːnɪŋ/ noun [U] **1** the process of gaining knowledge and experience, for example by studying **2** knowledge that someone has gained, especially by studying

learning ,curve noun [C] the rate at which you learn something: *I've never done this kind of work before, so I'm on a steep learning curve* (=I have to learn a lot in a short time).

learnt /lɜːnt/ a British past tense and past participle of **learn**

lease¹ /liːs/ noun [C] a legal contract in which you agree to pay to use someone else's building, land, or equipment for a particular period of time
   PHRASE **a new lease of life 1** new energy and enthusiasm, or better health **2** a change to something that makes it more modern or useful

lease² /liːs/ verb [T] to have a legal agreement in which someone pays you to use your building, land, or equipment

leash /liːʃ/ noun [C] a LEAD for a dog

least /liːst/ grammar word ★★★

Least can be:
■ a **determiner**: *This method takes the least time.*
■ a **pronoun**: *Of all the girls, she seemed to know the least.*

■ an **adverb**: *Doug is probably the least suitable person for the job.*
■ an **adjective**: *At the least sign of trouble, he gives up.*

1 a smaller amount than any other ≠ MOST: *I earn the least out of all of us.* ♦ *His most popular songs are always the ones he spends the least time on.* ♦ *Let me pay for the dinner – it's **the least I can do** (=I should probably do more).*

2 to a smaller degree or less often than any other, or than at any other time: *This is one of the least polluted industrial cities.* ♦ *Troubles come when you least expect them.* ♦ *The new taxes hurt those who are least able to pay.*

   PHRASES **at least 1** not less than a particular amount or number: *The disease killed at least 120 people in England last year.* ♦ *The journey will take a year, **at the very least** (=a year is the shortest time possible).* **2** even if nothing else happens or is true: *At least no one can accuse me of hiding the truth.* ♦ *You might at least have waited for me.* **3** used for talking about an advantage that exists despite something else: *The work is difficult, but at least the pay is good.* **4** used when you are saying something that changes or limits what you have just said: *No one saw anything, or at least they say they didn't.*

in the least or **the least bit** used for emphasizing a negative statement or question: *I'm not interested in him in the least.* ♦ *Aren't you the least bit worried?*

least of all used after a negative statement for saying that something applies to a particular person, thing, or group more than any other: *There is not much there to attract tourists, least of all the weather.*

not least used for emphasizing the importance of a particular aspect of a situation: *George is an excellent manager, not least because he is genuinely willing to listen.*

to say the least used for suggesting that something is worse or more extreme than you are saying: *He was a difficult person to deal with, to say the least.*

leather /ˈleðə/ noun [C] ★ a strong material made from animal skin that is used for making shoes, clothes, bags etc: *a black leather jacket*

leave¹ /liːv/ (past tense and past participle **left** /left/) verb ★★★

1 go away from place	**8** cause a feeling/opinion
2 go away permanently	**9** not do sth
3 stop doing sth	**10** let sb decide
4 cause sth that remains	**11** not use sth
5 forget to take sth	**12** give sth when you die
6 end relationship	**+ PHRASES**
7 put sth somewhere	**+ PHRASAL VERBS**

1 [I/T] to go away from a place: *We left London at three in the afternoon.* ♦ *Your plane leaves in ten minutes.* ♦ *She **leaves for** work at 7.30 every morning.*

2 [I/T] to go away from a place permanently: *He didn't leave home until he was 24.*

3 [I/T] to stop working for an organization, or to stop going to school or college: *He decided to leave the company after 15 years.*

4 [T] to produce something that remains after you have gone: *The government left the economy in ruins.* ♦ *The ants leave a trail of chemicals for others to follow.*

5 [T] to put something somewhere and forget to take it away with you: *I left my homework on the bus.*

6 [I/T] to end a relationship with someone and stop living with them: *His wife has threatened to leave him.*

7 [T] to put something somewhere, especially in a place where it will stay: *Leave your things by the door.* ♦ *I'll leave a note for Leigh.*

8 [T] to produce a feeling or opinion: **leave sb with sth** *I was left with the feeling that she wasn't being quite honest.* ♦ **leave sb doing sth** *Kate's sudden departure left us all wondering what was going to happen.*

9 [T] to not do something that can be done later, or that can be done by someone else: *Leave the dishes and do them in the morning.* ♦ **leave sth to sb** *Don't worry – just leave everything to me.*

10 [T] to not make a decision and let someone else make it: *Leave questions of guilt or innocence to the jury to decide.*

11 [T] to not use something: *I hope you've left enough hot water for me to have a shower.* ♦ *You've left half your dinner.* ♦ *There was some material left over when I'd finished making the dress.* ♦ **have sth left** *We don't have much money left.*

12 [T] to say that you want someone to have your money, property etc after you die: **leave sth to sb** *She left her jewels to her favourite niece.* ♦ **leave sb sth** *He left her all his money.*

<u>PHRASES</u> **leave it at that** to not do anything more about something

leave a lot to be desired to be of a very low quality or standard: *The food left a lot to be desired.*

<u>PHRASAL VERBS</u> **,leave sb/sth be'hind 1** to forget to take someone or something with you: *When she was halfway home, she realized that she'd left her purse behind.* **2** to improve or progress much faster than someone or something else

,leave sb/sth 'out to not include someone or something: *We decided to leave the chapter out of the book altogether.* ♦ *She feels left out because the other children don't play with her.*

Other ways of saying leave

- **depart** (*formal*) to leave a place: used mainly about planes, trains, and other types of transport

- **go** a general word used for talking about leaving a place or situation

- **go away** to leave a place: often used for ordering someone to leave

---

- **set off** to leave a place at the beginning of a journey

- **storm out** to leave a place in an angry way

- **walk out** to leave a job or relationship suddenly

- Both **forget** and **leave** can be used to talk about not taking something that you need with you.

- Use **leave**, not **forget**, when you mention the place where the thing is: *Oh no, I've forgotten my keys.* ♦ *Don't forget your wallet.* ♦ *I can't find my keys – I must have left them somewhere.* ♦ *Don't leave your bag in your hotel room.*

leave² /liːv/ noun [U] a period of time when you are officially away from your job or the armed forces: *You are entitled to six weeks annual leave.*

leaves the plural of **leaf¹**

lecherous /ˈletʃərəs/ adj behaving in an unpleasant way that shows you are sexually interested in someone

lecture¹ /ˈlektʃə/ noun [C] ★

1 a talk to a group of people about a particular subject, especially at a college or university: *a lecture on Dickens* ♦ *Tomorrow she will be giving a lecture at London University.*

2 *showing disapproval* a long serious talk that criticizes or warns someone: *I don't need any lectures from you about being late!*

lecture² /ˈlektʃə/ verb **1** [I] to give a lecture or a series of lectures **2** [T] *showing disapproval* to talk to someone seriously in order to criticize or warn them about something

lecturer /ˈlektʃərə/ noun [C] **1** someone who gives a lecture **2** *British* a teacher at a university or college

led the past tense and past participle of **lead¹**

ledge /ledʒ/ noun [C] **1** a narrow surface that sticks out from the side of a cliff or wall **2** a narrow shelf at the bottom of a window =SILL

ledger /ˈledʒə/ noun [C] a book that contains the financial records of a business

leech /liːtʃ/ noun [C] a small soft creature that sticks to the skin of other animals in order to feed on their blood

leek /liːk/ noun [C] a long thin vegetable that tastes similar to an onion and is white at one end with green leaves at the other

leer /lɪə/ verb [I] to look at someone in an unpleasant way that shows you are sexually interested in them —**leer** noun [C]

leeway /ˈliːweɪ/ noun [U] the amount of freedom that someone has to make their own decisions or to take action

left¹ /left/ adj ★★★

1 on the side of your body that is opposite to the right ≠ RIGHT: *He wore a wedding ring on his left hand.*

2 on the left side of something: *the bottom left corner of the screen* ♦ *We took a left turn when we should have gone right.*

left² /left/ noun [singular] ★★

1 the left side or direction: *On the left of the*

picture you can see his grandmother. ♦ *My office is the third door on your left.* ♦ *The car swerved to the left.*

2 the left or **the Left** people or groups with left-wing political opinions: *He received strong criticism from the left of the party.*

left³ /left/ adv **1** towards the left side: *Turn left at the end of the street.* **2** towards the left in politics

left⁴ the past tense and past participle of **leave**¹

'left-click verb [I] *computing* to press the button on the left side of a computer MOUSE with your finger

'left-hand adj on the left side ≠ RIGHT-HAND: *The plates are on the left-hand side of the cupboard.*

left-handed /ˌleft ˈhændɪd/ adj **1** born with a natural tendency to use the left hand to do things ≠ RIGHT-HANDED **2** designed for or done with the left hand ≠ RIGHT-HANDED
—**left-handedness** noun [U]

ˌleft ˈluggage ˌoffice noun [C] *British* a place at an airport, railway station, or bus station where you can pay to leave your bags for a short time

leftover /ˈleftˌəʊvə/ adj remaining after you have finished using the amount that you want or need

leftovers /ˈleftˌəʊvəz/ noun [plural] the food that remains at the end of a meal after you have finished eating

ˌleft ˈwing, the noun [singular] the members of a political organization whose aims and ideas are more SOCIALIST than the other members, because they believe that property, money, and power should be shared more equally

ˌleft-ˈwing adj someone who is left-wing believes that property, money, and power should be shared more equally ≠ RIGHT-WING —**ˌleft-ˈwinger** noun [C]

lefty /ˈlefti/ noun [C] *British informal* someone who is left-wing

leg /leg/ noun [C] ★★★

1 part of body	**4** part of furniture
2 clothing covering leg	**5** part of journey/race
3 meat from animal leg	**+ PHRASE**

1 one of the parts of a person's or animal's body to which the feet are attached: *an exercise to strengthen the leg muscles* ♦ *She sat down and crossed her legs.* —*picture* → C14

2 the part of a piece of clothing that covers one of your legs: *There was dirt on his trouser leg.*

3 a piece of meat that comes from an animal's leg: *roast leg of lamb*

4 the part of a piece of furniture that supports it and raises it off the floor: *a stool with three legs* ♦ *a table leg*

5 a part of a journey, race, or competition

PHRASE **not have a leg to stand on** *informal* to not have any way of proving that you are right about something
→ PULL¹, STRETCH¹

legacy¹ /ˈleɡəsi/ noun [C] **1** money or property

that you arrange for someone to have after you die **2** something such as a tradition or problem that exists as a result of something that happened in the past

legacy² /ˈleɡəsi/ adj *computing* legacy software or equipment is still in use, but is not the most recent or advanced type that is available

legal /ˈliːg(ə)l/ adj ★★★
1 relating to the law or lawyers: *You may wish to seek legal advice before signing the contract.* ♦ *China's legal system* ♦ *Parents are taking legal action to challenge the school's closure.*
2 allowed by the law or done according to the law ≠ ILLEGAL: *It is perfectly legal to import these goods under European law.* ♦ *the child's legal guardians*
—**legally** /ˈliːɡəli/ adv

ˌlegal ˈaid noun [U] a system in which the government pays for people to get legal help when they do not have much money

legality /lɪˈɡæləti/ noun [U] the fact that something is legal ≠ ILLEGALITY

legalize /ˈliːɡəˌlaɪz/ verb [T] to make something legal by creating a new law
—**legalization** /ˌliːɡəlaɪˈzeɪʃ(ə)n/ noun [U]

legend /ˈledʒ(ə)nd/ noun [C] **1** an old story about imaginary people and events in the past: *Greek myths and legends* **2** someone who a great many people know about and admire: *the Hollywood legend, Elizabeth Taylor*

legendary /ˈledʒ(ə)nd(ə)ri/ adj **1** very famous or well known for a long time **2** mentioned or described in a legend

leggings /ˈleɡɪŋz/ noun [plural] trousers worn by women and girls that stretch and fit very closely to their legs —*picture* → C4

legible /ˈledʒəb(ə)l/ adj legible writing is clear and tidy enough to be read ≠ ILLEGIBLE
—**legibly** adv

legion /ˈliːdʒ(ə)n/ noun **1** [C] a large group of soldiers forming part of an army **2 legions** [plural] a large group or number of people: *The band has legions of fans.*

legislate /ˈledʒɪˌsleɪt/ verb [I] to create a new law and have it officially accepted
—**legislator** /ˈledʒɪˌsleɪtə/ noun [C]

legislation /ˌledʒɪˈsleɪʃ(ə)n/ noun [U] a law, or a set of laws: *a complex piece of legislation* ♦ *The government should pass legislation to limit the powers of the police.*

legislative /ˈledʒɪslətɪv/ adj **1** relating to laws or to the process of creating new laws: *the legislative power of the upper house* **2** used for talking about groups of people who have the power to create new laws: *a legislative body*

legislature /ˈledʒɪslətʃə/ noun [C] the part of a government that has the power to create laws

legitimate /lɪˈdʒɪtəmət/ adj **1** fair and reasonable: *Did he have a legitimate excuse for being late?* **2** allowed by the law, or correct according to the law: *Are the premises being used for legitimate business*

purposes? **3** a legitimate child is born to parents who are legally married
≠ ILLEGITIMATE —**legitimacy** /lɪˈdʒɪtɪməsi/ noun [U], **legitimately** adv

leisure /ˈleʒə/ noun [U] **1** activities that you do in order to relax or enjoy yourself: *My busy schedule leaves little time for leisure.* ♦ *leisure pursuits/activities* **2** the time when you are not working or are not busy: *I'm looking forward to more leisure time in my retirement.*
PHRASE **at your leisure** when you have free time and it is convenient for you: *Read it at your leisure.*

leisure ,centre noun [C] *British* a large building with a swimming pool and areas for exercising and playing different sports

leisurely /ˈleʒəli/ adj slow and relaxed

lemon /ˈlemən/ noun [C/U] a fruit with a hard yellow skin and sour juice: *Add the juice of half a lemon.* —*picture* → C10

lemonade /ˌleməˈneɪd/ noun [C/U] a drink that has a lemon flavour, or a glass of this drink

lend /lend/ (past tense and past participle **lent** /lent/) verb ★★★
1 [T] to give someone something for a short time, expecting that they will give it back to you later: *The local library will lend books for a month without charge.* ♦ **lend sb sth** *She lent me her very expensive coat.* ♦ **lend sth to sb** *Joe lent this car to us for the weekend.* → BORROW
2 [I/T] to give someone money that you expect them to pay back later: **lend sth to sb** *Banks will lend large amounts of money to new businesses.*
3 [T] to give something a particular quality: **lend sth sth** *The smile lent his face a certain boyish charm.*
4 [T] to give someone support or help: *Patricia is always ready to lend a hand.*
PHRASE **lend itself to sth** to be suitable for a particular purpose: *The story lends itself to being adapted for film.*

lender /ˈlendə/ noun [C] a person or financial institution that lends money

length /leŋθ/ noun ★★★

1 how long in size	**4** how long book is
2 distance end to end	**5** long thin piece
3 how long in time	**+** PHRASES

1 [C/U] a measurement of how long something is in size: *The boat was 16 feet in length.*
2 [C] the distance from one end of something to the other: *Carter ran half the length of the pitch to score a brilliant goal.*
3 [C/U] a measurement of how long something takes to do or of how long it lasts: *The length of your talk must be at least 10 minutes.*
4 [C/U] a measurement of how big a book or piece of writing is: *His latest novel is twice the length of his previous one.*
5 [C] a piece of something that is long and thin: *a length of pipe/rope/string*
PHRASES **at (great/some) length** for a long

time and with a lot of detail: *Austin was questioned at length by detectives.*
at length *literary* after a long time
go to great/extreme/any etc lengths to try in a very determined way to achieve something: *They have gone to great lengths to make us feel welcome.*
the length and breadth of sth every part of a large area

lengthen /ˈleŋθ(ə)n/ verb [I/T] to become longer, or to make something longer

lengthways /ˈleŋθˌweɪz/ or **lengthwise** /ˈleŋθˌwaɪz/ adv in the direction of the longest side of something

lengthy /ˈleŋθi/ adj continuing for a long time, especially for too long: *a lengthy period of negotiation*

lenient /ˈliːniənt/ adj punishing someone less severely than they deserve —**leniency** /ˈliːniənsi/ noun [U], **leniently** adv

lens /lenz/ noun [C] **1** a thin piece of curved glass or plastic that makes things seem smaller, bigger, or clearer **2** the part of the eye that bends light to produce an image on the RETINA **3** a CONTACT LENS

lent the past tense and past participle of **lend**

Lent /lent/ the period of 40 days before Easter, when for religious reasons some Christians stop doing or eating something that they enjoy

lentil /ˈlentɪl/ noun [C/U] a small round flat dried seed that you boil before you eat it

Leo /ˈliːəʊ/ noun [C/U] one of the 12 signs of the ZODIAC. A **Leo** is someone who was born between 23 July and 22 August.

leopard /ˈlepəd/ noun [C] a large wild animal from Africa and Southern Asia that has yellow fur with black spots —*picture* → C12

leotard /ˈliːəˌtɑːd/ noun [C] a piece of clothing that covers the body tightly from the neck to the top of the legs and is used for dancing or exercising

leper /ˈlepə/ noun [C] someone who has leprosy

leprosy /ˈleprəsi/ noun [U] a serious disease that affects the skin, nerves, and bones and can cause people's fingers and toes to fall off

lesbian /ˈlezbiən/ noun [C] a woman who is sexually attracted to women —**lesbian** adj

lesion /ˈliːʒ(ə)n/ noun [C] *medical* an area of damaged skin=WOUND

less /les/ grammar word ★★★

Less can be:
■ a **determiner**: *Schools put less emphasis on being creative.*
■ a **pronoun**: *Connie did less than anyone else.* ♦ *He seemed to spend less of his time with her.*
■ an **adverb**: *The red jacket is less expensive.*

1 a smaller amount ≠ MORE: *You should eat less and exercise more.* ♦ *The industry operates with less government control these days.* ♦ *The new Ford is designed to use less fuel than earlier models.* ♦ *I aim to spend less of my time travelling.* ♦ *I wish you'd do a bit less talking and a bit more work.*

2 to a smaller degree, or not as often ≠ MORE: *We've been trying to use the telephone less this month.* ♦ *The homework was less difficult than I expected.* ♦ *My husband worries about things less than I do.* ♦ *We talk a lot less than we used to.*

PHRASES **less and less** gradually getting smaller in amount or degree: *Fishing was growing less and less profitable.*

the less...the less/more used for saying that when a particular activity, feeling etc is reduced, it causes something else to change at the same time: *Sometimes it seems like the less I do, the more tired I feel.*

no less than used before a number or amount for showing that it is large and surprising: *Exports have risen by no less than 80% in the last ten years.*

> Both **fewer** and **less** can be used to refer to an amount that is smaller than another amount.
> - Use **fewer** before plural nouns: *Fewer people turned up than expected.*
> - Use **less** before uncountable nouns: *You'll get a smoother finish if you use less paint.*
> - In informal English, some people now use **less** rather than **fewer** before plural nouns, although many people think that this is not correct.

lessen /'les(ə)n/ verb [I/T] to become smaller in amount, level, or importance, or to make something do this

lesser[1] /'lesə/ adj *formal* smaller, less important, or less serious than something else: *She was encouraged by her mother and, to a lesser extent, her father.*

PHRASE **the lesser of two evils** the less unpleasant or harmful of two possible choices

lesser[2] /'lesə/ adv less: *one of the lesser known English poets*

lesson /'les(ə)n/ noun [C] ★★★
1 *British* a period of time in which students are taught about a subject in school =CLASS: *a French/English/maths/history lesson*

2 a period of time in which someone is taught a skill: *a driving/dancing/swimming lesson*

3 something that you learn from life, an event, or an experience: *I hope you've learnt a lesson from this!* ♦ *the lessons of war/history/experience*

let /let/ (past tense and past participle **let**) verb ★★★

1 [T] to allow something to happen, or to allow someone to do something: **let sb/sth do sth** *Alice's mum won't let her come with us.* ♦ *I stepped back and let him pass.* ♦ **let sth in/out/through etc** *The large windows let in a lot of light.*

2 [T] used for offering to do something: *Here, let me help you.*

3 [I/T] *British* to rent a room, flat, house etc to someone: *There are three flats to let* (=available to be rented) *in the building.* ♦ **let sth to sb** *He's let his cottage to some people from London.*

PHRASES **let alone** used for saying that something is even less likely to happen than another unlikely thing: *I hardly have time to think these days, let alone relax.*

let sb go 1 to allow a person or animal to go free=RELEASE: *The police had to let her go because of insufficient evidence.* **2** *informal* to officially tell someone that they can no longer work at a job: *We have had to let several staff go.*

let (sb/sth) go to stop holding someone or something: *Let me go!* ♦ *Reluctantly, he let go of her arm.*

let sth go/pass to not react to something annoying that someone says: *The remark made me furious, but I let it pass.*

let sb have it *informal* to attack or criticize someone severely

let sb know to tell someone something: *Let us know what time your plane arrives.*

let's 1 used for suggesting that you and one or more other people do something: *Let's eat now.* **2 let's face it** used for saying that someone must admit that a situation exists: *Let's face it – he just can't do this job.* **3 let's hope** used for saying that you hope something is true or will happen: *Let's hope she never finds out the truth.* **4 let's say/ suppose (that)** used for suggesting that a possible situation needs to be considered: *Let's say you lose. What will you do then?*

let's see 1 used for suggesting that you and one or more other people should find the answer to something: *Let's see if it works.* **2 let's see** or **let me see** *spoken* used for saying that you need a moment to think about something: *Let's see – where was I?*

let yourself go *informal* **1** to relax and stop trying to control your emotions or behaviour **2** to stop caring about your health or appearance: *He's really let himself go in the past few years.*

PHRASAL VERBS **let sb 'down** to make someone feel disappointed by not doing something that they are expecting you to do: *The families of the victims feel that the justice system has let them down.*

let sb 'in 1 to allow someone to enter a house, room etc **2 let yourself in for sth** *informal* to put yourself in a difficult situation: *She didn't know what she was letting herself in for when she married John.*

let sb 'in on sth to tell someone a secret: *They were planning something, but they wouldn't let me in on it.*

let sb 'off to give someone little or no punishment for something that they did wrong: *I was pulled over for speeding, but I was let off with a warning.*

let 'on *informal* to talk about something that is intended to be a secret: *He knows more than he lets on.*

let sb/sth 'out to allow a person or animal to leave a place

let sth 'out to make a noise: *As he walked away, he let out a sigh of relief.*

let 'up if something bad or unpleasant lets up, it slows down or stops: *The icy wind never let up for a moment.*

letdown /ˈletˌdaʊn/ noun [singular] something that makes you feel disappointed because it is not as good as you expected

lethal /ˈliːθl/ adj very dangerous and capable of killing you

lethargic /ləˈθɑːdʒɪk/ adj lacking energy and not wanting to do anything

lethargy /ˈleθədʒi/ noun [U] the feeling of being lethargic

letter /ˈletə/ noun [C] ★★★
1 a piece of paper that you write a message on and send to someone: *Most of the soldiers wrote long letters home.* ♦ *I get letters from them every week.* ♦ *I sent them a letter complaining about it.* ♦ *a letter to a friend*
2 a symbol used for writing words: *the letter J*
PHRASE **follow/obey sth to the letter** to do exactly what you are told to do

letterbox /ˈletəˌbɒks/ noun [C] British 1 a small hole in a door where letters can be delivered —*picture* → C1 2 a POSTBOX

lettuce /ˈletɪs/ noun [C/U] a vegetable with large thin green leaves that you eat raw in a salad —*picture* → C11

let-up noun [singular] a pause or reduction in something unpleasant

leukaemia /luːˈkiːmiə/ noun [U] a type of cancer that affects your blood

leukemia /luːˈkiːmiə/ the American spelling of **leukaemia**

level¹ /ˈlev(ə)l/ noun ★★★

1 amount	4 part/stage of system
2 height of sth	5 floor in building
3 standard	6 way of understanding

1 [C] the amount of something that exists at a particular time: *Unemployment is now at its lowest level for 15 years.* ♦ *Many people have to cope with high levels of stress at work.*
2 [C] the height of something in a container or on a surface: *The river is at its highest level for several years.* ♦ *Check the level of fluid in the tank.*
3 [C/U] a standard of academic ability: *This is an excellent book for advanced level students.*
4 [C/U] a part or stage in a system that has several parts or stages: *Decisions should be taken at local, not national, level.* ♦ *These social changes will affect everyone, at all levels of society.*
5 [C/U] one of the floors in a building: *a garage at basement level*
6 a particular way of relating to someone or something: *I get on with Frank very well on a personal level, but we just can't work together.*

level² /ˈlev(ə)l/ adj ★★
1 flat, smooth, and not sloping up or down: *We found a nice level spot for a picnic.* ♦ *Add two level teaspoons of salt.*
2 at the same height: *They stood so that their shoulders were level.* ♦ *My head was level with George's chin.*
3 equal in a competition: *At half time the*

two sides were level on 15 points each.

level³ /ˈlev(ə)l/ verb [T] 1 to make something flat: *Level the ground carefully before you lay the paving stones.* 2 to destroy a building or group of buildings 3 to make something equal: *James' goal levelled the score at three all.*
PHRASAL VERBS **ˈlevel sth aˌgainst sb** *same as* **level sth at sb** 2
ˈlevel sth at sb 1 to point a weapon at someone 2 to criticize or accuse someone: *Several criticisms have been levelled at the company's board of directors.*
ˌlevel ˈoff or **ˌlevel ˈout** 1 to stop sloping or moving up or down 2 to stop becoming more or less, and remain the same: *Oil prices should level out now that the war is over.*
ˈlevel sth ˈoff or **ˈlevel sth ˈout** to make something flat
ˈlevel with sb *informal* to be honest with someone

ˌlevel ˈcrossing noun [C] British a place where a road crosses a railway and gates are used to stop cars when a train is coming

ˌlevel-ˈheaded adj behaving in a calm sensible way, even in a difficult situation

ˌlevel ˈplaying-ˈfield noun [singular] a situation that is fair for all the people involved

lever¹ /ˈliːvə/ noun [C] 1 a long handle that you pull or push to operate a machine 2 a long metal bar that you put under a heavy object to move it

lever² /ˈliːvə/ verb [T] to move something using a lever

leverage /ˈliːvərɪdʒ/ noun [U] 1 the power to make someone do what you want 2 the power that a lever gives you to move things

levitate /ˈlevɪˌteɪt/ verb [I/T] to rise and float in the air as if by magic, or to make something do this —**levitation** /ˌlevɪˈteɪʃ(ə)n/ noun [U]

levy¹ /ˈlevi/ noun [C] an amount of money that you have to pay, for example as a tax

levy² /ˈlevi/ verb [T] to officially request payment of something such as a tax

lewd /luːd/ adj referring to sex in a rude or unpleasant way

liability /ˌlaɪəˈbɪləti/ noun 1 [U] legal responsibility for causing damage or injury, or for paying something 2 [C] someone or something that causes problems for someone

liable /ˈlaɪəb(ə)l/ adj legally responsible for causing damage or injury, so that you have to pay something or be punished: *The hospital was held liable for negligence.*
PHRASES **liable to sth** likely to suffer from something unpleasant: *Many parts of the country are liable to flooding.*
liable to do sth likely to do something bad or unpleasant: *The handle is liable to break.*

liaise /liˈeɪz/ verb [I] British if two or more people liaise, they tell each other what they are doing, so that they can work together effectively

liaison /liˈeɪz(ə)n/ noun 1 [singular/U] an exchange of information between people or organizations, so that they understand each other and work well together **2** [C] a secret sexual or romantic relationship between two people

liar /'laɪə/ noun [C] someone who tells lies

Lib Dem /ˌlɪb 'dem/ noun [C] Liberal Democrat

libel¹ /'laɪb(ə)l/ noun [C/U] the illegal act of writing bad things that are not true about someone → SLANDER —**libellous** /'laɪbələs/ adj

libel² /'laɪb(ə)l/ verb [T] to write bad things that are not true about someone → SLANDER

liberal¹ /'lɪb(ə)rəl/ adj **1** willing to accept ideas and ways of behaving that are different from your own: *Their views on marriage and divorce are rather liberal.* **2** believing that people should have social and political freedom, and that they should be allowed to make their own decisions about moral issues: *liberal politicians* **3** giving or consisting of a larger amount than is usual —**liberalism** /'lɪb(ə)rəˌlɪz(ə)m/ noun [U], **liberally** adv

liberal² /'lɪb(ə)rəl/ noun [C] someone who has liberal social or political beliefs

Liberal Democrat noun [C] a member of the Liberal Democrat party of the UK —**Liberal Democrat** adj

Liberal Democrats, the one of the three main political parties in the UK

liberalize /'lɪb(ə)rəˌlaɪz/ verb [T] to make laws or rules less strict —**liberalization** /ˌlɪb(ə)rəlaɪ'zeɪʃ(ə)n/ noun [U]

liberate /'lɪbəˌreɪt/ verb [T] **1** to make a place or the people in it free from soldiers who have been controlling it **2** to give someone the freedom to do what they want —**liberation** /ˌlɪbə'reɪʃ(ə)n/ noun [U], **liberator** noun [C]

liberated /'lɪbəˌreɪtɪd/ adj not accepting traditional ideas or rules about the way you should behave

liberating /'lɪbəˌreɪtɪŋ/ adj making you feel that you have more freedom to do what you want to do

liberty /'lɪbəti/ noun [U] **1** the freedom to think or behave in the way that you want and not be controlled by anyone else **2** freedom from being kept in prison

PHRASES be at liberty to do sth *formal* to be allowed to do something

I took the liberty of doing sth used for telling someone that you have done something without their permission but you hope that they will approve of this

libido /lɪ'biːdəʊ/ noun [C/U] *formal* someone's level of sexual energy and enthusiasm

Libra /'liːbrə/ noun [C/U] one of the 12 signs of the ZODIAC. A **Libra** or **Libran** is someone who was born between 23 September and 22 October.

librarian /laɪ'breəriən/ noun [C] someone who works in a library, or who is in charge of a library

library /'laɪbrəri/ noun [C] ★★★
1 a place where books, documents, CDs etc are available for you to look at or borrow: *the university/school library*
2 a private collection of books, or the room that it is kept in

lice /laɪs/ noun [plural] small insects that live on people's skin and in their hair. Lice is the plural of LOUSE.

licence /'laɪs(ə)ns/ noun ★★
1 [C] an official document that gives you permission to do or use something: *He was charged with possessing a shotgun without a licence.*
2 [U] freedom to say or do what you want: *The designers were allowed a lot of creative licence.*

license¹ /'laɪs(ə)ns/ verb [T] **1** if someone is licensed to do something, they have official permission to do it **2** if something is licensed, people have official permission to use it

license² /'laɪs(ə)ns/ the American spelling of licence

licensed /'laɪs(ə)nst/ adj **1** a place that is licensed has official permission to sell alcoholic drinks **2** someone who is licensed has official permission to do something, for example to work in a particular job **3** licensed products are products that someone has official permission to use or to own

licensee /ˌlaɪs(ə)n'siː/ noun [C] someone who has a licence to sell alcoholic drinks

license plate noun [C] *American* a NUMBER PLATE

licensing laws /'laɪs(ə)nsɪŋ ˌlɔːz/ noun [plural] *British* the laws that control when and where alcohol can be sold in the UK

lichen /'laɪkən, 'lɪtʃ(ə)n/ noun [C/U] a small soft plant that grows on surfaces such as trees and walls

lick¹ /lɪk/ verb [I/T] to move your tongue across something: *The boy licked his ice cream.*

lick² /lɪk/ noun [C] the action of licking something

PHRASE a lick of paint a layer of paint that you put on something to make it look better

lid /lɪd/ noun [C] ★
1 a cover for a container: *a saucepan lid*
2 the piece of skin that covers your eye when it is closed = EYELID

lie¹ /laɪ/ (present participle **lying** /'laɪɪŋ/; past tense **lay** /leɪ/; past participle **lain** /leɪn/) verb [I] ★★★

1 be/put yourself flat	5 be in particular state
2 be on surface	6 say sth that is not true
3 be in position/place	+ PHRASES
4 consist of	+ PHRASAL VERBS

1 to be or put yourself in a position in which your body is flat on a surface such as the floor or a bed: *She was lying on the beach reading a book.* ♦ *Emma was lying on her stomach on the couch.* → LAY —*picture* → POSTURE

2 to be on a particular surface: *The gun was lying on the ground next to him.*

3 to be in a particular position or place: *The farm lay a few miles to the north.*

4 used for talking about things such as plans, ideas, and qualities and what they consist of: *The difficulty lies in knowing what to do next.*

5 if something lies in a particular state, it is in that state: *The castle lay in ruins.*

6 (past tense and past participle **lied** /laɪd/) to deliberately say something that is not true: *It was obvious that she was lying.* ♦ *He had to lie about his age to get into the army.* ♦ *She admitted lying to the police.*

PHRASES **lie ahead** to be going to happen in the future: *A grand future lies ahead of him.*
lie in wait (for sb) to hide so that you can attack someone when they pass you
lie low to hide, or to try to avoid attracting attention to yourself

PHRASAL VERBS **lie a'bout** or **lie a'round 1** to have been left somewhere instead of being put in the correct place: *Never leave cash or other valuables just lying around.* **2** to spend a lot of time relaxing: *We lay around all day playing cards and watching television.*
lie 'back to move from a sitting position into a position in which you are lying on a surface
lie be'hind sth to be the real reason for a decision or action: *We'd like to know what lay behind her decision to change her will.*
lie 'down 1 to put yourself in a position in which your body is flat on a surface, especially in order to rest or to sleep: *I'm going to go and lie down for a while.* **2 not take sth lying down** to not accept unfair treatment, by complaining about it or trying to change it
lie 'in *British* to stay in bed in the morning for longer than usual
'lie with sb to be someone's responsibility

lie² /laɪ/ noun [C] ★★ something that you say or write that is not true and that you know is not true: *He told them he could drive, but it was a lie.* ♦ *All children tell their parents little lies sometimes.*

'lie de,tector noun [C] a piece of equipment that is used for checking whether someone is telling the truth

'lie-,in noun [singular] *British* a time when you stay in bed longer than usual in the morning

lieu /luː/ noun **in lieu (of)** instead, or instead of

lieutenant /lefˈtenənt, *American* luːˈtenənt/ noun [C] an officer of low rank in most armed forces

life /laɪf/ (plural **lives** /laɪvz/) noun ★★★

1 time sb is alive	5 time sth exists/lasts
2 way of living	6 activity/excitement
3 state of being alive	7 punishment
4 living things	+ PHRASES

1 [C/U] the period of time from someone's birth until their death: *He had a long and happy life.* ♦ *Don't spend your whole life*

worrying about money. ♦ *She's lived in California all her life.*

2 [C/U] your particular way of living and the experiences that you have: *His life revolves around his children.* ♦ *I never liked city life* (=the experiences people have in a city). ♦ *The life of a film star is not always a glamorous one.* ♦ *I just want to be able to lead a normal life.*

3 [C/U] the state of being alive: *He believed his life was in danger.* ♦ *They risk their lives to protect the people they love.* ♦ *Thousands of people lost their lives* (=died) *in the earthquake.* ♦ *It was a police officer who saved her life.*

4 [U] living things such as plants and animals: *Is there life on other planets?* ♦ *the great variety of bird life in the area*

5 [C] the period of time during which something exists or continues: *The average life of a television is about ten years.* ♦ *During the life of this government, unemployment has increased by 5%.*

6 [U] the quality of being lively or exciting: *There's not much life in this village.*

7 [U] *informal* a punishment in which someone is sent to prison for the rest of their life

PHRASES **bring sth to life** to make something exciting or interesting: *a book that brings the subject to life*
come to life to start to be exciting or interesting: *a new TV series in which history really comes to life*
get a life *spoken* used for telling someone that they are boring
not on your life *spoken* used for telling someone that you will certainly not do something
that's life used for encouraging someone to accept that bad things happen to everyone, not just them
the time of your life a very enjoyable experience: *The children were having the time of their lives.*

→ MATTER¹

lifebelt /ˈlaɪfbelt/ noun [C] *British* a large rubber ring that you throw to someone to save them when they have fallen into water

lifeboat /ˈlaɪfbəʊt/ noun [C] a small boat that is kept on a ship for emergencies

lifebuoy /ˈlaɪfbɔɪ/ noun [C] something that you throw to someone to save them when they have fallen into water

'life ,cycle noun [C] the series of changes that happen to an animal or plant during its life

life ex'pectancy noun [C/U] the length of time that someone is likely to live

lifeguard /ˈlaɪfgɑːd/ noun [C] someone whose job is to save swimmers who are in danger

'life in,surance noun [U] a type of insurance that pays money to your family when you die

lifejacket /ˈlaɪfˌdʒækɪt/ noun [C] something you wear on a boat to make you float if you fall into the water

lifeless /ˈlaɪfləs/ adj **1** not interesting or

exciting **2** dead, or seeming to be dead **3** without any living or growing things

lifelike /ˈlaɪflaɪk/ adj a lifelike picture, model etc looks real

lifeline /ˈlaɪflaɪn/ noun [C] someone or something that you depend on to help you when you are in a difficult situation

lifelong /ˈlaɪflɒŋ/ adj continuing all through your life: *a lifelong friendship*

lifesaving /ˈlaɪfˌseɪvɪŋ/ or **ˈlife-saving** adj done in order to prevent someone from dying

life ˈsentence noun [C] a punishment in which someone is sent to prison for the rest of their life, or for a very long time

ˈlife-ˌsize adj a life-size picture, model etc of something is the same size as the real thing

lifespan /ˈlaɪfˌspæn/ noun [C] the length of time that someone lives for, or the length of time that something exists

ˈlife ˌstory noun [C] a description of all the things that have happened to someone during their life

lifestyle /ˈlaɪfˌstaɪl/ noun [C/U] the type of life that someone has, for example the type of things that they own and the type of activities that they do: *a healthy, outdoor lifestyle*

ˈlife-ˌthreatening adj a life-threatening disease or situation is one that could kill you

lifetime /ˈlaɪfˌtaɪm/ noun [C] **1** the period of time when someone is alive **2** the length of time that something exists or works

lift¹ /lɪft/ verb ★★★

1 [T] to move something to a higher position: *Lie on the floor and lift your legs slowly.* ♦ *The phone rang and he lifted the receiver immediately.* ♦ *Always bend your knees when lifting heavy loads.* —picture → CARRY

2 [T] to improve the situation that someone or something is in, or to make someone feel happier: **lift sb out of sth** *economic measures designed to lift the country out of recession* ♦ *Being outdoors can really lift your spirits.*

3 [T] to officially end a rule or law that stopped someone from doing something: *They're hoping to get the **ban** lifted soon.*

4 [I] if something such as cloud or FOG lifts, it disappears

> **PHRASE** **not lift a finger** *informal* to not help at all in a situation in which someone else is working

> **PHRASAL VERB** ˈlift **off** if a space vehicle lifts off, it goes up from the ground into the air

lift² /lɪft/ noun [C] ★

1 an occasion when someone takes you somewhere in their car: *I can **give you a** lift into town.*

2 *British* a machine that carries people up or down between different levels of a tall building

3 a movement in which something is lifted

ˈlift-ˌoff noun [C/U] the time when a space vehicle goes up from the ground into the air

ligament /ˈlɪgəmənt/ noun [C] a part inside your body that holds bones together or keeps organs in place

light¹ /laɪt/ noun ★★★

1 [U] brightness from the sun or from a light, which allows you to see things: *a beam/flash/ray of light* ♦ *The house could be clearly seen **by the light** of the moon.*

2 [C] a piece of electrical equipment that produces brightness: *Could somebody put **the light on**? ♦ I turned the lights off and shut the door. ♦ All the lights went out.*

3 [C] a TRAFFIC LIGHT: *Turn left at **the lights**.*

4 [singular] something that is used for lighting a cigarette: *Have you got a light?*

> **PHRASES** **bring sth to light** or **come to light** if facts are brought to light or come to light, people discover them

> **in a bad/new/different etc light** used for talking about someone's opinion of a particular person or thing: *This incident made me see him in a completely different light.*

> **in (the) light of sth** because of a particular fact: *In light of your good record, we've decided to overlook this offence.*

> **light at the end of the tunnel** something that makes you think that a difficult situation will improve

> **see the light** to suddenly realize or understand something

> **see the light (of day) 1** if an object sees the light of day, it is brought out of a place where it has been for a long time **2** if something such as an idea, plan, or rule sees the light of day, it starts to exist

> **set light to sth** to make something start burning

> **throw/shed/cast light on sth** to provide new information that helps you to understand something

light² /laɪt/ adj ★★★

1 bright/well lit	**7** not severe
2 not dark	**8** gentle
3 pale in colour	**9** not serious
4 not weighing much	**10** about sleep
5 about clothes	**+ PHRASE**
6 small/not much	

1 very bright because of light from the sun ≠ DARK: *The room is light and airy.*

2 if it is light, you can see because it is day and not night ≠ DARK: *It gets light around 5 am.*

3 pale in colour, not dark ≠ DARK: *a **light blue** shirt*

4 not weighing much, or weighing less than you expect ≠ HEAVY: *The table is a lot lighter than it looks.*

5 light clothes are made of thin cloth and are not very warm ≠ HEAVY: *a light summer jacket*

6 not much in quantity: *Traffic was fairly light as we left the city.* ♦ *a light frost* ♦ *light refreshments*

7 a light punishment is not very severe ≠ HARSH: *a light prison sentence*

8 not strong, hard, or loud: *a light breeze* ♦

a light kiss on the cheek ♦ *She heard a light knock at the window.*

9 enjoyable and not very serious or difficult: *a little light reading*

10 a light sleep is one in which you wake up often ≠ DEEP

PHRASE **make light of sth** to treat something as not being very serious

light³ /laɪt/ (past tense and past participle **lit** /lɪt/) verb ★★

1 [I/T] to start to burn, or to make something start to burn: *The fire won't light if the wood is wet.* ♦ *Amy lit a cigarette.*

2 [T] to make a place brighter by giving it light: *dimly lit corridors* ♦ *The room was lit by candlelight.*

3 [T] if you light someone's way, you use a light to lead them through a dark place

PHRASAL VERBS **light up** to start to shine: *A warning signal lit up on the dashboard.*

light (sth) up 1 *informal* to light a cigarette **2** if someone's face or eyes light up, they express a strong emotion, usually happiness or excitement: *a smile that lit up her whole face* ♦ *Antony's eyes lit up when Keiko walked into the room.*

light⁴ /laɪt/ adv if you travel light, you do not take many things with you

light aircraft noun [C] a very small plane

light bulb noun [C] a glass object that you put in an electric light to produce light

lighten /ˈlaɪt(ə)n/ verb **1** [I/T] if a situation or someone's mood lightens, or if something lightens the mood, it becomes more relaxed **2** [I/T] to become brighter or lighter in colour, or to make something brighter or lighter in colour **3** [T] to reduce an amount of work **4** [I/T] to become less heavy, or to make something less heavy

PHRASAL VERB **lighten (sth) up** *same as* **lighten** 1

light entertainment noun [U] entertainment that involves things such as singing, dancing, and telling jokes

lighter /ˈlaɪtə/ noun [C] a small object that produces a flame, used for lighting cigarettes

light-headed adj feeling as though you might fall down or become unconscious, for example because you are drunk

light-hearted /ˌlaɪt ˈhɑːtɪd/ adj **1** funny and not intended to be serious **2** happy and not worried about anything

lighthouse /ˈlaɪthaʊs/ noun [C] a tower that is built next to the sea with a powerful light that warns ships of danger

light industry noun [U] industry in which small goods are produced, for example electronic equipment → HEAVY INDUSTRY

lighting /ˈlaɪtɪŋ/ noun [U] light of a particular type or quality, or the equipment that produces it

lightly /ˈlaɪtli/ adv

1 without much force	4 cooked for a short time
2 without thought	5 waking up very easily
3 in small amounts	♦ PHRASE

1 without using much force or pressure **2** without considering something carefully and seriously: *The decision was not taken lightly.* **3** in small amounts, or using only a small amount of something **4** cooked for a short time: *a lightly boiled egg* **5** if you sleep lightly, you wake up very easily

PHRASE **get off/be let off lightly** to not be harmed or punished as severely as you might have been

lightning /ˈlaɪtnɪŋ/ noun [U] the bright flashes of light that you see in the sky during a storm: *The ship was struck by lightning soon after it left the port.* ♦ *She lay awake, listening to the thunder and lightning.*

lightning

lightweight¹ /ˈlaɪtweɪt/ adj weighing less than other similar things

lightweight² /ˈlaɪtweɪt/ noun [C] **1** someone who is not important or does not have much influence **2** a BOXER or WRESTLER who belongs to one of the lower weight groups

light year noun **1** [C] the distance that light travels in a year, used as a unit for measuring distances in space **2** light years [plural] *informal* a very long way in time, distance, or quality

like¹ /laɪk/ grammar word ★★★

Like can be:
- a **preposition**: *He looks like his father.*
- a **conjunction**: *She looked like she was about to cry.*
- an **adverb**: *I said, like, you can't do this to me.*

1 similar similar to someone or something else: *No one could play the trumpet like he did.* ♦ *I went and bought myself a new pen just like yours.* ♦ *Doesn't he look like Mark?* ♦ *The cloth felt like silk against her skin.* ♦ *Once it's washed and ironed it'll be like new.* ♦ *an animal something like a shark*

2 such as used for introducing an example of someone or something that you have just mentioned: *It eats small animals like birds and mice.*

3 typical typical of a particular person: *It's not like him to lie.*

4 as if *spoken* used for saying that something seems to be true but may not be: *He sounded like he'd only just woken up.*

5 when you pause *spoken* used when you pause while you are speaking: *He hasn't phoned me in, like, three weeks.*

PHRASES **like crazy/mad** in a very extreme, noticeable, or fast way: *His new book is selling like crazy.*

like I say/said _spoken_ used when you are saying something again that you have already said: _It's unfortunate but, like I said, it's a decision we have to make._
like this used when showing someone exactly how to do something: _Click on the 'Mail' icon, like this._
more like used for giving a number or amount that you think is more accurate than another one: _I'd guess it's more like 40 per cent than 60 per cent ._
what is sb/sth like? used for asking or talking about the qualities or features that someone or something has: _I haven't met Alan – what's he like? ♦ She took Andrew with her to show him what the club was like._
→ ANYTHING

like² /laɪk/ verb [T] ★★★
1 to enjoy something, or to think that someone or something is pleasant or attractive: _Do you like my new hairstyle? ♦ You never did like John, did you? ♦ Which of her novels did you like best? ♦ Jamie doesn't like it when you correct him. ♦ like doing sth I like going to parties. ♦ like to do sth He always liked to sleep late on Sundays. ♦ 'How did you like Paris?''I loved it!'_
2 to prefer to do something in a particular way, or to prefer to have something done in a particular way: _How do you like your eggs? ♦ like sb to do sth She likes us to hand our work in on time. ♦ like to do sth I don't like to interrupt her when she's in a meeting._
PHRASES **if you like** _spoken_ **1** used when you are making an offer or suggestion: _We'll go to the beach tomorrow, if you like._ **2** used for showing that you agree to a suggestion although it is not what you would choose to do: _'Let's just sit here for a minute.' 'OK, if you like.'_
(whether you) like it or not used for saying that you cannot change a situation even if it is unpleasant: _Whether we like it or not, we are part of a global economy._
would like used for stating politely what someone wants: _I'd like a large whisky, please. ♦ would like to do sth I'd like to thank everyone who made this evening a success._
would you like...? used for offering something to someone or for inviting them to do something: _Would you like some cake? ♦ would you like to do sth? Would you like to go for a drink? ♦ would you like sb/sth to do sth Would you like me to help you with your homework?_

Other ways of saying like
■ **adore** (_informal_) to like someone or something very much
■ **be crazy/mad about** (_informal_) to like someone or something very much
■ **be fond of** to like someone or something very much
■ **be keen on** to be enthusiastic about a particular person, thing, or activity
■ **enjoy** to like doing a particular activity

■ **love** to like something very much. **Love** is also used for saying that you care about someone very much
■ **prefer** to like one thing more than another

like³ /laɪk/ noun
PHRASES **sb's likes and dislikes** the things that someone likes or does not like
the likes of _informal_ people or things of a particular type
-like /laɪk/ suffix similar to something: _a childlike face ♦ The illness causes flu-like symptoms._
likeable /ˈlaɪkəb(ə)l/ adj pleasant, friendly, and easy to like
likelihood /ˈlaɪklihʊd/ noun [singular/U] the chance that something might happen: _The likelihood of developing cancer is increased in people who smoke. ♦ a strong likelihood that he will run for president_
likely¹ /ˈlaɪkli/ adj ★★★
1 probably going to happen, or probably true ≠ UNLIKELY: **likely to do sth** _Is anyone likely to see Fran? ♦ +(that) It seems likely that interest rates will rise._
2 suitable, or almost certain to be successful ≠ UNLIKELY: _a likely candidate for the job_
likely² /ˈlaɪkli/ adv probably: _They'll quite likely ask you to pay._
like-minded adj like-minded people have similar interests and opinions
liken /ˈlaɪkən/ PHRASAL VERB ˈliken sb/sth to sb/sth _formal_ to say that someone or something is similar to someone or something else
likeness /ˈlaɪknəs/ noun **1** [C/U] the quality of being similar to someone or something else **2** [C] a picture, model etc of someone that looks just like them
likewise /ˈlaɪkwaɪz/ adv _formal_ in a similar way: _Most fathers said that they had too little time with their children. Likewise, kids wanted more time with their dads._
liking /ˈlaɪkɪŋ/ noun [singular] a feeling of enjoying something: _a liking for science subjects_
PHRASES **for sb's liking** if something is too expensive, too dark etc for someone's liking, they do not like it because it is too expensive, too dark etc
take a liking to to begin to like someone or something
to sb's liking if something is to someone's liking, they like it
lilac /ˈlaɪlək/ noun [C/U] a small tree with pale purple or white flowers
lilt /lɪlt/ noun [singular] a pleasant rising and falling pattern of sounds in the way that someone talks or in a piece of music —**lilting** adj
lily /ˈlɪli/ noun [C] a large flower in the shape of a bell —_picture_ → C9
limb /lɪm/ noun [C] an arm, or a leg
PHRASE **out on a limb** in a situation where you have no support from other people
limbo /ˈlɪmbəʊ/ noun **in limbo** in a situation where you have to wait to find out what will happen next

lime /laɪm/ noun **1** [C/U] a fruit with a hard green skin and sour juice —*picture* → C10
2 [U] a white substance used for making CEMENT

limelight, the /ˈlaɪmˌlaɪt/ noun [singular] a situation in which you are getting a lot of public attention: *DiCaprio has been in the limelight since the age of 12.*

limerick /ˈlɪmərɪk/ noun [C] a humorous poem with five lines

limit¹ /ˈlɪmɪt/ noun [C] ★★★
1 the greatest amount or level of something that is possible or allowed: *The speed limit here is forty miles an hour.* ♦ *There is a limit to what we can do in two weeks.*
2 the outer edge of an area: *No bombs landed within the city limits.*
PHRASE off limits 1 if a place is off limits, you are not allowed to go there **2** not allowed or approved of: *Discussion of these subjects is off limits.*

Words often used with limit

Nouns often used with limit (noun, sense 1)
- **age, speed, time, weight** + LIMIT: nouns that can come immediately before limit
Verbs often used with limit (noun, sense 1)
- **impose, place, put** + LIMIT + ON: limit something
- **define, set, specify** + LIMIT: say what the limits are
- **extend, raise** + LIMIT: increase the limit
- **lower, reduce** + LIMIT: make the limit lower

limit² /ˈlɪmɪt/ verb [T] ★★★
1 to prevent a number, amount, or effect from increasing past a particular point: *The new laws should limit environmental damage.* ♦ **limit sth to sth** *We want to limit classes to a maximum of 30 pupils.*
2 to reduce or control someone's freedom or ability to be effective =RESTRICT: **be limited by sth** *They were limited by the amount of money they could spend on the production.* ♦ **limit sb to sth** *Try to limit yourself to two or three glasses of wine a week.*
3 **be limited to** if something is limited to a particular place or group, it happens only in that place or within that group: *The right to vote was limited to men.*

limitation /ˌlɪmɪˈteɪʃ(ə)n/ noun **1** [C/U] a rule or situation that puts a limit on something, or the process of limiting something: *a limitation on the use of cars in the city*
2 limitations [plural] weak points that make someone or something less effective: *There are several limitations to this method.*

limited /ˈlɪmɪtɪd/ adj ★★
1 not allowed to go above a particular number, amount, or level ≠ UNLIMITED: *The promotional pack will be on sale for a limited period only.*
2 not very good, or not very great in amount: *a limited grasp of economics*
3 *British* used after the name of a company to show that it is a limited company

limited company noun [C] a company, especially in the UK, whose owners are legally responsible for only a limited amount of its DEBTS

limiting /ˈlɪmɪtɪŋ/ adj preventing someone or something from developing or improving

limitless /ˈlɪmɪtləs/ adj very great, or without any limits

limousine /ˌlɪməˈziːn/ noun [C] a large expensive comfortable car in which a rich or important person travels

limp¹ /lɪmp/ verb [I] to walk with difficulty because of an injured leg or foot —**limp** noun [singular]

limp² /lɪmp/ adj not firm, stiff, or strong

line¹ /laɪn/ noun ★★★

1 long thin mark	**8** direction/path
2 row of people/things	**9** series of events etc
3 on someone's skin	**10** imaginary limit
4 series of words	**11** way of thinking etc
5 string/rope/wire	**12** people waiting
6 telephone connection	**+ PHRASES**
7 part of railway system	

1 [C] a long thin mark on the surface of something: *Draw a straight line.* ♦ *It was hard to tell whether the ball had crossed the line.*
2 [C] a row of people or things: *a line of palm trees*
3 [C] a thin mark on someone's skin that appears especially as they get older =WRINKLE
4 [C] a series of words in a book, song, play etc: *The actors kept forgetting their lines.* ♦ *a line of poetry*
5 [C] a piece of string, rope, or wire used for a particular purpose: *a washing line*
6 [C] a telephone connection or service: *an advice line* ♦ *It's a very bad line – I'll call you back.*
7 [C] a part of a railway system: *the London to Brighton line*
8 [C] the direction or path along which someone or something moves or looks: *He was so drunk he couldn't walk in a straight line.*
9 [C] a series of people or events that are connected: *the latest in a long line of scandals*
10 [C] an imaginary limit or border between two situations or conditions: *There is a fine line between helping and interfering.*
11 [C] a way of thinking, talking, or finding out about something: *a persuasive line of argument* ♦ *The government is taking a hard line on street crime* (=dealing with it firmly).
12 [C/U] a QUEUE of people waiting for something: *We stood in line for an hour.*
PHRASES along the lines of similar to, or based on: *an ad campaign along the lines of the one we did last year*
along similar/different/the same lines in a way that is similar/different/the same
be in line for to be likely to receive something
bring sb/sth into line to make someone or something similar to another person or thing: *The new ruling brings this country into line with the rest of Europe.*

L

down the line at a later stage in a process: *The situation will be very different two months down the line.*

in/out of line with 1 similar to/different from someone or something: *The costs were very much in line with what we expected.* **2** changing/not changing in the same way as another thing: *The increase in pay is in line with the cost of living.*

on line connected to a computer system or to the Internet → ONLINE

on the line 1 at risk: *His job could be on the line if results do not improve.* **2** on the telephone: *We have a caller on the line from California.*

out of line behaving in a way that other people do not approve of: *That comment was way out of line.*

line² /laɪn/ verb [T] **1** to cover the inside of something with a layer of something else: **line sth with sth** *Line the baking tray with greaseproof paper.* ♦ *He wore a black coat lined with dark grey silk.* **2** to form rows along the sides of something: *Crowds lined the streets to watch the parade.*

PHRASE **line your pockets** to obtain money, especially by acting dishonestly

PHRASAL VERBS **line (sb/sth) up** to form a row, or to put people or things in a row: *The books are lined up on a shelf above the desk.* ♦ *All children must line up when the whistle goes.*

line sth up to organize or prepare things for an event: *We have a series of activities lined up to keep you entertained.*

linear /ˈlɪniə/ adj *formal* consisting of lines, or of a straight line

lined /laɪnd/ adj **1** clothing that is lined has another layer of cloth on the inside **2** lined skin has a lot of lines on it =WRINKLED **3** lined paper has lines printed on it

line ˌmanager noun [C] *British* a manager at a higher level than you who is in charge of the work that you do

linen /ˈlɪnɪn/ noun [C/U] **1** a cloth like thick cotton that CREASES easily **2** things made of cloth that are used in the house, such as sheets and TABLECLOTHS

liner /ˈlaɪnə/ noun [C] **1** a large passenger ship that people travel on for pleasure **2** something that you use inside another thing to keep it clean or protect it: *a bin liner*

line-up noun [C] **1** a team of players who play in a particular sports game **2** a set of television or radio programmes that are broadcast one after another

linger /ˈlɪŋɡə/ verb [I] **1** to stay somewhere for a long time, or to do something for a long time: *I like to linger over breakfast and read the newspapers.* **2** to continue for a long time: *Doubts still linger about his honesty.*

PHRASAL VERB **linger on** same as **linger 2**

lingerie /ˈlænʒəri/ noun [U] women's underwear

lingering /ˈlɪŋɡərɪŋ/ adj lasting for a long time: *lingering doubts/fears*

linguist /ˈlɪŋɡwɪst/ noun [C] **1** someone who studies and speaks a lot of languages **2** someone who teaches or studies LINGUISTICS

linguistic /lɪŋˈɡwɪstɪk/ adj relating to languages, words, or linguistics

linguistics /lɪŋˈɡwɪstɪks/ noun [U] the study of language and how it works

lining /ˈlaɪnɪŋ/ noun [C/U] **1** a piece of cloth that is fastened to the inside of something such as clothes or curtains to make them thicker **2** something that you put on the inside of another thing to keep it clean or protect it

link¹ /lɪŋk/ verb [T] ★★★
1 if people, things, or events are linked, they are related to each other in some way: *Police suspect that the two murder cases are linked.* ♦ **be linked to/with sth** *Rock music has often been linked with the drug culture.* **2** to say or show that two things are related, or that one of the things causes the other: **link sb/sth to sth** *Scientists have linked certain types of cancer to people's diets.* **3** to connect two or more places or things: *Several new roads will link the southern and northern regions of the country.* ♦ **link sth to/with sth** *Link the supply cable to the fitting at the rear of the machine.*

PHRASAL VERB **link up** to make a connection between two or more things: *The space shuttle will link up with the space station this afternoon.*

link² /lɪŋk/ noun [C] ★★★

1 a connection	**4** on the Internet
2 a relationship	**5** ring in a chain
3 way to travel etc	

1 a connection between two or more people, places, facts, or events: *They are studying the links between carbon emissions and climate change.*

2 a relationship between two or more people, organizations, or countries: *Back in the 1980s, the bank was criticized for its links with South Africa.*

3 a means of travel or communication that connects two or more places: *a rail link between Edinburgh and London*

4 *computing* a connection between one Internet file or section and another, for example on a WEBSITE =HYPERLINK: *Click on this link to find out more.*

5 one of the rings that are connected to each other to form a chain

linking ˌverb noun [C] *linguistics* a verb such as 'be' or 'seem' that connects the subject of a sentence with its COMPLEMENT (=the part of the sentence that describes the subject)

link-up noun [C] **1** a connection between machines or electronic equipment **2** an agreement between two companies to work together or to become business partners

linoleum /lɪˈnəʊliəm/ or **lino** /ˈlaɪnəʊ/ *British* noun [U] a hard flat substance with a shiny surface, used for covering floors

L

lion /ˈlaɪən/ noun [C] a large African wild cat with yellow fur —*picture* → C12

lioness /ˈlaɪənes/ noun [C] a female lion

lip /lɪp/ noun [C] ★★★
1 one of the two edges that form the top and bottom parts of your mouth —*picture* → C14
2 the place on the edge of a glass or container where you pour out liquid
PHRASES **on everyone's lips** if something is on everyone's lips, a lot of people are talking about it
pay lip service to sth to say publicly that you agree with an idea, but not do anything to support it

lip-read /ˈlɪp riːd/ verb [I] to look at someone's lips in order to understand what they are saying because you cannot hear them

lipstick /ˈlɪpˌstɪk/ noun [C/U] a coloured substance in the form of a small stick that women put on their lips, or a stick of this —*picture* → MAKE-UP

liquefy /ˈlɪkwɪˌfaɪ/ verb [I/T] to become a liquid, or to make something become a liquid

liqueur /lɪˈkjʊə/ noun [C/U] a sweet strong alcoholic drink that you have at the end of a meal

liquid¹ /ˈlɪkwɪd/ noun [C/U] ★★ a substance such as water that can flow and is not a solid or gas: *a glass of colourless liquid*

liquid² /ˈlɪkwɪd/ adj ★ in the form of a liquid: *liquid detergent*

liquid 'assets noun [plural] *business* the money that a company has, and anything else that can easily be exchanged for money

liquidate /ˈlɪkwɪˌdeɪt/ verb [I/T] to close a business and sell everything that it owns in order to pay money that it owes —**liquidation** /ˌlɪkwɪˈdeɪʃ(ə)n/ noun [U]

liquidizer /ˈlɪkwɪˌdaɪzə/ noun [C] *British* a piece of electrical equipment that turns solid food into a liquid=BLENDER —**liquidize** verb [T]

liquor /ˈlɪkə/ noun [U] *American* strong alcoholic drinks=SPIRITS

liquorice /ˈlɪkərɪs, ˈlɪkərɪʃ/ noun [U] a black substance with a strong flavour, used for making sweets and medicines

'liquor ˌstore noun [C] *American* an OFF-LICENCE

lisp /lɪsp/ noun [singular] if someone has a lisp, they pronounce 's' sounds as 'th' —**lisp** verb [I/T]

list¹ /lɪst/ noun [C] ★★★
1 a set of names, numbers etc that are written or printed one below another: *a shopping list* ♦ *I'd better make a list, or I'll forget who I've invited.* ♦ *I couldn't see my name on the list.* ♦ *a list of the world's richest people*
2 a set of things that you put in a particular order in your mind, according to how important they are: *Decorating the house is high on our list of things to do.*

list² /lɪst/ verb ★★
1 [T] to mention or write things one after another: *The ingredients in food must be*

listed on the packet. ♦ *Chris lists his hobbies as cycling, gardening, and chess.*
2 [T] if a telephone number is listed, it is published in a book
3 [I] if a ship lists, it leans to one side

listen /ˈlɪs(ə)n/ verb [I] ★★★
1 to pay attention to a sound, or to try to hear a sound: *Do you like listening to music?* ♦ *Listen carefully to the instructions.* ♦ *She was listening for the sound of his key in the lock.* → HEAR
2 to pay attention to what someone tells you and do what they suggest: *I've tried to give Jerry advice, but he just won't listen.* ♦ *Don't listen to him – he doesn't know anything about it.*
PHRASAL VERBS ˌlisten 'in to secretly listen to what someone says=EAVESDROP: *Rachel was listening in on our conversation.*
ˌlisten 'out for sth *British* to listen carefully to try and hear a sound: *I was listening out for their footsteps.*
ˌlisten 'up *spoken* used for getting the attention of a noisy group of people: *Hey, listen up everybody!*

> **Words often used with listen**
>
> *Adverbs often used with listen (sense 1)*
> ■ LISTEN + **attentively, carefully, closely, hard, intently**: used for saying that someone is giving all their attention

listener /ˈlɪs(ə)nə/ noun [C] **1** someone who listens to the radio, or to a particular radio programme or radio station **2** someone who listens to a person speaking

listing /ˈlɪstɪŋ/ noun **1** [C] a list, or a position on a list **2 listings** [plural] a list of things such as films, plays, and exhibitions printed in a newspaper

listless /ˈlɪstləs/ adj feeling as if you have no energy and no interest in anything

listserv /ˈlɪstˌsɜːv/ *trademark* a piece of software that automatically sends a copy of every email received to all members of a group

lit the past tense and past participle of **light³**

lite /laɪt/ adj a spelling of 'light' that is often used in the names of foods and drinks that contain less sugar, fat, or alcohol than usual

liter /ˈliːtə/ the American spelling of **litre**

literacy /ˈlɪtərəsi/ noun [U] the ability to read and write

literal /ˈlɪt(ə)rəl/ adj **1** the literal meaning of a word is its most basic meaning
→ FIGURATIVE **2** a literal translation is one in which each word is translated separately in a way that does not sound natural

literally /ˈlɪt(ə)rəli/ adv **1** used for showing that what you are saying is really true: *Now there are literally thousands of companies using our software.* **2** used when you are describing something in an extreme way that cannot be true: *When I told him the news he literally exploded.* **3** in the most basic, obvious meanings of the words that are used: *There's an Italian dessert called tiramisu, which literally means 'pull me up'.*

4 if you translate something literally, you translate each word separately in a way that does not sound natural

literary /ˈlɪt(ə)rəri/ adj **1** relating to literature **2** typical of words that are used only in stories or poems, and not in normal writing or speech

literate /ˈlɪt(ə)rət/ adj able to read and write ≠ ILLITERATE

literature /ˈlɪtrətʃə/ noun [U] ★★
1 stories, poems, and plays, especially those that are considered to have value as art: *She is studying German literature.*
2 books or other printed information about a subject: *Police discovered racist literature in his home.*

lithe /laɪð/ adj moving and bending in a graceful way

litigation /ˌlɪtɪˈɡeɪʃ(ə)n/ noun [U] use of the legal system to settle a disagreement

litmus test /ˈlɪtməs ˌtest/ noun [C] an event, decision etc that provides a clear sign of what someone is really like, or of what their intentions are

litre /ˈliːtə/ noun [C] **1** a unit for measuring an amount of liquid or gas in the METRIC SYSTEM, containing 1000 millilitres **2** a unit for measuring the size of a vehicle's engine

litter¹ /ˈlɪtə/ noun **1** [U] things that people have dropped on the ground in a public place, making it untidy **2** [C] a group of baby animals that are born at the same time

litter² /ˈlɪtə/ verb [T] **1 be littered with** if a place is littered with things, they are spread around there: *The room was littered with books and papers.* **2 be littered with** if something is littered with things, there are many of them in it: *The book is littered with references from the Bible.*

little¹ /ˈlɪt(ə)l/ (comparative **less** /les/; superlative **least** /liːst/) grammar word ★★★

> **Little** can be:
> ■ a **determiner**: *Little progress has been made.*
> ■ a **pronoun**: *They manage to survive on very little.*
> ■ an **adverb**: *I go there very little.*

1 an extremely small amount of something: *They made little effort to explain.* ♦ *Little has been revealed about his background.* ♦ *He's an excellent manager, so there's very little tension in the office.* ♦ *There was too much rain and too little sun.* ♦ *The company did little to prevent the disaster.*
2 not very often, or only to a small degree: *In her last years I saw her very little.* ♦ *They spoke of him as little as possible.* ♦ *a little known fact* (=not known by many people)
> **PHRASES a little 1** a small amount: *We managed to save a little money.* ♦ *Mix in a little of the flour.* ♦ *Doesn't Helen speak a little bit of Chinese?* ♦ *I have a little more patience than you.* **2** to a small degree: *I held her a little closer.* ♦ *This may be a little bit painful.* **3** for a short time: *You should rest a little.* ♦ *Come and talk with me for a little bit.*

little by little very gradually: *Little by little his eyes adjusted to the light.*

> **Little** and **a little** are both used for talking about a small amount of something. But they have slightly different meanings.
> ■ **Little** means 'not much' or 'not enough', and is used when you would like there to be more of something: *There is little hope of finding survivors.* ♦ *There has been little change since this morning.*
> ■ **A little** means 'some', and is used for emphasizing that an amount is small, but greater than you might expect: *There is still a little time to finish the game.* ♦ *I had a little money left so I took a taxi.*

little² /ˈlɪt(ə)l/ adj ★★★
1 small in size or number: *Use the little pan for making the sauce.* ♦ *There's a little group of us who meet once a week.* ♦ *a tiny little garden* → SMALL
2 young, and often small ≠ BIG: *a little boy/ girl/child* ♦ *When I was little, we didn't have computers at school.* ♦ *Is this your little brother?* (=younger brother)? ♦ *My little girl* (=my daughter) *is three years old.*
3 short in time or distance: *Molly carried her a little way towards the house.* ♦ *I'll be with you in a little while.*
4 not important ≠ MINOR: *There are just some little details to sort out.*

little finger noun [C] the smallest finger on your hand —*picture* → C14

livable /ˈlɪvəb(ə)l/ adj **1** nice enough to live in **2** if something is livable, you can bear it but it is not very nice or enjoyable

live¹ /lɪv/ verb ★★★
1 [I] to have your home in a particular place: *Paris is a nice place to live.* ♦ *They lived in a flat in South London.* ♦ *I think he lives somewhere near Bath.* ♦ *Do you still live at home* (=in your parents' home)?
2 [I/T] to have a particular kind of life: *Food is inexpensive here, so you can live quite cheaply.* ♦ *people living in poverty* ♦ *Millions of families are living on benefits.* ♦ *Now they have retired and want to live a quiet life.*
3 [I] to be alive, or to stay alive: *Aunt Joan lived to be 86.* ♦ *live to do sth* (=live long enough to do it) *He lived to see the first talking pictures.* ♦ *Hippodamus lived in the early fifth century BC.*
4 [I] to have an interesting and exciting life: *Come on, you have to live a little!*
> **PHRASES can live with sth** used for saying that you can accept something: *It's a little less than I asked for, but I can live with that.*
> **live it up** to do enjoyable and exciting things that involve spending a lot of money
> **PHRASAL VERBS live by sth** to behave according to a particular set of beliefs or principles: *Even criminals have standards that they live by.*
> **live sth down** to make people forget about something embarrassing or silly that you have done: *I'm never going to live this down!*
> **live for sb/sth** to think that someone or something is so important that they are

your main reason for living: *She lives for her work.*

live 'in to live at the place where you work or study: *Their nanny lives in.*

'live off sb/sth to depend on someone or something for the money or food that you need: *He's 25 and still living off his parents.*

live 'on to continue to be alive, or to continue to exist: *These traditions live on in the villages in the mountains.*

'live on sth 1 to have a particular amount of money to buy the things that you need to live: *They have to live on a pension of £350 a month.* **2** to eat a particular kind of food: *These fish live on small sea creatures such as shrimp.*

'live through sth to experience a dangerous or unpleasant situation and still be alive after it

'live to,gether if two people live together, they are not married but live in the same house and have a sexual relationship

live 'up to sth to be as good as what was expected or promised: *The beautiful scenery certainly lived up to expectations.*

'live with sb to live in the same house and have a sexual relationship with someone that you are not married to

'live with sth to accept something unpleasant that you cannot change: *How does she live with the guilt?*

live² /laɪv/ adj ★

1 living	4 with electricity
2 broadcast	5 bullets
3 performance	

1 living and not dead: *The law deals with the transport of live animals.*

2 a live television or radio programme shows something that is happening at the same time as you are watching it or listening to it

3 a live performance is given in front of an audience: *We found a bar that has **live music** on Friday nights.*

4 a live wire or piece of equipment is connected to the electricity supply and has electricity going through it

5 live bullets or AMMUNITION are real, rather than BLANKS or rubber or plastic bullets

live³ /laɪv/ adv **1** if something is broadcast live, it is happening at the same time as you are watching it or listening to it **2** if something is performed live, it is performed in front of an audience

livelihood /ˈlaɪvlihʊd/ noun [C/U] something such as your work that provides the money that you need to live

lively /ˈlaɪvli/ adj **1** full of energy and enthusiasm: *a lively group/debate/ discussion* **2** full of people: *lively bars and restaurants*

liven /ˈlaɪv(ə)n/ PHRASAL VERB **liven (sth) 'up** to make something more interesting or exciting, or to become more interesting or exciting: *We need some music to liven things up.*

liver /ˈlɪvə/ noun **1** [C] the organ in your body

that cleans your blood **2** [C/U] the liver of some animals eaten as food

Liverpudlian /ˌlɪvəˈpʌdliən/ noun [C] someone from Liverpool, England

lives the plural of **life**

livestock /ˈlaɪvˌstɒk/ noun [plural] animals such as cows, sheep, and pigs that are kept on farms

livid /ˈlɪvɪd/ adj *informal* extremely angry

living¹ /ˈlɪvɪŋ/ adj [C] ★★

1 alive at the present time: *He has no living relatives.*

2 living things are animals or plants that are alive, rather than objects such as rocks

PHRASE **in living memory** during the time that anyone still alive can remember: *the worst storm in living memory*

living² /ˈlɪvɪŋ/ noun **1** [C] money that you earn to live on: *Do you know what she does for a living* (=does as a job)? ♦ *She makes a living as a music teacher.* **2** [U] a particular type of life: *the stresses of modern living*

'living ,room noun [C] the main room in a house where you usually relax in comfortable chairs = SITTING ROOM, LOUNGE

'living ,standards noun [plural] the way in which people live, for example how comfortable their houses are or how much money they have to spend

lizard /ˈlɪzəd/ noun [C] a small REPTILE with a long tail —*picture* → C13

load¹ /ləʊd/ noun [C] ★★

1 something that a person, animal, or vehicle carries: *a lorry carrying **a load of** wood*

2 an amount of work that a person, piece of equipment, or system has to do at one time = WORKLOAD: *Teaching loads have increased this year.*

3 a quantity of clothes that you put in a washing machine

PHRASE **a load of/loads of sth** *informal* a lot of something: *I've got loads of things to do today.*

load² /ləʊd/ verb ★

1 [I/T] to put a load onto or into something such as a vehicle or container: *Down at the docks, ships were loading and unloading.*

2 [T] to put something into a piece of equipment so that it is ready to use: *Did you **load the dishwasher**? ♦ **load sth with/into sth** My camera is loaded with a colour film.*

3 [T] to put bullets into a gun

PHRASAL VERBS **load sb 'down 1** if you are loaded down with a lot of heavy things, you are carrying them: *She was loaded down with luggage.* **2** if you are loaded down with responsibilities, problems or work, you have more than you can deal with

load (sth) 'up *same as* **load²** 1: *The trucks were being loaded up and driven away.*

loaded /ˈləʊdɪd/ adj

1 carrying a load	4 with second meaning
2 very full	5 very rich
3 containing bullets	

1 carrying a load: *a truck loaded with fruit*

2 having a large amount of a particular thing or quality: *mass-produced cakes that are loaded with fat and sugar* **3** a loaded gun has bullets in it **4** a loaded question, word, statement etc has a hidden or second meaning **5** *informal* very rich

loaf /ləʊf/ (plural **loaves** /ləʊvz/) noun [C] bread in a long, round, or square shape that you cut into SLICES (=thin flat pieces) for eating

loan¹ /ləʊn/ noun ★
  1 [C] an amount of money that a person, business, or country borrows, especially from a bank: *How soon do you have to pay off the loan?* ♦ *Jim took out a loan to pay for his car*.
  2 [singular] a situation in which someone lends something to someone: *He had accepted Tom's offer of the loan of his cottage*.
  PHRASE **on loan** if something is on loan, someone has borrowed it: *That book is already out on loan*. ♦ *These paintings are on loan from the Guggenheim in Bilbao*.

loan² /ləʊn/ verb [T] to lend something to someone

loath /ləʊθ/ adj *formal* very unwilling to do something=RELUCTANT

loathe /ləʊð/ verb [T] to dislike someone or something very much=DETEST —**loathing** noun [U]

loathsome /ˈləʊðs(ə)m/ adj very bad or unpleasant=VILE

loaves the plural of **loaf**

lob /lɒb/ verb [T] **1** to throw, hit, or kick something so that it goes high into the air **2** to hit or kick a ball high into the air and usually over the head of another player —*picture* → C15

lobby¹ /ˈlɒbi/ noun [C] **1** an organized group of people who try to influence politicians **2** the area just inside the entrance to a hotel, theatre, or other large building=FOYER

lobby² /ˈlɒbi/ verb [I/T] to try to influence politicians

lobbyist /ˈlɒbiɪst/ noun [C] someone who lobbies politicians

lobster /ˈlɒbstə/ noun [C/U] a large SHELLFISH with a long body and eight legs, or the meat from this fish

local¹ /ˈləʊk(ə)l/ adj ★
  1 in or related to a particular area, especially the place where you live: *Ask for the book in your local library*. ♦ *Local calls cost 2p a minute*.
  2 affecting only a small area of the body: *a local infection*

local² /ˈləʊk(ə)l/ noun [C] **1** someone who lives in a particular place **2** *British informal* a PUB that is near your home

local anaes'thetic noun [C/U] a drug which is given to you to stop you feeling pain in one part of your body ⇒ GENERAL ANAESTHETIC

local ,area 'network noun [C] *computing* a LAN

local au'thority noun [C] *British* an organization in the UK that provides public services in a particular area

local 'government noun [U] the organizations that provide public services in a particular town or area, controlled by officials chosen in local elections

locality /ləʊˈkæləti/ noun [C] *formal* a particular area or district

localized /ˈləʊkəlaɪzd/ adj *formal* existing only in a particular area

locally /ˈləʊk(ə)li/ adv in the area where you live or that you are talking about

local 'time noun [U] the time in a particular part of the world

locate /ləʊˈkeɪt/ verb [T] ★
  1 to find out the exact place where someone or something is: *Engineers are still trying to locate the fault*.
  2 to establish something in a particular place: *The company wants to locate the factory near the railway*.
  PHRASE **be located** to exist in a particular place: *The centre is conveniently located close to many historical sites*. ♦ *The hotel is located in Wolverhampton town centre*.

location /ləʊˈkeɪʃ(ə)n/ noun ★★
  1 [C] the place or position where someone or something is, or where something happens: *The talks are taking place at a secret location*.
  2 [C/U] a place where a film or TV programme is made, away from a STUDIO: *a thriller filmed entirely on location*

loch /lɒx, lɒk/ noun [C] *Scottish* a lake

lock¹ /lɒk/ verb [I/T] ★★
  1 to fasten something such as a door with a key, or to be fastened with a key ≠ UNLOCK: *Have you locked the car?* ♦ *This drawer won't lock*. ♦ *lock sth in sth She locked the documents in the safe*. —*picture* → CLOSE
  2 to become fixed in one position, or to fix something in one position: *The brakes locked and the car spun off the road*. ♦ *He locked his arms around her waist*.
  PHRASE **locked in a debate/dispute etc** involved in a discussion or argument that lasts a long time: *The two sides were locked in fierce debate*.
  PHRASAL VERBS **lock sth a'way** to put something in a place or container that you fasten with a lock: *Valuable items should be locked away*.
  lock sb 'in to put someone in a room and lock the door so that they cannot leave: *She went to her room and locked herself in*.
  lock sb 'out to prevent someone from coming into a room or building by locking the door: *I've locked myself out again – could I use your phone?*
  lock sb 'up to put someone in prison: *He was locked up for 12 years for armed robbery*.
  lock (sth) 'up to lock all the doors and windows of a building so that no one can get in: *I locked up and went to bed*. ♦ *The last person to leave locks up the shop*.

lock² /lɒk/ noun [C] ★
  1 the thing that is used for fastening a door, drawer etc so that no one can open it: *All the windows were fitted with locks*.

2 a piece of equipment used for preventing someone from using a vehicle, machine etc: *a bicycle lock*

3 a place on a river or CANAL that allows boats to move to a higher or lower water level

4 a small piece of hair on your head: *She cut off a lock of his hair.*

PHRASE **under lock and key** in a room or container that is fastened with a lock

locker /'lɒkə/ noun [C] a cupboard that you store clothes, books, and other personal things in temporarily, for example while you are at school

locket /'lɒkɪt/ noun [C] a piece of jewellery that consists of a very small case that you wear round your neck on a chain

locomotive /ˌləʊkəˈməʊtɪv/ noun [C] the vehicle that pulls a train=ENGINE

lodge¹ /lɒdʒ/ verb **1** [T] to formally make something such as a complaint or claim: *She lodged a complaint with the city council.* **2** [I/T] to become firmly fixed somewhere, usually accidentally: *A piece of meat lodged in his throat.* **3** [I] to pay to live in someone else's house

lodge² /lɒdʒ/ noun [C] **1** a small house in the countryside that people stay in, for example when they go hunting or fishing **2** a small room at the entrance to a building such as a university

lodger /'lɒdʒə/ noun [C] someone who pays to live in a house with the person who owns it

lodging /'lɒdʒɪŋ/ noun [C/U] a place that you pay to live in for a short time

lodgings /'lɒdʒɪŋz/ noun [plural] a room or set of rooms in someone's house that you pay to live in

loft /lɒft/ noun [C] a room or space under the roof of a building —*picture* → C1

lofty /'lɒfti/ adj **1** very tall or high **2** lofty aims or principles are based on high moral standards=NOBLE

log¹ /lɒg/ noun [C] **1** a thick piece of wood that has been cut from a tree **2** a written record of things that happen, especially on a ship or a plane

log² /lɒg/ verb [T] to make an official record of things that happen

PHRASAL VERBS ˌlog ˈoff or ˌlog ˈout *computing* to finish using a computer system

ˌlog ˈon or ˌlog ˈin *computing* to start using a computer system, for example by typing a PASSWORD

loggerheads /'lɒgəhedz/ noun **at loggerheads (with sb)** disagreeing very strongly with someone

logic /'lɒdʒɪk/ noun [U] **1** the way that someone connects ideas when they are explaining something or giving a reason **2** the study of the way that ideas can be connected and used to explain things

logical /'lɒdʒɪk(ə)l/ adj sensible and reasonable ≠ ILLOGICAL: *a logical argument* ♦ *It seems like the most logical solution to the problem.* —**logically** /'lɒdʒɪkli/ adv: *She*

presented her ideas clearly and logically.

login /'lɒgɪn/ noun [C/U] *computing* the process of starting to use a computer program or system

logistics /ləˈdʒɪstɪks/ noun [plural] the practical arrangements that are necessary in order to organize something successfully —**logistical** adj

logo /'ləʊgəʊ/ noun [C] a symbol that represents an organization or company

loins /lɔɪnz/ noun [plural] *literary* the part of your body below your waist, where your sex organs are

loiter /'lɔɪtə/ verb [I] to stand or wait in a public place for no particular reason =HANG AROUND —**loitering** noun [U]

loll /lɒl/ verb [I] **1** to sit, stand, or lie in a relaxed position **2** if your tongue or your head lolls, it hangs down in an uncontrolled way

lollipop /'lɒlipɒp/ noun [C] a hard sweet on the end of a stick

lolly /'lɒli/ noun [C] *British* **1** an ICE LOLLY **2** a LOLLIPOP

lone /ləʊn/ adj **1** single, or alone **2** *British* without a husband, wife, or partner: *lone parents*

lonely /'ləʊnli/ adj ★
1 unhappy because you are alone or have no friends: *a lonely childhood* ♦ *She must feel desperately lonely with all her family in Scotland.*
2 a lonely place is far from where people live or go=REMOTE: *a lonely stretch of country road* —**loneliness** noun [U]

lonely 'hearts noun [plural] *mainly journalism* people who are looking for a romantic relationship

loner /'ləʊnə/ noun [C] someone who likes to be alone

lonesome /'ləʊns(ə)m/ adj LONELY

long¹ /lɒŋ/ adj ★★★

1 lasting a long time	**5** of document
2 not short	**6** of clothes
3 giving a measurement	**+ PHRASES**
4 seeming long	

1 lasting for a large amount of time ≠ SHORT: *He has a long history of mental illness.* ♦ *It's a long time since I saw Rachel.*
2 measuring a large amount from one end to the other ≠ SHORT: *It's the longest tunnel in Europe.* ♦ *There was a long queue outside the bank.* ♦ *a woman with long blonde hair*
3 used for saying how long something lasts, or how long something is from one end to the other: *The room was 3 metres long.* ♦ *How long was the film?*
4 seeming to last for a very long time because you are bored or tired: *It had been a long week.*
5 a long book, letter, report etc has a lot of pages ≠ SHORT
6 long dresses, trousers, sleeves etc cover your arms or legs ≠ SHORT: *a shirt with long sleeves*

PHRASES **go a long way towards doing sth** to help someone to achieve something: *The money will go a long way towards paying for her medical treatment.*

have come a long way to have achieved a lot of things and made progress: *Technology has come a long way since the days of telegrams.*

have a long way to go to need to do a lot more before you are successful: *We've raised £100 so far, but we still have a long way to go.*

in the long run/term not immediately, but at some time in the future: *In the long run, this will be a better solution for the company.*

long hours or **a long day** if you work long hours, or a long day, you work more than usual

a long shot *informal* an attempt or guess that is not likely to be successful but that is worth trying: *It's a long shot, but I'll ask her.*

not by a long way/chalk *informal* used for saying that something is not true at all: *We haven't finished yet – not by a long way.*

long² /lɒŋ/ adv ★★★
1 for a long period of time: *I hope you haven't been **waiting** long.* ♦ *People are **living** longer nowadays.*
2 much earlier or later than a particular event or period: ***long** before/after the war* ♦ *I should have ended the relationship **long** ago.*

PHRASES **all day/year/week etc long** for the whole day/year/week etc: *I don't think I could look after children all day long.*

as/so long as used before explaining the conditions that will make something else happen or be true: *My parents don't care what job I do as long as I'm happy.*

before long soon: *She joined the company in 1995, and before long she was promoted to sales manager.*

be/take long used for saying or asking whether you will have to wait a long time for someone or something: *Dinner won't be long now.* ♦ *Will you be long, or shall I wait?* ♦ *It didn't take long to get there.*

for long for a long period of time: *I haven't known them for long.*

no longer or **not any longer** used when something happened or was true in the past but is not true now: *He no longer plays in an orchestra.*

long³ /lɒŋ/ verb [I] to want something very much: *She longed for him again.*

long-awaited /ˌlɒŋ əˈweɪtɪd/ adj a long-awaited event has been expected for a long time

long-distance adj **1** travelling between two places that are far apart: *a long-distance runner* **2** a long-distance phone call is one that you make to someone far away —**long-distance** adv

long-drawn-out adj continuing for too long =PROTRACTED

long-haul adj travelling a long distance, especially by air ≠ SHORT-HAUL

longing /ˈlɒŋɪŋ/ noun [C/U] a strong feeling of wanting someone or something —**longingly** adv

longitude /ˈlɒndʒɪˌtjuːd, ˈlɒŋɡɪˌtjuːd/ noun [C/U] the position of a place in the world when it is measured in relation to east or west, not to north or south → LATITUDE

long jump, the noun [singular] a sports event in which each person tries to jump further than the other people

long-lasting adj continuing for a long time: *long-lasting damage/harm*

long-life adj *British* long-life products remain fresh or useful for longer than other products

long-lost adj a long-lost friend or relative is someone who you have not seen for a long time

long-range adj **1** continuing or looking far into the future: *a long-range weather forecast* **2** able to travel long distances: *long-range aircraft/missiles*

long-running adj having continued for a long time: *a long-running dispute/conflict*

long-sighted adj *British* not able to see things clearly when they are near to you ≠ SHORT-SIGHTED

long-standing adj having existed for a long time: *a long-standing tradition/arrangement/agreement*

long-suffering adj patient despite having problems, or despite being badly treated, over a long period of time

long-term adj **1** continuing to exist, be relevant, or have an effect for a long time in the future ≠ SHORT-TERM: *a good long-term investment* **2** having existed for a long time and unlikely to change: *long-term debt*

long-time adj having continued or existed as a particular thing for a long time: *his long-time girlfriend*

long wave noun [U] a radio wave of more than 1,000 metres used for broadcasting. The written abbreviation is **LW**. → MEDIUM WAVE, SHORT WAVE

long weekend noun [C] a weekend when you have one or two extra days free in addition to the usual Saturday and Sunday

longwinded /ˌlɒŋˈwɪndɪd/ adj using more words and taking more time than necessary to say something

loo /luː/ noun [C] *British informal* a toilet, or a room with a toilet

look¹ /lʊk/ verb ★★★

1 direct eyes at sb/sth	**5** for saying how likely
2 search for sb/sth	**6** pay attention
3 have an appearance	**+ PHRASES**
4 seem	**+ PHRASAL VERBS**

1 [I] to direct your eyes towards someone or something so that you can see them: *Dan **looked at** his watch.* ♦ *If you **look through** this window, you can see the cathedral.* → SEE
2 [I] to search for someone or something: *I don't know where the keys are. I've **looked** everywhere.* ♦ *I spent most of the morning **looking for** my passport.*

3 [linking verb] to have a particular appearance: *He looked about twenty.* ♦ *He looked very funny in his hat.* ♦ *It was a first date so Emily wanted to **look her best** (=as attractive as possible).*

4 [linking verb] to seem to be something: *That new film looks good.*

5 [linking verb] used for giving your opinion about how likely it is that something will happen or be true: *Martin looks certain to win.*

6 [I] *spoken* used when you want someone to look at something, or when you want them to pay attention to what you are going to say: *Look! There's John!* ♦ *Look, why don't we meet up for a drink and talk about it then?*

PHRASES **(I'm) just looking** *spoken* used for telling someone who works in a shop that you do not yet know whether you want to buy anything

look good/bad 1 to seem to be going to have a good/bad result: *Things aren't looking too good for him at the moment.* **2** to be considered a good/bad thing to do: *Do you think it will look bad if I don't go and see him?*

looking to do sth planning to do something: *We're looking to expand the business.*

look like 1 to have a particular appearance: *Most people say that Kathleen looks like her dad.* ♦ *I asked him what the house looks like.* **2** to seem likely: *It looks like Bill will be able to come too.* ♦ *She looks like beating every player in the tournament.*

look out *spoken* used for warning someone to be careful, especially because they are likely to have an accident

PHRASAL VERBS ,look ˈafter **1** to take care of someone or something: *It's hard work looking after three children all day.* **2** to be in charge of something: *Who's looking after the department while you're away?*

,look aˈhead to think about what is likely to happen, or to plan what you are going to do in the future: *Looking ahead, I think the company needs to develop some new services.*

,look aˈround (sth) *British* to walk around a room, building, or place and see what is there: *Do you want to look around the school?*

ˈlook at sb/sth if an expert looks at someone or something, they examine them and decide what to do: *I'd like a skin specialist to look at that rash of yours.*

ˈlook at sth **1** to think about a situation or subject in a particular way=CONSIDER: *We're looking carefully at all the options before we make our decision.* **2** to read something quickly: *Would you like me to look at your essay before you hand it in?*

,look ˈback to think about a time or event in the past: *Most people **look back on** their schooldays with fondness.*

,look ˈdown on sb/sth to think that you are better or more important than someone else

ˈlook for sb/sth **1** to hope to get something that you want or need: *He was looking for*

work as a builder. **2** to search for someone or something: *I'm looking for Jim. Have you seen him?*

,look ˈforward to sth to feel happy and excited about something that is going to happen

,look ˈinto sth to try to discover the facts about something such as a problem or crime=INVESTIGATE: *The airline have promised to look into the matter.*

,look ˈon to watch an activity or event without taking part in it: *Phil looked on in disbelief as Maggie got up on the table and started to dance.*

,look ˈout for sb/sth to look carefully at people or things around you in order to try to find a particular person or thing: *We were told to look out for a blue van.*

,look ˈover sth to examine something, usually quickly: *He'd been looking over the leaflets he'd picked up earlier.*

,look ˈround (sth) *British same as* **look around (sth)**

,look ˈthrough sth **1** to read something quickly: *I've just been looking through your cookery books for inspiration.* **2** to search for something among a lot of other things: *I'll look through these files and see if I can find a copy of my CV.*

,look ˈup if a situation is looking up, it is getting better: *Finally, **things are looking up** for me.*

,look sb ˈup to go and see someone who you know when you are visiting the place where they live: *Look me up next time you come to Sydney.*

,look sth ˈup to try to find a piece of information by looking in a book or on a list, or by using a computer: *I had to look the word up in a dictionary.*

,look ˈup to sb to admire and respect someone

look² /lʊk/ noun ★★★

1 act of looking at sb/sth	4 appearance/style
2 act of searching	5 appearance of sb's face
3 expression on face	6 act of thinking

1 [C] an act of looking at someone or something: *Can I **have a look at** your new skateboard?* ♦ *Come and **take a look at** this.*

2 [C] an act of searching for someone or something: *I don't know where the book is, but I'll **have a look for** it.*

3 [C] an expression that you have on your face or in your eyes: *I could tell **by the look on his face** that he was not happy.* ♦ *She saw **the look of** surprise on Nicky's face.* ♦ *She **gave** me a worried **look** (=looked at me in a worried way).*

4 [C] the appearance that someone or something has: *I don't like the look of him.* ♦ *Let us create a stylish modern look for your home.*

5 looks [plural] the attractive appearance of someone, especially their face: *She's got everything – looks, intelligence, and money.*

6 [C] an occasion when you think carefully about a problem or situation: *We need to **have a look at** the way we deal with orders.*

lookalike /ˈlʊkəlaɪk/ noun [C] someone who

is very similar in appearance to a famous person

lookout /ˈlʊkaʊt/ noun [C] someone who watches for danger and is ready to warn other people, or the place where they watch from

> **PHRASE** **be on the lookout for** or **keep a lookout for** to be watching carefully for someone or something

loom¹ /luːm/ verb [I] **1** to appear as a large shape that is not clear, usually in a threatening way: *Suddenly the mountains loomed up out of the mist.* **2** if something unpleasant or difficult looms, it seems likely to happen soon: *The government is denying that a crisis is looming.*

loom² /luːm/ noun [C] a machine used for making cloth

loony /ˈluːni/ noun [C] *informal* a crazy or strange person —**loony** adj

loop¹ /luːp/ noun [C] a shape made by a line that curls back towards itself, or something in this shape

> **PHRASES** **in the loop** *informal* part of the group that has information about something, and therefore knowing the information
> **out of the loop** not part of the group that has information about something, and therefore not knowing the information: *I can't give you an answer – I'm out of the loop on this one.*

loop² /luːp/ verb [I/T] to form a loop, or to make something into a loop

loophole /ˈluːphəʊl/ noun [C] a bad feature of a law or legal document that allows people to avoid obeying it

loose¹ /luːs/ adj ★

1 not firmly fixed	4 free to move
2 not grouped together	5 not exact/detailed
3 not tight	6 not official

1 not firmly fixed in position: *a loose tooth* ♦ *One of the screws had come loose.*
2 not kept together as part of a group or in a container: *Loose oranges are 60p each.*
3 loose clothes are large and do not fit your body tightly ≠ TIGHT
4 free to move around: *A large dog was loose in the garden.* ♦ *The woman managed to break loose (=escape) from her attacker.*
5 not exactly accurate in every detail: *This is a loose translation of the letter.*
6 not strictly organized or official: *a system in which political parties form a loose alliance*
→ HELL, LOOSE END

loose² /luːs/ noun **on the loose** if a dangerous person or animal is on the loose, they have escaped from where they were being kept

loose ˈcannon noun [C] a member of a group who does unexpected things that could cause problems for the other members

loose ˈchange noun [U] coins that you have with you

loose ˈend noun **at a loose end** with nothing to do

loose ˈends noun [plural] the final details or parts of something that you have not yet dealt with: *I have to tie up a few loose ends (=deal with them) before I go.*

loose-ˈleaf adj containing pages that can be put in or taken out

loosely /ˈluːsli/ adv **1** not firmly or tightly **2** not in an exact or detailed way: *loosely translated* **3** not according to a strict system or official set of rules: *a loosely organized group of criminal gangs*

loosen /ˈluːs(ə)n/ verb [I/T] to become less firmly fixed or fastened, or to make something less firmly fixed or fastened ≠ TIGHTEN: *The screws began to loosen.* ♦ *He loosened his tie.*

> **PHRASAL VERB** **loosen ˈup 1** *informal* to relax or become less serious **2** to exercise your muscles before you do physical activity

loot¹ /luːt/ noun [U] things that have been stolen, especially during a war

loot² /luːt/ verb [I/T] to steal things from houses or shops during a war, or after a DISASTER such as a fire —**looter** noun [C], **looting** noun [U]

lop /lɒp/ **PHRASAL VERB** **lop sth ˈoff (sth)** to cut something off something else in one smooth movement

lope /ləʊp/ verb [I] to run with long slow steps

lopsided /ˌlɒpˈsaɪdɪd/ adj not level because one side is higher than the other

lord /lɔːd/ noun **1** [C] a man who has a high rank in the British ARISTOCRACY (=highest social class) **2 the Lord** a name that Christians use for talking about God or Jesus Christ

Lords, the /lɔːdz/ the British HOUSE OF LORDS, or its members

lore /lɔː/ noun [U] traditional knowledge about nature and culture that people get from older people, not from books

lorry /ˈlɒri/ noun [C] *British* a TRUCK

lose /luːz/ (past tense and past participle **lost** /lɒst/) verb ★★★

1 stop having sth	6 waste time/chance
2 be unable to find	7 escape from sb
3 not win	8 confuse sb
4 have less than before	9 when clock is too slow
5 when sb dies	+ PHRASES

1 [T] to no longer have something: *Mike lost his job last year.* ♦ *The family lost everything when their home burned down.* ♦ *Peter lost a leg in a climbing accident.* ♦ *Jane started to lose interest in her schoolwork.* ♦ *We've lost all hope of finding him alive.*
2 [T] to be unable to find someone or something: *I've lost my bag. Have you seen it?* ♦ *You can easily lose a child in a busy street.*
3 [I/T] to not win a race or competition ≠ WIN: *England lost 2–1 to Germany.* ♦ *They lost by only one point.* ♦ **lose sb sth** (=make someone lose something) *Those comments may well have lost them the election.*
4 [T] to have less of something than before because some of it has gone: *The plane*

suddenly lost cabin pressure. ♦ *He's **lost** a lot of **weight** recently.*

5 [T] if you lose a member of your close family or a close friend, they die: *She lost her son in a car accident.*

6 [T] if you lose time or an opportunity, you waste it

7 [T] to manage to escape from someone who is following you

8 [T] to make someone confused when you are explaining something: *I'm sorry, **you've lost me** there. Who's Andrew?*

9 [T] if a clock or watch loses time, it is operating too slowly and shows a time that is earlier than the correct time

PHRASES have a lot/too much to lose to be in a position where something bad might happen if you are not successful

have nothing to lose used for saying that someone should try something because their situation will not be any worse if they fail

lose count 1 to forget a total when you are counting something: *Don't talk to me or I'll lose count.* **2** used for emphasizing that something has happened many times: *I've **lost count** of the times he's asked to borrow money.*

lose it *informal* **1** to suddenly become unable to behave or think in a sensible way **2** to suddenly become very angry

lose ground to go into a position where you are less advanced or successful than someone else

lose your life to die as a result of something such as an accident, war, or illness: *He lost his life in a sailing accident.*

lose your mind *informal* to become crazy or confused

lose touch (with sth) to not know the most recent information about something, so you no longer understand it completely

lose touch/contact (with sb) to not know what someone is doing because you have not talked to or communicated with them for a long time

loser /ˈluːzə/ *noun* [C] **1** someone who did not win a race or competition ≠ WINNER
2 *informal* someone who has never been successful and is never likely to be
3 someone or something that is affected in a negative way by something ≠ WINNER: *When parents split up the real losers are the children.*

loss /lɒs/ *noun* ★★★

1 no longer having sth	**5** sadness
2 having less of sth	**6** disadvantage
3 money lost	**+ PHRASE**
4 death of sb	

1 [C/U] the state of no longer having something: *job losses* ♦ *a loss of confidence* ♦ *The **loss** of his sight was a severe blow.*
2 [C/U] the state of having less of something than before: *a new treatment for hair loss* ♦ *Exercise and **weight loss** can help lower your blood pressure.*
3 [C/U] money that a person or company

loses when they spend more than they earn ≠ PROFIT: *The company reported **heavy losses** for last year.* ♦ *We **made a loss** on the house sale.*

4 [C/U] the death of someone: *Jean never recovered from **the loss** of her husband.* ♦ *There was only minor damage and no **loss of life** (=no one died).*

5 [U] a feeling of sadness that you have when someone leaves or dies, or when you no longer have something: *We all felt a tremendous **sense of loss** when Robin left.*

6 [singular] a disadvantage that you have when you do not have something any longer: *If the school closes, it will be **a great loss to** the community.*

PHRASE at a loss (to do sth) not understanding something, or not knowing what to do: *I was at a loss to understand what had happened.*
→ CUT¹

lost¹ /lɒst/ *adj* ★

1 not knowing your way	**4** not relaxed/confident
2 when sth is missing	**5** unable to understand
3 no longer existing	**+ PHRASES**

1 if you are lost, you do not know where you are: *They decided to drive to York and ended up **getting lost**.*
2 if something is lost, you cannot find it: *The keys are lost somewhere in the house.*
3 if something is lost, you no longer have it: *The strike has cost the airline £3 million in lost profits.* ♦ *lost youth/innocence*
4 someone who feels lost does not feel confident or relaxed because they are in a new situation
5 unable to understand something: *I was completely lost after the first paragraph.*

PHRASES get lost *spoken* used for telling someone rudely to go away
lost on sb if something is lost on someone, they do not understand it or are not influenced by it: *The joke was lost on Alex.*

lost² the past tense and past participle of **lose**

lost 'cause *noun* [C] someone or something that will never succeed or improve

lot¹ /lɒt/ *grammar word* ★★★

> **A lot** can be:
> ■ an **adverb**: *He seems to like her a lot.* ♦ *I feel a lot better.*
> ■ a **pronoun**: *We didn't get paid a lot, but we had fun.* ♦ *A lot of people don't like the idea much.*
> **Lots** can be a **pronoun** like **a lot** but is more informal: *She knows lots about it.*

PHRASE a lot 1 to a great or greater degree: *I liked her a lot.* ♦ *I can run a lot faster than you.* **2 a lot** or **lots** a large number, amount, or quantity: *We're paying her a lot for her services.* ♦ *There's a lot to see in Paris.* ♦ *Have another piece of cake – there's **lots more** in the kitchen.* ♦ *Bob used to have **a lot of** friends in New York.* ♦ *The idea has attracted **lots of** publicity.* → MANY **3** often: *He's a sensitive child who cries a lot.* ♦ *I think about him a lot.* → MUCH

lot² /lɒt/ noun ★★★

1 [C] *British* a group of people or things: *I've just finished typing one lot of letters. ♦ It can be a bit difficult when there are two lots of parents involved.*

2 [C] a thing or group of things that are to be sold in an AUCTION

3 the lot [singular] *spoken* the whole of a number or amount that you have just mentioned: *I offered him half, but he wanted the lot.*

lotion /ˈləʊʃ(ə)n/ noun [C/U] a thick liquid that you put on your skin to make it feel softer

lottery /ˈlɒtəri/ noun **1** [C] a game in which people win money if they guess the correct numbers **2** [singular] *showing disapproval* a situation where everything depends on luck

loud¹ /laʊd/ adj ★★

1 a loud sound is strong and very easy to hear ≠ SOFT: *There was a loud knocking on the door. ♦ The music is deafeningly loud.*

2 someone who is loud talks in a loud and confident way that annoys other people ≠ QUIET

3 very bright in a way that does not show good taste = GAUDY: *a loud shirt*
—**loudly** adv

loud² /laʊd/ adv loudly
PHRASE **out loud** in a way that other people can hear

loudspeaker /ˌlaʊdˈspiːkə/ noun [C] a piece of electrical equipment that allows someone's voice to be heard far away

lounge¹ /laʊndʒ/ noun [C] **1** *British* a comfortable room in a house where people sit and relax = LIVING ROOM, SITTING ROOM **2** an area in an airport, hotel, or other public building for sitting and relaxing in

lounge² /laʊndʒ/ verb [I] to lie, sit, or lean in a relaxed or lazy way
PHRASAL VERB **lounge aˈround** or **lounge aˈbout** *British* to spend time relaxing or doing nothing when you should be doing something

lousy /ˈlaʊzi/ adj *informal* bad, or unpleasant

lout /laʊt/ noun [C] an unpleasant young man who behaves badly in public —**loutish** adj

lovable /ˈlʌvəb(ə)l/ adj attractive and easy to like

love¹ /lʌv/ verb [T] ★★★

1 to be very strongly attracted to someone in an emotional and sexual way: *I love you. ♦ We love each other, and we're getting married.*

2 to care very much about someone or something: *She loved her children with all her heart. ♦ She went back to the country she loved.*

3 to like or enjoy something very much: *She loves all types of music. ♦ I would love a glass of wine* (=would like one very much). **♦ love to do sth** *I would love to see them again.* **♦ love doing sth** *Bert loves playing the piano.*
PHRASE **I'd love to** *spoken* used for saying that you would like to do what someone has suggested: *'Do you want to come?' 'I'd love to!'*

love² /lʌv/ noun ★★★

1 romantic feeling	5 used for talking to sb
2 feeling of liking/caring	6 used at end of letter
3 sb in relationship	7 no points in tennis
4 sth you enjoy	**+ PHRASE**

1 [U] a very strong emotional and sexual feeling for someone: *I think I'm in love. ♦ They met and fell in love* (=started to love each other) *at college. ♦ the speech in which Romeo expresses his love for Juliet*

2 [U] the feeling of caring about someone or something very much ≠ HATE: *Children need a lot of love and affection. ♦ his love for his brother ♦ a great love of life*

3 [C] someone that you have a sexual or romantic relationship with: *the boy who was her first love*

4 [C] something that you enjoy very much: *Music was his greatest love.*

5 [singular] *British* used for talking to someone that you love, or for talking to anyone in a friendly way: *Did that letter arrive, love?*

6 [U] used at the end of a letter to someone you know well: *Hope to see you soon. Love, Ray. ♦ Take care. Lots of love, Helen. ♦ I can't wait to see you. All my love, Douglas.*

7 [U] a score of no points in tennis
PHRASE **make love** to have sex with someone

love afˌfair noun [C] a romantic sexual relationship between people who are not married to each other

loved ones /ˈlʌvd ˌwʌnz/ noun [plural] members of your family

love ˌlife noun [singular] the romantic or sexual relationships in a person's life

lovely /ˈlʌvli/ adj **1** very attractive = BEAUTIFUL: *a city surrounded by lovely countryside ♦ She had lovely hair.* **2** enjoyable or nice = WONDERFUL: *We've had a lovely evening. ♦ It's lovely to see you again. ♦ He's a lovely little boy.*

lover /ˈlʌvə/ noun [C] **1** someone that you have a sexual relationship with, often when you are married to someone else **2** someone who likes something very much: *a dog/music lover*

loving /ˈlʌvɪŋ/ adj feeling or showing love

lovingly /ˈlʌvɪŋli/ adv **1** in a way that expresses love **2** with great care and interest: *The old church has been lovingly restored.*

low¹ /ləʊ/ adj ★★★

1 small in height, or not far above the ground: *a low wall/bridge ♦ low cloud ♦ The water level was very low.*

2 small in amount or level ≠ HIGH: *The bigger shops are able to keep their prices low. ♦ low standards/expectations ♦ people on low incomes ♦ Vegetables are low in fat and high in nutrition.*

3 someone who is low feels unhappy and does not have much hope or confidence ≠ HIGH: *It was unlike her to be in such low spirits. ♦ She'd been feeling low for a few days.*

4 a low voice or sound is quiet and difficult to hear ≠ HIGH

low² /ləʊ/ adv **1** in or to a low position ≠ HIGH **2** quietly, or in a deep voice: *I asked them to turn the volume down low.* ♦ *She can sing high or low.* → LIE¹

low³ /ləʊ/ noun [C] **1** the lowest level, value, or price ≠ HIGH: *Share prices hit an all-time low.* **2** a bad time in your life ≠ HIGH: *He's experienced all the highs and lows of an actor's life.*

lowbrow /ˈləʊbraʊ/ adj used for describing things such as books and television programmes that are intended for people who are not well educated ≠ HIGHBROW

low-ˈcalorie or **low-ˈcal** adj low-calorie foods or drinks help people to lose weight because they do not contain many CALORIES

low-ˈcut adj a low-cut dress or BLOUSE shows a woman's chest and the top part of her breasts because it has a low NECKLINE

lowdown, the /ˈləʊˌdaʊn/ noun [singular] *informal* the important or interesting information you need to know about someone or something

lower¹ /ˈləʊə/ adj **1** below another thing of the same kind ≠ UPPER: *the upper and lower lips* **2** fairly near the bottom of something: *the lower floors of the building* **3** fairly low in status or importance ≠ HIGHER: *the lower ranks of the army*

lower² /ˈləʊə/ verb [T] ★
1 to move something or someone slowly down from a higher position ≠ RAISE: *He lowered himself into the chair.*
2 to reduce something in number, amount, value, or strength: *The voting age was lowered from 21 to 18 years.* ♦ *Less fat in your diet lowers the risk of heart disease.*

lower ˈcase noun [U] the ordinary small form in which letters are written → UPPER CASE

lower ˈclass noun the **lower class** or the **lower classes** people who have the lowest social status → MIDDLE CLASS, UPPER CLASS, WORKING CLASS

low-ˈfat adj low-fat food contains only a small amount of fat

low-ˈkey adj without much activity or excitement: *his usual low-key manner*

lowlands /ˈləʊləndz/ noun [plural] the part of a country that is fairly low and flat ≠ HIGHLANDS

low-ˈlevel adj **1** without much importance, power, or difficulty: *a low-level sales position* **2** in a low position

lowly /ˈləʊli/ adj with a low status or position: *a lowly office clerk*

low-ˈlying adj in a position which is close to the level of the sea or the ground

low-ˈpaid adj not receiving or offering much pay

low ˈpoint noun [C] the worst moment in a situation

low ˈprofile noun [C] behaviour that deliberately does not attract attention: *I've been trying to keep a low profile.* —**low-ˈprofile** adj

low-ˈrise adj a low-rise building has only a few levels ≠ HIGH-RISE

low ˈseason noun [singular] *British* the time of year when a place or business is least busy, for example because there are not many tourists ≠ HIGH SEASON

low-tech /ləʊ ˈtek/ adj low-tech equipment is simple and usually old-fashioned ≠ HI-TECH

low ˈtide noun [C/U] the time when the sea is at its lowest level

loyal /ˈlɔɪəl/ adj someone who is loyal continues to support a person, organization, or principle in difficult times =FAITHFUL ≠ DISLOYAL: *a loyal friend/ customer/employee* ♦ *people who have remained loyal to the company for years* —**loyally** adv

loyalist /ˈlɔɪəlɪst/ noun [C] someone who supports their government

loyalties /ˈlɔɪəltiz/ noun [plural] feelings of friendship and support

loyalty /ˈlɔɪəlti/ noun [U] support that you always give to someone or something ≠ DISLOYALTY: *I was impressed by his loyalty to his brother.*

lozenge /ˈlɒzɪndʒ/ noun [C] **1** a sweet that contains medicine for a sore throat **2** a shape with four sloping sides

L-plate /ˈel ˌpleɪt/ noun [C] *British* a white sign with a red 'L' that you put on a car to show people that the driver is learning to drive

LSD /ˌel es ˈdiː/ noun [U] a powerful illegal drug that makes people see things that are not real =ACID

Ltd abbrev Limited: used after the name of some companies

lubricate /ˈluːbrɪˌkeɪt/ verb [T] to put oil on the parts of a machine in order to make them move more smoothly —**lubrication** /ˌluːbrɪˈkeɪʃ(ə)n/ noun [U]

lucid /ˈluːsɪd/ adj **1** describing things in a clear, simple way **2** capable of thinking clearly

luck /lʌk/ noun [U] ★★
1 success that you have by chance: *John never had much luck with girls.* ♦ *We'd all like to wish you luck in your new job.*
2 an influence that seems to make good things happen to people for no particular reason: *He's had nothing but bad luck since moving to New York.* ♦ *It's a custom that is believed to bring good luck.* ♦ *Their luck is bound to run out* (=end) *sometime.*

PHRASES **any luck?** *spoken* used for asking someone if they succeeded in doing something they wanted

good luck or **best of luck** used for telling someone that you hope that they will be successful: *Good luck in your driving test!*

in luck able to do something that did not seem likely: *You're in luck. We've got one pair of shoes left in your size.*

just my luck *spoken* used for saying that something bad happened because you are not a lucky person

out of luck unable to do something that you wanted

with any luck or **with a bit of luck** used for saying that you hope a particular thing happens: *With any luck, this time next year I'll be living in France.*
→ POT LUCK

luckily /'lʌkɪli/ adv used for saying that something good happens in a lucky way =FORTUNATELY: *Luckily he wasn't injured.*

lucky /'lʌki/ adj ★★ if you are lucky, something good happens to you as a result of luck=FORTUNATE: *Five lucky winners will each receive £1,000.* ♦ *None of his sisters had been lucky with men.* ♦ +(that) *You're lucky that he was there.* ♦ **it is lucky (that)** *It's lucky that I arrived when I did.* ♦ **be lucky to do sth** *You're really lucky to be alive.*

lucrative /'lu:krətɪv/ adj bringing a lot of money=PROFITABLE

ludicrous /'lu:dɪkrəs/ adj extremely silly =ABSURD: *a ludicrous new rule* —**ludicrously** adv: *ludicrously expensive*

lug /lʌg/ verb [T] *informal* to carry something with difficulty because it is very heavy

luggage /'lʌgɪdʒ/ noun [U] bags and suitcases that you take on a journey=BAGGAGE

> **Luggage** is never used in the plural and cannot be used with **a**: *Someone had left* **a piece of luggage** (NOT a luggage) *in the taxi.* ♦ *Do you have* **any luggage**? ♦ *There was* **some luggage** *lying around in the hall.*

lukewarm /ˌluːkˈwɔːm/ adj **1** not hot or cold enough to be enjoyable **2** not very enthusiastic or interested

lull¹ /lʌl/ noun [C] a short period during which noise or activity stops

lull² /lʌl/ verb [T] **1** to make someone feel so relaxed or confident that they are not prepared when something unpleasant happens **2** to make someone relaxed enough to go to sleep

lumber /'lʌmbə/ verb **1** [T] to give someone a job or responsibility that they do not want: *I'm sorry you've been lumbered with all the dirty jobs.* **2** [I] to walk with slow heavy steps

lumberjack /'lʌmbəˌdʒæk/ noun [C] someone whose job is to cut down trees for wood

luminous /'lu:mɪnəs/ adj something that is luminous shines brightly in the dark

lump¹ /lʌmp/ noun [C] **1** a solid piece of something that does not have a regular shape: *a lump of metal/coal/concrete* **2** a solid piece in a substance that should be smooth or liquid: *Stir the sauce to get rid of any lumps.* **3** a small hard part on or under your skin, that is caused by illness or injury

lump² /lʌmp/ verb [T] to put people or things into the same group, although they do not really belong together: *Singing and dancing tend to be lumped together as 'performing arts'.*

lump ˈsum noun [C] money in a single large payment rather than separate small payments

lumpy /'lʌmpi/ adj full of lumps: *a lumpy sauce/pillow*

lunacy /'lu:nəsi/ noun [U] stupid ideas or behaviour=MADNESS

lunar /'lu:nə/ adj relating to the moon

lunatic /'lu:nətɪk/ noun [C] someone who behaves in an extreme or dangerous way —**lunatic** adj

lunch /lʌntʃ/ noun [C/U] ★★★ a meal that you eat in the middle of the day: *I'll get a sandwich for lunch.* ♦ *Let's have lunch at that new restaurant.* ♦ *She's usually at lunch from twelve till one.* ♦ *Mr. Miller's already gone to lunch.*

lunchtime /'lʌntʃˌtaɪm/ noun [U] the time in the middle of the day when people usually eat lunch: *I'm going swimming at lunchtime.* ♦ *the lunchtime news*

lung /lʌŋ/ noun [C] one of the organs in your chest that fill with air when you breathe

lunge /lʌndʒ/ verb [I] to move suddenly and with a lot of force —**lunge** noun [C]

lupin /'lu:pɪn/ noun [C] a tall plant with several stems and rows of small flowers on each stem —*picture* → C9

lurch¹ /lɜːtʃ/ verb [I] **1** to move suddenly in a way that is not smooth or controlled **2** if your heart or stomach lurches, it seems to jump suddenly because you are excited or upset

lurch² /lɜːtʃ/ noun [C] a sudden uncontrolled movement

> **PHRASE** **leave sb in the lurch** to leave someone in a difficult situation without helping them

lure¹ /ljʊə/ verb [T] to persuade someone to do something by making it look very attractive

lure² /ljʊə/ noun [C] something that attracts someone into a situation

lurid /'ljʊərɪd, 'lʊərɪd/ adj **1** full of shocking or unpleasant details **2** a lurid colour is very bright in an ugly way

lurk /lɜːk/ verb [I] **1** to hide somewhere and wait to frighten or attack someone **2** if something is lurking, it is likely to threaten, harm, or upset you

luscious /'lʌʃəs/ adj **1** very attractive in a sexual way **2** luscious food looks, smells, and tastes especially good=DELICIOUS

lush /lʌʃ/ adj a lush plant or area looks very green and healthy

lust¹ /lʌst/ noun [U] **1** a strong feeling of wanting to have sex=DESIRE **2** great enthusiasm for something=PASSION

lust² /lʌst/ **PHRASAL VERB** ˈlust after sb to want to have sex with a particular person
ˈlust after sth to want something very much

luxurious /lʌgˈzjʊəriəs/ adj very expensive and comfortable

luxury¹ /'lʌkʃəri/ noun **1** [U] a situation in which you are very comfortable because you have the best and most expensive things: *They live a life of absolute luxury.* **2** [C] something expensive that you enjoy but do not really need **3** [C] something that you enjoy very much but do not have very often: *An evening at home was a real luxury.*

luxury² /'lʌkʃəri/ adj very expensive and of the highest quality: *a luxury hotel/item/car*

L

Lycra /ˈlaɪkrə/ *trademark* cloth made from artificial fibres that is used for making sports clothes

lynch /lɪntʃ/ verb [T] if a group of angry people lynch someone, they kill that person by hanging them by the neck —**lynching** noun [C/U]

lyrical /ˈlɪrɪk(ə)l/ adj expressing emotions in a beautiful way

lyrics /ˈlɪrɪks/ noun [plural] the words of a song

M m

m¹ or **M** /em/ noun [C/U] the 13th letter of the English alphabet

m² abbrev **1** metre **2** mile

M abbrev **1** motorway: used in the names of motorways in the UK **2** medium: used on clothes labels

MA /ˌem ˈeɪ/ noun [C] Master of Arts: an advanced degree from a college or university in a subject such as languages or history

ma'am /mæm, mɑːm/ *American* used for talking politely to a woman whose name you do not know

mac /mæk/ noun [C] *British* a coat that stops you from getting wet in the rain=RAINCOAT

macabre /məˈkɑːbrə/ adj something that is macabre is frightening because it involves death or violence

macaroni /ˌmækəˈrəʊni/ noun [U] a type of pasta in the form of short curved tubes

machete /məˈʃeti/ noun [C] a large knife that can be used as a weapon or a tool

machine /məˈʃiːn/ noun [C] ★★★
1 a piece of equipment with moving parts that does a particular job: *Sue showed him how to operate the washing machine.* ♦ *These companies do everything by machine these days.*
2 the people and things that are used for achieving a particular aim: *the British war machine*

ma'chine ,gun noun [C] a gun that fires a lot of bullets very quickly

ma,chine-'readable adj able to be used by a computer

machinery /məˈʃiːnəri/ noun [U] **1** machines: *agricultural/industrial machinery* **2** an established system for doing something: *the company's decision-making machinery*

macho /ˈmætʃəʊ/ adj *showing disapproval* behaving in a way that is considered typical of a man, for example by being strong and not showing your feelings

mackerel /ˈmækrəl/ noun [C/U] a sea fish that is eaten as food

macro /ˈmækrəʊ/ noun [C] a short computer program that performs a longer series of operations

mad /mæd/ adj ★
1 *British* very silly or stupid=CRAZY: *You'll think I'm mad – I've just left my job.* ♦ **be mad to do sth** *You're mad to spend so much money on clothes.*
2 *informal* angry: *My boss is **mad with** me for missing the meeting.*
3 done quickly or without thinking, in a way that is badly organized: *It was **a mad rush** to get the job finished.*
4 *British informal* an offensive way of describing someone who is mentally ill

PHRASES **drive sb mad** *informal* to make someone feel angry, upset, or very impatient

go mad *informal* **1** to become extremely excited and happy: *The waiting crowd went mad when she stepped out of the car.* **2** to become crazy, for example because you are extremely bored: *I would go mad if I had to stay in bed for three weeks.* **3** to become extremely angry: *Dad went mad when he saw what I'd done to the car.*

like mad *informal* very quickly and with great effort: *We had to work like mad to finish on time.*

mad about/on sth *British informal* very enthusiastic about something

→ MADLY, MADNESS

madam /ˈmædəm/ used for talking or writing politely to a woman whose name you do not know

mad 'cow di,sease noun [U] *informal* BSE

maddening /ˈmæd(ə)nɪŋ/ adj making you feel very angry=INFURIATING —**maddeningly** adv

made¹ /meɪd/ adj

PHRASES **be made for each other** *informal* if two people are made for each other, they are perfect partners for each other

have (got) it made *spoken* to be in a very good situation: *She won all that money – she's got it made!*

made² the past tense and past participle of **make¹**

made-'up adj **1** imaginary or false **2** wearing MAKE-UP on your face

madhouse /ˈmædhaʊs/ noun [C] a place that is very noisy or busy

madly /ˈmædli/ adv **1** in a very excited or uncontrolled way **2** very, or very much: *He fell madly in love with her at first sight.* ♦ *madly jealous*

madman /ˈmædmən/ (plural **madmen** /ˈmædmən/) noun [C] a man who behaves in a crazy way

madness /ˈmædnəs/ noun [U] ideas and actions that show a lack of good judgment and careful thought: *It would be madness to give up your job just now.*

maestro /ˈmaɪstrəʊ/ noun [C] a musician who people admire and respect a lot

Mafia, the /ˈmæfiə/ a secret criminal organization that is involved in illegal activities, especially in Italy and the US

mag /mæg/ noun [C] *informal* a MAGAZINE

magazine /ˌmæɡəˈziːn/ noun [C] ★★ a large thin book with a paper cover that is usually published once a month or once a week: *a fashion/gardening/motoring magazine* ♦ *a magazine article*

maggot /ˈmæɡət/ noun [C] a small soft creature that develops into a fly and is sometimes found in old meat

magic¹ /ˈmædʒɪk/ noun [U] ★
1 a mysterious power that makes impossible things happen if you do special actions or say special words → BLACK MAGIC
2 mysterious tricks that an entertainer performs, for example making things disappear
3 a special attractive quality that something has: *the magic of Christmas/Hollywood*
PHRASES **as if by magic** in a surprising or sudden way that is impossible to explain: *I mentioned his name, and he appeared as if by magic.*
like magic *informal* in a very effective or quick way: *This medicine works like magic.*

magic² /ˈmædʒɪk/ adj **1** able to make impossible things happen: *a magic spell/box* **2** involving mysterious tricks performed by an entertainer: *a magic show/trick* **3** *informal* very good or pleasant

magical /ˈmædʒɪk(ə)l/ adj **1** involving magic: *magical powers* **2** especially enjoyable or attractive: *It was a truly magical evening.* —**magically** /ˈmædʒɪkli/ adv

magic bullet noun [C] *informal* a quick and easy solution to a difficult problem

magician /məˈdʒɪʃ(ə)n/ noun [C] someone whose job is to entertain people by performing magic tricks

magistrate /ˈmædʒɪˌstreɪt/ noun [C] a judge in a court for minor crimes

magnanimous /mæɡˈnænɪməs/ adj *formal* willing to forgive people, or willing to be kind and fair

magnate /ˈmæɡneɪt/ noun [C] a successful and powerful person in a particular industry =TYCOON: *an oil magnate*

magnesium /mæɡˈniːziəm/ noun [U] a light grey metal that burns very brightly

magnet /ˈmæɡnɪt/ noun [C] **1** a piece of iron that can make other iron objects stick to it **2** someone or something that attracts people

magnetic /mæɡˈnetɪk/ adj **1** able to attract iron objects **2** able to attract and interest people: *his magnetic personality* —**magnetically** /mæɡˈnetɪkli/ adv

magnetism /ˈmæɡnəˌtɪz(ə)m/ noun [U] **1** the power that a MAGNET has to make iron objects stick to it **2** a special ability to attract and interest people

magnification /ˌmæɡnɪfɪˈkeɪʃ(ə)n/ noun [U] the power of a piece of equipment to make something appear bigger than it really is

magnificent /mæɡˈnɪfɪs(ə)nt/ adj very impressive and beautiful, good, or skilful: *It was so exciting to see these magnificent animals in the wild.* ♦ *She gave a magnificent performance.* —**magnificence** noun [U], **magnificently** adv

magnify /ˈmæɡnɪˌfaɪ/ verb [T] **1** to make something appear bigger than it really is **2** to make something appear more important or serious than it really is

magnifying glass /ˈmæɡnɪfaɪɪŋ ˌɡlɑːs/ noun [C] a small circle of glass with a handle that makes things appear bigger when you look through it

magnitude /ˈmæɡnɪtjuːd/ noun [U] great size or importance

magnolia /mæɡˈnəʊliə/ noun **1** [C] a small tree with large white or pink flowers, or a flower from this tree —*picture* → C9 **2** [U] *British* a white colour that looks slightly yellow

magpie /ˈmæɡpaɪ/ noun [C] a noisy black and white bird with a long tail

mahogany /məˈhɒɡəni/ noun [U] a hard brown-red wood that is used for making furniture

maid /meɪd/ noun [C] a woman whose job is to clean rooms in a hotel or large house

maiden¹ /ˈmeɪd(ə)n/ noun [C] an old word meaning a girl or young woman who is not married

maiden² /ˈmeɪd(ə)n/ adj done for the first time: *a maiden flight*

maiden name noun [C] the original family name of a woman who uses her husband's family name now

mail¹ /meɪl/ noun ★
1 [U] letters and parcels that are delivered by the post office =POST: *The mail arrived early today.* ♦ *I haven't had a chance to open my mail yet.* ♦ *There was nothing interesting in the mail this morning.*
2 [U] the system for sending and delivering letters and parcels =POST: *All our goods can be ordered by mail.* ♦ *The letter must have got lost in the mail.*
3 [C/U] email, or an email message: *You've got mail.* ♦ *Did you read that mail from Cindy?*

mail² /meɪl/ verb [T] **1** to POST a letter or parcel to someone **2** *American* to send a message to someone by email

mailbox /ˈmeɪlˌbɒks/ noun [C] **1** *computing* the part of a computer's memory where email is stored **2** *American* a POSTBOX **3** *American* a LETTERBOX for putting letters in when they are delivered to a house

mailing list noun [C] *business* a list of all the people that letters or email messages are sent to

mail order noun [U] a way of buying goods in which you order them by post or telephone and they are posted to you

maim /meɪm/ verb [T] to injure someone severely and permanently

main¹ /meɪn/ adj ★★★ most important, or largest: *We eat our main meal in the evening.* ♦ *The main entrance to the building is on George Street.*
PHRASE **the main thing** *spoken* used for saying what is most important: *The main thing is that you're not injured.*

main² /meɪn/ noun **1** [C] a large pipe or wire that is used for carrying water, gas, or

M

electricity **2 the mains** [plural] *British* the point where the supply of gas, electricity, or water enters a building

main 'clause noun [C] *linguistics* a CLAUSE that can be a sentence on its own

'main 'course noun [C] the biggest part of a meal

mainframe /ˈmeɪnˌfreɪm/ noun [C] *computing* a large powerful computer that has several smaller computers connected to it

mainland, the /ˈmeɪnˌlænd/ noun [singular] a large mass of land that forms the main part of a country but does not include any islands —**mainland** adj

main 'line noun [C] an important railway between two cities

mainly /ˈmeɪnli/ adv ★★★
1 used for talking about the largest or most important part of something: *This sauce is made mainly of milk and flour.* ♦ *We spent four days there – mainly visiting family.* ♦ *I didn't come mainly because I didn't feel very well.*
2 in most cases: *Our customers are mainly young mothers.*

main 'road noun [C] a wide road that has a lot of traffic

mainstay /ˈmeɪnˌsteɪ/ noun [C] the person or thing that something depends on in order to continue or be successful

mainstream /ˈmeɪnˌstriːm/ adj considered normal, and used or accepted by most people: *mainstream ideas/schools/political parties*

mainstream, the /ˈmeɪnˌstriːm/ noun [singular] ideas or methods that most people think are normal

maintain /meɪnˈteɪn/ verb [T] ★★
1 to make something stay the same＝KEEP: *It's important that you maintain your current weight.* ♦ *Regular inspections ensure that high safety standards are maintained.*
2 to make regular repairs to something, so that it stays in good condition: *The car had been very well maintained.*
3 to continue to say that something is true, even though other people do not believe you＝ASSERT: *She maintained her innocence throughout the trial.* ♦ *+(that) The company still maintains that the drug is safe.*
4 to provide someone with the money and other things that they need in order to live

maintenance /ˈmeɪntənəns/ noun [U] **1** work that is done to keep something in good condition: *aircraft maintenance* **2** the process of continuing something: *the maintenance of international peace and security* **3** money that you pay to your EX-WIFE or EX-HUSBAND after you are divorced

maisonette /ˌmeɪzəˈnet/ noun [C] *British* a flat with two levels in a building

maize /meɪz/ noun [U] *British* a tall plant that produces yellow seeds that are cooked and eaten

majestic /məˈdʒestɪk/ adj very beautiful or impressive —**majestically** /məˈdʒestɪkli/ adv

majesty /ˈmædʒəsti/ noun [U] the quality of

being very beautiful or impressive

> **PHRASE** **Your/His/Her Majesty** used for talking formally to a king or queen

major¹ /ˈmeɪdʒə/ adj ★★★
1 important, large, or great: *one of the major problems facing our planet* ♦ *The major attraction is a huge clock in the entrance hall.* ♦ *Age is a major factor affecting chances of employment.*
2 in the musical SCALE that is used for most tunes in western music → MINOR

> **Words often used with major**
>
> *Nouns often used with **major** (adj, sense 1)*
> - MAJOR + **drawback, obstacle, problem, setback**: used about problems that are serious
> - MAJOR + **cause, factor, influence, source**: used about factors that are important
> - MAJOR + **change, shake-up, shift, upheaval**: used about changes that have a big effect

major² /ˈmeɪdʒə/ noun [C] **1** an officer of middle rank in the armed forces **2** a student's main subject at a college or university

major³ /ˈmeɪdʒə/ **PHRASAL VERB** 'major in sth to study something as your main subject at college or university

majority /məˈdʒɒrəti/ noun ★★★
1 [singular] most of the people or things in a group ≠ MINORITY: *The majority of our employees are women.* ♦ *The vast majority (=nearly everyone) had never travelled outside the United States.* ♦ *Young women are in the majority in the fashion industry.* ♦ *The majority view is that the election was unfair.* ♦ *We have to accept the majority decision.*
2 [C] the number of votes by which someone wins an election

make¹ /meɪk/ (past tense and past participle **made** /meɪd/) verb ★★★

1 create/produce sth	**7** give a total
2 do sth	**8** cause sth to succeed
3 cause sth to happen	**9** have right qualities for
4 force sb to do sth	**10** reach place
5 arrange sth	**+ PHRASES**
6 earn/get money	**+ PHRASAL VERBS**

1 [T] to create or produce something: *The nail made a hole in my shirt.* ♦ *Jane was making coffee.* ♦ *This furniture is made in South America.* ♦ *a bowl made of metal/plastic/wood* ♦ **make sth from sth** *They make paper from old rags.* ♦ **make sth out of sth** *We made curtains out of some old material we found.* ♦ **make sb sth** *Joan made me a beautiful dress for my wedding.*
2 [T] used with some nouns for showing that someone performs an action: *Have you made a decision?* ♦ *Nobody's perfect – we all make mistakes.* ♦ *Helen made an attempt to stop him.* ♦ *We've made some progress, but there's still a long way to go.* ♦ *People can eat more healthily without making major changes to their diet.* ♦ *Stop making so much noise!* ♦ *Matthew made a note of*

the car's number (=kept a written record of it) *and informed the police.*

3 [T] to cause someone or something to be in a particular state: *The noise in the school makes learning difficult.* ♦ *Listening to the news just* **makes** *me* **angry** *these days.* ♦ *The smell of fish* **makes** *me* **feel** *ill.* ♦ *That haircut* **makes** *you* **look** *ten years younger.* ♦ *I'd like to* **make it clear that** *I had nothing to do with this.* ♦ **make sb do sth** *This film always makes me cry.*

4 [T] to force someone to do something: **make sb do sth** *They made us work for 12 hours a day.*

5 [T] to arrange or organize something: *I've* **made an appointment** *with the doctor.*

6 [T] to earn or get money: *She makes about £2,000 a month.* ♦ *You can* **make** *a lot of* **money** *playing the stock market.* ♦ *Can you* **make a living** *from painting?* ♦ *The company* **made** *a small* **profit** *in its first year.*

7 [linking verb] to give a particular total when added together: *Four multiplied by two makes eight.*

8 [T] to cause something to be successful: *It was the children's singing that really made the performance.*

9 [linking verb] to have the right qualities for a particular job or purpose: *Don't you think the novel would make a great film?*

10 [T] *informal* to reach a place, or to be present in a place: *At this rate we won't make York before midnight.* ♦ *I won't be able to make tomorrow's meeting.*

PHRASES **make believe** to pretend that something is real

make do (with/without sth) to succeed in dealing with a situation by using what is available, or despite not having something: *There wasn't much food, but we made do.*

make it 1 to succeed in a particular activity: *She made it in films when she was still a teenager.* **2** to manage to arrive on time: *We just made it in time for the wedding.* **3** to be able to be present at a particular event: *I can't make it on Friday.* ♦ *We made it to the meeting.*

make way (for) 1 to move away so that someone or something can get past you: *We were asked to make way for the bride and groom.* **2** to be replaced by someone or something: *Most of the old buildings have made way for hotels and offices.*

PHRASAL VERBS **make for sth 1** to move towards a place: *He picked up his umbrella and made for the door.* **2** to help to make something possible: *The new computers make for much greater efficiency.*

'**make sb/sth ,into sth** to change someone or something so that they become something else: *The story was made into a film two years ago.*

'**make sth ,of sb/sth 1** to understand someone or the meaning of something in a particular way: *I don't know what to make of our new teacher.* ♦ *What do you make of this news?* **2 make the best of sth** to try to get a good

result despite a bad situation: *It rained all day, but we made the best of it.* **3 make the most of sth** to use a good situation to get the best possible result: *It's a beautiful day today. Let's make the most of it.*

,**make** '**off** to leave quickly, especially after doing something wrong: *The kids made off when they heard us coming.*

,**make** '**off with sth** to leave with something that you have stolen: *They made off with our television.*

,**make sth** '**out 1** to see, hear, or understand something with difficulty: *I can just make a few words out on this page.* ♦ *I couldn't make out what he was saying.* **2** to write all the necessary information on a cheque or other document **3 make out (that)** *informal* to pretend that something is true when it is not: *He made out that he'd won the lottery.* **4 make sb out to be sth** to say that someone is a particular type of person when this is not true: *He made me out to be a liar.*

,**make** '**up** to become friendly with someone again after an argument: *Why don't you two forget your differences and make up?* ♦ *Tom still hasn't* **made up with** *Alice.*

,**make sth** '**up 1** to invent something such as a story or an explanation: *He made up some excuse about the dog eating his homework.* ♦ *She's good at making up stories for the children.* **2 make it up to sb** to do something good that helps someone to feel better after you did something bad to them

,**make** '**up for sth 1** to take the place of something that has been lost or damaged: *Nothing can make up for the loss of a child.* **2** to provide something good, so that something bad seems less important: *He bought her some flowers to make up for being late.*

Words that you can use instead of **make**

Make is a very general word. Here are some words with more specific meanings that sound more natural and appropriate in particular situations.

things made in factories	assemble, build, manufacture, mass-produce, produce, turn out
buildings/structures	build, erect, put up
power/heat/light	emit, generate, give off, produce
problems/changes/ effects	cause, create, generate, produce
new things	come up with, create, design, develop, invent
things that are made quickly and not very well	churn out, cobble together, throw together

---

make² /meɪk/ noun [C] a product that is made by a particular company = BRAND: *a very popular make of car*

'**make-be,lieve** noun [U] the activity of pretending that something is real —**make-be,lieve** adj

makeover /ˈmeɪkˌəʊvə/ noun [C] changes that make a person or thing look much better

M

maker /ˈmeɪkə/ noun [C] a person, company, or machine that produces something

makeshift /ˈmeɪkʃɪft/ adj made using whatever is available and therefore not very good

ˈmake-up noun [U] substances that people put on their faces to make them look attractive =COSMETICS: *Gina wears no make-up at all.* ♦ *Rachel was still putting on her make-up when the taxi arrived.*

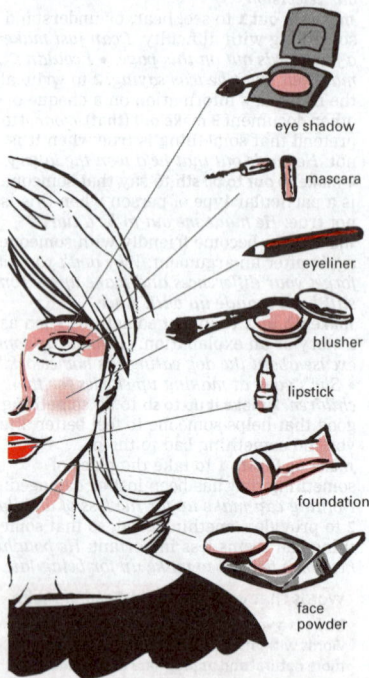

eye shadow

mascara

eyeliner

blusher

lipstick

foundation

face powder

make-up

making /ˈmeɪkɪŋ/ noun [U] the activity or process of creating something

PHRASES **have the makings of** to have the qualities that are necessary to become a particular type of thing or person: *I believe you have the makings of a great artist.*

in the making in the process of being created or produced: *We are witnessing a piece of history in the making.*

malaise /məˈleɪz/ noun [singular/U] *formal* a situation in which a society or organization is not operating effectively

malaria /məˈleəriə/ noun [U] a serious illness that you can get in a hot country if you are bitten by a MOSQUITO

male¹ /meɪl/ adj ★★★
1 belonging to the sex that does not give birth ≠ FEMALE: *male colleagues/workers* ♦ *a male elephant*
2 relating to men ≠ FEMALE: *ideas about female and male sexuality*

male² /meɪl/ noun [C] **1** a male animal

≠ FEMALE **2** *formal* a man ≠ FEMALE

ˌmale ˈchauvinist *see* chauvinist

malevolent /məˈlevələnt/ adj showing that you want to do something bad to someone

malfunction /mælˈfʌŋkʃ(ə)n/ noun [C/U] an occasion when something does not operate correctly —**malfunction** verb [I]

malice /ˈmælɪs/ noun [U] a strong feeling of wanting to hurt someone or be unkind to them

malicious /məˈlɪʃəs/ adj intended to hurt or upset someone —**maliciously** adv

malignant /məˈlɪɡnənt/ adj *medical* a TUMOUR that is malignant is dangerous and could cause death ≠ BENIGN —**malignancy** noun [C/U], **malignantly** adv

mall /mɔːl, mæl/ noun [C] a large building with a lot of shops in it

malleable /ˈmæliəb(ə)l/ adj **1** a malleable metal is easy to press into different shapes **2** a malleable person is easy to persuade or influence

mallet /ˈmælɪt/ noun [C] a wooden hammer

malnourished /ˌmælˈnʌrɪʃt/ adj weak or ill because you do not eat enough, or you do not eat enough of the right foods

malnutrition /ˌmælnjuˈtrɪʃ(ə)n/ noun [U] a medical condition in which you are very weak or ill because you do not have enough to eat, or you do not eat enough of the right foods

malpractice /mælˈpræktɪs/ noun [C/U] careless or illegal behaviour by someone with a professional or official job

malt /mɔːlt/ noun [U] a grain such as BARLEY that is kept in water until it begins to grow, and is then dried. It is used for making beer, WHISKY, and VINEGAR.

maltreat /mælˈtriːt/ verb [T] to be violent or cruel to a person or animal, especially when you should be responsible for them —**maltreatment** noun [U]

mama /ˈmæmə, məˈmɑː/ noun [C] *informal* a mother. This word is used mainly by young children talking to or about their mothers.

mammal /ˈmæm(ə)l/ noun [C] an animal that is born from its mother's body, not from an egg, and drinks its mother's milk as a baby

mammoth¹ /ˈmæməθ/ adj very big: *a mammoth task/corporation*

mammoth² /ˈmæməθ/ noun [C] an animal similar to an elephant with long hair that lived a very long time ago

man¹ /mæn/ (plural **men** /men/) noun ★★★
1 [C] an adult male human: *a jury of nine men and three women* ♦ *a man's overcoat* ♦ *a man of 64* (=who is 64 years old) ♦ *a nice young man*
2 [U] people in general. Some people avoid this word because it suggests that women are not included, or that men are more important than women. They use the word **humans** instead.
3 [C] a husband, boyfriend, or sexual partner: *Have you met Jessica's new man?*
4 [C] someone who is strong and brave, as a

man is traditionally expected to be

man² /mæn/ verb [T] to provide a place, machine, or system with the people who are needed to operate it. Some people avoid using this word because it suggests that women are not included. They use the word **staff** instead.

manage /ˈmænɪdʒ/ verb ★★★

1 succeed in doing sth	**4** be available for sth
2 organize and control	**5** live on limited money
3 be able to provide sth	

1 [I/T] to succeed in doing or dealing with something, especially something difficult or something that needs a lot of effort: *I don't think I can manage a long walk today.* ♦ *We couldn't have managed without your help.* ♦ *techniques for managing stress in the workplace* ♦ **manage to do sth** *She managed to escape by diving into the river.*
2 [T] to be in charge of a company, an area, or people that you work with: *He manages the family business.* ♦ *a well-managed restaurant* ♦ *Smith says he wants to manage the football team next year.*
3 [T] to be able to provide something such as money or time: *We can only manage £100 a week for rent.*
4 [T] to be available to do something at a particular time: *Can you manage 5 o'clock next Monday?*
5 [I] to be able to live with only a limited amount of money: *I don't know how he manages on what he earns.*

manageable /ˈmænɪdʒəb(ə)l/ adj able to be dealt with or controlled ≠ UNMANAGEABLE

management /ˈmænɪdʒmənt/ noun ★★
1 [U] the control and operation of a business or organization: *In this company we have a new approach to management.* ♦ *a diploma in management*
2 [U] the process of controlling or managing something: *stress management* ♦ *an attack on the government's **management** of the economy*
3 [singular/U] the people who are in charge of a business or organization, or of the people who work there: *the company's senior management* ♦ *Talks between the workers' union and management broke down today.*

In British English, **management** can be used with a singular or plural verb. You can say: *The management **was** responsible.* OR: *The management **were** responsible.*

manager /ˈmænɪdʒə/ noun [C] ★★
1 someone whose job is to organize and control the work of a business, a department, or the people who work there: *I'd like to speak to the manager.* ♦ *a marketing/project/sales/office manager* ♦ *For three years I was **the manager of** a radio station.*
2 someone whose job is to look after the business activities of an entertainer or sports player
3 someone whose job is to organize and train a sports team

manageress /ˌmænɪdʒəˈres/ noun [C] *British old-fashioned* a woman whose job is to run a shop or small business

managerial /ˌmænəˈdʒɪəriəl/ adj relating to the job of a manager, especially in a company

managing diˈrector noun [C] someone in charge of a company

Mandarin /ˈmændərɪn/ noun [U] the official language of China

mandate /ˈmændeɪt/ noun [singular] the authority of an elected government or official to do the things that they promised to do before an election: *He was elected with a clear mandate to reduce taxes.*

mandatory /ˈmændət(ə)ri/ adj something that is mandatory has to be done because of a law or rule: *a mandatory meeting for all employees*

mane /meɪn/ noun [C] the long hair on the neck of a horse or lion

maneuver /məˈnuːvə/ the American spelling of **manoeuvre**

manger /ˈmeɪndʒə/ noun [C] a long low open container that horses or cows eat from

mangle /ˈmæŋg(ə)l/ verb [T] to damage or hurt something seriously by twisting or crushing it —**mangled** /ˈmæŋg(ə)ld/ adj

mango /ˈmæŋgəʊ/ noun [C/U] a soft sweet tropical fruit with a red or green skin and yellow flesh —*picture* → C10

mangrove /ˈmæŋgrəʊv/ noun [C] a tropical tree that grows beside water and has roots that begin above the ground

manhandle /ˈmænˌhænd(ə)l/ verb [T] to touch, push, or pull someone in a rough way

manhole /ˈmænˌhəʊl/ noun [C] a hole in the surface of a road or street, covered with a metal lid and used for entering an underground passage

manhood /ˈmænhʊd/ noun [U] *formal* the time when a boy becomes a man

manhunt /ˈmænˌhʌnt/ noun [C] a search that is organized to catch someone that the police think has committed a crime or a prisoner who has escaped

mania /ˈmeɪniə/ noun [C/U] an extremely strong enthusiasm for something, especially among a lot of people: *World Cup mania*

maniac /ˈmeɪniˌæk/ noun [C] *informal* someone who behaves in a stupid and dangerous way = LUNATIC

manic /ˈmænɪk/ adj behaving in an unusually excited way —**manically** /ˈmænɪkli/ adv

manic deˈpression noun [U] a serious mental illness in which you experience extreme changes in mood

manicure /ˈmænɪkjʊə/ noun [C] a beauty treatment for your hands and nails —**manicure** verb [T]

manifest /ˈmænɪˌfest/ verb [T] *formal* to show something such as a feeling, attitude, or ability

manifestation /ˌmænɪfeˈsteɪʃ(ə)n/ noun [C/U] **a manifestation of sth** *formal* evidence that something exists or is present

M

manifestly /ˈmænɪˌfestli/ adv *formal* clearly and without any doubt=OBVIOUSLY

manifesto /ˌmænɪˈfestəʊ/ (plural **manifestoes**) noun [C] a formal statement describing the aims and plans of an organization, especially a political party

manipulate /məˈnɪpjʊˌleɪt/ verb [T] **1** to influence someone, or to control something, in a clever or dishonest way **2** to skilfully handle, control, or use something —**manipulation** /məˌnɪpjʊˈleɪʃ(ə)n/ noun [U]

manipulative /məˈnɪpjʊlətɪv/ adj *showing disapproval* someone who is manipulative makes people do what they want by influencing them in a clever or dishonest way

mankind /mænˈkaɪnd/ noun [U] all humans considered as a single group. Some people avoid using this word because it seems not to include women, and they use **humankind** instead.

manly /ˈmænli/ adj typical of traditional good male qualities, for example by being strong and brave —**manliness** noun [U]

man-made adj something that is man-made has been made by people and does not exist naturally ≠ NATURAL: *Rayon is a man-made fibre.*

M

manned /mænd/ adj a manned vehicle or place has people working in or on it ≠ UNMANNED: *a manned space flight*

manner /ˈmænə/ noun ★★
1 [singular] the way that you do something, or the way that something happens: *The manner of his death aroused a lot of interest in the media.* ♦ *Things had been done in the same manner for centuries.*
2 [singular] the way that you behave towards someone: *The salesman's aggressive manner put us off.*
3 **manners** [plural] traditionally accepted ways of behaving that show a polite respect for other people: *Children learn manners by observing their parents.* ♦ *It's **bad manners** to interrupt someone.*
PHRASE **all manner of sth** a great variety of people or things

mannerism /ˈmænərɪz(ə)m/ noun [C] a particular way of speaking or moving that someone has

manoeuvre¹ /məˈnuːvə/ noun **1** [C] an action or movement that you need care or skill to do **2** [C] a clever or dishonest action that you do in order to get something that you want **3** **manoeuvres** [plural] a military training operation

manoeuvre² /məˈnuːvə/ verb [I/T] to move someone or something in a situation that needs care or skill

manor /ˈmænə/ or **'manor ˌhouse** noun [C] a large house with a lot of land and small buildings around it

manpower /ˈmænˌpaʊə/ noun [U] all the people who are available to do a particular job or to work in a particular place

mansion /ˈmænʃən/ noun [C] a very large house

manslaughter /ˈmænˌslɔːtə/ noun [U] *legal* the crime of causing someone's death illegally but without intending to → MURDER

mantelpiece /ˈmænt(ə)lˌpiːs/ noun [C] a shelf above a FIREPLACE

mantle /ˈmænt(ə)l/ noun [singular] the authority or responsibility connected with someone's position, duties, or beliefs

mantra /ˈmæntrə/ noun [C] a sound, word, or phrase that is continuously repeated as a prayer

manual¹ /ˈmænjʊəl/ noun [C] a book that contains instructions for doing something, especially for operating a machine

manual² /ˈmænjʊəl/ adj **1** involving the use of your hands, or doing work with your hands: *The job requires manual skill.* ♦ *manual labour* **2** operated by people rather than automatically or using computers —**manually** adv

manufacture¹ /ˌmænjʊˈfæktʃə/ verb [T] ★ to make goods in large quantities in a factory: *The firm manufactures women's clothing.*

manufacture² /ˌmænjʊˈfæktʃə/ noun [U] the process of making goods in large quantities in a factory

manufacturer /ˌmænjʊˈfæktʃərə/ noun [C] a person or company that makes a particular type of product, especially in a factory

manufacturing /ˌmænjʊˈfæktʃərɪŋ/ noun [U] the business of making goods in large quantities, especially in factories

manure /məˈnjʊə/ noun [U] solid waste from farm animals, often mixed with other substances and used on crops to help them to grow

manuscript /ˈmænjʊˌskrɪpt/ noun [C] **1** a writer's original pages of a book, article, or document before it is published **2** a very old book or document that was written by hand before books began to be printed

many /ˈmeni/ (comparative **more** /mɔː/; superlative **most** /məʊst/) grammar word ★★★

Many can be:
- a **determiner**: *It happened many years ago.*
- a **pronoun**: *'Did he write any other books?' 'Not many.'* ♦ *Many of you will be going on to university.*
- an **adjective**: *He said goodbye to his many friends.*

1 a large number of people, things, places etc: *I've been to their house many times.* ♦ *I haven't told many people that I am pregnant.* ♦ *Did you get many replies to your advertisement?* ♦ ***Many of** the world's leading doctors have been trained here.* ♦ *There are **too many** rules and regulations.* ♦ *He has **so many** books, he couldn't possibly read them all.* ♦ ***Not very many** companies can afford the high cost of introducing new technology.* ♦ *We've lived here for **a good many** years.*
2 used for asking or talking about the number of people, things etc that there are: *How many students are taking the test?* ♦ *It's surprising how many different varieties of pasta there are.* ♦ **How many of** you can

remember your first day at school? ♦ They try to interview **as many** *candidates* **as** *possible.*

PHRASE **as many as** used before a number for showing how large and surprising it is: *As many as 500,000 people may have become infected with the virus.*

→ WORD¹

> **Many**, **a lot**, and **lots** can be used for referring to a large number of things or people.
> ■ In ordinary spoken English **many** is mainly used in negative sentences and in questions. It is also used in positive sentences after 'too', 'so', or 'as': *We didn't sell many tickets. ♦ Were there many children in the audience? ♦ You're trying to do too many things at once.*
> ■ In positive statements **a lot of** is usually used instead of **many**: *A lot of people came.*
> ■ In written English and in formal spoken English **many** is used in sentences of all types: *Many disabled people use public transport.*
> ■ In informal English, **lots** is often used instead of **a lot of**: *Lots of people get divorced these days.*

Maori /ˈmaʊri/ noun [C] someone who belongs to the race of people who were living in New Zealand before Europeans arrived, or the language that they speak —**Maori** adj

map¹ /mæp/ noun [C] ★★
1 a drawing of an area that shows the positions of things such as countries, rivers, cities, and streets: *a map of northern Europe/the London Underground/New York City ♦ They never taught us how to read a map at school.*
2 a drawing that shows the position of things in relation to each other: *a map of the human genome*

map² /mæp/ verb [T] **1** to make a map of an area **2** to find the position of something, or to find the positions of the parts of something: *Scientists have succeeded in mapping the human genome.*
PHRASAL VERB **map sth out** to plan or describe in detail how something will happen

maple /ˈmeɪp(ə)l/ noun [C] a tree that grows mainly in northern countries and has wide leaves that turn red and yellow in the autumn

mar /mɑː/ verb [T] to spoil something

Mar. abbrev March

marathon /ˈmærəθ(ə)n/ noun [C] **1** a race that is run for 42 kilometres or about 26 miles **2** an activity or event that takes a long time to complete: *The meeting turned out to be a bit of a marathon.*

marauding /məˈrɔːdɪŋ/ adj going from place to place in order to attack people or to steal or destroy things —**marauder** noun [C]

marble /ˈmɑːb(ə)l/ noun **1** [U] a hard smooth stone that is used for building and making STATUES **2** [C] a small coloured glass ball, used in children's games

march¹ /mɑːtʃ/ verb [I] **1** when soldiers march, they walk in a group with each person

matching the speed and movements of the others **2** to walk somewhere quickly and in a determined, confident, or angry way **3** to walk to a place as part of an organized group protesting about something —**marcher** noun [C]

march² /mɑːtʃ/ noun [C] **1** a long walk by an organized group, especially soldiers **2** a walk by a group of people to a place in order to protest about something

March /mɑːtʃ/ noun [C/U] ★★★ the third month of the year, between February and April: *His birthday is in March. ♦ The concert is on 29 March.*

mare /meə/ noun [C] an adult female horse

margarine /ˌmɑːdʒəˈriːn/ noun [C/U] a yellow substance made from vegetable oil or animal fat that can be used instead of butter

margin /ˈmɑːdʒɪn/ noun [C] ★
1 the space at the left or right side of a page that is usually left empty: *I made a couple of notes in the margin.*
2 the amount by which a competition or election is won: *Danes voted by a narrow margin* (=a small amount) *to keep their own currency.*
3 an additional amount of time, space, money etc that you include to be certain that you will be safe or successful: *There's no margin for error – we have to win. ♦ It's a business that operates with very small profit margins* (=the difference between the cost of providing a product, and the amount that you can charge for providing it).
4 the edge of an area

marginal /ˈmɑːdʒɪn(ə)l/ adj **1** very small **2** not important or relevant

marginalize /ˈmɑːdʒɪnəlaɪz/ verb [T] to make someone or something seem not important or relevant

marginally /ˈmɑːdʒɪn(ə)li/ adv by only a very small amount

marijuana /ˌmærɪˈwɑːnə/ noun [U] CANNABIS

marina /məˈriːnə/ noun [C] an area of water beside the sea or a lake for keeping small boats in

marinade /ˌmærɪˈneɪd/ noun [C/U] a liquid that you put food into to give it a special flavour before cooking it

marinate /ˈmærɪneɪt/ or **marinade** /ˈmærɪneɪd/ verb [I/T] to put meat, fish, or vegetables in a marinade

marine¹ /məˈriːn/ adj **1** living in, relating to, or happening in the sea: *marine life/animals/biology* **2** involving ships or the business of moving people and goods in ships

marine² /məˈriːn/ noun [C] a soldier whose job is to fight on both land and sea

Marine Corps, the the part of the US armed forces whose members are trained to operate on both land and sea

Marines, the /məˈriːnz/ noun [plural] **1** the ROYAL MARINES **2** the US MARINE CORPS

marital /ˈmærɪt(ə)l/ adj relating to marriage

marital status noun [U] *formal* your marital

M

status is whether you are married, divorced, SINGLE, or WIDOWED

maritime /ˈmærɪˌtaɪm/ adj **1** involving ships or the business of moving people and goods in ships **2** close to the sea

mark¹ /mɑːk/ noun [C] ★★★

1 area of dirt/damage	**4** sth printed/written
2 school score	**5** official sign on sth
3 level/stage/total etc	**+ PHRASES**

1 a small area of something such as dirt, oil, or damage on the surface of something: *There was a greasy mark on his shirt.* ♦ *There were burn marks all over her hands.*

2 *British* a score or GRADE that you are given for school work or for how you perform in a competition: *What mark did you get for your essay?*

3 a particular level, stage, total etc that something reaches: *Chicago was the halfway mark on our trip across the country.* ♦ *Average earnings had not yet reached the £18,000 mark.* → POINT

4 a printed or written symbol that is not a letter or a number: *Put a mark by the names of the most interesting candidates.*

5 an official sign on something that shows who made it, who it belongs to, or that it is of a particular standard or quality: *We suggest you only buy toys that carry the safety mark.*

PHRASES **leave your/a mark (on)** to have a very strong and noticeable effect on someone or something, usually a bad one: *Years of war have left their mark on these pretty islands.*

wide of the mark or **(way) off the mark** incorrect: *Her theory turned out to be pretty wide of the mark.*

mark² /mɑːk/ verb ★★★

1 make mark on surface	**5** show sth is happening
2 write/draw on sth	**6** celebrate sth
3 judge student's work	**7** stay close to opponent
4 show position of sth	**+ PHRASAL VERBS**

1 [T] to make a mark on the surface of something so that its appearance is spoiled or damaged: **be marked with sth** *Her cheek was marked with scratches.*

2 [I/T] to write or draw words, letters, symbols etc on something for a particular purpose: *We entered through a door marked 'Private'.* ♦ *The teacher marked six of the answers wrong* (=put a symbol by them to show they were wrong). ♦ **mark sth with sth** *Foods marked with a red star are included in the recipe section.* ♦ **mark sth on sth** *His job is to mark lines on roads.*

3 [I/T] *British* to judge the quality of a student's work and write a mark on it: *I spent the evening marking first-year essays.*

4 [T] to show the position of something: *A memorial plaque will mark the spot where he died.*

5 [T] to show that something is happening: *This tournament marks the official start of the season.*

6 [T] to celebrate something: *A ceremony was held to mark the occasion.*

7 [T] to stay close to a member of the other team in a game such as football in order to prevent them from getting the ball

PHRASAL VERBS **mark sth down** to reduce the price of something: *They've marked down the shoes to £20.*

mark sth off to show the limits of an area using a line, fence, rope etc: *The crime scene was marked off with official police tape.*

mark sth out to show the shape of something by drawing it on a surface: *The shape of the pond is marked out first with a spade.*

mark sth up to increase the price of something in order to increase your profits: *Foreign cars are often marked up by 40 per cent for the British market.*

markdown /ˈmɑːkˌdaʊn/ noun [C] a reduction in the price of something

marked /mɑːkt/ adj clear and noticeable =DISTINCT —**markedly** /ˈmɑːkɪdli/ adv

marker /ˈmɑːkə/ noun [C] **1** an object that is used for showing where something is or where you should go **2** a pen with a thick soft point

market¹ /ˈmɑːkɪt/ noun ★★

1 [C] a place, especially outside, where people sell goods: *a flower/fish/antiques market* ♦ *a street market* ♦ *a market trader*

2 [singular] trade in goods of a particular type: *Changes in the weather affect the market in fruit and vegetables.* ♦ *We're hoping to increase our share of the market.*

3 [C] a particular place or group of people that a product is sold to: *overseas markets* ♦ *France is the main market for our shellfish.*

4 [C] a STOCK MARKET: *Trading has been slow on the New York and Tokyo markets this morning.*

PHRASES **be in the market for sth** to want to buy something: *Most people are not in the market for this kind of product.*

on the market available to buy: *Computers as powerful as this are not yet on the market.*

market² /ˈmɑːkɪt/ verb [T] to use advertising and other methods to persuade people to buy something

marketable /ˈmɑːkɪtəb(ə)l/ adj **1** a marketable product can be sold because people want to buy it **2** marketable skills are those that employers are likely to want people to have

market economy noun [C] *business* an economic system in which prices, salaries, and the supply of goods are controlled by what and how much people buy, not by the government

market forces noun [plural] *business* the economic influences that affect prices, salaries, and the number of jobs available, and that are not controlled by governments

market garden noun [C] *British* a small farm where fruit and vegetables are grown to be sold —**market gardener** noun [C], **market gardening** noun [U]

marketing /ˈmɑːkɪtɪŋ/ noun [U] the ways in which a company encourages people to buy its products

M

marketplace /ˈmɑːkɪtˌpleɪs/ noun **1** [C] a place where people buy and sell goods in an outdoor market **2 the marketplace** [singular] *business* the part of the economy that involves buying and selling

market reˈsearch noun [U] the process of collecting information about what products people like to buy, or what people like or dislike about a particular product

market ˈshare noun [C/U] *business* the percentage of the total amount of sales of a particular product that a company has

marking /ˈmɑːkɪŋ/ noun **1** [C] a pattern of marks on the surface of something, for example the skin, fur, or feathers of an animal or bird **2** [U] the process of checking students' written work and giving it a mark

marksman /ˈmɑːksmən/ (plural **marksmen** /ˈmɑːksmən/) noun [C] someone who is skilful at shooting with a gun

ˈmark-ˌup noun [C] an amount of money that is added to the price of goods in order to make a profit

marmalade /ˈmɑːməleɪd/ noun [C/U] a sweet food that is made from cooked fruit, especially oranges. It is usually spread on TOAST.

maroon /məˈruːn/ adj dark red-brown in colour

marooned /məˈruːnd/ adj left in a place and unable to leave

marquee /mɑːˈkiː/ noun [C] a large tent that is used for an outdoor party or event

marriage /ˈmærɪdʒ/ noun ★★★
1 [C/U] the relationship between two people who are husband and wife: *a long and happy marriage ♦ Anne's marriage to Daniel lasted ten years.*
2 [C] a WEDDING: *Their marriage is planned for September.*

married /ˈmærid/ adj ★★★ a married person has a husband or wife ≠ SINGLE: *a married woman/man ♦ He's married to my older sister. ♦ We're getting married next year.*

marrow /ˈmærəʊ/ noun **1** [C/U] *British* a large long vegetable that has a dark green skin and is white inside **2** [U] the soft substance inside bones, where blood cells develop =BONE MARROW

marry /ˈmæri/ verb ★★
1 [I/T] to become someone's husband or wife: *Marge married a lawyer. ♦ They married in 1996.*
2 [T] to perform the ceremony in which two people become husband and wife

marsh /mɑːʃ/ noun [C] an area of soft wet land

marshal[1] /ˈmɑːʃ(ə)l/ noun [C] **1** someone whose job is to control a public or sports event **2** a police or FIRE BRIGADE officer of the highest rank in some parts of the US

marshal[2] /ˈmɑːʃ(ə)l/ verb [T] to organize people or things so that they can be used in an effective way

marshmallow /ˌmɑːʃˈmæləʊ/ noun [C/U] a soft white sweet with a thick round shape

marsupial /mɑːˈsuːpiəl/ noun [C] an animal whose babies live in a pocket in their mother's skin until they are completely developed

martial /ˈmɑːʃ(ə)l/ adj *formal* relating to war or fighting

martial ˈart noun [C] a sport that is a traditional Asian form of fighting such as KARATE or JUDO

martial ˈlaw noun [U] direct control of a country or area by the armed forces

Martian /ˈmɑːʃ(ə)n/ noun [C] an imaginary creature from Mars

martyr /ˈmɑːtə/ noun [C] **1** someone who suffers or is killed because of their religious or political beliefs **2** *showing disapproval* someone who talks a lot about how much they are suffering, because they want sympathy

martyrdom /ˈmɑːtədəm/ noun [U] a martyr's pain or death

marvel[1] /ˈmɑːv(ə)l/ verb [I/T] to show or feel surprise or admiration

marvel[2] /ˈmɑːv(ə)l/ noun [C] someone or something that is very surprising or impressive

marvellous /ˈmɑːvələs/ adj extremely enjoyable, good, or impressive: *a marvellous performance/trip/party* —**marvellously** adv

marvelous /ˈmɑːvələs/ the American spelling of **marvellous**

Marxism /ˈmɑːksɪz(ə)m/ noun [U] the political and economic theories of Karl Marx, from which Communist and SOCIALIST political systems developed

Marxist /ˈmɑːksɪst/ adj relating to or based on Marxism —**Marxist** noun [C]

marzipan /ˌmɑːzɪˈpæn/ noun [U] a sweet food made from sugar and ALMONDS that is used for decorating cakes

mascara /mæˈskɑːrə/ noun [C/U] a substance that is used to make EYELASHES look darker or longer —*picture* → MAKE-UP

mascot /ˈmæskɒt/ noun [C] an animal, person, or object that is thought to be lucky or that is used as a symbol of a team or organization

masculine /ˈmæskjʊlɪn/ adj **1** with qualities that are considered typical of men ≠ FEMININE **2** *linguistics* in some languages, masculine nouns, pronouns, and adjectives have different forms from FEMININE or NEUTER words

masculinity /ˌmæskjʊˈlɪnəti/ noun [U] the qualities that are considered typical of men ≠ FEMININITY

mash /mæʃ/ verb [T] to crush food so that it is a soft mass: *Mash the potatoes with a little milk.*

mask[1] /mɑːsk/ noun [C] something that you wear in order to cover part or all of your face

mask[2] /mɑːsk/ verb [T] **1** to cover something in order to hide it **2** to hide the smell, taste, or sound of something with a stronger smell or taste or a louder sound

masked /mɑːskt/ adj wearing a mask

masochism /ˈmæsəˌkɪz(ə)m/ noun [U] sexual

M

behaviour in which someone gets pleasure from being hurt —**masochist** noun [C], **masochistic** /ˌmæsəˈkɪstɪk/ adj

mason /ˈmeɪs(ə)n/ noun [C] someone whose job is to cut stones into pieces that can be used in building

masonry /ˈmeɪsənri/ noun [U] the bricks or stones that make a building, wall, or other structure

masquerade /ˌmæskəˈreɪd/ verb [I] to pretend to be someone or something that you are not

mass¹ /mæs/ noun ★★

1 large quantity	4 ordinary people
2 sth without shape	5 scientific use
3 a lot	

1 [C] a large quantity, number, or amount: *The police had a mass of evidence.* ♦ *a mass of fallen leaves*

2 [C] a lump or amount of a substance that does not have a clear or definite shape: *The vegetables had turned into a sticky mass at the bottom of the pan.*

3 masses [plural] *British informal* a lot: *Masses of people attended the meeting.* ♦ *There was masses of food.*

4 the masses [plural] ordinary people who are not highly educated or rich

5 [U] *science* the amount of MATTER (=physical substance) that something contains
→ CRITICAL MASS

mass² /mæs/ adj ★ involving or affecting a large number of people: *the problem of mass unemployment* ♦ *weapons of mass destruction*

Words often used with mass

Nouns often used with mass (adj)
■ MASS + **demonstration, destruction, killings, murder, protest**: used about things that involve a large number of people

mass³ /mæs/ verb [I/T] to come together, or to bring people together, in order to form a large group

Mass /mæs/ noun **1** [C/U] the main religious ceremony of the Roman Catholic Church **2** [C] a piece of music that was written to be played at a Mass

massacre /ˈmæsəkə/ noun [C/U] the action of killing a lot of people —**massacre** verb [T]

massage /ˈmæsɑːʒ/ noun [C/U] the action of pressing, squeezing, and rubbing someone's body in order to reduce pain in their muscles or to make them relax —**massage** verb [T]

massive /ˈmæsɪv/ adj ★
1 very large: *a massive amount of money*
2 very severe: *a massive heart attack*
—**massively** adv

mass-ˈmarket adj produced in large quantities in order to be sold to many customers

mass ˈmedia, the noun [plural] the newspapers, television, and radio that communicate news and information to large numbers of people

mass-produced /ˌmæs prəˈdjuːst/ adj made in large quantities using machines —**mass-produce** verb [T]

mast /mɑːst/ noun [C] **1** a tall pole that the sails hang from on a ship **2** a tall metal structure that is used for broadcasting radio and television signals

master¹ /ˈmɑːstə/ noun [C] **1** a man who has control over servants, other people, or an animal **2** a man who is very good at something: *He's a master of the clever remark.* **3** a document, photograph, or RECORDING from which copies are made =ORIGINAL **4** *British* a male teacher

master² /ˈmɑːstə/ verb [T] **1** to learn something so that you know it or can do it very well **2** to manage to control a difficult situation or a strong emotion

mastermind¹ /ˈmɑːstəmaɪnd/ verb [T] to plan and organize a difficult or complicated operation

mastermind² /ˈmɑːstəmaɪnd/ noun [C] someone who plans a difficult or complicated operation, especially a crime

masterpiece /ˈmɑːstəpiːs/ noun [C] an excellent work of art, or the best work of art from a particular artist, writer, or musician

ˈmaster's deˌgree noun [C] a university degree that a student gets if they study for one or two years after their first degree

mastery /ˈmɑːstəri/ noun [U] **1** great knowledge or skill **2** power or control over someone or something

masturbate /ˈmæstəbeɪt/ verb [I] to rub your sexual organs in order to get sexual pleasure —**masturbation** /ˌmæstəˈbeɪʃ(ə)n/ noun [U]

mat¹ /mæt/ noun [C] **1** a piece of thick cloth that is put on a floor to protect it or for decoration **2** a small piece of plastic, cloth, or other material that you put on a table or other surface to protect it **3** a piece of a thick soft material like rubber that you use when doing exercises —*picture* → C16

mat² /mæt/ an American spelling of **matt**

match¹ /mætʃ/ noun ★★★
1 [C] a small stick that produces a flame when it is rubbed against a rough surface: *a box of matches* ♦ *He lit a match* (=made it light).

2 [C] a game in which players or teams compete against each other: *a football match* ♦ *They lost the match on Saturday.*

3 [singular] a thing that forms an attractive combination with something else: *The curtains are a good match for the sofa.*

4 [C] something that looks the same as something else: *It was difficult to get an exact match for the paint.*

PHRASE be no match for sb to be not as good, strong, clever etc as someone

match² /mætʃ/ verb ★★
1 [I/T] if one thing matches another, or if they match, they are the same or have similar qualities: *The two signatures match.* ♦ *He matches the description of a man seen in the area.*

M

2 [I/T] to be equal to something else in amount or level, or to provide something that is equal: *The school promised to match whatever amount we could raise.* ♦ *The rise in student numbers has not been matched by an increase in teaching staff.*

3 [I/T] if one thing matches another, or they match, they form an attractive combination: *She wore a green dress and a hat to match.*

4 [T] to choose or provide something that is suitable for a particular situation, person, or purpose: **match sth to sth/sb** *It is important to match the software to the task.* ♦ **match sth with sth/sb** *The children were asked to match words with pictures.*

PHRASAL VERBS **match up** if two things match up, they are the same or have similar qualities

match up to sb/sth to be as good as someone or something: *The hotel didn't really match up to the description on the website.*

matchbox /'mætʃbɒks/ noun [C] a small box that contains matches

matching /'mætʃɪŋ/ adj with the same colour, pattern, or design

mate¹ /meɪt/ noun [C] **1** *British informal* a friend **2** *British* used for talking in a friendly way to someone, usually a man **3** an animal's sexual partner

mate² /meɪt/ verb [I] if one animal mates with another, or if two animals mate, they have sex

material¹ /mə'tɪəriəl/ noun ★★★
1 [C/U] cloth = FABRIC: *What sort of material is your dress made from?*
2 [C/U] a substance that is used for a particular purpose: *Brick was used as the main building material.*
3 [U] information or ideas that are used as the subject of a book, film, or song: *Newspaper articles are* **a** *good* **source of** *material for stories.*
4 [C/U] documents, or other things for presenting information, that are used for a particular activity: *publicity material* ♦ *teaching materials*

material² /mə'tɪəriəl/ adj **1** relating to things such as money and possessions that affect your physical life rather than your thoughts or emotions **2** *legal* important enough to have an effect: *information material to the decision*

materialism /mə'tɪəriə,lɪz(ə)m/ noun [U] the belief that money and possessions are the most important aspects of human existence —**materialistic** /mə,tɪəriə'lɪstɪk/ adj

materialize /mə'tɪəriə,laɪz/ verb [I] **1** to happen, or to become real **2** to appear suddenly and unexpectedly

maternal /mə'tɜːn(ə)l/ adj **1** typical of a kind and caring mother **2** a maternal relative is related to you through your mother

maternity /mə'tɜːnəti/ adj designed or provided for women who are pregnant or who have just had a baby: *maternity pay/benefits* ♦ *maternity clothes*

math /mæθ/ noun [U] *American* mathematics

mathematical /,mæθə'mætɪk(ə)l/ adj relating to or involving mathematics
—**mathematically** /,mæθə'mætɪkli/ adv

mathematician /,mæθ(ə)mə'tɪʃ(ə)n/ noun [C] someone who studies or teaches mathematics

mathematics /,mæθə'mætɪks/ noun [U] *formal* the study or use of numbers and shapes to calculate, represent, or describe things

maths /mæθs/ noun [U] *British* mathematics

matinee /'mætɪneɪ/ noun [C] an afternoon performance of a play or a film

matriarch /'meɪtriˌɑːk/ noun [C] a female leader of a family or community

matrimony /'mætrɪməni/ noun [U] *formal* marriage —**matrimonial** /,mætrɪ'məʊniəl/ adj

matt or **matte** /mæt/ adj with a dull surface that is not shiny ≠ GLOSSY, SHINY

matted /'mætɪd/ adj matted hair or fur is twisted or stuck together

matter¹ /'mætə/ noun ★★★

1 sth being dealt with	**5** substance/thing
2 problem/bad situation	**6** all substances
3 situation that sb is in	**+** PHRASES
4 when time is short	

1 [C] something that you are discussing, considering, or dealing with: *an extremely important matter* ♦ *Teachers feel this is a matter for discussion with parents.*
2 the matter [singular] used for talking about problems or bad situations: *You look sad. What's the matter?* ♦ *What's the matter with the car?* ♦ *I think there's something the matter with the printer.* ♦ *There's nothing the matter* (=there is no problem) *with you – you're just tired.*
3 matters [plural] a situation that someone is involved in = THINGS: *Her angry attitude didn't improve matters.* ♦ *To make matters worse, his wife is ill.*
4 [singular] **a matter of sth** used for emphasizing how short a period of time is: *The school could close in a matter of a few weeks.*
5 [U] a particular type of substance or thing: *organic matter* ♦ *Is this suitable* **reading matter** *for a young child?*
6 [U] *science* the physical substances that everything in the universe is made of
PHRASES **as a matter of fact 1** used when you are going to give more details about something: *I haven't been here long. As a matter of fact, I just got off the plane yesterday.* **2** used when you are going to disagree with or correct what has just been said: *'Was he in a bad mood?' 'No, as a matter of fact, he seemed quite cheerful.'*
as a matter of routine/course done as a habit or as the usual way of doing things
for that matter *spoken* used for emphasizing that something else is also true: *He doesn't like young women, or any women for that matter.*
a matter of life and death a serious or dangerous situation

M

a matter of opinion/taste something that different people have different opinions about

a matter of time used for saying that something will certainly happen eventually: *It was only a matter of time before she left the company.*

matter² /ˈmætə/ verb [I] ★★★ to be important: *Education matters.* ♦ *Does it matter if I don't take a present?* ♦ *It doesn't really matter if we're a bit late.* ♦ **sth matters to sb** *Winning this award matters a lot to me.*

matter-of-fact adj calm and showing no emotion when dealing with something —**matter-of-factly** adv

matting /ˈmætɪŋ/ noun [U] strong rough material that is used as a floor cover

mattress /ˈmætrəs/ noun [C] the thick soft part of a bed that you lie on

mature¹ /məˈtʃʊə/ adj **1** behaving in the sensible way that you would expect an adult to behave ≠ IMMATURE **2** fully developed or fully grown

mature² /məˈtʃʊə/ verb [I] **1** to start behaving like an adult and become more sensible **2** to grow to full adult size

maturity /məˈtʃʊərəti/ noun [U] **1** the qualities and behaviour that you would expect of a sensible adult **2** full growth, or completed development

maudlin /ˈmɔːdlɪn/ adj talking in a sad and emotional way that seems silly

maul /mɔːl/ verb [T] **1** if an animal mauls someone, it attacks them, usually causing serious injury **2** *British* to touch someone in a rough unpleasant way

mausoleum /ˌmɔːsəˈliːəm/ noun [C] a large impressive TOMB (=stone structure in which someone is buried)

mauve /məʊv/ adj pale purple in colour —**mauve** noun [U]

maverick /ˈmævərɪk/ noun [C] an independent person who has ideas and behaviour that are very different from other people's

max¹ /mæks/ adv *informal* at the most: *Fixing it should cost about £20 max.*

max² /mæks/ abbrev maximum

maxim /ˈmæksɪm/ noun [C] a phrase or saying that includes a rule or moral about how you should behave

maximize /ˈmæksɪˌmaɪz/ verb [T] to make something as large as possible ≠ MINIMIZE

maximum¹ /ˈmæksɪməm/ adj ★★ the largest in amount, size, or number that is allowed or possible ≠ MINIMUM: *The maximum amount of cash you can withdraw is £500.*

maximum² /ˈmæksɪməm/ noun [C] ★ the largest number, amount, or degree that is allowed or is possible ≠ MINIMUM: *20 kg of luggage is the maximum we allow on the flight.* ♦ *Give yourself a maximum of 15 minutes to read the questions.*

maximum³ /ˈmæksɪməm/ adv up to a particular amount, size, or number but no more ≠ MINIMUM: *You can invite 25 people maximum.*

may /meɪ/ modal verb ★★★

- **May** is usually followed by an infinitive without 'to': *It may rain.*
- Sometimes it is used without a following infinitive: *I'd like to make one or two comments, if I may.*
- **May** has no tenses, no participles, and no infinitive form. It does not change its form, so the third person singular form does not end in '-s': *He may arrive this afternoon.*
- Questions and negatives are formed without 'do': *May I make a suggestion?* ♦ *She may not understand.*

1 used for saying that something is possibly true, or that something will possibly happen: *I may not be able to play on Saturday.* ♦ *The injury may have caused brain damage.* ♦ *What you say* **may very well be** *true* (=it is fairly likely).

2 used for saying or asking whether something is allowed: *May I use your phone?* ♦ *Visitors may use the swimming pool between 5.30 and 7.30 pm.*

3 *spoken* used when making a polite request or offer: *May I see your ticket, please?* ♦ *May we offer you a glass of wine?* → CAN

May /meɪ/ noun [C/U] ★★★ the fifth month of the year, between April and June: *We're taking an early holiday in May.* ♦ *They were married on 17th May.*

maybe /ˈmeɪbi/ adv ★★★

1 used for showing that you are not sure whether something is true or correct, or whether something will happen: *Maybe it will snow tonight.* ♦ *'Do you think he really loves you?' 'Maybe. I'm not sure.'* ♦ *The whole process takes maybe ten or fifteen minutes.* ♦ *Maybe things will improve, but then again,* **maybe not***.

2 *spoken* used for making a suggestion when you are not sure what to do: *Maybe we should call a doctor.*

mayhem /ˈmeɪhem/ noun [U] a very confused situation =CHAOS

mayonnaise /ˌmeɪəˈneɪz/ noun [U] a thick white sauce made from eggs and oil

mayor /meə/ noun [C] the most important elected official in a town or city —**mayoral** adj

maze /meɪz/ noun **1** [C] an arrangement of closely connected paths that are separated by tall bushes, walls, or trees, that is designed to be difficult to find your way through **2** [singular] a set of many small streets or paths that is easy to get lost in **3** [singular] a set of closely connected but complicated rules, issues, or ideas: *a maze of new legislation*

MB /ˌem ˈbiː/ noun [C] megabyte

MBA /ˌem biː ˈeɪ/ noun [C] Master of Business Administration: a MASTER's degree in business management

MD /ˌem ˈdiː/ noun [C] **1** *British informal* the MANAGING DIRECTOR of a company **2** Doctor of Medicine: an advanced degree in medicine

M

me /weak mi, strong miː/ pronoun ★★★ the object form of 'I', used for referring to yourself when you are the person who is speaking or writing: *I think Darren really likes me.* ♦ *She wrote me a letter.* ♦ *You can come with me.*

ME /ˌem ˈiː/ noun [U] British an illness that makes you feel tired and weak all the time

meadow /ˈmedəʊ/ noun [C] a field where grass and wild flowers grow

meager /ˈmiːɡə/ the American spelling of **meagre**

meagre /ˈmiːɡə/ adj smaller or less than you want or need: *a meagre food supply*

meal /miːl/ noun [C] ★★★ an occasion when you eat, such as breakfast or lunch, or the food that you eat at that time: *He cooked us a delicious meal.* ♦ *We could see a film or go out for a meal* (=go to a restaurant).
→ SQUARE MEAL

mealtime /ˈmiːltaɪm/ noun [C] a time when you eat a meal

mean¹ /miːn/ (past tense and past participle **meant** /ment/) verb [T] ★★★

1 have a meaning	4 make sth happen
2 intend a meaning	5 be evidence of sth
3 intend sth	+ PHRASES

1 to have a particular meaning: *What does 'maudlin' mean?* ♦ *The word 'serviette' means something different in French.*
2 to intend to communicate a particular meaning: *By 'partner', I mean your wife, your husband, or someone you live with.* ♦ *Don't be offended, she meant it as a joke.* ♦ **+(that)** *She didn't reply to our invitation, which probably means she isn't coming.*
3 to intend something, or to intend to do something: *She had never meant him any real harm.* ♦ **mean to do sth** *I didn't mean to step on your toe.*
4 to make something happen, or to have a particular result: **+(that)** *The company's failure could mean that hundreds of workers lose their jobs.* ♦ **sth means doing sth** *The new contract will mean starting the whole project again.*
5 to be evidence that something exists: *That dark patch means that water is coming in.*
  PHRASES **be meant for** to be intended, designed, or suitable for something or someone: *These books are not meant for primary school students.*
be meant to do sth to have a particular responsibility, duty, or purpose: *You were meant to keep the children out of trouble.*
(do) you mean...? spoken used for saying what someone else has said using different words, as a way of asking them if you have understood it correctly: *You mean we do the work and you get the money?*
I know what you mean spoken used for telling someone that you understand their situation very well
I mean spoken **1** used for adding a comment, or for explaining what you have just said: *We couldn't live on that! I mean, it's*

ridiculous. **2** used for correcting a mistake in something you have just said: *Let's ask Mark. I mean Marco.*
I see what you mean spoken used for telling someone that you understand what they are saying
mean nothing to have no importance: *He spoke in a relaxed, slow way, as if time meant nothing to him.*
what do you mean? spoken **1** used for asking someone to explain what they have said **2** used for showing that you are shocked or annoyed about something that someone has told you: *What do you mean you can't find the keys?*

mean² /miːn/ adj ★
1 cruel or unkind: *Don't do that – it's mean.* ♦ *The older kids were mean to him.*
2 British not willing to spend money = STINGY: *She was too mean to put the heating on.*
3 technical average: *the mean annual temperature*
4 informal very good: *She plays a mean game of tennis.*
  PHRASE **no mean feat/achievement** very impressive: *She won her first championship at age 17, which is no mean achievement.*

mean³ /miːn/ noun [C] technical an average number or amount

meander /miˈændə/ verb [I] **1** if a river or road meanders, it has a lot of turns and curves **2** to move slowly without a particular direction or purpose

meaning /ˈmiːnɪŋ/ noun ★★★
1 [C/U] the thing, action, feeling, or idea that a word represents: *The dictionary gives two meanings for this word.* ♦ *The poem's real meaning has always been a puzzle.*
2 [singular/U] the special importance or purpose of something: *Times change and old customs lose their meaning.* ♦ *The book tackles important questions, such as the meaning of life.*

meaningful /ˈmiːnɪŋf(ə)l/ adj **1** serious, useful, or important: *a meaningful debate/discussion* **2** expressing a clear feeling or thought, but without using words: *a meaningful look/glance*
—**meaningfully** adv

meaningless /ˈmiːnɪŋləs/ adj **1** without any clear purpose or importance: *My life seems meaningless since Jim died.* **2** without a clear meaning: *a series of meaningless phrases*

means /miːnz/ (plural **means**) noun ★★★
1 [C] a method for doing or achieving something = METHOD: *Information is not easily obtained by any other means.* ♦ *The telephone was our only means of communication.* ♦ *We had no means of warning them.*
2 [plural] formal the money that someone has or gets: *She doesn't have the means to support herself.*
  PHRASES **by all means** spoken used for politely giving permission: *'Do you mind if I invite a few friends?' 'By all means.'*
by no means or **not by any means** not at all: *He was by no means certain that his plan would be successful.*

M

a means to an end a way of getting or achieving something you want

'means test noun [C] an examination of your income in order to find out whether you have the right to receive any extra money from the government —**'means-test** verb [I/T], **'means-tested** adj

meant the past tense and past participle of **mean¹**

meantime /'miːnˌtaɪm/ noun **in the meantime** during the time between two events, or between the present time and a future event

meanwhile /'miːnˌwaɪl/ adv ★ between the time that two things happen, or while something is happening: *Put the eggs on to boil and meanwhile slice the onions.*

measles /'miːz(ə)lz/ noun [U] an infectious disease in which you have red spots all over your body and a high temperature
→ GERMAN MEASLES

measly /'miːzli/ adj *informal* too small

measurable /'meʒ(ə)rəb(ə)l/ adj large enough to be measured, noticed, or important —**measurably** adv

measure¹ /'meʒə/ noun [C] ★★★
1 an action that is intended to achieve something or deal with something: *This is a temporary measure to stop the problem from getting any worse.* ♦ **take measures to do sth** *Stronger measures will have to be taken to bring down unemployment.*
2 an amount of a particular quality that is neither large nor small: *The system gives people a measure of protection against dishonest salesmen.*
3 a way of judging something: *The tests are not an accurate measure of performance.*
4 a unit used for measuring things
PHRASE **for good measure** as a way of making something complete or better: *Throw in a splash of red wine for good measure.*

Words often used with **measure**

Adjectives often used with measure (noun, sense 1)
■ **drastic, harsh, severe, strong** + MEASURE: used about measures that are severe
Verbs often used with measure (noun, sense 1)
■ **adopt, implement, introduce, take** + MEASURE: take measures in order to do something

---

measure² /'meʒə/ verb ★★★
1 [I/T] to find the exact size, amount, speed, or rate of something: *We measured from the back of the house to the fence.* ♦ *a device for measuring the flow of water through a pipe*
2 [T] to form an opinion about how good or bad something is: **measure sth by sth** *Success isn't measured by how much money you have.* ♦ *Their rate of economic growth is not very impressive, when you measure it against* (=compare it with) *that of the neighbouring countries.*
3 [linking verb] to be a particular size: *The room measures approximately 12 feet by 13 feet.*

M

PHRASAL VERBS **,measure 'out** to take a particular amount of something from a larger amount: *Measure out 10 grams of sugar.*
,measure 'up to be good enough: *The machines that we tested didn't measure up.* ♦ *Will he measure up to the challenges that lie ahead of him?*

measurement /'meʒəmənt/ noun **1** [C] the exact size, amount, speed, or rate of something, expressed in standard units: *They took measurements of noise levels inside the building.* **2** [U] the process of measuring something

meat /miːt/ noun [U] ★★★ the flesh of an animal or bird that is eaten as food

---

Talking or writing about **meat**

■ **beef** the meat of a cow
■ **chicken** the meat of a chicken
■ **game** the meat of a wild animal or bird
■ **lamb** the meat of a young sheep
■ **pork** the meat of a pig
■ **poultry** the meat of a chicken, duck, or other farm bird
■ **veal** the meat of a young cow
■ **red meat** meat that is red in colour, such as beef or lamb
■ **white meat** meat that is a light colour, such as chicken or turkey

---

meaty /'miːti/ adj containing a lot of meat

mecca /'mekə/ noun [C/U] a place that a lot of people visit

Mecca /'mekə/ a city in Saudi Arabia that is holy for Muslims

mechanic /mɪ'kænɪk/ noun **1** [C] someone whose job is to repair vehicles and machines **2** **mechanics** [plural] the way in which something works or is done: *the mechanics of newspaper reporting* **3** **mechanics** [U] the area of physics that deals with the forces such as GRAVITY that affect all objects

mechanical /mɪ'kænɪk(ə)l/ adj **1** operated by a machine, or relating to machines: *a mechanical device* **2** done without thinking, or without any attempt to be original: *her mechanical responses to my questions* —**mechanically** adv

mechanism /'mekəˌnɪz(ə)m/ noun [C] **1** a machine, or a part of a machine: *a locking mechanism* **2** a method or process for getting something done: *a mechanism for settling disputes*

mechanize /'mekəˌnaɪz/ verb [I/T] to start using machines to do something that was previously done by people

medal /'med(ə)l/ noun [C] a small flat piece of metal that you are given for winning a competition or for doing something that is very brave

medallion /mə'dæliən/ noun [C] a round flat piece of metal that you wear round your neck on a chain as jewellery

medallist /'med(ə)lɪst/ noun [C] someone who has won a MEDAL in a competition

meddle /'med(ə)l/ verb [I] to become involved

in a situation that does not affect you, in a way that is annoying=INTERFERE

media a plural of **medium**

media, the /ˈmiːdiə/ noun ★★★ radio, television, newspapers, the Internet, and magazines, considered as a group: *The story has been widely reported in the media.*
→ MASS MEDIA, MULTIMEDIA

> In British English, **media** can be used with a singular or plural verb. You can say: *The media **has** exaggerated the issue.* OR: *The media **have** exaggerated the issue.*

mediaeval /ˌmediˈiːvl/ another spelling of **medieval**

median /ˈmiːdiən/ adj *technical* in the middle of a set of numbers when they are arranged in order

mediate /ˈmiːdieɪt/ verb [I/T] to try to end a disagreement between two people or groups —**mediation** /ˌmiːdiˈeɪʃ(ə)n/ noun [U], **mediator** noun [C]

medic /ˈmedɪk/ noun [C] *British informal* a doctor or medical student

medical¹ /ˈmedɪk(ə)l/ adj ★★★ relating to medicine and the treatment of injuries and diseases: *a career in the medical profession* ♦ *a man in need of urgent **medical care*** —**medically** /ˈmedɪkli/ adv

medical² /ˈmedɪk(ə)l/ noun [C] *British* a complete examination of your body by a doctor=PHYSICAL

medication /ˌmedɪˈkeɪʃ(ə)n/ noun [C/U] drugs that you take to treat or cure an illness

medicinal /məˈdɪs(ə)nəl/ adj capable of treating an illness: *medicinal herbs*

medicine /ˈmed(ə)s(ə)n/ noun ★★
1 [C/U] a substance that you take to treat an illness: *cough medicine* ♦ *You have to **take** the **medicine** three times a day.*
2 [U] the study and practice of treating or preventing illnesses and injuries: *He went on to study medicine at Edinburgh University.*

> ### Words often used with **medicine**
> *Adjectives often used with **medicine** (sense 2)*
> ■ **alternative, complementary, conventional, herbal, traditional** + MEDICINE: used about different types of medicine

medieval /ˌmediˈiːv(ə)l/ adj relating to the period of European history between about the year 1000 AD and the year 1500 AD: *a medieval church*

mediocre /ˌmiːdiˈəʊkə/ adj not very good: *a mediocre performance* —**mediocrity** /ˌmiːdiˈɒkrəti/ noun [U]

meditate /ˈmedɪteɪt/ verb [I] to make your mind empty in order to relax, or as a religious exercise —**meditation** /ˌmedɪˈteɪʃ(ə)n/ noun [U]

Mediterranean /ˌmedɪtəˈreɪniən/ adj relating to the countries that surround the Mediterranean, or to the culture of the people in those countries

Mediterranean, the /ˌmedɪtəˈreɪniən/ **1** the sea that has Europe to the north and North

Africa to the south **2** the countries that surround the Mediterranean Sea

medium¹ /ˈmiːdiəm/ adj ★
1 between small and large in size or amount: *Use six medium tomatoes.* ♦ *medium-length blond hair* ♦ *She's slim, **of medium height**, with dark hair.*
2 neither light nor dark in colour: *medium-brown hair*

medium² /ˈmiːdiəm/ noun [C] ★
1 something such as a piece of clothing that is between small and large in size: *Have you got a medium in this style?*
2 (plural **media** /ˈmiːdiə/) a way of communicating information and ideas: *Patients can express their emotions through the medium of drama.*
3 someone who communicates with the spirits of dead people
→ MEDIA

medium-sized /ˌmiːdiəm ˈsaɪzd/ adj neither large nor small: *Use a medium-sized saucepan.* ♦ *a medium-sized business*

medium term, the noun [singular] the period of time that lasts a few months or years from now —**medium-term** adj: *the medium-term effects of the plan*

medium wave noun [U] a range of radio waves between 100 and 1000 metres in length, used for broadcasting → LONG WAVE, SHORT WAVE

medley /ˈmedli/ noun [C] **1** a piece of music that consists of tunes from other pieces of music **2** a mixture of things: *an interesting medley of flavours*

meek /miːk/ adj quiet, gentle, and easy to persuade —**meekly** adv

meet /miːt/ (past tense and past participle **met** /met/) verb ★★★

1 come together with sb	**6** do sth necessary
2 for discussions	**7** do sth planned
3 meet by accident	**8** of roads/lines
4 be introduced to sb	**9** look into sb's eyes
5 experience result	**+ PHRASAL VERBS**

1 [I/T] to come together in order to spend time with someone who you have arranged to see: *I'll meet you in the bar later.* ♦ *We're meeting for lunch tomorrow.* ♦ **meet to do sth** *Sally and I met after work to go and see a film.*
2 [I/T] to come together with other people in order to discuss something formally: *The president is meeting world leaders in Brussels.* ♦ **meet to do sth** *The council meets today to decide what action to take.*
3 [T] to see someone and speak to them without planning to: *You'll never guess who I met on the plane.*
4 [I/T] to be introduced to someone that you do not know: *Have you met my wife?* ♦ *I think they met at college.*
5 [T] to get a particular result or reaction: *The plans met strong opposition from local people.*
6 [T] to do what is necessary: *This technology can meet the challenges of the 21st century.*

M

♦ *The water won't* **meet the needs** *of the local population.*

7 [T] to do what you planned or promised to do=ACHIEVE: *Will the government be able to meet their spending targets?*

8 [I] if things such as roads or lines meet, they join each other: *The two rivers meet just north of the town.*

9 [I] if two people's eyes meet, they look directly into each other's eyes

PHRASAL VERBS **meet up** to come together with someone as you have planned to do: *We usually* **meet up** *for coffee after lunch.* **meet with sth** *same as* **meet 5**: *Experiments with the new drug have met with some success.*

meeting /ˈmiːtɪŋ/ noun [C] ★★★
1 an occasion when people come together in order to discuss things and make decisions: *We're* **holding a meeting** *for people who want to join the club.* ♦ *European leaders* **attended a meeting** *on air pollution.* ♦ *our* **meeting with** *the ambassador*
2 an occasion when two people meet
3 an occasion when two teams or players compete

megabyte /ˈmegəbaɪt/ noun [C] *computing* a unit for measuring the size of a computer's memory, equal to just over one million BYTES

megahertz /ˈmegəhɜːts/ (plural **megahertz**) noun [C] *computing* a unit for measuring the speed of a computer, equal to one million HERTZ

megalomaniac /ˌmegələʊˈmeɪniˌæk/ noun [C] someone who loves power over other people and always wants more of it

megaphone /ˈmegəfəʊn/ noun [C] a piece of equipment that is used for making your voice louder when you are talking to a crowd

melancholy /ˈmelənkəli/ noun [U] *literary* a feeling of being very sad and having no hope —**melancholy** adj: *a melancholy tone of voice*

melanin /ˈmelənɪn/ noun [U] a substance in your skin, eyes, and hair that gives them their colour

melanoma /ˌmeləˈnəʊmə/ noun [C] *medical* a serious type of skin cancer

melee /ˈmeleɪ/ noun [C] *literary* a noisy, confusing, or violent situation

mellow¹ /ˈmeləʊ/ adj **1** relaxed and satisfied **2** mellow colours are soft and warm **3** a mellow sound is soft, flowing, and pleasant **4** with a full pleasing taste

mellow² /ˈmeləʊ/ verb [I] if you mellow, you become gentler and wiser

melodic /məˈlɒdɪk/ adj pleasant to listen to

melodrama /ˈmelədrɑːmə/ noun [C/U] a story, play, or film in which the characters express extreme emotions

melodramatic /ˌmelədrəˈmætɪk/ adj *showing disapproval* behaving in a way that is too emotional or too serious

melody /ˈmelədi/ noun **1** [C] a tune or song **2** [C/U] *technical* the main tune in a piece of music

melon /ˈmelən/ noun [C/U] a large round fruit with orange, green, or white flesh —*picture* → C10

melt /melt/ verb ★
1 [I/T] to change a solid substance into a liquid, or to be changed from a solid into a liquid: *Melt the butter in a small saucepan.* ♦ *The ice will* **melt** *quickly in direct sunlight.*
2 [I] to disappear: *My fears melted when I saw his kind expression.*
3 [I/T] to make someone more sympathetic, or to become more sympathetic

meltdown /ˈmeltdaʊn/ noun [C/U] **1** a sudden complete failure of a company, organization, or system: *a global financial meltdown* **2** an accident in which nuclear fuel melts through its container

melting pot noun [C] a situation in which there are many different types of people or ideas existing together

member /ˈmembə/ noun [C] ★★★
1 someone who belongs to a group or an organization: *a trade union member* ♦ *She was the only* **member of** *the family who visited him.*
2 a plant or animal that belongs to a particular group of plants or animals: *members of the cat family*

Member of Parliament noun [C] a politician who represents people in a parliament

membership /ˈmembəʃɪp/ noun ★
1 [U] the fact of being a member of a club, organization, or group: *Several countries have applied for* **membership of** *the EU.*
2 [singular] the members of a club, organization, or group: *Our membership will vote on the proposal in May.*

membrane /ˈmembreɪn/ noun [C] a thin piece of skin inside your body

memento /məˈmentəʊ/ (plural **mementoes**) noun [C] an object that you keep to remind you of someone or something: *a memento of our trip*

memo /ˈmeməʊ/ noun [C] a short note about work that you send to someone that you work with

memoirs /ˈmemwɑːz/ noun [plural] a book that someone famous writes about their own experiences

memorabilia /ˌmem(ə)rəˈbɪliə/ noun [plural] objects that people collect because they are connected with someone famous or something interesting: *Beatles memorabilia*

memorable /ˈmem(ə)rəb(ə)l/ adj worth remembering, or easy to remember: *a memorable experience*

memorandum /ˌmeməˈrændəm/ noun [C] a short official note from someone in a government or organization

memorial /məˈmɔːriəl/ noun [C] a structure that is built to remind people of a famous person or event: *the Vietnam War Memorial* —**memorial** adj: *a memorial service/ceremony*

memorize /ˈmeməraɪz/ verb [T] to learn something so that can you remember it perfectly: *The children had memorized a poem.*

M

memory /ˈmem(ə)ri/ noun ★★★
1 [C] something that you remember: *What are your most vivid memories* (=very clear memories) *of that period?* ♦ *I have very fond memories of my childhood.*
2 [singular] the ability to remember things: *Your memory tends to get worse as you get older.* ♦ *I've never had a very good memory for names* (=I can't remember names very well).
3 [C] the part of a computer in which information is stored
PHRASES **do sth from memory** to do something that you remember learning in the past but have not done recently: *The three of us sang the whole song from memory.*
in memory of sb something that is done in memory of someone is done so that people will remember them

> ### Words often used with **memory**
> *Adjectives often used with **memory** (sense 1)*
> ■ **fond, happy, painful** + MEMORY: used about memories that make you feel happy or sad
> ■ **abiding, clear, distant, vague, vivid** + MEMORY: used about things that you remember well or badly
> *Verbs often used with **memory** (sense 1)*
> ■ **arouse, evoke, recall, rekindle, revive, stir, trigger** + MEMORY: make you remember something

men the plural of **man**
menace¹ /ˈmenəs/ noun **1** [C] someone or something that is dangerous or very annoying: *the growing menace of global pollution* **2** [U] a threatening quality or feeling
menace² /ˈmenəs/ verb [T] to threaten someone or something
menacing /ˈmenəsɪŋ/ adj intended to threaten someone: *a menacing look* —**menacingly** adv
mend¹ /mend/ verb [T] British to repair something that is broken or damaged: *Have you mended the gate?*
mend² /mend/ noun **be on the mend** to be getting better after an illness
menial /ˈmiːniəl/ adj menial work does not need much skill
meningitis /ˌmenɪnˈdʒaɪtɪs/ noun [U] medical a serious illness that affects your brain
menopause /ˈmenəpɔːz/ noun [singular] the time in a woman's life when her PERIODS stop and she is no longer capable of getting pregnant
menstrual /ˈmenstruəl/ adj relating to the time each month when a woman menstruates
menstruate /ˈmenstrueɪt/ verb [I] formal when a woman menstruates, blood flows out from her WOMB each month —**menstruation** /ˌmenstruˈeɪʃ(ə)n/ noun [U]
mental /ˈment(ə)l/ adj ★★
1 existing in the mind, or relating to the mind: *a child's mental development* ♦ *mental health/illness/problems*
2 offensive crazy or stupid

PHRASES **go mental** British informal to suddenly become extremely angry
make a mental note to pay special attention to something so that you will remember it —**mentally** adv: *mentally ill*
mentality /menˈtæləti/ noun [C] a particular way of thinking: *a destructive mentality*
mention¹ /ˈmenʃ(ə)n/ verb [T] ★★★ to refer to something, but not discuss it much: *He didn't mention her all evening.* ♦ **mention sth to sb** *I'll mention the problem to her.* ♦ **+(that)** *Did I mention that I've got a new job?*
PHRASES **don't mention it** spoken used as a polite answer to someone who has just thanked you for something
not to mention used for referring to something else that emphasizes what you have just said: *The fire caused terrible loss of life, not to mention all the damage to the buildings.*
mention² /ˈmenʃ(ə)n/ noun [singular/U] the act of referring to someone or something =REFERENCE: *There's no mention of these costs in the contract.*
mentor /ˈmentɔː/ noun [C] an experienced person who gives advice to someone with less experience —**mentoring** noun [U]
menu /ˈmenjuː/ noun [C] ★
1 a list of the food that is available in a restaurant: *Do you see anything you like on the menu?*
2 computing a list of choices on a computer screen: *the Edit menu*
MEP /ˌem iː ˈpiː/ noun [C] Member of the European Parliament: a politician who represents one of the regions of a country in the European Union
mercenary¹ /ˈmɜːs(ə)n(ə)ri/ adj showing disapproval interested only in the money or other personal advantages that you can get from something
mercenary² /ˈmɜːs(ə)n(ə)ri/ noun [C] a soldier who fights for any army that will pay him or her
merchandise /ˈmɜːtʃ(ə)nˌdaɪz/ noun [U] formal goods that people buy and sell
merchandising /ˈmɜːtʃ(ə)nˌdaɪzɪŋ/ noun [U] the business of selling products that are related to a popular film, television programme, sports team etc
merchant /ˈmɜːtʃ(ə)nt/ noun [C] formal a person or business that buys and sells goods
merchant bank noun [C] British a bank that provides financial services to companies, not to individual people —**merchant banker** noun [C], **merchant banking** noun [U]
merchant navy noun [U] British a country's ships that carry goods, not soldiers and weapons
merciful /ˈmɜːsɪf(ə)l/ adj **1** showing kindness, even when other people are unkind
2 making you feel grateful and lucky by ending something that is bad: *a merciful and painless death*
mercifully /ˈmɜːsɪf(ə)li/ adv used for saying that you feel grateful and lucky that something bad has ended

M

merciless /'mɜːsɪləs/ adj very cruel or severe: *a merciless beating* —**mercilessly** adv

mercury /'mɜːkjʊri/ noun [U] a silver liquid metal that is used in THERMOMETERS

mercy /'mɜːsi/ noun [U] the act of treating someone in a kind way when you could have punished them: *the mercy of God* — **PHRASE** **at the mercy of** in a situation that is controlled by someone or something that can harm you

mere /mɪə/ adj **1** used for emphasizing that something is small or unimportant: *Her comments are mere opinion, not fact.* **2** used for emphasizing the major effect of something that seems unimportant: *The mere fact that he came to see her made her happy.*

merely /'mɪəli/ adv **1** used for emphasizing that something is small or unimportant =ONLY: *This job is merely a way to pay my bills.* **2** used for emphasizing that something is not as bad, severe, or important as someone thinks it is =ONLY: *I'm not angry, I'm merely trying to explain it to you.*

merge /mɜːdʒ/ verb [I] **1** if two organizations merge, they combine to form one bigger organization: *Small publishers were forced to merge with larger companies.* **2** if two things merge, they combine so that you can no longer tell the difference between them: *The hills merged into the dark sky behind them.*

merger /'mɜːdʒə/ noun [C] *business* an occasion when two companies combine to form a bigger company

meridian /mə'rɪdiən/ noun [C] one of the lines on a map that goes around the Earth from the North Pole to the South Pole

meringue /mə'ræŋ/ noun [C/U] a sweet food made from a mixture of sugar and the white part of eggs

merit¹ /'merɪt/ noun [C/U] a good quality that makes you admire something: *Attention to detail is one of the great merits of the book.*

merit² /'merɪt/ verb [T] *formal* to deserve something: *The case merits further investigation.*

mermaid /'mɜːmeɪd/ noun [C] an imaginary sea creature that has the body of a woman and the tail of a fish

merrily /'merəli/ adv **1** in a happy or lively way **2** without knowing or thinking about any problems =GAILY

merry /'meri/ adj **1** *British informal* slightly drunk **2** *old-fashioned* happy and lively — **PHRASE** **Merry Christmas** used for wishing someone a happy time at Christmas

merry-go-round noun [C] a machine with models of animals that children ride on as it turns round

mesh¹ /meʃ/ noun [C/U] a piece of material that is like a net made of wires or strings

mesh² /meʃ/ verb [I] if two things or people mesh, they work well together

mesmerize /'mezmə,raɪz/ verb [T] to attract or interest you so much that you do not notice anything else

mess¹ /mes/ noun ★
1 [C/U] a situation in which a place is dirty, untidy, or in bad condition: *The garden was a real mess.* ♦ *Try not to make a mess because I've been cleaning.* ♦ *His papers were in a terrible mess.*
2 [singular] a difficult situation with a lot of problems: *an economic mess* ♦ *The company was in a complete mess.* ♦ *I don't know how we got into this mess.* ♦ *Tom felt he had made a mess of his life.*
3 [singular] *informal* someone who has so many problems that they cannot have a normal life: *I was a complete mess after the divorce.*
4 [C] a room where people have their meals in the armed forces

mess² /mes/ **PHRASAL VERB** **mess a'bout** or **mess a'round** *informal* **1** to behave in a silly way, or to waste time doing things that are not important: *We have to stop messing around, or we won't finish.* **2** to spend time doing things in a relaxed way: *We spent the weekend messing about on John's boat.*
mess sb a'bout or **mess sb a'round** *British informal* to treat someone badly by not doing what you promised
mess (sth) 'up to make a mistake, or to do something badly: *She says she messed up the interview.*
mess sth 'up 1 to make something dirty or untidy: *The wind had messed his hair up.* **2** to damage or spoil something: *I'm not going to let him mess up my life.*
mess with sth or **mess a'round with sth** *informal* to become involved with something that is dangerous: *A lot of the kids had been messing around with drugs.*

message /'mesɪdʒ/ noun ★★★
1 [C] a piece of written or spoken information that you give or send to someone: *I got your email message, thank you.* ♦ *If I'm not there, just leave a message with Chris.* ♦ *She's not here at the moment – can I take a message?*
2 [singular] the main idea that is contained in something such as a speech or an advertisement: *The film sends a clear message about the dangers of drug-taking.* — **PHRASE** **get the message** *informal* to understand what someone is trying to tell you

messaging /'mesɪdʒɪŋ/ noun [U] *computing* the process of sending and receiving electronic messages by computer or mobile phone

messenger /'mes(ə)ndʒə/ noun [C] someone who delivers messages to people

messiah /mə'saɪə/ noun **1** [C] someone who will save people from a difficult situation **2** [C] a religious leader who is sent by God to save the world **3 the Messiah** a name that Christians use for Jesus Christ

Messrs /'mesəz/ the plural of **Mr**

messy /'mesi/ adj **1** dirty or very untidy **2** complicated, difficult, and unpleasant to deal with: *a messy divorce/relationship*

met the past tense and past participle of **meet**

M

metabolism /mə'tæbə,lɪz(ə)m/ noun [C/U] the chemical processes in your body that change food and drink into energy —**metabolic** /,metə'bɒlɪk/ adj

metal /'met(ə)l/ noun [C/U] ★★★ a hard shiny substance such as steel or iron that is used to make things such as tools and machines: *a metal frame/bucket/rod*

metallic /me'tælɪk/ adj consisting of metal, or similar to metal

metamorphosis /,metə'mɔːfəsɪs/ (plural **metamorphoses** /,metə'mɔːfəsiːz/) noun [C/U] *formal* a major change that makes someone or something very different

metaphor /'metəfə, 'metəfɔː/ noun [C/U] a way of describing something in which you refer to it as something else with similar qualities: *Writers often use war as a metaphor for business activity and competition.* —**metaphorical** /,metə'fɒrɪk(ə)l/ adj, **metaphorically** /,metə'fɒrɪkli/ adv
→ SIMILE

metaphysical /,metə'fɪzɪk(ə)l/ adj relating to ideas about life, existence, and other things that are not part of the physical world

mete /miːt/ PHRASAL VERB **mete sth 'out** *formal* to give a punishment to someone

meteor /'miːtiə, 'miːtiɔː/ noun [C] a large piece of rock from space that appears as a bright light in the sky

meteoric /,miːti'ɒrɪk/ adj becoming very successful very quickly: *his meteoric political career*

meteorite /'miːtiə,raɪt/ noun [C] a piece of rock that has fallen from space and landed on the Earth

meteorology /,miːtiə'rɒlədʒi/ noun [U] the scientific study of weather —**meteorological** /,miːtiərə'lɒdʒɪk(ə)l/ adj, **meteorologist** noun [C]

meter¹ /'miːtə/ noun [C] **1** a piece of equipment for measuring how much electricity or gas you have used **2** a PARKING METER

meter² /'miːtə/ verb [T] to measure something with a meter

meter³ /'miːtə/ the American spelling of **metre**

methadone /'meθə,dəʊn/ noun [U] a strong drug that is often taken by people who want to stop using the drug HEROIN

methane /'miː,θeɪn/ noun [U] a gas with no colour or smell that is used as a fuel

method /'meθəd/ noun [C] ★★★ a way of doing something, especially a planned or established way: *a rug produced by traditional methods* ♦ *We developed new methods of pollution control.* ♦ **method of doing sth** *a reliable method of detecting breast cancer*

Words often used with **method**

Adjectives often used with method
■ **effective, efficient, good, reliable, successful** + METHOD: used about methods that achieve the result you want

Verbs often used with method
■ **adopt, apply, choose, employ, use** + METHOD: use a particular method to do something
■ **develop, devise, pioneer** + METHOD: invent a particular method of doing something

---

methodical /mə'θɒdɪk(ə)l/ adj always careful to do things in an organized way, or done in an organized way: *a methodical worker* —**methodically** /mə'θɒdɪkli/ adv

Methodist /'meθədɪst/ noun [C] a member of a Protestant Christian church that was formed by John Wesley in the 18th century —**Methodist** adj

methodology /,meθə'dɒlədʒi/ noun [C/U] *formal* the methods and principles that are used for doing research or other work —**methodological** /,meθədə'lɒdʒɪk(ə)l/ adj

meticulous /mɪ'tɪkjʊləs/ adj done with careful attention to detail: *a meticulous piece of research* —**meticulously** adv

metre /'miːtə/ noun [C] ★★★ a unit for measuring length in the METRIC SYSTEM, equal to 100 centimetres

metric /'metrɪk/ adj using or relating to the metric system of measurements
→ IMPERIAL 2

'metric ,system, the noun [singular] the system of measurement in which the basic units are metres and kilograms

metro /'metrəʊ/ noun [C] an underground railway system in a city

metropolis /mə'trɒpəlɪs/ noun [C] a big city

metropolitan /,metrə'pɒlɪt(ə)n/ adj belonging to a big city or typical of big cities: *the metropolitan area*

mg abbrev milligram

MHz abbrev megahertz

miaow /mjaʊ/ verb [I] if a cat miaows, it makes a short high sound —**miaow** noun [C]

mice the plural of **mouse**

mickey /'mɪki/ noun **take the mickey** *British informal* to say something funny in order to make someone seem silly

microbe /'maɪkrəʊb/ noun [C] a MICROORGANISM

microchip /'maɪkrəʊ,tʃɪp/ noun [C] a very small piece of SILICON that contains the electronic connections for making a computer work

microcosm /'maɪkrəʊ,kɒz(ə)m/ noun [C] *formal* something small that contains all the features of something larger

microorganism /,maɪkrəʊ'ɔːgənɪz(ə)m/ noun [C] a very small living thing that you can see only with a MICROSCOPE

microphone /'maɪkrə,fəʊn/ noun [C] a piece of equipment for making someone's voice louder when they are performing or recording something

microprocessor /'maɪkrəʊ,prəʊsesə/ noun [C] *computing* a piece of electronic equipment inside a computer that makes it work

microscope /'maɪkrə,skəʊp/ noun [C] a piece of scientific equipment for looking at things that are too small to see normally

microscopic /,maɪkrə'skɒpɪk/ adj very small: *microscopic life*

M

microwave¹ /ˈmaɪkrəˌweɪv/ or **microwave ˈoven** noun [C] an oven that cooks food very quickly by using ELECTROMAGNETIC waves rather than heat —*picture* → C2

microwave² /ˈmaɪkrəˌweɪv/ verb [T] to cook food in a microwave —**microwavable** adj

mid-ˈair noun in mid-air while someone or something is in the air
—**mid-ˈair** adj: *a mid-air collision*

midday /ˌmɪdˈdeɪ/ noun [U] 12 o'clock, when the morning ends and the afternoon begins
=NOON

middle¹ /ˈmɪdl/ noun ★★★
1 the middle [singular] the part of something that is furthest from the sides, edges, or ends =CENTRE: *a sheet with a blue stripe down the middle* ♦ *There was a large cat sitting in the middle of the road.*
2 the middle [singular] the part that is between the beginning and the end of a period of time or an event: *the middle of the 15th century* ♦ *He fell asleep in the middle of the film.*
3 [C] your waist and the part of your body around your waist: *Ben was holding a towel around his middle.*

PHRASES **in the middle of (doing) sth** busy doing something: *He was in the middle of cooking dinner when I arrived.*
in the middle of nowhere a long way from any town or city

middle² /ˈmɪdl/ adj ★★
1 nearest the centre: *The map's in the middle drawer.* ♦ *middle-income families*
2 between the beginning and end of something: *The middle section of the book deals with training a dog.*

middle-ˈaged adj no longer young but not yet old, usually between 40 and 60 years of age —**middle ˈage** noun [U]

Middle ˈAges, the the period in European history between about 1000 AD and 1500 AD

middle ˈclass noun **the middle class** or **the middle classes** the social class that consists mostly of educated people who have professional jobs and are neither very rich nor very poor → LOWER CLASS, UPPER CLASS, WORKING CLASS

middle-ˈclass adj belonging or relating to the middle class: *middle-class families*

Middle ˈEast, the the region of the world that consists of the countries east of the Mediterranean Sea and west of India

Middle ˈEngland noun [U] middle-class people in England who have conservative opinions about political and social issues

middle ˈground noun [singular/U] opinions and attitudes that most people agree with because they are not extreme: *a party that occupies the middle ground of politics*

middleman /ˈmɪdlˌmæn/ (plural **middlemen** /ˈmɪdlˌmen/) noun [C] **1** a person or company that buys things from producers and sells them to customers **2** someone who helps to arrange business deals and discussions between other people

middle ˈmanagement noun [U] *business*

managers who are in charge of parts of an organization and have less authority than senior managers —**middle ˈmanager** noun [C]

middle ˈname noun [C] a second name that some people have between their first name and their family name

middle-of-the-ˈroad adj not unusual or extreme

middle ˈschool noun [C/U] **1** a school in the UK for children between the ages of 8 and 12 **2** a school in the US for children between the ages of 11 and 14

midfield /ˈmɪdfiːld/ noun [U] the middle part of the field in football, HOCKEY, and other ball games

midfielder /ˈmɪdfiːldə/ noun [C] a player who plays in the midfield

midget /ˈmɪdʒɪt/ noun [C] *offensive* an adult who has not grown to a normal size. A more polite expression is **person of restricted growth**.

midnight /ˈmɪdˌnaɪt/ noun [U] ★ 12 o'clock at night

midriff /ˈmɪdrɪf/ noun [C] the front part of your body between your waist and your chest

midst /mɪdst/ noun **in the midst of sth** *formal* while something else is happening or affecting you: *The President went to China in the midst of a crisis at home.*

midsummer /ˌmɪdˈsʌmə/ noun [U] the middle part of summer, when the weather is usually hottest: *a midsummer morning*

midterm /ˌmɪdˈtɜːm/ adj happening in the middle part of a government's time in power or in the middle part of a school TERM: *midterm elections* ♦ *midterm examinations*

midway /ˌmɪdˈweɪ/ adj, adv **1** in a position that is HALFWAY between two places: *He stopped midway across the room.* **2** at a time in the middle of an event or period: *Our problems started midway through the first year.*

midweek /ˌmɪdˈwiːk/ adj, adv in the middle of the week, usually from Tuesday to Thursday: *a midweek game*

Midwest, the /ˌmɪdˈwest/ the states in the north central region of the US —**Midwestern** adj

midwife /ˈmɪdˌwaɪf/ (plural **midwives** /ˈmɪdˌwaɪvz/) noun [C] a nurse whose job is to look after women when they are having a baby

midwinter /ˌmɪdˈwɪntə/ noun [U] the middle part of winter, when the weather is usually coldest

miffed /mɪft/ adj *informal* slightly annoyed or offended

might¹ /maɪt/ modal verb ★★★

■ **Might** is usually followed by an infinitive without 'to': *I might change my mind.* Sometimes it is used without a following infinitive: *I don't think we'll need any more help, but we might.*

M

- **Might** has no tenses, no participles, and no infinitive form. It does not change its form, so the third person singular form does not end in '-s': *She might be late.*
- Questions and negatives are formed without 'do': *Might I make a suggestion?* ♦ *Your plan might not work.* The negative short form **mightn't** can also be used.

1 used for saying that there is a small possibility that something is true or will happen: *You never know what might happen in the future.* ♦ *I was afraid that someone might recognize me.* ♦ *Did you say anything that might have upset her?* ♦ *We **might just** get there in time if we hurry.*
2 *spoken* used for very politely asking permission to do something: *Might I ask the president a question?*
3 used as the past tense of 'may' when you are reporting what someone said: *Roger said they might not be able to come.*
PHRASES I might have known/guessed *British spoken* used for saying that you are not surprised at a situation: *I might have known he would be late.*
might have done sth used when something was possible but did not in fact happen: *With a bit more effort we might have won the match.*
might (just) as well *informal* **1** used for making a suggestion when you cannot think of anything better to do: *We might as well sit down while we're waiting.* **2** used for saying that it would not make any difference if you did something else: *The meeting was a complete waste of time. I might just as well have stayed at home.*

might² /maɪt/ noun [U] great power or strength

mightn't /ˈmaɪt(ə)nt/ short form the usual way of saying 'might not' in questions: *It might be nice to get out of the city for a while, mightn't it?*

mighty /ˈmaɪti/ adj very large, powerful, or impressive: *a mighty empire*

migraine /ˈmiːɡreɪn, ˈmaɪɡreɪn/ noun [C] a very severe HEADACHE

migrant /ˈmaɪɡrənt/ noun [C] someone who travels to another place in order to find work: *migrant workers/labourers*

migrate /maɪˈɡreɪt/ verb [I] **1** if a bird or animal migrates, it travels to another part of the world for warmer weather **2** to go to another place in order to find work —**migration** /maɪˈɡreɪʃ(ə)n/ noun [U]

mike /maɪk/ noun [C] *informal* a MICROPHONE

mild /maɪld/ adj ★
1 not strong, serious, or severe: *They were both suffering from a mild bout of flu.* ♦ *There was a note of mild alarm in her voice.* ♦ *a mild recession*
2 mild weather is warm and pleasant: *a mild winter*
3 without a strong taste: *a mild curry*
4 very gentle and not likely to have any bad effects: *a mild soap*

mildly /ˈmaɪldli/ adv slightly but not very:

Some of the stories were mildly amusing.
PHRASE to put it mildly *spoken* used for saying that the words you have chosen are not as extreme as they could have been: *The pay cut was unpopular, to put it mildly.*

mile /maɪl/ noun ★★★
1 [C] a unit for measuring distance, equal to 1.609 kilometres or 1760 YARDS: *We drove about 900 miles in two days.* ♦ *The island is 13 miles long.* ♦ *The car was travelling at 50 miles per hour.*
2 miles [plural] a long distance: *They live miles from the nearest town.* ♦ *The beach stretched for miles in each direction.*

mileage /ˈmaɪlɪdʒ/ noun **1** [singular/U] the number of miles that a vehicle has travelled: *a car with high mileage*
2 [singular/U] the number of miles that a vehicle can travel using one GALLON or one litre of petrol **3** [U] *informal* an advantage or opportunity that you get from something: *He has got a lot of mileage out of his friendship with the mayor.*

mileometer /maɪˈlɒmɪtə/ noun [C] *British* a piece of equipment fitted to a vehicle that shows how many miles the vehicle has travelled —*picture* → C6

milestone /ˈmaɪlstəʊn/ noun [C] an event or achievement that marks an important stage in a process

milieu /ˈmiːljɜː/ noun [C] *formal* the type of society that you live in, or the type of people that you spend time with

militant¹ /ˈmɪlɪtənt/ adj using violence or extreme methods in order to achieve political change: *The militant group claimed to have killed two soldiers.* —**militancy** noun [U]

militant² /ˈmɪlɪtənt/ noun [C] someone who uses militant methods to achieve something

military /ˈmɪlɪt(ə)ri/ adj ★★ relating to armed forces, or using armed forces: *military service* ♦ *The government is prepared to take military action.* ♦ *a huge military operation*

military, the /ˈmɪlɪt(ə)ri/ noun [singular] a country's armed forces: *The military does not have the weapons it needs to defeat the rebels.*

militia /məˈlɪʃə/ noun [C] a group of ordinary people who are trained as soldiers to fight in an emergency

milk¹ /mɪlk/ noun [U] ★★★
1 a white liquid that women and female animals produce to feed their babies. People drink the milk of cows, goats, and sheep and use it in cooking: *a carton/glass of milk*
2 a white liquid that some plants produce

milk² /mɪlk/ verb [T] **1** to take milk from a cow, goat, or sheep **2** to get a lot of personal advantage from something: *Both parties have milked the political situation for all it's worth.*

milkman /ˈmɪlkmən/ (plural **milkmen** /ˈmɪlkmən/) noun [C] a man whose job is to deliver milk to people's homes

M

milkshake /ˈmɪlkʃeɪk/ noun [C] a sweet drink made by mixing milk with chocolate or fruit

milky /ˈmɪlki/ adj **1** containing milk or a liquid that looks like milk: *milky drinks* **2** white like milk

mill¹ /mɪl/ noun [C] **1** a building with a machine that is used for crushing grain into flour **2** a factory where a product such as cotton, wool, or steel is made: *a textile mill* **3** a small machine or tool that you use in the kitchen for crushing substances into powder: *a coffee/pepper mill*

mill² /mɪl/ verb [T] to crush grain into flour

PHRASAL VERB ˌmill aˈround or ˌmill aˈbout *informal* to move about in large numbers in a confused way with no particular purpose

millennium /mɪˈleniəm/ (plural **millennia** /mɪˈleniə/) noun [C] a period of 1000 years —**millennial** adj

milligram /ˈmɪlɪˌɡræm/ noun [C] a unit for measuring weight. There are 1000 milligrams in a **gram**.

millilitre /ˈmɪlɪˌliːtə/ noun [C] a unit for measuring an amount of liquid. There are 1000 millilitres in a **litre**.

millimetre /ˈmɪlɪˌmiːtə/ noun [C] a unit for measuring length. There are 1000 millimetres in a **metre**.

million /ˈmɪljən/ number ★★ **1** the number 1,000,000 **2 millions** or **a million** a large number of people or things: *I've got a million things to do before I leave.* ♦ *They received **millions of** letters asking for information.* —**millionth** /ˈmɪljənθ/ number

millionaire /ˌmɪljəˈneə/ noun [C] someone who has more than a million pounds or dollars

millisecond /ˈmɪlɪˌsekənd/ noun [C] a unit for measuring extremely short periods of time. There are 1000 milliseconds in a second.

mime /maɪm/ verb [I/T] to tell a story using only the movements of your body and face, not using words —**mime** noun [U]

mimic¹ /ˈmɪmɪk/ (present participle **mimicking**; past tense and past participle **mimicked**) verb [T] to copy someone's voice, behaviour, or appearance=IMITATE: *She mimicked his accent.* —**mimicry** noun [U]

mimic² /ˈmɪmɪk/ noun [C] someone who is able to copy the voice, behaviour, or appearance of someone else

min abbrev **1** minute **2** minimum

mince¹ /mɪns/ verb [T] to cut meat into very small pieces using a machine

PHRASE **not mince (your) words** *informal* to say exactly what you think and not care about other people's reactions

mince² /mɪns/ noun [U] *British* meat that has been cut into very small pieces using a machine

mincemeat /ˈmɪnsˌmiːt/ noun [U] a sweet food made by mixing small pieces of DRIED FRUIT and SPICES

PHRASE **make mincemeat (out) of sb** *informal* to defeat someone thoroughly in a game, fight, or argument

mince ˈpie noun [C] a small PIE that is filled with mincemeat. People usually eat mince pies at Christmas.

mind¹ /maɪnd/ noun [C/U] ★★★ your thoughts and attention, or the part of you that thinks, knows, and remembers things: *You never know what's going on **in her mind**.* ♦ *I can't **keep my mind on** work when it's so sunny outside.* ♦ *She's never been able to **get him out of her mind** (*=stop thinking about him). ♦ *She shouldn't drive in her present **state of mind** (*=the way she is thinking and feeling). ♦ *Just try to **put** the problem **out of your mind**.* ♦ *A good night out will help you **take your mind off** your exams (*=help you to stop thinking about them).*

PHRASES **at the back of your mind** if something is at the back of your mind, you are not thinking about it now, but you still remember it or know about it: *At the back of her mind, she knew he was lying.*

be/go out of your mind *informal* to be/become crazy or confused: *You must be out of your mind to want to see him again.*

be in two minds (about sth) to not be certain about something, or to have difficulty in making a decision: *I'm in two minds about accepting the job.*

come/spring to mind if something comes to mind, you suddenly remember it or start to think about it

have sb/sth in mind to know the person or thing that you want: *Who do you have in mind for the job?*

have/keep an open mind to be willing to listen to other people's opinions: *I told the committee that I had an open mind on the matter.*

keep/bear sth in mind to remember or consider something: *Keep that in mind when you come to make your decision.*

keep sb in mind to remember someone because they might be suitable for something in the future: *Keep me in mind if you need some help.*

make up your mind to make a decision: *I can't make up my mind whether to go or not.* ♦ *My mind's made up. Nothing will make me change it.*

on your mind if something is on your mind, you are thinking or worrying about it: *She isn't usually so rude; she's got **a lot on her mind**.*

put your mind to sth to decide to do something and try very hard to achieve it

mind² /maɪnd/ verb ★★★ **1** [I/T] to feel annoyed, upset, or unhappy about something: *We had to cancel, but Rosa didn't seem to mind.* ♦ *I don't mind the heat (*=the heat is not a problem to me).* ♦ *I don't mind going to the shops (*=I'm willing to go) if no one else wants to.* ♦ *He won't mind if we're a bit late.* **2** [T] *British* to be careful about something: *Mind the step (*=do not fall over it).* ♦ *+(that) Mind you don't spill that drink.* **3** [T] *British* to look after someone or something for a short time: *Could you mind* *the children for me for five minutes?*

PHRASES **do you mind if I do sth?** used for politely asking someone's permission to do something

if you don't mind me/my saying so a polite way of saying that you hope someone is not offended by what you are saying: *You were a bit rude, if you don't mind me saying so.*

I wouldn't mind sth used for asking for something politely: *I wouldn't mind a cold drink if you've got one.*

mind your own business *spoken* a rude way of telling someone not to ask questions about something that you do not not want them to know about: *'Where do you think you're going?' 'Mind your own business!'*

never mind 1 *spoken* used for telling someone not to feel upset about something, because you do not think it is important enough to worry about: *'We've missed the show!' 'Never mind, we can go next week.'* **2** used for saying that you do not want to repeat something that you said, or that you want someone to ignore it: *Where's my hat? Oh, never mind, I found it!*

would you mind used for asking politely for something: *Would you mind if I brought a friend to the party?* ♦ **would you mind doing sth** *Would you mind closing that window?*

mind-blowing /ˈmaɪnd ˌbləʊɪŋ/ adj *informal* extremely impressive, exciting, or shocking

minder /ˈmaɪndə/ noun [C] *British* someone whose job is to protect someone else

mindful /ˈmaɪn(d)f(ə)l/ adj careful about something, or conscious of something: *Travellers ought to be mindful of their surroundings.*

mindless /ˈmaɪn(d)ləs/ adj **1** done without a reason, or without thinking about the results: *mindless vandalism* **2** not needing any thought or intelligence: *a mindless task*

mindset /ˈmaɪn(d)ˌset/ noun [C] a way of thinking about things: *The company will have to change its whole mindset if it is to survive.*

mine¹ /maɪn/ pronoun ★★★ used for referring to people or things that belong to you or are connected with you, when you are the person speaking or writing: *Can I borrow your keys? I can't find mine.* ♦ *This must be your T-shirt. Mine has stains on it.* ♦ *I got the idea from a friend of mine.*

mine² /maɪn/ noun [C] ★

1 a large hole or tunnel in the ground from which people take coal, gold etc

2 a bomb that is hidden under the ground or under water and explodes when it is touched

mine³ /maɪn/ verb **1** [I/T] to dig a large hole or tunnel in the ground in order to get coal, gold etc: *People still mine for coal in this area.* **2** [T] to hide bombs under the ground or under water

minefield /ˈmaɪnˌfiːld/ noun **1** [singular] a situation with many possible problems or

dangers: *The issue of tax cuts is a potential minefield for the government.* **2** [C] an area where bombs have been hidden under the ground or under water

miner /ˈmaɪnə/ noun [C] someone whose job is to dig coal from a mine

mineral /ˈmɪn(ə)rəl/ noun [C] **1** a natural substance in the earth, for example coal, salt, or gold **2** a natural substance in some foods that you need for good health, for example iron and CALCIUM

ˈmineral ˌwater noun [U] water that comes from under the ground and contains minerals

mingle /ˈmɪŋɡ(ə)l/ verb [I] **1** if things such as smells or feelings mingle, they become mixed together: *Polly felt hope mingled with fear.* **2** to move around and talk to a lot of people during a social event: *Try to get the guests to mingle.*

mini- /ˈmɪni/ prefix smaller or shorter than other things of the same kind: *a miniskirt*

miniature¹ /ˈmɪnətʃə/ adj much smaller than things of the same kind: *a miniature railway*

miniature² /ˈmɪnətʃə/ noun [C] a very small painting or photograph

PHRASE **in miniature** the same in appearance as someone or something else but much smaller

minibar /ˈmɪniˌbɑː/ noun [C] a small cupboard of alcoholic drinks for guests in a hotel room

minibus /ˈmɪniˌbʌs/ noun [C] a small bus for about 10 to 15 people —*picture* → C7

minicab /ˈmɪniˌkæb/ noun [C] *British* a car that is used as a taxi. You must call for it by telephone and you cannot stop it in the street.

minimal /ˈmɪnɪm(ə)l/ adj extremely small in amount or degree: *a minimal increase* ♦ *minimal damage* —**minimally** adv

minimalism /ˈmɪnɪm(ə)lˌɪz(ə)m/ noun [U] a style of art that developed in the 1960s and uses a small number of simple shapes and colours

minimalist /ˈmɪnɪməlɪst/ adj relating to minimalism

minimize /ˈmɪnɪˌmaɪz/ verb [T] **1** to make the amount of something bad as small as possible ≠ MAXIMIZE: *We must minimize the damage to innocent civilians.* **2** to make something seem much less important than it really is ≠ EXAGGERATE: *I don't want to minimize their role in the campaign.* **3** to make a computer program appear as only a small picture on your computer screen when you are not using it

minimum¹ /ˈmɪnɪməm/ adj ★★ as small in amount or degree as possible ≠ MAXIMUM: *the minimum voting age* ♦ *the minimum requirements for entry to college*

minimum² /ˈmɪnɪməm/ noun [singular] ★ the smallest amount or degree of something that is necessary or possible ≠ MAXIMUM: *The project will take a minimum of six weeks.* ♦ **keep sth to a minimum** *We need to keep costs to a minimum.*

M

minimum wage noun [singular/U] the smallest amount of money that an employer is legally allowed to pay a worker

mining /ˈmaɪnɪŋ/ noun [U] the process of getting coal, gold etc from under the ground

miniskirt /ˈmɪniˌskɜːt/ noun [C] a very short skirt

minister /ˈmɪnɪstə/ noun [C] ★★
1 an official who is in charge of a government department in the UK and in other countries: *a meeting of trade ministers* ♦ *the Minister for Education*
2 a priest in some Protestant churches

ministerial /ˌmɪnɪˈstɪəriəl/ adj relating to the job of being a government minister: *ministerial powers/colleagues/meetings*

ministry /ˈmɪnɪstri/ noun ★★
1 [C] a government department in the UK and in other countries: *the Dutch foreign ministry* ♦ *the Ministry of Defence*
2 the ministry [singular] the profession or work of a church MINISTER

minivan /ˈmɪniˌvæn/ noun [C] a small van with seats for about eight people

mink /mɪŋk/ noun [C/U] a small animal that is kept for its thick dark fur, or the fur of this animal

minnow /ˈmɪnəʊ/ noun [C] a small fish that lives in rivers and lakes

minor¹ /ˈmaɪnə/ adj ★★
1 not very important in comparison with people or things of the same type: *The damage here was only minor.* ♦ *a minor crime/offence* ♦ *Some minor changes may be necessary.*
2 relating to one of the two types of musical KEYS (=set of notes)
→ MAJOR

minor² /ˈmaɪnə/ noun [C] legal a young person who is not yet an adult, according to the law

minority¹ /maɪˈnɒrəti/ noun [C] ★★
1 a group of people or things that forms less than half of a larger group ≠ MAJORITY: *In a small minority of cases, the treatment does not help.* ♦ *Women are in the minority in the top ranks of government.*
2 a part of a population that is different in race, religion, or culture from most of the population: *The regulations are intended to prevent discrimination against minorities.* ♦ *Members of ethnic minorities are represented on the committee.* ♦ *a religious minority*

minority² /maɪˈnɒrəti/ adj **1** relating to a minority or forming a minority: *They hold a minority interest in the company.*
2 belonging to a RACIAL minority: *kids from minority backgrounds*

mint¹ /mɪnt/ noun **1** [U] a small plant with green leaves that have a strong smell and a cool pleasant taste **2** [C] a sweet with a strong fresh taste **3** [C] the place where a country makes its coins

mint² /mɪnt/ verb [T] to make a coin from metal

minus¹ /ˈmaɪnəs/ grammar word ★

Minus can be:
■ a **preposition**: *17 minus 9 is 8.*
■ an **adjective**: *It was minus 12 degrees this morning.*

1 used in mathematics for showing that you are taking one number from another. This word is usually represented by the symbol − ≠ PLUS: *72 minus 5 equals 67.*
2 used before a number to show that a number or temperature is less than zero: *The temperature fell to minus 15 degrees last night.*
3 informal without something that you had in the past or usually have: *Anthony returned to work minus his beard.*
PHRASE A minus/B minus etc marks given for students' work that are lower than the marks A, B etc. These marks are usually written 'A-', 'B-' etc.

minus² /ˈmaɪnəs/ noun [C] informal a disadvantage: *Before I decide, I need to weigh up all the pluses and minuses.*

minuscule /ˈmɪnəˌskjuːl/ adj extremely small in size or amount: *The risk to public health is minuscule.*

minus sign noun [C] the symbol −

minute¹ /ˈmɪnɪt/ noun [C] ★★★
1 a period of 60 seconds. There are 60 minutes in one hour: *I'll meet you downstairs in ten minutes.* ♦ *The train leaves at six minutes past ten.*
2 informal a very short period of time: *It will only take a minute.* ♦ *For a minute I thought she had left.* ♦ *I'll be ready in a minute* (=very soon). ♦ *Within minutes I realized I was on the wrong train.*
PHRASES any minute very soon: *Jack should be here any minute.*
the last minute the latest possible time for doing something: *Jane always waits until the last minute to write her paper.*
the minute you do sth as soon as you do something: *Please call me the minute you get home.*
this minute informal immediately: *Turn off that television this minute!*
wait/just a minute spoken **1** used for asking someone to wait or be patient: *Just a minute, sir, and I'll take your order.* **2** used when you are about to disagree with what someone has said: *Wait a minute – that can't be right.*

minute² /maɪˈnjuːt/ adj **1** very small: *The soil contained minute quantities of uranium.*
2 very careful and detailed: *a minute examination of the evidence*

minutes /ˈmɪnɪts/ noun [plural] an official written record of the decisions that people make at a formal meeting: *Carl usually takes the minutes but he's not here tonight.*

miracle /ˈmɪrək(ə)l/ noun [C] **1** something that is extremely lucky and that would not normally be possible: *It's a miracle that no one was killed.* **2** an event that cannot be explained according to the laws of nature and is considered to be an act of God

PHRASE perform/work miracles to achieve extremely impressive results

miraculous /mə'rækjʊləs/ adj extremely lucky and unexpected —**miraculously** adv

mirage /'mɪrɑːʒ/ noun [C] a strange effect in a desert in which you see something that is not really there

mirror¹ /'mɪrə/ noun [C] ★★ a piece of special glass in which you can see yourself or what is behind you: *a bathroom mirror* ♦ *Rachel looked at herself in the mirror.*

mirror² /'mɪrə/ verb [T] to match or express the qualities, features, or feelings of someone or something

mirth /mɜːθ/ noun [U] *literary* happy laughter

misapprehension /ˌmɪsæprɪ'henʃ(ə)n/ noun [C] *formal* a belief that is not correct

misbehave /ˌmɪsbɪ'heɪv/ verb [I] to behave badly

misbehavior /ˌmɪsbɪ'heɪvjə/ the American spelling of **misbehaviour**

misbehaviour /ˌmɪsbɪ'heɪvjə/ noun [U] bad behaviour

misc. abbrev miscellaneous

miscalculate /ˌmɪs'kælkjʊˌleɪt/ verb [I/T] 1 to make a mistake in calculating numbers 2 to make a wrong judgment about what will happen or what to do in a situation —**miscalculation** /ˌmɪskælkjʊ'leɪʃ(ə)n/ noun [C/U]

miscarriage /'mɪskærɪdʒ/ noun [C/U] the process of giving birth to a baby before it has developed enough to live

PHRASE miscarriage of justice a situation in which a court of law punishes someone for a crime that they did not commit

miscarry /ˌmɪs'kæri/ verb [I/T] to give birth to a baby before it has developed enough to live

miscellaneous /ˌmɪsə'leɪniəs/ adj consisting of various kinds of people or things

mischief /'mɪstʃɪf/ noun [U] behaviour or play, especially of children, that causes trouble but not serious harm

mischievous /'mɪstʃɪvəs/ adj a mischievous person, especially a child, enjoys having fun by causing trouble —**mischievously** adv

misconception /ˌmɪskən'sepʃ(ə)n/ noun [C/U] a wrong belief or opinion that is the result of not understanding something

misconduct /ˌmɪs'kɒndʌkt/ noun [U] *formal* bad or dishonest behaviour by someone who has a position of responsibility

misdeed /ˌmɪs'diːd/ noun [C] *formal* an action that is wrong or illegal

misdemeanor /ˌmɪsdɪ'miːnə/ the American spelling of **misdemeanour**

misdemeanour /ˌmɪsdɪ'miːnə/ noun [C] *formal* an action that is bad or wrong, but not in a serious way

miserable /'mɪz(ə)rəb(ə)l/ adj 1 extremely unhappy: *He looked cold and miserable.* 2 making you feel very unhappy: *The weather was miserable.* 3 a miserable amount of something is very small and not enough —**miserably** adv

misery /'mɪzəri/ noun [U] the state of being

extremely unhappy or uncomfortable

PHRASES make sb's life a misery *British* to cause someone to suffer or be unhappy for a long period

put sb/sth out of their misery 1 to end the life of an animal that is suffering 2 *humorous* to tell someone something that they are very keen to know, so that they stop worrying about it

misfire /mɪs'faɪə/ verb [I] 1 if a plan or activity misfires, it does not have the result that you wanted 2 if a gun misfires, the bullet does not come out

misfit /'mɪsfɪt/ noun [C] someone who does not seem to belong to a group, or who is not accepted by a group

misfortune /mɪs'fɔːtʃ(ə)n/ noun [C/U] bad luck, or a situation in which you have bad luck

misgiving /mɪs'gɪvɪŋ/ noun [C/U] a feeling of doubt about whether something is right or will have a good result: *Richard expressed grave misgivings about the deal.*

misguided /mɪs'gaɪdɪd/ adj based on judgments or opinions that are wrong

mishandle /mɪs'hænd(ə)l/ verb [T] to deal with a situation or process badly

mishap /'mɪshæp/ noun [C/U] a minor mistake or accident

mishmash /'mɪʃmæʃ/ noun [singular] *informal* an untidy or confused mixture of different things

misinform /ˌmɪsɪn'fɔːm/ verb [T] to give someone false or incorrect information —**misinformation** /ˌmɪsɪnfə'meɪʃ(ə)n/ noun [U]

misinterpret /ˌmɪsɪn'tɜːprɪt/ verb [T] to understand or explain something wrongly —**misinterpretation** /ˌmɪsɪntɜːprɪ'teɪʃ(ə)n/ noun [C/U]

misjudge /mɪs'dʒʌdʒ/ verb [T] 1 to make a wrong judgment about a person or situation 2 to make a mistake in calculating something —**misjudgment** noun [C/U]

mislay /mɪs'leɪ/ (past tense and past participle **mislaid** /mɪs'leɪd/) verb [T] to lose something for a short time, because you cannot remember where you put it

mislead /mɪs'liːd/ (past tense and past participle **misled** /mɪs'led/) verb [T] to make someone believe something that is incorrect or not true

misleading /mɪs'liːdɪŋ/ adj intended or likely to make someone believe something that is incorrect or not true: *He had made misleading statements to the committee.*

mismanagement /mɪs'mænɪdʒmənt/ noun [U] the process of managing something badly: *the mismanagement of public funds* —**mismanage** verb [T]

mismatch /'mɪsmætʃ/ noun [C] a difference or disagreement between two facts or two aspects of a situation

misnomer /mɪs'nəʊmə/ noun [C] a name or description that is incorrect or unsuitable

misogynist /mɪ'sɒdʒənɪst/ noun [U] a man who hates women

misplaced /ˌmɪs'pleɪst/ adj a misplaced feeling or opinion is not suitable for a particular situation, or is directed towards

M

the wrong person: *misplaced fears/ loyalty/trust*

misprint /ˈmɪsˌprɪnt/ noun [C] a mistake such as a wrong spelling in a book, newspaper etc

mispronounce /ˌmɪsprəˈnaʊns/ verb [T] to pronounce a word wrongly

misquote /mɪsˈkwəʊt/ verb [T] to report wrongly what someone said or wrote

misread /mɪsˈriːd/ (past tense and past participle **misread** /mɪsˈred/) verb [T] **1** to read something wrongly **2** to understand or judge a person or situation wrongly

misrepresent /ˌmɪsreprɪˈzent/ verb [T] to deliberately give a false or incorrect description of someone or something —**misrepresentation** /mɪsˌreprɪzenˈteɪʃ(ə)n/ noun [C/U]

miss¹ /mɪs/ verb ★★★

1 not reach	5 opportunity/chance
2 not be present at	6 avoid sth bad
3 be too late for	7 feel sad about
4 not notice/understand	+ PHRASAL VERBS

M

1 [I/T] to fail to catch, hit, or reach something: *I tried to catch the ball but missed.* ♦ *An official said that the missiles had missed their targets.* —picture → C14

2 [T] to fail to be present for someone or something: *I had to miss a week of school.* ♦ *We must have missed each other by about an hour.* ♦ *I wouldn't miss your party for the world* (=I really want to go to it).

3 [T] to be too late for something such as a train or bus: *I missed the last train home again.* ♦ *If you don't go now you'll miss the post.*

4 [T] to fail to notice or understand something: *I missed most of what she said.* ♦ *Sue had missed the point* (=not understood what someone meant) *entirely.* ♦ *The house is next to the station – you can't miss it* (=it is very easy to notice).

5 [T] to fail to take advantage of an opportunity: *She realized she had missed a chance to speak to Brian.*

6 [T] to escape something that is unpleasant or uncomfortable: *If I leave at eight, I miss the traffic.*

7 [T] to feel sad because someone is not with you any longer, or because you do not have or cannot do something any longer: *We miss him enormously.* ♦ *I'm missing our lunchtime drinks on Friday.* ♦ **miss doing sth** *I miss watching her ride her horse.*

PHRASAL VERBS **miss 'out** to lose an opportunity to do or have something: *We will be repeating the questions later, so you won't miss out.* ♦ *Come with us or you'll miss out on all the fun.*

ˌmiss sth 'out *British* to fail to include someone or something: *An important fact had been missed out.*

miss² /mɪs/ noun **1 Miss** a title used in front of the last name or whole name of a girl or woman who is not married → MRS, MS **2** *formal* used for talking politely to a girl or young

woman whose name you do not know **3** *British* a title used by children when talking to a woman teacher **4** [C] a failure to hit or catch something, or to score in a game

PHRASE **give sth a miss** *British informal* to decide not to do something that you usually do

missile /ˈmɪsaɪl, ˈmɪs(ə)l/ noun [C] **1** a weapon that travels long distances and explodes when it hits something: *a nuclear missile* → BALLISTIC MISSILE, CRUISE MISSILE **2** an object that is thrown or fired at someone or something

missing /ˈmɪsɪŋ/ adj ★★

1 if someone or something is missing, they are not where they should be and you do not know where they are: *We need to look to see if anything is missing.* ♦ *a missing dog* ♦ *The young woman's boyfriend had already reported her missing.* ♦ *Important documents have mysteriously gone missing.* ♦ *The key was missing from its usual place.*

2 if someone or something is missing, they are not included in something although you would expect them to be there: *Candidates' names were missing from ballot papers.*

3 not found after a battle or accident, but not known to be dead or taken prisoner: *Five other passengers are missing, presumed dead.* ♦ *Over 8,000 American soldiers are listed as missing in action.*

mission /ˈmɪʃ(ə)n/ noun

1 important work	4 flight into space
2 group sent to do sth	5 important aim
3 military operation	6 religious work

1 [C] an important piece of work that a person or group of people has to do for a government or large organization, especially one that involves travel: *a fact-finding/rescue mission* **2** [C] a group of people who have been sent to do an important piece of work: *members of the trade mission to Russia* **3** [C] a military operation, especially one by aircraft: *He was shot down during a mission over the Balkans.* **4** [C] a flight into space: *the possibility of a manned mission to Mars* **5** [singular] an aim that is very important to a person or organization: *Helping homeless people was Gina's mission in life.* ♦ *a mission statement* **6** [C/U] the work of religious people who go to other countries in order to make people believe in their religion, or the building where they do this

missionary /ˈmɪʃ(ə)n(ə)ri/ noun [C] someone who has been sent to a foreign country by a religious organization to teach people about a particular religion

ˈmission ˌstatement noun [C] a short official statement that an organization makes about the work it does and why it does it

misspell /mɪsˈspel/ verb [T] to spell a word wrongly —**misspelling** noun [C/U]

mist¹ /mɪst/ noun [C/U] a mass of small drops of water in the air close to the ground → FOG¹

mist² /mɪst/ or ,**mist 'up** verb [I] to become covered with small drops of water

mistake¹ /mɪˈsteɪk/ noun [C] ★★
1 something that you have not done correctly, or something you say or think that is not correct: *spelling/grammar mistakes*
2 something that you do that you later wish you had not done, because it causes a lot of problems: *You're **making a big mistake**.* ♦ **it would be a mistake to do sth** *It would be a mistake to think that the trouble is over.* ♦ **make the mistake of doing sth** *I made the mistake of inviting Jennifer to the party.* **PHRASE** **by mistake** if you do something by mistake, you do it accidentally =BY ACCIDENT ≠ ON PURPOSE: *I'm sorry, I opened one of your letters by mistake.*

> **Words often used with mistake**
>
> *Adjectives often used with **mistake** (noun, sense 2)*
>
> ■ **bad, big, costly, dreadful, expensive, fatal, serious, terrible** + **MISTAKE**: used about mistakes that have bad results

mistake² /mɪˈsteɪk/ (past tense **mistook** /mɪˈstʊk/; past participle **mistaken** /mɪˈsteɪkən/) verb [T] to not understand something correctly: *I'm afraid I mistook the nature of our relationship.*
PHRASAL VERB **mi'stake sb/sth for sb/sth** to think that a person or thing is someone or something else: *I had mistaken friendship for love.*

mistaken /mɪˈsteɪkən/ adj **1** if someone is mistaken, they are wrong about something: *If you think I'm going to help, you're sadly mistaken.* **2** a mistaken belief, idea, opinion etc is not correct —**mistakenly** adv: *He mistakenly believed that she was married.*

mister /ˈmɪstə/ *American spoken* used for talking to a man whose name you do not know

mistletoe /ˈmɪs(ə)lˌtəʊ/ noun [U] a plant with small white fruits. It is often used as a Christmas decoration.

mistook the past tense of **mistake²**

mistreat /mɪsˈtriːt/ verb [T] to treat someone in an unfair or cruel way: *She felt she had been mistreated by the police.* —**mistreatment** noun [U]

mistress /ˈmɪstrəs/ noun [C] a woman who is having a sexual relationship with a married man

mistrust /mɪsˈtrʌst/ noun [singular/U] a feeling that you should not trust someone or something: *Many voters have a deep mistrust of the government.* —**mistrust** verb [T]

misty /ˈmɪsti/ adj it is misty when a mass of small drops of water is in the air close to the ground

misunderstand /ˌmɪsʌndəˈstænd/ (past tense and past participle **misunderstood** /ˌmɪsʌndəˈstʊd/) verb [I/T] to not understand someone or something correctly: *I think he has misunderstood the nature of the problem.*

misunderstanding /ˌmɪsʌndəˈstændɪŋ/ noun

1 [C/U] a failure to understand someone or something correctly: *There's been a misunderstanding: Mr Jones isn't expecting you until tomorrow.* **2** [C] an argument that is not very serious

misunderstood¹ /ˌmɪsʌndəˈstʊd/ adj if someone or something is misunderstood, people do not realize what they are really like

misunderstood² the past tense and past participle of **misunderstand**

misuse /mɪsˈjuːs/ noun [C/U] the use of something in the wrong way or for the wrong purpose: *a misuse of government money* —**misuse** /mɪsˈjuːz/ verb [T]

mite /maɪt/ noun [C] **1** a very small insect that lives in foods, on plants, or on animals **2** *spoken* a young child or animal that you feel sorry for
PHRASE **a mite** *old-fashioned* slightly: *He looked a mite upset.*

mitigate /ˈmɪtɪˌɡeɪt/ verb [T] *formal* to reduce the harmful effects of something —**mitigation** /ˌmɪtɪˈɡeɪʃ(ə)n/ noun [U]

mitigating /ˈmɪtɪˌɡeɪtɪŋ/ adj **mitigating circumstances** facts which help to explain a crime or mistake and make it seem less bad

mitt /mɪt/ noun [C] a baseball GLOVE, used for catching the ball

mitten /ˈmɪt(ə)n/ noun [C] a type of GLOVE with one part for your thumb and another part for your fingers —*picture* → C4

mix¹ /mɪks/ verb ★★
1 [I/T] to combine two or more substances so that they become a single substance: *Add the eggs and mix thoroughly.* ♦ *Oil and water don't mix.* ♦ **mix sth with sth** *Mix the flour with the eggs and butter.* ♦ **mix sth together** *Mix the paint and water together.* —*picture* → C2
2 [T] to make something by combining two or more substances: *Phil was mixing a cocktail.*
3 [T] to combine things such as activities, ideas, or styles: *In this room, antique and modern furniture have been successfully mixed.* ♦ **mix sth with sth** *Their mood was one of relief mixed with sadness.*
4 [I] to meet other people in social situations and talk to them: *The party gave me a chance to mix with the other students.*
PHRASAL VERBS ,**mix sb 'up** to think that someone or something is another person or thing: *They look so alike that it's easy to mix them up.* ♦ *I think I'm mixing him up with someone else.*
,**mix sth 'up** to put things together without any order: *I sorted all the papers and you've mixed them up again.*

mix² /mɪks/ noun **1** [singular] a combination of different types of people or things: *There was a good mix of people at the party.* **2** [C/U] a powder that you buy and mix with liquid to make a particular type of food: *a cake mix*

mixed /mɪkst/ adj ★
1 consisting of different things: *a mixed salad*

2 involving people of different ages, abilities, races etc: *a mixed population* ♦ *students of mixed abilities* ♦ *a mixed marriage*

3 for men and women, or for boys and girls: *Lucy goes to a mixed school.*

4 partly good and partly bad: *Reactions to the new policy have been mixed.* ♦ *mixed reviews of the new film*

PHRASE **mixed feelings/emotions** mixed feelings or emotions make you not certain how you feel about someone or something

,**mixed 'blessing** noun [C] something that has both advantages and disadvantages

,**mixed-'race** adj involving people of different races: *mixed-raced marriage* ♦ *a mixed-race child* (=with parents who are different races)

,**mixed 'up** adj **1** confused: *I got mixed up with the dates and went on the wrong day.*

2 *informal* someone who is mixed up has a lot of emotional problems

PHRASES **be/get mixed up in sth** *informal* to be or become involved in something bad or embarrassing

be/get mixed up with sb *informal* to spend time with someone who has a bad influence on you

mixer /ˈmɪksə/ noun [C] **1** a machine that mixes something: *a cement mixer* **2** a drink without alcohol that you mix with an alcoholic drink

mixture /ˈmɪkstʃə/ noun ★★

1 [singular] a combination of two or more different people or things: *Her face showed a mixture of fear and excitement.* ♦ *a mixture of volunteers and paid staff*

2 [C/U] a substance such as food that is the result of mixing different things: *Spoon the mixture into the cake tins.*

,**mix-'up** noun [C] *informal* a mistake or problem that happens because someone is confused about details

ml abbrev millilitre

mm abbrev millimetre

moan¹ /məʊn/ verb [I/T] **1** to complain about something in an annoying way **2** to make a long low sound because of pain, sadness, or pleasure —**moaner** noun [C]

moan² /məʊn/ noun [C] a long low sound that you make because of pain, sadness, or pleasure

moat /məʊt/ noun [C] a deep wide hole filled with water that surrounds a castle

mob¹ /mɒb/ noun [C] **1** a large crowd of people that is dangerous or difficult to control **2** the **Mob** *informal* the MAFIA

mob² /mɒb/ verb [T] if a large group of people mob someone or something, they surround them in an angry or excited way

mobile¹ /ˈməʊbaɪl, ˈməʊb(ə)l/ adj ★

1 easily moved	**4** owning vehicle
2 contained in vehicle	**5** changing job/class
3 able to move	**6** relating to phones

1 easy to move and use in different places: *a mobile X-ray unit*

2 a mobile shop, library etc is in a vehicle so that it can be moved from one place to another

3 able to move and walk: *He's got a broken leg and isn't very mobile.*

4 able to travel from one place to another because you have a vehicle

5 able to move easily from one job, social class, or place to another

6 *British* relating to MOBILE PHONES: *Mobile communications can now reach any part of the planet.*

mobile² /ˈməʊbaɪl/ noun [C] **1** *British* a MOBILE PHONE **2** a decoration with parts that hang down and move in the air

,**mobile 'home** noun [C] *British* a large CARAVAN that people live in as their home

,**mobile 'phone** noun [C] *British* a small phone that you can carry around with you =MOBILE —*picture* → C3

mobility /məʊˈbɪləti/ noun [U] **1** the ability to move a part of your body **2** the ability to travel from one place to another **3** the tendency to move between places, jobs, or social classes

mobilize /ˈməʊbəlaɪz/ verb [I/T] **1** to bring together a large group of people, or to be brought together, in order to achieve something **2** to prepare an army to fight a war, or to be prepared to do this —**mobilization** /ˌməʊbəlaɪˈzeɪʃ(ə)n/ noun [U]

mobster /ˈmɒbstə/ noun [C] a member of the MAFIA

mocha /ˈmɒkə/ noun [C/U] a drink made by mixing coffee and chocolate together, or a cup of this drink

mock¹ /mɒk/ adj **1** not real but intended to look or seem real =FAKE **2** a mock feeling is one that you pretend to have, usually as a joke **3** a mock test, interview etc is one that you do in order to practise for a real one

mock² /mɒk/ verb [I/T] to make someone or something look stupid by laughing at them or copying them

mock³ /mɒk/ noun [C] *British* an examination that you do for practice before an important examination

mockery /ˈmɒkəri/ noun [U] remarks or behaviour intended to make someone seem stupid

PHRASE **make a mockery of** to make someone or something seem stupid or useless

mockup /ˈmɒkʌp/ noun [C] a model of something that is the same size as the real thing

,**modal 'verb** or ,**modal aux'iliary** or ,**modal** /ˈməʊd(ə)l/ noun [C] *linguistics* a verb such as 'can', 'may', 'should' etc that is used with another verb to express ideas such as possibility, permission, or intention

mode /məʊd/ noun [C] **1** a particular way of doing something **2** one of a series of ways that a machine can be made to work

model¹ /ˈmɒd(ə)l/ noun [C] ★★★

1 small copy of sth	**4** for artist
2 good example	**5** type of vehicle etc
3 sb who shows clothes	

1 a small copy of something such as a building, vehicle, or machine: *a model of the Eiffel Tower*

2 someone or something that is such a good example of a particular quality or method that people should copy them: *Daisy was a model of good manners.* ♦ *The school was a model of excellence.* ♦ *The system has been used as a model for other organizations.*

3 someone whose job is to show clothes, MAKE-UP etc by wearing them at FASHION SHOWS or for magazine photographs: *a fashion model*

4 someone whose job is to be drawn or painted by an artist or photographed by a photographer

5 a particular type of vehicle or machine that a company makes: *Fiat launched a new model last week.*

model² /ˈmɒd(ə)l/ (present participle **modelling**; past tense and past participle **modelled**) verb
1 [I/T] to show clothes by wearing them at FASHION SHOWS, in magazine photographs etc, especially as a job **2** [T] to copy a method or system: *Their economic structure is closely modelled on the British system.* **3** [I] to allow an artist or photographer to draw, paint, or photograph you, especially as your job

PHRASE **model yourself on sb** to copy the way someone behaves because you admire them

model³ /ˈmɒd(ə)l/ adj **1** a model railway, aircraft, boat etc is a small copy of a real one **2** a model student, husband etc behaves in the way a perfect student, husband etc would behave

modeling /ˈmɒd(ə)lɪŋ/ an American spelling of **modelling**

modelling /ˈmɒd(ə)lɪŋ/ noun [U] the job of working as a fashion model

modem /ˈməʊˌdem/ noun [C] *computing* a piece of equipment that allows you to connect a computer to a telephone line

moderate¹ /ˈmɒd(ə)rət/ adj **1** neither very big nor very small in amount, size, strength, or degree: *Cook the spinach over a moderate heat.* ♦ *a moderate increase in house prices* **2** reasonable and avoiding extreme opinions or actions: *a moderate political party* ♦ *The tone of his speech was quite moderate.*
—**moderately** /ˈmɒd(ə)rətli/ adv

moderate² /ˈmɒdəˌreɪt/ verb [I/T] to make something less extreme, or to become less extreme

moderate³ /ˈmɒd(ə)rət/ noun [C] someone whose opinions and actions are reasonable and not extreme, especially in politics

moderation /ˌmɒdəˈreɪʃ(ə)n/ noun [U] sensible behaviour, especially behaviour that involves not eating or drinking too much of something: *In moderation, red wine is still thought to be good for health.*

modern /ˈmɒd(ə)n/ adj ★★★
1 relating to or belonging to the present time: *the role of women in modern society*
2 using the most recent methods, ideas,

designs, or equipment: *We should replace the equipment with something more modern.*
3 using new styles that are very different from the styles of the past = CONTEMPORARY: *The architecture of the hotel is strikingly modern.*

modern-day adj existing or happening in the present

modernity /mɒˈdɜːnəti/ noun [U] ideas and practices that use modern methods, styles, or equipment

modernize /ˈmɒdəˌnaɪz/ verb [I/T] to become less old-fashioned, or to make something become less old-fashioned, as a result of new methods, equipment, or ideas
—**modernization** /ˌmɒdənaɪˈzeɪʃ(ə)n/ noun [U]

modern languages noun [plural] languages that are still spoken today

modest /ˈmɒdɪst/ adj ★
1 fairly small in size, degree, or value: *He earned a modest income.* ♦ *She has had some modest success with her short stories.*
2 a modest person does not like to talk about themselves, their achievements, or their abilities, even if they are successful ≠ BOASTFUL: *Campese is genuinely modest about his achievements.*
3 feeling shy or embarrassed about other people seeing your body
—**modestly** adv

modesty /ˈmɒdɪsti/ noun [U] **1** the tendency not to talk about yourself, your achievements, or your abilities even if you are successful **2** a feeling of being shy or embarrassed about other people seeing your body

modicum /ˈmɒdɪkəm/ noun **a modicum of sth** *formal* a small amount of something good

modification /ˌmɒdɪfɪˈkeɪʃ(ə)n/ noun *formal*
1 [C/U] a small change to something = ALTERATION **2** [U] the process of changing something slightly

modifier /ˈmɒdɪˌfaɪə/ noun [C] *linguistics* a word or phrase that slightly changes the meaning of another word or phrase by giving more information about it

modify /ˈmɒdɪˌfaɪ/ verb **1** [T] *formal* to change something slightly in order to improve it or in order to make it less extreme = ALTER **2** [I/T] *linguistics* to slightly change the meaning of another word or a phrase by giving more information about it

modular /ˈmɒdjʊlə/ adj **1** *British* a modular course of study is divided into modules **2** modular buildings, furniture, or other structures are made in separate sections that fit together

module /ˈmɒdjuːl/ noun [C] ★
1 *British* one of the separate units of a course of study
2 one of several parts that are made separately and then joined together in order to make a building or other structure
3 a part of a space vehicle that is used separately for doing a particular job

mogul /ˈməʊɡ(ə)l/ noun [C] an important powerful person in a particular activity or industry

M

mohair /'məʊˌheə/ noun [U] soft wool made from the hair of a particular type of goat

moist /mɔɪst/ adj slightly wet

moisten /'mɔɪs(ə)n/ verb [T] to make something slightly wet

moisture /'mɔɪstʃə/ noun [U] very small drops of water or another liquid in the air, on the surface of something, or in a substance

moisturise /'mɔɪstʃəˌraɪz/ a British spelling of **moisturize**

moisturize /'mɔɪstʃəˌraɪz/ verb [I/T] to make your skin less dry by using moisturizer

moisturizer /'mɔɪstʃəˌraɪzə/ noun [C/U] a cream that you put on your skin to make it less dry

molar /'məʊlə/ noun [C] one of the large teeth at the back of your mouth that you use for CHEWING food

molasses /mə'læsɪz/ noun [U] American TREACLE

mold /məʊld/ the American spelling of **mould**

molding /'məʊldɪŋ/ the American spelling of **moulding**

moldy /'məʊldi/ the American spelling of **mouldy**

mole /məʊl/ noun [C] **1** a small animal with dark fur that digs underground and cannot see well —*picture* → C13 **2** a dark brown lump or spot on your skin that is permanent **3** *informal* someone who joins or works for an organization in order to give secret information about it to its enemies

molecule /'mɒlɪˌkjuːl/ noun [C] a very small group of atoms that form a particular substance —**molecular** /mə'lekjʊlə/ adj

molest /mə'lest/ verb [T] to hurt someone, especially a child, by touching them in a sexual way or forcing them to do sexual acts —**molester** noun [C]

mollify /'mɒlɪˌfaɪ/ verb [T] *formal* to make someone feel less angry or upset

mollusc /'mɒləsk/ noun [C] a type of animal that has a soft body with no bones and is usually covered by a hard shell

mollycoddle /'mɒlɪˌkɒd(ə)l/ verb [T] to make someone's life too easy by doing too much for them

molt /məʊlt/ the American spelling of **moult**

molten /'məʊltən/ adj molten rock, metal, or glass has become liquid because it is very hot

mom /mɒm/ noun [C] American informal your mother

moment /'məʊmənt/ noun [C] ★★★
1 a particular point in time when something happens: *At that moment there was a knock on the door.* ♦ *Ellie had never really given it much thought up until that moment.* ♦ *This is the proudest moment of my career.*
2 a very short period of time: *A moment later Jane had completely disappeared.* ♦ *He paused for a moment before giving his answer.*
3 a short period of time when you have the opportunity to do something: *As he stood up, James knew his big moment had arrived.*
♦ *I saw he was alone and seized the moment.*

♦ *She waited until the last possible moment to cancel her flight.*

PHRASES any moment (now) very soon: *They should be here any moment now.*
at the moment now: *They're very upset and don't want to talk at the moment.*
for the moment at the present time, but possibly not in the future: *I thought it was best to say nothing about it for the moment.*
have its/your moments 1 to have some good periods or parts: *Although the film has its moments, it's not really worth seeing.* **2** to sometimes have problems or cause trouble
in a moment used for telling someone that you will do something very soon: *'Come and see this.' 'In a moment.'*
just/wait a moment 1 used for telling someone that you will do something very soon: *'Can you give me a hand?' 'Just a moment.'* **2** used for asking someone to give you their attention for a short time: *Just a moment, I want to ask you something.*
the moment (that) as soon as: *The moment he said that, everything became clear to me.*
→ FOR, HEAT¹

momentarily /'məʊmənt(ə)rəli, ˌməʊmən'terəli/ adv **1** for a moment **2** American very soon

momentary /'məʊmənt(ə)ri/ adj lasting for only a very short time

momentous /məʊ'mentəs/ adj very important because of having an effect on future events

momentum /məʊ'mentəm/ noun [U] **1** progress or development that is becoming faster or stronger **2** the speed with which a moving object keeps moving or moves faster

mommy /'mɒmi/ noun [C] American informal your mother

Mon. abbrev Monday

monarch /'mɒnək/ noun [C] a king or queen

monarchy /'mɒnəki/ noun **1** [C/U] a system of government in which a country is ruled by a king or queen **2** [C] a country that is ruled by a king or queen

monastery /'mɒnəst(ə)ri/ noun [C] a building where a group of MONKS (=religious men) lives and works

monastic /mə'næstɪk/ adj relating to MONKS or MONASTERIES

Monday /'mʌndeɪ/ noun [C/U] ★★★ the day after Sunday and before Tuesday: *This year's Oscar ceremony will be on a Monday.* ♦ *Let's meet for lunch on Monday.* ♦ *You can start work next Monday.* ♦ *The group meets on Mondays* (=every Monday) *at 8 pm.*

monetary /'mʌnɪt(ə)ri/ adj relating to money

money /'mʌni/ noun [U] ★★★ the coins and pieces of paper that you earn, save, invest, and use for paying for things: *I haven't got any money.* ♦ *We've spent a lot of money on this house.* ♦ *It would have cost us a lot of money to cancel the event.* ♦ *I have had to borrow money from my family.* ♦ *The business has made more money this year.* ♦ *You can save money* (=avoid spending it) *by*

M

taking your own lunch. ♦ *They're trying to* **save money** *(=keep it so that they can spend it later) so that they can have a holiday.* ♦ *Have you got any* **money on you** *(=in your pocket/bag)?*

PHRASES **get your money's worth** to feel that something that you have got is worth the amount that you paid for it: *Get there early to make sure you get your money's worth.*
put money on sth *informal* **1** to BET on something so that you will win money if you are right, but will lose it if you are wrong **2** used for emphasizing that you are completely certain that something will happen: *She'll be late. You can put money on it .*
→ POCKET MONEY, ROLL¹

'**money ,market** noun [C] *business* business activities in which banks and other financial institutions lend money to other organizations in order to make more money

'**money ,order** noun [C] an official document that you buy at a bank as a safe way of sending money to someone

mongrel /'mʌŋgrəl/ noun [C] a dog that is a mixture of different BREEDS (=types with particular features)

monitor¹ /'mɒnɪtə/ verb [T] ★ to regularly check something or watch someone in order to find out what is happening: *a special machine to monitor the baby's breathing* ♦ *Staff will* **monitor his progress**.

monitor² /'mɒnɪtə/ noun [C] **1** a screen that shows pictures or information, especially on a computer, or the piece of equipment that contains the screen —*picture* → C3 **2** a piece of equipment that shows and records what is happening in a particular part of someone's body **3** someone who checks to see that something is done fairly or correctly

monk /mʌŋk/ noun [C] a man who lives in a religious community away from other people → NUN

monkey /'mʌŋki/ noun [C] an animal with a long tail that climbs trees and uses its hands in the same way that people do —*picture* → C12

'**monkey ,business** noun [U] *informal* dishonest or bad behaviour

'**monkey ,wrench** noun [C] a SPANNER that you use for turning NUTS of different sizes

monochrome /'mɒnəkrəʊm/ adj able to show or produce only black, white, and grey

monogamous /mə'nɒgəməs/ adj having only one husband, wife, or sexual relationship at a time

monogamy /mə'nɒgəmi/ noun [U] the practice of having only one husband, wife, or sexual relationship at a time → BIGAMY

monogram /'mɒnəgræm/ noun [C] a design using the first letter of each of someone's names —**monogrammed** /'mɒnəgræmd/ adj

monolingual /ˌmɒnəʊ'lɪŋgwəl/ adj speaking, writing, or using only one language → BILINGUAL

monolith /'mɒnəlɪθ/ noun [C] **1** a very large piece of stone standing on one end that was put in position in ancient times **2** a large and very powerful organization or system that is not willing to change

monolithic /ˌmɒnə'lɪθɪk/ adj a monolithic organization or system is large, very powerful, and not willing to change

monologue /'mɒnəlɒg/ noun [C] **1** a speech made by someone who talks for a long time and does not let anyone else say anything **2** a long speech made by someone in a play or film

monopolize /mə'nɒpəlaɪz/ verb [T] to control something completely and prevent other people or organizations from being involved in it or using it

monopoly /mə'nɒpəli/ noun **1** [C/U] complete control over something by one organization or person **2** [C] a company that has complete control of the product or service it provides because it is the only company that provides it **3** [singular] something that only one person or group of people has

monorail /'mɒnəʊˌreɪl/ noun [C] a railway system in which trains travel on a single metal track, or a train on this system

monosyllabic /ˌmɒnəʊsɪ'læbɪk/ adj using very few short words

monosyllable /'mɒnəʊˌsɪləb(ə)l/ noun [C] *linguistics* a short word with only one SYLLABLE

monotone /'mɒnətəʊn/ noun [singular] a way of talking that is boring because the sound of your voice does not change

monotonous /mə'nɒtənəs/ adj **1** a monotonous sound or voice is boring because it does not change **2** a monotonous job is boring because you have to keep repeating the same activity —**monotonously** adv

monotony /mə'nɒtəni/ noun [U] the fact that something never changes, so that it is boring

monsoon /mɒn'suːn/ noun [C] a period of heavy rain in India and Southeast Asia

monster¹ /'mɒnstə/ noun [C] **1** an imaginary creature that is large, ugly, and frightening **2** something that is very large **3** someone who is very cruel

monster² /'mɒnstə/ adj *informal* very large

monstrosity /mɒn'strɒsəti/ noun [C] something that is very large and ugly

monstrous /'mɒnstrəs/ adj **1** cruel, unfair, or morally wrong **2** very large and ugly or frightening —**monstrously** adv

month /mʌnθ/ noun ★★★
1 [C] one of the 12 periods that a year is divided into, for example January or February: *Could we meet earlier in the month?* ♦ *They aim to finish by the end of the month.* ♦ *A man was arrested last month in connection with the robbery.* ♦ *I give my daughter £50 a month (=each month).*
2 [C] a period of about four weeks: *They're*

M

M

getting married in a month's time. ♦ *I'll be leaving a month from today.* ♦ *a three-month-old baby*

3 months [plural] a long time: *It'll take months to finish the work on the house.* ♦ *We haven't been to the cinema for months.*

monthly¹ /'mʌnθli/ adj happening or published once a month —**monthly** adv

monthly² /'mʌnθli/ noun [C] a magazine that is published once a month

monument /'mɒnjʊmənt/ noun [C] **1** a structure that is built in a public place in order to celebrate an important person or event **2** a place of historical importance
PHRASE **a monument to sth** something that reminds people of something

monumental /ˌmɒnjʊ'ment(ə)l/ adj very great in size, degree, or importance

monumentally /ˌmɒnjʊ'mentəli/ adv extremely: *monumentally stupid*

moo /muː/ verb [I] to make the long deep sound that a cow makes —**moo** noun [C]

mood /muːd/ noun ★★
1 [C/U] the way that someone is feeling, or the way that a group of people is feeling at a particular time: *Politicians have to be in touch with the public mood.* ♦ *I had never seen Ann in such a good mood before.* ♦ *Jeff's been in a bad mood all day.* ♦ *a mood of optimism*
2 [C] a period when you feel unhappy or angry: *She refused to put up with her husband's moods.* ♦ *Just leave her on her own when she's in a mood.*
3 [C/U] a quality that something such as a place, film, or piece of music has that makes you have a particular feeling: *a collection of stories that vary in mood and style* ♦ *Lighting was particularly important in setting the mood of the play.*
4 [C] *linguistics* a group of verb forms that are used to show whether, for example, a sentence is a statement, question, or order
PHRASES **be/feel in the mood (for sth)** to want to do something: *I'm in the mood for dancing.*
be in no mood for sth/to do sth to really not want to do something: *Dad was in no mood for joking.*

moody /'muːdi/ adj **1** likely to become unhappy or angry for no particular reason **2** creating a feeling of sadness or mystery

moon /muːn/ noun ★★
1 the Moon or **the moon** the object similar to a planet that goes round the Earth and that you can see shining in the sky at night: *The moon was shining brightly.*
2 [C] an object similar to a planet that goes round another planet: *How many moons has Jupiter got?*
PHRASES **be over the moon (about sth)** *British informal* to be very happy about something: *Keith was over the moon about becoming a father.*
once in a blue moon used for emphasizing that something does not happen very often: *We only go out once in a blue moon.*

moonbeam /'muːnˌbiːm/ noun [C] a RAY (=thin line) of light from the moon

moonlight /'muːnˌlaɪt/ noun [U] light from the moon

moonlighting /'muːnˌlaɪtɪŋ/ noun [U] *informal* the activity of working at a second job in the evenings or at weekends

moonlit /'muːnˌlɪt/ adj provided with light from the moon

moor¹ /mɔː, mʊə/ verb [I/T] to stop a ship or boat from moving by fastening it to a place with ropes or chains, or by using an ANCHOR

moor² /mɔː, mʊə/ noun [C] *British* a large area of high land that is covered with grass, bushes, and HEATHER, and has soil that is not good for growing crops

mooring /'mɔːrɪŋ, 'mʊərɪŋ/ noun **1 moorings** [plural] ropes, chains, or ANCHORS that you use to moor a ship or boat **2** [C] a place where a ship or boat is moored with ropes, chains, or ANCHORS

moose /muːs/ (plural **moose**) noun [C] a large DEER that lives in North America, northern Europe, and Asia

moot¹ /muːt/ adj a moot point, question, or issue is one that people disagree about

moot² /muːt/ verb [T] *formal* to suggest something as a subject for discussion

mop¹ /mɒp/ noun [C] **1** an object that has a long handle and is used for washing floors **2** a lot of thick untidy hair

mop² /mɒp/ verb **1** [I/T] to wash a floor using a mop **2** [T] to wipe SWEAT from your face with a cloth when you are very hot or ill **3** [T] to clean liquid or dirt from a surface using a mop, cloth, or something soft
PHRASAL VERB **ˌmop sth 'up** *same as* **mop²** 3

mope /məʊp/ verb [I] to feel bored or unhappy and show no interest in doing anything
PHRASAL VERB **ˌmope aˈround** or **ˌmope aˈbout** *British* to spend time somewhere with no no particular purpose, feeling bored or unhappy

moped /'məʊˌped/ noun [C] a type of MOTORCYCLE with an engine that is not powerful and PEDALS like a bicycle —*picture* → C7

moral¹ /'mɒrəl/ adj ★
1 relating to right and wrong and the way that people should behave: *moral standards/principles/values* ♦ *our children's religious and moral education*
2 a moral person always tries to behave in the right way
—**morally** adv

moral² /'mɒrəl/ noun **1 morals** [plural] principles of right or wrong behaviour that are generally accepted by a society: *He's shown that he has no morals at all.*
2 [singular] something that you can learn from a story or an experience

morale /mə'rɑːl/ noun [U] the amount of enthusiasm that someone feels about the situation that they are in

moralise /'mɒrəˌlaɪz/ a British spelling of moralize

moralistic /ˌmɒrə'lɪstɪk/ adj *showing disapproval*

expressing firm opinions about what is right or wrong

morality /məˈræləti/ noun [U] **1** principles of right or wrong behaviour: *standards of morality* **2** the degree to which something is thought to be right or wrong: *the continuing debate about the morality of foxhunting*

moralize /ˈmɒrəlaɪz/ verb [I] *showing disapproval* to tell people how they should behave and what is right and wrong

moral sup'port noun [U] if you give someone moral support, you try to make them more confident

moratorium /ˌmɒrəˈtɔːriəm/ noun [C] an official agreement to stop an activity for a short time

morbid /ˈmɔːbɪd/ adj interested in subjects such as death that most people think are unpleasant

more /mɔː/ grammar word ★★★

> **More** is the comparative form of **much** and **many**. It can be:
> ■ a **determiner**: *He wants to spend more time with his family.*
> ■ a **pronoun**: *I wish I could do more to help.* ♦ *I'm not going to listen to any more of your lies.*
> ■ an **adverb**: *The stereos are more expensive in Japan than they are here.* ♦ *I'd like to travel more.*
> ■ used after numbers or expressions of quantity: *You'll have to wait a few more minutes.*

1 to a greater degree ≠ LESS: *Scotland has become more prosperous in recent years.* ♦ *The storm was more violent than we expected.* ♦ *Lizzie is obviously a lot more intelligent than the other girls.* ♦ *Could you speak a little more slowly?*

> ■ **More** is used to form the comparative with adjectives and adverbs with three or more syllables, such as 'important', and many adjectives and adverbs with two syllables, such as 'often'.
> ■ Adjectives and adverbs with only one syllable form the comparative by adding **-er**, and not with **more**.

2 a larger amount or number ≠ LESS: *No matter what her brother gets, she always wants more.* ♦ *Ken already earns more than his father ever did.* ♦ *The merger has created far more problems than it has solved.* ♦ *People in the UK are spending more than ever on health and fitness.*

3 happening or doing something a greater number of times, for longer periods, or to a greater degree: *You should get out more and meet other people.* ♦ *Rural life has changed more in the last 40 years than at any other time.*

4 an additional amount or number ≠ LESS: *If you need more paper, there's some in the drawer.* ♦ *We'll have to wait for two more days.* ♦ *That's all I know. I can't tell you any more.* ♦ *I'm not wasting any more of my money on lottery tickets.* ♦ *There are no more eggs.*

PHRASES **more and more** used for saying that something is increasing in number or degree all the time: *More and more people are choosing to spend their holidays abroad.* ♦ *As the situation grew steadily worse, he became more and more depressed.*

the more...the more/less used for saying that when a particular activity, feeling etc increases, it causes something else to change at the same time: *The more I thought about Carrie's suggestion, the more doubtful I became.*

more or less almost: *The team is more or less the same as it was last season.*

not any more used for saying that something which used to happen in the past does not happen now: *Mr Carling doesn't work here any more.*

→ OFTEN, ONCE, WHAT

moreover /mɔːˈrəʊvə/ adv *formal* used for introducing an additional important fact that supports or emphasizes what you have just said: *There is growing opposition to capital punishment. Moreover, there is now evidence that many executed prisoners were innocent.*

morgue /mɔːg/ noun [C] a building or room where dead bodies are kept for a short time

morning[1] /ˈmɔːnɪŋ/ noun [C/U] ★★★
1 the part of the day from when the sun rises until midday: *What time did you get up this morning?* ♦ *Call me at my office on Monday morning.* ♦ *We spent the morning walking in the park.* ♦ *Let's talk about this in the morning* (=during the morning of the next day).
2 the part of the day between midnight and midday: *The phone woke me at 2 o'clock in the morning.* ♦ *I was working until the early hours of the morning.*

morning[2] /ˈmɔːnɪŋ/ interjection *informal* used for saying hello to someone in the morning

moron /ˈmɔːrɒn/ noun [C] *informal* an insulting word for someone who behaves in a stupid way

morose /məˈrəʊs/ adj unhappy and unfriendly —**morosely** adv

morphine /ˈmɔːfiːn/ noun [U] a powerful drug that is used for reducing pain

morsel /ˈmɔːs(ə)l/ noun [C] **1** *formal* a small piece of food **2** a small amount of something

mortal[1] /ˈmɔːt(ə)l/ adj **1** human and not able to live for ever ≠ IMMORTAL **2** serious enough to cause death **3** used for emphasizing that a particular feeling is extremely strong: *people living in mortal fear*

mortal[2] /ˈmɔːt(ə)l/ noun [C] a normal person, as opposed to a god or people who are thought to be very important

mortality /mɔːˈtæləti/ noun [U] **1** the number of deaths in a particular area or group of people **2** the fact that your life will end ≠ IMMORTALITY

mortally /ˈmɔːt(ə)li/ adv in a way that is likely to cause death: *mortally wounded/injured*

mortar /ˈmɔːtə/ noun **1** [U] a substance that is used in building for joining bricks **2** [C] a

M

large gun that soldiers use for firing bombs over short distances

mortgage¹ /ˈmɔːgɪdʒ/ noun [C] money that you borrow from a bank and use to buy a house

mortgage² /ˈmɔːgɪdʒ/ verb [T] if you mortgage property, you borrow money from a bank and agree to give the property to the bank if you do not pay back the money

mortified /ˈmɔːtɪˌfaɪd/ adj feeling extremely embarrassed or ashamed —**mortify** verb [T]

mortuary /ˈmɔːtjuəri/ noun [C] British a place where dead bodies are kept for a short time

mosaic /məʊˈzeɪɪk/ noun [C] a pattern made of small pieces of coloured stone or glass

mosque /mɒsk/ noun [C] a building in which Muslims worship

mosquito /mɒˈskiːtəʊ/ (plural **mosquitos** or **mosquitoes**) noun [C] a small flying insect that bites people and can give them diseases —*picture* → C13

moss /mɒs/ noun [U] a soft green or brown plant that grows in a layer on wet ground, rocks, or trees —**mossy** adj

most /məʊst/ grammar word ★★★

Most is the superlative form of **much** and **many**. It can be:
- an **adverb**: *Love is what these children need most.* ♦ *Angie looks like her father the most.*
- a **determiner**: *Most shops will be closed over Christmas.* ♦ *Which athlete won the most medals?*
- a **pronoun**: *All the victims were male, and most were between the ages of 15 and 25.* ♦ *Most of my friends live in this area.*

1 used for comparing people, places, things etc to a greater degree than anyone or anything else ≠ LEAST: *Zurich is Switzerland's most important city.* ♦ *Who do you think is most likely to win the next presidential election?* ♦ *The English Patient was one of the most successful films ever made.*

- **Most** is used to form the superlative with adjectives and adverbs with three or more syllables, such as 'important', and many adjectives and adverbs with two syllables, such as 'often'.
- Adjectives and adverbs with only one syllable form the comparative by adding -est, and not with **most**.

2 the largest part the largest part of something, or the majority of people or things ≠ LEAST: *Most people think of robots as machines that look like people.* ♦ *A few of the moths are grey, but most are white.* ♦ *Johnson spent most of his life in London.* ♦ *Most of the time we sit around playing cards.*
3 the largest amount a larger amount or number than any other: *Those who earn most pay most tax.* ♦ *We chose the option that would help the most people.*
4 happening most happening or doing something more often or to a greater degree than anyone or anything else ≠ LEAST: *Of the three boys, Eric had changed the most.* ♦ *What I want most of all is to spend more time with my little girl.*

5 very formal used for emphasizing a particular quality: *We spent a most enjoyable afternoon at the races.*

PHRASES **at (the) most** used for showing that you are mentioning the largest possible amount and that the real amount may be less: *The whole process will take half an hour at the most.*

for the most part used for saying that something is mainly true but not completely true: *For the most part we were happy to live alongside each other.*

mostly /ˈməʊs(t)li/ adv ★★
1 most of the time, or in most situations: *We listen to rock music mostly.* ♦ *Mostly, he avoids arguments.*
2 used for saying what the largest part of something consists of: *a group of journalists, mostly American* ♦ *The group is made up mostly of local businesspeople.*
3 used for emphasizing the main reason or purpose of something = MAINLY: *People work mostly because they need the money.* ♦ *This machine was used mostly for agricultural work.*

MOT /ˌem əʊ ˈtiː/ noun [C] in the UK, an official test to check that a car is safe to drive

motel /məʊˈtel/ noun [C] a hotel for people who are travelling by car

moth /mɒθ/ noun [C] a flying insect that flies mainly at night —*picture* → C13

mother¹ /ˈmʌðə/ noun [C] ★★★ your female parent: *My mother and father live in Rome.* —*picture* → FAMILY TREE

mother² /ˈmʌðə/ verb [T] to give someone a lot of care and protection

motherboard /ˈmʌðəbɔːd/ noun [C] computing the main CIRCUIT BOARD in a computer

motherhood /ˈmʌðəhʊd/ noun [U] the state of being a mother

mother-in-law (plural **mothers-in-law**) noun [C] the mother of your husband or wife —*picture* → FAMILY TREE

motherly /ˈmʌðəli/ adj kind, like a good mother

Mother Nature nature, or natural forces

mother-of-pearl noun [U] the shiny layer inside some shells that is used for making jewellery

Mother's Day noun [C/U] a day when people give cards and presents to their mothers to show their love

mother tongue noun [C] the first language that you learn to speak

motif /məʊˈtiːf/ noun [C] **1** a shape that is repeated in a design **2** an idea or subject that is frequently repeated in a piece of literature or art

motion¹ /ˈməʊʃ(ə)n/ noun ★★
1 [U] the process or action of moving: *photographs of animals in motion* ♦ *He studied the motion of the planets.*
2 [C] a movement that someone or something makes: *Rub the horse's coat with a circular motion.*
3 [C] a suggestion that you make at a formal meeting: *propose a motion* (=suggest something for discussion)

PHRASES **go through the motions** to do something without any interest or enthusiasm

in motion if something is in motion, it has already started to happen

motion² /ˈməʊʃ(ə)n/ verb [I] to move your hand in a particular direction, for example in order to point to something: *He motioned for the waiter to bring the bill.*

motionless /ˈməʊʃ(ə)nləs/ adj not moving at all =STILL

motion picture noun [C] *American* a film that is made for the cinema =MOVIE

motivate /ˈməʊtɪˌveɪt/ verb [T] **1** to make someone behave in a particular way: *The crime appears to have been motivated by hatred.* **2** to make someone feel enthusiastic about doing something or determined to do something: *We must motivate students to take charge of their own learning.* —**motivator** noun [C]

motivated /ˈməʊtɪˌveɪtɪd/ adj **1** enthusiastic about doing something or determined to do something: *highly motivated teachers* **2** caused by a particular belief or emotion: *a racially motivated crime*

motivation /ˌməʊtɪˈveɪʃ(ə)n/ noun **1** [U] a feeling of enthusiasm about something, or a feeling of determination to do something: *Some of the students lack motivation.* **2** [C] a reason for doing something: *Our real motivation is to make a profit.* —**motivational** adj

motive /ˈməʊtɪv/ noun [C] ★ a reason for doing something: *The motive for the attack is still unknown.*

motley /ˈmɒtli/ adj consisting of many different types of people or things that do not seem to belong together

motor¹ /ˈməʊtə/ noun [C] ★★ the part of a machine or vehicle that makes it work: *The pump is powered by an electric motor.*

motor² /ˈməʊtə/ adj **1** operated by a motor **2** relating to cars: *motor insurance*

motorbike /ˈməʊtəˌbaɪk/ noun [C] a road vehicle that has two wheels and an engine → MOPED

motorboat /ˈməʊtəˌbəʊt/ noun [C] a small boat that has an engine

motorcade /ˈməʊtəˌkeɪd/ noun [C] a group of cars that includes a car that an important person is travelling in

motor car noun [C] *British old-fashioned* a car

motorcycle /ˈməʊtəˌsaɪk(ə)l/ noun [C] *formal* a MOTORBIKE

motoring /ˈməʊtərɪŋ/ noun [U] *old-fashioned* the activity of driving a car

motorist /ˈməʊtərɪst/ noun [C] someone who drives a car

motorized /ˈməʊtəˌraɪzd/ adj something that is motorized has a motor that makes it move

motor neurone disease noun [U] a serious illness in which the part of a person's NERVOUS SYSTEM that controls movement is gradually destroyed

motor racing noun [U] *British* a sport in which fast cars race on a track

motor vehicle noun [C] *formal* a road vehicle that has an engine

motorway /ˈməʊtəˌweɪ/ noun [C] *British* a wide fast road with several LANES of traffic going in each direction

mottled /ˈmɒt(ə)ld/ adj covered with areas of light and dark colours

motto /ˈmɒtəʊ/ (plural **mottos** or **mottoes**) noun [C] a short statement that expresses a principle or aim

mould¹ /məʊld/ noun **1** [U] a green, blue, or white substance that grows on food that is not kept fresh or on other things that are not kept clean and dry **2** [C] a container into which you pour a liquid that then becomes solid in the shape of the container

PHRASE **break the mould** to change a situation by doing something completely new and different

mould² /məʊld/ verb [T] **1** to give something a particular shape: *Mould the dough into loaves.* **2** to influence someone strongly so that they will have particular qualities or behave in a particular way: *The coach must mould the group into a team.*

moulding /ˈməʊldɪŋ/ noun [C/U] a decorated edge around something such as a door or picture frame

mouldy /ˈməʊldi/ adj covered with mould: *mouldy bread*

moult /məʊlt/ verb [I] if an animal or bird moults, it loses its outer layer of skin or feathers so that a new layer can replace it

mound /maʊnd/ noun [C] **1** a pile of something such as earth or stones **2** a large amount of something in a pile: *a mound of papers*

mount¹ /maʊnt/ verb ★

1 increase	4 get on horse
2 prepare for and begin	5 climb up
3 fix sth in position	+ PHRASAL VERB

1 [I] if a particular feeling mounts, it gets stronger: *Tension continues to mount between the two parties.*

2 [T] to prepare and begin an activity: *We are mounting a campaign to recruit more volunteers.* ♦ *Government forces have mounted an attack on a rebel base.*

3 [T] to fix something in position: *A machine gun was mounted on the roof.* ♦ *Each photograph is mounted on cardboard.*

4 [T] to get on a horse

5 [T] *formal* to go up stairs, or to climb up somewhere

PHRASAL VERB **mount up** to increase a lot: *The costs are beginning to mount up.*

mount² /maʊnt/ noun [C] a base that something is fixed to

Mount /maʊnt/ a word used in the names of mountains: *Mount Everest*

mountain /ˈmaʊntɪn/ noun [C] ★★★
1 a very high hill: *They went walking and climbing in the mountains.* ♦ *There was still snow on the mountain tops.*
2 a large pile or amount of something: *a mountain of paperwork*

PHRASE **make a mountain out of a molehill** to

treat a minor problem as if it were a very serious problem

'mountain bike noun [C] a strong bicycle with wide tyres, used on rough ground

mountaineer /ˌmaʊntɪˈnɪə/ noun [C] someone who climbs mountains

mountaineering /ˌmaʊntɪˈnɪərɪŋ/ noun [U] the activity of climbing mountains

mountainous /ˈmaʊntɪnəs/ adj covered with mountains

mounted /ˈmaʊntɪd/ adj riding on a horse: *mounted police*

mounting /ˈmaʊntɪŋ/ adj becoming stronger, greater, or worse: *mounting anger/costs/debts*

mourn /mɔːn/ verb [I/T] **1** to feel extremely sad because someone has died **2** to be sad because something no longer exists

mourner /ˈmɔːnə/ noun [C] someone who is at a funeral

mournful /ˈmɔːnf(ə)l/ adj feeling sad, or expressing sadness

mourning /ˈmɔːnɪŋ/ noun [U] **1** expressions of sadness because someone has died **2** *old-fashioned* black clothes that people wear when someone has died

mouse /maʊs/ (plural **mice** /maɪs/) noun [C] ★★

1 a small furry animal with a long tail —*picture* → C13

2 (plural **mouses** or **mice**) a small object connected to a computer that you move in order to do things on the computer screen: *Click on the left mouse button.* —*picture* → C3

'mouse mat noun [C] *British* a piece of soft material that you move a computer mouse around on —*picture* → C3

mousse /muːs/ noun [U] **1** a cold sweet food made with cream, eggs, and fruit or chocolate **2** a white substance that you put in your hair in order to hold it in a particular style

moustache /məˈstɑːʃ/ noun [C] hair that grows above a man's mouth

mousy /ˈmaʊsi/ adj **1** mousy hair is a dull pale brown colour **2** a mousy person is quiet and prefers not to be noticed

mouth¹ /maʊθ/ (plural **mouths** /maʊðz/) noun [C] ★★★

1 the part of your face that you use when you eat or speak: *She opened her mouth to speak.* ♦ *I've got a funny taste in my mouth.* —*picture* → C14

2 the place where a river is widest and joins the sea

3 the entrance to a tunnel or CAVE

PHRASES **big mouth** used as a criticism of someone when they say things they should not say: *You should have kept your big mouth shut.*

open your mouth to speak: *She didn't open her mouth once during the meeting.*

mouth² /maʊð/ verb [T] **1** to form words with your mouth but not make any sound **2** to say something without really meaning or understanding what you say

PHRASAL VERB **,mouth 'off** *informal* to give

your opinions about something in an annoying way

mouthful /ˈmaʊθfʊl/ noun [C] **1** an amount of food or drink that you put in your mouth at one time **2** *informal* a word or phrase that is very long or is hard to pronounce

'mouth ,organ noun [C] a HARMONICA

mouthpiece /ˈmaʊθpiːs/ noun [C] **1** *informal* a person or newspaper that expresses the opinions of an organization **2** the part of something that you put in or near your mouth

mouthwash /ˈmaʊθwɒʃ/ noun [C/U] a liquid that you use for cleaning your mouth

'mouth-,watering adj mouth-watering food smells or looks very good

movable /ˈmuːvəb(ə)l/ adj able to be moved easily

move¹ /muːv/ verb ★★★

1 change position	5 affect sb emotionally
2 progress/change	6 spend time with group
3 live in a different place	+ PHRASAL VERBS
4 do sth	

1 [I/T] to change position, or to make someone or something change position: *Could you help me move the bookcase away from the wall?* ♦ *The traffic was barely moving.* ♦ *She moved quickly towards the door.*

2 [I] to progress or change in a particular way: *Events were moving rapidly.* ♦ *The country has only recently begun **moving towards** democracy.* ♦ *We need to **move to** the next item on the agenda.*

3 [I/T] to begin to live in a different house or area: *We're moving next week.* ♦ *Moving house can be quite a stressful experience.*

4 [I] to do something in order to achieve an aim or solve a problem: *The police moved swiftly to prevent a riot.*

5 [T] to make someone feel sad or sympathetic: *You can't fail to be moved by the plight of these people.* ♦ *Her songs can move me to tears.*

6 [I] to spend time with people who belong to a particular group: *We move in such different circles I'm surprised we ever met.*

PHRASAL VERBS **,move 'in 1** to start living in a different house: *We're moving in next week.* **2** to start living in the same place as someone else: *He's **moving in with** his friends from college.*

,move 'into sth 1 to start living or working in a place: *We're moving into new offices by the river.* **2** to begin a new business or a new type of business: *They're planning to move into publishing.*

,move 'off if a vehicle moves off, it starts to move

,move 'on 1 to leave one place and travel to another: *They stay for only a few days before moving on.* **2** to stop doing one thing and begin doing another thing: *Let's move on to the next question.* **3** to have a new opinion or way of behaving that is better than the old one: *Public opinion has moved on a great deal since then.*

move out to leave your house and start to live somewhere else

move over to change your position in order to make space for someone or something else: *She moved over to let me pass.*

move up 1 *British* to change your position in order to make space for someone or something: *Could everyone move up a bit, please?* **2 move up in the world** *humorous* to improve your social status, for example by getting a better job

move (sb) up to go to a better job or position, or to put someone in a better job or position: *He's been moved up to the position of manager.*

move² /muːv/ noun [C] ★★★
1 something that you do in order to achieve an aim or solve a problem: *Getting rid of the tax would be a welcome move.* ♦ *She's going to have to plan her next move carefully.*

2 a change in an activity or situation: *an upward move in the value of the company* ♦ *The new law is a move towards equality.* ♦ *He's considering a move into politics.*

3 a change in the place where you live or work: *We're considering a move to the city.*

PHRASES **get a move on** *spoken* used for telling someone to hurry

make a move 1 to move: *Don't make a move or they'll see you.* ♦ *He made a quick move for his gun.* **2** to start doing something to achieve an aim or solve a problem: *No one made a move to help.*

on the move 1 travelling from one place to other places **2** *informal* developing or progressing quickly: *It's an industry on the move.* **3** *informal* busy or active all the time: *He's always on the move.*
→ FIRST

moveable /ˈmuːvəb(ə)l/ another spelling of **movable**

movement /ˈmuːvmənt/ noun ★★★

1 group with same aim	**4** change of place
2 way of moving	**5** sb's activities
3 change in situation	**6** part of classical music

1 [C] a group of people who work together in order to achieve a particular aim: *the peace movement* → LABOUR MOVEMENT

2 [C/U] a way of moving your body, or the ability to move your body: *rhythmic movements* ♦ *The injury has restricted movement in his arm.*

3 [C/U] change or progress in a situation: *There has been little movement in the peace talks.*

4 [C/U] the process of moving something from one place to another: *The agreement governs the free movement of goods between countries.*

5 movements [plural] someone's activities over a period of time: *Their job is to monitor the movements of suspected terrorists.*

6 [C] one of the main parts of a SYMPHONY

movie /ˈmuːvi/ noun [C] ★ a film shown in a cinema or on television

movies, the /ˈmuːviz/ noun [plural] the cinema, or the film industry

movie star noun [C] *American* a famous film actor

movie theater noun [C] *American* a CINEMA

moving /ˈmuːvɪŋ/ adj **1** making you feel sad or sympathetic **2** a moving object is something that moves: *He was pushed from a moving train.* ♦ *the moving parts of a machine* —**movingly** adv

mow /məʊ/ (past tense **mowed** /məʊd/; past participle **mown** /məʊn/ or **mowed**) verb [T] to cut grass using a machine with blades
PHRASAL VERB **mow sb down** *informal* to kill a person or a crowd of people quickly and violently

mower /ˈməʊə/ noun [C] a machine that is used for cutting grass = LAWNMOWER

MP /ˌem ˈpiː/ noun [C] **1** Member of Parliament: a politician who represents people in a parliament **2** a member of the military police

MP3 /ˌem piː ˈθriː/ noun [C/U] *computing* a computer program that is used for sending music by email

mpg abbrev miles per gallon: the distance in miles that a vehicle can travel using one GALLON of petrol

mph /ˌem piː ˈeɪtʃ/ abbrev miles per hour: a unit for measuring the speed at which a vehicle is travelling

MPV /ˌem piː ˈviː/ noun [C] *British* multi-purpose vehicle: a private road vehicle that can take more passengers than an ordinary car

Mr /ˈmɪstə/ ★★★ a polite or formal title used in front of a man's name: *Mr Jones* ♦ *Mr Samuel Smith*

MRI /ˌem ɑːr ˈaɪ/ noun [C/U] magnetic resonance imaging: a medical test that produces images of the organs inside your body

Mr Right a man who would be a perfect partner in a relationship

Mrs /ˈmɪsɪz/ ★★★ a polite or formal title used in front of the name of a married woman: *Mrs Grace Talbot*

Ms /məz, mɪz/ ★★★ a polite or formal title used in front of the name of a woman, whether she is married or not: *Ms Gloria Johnson* ♦ *Can I help you, Ms Jones?*

Words that avoid giving offence: Ms

Ms can be used as a title for all women, whether they are married or not. **Mrs** is usually used only for married women who have the same surname as their husband. **Miss** is used as a title for women who are not married, and **Miss** is sometimes also used for married women who did not change their name when they got married. However, many women prefer to use **Ms** as their title. **Ms** is more common in American English than in British English.

MS /ˌem ˈes/ noun [U] MULTIPLE SCLEROSIS

MSc /ˌem es ˈsiː/ noun [C] Master of Science: an advanced degree from a college or university in a subject such as physics or biology

MSP /ˌem es ˈpiː/ noun [C] Member of the Scottish Parliament: a politician who represents people in the Scottish Parliament

Mt abbrev Mount or Mountain: used in the names of mountains

MTV /ˌem tiː ˈviː/ trademark music television: a US television company that broadcasts music videos

much /mʌtʃ/ (comparative **more** /mɔːr/; superlative **most** /məʊst/) grammar word ★★★

> **Much** can be:
> ■ a **determiner**: *There isn't much time left.*
> ■ a **pronoun**: *He didn't say much.* ♦ *Much of the work has already been completed.*
> ■ an **adverb**: *Things haven't changed much.* ♦ *The exam was much easier than I had expected.*

1 a large amount of something: *It's a small car that doesn't use much fuel.* ♦ *I don't know much about art.* ♦ *It wouldn't cost very much to have your old bike repaired.* ♦ *Much of the evidence was gathered in 1991.* ♦ *We can't talk here. There's too much noise.* ♦ *He spent so much time with Claudia, it seemed as if they were never apart.*

2 used for asking or saying what the amount of something is: *How much stuff is she taking with her?* ♦ *How much were the tickets?* ♦ *We didn't spend as much time at the museum as I had hoped.*

3 used for emphasizing that someone or something is a lot bigger, better, worse etc: *Richard's much happier now that he's got a permanent job.* ♦ *You will have to try much harder.*

4 a lot, or to a great degree: *People here don't use public transport much.* ♦ *The trouble with Jean is she talks too much.* ♦ *Aunt Edie laughed so much that her sides ached.* ♦ *We don't go out as much as we used to.* ♦ *It's amazing how much she's changed.* ♦ *It's obvious that they love each other very much.*

PHRASES **as much as** used before an amount for showing how large and surprising it is: *You can pay as much as £300,000 for a one-bedroom flat in central London.*

be too much for sb to be too difficult or tiring for someone to deal with

much less used for saying that something is even less likely or true than something else: *I wouldn't have dinner with him, much less spend the weekend with him.*

not much of a informal used for saying that someone or something is not a very good example of something: *We haven't had much of a summer this year.*

not/nothing much spoken used for saying that something is not very important, good, or serious: *'What are you doing tomorrow?' 'Nothing much.'* ♦ *There's not much to get excited about.*

→ BIT¹

> Both **much** and **a lot** can be used for referring to a large amount or a great degree.

> ■ **Much** is mainly used in questions and negative sentences, or in positive statements after 'so', 'too', and 'as': *He drinks too much.*
> ■ **A lot** is usually used instead of **much** in positive statements: *They waste a lot of time.*

muck¹ /mʌk/ noun [U] **1** informal dirt **2** solid waste from animals **3** informal something unpleasant or of no value: *Why do you read this muck?*

muck² /mʌk/ PHRASAL VERB ˌmuck aˈbout or ˌmuck aˈround British informal to waste time when you should be doing something useful or paying attention to something
ˌmuck ˈin British informal to join a group of people who are doing work
ˌmuck sth ˈup informal to spoil something

mucky /ˈmʌki/ adj informal covered with dirt

mucus /ˈmjuːkəs/ noun [U] a liquid that is produced inside your nose and other parts of your body

mud /mʌd/ noun [U] very soft wet earth

muddle¹ /ˈmʌd(ə)l/ noun [singular] a confused situation in which mistakes happen: *She died leaving her financial affairs in a muddle.*

muddle² /ˈmʌd(ə)l/ PHRASAL VERB ˌmuddle aˈlong or ˌmuddle ˈon to continue living or doing something in a confused way without planning
ˌmuddle ˈthrough to succeed in doing something despite having no clear plan or method
ˌmuddle sb/sth ˈup to become confused about who someone is or what something is: *I always get the children's names muddled up.*
ˌmuddle sth ˈup to put things in the wrong order

muddled /ˈmʌd(ə)ld/ adj not clear or effective

muddy¹ /ˈmʌdi/ adj covered with MUD, or full of mud

muddy² /ˈmʌdi/ verb [T] to make something muddy
PHRASE **muddy the issue** to make a situation more complicated or difficult than it needs to be

mudflap /ˈmʌdflæp/ noun [C] a piece of rubber that hangs behind a wheel of a vehicle and stops dirt from the road from hitting the vehicle —*picture* → C6

muesli /ˈmjuːzli/ noun [U] a food consisting of nuts, seeds, and dried fruit that people eat with milk for breakfast

muffin /ˈmʌfɪn/ noun [C] **1** a small sweet cake that often contains fruit **2** British a flat round type of bread that is eaten hot with butter

muffle /ˈmʌf(ə)l/ verb [T] to make a sound quieter and less easy to hear —**muffled** /ˈmʌf(ə)ld/ adj

mug¹ /mʌg/ noun [C] **1** a cup with straight sides and no SAUCER —*picture* → CUP **2** informal someone who does not realize that they are being tricked

mug² /mʌg/ verb [T] to attack someone in a public place and steal their money or possessions —**mugger** noun [C], **mugging** noun [C/U]

muggy /ˈmʌgi/ adj muggy weather is warm in an unpleasant way because the air feels wet

ˈmug ˌshot noun [C] *informal* a photograph of someone's face that is taken by the police for their records

mule /mjuːl/ noun [C] an animal that has a horse as its mother and a DONKEY as its father

mull /mʌl/ **PHRASAL VERB ˌmull sth ˈover** to think carefully about something over a period of time

mullah /ˈmʌlə, ˈmʊlə/ noun [C] a Muslim leader or religious teacher

multicultural /ˌmʌltiˈkʌltʃərəl/ adj consisting of people of different cultures —**multiculturalism** noun [U]

multigym /ˈmʌltiˌdʒɪm/ noun [C] a piece of exercise equipment that is designed so that you can perform many different exercises on it —*picture* → C16

multilateral /ˌmʌltiˈlæt(ə)rəl/ adj involving several groups or countries: *a multilateral agreement/treaty* → UNILATERAL, BILATERAL

multimedia /ˌmʌltiˈmiːdiə/ adj multimedia computers and software produce both pictures and sounds —**multimedia** noun [U]

multimillionaire /ˌmʌltiˌmɪljəˈneə/ noun [C] someone who has money or property worth many millions of pounds

multinational¹ /ˌmʌltiˈnæʃ(ə)nəl/ adj **1** a multinational company has offices or factories in several countries **2** involving people from many different countries

multinational² /ˌmʌltiˈnæʃ(ə)nəl/ noun [C] a multinational company

multiple¹ /ˈmʌltɪp(ə)l/ adj involving many people, things, or parts

multiple² /ˈmʌltɪp(ə)l/ noun [C] a number that you can divide by a smaller number an exact number of times: *12 is a multiple of 4.*

ˌmultiple-ˈchoice adj giving you several answers from which you choose the correct answer

multiple sclerosis /ˌmʌltɪp(ə)l skləˈrəʊsɪs/ noun [U] a serious illness that gradually makes you unable to move, speak, or see

multiplex /ˈmʌltiˌpleks/ noun [C] a large building that contains several cinema screens

multiplication /ˌmʌltɪplɪˈkeɪʃ(ə)n/ noun [U] the process of adding a number to itself a particular number of times

multiplicity /ˌmʌltɪˈplɪsəti/ noun [singular] *formal* a large quantity or variety of things

multiply /ˈmʌltɪˌplaɪ/ verb [I/T] **1** to increase, or to increase something **2** to add a number to itself a particular number of times: *If you multiply 3 by 3, you get 9.*

ˌmulti-ˈpurpose adj able to be used for several different purposes

multiracial /ˌmʌltiˈreɪʃ(ə)l/ adj involving people of many different races

ˌmulti-ˈstorey adj *British* a multi-storey building has several levels

multitasking /ˌmʌltiˈtɑːskɪŋ/ noun [U] the activity of doing more than one thing at the same time

multitude /ˈmʌltɪˌtjuːd/ noun **a multitude of** *formal* a very large number of people or things

mum /mʌm/ noun [C] *British informal* ★★ your mother: *It's my mum's birthday tomorrow.* ♦ *What's for dinner, Mum?*

mumble /ˈmʌmb(ə)l/ verb [I/T] to speak in a way that is not loud enough or clear enough for people to hear

mumbo-jumbo /ˌmʌmbəʊ ˈdʒʌmbəʊ/ noun [U] *informal* ideas, beliefs, or customs that you think are nonsense

mummy /ˈmʌmi/ noun [C] **1** *British informal* your mother. This word is used especially by or to young children. **2** a dead body that was preserved in special oils and wrapped in cloth in ancient Egypt

mumps /mʌmps/ noun [U] a children's disease that makes the neck swollen and painful

munch /mʌntʃ/ verb [I/T] to eat something in a noisy way

mundane /ˌmʌnˈdeɪn/ adj ordinary and not interesting or exciting

municipal /mjuːˈnɪsɪp(ə)l/ adj relating to a town: *municipal elections* ♦ *a municipal swimming pool*

munitions /mjuːˈnɪʃ(ə)nz/ noun [plural] military weapons and equipment

mural /ˈmjʊərəl/ noun [C] a large painting done on a wall

murder¹ /ˈmɜːdə/ noun [C/U] ★★ the crime of deliberately killing someone: *The murder was committed over five years ago.*
→ MANSLAUGHTER

PHRASES be murder *informal* to be very difficult or unpleasant: *The traffic out there is murder.*
get away with murder *informal* to do something bad without being stopped or punished: *They let their children get away with murder.*

murder² /ˈmɜːdə/ verb [T] ★
1 to commit the crime of deliberately killing someone
2 *informal* to do something so badly that you spoil it completely = RUIN: *She's murdering that song!*

murderer /ˈmɜːdərə/ noun [C] someone who commits murder

murderous /ˈmɜːdərəs/ adj likely to kill someone, or intending to kill someone

murky /ˈmɜːki/ adj **1** dark and difficult to see through: *murky water* **2** involving activities that are dishonest or morally wrong: *We suspected he had a murky past.*

murmur /ˈmɜːmə/ verb [I/T] to say something in a very quiet voice: *Frances murmured an apology as she left.* ♦ *'How strange', she murmured.* —**murmur** noun [C]

muscle¹ /ˈmʌs(ə)l/ noun ★★
1 [C/U] a piece of flesh that connects bones and moves a particular part of your body: *These exercises are good for your stomach muscles.*
2 [U] power or strength: *financial/political muscle*

M

muscle

muscle² /ˈmʌs(ə)l/ **PHRASAL VERB** ,muscle ˈin
to use your power or influence to become
involved in something

muscular /ˈmʌskjʊlə/ adj **1** having big
muscles: *muscular arms/legs* **2** affecting
your muscles

muse /mjuːz/ verb [I] to think about
something in a careful slow way

museum /mjuːˈziːəm/ noun [C] ★★★ a
building where valuable and important
objects are kept for people to see and study

mush /mʌʃ/ noun [singular/U] a solid substance
that is much softer than it should be
—**mushy** adj

mushroom¹ /ˈmʌʃruːm/ noun [C] a small
white or brown FUNGUS with a short stem
and a round top that is often eaten as a
vegetable → TOADSTOOL —*picture* → C11

mushroom² /ˈmʌʃruːm/ verb [I] to increase or
develop very quickly

music /ˈmjuːzɪk/ noun [U] ★★★
1 pleasant sounds made by voices or
instruments: *She prefers listening to
classical music.* ♦ *She writes music for films.*
♦ *We need to play a new piece of music for
the concert.*
2 the activity of writing, performing, or
studying music: *She's planning to do a
degree in music.* ♦ *a music teacher*
3 the printed symbols that represent music:
I'm learning to read music.

musical¹ /ˈmjuːzɪk(ə)l/ adj ★
1 involving music, or relating to music:
musical instruments ♦ *an evening of musical
entertainment*
2 a musical sound is pleasant to listen to
3 good at playing or singing music: *They're
a very musical family.*
—**musically** /ˈmjuːzɪkli/ adv

musical² /ˈmjuːzɪk(ə)l/ noun [C] a play or film
in which there are a lot of songs

musician /mjuːˈzɪʃ(ə)n/ noun [C] ★ someone
who performs or writes music, especially
as their job

Muslim /ˈmʊzləm/ noun [C] ★ someone whose
religion is Islam —**Muslim** adj

muslin /ˈmʌzlɪn/ noun [U] a type of thin cotton
cloth

mussel /ˈmʌs(ə)l/ noun [C] a small SHELLFISH
with a black shell and a soft body that can
be eaten

must¹ /weak məst, strong mʌst/ modal verb ★★★

- **Must** is usually followed by an infinitive
  without 'to': *You must stop at the red light.*
  Sometimes it is used without a following
  infinitive: *We will act alone if we must.*
- **Must** has no tenses, no participles, and no
  infinitive form. It does not change its form,
  so the third person singular form does not
  end in '-s': *She must be asleep.*
- Questions and negatives are formed without
  'do': *Must we wear our uniforms?*
- The negative form **must not** is used for saying
  that something should not be done. This is
  often shortened in conversation or informal
  writing to **mustn't**: *You mustn't use the office
  phone for private calls.* For saying that it is not
  necessary to do something **not have to, not
  need to**, or **needn't** is used: *Children don't
  have to pay to go in.*

1 used for saying that you think something
is probably true because nothing else
seems possible: *You must be tired after your
long journey.* ♦ *There must be some mistake –
no one called Shaw lives here.* ♦ *I must have
fallen asleep.*
2 used for saying that something is
necessary or important to do: *You must
answer all the questions.* ♦ *We mustn't be
late.*
3 used for suggesting to someone that they
should do something because it would be
enjoyable or interesting: *You must come and
visit us again some time.*
→ SAY¹

must² /mʌst/ noun **a must** something that you
definitely need in a particular situation:
*Good binoculars are a must for any serious
birdwatcher.*

mustache /məˈstɑːʃ/ an American spelling of
moustache

mustard /ˈmʌstəd/ noun [U] a thick yellow
sauce with a hot taste

muster /ˈmʌstə/ verb [T] to try to make
yourself feel something as strongly as
possible: *The job would need all the energy
I could muster.*

mustn't /ˈmʌs(ə)nt/ short form the usual way
of saying or writing 'must not'. This is not
often used in formal writing: *I mustn't forget
to phone Jenny.*

musty /ˈmʌsti/ adj smelling unpleasant and
not fresh

mutant /ˈmjuːt(ə)nt/ noun [C] a plant or
animal that is different from others of its
type because of a change in its genes
—**mutant** adj

mutate /mjuːˈteɪt/ verb [I] to become
physically different from other plants or
animals of the same type because of a
genetic change —**mutation** /mjuːˈteɪʃ(ə)n/
noun [C/U]

mute /mjuːt/ adj **1** saying nothing, or not
willing to speak **2** old-fashioned unable to
speak. People now think that this word is
offensive and prefer to use the expression
speech-impaired.

muted /'mju:tɪd/ adj not very strong, loud, or bright

mutilate /'mju:tɪˌleɪt/ verb [T] to damage someone's body permanently by cutting it or cutting off part of it —**mutilation** /ˌmju:tɪ'leɪʃ(ə)n/ noun [C/U]

mutinous /'mju:tɪnəs/ adj refusing to obey someone who is in a position of authority

mutiny /'mju:təni/ noun [C/U] an occasion when people refuse to obey someone in a position of authority —**mutiny** verb [I]

mutter /'mʌtə/ verb [I/T] to say something in a quiet voice, especially because you are annoyed

mutton /'mʌt(ə)n/ noun [U] the meat from an adult sheep → LAMB

mutual /'mju:tʃuəl/ adj 1 felt or done in the same way by each person: *mutual respect/support/understanding* ♦ *His contract was cancelled by mutual agreement.* 2 belonging to two or more people: *They were introduced by a mutual friend.* ♦ *We have a mutual interest in hiking.*

mutually /'mju:tʃuəli/ adv to or for each person equally

muzzle¹ /'mʌz(ə)l/ noun [C] 1 the nose and mouth of an animal such as a dog or horse 2 something that you put around the nose and mouth of a dog to prevent it from biting people 3 the end of a gun BARREL where the bullets come out

muzzle² /'mʌz(ə)l/ verb [T] 1 to prevent someone from expressing their opinions publicly 2 to put a muzzle on a dog

my /maɪ/ determiner ★★★ belonging to or connected with you, when you are the person who is speaking or writing: *I shut my eyes.* ♦ *I want you to meet my parents.* ♦ *When my sister went to college I got my own room.*

MYOB abbrev mind your own business: used in emails and TEXT MESSAGES

myriad /'mɪriəd/ noun **a myriad of sth** *literary* an extremely large number of people or things —**myriad** adj

myself /maɪ'self/ pronoun ★★★
1 the REFLEXIVE form of 'I', used for showing that an action that you do affects you: *I fell and hurt myself.* ♦ *I was starting to enjoy myself.* ♦ *I'm going to pour myself another coffee.*
2 used for emphasizing that you are referring to yourself and not to anyone else: *I myself was once a prisoner.*
3 used instead of 'I' or 'me' when you are trying to be polite. Many people think that this use is incorrect: *Lindsey or myself will be happy to answer any of your questions.*
PHRASES **(all) by myself 1** alone: *I like to spend a little time by myself at weekends.* 2 without help from anyone else: *I made the whole meal all by myself.*
(all) to myself not sharing something with anyone else: *I had the whole beach to myself.*
be/feel myself to be in your normal mental or physical state: *I'm sorry if I shouted. I'm just not myself today.*

mysterious /mɪ'stɪəriəs/ adj 1 not explained, understood, or known: *They are investigating the mysterious disappearance of a young man.* ♦ *He died in mysterious circumstances.* 2 keeping things secret in a way that makes other people want to discover what they are —**mysteriously** adv

mystery¹ /'mɪst(ə)ri/ noun ★
1 [C] something that you cannot understand, explain, or get information about: *The exact origin of the universe remains a mystery.* ♦ *Why she left is still a mystery to him.*
2 [U] a quality that makes someone or something difficult to explain, understand, or get information about, in a way that makes them seem interesting or exciting: *a woman with an air of mystery about her* ♦ *His past is shrouded in mystery.*
3 [C] a story, film, or play in which events take place that are not explained until the end: *a murder mystery*

mystery² /'mɪst(ə)ri/ adj a mystery person is someone who you do not know

mystic /'mɪstɪk/ noun [C] someone who practises MYSTICISM

mystical /'mɪstɪk(ə)l/ adj 1 relating to MYSTICISM 2 involving mysterious religious or spiritual powers

mysticism /'mɪstɪˌsɪz(ə)m/ noun [U] the belief that you can understand God directly by praying and MEDITATING

mystify /'mɪstɪˌfaɪ/ verb [T] if something mystifies you, you cannot understand or explain it —**mystifying** adj

mystique /mɪ'sti:k/ noun [U] an attractive quality that something has because it seems mysterious and special in an exciting way

myth /mɪθ/ noun [C] 1 an ancient traditional story about gods, magic, and HEROES 2 something that people wrongly believe to be true

mythical /'mɪθɪk(ə)l/ adj 1 existing only in MYTHS: *mythical creatures* 2 *formal* imaginary, or not real: *Has anyone ever met this mythical boyfriend of hers?*

mythology /mɪ'θɒlədʒi/ noun [C/U] ancient MYTHS: *Roman mythology* —**mythological** /ˌmɪθə'lɒdʒɪk(ə)l/ adj

Nn

n¹ or **N** /en/ noun [C/U] the 14th letter of the English alphabet

n² abbrev noun

N abbrev 1 north 2 northern

'n' /ən/ conjunction *informal* a way of writing 'and' that shows how it sounds in informal conversation

n/a abbrev not applicable: used on forms for showing that a particular question is not relevant to you

nab /næb/ verb [T] *informal* to quickly take or steal something

naff /næf/ adj *British informal* stupid, or not fashionable

nag /næg/ verb [T] **1** to annoy someone by frequently criticizing them or telling them to do something: *My mum keeps nagging me to tidy my room.* **2** if a doubt, worry, or fear nags you, you cannot stop thinking about it

nagging /'nægɪŋ/ adj **1** continuously hurting you or making you feel worried: *a nagging doubt/fear/pain* **2** annoying you by frequently criticizing you or telling you to do something

nail¹ /neɪl/ noun [C] ★
1 a thin pointed piece of metal that you use for fixing one thing to another by hitting it with a hammer
2 the smooth hard part that grows over the ends of your fingers and toes
PHRASES a nail in the coffin one of a series of events or actions that seriously harm someone or something: *These job losses are the final nail in the region's coffin.*
on the nail *British informal* if you pay on the nail, you pay immediately
→ HIT¹

nail² /neɪl/ verb [T] to fix something with nails

nail-biting adj a nail-biting situation makes you very excited or worried

nail file noun [C] a thin piece of metal with a rough side that you use for shaping your nails

nail polish noun [U] NAIL VARNISH

nail varnish noun [U] *British* a shiny coloured liquid that women put on their nails

naive /naɪ'iːv/ adj lacking experience of life, and extremely willing to trust and believe people —**naively** adv, **naivety** /naɪ'iːvəti/ noun [U]

naked /'neɪkɪd/ adj ★
1 not wearing any clothes=BARE: *a drawing of a naked woman*
2 not covered: *a naked flame/bulb*
3 a naked emotion is very strong and can be clearly seen in someone's expression
PHRASE the naked eye if you can see something with the naked eye, you can see it without using an instrument such as a TELESCOPE or a MICROSCOPE

name¹ /neɪm/ noun ★★★
1 [C] a word or set of words used for referring to a person or thing: *My name is Judith Kramer.* ♦ *What's the name of this flower?* ♦ *I think it's a great name for a band.*
2 [singular] a reputation: *These people have ruined the school's good name.* ♦ *He first made a name for himself as a singer.*
3 [C] a famous person or organization: *She's one of the most famous names in country music.* ♦ *This role has turned him into a household name* (=known by everyone).
→ BIG NAME

PHRASES call sb names to insult someone by using unpleasant words to refer to them
in the name of representing someone or something
the name of the game *informal* something that you must do if you want to be successful at a particular activity: *Personality is the name of the game in sales.*

Talking or writing about names

- **alias** a false name that a criminal uses
- **first name/Christian name** a personal name that you are given when you are born
- **last name/surname** your family name
- **maiden name** a woman's last name before she was married
- **nickname** an invented name that other people call you
- **second/middle name** the name that comes after your first name

---

name² /neɪm/ verb [T] ★★
1 to give someone or something a name: *Have you named the baby yet?* ♦ **name sb/sth sth** *We named our puppy Patch.*
2 to know and say what the name of someone or something is: *How many world capitals can you name?*
3 to make a decision about a date, time, place, or price, and say what it is: *Name a time, and I'll be there.*
4 to choose someone for a particular job, position, or prize: **name sb sth** *He was named player of the year.*
PHRASE you name it *informal* used after a list for saying that many other things of the same type are also available
PHRASAL VERB name sb/sth after sb/sth to give someone or something the same name as someone or something else: *Albert was named after his grandfather.*

name-dropping noun [U] the act of mentioning famous people who you know in order to impress other people

nameless /'neɪmləs/ adj not having a name, or not having a name that you know
PHRASE who shall remain nameless *often humorous* used for saying that you are not going to name the person who has done something: *Someone, who shall remain nameless, broke the lock.*

namely /'neɪmli/ adv used for introducing more detailed information about a subject that you are discussing: *Some groups, namely students and pensioners, will benefit from the new tax.*

namesake /'neɪmˌseɪk/ noun [C] a person or thing with the same name as someone or something else

nan /næn/ or **nana** /'nænə/ noun [C] *British informal* your grandmother

nanny /'næni/ noun [C] a woman whose job is to look after someone else's children

nap /næp/ noun [C] a short sleep, usually during the day —**nap** verb [I]

nape /neɪp/ noun [singular] the back of your neck

napkin /'næpkɪn/ noun [C] a piece of cloth or

paper that you use for protecting your clothes and wiping your mouth and hands when you are eating=SERVIETTE

nappy /ˈnæpi/ noun [C] *British* a thick piece of soft cloth or paper that a baby wears to catch solid and liquid waste

narcissism /ˈnɑːsɪsɪz(ə)m/ noun [U] the attitude of people who admire themselves a lot —**narcissist** /ˈnɑːsɪsɪst/ noun [C], **narcissistic** /ˌnɑːsɪˈsɪstɪk/ adj

narcotic /nɑːˈkɒtɪk/ noun [C] *American* an illegal drug

narrate /nəˈreɪt/ verb [T] to give information about what is happening in a television programme or a film without appearing on the screen

narration /nəˈreɪʃ(ə)n/ noun [U] spoken information about what is happening in a television programme or a film, given by someone who you do not see

narrative /ˈnærətɪv/ noun [C] a story or an account of something that has happened =STORY, TALE

narrator /nəˈreɪtə/ noun [C] **1** someone who tells the story in a novel **2** someone whose voice explains what is happening in a television programme or a film, but who you do not see

narrow¹ /ˈnærəʊ/ adj ★★★
 1 if something is narrow, there is only a short distance from one side of it to the other ≠ WIDE: *narrow streets*
 2 limited ≠ BROAD: *a narrow range of options*
 3 used about something that you succeed in doing but nearly failed to do: *a narrow victory/escape*

narrow² /ˈnærəʊ/ verb [I/T] to become narrower, or to make something narrower ≠ WIDEN

 PHRASAL VERB **narrow sth down** to reduce the number of possibilities or choices

narrowly /ˈnærəʊli/ adv by a very small amount: *Three teenagers narrowly escaped death in the crash.*

narrow-minded adj not interested in ideas or cultures that are different from your own ≠ BROAD-MINDED

nasal /ˈneɪz(ə)l/ adj **1** relating to your nose **2** someone with a nasal voice sounds as if they are speaking through their nose

nasty /ˈnɑːsti/ adj **1** very unpleasant =HORRIBLE: *a nasty cold wind* ♦ *cheap and nasty red wine* **2** unkind, offensive, or violent: *She said some very nasty things about him.* **3** serious or dangerous: *a nasty accident/cough* —**nastily** adv

nation /ˈneɪʃ(ə)n/ noun [C] ★★★
 1 a country: *the leaders of the main industrial nations*
 2 the people of a particular country: *We want government to serve the whole nation.*

national¹ /ˈnæʃ(ə)nəl/ adj ★★★
 1 relating to one particular nation: *the national and international news*
 2 relating to the whole of a nation: *House prices in London are 5% higher than the national average.*

3 owned or controlled by the government: *the National Museum of Wales* ♦ *a national park/monument*
—**nationally** adv

Word family: **national**
*Words in the same family as **national***
■ nation *n* ■ international *adj*
■ nationalize *v* ■ nationalized *adj*
■ nationalism *n* ■ nationalistic *adj*
■ nationality *n* ■ multinational *adj,n*

national² /ˈnæʃ(ə)nəl/ noun [C] a citizen of a particular country

national anthem noun [C] the official national song of a country

national curriculum noun [singular] a country's official programme of subjects that children must learn at school

National Health Service, the the system in the UK that provides free medical care for everyone=NHS, THE

National Insurance noun [U] a tax that all workers and employers in the UK pay

nationalism /ˈnæʃ(ə)nə,lɪz(ə)m/ noun [U] **1** the attitude of people who want political independence from a country that rules them **2** the belief that your country is better than all other countries

nationalist /ˈnæʃ(ə)nəlɪst/ noun [C] **1** a member of a group of people who want political independence from a country that rules them **2** someone who believes that their own country is better than all other countries —**nationalist** adj

nationalistic /ˌnæʃ(ə)nəˈlɪstɪk/ adj extremely proud of your own country and believing that it is better than all other countries

nationality /ˌnæʃəˈnæləti/ noun ★
 1 [U] the legal status of being a citizen of a particular country: *British/American/German nationality*
 2 [C] a group of people who have the same race, language, or culture: *There may be as many as 20 different nationalities in a school.*

nationalize /ˈnæʃ(ə)nə,laɪz/ verb [T] if a government nationalizes a large company or industry, it takes control of it and owns it ≠ PRIVATIZE —**nationalization** /ˌnæʃ(ə)nəlaɪˈzeɪʃ(ə)n/ noun [U]

national park noun [C] a large area of countryside that is protected by the government in order to preserve its natural beauty

national security noun [U] the protection or safety of a country

national service noun [U] a period of time that young people in some countries must spend in the armed forces

nation state noun [C] an independent country, especially one in which all the people share the same language and culture

nationwide /ˌneɪʃ(ə)nˈwaɪd/ adj, adv in all parts of a country: *a nationwide strike*

native¹ /ˈneɪtɪv/ adj ★
 1 living in a particular country or area since birth: *My wife's a native New Yorker, but I'm from Atlanta.* ♦ *After a long stay in*

England he's back in his **native land** (=the country that he was born in). **2** native plants, animals, or people have always existed in a place: *the native population* ♦ *Elephants are native to Africa and Asia.* **3** your native language or TONGUE is the first language that you learn

native² /'neɪtɪv/ noun [C] **1** someone who was born in a particular place: *He's a native of Edinburgh but now lives in London.* **2** *offensive* an offensive word for a member of a group of people who lived in a place before Europeans arrived there

Native A'merican noun [C] a member of one of the groups of people who lived in America before Europeans arrived

native 'speaker noun [C] someone who speaks a particular language as their first language

NATO /'neɪtəʊ/ North Atlantic Treaty Organization: an organization of North American and European countries that provides military support for its members

natter /'nætə/ noun [singular] *British informal* a conversation with a friend about unimportant things = CHAT —**natter** verb [I]

natural¹ /'nætʃ(ə)rəl/ adj ★★★ **1** existing in nature, and not produced by people: *This cloth is made from natural fibres.* ♦ *areas of great natural beauty* ♦ *The earthquake is the worst natural disaster that Japan has experienced.* ♦ *Mr Johnson died from natural causes* (=not as a result of an accident or crime). **2** reasonable in a particular situation: *His anger was an entirely natural reaction.* ♦ *It's only natural to worry about your child's diet.* **3** existing in someone from an early age: *The best players have natural talent.* **4** behaving in a relaxed and sincere way

natural² /'nætʃ(ə)rəl/ noun [C] someone with a lot of skill that has developed very quickly and easily

natural 'gas noun [U] a gas that is found underground and is used for heating and cooking

natural 'history noun [U] the study of plants and animals

naturalist /'nætʃ(ə)rəlɪst/ noun [C] someone who studies plants and animals

naturalize /'nætʃ(ə)rə,laɪz/ verb [T] to make someone an official citizen of a country that they were not born in —**naturalization** /ˌnætʃ(ə)rəlaɪ'zeɪʃ(ə)n/ noun [U], **naturalized** /'nætʃ(ə)rə,laɪzd/ adj

naturally /'nætʃ(ə)rəli/ adv ★ **1** as most people would expect or understand = OBVIOUSLY: *Naturally, I was very keen to make a good first impression.* ♦ *His death has naturally come as a shock to us all.* **2** as a basic feature: *Her hair is naturally curly.* ♦ *Many herbs grow naturally in poor dry soils.* **3** in a normal way: *Try to act naturally in front of the camera.*

PHRASE **come naturally (to sb)** to be easy for someone to learn or do: *Being funny comes naturally to him.*

natural re'sources noun [plural] useful substances such as coal and oil that exist in a country

nature /'neɪtʃə/ noun ★★★ **1** [U] the physical world and all the living things in it: *the beauty of nature* **2** [C/U] the character, qualities, or features of someone or something: *The pony has a very gentle nature.* ♦ *It isn't in my nature to be aggressive.* ♦ *Apes are curious by nature.* ♦ *It's the nature of plastic to melt at high temperatures.* **3** [singular] a particular type of thing: *His behaviour was inappropriate for a meeting of this nature.*

'nature re,serve noun [C] an area of land in which the animals and plants are protected

naughty /'nɔːti/ adj **1** a naughty child behaves badly **2** *British informal* sexual in a rude but funny way —**naughtily** adv

nausea /'nɔːsiə, 'nɔːziə/ noun [U] the feeling that you are going to VOMIT

nauseating /'nɔːsiˌeɪtɪŋ, 'nɔːziˌeɪtɪŋ/ adj **1** making you feel as if you are going to VOMIT **2** very unpleasant = DISGUSTING —**nauseatingly** adv

nauseous /'nɔːsiəs, 'nɔːziəs/ adj feeling as if you want to VOMIT

nautical /'nɔːtɪk(ə)l/ adj relating to ships, or to sailing them

naval /'neɪv(ə)l/ adj relating to a country's navy

navel /'neɪv(ə)l/ noun [C] the small round place in the middle of the skin on your stomach

navigable /'nævɪɡəb(ə)l/ adj deep and wide enough for ships to travel through

navigate /'nævɪˌɡeɪt/ verb **1** [I] to use maps or other equipment in order to decide which way to go in a ship, plane, or car **2** [T] to follow a path through a difficult place **3** [T] *formal* to deal effectively with a complicated situation

navigation /ˌnævɪ'ɡeɪʃ(ə)n/ noun [U] **1** the movement of a ship or an aircraft along a planned path **2** the skill of using maps or other equipment in order to decide which way to go

navigator /'nævɪˌɡeɪtə/ noun [C] someone whose job is to plan the direction in which a ship, plane, or car should travel

navy /'neɪvi/ noun **1** [C] the part of a country's armed forces that uses ships **2** [U] navy blue

navy 'blue adj very dark blue —**navy 'blue** noun [U]

Nazi /'nɑːtsi/ noun [C] someone who belonged to the political party that governed Germany during the Second World War —**Nazi** adj, **Nazism** noun [U]

NB abbrev nota bene: used for saying that someone should pay particular attention to the information that follows

NE abbrev north-east

near¹ /nɪə/ grammar word ★★★

Near can be:
- a **preposition**: *I lived near the school.*
- an **adverb**: *Come nearer, and I'll tell you the whole story.*
- an **adjective**: *I went into the nearest room.*

1 close close to someone or something: *A group of students were standing near the entrance.* ♦ *The shops are quite near.* ♦ *They live in a small cottage 15 miles from the nearest village.* ♦ *Rosa moved a little **nearer** to the fire.*

2 not long from then/now close to a particular time or event: *The incident occurred near the end of the war.* ♦ *It was nearer three than two o'clock when he finally arrived.* ♦ *The date of the election was **drawing near**.* ♦ *They plan to start a family sometime **in the near future** (=soon).*

3 close to a state or situation getting close to a particular state or situation: *Julian was **near to** panic as he suddenly realized that he was trapped.* ♦ **near to doing sth** *They are near to solving the puzzle.*

4 similar very similar to something: *It was **the nearest thing to** a home that he had ever had.*

5 not much less only a little less than a particular amount or number: *The temperature fell to near zero.*

PHRASES from near and far from a very wide area

not go near to avoid someone or something: *Dad doesn't go near red meat since his heart attack.*

nowhere/not anywhere near 1 far from a particular point or place: *The photographers were nowhere near the crash when it happened.* **2** not nearly: *She doesn't look anywhere near as old as Rebecca.*

near² /nɪə/ verb [T] to come closer to a place or time: *a man nearing the age of 60*

nearby¹ /ˌnɪəˈbaɪ/ adj a nearby place is not far away

nearby² /ˌnɪəˈbaɪ/ adv not far from where you are: *My cousin lives nearby.*

nearly /ˈnɪəli/ adv ★★★ almost: *It took nearly six hours to do the work.* ♦ *I tripped and nearly fell down the stairs.*

PHRASE not nearly (as/so) much less than: *It's not nearly so cold today.* ♦ *There isn't nearly enough food for everyone.*

neat /niːt/ adj ★

1 things that are neat look nice because they have been arranged carefully = TIDY: *She arranged the papers into three neat piles on her desk.* ♦ *The house was always **neat and tidy**.*

2 someone who is neat tends to keep things carefully arranged

3 producing a result in a simple but intelligent way: *a neat way of solving the problem*

4 a neat alcoholic drink is served without any ice and is not mixed with any other liquid

—**neatly** adv

necessarily /ˈnesəsərəli, ˌnesəˈserəli/ adv ★ always, or in every situation

PHRASE not necessarily not always, or not in every situation: *Our customers will not necessarily understand why we are raising our prices.*

necessary /ˈnesəs(ə)ri/ adj ★★★ if something is necessary, you must have it or must do it: *I don't want to be disturbed unless it's absolutely necessary.* ♦ *I can take your place at the meeting tomorrow **if necessary**.* ♦ *What type of clothing is **necessary for** a walk in the mountains?* ♦ **it is necessary for sb to do sth** *It was necessary for all students to attend classes regularly.*

PHRASE a necessary evil something that you do not like but cannot avoid: *Paying taxes is a necessary evil.*

Word family: **necessary**

*Words in the same family as **necessary***
- **necessity** n
- **necessarily** adv
- **necessitate** v
- **unnecessary** adj
- **unnecessarily** adv

necessitate /nəˈsesɪˌteɪt/ verb [T] formal to make something necessary

necessity /nəˈsesəti/ noun **1** [U] the fact that something is necessary: *the necessity for a quick solution to the problem* ♦ *doubts about the necessity of the war* **2** [C] something that you must have or must do ≠ LUXURY: *They lacked even the bare necessities (=the basic things that everyone needs).*

neck /nek/ noun [C] ★★★

1 the part of your body that joins your head to the rest of your body —*picture →* C14

2 the part of a piece of clothing that fits around your neck

3 a long narrow part of something such as a bottle or a musical instrument

PHRASES neck and neck with each person or group competing as well as the other and equally likely to win

up to your neck in sth informal very involved or busy with something

→ BREATHE

necklace /ˈnekləs/ noun [C] a piece of jewellery that hangs round your neck —*picture →* JEWELLERY

neckline /ˈnekˌlaɪn/ noun [C] the shape of a piece of clothing around your neck

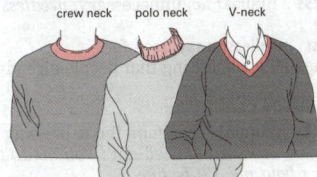

crew neck   polo neck   V-neck

necklines

nectar /ˈnektə/ noun [U] a sweet liquid in flowers that insects and birds drink

nectarine /ˈnektəˌriːn/ noun [C] a fruit with a smooth red and yellow skin. It is yellow

N

inside and has a large seed. —*picture* → C10

need¹ /niːd/ verb [T] ★★★

1 if you need something, you must have it because it is necessary: *You'll need some warm clothes for the winter.* ♦ *I don't need any advice from you.* ♦ **need sb to do sth** *I need someone to help me carry these books downstairs.*

2 used for saying whether it is necessary for something to be done or to exist: **need to do sth** *I'll need to know your decision by next week.* ♦ **sth needs doing/to be done** *The bathroom needs cleaning.*

need² /niːd/ noun ★★★

1 [singular/U] a situation in which it is necessary for something to be done: *I'll ask someone to help you, **if need be** (=if it becomes necessary).* ♦ *He recognizes the **need for** immediate action.* ♦ **a need to do sth** *We feel there is a need to do more research.*

2 [C] something that you need in order to be healthy, comfortable, successful etc: *People with mental health problems **have special needs**.*

> **PHRASES in need** not having enough food, money, clothing, or other things that are necessary: *families in need*
>
> **in need of sth** needing something: *He was tired and hungry, and badly in need of a bath.*
>
> **there is no need (for sb) to do sth** or **there is no need for sth** used for saying that something does not have to be done or should not be done: *There's no need for you to stay late – I can finish this.* ♦ *There's no need for all this violence.*

needle¹ /ˈniːd(ə)l/ noun [C] ★

1 a thin sharp metal tube that is used for putting medicine or drugs into your body through your skin

2 a thin metal tool that you use for sewing or KNITTING

3 the part of a piece of equipment that points to a number in order to show a measurement: *a compass needle*

4 a very thin sharp leaf that grows on some trees: *pine needles*

needle² /ˈniːd(ə)l/ verb [T] *informal* to say things that are intended to make someone angry or embarrassed

needless /ˈniːdləs/ adj unnecessary: *needless waste*

> **PHRASE needless to say** used for emphasizing something that people already know

—**needlessly** adv

needn't /ˈniːd(ə)nt/ short form the usual way of saying or writing 'need not': *You needn't worry about me, I'll be fine.*

needy /ˈniːdi/ adj **1** without enough money, food, or clothes **2 the needy** people who are poor

negate /nɪˈɡeɪt/ verb [T] *formal* to make something have no effect —**negation** /nɪˈɡeɪʃ(ə)n/ noun [U]

negative¹ /ˈneɡətɪv/ adj ★★

1 saying you disagree	**5** expressing 'no'
2 harmful/bad	**6** less than zero
3 emphasizing bad part	**7** about electrical charge
4 of medical test	

1 expressing disagreement or criticism ≠ POSITIVE: *a negative response*

2 harmful, or bad: *I hope the divorce won't have **a negative effect** on the children.*

3 giving more attention or emphasis to bad aspects than good ones ≠ POSITIVE: *The article presents a rather **negative view** of professional sports.*

4 showing that someone does not have a particular disease or condition: *Her pregnancy test was negative.* ♦ *He **tested negative** for drugs.*

5 *linguistics* a negative word expresses 'no' or 'not', for example 'don't' or 'never'

6 a negative number or amount is less than zero ≠ POSITIVE

7 *technical* with the same electrical charge as an ELECTRON ≠ POSITIVE

—**negatively** adv

negative² /ˈneɡətɪv/ noun [C] **1** an image on film in which dark things appear light, and light things appear dark **2** *linguistics* a word or expression that means 'no'

neglect¹ /nɪˈɡlekt/ verb [T] **1** to not look after someone or something: *parents who neglect their children* ♦ *The building had been neglected for years.* **2** to not do something that you should do: *He couldn't neglect his duties as an officer.* ♦ *She had neglected to inform me that the company was having financial problems.* **3** to not pay attention to something such as the work of a writer or an artist —**neglected** adj

neglect² /nɪˈɡlekt/ noun [U] the failure to give someone or something the care that they need: *Our roads have suffered from years of neglect.*

neglectful /nɪˈɡlektf(ə)l/ adj not doing something that you should do

negligence /ˈneɡlɪdʒ(ə)ns/ noun [U] the failure to be careful enough, so that something bad happens

negligent /ˈneɡlɪdʒ(ə)nt/ adj failing to be careful enough, so that something bad happens —**negligently** adv

negligible /ˈneɡlɪdʒəb(ə)l/ adj very unimportant or small=INSIGNIFICANT

negotiable /nɪˈɡəʊʃiəb(ə)l/ adj able to be changed through discussion by the people involved

negotiate /nɪˈɡəʊʃieɪt/ verb ★

1 [I/T] to try to reach an agreement by discussing something formally: *The two sides have shown their willingness to negotiate.* ♦ *Negotiating a peace deal will not be an easy task.* ♦ **negotiate sth with sb** *The airline is negotiating a new contract with the union.*

2 [T] to successfully travel on a road or path that is difficult to travel on or travel through: *Only 4-wheel-drive vehicles can*

negotiate the rough roads around here.
—**negotiator** noun [C]

negotiation /nɪˌgəʊʃiˈeɪʃ(ə)n/ noun [C/U] formal discussions in which people try to reach an agreement

neigh /neɪ/ verb [I] to make the high loud sound that a horse makes —**neigh** noun [C]

neighbor /ˈneɪbə/ the American spelling of **neighbour**

neighborhood /ˈneɪbəˌhʊd/ the American spelling of **neighbourhood**

neighboring /ˈneɪbərɪŋ/ the American spelling of **neighbouring**

neighborly /ˈneɪbəli/ the American spelling of **neighbourly**

neighbour /ˈneɪbə/ noun [C] ★★
1 someone who lives near you: *friends and neighbours*
2 a person or place that is next to another person or place: *She whispered to her neighbour that she thought the play was too long.* ♦ *Turkey and its European neighbours*

neighbourhood /ˈneɪbəˌhʊd/ noun [C] a particular area of a town

neighbouring /ˈneɪbərɪŋ/ adj next to each other: *neighbouring towns/countries*

neighbourly /ˈneɪbəli/ adj showing a helpful and friendly attitude towards people who live near you

neither /ˈnaɪðə, ˈniːðə/ grammar word ★★★

> **Neither** can be:
> ■ an **adverb**: *I can't play tennis, but neither can you.*
> ■ a **conjunction** with **nor**: *Neither Simon nor Sally can swim.*
> ■ a **determiner**: *Neither woman seemed sure of what to say.*
> ■ a **pronoun**: *There were two witnesses, but neither would make a statement.* ♦ *Neither of us knew what to do.*

1 used for showing that a negative statement also applies to someone or something else: *Adams was not invited, and neither were any of his friends.* ♦ *'I don't like him.' 'Neither do I.'* ♦ *'I don't feel like going to the party.' 'Me neither.'*
2 used for referring to each of two people or things when saying something negative that applies to both of them: *Neither side trusts the other.* ♦ *Neither company could succeed on its own.* ♦ *It was an experience that neither of us will ever forget.*
PHRASES **neither here nor there** not important or relevant: *Whether I agree with you is neither here nor there.*
neither...nor used for showing that something is not true of two people or things: *Neither his son nor his daughter were at the funeral.* ♦ *Ron's neither as young nor as fit as the other members of the team.*

> When **neither** is the subject of a sentence, it is usually used with a singular verb: *Neither of the books was published in this country.* But in spoken English a plural verb is sometimes used: *Neither of us are planning to go.*

neon /ˈniːɒn/ noun [U] a gas that is used in lights and signs

nephew /ˈnefjuː, ˈnevjuː/ noun [C] a son of your brother or sister, or a son of your husband's or wife's brother or sister
—*picture* → FAMILY TREE

nepotism /ˈnepəˌtɪz(ə)m/ noun [U] the practice of giving jobs to your family and friends

nerd /nɜːd/ noun [C] *informal* someone who is boring and not fashionable —**nerdy** adj

nerve /nɜːv/ noun ★
1 [C] one of the groups of fibres in your body that carry messages to and from your brain
2 nerves [plural] the worried feeling that you will do something badly: *He asked for a drink to calm his nerves before heading out to the plane.*
3 [U] the ability to control your fear and stay determined when you are doing something that is difficult=COURAGE: *Suddenly I lost my nerve and I couldn't move.* ♦ **the nerve to do sth** *After months of agonizing, she finally found the nerve to tell him he was wrong.*
4 [U] a rude attitude that makes other people angry: **have the nerve to do sth** *She had the nerve to call me a liar after everything I've done for her.*
PHRASE **get on sb's nerves** to annoy someone

nerve-wracking or **nerve-racking** /ˈnɜːv ˌrækɪŋ/ adj making you very nervous or worried

nervous /ˈnɜːvəs/ adj ★★
1 feeling excited and worried, or slightly afraid=ANXIOUS: *Driving on mountain roads always makes me nervous.* ♦ *a nervous laugh* ♦ *I got very nervous waiting for my turn to be called.* ♦ *She was nervous about walking home so late.*
2 a nervous person easily becomes excited or upset because they are not relaxed
3 relating to the nerves in your body: *a nervous condition*
—**nervously** adv

nervous breakdown noun [C] a mental condition in which you are so upset or unhappy that you cannot look after yourself

nervous system, the noun [singular] the system of nerves that control your body and your mind

nest¹ /nest/ noun [C] **1** a structure that birds make to keep their eggs and babies in **2** a home that insects or small animals make for themselves

nest² /nest/ verb [I] to build or use a nest

nestle /ˈnes(ə)l/ verb [I] **1** to put yourself into a comfortable and safe position **2** *literary* to be in a protected position: *a pretty village nestling among rolling hills*

net¹ /net/ noun ★★
1 [C/U] a material made of string or rope that is woven into a loose pattern with spaces in it
2 [C] in some sports, an object made of net that you hit, kick, or throw the ball over or into —*picture* → C15
3 [C] a bag made of net that you use for catching fish or other animals

N

4 the Net the INTERNET: *He spends hours surfing the Net.*

net² /net/ adj **1** a net amount of money is the total amount after taxes or costs have been removed → GROSS **2** a net effect or result is the final one, after everything has been considered **3** the net weight of something is its weight without its container

net³ /net/ verb [T] **1** to manage to get or do something **2** to earn a particular amount of money as profit → GROSS

netball /'netbɔːl/ noun [U] a women's game that is similar to basketball

netting /'netɪŋ/ noun [U] a material made of string or rope that is woven into a loose pattern with spaces in it =NET

nettle /'net(ə)l/ noun [C] a wild plant with pointed leaves and small hairs that sting you if you touch them

network¹ /'netwɜːk/ noun [C] ★★
1 a number of computers that are connected to each other
2 a system of things such as roads, rivers, or wires that are connected to each other: *a mobile phone network ♦ a network of canals*
3 a group of people or organizations that work together: *We have a nationwide network of financial advisors.*
4 a group of companies that broadcast the same television or radio programmes in all parts of a large area

Words often used with network

Adjectives often used with network (noun, sense 3)
■ **extensive, global, international, national, nationwide, wide, worldwide** + NETWORK: used about networks that cover a large area
Verbs often used with network (noun, sense 3)
■ **build, construct, create, develop, expand, form** + NETWORK: create a network

network² /'netwɜːk/ verb **1** [I] to meet people in order to make friends who will be useful for your business **2** [I/T] to connect computers together —**networking** noun [U]

neural /'njʊərəl/ adj *technical* relating to your nerves or your NERVOUS SYSTEM

neurology /njʊˈrɒlədʒi/ noun [U] *medical* the study of your NERVOUS SYSTEM and the diseases that affect it —**neurological** /ˌnjʊərəˈlɒdʒɪk(ə)l/ adj

neurosis /njʊˈrəʊsɪs/ (plural **neuroses** /njʊˈrəʊsiːz/) noun [C/U] *medical* a mental illness that makes you behave or think in an unreasonable way

neurotic /njʊˈrɒtɪk/ adj extremely worried about something in an unreasonable way

neuter¹ /'njuːtə/ verb [T] to perform an operation on an animal's sexual organs so that it cannot have babies

neuter² /'njuːtə/ adj *linguistics* a neuter word has a different form and behaviour from MASCULINE or FEMININE words in some languages

neutral¹ /'njuːtrəl/ adj ★
1 not supporting a particular person, group, or country in an argument, competition, or war: *a neutral country ♦ The television coverage was by no means neutral.*
2 not showing strong feelings or opinions in the way you speak or behave: *Her voice remained neutral as she spoke.*
3 neutral colours are not very strong or bright
—**neutrally** adv

neutral² /'njuːtrəl/ noun [U] the position of the GEARS in a car when the car cannot move

neutrality /njuːˈtræləti/ noun [U] the attitude of someone who does not support either side in a war or disagreement

neutralize /'njuːtrəlaɪz/ verb [T] to stop something from having any effect

neutron /'njuːtrɒn/ noun [C] *science* a part of an atom that does not have an electrical charge

never /'nevə/ adv ★★★
1 at no time, or not at all: *I've never been in love before. ♦ You'll never guess who I saw today! ♦ He never even said goodbye. ♦ I never knew you two were cousins. ♦ I went sailing once, but never again.*
2 *British spoken* used for saying that you are very surprised or shocked by what someone has said to you: *'She had the baby nine weeks early.' 'Never!'*
PHRASE **you never know** used for saying that something might happen even though it does not seem likely: *You never know – he might offer you a part in his film.*

nevertheless /ˌnevəðəˈles/ adv ★★ despite a fact or idea that you have just mentioned: *It's a difficult race. Nevertheless, about 1,000 runners participate every year.*

new /njuː/ adj ★★★

1 recently made	4 replacing sb/sth
2 recently bought	5 recently arrived
3 not used	6 not previously known

1 recently made, invented, or developed ≠ OLD: *They are going to build a new office block here. ♦ the new Tom Cruise film ♦ I was full of new ideas.*
2 recently bought or obtained ≠ OLD: *Have you seen my new car? ♦ When do you start your new job?*
3 never used or owned by anyone before: *I don't need a new printer – a used one is good enough.* → SECOND-HAND
4 replacing someone or something else ≠ OLD: *I need to get a new passport – my old one's expired.*
5 recently arrived in a new place or situation: *Many firms help new employees with finding accommodation. ♦ We are new to the London area.*
6 not previously known or discovered: *Police have now been given some new information.*
→ GOOD¹

Words that you can use instead of **new**

New is a very general word. Here are some words with more specific meanings that sound more natural and appropriate in particular situations.

equipment, computers etc made using the latest ideas and technology	advanced, cutting-edge, modern, newfangled (*showing disapproval*), state-of-the-art, up-to-date
ideas, methods etc that are new and not like anything that has existed before	innovative, fresh, novel, original, revolutionary
films, books etc that have just become available	latest, recent, just out
something you have just bought that has never been used	brand new

,New 'Age adj not connected with the main religions or with traditional ideas and methods

newborn /'njuːˌbɔːn/ adj recently born

newcomer /'njuːˌkʌmə/ noun [C] someone who has recently arrived somewhere

,New 'England the group of states in the NORTH-EASTERN part of the US

newfangled /ˌnjuːˈfæŋɡ(ə)ld/ adj *showing disapproval* very modern and complicated

'new-found adj recently gained: *a new-found confidence*

newly /'njuːli/ adv recently: *the newly appointed chairperson of the company*

newlyweds /'njuːliˌwedz/ noun [plural] two people who have not been married for long

news /njuːz/ noun ★★★
1 [U] information about something that has happened recently: *I'm afraid I've got some bad news.* ♦ *She was delighted by this piece of news.* ♦ *Have you heard the good news? Michael's got the job!* ♦ *Friends expressed shock at the news of his death.* ♦ *The leaflet is full of up-to-date news on the environment.*
2 [U] information about recent events that is reported in newspapers or on television or radio: *foreign/sports/financial news* ♦ *a news item* ♦ *Farming methods are back in the news this week.*
3 the news [singular] a television or radio broadcast that gives you information about recent events: *I always listen to the nine o'clock news.* ♦ *Did you see Tony Blair on the news last night?*
PHRASE **be news to sb** *spoken* to be a piece of information that surprises someone: *'Sally says she's borrowing your car tomorrow.' 'That's news to me!'*

News looks like a plural, but it is never used with a plural verb and cannot be used with a: *I've got a wonderful piece of news* (NOT *a wonderful news*) *for you.* ♦ *Do you have any news about Laura's baby?* ♦ *Here's some news about the World Cup.*

newsagent /'njuːˌzeɪdʒ(ə)nt/ noun [C] *British*
1 someone whose job is to sell newspapers and magazines **2 newsagent** or **newsagent's** a shop that sells newspapers and magazines

newsflash /'njuːzˌflæʃ/ noun [C] *British* a short broadcast of an important piece of news in the middle of a television or radio programme

newsgroup /'njuːzˌɡruːp/ noun [C] *computing* a place on the Internet where people can leave messages about a subject or activity that interests them

newsletter /'njuːzˌletə/ noun [C] a short simple magazine with information for members of an organization

newspaper /'njuːzˌpeɪpə/ noun ★★★
1 [C] a set of large printed sheets of folded paper containing news, articles, and other information that is published every day or every week: *a local newspaper* ♦ *a newspaper article* ♦ *I saw an interesting article in the newspaper this morning.*
2 [U] sheets of paper from a newspaper: *vegetables wrapped in newspaper*

newsprint /'njuːzˌprɪnt/ noun [U] the ink and paper that are used for printing newspapers

newsreader /'njuːzˌriːdə/ noun [C] *British* someone whose job is to read the news on television or radio

newsstand /'njuːzˌstænd/ noun [C] a place in the street where you can buy newspapers and magazines

newsworthy /'njuːzˌwɜːði/ adj interesting or important enough to be included in a news report

,New 'Testament, the the part of the Christian Bible that describes Jesus Christ's life

,new 'wave noun [singular/U] a form of art that uses new styles and ideas —,new 'wave adj

,New 'World, the North, Central, and South America

,New Year's 'Day noun [C] 1st January, the first day of the year

,New Year's 'Eve noun [C] 31st December

next /nekst/ grammar word ★★★

Next can be:
■ a **determiner**: *I'll see you next week.*
■ an **adjective**: *I'm leaving town on the next train.*
■ a **pronoun**: *You're the next in line.*
■ an **adverb**: *What happens next?*
■ used in the preposition phrase **next to**: *Come and sit next to me.*

1 used for referring to the time, event, or person that comes after this one, or that comes after another one: *He said he was leaving for Rome the next day.* ♦ *The next train to arrive at platform three is the 10.40 to Liverpool.* ♦ *I'll call you the next time I'm in town.* ♦ *Who's next in the queue?* ♦ *I knew exactly what was going to happen next.* ♦ *I'll see you next Friday.* ♦ *A meeting has been arranged for the weekend after next.*
2 used for referring to the place that is closest to where you are: *I could hear the sound of laughter in the next room.*
PHRASES **the next best/largest/smallest etc** one that is almost as good/large/small etc

N

as another one that you are mentioning: *Britain is Europe's next largest oil producer after Norway.* ♦ *This video game is the next best thing to flying a real plane.*

next of kin your closest relative or relatives

next to 1 beside, or very near to, someone or something, with no other person or thing in between: *She sat down next to me.* ♦ *Steve lives next to a lake, so we'll be able to go swimming.* **2** used before negative words to mean 'almost, but not completely': *It will be next to impossible to win.* ♦ *She earns next to nothing.*

next 'door adv in the building, room, or position next to yours, or next to another: *The restaurant is next door to the bank.*

next-'door adj **1** the next-door flat, garden, office etc is the one next to yours **2** your next-door neighbour lives in the house next to yours

NHS, the /ˌen eɪtʃ 'es/ the NATIONAL HEALTH SERVICE:

nib /nɪb/ noun [C] the part of a pen that the ink comes out of

nibble /'nɪb(ə)l/ verb [I/T] to eat something by taking a lot of small bites —**nibble** noun [C]

nice /naɪs/ adj ★★★

1 attractive, enjoyable, or pleasant: *London is a much nicer place to live nowadays.* ♦ *a nice big smile* ♦ *Your hair looks nice.* ♦ *It's nice and quiet in here.*

2 friendly, kind, and pleasant: *She's a nice girl.* ♦ *He's always been nice to me.* ♦ **it is nice of sb (to do sth)** *It was nice of you to come.*

PHRASE **nice to meet you** *spoken* used for saying hello or goodbye to someone when you meet them for the first time

Words that you can use instead of **nice**	
Nice is a very general word. Here are some words with more specific meanings that sound more natural and appropriate in particular situations.	
people	easy-going, easy to get on with, friendly, good fun, kind, lovely, sweet
behaviour	helpful, kind, thoughtful
something that happens or something that you do	good, great, lovely, marvellous, wonderful
weather	fantastic, fine, glorious, good, lovely, pleasant
clothes	beautiful, flattering, smart, stylish
food/flowers/gifts/places	beautiful, delightful, fantastic, great, lovely

nice-looking /ˌnaɪs 'lʊkɪŋ/ adj *informal* attractive

nicely /'naɪsli/ adv **1** in a satisfactory or suitable way: *That story illustrates the point nicely.* **2** in an attractive way: *a nicely furnished flat* **3** in a polite or friendly way: *If you ask Bob nicely, I'm sure he'll help.*

nicety /'naɪsəti/ noun [C] a very small difference or detail

niche /niːʃ/ noun [C] **1** a job or activity that is very suitable for you: *She's never really found her niche in life.* **2** *business* an opportunity to sell a particular product or service that no one else is selling **3** a small space in a wall where you can put small objects

nick¹ /nɪk/ verb [T] **1** *British informal* to steal something =PINCH **2** to cut the surface of something slightly: *He nicked his finger opening a tin.*

nick² /nɪk/ noun [C] a small cut on the surface of something

PHRASES **in good/bad etc nick** *British informal* in good/bad etc condition

in the nick of time just in time to prevent something bad from happening: *The swimmers were rescued in the nick of time.*

nickel /'nɪk(ə)l/ noun **1** [U] a hard silver metal **2** [C] a coin in the US and Canada that is worth five CENTS

nickname¹ /'nɪkˌneɪm/ noun [C] an informal name that your friends or family call you that is not your real name

nickname² /'nɪkˌneɪm/ verb [T] to give someone a nickname

nicotine /'nɪkəˌtiːn/ noun [U] the drug in tobacco that makes people ADDICTED to it

niece /niːs/ noun [C] a daughter of your brother or sister, or a daughter of your husband's or wife's brother or sister —*picture* → FAMILY TREE

nifty /'nɪfti/ adj *informal* well designed, effective, or easy to use

niggle /'nɪg(ə)l/ verb [I/T] **1** *British* to worry or annoy someone slightly but continuously **2** to argue with someone, or to criticize them about something unimportant —**niggle** noun [C]

niggling /'nɪg(ə)lɪŋ/ adj causing you slight worries or small problems for a long period of time

nigh /naɪ/ adv *literary* near

PHRASE **nigh on/well nigh sth** *old-fashioned* almost

night /naɪt/ noun ★★★

1 [C/U] the part of each 24-hour period when it is dark ≠ DAY: *It was a lovely warm night.* ♦ *I woke up in the middle of the night.* ♦ *It rained all night (long).* ♦ *The attacks usually take place at night.* ♦ *Owls hunt by night.*

2 [U] the time between the end of the afternoon and the time when people go to bed =EVENING: *Most nights Jan helps the kids with their homework.* ♦ *What are you doing Friday night?* ♦ *Did you watch the football on TV last night?*

PHRASES **an early/late night** an occasion when you go to bed earlier or later than usual

night and day or **day and night** all the time

a night out an evening when you go out to a place such as a cinema or theatre: *It's ages since we had a night out.*

Words often used with **night**

Noun often used with night (sense 1)
- **cold, cool, frosty, mild, warm** + NIGHT: used for saying how hot or cold a night is
- **dark, moonlit, starlit, starry** + NIGHT: used for saying how much light there is on a particular night

nightclub /'naɪtˌklʌb/ noun [C] a place where people go in the evening in order to dance and drink alcohol = CLUB

nightdress /'naɪtˌdres/ noun [C] *British* a loose dress that women wear for sleeping in = NIGHTIE —*picture* → C5

nightfall /'naɪtˌfɔːl/ noun [U] *literary* the time in the evening when it starts to become dark

nightgown /'naɪtˌɡaʊn/ noun [C] *old-fashioned* a NIGHTDRESS

nightie /'naɪti/ noun [C] *informal* a NIGHTDRESS

nightingale /'naɪtɪŋˌɡeɪl/ noun [C] a small bird that is known for the beautiful way that it sings at night

nightlife /'naɪtˌlaɪf/ noun [U] evening entertainment that you get in places such as NIGHTCLUBS and bars

nightly /'naɪtli/ adj, adv happening every night

nightmare /'naɪtˌmeə/ noun [C] **1** a very difficult or frightening situation: *The journey to work was a nightmare.* **2** a very frightening and unpleasant dream: *I still have terrible nightmares about the crash.* —**nightmarish** /'naɪtˌmeərɪʃ/ adj

nightshirt /'naɪtˌʃɜːt/ noun [C] a long loose shirt, used for sleeping in

nighttime /'naɪtˌtaɪm/ noun [U] the period of time when it is night

night ˈwatchman noun [C] someone whose job is to guard a building during the night

nil /nɪl/ noun [U] **1** *British spoken* the number 0 in the result of a game: *Birmingham won three nil.* **2** used for saying that something does not exist: *Their chances of survival are virtually nil.*

nimble /'nɪmb(ə)l/ adj able to move quickly and easily —**nimbly** /'nɪmbli/ adv

nine /naɪn/ number the number 9

nineteen /ˌnaɪn'tiːn/ number the number 19 —**nineteenth** number

nine-to-five adj a nine-to-five job is a normal office job, in which you usually work from nine o'clock until five o'clock

ninety /'naɪnti/ number the number 90
  PHRASES **be in the nineties** if the temperature is in the nineties, it is in the range of 90 to 99 degrees Fahrenheit
  be in your nineties to be an age in the range of 90 to 99
  the nineties the years from 1990 to 1999 —**ninetieth** number

ninth /naɪnθ/ number **1** in the place or position counted as number nine: *the ninth of January* **2** one of nine equal parts of something

nip /nɪp/ verb **1** [I] *British informal* to go somewhere quickly and for only a short time: *She's just nipped out for some milk.* **2** [I/T] to bite someone gently

PHRASE **nip sth in the bud** *informal* to stop a bad situation from becoming worse by taking action at an early stage of its development
—**nip** noun [C]

nipple /'nɪp(ə)l/ noun [C] a small round raised area of flesh on each side of your chest

nirvana /nɪə'vɑːnə/ noun [U] a state of complete spiritual happiness that Buddhists and Hindus try to achieve

nitpick /'nɪtˌpɪk/ verb [I/T] to criticize unimportant details in an annoying way —**nitpicking** noun [U]

nitrate /'naɪtreɪt/ noun [C/U] a chemical substance that is used for improving the quality of soil

nitrogen /'naɪtrədʒ(ə)n/ noun [U] a gas with no colour or smell that exists in large quantities in the air

nits /nɪts/ noun [plural] the eggs of insects called LICE that people sometimes have in their hair

nitty-gritty, the /ˌnɪti 'ɡrɪti/ noun [singular] *informal* the most basic aspects of a situation or an activity that must be dealt with

nitwit /'nɪtˌwɪt/ noun [C] *informal* a stupid person

no¹ /nəʊ/ grammar word ★★★

N

No can be:
- an **adverb**: *'Would you like some tea?' 'No, thanks.'* ♦ *She's no taller than Jerry.*
- a **determiner**: *There's no butter in the fridge.* ♦ *No smoking.*

1 giving a negative answer used for giving a negative answer to a question or an offer: *'Are you still working at the clinic?' 'No, I work at the hospital now.'* ♦ *'Do you want another cup of coffee?' 'No, thanks.'* ♦ *I asked Marla to come and help, but she said no.*

2 disagreeing with sb used for saying that a statement that someone has made is not true: *'You blame me whenever something goes wrong.' 'No, I don't.'*

3 agreeing with a negative used for agreeing with a negative statement, or agreeing to a negative request: *'Don't forget to make the reservation.' 'No, I won't.'* ♦ *'We're not as young as we used to be.' 'No, we're certainly not.'*

4 not any used for saying that there is not even one person or thing, or not any amount of something: *There was no hospital in the town.* ♦ *I have no living cousins that I know about.* ♦ *There's no time to stop and talk.*

5 telling sb not to do sth used for telling someone not to do something: *No! Don't touch that – it's hot.*

6 not allowed used on signs or in instructions in order to say that something is not allowed: *No smoking.*

7 not at all used for saying that someone or something cannot be described in a particular way: *It is no surprise that the company failed.* ♦ *He's no fool – he can see what you're trying to do.*

PHRASES **in no time** in a very short time:

I'll have it fixed for you in no time.
no more/less/better etc not more/less/better etc than someone or something else: *The painting was no more than a few inches square.* ♦ *In the end, he got no further than the station.*

no² /nəʊ/ (plural **noes**) noun [C] a negative answer or vote: *His answer was a firm no.*

no. abbrev number

nobility /nəʊˈbɪləti/ noun **1** [U] an honest and brave way of behaving that people admire **2 the nobility** [singular] the people in the highest social class in some countries

noble¹ /ˈnəʊb(ə)l/ adj **1** behaving in an honest and brave way that other people admire **2** belonging to the nobility —**nobly** /ˈnəʊbli/ adv

noble² /ˈnəʊb(ə)l/ noun [C] a member of the nobility

nobleman /ˈnəʊb(ə)lmən/ noun [C] a man who is a member of the NOBILITY

noblewoman /ˈnəʊb(ə)lˌwʊmən/ noun [C] a woman who is a member of the NOBILITY

nobody¹ /ˈnəʊbɒdi/ pronoun ★★★ no one: *Nobody understands me.* ♦ *Nobody else knows our secret.*

nobody² /ˈnəʊbɒdi/ noun [C] a person who is not at all important: *I'm tired of everyone treating me like a nobody.*

nocturnal /nɒkˈtɜːn(ə)l/ adj **1** nocturnal animals are active at night **2** *formal* happening at night

nod /nɒd/ verb ★
1 [I/T] to move your head up and down in order to answer 'yes' or to show that you agree, approve, or understand ≠ SHAKE YOUR HEAD: *I expected an argument, but she merely nodded and went out.* ♦ *Alison smiled and nodded in agreement.* ♦ *Luke was nodding his head thoughtfully.*
2 [I] to move your head once in order to make someone look at something, in order to greet someone, or in order to give someone a signal to do something: *'They're having fun', she said, nodding towards the kids on the beach.* ♦ *I nodded to my friend and she rang the bell.*
—**nod** noun [C]

PHRASAL VERB **nod off** *informal* to go to sleep when you do not intend to

nodule /ˈnɒdjuːl/ noun [C] a small round lump

no-go area noun [C] *British* an area of a city that is not safe because there is a lot of crime and violence there

noise /nɔɪz/ noun [C/U] ★★★ a loud or unpleasant sound: *The dog made a deep growling noise in his throat.* ♦ *The neighbours said that we were making too much noise.* ♦ *We heard the noise of breaking glass.*

noiseless /ˈnɔɪzləs/ adj not making any sound —**noiselessly** adv

noise pollution noun [U] dangerous or annoying levels of noise

noisy /ˈnɔɪzi/ adj ★ making a lot of noise, or full of noise: *noisy neighbours* ♦ *a noisy crowded bar* —**noisily** adv

nomad /ˈnəʊˌmæd/ noun [C] someone who belongs to a group of people who do not

live in one place but move from place to place —**nomadic** adj

no-man's-land noun [singular/U] an area of land between two countries or armies that is not controlled by either of them

nominal /ˈnɒmɪn(ə)l/ adj **1** a nominal amount of money is very small and is much less than the real cost of something: *Transport can be provided for a nominal fee.* **2** officially described in a particular way, although this is not really true or correct: *He is still the nominal leader of the organization.*

nominally /ˈnɒmɪn(ə)li/ adv officially described as being or doing something, although this is not really true or correct: *John Robbins is nominally in charge of the investigation.*

nominate /ˈnɒmɪneɪt/ verb [T] to officially suggest that someone should be given a job, or that someone or something should receive a prize —**nomination** /ˌnɒmɪˈneɪʃ(ə)n/ noun [C/U]

nominee /ˌnɒmɪˈniː/ noun [C] someone who has been officially suggested for a position or prize

non- /nɒn/ prefix not: *a non-alcoholic drink* ♦ *a non-smoker*

non-aggression noun [U] a policy of not attacking other countries

non-alcoholic adj a non-alcoholic drink does not contain alcohol

nonchalant /ˈnɒnʃ(ə)lənt/ adj relaxed and not worried about anything —**nonchalance** noun [U], **nonchalantly** adv

non-combatant noun [C] someone who is not involved in fighting during a war

non-committal /ˌnɒnkəˈmɪt(ə)l/ adj avoiding stating clearly what you think or what you plan to do: *He was non-committal about any future plans.*

nonconformist /ˌnɒnkənˈfɔːmɪst/ noun [C] someone who does not think or behave in the way that most people do —**nonconformist** adj

non-count adj *linguistics* a non-count noun is UNCOUNTABLE

nondescript /ˈnɒndɪˌskrɪpt/ adj very ordinary, and not interesting or attractive

none /nʌn/ grammar word ★★★

None can be:
■ a **pronoun**: *I asked for some more cake, but there was none left.* ♦ *None of my friends will help me.*
■ an **adverb**: *She looked none too pleased.*

1 not any of a group of people or things, or no amount of something: *I thought there was some coffee in the cupboard, but there's none there.* ♦ *The driver was killed, but none of the passengers was hurt.* ♦ *Some people might have only mild symptoms or none at all.*

PHRASES **none the better/worse etc** no better, worse etc than before
none the less *British see* **nonetheless**
none other than used for saying who someone is when this is surprising: *The songwriters are none other than Sir Tim Rice and Sir Elton John.*

none too not at all: *Hugo was none too happy when I told him I was leaving.*

→ SECOND[1]

> When **none** is the subject of a sentence and refers to members of a group of people or things, it can be used with a singular or plural verb. Some people think that it is more correct to use a singular verb in these cases: *None of his friends lives nearby. ♦ None of the plates were broken.*

nonentity /nɒˈnentəti/ noun [C] someone who is not at all important or interesting

nonetheless /ˌnʌnðəˈles/ adv *formal* despite what has just been said: *Everyone worked very hard. There were still problems, nonetheless.*

non-eˈvent noun [C] an event that is not as exciting as you expected it to be

non-exˈistent adj not real or present: *Wildlife is virtually non-existent in this area.*

non-ˈfiction noun [U] writing that is about real people and events, not imaginary ones —**non-ˈfiction** adj

non-ˈflammable adj not able to be burned easily

non-ˈgovernˈmental adj a non-governmental organization is not part of a government, but may work with government departments

non-interˈvention noun [U] a policy of not getting involved in a disagreement between other people or countries

non-inˈvasive adj non-invasive medical tests or treatments do not involve cutting your body or putting things inside it

non-ˈmember noun [C] someone who does not belong to a particular organization

ˈno-ˌno noun [singular] *informal* something that most people do not approve of

ˌno-ˈnonsense adj doing things quickly and effectively without worrying too much about people's feelings: *a no-nonsense approach/performance*

non-ˈpayment noun [U] a failure or a refusal to pay for something

nonplussed /ˌnɒnˈplʌst/ adj so surprised and confused that you do not know what to do or say

non-ˈprofit or **non-ˈprofit-ˌmaking** adj a non-profit organization works in order to help people in some way, rather than in order to make a profit

non-proˈlifeˈration noun [U] a policy of not increasing the number of nuclear or chemical weapons in the world

non-reˈfundable adj if the money that you pay for something is non-refundable, you cannot get the money back for any reason: *non-refundable tickets*

non-reˈnewable adj non-renewable types of energy exist in limited amounts, and when these are all used there will be none left

non-ˈresident noun [C] **1** *British* someone who is not staying at a particular hotel: *The restaurant is open to non-residents.*

2 someone who is not based in a particular country —**non-ˈresident** adj

nonsense /ˈnɒns(ə)ns/ noun [U] ★
1 ideas, behaviour, or statements that are not true or sensible: *So you believe the nonsense about ghosts? ♦ That's a load of nonsense. ♦ These latest accusations are absolute nonsense.*
2 unreasonable or annoying behaviour: *I won't stand any nonsense from anybody.*
3 words or sounds that seem like ordinary words but have no meaning: *a nonsense poem*
—**nonsensical** /nɒnˈsensɪk(ə)l/ adj

non sequitur /ˌnɒn ˈsekwɪtə/ noun [C] a statement that has no connection with what was said before

non-ˈsmoker noun [C] someone who does not smoke

non-ˈsmoking adj a non-smoking area is one where you are not allowed to smoke

non-ˈstandard adj *linguistics* non-standard forms of language are different from those that are usually thought to be correct

non-ˈstarter noun [C] an idea that has no chance of succeeding

non-ˈstick adj non-stick cooking pans have a surface that food will not stick to

non-ˈstop adj, adv without stopping: *a non-stop flight from Los Angeles to London ♦ The president spoke non-stop for two hours.*

non-ˈviolent adj **1** using peaceful methods to achieve political change: *a campaign of non-violent resistance* **2** non-violent crime does not involve physically hurting people —**non-ˈviolence** noun [U]

noodles /ˈnuːd(ə)lz/ noun [plural] a type of long thin pasta

nook /nʊk/ noun [C] a small corner, or a quiet place that is protected from bad weather
PHRASE **every nook and cranny** every part of a place

noon /nuːn/ noun [U] 12 o'clock in the middle of the day=MIDDAY: *We should be there by noon.*

ˈno ˌone or **ˈno-ˌone** pronoun ★★★ not any person=NOBODY: *There was no one around. ♦ No one else wanted the job.*

noose /nuːs/ noun [C] a piece of rope that is put around someone's neck and used for killing them by hanging them

nope /nəʊp/ adv *informal* used for saying 'no' when someone asks you a question

nor /nɔː/ conjunction ★★★ used after a negative statement when adding another negative statement: *I have not been asked to resign, nor do I intend to do so. ♦ She did not return that night, nor the night after.*

norm /nɔːm/ noun **1 the norm** [singular] something that is average, usual, or expected: *Students who fall below the norm should be encouraged to improve. ♦ Fast cars have become the norm.* **2 norms** [plural] standards of behaviour that are accepted in a particular society: *Each culture develops its own social norms.*

normal /ˈnɔːm(ə)l/ adj ★★★
1 as expected, and not unusual or surprising

in any way: *Temperatures are higher than normal.* ♦ *He didn't like anything to interrupt his normal daily routine.* ♦ *Life is beginning to get back to normal after the fire.* ♦ *Under normal circumstances, candidates are interviewed by the head of the department.* ♦ *it is normal to do sth It's normal to be nervous before an interview.*

2 thinking, behaving, or looking like most people: *He's no hero – just a normal human being.* ♦ *She's a perfectly normal messy child!*

normality /nɔːˈmæləti/ noun [U] a situation in which everything is normal

normalize /ˈnɔːməlaɪz/ verb [I/T] to make something normal, or to become normal: *The United States had decided to normalize relations with Vietnam.* —**normalization** /ˌnɔːməlaɪˈzeɪʃ(ə)n/ noun [U]

normally /ˈnɔːm(ə)li/ adv ★★★
1 in most situations or cases=USUALLY: *Normally it takes about six days to arrange a visit.* ♦ *She's not normally late.*
2 in the usual way: *Bus services are operating normally.*

north¹ /nɔːθ/ noun ★★★
1 [U] the direction that is on your left when you are facing the rising sun: *We were driving from north to south.*
2 the north [singular] the part of a place that is in the north: *How do you like living in the north?* ♦ *She grew up in the north of France.*

north² /nɔːθ/ adv towards the north: *The geese will soon be flying north.* ♦ *It's a lot colder up north.* ♦ *a village 10 miles north of here*

north³ /nɔːθ/ adj **1** in the north, or facing towards the north **2** a north wind blows from the north

northbound /ˈnɔːθbaʊnd/ adj going towards the north

north-ˈeast¹ noun **1** [U] the direction that is between north and east **2 the north-east** [singular] the part of a place that is in the north-east —**north-ˈeastern** adj

north-ˈeast² adj in the north-east, or facing towards the north-east —**north-ˈeast** adv

north-ˈeasterly adj **1** a north-easterly wind blows from the north-east **2** towards or in the north-east

northerly /ˈnɔːðəli/ adj **1** a northerly wind blows from the north **2** towards or in the north

northern /ˈnɔːð(ə)n/ adj ★★ in or from the north of a country or place: *northern Italy*

northerner /ˈnɔːð(ə)nə/ noun [C] someone who lives in or was born in the northern part of a country

northern ˈhemisphere, the noun [singular] the northern half of the Earth, north of the EQUATOR

northernmost /ˈnɔːðn̩məʊst/ adj furthest towards the north

North ˈPole, the noun the place on the surface of the Earth that is the furthest north

northward /ˈnɔːθwəd/ adj towards or in the north

northwards /ˈnɔːθwədz/ or **northward** /ˈnɔːθwəd/ adv towards the north

north-ˈwest¹ noun **1** [U] the direction that is between north and west **2 the north-west** [singular] the part of a place that is in the north-west —**north-ˈwestern** adj

north-ˈwest² adj in the north-west, or facing towards the north-west —**north-ˈwest** adv

north-ˈwesterly adj **1** a north-westerly wind blows from the north-west **2** towards or in the north-west

nose¹ /nəʊz/ noun [C] ★★★ the part of your face that is above your mouth that you use for smelling and breathing: *I'd like to punch him on the nose.* ♦ *Can you pass me a tissue – my nose is running* (=liquid is coming out of it). ♦ *Excuse me, I just need to blow my nose* (=force liquid from it). —*picture* → C14

PHRASES look down your nose at to behave in a way that shows that you think someone or something is not good enough for you: *She looks down her nose at most men.*

poke/stick your nose into sth to become interested or involved in something when you have no right to do this: *You have no right to poke your nose into my affairs!*

turn your nose up at sth *informal* to refuse to accept something because you do not think that it is good enough

under sb's nose if something happens under someone's nose, it happens in a place or situation where they should notice it, but they do not: *They were dealing drugs right under the noses of the police.*

nose² /nəʊz/ verb [I] if a vehicle noses forward, it moves forward slowly and carefully: *The ambulance nosed its way out of the crowd.*

PHRASAL VERB nose aˈround (sb/sth) or **nose aˈbout (sb/sth)** *British* to try to find out information about someone or something: *I found two men nosing around the boat.*

nosebleed /ˈnəʊzbliːd/ noun [C] an occasion when blood comes out of someone's nose

nosedive /ˈnəʊzdaɪv/ noun [C] **1** a sudden reduction in things such as prices or profits: *The value of the pound took a nosedive today.* **2** an occasion when a plane suddenly falls out of the sky with its front end pointing down —**nosedive** verb [I]

nosey /ˈnəʊzi/ another spelling of **nosy**

nostalgia /nɒˈstældʒə/ noun [U] thoughts about happy times in your past that make you want to be back in the past

nostalgic /nɒˈstældʒɪk/ adj remembering happy times in the past —**nostalgically** /nɒˈstældʒɪkli/ adv

nostril /ˈnɒstrəl/ noun [C] one of the two holes at the end of your nose

nosy /ˈnəʊzi/ adj *showing disapproval* wanting to know about things that involve other people but not you —**nosiness** noun [U]

not /nɒt/ adv ★★★
1 used for giving a negative or opposite meaning to a sentence, expression, or word: *He would not listen to anything she said.* ♦ *Barbara's not coming to the party.* ♦ *I don't*

feel sorry for her. ♦ *Not surprisingly, Greg forgot to bring the key.* ♦ *They told me not to worry.* ♦ *Not all children enjoy sport.* ♦ *The teacher could not even remember my name.* ♦ *My parents were **not at all** pleased with my exam results.*

2 used instead of repeating something in the negative: *Are you coming with me **or not**?* ♦ *I'll probably see you on Sunday; **if not**, it'll be Monday.* ♦ *'Is it going to be very expensive?' '**I hope not**.'*

3 *spoken* used for forming a question when you expect the answer to be 'yes': *Isn't it a beautiful day?* ♦ *That was easy, wasn't it?*

PHRASES **not one** or **not a single** used for emphasizing that there are none of the people or things you are talking about: *Not one member voted in favour.*

not that used for adding a negative statement that reduces the effect of what you have just said: *You're using my pen – not that I mind* (=I don't mind).

In spoken and informal English **not** is often shortened to **n't** on the end of auxiliary verbs ('be', 'do', and 'have') and modal verbs. For example, **was not** is shortened to **wasn't**.

notable /ˈnəʊtəb(ə)l/ adj unusual or interesting enough to be mentioned or noticed

notably /ˈnəʊtəbli/ adv *formal* especially

notation /nəʊˈteɪʃ(ə)n/ noun [U] a set of written signs or shapes that are used in something such as music or mathematics

notch¹ /nɒtʃ/ noun [C] a small cut on the edge or surface of something

notch² /nɒtʃ/ **PHRASAL VERB** ˌnotch sth ˈup *informal* to win or achieve something

note¹ /nəʊt/ noun [C] ★★★

1 short message	**5** sound/sign in music
2 sth that reminds	**6** feeling/thought
3 detailed information	**+ PHRASES**
4 piece of paper money	

1 a short written message to someone: *I've written him a note asking him to meet me tonight.* ♦ *We left them a note saying dinner was in the fridge.*

2 something that you write on a piece of paper in order to remind yourself of something: *I've **made a note** of what needs to be repaired.*

3 **notes** [plural] details from something such as a lecture or a book that you write on a piece of paper so that you can remember them: *It'll help you later if you **take notes**.*

4 *British* a piece of paper money: *a £5 note*

5 an individual sound in music, or a written sign that represents it: *See if you can **sing** this **note**.* ♦ *He **played** a few **notes** on the piano.*

6 a feeling or mood that is shown in the way that someone speaks or writes: *I'd like to end the discussion on a more cheerful note.* ♦ *There was **a note of** impatience in her voice.*

PHRASES **of note** *formal* important, or famous: *Several writers of note will be at the conference.*

take note to notice something and try to remember it because you think that it is important: *When the people speak with such passion, politicians should take note.* ♦ *I **took note** of what she said.*

→ COMPARE

note² /nəʊt/ verb [T] ★★

1 *formal* to notice or realize something: *Liz noted the changes with satisfaction.* ♦ **+(that)** *Please note that all travellers must have a valid passport.*

2 to write something on a piece of paper so that you will have a record of it: *Isabel noted the details in her diary.*

PHRASAL VERB ˌnote sth ˈdown same as note² 2

notebook /ˈnəʊtbʊk/ noun [C] **1** a book with empty pages that you use for writing notes **2** a small flat computer that is easy to carry

noted /ˈnəʊtɪd/ adj well known and admired: *a noted British scientist* ♦ *He is particularly noted for his short stories.*

notepad /ˈnəʊtpæd/ noun [C] several sheets of paper that are joined together along one edge and used for writing notes —*picture* → C3

notepaper /ˈnəʊtˌpeɪpə/ noun [U] paper that you use for writing letters

noteworthy /ˈnəʊtˌwɜːði/ adj worth giving special attention or praise to: *a noteworthy performance*

N

nothing /ˈnʌθɪŋ/ pronoun ★★★

1 not anything: *There was nothing in the room except for a chair.* ♦ *She waited, but nothing happened.* ♦ *I saw nothing strange in the situation.* ♦ *I knew **nothing at all about** looking after babies.* ♦ *If there's **nothing else** you want, can we go?* ♦ *The kids complain that there's **nothing to do** there.*

2 not anything that is important or worth thinking about: *You're just making a fuss about nothing.* ♦ *Do I mean nothing to you?* ♦ *A minor headache is **nothing to worry about**.* ♦ *The beach is **nothing special**, but we like it.*

PHRASES **be nothing like** to not be similar to someone or something in any way: *Her two daughters are nothing like each other.*

for nothing 1 without any payment: *Some of the men volunteered to work for nothing.* **2** without a reason or purpose: *Why did you call me down here for nothing?*

have/be nothing to do with 1 to not be connected with a particular fact or situation: *His resignation has nothing to do with his health.* **2** used for saying that someone has no reason to know about something or to be interested in it: *What I do in my own time has nothing to do with you.*

if nothing else used for mentioning what you think may be the only good aspect of something or the only good reason for doing something: *Andrea's work has always been neat and tidy, if nothing else.*

nothing but only: *He has nothing but praise*

for the managers at his company.

there's nothing better/worse/more exciting etc than used for emphasizing how good/bad/exciting etc something is: *There's nothing worse than not being able to sleep at night.*

there's nothing like sth used for saying that something is very good, enjoyable, or effective: *There's nothing like a cold drink on a hot day.*

there's nothing to it *spoken* used for saying that something is very easy to do
→ STOP¹

notice¹ /'nəʊtɪs/ verb [T] ★★★ to become conscious of someone or something by seeing, hearing, or feeling them: *After a few days here you hardly notice the rain!* ♦ *Did you notice how pale he looks?* ♦ *+(that) I noticed that the door was open.*

notice² /'nəʊtɪs/ noun ★★★

1 [C] a written sign or announcement that gives information or that warns people about something: *They put up a notice on the door saying they'd gone out of business.* ♦ *Have you read the notice on the board about next week's class?*

2 [U] information or a warning about something that is going to happen: *I need a month's notice if you're planning to move out.* ♦ *If you want to arrive early you must give advance notice.* ♦ *Finding a replacement could prove difficult at short notice.* ♦ *Lucy was ready to leave at a moment's notice.*

3 [U] *British* the fact that someone pays attention to something, or finds out about something: *Their working conditions were only brought to public notice last year.* ♦ *It has come to our notice that some cash is missing.* ♦ *It may have escaped your notice, but some of us are trying to work.*

PHRASES **give in/hand in your notice** to tell your employer that you are leaving your job

take notice to pay attention to something: *Wear what you like – no one seems to take any notice.* ♦ *Take no notice of him – he always behaves like that.*

until further notice until someone announces that a situation has changed or no longer exists: *The road is closed to traffic until further notice.*

noticeable /'nəʊtɪsəb(ə)l/ adj easy to see, hear, or feel: *There was a noticeable chill in the air.* —**noticeably** adv

noticeboard /'nəʊtɪsˌbɔːd/ noun [C] *British* a board that has announcements and other information on it

notification /ˌnəʊtɪfɪ'keɪʃ(ə)n/ noun [U] an official announcement about something

notify /'nəʊtɪˌfaɪ/ verb [T] to tell someone officially about something: *Winners will be notified as soon as possible.*

notion /'nəʊʃ(ə)n/ noun [C] ★ an idea or belief that is wrong or silly: *Somehow he got the notion that I was interested in going out with him.*

notoriety /ˌnəʊtə'raɪəti/ noun [U] a situation in which someone or something is famous for something that is bad

notorious /nəʊ'tɔːriəs/ adj famous for something that is bad: *This part of the city is notorious for its high crime rate.* —**notoriously** adv

notwithstanding /ˌnɒtwɪð'stændɪŋ/ adv, preposition *formal* despite something: *Notwithstanding his wealth, his house was simple inside.*

nougat /'nuːgaː/ noun [U] a sweet food made of sugar, nuts, and small pieces of fruit

nought /nɔːt/ noun [C] **1** zero **2** nothing

PHRASE **noughts and crosses** *British* a game for two players in which they take turns writing an X or an O in one of nine boxes until one player gets three Xs or three Os in a row —*picture* → C16

noun /naʊn/ noun [C] *linguistics* ★ a word or group of words used for referring to a person, thing, place, or quality

'noun phrase noun [C] *linguistics* a phrase that is used in a sentence in the same way that a noun is used

nourish /'nʌrɪʃ/ verb [T] to give a person, animal, or plant the food or the substances in food that they need to live, grow, and be healthy

nourishing /'nʌrɪʃɪŋ/ adj nourishing food provides the substances that you need to live, grow, and be healthy

nourishment /'nʌrɪʃmənt/ noun [U] food or the substances in food that you need to live, grow, and be healthy

novel¹ /'nɒv(ə)l/ noun [C] ★ a long written story about imaginary characters and events

novel² /'nɒv(ə)l/ adj new, or unusual

novelist /'nɒvəlɪst/ noun [C] someone who writes novels

novelty /'nɒv(ə)lti/ noun **1** [C] something that is new and unusual **2** [U] the excitement or interest that something that is new or unusual creates

November /nəʊ'vembə/ noun [C/U] ★★★ the eleventh month of the year, between October and December: *She's arriving in November.* ♦ *The play opens on November 15th.*

novice /'nɒvɪs/ noun [C] someone who is just beginning to learn a skill or subject
=BEGINNER

now /naʊ/ grammar word ★★★

Now can be:
■ an **adverb**: *We'd better leave now.*
■ a **conjunction**, often with 'that': *Now that I'm married, I don't go out so much.*

1 at the present time: *He is now 48 years old.* ♦ *She's been very ill, but she's much better now.* ♦ *The meeting should have finished by now.* ♦ *Nancy will be working full-time from now on* (=starting now). ♦ *Prices will remain unchanged for now* (=from now until some future time). ♦ *'Can I ask you a question?' 'Not now – I'm busy.'*

2 immediately, or very soon: *If everyone else has finished in the bathroom, I'll have my shower now.* ♦ *'Can you call me back?' 'No, I need to talk to you right now.'*

3 used when you are saying that something happens as a result of something else: *Now I understand why she was so upset.* ♦ *+(that) Now that the war is over, there is a lot more food in the shops.*

4 *spoken* used when you want to get people's attention, or when you are going to talk about something new: *Now, listen everybody.* ♦ *Now then, are there any more questions?*

PHRASES **(every) now and then/again** sometimes, but not regularly or often: *Now and then I receive letters from my former students.*

just now 1 a very short time ago: *'When did you see him?' 'Just now.'* **2** *British* at the present time: *Mrs Collins is busy just now.*

nowadays /ˈnaʊədeɪz/ adv ★★ at the present time: *Lots of people get divorced nowadays.*

no way adv *spoken* used for saying that you will definitely not do something

nowhere /ˈnəʊweə/ adv ★

1 not in any place, or not to any place: *Nowhere does it say that we cannot have guests in our rooms.* ♦ *There is nowhere else for me to stay.*

2 in or to no particular place: *The old railway tracks lead nowhere.*

PHRASES **get/go nowhere** to not be successful in what you are trying to achieve: *Our investigation got nowhere.* ♦ *get sb nowhere All this talk is getting us nowhere.*

nowhere near 1 not nearly: *His latest album is nowhere near as good as his last.* **2** a long way away from somewhere

nowhere to be seen/in sight/to be found impossible to see or find: *The children were nowhere in sight.*

out of/from nowhere appearing, arriving, or happening very quickly or unexpectedly: *The car seemed to come out of nowhere.*
→ MIDDLE¹

no-win situation noun [C] a situation in which there is no chance of success

noxious /ˈnɒkʃəs/ adj harmful, or poisonous

nozzle /ˈnɒz(ə)l/ noun [C] a narrow part at the end of a tube through which a liquid flows

nuance /ˈnjuːɒns/ noun [C] a slight difference: *A translator has to be alert to every nuance of meaning.*

nuclear /ˈnjuːkliə/ adj ★★★

1 relating to energy that is produced by changing the structure of the central part of an atom =ATOMIC: *nuclear power/energy* ♦ *nuclear weapons/arms* ♦ *a nuclear war* ♦ *Are you in favour of nuclear disarmament* (=getting rid of nuclear weapons)?

2 relating to the central part of an atom: *nuclear physics*

nuclear family noun [C] a family unit that consists of a mother, a father, and their children

nuclear reactor noun [C] a machine used for producing nuclear energy, usually in the form of electricity

nucleus /ˈnjuːkliəs/ (plural **nuclei** /ˈnjuːkliaɪ/)

noun [C] **1** *science* the central part of an atom **2** *science* the central part of a living cell **3** the central or basic part of something: *These groups formed the nucleus of a new political party.*

nude¹ /njuːd/ adj not wearing clothes =NAKED

nude² /njuːd/ noun [C] a painting or other work of art showing someone who is not wearing clothes

PHRASE **in the nude** not wearing clothes

nudge /nʌdʒ/ verb [T] to use a part of your body, especially your elbow, to give a little push to someone or something —**nudge** noun [C]

nudism /ˈnjuːdɪz(ə)m/ noun [U] the practice of wearing no clothes outside, for example on a beach

nudist /ˈnjuːdɪst/ noun [C] someone who prefers to wear no clothes —**nudist** adj

nudity /ˈnjuːdəti/ noun [U] the state of not wearing clothes, or of not covering a part of the body that is traditionally covered

nugget /ˈnʌɡɪt/ noun [C] a rough lump of gold or another metal that is found in the earth

nuisance /ˈnjuːs(ə)ns/ noun [C] someone or something that annoys you or causes problems for you

nuke¹ /njuːk/ verb [T] *informal* to attack an enemy with nuclear weapons

nuke² /njuːk/ noun [C] *informal* a nuclear weapon

nullify /ˈnʌlɪfaɪ/ verb [T] to make something lose its value or effect

numb¹ /nʌm/ adj **1** a part of your body that is numb has no feeling **2** not able to react or to show your emotions, often because of shock —**numbly** adv

numb² /nʌm/ verb [T] to make a part of your body lose its ability to feel

number¹ /ˈnʌmbə/ noun ★★★

1 sign/word for amount	4 for marking sth
2 for showing position	5 a quantity
3 telephone number	

1 [C] a sign or word that represents an amount or quantity: *Can you read the numbers on the chart?* ♦ *a number between one and ten*

2 [C] used for showing the position of something in a series: *The local trains will be arriving at platform number 4.*

3 [C] a telephone number: *Call this number to get a taxi.* ♦ *I must have dialled the wrong number.*

4 [C] a number that is given to a particular thing in order to show which one it is out of many others: *Your account number is printed on every cheque.*

5 [C/U] a quantity of people or things: *a small number of shops* → AMOUNT

number² /ˈnʌmbə/ verb [T] **1** to give a number to something **2** *formal* to consist of a particular quantity of people or things

Number 10 /ˌnʌmbə ˈten/ noun [U] *British informal* **1** 10 Downing Street, the official home in London of the Prime Minister of the UK **2** the Prime Minister of the UK

,**number 'one**¹ noun [singular] **1** the person or thing that is the first, best, or most important **2** in popular music, the CD or record that has sold the most copies in a particular week

,**number 'one**² adj first, best, or most important: *the world's number one female tennis player*

'**number ,plate** noun [C] *British* an official sign on the front and back of a car or truck, with numbers and letters on it —*picture* → C6

numbing /'nʌmɪŋ/ adj making you lose feeling in a part of your body

numbness /'nʌmnəs/ noun [U] the condition of having no feeling in a part of your body

numeracy /'njuːmərəsi/ noun [U] the ability to use numbers in mathematics

numeral /'njuːmərəl/ noun [C] a symbol that represents a number

numerate /'njuːmərət/ adj able to use and calculate numbers

numerical /njuːˈmerɪk(ə)l/ adj expressed as numbers, or consisting of numbers —**numerically** /njuːˈmerɪkli/ adv

numerous /'njuːmərəs/ adj ★ existing in large numbers=MANY: *The car was seen in the area on numerous occasions.*

nun /nʌn/ noun [C] a woman who belongs to a religious community of women → MONK

nurse¹ /nɜːs/ noun [C] ★★ someone who is trained to look after ill or injured people, usually in a hospital

nurse² /nɜːs/ verb **1** [I/T] to look after someone who is ill or injured **2** [T] to feel a strong emotion for a long time: *He had nursed a grudge* (=had angry feelings) *against them for ages.* **3** [T] to help yourself to get better after an illness or injury, for example by resting or getting medical treatment: *I took over as captain while she nursed a strained muscle.* ♦ *I'm nursing a cold.* **4** [T] if a woman nurses a baby, she feeds it by letting the baby suck milk from her breasts =BREASTFEED

nursery /'nɜːs(ə)ri/ noun [C] **1** a school or a place where very young children are looked after **2** a place where plants and young trees are grown

'**nursery ,rhyme** noun [C] a short poem or song for young children

'**nursery ,school** noun [C/U] a school for very young children

nursing /'nɜːsɪŋ/ noun [U] the job or skills of a nurse

'**nursing ,home** noun [C] a place where old people live when they are too old or ill to look after themselves without help

nurture /'nɜːtʃə/ verb [T] **1** to provide the care and attention that are needed for a young child, animal, or plant to grow and develop **2** to help someone or something to develop

nut /nʌt/ noun [C] ★

1 dry fruit with shell	**4** enthusiastic person
2 for fastening things	**5** head/brain
3 crazy person	

1 a dry fruit that grows inside a hard shell on some types of tree. Many kinds of nut can be eaten: *Do you want some nuts and raisins?*

2 a small metal object with a hole in the middle that you screw a BOLT through in order to fasten things together

3 *informal* someone who is crazy, or who behaves in a crazy way

4 *informal* someone who is extremely enthusiastic about a particular activity, sport, or subject: *a football nut*

5 *informal* your head, or your brain

nutcracker /'nʌt,krækə/ noun [C] a tool for breaking open the shells of nuts

nutrient /'njuːtriənt/ noun [C] a substance in food that plants, animals, and people need in order to live, grow, and be healthy

nutrition /njuːˈtrɪʃ(ə)n/ noun [U] **1** the food that you eat and its effects on your health and growth **2** the science of food and its effect on health and growth —**nutritional** /njuːˈtrɪʃən(ə)l/ adj, **nutritionally** /njuːˈtrɪʃən(ə)li/ adv

nutritionist /njuːˈtrɪʃ(ə)nɪst/ noun [C] someone who is an expert on nutrition

nutritious /njuːˈtrɪʃəs/ adj nutritious food provides the substances that you need in order to live, grow, and be healthy

nuts /nʌts/ adj *informal* crazy: *He'd be nuts to take that job.*

PHRASES **drive sb nuts** to make someone very annoyed

go nuts to suddenly become extremely angry

nuts about/over extremely enthusiastic about something or very attracted to someone

nutshell /'nʌtʃel/ noun [C] the hard shell around a nut

PHRASE **in a nutshell** *spoken* used for saying that you are going to explain something in a simple direct way

nutter /'nʌtə/ noun [C] *British informal* someone who is crazy, or who behaves in a crazy way

nutty /'nʌti/ adj **1** *informal* crazy, or very strange: *He had this nutty idea about buying a castle in Scotland.* **2** containing nuts, or having the taste of nuts

nuzzle /'nʌz(ə)l/ verb [I/T] to press your nose or face gently against something

NW abbrev north-west

nylon /'naɪlɒn/ noun [U] a strong artificial substance that is used in making plastic and clothes

nymph /nɪmf/ noun [C] in ancient Greek and Roman stories, one of the female spirits who live in rivers, mountains, or forests

nymphomaniac /,nɪmfəˈmeɪniæk/ noun [C] a woman who is always thinking about sex, or is always wanting to have sex —**nymphomania** /,nɪmfəˈmeɪniə/ noun [U]

LANGUAGE STUDY

These pages have been designed to help you to improve your knowledge and use of the English language. They contain information on how words are formed (Word Formation) and how new meanings develop (Metaphor), how words relate to each other (Collocation, Register, Text Types) and how they are pronounced (Pronunciation).

Increasing your vocabulary is an essential part of learning a foreign language – and remembering new words and phrases is often the hardest part. We have included an eight-page section (Topic Vocabulary) that brings together words and phrases that will help you to talk and write about key topic areas.

Throughout this section there is advice on how to improve your learning strategies, activities to practise these strategies, and exercises to test what you have learnt. We hope that you will find these pages informative, useful – and, above all, enjoyable.

Contents

COLLOCATION

What is collocation?

Why do we say 'to do your homework' and not 'to make your homework'? And why do we go somewhere 'by car' or 'by train' but 'on foot'? The reason is 'collocation'. Collocation means the way that words form predictable relationships with other words. Knowing the 'meaning' of a word is not only knowing its dictionary definition but also knowing the kind of words with which it is often associated.

We say, for example, 'take a look' and 'have a look' but not 'make a look' or 'get a look'. There is no reason or rule that tells us why we use some words with 'look' but not others. Looking up the meaning of **take** or **have** in the dictionary won't help us find the answer. Collocations, either fixed or more flexible, are the result of many years of habitual use by fluent speakers of the language.

Why is collocation important?

Collocation is important because:

- it makes speech sound natural and alive
- it provides 'chunks' of English that are ready to use
- it saves us a lot of time and effort when we are trying to express ourselves

These pages give you examples of the main kinds of collocation, and some ideas about how to improve your ability to use collocation.

In the case of grammar, once we know the rules we can make new correct sentences all the time, simply by 'slotting in' new vocabulary in the right places. But with collocation, there are limits to the changes we can make to a combination of words. In some cases those limits can be very strict, but in others there is more freedom to choose which words can go together.

A collocation may consist of two or more words. Look at this example:

Last year, we spent our summer holiday in Oxford.

This sentence is made up of nine separate words, but if we look more carefully we can identify four groups of words or 'collocations':

- *last + year* – we can also say 'last summer/last night/last week', or 'next year/this year/every year'. But we cannot say 'last hour' or 'past summer'.
- *spend + holiday* – we can also say 'spend a week/a month/the winter'. But we cannot say 'pass our holidays'.
- *summer + holiday* – we can also say 'winter holiday/skiing holiday/ walking holiday' and so on.
- *in + Oxford* – we often use the preposition **in** with the names of towns and countries. If you say that you spent time '**at** Oxford' the meaning changes completely. You mean that you studied at the university!

So when we are learning English, it is not enough to know the meaning of words like **spend** and **pass** on their own – the *meanings* of such words may be similar, but the way that they *combine* with other words may be very different.

Fixed phrases

The relationship between two or more words can be very close. For example, the word **kith** is never seen anywhere but in the company of **kin**, in the phrase 'kith and kin' (a rather old-fashioned way of referring to your relatives). **Kin**, however, also appears with **next** in 'next of kin'. But both words have very little freedom to combine with other words in English. If you learn these words, it is best to learn them together, as fixed phrases. Other words that form strong partnerships like this are: **ajar** (*she left the **door** ajar* – which means 'she left the door open') and **amends** (*she was sorry for what she had done and decided to **make amends*** – which means 'she decided to try to make the situation better').

Idioms

Many idioms in English are examples of strong collocations. There is very little, if any, room for changing the words that make up expressions such as the following:

- under the weather
- lose face
- spill the beans

Sometimes we can guess the meaning of an idiom if we understand all the individual words that it is formed from. But in many cases, this is not possible. For example, it is difficult to see why 'spill the beans' should mean 'to give away secret information'. The words and grammar that make up these idioms are almost impossible to change, without changing the meaning. We cannot say 'on top of the weather' (but we can say 'on top of the world'). We cannot say 'find face' or 'lose faces' (but we can say 'save face') and 'spill *the peas*' is not an idiomatic expression. A small error in the use of these fixed collocations makes a big difference to their meaning – and will often make them meaningless.

Phrasal verbs

A special feature of English which is not found in many other languages is the use of combinations of verb + adverb or preposition (particle). These combinations are known as phrasal verbs: **pick up**, **take up**, **bump into**, **set off**, **put up with.**

Phrasal verbs are very common in English and many verbs combine with several different particles. Like other verbs, they also have particular 'friends':

- **take up** + an offer/a job/a hobby
- **pick sb up** + from the airport/in your car/at midday
- **run into** + difficulties/an old friend

Thus, there are two layers of collocation to get right if we want to use phrasal verbs correctly. First, we have to choose the correct particle to go with the verb, and then we have to choose the right kind of word or phrase to express the meaning we want.

A final point about word order: changing the position of the particle in a phrasal verb can have a major effect on the meaning. Compare *She couldn't get over the message* (She was very surprised by it), and *She couldn't get the message over* (She couldn't make other people understand it). For more information about phrasal verbs, see page 860.

Less fixed combinations

'Verb + noun' collocations

These are very common in English. In such cases, we have more freedom to make combinations, but there are certain restrictions on what is possible or probable.

Let's take **make**, a verb which has many 'friends'. We **make**:

- a mistake
- the bed
- (the) dinner
- an effort
- friends

It is difficult to say exactly what **make** means in all these different collocations. We can look up the meaning of **screwdriver** or **digest** in a dictionary and be fairly sure what they refer to, but this strategy does not work very well with **make**. One important part of the meaning of **make** is that it contrasts with the verb **do**. These two verbs tend to have very different friends. For example, we **do**:

- the shopping
- the dishes
- our best
- someone a favour

So we can see that there are many ways of combining **make** and **do** with nouns. There are limits to the number of collocations they have and they don't often share the same collocates.

There are several other very common verbs in English like **make** and **do** (such as **get**, **have**, and **take**) that do not have much meaning on their own. To really get a feel for the way these very common verbs are used, you need to know the phrases they form with other words and the contexts in which we use them.

Other common grammatical combinations

There are a number of other common grammatical combinations that form collocations in English:

noun + verb:	temperatures **rise**; prices **fall**; dogs **bark**; cats **miaow**
adverb + adjective:	**bitterly** cold; **hugely** enjoyable; **deeply** upset
adjective + noun:	**strong** tea; a **powerful** engine; a **heavy** smoker
verb + adverb:	sleep **soundly**; walk **briskly**; rely **heavily** on
adverb + verb:	**distinctly** remember; **flatly** refuse; **hotly** deny

You can find many examples of combinations like these in the 130 'Collocation Boxes' in this dictionary: see for example the boxes at the entries for **cost**, **environment**, **influence**, and **suggestion**.

Functional expressions

In everyday conversation, there are many collocations that occur with particular grammatical structures. These structures are like frames, into which we can put different words in order to perform a variety of communicative acts. Here are some examples:

- **I'd like** a return ticket to/a ham sandwich... [buying something]
- **I don't suppose you could** tell me the way/open the window... [making requests]
- **Have you got** the time/change for a pound... [asking for information, asking a favour]
- **Could you** tell me the way to... [asking for directions]
- **By the way**, ... [introducing a new topic of conversation]
- **Well, it's time** we were going/ **Well, I'll be** going now... [saying goodbye, ending a conversation]

There are thousands of such sentence frames in English and many are explained in this dictionary. They are one way in which expert users of English manage to sound so fluent.

Learning collocation

The fact that you are using this dictionary probably means that you would like to be a fluent user of spoken and written English. Here are some techniques to help you to acquire greater 'collocational fluency' in English:

- Read widely in English – begin with simplified texts and as quickly as possible go on to authentic, unsimplified texts: newspapers, magazines, stories etc.

- Use highlighters of different colours to make the new collocations stand out.

- As you read, connect keywords and their collocations by drawing lines between them.

- Copy out the examples you come across in your reading into a special notebook.

- Organize your notebook into topics (travel, sport etc) and add collocations connected with the topic as you come across them in your reading.

- Organize your notebook into collocational patterns:

Verb + noun
Noun + verb
Adverb + adjective
Verb + adverb
Adjective + noun
Functional expressions
Idioms
Phrasal verbs

- Organize your notebook into common keywords (**get**, **take**, **come**, **make**, **do** etc), and add collocations as you come across them in your reading.

- Make a chart showing common verbs and their collocations:

	a trip	a break	a date	the dishes	a walk	lunch
take	✓	✓			✓	
make			✓			✓
do				✓		
have		✓	✓			✓

- Use your dictionary to enrich your knowledge of collocations. For example, before you use a dull collocation such as 'a big storm', look up the word **storm** in your dictionary and try to choose a more interesting adjective (e.g. fierce, raging, terrible, violent).

ACTIVITY

Read the following passage and:

- underline any collocations you find
- organize them into separate groups (for example, verb+noun collocations, adverb+adjective collocations, phrasal verbs, idioms, and functional expressions)

England's decisive victory over Bulgaria yesterday was overshadowed by news that Phil Harper's knee injury could keep him out of the game for up to three months. By deciding to play in last night's game, the England midfielder had disregarded the advice of his doctor, and it was clear – even as the team was warming up before the game – that he was not fully fit. After 30 minutes, he limped off the field in agony, and it is now highly unlikely that he will take any further part in the European competition.

Harper has made an outstanding contribution to England's recent successes, and without him they face a daunting challenge as they gear up for the next round of the tournament. Said team coach Alex Murphy, 'Obviously we're bitterly disappointed, but to be honest, it was always on the cards that Phil's knee would cause him problems.'

ANSWERS

adjective + noun
decisive victory
outstanding contribution
daunting challenge
next round

noun + preposition
victory over
contribution to

preposition + noun
in agony
up to three months

noun + noun
knee injury
team coach

verb + noun
disregard advice

adjective + noun
make a contribution
face a challenge
cause problems

adverb + adjective
fully fit
highly unlikely
bitterly disappointed

phrasal verbs
keep sb out of sth
warm up
gear up for

idioms
take part in
on the cards

functional expressions
to be honest

TOPIC VOCABULARY: ENTERTAINMENT

The following eight pages contain short texts about different topics. Each text is accompanied by a list of vocabulary taken from it along with explanations. There are also some suggestions of other related words and phrases that you might need when talking or writing about one of the topics. Use this dictionary to check their meanings – and add more related words to these lists when you find them in your own reading.

Going to the cinema

I love going to the cinema and I'm lucky because there's a big new **multiplex** close to where I live. I always enjoy a good **thriller** – the **nail-biting** type where there's lots of **suspense** and you find yourself gripping the arm of the chair. I'm not very keen on **westerns** or war films – they usually involve a bit too much violence for my taste. But I enjoy **blockbuster sci-fi** movies, especially if the **special effects** are well done. I really like to watch foreign films too, although I hate it if they've been **dubbed** – I prefer the original versions with **subtitles**.

multiplex: a large building with several cinema screens
thriller: an exciting film about crime, murder etc
nail-biting: making you feel nervous and excited
suspense: the nervous, excited feeling that you have when you are waiting to see what will happen next
western: a film about cowboys and the American West in the 19th century
blockbuster: a very successful film
sci-fi: science fiction – stories about space travel and the future
special effects: exciting images that have been created using computers and other technical methods
dubbed: with the words spoken by actors speaking your own language, not by the film's original actors
subtitles: written words at the bottom of the cinema screen, which translate what is being said

Other useful vocabulary

You can use the dictionary to check the meanings of these words and expressions.

Types of film
action film
romantic comedy
horror film
sequel

People
director
producer
film star
cast

Other related vocabulary
script   be set in (Chicago/
scene   the future/ancient
flashback   Rome etc)

Going out

I don't **go out** much during the week. Occasionally I go to the cinema or meet friends in a bar. But usually I stay in and relax. Sometimes I just read a book or watch television, but now and again I order a **takeaway** from a local restaurant and rent a **video**. I have a lot more **free time** at the weekend so I do all kinds of things. I try to go to the gym on Saturday mornings and then in the afternoon I often **go shopping**. I meet up with friends and we go to the big **out-of-town shopping centre** together. We usually **go clubbing** on a Saturday night so we go round the clothes shops looking for something new to wear. Every couple of months I try to take a few days off work so that I can have a **long weekend** and go away somewhere nice.

go out: to go somewhere to do something enjoyable, instead of staying at home
takeaway: a meal that you buy from a restaurant or shop to eat at home
video: a film on videotape that you watch on your own TV
free time: time when you do not have to work or study
go shopping: to go out to different shops
out-of-town shopping centre: a large place that is just outside a city, where there are lots of different shops
go clubbing: to go to a place where you can dance and listen to music
long weekend: a weekend when you are also free on the Friday or Monday

PEOPLE AND RELATIONSHIPS

Families

Jake comes from a very **close family**. He spends a lot of time with his **immediate family** – his parents and his brothers and sisters – and he often sees his relatives when they get together for one of their **family reunions**. He has a large **extended family** too with lots of cousins, aunts, and uncles. His friend, Simon, is always telling Jake how lucky he is. Simon is an **only child** and so are both his parents, which means he has very few **close relatives**.

close family: a family in which everyone has a good relationship and talks to each other a lot
immediate family: family members who are most closely related to you
family reunion: a party when family members get together, especially when they have not seen each other for a long time
extended family: family members apart from your immediate family
only child: a child who has no brothers or sisters
close relatives: family members who are closely related to you such as brothers, sisters and cousins

Friends

I've never had trouble **making friends**. I have lots of friends, but there aren't many that I would call **close friends**. Paula's my **best friend**. We **got to know** each other when we were at university. I knew we'd **get on with** each other as soon as we met – we have so much in common. And I was right. We've been friends now for five years, and we've never **fallen out**.

make friends: when two people make friends with each other, they become friends
close friend: a friend that you know well and spend a lot of time with
best friend: the friend that you like best
get to know: to become friendly with someone that you have recently met
get on with: to like someone and have a friendly relationship with them
fall out: to stop being someone's friend, for example after arguing with them

Romantic relationships

Danuta and Marek first started **going out with** each other when they were 19. Danuta had **fancied** Marek for a long time, and she'd told all her friends how attractive she thought he was. So of course she was really pleased when he **asked her out**. They went to the cinema on their first **date**. Their relationship lasted two years and then they **split up**. A few months later, Danuta met Damien and **fell in love with** him straight away. Damien **proposed to** her and now they're **engaged**. They're **living together** and plan to get married some time next year.

go out with: to have a romantic relationship with someone
fancy: to think someone is very attractive, and want to be their boyfriend or girlfriend
ask sb out: to invite someone to go with you to a cinema, restaurant etc, because you want to start a relationship with them
date: a romantic meeting with someone
split up: to end a romantic relationship
fall in love with: to feel very strongly attracted to someone
propose to: to ask someone to marry you
engaged: if two people are engaged, they have agreed to get married
live together: to live together in a sexual relationship, but without being married

Other useful vocabulary

You can use the dictionary to check the meanings of these words and expressions.

Families
distant (relative/cousin)
single parent
be related to

Friends
old friend
circle of friends
classmate
flatmate/housemate

Romantic relationships
boyfriend/girlfriend
partner
fiancé/fiancée
single
separated
divorced
have an affair (with sb)

TRAVEL AND TOURISM

Choosing a holiday

If you want to go on holiday but you're not sure where you want to go, it's a good idea to start by going to a **travel agent's**. Take some holiday **brochures** home with you so that you can look at what's available. Think about what sort of **accommodation** you'd like to stay in. Do you enjoy the convenience of a **package holiday** or do you prefer to travel independently? Would you prefer an **all-inclusive** holiday, or would you be happier with a **self-catering** arrangement? Do you like staying in hotels or would an apartment or private **villa** be more your type of thing? Most of all though, you should think carefully about your **destination**. Find out what the weather is like there and try to get as much information about the different **resorts**. Are you looking for somewhere quiet, or would you prefer somewhere with plenty of **nightlife**? When you've answered all these questions, you can go ahead and **book** your holiday.

travel agent's: a business that provides information for travellers and helps them to arrange holidays
brochure: a type of magazine with a lot of pictures, giving information about places where you can go on holiday
accommodation: places to stay, such as hotels or rented apartments
package holiday: a holiday where everything is organized for you for a single fixed price
all-inclusive: including meals, hotel costs, entertainment etc
self-catering: when you do your own cooking and buy food from local shops
villa: a holiday house, especially near the sea or in the country
destination: the place that you are going to
resort: a town where many people go for holidays
nightlife: evening entertainment in nightclubs, bars etc
book (a holiday): to make reservations

My first holiday

When I was 18 I decided to go travelling with some friends. We really wanted to go to Australia, but we couldn't afford it. So, we decided to buy **rail passes** for Europe instead. We spent ages working out our **itinerary**, deciding which places we'd like to visit in each country. We bought some **guidebooks** to find out more about the countries we were going to and a couple of small **phrase books** so that at least we'd be able to buy food and ask for directions. As we didn't have much money, we planned to stay mainly in **youth hostels** or cheap **bed and breakfasts**. Although we all wanted to do a lot of **sightseeing**, we also agreed that it would be interesting to get away from the **touristy** areas and try to discover more about the real way of life in our chosen countries.

rail pass: a ticket that allows you to make as many train journeys as you want within a particular period
itinerary: a plan of a journey
guidebook: a book for tourists, giving information about a particular place or country
phrase book: a book that gives translations of useful words and phrases
youth hostel: a type of inexpensive hotel for young travellers
bed and breakfast: a small inexpensive hotel that provides rooms and breakfast
sightseeing: the activity of visiting well-known places, museums etc
touristy: full of tourists

Other useful vocabulary

You can use the dictionary to check the meanings of these words and expressions.

Types of holiday	Accommodation
beach holiday	full board
walking holiday	half board
skiing holiday	B&B
adventure holiday	

Money

foreign currency	change money
traveller's cheques	

Other related vocabulary

do your packing	travel insurance
go backpacking	visa

Working for a big company

I'm a sales representative. I work for a big **multinational**. I earn about £35,000 a year and get other **benefits** such as a **company car** and a **company pension**. I enjoy what I do even though I often have to **work** very **long hours**. Sometimes I wish I had a **nine-to-five job**, but I enjoy travelling and would hate to be stuck in the office all the time. I'm hoping that I'll **be promoted** to area manager next year – a senior **position** that would be a lot more **challenging**.

multinational: a large company that operates in many different countries
benefits: extra things that you get from your employer, in addition to your salary
company car: a car that your company pays for and provides for you to use
company pension: a system by which you and your company both invest money to provide you with an income when you stop working
work long hours: to work more hours than the usual working day
nine-to-five job: a job in which your working day has fixed hours
be promoted: to be given a more important job, usually with a higher salary
position: a specific job in an organization
challenging: difficult, but also interesting and enjoyable

Applying for a job

I have just finished university and am now **applying for jobs**. I'd like to work as a recruitment consultant. There have been quite a few **vacancies** advertised in the national newspapers recently. Most of them ask you to send your CV and a letter saying why you think you are suitable for the **post**. Some ask you to send for their **application form** which you then have to **fill in**. Out of the ten companies I've contacted so far, I've already had three **rejections**. I have two interviews next week though, so I hope it won't be long before I'm **offered a job**.

apply for a job: to write to an organization to tell them that you want a job that they have advertised
vacancy: a job that is available for people to apply for
CV: a document that gives details of your qualifications, skills, and experience
post: a job that you can apply for
application form: a paper with questions for you to answer when you are applying for a job
fill in: to provide all the necessary information on a form
rejection: when an organization tells you that your application has not been successful
be offered a job: to be told by someone that they want you to work for them

Other useful vocabulary

You can use the dictionary to check the meanings of these words and expressions.

CVs	Working hours
reference	full-time
qualifications	part-time
communication/	permanent
organizational/	temporary
interpersonal skills	flexitime
	overtime

Other related vocabulary

train as (a	pay rise
nurse/airline	career
pilot/chef etc)	job offer

ACTIVITY

Rewrite these sentences using words from the reading passage so that the second sentence means the same as the first. You can find the answers on page LS13.

1 I get all sorts of things in addition to my salary – free health insurance for example.
  I get all sorts of .... in addition to my salary – free health insurance for example.

2 They want me to send them all the details about my qualifications and work experience.
  They want me to send them my ....

3 My job involves a lot of hard work, but it's interesting and I enjoy it.
  I have quite a .... job.

4 Please write all your details on the application form and return it to us.
  Please .... the application form and return it to us.

NEW TECHNOLOGY

Communication

It wasn't such a long time ago that no one had even heard of **mobile phones**. These days, they are part of everyday life and one of the main ways we communicate with each other. People use their mobiles to make **personal calls** as well as **business calls**. They are a valuable **form of communication**, enabling people to **be contacted** wherever they are. And you don't always have to speak to someone – you can use a mobile phone to send someone a **text message**. **Texting** is a quick and easy way to **get in touch with** someone about something when you don't actually need to talk to them, for example to let them know that you are going to be late. The other option is to leave a message on their **voicemail** – your call gets automatically **diverted to** that if they don't answer the phone.

mobile or **mobile phone**: a phone that you carry around with you
personal calls: calls to your friends or family
business calls: calls that you make as part of your job
form of communication: any of the ways that people use to exchange information with each other
be contacted: to be reached by someone who wants to talk to you
text message: a short written message that you send using a mobile phone
texting: the activity of communicating by text messages
get in touch with: to talk to, write to, or send a message to someone
voicemail: a system for recording and storing spoken messages
be diverted to: to be sent to another part of a phone system

ACTIVITY
Complete these sentences using words from the reading passage. You can find the answers on page LS13.

1 I won't be at home all day but you can call me on my ....

2 If I don't answer the phone, just leave a message on my ....

3 You're not supposed to use your phone at work to make ....

4 I often use my mobile to send someone a .... – it's not always necessary to talk to them directly.

Other useful vocabulary
Common abbreviations used for texting
CUL8R: see you later
B4: before
GR8: great
BTW: by the way
2day: today

Emoticons
:) shows that you are pleased
:)) shows that you are very happy
:(shows that you are annoyed or sad
:0 shows that you are surprised
:-D shows that you think that something is funny
;) a wink – shows that you are making a joke

Computers and the Internet

Everyone I know has a home computer so I decided it was time I got one too. I thought it would be best to get a **laptop** as they don't take up so much room. I got a bit carried away and bought all the extras – a printer, a **scanner**, a **webcam** and lots of **software** that I didn't really need. Most importantly though, I wanted to have **Internet access** so I arranged a **broadband connection** as I was told that it would make everything much easier and faster.

laptop or **notebook**: a small computer that you can carry around with you
scanner: a device that converts pictures or documents into computer files
webcam: a small camera attached to a computer. It takes moving pictures that can be seen on a website.
software: computer programs, such as word-processors and web browsers
Internet access: the ability to use the Internet
broadband connection: an Internet connection that allows data to be sent and received at very high speeds

Now I spend a lot of my spare time **going online**. I love **logging on to** some of the **chat rooms**. You can meet some really interesting people. The biggest change for me though has been the **online shopping**. Many of the big shops have great websites and it saves me so much time. The other thing I love is being able to send and receive **emails** – it's such an easy way to **keep in touch** with people.

go online: to connect your computer to the Internet
log on to: to enter a particular area of the Internet
chat room: an area on the Internet where several people can have a discussion
online shopping: to buy things using the Internet
email: a written message sent from one computer to another by means of the Internet
keep in touch: to phone or write to someone regularly

Computers are really changing the way we live our lives. Some of my friends now work from home. They use their computers to **download** work from their offices and then send it back as an email **attachment** when they've finished. I know they worry a little about getting computer **viruses** but there is plenty of good anti-virus software that you can **install**.

download: to use the Internet to transfer data from another computer system to your own computer
attachment: a computer file that is sent with an email
virus: a computer program that has been deliberately created to cause damage to other people's files
install: to add a new piece of software to your computer system

ACTIVITY
Complete the following paragraph using words from the reading passage. You can find the answers on page LS13.

If you want a computer that you can take anywhere with you, it'd be a good idea to buy a (1)............... . You can use

it like an ordinary computer and attach any of the usual things to it, such as a (2)............... if you need to send letters to people. You can use it to do some (3)............... if you don't have time to go to the shops yourself, or you can connect to an Internet (4)............... if you want to talk to other people about something that you're interested in. I mainly use my computer to send and receive (5)............... because it's such a convenient way of exchanging information.

Other useful vocabulary
You can use the dictionary to check the meanings of these words and expressions.

Computers
PC
computer-literate
hardware
hard disk/hard drive
memory
folder
document
program
menu
upgrade

Internet
ISP (Internet Service Provider)
home page
link
search engine
browser

Commands and Actions
edit
delete
save
copy
cut
paste
scroll up/down
click on
right-click/left-click/double-click

MEDIA

Newspapers

People don't seem to want **hard news** in their daily newspapers. These days, it's **exclusives** about film stars, pop stars, and television celebrities that **make the headlines**. And no story is complete without those **intrusive** photographs taken by the **paparazzi**. And it's not just the **tabloids**. Even the **broadsheets** put **sensationalist** stories on their front pages instead of real **investigative journalism** or international news. Most of the weekend newspapers now come with free **colour supplements** packed with yet more **trivia**, **gossip columns,** and lifestyle **features** on things like gardening, cooking, and DIY.

hard news: news about important national and international events
exclusive: a story reported in only one newspaper
make the headlines or **hit the headlines**: to get a lot of attention in the newspapers
intrusive: disturbing people's private lives
paparazzi: photographers who follow famous people around to take photos of them
tabloids: small newspapers that are full of stories about celebrities, sport, etc. but not much serious news
broadsheets: larger newspapers with a lot of serious news stories
sensationalist: deliberately making facts seem as shocking as possible
investigative journalism: news stories that are based on serious research that tries to find the truth about something
colour supplement: a type of magazine that is given free with a newspaper
trivia: very unimportant stories
gossip column: an article that is full of stories about famous people
feature: an article that deals with a particular subject, but not with a news story

Other useful vocabulary
You can use the dictionary to check the meanings of these words and expressions.

People
journalist	editor
reporter	columnist
correspondent	

Sections of a newspaper
sports news	letters page
business news	horoscope
editorial	

Other related vocabulary
the press	the papers
the media	press coverage

ACTIVITY
Rewrite these sentences using words from the reading passage so that the second sentence means the same as the first. You can find the answers on page LS13.

1 I like reading the serious newspapers.
   I like reading the ....
2 My favourite part of the paper is where you read about all the things famous people have been doing.
   My favourite part of the paper is the ....
3 If it's true that their marriage is breaking up, all the newspapers will have stories about it.
   Their marriage break-up is sure to ....
4 The story about his illness was only in *The Daily Star*.
   The Daily Star had an .... about his illness.
5 The paper reported his drug problem with a lot of shocking details.
   The paper reported his drug problem in a very .... way.

Television

If we're watching TV together and Miguel has the **remote control**, he spends the whole time **zapping**. I'm never allowed to watch the latest **reality show**, listen to a whole interview on a **chat show** or find out who wins the big prize on a **game show**. When the **adverts** come on, he always **switches over** to see what's on the other **channels**. He usually falls asleep during the news or a **documentary**. So I **turn the volume down**, put the **subtitles** on, and enjoy a complete episode of my favourite **soap**.

remote control or **remote**: a device that you hold in your hand and use for changing the channel on your TV

zapping: the activity of continually changing from one TV programme to another

reality show: a TV programme involving ordinary people, not using professional actors or presenters

chat show: a show in which a presenter interviews famous people

game show: a show in which people win prizes by playing games and answering questions

adverts: advertisements that are shown between TV programmes or in the middle of programmes

switch over: to change to another channel

channels: the different television stations and their programmes

documentary: a serious programme about subjects such as science, history, or politics

turn the volume down: to reduce the level of sound

subtitles: written words at the bottom of the TV screen, which show what is being said

soap or **soap opera**: a drama series broadcast several times a week, about the lives of a group of imaginary people

Other useful vocabulary

You can use the dictionary to check the meanings of these words and expressions.

People
presenter
newsreader
viewer

Types of television or programme
cable TV
satellite TV

series
sitcom
weather forecast

Actions
turn on/off
turn up/down
turn over

ACTIVITY

Rewrite these sentences using words from the reading passage so that the second sentence means the same as the first. You can find the answers at the bottom of this page.

1 On a Friday night I usually watch that programme where people try to win prizes.
On Friday night I usually watch that ....

2 Don't change to another channel. I was watching that.
Don't .... I was watching that.

3 They are showing a programme about the history of Caribbean music.
They are showing a .... about Caribbean music.

4 Install our new satellite dish, and you can watch shows from over 40 different TV stations.
Install our new satellite dish, and you can watch over 40 different ....

5 I was working in the evening on Tuesday and Thursday, so I missed my favourite drama series.
I was working in the evening on Tuesday and Thursday, so I missed my favourite ....

ANSWERS

Television
1 game show
2 switch over
3 documentary
4 channels
5 soap (opera)

PRONUNCIATION

Transcription

The words in this dictionary are followed by a **transcription** to show the pronunciation:

- *come* /kʌm/, *home* /həʊm/

Often the number of **symbols** in the transcription will be different from the number of **letters** in the written word. This is because symbols in a transcription represent the **sounds** rather than the letters.

Written letters may correspond to a number of different sounds – or to no sound at all! But symbols always represent the same sound. Look at the following groups of words. They all contain the same vowel sound – but the spelling is different:

- *come* /kʌm/, *sum* /sʌm/, *dumb* /dʌm/
- *home* /həʊm/, *roam* /rəʊm/, *comb* /kəʊm/

Some symbols are familiar and easy to recognise, for example / p, b, t, d, k, g, f /. Others are less easy. The 'ng' sound in words such as *song* /sɒŋ/ and *thing* /θɪŋ/ is represented by the single symbol /ŋ/. And the symbols for 'th' show that this pair of letters can cover two different sounds. Compare:

- *thing* /θɪŋ/ and *this* /ðɪs/

If you want to check the sound of a new symbol, look at the list of symbols and words on the inside back cover.

The schwa sound /ə/

The **schwa** represents the most common sound in English. It is the first sound in *above* /əˈbʌv/ and the last sound in *under* /ˈʌndə/. In fact, almost any written vowel can, when unstressed, be sounded as a schwa:

- *allow* /əˈlaʊ/, *perform* /pəˈfɔːm/, *commit* /kəˈmɪt/, *supply* /səˈplaɪ/.

Stress

Both *above* /əˈbʌv/ and *under* /ˈʌndə/ have two **syllables**. But they are different in terms of the relative importance of the syllables. In *above* the first syllable is relatively short and weak, while the second syllable is relatively strong and long. In *under*, by contrast, it is the first syllable that is relatively strong and long. In other words, the first syllable in *under* is **stressed**, and we indicate this in the dictionary by using the symbol /ˈ/ directly before the stressed syllable. You can imagine these two words written as aBOVE and UNder.

It is useful to know that:

- most two-syllable nouns and adjectives have **front stress** (the first syllable is stressed): FLOWer, LITTLe, VILLage, PREtty, BOdy, FOrest etc.

- most two-syllable verbs have **end stress** (the second syllable is stressed): forGIVE, aLLOW, coMMIT etc.

It is worth checking the pronunciation in the dictionary, especially if a two-syllable word can be both a noun and a verb. In such cases one of two things can happen:

- *either* there is no change in the pronunciation or in the stress, for example: *reply* /rɪˈplaɪ/, *damage* /ˈdæmɪdʒ/, and *wonder* /ˈwʌndə/

- *or* the written form stays the same, but the stress changes, often causing a change in the vowel sound: compare *permit* (noun) /ˈpɜːmɪt/ and *permit* (verb) /pəˈmɪt/, *record* (noun) /ˈrekɔːd/ and *record* (verb) /rɪˈkɔːd/, and *import* (noun) /ˈɪmpɔːt/ and *import* (verb) /ɪmˈpɔːt/.

		weak	secondary	weak	primary	weak
		o	■	o	■	o
station	/ˈsteɪʃ(ə)n/				STA	tion
reaction	/rɪˈækʃ(ə)n/			re	AC	tion
satisfaction	/ˌsætɪsˈfækʃ(ə)n/		SA	tis	FAC	tion
pronunciation	/prəˌnʌnsɪˈeɪʃ(ə)n/	pro	NUN	ci	A	tion

Primary and secondary stress

In words of three or more syllables, there are sometimes two levels of stress: **primary** and **secondary**. When this happens, we use the symbol /ˌ/ before the secondary stressed syllable. Look at the examples in the table above.

Making sure that people understand you when you speak

If you want to be easily understood, then the first thing to do is to make sure that your **consonant sounds** are as clear and accurate as possible.

In the case of **vowel sounds**, you should pay special attention to vowel **length**. In British English, the difference between the short vowels (the schwa, in particular) and the long ones is much greater than in most languages. There are two types of long vowel: firstly, those where the vowel symbol is followed by /ː/, the symbol that indicates length. So pay particular attention to vowel length in pairs such as:

- *cat* = /kæt/ and *cart* = /kɑːt/
- *sit* = /sɪt/ and *seat* = /siːt/
- *shot* = /ʃɒt/ and *short* = /ʃɔːt/

The other long vowels, the **diphthongs**, are indicated by double symbols, for example:

- *day* /deɪ/, *nice* /naɪs/, *boy* /bɔɪ/, *go* /goʊ/

In all of these the tongue moves from one position to another as the vowel sound continues.

You should also make sure that your **word stress** is as accurate as possible. You will see that the dictionary shows the stress patterns of compound words and phrasal verbs, for example:

- ˈquestion ˌmark
- ˌput ˈup with sb/sth

Understanding native speakers

The dictionary shows the pronunciations of words spoken in their slow, careful form. But in normal rapid speech, this changes, particularly in the following ways:

1 It is sometimes difficult to hear when one word ends and the next begins. Here are examples of the four main types of **word linking**.

- *an apple* sounds like *a napple*
- *two apples* sounds like *two wapples*
- *three apples* sounds like *three yapples*
- *four apples* sounds like *four rapples*

2 The schwa can disappear between certain consonants. This means that *support* /səˈpɔːt/ may sound like *sport* /spɔːt/ and *parade* /pəˈreɪd/ like *prayed* /preɪd/. The consonants /t/ and /d/ may disappear when found between two other consonants. So *facts* may sound like *fax* and *friendly* like *frienly*.

If you see a symbol in brackets in this dictionary, (as in /ˈsteɪʃ(ə)n/ or /fren(d)li/) it means that the sound may disappear in normal rapid speech.

3 Finally, consonants may change to make it easier to produce the next sound. Sometimes words change permanently, as with *handkerchief* where the /d/ has disappeared completely and it now sounds like *hangkerchief*. Other words change when spoken fast, such as *handbag* which is on its way to sounding permanently like *hambag*.

METAPHOR

You may think that metaphor is only used in poetry and creative writing, but this is not the case. Many words in English have more than one meaning, and these other meanings are often connected to the main meaning in metaphorical ways.

Most of the words that we use for describing familiar objects and familiar experiences also have metaphorical meanings. Groups of metaphors come from many different areas of human life. Here are some examples.

Metaphors about the body

Some of the first words that you learn in English are for the parts of the body: **hand**, **head**, **eye**, and so on. But these words will sometimes be used in ways that don't fit the meanings that you know:

*Could you give Jill a **hand** with these boxes?*
*It's very important for us all to put our **heads** together.*
*Can you keep an **eye** on things here until I get back?*

If you know only the basic meanings of these words, you will find these sentences strange. Does the first speaker want someone to cut off their hand and give it to Jill, together with the boxes? Does the second speaker want to put their head next to other people's heads? Of course not. The first speaker is asking for help. The second speaker is suggesting that everyone should work together in order to solve a problem. In these sentences, the body parts are being used in ways that are not *literal* but *metaphorical*.

Although the sentences above do not refer literally to body parts, their meanings are influenced by the literal meanings. We use our hands to help people, so to help someone is to **give them a hand**. Our brains are inside our heads, so the head is associated with people thinking. We look at things with our eyes, so if we **keep an eye on something**, we watch it carefully to make sure that it is being done correctly.

Metaphors about the weather

Most people like sunny weather so, as you might guess, a **sunny** smile or a **sunny** nature or personality are good, positive things.

Storms are powerful and impossible to control, so a **storm** of protest or criticism is difficult to deal with.

Warm weather is pleasant and comfortable, and a **warm** person is kind and friendly in a way that makes other people feel comfortable.

Cold weather, on the other hand, is often less pleasant, and a **cold** person is unfriendly and makes us feel uncomfortable.

ACTIVITY
Have a look in the dictionary at the literal and metaphorical meanings of the following words, and try to find the connections between them:

- cool, icy, heated, hot
- hail, gale, flood, torrent
- to rain, to cloud over

ACTIVITY
Try to think of some more English words connected with temperature and the weather that have metaphorical meanings.

ACTIVITY
There are many metaphors relating to animals in English. Try to find the metaphorical meanings associated with common animals such as **pigs**, **sheep**, **donkeys**, and **rats**.

Are animal metaphors the same in your language as they are in English? Think of some in your own language, and compare them.

Metaphor and the creation of new meanings

When new words are needed in order to describe things that did not exist before, they are often created by means of metaphor. With the growth of computer technology, we need words to describe many new objects and activities – and most of these new words have been produced metaphorically:

> When you want to spend some time **surfing** the **Net,** you get connected and start to **browse**. You notice a **website** that looks interesting, and use your **mouse** to click on the **link** that takes you to the website. The **site's home page** may have a **menu** with links to different areas of the site. Having **visited** the site, you like it so much that you will want to return, so you **bookmark** it.

> The first thing I do when I switch on my computer is to check my **mailbox** for any new **emails**. I get about 20 a day but try to keep my **inbox** as tidy as possible by **filing** them in a number of different **folders**.

If you look in a dictionary that is over 10 years old, you will find most of the bold words above. But you will not find the meanings that are used here.

Although a website is not a physical place, we can **visit** it as we would visit a friend or a place of interest. Similarly, a **mailbox** can now mean the part of a computer's memory where email is stored. Thinking of it as the physical place where letters written on paper are delivered helps us to understand the technology.

ACTIVITY
The metaphors that are used in computer language come from many different areas of life. Which areas do the following terms come from?

● **virus, window, exit, memory, icon**

ACTIVITY
Many computer metaphors come from the language we use to talk about **books**, the **office**, and the traditional **postal system**. Look at the words highlighted in the text above, and try to decide whether they fit into any of these categories.

How awareness of metaphor can help your language learning

We use metaphors almost every time we write or speak, often without realizing it. Becoming aware of how language works – a process known as 'language awareness' – is an essential part of successful language learning.

Here are two ways in which awareness of metaphor can help you to increase your understanding of how English works:

● When you read a piece of English, notice the metaphors, and think about the ways in which *metaphorical* meanings are connected with *literal* meanings.

● Try to relate new words and expressions that you come across in your reading to the words you already know. Thinking about the connections between familiar items of vocabulary and new, unfamiliar ones will help you to remember the new meanings you have learned.

If you develop the habit of thinking about language in this way, you will be able to learn and remember new vocabulary more effectively.

ANSWERS
system; filing; office; folders: office
bookmark: books; mailbox: postal
page: books; menu: restaurants;
surfing: sport; browse: books; home
psychology; icon: religion
exit: architecture; memory;
virus: medicine; window: architecture;

WORD FORMATION

Word families

Look at this group of words and decide what they have in common:

ability   *disability*
disabled   *enable*
inability   *unable*

All of the above words are formed from – and are related to – the adjective **able**. So we can call **able** the 'base word' from which all these other words are developed. Can you guess which word is the base word for this next group?

destroyer   *destructive*
destruction   *indestructible*

All these words are formed from the base word **destroy**. We call these groups of related words 'word families'. Like members of real families, the words that make up a word family share some of the same features: they all share some of the letters of the base word, and their meanings are related too.

ACTIVITY

Look at the following groups of words and try to decide in each case what the base word is. The answers are on page LS19. Then try to guess the meaning of each word. Check in the dictionary to see if you are right.

discomfort   *uncomfortable*
comfortable   *comforting*

decision   *decisive*
undecided   *indecisive*
indecision

impure   *purify*
purist   *impurity*

How are words formed?

Many English words are formed from combinations of other words, or from combinations of words and prefixes or suffixes. So if you know what each of the parts means, you will often be able to guess the meaning of a new word.

What are prefixes and suffixes?

A *prefix* is added to the *beginning* of a word to make another word. A prefix can be either a short word, or a group of letters that is not a word. An example of the first type is **self-**. **Self-** means 'yourself' or 'itself', so if you are **self-employed**, you work for yourself, and if something **self-destructs**, it destroys itself. An example of the second type is **non-**, which means 'not'. So a **non-violent** protest is a protest that does not involve violence.

A *suffix* is added to the *end* of a word to make another word. A suffix can be either a short word, or a group of letters that is not a word. An example of the first type is **-rich**, which is added to nouns to make adjectives for describing something that 'contains a lot' of something. So **oil-rich** rocks are full of oil, and **vitamin-rich** foods contain a lot of vitamins. An example of the second type is **-ish**, which means 'slightly' or 'rather'. So **greenish** water looks slightly green.

ACTIVITY

Look at the words in **bold** in the following sentences and see if you can guess what they mean. After you have guessed, you can check the meanings in the dictionary. All the prefixes and suffixes used in these sentences (and shown here in red) have their own entries in the dictionary.

*The software is **overpriced** and doesn't offer anything more than its rivals.*

*Local residents are calling for the police to crack down on **antisocial** behaviour by troublemakers, some of whom are as young as ten.*

***E-commerce** now accounts for 84 per cent of the company's sales.*

*The machines are very **user-friendly** and they tell you how hard you are working and how many calories you have used up.*

*The new district health boards will be required to act in an efficient and **businesslike** way.*

ACTIVITY
See if you can make some more words using these prefixes and suffixes. Check in the dictionary to see if your words are there.

Compounds

Using prefixes and suffixes is not the only way to form new words. Many English words are *compounds*. Compounds are formed by combining two or three words. Sometimes these combinations remain as two or three separate words and sometimes they combine to form one new word. For example, the word **troublemakers** in the second example above has been formed by combining the two nouns **trouble** and **maker**. This has created a new word meaning 'someone who makes (=causes) trouble'.

Most compounds are treated as separate entries in this dictionary, so that you can see immediately that they have a meaning of their own that is different from the meanings of the words from which they are formed. Sometimes these meanings are easy to guess. For example, a **bus stop** is a place where buses stop to pick up passengers, and a **bookshop** is a place where you buy books. However, a **soap opera** does not contain any singing and has nothing to do with soap: it is a television or radio show that is broadcast several times a week, and tells the story of the lives of a group of ordinary people.

Other ways of forming words

Some new words are formed by combining part of one word with part of another. For example, **brunch** is a meal you eat in the late morning that combines **breakfast** and **lunch**, and **edutainment** is something such as a video, television programme, or software program that combines **education** and **entertainment**.

ACTIVITY
Can you guess which words have combined to form the following computer terms: **emoticon**, **netiquette**, **netizen**, **technophobe**?

And can you guess their meanings from the words that have combined to form them? The answers are at the bottom of this page.

Other new words are formed from the first letters of the words in a compound or phrase. Examples of this are **CD-ROM** (**c**ompact **d**isc **r**ead-**o**nly **m**emory), **FAQs** (**f**requently-**a**sked **q**uestions), and **IT** (**i**nformation **t**echnology). These new words are called *acronyms*.

ACTIVITY
Think about how new words are formed in your own language. Are they formed mainly by using *prefixes* and *suffixes*, by combining words to form *compounds*, by means of *acronyms*, or in other ways?

Spelling note: Words that are formed from combinations of other words, whether these are compounds or words formed from prefixes or suffixes, are often written in several different ways. You may see them written as separate words, or with hyphens, or as single words. For example: **hard hat**, **hard-hat**, or **hardhat**. Although one form is often more frequent than others, you shouldn't worry too much about which is correct. If you want to be sure, write the word using the form that you find in this dictionary.

ANSWERS

The base words are *comfort, decide, pure*

emoticon: emotion + *icon* (=a symbol such as :-) or :-(that you type in an email or text message to show how you are feeling)

netiquette: Internet + *etiquette* (=the rules of polite behaviour, used when communicating with people on the Internet)

netizen: Internet + *citizen* (=someone who spends a lot of time using the Internet)

technophobe: technology + *-phobe* (=someone who does not like to use new technology, especially computers)

REGISTER

Saying the right thing at the right time

I recently received an email from a business colleague that began like this:

How are things with you? And your mum? How is she?

She knew that my mother was in hospital at the time, and wanted to show concern. It was a rather chatty beginning to a letter, which was fine since we are colleagues. What was perhaps less appropriate was her use of the word **mum**. And the reason this sounded a little strange relates to the issue of 'register'.

Register

The word **mum** has exactly the same *meaning* as **mother**, but it sounds too informal to use in a professional context. Even when trying to sound friendly, you should use the more 'neutral' word **mother**, unless you know the person that you are referring to very well. It is a good example of how using the wrong register can make an otherwise successful piece of communication sound strange.

Register in the dictionary

This dictionary helps learners of English to avoid these (sometimes embarrassing) misuses. At some entries, you will see register 'labels', which show that the word is not neutral. Look at the entries for *mother* and *mum*. Notice that *mother* has no register label: this means that it is neutral and safe to use in almost any context. But *mum* is labelled *informal*, which means that you should pay extra attention to when and where you use it.

There are many examples of register labels in the dictionary. These three words express the same idea, for example, but with three different levels of formality:

strike	formal
hit	neutral
bash	informal

Grammatically, they all function in the same way:

	struck	the nail
He	hit	with a
	bashed	hammer.

Which should you use? There is no fixed rule, but when you are not sure which register to use, think of how you want to *sound*.

	Formal	Informal	Neutral
I want to sound friendly.	No	Maybe	OK
I want to sound official.	Yes	No	OK
I want to sound serious.	Yes	No	OK
I want to use the least risky word.	No	No	Yes
I don't want to sound too serious.	No	Yes	No

This concept of formality affects expressions as well as individual words. Consider these:

*They found it **most agreeable**.*   formal

*They really **enjoyed themselves**.*   neutral

*They **had a ball**.*   informal

Additional care should be taken before attempting to say a word or expression that is labelled *informal*. Informal words and expressions can sometimes sound strange when spoken by a non-native speaker of English. If you feel that your accent is native-like, a word that is labelled *informal* might be OK to use. Otherwise, be careful.

Domain labels

Imagine that you are jogging with a friend. She turns to you and says:

*Wait. I'm short of **respiration**.*

Then you pass a cashpoint and she says:

*I'm just going to take out some **liquid assets**.*

Finally, you invite her to have lunch and she says:

*No, thanks. I'm having lunch in my **abode**.*

If this sounds strange to you, it's because some of the words that your friend is using are not neutral, but belong to specific 'domains'. The word **respiration** means the same as 'breath' or 'breathing', but is used mainly by doctors and nurses. In other words, it belongs to the *medical* domain. Similarly, **liquid assets** is a *business* term, and **abode** is *literary*.

When a word belongs to a specific domain, this dictionary shows this by giving 'domain labels'. These include: *science, journalism, literary,* and *computing*. You can find a list of all the labels on page 861.

Here are some examples that illustrate the contrast between neutral and domain-specific registers:

Domain-specific term	Domain	Neutral term
respiration	*medical*	breath, breathing
liquid assets	*business*	money
abode	*literary*	home, house
minor	*legal*	child, young person
ferrous	*science*	containing iron

So, instead of *short of respiration*, it is more natural to say *short of breath* in a social situation. Similarly, *take out some money* and *at home* are more natural than *take out some liquid assets* and *in my abode*.

Like formal and informal words, words that belong to specific domains have a more limited use. But they do have a role in the right context. It would sound strange to talk about *minors* if you were talking to a friend, but it would sound completely normal if used in a court of law. The important thing is to know which word to choose to suit the situation.

Conclusion

The register and domain labels given in this dictionary are guides, but there is never a fixed rule as to which register is appropriate to any given situation. Could someone communicate without paying attention to register? Of course. After all, I understood what my colleague was trying to say in her email. However, by using the word **mum**, her message sounded a little strange.

By using the 'wrong' register, you may (at best) fail to convey the correct message or (at worst) even cause offence. So when you see a label like *informal* or *literary* next to a word or expression in this dictionary, be careful how you use it. It might help you to avoid uncomfortable situations.

TEXT TYPES

Texts are written for a purpose. The purpose might be to get or give information, to discuss a topic, to present an opinion, or to persuade someone to do something. Writers organize texts in various ways to do these particular jobs. They use different grammar structures and vocabulary depending on the purpose of a text.

Narratives

A narrative tells a story or gives an account (real or imagined) of something that has happened. The events are usually given in the order that they happen.

Past tenses are the most common grammar structures in narratives. The main events are usually told in sentences using the past simple and past continuous tenses. The details or extra information about the story are often in the present or past perfect tenses. Direct speech is used to add variety and interest.

Ordering events: useful vocabulary

after that, afterwards, at first, before, during, in the end, eventually, finally, for, later, meanwhile, next, since, then, till, until, when, while

> *Fran Miller, who works as an acrobat in a circus, went into a charity shop in Edinburgh. She left her bike at the door. While she was in the shop, one of the assistants sold her bike for ten pounds. Ms. Miller had paid £1,200 for it. When she came out of the shop and discovered what had happened, she was shocked. 'At first I thought someone had moved it. Then my knees turned to jelly and I fell down. I felt like I'd been kicked in the stomach,' she said.*

ACTIVITY

Write a short account of Nelson Mandela's life based on the information below, using some of the useful vocabulary from the Narratives section.

Nelson Mandela Timeline

1918	born in a village in the Transkei
1940	expelled from Fort Hare University for leading a strike
1942	joined the African National Congress, formed the African National Congress Youth League with fellow ANC members
1952	became a lawyer, opened the first black legal firm in the country with Oliver Tambo
1960	Sharpeville Massacre, Mandela detained until 1961
1962	jailed for 5 years
1964	sentenced to life imprisonment while serving the 5-year sentence
1990	released
1990	elected President of the ANC
1993	shared Nobel Peace Prize with President FW de Clerk
1994	became President of South Africa
1999	retired as President of South Africa

Descriptions

A description gives details about what someone or something is like or how something is done.

Descriptions often use present tenses, but they also use past tenses to give background information. Fictional and historical descriptions often use past tenses.

Adjectives

When we are describing people and things, we often use a series of adjectives. The usual order for adjectives before nouns is:

opinion, number	other (size, shape, age etc)	colour	origin	material	purpose	
a strange	old	red	Moroccan	leather	money	bag
lovely	fluffy	white				clouds
several	tall	grey		concrete	office	blocks

Describing a person: useful vocabulary

Describing a person's appearance
he/she is tall/short/fair/dark
he/she has curly/straight/wavy hair
he's got a beard/moustache
he/she wears glasses
he/she has wrinkles/freckles/a dimple
he/she has a round/oval/long face
he/she looks/seems/appears nervous/relaxed/troubled

> ### My friend Jane (Part 1)
> *My friend Jane is fair with short, curly hair. She's got an oval face, beautiful green eyes, and a few freckles on her nose. She's about average height for her age – 14. Today she's wearing her school uniform – a grey skirt, a long-sleeved white blouse, and black shoes.*

Describing a person's character
he/she has an outgoing personality/ easygoing manner
she/he can be stubborn/difficult/ charming

> ### My friend Jane (Part 2)
> *Jane is sitting at her desk, staring out the window and seems to be thinking about something else. She is not paying attention to what the teacher is saying. She's often very quiet and doesn't say much in class. Her teachers say that she is a good student – hardworking and intelligent – just not very outgoing.*

ACTIVITY
Write a description of a person that you know and/or admire. Write about their appearance and character.

Describing a scene: useful vocabulary
there is/are
in the centre/middle
to the right/left, to one side
in the foreground/background
above, behind, between, beyond, in front of, near, over, under

> ### The view from my bedroom
> *The clouds look like dark mountains in the distance. There is a small white house to the right with smoke coming out of the chimney. One of the upstairs windows is open and there is a cat asleep on the porch. The trees are beginning to lose their leaves. An old rusty red pickup truck is slowly climbing the rocky road to the house. There is a long wooden table and several cardboard boxes in the back of the truck.*

Describing how to do something: useful vocabulary
first, next, then, before doing something, when/once you have done something

> ### Hot peanut sauce
> *First heat the coconut milk until it boils. Then add the two kinds of curry paste and stir-fry for three minutes. When the mixture has cooked, add peanut butter, sugar, salt, and lemon juice. Mix all the ingredients thoroughly, then return to a low heat, stirring continuously.*

Reviews
A review is an article in which someone gives their opinion about a book, play, film, exhibition etc. Film and book reviews often summarize main events in the story or plot.

The film is set in the early days of the 24th century. Science, technology, and hard work have solved most of the problems humanity faces today but life has become so serious that there is no fun in the world. A team of scientists is sent on a mission to the past to find a sense of humour. This is a delightful, upbeat 'feel-good' movie that will leave you laughing.

ACTIVITY

Write a short review of a film or play that you have seen recently.

Discussions and arguments

A discursive text presents and discusses issues and opinions. The purpose may be to convince or persuade someone that a particular course of action is important or necessary, or simply to present all sides of an argument.

Discursive texts usually:
- compare or contrast two or more things,
- present a problem and suggest a solution, or
- present arguments for or against an action.

The **opening** or **introductory section** may describe the present situation or different sides of an argument. This is followed by a **development section** that describes and illustrates different points. The development section may also consider other points of view or objections. The **closing section** sums up the options or solutions.

Presenting a discussion: useful vocabulary

expressing opinions: in my view/ opinion, I think/feel
ordering ideas: first/firstly/in the first place/to begin with, next/secondly, lastly/finally
giving additional information or reasons: additionally, equally, in fact,

moreover, what is more, furthermore
giving examples: for example, for instance, such as
showing cause and effect: as a result, consequently, resulting in
contrasting and comparing: compared with/to, however, in contrast, on the one hand … on the other hand, similarly, whereas, while, yet
summing up: on balance, in conclusion, to sum up

Discuss the following statement:

Ecotourism is responsible for causing many of the problems that it originally set out to solve.

Ecotourism is defined by TIES (The International Ecotourism Society) as 'responsible travel to natural areas that conserves the environment and sustains the well-being of local people'. This 'environmentally friendly' form of tourism aims to help fund environmental protection programmes, stimulate the incomes of the local people, especially those on very low incomes, and promote intercultural understanding. These are commendable goals.

Unfortunately, in my view, they are not being achieved. For example, recent reports from a number of developing countries state that locals have been evicted from their houses. These people are being driven from their homes to make way for the development of eco-parks, resorts, and hotels.

While much valuable work has been done and, no doubt, with the best intentions, ecotourism has made many local people homeless.

ACTIVITY

Choose one of the topics below to discuss in writing:

- Smoking should be banned in all public places.
- Parents should control their children's access to the Internet.
- Film censorship is a waste of time.

Oo

o or **O** /əʊ/ noun **1** [C/U] the 15th letter of the English alphabet **2** [C/U] *spoken* a way of saying 'zero' **3** O [U] a common BLOOD GROUP

oak /əʊk/ noun **1** [C] a large tree that can live for a very long time and that produces small hard fruits —*picture* → c9 **2** [U] the wood from an oak tree

OAP /ˌəʊ eɪ ˈpiː/ noun [C] *British* old age pensioner: someone who no longer works and is old enough to receive a pension

oar /ɔː/ noun [C] a long stick with a wide flat blade at one end, used for ROWING a boat

oasis /əʊˈeɪsɪs/ noun [C] a place in a desert where there is water and where plants and trees grow

oath /əʊθ/ (plural **oaths** /əʊðz/) noun [C] a formal promise: *an oath of loyalty*
 PHRASE **under oath** if someone is under oath, they have officially promised to tell the truth in a court of law

oatmeal /ˈəʊtmiːl/ noun [U] crushed OATS that are used in cooking

oats /əʊts/ noun [plural] a type of grain that people and animals eat

obedient /əˈbiːdiənt/ adj doing what a person, law, or rule says that you must do ≠ DISOBEDIENT —**obedience** noun [U], **obediently** adv

obese /əʊˈbiːs/ adj extremely fat

obesity /əʊˈbiːsəti/ noun [U] a condition in which someone is extremely fat

obey /əˈbeɪ/ verb [I/T] ★ to do what a person, law, or rule says that you must do: *Officers expect their troops to obey them without question.* ♦ *Drivers are not obeying the new traffic laws.* ♦ *The soldiers were used to obeying orders.*

Word family: obey

Words in the same family as obey
- **obedience** *n*
- **obedient** *adj*
- **disobey** *v*
- **disobedience** *n*
- **disobedient** *adj*

obituary /əˈbɪtʃuəri/ noun [C] a report in a newspaper that announces someone's death and that gives a short description of their life and achievements

object¹ /ˈɒbdʒɪkt/ noun [C] ★★★
 1 a thing that you can see and touch that is not living: *candles, vases, and other household objects* ♦ *There are 6,000 objects in the museum's collection.*
 2 something that you plan to achieve: *His object was to gain time until help could arrive.* ♦ *The decision was made with the object of cutting costs.*
 3 **object of sth** the person or thing that something happens to, or that people have a particular feeling about: *The band is currently the object of much media attention.*

 4 *linguistics* a noun, pronoun, or phrase that is affected by the action of a verb, for example 'the report' in 'I've read the report'

object² /əbˈdʒekt/ verb [I] ★ to be opposed to something, or to say that you oppose it: *I'll take care of it, unless anyone objects.* ♦ *China and India formally objected to the peace plan.* ♦ **object to doing sth** *I object to paying that much for milk.*

objection /əbˈdʒekʃ(ə)n/ noun [C/U] ★ a statement that shows that you disagree with a plan, or a reason for your disagreement: *I think I'll go home now, if you have no objection.* ♦ *I would like to put forward several objections to this proposal.* ♦ *They raised an objection* (=expressed an objection) *to the plan.*

objectionable /əbˈdʒekʃ(ə)nəb(ə)l/ adj unpleasant and offensive

objective¹ /əbˈdʒektɪv/ noun [C] ★ something that you plan to achieve: *I'm not sure I understand the objective of this exercise.* ♦ *The main objective of our department is to identify market opportunities.*

Words often used with objective

Adjectives often used with objective (noun)
- **key, main, overriding, primary, prime, principal, ultimate** + OBJECTIVE: used for saying that a particular objective is the most important one

Verbs often used with objective (noun)
- **accomplish, achieve, attain, fulfil, meet, reach** + OBJECTIVE: achieve an objective

objective² /əbˈdʒektɪv/ adj based only on facts and evidence, and not influenced by personal feelings or beliefs —**objectively** adv

objectivity /ˌɒbdʒekˈtɪvəti/ noun [U] **1** a state or situation in which something is based only on facts and evidence **2** the ability to make decisions that are based on facts rather than on your own personal feelings or beliefs

objector /əbˈdʒektə/ noun [C] someone who disagrees with or opposes something

obligated /ˈɒblɪɡeɪtɪd/ adj **be/feel obligated to do sth** *formal* if you are obligated to do something, you must do it because it is your duty, or because it is morally right

obligation /ˌɒblɪˈɡeɪʃ(ə)n/ noun [C/U] ★
 1 something that you must do for legal or moral reasons: *You are under no obligation to give anyone personal information.* ♦ *The firm has an obligation to its customers.* ♦ *He felt a certain moral obligation to help.*
 2 a grateful feeling that you have towards someone who has done something for you: *She felt a certain obligation towards him.*

Words often used with obligation

Adjectives often used with obligation (sense 1)
- **contractual, financial, legal, professional, statutory** + OBLIGATION: used about obligations that are legal or moral

Verbs often used with **obligation** (sense 1)
■ fulfil, honour, undertake + OBLIGATION:
perform an obligation

obligatory /əˈblɪɡət(ə)ri/ adj formal something that is obligatory must be done in order to obey a law or rule

oblige /əˈblaɪdʒ/ verb ★
1 [T] formal to force someone to do something because it is the law, a rule, or a duty: They felt obliged to offer him hospitality. ♦ be/feel obliged to do sth You are legally obliged to pay this fine.
2 [I/T] to help someone by doing something that they have asked you to do: If there's anything else I can do, I'm always happy to oblige.

obliging /əˈblaɪdʒɪŋ/ adj willing to help someone

oblique /əˈbliːk/ adj not expressing something directly —obliquely adv

obliterate /əˈblɪtəreɪt/ verb [T] to destroy something completely —obliteration /əˌblɪtəˈreɪʃ(ə)n/ noun [U]

oblivion /əˈblɪviən/ noun [U] 1 a situation in which someone or something has been completely forgotten 2 a state in which you do not notice what is happening around you

oblivious /əˈblɪviəs/ adj not noticing something, or not knowing about it

oblong /ˈɒblɒŋ/ noun [C] a shape that is longer than it is wide —oblong adj

obnoxious /əbˈnɒkʃəs/ adj very rude, offensive, or unpleasant

oboe /ˈəʊbəʊ/ noun [C] a musical instrument that you play by blowing air through a REED —picture → WOODWIND

obscene /əbˈsiːn/ adj 1 offensive in a sexual way 2 extremely unfair or immoral

obscenely /əbˈsiːnli/ adv extremely, in a way that makes you angry: obscenely rich

obscenity /əbˈsenəti/ noun 1 [U] behaviour or language that is sexually offensive 2 [C] a word or action that is sexually offensive

obscure¹ /əbˈskjʊə/ adj 1 not known about, or not well known 2 not clearly expressed, or not easy to understand —obscurely adv

obscure² /əbˈskjʊə/ verb [T] 1 to cover something so that it cannot be seen 2 to make something difficult to understand

obscurity /əbˈskjʊərəti/ noun [U] a state in which a person or thing is not well known, or is not remembered

observance /əbˈzɜːv(ə)ns/ noun [U] the practice of obeying a law or rule, or of doing something according to a tradition

observant /əbˈzɜːv(ə)nt/ adj noticing the things that happen around you

observation /ˌɒbzəˈveɪʃ(ə)n/ noun ★
1 [U] the process of watching someone or something carefully in order to find something out: She's been admitted to hospital for observation.
2 [C] a written or spoken comment about something that you have seen, heard, or felt

3 [U] the ability to notice things: Most children have great powers of observation.
4 [U] the practice of obeying a law, rule, or custom
—observational adj

observatory /əbˈzɜːvətri/ noun [C] a building with a TELESCOPE that scientists use to study the stars and planets

observe /əbˈzɜːv/ verb [T] ★
1 to notice or watch someone who is doing something, or something that is happening: Similar trends may be observed in most modern societies. ♦ All evening Jane observed his behaviour closely.
2 to accept and obey something such as a rule or agreement: The proper procedures must be strictly observed.
3 formal to make a written or spoken comment about someone or something

observer /əbˈzɜːvə/ noun [C] someone who watches, sees, or notices something

obsess /əbˈses/ verb 1 [T] if someone or something obsesses you, you are unable to stop thinking about them all the time: The thought of seeing him again completely obsessed her. 2 [I] to worry about something all the time

obsessed /əbˈsest/ adj unable to stop thinking about someone or something all the time

obsession /əbˈseʃ(ə)n/ noun 1 [U] an emotional condition in which someone or something is so important to you that you are always thinking about them 2 [C] someone or something that you cannot stop thinking about

obsessive /əbˈsesɪv/ adj unable to stop thinking about someone or something in a way that is extreme —obsessively adv

obsolete /ˈɒbsəliːt, ˌɒbsəˈliːt/ adj something that is obsolete is no longer used because it has been replaced by something newer

obstacle /ˈɒbstək(ə)l/ noun [C] 1 a difficulty or problem that prevents you from achieving something=BARRIER 2 an object that you must remove or go around in order to move forwards=BARRIER

obstetrician /ˌɒbstəˈtrɪʃ(ə)n/ noun [C] a doctor whose job is to check the health of a woman who is pregnant, and to help with the birth of her child

obstetrics /əbˈstetrɪks/ noun [U] the part of medicine that deals with pregnant women and the birth of children —obstetric adj

obstinate /ˈɒbstɪnət/ adj not willing to be reasonable and change your ideas or behaviour=STUBBORN —obstinacy noun [U], obstinately adv

obstruct /əbˈstrʌkt/ verb [T] 1 to block a path, passage, door etc so that it is difficult or impossible to get past 2 to take action in order to prevent something from happening

obstruction /əbˈstrʌkʃ(ə)n/ noun 1 [C] something that blocks a path, passage, door etc so that it is difficult or impossible to get past 2 [U] the process of taking action in order to prevent something from happening

obstructive /əbˈstrʌktɪv/ adj trying to

obtain /əb'teɪn/ verb [T] ★★★ to get something that you want or need: *She has to obtain her father's permission before she does anything.* ♦ **obtain sth from sb/sth** *Details can be obtained from the Department for Education.*

obtainable /əb'teɪnəb(ə)l/ adj able to be obtained

obtrusive /əb'truːsɪv/ adj attracting attention in a way that is not pleasant or welcome ≠ UNOBTRUSIVE

obtuse /əb'tjuːs/ adj technical an obtuse angle is between 90° and 180° —*picture* → C8

obvious /'ɒbviəs/ adj ★★★ clear to almost anyone: *an obvious mistake* ♦ **For obvious reasons, I won't go into details.** ♦ **+(that)** *It's pretty obvious he's crazy about you.*

obviously /'ɒbviəsli/ adv ★★★
1 in a way that is clear for almost anyone to see or understand=CLEARLY: *Richards was obviously disappointed at being left out of the team.* ♦ *'Isn't he afraid?' 'Obviously not.'*
2 as most people would expect or understand=NATURALLY: *Obviously, I'll have to think about your offer carefully.*

occasion /ə'keɪʒ(ə)n/ noun [C] ★★★
1 a time at which something happens: *On one occasion* (=once) *the defendant was seen trying to get in through a window.* ♦ *He continues to work with us on occasion* (=sometimes).
2 a special or important time or event: *a great occasion in the nation's history* ♦ *This dress is perfect for a special occasion.*

occasional /ə'keɪʒ(ə)nəl/ adj ★ happening sometimes, but not frequently or regularly: *Chocolate is best kept as an occasional treat.* ♦ *He made occasional visits to London.*

occasionally /ə'keɪʒ(ə)nəli/ adv ★★ sometimes, but not frequently or regularly: *Simmer the sauce for ten minutes, stirring occasionally.*

occult, the /ə'kʌlt, 'ɒkʌlt/ noun [singular] magic or SUPERNATURAL forces and events —**occult** adj

occupancy /'ɒkjʊpənsi/ noun [U] formal the use of a place, or the period of time for which it is used

occupant /'ɒkjʊpənt/ noun [C] someone who is living in or using a place: *the current occupants of the building*

occupation /ˌɒkjʊ'peɪʃn/ noun ★
1 [C/U] a job: *Please give your name, address, and occupation.*
2 [C] something that you do in your free time: *Walking is now Dad's favourite occupation.*
3 [U] the act of living or staying in a building, room, or other place: *The new homes will be ready for occupation in August.*
4 [U] the action of using military force to go into a place and take control away from the people or government there: *the Roman occupation of Britain*

occupational /ˌɒkjʊ'peɪʃ(ə)nəl/ adj relating to, or caused by, your job

occupied /'ɒkjʊpaɪd/ adj **1** a seat, room etc that is occupied has someone using it **2** an area or country that is occupied has foreign military forces in it that are controlling it **3** busy doing something: *The game kept them occupied for the rest of the afternoon.*

occupier /'ɒkjʊpaɪə/ noun [C] **1** British someone who lives in, works in, or uses a room, building, or area of land **2** someone who is in control of a place that they have entered in a group using military force

occupy /'ɒkjʊpaɪ/ verb [T] ★★
1 to be using or in a room, building, or other place: *The Smith family have occupied this farm for over a hundred years.*
2 to be in control of a place that you have entered in a group using military force: *The region was quickly occupied by foreign troops.*
3 to keep someone busy at an activity: *I need some way to occupy the kids for an hour.*

occur /ə'kɜː/ verb [I] ★★★
1 to happen: *The police said that the accident occurred at about 4.30 pm.*
2 formal to exist or be found somewhere: *Radon gas occurs naturally in rocks such as granite.*
PHRASAL VERB **occur to sb** if a thought or idea occurs to you, you suddenly start to think about it: *The thought of giving up never occurred to me.* ♦ **it occurs to sb that** *It suddenly occurred to her that Joe was afraid of being alone.*

occurrence /ə'kʌrəns/ noun [C/U] something that happens

ocean /'əʊʃ(ə)n/ noun ★
1 [C] one of the large areas of salt water that cover most of the Earth: *the Atlantic/Pacific/Indian Ocean*
2 **the ocean** [singular] a large area of salt water that lies along the coast of a country → DROP², SEA

o'clock /ə'klɒk/ adv ★★
PHRASE **one o'clock/four o'clock etc** used for saying what time it is when a clock shows the exact hour

octagon /'ɒktəgən/ noun [C] a shape with eight straight sides —*picture* → C8 — **octagonal** /ɒk'tægən(ə)l/ adj

octave /'ɒktɪv/ noun [C] a series of eight musical notes in a musical SCALE

October /ɒk'təʊbə/ noun [C/U] ★★★ the tenth month of the year, between September and November: *We're going to Boston in October.* ♦ *The next meeting will be on October 9th.*

octopus /'ɒktəpəs/ noun [C] a sea animal with a soft round body and eight long arms —*picture* → C13

OD /ˌəʊ'diː/ noun [C] informal an OVERDOSE of a dangerous drug —**OD** verb [I]

odd /ɒd/ adj ★★
1 unusual, or strange: *Harry's behaviour did seem a little odd.* ♦ **it is odd (that)** *It's very odd that he hasn't sent you a birthday present.*

O

2 not happening frequently or regularly =OCCASIONAL: *The weather will remain cloudy with odd showers here and there.*
3 an odd number is a WHOLE NUMBER that cannot be divided exactly by two, for example 1, 3, 5, 7 etc ≠ EVEN
4 without the other thing from a pair of things: *odd socks/shoes/gloves*

PHRASE **the odd one/man out** someone or something that is different from the others in a group or list
→ ODDS

oddity /ˈɒdəti/ noun [C] someone or something that seems strange or unusual

odd jobs noun [plural] small jobs of various types that you do in your home, such as repairing things

oddly /ˈɒdli/ adv **1** in an unusual way that attracts your interest or attention **2 oddly** or **oddly enough** used for saying that something is not what you would expect in a particular situation

odds /ɒdz/ noun [plural] **1** the chances of something happening: *The odds are* (=it is likely that) *they won't succeed.* **2** the chances that are used for calculating how much money you will get if the person or thing you BET on wins a race or competition

PHRASES **against all (the) odds** if you succeed in doing something against all odds, you succeed in it despite problems and difficulties

at odds (with) 1 disagreeing with someone: *She continued to find herself at odds with the chairman.* **2** if things are at odds with each other, they are different or opposite when they should be the same: *This statement is completely at odds with what was said last week.*

odds and ends small things that are all different and that are not valuable or important

ode /əʊd/ noun [C] a poem that has been written for or about a particular person, thing, or event

odor /ˈəʊdə/ the American spelling of **odour**

odour /ˈəʊdə/ noun [C] a smell, especially one that is unpleasant

odourless /ˈəʊdələs/ adj with no smell

odyssey /ˈɒdəsi/ noun [C] *literary* a long journey during which many things happen

oestrogen /ˈiːstrədʒ(ə)n/ noun [U] a HORMONE that makes women develop typical female sexual features

of /əv, *strong* ɒv/ preposition ★★★
1 connected with or part of sb/sth belonging to, connected with, or forming part of someone or something: *the colour of the sky* ♦ *I don't remember the name of the street.* ♦ *The roof of the church was damaged.* ♦ *the President of Syria* ♦ *Lori is the daughter of my father's sister.* ♦ *a good friend of mine*
2 showing or describing sb/sth concerning or showing someone or something: *She had a photograph of him beside her bed.* ♦ *It was a tale of war and bravery.* ♦ *a history of Russia*

3 containing or consisting of sth containing, including, or formed from a particular type of person or thing: *He handed her a glass of water.* ♦ *a box of chocolates* ♦ *a kilo of rice* ♦ *a collection of poems* ♦ *a group of teenage girls* ♦ *a sheet of paper*
4 saying which specific thing used after a general word for giving a specific example: *I had a feeling of duty towards him.* ♦ *She seemed to like the idea of having children.* ♦ *the month of April* ♦ *the city of Rome*
5 from a particular group coming from a particular group: *She's one of my best friends.* ♦ *Three of us went on holiday together.* ♦ *Several of the flats cannot be lived in.*
6 saying who or what does sth used after nouns that refer to actions for saying who or what does the action, or who or what is affected by the action: *the shouts of excited children* ♦ *the arrival of our train* ♦ *the removal of a tumour*
7 giving a specific number used for giving a specific number or value: *She met Charles at the age of 20.* ♦ *Teachers are asking for a pay rise of 4 per cent.*
8 created by sb written or produced by someone: *the paintings of Picasso* ♦ *the plays of Harold Pinter*
9 giving the cause of sth used for saying what causes something: *He died of lung cancer.* ♦ *As a result of pollution, many species have died out.*
10 in dates used for saying dates: *the 27th of November*
11 saying who has a quality used for saying who shows a particular quality in a situation: *It was nice of you to help me.* ♦ *It was stupid of me to think they would agree.*

of course adv ★★★
1 used for saying 'yes' very definitely, in answer to a question
2 used for agreeing or disagreeing with someone: *'I'm sure everything's going to be OK.' 'Of course it is.'*
3 used for saying something that someone probably already knows or will not be surprised about: *He finally found out that Doug had lied, of course.*
4 used when you have just realized something: *Of course! Now I understand.*

PHRASE **of course not 1** used for saying 'no' very definitely, in answer to a question
2 used for agreeing or disagreeing with someone: *'I don't think we should tell anyone.' 'Of course not.'*

off /ɒf/ grammar word ★★★

Off can be:
■ an **adverb**: *He waved and drove off.*
■ a **preposition**: *She got off the bus at the next stop.*
■ an **adjective**: *I'm having an off day.*

1 not on sth not on the top or surface of something, especially after being on it: *The wind blew a flowerpot off the balcony.* ♦ *Hold on tight so you don't slip off.*

2 no longer attached no longer attached to someone or something: *They cut a branch off the tree.* ♦ *One of the doll's legs fell off.*
3 away from sth leaving a place, or going away from something: *I'd never let an 11-year-old kid go off on his own.* ♦ *If you don't need me any more, you can be off.*
4 going out of a vehicle leaving a plane, train, bus etc: *Let's get off at the next bus stop.* ♦ *They didn't see each other till they got off the plane.*
5 close to sth near an area of land, a room, or a road, or connected to it: *an island five miles off the coast* ♦ *There is a bathroom off the bedroom.* ♦ *We live just off the main road.*
6 not working a machine or piece of electrical equipment that is off is not switched on: *The lights were off in the house.*
7 when clothes are removed used for saying that clothes or shoes are removed: *Take off your wet clothes.* ♦ *She kicked off her shoes and sat down.*
8 not at school or work not at school or work, for example because you are not well or because it is not a normal working day: *I took two weeks off in August.* ♦ *I'm thinking of having some time off work.* ♦ *Today is my day off.* ♦ *She's off sick today.*
9 no longer planned used for saying that an event is no longer going to take place as planned: *Sorry, but the meeting's off.*
10 reduced reduced in price by a particular amount: *There's now 30% off all swimsuits.*
11 a particular time or distance away used for saying how long it will be until something happens, or how far away something is: *Christmas is only three weeks off.* ♦ *We could see a house a few miles off.*
12 no longer good food that is off is no longer fresh and is not good to eat
    PHRASE **off and on** or **on and off** sometimes but not regularly: *She's been seeing him off and on since she was 16.*

offal /'ɒfl/ noun [U] the organs of animals that are eaten

off-'balance adj in a position in which you feel that you are going to fall down

offbeat /'ɒf,biːt/ adj *informal* unusual, often in an interesting way

off-'centre adj not exactly in the middle of an area or a thing

off-'chance noun **on the off-chance** in the hope that something will happen or succeed, although it seems unlikely: *I called on the off-chance he'd be at home.*

off-'colour adj feeling slightly ill

off-'duty adj not working: *an off-duty police officer*

offence /ə'fens/ noun ★★
1 [C] a crime or illegal activity for which there is a punishment: *motoring/firearms/public order offences* ♦ *The usual fine is £15 to £100 for a first offence.* ♦ *Killing these animals is a criminal offence.* ♦ *minor offences such as vandalism* ♦ *She had committed no offence under military law.* ♦

Those arrested have been charged with public order offences. ♦ **be an offence (for sb) to do sth** *It is a criminal offence for a company to use a misleading name.* ♦ **convict sb of an offence** *Walker was convicted of a similar offence in 1997.*
2 [U] the feeling of being angry, upset, or insulted by something that someone says or does: *advertisements that cause offence*
3 [C] something that makes you feel angry and upset because it is insulting, unfair, or morally wrong: *This law is an offence to working people.*
    PHRASES **no offence** *spoken* used for telling someone that you hope that what you are saying will not upset them
    take offence (at sth) to feel angry and upset because of something that someone has said or done

offend /ə'fend/ verb **1** [T] to make someone angry and upset by doing or saying something: *They avoided saying anything that might offend their audience.* **2** [I] *formal* to commit a crime —**offended** adj: *We feel saddened and offended.*

offender /ə'fendə/ noun [C] someone who has committed a crime: *young offenders* ♦ *sex offenders*

offense /ə'fens/ the American spelling of **offence**

offensive¹ /ə'fensɪv/ adj ★
1 unpleasant or insulting, and likely to make people upset or embarrassed ≠ INOFFENSIVE: *offensive language* ♦ *offensive odours* ♦ *The advertisement was offensive to many women.*
2 used for attacking ≠ DEFENSIVE: *offensive weapons*
—**offensively** adv

offensive² /ə'fensɪv/ noun [C] a major military attack
    PHRASE **be on the offensive** to be ready to attack or criticize people

offer¹ /'ɒfə/ verb [T] ★★★
1 to let someone know that you will give them something or do something for them if they want it: **offer sb sth** *They haven't offered me the job yet.* ♦ **offer sth to sb** *He had offered cocaine to an undercover police officer.* ♦ **offer to do sth** *Thank you for offering to help.*
2 to say that you will pay a particular price for something: **offer sb sth for sth** *I offered Jim £5,000 for his car.* ♦ **offer sth to sb** *Police are offering a reward to anyone with information.*
3 to provide something such as a product or service: *Smaller hotels can offer comfort at lower prices.* ♦ *The city has a lot to offer* (=has many attractive features for) *the business traveller.*
4 to express your feelings towards someone: *offer sympathy/regrets/thanks* ♦ *He called the team manager to offer his congratulations.*

offer² /ˈɒfə/ noun [C] ★★★

1 a statement in which you offer to give, pay, or do something if someone wants it: *a job offer* ♦ *I've decided to accept your offer*. ♦ *Did she make you an offer for* (=tell you how much she would pay for) *the bike?* ♦ *the government's offer of financial aid*

2 a special price that is lower than the usual price for something: *a half-price offer*

PHRASE **on offer** British **1** available, for example for people to buy or use: *These are just some of the films on offer this week.* **2** being sold for a lower price for a short time

---

Words often used with **offer**

Verbs often used with offer (noun, sense 1)
- **make, put in, submit** + OFFER: make someone an offer
- **accept, take, take up, welcome** + OFFER: accept someone's offer
- **decline, refuse, reject, turn down** + OFFER: not accept someone's offer

---

offering /ˈɒf(ə)rɪŋ/ noun [C] something that people give

off-'guard adj surprised by something unexpected: *The questions caught her completely off-guard.*

offhand¹ /ˈɒfˈhænd/ adj **1** unfriendly in the way that you treat someone **2** an offhand remark is one that you do not think carefully about

offhand² /ˈɒfˈhænd/ adv immediately and without checking the facts: *I can't remember their names offhand.*

office /ˈɒfɪs/ noun ★★★

1 [C] a room or building where the people in an organization or department work, or the people who work there: *the company's Los Angeles office* ♦ *Our offices are on the third floor.* ♦ *office furniture* ♦ *I share an office with my secretary.* ♦ *I left the office before 6.00 pm.*

2 [C] a room or building where you go for a particular service: *a tourist information office*

3 [C] a government department: *the unemployment/tax office* ♦ *the Foreign/Home Office*

4 [C/U] a position in a large powerful organization, especially a government: *the office of President* ♦ *Bob plans to run for office* (=try to be elected) *next year.*

office ,block noun [C] British a large building that contains many offices

office 'hours noun [plural] the times when a business or other organization is open during the day

officer /ˈɒfɪsə/ noun [C] ★★★

1 someone with a position of power and authority in the armed forces: *an army officer*

2 a POLICE OFFICER

3 someone with a position of authority in an organization

official¹ /əˈfɪʃ(ə)l/ adj ★★★

1 decided or done by people in authority, especially a government ≠ UNOFFICIAL: *the country's official language* ♦ *There will be an official investigation into last week's accident.*

2 relating to a job in which you have authority or represent other people: *a list of my official duties*

official² /əˈfɪʃ(ə)l/ noun [C] ★★ someone with an important position in an organization: *a senior government official*

officially /əˈfɪʃəli/ adv ★

1 publicly and formally: *The school won't be officially opened until next month.*

2 according to what governments or people in authority say, although it may not be true: *Officially, the government claims no knowledge of the subject.*

officious /əˈfɪʃəs/ adj too serious about your job and duties, in a way that is annoying

off-'key adj, adv music or singing that is off-key does not sound good because the notes are slightly wrong

off-'licence noun [C] British a shop that sells alcoholic drinks

off-'limits adj if a place is off-limits, you are not allowed to go there

offline /ˈɒfˈlaɪn/ adj, adv computing **1** not directly connected to a computer **2** working on a computer but not connected to the Internet → ONLINE

off-'peak adj, adv at times when prices are lower because a service is not usually used by many people: *off-peak hours/prices/electricity*

off-putting /ˈɒf ˌpʊtɪŋ/ adj British used for describing something that you want to avoid because it is unpleasant

offset /ˈɒfˌset/ (past tense and past participle **offset**) verb [T] to balance the effect of something, with the result that there is no real change or difference: *Falling sales were offset by strong performances in other markets.*

offshoot /ˈɒfˌʃuːt/ noun [C] a company, group, or organization that has developed from a larger one

offshore /ˈɒfˈʃɔː/ adj, adv **1** in the sea, not on the land ≠ ONSHORE: *an offshore oil rig* ♦ *They're going to be working offshore.* **2** involving money that is invested in another country, or referring to a business that is in another country: *offshore banking* ♦ *offshore investments*

offside /ˈɒfˈsaɪd/ adj, adv in the wrong position according to the rules in a game such as football or HOCKEY

offspring /ˈɒfˌsprɪŋ/ (plural **offspring**) noun [C] someone's child, or the baby of an animal

offstage /ˈɒfˈsteɪdʒ/ adj, adv in or towards the area behind a theatre stage where the audience cannot see ≠ ONSTAGE: *He rushed offstage.*

off-the-'cuff adj, adv if you say something off-the-cuff, you do not think about it first: *an off-the-cuff reply*

off-the-record adj, adv said to someone in a private way and not intended as part of an official statement: *an off-the-record remark*

off-the-wall adj strange, often in a funny or interesting way

off-white adj close to white in colour, but with slightly more yellow or grey

often /ˈɒf(ə)n/ adv ★★★
1 on many occasions or in many situations: *Boredom often leads to poor behaviour.* ♦ *Very often the student can't understand the question.* ♦ *It's quite often impossible to park in town.*
2 used for talking about how many times something happens in a particular period of time: *How often do you eat meat?*
PHRASES **all too often** used for saying that something happens more often than you think it should: *All too often, parents leave their children at home alone.*
every so often sometimes, but not frequently: *She still phones me every so often.*
more often than not on most occasions, or in most situations: *More often than not, arguments can be avoided.*

ogle /ˈəʊɡ(ə)l/ verb [I/T] *showing disapproval* to look at someone in a way that shows you think they are sexually attractive

ogre /ˈəʊɡə/ noun [C] a cruel frightening person

oh¹ /əʊ/ interjection **1** used at the beginning of an answer or reply for showing that you understand or accept new information: *'Joe is her brother, not her boyfriend.' 'Oh, I see!'* ♦ *'He just resigned.' 'Oh, did he?'* **2** used for expressing an emotion such as surprise, anger, or happiness: *Oh, what a beautiful view!* ♦ *Oh no! I've left my keys in the car.*
3 used when you start telling someone something, for example something that you have just remembered: *Oh darling, did you see that note I left you?*

oh² /əʊ/ number *spoken* a way of saying 'zero', for example in saying telephone numbers or a date, such as 1908

oil¹ /ɔɪl/ noun ★★★
1 [U] a thick dark smooth liquid used for making petrol and other fuels: *The house is heated with oil.* ♦ *oil prices/companies*
2 [C/U] a thick smooth liquid, used in cooking and medicines: *Cook the chicken in oil.* ♦ *vegetable/olive/sunflower oil*
3 [C/U] a thick liquid used in an engine so that it will work smoothly
4 [C/U] a thick clear liquid used for protecting your skin or making it soft: *massage/bath/suntan oil* ♦ *baby oil*

oil² /ɔɪl/ verb [T] to put oil on something

oilfield /ˈɔɪlfiːld/ noun [C] an area where there is oil underground

oil paint noun [C/U] a thick paint used by artists, that contains oil

oil painting noun [C/U] a picture painted with oil paint, or the art of painting this type of picture

oil rig noun [C] a large structure with equipment on it for getting oil out from underground

oil slick noun [C] a layer of oil on the surface of a large area of water, after an accident

oil tanker noun [C] a large ship that carries oil

oil well noun [C] a deep narrow hole that is dug in order to obtain oil

oily /ˈɔɪli/ adj **1** covered with oil, containing oil, or like oil: *an oily rag* ♦ *oily fish* ♦ *an oily texture* **2** very polite in a way that does not seem sincere

ointment /ˈɔɪntmənt/ noun [C/U] a thick smooth substance that you put on sore or injured skin

OK¹ /əʊˈkeɪ/ interjection ★★★
1 used for showing that you agree, approve, or understand. This is also used to ask if someone agrees, approves, or understands: *'I'd like to buy some new clothes.' 'OK.'* ♦ *So 'C' is the best answer. OK?*
2 used when you want to start or continue talking about something: *OK. Is everyone ready?*
3 used for showing that you want to end a conversation or argument: *OK! I'll try to do better next time.*

OK² /əʊˈkeɪ/ adj *spoken* **1** satisfactory, but not usually the best possible: *The food was OK.*
2 allowed, suitable, or not likely to make you upset: *The teacher said it was OK for me to leave class early.* **3** not injured, damaged, ill, or upset: *Are you OK? You look tired.*
PHRASE **it's/that's OK** *spoken* used for saying that something does not make you angry, upset, or sad: *'I'm sorry I said that.' 'That's OK.'*
—**OK** adv: *I think I did OK in the exam.*

okay /əʊˈkeɪ/ another spelling of **OK**

old /əʊld/ adj ★★★
1 used for talking about the age of someone or something: *I'm older than my brother.* ♦ *She's the oldest girl in the class.* ♦ *A woman stood watching with her 3-year-old* (=child who is 3). ♦ *How old are you? I'm 5 years old.* ♦ **old enough to do sth** *He's not old enough to see this film.*
2 someone who is old has lived a long time ≠ YOUNG: *A lot of old people live alone.* ♦ *I hope I'll still be able to play golf when I get old.*
3 something that is old has existed or been used for a long time: *an old belief* ♦ *I finally replaced my old sewing machine.* ♦ *Trees are the oldest living things on the planet.* ♦ *I'm meeting an old friend for lunch.*
4 used for describing something that existed, happened, or was used in the past: *'Thy' is an old way of saying 'your'.* ♦ *The old motorway only had two lanes.* ♦ *I still get letters from some of my old students* (=people that I taught in the past).
PHRASES **for old times' sake** so that you can remember a happy time in the past
your old self the way you normally were in the past, before something happened: *Now you sound like your old self again!*

O

,old 'age noun [U] the period of time when you are old

,old age 'pension noun [C] British a PENSION that you receive from the government when you are old and have stopped working

,old age 'pensioner noun [C] British an OAP

old-fashioned /ˌəʊld ˈfæʃ(ə)nd/ adj ★
1 no longer modern or fashionable: *an old-fashioned leather briefcase*
2 no longer useful or suitable in the modern world =OUTDATED: *old-fashioned ideas about raising children*
3 used for referring to nice things from the past that still exist: *good old-fashioned home baking*

,old 'flame noun [C] someone who you had a romantic relationship with in the past

'old ,guard, the noun [singular] the people in an organization who have been there for a long time and do not like changes

,old 'hand noun [C] someone who has been doing something for a long time and is very good at it

,old 'hat adj *informal* old-fashioned and boring

,old 'people's ,home noun [C] a place where old people live and are looked after

'old ,school, the noun [singular] people who have traditional or old-fashioned ideas — 'old ,school adj

,Old 'Testament, the the first part of the Christian Bible → NEW TESTAMENT

'old-time adj old-fashioned in a way that you admire

,old 'wives' ,tale noun [C] a traditional belief that many people think is silly because there is no scientific proof of it

'old-,world adj old-fashioned in a pleasant and attractive way: *the town's old-world charm*

olive[1] /ˈɒlɪv/ noun 1 [C] a small black or green fruit that is eaten or used for its oil 2 olive or olive green [U] a dark yellow-green colour

olive[2] /ˈɒlɪv/ adj 1 olive skin is yellowish brown in colour 2 dark yellowish green in colour

'olive ,branch noun [singular] something that someone does in order to show that they want to stop arguing

,olive 'oil noun [C/U] a type of cooking oil that is made from OLIVES

Olympic /əˈlɪmpɪk/ adj relating to the Olympic Games

O,lympic 'Games, the or the Olympics an international sports event that takes place every four years

omelette /ˈɒmlət/ noun [C] a flat round food made by mixing eggs together and cooking them —*picture* → EGG

omen /ˈəʊmən/ noun [C] something that shows whether good or bad things will happen in the future: *He was convinced that losing his bag was a bad omen.*

ominous /ˈɒmɪnəs/ adj making you think that something bad will happen: *an ominous silence* —ominously adv

omission /əʊˈmɪʃ(ə)n/ noun [C/U] someone or something that has not been included, or the fact of not including something: *I did notice one or two surprising omissions from the list.*

omit /əʊˈmɪt/ verb [T] to fail to include someone or something: *Important details had been omitted from the article.*

omnipotent /ɒmˈnɪpətənt/ adj *formal* powerful enough to do everything —omnipotence noun [U]

on /ɒn/ grammar word ★★★

On can be:
- a preposition: *She was lying on the floor.*
- an adverb: *When the bus stopped, he got on.*
- after the verb 'to be': *Is the central heating on?*

1 **supported by a surface** supported by something, or touching the top of it: *Chad was asleep on the floor.* ♦ *He left a note for you on the kitchen table.*
2 **sticking to sth** touching, sticking to, or hanging from something: *There were several posters on the wall.* ♦ *The key is hanging on a hook in the hall.* ♦ *Evelyn kissed him on the cheek.*
3 **at a particular time** used for stating the day or date when something happens: *He's coming home on Wednesday.* ♦ *My birthday is on the 27th of November.*
4 **in an area** in a particular area or on a particular type of land: *The house was built on a beautiful piece of land.* ♦ *Wilson grew up on a farm.*
5 **in a particular place** at the side of a road, river, or area of water: *Gordie's grandparents live on Crescent Drive.* ♦ *a town on the Mississippi*
6 **as part of a page or list** included as part of a page of a book, or as part of a list: *Look at the picture on page 94.* ♦ *Why isn't my name on the list?*
7 **wearing or carrying sth** wearing or carrying a particular thing on a part of your body: *Put your shoes on.* ♦ *She wore a ring on her left hand.* ♦ *You look funny with glasses on.* ♦ *Have you got any cash on you?*
8 **being broadcast** being broadcast by radio or television: *I usually listen to the news on the radio.* ♦ *What time is the football match on?*
9 **saying who or what is affected** used for saying who or what is affected by something: *the effect of interest rates on the housing market* ♦ *The attacks on Walters are very unfair.*
10 **about sth** concerning a particular subject: *a report on the Civil War*
11 **continuing** continuing to do something or to happen: *Read on to find out the rest of the story.* ♦ *The opera seemed to go on and on for hours.*

12 in or into a vehicle in or into a bus, train, plane etc: *We got on the train at Bournville.* ♦ *I'll get some work done while I'm on the plane.*

13 using particular equipment used for saying what type of machine or equipment is used for doing something: *The work is done on computer.* ♦ *I recorded our conversation on my tape recorder.*

14 working if a machine or piece of electrical equipment is on, it is working: *Who left the TV on?*

15 taking part in a journey used for saying that someone takes part in an activity in which they travel or see something: *I'll take you on a tour of the factory.* ♦ *I met him when I was on a Mediterranean cruise.*

16 using a drug using a particular drug: *She's on antibiotics for an eye infection.* ♦ *He seemed to be on drugs.*

17 being a member of sth if someone is on a team or committee, they are a member of it: *There are only three directors on the board.*

18 happening happening, or planned to happen: *There's a wedding on at the church.* ♦ *Have you got anything on this weekend?*

19 happening immediately *formal* immediately after another event, or at the same time as another event: *Report to the reception desk on arrival.*

20 giving phone numbers *British* used for giving the phone number where someone can be contacted: *Call us on 0800 0900017.*

21 paid for by sb *spoken* used for saying who will pay for something: *Drink up! The next one is on me.*

PHRASES **be/go on about sb/sth** or **be/go on at sb** *informal* to keep talking about someone or something in a way that annoys other people: *She's always on about her children.*

from now/then/that moment etc on starting at a particular time and continuing to happen: *The new rules will apply to all members from now on.*

sth is not on *British informal* used for saying that something is wrong or cannot be allowed

on sb's face used for saying that someone's face has a particular expression: *There was a look of horror on her face.*

on the left/right at or to the left/right side of someone or something: *His office is the last door on the left.*

→ FULL-ON, HEAD-ON

on-air adj broadcast during a radio or television programme

once /wʌns/ grammar word ★★★

Once can be:
■ an **adverb**: *I only met him once.*
■ a **conjunction**: *Once you get there, you'll love it.*
■ a **noun**: *For once I wish you'd tell me the truth.* ♦ *Yes, I met him, but just the once.*

1 on one occasion only: *Cathy's only been to visit us once.* ♦ *I'd seen the show once before.* ♦ *The class meets once a week.* ♦ *You should*

take two pills *once every six hours.* ♦ *We met just the once, but I remember him well.*

2 used for saying that a particular situation existed in the past, but it does not exist any longer: *Did you know that Dan was once a policeman?* ♦ *Louise bought the house where her grandparents had once lived.*

3 used for saying that as soon as one thing happens, something else happens: *You'll be very happy here once you get to know everyone.*

PHRASES **all at once 1** happening suddenly when you are not expecting it: *All at once thunder shook the whole house.* **2** at the same time: *Everybody started speaking all at once.*

at once 1 immediately: *Bake for 35 minutes and then serve at once.* **2** at the same time: *You're trying to do too many things at once.*

(every) once in a while sometimes, but not very often: *I still see Ken once in a while.*

(just) for once *spoken* used for saying that you would like something to happen, and you think it should happen more often: *You can pay the bill for once.*

once again/more 1 used for saying that something happens again: *The fair was once again a tremendous success.* **2** used for saying that a situation becomes as it was before it changed: *We look forward to the day when there will be peace once more.*

once and for all completely and finally: *The Supreme Court's ruling should decide this matter once and for all.*

once or twice a few times, but not very often: *Martin's gone hunting once or twice, but I don't think he really liked it.*

once upon a time used for starting children's stories

→ BLUE¹

oncoming /ˈɒnˌkʌmɪŋ/ adj moving towards you: *oncoming traffic/vehicles*

one /wʌn/ grammar word ★★★

One can be:
■ a **number**: *We have one child.*
■ a **determiner**: *He grew roses on one side of his garden, and vegetables on the other.*
■ a **pronoun**: *They are the ones who suffered.* ♦ *Sydney is one of the world's most exciting cities.*

1 number the number 1: *I've only got one hour free.* ♦ *They have one daughter and five sons.*

2 a single person or thing used for referring to a single person or thing when there are others of the same type: *I bought three T-shirts – do you want one?* ♦ *One passenger said she had been waiting for 13 hours.* ♦ *I met one of her brothers.* ♦ *one of the best Japanese restaurants in town*

3 (plural **ones**) used for referring to things used for referring to something when that type of thing has already been mentioned: *It was a problem, but not a major one.* ♦ *Your experiences are ones that are shared by many other parents.* ♦ *I'm going to keep those boxes. The ones I want to get rid of are in the garage.* ♦ *I'd never seen a game like that one.*

4 the one (plural **the ones**) used for referring to people used for referring to someone

O

who is part of a group: *David and I are the only ones left who are not married.* ♦ *Who is the one with the beard?*

5 in general statements *British formal* used instead of 'you' when you are making a statement about people in general, that also applies to yourself: *One cannot be sure what lies ahead.*

6 the only the only person or thing of a particular type: *My one concern is that not everyone will be able to attend.* ♦ *We're going to have to play **the one** team we did not want to play.*

7 used for emphasis used for emphasizing a particular fact, person, or thing: *There's one thing you can be sure of – you won't get any help from him.* ♦ *One person who won't be invited is her ex-husband.*

8 used for comparison used for mentioning the first of two or more similar people or things, especially when you are comparing them: *She had a glass in **one** hand and an empty bottle in **the other**.*

PHRASES **(all) in one** used for saying that someone or something can do many different things at the same time: *The device will give you telephone, television, and Internet all in one.*

one after another or **one after the other** used for saying that actions are done or things happen with very little time between them: *They had four children one after another.*

the one and only used for introducing a famous person, or for saying that someone is very famous

one by one first one, then the next, then the next, separately: *Add the eggs one by one.*

one day/night/year etc 1 on a particular day/night/year etc in the past: *One evening Sam didn't come home.* **2** on any day/night/year etc in the future: *She knew that one day she'd get married.*

one or two a small number of people or things: *Carla said she had one or two ideas of her own.*

,**one a'nother** pronoun used for saying that each of two or more people does the same thing to the other, or has the same relationship with the other=EACH OTHER: *They all shook hands with one another.* ♦ *We respect one another's privacy.*

'**one-,man** adj **1** made for just one person. Many people prefer to use the word ONE-PERSON: *a one-man tent* **2** involving just one person. Many people prefer to use the word ONE-PERSON: *a one-man show*

,**one-night 'stand** noun [C] a situation in which two people have sex once but do not have a relationship

,**one-'off** adj *British* happening, done, or made only once —**one-'off** noun [C]

,**one-on-'one** adj, adv *American* happening between only two people: *a one-on-one interview*

'**one-,person** adj involving one person, or made for one person: *a one-person household*

oneself /wʌn'self/ pronoun *British formal* **1** the REFLEXIVE form of 'one', used for showing that people in general, including yourself, are affected by something that they do: *One*

has to think of oneself in these matters. **2** used for emphasizing that you do something, not anyone else: *It's important to complete the application forms oneself.*

one-sided /,wʌn 'saidid/ adj **1** unfair because of only showing one aspect of something: *a one-sided account of the conflict* **2** in a one-sided activity, one of the people or groups involved has a lot more skill, power etc than the other: *a one-sided contest/game/match*

'**one-,time** adj used for saying what someone or something was in the past=FORMER: *the one-time Communist party leader*

,**one-to-'one** adj, adv *British* involving only two people

,**one-track 'mind** noun [C] someone with a one-track mind thinks about one particular thing all the time

one-upmanship /wʌn 'ʌpmənʃɪp/ noun [U] attempts to get an advantage by appearing to be more skilful, important etc than other people

'**one-,way** adj **1** with cars travelling in one direction only: *a one-way street* **2** a one-way ticket allows you to travel from one place to another but not back again ≠ RETURN

'**one-,woman** adj involving only one woman: *a one-woman comedy act*

ongoing /'ɒn,gəʊɪŋ/ adj still happening or being done: *an ongoing discussion*

onion /'ʌnjən/ noun [C] a round vegetable with thin dry skin, many layers inside, and a strong smell —*picture* → C11

online /'ɒnlaɪn/ adj, adv *computing* connected to or available through a computer or a computer NETWORK such as the Internet: *an online bookshop* ♦ *online banking* —**online** /ɒn'laɪn/ adv: *Just go online and order it.*

onlooker /'ɒn,lʊkə/ noun [C] someone who watches something happen but does not take part in it

only /'əʊnli/ grammar word ★★★

> **Only can be:**
> ■ an **adverb**: *She's only 18.*
> ■ an **adjective**: *You're the only person who can help me.*
> ■ a **conjunction**: *You can come, only make sure you're on time.*

1 nothing, no one, nowhere etc except used for showing that a statement does not apply to anyone or anything else except the person or thing that you are mentioning: *The flowers grow only on the island of Maui.* ♦ *Everyone promised to come, but only Ted turned up.* ♦ *I only design the dresses, I don't actually make them.*

2 when there are no others used for showing that there are no other things or people of the same kind as the one or ones that you are mentioning: *This is **the only** letter my father ever wrote to me.* ♦ *David's **the only one** of us who has a computer.* ♦ *My **only** reason for coming here was to see you.*

3 showing that an amount is small used for emphasizing that an amount, distance, or time is small: *She was only 18 when she got married.* ♦ *The police station was only 150 yards away.* ♦ *The two men spoke with each other only briefly.*

4 not better, worse etc than sth used for saying that something is not better, worse, more important etc than you are stating: *'What was that noise?' 'Don't worry – it's only the wind.'* ♦ *We are only trying to help.*
5 no earlier than sth not before a particular time, or not before a particular thing has happened: *I met him for the first time only last week.* ♦ *You pay the agent only when you sell the house.*
6 but used for adding a comment to something that you have just said that makes it less true or correct: *Her car is like mine, only it has four doors.* ♦ *I'd love to come. **The only thing is,** I'll have to leave early.*
PHRASE **only just 1** a very short time ago: *The film's only just started, so you haven't missed much.* **2** by a small degree or a small amount: *I've got only just enough money to last me the month.*
→ ONE

,only 'child noun [C] a child who has no brothers or sisters

'on-,off adj *British* happening, stopping, and then happening again, several times: *an on-off relationship*

'on-,screen adj, adv **1** on a computer screen: *The work is edited on-screen.* **2** happening or being in a television programme or film: *She plays his on-screen wife, Nancy.*

onset /'ɒn,set/ noun **the onset of sth** the beginning of something, especially something bad: *the onset of the disease*

onshore /'ɒnʃɔː/ adj on land rather than on the sea ≠ OFFSHORE

onslaught /'ɒn,slɔːt/ noun [C] **1** large numbers of people or things that come at the same time and are difficult to deal with **2** an attack

onstage /'ɒn,steɪdʒ/ adj, adv on the stage of a theatre ≠ OFFSTAGE

onto /'ɒntə/ preposition ★★★
1 into a position on an object or surface: *A tree fell onto a car, trapping the people inside.* ♦ *Marilyn emptied her shopping bag onto the carpet.*
2 into a bus, train, aircraft etc: *Slater tried to carry a gun onto the plane.* ♦ *The refugees were put onto buses.*
3 into an area that you consider to be a surface: *A spectator ran onto the field and attacked the referee.*
4 used for saying that something is added to a list, statement, word etc: *To form the plural, just add 's' or 'es' onto the end.*
PHRASES **be onto sb** to have found out that someone has done something wrong: *He knew the police were onto him.*
be onto sth to have information that will help you to make an important discovery: *I think you could be onto something here.*

onus /'əʊnəs/ noun [singular] *formal* if the onus is on someone to do something, it is their responsibility or duty to do it

onward[1] /'ɒnwəd/ adj moving forwards, or continuing

onward[2] /'ɒnwəd/ adv *American* onwards

onwards /'ɒnwədz/ adv if something happens or exists from a particular time onwards, it starts at that time and continues to happen or exist: *Most nights are busy from about 7 pm onwards.*

ooh /uː/ interjection used for showing surprise, excitement, or pleasure

oops /ʊps, uːps/ interjection used when a small mistake or slight accident has happened

ooze /uːz/ verb [I/T] **1** if a thick liquid oozes from something, or if something oozes a liquid, a small amount of it flows out slowly: *Juice oozed from the grapes.* **2** if someone or something oozes a particular quality, or if it oozes from them, they show that quality in a very obvious way: *Her brother oozes charm.*

opal /'əʊp(ə)l/ noun [U] a smooth white stone used in jewellery

opaque /əʊ'peɪk/ adj **1** opaque glass, liquid etc is difficult to see through **2** difficult to understand

OPEC /'əʊpek/ Organization of Petroleum Exporting Countries: an organization that controls the supply and price of oil in the world market

open[1] /'əʊpən/ adj ★★★

1 when public can visit	7 anyone can see/join
2 when you can see in	8 considering ideas
3 of a door/window	9 not decided
4 not blocked	10 when sth can be done
5 not covered/enclosed	+ PHRASE
6 honest	

1 if a shop, restaurant etc is open, the public can use it or visit it ≠ CLOSED, SHUT: *The bar stays open all night.* ♦ *the campaign to keep the hospital open* ♦ *The house is only **open to the general public** for three weeks each year.*
2 something that is open has no cover, or has its edges separated, so that you can see what is inside: *an open drawer* ♦ *The kids were tearing open presents.* ♦ *A **book** lay open on the table.* ♦ *The baby's eyes were open.*
3 in a position that allows someone or something to pass through: *The bedroom door was open.* ♦ *Someone has left the gate wide open.*
4 if a road or method of communication is open, it is available for people to use
5 an open space or area is not covered or enclosed, or does not have many buildings, trees etc: *The top deck of the bus is open.* ♦ *the **wide open spaces** of the American West*
6 not keeping anything secret: *an open and honest discussion* ♦ *He has always been **open about** his drinking problem.*
7 available for anyone to take part in or see: *The meeting is **open to** the public.*
8 willing to consider many different possibilities: *Police are **keeping an open mind** about the cause of her disappearance.* ♦ *I have some ideas about where to go, but I'm **open to** suggestions.*
9 a situation that is open has at least two possible results: *Shall we **leave it open** for now, and decide at the meeting?*
10 if something is open to criticism, doubt etc, it is possible or reasonable to criticize it, doubt it etc: *The system is **open to** abuse.*
PHRASE **welcome sb/sth with open arms** to be very happy to see someone or receive something

O

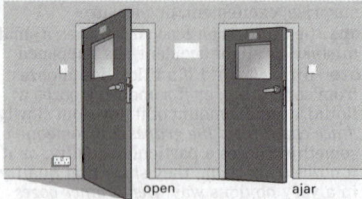

open ajar

open² /ˈəʊpən/ *verb* ★★★

1 move sth to see inside	**5** first become available
2 of a door/window	**6** begin
3 move part of body	**+ PHRASES**
4 allow people in	**+ PHRASAL VERB**

1 [T] to separate the edges of something, or take off its cover, so that you can see what is inside: *She opened her shopping bag and took out an umbrella.* ♦ *Can you open this jar?* ♦ *Open your books at page 25.*

2 [I/T] if you open a door or window, or if it opens, you move it into a position that allows people or things to pass through: *Do you mind if I open a window?*

3 [I/T] if parts of your body open, or if you open them, they move to their widest position: *Open your mouth wide.* ♦ *Her eyes opened slowly.*

4 [I/T] if a shop, public building etc opens at a particular time, or if someone opens it, it becomes available for people to use or visit at that time: *The library doesn't open till 9.30.*

5 [I/T] if a new business, building etc opens, or if someone opens it, it becomes available for people to use for the first time: *They decided to move to Spain and open a bar.*

6 [T] to begin something: *I opened an account at the local bank.* ♦ *He opened his talk with a quotation from Shakespeare.* ♦ *The police have opened an investigation into his business affairs.*

7 [I] if a film or play opens, it starts being shown to the public

8 [I] if a flower opens, it moves into its widest position

PHRASES **open the door** to make it possible for something to happen

open doors to give someone opportunities

open sb's eyes to make someone realize the truth about something

open fire to start shooting a gun

PHRASAL VERB **open (sth) up 1** to open a locked door, container, or building: *He opens up the shop every morning.* **2** *same as* **open²** 5: *Donald wants to open up a bookshop.* **3** to make a situation possible or make something available to people, or to become possible or available in this way: *New markets are opening up every day.* ♦ *The job opened up a lot of opportunities for me.*

open, the /ˈəʊpən/ *noun* [singular] any place that is outside, not in a building: *It's cold out here in the open.*

PHRASE **(out) in the open** known about and not secret

open air, the *noun* [singular] any place that is outside

open-air *adj* happening or existing outside

open day *noun* [C] *British* an occasion when an organization such as a school allows people to visit and see what is done there

open-ended /ˌəʊpən ˈendɪd/ *adj* something that is open-ended has no limits: *an open-ended ticket*

opener /ˈəʊp(ə)nə/ *noun* [C] a tool or machine that is used for opening something

open house *noun* [C] a period of time when people are encouraged to visit a place

opening¹ /ˈəʊp(ə)nɪŋ/ *noun* ★★

1 (hole) where sth opens	**4** when shops are open
2 opportunity	**5** beginning
3 a job	

1 [C] a hole or place where something opens: *a narrow opening in the hedge* ♦ *The doctors had to make an opening in her windpipe.*

2 [C] an opportunity to do something: *His comments created an opening for efforts to resolve the crisis.*

3 [C] a job that has become available: *There's an opening in the sales department.*

4 [U] times when shops and businesses are open: *Staff at the supermarket campaigned against Sunday opening.*

5 [C] the beginning of a performance or film: *the opening of the play*

opening² /ˈəʊp(ə)nɪŋ/ *adj* **1** showing that something is open or has begun: *the opening ceremony of the Olympic Games* **2** the first of several similar things: *the opening paragraph*

opening hours *noun* [plural] *British* the hours that a shop, business etc is open

opening night *noun* [C] the first night that a play or other entertainment is performed

open invitation *noun* [C] an invitation to do something at any time

openly /ˈəʊpənli/ *adv* in a direct or honest way that makes something obvious: *The report openly criticizes the military leadership.*

open market *noun* [C] *business* a situation in which people can buy and sell things without any official rules about prices: *The land will be sold on the open market.*

open-minded *adj* willing to consider new ideas

open-mouthed /ˌəʊpən ˈmaʊðd, ˌəʊpən ˈmaʊθt/ *adj, adv* with your mouth wide open in surprise

openness /ˈəʊpənnəs/ *noun* [U] **1** an honest way of talking or behaving **2** a tendency to accept new ideas, methods, or changes

open-plan *adj* an open-plan office, house, etc has few walls and a lot of open space

opera /ˈɒp(ə)rə/ *noun* [C/U] a type of play that is performed by singers and an orchestra, or the art of performing these plays
—**operatic** /ˌɒpəˈrætɪk/ *adj* → SOAP OPERA

opera house *noun* [C] a theatre where operas are performed

operate /ˈɒpəreɪt/ *verb* ★★★

1 [I/T] if equipment operates, or if you operate it, you use or control it and it works in the way it should: *The equipment was not operating properly.* ♦ *The motor operates at very high speeds.* ♦ *Do not operate machinery after taking this medication.*

2 [I/T] if an organization, company, service, or system operates, or if it is operated, it does its work: *The company has been operating in Europe for two years.* ♦ *Flights operate every day from Birmingham.*
3 [I] to cut into part of someone's body for medical reasons: *Surgeons had to operate to remove the bullet.* ♦ *We may have to operate on your leg.*
4 [I] if something such as a rule, idea, or fact operates, it exists and has an effect in a particular situation: *Racism operates at many levels, conscious and unconscious.*

'**operating ,system** noun [C] *computing* the software that tells the parts of a computer how to work together and what to do

'**operating ,theatre** noun [C] a room in a hospital where doctors perform medical operations

operation /ˌɒpəˈreɪʃ(ə)n/ noun ★★★

1 planned activity	**4** (part of) company
2 actions to achieve sth	**5** way sth operates
3 cutting body medically	**+ PHRASES**

1 [C] a planned activity involving a lot of people, especially soldiers or police officers: *the biggest military operation for 20 years*
2 [C] an action or set of actions that is necessary to achieve something: *Connecting the water supply is a very simple operation.*
3 [C] the process of cutting into someone's body for medical reasons: *She may need an operation on her knee.* ♦ *The baby had to have an operation.* ♦ *A very experienced surgeon will perform the operation.*
4 [C] a company, or a part of a large company: *the company's UK operations*
5 [U] the way that something operates: *We are here to explain the operation of the new exam system.*

PHRASES **go/come into operation** to start to work or become effective: *The new production plant went into operation last month.*
in operation 1 working in the normal way: *Only one of our telephone lines is currently in operation.* **2** existing and having an effect in a situation: *Guidelines governing the use of email are now in operation.*

operational /ˌɒpəˈreɪʃ(ə)nəl/ adj **1** working correctly and able to be used: *The new computer system is fully operational.*
2 relating to the way something works, especially a system or business: *operational efficiency*

operative /ˈɒp(ə)rətɪv/ adj working correctly and having the right effect

operator /ˈɒpəˌreɪtə/ noun [C] **1** someone who works for a telephone company and helps people with calls **2** someone whose job is to operate a machine or piece of equipment: *a crane operator* **3** a person or company that runs a business: *bus/ferry/coach operator*

ophthalmologist /ˌɒfθælˈmɒlədʒɪst/ noun [C] a doctor who is an expert in illnesses of the eyes —**ophthalmology** /ˌɒfθælˈmɒlədʒi/ noun [U]

opinion /əˈpɪnjən/ noun [C] ★★★ the attitude that someone has towards something,

especially about how good it is: *What is your opinion of her latest novel?* ♦ *Professor Wright has a high opinion of your work* (=thinks your work is good). ♦ *The students all gave their opinions.* ♦ *Despite our differences of opinion, we remained good friends.* ♦ *The book was a waste of time, in my opinion.* ♦ *Public opinion has turned against the government in recent months.*

opinionated /əˈpɪnjəˌneɪtɪd/ adj having very strong opinions that do not change even when they are unreasonable

o'pinion ,poll noun [C] an attempt to find out what people in general think about a subject by asking a number of people questions about it

opium /ˈəʊpiəm/ noun [U] a powerful illegal drug made from the seeds of a type of POPPY (=flower)

opponent /əˈpəʊnənt/ noun [C] ★★
1 someone who is competing against you: *His opponent received only 36 per cent of the vote.*
2 someone who disagrees with something and tries to change or stop it: *opponents of the legislation*

opportune /ˈɒpətjuːn/ adj *formal* an opportune moment or time is a good or lucky time for something to happen

opportunist /ˌɒpəˈtjuːnɪst/ noun [C] someone who is always trying to gain an advantage and is willing to behave in an unfair way —**opportunism** noun [U]

opportunistic /ˌɒpətjuːˈnɪstɪk/ adj looking for and taking an opportunity, often in a way that is unfair or harms someone else: *opportunistic crimes*

opportunity /ˌɒpəˈtjuːnəti/ noun ★★★
1 [C/U] a chance to do something, or a situation in which it is easy for you to do something: *The trip sounds like a wonderful opportunity.* ♦ *We have given them ample opportunity* (=a lot of chances) *to voice their complaints.* ♦ *I'd like to take this opportunity to thank all of you for coming.* ♦ *We will inform you of any changes at the earliest opportunity* (=as soon as possible). ♦ *an opportunity for career advancement* ♦ **give sb the opportunity to do sth** *The programme gives students the opportunity to learn more about global warming.*
2 [C] a job that is available: *There are good opportunities in the marketing division.*

Words often used with opportunity

Adjectives often used with opportunity (sense 1)
■ **excellent, golden, good, great, ideal, perfect, rare, unique, wonderful** + OPPORTUNITY: used about opportunities that are good

oppose /əˈpəʊz/ verb [T] ★ to disagree with a plan or policy, and to try to stop it: *a group that opposes the death penalty* ♦ *There was a campaign to oppose the building of a nuclear reactor.*

opposed /əˈpəʊzd/ adj ★
1 someone who is opposed to something thinks that it should not happen: *He was bitterly opposed to the war.*
2 completely different: *The two ideas are directly opposed.*
PHRASE **as opposed to** used for referring to

O

something that is very different from the thing that you have just mentioned: *The cost of these planes is £3 million, as opposed to the £2 million charged by their competitors.*

opposing /əˈpəʊzɪŋ/ adj **1** competing against someone else or against each other **2** opposing facts, opinions, or ideas are completely different from each other

opposite¹ /ˈɒpəzɪt/ adj ★★
1 across from, or on the other side of, someone or something: *They sat at* **opposite ends** *of the room.* ♦ *On the* **opposite side** *of the road from the school was the church.*
2 completely different: *The car smashed into a lorry coming* **in the opposite direction**.

opposite² /ˈɒpəzɪt/ preposition ★ across from, or facing someone or something: *the bus stop opposite the cinema* ♦ *Adam took the seat opposite her.*

opposite³ /ˈɒpəzɪt/ adv British on the other side of an area from someone or something and facing towards them: *Jim and Rachel live opposite* (=on the other side of the road).

opposite⁴ /ˈɒpəzɪt/ noun [C] someone or something that is completely different from someone or something else: *Whatever I suggested, they would go and do the opposite.*

opposite ˈsex, the noun [singular] for men, women are the opposite sex, and for women, men are the opposite sex

opposition /ˌɒpəˈzɪʃ(ə)n/ noun ★★★
1 [U] strong disagreement with a plan or policy: *Public* **opposition to** *the government is growing.*
2 the opposition [singular] a person, organization etc that someone is competing against
3 the opposition [singular] the political parties in a country that are not part of the government

oppress /əˈpres/ verb [T] to treat people who are less powerful in an unfair and cruel way —**oppression** /əˈpreʃ(ə)n/ noun [U]

oppressed /əˈprest/ adj suffering from unfair and cruel treatment

oppressive /əˈpresɪv/ adj **1** unfair and cruel **2** hot in an unpleasant way

oppressor /əˈpresə/ noun [C] a powerful leader or government that treats people in an unfair and cruel way

opt /ɒpt/ verb [I] to choose from a range of possibilities: *We opted for the less expensive car.*
PHRASAL VERB **opt ˈout** to decide not to take part in something, or to stop taking part in it

optic /ˈɒptɪk/ adj medical relating to the eyes

optical /ˈɒptɪk(ə)l/ adj relating to sight, or to light

optical ilˈlusion noun [C] something that looks very different from what it really is, usually because of the way it is drawn or lit

optician /ɒpˈtɪʃ(ə)n/ noun [C] British someone whose job is to test people's sight and make and sell glasses

optics /ˈɒptɪks/ noun [singular] the scientific study of sight and light

optimal /ˈɒptɪm(ə)l/ adj OPTIMUM

optimism /ˈɒptɪmɪzəm/ noun [U] a tendency

to be hopeful and to expect that good things will happen ≠ PESSIMISM

optimist /ˈɒptɪmɪst/ noun [C] someone who tends to be hopeful and expect that good things will happen ≠ PESSIMIST

optimistic /ˌɒptɪˈmɪstɪk/ adj someone who is optimistic is hopeful about the future and tends to expect that good things will happen ≠ PESSIMISTIC: *She said that she was optimistic about the outcome of the trial.* —**optimistically** /ˌɒptɪˈmɪstɪkli/ adv

optimize /ˈɒptɪˌmaɪz/ verb [T] to make something as good or as effective as possible

optimum /ˈɒptɪməm/ adj best, or most suitable

option /ˈɒpʃ(ə)n/ noun [C] ★★★
1 something that you can choose to do: *We discussed all the marketing options and chose television advertising.* ♦ *She* **had no option but** *to admit the truth* (=she had to admit the truth).
2 an extra feature on a new product such as a car, that you can choose when you buy it
PHRASE **keep/leave your options open** to avoid making a decision now so that you will still have choices later

optional /ˈɒpʃ(ə)nəl/ adj something that is optional is available if you want it, but you do not have to have it ≠ COMPULSORY: *The history course is optional.*

optometrist /ɒpˈtɒmətrɪst/ noun [C] an OPTICIAN

opulent /ˈɒpjʊlənt/ adj formal very impressive and expensive —**opulence** noun [U]

or /ɔː/ conjunction ★★★
1 showing possibilities or choices used for connecting possibilities or choices. In a list, 'or' is usually used only before the last possibility or choice: *Which colour do you want – red, green, yellow, or blue?* ♦ *He's probably at lunch or in a meeting.* ♦ *'When will you get the results?' '****Either** tomorrow **or** the day after.'* ♦ *The jury must decide whether the prisoner is guilty* **or not**.
2 and not used for including someone or something else in a negative statement: *She's had nothing to eat or drink all day.* ♦ *I never had any help or advice from my parents.*
3 when amounts are not exact used between two similar numbers or before 'so' for showing that you do not know what the exact number is: *I can photocopy your notes. It'll only take a minute or two.* ♦ *They spent an hour* **or so** *searching for the missing file.*
4 in warnings, threats, or advice used for saying what will happen if someone does not do something: *The soldiers told everyone to leave* **or** *they would be shot.* ♦ *We must deal with the problem now,* **or else** *it will be too late.*
5 correcting or explaining what you have said used for introducing a comment that corrects or adds more information to what you have just said: *He spent time in the Soviet labour camps, or Gulags, as they were called.*

oral¹ /ˈɔːrəl/ adj ★
- **1** spoken, not written: *an oral agreement*
- **2** relating to the mouth: *oral health/hygiene*
—**orally** adv: *The medicine is taken orally.*

oral² /ˈɔːrəl/ noun [C] a spoken examination, especially in a foreign language

orange¹ /ˈɒrɪndʒ/ noun ★★
- **1** [C] a round fruit that has a thick orange-coloured skin —*picture* → C10
- **2** [U] a colour that is between red and yellow

orange² /ˈɒrɪndʒ/ adj between red and yellow in colour

orang-utan or **orang-utang** /ɔːˈræŋ əˌtæn, əˈræŋ uːˌtæn/ noun [C] an APE (=a large monkey without a tail) with long orange hair

orator /ˈɒrətə/ noun [C] someone who is skilled at making speeches in public

oratory /ˈɒrət(ə)ri/ noun [U] the skill of making effective and impressive speeches in public

orbit¹ /ˈɔːbɪt/ noun [C] the path that is taken by an object that is moving around a larger object in space

orbit² /ˈɔːbɪt/ verb [I/T] to move around a large object in space such as a planet

orchard /ˈɔːtʃəd/ noun [C] a place where fruit trees are grown

orchestra /ˈɔːkɪstrə/ noun [C] ★ a large group of musicians who use many different instruments in order to play mostly classical music —**orchestral** /ɔːˈkestrəl/ adj

orchestrate /ˈɔːkɪˌstreɪt/ verb [T] to organize a complicated event or course of action so that you achieve the result that you want

orchid /ˈɔːkɪd/ noun [C] a tropical flower with an unusual shape —*picture* → C9

ordain /ɔːˈdeɪn/ verb [T] to make someone a priest, MINISTER, or RABBI in an official religious ceremony → ORDINATION

ordeal /ɔːˈdiːl/ noun [C] an extremely unpleasant experience: *They have suffered a terrible ordeal.*

order¹ /ˈɔːdə/ noun ★★★

1 arrangement	**5** organized situation
2 request by customer	**6** general situation
3 official instruction	**7** group of people
4 when law is obeyed	**+** PHRASES

- **1** [C/U] the way in which a set of things is arranged or done so that it is clear which thing is first, second, third etc: *Please try to keep the pictures in order* (=in the correct order). ◆ *Some of the names on the list are out of order* (=in the wrong order).
- **2** [C] a request for something to be made for you or brought to you: *May I take your order* (=write down what you want to eat or drink)? ◆ *A major order for six new ships will guarantee the company's future.*
- **3** [C] an instruction that is given by someone in a position of authority: *Try to persuade your employees – don't just give orders.* ◆ *Soldiers must obey orders.* ◆ *I don't have to take orders from you* (=obey you).
- **4** [U] a situation in which people obey the law: *The new president's most urgent task will be to maintain order.*
- **5** [U] a situation in which everything is well organized or arranged: *I'm trying to bring a bit of order to the garden.*

- **6** [singular] the general situation at a particular time, especially the existing political, economic, or social system: *The old social order was slowly breaking down.*
- **7** [C] a group of people, especially a religious group, who live according to special rules: *a Buddhist order*

PHRASES **in order** legally or officially correct: *All your papers seem to be in order.*
in order (for sb/sth) to do sth so that someone can do something, or so that something can happen: *What do I have to do in order to convince them?*
out of order 1 a machine or piece of equipment that is out of order is not working correctly **2** *British* if someone is out of order, they have done something to annoy or offend someone else

order² /ˈɔːdə/ verb ★★★
- **1** [T] to tell someone to do something, in a way that shows that you have authority: *The government has **ordered an investigation** into the cause of the accident.* ◆ **order sb to do sth** *The judge ordered Hill to serve five years in prison for the robbery.*
- **2** [I/T] to ask for something to be brought to you or be made for you: *Are you ready to order?* ◆ *We sat down and ordered some beers.* ◆ *The airline has ordered 35 new planes.*
- **3** [T] to put things in a particular order: *The list of books is ordered alphabetically.*

PHRASAL VERB ˌorder sb aˈround or ˌorder sb aˈbout *British* to keep telling someone what to do, in an annoying way

orderly¹ /ˈɔːdəli/ adj **1** correctly or neatly organized **2** well-behaved, or well-controlled

orderly² /ˈɔːdəli/ noun [C] someone with no special medical training who works in a hospital, doing jobs such as moving people around

ordinarily /ˈɔːd(ə)n(ə)rəli, ˌɔːd(ə)n(ə)rerəli/ adv usually=NORMALLY

ordinary /ˈɔːd(ə)n(ə)ri/ adj ★★★
- **1** normal or average, and not unusual or special: *It was just an ordinary Saturday morning.* ◆ *I didn't notice anything out of the ordinary* (=unusual).
- **2** not especially good, interesting, or impressive: *The inside of the house is rather ordinary.*

ordination /ˌɔːdɪˈneɪʃ(ə)n/ noun [C/U] the process or religious ceremony by which someone is officially made a priest, MINISTER, or RABBI

ore /ɔː/ noun [C/U] rock or earth from which metal can be obtained

oregano /ˌɒrɪˈɡɑːnəʊ/ noun [U] a plant whose leaves are used in cooking for giving a special flavour to food

org /ɔːɡ/ abbrev private organization: used in Internet addresses

organ /ˈɔːɡən/ noun [C] ★★
- **1** a part of your body that does a particular job, such as your heart or brain: *organ transplant operations*
- **2** a large musical instrument with pipes of different lengths, played by pressing KEYS (=narrow bars) on it —*picture* → PIANO
- **3** an electronic instrument like a piano

organic /ɔːˈɡænɪk/ adj ★
1 organic food or drink is produced without using artificial chemicals: *organic apples/ meat* ♦ *organic farming*
2 relating to, or produced by, living things: *organic material/waste/matter*
3 happening or developing as a natural and continuous process: *The business has expanded by 70% through organic growth.*
—**organically** /ɔːˈɡænɪkli/ adv

organisation /ˌɔːɡənaɪˈzeɪʃ(ə)n/ a British spelling of **organization**

organise /ˈɔːɡənaɪz/ a British spelling of **organize**

organism /ˈɔːɡənɪz(ə)m/ noun [C] a living thing

organist /ˈɔːɡənɪst/ noun [C] someone who plays the organ

organization /ˌɔːɡənaɪˈzeɪʃ(ə)n/ ★★★
1 [C] an officially organized group of people who work together or have the same aims, for example a company or a political party: *the human rights organization Amnesty International* ♦ *She belongs to a number of political and charitable organizations.*
2 [U] the way in which the different parts of something are arranged=STRUCTURE: *scientists investigating **the organization of** the human brain* ♦ *Officials have asked for help with **the organization of** the elections.*
—**organizational** adj: *her excellent organizational skills*

organize /ˈɔːɡənaɪz/ verb ★★
1 [T] to prepare or arrange an activity or event: *Who's organizing the conference?*
2 [T] to put things into a sensible order, or to create a system in which all the parts work well together: *Let's organize this agenda a little better.*
3 [I/T] to form a TRADE UNION (=an organization that protects workers' rights)

organized /ˈɔːɡənaɪzd/ adj **1** planned carefully and effectively ≠ DISORGANIZED **2** an organized person arranges and plans activities carefully and effectively ≠ DISORGANIZED

organized crime noun [U] criminal activities that are controlled by a large powerful secret organization

organizer /ˈɔːɡənaɪzə/ noun [C] someone who makes all the arrangements for an event or activity

orgasm /ˈɔːɡæz(ə)m/ noun [C/U] the stage of sexual activity when sexual pleasure is strongest

orgy /ˈɔːdʒi/ noun [C] **1** a party at which there is a lot of drinking and sexual activity **2 an orgy of sth** an occasion on which someone does something a lot, especially something bad: *an orgy of killing*

Orient, the /ˈɔːriənt/ *old-fashioned* the countries of eastern Asia

oriental /ˌɔːriˈent(ə)l/ adj of eastern Asia, or from eastern Asia

orientated /ˈɔːriənˌteɪtɪd/ adj *British* mainly concerned with a particular activity: *He's very career-orientated.*

orientation /ˌɔːriənˈteɪʃ(ə)n/ noun **1** [C/U] someone's basic attitudes or beliefs → SEXUAL ORIENTATION **2** [U] information or training that you are given before you start a new job or activity

origin /ˈɒrɪdʒɪn/ noun ★★
1 [C] the place or moment at which something begins to exist: *Meteorites may hold clues about **the origin of** life on Earth.* ♦ *The college can **trace its origins** back to the 18th century.*
2 [C/U] the country, race, or social situation that someone comes from=BACKGROUND: *She tries to hide her upper-class origins, but her accent gives her away.*

original¹ /əˈrɪdʒ(ə)nəl/ adj ★★★
1 existing at the beginning of a period or process, before any changes have been made=FIRST: *Do you know who the car's original owner was?* ♦ *The house still has its original doors.*
2 new, interesting, and different from anything else: *a highly original design* ♦ *a very original songwriter*
3 not copied from something else: *The original painting is in a museum in Vienna.*

original² /əˈrɪdʒ(ə)nəl/ noun [C] something such as a document or painting that is not a copy

originality /əˌrɪdʒəˈnæləti/ noun [U] the quality of being new, interesting, and different

originally /əˈrɪdʒ(ə)nəli/ adv ★★ at first: *His novels were originally published in magazines.* ♦ *He's from Germany originally.*

originate /əˈrɪdʒəneɪt/ verb **1** [I] to begin to exist or appear for the first time **2** [T] to create or start something

originator /əˈrɪdʒəneɪtə/ noun [C] the first person to create or start something

ornament /ˈɔːnəmənt/ noun [C] a small attractive object that is used for decoration

ornamental /ˌɔːnəˈment(ə)l/ adj designed to be used as decoration

ornate /ɔːˈneɪt/ adj decorated with complicated patterns or shapes

ornithology /ˌɔːnɪˈθɒlədʒi/ noun [U] the scientific study of birds —**ornithologist** noun [C]

orphan¹ /ˈɔːf(ə)n/ noun [C] a child whose parents have died

orphan² /ˈɔːf(ə)n/ verb **be orphaned** to become an orphan

orphanage /ˈɔːf(ə)nɪdʒ/ noun [C] a building where orphans live and are looked after

orthodox /ˈɔːθədɒks/ adj **1** accepted by most people as the correct or usual idea or practice ≠ UNORTHODOX **2** accepting and obeying traditional religious beliefs and practices: *orthodox Judaism*

orthodoxy /ˈɔːθədɒksi/ noun [C/U] an idea or practice that is accepted by most people as being correct or usual

orthopaedic /ˌɔːθəˈpiːdɪk/ adj *medical* relating to the treatment of injuries and diseases that affect people's bones and muscles: *an orthopaedic surgeon*

Oscar /ˈɒskə/ *trademark* a prize that is given to people working in the film industry

oscillate /ˈɒsɪleɪt/ verb [I] *science* to move quickly from side to side at a steady speed —**oscillation** /ˌɒsɪˈleɪʃ(ə)n/ noun [C/U]

osmosis /ɒzˈməʊsɪs/ noun [U] *science* the process by which a liquid slowly passes through a thin layer of something

ostensible /ɒˈstensəb(ə)l/ adj seeming to be true, or said by someone to be true, but possibly false: *The ostensible reason for the army's presence was to keep the peace.* —**ostensibly** adv

ostentatious /ˌɒstenˈteɪʃəs/ adj *showing disapproval* intended to impress people: *an ostentatious display of wealth* —**ostentation** noun [U], **ostentatiously** adv

osteopathy /ˌɒstiˈɒpəθi/ noun [U] *medical* a treatment for conditions such as back pain or muscle injury —**osteopath** noun [C]

osteoporosis /ˌɒstiəʊpəˈrəʊsɪs/ noun [U] *medical* a condition in which your bones become more likely to break

ostracize /ˈɒstrəsaɪz/ verb [T] to no longer accept someone as a member of your social group

ostrich /ˈɒstrɪtʃ/ noun [C] a large African bird that runs very fast but that cannot fly

other /ˈʌðə/ grammar word ★★★

> **Other** can be:
> ■ a **determiner**: *He doesn't like other people interfering.*
> ■ an **adjective**: *She invited all her other friends.*
> ■ a **pronoun**: *He swerved from one side of the road to the other.* ♦ *Some systems are better than others.*

1 additional used for referring to additional people or things of the type that has already been mentioned: *Apart from the victim's name and age, no other details were given.* ♦ *a book aimed at teachers and others working in education* ♦ **Among other things**, *she enjoys reading and tennis.*
2 different used for referring to a different person or thing from the one that has already been mentioned: *I wanted to go camping, but Kerry had other ideas.* ♦ *Not now. We'll talk about it some other time.*
3 second of two used for referring to the second of two people or things: *I held onto the rope with my other hand.* ♦ *He sat in front of the fire rubbing one bare foot against the other.* ♦ *One of the twins was Reggie. What was the other one called?*
4 the rest of a group used for referring to the rest of the people or things in a group: *Beethoven's Ninth is much longer than his other symphonies.* ♦ *We stayed until all the other guests had gone home.* ♦ *One boy fell off his chair and the others laughed.*
5 people in general used for referring to people in a general way when you are not including yourself as one of them: *I don't care what others think.*
6 opposite opposite, or furthest from you: *Ashley sat at the other end of the sofa.* ♦ *A car was coming in the other direction.* ♦ *I tried to attract her attention, but she was looking the other way.* ♦ *Did the boys do better than the girls or the other way round?*
PHRASES **the other day/night etc** two or three days/nights etc ago: *I had a phone call from Mandy the other day.*
other than except for someone or something: *I don't have time to read anything other than the newspaper.*

someone/something/somewhere etc or other used when you are not saying exactly which person, thing, place etc that you mean: *He's always complaining about something or other.*
→ ANOTHER, HAND¹, NONE, WORD¹

otherwise /ˈʌðəwaɪz/ adv ★★★
1 used for saying that if one thing does not happen or is not true, something else will happen, usually something bad: *I hope the weather improves. Otherwise, we'll have to cancel the picnic.* ♦ *The programme has saved thousands of children who would otherwise have died.*
2 in a different or opposite way from what has been mentioned: *I plan to wait here unless someone tells me otherwise.*
3 used for saying that something is true except for the fact you have just mentioned: *The show was a little long, but otherwise it was very good.*

OTT /ˌəʊ tiː ˈtiː/ adj *spoken* over-the-top: extreme, or unreasonable

otter /ˈɒtə/ noun [C] an animal that has a long body covered in brown fur and that can swim very well

ouch /aʊtʃ/ interjection *spoken* used for expressing a feeling of sudden pain

ought /ɔːt/ modal verb ★★★

> ■ **Ought** is usually followed by 'to' and an infinitive: *You ought to tell the truth.* Sometimes it is followed by 'to' but no following infinitive: *I don't spend as much time with them as I ought to.*
> ■ **Ought** has no tenses, no participles, and no infinitive form. It does not change its form, so the third person singular form does not end in '-s': *She ought to try a little harder.*
> ■ Questions and negatives are formed without 'do': *You ought not to be here.* ♦ *Ought I to tell my parents?* The negative short form **oughtn't** can also be used, and this is less formal.

1 ought to (do sth) used for saying what is the right or sensible thing to do, or the right way to behave: *You ought to get up earlier.* ♦ *Teachers ought not to swear in front of the children.* ♦ *You ought to have listened to the warnings.*
2 ought to (do sth) used when you have strong reasons for believing or expecting something: *France ought to win this game.*

> **Should** can be used in the same way as **ought to** and is more common, especially in negatives and questions.

oughtn't /ˈɔːt(ə)nt/ short form a way of saying or writing 'ought not'. This is not often used in formal writing: *You oughtn't to make promises you can't keep.*

ounce /aʊns/ noun [C] a unit for measuring weight, equal to 28.35 grams. The written abbreviation for ounce is **oz**.

our /aʊə/ determiner ★★★ belonging to or connected with you and the group that you are a part of, when you are the person speaking or writing: *When is our next meeting?* ♦ *Most of our friends live in the suburbs.* ♦ *We want to make our own decisions.*

O

ours /aʊəz/ pronoun ★★ used for referring to something that belongs to or is connected with you and the group that you are a part of, when you are the person speaking or writing: *Ours is the third house on the left.*
♦ *If you don't have a barbecue, you can borrow ours.* ♦ *Friends of ours are coming to visit.*

ourselves /aʊəˈselvz/ pronoun ★★
1 the REFLEXIVE form of 'we', used for showing that both you and the group that you are a part of are affected by what you do together: *We kept ourselves awake by playing card games.* ♦ *We are doing this for ourselves and our families.*
2 used for emphasizing that you are referring to yourself and your group, and not to anyone else: *If nobody will help us, we will do it ourselves.*
PHRASES **(all) by ourselves 1** alone: *We had dinner by ourselves in our hotel room.*
2 without help from anyone: *We knew that we couldn't organize such a big event all by ourselves.*
(all) to ourselves not sharing something with anyone else: *Freddy's folks were away, so we had the place all to ourselves.*

oust /aʊst/ verb [T] to remove someone from a position of power

out¹ /aʊt/ grammar word ★★★

Out can be:
■ an **adverb**: *We went out into the garden.*
■ used after the verb 'to be': *You were out when I called.*
■ used in the preposition phrase **out of**: *I got out of bed and went downstairs.*
■ a **preposition**, although many British people consider that this use is not correct: *I looked out the window.*

1 outside not inside a building or vehicle: *Is it cold out?* ♦ *The children are out in the garden.* ♦ *He leaned out of his car and called to me.*
2 not at home or work away from your home or place of work: *Dr Hammond's out just now, visiting a patient.* ♦ *Try to get out more – make new friends.* ♦ **take sb out** *Why don't you take Dad out for a drink?*
3 from inside sth from inside a container, building, or place: *He opened the drawer and took out a large brown envelope.* ♦ *She went out, slamming the door behind her.* ♦ *Take that chewing gum out of your mouth.*
4 none left with none of something left: *We're out of bread.* ♦ *I'm running out of ideas – can you suggest anything?*
5 no longer in a situation used for saying that someone is no longer in a bad situation: *We are facing a major crisis and there is no easy way out.* ♦ *Parents will be relieved that their children are out of danger.*
6 publicly available available for the public to buy, see, or know about: *Their new album comes out next week.*
7 far away used for saying that someone or something is in another place that is far away: *They live way out in the countryside.*
8 unconscious used for saying that someone is unconscious: *Arthur had hit his head on a beam and knocked himself out.* ♦ *I must have been out for five minutes.*

9 no longer in a competition not allowed to continue taking part in a game or competition: *If we don't win today, we'll be out of the championships.*
10 when the sun can be seen if the sun or moon is out, it is not behind clouds
11 not burning no longer burning or shining: *It got so cold when the fire went out.* ♦ *The children were in bed and the lights were out.*
12 not wanted or not possible *informal* if a particular idea, suggestion, or activity is out, it is not possible, or it cannot be accepted
13 not correct *British* used for saying that a number is not correct: *Their calculations were out by about two million pounds.*
14 when the sea is low if the TIDE is out, the sea is at a lower level on the land
PHRASES **be out to do sth** or **be out for sth** to be aiming to do something or get something: *These are dangerous men, and they are out for revenge.*
one out of ten/99 out of 100 etc used for saying how large a part of a group or number is: *Only one out of ten graduates goes into the teaching profession.*
out of interest/respect/pity etc because of a particular feeling or attitude: *I went there out of curiosity, really.*
out of it *informal* not conscious of what is happening because you are drunk or have taken drugs

out² /aʊt/ adj a gay person who is out has told other people that he or she is gay

out³ /aʊt/ verb [T] to make it publicly known that someone is gay

outback, the /ˈaʊtˌbæk/ noun [singular] the large areas of land in Australia that are far away from any city or town

outbid /aʊtˈbɪd/ (past tense and past participle **outbid**) verb [T] to offer to pay more than someone else for something that you want to buy

outbox /ˈaʊtˌbɒks/ noun [C] *computing* the place on an email program where emails are stored before you send them

outbreak /ˈaʊtˌbreɪk/ noun [C] the sudden start of war, disease, violence etc

outburst /ˈaʊtˌbɜːst/ noun [C] a sudden spoken expression of a strong feeling, especially anger

outcast /ˈaʊtˌkɑːst/ noun [C] someone who other people will not accept as a member of society or of a particular group

outclass /ˌaʊtˈklɑːs/ verb [T] to be much better than someone or something else

outcome /ˈaʊtˌkʌm/ noun [C] ★ the final result of a process or activity: *A second game will be played to determine the outcome.*

outcrop /ˈaʊtˌkrɒp/ noun [C] a rock, or a group of rocks, that sticks up out of the ground

outcry /ˈaʊtˌkraɪ/ noun [C/U] an angry expression of protest or shock by a lot of people

outdated /ˌaʊtˈdeɪtɪd/ adj not modern enough to be useful

outdo /ˌaʊtˈduː/ (past tense **outdid** /ˌaʊtˈdɪd/; past participle **outdone** /ˌaʊtˈdʌn/) verb [T] to be better than someone else at doing something

outdoor /ˌaʊtˈdɔː/ adj done, used, or existing outside ≠ INDOOR

outdoors¹ /ˌaʊtˈdɔːz/ adv not in a building = OUTSIDE ≠ INDOORS

outdoors² /ˌaʊtˈdɔːz/ noun **the (great) outdoors** the countryside, especially considered as somewhere that you visit in order to take part in activities such as walking

outer /ˈaʊtə/ adj ★
1 on or around the outside of something ≠ INNER: *The outer walls of the castle were over six feet thick.*
2 furthest away from the centre of something ≠ INNER: *the outer limits of the solar system*

outermost /ˈaʊtəˌməʊst/ adj furthest away from a particular place or from the centre of something ≠ INNERMOST

outer space noun [U] the area outside the Earth's atmosphere that contains the stars and planets

outfit¹ /ˈaʊtfɪt/ noun [C] **1** a set of clothes that are worn together **2** *informal* an organization, especially a small firm

outfit² verb [T] to provide someone or something with the clothes or equipment that they need

outflank /ˌaʊtˈflæŋk/ verb [T] to get an advantage over someone, for example in business or politics

outgoing /ˌaʊtˈɡəʊɪŋ/ adj **1** someone who is outgoing is friendly and enjoys meeting and talking to people = SOCIABLE **2** soon to leave a position of authority or power ≠ INCOMING: *the outgoing prime minister* **3** going out of or away from a place ≠ INCOMING: *outgoing flights*

outgoings /ˈaʊtˌɡəʊɪŋz/ noun [plural] amounts of money that you have to spend regularly, for example on food

outgrow /ˌaʊtˈɡrəʊ/ (past tense **outgrew** /ˌaʊtˈɡruː/; past participle **outgrown** /ˌaʊtˈɡrəʊn/) verb [T] **1** if you outgrow a piece of clothing, it is too small for you because you have grown **2** if you outgrow an activity or relationship, you have developed and it is now no longer suitable for you

outing /ˈaʊtɪŋ/ noun **1** [C] a short journey that you take for enjoyment **2** [C/U] a public announcement saying that someone, especially a famous person, is gay

outlandish /aʊtˈlændɪʃ/ adj extremely strange and unusual

outlast /ˌaʊtˈlɑːst/ verb [T] to last longer than someone or something else: *This system has outlasted many of its rivals.*

outlaw¹ /ˈaʊtlɔː/ verb [T] to make something illegal: *They signed an agreement outlawing chemical weapons.*

outlaw² /ˈaʊtlɔː/ noun [C] *old-fashioned* a criminal

outlay /ˈaʊtleɪ/ noun [C/U] the amount of money that you must spend in order to buy something or in order to start a new business or project

outlet /ˈaʊtlet/ noun [C] **1** a shop or place where a particular product is sold **2** a way of expressing strong feelings, or of using extra physical energy **3** a pipe or hole through which gas or liquid flows out

outline¹ /ˈaʊtlaɪn/ verb [T] **1** to give the main ideas of a plan or a piece of writing: *The document outlines our company's recycling policy.* **2** to draw a line around the edge of something

outline² /ˈaʊtlaɪn/ noun [C] ★
1 an explanation that includes the general points about something, but not the details: *The chairman gave them a brief outline of the museum's history.*
2 a line that shows the outer edge or shape of something: *Through the mist we could see the outline of the island.*

Words often used with outline

Adjectives often used with outline (noun, sense 1)
■ **bare, basic, brief, broad, general, rough, vague** + OUTLINE: used for emphasizing that an outline lacks details

---

outlive /ˌaʊtˈlɪv/ verb [T] **1** to live longer than someone else **2** to continue to exist after something else has stopped

outlook /ˈaʊtlʊk/ noun [singular] **1** an idea about what a situation will be like in the future: *The outlook for the economy is still uncertain.* **2** your general attitude to things: *a positive outlook on life*

outlying /ˈaʊtˌlaɪɪŋ/ adj existing away from a particular place: *outlying islands*

outmanoeuvre /ˌaʊtməˈnuːvə/ verb [T] to defeat or gain an advantage over someone by being more clever or skilful than they are

outmoded /ˌaʊtˈməʊdɪd/ adj no longer modern or useful

outnumber /ˌaʊtˈnʌmbə/ verb [T] if one group outnumbers another, there are more in the first group than in the second

out-of-date adj old and no longer useful

out-of-the-way adj a long way from other places

out-of-town adj in the countryside outside a town or city, but intended to be used by the people who live in that town or city: *out-of-town shopping*

outpatient /ˈaʊtˌpeɪʃ(ə)nt/ noun [C] someone who receives medical treatment at a hospital, but does not stay there for the night → INPATIENT

outperform /ˌaʊtpəˈfɔːm/ verb [T] to do something better than someone or something else

outplay /ˌaʊtˈpleɪ/ verb [T] to play much better than your opponent in a sport

outpost /ˈaʊtpəʊst/ noun [C] **1** a military camp that is far away from the army **2** a small town that is far away from other towns

outpouring /ˈaʊtˌpɔːrɪŋ/ noun [C/U] the act of expressing a strong emotion

output¹ /ˈaʊtpʊt/ noun [C/U] **1** the amount of something that a person, organization, or system produces ≠ INPUT: *Industrial output increased by four per cent last year.* **2** the information that is shown on a screen or printed on paper by a computer: *graphics output*

output² /ˈaʊtpʊt/ (past tense and past participle **output**; present participle **outputting** /ˈaʊtpʊtɪŋ/) verb [T] to produce information

O

from a computer, for example by showing it on a screen or printing it **≠** INPUT

outrage¹ /ˈaʊtreɪdʒ/ noun [C/U] a strong feeling of anger and shock, or something that causes this feeling

outrage² /ˈaʊtreɪdʒ/ verb [T] to make someone extremely angry and shocked

outrageous /aʊtˈreɪdʒəs/ adj **1** very shocking or unreasonable **2** extremely unusual and likely to shock people or make them laugh —**outrageously** adv

outright¹ /ˌaʊtˈraɪt/ adv **1** completely in a single process: *They can't afford to buy the house outright.* **2** without hiding your feelings: *I told them outright that they had to leave.*

outright² /ˈaʊtraɪt/ adj **1** clear and direct: *outright hostility* **2** complete and total: *an outright lie*

outset /ˈaʊtset/ noun [singular] the start of something: *You are going to love this book from the outset.*

outside /aʊtˈsaɪd/ grammar word ★★★

Outside can be:
- a **preposition**: *He was sitting at a table outside the café.*
- an **adverb**: *Why don't you go and play outside?*
- an **adjective**: *the outside wall of the building*
- a **noun**: *The house doesn't look very impressive from the outside.*

1 not inside or within a room, building, or area **≠** INSIDE: *Outside the sun was shining.* ♦ *I went to the window and looked outside.* ♦ *Three police cars were parked outside their house.* ♦ *Could you wait outside in the corridor?* ♦ *Her name is almost unknown outside of Latin America.*
2 used for referring to the outer part or surface of something **≠** INSIDE: *The outside of the house is in urgent need of repair.*
3 not within the limits of a particular time, range, or situation **≠** INSIDE: *classes held outside normal school hours* ♦ *Until then love was something outside my experience.*
4 used for referring to people who do not belong to a particular group or organization: *The company brought in advisers from outside.*
PHRASE **an outside chance** a situation in which something is possible but unlikely: *There's an outside chance that we'll both arrive on the same day.*

outsider /aʊtˈsaɪdə/ noun [C] someone who does not belong to a particular group

outsize /ˈaʊtsaɪz/ or **outsized** /ˈaʊtsaɪzd/ adj much larger than usual=OVERSIZED

outskirts, the /ˈaʊtskɜːts/ noun [plural] the areas of a town or city that are furthest away from the centre: *a park on the outskirts of Edinburgh*

outspoken /aʊtˈspəʊkən/ adj an outspoken person states their opinion honestly, even if other people do not like it=FORTHRIGHT

outstanding /aʊtˈstændɪŋ/ adj **1** extremely good or impressive: *an outstanding example of Indian art* ♦ *an area of outstanding natural beauty* **2** not yet completed, dealt with, or paid: *Some tasks are still outstanding.* —**outstandingly** adv

outstay /aʊtˈsteɪ/ *see* **welcome**³

outstretched /ˌaʊtˈstretʃt/ adj stretched out

outstrip /ˌaʊtˈstrɪp/ verb [T] to go faster, do something better, or become larger than someone or something else: *Demand for the new computers has outstripped supply.*

'out tray noun [C] *British* a container on your desk where you keep letters or documents that are ready to be sent or put somewhere else —*picture* → C3

outward¹ /ˈaʊtwəd/ adj **1** relating to something that you can see or notice =EXTERNAL **≠** INWARD: *He had no outward signs of the illness.* **2** an outward journey is one in which you are going away from home

outward² /ˈaʊtwəd/ adv OUTWARDS

outwardly /ˈaʊtwədli/ adv according to the way that something seems, that is not always the same way that it really is **≠** INWARDLY

outwards /ˈaʊtwədz/ adv away from the centre of something, or towards the outside of it **≠** INWARDS

outweigh /ˌaʊtˈweɪ/ verb [T] to be more important, useful, or valuable than something else: *The possible benefits outweigh the risks involved.*

outwit /ˌaʊtˈwɪt/ verb [T] to gain an advantage over someone by using a clever or dishonest trick

oval /ˈəʊv(ə)l/ adj with a shape like a long narrow circle —*picture* → C8 —**oval** noun [C]

ovary /ˈəʊv(ə)ri/ noun [C] one of the two organs in a woman's body that produce eggs

ovation /əʊˈveɪʃ(ə)n/ noun [C] *formal* if an audience gives someone an ovation, they CLAP their hands to express their admiration or enjoyment

oven /ˈʌv(ə)n/ noun [C] ★ a large piece of equipment in a kitchen that you cook food in: *Preheat the oven to 220°C, Gas mark 7.* —*picture* → C2

ovenproof /ˈʌv(ə)nˌpruːf/ adj ovenproof plates, dishes etc can be used in an oven without breaking

over¹ /ˈəʊvə/ grammar word ★★★

Over can be:
- a **preposition**: *a bridge over the river* ♦ *It happened over a hundred years ago.*
- an **adverb**: *He fell over and broke his arm.*
- used after the verb 'to be': *The exams will be over soon.*

1 above sb/sth in a higher position above someone or something, without touching them **≠** UNDER: *Perry glanced at the clock over the door.* ♦ *The Simpsons live in a flat over the shop.* ♦ *Birds circled over their heads.*
2 on sb/sth covering someone or something: *She put her hands over her ears.* ♦ *She spilled coffee all over my new dress.*
3 from one side to the other across from one side of something to the other: *Several bridges over the River Danube were destroyed.* ♦ *I crossed over to the other side of the street.* ♦ *Three prisoners had climbed over the fence.*
4 on the opposite side of sth on the opposite side of an area, line, road, river etc:

*Sandra's brother lives just **over the road** from our house.*

5 into the opposite position moving into a position so that the side that was facing down now faces up: *He turned the card over.* ◆ *Roll over onto your back.*

6 in or to many parts of sth in, to, or from many different parts of an area: *The drought has spread over much of the southern US.* ◆ *The festival attracts music lovers from **all** over the world.*

7 towards the side towards the side: *The main entrance is further over on the left.* ◆ *She leaned over and whispered in my ear.*

8 in or to a place in or to a particular place, for example someone's home: *Why don't you come over and have dinner with us sometime?* ◆ *Lawrence walked over to the window and looked out.*

9 moving downwards falling or bending down from an upright position: *Carey fell over and broke his leg.* ◆ *I bent over to tie my shoe.*

10 concerning sth used for talking about the cause of a feeling or argument: *There are worries over the future of the steel industry.* ◆ *We spent a whole hour arguing over the meaning of two words.*

11 down from an edge falling, hanging, or looking down from the edge of something: *Lava flowed over the rim of the volcano.*

12 ended used for saying that a particular event, situation, or period of time has ended: *Moore's fourth marriage was over after only 18 months.* ◆ *We're all so relieved that the trial is over and done with.*

13 no longer affected no longer upset or affected by an illness or a bad experience: *She still isn't over the shock of her brother's death.* ◆ *He'll soon **get over** his disappointment.*

14 controlling or influencing sb/sth used for stating who or what is controlled or influenced by someone or something: *The Church today has little influence over the way people lead their lives.*

15 during during a period of time: *Over the last few years we've become friends.* ◆ *Most hotels are fully booked over the holiday weekend.*

16 more than more than a particular amount or age ≠ UNDER: *Yeltsin was elected with over 45 million votes.* ◆ *The pension will be paid to people aged 65 **and over**.*

PHRASES all over again used for saying that you do the whole of something again starting from the beginning, or that the whole of a long process happens again: *I had to do my essay all over again.*

over and over (again) many times: *They keep asking the same questions over and over again.*

→ ABOVE

over² /ˈəʊvə/ noun [C] *British* in CRICKET, a series of six actions of BOWLING

overall¹ /ˌəʊvərˈɔːl/ adj ★★
1 considering something as a whole, rather than its details: *My **overall impression** of the town was not very good.*
2 including everything: *What were the overall costs of the project?*

overall² /ˌəʊvərˈɔːl/ adv when everything is considered: *Overall, our position is stronger than it was last year.*

overall³ /ˈəʊvərˌɔːl/ noun **1** [C] *British* a light coat that is worn over your clothes to protect them when you are working
2 overalls [plural] *British* a single piece of clothing with trousers and long sleeves, worn over your clothes to protect them when you are working **3 overalls** [plural] *American* DUNGAREES

overawed /ˌəʊvərˈɔːd/ adj feeling slightly afraid of something that is extremely impressive or powerful

overbearing /ˌəʊvəˈbeərɪŋ/ adj an overbearing person tries to control other people's behaviour and ignores their feelings

overboard /ˈəʊvəbɔːd/ adv off a boat or ship and into the water
PHRASE go overboard *informal* to do or say more than is reasonable or necessary, for example because you are excited

overcast /ˌəʊvəˈkɑːst/ adj an overcast sky is covered in clouds

overcharge /ˌəʊvəˈtʃɑːdʒ/ verb [I/T] to charge someone too much money for something

overcoat /ˈəʊvəkəʊt/ noun [C] a long warm coat

overcome /ˌəʊvəˈkʌm/ (past tense **overcame** /ˌəʊvəˈkeɪm/; past participle **overcome**) verb [T] ★
1 to succeed in dealing with a problem: *Jimmy overcame his difficulties to graduate with a first-class degree.*
2 to make someone very emotional, ill, or unconscious: *The entire family was overcome with grief.* ◆ *Two men died when they were overcome by smoke.*
3 to defeat someone or something: *Government troops have finally overcome rebel forces in the north.*

> **Words often used with overcome**
>
> *Nouns often used with **overcome** (sense 1)*
> ■ OVERCOME + **difficulty, disadvantage, fear, obstacle, problem, resistance**: deal successfully with a problem

overcompensate /ˌəʊvəˈkɒmpənˌseɪt/ verb [I] to do more than you need to do in trying to correct a fault

overcrowded /ˌəʊvəˈkraʊdɪd/ adj containing too many people or things: *overcrowded schools*

overcrowding /ˌəʊvəˈkraʊdɪŋ/ noun [U] unpleasant conditions that are caused by too many people or things being in the same place

overdo /ˌəʊvəˈduː/ (past tense **overdid** /ˌəʊvəˈdɪd/; past participle **overdone** /ˌəʊvəˈdʌn/) verb [T] to do or use more of something than you should: *Don't overdo it* (=work too hard) *or you'll make yourself ill.*

overdone /ˌəʊvəˈdʌn/ adj cooked for too long ≠ UNDERDONE

overdose /ˈəʊvədəʊs/ noun [C] too much of a drug that is taken at one time —**overdose** verb [I]

O

overdraft /ˈəʊvəˌdrɑːft/ noun [C] an agreement with your bank that allows you to spend money when you have no money left in your account

overdrawn /ˌəʊvəˈdrɔːn/ adj if you are overdrawn, you have spent more money than the amount that you had in your bank account

overdue /ˌəʊvəˈdjuː/ adj if something is overdue, it should have been done before now

overestimate /ˌəʊvərˈestɪˌmeɪt/ verb [T] to think that something is better or bigger than it really is ≠ UNDERESTIMATE —**overestimate** /ˌəʊvərˈestɪmət/ noun [C]

overflow¹ /ˌəʊvəˈfləʊ/ verb **1** [I/T] to flow over the top of a container because it is too full **2** [I/T] if a river or lake overflows, it floods the land next to it **3** [I] if a place is overflowing with people or things, there are too many of them to fit into it

overflow² /ˈəʊvəˌfləʊ/ noun [C] a hole or pipe that allows a substance to flow out of a container when it gets too full

overgrown /ˌəʊvəˈɡrəʊn/ adj covered with plants that have been allowed to grow in an uncontrolled way

overhang /ˌəʊvəˈhæŋ/ (past tense and past participle **overhung** /ˌəʊvəˈhʌŋ/) verb [I/T] to stick out from an edge above something —**overhang** /ˈəʊvəˌhæŋ/ noun [C]

overhaul /ˌəʊvəˈhɔːl/ verb [T] to repair or change a machine or system in order to make it work better —**overhaul** /ˈəʊvəˌhɔːl/ noun [C]

overhead /ˌəʊvərˈhed/ adj, adv above your head

overheads /ˈəʊvəˌhedz/ noun [plural] money that you pay regularly as the costs of operating a business or organization

overhear /ˌəʊvəˈhɪə/ (past tense and past participle **overheard** /ˌəʊvəˈhɜːd/) verb [I/T] to hear what people are saying during a conversation that you are not involved in

overheat /ˌəʊvəˈhiːt/ verb [I/T] to become too hot, or to make something too hot

overjoyed /ˌəʊvəˈdʒɔɪd/ adj extremely pleased

overkill /ˈəʊvəˌkɪl/ noun [U] much more of something than is needed or wanted: *I really did think that four hours of speeches amounted to overkill.*

overland /ˈəʊvəˌlænd/ adj, adv on land rather than by boat or plane: *an overland journey*

overlap /ˌəʊvəˈlæp/ verb [I/T] **1** if two objects overlap, or if one overlaps the other, part of one object covers part of the other **2** if subjects, activities, or ideas overlap, they are partly the same as each other —**overlap** /ˈəʊvəˌlæp/ noun [C/U], **overlapping** adj

overleaf /ˌəʊvəˈliːf/ adv formal on the other side of the page

overload /ˌəʊvəˈləʊd/ verb [T] **1** to put too many people or things in or on something **2** to give someone too much work to do **3** to damage a piece of electrical equipment by putting too much electricity through it —**overload** /ˈəʊvəˌləʊd/ noun [C/U], **overloaded** /ˌəʊvəˈləʊdɪd/ adj

overlook /ˌəʊvəˈlʊk/ verb [T] **1** to fail to notice or do something: *Accidents happen when safety checks are overlooked.* **2** to forgive or ignore a mistake or bad behaviour: *I'm prepared to overlook what you said.* **3** to have a view of something from above: *Our hotel overlooked the river.* **4** to not consider someone or something: *Sean Connery was once again overlooked in the New Year's Honours list.*

overly /ˈəʊvəli/ adv formal very much, or too much: *It is a problem, but we're not overly worried about it.*

overnight¹ /ˌəʊvəˈnaɪt/ adv **1** during the night, or for one night: *They stayed overnight at the hotel.* **2** in a very short time: *Don't expect to become famous overnight.*

overnight² /ˈəʊvəˌnaɪt/ adj **1** working or happening during the night: *the overnight train/flight/ferry* **2** happening after a very short time: *an overnight success*

overpower /ˌəʊvəˈpaʊə/ verb [T] **1** to control or defeat someone using physical strength: *Two police officers overpowered him and took the gun.* **2** to affect someone so strongly that they cannot think or behave normally

overpowering /ˌəʊvəˈpaʊərɪŋ/ adj **1** very strong, so that you do not notice or feel anything else: *an overpowering smell of fish* **2** able to control people because of having a very strong personality

overpriced /ˌəʊvəˈpraɪst/ adj worth less than the price that is being charged

overran the past tense of **overrun**

overrated /ˌəʊvəˈreɪtɪd/ adj not as good or important as some people believe ≠ UNDERRATED

overreact /ˌəʊvəriˈækt/ verb [I] to be more worried, annoyed, or offended than you should be

override /ˌəʊvəˈraɪd/ (past tense **overrode** /ˌəʊvəˈrəʊd/; past participle **overridden** /ˌəʊvəˈrɪd(ə)n/) verb [T] **1** to be much more important than something else: *Passenger safety overrides all other concerns.* **2** to officially change someone else's decision

overriding /ˌəʊvəˈraɪdɪŋ/ adj more important than anything else

overrode the past tense of **override**

overrule /ˌəʊvəˈruːl/ verb [T] to officially change someone else's decision

overrun /ˌəʊvəˈrʌn/ (past tense **overran** /ˌəʊvəˈræn/; past participle **overrun**) verb **1** [I/T] British to take more time or money than was intended **2** [T] to be present in a place in very large numbers, in a way that is unpleasant: *The mall was overrun with holiday shoppers.*

oversaw the past tense of **oversee**

overseas¹ /ˌəʊvəˈsiːz/ adj ★ existing in, or coming from, a country that is across the sea from your country: *overseas visitors/ students/markets*

overseas² /ˌəʊvəˈsiːz/ adv to or in a country that is across the sea from your country: *There are plans to move production overseas.*

oversee /ˌəʊvəˈsiː/ (past tense **oversaw** /ˌəʊvəˈsɔː/; past participle **overseen** /ˌəʊvəˈsiːn/) verb [T] to watch something in order to check that it happens in the way that it should

overshadow /ˌəʊvəˈʃædəʊ/ verb [T] **1** to be a negative feature that spoils something: *Violent protests overshadowed the president's visit.* **2** to make someone or something seem less important

overshoot /ˌəʊvəˈʃuːt/ (past tense and past participle **overshot** /ˌəʊvəˈʃɒt/) verb [I/T] to stop or fall at a point that is further forward than was intended: *The plane seemed in danger of overshooting the runway.*

oversight /ˈəʊvəsaɪt/ noun [C] something that you do not think of that causes problems later

oversized /ˈəʊvəsaɪzd/ or **oversize** /ˈəʊvəsaɪz/ adj much larger than usual

overspend /ˌəʊvəˈspend/ (past tense and past participle **overspent** /ˌəʊvəˈspent/) verb [I/T] to spend more money than you intended to — **overspend** /ˈəʊvəspend/ noun [C], **overspending** noun [U]

overstep /ˌəʊvəˈstep/ verb [T] to do something that is not allowed or that is not acceptable: *The committee had overstepped the bounds of its authority.*

overt /əʊˈvɜːt/ adj not hidden or secret ≠ COVERT: *overt racism/hostility* —**overtly** adv

overtake /ˌəʊvəˈteɪk/ (past tense **overtook** /ˌəʊvəˈtʊk/; past participle **overtaken** /ˌəʊvəˈteɪkən/) verb **1** [T] to become better, bigger, or faster than someone or something else: *The women students seem to be overtaking the men.* **2** [I/T] British to go past another vehicle that is travelling in the same direction: *That's a dangerous place to overtake.*

ˌover-the-ˈcounter adj, adv over-the-counter medicine can be bought without a PRESCRIPTION from a doctor

overthrow /ˌəʊvəˈθrəʊ/ (past tense **overthrew** /ˌəʊvəˈθruː/; past participle **overthrown** /ˌəʊvəˈθrəʊn/) verb [T] to force a leader or government out of their position of power —**overthrow** /ˈəʊvəθrəʊ/ noun [singular]

overtime /ˈəʊvətaɪm/ noun [U] extra hours that someone works at their job, or money that is paid for working extra hours

overtone /ˈəʊvətəʊn/ noun [C] a quality that is noticeable but not obvious

overtook the past tense of **overtake**

overture /ˈəʊvətjʊə/ noun [C] the first part of a long piece of classical music

overturn /ˌəʊvəˈtɜːn/ verb **1** [I/T] if something overturns, or if you overturn it, it moves so that its bottom or side is upwards **2** [T] to officially change a decision or law

overvalue /ˌəʊvəˈvæljuː/ verb [T] to give something a higher price than it should have

overview /ˈəʊvəvjuː/ noun [C] a description of the main features of something: *The book gives a good overview of the subject.*

overweight /ˌəʊvəˈweɪt/ adj heavier than you should be ≠ UNDERWEIGHT

overwhelm /ˌəʊvəˈwelm/ verb [T] **1** to affect someone's emotions in a very powerful way: *Her beauty completely overwhelmed him.* **2** to be too much for someone or something to deal with: *In June the town is overwhelmed by tourists.*

overwhelming /ˌəʊvəˈwelmɪŋ/ adj ★ **1** making you feel a very strong emotion that you cannot control: *I had the overwhelming desire to get up and leave.* **2** much larger or more important than anything else in a situation: *An overwhelming majority voted against his proposal.* —**overwhelmingly** adv

> **Words often used with overwhelming**
>
> *Nouns often used with* **overwhelming** *(sense 1)*
> ■ OVERWHELMING + **desire, emotion, feeling, longing, need, temptation**: used about feelings that are very strong

overworked /ˌəʊvəˈwɜːkt/ adj forced to work too hard

overwrite /ˌəʊvəˈraɪt/ (past tense **overwrote** /ˌəʊvəˈrəʊt/; past participle **overwritten** /ˌəʊvəˈrɪt(ə)n/) verb [T] computing to get rid of information in a computer file by replacing it with other information

overzealous /ˌəʊvəˈzeləs/ adj showing disapproval doing something to an unnecessary degree

ˌover-ˈzealous adj showing disapproval doing something to an unnecessary degree

ow /aʊ/ interjection used for expressing a feeling of sudden pain

owe /əʊ/ verb [T] ★★ **1** to have to give someone a particular amount of money because you have bought something from them or have borrowed money from them: **owe sb sth** *Pam still owes me £5.* ♦ **owe sb sth for sth** *How much do we owe you for the tickets?* ♦ **owe sth to sb** *The companies owe as much as £200 billion to foreign lenders.* **2** to have an obligation to do something for someone or to give them something: **owe sb sth** *I think you owe her an apology.* ♦ **owe it to sb to do sth** *They owe it to their children to try to save the marriage.* **3** to have something because someone or something has helped you: **owe sth to sb/sth** *The company owes its success to its excellent training programme.* **4** to feel grateful to someone because of the way that they have helped you: **owe sb sth** *We really owe you a great deal for all your hard work this year.*

owing to /ˈəʊɪŋ ˌtuː/ preposition because of something: *Owing to the rising cost of fuel, more people are using public transport.*

owl /aʊl/ noun [C] a large bird with a big head and eyes and a small sharp beak. Owls hunt at night.

own¹ /əʊn/ grammar word ★★★

> **Own can be:**
> ■ an **adjective**: *We grow our own vegetables.*
> ■ a **pronoun**: *Her sister's house is bigger than her own.*

1 belonging to a particular person or thing and not to any other: *You are free to do what you like in your own home.* ♦ *She has two small children of her own.* ♦ *The club now has its very own radio station.* **2** done or caused by a particular person and not by anyone else: *Alan had always done his own cooking and cleaning.* ♦ *It's my own fault I didn't get the job.*

O

PHRASES **(all) on your own 1** alone: *You shouldn't be out on your own at this time of night.* **2** without any help: *Your grandfather did it all on his own.* → YOURSELF
get your own back *British informal* to do something bad to someone because they did something bad to you
→ HOLD¹

own² /əʊn/ verb [T] ★★★ to legally have something, especially because you have bought it: *Who owns that house by the lake?* ♦ *Larry doesn't own a car.*
PHRASAL VERB **own up** to admit that you have done something that is bad or embarrassing: *Two local students later owned up to the prank.*

owner /ˈəʊnə/ noun [C] ★★★ someone who owns something: *a restaurant/ supermarket/hotel owner* ♦ *I am the owner of three cars.*

ownership /ˈəʊnəʃɪp/ noun [U] legal possession of something

own goal noun [C] *British* **1** a goal that you accidentally score against your own team **2** something you do that accidentally harms you

ox /ɒks/ (plural **oxen** /ˈɒks(ə)n/) noun [C] a large type of male cow that is used for pulling or carrying things

oxide /ˈɒksaɪd/ noun [U] *science* a chemical that consists of oxygen mixed with another substance

oxygen /ˈɒksɪdʒ(ə)n/ noun [U] a gas in the air that has no smell or taste, and that all animals need in order to breathe

oyster /ˈɔɪstə/ noun [C] a type of SHELLFISH with a rough shell that is eaten as food, often raw

oz abbrev ounce

ozone /ˈəʊzəʊn/ noun [U] a type of oxygen that exists high in the Earth's atmosphere

ozone layer noun [singular] a layer of OZONE in the Earth's atmosphere that protects the Earth from the harmful effects of the Sun

P p

p¹ or **P** /piː/ noun [C/U] the 16th letter of the English alphabet

p² /piː/ abbrev **1** page **2** pence **3** penny

p & p /ˌpiː ən ˈpiː/ abbrev *British* postage and packing

PA /ˌpiː ˈeɪ/ noun [C] **1** personal assistant: someone whose job is to help a manager by writing business letters, organizing meetings etc **2** public address system: a piece of electrical equipment for making announcements or for playing music in a public place

pace¹ /peɪs/ noun ★
1 [singular/U] the speed at which something happens or is done: *The pace of*

technological change increased steadily during the 20th century. ♦ *The course allows students to progress at their own pace.*
2 [singular/U] the speed at which you move: *a player with skill and pace* (=the ability to move fast) ♦ *We wandered along at a leisurely pace.*
3 [C] a step that you take when you walk or run: *I took a few paces towards her.*
PHRASES **gather pace** *British* **1** to start to happen more quickly and have more success: *After 1946, support for European unity began to gather pace.* **2** to start to move more quickly
keep pace with sth to develop or progress at the same rate as something else: *The government is not allowing salaries to keep pace with inflation.*
put sb/sth through their/its paces to make a person or machine show how good they are at doing something
set the pace to establish a rate or standard that others have to achieve

pace² /peɪs/ verb **1** [I/T] to walk with regular steps around a small area, because you are worried, nervous, or impatient **2** [T] to make the story in a book, film etc develop in a particular way: *His films were always well paced and exciting.*
PHRASE **pace yourself** to avoid using all your energy too quickly, so that you have enough left to complete an activity

pacemaker /ˈpeɪsˌmeɪkə/ noun [C] a small piece of electronic equipment that is put in someone's heart in order to help the muscles to move regularly

Pacific /pəˈsɪfɪk/ adj relating to the Pacific Ocean

Pacific Rim, the the countries around the Pacific Ocean, considered as a political or economic group

pacifism /ˈpæsɪˌfɪz(ə)m/ noun [U] the belief that violence is wrong and that people should refuse to fight in wars

pacifist /ˈpæsɪfɪst/ noun [C] someone who believes that violence is wrong and refuses to fight in wars —**pacifist** adj

pacify /ˈpæsɪˌfaɪ/ verb [T] to make someone who is angry, worried, or upset feel calm

pack¹ /pæk/ verb ★
1 [I/T] to put your possessions into a bag, case, or box so that you can take or send them somewhere ≠ UNPACK: *It didn't take her long to pack a few clothes.* ♦ *Haven't you packed yet?* ♦ *He was still packing his suitcase when the taxi came.* ♦ **pack sb sth** *I've packed you a few sandwiches in case you get hungry.*
2 [T] to put goods into containers so that they can be sent somewhere and sold: *This is where the fruit is packed.* ♦ **pack sth in sth** *They pack the anchovies in salt.*
3 [T] to fill a place completely: *Eager spectators packed the courtroom.*
4 [T] to press something such as soil or snow into a solid hard mass
PHRASAL VERBS **pack sth away** to put something back into the place where it is stored: *We packed away the picnic things.*
pack sth in 1 *British informal* to stop doing something: *A year ago, she packed in her*

job to join the band. **2** to fill a period of time with a lot of activities: *He packed in an amazing amount in such a short life.*

pack sth 'into sth to fit a lot of activities into a period of time: *The festival offers 16 different shows, all packed into one weekend.*

pack 'up *informal* to finish work for the day by putting work or equipment away: *The workmen have already packed up and left.*

pack (sth) 'up to put things into a bag, case, or box so that you can take or send them somewhere: *He simply packed up his belongings and moved out.*

pack² /pæk/ noun [C] ★

1 set of things	**4** group of animals
2 box of cards/cigarettes	**5** group of people/things
3 bag	

1 a set of things such as products or documents that are wrapped together: *On registration we will send you a membership pack.* ♦ *Envelopes are cheaper if you buy them in **packs of** 100.*

2 a paper or card box for something such as PLAYING CARDS or cigarettes

3 a bag that you carry on your back

4 a group of animals that live and hunt together: *a pack of wolves*

5 *showing disapproval* a group of people or things: *There was a **pack** of reporters waiting outside.* ♦ *The whole story is **a pack of lies** (=completely untrue).*

package¹ /'pækɪdʒ/ noun [C] ★★★
1 an object or set of objects that is wrapped in a box or in paper and sent to someone =PARCEL: *a package full of Christmas presents*

2 a plan or offer that is intended to deal with a problem: *a package designed to stabilize the economy*

3 money and other benefits, for example a car, that someone gets from their employer

4 *computing* a set of computer software that is sold as one unit: *the best new graphics package on the market*

package² /'pækɪdʒ/ verb [T] **1** to put things into boxes, or to wrap them, so that they can be sold **2** to try to make a product, idea, or person attractive to the public: *Politicians these days are packaged to appeal to a mass market.*

'package ,holiday noun [C] *British* a holiday arranged by a travel company for a fixed price that includes the cost of your hotel and transport, and sometimes meals and entertainment

packaging /'pækɪdʒɪŋ/ noun [U] the boxes, plastic etc that are used for wrapping products

packed /pækt/ adj **1** extremely crowded: *The cinema was packed.* **2** *informal* containing a lot of something: *This new series is packed with drama.*

packet /'pækɪt/ noun [C] ★
1 *British* a box, bag, or piece of plastic wrapping, containing food that is ready to be sold: *The ingredients should be listed on the packet.* ♦ *an empty crisp packet* ♦ *a 500g packet of spaghetti*

2 a small parcel or envelope containing a set of similar things: *A **packet of** brochures arrived in the post.*

packing /'pækɪŋ/ noun [U] the activity of putting your possessions into bags, cases, or boxes so that you can take or send them somewhere: *I haven't done my packing yet.*

pact /pækt/ noun [C] an agreement between two or more people or organizations in which they promise to do something

pad¹ /pæd/ noun [C] **1** a set of sheets of paper that are fastened together along the top or along one side: *a note pad* **2** a thick piece of a soft substance that you use for protecting something, making it more comfortable, or changing its shape: *knee/elbow/shin pads* ♦ *a foam pad* **3** an area of soft flesh on the end of your finger or thumb

pad² /pæd/ verb **1** [I] to walk with quiet light steps **2** [T] to cover or fill something with a soft substance in order to protect it, make it more comfortable, or change its shape —**padded** adj: *a warm padded jacket*

padding /'pædɪŋ/ noun [U] a thick soft substance that is used for protecting something, making it more comfortable, or changing its shape

paddle¹ /'pæd(ə)l/ noun [C] **1** a short pole with a flat end or with two flat ends that is used for moving a small boat such as a CANOE **2** *British* an act of playing or walking in water that is not very deep

paddle² /'pæd(ə)l/ verb **1** [I] *British* to play or walk in water that is not very deep **2** [I/T] to move a small boat through the water using a paddle

paddock /'pædək/ noun [C] a small field where horses are kept

'paddy ,field or **paddy** /'pædi/ noun [C] a field of rice growing in water

padlock /'pædlɒk/ noun [C] a lock that you can fix to something such as a gate or suitcase. It has a curved bar on top that moves when you open the lock. —**padlock** verb [T]

paediatric /,pi:di'ætrɪk/ adj relating to the part of medicine that deals with children and their illnesses

paediatrician /,pi:diə'trɪʃ(ə)n/ noun [C] a doctor who deals with children and their illnesses

paediatrics /,pi:di'ætrɪks/ noun [U] the part of medical science that deals with children and their illnesses

paedophile /'pi:dəfaɪl/ noun [C] an adult who is sexually attracted to children —**paedophilia** /,pi:də'fɪliə/ noun [U]

pagan /'peɪgən/ adj relating to any religion that is not one of the main religions of the world —**pagan** noun [C]

page¹ /peɪdʒ/ noun [C] ★★★
1 a sheet of paper in a book, newspaper, or magazine: *the poem **on page** 125* ♦ *For information on hotels in Amsterdam, **see page** 20.* ♦ *She **turned a page** of the book in her lap.* ♦ *The football scores are on the **back page**.* ♦ *Lawrence was eating breakfast while glancing at the **sports page**.* ♦ *She sat on the grass, slowly **turning the pages** of a magazine.*

2 a piece of paper: *Chris wrote her name at the top of the page.*

3 the writing or pictures on a computer screen that you can see at one time, for example as part of a WEBSITE: *Click 'Back' to return to the previous page.*

page² /peɪdʒ/ verb [T] **1** to communicate with someone by sending a message to their PAGER **2** to call someone's name in a public place using a PA

pageant /'pædʒ(ə)nt/ noun [C] a play, concert, or other performance that is based on a historical or religious event

pager /'peɪdʒə/ noun [C] a small piece of equipment that makes a noise to tell you to phone someone or go somewhere=BEEPER

pagoda /pə'gəʊdə/ noun [C] a Buddhist religious building with several roofs built on top of each other

paid¹ /peɪd/ adj **1** a paid period of time is one when you receive pay although you are not at work ≠ UNPAID: *paid holidays* **2** earning a particular amount of money: *highly paid managers* ♦ *a new deal for low-paid workers* **3** working or done in exchange for pay: *paid campaign workers* ♦ *paid work*

paid² the past tense and past participle of **pay¹**

pail /peɪl/ noun [C] *old-fashioned* a BUCKET

pain¹ /peɪn/ noun [C/U] ★★★
1 a bad feeling in part of your body when you are hurt or become ill: *An old injury was causing him intense pain.* ♦ *He heard Leo scream in pain.* ♦ *I don't think she's in any pain.* ♦ *I'm having terrible pains in my chest.*
2 a feeling of being very upset or unhappy: *He found it hard to cope with the pain of being separated from his children.* ♦ *The incident must have caused my parents great pain.*
PHRASES **be a pain (in the neck)** *informal* to be very annoying
go to/take great pains to make a lot of effort to do something well and with care

Words often used with **pain**
Adjectives often used with **pain** *(noun, sense 1)*
■ **excruciating, intense, searing, severe, sharp, stabbing, terrible, unbearable** + PAIN: used about pains that are very strong
Verbs often used with **pain** *(noun, sense 1)*
■ **cause, inflict** + PAIN: make someone feel pain
■ **alleviate, deaden, dull, ease, lessen, relieve, soothe** + PAIN: make a pain less severe
■ **bear, endure, stand, put up with** + PAIN: be able to suffer pain

pain² /peɪn/ verb [T] *formal* to make someone feel very upset, ashamed, or unhappy

pained /peɪnd/ adj showing that you feel very upset or unhappy

painful /'peɪnf(ə)l/ adj ★
1 making you feel upset, ashamed, or unhappy: *painful memories of her unhappy childhood*
2 causing physical pain: *The sting can be excruciatingly painful.* ♦ *I have a sore throat, and it's really painful when I swallow.*

painfully /'peɪnf(ə)li/ adv in a way that makes you feel upset, ashamed, or unhappy: *She was painfully aware of his embarrassment.* ♦ *She looked painfully thin.*

painkiller /'peɪnˌkɪlə/ noun [C] a medicine that reduces pain

painless /'peɪnləs/ adj **1** not causing any

physical pain **2** less difficult or unpleasant than you expected: *I was dreading the interview, but in fact it was pretty painless.*

painstaking /'peɪnzˌteɪkɪŋ/ adj done or doing something very carefully and slowly =METICULOUS —**painstakingly** adv

paint¹ /peɪnt/ noun ★
1 [U] a coloured substance that you use for changing the colour of a surface or for making a picture: *The paint was peeling off the doors.* ♦ *You need to apply two coats of paint.*
2 paints [plural] a set of small blocks or tubes containing paint that you use for making pictures

paint² /peɪnt/ verb ★★
1 [I/T] to put paint onto something in order to change its colour: *Wash the walls before you start to paint.* ♦ *Will you help me paint the kitchen?*
2 [I/T] to create a picture of something using paints: *I painted a view of the lake.*
3 [T] to describe someone or something in a particular way: *The film paints a picture of what life was like during the war.*

paintbrush /'peɪntˌbrʌʃ/ noun [C] a brush used for painting

painter /'peɪntə/ noun [C] **1** an artist who paints pictures **2** someone whose job is to paint the inside or outside of buildings

painting /'peɪntɪŋ/ noun ★★
1 [C] a picture made using paint: *a painting by Picasso*
2 [U] the activity of using paint to make a picture or cover a surface: *After retirement he took up painting.*

paintwork /'peɪntˌwɜːk/ noun [U] *British* the painted surface of something such as a car or the inside of a building

pair¹ /peə/ noun [C] ★★★
1 a set of two things of the same type: *The vases were sold as a pair.* ♦ *a pair of shoes/socks/gloves*
2 a single unit made up of two similar parts joined together: *My glasses are getting old and I probably need a new pair.* ♦ *a pair of scissors/binoculars/pliers* ♦ *a pair of trousers/pants/tights*
3 two people who are connected or who do something together: *The pair became good friends.* ♦ *a pair of identical twins* ♦ *The students worked in pairs.*

pair² /peə/ **PHRASAL VERB** **pair (sb) up** to form a pair, or to make two people form a pair

pal /pæl/ noun [C] *informal old-fashioned* a friend

palace /'pæləs/ noun [C] a very large building that is the official home of a royal family, president, or religious leader

palatable /'pælətəb(ə)l/ adj **1** tasting good enough to eat or drink **2** acceptable

palate /'pælət/ noun [C] **1** the inside upper part of your mouth **2** the ability to taste and judge flavours

palatial /pə'leɪʃ(ə)l/ adj a palatial building is very large and impressive

pale¹ /peɪl/ adj ★★
1 light and not bright in colour: *pale blue/yellow/green* ♦ *a pale sky*
2 a pale person has skin that is lighter than usual because they are ill, shocked, or

worried: *He looked pale and weary.*

pale² /peɪl/ verb [I] to seem less important or serious: *The devastating floods of two years ago go pale in comparison with last week's storms.*

palette /ˈpælət/ noun [C] a board that an artist uses for mixing paints on

pall¹ /pɔːl/ noun [singular] something such as smoke, dust, or cloud that covers an area and makes it darker

PHRASE **cast a pall over sth** to create an unpleasant situation or mood: *His comments cast a pall over the meeting.*

pall² /pɔːl/ verb [I] if something palls, it becomes less interesting or less exciting because you have experienced it many times

pallid /ˈpælɪd/ adj very pale in a way that does not look healthy

pallor /ˈpælə/ noun [singular] the very pale colour that your skin has when you are ill or worried

palm¹ /pɑːm/ noun [C] **1** the inside part of your hand, between your fingers and your wrist —*picture* → C14 **2** a PALM TREE

palm² /pɑːm/ PHRASAL VERB ˌpalm sb/sth ˈoff *informal* to get rid of someone or something that you do not want by persuading someone else to take or buy them from you

ˈpalm ˌtree noun [C] a tropical tree without branches that has large wide leaves growing from the top of its TRUNK —*picture* → C9

palpable /ˈpælpəb(ə)l/ adj obvious, or very easily noticed

paltry /ˈpɔːltri/ adj not at all big or important

pamper /ˈpæmpə/ verb [T] to look after someone very well, especially by making them feel very comfortable

pamphlet /ˈpæmflət/ noun [C] a very thin book with a paper cover

pan¹ /pæn/ noun [C] ★
1 a round metal container with a handle that is used for cooking → DUSTPAN
2 the contents of a pan, or the amount that a pan holds: *a pan of hot water* → FLASH²

pan² /pæn/ verb **1** [I] if a camera pans, it moves sideways slowly to photograph something **2** [T] *informal* to criticize someone or something very strongly

PHRASAL VERB ˌpan ˈout *informal* if a situation pans out in a particular way, it develops in that way

panacea /ˌpænəˈsiːə/ noun [C] something that people think will solve all their problems

panache /pəˈnæʃ/ noun [U] an impressive way of doing something that shows great skill and confidence

pancake /ˈpænˌkeɪk/ noun [C] *British* a thin round flat food made by cooking a mixture of flour, eggs, and milk = CREPE

panda /ˈpændə/ noun [C] a large Chinese wild animal with black and white fur —*picture* → C12

pandemonium /ˌpændəˈməʊniəm/ noun [C/U] a very noisy and confused situation that is caused by a lot of angry or excited people = CHAOS

pander /ˈpændə/ PHRASAL VERB ˈpander to

sb/sth *showing disapproval* to do or say what someone wants in order to please them: *The president was accused of pandering to racial prejudice.*

pane /peɪn/ noun [C] a flat piece of glass in a window or door

panel /ˈpæn(ə)l/ noun [C] ★★
1 a group of people who make decisions or judgments: *an interview panel* ♦ *a panel of judges*
2 a group of well-known people who discuss subjects on television or radio programmes
3 a flat piece of wood, glass, or other material that forms part of something such as a door or wall: *a door with stained glass panels*
4 the part of a vehicle or machine that contains the switches and other instruments: *a control/instrument panel*

paneling /ˈpæn(ə)lɪŋ/ the American spelling of **panelling**

panelist /ˈpæn(ə)lɪst/ the American spelling of **panellist**

panelling /ˈpæn(ə)lɪŋ/ noun [U] pieces of wood that cover the walls of a room for decoration

panellist /ˈpæn(ə)lɪst/ noun [C] a member of a PANEL of people who discuss things on television or radio

pang /pæŋ/ noun [C] a sudden unpleasant physical feeling or emotion: *a pang of guilt*

panic¹ /ˈpænɪk/ noun **1** [singular/U] a sudden strong feeling of fear or worry that makes you unable to think clearly or calmly: *Panic spread quickly through the city.* ♦ *People are fleeing the area in panic.* ♦ *She gets in a panic whenever she has to speak in public.* **2** [C/U] a situation in which a lot of people are hurrying to do something because they are frightened or worried: *News of the incident caused a panic.* —**panicky** /ˈpænɪki/ adj

panic² /ˈpænɪk/ (present participle **panicking**; past tense and past participle **panicked**) verb [I/T] to have a sudden strong feeling of fear or worry and be unable to think clearly or calmly, or to make someone do this

ˈpanic-ˌstricken adj feeling so afraid or worried that you cannot think clearly or calmly

panorama /ˌpænəˈrɑːmə/ noun [C] a view of a large area of land or sea —**panoramic** /ˌpænəˈræmɪk/ adj

pansy /ˈpænzi/ noun [C] a small plant with large flowers

pant /pænt/ verb [I] to breathe very loudly with your mouth open, for example when you have been running —**pant** noun [C]

panther /ˈpænθə/ noun [C] a LEOPARD with black fur

panties /ˈpæntiz/ noun [plural] a piece of women's underwear that covers the part of the body from the waist to the top of the legs = KNICKERS, PANTS

panto /ˈpæntəʊ/ noun [C/U] *British informal* a PANTOMIME for children

pantomime /ˈpæntəˌmaɪm/ noun [C/U] in the UK, a funny play for children that is based on a traditional story and is performed at Christmas

P

pantry /ˈpæntri/ noun [C] a small room for storing food =LARDER

pants¹ /pænts/ noun [plural] **1** British a piece of underwear that covers the part of the body from the waist to the top of the legs **2** American TROUSERS

pants² /pænts/ adj British informal of very low quality

papacy, the /ˈpeɪpəsi/ noun [singular] the position of being the POPE

papal /ˈpeɪp(ə)l/ adj relating to the POPE

paparazzi /ˌpæpəˈrætsi/ noun [plural] photographers who follow famous people in order to take photographs of them

papaya /pəˈpaɪə/ noun [C/U] a fruit with green and yellow skin, orange flesh, and small black seeds inside —picture → C10

paper¹ /ˈpeɪpə/ noun ★★★

1 for writing/wrapping	**5** academic writing/talk
2 newspaper	**6** writing by student
3 documents	+ PHRASE
4 examination	

1 [U] the thin flat substance that you use for writing on or wrapping things in: *a parcel wrapped in brown paper* ♦ *Stuart handed me* ***a piece of paper*** *with an address written on it.*

2 [C] a newspaper: *Is that today's paper?* ♦ *He sat down and* ***read the paper****.* ♦ *The story was* ***in all the papers***.

3 **papers** [plural] official documents such as your passport, or documents relating to work, study, or personal matters: *We had to show our papers at the security desk.* ♦ *Some important papers are missing from the files.*

4 [C] British a document containing a set of examination questions, or the answers that a student has written to them: *I had a maths paper in the afternoon.* ♦ *Please hand your papers in now.*

5 [C] a piece of writing or talk by an expert on an academic subject: *He has published many* ***papers on*** *the subject.*

6 [C] a piece of writing done by a student as part of a course: *I have to write* ***a paper on*** *the Cuban Revolution.*

PHRASE **on paper 1** in writing: *We need to have something on paper that people can take away with them.* **2** used for saying that something appears to be true but may not in fact be true: *On paper they are the best team in the Premier League.*

paper² /ˈpeɪpə/ adj made of paper

paper³ /ˈpeɪpə/ verb [T] to cover the walls of a room with WALLPAPER

paperback /ˈpeɪpəˌbæk/ noun [C] a book with a cover made of thick paper → HARDBACK

paper boy noun [C] a boy who earns money by delivering newspapers to people's homes

paperclip /ˈpeɪpəˌklɪp/ noun [C] a small piece of bent wire that is used for holding pieces of paper together —picture → C3

paper girl noun [C] a girl who earns money by delivering newspapers to people's homes

paperweight /ˈpeɪpəˌweɪt/ noun [C] a small heavy object that you put on top of pieces of paper to keep them in place

paperwork /ˈpeɪpəˌwɜːk/ noun [U] **1** the part of a job that involves producing reports, keeping records, and writing letters **2** the documents that you need for a particular activity or occasion

paprika /ˈpæprɪkə, pəˈpriːkə/ noun [U] a red powder that is used in cooking for adding a slightly hot flavour to food

par /pɑː/ noun [U] **1** the usual or expected standard: *His performance was well below par* (=not as good as usual). **2** in golf, the number of times that a player is expected to hit the ball to get it into the hole, or into all of the holes

PHRASES **on a par with** of the same quality as, or at the same level as someone or something

par for the course informal usual or expected in a particular situation: *For a footballer, that kind of injury is par for the course.*

par. or **para.** abbrev paragraph

parable /ˈpærəb(ə)l/ noun [C] a simple story with a moral or religious purpose, especially one told by Jesus Christ in the Bible

paracetamol /ˌpærəˈsiːtəmɒl, ˌpærəˈsetəmɒl/ noun [C/U] a common type of PAINKILLER (=drug for curing minor pains)

parachute¹ /ˈpærəˌʃuːt/ noun [C] a large piece of cloth joined to heavy strings that is used by someone jumping out of a plane

parachute² /ˈpærəˌʃuːt/ verb [I] to jump from a plane wearing a parachute

parade¹ /pəˈreɪd/ noun [C] **1** a public celebration in which a large group of people moves through an area, often with decorated vehicles and bands playing music **2** a public ceremony in which a large group of soldiers marches together

parade² /pəˈreɪd/ verb **1** [I] to walk as part of an organized group in order to celebrate or publicly protest about something **2** [I] showing disapproval to walk around so that people will look at you and admire you **3** [T] to publicly show something that you are proud of

paradigm /ˈpærəˌdaɪm/ noun [C] formal **1** a typical example or model of something **2** a set of ideas that are used for understanding or explaining something, especially in a particular subject

paradise /ˈpærədaɪs/ noun **1** [C/U] a perfect place or situation **2** Paradise Heaven, the place where some people believe that you go when you die if you have lived a good life

paradox /ˈpærəˌdɒks/ noun [C] a situation or idea that is strange because it has features or qualities that you would not expect to exist together: *the paradox of people with the best qualifications not being able to get jobs*

paradoxical /ˌpærəˈdɒksɪk(ə)l/ adj strange because of being the opposite of what you expect —**paradoxically** /ˌpærəˈdɒksɪkli/ adv

paraffin /ˈpærəfɪn/ noun [U] British a clear oil with a strong smell that is used for fuel

paragon /ˈpærəɡən/ noun [C] formal someone who is perfect, or who is the best possible example of a particular quality

paragraph /ˈpærəɡrɑːf, ˈpærəɡræf/ noun [C]
★★★ a section of a piece of writing that
begins on a new line and contains one or
more sentences

parallel¹ /ˈpærəlel/ adj **1** lines that are
parallel are the same distance apart at
every point along their length: *He leaned
forward so that his body was almost parallel
to the ground.* ♦ *The river flows parallel with
the high street.* —picture ➔ C8 **2** happening at
the same time or in the same way but
separately: *Taxes are going up in the US,
and in a parallel development, Germany is
also raising taxes.*

parallel² /ˈpærəlel/ noun [C] **1** a way in which
separate things or people are similar to
each other: *There are some interesting
parallels between the two wars.* ♦ *Some
writers have drawn parallels between
computers and the human brain* (=shown
how they are similar). **2** someone or
something that is similar to another person
or thing: *The proposed reforms have
parallels in several other countries.* ♦ *Woods
is a golfer without parallel* (=no one is
better).
PHRASE **in parallel** connected and
happening at the same time: *Advertising has
developed in parallel with modern industry
and the mass media.*

parallel³ /ˈpærəlel/ verb [T] to be similar or
equal to something

parallelogram /ˌpærəˈleləɡræm/ noun [C] a
shape with four straight sides in which
opposite sides are of equal length and are
parallel to each other —picture ➔ C8

paralyse /ˈpærəlaɪz/ verb [T] **1** to make
someone lose the ability to move their body
or a part of it **2** to make something unable
to operate normally

paralysed /ˈpærəlaɪzd/ adj **1** unable to move
your body or part of it because of an injury
or illness **2** temporarily unable to move or
think clearly **3** completely unable to operate
normally

paralysis /pəˈræləsɪs/ noun [U] **1** the loss of the
ability to move your body or a part of it
2 the state of being completely unable to
operate normally

paralyze /ˈpærəlaɪz/ the American spelling of
paralyse

paramedic /ˌpærəˈmedɪk/ noun [C] someone
who is not a doctor but is trained to give
medical treatment to people at the place
where an accident has happened

parameter /pəˈræmɪtə/ noun [C] a limit that
affects how something can be done

paramilitary /ˌpærəˈmɪlɪt(ə)ri/ adj organized
and operating like an army, but not part of
an official army —**paramilitary** noun [C]

paramount /ˈpærəmaʊnt/ adj more
important than all other things

paranoia /ˌpærəˈnɔɪə/ noun [U] **1** the worried
feeling that other people do not like you and
are trying to harm you, although you have
no proof of this **2** *medical* a mental illness
that makes people believe that other people
do not like them and want to harm them

paranoid /ˈpærənɔɪd/ adj **1** worrying that
people do not like you and are trying to
harm you, although you have no proof of

this **2** *medical* suffering from the mental
illness PARANOIA

paranormal, the /ˌpærəˈnɔːm(ə)l/ noun
[singular] mysterious events or facts that
cannot be explained by science

paraphernalia /ˌpærəfəˈneɪliə/ noun [U] a set
of objects that are used for a particular
activity

paraphrase /ˈpærəfreɪz/ verb [T] to express
what someone else has said or written
using different words in order to make it
shorter or clearer —**paraphrase** noun [C]

paraplegic /ˌpærəˈpliːdʒɪk/ noun [C] someone
who cannot move the parts of their body
below their waist —**paraplegic** adj

parasite /ˈpærəsaɪt/ noun [C] **1** a plant or
animal that lives in or on another type of
animal and feeds on it **2** a lazy person who
lives by getting things such as money or
food from other people —**parasitic**
/ˌpærəˈsɪtɪk/ adj

parasol /ˈpærəsɒl/ noun [C] a type of
UMBRELLA that provides protection from
the sun

paratrooper /ˈpærəˌtruːpə/ noun [C] a soldier
who is trained to jump out of planes
wearing a PARACHUTE

paratroops /ˈpærəˌtruːps/ noun [plural]
soldiers who are paratroopers

parcel /ˈpɑːs(ə)l/ noun [C] something wrapped
in paper or in a large envelope so that it
can be sent by post=PACKAGE ➔ PART¹

parched /pɑːtʃt/ adj **1** extremely dry because
of hot weather **2** *informal* very thirsty

pardon¹ /ˈpɑːd(ə)n/ interjection **1** used for
politely asking someone to repeat
something that you did not hear or did not
understand **2** used for saying 'sorry' when
you make a rude noise with your body

pardon² /ˈpɑːd(ə)n/ verb [T] to officially
forgive someone for committing a crime
and free them from prison
PHRASE **pardon me** used for saying 'sorry'
when you do something rude, for example
when you interrupt someone or make a
rude noise with your body

pardon³ /ˈpɑːd(ə)n/ noun [C] an official
decision to forgive someone for committing
a crime and to free them from prison ➔ BEG

pare /peə/ verb [T] to reduce the total number
or amount of something

parent /ˈpeərənt/ noun [C] ★★★ your mother
or father: *Has Joe met your parents yet?*

parentage /ˈpeərəntɪdʒ/ noun [U] your
parents considered as belonging to a
particular country, religion, or social class:
*He is of mixed Italian and English
parentage.*

parental /pəˈrent(ə)l/ adj involving or
provided by parents

parent company noun [C] *business* a company
that owns or controls a smaller company
of the same type ➔ SUBSIDIARY

parentheses /pəˈrenθəsiːz/ noun [plural] the
symbols (and), used in writing for
separating a word, phrase, or number from
the rest of a sentence: *The students'
nationalities are shown in parentheses.*

parenthood /ˈpeərənthʊd/ noun [U] the fact
of being a parent

P

parenting /ˈpeərəntɪŋ/ noun [U] the activities that are involved in being a parent and bringing up children

parish /ˈpærɪʃ/ noun **1** [C] in some Christian churches, a district that has its own church building and priest **2** [singular] the people who live in a parish

parishioner /pəˈrɪʃ(ə)nə/ noun [C] someone who lives in a particular parish and regularly goes to church

parity /ˈpærəti/ noun [U] a situation in which different people or things are equal

park¹ /pɑːk/ noun [C] ★★
1 an open public area with grass and trees in a town. Parks often have sports fields or places for children to play.
2 an area in the countryside that is protected by the government for people to enjoy. Parks often have important natural features such as lakes or mountains: *Yellowstone National Park*

park² /pɑːk/ verb [I/T] ★ to move a vehicle into a place where you are going to leave it for a period of time: *Mary **parked** the car at the side of the road.*

parka /ˈpɑːkə/ noun [C] a long warm jacket with a HOOD (=a part to cover your head) —*picture* → C4

parking /ˈpɑːkɪŋ/ noun [U] **1** the process of putting a vehicle into a place and leaving it there **2** space where vehicles can be left

parking lot noun [C] *American* a CAR PARK

parking meter noun [C] a machine in the street that you put coins into in order to pay for leaving your car there

parking ticket noun [C] an official document that is put on your car telling you that you have broken a rule about parking and must pay a FINE

Parkinson's disease /ˈpɑːkɪnsənz dɪˌziːz/ noun [U] a serious illness that affects your nerves and makes you shake and move slowly

parliament /ˈpɑːləmənt/ noun ★★★
1 [C] an official elected group of people in some countries who meet to make the laws of the country and discuss national issues: *the Russian parliament*
2 Parliament [U] the main law-making institution in some countries such as the UK: *The party has a large majority in Parliament.* ♦ *He entered Parliament in 1997.* → MEMBER OF PARLIAMENT
3 [C/U] the period of time during which a particular parliament meets: *The bill would be discussed in the next parliament.*

parliamentary /ˌpɑːləˈment(ə)ri/ adj relating to a parliament, or suitable for a parliament

Parmesan /ˈpɑːmɪzæn/ or **Parmesan cheese** noun [U] a hard Italian cheese with a strong flavour, often used on pasta

parochial /pəˈrəʊkiəl/ adj *showing disapproval* not interested in things that do not affect your own local area

parody¹ /ˈpærədi/ noun [C/U] a literary or musical work that copies a serious work in a humorous way

parody² /ˈpærədi/ verb [T] to copy someone or something in a way that makes people laugh

parole¹ /pəˈrəʊl/ noun [U] permission for a prisoner to leave prison before the official time, if they promise to obey particular rules: *He could be out on parole in two years.*

parole² /pəˈrəʊl/ verb [T] to give a prisoner parole

parrot /ˈpærət/ noun [C] a brightly coloured tropical bird that is often kept as a pet and can be taught to copy what people say

parrot-fashion adv *British* copying or repeating what someone says without thinking about it or understanding it properly

parsley /ˈpɑːsli/ noun [U] a small plant that you use for decorating food or giving it a fresh flavour

parsnip /ˈpɑːsnɪp/ noun [C/U] a long white hard vegetable that grows under the ground —*picture* → C11

part¹ /pɑːt/ noun ★★★

1 piece/section/aspect	**5** piece for machine
2 person played by actor	**6** relative quantity
3 being involved in sth	**7** place/area
4 section of book/play	**+** PHRASES

1 [C] one of the pieces, sections, or aspects that something consists of: *The top **part** of the shoe is made of leather.* ♦ *We walked **part** of the way, then took a bus.* ♦ *The hardest **part** of my job is controlling the budgets.* ♦ *This is one of the nicest **parts** of San Francisco.*
2 [C] the person played by an actor in a film, play, or television programme, or the words that the actor speaks: *She'd be really good for that part.* ♦ *He had just two weeks to learn his part.*
3 [singular] the way in which someone is involved in an activity or event, and the effect that they have on what happens: *He was jailed for 10 years for **his part in** the crime.*
4 [C] a section of a book, magazine, play, television series etc: *a new 12-part drama starting tonight on ITV*
5 [C] an individual piece of a machine or vehicle: *We're waiting for a part to come from Germany.*
6 [C] a particular quantity that is used for measuring equal amounts of different substances to form a mixture: *Use a mixture of one part milk to four parts water.*
7 parts [plural] *old-fashioned* a place or area: *This is the worst summer we've had in **these parts** for years.*

PHRASES be part and parcel of sth to be an aspect of something that has to be accepted: *These little arguments were part and parcel of their relationship.*
the best/better part of sth almost all of something: *The journey will take him the best part of a year.*
for the most part in most cases, or generally: *There were a few complaints, but for the most part people seemed to enjoy themselves.*
have/play a part (in sth) to be involved in a particular situation or activity and influence its development: *They have worked very hard, but luck has played a part too.*
in part to some degree: *The accidents were due in part to the bad weather.*

look/dress the part to have an appearance or wear clothing that is usual or expected for a particular situation, activity, or job

on sb's part or **on the part of sb** done or experienced by someone: *a mistake on the part of the authorities*

part of me used for saying that you are not completely sure about what you think or feel about something: *Part of me still wants to believe you.*

part of speech *linguistics* one of the main GRAMMATICAL groups that a particular word belongs to, for example noun, verb, adjective, or adverb

take part (in sth) to be involved in an activity with other people: *They will be taking part in the discussions.*

part² /pɑːt/ verb **1** [I/T] to move apart, or to move two things or two sections of a single unit away from each other: *The crowd parted to let them through.* ♦ *Tony parted the curtains and looked out.* **2** [I] if two people part, they go away from each other: *They parted at the train station.* ♦ *The marriage failed, but they parted on good terms.* **3** [T] to make a line on your head by brushing or COMBING your hair in two different directions: *Her dark hair was parted down the middle.*

PHRASES **be parted (from sb)** to be prevented from being with someone who you want to be with: *Being parted from his family made him depressed.*

part company (with sb) 1 to go away from each other: *We parted company at York.* **2** to end a relationship

PHRASAL VERB **ˈpart with sth** to give something to someone although you would prefer to keep it

part³ /pɑːt/ adv **part..., part...** a mixture of two things: *I am part Russian, part English.*

ˌpart exˈchange noun [U] *British* a method of buying something new such as a car by giving your old one as part of the payment for the new one

partial /ˈpɑːʃ(ə)l/ adj **1** not complete: *a partial withdrawal from enemy territory* **2** supporting one person, group, or opinion more than others, instead of being fair to everyone ≠ IMPARTIAL

PHRASE **be partial to** to like someone or something: *I'm very partial to bacon and eggs.*

partially /ˈpɑːʃəli/ adv not completely =PARTLY: *A partially clothed body was discovered in the woods.*

participant /pɑːˈtɪsɪpənt/ noun [C] someone who takes part in something

participate /pɑːˈtɪsɪˌpeɪt/ verb [I] to take part in something: *The rebels have agreed to participate in the peace talks.* —**participation** /pɑːˌtɪsɪˈpeɪʃ(ə)n/ noun [U]

participle /pɑːˈtɪsɪp(ə)l, ˈpɑːtɪsɪp(ə)l/ noun [C] *linguistics* the form of a verb used in COMPOUND tenses and as an adjective. English uses the **present participle**, which ends in '-ing', and the **past participle**, which usually ends in '-ed'.

particle /ˈpɑːtɪk(ə)l/ noun [C] **1** an extremely small piece or amount of something **2** *linguistics* an adverb or preposition used

with a verb to form a PHRASAL VERB. For example in the sentence 'He quickly put on his clothes', 'on' is a particle.

particular¹ /pəˈtɪkjʊlə/ adj ★★★
1 used for emphasizing that you are talking about one specific person or thing and not anyone or anything else=SPECIFIC: *Are there any particular topics that you would like me to explain further?*
2 especially great=SPECIAL: *Two matters need to be given particular attention.*
3 someone who is particular has very clear ideas about what they like and dislike, and is difficult to please: *She's very particular about what she eats.*
4 clearly different and belonging to just one person or thing=DISTINCTIVE

particular² /pəˈtɪkjʊlə/ noun
PHRASE **in particular 1** especially: *I liked the last candidate in particular.* **2** special, or important: *'What are you doing tonight?' 'Nothing in particular.'*
→ PARTICULARS

particularly /pəˈtɪkjʊləli/ adv ★★★
1 very, or very much: *His remarks were particularly helpful.* ♦ *'Did you have a good time?' 'Not particularly.'*
2 especially: *The environment has become a major political issue, particularly in the past decade.*
3 in a clear and specific way: *He particularly asked for you to be at the meeting.*

particulars /pəˈtɪkjʊləz/ noun [plural] information and details about someone or something

parting¹ /ˈpɑːtɪŋ/ adj done or said by someone when they are leaving: *a parting gift/comment*

parting² /ˈpɑːtɪŋ/ noun **1** [C/U] the act of leaving someone **2** [C] *British* a line on your head that you make by brushing or COMBING your hair in two different directions
PHRASE **a parting of the ways** a point at which two people or groups decide to separate or stop working together

ˌparting ˈshot noun [C] an unpleasant or angry remark made at the end of a conversation by someone when they are leaving

partisan¹ /ˌpɑːtɪˈzæn/ adj showing strong and usually unfair support for one particular person, group, or idea

partisan² /ˈpɑːtɪzən/ noun [C] **1** someone who gives strong support to a particular person, group, or idea **2** a member of a group that continues to fight secretly against an enemy who has taken control of its country

partition /pɑːˈtɪʃ(ə)n/ noun **1** [C] a wall, screen, or piece of glass that is used for separating one area from another in a room **2** [U] the process of dividing a country into two or more separate countries —**partition** verb [T]

partly /ˈpɑːtli/ adv ★★ to some degree, but not completely: *I'll admit I was partly to blame.* ♦ *We get on well together, partly because we share the same sense of humour.*

partner¹ /ˈpɑːtnə/ noun [C] ★★★
1 someone who you live with and have a sexual relationship with: *Are partners invited to the office party?*
2 someone who you do a particular activity with: *John is my tennis partner.* ♦ *Take your partners for the last dance.*

P

3 one of two or more people who own a company and share its profits and losses: *He became **a partner in** his father's law firm.*

4 a business, organization, or country that has an agreement with another business, organization, or country: *China is one of our major trading partners.*

> ### Words that avoid giving offence: partner
>
> In British English, you can use **partner** to refer to the husband or wife of someone, or to refer to a person who lives with someone and has a sexual relationship with them, but is not married to them. In American English, some people use **partner** only about unmarried people, and many people use **partner** only about gay people.

partner² /ˈpɑːtnə/ verb [T] to be someone's partner in an activity

partnership /ˈpɑːtnəʃɪp/ noun **1** [U] the position of being one of two or more people who own a company as partners **2** [C] a company that is owned by two or more partners **3** [C/U] a relationship between two or more people, groups, or countries that are involved in an activity together

part-time adj **1** done for only part of the time that an activity is usually performed: *a part-time job* **2** doing part-time work or study: *a part-time student* —**part-time** adv
→ FULL-TIME

party¹ /ˈpɑːti/ noun [C] ★★★

1 a social event at which people meet in order to celebrate something or have fun: *Did you invite her to your birthday party?* ♦ *We're **having a party** on Saturday night.*

2 an organized group of people who share the same ideas about how a country should be governed, and who try to get elected: *the two main political parties*

3 a group of people who are going somewhere together, or who are involved in the same activity: *a rescue party* ♦ *a party of tourists*

4 *formal* a person or group involved in a contract or legal case with another person or group: *the guilty/innocent party* (=the person responsible/not responsible for something wrong or illegal) ♦ *the parties to the 1930 agreement*

party² /ˈpɑːti/ verb [I] *informal* to have fun eating and drinking, dancing etc with other people

pass¹ /pɑːs/ verb ★★★

1 go past sth	**10** kick/hit ball to sb
2 move somewhere	**11** go above amount
3 be successful in test	**12** happen
4 accept in test	**13** give opinion
5 let sb have sth	**14** of body waste
6 make law etc official	**15** change owner
7 be spent	✦ PHRASE
8 spend time	✦ PHRASAL VERBS
9 stop happening	

1 [I/T] to go past something: *The procession slowly passed us.* ♦ *They stopped at the crossing, waiting for the train to pass.*

2 [I/T] to move, or to move something, in a particular direction or to a particular place or position: *The railway line **passes through***

Darlington, Newcastle, and Berwick. ♦ *Two large birds **passed over** our heads.* ♦ **pass sth across** sth *He passed his hand across his forehead.*

3 [I/T] to be successful in an examination or test, by achieving a satisfactory standard ≠ FAIL: *Do you think you'll pass?* ♦ *She passed her driving **test**.*

4 [T] to officially decide that someone has been successful in an examination or test ≠ FAIL: *The examiners passed only 40% of the candidates.*

5 [T] to put something into someone's hand or into a position where they can take it: *Pass the salt, please.* ♦ **pass sb sth** *Could you pass me that newspaper?* ♦ **pass sth to sb** *He passed the camera to her.*

6 [T] to make a law or proposal become official by voting to accept it: *one of the worst **laws** ever **passed***

7 [I] if time passes, it happens and comes to an end: *The summer holidays passed quickly, as usual.*

8 [T] to spend time doing something: *We passed the day swimming and lying in the sun.* ♦ *They watched videos to **pass the time** (=make it seem shorter).*

9 [I] to come to an end: *I felt a sharp pain, but it soon passed.*

10 [I/T] to kick, hit, or throw the ball to another player in a sports team: **pass sth to sb** *He **passed the ball** to Scholes who shot wide of the goal.*

11 [T] to become more than a particular amount: *The death toll has already passed 200.*

12 [I] to happen, or to be allowed to happen: *Her mistake seemed to have **passed unnoticed**.* ♦ *The rest of the meeting **passed without incident** (=without anything unpleasant happening).* ♦ *Andrew was furious and wasn't going to **let** this one **pass** (=not react to something annoying).*

13 [T] to make a comment or give an opinion: *He was asked for his opinion but refused to **pass comment**.*

14 [T] *formal* to make something leave your body as a waste product: *difficulty in passing water* (=making liquid waste leave the body)

15 [I] to stop being owned or controlled by one person and start being owned or controlled by another: **pass from sb to sb** *The estate has passed from father to son for generations.*

PHRASE **pass (a) sentence (on sb)** to officially say in a court of law what a criminal's punishment will be
→ BUCK

PHRASAL VERBS **,pass sth a'round** *same as* **pass sth round**

,pass sth/sb 'off *same as* **pass for sb/sth**

,pass a'way to die. This word is used to avoid saying 'die' when you think it might upset someone.

,pass 'by (sth) to go past: *Three buses passed by, but mine never came.* ♦ *I pass by her house every day on my way to school.*

,pass sb 'by if something passes you by, it happens, but you get no advantage from it: *Sometimes I feel that life is just passing me by.*

pass sth 'down to give knowledge, or to teach skills, to your children or to younger people

'pass for sb/sth to be accepted, wrongly, as being a particular type of person or thing: *He's nearly forty, but he could pass for twenty-five.*

pass sb/sth 'off as sth to make people believe that a person or thing is something else: *He put on a suit, intending to pass himself off as a businessman.*

pass 'on *same as* **pass away**

pass sth 'on 1 to give someone something that someone else has given you: *When you've read this message, please pass it on.* **2** to give someone an infectious illness

pass 'out to suddenly become unconscious =FAINT

pass sth 'round *British* to give something to one person in a group, who gives it to someone else, who then gives it to someone else etc

pass sth 'up *informal* to not take advantage of an opportunity

pass² /pɑːs/ noun [C] ★

1 an official document that gives you permission to enter a place or to use a particular form of transport without having to pay each time: *You always have to show your pass before they'll let you in.*

2 a successful result in an examination or test: *She got a pass in maths.*

3 a kick, hit, or throw of the ball to another player in your sports team: *a perfect pass from Ince to Owen*

4 a path or road that goes through an area of mountains

passable /'pɑːsəb(ə)l/ adj **1** satisfactory, but not of high quality **2** if a road or a river is passable, it is not blocked and can be travelled on ≠IMPASSABLE

passage /'pæsɪdʒ/ noun ★★

1 [C] a long narrow area with walls on each side that leads from one room or place to another: *He left his bike in the passage between the kitchen and the back door.*

2 [C] a short section of a book, article, poem, or piece of music, considered on its own =EXCERPT: *He read me a passage from his favourite book.*

3 [U] movement past, over, or through a place: *The passage of heavy guns had left deep ruts in the field.*

4 [C] a tube in your body for air or liquid to pass through: *Her air passages were blocked.*

PHRASE **the passage of time** the process by which time passes: *Her beauty had not faded with the passage of time.*

passageway /'pæsɪdʒweɪ/ noun [C] a passage from one room or place to another =PASSAGE

passé /'pɑːseɪ, 'pæseɪ/ adj no longer fashionable or relevant

passenger /'pæsɪndʒə/ noun [C] ★★ someone who travels in a vehicle, aircraft, train, or ship but is not the driver or one of the people who works on it

passerby /pɑːsə'baɪ/ (plural **passersby** /pɑːsəz'baɪ/) noun [C] someone who is walking past a place

passing¹ /'pɑːsɪŋ/ adj **1** moving past: *He was found by a passing motorist.* **2** lasting only a short time, and usually not very important or serious: *a passing craze/fashion*

passing² /'pɑːsɪŋ/ noun [U] the process by which time passes: *Even with the passing of time, nothing had happened to change his view.*

PHRASE **in passing** if you say something in passing, you mention it while you are talking about something else

passion /'pæʃ(ə)n/ noun ★

1 [C/U] a powerful emotion such as love or anger: *She spoke with great passion about the plight of the refugees.*

2 [C/U] a very strong feeling of sexual love: *I was suddenly seized by an overwhelming passion for him.*

3 [C] a strong enthusiasm or interest: *a passion for classical music*

passionate /'pæʃ(ə)nət/ adj **1** showing or expressing powerful emotions or very strong beliefs **2** involving or affected by very strong feelings of sexual excitement

—**passionately** adv

passive /'pæsɪv/ adj ★★

1 accepting what happens without trying to change events or react to things: *a helpless and passive victim*

2 *linguistics* in a passive sentence, the subject is the person or thing that is affected by the action of the verb. 'He was examined by another doctor' is a passive sentence.

→ ACTIVE 3

—**passively** adv

passive, the /'pæsɪv/ or **passive 'voice, the** noun [singular] *linguistics* the passive form of a verb

passive 'smoking noun [U] the act of breathing other people's tobacco smoke into your lungs

Passover /'pɑːsəʊvə/ noun [C/U] a Jewish religious festival that lasts for seven or eight days in March or April

passport /'pɑːspɔːt/ noun [C] ★

1 an official document that contains your photograph and shows which country you are a citizen of: *Bill has a Canadian passport.* ♦ *You must hold a valid passport.*

2 a passport to sth something that makes it possible for you to achieve something good: *In those days a university degree was a passport to a secure job.*

passport con'trol noun [U] an area in an airport where your passport is checked

password /'pɑːswɜːd/ noun [C] **1** a secret word or phrase that you need in order to get into a room, building, or area **2** *computing* a set of numbers or letters that you have to type in order to use a computer system

past¹ /pɑːst/ adv, preposition ★★★

1 after a particular time later than a particular time: *It was past midnight by the time we arrived.*

2 passing sb/sth moving near someone or something and then beyond them: *I walked past several hotels on my way to the petrol station.* ♦ *She heard music coming from inside the van as it drove past.*

3 further away than a place further than a particular place along a road, path, river etc: *Turn right a mile past the graveyard and you'll see the church.*

P

4 after a particular stage used for saying that someone or something has passed a particular stage or point: *I tried to read the book, but couldn't get past the first chapter.* ♦ *He was past his prime as a player by then.*
5 when time passes used for saying that a period of time passes: *The months went past, and still no word from her.*
6 used for saying the time used for saying what time it is when it is not more than thirty minutes after one, two etc o'clock: *I'll meet you at half past five.* ♦ *It's exactly ten past three* (=3.10).

PHRASE **past it** *British informal* no longer able to do what you used to do because you are too old

→ PUT

past² /pɑːst/ noun ★★★
1 the past [singular] the time before the present, and everything that happened then: *Archaeology helps us to understand the past.* ♦ *He has made similar promises* **in the past.**
2 [C] all the things that someone has done before now: *My past as a player has helped me in my career as a coach.*
3 the past [singular] *linguistics* the form of a verb that is used for describing states that existed or things that happened before the present time

past³ /pɑːst/ adj ★★★
1 happening or existing in the period immediately before now: *He has spent the past two weeks travelling around the country.*
2 happening or existing at any earlier time: *He is a past president of the Union.* ♦ *I know from* **past experience** *that this work is very time-consuming.*
3 ended, or no longer existing: *My running days are long past.*

pasta /ˈpæstə/ noun [C/U] an Italian food made in many different shapes from flour and water, and sometimes eggs

paste¹ /peɪst/ noun [U] **1** a glue that is used for making something stick to a surface **2** a food that is made by crushing meat, fish, or vegetables. It is spread on bread or added to other food in cooking.

paste² /peɪst/ verb [I/T] **1** to glue paper onto a surface using paste **2** *computing* to copy or move words, pictures etc on a computer screen from one place to another

pastel /ˈpæst(ə)l/ adj pale and not strong in colour —**pastel** noun [C]

pasteurized /ˈpɑːstʃəˌraɪzd/ adj a pasteurized liquid such as milk has been heated to a temperature that kills all the harmful bacteria —**pasteurization** /ˌpɑːstʃəraɪˈzeɪʃ(ə)n/ noun [U]

pastime /ˈpɑːsˌtaɪm/ noun [C] something that you do regularly for fun in your free time

pastor /ˈpɑːstə/ noun [C] a priest in some Christian churches

pastoral /ˈpɑːst(ə)rəl/ adj **1** pastoral work or activities involve giving help and advice to people about personal problems **2** *literary* relating to life in the countryside

past participle noun [C] *linguistics* the form of a verb that is used for making perfect tenses and passive forms of verbs. Past participles are also sometimes used as

adjectives, for example 'cooked' in the phrase 'cooked vegetables'.

past perfect, the noun [singular] *linguistics* a verb tense that is formed in English with 'had' and a past participle. It is used to express an action that was completed before a particular time in the past, for example 'had finished' in the sentence 'She offered to help but I had already finished'.

pastry /ˈpeɪstri/ noun **1** [U] a food made by mixing flour, fat, and water. The mixture is rolled flat and used for making PIES and other food. **2** [C] a type of cake made from sweet pastry

past tense, the noun [singular] *linguistics* the form of a verb that is used for expressing what existed or happened in the past, for example 'lived' in the sentence 'We lived in France until I was seven'.

pasture /ˈpɑːstʃə/ noun [C/U] land covered with grass where sheep or cows are kept

pasty /ˈpeɪsti/ adj looking pale and not very healthy

pat¹ /pæt/ verb [T] to touch a person or animal gently several times with a flat hand in a friendly way

pat² /pæt/ noun [C] the action of gently touching a person or animal several times with a flat hand in a friendly way
PHRASE **a pat on the back** *informal* praise for having done something good

pat³ /pæt/ adj pat answers or explanations sound as though they have been used many times before and are not sincere

patch¹ /pætʃ/ noun [C]

1 different part of sth	4 cover for eye
2 piece of ground	5 piece of software
3 piece of cloth	**+ PHRASES**

1 an area that is different from what surrounds it: *There were damp patches on the ceiling.* **2** a piece of ground, especially one where you grow fruit or vegetables, or where a particular plant grows: *a patch of grass* **3** a piece of cloth that you sew over a hole in clothes, or over a part where holes might form **4** a cover that you wear over an injured eye **5** *computing* a piece of software that you add to a computer program in order to improve it or remove a fault
PHRASES **a bad/rough patch** a time when your life is difficult or unpleasant
not a patch on sth *British informal* much less good than something

patch² /pætʃ/ verb [T] to cover a hole in clothes by sewing a patch over it
PHRASAL VERB **patch sth 'up 1** to become friendly with someone again after a disagreement **2** to repair something quickly and not very well

patchwork /ˈpætʃˌwɜːk/ noun **1** [singular] something that consists of many different parts **2** [U] the art of sewing pieces of cloth of different colours together to make a pattern or picture

patchy /ˈpætʃi/ adj **1** happening or existing in some places but not in other places: *patchy rain* **2** not detailed enough or complete enough to be useful: *a patchy knowledge of Spanish history* **3** if someone's performance or work is patchy, it is good sometimes but not always

P

pâté /'pæteɪ/ noun [C/U] a soft food made from meat, fish, or vegetables that you spread on bread

patent¹ /'peɪt(ə)nt, 'pæt(ə)nt/ noun [C] an official document that gives someone who has invented something the legal right to make or sell that thing for a particular period of time, and prevents anyone else from doing so

patent² /'peɪt(ə)nt, 'pæt(ə)nt/ verb [T] to get a patent for something

patent³ /'peɪt(ə)nt/ adj extremely obvious —**patently** /'peɪt(ə)ntli/ adv

patent leather noun [U] very shiny leather, used for making bags and shoes

paternal /pə'tɜːn(ə)l/ adj **1** relating to being a father **2** a paternal relative is related to you through your father **3** typical of a kind and caring father —**paternally** adv

paternity /pə'tɜːnəti/ noun [U] legal the fact of being the father of a child

paternity leave noun [U] a period of time when a father is allowed to be away from work after the birth of his child

path /pɑːθ/ noun [C] ★★★
1 a way from one place to another that people can walk along: Amy walked up the path to the house. → ROAD —picture → C1
2 a way from one place to another passing through a lot of people or objects: Police tried to **clear a path through** the rush hour traffic.
3 the direction that someone or something is moving in: She ran into the path of an oncoming car.
4 the way that someone takes to achieve something, or the way that their life develops: Our lives began to follow separate paths.
PHRASE **our/your/their paths cross** if two people's paths cross, they meet each other by chance

pathetic /pə'θetɪk/ adj **1** useless or not effective in an annoying way **2** if someone or something looks or sounds pathetic, you feel sympathy for them=PITIFUL —**pathetically** /pə'θetɪkli/ adv

pathological /ˌpæθə'lɒdʒɪk(ə)l/ adj
1 pathological behaviour or feelings are not based on ordinary practical reasons, and cannot be controlled by the person experiencing them **2** relating to pathology —**pathologically** /ˌpæθə'lɒdʒɪkli/ adv

pathologist /pə'θɒlədʒɪst/ noun [C] a scientist who studies the causes of diseases and how they affect people, especially one who studies the causes of a person's death

pathology /pə'θɒlədʒi/ noun [U] the study of the causes of diseases and how they affect people

pathos /'peɪθɒs/ noun [U] a quality in a person or situation that makes you feel sad or sorry for them

pathway /'pɑːθ,weɪ/ noun [C] a PATH that you can walk on

patience /'peɪʃ(ə)ns/ noun [U] ★
1 the ability to continue doing something for a long time without losing interest: Photography **requires** a lot of **patience**.
2 the ability to remain calm and not get angry, especially when something is

annoying or takes too long: I'm afraid I've no patience with people like them. ♦ After waiting for an hour, I was beginning to **run out of patience** (=stop having any). ♦ She was quickly **losing patience with** the whole wretched situation.
3 British a card game for one person in which you have to place the cards in a particular order

patient¹ /'peɪʃ(ə)nt/ noun [C] ★★★ someone who is receiving medical treatment

patient² /'peɪʃ(ə)nt/ adj ★★ someone who is patient is able to wait for a long time or deal with a difficult situation without becoming angry or upset ≠ IMPATIENT: Susan's very **patient with** the children. —**patiently** adv

patio /'pætiəʊ/ noun [C] a flat area covered with stone or brick at the back of a house, where people can sit outside

patriotic /ˌpætri'ɒtɪk, ˌpeɪtri'ɒtɪk/ adj feeling a lot of love, respect, and duty towards your country ≠ UNPATRIOTIC —**patriot** /'pætriət, 'peɪtriət/ noun [C], **patriotism** /'pætriəˌtɪz(ə)m, 'peɪtriəˌtɪz(ə)m/ noun [U]

patrol¹ /pə'trəʊl/ noun **1** [C] a group of people or vehicles that move regularly around a place in order to prevent trouble or crime **2** [C/U] the movement of a patrol around a place: Police officers will be on patrol during the carnival.

patrol² /pə'trəʊl/ (present participle **patrolling**; past tense and past participle **patrolled**) verb [I/T] to move regularly around a place in order to prevent trouble or crime

patron /'peɪtrən/ noun [C] **1** someone who supports the work of writers, artists, or musicians by giving them money **2** a famous person who supports an organization and allows it to use their name in its advertising **3** formal someone who uses a particular restaurant, hotel, or other business

patronage /'pætrənɪdʒ/ noun [U] help or money that is given by a patron

patronize /'pætrəˌnaɪz/ verb **1** [I/T] to behave or talk in a way that shows that you think that you are more intelligent or important than someone else **2** [T] formal to use a restaurant, hotel, or other business

patronizing /'pætrəˌnaɪzɪŋ/ adj behaving or speaking in a way that shows that you think that you are more intelligent or important than someone else

patron saint noun [C] a SAINT (=a dead holy person) who is believed to protect a particular place, activity, or group of people

patter /'pætə/ noun **1** [singular] a series of short quiet sounds caused by something falling onto or hitting a surface, or by someone walking or running along it **2** [singular/U] very fast continuous talk from someone who is entertaining people or trying to sell something

pattern /'pæt(ə)n/ noun [C] ★★★
1 a series of actions or events that together show how things normally happen or are done: The study examined **patterns of** behaviour in young children. ♦ The four murders all seemed to **follow** the same **pattern**.
2 a set of lines, shapes, or colours that are

P

repeated regularly: *a carpet with a pretty pattern*

3 a drawing or shape that you use when you are making something, so that you get the shape and size correct

patterned /ˈpæt(ə)nd/ adj decorated with a pattern

paunch /pɔːntʃ/ noun [C] a fat stomach that a man has

pause¹ /pɔːz/ verb ★

1 [I] to stop moving or doing something for a short time before starting again: *She paused at the door and then left.*

2 [I/T] to make a CD, video, or computer program stop for a short time by pressing a button

pause² /pɔːz/ noun **1** [C] a short time when someone stops moving or doing something before starting again **2** [U] a button that stops a CD, video, or computer game for a short time

pave /peɪv/ verb [T] to put a hard flat surface on an area of ground, using bricks, blocks of stone, CONCRETE etc

PHRASE **pave the way for sth** to create a situation that makes it possible for something important to happen

pavement /ˈpeɪvmənt/ noun [C] British ★ a path with a hard surface beside a road

pavilion /pəˈvɪliən/ noun [C] **1** British a building beside a sports field for players or club members to use **2** a building in a park or large garden for people to sit in **3** a building or tent at an exhibition or show

paving ˌstone noun [C] a flat square piece of stone or CONCRETE that is used for covering a path or area of ground

paw¹ /pɔː/ noun [C] the foot of some animals such as cats, dogs, and bears

paw² /pɔː/ verb [I/T] to touch something several times with a paw

pawn¹ /pɔːn/ noun [C] **1** a person who is used by someone who is more powerful so that they can achieve an aim **2** one of the eight least important pieces that each player has in a game of CHESS —*picture* → C16

pawn² /pɔːn/ verb [T] to give something valuable to a pawnbroker, so that you can borrow some money

pawnbroker /ˈpɔːnˌbrəʊkə/ noun [C] someone whose job is to lend money to people in exchange for a valuable object that they can sell if the person does not return the money

pay¹ /peɪ/ (present participle **paying**; past tense and past participle **paid** /peɪd/) verb ★★★

1 buy goods	**5** suffer for sth
2 give money for job	✦ PHRASES
3 give money owed	✦ PHRASAL VERBS
4 have good result	

1 [I/T] to give money in order to buy something: *Let me pay for dinner.* ♦ *Will you be paying by cash, cheque, or credit card?* ♦ *Can I pay in dollars?* ♦ *There's a reduction if you pay cash.* ♦ **pay sb for sth** *Can I pay you for this?*

2 [I/T] to give money to someone for a job that they do for you or as their salary: **pay sb for sth** *We still haven't paid them for the repairs to the roof.* ♦ **pay sb sth to do sth** *We had to pay them over £100 to sort it out.* ♦

Some of the workers haven't been paid for weeks. ♦ **pay to have/get sth done** *Now I'll have to pay to get the car fixed.*

3 [I/T] to give money that you owe for something: *Did you pay the gas bill?*

4 [I/T] to have a good result: *The message is simple: crime doesn't pay.* ♦ **it pays to do sth** *It pays to cover the pool to keep out falling leaves.*

5 [I] to suffer because of something that you have done: *They had made him look like a fool and now they were going to pay for it.*

PHRASES **pay attention (to)** to listen to, watch, or think about someone or something very carefully

pay sb a compliment to say something nice about someone

pay the penalty/price for sth to have to deal with the bad effects of something that you have done

pay tribute to sb to say or do something that shows that you respect and admire someone a lot

pay sb/sth a visit to visit someone or something

pay your way to pay for everything that you need or use, instead of allowing or expecting other people to pay for you

PHRASAL VERBS **ˌpay sb ˈback 1** to give someone the same amount of money that you borrowed from them **2** to do something bad to someone because they have done something bad to you: *She was determined to pay them back for the trouble they had caused.*

ˌpay sth ˈin to put money into your bank account

ˌpay ˈoff if something that you do pays off, it brings you some benefit

ˌpay sth ˈoff to give back all the money that you borrowed in order to buy something: *In another two years, we will have paid off our mortgage.*

ˌpay sth ˈout to spend or pay a lot of money

ˌpay ˈup to pay money that you owe, especially when you are unwilling to pay

pay² /peɪ/ noun [U] ★★ money that you receive for doing your job: *They were demanding higher pay.* ♦ *holiday pay* ♦ *a pay rise*

payable /ˈpeɪəb(ə)l/ adj an amount of money that is payable must be paid

PHRASE **payable to sb** a cheque that is payable to someone has that person's name written on it

paycheck /ˈpeɪtʃek/ the American spelling of **pay cheque**

ˈpay ˌcheque noun [C] a cheque from your employer for work that you have done

ˈpay ˌday noun [C/U] the day when you get your pay

payee /ˌpeɪˈiː/ noun [C] the person who you pay a cheque or money to

payment /ˈpeɪmənt/ noun ★★★

1 [C] an amount of money that you pay or receive: *The first payment is due on 31 January.*

2 [U] the process of paying money: *We require prompt payment of all bills.*

payoff /ˈpeɪˌɒf/ noun [C] the benefit that you get from doing something

payphone /ˈpeɪˌfəʊn/ noun [C] a telephone in a public place that you pay to use

payroll /ˈpeɪˌrəʊl/ noun [C] a list of all the people that a company employs and the money that each of them earns
PHRASE on the payroll employed by a particular company

PC¹ /ˌpiː ˈsiː/ noun [C] **1** personal computer: a computer that is designed to be used by one person at home or in an office **2** British police constable: a police officer of the lowest rank

PC² /ˌpiː ˈsiː/ adj POLITICALLY CORRECT

PE /ˌpiː ˈiː/ noun [U] physical education: a school subject in which you exercise and play sports

pea /piː/ noun [C] a very small round green vegetable that grows in a long narrow POD —*picture* → C11

peace /piːs/ noun [U] ★★★
1 a situation in which there is no war between countries or groups: *For many years the agreement maintained peace in Europe.* ♦ *peace talks/negotiations* ♦ *The UN Secretary General urged the two sides to* **make peace.** ♦ *The agreement brought* **peace between** *the two countries.*
2 a calm quiet situation in which you are not annoyed by noise or other people: *He just wanted to read his newspaper* **in peace.** ♦ *It's not the holiday to choose if you're looking for* **peace and quiet.**
3 a state when you are calm and have no worries: *With this type of insurance, you're buying* **peace of mind.**
PHRASE make (your) peace (with sb) to end an argument with someone and stop feeling angry towards them

peaceful /ˈpiːsf(ə)l/ adj ★
1 not involving war or violence: *talks aimed at finding a* **peaceful solution** *to the crisis*
2 calm and quiet: *The hotel is set in peaceful surroundings.*
—**peacefully** adv: *The baby was sleeping peacefully.*

peacekeeper /ˈpiːsˌkiːpə/ noun [C] a soldier in a military force that has been sent to a place in order to prevent war between groups who have been fighting there
—**peacekeeping** /ˈpiːsˌkiːpɪŋ/ noun [U]

peacetime /ˈpiːsˌtaɪm/ noun [U] the time when a country is not involved in a war ≠ WARTIME

peach /piːtʃ/ noun **1** [C/U] a fruit with a furry yellow-pink skin that is yellow inside and has a large hard seed —*picture* → C10 **2** [U] a yellow-pink colour

peacock /ˈpiːˌkɒk/ noun [C] a large brightly-coloured male bird with long blue-green tail feathers that it can spread out and up

peak¹ /piːk/ noun [C] ★
1 the time when something is at its highest or greatest level: *The traffic* **reaches its peak** *at about 8.30 in the morning.*
2 the top of a mountain: *snow-covered peaks*
3 *literary* a mountain: *one of the hardest peaks in Europe for climbers*
4 the flat curved part of a CAP that continues beyond the main part at the front above your eyes

peak

peak² /piːk/ adj **1** a peak period of time is when the largest number of people are doing or using something **2** a peak level of something is when it is highest

peak³ /piːk/ verb [I] to reach the highest amount, level, or standard before becoming lower

peal /piːl/ noun [C] **1** a sound of several bells ringing **2** a loud sound of laughter or THUNDER —**peal** verb [I/T]

peanut /ˈpiːnʌt/ noun [C] a type of nut that you can eat that grows under the ground inside a thin shell

peanut butter noun [U] a soft food made by crushing peanuts

peanuts /ˈpiːˌnʌts/ noun [U] *informal* a very small amount of money

pear /peə/ noun [C/U] a fruit that is smaller towards the stem end, is white inside, and has yellow, green, or brown skin —*picture* → C10

pearl /pɜːl/ noun [C] a small round jewel that is white and shiny. Pearls grow inside the shells of OYSTERS.

pear-shaped adj **go pear-shaped** British informal if something such as a plan goes pear-shaped, it does not have the result that you wanted

peasant /ˈpez(ə)nt/ noun [C] a poor person who works on another person's farm or on their own small farm, especially in the past

peat /piːt/ noun [U] a type of soil that consists of decaying plants. It can be used as fuel.

pebble /ˈpeb(ə)l/ noun [C] a small stone made smooth by water

pecan /ˈpiːkæn, ˈpiːkən/ noun [C] a sweet nut with a hard thin smooth shell

peck /pek/ verb **1** [I/T] when a bird pecks, or when it pecks something, it moves its beak quickly forward to hit or bite something **2** [T] to kiss someone in a quick light way: *She pecked him on the cheek.* —**peck** noun [C]

peckish /ˈpekɪʃ/ adj British informal slightly hungry

peculiar /pɪˈkjuːliə/ adj **1** strange, often in an unpleasant way: *a peculiar smell*
2 especially true or typical of a particular person, thing, or situation = PARTICULAR: *features of the environment that are peculiar to the tropics*

peculiarity /pɪˌkjuːliˈærəti/ noun [C] **1** a quality or feature that belongs to a particular person, thing, or situation **2** something strange in the way that a person or animal behaves, or in their appearance

peculiarly /pɪˈkjuːliəli/ adv **1** in a strange or unusual way: *He's been behaving very peculiarly lately.* **2** in a way that is true or

P

typical of a particular person, thing, or situation: *a peculiarly British attitude* **3** extremely: *a peculiarly difficult problem*

pedagogical /ˌpedəˈgɒdʒɪk(ə)l/ adj *formal* relating to educational methods and principles

pedal /ˈped(ə)l/ noun [C] a part of a bicycle, vehicle, or machine that you push with your foot in order to operate it —**pedal** verb [I/T]

pedantic /pɪˈdæntɪk/ adj *showing disapproval* giving too much importance to details and formal rules, especially of grammar —**pedantically** /pɪˈdæntɪkli/ adv

peddle /ˈped(ə)l/ verb [T] **1** to sell something in the street or by going from place to place in order to find customers **2** to sell illegal drugs

pedestal /ˈpedɪst(ə)l/ noun [C] a base on which something such as a STATUE stands

PHRASE **put sb on a pedestal** to admire or love someone so much that you believe that they have no faults

pedestrian¹ /pəˈdestriən/ noun [C] someone who is walking, especially in a town or city, instead of driving or riding

pedestrian² /pəˈdestriən/ adj **1** used by people who are walking **2** ordinary and boring

pe,destrian 'crossing noun [C] *British* an area where vehicles must stop for people who are walking across the street

pediatrician /ˌpiːdiəˈtrɪʃ(ə)n/ the American spelling of **paediatrician**

pediatrics /ˌpiːdiˈætrɪks/ the American spelling of **paediatrics**

pedicure /ˈpedɪkjʊə/ noun [C/U] a treatment for your feet and TOENAILS that makes them look and feel good

pedigree¹ /ˈpedɪgriː/ noun **1** [C] all the past experiences, achievements, and successes of someone or something: *an investment analyst with a remarkable pedigree* **2** [C/U] the parents, grandparents etc of an animal

pedigree² /ˈpedɪgriː/ adj a pedigree animal comes from a family whose members are all of the same type

pee¹ /piː/ verb [I] *informal* to pass liquid waste from your body

pee² /piː/ noun *informal* **1** [singular] the action of passing liquid waste from your body **2** [U] the liquid waste that you pass from your body

peek¹ /piːk/ noun [C] a quick look at something: *Emma took a quick peek inside the box.*

peek² /piːk/ verb [I] to look at something quickly

peel¹ /piːl/ verb **1** [T] to remove the skin from a fruit or vegetable —*picture* → C2 **2** [I] if something peels, small pieces of it start to fall off: *Paint was peeling off the walls.*

PHRASAL VERB ,peel sth 'off to remove a tight or wet piece of clothing

peel² /piːl/ noun [U] the skin of a fruit or vegetable

peep¹ /piːp/ verb [I] **1** to look at something quickly and secretly **2** to appear from behind or under something: *His head peeped out from under the blanket.*

peep² /piːp/ noun [C] a quick look at something

peer¹ /pɪə/ noun [C] **1** someone who is the same age or who belongs to the same social or professional group as another person **2** someone who is from a high social class in the UK and has a title such as 'Lord'

peer² /pɪə/ verb [I] to look very carefully at something because it is difficult to see

'peer ,pressure noun [U] the influence that other people of your own age or social class have on the way that you behave or dress

peeved /piːvd/ adj annoyed

peg¹ /peg/ noun [C] **1** *British* a wooden or plastic object that you use for fastening wet clothes onto a line so that they will dry **2** an object that is fixed to a wall or door and used for hanging things on **3** an object that is used for fastening things together: *The furniture is built using wooden pegs instead of nails.* **4** peg or tent peg an object that is pushed or hit into the ground to keep a tent in position

peg² /peg/ verb [T] **1** to fasten something, or to keep something in position, with pegs **2** to keep prices, salaries, or amounts at a particular level

pelican /ˈpelɪkən/ noun [C] a large bird with a bag of skin that hangs from its beak

pellet /ˈpelɪt/ noun [C] a small round piece of a substance

pelt¹ /pelt/ verb **1** [T] to throw a lot of things at someone or something: *Some of the players were pelted with cans and bottles.* **2** [I] to run somewhere very fast

pelt² /pelt/ noun [C] the skin or fur of an animal

pelvic /ˈpelvɪk/ adj relating to your pelvis

pelvis /ˈpelvɪs/ noun [C] the large circular bones that support the lower part of your back. They are connected to the bones of your legs.

pen¹ /pen/ noun [C] ★★
1 an object that you use for writing or drawing with ink: *a felt-tip pen*
2 a small area with a fence around it, used for keeping animals in

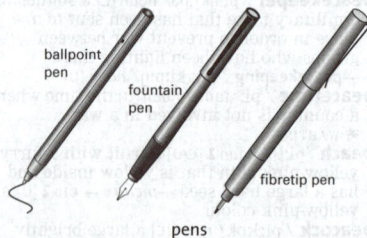

ballpoint pen

fountain pen

fibretip pen

pens

pen² /pen/ verb [T] **1** *mainly journalism* to write something **2** to shut an animal in a small area with a fence around it

penal /ˈpiːn(ə)l/ adj relating to the punishment of criminals

penalize /ˈpiːnəlaɪz/ verb [T] **1** to treat someone in an unfair way and make them have a disadvantage: *The tax system seems to penalize people who save for their old age.* **2** to punish someone for breaking a rule or law

penalty /ˈpen(ə)lti/ noun [C] ★
1 a punishment for breaking a rule or law: *the death penalty* ♦ *The maximum penalty for the offence is two years' imprisonment.*
2 a chance to score a goal in a sports match when the other team has broken a rule: *Southgate missed a penalty that would have won them the match.* ♦ *the penalty area* (=area where a penalty can be given) ♦ *the penalty spot* (=place from where a penalty is taken) —*picture* → C15

penance /ˈpenəns/ noun [C/U] punishment or suffering that you accept in order to show that you are sorry

pence /pens/ *British* a plural of **penny**

penchant /ˈpɒʃɒ̃/ noun **a penchant for sth** a feeling of liking something very much or a tendency to do something a lot

pencil¹ /ˈpens(ə)l/ noun [C] ★★ a long thin wooden object that you use for writing or drawing: *a coloured pencil*

pencil² /ˈpens(ə)l/ (present participle **pencilling**; past tense and past participle **pencilled**) verb [T] to write or draw something with a pencil
PHRASAL VERB **pencil sb/sth in** to decide or arrange something that may have to be changed later: *The meeting has been pencilled in for next Friday.*

pencil sharpener noun [C] an object with a blade inside, used for making a pencil sharper

pendant /ˈpendənt/ noun [C] a piece of jewellery that hangs from a chain around your neck

pending¹ /ˈpendɪŋ/ adj **1** waiting to be dealt with **2** likely to happen soon

pending² /ˈpendɪŋ/ preposition *formal* while you are waiting for something to be dealt with

pendulum /ˈpendjʊləm/ noun [C] a long thin bar with a weight at the lower end that swings from side to side, usually in order to keep a clock working

penetrate /ˈpenətreɪt/ verb [I/T] to get inside something, get past something, or get through something: *A piece of glass had penetrated the skin.* —**penetration** /ˌpenəˈtreɪʃ(ə)n/ noun [U]

penetrating /ˈpenətreɪtɪŋ/ adj **1** a person who gives you a penetrating look seems to know what you are thinking=PIERCING
2 intelligent and quick to solve problems or to understand things **3** a penetrating voice or sound is so high or loud that it makes you slightly uncomfortable —**penetratingly** adv

pen friend noun [C] *British* someone who you regularly write friendly letters to but have never met

penguin /ˈpeŋgwɪn/ noun [C] a black and white bird that cannot fly. Penguins live by the sea, especially around Antarctica. —*picture* → C13

penicillin /ˌpenəˈsɪlɪn/ noun [U] a drug used for treating illnesses that are caused by bacteria

peninsula /pəˈnɪnsjʊlə/ noun [C] a long piece of land that is mostly surrounded by water but that is joined at one end to a larger area of land —**peninsular** adj

penis /ˈpiːnɪs/ noun [C] the part of a man's body that he uses for having sex and for getting rid of liquid waste

penitent /ˈpenɪtənt/ adj sorry for something bad that you have done and willing to change your behaviour —**penitence** noun [U]

penitentiary /ˌpenɪˈtenʃəri/ noun [C] a prison in the US

penknife /ˈpennaɪf/ (plural **penknives** /ˈpennaɪvz/) noun [C] a small knife with one or more blades that fold into the handle

pen name noun [C] a name that a writer uses instead of their real name

penniless /ˈpenɪləs/ adj someone who is penniless has no money

penny /ˈpeni/ noun [C] **1** (plural **pence**) a small unit of money in the UK There are 100 pence in one pound. **2** (plural **pennies**) a small coin in the US or Canada that is worth one CENT
PHRASES **every penny** all of an amount of money: *The legal case cost them every penny they had.*
not a penny no money at all: *He never gave us a penny.*

pension /ˈpenʃ(ə)n/ noun [C] ★★ an amount of money that someone receives regularly when they no longer work because of their age or because they are ill

pensioner /ˈpenʃ(ə)nə/ noun [C] someone who receives a pension

pensive /ˈpensɪv/ adj someone who is pensive seems to be thinking carefully about something —**pensively** adv

pentagon /ˈpentəgən/ noun [C] a shape that has five straight sides —*picture* → C8

Pentagon, the /ˈpentəgən/ the department of defence in the US government, or the building that belongs to this department

pentathlon /penˈtæθlən/ noun [C] a sports event that consists of five different sports → DECATHLON

penthouse /ˈpenthaʊs/ noun [C] an expensive flat at the top of a tall building

pent up /ˌpent ˈʌp/ adj pent up emotions are strong feelings that you have not expressed

penultimate /pəˈnʌltɪmət/ adj *formal* just before the last in a series

people¹ /ˈpiːp(ə)l/ noun ★★★
1 [plural] the plural of **person**: *The accident left three people dead and many injured.* ♦ *People were running everywhere.* ♦ *a magazine full of gossip about famous people*
2 **the people** [plural] ordinary people who are not members of the government or the upper classes: *On this issue, government has failed to listen to the people.*
3 [C] everyone who belongs to a particular nation, religion, or race: *The Mongols were regarded as a very warlike people.*
PHRASE **of all people** used to express surprise that a particular person did something

people² /ˈpiːp(ə)l/ verb **be peopled with** to be filled with a particular type of person

pepper¹ /ˈpepə/ noun **1** [U] a black or white powder that adds a strong flavour to food **2** a green, red, or yellow vegetable with small white seeds inside it —*picture* → C11

pepper² /ˈpepə/ verb **be peppered with sth** to be full of something: *His conversation was peppered with anti-American comments.*

P

peppermint /ˈpepəˌmɪnt/ noun **1** [U] a strong fresh flavour that is obtained from a MINT plant and is used in medicines or drinks **2** [C] a sweet with a peppermint flavour

pep talk /ˈpep ˌtɔːk/ noun [C] *informal* a talk during which someone encourages you to do something better or to work harder

per /*weak* pə, *strong* pɜː/ preposition ★ used for stating the rate or cost for each unit of time, quantity, distance etc: *He is paid £10 per hour for the job.* ♦ *Ellen can type 100 words per minute.*

per annum /pər ˈænəm/ adv *formal* for each year

per capita /pə ˈkæpɪtə/ adj, adv *formal* based on calculations that show the average amount for each person affected

perceive /pəˈsiːv/ verb [T] ★
1 to understand or think about something in a particular way: **perceive sb/sth as sth** *New technology is often perceived as a threat.*
♦ **perceive sb/sth to be sth** *The organization is generally perceived to be inefficient.*
2 *formal* to notice or realize something: **+that** *He quickly perceived that there was a problem with the figures.*

per cent¹ /pəˈsent/ noun [singular] ★★★ one part of every 100. Per cent is often shown using the symbol %: *Women now represent 50 per cent of the workforce.* ♦ *He only owns 20% of the business.*

per cent² /pəˈsent/ adj, adv ★★ equal to part of a total that has been divided by 100: *Sales increased thirty per cent compared to last year.*

percentage /pəˈsentɪdʒ/ noun ★
1 [C/U] an amount that is equal to a particular part of a total that has been divided by 100: *Calculate what percentage of your income you spend on food.*
2 [C] a part of the profit from something

perceptible /pəˈseptəb(ə)l/ adj able to be noticed ≠ IMPERCEPTIBLE —**perceptibly** adv

perception /pəˈsepʃ(ə)n/ noun **1** [C/U] a particular way of understanding or thinking about something: *There is a perception among workers that management only wants to cut costs.* **2** [U] the ability to notice something by seeing, hearing, smelling etc

perceptive /pəˈseptɪv/ adj good at noticing or understanding things quickly and easily: *Children are often very perceptive about adults' moods.*

perch¹ /pɜːtʃ/ verb [I/T] **1** to sit on something that is narrow or small, or to sit on the edge of something **2** to put something high up or on the edge of something, or to be in this position

perch² /pɜːtʃ/ noun [C] an area or object that a bird uses for resting on

percolate /ˈpɜːkəˌleɪt/ verb [I] if a liquid or gas percolates through a substance, it gradually passes through it —**percolation** /ˌpɜːkəˈleɪʃ(ə)n/ noun [U]

percussion /pəˈkʌʃ(ə)n/ noun [U] musical instruments such as drums that you play by hitting them

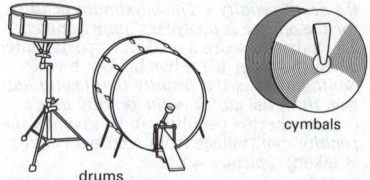

cymbals

drums

triangle

xylophone

percussion instruments

perennial¹ /pəˈreniəl/ adj **1** always existing, or never seeming to change **2** a perennial plant lasts for several years —**perennially** adv

perennial² /pəˈreniəl/ noun [C] a plant that lasts for several years

perfect¹ /ˈpɜːfɪkt/ adj ★★
1 as good, accurate, or complete as possible, with no faults=FLAWLESS: *Her English was perfect.* ♦ *These recipes give perfect results every time.*
2 completely suitable or right=IDEAL: *It seemed like the perfect gift.* ♦ *Their house is absolutely perfect for parties.*
3 used for emphasizing what you are saying: *I don't want to share a room with a perfect stranger.*
4 *linguistics* the perfect form of a verb is used for talking about an action that has been completed before the present time
→ PERFECT TENSE

perfect² /pəˈfekt/ verb [T] to make something completely free from faults, or to make it as good as it can be

perfect, the /ˈpɜːfɪkt/ noun [singular] *linguistics* the PERFECT TENSE

perfection /pəˈfekʃ(ə)n/ noun [U] a state in which someone or something is perfect

perfectionist /pəˈfekʃ(ə)nɪst/ noun [C] someone who always wants things to be done in a perfect way

perfectly /ˈpɜːfɪktli/ adv **1** in a way that could not be better **2** used for emphasizing a particular quality=COMPLETELY

perfect tense, the noun [singular] *linguistics* the form of a verb that is used for talking about an action that has been completed before the present time. It is formed in English with 'have' and a past participle.
→ FUTURE PERFECT, PAST PERFECT, PRESENT PERFECT

perforated /ˈpɜːfəˌreɪtɪd/ adj **1** with a lot of small holes in the surface **2** if an organ or tube inside your body is perforated, it has a small hole or cut in its surface —**perforation** /ˌpɜːfəˈreɪʃ(ə)n/ noun [C]

P

perform /pəˈfɔːm/ verb ★★★
1 [T] to complete an action or activity: *He's a surgeon who has performed many heart transplant operations.* ♦ *a robot that can perform routine tasks in the home*
2 [I/T] to do something in front of an audience in order to entertain them: *The opera was first performed in 1992.* ♦ *Akram went on to perform on stage in England and India.*
3 [I] to do something with a particular amount of success: *The tyres perform well in wet or snowy conditions.*

performance /pəˈfɔːməns/ noun ★★★
1 [C] the act of performing a play, dance, or other form of entertainment: *The first performance of the opera was in 1936.*
2 [C/U] the standard of success that someone or something achieves: *A healthy diet can improve a child's performance in school.* ♦ *We need to test the performance of the equipment.*
3 [C/U] *formal* the process of doing a job or action

performer /pəˈfɔːmə/ noun [C] someone who performs in front of an audience, for example an actor or a musician

performing arts, the /pərˌfɔːmɪŋ ˈɑːts/ noun [plural] types of art that are performed in front of an audience, such as plays, music, and dance

perfume /ˈpɜːfjuːm/ noun **1** [C/U] a liquid with a pleasant smell that you put on your skin **2** [C] *literary* the pleasant smell of something such as a flower or plant —**perfumed** /ˈpɜːfjuːmd/ adj

perhaps /pəˈhæps/ adv ★★★
1 used for saying that you are not certain whether something is true: *I haven't seen them for months – perhaps they've moved away.* ♦ *There were perhaps a dozen women in the audience.*
2 *spoken* used when you are making a suggestion, giving advice, or making a polite request: *You don't look well – perhaps you should go to the doctor.*

peril /ˈperəl/ noun [U] *literary* serious danger
perilous /ˈperələs/ adj *literary* very dangerous —**perilously** adj

perimeter /pəˈrɪmɪtə/ noun [C] the outer edge of an enclosed area of ground such as a field

period¹ /ˈpɪəriəd/ noun [C] ★★★
1 an amount of time: *The long dry period ended with heavy rain.* ♦ *a period of three months*
2 the time about once a month when a woman who is not pregnant MENSTRUATES (=loses blood)
3 a part of a school day when a particular subject is taught=LESSON
4 *American* a FULL STOP

period² /ˈpɪəriəd/ adj typical of a particular historical time: *period costumes/furniture*

periodic /ˌpɪəriˈɒdɪk/ adj happening regularly though not frequently —**periodically** /ˌpɪəriˈɒdɪkli/ adv

periodical /ˌpɪəriˈɒdɪk(ə)l/ noun [C] a magazine on a particular subject that is published regularly

peripheral¹ /pəˈrɪf(ə)rəl/ adj connected with something but not a necessary or important part of it=MARGINAL
peripheral² /pəˈrɪf(ə)rəl/ noun [C] *computing* a piece of equipment that you can connect to a computer, for example a printer
periphery /pəˈrɪf(ə)ri/ noun [C] the outer part of an area
perish /ˈperɪʃ/ verb [I] *literary* to die
perishable /ˈperɪʃəb(ə)l/ adj perishable food decays after a short time
perjury /ˈpɜːdʒəri/ noun [U] *legal* the crime of lying when you give evidence in a court of law
perk¹ /pɜːk/ noun [C] an extra payment or benefit that you get in your job
perk² /pɜːk/ **PHRASAL VERB** **perk (sb) up** if someone perks up, or if something perks them up, they begin to feel happier or more lively
perky /ˈpɜːki/ adj *informal* lively and happy
perm /pɜːm/ noun [C] a chemical treatment for hair that makes straight hair become curly —**perm** verb [T]
permanent /ˈpɜːmənənt/ adj ★★ happening or existing for a long time, or for all time in the future ≠ TEMPORARY: *The illness can cause permanent blindness.* ♦ *They've offered me a room until I can find something more permanent.* ♦ *I don't have a permanent job.* —**permanently** adv: *She complained of feeling permanently exhausted.* ♦ *the decision to close down the factory permanently*
permeate /ˈpɜːmieɪt/ verb [I/T] to spread gradually through every part of something
permissible /pəˈmɪsəb(ə)l/ adj *formal* if something is permissible, you are allowed to do it
permission /pəˈmɪʃ(ə)n/ noun [U] ★★ the right to do something that is given to you by someone in authority: *You are not allowed to camp here without permission.* ♦ *Children should ask their parents' permission before making phone calls.* ♦ *permission to do sth Who gave you permission to come in here?*

> ### Words often used with **permission**
> *Verbs often used with permission*
> ■ **ask, request, seek** + PERMISSION: ask someone to allow you to do something
> ■ **gain, get, obtain, receive** + PERMISSION: be allowed to do something
> ■ **give, grant** + PERMISSION: allow someone to do something
> ■ **deny, refuse** + PERMISSION: not allow someone to do something

permissive /pəˈmɪsɪv/ adj allowing people a lot of freedom to behave as they want to
permit¹ /pəˈmɪt/ verb ★★
1 [T] *formal* to allow someone to do something, or to allow something to happen: *The use of mobile phones is not permitted inside the aircraft.* ♦ **permit sb to do sth** *The new law permits gay people to serve in the armed forces.*
2 [I/T] to make something possible: *The game starts at 11 o'clock, weather permitting (=if the weather is good enough).*

permit² /'pɜːmɪt/ noun [C] an official document that gives you permission to do something

permutation /ˌpɜːmjʊˈteɪʃ(ə)n/ noun [C] one of the various ways in which you can combine or arrange a group of things

pernicious /pəˈnɪʃəs/ adj formal dangerous or harmful

perpendicular /ˌpɜːpənˈdɪkjʊlə/ adj **1** completely upright **2** forming a 90° angle with another surface or line: *Line A is perpendicular to line B.*

perpetrate /'pɜːpətreɪt/ verb [T] formal to do something that is harmful, illegal, or dishonest —**perpetrator** noun [C]

perpetual /pəˈpetʃuəl/ adj happening or continuing all the time —**perpetually** adv

perpetuate /pəˈpetʃueɪt/ verb [T] to make a situation or process continue for a long time, especially a bad or dangerous situation

perplexed /pəˈplekst/ adj confused because you cannot understand something =BEWILDERED

persecute /'pɜːsɪkjuːt/ verb [T] to treat someone very badly because of their race, religion, or political beliefs —**persecution** /ˌpɜːsɪˈkjuːʃ(ə)n/ noun [U], **persecutor** noun [C]

perseverance /ˌpɜːsɪˈvɪərəns/ noun [U] a determined attitude that makes you continue trying to achieve something that is difficult

persevere /ˌpɜːsɪˈvɪə/ verb [I] to continue trying to achieve something that is difficult

persist /pəˈsɪst/ verb [I] **1** to continue to do or say something in a determined way, especially something bad or annoying **2** formal to continue to exist: *Despite yesterday's stock market falls, optimism persists among investors.*

persistent /pəˈsɪstənt/ adj **1** continuing to do something in a determined way, especially something bad or annoying **2** continuing to exist —**persistence** noun [U], **persistently** adv

person /'pɜːs(ə)n/ noun [C] ★★★ an individual human. The plural is **people**, but in formal or official language the form **persons** is used: *Every single person in the room stopped talking.* ♦ *Some people hate camping.* ♦ *Voting is obligatory for all persons between the ages of 18 and 70.*

> PHRASES **do sth in person** to do something by going to a place yourself, rather than by writing, telephoning, or sending someone else: *You have to collect your tickets in person.*

first/second/third person linguistics the forms of pronouns and verbs that show who is being referred to. People use the **first person** (I/we) to refer to themselves, the **second person** (you) to refer to the person or people that they are talking to, and the **third person** (he/she/they) to refer to anyone else.

persona /pəˈsəʊnə/ noun [C] the part of your personality that you deliberately show to most people

personable /'pɜːs(ə)nəb(ə)l/ adj friendly, or nice

personal /'pɜːs(ə)nəl/ adj ★★★
1 involving you or belonging to you, not to anyone else: *My own personal view is that boxing should be banned.* ♦ *Most writers use **personal experience** as the basis for their novels.* ♦ *Many of Tim's **personal belongings** had been stolen.*
2 private and not known or available to most people: *This is **a personal matter** and does not concern you.* ♦ *She resigned from her job for **personal reasons**.* ♦ *My **personal life** is not your concern.*
3 aimed at one particular person, in an unfriendly or offensive way: *He saw her comments as a personal attack.*
4 done by a person directly, rather than by a representative: *The members of REM will be making a **personal appearance** at the awards ceremony.* ♦ *the president's **personal involvement** in the project*

ˌpersonal comˈputer noun [C] the usual type of computer, designed to be used by one person on his or her desk

personality /ˌpɜːsəˈnælɪti/ noun ★★
1 [C/U] the part of a person that makes them behave in a particular way in social situations: *He has a very outgoing personality and makes friends very easily.* ♦ *a personality disorder*
2 [U] confidence and lively behaviour that make people like you and consider you interesting: *Mary has lots of personality.*
3 [C] a famous or well-known person =CELEBRITY: *a TV personality*

Words often used with personality

*Adjectives often used with **personality** (sense 1)*
- **charismatic, dominant, dynamic, engaging, extrovert, forceful, outgoing, strong +** PERSONALITY: used about personalities that have a strong effect on other people

---

personalized /'pɜːs(ə)nəlaɪzd/ adj made or changed in order to be especially suitable for a particular person

personally /'pɜːs(ə)nəli/ adv ★
1 spoken used for emphasizing that you are giving your own opinion: *Personally, I think we should stick with our original plan.* ♦ *I personally prefer pizza to burgers.*
2 used for emphasizing that you are referring to a particular person, not to anyone else: *Were you personally involved in this decision?* ♦ *I have never met the man personally.*
3 in a way that is intended for you only, rather than for a group of people that you belong to: *The invitation was made to me personally, not to the committee.*

> PHRASE **take sth personally** to feel that a failure or unpleasant situation is your fault and to be upset about it

ˌpersonal ˈorganizer noun [C] a small book or simple computer that you use for keeping addresses, telephone numbers, and dates

ˌpersonal ˈpronoun noun [C] linguistics a pronoun such as 'I', 'you', 'them', or 'it' that refers to a specific person, thing, or group of people or things

,personal 'trainer noun [C] someone whose job is to show you how to exercise effectively —picture → C16

personify /pəˈsɒnɪˌfaɪ/ verb [T] to be a very clear example of a particular quality: *He personifies Russia's dynamic new business class.* —**personification** /pəˌsɒnɪfɪˈkeɪʃ(ə)n/ noun [C/U]

personnel /ˌpɜːsəˈnel/ noun **1** [plural] the people who work for a company or organization **2** [U] the department in an organization that is responsible for looking after all of the people who work there, and for choosing new workers=HUMAN RESOURCES

perspective /pəˈspektɪv/ noun ★
1 [C] a way of thinking about something: *You can call it brave or foolish, depending on your perspective.*
2 [U] a sensible way of judging something without making it seem too important: *It's important to* **keep** *things* **in perspective** *and not worry too much.* ♦ *This kind of tragedy* **puts** *a mere football match* **into perspective.*
3 [U] a method of showing distance in a picture by making far away objects smaller

perspiration /ˌpɜːspəˈreɪʃ(ə)n/ noun [U] the liquid that your skin produces when you are hot, ill, or nervous=SWEAT

perspire /pəˈspaɪə/ verb [I] to produce liquid on your skin as a result of being hot, ill, or nervous=SWEAT

persuade /pəˈsweɪd/ verb [T] ★★
1 to make someone agree to do something by giving them reasons why they should: *He did finally come with us, although it took a long time to persuade him.* ♦ **persuade sb to do sth** *Nobody could persuade her to change her mind.*
2 to make someone believe that something is true=CONVINCE: **persuade sb (that)** *I managed to persuade him that it was not his fault.* ♦ **persuade sb of sth** *There was no way she could persuade him of her innocence.*

persuasion /pəˈsweɪʒ(ə)n/ noun [U] the process of persuading someone to do or believe something

persuasive /pəˈsweɪsɪv/ adj good at making people agree to do or believe what you want them to —**persuasively** adv

pertain /pəˈteɪn/ PHRASAL VERB **per'tain to sth** *formal* to be directly related to something

pertinent /ˈpɜːtɪnənt/ adj *formal* relevant

perturbed /pəˈtɜːbd/ adj worried, or upset ≠ UNPERTURBED —**perturb** verb [T]

peruse /pəˈruːz/ verb [T] *formal* to read something —**perusal** noun [C/U]

pervade /pəˈveɪd/ verb [T] *formal* to spread through the whole of something

pervasive /pəˈveɪsɪv/ adj spreading through the whole of something: *a pervasive culture of official corruption*

perverse /pəˈvɜːs/ adj behaving in an unreasonable way, by deliberately doing what people do not expect you to do —**perversely** adv

perversion /pəˈvɜːʃ(ə)n/ noun [C/U] **1** sexual behaviour that is thought to be wrong or not normal **2** the process of changing something that is good or right into something that is bad or wrong

pervert¹ /pəˈvɜːt/ verb [T] to change something that is good or right into something that is bad or wrong

pervert² /ˈpɜːvɜːt/ noun [C] an insulting word for someone whose sexual behaviour is thought to be wrong or not normal

perverted /pəˈvɜːtɪd/ adj relating to sexual behaviour that is considered to be wrong or not normal

pessimism /ˈpesəˌmɪzəm/ noun [U] the attitude of someone who expects the worst thing to happen in every situation ≠ OPTIMISM

pessimist /ˈpesəmɪst/ noun [C] someone who expects the worst thing to happen in every situation ≠ OPTIMIST

pessimistic /ˌpesəˈmɪstɪk/ adj expecting the worst thing to happen in every situation ≠ OPTIMISTIC: *Doctors are pessimistic about his chances of making a full recovery.*

pest /pest/ noun [C] **1** *informal* someone who keeps annoying you=NUISANCE **2** an insect or small animal that damages plants or supplies of food

pester /ˈpestə/ verb [T] to keep annoying someone by asking them for something, or by asking them to do something=NAG

pesticide /ˈpestɪˌsaɪd/ noun [C] a chemical used for killing insects that damage crops

pet¹ /pet/ noun [C] ★ an animal that you keep in your home and look after: *a pet dog*

pet² /pet/ adj liked more than anything else: *Getting kids to do more sport is one of his pet projects.*

pet³ /pet/ verb **1** [T] to touch an animal in a gentle way that shows that you like them **2** [I/T] to hold and touch someone in a sexual way

petal /ˈpet(ə)l/ noun [C] one of the coloured parts around the centre of a flower

peter /ˈpiːtə/ PHRASAL VERB **,peter 'out** to gradually become smaller or weaker before ending or disappearing completely

,pet 'hate noun [C] *British* something that you dislike very much

petite /pəˈtiːt/ adj a petite woman is small and thin in an attractive way

petition¹ /pəˈtɪʃ(ə)n/ noun [C] a document that is signed by many people that asks someone in authority to do something

petition² /pəˈtɪʃ(ə)n/ verb [I/T] to ask someone in authority to do something by using a petition

petrified /ˈpetrɪˌfaɪd/ adj extremely frightened

petrol /ˈpetrəl/ noun [U] *British* ★ a liquid that is used as a fuel for cars and other vehicles

petroleum /pəˈtrəʊliəm/ noun [U] oil that is found under the ground or under the bottom of the sea. It is used for making petrol for cars and chemical products.

'petrol ,station noun [C] *British* a garage that sells petrol for your car

petty /ˈpeti/ adj **1** not important and not worth worrying about: *petty arguments* **2** behaving badly towards other people, because you care too much about

P

something that is not really important
3 minor: *a petty criminal/thief/offender*

petulant /ˈpetjʊlənt/ adj behaving in an
unreasonable way because you cannot get
what you want —**petulance** noun [U]

pew /pjuː/ noun [C] a long wooden seat in a
church

PG /ˌpiː ˈdʒiː/ adj parental guidance: used for
describing a film that contains scenes,
subjects, or language that is considered
unsuitable for children unless they have a
parent with them

pH /ˌpiː ˈeɪtʃ/ noun [singular/U] *science* a number
that describes how ACID or ALKALINE a
substance is: *Most unpolluted rainwater has
a pH of around 5.0.*

phantom¹ /ˈfæntəm/ noun [C] the spirit of a
dead person that someone sees=GHOST

phantom² /ˈfæntəm/ adj imagined, not real:
Sailors often see phantom ships in the fog.

pharmaceutical /ˌfɑːməˈsjuːtɪk(ə)l/ adj
relating to medicines and drugs: *the
pharmaceutical industry*

pharmacist /ˈfɑːməsɪst/ noun [C] someone
whose job is to prepare and sell medicines
=CHEMIST

pharmacology /ˌfɑːməˈkɒlədʒi/ noun [U] the
scientific study of medicines and drugs
—**pharmacologist** noun [C]

pharmacy /ˈfɑːməsi/ noun [C] a place where
medicines are prepared and sold=CHEMIST

phase¹ /feɪz/ noun [C] ★ a particular period
of time during the development of
something: *The first phase of the project will
be completed by 2010.* ♦ *Tim went through
a phase of being aggressive at school.* ♦ *a
depressing phase in our history*

phase² /feɪz/ PHRASAL VERB ˌphase sth ˈin to
gradually start using something: *The new
regulations can be phased in over six months.*
ˌphase sth ˈout to gradually stop using
something: *Over the following three years,
the use of the drug will be phased out.*

PhD /ˌpiː eɪtʃ ˈdiː/ noun [C] Doctor of
Philosophy: the highest university degree,
or someone who has this degree

pheasant /ˈfez(ə)nt/ noun [C/U] a large bird
with a long tail that is hunted for sport and
food, or the meat from this bird

phenomenal /fəˈnɒmɪn(ə)l/ adj extremely
impressive or surprising: *the phenomenal
success of the film* —**phenomenally** adv

phenomenon /fəˈnɒmɪnən/ (plural
phenomena /fəˈnɒmɪnə/) noun [C] **1** an event
or situation: *Some people see 'reality TV'
shows as a disturbing new phenomenon.*
2 someone or something that is very
impressive or surprising: *a publishing
phenomenon*

phew /fjuː/ interjection *spoken* used for
showing that you feel hot, tired, or no
longer worried about something: *Phew,
that's a relief!*

philanthropist /fɪˈlænθrəpɪst/ noun [C]
someone who spends a lot of their money
on things that benefit society or poor
people —**philanthropic** /ˌfɪlənˈθrɒpɪk/ adj

philistine /ˈfɪlɪstaɪn/ noun [C] *showing
disapproval* someone who does not

understand or care about serious art,
literature, or music

philosopher /fɪˈlɒsəfə/ noun [C] someone who
studies and writes about the meaning of
things such as life, knowledge, or beliefs

philosophical /ˌfɪləˈsɒfɪk(ə)l/ adj **1** relating to
philosophy: *a philosophical argument* **2** able
to accept an unpleasant situation calmly
because you know that you cannot change
it —**philosophically** /ˌfɪləˈsɒfɪkli/ adv

philosophy /fɪˈlɒsəfi/ noun ★
1 [C/U] the study of theories about the
meaning of things such as life, knowledge,
and beliefs, or a particular theory that
results from this study: *He studied politics
and philosophy.* ♦ *a professor of philosophy*
♦ *Eastern philosophies*
2 [C] a belief that influences someone's
decisions and behaviour: *the latest
philosophies of management* ♦ *My
philosophy is 'live and let live'.*

phlegm /flem/ noun [U] a thick substance
that you get in your nose and throat,
especially when you have a cold

phlegmatic /fleɡˈmætɪk/ adj able to be calm
in a dangerous or frightening situation

phobia /ˈfəʊbiə/ noun [C] a very strong feeling
of fear or dislike for something: *a phobia
about spiders* —**phobic** /ˈfəʊbɪk/ adj

phone¹ /fəʊn/ noun [C] ★★★ a telephone: *The
phone rang five times in the next hour.* ♦ *I
called his house but his mother **answered
the phone** (=picked it up when it rang).* ♦
*Our teenagers spend hours **on the phone**
(=using the phone) every day.* ♦ *We take
orders **by phone** or by email.*

phone² /fəʊn/ verb [I/T] ★★ to use a telephone
to call someone=CALL: *Phone me if you
have any questions.*
PHRASAL VERB ˌphone (sb) ˈup *same as*
phone²: *He phoned up the editor and told
her what he thought of her.*

ˈphone ˌbook noun [C] a book that contains
lists of names of people, businesses, and
organizations with their addresses and
phone numbers=TELEPHONE DIRECTORY

ˈphone ˌbox noun [C] *British* a small structure
with a telephone inside it that you pay to
use=CALL BOX

ˈphone ˌcall noun [C] an act of telephoning
someone: *Excuse me, I have to make a phone
call.*

ˈphone ˌcard noun [C] a plastic card that you
can use instead of money for paying for a
telephone call

ˈphone-ˌin noun [C] *British* a radio or television
programme that people phone with their
questions or comments

ˈphone ˌnumber noun [C] a series of numbers
that you press on a telephone in order to
call someone=TELEPHONE NUMBER

phonetic /fəˈnetɪk/ adj *linguistics* relating to the
sounds used in speech, or using special
symbols to show speech sounds: *the phonetic
alphabet* —**phonetically** /fəˈnetɪkli/ adv

phonetics /fəˈnetɪks/ noun [U] *linguistics* the
study of the sounds that are used in speech

phoney /ˈfəʊni/ adj *informal* **1** not real and
intended to trick people=FAKE: *a phoney*

P

ID card **2** pretending to be friendly, clever, kind etc in order to impress or trick people =INSINCERE

photo /ˈfəʊtəʊ/ *noun* [C] ★★ a PHOTOGRAPH: *photos of her grandchildren* ♦ *Shall I take a photo of the cathedral?*

photocopier /ˈfəʊtəʊˌkɒpiə/ *noun* [C] a machine that copies documents or pictures from one piece of paper to another —*picture* → C3

photocopy /ˈfəʊtəˌkɒpi/ *noun* [C] a copy made by a photocopier —**photocopy** *verb* [T]

photogenic /ˌfəʊtəʊˈdʒenɪk/ *adj* someone who is photogenic looks good in photographs

photograph¹ /ˈfəʊtəɡrɑːf/ *noun* [C] ★★★ a picture of something that you make with a camera: *black and white photographs* ♦ *These are photographs of the Earth, taken from space.* ♦ *We took lots of photographs on holiday.*

photograph² /ˈfəʊtəɡrɑːf/ *verb* [T] to make a photograph of someone or something: *They were photographed shaking hands.*

photographer /fəˈtɒɡrəfə/ *noun* [C] someone who takes photographs, especially as their job

photographic /ˌfəʊtəˈɡræfɪk/ *adj* relating to photographs or photography: *photographic images/equipment*

photography /fəˈtɒɡrəfi/ *noun* [U] **1** the skill, job, or process of taking photographs **2** the photographic images in books, magazines, films, and television: *fashion/wildlife photography*

photo oppoṟtunity *noun* [C] an occasion when a politician or famous person appears in public and people take photographs of them

phrasal verb /ˌfreɪz(ə)l ˈvɜːb/ *noun* [C] *linguistics* a combination of words that is used like a verb. It consists of a verb and an adverb or preposition, for example 'give in' or 'come up with'.

phrase¹ /freɪz/ *noun* [C] ★★★
1 a group of words that are used together in a fixed expression: *Several of those interviewed used the phrase 'being my own boss'.*
2 *linguistics* a group of words that form a unit within a CLAUSE (=a group of words containing a subject and verb) → COIN²

phrase² /freɪz/ *verb* [T] to express something in a particular way in speech or writing

phrase ̱book *noun* [C] a small book that contains useful words and phrases in a particular foreign language

physical /ˈfɪzɪk(ə)l/ *adj* ★★★
1 relating to your body rather than to your mind: *children who have physical disabilities* ♦ *hard physical work* → MENTAL
2 real and able to be seen, touched, or felt: *There was no physical evidence to connect Whitman with the crime.*
3 used about activities or relationships that involve people touching or hitting each other a lot: *Rugby is a very physical game.*
♦ *There was little physical contact* (=touching) *between mother and children.*

4 involving sex: *Did they have a physical relationship?*

physical edu̱cation *noun* [U] PE

physically /ˈfɪzɪkli/ *adv* **1** in a way that is related to your body or appearance: *physically attractive* ♦ *physically active/fit*
2 used about things in the real world, rather than in your imagination or in stories: *It is physically impossible to be in two places at the same time.*

physical ̱science *noun* [C] a science such as geography or physics that deals with things that are not alive

physician /fɪˈzɪʃ(ə)n/ *noun* [C] *formal* a DOCTOR

physics /ˈfɪzɪks/ *noun* [U] ★ the science that deals with heat, light, and other forms of energy and how they affect objects —**physicist** /ˈfɪzɪsɪst/ *noun* [C]

physiological /ˌfɪziəˈlɒdʒɪk(ə)l/ *adj* relating to the way that the body of a living thing operates

physiology /ˌfɪziˈɒlədʒi/ *noun* [U] **1** the science that deals with the way that the bodies of living things operate **2** the way that the body of a particular living thing operates

physiotherapy /ˌfɪziəʊˈθerəpi/ *noun* [U] *British* the treatment of injuries using special physical exercises —**physiotherapist** *noun* [C]

physique /fɪˈziːk/ *noun* [C] the shape of someone's body: *a boxer with an impressive, muscular physique*

pianist /ˈpiːənɪst/ *noun* [C] someone who plays the piano

piano /piˈænəʊ/ *noun* [C] ★★ a large musical instrument with a row of black and white KEYS that you press: *Do you play the piano?* ♦ *She was accompanied by Helen on piano.*

piano   organ

piano

piccolo /ˈpɪkələʊ/ *noun* [C] a musical instrument like a small FLUTE —*picture* → WOODWIND

pick¹ /pɪk/ *verb* [T] ★★★
1 to choose someone or something from a group: *Each month we pick a novel, and we all read it and discuss it.* ♦ *pick sb/sth for sth The following season he was picked for the national team.*
2 to get flowers or fruit by breaking them off their stems: *They spent the summer picking strawberries.*
3 to keep pulling something with your FINGERNAILS: *She sits and picks the loose skin on her feet.*

PHRASES **pick and choose (sth)** to choose the things you prefer, rather than simply accepting what you are given: *We cannot pick and choose which laws to obey.*

P

pick sb's brains *informal* to ask someone questions because they have a lot of information or knowledge

pick a fight/quarrel with sb to start a fight or argument with someone

pick a lock to open a lock without a key, for example with a piece of wire

pick your nose to use your finger to remove MUCUS from inside your nose

pick sb's pocket to steal things from someone's pocket or bag in a crowded place

PHRASAL VERBS **pick at sth 1** to eat only small amounts of a meal when you are not hungry: *Most of the time he just picks at his food.* **2** same as **pick**¹ 3: *He picked at a loose thread on his coat.*

pick on sb to keep treating someone badly or unfairly, especially by criticizing them: *Why do you always pick on Jill?*

pick sb/sth out to choose one thing or person from a group: *The police organized a lineup, and I had to pick out the man who attacked me.*

pick up to improve: *The economy picked up slightly towards the end of the year.*

pick sb up *informal* to start a relationship with someone because you want to have sex with them: *She picked up some guy in a bar.*

pick sth up 1 to learn a new skill, or to start to have a habit, without intending to: *She picked up a few German phrases while staying in Berlin.* **2** *informal* to get an illness =CATCH: *I must have picked up a bug on holiday.* **3** *informal* to receive an electronic signal on a radio or similar piece of equipment **4 pick up the bill/tab** *informal* to pay for something: *Her father picks up the tab for her expensive lifestyle.* **5 pick up speed** if something picks up speed, it starts to move faster =ACCELERATE

pick sb/sth up 1 to lift someone or something up from a surface: *She rushed to pick up the baby.* ♦ *Please pick those toys up and put them away.* —picture → CARRY **2** to go to a place in order to get someone or something and take them somewhere, usually in a car: *Will you pick me up at 11.00?* ♦ *Can I pick up my luggage tomorrow?*

pick up on sth to notice something that is not very obvious: *These are mistakes that you would expect an experienced teacher to pick up on.*

pick² /pɪk/ noun [C] a tool with a heavy curved blade, used for breaking hard surfaces

PHRASES **have your pick of sth** to be able to choose anyone or anything that you want from a group

the pick of sth the best people or things in a particular group

take your pick to choose someone or something

picket¹ /ˈpɪkɪt/ or **picket line** noun [C] a group of people who are protesting outside a building, especially a group of workers who are on STRIKE

picket² /ˈpɪkɪt/ verb [I/T] to take part in a protest outside a building: *About 100 people picketed the US embassy on Thursday.*
—picketing noun [U]

pickle¹ /ˈpɪk(ə)l/ noun [U] *British* a thick sauce that consists of vegetables or fruit preserved in VINEGAR. You eat it cold.

pickle² /ˈpɪk(ə)l/ verb [T] to preserve food in VINEGAR or salt water —**pickled** /ˈpɪk(ə)ld/ adj

pickpocket /ˈpɪkˌpɒkɪt/ noun [C] someone who steals things from people's pockets and bags in crowded places

pickup /ˈpɪkʌp/ noun **1** [C] a place or time at which people, goods, or other things are collected =COLLECTION **2** [singular] *informal* an improvement or increase in something =RECOVERY **3 pickup** or **pickup truck** [C] a truck with an open back and low sides

picky /ˈpɪki/ adj *informal* someone who is picky only likes things that are correct or suitable in every detail =FUSSY

picnic¹ /ˈpɪknɪk/ noun [C] a meal that you eat outside

picnic² /ˈpɪknɪk/ (present participle **picnicking**; past tense and past participle **picnicked**) verb [I] to have a picnic

pictorial /pɪkˈtɔːriəl/ adj consisting of pictures: *a pictorial history of the Shetland Islands*

picture¹ /ˈpɪktʃə/ noun ★★★

1 drawing/painting etc	**5** image on screen
2 description	**6** film
3 mental image	✦ PHRASES
4 situation	

1 [C] a drawing, painting, or photograph: *I'll stand over here, and you can take the picture* (=make a photograph with a camera). ♦ *a picture of the house where I was born* ♦ *She asked children to draw pictures of their family.*

2 [C] a description or idea of what someone or something is like: *The book paints a picture of* (=gives a description of) *a man with a very lonely life.*

3 [C] an image in your mind: *I have this picture in my head of Sam when he realized it was a joke.*

4 [singular] a situation: *The picture has changed a lot recently.*

5 [singular] the image on a television or film screen, or the quality of the image: *The picture isn't very good on this channel.*

6 [C] *American* a film: *It won the award for Best Picture.*

PHRASES **the big picture** a whole situation, not just one part of it

get the picture *informal* to understand something

put sb in the picture *British informal* to give someone the information that they need in order to understand something

Talking or writing about **pictures**

- **drawing** a picture that is made using a pen or pencil
- **graphics** the pictures in a magazine or a computer document
- **illustration** a picture that appears in a book or magazine
- **painting** a picture that is made using paints
- **photograph/photo** a picture that is taken with a camera

P

- **portrait** a picture of a person
- **sketch** a picture that you create quickly, often in preparation for a more detailed drawing or painting

picture² /ˈpɪktʃə/ verb [T] **1** to imagine something: *Try to picture what life was like in those days.* ♦ *I pictured myself lying in the sun on a beach.* **2** to show someone in a photograph, painting etc: *Pictured above are some of the clothes from the new collection.*

picturesque /ˌpɪktʃəˈresk/ adj a picturesque place or scene is attractive

pie /paɪ/ noun [C/U] a food that consists of meat, vegetables, or fruit cooked inside a case of PASTRY

PHRASE **a piece/share/slice of the pie** a share of the available money, benefits etc
→ PIE CHART

piece¹ /piːs/ noun [C] ★★★

1 individual object	**5** writing/art etc
2 one of a particular type	**6** object in board game
3 part of sth	**+ PHRASES**
4 used to make sth	

1 an individual object of a particular type: *I've used four pieces of paper already.* ♦ *a piece of equipment/furniture* ♦ *Police found several pieces of clothing.*
2 a single instance or amount of something of a particular type: *a piece of information/advice/evidence/legislation* ♦ *an impressive piece of work* ♦ *I have another piece of news for you.*
3 a part that has been cut, broken, or separated from something larger: *Can I offer you another piece of cake?* ♦ *a piece of land* ♦ *Jerry tore the letter to pieces* (=tore it until it was destroyed) *and threw it out.*
4 a part that you fit together with other parts to make something: *a jigsaw with 500 pieces* ♦ *I didn't expect the furniture to arrive in pieces.*
5 something that a writer, musician, or artist has produced
6 an object that you move in a BOARD GAME: *chess pieces*

PHRASES **give sb a piece of your mind** *informal* to speak angrily to someone about something they have done
go to pieces *informal* to be so nervous or worried that you cannot behave in a sensible way
in one piece not badly damaged or injured
a piece of the action *informal* the chance to be involved in something exciting
a piece of cake *informal* something that is very easy to do
pull/rip/tear etc sb/sth to pieces to criticize someone or something severely
→ BIT², SET PIECE

piece² /piːs/ PHRASAL VERB **piece sth together 1** to learn the truth about something by considering all the separate bits of information that you have **2** to make something by combining separate bits

piecemeal /ˈpiːsmiːl/ adj, adv made or done in separate stages rather than being planned and done as a whole: *a piecemeal approach to the problem*

pie chart noun [C] a circle divided into sections, used in order to show how something is divided into different amounts

pier /pɪə/ noun [C] a structure that is built out from the land over water. It is used for getting on and off boats, fishing, walking etc

pierce /pɪəs/ verb [T] **1** to make a hole in something using a sharp object =PENETRATE: *The knife pierced his skin.* **2** if you have a part of your body pierced, you have a small hole made in it so that you can wear jewellery in it: *I had my ears pierced years ago.*

piercing¹ /ˈpɪəsɪŋ/ adj **1** very loud, high, and unpleasant =PENETRATING: *a piercing scream/whistle* **2** piercing wind or cold air is so cold that it hurts you **3** *literary* piercing eyes or looks seem to show that someone understands everything

piercing² /ˈpɪəsɪŋ/ noun [U] the practice of making holes in people's skin for jewellery to fit through

pig¹ /pɪg/ noun [C] ★
1 an animal with no fur and a curly tail that is kept by farmers for its meat —*picture* → C12
2 an insulting word for someone who behaves in an unpleasant way or eats too much

pig² /pɪg/ PHRASAL VERB **pig out** *informal* to eat an extremely large amount of food at one time

pigeon /ˈpɪdʒ(ə)n/ noun [C] a brown or grey bird that often lives in cities

pigeonhole¹ /ˈpɪdʒ(ə)nˌhəʊl/ noun [C] one of the open boxes in a desk or on a wall where you can put papers, letters, messages etc

pigeonhole² /ˈpɪdʒ(ə)nˌhəʊl/ verb [T] *showing disapproval* to decide that someone or something belongs to a particular type or group

pigeon-toed /ˌpɪdʒ(ə)n ˈtəʊd/ adj having feet that point inwards

piggyback /ˈpɪɡiˌbæk/ noun [C] if you give someone a piggyback, you carry them on your back with your arms supporting their legs

piglet /ˈpɪɡlət/ noun [C] a young pig

pigment /ˈpɪɡmənt/ noun [C/U] a natural substance that gives colour to something such as paint, skin, or hair

pigmentation /ˌpɪɡmenˈteɪʃ(ə)n/ noun [U] *formal* the natural colour of something, for example someone's skin

pigsty /ˈpɪɡstaɪ/ noun [C] **1** a small building on a farm where pigs are kept **2** *informal* a place that is very dirty or untidy

pigtails /ˈpɪɡteɪlz/ noun [plural] a hairstyle in which the hair is twisted into PLAITS that hang at each side of the head —*picture* → HAIRSTYLE

pike /paɪk/ noun [C] a large fish that lives in rivers and lakes

pile¹ /paɪl/ noun ★
1 [C] a number of things that are put on top of each other in an untidy way: *Rubbish lay in piles in the street.* ♦ *a pile of books and papers*
2 [C] *informal* a large amount of something: *By the time he was 40, he'd made piles of money.*

3 piles [plural] *informal* HAEMORRHOIDS

pile² /paɪl/ verb [T] to put a large number of things on top of each other: *A group of boys were piling branches in a heap for their bonfire.* ♦ *a plate piled high with food*

PHRASAL VERBS **pile 'in** to enter a place in large numbers, all at the same time: *They opened the doors and all fifteen of us piled in.*

,pile 'into sth to enter a place in large numbers, all at the same time: *Four huge men piled into the back of the car.*

,pile 'up if something piles up, the amount of it increases a lot: *The bills were piling up.*

pile sth'up *same as* **pile²**: *Newspapers were piled up on the floor.*

'pile-up noun [C] an accident in which several vehicles crash into each other

pilfer /'pɪlfə/ verb [I/T] to steal things, especially from the place where you work

pilgrim /'pɪlgrɪm/ noun [C] **1** someone who travels to a holy place that is important in their religion **2 Pilgrim** one of the people who left England and went to live in what is now the US in the early 17th century

pilgrimage /'pɪlgrɪmɪdʒ/ noun [C/U] a journey that a religious person makes to a holy place

pill /pɪl/ noun ★

1 [C] a small piece of solid medicine that you swallow with water=TABLET: *vitamin pills* ♦ *Did you remember to take your pills this morning?*

2 the pill [singular] a pill that a woman swallows every day to prevent her from becoming pregnant: *Are you on the pill (=taking it)?*

pillage /'pɪlɪdʒ/ verb [I/T] to steal things from a place using force during a war

pillar /'pɪlə/ noun [C] a thick strong upright post that supports part of a building

PHRASE **pillar of the community/nation/ church** someone who is important and respected in society or in an organization

pillow /'pɪləʊ/ noun [C] a soft object on which you rest your head in bed

pillowcase /'pɪləʊ,keɪs/ noun [C] a cloth cover for a pillow

pilot¹ /'paɪlət/ noun [C] ★

1 someone who flies an aircraft: *an airline pilot*

2 a television programme that is broadcast to find out if people would enjoy a whole series

—**pilot** verb [T]

pilot² /'paɪlət/ adj done with only a few people in order to find out if something will be successful or popular: *a pilot study/project*

pimp /pɪmp/ noun [C] a man who earns money by finding customers for PROSTITUTES

—**pimp** verb [I]

pimple /'pɪmp(ə)l/ noun [C] a small red lump on your skin, especially on your face=SPOT

pin¹ /pɪn/ noun [C] ★

1 a small thin piece of metal with a sharp point, used for holding cloth in place while you are sewing

2 a thin piece of metal or wood used for holding things together

3 one of the tall objects that you knock over in the game of BOWLING

PHRASE **pins and needles** the slightly

painful feeling that you get in a part of your body when you move it after it has been in an uncomfortable position for a long time

pin² /pɪn/ verb [T] to fasten something, or hold it in place, using pins: *Lucy pinned back her hair.* ♦ *Maps were pinned to the walls.* ♦ *She pinned the badge on her jacket.*

PHRASE **pin your hopes on** to hope very much that someone or something will succeed when everyone or everything else has failed

PHRASAL VERBS **,pin sb 'down 1** to force someone to make a decision about something: *We finally pinned him down and got him to agree to a meeting.* **2** to hold someone firmly on the ground so that they cannot move

,pin sth 'down to understand or describe something exactly: *Officials are trying to pin down the cause of the power cuts.*

,pin sth 'on sb to blame someone for something, often when they are not responsible: *He has managed to pin the blame on the previous government.*

,pin sth 'up to fix a picture or notice to a wall

PIN /pɪn/ noun [C] personal identification number: a set of four numbers that you put into a CASH MACHINE in order to take money out of your bank account

pinball /'pɪn,bɔ:l/ noun [U] a game that you play on a machine with a board that slopes. You use controls to hit a ball into TARGETS on the board.

pincer /'pɪnsə/ noun [C] a large part like a hand on some insects and SHELLFISH. It is used for attacking and for holding things.

pinch¹ /pɪntʃ/ verb **1** [T] to squeeze someone's skin between your thumb and finger so that it hurts them: *Roger pinched my arm.* **2** [I/T] if shoes or clothes pinch, they hurt you because they fit too tightly **3** [T] *British informal* to steal something=NICK

pinch² /pɪntʃ/ noun [C] **1** a small amount of something that you can hold between your finger and thumb: *Add a pinch of salt.* **2** the action of squeezing someone's skin between your thumb and finger so that it hurts them

PHRASES **at a pinch** *informal* if it becomes necessary and you have no choice

feel the pinch *informal* to have less money than you need

take sth with a pinch of salt *informal* to doubt that something is completely true

pine¹ /paɪn/ noun **1** [C] a tall tree with long thin sharp leaves that do not fall off in winter —*picture* → C9 **2** [U] the wood of a pine tree

pine² /paɪn/ verb [I] to feel very sad because you cannot be with someone who you love

pineapple /'paɪn,æp(ə)l/ noun [C/U] a large fruit that is yellow inside and has a thick brown skin with sharp points on it —*picture* → C10

'pine ,cone noun [C] the brown hard fruit of a PINE tree

'pine ,needle noun [C] the thin sharp leaf of a PINE tree

'pine ,tree noun [C] a PINE

ping /pɪŋ/ verb [I] to make a short high sound like the sound of a small bell —**ping** noun [C]

pink¹ /pɪŋk/ adj between red and white in colour: *His cheeks turned pink with embarrassment.*

pink² /pɪŋk/ noun [U] a colour that is between red and white

pinkish /ˈpɪŋkɪʃ/ adj similar to pink

pinnacle /ˈpɪnək(ə)l/ noun [C] *literary* **1** the most successful or exciting part of someone's life: *the pinnacle of her acting career* **2** the top of a very high mountain

pinpoint¹ /ˈpɪnˌpɔɪnt/ verb [T] to discover or explain exactly what or where something is: *We couldn't pinpoint the source of the problem.*

pinpoint² /ˈpɪnˌpɔɪnt/ adj very accurate and exact: *The missiles can be fired with pinpoint accuracy.*

pinstripe /ˈpɪnˌstraɪp/ noun [C/U] a thin line in cloth, or cloth with thin lines in it —**pinstriped** /ˈpɪnˌstraɪpt/ adj

pint /paɪnt/ noun [C] **1** a unit for measuring liquid, equal to 0.57 litres in the UK and 0.48 litres in the US **2** *British informal* a pint of beer

pin-up noun [C] *informal* a sexually attractive person who appears in photographs that people hang on their walls, or a photograph of this person

pioneer¹ /ˌpaɪəˈnɪə/ noun [C] **1** one of the first people to do something important that is later developed by other people: *the pioneers of early colour photography* **2** one of the first people to travel to a new place and start living there, especially one of the first Europeans to start living in unknown parts of North America —**pioneering** adj: *pioneering work/research/studies*

pioneer² /ˌpaɪəˈnɪə/ verb [T] to do something that no one else has ever done: *The approach was pioneered by Dr Bruce Fisher.*

pious /ˈpaɪəs/ adj **1** strict in your religious beliefs and practices **2** *showing disapproval* done or said with the intention of seeming religious and moral —**piously** adv

pip /pɪp/ noun [C] *British* a small seed in a piece of fruit

pipe¹ /paɪp/ noun [C] ★
1 a tube that carries liquid or gas from one place to another: *A pipe runs to the hot water tap in the kitchen.* ♦ *Workers were laying water pipes outside the house.*
2 an object used for smoking tobacco, consisting of a tube with a small bowl at the end
3 a musical instrument with one or more tubes that you blow through
→ PIPING

pipe² /paɪp/ verb [T] to send liquid or gas through a pipe from one place to another
→ PIPING
PHRASAL VERB **pipe up** *informal* to enter a conversation that other people are having

pipeline /ˈpaɪpˌlaɪn/ noun [C] a long underground pipe that carries water, gas etc from one place to another: *a 500-kilometre oil pipeline*
PHRASE **in the pipeline** something that is being planned and will happen or be available soon

piping /ˈpaɪpɪŋ/ noun [U] long tubes that are

cut to make pipes, or a system of pipes made from these tubes

piping hot adj food or drink that is piping hot is very hot

piqued /piːkt/ adj feeling annoyed and offended because someone has been rude to you

piracy /ˈpaɪrəsi/ noun [U] **1** the crime of making and selling illegal copies of computer programs, books, videos, or CDs **2** the crime of stealing things from ships while they are sailing

piranha /pəˈrɑːnə/ noun [C] a small South American river fish that has sharp teeth and eats meat

pirate¹ /ˈpaɪrət/ noun [C] someone who steals things from ships while they are sailing

pirate

pirate² /ˈpaɪrət/ verb [T] to illegally make copies of computer programs, books, videos, or CDs —**pirated** adj

Pisces /ˈpaɪsiːz/ noun [C/U] one of the 12 signs of the ZODIAC. A **Pisces** is someone who was born between 20 February and 20 March.

pistachio /pɪˈstɑːʃiəʊ, pɪˈstæʃiəʊ/ noun [C/U] a small green nut

pistol /ˈpɪst(ə)l/ noun [C] a small gun

piston /ˈpɪstən/ noun [C] the part of an engine that moves up and down to create power

pit¹ /pɪt/ noun ★
1 [C] a large hole in the ground: *a gravel pit*
2 [singular] *informal* an extremely untidy place: *Her room was an absolute pit.*
3 **the pits** [plural] *British* the area beside a race track where cars are repaired during a race
PHRASES **be the pits** *informal* to be very bad: *Having to work on Saturday night is the pits.*
the pit of your stomach the place in your stomach where you experience unpleasant feelings when you are worried, upset, or frightened

pit² /pɪt/ **PHRASAL VERB** **pit sb/sth against sb/sth** to make someone compete or fight against someone or something else → PITTED

pit bull or **pit bull terrier** noun [C] a type of small very strong dog

pitch¹ /pɪtʃ/ noun ★

1 sports ground	4 attempt to persuade
2 strength of emotions	5 slope of roof etc
3 how high/low sound is	

1 [C] *British* a flat area of ground that is used for playing sports on: *a football/cricket/rugby pitch* ♦ *Hundreds of fans invaded the pitch at the end of the game.* —*picture* → C15
2 [singular/U] the level of someone's

emotions: *Excitement and enthusiasm rose to fever pitch* (=reached a high level).
3 [singular/U] the high or low quality of a sound or musical note: *Many actors have been trained to lower the pitch of their voice.*
4 [C] the things that you say to persuade someone to buy something or support you: *Most people do not like a very obvious sales pitch.*
5 [singular/U] the slope of something such as a roof

pitch² /pɪtʃ/ verb **1** [T] to make something such as a speech or explanation suitable for people who are a particular age or level of ability: *Her book is pitched at a teenage audience.* **2** [T] to throw something using a lot of force=FLING: *Jan pitched her books over the fence.* **3** [T] to try to sell something, or to try to persuade someone to do something: *He tried to pitch the film to all the major Hollywood studios.* **4** [I] to fall suddenly in a particular direction=PLUNGE: *He tripped and pitched head first into the water.*

PHRASE **pitch a tent** to make a tent ready to use

pitch-black adj completely black or dark
pitch-dark adj completely dark

pitcher /ˈpɪtʃə/ noun [C] *American* a container for serving drinks, with a handle and a SPOUT

pitfall /ˈpɪtfɔːl/ noun [C] a problem that is likely to happen in a particular situation: *the pitfalls involved in starting a business*

pithy /ˈpɪθi/ adj a pithy statement or piece of writing is short and very effective

pitiful /ˈpɪtɪf(ə)l/ adj **1** someone who is pitiful looks or sounds so unhappy that you feel sympathy for them **2** extremely bad: *a pitiful performance* ♦ *a pitiful excuse* **3** a pitiful amount of something is very small and not enough: *pitiful wages* —**pitifully** adv

pitiless /ˈpɪtɪləs/ adj *literary* cruel and showing no sympathy=MERCILESS

pitta bread /ˈpɪtə ˌbred, ˈpiːtə ˌbred/ or **pitta** /ˈpɪtə, ˈpiːtə/ noun [C/U] a type of flat bread that is hollow inside

pittance /ˈpɪt(ə)ns/ noun [singular] an amount of money that is so small that it seems unfair

pitted /ˈpɪtɪd/ adj a pitted surface has small marks or holes in it

pity¹ /ˈpɪti/ noun [U] ★ a strong feeling of sympathy that you have for someone because they are very unhappy or in a bad situation: *She looked at him with a mixture of pity and disgust.*

PHRASES **(it's a) pity** used for saying that you are disappointed about something:
+**that** *It's a pity we couldn't stay longer in Boston.* ♦ **it's a pity to do sth** *It seems a pity to waste this food.*

take pity on sb to feel sorry for someone and try to help them

pity² /ˈpɪti/ verb [T] to feel sorry for someone because they are in a bad situation: *I pity the poor person who has to clean this mess up.*

pivot¹ /ˈpɪvət/ noun [C] **1** a fixed point or pin that something turns on or balances on

2 the most important thing that something is based on or depends on

pivot² /ˈpɪvət/ verb [I/T] to turn or balance on a central point, or to make something do this

pivotal /ˈpɪvət(ə)l/ adj extremely important

pixel /ˈpɪks(ə)l/ noun [C] *computing* the smallest unit of an image on a computer screen

pizza /ˈpiːtsə/ noun [C/U] a food that consists of flat round bread with tomato, cheese, vegetables, meat etc on it

pizzeria /ˌpiːtsəˈriːə/ noun [C] a restaurant that serves pizza

pl. abbrev plural

placard /ˈplækɑːd/ noun [C] a large sign that is used for advertising something, or is carried in the street by someone who is protesting against something

placate /pləˈkeɪt/ verb [T] *formal* to stop someone feeling angry or offended by being nice to them=PACIFY

place¹ /pleɪs/ noun [C] ★★★

1 area/position	**5** position in a race etc
2 town/building etc	**6** importance to people
3 chance to be in sth	**7** point in book etc
4 seat/position	**+ PHRASES**

1 an area or position: *Carl went back to his place* (=the position where he usually is) *and sat down.* ♦ *Keep your credit cards in a safe place.* ♦ *She pushed the couch back into place* (=into the correct position). ♦ *The road is very narrow and quite dangerous in places* (=in some areas but not all).
2 a particular town, country, building, shop etc: *They live in a small place called Clovelly.* ♦ *We went back to Jon's place* (=where Jon lives) *after the film.* ♦ *Cyprus is a great place for a holiday.* ♦ **a place to do sth** *Is this a safe place to swim?*
3 an opportunity to join an organization, team, university etc: *nursery places for children* ♦ *The organizers are expecting all the places on the course to be filled.* ♦ *Lewis has earned a place in the Olympic team.*
4 a seat on a train, on a bus, in a theatre etc, or a position in a QUEUE: *There's no place to sit.* ♦ *Would you mind saving my place for a minute?*
5 the position that you achieve in a race or competition: *Brian finished the race in third place.*
6 the importance that someone or something has in people's lives: *a discussion about the place of religion in society*
7 the point that you have reached in a book, speech etc

PHRASES **all over the place 1** in or to many different places=EVERYWHERE: *I travel all over the place in my job.* **2** in an untidy state: *His papers were all over the place.* **3** *British* not well planned or organized

change places (with sb) to take someone's position while they take yours

fall into place 1 if something falls into place, you suddenly understand something that you did not understand before **2** if things fall into place, they start to happen in the way that you want them to

in place existing and capable of being used: *We didn't have the systems in place to deal with so many orders.*

P

in place of instead of
out of place 1 if someone feels out of place, they are uncomfortable because they feel that they are not like other people around them **2** if something looks out of place, it is in a position where it does not belong or look good
place of work/business/worship *formal* the area where you work/have your business/practise your religion
take sb's/sth's place or **take the place of sb/sth** to do something instead of someone else, or to be used instead of something else: *Joe resigned as chairperson in 1999 and I took his place.*

> Use **room** or **space**, not **place**, to mean an empty area or part of something where people or things can fit: *Is there any room* OR *any space for me in your car? ◆ I wanted a big table in here, but there wasn't enough room* OR *enough space.*

place² /pleɪs/ verb [T] ★★★

1 put sth somewhere	**4** remember/recognize
2 put sb in situation	**5** of advertisement etc
3 decide importance	

1 to put something somewhere, usually in a careful way: **place sth on/under/into etc sth** *Ella placed the dish on the table.*
2 to put someone or something in a particular situation or state: **place sb in/at/under sth** *Her decision places me in an awkward situation. ◆ At the end of the war, the island was placed under French control.*
3 to decide how good or important something is in comparison with other things: *The school places great importance on the welfare of its students. ◆ place sth above sth The company was accused of placing profits above safety.*
4 if you can't place someone, you do not remember them or you cannot remember their name: *He looks familiar, but I can't place him.*
5 if you place an advertisement, an order, or a BET, you give it to someone formally

placebo /pləˈsiːbəʊ/ noun [C] a substance that a doctor pretends is medicine and gives to a patient, either as part of an experiment or in order to help the patient without drugs
placement /ˈpleɪsmənt/ noun **1** [U] the process of finding someone a place where they can live, work, or study: *job placement schemes* **2** [C/U] *British* a temporary job that is part of a course of study and gives you experience of the work that you hope to do at the end of the course: *a three-month placement with the BBC* **3** [C/U] the act of putting something into a position, or the position it is in
placid /ˈplæsɪd/ adj someone who is placid is not often angry or excited
plagiarism /ˈpleɪdʒərɪz(ə)m/ noun [U] the process of taking another person's work, ideas, or words, and using them as if they were your own
plagiarize /ˈpleɪdʒəraɪz/ verb [I/T] to take someone else's work, ideas, or words, and use them as if they were your own
plague¹ /pleɪɡ/ noun [C] **1** any serious disease that spreads quickly and usually ends in

death **2** an uncontrolled increase in the numbers of an animal or insect in a place
plague² /pleɪɡ/ verb [T] to cause a lot of problems for someone or something for a long period of time: *The east coast has been plagued by blizzards all this month.*
plaice /pleɪs/ noun [C/U] a thin flat brown sea fish with orange spots, or the meat from this fish
plaid /plæd/ noun [U] a type of cloth that has a pattern of squares, especially one that is traditional in Scotland
plain¹ /pleɪn/ adj ★
1 simple, with no decoration or with nothing extra added: *a plain wooden table ◆ a plain white T-shirt ◆ plain yoghurt*
2 easily seen or understood=OBVIOUS: **it is plain to sb (that)** *It was plain to everyone that Maude was not happy. ◆ Her disappointment was plain to see. ◆ Sykes made it plain that he had no intention of resigning.*
3 expressing what you think honestly, using simple, direct language: *She was admired for her plain speaking.*
4 not very attractive
PHRASE **plain and simple** used for emphasizing that something is completely true and cannot be described as anything else: *It was cheating plain and simple.*
plain² /pleɪn/ noun [C] a large flat area of land
plain³ /pleɪn/ adv used for emphasizing that someone or something has a particular negative quality: *It was just plain stupid of him to get involved.*
plain chocolate noun [U] *British* chocolate made without milk and with very little sugar
plain-clothes adj plain-clothes police wear ordinary clothes, so that people do not know who they are
plainly /ˈpleɪnli/ adv **1** in a way that is easy to see, hear, or notice=CLEARLY: *The climbers were plainly visible on the hillside. ◆ Something was plainly wrong with the engine.* **2** in a direct and honest way: *Albright told us plainly what the situation was like.* **3** without much decoration
plaintiff /ˈpleɪntɪf/ noun [C] *legal* someone who brings a legal case against someone else in a court of law
plaintive /ˈpleɪntɪv/ adj a plaintive sound is high and sad —**plaintively** adv
plait¹ /plæt, *American* pleɪt/ noun [C] a length of hair that is formed by twisting three separate lengths over each other —*picture* → HAIRSTYLE
plait² /plæt, *American* pleɪt/ verb [T] to twist three lengths of hair or rope over and under each other in order to make one single piece
plan¹ /plæn/ noun [C] ★★★
1 an idea about what you will do in the future, usually including details about how you will do it: *a five-year business plan ◆ We need to make a plan before we start. ◆ We don't have any plans for our holiday yet. ◆ Everything went according to plan* (=there were no problems). ◆ **a plan to do sth** *plans to reduce the use of pesticides in food production*
2 a drawing that shows what something is

P

like or how it will be made=DESIGN: *plans for the new public gardens*

plan² /plæn/ verb ★★★

1 [I/T] to think carefully about a series of actions that you need to take in order to achieve something: *They had been planning their trip to Africa for months.* ♦ *We'll need to plan ahead if we want to take a year off for travelling.* ♦ *Officials are planning for every possibility.* ♦ **plan sth for sth** *The meeting has been planned for next week.*
2 [T] to intend to do something: **plan to do sth** *My boss is planning to retire at 50.*
3 [T] to think about something that you intend to build or make, and draw a picture of how it will look

PHRASAL VERB ˈplan on sth to intend to do something, or to expect something to happen: *We hadn't planned on so many people coming.*

Plan 'A noun [singular] the first plan that someone tries

Plan 'B noun [singular] a plan that you intend to use if your first plan fails

plane /pleɪn/ noun [C] ★★★
1 an aircraft with wings and an engine or engines: *Most of the passengers got off the plane in Dublin.* ♦ *We travelled by plane from Mexico City.* —*picture* → C7
2 a level in society, or a level of intelligence or ability=LEVEL: *The top players are on a higher plane than the rest.*
3 a tool that is used for making wooden surfaces smooth
4 *technical* a flat surface

planet /ˈplænɪt/ noun ★
1 [C] a very large round object that moves around the sun or around another star: *planet Earth* ♦ *Mars is sometimes known as the red planet.*
2 **the planet** [singular] the planet Earth and everything on it: *policies to protect the future of the planet*
—**planetary** /ˈplænət(ə)ri/ adj

plank /plæŋk/ noun [C] **1** a long narrow piece of wood that is used for making structures such as floors **2** an important aspect of something, on which it is based: *the main plank of the party's defence policy*

plankton /ˈplæŋktən/ noun [U] very small animals and plants that live in water and are eaten by fish

planner /ˈplænə/ noun [C] someone whose job is to decide where buildings and roads should be built

planning /ˈplænɪŋ/ noun [U] ★
1 the process of deciding how you will do something before you do it: *There was very little planning done for this project.*
2 the job of deciding where buildings and roads should be built: *urban planning departments*

plant¹ /plɑːnt/ noun ★★★
1 [C] a living thing that grows in soil and has leaves and roots: *a strawberry plant*
2 [C] a large factory: *a nuclear/chemical plant*
3 [U] *British* large machines and equipment that are used in industry: *plant hire* (=industrial machines for rent)

plant² /plɑːnt/ verb [T] ★

1 of seeds etc	4 hide bomb
2 put firmly in position	5 give sb an idea
3 put sth on sb secretly	

1 to put trees, plants, or seeds in soil so that they will grow there: *I've planted a small apple tree in the garden.*
2 to put someone or something firmly in a particular place or position: *Henry planted himself in the seat next to me.*
3 to secretly put something that is illegal or stolen in someone's clothes so that they appear to be guilty when it is found: *Someone must have planted the gun on him.*
4 if someone plants a bomb, they hide it where they want it to explode
5 if you plant an idea in someone's mind, you mention it so that they begin to think about it

plantation /plɑːnˈteɪʃ(ə)n/ noun [C] a large farm where crops such as tea, coffee, cotton, and sugar are grown

plaque /plæk, plɑːk/ noun **1** [C] a flat piece of metal or stone that is hung on a wall for decoration, or to give information **2** [U] a substance that forms on your teeth and in which bacteria can grow

plasma /ˈplæzmə/ noun [U] *medical* the yellowish liquid that is part of blood

plasma ˈscreen noun [C] a type of television or computer screen made by putting a mixture of gases between two sheets of glass

plaster¹ /ˈplɑːstə/ noun **1** [U] a substance that is spread onto walls and ceilings to form a hard smooth surface **2** [C] *British* a thin piece of cloth or plastic that sticks to your skin to cover a cut

PHRASE in plaster *British* enclosed in a hard cover that protects a broken bone: *One man had his leg in plaster.*

plaster² /ˈplɑːstə/ verb [T] **1** to cover a surface with labels, advertisements, pictures etc: *He has posters of rock stars plastered all over the walls of his room.* **2** to cover a wall or ceiling with wet plaster or a similar substance **3** to make something lie flat against something else: *The rain had plastered her hair to her forehead.*

plastic¹ /ˈplæstɪk/ noun [C/U] ★★ a very common light, strong substance that is produced by a chemical process and used for making many different things

plastic² /ˈplæstɪk/ adj ★★★ made of plastic: *plastic bags*

plastic ˈsurgery noun [U] medical operations to improve the appearance of a part of someone's body → COSMETIC SURGERY
—**plastic ˈsurgeon** noun [C]

plate /pleɪt/ noun ★★★

1 flat round dish	5 thin silver/gold layer
2 amount of food	6 picture in book
3 metal/plastic sign	+ PHRASE
4 sth flat and hard	

1 [C] a flat round dish that you put food on
2 [C] the amount of food that a plate will hold: *a plate of sandwiches*
3 [C] a small piece of metal or plastic that is fixed to something and used for showing information such as someone's name or a

P

number: *He read the name on the brass plate on the door.* → NUMBER PLATE

4 [C] a flat piece of metal or other hard substance: *steel/glass plates*

5 [U] a thin layer of silver or gold that covers a less valuable metal to improve its appearance

6 [C] a picture that is printed on special paper in a book: *The book contains 35 colour plates.*

PHRASE **have a lot on your plate** to have a lot of things to worry about or deal with

plateau /ˈplætəʊ/ *noun* [C] **1** a large flat area of land that is higher than the land around it **2** a period of time when something stops increasing or improving: *The recent boom in mobile phone sales seems to have reached a plateau.*

plated /ˈpleɪtɪd/ *adj* a metal object that is plated is covered with a thin layer of silver or gold

plateful /ˈpleɪtfʊl/ *noun* [C] the amount of food that a plate will hold

platform /ˈplætˌfɔːm/ *noun* [C] ★

1 raised structure	4 policies/aims of party
2 where you get on train	5 in computing
3 chance to express sth	

1 a raised structure for people to stand on so that they can be seen by an audience: *The two candidates shared the platform for the question and answer session.*

2 an area next to a railway track where passengers get onto and off trains: *The next train to Brussels will depart from platform 3.*

3 an opportunity to express your ideas or opinions: *Radio phone-ins provide a platform for people with strong opinions.*

4 the policies and aims of a political party, especially the ones they state in order to get people to vote for them: *the Labour party's election platform*

5 *computing* the type of computer system you have and the programs you can use with it

platinum /ˈplætɪnəm/ *noun* [U] a silver-grey metal that is used in industry and for making expensive jewellery

platitude /ˈplætɪˌtjuːd/ *noun* [C] something that has been said so often that it is no longer interesting and shows a lack of imagination

platonic /pləˈtɒnɪk/ *adj* a platonic relationship is friendly but does not involve sex

platoon /pləˈtuːn/ *noun* [C] a small group of soldiers

platter /ˈplætə/ *noun* [C] a large plate that is used for serving food

plaudits /ˈplɔːdɪts/ *noun* [plural] *formal* praise

plausible /ˈplɔːzəb(ə)l/ *adj* likely to be true =REASONABLE ≠ IMPLAUSIBLE —**plausibility** /ˌplɔːzəˈbɪləti/ *noun* [U], **plausibly** *adv*

play¹ /pleɪ/ *verb* ★★★

1 take part in game	5 have part in play etc
2 compete against sb	6 of children
3 make music	+ PHRASES
4 produce sounds	+ PHRASAL VERBS

1 [I/T] to take part in a sport or game: *The children were playing football in the park.*

♦ *He played for AC Milan before he was transferred to Arsenal.*

2 [I/T] to compete against someone in a sport or game: *She plays the winner of tomorrow's match.* ♦ *England will be playing against Brazil in the next round.*

3 [I/T] to perform music, or to use an instrument to make music: *He played several organ pieces by Bach.* ♦ *Gloria plays the violin in the London Philharmonic.*

4 [I/T] to produce sounds, or to make something such as a radio or CD produce sounds: *They played the CD at full volume.* ♦ *I could hear a radio playing in the flat above.*

5 [T] to have a particular part in a play or film: *She played Blanche in* A Streetcar Named Desire.

6 [I] if children play, they do things that they enjoy, for example using toys: *The children were out playing in the garden.* ♦ *Which toys do you want to play with today?*

PHRASES **be playing with fire** to be doing something dangerous or risky that could cause lots of problems for you

play ball (with sb) *informal* to agree to do something that someone wants you to do

play the fool to pretend that you do not understand something

play for time to deliberately delay doing something, or to do something more slowly than usual, so that you have more time to decide what to do

play games to behave in a silly way by not saying what you really think or by not being serious enough

play it cool *informal* to behave calmly and not show that you are worried about something

play (it) safe to avoid taking any risks

PHRASAL VERBS ˌplay aˈbout to behave in a silly way, especially when you should be doing something else=MESS ABOUT

ˌplay aˈround **1** *same as* **play about**: *The kids played around in the pool.* **2** *informal* if someone who is married or has a partner plays around, they have sexual relationships with other people **3** to behave in a silly way, especially when you should be doing something else: *The kids were playing around in the pool.*

ˈplay at sth **1** to do something without being very serious about it **2** what is he/she playing at? used when you think that someone is behaving in a stupid or careless way

ˌplay sth ˈback to play a message or video that has been recorded in order to listen to or watch it

ˌplay sth ˈdown to try to make a problem or difficult situation seem less important than it is: *At first the government played down the threat to public health.*

ˌplay sb ˈoff against sb if you play two people off against each other, you try to cause an argument between them in order to get more control in a situation

ˈplay on sth to use a situation or emotions such as fear or worry in order to get what you want: *She plays on the fact that people feel sorry for her.*

ˌplay (sb) ˈup to cause difficulties or pain for someone: *The printer's playing up again.*

ˌplay sth ˈup to try to persuade people to

P

believe that something is more important than it is: *The newspapers have really played up the government's poor election results.*
'**play with sth** to keep touching something, especially because you are bored

play² /pleɪ/ noun ★★★
1 [C] a piece of writing that is intended to be performed by actors in a theatre or on television or the radio: *a Shakespeare/West End play* ♦ *The school's going to **put on a play** this Christmas.*
2 [U] activities that are done because they are enjoyable and fun, especially by children: *She watched the children **at play** in the park.*
3 [U] the action in a sport or game: *Rain stopped play again this afternoon.*
> PHRASES **bring sth into play** to make something start to have an effect
come into play to start to happen or have an effect
a play on words a clever or funny use of a word that has two different meanings
→ FOUL PLAY

playboy /'pleɪˌbɔɪ/ noun [C] a man who is rich and spends his time enjoying himself instead of working

player /'pleɪə/ noun [C] ★★★
1 someone who plays a particular game or sport: *a tennis/cricket player*
2 someone who plays a musical instrument: *a piano player*
3 a person or organization that influences a situation: *Germany is seen as **a key player** within the European Union.*

playful /'pleɪf(ə)l/ adj **1** lively and full of fun: *playful kittens* **2** intended to be funny or friendly rather than serious: *a playful pat on the back* —**playfully** adv

playground /'pleɪˌɡraʊnd/ noun [C] an area of land where children can play, especially at a school

playgroup /'pleɪˌɡruːp/ noun [C/U] *British* a place where children between the ages of two and four go to play and learn

playing card /'pleɪɪŋ ˌkɑːd/ noun [C] a card that is used for playing card games

playing field /'pleɪɪŋ ˌfiːld/ noun [C] a piece of land with lines marked on it where a particular sport is played

playmate /'pleɪˌmeɪt/ noun [C] a child who another child plays with

'**play-off** noun [C] an extra game that is played to decide who the winner will be after a game or series of games ends with an equal score

playroom /'pleɪˌruːm/ noun [C] a room for children to play in and keep their toys in

plaything /'pleɪˌθɪŋ/ noun [C] **1** someone or something that you are only interested in when you want pleasure or entertainment and do not care about the rest of the time
2 *formal* a toy

playtime /'pleɪˌtaɪm/ noun [C/U] a period of time at school when children can play outside

playwright /'pleɪˌraɪt/ noun [C] someone who writes plays

plc /ˌpiː el 'siː/ noun [C] *British* public limited company: a company in the UK that has SHARES that ordinary people can buy

plea /pliː/ noun [C] **1** an urgent or emotional request for something: *The police ignored her pleas for help.* **2** *legal* a statement that someone makes in a court of law to say whether they are guilty or not

plead /pliːd/ verb **1** [I] to make an urgent or emotional request: *She pleaded with him to stay, but he would not.* **2** [I/T] *legal* to say in a court of law whether you are guilty of a crime or not: *Both defendants pleaded not guilty.* **3** [T] to mention something as an excuse for doing or not doing something: *Ellie pleaded tiredness and went to bed very early.* **4** [T] to try to show that something is important or worth trying to achieve: *He pleaded the case for continued cooperation with the Russians.*

pleasant /'plez(ə)nt/ adj ★
1 enjoyable, or attractive ≠ UNPLEASANT, UNPLEASANT: *They spent a pleasant evening together.*
2 a pleasant person is friendly and behaves correctly in social situations ≠ UNPLEASANT, UNPLEASANT
—**pleasantly** adv: *I was pleasantly surprised by the results of the survey.*

pleasantries /'plez(ə)ntriz/ noun [plural] friendly remarks that you make in order to be polite

please¹ /pliːz/ interjection ★★★
1 used as a polite way of asking for something, or of asking someone to do something: *Would you help me, please?* ♦ *Could I have change for a pound, please?*
2 used for emphasizing a request, an order, or a statement: *Please stop making all that noise!*
3 used as a polite way of accepting something that someone has offered you: *'Would you like more coffee?' 'Yes, please.'*

please² /pliːz/ verb [I/T] ★ to make someone feel happy and satisfied: *He'll do anything to please her.* ♦ *Some of our customers can be very **difficult to please**.*
> PHRASES **please yourself** used for telling someone that you do not care whether they do a particular thing or not: *'I can't finish my dinner.' 'Please yourself, but don't complain to me when you're hungry later on.'*
whatever/wherever/whenever etc sb pleases whatever/wherever/whenever etc someone wants: *You can go whenever you please.*

pleased /pliːzd/ adj ★★ happy and satisfied: *Are you **pleased with** the way things went yesterday?.* ♦ *I'm really **pleased about** your new job.* ♦ +(that) *We're very pleased that you've accepted our offer.* ♦ *be pleased to do sth You'll be pleased to hear that Dave can come tonight!*
> PHRASE **pleased to meet you** *spoken* used as a polite way of greeting someone when you meet them for the first time: *'Tony, this is Mr Wilkins.' 'Pleased to meet you.'*

pleasing /'pliːzɪŋ/ adj *formal* **1** pleasant and enjoyable: *a pleasing aroma* **2** making you feel happy and satisfied: *pleasing news*

pleasurable /'pleʒ(ə)rəb(ə)l/ adj *formal* giving you a feeling of happiness, enjoyment, or satisfaction = ENJOYABLE

pleasure /ˈpleʒə/ noun ★★
1 [U] a feeling of happiness, enjoyment, or satisfaction: *He smiled with pleasure when she walked in.* ♦ **give/bring pleasure to sb** *His books have given enormous pleasure to many people.* ♦ **take pleasure in (doing) sth** *He took great pleasure in pointing out my mistakes.*
2 [C] something that makes you feel happy and satisfied: *Music is one of the greatest pleasures in life.* ♦ **it's a pleasure to do sth** *It's a pleasure to meet you.*
3 [U] the activity of relaxing and enjoying yourself rather than working: *Are you travelling for business or pleasure?*
PHRASE **(it's) my pleasure** *spoken formal* used when someone thanks you as a polite way of saying that you were happy to help them: *'Thanks so much for helping us with our bags.' 'My pleasure.'*

pleated /ˈpliːtɪd/ adj a pleated piece of clothing has regular folds in it

plebiscite /ˈplebɪˌsaɪt, ˈplebɪsɪt/ noun [C] a vote by everyone in a country about a very important issue

pledge /pledʒ/ verb [T] to promise seriously and publicly to do something =PROMISE —**pledge** noun [C]

plentiful /ˈplentɪf(ə)l/ adj present or available in large quantities ≠ SCARCE

plenty /ˈplenti/ pronoun ★★★ a lot, or enough: *'How much money will I need?' 'Five pounds should be plenty.'* ♦ *There's plenty of room for luggage behind the seats.* ♦ *They had plenty of chances to win the game.* ♦ *There's plenty more ice cream in the freezer.* ♦ **plenty to do** *She always has plenty to say.*

plethora /ˈpleθərə/ noun [singular] *formal* a greater amount than you need or want =PROFUSION ≠ DEARTH

pliable /ˈplaɪəb(ə)l/ adj able to bend or change shape easily without breaking

pliers /ˈplaɪəz/ noun [plural] a metal tool that looks like a strong pair of scissors, used for holding small objects or for bending or cutting wire —*picture →* TOOL

plight /plaɪt/ noun [C] a sad, serious, or difficult situation

plod /plɒd/ verb [I] to walk with slow heavy steps =TRUDGE

plonk¹ /plɒŋk/ verb [T] *British informal* to put something down somewhere in a careless way
PHRASE **plonk yourself down** *British informal* to sit or lie down on something in a careless way

plonk² /plɒŋk/ noun [U] *British informal* cheap wine of low quality

plop¹ /plɒp/ verb [I] to fall with a short sound like the sound made by a small object falling into a liquid

plop² /plɒp/ noun [C] a short sound like the sound made by a small object falling into a liquid

plot¹ /plɒt/ noun ★
1 [C/U] a series of related events that make up the main story in a book, film etc
2 [C] a secret plan to do something bad, made by two or more people: *a kidnap plot* ♦ *a plot against the government* ♦ **a plot to do sth** *a plot to kill the president*

3 [C] a piece of land that is used for a particular purpose: *a building/burial plot*

plot² /plɒt/ verb **1** [I/T] to make a secret plan with other people to do something bad =SCHEME **2** [T] to make marks on a map or GRAPH to show the movement or development of something

plough¹ /plaʊ/ verb [I/T] to turn over the soil with a plough before putting seeds into it
PHRASAL VERBS **plough sth back** to put back profits into a business in order to make it more successful
plough into sb/sth to crash into someone or something with force because you are moving or driving too quickly
plough on to continue doing something that takes a lot of effort or is likely to cause you problems
plough through sth to finish something that takes a long time and is difficult or boring =WADE THROUGH STH

plough² /plaʊ/ noun [C] a piece of equipment that farmers use for turning over the soil before putting seeds into it

plow /plaʊ/ the American spelling of **plough**

ploy /plɔɪ/ noun [C] a way of tricking someone in order to get an advantage, or to make them do what you want them to do =RUSE

PLS abbrev please: used in emails and TEXT MESSAGES

pluck /plʌk/ verb **1** [T] to take someone or something quickly from a particular place: *Rescue crews plucked survivors from the sea.* **2** [T] to pull the feathers off the body of a dead bird so that it can be cooked **3** [I/T] to pull the strings of a musical instrument with your fingers in order to produce a sound **4** [T] *literary* to pull a piece of fruit from a tree, or a flower or leaf from a plant =PICK
PHRASES **pluck your eyebrows** to pull hairs out from around the edges of your EYEBROWS in order to make them look tidier
pluck up (the) courage (to do sth) to persuade yourself to do something that frightens you

plucky /ˈplʌki/ adj brave and determined, especially when success is unlikely =GUTSY

plug¹ /plʌg/ noun [C] **1** an object that is used for connecting a piece of equipment to an electricity supply **2** an attempt to make people interested in a book, film etc by talking about it in an enthusiastic way on a radio or television programme **3** a small round plastic or rubber object that prevents water from flowing out of the hole in a SINK or bath
PHRASE **pull the plug (on sth)** to stop an activity, especially by no longer providing money for it

plug² /plʌg/ verb [T] **1** to fill a hole so that nothing can get through it: *Plug the hole with newspaper before applying the cement.* **2** to try to make people interested in a book, film, idea etc by talking about it in an enthusiastic way on a radio or television programme
PHRASAL VERBS **plug away (at sth)** to continue doing something in a determined way despite difficulties
plug sth in to connect a piece of equipment to an electricity supply or to another piece

P

of equipment: *I realized I hadn't plugged the TV in.*

plug (sth) into sth to connect a piece of equipment to an electricity supply or to another piece of equipment, or to be connected in this way: *First plug the keyboard into your computer.*

plughole /ˈplʌghəʊl/ noun [C] *British* a hole at the bottom of a SINK or bath where water flows out and where you put a plug

plum /plʌm/ noun [C] a small round fruit with purple, red, or yellow skin and a large hard seed inside —*picture* → C10

plumage /ˈpluːmɪdʒ/ noun [U] a bird's feathers

plumber /ˈplʌmə/ noun [C] someone whose job is to fit and repair the pipes and equipment that are used for supplying and storing water

plumbing /ˈplʌmɪŋ/ noun [U] **1** the job of fitting and repairing the pipes and equipment that are used for supplying and storing water **2** the system of pipes and equipment that are used for supplying and storing water in a building

plume /pluːm/ noun [C] **1** a long narrow cloud of dust, smoke etc that moves upwards **2** a large feather or group of feathers, used especially for decorating a hat

plummet /ˈplʌmɪt/ verb [I] **1** if something such as an amount, rate, or value plummets, it suddenly becomes much lower: *Share prices plummeted on the New York stock exchange today.* → CRASH, NOSEDIVE **2** to fall straight down very quickly from a high position =PLUNGE

plump¹ /plʌmp/ adj **1** slightly fat, in a pleasant way ≠ SKINNY **2** large and round in an attractive way: *plump strawberries*

plump² /plʌmp/ **PHRASAL VERB** **plump for sb/sth** *informal* to choose someone or something after being unable to decide what to do

plunder /ˈplʌndə/ verb [I/T] to take valuable things from a place using force —**plunder** noun [U]

plunge¹ /plʌndʒ/ verb [I] **1** to fall quickly from a high position =PLUMMET: *The helicopter plunged 500 feet into the sea.* **2** if an amount or level plunges, it suddenly becomes much lower =PLUMMET: *The temperature is expected to plunge below zero tonight.*

PHRASAL VERBS **plunge into sth** to suddenly start doing something with energy and enthusiasm

plunge sb/sth into sth to suddenly put someone or something in a particular state or situation: *The city was plunged into total darkness when the entire electrical system failed.*

plunge sth into sth to quickly push something a long way into something else

plunge² /plʌndʒ/ noun [C] **1** a sudden reduction in the amount or level of something: *the plunge in oil prices* **2** a quick fall from a high position: *the plane's plunge into the sea*

PHRASE **take the plunge** to finally do something that is important, difficult, or dangerous, after thinking about it carefully

pluperfect, the /ˌpluːˈpɜːrfɪkt/ noun [singular]

linguistics the PAST PERFECT tense of a verb

plural¹ /ˈplʊərəl/ adj *linguistics* ★ a plural word or form is used for referring to more than one person or thing

plural² /ˈplʊərəl/ noun [C] *linguistics* a word or form that is used for referring to more than one person or thing. For example, 'students' is the plural of 'student', and 'mice' is the plural of 'mouse'.

pluralism /ˈplʊərəlɪz(ə)m/ noun [U] *formal* a situation in which people of different races, religions, cultures, politics etc live together in a society —**pluralist** adj

plus¹ /plʌs/ grammar word ★

> **Plus** can be:
> ■ a **preposition**: *Two plus seven is nine.*
> ■ a **conjunction**: *You can have this bread, plus there's cheese in the fridge.*
> ■ an **adjective**: *There are 30 plus students in every class.*

1 used for showing that one number or amount is added to another. This word is usually represented in mathematics by + ≠ MINUS: *36 plus 5 is 41.* ♦ *You have to pay back £100 a month, plus interest.*
2 used when mentioning an additional thing or fact: *He came along with his five children, plus their partners, and his grandchildren.*
3 used after you mention a number or quantity to show that the actual number or quantity may be larger: *Ray Charles' 40-year plus career began in 1954.*

PHRASE **A plus/B plus/C plus/D plus** a mark for a student's work that is higher than a mark of A, B, C, and D. These marks are usually written A+, B+ etc.

plus² /plʌs/ noun [C] an advantage: *For this job, experience in telecommunications is a plus.*

plush /plʌʃ/ adj expensive, comfortable, and attractive

plus sign noun [C] the symbol +

plutonium /pluːˈtəʊniəm/ noun [U] a RADIOACTIVE substance that is used in making nuclear power

ply /plaɪ/ verb **ply your trade** *literary* to do your job

PHRASAL VERB **ply sb with sth** to keep giving someone a lot of presents, food, or drinks

plywood /ˈplaɪwʊd/ noun [U] a type of board that is used in building houses, furniture etc, made by sticking thin layers of wood together with glue

pm /ˌpiːˈem/ abbrev used after a time for showing that it is between noon and midnight: *3.30 pm*

PM /ˌpiːˈem/ noun [C] *British informal* a prime minister

PMS /ˌpiː em ˈes/ noun [U] premenstrual syndrome: the pain and unpleasant feelings that some women have just before their PERIOD every month

PMT /ˌpiː em ˈtiː/ noun [U] *British* premenstrual tension: another name for **PMS**

pneumatic /njuːˈmætɪk/ adj **1** filled with air or gas **2** a pneumatic tool or piece of equipment works by using air

pneumonia /njuːˈməʊniə/ noun [U] a serious illness that affects your lungs

PO /ˌpiːˈəʊ/ abbrev post office

P

poach /pəʊtʃ/ verb **1** [T] to cook something in liquid that is boiling gently **2** [I/T] to illegally catch or kill an animal, bird, or fish on someone else's property **3** [T] to persuade someone to leave a group or organization and become a member of yours

poacher /ˈpəʊtʃə/ noun [C] someone who illegally catches or kills animals, birds, or fish on someone else's property

PO Box /ˌpiː ˈəʊ ˌbɒks/ noun [C] post office box: used in an address showing the number of a small box at a POST OFFICE where your letters can be sent

pocket¹ /ˈpɒkɪt/ noun [C] ★★
1 a small bag that forms part of a piece of clothing and is used for holding small objects: *She searched her pockets for the car keys.*
2 a small bag or other container that forms part of an object: *The safety instructions are in the pocket of the seat in front of you.*
3 a supply of money that is available for spending: *Our boss expects us to pay for the trip out of our own pockets* (=using our own money)*!*
4 a small area with a particular quality that makes it different from the areas around it: *pockets of resistance to government forces*
PHRASE **be out of pocket** to have lost money as the result of a business deal
→ LINE

pocket² /ˈpɒkɪt/ verb [T] **1** to put something into your pocket: *He locked the door and pocketed the key.* **2** to take money for yourself that does not belong to you: *He said the officials pocketed some of the taxes they collected.*

pocket³ /ˈpɒkɪt/ adj small enough to fit into your pocket: *a pocket dictionary/diary*

pocketful /ˈpɒkɪtˌfʊl/ noun [C] the amount of something that can be put in a pocket

pocket ˌmoney noun [U] *British* money that parents regularly give to their children

pod /pɒd/ noun [C] the long narrow part that holds the seeds of a bean plant or similar plant

podiatrist /pəʊˈdaɪətrɪst/ noun [C] someone whose job is to take care of people's feet and to treat foot diseases —**podiatry** noun [U]

podium /ˈpəʊdiəm/ noun [C] a small raised area where someone stands to give a speech or receive a prize

poem /ˈpəʊɪm/ noun [C] ★ a piece of writing that uses beautiful or unusual language. It is arranged in lines that have a particular beat and often RHYME.

poet /ˈpəʊɪt/ noun [C] someone who writes poetry

poetic /pəʊˈetɪk/ adj connected with poetry, or having the qualities of poetry

poetry /ˈpəʊɪtri/ noun [U] ★ poems: *the poetry of Walt Whitman ♦ a poetry book*

poignant /ˈpɔɪnjənt/ adj giving you feelings of sadness —**poignancy** noun [U], **poignantly** adv

point¹ /pɔɪnt/ noun ★★★

1 idea/opinion	**7** particular place
2 what you want to say	**8** unit for game score
3 reason	**9** unit of measurement
4 particular time	**10** sharp end of sth
5 stage in process	**11** decimal point
6 aspect/feature	**+ PHRASES**

1 [C] one idea or opinion among a number of others: *I disagree with you on a couple of points.*
2 [singular] the thing that you are trying to say: *My point is that we're spending too much time on details. ♦ I take your point* (=understand it), *but I still think we should go ahead with the changes. ♦ She missed the point* (=did not understand it) *and thought I was blaming her.*
3 [singular] the reason for something: *I see no point in discussing this any further. ♦ What is the point of your visit? ♦ I'm sorry – I just don't see the point of doing this* (=understand the reason).
4 [C] a particular moment in time: *At that point I left the room. ♦ At this point in time we can't afford to hire any more people.*
5 [C] a particular stage in a process: *the freezing/boiling point of water ♦ We're just trying to reach a point where both sides will sit down together and talk.*
6 [C] an aspect or feature: *Patience is not one of his strong points.*
7 [C] a particular place: *We'll meet at a point halfway between here and your hotel.*
8 [C] a unit for counting the score in a game or sport: *Our team is two points behind.*
9 [C] a unit of measurement: *Interest rates fell by 2 percentage points.*
10 [C] the sharp end of something: *The potatoes should be soft when pierced with the point of a knife.*
11 [C] the word for a DECIMAL POINT, used when saying a number. For example, 6.3 is said as 'six point three'.

PHRASES **beside the point** not relevant to what is happening or being said
come/get to the point to stop talking about unimportant details and say what is most important
have (got) a point to have made an important statement
make a point of doing sth to be certain that you do something, usually in an obvious way: *He now made a point of avoiding her.*
on the point of doing sth about to do something: *We were on the point of leaving when the phone rang.*
the point of no return the moment at which it becomes impossible to change or stop something
point of view a way of judging a situation, based on a particular aspect
to the point relevant and worth paying attention to
up to a point to some degree but not completely

Words often used with **point**

Adjectives often used with point (noun, sense 1)
■ **crucial, fundamental, important, key, main** + POINT: used about points that are important for what you are trying to say

point² /pɔɪnt/ verb ★★★
1 [I/T] to show something by holding out your finger or a long thin object: *Don't point. They'll know we're looking at them. ♦ He pointed his stick in the direction of the path. ♦ 'What's through there?' he asked, pointing at the door.*

P

2 [I] to show a particular direction or place, usually using a sign or symbol: *The arrow pointed left towards the exit door.*
3 [I/T] to aim an object at someone or something, or to be aimed at someone or something: *All you have to do is point the camera and shoot.* ♦ **point sth at/towards sb/sth** *He pointed his rifle at the deer.*
4 [I/T] to show someone the direction in which they should go: *Could you point me in the direction of the exit?*

PHRASE **point the/a finger (at sb)** to accuse someone of something

PHRASAL VERBS **,point sth 'out** to tell someone something: *Thank you for pointing that out.* ♦ **+that** *He pointed out that we had two hours of free time before dinner.* **,point sb/sth 'out** to show someone who a person is or where something is: *Which one is Jane's brother? Can you point him out to me?* ♦ *He pointed out the best beaches on the map.*
'point to sth to show the truth or importance of something: *The evidence clearly points to her guilt.*

,point-'blank adj, adv in a very firm and direct way: *Polly refused point-blank to let me use the car.*

PHRASE **at point-blank range** if you shoot someone at point-blank range, you hold the gun very close to their body

pointed /'pɔɪntɪd/ adj **1** with a point at the end **2** done in a way that shows that you are annoyed or do not agree: *a pointed comment/remark* —**pointedly** adv

pointer /'pɔɪntə/ noun [C] **1** *informal* a piece of advice or information **2** a pole or stick for pointing at something such as a map or picture

pointless /'pɔɪntləs/ adj lacking any purpose or use —**pointlessly** adv, **pointlessness** noun [U]

poise /pɔɪz/ noun [U] **1** a controlled and relaxed way of behaving **2** a graceful and calm way of moving, standing, or sitting

poised /pɔɪzd/ adj **1** about to do or achieve something after preparing for it: *Japan was poised to become the biggest foreign investor in Vietnam.* **2** waiting in a position where you can make a movement as soon as you need to: *Two guards stood poised with their hands on their guns.* **3** behaving in a controlled and relaxed way

poison¹ /'pɔɪz(ə)n/ noun [C/U] a substance that can kill you or make you ill if you eat, drink, or breathe it

poison² /'pɔɪz(ə)n/ verb [T] **1** to kill someone, or make them very ill, by giving them poison: *He was suspected of poisoning his wife.* **2** to put poison in something: *Waste from the factories is poisoning the water supply.* **3** to have a bad effect on something: *The decision had poisoned relations between Britain and France.*

poisoning /'pɔɪz(ə)nɪŋ/ noun [C/U] an occasion when someone is affected by poison

poisonous /'pɔɪz(ə)nəs/ adj **1** containing poison: *poisonous gases/plants* **2** capable of producing poison: *a poisonous snake*

poke¹ /pəʊk/ verb **1** [I/T] to push something quickly with your finger or a pointed

object: *Jane poked me in the arm to get my attention.* **2** [T] to put something into a space: *The kid was poking a stick down a drain.* ♦ *Dad poked his head into my room and said dinner was ready.*

PHRASE **poke fun (at)** to make unkind jokes about someone or something

poke² /pəʊk/ noun [C] a quick push with your finger or a pointed object

poker /'pəʊkə/ noun **1** [U] a card game in which players try to win money **2** [C] a metal stick for moving the coal or wood of a fire around

poky /'pəʊki/ adj small and uncomfortable

polar /'pəʊlə/ adj coming from or relating to an area near the North Pole or the South Pole

'polar ,bear noun [C] a large white bear that lives in areas near the North Pole

polarize /'pəʊlə,raɪz/ verb [I/T] to form two very different groups, opinions, or situations that are completely opposite to each other, or to cause this to happen —**polarization** /,pəʊləraɪ'zeɪʃ(ə)n/ noun [U]

Polaroid /'pəʊlərɔɪd/ *trademark* a type of camera that produces photographs immediately, or a photograph from this type of camera

pole /pəʊl/ noun [C] ★
1 a long thin stick, often used for holding or supporting something: *There were rows of poles supporting young bean plants.*
2 one of the points on the very top or bottom of the Earth, called the North Pole and the South Pole

PHRASE **poles apart** completely different

polemic /pə'lemɪk/ noun [C/U] *formal* a strong statement of opinion, especially negative opinion —**polemical** adj

'pole ,vault, the noun [singular] a sport in which you use a long pole to push yourself over a high bar

police¹ /pə'liːs/ noun [plural] ★★★ the official organization that tries to catch criminals and checks that people obey the law, or the people that work for this organization: *traffic/riot police* ♦ *a police car* ♦ *If you don't leave, I'll call the police.*

police² /pə'liːs/ verb [T] to use police officers to control an area or event

po'lice ,constable noun [C] *British* a police officer of the lowest rank

po'lice ,force noun [C] an organized group of police officers in charge of a country or a particular area

policeman /pə'liːsmən/ (plural **policemen** /pə'liːsmən/) noun [C] a male police officer

po'lice ,officer noun [C] a member of the police

po'lice ,state noun [C] a country where the government controls people and limits their freedom very severely

po'lice ,station noun [C] the building where the police of a particular place work

policewoman /pə'liːs,wʊmən/ (plural **policewomen** /pə'liːs,wɪmɪn/) noun [C] a female police officer

policy /'pɒləsi/ noun ★★★
1 [C/U] a set of plans or actions that are agreed on by a government, political party, business, or other organization: *the*

government's economic policy ◆ It is not the hospital's policy to disclose the names of patients. ◆ What is the party's **policy on** immigration?
2 [C] a contract between an insurance company and a person or organization: Read the wording of your policy very carefully.

polio /ˈpəʊliəʊ/ noun [U] a serious infectious disease that mostly affects children and destroys muscles

polish¹ /ˈpɒlɪʃ/ verb [T] **1** to rub the surface of something in order to make it shine: They spend most of their time polishing shoes. **2** to improve a skill by practising: He'd spent the summer polishing his flying skills.
PHRASAL VERBS ˌpolish sth ˈoff informal to eat or drink something until it is finished: Well, it didn't take us long to polish off the ice cream.
ˌpolish sth ˈup same as **polish¹** 3: I could do the job if I spent some time polishing up my Spanish.

polish² /ˈpɒlɪʃ/ noun **1** [C/U] a substance that you rub onto an object to make it shine: furniture/shoe polish **2** [singular] an act of rubbing an object to make it shine: This table needs a good polish.

polished /ˈpɒlɪʃt/ adj **1** clean and shiny because of being rubbed: a highly polished wooden floor **2** of very high quality: a polished performance

polite /pəˈlaɪt/ adj ★ behaving towards other people in a pleasant way that follows all the usual rules of society = COURTEOUS ≠ RUDE: a polite refusal ◆ It's not polite to talk with your mouth full of food. ◆ You must be more polite to the customers. —**politely** adv, **politeness** noun [U]

political /pəˈlɪtɪk(ə)l/ adj ★★★
1 relating to politics: the importance of political stability ◆ the political system in the US ◆ political leaders/opponents/parties
2 interested or involved in politics: I'm really not very political at all.
3 relating to relationships of power that exist between people in an organization: It was a purely political decision to give him the job.
—**politically** /pəˈlɪtɪkli/ adv

poˌlitically corˈrect adj using language or behaviour that is not offensive to groups of people who have often been affected by DISCRIMINATION (=unfair treatment) —poˌlitical corˈrectness noun [U]

poˌlitical ˈprisoner noun [C] someone who is sent to prison for opposing their government

poˌlitical ˈscience noun [U] the study of politics and the way that political power is used in a country

politician /ˌpɒləˈtɪʃ(ə)n/ noun [C] ★★ someone who has a job in politics

politicize /pəˈlɪtɪsaɪz/ verb [T] **1** to cause something to become involved with politics: The tobacco issue is becoming too politicized. **2** to make someone more interested and involved in politics

politics /ˈpɒlətɪks/ noun ★★★
1 [U] the ideas and activities that are involved in getting power in an area or

governing it: She's heavily involved in **local politics**.
2 [plural] your beliefs and attitudes about how government should work: Her politics became more conservative as she grew older.
3 [U] the profession of being a politician: He entered politics at the age of 21.
4 [U] the ideas and activities that people within a particular group use to try to get power: Now that I'm self-employed, I don't have to worry about office politics.

> **Word family: politics**
>
> *Words in the same family as **politics**:*
> - **political** adj
> - **politically** adv
> - **politician** n
> - **apolitical** adj
> - **politicize** v

polka /ˈpɒlkə/ noun [C] a fast lively dance, or the music for this dance

poll¹ /pəʊl/ noun ★
1 [C] an occasion when a lot of people are asked their opinions about something, usually as research for a political party, television programme etc: A recent poll indicated that most people supported a ban on tobacco advertising. ◆ According to a poll conducted last week, 75% of the public support the Prime Minister.
2 the polls [plural] the place where people vote: The polls close at ten o'clock. ◆ Citizens across the country will be **going to the polls** (=voting in an election) tomorrow.

poll² /pəʊl/ verb [T] **1** to ask a lot of people their opinions about something, especially a political issue: Over half of those polled said that they were satisfied with the government's performance. **2** to get a particular number or percentage of votes in an election

pollen /ˈpɒlən/ noun [U] a powder that flowers produce. It is carried by the wind or by insects to other flowers so that they can produce seeds.

ˈpollen ˌcount noun [C] a measurement of how much pollen there is in the air

ˈpolling ˌstation noun [C] a building where people go to vote in an election

pollster /ˈpəʊlstə/ noun [C] mainly journalism a person or organization that prepares a POLL

pollutant /pəˈluːt(ə)nt/ noun [C/U] a substance that is harmful to the environment

pollute /pəˈluːt/ verb [T] to make air, water, or land dirty and dangerous: The oil spillage has polluted the harbour. —**polluted** adj: heavily/badly polluted rivers —**polluter** noun [C]

pollution /pəˈluːʃ(ə)n/ noun [U] ★★ chemicals and other substances that have a harmful effect on air, water, or land: new measures to prevent pollution levels from rising ◆ The agency is responsible for controlling air pollution.

> **Words often used with pollution**
>
> *Verbs often used with pollution*
> - **combat, control, prevent, tackle** + POLLUTION: stop pollution from happening
> - **cut, limit, reduce** + POLLUTION: make the amount of pollution less

P

polo /ˈpəʊləʊ/ noun [U] a game in which two teams of players ride horses and hit a ball with long wooden hammers

'polo ,neck noun [C] British a SWEATER with a high neck that folds over —picture → NECKLINE —**'polo-,neck** adj

'polo ,shirt noun [C] a cotton shirt with a collar, a few buttons at the neck, and short sleeves

polyester /ˌpɒliˈestə/ noun [U] a light cloth made from artificial fibres

polyp /ˈpɒlɪp/ noun [C] a small lump that grows inside your body

polystyrene /ˌpɒliˈstaɪriːn/ noun [U] a very light artificial substance, used especially for making containers or for protecting the things in a box

polythene /ˈpɒlɪθiːn/ noun [U] British a strong light plastic, used especially for wrapping food in and keeping it fresh

pomegranate /ˈpɒmɪˌɡrænət/ noun [C] a round fruit that has a hard skin and a lot of thick seeds inside

pomp /pɒmp/ noun [U] formal ceremony, especially involving expensive clothes and special traditions

pompous /ˈpɒmpəs/ adj showing disapproval speaking or behaving in a very serious and formal way that shows that you think you are very important —**pomposity** /pɒmˈpɒsəti/ noun [U]

pond /pɒnd/ noun [C] an area of water that is smaller than a lake: a garden pond

ponder /ˈpɒndə/ verb [I/T] formal to think carefully about something for a long time before making a decision: Mike pondered what he should say to his wife.

ponderous /ˈpɒndərəs/ adj literary **1** moving slowly because of being big and heavy **2** ponderous writing or speech is serious and boring

pontificate /pɒnˈtɪfɪkeɪt/ verb [I] formal to give your opinions in an annoying way that shows that you think you know a lot

pony /ˈpəʊni/ noun [C] a small horse

ponytail /ˈpəʊniteɪl/ noun [C] long hair that is tied at the back of your head and hangs down —picture → HAIRSTYLE

poo /puː/ noun [C/U] British informal solid waste that comes out of your body when you use the toilet. This word is used especially by and to children. —**poo** verb [I]

poodle /ˈpuːd(ə)l/ noun [C] a dog with thick curly fur

pool¹ /puːl/ noun ★★

1 water to swim in	4 light shining on area
2 area of liquid	5 group of people
3 name of game	6 competition

1 [C] a large structure filled with water for people to swim in=SWIMMING POOL: a heated indoor pool

2 [C] a small area of liquid: The water collected in a little pool on the floor. ♦ a muddy road dotted with pools of rainwater ♦ a pool of blood

3 [U] a game in which two players hit balls into holes at the edges of a table using a cue (=long stick)

4 [C] a small area of light: The sun cast a small pool of light on the dirty floor.

5 [C] a group that shares something, or that

someone or something can be chosen from: a car pool ♦ The training programme is helping to establish a pool of local qualified craftsmen.

6 the pools [plural] British a national competition in which people try to win money by guessing the results of football matches each week

pool² /puːl/ verb [T] to share something such as money, ideas, equipment etc with a group of people: It seemed sensible for us to pool our resources.

poor /pɔː/ adj ★★★

1 lacking money	4 not skilful
2 people without money	5 lacking sth important
3 of low quality	6 feeling sorry for sb

1 having little money and few possessions ≠ RICH: a poor family/area/country ♦ We were very poor and could barely afford the necessities of life.

2 the poor people who have little money and few possessions

3 not as good as expected or needed=BAD: poor health/eyesight/hearing ♦ The buildings were all in poor condition.

4 formal not skilful or clever ≠ GOOD: I was always put with the poorest students in the class.

5 not having enough of something important: a country poor in natural resources

6 spoken used for showing that you feel sorry for someone: The poor child had lost both his parents.

poorly¹ /ˈpɔːli/ adv badly: a poorly written essay

poorly² /ˈpɔːli/ adj British informal ill

pop¹ /pɒp/ noun ★

1 [U] POP MUSIC: Her music combines funk and pop.

2 [C] a sudden short sound like a small explosion: The balloon burst with a loud pop.

3 [U] informal a sweet drink containing many BUBBLES

pop² /pɒp/ adj **1** created for, or popular with, a very large number of people: pop psychology **2** relating to POP MUSIC: a pop singer/record/song

pop³ /pɒp/ verb ★

1 make sudden noise	5 ears feel pressure
2 burst	6 when eyes open wide
3 go/move quickly	+ PHRASE
4 put sth somewhere	+ PHRASAL VERB

1 [I/T] to make a sudden noise like a small explosion, or to make something do this: Champagne corks were popping.

2 [I/T] if something such as a BALLOON pops, or if you pop it, it bursts

3 [I] informal to go somewhere quickly or for a short time: I'm just popping round to Mary's to borrow some milk. ♦ He kept popping in and out, asking all kinds of questions.

4 [T] to move something quickly to a particular position: She picked a berry and popped it into her mouth.

5 [I] if your ears pop, you feel a sudden change of pressure in them

P

6 [I] *informal* if your eyes pop, they open very wide in surprise or excitement

PHRASE **pop the question** *informal* to ask someone to marry you

PHRASAL VERB **,pop 'up** to appear very quickly or suddenly: *The daffodils and tulips are popping up everywhere.*

popcorn /ˈpɒpkɔːn/ *noun* [U] a food made from dried grains that swell when they are heated. You can eat it with sugar or salt.

Pope /pəʊp/ *noun* [C] the leader of the Roman Catholic Church

poplar /ˈpɒplə/ *noun* [C] a tall thin tree

pop ,music *noun* [U] a type of music that is popular with many people, especially young people

poppy /ˈpɒpi/ *noun* [C] a red flower with a black centre that produces small black seeds —*picture* → C9

populace /ˈpɒpjʊləs/ *noun* [U] *formal* the people who live in a particular country or area

popular /ˈpɒpjʊlə/ *adj* ★★★
1 liked by many people ≠ UNPOPULAR: *Jenny is one of the most popular girls in the school.* ♦ *a popular brand of breakfast cereal*
2 a popular belief, feeling, attitude etc is one that many people have: *It's a popular misconception that all women love shopping.*
3 intended for, or involving, ordinary people rather than experts or leaders: *popular science/psychology* ♦ *There is little* **popular support** *for their economic reform policies.*

popularity /ˌpɒpjʊˈlærəti/ *noun* [U] a situation in which someone or something is popular with many people: *The popularity of professional sports has been increasing steadily.*

popularize /ˈpɒpjʊləraɪz/ *verb* [T] to make something popular with many people: *The Beatles popularized British rock in the early 1960s.* —**popularization** /ˌpɒpjʊləraɪˈzeɪʃ(ə)n/ *noun* [U]

popularly /ˈpɒpjʊləli/ *adv* by most people, or in most situations: *The duchess is popularly known as 'Fergie'.*

populate /ˈpɒpjʊleɪt/ *verb* **be populated** if an area is populated by people or animals, they live there: *Burundi is one of the most densely populated countries in the world.*

population /ˌpɒpjʊˈleɪʃ(ə)n/ *noun* [singular] ★★★
1 the number of people who live in a particular area: *Los Angeles has* **a population of** *over 3 million.* ♦ *Better health care and agriculture have led to rapid* **population growth.**
2 all the people who live in a particular area: *Less than 40% of the population voted in the last election.* ♦ *the* **ageing population** *of the US*

populist /ˈpɒpjʊlɪst/ *adj* representing the interests and opinions of ordinary people —**populist** *noun* [C]

populous /ˈpɒpjʊləs/ *adj* a populous area has many people living in it

porcelain /ˈpɔːs(ə)lɪn/ *noun* [U] a hard shiny white substance that is used for making things such as dishes, cups, and

decorations, or the things that are made from this substance

porch /pɔːtʃ/ *noun* [C] **1** *British* a small area covered by a roof at the entrance to a house or other building —*picture* → C1 **2** *American* a VERANDA

pore¹ /pɔː/ *noun* [C] one of the very small holes in the surface of your skin

pore² /pɔː/ **PHRASAL VERB** **ˈpore over sth** to examine or read something very carefully and in a lot of detail: *Ben was poring over computer printouts with an engineer.*

pork /pɔːk/ *noun* [U] the meat from a pig: *pork chops* → BACON, HAM

porn /pɔːn/ *noun* [U] *informal* PORNOGRAPHY

pornography /pɔːˈnɒgrəfi/ *noun* [U] films, pictures, magazines etc that show sexual activities in a very obvious way that is intended to make people sexually excited —**pornographic** /ˌpɔːnəˈgræfɪk/ *adj*

porous /ˈpɔːrəs/ *adj* with a lot of very small holes that air and water can pass through

porpoise /ˈpɔːpəs/ *noun* [C] a large sea animal, similar to a DOLPHIN

porridge /ˈpɒrɪdʒ/ *noun* [U] *British* a hot food made from OATS (=a type of grain) and milk or water, often eaten at breakfast

port /pɔːt/ *noun* ★★
1 [C/U] an area of water on the coast where ships stop, or a city with a port: *New York is the busiest port on the East Coast.* ♦ *At dusk they docked at* **the port of** *Monaco.* ♦ *We'll have to spend 10 days* **in port** *for repairs.*
2 [C] *computing* a part of a computer where you can connect another piece of equipment
3 [U] a strong sweet wine made in Portugal
4 [U] the left side of a ship or plane

portable /ˈpɔːtəb(ə)l/ *adj* easy to carry or move: *a portable television/heater*

portal /ˈpɔːt(ə)l/ *noun* [C] *computing* a WEBSITE that has LINKS (=connections) to other WEBSITES

porter /ˈpɔːtə/ *noun* [C] someone in a station, airport, or hotel whose job is helping people with their bags and showing them where to go

portfolio /pɔːtˈfəʊliəʊ/ *noun* [C] **1** a collection of pictures, photographs, or documents that you use as examples of work that you have done **2** all the INVESTMENTS that a person or company has made

porthole /ˈpɔːthəʊl/ *noun* [C] a small round window in the side of a ship or plane

portion /ˈpɔːʃ(ə)n/ *noun* [C] **1** a part of something: *Only a small portion of the population could read.* **2** the amount of food that one person eats at a meal: *If you eat smaller portions, you will begin to lose weight.*

portly /ˈpɔːtli/ *adj* a portly person is fairly fat=STOUT

portrait /ˈpɔːtrɪt/ *noun* ★
1 [C] a painting, drawing, or photograph of someone: *A* **portrait of** *her three children hangs behind her desk.*
2 [C] a description of someone or something, for example in a book: *an interesting* **portrait of** *life under communism*
3 [U] a way of arranging a page so that its

P

short sides are at the top and bottom
→ LANDSCAPE

portray /pɔːˈtreɪ/ verb [T] **1** to show or describe someone or something in a particular way: *Opponents portray the president as weak and ineffectual.* **2** to play the part of a particular person in a film, play etc —**portrayal** noun [C/U]

pose¹ /pəʊz/ verb **1** [T] to create a difficult or dangerous situation: *The oil spill poses a threat to marine life in the area.* **2** [I] to sit or stand somewhere so that someone can take a photograph of you or paint a picture of you **3** [I] to dress or behave in a particular way to make people notice you, admire you, or be impressed by you

> **PHRASE** **pose a question** *formal* to ask a question

> **PHRASAL VERB** **pose as sb/sth** to pretend to be a particular person or type of person in order to trick people: *Police officers posing as customers were sold some of the stolen items.*

pose² /pəʊz/ noun [C] **1** the position that you keep your body in when someone is taking your photograph or painting your picture **2** behaviour that is not natural or sincere and is intended to impress or trick people: *You get the feeling that his apparently strong religious faith is just a pose.*

posh /pɒʃ/ adj *informal* **1** expensive and attractive: *a posh home/hotel/restaurant* **2** *British* talking or behaving in a way that is typical of people from a high social class

position¹ /pəˈzɪʃ(ə)n/ noun [C] ★★★

1 way sth is placed	**5** job in company
2 general situation	**6** rank/status
3 where sth is	**7** place in list etc
4 opinion about issue	**8** where sb plays

1 the way that someone's body or an object is placed: *First, get yourself into a comfortable position.* ♦ *He managed to push the vehicle back to an upright position.*
2 the situation that someone is in: *What would you do if you were in my position?* ♦ *I'm not **in a position** to say who my sources are.*
3 where something is in relation to other things: *Place the plant in a bright sunny position.* ♦ *Here is a chart showing the **positions** of the planets.* ♦ *Put the photographs **into position** on the page.*
4 an opinion about an important issue: *No one was sure of his **position** on any issue.* ♦ *The President will consider the facts carefully before **taking a position** on this case.*
5 a job in a company: *There are 12 women in **management positions** within the company.* ♦ *I'm sorry, **the position has already been filled** (=someone has already been chosen to do the job).*
6 someone's rank or status in an organization or in society: *Such behaviour was clearly not acceptable for someone in a **position of authority**.*
7 the place that someone or something has in a list or competition: *Following behind in fourth position is car number 47.*
8 in team sports, the part of the field where a particular player plays

position² /pəˈzɪʃ(ə)n/ verb [T] to put someone or something in a particular place: *Position the microphone as close as possible to the source of sound.*

positive /ˈpɒzətɪv/ adj ★★★

1 completely certain	**4** situation etc: good
2 expecting good things	**5** showing condition
3 showing agreement	**6** number: above zero

1 completely certain: *We'd met before – I was **positive about** that.* ♦ **+(that)** *Are you positive that there's been no mistake?*
2 believing that good things will happen, or that a situation will get better ＝OPTIMISTIC ≠ NEGATIVE: *a positive attitude* ♦ *Try to think positive thoughts.*
3 showing agreement or approval ≠ NEGATIVE: *We couldn't be sure if her reaction would be positive.*
4 a positive experience, situation, result etc is a good one ≠ NEGATIVE: *School was **a totally positive experience** for me.* ♦ *The **positive aspects** of parenthood are rarely written about.*
5 a positive result in a medical test means that the person has the disease or condition that was tested for ≠ NEGATIVE
6 *technical* a positive number is higher than zero ≠ NEGATIVE

> **Words often used with positive**
>
> *Nouns often used with positive (sense 2)*
> ■ POSITIVE + **approach, attitude, outlook, view**: used about attitudes that emphasize the good aspects of something
> *Nouns often used with positive (sense 3)*
> ■ POSITIVE + **feedback, reaction, response**: used about reactions that show that you approve of someone or something

positively /ˈpɒzətɪvli/ adv **1** used for emphasizing that something is true: *His voice changed and became positively angry.* **2** in a way that shows that you approve or agree with something: *Most people reacted quite positively to the proposal.* **3** in a way that is likely to have good results: *We need to approach this problem positively.*

possess /pəˈzes/ verb [T] *formal* ★★ to own or have something: *Kate is a woman who possesses a rare intelligence.* ♦ *They were all found guilty of illegally possessing firearms.*

> **PHRASE** **what possessed you (to do sth)** *spoken* used for asking someone why they did something when you think that they made a serious mistake: *What possessed you to get involved with such a ridiculous scheme?* —**possessor** noun [C]

possessed /pəˈzest/ adj controlled by an evil spirit

possession /pəˈzeʃ(ə)n/ noun ★★
1 [C] something that you own: *Their family home and possessions were destroyed in the fire.* ♦ *Her most **prized possession** is a locket that she wears constantly.*
2 [U] *formal* a situation in which you have or own something: *The seller is entitled to retain **possession** of the goods until they are paid for.* ♦ *The town of Winterset **took possession of** (=started owning) the castle in 1947.* ♦ *Unfortunately, we no longer have those records **in our possession**.* ♦ *The*

P

brothers were caught in possession of stolen property.

possessive /pəˈzesɪv/ adj **1** wanting to have all of someone's love and attention: *a jealous and possessive boyfriend* **2** not willing to share things **3** *linguistics* a possessive word or form of a word is a word such as 'her', 'its', 'Jan's', or 'dog's' that shows who or what someone or something belongs to or is connected with: *a possessive pronoun* —**possessively** adv, **possessiveness** noun [U]

possibility /ˌpɒsəˈbɪləti/ noun ★★★
1 [C/U] something that might happen or be true: *Is everyone aware of the possibility of injury when skateboarding?* ♦ +(that) *There is a strong possibility that they will win the next election.*
2 [C] a likely or suitable choice among several possible people or things: *We need to examine other possibilities before we make a final decision.*
3 possibilities [plural] opportunities to develop in a successful, interesting, or exciting way: *This old building has some intriguing possibilities.*

possible /ˈpɒsəb(ə)l/ adj ★★★
1 able to be done, or capable of happening or being true ≠ IMPOSSIBLE: *The task will not be possible without access to the Internet.* ♦ *We need to avoid delay if at all possible.* ♦ *I relax with a good book whenever possible.* ♦ *Get as much information as possible.* ♦ **it is possible (that)** *I suppose it's possible she didn't know, but I'm fairly sure I told her.* ♦ **it is possible to do sth** *It is possible to see as far as Corsica on a clear day.*
2 likely or suitable in a particular situation or for a particular purpose: *a possible explanation* ♦ *a possible site for the new school building*
3 used with a SUPERLATIVE for emphasizing that something has the most or least of a particular quality: *Deb scored the highest score possible on the test.* ♦ *He arrived at the worst possible time.*
PHRASE is it/would it be possible? *spoken* used for asking politely if you can do something or have something: *Would it be possible to have a look at your newspaper?*

possibly /ˈpɒsəbli/ adv ★★★ likely to happen or be true, but not certain: *There is a chance of showers today and possibly a thunderstorm.* ♦ *'Do we have enough money to get a car?' 'Possibly.'* ♦ *He is quite possibly the most experienced climber in the world.*
PHRASES can/could possibly 1 used for emphasizing what is or is not possible: *There was nothing more we could possibly do under the circumstances.* ♦ *You can't possibly ask them to risk their lives.* **2** used for emphasizing your surprise or shock at something: *How can anyone possibly spend an hour in the shower?*
can/could sb possibly do sth? *spoken* used for asking someone to do something that you think might not be convenient for them: *Could you possibly give me a lift to work?*

post¹ /pəʊst/ noun ★★★
1 [U] *British* the letters and parcels that are delivered to someone, or the system used

for collecting, carrying, and delivering them =MAIL: *There was no post for you today.* ♦ *I never send anything valuable through the post.* ♦ *Did you send the parcel by post or by courier?*
2 [C] a job, especially one with a lot of responsibility: *The Prime Minister appointed her to the post of ambassador.*
3 [C] a strong thick pole made of wood or metal that is put upright in the ground
4 [C] a place where a soldier or guard must remain in order to do their job

post² /pəʊst/ verb [T] ★
1 *British* to send a letter or parcel to someone in the post
2 to put information or a message where the public can see it, for example on a wall: *The menu and prices are posted outside the door.*
3 *computing* to put information on the Internet: *New job openings are posted every day on their website.*
4 to send someone somewhere to do a job, especially in another country =STATION: *a United Nations plan to post troops along Croatia's borders*
PHRASE keep sb posted to regularly give someone information about how something is developing or changing: *We'll keep you posted on the weather situation.*

post- /pəʊst/ prefix after or later than: *a post-match interview*

postage /ˈpəʊstɪdʒ/ noun [U] money that you pay in order to send letters and parcels in the post

'postage ,stamp noun [C] *formal* a stamp that is put on an envelope

postal /ˈpəʊst(ə)l/ adj **1** relating to the system that takes the post to the people it is addressed to: *postal deliveries* **2** *British* done in a way that involves sending things by post: *a postal vote*

'postal ,order noun [C] *British* an official document that you buy in a POST OFFICE as a safe way of sending money to someone

postbox /ˈpəʊs(t)ˌbɒks/ noun [C] *British* a container in a public place where you can put post that you want to send

postcard /ˈpəʊs(t)ˌkɑːd/ noun [C] a small card that you write on one side of and send to someone in the post

postcode /ˈpəʊs(t)ˌkəʊd/ noun [C] *British* a group of letters and numbers that you write at the end of a person's address

poster /ˈpəʊstə/ noun [C] a large printed notice or picture that you put on a wall for decoration or to advertise something

posterity /pɒˈsterəti/ noun [U] the people who will live in the future after you are dead: *We have a duty to preserve great works of art for posterity.*

postgraduate /ˌpəʊs(t)ˈɡrædʒuət/ adj **1** *British* relating to study that you do after receiving your first university degree **2** *American* relating to work or studies that you do after receiving an advanced degree such as an MA or a PHD —**postgraduate** noun [C]

posthumous /ˈpɒstjʊməs/ adj given or happening after someone's death: *posthumous awards for bravery* —**posthumously** adv

P

posting /ˈpəʊstɪŋ/ noun [C] **1** a public notice, especially one advertising a job **2** computing a message put on the Internet **3** a job that someone is sent somewhere to do, usually in another country

Post-it trademark a small piece of paper with a sticky substance on the back that is used for sticking notes on other papers and surfaces —picture → C3

postman /ˈpəʊs(t)mən/ (plural **postmen** /ˈpəʊs(t)mən/) noun [C] someone whose job is to collect and deliver post

postmark /ˈpəʊs(t)mɑːk/ noun [C] an official mark that the POST OFFICE puts on a letter or parcel to show when and where it was posted —**postmark** verb [T]

postmortem /ˌpəʊs(t)ˈmɔːtəm/ noun [C] a medical examination of a dead body to find out why the person died=AUTOPSY

postnatal /ˌpəʊs(t)ˈneɪt(ə)l/ adj relating to the period of time after the birth of a baby: postnatal depression → ANTENATAL

post office noun [C] a place where you can buy stamps, send letters and parcels, collect money given to you by the government etc

postpone /ˈpəʊs(t)pəʊn/ verb [T] to decide that something will not be done at the time when it was planned for, but at a later time: Bad weather forced us to postpone Friday's game. —**postponement** noun [C/U]

postscript /ˈpəʊs(t)skrɪpt/ noun [C] information that is added at the end of a letter, email, or other piece of writing

posture /ˈpɒstʃə/ noun [C/U] the position that your body is in when you sit, stand, or walk: Exercise can improve your posture.

post-war or **postwar** /ˈpəʊs(t)ˈwɔː/ adj

happening or existing in the period of time immediately after a war, especially the Second World War

pot¹ /pɒt/ noun [C] ★★
1 a deep round metal container that you cook food in: a set of **pots and pans**
2 a container used for making or serving hot drinks, or the amount of a drink that a pot contains: a pot of tea/coffee
3 a container that you grow plants in: a plant pot
4 a container made of glass or clay that is used for storing food=JAR: a pot of jam/ honey

pot² /pɒt/ verb [T] to put a plant in a container with soil

potassium /pəˈtæsiəm/ noun [U] a soft white metal element that is used for making soap and FERTILIZER

potato /pəˈteɪtəʊ/ (plural **potatoes**) noun [C/U] ★★ a hard round vegetable that grows under the ground: baked potatoes ♦ potato salad —picture → C11

potato chips noun [plural] American CRISPS

potent /ˈpəʊt(ə)nt/ adj powerful or effective: a potent painkiller —**potency** noun [U]

potential¹ /pəˈtenʃ(ə)l/ adj ★ possible or likely in the future: a potential disaster ♦ The disease is a potential killer. —**potentially** adv: a potentially harmful drug

potential² /pəˈtenʃ(ə)l/ noun ★
1 [U] the possibility to develop or achieve something in the future: As a composer, she still hasn't **realized her potential**.
2 [singular] a possibility that something will happen: With this many people involved, there is always **a potential for** conflict.

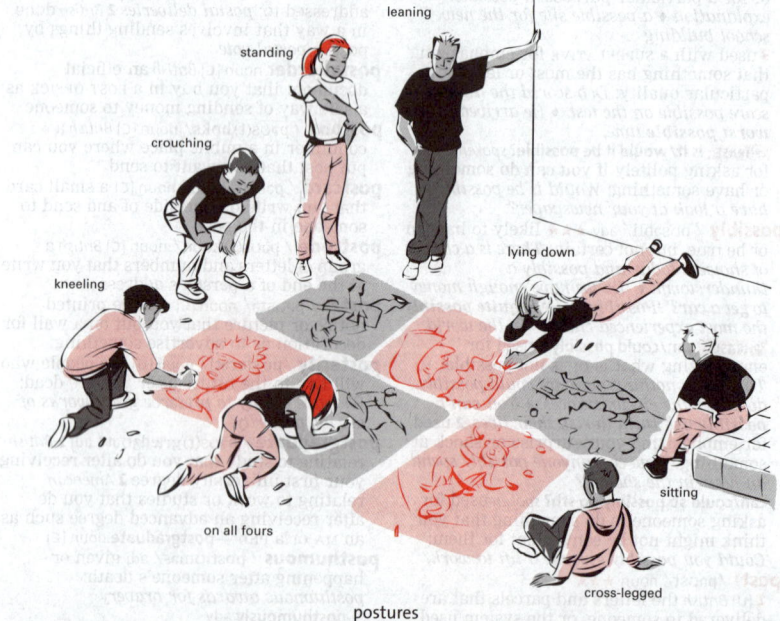

leaning

standing

crouching

lying down

kneeling

sitting

on all fours

cross-legged

postures

pothole /ˈpɒtˌhəʊl/ noun [C] a hole in a road
—**potholed** /ˈpɒtˌhəʊld/ adj

potholing /ˈpɒtˌhəʊlɪŋ/ noun [U] *British* the
sport of going into holes in mountains or
underground

potion /ˈpəʊʃ(ə)n/ noun [C] a drink that is
believed to be magic, poisonous, or useful
as a medicine

pot ˈluck noun **take pot luck** to choose
something when you do not know what
you will get

potted /ˈpɒtɪd/ adj *British* **1** giving a short
summary of the facts: *a potted history*
2 potted food is preserved in a POT **3** growing
in a pot: *a potted plant*

potter¹ /ˈpɒtə/ noun [C] someone who makes
pottery

potter² /ˈpɒtə/ verb [I] *British* to do things in a
slow and enjoyable way: *Jo spent the day
pottering around the garden.*

pottery /ˈpɒtəri/ noun [U] **1** objects such as
plates and cups that are made out of baked
clay **2** the activity of making pottery

potty¹ /ˈpɒti/ noun [C] a container that is
used as a toilet by young children

potty² /ˈpɒti/ adj *British informal* crazy

pouch /paʊtʃ/ noun [C] **1** a small bag made of
cloth or thin leather **2** a fold of skin on the
body of an animal, for example the place
where a KANGAROO carries its baby

poultry /ˈpəʊltri/ noun [U] birds such as
chickens that are used for meat or eggs, or
the meat of these birds

pounce /paʊns/ verb [I] **1** to quickly jump on
or hold someone or something: *They
pounced on their suspect.* **2** to react in a very
sudden way, especially by criticizing
someone: *White House aides pounced on the
remark.*

pound¹ /paʊnd/ noun [C] ★★★
1 a unit of money that is used in the UK
and several other countries. Its symbol is
£: *a pound coin* ♦ *a ten pound note*
2 a unit for measuring weight, used in
several countries including the US and the
UK, containing 16 OUNCES and equal to 0.454
kilograms: *half a pound of cheese* ♦ *The baby
weighed over 10 pounds.*
3 a place where pets that are lost or not
wanted are kept

pound² /paʊnd/ verb **1** [I/T] to hit something
many times with a lot of force: *I could hear
them pounding on the door.* **2** [I] if your heart
pounds, it beats strongly and quickly
because you are nervous, excited, or afraid
3 [I] to walk or run with heavy and regular
steps: *She pounded down the hall to see what
had happened.*

pour /pɔː/ verb ★★
1 [T] to make a liquid or substance flow out
of a container that you are holding: **pour sb
sth** *Sit down and I'll pour you a drink.* ♦
pour sth into/over/down sth *Pour the mixture
into a dish and bake for 45 minutes.*
2 [I] to flow continuously and in large
amounts: *The village was evacuated as lava
poured from the volcano.* ♦ *Tears were
pouring down her face.*
3 [I] to rain very hard: *The thunder and
lightning stopped, but it continued to pour.*

4 [I] to arrive or go somewhere quickly in a
large group or in large amounts: *People
poured out of the train.* ♦ *Election results
are beginning to pour in.*

PHRASAL VERBS ˈpour ˌdown same as **pour** 3:
The rain poured down in torrents.
ˈpour sth ˌinto sth to give a lot of effort, money,
or help: *They've already poured a lot of time
and money into this project.*
ˈpour sth ˈout to tell someone everything that
you are feeling: *She began pouring out her
fears about the future.*

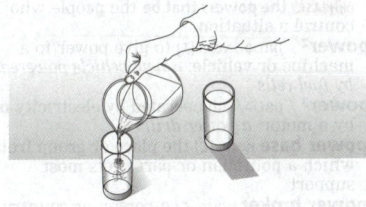

pour

pout /paʊt/ verb [I] to push your lips out in
order to show that you are annoyed, or in
order to look more sexually attractive
—**pout** noun [C]

poverty /ˈpɒvəti/ noun [U] a situation in
which someone does not have enough
money to pay for their basic needs
≠ WEALTH: *Half the world's population is
living in poverty.*

ˈpoverty ˌline, the noun [singular] the amount
of money that is considered necessary to
live

ˈpoverty-stricken adj extremely poor

POW /ˌpiː əʊ ˈdʌb(ə)ljuː/ noun [C] a PRISONER
OF WAR

powder¹ /ˈpaʊdə/ noun [C/U] ★ a soft dry
substance that looks like dust or sand:
chilli powder —**powdery** adj

powder² /ˈpaʊdə/ verb [T] to put powder on
your face or body

powdered /ˈpaʊdəd/ adj in the form of
powder: *powdered milk*

power¹ /ˈpaʊə/ noun ★★★

1 ability to influence	**6** physical force
2 ability to achieve	**7** strong country
3 political control	**8** natural ability
4 legal authority	+ PHRASE
5 energy/electricity	

1 [U] the ability to influence or control
people: *a power struggle within the party*
(=an attempt by each of two people or
groups to get control) ♦ *Her parents still
have a lot of power over her.* ♦ *Don't
underestimate the power of advertising.*
2 [U] the ability to achieve something or
make something happen: *purchasing/
bargaining power* ♦ *Willis did everything
within his power for his client.*
3 [U] political control of a country or
government: *The ruling Social Democratic
party has been in power for ten years.* ♦
*Later that year, the generals seized power
in a bloody coup.*

4 [C/U] official or legal authority to do something: *A high court has* **power to** *overturn the lower court's decision.*
5 [U] energy that is used for operating equipment and machines: *solar power*
6 [U] physical force or strength: *The boy was thrown backwards by the power of the blast.*
7 [C] a strong country that is able to influence other countries: *China has emerged as a major economic power.*
8 [C/U] a natural or unusual ability for doing something: *He has amazing powers of concentration.*

PHRASE **the powers that be** the people who control a situation

power² /'paʊə/ verb [T] to give power to a machine or vehicle: *a new vehicle powered by fuel cells*

power³ /'paʊə/ adj operated by electricity or by a motor: *a power drill*

power base noun [C] the place or group from which a politician or party gets most support

power broker noun [C] a person or country that has a lot of influence and uses it in order to control other people or countries

power cut noun [C] *British* a period when the electricity supply stops

powerful /'paʊəf(ə)l/ adj ★★★
1 able to influence or control what people do or think ≠ WEAK: *We live in a society where the media are extremely powerful.* ♦ *a powerful argument in favour of gun control*
2 with a lot of physical strength or force: *a powerful explosion* ♦ *a powerful athlete* ♦ *The new model has a more powerful engine.*
3 with a strong effect: *powerful drugs*
—**powerfully** adv

powerless /'paʊələs/ adj not able to control or prevent something: *She was powerless to stop him.* —**powerlessness** noun [U]

power station noun [C] *British* a large building that contains machines that produce power, especially electricity

power steering noun [U] a system that makes it easy to turn a car with small movements of the STEERING WHEEL

power tool noun [C] a tool that uses electricity or a motor

pp abbrev pages

PR /ˌpiː 'ɑː/ abbrev **1** public relations
2 proportional representation

practicable /'præktɪkəb(ə)l/ adj *formal* able to be done or used successfully

practical¹ /'præktɪk(ə)l/ adj ★★★
1 involving, or relating to, real situations rather than theories or ideas alone: *Unfortunately this research has no practical use.* ♦ **Practical experience** *can be as valuable as academic qualifications.*
2 making sensible decisions and choices based on what can be successfully achieved ≠ IMPRACTICAL: *Despite their wealth, they were always practical about money.* ♦ *a practical attitude to marriage*
3 intended to be useful or suitable, not just fashionable or attractive: *a practical car for the family*
4 able to make repairs or do things with your hands in a skilful way

practical² /'præktɪk(ə)l/ noun [C] *British* an examination or lesson in which you make things or do experiments

practicality /ˌpræktɪ'kæləti/ noun **1** [U] the quality of being useful or suitable for a particular purpose or situation
2 practicalities [plural] the things that need to be dealt with, planned for, or done in order to achieve something

practical joke noun [C] a trick that is intended to surprise someone or make them look silly

practically /'præktɪkli/ adv **1** almost: *I was practically begging him to think again.*
2 in a way that is useful, sensible, or practical

practice¹ /'præktɪs/ noun [C/U] ★★★
1 occasions when you do something in order to become better at it, or the time that you spend doing this: *piano/basketball practice*
♦ *Your typing will improve* **with practice**.
2 a way of doing something, or something that is regularly done: *It is* **good practice** *to check your work before handing it in.* ♦ *Bribery is* **common practice** *in many countries.*
3 the business or profession of a doctor, lawyer, or other professional person

PHRASES **in practice** used for talking about what really happens rather than what you think will or should happen: *It's a good idea, but I don't think it would work in practice.*
out of practice bad at doing something because you have not been doing it regularly

practice² /'præktɪs/ the American spelling of **practise**

practiced /'præktɪst/ the American spelling of **practised**

practise /'præktɪs/ verb ★★
1 [I/T] to repeat an activity regularly so that you become better at it: *How many hours a day do you practise?* ♦ *Practise doing sth Practise putting your tent up in the garden several times.*
2 [T] to do something regularly or in a particular way: *The earliest colonists seem to have practised farming.*
3 [I/T] to work in a particular profession, especially in the medical or legal profession: *She completed her medical training, though she never practised.* ♦ *He is no longer allowed to* **practise law**.

PHRASE **practise what you preach** to behave in the same way that you try to persuade other people to behave

practised /'præktɪst/ adj skilful in something as a result of experience

practising /'præktɪsɪŋ/ adj active in a particular profession, religion, or way of life

practitioner /præk'tɪʃ(ə)nə/ noun [C] *formal* someone who works in a particular profession, especially medicine or law

pragmatic /præg'mætɪk/ adj involving or emphasizing practical results rather than theories and ideas: *a pragmatic approach to problem solving* —**pragmatically** /præg'mætɪkli/ adv, **pragmatism** /'prægmətɪz(ə)m/ noun [U], **pragmatist** /'prægmətɪst/ noun [C]

P

prairie /ˈpreəri/ noun [C] a large flat area in central North America that is covered with grass and farms but that has no trees

praise¹ /preɪz/ verb [T] to express strong approval or admiration for someone or something: *If you never praise your kids, how can they know when they're doing something right?* ♦ *The painting was highly praised.*

praise² /preɪz/ noun [U] an expression of strong approval or admiration

praiseworthy /ˈpreɪzˌwɜːði/ adj formal deserving praise or admiration

pram /præm/ noun [C] a small vehicle with four wheels that you push a baby in while you are walking

prance /prɑːns/ verb [I] showing disapproval to move around in a lively way that seems silly to other people

prank /præŋk/ noun [C] a silly trick that you play on someone in order to surprise them

prattle /ˈpræt(ə)l/ verb [I] to talk in a silly way for a long time about unimportant things
—**prattle** noun [U]

prawn /prɔːn/ noun [C] a SHELLFISH (=a small sea animal with a hard shell) that can be eaten

pray /preɪ/ verb ★
1 [I/T] to speak to God or a SAINT, for example to give thanks or to ask for help: *They prayed for peace.* ♦ *He prayed to God to save him.* ♦ +(that) *We all prayed that she would soon return.*
2 [I] to hope or wish very strongly for something: +(that) *Everyone prayed that the war wouldn't last long.*

prayer /preə/ noun ★
1 [C] something that you say when you speak to God: *a prayer for peace* ♦ *He said a prayer for their safety.*
2 [U] the practice of speaking to God: *the power of prayer*

prayer book noun [C] a book that contains prayers

prayer mat noun [C] a small carpet that Muslims put on the floor under their knees when they pray

pre- /priː/ prefix before: *pre-war fashions* ♦ *pre-school programmes* (=for children who are too young for school)

preach /priːtʃ/ verb **1** [I/T] to talk about a religious subject to a group of people, especially in a church **2** [I] showing disapproval to tell people how to behave=LECTURE

preacher /ˈpriːtʃə/ noun [C] someone whose job is to give religious speeches or lead religious ceremonies in some Christian churches

prearranged /ˌpriːəˈreɪndʒd/ adj planned or agreed to at an earlier time

precarious /prɪˈkeəriəs/ adj likely to change or become dangerous without warning: *For the refugees life was always precarious.*
—**precariously** adv

precaution /prɪˈkɔːʃ(ə)n/ noun [C] something that you do in order to protect people or things against possible harm or trouble: *Doctors recommend taking precautions to protect your skin from the sun.*

precautionary /prɪˈkɔːʃ(ə)n(ə)ri/ adj done or used for protection against possible harm or trouble: *a precautionary step/measure*

precede /prɪˈsiːd/ verb [T] formal to happen or exist before another person or thing: *These exercises must always be preceded by a warm-up.*

precedence /ˈpresɪdəns/ noun **take precedence (over)** if something takes precedence over something else, it is more important and should be dealt with first

precedent /ˈpresɪdənt/ noun [C/U] an action or event in the past that is used as an example when someone wants to do the same thing again: *This decision could set a dangerous precedent.*

preceding /prɪˈsiːdɪŋ/ adj existing or coming immediately before someone or something else

precinct /ˈpriːsɪŋkt/ noun [C] **1** British a part of a town that has a particular use, especially an area where no cars are allowed: *a shopping precinct* **2** American a district in a town or city, usually organized for voting, police, or government purposes

precious¹ /ˈpreʃəs/ adj ★ very valuable: *a precious jewel* ♦ *Our freedom is the most precious thing we have.*

precious² /ˈpreʃəs/ adv **precious little/few** used for emphasizing how little there is of something

precious metal noun [C] a valuable metal such as gold or silver

precious stone noun [C] a valuable stone such as a DIAMOND or RUBY

precipice /ˈpresəpɪs/ noun [C] a very steep high CLIFF

precipitate /prɪˈsɪpɪˌteɪt/ verb [T] formal to make something happen or begin to exist: *Such headaches can be precipitated by certain foods as well as stress.*

precipitation /prɪˌsɪpɪˈteɪʃ(ə)n/ noun [U] technical rain, snow, HAIL etc

précis /ˈpreɪsiː/ noun [C] (plural **précis**) a short summary of a speech or piece of writing

precise /prɪˈsaɪs/ adj ★ exact and accurate: *The precise date and place of his birth are unknown.* ♦ *Lara was able to tell me everything that had happened in precise detail.*

> **PHRASE** **to be precise** used for saying that the information that you are giving about something is more exact than what you have said before=EXACT: *It's her 70th birthday soon, in March to be precise.*

precisely /prɪˈsaɪsli/ adv ★
1 exactly: *He knows precisely what we want.*
2 clearly: *Dartman spoke very precisely.*
3 used for adding emphasis to a reason or explanation: *They have the best medical care precisely because of high taxes.*
4 spoken used for showing that you completely agree with what someone says: *'You mean he took the money for himself?' 'Precisely.'*

precision /prɪˈsɪʒ(ə)n/ noun [U] the quality of being accurate and exact

preclude /prɪˈkluːd/ verb [T] formal if one thing precludes another, the first thing prevents the second one from happening

P

precocious /prɪˈkəʊʃəs/ adj a precocious child is more intelligent or behaves in a more developed way than is normal for their age

preconceived /ˌpriːkənˈsiːvd/ adj a preconceived idea or opinion is formed before you have all the facts

preconception /ˌpriːkənˈsepʃ(ə)n/ noun [C] an idea or opinion about something that you form before you have all the facts

precondition /ˌpriːkənˈdɪʃ(ə)n/ noun [C] something that must happen before something else can happen

precursor /priːˈkɜːsə/ noun [C] something that exists before something else

predate /ˌpriːˈdeɪt/ verb [T] to exist or happen earlier than something else

predator /ˈpredətə/ noun [C] **1** an animal that kills and eats other animals **2** business a company that tries to take control of other companies —**predatory** /ˈpredət(ə)ri/ adj: a predatory takeover bid

predecessor /ˈpriːdɪˌsesə/ noun [C] the person who had a job before someone else

predetermined /ˌpriːdɪˈtɜːmɪnd/ adj decided in advance

predicament /prɪˈdɪkəmənt/ noun [C] a difficult or unpleasant situation that is not easy to get out of

predicative /prɪˈdɪkətɪv/ adj linguistics predicative adjectives and phrases follow a verb, for example 'tired' in the sentence 'We were tired'

predict /prɪˈdɪkt/ verb [T] ★ to say what you think will happen in the future: They're predicting heavy rain for tomorrow. ♦ +(that) Industry leaders predict that another 8,000 jobs could be lost by the end of the year.

predictable /prɪˈdɪktəb(ə)l/ adj **1** something that is predictable happens in the way that you expect it to=FORESEEABLE **2** someone who is predictable always behaves or reacts in the same way ≠ UNPREDICTABLE —**predictably** adv

prediction /prɪˈdɪkʃ(ə)n/ noun [C] a statement about what you think will happen in the future

predisposed /ˌpriːdɪsˈpəʊzd/ adj **predisposed to/towards sth** likely to think, feel, or behave in a particular way, or to develop a particular medical condition

predisposition /ˌpriːdɪspəˈzɪʃ(ə)n/ noun **have a predisposition to/towards sth** to be likely to think or behave in a particular way, or to develop a particular medical condition

predominant /prɪˈdɒmɪnənt/ adj **1** most common, or greatest in number or amount **2** most important or powerful —**predominance** noun [U]

predominantly /prɪˈdɒmɪnənt(ə)li/ adv mainly: a predominantly Catholic country

predominate /prɪˈdɒmɪneɪt/ verb [I] formal to be more important, or greater in number or amount, than other things or people

pre-ˈeminent adj best at a particular activity: Spain's pre-eminent guitarist

pre-empt /priːˈempt/ verb [T] to do something in order to try to prevent something from happening

pre-emptive /priːˈemptɪv/ adj said or done before someone else has a chance to act or attack so that their plans or actions are prevented from happening

preen /priːn/ verb [I/T] if a bird or animal preens, or if it preens itself, it cleans and arranges its feathers or fur

prefabricated /priːˈfæbrɪˌkeɪtɪd/ adj a prefabricated building is built in sections that can be moved and put together quickly

preface /ˈprefəs/ noun [C] an introduction to a book or a speech

prefect /ˈpriːfekt/ noun [C] in some schools in the UK, an older student who controls the activities of younger students and helps them to obey the rules

prefer /prɪˈfɜː/ verb [T] ★★★ to like or want someone or something more than someone or something else: Which do you prefer, the red or the blue one? ♦ **prefer sb/sth to sb/sth** Even today, most Americans prefer coffee to tea. ♦ **prefer to do sth** Do you prefer to exercise indoors or out of doors? ♦ **prefer doing sth** I prefer working alone.

preferable /ˈpref(ə)rəb(ə)l/ adj more suitable or useful than something else

preferably /ˈpref(ə)rəbli/ adv used for saying what would be best in a particular situation even if it is not possible: The successful candidate should have a degree, preferably in a foreign language.

preference /ˈpref(ə)rəns/ noun [C/U] ★ someone or something that you prefer to something else: Either tomorrow or Wednesday is fine for me. Do you **have a preference?** ♦ It's really just a matter of **personal preference** which you choose.
PHRASE **in preference to** instead of someone or something else that you like or want less: They drink beer in preference to wine.

preferential /ˌprefəˈrenʃ(ə)l/ adj giving one person or group an advantage over all others: Neither sex should get preferential treatment.

prefix /ˈpriːfɪks/ noun [C] linguistics a group of letters that is added to the beginning of a word in order to change its meaning. For example, the prefix 'un-' is added to the word 'tidy' in order to form the word 'untidy'.

pregnancy /ˈpregnənsi/ noun [C/U] the condition of being pregnant, or the period of time when a woman is pregnant

pregnant /ˈpregnənt/ adj ★ if a woman is pregnant, she has a baby developing inside her body: I was only 19 when I **got pregnant.** ♦ She was **pregnant with twins.**

preheat /ˌpriːˈhiːt/ verb [T] to heat an oven so that it is the correct temperature for cooking something

prehistoric /ˌpriːhɪˈstɒrɪk/ adj relating to the period of time before anything was written down by humans: prehistoric animals

prejudge /ˌpriːˈdʒʌdʒ/ verb [T] to form an opinion about someone or something before you know everything about them

prejudice¹ /ˈpredʒʊdɪs/ noun [C/U] an unreasonable opinion or feeling, especially the feeling of not liking a particular group of people: We've been working hard to

P

overcome prejudice against women in politics.

prejudice² /ˈpredʒʊdɪs/ *verb* [T] to make someone form an opinion about someone or something before they have enough information

prejudiced /ˈpredʒʊdɪst/ *adj* someone who is prejudiced has an unreasonable opinion or feeling about someone or something, especially about a particular group of people

preliminary /prɪˈlɪmɪn(ə)ri/ *adj* coming before the main or most important part of something: *a preliminary agreement/ discussion*

prelude /ˈprelju:d/ *noun* [C] **1** an event that happens before a more important event **2** a short piece of music that introduces a longer piece of music

premature /ˈpremətʃə/ *adj* **1** happening too soon or before the usual time **2** a premature baby is born before it should be —**prematurely** *adv*

premeditated /priːˈmedɪteɪtɪd/ *adj* a premeditated crime is deliberately planned —**premeditation** /priːˌmedɪˈteɪʃ(ə)n/ *noun* [U]

premenstrual /priːˈmenstruəl/ *adj* happening in the days before a woman's PERIOD

premier¹ /ˈpremiə, *American* prɪˈmɪr/ *adj* best, largest, or most important

premier² /ˈpremiə, *American* prɪˈmɪr/ *noun* [C] a PRIME MINISTER

premiere /ˈpremieə, *American* prɪˈmɪr/ *noun* [C] the first public performance of a play or a film —**premiere** *verb* [I/T]

premiership /ˈpremiəʃɪp/ *noun* [U] the position of being Prime Minister, or the period of time that someone is Prime Minister

Premiership, the /ˈpremiəʃɪp/ the LEAGUE (=group of sports teams) in which the best English football teams compete

premise /ˈpremis/ *noun* [C] *formal* a principle or statement that you consider to be true, on which you base other theories and actions

premises /ˈpremisiz/ *noun* [plural] the buildings and land that a business or organization uses

premium¹ /ˈpriːmiəm/ *noun* [C] an amount of money that you pay regularly for an insurance policy

PHRASE **at a premium** if something is at a premium, a lot of people want it so that it is difficult to get

premium² /ˈpriːmiəm/ *adj* more expensive or of higher quality than other similar things

premonition /ˌpreməˈnɪʃ(ə)n/ *noun* [C] a strong feeling that something bad is going to happen

prenatal /priːˈneɪt(ə)l/ *adj* relating to the period of time when a woman is pregnant

preoccupation /priːˌɒkjʊˈpeɪʃ(ə)n/ *noun* **1** [singular/U] a state in which you think much about something so much that you do not think about other things: *a preoccupation with death* **2** [C] something that you think

about and want to do because it is important=CONCERN

preoccupied /priˈɒkjʊpaɪd/ *adj* thinking about something so much that you do not notice other things or cannot think about other things —**preoccupy** *verb* [T]

prepackaged /ˌpriːˈpækɪdʒd/ or **prepacked** /ˌpriːˈpækd/ *adj* prepackaged products are already wrapped or in a box when you buy them

prepaid /ˌpriːˈpeɪd/ *adj* something that is prepaid has already been paid for before you use it: *prepaid postage*

preparation /ˌprepəˈreɪʃ(ə)n/ *noun* ★ **1** [U] the process of making someone or something ready for something: *The experience was good **preparation for** a career in journalism.* ◆ *The flowers were ordered **in preparation for** the wedding.* **2 preparations** [plural] things that you do so that you are ready for something: *The US continued its military preparations.* ◆ *Organizers are **making final preparations** for next week's festival.*

preparatory /prɪˈpærət(ə)ri/ *adj* done as preparation for something else

prepare /prɪˈpeə/ *verb* ★★★ **1** [I/T] to get ready for something, or to make someone or something ready: **prepare sth for sb/sth** *Wendy helped Karen prepare the room for their guests.* ◆ **prepare to do sth** *Medical teams are preparing to fly to the area tomorrow.* **2** [T] to make food ready to be cooked or eaten: *You can prepare this dish in advance and freeze it.*

PHRASE **prepare the way/ground for** to do things that make it possible or easier for something to happen: *Her research prepared the way for later advances.*

prepared /prɪˈpeəd/ *adj* **1** ready and able to do something ≠ UNPREPARED: *We have to be prepared for anything.* **2** ready for use: *Make sure the room is prepared before they get there.* **3** done or made earlier: *Bonner read from a prepared statement.*

PHRASE **prepared to do sth** willing and able to do something: *I'm not prepared to listen to excuses.*

prepayment /priːˈpeɪmənt/ *noun* [C/U] money that you pay before you can use a service

preponderance /prɪˈpɒnd(ə)rəns/ *noun* [singular] *formal* most of the people or things in a group

preposition /ˌprepəˈzɪʃ(ə)n/ *noun* [C] *linguistics* a word that usually comes before a noun or a pronoun and that shows its relation to another part of the sentence. In the sentences 'I left it on the table' and 'She came out of the house', the words 'on' and 'out of' are prepositions. —**prepositional** *adj*

preposterous /prɪˈpɒst(ə)rəs/ *adj* *formal* extremely unreasonable or silly=ABSURD

pre-program *verb* [T] to give a computer, VCR, or other machine a set of instructions so that it will do what you want it to do at a later time

prep school /ˈprep ˌsku:l/ *noun* [C/U] **1** in the UK, a private school for children between

P

the ages of 7 or 8 and 11 or 13 **2** in the US, a private school for children over the age of 11 that prepares them for college

prequel /ˈpriːkwəl/ noun [C] a book or film that is about events that happened before the events in another book or film that was written or made earlier

prerecorded /ˌpriːrɪˈkɔːdɪd/ adj prerecorded messages, music, or television or radio programmes have been recorded so that they can be used later —**prerecord** verb [T], **prerecording** noun [C]

prerequisite /ˌpriːˈrekwəzɪt/ noun [C] formal something that must exist or happen before something else is possible

pre-school adj relating to children who are too young to go to school

prescribe /prɪˈskraɪb/ verb [T] if a doctor prescribes a drug or treatment, they say that you should have it

prescription /prɪˈskrɪpʃən/ noun [C] a piece of paper that a doctor gives you that says what type of medicine you need: *The drug is only available on prescription* (=if you have a prescription).

preseason /priːˈsiːsən/ adj relating to the time before the SEASON for a particular sport begins: *a preseason game*

presence /ˈprez(ə)ns/ noun ★★★
1 [U] the fact of being in a particular place at a particular time: *Mr Reese didn't even acknowledge my presence.* ♦ *a device for detecting the presence of submarines*
2 [singular] a group of people who are in a place for a particular purpose: *There is still a large military presence in the region.*
3 [singular/U] an impressive appearance or way of behaving or speaking
PHRASE **presence of mind** the ability to think quickly and clearly in a difficult situation

present¹ /ˈprez(ə)nt/ adj ★★★
1 existing or happening now: *The present situation cannot be allowed to continue.* ♦ *The present owners purchased the farm in 1976.*
2 at an event, or in a place: *Among those present at the ceremony were the ambassador and his wife.*
PHRASE **the present day** now: *It's a tradition that has survived right up till the present day.*

present² /prɪˈzent/ verb [T] ★★★

1 give formally/officially	**5** introduce programme
2 cause situation etc	**6** produce/organize sth
3 offer to be considered	**7** show sth to an official
4 describe sb/sth	

1 to give something to someone formally or officially: *Who will be **presenting** the prizes?* ♦ **present sb with sth** *We are very pleased to have been presented with this award.* ♦ **present sth to sb** *Finally the mayor presented the medals to the winners.*
2 to cause something such as a problem, threat, or opportunity: *The group's activities **presented a threat** to national security.*

3 to offer something for people to consider: *The commission **presented** its **report** in October.*
4 to show someone or something in a particular way: *The film **presents** a disturbing **image** of youth culture.*
5 British to introduce a television or radio programme: *The show will be presented by Trevor McDonald.*
6 to produce or organize something such as a play, film, or exhibition
7 to show something such as a passport to someone in an official position

present³ /ˈprez(ə)nt/ noun ★★★
1 [C] something that you give to someone, for example on their birthday =GIFT: *a wedding/birthday/Christmas present* ♦ *Yuki was wrapping **a present for** her mother.*
2 the present [singular] the period of time that is happening now: *We must learn to **live in the present**, not in the past.*
3 the present [singular] linguistics the PRESENT TENSE
PHRASE **at present** now: *At present there seems to be no solution to the crisis.*

presentable /prɪˈzentəb(ə)l/ adj looking good enough for people to see

presentation /ˌprez(ə)nˈteɪʃ(ə)n/ noun ★
1 [U] the way in which something is shown, arranged, or explained: *Using a computer helped with the spelling and **presentation** of his school work.*
2 [C] a ceremony at which something such as a prize is given to someone: *He will receive the prize at a presentation on Saturday.*
3 [C] a formal talk in which you describe or explain something to a group of people: *I'm going to ask each of you to **give a presentation**.*

present-day adj relating to a situation or place as it exists now: *The novel is set in present-day Russia.*

presenter /prɪˈzentə/ noun [C] British someone who introduces a television or radio programme

presently /ˈprez(ə)ntli/ adv **1** formal at the present time **2** old-fashioned soon

present participle noun [C] linguistics in English, the form of a verb that ends in 'ing' and that expresses continuing action, for example the word 'fishing'. It can sometimes be used as an adjective, for example in 'the screaming baby'.

present perfect, the noun [singular] linguistics in English, a verb tense that expresses an action that was completed at some time in the past, or that started in the past and continues. The tense is formed by combining the present tense of 'have' and the past participle of a verb, as in the sentence 'She has paid the bill'.

present tense, the noun [singular] linguistics the form of a verb that expresses what exists now, what is happening now, or what happens regularly

preservation /ˌprezəˈveɪʃ(ə)n/ noun [U] the process of working to protect something so that it is not damaged or destroyed

preservative /prɪˈzɜːvətɪv/ noun [C/U] a chemical substance used for preventing food or wood from decaying

preserve¹ /prɪˈzɜːv/ verb [T] ★

1 to take care of something in order to prevent it from being harmed or destroyed: *The society works to preserve historic buildings.*

2 to keep food fresh for a long time, for example by adding salt or chemicals to it

preserve² /prɪˈzɜːv/ noun **1** [C] *formal* a place or activity that is considered to belong to a particular person or group: *Sailing is no longer the preserve of the rich.* **2** [C/U] a sweet food made by boiling fruit and sugar together=JAM

preside /prɪˈzaɪd/ verb [I] to be in charge of an official meeting, ceremony, or other event

  PHRASAL VERB pre'side **over sth** to be in a position of power while important things are happening

presidency /ˈprezɪdənsi/ noun [C] the job of being president, or the period of time that someone has this job

president /ˈprezɪdənt/ noun [C] ★★★

1 the political leader of a country that does not have a king or queen: *President Lincoln ♦ the French president ♦ Clinton was elected president in 1992.*

2 the person who has the highest position in an organization or institution: *Lily Chang, our club president*

3 *American* the person in charge of a business or university: *the president of Citibank Corporation*

presidential /ˌprezɪˈdenʃ(ə)l/ adj **1** relating to a president: *a presidential election/ campaign/candidate* **2** behaving like a president or an important leader

press¹ /pres/ noun ★★★

1 newspapers etc	5 for crushing fruit etc
2 machine for printing	6 single push on sth
3 publishing business	+ PHRASE
4 for making sth flat	

1 the press newspapers and news magazines, or the journalists who work on them: *the national/local/American press ♦ the popular/tabloid press ♦ She has been criticized in the press for not speaking out on this issue.*

2 [C] a machine that is used for printing newspapers, books, or magazines
→ PRINTING PRESS

3 [C] a business that publishes books: *Edinburgh University Press*

4 [C] a piece of equipment that is used for making something flat or smooth: *a trouser press*

5 [C] a piece of equipment that is used for squeezing the juice or oil out of fruit or vegetables: *a garlic press*

6 [C] a single push on something such as a button or switch: *Internet shopping brings the shop to your door at the press of a button.*

  PHRASE give **sth** a press to make a piece of clothing smooth using an iron

> In British English, **the press** can be used with a singular or plural verb when it means all of the journalists who work on a newspaper or magazine . You can say *The press **was** out in force.* OR *The press **were** out in force.*

press² /pres/ verb ★★★

1 [I/T] to push one thing against another: **press sth against sth** *Children were pressing their faces against the window.* ♦ **press sth to sth** *Even with the phone pressed to his ear, he couldn't hear what she was saying.* ♦ *He felt the enormous weight of the man **pressing down on** his back.*

2 [T] to push something such as a button or switch in order to make a piece of equipment do something: *To read your email, press the return key.*

3 [I] to move as a group by pushing together in a particular direction: *A wave of protesters **pressed forward** towards the building.*

4 [T] to make clothes smooth using a hot iron=IRON

  PHRASE press charges (against sb) to officially accuse someone of committing a crime and make them go to court for a trial

  PHRASAL VERBS press a'head to continue doing something in a determined way: *They pressed ahead regardless of objections from local people.*

'press **sb for sth** to try in a determined way to get something from someone: *The more she pressed him for an explanation, the more he refused to speak.*

,press 'on *same as* press ahead

press

'press ,conference noun [C] an official meeting where someone makes a formal statement about something to journalists and answers questions about it

pressed /prest/ adj in a difficult situation because you do not have enough time, money, or other things that you need

pressing /ˈpresɪŋ/ adj very important and urgent

'press ,office noun [C] a department of a government or other organization that is responsible for dealing with journalists

'press re,lease noun [C] an official statement or report that an organization gives to journalists

'press-,up noun [C] *British* a physical exercise in which you lie down with your face towards the floor and use your arms to raise and lower your body

pressure¹ /ˈpreʃə/ noun ★★★
1 [C/U] attempts to persuade or force someone to do something: *Pressure for political change increased in the 1990s.* ♦ **be/come under pressure to do sth** *The council is still under pressure to reduce spending.* ♦ *There is now greater pressure on the White House to take action.* ♦ *He did not put any pressure on her to take the job.*
2 [U] a physical force that is pressing on someone or something: *She became aware of the pressure of his hand on her shoulder.*
3 [U] the force that a liquid, air, or gas produces in an area or a container: *You should check your tyre pressure at least once a month.*
4 [C/U] a worried feeling that you get when you have to deal with a difficult or complicated situation=STRESS: *With greatly increased workloads, everyone is under pressure now.* ♦ *The pressure on teachers has increased dramatically.*

pressure² /ˈpreʃə/ verb [T] to try to make someone do something that they do not want to do: *Don't be pressured into making any rash decisions.*

pressured /ˈpreʃəd/ adj worried because you have a lot of problems or responsibilities

pressure group noun [C] an organized group of people who try to persuade people and influence political decisions about a particular issue

pressurize /ˈpreʃəˌraɪz/ verb [T] **1** *British* to try to make someone do something that they do not want to do **2** to make the pressure inside something such as a container different from the pressure outside

pressurized /ˈpreʃəˌraɪzd/ adj **1** with air pressure that is controlled so that it is different from the air pressure outside, for example in a plane **2** a pressurized container forces a substance out when the container is opened

prestige /preˈstiːʒ/ noun [U] the good reputation and respect that someone or something has, based on their achievements, high social status etc

prestigious /preˈstɪdʒəs/ adj admired and respected by a lot of people

presumably /prɪˈzjuːməbli/ adv used for saying that you think something is true, although you are not completely sure: *They are students, so presumably they don't have a lot of money.*

presume /prɪˈzjuːm/ verb **1** [T] to think that something is true because it is likely, although you cannot be certain: *I presume you've already ordered lunch.* **2** [I] to behave as though you have the right to behave in a particular way when you do not: *He would never presume to tell me what to do.* **3** [T] *legal* to accept that something is true unless someone proves that it is not true: *Everyone should be presumed innocent until proven guilty.*

presumption /prɪˈzʌmpʃ(ə)n/ noun [C] a belief that something is true because it seems reasonable or likely

presumptuous /prɪˈzʌmptʃuəs/ adj *showing disapproval* showing too much confidence and not enough respect

presuppose /ˌpriːsəˈpəʊz/ verb [T] *formal* if one thing presupposes another, it cannot exist or happen unless the other thing is also true —**presupposition** /ˌpriːsʌpəˈzɪʃ(ə)n/ noun [C/U]

pre-tax adj used for describing an amount of money before taxes are taken out

pre-teen adj relating to children between 9 and 12 years old

pretence /prɪˈtens/ noun [C/U] a way of behaving that does not honestly express your real feelings, thoughts, or intentions

pretend¹ /prɪˈtend/ verb [I/T] ★
1 to behave in a particular way because you want someone to believe that something is true when it is not: *We were never going to make the marriage work, so why pretend?* ♦ **+(that)** *I'm sorry, but I can't just pretend it hasn't happened.* ♦ **pretend to do sth** *She closed her eyes and pretended to be asleep.*
2 to imagine that something is true when you are playing a game: **+(that)** *They're pretending they're astronauts again.* ♦ **pretend to be sb/sth** *The little girl was pretending to be a lion.*

pretend² /prɪˈtend/ adj imaginary

pretended /prɪˈtendɪd/ adj not real or sincere

pretense /prɪˈtens/ the American spelling of pretence

pretentious /prɪˈtenʃəs/ adj *showing disapproval* trying to seem more important, intelligent etc than you really are ≠ UNPRETENTIOUS

pretext /ˈpriːˌtekst/ noun [C] a reason that you pretend to have for doing something, that is given in order to hide your real reason or intention

prettily /ˈprɪt(ə)li/ adv in a pretty way

pretty¹ /ˈprɪti/ adv *spoken* ★
1 fairly: *My TV's getting pretty old now.* ♦ *Tom looks pretty tired.*
2 very: *The weather's been pretty awful, hasn't it?* ♦ *I can see they've made a pretty good job of it.*
PHRASE **pretty much/well/nearly** almost: *They look pretty much the same, don't they?*

pretty² /ˈprɪti/ adj ★
1 a pretty child, girl, or woman is attractive: *His girlfriend's very pretty.*
2 attractive or nice to look at or listen to: *It's one of the prettiest villages on the south coast.* ♦ *a pretty tune* ♦ *a pretty little cottage*
PHRASE **not just a pretty face** *spoken* used humorously for saying that someone is intelligent or skilful as well as being attractive
—**prettiness** noun [U]

prevail /prɪˈveɪl/ verb [I] *formal* **1** to exist at a particular time or in a particular situation: *A friendly atmosphere prevailed among the crowd.* **2** to be the strongest influence or element in a situation: *We hope that common sense will prevail in the dispute.* **3** to defeat someone in a game, competition, argument etc

prevailing /prɪˈveɪlɪŋ/ adj existing or having influence at a particular time or in a particular place: *Our markets were affected by the prevailing economic environment.*

preˈvailing ˈwind noun [C] a wind that blows in a particular area at a particular time of year

prevalent /ˈprevələnt/ adj very common in a particular place or among a particular group —**prevalence** noun [U]

prevent /prɪˈvent/ verb [T] ★★★
 1 to stop something from happening: **prevent sth (from) happening** *Rubber seals are fitted to prevent gas from escaping.*
 2 to stop someone from doing something: **prevent sb (from) doing sth** *The owner is prevented by law from making any major changes.*

preventable /prɪˈventəb(ə)l/ adj capable of being prevented

preventative /prɪˈventətɪv/ adj PREVENTIVE

prevention /prɪˈvenʃ(ə)n/ noun [U] the act of preventing something, or things that people do in order to prevent something: *the prevention of cancer ♦ crime prevention*

preventive /prɪˈventɪv/ adj done so that something does not become worse or turn into a problem

preview /ˈpriːvjuː/ noun [C] **1** an opportunity to see something such as a play, film, or work of art before it is shown to the public **2** a short description of something that will happen or will be available later —**preview** verb [T]

previous /ˈpriːviəs/ adj ★★★ a previous event, period, or thing happened or existed before the one that you are talking about: *Mark has two children from a previous marriage. ♦ All the other guests had arrived the previous day. ♦ No previous experience is required.*

previously /ˈpriːviəsli/ adv ★★★ before the present time, or before the time that you are discussing: *She was previously employed as a nurse.*

ˈpre-ˈwar adj from a time before a particular war

prey¹ /preɪ/ noun [U] **1** an animal that is caught by another animal and eaten → BIRD **2** someone who is attacked, cheated, or harmed by a criminal or dishonest person =VICTIM

prey² /preɪ/ **PHRASAL VERB** ˈprey on sb or ˈprey uˌpon sb to harm someone who is weak or cannot defend themselves

price¹ /praɪs/ noun ★★★
 1 [C] the amount of money that you have to pay in order to buy something: *Oil was at its lowest price in 30 years. ♦ For a limited period only, all our carpets are being sold at half price. ♦ They'll do the work for you, at a price* (=for a lot of money).
 2 [singular] the bad things that you have to accept in order to achieve something that you want: *For some of these young athletes, success comes at a heavy price. ♦ She has fulfilled her dream, but at what price?*
 PHRASE **at any price 1** if you want something at any price, you are determined to get it,

even if this brings severe problems **2** if you refuse to do something at any price, you refuse to do it, even for a lot of money or other benefits

---

Words often used with **price**

*Verb often used with **price** (noun, sense 1)*
 ■ **cut, lower, reduce, slash** + PRICE: make the price of something less
 ■ **increase, put up, raise** + PRICE: make the price of something greater
 ■ PRICE + **come down, fall, plummet, tumble**: become lower in price
 ■ PRICE + **go up, increase, rise, rocket, soar**: become higher in price

---

price² /praɪs/ verb [T] to set the price of a product or service: *The farmhouse is priced at £195,000.*

priceless /ˈpraɪsləs/ adj **1** very valuable and impossible to replace **2** extremely useful in helping you to achieve something

ˈprice ˌtag noun [C] **1** a label on a product that says how much it costs **2** *informal* the cost of something very big and expensive

pricey /ˈpraɪsi/ adj *informal* expensive=DEAR

prick¹ /prɪk/ verb [T] to make a very small hole in the surface of something with a sharp object
 PHRASE **prick (up) your ears** to start listening to something very carefully because it sounds interesting

prick² /prɪk/ noun [C] a quick feeling of sharp pain, caused by a sharp object making a hole in your skin

prickle¹ /ˈprɪk(ə)l/ verb [I/T] if your skin prickles, or if something prickles it, you feel as if something sharp is touching it

prickle² /ˈprɪk(ə)l/ noun [C] **1** an uncomfortable stinging feeling on your skin **2** a sharp pointed part on a plant or animal

prickly /ˈprɪkli/ adj **1** covered with prickles **2** *informal* a prickly person becomes angry very quickly **3** *informal* a prickly issue makes people disagree

pricy /ˈpraɪsi/ another spelling of **pricey**

pride¹ /praɪd/ noun ★
 1 [U] a feeling of pleasure at your own achievements or those of someone you love: *They take a lot of pride in their daughter's career.*
 2 [U] a feeling of respect for yourself =DIGNITY: *Their win has restored national pride.* → SWALLOW¹
 3 [U] a feeling that you are better than other people
 4 [C] a group of lions
 PHRASES **sb's pride and joy** a person or possession that gives someone a lot of happiness and satisfaction
 pride of place the most central or important position: *The clock now sits in pride of place in my sitting room.*

pride² /praɪd/ verb **pride yourself on sth** to feel proud about an achievement, skill, or special quality that you have

priest /priːst/ noun [C] ★
 1 someone whose job is to perform religious duties and ceremonies in some Christian

P

churches: *a Roman Catholic priest*
2 a man who performs religious duties in some religions that are not Christian
—**priestly** adv

priestess /ˌpriːˈstes/ noun [C] a woman who performs religious duties in some religions that are not Christian

priesthood /ˈpriːsthʊd/ noun **1 the priesthood** [singular] the work and responsibility of being a priest **2** [C/U] all the priests of a particular religion

prim /prɪm/ adj very careful about your behaviour and easily shocked —**primly** adv

prima donna /ˌpriːmə ˈdɒnə/ noun [C] someone who thinks that they are very important, and who is very difficult to please

primal /ˈpraɪm(ə)l/ adj relating to something that is very basic, especially very basic needs or emotions = PRIMITIVE

primarily /ˈpraɪm(ə)rəli, praɪˈmerəli/ adv mainly

primary¹ /ˈpraɪməri/ adj ★★
1 most important = MAIN: *Dealing with crime is our primary concern.*
2 relating to the education of children between the ages of about five and eleven: *primary education*
3 coming or happening before other things: *primary sources of information*

primary² /ˈpraɪməri/ noun [C] an election in which people in a particular state or area in the US choose their CANDIDATE for a political position

primary care noun [U] medical treatment and advice that you get in your local community

primary colour noun [C] one of the colours red, blue, or yellow that are combined to make other colours

primary election noun [C] a PRIMARY

primary school noun [C/U] a school for children between the ages of four or five and eleven

primate /ˈpraɪmeɪt/ noun [C] any animal belonging to the same group as humans, including monkeys and APES

prime¹ /praɪm/ adj **1** most important = PRIMARY: *Our prime concern was the safety of our customers.* **2** of the highest quality: *prime beef* **3** most likely to be chosen or to be suitable for something: *the prime suspect in a murder case*

prime² /praɪm/ verb [T] **1** to prepare someone to behave or react in a particular way **2** to get a weapon or bomb ready to fire or explode **3** to prepare a surface for paint or some other substance

prime³ /praɪm/ noun [singular] the stage in your life when you are most active or most successful

prime minister noun [C] ★★ the political leader in countries such as the UK that are governed by a parliament

primer /ˈpraɪmə/ noun **1** [U] a substance that is used for preparing a surface for paint **2** [C] a book that gives very simple instructions or basic information about something

prime time noun [U] the most popular time for watching television, which is in the middle of the evening

primeval /praɪˈmiːv(ə)l/ adj relating to the period when the universe or the Earth first began to exist

primitive /ˈprɪmətɪv/ adj **1** relating to a very early stage in the development of people, animals, or plants: *primitive fish* **2** very simple or old-fashioned: *a primitive computer* **3** natural, and done or experienced without thinking: *a primitive instinct*

primrose /ˈprɪmˌrəʊz/ noun [C] a pale yellow flower that grows wild

prince /prɪns/ noun [C] **1** a male member of a royal family who is not the king **2** the male royal leader of some small countries

princely /ˈprɪns(ə)li/ adj **1** very large, beautiful, or impressive **2** belonging or relating to a prince

Prince of Wales, the /ˌprɪns əv ˈweɪlz/ a title given to the first son of the British king or queen

princess /ˌprɪnˈses/ noun [C] **1** a female member of a royal family who is not the queen **2** the wife of a prince

principal¹ /ˈprɪnsəp(ə)l/ adj ★ main or most important: *The principal aim of the project is to provide an answer to this question.*

principal² /ˈprɪnsəp(ə)l/ noun ★
1 [C] *British* the head of a college or university: *the Principal of Glasgow University*
2 [C] the head of a school in countries other than the UK
3 [singular] the original amount of money that someone borrows

principality /ˌprɪnsəˈpæləti/ noun [C] a country that is ruled by a prince

principally /ˈprɪnsəp(ə)li/ adv mainly

principle /ˈprɪnsəp(ə)l/ noun ★★★
1 [C] a basic belief, theory, or rule that has a major influence on the way in which something is done: *It is a basic principle of English law that a person is innocent until proven guilty.* ♦ +**that** *the principle that education should be free to everyone*
2 [C/U] a basic rule or belief about what is right, that influences the way you behave: *We are opposed on principle to any further building in the valley.* ♦ *It was against their principles to join the armed forces.*
3 [C] a scientific theory or basic natural law that explains the way something works: *Windmills differ in design, but all operate on exactly the same principle.*
PHRASE **in principle** used for saying that something is possible in theory, although it has not been tried

principled /ˈprɪnsəp(ə)ld/ adj honest and responsible ≠ UNPRINCIPLED

print¹ /prɪnt/ verb ★★

1 produce on paper	4 press surface
2 publish	5 produce photograph
3 write by hand	+ PHRASAL VERB

1 [I/T] to produce words, numbers, pictures etc on paper, using a printer or PRINTING PRESS: **print sth on sth** *The book is beautifully printed on quality paper.*

2 [T] to publish something in a newspaper or magazine: *They refused to print my letter.*
3 [I/T] to write by hand using individual letters that are not joined together: *Please be sure to **print your name** next to your signature.*
4 [T] to create a mark on a surface by pressing something into it
5 [I/T] to produce a photograph on paper
PHRASAL VERB ,print sth 'out or ,print sth 'off to produce a copy of a computer document from a printer

print² /prɪnt/ noun ★

1 mark	**4** picture
2 of fingers	**5** photograph
3 letters	**+** PHRASES

1 [C] a mark made by pressing something onto a surface: *There were huge paw prints right outside our tent.*
2 [C] a FINGERPRINT
3 [U] letters or other symbols made by pressing ink, paint etc on paper or a similar surface: *The print is too small to read.*
4 [C] an image that is created by pressing a raised design onto paper, or by copying an existing image: *a limited edition print*
5 [C] a photograph: *old black and white prints*
PHRASES **in print 1** printed in a book, magazine or newspaper **2** a book that is in print is still available to buy from the company that published it
out of print a book that is out of print is no longer being published

printer /'prɪntə/ noun [C] ★
1 a piece of equipment that you use for printing documents that you have created on a computer —*picture* → C3
2 a person or business that prints books, newspapers etc

printing /'prɪntɪŋ/ noun **1** [U] the process of making books, newspapers etc, using a printing press **2** [C] the number of copies of something such as a book or newspaper that are printed at one time

'printing ,press noun [C] a machine that is used for printing newspapers, books etc

'print ,media, the noun [plural] newspapers and magazines

printout /'prɪnt,aʊt/ noun [C/U] paper that is printed with information from a computer file

prior /'praɪə/ adj *formal* ★ happening, existing, or done before a particular time=PREVIOUS: *I'm afraid I won't be able to come. I've got a prior engagement.* ♦ *students with no prior knowledge of English*
PHRASE **prior to sth** before something happened or existed: *The plane appeared to catch fire a few seconds prior to taking off.*

prioritize /praɪ'ɒrɪ,taɪz/ verb **1** [I/T] to decide in what order you should do things, based on how important or urgent they are **2** [T] to treat a particular job or issue as being more important than any others

priority /praɪ'ɒrəti/ noun ★★
1 [C] something important that must be done first, or that needs more attention than

anything else: *Health insurance will be our top priority.*
2 [U] the importance that you give to something that must be done: *Their marriage took priority over everything else.* ♦ *Safety must be given the highest priority.*
3 [U] the right to go before someone or something else, or to receive something before they do: *Buses take priority over other vehicles on the road.*

prism /'prɪz(ə)m/ noun [C] **1** any solid object that has a regular shape with flat sides and straight edges **2** a glass object in the shape of a prism, used for dividing light into its different colours

prison /'prɪz(ə)n/ noun [C/U] ★★★ an institution where people are kept as a punishment for committing a crime: *He's currently in prison for tax fraud.* ♦ *You can go to prison for that, you know.* ♦ *He was sent to prison for armed robbery.* ♦ *She could face a ten-year prison term* (=period in prison).

'prison ,camp noun [C] a place where prisoners are kept during a war

prisoner /'prɪz(ə)nə/ noun [C] ★★ someone who is in prison: *He was taken prisoner during the battle.*
PHRASE **prisoner of war** someone who is held as a prisoner by the enemy during a war=POW

pristine /'prɪstiːn/ adj something that is pristine looks very clean, tidy, or new

privacy /'prɪvəsi, 'praɪvəsi/ noun [U] the freedom to do things without other people watching you or knowing what you are doing

private¹ /'praɪvət/ adj ★★★

1 not for everyone	**5** not government
2 secret	**6** not public
3 person	**+** PHRASE
4 not work	

1 used only by a particular person or group, or available only to them: *a private bathroom/plane*
2 used about places or situations where other people cannot see or hear you: *They found a private spot where they could talk.*
3 a private person does not talk to other people about their personal life or feelings
4 not connected with someone's work or their public position: *What you do in your private life has nothing to do with your boss.*
5 controlled or owned by individual people or companies, rather than by the government ≠ PUBLIC: *a private hospital*
6 with no position in government or public life: *a private citizen*
PHRASE **in private** in a place or situation where other people cannot watch or listen: *I'd like to talk with you in private, if you don't mind.*

private² /'praɪvət/ noun [C] the lowest rank of soldier in the army

private 'company noun [C] a company that is owned by a person or group of people who do not sell SHARES (=the right to share profits) to the public

P

private de'tective noun [C] someone who is paid to follow people secretly or to find out information about their lives

private 'enterprise noun [C/U] business or industry that is owned and managed by independent people or businesses, rather than by the government

private in'vestigator noun [C] a PRIVATE DETECTIVE

privately /ˈpraɪvətli/ adv 1 in a place where no other people can see or hear you: *We wanted to speak privately.* 2 used about thoughts or feelings that you do not express: *Privately, he hoped they would refuse.* 3 by people who provide money themselves, rather than by governments: *privately owned businesses*

private 'practice noun [C] a business that is managed and owned by a professional person such as a doctor or lawyer

private 'school noun [C] a school that the children's parents pay for directly to the school

private 'secretary noun [C] someone who works as a secretary for an important person in business or government

'private ,sector, the noun [singular] all the businesses, industries, and services that are not owned or managed by the government

privatize /ˈpraɪvətaɪz/ verb [T] to sell a business or industry that was owned and managed by the government so that it becomes a private business ≠ NATIONALIZE —**privatization** /ˌpraɪvətaɪˈzeɪʃ(ə)n/ noun [C/U]

privet /ˈprɪvət/ noun [C/U] a bush with small, dark green leaves that is often used for making HEDGES

privilege /ˈprɪvəlɪdʒ/ noun 1 [C] a special benefit that is available only to a particular person or group: *Cheap air travel is one of the privileges of working for the airline.* 2 [C] something nice that you feel lucky to have: *It's been a privilege to be involved in such an interesting project.* 3 [U] a way of life that involves having many advantages and opportunities, without working hard for them: *a life of privilege*

privileged /ˈprɪvəlɪdʒd/ adj having advantages and opportunities that other people do not have: *a privileged background/upbringing*

prize¹ /praɪz/ noun [C] ★★ a reward that you get for being successful in a competition, or for being good at something: *the Nobel Prize for chemistry* ♦ *Peter Turnbull won first prize* (=the prize that is given to the person who is first in a competition).

prize² /praɪz/ adj good enough to deserve or win a prize

prize³ /praɪz/ verb [T] to think that something is very important and special

pro /prəʊ/ noun [C] *informal* someone who plays a sport or takes part in an activity as a job rather than for enjoyment = PROFESSIONAL

PHRASE **pros and cons** advantages and disadvantages

pro- /prəʊ/ prefix supporting or approving of something: *pro-democracy groups*

proactive /prəʊˈæktɪv/ adj taking action and making changes before they need to be made, instead of waiting until problems develop

probability /ˌprɒbəˈbɪləti/ noun 1 [singular/U] a measure of how likely something is to happen: *What is the probability of success?* 2 [C] something that is likely to happen or be true: *War is now a probability rather than a possibility.*

PHRASE **in all probability** used for saying that you think that something is very likely

probable /ˈprɒbəb(ə)l/ adj likely to happen or be true ≠ IMPROBABLE: *It seems probable that the chairman will resign.*

probably /ˈprɒbəbli/ adv ★★★ used for saying that you think that something is likely: *You'll probably be gone by the time I get back.* ♦ *'Are you going to accept their offer?' 'Probably not.'*

probation /prəˈbeɪʃ(ə)n/ noun [U] 1 a system by which someone who has committed a crime is not sent to prison if they promise to behave well for a specific period of time 2 a period of time during which someone who has a new job is watched to see whether they can do the job well

probationary /prəˈbeɪʃ(ə)n(ə)ri/ adj relating to someone who has a new job, or to the period during which they are watched to see whether they can do the job well

pro'bation ,officer noun [C] someone whose job is to give help and advice to people on PROBATION and to check that they are behaving well

probe¹ /prəʊb/ verb 1 [I/T] to try to find out the truth about something, especially by asking a lot of questions 2 [T] to examine something by using your fingers or a tool —**probing** adj

probe² /prəʊb/ noun [C] 1 a long thin medical instrument that is used for examining things inside your body 2 a SPACE PROBE 3 *mainly journalism* an attempt to find out the truth about an issue, problem, or accident = INQUIRY

problem /ˈprɒbləm/ noun [C] ★★★ 1 something that causes trouble or difficulty: *the problem of unemployment* ♦ *We've been having problems with our neighbours.* ♦ *They're the best cameras on the market. The only problem is they're incredibly expensive.* 2 a question that someone is given to answer as a test of their ability: *mathematical problems*

PHRASES **no problem** *spoken* 1 used for saying that you will be happy to do what someone is asking you to do: *'Can you look after the children for an hour or so?' 'No problem.'* 2 used as a polite way of answering someone who has thanked you for something, or said that they are sorry for something: *'You did a good job today – thanks'. 'No problem.'*

not be sb's problem *spoken* used for saying that someone is not responsible for a difficulty and does not have to worry about it

that's your problem *spoken* used for saying in an unkind way that you are not going to help someone

> Words often used with **problem**
>
> *Adjectives often used with **problem** (sense 1)*
> ■ **big, fundamental, important, major, pressing, serious** + PROBLEM: used about problems that are very difficult to deal with

problematic /ˌprɒbləˈmætɪk/ or **problematical** /ˌprɒbləˈmætɪk(ə)l/ adj involving or causing problems

procedure /prəˈsiːdʒə/ noun [C] ★ a way of doing something, especially the correct or usual way: *Those ticket holders who followed the proper procedure will receive a full refund.* ♦ *The procedure for doing this is explained fully in the next chapter.* —**procedural** /prəˈsiːdʒ(ə)rəl/ adj

proceed /prəˈsiːd/ verb [I] ★
1 *formal* to continue doing something: *The council is proceeding with its plan to move the stadium.*
2 *formal* to go in a particular direction: *Passengers for flight 406 to New York should proceed to Gate 32.*
3 used for telling other people about a surprising or annoying thing that someone has done: **proceed to do sth** *He placed the remainder of the apple in his mouth and proceeded to eat the core, stalk and pips.*

proceedings /prəˈsiːdɪŋz/ noun [plural] **1** the actions that are taken to settle a legal matter, usually in court **2** an event, or series of related events

proceeds /ˈprəʊsiːdz/ noun [plural] money that a person or organization makes from selling or winning something, or from organizing an event

process¹ /ˈprəʊses/ noun [C] ★★★
1 a series of things that happen naturally and that have a particular result: *Changes occur in the body because of **the process of** ageing.*
2 a series of actions that you take that have a particular result: *Learning a language is a slow process.* ♦ *an industrial process*
 PHRASE **in the process of doing sth** involved in doing something at the present time

process² /ˈprəʊses/ verb [T] ★
1 to treat food or another substance with chemicals or machines: *processed meat/ cheese*
2 to put information into a computer in order to organize it: *Data is processed as it is received.*
3 to deal with a document officially: *28,000 applications have still to be processed.*
4 to make photographs from film by treating it with chemicals
—**processing** noun [U]: *the food processing industry*

procession /prəˈseʃ(ə)n/ noun [C] **1** a line of people or vehicles that are moving in a slow formal way as part of an event **2** a series of people or things

processor /ˈprəʊsesə/ noun [C] **1** *computing* the

part of a computer that controls and performs all its operations **2** a FOOD PROCESSOR

proclaim /prəˈkleɪm/ verb [T] to announce or state something officially or publicly

proclamation /ˌprɒkləˈmeɪʃ(ə)n/ noun [C/U] an official announcement, or the act of making an official announcement

procrastinate /prəʊˈkræstɪˌneɪt/ verb [I] to delay doing something until later because you do not want to do it —**procrastination** /prəʊˌkræstɪˈneɪʃ(ə)n/ noun [U]

procure /prəˈkjʊə/ verb [T] *formal* to obtain something, especially with effort or difficulty

prod /prɒd/ verb [I/T] **1** to push someone or something quickly with your finger, or with an object that has a long thin end **2** to persuade or encourage someone to do something —**prod** noun [C]

prodigious /prəˈdɪdʒəs/ adj very great, or impressive

prodigy /ˈprɒdədʒi/ noun [C] a young person who has a natural ability to do something extremely well

produce¹ /prəˈdjuːs/ verb ★★★
1 [T] to make or grow something: *We are now producing the same quantity of goods with far fewer workers.* ♦ *The body produces chemicals to control the pain.* ♦ *The region produces some of the best wine in France.*
2 [T] to cause something to happen: *I managed to produce the opposite effect from the one I had intended.*
3 [T] to show or offer something so that it can be examined or used by someone else: *They produced very little evidence in support of their argument.*
4 [I/T] to organize the work and money that are involved in making a film, play, television or radio programme, CD etc: *Steve McQueen produced and starred in* The Getaway.

> Word family: **produce**
>
> *Words in the same family as **produce***
> ■ **producer** *n*   ■ **reproduce** *v*
> ■ **product** *n*   ■ **reproduction** *n*
> ■ **production** *n*   ■ **reproductive** *adj*
> ■ **productive** *adj*   ■ **unproductive** *adj*
> ■ **productivity** *n*

produce² /ˈprɒdjuːs/ noun [U] fruit, vegetables, and other things that farmers grow

producer /prəˈdjuːsə/ noun [C] ★
1 someone whose job is to organize the work and money that are involved in making a film, play, television or radio programme, CD etc
2 a person, company, or country that grows food or makes goods to be sold: *an oil/ grain/wine producer*

product /ˈprɒdʌkt/ noun ★★★
1 [C/U] something that is made, grown, or obtained in large quantities so that it can be sold: *dairy/pharmaceutical/software products*
2 [C] something or someone that is the result of particular actions, events, or influences:

P

*The system we have now is **the product of** years of research.*

3 [C] *technical* a number that is the result of multiplying two other numbers

production /prəˈdʌkʃ(ə)n/ *noun* ★★★

1 [U] the process of making or growing things in large quantities so that they can be sold: ***the production of** goods for sale in the Far East*

2 [U] the natural process of making a substance: *the body's **production of** hormones*

3 [C/U] a film, play, television or radio programme, CD etc, or the process of making it: *the Royal Shakespeare Company's **production of** Macbeth*

pro'duction line *noun* [C] a system for making products in a factory. Each worker or machine does a single job as the product moves past them=ASSEMBLY LINE

productive /prəˈdʌktɪv/ *adj* **1** making or growing things in large quantities: *This is highly productive farming country.*
2 producing or achieving a lot ≠ UNPRODUCTIVE: *a very productive meeting* —**productively** *adv*

productivity /ˌprɒdʌkˈtɪvəti/ *noun* [U] the rate at which goods are produced, especially in relation to the time, money, and workers that are needed to produce them

Prof. /prɒf/ *abbrev* Professor: used in writing before the name of a professor

profess /prəˈfes/ *verb* [T] *formal* **1** to claim that something is true, especially when it is not
2 to admit publicly that you have a particular feeling or belief

profession /prəˈfeʃ(ə)n/ *noun* [C] ★
1 a job that you need special skills and qualifications to do: *Her father discouraged her from going into **the legal profession**.* ♦ *He was a teacher **by profession** (=as his job).*
2 all the people who work in a particular profession: ***The medical profession** is always telling us we should exercise more.*

professional¹ /prəˈfeʃ(ə)nəl/ *adj* ★★★
1 relating to work that needs special skills and qualifications: *Teachers must be free to exercise their **professional judgment**.*
2 playing a sport or taking part in an activity as a job rather than for enjoyment ≠ AMATEUR: *a professional actor/ photographer* ♦ *professional football/ boxing*
3 showing a high level of skill or training ≠ UNPROFESSIONAL: *They did **a** thoroughly **professional job**.*

professional² /prəˈfeʃ(ə)nəl/ *noun* [C]
1 someone who needs a job that you need special skills and qualifications to do: *doctors and other professionals* **2** someone who plays a sport or takes part in an activity as a job rather than for enjoyment ≠ AMATEUR **3** someone who has a lot of skill or training ≠ AMATEUR: *You've got the makings of a real professional.*

professionalism /prəˈfeʃ(ə)nəlɪz(ə)m/ *noun* [U] the qualities and skills that someone with a professional job is expected to have

professionally /prəˈfeʃ(ə)nəli/ *adv* **1** with the formal qualifications that are necessary for a particular profession: *professionally qualified staff* **2** showing the type of behaviour and skills that someone with a professional job is expected to have: *She hasn't behaved very professionally, has she?*
3 in a way that is connected with your work: *Without Nina's help I wouldn't be where I am today professionally.* **4** as a job rather than for enjoyment: *She has been acting professionally since she was 17.*

professor /prəˈfesə/ *noun* [C] ★
1 *British* a senior teacher in a college or university: *a **professor of** English*
2 *American* a teacher in a college or university

proffer /ˈprɒfə/ *verb* [T] *formal* to offer something to someone

proficiency /prəˈfɪʃ(ə)nsi/ *noun* [U] great skill

proficient /prəˈfɪʃ(ə)nt/ *adj* very good at something —**proficiently** *adv*

profile¹ /ˈprəʊfaɪl/ *noun* [C] **1** the public image of a person or organization, and the attention that they get from the public or journalists: *We have done a lot to change the profile of the company.* ♦ *She's trying to keep **a low profile** (=avoid being noticed).*
2 a short article or television or radio programme about someone: *a profile of the British royal family* **3** the shape of someone's face when you look at them from the side: *She turned his head so she could see his profile.*

profile² /ˈprəʊfaɪl/ *verb* [T] to give a description of someone in an article or in a television or radio programme

profit¹ /ˈprɒfɪt/ *noun* ★★★
1 [C/U] money that you get when you sell something for a price that is higher than the cost of making it or buying it ≠ LOSS: *Investors have **made a** 14% **profit** in just 3 months.* ♦ *the practice of killing whales **for profit** (=in order to make money)* ♦ *They were buying computers and reselling them **at a profit** (=so that you make a profit).* ♦ *The **profit on** that deal was £21 million.* ♦ *All the **profits from** the sales of the CD will go to charity.* ♦ *The company's **profits rose** to £144 million last year.*
2 [U] *formal* the advantage that you get from a situation

profit² /ˈprɒfɪt/ *noun* **PHRASAL VERB** **'profit from sth** or **'profit by sth** to get an advantage from a situation

profitable /ˈprɒfɪtəb(ə)l/ *adj* **1** making a profit ≠ UNPROFITABLE: *a profitable business/company/investment* **2** giving you a benefit or advantage: *The trip should be an enjoyable and profitable experience.* —**profitability** /ˌprɒfɪtəˈbɪləti/ *noun* [U], **profitably** *adv*

profiteering /ˌprɒfɪˈtɪərɪŋ/ *noun* [U] the behaviour of companies that make large profits by charging people unfairly high prices

'profit-making *adj* a profit-making organization exists in order to make a profit

profound /prəˈfaʊnd/ adj **1** very great: *My grandfather's death had a profound effect on my father.* **2** showing intelligence and serious thought: *a very profound statement* —**profoundly** adv

profuse /prəˈfjuːs/ adj existing in large amounts —**profusely** adv

profusion /prəˈfjuːʒ(ə)n/ noun [singular] *formal* a large quantity of something

prognosis /prɒɡˈnəʊsɪs/ (plural **prognoses** /prɒɡˈnəʊsiːz/) noun [C] **1** *medical* a doctor's opinion about how a disease is likely to develop **2** *formal* a statement about what is likely to happen in a particular situation → DIAGNOSIS

program¹ /ˈprəʊɡræm/ noun [C] ★★
1 *computing* a series of instructions that makes a computer do something: *a word processing/graphics/spreadsheet program* **2** the American spelling of **programme**

program² /ˈprəʊɡræm/ verb [T] to make a computer or other piece of equipment do something automatically —**programmable** /prəʊˈɡræməb(ə)l, ˈprəʊɡræməb(ə)l/ adj

programme¹ /ˈprəʊɡræm/ noun [C] ★★★
1 a plan of activities for achieving something: *a training/development/ research programme* ♦ *an ambitious programme of educational expansion* ♦ *the government's programme for economic recovery*
2 a series of planned events: *a festival with an exciting musical programme*
3 a television or radio broadcast: *More people watch the news than any other programme.*
4 a document that tells you what will happen in a performance or event

programme² /ˈprəʊɡræm/ verb [T] **1** to make a person or animal behave in a particular way **2** to plan something → PROGRAM²

programmer /ˈprəʊɡræmə/ noun [C] *computing* someone whose job is to create computer programs

programming /ˈprəʊɡræmɪŋ/ noun [U] *computing* the activity of creating computer programs

progress¹ /ˈprəʊɡres/ noun [U] ★★★
1 the process of developing or improving: *Keep me informed about the progress of the project.* ♦ *I'm worried about my son's lack of progress in English.* ♦ *Negotiators have made considerable progress in the peace talks.*
2 forward movement: *the ship's slow progress across the harbour*
PHRASE in progress happening, or being done: *The road will be closed while the maintenance work is in progress.*

Words often used with **progress**
Verbs often used with progress (noun, sense 1)
■ **assess, evaluate, review** + PROGRESS: judge how much progress has been made
■ **chart, check, follow, monitor, track, watch** + PROGRESS: watch how something develops
■ **hamper, hinder, impede, obstruct, slow** + PROGRESS: stop something from developing

progress² /prəˈɡres/ verb [I] ★
1 to continue to develop: *Work on the project is progressing well.*
2 to move forward in space or time: *The situation improved as the century progressed.*

progression /prəˈɡreʃ(ə)n/ noun [U] gradual change or development=PROGRESS: *The drug can slow the progression of the disease.*

progressive /prəˈɡresɪv/ adj **1** involving political change that aims to make society fairer: *a progressive tax system* **2** developing gradually: *The disease causes progressive deterioration of the nervous system.* **3** using the most modern ideas or methods: *progressive music* **4** *linguistics* the progressive form of a verb is used for showing that an action is continuing=CONTINUOUS —**progressively** adv

prohibit /prəˈhɪbɪt/ verb [T] to officially stop people from doing something=BAN: *Smoking is prohibited inside the building.* ♦ *a rule prohibiting doctors from advertising their services* —**prohibition** /ˌprəʊɪˈbɪʃ(ə)n/ noun [C/U]

prohibitive /prəˈhɪbɪtɪv/ adj a prohibitive price is so high that it prevents people from buying something —**prohibitively** adv

project¹ /ˈprɒdʒekt, ˈprəʊdʒekt/ noun [C] ★★★
1 an organized attempt to achieve something=SCHEME: *The first phase of the project is now complete.* ♦ *a project to do sth an ambitious project to modernize the road network*
2 a piece of work that involves collecting information: *The university has set up a new research project to study language development in babies.* ♦ *Students must complete a project on a topic of their choice.*

Words often used with **project**
Adjectives often used with project (noun, sense 1)
■ **ambitious, innovative, major, large-scale** + PROJECT: used about projects that are intended to achieve a lot

project² /prəˈdʒekt/ verb **1** [T] to calculate how big something will become in the future, using information that is available now =FORECAST, PREDICT: *It is projected that the population will rise by one million by 2008.*
2 [I] to stick out past the edge or surface of something: *The edges of the roof project outwards and keep the rain away from the walls.* **3** [T] to make people believe that someone or something has a particular quality: *Ending the talks now would project an image of failure.* **4** [T] to send an image to a screen or other surface

projectile /prəˈdʒekˌtaɪl/ noun [C] *formal* an object that is shot or thrown as a weapon =MISSILE

projection /prəˈdʒekʃ(ə)n/ noun **1** [C] a calculation of the way that something will develop **2** [U] the action of sending an image to a screen **3** [C] something that sticks out from a surface

projector /prəˈdʒektə/ noun [C] a piece of equipment that is used for showing films or SLIDES on a screen

P

proliferate /prəˈlɪfəˌreɪt/ verb [I] *formal* to quickly increase in number or amount

proliferation /prəˌlɪfəˈreɪʃ(ə)n/ noun [singular/U] *formal* a sudden increase in number or amount

prolific /prəˈlɪfɪk/ adj producing a lot of something: *a prolific writer/artist*

prolog /ˈprəʊlɒg/ an American spelling of **prologue**

prologue /ˈprəʊlɒg/ noun [C] a short part at the start of a book, play, or film that introduces the story

prolong /prəˈlɒŋ/ verb [T] to make something last longer ≠ CURTAIL

prolonged /prəˈlɒŋd/ adj continuing for a long time: *a prolonged period of silence*

prom /prɒm/ noun [C] in the US, a formal party for students at SECONDARY SCHOOL

promenade /ˌprɒməˈnɑːd/ noun [C] a wide path that is next to a beach

prominence /ˈprɒmɪnəns/ noun [U] the state of being important or well known: *a young actor who came to prominence last year*

prominent /ˈprɒmɪnənt/ adj **1** important and well known: *a prominent member of the government* **2** easy to see or notice: *prominent cheekbones* ♦ *a prominent feature of the landscape* —**prominently** adv

promiscuous /prəˈmɪskjuəs/ adj someone who is promiscuous has a lot of sexual partners —**promiscuity** /ˌprɒmɪˈskuːəti/ noun [U]

promise¹ /ˈprɒmɪs/ verb [I/T] ★★★
1 to tell someone that you will definitely do something: *The police chief promised tougher action against young criminals.* ♦ *She phoned at 9 am, as promised.* ♦ **promise to do sth** *Peter wished he'd never promised to help them.* ♦ **promise sth to sb/promise sb sth** *Relief organizations are promising aid to the country.* ♦ **promise sb (that)** *Promise me you'll be home before dark.*
2 *formal* to make something seem likely: *This evening promises to be a lot of fun.*

promise² /ˈprɒmɪs/ noun ★★
1 [C] a statement in which you say that you will definitely do something: *the party's election promises* ♦ *I'll try to come, but I'm not making any promises!* ♦ *He swore he would return one day, and he kept his promise.* ♦ **a promise to do sth** *You made a promise to deal with it immediately.* ♦ *The army broke its promise to bring peace back to the country.*
2 [U] signs that someone or something is likely to be successful in the future =POTENTIAL: *Life was hopeful and full of promise.* ♦ *He shows great promise as a writer.*

promising /ˈprɒmɪsɪŋ/ adj likely to be successful or very good: *a highly promising young artist* —**promisingly** adv

promo /ˈprəʊməʊ/ noun [C] *informal* an advertisement

promontory /ˈprɒmənt(ə)ri/ noun [C] a narrow piece of land that sticks out into the sea

promote /prəˈməʊt/ verb [T] ★★
1 to support something, or to help something to develop: *a campaign to promote recycling* ♦ *Young plants are exposed to bright light to promote growth.*
2 to attract people's attention to a product or event, for example by advertising: *They are going on tour to promote their new album.*
3 to move someone to a job at a higher level: **promote sb to sth** *Steve Burrows was recently promoted to senior manager.*

> **Words often used with promote**
>
> *Adverbs often used with promote (sense 1)*
> ■ **actively, heavily, strongly, vigorously** + PROMOTE: promote something in a determined way
> *Nouns often used with promote (sense 1)*
> ■ PROMOTE + **awareness, competition, development, efficiency, growth, interest, understanding, use**: increase the level of something

promoter /prəˈməʊtə/ noun [C] **1** someone whose job is to arrange and advertise concerts and sports events **2** someone who tries to make people support an idea or issue

promotion /prəˈməʊʃ(ə)n/ noun ★
1 [C/U] a move to a job at a higher level: *His main objective is to get promotion.* ♦ *his promotion to a position of leadership*
2 [U] the activity of encouraging or supporting something: *The campaign is concerned with the promotion of health.*
3 [U] the process of advertising something: *a ban on the promotion of tobacco products*

promotional /prəˈməʊʃ(ə)nəl/ adj used for advertising something

prompt¹ /prɒmpt/ verb [T] **1** to cause something to happen: *The birth of my first child prompted me to write this article.* **2** to encourage someone to say something: *Without being prompted, she began to apologize.* **3** to remind an actor which words to say next —**prompting** /ˈprɒmptɪŋ/ noun [U]

prompt² /prɒmpt/ adj **1** immediate or quick: *Prompt action is required.* **2** happening or arriving at exactly a particular time: *The meeting got off to a prompt start at ten o'clock.* —**promptly** adv, **promptness** noun [U]

prompt³ /prɒmpt/ adv at a particular time exactly: *We begin at 9.00 prompt.*

prompt⁴ /prɒmpt/ noun [C] **1** *computing* a sign on a computer screen that shows that the computer is ready for you to KEY something **2** a word or words that someone says to remind an actor what to say next

prone /prəʊn/ adj **1** likely to do something bad, or likely to be affected by something bad: *The region is prone to earthquakes.* ♦ *He's prone to gain weight.* ♦ *an accident-prone child* **2** *formal* lying flat with the front of your body facing downwards

prong /prɒŋ/ noun [C] one of the sharp points on a fork

pronoun /ˈprəʊnaʊn/ noun [C] *linguistics* a word used instead of a noun that has been mentioned earlier, for example 'she', 'this', and 'yourself'

pronounce /prəˈnaʊns/ verb [T] ★
1 to say the sounds of words: *I find some Japanese words very difficult to pronounce.* ♦ *Did I pronounce your name correctly?*
2 *formal* to state an official opinion or decision: *The court pronounced her innocent of all charges.*

pronounced /prəˈnaʊnst/ adj very obvious or noticeable: *a pronounced German accent*

pronouncement /prəˈnaʊnsmənt/ noun [C] *formal* an official public statement

pronunciation /prəˌnʌnsiˈeɪʃ(ə)n/ noun [C/U] ★ the way in which a word or language is pronounced: *a guide to French pronunciation* ♦ *What is the correct pronunciation of 'rabid'?*

proof /pruːf/ noun ★
1 [U] information or evidence that shows that something is definitely true: *We were unable to establish proof of her innocence.* ♦ *Do you have any proof of identity* (=a document that proves who you are)*?* ♦ **+(that)** *Do you have any proof that this is true?*
2 [U] the strength of an alcoholic drink
3 [C] *technical* a copy of a book or article that someone reads and corrects before the final copy is made

> **Words often used with proof**
>
> *Adjectives often used with proof (sense 1)*
> ■ **ample, clear, conclusive, final, irrefutable, tangible** + PROOF: used about proof that is good enough to show that something is true

proofread /ˈpruːfriːd/ (past tense and past participle **proofread** /ˈpruːfred/) verb [I/T] to correct the mistakes in a piece of writing before the final copy is printed
—**proofreader** /ˈpruːfriːdə/ noun [C]

prop¹ /prɒp/ verb [T] to hold something in position by putting an object under or against it, or by leaning it against an object: *I noticed a red bicycle propped against the wall.* ♦ *Prop the door open behind you so we don't get locked out.*
PHRASAL VERB **prop sth up 1** to stop something from falling by putting an object under it or against it: *The wall was propped up with wooden poles.* **2** to help something such as a government or an organization to continue to exist

prop² /prɒp/ noun [C] **1** something you put under or against an object in order to hold it up **2** an object that is used in a play or film

propaganda /ˌprɒpəˈɡændə/ noun [U] information that a government or an organization spreads in order to influence people's opinions

propagate /ˈprɒpəɡeɪt/ verb [T] **1** to spread ideas or beliefs to a lot of people **2** *technical* to make a plant produce more plants
—**propagation** /ˌprɒpəˈɡeɪʃ(ə)n/ noun [U]

propel /prəˈpel/ verb [T] **1** to move something forward: *a car propelled by solar energy* **2** to quickly put someone into a particular situation: *The film's success propelled him to stardom.*

propeller /prəˈpelə/ noun [C] the part of a

plane or ship that has blades that spin round to make it move

propensity /prəˈpensəti/ noun [C] a natural tendency to behave in a particular way

proper /ˈprɒpə/ adj ★★
1 suitable for a particular purpose or situation: *You have to have the proper tools for the job.* ♦ *That's not the proper way to do it!*
2 *British* considered to be real or serious: *Start the day with a proper breakfast.* ♦ *When are you going to get a proper job?*
3 behaving in a way that is morally right or polite: *It's only right and proper that his family should be present.*
4 understood in its most exact meaning: *Does he live in Swansea proper or in the suburbs?*

properly /ˈprɒpəli/ adv ★★ in a correct or suitable way: *You're not properly dressed for this weather.* ♦ *If she doesn't behave properly, send her home.*

proper noun noun [C] *linguistics* a noun that is the name of a person, place, or thing

property /ˈprɒpəti/ noun ★★★
1 [U] the things that you own: *The books are my personal property.* ♦ *The police found a lot of stolen property in his house.*
2 [C/U] land and the buildings on it: *He owns several properties in London.* ♦ *The sign said 'Private Property, Keep Out'.* ♦ *Property prices are falling.*
3 [C] a quality or feature of something: *The plants are believed to have healing properties.*

prophecy /ˈprɒfəsi/ noun [C] a statement about what will happen in the future

prophesy /ˈprɒfəsaɪ/ verb [T] to say what will happen in the future

prophet /ˈprɒfɪt/ noun **1** [C] someone who is believed to have been sent by God to lead people and teach religious beliefs **2 the Prophet** Muhammad, the FOUNDER of Islam

prophetic /prəˈfetɪk/ adj saying what will happen in the future

proponent /prəˈpəʊnənt/ noun [C] someone who publicly supports something

proportion /prəˈpɔːʃ(ə)n/ noun ★★

1 part of whole amount	**4** importance
2 relative quantity	**5** size or shape
3 of appearance	**+** PHRASES

1 [C] a quantity of something that is a part of the whole: *Only a small proportion of graduates fail to get a job.*
2 [U] the relationship between two or more quantities or parts of a whole: **the proportion of sth to sth** *The proportion of trucks to cars on the roads has changed dramatically.*
3 [C] the correct or most attractive relationship between things: *Everything about the room is beautifully in proportion.* ♦ *His head is large in proportion to his body.* ♦ *The figures in the painting are completely out of proportion with their surroundings.*
4 [U] the importance of something in comparison with other things: *We need to keep a sense of proportion about what really matters.*

P

5 proportions [plural] the size or shape of something: *a chair of graceful proportions* ♦ *The tree can grow to massive proportions.*
PHRASES **blow sth up out of (all) proportion** to make a situation seem much worse than it really is
out of (all) proportion (to sth) too strong or serious for a particular situation

proportional /prəˈpɔːʃ(ə)nəl/ adj **1** two things that are proportional to each other keep the same relationship to each other when they change in size or amount: *Proportional increases in income maintain the gap between rich and poor.* **2** not too big or too severe in relation to something else = PROPORTIONATE —**proportionally** /prəˈpɔːʃ(ə)nəli/ adv

proportionate /prəˈpɔːʃ(ə)nət/ adj **1** not too big or too severe in relation to something else: *a punishment that is proportionate to the crime* **2** keeping the same relationship of size or amount to something else = PROPORTIONAL —**proportionately** adv

proposal /prəˈpəʊz(ə)l/ noun [C] ★
1 an official plan or suggestion: *Proposals for a new health service are under discussion.* ♦ **a proposal to do sth** *a government proposal to impose a tax on fuel*
2 an occasion when you ask someone to marry you

propose /prəˈpəʊz/ verb **1** [T] *formal* to suggest something: *She is proposing that we sell the house.* **2** [T] to make a formal suggestion, especially in a meeting: *I propose Sue Wilson for chairman.* ♦ *It was proposed that we postpone the next meeting.* ♦ *France has proposed creating an international force to deal with the crisis.* **3** [I] to ask someone to marry you: *He proposed to her in August.* **4** [T] *formal* if you propose to do something, you intend to do it

proposition[1] /ˌprɒpəˈzɪʃ(ə)n/ noun [C] **1** an offer or suggestion **2** a statement that people can examine in order to decide whether it is true

proposition[2] /ˌprɒpəˈzɪʃ(ə)n/ verb [T] to offer to have sex with someone, especially in an offensive way

proprietor /prəˈpraɪətə/ noun [C] *formal* someone who owns a business

propriety /prəˈpraɪəti/ noun [U] *formal* behaviour that most people think is morally or socially correct ≠ IMPROPRIETY

propulsion /prəˈpʌlʃ(ə)n/ noun [U] *technical* the force that makes something move forwards

pro rata /ˌprəʊ ˈrɑːtə/ adj, adv *business* calculated according to how long someone works or how much of an amount is used

prosaic /prəʊˈzeɪɪk/ adj not interesting or exciting

prose /prəʊz/ noun [U] ordinary written language, not poetry

prosecute /ˈprɒsɪkjuːt/ verb **1** [T] to officially accuse someone of a crime and ask a court of law to judge them **2** [I/T] to try to prove as a lawyer in court that someone is guilty of a crime

prosecution /ˌprɒsɪˈkjuːʃ(ə)n/ noun **1** [U] the act of accusing someone of a crime and

asking a court of law to judge them **2 the prosecution** [singular] the lawyers in a court who try to prove that someone is guilty ≠ DEFENCE

prospect[1] /ˈprɒspekt/ noun ★
1 [U] the possibility that something good will happen: *Doctors say there is little prospect of any improvement in his condition.* ♦ *We have an exciting match in prospect.*
2 [singular] something that you expect to happen in the future, or the thought of this: *Spending a week at his cousin's farm was an exciting prospect.* ♦ *We were very excited at the prospect of going home.*
3 prospects [plural] chances of success in a career: *Your employment prospects would be much better if you finished your degree.*

> ### Words often used with **prospect**
> *Adjectives often used with **prospect** (noun, sense 2)*
> ■ **attractive, bright, exciting, inviting** + PROSPECT: used about a prospect that makes you confident or excited about what will happen
> ■ **bleak, daunting, gloomy, grim, terrifying** + PROSPECT: used about a prospect that makes you worried or frightened about what will happen

prospect[2] /prəˈspekt/ verb [I] to search for gold, oil, or another valuable substance

prospective /prəˈspektɪv/ adj likely to become a particular thing: *a prospective client/employee*

prospectus /prəˈspektəs/ noun [C] **1** a small book that describes a school or university and its courses **2** a document that provides details about a business to people who are interested in investing in it

prosper /ˈprɒspə/ verb [I] to be successful, or to become rich

prosperity /prɒˈsperəti/ noun [U] the situation of being successful and having a lot of money

prosperous /ˈprɒsp(ə)rəs/ adj rich and successful

prostitute /ˈprɒstɪtjuːt/ noun [C] someone who has sex with people as their job

prostitution /ˌprɒstɪˈtjuːʃ(ə)n/ noun [U] the job of having sex with people

prostrate /ˈprɒstreɪt/ adj *formal* lying completely flat on the ground with your face downwards

protagonist /prəˈtæɡənɪst/ noun [C] the main character in a play, film, or book

protect /prəˈtekt/ verb [T] ★★★ to keep someone or something safe: *Are you prepared to protect yourself in case of attack?* ♦ **protect sb/sth from sth** *The hat will protect his face from the sun.* ♦ **protect sb/sth against sth** *The jacket protected him against the cold.* —**protector** noun [C]

protected /prəˈtektɪd/ adj used about animals, plants, and other things that the law prevents people from harming

P

oak

chestnut

sycamore

holly

willow

palm tree

redwood

fir

magnolia

pine

buttercup

daisy

dandelion

carnation

hyacinth

poppy

iris

daffodil

geranium

lupin

rose

lily

tulip

fuchsia

orchid

sunflower

chrysanthemum

FRUIT

orange

lemon

lime

grapefruit

apple

pear

peach

apricot

nectarine

plum

grapes

cherries

strawberries

raspberries

blueberries

watermelon

melon

papaya

avocado

banana

fig

coconut

kiwi fruit

mango

pineapple

sweet potato

parsnip

potato

carrot

beetroot

radish

ginger

shallots

garlic

onion

spring
onions

tomato

courgette

pumpkin

mushrooms

peppers

cucumber

lettuce

celery

fennel

broccoli

Brussels sprouts

aubergine

cabbage

asparagus

corn on the cob

green beans

cauliflower

peas

kidney beans

ANIMALS

leopard

cheetah

koala

lion

elephant

gorilla

zebra

tiger

rhinocerous

hippopotamus

monkey

giraffe

panda

duck

goose

deer

chicken

bull

pig

goat

sheep

cow

donkey

shark

octopus

kangaroo

penguin

whale

fox

iguana

rat

mole

badger

mouse

squirrel

wasp

rabbit

moth

fly

ant

butterfly

caterpillar

lizard

bee

snake

ladybird

cockroach

crocodile

grasshopper

mosquito

beetle

BODY

head

hand

arm

neck

back

chest

breast

waist

elbow

hip

buttocks

shoulder

stomach

leg

knee

foot

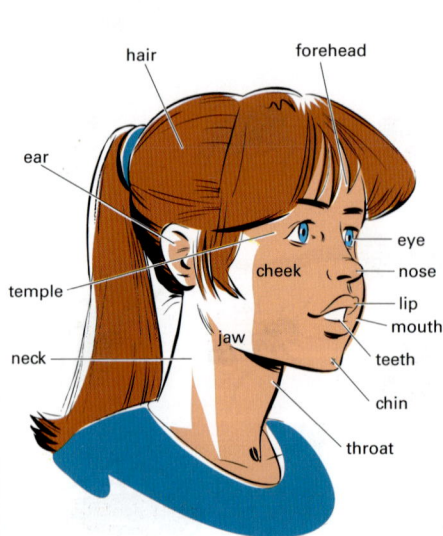

hair

forehead

ear

eye

temple

cheek

nose

jaw

lip

mouth

neck

teeth

chin

throat

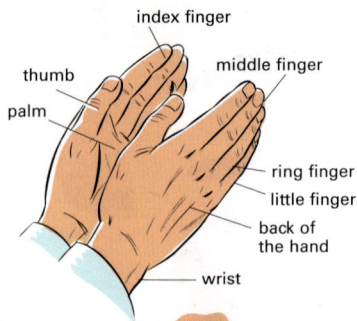

index finger

thumb

middle finger

palm

ring finger

little finger

back of
the hand

wrist

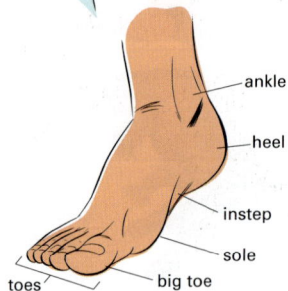

ankle

heel

instep

sole

toes

big toe

Football

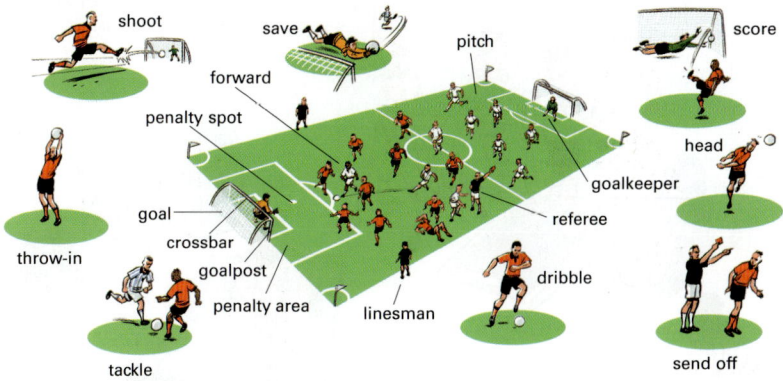

shoot

save

pitch

score

forward

penalty spot

head

goalkeeper

goal

crossbar

referee

throw-in

goalpost

dribble

penalty area

linesman

tackle

send off

Golf

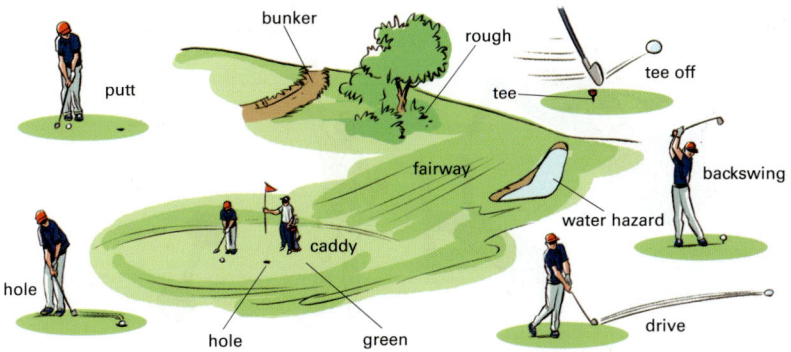

bunker

rough

putt

tee off

tee

fairway

backswing

water hazard

caddy

hole

drive

hole

green

Tennis

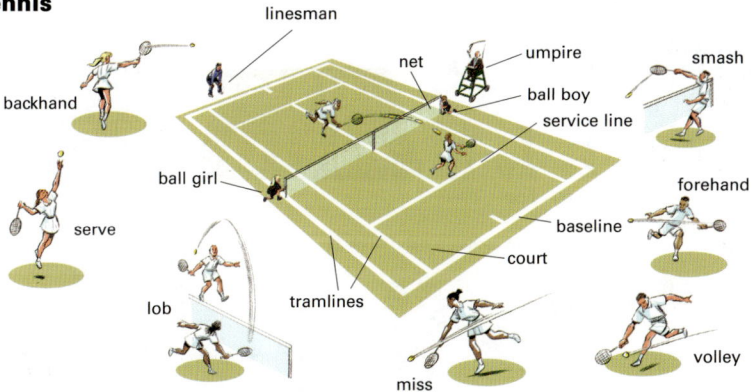

linesman

umpire

smash

net

backhand

ball boy

service line

ball girl

forehand

serve

baseline

court

lob

tramlines

volley

miss

GYM

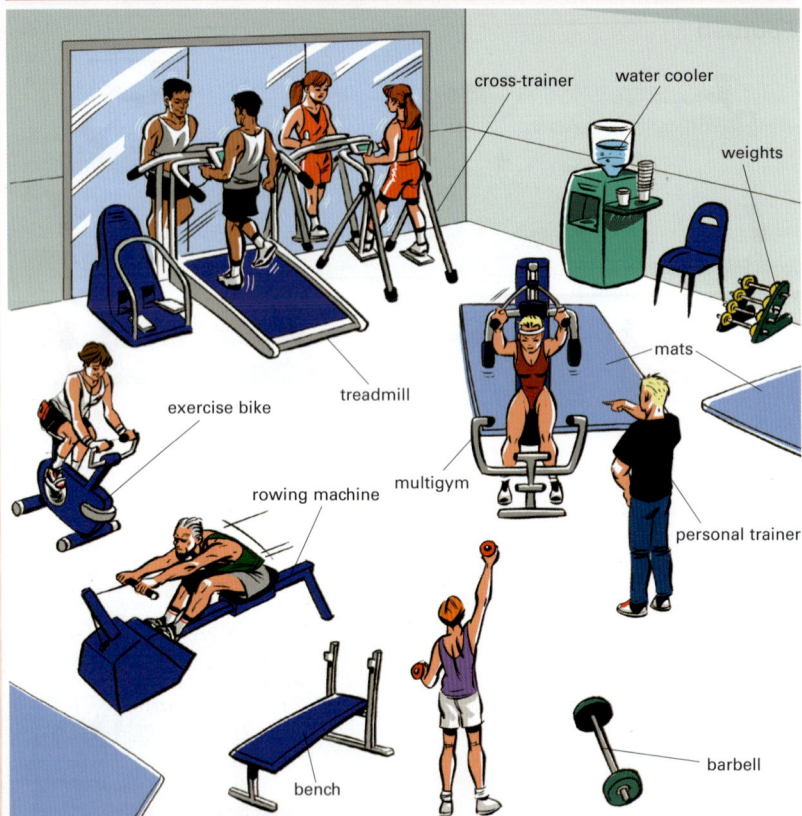

cross-trainer

water cooler

weights

mats

treadmill

exercise bike

multigym

personal trainer

rowing machine

bench

barbell

GAMES

chess
chessboard

chessmen

castle/ knight bishop
rook

queen king pawn

backgammon
dice/die   counter

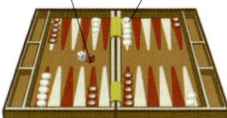

draughts
counter

noughts and crosses

cards
a pack/deck of cards

a hand of cards

suits

♠ spade

♥ heart

♦ diamond

♣ club

jack/knave   queen   king

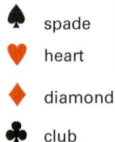

ace   joker

protection /prəˈtekʃ(ə)n/ noun [U] ★★★ the process of keeping someone or something safe: *the **protection** of the countryside* ◆ *A healthy diet should provide **protection** against disease.* ◆ *White clothes give your skin good **protection** from the sun.*

protective /prəˈtektɪv/ adj **1** wanting to protect someone from being harmed or hurt: *He's very protective towards his sister.* **2** providing protection against something harmful or dangerous: *protective clothing*

protégé /ˈprɒtəʒeɪ/ noun [C] a young person who receives help or training from an older experienced person

protein /ˈprəʊtiːn/ noun [U] a substance in foods such as meat, eggs, and milk that keeps you healthy

protest¹ /ˈprəʊtest/ noun ★★
1 [C/U] a strong complaint or disagreement: *a formal **protest** against the nuclear testing* ◆ *She resigned **in protest** during the scandal.*
2 [C] an occasion when people show strong public opposition to something: *a protest march* ◆ *Students will **stage a protest** this weekend outside Parliament.*
PHRASE **under protest** if you do something under protest, you do it but you tell people that you think that it is unfair

> ### Words often used with **protest**
> *Adjectives often used with **protest** (noun, sense 2)*
> ■ **mass, peaceful, public, violent** + PROTEST: used about a particular type of protest
> *Verbs often used with **protest** (noun, sense 2)*
> ■ **hold, organize, stage** + PROTEST: to arrange for a protest to take place

protest² /prəˈtest/ verb ★
1 [I] to show publicly that you oppose something: *Workers are **protesting against** high unemployment.* ◆ *Prisoners began **protesting at** their conditions.*
2 [T] to try to make other people believe that something is true=SWEAR: *She still protests her innocence.*

Protestant /ˈprɒtɪstənt/ noun [C] a member of a group of Christian churches that separated from the Roman Catholic church in the 16th century —**Protestant** adj

protestation /ˌprɒtɪˈsteɪʃ(ə)n/ noun [C] *formal* a statement that shows that you strongly disagree with something

protester /prəˈtestə/ noun [C] someone who publicly shows their opposition to something

protocol /ˈprəʊtəʊˌkɒl/ noun [U] rules for correct behaviour

prototype /ˈprəʊtəˌtaɪp/ noun [C] the first form of something new that is made before it is produced in large quantities

protracted /prəˈtræktɪd/ adj *formal* continuing for a longer time than normal or necessary =LONG, LENGTHY

protrude /prəˈtruːd/ verb [I] to stick out from a surface

protrusion /prəˈtruːʒ(ə)n/ noun [C] a part of something that sticks out from a surface

proud /praʊd/ adj ★
1 feeling happy about your achievements, your possessions, or people who you are connected with: *We're so **proud of** her for telling the truth.* ◆ *+(that)* *We're proud that*

they chose our hotel for their conference. ◆ **be proud to do sth** *I'm proud to say we made the right decision.*
2 a proud person does not like other people to help them or to think that they are weak ≠ HUMBLE: *a proud and independent nation* ◆ **be too proud to do sth** *I was too proud to admit I didn't understand.*
3 someone who is proud thinks that they are better than other people=ARROGANT —**proudly** adv

prove /pruːv/ (past participle **proved** or **proven** /ˈpruːv(ə)n, ˈprəʊv(ə)n/) verb ★★★
1 [T] to provide evidence that shows that something is true: *He is still fighting to **prove** his innocence.* ◆ *+(that)* *You have to prove you are sorry for what you've done.* ◆ **prove sth to sb** *She was determined to prove to her parents that she could live on her own.* ◆ **prove sb right/wrong** *Recent excellent results have proved their critics wrong.*
2 [linking verb] if something proves to have a particular quality, things happen that show that it has that quality: *My decision proved to be a good one.* ◆ *The film is proving very profitable.*
PHRASES **have sth to prove** to try to show people how good you are because you think that they do not realize it
prove yourself to show how good you are at doing something

proven¹ /ˈpruːv(ə)n, ˈprəʊv(ə)n/ adj shown to be true, real, or effective

proven² a past participle of **prove**

proverb /ˈprɒvɜːb/ noun [C] a short well-known statement that gives practical advice about life=ADAGE, SAYING

provide /prəˈvaɪd/ verb [T] ★★★ to give someone something that they want or need: *Our office can **provide information** on the local area.* ◆ **provide sb with sth** *The lecture provided him with an opportunity to meet one of his heroes.* ◆ **provide sth for sb** *The hotel provides a playroom for children.* ◆ **provide sth to sb** *We provide legal advice to our clients.*
PHRASAL VERBS **proˈvide for sb** to look after someone by making money in order to buy the things that they need: *She has always provided for her children.*
proˈvide for sth to make it possible for something to happen in the future: *The budget provides for a salary increase after one year.*

provided /prəˈvaɪdɪd/ or **proˈvided that** conjunction ★★ only if a particular thing happens or is done=PROVIDING: *You can go out to play provided that you finish your homework first.*

providence /ˈprɒvɪdəns/ noun [U] *literary* a powerful force that some people believe causes everything that happens to us =DESTINY, FATE

provider /prəˈvaɪdə/ noun [C] a company that provides a service

providing /prəˈvaɪdɪŋ/ or **proˈviding that** conjunction only if a particular thing happens or is done=PROVIDED: *We'll all be there providing that Al can get time off work.*

P

province /ˈprɒvɪns/ noun **1** [C] one of the large areas that some countries are divided into **2 the provinces** [plural] the parts of a country that are outside the capital city or the large cities

provincial /prəˈvɪnʃ(ə)l/ adj **1** in the parts of a country that are not the capital city or the large cities **2** old-fashioned or conservative: *provincial attitudes to modern art*

provision /prəˈvɪʒ(ə)n/ noun **1** [U] the act of providing something that someone needs **2** [C/U] plans to provide things that you will need in the future: *We've made provision for our grandchild's education.* **3** [C] a part of a law that deals with a particular problem **4 provisions** [plural] food and other necessary supplies, especially for a journey

provisional /prəˈvɪʒ(ə)nəl/ adj intended to be temporary and therefore likely to be changed —**provisionally** adv

proviso /prəˈvaɪzəʊ/ noun [C] something that someone must agree to do before you will agree to do something else

provocation /ˌprɒvəˈkeɪʃ(ə)n/ noun [C/U] something that makes you react in an angry or violent way

provocative /prəˈvɒkətɪv/ adj **1** intended to make you angry or upset **2** intended to make you sexually excited —**provocatively** adv

provoke /prəˈvəʊk/ verb [T] **1** to deliberately try to make someone angry: *He's just trying to provoke you.* **2** to cause a particular reaction, especially an angry one: *The Minister's speech has provoked a furious reaction.*

prow /praʊ/ noun [C] the front of a ship

prowess /ˈpraʊəs/ noun [U] great skill, or great ability

prowl¹ /praʊl/ verb [I/T] to move around an area quietly, especially because you are planning to do something bad

prowl² /praʊl/ noun **on the prowl** looking for someone or something

prowler /ˈpraʊlə/ noun [C] someone who moves around an area quietly, looking for an opportunity to commit a crime

proximity /prɒkˈsɪməti/ noun [U] *formal* the state of being near someone or something

proxy /ˈprɒksi/ noun **do sth by proxy** if you do something by proxy, someone else does it for you

prude /pruːd/ noun [C] *showing disapproval* someone who is easily shocked or embarrassed by anything relating to sex —**prudish** adj

prudent /ˈpruːd(ə)nt/ adj careful, and using good judgment —**prudence** noun [U], **prudently** adv

prune¹ /pruːn/ verb [T] to cut off parts of a tree or plant

prune² /pruːn/ noun [C] a dried PLUM (=type of fruit)

pry /praɪ/ verb **1** [I] to be interested in someone's personal life in a way that is annoying or offensive: *I just glanced at the letter; I didn't mean to pry.* ♦ *The press continues to pry into their affairs.* **2** [T] to force something open, or to force things apart

PS /ˌpiː ˈes/ abbrev postscript: used for introducing additional information at the end of a letter after you have signed your name

psalm /sɑːm/ noun [C] a song or poem from the Bible that praises God

pseudonym /ˈsjuːdənɪm/ noun [C] a false name that someone uses, especially when they write a book

psych /saɪk/ PHRASAL VERB ,**psych sb ˈup** *informal* to try to make someone feel confident and ready for something

psyche /ˈsaɪki/ noun [C] the part of your mind that controls your attitudes and behaviour

psychedelic /ˌsaɪkəˈdelɪk/ adj **1** psychedelic drugs make you see things that are not really there **2** psychedelic clothes or designs are very brightly coloured and have big unusual patterns

psychiatrist /saɪˈkaɪətrɪst/ noun [C] a doctor who treats people with mental illnesses

psychiatry /saɪˈkaɪətri/ noun [U] the study and treatment of mental illness —**psychiatric** /ˌsaɪkiˈætrɪk/ adj

psychic /ˈsaɪkɪk/ adj **1** someone who is psychic claims to be able to know what other people are thinking or what is going to happen to them **2** connected with mysterious mental powers that cannot be explained by science: *psychic energy* —**psychic** noun [C]

psycho /ˈsaɪkəʊ/ noun [C] *informal* someone who is crazy and behaves in a frightening and violent way

psychoanalysis /ˌsaɪkəʊəˈnæləsɪs/ noun [U] medical treatment in which someone talks to a psychoanalyst about their feelings in order to solve their mental problems —**psychoanalyse** /ˌsaɪkəʊˈænəˌlaɪz/ verb [T]

psychoanalyst /ˌsaɪkəʊˈænəlɪst/ noun [C] a doctor whose job is to talk to people about their feelings in order to solve their mental problems

psychological /ˌsaɪkəˈlɒdʒɪk(ə)l/ adj ★ **1** involving or affecting your mind: *Harry's problems are more psychological than physical.* **2** connected with the study of how your mind works: *psychological theories* —**psychologically** /ˌsaɪkəˈlɒdʒɪkli/ adv

psychologist /saɪˈkɒlədʒɪst/ noun [C] someone who studies how people's minds work and how this affects their behaviour

psychology /saɪˈkɒlədʒi/ noun [U] ★ **1** the study of the mind and how it affects behaviour **2** the way that the mind affects behaviour in a particular person or group of people: *a book on the psychology of murderers*

psychopath /ˈsaɪkəʊˌpæθ/ noun [C] someone who has a serious mental illness that makes them behave in a very violent way —**psychopathic** /ˌsaɪkəʊˈpæθɪk/ adj

psychosis /saɪˈkəʊsɪs/ (plural **psychoses** /saɪˈkəʊsiːz/) noun [C/U] *medical* a serious mental illness

psychosomatic /ˌsaɪkəʊsəʊˈmætɪk/ adj a psychosomatic illness is caused by a problem in your mind

psychotherapy /ˌsaɪkəʊˈθerəpi/ noun [U] a treatment for people with mental illness that involves talking to them instead of giving them drugs —**psychotherapist** noun [C]

psychotic /saɪˈkɒtɪk/ adj someone who is psychotic behaves in a dangerous or violent way because they have a serious mental illness —**psychotic** noun [C]

pt abbrev **1** pint **2** point

PTA /ˌpiː tiː ˈeɪ/ noun [C] Parent-Teacher Association: an organization of parents and teachers who work together in order to improve their school

PTO /ˌpiː tiː ˈəʊ/ abbrev please turn over: used at the bottom of a page when there is more writing on the other side

pub /pʌb/ noun [C] ★★ a place where people go to drink alcohol

puberty /ˈpjuːbəti/ noun [U] the period in a person's life when their body changes from a child's body to an adult's body

pubic /ˈpjuːbɪk/ adj relating to the area around the sexual organs

public¹ /ˈpʌblɪk/ adj ★★★
1 owned by the government, not by a private company ≠ PRIVATE: *public money/ institutions*
2 available for people in general to use ≠ PRIVATE: *a public library* ♦ *the city's public parks*
3 involving a lot of people, or involving people in general: *a public nuisance/hazard* ♦ *The scheme has a lot of* **public support**.
4 used about places and situations where other people can see you: *Can we go somewhere a little less public?* ♦ *She keeps her public and private lives very separate.*
PHRASES **in the public eye** well known to people in general: *Her job keeps her in the public eye.*
make sth public to tell everyone about something: *The government has decided to make the results of the inquiry public.*

public² /ˈpʌblɪk/ noun ★★★ **the public** people in general: *The palace was opened to the public in the 1950s.* ♦ *The decision was not in the best interests of the travelling public.* ♦ *The police should be trained to deal politely with* **members of the public**. → GENERAL PUBLIC
PHRASE **in public** if you do something in public, people in general hear about it or see it ≠ IN PRIVATE: *It's unprofessional to criticize your colleagues in public.*

In British English, **the public** can be used with a singular or plural verb. You can say *The public* **wants** *tougher sentences for terrorists.* OR *The public* **want** *tougher sentences for terrorists.*

public-adˈdress ˌsystem noun [C] a PA system

publican /ˈpʌblɪkən/ noun [C] British someone who owns or manages a PUB

publication /ˌpʌblɪˈkeɪʃ(ə)n/ noun ★
1 [U] the process of producing a book for people to buy: *She became famous after* **the publication of** *her first novel.*
2 [C] a magazine, newspaper, or book: *a weekly financial publication*
3 [U] the process of making information available to the public: **Publication of** *the report is expected next week.*

public ˈfigure noun [C] a well-known person

public ˈholiday noun [C] a BANK HOLIDAY

publicist /ˈpʌblɪsɪst/ noun [C] someone whose job is to make a person or thing well known

publicity /pʌbˈlɪsəti/ noun [U] ★ attention in newspapers and on television: *a publicity campaign* (=an attempt to get publicity) ♦ *Her behaviour during the filming attracted a lot of* **publicity**.

Words often used with **publicity**

Adjectives often used with **publicity**
■ **adverse, bad, negative, unfavourable, unwelcome** + PUBLICITY: used about bad publicity
■ **considerable, extensive, enormous, massive, maximum, widespread** + PUBLICITY: used about publicity that a large number of people see or hear

Verbs often used with **publicity**
■ **attract, gain, generate, get, receive** + PUBLICITY: get publicity
■ **avoid, shun** + PUBLICITY: try not to get publicity

publicize /ˈpʌblɪsaɪz/ verb [T] to publish or broadcast information about someone or something

publicly /ˈpʌblɪkli/ adv **1** in a way that many people notice ≠ PRIVATELY: *Kent publicly disagreed with his fellow doctors on many occasions.* **2** by the government, or by or for people in general: *a publicly owned health service* ♦ *publicly available information*

public reˈlations noun [U] the job of giving people information about something and making it popular = PR

public ˈschool noun [C/U] **1** British an expensive private school **2** American a school that is controlled and paid for by the government

public ˈsector noun [singular] the industries and services that are controlled by the government

public ˈservice noun **1** [C] a service that the government pays for, such as education or health care **2** [U] the work that is done by people who are employed by the government **3** [C] a service that helps people without charging them any money

public ˈtransport noun [U] British buses, trains etc that everyone can use

public transporˈtation noun [U] American PUBLIC TRANSPORT

publish /ˈpʌblɪʃ/ verb [T] ★★★
1 to produce many copies of a book, magazine, or newspaper for people to buy: *Their company publishes a wide selection of books.*
2 to make information available for everyone to read: *The department's* **report** *was* **published** *in June.*
3 to have something that you have written printed and sold: *In 1934 he published another successful novel.*
4 to include something such as a letter in a newspaper or magazine: *Our* **research** *is being* **published** *in a well-known medical journal.*

publisher /ˈpʌblɪʃə/ noun [C] a person or company that produces and sells books

publishing /ˈpʌblɪʃɪŋ/ noun [U] the business of producing books

P

pudding /ˈpʊdɪŋ/ noun **1** [C] *British* a soft sweet food that you eat at the end of a meal: *a sponge pudding* **2** [U] *British* the last part of a meal when you eat sweet foods=DESSERT: *What's for pudding?* **3** [C/U] *American* a cold, soft, sweet food, flavoured, for example, with chocolate

puddle /ˈpʌd(ə)l/ noun [C] a small pool of water that is left on the ground after it has rained

puff¹ /pʌf/ verb **1** [I/T] to smoke a cigarette **2** [I] to breathe noisily after running or doing something else that is physically hard

PHRASAL VERBS **puff sth ˈout** if you puff out your cheeks or your chest, you fill them with air so that they look bigger
puff ˈup to swell because of an injury or illness: *The next day his face had really puffed up.*

puff² /pʌf/ noun [C] **1** the action of breathing in smoke from a cigarette **2** a small amount of smoke, wind, or air

puffy /ˈpʌfi/ adj slightly swollen

pugnacious /pʌɡˈneɪʃəs/ adj *formal* quick to argue or fight with people

puke /pjuːk/ verb [I/T] *informal* to VOMIT food from your stomach out through your mouth=THROW (STH) UP —**puke** noun [U]

pull¹ /pʊl/ verb ★★★

1 move sth towards you	**6** injure muscle
2 remove sth fixed	**7** take gun/knife out
3 move body with force	**+ PHRASES**
4 take sth behind vehicle	**+ PHRASAL VERBS**
5 attract people	

1 [I/T] to move someone or something towards you using your hands ≠ PUSH: *The little girl pulled gently at my sleeve.* ♦ **pull sb/sth away from/out of/into etc sth** *I climbed into bed and pulled the duvet over my head.* ♦ *A lifeguard had to pull her out of the water.* ♦ **pull sth open/shut** *Jane pulled the door open.* ♦ **pull sth tight** *Don't pull the string too tight.*

2 [T] to use force to remove something that is fixed somewhere: **pull sth up** *She was pulling up the weeds in the garden.* ♦ **pull sth off sth** *Someone pulled the handle off the door.*

3 [T] to move your body or part of your body using effort or force: *He needed all his energy to pull himself up off the ground.*

4 [T] to move something along behind your vehicle by fixing it to the vehicle: *Two horses were pulling the plough.*

5 [T] to attract customers, VOTERS, or an audience: *The show is pulling huge audiences all over America.*

6 [T] to injure a muscle by stretching it too much

7 [T] to take a gun or a knife out of your pocket and be ready to use it: **pull sth on sb** *His attacker suddenly pulled a knife on him.*

PHRASES **pull sb's leg** to tell someone a lie as a joke

pull out all the stops to make a big effort so that something happens or is successful: *Her parents pulled out all the stops for her wedding.*

pull your socks up *British informal* used for telling someone to work harder or try harder

pull strings to use your influence in order to get something: *We might be able to get tickets if I pull a few strings.*

pull the strings if someone is pulling the strings, they are secretly controlling a situation

pull sb/sth to pieces/to bits 1 to separate the connected pieces of something **2** to criticize someone or something severely

pull up a chair to move a seat near to where someone is sitting, and sit on it

pull your weight to work as hard as the other people who are involved in something

pull the wool over sb's eyes to try to trick someone by giving them wrong information

pull yourself together to start to control your emotions after being very upset or angry

→ PLUG¹, PUNCH²

PHRASAL VERBS **pull sb aˈpart** to separate two people or animals that are fighting
pull sb/sth aˈpart to criticize someone or something severely
pull sth aˈpart to destroy something by violently pulling it into pieces
pull aˈway 1 if a vehicle pulls away, it starts to move away from a place: *The bus pulled away from the station around noon.* **2** to move away from someone who is trying to hold you: *When he tried to kiss her, she pulled away.*
pull ˈback 1 to decide not to do something that you said you would do: *The government has pulled back from sending the navy there.* **2** to move away from someone who is trying to hold you
pull sth ˈdown to destroy a building that is old or dangerous=DEMOLISH
pull ˈin if a vehicle pulls in, it arrives or stops somewhere
pull ˈinto sth if a vehicle pulls into a place, it stops there: *The train pulled into Central Station.*
pull sth ˈoff to succeed in doing something that is difficult: *Hanley pulled off a surprise victory in the semi-final.* ♦ *They nearly managed to get the loan but just failed to pull it off.*
pull ˈoff sth if a vehicle pulls off a road, it stops by the side of it
pull sth ˈon to put clothes on quickly
pull ˈout 1 to leave a place: *The troops are expected to pull out tomorrow.* **2** to decide not take part in something: *The Columbian team pulled out at the last minute.* **3** if a train pulls out, it leaves a station **4** if a vehicle pulls out, it moves onto a road or onto a part of a road where the traffic is moving faster: *She just pulled out in front of me without indicating!*
pull (sth) ˈover to stop at the side of the road, or to make a vehicle stop at the side of the road
pull ˈthrough to manage to stay alive after you have been very ill or badly injured
pull (sb) ˈthrough to succeed in a very difficult situation, or to help someone to do this: *It was a difficult year financially, but we pulled through.*
pull toˈgether if people pull together, they work together to achieve something: *The community pulled together to help the flood victims.*

,**pull 'up** if a vehicle pulls up, it stops: *Their taxi pulled up outside the church.*

pull² /pʊl/ noun **1** [C] the act of moving someone or something towards you **2** [singular] a strong physical force that causes things to move in a particular direction: *the pull of gravity* **3** [singular] the power that something has to attract people

'**pull-down ,menu** noun [C] *computing* a list of choices on a computer screen that you get by CLICKING on something → DROP-DOWN MENU

pulley /'pʊli/ noun [C] a piece of equipment used for lifting heavy things, consisting of a wheel with a rope around it

pullout /'pʊlaʊt/ noun [C] an occasion when an army or business leaves a place

pullover /'pʊləʊvə/ noun [C] a warm piece of KNITTED clothing without buttons that you wear on the top part of your body=JUMPER, SWEATER

pulmonary /'pʌlmən(ə)ri/ adj *medical* affecting your lungs

pulp /pʌlp/ noun **1** [U] the inside of a fruit or vegetable=FLESH **2** [singular/U] a thick soft substance made by crushing something

pulpit /'pʊlpɪt/ noun [C] the place where a priest stands to talk to people in a church

pulsate /pʌl'seɪt/ verb [I] to make strong regular movements or sounds —**pulsating** adj

pulse¹ /pʌls/ noun [C] the regular movement of blood as your heart pumps it round your body: *The first thing the doctor does is take your pulse* (=check how fast your heart is beating).

pulse² /pʌls/ verb [I] **1** to move with a strong regular movement **2** to fill a person or place with a quality: *a city pulsing with life*

pulses /'pʌlsɪz/ noun [plural] beans, PEAS, and other seeds that you can cook and eat

pulverize /'pʌlvə,raɪz/ verb [T] to crush something into very small pieces

pummel /'pʌm(ə)l/ verb [T] to hit someone or something many times

pump¹ /pʌmp/ noun [C] ★ a piece of equipment for sending a liquid or gas into or out of something: *a fuel pump ♦ a hand/foot pump* (=operated with your hand or foot)

pump² /pʌmp/ verb ★
1 [T] to send liquid or gas somewhere, especially by using a pump: *Poisonous gases are pumped into the atmosphere every day.*
2 [I/T] to move up and down with a lot of force, or to move something up and down with a lot of force: *Liz pumped the accelerator and tried to start the car. ♦ His legs were really pumping.*
3 [T] *informal* to try to get information from someone

PHRASAL VERBS '**pump sth into sth** to invest a lot of money in something
,**pump sth 'out 1** to make liquid or gas escape from a place: *Huge generators were pumping out black smoke.* **2** *informal* to produce a lot of something
,**pump sth 'up** to fill something with air, using a pump

pumpkin /'pʌmpkɪn/ noun [C/U] a large round vegetable with a thick orange skin —*picture* → C11

pumps /pʌmps/ noun [plural] *British* flat shoes that do not fasten and are worn for dancing

pun /pʌn/ noun [C] a joke using words that have two meanings

punch¹ /pʌntʃ/ verb [T] **1** to hit someone or something with your FIST (=closed hand) **2** to make a hole in something with a tool or machine

punch

punch² /pʌntʃ/ noun **1** [C] the action of hitting someone or something with your FIST (=closed hand) **2** [U] a sweet drink made with fruit juice and alcohol **3** [C] a tool for making a hole in something

PHRASE **not pull any/your punches** to criticize someone or something in a very direct honest way

'**punch ,line** noun [C] the funny last part of a joke

punctual /'pʌŋktʃuəl/ adj someone who is punctual arrives at the time that they should arrive at —**punctuality** /,pʌŋktʃu'æləti/ noun [U], **punctually** adv

punctuate /'pʌŋktʃueɪt/ verb [I/T] to use FULL STOPS, COMMAS, and other PUNCTUATION MARKS in your writing

PHRASE **be punctuated by/with sth** to be frequently interrupted by something: *a 15-minute speech punctuated by applause*

punctuation /,pʌŋktʃu'eɪʃ(ə)n/ noun [U] **1** the use of marks such as FULL STOPS and COMMAS in writing **2** punctuation marks

punctu'ation ,mark noun [C] a mark such as a FULL STOP, COMMA, or QUESTION MARK that you use in order to write in a clear style

puncture¹ /'pʌŋktʃə/ noun [C] **1** a small hole made with a sharp point **2** a small hole that is made by accident in a tyre

puncture² /'pʌŋktʃə/ verb [T] to make a small hole in something

pundit /'pʌndɪt/ noun [C] an expert who gives their opinions in newspapers and on television and radio programmes

pungent /'pʌndʒənt/ adj a pungent taste or smell is very strong and sharp

punish /'pʌnɪʃ/ verb [T] ★ to do something unpleasant to someone because they have done something bad or illegal: **punish sb for (doing) sth** *He was punished for stealing.*

PHRASE **punish yourself** to do something that makes you suffer: *Why punish yourself by working harder than you need to?*

punishable /ˈpʌnɪʃəb(ə)l/ adj if someone does something punishable, they can be punished for doing it

punishing /ˈpʌnɪʃɪŋ/ adj extremely difficult or tiring

punishment /ˈpʌnɪʃmənt/ noun ★
1 [C] a way in which someone is punished: *He had to clean up the mess as a punishment.*
2 [U] the process of punishing someone: *He has cheated people and escaped punishment.*

punitive /ˈpjuːnətɪv/ adj relating to punishment, or intended as a punishment

Punjabi¹ /pʌnˈdʒɑːbi/ noun [U] the language most people speak in the Punjab region of India and Pakistan

Punjabi² /pʌnˈdʒɑːbi/ adj 1 someone who is Punjabi is from Punjab 2 relating to Punjab, or its language or culture

punk /pʌŋk/ noun 1 punk or punk rock [U] a type of loud fast music with angry words 2 punk or punk rocker [C] someone who likes punk music, or who dresses in the style of punk musicians

punt¹ /pʌnt/ noun [C] a long flat boat that you move by pushing a long pole against the bottom of the river

punt² /pʌnt/ verb [I] to travel on a river in a punt

punter /ˈpʌntə/ noun [C] *British informal* 1 a customer 2 someone who BETS (=risks their money) on the result of a race

puny /ˈpjuːni/ adj a puny person or animal is small, thin, and weak

pup /pʌp/ noun [C] a PUPPY

pupil /ˈpjuːp(ə)l/ noun [C] ★★★
1 someone who goes to school or who has lessons in a particular subject → STUDENT
2 the black round part in the middle of your eye

puppet /ˈpʌpɪt/ noun [C] 1 a toy that looks like a person or animal that you move by pulling wires or strings, or by putting your hand inside it 2 someone who is controlled by someone else

puppeteer /ˌpʌpɪˈtɪə/ noun [C] someone who performs using puppets

puppy /ˈpʌpi/ noun [C] a very young dog

purchase¹ /ˈpɜːtʃəs/ verb [T] *formal* to buy something: *She purchased shares in the company.*

purchase² /ˈpɜːtʃəs/ noun *formal* 1 [U] the process of buying something: *the purchase of new computers* 2 [C] something that you buy: *Her latest purchase was a long black coat.*

pure /pjʊə/ adj ★★
1 a pure substance has nothing mixed with it that might spoil its quality ≠ IMPURE: *pure gold/alcohol* ♦ *clean, pure drinking water*
2 used for emphasis: *a smile of pure happiness* ♦ *Perhaps it was pure chance that the other woman happened to be there.*
3 morally good ≠ IMPURE: *He seems to have led a pure life.*
4 a pure science deals only with theory and not with the way the theory is used: *pure mathematics*

Word family: pure

Words in the same family as pure
- **purely** *adv*
- **purify** *v*
- **purity** *n*
- **purist** *n*
- **impure** *adj*
- **impurity** *n*

---

purée /ˈpjʊəreɪ/ noun [C/U] food that has been mixed or crushed to form a thick smooth sauce —**purée** verb [T]

purely /ˈpjʊəli/ adv ★ completely, or only: *What I'm saying is purely my own point of view.* ♦ *We meet purely for business reasons.*

purgatory /ˈpɜːgət(ə)ri/ noun [U] 1 the place where Roman Catholics believe that people go to suffer after they die before they are allowed to go to heaven 2 an unpleasant place or experience

purge /pɜːdʒ/ verb [T] 1 to force people to leave an organization 2 to get rid of bad feelings —**purge** noun [C]

purify /ˈpjʊərɪfaɪ/ verb [T] to make something clean by removing dirty or harmful substances from it —**purification** /ˌpjʊərɪfɪˈkeɪʃ(ə)n/ noun [U]

purist /ˈpjʊərɪst/ noun [C] someone who wants people to follow rules carefully

puritan /ˈpjʊərɪtən/ noun [C] *showing disapproval* someone who does not approve of pleasures such as sex and drinking alcohol —**puritanical** /ˌpjʊərɪˈtænɪk(ə)l/ adj

purity /ˈpjʊərəti/ noun [U] the condition of being pure ≠ IMPURITY

purple¹ /ˈpɜːp(ə)l/ adj between red and blue in colour

purple² /ˈpɜːp(ə)l/ noun [U] a colour that is between red and blue

purport /pəˈpɔːt/ verb [I] *formal* to claim to do something

purpose /ˈpɜːpəs/ noun [C] ★★★ an aim or use: *The purpose of this dictionary is to help students of English.* ♦ *Another meeting would serve absolutely no purpose.* ♦ **for the purpose of doing sth** *He went there for the purpose of making business contacts.*
PHRASE **on purpose** deliberately: *They think the fire was started on purpose.*
→ ALL-PURPOSE

purpose-built adj *British* made for one particular purpose

purposeful /ˈpɜːpəsf(ə)l/ adj showing that you are determined to do something

purposely /ˈpɜːpəsli/ adv deliberately

purr /pɜː/ verb [I] 1 if a cat purrs, it makes a continuous low sound because it is happy 2 if a machine purrs, it makes a continuous quiet sound because it is operating correctly —**purr** noun [C]

purse¹ /pɜːs/ noun [C] ★
1 *British* a small bag for carrying money
2 *American* a woman's HANDBAG

purse² /pɜːs/ verb **purse your lips** to press your lips together and outwards because you are angry or you are thinking

purse strings, the noun [plural] the way in which money is controlled and spent by a group or organization: *Who controls the purse strings?*

pursue /pəˈsjuː/ verb [T] ★
1 to do something, or to try to achieve something: *We're persuading both countries to pursue a peaceful solution.* ♦ *He wants to*

pursue a career in medicine. ♦ *I intend to pursue the matter* (=continue to try to achieve my aim).
2 to chase someone

pursuit /pəˈsjuːt/ noun **1** [U] the process of trying to achieve something: *the pursuit of happiness* **2** [U] the process of chasing someone: *Several police officers are in pursuit of the stolen car.* **3** [C] *formal* an activity that you enjoy: *his artistic pursuits*

pus /pʌs/ noun [U] a thick yellow liquid that your body produces when you have an infection

push[1] /pʊʃ/ verb ★★★

1 move sb/sth away	5 force sb
2 press button	6 make sb work hard
3 move through group	7 make impatient
4 make sth reach level	+ PHRASAL VERBS

1 [I/T] to move someone or something away from you using your hands ≠ PULL: *Push as hard as you can.* ♦ **push sb/sth away** *She gently pushed him away.* ♦ **push sth open/shut** *I pushed open the door.*
2 [I/T] to press a button on a machine: *To turn on the television, you push this switch.*
3 [I/T] to move through a group of people using the force of your body: *Stop pushing and just wait your turn.* ♦ *He just pushed past Fred and left.* ♦ *I was pushing my way through the crowd.*
4 [T] to make something reach a particular level or standard: **push sth into/towards sth** *The strong sun pushed temperatures into the nineties.* ♦ **push sth up/down** *The Bank of England had pushed up interest rates sharply to protect the pound.*
5 [T] to force someone to do something: **push sb into (doing) sth** *The police pushed her into giving evidence.*
6 [T] to make someone work very hard: *Some parents really push their children.* ♦ *You shouldn't push yourself so hard.*
7 [T] to make someone impatient or annoyed by behaving in an unreasonable way: *If you push him too far, he'll resign.*
PHRASAL VERBS ˌpush aˈhead to continue trying to achieve something
ˌpush sb aˈround *informal* to keep telling someone what to do in an unfair and unpleasant way
ˌpush sth aˈside to refuse to think about something unpleasant: *She pushed her doubts aside and carried on.*
ˈpush for sth to try hard to get or achieve something: *They continue to push for more pay.*
ˌpush ˈin *British* to unfairly stand in front of people who have been waiting longer than you
ˌpush ˈoff *British informal* used for telling someone rudely and angrily to go away
ˌpush ˈon **1** to continue a journey after stopping for a time **2** to continue doing something
ˌpush sb/sth ˈover to push someone or something hard so that they fall to the ground
ˌpush sth ˈthrough to succeed in making people accept something such as an agreement or a new law
ˌpush sth ˈup to increase the price or level of something

push[2] /pʊʃ/ noun ★
1 [C] a movement in which you push someone or something: **give sb/sth a push** *Jan helped me give the car a push.*
2 [C] a determined attempt to do something: **a push to do sth** *The two sides began a final push to reach an agreement before the deadline.*
3 [singular] an occasion when you encourage or force someone to do something: **give sb a push (to do sth)** *I knew I could do it – I just needed someone to give me an extra push.* ♦ **need a push (to do sth)** *Some people need a little push to make new friends.*
PHRASES **at a push** *British informal* used for saying that something is possible, but very difficult: *I can afford to pay fifty pounds at a push.*
give sb the push *British informal* **1** if your employer gives you the push, they force you to leave your job **2** to end a sexual or romantic relationship with someone: *I finally gave him the push last night.*
if/when push comes to shove if or when you are forced to make a decision or to do something difficult

ˈpush-button adj operated by pressing a button or switch

pushchair /ˈpʊʃˌtʃeə/ noun [C] *British* a small chair with wheels that a small child sits in and is pushed along

pusher /ˈpʊʃə/ noun [C] *informal* someone who sells illegal drugs

pushover /ˈpʊʃˌəʊvə/ noun [C] **1** someone who is easy to persuade or defeat **2** something that is easy to achieve

pushy /ˈpʊʃi/ adj *informal* extremely determined to get what you want, even if it annoys other people

pussy /ˈpʊsi/ or **pussycat** /ˈpʊsikæt/ noun [C] *informal* a cat. This word is used especially by children.

pussyfoot /ˈpʊsiˌfʊt/ verb [I] *informal* to avoid saying or doing anything definite because you are afraid

put /pʊt/ (past tense and past participle **put**) verb [T] ★★★

1 move sth to position	6 place somewhere
2 cause to be in situation	7 give position on list
3 write/print sth	8 state sth
4 make sb go to place	+ PHRASES
5 say in particular way	+ PHRASAL VERBS

1 to move something to a particular position using your hands: *Where did you put the newspaper?* ♦ **put sth in/on/through etc sth** *Did I put my wallet in your bag?* ♦ *She put her hand on Cliff's arm.*
2 to cause someone or something to be in a particular situation: *She was **put in charge of** the marketing department.* ♦ *The information you've given me puts me **in a really difficult position**.* ♦ *I hate being **put under** so much **pressure**.* ♦ *That argument put me **in a bad mood** for the rest of the day.* ♦ *Supermarkets have put many smaller shops **out of business**.*
3 to write or print something somewhere: *Put a tick by the correct answer.* ♦ *I'll put a note at the bottom of the card.* ♦ *You've put the comma in the wrong place.*

P

4 to make someone go to a place: *The government has promised to put more police officers on the street.* ♦ *What time do you put the kids to bed?*

5 to say or write something in a particular way: *She put it very well when she described him as 'brilliant but lazy'.*

6 to build or place something somewhere: *There are plans to put ten new houses on the site.* ♦ *We decided to put the office upstairs.*

7 to give something a particular position on a list according to importance, quality, or value: *I'd put Monet among the best artists of the century.* ♦ *They're so different, you can't even put them in the same category.*

8 to state or explain something: *You will get plenty of opportunity to put your point of view.*

PHRASES **not put it past sb (to do sth)** used for saying that you think someone is capable of doing something bad or dishonest: *'Do you think Jake took the money?' 'I wouldn't put it past him.'*

put sth behind you to stop thinking about something unpleasant that has happened to you: *I was upset at the time, but I've managed to put it behind me.*

put a stop/end to sth to make something stop happening: *You ought to put a stop to that sort of behaviour.*

→ STAY¹

PHRASAL VERBS **put sth across** to explain something in a way that people can understand: *Television can be a useful way of putting across information.*

put sth aside 1 to save money for the future **2** to not allow yourself to be affected by a problem or argument, so that you can achieve something more important: *Both sides need to put aside their differences and continue the peace talks.*

put sth away to put something in the place where you usually keep it: *He put the notebook away and stood up.*

put sth back 1 to put something in the place where it was before it was moved: *Can you put the book back when you've finished with it?* **2** to make something happen at a later time or date than you originally planned: *We've put the trip back until June now.* **3** to change the time of a clock or watch to an earlier time

put sth by *same as* **put sth aside**

put sb down 1 to criticize someone in a way that makes them feel stupid **2** to write someone's name on a list so that they can take part in a particular activity

put sth down 1 to put something onto a surface such as the floor or a table: *Emma put her bag down and went upstairs.* **2** to kill an animal using a drug because it is very old, ill, or dangerous **3** to write something on a piece of paper: *I put my name down on the list.* **4 put the phone down** to put the telephone RECEIVER back onto its base after you have finished talking to someone

put sth down to sth to think that something happened for a particular reason: *I put his bad mood down to tiredness.*

put sb forward to officially suggest that someone should be considered for a particular job: *Your name was put forward as a possible team leader.*

put sth forward 1 to suggest something so that people can discuss it and make a decision: *He rejected all the proposals put forward by the committee.* **2** to change the time of a clock or watch to a later time

put sth in 1 to spend time or effort doing something: *Wendy has been putting in more hours at the office recently.* **2** to put equipment somewhere and make it ready to use: *We're having a burglar alarm put in.* **3** to make an official request, claim, offer etc: *Why don't you put in a claim for the damage?* → APPEARANCE

put sth into sth 1 to spend time or effort in order to do something: *I put a lot of work into the speech.* **2** to invest money in something: *How much are you prepared to put into the business?*

put sb off 1 to prevent someone from concentrating on something: *Stop laughing – you'll put her off.* **2** to tell someone that you cannot see them or do something until a later time: *We'll have to put George off if your mother's coming on Thursday.*

put sb off (sb/sth) to make someone not like someone or something or not want to do something: *Robert's attitude towards women really puts me off.* ♦ *I put him off the idea of going shopping with me.*

put sth off 1 to delay doing something that you do not want to do: *You can't put the decision off any longer.* ♦ **put off doing sth** *He was glad to have an excuse to put off telling her the news.* **2** to arrange to do something at a later time than you originally planned: *They had to put the wedding off because the bride's mother had an accident.* ♦ **put off doing sth** *I'll put off going to Scotland until you're well enough to look after yourself again.* **3** to switch off a piece of equipment

put sb on to pass the telephone to someone so that they can speak to the person that you have been talking to

put sth on 1 to cover a part of your body with a piece of clothing or jewellery so that you are wearing it ≠ TAKE STH OFF: *Dorothy put on her coat and went out.* —picture → DRESS **2** to make equipment start working: *Can you put the light on, please?* **3** to organize an event: *We're putting on a concert.* **4** if you put on weight, you become fatter **5** to pretend to have a particular feeling or a particular way of speaking or behaving: *She's not really upset – she's just putting it on.*

put sb out to cause problems for someone by making them do something for you: *It would be lovely to stay with you, but I don't want to put you out.*

put sth out 1 to make something stop burning **2** to switch off a light **3** to put something in a place where someone will see it, so that they can use it or take it: *I put out food for the birds in cold weather.*
→ PUT OUT

P

,put sth 'over *same as* **put sth across**: *I don't think I put my point over very clearly.*

,put sb 'through sth to make someone do something difficult or unpleasant: *The team are put through a daily fitness programme.*

,put sb/sth 'through if you put a person or a telephone call through, you connect someone to the person that they want to speak to on the telephone: *Can you put me through to the accounts department, please?*

'put sth to sb **1** to suggest something so that people can discuss it or consider it: *I put the resolution to the meeting.* ♦ *I put it to her that she was mistaken.* **2** to ask someone a question: *The questions they put to me were quite difficult.*

,put sth to'gether **1** to produce or organize something using many different things: *The exhibition has been put together by a group of young artists.* **2** to make something by joining all its parts: *Will you help me put this desk together?*

,put sb 'up to let someone stay in your house: *Could you put me up for the night when I come to London?*

,put sth 'up **1** to increase the value or price of something **2** to build something such as a wall, fence, or house **3** to fix something to a wall: *The teachers will put a notice up about the new courses.*

,put sb 'up to sth to encourage someone to do something stupid or wrong: *One of the older boys must have put him up to it.*

,put 'up with sb/sth to accept someone or something unpleasant in a patient way: *How has Jan put up with him for so long?*

'put-,down noun [C] a comment that is intended to make someone feel stupid

,put 'out adj annoyed, offended, or upset

putrid /'pju:trɪd/ adj *formal* decaying and smelling very bad

putt /pʌt/ noun [C] in golf, a gentle hit of the ball along the ground towards the hole —*picture* → C15 —**putt** verb [I/T]

putty /'pʌti/ noun [U] a soft grey substance that is used for fixing glass into windows

puzzle[1] /'pʌz(ə)l/ verb [T] if something puzzles you, you cannot understand it

PHRASAL VERB 'puzzle ,over sb/sth to think hard about something and try to understand it

puzzle[2] /'pʌz(ə)l/ noun [C] **1** someone or something that you cannot understand **2** a game or toy that is designed to test your intelligence

puzzled /'pʌz(ə)ld/ adj confused because you cannot understand something

puzzling /'pʌz(ə)lɪŋ/ adj confusing or difficult to understand

PVC /,pi: vi: 'si:/ noun [U] a type of plastic that is used for making clothes and cloth

pyjamas /pə'dʒɑ:məz/ noun [plural] comfortable trousers and a shirt that you wear in bed —*picture* → C5

pylon /'paɪlən/ noun [C] a tall metal tower that holds electricity wires high above the ground

pyramid /'pɪrəmɪd/ noun [C] **1** a large pointed stone structure with a square base and TRIANGULAR sides **2** an object with the shape of a pyramid —*picture* → C8

pyre /paɪə/ noun [C] a high pile of wood for burning a dead body in a funeral ceremony

python /'paɪθn/ noun [C] a large snake that kills animals by wrapping itself around them

Q q

q or **Q** /kju:/ noun [C/U] the 17th letter of the English alphabet

QC /,kju: 'si:/ noun [C] Queen's Counsel: in the UK, a lawyer of high status

quack[1] /kwæk/ noun [C] **1** the sound that a DUCK makes **2** *informal* a bad doctor, or someone who pretends to be a doctor

quack[2] /kwæk/ verb [I] to make the sound that a DUCK makes

quadruple /'kwɒdrʊp(ə)l, kwɒ'dru:p(ə)l/ verb [I/T] if a number or an amount quadruples, or if you quadruple it, it becomes four times bigger than it was

quagmire /'kwæɡmaɪə, 'kwɒɡmaɪə/ noun [C] **1** a situation that is so difficult or complicated that you cannot make much progress **2** an area of very wet land that is too soft to walk on

quaint /kweɪnt/ adj interesting or attractive with a slightly strange and old-fashioned quality

quake[1] /kweɪk/ verb [I] **1** to feel so afraid that your body shakes slightly **2** if something such as a building quakes, it shakes violently

quake[2] /kweɪk/ noun [C] *informal* an EARTHQUAKE

Quaker /'kweɪkə/ noun [C] a member of a Christian religious group whose members avoid violence and hold simple religious services with no priests

qualification /,kwɒlɪfɪ'keɪʃ(ə)n/ noun ★
1 [C] *British* something such as a degree or a DIPLOMA that you get when you successfully finish a course of study: *Simon left school with no qualifications.* ♦ *Young people are encouraged to achieve better skills and qualifications.* ♦ *She has a qualification in teaching.*
2 [C] an ability or quality that you need in order to do a particular job or activity: *Good communication skills are an essential qualification for the job.*
3 [U] the action or process of qualifying for something: *Their chances of World Cup qualification are high.*
4 [C/U] something that you add to a statement or rule in order to show that it is not true in some situations

qualified /'kwɒlɪfaɪd/ adj **1** successfully trained for a particular job: *a qualified*

Q

doctor/nurse/teacher **2** able to do something, because you have the knowledge, skill, or experience that is needed: **qualified to do sth** *She is particularly well qualified to give an opinion.* **3** qualified support or agreement is not completely positive because someone has some doubts or criticisms

qualifier /ˈkwɒlɪˌfaɪə/ noun [C] **1** a game that is played to decide which team or player may enter a competition **2** a team or person who competes successfully in an early stage of a competition and is able to go on to the next stage

qualify /ˈkwɒlɪˌfaɪ/ verb ★
1 [I/T] to become a member of a particular profession after a period of training or study, or to decide that someone can be a member of a particular profession: *Andrew qualified as a teacher in 1995.* ♦ *After qualifying in medicine, he worked for a time at City Hospital.* ♦ **be qualified to do sth** *At the end of the course, you will be qualified to practise law.*
2 [I/T] to have the right qualities to be or to do something: *Twenty percent of Americans qualify as rich.* ♦ *To* **qualify for** *Olympic status, a sport must be played in 50 countries and on three continents.* ♦ **be qualified to do sth** *Only people over the age of 18 are qualified to vote.* ♦ **qualify sb to do sth** *The fact that his grandparents were Irish qualified him to play in the Irish national team.*
3 [I] to reach a particular stage of a competition by competing successfully in an earlier stage: *It would be incredible if Brazil failed to qualify.* ♦ *What are your team's chances of qualifying for the finals?*

> **Word family: qualify**
>
> *Words in the same family as* **qualify**
> - **qualification** *n*
> - **qualified** *adj*
> - **disqualified** *adj*
> - **qualifier** *n*
> - **unqualified** *adj*
> - **disqualify** *v*

quality¹ /ˈkwɒləti/ noun ★★★
1 [C/U] the quality of something is how good or how bad it is: *poor-quality workmanship* ♦ *This cut in funding will affect* **the quality** *of education in our schools.* ♦ *The food is* **of the highest quality**.
2 [U] a high standard: *a company with a reputation for quality and reliability*
3 [C] a positive feature of a person's character: *What is the quality you most admire in others?* ♦ *Do you possess the right* **personal qualities** *to be a teacher?* ♦ *a woman with strong* **leadership qualities** (=the ability to be a good leader)
4 [C] a feature of something: *the addictive qualities of tobacco*

quality² /ˈkwɒləti/ adj of a high standard

ˈquality ˌtime noun [U] time that you spend with someone, usually your child, doing enjoyable things together so that your relationship remains strong

qualms /kwɑːmz/ noun [plural] thoughts that what you are doing might be bad or wrong

quandary /ˈkwɒndəri/ noun **be in a quandary** to not be certain what decision to take about something

quantifier /ˈkwɒntɪˌfaɪə/ noun [C] *linguistics* a word or phrase such as 'much' or 'a few' that is used with another word in order to show quantity

quantify /ˈkwɒntɪˌfaɪ/ verb [T] *formal* to measure or describe something as a quantity —**quantifiable** /ˈkwɒntɪˌfaɪəb(ə)l/ adj, **quantification** /ˌkwɒntɪfɪˈkeɪʃ(ə)n/ noun [U]

quantity /ˈkwɒntəti/ noun **1** [U] the amount of something: *They check both the quantity and quality of materials used.* **2** [C/U] a particular amount of something: *a small quantity of drugs* ♦ *large quantities of water*

quantum leap /ˌkwɒntəm ˈliːp/ noun [C] a very big change or improvement

quarantine /ˈkwɒrənˌtiːn/ noun [U] a situation in which a person or animal that might have a disease is kept separate from other people or animals —**quarantine** verb [T]

quarrel¹ /ˈkwɒrəl/ noun [C] an argument
   PHRASE **have no quarrel with** to have no reason for being unfriendly or for disagreeing with a person, idea, plan, or decision

quarrel² /ˈkwɒrəl/ (present participle **quarrelling**; past tense and past participle **quarrelled**) verb [I] to have an argument

quarrelsome /ˈkwɒrəls(ə)m/ adj tending to argue with people

quarry¹ /ˈkwɒri/ noun **1** [C] a place where stone is dug up out of the ground **2** [singular] *formal* a person or animal that someone is trying to catch

quarry² /ˈkwɒri/ verb [T] to dig stone out of the ground

quart /kwɔːt/ noun [C] a unit for measuring an amount of liquid, containing two PINTS

quarter /ˈkwɔːtə/ noun [C] ★★★

1 one of four equal parts	**5** person/group
2 period of 15 minutes	**6** coin worth 25 cents
3 period of 3 months	**+ PHRASES**
4 part of town	

1 one of four equal parts of something: *Over* **a quarter** *of our income goes on food.*
2 one of four periods of 15 minutes that an hour is divided into when you are telling the time
3 one of four periods of three months that the year is divided into, especially when you are talking about financial accounts: *The company's profits fell in the third quarter.*
4 a part of a town where you find particular buildings, activities, or people: *the Chinese quarter of the city*
5 *formal* a particular person or group of people: *I knew there would be a lot of trouble* **from that quarter**. ♦ *Concern has been expressed* **in some quarters** (=among some people or groups) *about this policy.* ♦ *He has won support* **from all quarters** (=from all people or groups).
6 a coin that is worth one quarter of an

American or Canadian dollar, or 25 CENTS

PHRASES **quarter past five/six etc** 15 minutes past five o'clock/six o'clock etc

quarter to five/six etc 15 minutes before five o'clock/six o'clock etc

→ QUARTERS

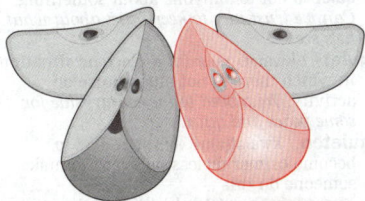

quarter

quarter-'final noun [C] one of the four games that are played between the eight players or teams that are still left in a competition

quarterly /'kwɔːtəli/ adj, adv done or produced four times a year

quarters /'kwɔːtəz/ noun [plural] *formal* rooms or buildings for people to live in

quartet /kwɔːˈtet/ noun [C] a group of four musicians or singers, or a piece of music for a quartet to perform

quartz /kwɔːts/ noun [U] a hard shiny stone that is often used inside electronic equipment and watches

quash /kwɒʃ/ verb [T] *formal* **1** to stop something from continuing **2** to say officially that a decision taken by another court was wrong and has no legal force

quaver /'kweɪvə/ verb [I] if your voice quavers, it is not steady because you are feeling nervous or afraid

quay /kiː/ noun [C] a hard surface next to the sea or a river, where boats can stop

queasy /'kwiːzi/ adj feeling that you are going to VOMIT (=get rid of food from your stomach through your mouth)

queen /kwiːn/ noun [C] ★★★

1 woman who rules	4 in cards
2 king's wife	5 in chess
3 female insect	

1 a woman who belongs to a royal family and who rules a country: *Queen Elizabeth* ♦ *She was crowned queen in 1953.*

2 a woman who is married to a king

3 a large female insect that can lay eggs: *a queen bee*

4 in a game of CARDS, a card with a picture of a queen on it —*picture* → C16

5 a piece that can move in any direction in a game of CHESS —*picture* → C16

queer¹ /kwɪə/ adj **1** *old-fashioned* strange **2** *offensive* an offensive word used for describing gay people

queer² /kwɪə/ noun [C] *offensive* an offensive word for someone who is gay

quell /kwel/ verb [T] *formal* **1** to get rid of unpleasant thoughts or feelings **2** to cause a violent situation to end

quench /kwentʃ/ verb **quench your thirst** to

drink something so that you no longer feel THIRSTY

query¹ /'kwɪəri/ noun [C] a question

query² /'kwɪəri/ verb [T] to ask a question

quest /kwest/ noun [C] *literary* a long difficult search

question¹ /'kwestʃ(ə)n/ noun ★★★

1 [C] something that someone asks you when they want information: *Why won't you answer my question?* ♦ *I wish I hadn't asked that question.* ♦ *Does anyone have any questions about the trip?*

2 [C] something that you are asked in a test or competition: *Only one person answered all three questions correctly.*

3 [C] an issue that needs to be discussed and dealt with: *Recent incidents are bound to raise questions about the level of violence in football.* ♦ *His report did not address the question of air warfare.*

4 [C/U] a feeling of doubt about something: *This information began to raise questions in her mind about Jack's innocence.* ♦ *New evidence has called into question* (=made people have doubts about) *the testimony of this witness.* ♦ *There had been some question about whether to interview the boy.*

PHRASES **be out of the question** used for saying that something is definitely not a possibility: *Taking a holiday then is out of the question.*

be a/the question of used for saying what the most important issue is in a situation: *There would definitely be some job losses; it was just a question of how many.* ♦ *We all want to go ahead with the project, but there's the question of finance.*

in question the person, thing, time etc in question is the one that you are talking about: *The photograph in question was taken long before I met you.*

(that's a) good question *spoken* used as a way of saying that you do not know something

there is no question of sth if there is no question of something, it definitely will not happen

without question 1 used for saying that something is definitely true: *He is without question the best player in our team.* **2** if someone does something without question, they do it without asking any questions: *He expected the children to obey without question.*

question² /'kwestʃ(ə)n/ verb [T] ★★

1 to ask someone questions: *A man is being questioned by detectives in connection with a murder.* ♦ *A hundred employers were questioned in the survey.* ♦ **question sb about sth** *Curious friends questioned me about the case.*

2 to have or express doubts about something: *I have never questioned her honesty.*

questionable /'kwestʃ(ə)nəb(ə)l/ adj **1** possibly not true, accurate, or complete: *The results of the test seem highly questionable.* **2** probably not good, honest, or worth admiring: *questionable behaviour/ conduct/practices* —**questionably** adv

questioning /ˈkwestʃ(ə)nɪŋ/ noun [U] a situation in which people ask someone questions

ˈ**question ˌmark** noun [C] the symbol ? that is used at the end of a sentence in order to show that it represents a question

questionnaire /ˌkwestʃəˈneə/ noun [C] a set of questions that a lot of people are asked as a way of getting information about what people generally think or do

ˈ**question ˌtag** noun [C] *linguistics* a word or phrase such as 'isn't it?' or 'haven't you?' that you can add to a sentence in order to make a question

queue¹ /kjuː/ noun [C] *British* ★ a line of people that are waiting for something: *There was a long queue for tickets.* ♦ *We stood in a queue for over an hour.* ♦ **a queue to do sth** *a queue to get into the museum*

queue² /kjuː/ (present participle **queuing** or **queueing**) or ˌ**queue ˈup** verb [I] *British* to wait for something in a queue

quibble /ˈkwɪb(ə)l/ verb [I] to argue or complain about things that are not important —**quibble** noun [C]

quiche /kiːʃ/ noun [C/U] a food with a PASTRY base that is filled with a mixture of eggs and milk and other foods such as cheese and vegetables or meat

quick¹ /kwɪk/ adj ★★★
1 able to move fast or to do something fast: *He's surprisingly quick for such a big man.* ♦ *a quick worker*
2 done or happening in a short time: *He took a quick glance over his shoulder.* ♦ *a quick decision*
3 able to understand things very easily: *a quick learner*
| **PHRASES** **be quick** to hurry
be quick to do sth to do something very quickly: *Townsend was quick to point out that it has been a team effort.*

quick² /kwɪk/ adv *spoken* quickly

quicken /ˈkwɪkən/ verb [I/T] *formal* if something quickens, or if you quicken it, it happens or moves more quickly

quickie /ˈkwɪki/ noun [C] *informal* something that you do quickly —**quickie** adj

quickly /ˈkwɪkli/ adv ★★★
1 at a fast speed: *We have to work quickly.* ♦ *She walked quickly out of the room.*
2 after only a short time, or lasting only a short time: *Something has to be done about this quickly.* ♦ *Let me explain very quickly what I mean.*

quicksand /ˈkwɪkˌsænd/ noun [U] soft wet sand that is dangerous to walk on because it pulls your body down into it

quid /kwɪd/ (plural **quid**) noun [C] *British informal* a pound in money

quiet¹ /ˈkwaɪət/ adj ★★★
1 making very little or no noise: *some quiet soothing music* ♦ *Be quiet, please. I'm trying to read.*

2 not talking, or not usually talking: *He's a quiet sensitive boy.*
3 not very busy, or with not much activity: *a quiet little seaside town* ♦ *a quiet and relaxing holiday*
| **PHRASE** **keep quiet about sth** or **keep sth quiet** to not tell anyone about something: *Can we trust him to keep quiet about what he's seen?*

quiet² /ˈkwaɪət/ noun [U] a place or situation in which there is not much noise or activity: *We moved to the countryside for some peace and quiet.*

quieten /ˈkwaɪət(ə)n/ verb [I/T] *British* to become calmer or less noisy, or to make someone do this
| **PHRASAL VERB** ˌ**quieten (sb/sth) ˈdown** same as **quieten**

quietly /ˈkwaɪətli/ adv ★★★
1 in a way that does not make much noise: *He closed the door quietly behind him.*
2 in a quiet voice: *'Listen,' she said quietly, 'I want to tell you something.'*
3 in a way that is not obvious to other people: *Sandra stood by, quietly amused.*

quilt /kwɪlt/ noun [C] a thick cover for a bed

quintessential /ˌkwɪntɪˈsenʃ(ə)l/ adj *formal* perfect as an example of a type of person or thing —**quintessentially** adv

quintet /kwɪnˈtet/ noun [C] a group of five musicians or singers, or a piece of music for a quintet to perform

quip /kwɪp/ verb [T] to say something that is funny or clever —**quip** noun [C]

quirk /kwɜːk/ noun [C] **1** a strange or annoying habit **2** something strange that happens

quirky /ˈkwɜːki/ adj slightly strange

quit /kwɪt/ (past tense and past participle **quit**) verb ★
1 [T] *informal* to stop doing something
2 [I/T] *informal* to leave a job or school permanently
3 [T] *formal* to leave a place

quite /kwaɪt/ grammar word ★★★

> **Quite** can be:
> ■ an **adverb**: *I was quite angry with her.*
> ■ a **determiner**: *I was taking quite a risk when I decided to talk to him.*

1 fairly but not very: *I was feeling quite tired after our walk.* ♦ *They said the dog was quite badly injured.* ♦ *He was **quite a good** musician.* ♦ *I **quite like** his films.*
2 completely, or very: *The food was quite disgusting.* ♦ *We haven't quite finished.* ♦ *Are you **quite sure** you know what to do?* ♦ *'Are you ready?' 'Not quite.'*
3 *British spoken* used for showing that you agree with what someone has said: *'Some laws are meant to be broken.' '**Quite right**.'*
| **PHRASES** **quite a lot/a bit/a few** a large number or amount: *My family have moved around quite a bit since then.* ♦ *Quite a few people asked questions.*
quite a or **quite some** used before a noun for emphasizing that something is unusual or interesting: *The news came as quite a*

surprise. ♦ *He's been renting the house for quite some time.*

that's quite all right *spoken* used when you reply to someone who has said that they are sorry, in order to show them that you do not mind

quiver /ˈkwɪvə/ verb [I] to shake with short quick movements —**quiver** noun [C]

quiz¹ /kwɪz/ noun [C] a test or competition in which you answer questions

quiz² /kwɪz/ verb [T] to ask someone a lot of questions

quizzical /ˈkwɪzɪk(ə)l/ adj showing that you are confused or surprised by something that is rather strange — **quizzically** /ˈkwɪzɪkli/ adv

quorum /ˈkwɔːrəm/ noun [singular] *technical* the smallest number of people who must be present at a meeting in order to allow official decisions to be made

quota /ˈkwəʊtə/ noun [C] an amount of something that someone is allowed or should do

quotation /kwəʊˈteɪʃ(ə)n/ noun [C] **1** words from a book, play, film etc that are used by someone else **2** the price that someone says that they will charge you for doing a job

quotation marks noun [plural] the symbols ' and ' that are used in writing before and after a quotation or the words that someone speaks=INVERTED COMMAS

quote¹ /kwəʊt/ verb ★
1 [I/T] to say or write words that someone else has said or written: *He was quoted as saying that he was shocked by the judge's decision.* ♦ *Robert quoted from one of Churchill's speeches.*
2 [T] to give something as an example to support what you are saying: *He quoted the example of a 40-year-old man who has been waiting nearly two years for an operation.*
3 [T] to tell someone what price you would charge them to do a particular piece of work: **quote sb sth** *They quoted us £500 to replace the whole window.*

quote² /kwəʊt/ noun [C] *informal* a QUOTATION

Rr

r or **R** /ɑː/ noun [C/U] the 18th letter of the English alphabet

R abbrev are: used in emails and TEXT MESSAGES

R & B /ˌɑːr ən ˈbiː/ noun [U] rhythm and blues: a type of music that combines BLUES and SOUL styles with modern beats

rabbi /ˈræbaɪ/ noun [C] a Jewish religious leader

rabbit /ˈræbɪt/ noun [C] a small animal with long ears, soft fur, and a short tail —*picture* → C13

rabble /ˈræb(ə)l/ noun [singular] a noisy or violent crowd of people

rabid /ˈræbɪd/ adj a rabid animal has rabies

rabies /ˈreɪbiːz/ noun [U] a very serious disease that humans can get if they are bitten by an animal with the disease

race¹ /reɪs/ noun ★★★
1 [C] a competition that decides who is the fastest at doing something: *He is training for a big race.* ♦ *Marlene needs to win the race to keep her title.*
2 [C] a competition in which a person, organization, business, or country tries to win something or to be the first to do something: *There are three candidates in the race for the presidency.* ♦ **a race to do sth** *We are losing the race to find a cure for AIDS.*
3 [C/U] a group of people who are similar because they have the same skin colour or other physical features, or because they speak the same language or have the same history or customs: *We do not discriminate on the basis of race or gender.* ♦ *a disaster that could mark the end of the human race* (=all of the people of the world, considered as a single group)
4 **the races** [plural] a series of horse races: *a day at the races*
PHRASE **a race against time** a situation in which someone must do or finish something very quickly because they only have a limited amount of time to do it

race² /reɪs/ verb ★★
1 [I/T] to compete in a race: *The gun sounded and they started to race.* ♦ *I raced my brother down the street.*
2 [I] to move very quickly: *He raced to the bathroom when he heard Cheryl scream.* ♦ *Thoughts were racing through her mind.*
3 [T] to take someone somewhere quickly: *We raced the children to hospital.*
4 [I] to work or move at a faster speed than usual: *Her heart began to race madly.*

racecourse /ˈreɪsˌkɔːs/ noun [C] a track that is used for horse races

racehorse /ˈreɪsˌhɔːs/ noun [C] a horse that is trained to run in races

race relations noun [plural] the relationships between people of different races who live in the same community

racetrack /ˈreɪsˌtræk/ noun [C] **1** a track that is used for racing cars **2** a RACECOURSE

racial /ˈreɪʃ(ə)l/ adj **1** happening between people of different races **2** relating to someone's race —**racially** adv

racing /ˈreɪsɪŋ/ noun [U] a sport in which cars, boats, or horses or other animals race against each other —**racing** adj

racism /ˈreɪˌsɪz(ə)m/ noun [U] a way of behaving or thinking that treats people belonging to some races unfairly

racist /ˈreɪsɪst/ noun [C] someone who thinks that their race is better than others —**racist** adj

R

rack¹ /ræk/ noun [C] an object with shelves, spaces, or hooks, used for storing things

rack² /ræk/ verb [T] if you are racked by pain or unpleasant feelings, you suffer because of them

PHRASE **rack your brains** to try hard to think of something

racket /'rækɪt/ noun **1** [singular] *informal* a loud annoying noise **2** [C] an object used for hitting the ball in games such as tennis **3** [C] *informal* an illegal activity that makes money

racy /'reɪsi/ adj a racy story, film, or play is slightly shocking in the way that it describes or shows sex

radar /'reɪdɑː/ noun [C/U] a system that uses radio signals in order to find the position of something such as an aircraft or ship

radiance /'reɪdiəns/ noun [singular/U]
1 happiness that you can see in someone's appearance or smile **2** light that shines from something

radiant /'reɪdiənt/ adj **1** someone who is radiant looks extremely happy **2** very bright —**radiantly** adv

radiate /'reɪdieɪt/ verb **1** [I/T] to show a particular feeling or attitude: *John radiated charm.* **2** [I/T] to produce heat, light, or energy **3** [I] if lines, paths, or roads radiate from a central point, they spread out from it

radiation /ˌreɪdi'eɪʃ(ə)n/ noun [U] **1** a form of energy that is produced during a nuclear reaction, used for making electrical power **2** heat or light that is sent out but that you cannot see → RADIOACTIVE

radiator /'reɪdieɪtə/ noun [C] **1** a large metal object on a wall, used for heating a room **2** the part of an engine that keeps it from getting too hot

radical¹ /'rædɪk(ə)l/ adj **1** a radical change or way of doing something is new and very different from the usual way: *a radical solution to the problem of juvenile crime* ♦ *a programme of radical reforms in schools* **2** believing that important political and social changes are necessary: *a radical left-wing group* ♦ *He surprised us all with his radical views.*

radical² /'rædɪk(ə)l/ noun [C] someone who believes that important political and social changes are necessary

radically /'rædɪkli/ adv if something changes radically, it changes completely or in a way that is very noticeable

radio¹ /'reɪdiəʊ/ noun ★★★

1 broadcasting system	4 message system
2 broadcast equipment	5 message equipment
3 programmes	

1 [U] a system of broadcasting information and programmes that people can listen to: *an independent radio station* ♦ *Radio and television have had an enormous effect on people's lives.* ♦ *She began her career in local radio.*

2 [C] a piece of equipment that you use for listening to radio programmes: *a car radio* ♦ *Let's turn on the radio.*

3 the radio [singular] programmes that are broadcast for people to listen to: *Joe's listening to the radio.* ♦ *What's on the radio?*

4 [U] a system of sending and receiving spoken messages by using electronic signals: *We remained in constant radio contact.*

5 [C] the piece of equipment that is used for sending or receiving spoken messages using electronic signals: *a two-way radio*

radio² /'reɪdiəʊ/ verb [I/T] to communicate with someone using a radio

radioactive /ˌreɪdiəʊ'æktɪv/ adj containing RADIATION (=energy that is produced during nuclear reactions)

radioactivity /ˌreɪdiəʊæk'tɪvəti/ noun [U] the ability that some substances have to produce energy in the form of RADIATION

radiography /ˌreɪdi'ɒgrəfi/ noun [U] the process of taking X-RAY photographs of someone's body as part of a medical treatment —**radiographer** noun [C]

radish /'rædɪʃ/ noun [C] a small white or red vegetable that is eaten raw in salads —*picture* → C11

radius /'reɪdiəs/ (plural **radii** /'reɪdiaɪ/ or **radiuses**) noun [C] **1** the distance from the centre of a circle to its edge, or a straight line from the centre to the edge —*picture* → C8 **2** a particular distance in all directions from a central point: *Delivery is free within a five mile radius of the city centre.*

raffle /'ræf(ə)l/ noun [C] a competition in which you win a prize if the number on your ticket is the same as the number on the prize

raft /rɑːft/ noun [C] **1** a simple flat boat made by tying long pieces of wood together **2** a small light boat made of rubber or plastic

PHRASE **a raft of** *informal* a very large number of things or people

rafter /'rɑːftə/ noun [C] a large piece of wood that supports a sloping roof

rafting /'rɑːftɪŋ/ noun [U] the activity of travelling on a river in a small boat

rag /ræg/ noun **1** [C] a piece of old cloth that is used for cleaning or wiping something **2** **rags** [plural] clothes that are old, torn, and dirty: *The little girl was dressed in rags.*

rage¹ /reɪdʒ/ noun **1** [C/U] a very strong feeling of anger: *Her eyes filled with tears of rage and frustration.* **2** [U] angry violent behaviour in a public situation

PHRASE **(all) the rage** *informal* very popular

rage² /reɪdʒ/ verb [I] **1** to continue with a lot of force, violence, or angry arguments: *Fierce fighting raged for several days.* **2** to shout angrily at someone

ragged /'rægɪd/ adj **1** torn and dirty: *a pair of ragged shorts* **2** wearing old dirty clothes: *ragged children playing in the street* **3** not smooth or regular: *a ragged edge*

raging /'reɪdʒɪŋ/ adj **1** happening with a lot of force or violence: *a raging battle* **2** very serious, painful, or strong: *a raging fever/headache/thirst*

rags-to-riches adj used for describing the life of someone who was born into a poor family but later became very rich and successful

raid¹ /reɪd/ noun [C] **1** a sudden short military attack: *Soldiers carried out raids on enemy targets.* **2** an action by police officers in which they suddenly enter a place in order to arrest people or search for something **3** a crime in which someone suddenly enters a place and uses force or threats to steal something

raid² /reɪd/ verb [T] **1** to use force to enter a place in order to search for something **2** to suddenly attack a place and cause a lot of damage **3** *informal* to take or steal things from a place: *hungry teenagers raiding the fridge*

raider /ˈreɪdə/ noun [C] someone who attacks a place using force

rail /reɪl/ noun ★★
1 [C] a metal bar that is used for hanging clothes and other things on: *a clothes/towel rail*
2 [C] a metal or wooden bar that you can hold onto to stop yourself from falling: *a safety rail*
3 [U] the system of travelling by train: *We ought to transport more heavy goods by rail.* ♦ *an increase in rail fares*
4 [C] one of the pair of metal bars that a train travels on

railing /ˈreɪlɪŋ/ noun [C] a fence made of narrow posts supporting an upper bar

railroad /ˈreɪlˌrəʊd/ noun [C] American a RAILWAY

railway /ˈreɪlweɪ/ noun [C] British ★★★
1 the system of travelling by train, and all the people and things that are connected with it: *a railway station/carriage* ♦ *She's worked on the railways all her life.*
2 railway or **railway line** the metal track that trains travel on: *The path continues along a disused railway.*

rain¹ /reɪn/ noun ★★★
1 [U] water that falls in drops from clouds in the sky: *Visibility was good, with only occasional light rain.* ♦ *People were standing in the rain.*
2 the rains [plural] the large amounts of rain that fall in tropical regions during a particular season

rain² /reɪn/ verb [I] ★
1 if it rains, water falls from clouds in the sky: *Just as we were leaving home it started to rain.* ♦ *It had been raining heavily all day.*
2 to fall from the air in large amounts
PHRASE **rained off** if a sports game or other outside event is rained off, it does not happen because of rain
PHRASAL VERB **rain down** *same as* **rain²** 2: *Sparks from the fire rained down on the frightened spectators.*

rainbow /ˈreɪnˌbəʊ/ noun [C] a curved line of colours that appears in the sky when the sun shines while it is raining

raincoat /ˈreɪnˌkəʊt/ noun [C] a long coat made of light material that you wear when it is raining —*picture* → C4

raindrop /ˈreɪnˌdrɒp/ noun [C] a drop of rain

rainfall /ˈreɪnˌfɔːl/ noun [C/U] the amount of rain that falls in a particular area during a particular period of time

rainforest /ˈreɪnˌfɒrɪst/ noun [C/U] a forest in a tropical region of the world where it rains a lot

rainstorm /ˈreɪnˌstɔːm/ noun [C] a storm with a lot of rain

rainwater /ˈreɪnˌwɔːtə/ noun [U] water that falls to the ground in the form of rain

rainy /ˈreɪni/ adj a rainy day is one on which it rains a lot
PHRASE **the rainy season** the part of the year in tropical regions when large amounts of rain fall

raise¹ /reɪz/ verb [T] ★★★

1 lift to higher position	6 cause feelings
2 lift yourself	7 take care of children
3 increase	8 of animals/crops
4 collect money	✦ PHRASE
5 mention sth	

1 to lift something to a higher place or position: *A number of children raised their hands.* ♦ *He slowly raised the cup to his lips.*
2 to lift yourself from a sitting or lying position: *She could barely raise herself out of the chair.*
3 to increase a number, amount, or level: *They had raised their prices to unreasonable levels.*
4 to collect money for a particular purpose: *We need your help to raise money for medical research.*
5 to mention something so that it can be discussed: *Are there any other questions you would like to raise at the meeting?* ♦ **raise sth with sb** *We will raise the issue of working hours with the manager.*
6 to make someone have a particular feeling or reaction: *Doubts have been raised about the company's right to use this land.*
7 to take care of children while they are growing up: *For most parents, raising a family is a positive challenge.* ♦ *This seems strange to someone born and raised in the city.*
8 to keep a particular type of animal, or to grow a particular crop: *She's been raising sheep for over 40 years.*
PHRASE **raise your voice** to speak in a loud angry way
→ ALARM¹, EYEBROW

raise² /reɪz/ noun [C] American a RISE in the amount that you are paid for work

raisin /ˈreɪz(ə)n/ noun [C] a dried GRAPE

rake¹ /reɪk/ verb **1** [I/T] to use a rake in order to make an area of soil level or to remove leaves from the ground **2** [T] to pull your fingers through or along something
PHRASE **be raking it in** to be earning a lot of money

rake² /reɪk/ noun [C] a tool for making soil level and for removing leaves from the ground. It has a long handle with a row of sharp points on one end.

rally¹ /ˈræli/ noun **1** [C] a public meeting that a lot of people go to in order to support something or protest against something **2** [C] a car race **3** [singular] an increase or improvement in something

rally² /ˈræli/ verb **1** [I/T] to join other people in order to support someone or something **2** [I] to increase or improve after being low, weak, or ill

ram¹ /ræm/ verb **1** [I/T] if a vehicle or boat rams something, it hits it very hard **2** [T] to push something into a place with great force: *He rammed his fist through a window.*

ram² /ræm/ noun [C] a male sheep

RAM /ræm/ noun [U] *computing* random access memory: the part of a computer that programs are loaded into while you are using them

Ramadan /ˈræməˌdɑːn/ the ninth month of the Muslim year, when Muslims do not eat or drink anything during the day

ramble¹ /ˈræmb(ə)l/ verb [I] **1** to talk for a long time in a confused way **2** to go for a long walk —**rambling** adj: *a rambling speech*

ramble² /ˈræmb(ə)l/ noun [C] a long walk

ramifications /ˌræməfɪˈkeɪʃ(ə)nz/ noun [plural] *formal* the complicated or unexpected effects of something

ramp /ræmp/ noun [C] a slope connecting two levels of a building or road

rampage¹ /ˈræmpeɪdʒ/ verb [I] to behave in an uncontrolled way, damaging property over a wide area

rampage² /ˈræmpeɪdʒ/ noun [C] uncontrolled behaviour involving damage to property

rampant /ˈræmpənt/ adj existing or spreading in an uncontrolled way: *Official corruption here is rampant.*

ramparts /ˈræmpɑːts/ noun [plural] high hills or walls built around a building or town in the past in order to protect it

ramshackle /ˈræmˌʃæk(ə)l/ adj in bad condition and likely to fall down

ran the past tense of **run¹**

ranch /rɑːntʃ/ noun [C] a very large farm where cows, horses, or sheep are kept

rancour /ˈræŋkə/ noun [U] *formal* a feeling of hate or anger that lasts a long time

random /ˈrændəm/ adj chosen or happening without any particular method or pattern: *a random sample of voters* ♦ *Winning tickets will be chosen at random.* —**randomly** adv

randomize /ˈrændəˌmaɪz/ verb [T] *technical* to choose people or things for a test or experiment in a RANDOM way

rang the past tense of **ring¹**

range¹ /reɪndʒ/ noun ★★★

1 things of same type	4 distance for sth
2 numbers, ages etc	5 group of mountains
3 of responsibility etc	

1 [C] a number of different things that are of the same general type: *We discussed a range of issues affecting professional women.* ♦ *We stock a wide range of office furniture.*

2 [C] all the numbers, ages, measurements etc that are included within particular fixed limits: *books for children in the 11-to-14 age range* ♦ *Temperatures are expected to be in the range of 75 to 85 degrees.*

3 [singular] the limits within which a person or organization is able to deal with something=SCOPE: *Such a decision is not within the range of my responsibility.*

4 [singular/U] the distance within which you can see, hear, or reach something: *The children turned their cameras on anyone in range.* ♦ *It's best to stay out of range of recording equipment.*

5 [C] a number of mountains considered as a group

range² /reɪndʒ/ verb **1** [I] to be included in a group of numbers, ages, measurements etc with particular fixed limits: *Costs range from 50 to several hundred pounds.* ♦ *The team contained ten players whose ages ranged between 10 and 16.* **2** [I] to include a variety of things: *products ranging from televisions to computer software* **3** [I/T] to move with complete freedom around a large area: *There were buffalo ranging the plains of North America.*

rank¹ /ræŋk/ noun ★★

1 [C/U] someone's position in an organization or in society: *Her rank when she retired was captain.* ♦ *She had reached the rank of junior minister by the time she was 30.*

2 ranks [plural] all the people within a group or organization: *a dispute within the party ranks* ♦ *Another Republican senator joined the ranks of the presidential candidates.*

PHRASES break ranks to stop belonging to or supporting a group

close ranks if members of a group close ranks, they support each other against people who are trying to defeat or criticize them

the rank and file all the members of a group or organization except the leaders or officers

rank² /ræŋk/ verb **1** [I] to have a particular quality compared with other similar things: *This must rank as one of the most violent films ever made.* **2** [T] to put someone or something into a position according to their success, importance, size etc: *The survey ranked schools according to their exam results.*

ranking /ˈræŋkɪŋ/ noun [C] a position on a list that shows how good someone or something is compared to others

rankle /ˈræŋk(ə)l/ verb [I/T] if an action rankles, or if it rankles you, it continues to annoy or upset you for a long time

ransack /ˈrænsæk/ verb [T] to go through a place stealing or damaging things

ransom /ˈræns(ə)m/ noun [C/U] an amount of money that someone asks for, in exchange for a person who they are keeping as a prisoner

rant /rænt/ verb [I] to complain or talk loudly and angrily for a long time: *He was ranting about taxes.*

rap¹ /ræp/ noun **1** [U] a type of music in which words are spoken over a strong beat **2** [C] a quick hard hit, or the sound of this

rap² /ræp/ verb **1** [I/T] to hit something hard and quickly **2** [I] to perform by speaking over a strong musical beat **3** [T] *mainly journalism* to criticize someone

rape /reɪp/ noun [C/U] the crime of forcing someone to have sex by using violence —**rape** verb [T]

rapid /'ræpɪd/ adj ★ happening, moving, or acting quickly: *We are seeing a rapid growth in the use of the Internet.* ♦ *the rapid movement of troops into the area* —**rapidity** /rə'pɪdəti/ noun [U], **rapidly** adv: *a rapidly expanding population*

> **Words often used with rapid**
>
> *Nouns often used with rapid*
> ■ RAPID + **change, decline, deterioration, expansion, growth, increase, progress, rise, succession**: used about things that happen quickly

rapids /'ræpɪdz/ noun [plural] a part of a river where the water moves extremely quickly over rocks

rapist /'reɪpɪst/ noun [C] someone who forces someone else to have sex with them

rapper /'ræpə/ noun [C] someone who performs RAP music

rapport /ræ'pɔː/ noun [singular/U] a relationship in which people like, understand, and respect each other

rapt /ræpt/ adj *literary* completely interested and involved in something

rapture /'ræptʃə/ noun [U] *literary* a feeling of great happiness or excitement

rare /reə/ adj ★★
1 not happening very often: *I am late only on rare occasions.* ♦ **it is rare (for sb) to do sth** *It's extremely rare for her to lose her temper.*
2 not often seen or found, and therefore valuable: *rare birds* ♦ *He has a rare talent for managing people.*
3 rare meat has been cooked for only a short time and is red inside
→ RARITY

rarely /'reəli/ adv ★★ not often ≠ FREQUENTLY: *My mother very rarely wears jewellery.*

rarity /'reərəti/ noun [C] something that is unusual or does not happen often

rash¹ /ræʃ/ noun [C] **1** an area of small red spots on your skin that is caused by an illness or a reaction to something **2** a lot of events of the same type taking place in a short period of time

rash² /ræʃ/ adj acting or done too quickly, without thinking —**rashly** adv

rasher /'ræʃə/ noun [C] a thin flat piece of BACON (=meat from a pig)

rasp /rɑːsp/ verb [I/T] to make an unpleasant sound as if two rough surfaces were rubbing together

raspberry /'rɑːzbəri/ noun [C] a small soft red fruit that grows on a bush —*picture* → C10

Rastafarian /ˌræstəˈfeəriən/ noun [C] a member of a religious group based in Jamaica whose main religious leader was Emperor Haile Selassie of Ethiopia

rat /ræt/ noun [C] an animal like a large mouse with a long tail —*picture* → C13

rate¹ /reɪt/ noun [C] ★★★
1 the number of times that something happens, or the number of examples of something within a particular period of time: *a rising birth rate* ♦ *areas where the rate of unemployment is high*
2 the speed at which something happens within a particular period of time: *The population was growing at an alarming rate.* ♦ *Doctors monitor the patient's heart rate.*
3 an amount of money that is paid or charged: *tax rates* ♦ *They increased the hourly rate of pay to £8.50.*

PHRASES **at any rate** *spoken* used for changing a statement, and telling someone that one part of what has been mentioned is true: *They agree with me – well, at any rate, Maggie does.*

at this rate *spoken* used for saying what will happen if the present situation continues: *At this rate the factory will be closed down by Christmas.*

the going rate the usual amount of money that people pay for something
→ FIRST-RATE, SECOND-RATE, THIRD-RATE

rate² /reɪt/ verb **1** [T] to consider that someone or something has a particular quality or has achieved a particular standard or level: *Many voters rate the environment as the number one issue.* ♦ *She is rated very highly by her colleagues* (=they approve of her). **2** [I] to have a particular quality compared with other similar things: *The exhibition rates as one of the most successful for this museum.* **3** [T] to deserve something: *That should rate a mention in the local newspaper!*

rather /'rɑːðə/ adv ★★★
1 to a fairly large degree=QUITE: *Matt left rather suddenly without any explanation.* ♦ *He was a rather handsome boy.* ♦ *I realize that I've been rather stupid and selfish.*
2 used for correcting or explaining what you have just said: *He couldn't help us, or rather he didn't want to.*

PHRASES **rather than** instead of: *Doug chose to quit rather than admit that he'd made a mistake.* ♦ *Rather than criticizing your husband, why not find out if there's something wrong?*

would rather used for saying what you would prefer: *He doesn't want to learn – he'd rather stay at home and play video games.* ♦ *They said they would rather die than abandon their homes.* ♦ *You don't need to come if you'd rather not.*

ratify /'rætɪfaɪ/ verb [T] to make an agreement official by signing it or formally approving

R

it —**ratification** /ˌrætɪfɪˈkeɪʃ(ə)n/ noun [U]

rating /ˈreɪtɪŋ/ noun **1** [C] a measurement of how good or popular someone or something is: *Labour's popularity rating fell for the first time.* **2** [C] a letter or number that shows how old someone needs to be before they are allowed to see a particular film **3 ratings** [plural] the number of people who watch or listen to a particular television or radio programme: *Her new series had high ratings right from the start.*

ratio /ˈreɪʃiəʊ/ noun [C] ★ a relationship between two things that is expressed as two numbers or amounts: *a teacher-student ratio of 1:20* (=1 teacher for every 20 students) ♦ *The ratio of men to women was 4:1.*

ration¹ /ˈræʃ(ə)n/ noun [C] a limited amount of something that you are allowed to have when there is not much available

ration² /ˈræʃ(ə)n/ verb [T] to control the supply of something so that people are allowed only a fixed amount —**rationing** noun [U]

rational /ˈræʃ(ə)nəl/ adj a rational person makes decisions based on sensible practical reasons, rather than emotions ≠ IRRATIONAL: *There was no rational explanation for his actions.* ♦ *She was perfectly calm and rational.* —**rationally** adv

rationale /ˌræʃəˈnɑːl/ noun [C] the set of reasons that a plan, decision, or belief is based on

rationalize /ˈræʃ(ə)nəlaɪz/ verb [I/T] **1** to try to find a reasonable explanation for your feelings or behaviour **2** to change the way a business is organized in order to make it more effective —**rationalization** /ˌræʃ(ə)nəlaɪˈzeɪʃ(ə)n/ noun [C/U]

rattle¹ /ˈræt(ə)l/ verb **1** [I/T] to make short sharp knocking sounds, or to move or shake things so that they make these sounds: *The house shook and the windows rattled.* ♦ *She rattled her keys impatiently.* **2** [T] *informal* to make someone feel nervous or angry

PHRASAL VERB ˌrattle sth ˈoff to say something quickly

rattle² /ˈræt(ə)l/ noun [C] **1** the sound that something makes when it rattles **2** a baby's toy that rattles when it is shaken

raucous /ˈrɔːkəs/ adj a raucous voice is loud and sounds rough —**raucously** adv

ravage /ˈrævɪdʒ/ verb [T] to destroy something, or to damage it very badly

ravages /ˈrævɪdʒɪz/ noun **the ravages of sth** the damage or destruction caused by something

rave¹ /reɪv/ verb [I] **1** to speak or write in a very enthusiastic way about something or someone: *The critics are raving about her performance.* **2** to talk in an angry and uncontrolled way

rave² /reɪv/ noun [C] a very large party where people dance to loud music

raven /ˈreɪv(ə)n/ noun [C] a large bird with shiny black feathers

ravenous /ˈræv(ə)nəs/ adj very hungry

ravine /rəˈviːn/ noun [C] a very deep narrow valley with steep sides

raving /ˈreɪvɪŋ/ adj *informal* behaving or talking in a crazy way: *a raving lunatic*

ravishing /ˈrævɪʃɪŋ/ adj *literary* very beautiful

raw /rɔː/ adj ★

1 not cooked	5 not examined
2 strong/natural	6 not trained
3 not processed	✦ PHRASE
4 sore	

1 raw food has not been cooked: *raw meat* ♦ *The chicken is still raw.*

2 a raw quality is strong and natural, without being controlled or made more pleasant: *Her performance was filled with raw emotion.*

3 raw substances have not been processed or treated in any way: *raw silk/cotton* ♦ *There was raw sewage on the beach.* → RAW MATERIALS

4 if your skin is raw, it is very sore: *I scrubbed my hands until they were raw.*

5 raw DATA consists of information that has not been examined or organized

6 not trained or experienced: *raw recruits*

PHRASE a raw deal unfair treatment

ˌraw maˈterials noun [plural] substances that are in their natural state before being processed or made into something

ray /reɪ/ noun [C] a line of light, heat, or energy

PHRASE a ray of hope something that makes you feel slightly more hopeful in a difficult situation

raze /reɪz/ verb [T] to completely destroy a building or town

razor /ˈreɪzə/ noun [C] a small tool or piece of electrical equipment that you use for SHAVING (=removing hair from your skin)

ˈrazor ˌblade noun [C] a thin flat blade with a very sharp edge that you put in a razor

Rd abbrev Road: used in addresses

re /riː/ preposition used in business letters for introducing the subject that you are going to write about

re- /riː/ prefix again: *the re-election of the Mayor* ♦ *reheated soup* ♦ *She reappeared a few minutes later.*

reach¹ /riːtʃ/ verb ★★★

1 arrive somewhere	6 achieve sth
2 get to point/stage	7 be seen/heard
3 get to level/amount	8 talk by phone
4 move hand towards	✦ PHRASAL VERBS
5 manage to touch sth	

1 [T] to arrive somewhere: *We hoped to reach the camp before dark.* ♦ *The money should reach your bank account within three days.* → ARRIVE

2 [T] to get to a particular point in time, or to a particular stage in a process: *You reach a point where medicine can't help.* ♦ *The children have reached the age when they want more privacy.*

3 [T] to get as high as a particular level or amount: *Temperatures here can reach 120 degrees Fahrenheit.*

R

4 [I] to move your hand towards something you are trying to touch or pick up: *He turned round and reached for the phone.* ♦ *Travis reached into his pocket to get his car keys.* ♦ *I reached across the table and took Alice's hand.*

5 [I/T] to manage to touch something or pick it up by stretching out your arm: *We keep the bottles up here so the children can't reach them.*

6 [T] to achieve something after discussing it or thinking about it for a long time: *Ministers must reach a decision before next month.*

7 [T] if something such as a programme or message reaches people, they see or hear it: *The advertisement reached an audience of over 19 million.*

8 [T] to succeed in talking to someone by phone: *I'll leave you a number where I can be reached in an emergency.*

PHRASAL VERBS ,reach (sth) ꞌout to stretch out your arm to try to touch or hold something: *She reached out to touch his face.* ,reach ꞌout to sb to show someone that you are sympathetic and want to communicate with them

reach

reach² /riːtʃ/ noun [U] **1** the distance within which you can touch something by stretching out your arm: *Put the books within reach of your desk.* ♦ *I kicked the knife out of reach.* **2** the distance that you travel to get somewhere: *The hotel is within easy reach of the town centre.*

PHRASE **within/beyond sb's reach** used for saying that someone can/cannot have or do something: *Achievements like these are beyond the reach of ordinary players.* ♦ *Reduced ticket prices put the best seats within everyone's reach.*

react /riꞋækt/ verb [I] ★

1 to behave in a particular way because of things that are happening around you or things that other people are doing to you: *I wasn't sure how you would react.* ♦ *Workers reacted angrily to the news of more job cuts.*

2 if a chemical substance reacts with another substance, it changes as they are mixed together: *Car emissions react with sunlight to form ozone.*

3 to become ill when you eat a particular food or medicine: *Some people react badly to nuts.*

reaction /riꞋækʃ(ə)n/ noun ★★★

1 how you react to sth	**4** chemical change
2 bad effect on body	**5** interest in change
3 ability to act quickly	

1 [C] the way that you feel or behave as a result of something that happens: *My mother's reaction was quite unexpected.* ♦ *Shock is a natural reaction to such bad news.* → KNEE-JERK

2 [C] a bad effect on your body caused by food, medicine, or another substance: *an allergic reaction to dust*

3 reactions [plural] your ability to think and act quickly in a difficult or dangerous situation: *A tragedy was prevented by the driver's quick reactions.*

4 [C] *science* a process in which a chemical change happens: *Temperature can affect the rate of a chemical reaction.* → CHAIN REACTION

5 [singular] an attitude of wanting to do things in a different way from the way that they were done in the past: *The reaction against traditional styles continued for another 50 years.*

Words often used with reaction

Verbs often used with reaction (sense 1, 2)
■ **cause, produce, provoke, trigger** + REACTION: make a reaction happen

reactionary /riꞋækʃ(ə)n(ə)ri/ adj strongly opposed to any political change or social progress —**reactionary** noun [C]

reactor /riꞋæktə/ noun [C] a NUCLEAR REACTOR

read¹ /riːd/ (past tense and past participle **read** /red/) verb ★★★

1 understand words	**7** know what sb thinks
2 speak written words	**8** contain words
3 get information	**9** show number etc
4 understand symbols	+ PHRASE
5 examine/copy data	+ PHRASAL VERBS
6 interpret meaning	

1 [I/T] to look at and understand words in a letter, book, newspaper etc: *I read a few chapters every night.* ♦ *He was sitting reading in the waiting room.* ♦ *By the age of five, he was able to read and write.*

2 [I/T] to speak the words that you are looking at: *I'm going to read this poem aloud.* ♦ **read (sth) to sb** *Reading to young children helps develop their language skills.* ♦ **read sb sth** *Read me that last sentence again.*

3 [I/T] to get information from books, newspapers etc: *He likes reading about wildlife.* ♦ **read sth in sth** *We read it in the local paper.*

4 [T] to look at and understand the information, symbols, or numbers on a map or a piece of measuring equipment: *Has the man been to read the gas meter?*

5 [T] if a computer or other piece of electronic equipment reads something, it examines the information on it or copies it to a particular place

6 [T] to understand something in a

R

particular way=INTERPRET: *They had read the situation accurately.* ♦ **read sth as sth** *We had read their decision as an admission of failure.*

7 [T] to be able to understand what someone is like or what they are thinking: *It was difficult to read his expression.* ♦ **read sb's mind** *Her next comment surprised me. It was as if she had read my mind.*

8 [T] if a short piece of writing reads something, it contains those particular words: *The label read, 'Suitable only for children over three'.*

9 [T] if a piece of measuring equipment reads something, it shows a particular number or amount: *The thermometer has been reading over 90 degrees all day.*

PHRASE **read between the lines** to guess something that is not expressed directly

PHRASAL VERBS **,read sth 'into sth** to find an extra meaning in someone's words or actions that is not obvious or does not exist: *I think you're reading too much into his remark.*

,read sth 'out to say the words that you are reading so that people can hear them: *He read the list of names out.*

,read sth 'through to read all of a piece of writing in order to check or correct it: *Read the contract through carefully before you sign.*

,read 'up on sth to get information on a particular subject by reading a lot about it: *I need to read up on my British history.*

read² /riːd/ noun [singular] an act of reading something, or a period of time spent reading something

readable /ˈriːdəb(ə)l/ adj **1** easy and pleasant to read **2** clear and able to be read

R **reader** /ˈriːdə/ noun [C] ★★★

1 someone who reads: *I am an avid reader of detective novels.*

2 someone who reads a particular newspaper, book, or magazine: *The books provide the reader with an introduction to natural history.* ♦ *Readers of our magazine will be familiar with her column.*

3 someone who reads in a particular way or with a particular level of skill: *a special programme for slow readers*

4 a book containing simple pieces of writing for people who are learning to read or who are learning a language

readership /ˈriːdəʃɪp/ noun [singular/U] the group or number of people who read a particular newspaper, book, or magazine

readily /ˈredɪli/ adv **1** easily: *The equipment was cheap and readily available.* **2** in a way that shows that you are willing: *She had readily agreed to the interview.*

readiness /ˈredinəs/ noun **1** [U] a state of being ready and able to deal with what might or will happen **2** [singular/U] the state of being willing to do something

reading /ˈriːdɪŋ/ noun ★★

1 [U] the process of recognizing written or printed words and understanding their

meaning: *My little boy is having difficulty with his reading.*

2 [singular/U] the act of reading or studying a book, newspaper, document etc: *I haven't done much reading lately.* ♦ *a list of suggestions for further reading*

3 [C] an event at which someone reads something to a group of people: *a poetry reading*

4 [C] a number or amount shown on a piece of measuring equipment: *compass readings*

readjust /ˌriːəˈdʒʌst/ verb **1** [I] to become capable of dealing with a new situation or feeling comfortable in it **2** [T] to make a slight change to something —**readjustment** noun [C/U]

read-out /ˈriːd ˌaʊt/ noun [C] a record of information that has been produced by a piece of electronic equipment

ready /ˈredi/ adj ★★★

1 prepared for what is going to happen: *We'll never be ready in time.* ♦ *She was ready for a new challenge.* ♦ **ready to do sth** *Are you ready to go yet?*

2 in a suitable condition for use: *Is dinner ready?* ♦ **get sth ready** *I'd just got tea ready when they called.* ♦ **have sth ready** *We can have your order ready by 5.00.*

3 willing or likely to do something: *You are too ready to find fault with other people.* ♦ **ready to do sth** *Jack was always ready to work extra hours if necessary.*

,ready-'made adj already made or prepared and ready to be used

real /rɪəl/ adj ★★★

1 in physical world	5 important/serious
2 not false/artificial	6 the most important
3 with true qualities	7 for emphasis
4 true, not just claimed	+ PHRASES

1 existing in the physical world, not just in someone's imagination or in stories: *Children believe that these characters are real.* ♦ *I had never met a real live pop star before.*

2 not false or artificial=GENUINE: *Is that a real diamond?* ♦ *You'd pay a lot more for the real thing.*

3 used for emphasizing that someone or something has the true qualities of a particular type of person or thing: *Few tourists see the real Spain.* ♦ *He had no real friends.*

4 true, and not just according to what someone claims: *We all know the minister's real reason for refusing to speak.*

5 important or serious enough to be worth thinking or worrying about: *The committee had little real power.* ♦ *The journey was difficult, but we were never in any real danger.*

6 most important: *Let's deal with the real issue.*

7 *informal* used for emphasizing that a description of someone or something is very accurate: *This walk is a real treat for anyone interested in birds.*

PHRASES **for real** *informal* if something is for

real, you are doing it seriously, not just practising or pretending

get real *spoken* used for telling someone to start thinking about something in a sensible way and stop being silly or unreasonable about it

'real es,tate noun [U] *American* land and the buildings on it

realism /'rɪəlɪz(ə)m/ noun [U] **1** the ability to accept events and situations as they really exist and to deal with them in a practical way **2** a style in art and literature that shows life as it really is

realist /'rɪəlɪst/ noun [C] **1** someone who accepts events and situations as they really are and deals with them in a practical way **2** an artist or writer whose work shows life as it really is

realistic /ˌrɪə'lɪstɪk/ adj **1** based on facts and situations as they really are ≠ UNREALISTIC: *Changing your job is the only realistic solution.* ♦ *He has a realistic chance of winning the election.* ♦ *I don't think it's very realistic to expect her to help us.* **2** able to understand and accept things as they really are: *He's never going to agree to that. Be realistic!* ♦ *The recession has made people more realistic about what they can afford to buy.* **3** made to seem natural or real ≠ UNREALISTIC: *The troops staged a realistic attack using blank ammunition.*
—**realistically** /ˌrɪə'lɪstɪkli/ adv

reality /ri'æləti/ noun ★★

1 [U] the real character or nature of things, not what you imagine or think is possible: *What she had to do, finally, was face reality.* ♦ *Her version of events bore no relation to reality.* ♦ *This is a man who has lost touch with reality.*

2 [C] a fact, event, or situation as it really exists: *After years of hard work, his dream has become a reality.* ♦ *the grim realities of war*

PHRASE **in reality** used for saying that the true situation is different from what has been said or thought: *Reports put the death toll at 50, when in reality it was closer to 200.*

realization /ˌrɪəlaɪ'zeɪʃ(ə)n/ noun [singular/U] **1** the process of understanding something, or the moment when this happens **2** the process of achieving something that you have planned or hoped for, or the moment when this happens

realize /'rɪəlaɪz/ verb ★★★

1 [I/T] to know and understand something: **+(that)** *We realize that this is upsetting for you, but it's for the best.* ♦ *It's important to realize that this situation is only temporary.* ♦ **+what/how etc** *At the time I never even realized how unhappy I was.*

2 [T] to gradually begin to understand something that you did not know or notice before: *I soon realized my mistake.* ♦ **+(that)** *It was some time before he realized he'd offended them.* ♦ **+why/how etc** *I've just realized how much I miss him.*

3 [T] *formal* to achieve something that you have planned or hoped for: *He finally realized his dream to become a dancer.*

really /'rɪəli/ adv ★★★

1 **very** *spoken* very, or very much: *I'm really hungry.* ♦ *She really enjoys working with young children.* ♦ *We've all been working really hard.*

2 **for emphasis** used for emphasizing what you are saying: *I really must see that film.* ♦ *There's really no need to worry.*

3 **completely** completely: *Rigby had never really recovered from his knee injury.* ♦ *Are you really sure that you want to marry this man?*

4 **for saying what is true** used for talking about what is in fact true, when something else seems to be true: *Hamlet isn't really mad – he's just pretending to be.* ♦ *We'll never know what really happened.*

5 **for showing surprise or interest** *spoken* used for showing that you are surprised by or interested in what someone has just told you: 'I've decided to move back to York.' 'Really? But why?'

PHRASE **not really** used for saying 'no' without being very definite: 'Was he sorry for what he'd done?' 'Not really.'

realm /relm/ noun [C] **1** *formal* a particular area of knowledge, experience, interest etc **2** *literary* a country ruled by a king or queen

'real ,time noun [U] if a computer deals with information in real time, it deals with it immediately —**'real-,time** adj

reap /riːp/ verb [T] **1** to get something as a result of something else that you do **2** to cut and gather a crop

reappear /ˌriːə'pɪə/ verb [I] to appear again —**reappearance** noun [C/U]

rear[1] /rɪə/ noun **1 the rear** [singular] the back part of a place or thing: *The main entrance is at the rear.* **2** [C] *informal* the part of your body that you sit on

PHRASE **bring up the rear** to be the last in a line or group

rear[2] /rɪə/ verb **1** [T] to look after a child or young animal until it is fully grown: *Most farmers in the area rear sheep.* **2** [I] if a horse rears, it lifts its front legs up into the air

PHRASAL VERB **'rear up** *same as* **rear**[2] 2

rear[3] /rɪə/ adj at the back of something

rearrange /ˌriːə'reɪndʒ/ verb [T] **1** to arrange people or things in a different way **2** to arrange for an event or meeting to take place at a different time

,rear-view 'mirror noun [C] a mirror fixed to the front window of a car that lets the driver see what is happening behind the car —*picture* → C6

reason[1] /'riːz(ə)n/ noun ★★★

1 [C] a fact, situation, or intention that explains why something happened, why someone did something, or why something is true: *The police asked her the reason for her visit.* ♦ *The council gave no reason for its decision.* ♦ **reason for doing sth** *Could you explain your reasons for choosing this*

R

particular course? ✦ **+why** *The reason why so many people caught the disease is still not clear.* ✦ **+(that)** *The reason these cars are so expensive is that they are largely built by hand.*

2 [U] a good or clear cause for doing something or thinking something: *Sometimes the dog would bark for no reason.* ✦ *With plenty of orders coming in, there is reason for optimism about the company's future.*

3 [U] a way of behaving that most people accept as sensible: *He finally saw reason and gave me the gun.* ✦ *Let your children have their freedom, within reason.*

4 [U] the human ability to think in an intelligent way, make sensible decisions, and form clear arguments: *His assessment of the situation is based on sheer emotion, not reason.*

PHRASES **all the more reason** used for emphasizing that what someone has said or done is another reason why they should do a particular thing
for some reason used for saying that you do not know why something happened: *For some reason, they wouldn't let me help them.*
→ STAND¹

Other words that mean **reason**

- **cause** the reason that something happens, or the reason that you feel a particular emotion
- **excuse** a reason that you give in order to explain why you did something bad
- **explanation** a set of facts that tell you why something happened
- **grounds** a good or fair reason for doing something. This word is used in official or legal situations
- **motivation** someone's personal reason for doing something
- **motive** someone's personal reason for doing something
- **pretext** a false reason that you give in order to hide your real reason for doing something
- **purpose** something that you want to achieve

reason² /ˈriːz(ə)n/ verb [T] *formal* to make a particular judgment after you have thought about the facts of a situation in an intelligent and sensible way

PHRASAL VERB ˈreason with sb to try to persuade someone to do something by explaining why you think it is sensible

reasonable /ˈriːz(ə)nəb(ə)l/ adj ★★
1 sensible and fair: *We have taken all reasonable precautions to avoid an accident.* ✦ *Come on, be reasonable – I didn't mean to do it!*
2 if something is reasonable, there are good reasons for thinking it is true or correct: *I'm sure there's a reasonable explanation for his absence.* ✦ **it is/seems reasonable to do sth** *It's reasonable to assume that these measures will prove successful.*
3 fairly good, although not extremely good =ACCEPTABLE: *a reasonable standard of accommodation*

4 not too high or great: *The hotel is situated within a reasonable distance of the beach.* ✦ *reasonable prices*

reasonably /ˈriːz(ə)nəbli/ adv **1** to a fairly high degree, level, or standard: *He did reasonably well in maths.* **2** in a sensible and fair way: *She behaved very reasonably.*

reasoned /ˈriːz(ə)nd/ adj thought about and expressed in an intelligent and sensible way

reasoning /ˈriːz(ə)nɪŋ/ noun [U] the process of thinking about something in an intelligent and sensible way

reassure /ˌriːəˈʃʊə/ verb [T] to make someone feel less worried about something —**reassurance** noun [C/U]

reassuring /ˌriːəˈʃʊərɪŋ/ adj making you feel less worried —**reassuringly** adv

rebate /ˈriːbeɪt/ noun [C] an amount of money that is officially given back to someone

rebel¹ /ˈreb(ə)l/ noun [C] **1** someone who tries to remove a government or leader by using force **2** someone who opposes people in authority or opposes accepted ways of doing things

rebel² /rɪˈbel/ verb [I] **1** to try to remove a government or leader by using organized force **2** to oppose someone in authority, or to oppose accepted ways of doing things

rebellion /rɪˈbeljən/ noun **1** [C/U] an attempt to remove a government or leader by force =REVOLT, UPRISING **2** [U] opposition to someone in authority or to accepted ways of doing things

rebellious /rɪˈbeljəs/ adj **1** fighting to remove a government or leader by force **2** opposing authority or the accepted rules of society

rebirth /riːˈbɜːθ/ noun [singular/U] a situation in which something becomes popular, important, or effective again

reboot /riːˈbuːt/ verb [I/T] if a computer or system reboots, or if someone reboots it, it starts again after it has been turned off

rebound¹ /rɪˈbaʊnd/ verb [I] **1** to hit a surface and then move quickly backwards again **2** if something bad that you try to do to someone rebounds on you, it harms you instead of them

rebound² /ˈriːbaʊnd/ noun **on the rebound** feeling sad because a romantic relationship has ended and impatient to start a new one

rebuff /rɪˈbʌf/ verb [T] *formal* to refuse to talk to someone or do what they suggest —**rebuff** noun [C]

rebuild /riːˈbɪld/ (past tense and past participle **rebuilt** /riːˈbɪlt/) verb [T] **1** to build something again after it has been damaged or destroyed **2** to improve a situation so that it is as good as it was in the past

rebuke /rɪˈbjuːk/ verb [T] *formal* to tell someone angrily that they have behaved badly —**rebuke** noun [C]

rebut /rɪˈbʌt/ verb [T] *formal* to show or say that something is not true =REFUTE

recalcitrant /rɪˈkælsɪtrənt/ adj *formal* refusing to obey orders —**recalcitrance** noun [U]

R

recall /rɪˈkɔːl/ verb ★
1 [I/T] to remember something: +who/where/
why etc *He couldn't recall what had
happened.* ♦ **recall doing sth** *I don't recall
seeing the document.*
2 [T] to order someone to return to their
country or the place where they work:
*Spain immediately recalled its ambassador
for consultations.*
3 [T] to ask for a product that people have
bought to be returned because there is
something wrong with it
—**recall** /rɪˈkɔːl, ˈriːkɔːl/ noun [singular/U]

recap /ˌriːˈkæp, ˈriːˌkæp/ verb [I/T] to describe
what has already been done or decided,
without repeating the details —**recap**
/ˈriːˌkæp/ noun [C]

recapture /riːˈkæptʃə/ verb [T] **1** to use force to
get an area into your control again **2** to
have a memory or feeling again **3** to catch
an animal or person that has escaped

recede /rɪˈsiːd/ verb [I] **1** to move further away
2 to become less strong or likely **3** if a man's
hair is receding, less and less of it is
growing at the front

receipt /rɪˈsiːt/ noun ★
1 [C] a document that you get from someone
showing that you have given them money
or goods: *Keep all your credit card receipts.*
♦ *Make sure you get **a receipt for** the taxi
fare.*
2 [U] *formal* the act of receiving something:
*Please acknowledge **receipt of** this letter.*
3 receipts [plural] *business* the total amount of
money that a business or organization
receives in a particular period of time

receive /rɪˈsiːv/ verb [T] ★★★
1 to get something that someone gives or
sends you: *We have not received your letter.*
♦ **receive sth from sb** *The head teacher has
received several calls from angry parents.*
2 to have a particular type of treatment or
experience: *Several of the victims are
receiving hospital **treatment**.*
3 to react to something in a particular way:
*Heather's proposals were received without
much enthusiasm.*
4 to formally welcome a visitor: *Her Royal
Highness was received by the Deputy Mayor.*
PHRASE **at/on the receiving end (of sth)**
affected by something unpleasant

> **Word family: receive**
>
> *Words in the same family as **receive***
> ■ receipt *n*   ■ reception *n*
> ■ receiver *n*   ■ receptive *adj*

receiver /rɪˈsiːvə/ noun [C] **1** the part of a
phone that you pick up in order to hear
and speak **2** the part of a television or radio
that receives electronic signals and
changes them into pictures and sounds **3** an
official who is put in charge of a business
with financial problems by a court

recent /ˈriːs(ə)nt/ adj ★★★ happening or
starting a short time ago: *a recent discovery*
♦ *Business has boomed **in recent years**.*

recently /ˈriːs(ə)ntli/ adv ★★★ not long ago:
*She **only recently** discovered the truth.* ♦

*He's been back to America fairly **recently**.*

receptacle /rɪˈseptək(ə)l/ noun [C] *formal* a
container

reception /rɪˈsepʃ(ə)n/ noun ★
1 [U] the part of a building where there is
someone whose job is to welcome visitors,
deal with questions etc: *Visitors must **report
to reception** first.*
2 [C] a formal party to welcome someone or
to celebrate something: *a wedding reception*
3 [singular] the reaction of people to someone
or something: *a friendly reception* ♦
*Crawford's performance had **a mixed
reception** from the critics.*
4 [U] the quality or strength of the picture
or sound you receive on a television, radio,
or mobile phone: *Mobile phone users were
complaining of **poor reception**.*

receptionist /rɪˈsepʃ(ə)nɪst/ noun [C] someone
who works in reception at a hotel or office
and whose job is to welcome visitors, deal
with questions etc

receptive /rɪˈseptɪv/ adj willing to listen or
consider suggestions

recess /ˈriːses, ˈriːˌses/ noun **1** [C/U] a short time
between periods of work in a court of law
or parliament **2** [C] a space in a room where
part of a wall is further back than the rest
of it **3** [U] *American* a BREAK between school
lessons

recession /rɪˈseʃ(ə)n/ noun [C/U] a period when
trade and industry are not successful and
there is a lot of unemployment

recharge /riːˈtʃɑːdʒ/ verb [T] to put more
power into a BATTERY
PHRASE **recharge your batteries** to rest after
being very busy, so that you will be ready
to start working again

recipe /ˈresəpi/ noun [C] ★ a set of instructions
for cooking or preparing a particular food:
a recipe for apple pie
PHRASE **be a recipe for sth** to make it
extremely likely that something will
happen: *Giving your kids too much freedom
can be **a recipe for disaster**.*

recipient /rɪˈsɪpiənt/ noun [C] *formal* someone
who receives something

reciprocal /rɪˈsɪprək(ə)l/ adj done according
to an arrangement by which you do
something for someone who does the same
thing for you

reciprocate /rɪˈsɪprəˌkeɪt/ verb [I/T] *formal* to do
the same thing for someone that they have
done for you

recital /rɪˈsaɪt(ə)l/ noun [C] a performance of
music or poetry

recite /rɪˈsaɪt/ verb [I/T] to say a poem or story
that you have learnt to an audience
—**recitation** /ˌresɪˈteɪʃ(ə)n/ noun [C/U]

reckless /ˈrekləs/ adj not thinking about the
possible bad effects of your actions: *reckless
driving* —**recklessly** adv, **recklessness** noun [U]

reckon /ˈrekən/ verb *spoken* ★
1 [I/T] *British* to believe that something is true:
+(that) *I reckon there's something wrong
with him.* ♦ **be reckoned to be sth** *It is
generally reckoned to be the best restaurant
in town.*

2 [T] to have a particular opinion about someone or something: *I think it'll work. What do you reckon?*

PHRASAL VERBS 'reckon on sth to expect something to happen and plan for it
'reckon with sth to consider something important when you are making plans

reckoning /'rekənɪŋ/ noun [C/U] a calculation or measurement

reclaim /rɪ'kleɪm/ verb [T] **1** to get something back that someone has taken from you: *He wants to reclaim the world championship title.* **2** to improve an area of land so that it can be used —**reclamation** /ˌrekləˈmeɪʃ(ə)n/ noun [U]

recline /rɪ'klaɪn/ verb [I] **1** to lie or lean in a comfortable position with your back supported by something **2** if a chair reclines, you can make the back of it lean backwards to be more comfortable

recluse /rɪ'kluːs, *American* 'reklu:s/ noun [C] someone who lives alone and avoids seeing other people —**reclusive** /rɪ'kluːsɪv/ adj

recognise /'rekəgnaɪz/ a British spelling of recognize

recognition /ˌrekəgˈnɪʃ(ə)n/ noun ★
1 [singular/U] agreement that something is true or important: *official recognition of the need for affordable childcare*
2 [singular/U] praise, respect, or admiration for something that you have done: *His work has gained international recognition.* ♦ *She received the award in recognition of her work in the community.*
3 [U] the ability to recognize a person or thing: *She looked at me without recognition.*

recognize /'rekəgnaɪz/ verb [T] ★★★
1 to know someone or something because you have seen, heard, or met them before: *I recognized the house from your description.* ♦ *I thought I recognized the voice!*
2 to accept that something is true or important: *We recognize the need for improvement in our performance.* ♦ +(that) *I recognize that there are some problems with the current system.*
3 to give praise or approval to someone for something they have done: *Her achievement was recognized with a medal.*
4 to accept the authority or status of someone or something: *Many countries refused to recognize the new regime.*
—**recognizable** /'rekəgnaɪzəb(ə)l/ adj, **recognizably** adv

recoil /rɪ'kɔɪl/ verb [I] to move quickly back from someone or something frightening or unpleasant

recollect /ˌrekə'lekt/ verb [I/T] to remember something that has happened

recollection /ˌrekə'lekʃ(ə)n/ noun **1** [U] the ability to remember something that has happened **2** [C] something that you remember

recommend /ˌrekə'mend/ verb [T] ★★
1 to advise that something should happen: +(that) *I recommend that you buy a more powerful computer.* ♦ **recommend doing sth**

We strongly recommend booking early. ♦ **recommend sb for sth** *He was recommended for the job.* ♦ **recommend sb to do sth** *Students are recommended to read the following books.*
2 to say that someone or something is good and worth using, having, or experiencing: *Can you recommend a good restaurant?* ♦ **recommend sb/sth to sb** *Please recommend our shop to your friends.*

Words often used with **recommend**
*Adverbs often used with **recommend** (sense 2)*   ■ **heartily, highly, thoroughly, wholeheartedly**   + RECOMMEND: say that someone or something is very good

recommendation /ˌrekəmenˈdeɪʃ(ə)n/ noun [C/U] **1** a suggestion or piece of advice about how to solve a problem, deal with a situation etc **2** a suggestion that someone or something is especially suitable or useful for a particular situation

recompense /'rekəmˌpens/ noun [U] *formal* payment that you give to someone who has done something for you or who has suffered injury or loss because of you —**recompense** verb [T]

reconcile /'rekənˌsaɪl/ verb **1** [T] to make things that are opposed to each other capable of existing together: *We can't reconcile the two versions of what happened.* **2** [I/T] if you reconcile two people or groups, or if they reconcile, they become friendly again after a disagreement **3** [T] to force someone to accept a situation that they do not like: *She couldn't reconcile herself to the idea of just giving up.*

reconciliation /ˌrekənsɪliˈeɪʃ(ə)n/ noun [singular/U] **1** a new and friendly relationship with someone who you have argued with or fought with **2** a way of making it possible for things that are opposed to each other to exist together

reconnaissance /rɪ'kɒnɪs(ə)ns/ noun [C/U] the use of soldiers or aircraft to go into an area and get information about an enemy

reconsider /ˌriːkən'sɪdə/ verb [I/T] to think again about a decision in order to decide whether you should change it

reconstitute /riː'kɒnstɪˌtjuːt/ verb [T] **1** to change the form or structure of something **2** to add a liquid to dried food so that you can eat it

reconstruct /ˌriːkən'strʌkt/ verb [T] **1** to build something again **2** to form an idea of something that happened by connecting pieces of information

reconstruction /ˌriːkən'strʌkʃ(ə)n/ noun **1** [U] the process of building something again **2** [C/U] a situation in which you try to form an idea of something that happened by making something similar happen again

record¹ /'rekɔːd/ noun ★★★
1 [C] information that is kept about something that has happened: *medical/historical records* ♦ *Try to keep a record of everything you eat this week.* ♦ *This*

*summer has been the hottest **on record*** (=hotter than ever before).

2 [singular] the things that someone has done that give an idea of what they are like: *The company has a reasonably good **safety record**.*

3 [C] the best achievement so far in a particular activity, especially a sport: *She **holds the** world **record** in the 800 metres.* → BREAK¹

4 [C] a large circular black piece of plastic containing music or other sounds: *an original Beatles' record*

PHRASES **(just) for the record** used for giving a piece of information that you want people to know: *It doesn't matter now, but just for the record – you were wrong.*

off the record used for saying that a remark is not official or is not intended to be made public

on (the) record used for stating that you are saying something officially or publicly

set/put the record straight to tell the truth about something after someone else has not told the truth about it

record² /rɪˈkɔːd/ verb ★★★
1 [T] to make a record of something that has happened, usually by writing it down: *They were asked to record the time at which the attack happened.*
2 [I/T] to put sounds or images onto a CASSETTE, CD, or video: *Can you record the football for me at 10 o'clock?*
3 [T] if a piece of equipment records an amount, it measures it and shows it: *Temperatures as low as –70 degrees Celsius have been recorded.*

record³ /ˈrekɔːd/ adj more, better, worse, faster etc than ever before: *I made it back to the office in record time.*

record-breaking /ˈrekɔːd ˌbreɪkɪŋ/ adj faster, longer, larger etc than anything that has been done before

recorder /rɪˈkɔːdə/ noun [C] a musical instrument that you play by blowing into a hole at the top while putting your fingers over other holes —*picture* → WOODWIND

recording /rɪˈkɔːdɪŋ/ noun **1** [C] a piece of music or speech that has been recorded **2** [U] the process of making recordings

recount¹ /rɪˈkaʊnt/ verb [T] formal **1** to say what happened **2** to count something again

recount² /ˈriːkaʊnt/ noun [C] an occasion when the votes in an election are counted again

recoup /rɪˈkuːp/ verb [T] to get back money that you have invested or lost

recourse /rɪˈkɔːs/ noun [U] formal the use of something that you can get what you want or need in a difficult situation

recover /rɪˈkʌvə/ verb ★★
1 [I] to become fit and healthy again after an illness or injury: *I haven't fully **recovered from** the flu.*
2 [T] to get back something that has been lost or stolen or is owed: *The thieves were caught, but many of the items were never recovered.*

3 [I] to return to a previous state after a difficult period or unpleasant experience: *The housing market appears to be recovering from the recession.*
4 [T] to get back the ability to do or feel something: *Simon never recovered the use of his arm after the crash.* ♦ *Darren was rushed to hospital, but he never **recovered consciousness**.*

recovery /rɪˈkʌv(ə)ri/ noun ★
1 [singular/U] the process of becoming fit and healthy again after an illness or injury: *The doctors expect Josie to **make a full recovery**.*
2 [singular/U] the process of returning to normal activity after a period of slow activity: *signs of **economic recovery***
3 [U] the act of getting something back that has been lost or stolen or is owed: *the **recovery** of stolen property*

recreate /ˌriːkriˈeɪt/ verb [T] to make something exist again

recreation /ˌrekriˈeɪʃ(ə)n/ noun [C/U] formal things that you do to enjoy yourself —**recreational** adj

recrimination /rɪˌkrɪmɪˈneɪʃ(ə)n/ noun **1** [U] a situation in which people are accusing or criticizing each other **2** [C] a statement accusing or criticizing someone who has accused or criticized you

recruit¹ /rɪˈkruːt/ verb [I/T] to get someone to join a company, an organization, or the armed forces —**recruitment** noun [U]

recruit² /rɪˈkruːt/ noun [C] a new member of a company, an organization, or the armed forces

rectangle /ˈrekˌtæŋɡ(ə)l/ noun [C] a shape with four straight sides and four angles of 90° —*picture* → C8 —**rectangular** /rekˈtæŋɡjʊlə/ adj

rectify /ˈrektɪfaɪ/ verb [T] formal to correct a problem or mistake, or to make a bad situation better

rector /ˈrektə/ noun [C] **1** a priest in an Anglican church **2** the person in charge in some schools, colleges, and universities

rectum /ˈrektəm/ noun [C] medical the lowest part of the tube through which solid waste leaves your body —**rectal** adj

recuperate /rɪˈkuːpəreɪt/ verb [I] to get better after being ill or injured —**recuperation** /rɪˌkuːpəˈreɪʃ(ə)n/ noun [U]

recur /rɪˈkɜː/ verb [I] to happen again, once or several times —**recurrence** /rɪˈkʌrəns/ noun [C/U], **recurrent** /rɪˈkʌrənt/ adj

recycle /riːˈsaɪk(ə)l/ verb [T] **1** to treat waste materials so that they can be used again **2** to use something again, often for a different purpose —**recyclable** adj, **recycling** noun [U]

red¹ /red/ adj ★★★
1 something that is red is the same colour as blood: *bright red lipstick*
2 red hair is a red-brown or orange colour
3 red wine is dark red or purple in colour
PHRASES **go red** to become red in the face because you are embarrassed

R

roll out the red carpet for sb to give special treatment to an important visitor

red² /red/ noun [C/U] ★ the colour of blood: *She was dressed all in red.*

PHRASES **in the red** with more money being spent than there is available: *Their bank account was in the red again.*

see red to become very angry

,red 'card noun [C] in football, a card that is used for telling a player that they have done something wrong and that they must leave the field → YELLOW CARD

redden /'red(ə)n/ verb [I/T] to become red, or to make something become red

reddish /'redɪʃ/ adj similar to red

redeem /rɪ'diːm/ verb [T] **1** to improve something that is not very good by including something that is good: *A difficult year for the company was redeemed by a successful deal.* **2** to make someone free from the power of evil, especially in the Christian religion

PHRASE **redeem yourself** to do something good because you have behaved badly, so that people will realize that you are not a bad person

redemption /rɪ'dempʃ(ə)n/ noun [U] the state of being made free from the power of evil, especially in the Christian religion =SALVATION

PHRASE **beyond/past redemption** too bad to be used or made good

redeploy /ˌriːdɪ'plɔɪ/ verb [T] *formal* to move someone or something to a different place or job —**redeployment** noun [U]

redevelop /ˌriːdɪ'veləp/ verb [T] to improve an area in bad condition by destroying or improving old buildings and building new ones —**redevelopment** noun [U]

red-handed /ˌred 'hændɪd/ adj **be caught red-handed** to be caught doing something wrong

redhead /'red,hed/ noun [C] someone with red hair

,red 'herring noun [C] something that is not relevant that makes you confused or takes your attention away from what you should be concentrating on

,red-'hot adj extremely hot

redial /ˌriː'daɪəl/ verb [I/T] to press one or more buttons in order to make a phone call for a second time

redid the past tense of **redo**

redirect /ˌriːdɪ'rekt/ verb [T] **1** to send someone or something to a different place **2** to use money or effort for a different purpose: *The money we save will be redirected to other parts of the business.*

redistribute /ˌriːdɪ'strɪbjuːt/ verb [T] to change the way that something is shared between people —**redistribution** /ˌriːdɪstrɪ'bjuːʃ(ə)n/ noun [U]

,red 'meat noun [U] meat such as BEEF or LAMB that is red before it is cooked

redo /ˌriː'duː/ (past tense **redid** /ˌriː'dɪd/; past participle **redone** /ˌriː'dʌn/) verb [T] to do something again in a different way in order to correct or improve it

redress /rɪ'dres/ verb [T] *formal* to improve a bad situation that you are responsible for by doing something for someone or by giving them money =MAKE UP FOR STH —**redress** noun [U]

,red 'tape noun [U] documents, rules, or processes that cause delays

reduce /rɪ'djuːs/ verb [T] ★★★ to make something smaller or less in size, amount, importance, price etc =CUT (STH) DOWN: *Try to reduce the amount of fat in your diet.* ♦ **reduce sth to sth** *All children's shoes are now reduced to £10 a pair.*

PHRASAL VERB **re'duce sb/sth to sth** to put someone or something into a particular unpleasant state or situation: *The building was reduced to rubble by the explosion.* ♦ *Her remarks had reduced him to tears.*

Words often used with **reduce**

Adverbs often used with reduce
■ REDUCE + **considerably, dramatically, drastically, greatly, sharply, significantly, substantially**: reduce sth by a large amount

---

reduction /rɪ'dʌkʃ(ə)n/ noun [C/U] ★★ the process or result of making something smaller or less in amount, size, price, importance etc: *a £50 reduction for all hotel guests* ♦ *a dramatic reduction in the birth rate*

Words often used with **reduction**

Adjectives often used with reduction
■ **considerable, dramatic, drastic, large, marked, sharp, significant, substantial** + REDUCTION: used about reductions that are large

---

redundancy /rɪ'dʌndənsi/ noun [C/U] **1** *British* a situation in which someone is told to leave their job because they are no longer needed **2** a situation in which something is not needed, because the same thing or a similar thing already exists

redundant /rɪ'dʌndənt/ adj **1** *British* if someone is made redundant, they have been told that they must leave their job because they are no longer needed **2** not needed because the same thing or a similar thing already exists

redwood /'red,wʊd/ noun [C/U] a very large tree with red wood that grows in the US —*picture* → C9

reed /riːd/ noun **1** [C/U] a tall thin plant that grows near water **2** [C] a thin piece of wood in the top of some musical instruments that makes a sound when you blow over it

reef /riːf/ noun [C] a long line of rock or CORAL in the sea, with its top just below or just above the surface

reek /riːk/ verb [I] to have a strong unpleasant smell =STINK —**reek** noun [singular]

reel¹ /riːl/ noun [C] an object shaped like a WHEEL that you wind string, THREAD, wire, or film around in order to store it

reel² /riːl/ verb [I] **1** to move in a way that is not steady =LURCH **2** to feel very shocked, upset, or confused

PHRASAL VERB ‚reel sth 'off to say a list of things quickly and without much effort

‚re-e'lect verb [T] to elect someone again
—‚re-e'lection noun [U]

‚re-'entry noun [C/U] the moment when a SPACECRAFT enters the Earth's atmosphere again

ref /ref/ noun [C] informal a REFEREE

refer /rɪ'fɜː/ verb ★★★

PHRASAL VERBS re'fer to sth 1 to describe something, or to be about something: These notes refer to the case of a teenage murderer. 2 formal to look at a book, map etc for information: Please refer to our catalogue for details.

re'fer to sb/sth to mention someone or something when you are speaking or writing: She referred to the subject several times during her speech.

re'fer sb to sb/sth to send someone to another person or place in order to get help, information, or advice: The doctor referred me to a skin specialist.

referee[1] /‚refə'riː/ noun [C] someone whose job is to make sure that players in a game obey the rules —picture → C15

referee[2] /‚refə'riː/ verb [I/T] to be a referee in a game

reference /'ref(ə)rəns/ noun ★★
1 [C/U] a comment that mentions someone or something = MENTION: He made no reference to my untidy appearance.
2 [C] a statement giving information about you that you ask someone who knows you or has worked with you to provide when you apply for a new job: Her former employer provided a reference for her.
3 [C/U] the process of looking at something in order to get information: The sentences are numbered for ease of reference.
→ FUTURE[2]

'reference ‚book noun [C] a book that contains facts and information

referendum /‚refə'rendəm/ noun [C/U] an occasion on which everyone in a country can vote to make a decision about one particular subject

refill /riː'fɪl/ verb [T] to put another amount of something into a container that was full but is now empty —refill /'riː.fɪl/ noun [C]

refine /rɪ'faɪn/ verb [T] 1 to make some changes to something in order to improve it: We've refined the system since it was first launched. 2 to remove things from a natural substance in order to make it pure

refined /rɪ'faɪnd/ adj 1 pure, because other things have been removed: refined sugar/oil 2 someone who is refined is very polite and enjoys art, music etc = CULTURED

refinement /rɪ'faɪnmənt/ noun 1 [C/U] a small change that is made to something in order to improve it 2 [U] the quality of being very polite and enjoying art, music etc 3 [U] the process of removing things from a natural substance so that it is pure

refinery /rɪ'faɪnəri/ noun [C] a factory where things are removed from a natural substance to make it pure

reflect /rɪ'flekt/ verb ★★★
1 [T] if a surface reflects something, you can see the image of that thing on the surface: I caught a glimpse of them reflected in the mirror.
2 [I/T] if something reflects light, heat etc, the light, heat etc comes back off it: Pale colours reflect light.
3 [T] to show that something is true of a particular situation or person: He said that the statement did not reflect his own views.
4 [I] to think about something carefully and seriously

PHRASE reflect well/badly on sb to give people a good or bad opinion of someone

reflection /rɪ'flekʃ(ə)n/ noun ★
1 [C] an image that you see when you look in a mirror or at a shiny surface: Anna stared at her reflection in the hall mirror.
2 [U] careful thought about something = CONSIDERATION: At the time I thought I was right, but on reflection I think perhaps I wasn't.
3 [C] something that shows that something is true of a particular person or situation: Your choice of clothes is a reflection of your personality.
4 [U] the process of reflecting light, sound, or images

PHRASE be a reflection on to show the faults of someone or something: These crimes are a sad reflection on modern society.

reflective /rɪ'flektɪv/ adj able to reflect light

reflector /rɪ'flektə/ noun [C] an object that reflects light and shines when light shines onto it

reflex /'riː.fleks/ noun [C] 1 a movement that one of your muscles makes without you thinking about it or being able to control it 2 a quick way of reacting to something, without thinking about it

reflexive /rɪ'fleksɪv/ adj linguistics a reflexive verb or pronoun refers back to the subject of the verb. In English, 'to enjoy yourself' is a reflexive verb and 'yourself' is a reflexive pronoun.

re'flexive 'verb noun [C] linguistics a verb whose object is the same thing or person as the subject. In English, the verb 'to enjoy yourself' is a reflexive verb.

reflexology /‚riː.flek'sɒlədʒi/ noun [U] a type of treatment in which a person's feet are rubbed and pressed in order to make other parts of their body more healthy, or to help the person to relax

reform[1] /rɪ'fɔːm/ noun [C/U] ★★ a change that is made in order to improve a situation or system: economic reforms ♦ the most important reform of the police service in over 30 years

R

Words often used with **reform**

Adjectives often used with **reform** (noun)
■ far-reaching, fundamental, important, major, radical, sweeping + REFORM: used about reforms that change things a lot

reform[2] /rɪ'fɔːm/ verb 1 [T] to change a

situation or system in order to improve it
2 [I/T] to improve your own or someone
else's behaviour

Reformation, the /ˌrefəˈmeɪʃ(ə)n/ a period of
religious change in Europe in the 16th
century, in which the Protestant Church
was started

reformer /rɪˈfɔːmə/ noun [C] someone who
tries to change and improve a political or
social system

refrain /rɪˈfreɪn/ verb [I] formal to stop yourself
from doing something

refresh /rɪˈfreʃ/ verb [T] **1** to make you feel that
you have more energy again, when you are
tired or hot **2** computing to make an Internet
or other computer document show the most
recent changes to it
PHRASE **refresh sb's memory** to make
someone remember something

refreshing /rɪˈfreʃɪŋ/ adj **1** making you feel
more lively when you have been feeling
tired or hot **2** showing approval newer, more
interesting, or more exciting than other
things that have come before: a refreshing
change —**refreshingly** adv

refreshments /rɪˈfreʃmənts/ noun [plural] food
and drinks that are provided at an event

refrigerate /rɪˈfrɪdʒəˌreɪt/ verb [T] to keep food
or drinks cold by putting them in a
refrigerator —**refrigeration** /rɪˌfrɪdʒəˈreɪʃ(ə)n/
noun [U]

refrigerator /rɪˈfrɪdʒəˌreɪtə/ noun [C] a
machine that keeps food and drinks cold

refuel /riːˈfjuːəl/ verb [I/T] if you refuel a
vehicle or aircraft, or if it refuels, you put
more fuel in it

refuge /ˈrefjuːdʒ/ noun [C/U] a place you go to
in order to protect yourself from something
dangerous or threatening=SHELTER

refugee /ˌrefjʊˈdʒiː/ noun [C] someone who
leaves their country because of a war or
other threatening event

refund¹ /ˈriːfʌnd/ noun [C] money that you
get back because you have paid too much
for something, or because you have decided
that you do not want it

refund² /rɪˈfʌnd/ verb [T] to give money back
to someone because they have paid too
much for something or have decided that
they do not want it

refurbish /riːˈfɜːbɪʃ/ verb [T] to improve a room
or a building by cleaning and painting it,
by adding new furniture or equipment etc
—**refurbishment** noun [C/U]

refusal /rɪˈfjuːz(ə)l/ noun [C/U] ★ the act of
refusing to do or accept something, or of
not allowing someone to do something:
refusal to do sth The rebels' refusal to
surrender led to further bloodshed.

refuse¹ /rɪˈfjuːz/ verb [I/T] ★★★ to say that you
will not do or accept something, or will not
let someone do something: I asked him to
apologize, but he refused. ♦ **refuse to do sth**
He couldn't refuse to help his own son. ♦
refuse sb sth Judge Mackey refused the
defendant the right to appeal.

refuse² /ˈrefjuːs/ noun [U] formal rubbish

refute /rɪˈfjuːt/ verb [T] formal to prove or say
that a statement is false=DISPROVE

regain /rɪˈgeɪn/ verb [T] to get back something
that you had lost

regal /ˈriːg(ə)l/ adj typical of or suitable for a
king or queen —**regally** adv

regard¹ /rɪˈgɑːd/ verb [T] ★★★
1 to think of someone or something in a
particular way: **regard sb/sth as sth** I regard
him as a friend.
2 literary to look at someone or something
PHRASE **as regards** formal concerning
someone or something
→ REGARDING

regard² /rɪˈgɑːd/ noun ★
1 [U] attention or care that you give to
someone or something: The road was built
without regard for the safety of residents.
2 [U] respect and admiration for someone or
something=ESTEEM: I have very high
regard for her.
3 regards [plural] greetings: **Give my regards**
to your parents.
PHRASES **in this/that regard** relating to this
or that
in/with regard to concerning a particular
subject

regarding /rɪˈgɑːdɪŋ/ preposition ★ concerning
a particular subject: Davis had very little to
say regarding the accident.

Regarding is often used to introduce the subject
of a business letter or document: Regarding
your inquiry of 12 September...

regardless /rɪˈgɑːdləs/ adv without being
affected or influenced by something: It
seemed an impossible task, but we carried
on, regardless. ♦ There must be equality for
all citizens, regardless of nationality.

regenerate /rɪˈdʒenəˌreɪt/ verb [T] to develop
something again, or to bring it back to its
original state —**regeneration**
/rɪˌdʒenəˈreɪʃ(ə)n/ noun [U]

reggae /ˈregeɪ/ noun [U] a type of popular
music that developed in Jamaica in the
1960s

regime /reɪˈʒiːm/ noun [C] ★ a system of
government, especially a strict or unfair
one: a military regime

regiment /ˈredʒɪmənt/ noun [C] a large group
of soldiers made up of several
BATTALIONS —**regimental** /ˌredʒɪˈment(ə)l/ adj

regimented /ˈredʒɪˌmentɪd/ adj organized and
controlled by strict rules

region /ˈriːdʒ(ə)n/ noun [C] ★★★
1 a large area of land: Peru's eastern jungle
region
2 a particular area of your body: pain in the
abdominal region
PHRASE **in the region of** used before a
number for saying that it is not exact

regional /ˈriːdʒ(ə)nəl/ adj ★★★ relating to or
typical of a particular region: a regional
council/newspaper/accent

register¹ /ˈredʒɪstə/ verb ★

1 put information on list	**4** show feelings
2 show measurement	**5** make opinion known
3 realize/notice sth	

R

1 [I/T] to put a name or other information on an official list: *Births must be registered within 42 days.* ♦ *Have you registered for the English exam yet?* ♦ *When you move house you need to register with a local doctor.*

2 [T] to show something as a measurement on a piece of equipment: *an earthquake registering 5.1 on the Richter scale*

3 [I/T] to realize or notice something, or to be realized or noticed: *She did tell me she'd be out, but it didn't register.*

4 [T] *formal* to show your feelings about something in your face or voice: *George's look registered his confusion.*

5 [T] *formal* to make your opinion known publicly or officially: *I decided to register a complaint with the manager.*

register² /ˈredʒɪstə/ noun ★
1 [C] an official list or record of a particular type of thing: *the register of births, deaths, and marriages* ♦ *All guests must sign the hotel register.*

2 [C/U] *linguistics* the type of language that you use in a particular situation or when you are communicating with a particular group of people

3 [C] a CASH REGISTER

register ,office noun [C] A REGISTRY OFFICE

registrar /ˌredʒɪˈstrɑː/ noun [C] **1** someone whose job is to keep official records **2** *British* a doctor in a hospital who is training to be a CONSULTANT

registration /ˌredʒɪˈstreɪʃ(ə)n/ noun [U] the process of recording names or information on an official list

regis'tration ,number noun [C] *British* the official set of numbers and letters on a car's NUMBER PLATE —*picture* → C6

registry /ˈredʒɪstri/ noun [C] a collection of official records, or the place where it is kept

registry ,office noun [C] in the UK, a place where births, deaths, and marriages are officially recorded, and where you can get married without a religious ceremony

regress /rɪˈgres/ verb [I] to return to a previous and usually less developed state
—**regression** /rɪˈgreʃ(ə)n/ noun [U]

regret¹ /rɪˈgret/ verb [T] ★★ to feel sorry or sad about something that has happened, or about something that you have done: *We regret any inconvenience caused by the delay.* ♦ *+(that)* *I regret that I cannot attend your wedding.* ♦ **regret doing sth** *I don't regret moving to New York.*

> **PHRASE** **I/we regret to inform/tell you that** *formal* used when you are giving someone bad news

regret² /rɪˈgret/ noun [C/U] a feeling of sadness about something that has happened or something that you have done —**regretful** adj, **regretfully** adv

regrettable /rɪˈgretəb(ə)l/ adj used for talking about something that you wish had not happened —**regrettably** adv

regular¹ /ˈregjʊlə/ adj ★★★

1 arranged evenly	**4** with even shape
2 doing sth often	**5** with normal grammar
3 ordinary	**6** of professional army

1 arranged so that there is the same amount of time or space between things: *regular monthly meetings* ♦ *They come here on a regular basis.*

2 doing something or done frequently: *a regular customer* ♦ *regular exercise*

3 ordinary, or of average size: *regular unleaded petrol*

4 arranged to form an even shape: *He was a handsome man, with strong regular features.*

5 *linguistics* following the normal patterns of grammar ≠ IRREGULAR: *regular verbs*

6 relating to or belonging to a professional army
—**regularity** /ˌregjʊˈlærəti/ noun [U]

regular² /ˈregjʊlə/ noun [C] a customer who often goes to the same bar, restaurant, or shop

regularly /ˈregjʊləli/ adv ★★
1 after equal amounts of time have passed: *The committee meets regularly.*
2 frequently: *The equipment needs to be checked regularly.*

regulate /ˈregjʊleɪt/ verb [T] **1** to officially control an activity, process, or industry **2** to control something so that it operates effectively

regulation /ˌregjʊˈleɪʃ(ə)n/ noun ★★
1 [C] an official rule that controls the way things are done: *building/safety regulations*
2 [U] official control of an activity, process, or industry: *the government's regulation of the steel industry*

rehab /ˈriːhæb/ noun [U] *informal* the process of helping someone to give up drugs or alcohol

rehabilitate /ˌriːəˈbɪlɪteɪt/ verb [T] to help someone to return to a normal life after they have been in prison, or after they have been ADDICTED to drugs or alcohol
—**rehabilitation** /ˌriːəbɪlɪˈteɪʃ(ə)n/ noun [U]

rehash /ˌriːˈhæʃ/ verb [T] to repeat or use something again without adding anything new

rehearsal /rɪˈhɜːs(ə)l/ noun [C/U] an occasion when you practise for the performance of a play, concert etc

rehearse /rɪˈhɜːs/ verb [I/T] to practise a play, concert etc before giving a performance

rehouse /ˌriːˈhaʊz/ verb [T] to provide a new house for someone

reign¹ /reɪn/ noun [C] **1** the period of time when a king or queen rules a country **2** a period of time during which a particular person, group, or thing is very powerful or popular

reign² /reɪn/ verb [I] **1** if a king or queen reigns, they officially rule a country **2** to be very powerful or popular at a particular time **3** to be the most important feature in a situation: *For weeks, confusion reigned at the office.*

R

reimburse /ˌriːɪmˈbɜːs/ verb [T] to give someone back money that they have spent =PAY SB BACK —**reimbursement** noun [C/U]

rein /reɪn/ noun [C] a piece of leather fastened to a horse's head that a rider uses to control the horse → TIGHT¹

reincarnated /ˌriːɪnkɑːˈneɪtɪd/ adj born again as a different person, animal, or thing after death, according to some religions

reincarnation /ˌriːɪnkɑːˈneɪʃ(ə)n/ noun **1** [U] the belief that after you die you can be born again as a different person, animal, or thing **2** [C] someone who has been born again as a different person, animal, or thing after their death

reindeer /ˈreɪndɪə/ noun [C] an animal like a DEER with large ANTLERS

reinforce /ˌriːɪnˈfɔːs/ verb [T] **1** to make an idea, belief, or feeling stronger: *The figures reinforce the view that economic growth is slowing.* **2** to make a building, structure, or object stronger: *Crews started work to reinforce the damaged bridge.* —**reinforced** /ˌriːɪnˈfɔːst/ adj

reinforcement /ˌriːɪnˈfɔːsmənt/ noun **1 reinforcements** [plural] extra soldiers or police officers who go to help an existing group of soldiers or police officers **2** [U] the process of REINFORCING something

reinstate /ˌriːɪnˈsteɪt/ verb [T] **1** to give someone back their previous job or position **2** to bring back something such as a law or benefit that had been stopped =RESTORE —**reinstatement** noun [U]

reinvent /ˌriːɪnˈvent/ verb [T] to change something that already exists and give it a different form or purpose

PHRASES reinvent the wheel to waste time and effort trying to do something that someone else has already done well **reinvent yourself** to change things about yourself, so that people think of you as a different type of person

reiterate /riˈɪtəˌreɪt/ verb [T] *formal* to repeat something in order to emphasize it —**reiteration** /riˌɪtəˈreɪʃ(ə)n/ noun [C/U]

reject¹ /rɪˈdʒekt/ verb [T] ★★
1 to not accept or agree with something such as an offer or an argument: *Our proposal was rejected.*
2 to refuse to accept someone for a job or a course of study
3 to behave in an unkind way to someone who wants kindness or love from you

> **Words often used with reject**
>
> *Adverbs often used with reject (verb, sense 1)*
> ■ REJECT + **categorically, firmly, flatly, outright, totally, vigorously**: reject something in a very clear and definite way

reject² /ˈriːdʒekt/ noun [C] something or someone that is not accepted because they have not reached the necessary standard

rejection /rɪˈdʒekʃən/ noun **1** [C/U] a refusal to accept or agree with something such as an offer or an argument ≠ ACCEPTANCE: *the rejection of the peace plan* **2** [C] a letter that

tells you that you have not got a job or a place on a course of study **3** [C/U] a refusal to show someone the love or kindness that they need or expect: *fear of rejection*

rejoice /rɪˈdʒɔɪs/ verb [I] *literary* to celebrate and express feelings of great happiness —**rejoicing** noun [U]

rejoin /ˌriːˈdʒɔɪn/ verb [T] to return to a person or organization that you were with before

rejuvenate /rɪˈdʒuːvəˌneɪt/ verb [T] to make someone feel or look younger —**rejuvenation** /rɪˌdʒuːvəˈneɪʃ(ə)n/ noun [U]

rekindle /ˌriːˈkɪnd(ə)l/ verb [T] to make you start feeling or thinking about something again

relapse /ˈriːlæps/ noun [C/U] **1** a period of illness after you had been getting better **2** a return to a worse state after a period of improvement —**relapse** /rɪˈlæps/ verb [I]

relate /rɪˈleɪt/ verb ★★★
1 [I/T] to show how one thing has a connection with another, or to be connected with another thing: *I can't really see how the two issues relate.* ♦ **relate sth to sth** *We offer courses that relate English literature to other subjects.*
2 [T] *formal* to tell someone about something that has happened: *Philip began to relate the horrors of his childhood.*

PHRASAL VERB re'late to sth 1 to be about something, or to be connected with something: *We're only interested in events that relate directly to the murder.* **2** to be able to understand a situation or the way that someone feels and thinks: *The programme deals with subjects that ordinary people can relate to.*

related /rɪˈleɪtɪd/ adj ★
1 connected ≠ UNRELATED: *We think the two crimes are related in some way.*
2 belonging to the same family: *Annie's related to the director.*

relation /rɪˈleɪʃ(ə)n/ noun ★★★
1 relations [plural] the relationship between countries, people, or organizations: *international relations* ♦ *better relations between Japan and China* ♦ *We have very good relations with the local police.*
2 [C/U] a connection between two or more people or things: *The study found a direct relation between smoking and lung cancer.* ♦ *The tax bears no relation to people's ability to pay.*
3 [C] a member of your family =RELATIVE: *All our friends and relations came to our wedding.*

PHRASE in relation to 1 in comparison to something: *Unemployment here is high in relation to national levels.* **2** concerning something: *I have nothing further to say in relation to this matter.*

> **Word family: relation**
>
> *Words in the same family as relation*
> ■ **relate** v
> ■ **related** adj
> ■ **relationship** n
> ■ **relative** adj, n
> ■ **relatively** adv
> ■ **unrelated** adj

R

relationship /rɪˈleɪʃ(ə)nʃɪp/ noun [C] ★★★
1 the way in which two or more people or things are connected: *There is a close relationship between poverty and crime.*
2 the way in which two or more people or groups behave towards each other: *The relationships between players from the two teams were pretty friendly.* ♦ *What was your relationship with your mother like?*
3 a situation in which two people are sexual or romantic partners: *I was already in a relationship when I met Ben.*

relative¹ /ˈrelətɪv/ adj ★★ used for comparing one situation with a more extreme one: *There was relative calm after the violence of the previous night.*
— **PHRASE** **relative to** compared with

relative² /ˈrelətɪv/ noun [C] ★ a member of your family, especially one who does not live with you=RELATION

relative ˈclause noun [C] *linguistics* a CLAUSE that is joined to a previous one by words such as 'who', 'that', or 'which'

relatively /ˈrelətɪvli/ adv ★★★ in comparison with someone or something similar
=COMPARATIVELY: *a relatively small flat*

relative ˈpronoun noun [C] *linguistics* a pronoun such as 'who', 'that', or 'which' that introduces a RELATIVE CLAUSE

relax /rɪˈlæks/ verb ★★
1 [I] to rest and become calm: *Just sit down and try to relax for half an hour.*
2 [I/T] to make your muscles or a part of your body feel less tight and more comfortable, or to become less tight and more comfortable: *Relax your stomach muscles, then repeat the exercise.*
3 [T] to make rules, controls, conditions etc less strict: *Some firms have relaxed their rules about unpaid leave.*
— **relaxation** /ˌriːlækˈseɪʃ(ə)n/ noun [C/U]

relaxed /rɪˈlækst/ adj ★
1 calm and not worried: *Bill came back from his holiday looking relaxed and tanned.*
2 friendly, informal, and comfortable: *The atmosphere in our office is very relaxed.*

relaxing /rɪˈlæksɪŋ/ adj pleasant and making you feel relaxed

relay¹ /ˈriːleɪ, ˈriːˌleɪ/ verb [T] **1** to communicate information to someone **2** to send out television or radio signals to be broadcast

relay² /ˈriːˌleɪ/ or **relay ˈrace** noun [C] a race between two or more teams where each member of the team does part of the race and then another member continues

release¹ /rɪˈliːs/ verb [T] ★★★

1 let sb leave	4 offer product
2 stop holding sth	5 get rid of feeling
3 give information	6 move held equipment

1 to let someone leave a place where they have been kept=FREE: *The authorities had recently released two suspects.* ♦ **release sb from sth** *He was released from prison in July.*
2 to stop holding someone or something
=LET: *She slowly released her grip on Louisa's hand.*

3 to make information or documents available: *Managers have released few details from yesterday's meeting.*
4 to make a film, video, or CD available for people to see or buy: *They have just released their second album.*
5 to get rid of a negative feeling, especially by expressing it: *Exercise will release all that tension.*
6 to move a piece of equipment from the position it is held in: *Don't forget to release the brake.*

release² /rɪˈliːs/ noun ★★

1 letting sb leave	4 making sth available
2 letting sth into area	5 new film/CD
3 feeling of calm	+ PHRASE

1 [U] the act of letting someone leave a place such as a prison or hospital: *The release of Nelson Mandela was watched by millions of people on TV.*
2 [U] a situation in which something such as a chemical spreads into the area around it: *We're doing all we can to prevent the release of toxic waste into the oceans.*
3 [singular/U] a feeling of being happier and calmer that you have after a difficult experience
4 [U] the act of making information or documents available: *the release of secret government information*
5 [C] a new film, video, or CD that is available for people to see or buy
— **PHRASE** **on (general) release** available to be seen in cinemas

relegate /ˈreləgeɪt/ verb [T] to move someone or something to a less important position
— **relegation** /ˌreləˈgeɪʃ(ə)n/ noun [U]

relent /rɪˈlent/ verb [I] **1** to change your mind about not letting someone do something **2** if rain or snow relents, it stops being so severe

relentless /rɪˈlentləs/ adj **1** never seeming to stop or improve **2** determined and never stopping your attempts to achieve something — **relentlessly** adv

relevance /ˈreləv(ə)ns/ noun [U] the quality of being connected with and important to something else

relevant /ˈreləv(ə)nt/ adj ★★★ important and directly connected with what is being discussed or considered ≠ IRRELEVANT: *How is that relevant to this discussion?*

reliable /rɪˈlaɪəb(ə)l/ adj ★ able to be trusted =DEPENDABLE ≠ UNRELIABLE: *a reliable workman/car* ♦ *reliable information/ evidence* — **reliability** /rɪˌlaɪəˈbɪləti/ noun [U], **reliably** adv

reliance /rɪˈlaɪəns/ noun [U] the state of depending on someone or something
=DEPENDENCE

reliant /rɪˈlaɪənt/ adj depending on someone or something=DEPENDENT

relic /ˈrelɪk/ noun [C] an object, system, or rule that belongs to the past

relief /rɪˈliːf/ noun ★★★
1 [singular/U] a relaxed happy feeling that you get because something bad has ended

R

or has not happened: *It's **a huge relief** to know that everyone is safe.* ♦ *To her relief, someone had found her keys.*

2 [U] the reduction of pain or the effects of an illness: *The patients experienced no **relief from** their symptoms.*

3 [U] food, clothes, and money that is given to people who are in need of help: *flood/disaster/earthquake relief*

4 [U] the right to not have to pay the full amount of tax or interest on an amount of money

relieve /rɪˈliːv/ verb [T] ★
1 to make an unpleasant feeling or situation less severe or unpleasant: *Use a cooling gel to relieve the discomfort of sunburn.* ♦ *Reading helped to **relieve the boredom.***
2 to replace someone when they finish work

PHRASE **relieve sb of sth** *formal* to take something from someone

relieved /rɪˈliːvd/ adj happy and relaxed because something bad has ended or did not happen: *I'm so relieved to know the truth.*

religion /rɪˈlɪdʒ(ə)n/ noun [C/U] ★★★ belief in a god or in gods, or a particular system of beliefs in a god or in gods: *the Christian/Hindu/Muslim religion*

religious /rəˈlɪdʒəs/ adj ★★★
1 relating to religion: *religious beliefs*
2 believing strongly in your religion =DEVOUT: *a deeply religious man*

religiously /rəˈlɪdʒəsli/ adv if you do something religiously, you do it regularly and are very serious about it

relinquish /rəˈlɪŋkwɪʃ/ verb [T] *formal* to give up your power, position, or an advantage

relish¹ /ˈrelɪʃ/ verb [T] to get great pleasure or satisfaction from something

relish² /ˈrelɪʃ/ noun **1** [U] great pleasure and satisfaction **2** [C/U] a cold sauce that you put on meat

relive /riːˈlɪv/ verb [T] to remember an experience so clearly that you seem to be in the same situation again

reload /riːˈləʊd/ verb [I/T] to put something into an object such as a gun or camera so that it is ready to use again

relocate /ˌriːləʊˈkeɪt/ verb [I/T] to move to a different place, or to make someone do this —**relocation** /ˌriːləʊˈkeɪʃ(ə)n/ noun [U]

reluctant /rɪˈlʌktənt/ adj ★ not willing to do something: **reluctant to do sth** *She was reluctant to leave.* —**reluctance** noun [U], **reluctantly** adv

rely /rɪˈlaɪ/ verb ★★
PHRASAL VERBS **reˈly on sth** to need something in order to continue living, existing, or operating: **rely on sth to do sth** *The museum relies on voluntary donations to keep open.*
reˈly on sb/sth to trust someone or something to do something for you: *Sometimes you just have to rely on your own judgment.* ♦ **rely on sb/sth to do sth** *Can we rely on him to support us?*

remain /rɪˈmeɪn/ verb ★★★
1 [linking verb] to continue to be in a

particular situation or condition: *The dictator has remained in power for over 20 years.* ♦ *The economy remains fragile.*
2 [I] to stay in a particular place or position and not leave it: *You must **remain in bed** for three days after surgery.*
3 [I] to continue to exist after other things have gone or have been dealt with: *Only a handful of these rare fish remain in Scotland.*
PHRASE **it remains to be seen (whether/what/how)** used for saying that you do not know yet whether something will happen or will be possible

remainder, the /rɪˈmeɪndə/ noun [singular] the part of something that is left after the rest has gone or been finished

remaining /rɪˈmeɪnɪŋ/ adj still left after other people or things have gone or been dealt with

remains /rɪˈmeɪnz/ noun [plural] **1** the part of something that is left after the rest has been finished, used, or destroyed **2** the body of a person or animal that has died

remake /ˈriːˌmeɪk/ noun [C] a film that uses the same story as a previous film —**remake** /riːˈmeɪk/ verb [T]

remand¹ /rɪˈmɑːnd/ verb **be remanded in custody** *legal* to be put in prison until your trial

remand² /rɪˈmɑːnd/ noun **on remand** *legal* in prison waiting for your trial

remark¹ /rɪˈmɑːk/ noun [C] ★ a few words that give the facts or give your opinion about something =COMMENT: *Nicholas **made a** rude **remark about** her hair.*

remark² /rɪˈmɑːk/ verb [T] to make a comment about something
PHRASAL VERB **reˈmark on sth** to make a comment about something that you have noticed

remarkable /rɪˈmɑːkəb(ə)l/ adj ★★ unusual in a way that surprises or impresses you: *The play has been a remarkable success.*

remarkably /rɪˈmɑːkəbli/ adv in an unusual or surprising way: *All the students did remarkably well.*

remarry /riːˈmæri/ verb [I/T] to get married again —**remarriage** /riːˈmærɪdʒ/ noun [C]

remedial /rɪˈmiːdiəl/ adj **1** intended to improve or correct something **2** intended to help people who have difficulty learning basic skills such as reading and writing

remedy¹ /ˈremədi/ noun [C] ★
1 a solution to a particular problem: *There are no easy **remedies for** learning difficulties.*
2 a cure for pain or for a minor illness: *homeopathic/herbal remedies*

remedy² /ˈremədi/ verb [T] to correct or improve a situation

remember /rɪˈmembə/ verb ★★★
1 [I/T] to have an image in your mind of a person, a place, or something that happened in the past: *I can still remember every word of our conversation.* ♦ **remember doing sth** *She remembers seeing him there.* ♦ **+(that)** *I remember that I was really nervous*

R

on my first day at school. ♦ **+when/where/ how etc** Try to remember where you put the keys.

2 [T] to not forget to do something: I hope she remembers my book (=brings it with her). ♦ **remember to do sth** He never remembers to lock the door when he goes out.

remembrance /rɪˈmembrəns/ noun [U] a way of showing respect for someone who has died or for an important event

remind /rɪˈmaɪnd/ verb [T] ★★ to help someone to remember something: **remind sb of/about sth** Can you remind us about your plans for the building? ♦ **remind sb to do sth** Remind Jenny to bring my CD when she comes. ♦ **remind sb (that)** She reminded me that we had met before. ♦ **remind sb what/when/ where/how etc** I need the notes to remind me what to say.

PHRASE **remind sb of sb/sth** to be very similar to someone or something else: She reminded me of my cousin Sarah.

reminder /rɪˈmaɪndə/ noun [C] something that reminds you of something

reminisce /ˌremɪˈnɪs/ verb [I] to talk, think, or write about enjoyable experiences in your past —**reminiscence** /ˌremɪˈnɪs(ə)ns/ noun [C]

reminiscent /ˌremɪˈnɪs(ə)nt/ adj reminding you of someone or something similar

remission /rɪˈmɪʃ(ə)n/ noun [C/U] a period of time when an illness or disease becomes less severe: Her sister's cancer is in remission.

remittance /rɪˈmɪt(ə)ns/ noun [C/U] formal payment for goods or services

remnant /ˈremnənt/ noun [C] a small remaining part of something

remodel /ˌriːˈmɒd(ə)l/ verb [T] to change the structure or appearance of something

remonstrate /ˈremənˌstreɪt/ verb [I] formal to argue with, complain to, or criticize someone about something

remorse /rɪˈmɔːs/ noun [U] a strong sad and guilty feeling about something bad that you have done —**remorseful** adj, **remorsefully** adv

remorseless /rɪˈmɔːsləs/ adj **1** not feeling sad or guilty for having done something bad **2** continuing without stopping, or continuing to get worse=RELENTLESS —**remorselessly** adv

remote¹ /rɪˈməʊt/ adj ★
1 distant in space or time=ISOLATED: a remote village in China ♦ the remote past
2 slight: You have only **a remote chance** of winning.
3 not showing any friendly interest in other people=ALOOF
—**remoteness** noun [U]

remote² /rɪˈməʊt/ noun [C] a REMOTE CONTROL

re,mote con'trol noun **1** [C] a piece of equipment that you use for controlling something such as a television from a short distance away **2** [U] a system of controlling a machine or a vehicle from a distance —**re,mote-con'trolled** adj

remotely /rɪˈməʊtli/ adv in a very small way:

He wasn't even remotely interested in anything we had to say.

removable /rɪˈmuːvəb(ə)l/ adj easily removed =DETACHABLE

removal /rɪˈmuːv(ə)l/ noun [C/U] the process of removing someone or something

remove /rɪˈmuːv/ verb [T] ★★★
1 to take someone or something away from a place: **remove sb/sth from sth** Medical crews removed two people from the collapsed building.
2 to take off a piece of clothing: She removed her coat and sat down.
3 to get rid of a problem, difficulty, or something that annoys you: We need to remove any obstacles to a peaceful solution.
4 to take away someone's power or position, especially in politics: Officials who were involved in the scandal were removed from office.

removed /rɪˈmuːvd/ adj **1** different from something: Paris is far removed from the little town I grew up in. **2** distant in time or space

remover /rɪˈmuːvə/ noun [C/U] a substance used for removing paint, STAINS, NAIL POLISH etc

remuneration /rɪˌmjuːnəˈreɪʃ(ə)n/ noun [U] formal payment that you get for your work —**remunerate** /rɪˈmjuːnəˌreɪt/ verb [T]

renaissance /rɪˈneɪs(ə)ns, American ˈrenəsɑːns/ noun **1** [singular] a situation in which something becomes popular again **2 the Renaissance** the period in Europe between the 14th and 16th centuries when there was increased interest in art, literature, and science

rename /riːˈneɪm/ verb [T] to change the name of someone or something

render /ˈrendə/ verb [T] formal **1** to provide a service, or to help someone **2** to make something be in a particular condition or state: Failure to supply the information will render the contract invalid.

rendezvous /ˈrɒndɪˌvuː/ (plural **rendezvous** /ˈrɒndɪˌvuːz/) noun [C] a meeting that is arranged for a particular time and place, or the place where the meeting happens —**rendezvous** verb [I]

rendition /renˈdɪʃ(ə)n/ noun [C] a particular way of performing a song, poem, piece of music etc

renege /rɪˈneɪg, rɪˈniːg/ verb [I] formal to not do something that you promised to do

renew /rɪˈnjuː/ verb [T] **1** to arrange for something to continue **2** to do something again after a pause **3** to replace something that is old or damaged —**renewal** noun [C/U]

renewable /rɪˈnjuːəb(ə)l/ adj **1** a renewable contract or arrangement can be continued for a longer period of time ≠ NON-RENEWABLE **2** renewable energy and natural materials replace themselves by natural processes, so that they are never completely used up ≠ NON-RENEWABLE

renewed /rɪˈnjuːd/ adj happening again after a pause, and with more energy or enthusiasm than before

R

renounce /rɪˈnaʊns/ verb [T] formal **1** to say formally that you no longer support or believe in something **2** to say formally that you want to give up a right, title, or position —**renunciation** /ˌrɪnʌnsiˈeɪʃ(ə)n/ noun [C/U]

renovate /ˈrenəˌveɪt/ verb [T] to make something old look new again by repairing and improving it —**renovation** /ˌrenəˈveɪʃ(ə)n/ noun [C/U]

renowned /rɪˈnaʊnd/ adj famous for a special skill or achievement —**renown** noun [U]

rent¹ /rent/ noun [C/U] ★★ an amount of money that you pay regularly for using a house, room, office etc that belongs to someone else: *After she'd paid her rent, Jan had no money left for food.*

rent² /rent/ verb ★
1 [I/T] to pay money regularly to use a house, room, office etc that belongs to someone else: *How long have you been renting this place?*
2 [I/T] to pay money to use a vehicle, piece of equipment etc for a short time
3 [T] to allow a house, room, office etc that you own to be used by someone who pays you regularly for using it: *All the rooms are rented out to students.*

PHRASAL VERB ,rent sth ˈout same as **rent²** 3

rental /ˈrent(ə)l/ noun [C/U] the process of renting something, or an amount of money that you pay for renting something —**rental** adj

rented /ˈrentɪd/ adj used by someone who pays rent to the owner

reopen /riːˈəʊpən/ verb [I/T] if a process reopens, or if someone reopens it, it begins again after stopping for a time

reorganize /riːˈɔːɡəˌnaɪz/ verb [I/T] to organize something in a different way —**reorganization** /riˌɔːɡənaɪˈzeɪʃ(ə)n/ noun [C/U]

rep /rep/ noun [C] someone who works for a company and whose job it is to deal directly with customers: *a sales/holiday rep*

repair¹ /rɪˈpeə/ verb [T] ★
1 to fix something that is broken or damaged: *The cost of repairing the damage was much higher than we thought.*
2 to improve a bad situation: *an attempt to repair the relationship between the two countries*

repair² /rɪˈpeə/ noun ★
1 [C/U] work that is done to fix something that is broken or damaged: *How much will the repairs cost?* ♦ *Unfortunately the engine is beyond repair* (=so badly damaged that it cannot be repaired). ♦ *Both church and tower were in need of repair.*
2 [C] a part of something that has been repaired
PHRASE in good/bad repair in a good or a bad condition: *Most of the paintings are in good repair.*

reparations /ˌrepəˈreɪʃ(ə)nz/ noun [plural] money paid by the country that loses a war for the damage that it has caused to other countries

repatriate /ˌriːˈpætrieɪt/ verb [T] to send someone back to the country that is legally their own —**repatriation** /riːˌpætriˈeɪʃ(ə)n/ noun [U]

repay /rɪˈpeɪ/ (past tense and past participle **repaid** /rɪˈpeɪd/) verb [T] **1** to give someone back the money that you borrowed from them **2** to reward someone who has helped you

repayment /rɪˈpeɪmənt/ noun [C] an amount of money that you pay back to the person that you borrowed it from

repeal /rɪˈpiːl/ verb [T] legal to officially end a law —**repeal** noun [U]

repeat¹ /rɪˈpiːt/ verb [T] ★★★
1 to say or do something again: *Can you repeat what you just said, please?* ♦ *Repeat the exercise eight times with each leg.*
2 to tell someone something that someone else has told you: **repeat sth to sb** *I'll tell you a secret, but please don't repeat it to anyone.*
3 to say or write something that you have heard or read because you are trying to learn or understand it: **repeat sth after sb** *The students carefully repeated the words after the teacher.*
4 to broadcast a television or radio programme again
PHRASE repeat yourself to say the same words or idea that you said before, often without realizing you are doing it: *Sally sometimes gets confused and repeats herself.*

Word family: repeat
Words in the same family as repeat
■ **repetition** *n*   ■ **repetitive** *adj*
■ **repeated** *adj*   ■ **repeatedly** *adv*
■ **repetitious** *adj*

repeat² /rɪˈpiːt/ noun [C] **1** a television or radio programme that is broadcast again **2** an event or situation that happens again

repeated /rɪˈpiːtɪd/ adj done many times —**repeatedly** adv

repel /rɪˈpel/ verb [T] **1** if something repels you, you think that it is extremely unpleasant **2** to keep someone or something away, or to prevent them from attacking you **3** if one thing repels another, an electrical or MAGNETIC force pushes them away from each other

repellent¹ /rɪˈpelənt/ noun [C/U] a substance that keeps insects or animals away

repellent² /rɪˈpelənt/ adj very unpleasant

repent /rɪˈpent/ verb [I/T] formal to be very sorry for something bad that you have done —**repentance** noun [U], **repentant** adj

repercussions /ˌriːpəˈkʌʃ(ə)nz/ noun [plural] the bad effects that something causes

repertoire /ˈrepəˌtwɑː/ noun [C] all the songs, pieces of music etc that a performer knows

repetition /ˌrepəˈtɪʃ(ə)n/ noun **1** [U] a situation in which someone repeats something **2** [C] something that happens in the same way as an earlier event

repetitive /rɪˈpetətɪv/ or **repetitious** /ˌrepəˈtɪʃəs/ adj repeating the same thing, especially in a way that is boring or annoying

R

rephrase /ˌriːˈfreɪz/ verb [T] to say or write the same thing, using different words

replace /rɪˈpleɪs/ verb [T] ★★★
1 to get rid of someone or something and put a new person or thing in their place: *We'll have to replace all the furniture that was damaged in the flood.* ◆ **replace sth with sth** *The plan is to replace state funding with private money.*
2 to do the same job that someone or something did before: *Have they found anyone to replace me yet?* ◆ *Email has largely replaced traditional letters.*
3 to put something back in its correct place or position: *She carefully replaced the plate on the shelf.*

replacement /rɪˈpleɪsmənt/ noun [C/U] someone or something that takes the place of another person or thing, or the process of replacing someone or something: *Have you found a replacement for your assistant?*

replay /ˈriːˌpleɪ/ noun [C] **1** part of a sports match that is broadcast again **2** a game that is played again because neither team won the first time —**replay** /ˌriːˈpleɪ/ verb [T]

replenish /rɪˈplenɪʃ/ verb [T] *formal* to make something full again, or to bring it back to its previous level by replacing what has been used

replica /ˈreplɪkə/ noun [C] an accurate copy of something

replicate /ˈreplɪˌkeɪt/ verb [T] *formal* to do or make something again in the same way as before —**replication** /ˌreplɪˈkeɪʃ(ə)n/ noun [U]

reply¹ /rɪˈplaɪ/ verb ★★★
1 [I/T] to say, write, or do something as an answer: *'I know,' Corbett replied quietly.* ◆ *It took them a week to reply to my letter.* ◆ **+(that)** *When I asked where he was going, he replied that it was none of my business.*
2 [I] to do something as a reaction to what someone else has done=RESPOND

reply² /rɪˈplaɪ/ noun [C] ★★
1 something that you say or write as an answer: *I wrote to him, but I got no reply.* ◆ *We received a reply from the minister herself.* ◆ *I still haven't had a reply to my email.* ◆ *I am writing in reply to your letter of 7 August.*
2 something that you do as a reaction to what someone else has done=RESPONSE

report¹ /rɪˈpɔːt/ noun [C] ★★★
1 a spoken or written description of a particular subject, situation, or event: *A new report shows violent crime is on the increase.* ◆ *We're getting reports of more fighting in the area.* ◆ *the company's annual report* ◆ *We have to write a short report on the conference.*
2 an article or broadcast that gives information about something in the news: *Did you see that report about house prices in London?*
3 *British* a document that is written by a teacher, giving details of a student's school work

report² /rɪˈpɔːt/ verb ★★★
1 [T] to provide information about something, especially to people in authority: *Supermarkets report a sharp increase in sales of organic vegetables.* ◆ **report doing sth** *Witnesses reported hearing a loud noise before the plane crashed.* ◆ **report sth to sb** *If you see anything suspicious, report it to the police.*
2 [I/T] to give information about something in a news article or broadcast: *Three journalists were sent to report on the conflict.* ◆ **+that** *Correspondents reported that the president had lost control of the country.*
3 [T] to produce an official statement or a written document about a particular subject: *The committee will report the results of its investigation tomorrow.*

PHRASAL VERB **re'port to sb** if you report to someone at work, they are responsible for telling you what to do

reportedly /rɪˈpɔːtɪdli/ adv used for showing that you are not certain that something you are reporting is true

reported speech /rɪˌpɔːtɪd ˈspiːtʃ/ noun [U] *linguistics* a way of saying what someone has said that does not repeat their actual words =INDIRECT SPEECH

reporter /rɪˈpɔːtə/ noun [C] someone whose job is to write articles or make broadcasts about events in the news=JOURNALIST

reporting /rɪˈpɔːtɪŋ/ noun [U] the job of producing written reports or broadcasts about events in the news

repose /rɪˈpəʊz/ noun [U] *literary* a calm or relaxed state

repossess /ˌriːpəˈzes/ verb [T] to take back something that someone had promised to pay for, because they are unable to pay for it —**repossession** /ˌriːpəˈzeʃ(ə)n/ noun [C/U]

reprehensible /ˌreprɪˈhensəb(ə)l/ adj *formal* very bad

represent /ˌreprɪˈzent/ verb [T] ★★★

1 speak/act for sb	**4** be example of
2 be sth	**5** in sport
3 be sign/symbol of	**6** be picture/image of

1 to officially speak or do something for another person or group: *The vice-president will represent the United States at the ceremony.*
2 [linking verb] if something represents another thing, it consists of that thing =CONSTITUTE: *Albanians represent about 90 per cent of the population in Kosovo.*
3 to be a sign or symbol of something: *The colour red commonly represents danger.*
4 to be an example of a particular quality or type: *His attitude represents everything I dislike about this country.*
5 to take part in a sport as a member of a particular team, country etc: *Ben's ambition is to represent Britain at the Olympics.*
6 to be a picture or image of something =DEPICT: *The statue represents Jefferson as a young man.*

representation /ˌreprɪzenˈteɪʃ(ə)n/ noun **1** [C] a sign, symbol, or picture of something **2** [U]

R

a person or group that officially speaks or does something for someone else
—**representational** adj

representative[1] /ˌreprɪˈzentətɪv/ noun [C] ★★ someone who has been chosen by a person or group to vote, speak, or make decisions for them: *an elected/political representative* ♦ *The new government sent a representative to the talks.*

representative[2] /ˌreprɪˈzentətɪv/ adj **1** typical of people or things in a particular group ≠ UNREPRESENTATIVE: *His views are not representative of the majority of the population.* **2** a representative form of government is one in which people vote for their politicians

repress /rɪˈpres/ verb [T] **1** to prevent yourself from showing a feeling **2** to use force to control people —**repression** noun [U]

repressed /rɪˈprest/ adj having feelings that you do not show or do not admit that you have

repressive /rɪˈpresɪv/ adj ruling or controlling people with force or violence

reprieve /rɪˈpriːv/ noun [C] **1** a stop or delay in something bad or unpleasant **2** an official decision not to kill someone who was going to be killed as a punishment for a crime —**reprieve** verb [T]

reprimand /ˈreprɪˌmɑːnd/ verb [T] to tell someone officially that something that they have done is wrong —**reprimand** noun [C]

reprint[1] /ˌriːˈprɪnt/ verb [T] to make more copies of a book

reprint[2] /ˈriːˌprɪnt/ noun [C] a book that has been reprinted

reprisal /rɪˈpraɪz(ə)l/ noun [C/U] something unpleasant that is done to punish an enemy for something that they have done to you

reproach[1] /rɪˈprəʊtʃ/ verb [T] to criticize someone for something that they have done

reproach[2] /rɪˈprəʊtʃ/ noun [C/U] a criticism that you make of someone because of something bad that they have done

PHRASE **beyond reproach** impossible to criticize because of being so good —**reproachful** adj, **reproachfully** adv

reprocess /ˌriːˈprəʊses/ verb [T] to process a waste substance so that it can be used again

reproduce /ˌriːprəˈdjuːs/ verb **1** [T] to make a copy of something, or to repeat something **2** [I/T] to have babies, or to produce young animals or plants

reproduction /ˌriːprəˈdʌkʃ(ə)n/ noun **1** [U] the process of having babies or producing young animals or plants **2** [C] a copy of something, especially a work of art

reproductive /ˌriːprəˈdʌktɪv/ adj relating to sex, or to the process of having babies or producing young animals or plants

reptile /ˈreptaɪl/ noun [C] a type of animal such as a snake or LIZARD that lays eggs, and whose body is covered in SCALES (=flat hard pieces of skin) —**reptilian** /repˈtɪliən/ adj

republic /rɪˈpʌblɪk/ noun [C] ★ a country that is not ruled by a king or queen

republican /rɪˈpʌblɪkən/ noun [C] someone

who thinks that their country should not have a king or queen —**republican** adj

Republican /rɪˈpʌblɪkən/ noun [C] someone who supports the US Republican Party —**Republican** adj

Re'publican ,Party, the one of the two main political parties in the US

repudiate /rɪˈpjuːdieɪt/ verb [T] *formal* to say formally that something is not true, or that you do not accept it —**repudiation** /rɪˌpjuːdiˈeɪʃ(ə)n/ noun [U]

repugnant /rɪˈpʌgnənt/ adj *formal* extremely unpleasant or offensive —**repugnance** noun [U]

repulse /rɪˈpʌls/ verb [T] *formal* **1** to stop a military attack **2** if someone or something repulses you, you think that they are very unpleasant

repulsion /rɪˈpʌlʃ(ə)n/ noun [U] a strong feeling of dislike

repulsive /rɪˈpʌlsɪv/ adj extremely unpleasant=DISGUSTING

reputable /ˈrepjʊtəb(ə)l/ adj generally considered to be honest and reliable

reputation /ˌrepjʊˈteɪʃ(ə)n/ noun [C/U] ★★ the opinion people have about how good or bad someone or something is: *The town has a bad reputation.* ♦ *Clark had a reputation for arrogance.* ♦ *Our university has an international reputation as a centre of excellence.*

Words often used with **reputation**

Verbs often used with reputation

■ acquire, build, develop, earn, establish, gain, get + REPUTATION: get a reputation

repute /rɪˈpjuːt/ noun [U] *formal* the reputation that someone or something has

reputed /rɪˈpjuːtɪd/ adj *formal* said or believed by a lot of people, but not definitely true —**reputedly** adv

request[1] /rɪˈkwest/ noun [C] ★★
1 an act of asking for something in a polite or formal way: *Evening meals are available on request* (=if you ask). ♦ *Requests for visas will be dealt with immediately.* ♦ *I've made a request for the names of the previous owners.* ♦ *at sb's request/at the request of sb No photographs of the girl were printed, at her parents' request.*
2 a piece of music that you ask a musician or a DJ to play

request[2] /rɪˈkwest/ verb [T] to ask for something, or to ask someone to do something, in a polite or formal way

require /rɪˈkwaɪə/ verb [T] ★★★
1 to need someone or something: *Working with these children requires a great deal of patience.* ♦ *a medical condition requiring treatment*
2 if a rule, law, contract etc requires something, you must do that thing: *Car insurance is required by law.*

requirement /rɪˈkwaɪəmənt/ noun [C] ★★★ something that is necessary, or that a rule or law says that you must do: *a list of safety requirements* ♦ *Check the car's fuel requirements.*

Words often used with requirement

Adjectives often used with requirement

- **basic, essential, legal, minimum, statutory** + REQUIREMENT: used about different types of requirement
- **comply with, fulfil, match, meet, satisfy, suit** + REQUIREMENT: do what is necessary

---

requisite /ˈrekwɪzɪt/ adj *formal* necessary for a particular purpose

re-re'lease verb [T] to make something such as a film or CD available to the public for a second time —**re-re,lease** noun [C/U]

re-'route verb [T] to send something such as a vehicle or an email by a different way

rerun /ˈriːrʌn/ noun [C] **1** a film or television programme that is being shown again **2** something that happens again in a similar way as before

resale /ˈriːseɪl/ noun [U] a situation in which someone sells something that they have bought previously

reschedule /ˌriːˈʃedjuːl/ verb [T] to change the time when something is planned to happen

rescue¹ /ˈreskjuː/ verb [T] ★
1 to save someone from a dangerous or unpleasant situation: *The crew of the ship were rescued just before it sank.*
2 to prevent a business, project etc from failing: *an attempt to rescue the peace process*
—**rescuer** noun [C]

rescue

rescue² /ˈreskjuː/ noun [C/U] ★ an act of saving someone or something from danger or from an unpleasant situation: *Soldiers carried out a dramatic rescue of the hostages last night.* ♦ *a rescue operation/attempt*

research¹ /rɪˈsɜːtʃ, ˈriːsɜːtʃ/ noun [U] ★★ the detailed study of something in order to discover new facts: *medical/historical/linguistic research* ♦ *a research project/programme* ♦ *He did some research into the causes of lung cancer.* ♦ *Scientists have carried out extensive research into the effects of these drugs.* → MARKET RESEARCH

Words often used with research

Verbs often used with research (noun)

- **carry out, conduct, undertake** + RESEARCH: to do research

---

research² /rɪˈsɜːtʃ, ˈriːsɜːtʃ/ verb [T] to make a

detailed study of something in order to discover new facts —**researcher** noun [C]

resell /ˌriːˈsel/ (past tense and past participle **resold** /ˌriːˈsəʊld/) verb [T] to sell something that you previously bought

resemblance /rɪˈzembləns/ noun [C/U] if there is a resemblance between two people or things, they are similar

resemble /rɪˈzemb(ə)l/ verb [T] to be similar to someone or something: *The animals make a sound that resembles a cat's miaow.*

resent /rɪˈzent/ verb [T] to feel angry because you think that you have been treated unfairly

resentful /rɪˈzentf(ə)l/ adj feeling angry because you think that you have been treated unfairly

resentment /rɪˈzentmənt/ noun [U] an angry feeling that you have when you think that you have been treated unfairly: *The decision caused a lot of resentment among the staff.*

reservation /ˌrezəˈveɪʃ(ə)n/ noun **1** [C] an arrangement to have something such as a room in a hotel or a seat in a theatre kept for you to use=BOOKING **2** [C/U] a feeling of doubt about whether something is good or right

reserve¹ /rɪˈzɜːv/ noun **1** [C] a supply of something that a country, an organization, or a person can use: *Norway's oil reserves* ♦ *We discovered reserves of strength that we didn't realize we had.* **2** [C] a player who has not been chosen to play in a particular match but who is available to play if they are needed=SUBSTITUTE **3** [U] the behaviour of someone who tends not to talk about or show their feelings **4** [C] *British* an area of land where wild animals or plants are officially protected

PHRASE **in reserve** available to be used: *Keep a few pounds in reserve to cover unexpected costs.*

reserve² /rɪˈzɜːv/ verb ★
1 [I/T] to make an arrangement so that something such as a room in a hotel or a seat in a theatre is kept for you to use: *We've reserved a table for 7.30.*
2 [T] to keep something for a particular person, purpose, or situation: **reserve sth for sb/sth** *This area is reserved for non-smokers.*
PHRASE **reserve judgement** to not form an opinion about someone or something until you have more information

reserved /rɪˈzɜːvd/ adj **1** available to be used only by a particular person or group **2** someone who is reserved tends not to talk about or show their feelings

reservoir /ˈrezəvwɑː/ noun [C] **1** a lake, often an artificial one, where water is stored so that it can be supplied to houses, factories etc **2** a container, often part of a machine, where liquid is kept for a particular purpose

reset /ˌriːˈset/ (past tense and past participle **reset**) verb [T] **1** to press a special button, or to make changes, so that a machine will work again or will work in a different way

R

2 to put a broken bone back into its correct position

resettle /ˌriːˈset(ə)l/ verb [I/T] to go to live in a different region or country, or to be moved to a different region or country
—**resettlement** noun [U]

reshape /ˌriːˈʃeɪp/ verb [T] **1** to change the way that something operates **2** to change the shape of something

reshuffle /ˌriːˈʃʌf(ə)l/ verb [T] to change the jobs of the people in an organization
—**reshuffle** /ˈriːʃʌf(ə)l/ noun [C]

reside /rɪˈzaɪd/ verb [I] formal to live in a particular place

residence /ˈrezɪd(ə)ns/ noun [C] formal ★ a house or other place where someone lives: *the President's official residence*
PHRASE **in residence** living or working somewhere

residency /ˈrezɪd(ə)nsi/ noun [U] the legal right to live in a country

resident /ˈrezɪd(ə)nt/ noun [C] ★★ someone who lives in a particular place: *Many local residents have objected to the new road.* ♦ *They are both residents of the same village.* —**resident** adj

residential /ˌrezɪˈdenʃ(ə)l/ adj **1** a residential area is one in which most of the buildings are houses **2** relating to the fact that someone lives in a place

residual /rɪˈzɪdjuəl/ adj remaining after the rest of something has gone

residue /ˈrezɪˌdjuː/ noun [C] the part of something that remains after the rest has gone

resign /rɪˈzaɪn/ verb [I/T] ★ to state formally that you are leaving your job: *He made it clear that he was not resigning from active politics.* ♦ *He was forced to resign as mayor.*
PHRASE **resign yourself (to sth)** to accept that something unpleasant must happen and that you cannot change it: *I resigned myself to the fact that I'd never be thin.*

resignation /ˌrezɪɡˈneɪʃ(ə)n/ noun **1** [C/U] the act of leaving a job permanently: *Rebel groups have demanded the resignation of the government.* ♦ *The scandal resulted in Allen's resignation from his post.* **2** [U] the attitude of someone who accepts that something unpleasant must happen and that they cannot change it

resigned /rɪˈzaɪnd/ adj accepting that something unpleasant must happen and that you cannot change it

resilient /rɪˈzɪliənt/ adj **1** able to quickly become healthy or strong again after an illness or a problem **2** a resilient substance or object can return to its original shape after being bent, stretched, or pressed
—**resilience** noun [U]

resin /ˈrezɪn/ noun [U] a transparent sticky substance that is used for making paints, glue, and plastic

resist /rɪˈzɪst/ verb ★★
1 [I/T] to stop yourself from doing something that you would like to do: *It's difficult to resist a challenge like that.* ♦ *resist doing sth*

She couldn't resist asking him about his date.
2 [T] to oppose someone or something, or to fight against them: *Antibodies help us resist infection.* ♦ *One protester was injured while resisting arrest.*
3 [T] to not be affected or harmed by something: *The shelters are designed to resist heat.*

resistance /rɪˈzɪst(ə)ns/ noun ★★

1 not being affected	4 force
2 refusal of sth new	5 opposition group
3 opposition to sb/sth	

1 [singular/U] the ability not to be affected or harmed by something: *water resistance* ♦ *Vitamin A helps build resistance to infection.*
2 [singular/U] a refusal to accept something: *political resistance* ♦ *This proposal is meeting some resistance* (=some people do not accept it) *at the UN.*
3 [singular/U] military opposition to someone who is attacking you: *There was some resistance in the north.*
4 [U] a force that slows down a moving object: *wind resistance*
5 [singular] a secret organization that fights against the group that controls their country

resistant /rɪˈzɪst(ə)nt/ adj **1** not harmed or affected by something: *a flame-resistant material* **2** opposed to something

resit¹ /ˌriːˈsɪt, ˈriːsɪt/ (past tense and past participle **resat** /ˌriːˈsæt, ˈriːsæt/) verb [T] British to take an examination again

resit² /ˈriːsɪt/ noun [C] British an examination that you take again because you failed it the first time

resold the past tense and past participle of resell

resolute /ˈrezəluːt/ adj extremely determined —**resolutely** adv

resolution /ˌrezəˈluːʃ(ə)n/ noun ★
1 [C] a formal proposal that is considered by an organization and then voted on: *The UN passed a resolution* (=formally accepted it) *condemning the country's actions.*
2 [U] the act of solving a problem or of dealing with a disagreement: *a peaceful resolution of the conflict*
3 [C] a serious decision to do something: *Make a resolution to go to the gym once a week.*
4 [U] technical the amount of detail that you can see on a television or computer screen

resolve¹ /rɪˈzɒlv/ verb **1** [T] to solve a problem, or to find a way of dealing with a disagreement **2** [I] formal to make a determined decision to do something

resolve² /rɪˈzɒlv/ noun [U] formal determination

resort¹ /rɪˈzɔːt/ noun [C] a place where people go for a holiday: *a ski resort*
PHRASE **(as) a last resort** used for saying that you will do something only after trying everything else to solve a problem: *We*

R

would only expel a student as a last resort.

resort² /rɪˈzɔːt/ **PHRASAL VERB** re'sort to sth
to do something extreme or unpleasant in order to solve a problem: *protest groups that resort to violence*

resounding /rɪˈzaʊndɪŋ/ adj **1** a resounding victory, success, defeat etc is a very definite one **2** very loud

resource /rɪˈzɔːs/ noun ★★★
1 [C] something that you can use to achieve something: *We are increasing resources for the health service.* ♦ *The Internet has become a valuable resource in schools.* ♦ *a lack of educational resources*
2 [C] things that exist in nature and can be used by people: *Many of these countries are rich in mineral resources.*
3 resources [plural] the skills that someone has that they can use for dealing with problems: *He needed all his resources to escape alive.*

resourceful /rɪˈzɔːsf(ə)l/ adj good at finding effective ways to deal with problems

respect¹ /rɪˈspekt/ noun [U] ★★★
1 the attitude that someone is important and should be admired, and that you should treat them politely: *She has worked hard to gain the respect of her colleagues.* ♦ *Students show their respect for the teacher by not talking.* ♦ *Children should treat their parents with respect.*
2 respect for sth a feeling that something is important and deserves serious attention: *a healthy respect for the law*
3 an aspect of something: *In many respects, we are no different from other people.*
PHRASES in respect of or with respect to *formal* concerning: *The two groups are very similar with respect to age.*
with all (due) respect or with the greatest respect used for showing that you are going to disagree with someone in a polite way: *With all due respect, I think you're missing the point.*

respect² /rɪˈspekt/ verb [T] ★★
1 to treat someone in a way that shows that you think they are important and should be admired: *He is highly respected in his profession.* ♦ respect sb for (doing) sth *People will respect you for telling the truth.*
2 to understand the importance of something: *We expect all governments to respect the rights of minorities.*

Word family: respect

Words in the same family as respect
- respectable *adj*
- respectful *adj*
- respectability *n*
- disrespectful *adj*
- respectably *adv*
- respectfully *adv*
- respected *adj*
- disrespect *n*

respectable /rɪˈspektəb(ə)l/ adj **1** keeping to the accepted moral standards of your society, and not doing anything shocking or illegal **2** if an amount is respectable it is enough: *a respectable salary* —**respectability** /rɪˌspektəˈbɪləti/ noun [U], **respectably** adv

respected /rɪˈspektɪd/ adj admired and approved of by many people

respectful /rɪˈspektf(ə)l/ adj treating someone with respect —**respectfully** adv

respective /rɪˈspektɪv/ adj belonging to each of the people or things that you mentioned previously: *Jane and Patrick talked about their respective childhoods.*

respectively /rɪˈspektɪvli/ adv in the same order as the people or things you have mentioned: *Walsh and O'Neill were jailed for 12 and 11 years respectively.*

respirator /ˈrespəˌreɪtə/ noun [C] a machine that is used for helping people to breathe

respiratory /rɪˈspɪrət(ə)ri, ˈresp(ə)rət(ə)ri/ adj *medical* relating to the process of breathing —**respiration** /ˌrespəˈreɪʃ(ə)n/ noun [U]

respite /ˈrespɪt, ˈrespaɪt/ noun [singular/U] a short period of time in which a difficult or unpleasant situation stops ★★

respond /rɪˈspɒnd/ verb [I] ★★
1 to react to something by doing or saying something: *She hugged him, but he didn't respond.* ♦ *Protesters threw stones at police, who responded with rubber bullets.*
2 to reply, especially in writing: *Thousands of readers responded to our questionnaire.*
3 to react well to medical treatment: *The infection should respond to antibiotics.*

response /rɪˈspɒns/ noun [C] ★★★
1 a reaction: *Her response was to leave the room and slam the door.* ♦ *There was an enthusiastic response to the suggestions.* ♦ *In response to complaints, the company reviewed its safety procedures.*
2 an answer to a question in a test: *I'm sorry; the correct response was 'B'.*
3 a reply to a question or letter: *I've left messages, but there's been no response.*

responsibility /rɪˌspɒnsəˈbɪləti/ noun [U] ★★★
1 something that you have to do as a duty or a job: *She has a lot of responsibility as a nurse.* ♦ *Overall responsibility for the school lies with the head teacher.* ♦ *You will have responsibility for marketing.* ♦ *People in positions of responsibility cannot behave like this.*
2 blame for something bad that has happened: *Allan has got to take responsibility for the failure of the deal.* ♦ *No one has accepted responsibility for the attack on the embassy.*

responsible /rɪˈspɒnsəb(ə)l/ adj ★★★
1 if you are responsible for something that has happened, you caused it, or you deserve to be blamed for it: *Parents feel responsible when things go wrong.* ♦ *He was responsible for the accident.* ♦ *The farmer was held responsible for the damage done by his animals.*
2 in charge of someone or something: *The manager is responsible for the running of the theatre.*
3 sensible, reliable, and able to be trusted ≠ IRRESPONSIBLE: *She may be only 14, but she's very responsible.*
PHRASE be responsible to sb if you are responsible to someone, they are in a position of authority over you: *The prime*

R

minister and his ministers are responsible to Parliament.

responsibly /rɪˈspɒnsəbli/ adv in a sensible way that shows that you can be trusted

responsive /rɪˈspɒnsɪv/ adj **1** quick to react in the way that is right for a particular situation **2** willing to reply to a question or talk about something

rest¹ /rest/ noun ★★★

1 [singular] the part of something that remains, or the people or things that remain: *I'm not really hungry – do you want the rest?* ♦ *Rain will spread to the rest of the country by evening.* ♦ *The rest of the attackers were in jail.*

2 [C/U] a period of time that you spend relaxing or sleeping: *Can we stop for a minute? I need a rest.* ♦ *She has a rest after lunch.* ♦ *She took a well-earned rest from her studies.*

3 [C] an object that is used for supporting something → HEADREST

PHRASES **come to rest** to finally stop moving: *The car skidded across the road before coming to rest against a wall.*

lay/put sth to rest to finally show that something is not true

set/put sb's mind at rest to stop someone from worrying: *Tell me what happened, just to put my mind at rest.*

rest² /rest/ verb ★★★

1 [I] to spend a period of time relaxing or sleeping: *It would be nice to sit down and rest for a while.*

2 [T] to put something somewhere for support, especially a part of your body: *John was asleep, with his head resting on my shoulder.* ♦ *He rested the bag on the desk.*

3 [T] to not use a part of your body that is tired or injured, so that it can get better: *You'll need to rest your foot for at least two days.*

PHRASE **let sth rest** to stop discussing, examining, or dealing with something → ASSURED

PHRASAL VERBS **ˈrest on sth** or **ˈrest u͵pon sth** to be based on something: *The theory rests on the assumption that there are enough jobs for everyone.*

ˈrest with sb if a decision or responsibility rests with someone, they are the person that should decide it or deal with it: *Responsibility for child care rests with social services.*

restaurant /ˈrest(ə)rɒnt/ noun [C] ★★★ a building or room where meals and drinks are sold to customers sitting at tables: *an Italian/Mexican restaurant* ♦ *a chain of restaurants* → CAFÉ

rested /ˈrestɪd/ adj feeling full of energy again because you have had a rest

restful /ˈrestf(ə)l/ adj relaxing and peaceful

restless /ˈres(t)ləs/ adj **1** not willing or not able to keep still **2** not satisfied with the way that you are living and wanting to have new experiences —**restlessly** adv, **restlessness** noun [U]

restore /rɪˈstɔː/ verb [T] ★★

1 to make something exist again: *The lesson continued when order had been restored.* ♦ *The government is trying to restore confidence in the country's economy.* ♦ *Doctors say there's a possibility that his sight can be restored.*

2 to clean and repair something that is old and dirty or damaged: *The church has now been beautifully restored.*

3 to give something back to the person that it belongs to after it has been lost, taken, or stolen: *Most of the land has been restored to its original owners.*

—**restoration** /ˌrestəˈreɪʃ(ə)n/ noun [C/U]

restrain /rɪˈstreɪn/ verb [T] **1** to stop yourself or someone else from doing something **2** to control the movements of a person or animal

restrained /rɪˈstreɪnd/ adj controlled and not emotional

restraint /rɪˈstreɪnt/ noun **1** [U] an attempt to control your emotions, or to not do what you would like to do **2** [C/U] something that limits what you can do

restrict /rɪˈstrɪkt/ verb [T] ★★

1 to keep something within strict limits: **restrict sth to sth** *Doctors have restricted the number of visits to two per day.*

2 to physically limit or control the movement of something: *The drug restricts blood flow.*

restricted /rɪˈstrɪktɪd/ adj **1** not able to develop, to happen, or to do things freely: *Freedom of the press is restricted here.* **2** a restricted area is one that only particular people can go into: *This is a restricted area.*

restriction /rɪˈstrɪkʃ(ə)n/ noun [C] something, for example a law, that limits what you can do

restrictive /rɪˈstrɪktɪv/ adj strictly limiting or controlling something

restructure /ˌriːˈstrʌktʃə/ verb [T] to change the way that a company is organized —**restructuring** noun [C/U]

result¹ /rɪˈzʌlt/ noun ★★★

1 sth caused by sth else	**5** success from actions
2 score	**6** financial document
3 information obtained	**7** votes in election
4 mark in examination	

1 [C/U] something that is caused directly by something else: *He said the argument was the result of a misunderstanding.* ♦ *York Road will be closed and delays are likely as a result.* ♦ *Colby died as the result of a heart attack.* ♦ *Whichever method you use, the end result is the same.*

2 [C] the final score in a sports game, the number of votes that someone gets in an election, or the number of points that someone gets in a competition: *The election result was a disaster for the party.*

3 [C] a piece of information that you get by examining, studying, or calculating something: *The results of the survey will be published shortly.*

4 [C] *British* the mark that a student gets in an examination: *You should get your **exam results** next week.*

5 results [plural] success that you achieve: *He breaks rules, but he **gets results**.*

6 results [plural] *business* a financial document that shows how well a company has done over a particular period of time

7 results [plural] the number of votes that someone gets in an election: *We'll see who controls Congress **when the results are in*** (=when the winner is announced).

result² /rɪˈzʌlt/ verb [I] ★★★ to be caused directly by something that happened previously: *The arrests **resulted from** an anonymous telephone call.*

PHRASAL VERB re**sult in sth** to cause or produce something: *The crash resulted in the deaths of 14 passengers.*

resume /rɪˈzjuːm/ verb [I/T] *formal* to start something again after stopping temporarily, or to be started again after stopping temporarily: *Tom resumed his work.* ♦ *Talks will resume today.*

résumé /ˈrezjuːˌmeɪ/ noun [C] **1** a summary **2** *American* a CV

resumption /rɪˈzʌmpʃ(ə)n/ noun [singular/U] *formal* the act of starting something again after it had stopped

resurface /ˌriːˈsɜːfɪs/ verb **1** [I] to start to be noticed, or to start to be seen again: *Old tensions between the two countries have recently resurfaced.* **2** [I] to come back up to the surface of water **3** [T] to replace the surface of something such as a road

resurrect /ˌrezəˈrekt/ verb [T] **1** to make something exist again or start to be used again **2** to bring someone back to life after they are dead —**resurrection** noun [singular/U]

resuscitate /rɪˈsʌsɪˌteɪt/ verb [T] to make an unconscious person start to breathe again —**resuscitation** /rɪˌsʌsɪˈteɪʃ(ə)n/ noun [U]

retail¹ /ˈriːteɪl/ adj relating to the sale of goods directly to the public for their own use: *a retail outlet* (=a shop) → WHOLESALE —**retail** adv

retail² /ˈriːteɪl/ noun [U] the sale of goods directly to the public for their own use

retail³ /ˈriːteɪl/ verb [I/T] *business* to sell goods directly to the public for their own use, or to be sold directly to the public → WHOLESALE

retailer /ˈriːˌteɪlə/ noun [C] a person or company that sells goods directly to the public ≠ WHOLESALER

retailing /ˈriːˌteɪlɪŋ/ noun [U] the business of selling goods directly to the public

retain /rɪˈteɪn/ verb [T] *formal* **1** to keep someone or something: *We're trying to recruit and retain skilled staff.* **2** to remember ideas or information

retake /ˌriːˈteɪk/ (past tense **retook** /ˌriːˈtʊk/; past participle **retaken** /ˌriːˈteɪkən/) verb [T] **1** to take control of something, or to get something again, after you have lost it: *The army launched an operation to retake land captured by rebels.* **2** to take an examination again because you did not pass it the first time

retaliate /rɪˈtæliˌeɪt/ verb [I] to do something unpleasant to someone because they did something unpleasant to you —**retaliation** /rɪˌtæliˈeɪʃ(ə)n/ noun [U]

retention /rɪˈtenʃ(ə)n/ noun [U] *formal* **1** the act of keeping something **2** the ability to remember ideas or facts

rethink /ˌriːˈθɪŋk/ (past tense and past participle **rethought** /ˌriːˈθɔːt/) verb [I/T] to think about something such as an idea, plan, or system again in order to change it —**rethink** /ˈriːˌθɪŋk/ noun [C]: *a rethink of government security measures*

reticent /ˈretɪs(ə)nt/ adj not willing to talk to or provide information about something —**reticence** noun [U]

retina /ˈretɪnə/ noun [C] the part at the back of your eye that sends light signals to the brain

retinue /ˈretɪˌnjuː/ noun [C] a group of people who travel with and look after an important person

retire /rɪˈtaɪə/ verb [I] ★★
1 to stop working permanently, especially when you are old: *He **retired from** the army last month.* ♦ *Mrs Kenny **retired as** headteacher in July.*
2 *formal* to leave a place in order to go somewhere quieter: *In the evenings, Lloyd **retired to** his study to write.*
3 *literary* to go to bed at the end of the day

retired /rɪˈtaɪəd/ adj no longer working at a job, especially when you are old: *a retired teacher/police officer*

retirement /rɪˈtaɪəmənt/ noun [C/U] the time after you permanently stop working, or the act of permanently stopping work: *her retirement from politics*

retiring /rɪˈtaɪərɪŋ/ adj shy and not likely to enjoy social activities

retook the past tense of **retake**

retort /rɪˈtɔːt/ verb [T] to reply immediately in an angry or humorous way —**retort** noun [C]

retrace /rɪˈtreɪs/ verb **retrace your steps** to return along the same path that you have just travelled along

retract /rɪˈtrækt/ verb [I/T] to say that something that you previously said is not true —**retraction** /rɪˈtrækʃ(ə)n/ noun [C/U]

retrain /ˌriːˈtreɪn/ verb [I/T] to learn, or to teach someone, new skills that are needed for a job —**retraining** noun [U]

retreat¹ /rɪˈtriːt/ verb [I] **1** to move back in order to avoid a dangerous or unpleasant situation: *The army was forced to retreat.* **2** to change your previous opinion or decision about something, especially because of opposition to it

retreat² /rɪˈtriːt/ noun **1** [C] a peaceful and private place where you can go in order to rest **2** [C/U] an act of moving back in order to avoid a dangerous or unpleasant situation **3** [C/U] a change in someone's opinion or decision, especially because there is opposition to it

retrial /ˈriːˌtraɪəl/ noun [C] a second trial in a

R

court of law because the first one was unfair, or because it did not have a definite result

retribution /ˌretrɪˈbjuːʃ(ə)n/ noun [U] severe punishment for something bad, especially one that you think someone deserves

retrieve /rɪˈtriːv/ verb [T] **1** formal to go and get something back: *Bobby waded out into the lake to retrieve the ball.* **2** computing to find information that is stored in a computer —**retrieval** noun [U]

retrospect /ˈretrəʊˌspekt/ noun **in retrospect** used for saying that, when you think about a situation in the past, you would have done something differently if you had known then what you know now: *In retrospect, I should have told her the truth.*

retrospective¹ /ˌretrəʊˈspektɪv/ adj relating to things that have already happened or that have already been done: *a retrospective study/analysis* —**retrospectively** adv

retrospective² /ˌretrəʊˈspektɪv/ noun [C] an exhibition that includes examples of an artist's work from their whole career

retry /ˌriːˈtraɪ/ verb **1** [T] to judge someone in a court of law again because a previous trial was unfair, or because it ended without a definite result **2** [I] to try to do something again after the first attempt was not successful

return¹ /rɪˈtɜːn/ verb ★★★

1 go/come back	**4** go back to activity
2 put/send sth back	**5** do/say sth similar back
3 start to happen again	**+** PHRASE

1 [I] to go back to a place where you were earlier, or to come back from a place where you have just been: *He returned home around midnight.* ♦ *Seven years later we returned to the village.* ♦ *And when do you return from Paris?*

2 [T] to put, send, or take something back to the place where it came from: *She had to return the dress because it didn't fit.* ♦ **return sth to sb** *Please complete the questionnaire and return it to the personnel department.*

3 [I] to go back to a previous state or situation: *Once the holidays were over, our lives returned to normal.*

4 [I] to go back to a previous activity or subject: *She looked up, then returned to her reading.* ♦ *I'd like to return to what David was saying earlier.*

5 [T] to do or say something to someone that is similar to something that they have done or said to you: *I'm sorry I wasn't able to return your phone call earlier.* ♦ *Thanks for helping me. I'll try to return the favour some day.*

PHRASE **return a verdict** to say whether someone is guilty or not guilty of a crime in a court of law: *After several hours the jury returned a verdict of not guilty.*

return² /rɪˈtɜːn/ noun ★★★

1 going/coming back	**5** ticket
2 of activity/condition	**6** official (tax) form
3 sending etc sth back	**+** PHRASES
4 profit	

1 [singular/U] a situation in which you go back to a place or come back from a place: *Harry met Olivia shortly after his return from India.* ♦ *John was packing for his return to London.*

2 [singular/U] a situation in which a previous activity or condition starts again: *the country's return to democratic rule* ♦ *After a long winter, they eagerly awaited the return of spring.*

3 [C/U] the action of putting, sending, or taking something back to the place where it came from: *A reward is offered for the safe return of the medal.*

4 [C/U] a profit on money that you have invested: *We were able to get a return of 10% on our investment.*

5 [C] British a ticket that allows you to travel to a place and back again

6 [C] an official form on which you say how much your income is, so that the amount of tax that you owe can be calculated

PHRASES **in return** as a payment, exchange, or way of thanking someone: *What can we do in return for your kindness?*

many happy returns used as a greeting on someone's birthday

return³ /rɪˈtɜːn/ adj British relating to a trip to a place and back again, or to the trip that you take on the way back: *a return trip/ticket/journey*

reunification /ˌriːjuːnɪfɪˈkeɪʃ(ə)n/ noun [U] the process of joining together parts of a country that were divided, so that they form one country again

reunion /riːˈjuːnɪən/ noun **1** [C] a social event for people who have not seen each other for a long time: *a family reunion* **2** [C/U] a situation in which people meet again after a time when they have been separated

reunite /ˌriːjuːˈnaɪt/ verb [I/T] to bring people or groups together again after they have been separated for a time, or to be brought together again after being separated for a time

reuse /riːˈjuːz/ verb [T] to use something again —**reusable** adj

rev /rev/ or **rev (sth) 'up** verb [I/T] if you rev an engine, or if it revs, you press the ACCELERATOR with your foot when the vehicle is not moving in order to make the engine operate faster

Rev. abbrev Reverend

revamp /ˌriːˈvæmp/ verb [T] informal to improve the way that something looks or operates by making major changes to it —**revamp** noun [C]

reveal /rɪˈviːl/ verb [T] ★★★

1 to let something become known that was previously not known: *Cockpit recordings may reveal the cause of the crash.* ♦ *Neither side revealed what was discussed in the meeting.* ♦ **reveal sth to sb** *Plans for re-routing traffic have been revealed to residents.* ♦ **+(that)** *The survey revealed that many consumers are aware of the risks involved.*

2 to show something that was covered or

hidden: *She pulled back the curtain to reveal a table.*

revealing /rɪˈviːlɪŋ/ adj **1** providing new, surprising, or important information **2** showing a part of someone's body that is usually covered

revel /ˈrevl/ PHRASAL VERB ˈrevel ˌin sth to enjoy something very much

revelation /ˌrevəˈleɪʃ(ə)n/ noun **1** [C] a surprising piece of information: *revelations about his private life* **2** [singular] a surprising and enjoyable experience that makes you realize something that you previously had not known: *His piano-playing was a revelation.*

reveller /ˈrevələ/ noun [C] someone who enjoys themselves at a lively and noisy party or celebration

revenge /rɪˈvendʒ/ noun [U] something that you do in order to hurt or punish someone because they have hurt you or someone else: *I wanted to get revenge for the trouble she had caused.*

revenue /ˈrevəˌnjuː/ noun [C/U] income from business activities or taxes

reverberate /rɪˈvɜːbəˌreɪt/ verb [I] if a sound reverberates, it is repeated many times as it hits two opposite surfaces —**reverberation** /rɪˌvɜːbəˈreɪʃ(ə)n/ noun [C/U]

revere /rɪˈvɪə/ verb [T] *formal* to have a lot of respect and admiration for someone or something

reverence /ˈrev(ə)rəns/ noun [U] a strong feeling of respect and admiration

Reverend /ˈrev(ə)rənd/ a title that is used for some Christian priests and MINISTERS

reverie /ˈrevəri/ noun [C/U] *literary* pleasant thoughts that make you forget what is happening around you

reversal /rɪˈvɜːs(ə)l/ noun [C/U] a change in something, so that it becomes the opposite of what it was: *The decision was a complete reversal of government policy.*

reverse¹ /rɪˈvɜːs/ verb ★

1 [T] to change something such as a process, situation, decision, or policy so that it becomes the opposite of what it was: *The judge reversed the court's previous decision.* ♦ *products that claim to reverse the effects of aging*

2 [I/T] to go BACKWARDS in a vehicle, or to make a vehicle do this: *She reversed into the parking space.*

3 [T] to exchange your status with that of another person: *He's always taught me, but now the roles are reversed and I can teach him.*

4 [T] to turn something so that the part that is usually on the outside is on the inside: *You can reverse the jacket so that the pattern is on the outside.*

reverse² /rɪˈvɜːs/ adj opposite to what is usual or to what existed previously: *Now arrange the numbers in reverse order.*

reverse³ /rɪˈvɜːs/ noun **1 the reverse** [singular] the opposite of something: *The situation is the reverse of what it seems.* **2 the reverse**

[singular] the back side of a flat object **3** [U] the position in which you put a GEAR in a vehicle in order to make it go BACKWARDS: *Put the car in reverse.*

reversible /rɪˈvɜːsəb(ə)l/ adj **1** able to return or to be changed to a previous state ≠ IRREVERSIBLE: *The effects of the treatment are reversible.* **2** able to be used or worn with either side facing out: *a reversible jacket*

reversing light /rɪˈvɜːsɪŋ ˌlaɪt/ noun [C] *British* a light at the back of a car that warns other drivers that it is going backwards —*picture* → C6

revert /rɪˈvɜːt/ PHRASAL VERB reˈvert to sth to return to a previous state or way of behaving: *If you revert to your old eating habits, you'll gain weight again.*

review¹ /rɪˈvjuː/ noun ★★

1 [C/U] the process of examining something again in order to check it or make a decision about it: *Several aspects of prison practices are currently under review.* ♦ *A review of all government policy affecting the environment was announced.*

2 [C] an article in which someone gives their opinion of a play, book, exhibition etc: *The film got really good reviews.*

review² /rɪˈvjuː/ verb [T] ★★

1 to examine something again in order to check it or make a decision about it: *After reviewing the evidence, the committee decided he had a strong case.* ♦ *The progress of each child must be regularly reviewed.*

2 to write an article giving your opinion of a play, book, exhibition etc

reviewer /rɪˈvjuːə/ noun [C] someone whose job is to write articles giving their opinion about plays, books, exhibitions etc

revile /rɪˈvaɪl/ verb [T] *formal* to hate and criticize someone or something very much

revise /rɪˈvaɪz/ verb **1** [T] to change, improve, or make additions to something: *a revised draft of the treaty* **2** [I/T] *British* to study your notes and information again in order to prepare for an examination

revision /rɪˈvɪʒ(ə)n/ noun **1** [C/U] the process of changing, improving, or making additions to something: *He intends to undertake a major revision of the constitution.* ♦ *The article was published with a few revisions.* **2** [U] *British* the work of studying for an examination: *I can't go out – I've got to do some revision for my exams.*

revitalize /riːˈvaɪtəlaɪz/ verb [T] **1** to make something that is failing or weak become strong and successful again **2** to make someone feel or look healthy again

revival /rɪˈvaɪv(ə)l/ noun **1** [C/U] the process of becoming active, successful, or popular again: *a revival of interest in the subject* **2** [C] a new performance of something that has not been performed for a long time, such as a play

revive /rɪˈvaɪv/ verb [I/T] **1** to make someone become conscious or alive again, or to become conscious or alive again: *She had*

R

fainted, but soon revived. **2** to become active, successful, or popular again, or to make something do this: *His TV series revived interest in British history.*

revoke /rɪˈvəʊk/ verb [T] to officially say that a law or legal right no longer exists

revolt[1] /rɪˈvəʊlt/ verb **1** [I] to try to remove the government of your country by using force **2** [I] to say that you will not accept someone's authority **3** [T] if someone or something revolts you, they are so unpleasant that you feel slightly ill =DISGUST

revolt[2] /rɪˈvəʊlt/ noun [C/U] **1** an attempt to remove the government of a country by using force=REBELLION **2** a refusal to accept someone's authority

revolting /rɪˈvəʊltɪŋ/ adj extremely unpleasant=DISGUSTING

revolution /ˌrevəˈluːʃ(ə)n/ noun ★
1 [C/U] a situation in which people completely change their government or political system, usually by force: *the French/Russian Revolution* ♦ *a group committed to promoting revolution*
2 [C] a sudden or major change, especially in ideas or methods: *a sexual/cultural revolution* ♦ *the revolution in information technology*
3 [C/U] the movement of something in a circle around something else

revolutionary[1] /ˌrevəˈluːʃ(ə)n(ə)ri/ adj
1 relating to or supporting a political revolution: *a revolutionary movement* **2** new and completely changing the way that something is done or thought about: *a revolutionary idea*

revolutionary[2] /ˌrevəˈluːʃ(ə)n(ə)ri/ noun [C] someone who supports or takes part in a revolution

revolutionize /ˌrevəˈluːʃənaɪz/ verb [T] to completely change the way that something is done or thought about

revolve /rɪˈvɒlv/ verb [I/T] to turn or spin around a central point, or to make something do this —**revolving** /rɪˈvɒlvɪŋ/ adj

PHRASAL VERB **reˈvolve aˌround sth** to have something as a very important part or purpose: *little villages where life still revolves around the old church square*

revolver /rɪˈvɒlvə/ noun [C] a small gun that holds several bullets

revulsion /rɪˈvʌlʃ(ə)n/ noun [U] a feeling of dislike for someone or something that is enough to make you feel slightly ill =DISGUST

reward[1] /rɪˈwɔːd/ noun ★
1 [C/U] something good that happens or that you receive because of something that you have done: *Nursing is a tough job, but it has its rewards.* ♦ *You deserve a day off as a reward for working so hard.*
2 [C] money that is offered for help in finding someone or something: *There's a substantial reward for information leading to his capture.*

reward[2] /rɪˈwɔːd/ verb [T] to give someone

something such as praise or money as a reward

rewarding /rɪˈwɔːdɪŋ/ adj giving you satisfaction, pleasure, or profit
≠ UNREWARDING: *rewarding work*

rewind[1] /ˌriːˈwaɪnd/ (past tense and past participle **rewound** /ˌriːˈwaʊnd/) verb [I/T] if you rewind a video or a TAPE, or if it rewinds, it goes BACKWARDS to the beginning or to an earlier place

rewind[2] /ˌriːˈwaɪnd/ noun [singular/U] the button that you use in order to rewind a video or a TAPE

rework /ˌriːˈwɜːk/ verb [T] to make changes to something in order to improve it or use it for a new purpose

rewound the past tense and past participle of rewind[1]

rewrite[1] /ˌriːˈraɪt/ (past tense **rewrote** /ˌriːˈrəʊt/; past participle **rewritten** /ˌriːˈrɪt(ə)n/) verb [T] to make changes to a piece of writing, a computer program, or a law

rhetoric /ˈretərɪk/ noun [U] a style of speaking or writing that is intended to influence people: *anti-American rhetoric* —**rhetorical** /rɪˈtɒrɪk(ə)l/ adj, **rhetorically** /rɪˈtɒrɪk(ə)li/ adv

rheˌtorical ˈquestion noun [C] a question that you ask without expecting or wanting an answer

rheumatism /ˈruːmətɪz(ə)m/ noun [U] an illness affecting your JOINTS (=where bones are joined) or muscles so that they swell and become stiff and painful

rhinoceros /raɪˈnɒs(ə)rəs/ or **rhino** /ˈraɪnəʊ/ noun [C] a large animal with very thick grey skin and one or two horns on its nose —*picture* → C12

rhododendron /ˌrəʊdəˈdendrən/ noun [C/U] a large bush with big flowers and leaves that stay green all year

rhombus /ˈrɒmbəs/ noun [C] technical a shape with four straight sides of equal length and angles that are not 90° —*picture* → C8

rhubarb /ˈruːbɑːb/ noun [U] a plant with long red or pink stems that is cooked and eaten as a fruit

rhyme[1] /raɪm/ noun **1** [C] a short poem, often for children, that has lines ending in the same sound **2** [C] a word that ends with the same sound as another word **3** [U] the use of words that are rhymes, especially in poetry

rhyme[2] /raɪm/ verb [I] if two words or lines of poetry rhyme, they end with a similar sound: *'Boy' rhymes with 'toy'.*

rhythm /ˈrɪðəm/ noun [C] ★ a regular pattern of sounds in music: *He tapped out the rhythm on the table.* —**rhythmic** /ˈrɪðmɪk/ adj, **rhythmical** /ˈrɪðmɪkl/ adj, **rhythmically** /ˈrɪðmɪkli/ adv

rib /rɪb/ noun [C] one of the long curved bones in your chest

ribbed /rɪbd/ adj ribbed material has raised parallel lines on it

ribbon /ˈrɪbən/ noun **1** [C/U] a long narrow piece of coloured cloth or paper that is used for decorating or tying things **2** [C] a small piece of coloured cloth that is worn on a uniform as a military honour

'rib ,cage noun [C] the bones that curve around and protect the organs in your chest

rice /raɪs/ noun [U] ★ a food consisting of small white or brown grains that are eaten cooked

rich /rɪtʃ/ adj ★★★

1 having a lot of money	**5** of land/soil
2 rich people	**6** strong and attractive
3 having a lot of sth	**7** interesting
4 about food	

1 having a lot of money, property, or valuable possessions = WEALTHY ≠ POOR: *a rich man* ♦ *one of the world's richest countries* ♦ *People wanted to get rich by investing in Internet companies.*
2 the rich people who have a lot of money, property, or valuable possessions
3 containing a large quantity of something: *a rich source of protein* ♦ *an area rich in natural resources*
4 containing a lot of things such as butter, eggs, or cream that make your stomach feel full very quickly: *a rich chocolate dessert*
5 containing a lot of substances that are good for growing plants ≠ POOR: *rich agricultural land*
6 a rich colour, sound, or smell is strong in a nice way
7 interesting, with a lot of different qualities, experiences, or events: *a town with a rich cultural life*
—**richness** noun [U]

-rich /rɪtʃ/ suffix full of something: *an oil-rich country*

riches /'rɪtʃɪz/ noun [plural] *literary* large amounts of money, property, or valuable possessions

richly /'rɪtʃli/ adv **1** in a beautiful and expensive way: *a richly decorated palace* **2** with pleasant strong colours, flavours, or smells: *richly coloured silks* **3** completely: *He gave them the credit that they very richly deserved.* **4** with a lot of money or benefit: *He was richly rewarded for the help he gave.*

rickety /'rɪkəti/ adj a rickety structure or piece of furniture is likely to break if you put any weight on it

rickshaw /'rɪkʃɔː/ noun [C] a small vehicle with two wheels that is used for carrying passengers and is pulled by someone riding a bicycle or walking

ricochet /'rɪkəʃeɪ/ verb [I] to hit a surface at an angle and immediately move away from it at a different angle —**ricochet** noun [C]

rid¹ /rɪd/ adj ★★
PHRASES **be rid of** to be no longer affected by someone or something that is annoying, unpleasant, or not wanted: *Just give him the money and you can be rid of him.*
get rid of 1 to throw away, give away, or sell something that you no longer want or need: *We're moving, so we have to get rid of a lot of our furniture.* **2** to do something so that

you stop being affected by someone or something that is annoying or unpleasant: *I wish I could get rid of this cold.* ♦ *I'm sure he knew we were trying to get rid of him!*

rid² /rɪd/ (past tense and past participle **rid**)
PHRASAL VERB **'rid sb/sth of sb/sth** to stop a person or thing being affected by something that is annoying, unpleasant, or harmful, by removing it: *a movement to rid the world of nuclear weapons*

riddance /'rɪd(ə)ns/ noun **good riddance (to)** used for saying that you are pleased to be free of someone or something that is annoying or unpleasant

ridden the past participle of **ride¹**

riddle /'rɪd(ə)l/ noun [C] **1** a question that seems impossible or silly but that has a clever or funny answer **2** someone or something that is mysterious or confusing

riddled /'rɪd(ə)ld/ adj containing a lot of things that are bad or not wanted: *a project riddled with problems*

ride¹ /raɪd/ (past tense **rode** /rəʊd/; past participle **ridden** /'rɪd(ə)n/) verb ★★
1 [I/T] to sit on a bicycle, MOTORCYCLE, or an animal such as a horse and control it as it moves: *I learned to ride a bike when I was five.* ♦ *Have you ever ridden on a camel?*
→ DRIVE
2 [I] to be a passenger in a vehicle, especially a car or bus: *They rode to the wedding in a carriage.*
3 [I/T] to take part in a race on a horse, bicycle, MOTORCYCLE etc: *Are you riding in tomorrow's race?*
4 [I/T] to float, or to appear to float, on water or in the air: *Surfers rode the huge waves.*
PHRASAL VERBS **'ride on sth** to depend on something for success: *I feel as though my whole future is riding on this interview.*
,ride sth 'out to get to the end of a difficult or dangerous period or situation without any serious problems

ride² /raɪd/ noun [C] ★
1 a journey on a horse or other animal, on a bicycle or MOTORCYCLE, or in a vehicle: *The bus ride from the airport was very pleasant.* ♦ *I went for a ride in Jason's new car.* ♦ *Joe let us have a ride on his horse.*
2 a machine at an AMUSEMENT PARK (=a place outside where there are games and other activities) that people ride in for fun
PHRASES **a rough ride** or **not an easy ride** a period of time when you experience a lot of problems
take sb for a ride to trick, cheat, or lie to someone

rider /'raɪdə/ noun [C] someone who rides on an animal such as a horse, or on a vehicle such as a bicycle or MOTORCYCLE

ridge /rɪdʒ/ noun [C] **1** the long narrow top of a mountain or group of mountains **2** a long narrow raised line along the surface of something

ridicule¹ /'rɪdɪˌkjuːl/ verb [T] to try to make someone or something seem silly by making fun of them in an unkind way

R

ridicule[2] /ˈrɪdɪˌkjuːl/ noun [U] remarks or behaviour that are intended to make someone or something seem silly by making fun of them in an unkind way

ridiculous /rɪˈdɪkjʊləs/ adj silly or unreasonable and deserving to be laughed at=ABSURD: *a ridiculous idea* ♦ *She looks absolutely ridiculous in that hat.*
—**ridiculously** adv: *The test was ridiculously easy.*

riding /ˈraɪdɪŋ/ noun [U] the activity or sport of riding horses

rife /raɪf/ adj if something that is bad is rife, there is a lot of it

rifle[1] /ˈraɪf(ə)l/ noun [C] a large gun with a long BARREL

rifle[2] /ˈraɪf(ə)l/ or ˌ**rifle ˈthrough sth** verb [T] to search quickly through something in order to find something

rift /rɪft/ noun [C] **1** a disagreement between two people or groups **2** a crack or long narrow space that forms in a large mass of something such as rock

rig[1] /rɪg/ verb [T] to influence something such as an election in a dishonest way in order to produce a particular result
PHRASAL VERB ˌ**rig sth ˈup** to make something quickly out of whatever you can find

rig[2] /rɪg/ noun [C] a tall structure with equipment for getting oil or gas out of the ground

rigging /ˈrɪgɪŋ/ noun [U] the ropes and chains that are used for supporting a ship's sails and MASTS

right[1] /raɪt/ adv ★★★

1 exactly	4 towards the right
2 immediately	5 correctly/accurately
3 all the way	+ PHRASE

1 exactly: *Their office is right in the middle of town.* ♦ *'Am I late?' 'No, you're right on time.'* ♦ *Don't worry – I'm right behind you.*
2 immediately: *I liked her right from the start.* ♦ *Paul arrived right after me.* ♦ *She called and asked me to come over right away.* ♦ *Just a minute – I'll be right there.*
3 all the way or completely: *My foot went right through the floorboards.*
4 in the direction of your right side: *Turn right at the corner.*
5 correctly, or accurately: *You did it right the first time.*
PHRASE **right now** *spoken* **1** at the present time: *We're working on it right now.* **2** immediately: *Go to bed right now!*
→ RIGHTLY, SERVE[1]

right[2] /raɪt/ adj ★★★

1 correct	5 with needed qualities
2 morally correct	6 complete
3 in correct state etc	+ PHRASE
4 on one side of body	

1 correct according to the facts ≠ WRONG: *'D' is the right answer.* ♦ *Is this the right way to the station?* ♦ *You were absolutely right. My sweater was in the car.* ♦ *I think*

you were right about the colour – it doesn't match.
2 morally correct ≠ WRONG: *You did the right thing by telling them you had lied.* ♦ **it is only right to do sth** *I think it's only right to warn you that I'm looking for another job.* ♦ **it is right (of sb) to do sth** *It wasn't right of her to take it without asking.*
3 in the position, state, or situation that you would normally expect someone or something to be in ≠ WRONG: *She hadn't been feeling right for weeks.* ♦ *I noticed that some of the pictures weren't in the right place.*
4 on or relating to the side of your body that is towards the east when you are facing north ≠ LEFT: *Hold the bat in your right hand.*
5 the right person or thing has exactly the qualities that you want or need ≠ WRONG: *I'm not sure this is the right time to go on holiday.* ♦ *Harry's definitely the right person for the job.*
6 *British spoken* complete: *You've made a right mess of things.*
PHRASE **that's right** *spoken* used instead of 'yes' as an answer to a question or statement: *'So you're seeing James again tomorrow?' 'That's right.'*
→ ALL RIGHT[1], MR RIGHT

right[3] /raɪt/ noun ★★★

1 good behaviour	5 a turn to the right
2 sth that is allowed	6 in politics
3 permission to publish	+ PHRASES
4 side of your body	

1 [U] behaviour that is considered good or moral ≠ WRONG: *Do children of that age know the difference between right and wrong?*
2 [C] something that you are morally or legally allowed to do or have: *We are fighting for workers' rights.* ♦ *equal rights for women* ♦ *the right to political asylum* ♦ *We have every right to complain.* ♦ *You have no right to come barging in here like that.*
→ CIVIL RIGHTS
3 **rights** [plural] the legal authority to publish a book, play, film, piece of music etc, or to use it for a performance or production: *the film rights to her book*
4 [singular] the side of your body that is towards the east when you are facing north, or this direction ≠ LEFT: *Could you move a little to the right?* ♦ *It's the second door on your right.*
5 [C] a turn towards the right that is made by someone who is walking or driving: *Take a right at the art gallery.* ♦ *It's the first right (=the first street where you can turn right) after the supermarket.*
6 **the right** [singular] the political party or the group of people within a society who are conservative in their political views
PHRASES **in your own right** as a result of your own ability, achievements, qualifications etc and not because of anyone else: *Her father's a well-known author, but*

she's an excellent writer in her own right.
right of way 1 the legal right to pass in front of other vehicles when you are entering or crossing a road **2** the legal right to go across someone's private land **3** a path by which you can legally go across someone's private land

right⁴ /raɪt/ interjection ★
1 used for making someone pay attention before you say something: *Right! Is everybody ready to start?*
2 used for asking whether what you have said is correct: *You told everyone about tomorrow's meeting, right?*
3 used for saying that you agree with a statement or accept a suggestion or an order: *'Get some more milk when you're out.' 'Right.'*

right⁵ /raɪt/ verb [T] to put someone or something back into their usual upright position
PHRASE right a wrong to correct something that is bad or wrong that someone has done

right ˌangle noun [C] an angle of 90° —*picture* → C8 —**right-ˌangled** adj

right-ˈclick verb [I] *computing* to press the button on the right side of a computer **MOUSE**

righteous /ˈraɪtʃəs/ adj **1** righteous feelings of anger are caused by a belief that you are right to feel angry **2** *literary* morally good or correct

rightful /ˈraɪtf(ə)l/ adj *formal* officially or legally accepted as right or correct —**rightfully** adv

right-ˈhand adj on the right, or towards the right of someone or something ≠ LEFT-HAND: *the right-hand side of the bed*

right-ˈhanded /ˌraɪt ˈhændɪd/ adj naturally tending to use your right hand rather than your left to do things such as writing ≠ LEFT-HANDED —**right-ˈhanded** adv

right-hand ˈman noun [singular] the person that you regularly depend on to help you

rightly /ˈraɪtli/ adv **1** for a good reason: *Voters are rightly concerned about what is going to happen.* **2** correctly, or accurately: *As you rightly say, we must work carefully.*

ˌright ˈwing, the noun [singular] the most conservative group within a political party

right-ˈwing adj conservative in your political views ≠ LEFT-WING —**right-ˈwinger** noun [C]

rigid /ˈrɪdʒɪd/ adj **1** not easily changed: *a rigid class system* **2** done or applied in a strict and unreasonable way: *rigid discipline* **3** stiff, hard, and difficult to bend or move **4** not willing to change your ideas, attitudes, opinions etc —**rigidity** /rɪˈdʒɪdəti/ noun [U], **rigidly** adv

rigmarole /ˈrɪɡmərəʊl/ noun [singular] a long complicated process that seems unnecessary or silly

rigor /ˈrɪɡə/ the American spelling of **rigour**

rigorous /ˈrɪɡərəs/ adj **1** thorough and careful **2** strict, or severe —**rigorously** adv

rigour /ˈrɪɡə/ noun [U] **1** the quality of being thorough and careful **2** the quality of being strict or severe

PHRASE the rigours of sth the difficult and unpleasant aspects of a situation

rile /raɪl/ verb [T] to annoy someone

rim /rɪm/ noun [C] the edge of an open container or circular object → PACIFIC RIM

rind /raɪnd/ noun [C/U] **1** the outer skin of a fruit such as a lemon or orange **2** the hard outer edge of BACON or some types of cheese

ring¹ /rɪŋ/ (past tense **rang** /ræŋ/; past participle **rung** /rʌŋ/) verb ★★★

1 phone sb	6 surround sb/sth
2 of telephone	7 draw circle around sth
3 of bell	+ PHRASES
4 of ears	+ PHRASAL VERBS
5 of sound in a place	

1 [I/T] *British* to call someone on the telephone =CALL, PHONE, TELEPHONE: *Ring me at home later.* ♦ *Sarah rang to say she couldn't come tonight.* ♦ *I'm **ringing about** the vacancy you advertised.*
2 [I] if a telephone rings, it makes a sound in order to show that someone is calling: *The **phone rang** again immediately.*
3 [I/T] if a bell rings, or if you ring it, it makes a sound: *He rang the doorbell.* ♦ *The **bell rang**, and the children stood up.*
4 [I] if your ears are ringing, you continue to hear a loud sound in your head, for example after a loud noise
5 [I] if a sound rings in a place, or if a place rings with sound, the sound is loud and you can hear it clearly: *A great cheer rang through the hall.*
6 [T] to surround someone or something, especially in order to protect them or to prevent them from escaping: *Protesters carrying signs ringed the hotel.* ♦ *Ringed by soldiers for protection, he tried to address the crowd.*
7 [T] to draw a circle around something =CIRCLE: *She ringed the date on the calendar in the kitchen.*
PHRASES ring a bell *informal* to sound familiar to you: *The name rings a bell. Isn't he an architect?*
ring true to sound true or sincere: *I didn't think Green's explanation rang true.*
PHRASAL VERBS ˌring ˈback *British* to phone someone again later: *I'll ring back later.*
ˌring sb ˈback to phone someone who phoned you earlier: *Can you ask him to ring me back when he gets home?*
ˌring ˈin *British* to phone a place, especially the place where you work or a television or radio station: *John's **rung in sick** (=phoned his place of work in order to say that he is ill).*
ˌring ˈoff *British* to finish a phone call
ˌring ˈout *literary* to produce a loud clear sound
ˌring (sb) ˈup *British* same as **ring¹**1: *She rang up yesterday to make an appointment.*

ring² /rɪŋ/ noun ★★★

1 jewellery	5 group doing activity
2 sth shaped like circle	6 quality
3 bell sound	+ PHRASE
4 in boxing/wrestling	

1 [C] a piece of jewellery in the form of a circle that you wear on a finger: *She had a ring on every finger.* —picture → JEWELLERY

2 [C] something that is in the shape of a circle: *onion rings* ♦ *Kate had dark rings under her eyes.* ♦ *The kids sat in a ring around the fire.*

3 [C] the sound that a bell or telephone makes: *the ring of the doorbell* ♦ *I answered the phone on the first ring.*

4 [C] a raised area that is surrounded by ropes where people take part in BOXING or WRESTLING

5 [C] a group of people who are involved in an illegal activity: *an international drugs ring*

6 [singular] a particular quality that something such as a statement seems to have: *His version of events had a ring of truth.*

PHRASE **give sb a ring** British informal to call someone on the telephone: *Give me a ring tomorrow.*

ring finger noun [C] the third finger on your left hand, on which a WEDDING RING is traditionally worn —picture → C14

ringleader /'rɪŋliːdə/ noun [C] a leader of a group of people who are doing something that is illegal or wrong

ringlet /'rɪŋlət/ noun [C] a piece of long hair that hangs down in curls

ring road noun [C] British a road that is built around a large town or city in order to keep traffic away from the town centre

rink /rɪŋk/ noun [C] a large flat area where people go to SKATE

rinse¹ /rɪns/ verb [T] to wash something quickly in clean water in order to remove soap or dirt

PHRASAL VERB **rinse sth out** to wash the inside of something quickly with clean water

rinse² /rɪns/ noun **1** [C] a quick wash in clean water **2** [C/U] something that you put on your hair to change its colour for a short time

riot¹ /'raɪət/ noun [C/U] a violent protest by a crowd of people

PHRASE **run riot 1** to behave in a noisy and uncontrolled way **2** if your imagination or emotions run riot, you cannot control them

riot² /'raɪət/ verb [I] if people riot, they protest violently about something —**rioter** noun [C], **rioting** noun [U]

riotous /'raɪətəs/ adj **1** very lively and noisy: *riotous laughter* **2** behaving in a noisy and violent way: *The crowd was becoming riotous.*

rip¹ /rɪp/ verb **1** [I/T] to tear something quickly and with a lot of force, or to be torn in this way: *Stop pulling my shirt – it's going to rip.* ♦ *Jodie ripped the letter open.* ♦ **rip sth on sth** *I ripped my jeans on a sharp nail.* **2** [T] to remove something quickly by pulling hard: *We've ripped out the old fireplace.*

PHRASAL VERBS **rip sb off** informal to cheat someone by charging them too much money for something

rip through sth if something such as a fire, storm, or bomb rips though a place, it damages or destroys the place very quickly

rip sth up to tear something into small pieces

rip² /rɪp/ noun [C] a hole in something that is produced by tearing=TEAR: *My shirt has a big rip in it.*

ripe /raɪp/ adj ripe fruit or crops have grown to their full size and are ready to eat or use

PHRASES **be ripe for sth** to be ready for something, especially a change: *Some of the smaller firms are ripe for takeover.*

ripe old age an age at which someone is very old: *She lived to the ripe old age of 103.* —**ripeness** noun [U]

ripen /'raɪpən/ verb [I/T] to become ripe, or to make something become ripe

rip-off noun [C] informal something that is more expensive than it should be

ripple¹ /'rɪp(ə)l/ noun [C] **1** a small wave or series of small waves on the surface of a liquid **2** an emotion or reaction that spreads gradually through a person or a group: *a ripple of laughter/applause*

ripple² /'rɪp(ə)l/ verb [I/T] to move like small waves, or to make something move like small waves

rise¹ /raɪz/ (past tense **rose** /rəʊz/; past participle **risen** /'rɪz(ə)n/) verb [I] ★★★

1 move upwards	**7** be tall/high
2 increase	**8** oppose government
3 achieve success	**9** bread/cake grows
4 stand up	**+ PHRASE**
5 voice gets higher	**+ PHRASAL VERBS**
6 water increases	

1 to move upwards or to a higher position: *The aircraft rose slowly into the air.* ♦ *Thick black smoke rose from the middle of the town.* ♦ *As the sun rose in the sky, the clouds disappeared.*

2 to increase in size, amount, quality, or strength: *Temperatures will rise steadily towards the end of the week.* ♦ *Rising unemployment is our biggest problem.* ♦ *Tensions rose in the city as the day went on.* ♦ *Interest rates rise and fall according to the health of the economy.*

3 to achieve success, power, or a higher status: *I am sure she will rise to the top of her profession.* ♦ *He rose to power as a leader of the miners' union.*

4 formal to stand from a sitting, KNEELING, or lying position: *He rose and went to the window.*

5 if your voice rises, it gets higher, often because of a strong feeling

6 if an area of water rises, its level goes up: *The river rose and burst its banks.*

7 if something such as a building or mountain rises somewhere, it is tall or high and can be seen clearly: *Grey mountains rose above the lakes.*

8 to start to protest and fight against a government or leader=REBEL, REVOLT: *Eventually the people rose against the regime.*

9 if something such as bread or a cake rises, it increases in size when it is cooked

PHRASE **rise to the challenge/occasion** to deal successfully with a difficult problem or situation

PHRASAL VERBS ,rise a'bove sth to not let something bad affect you, because you have a strong character

,rise 'up *same as* **rise¹** 8: *The peasants rose up in revolt.*

Words often used with rise

Adverbs often used with rise (verb, sense 2)
■ RISE + **dramatically, markedly, quickly, rapidly, sharply, significantly, steeply, substantially, suddenly**: rise quickly or by a large amount in a short time

---

rise² /raɪz/ noun ★★★
1 [C] an increase in size, amount, quality, or strength: *The proposed tax rise was not unexpected.* ◆ *Serious crime is once again on the rise.* ◆ *the rise and fall of share prices* ◆ *the threat of a sudden rise in oil prices*
2 [singular] an increase in the power or influence of someone or something: *Fidel Castro's rise to power* ◆ *the rise of nationalism in the 1930s* ◆ *The series covers the rise and fall of the Third Reich.*
3 [C] *British* an increase in pay: *I'm going to ask for a rise next week.*
4 [singular] a movement upwards
PHRASE **give rise to sth** to make something happen or begin, especially something that is unpleasant or unexpected

---

Words often used with rise

Adjectives often used with rise (noun, sense 1)
■ **dramatic, marked, rapid, sharp, significant, spectacular, steep, substantial, sudden** + RISE: used about rises that are large and happen quickly

---

riser /'raɪzə/ noun **an early/late riser** someone who usually gets out of bed early/late

risk¹ /rɪsk/ noun ★★★
1 [C/U] the possibility that something unpleasant or dangerous might happen: *The risks to consumers are being analysed.* ◆ *There is a serious risk of a major nuclear accident.* ◆ **the risk of doing sth** *the risk of developing lung cancer* ◆ **+(that)** *There is a risk that the virus can be transferred from patient to doctor.*
2 [C] someone or something that is likely to be a danger or problem in the future: *a possible fire risk* (=something that could cause fire)
PHRASES **at your own risk** if you do something at your own risk, you are responsible for any harm or damage that you suffer as a result
at risk in a situation in which something that is unpleasant or dangerous could happen to you: *The laws will put many small businesses at risk.*
at the risk of doing sth used for saying that you realize that something bad or unpleasant may happen as a result of what

you are going to say: *At the risk of seeming boring, I don't think we should try it.*
a good/bad risk a person or company that is safe/not safe to lend money to or to give CREDIT to
run the risk (of sth) to be in a situation in which something that is bad could happen: *I didn't want to run the risk of seeing Neil again.*
take a risk to do something although you know that something that is unpleasant or dangerous could happen: *A good pilot never takes a risk.* ◆ **take the risk of doing sth** *I didn't want to take the risk of leaving John alone.*

risk² /rɪsk/ verb [T] ★★ to do something although you know that something that is bad could happen as a result: **risk sth on sth** *He risked a lot of money on the company.* ◆ **risk doing sth** *We don't want to risk becoming involved in a civil war.*
PHRASE **risk your life** to put yourself in a situation in which you could be killed

risky /'rɪski/ adj involving the possibility of danger, harm, or failure

risqué /'rɪskeɪ/ adj likely to offend some people, especially by referring to sex

rite /raɪt/ noun [C] a traditional ceremony, especially a religious one

ritual /'rɪtʃuəl/ noun [C/U] **1** a formal ceremony **2** something that you do regularly and always in the same way: *Their meetings became a weekly ritual.* —**ritual** adj

rival¹ /'raɪv(ə)l/ noun [C] ★
1 a person, team, or business that competes with another: *She scored twice as many points as her rival.*
2 someone or something that is as good as someone or something else: *The band has few rivals in the pop music world.*
—**rival** adj: *rival companies*

rival² /'raɪv(ə)l/ (present participle **rivalling**; past tense and past participle **rivalled**) verb [T] to be as good as someone or something else: *This small restaurant rivals any that you will find in the city.*

rivalry /'raɪv(ə)lri/ noun [C/U] a situation in which people, teams, businesses etc compete with one another

river /'rɪvə/ noun [C] ★★★ a large area of water that flows towards the sea: *They were swimming in the river.* ◆ *the River Nile*

riverside /'rɪvə,saɪd/ noun [singular] the land at the side of a river

rivet¹ /'rɪvɪt/ verb **be riveted by/to sth** to be so interested in something that you pay complete attention to it: *I was totally riveted by the pictures.*

rivet² /'rɪvɪt/ noun [C] a metal pin used for joining pieces of metal together

riveting /'rɪvɪtɪŋ/ adj extremely interesting or exciting: *a riveting performance*

road /rəʊd/ noun [C] ★★★ a way that leads from one place to another that cars and other vehicles can use: *He was driving on the wrong side of the road.* ◆ *They live on Lockwood Road.* ◆ *The journey is about three*

R

hours by road. ♦ *There's a supermarket just up the road* (=not far away on the same road).

PHRASES down the road *informal* used for talking about what may happen in the future: *Two years down the road, you might feel very differently.*

on the road travelling in a car, bus, or truck, especially for a long distance or a long period of time

the road to sth a process or series of events that will achieve something or have a particular result: *It's an important step on the road to democracy.*

→ HIT¹

■ A **road** is built for vehicles to travel along and can have buildings on each side. It can be wide or narrow, and it can be in a town or can join different towns: *My school is just down the road.* ♦ *the road from Oxford to Bath*

■ A **street** is a road in a town, with buildings such as houses and shops along its sides: *They live on a busy street.*

■ A **path** is a way from one place to another for people to walk along: *a path leading into the forest*

roadblock /'rəʊdˌblɒk/ noun [C] a part of a road where police or soldiers stop traffic

road map noun [C] a map that shows all the main roads and motorways in a region or country

road rage noun [U] violent behaviour by a driver towards another driver

roadside /'rəʊdˌsaɪd/ noun [C] the area at the edge of a road

roadway /'rəʊdˌweɪ/ noun [C] the part of a road that you drive on

roadworks /'rəʊdˌwɜːks/ noun [plural] *British* repairs that are done to the surface of a road

roadworthy /'rəʊdˌwɜːði/ adj safe to drive

roam /rəʊm/ verb [I/T] to move or travel with no particular purpose: *Young men roamed the streets.*

roar¹ /rɔː/ verb **1** [I/T] to shout, speak, or laugh very loudly: *The crowd roared as the team ran onto the pitch.* ♦ *Barney roared with laughter.* **2** [I] to make a continuous very loud noise: *Military planes roared overhead.* **3** [I] if a lion roars, it makes a deep loud sound **4** [I] if a vehicle roars somewhere, it travels there very quickly and noisily: *We sat and waited as the traffic roared past.*

roar² /rɔː/ noun [C] **1** a loud continuous sound: *the roar of the waves* ♦ *a roar of anger* **2** the loud deep sound that a lion makes

roaring /'rɔːrɪŋ/ adj **1** a roaring fire burns very brightly and produces a lot of heat **2** making a loud deep noise: *a roaring waterfall*

PHRASES be a roaring success *British* to be very successful

do a roaring trade (in sth) to sell large quantities of something in a short period of time

roast¹ /rəʊst/ verb [I/T] to cook meat or vegetables in an oven

roast² /rəʊst/ noun [C] a large piece of meat that has been cooked in an oven

roast³ /rəʊst/ adj cooked in an oven: *roast beef*

rob /rɒb/ verb [T] **1** to take money or property from someone illegally: *They were planning to rob the museum.* **2** to take something such as an opportunity, ability, or quality from someone: *The shock had robbed her of the power of speech.*

robber /'rɒbə/ noun [C] someone who steals money or property

robbery /'rɒbəri/ noun [C/U] the crime of stealing money or property → DAYLIGHT ROBBERY

robe /rəʊb/ noun [C] **1** a DRESSING GOWN **2** a long loose piece of clothing that is worn by a priest or other important person

robin /'rɒbɪn/ noun [C] a small brown European bird with a red chest

robot /'rəʊbɒt/ noun [C] a machine that can do work by itself, often work that humans do —**robotic** /rəʊ'bɒtɪk/ adj

robust /rəʊ'bʌst/ adj **1** a robust person is strong and healthy **2** a robust object is strong and unlikely to break **3** firm and determined: *a robust approach*

rock¹ /rɒk/ noun ★★★

1 [C/U] the hard solid substance that forms part of the Earth's surface, or a piece of this substance on the ground: *a layer of rock* ♦ *a castle built on a rock* ♦ *The waves crashed against the rocks.*

2 [U] ROCK MUSIC: *a rock star* ♦ *rock concerts*

PHRASE rock 'n' roll or **rock and roll** music for dancing that is played on guitars. It was popular in the 1950s.

rock² /rɒk/ verb **1** [I/T] to move gently BACKWARDS and forwards or from side to side, or to make someone or something do this: *He sat and rocked the baby to sleep.* ♦ *Hold your knees close to your chest and rock from side to side.* **2** [T] *mainly journalism* to shock, surprise, or frighten someone: *Spain has been rocked by another political scandal.* **3** [T] if an explosion or EARTHQUAKE rocks something, it makes it shake violently: *The blast rocked the houses in the street.*

PHRASE rock the boat *informal* to cause problems by changing a situation that other people do not want to change

rock bottom noun [U] the lowest possible level: *Confidence in the company is at rock bottom.* —**rock-bottom** adj: *rock-bottom prices*

rocket¹ /'rɒkɪt/ noun **1** [C] a vehicle that is shaped like a tube that travels in space **2** [C] a weapon that is shaped like a tube that flies through the air and explodes when it hits something **3** [C] a FIREWORK that is shaped like a tube that flies up into the air when you light it and then explodes **4** [U] *British* a vegetable with leaves with a strong flavour that are eaten raw in salads

rocket² /'rɒkɪt/ verb **1** [I/T] *informal* to suddenly become very successful, or to make someone do this **2** [I] to increase suddenly

R

'rocking ,chair noun [C] a chair on two curved pieces of wood that moves gently BACKWARDS and forwards when you are sitting in it

'rock ,music noun [U] music that has a heavy regular beat and that is played on electric guitars

rocky /'rɒki/ adj covered with rocks, or made of rock

rod /rɒd/ noun [C] a long thin bar or stick made of metal, plastic, or wood

rode the past tense of **ride**[1]

rodent /'rəʊd(ə)nt/ noun [C] a type of small animal that has long sharp front teeth, for example a mouse

rodeo /rəʊ'deɪəʊ, 'rəʊdiəʊ/ (plural **rodeos**) noun [C] a sports event in which COWBOYS compete by riding wild horses or catching CATTLE with ropes

roe /rəʊ/ noun [U] fish eggs that are eaten as food

rogue[1] /rəʊg/ noun [C] someone who behaves badly but is liked by other people

rogue[2] /rəʊg/ adj a rogue member of a group does not behave in the same way as its other members and is considered dangerous: *a rogue state*

role /rəʊl/ noun [C] ★★★
1 the purpose or influence that someone or something has: *It's not my role to tell the politicians what to do. ♦ The book examines* **the role of** *food and drink in society. ♦ We expect parents to have* **a key role in** *this discussion. ♦ Trade unions have* **played a** *significant* **role** *in the recent debate.*
2 the character that is played by a particular actor in a film or play=PART: *Who is playing the role of Hamlet?*

> **Words often used with role**
>
> *Adjectives often used with role (sense 1)*
> ■ **central, crucial, important, key, leading, major, prominent, significant, vital** + ROLE: used about roles that have an important influence on a situation

'role ,model noun [C] someone whose behaviour is a good example for other people to copy

'role-play noun [C/U] an activity in which you pretend to be someone else, especially in order to learn new skills

roll[1] /rəʊl/ verb ★★★

1 move while turning	**6** flow
2 move on wheels	**7** make substance flat
3 move from side to side	**8** machine: work
4 change body position	**+ PHRASES**
5 wrap sth around itself	**+ PHRASAL VERBS**

1 [I/T] to move forwards while turning over and over, or to make something do this: *The pencil went rolling across the floor. ♦ Men were rolling tyres across the yard.*
2 [I/T] to move on wheels, or to move something that is on wheels: *The car rolled to a stop at the side of the road. ♦ We rolled the piano to the front of the stage.*

3 [I] to move from side to side: *The pigs were rolling in the mud.*
4 [I] to change the position of your body when you are lying down: *He rolled onto his back and looked up at me.*
5 [T] to fold something or wrap it around itself so that it forms a tube or a ball: *I always roll my clothes when I pack them. ♦* **roll sth into sth** *Take a piece of the mixture and roll it into a ball.*
6 [I] if a drop of liquid rolls, it moves across a surface without stopping: *Rain drops rolled down the window.*
7 [T] to make a substance flat by pushing something across it: *Roll the dough very thinly.*
8 [I] if a machine such as a camera is rolling, it is working: *Although the interview had ended, the cameras were still rolling.*

PHRASES **(all) rolled into one** if someone is several things rolled into one, they are all of those things at the same time
be rolling in money/it *informal* to have a lot of money
roll your eyes to move your eyes upwards in order to show that you are annoyed or impatient
→ BALL

PHRASAL VERBS **,roll 'in** to arrive in large numbers or amounts
,roll 'up *informal* to arrive somewhere late: *They eventually rolled up at lunchtime.*
,roll sth 'up 1 if you roll your sleeves or the legs of your trousers up, you fold the cloth several times until they are shorter **2** *same as* **roll**[1] 5: *She rolled her scarf up and put it into her bag.*

roll

roll[2] /rəʊl/ noun [C] ★

1 sth rolled into tube	**4** official list of names
2 small loaf of bread	**5** continuous low sound
3 action of rolling	**+ PHRASE**

1 a long piece of something such as paper or carpet that is rolled into the shape of a tube: *We used ten* **rolls** *of wallpaper.*
2 bread in the form of a small round or long shape → SAUSAGE ROLL
3 the action of turning over or rolling from side to side: *The constant roll of the ship made her feel ill.*
4 an official list of names
5 a continuous low sound made by drums or THUNDER

PHRASE **be on a roll** *informal* to be having a lot of success or good luck

R

roll call noun [C/U] the process of reading out an official list of people's names in order to see who is present

roller /'rəʊlə/ noun [C] **1** something that is shaped like a tube that goes over a surface in order to make it flat or in order to crush, spread, or print something **2** a small tube that you wind some of your hair around in order to make a curl = CURLER

Rollerblades /'rəʊləˌbleɪdz/ trademark boots with a single row of small wheels along the bottom

roller coaster noun [C] **1** a structure like a tall railway with steep slopes that people ride on for fun at an AMUSEMENT PARK **2** a situation in which there are many big and sudden changes

roller skates noun [plural] boots with four small wheels on the bottom —**roller-skate** verb [I], **roller skating** noun [U]

rolling /'rəʊlɪŋ/ adj rolling land has a lot of gentle slopes

rolling pin noun [C] a piece of kitchen equipment that you roll over PASTRY in order to make it flat and thin

ROM /rɒm/ noun [U] computing read-only memory: the part of a computer's memory that is permanent and cannot be changed

Roman[1] /'rəʊmən/ adj of ancient Rome or its EMPIRE, or from ancient Rome or its EMPIRE

Roman[2] /'rəʊmən/ noun [C] someone from ancient Rome or its EMPIRE

Roman Catholic noun [C] a member of the part of the Christian Church that has the POPE as its leader —**Roman Catholic** adj, **Roman Catholicism** noun [U]

romance /rəʊ'mæns/ noun **1** [C] a short exciting romantic relationship **2** [U] the behaviour that is typical of two people who love each other: She wasn't in a mood for romance. **3** [C] a book or film about a romantic relationship **4** [U] a feeling of excitement that you get from a particular place, activity, or experience: the romance of travel

Roman numeral noun [C] one of the letters 'I', 'V', 'X', 'L', 'C', 'D', and 'M' that are sometimes used for representing numbers

romantic[1] /rəʊ'mæntɪk/ adj **1** involving love, or making you have feelings of love: We had a romantic dinner in an expensive restaurant. ♦ romantic relationships **2** tending to believe that things are better or more exciting than they really are: a romantic vision of life on a farm —**romantically** /rəʊ'mæntɪkli/ adv

romantic[2] /rəʊ'mæntɪk/ noun [C] **1** someone who does things that show their love **2** someone who believes that things are better or more exciting than they really are

romanticize /rəʊ'mæntɪˌsaɪz/ verb [T] to think that something is better or more exciting than it really is

Romany /'rɒməni, 'rəʊməni/ noun [C] a member of a group of people who originally came from India and who sometimes travel around rather than live in one place

romp /rɒmp/ verb [I] to play in a lively way —**romp** noun [singular]

roof /ruːf/ noun [C] ★★★
1 the top outer part of a building or vehicle: The roof is leaking again. —picture → C1
2 the hard top part of the inside of your mouth

PHRASES **go through the roof 1** informal to increase quickly to a very high level **2** informal to suddenly become extremely angry

a roof over your head a place to live
→ HIT[1]

roofing /'ruːfɪŋ/ noun [U] **1** material used for making roofs **2** the process of building or repairing roofs

roof rack noun [C] British a frame on the roof of a car that is used for carrying large objects —picture → C6

rooftop /'ruːfˌtɒp/ noun [C] the roof of a building

rook /rʊk/ noun [C] **1** a large black European bird like a CROW **2** a piece in the shape of a tower used in CHESS —picture → C16

rookie /'rʊki/ noun [C] American informal someone who has just started doing a job and does not have much experience

room /ruːm/ noun ★★★
1 [C] a part of a building with a floor, walls, and a ceiling: Annie ran out of the room.
2 [C] a bedroom in a home or a hotel: My mum told me to tidy my room. ♦ I'm staying in Room 52.
3 [U] the amount of space that you need for a particular purpose: There isn't much room in here. ♦ This table takes up too much room. ♦ Is there room for another person in your car? ♦ room to do sth The band was good, but there was no room to dance. → PLACE
4 [U] the possibility for something to happen: There is room for improvement in his work (=it is not very good).

roommate /'ruːmˌmeɪt/ noun [C] someone who you share a room with

room service noun [U] the service that you use when you ask a hotel to bring food and drinks to your room

roomy /'ruːmi/ adj large and providing you with a lot of space: a roomy car

roost /ruːst/ noun [C] a place where birds rest and sleep
PHRASE **rule the roost** to control a situation —**roost** verb [I]

rooster /'ruːstə/ noun [C] a male chicken

root[1] /ruːt/ noun ★★
1 [C] the part of a plant that grows under the ground: Olive trees have deep roots. —picture → TREE
2 [C] the part of a hair, tooth, or nail that is under your skin
3 [C] a basic cause or idea: We need to get to the root of the problem.
4 roots [plural] the place, culture, or family that someone comes from originally
PHRASES **put down roots** to become a part of the community where you live by

R

making friends and taking part in local activities

take root if an idea or system takes root, it becomes established

root² /ruːt/ verb [I] to search for something by putting your hand deep into a place and pushing things around: *He rooted around in his coat pocket for some change.*

PHRASAL VERBS 'root for sb *informal* to support someone in a game or competition ,root sth 'out to find something that is bad and get rid of it

rooted /'ruːtɪd/ adj **rooted in sth** if one thing is rooted in another, it is based on it or it has developed from it

PHRASE be rooted to the spot to be unable to move because you are suddenly very frightened or surprised

rope¹ /rəʊp/ noun ★★
1 [C/U] a type of very thick string that can be used for tying or pulling things
2 the ropes [plural] the correct way of doing something: *You spend the first few days learning the ropes.* ♦ *One of our most experienced workers will show you the ropes.*

PHRASE on the ropes *informal* affected by serious problems, and likely to fail

rope² /rəʊp/ verb [T] to tie people or things together with a piece of rope

PHRASAL VERBS ,rope sb 'in *informal* to persuade someone to do something that they do not really want to do
,rope sth 'off to put ropes around an area in order to prevent people from entering it

ropey or **ropy** /'rəʊpi/ adj *informal* not very good

rosary /'rəʊzəri/ noun [C] a set of BEADS used by Catholics for counting prayers

rose¹ /rəʊz/ noun [C] ★ a flower that has a sweet smell and sharp THORNS on its stem, or the bush that it grows on —*picture* → C9

rose² the past tense of **rise¹**

rosé /'rəʊzeɪ/ noun [U] a type of wine that is pink

rosemary /'rəʊzməri/ noun [U] a bush with narrow leaves that are used as a HERB in cooking

rosette /rəʊ'zet/ noun [C] a circular decoration that is given to someone as a prize or worn by supporters of a political party

roster /'rɒstə/ noun [C] a list of people's names that shows when each person has to do a particular job

rostrum /'rɒstrəm/ noun [C] a small raised area that you stand on so that an audience can see you

rosy /'rəʊzi/ adj **1** pink **2** likely to be successful or happy: *a rosy future*

rot¹ /rɒt/ verb [I/T] to decay, or to make something decay

rot² /rɒt/ noun **1** [U] decayed material, or the process of decaying **2 the rot** [singular] the process by which a situation gradually gets much worse: *This government has got to stop the rot in the health service.* ♦ *Once*

officers start accepting money, that's when the rot sets in (=starts).

rota /'rəʊtə/ noun [C] *British* a list of people's names that shows when each person has to do a particular job

rotary /'rəʊtəri/ adj with parts that turn around a central point

rotate /rəʊ'teɪt/ verb [I/T] **1** to move in a circle around a central point, or to move something in this way: *The Earth rotates 360 degrees every 24 hours.* **2** if people or things rotate, or if you rotate them, you change them regularly in a fixed order

rotation /rəʊ'teɪʃ(ə)n/ noun **1** [C/U] movement in a circle around a central point **2** [U] the process of regularly changing people or things in a fixed order

rote /rəʊt/ noun **learn sth by rote** to learn something by repeating it many times rather than by understanding it

rotten /'rɒt(ə)n/ adj **1** decayed: *rotten eggs/fruit/teeth* **2** *informal* unpleasant: *They were really rotten to him!* ♦ *If it rains all the time, we'll have a rotten holiday.* **3** *informal* of a low quality, standard, or ability: *She's a rotten singer.* **4** *informal* used for emphasizing what you are saying when you are annoyed: *I didn't want the rotten job anyway!*

rottweiler /'rɒt,waɪlə/ noun [C] a large strong dog with smooth black and brown hair

rough¹ /rʌf/ adj ★★

1 not smooth	4 with crime/violence
2 difficult	5 not finished/exact
3 not gentle	6 not feeling well

1 with a surface that is not smooth: *The walls were built of dark rough stone.* ♦ *a rough dirt track* ♦ *strong winds and rough seas*
2 *informal* difficult and full of problems: *I've had a really rough day at the office.*
3 not gentle ≠ GENTLE: *Don't be so rough with her, James. She's only a baby.*
4 a rough place is not pleasant because there is a lot of crime or violence there
5 not completely finished, or not exact: *Can you give me a rough idea of the cost?* ♦ *Here is a rough draft for you to read.*
6 *British informal* if someone feels rough, they do not feel well
—**roughness** noun [U]
→ ROUGHLY

rough² /rʌf/ verb **rough it** *informal* to live for a short time without things that you usually live with, for example water or electricity

PHRASAL VERB ,rough sb 'up *informal* to physically attack someone

rough³ /rʌf/ noun [singular] the part of a GOLF COURSE where the grass is tall and not cut —*picture* → C15

PHRASES in rough if you do a piece of written work in rough, you do it in a form that you will finish or improve at a later time

take the rough with the smooth to accept the bad things that happen as well as the good things

R

rough⁴ /rʌf/ adv **sleep/live rough** British to sleep or live outside because you do not have a home

,rough-and-'tumble noun [U] **1** the rough way in which a particular activity is usually done: *the rough-and-tumble of a political campaign* **2** the rough behaviour of children who are playing

roughen /'rʌf(ə)n/ verb [T] to make something rough

roughly /'rʌfli/ adv ★
1 used for showing that an amount or number is not exact=APPROXIMATELY: *The meeting lasted roughly 45 minutes.*
2 in a way that is not gentle: *He pushed roughly past her.*
PHRASE roughly speaking used for giving information that is not exact: *There are, roughly speaking, three possible solutions to our problem.*

roughshod /'rʌfʃɒd/ adv **ride roughshod over** to behave in a way that shows that you have no respect for someone or something

roulette /ru:'let/ noun [U] a game in which a small ball is thrown onto a moving wheel. People try to win money by guessing where the ball will stop.

round¹ /raʊnd/ adv, preposition British ★★★
1 in circles moving in a circular way: *The children were dancing round in a circle.* ♦ *The bird flew round and round the room, unable to escape.*
2 in or to many places in or to many different parts or areas: *He wandered round the town, looking in shop windows.* ♦ *Books and papers were scattered round the room.* ♦ *All round the country factories are closing.*
3 into the opposite direction moving so that you face in the opposite direction: *Katharine spun round to face him.* ♦ *The car stopped, turned round, and came back towards us.*
4 to the opposite side moving so that you can get to the opposite side of something: *He walked round to the back of the building.*
5 near a place in or close to a particular place or area: *She loved the countryside round Oxford.* ♦ *Do you live round here?*
6 surrounding sb/sth surrounding someone or something: *He tied one end of the rope round his waist.* ♦ *There was a high brick wall round the garden.* ♦ *The children crowded round to see what was happening.*
7 not doing anything spending time in a place and not doing much: *They spend all their time sitting round drinking coffee.*
8 at sb's house at or to someone's house: *She's round at Patrick's.* ♦ *Why don't you invite him round for dinner?*
PHRASE round about informal used for showing that you are guessing a time or number: *We got there round about half past nine.*
→ ABOUT, AROUND, CIRCLE¹, CORNER¹

round² /raʊnd/ adj ★★★
1 shaped like a circle or a ball: *a round table*
2 not exact, but given as a WHOLE NUMBER or as a number ending in zero: *They quoted*

a round figure of £100 million.
—**roundness** noun [U]

round³ /raʊnd/ noun [C] ★★

1 (one of) a series	**5** drink for all in group
2 stage in competition	**6** part of boxing match
3 series of visits	**7** complete game of golf
4 bullet/shot	✦ PHRASE

1 one of a series of similar events: *The next round of peace talks will be held in Rome.*
2 a stage in a competition or election: *Brazil beat the United States in the second round of the World Cup.*
3 a series of visits to different people or places that is made as part of someone's job: *Both doctors were out on their rounds.* ♦ *The bag was found by a postman on his morning delivery round.*
4 a bullet or a shot that is fired from a weapon: *Those guns are capable of firing 1,250 rounds per minute.*
5 a drink for each of the people in a group: *Tom bought a round of drinks.*
6 one of the periods of fighting in a BOXING or WRESTLING match: *He knocked out his opponent in the fourth round.*
7 a complete game of golf: *He likes to play a round of golf on Saturdays.*
PHRASE a round of applause a period of time when an audience reacts by CLAPPING their hands

round⁴ /raʊnd/ verb [T] to go round something: *The van had just rounded the corner.*
PHRASAL VERBS ,round sth 'down to reduce a number to the nearest WHOLE NUMBER, or to the nearest number ending in zero
,round sth 'off 1 to end something in a satisfactory way: *They rounded off their six-match tour with a brilliant victory.* **2** to make an angle or surface curved and smooth: *Use a sharp knife to round off the edges.*
,round sth 'up to increase a number to the nearest WHOLE NUMBER, or to the nearest number ending in zero
,round sb/sth 'up to bring people or animals together in one place for a particular purpose

roundabout¹ /'raʊndə,baʊt/ noun [C] British **1** a circular area where three or more roads meet **2** a circular structure in a PLAYGROUND that children sit on while someone pushes it round → SWING²

roundabout² /'raʊndə,baʊt/ adj not direct, simple, or short: *a roundabout route*

rounded /'raʊndɪd/ adj something that is rounded has a curved shape or surface

rounders /'raʊndəz/ noun [U] a game played in the UK that is similar to baseball

roundly /'raʊndli/ adv in a strong clear way: *Their tactics were roundly condemned.*

,round-the-'clock adj happening all day and all night

,round 'trip noun [C] a journey to a place and back again

'round-up noun [C] **1** a summary of the news **2** an occasion when people or animals are forced together into one place

rouse /raʊz/ verb [T] **1** to make someone have strong feelings, or to make someone want to take strong action **2** *formal* to wake someone up

rousing /ˈraʊzɪŋ/ adj making people have strong feelings: *a rousing speech/song*

rout /raʊt/ verb [T] to completely defeat someone in a battle, competition, or election —**rout** noun [C]

route¹ /ruːt/ noun [C] ★★
1 the roads or paths that you use when you go from one place to another: *The tunnel is the route taken by most drivers.* ♦ *The most direct route from the house to the school is through the town centre.*
2 a way of doing something: *I'll need to think carefully before deciding what route to take next.* ♦ *the route to success/happiness*
→ EN ROUTE

route² /ruːt/ verb [T] to send someone or something along a particular route

routine¹ /ruːˈtiːn/ noun ★
1 [C/U] your usual way of doing things: *It shouldn't take too long to get back to our old routine.*
2 [C] a set of things such as jokes or songs that a performer uses regularly: *a comedy/dance routine*

routine² /ˌruːˈtiːn/ adj **1** usual and not done for any special reason: *a routine check*
2 ordinary and not interesting or special: *routine, repetitive work*

routinely /ruːˈtiːnli/ adv as part of the normal way of doing something

roving /ˈrəʊvɪŋ/ adj travelling around from place to place: *a roving reporter*

row¹ /rəʊ/ noun [C] ★★★
1 a series of people or things that are arranged in a straight line: *a row of houses/shops/chairs*
2 a line of seats in a theatre or cinema
PHRASE **in a row 1** in a straight line: *The children stood in a row against the wall.*
2 one after another, without anything different happening in between: *His job allows him to take several days off in a row.*

row² /rəʊ/ verb [I/T] to move a boat through water using poles with flat ends called **oars**

row³ /raʊ/ noun *British* **1** [C] an argument or disagreement between people, organizations, or countries: *I had a row with my boyfriend last night.* ♦ *the continuing row over the terms of the ceasefire* **2** [singular] noisy behaviour

row⁴ /raʊ/ verb [I] *British* if people row, they have a noisy argument with each other

rowdy /ˈraʊdi/ adj noisy and causing trouble

rowing boat /ˈrəʊɪŋ ˌbəʊt/ noun [C] *British* a small boat that you move by pulling on two poles with flat ends called **oars**

rowing machine /ˈrəʊɪŋ məˌʃiːn/ noun [C] an exercise machine that you sit on and use as if you were ROWING a boat —*picture* → C16

royal¹ /ˈrɔɪəl/ adj ★★ relating to a king or queen, or to their family: *the royal palace* ♦ *a royal wedding*

royal² /ˈrɔɪəl/ noun [C] *mainly journalism* a member of a royal family

royal 'blue adj deep blue —**royal 'blue** noun [U]

Royal 'Highness noun **Your/His/Her Royal Highness** used for speaking to or about a prince or princess

Royal Ma'rines, the a part of the British navy that is trained to fight on land or at sea

royalist /ˈrɔɪəlɪst/ noun [C] someone who believes that their country should have a king or queen

royalties /ˈrɔɪəltiz/ noun [plural] money that a writer or performer gets each time their work is sold or performed

royalty /ˈrɔɪəlti/ noun [U] kings and queens and their families

rpm /ˌɑː piː ˈem/ abbrev revolutions per minute: a unit for measuring the speed at which something goes round in a circle

RSI /ˌɑːr es ˈaɪ/ noun [U] repetitive strain injury: a painful condition of the hands that is caused by doing repeated small movements

RSVP /ˌɑːr es viː ˈpiː/ abbrev used on written invitations for asking for a reply

RTF /ˌɑːr tiː ˈef/ abbrev *computing* rich text format: a way of storing a computer document so that when you send it to someone, it will look exactly the same on their computer screen

rub¹ /rʌb/ verb ★
1 [I/T] to move your hands or an object over a surface firmly: *Scott gently rubbed her back until the pain went away.* ♦ *Rub your hands together – it will help you to stay warm.*
2 [T] to spread a liquid or substance onto the surface of something: **rub sth on sth** *She rubbed some tanning oil on his back.* ♦ **rub sth with sth** *Rub the chicken with garlic before putting it in the oven.*
3 [I] *British* to hurt or damage something by continuously pressing and moving against it: *Cindy's new shoes were rubbing and giving her blisters.*
PHRASES **rub it in** *spoken* to remind someone of something that is stupid or bad that they have done
rub shoulders with sb *informal* to meet and talk to someone who is important or famous
rub sb up the wrong way *informal* to do or say things that annoy someone
PHRASAL VERBS **rub sb/sth 'down** to dry someone or something by rubbing them with a TOWEL
rub (sth) 'off if you rub something off, or if it rubs off, you remove it by rubbing it
rub 'off on sb if something such as a good quality that you have rubs off on someone, they start to develop it too: *Hopefully her enthusiasm will rub off on the rest of the team.*
rub sth 'out *British* to use a RUBBER to remove something that you have written or drawn in pencil

rub² /rʌb/ noun [singular] the action of rubbing something: *Let the polish dry then give the shoes a good rub.*

R

rubber /'rʌbə/ noun **1** [U] a strong substance that bends easily and is used for making things such as tyres and boots **2** [C] British a small piece of rubber that you use for removing pencil marks from paper —*picture* → C3

rubber 'band noun [C] a thin circle of rubber that you use for holding things together

rubber-'stamp verb [T] to give official approval for something without thinking about it at all

rubbery /'rʌbəri/ adj similar to rubber

rubbish /'rʌbɪʃ/ noun [U] British ★
1 things that you throw away because they are no longer useful: *The streets were* **littered** *with rubbish.*
2 things that someone says or writes that are not reasonable or sensible =NONSENSE: *As usual, he was* **talking** *complete* **rubbish.**
3 something that is of very low quality =JUNK: *Critics have described the paintings as worthless rubbish.*

rubble /'rʌb(ə)l/ noun [U] broken pieces of stone and brick from buildings that have been destroyed

rubella /ruː'belə/ noun [U] *medical* a minor infectious disease that causes red spots on the skin =GERMAN MEASLES

ruby /'ruːbi/ noun [C] a valuable red jewel

rucksack /'rʌk,sæk/ noun [C] a bag that you carry on your back =BACKPACK

rudder /'rʌdə/ noun [C] a flat part at the back of a boat or plane that you move in order to turn the boat or plane

ruddy /'rʌdi/ adj *literary* a ruddy face is pink and looks healthy

rude /ruːd/ adj ★
1 not polite: *I don't want to seem rude, but I'd rather be alone.* ♦ *it is rude to do sth It's rude to keep people waiting.*
2 offensive because of referring to sex or using the toilet: *a rude word/joke*
—**rudely** adv: *I can't remember what I was saying before I was so rudely interrupted!*
—**rudeness** noun [U]

rudimentary /,ruːdɪ'ment(ə)ri/ adj basic: *rudimentary knowledge*

rudiments /'ruːdɪmənts/ noun **the rudiments of sth** the basic skills or information that are needed for an activity or subject

rueful /'ruːf(ə)l/ adj showing that you are sorry that something has happened
—**ruefully** adv

ruffle /'rʌf(ə)l/ verb [T] **1** to move or shake something so that it is no longer smooth **2** to make someone feel nervous or upset

rug /rʌg/ noun [C] **1** a small carpet that covers part of a floor **2** British a cloth made of wool that you use to keep yourself warm

rugby /'rʌgbi/ noun [U] a game that is played by two teams of players with a ball that is shaped like an egg

rugged /'rʌgɪd/ adj **1** not smooth or flat: *a rugged landscape* **2** strong and able to deal with difficult conditions: *a rugged piece of equipment* **3** with a strong attractive appearance: *He had a tanned rugged face.*

ruin¹ /'ruːɪn/ verb [T] **1** to spoil or destroy something: *She had ruined her mother's chances of getting a job.* **2** to make someone lose all their money or power: *The scandal that totally ruined him.*

ruin² /'ruːɪn/ noun **1 ruins** [plural] the parts of a building that remain after it has been severely damaged: *Roman ruins* ♦ *People had built shelters among the ruins of the city.* **2** [U] the loss of all your money or power: *Many of these companies are facing ruin.*

PHRASE in ruins destroyed, or severely damaged: *His marriage was over and his career was in ruins.*

ruinous /'ruːɪnəs/ adj **1** causing severe damage **2** something that is ruinous costs so much money that it causes a lot of problems for you

rule¹ /ruːl/ noun ★★★
1 [C] a statement that explains what you can or cannot do in a particular situation: *grammatical rules* ♦ *Players who* **break the rules** *are sent off the field.* ♦ *You should always* **follow** *these simple* **rules** *when using electrical equipment.* ♦ *You can't do that, it's* **against the rules!** ♦ *the basic* **rules** *of the game*
2 [U] the person, group, or country that officially controls a place: *In 1999 Hong Kong went back to Chinese rule.*

PHRASES as a rule usually: *As a rule, I stay in on Friday nights.*
bend/stretch the rules to allow something that is not normally allowed
be the rule to be what usually happens, or what is thought to be normal: *Sunny skies are the rule at this time of year.*
rule of thumb a simple method or principle that is not exact, but that is effective
→ GOLDEN RULE, HOME RULE

> ### Words often used with **rule**
> *Verbs often used with* **rule** *(noun, sense 1)*
> ■ **bend, break, flout, stretch** + RULES: not accept rules
> ■ **follow, obey, play by, stick to** + RULES: accept rules

rule² /ruːl/ verb ★★
1 [I/T] to officially control a country or area =GOVERN: *Portugal ruled East Timor for nearly four centuries.*
2 [I/T] to make and announce an official decision: *The judge still has not* **ruled on** *the case.* ♦ **+(that)** *The court ruled that the strike was illegal.*
3 [T] to control someone's thoughts or actions: *Money and music rule Charlie's world.* ♦ *We must not allow ourselves to be ruled by personal feelings.*

PHRASAL VERB ,rule sb/sth 'out to stop considering someone or something as a possibility: *The president has ruled out the use of US troops.*

ruled /ruːld/ adj ruled paper has straight lines printed on it for writing on

ruler /'ruːlə/ noun [C] ★
1 someone who controls a country: *Haiti's former military rulers*

2 a long flat object that you use for measuring or for drawing straight lines

ruling¹ /ˈruːlɪŋ/ adj in control of a country or group: *members of the ruling party*

ruling² /ˈruːlɪŋ/ noun [C] an official decision

rum /rʌm/ noun [U] a strong alcoholic drink made from SUGAR CANE

rumble /ˈrʌmb(ə)l/ verb [I] to make a continuous deep sound —**rumble** noun [C]

rumbling /ˈrʌmblɪŋ/ noun **1** [singular] a continuous deep sound **2 rumblings** [plural] signs that people are becoming unhappy about a situation

ruminate /ˈruːmɪˌneɪt/ verb [I] *formal* to think about something carefully

rummage /ˈrʌmɪdʒ/ verb [I] to search for something among a lot of other things

rumor /ˈruːmə/ the American spelling of **rumour**

rumored /ˈruːməd/ the American spelling of **rumoured**

rumour /ˈruːmə/ noun [C/U] something that people are saying that may or may not be true: *A student had been spreading rumours about the teachers.* ♦ *Rumour has it that* (=there is a rumour that) *he's seriously ill.* ♦ *Now there are rumours of wedding plans.* ♦ *He denied rumours that staff would lose their jobs.*

rumoured /ˈruːməd/ adj if something is rumoured, people are saying it, but it is not definitely true

rump /rʌmp/ noun [C] the part of an animal's body that is above its back legs

rumpled /ˈrʌmp(ə)ld/ adj something that is rumpled is untidy because it is not smooth or flat —**rumple** verb [T]

run¹ /rʌn/ (past tense **ran** /ræn/; past participle **run**) verb ★★★

1 move quickly	**11** exist in a place
2 control/organize	**12** use program
3 machine: work	**13** print in newspaper
4 take sb in car	**14** try to be elected
5 liquid: flow	**15** liquid/colour: spread
6 make water flow	**16** pay for car
7 be shown/performed	**17** do test/check
8 vehicle: travel	**+ PHRASES**
9 reach amount/rate	**+ PHRASAL VERBS**
10 move sth along sth	

1 [I] to move quickly using your legs and feet: *You'll have to run if you want to catch the bus.* ♦ *A cat ran across the road in front of me.* ♦ *I ran to the door and opened it.*

2 [T] to control and organize something such as a business, organization, or event =MANAGE: *He was the man who ran Clinton's election campaign.*

3 [I] if a machine or engine is running, it is operating: *Don't leave the car engine running.*

4 [T] to take someone somewhere in your car: *I'll run you there – it's no trouble.* ♦ **run sb to/into sth** *John kindly offered to run me into town.*

5 [I] if a liquid runs somewhere, it flows there: *Tears were running down his face.* ♦

The River Rhine runs into the North Sea.

6 [T] to make water flow from or into a container: *I'm going to run a bath.*

7 [I] if a play, film, or television programme runs, it continues to be performed or shown: *a soap opera that has been running for many years*

8 [I] if a bus or train runs, it travels somewhere at regular times: *The train only runs at weekends.*

9 [I] to continue at a particular amount or rate: *Inflation is running at 3%.*

10 [T] to move something through or along something else: **run sth through/across/down sth** *Fred ran his fingers gently through her hair.*

11 [I] if something such as a road or wall runs somewhere, it continues from one place to another: *There was a path running through the middle of the forest.*

12 [I/T] if you run a computer program, or if it runs, you start it or use it: *The software will run on any PC.*

13 [T] if newspapers run an article, advertisement, or photograph, they print it

14 [I] to try to be elected to an official job or position: *How many candidates are running?* ♦ *Jackson announced his intention to run for president.*

15 [I] if a piece of clothing or a colour runs, the colour spreads when you wash it

16 [T] to use and pay for a car: *I can't afford to run a car on my salary.*

17 [T] to perform something such as a test, or to check on someone or something: *He'd run a check on her through his London office.*

PHRASES **running late** if you are running late, you do something or arrive somewhere later than you planned

run rings round sb to do something much better than someone else

run short/low if you run short of something, or if you run low on something, you do not have enough of it left: *We're running low on milk.* ♦ *I'm running short of ideas.*

sth runs in the family if something such as a quality or disease runs in the family, a lot of people in the family have it

→ COURSE¹

PHRASAL VERBS **run across sb/sth** to meet someone or find something by chance

run after sb/sth to chase someone or something: *Velluci ran after the car waving his fists.*

run around to be very busy doing a lot of different things: *I've been running around all day.*

run away 1 to secretly leave a place because you are not happy there: *When I was 13, I ran away from home.* **2** to try to avoid dealing with a difficult or unpleasant situation: *You can't keep running away from the problem.*

run sth by sb to tell someone your ideas so that they can give you their opinion: *Can I run a few ideas by you?*

R

,**run (sth) 'down** if something such as a machine runs down, or if you run it down, it gradually stops working because it is losing power: *Switch your headlights off, or you'll run the battery down.*

,**run sb/sth 'down 1** to hit a person or animal with your car and injure or kill them: *She got run down outside school.* **2** to criticize someone or something unfairly → RUNDOWN

,**run 'into sb** to meet someone when you did not expect to: *Guess who I ran into this morning?*

,**run 'into sth 1** to start to experience something that is unpleasant: *The project soon ran into difficulties.* **2** to reach a particular amount: *The cost of paying for the flood damage could run into millions.*

,**run 'into sb/sth** to hit someone or something by accident while you are driving: *A truck ran into me (=hit my car) this morning.*

,**run 'off** to suddenly leave a place or person: *Their dad ran off when they were little.*

,**run 'off with sb** *informal* to secretly leave a place with someone in order to marry them or have a sexual relationship with them: *They said Phil had run off with his wife's best friend.*

,**run 'off with sth** to steal something, or to take it without permission

,**run 'out 1** to use all of something and not have any left: *Many hospitals are running out of money.* **2** if something such as money or time runs out, there is no more of it left: *They returned home from South Africa when their money ran out.* **3** to stop being legal on a particular date = EXPIRE: *My contract runs out next July.* ♦ *When does your passport run out?*

,**run sb/sth 'over** to hit someone or something with a vehicle: *Keeley was run over by a car outside her house.*

,**run 'round** same as **run around**

,**run 'through sth 1** to explain or read something quickly: *Do you want me to run through the details with you?* **2** to practise something so that it is correct for a performance or test: *Let's just run through the piece one more time.*

,**run 'up sth** if you run up a bill or a DEBT, you owe someone a lot of money: *My son ran up a huge phone bill.*

,**run 'up a,gainst sth** to have to deal with something that is difficult or unpleasant

run² /rʌn/ noun ★★★

1 race	4 amount produced
2 period of time	5 cricket point
3 a journey	+ PHRASES

1 [C] an act of running, or a race in which you run a long distance: *Lee is doing a six-mile run on Saturday.*

2 [singular] a period of time when something continues: *The play is enjoying a successful run on Broadway.* ♦ *We've had a run of bad luck recently.*

3 [singular] a journey in a vehicle: *We took the new car out for a run in the country.*

4 [C] the amount of something that a company or factory produces at one time:

The plates are a limited edition run of 250.
5 [C] one point in the game of CRICKET: *He has scored 90 runs in this match.*

PHRASES **in the long run** not immediately but at a time in the future: *In the long run, I think you're better off without him.*

in the short run for a short period of time from now: *Most diets produce weight loss only in the short run.*

make a run for sth to suddenly run towards something and try to reach it: *Mary made a run for the exit.*

on the run trying to hide or escape from the police

a run on sth a situation in which a lot of people want to buy something at the same time
→ RUNS

runaway¹ /'rʌnəweɪ/ adj **1** a runaway vehicle or animal is moving fast without anyone controlling it **2** happening or increasing very quickly: *runaway inflation* **3** a runaway person has left their home or has escaped from somewhere

runaway² /'rʌnəweɪ/ noun [C] a child who has secretly left their home

rundown /'rʌnˌdaʊn/ noun [C] a short report

,**run-'down** adj **1** so tired that you do not feel well **2** in bad condition because no one has spent money on repairs: *a run-down hotel*

rung¹ /rʌŋ/ noun [C] **1** one of the bars across a LADDER that you put your feet on when you climb up **2** a level of achievement: *You could be on the first rung of a great new career.*

rung² the past participle of **ring¹**

'run-in noun [C] *informal* an argument

runner /'rʌnə/ noun [C] **1** a person or animal that runs in a race, or someone who runs for pleasure **2** a narrow part on which something such as a drawer or SLEDGE slides **3** someone who carries drugs or weapons illegally from one place to another
→ FRONT RUNNER

'runner bean noun [C] a long green bean that is cooked and eaten

,runner-'up (plural **,runners-'up**) noun [C] someone who is second in a competition or race

running¹ /'rʌnɪŋ/ noun [U] **1** the activity of running for pleasure or as a sport **2** the activities that are involved in managing or organizing something: *The family is not involved in the day-to-day running of the company.*

PHRASE **be in/out of the running** to have some chance/no chance of success

running² /'rʌnɪŋ/ adv **four weeks/five years/ six times etc running** four weeks/five years/ six times etc, following one after another

,**running 'battle** noun [C] an argument that continues over a long period of time

'running ,costs noun [plural] the money that you spend regularly in order to operate a machine or service

'running ,total noun [C] a total amount that has new amounts added to it regularly

running water noun [U] water that is supplied by pipes into a building

runny /'rʌni/ adj **1** a runny nose has liquid coming out of it **2** like a liquid

run-of-the-mill adj ordinary and not interesting

runs, the /rʌns/ noun [plural] informal DIARRHOEA

run-up noun **the run-up to sth** the period of time just before an important event

runway /'rʌnweɪ/ noun [C] a long road that is used by planes when they land and TAKE OFF

rupture /'rʌptʃə/ verb [I/T] if something ruptures, or if you rupture it, it bursts or tears suddenly: *The impact ruptured both fuel tanks.* —**rupture** noun [C]

rural /'rʊərəl/ adj ★★ relating to the countryside, or in the countryside ≠ URBAN: *rural areas/roads/schools*

ruse /ruːz/ noun [C] a way of tricking someone =PLOY

rush¹ /rʌʃ/ verb [I/T] ★★
1 to go somewhere in a hurry, or to take someone or send something somewhere in a hurry: *Suddenly the door burst open and Joe rushed in.* ♦ *Ambulance crews rushed to the scene of the accident.* ♦ rush sb **to/into** sth *Frank was rushed to hospital with violent stomach pains.* ♦ rush sb sth *Can you rush me a copy of the report?*
2 to do something quickly, or to make someone do something quickly: *There's no need to rush. We've got plenty of time.* ♦ *Don't rush into a decision.* ♦ rush sb **into (doing) sth** *His parents rushed him into getting married.* ♦ rush **to do sth** *Hayley rushed to answer the phone.*
PHRASAL VERB **rush around** to try to do a lot of things in a short time

rush² /rʌʃ/ noun ★
1 [singular] a sudden strong movement forwards: *Everyone made a rush for the refreshments.* ♦ **a rush to do sth** *Commuters jostled in a rush to get off the train.*
2 [singular/U] a situation in which you hurry to do something: *Sorry, I can't stop. I'm in a rush.* ♦ *There was a mad rush to get the house tidy before they arrived.*
3 [singular] an occasion when a lot of people suddenly want to do something or have something: *We've had a rush on mobile phones this week.* ♦ **a rush to do sth** *There was a rush to buy tickets for the concert.*
4 the rush [singular] the time of day when a place is very busy and there is a lot of traffic: *Lee left London at six o'clock to avoid the rush.*

rushed /rʌʃt/ adj done in a hurry
PHRASE **rushed off your feet** British extremely busy

rushes /'rʌʃɪz/ noun [plural] tall plants like grass that grow in water

rush hour noun [C/U] the time of day when there is a lot of traffic because people are travelling to or from work

rust¹ /rʌst/ noun [U] the red substance that damages the surface of metal

rust² /rʌst/ verb [I/T] to become damaged by rust, or to make metal develop rust

rustic /'rʌstɪk/ adj made in the simple style of the countryside

rustle /'rʌs(ə)l/ verb [I/T] to produce a sound like the sound that leaves or sheets of paper make when they move, or to make something do this —**rustle** noun [singular]
PHRASAL VERB **rustle sth up** informal to quickly produce something such as a meal using whatever things are available

rusty /'rʌsti/ adj **1** covered in RUST **2** a skill that is rusty has not been used recently

rut /rʌt/ noun [C] **1** a situation that is boring and difficult to change: *If you're in a rut, change jobs.* **2** a deep narrow mark in the ground made by a wheel

ruthless /'ruːθləs/ adj willing to hurt other people in order to get what you want —**ruthlessly** adv

rye /raɪ/ noun [U] **1** plants that produce grain that is used for making bread and WHISKEY **2** bread or WHISKEY made from rye

S s

s or **S** /es/ noun [C/U] the 19th letter of the English alphabet

S abbrev **1** small: used on clothes labels **2** South **3** Southern

-'s¹ short form **1** a way of saying or writing 'is' and 'has'. This is not often used in formal writing: *She's in the kitchen.* ♦ *John's gone out.* **2** the usual way of saying or writing 'us' when you use it with 'let' to make a suggestion: *Let's not tell him now.*

-'s² suffix **1** used with nouns for showing who or what something belongs to: *I've never met Andy's wife.* ♦ *The dog's leg was badly cut.* ♦ *the evening's activities* (=activities that happen in the evening) **2** used for talking about the home of a particular person: *We all went back to Alan's for lunch.*

Sabbath, the /'sæbəθ/ noun [singular] a day when the people of some religions rest and pray

sabbatical /sə'bætɪk(ə)l/ noun [C/U] a period when a university teacher is away from work because they are doing research

sabotage /'sæbətɑːʒ/ verb [T] **1** to deliberately damage or destroy something that belongs to an enemy **2** to deliberately prevent something from being successful —**sabotage** noun [U]

saboteur /ˌsæbə'tɜː/ noun [C] someone who deliberately damages or destroys something that belongs to an enemy

sabre /'seɪbə/ noun [C] a sword with a curved blade

'sabre-rattling noun [U] a threat of violence or military action

saccharin /'sækərın/ noun [U] a chemical substance that is used instead of sugar for making food sweet

sachet /'sæʃeɪ/ noun [C] *British* a small flat plastic bag that contains a liquid or powder

sack¹ /sæk/ noun **1** [C] a large strong bag for storing and carrying things: *a sack of potatoes/flour* ♦ *The sack was too heavy to lift.* **2 the sack** [singular] *British informal* a situation in which someone is forced to leave their job: *We didn't want to risk getting the sack by going on strike.* ♦ *He ought to be given the sack.*

sack² /sæk/ verb [T] ★
1 *British informal* to force someone to leave their job=FIRE: *Hundreds of workers are to be sacked at the factory.*
2 if an army sacks a place, they steal property from it and destroy it

sacking /'sækɪŋ/ noun [C] *British informal* an act of forcing someone to leave their job

sacrament /'sækrəmənt/ noun [C] an important Christian ceremony such as marriage or BAPTISM

sacred /'seɪkrɪd/ adj **1** connected with religion: *sacred art* **2** holy: *Jerusalem is sacred to Christians, Muslims, and Jews.* **3** something that is sacred is so important that you should not change or criticize it: *He has broken one of the profession's most sacred rules.*

,sacred 'cow noun [C] something that is too important to change or criticize

sacrifice¹ /'sækrɪfaɪs/ noun [C/U] **1** a decision not to have or do something that is important to you, so that someone else will have a benefit or so that you will benefit later: *Making sacrifices is part of bringing up children.* **2** the act of killing a person or animal as part of a ceremony to honour a god or spirit —**sacrificial** /,sækrɪ'fɪʃ(ə)l/ adj: *a sacrificial animal*

sacrifice² /'sækrɪfaɪs/ verb [T] **1** to choose not to have something so that other people can have something else: *She sacrificed her career to bring up the children.* ♦ *Would you sacrifice some of your salary for more holiday time?* **2** to kill a person or animal as part of a ceremony to honour a god or spirit

sacrilege /'sækrəlɪdʒ/ noun [U] behaviour that shows that someone has no respect for something holy or important —**sacrilegious** /,sækrə'lɪdʒəs/ adj

sacrosanct /'sækrəʊ,sæŋkt/ adj too important to change or criticize

sad /sæd/ adj ★★
1 feeling unhappy, making you feel unhappy, or showing that you feel unhappy: *It was a sad day when we sold our home.* ♦ *sad eyes* ♦ *Reading her letter made us all feel a little sad.* ♦ *I felt sad about leaving him, but I had no choice.* ♦ *I feel sad for all the children growing up without a father at home.* ♦ *be sad to see/hear sth I was very sad to hear that your mother had died.*

2 very bad in a way that makes you feel angry, upset, or shocked: *The sad truth is that many people never learn to read.* ♦ *It's a sad state of affairs when people can't be bothered to vote any more.* ♦ *it is sad that/it's a sad fact that I think it's sad that children spend so much time watching television.*

3 *very informal* boring or not fashionable

> **Other ways of saying sad**
> - **depressed** feeling very negative about your situation
> - **down** (*informal*) slightly depressed
> - **gloomy** sad and having no hope for the future
> - **low** feeling negative about life, and lacking energy
> - **miserable** very sad because you are uncomfortable, lonely, or ill
> - **unhappy** a general word for 'sad'

sadden /'sæd(ə)n/ verb [T] *formal* to make someone feel sad

saddle¹ /'sæd(ə)l/ noun [C] **1** a leather seat that you put on a horse's back **2** the seat on a bicycle or MOTORCYCLE
   PHRASE **in the saddle** *informal* in control of something

saddle² /'sæd(ə)l/ verb [T] to put a saddle on a horse
   PHRASAL VERB **'saddle sb with sth** to give someone something that is difficult or unpleasant to deal with: *The company was saddled with a huge debt last year.*

sadhu /'sɑːduː/ noun [C] a Hindu holy man

sadist /'seɪdɪst/ noun [C] someone who likes to hurt people —**sadism** noun [U]

sadistic /sə'dɪstɪk/ adj someone who is sadistic likes to hurt people

sadly /'sædli/ adv **1** used for showing that you think that something is bad or wrong: *Sadly, they chose to ignore our advice.* **2** in a way that shows that you are sad, or that makes you feel sad: *She smiled sadly.* ♦ *Jim Perry was a wonderful employee and will be sadly missed.*

sadness /'sædnəs/ noun [U] the feeling of being unhappy: *Joan's childhood was filled with pain and sadness.* ♦ *It is with great sadness that we announce the death of Wilfred White.*

sae /,es eɪ 'iː/ noun [C] *British* stamped addressed envelope or self-addressed envelope: an envelope with your name, address, and a stamp on it that you give to someone so that they can easily send you something

safari /sə'fɑːri/ noun [C] a journey, especially to Africa, in order to see wild animals in their natural environment

safe¹ /seɪf/ adj ★★★
1 not likely to be harmed, lost, or stolen: *Will my car be safe if I park it in the street?* ♦ *It's difficult to make airports safe from terrorist attacks.* ♦ *keep sth safe Make sure to keep your credit card safe.*
2 not likely to cause damage or harm: *Travelling by plane is much safer than driving your own car.* ♦ *a safe environment for children*

3 not damaged, hurt, or lost: *Rescuers found the children safe but scared inside the house.* ♦ *Everyone arrived safe and sound.*
4 not involving a lot of risk: *a safe investment*

PHRASES **in safe hands** protected from harm or danger by a particular person or organization
on the safe side in a situation that involves very little risk because you have been very careful: *Just to be on the safe side, take an umbrella.*

safe² /seɪf/ noun [C] a strong metal box that is used for storing valuable things

safeguard /'seɪf.gɑːd/ verb [T] to protect something or someone: *We hope that world leaders can agree on a plan to safeguard the environment.* ♦ *Oil companies were blamed for failing to safeguard workers against dangerous chemicals.* —**safeguard** noun [C]

safe 'haven noun [C] a place where people are safe from danger or attack

safekeeping /ˌseɪfˈkiːpɪŋ/ noun [U] protection from being damaged or lost: *Sheila gave me the rings for safekeeping.*

safely /'seɪfli/ adv **1** in a way that will not cause damage or harm: *Remember to drive safely.* ♦ *Keep plastic bags safely out of the reach of children.* **2** without being damaged, hurt, or lost: *All the children have been returned safely to their parents.*

safe 'sex noun [U] sexual activity in which people are careful to avoid getting diseases

safety /'seɪfti/ noun [U] ★★★
1 the fact that something is safe to do or use: *Their cars have a reputation for safety and reliability.* ♦ *a safety helmet/harness* ♦ *The airline has a poor **safety record** (=a record of how safe something has been in the past).* ♦ *Do we know enough about **the safety of** these vaccines?*
2 a place or situation in which you are protected from danger: *Refugees walked for several days until they reached safety.* ♦ *We watched the storm from **the safety of** our home.*
3 a safe way of behaving: *We plan to have frequent training sessions on safety at work.*

'safety ,belt noun [C] a SEAT BELT

'safety de'posit ,box noun [C] a small box in a bank that a customer uses for storing valuable possessions

'safety ,net noun [C] **1** a plan or system that is designed to protect people or prevent serious problems **2** a net that you put under something in order to catch people if they fall

'safety ,pin noun [C] a curved pin with a cover that fits over the sharp point

saffron /'sæfrən/ noun [U] part of a flower that is used for adding flavour and yellow colour to food

sag /sæg/ verb [I] **1** to become soft and start to bend or hang downwards **2** to become weaker or less in amount or value

saga /'sɑːgə/ noun [C] **1** a story about what happens to a group of characters over a

long period of time **2** *informal* a long series of events, or a description of them

sage¹ /seɪdʒ/ noun **1** [U] a plant that is used for flavouring food **2** [C] *literary* someone who is wise

sage² /seɪdʒ/ adj *literary* wise —**sagely** adv

Sagittarius /ˌsædʒɪˈteəriəs/ noun [U] one of the twelve signs of the ZODIAC. A **Sagittarius** is someone who was born between 23 November and 21 December.

said the past tense and past participle of **say**¹

sail¹ /seɪl/ verb ★★
1 [I] to travel somewhere by boat or ship: *Sail to Greece aboard the SS Monterey.*
2 [I/T] to control the movement of a boat or ship, especially one that uses the wind to move it: *It's a great opportunity to learn to sail.*
3 [I/T] if a boat sails, it moves across the surface of water: *The yacht sailed into harbour.*
4 [I] to move quickly and easily: *The ball sailed over his head and into the goal.*

PHRASAL VERB **'sail ,through sth** to achieve a particular result very easily: *She sailed through the first interview.*

sail² /seɪl/ noun **1** [C] a large piece of strong cloth fixed to a tall pole on a boat. It uses the wind to move the boat across water.
2 [singular] a journey by boat or ship

sailboard /'seɪl.bɔːd/ noun [C] a long board with a MAST and sail, used for moving across water in the sport of WINDSURFING

sailing /'seɪlɪŋ/ noun [U] the sport or activity of travelling across water in a sailing boat

'sailing ,boat noun [C] *British* a small boat that uses a sail or sails to move along

sailor /'seɪlə/ noun [C] someone who works on a boat or ship, or who sails for pleasure

saint /seɪnt/ noun [C] **1** someone who the Christian Church officially honours after their death because they have lived a very holy life **2** someone who is very kind, patient, and helpful —**sainthood** /'seɪnt.hʊd/ noun [U]

saintly /'seɪntli/ adj very good or holy

sake /seɪk/ noun ★
PHRASES **for God's/goodness'/Heaven's/Pete's sake** *spoken* used for emphasizing what you are saying when you are annoyed or angry: 'for God's sake' is offensive to some people: *Oh, for goodness' sake, leave me alone!*
for sb's/sth's sake or **for the sake of sb/sth** for the benefit or good of someone or something: *He agreed to resign for the sake of the party.* ♦ *We hope for her sake that the wedding goes as planned.*
for the sake of sth for the purpose of doing, getting, or achieving something: *I hope you're not doing this just for the sake of the money.* ♦ *For clarity's sake, I'd like to reword my statement.*

salad /'sæləd/ noun [C/U] ★
1 a food containing a mixture of raw vegetables such as LETTUCE, tomatoes, and CUCUMBERS, usually served with a salad dressing: *a green salad*

S

2 food that has been cut into small pieces and mixed together, usually with a sauce, and served cold: *an egg salad sandwich ♦ a fruit salad*

salad ,dressing noun [C/U] a sauce that adds flavour to salads, usually made by mixing oil, VINEGAR, and HERBS or SPICES

salami /səˈlɑːmi/ noun [C/U] a type of SAUSAGE containing strong SPICES, cut into thin pieces and served cold

salaried /ˈsælərid/ adj paid a fixed amount of money for your job each month or year

salary /ˈsæləri/ noun [C] ★ a fixed amount of money that you earn each month or year from your job: *an annual salary of £25,000*

sale /seɪl/ noun ★★★

1 process of selling	**5** total sold
2 instance of selling	**6** selling department
3 event for selling	**+** PHRASES
4 when prices are lower	

1 [C/U] the process of selling goods or services for money: *a ban on the sale of arms*

2 [C] a single instance of selling goods or services: *I'm willing to lower the price in order to make a sale*.

3 [C] an event at which people meet to buy and sell things: *a second-hand book sale*

4 [C] an event or period of time during which a shop reduces the prices of some of its goods: *the start of the after-Christmas sales*

5 sales [plural] the total number of things that a company sells within a particular period of time, or the money that it earns by selling things: *Sales are up for the month of May*. ♦ *We hope to increase sales this year to £50 million*. ♦ *Do you have the sales figures yet?*

6 sales [plural] the department of a company that sells its goods or services: *Dave works in sales*.

S

PHRASES **for sale** available for people to buy: *That chair is not for sale*.

on sale 1 available for people to buy: *Tickets for the performance are on sale at the box office*. **2** *American* available for people to buy at a price that is less than the usual price: *Bedding usually goes on sale in January*.

up for sale available for people to buy: *We're putting the factory up for sale*.

saleable /ˈseɪləb(ə)l/ adj able to be sold

sales as,sistant noun [C] *British* someone whose job is to help customers and sell things in a shop

salesman /ˈseɪlzmən/ (plural **salesmen** /ˈseɪlzmən/) noun [C] a man whose job is to sell the products or services of a particular company

salesperson /ˈseɪlzˌpɜːs(ə)n/ (plural **salespeople** /ˈseɪlzˌpiːp(ə)l/) noun [C] someone whose job is to sell the products or services of a particular company

sales repre,sentative or **'sales ,rep** noun [C] someone whose job is to travel to different places and sell the products or services of a particular company

saleswoman /ˈseɪlzˌwʊmən/ (plural

saleswomen /ˈseɪlzˌwɪmɪn/) noun [C] a woman whose job is to sell the products or services of a particular company

salient /ˈseɪliənt/ adj *formal* very noticeable or relevant

saline /ˈseɪlaɪn/ adj *technical* containing salt

saliva /səˈlaɪvə/ noun [U] the liquid that is produced in your mouth = SPIT

salivate /ˈsælɪˌveɪt/ verb [I] to produce more than the usual amount of SALIVA, because you see or smell food

sallow /ˈsæləʊ/ adj sallow skin is a pale yellow colour and does not look healthy

salmon /ˈsæmən/ (plural **salmon**) noun [C/U] a large silver fish with pink flesh that is eaten as food

salmonella /ˌsælməˈnelə/ noun [C] a type of bacteria that is found in food. It can make you ill.

salon /ˈsælɒn/ noun [C] a place where you can have your hair cut and STYLED

saloon /səˈluːn/ noun [C] *British* a car with front and back seats for passengers and a boot for carrying things such as suitcases

salsa /ˈsælsə/ noun **1** [U] a sauce made from tomatoes, onions, and other herbs or spices. It is served with Mexican or Spanish food. **2** [C/U] a type of Latin-American dance music, or a dance performed to this music

salt¹ /sɔːlt/ noun ★

1 [U] a white substance that is often added to food to improve its flavour: *Add a pinch of salt*.

2 [C] *science* a chemical substance formed from an acid

PHRASE **take sth with a pinch of salt** to doubt the truth or value of something: *If I were you, I'd take his advice with a pinch of salt*.

salt² /sɔːlt/ verb [T] to add salt to food

'salt ,cellar noun [C] *British* a small container with a lid that has holes in it, used for pouring salt on food

saltwater /ˈsɔːltˌwɔːtə/ adj living in the sea or in water that contains salt ≠ FRESHWATER: *saltwater fish*

salty /ˈsɔːlti/ adj containing salt, or tasting like salt

salute /səˈluːt/ verb **1** [I/T] to put your hand to your head as a formal way of showing respect to a senior officer in the armed forces **2** [T] to express praise or respect for a person or an achievement, especially formally and in public —**salute** noun [C]

salvage /ˈsælvɪdʒ/ verb [T] **1** to save things from a ship or building that has been damaged or destroyed **2** to succeed in achieving something in a situation that has been a failure —**salvage** noun [U]

salvation /sælˈveɪʃ(ə)n/ noun [U] **1** according to the Christian religion, the act of being saved by God from evil = REDEMPTION **2** someone or something that helps you in a bad or dangerous situation

Sal,vation 'Army, the an international organization that teaches CHRISTIANITY and helps people who have problems

same /seɪm/ grammar word ★★★

> Same can be:
> ■ an **adjective**: *We both went to the same school.*
> ■ a **pronoun**: *I'd do the same if I had the chance.*
> ■ an **adverb**: *The twins always dress the same.*

1 the same used for saying that a particular person or thing is the one that you are referring to, and not a different one: *We were staying at **the same** hotel as our parents.* ♦ *Was this **the same** Timothy Evans **that** Carol had been at school with?* ♦ *I was born on **the very same** day that my father died.*

2 the same exactly like another person, thing, or way of doing something: *She did not want to make the same mistake again.* ♦ *The two pictures **look the same** to me – I can't tell them apart.* ♦ *Her eyes are **the same** colour as yours.*

3 the same used for saying that someone or something has not changed: *The Government's policy has **remained the same** since 1991.* ♦ *'How is Frances?' 'Oh, she's still **the same as** always.'* ♦ *The countryside looks **much the same** as it did 200 years ago.*

4 the same used for saying that one number, amount, price etc is equal to another: *The four sides of a square are all the same length.* ♦ *One centimetre is **the same as** ten millimetres.*

PHRASES all/just the same *spoken* despite what has been mentioned: *I'm sure he's safe, but all the same, I wish he'd come home.*
at the same time 1 used for saying that two or more things happen together: *The show will make you laugh and cry at the same time.* **2** used for introducing another fact or opinion that needs to be considered as well as the one that has just been stated: *I want to work hard for my family, but at the same time I want to spend time with them.*
same here *spoken* used for saying that you agree or that you have the same feeling: *'I've been looking forward to meeting you.' 'Same here.'*
the same old... familiar and not new or exciting: *Politicians repeat the same old phrases every election.*
→ BOAT

> **Other ways of saying same**
> ■ **alike** almost the same
> ■ **constant** remaining at the same level
> ■ **equal/equivalent** at the same level, or the same in quality or quantity
> ■ **identical** exactly the same, with no differences
> ■ **similar** almost the same, but with small differences

sample¹ /ˈsɑːmp(ə)l/ noun [C] ★
1 an example or small amount of something that shows you what all of it is like: *We had to bring some **samples** of our work to the interview.* ♦ *I took home some **samples of** curtain fabrics.*
2 a small amount of a substance that is used for scientific or medical tests: *Tests were performed on hair and blood samples.* ♦ *Researchers are **taking samples** of the air close to the factory.*
3 a group of people that is used for getting information about a larger group, or about the whole population: *The study took a sample of 100 students from 3 schools.*

sample² /ˈsɑːmp(ə)l/ verb [T] **1** to taste a small amount of food or drink in order to see what it is like: *They let us sample some of the wine.* **2** to try doing a new activity for a time: *Here you can relax and sample life in this island paradise.*

sanatorium /ˌsænəˈtɔːriəm/ noun [C] a hospital where people who have had a serious illness go so that doctors can take care of them until they get better

sanctimonious /ˌsæŋktɪˈməʊniəs/ adj *showing disapproval* trying to show that you have better moral or religious principles than other people

sanction¹ /ˈsæŋkʃ(ə)n/ noun **1** [C] an official order to stop communication, trade etc with a country that has broken international law: *economic/trade/international sanctions* ♦ *The Council wanted to impose sanctions* (=start to use them) *against the countries involved in the dispute.* **2** [U] official permission for taking action: *War was declared without the sanction of parliament.* **3** [C] a punishment for breaking a rule

sanction² /ˈsæŋkʃ(ə)n/ verb [T] *formal* to give approval or permission for something

sanctity /ˈsæŋktəti/ noun [U] the special importance that something has

sanctuary /ˈsæŋktʃuəri/ noun **1** [C/U] a place that provides official protection for someone: *Refugees sought sanctuary in Thailand.* **2** [C/U] a place where you feel safe or comfortable: *All she wanted now was the sanctuary of her own room.* **3** [C] a special area where animals live in a natural environment protected from people

sand¹ /sænd/ noun ★★
1 [U] a pale brown substance that you find at a beach or in the desert, formed from very small pieces of rock: *The children were playing in the sand.* ♦ *a grain of sand*
2 sands [plural] an area of sand

sand² /sænd/ verb [I/T] to make something such as wood very smooth by rubbing it with SANDPAPER

sandal /ˈsænd(ə)l/ noun [C] a light shoe that is partly open on top and does not cover your heel or toes —*picture* → SHOE

sandbag /ˈsæn(d)ˌbæg/ noun [C] a bag that is filled with sand, used for protecting a place from floods or explosions

sandcastle /ˈsæn(d)ˌkɑːs(ə)l/ noun [C] a pile of sand that is made in the shape of a castle or tower by children on a beach

ˈsand ˌdune noun [C] a hill of sand that is formed by the wind in a desert or near a beach

sandpaper /ˈsæn(d)ˌpeɪpə/ noun [U] strong paper with a rough surface that you rub

S

against wood or metal to make it smooth —**sandpaper** verb [T]

sandpit /'sæn(d)ˌpɪt/ noun [C] British a large low container that is filled with sand for children to play in

sandstone /'sæn(d)ˌstəʊn/ noun [U] a pale yellow stone that is used for building

sandstorm /'sæn(d)ˌstɔːm/ noun [C] a strong wind in the desert in which clouds of sand are blown into the air

sandwich¹ /'sæn(d)wɪdʒ/ noun [C] ★ two pieces of bread with a layer of food such as meat, cheese, or egg between them: *a ham/tuna/cheese sandwich* ♦ *I usually just have a sandwich for lunch.*

sandwich² /'sæn(d)wɪdʒ/ verb **be sandwiched between** to be in a small or tight space between two people or things that are larger: *The tiny kingdom was sandwiched between Austria and Czechoslovakia.*

sandy /'sændi/ adj covered with sand, or containing sand

sane /seɪn/ adj **1** able to think, speak, and behave in a reasonable and normal way ≠ INSANE **2** a sane action or decision is a sensible one

sang the past tense of **sing**

sanguine /'sæŋgwɪn/ adj formal confident and hopeful about what might happen =OPTIMISTIC

sanitary /'sænət(ə)ri/ adj **1** relating to people's health, especially to the system of supplying water and dealing with human waste **2** keeping things healthy and clean

'**sanitary ˌtowel** or '**sanitary ˌpad** noun [C] British a thick band of soft material that women put inside their underwear during MENSTRUATION

sanitation /ˌsænɪˈteɪʃ(ə)n/ noun [U] conditions and processes relating to people's health, especially the systems that supply water and deal with human waste

sanitize /'sænɪˌtaɪz/ verb [T] to remove information or details that might be offensive or unpleasant: *books that sanitize history*

sanity /'sænəti/ noun [U] the ability to think and speak in a reasonable way and to behave normally: *I was beginning to doubt my own sanity* (=think I was possibly mentally ill).

sank the past tense of SINK

Santa Claus /'sæntə ˌklɔːz/ or **Santa** /'sæntə/ an imaginary man with a long white BEARD and a red suit who brings presents for children at Christmas=FATHER CHRISTMAS

sap¹ /sæp/ noun [U] a sticky substance that is found in plants and trees

sap² /sæp/ verb [T] to make something become weak: *Years of illness had sapped his strength.*

sapling /'sæplɪŋ/ noun [C] a young tree

sapphire /'sæfaɪə/ noun [C/U] a clear blue jewel

sarcasm /'sɑːkæz(ə)m/ noun [U] the activity of saying or writing the opposite of what you mean, in order to make someone feel stupid or to show them that you are angry:

'Fascinating,' said Sheila, her voice heavy with sarcasm.

sarcastic /sɑːˈkæstɪk/ adj using sarcasm —**sarcastically** /sɑːˈkæstɪkli/ adv

sardine /sɑːˈdiːn/ noun [C] a small silver fish that is eaten as food

PHRASE **packed (in) like sardines** placed tightly together in a space so that there is no room to move

sardonic /sɑːˈdɒnɪk/ adj showing a lack of respect for what someone has said or done

sari /'sɑːri/ noun [C] a very long wide piece of cloth that women in South Asia wrap around their bodies to make a long dress

sash /sæʃ/ noun [C] **1** a long piece of cloth that you put around your waist or over one shoulder and across your chest, for example in an official ceremony **2** technical a piece of glass in a wooden frame that forms part of a window

sat the past tense and past participle of **sit**

Sat. abbrev Saturday

Satan /'seɪt(ə)n/ the most powerful evil spirit in many religions such as Christianity and Islam=DEVIL

satanic /səˈtænɪk/ adj **1** involving the worship of Satan as a god **2** very evil and cruel

satanism /'seɪt(ə)nˌɪz(ə)m/ noun [U] the worship of Satan as a god —**satanist** noun [C]

satchel /'sætʃəl/ noun [C] a bag with a long STRAP that goes over your shoulder, used for carrying school books

satellite /'sætəlaɪt/ noun ★
1 [C] an object that is sent into space to travel round the Earth in order to receive and send information: *a spy/ communications/weather satellite* ♦ *We have pictures of the disaster live via satellite* (=by satellite). ♦ *The new equipment will link vehicles by satellite to their office.*
2 [C] a natural object such as a moon that moves around a planet
3 [C] a country, city, or organization that depends on or is controlled by a larger, more powerful one: *She works in a satellite office.*
4 [U] SATELLITE TELEVISION

'**satellite ˌdish** noun [C] a piece of equipment in the shape of a dish that receives signals from a satellite —*picture* → C1

ˌ**satellite 'television** or ˌ**satellite TV** noun [U] television programmes that are sent to your television by SATELLITE

satin /'sætɪn/ noun [U] a very smooth shiny cloth that is used for making expensive clothes

satire /'sætaɪə/ noun **1** [U] the use of humour to criticize someone or something and make them seem silly **2** [C] a play, book, film etc that uses this humour

satirical /səˈtɪrɪk(ə)l/ adj using humour to criticize people or things and make them seem silly —**satirically** /səˈtɪrɪkli/ adv

satirist /'sætərɪst/ noun [C] someone who writes SATIRE

satirize /'sætəˌraɪz/ verb [T] to use SATIRE as a

way of criticizing people or things and making them seem silly

satisfaction /ˌsætɪsˈfækʃ(ə)n/ noun ★
1 [U] the feeling of pleasure that you get when you achieve or obtain something that you want ≠ DISSATISFACTION: *'My daughter is getting married,' she announced with satisfaction.* ♦ *He expressed **satisfaction with** the results.* ♦ *At least we **had the satisfaction of** knowing we had done our best.* ♦ *I get a lot of **satisfaction from** working in the garden.*
2 [C] something that gives you this feeling: *Being a parent is one of the great satisfactions in life.*
PHRASE **to sb's satisfaction** in the way that a particular person likes or wants: *The problem was resolved to everyone's satisfaction.*

satisfactory /ˌsætɪsˈfækt(ə)ri/ adj 1 good enough ≠ UNSATISFACTORY: *His work is far from satisfactory.* ♦ *I have still not received a satisfactory answer to my question.* ♦ *The patient was said to be in a satisfactory condition.* 2 enjoyable and pleasing: *a satisfactory outcome/conclusion/result* ♦ *This new arrangement proved highly satisfactory to us all.* —**satisfactorily** adv

satisfied /ˈsætɪsˌfaɪd/ adj 1 pleased with what has happened, or with what you have achieved: *a satisfied customer* ♦ *Honestly, some people are never satisfied!* ♦ *The President declared himself satisfied with the progress of the talks.* 2 if you are satisfied that something is true or correct, you do not need any more proof: *I am satisfied that they are doing all they can.*

satisfy /ˈsætɪsˌfaɪ/ verb ★★
1 [T] to please someone by giving them something that they want or need: *an agreement that is unlikely to satisfy environmental campaigners* ♦ *It's impossible to satisfy everyone.*
2 [I/T] to provide what is needed or wanted: *There's nothing like a cold drink to satisfy your thirst.* ♦ *I just want to satisfy my curiosity – why did he do it?*
3 [T] to have all the qualities or features that are necessary according to a rule, condition, or standard: *Students must satisfy all requirements to be accepted on the course.*
4 [T] to provide someone with the evidence that they need in order to be certain that something is true=CONVINCE: *The prosecution has to satisfy the jury that the defendant is guilty.*

satisfying /ˈsætɪsˌfaɪɪŋ/ adj making you feel pleased or happy because you have got what you want or need: *a satisfying result/achievement* ♦ *a satisfying meal*

SATS /sæts/ noun [plural] *British* Standard Assessment Tasks: in the UK, a set of tests in maths, English, and science that children take so that schools can judge their ability and progress

satsuma /sætˈsuːmə/ noun [C] a fruit similar to a small orange, but with a loose skin and without seeds

saturate /ˈsætʃəˌreɪt/ verb [T] 1 to make something completely wet 2 to fill something completely with a large number of things or a large amount of something —**saturation** /ˌsætʃəˈreɪʃ(ə)n/ noun [U]

saturated fat noun [C/U] fat from food such as meat or milk products that is difficult for the body to process, and is thought to be bad for your health

Saturday /ˈsætədeɪ/ noun [C/U] ★★★ the day after Friday and before Sunday: *I'm looking forward to the match next Saturday.* ♦ *Christmas is on a Saturday this year.* ♦ *See you on Saturday.* ♦ *I usually go for a walk on Saturdays* (=every Saturday).

sauce /sɔːs/ noun [C/U] ★ a liquid food that you put on other foods to give them a particular flavour: *tomato sauce* ♦ *ice cream and chocolate sauce*

saucepan /ˈsɔːspən/ noun [C] a round deep metal container with a long handle. It is used for cooking food on a COOKER. —*picture* → C2

saucer /ˈsɔːsə/ noun [C] a small round flat dish that you put a cup on → FLYING SAUCER

saucy /ˈsɔːsi/ adj referring to sex in a way that is funny

sauna /ˈsɔːnə/ noun [C] 1 a small hot wooden room that people sit in in order to SWEAT (=produce water from their skin) 2 a period of time spent in a sauna

saunter /ˈsɔːntə/ verb [I] to walk in a slow and relaxed way

sausage /ˈsɒsɪdʒ/ noun [C/U] a food that consists of a tube of skin containing meat mixed with SPICES

sausage roll noun [C] *British* a food that consists of a tube of PASTRY with sausage meat inside it

sauté /ˈsəʊteɪ/ verb [T] to cook something quickly in a small amount of fat or oil

savage¹ /ˈsævɪdʒ/ adj 1 extremely violent: *a savage attack/animal* 2 extremely severe: *savage cuts in public services* —**savagely** adv

savage² /ˈsævɪdʒ/ verb [T] 1 to criticize someone or something severely 2 if an animal savages someone, it attacks them and injures or kills them

savage³ /ˈsævɪdʒ/ noun [C] *old-fashioned* an insulting word for someone from a culture that is not advanced

savagery /ˈsævɪdʒ(ə)ri/ noun [U] extremely violent behaviour

save¹ /seɪv/ verb ★★★

1 help sb/sth avoid harm	7 collect things
2 help sb avoid doing sth	8 in computing
3 avoid using sth	9 in sport
4 put money in bank	+ PHRASE
5 keep sth for future	+ PHRASAL VERBS
6 keep sth for sb	

1 [T] to make it possible for someone or something to avoid danger, harm, injury etc: *campaigns to save the planet* ♦ *A cure for cancer would save thousands of lives each year.* ♦ *save sb/sth from sth Nothing can save this company from bankruptcy.*

S

2 [T] to make it possible for someone to avoid doing something: *Setting down clear rules from the start will save arguments later on.* ♦ **save sb sth** *If you get some milk on your way home, it'll save me a trip to the shops.* ♦ **save sb doing sth** *If you could tell her, that would save me phoning her.*

3 [T] to avoid using something such as money, time, or energy, or to use less of it: *You can save £25 if you buy your tickets before Saturday.* ♦ *Travelling by plane is more expensive, but it **saves time**.* ♦ **save sb sth** *Democrats argue their plan will save the government money in the future.*

4 [I/T] to regularly put money in a bank, or to invest it so that you can use it later: *Don't wait until you're 40 to start **saving for retirement**.* ♦ **save sth for sth** *I've managed to save almost £500 for my holiday.* ♦ **save to do sth** *We've been saving to buy a new car.*

5 [T] to keep or store something so that you can use it in the future: *Save some energy for the end of the race.* ♦ *Let's have one piece of cake now and **save the rest for later**.*

6 [T] to keep something for someone by making sure that other people do not take it: **save sth for sb** *Would you please save a place in the queue for me?* ♦ **save sb sth** *Save me some dinner and I'll have it when I get in.*

7 [T] to collect a set of things and keep them for a particular purpose: *Save eight tokens and you can get one of these amazing pens!*

8 [I/T] to make a computer keep information that you have put into it: *Where did you save the file you were working on?* ♦ *It's a good idea to save frequently.*

9 [I/T] if a GOALKEEPER saves a ball in a sport such as football, they prevent the ball from going into the net —*picture* → C15

> PHRASE **save face** to avoid seeming stupid or feeling embarrassed: *a compromise that allows both sides to save face*

> PHRASAL VERBS **save on sth 1** to spend less money on something than you would normally: *light bulbs that help you save on electricity bills* **2** to avoid using something, or to use less of it: *Keep your showers short to save on water.*
> ,save (sth) 'up *same as* save¹ 4: *I'm saving up for a new car.*
> ,save sth 'up *same as* save¹ 7: *You save up the tokens to get a prize.*

save² /seɪv/ noun [C] an action by a GOALKEEPER that prevents a ball from going into the net in a sport such as football

saver /ˈseɪvə/ noun [C] **1** someone who regularly puts money in a bank or BUILDING SOCIETY so that they can use it later **2** something that makes it possible for you to use or spend less of something: *Our new microwave is great – it's a real time saver.*

saving /ˈseɪvɪŋ/ noun ★
1 savings [plural] money that you have saved in a bank or invested so that you can use it later: *The money for the flight came out of my savings.*
2 [C] an amount of something that you

manage to avoid using or spending: *That could mean a **saving of** up to £500 for a family of four.* ♦ *At £350, this represents a considerable **saving on** the usual fee.*

,saving 'grace noun [singular] a good quality that makes it possible for you to accept someone or something that is bad in all other ways

saviour /ˈseɪvjə/ noun **1** [C] someone who saves someone or something from trouble or danger **2 the Saviour** or **Our Saviour** a name that Christians sometimes use for Jesus Christ

savour /ˈseɪvə/ verb [T] to enjoy an experience, activity, or feeling as much as you can and for as long as you can

savoury /ˈseɪvəri/ adj tasting of salt or SPICES and not sweet

savvy¹ /ˈsævi/ adj *informal* knowing a lot about something and able to make good judgments about it

savvy² /ˈsævi/ noun [U] *informal* the ability to understand and judge people and situations well

saw¹ /sɔː/ noun [C] a tool that is used for cutting wood or metal —*picture* → TOOL

saw² /sɔː/ (past participle **sawn** /sɔːn/) verb [I/T] to cut something with a saw

> PHRASAL VERB ,saw sth 'off to remove something by cutting through it with a saw or knife

saw³ the past tense of **see**

sawdust /ˈsɔːdʌst/ noun [U] very small pieces of wood like dust that are produced when you cut wood

sawmill /ˈsɔːmɪl/ noun [C] a building where wood is cut into boards using machines

sawn the past participle of **saw²**

sax /sæks/ noun [C] *informal* a SAXOPHONE

saxophone /ˈsæksəfəʊn/ noun [C] a musical instrument consisting of a long curved metal tube that you play by blowing into as you press its KEYS with your fingers —*picture* → WOODWIND —**saxophonist** /sækˈsɒfənɪst/ noun [C]

say¹ /seɪ/ (3rd person singular **says** /sez/; past tense and past participle **said** /sed/) verb ★★★

1 express with words	4 show sth
2 have opinion	5 imagine sth
3 give information	+ PHRASES

1 [I/T] to express something using words: *'Pleased to meet you,' he said with a smile.* ♦ *'When's he coming back?' 'He didn't say.'* ♦ *The committee **said yes** (=gave permission), so we can go ahead.* ♦ *What an odd **thing to say**, Carrie thought.* ♦ *I then **said goodbye** and left.* ♦ *I've already **said sorry** for hurting his feelings.* ♦ **+(that)** *She said that she liked dancing.* ♦ **+how/what/who etc** *Did he say who called?* ♦ **say sth to sb** *Tell me what he said to you.* ♦ **say sth on/about** *I want to say something on this subject.*

2 [T] to think something, or to have a particular opinion: *I think we should stop now. What do you say?* ♦ *'Will she meet the* deadline?' 'I would say so (=think it is likely).' ♦ +(that) He always said you'd be rich and famous one day. ♦ I say we go (=I think we should go) by car: it's quicker than the train. ♦ be said to do sth She is said to have great talent as an artist.

3 [T] to give information or orders in writing, numbers, pictures etc: My watch says quarter to twelve. ♦ Her letter says she's arriving at midday. ♦ +(that) The rules say that we need a two-thirds majority to win. ♦ +how/when/what etc Does it say on the box how much it costs?

4 [T] to show indirectly what someone or something is like: This problem says something about the way the company is run.

5 [T] to imagine what will happen in a particular situation: Say you get £2,000 for the car – you'll still need another thousand.

PHRASES go without saying (that) to be completely obvious or true: It goes without saying that I'm sorry.

have something/a lot/nothing etc to say for yourself to be fairly/very/not at all keen to talk about yourself and your reasons for doing something: He didn't have a lot to say for himself.

having said that spoken used for adding an opinion that seems to be the opposite of what you have just said, although you think both are true: It's expensive. Having said that, I admit that it is very well made.

I must say (that) used for emphasizing a statement: I'm not very impressed, I must say. ♦ I must say that the standard of play was awful.

I wouldn't say no (to sth) spoken used for admitting that you would like something: I wouldn't say no to another piece of cake.

say it all used for saying that something shows very clearly what someone's feelings are or what a particular situation is really like: The look on his face says it all.

say sth to yourself to think something: 'This is the real thing,' he said to himself. ♦ I keep saying to myself that I shouldn't do it.

say when spoken used for asking someone to tell you when you have given them enough food or drink

that is to say formal used for explaining something that you have just said in a more exact way: I'll deal with the second point first, that is to say the change to the club's rules.

to say the least used for saying that you could have expressed something in a much stronger way: I found the flight rather uncomfortable, to say the least.

you can say that again spoken used for expressing strong agreement with what someone has said: 'This is so boring!' 'You can say that again!'

you don't say spoken **1** used for saying that you are surprised by what someone has told you: 'He's just won the lottery.' 'You don't say!' **2** used for saying that you are not surprised by what someone has told you: 'He phoned in sick again this morning.' 'You don't say!'

■ You **say** something to someone. **Say** is followed by the words that someone uses, or by reported speech: She said no to me. ♦ 'Hello', he said. ♦ I said that I was cold.

■ You **tell** someone something when you give them information or an instruction. **Tell** is usually followed by the person who is spoken to: 'It's time to go', he told us. ♦ I told Kate to shut up.

■ **Speak** and **talk** mean to say something. They are not usually followed by an object: Don't interrupt me when I'm speaking. ♦ Jade and Adele were talking in the corner.

say² /seɪ/ noun [singular/U] the right to give your opinion and be involved in a discussion about something: The junior staff had no say in this decision.

PHRASE have your say to get the chance to say what you think about something

saying /ˈseɪɪŋ/ noun [C] a well-known statement about what often happens in life

scab /skæb/ noun [C] **1** a hard layer of dried blood that forms on a cut on your skin **2** offensive an insulting word for someone who continues to work while others are on STRIKE

scaffold /ˈskæfəʊld/ noun [C] **1** a structure consisting of poles and boards on the outside of a building. You stand on it when you are working on the building. **2** a structure on which criminals were killed in the past by being HANGED or BEHEADED

scaffolding /ˈskæfəʊldɪŋ/ noun [U] poles and boards used for making a scaffold on the outside of a building

scald /skɔːld/ verb [T] to burn your skin with very hot liquid or steam —**scald** noun [C]

scalding /ˈskɔːldɪŋ/ adj very hot

scale¹ /skeɪl/ noun ★★★

1 size/rate/level	5 for weighing
2 range	6 series of musical notes
3 set of marks	7 hard piece of skin
4 of map/model	

S

1 [singular/U] the size, rate, or level of something: Is the Government aware of **the scale of the problem** (=are they aware of how big it is)?

2 [C] a range of numbers or amounts forming a system for separating things into different groups: the Celsius scale of temperature ♦ The rich are at the top of the social scale. ♦ We were told to rate the films **on a scale of 1 to 10**.

3 [C] a set of marks on a piece of equipment or a drawing, used for measuring something: the vertical scale on the graph

4 [C/U] the relationship between the actual distance or size of something and how it is shown on a map or in a drawing or model: This map has a scale of 1:20,000.

5 scales [plural] a piece of equipment that you use for weighing people or things: a pair/set of scales ♦ He weighed himself on **the bathroom scales**. → TIP²

6 [C] a series of musical notes in a fixed order: She was **practising scales** on her new piano.

7 [C] one of the small hard flat pieces of skin on the body of a fish, snake, or similar animal

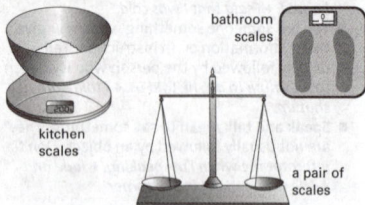

bathroom scales

kitchen scales

a pair of scales

scale² /skeɪl/ verb [T] to climb to or over the top of a mountain, wall etc

PHRASAL VERB ,scale sth 'down or ,scale sth 'back to make something smaller in size, amount etc

scallop /'skɒləp, 'skæləp/ noun [C] a SHELLFISH, eaten as food

scalp /skælp/ noun [C] the skin under the hair on your head

scalpel /'skælp(ə)l/ noun [C] a small sharp knife that a doctor uses for doing an operation

scaly /'skeɪli/ adj scaly skin is so dry that small pieces of it fall off

scam /skæm/ noun [C] informal a dishonest plan for getting money

scamper /'skæmpə/ verb [I] to move quickly with small light steps

scampi /'skæmpi/ noun [U] British large PRAWNS covered with BREADCRUMBS and cooked in hot oil

scan¹ /skæn/ verb **1** [T] to look at something very carefully in order to see a particular person or thing: *Ella scanned the crowd for any sign of Geoff.* **2** [I/T] to read something very quickly in order to get a general idea of its meaning or to find particular information: *She scanned the paper for any news of them.* **3** [I/T] to copy and store information in DIGITAL form using computer equipment **4** [T] to use a piece of equipment to produce a picture of the inside of an object or a part of your body

PHRASAL VERB 'scan ,through (sth) same as scan¹ 2

scan² /skæn/ noun [C] a medical test that uses a piece of equipment to produce a picture of the inside of your body

scandal /'skænd(ə)l/ noun **1** [C/U] a situation in which people behave in a dishonest or immoral way that shocks people: *a sex scandal* **2** [U] talk or reports in the newspapers or on television about shocking behaviour: *the endless stream of scandal offered by the tabloid press*

scandalize /'skænd(ə)l,aɪz/ verb [T] to do something that shocks someone

scandalous /'skænd(ə)ləs/ adj shocking and immoral or dishonest

scanner /'skænə/ noun [C] **1** a piece of equipment that you use for copying a picture or document into a computer **2** a

piece of equipment that is used for producing a picture of the inside of an object or a part of your body

scant /skænt/ adj very little, or not enough: *Peter had shown scant regard for her feelings.*

scantily /'skæntɪli/ adv **scantily clad/dressed** wearing clothes that do not cover much of your body

scapegoat /'skeɪp,gəʊt/ noun [C] someone who is blamed for something that is not their fault —**scapegoat** verb [T]

scar¹ /skɑː/ noun [C] **1** a permanent mark on your skin where you have been injured: *He has a scar under his left eye.* **2** a permanent effect on someone's mind, caused by an unpleasant experience: *She bore the scars of an unhappy childhood.*

scar² /skɑː/ verb [T] **1** to leave a permanent mark on someone's skin as the result of an injury **2** if an unpleasant experience scars someone, it has a permanent effect on the way that they think and live: *He got involved in drugs at an early age, and it scarred him for life.*

scarce /skeəs/ adj if something is scarce, there is not very much of it ≠ ABUNDANT: *Fresh water and medicines were scarce in the disaster area.*

scarcely /'skeəsli/ adv **1** almost not, or almost none=BARELY, HARDLY: *There was scarcely any traffic.* **2** only just=BARELY: *We had scarcely driven a mile when the car broke down.* **3** used for showing that something is certainly not true or possible=HARDLY: *I can scarcely refuse to help after all he's done for me.*

scarcity /'skeəsəti/ noun [singular/U] a situation in which there is not enough of something for the people who want or need it=SHORTAGE ≠ ABUNDANCE

scare¹ /skeə/ verb **1** [T] to make someone feel frightened: *I'm sorry, I didn't mean to scare you.* **2** [I] to become frightened

PHRASAL VERB ,scare sb a'way or ,scare sb 'off **1** to make someone feel so frightened or worried that they do not do something that they had planned to do **2** to make someone so frightened that they run away

scare² /skeə/ noun [C] **1** a situation that makes people suddenly feel frightened or worried about something: *a bomb scare* **2** a sudden feeling of fear: *It gave me quite a scare when the cat jumped on me.*

scarecrow /'skeə,krəʊ/ noun [C] an object in the shape of a person that farmers put in their fields to frighten birds away

scared /skeəd/ adj ★ frightened, or worried: *I'm scared stiff* (=extremely scared) *of having the operation.* ♦ *Louise is scared of flying.* ♦ **+(that)** *I'm scared I'll fail all my exams.* ♦ **be scared to do sth** *Mike was too scared to go bungee jumping.*

scarf /skɑːf/ (plural **scarves** /skɑːvz/) noun [C] a piece of cloth that you wear round your neck or head —*picture* → C4

scarlet /'skɑːlət/ adj bright red in colour —**scarlet** noun [U]

scarves the plural of **scarf**

scary /ˈskeəri/ adj frightening: *a scary story*

scathing /ˈskeɪðɪŋ/ adj criticizing someone or something in a very strong way

scatter /ˈskætə/ verb **1** [T] to throw or drop things so that they spread over an area **2** [I/T] if a group of people or animals scatter, or if something scatters them, they suddenly move away in different directions

scattered /ˈskætəd/ adj **1** spread over a large area: *My relatives are scattered all over the country.* **2** happening in only a few places: *scattered showers*

scattering /ˈskætərɪŋ/ noun [C] a small number of people or things that are spread over a large area

scavenge /ˈskævɪndʒ/ verb [I/T] **1** if an animal scavenges, it eats anything that it can find **2** to search through things that other people have thrown away in order to see if there is anything that you want —**scavenger** noun [C]

scenario /səˈnɑːriəʊ/ noun [C] a situation that could possibly happen: *The most likely scenario is that Brooks will resign.* ♦ *According to the worst-case scenario, global temperatures could rise by 8 degrees in the next 30 years.*

scene /siːn/ noun [C] ★★★

1 part of play/book etc	**4** activity/interest
2 view	**5** argument etc in public
3 where sth happens	**+ PHRASES**

1 a part of a play, book, film etc in which events happen in the same place or period of time: *a love scene* ♦ *the opening scene* of Macbeth

2 a view that you can see in a picture or from the place where you are: *She stood in the doorway surveying the scene.* ♦ *paintings that depict scenes of country life*

3 a place where something happens: *the scene of the crime/accident/attack* ♦ *The paramedics will be at the scene within a few minutes.*

4 a particular interest or activity, and the people and places that are involved in it: *an important figure on the political scene* ♦ *the music/rave/dance scene*

5 a noisy argument or a strong show of feelings in a public place: *Stop making such a scene!*

PHRASES behind the scenes secretly: *These agreements have been drafted by officials behind the scenes.*

set the scene 1 to create the conditions that make it possible for an event to happen: *These findings have set the scene for further debate on the system.* **2** to give someone the information that they need so that they can understand what is going to happen or be said: *Let me just set the scene by telling you a little about the school.*

scenery /ˈsiːnəri/ noun [U] **1** natural things such as trees, hills, and lakes that you can see in a particular place: *Switzerland has some valuable scenery.* **2** the furniture

and painted background on a theatre stage

scenic /ˈsiːnɪk/ adj providing beautiful views of nature

scent¹ /sent/ noun **1** [C] a pleasant smell: *an apple with a rich flavour and scent* **2** [C/U] a liquid that women put on their skin to make themselves smell nice=FRAGRANCE, PERFUME **3** [C/U] the smell that an animal or person has, that some animals can follow

PHRASE the scent of sth a feeling that a new situation is going to happen: *The scent of victory was in the air.*

scent² /sent/ verb [T] if an animal scents someone or something, it knows that they are there because of their smell

scented /ˈsentɪd/ adj having a pleasant smell

sceptic /ˈskeptɪk/ noun [C] someone who has doubts about things that other people think are true or right

sceptical /ˈskeptɪk(ə)l/ adj having doubts about something that other people think is true or right: *I'm very sceptical about the results of the survey.*

scepticism /ˈskeptɪˌsɪz(ə)m/ noun [U] doubts that someone has about something that other people think is true or right

schedule¹ /ˈʃedjuːl/ noun [C] ★ a plan of activities or events and when they will happen=TIMETABLE: *What's on your schedule today?* ♦ *Our MP has a very busy schedule.* ♦ *We're shooting the film on a very tight schedule* (=with many things to do in a short time). ♦ *a project completed ahead of schedule* (=before the time that was planned)

schedule² /ˈʃedʒuːl/ verb [T] to plan for something to happen at a particular time =TIMETABLE: *Let's schedule another meeting for July.* ♦ *The exhibition is scheduled to run from January until March.*

scheduled /ˈʃedʒuːld/ adj planned to happen at a particular time, or at the same time each day, week etc: *a scheduled lecture* ♦ *a scheduled flight*

scheme¹ /skiːm/ noun [C] ★★
1 *British* a plan that is developed by a government or large organization in order to provide a particular service for people: *a training scheme* ♦ *The proposed scheme should solve the parking problem.* ♦ *Have you joined the company pension scheme?*
2 a plan for achieving something, especially something illegal or dishonest: *a crazy money-making scheme*

scheme² /skiːm/ verb [I] to make secret plans to achieve something, especially in an illegal or dishonest way=PLOT: *She's convinced that they're scheming against her.* —**schemer** noun [C], **scheming** adj

schizophrenia /ˌskɪtsəʊˈfriːniə/ noun [U] a serious mental illness in which the way that you think and feel is not connected with what is really happening

schizophrenic /ˌskɪtsəʊˈfrenɪk/ adj relating to schizophrenia, or affected by it —**schizophrenic** noun [C]

scholar /ˈskɒlə/ noun [C] **1** someone who

S

studies a particular subject and knows a lot about it **2** someone who is given a SCHOLARSHIP to study at a particular school or university

scholarly /'skɒləli/ adj **1** based on serious academic study: *a scholarly discussion* **2** someone who is scholarly knows a lot about a particular subject or studies something seriously

scholarship /'skɒləʃɪp/ noun **1** [C] an amount of money that an organization gives to someone so that they can study at a particular school or university: *Sophie was awarded a scholarship to attend Boston University.* **2** [U] serious formal study and the knowledge that you get from it: *a work of great scholarship*

scholastic /skə'læstɪk/ adj *formal* connected with schools, teaching, or studying
=ACADEMIC, EDUCATIONAL

school /skuːl/ noun ★★★

1 where children learn	**6** people sharing ideas
2 period of education	**7** college/university
3 everyone in school	**8** large group of fish etc
4 department	**+** PHRASE
5 where skill is taught	

1 [C/U] a place where children go to be taught, or the time during the day when they are there: *the biggest school in the city* ♦ *The kids will be at school until 3.00 today.* ♦ *It's time to go to school.* ♦ *They go swimming after school.*
2 [U] the situation or period of years when you receive your education: *Both of my kids are still at school.* ♦ *I left school when I was fifteen.*
3 [singular] all the students and staff at a school: *The whole school assembled in the hall.*
4 [C/U] a university department or a college that teaches a particular subject: *the Slade School of Fine Art* ♦ *the School of Management* ♦ *medical/law school*
5 [C/U] a private institution that teaches a particular skill: *the Perkins School of Ballroom Dancing* ♦ *a driving school*
6 [C] a group of writers, artists etc whose work or ideas are similar: *the Impressionist school of painting*
7 [C/U] *American informal* a college or university: *Cornell is a very good school.*
8 [C] a large group of fish, DOLPHINS, WHALES etc

PHRASE **school of thought** a way of thinking about a particular subject or idea that is shared by a group of people

schoolboy /'skuːlˌbɔɪ/ noun [C] *old-fashioned* a boy who goes to school

schoolchild /'skuːlˌtʃaɪld/ (plural **schoolchildren** /'skuːlˌtʃɪldrən/) noun [C] a child who goes to school

schooldays /'skuːlˌdeɪz/ noun [plural] the time in your life when you go to school

schoolgirl /'skuːlˌgɜːl/ noun [C] *old-fashioned* a girl who goes to school

schooling /'skuːlɪŋ/ noun [U] the education that you get at school

school-leaver noun [C] *British* someone who has just left school and is looking for a job

schoolteacher /'skuːlˌtiːtʃə/ noun [C] a teacher who works in a school

schwa /ʃwɑː/ noun [C] *linguistics* a vowel sound used in UNSTRESSED SYLLABLES, for example the sound of 'a' in 'above'. Its symbol is /ə/.

science /'saɪəns/ noun ★★★
1 [U] the study and knowledge of the physical world and its behaviour, that is based on experiments and facts and is organized into a system: *recent advances in science* ♦ *a science teacher*
2 [C] a scientific subject such as chemistry, physics, or biology

science fiction noun [U] books and films about imaginary future events that often include space travel and creatures from other planets

scientific /ˌsaɪən'tɪfɪk/ adj ★★
1 relating to science, or based on the methods of science: *scientific research* ♦ *scientific instruments*
2 done in an organized way: *There's nothing scientific about the process they use to select people.*
—**scientifically** /ˌsaɪən'tɪfɪkli/ adv

scientist /'saɪəntɪst/ noun [C] ★★ someone who is trained in science, especially someone whose job is to do scientific research

sci-fi /'saɪ faɪ/ noun [U] *informal* SCIENCE FICTION

scintillating /'sɪntɪˌleɪtɪŋ/ adj very impressive, interesting, or clever

scissors /'sɪzəz/ noun [plural] a tool for cutting paper, with two blades that open and shut

scoff /skɒf/ verb **1** [I] to laugh or say things to show that you do not respect someone or something **2** [T] *British informal* to eat a lot of something very quickly

scold /skəʊld/ verb [T] *old-fashioned* to criticize someone angrily because they have done something that is wrong

scone /skɒn, skəʊn/ noun [C] a small soft cake that sometimes contains dried fruit. You usually eat scones with butter.

scoop¹ /skuːp/ verb [T] **1** to dig something out, or to pick something up, using an object or your curved hand: *He scooped some water from the stream.* **2** *mainly journalism* to earn or win something: *Advisors will scoop fees of up to one million pounds.*

scoop² /skuːp/ noun [C] **1** a tool like a spoon that is used for measuring or serving something, or the amount that this tool holds **2** *informal* an exciting or important news story that one news organization publishes or broadcasts before anyone else

scooter /'skuːtə/ noun [C] **1** a child's vehicle that consists of a board with two small wheels and an upright handle. You stand on the board with one foot and push with the other. **2** a vehicle with an engine and two small wheels that looks like a small MOTORCYCLE

scope /skəʊp/ noun [U] ★
1 the things that a particular activity,

organization, subject etc deals with =RANGE: *The new law is limited in scope.* ◆ *These issues are beyond the scope of this book.* ◆ *Responsibility for office services is not within the scope of the department.* **2** the opportunity or freedom to do something: *There is still much scope for improvement.*

scorch /skɔːtʃ/ verb [T] to burn something slightly so that it changes colour or is damaged on the surface

scorched /skɔːtʃt/ adj burnt on the surface

scorching /ˈskɔːtʃɪŋ/ adj extremely hot

score¹ /skɔː/ verb ★★
1 [I/T] to get a point in a game or sport: *No one scored in the first half.* ◆ *He scored the first goal after five minutes.* —picture → C15
2 [T] to achieve a particular amount, level etc in a test: *She's hoping to score full marks in the maths test.*
3 [I/T] to be successful in doing something: *She seems to have scored with her latest novel.* ◆ *They scored some big sales successes.*
4 [T] to mark a line into the surface of something: *Score the meat lightly with a knife.*

score² /skɔː/ noun ★★
1 [C] the number of points that someone gains in a game or test: *The average score for the test was 75.* ◆ *The final score was 4–3 to United.*
2 [C] a written copy of a piece of music
3 **scores** [plural] a large number of people or things: *Scores of volunteers offered to help.*
4 [C] *literary* a group of 20 people or things
PHRASES **know the score** *informal* to know the truth about something, especially when it is unpleasant: *You don't have to lie to me. I know the score.*
on that/this score concerning the thing that has just been mentioned: *We wanted to attract new recruits, and on that score, the campaign has been successful.*

scoreboard /ˈskɔːbɔːd/ noun [C] a large board that shows the score in a game or sports event

scorn¹ /skɔːn/ noun [U] a feeling that someone or something is not good enough to deserve your approval or respect

scorn² /skɔːn/ verb [T] to treat someone or something as if they do not deserve your approval or respect

scornful /ˈskɔːnf(ə)l/ adj feeling or expressing scorn —**scornfully** adv

Scorpio /ˈskɔːpiəʊ/ noun [C/U] one of the twelve signs of the ZODIAC. A **Scorpio** is someone who was born between 24 October and 22 November.

scorpion /ˈskɔːpiən/ noun [C] an animal like a large insect that has a curved tail with a poisonous part on the end

Scot /skɒt/ noun [C] someone from Scotland

Scotch /skɒtʃ/ noun [C/U] WHISKY that is produced in Scotland, or a glass of this drink

Scotland Yard /ˌskɒtlənd ˈjɑːd/ the department of the London police that deals with serious national crime, or the building where this department works

scoundrel /ˈskaʊndrəl/ noun [C] *old-fashioned* a man who behaves in an unfair or dishonest way

scour /ˈskaʊə/ verb [T] **1** to search a place or document thoroughly for something: *Police officers are scouring the area for the missing child.* **2** to clean something thoroughly by rubbing it hard with something rough

scourge /skɜːdʒ/ noun [C] *formal* something that causes a lot of trouble or harm

scout¹ /skaʊt/ noun [C] **1** a soldier who is sent by an army to get information about the position of the enemy **2** someone whose job is to find and employ people who have special abilities, for example in sports or entertainment: *a talent scout* **3** **scout** or **Scout** a BOY SCOUT

scout² /skaʊt/ verb [I/T] to search for someone or something

scowl /skaʊl/ verb [I] to put an angry expression on your face —**scowl** noun [C]

scrabble /ˈskræb(ə)l/ verb [I] to make a lot of small quick movements with your fingers, especially when you are trying to find something that you cannot see

scramble /ˈskræmb(ə)l/ verb [I] **1** to climb somewhere quickly using your feet and hands=CLAMBER: *She managed to scramble over the wall.* **2** to move somewhere quickly and in a way that is not graceful: *He scrambled awkwardly to his feet.* **3** to try very hard to get something that other people are also trying to get: *Companies are scrambling to recruit skilled workers.* —**scramble** noun [singular]

scrambled eggs /ˌskræmb(ə)ld ˈegz/ noun [plural] eggs that are cooked with their white and yellow parts mixed together —picture → EGG

scrap¹ /skræp/ noun **1** [C] a small piece of something: *a scrap of paper* ◆ *Every scrap of evidence has to be investigated.* **2** [U] old metal that can be used again after going through a special process: *The car was sold for scrap.* **3** [C] *informal* a fight or argument

scrap² /skræp/ verb [T] **1** *informal* to decide not to continue with something such as a plan or event=ABANDON **2** to get rid of something

scrapbook /ˈskræpbʊk/ noun [C] a book in which you stick pictures, articles etc

scrape¹ /skreɪp/ verb **1** [T] to remove something by pulling a hard tool across the surface it is on: *Scrape the mud off your boots before you come inside.* **2** [I/T] if a sharp edge or point scrapes a surface, or if you scrape it across the surface, it moves across a surface: *He felt the knife blade scrape against the back of his neck.* **3** [T] to injure a part of your body or damage something by rubbing it against a rough surface =GRAZE: *I scraped my elbow when I fell over.* ◆ *He scraped his van while he was parking it.* **4** [I] to make a rough unpleasant noise by rubbing against a hard surface: *Simon's chair scraped as he pushed it back.*
PHRASAL VERBS **scrape ˈby** to have just enough money to pay for the things that

S

you really need in order to live, but no more: *She just manages to scrape by on her teacher's salary.*

,scrape 'through sth to succeed in doing something, but not in a very impressive way: *I think he'll just scrape through the entrance exam.*

,scrape sth to'gether to succeed in getting enough of something by making a lot of effort: *They have trouble even scraping together their rent.*

scrape² /skreɪp/ noun **1** [C] a slight injury or mark caused by rubbing against a rough surface **2** [singular] the sound caused by something rubbing against a hard surface **3** [C] *informal* a difficult situation that you cause by being careless

scrapheap /ˈskræp,hiːp/ noun **on the scrapheap** no longer wanted or needed, although still capable of being useful

scrappy /ˈskræpi/ adj not done in an organized way

scratch¹ /skrætʃ/ verb **1** [I/T] to pull your nails along your skin, especially because you have an ITCH that makes you want to do this: *Scratch my back for me.* **2** [T] to damage a surface by cutting it slightly or marking it with something sharp or rough: *Don't worry: the cat won't scratch you.* ♦ *Someone's scratched my car door.* **3** [I/T] to move something sharp or rough against a hard surface and make a noise: *I could hear the dog scratching at the back door.*

scratch

scratch² /skrætʃ/ noun [C] **1** a narrow mark on your skin or on a surface that is caused by cutting it slightly or marking it with something sharp or rough **2** the action of pulling your nails along your skin, especially because you have an ITCH that makes you want to do this **3** a sound made by moving something sharp or rough against a hard surface

PHRASES from scratch from the beginning, doing everything yourself: *the travel company he built from scratch*
up to scratch *informal* good enough

scrawl /skrɔːl/ verb [T] to write something carelessly or in a hurry, so that it is difficult to read —**scrawl** noun [C]

scrawny /ˈskrɔːni/ adj very thin, in a way that is not attractive or healthy

scream¹ /skriːm/ verb ★
1 [I] to make a loud high cry because you are hurt, frightened, or excited: *She opened her mouth to scream.* ♦ *They were screaming*

with delight. ♦ *We could hear the passengers screaming in terror.* → SHOUT
2 [I] to make a very loud high noise: *screaming engines*
3 [I/T] to shout something in a very loud voice=YELL: *She heard Anna scream her name.* ♦ *Nobody heard them screaming for help.* ♦ *I felt like screaming at him.*

scream² /skriːm/ noun [C] **1** a loud high cry that you make because you are hurt, frightened, or excited=SHRIEK **2** a very loud high noise=SCREECH

PHRASE be a scream *informal* to be extremely funny

screech /skriːtʃ/ verb [I/T] to make a loud, high, and unpleasant cry or noise=SHRIEK: *Seagulls were screeching over our heads.* ♦ *The car screeched to a halt.* —**screech** noun [C]

screen¹ /skriːn/ noun ★★

1 on television etc	**4** for separating area
2 for showing film	**5** for keeping insects out
3 cinema	

1 [C] the flat surface on a computer, television, or piece of electronic equipment where words and pictures are shown: *Suddenly the screen went blank.*
2 [C] the flat surface in a cinema where the picture is shown: *a new 14-screen cinema*
3 [U] cinema in general: *a star of stage and screen*
4 [C] a flat structure that is used for separating one area of a room from another: *She got undressed behind a folding screen.*
5 [C] a wire or plastic net in a frame that fits in a door or window and lets air into a building but keeps insects out

screen² /skriːn/ verb [T] **1** to broadcast a television programme, or to show a film: *The series is currently being screened on BBC2 on Fridays.* **2** to hide someone or something by being in front of them: *A line of fir trees screened the house from the road.* **3** to get information about someone in order to decide whether they are suitable for a job=VET —**screening** noun [C/U]

PHRASAL VERB ,screen sth 'off to separate one part of a room from another with a screen

screenplay /ˈskriːn,pleɪ/ noun [C] a story that someone writes for a film

screen ,saver noun [C] a computer program that makes the screen black or shows a picture when the computer is on but not being used

screenwriter /ˈskriːn,raɪtə/ noun [C] someone whose job is to write stories for films

screw¹ /skruː/ verb [T] **1** to fasten one thing to another using screws ≠ UNSCREW: *The rails need to be firmly screwed to the wall.* **2** to put something into its position by turning it: *Make sure you screw the lid on firmly to keep the contents fresh.* **3** to make something into a smaller shape by squeezing or twisting it: *She was nervously screwing her tissue into a ball.*

S

PHRASAL VERBS ,screw (sth) 'up *very informal* to make a serious mistake or spoil something ≈MESS (STH) UP

,screw sth 'up **1** to make something into a smaller shape by squeezing or twisting it **2** if you screw up your eyes, you close them tightly

screw² /skruː/ noun [C] a thin pointed piece of metal that you push and turn in order to fasten one thing to another

screwdriver /'skruːˌdraɪvə/ noun [C] a tool used for turning screws —*picture* → TOOL

screwed up /ˌskruːd 'ʌp/ adj *informal* upset, unhappy, or confused as a result of bad experiences that you have had

scribble /'skrɪb(ə)l/ verb **1** [T] to write something quickly and carelessly **2** [I/T] to make marks or drawings with no meaning —**scribble** noun [C/U]

script¹ /skrɪpt/ noun ★
1 [C] the written words of a play, film, television programme, speech etc
2 [C/U] a system of written letters and symbols: *Roman script*

script² /skrɪpt/ verb [T] to write the words of something such as a film, television programme, or speech

scripture /'skrɪptʃə/ noun [C/U] the holy writings of a religion

scriptwriter /'skrɪptˌraɪtə/ noun [C] someone whose job is to write the words for films or television programmes

scroll¹ /skrəʊl/ noun [C] a long roll of paper with ancient writing on it

scroll² /skrəʊl/ verb [I/T] *computing* to move words or images up or down a computer screen in order to read or look at something: *It shouldn't take long to scroll through the document and check the spelling.*

'scroll ,bar noun [C] *computing* a long narrow area at the edge of a computer screen that is used for moving information up, down, or across the screen

scrooge /skruːdʒ/ noun [C] *informal* someone who hates spending money

scrounge /skraʊndʒ/ verb [I/T] *informal* to get something that you want by asking someone for it, instead of providing it or paying for it yourself

scrub¹ /skrʌb/ verb [I/T] to wash or clean something by rubbing it hard with a brush or cloth

scrub² /skrʌb/ noun **1** [U] small bushes and trees that grow in areas without much rain **2** [singular] a thorough wash or clean that you give something by rubbing it hard with a brush or cloth

scruff /skrʌf/ noun **by the scruff of the/sb's neck** by the back of the neck

scruffy /'skrʌfi/ adj untidy, or dirty

scrum /skrʌm/ noun [C] an arrangement of players in a game of RUGBY in which they all push together to try and get the ball

scrunch /skrʌntʃ/ or ,scrunch sth 'up verb [T] to press or squeeze something into a smaller shape

scruples /'skruːp(ə)lz/ noun [plural] moral

principles that prevent you from doing something that you think is bad

scrupulous /'skruːpjʊləs/ adj **1** very careful to be honest and to do what is morally right ≠ UNSCRUPULOUS **2** done very carefully, giving a lot of attention to details —**scrupulously** adv

scrutinize /'skruːtɪˌnaɪz/ verb [T] to examine someone or something very carefully

scrutiny /'skruːtəni/ noun [U] careful examination of someone or something: *The industry comes under scrutiny in tonight's programme.*

scuba diving /'skuːbə ˌdaɪvɪŋ/ noun [U] the activity of swimming under water with a container of air on your back and a tube for breathing through

scuff /skʌf/ verb [T] to make a mark on the surface of something, especially a shoe, by rubbing it against something rough

scuffle /'skʌf(ə)l/ noun [C] a fight that lasts for a short time and is not very violent —**scuffle** verb [I]

sculptor /'skʌlptə/ noun [C] an artist who makes sculptures

sculpture /'skʌlptʃə/ noun **1** [C/U] a solid object that someone makes as a work of art by shaping a substance such as stone, metal, or wood **2** [U] the art of making sculptures

scum /skʌm/ noun [U] **1** a layer of a dirty or unpleasant substance that forms on the surface of a liquid **2** *offensive* an insulting word for a person or people who you think are very unpleasant

scurry /'skʌri/ verb [I] to hurry to do something or get something

scuttle /'skʌt(ə)l/ verb [I] to move quickly with short steps

scythe /saɪð/ noun [C] a tool with a long curved metal blade for cutting long grass or grain

SE abbrev south east

sea /siː/ noun ★★★
1 [singular/U] the large area of salt water that covers most of the surface of the Earth: *He had a room overlooking the sea.* ♦ *Tim went swimming in the sea.* ♦ *We're renting a house by the sea* (=close to the sea). ♦ *He died in an accident at sea.* ♦ *Most of his belongings will be transported by sea.* ♦ *She rowed the boat out to sea.*
2 [C] the condition of the sea, especially the way it is affected by the weather: *A fishing boat is missing in rough seas off the Shetlands.*
3 [C] a large area of salt water: *The dam will create an enormous inland sea.*
PHRASE **a sea of sth** a large amount of something: *She looked out over a sea of smiling faces.*

■ In British English, **the sea** is the large area of salt water along the coast of a country: *They live by the sea.*
■ In American English, **the ocean** is the general word for this area of salt water: *He looked out at the ocean.*

S

■ In British and American English, an **ocean** is one of the very large seas that cover most of the Earth: *the Atlantic/Pacific Ocean*

'sea ,bed, the noun [singular] the ground at the bottom of the sea

'sea ,change noun [singular] a very important change

seafood /'si:fu:d/ noun [U] fish and SHELLFISH that you can eat

seafront /'si:frʌnt/ noun [singular] the part of a town that is close to the sea

seagull /'si:gʌl/ noun [C] a large grey and white bird that lives near the sea

seahorse /'si:hɔ:s/ noun [C] a small sea fish with a head that looks like a horse's head

seal¹ /si:l/ verb [T] **1** to close a container or space by covering it with something so that air or other substances cannot get in or out: *Small gaps can be sealed with wax.* **2** to close an envelope by sticking down the top edge

> **PHRASE** **seal a victory/deal/agreement** to make a victory/deal/agreement certain or complete: *We shook hands to seal the deal.*
> **PHRASAL VERB** **,seal sth 'off** to prevent people from entering an area or building: *Police sealed off the area so that the investigations could begin.*

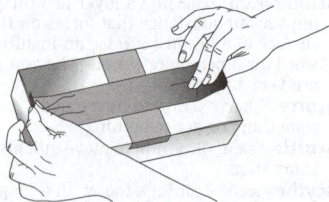

seal

seal² /si:l/ noun [C] **1** a large sea animal that eats fish and lives mainly in cold parts of the world **2** something that seals a container and that you have to break before you can open the container: *Make sure that the seal on the bottle is intact.* **3** something that stops air or other substances entering or leaving something: *I replaced the seal, but oil is still leaking out.* **4** a special mark that you put on a document, to show that it is legal or official

'sea ,level noun [U] the average level of the sea. It is used for measuring the height of parts of the land.

'sea ,lion noun [C] a large type of SEAL

seam /si:m/ noun [C] **1** a line of stitches that joins two pieces of cloth **2** a long thin layer of coal under the ground

seaman /'si:mən/ (plural **seamen** /'si:mən/) noun [C] a sailor

seamless /'si:mləs/ adj changing or continuing very smoothly and without stopping —**seamlessly** adv

seance /'seɪɒs, 'seɪɒns/ noun [C] a meeting in which people try to communicate with the spirits of dead people

seaport /'si:pɔ:t/ noun [C] a town by the sea with a large port

search¹ /sɜ:tʃ/ noun [C] ★★
1 an attempt to find something: *Despite a thorough search, they found no drugs on him.* ♦ *The authorities carried out several air searches for survivors of the crash.* ♦ *The police have conducted an extensive search of the area.* ♦ *Many people had left their homes to go in search of food.*
2 an attempt to find an answer: *The committee is involved in a search for solutions to key international problems.*
3 *computing* the process of using a computer to find information, especially on the Internet: *You can probably get the address by doing an Internet search.*
4 the process of examining official documents to find information: *A search of the parish records provided useful information.*

Words often used with **search**

*Adjectives often used with **search** (noun, sense 1)*
■ **careful, painstaking, systematic, thorough** + SEARCH: used about searches that are done with great care
■ **desperate, frantic** + SEARCH: used about searches by people who are very keen to find someone or something
■ **fruitless, unsuccessful** + SEARCH: used about searches that fail to find someone or something

*Verbs often used with **search** (noun, sense 1)*
■ **carry out, conduct, launch, make, mount, undertake** + SEARCH: look for someone or something

---

search² /sɜ:tʃ/ verb ★★
1 [I/T] to try to find something or someone by looking carefully: *After three days searching, I gave up.* ♦ *Detectives have been brought in to help search for clues.* ♦ *Rescue teams are still searching through the wreckage for survivors.*
2 [T] to carefully examine something or someone for something that is hidden: *The police have arrested a man after searching his house.*
3 [T] *computing* to use a computer to look for information, especially on the Internet: *I got most of the answers by searching the Net.*

'search ,engine noun [C] *computing* a computer program that is used for searching for information on the Internet

searcher /'sɜ:tʃə/ noun [C] someone who is looking for someone or something that is lost or missing

searching /'sɜ:tʃɪŋ/ adj intending to find out the truth: *searching questions*

'search ,party noun [C] a group of people that is organized to search for someone who is lost or missing

'search ,warrant noun [C] an official document that allows the police to search a place

searing /'sɪərɪŋ/ adj **1** extreme in degree or strength: *searing pain/heat* **2** severe in your judgment of someone or something

seashell /'siːʃel/ noun [C] the empty shell of a sea animal

seashore /'siːʃɔː/ noun [C] a piece of land next to the sea

seasick /'siːˌsɪk/ adj feeling ill from the movement of the boat that you are travelling on

seaside /'siːˌsaɪd/ noun [singular] an area that is near the sea, especially one where people go for a holiday: *This was their first family holiday together at the seaside.* ♦ *a seaside resort/town/hotel*

season¹ /'siːz(ə)n/ noun ★★★

1 one of 4 periods of year	**5** time for event
2 of weather	**6** period for films etc
3 period sport is played	**+** PHRASES
4 time for activity	

1 [C] one of the four periods into which the year is divided according to the weather: *She likes to paint the changing seasons in the garden.* ♦ *My mood is often affected by the season of the year.*

2 [singular] a period of the year when a particular type of weather is expected in some regions of the world: *the dry/rainy season*

3 [C] a period of the year when a particular sport is played: *The cricket season starts next week.*

4 [singular] a particular time or period of the year when something happens: *It's the peak of the holiday season, so the roads will be busy.* ♦ *Fruit trees need to be watered regularly during the growing season.*

5 [singular] a period of time when a particular event takes place: *This topic will be debated throughout the election season.*

6 [singular] a period of time when a series of films, plays, or television programmes are shown: *There is a short season of films by the French director Bertrand Tavernier.*

PHRASES **in/out of season** grown/not grown at the normal time or under normal conditions: *I don't like to use food that is out of season.*

season's greetings used as a greeting during the Christmas period, especially on cards

season² /'siːz(ə)n/ verb [T] to add salt, pepper, or other SPICES to food

seasonal /'siːz(ə)nəl/ adj available, or happening, at a particular time of year: *seasonal work* ♦ *seasonal changes in temperature* ♦ *seasonal vegetables*

seasoned /'siːz(ə)nd/ adj experienced in a particular activity or job

seasoning /'siːz(ə)nɪŋ/ noun [C/U] salt, pepper, or other SPICES that you add to food to improve the taste

season ticket noun [C] a ticket that you use several times within a particular period of time

season tickets noun [plural] a set of tickets that you use to see a series of performances or sports games during one year

seat¹ /siːt/ noun [C] ★★★
1 something that you can sit on: *Some of the*

vans have leather seats. ♦ *The seat next to me was empty.* ♦ *He was in the back seat of the car when the accident happened.* ♦ *She put her bag on the passenger seat* (=the seat next to the driver) *and started the car.* ♦ *I had a window seat on the plane.*

2 a seat that you pay for as a passenger on a vehicle or as a member of the audience in a theatre: *I managed to get us the best seats in the theatre.* ♦ *We tried to get on the Friday flight, but there were no seats left.*

3 the part of a chair that you sit on

4 a position as a member of a parliament or committee: *The Green Party won four seats in the new parliament.* ♦ *a permanent seat on the UN Security Council*

PHRASES **take a back seat** to have a less important position than someone or something else

take a seat to sit down: *Hi, come on in, take a seat.*

take your seat to sit down, especially in a place that has been kept for you: *They took their seats in the front row.*

seat² /siːt/ verb [T] **1** *formal* to put someone or yourself in a seat somewhere: *He seated himself behind his desk.* ♦ *The general seated them to his right.* **2** to have places for a particular number of people to sit: *The new stadium will seat up to 80,000 people.*

PHRASE **be seated** to be sitting down: *When she entered the room they were already seated.*

seat belt noun [C] a strong belt in a car or plane that you fasten around yourself
—*picture* → C6

seating /'siːtɪŋ/ noun [U] **1** the seats in a public place such as a cinema, or on a bus or train **2** the way in which seats are arranged

seaweed /'siːˌwiːd/ noun [U] a green or brown plant that grows in the sea

sec /sek/ noun [C] *informal* a very short time: *Wait a sec – I just have to brush my teeth.*

secluded /sɪ'kluːdɪd/ adj private, peaceful, and not near other people or places

seclusion /sɪ'kluːʒ(ə)n/ noun [U] a situation in which someone stays apart from other people

second¹ /'sekənd/ number ★★★

1 in the place or position counted as number two: *the second of October* ♦ *This is the second programme in a series on rural health.* ♦ *Gothenburg is Sweden's second largest city.* ♦ *He came second in the European championship this year.*

2 in addition to the first one: *The bookcase needs a second coat of paint.*

3 next in quality or importance after someone or something that is the best or most important: *She was our second choice for the job.* ♦ *In terms of scoring goals, he's second only to Davies.*

PHRASES **have second thoughts (about sth)** to begin to doubt a decision that you have made

on second thoughts used when you want to change something that you have just said,

S

often to say the opposite: *We don't need an umbrella. On second thoughts, maybe we do.*
second to none the best

second² /'sekənd/ noun [C] ★★★
1 a period of time that is one of the 60 parts in a minute: *Each commercial lasts for 30 seconds.*
2 an extremely short period of time: *Just give me a second to put my coat on.*
3 a product that is not perfect, that you can buy at a reduced price
4 a SECOND-CLASS university degree

second³ /'sekənd/ adv SECONDLY

second⁴ /'sekənd/ verb [T] **1** to officially support a proposal made by another person in a meeting **2** /sɪ'kɒnd/ *British* to send someone to work temporarily in another place

secondary /'sekənd(ə)ri/ adj ★
1 relating to the education of children between the ages of 11 and 16 or 18: *primary and secondary education* ♦ *secondary teachers/pupils*
2 less important than something else: *The colour of the car is secondary to its quality and price.*
3 happening after something else or as a result of it: *a secondary infection*

secondary school noun [C] a school for children between the ages of 11 and 16 or 18

second best noun [singular/U] **1** someone or something that is not what you wanted, or is not as good as others **2** someone or something that comes directly after the best in order of achievement or quality
—**second-best** adj

second class noun [U] **1** the ordinary method of sending post that is not urgent **2** the ordinary seats and service on a train or ship

second-class adj **1** low in quality or importance **2** relating to post that is sent by second class **3** travelling in second class **4** *British* a second-class university degree is a good degree, but not as good as a FIRST

second cousin noun [C] a child of your parent's COUSIN

second-generation adj **1** used for describing someone who was born in the country that they live in but whose parents were not born there **2** developed and improved from an earlier form

second-guess verb [T] to guess what someone is going to do, or what will happen

second-hand adj **1** owned or used by someone else before you: *second-hand books/clothing* **2** heard from someone who was not directly involved: *second-hand reports/information* —**second-hand** adv

second language noun [C] a language that you can speak but that is not your main language

secondly /'sekən(d)li/ adv used for introducing the second in a series of two or more things: *Firstly, I didn't know the neighbourhood and, secondly, it was night.*

second-rate adj not of good quality
=MEDIOCRE

secrecy /'siːkrəsi/ noun [U] a situation in which you keep something secret

secret¹ /'siːkrət/ noun [C] ★★
1 a piece of information that is known by only a small number of people, and is deliberately not told to other people: *I can't tell you what she said – it's a secret.* ♦ *Can you promise to keep a secret* (=not tell anyone)? ♦ **keep sth a secret (from sb)** *Mandela kept his work a secret from the prison authorities.*
2 something that cannot be explained or is difficult to understand: *What secrets of the universe will the new telescope reveal?*
3 a particular way of achieving something: *She always looks so slim – I wish I knew her secret.* ♦ *The secret of our success is having highly skilled staff.*
PHRASE **in secret** without anyone else knowing: *The negotiations were conducted in secret.*

secret² /'siːkrət/ adj ★★
1 deliberately not told to other people, or kept hidden from other people: *The diary records her most secret thoughts and feelings.* ♦ **keep sth secret** *Campaigners have accused the government of keeping the report secret.*
2 not known about by many people: *We love coming here because it's like a secret garden.* —**secretly** /'siːkrətli/ adv: *The videotapes were secretly recorded by the FBI.*

secret agent noun [C] someone whose job involves working for a government and finding out the secrets of other governments
=SPY

secretarial /ˌsekrə'teəriəl/ adj relating to the work or skills of a secretary

secretary /'sekrətri/ noun [C] ★
1 someone in an office who works for someone else and does jobs such as arranging meetings, making phone calls, and preparing letters
2 the member of a committee who writes letters and keeps records of meetings: *He was secretary of the local golf club.*
3 the politician in charge of a particular government department: *the Education Secretary*

Secretary of State noun [C] **1** the politician in charge of a particular government department in the UK **2** the senior US politician who deals with relations with other countries

secrete /sɪ'kriːt/ verb [T] **1** *science* to produce a liquid **2** *formal* to hide something

secretion /sɪ'kriːʃ(ə)n/ noun [C/U] a liquid that is produced by a plant or animal, or the process of producing this liquid

secretive /'siːkrətɪv, sɪ'kriːtɪv/ adj deliberately not telling people things

secret service noun [C] a government department that SECRET AGENTS work for

sect /sekt/ noun [C] a religious group whose beliefs are different from the beliefs of an established religion

S

sectarian /sek'teəriən/ adj caused by disagreements among people from different religious groups

section /'sekʃ(ə)n/ noun [C] ★★★
1 a person, group, part, or area that forms part of something larger: *The frozen-foods section is in the rear of the shop.* ♦ *A large section of the population lives in poverty.*
2 a part of a newspaper, book, or other piece of writing that may be considered separately: *The story was reported on the front page of the business section.*
3 *technical* an image that you would see if you cut through something and looked at the flat surface that is created by the cut: *Figure 2 shows a vertical section of the building.*

sector /'sektə/ noun [C] ★★
1 a part of a country's economic or business activity: *the manufacturing/industrial/ financial sector* ♦ *the private/public sector* ♦ *A number of key sectors of the economy are in trouble.*
2 a part of an area: *a UN-patrolled sector of Bosnia*
3 a group that is part of a larger group: *Some sectors of the community are opposed to the development plan.*

secular /'sekjʊlə/ adj not religious, or not connected with religion

secure¹ /sɪ'kjʊə/ verb [T] *formal* ★
1 to get or achieve something important: *The team secured their second victory of the season.*
2 to make an area or building safe: *We have done our best to secure the embassy against terrorist attacks.*
3 to hold something firmly in place by tying or fastening it: *Screws secure the steel bars to the window frame.*

secure² /sɪ'kjʊə/ adj ★
1 safe from attack, harm, or damage: *Make your home more secure with our burglar alarm system.* ♦ *No shop can be completely secure against theft.*
2 fastened firmly, in a safe way: *Make sure the pictures are secure.*
3 in a situation where you feel confident and do not need to worry ≠ INSECURE: *The important thing is that children feel secure about being loved.* ♦ *You can go home, secure in the knowledge that your car is safe.*
4 a secure situation or job is safe and reliable: *She wanted a job with a more secure future.*
—**securely** adv: *Please make sure that your seat belt is securely fastened.*

securities /sɪ'kjʊərətiz/ noun [plural] *business* documents showing that you own SHARES in a company

security /sɪ'kjʊərəti/ noun [U] ★★★
1 safety from attack, harm, or damage: *The information received is highly confidential and relates to national security.* ♦ *The meeting took place amid extremely tight security.*
2 a feeling of confidence and safety, or a situation in which you can feel confident

and safe: *A predictable routine gives children a sense of security.* ♦ *We were lulled into a false sense of security and failed to see what was coming.*
3 the department within an organization that protects buildings and workers: *If you won't leave, I'll have to call security.*
4 *business* property or goods that you agree to give to someone who has lent you money if you cannot pay the money back
→ SECURITIES

se'curity ,service noun [C] a government organization that deals with a country's security

sedan /sɪ'dæn/ noun [C] *American* a SALOON car

sedate¹ /sɪ'deɪt/ adj quiet or slow, and not likely to shock people or attract attention
—**sedately** adv

sedate² /sɪ'deɪt/ verb [T] to give someone a SEDATIVE

sedation /sɪ'deɪʃ(ə)n/ noun [U] the use of drugs to make someone calmer, or to make them sleep

sedative /'sedətɪv/ noun [C] a drug that makes someone calmer, or makes them sleep

sedentary /'sed(ə)nt(ə)ri/ adj involving a lot of sitting and not much exercise

sediment /'sedɪmənt/ noun [C/U] a layer of a substance that forms at the bottom of a liquid

seduce /sɪ'djuːs/ verb [T] **1** to persuade someone to have sex with you **2** to persuade someone to do something by making it seem easy or exciting —**seduction** /sɪ'dʌkʃ(ə)n/ noun [C/U]

seductive /sɪ'dʌktɪv/ adj **1** sexually attractive **2** attractive and likely to persuade you to do something that may be harmful or wrong —**seductively** adv

see /siː/ (past tense **saw** /sɔː/; past participle **seen** /siːn/) verb ★★★

1 notice with eyes	**8** find sth out
2 watch film etc	**9** experience sth
3 meet/visit sb	**10** go with sb
4 understand sth	**11** be in relationship
5 consider sb/sth	**+ PHRASES**
6 imagine sb/sth	**+ PHRASAL VERBS**
7 make sure	

1 [T] to notice someone or something using your eyes: *She laughed when she saw the expression on his face.* ♦ *She can't see a thing without her contact lenses.* ♦
+what/where/who *Did you see who it was?* ♦
+(that) *I could see she was upset.* ♦ **see sb/sth doing sth** *Didn't you see him talking to her earlier?*
2 [T] to watch something such as a film or television programme: *Have you seen American Beauty?*
3 [T] to meet or visit someone: *Are you seeing Jane tomorrow?* ♦ *See you at the station at 6 o'clock.* ♦ *When can Mr Martin see me?*
4 [I/T] to understand something: *I think I see the problem here.* ♦ *'You do it like this.' 'I see.'* ♦ *I see why you're angry.* ♦ **+what** *'It's not fair to go without him.' 'Yes, I see what you mean.'*

S

5 [T] to consider someone or something in a particular way: *A scientist sees things differently from an artist.* ♦ **see sb/sth as sth** *This was seen as an attempt to fool the voters.* ♦ *He seems to see me as a threat.*

6 [T] to imagine someone or something: *Where do you see yourself in five years' time?* ♦ **see sb as sth** *Can you really see her as the president?* ♦ **see sb/sth doing sth** *I just can't see them winning the game.*

7 [T] to make sure that someone does something or that something happens: **+that** *Could you see that everything's ready in time?*

8 [I/T] to find something out: *As we saw in Chapter 2, the reasons for the war were complex.* ♦ **+if/whether** *He went back to see whether they needed any help.* ♦ **+(that)** *If you read his report, you'll see that he recommends a cautious approach.* ♦ **+who/what/why** *I'll go and see what he wants.*

9 [T] to experience something: *The region has seen some of the fiercest fighting in the war.*

10 [T] to go with someone because you want to make sure that they arrive somewhere: *Can I see you home?*

11 [T] to be in a romantic relationship with someone: *Is she seeing anyone at the moment?*

PHRASES **I don't see why not** *spoken* used for saying yes when someone asks for your permission: *'Can Jason come too, Dad?' 'I don't see why not.'*

I'll see what I can do *spoken* used for saying that you will try to help: *Bring the car over tomorrow and I'll see what I can do.*

let me see/let's see *spoken* used for saying that you are thinking about something or trying to remember something: *It must have been, let me see, 10 years ago.*

see sth coming *spoken* to notice or realize that something is going to happen

see for yourself to check what someone has told you by looking at it: *It's all gone – see for yourself.*

see how it goes/things go *spoken* used for saying that a decision about a situation will be made after allowing it to develop for a period of time

see if you can do sth *spoken* to try to do something: *I'll see if I can find out what he's up to.*

see you *spoken* used for saying goodbye to someone you know when you expect to see them again soon

we'll see *spoken* used for saying that you will decide later: *'Can we go to the park this afternoon, Mum?' 'We'll see.'*

you'll see *spoken* used for telling someone that they will find out that you are right about something: *It will be wonderful, you'll see.*

you see *spoken* used when you are explaining something: *You see, Harry's coming this afternoon, so I can't come.*

→ DEAD¹, EYE¹, RED²

PHRASAL VERBS **see a'bout sth** to deal with or organize something: *I must go and see*

about this job. ♦ **see about doing sth** *Can you see about getting us a lift home?*

,**see sb 'off** to go somewhere such as a station or airport with someone in order to say goodbye to them: *Anne saw Terry off at the station.*

,**see sb/sth 'off** to successfully deal with something, or to easily defeat someone: *She saw off the challenge from her opponent.*

,**see sb 'out** to go with someone to the door when they are leaving in order to say goodbye to them: *My secretary will see you out.*

,**see 'through sb/sth** to recognize that someone is trying to trick you: *We can all see through your little game, Adam.*

,**see sth 'through** to continue doing something until it is finished: *Having come this far, she was determined to see things through.*

'**see to sb/sth** to deal with someone or something: *You try to get some sleep, I'll see to the children's breakfast.* ♦ *I should have seen to it that she was told.*

■ If you **see** someone or something, you become aware of them using your eyes: *I saw a flash of light.* ♦ *He saw someone run into the house.*

■ If you **look at** someone or something, you deliberately move your eyes towards them so that you can **see** them: *Look at that car!* ♦ *I dropped a glass and everyone turned to look at me.*

■ If you **watch** someone or something, you look at them for some time because they are moving or changing and you want to see what happens. You **watch** television or a piece of entertainment: *They were all watching the football match.* ♦ *He sat and watched her clean up.*

---

seed¹ /siːd/ noun ★★★

1 [C/U] a small hard part produced by a plant that can grow into a new plant of the same type: *a packet of seeds* ♦ *You can sow grass seed to cover the worn patches.* ♦ *I grew these herbs **from** seed.*

2 [C] a player who is given a number that shows how likely they are to win a competition: *number one seed, Venus Williams*

seed² /siːd/ verb **1** [T] to put seeds in the ground so that they can grow **2** [I] if a plant seeds, it produces seeds

PHRASE **be seeded third/tenth etc** to be in the third/tenth etc position in an official list of the best players in a competition

seedless /'siːdləs/ adj not containing any seeds

seedling /'siːdlɪŋ/ noun [C] a young plant that has grown from a seed

seedy /'siːdi/ adj connected with activities that are illegal or morally wrong

seeing /'siːɪŋ/ conjunction **seeing as** or **seeing (that)** *spoken* used for giving the reason why you are saying something: *Maybe we should throw a party, seeing that it's Dan's birthday next week.*

S

seek /siːk/ (past tense and past participle **sought** /sɔːt/) verb [T] *formal* ★★

1 to ask for something, or to try to get something: *Seek medical* **advice** *if symptoms last more than a week.* ♦ *Hundreds of people* **sought refuge** *in the British Embassy.* ♦ *You must first* **seek permission** *before publishing their names.*

2 to try to find something or someone that you need in your life: *To be eligible, you must show that you are actively seeking employment.* ♦ *Many single people are seeking that special someone.*

PHRASE **seek to do sth** *formal* to try to do something: *The law must seek to protect the democratic rights of citizens.*

—**seeker** /ˈsiːkə/ noun [C]

PHRASAL VERB ˌseek sb/sth ˈout to find someone or something by looking for them in a determined way: *Corbett promised to seek out the truth.*

seem /siːm/ linking verb [I] ★★★

1 to appear to be something or appear to have a particular quality: *Going out for lunch* **seemed like** *a good idea.* ♦ **seem happy/genuine etc to sb** *He seems happy enough to me.* ♦ **seem to do sth** *She seemed to take very good care of herself.* ♦ **seem (to be) sb/sth** *Susan seems a very sensible person.*

2 used when you want to say something in a more careful and less direct way: **seem to have done sth** *I seem to have forgotten your name.* ♦ **can't seem to do sth** *We can't seem to get this computer to work.*

PHRASE **it seems** used for saying that something appears to exist or be true: *It seems like their marriage is over.* ♦ **It seems as if** *everybody else knew except me.* ♦ **+(that)** *Standing there in the house, it seemed that he had never been away.* ♦ **it seems to sb (that)** *It seems to me this is his most important novel.*

seemingly /ˈsiːmɪŋli/ adv in a way that appears to have a particular quality, even though this is probably not true: *Heidi was seemingly calm when she left to take the test.*

seen the past participle of **see**

seep /siːp/ verb [I] to flow into or out of something through small holes: *Chemicals from the factory were seeping into the earth.*

seesaw /ˈsiːsɔː/ noun [C] a long board for children to play on. It is balanced on a support in the middle.

seethe /siːð/ verb [I] **1** to be extremely angry **2** to be full of a lot of people or animals that are moving around quickly

segment /ˈsegmənt/ noun [C] a part of something: *certain segments of the population* ♦ *orange/grapefruit segments*

segregate /ˈsegrɪˌgeɪt/ verb [T] to separate groups of people, especially according to race, sex, or religion —**segregation** /ˌsegrɪˈgeɪʃ(ə)n/ noun [U]

seismic /ˈsaɪzmɪk/ adj relating to EARTHQUAKES (=sudden shaking of the ground)

seize /siːz/ verb [T] **1** to suddenly and firmly hold someone or something: *'Listen,' he said, seizing my wrist.* ♦ *Before he could run away, she seized him by the collar.* **2** to take something using official power or force =CONFISCATE: *Customs officials have seized 100 kilos of cocaine.* **3** to take control of a place or situation: *Their opponents had seized control of the army.* ♦ *You must seize the initiative in discussions about salary.* **4** if a feeling or emotion seizes someone, it suddenly affects them very strongly: *A wave of panic seized me.*

PHRASE **seize the opportunity/chance to do sth** to act quickly in order to use an opportunity that may not be available later: *If he looks away, his opponent will seize the opportunity to attack.*

PHRASAL VERBS ˈseize on sth or ˈseize uˌpon sth to use something in an enthusiastic way in order to gain an advantage: *Companies were quick to seize on the possibilities offered by new technology.*

ˌseize ˈup to suddenly stop moving or working properly: *If you don't add oil, the engine will eventually seize up.*

seizure /ˈsiːʒə/ noun **1** [C/U] the action of taking something, or of taking control of something, using power or force **2** [C] a sudden attack of an illness that makes your body shake

seldom /ˈseldəm/ adv not often =RARELY ≠ FREQUENTLY: *We seldom see each other any more.*

select¹ /sɪˈlekt/ verb [T] ★

1 to choose someone or something from a group: *You can select one of four colours.* ♦ **select sb to do sth** *We're going to select two students to represent the school.* ♦ **select sb/sth for sth** *The group had been carefully selected for the study because of their lifestyles.*

2 *computing* to mark something on a computer screen before changing it: *You can select a word by double clicking on it.*

select² /sɪˈlekt/ adj **1** carefully chosen from a larger group: *Only a select few companies were allowed to compete for the contract.* **2** very good, or expensive: *a small, very select school*

selection /sɪˈlekʃ(ə)n/ noun ★★

1 [C/U] the process of choosing one person or thing from a group: *There are strict rules that govern* **the selection of** *political candidates.*

2 [C] a set of things for you to choose from: *a selection of local cheeses* ♦ *They have a* **wide selection** *of carpets to suit all tastes.*

3 [C] someone or something that you have chosen: *I'm very happy with my selection.*

selective /sɪˈlektɪv/ adj **1** careful about what you choose or accept: *He is very selective in his reading.* **2** accepting or using only some things or people: *selective schools* —**selectively** /sɪˈlektɪvli/ adv

selector /sɪˈlektə/ noun [C] someone on a committee whose job is to choose someone or something

S

self /self/ (plural **selves** /selvz/) noun [C/U] ★★
who you are and what you think and feel,
especially the conscious feeling of being
separate and different from other people:
*Young babies do not have a fully developed
sense of self.*

PHRASES **your old self** the type of person
you usually are, especially when you have
not been feeling as healthy or happy as
usual

your true/real self the type of person you are
when you are not trying to impress anyone

self- /self/ prefix relating to yourself or itself:
used with many nouns and adjectives: *self-
respect ♦ a self-cleaning oven*

self-assured adj confident and relaxed
because you are sure of your abilities
—**self-assurance** noun [U]

self-awareness noun [U] the quality of
understanding what your own true
thoughts, feelings, and abilities are
—**self-aware** adj

self-catering adj British a self-catering holiday
or place is one where you cook your own
food

self-centred adj too interested in yourself,
so that you do not think about what other
people feel or need

self-confessed adj admitting to being a
particular bad type of person

self-confidence noun [U] the feeling that you
can do things well and that people respect
you —**self-confident** adj

self-conscious adj 1 embarrassed or worried
about how you look or what other people
think of you 2 not successful in creating a
particular effect because of being too
obvious —**self-consciously** adv, **self-
consciousness** noun [U]

self-contained /ˌself kənˈtemd/ adj 1 a self-
contained flat is part of a larger house but
has its own kitchen and bathroom 2 not
needing the help or friendship of other
people

self-control noun [U] the ability to control
your behaviour and not show strong
emotions

self-defence noun [U] things that you do in
order to protect yourself from being
attacked: *Margaret claims she was acting in
self-defence when she shot him.*

self-destruct /ˌself dɪˈstrʌkt/ verb [I] if
something self-destructs, it destroys itself

self-destructive adj doing things that are
likely to harm yourself in some way
—**self-destruction** noun [U]

self-determination noun [U] the freedom of
the people in a country to choose their own
government and not be controlled by
another country

self-discipline noun [U] the ability to control
your behaviour so that you do what you
should do —**self-disciplined** adj

self-effacing /ˌself ɪˈfeɪsɪŋ/ adj someone who
is self-effacing does not want to be noticed
by other people and tends not to talk about
their abilities or achievements

self-employed /ˌself ɪmˈplɔɪd/ adj working
for yourself rather than being employed
directly by a company or organization
—**self-employment** noun [U]

self-esteem noun [U] the feeling that you are
as good as other people and that you
deserve to be treated well

self-evident adj obvious, and therefore not
needing any explanation —**self-evidently**
adv

self-explanatory adj easy to understand
without further explanation

self-governing adj something such as a
country or organization that is self-
governing controls itself —**self-government**
noun [U]

self-help noun [U] things that you do to solve
your own problems instead of depending
on other people

self-important adj behaving in a way that
shows you think you are very important

self-imposed /ˌself ɪmˈpəʊzd/ adj self-imposed
rules and conditions are those that you
have chosen for yourself, rather than those
that someone else has forced you to accept

self-indulgent adj doing things for your own
pleasure, rather than for any other
purpose: *an idle self-indulgent lifestyle*
—**self-indulgence** noun [U]

self-inflicted /ˌself ɪnˈflɪktɪd/ adj a self-
inflicted injury, condition etc is one that
you suffer from and that you have caused:
a self-inflicted gunshot wound

self-interest noun [U] the fact of caring only
about what will bring advantages for
yourself, rather than what will help other
people —**self-interested** adj

selfish /ˈselfɪʃ/ adj thinking only about
yourself and not caring about other people
≠ UNSELFISH: *a greedy selfish man* —**selfishly**
adv, **selfishness** noun [U]

selfless /ˈselfləs/ adj caring about other
people's needs and problems more than
your own = UNSELFISH —**selflessly** adv,
selflessness noun [U]

self-made adj a self-made person has become
successful despite starting with no
particular advantages: *a self-made
millionaire*

self-pity noun [U] the feeling that your
situation is worse than other people's and
that they should feel sorry for you
—**self-pitying** adj

self-portrait noun [C] a picture that you draw
or paint of yourself

self-preservation noun [U] the wish to stay
alive and protect yourself from things that
might hurt you

self-reliant adj able to do things for yourself
without depending on other people
—**self-reliance** noun [U]

self-respect noun [U] the feeling that you are
as important or as good as other people,
and that you should not allow them to treat
you badly —**self-respecting** adj

self-righteous adj too proud of your own
moral behaviour or beliefs, especially in a

way that annoys other people
—**self-righteously** adv

self-rule noun [U] government of a country or region by its own people

self-satisfied adj feeling pleased about your own situation in a way that annoys other people: *He gave her a self-satisfied smile.* —**self-satisfaction** noun [U]

self-service adj a self-service restaurant or petrol station is one where the customers have to serve themselves

self-sufficient adj able to provide everything that you need for yourself, without help from other people —**self-sufficiency** noun [U]

self-taught /ˌself ˈtɔːt/ adj having learnt a particular skill by yourself, instead of being taught by someone

sell¹ /sel/ (past tense and past participle **sold** /səʊld/) verb ★★★

1 [T] to let someone have something in exchange for money: *We've decided to sell our house and move to Spain.* ♦ *My uncle buys and sells second-hand books for a living.* ♦ **sell sb sth** *I sold Chris my old car.* ♦ **sell sth to sb** *Sheila sold her jewellery to an antiques dealer.*

2 [T] if a shop or company sells a particular product, people can buy that product from them: *Do you think they sell children's books here?*

3 [I] if a product sells, people buy it: *Her novel sold very well in the first six months.*

4 [T] *informal* to persuade someone to do, have, or use something: **sell sth to sb** *I don't think we could sell the idea to our partners.*

PHRASAL VERBS **sell sth off** to sell something quickly and for a low price, usually because you need the money

sell out 1 if a shop sells out of something, it sells all that it has so that there is no more available: *I went to get some bread, but the shop had sold out.* ♦ *On a hot day, we can sell out of ice cream in an hour.* **2** if products, tickets etc sell out, there are none left for people to buy because they have all been sold **3** *informal* to do something that shows you no longer have the same moral principles you used to have

sell² /sel/ noun *see* **hard sell**

sell-by date noun [C] *British* a date printed on food products to show that they should not be sold after that date because they will no longer be good to eat

seller /ˈselə/ noun [C] someone who sells something, especially as their job: *an ice-cream seller*

sell-off noun [C] *British* a situation in which a business or part of a business is sold

Sellotape /ˈseləˌteɪp/ *British trademark* clear plastic material that is sticky on one side and is used for sticking things together

sell-out noun [singular] **1** a performance, sports event etc for which all the tickets are sold **2** *informal* a situation in which someone does something that is the opposite of what they had promised, or is against their principles

selves the plural of **self**

semantic /sɪˈmæntɪk/ adj *linguistics* relating to the meaning of words —**semantically** /sɪˈmæntɪkli/ adv

semblance /ˈsembləns/ noun **a/some semblance of sth** a small amount of a particular quality: *The country was finally returning to some semblance of normality.*

semen /ˈsiːmən/ noun [U] the liquid that contains SPERM produced by the male sex organs

semester /sɪˈmestə/ noun [C] one of the two periods of about 18 weeks that the school year is divided into in some countries

semicircle /ˈsemiˌsɜːk(ə)l/ noun [C] **1** half of a circle **2** a group of people or things arranged in a curved line —**semicircular** /ˌsemiˈsɜːkjʊlə/ adj

semicolon /ˌsemiˈkəʊlɒn/ noun [C] the symbol ; used in writing for separating words in a list or two parts of a sentence that can be understood separately

semi-conscious adj someone who is semi-conscious is only partly conscious and not fully awake —**semi-consciousness** noun [U]

semi-detached /ˌsemidɪˈtætʃt/ adj a semi-detached house is joined to another house by one wall that they share —**picture** → C1

semifinal /ˌsemiˈfaɪn(ə)l/ noun [C] one of the two games that are played immediately before the last game in a sports competition

seminar /ˈsemɪnɑː/ noun [C] a meeting or class in which a small group of people discuss a subject

seminary /ˈsemɪnəri/ noun [C] a college in which priests or MINISTERS are trained

semitone /ˈsemiˌtəʊn/ noun [C] *British* an amount by which one sound is higher or lower than another, equal to $\frac{1}{12}$ of an OCTAVE

senate /ˈsenət/ noun **1** [C] the more senior part of a law-making institution that has two parts **2 the Senate** the more senior part of the US Congress

senator /ˈsenətə/ noun [C] someone who is a member of a senate

send /send/ (past tense and past participle **sent** /sent/) verb [T] ★★★

1 to arrange for something such as a letter or email to be delivered to someone in another place: *I sent the letters yesterday, so they should arrive today.* ♦ **send sb sth** *Send me an email when you get there!* ♦ **send sth to sb** *I forgot to send a birthday card to Amy.*

2 to arrange for someone or something to go to a place, or to tell someone to go to a place: **send sb/sth somewhere** *Two warships have been sent to the area.* ♦ *My mother sent me back to the shop to get the things I'd forgotten.*

3 to make someone move or fall suddenly: *The blow sent him crashing to the floor.*

4 to make a substance such as smoke or a chemical go out into the atmosphere: **send sth out/up** *Forest fires sent up smoke for miles around.*

S

PHRASAL VERBS ,send sb a'way to tell someone to leave a place: *His solicitor was sent away by the security guards.*
,send a'way for sth to write to an organization asking them to send something to you
,send sth 'back to return something to the person who sent it, especially because it is not satisfactory: *If you're not happy with it, you can always send it back.*
'send for sb/sth to ask or arrange for someone or something to come to you: *I think we should send for a doctor.*
,send sb 'in to arrange for people to go to a place, especially in order to help with a difficult situation: *Government forces were sent in to fight the rebellion.*
,send sth 'in to send a letter or document to an organization: *Keep sending your letters and suggestions in to the BBC.*
,send sb 'off *British* to tell a sports player officially to leave the sports field because they have done something that is not allowed by the rules —*picture* → C15
,send sth 'off to send a letter, email etc to someone: *I must get the parcel sent off tomorrow.*
,send sth 'out to send a lot of copies of the same document to a large number of people
,send sb 'up to make someone seem silly by pretending to speak or behave like them

sender /'sendə/ noun [C] the person who sent a letter, parcel, email etc

senile /'si:naɪl/ adj someone who is senile is confused, forgets things, or behaves in a strange way, because they are old —**senility** /sə'nɪləti/ noun [U]

senior¹ /'si:niə/ adj ★
1 with a high position within an organization, or a higher position than someone else ≠ JUNIOR: *a senior officer/ manager*
2 belonging to an older age group

senior² /'si:niə/ noun [C] **1** someone who is older than someone else, especially by a particular number of years **2** a SENIOR CITIZEN

,senior 'citizen noun [C] someone who is at or past the age when most people stop working

,senior 'high ,school or ,senior 'high noun [C] *American* a school in the US for children between the ages of 14 and 18

seniority /,si:ni'ɒrəti/ noun [U] greater age or a more important position

sensation /sen'seɪʃ(ə)n/ noun **1** [C/U] the ability to feel something, or something that you feel: *When she awoke she had lost all sensation in her legs.* ♦ *When applied, the cream may cause a slight burning sensation.*
2 [C] a feeling in your mind, especially a strange or uncomfortable one: *He had the eerie sensation that he was being watched.*
3 [singular] an event that causes a lot of excitement and interest: *The show caused a sensation when it was first performed.*

sensational /sen'seɪʃ(ə)nəl/ adj very exciting and impressive: *a sensational victory in the FA Cup* —**sensationally** adv

sensationalism /sen'seɪʃ(ə)nə,lɪz(ə)m/ noun [U] a way of reporting events, especially in a newspaper, that makes them seem as exciting or shocking as possible —**sensationalist** adj

sense¹ /sens/ noun ★★★

1 reasonable behaviour	4 natural ability
2 feeling/belief	5 meaning of word
3 way of understanding	+ PHRASES

1 [U] a reasonable way of thinking about something or doing something: **have the sense to do sth** *They must have had the sense to park the car in the shade.* ♦ **there's no sense in doing sth** *There's no sense in going ahead until the costs have been agreed.*
2 [C] a feeling or belief that you have, especially about yourself: *All children need to feel **a sense of** pride in their achievements.* ♦ *Beth read Jake's letter with an increasing sense of panic.*
3 [singular] a way of understanding something, although there may be other ways: *My family's from this area, so **in a sense** it's like coming home.* ♦ *In one sense, Robertson is a typical politician.*
4 [C] a natural physical ability that most people have, especially the ability to see, hear, smell, taste, and feel things: *Dogs have **a sense of smell** that is five times more sensitive than that of humans.*
5 [C] the meaning of a word or phrase: *The word 'bank' has a number of senses.*

PHRASES come to your senses to start to behave in a reasonable way: *At last she's come to her senses and realizes that we just can't afford it.*
make sense 1 to be practical and sensible: *It makes sense to keep such information on disk.* **2** to be easy to understand: *These instructions don't make any sense to me.*
make sense of sth to understand something that is complicated or unusual
sense of humour the ability to laugh at things and recognize when they are funny

sense² /sens/ verb [T] ★ to know about something through a natural ability or feeling, without being told: **+(that)** *I think she must have sensed there was something wrong.*

Words often used with sense

Nouns often used with sense (verb)
- SENSE + **atmosphere, danger, fear, mood, presence, tension, unease**: know that something exists without being told

---

senseless /'sensləs/ adj **1** happening or done for no purpose: *the senseless killing of innocent people* **2** unconscious —**senselessly** adv

sensibilities /,sensə'bɪlətiz/ noun [plural] the ability to be shocked or offended by something: *We have to consider the sensibilities of older people.*

sensible /'sensəb(ə)l/ adj ★ reasonable and practical: *This seems to be a sensible way of dealing with the problem.* ♦ **be sensible to do sth** *It would be sensible to consult the others first.* —**sensibly** adv

S

sensitive /'sensətɪv/ adj

1 reacting quickly	**4** easily damaged
2 easily upset	**5** secret
3 caring about feelings	**6** likely to offend sb

1 reacting quickly or strongly to something: *Bats have extremely sensitive ears.* ♦ *Coral is very sensitive to changes in water temperature.* **2** likely to become upset very easily: *Paul was always a very sensitive little boy.* **3** caring about someone's feelings and not wanting to offend or upset them ≠ INSENSITIVE: *This is a case that needs sensitive and skilful handling.* **4** needing to be protected because of being easy to harm or destroy: *sensitive skin* **5** sensitive information should be kept secret **6** a sensitive issue needs to be dealt with carefully because it is likely to upset or offend people —**sensitively** adv: *I thought she handled the situation very sensitively.*

sensitivity /,sensə'tɪvəti/ noun **1** [U] the quality of understanding how someone feels and being careful not to offend them: *Delivering bad news requires sensitivity on the doctor's part.* **2** [C/U] a tendency to have a strong physical reaction to something: *The drug can cause sensitivity to sunlight.*

sensor /'sensə/ noun [C] a piece of equipment that reacts to physical changes such as the amount of heat or light that there is in a place

sensory /'sensəri/ adj relating to the physical senses of sight, hearing, smell, taste, and touch

sensual /'sensjuəl/ adj relating to or providing physical pleasure, especially sexual pleasure —**sensuality** /,sensju'æləti/ noun [U]

sensuous /'sensjuəs/ adj relating to physical pleasure

sent the past tense and past participle of **send**

sentence¹ /'sentəns/ noun [C] ★★★
1 a group of words, usually including a subject and a verb, that expresses a statement, question, or instruction
2 a punishment that is officially given by a judge: *She received the maximum sentence of ten years.* ♦ *He is serving a three-year sentence for burglary.*

sentence² /'sentəns/ verb [T] if a judge sentences someone, they officially say what that person's punishment will be: *He was sentenced to 15 years in prison.*

sentiment /'sentɪmənt/ noun [C/U] *formal* a feeling or attitude

sentimental /,sentɪ'ment(ə)l/ adj making people experience feelings of sadness, sympathy, love etc, especially in a deliberate way that many people do not like: *a sentimental song/book/film*
PHRASE **sentimental value** something that has sentimental value is important because it reminds you of someone or something —**sentimentality** /,sentɪmen'tæləti/ noun [U], **sentimentally** adv

sentry /'sentri/ noun [C] a soldier who stands

at the entrance to a place and guards it

separable /'sep(ə)rəb(ə)l/ adj capable of being separated ≠ INSEPARABLE

separate¹ /'sep(ə)rət/ adj ★★★
1 not together: *My brother and I always had separate rooms.* ♦ *Clients' funds should be kept separate from the firm's own money.*
2 different or new: *Answer each question on a separate sheet of paper.*
3 not connected with something that is similar: *Police have arrested seven drug smugglers in three separate incidents this week.*
PHRASE **go your separate ways** to end a relationship with a partner and decide to live or work apart
—**separately** adv: *They arrived at the party separately.*

separate² /'sepəreɪt/ verb ★★★
1 [I/T] to keep people or things apart from each other, or to stop being joined to something else: *The army was called in to help separate the warring factions.* ♦ *The newly formed cells will separate from the main organism.* ♦ *separate sb from sb The child may be separated from his mother while she receives treatment.*
2 [T] to be between things or people so that they are kept apart: *separate sth from sth A large river separates the north of the city from the south.*
3 [I/T] to divide something, or to become divided, into different parts: *The two issues need to be separated to discuss them fairly.* ♦ *The story then separates into several different strands.*
4 [I] to stop living with your husband, wife, or sexual partner
PHRASAL VERB **separate (sth) out** same as **separate²** 3: *The material is processed to separate out any impurities.*

separated /'sepəreɪtɪd/ adj no longer living with your husband, wife, or sexual partner → DIVORCED

separation /,sepə'reɪʃ(ə)n/ noun **1** [C/U] a period of time that people who are usually together spend apart: *a baby's response to separation from its mother* **2** [U] the act of separating two or more things, or the fact that they are separated: *Quebec wanted some form of separation from the rest of Canada.* **3** [C/U] an arrangement in which a husband and wife live apart even though they are not divorced

separatist /'sep(ə)rətɪst/ noun [C] a member of a group of people who want to be independent of a national, religious, or other group to which they belong

Sept. abbrev September

September /sep'tembə/ noun [C/U] ★★★ the ninth month of the year, between August and October: *The last time I saw her was in September.* ♦ *The interview is on September 9th.*

septic /'septɪk/ adj infected with bacteria

sequel /'siːkwəl/ noun [C] a book, film, play etc that continues the story of an earlier one = FOLLOW-UP

S

sequence /'siːkwəns/ noun [C/U] ★★ a set of related things that happen or are arranged in a particular order: *A computer can store and repeat sequences of instructions.* ♦ *Are the numbers in sequence?* ♦ *Describe the exact sequence of events that evening.*

sequin /'siːkwɪn/ noun [C] a small shiny flat piece of plastic or metal that you sew onto clothes to decorate them

serene /sə'riːn/ adj calm, or peaceful
—**serenely** adv, **serenity** /sə'renəti/ noun [U]

sergeant /'sɑːdʒ(ə)nt/ noun [C] **1** an officer of middle rank in the army or air force **2** a police officer of middle rank

,**sergeant 'major** noun [C] an officer of middle rank in the army

serial /'sɪəriəl/ noun [C] a story that is broadcast or published in a series of separate parts

,**serial ,killer** noun [C] someone who murders several people one after the other, often in the same way

,**serial ,number** noun [C] a number that is printed on things such as electrical goods or paper money, so that each one can be recognized

series /'sɪəriːz/ (plural **series**) noun [C] ★★★
1 a set of similar things that come one after another: *We'll need to do a series of tests before we do anything else.*
2 a set of television or radio programmes that are all about a particular subject, person, or group of people: *Tonight's programme is the second in a three-part series.*
3 a set of things that are made with the same design, or made in the same way: *a popular new series of children's books*

serious /'sɪəriəs/ adj ★★★
1 bad or dangerous enough to make you worried: *It's not a serious problem.* ♦ *a serious head injury* ♦ *An accident like this poses a serious threat to the environment.*
2 meaning what you say or do, and not making a joke: *I'm sorry, I didn't realize you were being serious.* ♦ **serious about (doing) sth** *Do you think Mike's serious about going to live in New Zealand?*
3 thinking carefully about things and not laughing much: *Peter seems serious but he actually has a good sense of humour.*
4 if you are in a serious romantic relationship with someone, you intend to stay together for a long time
—**seriousness** noun [U]

seriously /'sɪəriəsli/ adv ★★
1 in a way that is bad or dangerous enough to make you worried: *Was anyone in the car seriously hurt?*
2 in a way that shows that you think something is important and should be thought about carefully: *We have to think seriously about what we do next.* ♦ *I'm seriously considering moving to France.*
3 *spoken* really: *Do you seriously think I'm going to lend you the car?*
4 *informal* very: *He must be seriously rich.*

PHRASE **take sb/sth seriously** to behave in a way that shows that you think that someone or something is important

sermon /'sɜːmən/ noun [C] a religious speech that is made by a priest in church

serotonin /ˌsɪərə'təʊnɪn/ noun [U] a substance in your body that affects your moods

serpent /'sɜːpənt/ noun [C] *literary* a snake

servant /'sɜːv(ə)nt/ noun [C] someone whose job is to cook, clean, or do other work in someone else's home

serve¹ /sɜːv/ verb ★★★

1 provide food/drink	**6** help customers
2 do work	**7** spend time in prison
3 be used for purpose	**8** give document
4 help achieve sth	**9** hit ball to start play
5 provide with sth useful	**+ PHRASE**

1 [I/T] to provide food or a drink for someone, especially at a meal: *A light meal will be served during the flight.* ♦ *Dinner is served between 7 and 10 pm.* ♦ **serve sb sth** *Carolyn served them tea and cake in the garden.*
2 [I/T] to do a job, or to perform duties for a person or organization: *He served more than 20 years in the army.* ♦ *Mr Russell served as president of the Association for fifteen years.* ♦ *Henry served on numerous committees and commissions.*
3 [I/T] to be used for a particular purpose: *Their spare room also serves as an office.* ♦ **serve to do sth** *His death serves to remind us how dangerous drugs can be.*
4 [T] to help to achieve something: **serve sb's interests** *They voted for a chairman who might better serve their interests.* ♦ **serve sb well** *His ability to get on with people served him well in setting up his own business.*
5 [T] to provide a group of people or an area with something useful: *These gas pipes serve the whole area.* ♦ *a new hospital to serve the needs of the local community*
6 [I/T] to help customers to buy goods in a shop
7 [T] to spend time in prison: *He's serving a life sentence for murder.*
8 [T] to officially give someone a legal document that orders them to do something: **serve sb with sth** *She was served with a summons to appear in court.*
9 [I/T] to hit a ball in order to start playing for a point in a game such as tennis
—*picture* → C15

PHRASE **it serves sb right (for doing sth)** used for saying that you think that someone deserves something unpleasant that happens to them

serve² /sɜːv/ noun [C] a hit of a ball in order to start playing for a point in a game such as tennis=SERVICE

server /'sɜːvə/ noun [C] *computing* a computer that stores information for all the computers in a NETWORK

service¹ /'sɜːvɪs/ noun ★★★

1 system to meet needs	**6** of vehicles/machines
2 help for customers	**7** religious ceremony
3 type of business	**8** the armed forces
4 government work	**9** in tennis etc
5 sb's work	

S

1 [C] a system that provides things that the public needs: *transport/education services*
→ HEALTH SERVICE

2 [U] help and advice that is given to customers in a shop, hotel, or business: *a shop with a reputation for excellent customer service*

3 [C] a business that provides help, information, or advice for the public: *financial/banking services* ♦ *the service sector*

4 [C] an organization that does work for a government: *the prison/diplomatic service*

5 [C/U] work that someone does as a job or in order to help other people: *Jack had given 25 years of loyal service.* ♦ *She was praised for her services to the community.*

6 [C] an occasion when a vehicle or machine is examined to check that it works correctly, and to make repairs: *I need to take the car in for a service.*

7 [C] a religious ceremony: *a church service*

8 the services [plural] the armed forces

9 [C] a hit of a ball in order to start playing for a point in a game such as tennis = SERVE

service² /'sɜːvɪs/ verb [T] to examine and repair a vehicle or machine as part of a regular check

'service charge noun [C] an amount of money added to your bill in a restaurant, that is for the person who brings your food

serviceman /'sɜːvɪsmən/ (plural **servicemen** /'sɜːvɪsmən/) noun [C] a man who is a member of the armed forces

'service pro,vider noun [C] *computing* a company that provides customers with a connection to the Internet = ISP

services /'sɜːvɪsɪz/ noun [C] *British* a place beside a motorway where petrol, food, drinks, and toilets are available

'service ,station noun [C] a business that sells petrol, oil, and other things for vehicles

servicewoman /'sɜːvɪsˌwʊmən/ (plural **servicewomen** /'sɜːvɪsˌwɪmɪn/) noun [C] a woman who is a member of the armed forces

serviette /ˌsɜːviˈet/ noun [C] *British* a piece of cloth or paper that you use for wiping your mouth during a meal = NAPKIN

serving /'sɜːvɪŋ/ noun [C] an amount of food for one person = HELPING

sesame /'sesəmi/ noun [U] a plant that produces seeds and oil that are used in cooking

session /'seʃ(ə)n/ noun [C] ★★
1 a period of time that is used for a particular activity: *a question-and-answer session* ♦ *a training/recording session*
2 a formal meeting of an institution such as a parliament or a court of law: *an emergency session of the UN Security Council*
PHRASE **in session** meeting to deal with business: *Parliament is not in session during August.*

set¹ /set/ (past tense and past participle **set**) verb ★★★

1 put sb/sth somewhere	8 put story in time/place
2 of equipment	9 when sun goes down
3 decide time/place	10 liquid: become solid
4 decide price/value	11 join broken bone
5 establish rule etc	+ PHRASE
6 give sb sth to do	+ PHRASAL VERBS
7 put sb/sth in state	

1 [T] to put someone or something in a position, or to be in a particular place or position: *Tea's ready, he told them and set down the tray.* ♦ *She set the baby on the floor to play.*

2 [T] to make a piece of equipment ready to operate, or ready to start at a particular time: **set sth to do sth** *The bomb was set to go off at eight o'clock.* ♦ *I'm setting the alarm for 6.30.*

3 [T] to decide where or when an event will happen: *Have they set a date for the wedding?*

4 [T] to decide the price, value, or level of something: *The central bank is responsible for setting interest rates.*

5 [T] to establish a rule, standard, limit etc that people must follow: *Their teacher sets high standards and expects everyone to meet them.* ♦ *Opposition parties have set conditions for cooperating with the government.* ♦ *You should set an example for your younger brothers.*

6 [T] to give something to someone to do or achieve: **set sb sth** *You'll never get anywhere if you don't set yourself any goals.* ♦ *The teacher set us an essay to do over the weekend.*

7 [T] to put someone or something in a particular state: *The suspect has been accused of setting the restaurant on fire.* ♦ *Don't set the dog loose.* ♦ *The hostages have been set free after 34 days in captivity.*

8 [T] if a play, book, film etc is set in a particular time or place, it happens in that time or place: *The film is set in 18th-century New England.*

9 [I] when the sun sets, it goes below the HORIZON at the end of the day ≠ RISE

10 [I] if a liquid sets, it forms a solid substance: *a type of concrete that sets in 15 minutes*

11 [I/T] to put the two ends of a broken bone back together, or to be joined in this way

PHRASE **set the stage for sth** to create the conditions in which something is likely to happen

PHRASAL VERBS **set a,bout sth** to begin doing something, especially in a determined or enthusiastic way: *She set about the problem with her usual energy.*

,set sb a'gainst sb to cause two people or groups to fight each other

,set sb/sth a'part to make someone or something different and special: *Graf's natural athleticism set her apart from other tennis players.*

,set sth a'side 1 to keep or save something

S

from a larger amount or supply in order to use it later: *Have you set aside some money for your child's education?* **2** to not let a particular feeling, opinion, or belief influence you, in order to achieve something more important: *They agreed to set aside their differences and work together for peace.*

,set sth 'back to delay the progress of something

,set sth 'down *formal* to state officially how something should be done

,set 'forth *literary* to start a journey

,set 'in if something unpleasant sets in, it starts to happen and is likely to continue: *If the wound is not kept clean, infection could set in.*

,set 'off to start a journey: *We set off early the next morning.*

,set sth 'off 1 to cause something to operate or to explode: *Jeff pushed open the front door, which set off the alarm.* **2** to cause a situation or a series of events to happen: *The price rises could set off mass protests.*

,set 'out 1 to start a journey: *The group set out from Grand Cayman five days ago.* **2** to start doing something, or trying to achieve something: **set out to do sth** *They set out to build their own house.*

,set sth 'out to explain, describe, or arrange something in a clear and detailed way

,set sb 'up *informal* to arrange for someone to be blamed for doing something illegal

,set sth 'up 1 to start something such as a business, organization, or institution **2** to organize or plan something: *I'll set up a meeting for Thursday.* **3** to make a piece of equipment ready for use: *Will you be able to set up my PC?*

set² /set/ noun [C] ★★★

1 group of things	4 part of tennis match
2 piece of equipment	5 songs performed
3 part of play/film	

1 a group of things that belong together: *Teachers are given a set of guidelines for dealing with violent students.* ♦ *a set of keys* ♦ *Winners will receive a complete set of REM albums.*

2 a piece of equipment that receives television or radio signals: *a TV set*

3 a theatre stage, or a place where a film or television programme is made: *This photograph was taken on the set of her latest film.*

4 a part of a tennis match consisting of at least six games

5 a series of songs that are played or sung in a performance

set³ /set/ adj ★

1 already decided	4 likely to do sth
2 not willing to change	5 necessary to study
3 ready to do sth	

1 already decided or agreed: *There's no set time limit for the job.* ♦ *He charges a set fee for his services.*

2 not willing to change your opinion or way of doing things: *He's old and stubborn and set in his ways.*

3 ready to do something: *Gillian is getting set to do a world tour.* ♦ *Are you all set for the party tonight?*

4 likely to do something: **be set to do sth** *Car repair costs are set to rise under the new proposals.*

5 a set book or TEXT contains information that students must study before an examination

setback /'setbæk/ noun [C] a problem that delays or stops progress

,set 'piece noun [C] a performance or action that is planned very carefully

settee /se'tiː/ noun [C] *British* a long comfortable chair for two or three people =COUCH, SOFA

setting /'setɪŋ/ noun [C] ★

1 the place where someone or something is, and all the things that are part of that place: *The classroom setting must be calm and safe.* ♦ *a hotel in a charming mountain setting*

2 the time or place in which the events of a play, book, film etc happen: *a love story in a tropical island setting*

3 a position on the controls of a piece of equipment: *To save energy, lower the thermostat setting at night.*

Words often used with **setting**

*Adjectives often used with **setting** (sense 1)*
■ **beautiful, ideal, idyllic, magnificent, perfect, picturesque, tranquil** + SETTING: used about settings that are pleasant

---

settle /'set(ə)l/ verb ★★★

1 end disagreement	6 pay money owed to sb
2 decide sth	7 become calm
3 make sb comfortable	+ PHRASE
4 fall & rest on ground	+ PHRASAL VERBS
5 go to live somewhere	

1 [T] to end an argument or legal disagreement: *The two sides are holding talks to settle the dispute.* ♦ *The case was settled out of court* (=without asking a law court to decide).

2 [T] to decide something definitely: *It was settled that they would leave before dark.*

3 [I/T] to make yourself or someone else comfortable and relaxed in a particular place or position: *I settled back into a comfortable chair and waited.*

4 [I] if something settles, it falls downwards and stays on the place where it has fallen: *Flakes of snow settled on the windscreen.*

5 [I] to go to live permanently in a particular place: *Her relatives had come to America and settled in Boston.*

6 [T] to pay all the money that you owe to a particular person or company: *He has 30 days to settle his bill.*

7 [I/T] to become calm after being upset, nervous, or excited, or to make someone do this: *The kids will settle after they've had a nap.*

PHRASE **settle a score (with sb)** to do something bad in order to harm someone, because they did something bad to you in the past

PHRASAL VERBS ,settle 'down to change your life by choosing to stay in one place or with one partner: *Are you ever going to settle down?*

,settle (sb) 'down *same as* **settle 7**
'settle for sb/sth to accept someone or something that is not exactly what you wanted: *Why settle for second best when you can have something better?*

,settle 'in to become familiar with a new way of life, place, or job: *She seems to have settled in quickly at her new company.*

'settle on sb/sth to make a decision between two or more people or things after not being certain which to choose

,settle 'up to pay all of an amount of money that you owe

settled /'set(ə)ld/ adj **1** happy and relaxed because you are in a familiar or permanent situation **2** if you have a settled way of life, you stay permanently in one place or job or with one person **3** not changing or likely to change

settlement /'set(ə)lmənt/ noun ★
1 [C/U] a formal agreement that ends a disagreement: *They are negotiating a peace settlement.* ◆ *the settlement of disputes between employers and employees*
2 [C] a place where people have come to live permanently: *They discovered the remains of an early Anglo-Saxon settlement.*

settler /'setlə/ noun [C] someone who goes to live in a place where not many people live

,set-top 'box noun [C] a piece of electronic equipment shaped like a box that you use for operating CABLE TELEVISION or DIGITAL TELEVISION

'set-up noun [C] **1** the way a particular group of people or things is organized **2** *informal* a situation in which someone cheats or tricks you

seven /'sev(ə)n/ number the number 7

seventeen /,sev(ə)n'ti:n/ number the number 17

seventeenth /,sev(ə)n'ti:nθ/ number **1** in the place or position counted as number 17 **2** one of 17 equal parts of something

seventh /'sev(ə)nθ/ number **1** in the place or position counted as number 7 **2** one of 7 equal parts of something

seventieth /'sev(ə)ntiəθ/ number **1** in the place or position counted as number 70 **2** one of 70 equal parts of something

seventy /'sev(ə)nti/ number the number 70

sever /'sevə/ verb [T] **1** to cut through a part of something so that it is separated completely from the main part **2** to end something such as a friendship or a connection completely and permanently

several /'sev(ə)rəl/ grammar word ★★★

Several can be:
- a **determiner**: *Several buildings were damaged by the explosion.*
- a **pronoun**: *If you want to see Edward's paintings, there are several in the city art gallery.* ◆ *I've introduced her to several of my friends.*
- an **adjective**: *These past several weeks have been difficult for the whole family.*

a number of people or things that is more than two or three, but not many: *He had been warned several times about speeding.* ◆ *There are only nine men in the programme, but several have drug problems.* ◆ *Several of the passengers were badly injured.*

severe /sɪ'vɪə/ adj ★★
1 very serious and bad, worrying, or unpleasant: *The housing shortage is severe.* ◆ *a severe thunderstorm* ◆ *John had suffered severe bruising and serious cuts.*
2 very strict or extreme=HARSH: *The most severe penalty he could get is ten years in prison.* ◆ *The country has come under severe criticism for its human rights record.*
3 unfriendly and not smiling: *a severe expression*
—**severely** adv, **severity** /sɪ'verəti/ noun [U]

sew /səʊ/ (past tense **sewed**; past participle **sewn** /səʊn/) verb [I/T] to make or repair clothes, or to fasten something, using a needle and THREAD

PHRASAL VERB ,sew sth 'up **1** *informal* to deal with something successfully, or to make certain that you will win something **2** to repair something such as a hole in a piece of cloth by sewing it

sewage /'su:ɪdʒ/ noun [U] waste from people's bodies that is removed from houses and other buildings by a system of large underground pipes

sewer /'su:ə/ noun [C] an underground pipe or passage that carries sewage

sewing /'səʊɪŋ/ noun [U] **1** work that you do using a needle and THREAD or a sewing machine **2** things such as clothes or curtains that you sew

'sewing ma,chine noun [C] a machine that you use for sewing clothes, curtains etc

sewn the past participle of **sew**

sex /seks/ noun ★★★
1 [U] the activity in which people kiss and touch each other's sexual organs, that may also include SEXUAL INTERCOURSE: *the impact of sex and violence in TV programmes* ◆ *Parents worry about their teenagers having sex.*
2 [C] males or females considered as separate groups: *equal treatment of the sexes* ◆ *The hostel has separate sleeping areas for each sex.*
3 [U] the fact that a person, animal, or plant is either male or female: *We don't want to know the sex of our baby before it is born.*

'sex ap,peal noun [U] the quality of being sexually attractive

S

sexism /'seks,ɪz(ə)m/ noun [U] unfair treatment of someone because they are a woman or a man —**sexist** adj

ˈsex ˌlife noun [C] someone's sexual relationships or activities

ˈsex ofˌfender noun [C] someone who has committed a crime involving sex

sexual /'sekʃuəl/ adj ★★★
1 involving or relating to sex: *a sexual relationship/partner* ♦ *sexual desire/feelings*
2 concerning relationships between men and women, or the way that people think that men and women should behave: *sexual stereotyping*
—**sexually** adv

ˌsexual ˈharassment noun [U] offensive or threatening behaviour that involves regularly making sexual comments or touching someone in a sexual way when they do not want this

ˌsexual ˈintercourse noun [U] *formal* the sexual actions between a man and a woman in which the man puts his PENIS inside the woman's VAGINA

sexuality /ˌsekʃuˈæləti/ noun [U] sexual feelings, attitudes, and activities

ˌsexual orienˈtation or **ˌsexual ˈpreference** noun [U] the state of preferring sexual relationships with people of one sex rather than the other

ˈsex ˌworker noun [C] a PROSTITUTE

sexy /'seksi/ adj sexually attractive, or causing feelings of sexual excitement

SGML noun [U] *computing* Standard Generalized Markup Language: a computer language that uses normal English words for publishing documents in electronic form

sh /ʃ/ interjection used for telling someone to stop talking or to be less noisy

shabby /'ʃæbi/ adj 1 old and in bad condition: *shabby clothes/furniture/buildings* 2 not fair or honest: *the government's shabby treatment of trade unions* —**shabbily** adv

shack /ʃæk/ noun [C] a small plain building

shackle /'ʃæk(ə)l/ verb **be shackled** to be prevented from doing what you want to do

shackles /'ʃæk(ə)lz/ noun [plural] a pair of connected metal rings that can be locked onto the wrists or legs of a prisoner

shade¹ /ʃeɪd/ noun ★

1 cool dark area	4 slightly different form
2 screen/cover	5 sunglasses
3 form of a colour	

1 [U] a slightly cool dark area where the light and heat from the sun does not reach: *I spent the afternoon reading under the shade of an umbrella.* ♦ *We sat in the shade and ate our lunch.*
2 [C] a screen or cover that protects something from the sun or from a light
3 [C] a particular form of a colour: *a brilliant shade of red*
4 [C] a slightly different form or type of something: *All shades of political opinion were represented.*

5 **shades** [plural] *informal* a pair of SUNGLASSES

shade² /ʃeɪd/ verb [T] to prevent light from shining directly onto or into something

shadow¹ /'ʃædəʊ/ noun [C/U] ★★ an area of darkness that is created when something blocks light: *The dogs are always trying to chase their own shadows.* ♦ *Even on a bright day, the room was in shadow.*

PHRASES **beyond/without a shadow of a doubt** used for saying that you are completely certain of something
in sb's shadow in a situation where your own qualities are not noticed or recognized because of someone who is more famous or powerful: *For years, she lived in her father's shadow.*

shadow² /'ʃædəʊ/ verb [T] to secretly follow someone wherever they go

shadowy /'ʃædəʊi/ adj 1 mysterious and secret, or not understood 2 hidden in darkness or shadows

shady /'ʃeɪdi/ adj 1 probably dishonest or illegal 2 sheltered from the hot sun

shaft /ʃɑːft/ noun [C] 1 a long narrow passage that goes down through a building or down through the ground: *a lift shaft* 2 the handle of a tool 3 *literary* a long thin line of light

shaggy /'ʃægi/ adj shaggy fur or hair is long, thick, and untidy

shake¹ /ʃeɪk/ (past tense **shook** /ʃʊk/; past participle **shaken** /'ʃeɪkən/) verb ★★★
1 [I/T] to make lots of quick small movements up and down, or from side to side, or to make someone or something do this: *Houses shook as a bomb exploded in the neighbourhood.* ♦ *An earthquake shook a wide area of southern Italy last year.* ♦ *'You're not listening!' she cried, shaking him.*
2 [T] to frighten someone, or to make them feel very shocked or upset: *The boy's tragic death shook the entire community.* ♦ *He was shaken and upset by the accident.*
3 [T] to make something less strong, powerful, or confident: *Violent conflicts between tribes have shaken the region.* ♦ *You must believe in yourself and not allow anyone to shake your confidence.*
4 [I] if your voice shakes, it sounds weak, nervous, or emotional

PHRASES **shake hands (with sb)** or **shake sb's hand** to hold someone's hand and move it up and down, as a way of greeting them or to show that you agree to something: *'Nice to meet you,' Larry said, shaking my hand.*
shake your head to say no by turning your head from side to side

PHRASAL VERBS **ˌshake sb ˈoff** to escape from someone who is following you
ˌshake sth ˈoff to get rid of something bad: *I haven't been able to shake this cold off for weeks.*
ˌshake sb ˈup to upset or frighten someone

shake² /ʃeɪk/ noun [C] 1 the action of shaking 2 a MILKSHAKE

ˈshake-up noun [C] an important change in the way that something such as a department or company is organized

S

shake

shaky /ˈʃeɪki/ adj **1** feeling weak or unable to walk or move without shaking, for example because you are ill **2** likely to fail or be unsuccessful: *The Canadian team overcame a shaky start to win the ice hockey championship.* —**shakily** adv

shall /ʃəl, *strong* ʃæl/ modal verb ★★★

- **Shall** is usually followed by an infinitive without 'to': *I shall explain everything later.* Sometimes it is used without a following infinitive: *I have never visited America and probably never shall.*
- **Shall** has no participles and no infinitive form. It does not change its form, so the third person singular form does not end in '-s': *The President shall appoint all ambassadors with the consent of the Senate.*
- Questions and negatives are formed without 'do': *Shall I come with you?*
- The negative form **shall not** can be shortened in conversation or informal writing to **shan't**.

1 *British* used after 'I' or 'we' for saying what you intend to do in the future: *I shall be busy all day tomorrow.* ♦ *If he gets violent, I shall phone the police.* ♦ *We shan't be able to stay with you very long.* ♦ *By nightfall we shall have achieved our objectives.*

In forming the future tense **shall** is only used with the subject 'I' or 'we'. **Will** or its short form '**ll** is much more common with all subjects. Both verbs are used to express intentions, but **will** also expresses willingness: *I'll come with you if you like.*

2 used for offering help, suggesting something, or asking someone what to do: *Shall we have some lunch?* ♦ *Shall I open the champagne?* ♦ *Where shall we meet?*
3 *legal* used in instructions and legal documents for saying that something must be done: *The Court shall have authority to demand the presence of witnesses.*

shallot /ʃəˈlɒt/ noun [C] a small vegetable similar to an onion —*picture* → C11

shallow /ˈʃæləʊ/ adj ★
1 with only a short distance from the top or surface to the bottom ≠ DEEP: *Move to the shallow end of the pool.* ♦ *He dug a shallow trench.*
2 not interested in serious ideas, strong feelings, or other important things =SUPERFICIAL

sham /ʃæm/ noun [singular] something that people pretend is good, serious, or honest, but is not

shambles /ˈʃæmb(ə)lz/ noun [singular]
1 something that is very badly organized
2 an extremely untidy place

shame¹ /ʃeɪm/ noun ★
1 [singular] a reason for feeling sad or disappointed: **it seems a shame to do sth** *It seems a shame to waste all this food.* ♦ **+(that)** *It was a shame that you couldn't come with us.*
2 [U] a guilty and embarrassed feeling that you have when you have behaved badly: *He speaks about his affair without shame.* ♦ *The people who let this happen should hang their heads in shame.*
  PHRASE **put sb/sth to shame** to make someone or something seem less good by comparison

shame² /ʃeɪm/ verb [T] to make someone feel guilty or embarrassed, especially so that they change their behaviour

shameful /ˈʃeɪmf(ə)l/ adj so bad that you feel ashamed —**shamefully** adv

shameless /ˈʃeɪmləs/ adj not feeling ashamed of behaving in a way that other people do not approve of: *a shameless womaniser* —**shamelessly** adv

shampoo /ʃæmˈpuː/ noun [C/U] a liquid that you use for washing your hair —**shampoo** verb [T]

shan't /ʃɑːnt/ short form *British* the usual way of saying or writing 'shall not'. This is not often used in formal writing: *I shan't be away for long.*

shanty town /ˈʃænti ˌtaʊn/ noun [C] an area where very poor people live in houses made from sheets of wood, metal, or other thin material

shape¹ /ʃeɪp/ noun ★★★
1 [C/U] the outer form of something: *Trace the shape onto the card and cut it out.* ♦ *There were balloons of all shapes and sizes in the sky.* ♦ *a flowerbed in the shape of a cross* ♦ *My favourite sweater was beginning to lose its shape.*
2 [C] something that you cannot see well because it is far away or there is not enough light: *Ghostly shapes loomed out of the fog.*
3 [U] the condition of something: *The economy is in bad shape.*
4 [U] the features or qualities of something: *It's part of a plan to change the shape of local government.*
  PHRASES **in/out of shape** in good/bad physical condition: *I can't believe how out of shape I am.* ♦ *I really want to get in shape before summer.*
  take shape to develop into something that can be recognized: *The idea began to take shape about two years ago.*

shape² /ʃeɪp/ verb [T] ★
1 to influence the way that a person, idea, or situation develops: *We have all been shaped by our past experiences.* ♦ *His generation firmly believed they could shape the future.*
2 to form something into a particular shape: **shape sth into sth** *Shape the mixture into cubes.*

S

PHRASAL VERB ,shape 'up to develop:
*Education is shaping up as the hottest issue
on the agenda.*

shaped /ʃeɪpt/ adj with a particular shape

shapeless /'ʃeɪpləs/ adj without a definite
shape

shapely /'ʃeɪpli/ adj attractive in shape

shard /ʃɑːd/ noun [C] a sharp piece of broken
glass, metal, or other hard substance

share¹ /ʃeə/ verb ★★★

1 use/have with sb	5 have same opinion
2 do sth with sb else	6 tell sb sth
3 give part to sb	+ PHRASAL VERB
4 let sb use/have sth	

1 [I/T] to use or to have something at the
same time as someone else: *Do you mind
sharing a table?* ♦ *There's only one copy left,
so we'll have to share.* ♦ **share sth with sb** *I
share this flat with five other people.*
2 [I/T] to do something, or to be responsible
for something, with someone else: *We **share
responsibility** for meeting the targets.*
3 [T] to give a part of something to someone
else: **share sth between/among sb** *The money
will be shared between 30 different
environmental organizations.*
4 [T] to allow someone to use or have
something that you own: **share sth with sb**
He would never share his toys with me.
5 [T] to have the same opinion or feeling as
someone else: *Not everyone will share your
enthusiasm for this scheme.*
6 [I/T] to tell someone something: *Thanks for
sharing.* ♦ *Newsgroups enable patients to
share information.*

PHRASAL VERB ,share sth 'out *same as* **share¹** 3

share² /ʃeə/ noun ★★★

1 [C] a part of a total number or amount of
something that is divided between two or
more people or things: *Britain's share of
world trade had steadily declined.* ♦ *He has
no right to **a share in** profits.*
2 [singular] a part of the total amount of work
or responsibility of several people: *He does
his **share** of the cooking.* ♦ *Jane has accepted
her **share** of the blame.*
3 [singular] a reasonable or normal amount
of something: *We certainly had our **share**
of good fortune.* ♦ *He has suffered more than
his **fair share** of disappointments.*
4 [C] *business* one of the equal parts of a
company that you can buy as a way of
investing money: *The scheme allows
employees to buy **shares** in the company.* ♦
Share prices fell on the Tokyo Stock
Exchange today.

shareholder /'ʃeəˌhəʊldə/ noun [C] someone
who owns shares in a company

shareware /'ʃeəˌweə/ noun [U] *computing*
computer software that you can use for a
period of time before paying for it

sharia /ʃəˈriːə/ noun [U] the traditional system
of Islamic law

shark /ʃɑːk/ noun [C] a very large fish with
sharp teeth that lives in the sea —*picture*
→ C13

S

sharp¹ /ʃɑːp/ adj ★★★

1 able to cut	6 showing sb is annoyed
2 sudden & big/severe	7 clearly different
3 turning suddenly	8 wind/frost: very cold
4 clear & with detail	9 higher in music
5 quick to notice/react	

1 a sharp object has an edge that can cut or
an end that is pointed: *a sharp knife* ♦ *sharp
teeth/claws* ♦ *a sharp pencil* ♦ *These scissors
aren't very sharp.*
2 sudden and very big or severe: *a sharp
rise in sales of organic produce* ♦ *a sharp
drop in unemployment* ♦ *I felt a sharp pain
in my foot.*
3 changing direction suddenly: *a sharp bend
in the road*
4 clear and seen in a lot of detail: *The new
high-definition TV offers razor-sharp
pictures and digital sound.*
5 intelligent and quick to notice something
or react to something: *Some of these kids
are pretty sharp when it comes to maths.* ♦ *a
sharp wit*
6 a sharp comment, voice, or expression
shows that someone is unfriendly or
annoyed: *The deal has come under sharp
criticism from the opposition parties.*
7 clearly recognized as different: *The warm
weather was in sharp contrast to last year's
cold temperatures.*
8 a sharp wind or FROST is very cold
9 used for showing that a musical note
should be played or sung a SEMITONE higher
than usual
—**sharply** /'ʃɑːpli/ adv: *Interest rates have
fallen sharply.* ♦ *The government has been
sharply criticized.* —**sharpness** noun [U]

sharp² /ʃɑːp/ adv **1** at a particular time
exactly: *We're leaving at 5 o'clock sharp.*
2 *British* in a way that changes direction
suddenly: *Turn sharp left after the bridge.*
3 at a higher than usual PITCH

sharp³ /ʃɑːp/ noun [C] a musical note that is
played or sung a SEMITONE higher than usual

sharpen /'ʃɑːpən/ verb [T] **1** to make something
such as a knife, tool, or pencil sharp **2** to
make something better, stronger, or more
noticeable

shatter /'ʃætə/ verb **1** [I/T] to break suddenly
into a lot of small pieces, or to break
something into a lot of small pieces: *The
blast shattered windows over a wide area.*
2 [T] to destroy or seriously damage
something: *His father's constant criticism
shattered his confidence.*

shattered /'ʃætəd/ adj **1** extremely upset
2 *British informal* extremely tired

shave¹ /ʃeɪv/ verb [I/T] to make a part of your
body smooth by cutting off the hair: *I cut
myself while I was shaving.* ♦ *shaving
cream/foam*

PHRASAL VERB ,shave sth 'off to remove hair
from a part of your body: *You've shaved off
your beard.*

shave² /ʃeɪv/ noun [singular] an act of making
a part of your body smooth by cutting off

the hair: *Did you have a shave this morning?*

PHRASE **a close shave** a situation in which you only just avoid something dangerous or unpleasant

shaven /ˈʃeɪv(ə)n/ adj *formal* with the hair shaved off → CLEAN-SHAVEN

shaver /ˈʃeɪvə/ noun [C] a small piece of electrical equipment used for cutting hair from a part of your body

shavings /ˈʃeɪvɪŋz/ noun [plural] thin pieces that have been cut from the surface of something

shawl /ʃɔːl/ noun [C] a large piece of material that is worn by a woman around her shoulders or on her head

she /weak ʃɪ, strong ʃiː/ pronoun ★★★ used for referring to a woman, girl, or female animal, when they have already been mentioned, or when it is obvious which one you are referring to: *I was with Lisa when she bought her wedding dress.*

s/he abbrev she or he

sheaf /ʃiːf/ (plural **sheaves** /ʃiːvz/) noun [C] **1** a large number of pieces of paper that are kept together **2** stems of grain that have been cut and tied together

shear /ʃɪə/ (past tense **sheared**; past participle **sheared** or **shorn** /ʃɔːn/) verb [T] to cut the wool from a sheep

shears /ʃɪəz/ noun [plural] a tool like a very large pair of scissors that is used for cutting grass or bushes

sheath /ʃiːθ/ (plural **sheaths** /ʃiːðz/) noun [C] a cover that is used for a knife or a sword

sheaves the plural of **sheaf**

she'd /ʃiːd/ short form **1** the usual way of saying or writing 'she had' when 'had' is an AUXILIARY VERB. This is not often used in formal writing: *She'd forgotten to lock the door.* **2** the usual way of saying or writing 'she would'. This is not often used in formal writing: *She'd like to have a holiday.*

shed¹ /ʃed/ (present participle **shedding**; past tense and past participle **shed**) verb [T] **1** to get rid of something that is not wanted: *The company shed a further 250 jobs this month.* **2** to let something fall off as part of a natural process: *Deciduous trees shed their leaves each autumn.*

PHRASES **shed blood** *literary* to cause death or injury

shed light on sth to suggest an explanation for something that is difficult to understand

shed tears to cry, or to feel very sad

shed² /ʃed/ noun [C] a small building that is used for storing things

sheen /ʃiːn/ noun [singular] a shine on the surface of something

sheep /ʃiːp/ (plural **sheep**) noun [C] ★★ an animal that is kept by farmers for its wool or meat —*picture* → C12 → BLACK SHEEP

sheepdog /ˈʃiːpˌdɒɡ/ noun [C] a dog that has been trained to guard and control sheep

sheepish /ˈʃiːpɪʃ/ adj embarrassed about something that you have done —**sheepishly** adv

sheepskin /ˈʃiːpˌskɪn/ noun [C/U] the skin of a sheep with the wool still on it

sheer /ʃɪə/ adj **1** used for emphasizing the amount or degree of something: *Maya succeeded through sheer hard work.* ♦ *We were overwhelmed by the sheer volume of work.* ♦ *The journey to work every day was sheer hell.* **2** extremely steep: *a sheer cliff face* **3** sheer cloth is very thin

sheet /ʃiːt/ noun [C] ★★★
1 a large piece of thin cloth that you put on your bed and use for lying on or for covering your body when you sleep: *I think the chambermaid is waiting to change the sheets* (=put clean sheets on the bed).
2 a thin flat piece of paper, metal, plastic, glass etc: *The answers are printed on a separate sheet.* ♦ *a sheet of cardboard*
3 a wide flat area of something such as water or ice
→ CLEAN¹

sheeting /ˈʃiːtɪŋ/ noun [U] large flat pieces of plastic or metal

sheik or **sheikh** /ʃeɪk, ʃiːk/ noun [C] a male leader in an Arab country

shelf /ʃelf/ (plural **shelves** /ʃelvz/) noun [C] ★★ a flat piece of wood or glass that is attached to a wall or is part of a piece of furniture. It is used for putting things on: *He took a book from the shelf.* ♦ *The plates are on the top shelf.*

PHRASE **off the shelf** available in a shop without being ordered or made for a particular customer

shelf life noun [singular] the amount of time that something can be kept in a shop before it is too old to sell

she'll /ʃiːl/ short form the usual way of saying or writing 'she will'. This is not often used in formal writing: *She'll be home in about an hour.*

shells

S

shell¹ /ʃel/ noun ★
1 [C/U] the hard outer part that protects the body of a sea creature or other animal: *a crab/tortoise/snail shell* ♦ *The kids were collecting shells on the beach.*
2 [C] a metal container filled with a substance that explodes when it is fired from a large gun: *anti-aircraft shells*

3 [C/U] the hard outer part of an egg or nut: *pieces of egg shell*

shell² /ʃel/ verb [T] **1** to attack or destroy a place by firing shells: *Army bases were shelled overnight by rebel forces.* **2** to remove the outer part that covers nuts or other foods

PHRASAL VERB ,shell (sth) 'out *informal* to spend a lot of money on something

shellfish² /'ʃel,fɪʃ/ (plural **shellfish**) noun [C/U] sea creatures with a hard shell around them

shelter¹ /'ʃeltə/ noun **1** [C] a place where people are protected from bad weather or from danger: *We built a temporary shelter out of branches.* ♦ *a bus shelter* ♦ *a bomb shelter* **2** [U] protection from bad weather or danger: *People stood and watched from the shelter of shop doorways.* ♦ *We took shelter from the rain in a nearby café.* **3** [C] a temporary place to live for people who do not have their own homes, or for animals who have been treated in a cruel way =REFUGE: *a women's shelter* **4** [U] a place to live, considered as a basic human need: *Everyone has the right to food, clothing, and shelter.*

shelter² /'ʃeltə/ verb **1** [T] to protect someone or something from bad weather: *Hills sheltered the town from the winds.* **2** [T] to protect someone from unpleasant experiences or danger: *You cannot shelter your children from the realities of life.* **3** [I] to stay somewhere where you are protected from danger or bad weather: *We sheltered in an old barn for the night.*

sheltered /'ʃeltəd/ adj **1** not affected by bad weather **2** protected from unpleasant experiences

shelve /ʃelv/ verb [T] to decide not to use something such as a plan or suggestion now, although you may use it later

shelves the plural of **shelf** → STACK² 2

shelving /'ʃelvɪŋ/ noun [U] a set of shelves

shenanigans /ʃə'nænɪɡənz/ noun [plural] *informal* silly, dishonest, or immoral behaviour

shepherd¹ /'ʃepəd/ noun [C] someone whose job is to look after sheep

shepherd² /'ʃepəd/ verb [T] to take someone to a place in order to make sure that they get there safely: *Carrie was shepherding a party of children towards the museum.*

sheriff /'ʃerɪf/ noun [C] in the US, the most senior police officer in a COUNTY

sherry /'ʃeri/ noun [C/U] a strong wine from southern Spain

she's /ʃiːz/ short form **1** the usual way of saying or writing 'she is'. This is not often used in formal writing: *She's a psychiatrist.* **2** the usual way of saying or writing 'she has' when 'has' is an AUXILIARY VERB. This is not often used in formal writing: *She's gone over to Kerry's house.*

shh /ʃ/ interjection used for telling someone to stop talking or to be less noisy

shield¹ /ʃiːld/ noun [C] **1** a large transparent plastic object that police officers carry to protect them when they are controlling crowds: *Riot police with shields had surrounded the building.* **2** someone or something that protects you from harm or bad experiences **3** an object that soldiers carried in the past to protect themselves from being hit **4** an object shaped like a shield that is given to the winner of a competition

shield² /ʃiːld/ verb [T] to protect something or someone from something that is dangerous or unpleasant

shift¹ /ʃɪft/ verb ★
1 [I/T] to change, or to change something: *Public opinion had shifted sharply to the left following the war.* ♦ *The government has shifted its attention away from the fight against crime.*
2 [I/T] to move, or to move something: *The children are shifting uncomfortably in their seats.* ♦ *She stared at him, then shifted her gaze to the suitcase on the bed.* ♦ *We'll need to shift this table over to the wall.*
3 [T] to make someone or something else responsible for something: *The lawyers want to shift the blame from their client to our company.*
4 [T] *British informal* to get rid of something: *There's still a stain on the carpet that I can't shift.*

shift² /ʃɪft/ noun [C] **1** a period of work time in a place where some people work during the day and some work at night: *a 12-hour shift* ♦ *Rudolfo works the day shift.* **2** a change in someone's ideas or opinions: *the government's latest policy shift* ♦ *shifts in consumer demand* **3** a SHIFT KEY on a computer keyboard

'shift ,key noun [C] the KEY that you press on a computer keyboard when you want to write a CAPITAL LETTER

shifty /'ʃɪfti/ adj *informal* looking dishonest

Shiite /'ʃiːaɪt/ noun [C] a Muslim who belongs to the Shia group within the religion of Islam

shilling /'ʃɪlɪŋ/ noun [C] a small unit of money that was used in the UK until 1971

shimmer /'ʃɪmə/ verb [I] to reflect a gentle light that seems to shake slightly

shin /ʃɪn/ noun [C] the lower front part of your leg that is between your knee and your foot

shine¹ /ʃaɪn/ (past tense and past participle **shone** /ʃɒn, *American* ʃoʊn/) verb ★

1 produce light	4 look happy/excited
2 appear bright	5 show lot of skill
3 point light somewhere	+ PHRASAL VERB

1 [I] to produce a bright light: *Lights were shining from the windows of a few of the houses.* ♦ *The sun was shining brightly.*
2 [I] to have a bright attractive appearance: *The wooden tables had been polished until they shone.* ♦ *Her hair shone like gold.*
3 [T] to make a light shine in a particular direction: *Kobe shone the torch slowly around the room.*
4 [I] if people's eyes or faces shine, they look extremely happy or excited

5 [I] to show that you have a lot of skill when you do something: *It's time we gave some of the younger players a chance to shine.*

PHRASAL VERB ,shine 'through if a good feeling or quality shines through, it is very noticeable

shine² /ʃaɪn/ noun [singular] the bright appearance that something such as wood, metal, or leather has when it is in good condition

shingle /'ʃɪŋg(ə)l/ noun [U] small stones on a beach

Shinto /'ʃɪntəʊ/ or **Shintoism** /'ʃɪntəʊˌɪz(ə)m/ noun [U] the traditional religion of Japan

shiny /'ʃaɪni/ adj something that is shiny has a bright surface that reflects light: *a shiny red apple*

ship¹ /ʃɪp/ noun [C] ★★★ a very large boat that is used for carrying people or goods long distances: *His ship sailed from Pearl Harbor on Monday.* ♦ *a cargo/cruise ship* ♦ *There were over 350 passengers aboard ship.*

ship² /ʃɪp/ verb [T] **1** to send goods to customers, usually by air or land **2** to send people somewhere by ship

shipbuilder /'ʃɪpˌbɪldə/ noun [C] a company that builds ships —**shipbuilding** noun [U]

shipment /'ʃɪpmənt/ noun **1** [C] an amount of goods carried on a ship, plane, train, or truck **2** [U] the process of taking goods from one place to another

shipping /'ʃɪpɪŋ/ noun [U] **1** the business of carrying goods **2** ships and boats that are sailing

shipwreck¹ /'ʃɪpˌrek/ noun [C/U] an accident in which a ship is destroyed during a journey

shipwreck² /'ʃɪpˌrek/ verb **be shipwrecked** to be involved in a shipwreck

shipyard /'ʃɪpˌjɑːd/ noun [C] a place where ships are built or repaired

shirk /ʃɜːk/ verb [I/T] to avoid doing something difficult, or to avoid accepting responsibility for something: *A good manager should never shirk difficult decisions.*

shirt /ʃɜːt/ noun [C] ★★★ a piece of clothing that covers the top part of your body. It usually has long sleeves and buttons down the front: *a cotton/silk/denim shirt* ♦ *One of his shirt buttons was missing.* —picture → C5

shiver /'ʃɪvə/ verb [I] to shake slightly because you are cold or frightened — **shiver** noun [C]

shiver

shoal /ʃəʊl/ noun [C] a group of fish that swim together

shock¹ /ʃɒk/ noun ★★

1 surprise from sth bad	4 electric flow in body
2 sth that surprises you	5 very thick hair
3 being weak and cold	

1 [singular/U] the feeling of being very surprised by something bad that happens unexpectedly: *Jessica's face was blank with shock.* ♦ *My mother got a shock when she saw my new haircut.* ♦ *give sb a shock It will give him a shock when he sees how much you've spent.*

2 [C] something that happens unexpectedly and makes you feel very surprised and upset: *The price of housing was quite a shock for us.* ♦ *The announcement came as a complete shock to me.* ♦ *It was a terrible shock to discover he was already married.*

3 [U] a medical condition in which you suddenly become very weak and cold after a serious accident or injury

4 [C] a sudden flow of electricity that goes through your body

5 [singular] hair that is very thick

shock² /ʃɒk/ verb ★

1 [T] if something bad and unexpected shocks someone, they are very surprised or upset by it: *The news shocked everyone.* ♦ *We were all shocked by the lies he told.*

2 [I/T] to make someone feel embarrassed or offended by saying or doing something that is offensive or immoral: *He only says things like that to shock you.*

—**shocked** /ʃɒkt/ adj: *We were deeply shocked to hear of his sudden death.* ♦ *They listened in shocked silence.*

shocking /'ʃɒkɪŋ/ adj **1** making you feel extremely surprised, upset, or embarrassed **2** British informal very bad —**shockingly** adv

'**shock ,wave** noun [C] a severe effect that something has on people

shod /ʃɒd/ adj formal wearing shoes of a particular type

shoddy /'ʃɒdi/ adj of a very low standard

shoe /ʃuː/ noun [C] ★★★

1 something that you wear on each foot,

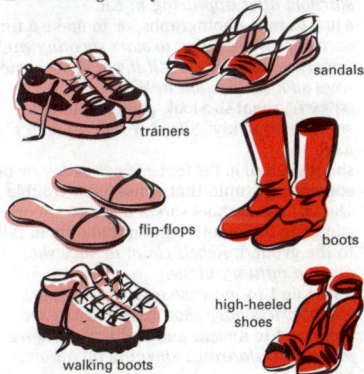

sandals

trainers

flip-flops

boots

high-heeled shoes

walking boots

shoes

S

usually over socks: *walking/running shoes*
♦ *She bought several pairs of shoes.* ♦ *shoe
polish*

2 a HORSESHOE

PHRASE **in sb's shoes** in the situation that
someone else is in: *What would you do if
you were in my shoes?*

shoelace /ˈʃuːleɪs/ noun [C] a thick string that
you use for fastening a shoe on your foot

shoestring /ˈʃuːstrɪŋ/ noun **on a shoestring**
using or having a very small amount of
money

shone the past tense and past participle of
shine

shoo /ʃuː/ verb [T] to tell an animal or a person
to go away, especially by saying 'shoo' and
waving your hands —**shoo** interjection

shook the past tense of **shake**[1]

shoot[1] /ʃuːt/ (past tense and past participle **shot**
/ʃɒt/) verb ★★★

1 fire gun	**5** suddenly achieve sth
2 hit with bullet	**6** take photographs etc
3 in sports	**+** PHRASES
4 move suddenly	**+** PHRASAL VERBS

1 [I/T] to fire a gun: *We were ordered not to
shoot until he gave the signal.* ♦ *They were
shooting at bottles on a wall.* ♦ *Armed
officers had instructions to shoot the
kidnapper on sight* (=as soon as they saw
him).

2 [T] to hit someone or something with a
bullet from a gun: *The man was shot in the
head as he left the bar.* ♦ *Two of our officers
were shot dead.* ♦ *The victim had been shot
at close range* (=by someone very close to
them).

3 [I/T] in sport, to throw or kick a ball in an
attempt to score points: *He shot the ball
straight at the goalkeeper.* ♦ *We were all
shouting for him to shoot.* —picture → C15

4 [I] to move somewhere very suddenly and
quickly: *The car shot across the road at
high speed.*

5 [I] *informal* to quickly and suddenly become
successful or famous: *Clooney shot to
stardom after appearing in ER.*

6 [I/T] to take photographs, or to make a film
or video: *We're going to start shooting early
tomorrow morning.* ♦ *All the outdoor scenes
were shot on location in Wales.*

PHRASES **shoot sb a look/glance** to look at
someone quickly: *She shot him an angry
look.*

shoot yourself in the foot *informal* to say or do
something stupid that causes you trouble

PHRASAL VERBS ˌshoot sb/sth ˈdown to shoot
someone or something and make them fall
to the ground: *Rebels claim to have shot
down a military plane.*

ˌshoot ˈup **1** to increase or grow quickly:
*Petrol prices have shot up in the last six
months.* **2** to appear suddenly: *There were
fast-food restaurants shooting up all over
town.*

shoot[2] /ʃuːt/ noun [C] **1** a very young plant,

shoot

or a new part growing on a plant **2** an
occasion when someone takes a series of
photographs or makes a film

shooting /ˈʃuːtɪŋ/ noun **1** [C/U] an occasion
when someone is attacked by a person with
a gun: *the fatal shooting of two teenagers*
2 [U] any sport or activity in which guns
are used: *hunting, shooting, and fishing*

ˌshooting ˈstar noun [C] a piece of rock that
makes a line of light as it falls through the
sky=METEOR

ˈshoot-out noun [C] a fight using guns

shop[1] /ʃɒp/ noun [C] ★★★
1 a place where you buy things or where
you pay for a service: *I'm just going to the
shop.* ♦ *We had lunch at a little coffee shop.*
♦ *The shops are closed on Sundays.*
2 a business where something is made or
repaired: *a shoe repair shop*

PHRASE **set up shop** to start a business or
activity

shop[2] /ʃɒp/ verb [I] to go to shops to look at
and buy things: *I like to shop at the local
supermarket.*

PHRASAL VERB ˌshop aˈround **1** to go to
several shops before you decide what
particular thing to buy: *I'm shopping
around for a new winter coat.* **2** to consider
several possibilities before making a
choice: *Shop around carefully before
investing your money.*

ˈshop asˌsistant noun [C] *British* someone whose
job is to serve people in a shop

ˌshop ˈfloor noun [C] **1** the area in a factory
where products are made **2** the workers in a
factory, not the managers

shopkeeper /ˈʃɒpˌkiːpə/ noun [C] someone
who owns or manages a shop

shoplifting /ˈʃɒpˌlɪftɪŋ/ noun [U] the crime of
stealing things from a shop —**shoplift** verb
[I/T], **shoplifter** noun [C]

shopper /ˈʃɒpə/ noun [C] someone who goes
to a shop in order to look at or buy the
things that are sold there

shopping /ˈʃɒpɪŋ/ noun [U] ★★
1 the activity of going to a shop to buy
things: *I don't like shopping very much.* ♦ *a
shopping list/trolley/basket* ♦ *I don't suppose
you've had a chance to go shopping yet?* ♦
Where do you go to do your shopping?
→ WINDOW SHOPPING

2 *British* all of the things that you have
bought in a shop, especially food and
products for cleaning the house: *Can you
help me bring the shopping in?*

ˈshopping ˌcentre noun [C] an area where

S

different types of stores and businesses are built next to each other

shopping mall noun [C] a MALL

shore¹ /ʃɔː/ noun [C/U] the land that is on the edge of a sea or lake: *Three of the sailors managed to swim to the shore.* ♦ *We stayed in a hotel on the shores of Lake Maggiore.*

- The **shore** is the land that is on the edge of a lake, river, or sea: *They managed to swim to the shore.* ♦ *a cabin on the shores of the lake*
- The **coast** is the land at the edge of a country, near the sea: *From the deck we could see the coast of Africa.* ♦ *a holiday cottage on the south coast*
- A **beach** is an area of sand or small stones next to the sea or by a river or lake, where people can sit and enjoy themselves: *Let's have a picnic on the beach.*

shore² PHRASAL VERB ,shore sth 'up **1** to give support or help to something that is having problems or is likely to fail **2** to support something such as a wall, in order to prevent it from falling

shoreline /'ʃɔːlaɪn/ noun [C] the edge of a sea or lake

shorn a past participle of **shear**

short¹ /ʃɔːt/ adj ★★★

1 small in height etc	**5** not having enough
2 of time	**6** about memory
3 with few words	**7** rude and unfriendly
4 with fewer letters	**+** PHRASES

1 measuring a small height, length, or distance: *She's short and slim, with light brown hair and blue eyes.* ♦ *The theatre is a relatively short distance from here.* ♦ *The sleeves are much too short.*
2 a short period of time does not last very long, or seems to pass quickly: *I'm sorry this has been such a short stay.* ♦ *He was here for a short while last week.* ♦ *It will be difficult to reach an agreement in such a short space of time.*
3 expressed in few words, or containing few pages: *Could you give us a short summary of what happened?* ♦ *It was a short book and she read it in one night.*
4 using fewer words or letters than the full form of something: *Memo is short for memorandum.* ♦ *My name is Elizabeth, or Liz for short.*
5 used for saying that you do not have enough of something: *Dad wasn't working and money was short.* ♦ *Skilled workers are in short supply around here.* ♦ *Many of our clients are short of money.* ♦ *He's very bright but a little short on personality.* ♦ *We were very poor then, and often went short of food.*
6 if you have a short memory, you are not able or willing to remember things
7 rude and unfriendly when speaking to someone

PHRASES **at short notice** without being given much warning before something happens: *I was asked to come at very short notice.*
in the short run/term during the period of time that is not very far into the future: *The policy served him well in the short term but later backfired.*

short² /ʃɔːt/ adv ★★ without reaching a particular place or position: *The plane came down just short of the runway.*

PHRASES **cut sth short** to end something before it is completely finished: *We cut our holiday short because Rachel fell ill.*
fall short of sth to fail to reach your aim or fail to reach a particular level: *Sales of the CD fell short of expectations.*
run short (of sth) used for saying that there is not much of something left: *Supplies were running short as winter came on.* ♦ *We're running short of time.*
short of (doing) sth except for: *Short of winning the lottery, I don't know how we'll pay for this.* ♦ *Nothing short of a miracle can save us now.*

short³ /ʃɔːt/ noun [C] **1** *British* a strong alcoholic drink served in small amounts **2** *informal* a film that lasts only a few minutes **3** a SHORT CIRCUIT

PHRASE **in short** used for introducing a summary of something that you have just said
→ SHORTS

shortage /'ʃɔːtɪdʒ/ noun [C/U] ★ a lack of something that you need or want: *Refugees are facing serious food and fuel shortages.* ♦ *a shortage of clean water*

short 'circuit noun [C] a bad electrical connection that prevents a piece of equipment from working —**short-'circuit** verb [I/T]

shortcoming /'ʃɔːtkʌmɪŋ/ noun [C] a fault that makes someone or something less effective

'short ,cut or **shortcut** /'ʃɔːtkʌt/ noun [C] **1** a path or ROUTE that is quicker and shorter than the usual way **2** a way of saving time or effort in doing something **3** *computing* a combination of keys on a keyboard that helps you to do something more quickly, or an ICON on the screen that lets you start a program

shorten /'ʃɔːt(ə)n/ verb [I/T] to become shorter, or to make something shorter

shortfall /'ʃɔːtfɔːl/ noun [C] a lack of something that you need or want, or the amount that you lack

shorthand /'ʃɔːthænd/ noun [U] a quick way of writing that uses symbols to represent letters, words, or phrases

'short-,haul adj travelling a short distance, especially by air ≠ LONG-HAUL

shortlist /'ʃɔːtlɪst/ noun [C] a list of people who have been chosen from a larger group by someone who is deciding who should get a job, prize etc —**shortlist** verb [T]

short-lived /ʃɔːt 'lɪvd/ adj lasting for a short period of time

shortly /'ʃɔːtli/ adv **1** soon, or happening within a short period of time of something: *We're going to break for lunch very shortly.* ♦ *Police arrived at the scene shortly after midnight.* **2** if you say something shortly, you sound annoyed or rude

shorts /ʃɔːts/ noun [plural] **1** short trousers

S

that end at or above the knees —*picture*
→ C4 **2** *American* men's underwear

short-'sighted adj **1** *British* not able to see things clearly if they are far away from you ≠ LONG-SIGHTED **2** failing to consider what will happen in the future

short 'story noun [C] a short piece of writing about an imaginary situation

short-'term adj lasting for a short period of time ≠ LONG-TERM: *a short-term solution*

'short ,wave noun [C] a type of radio wave that is used for broadcasting across large distances → LONG WAVE, MEDIUM WAVE

shot¹ /ʃɒt/ noun [C] ★★★

1 when gun is fired	**5** small alcoholic drink
2 throw/hit/kick of ball	**6** of drug
3 photograph/view	**+ PHRASES**
4 attempt to do/get sth	

1 an act of firing a gun, or the sound of a gun being fired: *The man **fired** two **shots** from a handgun.* ♦ *The neighbours say they **heard** four **shots**.*

2 an act of throwing, hitting, or kicking a ball: *That was another fine shot from Tiger Woods.* ♦ *They didn't manage to get a single **shot at** our goal.*

3 a photograph, or the view of something that you have because of the position of a camera: *The opening shot is of a man walking across a field.* ♦ *I got a great **shot** of the dogs playing together.*

4 a chance or attempt to do or get something: *This is her first **shot** at an international title.* ♦ *We had a shot at bringing the ship round into the harbour.* ♦ *Give it your best shot* (=try as hard as you can) – *that's all you can do.*

5 a small amount of a strong alcoholic drink

6 a medical treatment in which a small amount of a drug is put into your body with a needle

PHRASES **like a shot** *informal* immediately and very quickly

a shot in the arm *informal* something that quickly makes a bad situation much better → BIG SHOT, LONG¹

shot² the past tense and past participle of **shoot¹**

shotgun /ˈʃɒtˌɡʌn/ noun [C] a long gun that is used especially for hunting birds and animals

'shot ,put, the noun [singular] a sports event in which you throw a heavy metal ball as far as you can

should /ʃʊd/ modal verb ★★★

- **Should** is usually followed by an infinitive without 'to': *You should eat more fresh fruit.* Sometimes it is used without a following infinitive: *I don't always do everything I should.*
- **Should** has no tenses, no participles, and no infinitive form. It does not change its form, so the third person singular form does not end in '-s': *She should see a doctor about that cough.*
- Questions and negatives are formed without 'do': *Should we come back later?* ♦ *You should not bring up embarrassing topics.*
- The negative form **should not** is often shortened in conversation or informal writing to **shouldn't**: *Those kids shouldn't be in there.*

1 used for saying or asking about the right or sensible thing to do or the right way to behave: *It's an amazing book – you should read it.* ♦ *You shouldn't drive so fast.* ♦ *What should I do? Should I look for another job?* ♦ *You should have taken my advice.*

2 used when you have strong reasons for believing or expecting something: *There should be a knife in the drawer.* ♦ *There'll be lots of games, so it should be fun.* ♦ *That was disappointing – we should have won that game easily.*

3 used for describing a situation that may possibly happen: *Should you need help, do not hesitate to call me.* ♦ *If anything should happen to me, please give this letter to my wife.*

4 *British formal* used after 'I' or 'we' instead of 'would', for example in polite requests =WOULD: *I should like to introduce our guest speaker.*

shoulder¹ /ˈʃəʊldə/ noun [C] ★★★ one of the two parts of your body between your neck and the top of your arms: *She injured her shoulder in the accident.* ♦ *The man tapped my friend on the shoulder and asked for a cigarette.* ♦ *He just smiled and **shrugged his shoulders** (=moved them quickly up and down). —picture → C14*

PHRASE **a shoulder to cry on** someone who listens to you with sympathy when you talk about your problems → COLD¹

shoulder² /ˈʃəʊldə/ verb [T] **1** to deal with or accept something difficult **2** to push someone with your shoulder

'shoulder ,blade noun [C] one of the two flat bones at the top of your back, near your shoulders

'shoulder-length adj shoulder-length hair reaches down to your shoulders

shouldn't /ˈʃʊd(ə)nt/ short form the usual way of saying or writing 'should not'. This is not often used in formal writing: *We shouldn't assume that everyone will agree.*

shout¹ /ʃaʊt/ verb [I/T] ★★★

1 to say something in a loud voice: *He was one of those speakers who shout into the microphone.* ♦ *We **shouted to** the driver to tell him to switch off the engine.* ♦ *Donna **shouted at** the men furiously.*

2 to make a sudden loud noise because you are afraid or you feel pain: *A man in the next bed was shouting wildly in pain.*

PHRASAL VERBS **,shout sb 'down** to make it difficult to hear what someone says by shouting while they are speaking: *The minister was shouted down as he tried to justify the government's decision.*

,shout (sth) 'out to say something suddenly

in a very loud voice: *I wanted to shout out and stop her but she was already gone.* ♦ *An officer was shouting out orders.*

shout² /ʃaʊt/ noun [C] the sound of someone shouting, or the words that they shout: *They could hear angry shouts coming from the kitchen.*

shove /ʃʌv/ verb **1** [I/T] to push someone or something with force **2** [T] *informal* to move something, or put it somewhere, quickly and carelessly —**shove** noun [C]

shovel /'ʃʌv(ə)l/ noun [C] a tool that is used for lifting and moving something such as snow or soil. It consists of a long handle with a curved metal end. —**shovel** verb [I/T]

show¹ /ʃəʊ/ (past tense **showed**; past participle **shown** /ʃəʊn/) verb ★★★

1 prove sth is true	7 of film/programme
2 let sb see sth	8 put in exhibition etc
3 let sb know sth	9 lead sb somewhere
4 give information	+ PHRASES
5 be/make noticeable	+ PHRASAL VERBS
6 explain sth to sb	

1 [T] to prove that something exists or is true: *The study shows an increase in the disease among the elderly.* ♦ *Accidents like this show what can happen when drivers are not alert.* ♦ **+(that)** *The test results show that he could not have committed the murder.*

2 [T] to let someone see something: **show sth to sb** *This is the first time the painting has been shown to the public.* ♦ **show sb sth** *I couldn't wait to show him the letter.*

3 [T] to behave in a way that allows people to know your feelings, opinions, or personal qualities: *Try to show an interest in the customer's needs.* ♦ *They have shown what they think of our suggestion.* ♦ **+(that)** *The government has shown that it is not willing to compromise.*

4 [T] if a map, photograph, piece of equipment etc shows something, you can see or read that thing on it: *a map showing all the major tourist attractions* ♦ **+(that)** *The dial showed that the pressure had fallen to a dangerously low level.*

5 [I/T] to be easy to see or notice, or to make something easy to see or notice: *A deep sadness showed in his eyes.* ♦ *She had chosen a colour that really* **showed the dirt**.

6 [T] to explain something to someone by doing it once and letting them watch: **show sb how/what/which etc** *A young girl showed me how to operate the machine.* ♦ **show sb sth** *Can you show me the right way to do this?*

7 [I/T] if someone shows a film or television programme, or if it is showing, people can see it: *It was the first time the film was* **shown on television**. ♦ *Now showing at a cinema near you!*

8 [T] to put something such as a work of art, an animal, or a plant in an exhibition or competition: *Her work was first shown at a gallery in Munich.*

9 [T] to lead someone somewhere: **show sb to** sth *Let me show you to your room.*

PHRASES **have something/nothing to show for sth** to have achieved something/nothing as a result of your efforts: *They had absolutely nothing to show for weeks of hard work.*

show a profit/loss if a company, project etc shows a profit/loss, it makes a profit or a loss

PHRASAL VERBS ,**show sb a'round** to lead someone around a place for the first time, so that they can see all parts of it

,**show sb 'in** to lead someone into a room where they are going to meet other people

,**show 'off** *showing disapproval* to behave in a way that is intended to attract people's attention and make them admire you: *The children start showing off the minute anyone comes into the house.*

,**show sth 'off** to show people something that you are very proud of so that they will admire it: *Young musicians will get the chance to show off their musical skills.*

,**show sb 'out** to lead someone to the door when they are leaving a place

,**show sb 'round** *British same as* **show sb around**

,**show 'up 1** *informal* to arrive in a place where people are expecting you **2** if something shows up, people can see it: *The writing didn't show up very well on yellow paper.*

,**show sb 'up** *British* to behave in a way that makes someone who you are with feel embarrassed: *You're always showing me up in front of my friends.*

,**show sth 'up** to make it possible to see something: *The white seat covers showed up every speck of dirt.*

show² /ʃəʊ/ noun ★★★

1 theatre performance	4 making sth clear
2 TV/radio programme	5 pretending sth
3 exhibition	+ PHRASES

1 [C] a performance in a theatre: *the new show at the Aldwych Theatre*

2 [C] a television or radio programme: *It's the funniest comedy show on television.*

3 [C] an exhibition: *a fashion/flower show*

4 [singular] something that you do in order to make people realize what your opinions or intentions are: *The attack was clearly intended as a* **show of force**.

5 [singular/U] an occasion when you pretend to have particular feelings: *They put on a* **show of affection** *in front of the journalists.* ♦ *The friendly behaviour was clearly just for show.*

PHRASES **get the show on the road** *spoken* to begin an activity

on show available for people to see: *These are just some of the exciting works of art on show in Britain today.*

showbiz /'ʃəʊbɪz/ noun [U] *informal* SHOW BUSINESS

'**show ,business** noun [U] the entertainment industry, including films, television, radio, theatre, and music

showcase /'ʃəʊ,keɪs/ noun [C] an event that

S

emphasizes the good qualities of someone or something

showdown /'ʃəʊ,daʊn/ noun [C] a meeting, argument, or fight that finally settles a disagreement between people, or proves who is the best

shower¹ /'ʃaʊə/ noun [C] ★
1 a piece of equipment that forces small drops of water into the air and is used for washing your body, or a small area with a shower in it: *The shower isn't working.* ♦ *Is Sue still in the shower?*
2 the activity of washing yourself by standing under a shower: *I'm going to have a shower.*
3 a short period when it rains: *Tonight there's a 50% chance of showers.*
4 a large number of things moving through the air or falling together: *a shower of sparks*

shower² /'ʃaʊə/ verb **1** [I] to wash yourself in a shower **2** [T] to give a very large number of things to someone: *He showered her with flowers and jewellery.*

showery /'ʃaʊəri/ adj with frequent short periods of rain

showing /'ʃəʊɪŋ/ noun [C] **1** an occasion when something such as a film or television programme is shown **2** the amount of success that someone or something has in an event or during a particular period: *She had a strong showing in the local elections.*

'show ,jumping noun [U] a sport in which someone riding a horse jumps over a set of fences

showman /'ʃəʊmən/ (plural **showmen** /'ʃəʊmən/) noun [C] someone such as an entertainer or politician who does things in a lively and enthusiastic way that attracts attention —**showmanship** /'ʃəʊmənʃɪp/ noun [U]

shown the past participle of **show¹**

showoff /'ʃəʊ,ɒf/ noun [C] *informal showing disapproval* someone who tries to show how clever they are in order to get attention and praise from other people

showpiece /'ʃəʊ,piːs/ noun [C] the most impressive feature of something, or the most impressive example of a particular thing: *an architectural showpiece*

showroom /'ʃəʊruːm/ noun [C] a large room where you can look at cars or other large objects that are for sale

showy /'ʃəʊi/ adj **1** brightly coloured and attractive: *a plant with large showy flowers* **2** big and expensive in a way that seems ugly = OSTENTATIOUS: *a showy ring*

shrank a past tense of **shrink¹**

shrapnel /'ʃræpn(ə)l/ noun [U] small pieces of metal that fly out of a bomb or bullet when it explodes

shred¹ /ʃred/ noun [C] **1** a long thin piece that has been cut or torn from something **2** a very small amount of something: *There's not a shred of evidence to support his claim.*

shred² /ʃred/ verb [T] **1** to destroy a document by putting it into a shredder **2** to cut or tear something into long thin pieces

shredder /'ʃredə/ noun [C] a machine that destroys documents by cutting them into long thin pieces

shrewd /ʃruːd/ adj able to make good decisions and to judge people and situations very well —**shrewdly** adv

shriek /ʃriːk/ verb [I] to shout in a loud high voice because you are frightened, excited, or surprised = SCREAM —**shriek** noun [C]

shrill /ʃrɪl/ adj a shrill noise or voice is very loud, high, and unpleasant

shrimp /ʃrɪmp/ noun [C] a small SHELLFISH with a lot of legs

shrine /ʃraɪn/ noun [C] a religious place that has been built to remember a particular holy person or event

shrink¹ /ʃrɪŋk/ (past tense **shrank** /ʃræŋk/ or **shrunk** /ʃrʌŋk/; past participle **shrunk** /ʃrʌŋk/) verb **1** [I/T] to become smaller, or to make something become smaller: *Do you think this dress will shrink if I put it in the washing machine?* ♦ *Profits shrank from 32.5 per cent to 17 per cent.* **2** [I] to move back or away from someone or something because you are frightened or nervous: *He shrank away from her touch.*
PHRASAL VERB **shrink from sth** to not be willing to do something that is difficult or unpleasant

shrink² /ʃrɪŋk/ noun [C] *informal* a PSYCHIATRIST

shrinkage /'ʃrɪŋkɪdʒ/ noun **1** [U] the process of becoming smaller in size **2** [singular/U] a reduction in something

shrink-wrapped /'ʃrɪŋk ˌræpt/ adj wrapped very tightly in thin clear plastic

shrivel /'ʃrɪv(ə)l/ (present participle **shrivelling**; past tense and past participle **shrivelled**) or **,shrivel 'up** verb [I] if something such as a plant shrivels, it becomes smaller, thinner, and drier, and it does not look fresh and healthy —**shrivelled** /'ʃrɪv(ə)ld/ adj

shroud¹ /ʃraʊd/ noun [C] **1** a piece of cloth that is wrapped around a dead body before it is buried **2** *literary* something that covers or hides something

shroud² /ʃraʊd/ verb [T] to cover or hide something
PHRASE **be shrouded in secrecy/mystery** to be very secret or mysterious

shrub /ʃrʌb/ noun [C] a low thick bush

shrubbery /'ʃrʌbəri/ noun **1** [C] an area in a garden or park where shrubs are planted **2** [U] several shrubs growing together

shrug

shrug /ʃrʌg/ verb [I/T] to move your shoulders up and let them drop, in order to show that you do not know something or do not care —**shrug** noun [C]

PHRASAL VERB ,shrug sth 'off to not let something worry or upset you

shrunk the past tense and past participle of **shrink**¹

shrunken /'ʃrʌŋk(ə)n/ adj smaller than before, or smaller than is natural

shudder /'ʃʌdə/ verb [I] **1** if you shudder, your body shakes several times, for example because you suddenly feel cold or frightened **2** if something shudders, it shakes violently several times —**shudder** noun [C]

shuffle /'ʃʌf(ə)l/ verb **1** [I] to walk slowly and noisily without lifting your feet **2** [I/T] to keep moving your feet because you are nervous, embarrassed, or bored **3** [T] to change the order of papers or other things in a group **4** [I/T] to put cards into a different order before you DEAL (=give) them to players at the beginning of a game —**shuffle** noun [C]

shun /ʃʌn/ verb [T] to deliberately avoid a person, place, or activity

shunt /ʃʌnt/ verb [T] to move someone or something to a different place or position, especially to avoid dealing with them: *The children are constantly shunted around to various relatives.*

shush /ʃʊʃ/ interjection used for telling someone to be quiet

shut¹ /ʃʌt/ (past tense and past participle **shut**) verb [I/T] ★★★
1 to close something, or to become closed ≠ OPEN: *Sandra shut the book and put it down on the table.* ♦ **Shut the gate** or the dog will get out. ♦ *I heard the front **door shut**.*
2 *British* to close a business at the end of the working day or for a short period of time ≠ OPEN: *We shut at 6 o'clock.*

PHRASAL VERBS ,shut sb a'way to put someone in a place where they are kept apart from other people

,shut (sth) 'down **1** if a shop, school, factory, or business shuts down, or if someone shuts it down, it closes permanently **2** if a machine or computer shuts down, or if someone shuts it down, it stops operating

,shut sb/sth 'in to put a person or animal in a place that they cannot leave

,shut sth 'in sth to crush a part of someone's body by closing a door, window, drawer etc on it: *I stupidly shut my fingers in the door.*

,shut (sth) 'off if a machine shuts off, or if someone shuts it off, it stops working

,shut sth 'off to stop the flow of something such as water or electricity

,shut sb 'out to not allow someone to enter a particular place

,shut sth 'out if you shut something out, you stop yourself from seeing it, hearing it, or thinking about it: *He closed the door to* **shut out** *the noise.*

,shut (sb) 'up *impolite* to stop talking or making a noise, or to make someone stop talking or making a noise: *Why don't you shut up?* ♦ *Can't you shut the kids up for just five minutes?* ♦ *I wish he'd **shut up** about his holiday.*

shut² /ʃʌt/ adj ★
1 closed: *With the door shut, the room was hot and humid.*
2 *British* not open for business: *Are all the bars shut in this town?*

shutdown /'ʃʌt,daʊn/ noun [C] an occasion when a machine or factory stops working for a short time

shutter /'ʃʌtə/ noun [C] **1** a cover that can be closed over the outside of a window —*picture* → C1 **2** the part inside a camera that quickly opens and closes to let in light

shuttle¹ /'ʃʌt(ə)l/ noun [C] **1** a bus, train, or plane that makes frequent short journeys between two places **2** a SPACE SHUTTLE

shuttle² /'ʃʌt(ə)l/ verb [I/T] to travel frequently between two places, or to take people frequently between two places

shuttlecock /'ʃʌt(ə)l,kɒk/ noun [C] the object that you hit over the net in BADMINTON

shy¹ /ʃaɪ/ adj ★
1 nervous and embarrassed in the company of other people, especially people who you do not know: *I'd love to meet her but I'm too shy to introduce myself.* ♦ *He gave me a shy smile and looked away.*
2 nervous about doing something or being involved in something: *He's not **shy about** saying what he wants.*
—**shyly** adv, **shyness** noun [U]

shy² /ʃaɪ/ verb [I] if a horse shies, it moves suddenly away from something because it is afraid

PHRASAL VERB ,shy a'way to avoid someone, or to be unwilling to do something, because you are nervous, afraid, or not confident

sibling /'sɪblɪŋ/ noun [C] your siblings are your brothers and sisters

sic /sɪk/ adv *formal* written in BRACKETS after a word that is not spelled or used correctly in order to show that you have written it as someone else spelled or used it

sick /sɪk/ adj ★★
1 if you are sick, food that you have eaten suddenly comes out of your stomach through your mouth: *I'm going to be sick!* → SEASICK
2 if you are sick, you have an illness: *He stayed at home caring for his sick wife.*
3 unpleasant in a way that would upset some people: *sick humour/jokes*
4 the sick people who are ill

PHRASES **feel sick** to feel that food that you have eaten is going to come out of your stomach through your mouth

make sb sick *spoken* to make someone very angry or upset: *The way he treats her makes me sick.*

off sick *British* if you are off sick or you take time off sick, you do not go to work because you are ill

sick (and tired) of sth *spoken* angry or unhappy about something that keeps happening: *I'm sick of listening to your complaints.*

sicken /'sɪkən/ verb [T] to make you feel shocked and angry

sickening /'sɪk(ə)nɪŋ/ adj very unpleasant and shocking

S

'sick ,leave noun [U] a period of time during which you do not work because you are ill

sickly /'sɪkli/ adj **1** not healthy and often ill **2** a sickly smell or taste makes you feel sick

sickness /'sɪknəs/ noun **1** [U] a condition in which you have an illness **2** [C] a particular illness **3** [U] the feeling that you are going to bring up food from your stomach, or the act of doing this

side¹ /saɪd/ noun [C] ★★★

1 one part of area	7 aspect of situation
2 surface of object	8 of opposing groups
3 edge of sth flat	9 sports team
4 surface of sth flat	10 part of family
5 edge of body	11 television channel
6 slope of hill	+ PHRASES

1 either of the two parts or areas that something consists of: *Motorists in Japan drive on* **the left side** *of the road.*
2 a surface of an object or shape, especially one that is not its front, back, bottom, or top: *The ship was found lying on its side.* ♦ *A cube has six sides.* ♦ *The entrance is on* **the side** *of the building.*
3 any of the edges of a flat shape: *A square has four sides.*
4 either of the flat surfaces of something that is thin such as a piece of paper or a coin: *Use the lined side of the paper.*
5 the general area of your body from your shoulder down to your waist: *I had a sharp pain in my right side.* ♦ *His arms hung limply by his sides.*
6 the part of a hill that slopes and is between the top and the bottom
7 one aspect of a situation or subject: *I still haven't heard her side of the story.* ♦ *Fortunately, my boss saw the funny side of the situation.*
8 one of two or more groups of people who are opposing each other: *The agreement has been signed by both sides.* ♦ *Don't get annoyed with me – I'm on your side* (=supporting you)*!* ♦ *I'm not taking sides* (=showing support for one person and not another) *in this argument.* ♦ *Mary always takes your side* (=supports you)*.*
9 a sports team: *Our side lost.*
10 a part of your family, either your father's set of relatives or your mother's: *Which side of the family is his uncle from?* ♦ *Rose is my cousin on my mother's side.*
11 *British* a television CHANNEL: *Which side is the film on?*

   PHRASES **at/by sb's side 1** beside someone: *She sat by his side.* **2** supporting someone, or remaining loyal to them: *The family will be at her side throughout the trial.*
from all sides from all directions towards one object or person: *Suddenly the crowd came at him from all sides.*
from side to side moving from left to right, then from right to left, then back again
on the side in addition to what is usual: *The band's lead singer has been making solo appearances on the side.*
on the...side slightly, but not very: *It's a nice*

hotel, but the rooms are on the small side (=rather small).
   put sth to one side to not talk about something, deal with it, or use it now: *Let's put the question of blame to one side for a minute.*
   side by side directly next to each other: *The two girls stood side by side.*
   → COIN¹

side² /saɪd/ adj **1** not in or on the central part of something: *a side door* **2** less important or less relevant: *a side issue*

side³ /saɪd/ PHRASAL VERB **'side with sb** to agree with and support a particular person in an argument

sideboard /'saɪdˌbɔːd/ noun [C] a large piece of furniture with shelves and cupboards that you use for storing dishes, glasses etc

'side ef,fect noun [C] **1** an effect of a medicine that is not intended and could be unpleasant **2** an additional result that you did not expect or want

sidekick /'saɪdˌkɪk/ noun [C] *informal* the friend or ASSISTANT of someone who is more important

sidelight /'saɪdˌlaɪt/ noun [C] *British* one of the two small lights next to the main front lights on a car —*picture* → C6

sideline¹ /'saɪdˌlaɪn/ noun **1** [C] a job that you do in addition to your main job **2** the **sidelines** [plural] the area at the edge of a sports field
   PHRASE **be on the sidelines** or **watch from the sidelines** to watch something that is happening without being involved or being able to influence it

sideline² /'saɪdˌlaɪn/ verb [T] to prevent someone from being involved in something that they are normally involved in

sidelong /'saɪdˌlɒŋ/ adj a sidelong look is one in which you move your eyes to one side without moving your head much

sideshow /'saɪdˌʃəʊ/ noun [C] something that is less important than something else that is happening at the same time

sidestep /'saɪdˌstep/ verb [T] to avoid something that is difficult or unpleasant

'side ,street noun [C] a small street that is connected to a major street

sidetrack /'saɪdˌtræk/ verb [T] to delay the progress of something by causing people to waste time on something else that is less important: *It's easy to get sidetracked by talking about unimportant issues like this.*

sidewalk /'saɪdˌwɔːk/ noun [C] *American* the PAVEMENT by the side of a road

sideways /'saɪdweɪz/ adj, adv **1** to, towards, or from one side: *He moved sideways along the bench.* **2** with one side facing forwards: *A car was sideways across the road, blocking it.*

sidle /'saɪd(ə)l/ verb [I] to move slowly in a particular direction, because you are nervous or do not want to be noticed

siege /siːdʒ/ noun [C/U] **1** an attack in which an army surrounds a castle or city in order to prevent the people inside from receiving supplies **2** a situation in which a group of soldiers or police surround a building in order to force the people inside to come out

siesta /si'estə/ noun [C] a short period of sleep in the middle of the day=NAP

sieve /sIv/ noun [C] an object that you pour a liquid or mixture through in order to remove the large pieces —**sieve** verb [T]

sift /sIft/ verb [T] **1** to pour a dry substance through a sieve in order to remove the large pieces **2** to examine something carefully in order to find what you are looking for

> **PHRASAL VERB** **sift through sth** same as **sift** 2

sigh¹ /saI/ verb **1** [I] to breathe out slowly making a long soft sound, especially because you are disappointed, tired, annoyed, or relaxed: *Jan sighed heavily and shook her head.* **2** [T] to say something with a sigh: *'I wish you had told me earlier,' she sighed.*

sigh² /saI/ noun [C] a slow breath out that makes a long soft sound: *She let out a deep sigh.*

sight¹ /saIt/ noun ★★★

1 ability to see	**5** untidy person/place
2 act of seeing sb/sth	**6** places to visit
3 area you see	**7** part of a gun
4 sb/sth that you see	**+ PHRASES**

1 [U] the ability to see using your eyes =EYESIGHT, VISION: *people with poor sight*
2 [U] the act of seeing someone or something: *I don't know him personally, but I know him by sight* (=I know what he looks like). ♦ *The captain ordered us to shoot any strangers on sight* (=as soon as we saw them). ♦ *I can't stand the sight of blood.*
3 [U] any place that you can see from where you are=VIEW: *They passed behind the hill and out of sight.* ♦ *The rocket disappeared from sight.* ♦ *The ship sank within sight of the harbour.*
4 [C] a person or thing that you see that has a particular feature: *Windmills are a common sight in this part of the country.*
5 [singular] a person or place that is very unusual, untidy, or unpleasant to look at: *You look a sight!*
6 **sights** [plural] interesting places that people go to see: *We enjoyed seeing the sights of San Francisco.*
7 [C] the part of a gun or other piece of equipment that you look through in order to aim it

> **PHRASES** **catch sight of** to suddenly see someone or something: *As she stood up she caught sight of her reflection in the mirror.*
> **in/within sight 1** in a place that you can see from where you are: *There was nobody in sight.* **2** going to happen soon: *Political independence seemed to be in sight.*
> **lose sight of 1** to no longer be able to see something or someone **2** to forget something that is important, or to forget how important it is: *We shouldn't lose sight*

of the reasons why we started this campaign.
> **set your sights on sth** to decide that you want to get or achieve something: *The team has set its sights on the national championship.*

sight² /saIt/ verb [T] *formal* to see someone or something suddenly or in the distance

sighted /'saItId/ adj not blind

sighting /'saItIŋ/ noun [C] an occasion when you see someone or something that you do not often see

sightseeing /'saIt,si:Iŋ/ noun [U] the activity of travelling around a place in order to see the interesting things in it

sign¹ /saIn/ noun ★★★

1 piece of evidence	**4** written symbol
2 sth with information	**5** star sign
3 movement/sound	

1 [C/U] a piece of evidence that something exists or is happening=INDICATION: *I couldn't see any sign of progress.* ♦ **+that** *He had somehow missed the signs that she was upset.*
2 [C] a flat object with words or pictures on it, put in a public place in order to provide information or to advertise something: *a flashing neon sign* ♦ *Turn right and follow the signs to the zoo.*
3 [C] a movement or sound that you make in order to tell someone something =SIGNAL: **a sign to sb (to do sth)** *He made a sign to me to leave.*
4 [C] a written symbol that has a particular meaning, for example % meaning 'per cent' or $ meaning 'dollar': *a multiplication/ division sign*
5 [C] a STAR SIGN: *I'm a Scorpio. What sign are you?*

sign² /saIn/ verb ★

1 [I/T] to write your name on something in order to show that you have written it, or that you agree with what is written on it: *You haven't signed Rory's birthday card yet.* ♦ *Please sign and date the form.* ♦ *A trade agreement was signed today by the US and China.*
2 [T] to officially employ someone to work for a particular organization: *The team needs to sign some new players.*
3 [I/T] to communicate using SIGN LANGUAGE → DOTTED LINE

> **PHRASAL VERBS** **sign sth away** to agree that a property or a right to something no longer belongs to you, by writing your name on a document
> **sign for sth 1** to show that you have received something by writing your name on a document **2** *British* to agree to play for a sports club by signing a contract
> **sign (sb) in** to write your name, or someone else's name, on an official list when you or they arrive at a place ≠ SIGN (SB) OUT: *All visitors must sign in at the front desk.* ♦ *Mr Moore signed me in and showed me to his office.*
> **sign on** *British* to apply to receive money from

S

the government when you have lost your job

,sign (sb) 'out to write your name, or someone else's name, on an official list when you or they leave a place ≠ SIGN (SB) IN: *Please sign out when you leave.* ♦ *I'll sign both of us out.*

,sign sth 'over to officially give your property to someone by writing your name on a document: *He's nervous about signing over the whole farm.* ♦ **sign sth over to sb** *Her dad signed the car over to her.*

,sign 'up to agree to do something or to join a course or organization

,sign sb 'up *same as* **sign²** 2: *We have signed up two new players.*

signal¹ /'sɪɡn(ə)l/ noun [C] ★★★
1 a movement or sound that is made by someone and has a special meaning for another person: *We waited for them to give us the signal to move.*
2 a fact, event, or action that shows what someone intends to do, or that shows what is likely to happen = SIGN: *There were strong signals that she intended to resign.*
3 *technical* pictures, sounds, or other pieces of information that are sent by one piece of electronic equipment and received by another one: *a radio/electrical signal*
4 a piece of equipment with coloured lights on it that tells the driver of a vehicle to stop, go, or slow down = TRAFFIC LIGHTS: *The signal was at green.*

Words often used with signal

Adjectives often used with signal (noun, sense 2)
■ **clear, powerful, strong, unmistakable** + SIGNAL: used about signals that show clearly what is likely to happen

---

signal² /'sɪɡn(ə)l/ (present participle **signalling**; past tense and past participle **signalled**) verb
1 [I/T] to make a movement or sound that has a special meaning to another person: *The cyclist signalled and turned right.* ♦ *He signalled to his wife, who was on the other side of the room.* ♦ **signal (to) sb to do sth** *The driver signalled her to cross the road.* ♦ **+that** *He flashed his torch to signal that he was ready.* **2** [T] to show that something is happening or will happen: *This agreement signalled the end of the war.* **3** [T] to show what you intend to do about something: *The kidnappers have signalled their willingness to negotiate.*

signatory /'sɪɡnət(ə)ri/ noun [C] a person or organization that has signed an official agreement

signature /'sɪɡnətʃə/ noun [C] ★ a person's name that is written in a special way by that person: *Is this your signature on the letter?* → AUTOGRAPH

significance /sɪɡ'nɪfɪkəns/ noun [singular/U] ★
1 the importance that something has because it affects other things: *I do not think this case is really of great significance.* ♦ *the historical significance of these events*
2 the meaning of something, usually a

special meaning or a meaning that is not obvious: *I didn't realize the true significance of this comment at the time.*

Words often used with significance

Adjectives often used with significance (sense 1)
■ **considerable, crucial, enormous, great, immense, particular, real, special** + SIGNIFICANCE: used about significance that is great

---

significant /sɪɡ'nɪfɪkənt/ adj ★★★
1 very large or noticeable ≠ INSIGNIFICANT: *A significant proportion of the population never actually votes in elections.* ♦ *I think we can save a significant amount of time.*
2 very important: *one of the most significant musicians of the last century*
—**significantly** /sɪɡ'nɪfɪkəntli/ adv

signify /'sɪɡnɪfaɪ/ verb [T] to mean something: *What does this symbol signify?*

signing /'saɪnɪŋ/ noun **1** [U] the action of agreeing to a document by writing your name on it **2** [C] *British* a player who has recently signed a contract to join a sports team **3** [U] the use of sign language to communicate

'sign ,language noun [C/U] a way of communicating with people who cannot hear by making signals with your hands

signpost¹ /'saɪnpəʊst/ noun [C] a sign that is next to a road, that shows where something is

signpost² /'saɪnpəʊst/ verb [T] to mark something with signposts

Sikh /siːk/ noun [C] a member of an Indian religious group that separated from HINDUISM in the 16th century —**Sikh** adj, **Sikhism** /'siːkɪz(ə)m/ noun [U]

silence¹ /'saɪləns/ noun ★★
1 [U] complete quiet: *The silence was broken by the soft sound of rain.*
2 [C/U] a period of time when no one speaks: *Long silences make her uncomfortable.* ♦ *They drove home in silence.*
3 [singular/U] a refusal to talk about something or provide information: *Her silence on the subject has been interpreted as a sign of guilt.*

silence² /'saɪləns/ verb [T] **1** to stop someone or something from speaking or making a sound **2** to prevent someone from giving an opinion or criticizing you

silent /'saɪlənt/ adj ★★
1 not talking or making any noise: *a crowd of silent onlookers* ♦ *Everyone fell silent* (=stopped talking) *as the president walked in.*
2 a silent place is very quiet: *The old house was completely silent.*
3 refusing to talk about something: *If you are arrested, you have the right to remain silent* (=do not have to give information to the police). ♦ *For now, I prefer to stay silent on the matter.*
4 not pronounced: *The 'b' in 'thumb' is silent.*
—**silently** adv

S

silhouette /ˌsɪluˈet/ noun [C] the dark shape or shadow of someone or something with the light behind them

silhouetted /ˌsɪluˈetɪd/ adj seen only as a silhouette

silicon /ˈsɪlɪkən/ noun [U] a chemical element, used especially for making computer CHIPS

silicon chip noun [C] a small piece of silicon with a set of complicated electronic connections on it, used especially in computers

silk /sɪlk/ noun [U] a thin smooth cloth made from the fibres produced by insects called SILKWORMS: *a silk shirt*

silken /ˈsɪlkən/ adj *literary* very soft, smooth, and shiny

silky /ˈsɪlki/ adj very soft, smooth, and shiny

sill /sɪl/ noun [C] a narrow shelf at the bottom of a window = LEDGE

silly /ˈsɪli/ adj ★
1 not intelligent or sensible: *a silly mistake* ♦ *You've been very silly.*
2 not important: *Don't get upset over silly things that people say.*
3 unsuitable and annoying because it makes you seem stupid or like a child: *a silly hat*

silo /ˈsaɪləʊ/ noun [C] **1** a large underground structure, used for storing or protecting something **2** a tall round tower on a farm, used for storing things such as grain

silt /sɪlt/ noun [U] sand, dirt, and very small rocks that are carried from one place to another by moving water

silver¹ /ˈsɪlvə/ noun ★
1 [U] a light grey metal that is used for making jewellery, coins etc
2 [U] attractive objects made from silver that people collect: *They had some beautiful silver.*
3 [C/U] a SILVER MEDAL

silver² /ˈsɪlvə/ adj **1** made of silver **2** light grey in colour

silver medal noun [C] a round flat silver object that is given as a prize for being second in a competition

silverware /ˈsɪlvəweə/ noun [U] objects made from silver, especially objects used at meals

silver wedding noun [C] *British* the day when people celebrate 25 years of marriage

silvery /ˈsɪlvəri/ adj like silver in colour or appearance

SIM card /ˈsɪm ˌkɑːd/ noun [C] a small piece of plastic that is inside a mobile phone, that contains information about the person who uses the phone

similar /ˈsɪmɪlə/ adj ★★★ things that are similar are like each other but are not exactly the same ≠ DIFFERENT: *We have similar interests.* ♦ *A second study produced remarkably similar results.* ♦ *Their situation is very similar to ours.* ♦ *The two men are similar in appearance.*

similarity /ˌsɪməˈlærəti/ noun **1** [C/U] the degree to which one thing is similar to another thing, or the fact that they are similar: *The similarity between the two stories suggests Lowry wrote them both.* ♦ *a*

striking similarity of style ♦ *His signature bears absolutely no similarity to mine.* **2** [C] something that makes one thing seem like another: *There are many similarities between Ron and his father.* ♦ *His music shows several similarities to that of other modern composers.*

similarly /ˈsɪmələli/ adv ★
1 used for showing that two ideas are related or connected: *High inflation usually leads to high interest rates. Similarly, interest rates decline when inflation is low.*
2 in a similar way: *similarly priced cars*

simile /ˈsɪməli/ noun [C] a phrase that describes something by comparing it to something else using the word 'like' or 'as', for example 'His hands were as cold as ice'

simmer /ˈsɪmə/ verb [I/T] to cook slowly at a temperature that is near boiling, or to cook something in this way

simple /ˈsɪmp(ə)l/ adj ★★★
1 easy to understand or do: *Students were given a simple skills test.* ♦ **simple to do** *The machine is fairly simple to operate.*
2 plain, without any complicated features or decoration: *a simple meal* ♦ *simple tools*
3 used for emphasizing one important fact: *The simple truth is that I was scared.* ♦ *She came for the simple reason that she wanted to see you.*

simplicity /sɪmˈplɪsəti/ noun [U] the quality of being simple

simplify /ˈsɪmplɪˌfaɪ/ verb [T] to make something less complicated or difficult —**simplification** /ˌsɪmplɪfɪˈkeɪʃ(ə)n/ noun [C/U]

simplistic /sɪmˈplɪstɪk/ adj *showing disapproval* treating a complicated problem or situation in a way that makes it seem much simpler than it really is

simply /ˈsɪmpli/ adv ★★★
1 used for emphasizing one important fact: *He lost simply because he wasn't good enough.*
2 in a way that is not complicated or confusing: *I've stated my intention as simply as possible.*
3 in a very ordinary or plain way: *We live very simply and don't spend a lot of money.*

simulate /ˈsɪmjʊˌleɪt/ verb [T] to produce the features of something in a way that seems real but is not —**simulated** adj: *simulated leather/pearls*

simulation /ˌsɪmjʊˈleɪʃ(ə)n/ noun [C/U] something that produces the features of something in a way that seems real but is not

simulator /ˈsɪmjʊˌleɪtə/ noun [C] a piece of equipment that is used for training people to operate an aircraft or other vehicle, by SIMULATING different situations

simultaneous /ˌsɪm(ə)lˈteɪniəs/ adj happening or done at the same time —**simultaneously** adv

sin¹ /sɪn/ noun [C/U] an action, thought, or way of behaving that is wrong according to religious laws: *the sin of pride/greed*

sin² /sɪn/ verb [I] to do something that is

S

wrong according to religious laws

since /sɪns/ grammar word ★★★

Since can be:
- a **preposition**: *Everything has changed so much since last spring.*
- an **adverb**: *She left home in 1993 and hasn't been seen since.*
- a **conjunction**: *Paul's had several different jobs since he left school.*

1 from a particular point in the past until now, or until another point in the past: *I've known Joanna since she was born. ♦ Turkey has been a republic since 1923. ♦ I'd not seen her since she went to live in Oxford. ♦ Since arriving in New York, Thomas has had 15 job interviews. ♦ Paul started sailing in 1986 and he's been doing it **ever** since.*
2 used when giving a reason: *Since Barbara is no longer my wife, I'm not responsible for her debts.*

PHRASE **since when?** *spoken* used for showing that you are surprised or annoyed by something: *Since when has it been against the rules to have a coffee break?*

Both **since** and **for** are used for saying how long something has been happening.
- Use **since** to introduce a particular time or event when something started: *I've been working here since 1980.*
- Use **for** to introduce the period of time during which something has continued: *They've been married for over 40 years.*

sincere /sɪnˈsɪə/ adj showing that you really mean what you say ≠ INSINCERE: *His apology seemed sincere.*

sincerely /sɪnˈsɪəli/ adv really, or honestly: *I sincerely hope you will succeed.*
PHRASE **Yours sincerely** used before your name as a way of ending a formal letter

sincerity /sɪnˈserəti/ noun [U] an honest way of behaving that shows that you really mean what you say or do

sinful /ˈsɪnf(ə)l/ adj morally wrong according to religious laws

sing /sɪŋ/ (past tense **sang** /sæŋ/; past participle **sung** /sʌŋ/) verb ★★★
1 [I/T] to make music using your voice: *Grace was singing softly to herself. ♦ They **sang** several old familiar **songs**.*
2 [I] if a bird sings, it makes musical sounds
PHRASE **sing sb's/sth's praises** to talk about how good someone or something is
PHRASAL VERB **sing aˈlong** to sing a song with someone who is already singing

sing. abbrev singular

singe /sɪndʒ/ (present participle **singeing**; past tense and past participle **singed**) verb [I/T] to burn something slightly, so that only the edge or surface is affected

singer /ˈsɪŋə/ noun [C] someone who sings, especially someone who sings well or as their job

single¹ /ˈsɪŋɡ(ə)l/ adj ★★★
1 only one: *a single sheet of paper*
2 not married, or not in a romantic

relationship: *Please state whether you are single, married, or divorced.*
3 designed for one person or used by one person: *The room has two **single beds**.*
4 used for emphasizing one thing: *Drugs are the single biggest cause of crime here. ♦ Do we have to count **every single** penny we spend?*

PHRASE **not a single** not even one: *You didn't write a single letter the whole time you were away.*

single² /ˈsɪŋɡ(ə)l/ noun

1 short musical record	4 in tennis
2 room/bed	5 ticket for one way only
3 people not married	

1 [C] a musical record with only one song or piece of music on each side **2** [C] a room or bed for one person **3 singles** [plural] people who are not married, or who are not in a romantic relationship **4 singles** [plural] in tennis, a match that is played between two people **5** [C] *British* a ticket for travelling to a place, but not for returning from it

single³ /ˈsɪŋɡ(ə)l/ PHRASAL VERB ˌsingle sb/sth ˈout to choose one person or thing from a group for special attention: *In her article, three schools were singled out for particular criticism.*

ˌsingle ˈcurrency noun [singular] a system of money that is shared by several countries

single-handed /ˌsɪŋɡ(ə)l ˈhændɪd/ adj, adv done by one person without help from anyone else —**single-handedly** adv

ˌsingle-ˈminded adj with your attention fixed on only one thing = FOCUSED

ˌsingle ˈparent noun [C] a parent who raises their children alone, without a partner

singly /ˈsɪŋɡli/ adv separately: *You can buy stamps singly or in packs of ten.*

singular /ˈsɪŋɡjʊlə/ adj **1** *linguistics* the singular form of a word is used for referring to one person or thing **2** *formal* strange, or unusual

singular, the /ˈsɪŋɡjʊlə/ noun [singular] *linguistics* the form of a word that is used for referring to one person or thing

singularly /ˈsɪŋɡjʊləli/ adv in a noticeable way

sinister /ˈsɪnɪstə/ adj threatening to do something harmful or evil: *a sinister remark*

sink¹ /sɪŋk/ (past tense **sank** /sæŋk/; past participle **sunk** /sʌŋk/) verb ★★

1 go under water	6 become quiet
2 go below surface of sth	7 push sth sharp into sth
3 move to lower level	8 invest money
4 fall/sit/lie down	+ PHRASE
5 go down in amount	+ PHRASAL VERB

1 [I/T] to disappear below the surface of water, or to make something do this: *The ferry sank during a storm. ♦ The ship was sunk by an enemy submarine.*
2 [I] to go below the surface of a soft substance: *Our feet **sank into** the mud as we walked.*

3 [I] to move to a lower level: *The water level in the lake had sunk by several feet.* ♦ *We watched the sun sinking below the horizon.*

4 [I] to fall, sit, or lie down: *All I wanted to do was to **sink into** an armchair and rest.*

5 [I] to go down in value or amount: *Agricultural production had **sunk to** its lowest level in years.*

6 [I] to become quiet: *Their voices sank to a whisper.*

7 [T] to push something that is sharp into something that is solid: *The cat sank its claws into my leg.*

8 [T] to invest money in something: *We've sunk several thousand dollars into the project so far.*

> **PHRASE** **your spirits/heart sinks** if your spirits sink or your heart sinks, you become sad or lose hope

> **PHRASAL VERB** ,sink 'in to become completely understood: *She had to repeat her words several times before they finally sank in.*

sink

sink² /sɪŋk/ noun [C] a large open container for water that is fixed to a wall and connected to pipes that bring the water and carry it away —*picture* → C2

'**sinking ,feeling** noun [singular] a feeling that you get when you realize that something bad has happened or is going to happen

sinner /'sɪnə/ noun [C] someone who does not obey religious laws

Sinn Fein /ˌʃɪn 'feɪn/ a political organization in Northern Ireland that wants Ireland to become united and separate from the UK

sinus /'saɪnəs/ noun [C] one of several empty spaces that are in the bones of your face in the area behind your nose

sip¹ /sɪp/ verb [I/T] to drink in small amounts: *She sipped her lemonade.*

sip² /sɪp/ noun [C] a small amount of liquid that is taken into your mouth: *He took a sip of coffee.*

siphon /'saɪf(ə)n/ or '**siphon sth ,off** verb [T] **1** to move liquid from one container to another through a tube **2** to move money from one bank account to another illegally or dishonestly

sir / weak sə, strong sɜ:/ **1** spoken used as a polite way of speaking to a man **2** Sir used before the name of a man who is a KNIGHT

> **PHRASE** **Dear Sir** used for beginning a letter to a man whose name you do not know

siren /'saɪrən/ noun [C] a piece of equipment that makes a loud sound, used for warning people

sister /'sɪstə/ noun [C] ★★★

1 relative	4 woman friend
2 nurse	5 black woman
3 nun	+ PHRASE

1 a girl or woman who has the same parents as you: *He has two brothers and two sisters.* → HALF SISTER, STEPSISTER —*picture* → FAMILY TREE

2 British a female nurse in charge of a hospital WARD (=a room for people who are ill)

3 a NUN (=a woman who is a member of a religious community): *Sister Mary*

4 used by women for referring to a woman who they feel loyalty and friendship towards: *support for our sisters who are the victims of war*

5 a black woman. This word is mainly used by black people.

> **PHRASE** **sister organization/company etc** an organization that has close connections with another similar organization

'**sister-in-law** (plural **sisters-in-law**) noun [C] **1** the sister of your husband or wife —*picture* → FAMILY TREE **2** the wife of your brother

sisterly /'sɪstəli/ adj suitable for a sister, or typical of a sister

sit /sɪt/ (past tense and past participle **sat** /sæt/) verb ★★★

1 rest on seat	6 be member of sth
2 lower body into seat	7 meet officially
3 make someone sit	8 take an examination
4 be in situation etc	9 be model
5 be in particular place	+ PHRASAL VERBS

1 [I] to be in a position in which the lower part of your body rests on a seat or the ground, while the upper part of your body is upright: *Sit still* (=without moving) *while I brush your hair.* ♦ *I usually sit next to Andrew in history.* ♦ *They were sitting in a café drinking coffee.* ♦ *I was sitting at my computer when the phone rang.* ♦ *Matt sat on a park bench, eating his lunch.* ♦ *Six of us were sitting around the table talking.* —*picture* → POSTURE

2 [I] to lower your body into a sitting position: *He came over and sat on the sofa.*

3 [T] to put someone into a sitting position: *Joanna sat the child on her lap and read him a story.*

4 [I] to be in a particular situation or condition for a period of time: *I was sitting in traffic for over an hour.*

5 [I] to be in a particular place: *The house sits on top of a hill.*

6 [I] to be a member of a committee or other official group: *She sits on the boards of several large companies.*

7 [I] if a parliament, a court of law, or a committee sits, it has an official meeting

8 [T] British to take an examination: *I'm sitting my French exam tomorrow.*

9 [I] to be a model for a painter or a PHOTOGRAPHER

S

PHRASAL VERBS ,sit a'round to spend time doing nothing

,sit 'back to relax and stop making the effort to do something: *We can't just sit back and let them win.*

,sit 'by to take no action while something bad is happening: *Are we just going to sit by and let this happen?*

,sit 'down *same as* sit 2: *Please, sit down and make yourselves comfortable.*

,sit 'in on sth to go to a meeting or a class although you are not directly involved in it: *Do you mind if I sit in on your class this afternoon?*

'sit through sth to stay until the end of something, especially if you are not enjoying it: *If I have to sit through one more boring meeting, I think I'll scream.*

,sit 'up 1 to sit with your back straight and upright: *Sit up straight and pay attention.* 2 to go from a lying position to a sitting position: *Would you like to sit up and read for a while?*

,sit sb 'up to help someone to go from a lying position to a sitting position: *We sat her up in a chair.*

sitcom /'sɪt‚kɒm/ noun [C] a humorous television or radio series about a group of characters

site¹ /saɪt/ noun [C] ★★★
1 an area of land where something is being built or could be built: *a construction site*
2 a place where something interesting or important happened: *We visited the site of the Battle of Bosworth.*
3 a place used for a particular purpose: *a landing site for helicopters*
4 a WEBSITE

site² /saɪt/ verb [T] to put something in a particular place

sitter /'sɪtə/ noun [C] 1 someone who is painted or photographed by an artist 2 *informal* a BABYSITTER

sitting /'sɪtɪŋ/ noun [C] 1 a period of time during which a meal is served 2 a period of time when a parliament or court meets 3 a period of time when someone is being painted or photographed by an artist
PHRASE in/at one sitting during a single period of time while you are sitting: *He read the whole book in one sitting.*

'sitting ,room noun [C] a LIVING ROOM

situated /'sɪtʃueɪtɪd/ adj in a particular place

situation /‚sɪtʃu'eɪʃ(ə)n/ noun [C] ★★★ the set of conditions that exist at a particular time in a particular place: *The country is facing a very difficult economic situation.* ♦ *I found myself in an embarrassing situation.* ♦ *sb's situation* (=the conditions that affect their life at a particular time) *What prospects are there for a person in his situation?*

six /sɪks/ number the number 6
PHRASE six of one, (and) half a dozen of the other used for saying that two things are equally good or bad

sixteen /‚sɪks'tiːn/ number the number 16

sixteenth /‚sɪks'tiːnθ/ number 1 in the place

or position counted as number 16 2 one of 16 equal parts of something

sixth /sɪksθ/ number 1 in the place or position counted as number 6 2 one of 6 equal parts of something

'sixth ,form noun [C/U] the last stage of school in England and Wales for students between the ages of 16 and 18

sixties /'sɪkstiz/ noun [plural] 1 the years from 1960 to 1969: *music from the sixties* 2 the period of time from age 60 to age 69: *a woman in her sixties* 3 the numbers 60 to 69, especially as a temperature

sixtieth /'sɪkstiəθ/ number 1 in the place or position counted as number 60 2 one of 60 equal parts of something

sixty /'sɪksti/ number the number 60

sizable /'saɪzəb(ə)l/ another spelling of sizeable

size¹ /saɪz/ noun ★★★
1 [C/U] a measurement of how large or small something is: *balloons of all shapes and sizes* ♦ *The president has promised to reduce the size of the army.*
2 [C] one of a series of standard measurements according to which goods are made or sold: *What size shoes do you take?* ♦ *This dress is a size 12.*
3 [U] the fact that something is very large: *The size of the organization makes communication difficult.*

size² /saɪz/ **PHRASAL VERB** ,size sb/sth 'up to think carefully and form an opinion about a person or a situation

sizeable /'saɪzəb(ə)l/ adj fairly large

sizzle /'sɪz(ə)l/ verb [I] to make the sound of food that is cooking in hot oil —sizzle noun [singular]

sizzling /'sɪzlɪŋ/ adj *informal* very hot

skate¹ /skeɪt/ noun [C] 1 a type of shoe with a thin metal blade on the bottom, used for moving quickly on ice=ICE SKATE 2 a type of shoe with four thick wheels on the bottom, used for moving over a smooth surface=ROLLER SKATES

skate² /skeɪt/ verb [I] to move over a surface using skates → THIN —skater noun [C], skating noun [U]

skateboard /'skeɪt‚bɔːd/ noun [C] a board with four wheels on the bottom that you stand on and ride —skateboarder noun [C], skateboarding noun [U]

'skating ,rink noun [C] a place with an area of ice or a smooth floor, used for skating

skeletal /'skelɪt(ə)l/ adj 1 relating to a skeleton 2 extremely thin

skeleton /'skelɪt(ə)n/ noun [C] the set of bones that supports a human or animal body, or a model of this
PHRASE skeleton in the cupboard/closet an embarrassing secret about your past

sketch¹ /sketʃ/ noun [C] 1 a drawing that is made quickly that does not have many details 2 a short funny scene performed within a longer show

sketch² /sketʃ/ verb 1 [I/T] to draw a picture quickly and with few details —*picture*

S

→ DRAW **2** [T] to make a general plan of something, with only a few details

PHRASAL VERB ,sketch sth 'out *same as* sketch² 2: *I've just sketched out a rough proposal.*

sketchy /'sketʃi/ adj not detailed or complete =VAGUE: *a rather sketchy account*

skewed /skjuːd/ adj **1** results or judgments that are skewed are not accurate because they have been affected by something **2** not straight

skewer /'skjuːə/ noun [C] a long thin piece of metal or wood that you stick through food to hold it while it cooks

ski¹ /skiː/ noun [C] a long thin object that you fix to your boot so that you can slide easily over snow

ski² /skiː/ verb [I] to slide over snow on skis

skid /skɪd/ verb [I] to slide across the ground in an uncontrolled way —**skid** noun [C]

skier /'skiːə/ noun [C] someone who moves over snow on SKIS

skiing /'skiːɪŋ/ noun [U] the sport or activity of moving over snow on SKIS

skilful /'skɪlf(ə)l/ adj showing a lot of skill: *a skilful negotiator* ♦ *her skilful use of colour* —**skilfully** adv

skill /skɪl/ noun [C/U] ★★★ the ability to do something well, usually as a result of experience and training: *I admired the skill and dedication of the nursing staff.* ♦ *computer skills*

skilled /skɪld/ adj **1** skilful ≠ UNSKILLED: *a skilled craftsman* **2** a skilled job needs someone who has ability and experience

skillful /'skɪlf(ə)l/ the American spelling of skilful

skim /skɪm/ verb **1** [T] to remove a substance that is floating on the surface of a liquid: *Skim the fat off the soup.* **2** [I/T] to move quickly over the surface of something: *Water skiers skimmed across the lake.* **3** [I/T] to read something quickly and not very carefully

skimmed milk /ˌskɪmd 'mɪlk/ noun [U] milk that has had the cream removed from it

skimpy /'skɪmpi/ adj skimpy clothes fit very tightly and do not cover much of someone's body

skin¹ /skɪn/ noun [C/U] ★★★
1 the outer layer of a person's or animal's body: *She has beautiful soft skin.* ♦ *fair/ dark skin* ♦ *a skin disease*
2 the outer layer that is cut from an animal's body, used for making clothing and decorations =HIDE
3 the outer layer of a fruit or vegetable =PEEL: *banana skins*

PHRASE **get under sb's skin 1** to make someone very annoyed or upset **2** to make someone feel very attracted to you

skin² /skɪn/ verb [T] to remove the skin from an animal, fruit, or vegetable

skinhead /'skɪnˌhed/ noun [C] a young man whose hair has been cut extremely short, especially one who is part of a violent right-wing group

skinny /'skɪni/ adj *informal* very thin

skip¹ /skɪp/ verb **1** [I] to move forwards by jumping first on one foot and then the other: *Julie skipped along the pavement.* **2** [I] to jump over a rope that you or two other people swing above your head and then under your feet **3** [T] to not do or have something: *Let's skip that chapter and move on to the next one.* ♦ *It's not a good idea to skip breakfast.* **4** [I] to move quickly from one place or thing to another: *They kept skipping from one topic to another.*

skip

skip² /skɪp/ noun [C] **1** *British* a very large metal container that is used in the building industry for rubbish **2** the action of skipping

skipper /'skɪpə/ noun [C] *informal* **1** someone who is in charge of a small ship =CAPTAIN **2** *British* someone who is in charge of a team =CAPTAIN

skirmish /'skɜːmɪʃ/ noun [C] **1** a fight involving a small number of soldiers **2** an argument or disagreement

skirt¹ /skɜːt/ noun [C] ★★ a piece of clothing for a woman or girl. It hangs from the waist and is not joined between the legs: *She was wearing a long skirt.*

skirt² /skɜːt/ verb **1** [T] to go around the edge of a place or thing: *They skirted the field to avoid the mud.* **2** [I/T] to avoid talking about something that is unpleasant: *He just skirted around the subject.*

'ski ˌslope or **'ski ˌrun** noun [C] a part of a hill or mountain that you SKI on

skulk /skʌlk/ verb [I] to move around or wait somewhere in a secret way

skull /skʌl/ noun [C] the bones of the head

sky /skaɪ/ noun ★★★
1 [C/U] the space above the Earth that you see when you look up into the air: *a clear blue sky* ♦ *Black smoke rose into the sky.* ♦ *The night sky was filled with stars.*
2 **skies** [plural] a way of referring to the sky, used especially when talking about the weather: *Tomorrow we expect clear skies and sunshine.*

PHRASE **the sky's the limit** used for saying that there is no limit to what someone can do

S

Words often used with sky

Adjectives often used with sky (sense 2)
■ **cloudy, dark, dull, gloomy, grey, leaden, lowering, overcast** + SKIES: used about a sky that is not bright or sunny
■ **blue, clear, cloudless, sunny** + SKIES: used about a sky that has no clouds

skydiving /ˈskaɪˌdaɪvɪŋ/ noun [U] the sport of jumping out of a plane and falling for as long as possible before opening your PARACHUTE —**skydiver** noun [C]

skylight /ˈskaɪˌlaɪt/ noun [C] a window in a roof or ceiling —*picture* → C1

skyline /ˈskaɪˌlaɪn/ noun [C] the shapes made by buildings or mountains when you see them against the sky

skyscraper /ˈskaɪˌskreɪpə/ noun [C] a very tall building containing offices or flats

slab /slæb/ noun [C] a large flat piece of something, especially something hard: *a concrete slab* ♦ *a slab of chocolate*

slack¹ /slæk/ adj **1** loose and not pulled tight: *The rope suddenly went slack.* **2** not taking enough care to make sure that something is done well: *slack safety standards* **3** not as busy or successful as usual in business

slack² /slæk/ verb [I] to try to avoid working

slack³ /slæk/ noun [U] **1** people, equipment, or money that could be used more effectively in an organization **2** the fact that a rope is loose, rather than being pulled tight

slacken /ˈslækən/ verb [I/T] **1** to become slower or less active, or to make something become slower or less active **2** to become looser, or to make something looser

PHRASAL VERB ,**slacken (sth) ˈoff** *same as* **slacken** 1

slag¹ /slæg/ noun [U] waste that is produced after coal or a metal has been processed

slag² /slæg/ PHRASAL VERB ,**slag sb/sth ˈoff** *British informal* to criticize someone or something

slain the past participle of **slay**

slalom /ˈslɑːləm/ noun [C/U] a race, especially on SKIS, in which people move around a series of poles

slam /slæm/ verb **1** [I/T] if a door or lid slams, or if you slam it, it shuts with great force so that it makes a loud noise: *He ran from the room, slamming the door behind him.* ♦ *The heavy gate slammed shut.* **2** [T] to put, move, or hit something somewhere with great force: *He slammed the groceries down on the table.* ♦ *She slammed the brakes on.* **3** [I] to hit against something with great force: *The bicycle slammed into a tree.* **4** [T] *mainly journalism* to criticize someone or something severely: *The film has been slammed by critics.*

slander /ˈslɑːndə/ noun [C/U] *legal* the crime of saying something about someone that is not true and that is likely to damage their reputation —**slander** verb [T]

slang /slæŋ/ noun [U] words or expressions that are very informal and that are not considered suitable for formal situations

slant¹ /slɑːnt/ verb **1** [I] to be or move at an angle that is not 90 degrees: *Sunlight slanted through the curtains.* **2** [T] to give information or ideas in a way that gives more attention or support to a particular person, group, or opinion: *He was accused of slanting his reports to protect his colleagues.*

slant² /slɑːnt/ noun [singular] **1** the angle at which something slopes **2** a particular way of showing or considering information: *Her recipes give us a new slant on Italian cooking.*

slanted /ˈslɑːntɪd/ adj **1** at an angle that is not 90 degrees: *a room with a slanted ceiling* **2** done in a way that gives more attention or support to a particular person, group, or opinion: *The book is heavily slanted towards American business methods.*

slap¹ /slæp/ verb **1** [T] to hit someone or something quickly with the palm of the hand **2** [T] to put something down quickly and noisily: *Annie slapped down her cards.* **3** [I] to hit a surface with a sound that is like someone slapping something: *The waves slapped against the stone pier.* **4** [T] to put something on a surface quickly and without much attention: *Just slap some paint on the wall and it will look fine.*

slap² /slæp/ noun [C] a sharp hit with the palm of the hand

PHRASE **a slap in the face** an action or criticism that is unkind and that makes you feel sad or disappointed

slapstick /ˈslæpstɪk/ noun [U] humour that is based on physical actions such as people hitting each other or falling over

slash¹ /slæʃ/ verb **1** [T] *mainly journalism* to reduce something by a large amount: *The budget had been slashed by £3 million.* **2** [T] to cut something in a violent way: *The tyres on the car had been slashed.* **3** [I/T] to try to cut or hit something by making several swinging movements: *She slashed wildly at the ball.*

slash² /slæʃ/ noun [C] **1** a long deep cut **2** a quick swinging movement, especially with something sharp **3** a line (/) that separates numbers, letters, or words in writing

slat /slæt/ noun [C] a thin flat piece of wood, metal etc, used especially for making furniture or window BLINDS

slate /sleɪt/ noun **1** [U] a type of dark grey stone that breaks easily into flat thin pieces **2** [C] a single flat piece of slate that is used with others for covering a roof → CLEAN¹

slaughter¹ /ˈslɔːtə/ noun [U] **1** the violent killing of a large number of people **2** the killing of animals, usually for their meat

slaughter² /ˈslɔːtə/ verb [T] **1** to kill a large number of people in a violent way **2** to kill animals, usually for their meat **3** *informal* to defeat an opponent completely

slaughterhouse /ˈslɔːtəhaʊs/ noun [C] a building where animals are killed for their meat

slave¹ /sleɪv/ noun [C] someone who belongs by law to another person and who has to obey them and work for them

slave² /sleɪv/ or **slave aˈway** verb [I] to work very hard

slavery /ˈsleɪvəri/ noun [U] **1** the system of owning people as slaves **2** the condition of being a slave

S

slay /sleɪ/ (past tense **slew** /sluː/; past participle **slain** /sleɪn/) verb [T] *literary* to kill someone in a violent way

sleaze /sliːz/ noun [U] behaviour that is dishonest or immoral, especially in politics or business

sleazy /'sliːzi/ adj **1** dishonest or immoral **2** a sleazy place is dirty and unpleasant

sled /sled/ noun [C] a SLEDGE

sledge¹ /sledʒ/ noun [C] *British* a vehicle that you sit on to slide over snow. It moves on smooth pieces of wood or plastic.

sledge² /sledʒ/ verb [I] *British* to ride on a sledge

sleek /sliːk/ adj **1** sleek fur or hair is smooth and shiny **2** with a modern attractive smooth design: *a sleek red sports car*

sleep¹ /sliːp/ (past tense and past participle **slept** /slept/) verb ★★★
1 [I] to go into a natural state in which your body rests and you are unconscious, especially for several hours at night: *The baby usually sleeps in the afternoon.* ♦ *'Did you sleep well?' 'Yes, thanks.'* ♦ *We both slept badly and felt terrible the next day.*
2 [T] to have enough room or beds for a particular number of people to sleep in: *Our house at the beach sleeps six comfortably.*
PHRASE **sleep rough** *British* to sleep outside because you do not have anywhere to live
PHRASAL VERBS **sleep around** *informal* to have sexual relations with a lot of different people
sleep in to continue sleeping after the time that you usually wake up: *The whole family sleeps in on Sundays.*
sleep sth off to get rid of an unpleasant feeling by sleeping
sleep on sth to wait to make a decision until the next day, after you have rested and had more time to think: *Let me sleep on it and give you an answer tomorrow.*
sleep through sth to continue sleeping although there is a lot of noise around you: *He slept through the whole storm.*
sleep together if two people sleep together, they have sex, especially when they are not married
sleep with sb to have sex with someone, especially someone who you are not married to

sleep² /sliːp/ noun ★★
1 [U] a natural state in which your body rests and you are unconscious: *I can't get to sleep if there's any noise.* ♦ *You need to go home and get some sleep.* ♦ *The motion of the car sent me to sleep.* ♦ *You were talking in your sleep* (=while you were sleeping) *last night.*
2 [singular] a period of time when you are sleeping: *I think I'll have a sleep this afternoon.* ♦ *I haven't had a good night's sleep for over a week.* ♦ *She lay down and soon fell into a deep sleep.*
PHRASES **can do sth in your sleep** to be able to do something so easily that you do not need to think about it

go to sleep 1 to begin sleeping: *What time do the kids usually go to sleep?* **2** *informal* if a part of your body goes to sleep, you cannot feel it for a short time because it has not been getting enough blood
put sth to sleep to give an animal drugs so that it dies quickly without feeling any pain

sleeper /'sliːpə/ noun [C] **1** someone who is sleeping: *a light/heavy sleeper* (=someone who wakes/does not wake easily) **2** a train with beds for passengers to sleep in **3** *British* one of the large pieces of wood that support a railway track

sleeping bag noun [C] a warm bag that you sleep in, especially when camping

sleeping pill or **sleeping tablet** noun [C] a pill that you take in order to help you to sleep

sleepless /'sliːpləs/ adj without sleep, or unable to sleep: *a sleepless night*

sleepover /'sliːpˌəʊvə/ noun [C] a children's party at which the guests stay the night

sleepwalking /'sliːpˌwɔːkɪŋ/ noun [U] the action of walking and sometimes doing things while you are still sleeping

sleepy /'sliːpi/ adj **1** feeling tired and wanting to sleep **2** a sleepy place is very quiet and does not have much activity —**sleepily** adv

sleet /sliːt/ noun [U] a mixture of snow and rain —**sleet** verb [I]

sleeve /sliːv/ noun [C] **1** the part of a piece of clothing that covers your arm: *a dress with long sleeves* **2** a paper or plastic cover that protects something such as a record or book
PHRASE **have sth up your sleeve** to have a secret plan that you can surprise people with

sleeveless /'sliːvləs/ adj a sleeveless dress or shirt does not have sleeves

sleigh /sleɪ/ noun [C] a vehicle that is pulled by animals and used for travelling over snow

sleight of hand /ˌslaɪt əv 'hænd/ noun [singular/U] clever and slightly dishonest behaviour used for achieving something

slender /'slendə/ adj **1** tall or long and thin in an attractive way: *slender fingers* **2** very small in amount and only just enough: *They won by a slender majority.*

slept the past tense and past participle of **sleep¹**

slew the past tense of **slay**

slice¹ /slaɪs/ noun [C] ★
1 a flat piece of food that has been cut from something larger: *Cut the bread into thick slices.* ♦ *a slice of cake/pizza/cheese*
2 *informal* a part or share of something: *We want a bigger slice of the tourist trade.*

slice² /slaɪs/ verb **1** [T] to cut something into flat pieces: *I'll slice some bread.* —*picture* → C2 **2** [I] to cut something easily: *The saw quickly sliced through the board.*

slick¹ /slɪk/ adj **1** smooth and shiny or wet: *slick black hair* **2** clever and good at persuading people but probably not honest: *a slick car salesman* **3** done in an impressive

S

way that seems to need little effort: *a slick advertisement*

slick² /slɪk/ noun [C] an OIL SLICK

slick³ /slɪk/ verb [T] if you slick your hair back or down, you put oil or water on it in order to make it stay in place

slide¹ /slaɪd/ noun [C] **1** a structure for children to play on, with steps and a slope to slide down **2** a situation in which an amount gradually becomes less: *a slide in sales* **3** a small piece of film in a frame. You shine light through it in order to show the image on a screen. **4** a small thin piece of glass used for looking at things with a MICROSCOPE

slide² /slaɪd/ (past tense and past participle **slid** /slɪd/) verb ★
1 [I/T] to move smoothly and quickly across a surface, or to make something move in this way: *He slid down the hill on a sledge.* ♦ *The doors slid open.* ♦ *I slid the letter under her door.*
2 [I] to gradually get into a worse situation than before: *The company slid further into debt last year.*

slight /slaɪt/ adj ★★
1 small in size, amount, or degree: *a slight increase in temperature*
2 thin and small: *a slight young woman*
    PHRASE **not in the slightest** not at all

slightly /ˈslaɪtli/ adv ★★★ a little: *I feel slightly better today.* ♦ *He was limping slightly.* ♦ *'Do you know her?' 'Only slightly.'*

slim¹ /slɪm/ adj ★★
1 thin in an attractive way: *She had a slim youthful figure.*
2 very small: *There is still **a slim chance** that she may be alive.*

slim² /slɪm/ verb [I] *British* to try to lose weight by eating less
    PHRASAL VERB **ˌslim (sth) ˈdown** if you slim down an organization, or if it slims down, you reduce the number of staff in it

slime /slaɪm/ noun [U] a thick, wet, and unpleasant substance

slimming¹ /ˈslɪmɪŋ/ noun [U] *British* the process of losing weight by eating less

slimming² /ˈslɪmɪŋ/ adj **1** *British* designed to help you to lose weight **2** making you look thinner than you really are

slimy /ˈslaɪmi/ adj **1** thick, wet, and unpleasant to touch **2** *informal* friendly in a way that is unpleasant because it is not sincere

sling¹ /slɪŋ/ (past tense and past participle **slung** /slʌŋ/) verb [T] to put or throw something somewhere in a careless way: *Just sling all that stuff on the floor.* ♦ *He slung his jacket over one shoulder.*

sling² /slɪŋ/ noun [C] **1** a piece of cloth used for supporting your arm when it is injured **2** a set of belts or ropes used for supporting or lifting something heavy

slink /slɪŋk/ (past tense and past participle **slunk** /slʌŋk/) verb [I] to go somewhere slowly and quietly so that people will not notice you: *Ray slunk out of the building.*

---

slip¹ /slɪp/ verb ★★

1 (almost) fall	5 become less strong
2 slide out of position	+ PHRASES
3 go quickly and quietly	+ PHRASAL VERBS
4 slide sth somewhere	

1 [I] if you slip, your feet slide accidentally and you fall or lose your balance: *Margaret slipped and broke her arm.* ♦ *Be careful you don't **slip on** the wet floor.*
2 [I] if something slips, it slides out of the position it should be in: *The knife slipped and cut my finger.* ♦ *The ball **slipped out of** my hands.*
3 [I] to go somewhere quickly and quietly, without anyone noticing you or stopping you: *Several people managed to **slip past** the guards.* ♦ *I **slipped away** before the end of the meeting.*
4 [T] to slide something into a place or position, often so that other people do not notice: *John **slipped** his arm **around** his wife's waist.* ♦ *He **slipped** the money **into** his pocket.*
5 [I] to gradually become less strong or good: *Profits slipped by 13% last year.*
    PHRASES **let (it) slip** to tell someone something that is secret by mistake: *He let it slip that they intended to move to Canada.*
slip your mind if something slips your mind, you forget to do it
slip through your fingers if something such as an opportunity or a prize slips through your fingers, you fail to get it or to take advantage of it
slip through the net/cracks to fail to be caught or protected by the system that was intended to catch or protect you
    PHRASAL VERBS **ˌslip ˈinto sth** to quickly put on a piece of clothing: *I slipped into my pyjamas.*
ˌslip sth ˈoff to take a piece of clothing off quickly: *Slip your shirt off.*
ˌslip sth ˈon to put clothes on: *Ann slipped the jacket on.*
ˌslip ˈout if something slips out, you say it without intending to
ˌslip ˈup *informal* to make a careless mistake

slip

slip² /slɪp/ noun [C] **1** a small piece of paper: *I left the message for you on a slip of paper.* **2** a small mistake: *Tom played well, despite a few slips at the beginning.* **3** a small change from a higher level to a lower one: *a slip in the price of technology stocks* **4** a piece of women's underwear consisting of a loose skirt or dress with no sleeves

PHRASE **give sb the slip** *informal* to escape from someone who is following or chasing you

slipper /ˈslɪpə/ noun [C] a soft comfortable shoe that you wear in your house

slippery /ˈslɪpəri/ adj **1** a slippery surface or object is difficult to move on or hold because it is smooth or wet **2** *informal* clever but dishonest

slippery ˈslope noun [singular] *British* a problem or situation that will become extremely bad unless it is stopped

ˈslip ˌroad noun [C] *British* a road that you use to drive onto or off a motorway

slit¹ /slɪt/ noun [C] a long narrow space or cut in something: *a skirt with a slit up the side*

slit² /slɪt/ (past tense and past participle **slit**) verb [T] to make a long thin cut in something: *She grabbed the envelope and slit it open.*

slither /ˈslɪðə/ verb [I] to move along the ground like a snake

sliver /ˈslɪvə/ noun [C] a small thin piece of something: *slivers of glass*

slob /slɒb/ noun [C] *informal* someone who is lazy or untidy

slobber /ˈslɒbə/ verb [I] to have SALIVA coming out of your mouth

slog¹ /slɒɡ/ noun *British informal* **1** [singular/U] something that is difficult or boring and seems to take a long time **2** [singular] a long tiring walk

slog² /slɒɡ/ verb [I] *informal* **1** to work hard and for a long time doing something that is difficult or boring **2** to make a long tiring journey somewhere by walking there

slogan /ˈsləʊɡən/ noun [C] a short phrase that is used for advertising something, or for supporting someone in politics

slop /slɒp/ verb [I/T] if a liquid slops, or if you slop it, it moves inside its container, or some of it comes out of the container =SLOSH

slope¹ /sləʊp/ noun [C] ★
1 a surface or piece of ground that has one end higher than the other: *At the end of the garden there is a steep slope.*
2 the angle of a slope: *a 45-degree slope*

slope² /sləʊp/ verb [I] to have one end higher than the other: *The floor slopes a bit.*
—**sloping** adj

sloppy /ˈslɒpi/ adj **1** done in a very careless way: *a sloppy job* **2** sloppy clothes are loose and informal **3** expressing emotions in a way that seems silly or embarrassing

slosh /slɒʃ/ verb **1** [I/T] if a liquid sloshes, or if you slosh it, it moves inside its container, or some of it comes out of the container =SLOP **2** [I] to walk through something wet in a noisy way

slot¹ /slɒt/ noun [C] **1** a long narrow hole or space that you can fit something through or into: *He put a coin in the slot.* **2** a time between other events when it is arranged that something will happen: *We circled the airport waiting for a landing slot.*

slot² /slɒt/
PHRASAL VERBS **slot (sth) ˈin** to fit into a narrow space, or to fit something into a narrow space: *The last tile slotted in neatly.*
slot sb/sth ˈin to arrange a time for someone or something between other things that you have to do
slot (sth) ˈinto sth to fit something into a narrow space, or to fit into a narrow space: *She slotted another tape into the cassette player.*

ˈslot maˌchine noun [C] a machine that you put coins into in order to play a game or buy things

slouch /slaʊtʃ/ verb [I] to sit, walk, or stand with your shoulders bent forwards

slow¹ /sləʊ/ adj ★★★
1 not moving or happening fast: *This bus is really slow.* ♦ *a long slow walk to the top of the hill* ♦ *She's a slow worker, but reliable.* ♦ *Progress has been **painfully slow** (=very slow).* ♦ **slow to do sth** *The government has been slow to respond.*
2 not busy, interesting, or exciting: *The first part of the film is very slow.*
3 a watch or clock that is slow shows a time that is earlier than the correct time: *Your watch is 15 minutes slow.*
4 not intelligent, so that you need a lot of time in order to understand simple things

slow² /sləʊ/ verb [I/T] **1** if you slow something, or if it slows, you reduce the speed at which it happens or moves: *Drugs can slow the progress of the disease.* ♦ *Traffic on the motorway had slowed to walking pace.* **2** if you slow something, or if it slows, you reduce the level or amount of it: *Inflation slowed significantly in the 1990s.*
PHRASAL VERBS **slow (sb) ˈdown** if someone slows down, or if something slows them down, they become less active or effective: *For me, holidays are a time to slow down and relax.*
slow (sb/sth) ˈdown to move at a slower speed, or to make someone or something move at a slower speed: *Slow down! You're driving too fast.*
slow (sth) ˈdown same as **slow²** 1: *The new government is slowing down the pace of reform.*

slow³ /sləʊ/ adv *informal* at a slow speed: *Hurry up! You're driving too slow.*

slowdown /ˈsləʊˌdaʊn/ noun [C] a period when there is less activity: *an economic slowdown*

slowly /ˈsləʊli/ adv ★★★ moving or happening at a slow speed: *The city is slowly getting back to normal after a three-day transport strike.* ♦ *Could you **speak** a little more **slowly**?* ♦ *We're making progress – **slowly but surely** (=slowly but with definite results).*

ˌslow ˈmotion noun [U] action in a film or television programme that is shown more slowly than the real speed: *Let's see it again in slow motion.*

S

sludge /slʌdʒ/ noun [U] **1** a thick soft waste substance from an industrial process **2** an unpleasant thick wet substance

slug /slʌg/ noun [C] a small slow creature with no legs. It looks like a SNAIL without a shell.

sluggish /ˈslʌgɪʃ/ adj not moving, performing, or reacting as well as usual: *a sluggish economy* ♦ *Sasha woke up feeling tired and sluggish.*

sluice[1] /sluːs/ verb [T] to wash something with a flow of water

sluice[2] /sluːs/ noun [C] a passage that water flows along, with a gate that can be closed to control the flow

slum /slʌm/ noun [C] a poor area of a town where the houses are in very bad condition

slumber /ˈslʌmbə/ noun [U] *literary* sleep

slump[1] /slʌmp/ verb [I] **1** to suddenly fall to a much lower level: *Profits slumped to under $250 million.* **2** to suddenly fall or sit down because you are very tired or unconscious: *Sam's body slumped to the floor.*

PHRASE **be slumped in/over etc sth** to be sitting still in a position that is not upright: *They found him slumped over the wheel of his car.*

slump[2] /slʌmp/ noun [C] **1** a sudden large reduction in amount: *a slump in prices* **2** a period when someone or something is much less successful than before: *an economic slump*

slung the past tense and past participle of **sling**

slunk the past tense and past participle of **slink**

slur[1] /slɜː/ noun [C] a remark that is intended to insult someone or damage their reputation

slur[2] /slɜː/ verb [I/T] to speak without pronouncing the words clearly or separately —**slurred** /slɜːd/ adj: *slurred speech*

slurp /slɜːp/ verb [I/T] to make loud sucking noises as you drink something

slush /slʌʃ/ noun [U] snow that is starting to MELT (=become water)

sly /slaɪ/ adj clever at tricking people or at hurting them without them realizing it: *I noticed his sly smile.*

smack[1] /smæk/ verb [T] to hit someone with your flat hand or with a flat object

PHRASAL VERB **smack of sth** to be a sign of something bad: *Their decision smacked of discrimination.*

smack[2] /smæk/ noun [C] **1** a hit with your flat hand or with a flat object **2** a loud sound that is made when something hits a surface

smack[3] /smæk/ adv *informal* exactly in a particular place: *The ball hit me smack in the eye.*

small /smɔːl/ adj ★★★

1 not large in size, amount, or number: *These shoes are too small for me.* ♦ *I'd rather work for a smaller company.* ♦ *A small number of people have complained.*

2 not very important or difficult: *Can you do me a small favour?* ♦ *I noticed a few small mistakes.*

3 not worth a lot of money, or not involving a lot of money: *a new mutual fund that is ideal for small investors*

4 small children are very young
—**small** adv: *Write small so that everything will fit on one page.*
→ WONDER²

Both **small** and **little** can be used to describe something that is not big in size or number.

■ **Small** is a more general word: *a woman with a small dog* ♦ *Our house is fairly small.*

■ **Little** is usually used when you feel something about the thing that you are describing, for example when you like it, dislike it, or feel surprised that it is so small: *Look at that little baby!* ♦ *She has such little feet.*

---

small ad noun [C] *British* a CLASSIFIED AD

small intestine noun [C] the tube in your body that food goes into after it has passed through your stomach

smallpox /ˈsmɔːlpɒks/ noun [U] a serious disease in which your skin becomes covered in spots

small print, the noun [U] the details of something such as a contract that are printed in very small letters and often contain conditions that limit your rights

small-scale adj smaller or less important than other things of the same kind: *a small-scale operation/attack*

small talk noun [U] informal conversation about things that are not important

smart[1] /smɑːt/ adj ★

1 *British* clean and tidy in appearance and dressed in nice clothes: *smart new clothes* ♦ *Sandy's looking very smart today.*

2 intelligent: *Sophie is a smart hard-working student.* ♦ *Wilson made a few smart investments.*

3 *British* used by rich fashionable people: *Beverly Hills' smartest shopping district*

4 smart weapons and machines are very effective because they use computer technology
—**smartly** adv: *a smartly dressed young man*

smart[2] /smɑːt/ verb [I] **1** to hurt with a sudden sharp pain **2** to be very upset by something that someone has said or done

smart card noun [C] a small plastic card that stores information in electronic form

smarten /ˈsmɑːtn/ **PHRASAL VERB** **smarten (yourself) up** if you smarten up, or if you smarten yourself up, you make yourself look tidy and clean

smash[1] /smæʃ/ verb ★

1 [I/T] if something smashes, or if you smash it, it breaks noisily into many pieces when it falls or when you break it: *Someone had smashed a window.* ♦ *The bottle fell and smashed on the floor.*

2 [I/T] to hit against an object or surface with a lot of force, or to hit something against something in this way: *His car smashed into a tree.* ♦ *He fell and smashed his head on the pavement.*

3 [T] to completely destroy or defeat an organization, system etc

4 [T] in tennis, to hit a ball that is above your head downwards and very hard —*picture* → C15

PHRASE **smash a record** to do something much faster, better etc than it has ever been done before

PHRASAL VERB ,**smash sth 'up** *spoken* to destroy something completely by violently breaking it into many pieces: *She got angry and started smashing things up.*

smash² /smæʃ/ noun [C] informal **1** smash or **smash hit** something such as a play, film, or song that is extremely successful **2** a car crash

smashing /ˈsmæʃɪŋ/ adj British informal old-fashioned very good

smear¹ /smɪə/ verb [T] **1** to spread a soft substance on a surface in a untidy way: *The kids had smeared glue all over the floor.* ♦ *His face was smeared with mud.* **2** to try to damage someone's reputation by telling lies about them

smear² /smɪə/ noun [C] **1** a dirty mark made by rubbing something **2** an attempt to damage someone's reputation by telling lies about them

smell¹ /smel/ noun ★★

1 [C] the quality of something that you notice when you breathe in through your nose: *This paint has a very strong smell.* ♦ *the delicious smell of fresh bread* → AROMA

2 [U] the ability to notice or recognize smells: *Dogs have an excellent sense of smell.*

3 [C] an instance of smelling something: *Have a smell of this perfume.*

smell² /smel/ (past tense and past participle **smelled** or **smelt** /smelt/) verb ★

1 [linking verb] to have a particular smell: *That cake smells so good!* ♦ *The laboratory smelled strongly of chemicals.* ♦ *It smells like a bar in here.*

2 [I] to have an unpleasant smell: *It smells in here!* ♦ *His feet really smell.*

3 [T] to notice or recognize the smell of something: *Do you smell gas?*

4 [T] to experience the smell of something by putting your nose close to it: *Come and smell these roses.*

→ ROSE

smelly /ˈsmeli/ adj with an unpleasant smell

smelt a past tense and past participle of **smell²**

smile¹ /smaɪl/ verb [I] ★★★ to raise the corners of your mouth when you are happy or when you are being friendly: *James looked up and smiled at Karen.*

smile² /smaɪl/ noun [C] ★★★ an expression on your face in which you smile: *Tom had a huge smile on his face.* ♦ *a smile of satisfaction*

Words often used with smile

Adjectives often used with smile (noun)

■ **beaming, dazzling, faint, knowing, radiant, rueful, slight, wry** + SMILE: used about different types of smile

---

smirk /smɜːk/ verb [I] to smile in an

unpleasant way because something bad has happened to someone else —**smirk** noun [C]

smock /smɒk/ noun [C] a long loose shirt

smog /smɒg/ noun [U] polluted air that forms a cloud close to the ground

smoke¹ /sməʊk/ noun ★★

1 [U] a grey, black, or white cloud that is produced by something that is burning: *A column of black smoke slowly rose above the building.* ♦ *The air was thick with cigarette smoke.* ♦ *Exploding rockets sent up clouds of smoke.*

2 [C] informal a cigarette, or an act of smoking a cigarette: *I'm just going out for a smoke.*

PHRASE **go up in smoke** *informal* to be destroyed

smoke² /sməʊk/ verb ★★

1 [I/T] to suck smoke from a cigarette, pipe etc into your mouth and lungs: *Phil was reading the paper and smoking a cigarette.*

2 [I/T] to smoke cigarettes as a regular habit: *I didn't know you smoked!*

3 [I] to produce smoke: *By the time I got to the garage, the engine was smoking alarmingly.*

4 [T] to preserve and give flavour to food by hanging it in smoke

smoked /sməʊkt/ adj smoked food has a special flavour because it has been hung in smoke

smoker /ˈsməʊkə/ noun [C] someone who smokes cigarettes, a pipe etc ≠ NON-SMOKER

smokescreen /ˈsməʊkˌskriːn/ noun [C] something that you say or do as a way of hiding your real feelings, intentions, or activities

smoking /ˈsməʊkɪŋ/ noun [U] the activity of breathing smoke from cigarettes, pipes etc into your mouth and lungs

smoky /ˈsməʊki/ adj **1** with a lot of smoke in the air **2** tasting or smelling of smoke

smolder /ˈsməʊldə/ the American spelling of **smoulder**

smooth¹ /smuːð/ adj ★★

1 completely even with no rough areas or lumps ≠ ROUGH: *smooth skin*

2 moving in a way that is steady and well controlled: *With a smooth swing, he hit the ball.*

3 causing no difficulty, problems, or delays: *a smooth process* ♦ *We are changing systems, but we expect a smooth transition.*

4 showing disapproval relaxed and confident in a way that usually persuades people to do things: *Steven's a bit too smooth for my liking.* ♦ *a smooth operator* (=someone you cannot trust)

smooth² /smuːð/ verb [T] **1** to move your hand across the surface of something until it is flat and even: *Frances smoothed her skirt down over her knees.* **2** to carefully spread a substance over a surface: *Anne gently smoothed cream into the baby's skin.*

PHRASAL VERB ,**smooth sth 'over** to make a problem seem less serious

smoothie /ˈsmuːði/ noun [C] **1** showing disapproval an attractive, relaxed, and

S

confident man who is good at persuading people to do what he wants **2** a drink made from fruit and milk, cream, or ICE CREAM

smoothly /'smuːðli/ adv **1** without difficulty, problems, or delays **2** with a movement that is steady and well controlled

smother /'smʌðə/ verb [T]

1 cover sth	**4** not express sth
2 kill sb	**5** love too much
3 cover fire	

1 to cover something completely **2** to kill someone by covering their face until they stop breathing **3** to stop a fire burning by covering it **4** to try not to express a feeling **5** to express your love for someone too much

smoulder /'smʌuldə/ verb [I] **1** to burn slowly, producing smoke but no flames **2** to feel very strong emotions that you do not express in words

SMS /ˌes em 'es/ noun [U] short message service: a method of sending a written message using a mobile phone

smudge¹ /smʌdʒ/ noun [C] a small untidy mark made by a substance such as dirt or ink

smudge² /smʌdʒ/ verb [I/T] if you smudge something such as ink, or if it smudges, you make it spread in an untidy way by touching it

smug /smʌg/ adj *showing disapproval* too satisfied with your abilities or achievements —**smugly** adv, **smugness** noun [U]

smuggle /'smʌg(ə)l/ verb [T] to take someone or something secretly or illegally into or out of a place —**smuggler** noun [C], **smuggling** noun [U]

snack /snæk/ noun [C] a small amount of food that you eat between meals: *Coffee, tea, and snacks are available throughout the day.* —**snack** verb [I]

snag¹ /snæg/ noun [C] a problem or disadvantage

snag² /snæg/ verb [I/T] to damage something, especially clothing, with something that is sharp or rough

snail /sneɪl/ noun [C] a small animal that has a soft body, no legs, and a hard shell on its back

PHRASE at a snail's pace very slowly

'snail ˌmail noun [U] *informal* letters that are sent by post rather than by email

snake¹ /sneɪk/ noun [C] a long thin animal with no legs and a smooth skin —*picture* → C13

snake² /sneɪk/ verb [I] to move in a series of long curves: *The path snakes through the trees and up the hill.*

snap¹ /snæp/ verb

1 break with loud noise	**5** speak angrily
2 move sth with noise	**+** PHRASES
3 (try to) bite	**+** PHRASAL VERB
4 become angry/upset	

1 [I/T] to suddenly break something with a short loud noise, or to be broken in this

way: *When the rope snapped, Davis fell into the water.* ♦ *Ken snapped off the smaller branches.* **2** [I/T] to quickly move something, for example a light switch or something else that makes a short sound, or to be moved quickly in this way: *She quickly snapped her handbag shut.* ♦ *It's really simple to build – the bits just snap together.* **3** [I/T] if an animal such as a dog snaps at you, it bites you or tries to bite you: *A terrier was snapping at his heels.* **4** [I] to suddenly lose control and become extremely angry or upset: *She was bound to snap under all that pressure.* **5** [I/T] to speak to someone in a sudden angry way: *What do you want now? he snapped angrily.* ♦ *I'm sorry I snapped at you just now.*

PHRASES snap your fingers to make a short sound by pressing your middle finger against your thumb and moving them suddenly apart

snap out of it to make an effort to stop being unhappy or upset

PHRASAL VERB ˌsnap sth 'up 1 to buy something as soon as you see it: *By 10 o'clock most of the best bargains had been snapped up.* **2** to immediately take advantage of an opportunity

snap² /snæp/ noun **1** [singular] a short loud noise, made especially by something breaking or closing **2** [C] *British informal* a photograph that is taken without the use of professional equipment **3** [U] a card game in which players put down cards in piles and try to be the first to shout 'snap' when two cards are the same

PHRASE cold snap a short period of time when the weather is very cold

snap³ /snæp/ adj decided or arranged very quickly: *We mustn't be pushed into making a snap decision.*

snappy /'snæpi/ adj **1** tending to speak to people in an angry way **2** clever and using few words

snapshot /'snæpʃɒt/ noun [C] **1** a photograph that is taken without the use of professional equipment **2** a short explanation or description that tells you what a particular place or situation is like

snare¹ /sneə/ noun [C] a piece of equipment that is used for catching an animal

snare² /sneə/ verb [T] **1** to catch an animal using a snare **2** to trick someone into an unpleasant situation that they cannot escape from

snarl /snɑːl/ verb **1** [I/T] to speak in an unpleasant angry way **2** [I] if an animal snarls, it makes an angry sound in its throat and shows its teeth —**snarl** noun [C]

snatch¹ /snætʃ/ verb [T] **1** to quickly take something or someone away: *Her brother snatched the letter and tore it open.* **2** to take the opportunity to do something quickly: *They managed to snatch a few hours' sleep.* **3** to manage to get something that you almost did not get: *They snatched victory with a goal in the last minute.*

snatch² /snætʃ/ noun [C] a short piece of something that you hear: *a few snatches of conversation*

sneak¹ /sni:k/ (past tense and past participle **sneaked** /sni:kt/ or **snuck** /snʌk/) verb **1** [I] to move somewhere quietly and secretly so that no one can see you or hear you **2** [T] to take someone or something secretly or illegally

PHRASAL VERB ,sneak 'up to get very near to someone before they notice you

sneak² /sni:k/ noun [C] *informal showing disapproval* a person who tells someone in authority about something wrong that you have done

sneakers /'sni:kəz/ noun [plural] *American* TRAINERS

sneaking /'sni:kɪŋ/ adj a sneaking feeling is one that you are not sure about or do not want to have

sneaky /'sni:ki/ adj doing or saying things secretly, often in a dishonest or unfair way

sneer /snɪə/ verb [I/T] to smile or speak in an unpleasant way that shows that you do not respect someone or something —**sneer** noun [C]

sneeze /sni:z/ verb [I] to loudly blow air out of your nose in a sudden uncontrolled way —**sneeze** noun [C]

snide /snaɪd/ adj deliberately unkind in an indirect way

sniff /snɪf/ verb **1** [I] to breathe in noisily through your nose, for example because you have been crying: *Amanda sniffed and wiped her nose.* **2** [T] to breathe in through your nose in order to smell something: *He took off the lid and sniffed the contents of the jar.* —**sniff** noun [C]

sniffle /'snɪf(ə)l/ verb [I] to keep sniffing because you are crying or because you have a cold

snigger /'snɪgə/ verb [I] *British* to laugh quietly at something that is rude or at something that is unpleasant that has happened to someone —**snigger** noun [C]

snip /snɪp/ verb [T] to cut something in a short quick movement using scissors —**snip** noun [C]

sniper /'snaɪpə/ noun [C] someone who shoots at people from a hidden place —**snipe** verb [I]

snippet /'snɪpɪt/ noun [C] a small piece of information or news

snivel /'snɪv(ə)l/ verb [I] to cry or complain in a way that seems weak or annoying

snob /snɒb/ noun [C] *showing disapproval* someone who thinks that they are better than other people, usually because of their social class

snobbery /'snɒbəri/ noun [U] the attitudes or behaviour of someone who thinks that they are better than other people

snobbish /'snɒbɪʃ/ or **snobby** /'snɒbi/ adj behaving in a way that shows that you think you are better than other people

snog /snɒg/ verb [I/T] *British informal* if two people snog, or if one person snogs another,

they kiss each other for a period of time —**snog** noun [C]

snooker /'snu:kə/ noun [U] a game that you play on a large table that is covered with green cloth. Players try to hit coloured balls into holes with a long stick.

snoop /snu:p/ verb [I] to secretly try to get information that someone would not want you to have

snooze /snu:z/ verb [I] *informal* to sleep for a short period of time, especially during the day —**snooze** noun [C]

snore /snɔ:/ verb [I] to breathe noisily while you sleep —**snore** noun [C]

snorkel /'snɔ:k(ə)l/ noun [C] a piece of equipment with a tube that fits in your mouth so that you can breathe when you are looking into the water while swimming

snorkelling /'snɔ:k(ə)lɪŋ/ noun [U] the activity of swimming using a snorkel

snort /snɔ:t/ verb [I] to make a sudden loud noise through your nose, for example because you are angry or laughing —**snort** noun [C]

snot /snɒt/ noun [U] *impolite* the thick wet substance that is produced in your nose

snotty /'snɒti/ adj **1** *impolite* covered in snot **2** *informal* a snotty person thinks that they are better or more important than other people

snout /snaʊt/ noun [C] the long nose of a pig or a similar animal

snow¹ /snəʊ/ noun ★★

1 [U] small soft white pieces of ice that fall from the sky and cover the ground: *The path was hidden under a blanket of snow.* ♦ *Three inches of snow fell overnight.*
2 snows [plural] the snow that falls over a period of time: *The first snows of winter are here.*

snow² /snəʊ/ verb [I] if it snows, snow falls from the sky

PHRASES **snowed in** unable to leave a place because a lot of snow has fallen there
snowed under if you are snowed under, you have too much work to deal with

snowball¹ /'snəʊ,bɔ:l/ noun [C] a ball of snow that you can throw

snowball² /'snəʊ,bɔ:l/ verb [I] to develop quickly and become very big or serious

snowboarding /'snəʊ,bɔ:dɪŋ/ noun [U] a sport in which you stand with both feet on a large curved board and slide down a hill that is covered in snow —**snowboard** noun [C]

snowdrift /'snəʊ,drɪft/ noun [C] a deep pile of snow that is made by the wind

snowdrop /'snəʊ,drɒp/ noun [C] a type of small white flower that appears in early spring

snowfall /'snəʊ,fɔ:l/ noun [C/U] the amount of snow that falls during a particular period

snowflake /'snəʊ,fleɪk/ noun [C] a single piece of snow that falls from the sky

snowman /'snəʊmæn/ noun [C] a model of a person that children make using snow

snowplough /'snəʊ,plaʊ/ noun [C] a large

S

vehicle that pushes snow off the road

snowplow /ˈsnəʊˌplaʊ/ the American spelling of **snowplough**

snowstorm /ˈsnəʊˌstɔːm/ noun [C] a storm with a lot of snow and strong winds

snowy /ˈsnəʊi/ adj with a lot of snow

snub /snʌb/ verb [T] to insult someone by ignoring them or being rude to them —**snub** noun [C]

snuck a past tense and past participle of **sneak**

snuff¹ /snʌf/ noun [U] tobacco in the form of a powder that you breathe in through your nose

snuff² /snʌf/ PHRASAL VERB ˌsnuff sth ˈout to make a flame stop burning by squeezing it with your fingers or covering it

snug /snʌg/ adj **1** warm and comfortable =COSY **2** fitting closely —**snugly** adv

snuggle /ˈsnʌg(ə)l/ verb [I/T] to put yourself into a warm, comfortable, and safe position

so /səʊ/ grammar word ★★★

So can be:
- an **adverb**: *Why are you so angry this morning?* ♦ *'I'm hungry.' 'So am I.'*
- a **conjunction**: *There weren't enough beds, so I had to sleep on the floor.*
- used in the conjunction phrase **so that**: *He was standing in the shadow so that I could not see his face clearly.*

---

1 **for emphasis** used for emphasizing a quality, feeling, or amount: *I'm so glad you could come.* ♦ *The food's wonderful, but it's so expensive!* ♦ *The children couldn't sleep, they were so excited.* ♦ *Like so many great artists, he died young.* ♦ *The road surface became so hot that it melted.*

2 **used instead of repeating sth** used for referring back to what has just been said instead of repeating it: *You're in love with Rita, aren't you? I thought so.* ♦ *If you wanted to leave early, you should have said so.* ♦ *Does the President intend to go to Moscow? And if so, when?*

3 **also** used for saying that something that was just said is also true about another person or thing: *Heidi is planning to come, and so is Sylvia.* ♦ *My parents send their love, and so does Rachel.* ♦ *'I'd like to know what's happening out there.' 'So would I.'* ♦ *If I learned how to drive a car, so can you.*

4 **because of what has just been mentioned** used for saying that something happens because of what you have just mentioned: *A tree had fallen across the road, so they had to turn round and go back.*

5 **for stating a purpose** used for saying what the purpose of an action is: +**(that)** *He lowered his voice so that no one would hear.*

6 **for starting a new subject** *spoken* used for starting a new subject or starting to ask a question: *So, let's get down to business.* ♦ *So, what do you suggest we do next?*

7 **when showing sth** *spoken* used when showing someone what size something is or how something should be done: *She was about so tall.* ♦ *Tie the two ends together, like so.*

8 **for saying that sth is limited** used for saying that a number or amount is limited: *We have only so much time before the exams start.* ♦ *There are only so many police officers available.*

PHRASES **and so on/forth** used instead of mentioning more of a similar type of thing that has already been mentioned: *Employees were always complaining about their wages, their working conditions, and so forth.*

not so...(as) used for saying that one person or thing has less of a particular quality than another: *The Rosario family managed to flee, but others were not so lucky.* ♦ *The idea is not so silly as it sounds.*

or so used for showing that a number or amount is not exact: *The job won't take long – about twenty minutes or so.*

so (what)? *informal* used for saying in a slightly rude way that what someone has said is not important: *'Someone might see us.' 'So what? We're not doing anything illegal.'*

→ LONG²

soak /səʊk/ verb [I/T] **1** to put something into a liquid and leave it there for a period of time: *Leave the beans to soak overnight.* **2** to make something very wet, or to become very wet: *The rain poured in, soaking the cardboard boxes.*

PHRASAL VERB ˌsoak sth ˈup if a dry or soft substance soaks up a liquid, the liquid goes into it

soaked /səʊkt/ adj extremely wet

soaking /ˈsəʊkɪŋ/ adj extremely wet

so-and-so noun *informal* **1** [U] used for referring to someone whose name you do not know **2** [C] an unpleasant person

soap /səʊp/ noun ★★

1 [C/U] a substance that you use with water in order to wash your body or an object: *a bar of soap* ♦ *perfumed soaps*

2 [C] *informal* a SOAP OPERA

ˈsoap ˌopera noun [C] a television or radio series about the imaginary lives of a group of people

ˈsoap ˌpowder noun [C/U] soap in the form of a powder that you use for washing clothes

soapy /ˈsəʊpi/ adj covered in soap, or containing soap

soar /sɔː/ verb [I] **1** to quickly increase to a high level: *Unemployment has soared.* **2** to rise or fly high in the sky —**soaring** adj

sob /sɒb/ verb [I/T] to cry noisily while taking short breaths —**sob** noun [C]

sober¹ /ˈsəʊbə/ adj **1** not drunk **2** with a serious attitude **3** plain and not brightly coloured —**soberly** adv

sober² /ˈsəʊbə/ PHRASAL VERB ˌsober ˈup to become sober after being drunk

sobering /ˈsəʊbərɪŋ/ adj making you think about things in a serious way

so-called /ˈsəʊ ˌkɔːld/ adj **1** used for showing that you think a word used for describing something is not suitable: *His so-called friends betrayed him.* **2** used for saying that a particular word is usually used for referring to something: *They've found the flight recorder, the so-called black box.*

soccer /ˈsɒkə/ noun [U] the game of FOOTBALL

sociable /ˈsəʊʃəb(ə)l/ adj a sociable person is friendly and enjoys being with other people =OUTGOING ≠ UNSOCIABLE

social /ˈsəʊʃ(ə)l/ adj ★★★

1 about society	4 about behaviour
2 about position	5 about animals
3 about activities	

1 relating to society and to people's lives in general: *a period of enormous political and social change* ♦ *the social conditions of rural workers* ♦ *social problems such as unemployment*

2 relating to the position that someone has in society in relation to other people: *someone's social background* ♦ *The evidence shows a relationship between crime and social class.*

3 relating to activities that involve being with other people, especially activities that you do for pleasure: *a social activity/engagement* ♦ *The worst thing about working at home is the lack of social contact.* ♦ *This is not a social call. I'm afraid I have some bad news.*

4 relating to rules about behaviour with other people: *We need someone with excellent social skills.*

5 used for describing animals that live in groups rather than alone
—**socially** adv

socialism /ˈsəʊʃəlɪz(ə)m/ noun [U] a political system that aims to create a society in which everyone has equal opportunities and in which the most important industries are owned or controlled by the whole community —**socialist** adj, noun [C]

socialize /ˈsəʊʃəlaɪz/ verb [I] to spend time with other people socially

social ˈscience noun [C/U] the study of the way that people live in society, or one of the separate subjects that deal with the way that societies are organized —**social ˈscientist** noun [C]

social seˈcurity noun [U] **1** the system by which the government regularly pays money to people who do not have a job, or are too ill or too old to work **2** money that you receive from social security

social ˈservices noun [plural] the services that are provided by a government or local council for people with social problems

ˈsocial ˌworker noun [C] someone who is trained to give help and advice to people who have severe social problems —**ˈsocial ˌwork** noun [U]

society /səˈsaɪəti/ noun ★★★

1 [U] people in general living together in organized communities, with laws and traditions controlling the way that they behave towards each other: *Society has to be prepared to support its elderly people.* ♦ *The scheme aims to support prisoners who have been released into society.*

2 [C/U] a particular community or type of community, or the people who live in it: *The protesters were drawn from a broad cross section of society.* ♦ *Never forget that we live in a multicultural society.* ♦ *The novels reflect the values of Victorian society.*

3 [U] the group of people in a country who are rich and fashionable or from a high social class: *a big society wedding* ♦ *She moved in* **high society** *and had many aristocratic friends.*

4 [C] an organization or club for people who have a particular interest or who take part in a particular activity: *She joined the local history society and made some new friends.*
→ BUILDING SOCIETY

socioeconomic /ˌsəʊsiəʊ̩ekəˈnɒmɪk/ adj involving a combination of social and economic elements

sociology /ˌsəʊʃiˈɒlədʒi/ noun [U] the study of society, the way that it is organized, and the way that people behave in relation to each other —**sociological** /ˌsəʊʃiəˈlɒdʒɪk(ə)l/ adj, **sociologist** noun [C]

sock /sɒk/ noun [C] a soft piece of clothing that you wear on your foot inside your shoe: *a pair of yellow socks* —*picture* → C5 → PULL¹

socket /ˈsɒkɪt/ noun [C] **1** a place on a wall or machine with holes that you use for connecting a piece of electrical equipment **2** a curved space that something fits into

soda /ˈsəʊdə/ or **ˈsoda ˌwater** noun [C/U] water with gas in it that you add to an alcoholic drink

sodden /ˈsɒd(ə)n/ adj completely wet =SOAKING

sodium /ˈsəʊdiəm/ noun [U] a chemical element that is a silver-white metal and that is found in salt

sofa /ˈsəʊfə/ noun [C] a large soft comfortable seat with arms and a back that two or three people can sit on —*picture* → CHAIR

soft /sɒft/ adj ★★★

1 not hard/firm	5 not strict enough
2 not rough/stiff	6 kind/sympathetic
3 quiet/nice	7 about water
4 pale/gentle	+ PHRASE

1 a soft substance is easy to press or shape and is not hard or firm: *soft cheese* ♦ *The soil is fairly soft after the rain.*

2 a soft material or surface is nice to touch and not rough or stiff: *I want to get a nice soft carpet for the bedroom.* ♦ *Her skin felt soft to his touch.*

3 a soft sound is quiet and nice to listen to: *The engine noise was no more than a soft hum.*

4 a soft light or colour is pale, gentle, and nice to look at: *Her bedroom was decorated in soft shades of pink and blue.*

5 not strict enough with other people and allowing them to do things they should not do: *You're too soft – I wouldn't let them behave like that.* ♦ *They accused the minister of being soft on crime.*

S

6 kind and sympathetic: *He must have a soft heart beneath that stern exterior.*

7 soft water does not contain many MINERALS (=natural substances) and is easy to use with soap

PHRASE **have a soft spot for** to like someone or something a lot

—**softly** adv

soft copy noun [C/U] *computing* information that is in electronic form, not printed on paper

soft drink noun [C/U] a cold drink that does not contain any alcohol

soft drug noun [C] a type of illegal drug that is less harmful than other illegal drugs

soften /ˈsɒf(ə)n/ verb **1** [I/T] to become softer, or to make something become softer: *Simmer gently until the apple has softened.* **2** [I/T] to become kinder and less severe, or to make someone or something do this: *When Jack spoke to the children his voice softened.* **3** [T] to make something look nicer by making its colour or shape less strong: *The warm light softened her features.*

PHRASAL VERB **soften sb up** to make someone more likely to do what you want by being nice to them: *His strategy was to soften them up with compliments.*

soft-spoken adj speaking or said in a quiet gentle voice

soft touch noun [singular] *informal* someone who is easily persuaded to do something or to give something

software /ˈsɒf(t)ˌweə/ noun [U] *computing* ★★★ the programs used by computers for doing particular jobs: *word-processing software ♦ You log onto our website, then download and install the software. ♦ software companies/developers* → HARDWARE

soggy /ˈsɒgi/ adj wet and soft

soil¹ /sɔɪl/ noun [C/U] ★★★ the substance on the surface of the Earth in which plants grow: *She scraped away some soil and grasped the top of the root. ♦ The dry rocky soil is suitable for planting vines.*

PHRASE **on British/US/Japanese etc soil** in the UK, the US, Japan etc: *the presence of foreign troops on Canadian soil*

soil² /sɔɪl/ verb [T] *formal* to make something dirty —**soiled** /sɔɪld/ adj

solace /ˈsɒləs/ noun [singular/U] something that makes you feel better when you are sad or upset

solar /ˈsəʊlə/ adj relating to the Sun, or coming from the Sun

solar energy noun [U] energy that uses the power of the Sun's light and heat

solar panel noun [C] a piece of equipment that uses energy from the Sun in order to create power

solar system, the noun [singular] the Sun and the group of planets that move around it

sold the past tense and past participle of **sell¹**

soldier /ˈsəʊldʒə/ noun [C] ★★ someone who is a member of an army

sold out adj if an event is sold out, all the tickets for it have been sold

sole¹ /səʊl/ adj the sole person or thing is the only one of a particular type=ONLY: *She is the sole survivor of the crash. ♦ His sole purpose in going there was to see Kelly.*

sole² /səʊl/ noun **1** [C] the flat bottom part of your foot —*picture* → C14 **2** [C] the bottom part of your shoe that goes under your foot **3** [C/U] a flat fish that lives in the sea, or this fish eaten as food

solely /ˈsəʊlli/ adv involving nothing except the person or thing mentioned

solemn /ˈsɒləm/ adj involving serious behaviour, attitudes, or intentions —**solemnity** /səˈlemnəti/ noun [U], **solemnly** adv

solicit /səˈlɪsɪt/ verb **1** [T] *formal* to ask people for something such as money or support **2** [I/T] to offer to have sex with someone in exchange for money

solicitor /səˈlɪsɪtə/ noun [C] in the UK, a lawyer who gives legal advice, writes legal contracts, and represents people in the lower courts of law

solid¹ /ˈsɒlɪd/ adj ★★

1 not liquid/gas	**5** with no pauses
2 with no holes	**6** continuous
3 strong	**7** of one colour
4 with no bad parts	

1 a solid substance is firm and hard and is not a liquid or a gas: *The lake was frozen solid.*

2 a solid object or shape does not have any holes or empty space inside it: *a solid block of ice* → HOLLOW

3 strong enough not to break or become damaged easily: *the solid stone walls of the church ♦ The containers have to be solid enough to withstand pressure.*

4 completely good, with no mistakes or bad parts: *Would the evidence be solid enough to convince a jury? ♦ She gave another solid performance.*

5 with no pauses or interruptions: *It rained for a solid week. ♦ I can't believe I slept for twelve hours solid.*

6 a solid line is continuous, with no breaks in it: *a solid line of traffic*

7 consisting of one substance or one colour only: *a solid oak bookcase ♦ solid silver cutlery ♦ a solid blue screen* —**solidity** /səˈlɪdəti/ noun [U], **solidly** adv

solid² /ˈsɒlɪd/ noun **1** [C] *technical* a substance that is not a liquid or a gas **2** [C] a shape that is not flat but that can be measured in height, depth, and width **3 solids** [plural] food that is not liquid

solidarity /ˌsɒlɪˈdærəti/ noun [U] the support that people in a group give each other because they have the same opinions or aims

solidify /səˈlɪdɪˌfaɪ/ verb [I/T] to become solid, or to make something become solid

solitary /ˈsɒlɪt(ə)ri/ adj **1** tending to spend a lot of time alone **2** done or experienced by someone who is alone **3** in a place or situation where there are no other people or things of the same type

solitary con'finement noun [U] a punishment in which a prisoner is kept alone

solitude /'sɒlətjuːd/ noun [U] the state of being completely alone

solo[1] /'səʊləʊ/ noun [C] a piece of music that is performed by one person

solo[2] /'səʊləʊ/ adj, adv **1** done by one person alone **2** playing or singing alone

soloist /'səʊləʊɪst/ noun [C] someone who performs a musical solo

soluble /'sɒljʊb(ə)l/ adj able to mix with a liquid and become part of the liquid ≠ INSOLUBLE

solution /sə'luːʃ(ə)n/ noun [C] ★★
1 a way to solve a problem or deal with a bad situation: *Putting children in prison is not the solution.* ♦ *The committee has failed to come up with any **solutions for** the crisis.* ♦ *UN leaders are working hard to find a peaceful **solution to** the conflict.* ♦ *Solar energy **offers a** low cost **solution** to our fuel problems.*
2 the answer to a question in a game or a problem in mathematics
3 a liquid that is formed by mixing a liquid with another substance

> **Words often used with solution**
>
> *Adjectives often used with solution (sense 1)*
> ■ **ideal, peaceful, possible, practical, satisfactory, simple, workable** + SOLUTION: used about different types of solution

solve /sɒlv/ verb [T] ★★
1 to find a solution to something that is causing difficulties: *solve a crisis/dispute/conflict* ♦ *We can help you **solve** your financial **problems**.*
2 to find the reason or explanation for something: *solve a mystery/puzzle/riddle* ♦ *solve a case/crime/murder* (=find out who committed a crime)
3 to find the answer to a question in a game or a problem in mathematics: *solve an equation*

solvent[1] /'sɒlv(ə)nt/ noun [C] a liquid that you add to a substance in order to change it into a liquid

solvent[2] /'sɒlv(ə)nt/ adj able to pay money that you owe ≠ INSOLVENT

somber /'sɒmbə/ the American spelling of **sombre**

sombre /'sɒmbə/ adj **1** serious, or sad **2** dark in colour

some /weak səm, strong sʌm/ grammar word ★★★

> **Some can be:**
> ■ a **determiner**: *I brought her some flowers.* ♦ *She married some guy she met on the boat.*
> ■ a **pronoun**: *The cake's wonderful. Won't you have some?* ♦ *Some of the apples were rotten.*
> ■ an **adverb**: *The car stopped some twenty-five yards from where we were standing.*

1 an amount or number used for referring to an amount or number, without saying how much or how many: *Let me give you some advice.* ♦ *Tomatoes were only 80 pence*

a kilo, so I bought some. ♦ *I met some really interesting people at the party.* ♦ *I just wanted **some more** information about language courses.*

> ■ In negative sentences and questions **any** is usually used: *There aren't any lessons today.* ♦ *Have you any money?*
> ■ In positive statements and questions expecting the answer 'yes' **some** is usually used: *I have some news for you.* ♦ *Would you like some soup?*

2 part of an amount or number used for showing that you are only referring to part of an amount, group, or number and not all of it: *Some kids are more adventurous than others.* ♦ *Some people like cats and some don't.* ♦ *I've forgotten some of the details.*
3 a fairly large amount or number used for emphasizing that you are talking about a fairly large amount or number: *It took some courage to speak out against her employer.* ♦ *We've been waiting here **for some time** already.*
4 used for referring to a person or thing without being specific used for referring to a person or thing without saying exactly which one: *There must have been some mistake.* ♦ *Some fool drove into the back of my car.*
5 used before a number that is not exact used for showing that you are guessing a number: *York is a historic city of some 110,000 people.*

somebody /'sʌmbədi/ pronoun ★★★
someone: *Somebody phoned while you were out.* ♦ *When things go wrong, you always say it's somebody else's fault.*

someday /'sʌmˌdeɪ/ adv at some time in the future even though you do not know when: *Someday I'll meet the right woman and we'll get married.*

somehow /'sʌmhaʊ/ adv ★★
1 in some way, or by some method, that you do not know or understand exactly: *Somehow he managed to pass all his final exams.*
2 for some reason that you do not know or cannot explain: *Somehow, it was easier to deal with him when he was alone.*

someone /'sʌmwʌn/ pronoun ★★★ used for referring to a person when you do not know or do not say who the person is: *I can't find my calculator – someone must have taken it.* ♦ *I've invited someone special that I want you to meet.* ♦ *His wife told him she was in love with someone else.*

someplace /'sʌmpleɪs/ adv American somewhere

somersault /'sʌməsɔːlt/ noun [C] a movement in which you form your body into a ball and roll forwards or BACKWARDS on the ground —**somersault** verb [I]

something /'sʌmθɪŋ/ pronoun ★★★
1 used for referring to a thing, idea, fact etc when you do not know or do not say exactly what it is: *I need to buy something for Ted's birthday.* ♦ *Would you like something to drink?* ♦ *Be quiet – I have something*

S

important to tell you. ♦ *Jake looks pale – is there something wrong with him?* ♦ *I'd love to quit my job and do something else with my life.* ♦ *Why doesn't the government do something about fuel prices?* ♦ *We should call or something and make sure she's all right.* ♦ *He's always complaining about something or other.*

2 used for giving a description or amount that is not exact: *The house looks something like a castle.* ♦ *A small house in the area costs something around £80,000.*

PHRASES **be/have something to do with sth** used for saying that something is related to something else: *I can't always open my emails – it has something to do with the type of attachment they come with.*

be really/quite something *spoken* to be very impressive: *What Noreen's done with the business is quite something.*

be something of a 1 used for showing that you are not being very definite in a description: *Woods's performance in the tournament was something of a disappointment.* **2** used for emphasizing that someone is fairly good at something: *My grandmother was something of a poet.*

that's something *spoken* used for saying that one fact is good, although the general situation is not good: *'I've only enough money for basic necessities.' 'Well, that's something.'*

there is something about used for saying that someone or something has a particular quality but that you are not certain what it is: *There was something about his face that reminded me of my uncle.*
→ UP¹

sometime /ˈsʌmtaɪm/ adv at a time that you do not know exactly or have not yet decided: *I'd love to visit Norway sometime.* ♦ *Ewan returned from London sometime last week.*

S

sometimes /ˈsʌmtaɪmz/ adv ★★★ on some occasions, but not always: *Sometimes it's so cold I don't even want to leave the house.* ♦ *My dad cooks dinner sometimes, but usually my mum does it.*

somewhat /ˈsʌmwɒt/ adv to some degree, but not to a large degree: *The situation has improved somewhat during the past year.* ♦ *His behaviour has been somewhat unreasonable.*

somewhere /ˈsʌmweə/ adv ★★★

1 used for referring to a place when you do not know or do not say exactly where: *I think I've seen you before somewhere.* ♦ *I've lost my watch, but it must be somewhere in the house.* ♦ *Let's go somewhere nice for dinner.* ♦ *If we don't provide a good service, customers will go somewhere else.*

2 used when giving an amount that is not exact: *You will earn somewhere between £20,000 and £25,000.* ♦ *I'd say there were somewhere around 50 people at the meeting.*

PHRASE **be getting somewhere** to be making some progress: *I think at last we're getting somewhere.*

son /sʌn/ noun [C] ★★★ your male child: *My younger son is a doctor.* ♦ *He was the son of an eminent scientist.* —picture → FAMILY TREE

sonata /səˈnɑːtə/ noun [C] a piece of classical music for the piano, or for one instrument and a piano

song /sɒŋ/ noun ★★★

1 [C] a piece of music with words that you sing: *She knew the words to every song that came on the radio.* ♦ *a popular/patriotic/folk song* ♦ *He sang a beautiful love song.*

2 [U] the art or activity of singing: *festivals of traditional music and song*

3 [C/U] the musical sound that a bird makes

songwriter /ˈsɒŋˌraɪtə/ noun [C] someone who writes songs

sonic /ˈsɒnɪk/ adj *technical* relating to sound or sound waves

son-in-law noun [C] the husband of your daughter —picture → FAMILY TREE

sonnet /ˈsɒnɪt/ noun [C] a type of poem with 14 lines

soon /suːn/ adv ★★★

1 within a short time: *If we don't leave soon, we're going to miss our bus.* ♦ *Mum phoned to say she'd be home soon.* ♦ *If he doesn't show up pretty soon, I'm leaving.* ♦ *Danny showed up soon after you left.*

2 quickly: *How soon can this package be delivered to Brussels?* ♦ *Helen wants you to call her back as soon as possible.*

PHRASES **as soon as** immediately after something: *I'll call you as soon as I get home from work.*

I would just as soon do sth *spoken* used for saying what you would prefer to do: *I'd just as soon stay at home.*

sooner /ˈsuːnə/ adv earlier than expected: *The announcement came sooner than we expected.* ♦ *The investigation may be completed sooner than previously thought.*

PHRASES **I would sooner do sth** *spoken* used for saying what you would prefer to do: *I'd sooner marry no one than marry a fool like him.*

no sooner...than used for saying that something happens immediately after something else: *No sooner had I walked in the door than the phone rang.*

the sooner the better as soon as possible: *You'll have to face her, and the sooner the better.*

sooner or later definitely at some later time, although you do not know exactly when: *The whole thing was going to go wrong sooner or later.*

the sooner...the sooner... used for saying that you want something to happen soon so that something else can also happen: *The sooner you do your homework, the sooner you can go out.*

soot /sʊt/ noun [U] a dirty black powder that is produced when you burn something such as coal —**sooty** adj

soothe /suːð/ verb [T] **1** to make someone more calm when they are feeling worried or upset **2** to make something less sore or painful —**soothing** adj, **soothingly** adv

sophisticated /səˈfɪstɪˌkeɪtɪd/ adj **1** knowing and understanding a lot about a subject: *Consumers are getting more sophisticated.* **2** knowing a lot about things such as culture, fashion, and the modern world ≠ UNSOPHISTICATED: *sophisticated dinnertable conversation* **3** complicated and advanced in design ≠ UNSOPHISTICATED: *highly sophisticated electronic equipment* —**sophistication** /səˌfɪstɪˈkeɪʃ(ə)n/ noun [U]

sopping /ˈsɒpɪŋ/ or **sopping 'wet** adj *informal* completely wet=SOAKING

soprano /səˈprɑːnəʊ/ noun [C] a girl, woman, or boy with the highest type of voice for singing

sorcery /ˈsɔːsəri/ noun [U] magic that is done with the help of evil spirits

sordid /ˈsɔːdɪd/ adj immoral, dishonest, or unpleasant

sore[1] /sɔː/ adj painful and uncomfortable, usually as a result of an injury, infection, or too much exercise: *I always feel stiff and sore after gardening.* ♦ *a sore throat*
PHRASES **a sore point/spot/subject** something that makes you upset, angry, or embarrassed when someone mentions it
stick/stand out like a sore thumb to be very noticeable because of being different

sore[2] /sɔː/ noun [C] a small painful area of skin that is injured or infected

sorely /ˈsɔːli/ adv very much

sorrow /ˈsɒrəʊ/ noun **1** [U] great sadness **2** [C] an event or problem that makes someone feel very sad —**sorrowful** adj

sorry /ˈsɒri/ adj ★★★
1 ashamed, embarrassed, or unhappy about something that you have done: *Tell your sister you're sorry!* ♦ *He wasn't sorry for hitting the other boy.* ♦ **+(that)** *I'm sorry I behaved in such a childish way.*
2 feeling sadness or sympathy for someone because something bad has happened to them: *I am sorry to hear that your father died.* ♦ *I'm sorry about your losing your job.*
3 disappointed about a situation, and wishing you could change it: **+(that)** *I'm sorry you have decided to leave the company.*
PHRASES **feel sorry for sb** to feel sympathy for someone because they are in a difficult or unpleasant situation: *I feel sorry for the guys who have to work night shifts.*
feel sorry for yourself to feel sad about your life rather than trying to do things that could make you feel better: *Instead of sitting around feeling sorry for yourself, go out and socialize.*

sorry or **I'm sorry** *spoken* **1** used for telling someone that you are ashamed or unhappy about something that you have done that has hurt or upset them: *I'm sorry – I shouldn't have blamed you.* ♦ *Sorry, I didn't mean to step on your foot.* **2** used in a social situation as a way of asking someone to forgive you for doing something that is rude or embarrassing: *Sorry, I should have*

phoned to let you know I'd be late. ♦ *I'm sorry about the misunderstanding.* **3** used for politely interrupting someone, especially to ask them a question: *Sorry, do you know what time it is?* **4** used for politely asking someone to repeat something that they have said: *I'm sorry, what was your name again?* **5** used for interrupting yourself in order to correct a mistake that you have made while speaking: *You need to catch the number 3, sorry, the number 23 bus to Market Street.*

sort[1] /sɔːt/ noun [C] ★★★ a group or type of people or things with the same qualities or features=KIND, TYPE: *What sort are you looking for?* ♦ *Is this a joke of some sort?* ♦ *Mistakes of this sort happen every day.* ♦ *He was asking us all sorts of questions about you.* ♦ *In that sort of situation Tom tends to panic.*
PHRASES **of sorts** of a type that is not exactly the same as the actual thing, or not as good as the actual thing: *She's an artist of sorts.*
sort of *spoken* **1** slightly, or in some ways: *'Aren't you hungry?' 'Sort of. I'm mostly just tired.'* **2** similar, but not exactly the same: *It's sort of a shiny bluish grey colour.*

sort[2] /sɔːt/ verb [T] ★★
1 to arrange things in groups or in a particular order: **sort sth by sth** *Once the data is collected, the computer will sort it by date.* ♦ **sort sth into sth** *Sort the letters into three piles.*
2 *British informal* to solve a problem or deal with someone or something: *Don't worry about the bill. I'll sort it.* ♦ *Did you get the tickets sorted?*
PHRASAL VERBS **sort sth 'out 1** to get rid of things that you do not need and arrange things that you do need tidily: *I need to sort out the mess on my desk.* **2** to find an answer to a problem or mystery: **+how/what/why etc** *Investigators are still trying to sort out why the accident happened.* **3** to deal with a difficult situation successfully: *This matter could be sorted out if they would just sit down and talk.*
'sort through sth to look at a lot of things in order to find something. *Police are now sorting through boxes of documents trying to find evidence.*

'so-so adj, adv *informal* not good enough to be described as good

soufflé /ˈsuːfleɪ/ noun [C/U] a food that you make with eggs and bake into a high round shape

sought the past tense and past participle of seek

sought-after /ˈsɔːt ˌɑːftə/ adj wanted by many people but not easy to get

soul /səʊl/ noun ★
1 [C] the part of a person that is capable of thinking and feeling: *Deep in your heart and soul you must know that this is wrong.*
2 [C] the spiritual part of a person that most religions believe continues to exist after their body dies

S

3 [C] a person: *I promise I won't tell a soul.*
♦ *There wasn't a soul to be seen.*
4 soul or **soul music** [U] a type of African American music in which the voice of the singer and the words of the songs express deep emotions

soulful /'səʊlf(ə)l/ adj expressing deep emotions, especially sadness

soulless /'səʊlləs/ adj not at all interesting or attractive

soul-searching /'səʊl ,sɜːtʃɪŋ/ noun [U] careful thought about your beliefs or actions because you want to behave in a moral way

sound¹ /saʊnd/ noun ★★★
1 [C] something that you can hear: *Laura didn't make a sound as she left the room.* ♦ *the sound of voices/laughter/footsteps*
2 [U] the loudness of a radio, television etc =VOLUME: *Turn the sound up a bit – I can't hear.*

PHRASES **by the sound of it** used for saying that you are basing your ideas on what you have heard or read: *He's pretty ill by the sound of it.*
like the sound of sth to be pleased by something that you have heard or read: *A holiday in Greece? I like the sound of that!*

Types of **sound**

- **bang** a sound like an explosion
- **clank** a sound like two heavy pieces of metal knocking together
- **crash** a sound like a large object falling to the ground and breaking
- **creak** a sound like the sound that is made by an old door when you push it open slowly
- **rattle** a sound like a loose object hitting another object several times
- **squeak** a sound like the noise that a mouse makes
- **thud** a sound like something heavy falling to the ground

S

sound² /saʊnd/ verb ★★★
1 [linking verb] to seem good, bad, interesting, exciting etc based on what you have heard, read, or know: *It sounds as if he's never home.* ♦ *You make it sound as though he is the most boring man in the world.* ♦ *Malta sounds like a great place for a relaxing holiday.*
2 [linking verb] to show a particular emotion or quality in your voice: *He sounded a bit annoyed.* ♦ *It sounds as if you're getting a cold.*
3 [I/T] to produce a sound, or to make something produce a sound: *The sirens sounded, warning of a tornado.* ♦ *Trains are required to sound their whistles as they approach a crossing.*
4 [T] to express a particular attitude or opinion: *Officials sounded a hopeful note about building the new school.* ♦ *The aim of the scheme is to sound a warning to teenagers about the dangers of smoking.*
PHRASE **sounds good/great etc** *spoken* used for telling someone that their idea or suggestion seems like a good one: *'How about dinner and a film tonight?' 'Sounds great.'*

PHRASAL VERB **sound sb 'out** to try to find out someone's opinions by talking to them: *Candidates will be sounding out voters during the months before the election.*

sound³ /saʊnd/ adj

1 effective/reliable	4 in good condition
2 thorough	5 about sleep
3 healthy	

1 involving the use of good judgment, and therefore likely to be effective or reliable ≠ UNSOUND: *Administrators should make sure the programmes are legally sound.* ♦ *He will be able to offer you sound advice and guidance.* **2** thorough: *a sound understanding of basic teaching skills* **3** healthy: *a sound heart* **4** safe, or in good condition: *Investigators found the plane to be structurally sound.* **5** a sound sleep is one that is difficult to wake you from

Words often used with **sound**

Nouns often used with sound (adj, sense 1)
- SOUND + **advice, approach, decision, judgment, principle**: used about ways of thinking or behaving that are sensible and likely to be effective

sound⁴ /saʊnd/ adv **sound asleep** sleeping very well

'sound ,bite noun [C] a short comment by a politician or other famous person that gets people's attention

'sound ,card noun [C] *computing* a part inside a computer that changes information into sounds that you can hear

'sound ef,fects noun [plural] the special recorded sounds in a film, television programme, or radio show

soundly /'saʊn(d)li/ adv **1** if you sleep soundly, you sleep well and it is difficult to wake you **2** thoroughly: *soundly beaten/defeated/rejected*

soundtrack /'saʊn(d)ˌtræk/ noun [C] the music that is played during a film or television programme, or a CD of this music

soup /suːp/ noun [C/U] ★ a liquid food that is made by cooking meat, fish, or vegetables with water: *a bowl of soup* ♦ *chicken/tomato/potato soup*

'soup ,kitchen noun [C] a place where poor people can go in order to get a free hot meal

sour¹ /'saʊə/ adj **1** with a taste like a lemon **2** sour milk has an unpleasant taste or smell because it is no longer fresh **3** unpleasant, unfriendly, or in a bad mood: *a sour look*
PHRASE **go/turn sour** to be unsuccessful, or to develop in a way that is not satisfactory

sour² /'saʊə/ verb [I/T] to stop being successful or satisfactory, or to make something do this

source¹ /sɔːs/ noun [C] ★★
1 a person, place, or thing that provides something that you need or want: *a light/power/energy source* ♦ *A garden was the source of inspiration for the painting.*
2 someone who provides information for a journalist: *The article quoted a senior source at the UN.*

3 the cause of a problem, or the place where it began: *Her son was a constant source of worry to her.*
4 the beginning of a river or stream

source² /sɔːs/ verb [T] to get a product or basic material from somewhere: *All our timber is sourced from sustainable forests.*

south¹ /saʊθ/ noun ★★★
1 [U] the direction that is on your right when you are facing the rising sun: *driving from south to north*
2 the south [singular] the part of a place that is in the south: *Did you like living in the south?*
→ DEEP SOUTH

south² /saʊθ/ adv towards the south: *A room that faces south gets more sunlight.* ♦ *They live 20 minutes south of Manchester.*

south³ /saʊθ/ adj **1** in the south, or facing towards the south **2** a south wind blows from the south

southbound /ˈsaʊθˌbaʊnd/ adj going towards the south

south-east¹ noun **1** [U] the direction that is between south and east **2 the south-east** [singular] the part of a place that is in the south-east: *House prices are higher in London and the south-east.* —**south-eastern** adj

south-east² adj in the south-east, or facing towards the south-east —**south-east** adv

southerly /ˈsʌðəli/ adj **1** a southerly wind blows from the south **2** towards or in the south

southern /ˈsʌð(ə)n/ adj ★★ in or from the south of a place: *southern Europe* ♦ *the southern shore of the lake*

southerner /ˈsʌð(ə)nə/ noun [C] someone who lives or was born in the southern part of a country

southernmost /ˈsʌð(ə)nˌməʊst/ adj furthest towards the south

South Pole, the the point on the Earth that is the furthest south

southward /ˈsaʊθwəd/ adj towards or in the south

southwards /ˈsaʊθwədz/ adv towards the south

south-west¹ noun **1** [U] the direction that is between south and west **2 the south-west** [singular] the part of a country that is in the south-west: *They own a farmhouse in the south-west of France.*

south-west² adj in the south-west, or facing towards the south-west —**south-west** adv

south-western adj in or from the SOUTH-WEST of a country or place

souvenir /ˌsuːvəˈnɪə/ noun [C] something that you buy to remind you of a place that you visited on holiday or of a special event

sovereign¹ /ˈsɒvrɪn/ adj a sovereign nation rules itself

sovereign² /ˈsɒvrɪn/ noun [C] *formal* a king or queen

sovereignty /ˈsɒvrɪnti/ noun [U] **1** the right of a country to rule itself **2** the right to rule a country

Soviet /ˈsəʊviət, ˈsɒviət/ adj from or relating to the former USSR

sow¹ /səʊ/ (past participle **sown** /səʊn/ or **sowed** /saʊd/) verb [T] to plant seeds in the ground

sow² /saʊ/ noun [C] an adult female pig

sown a past participle of **sow¹**

soya bean /ˈsɔɪə ˌbiːn/ noun [C] the seed of a plant, used for making food and oil

soy sauce /ˌsɔɪ ˈsɔːs/ noun [U] a dark brown sauce made from soya beans

spa /spɑː/ noun [C] a place with a natural supply of MINERAL water where people go to improve their health

space¹ /speɪs/ noun ★★★

1 empty/available area	**4** area everything is in
2 area for purpose	**5** period of time
3 beyond atmosphere	**+** PHRASE

1 [C/U] an empty or available area: *We replaced the bath with a shower to create more space.* ♦ *Their voices sounded loud in the small space.* ♦ *What we really need is more green spaces in cities.* ♦ *The nursery has space for 48 children.* ♦ *You can grow herbs in the spaces between the plants.*
→ PLACE
2 [C/U] an area used for a particular purpose: *a parking space* ♦ *Newspapers make money from selling advertising space.*
3 [U] the whole of the universe outside the Earth's atmosphere: *a space mission* ♦ *The crew have been living in space for over three months.*
4 [U] the area in which everything exists: *different points in space and time*
5 [singular] a period of time: *It was an amazing achievement in such a short space of time.* ♦ *In the space of 36 hours, I had travelled halfway round the world.*
PHRASE **look/stare into space** to look ahead for a long time but not see anything, because you are thinking about something

space² /speɪs/ verb [T] to arrange objects, events etc so that they are a particular time or distance apart

spacecraft /ˈspeɪsˌkrɑːft/ (plural **spacecraft**) noun [C] a vehicle that can travel in space

space probe noun [C] a vehicle containing cameras and other equipment that is sent into space to collect information and send it back to Earth

spaceship /ˈspeɪsˌʃɪp/ noun [C] a SPACECRAFT

space shuttle noun [C] a vehicle that travels into space and back to Earth and that LANDS like a plane

space station noun [C] a laboratory in space where people can live for long periods

spacious /ˈspeɪʃəs/ adj with a lot of space inside

spade /speɪd/ noun **1** [C] a tool used for digging that consists of a handle and a flat part that you push into the earth **2** [C] a playing card with a pattern that is like a pointed black leaf —*picture* → C16 **3 spades** [plural] the SUIT (=group) of playing cards that has a pattern on them that is like a pointed black leaf: *the ace of spades*

S

spaghetti /spəˈgeti/ noun [U] a type of pasta that is in the form of long thin pieces like string

spam /spæm/ noun [U] computing emails that are sent to large numbers of people on the Internet, especially when these are not wanted

span¹ /spæn/ verb [T] **1** to last for a particular period of time: *His career spanned half a century.* **2** to cross or cover an area of water or land: *a bridge spanning the River Jordan*

span² /spæn/ noun [C] **1** the amount of time that something lasts: *Kids these days have a very limited attention span.* → LIFESPAN **2** the width of something

spaniel /ˈspænjəl/ noun [C] a type of small dog with long ears and long shiny hair

spank /spæŋk/ verb [T] to hit a child on their BOTTOM with an open hand

spanner /ˈspænə/ noun [C] British a metal tool that is used for turning small pieces of metal called NUTS —picture → TOOL

spar /spɑː/ verb [I] to practise fighting with someone

spare¹ /speə/ adj ★
1 kept in addition to other similar things, so that you can use it if you need it: *a spare key/battery* ♦ *Bring a towel and some spare clothes.*
2 available: *Have you got any spare room in your car?*

spare² /speə/ verb [T]

1 give/lend sth	4 use sth
2 have time available	5 not harm sb/sth
3 of bad experience	+ PHRASE

1 if you can spare something, you can give or lend it to someone because you do not need it: *Can you spare a couple of pounds?* ♦ *We can't spare the staff for training sessions.* **2** if you can spare time, you have it available: *Can you spare a couple of hours on Tuesday?* ♦ *We arrived at the airport with just 20 minutes to spare.* ♦ *It's kind of you to spare me a moment.* **3** to prevent someone from experiencing something that is unpleasant or painful: **spare sb sth** *I want to spare her the embarrassment of asking for money.* **4** if you do not spare something, you use a lot of it in order to make something succeed: *We will spare no effort to find the murderer.* ♦ *No expense was spared in organizing the conference.* **5** formal to not harm or kill someone or something: *The commander was so impressed by their bravery that he spared them.*
PHRASE **money/room/time etc to spare** more than enough money, room, time, etc: *We've got food to spare.*

spare³ /speə/ noun [C] something that you have in addition to other similar things, that you can use if you need it

sparingly /ˈspeərɪŋli/ adv in small quantities

spark¹ /spɑːk/ verb [I/T] **1** to make something start: *The verdict sparked riots all over the city.* **2** to start a fire or explosion, or to make a spark

spark² /spɑːk/ noun **1** [C] a very small fire or electrical flash **2** [C/U] a strong and exciting quality or feeling: *She felt a spark of enthusiasm.*

sparkle /ˈspɑːk(ə)l/ verb [I] **1** to shine with small points of reflected light **2** to be very lively and interesting —**sparkle** noun [C/U]

sparkling /ˈspɑːklɪŋ/ adj **1** shining with small points of reflected light **2** very lively and interesting **3** sparkling drinks are full of BUBBLES

ˈspark ˌplug noun [C] a small part in a car's engine that creates a SPARK that makes the fuel burn

sparrow /ˈspærəʊ/ noun [C] a small brown bird that is common in the US and in northern Europe

sparse /spɑːs/ adj existing in small amounts, or very spread out —**sparsely** adv

spartan /ˈspɑːt(ə)n/ adj very simple, rather than comfortable or pleasant

spasm /ˈspæz(ə)m/ noun [C/U] a sudden painful movement of a muscle

spat a past tense and past participle of **spit²**

spate /speɪt/ noun **a spate of sth** a large number of similar events that happen in a short period of time: *a spate of bombings*

spatial /ˈspeɪʃ(ə)l/ adj technical relating to the size, shape, and position of things and their relation to each other in space

spatter /ˈspætə/ verb [I/T] to throw small drops of a liquid onto a surface with a lot of force, or to be thrown onto a surface in this way

spawn¹ /spɔːn/ noun [U] the eggs of a FROG or fish

spawn² /spɔːn/ verb **1** [I/T] to produce spawn **2** [T] to create or produce something

speak /spiːk/ (past tense **spoke** /spəʊk/; past participle **spoken** /ˈspəʊkən/) verb ★★★
1 [I] to talk to someone about something: *We spoke yesterday.* ♦ *I phoned your office and spoke to your assistant.* ♦ *Let me speak with Jennifer and see what she thinks.* ♦ *He spoke movingly about his son's struggle with cancer.* ♦ *People spoke of their fear as the flood waters rose.* ♦ *I know I speak for all of us when I say how sorry I am.* → SAY, TALK
2 [I] to use your voice to talk: *There was a long pause before she spoke again.* ♦ *He spoke so softly it was difficult to hear what he said.*
3 [T] to be able to talk in a particular language: *Do you speak Chinese?* ♦ *He speaks three languages.*
4 [I] to give a formal speech: *The local MP will be speaking at our graduation ceremony.* ♦ *Petersen spoke to an audience of 2,000.*
PHRASES **broadly/generally speaking** used for showing that what you are saying is usually true, but not in every instance
no.../nothing to speak of used for saying that something is very small or unimportant: *She has no money to speak of.*
so to speak spoken used for showing that you have expressed something in an unusual way

speak for itself to be so clear or obvious that no argument is necessary: *His success as a lawyer speaks for itself.*

speaking of *spoken* used for introducing something new that is related to a subject that someone has just mentioned: *Speaking of money, have we paid our credit card bills yet?*

PHRASAL VERBS **speak 'out** to state your opinion firmly and publicly about something

speak 'up 1 to talk louder **2** to say what you think instead of saying nothing

---

Word family: speak

Words in the same family as speak
- **speaker** *n*
- **unspoken** *adj*
- **speech** *n*
- **unspeakable** *adj*
- **spoken** *adj*
- **outspoken** *adj*
- **speechless** *adj*
- **unspeakably** *adv*

---

speaker /'spiːkə/ noun [C] ★★
1 someone who talks about a subject to a group: *She's a very interesting speaker.*
2 someone who is able to speak a particular language: *an English speaker*
3 someone who is talking: *expressions that show the speaker is annoyed*
4 a piece of electrical equipment that sends out sound

spear¹ /spɪə/ noun [C] a long weapon that is like a stick with one sharp pointed end

spear² /spɪə/ verb [T] to push something that is sharp and pointed into something else

spearhead /'spɪəhed/ verb [T] to lead an organized effort or activity

special¹ /'speʃ(ə)l/ adj ★★★
1 different from and usually better than what is normal or ordinary: *The children can only stay up late on special occasions.* ♦ *You're very special to me.*
2 more than usual: *Special care must be taken in handling very old books.*
3 relating to one particular person, thing, or purpose: *Many sports have their own special equipment.*

special² /'speʃ(ə)l/ noun [C] something that is produced for a particular time or day, for example a type of food in a restaurant or a programme on television

special ef'fects noun [plural] the artificial images or sounds in a film that are created with technology

specialist /'speʃəlɪst/ noun [C] ★ someone whose training, education, or experience makes them an expert in a particular subject: *a web design specialist*

speciality /ˌspeʃiˈæləti/ noun [C] *British* **1** a food or drink that a region or restaurant is well known for and that you cannot always get in other places **2** a particular part of a wider subject that someone concentrates on or is an expert in

specialize /'speʃəlaɪz/ verb [I] to be an expert in a particular part of a subject or profession —**specialization** /ˌspeʃəlaɪˈzeɪʃ(ə)n/ noun [C/U]

specialized /'speʃəlaɪzd/ adj designed for a particular purpose, or concentrating on a particular subject

specially /'speʃ(ə)li/ adv in a particular way, or for a particular purpose: *These coats are specially treated to be water repellent.*

special 'needs noun [plural] the particular needs of people with disabilities

specialty /'speʃ(ə)lti/ noun [C] *American* a SPECIALITY

species /'spiːʃiːz/ (plural **species**) noun [C] ★★ a plant or animal group whose members all have similar general features and are able to produce young plants or animals together: *the human species* ♦ *Over 120 species of birds have been recorded in this National Park.*

specific /spəˈsɪfɪk/ adj ★★★
1 involving or limited to only one particular thing or purpose: *You have to enter the information in a specific order.* ♦ *problems that are specific to this type of work*
2 exact and detailed: *For specific instructions, please refer to the guide.* ♦ *Can you be more specific?*

specifically /spəˈsɪfɪkli/ adv ★
1 for one particular thing or purpose: *They bought the land specifically for the purpose of building a hotel.*
2 in an exact or detailed way: *She specifically stated that she went to the station because her brother told her to.*

specification /ˌspesɪfɪˈkeɪʃ(ə)n/ noun [C] an exact measurement or detailed plan about how something is to be made

specifics /spəˈsɪfɪks/ noun [plural] the details of something: *We'll leave the lawyers to deal with the specifics.*

specify /'spesɪfaɪ/ verb [T] to explain something in an exact and detailed way

specimen /'spesəmɪn/ noun [C] **1** a small amount of something such as blood or URINE that is taken from your body so that it can be examined **2** an example of something, especially of a plant or animal

speck /spek/ noun [C] a very small spot or mark

speckled /'spek(ə)ld/ adj covered with a lot of very small spots or marks

specs /speks/ noun [plural] *informal* glasses that you wear to help you to see better

spectacle /'spektək(ə)l/ noun [C/U] an unusual, exciting, or impressive event or sight

spectacles /'spektəklz/ noun [plural] *formal* glasses that you wear to help you to see better

spectacular /spek'tækjʊlə/ adj extremely impressive ≠ UNSPECTACULAR —**spectacularly** adv

spectator /spek'teɪtə/ noun [C] someone who watches a public activity or event

spectre /'spektə/ noun [C] the possibility of something unpleasant that might happen in the future

spectrum /'spektrəm/ noun [singular] **1** the whole range of ideas, qualities, situations etc that are possible **2** the complete range of colours into which light can be separated

S

speculate /ˈspekjʊˌleɪt/ verb **1** [I/T] to consider or discuss why something has happened **2** [I] to buy things such as SHARES and property, hoping to make a big profit later when you sell them —**speculator** noun [C]

speculation /ˌspekjʊˈleɪʃ(ə)n/ noun [C/U] guesses about why something has happened or what might happen

speculative /ˈspekjʊlətɪv/ adj **1** based on guesses or on only a little information **2** done in order to make a big profit, but with a high risk that money will be lost

sped the past tense and past participle of **speed**

speech /spiːtʃ/ noun ★★★
1 [C] a formal occasion when someone speaks to an audience, or the words that someone speaks to an audience: *He began his speech with a joke.* ♦ *She writes most of the president's speeches.* ♦ *She made a wonderful speech.*
2 [U] spoken language or the ability to speak: *A stroke can cause difficulties with speech.* ♦ *tapes of recorded speech* ♦ *speech development*

speechless /ˈspiːtʃləs/ adj so surprised or angry that you cannot think of anything to say

speed¹ /spiːd/ noun ★★★
1 [C/U] the rate at which something or someone moves or works: *They were working with incredible speed.* ♦ *The main advantage of this method is its speed.* ♦ *The device measures the speed and direction of the wind.*
2 [C] a GEAR: *a car with a 5-speed gearbox*
3 [U] an illegal drug that makes people feel as if they have a lot of energy
PHRASE up to speed **1** *informal* with all the information that you need **2** at the speed or level that is expected

speed² /spiːd/ (past tense and past participle **sped** /sped/ or **speeded**) verb **1** [I] to move somewhere quickly: *an endless stream of traffic speeding towards the city* ♦ *I heard a car speed away.* **2** [I] to drive a car faster than the speed that is allowed **3** [T] to make something happen more quickly: *Regular exercise will help speed your recovery.*
PHRASAL VERB speed (sth) up to move or happen faster, or to make something move or happen faster

speedboat /ˈspiːdˌbəʊt/ noun [C] a boat with a powerful motor that can go very fast

speeding¹ /ˈspiːdɪŋ/ noun [U] the offence of driving faster than the speed that is allowed in a particular area

speeding² /ˈspiːdɪŋ/ adj moving very fast

speed limit noun [singular] the fastest speed that is allowed for vehicles in a particular area

speedometer /spɪˈdɒmɪtə/ noun [C] the piece of equipment in a vehicle that shows how fast it is going —*picture* → C6

speedy /ˈspiːdi/ adj **1** happening very quickly **2** able to move very fast

spell¹ /spel/ (past tense and past participle **spelt** /spelt/ or **spelled**) verb ★
1 [I/T] to write or say the letters of a word

in the correct order: *Can you spell 'beautiful'?* ♦ *You've spelt my name wrong.*
♦ *Her writing is neat, but she can't spell.*
2 [T] to be the letters that make up a word: *L-O-V-E spells 'love'.*
3 [T] to show that something bad is going to happen: *That look on her face spells trouble.*
PHRASAL VERB spell sth 'out **1** to say or write the letters of a word in the correct order **2** *informal* to explain something so that it is very clear

spell² /spel/ noun [C] ★
1 a period of time, usually a short one: *After a short spell in the army, I went to college.*
♦ *a spell of rain*
2 words or actions that are believed to make magic things happen: *The witch cast a spell on him.*

spellbinding /ˈspelˌbaɪndɪŋ/ adj something that is spellbinding is so interesting that it holds your attention completely

spellbound /ˈspelˌbaʊnd/ adj so impressed by something that you do not pay attention to anything else

spellchecker /ˈspelˌtʃekə/ noun [C] *computing* a computer program that checks and corrects the way that you spell words

spelling /ˈspelɪŋ/ noun **1** [U] the ability to spell **2** [C] the correct way of writing a word

spelt a British past tense and past participle of **spell**

spend /spend/ (past tense and past participle **spent** /spent/) verb ★★★
1 [I/T] to use money to pay for things: *How much money did you spend?* ♦ **spend sth on sth** *You spend too much on clothes.*
2 [T] to stay somewhere, or to do something, for a period of time: *We spent the day at the beach.* ♦ **spend sth on sth** *We have spent too much time on this problem.* ♦ **spend sth with sb** *I'm going to spend Christmas with my family.* ♦ **spend sth doing sth** *He spent hours practising.*

spending /ˈspendɪŋ/ noun [U] money spent, especially by governments or large organizations

spending money noun [U] money for spending on things you want, not on things such as food and bills

spendthrift /ˈspendˌθrɪft/ noun [C] *showing disapproval* someone who is very careless about money and spends more than they need to

spent¹ the past tense and past participle of **spend**

spent² /spent/ adj **1** used, and therefore no longer useful: *spent nuclear fuel* **2** *literary* very tired

sperm /spɜːm/ (plural **sperm**) noun **1** [C] a cell from a man that FERTILIZES the egg inside a woman's body **2** [U] the liquid from a man's PENIS that contains sperm=SEMEN

spew /spjuː/ or **spew (sth) 'out** verb [I/T] to flow out with a lot of force, or to make something do this

SPF /ˌes piː ˈef/ abbrev sun protection factor: a

measurement of how much a product protects your skin from the sun

sphere /sfɪə/ noun [C] **1** an object that is round like a ball —*picture* → C8 **2** a particular area of interest, activity, or responsibility

spherical /'sferɪk(ə)l/ adj technical round like a ball

sphinx /sfɪŋks/ noun [C] an animal in ancient Greek and Egyptian MYTHS that has a lion's body and a human head

spice¹ /spaɪs/ noun **1** [C/U] a substance made from a plant and added to food to give it flavour **2** [U] extra interest or excitement

spice² /spaɪs/ PHRASAL VERB **spice sth up 1** to make something more interesting or exciting **2** to add spices to food to give it more flavour

spick and span /ˌspɪk ən ˈspæn/ adj informal very clean and tidy

spicy /'spaɪsi/ adj with a strong hot flavour

spider /'spaɪdə/ noun [C] a small creature with eight legs that weaves a WEB in order to catch insects

spidery /'spaɪdəri/ adj spidery writing is untidy and consists of long thin lines

spike /spaɪk/ noun [C] a sharp pointed piece of metal or wood —**spiky** adj

spill¹ /spɪl/ (past tense and past participle **spilled** or **spilt** /spɪlt/) verb ★
1 [I/T] if a liquid spills, or if you spill it, it accidentally flows out of its container: *Oil is still spilling from the ship.* ♦ **spill sth on/over sth** *I spilt coffee all over my desk.*
2 [I] if people spill out of a place, a lot of them leave at the same time

PHRASE **spill the beans** informal to tell someone something that should be kept secret

PHRASAL VERB **spill over** to spread to other areas: *The violence has spilled over to other parts of the city.*

spill

spill² /spɪl/ noun [C/U] an amount of liquid that has accidentally flowed out of its container: *an oil spill*

spilt a past tense and past participle of **spill**

spin¹ /spɪn/ (past tense and past participle **spun** /spʌn/) verb ★
1 [I/T] to turn round and round quickly, or to make something do this: *The dancers were spinning in circles.* ♦ *Spin the wheel with your hand.*
2 [I] when a washing machine spins, it squeezes water out of the clothes by turning them round and quickly

3 [I/T] to twist fibres into THREAD to make cloth

4 [T] if an insect or SPIDER spins something such as a WEB, it makes it from THREAD that it produces in its body

PHRASAL VERB **spin sth out** to make something last for a long time

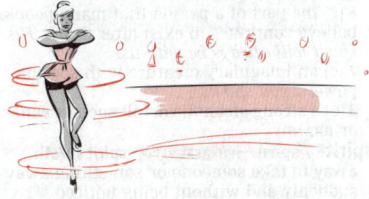

spin

spin² /spɪn/ noun **1** [C/U] a quick turning movement round and round **2** [singular/U] informal a way of giving information that makes something seem less bad **3** [C] informal a short journey for pleasure in a car

spinach /'spɪnɪdʒ/ noun [U] a vegetable with dark green leaves

spinal /'spaɪn(ə)l/ adj relating to your SPINE

spinal cord noun [C] the inner part of your SPINE

spin doctor noun [C] someone whose job is to give information to journalists in a way that gives people a good opinion of a politician, government, or organization

spin-dryer or **spin-drier** noun [C] British a machine that dries clothes by spinning them very fast

spine /spaɪn/ noun [C] **1** the row of bones down the middle of your back = BACKBONE **2** the edge of a book where all the pages are fixed together **3** a sharp point on a plant or animal

spineless /'spaɪnləs/ adj not brave or determined

spin-off noun [C] something good that happens unexpectedly as a result of something else

spiral¹ /'spaɪrəl/ noun [C] **1** a shape that looks like a set of circles and is made by one line curving around a central point **2** a situation that gets worse and worse: *the endless spiral of violence and hatred* —**spiral** adj

spiral² /'spaɪrəl/ (present participle **spiralling**; past tense and past participle **spiralled**) verb [I]
1 to move in the shape of a spiral **2** to become worse and worse: *Crime has begun to spiral out of control.*

spire /'spaɪə/ noun [C] the pointed top of a church tower

spirit¹ /'spɪrɪt/ noun ★

1 attitude of group	5 real meaning
2 determination	6 non-physical part of sb
3 mood	7 imaginary creature
4 sb's attitude	8 alcoholic drink

1 [singular/U] the attitude of people in a group: *a spirit of cooperation* ♦ *We need more team spirit*.
2 [U] an enthusiastic or determined attitude: *She showed a lot of spirit.*

S

3 spirits [plural] your mood at a particular time: *She tried singing to keep her spirits up.* ♦ *Dad's in high spirits today, isn't he?*
4 [C/U] your attitude to life or to other people: *He was always an independent spirit.*
5 [U] the general or real meaning of something: *Their actions go against the spirit of the agreement.*
6 [C] the part of a person that many people believe continues to exist after death: *His spirit will always be with us.*
7 [C] an imaginary creature with special powers: *evil spirits*
8 [C] a strong alcoholic drink such as WHISKY or BRANDY

spirit² /ˈspɪrɪt/ **PHRASAL VERB** ˌspirit sb/sth ˈaway** to take someone or something away suddenly and without being noticed

spirited /ˈspɪrɪtɪd/ adj showing a lot of determination and enthusiasm

spiritual /ˈspɪrɪtʃuəl/ adj **1** relating to the part of a person that many people believe continues to exist after death: *a spiritual experience* **2** religious: *spiritual leaders* —**spiritually** adv

spiritualism /ˈspɪrɪtʃuəˌlɪz(ə)m/ noun [U] the belief that dead people are able to communicate with people who are still alive —**spiritualist** noun [C]

spit¹ /spɪt/ (past tense and past participle **spat** /spæt/) verb [I/T] **1** to force something that is liquid or solid out from your mouth **2** *British* to rain slightly

PHRASE **spit it out** *spoken* used for telling someone to hurry and say something that they are nervous or embarrassed about saying

spit² /spɪt/ noun **1** [U] *informal* the clear liquid that is in your mouth=SALIVA **2** [C] a long sharp piece of metal that is used for holding and turning meat as it cooks over a fire

spite¹ /spaɪt/ noun [U] ★ a feeling of wanting to upset someone or to cause problems for them: *She refused out of spite.*

PHRASE **in spite of sth** used for referring to a fact that makes something else surprising =DESPITE: *In spite of feeling tired, we decided to go out.* ♦ *The house will certainly sell, in spite of the fact that it's overpriced.*

spite² /spaɪt/ verb [T] to deliberately upset someone or cause them problems

spiteful /ˈspaɪtf(ə)l/ adj deliberately trying to upset someone or cause problems for them —**spitefully** adv

ˌspitting ˈimage noun [C] *informal* someone who looks exactly like someone else

splash¹ /splæʃ/ verb **1** [I/T] if a liquid splashes, or if you splash it, it moves or hits something noisily **2** [I] to move around noisily in water

PHRASE **be splashed across sth** if words, a story, or pictures are splashed across a newspaper, they are large and easy to see

PHRASAL VERB ˌsplash ˈout** *British informal* to buy something expensive: *He's just splashed out on a brand new car.*

splash² /splæʃ/ noun [C] **1** the sound of liquid hitting something, or the sound of something falling into a liquid **2** a mark

made by a liquid splashing **3** a small amount of bright colour

splatter /ˈsplætə/ verb [I/T] if a liquid splatters, or if it splatters something, drops of it hit a surface violently

splay /spleɪ/ or ˌsplay (sth) ˈout** verb [I/T] to spread part of your body in a way that looks strange

splendid /ˈsplendɪd/ adj *formal* very good, impressive, or enjoyable=WONDERFUL —**splendidly** adv

splendor /ˈsplendə/ the American spelling of **splendour**

splendour /ˈsplendə/ noun [U] the impressive beauty of something

splice /splaɪs/ verb [T] to connect the ends of two pieces of something such as rope, so that they form one piece

splint /splɪnt/ noun [C] a piece of metal, plastic, or wood that is put next to a broken bone in order to hold it in place

splinter¹ /ˈsplɪntə/ noun [C] a small sharp piece of wood or glass that has broken off a bigger piece

splinter² /ˈsplɪntə/ verb [I/T] to break into small sharp pieces, or to make something do this

ˈsplinter ˌgroup noun [C] a group of people who have separated from a larger group because of a disagreement

split¹ /splɪt/ (past tense and past participle **split**) verb ★
1 [I/T] to divide something into several parts, or to be divided into several parts: *Let's split into groups and work separately.*
2 [T] to share something by dividing it into separate parts: *I suggest we split the bill* (=divide it into equal amounts).
3 [I/T] if something splits, or if you split it, a long thin cut or break forms in it: *How did you split your trousers?* ♦ *One of the boxes fell and split open.*

PHRASES **split the difference** *spoken* to agree on an amount that is the middle point between a larger amount and a smaller one
split hairs to argue or worry about unimportant details

PHRASAL VERB ˌsplit ˈup** to end a sexual or romantic relationship

split² /splɪt/ noun [C] **1** a long thin cut or break in something **2** a disagreement that causes a group to divide into smaller groups

ˌsplit ˈsecond noun [singular] an extremely small amount of time —**ˌsplit-ˈsecond** adj

ˌsplitting ˈheadache noun [C] a very bad pain in your head

splutter /ˈsplʌtə/ verb *informal* **1** [I/T] to make noises with your mouth because you suddenly cannot breathe or swallow normally, or to say something while doing this **2** [I] if something such as an engine splutters, it makes a series of short noises because it is not working well —**splutter** noun [C]

spoil /spɔɪl/ (past tense and past participle **spoiled** or **spoilt** /spɔɪlt/) verb ★
1 [T] to make something worse, less attractive, or less enjoyable: *Radio towers spoilt the view.* ♦ *I really hope it doesn't*

rain – that would spoil everything.

2 [T] to allow a child to get everything that they want, so that they behave badly if they do not get something: *His mother spoils him rotten* (=spoils him very much).

3 [T] to treat someone with a lot of care and kindness: *It's Mother's Day – let them spoil you a little!*

4 [I] if food spoils, it is not safe to eat because it is too old

spoiled /spɔɪld/ adj SPOILT

spoils /spɔɪlz/ noun [plural] *literary* the things that someone takes in a war or by stealing

spoilsport /ˈspɔɪlˌspɔːt/ noun [C] *informal* someone who spoils someone else's enjoyment

spoilt¹ /spɔɪlt/ adj a spoilt child behaves badly if they do not get what they want because people have always given them everything that they want

spoilt² a past tense and past participle of **spoil**

spoke¹ /spəʊk/ noun [C] one of the thin metal bars that connect the centre of a wheel to the outside part

spoke² the past tense of **speak**

spoken¹ /ˈspəʊkən/ adj said, instead of being written: *examples of spoken and written English*

spoken² the past participle of **speak**

spokesman /ˈspəʊksmən/ (plural **spokesmen** /ˈspəʊksmən/) noun [C] a male spokesperson

spokesperson /ˈspəʊksˌpɜːs(ə)n/ (plural **spokespeople** /ˈspəʊksˌpiːp(ə)l/) noun [C] someone whose job is to officially represent an organization and to speak to journalists

spokeswoman /ˈspəʊksˌwʊmən/ (plural **spokeswomen** /ˈspəʊksˌwɪmɪn/) noun [C] a female spokesperson

sponge¹ /spʌndʒ/ noun **1** [C] a piece of a soft substance that takes in water easily and that is used for cleaning things or for washing yourself **2** [C/U] *British* a SPONGE CAKE

sponge² /spʌndʒ/ verb [T] to wash someone or something with a sponge

PHRASAL VERB **sponge off sb** *informal* to ask for money and other things from someone and not give anything back or pay for anything yourself

sponge bag noun [C] *British* a small bag used for carrying things that you need for washing yourself

sponge cake noun [C/U] a very light cake made with flour, eggs, and sugar

spongy /ˈspʌndʒi/ adj light, soft, and full of small holes

sponsor¹ /ˈspɒnsə/ verb [T] ★
1 to pay for something such as an event or a radio or television programme as a way of advertising your company or products
2 to agree to give money to someone who is going to take part in a CHARITY event —**sponsorship** noun [U]

sponsor² /ˈspɒnsə/ noun [C] **1** a person or business that pays for something such as an event or a radio or television programme as a way of advertising their company or

products **2** someone who agrees to give money to someone who is taking part in a CHARITY event

sponsored /ˈspɒnsəd/ adj done in order to make money for a CHARITY: *a sponsored walk*

spontaneous /spɒnˈteɪniəs/ adj happening in a natural way without being planned or thought about: *spontaneous applause/cheers* —**spontaneity** /ˌspɒntəˈneɪəti/ noun [U], **spontaneously** adv

spoof /spuːf/ noun [C] a piece of entertainment that copies something in a way that is intended to make it seem funny or silly —**spoof** verb [T]

spooky /ˈspuːki/ adj *informal* strange and frightening

spool /spuːl/ noun [C] a round object with a hole in the middle that you wind something such as string around

spoon¹ /spuːn/ noun [C] ★ an object that you use for eating soup and other liquid foods and for mixing and preparing food

spoon² /spuːn/ verb [T] to eat or serve food with a spoon

spoon-feed verb [T] to provide someone with too much help so that they do not learn how to think for themselves

spoonful /ˈspuːnfʊl/ noun [C] the amount that a spoon contains

sporadic /spəˈrædɪk/ adj not regular or frequent —**sporadically** /spəˈrædɪkli/ adv

sport¹ /spɔːt/ noun ★★★
1 [C] a physical activity in which players or teams compete against each other: *Bob's favourite sport is tennis.* ♦ *the newspaper's sports section*
2 [U] *British* sports in general: *The school is keen to involve more young people in sport.*
3 [C] *informal* someone who always behaves in a reasonable way and is always willing to help: *Thanks, Shelly – you're always such a good sport.*

sport² /spɔːt/ verb [T] to wear something in a way that shows that you want people to notice it

sporting /ˈspɔːtɪŋ/ adj relating to sport

sports car noun [C] a small fast car, often with a roof that you can take off

sports centre noun [C] *British* a building where you can go to take part in sports

sportsman /ˈspɔːtsmən/ noun [C] a man who plays sport

sportsmanlike /ˈspɔːtsmənˌlaɪk/ adj fair and honest when playing sport

sportsmanship /ˈspɔːtsmənʃɪp/ noun [U] fair and honest behaviour in sport

sportswear /ˈspɔːtsˌweə/ noun [U] *British* clothes for playing sport

sportswoman /ˈspɔːtsˌwʊmən/ noun [C] a woman who plays sport

sporty /ˈspɔːti/ adj **1** a sporty car looks fast and expensive **2** a sporty person likes playing sport

S

spot¹ /spɒt/ noun [C] ★★

1 particular place	**5** on TV/radio
2 small area of colour	**6** small amount of sth
3 dirty mark	**7** spotlight
4 red lump on face	**+ PHRASES**

1 a particular place: *We found him sitting in a sunny spot in the garden.* ♦ *one of the region's best-known tourist spots*

2 a small round area of colour that is different from the colour of the area around it: *The flower is yellow with red spots.*

3 a small unpleasant or dirty mark on something

4 *British* a small red lump on someone's face =PIMPLE

5 *informal* a period of time in a television or radio programme that you get to use for a particular purpose

6 a spot of sth *British informal* a small amount of something: *We'd had a spot of trouble with the police.*

7 *informal* a SPOTLIGHT

PHRASES **on the spot 1** in the exact place where something is happening
2 immediately

put sb on the spot to ask someone a difficult or embarrassing question
→ BLIND SPOT, HOT SPOT

spot² /spɒt/ verb [T] to notice someone or something: *Maria spotted the book lying under the chair.*

spot check noun [C] an occasion when you check someone or something without a warning that you are going to do so

spotless /'spɒtləs/ adj extremely clean
—**spotlessly** adv

spotlight¹ /'spɒtlaɪt/ noun **1** [C] a powerful light that shines on a small area, for example in a theatre **2 the spotlight** [singular] a situation in which you get a lot of public attention

spotlight² /'spɒtlaɪt/ verb [T] **1** to shine a spotlight on someone or something **2** to make people pay a lot of attention to someone or something

spot on adj, adv *British informal* exactly right

spotted /'spɒtɪd/ adj covered with a pattern of spots

spotty /'spɒti/ adj **1** *British* someone who is spotty has a lot of small red lumps on their skin **2** covered with a pattern of spots

spouse /spaʊs/ noun [C] *formal* your husband or wife

spout¹ /spaʊt/ noun [C] a part of a container that is shaped like a tube and is used for pouring liquid

spout² /spaʊt/ verb **1** [I/T] if a liquid spouts from somewhere, or if something spouts it, a lot of it comes out fast and continuously **2** [T] *informal* to say something for a long time or in a boring way

sprain /spreɪn/ verb [T] to injure a JOINT such as your wrist by suddenly turning it too much —**sprain** noun [C], **sprained** /spreɪnd/ adj: *a sprained ankle*

sprang the past tense of **spring**²

sprawl /sprɔːl/ verb [I] **1** to sit or lie with your arms and legs stretched out in a relaxed or careless way **2** to stretch over or across something in an ugly and untidy way
—**sprawl** noun [singular/U]

spray¹ /spreɪ/ verb [I/T] **1** if you spray a liquid, or if it sprays, very small drops of it are forced out of a container through a small hole: *The chemical is sprayed onto the crops once a week.* **2** if something sprays very small drops or pieces of a substance, or if they spray, they are thrown into the air in different directions

spray² /spreɪ/ noun **1** [C/U] a liquid that is forced out of a container in very small drops when you push a button on it **2** [U] many small drops of water that are forced into the air

spread¹ /spred/ (past tense and past participle **spread**) verb ★★

1 affect larger area	**5** of information
2 open sth folded	**6** make happen in stages
3 put/be in wide area	**7** move arms/legs apart
4 cover with layer	**+ PHRASAL VERBS**

1 [I/T] to gradually affect a larger area or a large number of people or things, or to make something do this: *Rain will spread from the west this evening.* ♦ *Soldiers returning from the war spread the disease through the region.* ♦ *UN leaders hope to prevent the fighting from spreading.*

2 [T] to open something that is folded so that it covers a surface: *The map was spread on the floor.* ♦ **spread sth on/over sth** *We spread the blanket on the grass and sat down on it.*

3 [I/T] to put things in many parts of an area, or to be present in many parts of a large area: *There are 54 community colleges spread across California.*

4 [T] to cover a surface with a thin layer of a soft food: **spread sth on sth** *Maureen spread jam on her toast.* ♦ **spread sth with sth** *First, spread the bread with mayonnaise.*

5 [I/T] if information spreads, or if you spread it, it becomes known by more people than before: *Someone has been spreading nasty rumours about Stella's private life.*

6 [T] to make something happen at several times during a long period, instead of all at once: **spread sth over sth** *You can spread your payments over five years.*

7 [T] to move your arms, legs, or hands so that they are far apart =EXTEND

PHRASAL VERBS **spread out** if people in a group spread out, they move away from one another so that they cover a large area
spread sth out same as **spread**¹ 2: *We spread our papers out on the table.*

spread² /spred/ noun **1** [singular] the growth or development of something, so that it affects a larger area or a larger number of people: *There were concerns about the spread of fighting to other regions.* **2** [C/U] a soft food that you put on bread and similar foods: *a low-fat spread* **3** [C] a long article in a newspaper or magazine: *a double-page/two-page spread* **4** [singular] a number

S

of different things=RANGE: *You minimize risk by investing in a spread of companies.*

spreadsheet /'spredˌʃiːt/ noun [C] a CHART that is produced on a computer that shows numbers in a way that makes them easy to compare

spree /spriː/ noun [C] a short period that you spend doing a lot of an enjoyable activity

sprig /sprɪɡ/ noun [C] a stem or very small branch that is cut from a plant

sprightly /'spraɪtli/ adj healthy and full of energy despite being old

spring¹ /sprɪŋ/ noun ★★

1 [C/U] the season between winter and summer: *The garden is so beautiful in spring.*

2 [C] a place where water flows up from under the ground and forms a small stream or pool

3 [C] a long thin piece of metal that is twisted into the shape of a COIL that quickly returns to its original shape after you stop stretching it

4 [C] a quick jump forward or up

spring² /sprɪŋ/ (past tense **sprang** /spræŋ/; past participle **sprung** /sprʌŋ/) verb [I] **1** to jump or move quickly and with a lot of energy in a particular direction: *The young man turned to hit him, but Corbett sprang back.* ♦ *Robert sprang to his feet* (=stood quickly) *to shout at the referee.* ♦ *The door sprang open, and Jeremy appeared.* **2** to perform an action quickly and with energy or force: *'Let's get going,' my father cried, springing into action.* ♦ *'She was just trying to help!' said Eric, springing to her defence.* **3** to happen or appear somewhere suddenly or unexpectedly: *Tears sprang to his eyes as he thought of Helen.*

PHRASES **spring a leak** to crack or break so that water or another liquid can get in or out: *The boat sprang a leak and quickly sank.*

spring to life to begin to be active: *The game finally sprang to life in the second half.*

spring to mind if something springs to mind, you suddenly remember it

PHRASAL VERBS **'spring from sth** to come from a particular place, family, or situation

'spring sth on sb to tell someone something that they do not expect

ˌspring 'up to appear suddenly and quickly: *New Internet companies were springing up every day.*

springboard /'sprɪŋˌbɔːd/ noun [C] **1** something that helps you to become successful **2** a strong board used for helping you to jump in sports such as DIVING

ˌspring-'clean verb [I/T] *British* to clean a house completely —**ˌspring-'clean** noun [singular], **ˌspring-'cleaning** noun [singular/U]

ˌspring 'onion noun [C] *British* a small white onion with a long thin green stem that is often eaten raw in salads —*picture* → C11

springtime /'sprɪŋˌtaɪm/ noun [C] the season of spring

springy /'sprɪŋi/ adj something that is

springy quickly returns to its shape after you press it or walk on it

sprinkle /'sprɪŋk(ə)l/ verb [T] to shake small amounts of a liquid or a substance such as sugar over the surface of something: *Sprinkle the chicken with soy sauce.* ♦ *Sprinkle the grated cheese over the pasta, and serve.* —**sprinkle** noun [singular]

sprinkler /'sprɪŋklə/ noun [C] **1** a piece of equipment that is used for automatically sprinkling water on a garden **2** a piece of equipment on the ceiling that spreads water over the room if a fire starts

sprinkling /'sprɪŋklɪŋ/ noun [C] a small amount of a liquid or a substance such as sugar that is shaken over the surface of something

sprint /sprɪnt/ verb [I] to run at a very fast speed for a short period —**sprint** noun [C]

sprinter /'sprɪntə/ noun [C] a runner who takes part in short fast races

sprout¹ /spraʊt/ verb **1** [I/T] if a plant sprouts, or if it sprouts something, new leaves or SHOOTS begin to grow on it **2** [I] to suddenly appear or increase in number: *A lot of these modern buildings have sprouted suddenly along the shore of the lake.*

PHRASAL VERB **ˌsprout 'up** same as **sprout¹** 2: *New businesses began to sprout up across the country.*

sprout² /spraʊt/ noun [C] **1** *British* a BRUSSELS SPROUT **2** a new SHOOT on a plant

spruce¹ /spruːs/ noun [C] a tall tree with thin sharp leaves that do not fall off in winter

spruce² /spruːs/ **PHRASAL VERB** **ˌspruce sb/sth 'up** to improve the appearance of someone or something

sprung the past participle of **spring²**

spry /spraɪ/ adj healthy and full of energy despite being old

spud /spʌd/ noun [C] *British informal* a potato

spun the past tense and past participle of **spin¹**

spur¹ /spɜː/ noun [C] **1** a metal object on the heel of a rider's boot that the rider presses into a horse's side in order to make it go faster **2** something that encourages someone to do something

PHRASE **on the spur of the moment** if you do something on the spur of the moment, you do it suddenly and without planning it or thinking carefully about it

spur² /spɜː/ verb [T] **1** to encourage someone to do something **2** to cause something to happen

PHRASAL VERB **ˌspur sb 'on** same as **spur²** 1

spurious /'spjʊəriəs/ adj *formal* not based on true facts

spurn /spɜːn/ verb [T] *literary* to refuse to accept someone or something

spurt /spɜːt/ verb **1** [I/T] to come out in a sudden strong flow **2** [I] to suddenly increase in speed or energy —**spurt** noun [C]

sputter /'spʌtə/ verb **1** [I/T] to speak or say something in a confused way, because you are shocked or angry=SPLUTTER **2** [I] if an engine sputters, it makes noises like small

S

explosions and seems likely to stop
=SPLUTTER

spy¹ /spaɪ/ noun [C] someone whose job is to find out secret information about a country or an organization =AGENT

spy² /spaɪ/ verb **1** [I] to work as a spy **2** [T] literary to notice someone or something

PHRASAL VERB **spy on sb** to watch someone secretly so that you know everything that they do

spyhole /'spaɪˌhəʊl/ noun [C] a small hole in a door that you look through in order to see who is on the other side

sq. abbrev square

squabble /'skwɒb(ə)l/ verb [I] to argue with someone about something that is not important —**squabble** noun [C]

squad /skwɒd/ noun [C] **1** a small group of soldiers who do a particular job **2** a department in a police force that deals with a particular type of crime **3** a sports team **4** British a larger group of players from which a team is chosen

squad ˌcar noun [C] a car used by police officers

squadron /'skwɒdrən/ noun [C] a section of the armed forces, especially of the air force

squalid /'skwɒlɪd/ adj a place that is squalid is dirty and unpleasant

squall /skwɔːl/ noun [C] a storm that happens suddenly

squalor /'skwɒlə/ noun [U] dirty and uncomfortable conditions that people live in or work in

squander /'skwɒndə/ verb [T] to not use something such as money, time, or an opportunity in a sensible way

square¹ /skweə/ noun [C] ★★★
1 a shape with four straight sides of equal length and four RIGHT ANGLES: The flower beds form a perfect square. —picture → C8
2 an open area of land in the shape of a square with buildings around it: The hotel is in the main square. ♦ They have an office in Soho Square.
3 the number that is the result of multiplying one number by itself: The square of 3 is 9.

PHRASE **back to square one** in the same situation that you were in before you started to do something, so that you have made no progress

square² /skweə/ adj ★★
1 in the shape of a square: a small square garden
2 with edges or corners that are not as curved as usual: He had broad square shoulders.
3 used for talking about units for measuring the area of something: an area of over 200 square miles ♦ The room is less than four yards square.
4 informal if two people are square, neither person owes the other anything: You give me back six pounds - then we'll be square.

PHRASES **all square** British if a game is all square, both teams or players have the same number of points

a square deal informal fair treatment
→ FAIR³

square³ /skweə/ verb [T] to multiply a number by itself

PHRASAL VERBS **ˌsquare ˈup 1** if two people square up, one pays what they owe so that both people are equal **2** British to prepare to start competing or fighting
ˈsquare with sth if one idea, opinion, explanation etc squares with another, they both seem good or reasonable
ˈsquare sth with sb to get permission from someone to do something: I'll have to square it with the manager first.

squarely /'skweəli/ adv **1** in a clear and definite way: Responsibility for it rested squarely on her shoulders. **2** directly: She turned and looked him squarely in the eye.

ˌsquare ˈmeal noun [C] informal a large meal that makes you feel satisfied

ˌsquare ˈroot noun [C] a number that you multiply by itself in order to produce a particular number: The square root of 9 is 3.

squash¹ /skwɒʃ/ verb **1** [T] to damage something by pressing or crushing it so that it loses its normal shape **2** [I/T] to push someone or something so that they fit into a small space, or to fit into a small space with difficulty **3** [T] to prevent something from happening or being effective

squash² /skwɒʃ/ noun **1** [U] an indoor game in which two players use RACKETS in order to hit a small ball against a wall **2** [C/U] British a sweet drink made from fruit juice, sugar, and water **3** [singular] British a situation in which there are too many people in a small space **4** [C/U] a large hard vegetable with very thick skin

squat¹ /skwɒt/ verb [I] **1** to bend your knees and lower yourself towards the ground so that you balance on your feet =CROUCH **2** to live in a place without permission and without paying the owner

PHRASAL VERB **ˌsquat ˈdown** same as squat¹ 1

squat² /skwɒt/ noun [C] British a house where people live without permission and without paying the owner

squat³ /skwɒt/ adj wide and not very tall or high

squatter /'skwɒtə/ noun [C] someone who lives in a place without permission and without paying the owner

squawk /skwɔːk/ verb [I] when a bird squawks, it makes a loud unpleasant noise in its throat —**squawk** noun [C]

squeak /skwiːk/ verb [I] to make a short high noise —**squeak** noun [C]

squeaky /'skwiːki/ adj making a short high noise

ˌsqueaky ˈclean adj informal **1** always behaving in a completely moral and honest way **2** extremely clean

squeal /skwiːl/ verb [I] to make a long high sound —**squeal** noun [C]

squeamish /'skwiːmɪʃ/ adj easily upset by seeing something that is unpleasant

squeeze¹ /skwiːz/ verb ★
1 [I/T] to press something firmly: *Ruth smiled, squeezing his hand affectionately.*
2 [T] to press something such as a liquid out of something: *She squeezed some cream onto her hands.*
3 [I/T] to fit something into a small space, or to get through or into a small space: *We can only squeeze one more thing into the bag.* ♦ *He had squeezed through a hole in the fence.* ♦ *Passengers were trying to squeeze onto the bus.*
PHRASAL VERB ,squeeze sb/sth 'in to be able to do something or meet someone, even though you do not have much time: *I can squeeze a meeting in early tomorrow morning.*

squeeze² /skwiːz/ noun **1** [C] an act of squeezing something **2** [C] a small amount of a liquid that is squeezed out of something **3** [singular] a situation in which there are too many people or things in a small space **4** [singular] a situation in which there is strict control over money or goods

squelch /skweltʃ/ verb [I] to make the sound that your feet make when you walk on wet ground —**squelch** noun [C]

squid /skwɪd/ noun [C] a sea animal that is like an OCTOPUS but with ten arms instead of eight

squiggle /'skwɪg(ə)l/ noun [C] a line with a lot of curves in it —**squiggly** adj

squint /skwɪnt/ verb [I] to close your eyes slightly in order to try to see something more clearly —**squint** noun [C]

squirm /skwɜːm/ verb [I] **1** to look or feel embarrassed and uncomfortable **2** to move by twisting and turning in a small space

squirrel /'skwɪrəl/ noun [C] a grey or red-brown animal with a long thick tail. Squirrels live in trees. —*picture* → C13

squirt /skwɜːt/ verb **1** [I/T] if a liquid squirts somewhere, or if you squirt it, it comes out in a narrow stream with a lot of force **2** [T] to make someone or something wet by squirting a liquid —**squirt** noun [C]

squish /skwɪʃ/ verb [T] *informal* to press hard on something that is soft

squishy /'skwɪʃi/ adj *informal* extremely soft and easy to press or crush

Sr abbrev Senior: used after the name of someone who has a child with the same name

St abbrev **1** Saint **2** Street

stab¹ /stæb/ verb [T] to push a knife or other sharp object into someone or something
PHRASE stab sb in the back to do something that is not loyal to someone who trusts you

stab² /stæb/ noun [C] **1** an act of stabbing someone **2** *informal* an attempt to do something that is difficult to do or that you have never done: *They decided to have a stab at fixing the car themselves.* **3** a sudden feeling of a negative emotion: *a stab of jealousy*

stabbing¹ /'stæbɪŋ/ noun [C] an attack in which someone is stabbed

stabbing² /'stæbɪŋ/ adj sudden and very strong: *a stabbing pain*

stability /stə'bɪləti/ noun [U] a situation in which things continue without any major changes or problems ≠ INSTABILITY: *The rise of nationalism could threaten the stability of Europe.*

stabilize /'steɪbə,laɪz/ verb [I/T] to reach a state where there are no longer any major changes or problems, or to make something do this: *Oil prices have stabilized for now.* —**stabilization** /,steɪbəlaɪ'zeɪʃ(ə)n/ noun [U]

stable¹ /'steɪb(ə)l/ adj ★★
1 not changing frequently, and not likely to suddenly become worse ≠ UNSTABLE: *a stable economic situation* ♦ *Tonight the baby is in a stable condition in hospital.*
2 not likely to fall or move in the wrong way ≠ UNSTABLE: *The suspension keeps the car stable when cornering.*
3 with a healthy mental and emotional state =BALANCED

stable² /'steɪb(ə)l/ noun [C] a building where horses are kept

stack¹ /stæk/ noun [C] **1** a pile of things that are placed one on top of another: *a stack of unopened mail* **2** *informal* a large amount of something: *There's stacks of time left.*

stack² /stæk/ verb [T] **1** to arrange things by placing one on top of another: *Stack the chairs and put them in the corner when you're finished.* **2** to fill something by arranging things in piles or rows in or on it: *He got a job stacking shelves at the supermarket.*
PHRASAL VERB ,stack sth 'up same as stack² 1

stadium /'steɪdiəm/ noun [C] a large building, usually without a roof, where people watch sports events such as football matches or races

staff¹ /stɑːf/ noun [singular/U] ★★★ the people who work for a particular company, organization, or institution: *The embassy employs around 50 people on its full-time staff.* ♦ *She joined the staff in 1996.* ♦ *Peter became a very valued member of staff.*

In British English, **staff** can be used with a singular or plural verb. You can say: *The staff has worked very hard.* OR: *The staff have worked very hard.*

staff² /stɑːf/ verb [T] to provide an organization with workers

staffing /'stɑːfɪŋ/ noun [U] the activities connected with providing staff for an organization

stag /stæg/ noun [C] a male DEER

stage¹ /steɪdʒ/ noun ★★★
1 [C] a particular point in time during a process or series of events: *We were now on the last stage of our journey.* ♦ *They had the ball more often in the early stages of the game.* ♦ *There's no point arguing about it at this stage.*
2 [C] the part of a theatre where the actors or musicians perform: *They had now been on stage for over four hours.* ♦ *The band*

didn't take the stage (=come onto it) *until after ten o'clock.*

3 the stage [singular] the theatre: *She's written a number of works for the stage.*

4 the stage [singular] the profession of being an actor: *Do you think your children will go on the stage* (=become actors)?

Words often used with stage

Adjectives often used with stage (noun, sense 1)
■ **advanced, closing, early, final, formative, halfway, initial, last, late, preliminary** + STAGE: used for saying what stage a process has reached

---

stage² /steɪdʒ/ verb [T] **1** to organize an event: *They staged a protest in front of the embassy.* **2** to organize a performance of a play or opera —**staging** noun [C/U]

stagecoach /ˈsteɪdʒˌkəʊtʃ/ noun [C] a vehicle that is pulled by horses that was used in the past for carrying people, letters, and goods

stage fright noun [U] fear felt by an actor or singer before a performance, or by someone who is going to do something important

stage manager noun [C] someone who is in charge of the practical arrangements for a play or other show

stagger /ˈstæɡə/ verb **1** [I] to walk in an uncontrolled way, as if you are going to fall: *He gave her a slight push, and she staggered backwards.* **2** [T] to surprise and shock someone=ASTOUND: *Rory was staggered by his answer.* **3** [T] to arrange for events or activities to start at different times: *We have to stagger meal times because there are so many of us now.*

staggered /ˈstæɡəd/ adj extremely surprised

staggering /ˈstæɡərɪŋ/ adj extremely surprising —**staggeringly** adv

stagnant /ˈstæɡnənt/ adj **1** stagnant water does not flow and often smells bad **2** not growing or developing

stagnate /stæɡˈneɪt/ verb [I] **1** to stay the same without growing or developing **2** if water stagnates, it does not flow and becomes dirty —**stagnation** /stæɡˈneɪʃ(ə)n/ noun [U]

stag night or **stag party** noun [C] British an occasion when a group of men celebrate together because one of them is going to be married soon

staid /steɪd/ adj serious and rather boring

stain¹ /steɪn/ verb **1** [I/T] to leave a mark on something accidentally: *Sweat had stained his shirt.* **2** [T] to colour wood with a special liquid

stain² /steɪn/ noun **1** [C] a mark that is left accidentally on clothes or surfaces: *oil stains* **2** [C/U] a liquid that is used for colouring wood

stained glass /ˌsteɪnd ˈɡlɑːs/ noun [U] coloured glass that is traditionally used in church windows —**stained-glass** adj

stainless steel /ˌsteɪnləs ˈstiːl/ noun [U] steel that has been treated to stop RUST forming on its surface. It is used for making knives, tools etc. —**stainless-steel** adj

S

stair /steə/ noun ★★

1 stairs [plural] a set of steps that allow you to go from one level of a building to another: *I climbed the stairs to Charles's office.* ♦ *John raced down the stairs to answer the door.* ♦ *Someone was waiting at the top of the stairs.* —picture → C1

2 [C] one of the steps in a set of stairs: *He was standing on the bottom stair.*

staircase /ˈsteəˌkeɪs/ noun [C] a set of stairs in a building with a BANISTER that you hold onto when you go up or down

stairway /ˈsteəˌweɪ/ noun [C] a set of stairs inside or outside a building

stake¹ /steɪk/ noun ★

1 [C] business the part of a business that you own because you have invested money in it: *They took a 40% stake in the company last year.*

2 [C] an amount of money that you risk losing when you try to guess the result of a race or competition

3 stakes [plural] the things that you can gain or lose by taking a risk: *The Americans have raised the stakes* (=risked gaining or losing more) *in a bitter fight over imports.* ♦ *With such high stakes* (=a lot that could be won or lost), *the atmosphere was tense.*

4 [C] a wooden or metal post with a pointed end that is used for supporting or marking something

PHRASE at stake likely to be lost or damaged if something fails: *People's lives are at stake.*

stake² /steɪk/ verb [T] to risk losing or damaging something that is valuable in order to get or do something=GAMBLE: *The government has staked its reputation on eliminating the deficit.*

PHRASE stake a claim (to sth) to say or show clearly that you believe that something is yours

PHRASAL VERBS stake out sth to explain your opinion clearly and defend it in a determined way: *Political leaders are busy staking out their positions on this issue.*

stake sth out 1 to stay outside a building and watch it because something that is illegal or exciting is happening there: *The police are staking out his home in case he returns.* **2** to mark an area with fences or posts to show that it belongs to someone: *The settlers would arrive in a place and immediately stake out their territory.*

stale /steɪl/ adj **1** old and no longer fresh: *stale bread* **2** not smelling fresh or nice: *stale air* **3** not new, original, or interesting: *stale news* **4** someone who is stale has done something so often that they can no longer do it well or be interested in it

stalemate /ˈsteɪlˌmeɪt/ noun [C/U] **1** a situation in which progress is impossible because the people involved cannot agree: *Management and the unions have reached stalemate in their negotiations.* **2** the situation in CHESS when the game ends because neither player can win

stalk¹ /stɔːk/ noun [C] a long thin part of a plant with a flower, fruit, or leaf at the end

stalk² /stɔːk/ verb **1** [I] to walk in a way that shows that you feel angry or offended: *He shook his head in disgust and stalked off, muttering.* **2** [T] to hunt a person or animal by following them without being seen **3** [T] to follow and watch someone all the time in a threatening way, because of an extremely strong interest in them

stalker /ˈstɔːkə/ noun [C] someone who follows and watches another person all the time in a threatening way, because of an extremely strong interest in them

stall¹ /stɔːl/ noun [C] **1** a large table or a small building that is open at the front. Stalls are used for selling things or for giving people information. **2** a narrow space for one animal such as a horse or pig **3** stalls [plural] *British* the seats in front of the stage on the lowest level of a theatre, cinema etc

stall² /stɔːl/ verb [I/T] **1** if a vehicle's engine stalls, or if the driver stalls it, it suddenly stops working **2** if a process stalls, or if someone stalls it, it stops making progress: *Talks have stalled and both sides are preparing for war.* **3** to delay, or to delay someone, in order to gain more time: *If he calls again, try to stall him until I get there.*

stallion /ˈstæljən/ noun [C] an adult male horse

stalwart /ˈstɔːlwət/ adj very loyal: *a stalwart supporter* —**stalwart** noun [C]

stamina /ˈstæmɪnə/ noun [U] the ability to work hard over a long period of time without getting tired

stammer /ˈstæmə/ verb [I/T] to keep repeating a particular sound when trying to speak because you have a speech problem, or because you are nervous or excited —**stammer** noun [singular]

stamp¹ /stæmp/ noun ★★
1 [C] a small official piece of paper that you buy and stick on an envelope in order to pay for the cost of posting a letter or parcel =POSTAGE STAMP: *a first-class stamp*
2 [C] a small tool with a pattern or writing on one side that you press into ink and use for printing a mark on paper
3 [C] a mark that you make with a stamp: *Did you get a stamp in your passport?*
4 [singular] a particular quality that is clearly noticeable in someone or something: *The film bears the unmistakable stamp of its energetic director.* ♦ *He has a chance to put his stamp on government policy.*
PHRASE **stamp of approval** a statement that shows that you approve of someone or something

stamp² /stæmp/ verb ★
1 [I/T] to put your foot down hard and noisily on something: *Mary tried to stamp on the spider.* ♦ *He stamped his foot angrily.*
2 [I] to walk putting your feet down hard and noisily on the ground, usually because you are angry: *Riley stamped into the editor's office.*
3 [T] to put a mark on something using ink and a stamp: *They didn't stamp my passport.*
PHRASAL VERB **stamp sth out** to end something that is bad or unpleasant by taking strong and determined action

stamped addressed envelope /ˌstæmpt əˌdrest ˈenvələʊp/ noun [C] *British* an SAE

stampede /stæmˈpiːd/ noun [C] a situation in which a group of people or animals all start to run in a very fast uncontrolled way because they are frightened or excited —**stampede** verb [I/T]

stance /stæns/ noun [C] **1** an attitude or view about an issue that you state publicly =POSITION **2** a particular way of standing

stand¹ /stænd/ (past tense and past participle **stood** /stʊd/) verb ★★★

1 be upright on feet	10 be willing to accept
2 get up	11 have attitude
3 be/put sth upright	12 not be affected by sth
4 put foot on/in sth	13 try to be elected
5 be particular height	14 perform job/service
6 be in situation/state	15 buy sth for sb
7 of vehicle	✦ PHRASES
8 reach level/amount	✦ PHRASAL VERBS
9 still exist	

1 [I] to have your body in an upright position supported by your feet: *The train was full and we had to stand all the way to Edinburgh.* ♦ *Stand still* (=don't move) *and let me brush your hair.* ♦ *Mrs Carter was standing by the open window.* ♦ *The man standing behind him spoke.* ♦ *stand doing sth He stood looking at them in silence.* ♦ *stand and do sth The children stood and watched.* —*picture* → POSTURE

2 [I] to move from lying, sitting, or bending down into an upright position: *Everyone stood as the judge entered the court.*

3 [I/T] to put someone or something in an upright position, or to be in an upright position: *Stand the bookcase against the far wall.* ♦ *His statue stands in the city square.*

4 [I] to put your foot on or in something: *He apologized for standing on my foot.* ♦ *I just stood in something disgusting.*

5 [I] to be a particular height: *The structure stands 40 metres high.*

6 [I] to be in a particular situation or state: *How do negotiations stand at the moment?* ♦ *As it stands, the law doesn't allow local government to take such action.* ♦ *He might seem rude, but at least you know where you stand with him* (=understand your position).

7 [I] if a car, train, plane etc stands somewhere, it remains there without moving, waiting to be used: *Luckily, the train was still standing at the platform.*

8 [I] to reach a particular level or amount: *The total amount of money raised so far stands at over £3000.*

9 [I] to remain in existence or use: *Her world record has stood for nearly 20 years.* ♦ *Tell him my offer still stands.*

10 [T] to be willing to accept something that

S

is unpleasant: *How can you stand all that noise?* ♦ **stand sb doing sth** *I won't stand them interrupting me all the time.*

11 [I] to have a particular attitude or view about a person or subject: *Where does the Prime Minister stand on this issue?*

12 [T] to be good or strong enough not to be badly affected or damaged by something: *These are plants that do not stand the cold well.* ♦ *I wonder how many of these new businesses will stand the test of time.*

13 [I] *British* to take part in an election as a CANDIDATE (=someone who people vote for): *She's not intending to stand at the next election.* ♦ *She is intending to stand for parliament.* ♦ *He'll be standing as the candidate for Falkirk West.*

14 [T] to perform a particular job or service: *Two men were standing guard over the prisoners.*

15 [T] *informal old-fashioned* to buy food or drink for someone: **stand sb sth** *I'll stand you a cup of coffee if you've no money.*

PHRASES **sb can't stand sb/sth** used for saying that a person dislikes someone or something very much: *James just can't stand his mother-in-law.* ♦ *Sylvia couldn't stand the sight of blood.* ♦ **can't stand doing sth** *I can't stand waiting for buses.* ♦ **can't stand sb doing sth** *He couldn't stand anyone feeling sorry for him.* ♦ **can't stand to do sth** *She couldn't stand to see him leave.*

sb could stand sth used for saying that you think that someone should do something because it would be a good thing: *Those kids could stand a few lessons in good manners.* ♦ **sb could stand to do sth** *He could stand to lose a bit of weight.*

it stands to reason (that) used for saying that something is obvious because it is what most sensible people would expect: *If they don't like you, it stands to reason they won't give you the job.*

stand accused of sth to be the person who has been formally accused in a court of law of committing a crime

stand a chance (of doing sth) to be likely to achieve something: *Do they stand any chance of winning against France?*

stand in sb's way to try to stop someone from doing something

stand in the way of sth to try to prevent something from happening

stand on your own two feet to behave in an independent way, especially by not asking for financial help from anyone

stand to do sth to be in a particular situation or state that makes something likely to happen to you: *Many small companies stand to lose financially if the new law is introduced.*

stand trial (for sth) to be judged for a crime in a court of law

→ GROUND¹, LEG

PHRASAL VERB ˌstand aˈround or ˌstand aˈbout *British* to stand somewhere and do nothing

ˌstand aˈside **1** to move to one side in order to let someone go past you **2** to let someone

else have your job or position: *The trade secretary has been asked to stand aside in favour of her deputy.*

ˌstand ˈback to move away from something, or to stand at a distance from something

ˌstand ˈby **1** to be ready to do something: *A boat will be standing by in case of emergency.* **2** to not take action when you should: *We can't just stand by and watch her die.*

ˌstand ˈby sb to be loyal to someone who is in a difficult situation

ˌstand ˈby sth to continue to believe or support something although a situation has changed: *The doctors are standing by their claim that they are not at fault.*

ˌstand ˈdown to leave an important job or position: *She'll be standing down as president at the end of the year.*

ˈstand for sth **1** if an abbreviation or a symbol stands for something, that is what it means or represents: *The letters ERM stand for exchange-rate mechanism.* **2** if someone stands for a particular principle, they believe that that principle is important: *I hate them and everything they stand for.* **3** to be willing to accept something that someone does: *No one makes a fool of me. I won't stand for it!*

ˌstand ˈin to do someone else's job for a short time while they are not available to do it: *I'll be standing in for Peter while he's away.*

ˌstand ˈout **1** to be easy to see or notice because of being different: *His bright yellow tie stood out against his black suit.* **2** to be much more impressive or important than others: *It stands out in my mind as the most exciting day of my career.*

ˌstand ˈup **1** *same as* **stand¹** 1: *You have the chair. I don't mind eating standing up.* ♦ *Stand up straight and take your hands out of your pockets.* **2** *same as* **stand¹** 2: *A man at the back stood up to ask a question.* **3** to still seem true or correct after being examined carefully: *We all knew her story wouldn't stand up in court.*

ˌstand sb ˈup to not meet someone who you have arranged to meet, especially someone who you are having or starting a sexual or romantic relationship with

ˌstand ˈup for sb/sth to defend someone or something that is being criticized or attacked: *You've got to stand up for what you believe in.* ♦ *The only crime they've ever committed is to stand up for their rights.* ♦ *I learned how to stand up for myself early on in life.*

ˌstand ˈup to sb to not allow yourself to be treated badly by someone who is more powerful than you

stand² /stænd/ *noun* ★★

1 attitude/opinion	4 for holding sth
2 attempt to oppose	5 for watching sports
3 table	6 in court of law

1 [C] an attitude or opinion about something that you state publicly: *I couldn't vote for them because of their stand on social issues.*

♦ *The president has not **taken a stand** on this.*

2 [C] a determined attempt to oppose someone or something that you think is wrong: *support for their **stand against** racism* ♦ *The Prime Minister must **take a firm stand** against extremists in his party.*

3 [C] a large table or structure that is used for selling things or for providing information or services: *a hot-dog stand* ♦ *the Porsche stand at the Paris show*

4 [C] an object or a piece of furniture that is used for holding, supporting, or storing something: *a cake stand* ♦ *an umbrella stand*

5 [C] a part of a sports STADIUM where people sit or stand in order to watch a match or event

6 [singular] *American* the part of a court of law where people stand in order to answer lawyers' questions

→ ONE-NIGHT STAND

standard¹ /ˈstændəd/ noun ★★★

1 [C/U] a level of quality or achievement, especially one that most people think is normal or acceptable: *What can be done to **raise standards** in schools?* ♦ *The food was not **up to standard**.* ♦ *He **sets** himself **high standards**.* ♦ *higher **standards of service** in hospitals*

2 [C] a level of quality or achievement that is used for judging someone or something: *The first computers were terribly slow **by today's standards**.* ♦ *The building was still magnificent **by any standards**.*

3 **standards** [plural] traditional principles of good behaviour: *declining **moral standards***

PHRASE **standard of living** the type of life that a person or society has according to the amount of money that they have

standard² /ˈstændəd/ adj ★★★

1 generally used or accepted as normal: *It's a standard reply that the company sends out to applicants.* ♦ *It is **standard practice** for the school to inform the parents whenever a child is punished.*

2 made or done according to a generally accepted set of rules, measurements etc: *The promotional pack was 20 per cent bigger than the **standard size**.*

3 generally accepted as correct ≠ NON-STANDARD: *the teaching of **standard English***

standard assessment task /ˌstændəd əˈsesmənt ˌtɑːsk/ noun [C] *British* a test in a particular subject that is given to children in schools in the UK

standardize /ˈstændədaɪz/ verb [T] to make all the things of a particular type have the same features or level of quality
—**standardization** /ˌstændədaɪˈzeɪʃ(ə)n/ noun [U]

standby /ˈstæn(d)baɪ/ noun [C] someone or something that is always available to be used if they are needed

PHRASE **on standby 1** available to be used if needed: *The troops are on standby and can return at a moment's notice.* **2** ready to get on a plane if there is a seat left when it is about to take off: *The flight is sold out, but*

we can put you on standby.
—**standby** adj: *standby passengers*

stand-in noun [C] someone or something that takes the place of another person or thing for a short time, especially in order to do their job

standing¹ /ˈstændɪŋ/ noun [U] the status or reputation that someone or something has
PHRASE **of many/five/ten etc years' standing** used for saying how long something has been happening: *a friend of long standing*

standing² /ˈstændɪŋ/ adj always existing: *the members of the standing committee* ♦ *We've got a standing invitation to stay with Jen and Mike whenever we want.*

standing army noun [C] a professional army that a country has all the time, not just in a war

standing joke noun [C] something that happens regularly that a particular group of people find funny

standing order noun [C/U] *British* an instruction that you give a bank to take a particular amount of money out of your account on a particular day in order to pay a person or organization for you

standing ovation noun [C] an enthusiastic reaction to a performance or speech in which people stand and CLAP their hands

stand-off noun [C] a situation in a disagreement or fight in which neither opponent can do anything in order to win or to achieve their aim

standpoint /ˈstæn(d)pɔɪnt/ noun [C] a way of thinking about something

standstill /ˈstæn(d)stɪl/ noun [singular] a situation in which something stops moving or happening

stand-up adj consisting of one person standing in front of an audience and entertaining them by telling jokes: *stand-up comedy* —**stand-up** noun [U]

stank the past tense of **stink¹**

stanza /ˈstænzə/ noun [C] a group of lines in a poem that form a unit with a pattern that is repeated through the whole poem

staple¹ /ˈsteɪp(ə)l/ noun [C] **1** a small piece of wire that you press through pieces of paper with a STAPLER in order to fasten them together **2** an important food or product that people eat or use regularly

staple² /ˈsteɪp(ə)l/ adj a staple food or product is the most basic and important one for a particular place or group of people

staple³ /ˈsteɪp(ə)l/ verb [T] to fasten pieces of paper together with a staple

staple diet noun [singular] the main food or foods that a person or animal eats regularly

stapler /ˈsteɪplə/ noun [C] a small object used for fastening pieces of paper with a STAPLE
—*picture* → C3

star¹ /stɑː/ noun ★★★

1 small light in night sky	**5** the best in a group
2 sb famous and popular	**6** sign of quality
3 main actor	**7** sb's future
4 pointed object/shape	

S

1 [C] a very large hot ball of gas that appears as a small bright light in the sky at night

2 [C] a famous and popular actor, entertainer, or sports player: *a Hollywood/pop/soccer star*

3 [C] the main actor or performer in a film, play, television programme etc: *Today, he's the star of a hundred-million-dollar movie.*

4 [C] an object, shape, or sign with five or more points that looks like a star: *We always put a star at the top of our Christmas tree.* ♦ *the 50 stars on the US flag* ♦ *I've put stars next to the names I want you to check.* —picture → c8

5 [C] someone or something that is clearly better than all the other people or things in a group: *McAllister was most definitely the star of the Scottish team.* ♦ *Mick was a star pupil at his school.*

6 [C] a sign that is shaped like a star that is given to a hotel or restaurant in order to show what level of quality or importance it has: *a five-star hotel*

7 stars [plural] *British informal* a HOROSCOPE: *Have you read your stars today?*

star² /stɑː/ verb [I/T] ★★ if you star in a film, play, television programme etc, or if it stars you, you are the main actor or performer in it: The X-Files, *starring David Duchovny and Gillian Anderson* ♦ *He starred in the school play.*

starboard /ˈstɑːbəd/ noun [U] the right side of a ship when you are looking towards the front

starch /stɑːtʃ/ noun **1** [C/U] a white substance without any taste that is found in rice, potatoes, and other vegetables **2** [U] a substance that is used for making clothes stiff

starchy /ˈstɑːtʃi/ adj starchy foods have a lot of STARCH in them

stardom /ˈstɑːdəm/ noun [U] the state of being very famous and popular as an actor, entertainer, or sports player

stare /steə/ verb [I] ★★ to look at someone or something very directly for a long time: *It's rude to stare.* ♦ *He lifted his head and stared at her.* —**stare** noun [C]

starfish /ˈstɑːfɪʃ/ noun [C] a small flat sea animal with five or more arms that is shaped like a star

stark¹ /stɑːk/ adj **1** very clear and plain to look at, in a slightly unpleasant or frightening way: *stark brick walls* **2** very obvious or impossible to avoid: *The stark choice is between moving out or staying here and paying more.* **3** extreme and obvious: *His words were in stark contrast to what he had said earlier.* —**starkly** adv

stark² /stɑːk/ adv **stark naked** not wearing any clothes

starlight /ˈstɑːlaɪt/ noun [U] the light that comes from the stars

starling /ˈstɑːlɪŋ/ noun [C] a small bird with dark shiny feathers

starlit /ˈstɑːlɪt/ adj bright with light from the stars

starry /ˈstɑːri/ adj a starry sky or night is one with a lot of stars

starry-eyed /ˌstɑːri ˈaɪd/ adj someone who is starry-eyed has a lot of hopes or dreams about success in the future, but does not plan things in a sensible way

ˈstar ˌsign noun [C] one of the 12 signs of the ZODIAC that some people believe influences your character and your future

star-studded /ˈstɑː ˌstʌdɪd/ adj including a lot of famous people

start¹ /stɑːt/ verb ★★★

1 begin to happen	**7** be the limit of sth
2 begin to do sth	**8** be the lowest price
3 begin a journey	**9** make sth happen
4 begin job/education	**10** make machine work
5 begin a period of time	**+ PHRASES**
6 of business/project	**+ PHRASAL VERBS**

1 [I] to begin to happen: *The World Championships start in two weeks.* ♦ **start to do sth** *It's starting to rain.* ♦ **start doing sth** *The leaves have started falling off the trees.*

2 [I/T] to begin doing something: *Please start when you are ready.* ♦ *The class starts with some gentle stretching exercises.* ♦ **start to do sth** *I started to unpack my suitcase.* ♦ **start doing sth** *Everyone in the class started laughing.*

3 [I/T] to begin a journey: *We started early enough but got caught in the London traffic.*

4 [I/T] to begin a new job, career, or period of education: *I start work on Monday.* ♦ *Things were very different when I started in politics.*

5 [T] to begin a period of time in a particular way: *I always start the day with a cup of coffee.*

6 [T] to bring a business or project into existence: *He decided to quit his job and start his own business.*

7 [I] used for talking about the nearest end or edge of something: *The new houses start immediately beyond the bridge.*

8 [I] used for talking about the lowest price or number: *Prices for theatre tickets start from £10.*

9 [T] to cause something, or to be the first person to do something: *Who wants to start the discussion?* ♦ **start sb doing sth** *What she said started me thinking.*

10 [I/T] if you start a machine, or if it starts, it begins to work: *No matter how many times he tried, the car wouldn't start.* ♦ *Scott started the engine and drove off.*

PHRASES **back where you started** in the same place or situation where you were before, so that you have not made any progress

get started to begin doing something: *We couldn't wait to get started on the next job.*

get sb started to help or cause someone to begin doing something new: *It was his aunt who got him started in publishing.*

to start with 1 as a beginning, or as the first thing: *Let's have a few easy questions to start with.* **2** used for introducing the first or the most important point that supports an opinion: *Well, to start with, you haven't got the right qualifications.*

PHRASAL VERBS **ˌstart (sth) ˈoff** to begin, or to

cause something to begin: *Let's **start off** with a few questions from the audience.*
,start sb 'off to make someone begin doing something: **start sb off on sth** *What started you off on this new career?*
'start on sth to begin working on something or dealing with something: *We could have breakfast before we start on the painting.*
,start 'out 1 to begin as something before developing into something different: *Some businesses **start out as** hobbies.* **2** to begin a journey: *We started out at five o'clock and got there at eight.*
,start (sth) 'up if you start up a business or project, or if it starts up, you bring it into existence: *She left last year to start up her own business.*

start² /staːt/ noun ★★★

1 of period of time	5 in races and games
2 the way sb begins sth	6 new opportunity
3 of journey	7 advantage
4 of film/story	+ PHRASES

1 [C] the beginning of a period of time: *I hated her **right from the start**. ♦ The operation takes about 15 minutes **from start to finish**. ♦ **At the start of** the final year, students do work experience.*
2 [C] the way that someone begins a period of time or activity: *Hakkinen **made a good start** and was in second place by the first corner. ♦ Her election campaign **got off to a slow start**. ♦ There's no better **start to the** day than a healthy breakfast.*
3 [C] the beginning of a journey: *After an **early start**, we were soon out of the city.*
4 [C] the beginning of a film, story, show etc: *Let's take a look at **the start of** the story in more detail.*
5 [singular] the moment when a race begins, or the place where it begins: *The start has been brought forward by 30 minutes. ♦ The runners were all gathered **at the start**.*
6 [C] a big change or new opportunity in your life: *She travelled to Hong Kong, hoping for **a fresh start**.*
7 [singular] an advantage that you have, especially in a race or competition = HEAD START: *The women runners are given a 50-metre start.*
PHRASES for a start used for introducing the first point in a series, especially in an argument: *They are too young for a start.*
make a start (on sth) to begin doing something: *I'll make a start on the washing-up.*

starter /ˈstaːtə/ noun [C] **1** a small amount of food that is eaten at the start of a meal **2** an official who signals the start of a race

starting point /ˈstaːtɪŋ ˌpɔɪnt/ noun [C] **1** the place where a journey begins **2** something that you use as the first stage in a discussion or other activity

startle /ˈstaːt(ə)l/ verb [T] to make a person or animal suddenly feel frightened or surprised —**startled** /ˈstaːt(ə)ld/ adj, **startling** adj

'start-up noun [C/U] **1** the process of starting a business, or a small business that is just being started **2** *computing* the process of switching on a computer, or the action of doing this —**'start-up** adj

starvation /staːˈveɪʃ(ə)n/ noun [U] a situation in which people and animals suffer or die because they do not have enough to eat

starve /staːv/ verb [I/T] to suffer or die because you do not have enough food, or to make someone do this

starved /staːvd/ adj **1** prevented from having enough of what you need **2** *informal* very hungry

starving /ˈstaːvɪŋ/ adj **1** *informal* very hungry **2** ill or dying because you do not have enough food

stash¹ /stæʃ/ verb [T] *informal* to put something in a safe or secret place

stash² /stæʃ/ noun [C] *informal* an amount of something that you put in a safe or secret place

state¹ /steɪt/ noun ★★★

1 condition of sth	5 government
2 bad condition	6 USA
3 nation	+ PHRASE
4 region	

1 [C] the condition of something at a particular time: *Experts believe the painting can be restored to its original state. ♦ The British transport system is **in a sorry state** (=a very bad condition). ♦ We're collecting data on **the state of** the environment.*
2 [C] the physical or mental condition of a person, usually when this is bad: *By the time he got home, he was **in a terrible state**. ♦ I'd never seen you **in such a state** (=very upset or nervous). ♦ She was in **a state of panic**.*
3 [C] a nation, or country
4 [C] a region of a country that has its own government: *the state of Michigan*
5 [singular/U] the government of a country: *Should the state play a bigger role in industry?*
6 the States *informal* the United States of America
PHRASE state of mind the way that you are feeling at a particular time
→ STATE-OF-THE-ART

state² /steɪt/ verb [T] ★★★ to express something in speech or writing, especially in a definite or formal way: *'Jemma is going with me,' George stated firmly. ♦ **+that** He stated that the project would be completed by April.*

state³ /steɪt/ adj **1** a state occasion or event involves a country's government or leader **2** a state institution is one that is run by the government

stateless /ˈsteɪtləs/ adj not officially recognized as a citizen of any country

stately /ˈsteɪtli/ adj **1** stately movement is slow and steady **2** a stately person or thing is formal and impressive

,stately 'home noun [C] a large house in the UK that belongs to an important family

S

statement /'steɪtmənt/ noun [C] ★★★
1 something that you say or write, especially officially or in public: *He refused to make a statement to the press.*
2 an official document that lists the amounts of money that have been put in or taken out of a bank account

state-of-the-art adj very new and modern

state school noun [C] in the UK, a school that is paid for by the government and that provides free education

statesman /'steɪtsmən/ noun [C] an experienced political leader that many people respect —**statesmanlike** adj, **statesmanship** noun [U]

static¹ /'stætɪk/ adj something that is static does not move or change

static² /'stætɪk/ noun [U] the unpleasant noise that you hear on a radio, television, or telephone that is caused by electricity in the air

static electricity noun [U] electricity that is produced when two objects rub together

station¹ /'steɪʃ(ə)n/ noun [C] ★★★
1 a building or place where trains or buses stop so that passengers can get on or off: *It was dark when we arrived at the station.*
2 a building or place where a particular service or activity is based: *Astronomers at the Salyut Research Station discovered the star.*
3 a company that broadcasts television or radio programmes: *Listen to your local radio station for travel information.*

station² /'steɪʃ(ə)n/ verb [T] to send someone to a particular place in order to do a job, especially for the armed forces

stationary /'steɪʃ(ə)n(ə)ri/ adj not moving

stationer /'steɪʃ(ə)nə/ or **stationer's** noun [C] British a shop that sells stationery

stationery /'steɪʃ(ə)n(ə)ri/ noun [U] **1** things that you use for writing such as paper and pens **2** paper used for writing letters, often with the name of a company on it and envelopes that match

statistic /stə'tɪstɪk/ noun [C] a number that represents a fact or describes a situation

statistician /ˌstætɪ'stɪʃ(ə)n/ noun [C] someone whose job is to study and work with statistics

statistics /stə'tɪstɪks/ noun **1** [plural] a group of numbers that represent facts or describe a situation **2** [U] the science of using numbers to represent facts and describe situations —**statistical** /stə'tɪstɪk(ə)l/ adj, **statistically** /stə'tɪstɪkli/ adv

statue /'stætʃuː/ noun [C] an image of a person or animal that is made of stone, wood, metal etc

stature /'stætʃə/ noun [U] formal **1** the degree to which someone or something is respected or admired **2** someone's height

status /'steɪtəs/ noun ★★
1 [C/U] the legal position of someone or something: *Will I be officially self-employed, or will I have employee status?*
2 [U] someone's position in a profession or society, especially in comparison with

other people: *Our organization seeks to improve the **social status** of disabled people.*
3 [U] a high social position that makes other people respect and admire you: *a symbol of status and wealth*

status quo, the /ˌsteɪtəs 'kwəʊ/ noun [singular] the present situation, or the way that things usually are

status symbol noun [C] a possession that is a symbol of someone's money or power

statute /'stætʃuːt/ noun [C] formal a law, or a rule

statutory /'stætʃʊt(ə)ri/ adj formal controlled by a statute

staunch¹ /stɔːntʃ/ adj loyal and showing strong support

staunch² /stɔːntʃ/ verb [T] to stop the flow of something, especially blood

stave /steɪv/ PHRASAL VERB **stave sth off** to stop something that is unpleasant from happening

stay¹ /steɪ/ verb [I] ★★★
1 to remain in a particular place: *Stay right here, please.* ♦ *I have to **stay late** at work every Thursday.* ♦ *He wanted her to **stay at home** and look after the children.*
2 to remain in a particular situation or state: *Interest rates should stay low for the next few months.*
3 to live or remain in a place for a while as a guest or visitor: *How long is he planning to stay with you?*

PHRASES **sth is here to stay** used for saying that something is generally accepted and is part of all our lives: *Do you think high unemployment is here to stay?*
stay put spoken to remain where you are: *Stay put, I'll be back in a minute.*

PHRASAL VERBS **stay behind** to remain somewhere after everyone else has left: *Tony stayed behind and helped us clean the kitchen.*
stay in to remain in your home and not go out: *I think I'd rather stay in tonight.*
stay on to remain at a job, school, or place longer than you had intended to: *James promised to stay on for six months.*
stay out to remain out of your home for a period of time: *Please don't stay out all night again!*
stay out of sth to refuse to become involved in an argument or a bad situation: *He will go to jail if he doesn't stay out of trouble.*
stay up to not go to bed: *Josh could stay up all night without getting tired.*

stay² /steɪ/ noun [C] a period of time that you spend somewhere

STD /ˌes tiː 'diː/ abbrev sexually transmitted disease: a disease that you get from having sex with an infected person

stead /sted/ noun **stand sb in good stead** to be useful or helpful to someone

steadfast /'sted,fɑːst/ adj not changing your opinions or actions, because you have a strong belief in someone or something

steady¹ /'stedi/ adj ★
1 firmly held, without moving or shaking: *Hold the torch steady so I can see better.* ♦

You have to have a steady hand to be a surgeon.
2 slowly and gradually continuing to change, move, or happen: *A steady stream of people passed by.* ♦ *a steady increase in car sales*
3 staying at the same level, speed, value etc: *She listened to the steady rhythm of his breathing as he slept.*
4 likely to continue for a long period of time: *a steady boyfriend/girlfriend* ♦ *a steady relationship* ♦ *It would be nice to have a steady job.*
—**steadily** adv
steady² /ˈstedi/ verb [T] to hold something firmly without moving it
PHRASES **steady your nerves** to stop yourself from feeling nervous
steady yourself to try to get your balance again so that you will not fall
steak /steɪk/ noun [C/U] a large flat piece of meat or fish
steal /stiːl/ (past tense **stole** /stəʊl/; past participle **stolen** /ˈstəʊlən/) verb ★★
1 [I/T] to take something that belongs to someone else without permission: **steal sth from sb/sth** *She was caught stealing food from the supermarket.*
2 [I] to move somewhere quietly and secretly: *While Sara wasn't looking, I stole across the hall to make a call.*

Other ways of saying **steal**
■ **break into sth** to enter a building or vehicle illegally
■ **burgle** to steal from a house or flat that you have entered illegally
■ **mug** to attack a person in a public place and steal something from them
■ **nick** or **pinch** British (*informal*) to take something that belongs to someone else without their permission
■ **rob** to steal things from a place using violence, or threatening to use violence
■ **shoplift** to steal goods from a shop

stealth /stelθ/ noun [U] a quiet and secret way of behaving —**stealthily** adv, **stealthy** adj
steam¹ /stiːm/ noun [U] ★
1 the hot wet substance like a cloud that is produced when water is heated: *The steam from the window rose into the air.*
2 the power that is created when water is heated: *The equipment was originally powered by steam.* ♦ *a steam engine/locomotive/train*
PHRASES **let off steam** to express feelings of anger or excitement without harming anyone: *The meeting will be a chance for the protesters to let off steam.*
run out of steam to lose energy, enthusiasm, or importance
steam² /stiːm/ verb **1** [I/T] to cook food with steam **2** [I] to move using steam power
PHRASAL VERB **steam (sth) up** to cover something with steam, or to become covered with steam
steamer /ˈstiːmə/ noun [C] **1** a container used for cooking food with steam **2** a STEAMSHIP

steamroller¹ /ˈstiːmˌrəʊlə/ noun [C] a heavy vehicle that is used for making a road flat
steamroller² /ˈstiːmˌrəʊlə/ or **steamroll** /ˈstiːmˌrəʊl/ *informal* verb [T] *informal* **1** to defeat or destroy an opponent completely **2** to make sure that something happens by using all your power
steamship /ˈstiːmˌʃɪp/ noun [C] a ship that moves by steam power
steamy /ˈstiːmi/ adj **1** very hot and full of steam **2** *informal* sexually exciting
steel¹ /stiːl/ noun [U] ★ a strong metal made from a mixture of iron and CARBON
steel² /stiːl/ verb **steel yourself** to prepare yourself for something unpleasant
steelworks /ˈstiːlˌwɜːks/ (plural **steelworks**) noun [C] a factory where steel is made —**steelworker** noun [C]
steely /ˈstiːli/ adj showing a calm and firm attitude: *He had a look of steely determination in his eyes.*
steep¹ /stiːp/ adj ★
1 a steep slope goes up or down very quickly: *a steep hill/path* ♦ *Suddenly the plane went into a steep dive.*
2 a steep increase or fall in something is sudden and very big: *a steep rise in oil prices*
3 steep prices are very high
—**steeply** adv, **steepness** noun [U]
steep² /stiːp/ verb [T] to leave something in a liquid for some time
PHRASE **be steeped in sth** to have a lot of a particular quality or thing
steeple /ˈstiːp(ə)l/ noun [C] a tall pointed tower on a church
steer¹ /stɪə/ verb ★
1 [I/T] to control the direction in which a vehicle moves: *Jack steered while Ken gave directions.* ♦ *We steered the boat into the harbour.*
2 [T] to influence the way that something happens or the way that people behave: *Ruth attempted to steer the conversation well away from work.* ♦ *I try to steer my children towards healthier foods.*
3 [T] to control the direction in which someone moves with your hand: *He took her arm to steer her towards the door.*
PHRASE **steer clear (of)** *informal* to avoid someone or something that is dangerous or unpleasant: *Tourists are advised to steer clear of the area.*
steer² /stɪə/ noun [C] a young male cow
steering /ˈstɪərɪŋ/ noun [U] the parts of a vehicle that allow you to control the direction that it travels in
steering wheel noun [C] the wheel that you hold and turn in order to control the direction that a vehicle travels in —*picture* → C6
stem¹ /stem/ noun [C] **1** the long part of a plant from which the leaves and flowers grow **2** the long thin part of a wine glass that joins the bowl to the base
stem² /stem/ verb [T] to stop something from spreading or increasing

PHRASAL VERB ,stem from sth to be caused by something

stench /stentʃ/ noun [C] a very unpleasant smell

stencil[1] /ˈstens(ə)l/ noun [C] a piece of paper or plastic with a shape or letters cut out of it. You place it on a surface and paint over it in order to make a design on something.

stencil[2] /ˈstens(ə)l/ verb [T] to make a design on a surface using a stencil

step[1] /step/ noun [C] ★★★

1 movement or sound	**4** stage
2 one of series of actions	**5** dance movement
3 for walking up/down	**+** PHRASES

1 a movement made by putting one foot in front of the other, or the sound that your feet make while you are walking: *I could hear the steps coming closer.* ♦ *The postbox is just a few steps from my front door.* ♦ *Tom* ***took a step*** *backwards.*

2 one of a series of actions that you take in order to achieve a particular aim: *The government must* ***take steps*** *to control inflation.* ♦ *This agreement is an important* ***step towards*** *our goal.* ♦ *This new law is the first* ***step in*** *making our city safer.* ♦ *It's not the best deal for staff, but it's* ***a step in the right direction.*** ♦ *The new microchip is a major* ***step forward*** *(=improvement) in computer technology.*

3 a flat surface, usually one in a series, that you walk up or down in order to move to a different level: *I met him on the front steps of the bank.* ♦ *I climbed* ***a flight of steep steps*** *(=a set of steps).*

4 one of the stages in a process: *When you finish the exercise, repeat steps five to ten.* ♦ *Her new job is a big* ***step up*** *for her.* ♦ *Don't worry, we'll take things* ***one step at a time*** *(=gradually).* ♦ *She was congratulating herself on her cleverness, but he was* ***one step ahead*** *of her.*

5 a particular movement or set of movements that you make with your feet while dancing: *Juan was practising his new dance steps.*

PHRASES ***in step 1*** if people walk in step, each person moves their feet at exactly the same time as the others **2** if people or things are in step, they agree or move at the same rate: *Prices usually keep* ***in step with*** *inflation.*

out of step if people or things are out of step, they do not agree or move at the same rate

step[2] /step/ verb [I] ★★

1 to move somewhere by putting one foot down in front of the other: *I stepped onto the platform and started to speak.*

2 to move or walk a short distance: *Please* ***step*** *outside and wait for a moment.*

PHRASAL VERBS ,step aˈside to leave an official position or job, especially so that someone else can take your place

,step ˈdown *same as* **step aside**

,step ˈforward to offer help to someone who needs it: *Ron stepped forward and offered to change the tyre.*

,step ˈin to become involved in a discussion or argument, especially in order to make it stop: *It is time for the government to step in.*

,step sth ˈup to increase something: *The president has* ***stepped up the pressure*** *on the groups to come to an agreement.*

stepbrother /ˈstep,brʌðə/ noun [C] the son of your STEPFATHER or STEPMOTHER

,step-by-ˈstep adj a step-by-step plan or set of instructions explains each stage of a process in a clear way

stepchild /ˈstep,tʃaɪld/ noun [C] the son or daughter of your husband or wife from a previous relationship

stepdaughter /ˈstep,dɔːtə/ noun [C] the daughter of your husband or wife, who is not your child

stepfather /ˈstep,fɑːðə/ noun [C] the man who is married to your mother, but who is not your father

stepladder /ˈstep,lædə/ noun [C] a short LADDER consisting of two sloping parts, that can be folded and carried

stepmother /ˈstep,mʌðə/ noun [C] the woman who is married to your father, but who is not your mother

ˈstepping-ˌstone noun [C] **1** a step in a process that helps you to move forward to another part of it **2** a flat piece of rock in a river that you stand on in order to cross to the other side

stepsister /ˈstep,sɪstə/ noun [C] the daughter of your STEPFATHER or STEPMOTHER

stepson /ˈstep,sʌn/ noun [C] the son of your husband or wife, who is not your child

stereo /ˈsteriəʊ/ noun [C] a piece of electronic equipment with two SPEAKERS that you use for listening to the radio, CDs, and CASSETTES

PHRASE in stereo recorded or broadcast using a system that sends the sound through two SPEAKERS

—**stereo** adj

stereotype /ˈsteriə,taɪp/ noun [C] **1** a firm idea about what a particular type of person or thing is like, especially an idea that is wrong **2** someone who is exactly what many people expect a person of their particular class, NATIONALITY, profession etc to be like —**stereotype** verb [T], **stereotypical** /ˌsteriəˈtɪpɪk(ə)l/ adj

sterile /ˈsteraɪl/ adj **1** completely clean, with no bacteria ≠ DIRTY **2** not able to produce children **3** a sterile argument or discussion does not contain any interesting new ideas —**sterility** /stəˈrɪləti/ noun [U]

sterilize /ˈsterəlaɪz/ verb [T] **1** to kill all the bacteria on or in something and make it completely clean **2** to perform an operation on someone that makes them unable to produce children —**sterilization** /ˌsterəlaɪˈzeɪʃ(ə)n/ noun [C/U]

sterling[1] /ˈstɜːlɪŋ/ noun [U] **1** the standard unit of money in the UK **2** sterling or sterling silver silver that is of a standard quality

sterling[2] /ˈstɜːlɪŋ/ adj *formal* sterling work or

a sterling character is good, strong, and reliable

stern¹ /stɜːn/ adj serious and severe —**sternly** adv

stern² /stɜːn/ noun [C] the back part of a ship

steroid /'stɪərɔɪd, 'sterɔɪd/ noun [C] a drug that is used by doctors for treating conditions such as swelling, or, illegally, by ATHLETES for improving their performance

stethoscope /'steθəskəʊp/ noun [C] a piece of equipment that doctors use to listen to your heart or to your breathing

stew¹ /stjuː/ noun [C/U] a dish made by cooking vegetables, and usually meat or fish, slowly in a liquid

stew² /stjuː/ verb [T] to cook something slowly in a liquid

steward /'stjuːəd/ noun [C] **1** a man whose job is to look after the passengers on a plane, train, or ship **2** someone who helps to organize people at an event such as a football match or a horse race

stewardess /ˌstjuːə'des/ noun [C] old-fashioned a female FLIGHT ATTENDANT

stick¹ /stɪk/ (past tense and past participle **stuck** /stʌk/) verb ★★★

1 push sth long into sth	**5** become fixed
2 remain in sth	**6** accept sth unpleasant
3 fix to sth	**7** of name
4 put quickly	**+ PHRASAL VERBS**

1 [T] to push something that is long and thin into or through something else: *He **stuck** the end of the post **in** the ground.* ♦ *a piece of cloth with a pin **stuck through** it*

2 [I] if something sticks in, into, or through something else, its end remains in it or through it: *The knife missed its target and **stuck in** the door.* ♦ *Something sharp was **sticking into** my back.*

3 [I/T] to fix one thing to another, or to become fixed to something, especially using a sticky substance such as glue: *Can you **stick** the pieces of this vase back **together**?* ♦ *She was **sticking** posters **on** her bedroom wall.* ♦ *The pasta has **stuck to** the bottom of the pan.*

4 [T] informal to put something somewhere quickly and without taking much care =SHOVE: *Just **stick** the plates **in** the sink.*

5 [I] to become firmly fixed in one position, and therefore difficult or impossible to move: *The door is sticking, so give it a good push.* ♦ *The wheels had **stuck in** the mud.*

6 [T] British informal to accept something that is difficult or unpleasant in a patient way: *I don't know how she's **stuck** that job this long.*

7 [I] if a new name for someone or something sticks, it becomes accepted and used by everyone: *He'd been called 'Tufty' at school, and the name had **stuck**.*

PHRASAL VERBS ,stick a'round informal to remain in a particular place

'stick at sth British to continue to work at something that is difficult or unpleasant: *Just **stick at it** and I'm sure it'll get easier.*

'stick by sb informal to continue to support someone who is in a difficult situation

'stick by sth informal to do something that you promised or decided that you would do: *The head teacher is sticking by his decision to retire.*

,stick 'out **1** to continue further than the end of a surface or the main part of an object: *His ears stick out.* ♦ *A magazine was **sticking out** of his coat pocket.* **2** to be easy to notice or remember because of being unusual or different: *One face in particular stuck out.*
♦ *You **stick out like a sore thumb** in that uniform* (=look very different from everyone else).

,stick sth 'out **1** to push or stretch something forwards or away from you, especially a part of your body: *She stuck her arm out of the car window and waved.* ♦ *Ben **stuck out** his tongue at the little girl* (=as an insult). **2** to continue doing something difficult or unpleasant: *It was a tough course, but we **stuck it out**.*

'stick to sth **1** to do something that you promised or decided that you would do, or to do something that you should do: *We said we'd give her the cash, and we must stick to our agreement.* **2** to continue to do or use something, and not change it or stop it: *I think we should stick to our original plan.* ♦ *If you stick rigidly to your diet, you will lose weight.* ♦ *If everyone **sticks to the rules** (=obeys the rules), we shouldn't have any problems.* **3** **stick to your guns** informal to refuse to change what you are saying or doing

,stick to'gether informal if people stick together, they remain close together and support one another

,stick 'up to continue upwards further than the end of a surface or the main part of an object: *You've got a bit of hair sticking up at the back.*

,stick 'up for sb/sth informal to speak in support of someone or something, especially when no one else will do this

'stick with sb informal to stay close to someone and go with them wherever they go

'stick with sth informal to continue to do or use something, and not change it: *They're going to stick with the same team as last Saturday.*

stick² /stɪk/ noun [C] ★★

1 a thin piece of wood, especially one that has been broken or cut from a tree: *I went out to find some sticks for a fire.*

2 a long strong piece of wood, usually with a handle at the top, that you use for helping you to walk =WALKING STICK

3 a long thin piece of wood that is used for hitting or carrying something in a sport: *a hockey stick*

4 a long thin piece of something: *a stick of celery/dynamite*

sticker /'stɪkə/ noun [C] a piece of paper or plastic with a picture or writing on it, that you can stick to something

stickler /'stɪklə/ noun [C] someone who thinks that a particular thing is very important

sticks, the /stiks/ noun [plural] *informal* an area far from a town or city

sticky /'stiki/ adj **1** made of or covered with a substance that sticks to other things: *The dough should be soft but not sticky.* ♦ *sticky fingers* **2** sticky weather is hot and DAMP (=with a lot of water in the air) =HUMID **3** a sticky situation is difficult or dangerous =TRICKY

stiff¹ /stif/ adj ★

1 firm & difficult to bend	**5** of mixture
2 severe/difficult	**6** of wind
3 with pain in muscles	**7** with much alcohol
4 not moving easily	**8** formal/controlled

1 firm and difficult to bend: *a stiff piece of card* ♦ *a small stiff brush*
2 more severe or difficult than usual: *Jarvis is up against some stiff competition in this race.* ♦ *Those caught breaking the new law face stiff penalties.*
3 if a part of your body is stiff, you feel pain in your muscles and cannot move easily: *I've got a really stiff neck.*
4 not moving or operating as easily as you expect: *The drawer was rather stiff, so I pulled at it.*
5 a mixture that is stiff is very thick: *Whisk the egg whites until stiff.*
6 a stiff wind or BREEZE is fairly strong
7 a stiff drink contains a lot of alcohol
8 formal in a way that is not friendly or relaxed: *He looked stiff and awkward in his new suit.*
—**stiffly** adv, **stiffness** noun [U]

stiff² /stif/ adv **bored/scared/worried stiff** extremely bored/frightened/worried

stiffen /'stif(ə)n/ verb **1** [I] to suddenly hold your body in a stiff way, often because you are afraid or angry **2** [I/T] to become stiff, or to make something stiff

stifle /'staif(ə)l/ verb **1** [T] to stop something from happening or developing **2** [I/T] to stop someone from breathing, or to have difficulty in breathing =SUFFOCATE

stifling /'staif(ə)lɪŋ/ adj so hot that you feel uncomfortable and are unable to breathe easily

stigma /'stigmə/ noun [singular/U] a general attitude in which people treat something as wrong or embarrassing, especially in an unfair way

stigmatize /'stigmə,taiz/ verb [T] to treat something as wrong or embarrassing, especially in an unfair way

stiletto /sti'letəʊ/ (plural **stilettos** or **stilettoes**) noun [C] a shoe that has a thin high heel, or the heel on this kind of shoe

still¹ /stil/ adv ★★★
1 used for saying that a situation continues to exist up to and including a particular time: *Her hair was still damp from her walk in the rain.* ♦ *The car's doors were locked, but the motor was still running.* ♦ *Is Terry still in college?* → YET
2 used for emphasizing that a particular situation has not completely ended or changed: *I still have 50 pages to read before Friday.*

3 used for stating that something remains true despite what you have just said or done: *We knew we wouldn't win the game, but it was still exciting! ♦ I hadn't seen him for 25 years. Still, I recognized him immediately.*

still² /stil/ adj ★
1 not moving: *The water appeared still from a distance.* ♦ *Just sit still for a minute and let me tie your shoe.*
2 quiet and calm, with nothing happening: *By 10.00 the streets are quite still.*
3 without gas BUBBLES ≠ FIZZY: *still mineral water*

still³ /stil/ noun [C] **1** a photograph that is taken from one of the scenes in a film or video **2** a piece of equipment that is used for making strong alcohol

stillborn /'stilbɔːn/ adj a stillborn baby is born dead

still life (plural **still lifes**) noun [C/U] a type of art that represents objects instead of people, animals, or the countryside

stilted /'stiltid/ adj stilted movements or words are not relaxed or natural

stilts /stilts/ [plural] **1** a pair of long pieces of wood that you stand on so that you can walk high above the ground **2** a set of posts that a house is built on in order to raise it above the ground or above water

stimulant /'stimjʊlənt/ noun [C] a substance that makes you feel more lively or awake

stimulate /'stimjʊ,leit/ verb [T] **1** to encourage something to happen, develop, or improve: *The government should do more to stimulate investment in the north.* **2** to make someone feel interested in learning new things: *Such questions provide a useful way of stimulating students' interest.* —**stimulation** /,stimjʊ'leɪʃ(ə)n/ noun [U]

stimulating /'stimjʊ,leitɪŋ/ adj interesting and making you think

stimulus /'stimjʊləs/ (plural **stimuli** /'stimjʊlaɪ/) noun [C/U] **1** something that encourages something else to happen, develop, or improve **2** *science* something that produces a reaction in a person, animal, or plant

sting¹ /stɪŋ/ (past tense and past participle **stung** /stʌŋ/) verb **1** [I/T] if an insect, animal, or plant stings you, it hurts you by putting poison on or into your skin **2** [I/T] to be affected by a sudden pain or uncomfortable feeling, or to make something do this: *My eyes were stinging with the salt in the water.* **3** [T] to make someone feel angry and upset

sting² /stɪŋ/ noun [C] **1** the pain that you feel when an insect, animal, or plant stings you **2** a sudden pain or uncomfortable feeling

stinging /'stɪŋɪŋ/ adj strong enough to upset you: *a stinging attack on government policy*

stingy /'stɪndʒi/ adj *informal* unwilling to spend, give, or use a lot of money =MEAN ≠ GENEROUS

stink¹ /stɪŋk/ (past tense **stank** /stæŋk/ or **stunk** /stʌŋk/; past participle **stunk** /stʌŋk/) verb [I] *informal* **1** to smell very unpleasant or bad or dishonest **2** to be very bad

stink² /stɪŋk/ noun [singular] *informal* **1** a very

strong unpleasant smell **2** a situation in which you complain angrily about something

stint /stɪnt/ noun [C] a period of time that is spent doing something

stipulate /ˈstɪpjʊˌleɪt/ verb [T] formal to say what is allowed or what is necessary —**stipulation** /ˌstɪpjʊˈleɪʃ(ə)n/ noun [C]

stir¹ /stɜː/ verb ★

1 [I/T] to move food or a liquid around using a spoon or other object: Stir the sauce gently over a low heat.

2 [T] to make someone have a particular feeling or memory: This crime has stirred a lot of anger in the community. ♦ Seeing George again stirred old memories in me.

3 [I/T] to move slightly, or to make someone or something move slightly: The curtains stirred gently in the breeze. ♦ Mary was asleep and didn't stir.

PHRASAL VERB ˌstir sth ˈup same as stir¹ 2: He was accused of stirring up racial hatred.

stir² /stɜː/ noun [singular] **1** a situation in which a lot of people feel interested or angry: His speech caused quite a stir. **2** the movement that you make with a spoon or other object when you move food or a liquid around

ˈstir-ˌfry verb [T] to cook food quickly by moving it around in hot oil —**stir-ˌfry** noun [C]

stirring /ˈstɜːrɪŋ/ adj causing strong emotions

stirrup /ˈstɪrəp/ noun [C] a metal object that supports your foot when you ride a horse

stitch¹ /stɪtʃ/ noun **1** [C] one of the short pieces of THREAD that you can see on cloth when it has been sewn **2** [C] a short piece of THREAD that is used for joining someone's skin together after it has been cut **3** [C] a piece of wool that has been put round a needle when you are KNITTING **4** [singular/U] a sharp pain in the side of your body

PHRASE in stitches informal laughing a lot

stitch² /stɪtʃ/ verb [T] **1** to join pieces of cloth together by sewing them **2** to join someone's skin together with THREAD after it has been cut

PHRASAL VERB ˌstitch sth ˈup **1** to repair a piece of cloth that has been torn by sewing it **2** same as stitch² 2

stock¹ /stɒk/ noun ★★

1 amount kept	**4** worth of company
2 goods in shop	**5** for soups/sauces
3 shares in company	**+ PHRASE**

1 [C] an amount of something that is kept so that it can be used when it is needed: Their **stocks** of ammunition were running low.

2 [U] the goods that are available to buy in a shop: We're having some new stock delivered this afternoon. ♦ Do you have any of these batteries **in stock** (=available to buy) **at the moment?** ♦ I'm afraid that size is **out of stock** (=not available to buy).

3 [C/U] business a group of SHARES in an individual company: stocks and shares

4 [U] business the amount of money that a company is worth, represented by the total value of its SHARES

5 [C/U] a liquid made by boiling meat, bones, or vegetables that is used for making soups and sauces: chicken stock

PHRASE take stock (of sth) to spend some time thinking about the situation that you are in before you decide what to do next

stock² /stɒk/ verb [T] if a shop stocks goods, it has them available for sale

PHRASAL VERB ˌstock ˈup to get a lot of something so that it can be used when it is needed: We like to stock up on firewood before winter sets in.

stock³ /stɒk/ adj a stock answer, reply etc is one that someone always gives when they are asked a particular question

stockade /stɒˈkeɪd/ noun [C] a wall made of large wooden posts

stockbroker /ˈstɒkˌbrəʊkə/ noun [C] someone whose job is to buy and sell SHARES in companies for other people —**stockbroking** noun [U]

ˈstock exˌchange noun **1** [C] a place where people buy and sell SHARES in companies **2** the stock exchange [singular] the STOCK MARKET

stocking /ˈstɒkɪŋ/ noun [C] a very thin piece of clothing that is worn on a woman's foot and leg —picture → C5

stockist /ˈstɒkɪst/ noun [C] British a shop or business that sells a particular type of goods

ˈstock ˌmarket noun **1** [C] a STOCK EXCHANGE **2** the stock market [singular] the activities that are connected with buying and selling SHARES in companies

stockpile /ˈstɒkˌpaɪl/ verb [T] to collect large amounts of things that may be needed —**stockpile** noun [C]

stocktaking /ˈstɒkˌteɪkɪŋ/ noun [U] the process of counting a business's goods

stocky /ˈstɒki/ adj a stocky person looks strong but is not tall

stodgy /ˈstɒdʒi/ adj **1** stodgy food is solid and not pleasant to eat **2** boring and not willing to do things

stoical /ˈstəʊɪk(ə)l/ or **stoic** /ˈstəʊɪk/ adj accepting things without complaining —**stoically** /ˈstəʊɪkli/ adv, **stoicism** /ˈstəʊɪˌsɪz(ə)m/ noun [U]

stoke /stəʊk/ verb [T] **1** to add fuel to a fire **2** to make a feeling stronger

stole the past tense of **steal**

stolen the past participle of **steal**

stolid /ˈstɒlɪd/ adj acting or thinking in a slow serious way —**stolidly** adv

stomach¹ /ˈstʌmək/ noun [C] ★★

1 the soft part at the front of your body that is between your chest and your legs: A horse had kicked her in the stomach. —picture → C14

2 the organ inside your body where food goes when you have eaten it: She'll feel better when she has some food in her stomach.

PHRASES have the stomach for sth to have enough determination to do something that is unpleasant or dangerous

on an empty stomach if you do something on an empty stomach, you do not eat anything

S

before you do it: *It's not good to drink alcohol on an empty stomach.*

stomach² /'stʌmək/ verb [T] if you cannot stomach something, you cannot do it or deal with it because you dislike it very much

'stomach ache noun [C/U] pain in your stomach

stomp /stɒmp/ verb [I] to walk angrily making a lot of noise with your feet

stone¹ /stəʊn/ noun ★★★

1 rock	**4** unit of measurement
2 piece of rock	**5** jewel
3 seed in fruit	

1 [U] the hard substance that rocks are made of: *a cottage built of stone*
2 [C] a small piece of rock: *Children* **threw** *stones at him.*
3 [C] *British* a large hard seed that is inside a piece of fruit: *a peach stone*
4 (plural **stones** or **stone**) [C] *British* a unit for measuring weight that contains 14 pounds and is equal to 6.35 KILOGRAMS: *I've lost nearly two stone.*
5 [C] a jewel

stone² /stəʊn/ verb [T] to throw stones at someone in order to kill them

'Stone Age, the the period of history when people made tools and weapons from stone

stoned /stəʊnd/ adj *informal* affected by an illegal drug that makes you feel very relaxed

stony /'stəʊni/ adj **1** covered with stones, or containing stones **2** not friendly and not showing any emotion

stony-faced /ˌstəʊni 'feɪst/ adj looking unfriendly and not showing any emotion

stood the past tense and past participle of **stand¹**

stool /stuːl/ noun [C] **1** a seat that has legs but no support for your back or arms —*picture* → CHAIR **2** *technical* a piece of solid waste from your body

stoop¹ /stuːp/ verb [I] to bend the top half of your body downwards
PHRASAL VERB 'stoop to sth to do something that is bad in order to get what you want

stoop² /stuːp/ noun [singular] a way of standing or walking with your head and shoulders bent forwards and downwards

stop¹ /stɒp/ verb ★★★

1 prevent sth	**6** bus/train
2 no longer do sth	**7** pause to do sth
3 no longer move	**+** PHRASES
4 ask sb to stop	**+** PHRASAL VERBS
5 work no longer	

1 [T] to prevent someone from doing something, or to prevent something from happening: *Policies like this aren't going to stop crime.* ♦ **stop sb (from) doing sth** *A broken leg won't stop me from going to the concert.*
2 [I/T] to no longer do something, or to no longer happen: *When the rain stops, I'm going out.* ♦ **stop doing sth** *I want to stop smoking.*
3 [I] to no longer move: *The car stopped at the traffic lights.* ♦ *Lots of people stopped and stared at the accident.*

4 [T] to prevent someone from continuing to walk or drive so that you can talk to them: *I stopped a woman and asked her for directions.*
5 [I/T] to no longer work, or to cause something to no longer work: *My watch has stopped.* ♦ *Can you stop the engine?*
6 [I] if a bus or train stops somewhere, it stops moving in order to let passengers get on or off: *Does the train stop at Cambridge?*
7 [I] to pause while you are moving or doing something so that you can do something else: *He stopped and listened before opening the door.* ♦ **stop to do sth** *Jeff stopped to get a drink of water.*
PHRASES stop at nothing to do anything in order to get what you want, even if it is very bad
stop it/that used for telling someone not to do something that they are doing: *Stop it! You'll hurt him.*
stop short of (doing) sth to not do something, although you almost do it: *I stopped short of telling him what I really thought.*
PHRASAL VERBS ˌstop 'by to visit someone
ˌstop 'off to visit somewhere before continuing to another place

stop² /stɒp/ noun [C] ★
1 a place where you stop on a journey, or the time that you are there: *The president's first stop on his tour will be Honolulu.* ♦ *After a brief stop for coffee, we were on our way.*
2 a place where a bus or train stops in order to let passengers get on or off: *I'm getting off at the next stop.*
PHRASES come/jerk/skid etc to a stop to stop moving
put a stop to sth to prevent or end something → PULL¹

stopgap /'stɒpˌɡæp/ noun [C] a person or thing that provides a temporary solution

stoplight /'stɒpˌlaɪt/ noun [C] *American* a set of TRAFFIC LIGHTS

stopover /'stɒpˌəʊvə/ noun [C] a stop during a journey, especially during a flight

stoppage /'stɒpɪdʒ/ noun [C] a time when people stop working as a protest

stopper /'stɒpə/ noun [C] an object that is put into the top of a bottle in order to prevent the liquid from coming out

stopwatch /'stɒpˌwɒtʃ/ noun [C] a small clock that is used for measuring the exact time that it takes to do something

storage /'stɔːrɪdʒ/ noun [U] ★ the act of storing something, or the space where something is stored: *The area underneath provides useful storage.* ♦ *Most of our furniture is* **in storage.**

store¹ /stɔː/ noun [C] ★★
1 a supply of something that is kept so that it can be used later =STOCK: *a store of food for the winter*
2 *American* a shop: *a grocery store* ♦ *The store manager will be happy to assist you.*
PHRASES in store (for sb) if something is in store for you, it will happen to you in the future
set (great) store by sth to think that something is very important

store² /stɔː/ verb [T] ★★
1 to keep something in a particular place: *Store the cake in an airtight container.*
2 to save information in electronic form, for example in a computer's memory

storey /'stɔːri/ noun [C] British a level of a building

stork /stɔːk/ noun [C] a large bird with long legs and a long beak

storm¹ /stɔːm/ noun ★★
1 [C] an occasion when a lot of rain or snow falls very quickly, often with very strong winds or THUNDER and LIGHTNING: *A fierce storm hit the west coast of Florida early this morning.*
2 [singular] a situation in which many people are upset or excited: *His arrest provoked a storm of protest.*
PHRASE **take sth by storm** to be very successful in a particular place or among a particular group of people: *Jazz took London and Paris by storm in the 1920s.*

Words often used with storm

Adjectives often used with storm (noun, sense 1)
■ **fierce, freak, great, howling, raging, severe, terrible, violent** + STORM: used about storms that are severe
Verbs often used with storm (noun, sense 2)
■ **cause, create, provoke, raise, spark, unleash** + STORM: cause a storm by making many people upset or excited

storm² /stɔːm/ verb **1** [T] to use force to enter a place and take control of it **2** [I] to go somewhere very quickly because you are angry or upset: *Rob stormed out of the house and slammed the door.*

stormy /'stɔːmi/ adj **1** with a lot of rain or snow and strong winds **2** involving a lot of anger or arguments

story /'stɔːri/ noun [C] ★★★
1 a description of some events. Stories can be imaginary, traditional, or true: *She was reading a story to the children.* ♦ *a story about a princess and a frog* ♦ *stories of his travels in Asia* ♦ *He's written several children's stories.*
2 an account of events in a newspaper report or news programme: *tonight's main news stories*
3 an excuse or reason that is not true: *Do you expect me to believe that ridiculous story?*
4 the American spelling of **storey**
PHRASES **it's a long story** *spoken* used for saying that you do not want to talk about something because it is complicated
to cut a long story short *spoken* used for saying that you are not going to give all the details

storyteller /'stɔːriˌtelə/ noun [C] someone who tells stories

stout¹ /staʊt/ adj **1** slightly fat **2** strong and thick **3** very determined

stout² /staʊt/ noun [C/U] a type of dark beer

stove /stəʊv/ noun [C] a piece of equipment that provides heat for cooking or for heating a room

stow /stəʊ/ verb [T] to put something somewhere while you are not using it

stowaway /'stəʊəˌweɪ/ noun [C] someone who hides in a vehicle, ship, or plane in order to travel without permission

straddle /'stræd(ə)l/ verb [T] **1** to have one leg on either side of something **2** to be on both sides of something

straggle /'stræg(ə)l/ verb [I] to move more slowly than other people —**straggler** noun [C]

straight¹ /streɪt/ adj ★★

1 not bending/curving	**5** attracted to other sex
2 not leaning	**6** clean and tidy
3 honest and true	**7** having highest marks
4 one after the other	**+** PHRASES

1 without bends or curves: *a straight line/road* ♦ *She has long straight hair* (=no curls or waves).
2 in the correct position, not leaning to one side or the other: *The picture on that wall isn't straight.* ♦ *Make sure you keep your back straight.*
3 honest and true: *I want a straight answer.* ♦ *You have to be straight with her.*
4 happening one after the other: *It was the team's sixth straight win.* ♦ *There were five straight days of exams.*
5 *informal* sexually attracted to people of the opposite sex
6 clean and tidy: *I'll never get the house straight before my parents get home.*
7 a student who has straight A's has the highest mark in every subject or course: *She got straight A's this term.* ♦ *a straight-A student*
PHRASES **get sth straight** to correctly understand something: *Let me get this straight – you didn't know they had your car?*
a straight face if someone has a straight face, they look serious even though they are being funny or they are in a funny situation

straight² /streɪt/ adv ★★★
1 without a bend or curve: *The car was coming straight at me.* ♦ *He stared straight ahead.*
2 directly and immediately: *I decided I'd leave straight after breakfast.* ♦ *We decided to go straight home.* ♦ *I'll come straight to the point* (=say immediately what I want to say).
3 in an upright position, not leaning: *Sit up straight.*
4 without stopping: *We drove for five hours straight.*
PHRASE **straight out** said directly and immediately: *She asked straight out if I liked her.*

straight aˈway or **straightaway** /ˌstreɪtəˈweɪ/ adv British immediately: *They can't pay me straight away.*

straighten /'streɪt(ə)n/ verb [I/T] to make something straight, or to become straight: *He straightened his tie.*
PHRASAL VERBS **straighten sth ˈout** to deal with a problem or a confused situation
straighten ˈup to stand up straight

straightforward /ˌstreɪtˈfɔːwəd/ adj **1** not complicated or difficult to understand =UNCOMPLICATED: *a straightforward process* **2** clear and honest: *a straightforward answer*

S

strain¹ /streɪn/ noun **1** [C/U] worries or difficulties that are caused by a difficult situation: *This war will put a strain on the economy.* ♦ *She's been under a lot of strain since the divorce.* **2** [C/U] physical pressure or effort: *All that lifting is putting his back under severe strain.* **3** [C/U] an injury that is caused by twisting or stretching a muscle too much: *a thigh strain* **4** [C] a particular type or aspect of something: *a new strain of the flu virus*

strain² /streɪn/ verb

1 try hard to do sth	**4** separate solid & liquid
2 make relationship bad	**5** pull/push sth hard
3 injure muscle	

1 [I/T] to try very hard to do something: **strain to do sth** *I strained to hear what they were saying.* **2** [T] to cause problems in a relationship: *Relations between the two countries have been strained by trade disputes.* **3** [T] to injure yourself by twisting or stretching a muscle too much: *Reading in poor light can strain your eyes.* **4** [T] to separate a solid from a liquid by pouring it into a STRAINER **5** [I] to pull or push something very hard: *The elephants strained at their ropes.*

strained /streɪnd/ adj **1** not relaxed or friendly: *a strained atmosphere/silence* **2** done only by trying hard, in a way that is not natural: *a strained smile*

strainer /ˈstreɪnə/ noun [C] an object like a bowl with holes, used for separating the liquid and solid parts of food

strait /streɪt/ noun [C] a narrow area of water that joins two larger areas of water
PHRASE **in dire straits** in a very difficult situation, especially one that involves a lack of money

straitjacket /ˈstreɪtˌdʒækɪt/ noun [C] a jacket with very long arms that tie behind the back. It is put on someone who is violent in order to stop them from harming anyone.

strand /strænd/ noun [C] **1** a single thin piece of something: *a strand of hair/wire* **2** one of many aspects of something: *the different strands of the story*

stranded /ˈstrændɪd/ adj left in a place or situation that you cannot get away from: *The passengers were stranded at the airport overnight.*

strange /streɪndʒ/ adj ★★★
1 unusual or unexpected in a way that surprises, worries, or frightens you: *Ian is a very strange person.* ♦ *It seemed strange that she would leave so early.* ♦ *For some strange reason, she didn't even say 'hello'.*
2 not familiar or known to you: *When you arrive in a new country, everything seems strange.*
—**strangely** adv: *Everyone looked at him strangely.*

stranger /ˈstreɪndʒə/ noun [C] ★
1 someone who you do not know: *I didn't want to share a room with a complete stranger.*
2 someone who does not know a place well

PHRASE **be no stranger to sth** to have a lot of experience of something: *Davis is no stranger to tragedy.*

strangle /ˈstræŋɡ(ə)l/ verb [T] **1** to kill a person or an animal by squeezing their throat **2** to stop the development of something

stranglehold /ˈstræŋɡ(ə)lˌhəʊld/ noun [C] strong power over someone or something that prevents them from having any freedom

strap¹ /stræp/ noun [C] a narrow piece of cloth, plastic etc that you use for fastening or carrying something, or for holding something in position: *a bag with leather straps* ♦ *The dress had thin shoulder straps.*

strap² /stræp/ verb [T] to hold or keep something in position by fastening a strap around it: *He strapped down the lid of the basket.*

strata the plural of **stratum**

strategic /strəˈtiːdʒɪk/ adj **1** designed to achieve a particular goal in war, business, or politics: *strategic planning* ♦ *a strategic political move* **2** strategic weapons are designed to hit an enemy's home country
—**strategically** /strəˈtiːdʒɪkli/ adv: *a strategically located military base*

strategist /ˈstrætədʒɪst/ noun [C] someone who develops a business, military, or political plan

strategy /ˈstrætədʒi/ noun ★
1 [C] a plan or method for achieving something: *a strategy to reduce government spending* ♦ *successful language-learning strategies*
2 [U] the skill of planning how to achieve something: *experts in military strategy*

> **Words often used with strategy**
>
> *Verbs often used with strategy (sense 1)*
> ■ **adopt, develop, devise, evolve, formulate, plan, produce** + STRATEGY: invent a strategy for doing something
> ■ **follow, implement, pursue** + STRATEGY: use a strategy in order to do something

stratum /ˈstrɑːtəm/ (plural **strata** /ˈstrɑːtə/) noun [C] a group or class in society

straw /strɔː/ noun **1** [U] the yellow stems of dried crops such as wheat. It is given to animals to sleep on. **2** [C] a long thin tube that you use for drinking
PHRASE **the last/final straw** the last of a series of bad events that makes you decide to try to change a situation

strawberry /ˈstrɔːb(ə)ri/ noun [C] a small soft red fruit with a lot of very small seeds on its skin —*picture* → C10

stray¹ /streɪ/ verb [I] **1** to move away from the correct place or path: *The plane strayed into enemy airspace.* **2** to start talking about a new subject without intending to

stray² /streɪ/ adj **1** lost or without a home: *a stray cat/dog* **2** separated from a group or from the main part of something: *a stray curl of hair*

stray³ /streɪ/ noun [C] a pet that is lost or has left its home

streak¹ /striːk/ noun [C] **1** a line or long mark that is a different colour from the colour

S

surrounding it: *The bird has a dark streak on its breast.* ♦ *a streak of lightning* (=a long line of lightning) **2** a part of someone's character that is different from the rest of their character: *The child has a stubborn streak.*

PHRASE **a winning/losing streak** a series of wins/losses in a game or sport

streak² /striːk/ verb [I] to move very quickly: *Jet planes streaked overhead.*

PHRASE **be streaked (with sth)** to have lines or marks of a different colour: *Jim's face was streaked with paint.*

stream¹ /striːm/ noun [C] ★
1 a small narrow river
2 a continuous flow of liquid or gas: *A stream of blood was running down his face.*
3 a continuous flow of people or things: *a stream of visitors/traffic*
4 a group of school students of the same age and with the same level of abilities
PHRASE **on stream** ready to begin operating

stream² /striːm/ verb [I] **1** to flow continuously: *Tears streamed down his face.* **2** to move in large numbers in a continuous flow: *Students streamed into the building.* **3** to shine, or to give off light: *sunlight streaming through the windows*

streamer /ˈstriːmə/ noun [C] a long coloured piece of paper or cloth that is used for decoration

streaming /ˈstriːmɪŋ/ noun [U] *computing* a technology for sending sound or pictures to your computer through the Internet

streamline /ˈstriːmˌlaɪn/ verb [T] **1** to improve something such as an organization or process by making it more modern or simple **2** to design something with a smooth shape so that it will move quickly through air or water

street /striːt/ noun [C] ★★★ a road in a town or city with buildings along it: *Oxford Street/Fourth Street* ♦ *I just saw Bill walking down the street.* ♦ *Who lives across the street?* → ROAD

PHRASE **on the street(s) 1** with no house to live in: *After losing his job, then his family, he ended up on the streets.* **2** in public places in a town: *More police officers are being put on the streets.*
→ HIGH STREET

streetlamp /ˈstriːtˌlæmp/ or **streetlight** /ˈstriːtˌlaɪt/ noun [C] a light on top of a long pole in a street

streetwise /ˈstriːtˌwaɪz/ adj able to deal with difficult and dangerous situations in a confident way

strength /streŋθ/ noun ★★★

1 physical power	**5** sth sb does very well
2 ability not to break	**6** amount of influence
3 of sb's character	**+ PHRASE**
4 power of sth	

1 [U] the physical energy that someone has to lift or move things: *upper body strength* ♦ *The job requires a lot of physical strength.* ♦ *I didn't have the strength to get out of bed.*
2 [C/U] the ability of something to pull, push,

or support something without breaking: *Test the strength of the rope.*
3 [U] the ability to deal with difficult situations: *She has great strength of character.*
4 [U] power in a military, political, or economic situation: *the strength of the dollar against the euro*
5 [C] something that someone does very well =ABILITY: *Ron's main strength is his ability to motivate players.* ♦ *The test shows the students' strengths and weaknesses.*
6 [U] the amount of influence that a person or group has: *the strength of public opinion*
PHRASE **on the strength of** based on what you saw, heard, experienced etc: *I heard their new single, and on the strength of that I bought the album.*

strengthen /ˈstreŋθ(ə)n/ verb [I/T] ★ to make someone or something stronger, or to become stronger: *Aerobic exercise strengthens the heart.* ♦ *a sense of community that has strengthened over time*

strenuous /ˈstrenjuəs/ adj **1** using a lot of effort, energy, or strength: *strenuous exercise* **2** determined: *strenuous opposition/objections*

stress¹ /stres/ noun ★
1 [C/U] a worried or nervous feeling that makes you unable to relax, or a situation that makes you feel like this: *the stresses and strains of everyday living* ♦ *Carol's been under a lot of stress lately.*
2 [U] special importance that is given to something so that you pay more attention to it=EMPHASIS: *The course puts great stress on communication.*
3 [C/U] physical pressure that can make something break or change its shape: *Judo puts a lot of stress on your knee joints.*
4 [C/U] the emphasis that you put on a particular word or part of a word by saying it more loudly → INTONATION

> **Words often used with stress**
> *Verbs often used with stress (noun, sense 1)*
> ■ **cause, create, generate, produce** + STRESS: cause stress
> ■ **alleviate, combat, ease, manage, reduce, relieve** + STRESS: reduce stress or deal with it successfully

stress² /stres/ verb [T] ★
1 to emphasize something such as an idea, fact, or detail: *The Prime Minister stressed the importance of controlling spending.* ♦ +*that* *I want to stress that I accept responsibility for these mistakes.*
2 to say a particular word or part of a word more loudly

> **Words often used with stress**
> *Nouns often used with stress (verb, sense 1)*
> ■ STRESS + **desirability, importance, necessity, need, significance, urgency, value**: emphasize that something is important or necessary

stressed /strest/ or ˌstressed ˈout adj worried and unable to relax

S

stressful /'stresf(ə)l/ adj making you feel stressed: *My new job is much less stressful.*

'stress ˌmark noun [C] a mark that shows you which part of a word is pronounced more loudly

stretch¹ /stretʃ/ verb ★★

1 make longer/wider	5 use money/time etc
2 make smooth/tight	+ PHRASE
3 of body	+ PHRASAL VERBS
4 continue	

1 [I/T] if you stretch something, or if it stretches, it becomes longer or wider when you pull it: *Can you stretch the material a little?* ♦ *My jumper stretched the first time I washed it.*

2 [T] to pull something so that it becomes smooth, straight, and tight: *The canvas is stretched across a metal frame.*

3 [I/T] to make your arms, legs, or body as long as they can be: *I leaned back in the chair and stretched.* ♦ *Todd stretched his hand towards the rope.*

4 [I] to continue for a particular distance or time: *The beach stretches for miles in each direction.* ♦ *The team has a history that stretches back to 1895.*

5 [T] to use all the money, time, or ability that is available: *I don't think this new job stretches him much.* ♦ *Medical services were stretched to the limit.*

PHRASE stretch your legs to go for a walk after you have been sitting for a long time

PHRASAL VERBS ˌstretch 'out to lie down: *I'll just stretch out on the sofa.*

ˌstretch sth 'out same as **stretch¹** 3: *I stretched out a hand to touch her face.*

stretch² /stretʃ/ noun [C] **1** an area of land or water: *a narrow stretch of water* **2** a continuous period of time: *You can't learn it all in such a short stretch of time.* ♦ *He'll surf the Internet for six hours at a stretch* (=continuously). **3** a movement or exercise in which you make a part of your body as long as possible

PHRASE not by any stretch of the imagination used for emphasizing that you think that something is not true or possible

stretch³ /stretʃ/ adj stretch cloth becomes wider or longer when you pull it

stretcher /'stretʃə/ noun [C] a type of bed that is used for carrying someone who is injured or ill

strew /struː/ (past participle **strewn** /struːn/) verb **be strewn (with)** to be covered with things that are spread around in an untidy way: *One room was strewn with children's toys.*

stricken /'strɪkən/ adj damaged, destroyed, or affected by serious problems

strict /strɪkt/ adj ★

1 someone who is strict expects people to obey rules completely, or obeys rules completely themselves: *The coach is very strict about our diet.*

2 strict rules or conditions must be obeyed completely: *They operate within strict time limits.* ♦ *Lynn gave us strict instructions to be good.*

3 exact, or accurate: *He was not depressed in the strict sense of the word.*

strictly /'strɪk(t)li/ adv **1** in a strict way: *strictly enforced laws* **2** completely: *It's a strictly neutral organization.* ♦ *I'm not sure that what he said is strictly true.*

PHRASE strictly speaking used for showing that you are trying to be accurate, or trying to follow the rules: *Tomatoes are not, strictly speaking, vegetables.*

stride¹ /straɪd/ (past tense **strode** /strəʊd/; past participle **stridden** /'strɪd(ə)n/) verb [I] to walk with energy and confidence: *She strode onto the platform.*

stride² /straɪd/ noun [C] a long confident step

PHRASES get into your stride to begin to do something confidently and well

make strides to make progress towards a goal

take sth in your stride to not be upset by something

strident /'straɪd(ə)nt/ adj **1** expressing strong opinions in a way that offends some people: *a strident opponent of the treaty* **2** a strident voice or sound is loud and unpleasant

strife /straɪf/ noun [U] *formal* fighting or disagreement between people

strike¹ /straɪk/ (past tense and past participle **struck** /strʌk/) verb ★★

1 hit against	7 make flame
2 hit with hand etc	8 clock: make sound
3 protest by not working	9 make deal/agreement
4 affect sb/sth suddenly	10 find gold/oil etc
5 when you think sth	+ PHRASES
6 make violent attack	+ PHRASAL VERBS

1 [T] *formal* to hit against someone or something: *The car struck a tree.* ♦ *The ball struck her hard on the left shoulder.* ♦ *About 50 worshippers were inside the church when it was struck by lightning.*

2 [T] *formal* to hit someone or something with your hand, a tool, or a weapon: **strike sb on/in sth** *We watched helplessly as she struck the child in the face.*

3 [I] to refuse to work for a period of time as a protest about your pay or conditions of work: *Car workers were threatening to strike over the job losses.*

4 [I/T] if something unpleasant or dangerous strikes, or if it strikes someone or something, it happens to them suddenly and unexpectedly: *Three earthquakes struck Peru on April 5th and 6th.* ♦ *That same year, tragedy struck again.*

5 [T] if a thought or idea strikes you, it enters your mind suddenly: *The first thing that struck me about Alex was her self-confidence.*

6 [I] to make a sudden violent or illegal attack: *Police are worried the man could strike again.*

7 [I/T] to rub a match against a hard surface in order to produce a flame

8 [I/T] if a clock strikes, or if it strikes a particular time, it makes a sound to show what the time is: *The town hall clock struck midnight.*

9 [T] to make an agreement: *The two sides had just struck a deal.*

10 [T] to find something such as gold or oil by digging or DRILLING

PHRASES **strike sb as sth** to make someone have a particular opinion or feeling: *He didn't strike me as the jealous sort.* ♦ *It struck me as a little bit odd that she was always alone.*

strike a balance (between sth and sth) to find a solution that is more reasonable and fair than either of two extreme possibilities

within striking distance (of sth) close to something, or close to achieving something

PHRASAL VERBS ,strike 'back to attack, harm, or criticize someone who has attacked, harmed, or criticized you=RETALIATE: *They threatened to strike back against the UN forces.*

,strike sth 'off to remove something from a list or record

,strike 'out to try to hit, attack, or criticize someone or something

,strike 'up sth to start something such as a relationship or a conversation with someone: *The barman seemed to have struck up a friendship with Jane.*

strike² /straɪk/ noun ★★
1 [C/U] a period of time during which people refuse to work, as a protest: *A train strike has crippled the city.* ♦ *Workers have been on strike since Friday.* → HUNGER STRIKE
2 [C] a military attack: *a strike on the airfield*

striker /ˈstraɪkə/ noun [C] **1** a worker who is taking part in a strike **2** a football player whose job is to score goals

striking /ˈstraɪkɪŋ/ adj attracting your interest or attention because of an unusual feature: *a striking young woman* ♦ *There are some striking differences in the two theories.* —**strikingly** adv

string¹ /strɪŋ/ noun ★★
1 [C/U] thin rope that you use for tying things together: *a piece of string* ♦ *The balloon was attached to a long string.*
2 [C] a group of things or events: *He owns a string of restaurants in Wales.* ♦ *We had a string of burglaries in the area last month.*
3 [C] one of several long pieces of NYLON or wire on a musical instrument. You touch them in order to produce sound.
4 the strings [plural] the STRINGED INSTRUMENTS in an orchestra, or the people who play them

PHRASE **no strings (attached)** without any special conditions that limit an offer or agreement
→ PULL¹

string² /strɪŋ/ (past tense and past participle **strung** /strʌŋ/) verb [T] **1** to hang a string or rope somewhere, or to hang something that is like string or rope: *She strung a rope between two trees.* ♦ *Lights were strung all around the garden.* **2** to pass a string through several things in order to make a chain: *The children sat on the floor stringing beads.*

PHRASAL VERB ,string sth to'gether to arrange a group of things into a series: *He can hardly string a sentence together.*

stringed instrument /ˌstrɪŋd ˈɪnstrʊmənt/ noun [C] any musical instrument with strings that you touch to produce sound, for example a VIOLIN

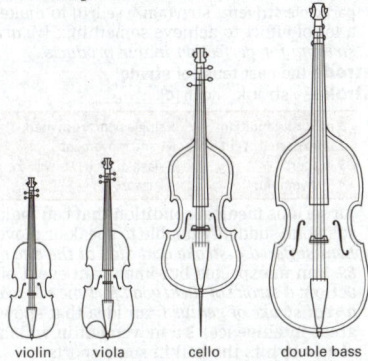

violin   viola   cello   double bass

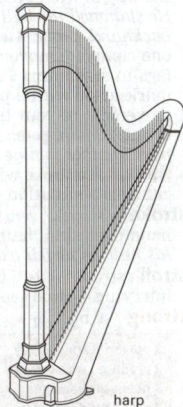

guitar   harp

stringed instruments

S

stringent /ˈstrɪndʒ(ə)nt/ adj stringent rules or conditions are strict —**stringently** adv

strip¹ /strɪp/ noun [C] ★ a long narrow piece of something: *a strip of land* ♦ *Cut the paper into strips.*

strip² /strɪp/ verb **1** [I/T] to take off all of your clothes, or to take off all of another person's clothes: *They all stripped and ran into the water.* **2** [T] to remove something that covers something: **strip sth off/from sth** *The wind had stripped the leaves from the trees.* **3** [T] to take something away using force or authority: **strip sb of sth** *They stripped the prisoners of weapons and cash.*

PHRASAL VERB ,strip 'off *spoken* to take off all your clothes

stripe /straɪp/ noun [C] a line of one colour on a background of a different colour: *a white shirt with red stripes*

striped /straɪpt/ adj with a pattern of stripes: *a blue and white striped tablecloth*

stripper /ˈstrɪpə/ noun [C] an entertainer who performs stripteases

striptease /ˈstrɪpˌtiːz/ noun [C/U] an

entertainment in which someone takes off their clothes while music is playing

strive /straɪv/ (past tense **strove** /strəʊv/; past participle **striven** /ˈstrɪv(ə)n/) verb [I] to make a lot of effort to achieve something: *We are striving for perfection in our products.*

strode the past tense of **stride**[1]

stroke[1] /strəʊk/ noun [C]

1 medical condition	5 single pen/brush mark
2 unexpected event	6 hand movement
3 in sport	7 slash mark (/)
4 in swimming	+ PHRASE

1 a serious medical condition that can make someone suddenly unable to speak or move: *Leni suffered a stroke and died at the age of 89.* **2** an unexpected but important event or action: *a stroke of luck/good fortune* ♦ *It was a real stroke of genius* (=an idea that shows great intelligence). **3** a movement in which someone hits the ball in some sports, or the way in which they make this movement: *He slammed the ball with a powerful backhand stroke.* **4** a style of swimming, or one complete movement of the arms and legs in swimming **5** a single short line or mark made with a pen or brush **6** a gentle movement of your hand across skin, hair, or fur **7** *British spoken* a SLASH mark (/): *My pass number is nine stroke three (9/3).*

PHRASE **at a stroke** with a single action that changes a situation completely

stroke[2] /strəʊk/ verb [T] to gently move your hand over skin, hair, or fur: *She stroked his hair as he fell asleep.*

stroll /strəʊl/ verb [I] to walk without hurrying —**stroll** noun [C]

strong /strɒŋ/ adj ★★★

1 powerful and healthy	6 firmly believed/felt
2 produced with power	7 of high degree/level
3 not easily damaged	8 with power/influence
4 with confidence etc	9 very noticeable
5 good at doing sth	+ PHRASES

1 physically powerful and healthy: *Are you strong enough to carry that?* ♦ *strong hands/arms/muscles* ♦ *Two weeks after her surgery she was **feeling** much **stronger**.* **2** done with a lot of power or force: *a strong punch/kick* **3** not easily broken, damaged, or destroyed: *a strong fabric/glue/rope* ♦ *a strong friendship/marriage/partnership* **4** someone who is strong has confidence, determination, and emotional strength: *You've got to be strong and not let their jokes bother you.* **5** good at doing something: *She's **a strong swimmer**.* **6** firmly believed or felt: *strong views/feelings/opinions* **7** of a high degree or level: *There's **a strong possibility** that they'll get married in the spring.* **8** with a lot of power or influence: *a strong leader/president* ♦ *Our lawyers say we have **a very strong case**.* **9** very noticeable: *a strong light/colour* ♦ *a strong British accent* ♦ *a strong smell/taste*

PHRASES **going strong** successful, or healthy: *The company was founded in 1860 and is still going strong.*
sb's strong point a good quality that makes someone or something effective: *Paula's ability to work quickly is one of her strongest points.* ♦ *Patience is not my strong point* (=I am not a patient person).

stronghold /ˈstrɒŋhəʊld/ noun [C] a place where the majority of people have the same political or religious beliefs

strongly /ˈstrɒŋli/ adv used for emphasizing that someone is very serious about what they say, feel, or believe: *I would strongly recommend that you don't pay him anything yet.* ♦ *I feel strongly that the trial was unfair.*

stroppy /ˈstrɒpi/ adj *British informal* a stroppy person gets angry very easily and is difficult to talk to

strove the past tense of **strive**

struck the past tense and past participle of **strike**[1]

structural /ˈstrʌktʃ(ə)rəl/ adj **1** related to the structure of something such as a building: *structural damage* **2** related to the way that something is organized: *structural changes in the industry* —**structurally** adv

structure[1] /ˈstrʌktʃə/ noun ★★★
1 [C/U] the way in which the parts of something are organized or arranged into a whole: *sentence structure* ♦ *the structure of DNA* ♦ *the changing structure of agriculture in this country*
2 [C] an organization or system that is made up of many parts: *a social/power/class structure*
3 [C] something large such as a building or a bridge that is built from different parts

structure[2] /ˈstrʌktʃə/ verb [T] to plan or organize something

struggle[1] /ˈstrʌg(ə)l/ verb [I] ★
1 to try hard to do something that is very difficult: **struggle to do sth** *She was struggling to cope with her work.* ♦ *a documentary about this species and its struggle for survival*
2 to try very hard to defeat someone or stop them having power over you: **struggle to do sth** *We have to struggle to win our freedom.* ♦ *women struggling against oppression*
3 to use your strength to fight against someone or something: *The man grabbed him, but he struggled free.*

struggle[2] /ˈstrʌg(ə)l/ noun ★
1 [C] an attempt to do something that takes a lot of effort over a period of time: *the struggle for democracy* ♦ *her struggle with the disease* ♦ *the community's struggle against racism*
2 [C/U] a fight, or a war: *the armed struggle against the government*
3 [singular] something that takes a lot of physical or mental effort: *Foreign languages were always a struggle for him.* ♦ *a struggle to do sth It was a struggle to get up the hill in the snow.*

strum /strʌm/ verb [T] to play a musical instrument such as a guitar by moving your fingers across its strings

strung the past tense and past participle of **string**[2]

strut /strʌt/ verb [I] to walk in a confident and proud way

stub[1] /stʌb/ verb [T] to hit your toe against something accidentally so that it hurts

PHRASAL VERB ,**stub sth 'out** to press a cigarette hard against a surface to make it stop burning

stub[2] /stʌb/ noun [C] the part of something that remains after you have used the rest: *a pencil/cigarette stub*

stubble /'stʌb(ə)l/ noun [U] **1** the short stiff hairs on a man's face that grow into a BEARD **2** the ends of plants that are left above ground after a farmer cuts a grain crop

stubborn /'stʌbən/ adj **1** not willing to change your ideas or decisions: *Stop being so stubborn!* ♦ *stubborn anger/pride* **2** very difficult to change, defeat, or remove: *stubborn opposition* ♦ *stubborn weeds/ stains* —**stubbornly** adv, **stubbornness** noun [U]

stubby /'stʌbi/ adj short and thick

stuck[1] /stʌk/ adj **1** caught or held in a position so that you cannot move: *Carl's car got stuck in the mud.* **2** unable to solve a problem that prevents you from continuing something: *I'm really stuck on this algebra problem.* **3** *informal* having to deal with someone or something that you do not like but cannot avoid: *I suppose I'm stuck with this haircut.*

stuck[2] the past tense and past participle of **stick**[1]

stud[1] /stʌd/ noun [C] **1** a small piece of jewellery on a short metal post that is worn through a part of your body **2** a small piece of metal that sticks up from a surface: *a jacket covered with metal studs* **3** a piece of plastic or rubber on the bottom of a boot that prevents you from slipping

stud[2] /stʌd/ verb **be studded with sth** to be covered or decorated with a lot of something: *a sky studded with stars*

student /'stjuːd(ə)nt/ noun [C] ★★★ someone who goes to a university, college, or school: *Jennifer is one of my best students.* ♦ *physics/ art student* ♦ *a student organization/ newspaper* ♦ *a first-year/final-year student*

■ In British English, a **student** usually means someone who goes to university or college. A child who goes to school is usually called a **pupil**.
■ In American English, a **student** means someone who goes to school, college, or university.

,**student 'loan** noun [C] money that a bank or institution lends to a student so that they can do their course

,**students' 'union** or ,**student 'union** noun [C] an organization at a university or college that helps students by providing services and places to meet or play sport

studio /'stjuːdiəʊ/ noun [C] ★★ **1** a room in which someone such as a painter or photographer works

2 a small flat that has only one main room
3 a company that produces films
4 a set of rooms where music or a film, television show, or radio show is recorded

studious /'stjuːdiəs/ adj **1** tending to study and read a lot **2** giving a lot of attention and care to what you are doing or learning —**studiously** adv

study[1] /'stʌdi/ noun ★★★
1 [U] the process of learning about a subject or problem: *the study of criminal behaviour* ♦ *a centre for* **the study of** *Asian languages*
2 [C] a research project that examines a problem or subject: *The study showed a link between the chemicals and cancer.*
3 studies [plural] the work that you do while you are at a college or university: *Sarah wants to continue her studies.*
4 [C] a room in a house where you can read or work quietly

study[2] /'stʌdi/ verb ★★★
1 [I/T] to learn about a subject by going to school, university etc: *She's studying history at university.* ♦ *Michael was* **studying to be** *a lawyer.* → LEARN
2 [I] to do work such as reading and homework: *You need to study hard if you want to pass.*
3 [T] to read or look at something very carefully: *I studied various maps of the area.*
4 [T] to learn about a problem or subject using scientific methods: *They will study the effect of technology on jobs.*

stuff[1] /stʌf/ noun [U] *informal* ★★★
1 objects, or things: *What's all this stuff on my desk?* ♦ *By the time we got to the sale, all the good stuff was gone.* ♦ *I spend most of my time doing really boring stuff.*
2 a material, or a substance: *The costumes were made of thin, gauzy stuff.* ♦ *What's that sticky stuff in your hair?*
3 general information: *I already know all that stuff.*

PHRASES ...**and stuff (like that)** *spoken* used for referring to things that are similar or related to the subject that you are discussing: *She wants us to smile more, and stuff like that.*
know your stuff *informal* to know a lot about something

stuff[2] /stʌf/ verb [T] **1** to push something soft into a space or container: *Alice quickly stuffed her clothes into a suitcase and left.* **2** to fill a container or space with something, especially something soft

stuffed /stʌft/ adj **1** full of things: *The drawer was stuffed with money.* **2** stuffed meat or vegetables have been filled with another type of food **3** *informal* having eaten until you are full or ill

stuffing /'stʌfɪŋ/ noun [U] **1** food that has been cut into small pieces and put inside meat or vegetables **2** soft material that is used for filling something such as a toy or a seat

stuffy /'stʌfi/ adj **1** a stuffy room is unpleasant to be in because it is too warm and there is no fresh air in it **2** *informal* with strict or old-fashioned attitudes —**stuffiness** noun [U]

stumble /'stʌmb(ə)l/ verb [I] **1** to fall, or almost

S

fall, while you are walking or running: *Derek stumbled over a fallen tree.* **2** to make a mistake when you are speaking

PHRASAL VERB ˈstumble aˌcross sb/sth or ˈstumble on sb/sth to find something or meet someone by accident

stumbling block /ˈstʌmblɪŋ ˌblɒk/ noun [C] a difficulty that causes mistakes or prevents progress

stump¹ /stʌmp/ noun [C] **1** the part of a tree that is left above the ground after it has been cut off at the base **2** the remaining part of someone's arm, leg, or finger after the rest is cut off **3** one of the three sticks that you try to hit in the game of CRICKET

stump² /stʌmp/ verb **be stumped by sth** to be unable to explain something mysterious, or to be unable to answer a question

PHRASAL VERB ˌstump (sth) ˈup *British informal* to give or pay money in an unwilling way

stun /stʌn/ verb [T] **1** to shock and surprise someone so much that they cannot react immediately: *His violent death stunned the nation.* **2** to hit someone so hard on the head that they are unable to move or to react for a short time —**stunned** /stʌnd/ adj

stung the past tense and past participle of **sting¹**

stunk the past tense and past participle of **stink¹**

stunning /ˈstʌnɪŋ/ adj **1** very impressive or beautiful: *The view from the top of the hill is stunning.* ♦ *a stunning man* **2** surprising, powerful, and effective —**stunningly** adv

stunt¹ /stʌnt/ noun [C] **1** something that is done in order to impress someone or to get their attention: *a publicity stunt* **2** something dangerous that is done to entertain people, often as part of a film

stunt² /stʌnt/ verb **stunt sb's/sth's growth** to stop someone or something from growing

stupendous /stjuːˈpendəs/ adj very impressive, large, or surprising

stupid /ˈstjuːpɪd/ adj ★★
1 not intelligent, or showing bad judgment: *What a stupid question!* ♦ *I didn't ask because I was afraid of looking stupid.*
2 silly or annoying: *He kept singing the same stupid song.* ♦ *Does this shirt look stupid?* —**stupidity** /stjuːˈpɪdəti/ noun [U], **stupidly** adv: *I stupidly loaned him some money.*

stupor /ˈstjuːpə/ noun [singular/U] the condition of being unable to think or act normally because you are not completely conscious

sturdy /ˈstɜːdi/ adj strong and thick or solid: *sturdy legs/shoes/plants*

stutter /ˈstʌtə/ verb [I/T] to repeat the sounds of words in an uncontrolled way when you speak, because you are nervous or you have a speech problem =STAMMER —**stutter** noun [singular]

sty /staɪ/ noun [C] a small building where pigs are kept on a farm

style¹ /staɪl/ noun ★★★
1 [C] the individual way that someone behaves and does things: *I really dislike her*

teaching style. ♦ *Picasso's **style of painting*** ♦ *Having big parties is **not my style**.*
2 [U] an attractive or impressive way of behaving or doing something: *Greg has a lot of style.*
3 [C/U] the way that something is made or done that is typical of a particular group, time, or place: *I don't like the style of dresses that are out now.* ♦ *traditional and modern styles of furniture*

PHRASES **in style 1** fashionable at a particular time **2** in a very comfortable, impressive, or expensive way: *Let's rent a big car and go in style.*
out of style not fashionable

style² /staɪl/ verb [T] to give something a particular shape or style

stylish /ˈstaɪlɪʃ/ adj attractive and fashionable: *stylish clothes* —**stylishly** adv

stylistic /staɪˈlɪstɪk/ adj relating to styles: *stylistic differences between the two books* —**stylistically** /staɪˈlɪstɪkli/ adv

stylized /ˈstaɪlaɪzd/ adj in a style that is artificial rather than REALISTIC (=like life)

suave /swɑːv/ adj confident and polite in a way that may not be sincere

sub /sʌb/ noun [C] *informal* **1** a SUBSTITUTE, especially someone who plays instead of another player in a sport **2** a SUBMARINE

sub- /sʌb/ prefix **1** one small part of a larger thing: *a subsection* **2** smaller or less important than someone or something: *a subheading* **3** below a particular level: *sub-zero temperatures*

subcommittee /ˈsʌbkəˌmɪti/ noun [C] a small group of people who are part of a larger committee and who meet to discuss one particular thing

subconscious¹ /ˌsʌbˈkɒnʃəs/ adj relating to thoughts or feelings that you have but do not think about, or that you do not realize that you have —**subconsciously** adv

subconscious² /ˌsʌbˈkɒnʃəs/ noun [singular] the part of your mind that contains thoughts and feelings that you do not think about, or that you do not realize that you have

subcontinent /ˌsʌbˈkɒntɪnənt/ noun [C] a large area of land that forms part of a CONTINENT, especially the part of Asia that contains the countries of India, Pakistan, and Bangladesh

subcontract /ˌsʌbˈkɒntrækt/ noun [C] a contract in which one person agrees to do some of the work that another person has agreed to do —**subcontract** /ˌsʌbkənˈtrækt/ verb [I/T], **subcontractor** /ˌsʌbkənˈtræktə/ noun [C]

subculture /ˈsʌbˌkʌltʃə/ noun [C] a group of people whose beliefs and ways of behaving make them different from the rest of society

subdivide /ˌsʌbdɪˈvaɪd/ verb [T] to divide the parts of something that has already been divided

subdivision /ˈsʌbdɪˌvɪʒ(ə)n/ noun [C] one small part of something that has already been divided into several larger parts

S

subdue /səbˈdjuː/ verb [T] **1** to make someone stop behaving in an uncontrolled or violent way **2** *formal* to defeat a place or a group of people, and take control of them

subdued /səbˈdjuːd/ adj **1** quiet and slightly sad or worried **2** not very loud or bright: *subdued lighting*

subgroup /ˈsʌbˌɡruːp/ noun [C] a small group of people who form part of a larger group

subheading /ˈsʌbˌhedɪŋ/ noun [C] the title of one section of a longer piece of writing

subject¹ /ˈsʌbdʒɪkt/ noun [C] ★★★

1 sth you discuss	**4** sb in scientific test
2 sth taught at school	**5** sth in picture
3 in grammar	**6** sb ruled by king/queen

1 something that you discuss or write about: *He's never mentioned the subject of money.* ♦ *Someone **raised the subject of** (=started talking about) sports facilities.* ♦ *Can we **change the subject** (=talk about something else), please?*
2 something that you learn or teach in a school, for example English, mathematics, or biology
3 *linguistics* in English grammar, the person, place, or thing that does what the verb describes. In the sentence 'Mary threw the ball', 'Mary' is the subject.
4 a person or animal that is used in a medical or scientific test
5 a person or thing that is shown in a picture
6 someone who lives in a country that is controlled by a king or queen: *a British subject*

subject² /ˈsʌbdʒɪkt/ adj **subject to sth 1** likely to be affected by something: *Train times are subject to change during bad weather.*
2 in a situation where you have to obey a rule or law: *All building firms are subject to tight controls.* **3** depending on whether something happens: *Goods will be sent out within 14 days, subject to availability.*

subject³ /səbˈdʒekt/ verb [T] to make someone experience something unpleasant: *Her husband subjected her to years of physical abuse.*

subjective /səbˈdʒektɪv/ adj based on your own feelings and ideas, and not on facts ≠ OBJECTIVE —**subjectively** adv, **subjectivity** /ˌsʌbdʒekˈtɪvəti/ noun [U]

ˈsubject ˌline noun [C] *computing* the place in an email where you can type what the email is about

ˈsubject ˌmatter noun [U] the things that a speech, a piece of writing, an article etc is about

subjunctive /səbˈdʒʌŋktɪv/ noun [singular] *linguistics* the form of a verb that is used for expressing doubts and wishes. For example, in the sentence 'I wish I were taller', 'were' is in the subjunctive. —**subjunctive** adj

sublime /səˈblaɪm/ adj **1** extremely good or beautiful **2** *formal* used for describing an extreme feeling or quality

submarine /ˈsʌbməriːn/ noun [C] a ship that

can travel both on the surface of the water and under water = SUB

submerge /səbˈmɜːdʒ/ verb [I/T] to go completely under water, or to put something completely under water —**submerged** /səbˈmɜːdʒd/ adj

submission /səbˈmɪʃ(ə)n/ noun **1** [U] *formal* the action of accepting that someone has defeated you or has power over you **2** [C/U] the process of giving a document to someone for them to consider, or the document that you give them **3** [C] a statement that you make to a judge or official committee

submissive /səbˈmɪsɪv/ adj willing to do what other people tell you to do without arguing —**submissively** adv, **submissiveness** noun [U]

submit /səbˈmɪt/ verb ★
1 [T] to formally give something to someone so that they can make a decision about it: *The plans will be submitted next week.*
2 [I/T] to accept that someone has power over you, and therefore to do what they want: *The rebels have refused to submit to the national government.* ♦ **submit yourself to sb** *Women were supposed to submit themselves totally to their husbands.*

subordinate¹ /səˈbɔːdɪnət/ adj **1** having less power or authority than someone else **2** less important than something else —**subordination** /səˌbɔːdɪˈneɪʃ(ə)n/ noun [U]

subordinate² /səˈbɔːdɪnət/ noun [C] someone who has less power or authority than someone else

subˌordinate ˈclause noun [C] *linguistics* a group of words that gives extra information about a sentence but cannot form a sentence by itself. For example, in the sentence 'Marla stayed at home because she was tired', 'because she was tired' is a subordinate clause.

subpoena /səˈpiːnə/ noun [C] an official legal document that says that you must come to a court of law to give evidence —**subpoena** verb [T]

subscribe /səbˈskraɪb/ verb [I] **1** to pay money regularly so that you will receive a product such as a magazine, or a service such as an Internet connection **2** *computing* to join an Internet NEWSGROUP ≠ UNSUBSCRIBE —**subscriber** noun [C]

PHRASAL VERB **subˈscribe to sth** to agree with an idea

subscription /səbˈskrɪpʃ(ə)n/ noun [C] an agreement to pay an amount of money so that you will receive something such as a magazine or a service, or the amount of money that you pay

subsection /ˈsʌbˌsekʃ(ə)n/ noun [C] a section within another section of something

subsequent /ˈsʌbsɪkwənt/ adj *formal* happening or coming after something else: *In subsequent interviews, he contradicted his original story.*

subsequently /ˈsʌbsɪkwəntli/ adv after something else happened: *The disease*

S

subsequently spread to the rest of the country.

subservient /səbˈsɜːviənt/ adj too willing to obey other people —**subservience** noun [U]

subset /ˈsʌbˌset/ noun [C] a small group of people or things that is a part of a larger group

subside /səbˈsaɪd/ verb [I] **1** to become weaker, less violent, or less severe: *Gradually the pain subsided.* **2** if flood water, land, or a building subsides, it sinks to a lower level

subsidence /ˈsʌbsɪd(ə)ns, səbˈsaɪd(ə)ns/ noun [U] the process by which land or buildings sink to a lower level

subsidiary¹ /səbˈsɪdiəri/ noun [C] a company that is owned by a larger company

subsidiary² /səbˈsɪdiəri/ adj *formal* related to something else, but less important than it

subsidize /ˈsʌbsɪˌdaɪz/ verb [T] to pay some of the cost of goods or services so that they can be sold to people at a lower price

subsidy /ˈsʌbsədi/ noun [C] an amount of money that the government or another organization pays to help to reduce the cost of a product or service

subsist /səbˈsɪst/ verb [I] to stay alive when you do not have much food or money —**subsistence** noun [U]

substance /ˈsʌbstəns/ noun ★★★
1 [C] a particular type of liquid, solid, or gas: *The wood is coated with a special substance that protects it from the sun.*
2 [U] the quality of being important, true, or useful: *The band is all show and no substance.* ♦ *There is no substance to his accusations* (=they are not true).
3 [C] a drug that people can become dependent on, especially an illegal drug
4 [U] the most important ideas or basic meaning of a discussion or piece of writing

substandard /ˌsʌbˈstændəd/ adj not as good as you would normally expect, or not good enough to be accepted

substantial /səbˈstænʃ(ə)l/ adj ★★
1 large in amount or degree=CONSIDERABLE: *A substantial number of people have called to complain.* ♦ *a substantial sum of money*
2 large and strongly built ≠ INSUBSTANTIAL: *a substantial brick building*

substantially /səbˈstænʃ(ə)li/ adv by a large amount or degree: *We have substantially increased the number of courses.*

substantiate /səbˈstænʃiˌeɪt/ verb [T] to provide evidence that proves something

substitute¹ /ˈsʌbstɪˌtjuːt/ verb **1** [T] to use something new or different instead of what is normally used: **substitute sth for sth** *You can substitute chicken for beef in this recipe.*
2 [T] to remove one thing and put something else in its place: **substitute sth for sth** *She substituted a photo of herself for the one already attached to the form.* **3** [I] **substitute for sb** to do someone else's job for a short period of time

substitute² /ˈsʌbstɪˌtjuːt/ noun [C] **1** something that is used instead of something else **2** someone who does someone else's job for a short time **3** a player who replaces

another member of his or her team during a sports game

PHRASE **there is no substitute for sth** used for saying that nothing else is good or useful enough to replace something: *There's no substitute for experience.*

substitution /ˌsʌbstɪˈtjuːʃ(ə)n/ noun [C/U] the action of replacing someone or something with someone or something else

subsume /səbˈsjuːm/ verb [T] *formal* to include something in a larger group

subterfuge /ˈsʌbtəˌfjuːdʒ/ noun [C/U] *formal* the use of lies and tricks=DECEIT

subterranean /ˌsʌbtəˈreɪniən/ adj under the ground

subtitle /ˈsʌbˌtaɪt(ə)l/ noun **1 subtitles** [plural] a translation of what people are saying in a foreign language film or television programme which appears at the bottom of the screen **2** [C] an additional title that appears after the main title of a piece of writing

subtle /ˈsʌt(ə)l/ adj **1** not obvious, and therefore difficult to notice: *subtle changes* ♦ *subtle threats/discrimination* ♦ *subtle advertising* (=that persuades people in a subtle way) ♦ *a subtle hint* **2** showing an ability to notice and understand small things that other people do not: *subtle arguments/humour* **3** delicate and complicated in an attractive way: *a subtle pattern/melody* **4** a subtle colour is pleasant because it is not too bright —**subtly** adv

subtlety /ˈsʌt(ə)lti/ noun **1** [U] the quality of being complicated, delicate, or difficult to notice **2** [C] a small detail or feature that is difficult to notice

subtract /səbˈtrækt/ verb [I/T] to take a number or amount from another number or amount —**subtraction** /səbˈtrækʃ(ə)n/ noun [U]

suburb /ˈsʌbɜːb/ noun [C] an area or town near a large city but away from its centre, where there are many houses

suburban /səˈbɜːbən/ adj in a suburb, relating to a suburb, or typical of a suburb → URBAN

suburbia /səˈbɜːbiə/ noun [U] SUBURBS in general, the people who live in them, or their way of life

subversive /səbˈvɜːsɪv/ adj intended to destroy the power or influence of a government or of an established principle

subvert /səbˈvɜːt/ verb [T] to attack or harm a government or established belief —**subversion** /səbˈvɜːʃ(ə)n/ noun [U]

subway /ˈsʌbˌweɪ/ noun [C] **1** *British* a tunnel that people can walk through to go under a road=UNDERPASS **2** *American* a railway that goes under the ground

sub-zero adj sub-zero temperatures are lower than zero degrees

succeed /səkˈsiːd/ verb ★★★
1 [I] to achieve something that you planned to do or attempted to do ≠ FAIL: *Everyone wants the peace process to succeed.* ♦ **succeed in (doing) sth** *We finally succeeded in getting some extra funding.*

S

2 [I] to do well in school, in your career, or in some other activity ≠ FAIL: *These days there is a lot of pressure on children to succeed.*

3 [T] to replace someone who was in a powerful job or position: *In 1603, Elizabeth was succeeded by James I.*

> **Word family: succeed**
>
> *Words in the same family as succeed*
> - **success** *n*
> - **successful** *adj*
> - **successfully** *adv*
> - **unsuccessful** *adj*
> - **unsuccessfully** *adv*

succeeding /səkˈsiːdɪŋ/ *adj* coming after something else

success /səkˈses/ *noun* ★★★
1 [U] the achievement of something that you planned to do or attempted to do ≠ FAILURE: *The chairman thanked all those who had contributed to **the success of** the company.* ◆ **success in (doing) sth** *How do you explain their success in reducing crime?*
2 [C] a plan or attempt that achieves good results: *She set up her own business and **made a success of** it.* ◆ *The party was **a great success**.*
3 [U] the fact that you are successful in your career: *Her success is due mainly to luck and determination.*

successful /səkˈsesf(ə)l/ *adj* ★★★
1 achieving the result that you want ≠ UNSUCCESSFUL: *The team has had a **highly successful** season.* ◆ **successful in (doing) sth** *We have been very successful in attracting top quality candidates.*
2 a successful person does well in their career ≠ UNSUCCESSFUL: *a successful businesswoman*
3 a successful business makes a lot of money ≠ UNSUCCESSFUL: *It was another very successful year for the bank.*
—**successfully** *adv*

succession /səkˈseʃ(ə)n/ *noun* **1** [singular] a series of people or things of the same type: *a succession of low-paid jobs* **2** [U] the process by which one person comes after another as a king, queen, or leader
> **PHRASE** **in succession** in a series: *Hankins has won the tournament five times in succession.*

successive /səkˈsesɪv/ *adj* coming or happening one after another in a series
—**successively** *adv*

successor /səkˈsesə/ *noun* [C] **1** someone who has an important position after someone else **2** an organization or machine that replaces something that did the same job before

suc'cess ,story *noun* [C] someone or something that becomes very successful

succinct /səkˈsɪŋkt/ *adj* expressed in a very short but clear way —**succinctly** *adv*

succulent /ˈsʌkjʊlənt/ *adj* succulent food is full of juice and tastes good

succumb /səˈkʌm/ *verb* [I] *formal* **1** to lose your ability to fight against someone or something **2** to become very ill, or to die from a disease

such /sʌtʃ/ *grammar word* ★★★

> **Such** can be:
> - a **determiner**: *She's such an intelligent woman.*
>   ◆ *We've had such awful weather lately.*
> - a **pronoun**: *I've never really had a career as such.*

1 of the type that is being mentioned: ◆ *On **such** a day **as** today, it's hard to imagine that things will ever be normal again.* ◆ *If this is not genuine champagne, it should not be labelled **as such**.*
2 used for emphasizing a special or unusual quality in someone or something: *If it's such a secret, why did you tell me?* ◆ *She's such a lovely person.*
> **PHRASES** **as such** used after a noun when you are referring to the usual meaning of the word: *She's not really a maid as such. She just helps out in the house sometimes.*
> **such and such** *spoken* used instead of giving an exact name or detail, when this is not important
> **such as** used for introducing more examples of the type of person or thing that you have just mentioned: *The money is used to buy basic foods such as flour, rice, and pasta.*
> **such (...) that** used for emphasizing the degree of a quality by stating its result: *We had such a good time that we're planning to go again next year.*
> **there's no such thing/person as** used for saying that a particular type of thing or person does not exist: *There's no such thing as luck.*

suck¹ /sʌk/ *verb* **1** [I/T] to pull liquid, air, or smoke into your mouth: *He sucked in a lungful of air, then jumped into the pool.*
2 [I/T] to put something in your mouth and move your tongue against it: *She sucked on a sweet and stared at us.* **3** [T] to pull something somewhere, especially with a lot of force: *The current nearly sucked us under the water.* **4** [I] *very informal* to be very bad, very annoying etc: *If your job really sucks, leave it.*
> **PHRASE** **be/get sucked into sth** *informal* to be unable to stop yourself from getting involved in something bad

suck² /sʌk/ *noun* [C] an act of sucking

sucker /ˈsʌkə/ *noun* [C] **1** *informal* someone who is easily tricked **2** a round structure on the bodies of some animals that allows them to stick to surfaces

suction /ˈsʌkʃ(ə)n/ *noun* [U] the process of sucking air or a liquid from somewhere by creating a space without air that it can flow into

sudden¹ /ˈsʌd(ə)n/ *adj* ★★ happening very quickly and without any sign that it is going to happen: *a sudden rise in violent crime* ◆ *She felt a sudden pain in her hip.*
—**suddenness** *noun* [U]

sudden² /ˈsʌd(ə)n/ *noun* **all of a sudden** if something happens all of a sudden, it happens quickly, and without any sign that it is going to happen: *All of a sudden, the door slammed shut.*

S

suddenly /'sʌd(ə)nli/ adv ★★★ quickly and without any warning: *A strange feeling suddenly came over him.* ♦ *Suddenly, the silence was broken by a loud explosion.*

sue /su:, sju:/ verb [I/T] to make a legal claim against someone, usually to get money from them because they have done something bad to you

suede /sweɪd/ noun [U] leather with a soft brushed surface

suet /'su:ɪt/ noun [U] hard fat from around an animal's kidneys that is used for cooking

suffer /'sʌfə/ verb ★★★

1 [I/T] to feel pain in your body or your mind: *When parents argue constantly, it's the children who suffer most.* ♦ *Don't worry, the animal won't **suffer** any **pain**.*

2 [T] **suffer from sth** to have a particular illness or physical problem: *patients suffering from heart disease*

3 [I/T] to experience something very unpleasant or painful: *In wars, it's usually innocent civilians that suffer.* ♦ *Our team **suffered** another humiliating **defeat** last night.*

4 [I] to become worse or less successful

sufferer /'sʌfərə/ noun [C] someone who has a particular problem or disease

suffering /'sʌfərɪŋ/ noun [C/U] mental or physical pain or problems

suffice /sə'faɪs/ verb [I] *formal* to be enough

sufficient /sə'fɪʃ(ə)nt/ adj ★★ as much as is needed =ENOUGH ≠ INSUFFICIENT: *The wages were not **sufficient** for people to live on.* ♦ **sufficient to do sth** *There is now sufficient evidence to prove his claims.* —**sufficiently** adv

suffix /'sʌfɪks/ noun [C] a letter or group of letters added to the end of a word to make a different word. For example, the suffix '-ness' is added to 'great' and 'happy' to make 'greatness' and 'happiness'.

suffocate /'sʌfəkeɪt/ verb [I/T] to die because you cannot breathe, or to kill someone in this way —**suffocation** /ˌsʌfə'keɪʃ(ə)n/ noun [U]

suffocating /'sʌfəkeɪtɪŋ/ adj so hot that you cannot breathe easily

suffrage /'sʌfrɪdʒ/ noun [U] the right to vote

sugar¹ /'ʃʊɡə/ noun ★★

1 [U] a sweet substance that is added to food or drinks to make them taste sweet: *Do you take sugar in your coffee?*

2 [C] the amount of sugar that is contained in a TEASPOON: *How many sugars do you take?*

sugar² /'ʃʊɡə/ verb [T] to add sugar to something, or to cover something with sugar

sugar cane noun [C/U] a tall tropical plant with thick stems that is used for producing sugar

sugary /'ʃʊɡəri/ adj tasting sweet from sugar

suggest /sə'dʒest/ verb [T] ★★★

1 to offer an idea or a plan for someone to consider: **+(that)** *He suggested that we have dinner first, and then watch the film.* ♦

suggest doing sth *If you have computer problems, we suggest phoning the manufacturer's helpline.*

2 to tell someone about something that may be suitable for a particular purpose =RECOMMEND: *Can you suggest a good restaurant?*

3 to make people think that something exists or is true =IMPLY: *Evidence suggests a link between asthma and pollution.* ♦ **+(that)** *I'm not suggesting that giving up smoking will be easy.*

suggestion /sə'dʒestʃ(ə)n/ noun ★★★

1 [C] an idea or plan that you offer for someone to consider: *Could I **make a suggestion?*** ♦ *People had some helpful **suggestions for** improving the service.* ♦ **+that** *The suggestion that only rich people go to the opera is inaccurate.*

2 [U] the act of suggesting something: **at sb's suggestion** *It was at Larry's suggestion that I attended the meeting.*

3 [singular] the possibility that something is true, or evidence that shows that something might be true: **+that** *The government rejected any suggestion that it was to blame.*

Words often used with suggestion

*Adjectives often used with **suggestion** (sense 1)*
- **alternative, constructive, helpful, positive, practical, sensible** + SUGGESTION: used about suggestions that are good

*Verbs often used with **suggestion** (sense 1)*
- **make, offer, put forward, submit, volunteer** + SUGGESTION: make a suggestion
- **accept, adopt, follow, take up, welcome** + SUGGESTION: accept a suggestion
- **oppose, reject** + SUGGESTION: not accept a suggestion

---

suggestive /sə'dʒestɪv/ adj **1** making you think of sex **2** making you think of, or making you remember, a particular thing

suicidal /ˌsu:ɪ'saɪd(ə)l/ adj **1** someone who is suicidal is likely to try to kill themselves **2** very dangerous, and likely to lead to serious problems or to death

suicide¹ /'su:ɪˌsaɪd/ noun **1** [C/U] the action of deliberately killing yourself: *Police believe he committed suicide.* **2** [U] something that you do that is likely to have very bad results for you

suicide² /'su:ɪˌsaɪd/ adj a suicide attack will kill the person who makes it: *a suicide bomber/bombing*

suicide note noun [C] a message left by someone who commits suicide

suit¹ /su:t/ verb [T] ★★★

1 to be convenient or suitable for someone: *It's important to find a form of exercise that suits your lifestyle.* ♦ *I work part time, which suits me fine.*

2 if a style or something you wear suits you, it makes you look good: *The new hairstyle really suits her.*

PHRASE suit yourself 1 used for telling someone to do what is convenient for them:

S

You can adapt the recipe to suit yourself.
2 *spoken* used for telling someone rather rudely to do whatever they want

suit² /suːt/ noun [C] ★★
1 a set of clothes made from the same cloth, usually a jacket with trousers or a skirt: *He was wearing a dark suit and a tie.* —*picture* → C4
2 a type of clothing that you wear for a particular activity: *a diving/jogging suit*
3 a claim or complaint that someone makes in a court of law=LAWSUIT
4 one of four sets of PLAYING CARDS that together make a PACK —*picture* → C16

suitability /ˌsuːtəˈbɪləti/ noun [U] the degree to which someone or something is suitable for a particular job or purpose

suitable /ˈsuːtəb(ə)l/ adj ★★★ right for a particular purpose, person, or situation ≠ UNSUITABLE: *It's difficult for students to find suitable accommodation.* ♦ *This film is not suitable for young children.*

suitably /ˈsuːtəbli/ adv **1** in a way that is right for a particular purpose or situation: *There is a shortage of suitably qualified and experienced teachers.* **2** used for saying that someone reacts in the way that you expected: *We all looked suitably impressed when she told us her exam results.*

suitcase /ˈsuːtˌkeɪs/ noun [C] a large bag with flat sides and a handle that you use for carrying clothes and other things when you travel

suite /swiːt/ noun [C] **1** a set of rooms → EN SUITE **2** *British* a set of matching pieces of furniture

suited /ˈsuːtɪd/ adj **1** right for a particular purpose or situation **2** if two people are suited, they are likely to have a successful relationship=COMPATIBLE

suitor /ˈsuːtə/ noun [C] *old-fashioned* a man who wants to get married to a particular woman

sulfur /ˈsʌlfə/ the American spelling of **sulphur**

sulk /sʌlk/ verb [I] to show that you are angry about being treated badly by looking unhappy and not talking to anyone —**sulk** noun [C]

sulky /ˈsʌlki/ adj feeling angry and unhappy, and not wanting to talk to anyone —**sulkily** adv

sullen /ˈsʌlən/ adj angry, unhappy, and not wanting to talk to anyone —**sullenly** adv

sulphur /ˈsʌlfə/ noun [U] a yellow chemical element that has a strong smell

sulphur dioxide /ˌsʌlfə daɪˈɒksaɪd/ noun [U] *science* a poisonous gas with a strong smell

sultan /ˈsʌltən/ noun [C] the leader in some Muslim countries

sultana /sʌlˈtɑːnə/ noun [C] a dried white GRAPE, used in cooking

sultry /ˈsʌltri/ adj sultry weather is unpleasant because the air is hot and wet

sum¹ /sʌm/ noun [C] ★★
1 an amount of money: *We already spend large sums of money on advertising.* ♦ *The painting was sold for the sum of £1.3 million.*

2 *British* a simple calculation
3 a total amount made by adding several numbers or amounts together: *What's the sum of those three numbers?*

sum² /sʌm/
PHRASAL VERBS ˌsum (sth) ˈup to give a summary of something
ˌsum sb/sth ˈup if something sums someone or something up, it shows exactly what they are like

summarily /ˈsʌmərɪli/ adv immediately, and without following the usual official methods or processes

summarize /ˈsʌməraɪz/ verb [I/T] to provide a short account of the most important facts or features of something

summary¹ /ˈsʌməri/ noun [C] ★★ a short account of something that gives only the most important information: *The text provides summaries of the plots of Shakespeare's plays.*

summary² /ˈsʌməri/ adj done immediately and without following the usual methods or processes: *summary executions*

summer /ˈsʌmə/ noun [C/U] ★★★ the season between spring and autumn, when the weather is hottest: *the summer of 1973* ♦ *a warm summer evening* ♦ *This room is cold even in summer.*

ˈsummer ˌcamp noun [C/U] a place where children can go to stay in the summer holiday and do various activities

ˌsummer ˈholiday noun [C] *British* a period of time in the summer when people do not work or go to school, college, or university

ˈsummer ˌhouse noun [C] a small building in a garden or park where you can sit in warm weather

ˈsummer ˌschool noun [C/U] a course of study held at a college or university during the summer holiday

ˈsummer ˌtime noun [U] *British* the system by which the time on clocks is changed in the summer in order to provide an extra hour of light in the evenings

summertime /ˈsʌmətaɪm/ noun [U] the period of the year when it is summer

ˌsummer vaˈcation noun [C] the period of time in the summer when universities are closed

summery /ˈsʌməri/ adj suitable for summer, or making you think of summer

summit /ˈsʌmɪt/ noun [C] ★
1 a meeting or series of meetings between leaders of two or more countries: *a summit of EU leaders*
2 the top of a mountain

summon /ˈsʌmən/ verb [T] **1** *formal* to officially order someone to come to a place: *He was urgently summoned to Washington for consultations.* **2** to manage to produce a quality or a reaction that helps you to deal with a difficult situation: *She could barely summon a smile.*
PHRASAL VERB ˌsummon sth ˈup *same as* **summon** 2

summons /ˈsʌmənz/ noun [C] an official document that orders someone to appear

S

in a court of law —**summons** verb [T]

sumo /ˈsuːməʊ/ or ˌsumo ˈwrestling noun [U] a Japanese sport in which two very large men WRESTLE —ˌsumo ˈwrestler noun [C]

sumptuous /ˈsʌmptʃuəs/ adj impressive, expensive, and of high quality —**sumptuously** adv

sun¹ /sʌn/ noun ★★★
1 **the Sun** or **the sun** the star in the sky that provides light and warmth to the Earth
2 [singular/U] the light and warmth that you feel from the sun: *Miriam was sitting in the sun reading a book.*
3 [C] a very bright star, especially one that a planet travels round

sun² /sʌn/ verb **sun yourself** if a person or animal suns themselves, they sit or lie in the sun

Sun. abbrev Sunday

sunbathe /ˈsʌnbeɪð/ verb [I] to sit or lie in the sun so that your skin becomes darker —**sunbather** noun [C], **sunbathing** noun [U]

sunbed /ˈsʌnbed/ noun [C] 1 a machine with special lights that you lie under to get a SUNTAN 2 a type of chair with a long seat that you can sit or lie on to enjoy the sun

sunburn /ˈsʌnbɜːn/ noun [U] sore red skin that is caused by staying in the sun for too long

sunburnt /ˈsʌnbɜːnt/ or **sunburned** /ˈsʌnbɜːnd/ adj skin that is sunburnt is red and sore from too much sun

Sunday /ˈsʌndeɪ/ noun [C/U] ★★★ the day after Saturday and before Monday: *Our next meeting is on a Sunday.* ♦ *I'm going to visit my parents next Sunday.* ♦ *Are you doing anything nice on Sunday?* ♦ *We usually go to church on Sundays* (=every Sunday).

ˈSunday ˌschool noun [C/U] religious lessons for children that are given in a church on Sundays

sundial /ˈsʌndaɪəl/ noun [C] an object that measures time by the position of a shadow made in sunny weather

sundown /ˈsʌndaʊn/ noun [U] the time when the sun goes below the HORIZON =SUNSET

sundry /ˈsʌndri/ adj *formal* sundry things or people are all different from each other and cannot be described as a group
PHRASE **all and sundry** everyone

sunflower /ˈsʌnˌflaʊə/ noun [C] a very tall plant that has large yellow flowers with a round brown centre —*picture* → C9

sung the past participle of **sing**

sunglasses /ˈsʌnˌɡlɑːsɪz/ noun [plural] dark glasses that you wear to protect your eyes when the sun is bright

sunk the past tense and past participle of **sink¹**

sunken /ˈsʌŋkən/ adj 1 lying at the bottom of the sea 2 lower than the level of the surrounding land or floor 3 sunken eyes or cheeks curve inwards, often showing that someone is ill or old

sunlight /ˈsʌnlaɪt/ noun [U] the light from the sun: *bright/strong sunlight*

sunlit /ˈsʌnlɪt/ adj brightly lit by the sun

Sunni /ˈsʊni/ noun [C/U] one of the two groups

within the religion of Islam, or a Muslim who belongs to this group → SHIITE

sunny /ˈsʌni/ adj 1 bright with light from the sun: *It was a beautiful sunny day.* 2 happy: *a sunny smile*

sunrise /ˈsʌnˌraɪz/ noun [C/U] the time in the early morning when the sun first appears in the sky, or the way the sky looks at this time → SUNSET

sunroof /ˈsʌnˌruːf/ noun [C] a part of a roof of a car that can be opened —*picture* → C6

sunscreen /ˈsʌnˌskriːn/ noun [C/U] a cream that you can rub onto your skin to stop it from being burned by the sun

sunset /ˈsʌnˌset/ noun [C/U] the time in the evening when the sun goes down below the HORIZON and night begins, or the way that the sky looks at this time =SUNDOWN → SUNRISE

sunshine /ˈsʌnˌʃaɪn/ noun [U] light from the sun: *We set off in bright sunshine.*

suntan /ˈsʌnˌtæn/ noun [C] the dark colour of your skin when you have spent time in the sun —**suntanned** /ˈsʌnˌtænd/ adj

ˈsuntan ˌlotion or ˈsuntan ˌoil noun [C/U] a substance that you rub onto your skin to stop it from being burned by the sun

super¹ /ˈsuːpə/ adj *informal old-fashioned* very good, nice, or enjoyable

super² /ˈsuːpə/ adv *informal* extremely: *a super luxurious hotel*

super- /ˈsuːpə/ prefix more, better, or bigger than usual: *a superhero* ♦ *supersonic*

superb /sʊˈpɜːb/ adj of the highest quality =EXCELLENT —**superbly** adv

supercomputer /ˈsuːpəkəmˌpjuːtə/ noun [C] a very powerful computer

superficial /ˌsuːpəˈfɪʃ(ə)l/ adj 1 affecting or involving only the surface or outside part of something =MINOR: *Her injuries were only superficial.* 2 not complete or thorough =CURSORY: *a superficial examination of the damage* 3 a superficial person does not think about serious or important things =SHALLOW —**superficially** adv

superfluous /suːˈpɜːfluəs/ adj not needed or wanted =UNNECESSARY

superhuman /ˌsuːpəˈhjuːmən/ adj superhuman qualities are much greater and more impressive than those of an ordinary person

superimpose /ˌsuːpərɪmˈpəʊz/ verb [T] 1 to put one image on top of another so that both can be seen 2 to add something such as a feature or idea from one system or situation to another

superintendent /ˌsuːpərɪnˈtendənt/ noun [C] 1 a senior police officer in the UK 2 someone whose job is to be in charge of an area or an activity

superior¹ /suːˈpɪəriə/ adj 1 of high quality, or better or bigger than something else: *The hotel's service is superior.* ♦ *The sound quality is superior to that on a regular CD.* 2 someone who is superior behaves as if they think that they are better than other people: *I can't stand that superior smile of* *his.* **3** having a higher status or position than someone or something else: *Rockwood was charged with disobeying a superior officer.*

superior[2] /suˈpɪəriə/ noun [C] someone who is senior to you in an organization or job

superiority /suˌpɪəriˈɒrəti/ noun [U] **1** the fact that one person or thing is better than another **2** a way of behaving that shows that you think you are better than other people

superlative[1] /suˈpɜːlətɪv/ adj **1** *linguistics* a superlative adjective or adverb is one that expresses the greatest degree of a particular quality. For example the superlative form of 'happy' is 'happiest'. → COMPARATIVE[1] **2** *formal* extremely good =SUPERB

superlative[2] /suˈpɜːlətɪv/ noun [C] *linguistics* the superlative form of an adjective or an adverb

supermarket /ˈsuːpəˌmɑːkɪt/ noun [C] ★ a very large shop that sells food and other products for the home

supermodel /ˈsuːpəˌmɒd(ə)l/ noun [C] a very famous and successful fashion model

supernatural /ˌsuːpəˈnætʃərəl/ adj used about things that seem to be caused by magic and do not have a natural or scientific explanation

supernatural, the /ˌsuːpəˈnætʃərəl/ noun [singular] supernatural events, forces, or creatures

superpower /ˈsuːpəˌpaʊə/ noun [C] a country that has great military, economic, and political power

supersede /ˌsuːpəˈsiːd/ verb [T] if one thing is superseded by another, it is replaced by it: *Steam trains were gradually superseded by diesel engines.*

supersonic /ˌsuːpəˈsɒnɪk/ adj faster than the speed of sound

superstar /ˈsuːpəˌstɑː/ noun [C] someone such as a film actor or musician who is extremely famous

superstition /ˌsuːpəˈstɪʃ(ə)n/ noun [C/U] a belief that things such as magic or luck have the power to affect your life —**superstitious** /ˌsuːpəˈstɪʃəs/ adj

superstore /ˈsuːpəˌstɔː/ noun [C] a very large shop that sells a wide range of different goods, usually on the edge of a town

supervise /ˈsuːpəˌvaɪz/ verb [I/T] to be in charge of people and check that they are behaving or working correctly: *His job was to supervise the loading of the ship.* —**supervision** /ˌsuːpəˈvɪʒ(ə)n/ noun [U]: *Here children can play safely under supervision.*

supervisor /ˈsuːpəˌvaɪzə/ noun [C] someone who is in charge of an activity, a place, or a group of people —**supervisory** /ˌsuːpəˈvaɪzəri/ adj

supper /ˈsʌpə/ noun [C/U] a meal that you eat in the evening → DINNER

supplant /səˈplɑːnt/ verb [T] *formal* to replace something or someone

supple /ˈsʌp(ə)l/ adj able to move and bend easily —**suppleness** noun [U]

supplement[1] /ˈsʌplɪˌment/ verb [T] **1** to add

something extra in order to improve something: *a balanced diet supplemented with vitamin tablets* **2** to add extra money to the amount that you normally earn: *He was able to supplement his income by writing stories.*

supplement[2] /ˈsʌplɪmənt/ noun [C] **1** something extra that you add to make something better **2** a separate part of a newspaper or magazine **3** an extra amount of money that you have to pay for special services, especially in a hotel

supplementary /ˌsʌplɪˈment(ə)ri/ adj additional

supplier /səˈplaɪə/ noun [C] a company, organization, or country that supplies or sells a product or service: *Colombia is our main supplier of coffee beans.*

supply[1] /səˈplaɪ/ noun ★★★

1 [C] an amount or quantity of something that is available to use: *The crops need a constant supply of water.* ♦ *electricity/gas/ oil supplies*

2 **supplies** [plural] things such as food, medicine, and equipment that you need to live or to perform a particular activity: *The trucks carried medicine and other supplies across the border.*

3 [U] the act or process of providing something that is needed: **the supply of sth to sth** *This muscle controls the supply of blood to the heart.*

PHRASE **in short supply** available only in small quantities, so that there is not enough: *Water was in short supply.*

supply[2] /səˈplaɪ/ verb [T] ★★★ to provide someone or something with something that they need or want: **supply sth to sb/sth** *Two huge generators supply power to farms in the area.* ♦ **supply sb/sth with sth** *They used the money to supply the school with new textbooks.*

support[1] /səˈpɔːt/ verb [T] ★★★

1 approve of and help	**5** help to prove sth
2 help a friend	**6** like a sports team
3 hold/bear weight	**7** be extra performer
4 provide sth necessary	

1 to approve of an idea or a person or organization, and help them to be successful: *The United Nations has supported efforts to return the refugees peacefully.* ♦ *Of course we all support the prime minister.*

2 to help someone and be kind to them when they are in a difficult situation: *My friends have supported me through the entire trial.*

3 to hold the weight of someone or something so that they do not move or fall: **support sth with sth** *The plants were supported with wire.* ♦ **be supported by sth** *She was sitting up in bed, supported by pillows.*

4 to provide someone with the money, food, shelter, or other things that they need in order to live: *How can we support our families on such low wages?* ♦ *She's been*

S

supporting herself since she was 18 years old.

5 to show that an idea, statement, theory etc is true or correct: *Our conclusions are supported by extensive research.*

6 to like a particular sports team and always want them to win: *I support West Ham – who do you support?* → SUPPORTER

7 to perform in a show or concert in addition to the main performer

Words often used with **support**

Nouns often used with support (verb, sense 5)
■ SUPPORT + **argument, claim, conclusion, hypothesis, idea, theory, view**: help to show that an idea or argument is true or correct

support² /sə'pɔːt/ noun ★★★

1 help/approval	4 sth that holds sth
2 money	5 proof
3 kindness	6 performers in show

1 [U] help and approval that you give to a particular idea, politician, organization etc: *I urge my colleagues to join me in support of this plan.*

2 [U] money that is provided to a person or organization in order to help them: *financial support for local bus services*

3 [U] help and kindness that you give to someone who is having a difficult time: *I am grateful to my family for their love and support.*

4 [C/U] something that holds the weight of an object, building, or structure so that it does not move or fall

5 [U] proof that something is true or correct: *Do you have any support for your theory?*

6 [U] someone who performs in a show or concert but is not the main performer

Words often used with **support**

Adjectives often used with support (noun, sense 1)
■ **active, complete, enthusiastic, full, strong, wholehearted** + SUPPORT: used about support that is strong
Verbs often used with support (noun, sense 1)
■ **attract, gain, get, receive, win** + SUPPORT: be thought to be a good idea
■ **enlist, mobilize, rally** + SUPPORT: get people to agree to support you
■ **give, lend, pledge** + SUPPORT: agree to support someone

supporter /sə'pɔːtə/ noun [C] ★★
1 someone who supports a particular idea, person, or group: *Jarvis is a strong supporter of the European Union.*
2 someone who likes to watch a particular sports team and wants that team to win =FAN: *Barcelona supporters*

sup'port ,group noun [C] a group that is organized by and for people who share a particular problem or medical condition

supporting /sə'pɔːtɪŋ/ adj **1** used about a part in a play or film that is important but is not the main part: *a supporting role*
2 holding the weight of something, especially in a building **3** helping to prove

that a theory or claim is true: *supporting evidence*

supportive /sə'pɔːtɪv/ adj helpful and sympathetic

suppose /sə'pəʊz/ verb [T] ★★★ to think that something is probably true, right, or possible: *I suppose she must be delighted about getting the job.* ♦ **+(that)** *You don't suppose that he's going to hurt anyone, do you?* ♦ *I suppose I had better get back to work.* ♦ *We have no **reason to suppose that** he's done anything illegal.*

PHRASES **be supposed to do/be sth 1** to be expected to behave in a particular way, especially according to a rule, an agreement, or someone in authority: *You're supposed to make a copy of the contract before you mail it.* **2** to be generally considered to have a particular quality or skill: *Latin America is supposed to be a pretty inexpensive place to travel.* **3** to be expected or intended to happen in a particular way or have a particular result: *The new regulations are supposed to help single parents.*

I don't suppose *spoken* **1** used as a polite way of making a request or asking a question, when you are not sure that you will get a positive answer: *I don't suppose you'd be willing to take me to the airport?* **2** used for saying that something is unlikely: *I don't suppose we'll ever be rich.*

I suppose (so) *spoken* **1** used for showing that you mainly agree with something but you have some doubts about it: *'It's a very busy road, isn' t it?' 'I suppose so.'* **2** used when you agree to do something but you are not completely willing to do it: *'Could you loan me £50?' 'Yes, I suppose.'*

suppose/supposing (that) used for introducing a possible situation or action and the results of it: *Suppose you won the lottery, what would you do with the money?*

supposed /sə'pəʊzd, sə'pəʊzɪd/ adj believed or said by some people to be true, although you may not agree with this: *the supposed economic benefits of lower taxes*

supposedly /sə'pəʊzɪdli/ adv as some people believe or say, although you may not agree with this: *The house is supposedly haunted.*

supposition /ˌsʌpə'zɪʃ(ə)n/ noun [C/U] something that you believe is true although you cannot prove it

suppress /sə'pres/ verb [T] **1** to stop political opposition, protests, or other forms of disagreement, especially by using force or strict laws: *The revolt was brutally suppressed.* **2** to stop yourself from feeling or showing an emotion: *suppressed anger* **3** to stop a physical process from happening or developing —**suppression** /sə'preʃ(ə)n/ noun [U]

supremacy /suː'preməsi/ noun [U] a situation in which one person, group, or thing has more power or influence than any other

supreme /suː'priːm/ adj **1** most important or powerful: *the Supreme Commander of the* *allied forces* **2** very great: *The Church was of supreme importance in medieval Europe.*

su,preme 'court noun [C] the most important court in some countries and in most states of the US

Su,preme 'Court, the the most powerful court in the US that has the authority to change the decisions made by other US courts

supremely /sʊˈpriːmli/ adv extremely, or to the highest possible degree

surcharge /ˈsɜːtʃɑːdʒ/ noun [C] an extra amount of money that you must pay for something

sure¹ /ʃɔː, ʃʊə/ adj ★★★
1 certain that something is real, true, or correct: *I think she's called Monica, but I'm not sure.* ♦ *If you're really sure about the facts, we'll publish them.* ♦ +(that) *I was sure I had left my keys on the counter.* ♦ **not sure how/why/if etc** *No one is really sure why he resigned.*
2 certain to happen or succeed: *Everyone thought that the deal was a sure thing* (=that it would definitely happen). ♦ **sure to do sth** *If you stay up late, you're sure to feel rotten in the morning.*
3 used about something that is definite and cannot be questioned or doubted: *Bill was chewing his nails, a sure sign that he was worried.*

PHRASES **be sure to do sth** *spoken* used for reminding someone to do something: *Be sure to fasten your seat belt.*
for sure definitely or definitely true: *I will call you tomorrow for sure.* ♦ *Ashe was an incredible tennis player, that's for sure.*
make sure 1 to check something, so that you can be sure about it: *Always make sure of your facts before accusing anyone.* ♦ +(that) *I just wanted to make sure you knew where to go.* **2** to take the action that is necessary for something to happen: +(that) *Police were there to make sure there was no violence.*
sure of yourself confident

sure² /ʃɔː, ʃʊə/ adv *spoken* ★★ used for saying yes or agreeing to something: *'Can I borrow your green jumper?' 'Sure, no problem.'*

PHRASE **sure enough** used for saying that something happened exactly as you thought it would: *I had a feeling we'd get lost, and sure enough, we did.*

sure-footed /ʃɔː ˈfʊtɪd/ adj **1** good at walking or climbing and unlikely to fall **2** dealing with a situation confidently and skilfully

surely /ˈʃɔːli, ˈʃʊəli/ adv ★★
1 used for showing that you think that something is very likely: *Surely you realized we were at home when you saw the lights on?*
2 *spoken* used for showing surprise or doubt: *'Did she tell you they've split up?' 'Surely not.'*

surf¹ /sɜːf/ verb **1** [I] to ride on waves in the sea on a SURFBOARD **2** [I/T] to look at various places one after another on the Internet or on television: *She spends hours every day just surfing the Net.*

surf

surf² /sɜːf/ noun [U] waves that are falling onto a beach

surface¹ /ˈsɜːfɪs/ noun ★★★
1 [C] the top layer or outside part of something: *a smooth/rough/hard surface* ♦ *Road surfaces are slippery from the rain.* ♦ *We saw fish swimming just under the surface of the water.*
2 [C] a flat area: *All surfaces in the kitchen should be carefully cleaned.* ♦ *Some players complained that the surface was too slippery.*
3 [singular] an appearance that is different from what someone or something is really like: *On the surface, they looked like a happily married couple.*

surface² /ˈsɜːfɪs/ verb **1** [I] if something surfaces, it appears or people start to notice it: *New information about the murder is slowly surfacing.* **2** [I] to come up to the surface of water: *The divers were forced to surface after their equipment was damaged.* **3** [T] to put a smooth surface on a road

surface³ /ˈsɜːfɪs/ adj **1** on the surface of something: *the surface temperature of the lake* **2** travelling on the surface of land or water, rather than through the air: *surface transport/mail*

surfboard /ˈsɜːfbɔːd/ noun [C] a board that you use for riding on waves

surfing /ˈsɜːfɪŋ/ noun [U] **1** a sport in which people ride on waves using surfboards **2** the activity of looking at different places on the Internet or on television in order to find something interesting

surge¹ /sɜːdʒ/ noun [singular] **1** a sudden increase in something: *a surge in spending* **2** a sudden movement of a large group of people **3** a sudden strong feeling: *a surge of emotion/desire/anxiety*

surge² /sɜːdʒ/ verb [I] **1** if a crowd of people surges, they all move forward together very quickly **2** to increase a lot very quickly **3** if a feeling surges, you start to feel it very strongly: *Panic surged inside her.*

PHRASAL VERB ,surge 'up *same as* surge² 3

surgeon /ˈsɜːdʒ(ə)n/ noun [C] a doctor who does operations

surgery /ˈsɜːdʒəri/ noun ★
1 [U] medical treatment in which a doctor cuts open someone's body
2 [C] *British* a place where people can visit a doctor or a DENTIST

surgical /ˈsɜːdʒɪk(ə)l/ adj connected with surgery

surly /ˈsɜːli/ adj unfriendly and rude

S

surmise /səˈmaɪz/ verb [T] *formal* to use information to make a guess about something

surmount /səˈmaʊnt/ verb [T] **1** to deal successfully with a difficult situation **2** to be on top of something

surname /ˈsɜːneɪm/ noun [C] the part of your name that is your family's name =FAMILY NAME, LAST NAME

surpass /səˈpɑːs/ verb [T] **1** to be better or bigger than something else =EXCEED: *Temperatures surpassed 42 degrees Celsius.* **2** to be even better than what was expected or hoped for: *Winning the gold medal surpassed my wildest dreams.*

surplus¹ /ˈsɜːpləs/ noun [C/U] more of something than is necessary: *a surplus of oil*

surplus² /ˈsɜːpləs/ adj more than is needed: *They should use the surplus cash to help people who need it.*

surprise¹ /səˈpraɪz/ noun ★★★
1 [C] an unusual event, or an unexpected piece of news: *The news came as a big surprise to everyone.* ♦ *Given the company's poor performance, the change of management came as no surprise.*
2 [U] the feeling that you have when something unusual or unexpected happens: *Many students expressed surprise at the news.* ♦ *Much to my surprise, the restaurant was actually very nice.*
PHRASE **take/catch sb by surprise** to surprise someone by happening unexpectedly: *The storm caught the fishermen completely by surprise.*

surprise² /səˈpraɪz/ verb [T] ★
1 to give someone a feeling of surprise: *Her angry tone of voice surprised me.* ♦ *It wouldn't surprise me if it snowed tonight.* ♦ *She surprised herself by finishing the race in less than 45 minutes.*
2 to attack someone when they do not expect it
3 to discover someone doing something bad or embarrassing: *A teacher surprised the boys smoking.*

surprised /səˈpraɪzd/ adj ★★
1 feeling surprise because something unexpected has happened: *We were surprised by Ben's reaction to the news.* ♦ *I wouldn't be surprised if he got married again soon.* ♦ **be surprised to do sth** *I wasn't surprised to hear that their marriage had ended.*
2 showing surprise: *a surprised look*

surprising /səˈpraɪzɪŋ/ adj ★★ unusual, or unexpected ≠ UNSURPRISING: *It's hardly surprising* (=not at all surprising) *that she's angry, considering what you said.* ♦ **it is surprising how/what/where etc** *It's surprising what you can achieve with so little money.* — **surprisingly** adv: *It's a small house, but the garden is surprisingly large.*

surreal /səˈrɪəl/ adj something surreal is so strange that you cannot believe that it is real

surrender¹ /səˈrendə/ verb **1** [I] if soldiers surrender, they stop fighting and officially admit that they have been defeated **2** [T] to give something to someone in authority because you have to: *She was ordered to surrender her passport.*

surrender² /səˈrendə/ noun [U] an occasion when soldiers stop fighting and officially admit that they have been defeated

surreptitious /ˌsʌrəpˈtɪʃəs/ adj done quietly or secretly so that other people will not notice —**surreptitiously** adv

surrogate mother /ˌsʌrəgət ˈmʌðə/ noun [C] a woman who gives birth to a baby for another woman who cannot have children

surround¹ /səˈraʊnd/ verb [T] ★★
1 to be all around something or someone: *Armed police quickly surrounded the building.* ♦ **surround sth with sth** *People are surrounding their homes with barbed wire fences.*
2 to be closely connected with a situation or an event: *Uncertainty surrounds the future of the industry.*
3 to be near someone all the time: *She grew up surrounded by older children.* ♦ **surround yourself with sb/sth** *She surrounds herself with talented people.*

surround² /səˈraʊnd/ noun [C] a border or edge around something

surrounding /səˈraʊndɪŋ/ adj around a place: *The hotel is ideally located for visiting the surrounding area.*

surroundings /səˈraʊndɪŋz/ noun [plural] a place and all the things in it: *She soon became accustomed to her new surroundings.*

surveillance /səˈveɪləns/ noun [U] if the police keep someone under surveillance, they watch them closely

survey¹ /ˈsɜːveɪ/ noun [C] ★★
1 a set of questions that you ask in order to find out people's opinions: *We carried out a survey of local housing needs.*
2 an examination of the condition of something, especially a house
3 an examination of land by someone who is making a map
4 a general book or programme about a subject

survey² /səˈveɪ, ˈsɜːveɪ/ verb [T] ★
1 to ask people questions in order to find out their opinions: *19% of those surveyed say they haven't decided who they will vote for.*
2 to look at something or examine something: *He sat quietly, surveying the scene around him.*

surveyor /səˈveɪə/ noun [C] **1** someone whose job is to measure land in order to make maps **2** *British* someone whose job is to examine a house or other building to see if it is in good condition, especially for someone who wants to buy it

survival /səˈvaɪv(ə)l/ noun [U] ★ the fact that someone is still alive, or the fact that something still exists: *survival equipment* ♦ *These animals face a constant fight for survival.*

survive /səˈvaɪv/ verb [I/T] ★★★
1 to continue to exist or live in a difficult situation: *Only one of the museum's paintings survived the fire.* ♦ *How does the family survive on such a small monthly wage?*
2 to stay alive after an injury, illness, or attack: *Doctors don't think the victims will survive.* ♦ *Just eight passengers survived the plane crash.*
3 to manage to deal with something difficult or unpleasant: *Don't worry about Molly – she'll survive.*

surviving /səˈvaɪvɪŋ/ adj still alive, or still existing

survivor /səˈvaɪvə/ noun [C] someone who is still alive after an accident, illness, or attack

susceptible /səˈseptəb(ə)l/ adj likely to be influenced or affected by something: *Children are particularly susceptible to the disease.* —**susceptibility** /səˌseptəˈbɪləti/ noun [U]

sushi /ˈsuːʃi/ noun [U] Japanese food that consists of cold rice with fish, egg, or vegetables

suspect¹ /səˈspekt/ verb [T] ★★
1 to believe that something is true: +(that) *Police suspected that she had some connection with the robbery.*
2 to think that someone might have done something bad: *He wrote a letter naming the people whom he suspected.* ♦ *suspect sb of sth men suspected of involvement in the bombing*
3 to think that something might be bad: *Carl seemed very kind, but she suspected his motives.*

> **Word family: suspect**
> *Words in the same family as suspect*
> ■ **suspected** *adj*   ■ **suspicion** *n*
> ■ **suspicious** *adj*   ■ **suspiciously** *adv*
> ■ **unsuspecting** *adj*

suspect² /ˈsʌspekt/ noun [C] **1** someone who might have committed a crime: *a murder suspect* **2** something that might have caused something bad

suspect³ /ˈsʌspekt/ adj **1** something that is suspect might not be good, honest, or reliable: *suspect motives* **2** a suspect object might be dangerous or illegal: *a suspect package*

suspected /səˈspektɪd/ adj if you have a suspected injury or illness, doctors think that you might have that injury or illness

suspend /səˈspend/ verb [T] ★
1 to order someone to leave their job or school for a short period of time as a punishment
2 to officially stop something for a short time: *Operations at the plant have been suspended because of safety concerns.*
3 *formal* to hang something from something else

suspenders /səˈspendəz/ noun [plural] **1** *British* a piece of clothing that holds STOCKINGS up

2 *American* BRACES for keeping trousers up

suspense /səˈspens/ noun [U] the excited or worried feeling that you have when you are waiting for something to happen: *Please don't keep me in suspense. I need to know!*

suspension /səˈspenʃ(ə)n/ noun **1** [C/U] the act of officially stopping something for a period of time: *the suspension of the peace talks* **2** [C/U] a punishment in which someone is forced to leave their job or school for a short period of time **3** [U] the equipment that makes a vehicle move smoothly when it goes over rough ground

susˈpension ˌbridge noun [C] a type of bridge that hangs from strong steel ropes that are fixed to towers

suspicion /səˈspɪʃ(ə)n/ noun **1** [C/U] a feeling that something bad has happened: *She had a suspicion that Mr Engel was not being completely honest.* ♦ *They were both arrested on suspicion of murder.* **2** [U] a feeling that you do not trust someone: *an atmosphere of suspicion and hostility*
> **PHRASE** **under suspicion** if someone is under suspicion, people think that they might have done something bad: *Several senior party members have come under suspicion.*

suspicious /səˈspɪʃəs/ adj **1** if you are suspicious, you do not trust someone or you think that something bad might have happened: *Colleagues became suspicious when he started acting strangely.* ♦ *a suspicious glance/look* ♦ *People are often suspicious of strangers.* **2** if something is suspicious, you think that it might be bad or dangerous: *Customers noticed a suspicious package by the door.*
—**suspiciously** adv

suss /sʌs/ or **ˌsuss sth ˈout** verb [T] *British informal* to discover something: *I've just sussed out how the system works.*

sustain /səˈsteɪn/ verb [T] **1** to provide the conditions that allow something to happen or exist: *Only two of the planets could sustain life.* ♦ *Can the country's economic growth be sustained?* **2** *formal* to give someone strength, energy, or hope: *A cup of coffee isn't enough to sustain you until lunchtime.* **3** *formal* to experience something bad=SUFFER: *One of the officers sustained minor injuries in the fire.*

sustainable /səˈsteɪnəb(ə)l/ adj **1** capable of continuing for a long time at the same level ≠ UNSUSTAINABLE **2** using methods that do not harm the environment

sustained /səˈsteɪnd/ adj continuing at the same level for a long time: *sustained economic growth*

sustenance /ˈsʌstənəns/ noun [U] *formal* food and drink

SW abbrev **1** southwest **2** southwestern

swab /swɒb/ noun [C] **1** a small piece of a soft substance that is used for cleaning injuries **2** a small amount of a substance from someone's body that a doctor is testing

swagger /ˈswægə/ verb [I] to walk in a proud confident way —**swagger** noun [singular]

S

Swahili /swɑːˈhiːli/ noun [U] a major language of eastern Africa

swallow¹ /ˈswɒləʊ/ verb ★

1 [I/T] to make food or drink go down your throat and into your stomach: *She quickly swallowed the rest of her coffee.* ♦ *I had a sore throat and it hurt to swallow.*

2 [I] to make a movement in your throat as if you are swallowing food: *Tim swallowed nervously before replying.*

3 [T] *informal* to believe something that is unlikely to be true

PHRASE **swallow your pride/disappointment/anger etc** to not allow your feelings to affect your behaviour: *He finally had to swallow his pride and ask for help.*

PHRASAL VERB **swallow sth up 1** if something is swallowed up, it becomes part of something larger: *The company was swallowed up in a corporate merger.* **2** to use a lot of something such as money, time, or effort

swallow² /ˈswɒləʊ/ noun [C] **1** a small bird whose tail has two long points **2** a movement in your throat that makes food or drink go down into your stomach

swam the past tense of **swim¹**

swamp¹ /swɒmp/ verb **1** [T] if someone is swamped, they have too much to deal with at one time: *Bookshops are always swamped with orders at Christmas.* **2** [T] if a place is swamped, there are very large numbers of people in it: *The hotel foyer was suddenly swamped by reporters and photographers.* **3** [I/T] to fill or cover something with water

swamp² /swɒmp/ noun [C/U] an area of land that is covered by water —**swampy** adj

swan /swɒn/ noun [C] a large white bird with a long neck that lives near water

swansong /ˈswɒnˌsɒŋ/ noun [C] the last performance of a performer's career

swap /swɒp/ verb [I/T] to give something to someone in exchange for something else: *If you like this one better, I'll swap with you.* ♦ *Members are encouraged to swap books with each other.*

PHRASE **swap places 1** if two people swap places, each person goes to the place where the other person was before **2** to be in the situation that another person is in —**swap** noun [singular]

swarm¹ /swɔːm/ verb [I] **1** to go somewhere as a large crowd: *Fans swarmed onto the pitch to celebrate.* **2** if insects swarm, they fly together in a large group

PHRASAL VERB **swarm with sth** if a place is swarming with people, insects, or animals, it is full of them

swarm² /swɔːm/ noun [C] **1** a large group of insects flying together **2** a large number of people moving together as a group

swarthy /ˈswɔːði/ adj someone who is swarthy has dark skin

swat /swɒt/ verb [T] to hit an insect and try to kill it

swathe /sweɪð/ noun [C] *formal* **1** a large area of land **2** a large number of people, or a large amount of something

swathed /sweɪðd/ adj covered or wrapped in something

sway¹ /sweɪ/ verb **1** [I] to move or swing gently from side to side: *Their bodies swayed to the music.* **2** [T] to change someone's opinion: *Do not allow yourselves to be swayed by these arguments.*

sway² /sweɪ/ noun [singular] a slow swinging movement from side to side

PHRASE **hold sway** *formal* **1** to be the main influence on people's opinions or behaviour **2** to control an area

swear /sweə/ (past tense **swore** /swɔː/; past participle **sworn** /swɔːn/) verb ★

1 [I] to use words that are deliberately offensive, for example because you are angry: *That's the first time I've ever heard him swear.* ♦ *She was shouting and swearing at everyone.*

2 [T] to make a sincere statement or promise: *I've never seen him before – I swear!* ♦ *Members have to swear an oath of secrecy.* ♦ **+(that)** *She swears that this is the man who attacked her.* ♦ **swear to do sth** *He swore to stay out of politics when he retired.*

PHRASE **could have sworn** *spoken* used for saying that you are sure that something happened: *I could have sworn I'd paid that bill.*

PHRASAL VERBS **'swear by sth** *informal* to believe that something is very effective: *My father swears by whisky as a cure for a cold.*

ˌswear sb 'in to make someone give a formal promise in a law court or at an official ceremony

swearword /ˈsweəˌwɜːd/ noun [C] an offensive word that people use when they swear

sweat¹ /swet/ noun [U] liquid that forms on your skin when you are hot: *She wiped the sweat off her forehead with a towel.*

PHRASES **in a (cold) sweat** very worried or nervous

no sweat *spoken* used for saying that you can easily do something

sweat² /swet/ verb [I] **1** to produce liquid on the surface of your skin when you are hot, nervous, or ill: *She could feel the palms of her hands sweating.* **2** *informal* to feel very nervous or worried **3** *informal* to work hard

PHRASE **sweat it out** to wait for something that you are nervous or worried about

sweater /ˈswetə/ noun [C] a warm piece of clothing that covers your upper body and arms —*picture* → C5

sweatshirt /ˈswetˌʃɜːt/ noun [C] a shirt made of thick soft cotton that some people wear for exercising —*picture* → C5

sweatshop /ˈswetˌʃɒp/ noun [C] *informal* a factory where people work very hard in bad conditions and earn very little money

sweaty /ˈsweti/ adj covered in SWEAT, or smelling of SWEAT

swede /swiːd/ noun [C/U] *British* a hard round yellow vegetable that grows under the ground

sweep¹ /swiːp/ (past tense and past participle **swept** /swept/) verb ★

1 [T] to clean a floor using a long brush: *Her*

S

work consisted mainly of making coffee and sweeping the floor.

2 [I/T] to move quickly or with a lot of force, or to take something somewhere quickly or with a lot of force: *Fire swept through the building.* ♦ *Disease has swept through this remote city.* ♦ *The flood waters swept the car downstream.*

3 [I] to go somewhere quickly and in a confident or angry way: *Several senior officials swept into the room.*

PHRASES **sweep to power** to win an election by a very large number of votes

sweep sth under the carpet to try to avoid dealing with a problem

PHRASAL VERBS **sweep sb/sth a'side** to ignore someone or something: *He swept aside all her objections.*

sweep sth a'way to destroy something, or to completely remove something: *Many people died when floods swept their homes away.*

sweep 'up to clean a floor using a long brush

sweep² /swiːp/ noun [C] **1** a long wide curved area of land or water **2** a long smooth curved movement

sweeping /ˈswiːpɪŋ/ adj **1** a sweeping change or development has a major effect **2** a sweeping statement is too general to be true in every case **3** with a wide impressive curved shape

sweepstake /ˈswiːpˌsteɪk/ noun [C] *British* a form of GAMBLING for a group of people. The winner gets all the money that everyone has BET.

sweet¹ /swiːt/ adj ★★
1 foods and drinks that are sweet taste like sugar ≠ SOUR: *I'd like something sweet, like a piece of cake.* ♦ *This tea is too sweet.*
2 something that is sweet has a nice smell, sound, or appearance: *The room is filled with the sweet fragrance of flowers.* ♦ *a sweet little kitten*
3 kind and gentle: *He's such a sweet man.* ♦ **sweet of sb to do sth** *It was so sweet of you to help me.*
—**sweetness** noun [U]
→ SWEET TOOTH

sweet² /swiːt/ noun **1** [C] *British* a small piece of sweet food made with sugar **2** [C/U] a sweet food that you eat at the end of a meal =DESSERT

sweetcorn /ˈswiːtˌkɔːn/ noun [U] *British* the small yellow seeds of some types of MAIZE plant that are cooked and eaten as a vegetable

sweeten /ˈswiːt(ə)n/ verb [T] **1** to make something taste sweeter **2** to make something such as an offer seem more attractive in order to persuade someone to accept it

sweetener /ˈswiːt(ə)nə/ noun **1** [C/U] a substance that is added to food or drink to make it taste sweeter **2** [C] *informal* something that you offer someone in order to persuade them to do something

sweetheart /ˈswiːtˌhɑːt/ noun [C] *spoken* used for talking to someone that you love

sweetly /ˈswiːtli/ adv **1** in a nice, kind, and gentle way **2** in a way that is nice to hear or smell

sweet 'pepper noun [C] a green, red, or yellow vegetable that does not have a strong flavour

sweet po'tato noun [C] a vegetable with a sweet taste that looks like a potato with pink skin —*picture* → C11

sweet 'tooth noun [singular] someone who has a sweet tooth likes to eat sweet food

swell¹ /swel/ (past tense **swelled** /sweld/; past participle **swollen** /ˈswəʊlən/) verb [I/T] **1** to become larger than normal, or to make something larger than normal: *My ankles tend to swell when I travel by air.* **2** to increase in amount or number, or to make something increase in amount or number

PHRASAL VERB **swell (sth) 'up** same as **swell¹** 1: *Her injured arm was swelling up.*

swell² /swel/ noun [singular] the movement of the waves in the sea

swelling /ˈswelɪŋ/ noun [C] an area of your body that has become bigger because of an injury or illness

sweltering /ˈswelt(ə)rɪŋ/ adj so hot that you feel uncomfortable

swept the past tense and past participle of **sweep¹**

swerve /swɜːv/ verb [I] to change direction suddenly in order to avoid something —**swerve** noun [C]

swift /swɪft/ adj **1** happening quickly or immediately **2** moving quickly —**swiftly** adv

swig /swɪg/ verb [I/T] *informal* to drink something carelessly and in large amounts —**swig** noun [C]

swill /swɪl/ verb [T] **1** to pour water over something in order to clean it **2** to drink a large amount of something

swim¹ /swɪm/ (past tense **swam** /swæm/; past participle **swum** /swʌm/) verb ★★
1 [I/T] to move through water by making movements with your arms and legs: *It's not safe to swim in the lake.* ♦ *Can you swim a length of the pool without stopping?*
2 [I] if your head is swimming, you cannot think or see clearly because you are tired or ill
3 [I] if things are swimming, they appear to be moving when you look at them, because you are tired or ill
—**swimmer** noun [C], **swimming** noun [U]: *I go swimming every evening.*

swim² /swɪm/ noun [singular] an occasion when you swim: *Why don't we go for a swim this afternoon?*

'swimming ,costume noun [C] *British* a SWIMSUIT

'swimming ,pool noun [C] a large structure filled with water for people to swim in

'swimming ,trunks noun [plural] *British* a piece of clothing that is worn by men for swimming

swimsuit /ˈswɪmˌsuːt/ noun [C] a piece of clothing that is worn by women for swimming —*picture* → C5

S

swindle /ˈswɪnd(ə)l/ verb [T] to cheat someone in order to get their money —**swindle** noun [C], **swindler** noun [C]

swine /swaɪn/ noun [C] **1** informal an extremely unpleasant man **2** (plural **swine**) an old word meaning a 'pig'

swing¹ /swɪŋ/ (past tense and past participle **swung** /swʌŋ/) verb [I/T] ★★
1 to move backwards and forwards from a point, or to make something move in this way: Swing your arms loosely at your sides. ♦ The rope bridge was swinging in the breeze.
2 to move with a wide curving movement, or to make something move in this way: The door **swung shut** with a loud bang. ♦ She **swung round** and stared angrily at us. ♦ **swing sth into/around/out** etc I swung the car into a narrow side street.
3 to change from one emotion or condition to another that is very different: Public opinion has begun to **swing the other way** (=away from what it was before).

swing² /swɪŋ/ noun [C] **1** an attempt to hit someone or something: I clenched my fist and took a swing at him. **2** a change from one emotion or condition to one that is very different: He suffers from severe mood swings. ♦ a swing away from traditional ideas of family life **3** a seat that hangs from chains or ropes and moves backwards and forwards
PHRASES **get into the swing of sth** informal to become used to a new situation and feel confident that you can deal with it
in full swing at a very busy or active stage: The party was in full swing when they arrived.
swings and roundabouts British informal used for describing a situation that has advantages and disadvantages

swipe¹ /swaɪp/ verb [T] **1** informal to steal something **2** to pass a plastic card through a piece of electronic equipment that reads the information on it **3** to swing your arm and hit someone or something

swipe² /swaɪp/ noun [C] **1** a movement in which you swing your arm and hit someone or something **2** informal an occasion when you criticize someone or something: Do you think he was taking a swipe at the President?

ˈswipe ˌcard noun [C] a plastic card that you pass through a piece of electronic equipment that reads the information stored on the card

swirl¹ /swɜːl/ verb [I] to move quickly in circles

swirl² /swɜːl/ noun [C] a fast circular movement, or a circular shape

swish /swɪʃ/ verb [I] to move quickly with a smooth gentle sound —**swish** noun [singular]

switch¹ /swɪtʃ/ verb ★★
1 [I/T] to change from one thing to another, or to make something do this: He used to vote Conservative, but he **switched to Labour** in 1997. ♦ Once you have learned the basics of word processing, **switching between**

different programs is quite easy. ♦ **switch sth (from sth) to sth** They announced that the tournament would be switched from March to December.
2 [T] to replace one object with another: He was accused of switching price labels.
3 [I/T] to do someone else's work and give them your work: Will you **switch with** me next week?
PHRASAL VERBS **ˌswitch ˈoff** informal to stop listening to someone, or to stop thinking about something: He just switches off and ignores me.
ˌswitch (sth) ˈoff if you switch off something such as a light or a machine, or if it switches off, it stops working: The heating has switched off. ♦ I parked the car and switched off the engine.
ˌswitch (sth) ˈon if you switch on something such as a light or a machine, or if it switches on, it starts working: Don't switch on the light. ♦ The machine switches on automatically.
ˌswitch ˈover British to start watching a different television programme or start listening to a different radio programme: Can't we **switch over** to Channel 4?

switch² /swɪtʃ/ noun [C] ★★
1 something such as a button or key that makes a piece of equipment work: a light switch ♦ an on-off switch
2 a change from one thing to another: a major policy switch by Washington ♦ He said **the switch from** electric to solar power would be made soon.

switchboard /ˈswɪtʃbɔːd/ noun [C] the electronic equipment that is used to connect telephone calls in a large business or organization

swivel /ˈswɪv(ə)l/ verb [I/T] to turn round a fixed point, or to make something turn in this way

swollen¹ /ˈswəʊlən/ adj **1** bigger than usual because of an injury or illness **2** a swollen river or stream contains more water than normal

swollen² the past participle of **swell¹**

swoop¹ /swuːp/ verb [I] **1** to move quickly and suddenly downwards through the air in order to attack something **2** to attack a place suddenly and unexpectedly

swoop² /swuːp/ noun [C] **1** a quick sudden movement downwards through the air **2** a sudden unexpected attack on a place
PHRASE **in/at one fell swoop** with one sudden action or on one single occasion

swop /swɒp/ a British spelling of **swap**

sword /sɔːd/ noun [C] a weapon with a short handle and a long sharp blade
PHRASE **a double-edged/two-edged sword** a situation that has bad aspects as well as good aspects

swordfish /ˈsɔːdfɪʃ/ (plural **swordfish**) noun [C] a large sea fish with a long upper jaw

swore the past tense of **swear**

sworn¹ /swɔːn/ adj **1** done by someone who promises to tell the truth: sworn testimony

2 sworn enemies hate each other

sworn² the past participle of **swear**

swot¹ /swɒt/ verb [I] *British informal* to study very hard: *She's swotting for her exams at the moment.*

swot² /swɒt/ noun [C] *British informal showing disapproval* a student who studies hard

swum the past participle of **swim¹**

swung the past tense and past participle of **swing¹**

sycamore /ˈsɪkəmɔː/ noun [C] a tall tree with large leaves —*picture* → C9

syllable /ˈsɪləb(ə)l/ noun [C] a part of a word that has only one vowel sound. For example, the word 'father' has two syllables.

syllabus /ˈsɪləbəs/ noun [C] a list of the main subjects in a course of study → CURRICULUM

symbol /ˈsɪmb(ə)l/ noun [C] ★
1 someone or something that represents a particular idea or quality: *Many Catholics saw him as a symbol of hope.*
2 a mark, letter, or number that is used to represent something, for example in chemistry or music
3 a picture or shape that is used to represent something

symbolic /sɪmˈbɒlɪk/ adj **1** representing something important: *This meeting has great symbolic importance for the people of Ireland.* **2** used as a symbol: *The wedding rings are symbolic of their love.*
—**symbolically** /sɪmˈbɒlɪkli/ adv

symbolism /ˈsɪmbəˌlɪz(ə)m/ noun [U] **1** the use of symbols to represent something **2** the fact that an action or event is a sign of something important

symbolize /ˈsɪmbəlaɪz/ verb [T] **1** to be a symbol of something: *The cross symbolizes Christianity.* **2** to be considered as a perfect example of something: *For many people, cars symbolize personal freedom.*

symmetrical /sɪˈmetrɪk(ə)l/ adj a symmetrical shape or object has two halves that are exactly the same —**symmetrically** /sɪˈmetrɪkli/ adv

symmetry /ˈsɪmətri/ noun [U] the fact that something has two halves that are exactly the same

sympathetic /ˌsɪmpəˈθetɪk/ adj **1** willing to understand someone's problems and help them ≠ UNSYMPATHETIC: *You're not being very sympathetic.* ◆ *Jill was a sympathetic listener.* **2** if you are sympathetic to something such as a plan, you support it ≠ UNSYMPATHETIC **3** a sympathetic character is easy to like ≠ UNSYMPATHETIC
—**sympathetically** /ˌsɪmpəˈθetɪkli/ adv

> **Sympathetic** and **friendly** have different meanings.
> ■ **Friendly** is a general word describing someone who is pleasant and wants to make friends with people: *I don't know Tim well, but he always seems friendly.*

> ■ **Sympathetic** means willing to listen to someone's problems and to try to understand them: *I asked my boss for some time off, but he wasn't very sympathetic.*

sympathize /ˈsɪmpəθaɪz/ verb [I] **1** to show that you understand someone's problems: *We sympathize deeply with the families of the victims.* **2** to support something: *Many people admit they sympathize with the rebels' demands.*

sympathizer /ˈsɪmpəθaɪzə/ noun [C] someone who supports something

sympathy /ˈsɪmpəθi/ noun ★
1 [U] a feeling of kindness and understanding that you have for someone who is experiencing problems: *It's his own fault, so he'll get no sympathy from me.* ◆ *We all have great sympathy for the victims of the flood.*
2 [C/U] support for something such as a plan or a political party: *journalists with left-wing sympathies* ◆ *Do you have any sympathy with his point of view?* ◆ *Darwin himself had little sympathy for these ideas.*
◆ **be out of/in sympathy with sb/sth** *The school should be entirely in sympathy with these aims.*

symphony /ˈsɪmfəni/ noun [C] a long piece of classical music played by an orchestra

symptom /ˈsɪmptəm/ noun [C] ★
1 a sign that someone has an illness: *The symptoms include fever and vomiting.* ◆ *The symptoms of flu may last several days.*
2 a sign of a larger problem: *The fighting is a symptom of growing insecurity in the region.*

symptomatic /ˌsɪmptəˈmætɪk/ adj *formal* showing that a bad situation exists

synagogue /ˈsɪnəgɒg/ noun [C] a building that is used by Jewish people for religious services

synchronize /ˈsɪŋkrənaɪz/ verb [T] to make two or more things happen at the same time or move at the same speed
—**synchronization** /ˌsɪŋkrənaɪˈzeɪʃ(ə)n/ noun [U]

syndicate /ˈsɪndɪkət/ noun [C] a group of people or organizations that work together to achieve something

syndrome /ˈsɪndrəʊm/ noun [C] **1** a medical condition that has a particular set of effects **2** a set of feelings or actions that are typical in a particular situation

synonym /ˈsɪnənɪm/ noun [C] a word that has the same meaning as another word
→ ANTONYM

synonymous /sɪˈnɒnɪməs/ adj **1** if one person or thing is synonymous with another, people think of one of them whenever they think of the other one **2** if two words are synonymous, they have the same meaning

synopsis /sɪˈnɒpsɪs/ (plural **synopses** /sɪˈnɒpsiːz/) noun [C] a short summary of a book, play, or film

syntax /ˈsɪntæks/ noun [U] *linguistics* the rules about how words are arranged to make phrases and sentences

S

synthesis /ˈsɪnθəsɪs/ (plural **syntheses** /ˈsɪnθəsiːz/) noun **1** [C] a new combination of ideas or styles **2** [C/U] *technical* the process of producing a substance by a chemical or BIOLOGICAL reaction

synthesize /ˈsɪnθəˌsaɪz/ verb [T] **1** *technical* to produce a new substance as a result of a chemical or BIOLOGICAL reaction **2** to combine different ideas or styles

synthesizer /ˈsɪnθəˌsaɪzə/ noun [C] an electronic machine that produces sounds for music

synthetic /sɪnˈθetɪk/ adj made from artificial substances

syphilis /ˈsɪfəlɪs/ noun [U] a serious disease that you can get by having sex with someone who has it

syphon /ˈsaɪf(ə)n/ another spelling of **siphon**

syringe /sɪˈrɪndʒ/ noun [C] a plastic tube with a needle that is used for putting medicine into your body through your skin

syrup /ˈsɪrəp/ noun [U] thick sweet liquid

system /ˈsɪstəm/ noun ★★★
1 [C] a set of connected things that work together: *a central heating system ◆ the public transport system ◆ the body's central nervous system ◆ a new computer system*
2 [C] a method of organizing things or doing things: *a legal/educational/political system ◆ the criminal justice system ◆ They are introducing a new system for delivering information to the public. ◆ a democratic system of government*
3 [C] your body: *The drug stays in your system for hours.*
4 the system [singular] rules that decide how a society should operate: *You can't beat the system.*
PHRASE get sb/sth out of your system *informal* to get rid of strong feelings about someone or something
→ IMMUNE SYSTEM

systematic /ˌsɪstəˈmætɪk/ adj done according to a careful plan —**systematically** /ˌsɪstəˈmætɪkli/ adv

systems analyst noun [C] someone whose job is to plan or improve the way that an organization uses computers —**systems analysis** noun [U]

t or **T** /tiː/ noun [C/U] the 20th letter of the English alphabet
PHRASE to a T exactly or completely
→ T-SHIRT

ta /tɑː/ interjection *British informal* thank you

tab¹ /tæb/ noun [C] **1 tab** or **tab key** a button on a computer keyboard that you press in order to move several spaces along the same line **2** a part that you pull to open something **3** a bill for the cost of a meal or drinks: *The company picked up the tab (=paid) for lunch.*
PHRASE keep tabs on *informal* to watch someone or something carefully

tab² verb [I] to press the tab on a computer keyboard

tabby /ˈtæbi/ noun [C] a cat with grey or brown and orange bands on its fur

tab key noun [C] a TAB on a computer keyboard

table¹ /ˈteɪb(ə)l/ noun [C] ★★★
1 a piece of furniture that consists of a flat surface that is supported by legs: *They sat around a long table in the conference room.*
2 a set of facts or numbers that are arranged in rows and COLUMNS on a page
PHRASES clear the table to take away from a table all the knives, forks, plates etc after people have finished eating
on the table if a proposal or offer is on the table, someone has suggested it officially and people are considering it
set the table to put knives, forks, plates etc on a table at each place where a person will eat
turn the tables (on sb) to succeed in gaining an advantage over someone who had the advantage before

table² /ˈteɪb(ə)l/ verb [T] **1** *British* to suggest something at a formal meeting **2** *American* to decide not to discuss something until later

tablecloth /ˈteɪb(ə)lˌklɒθ/ noun [C] a large cloth for covering a table

tablespoon /ˈteɪb(ə)lˌspuːn/ noun [C] **1** a large spoon that you use for serving food **2 tablespoon** or **tablespoonful** the amount of food that a tablespoon holds

tablet /ˈtæblət/ noun [C] ★
1 a small hard round piece of medicine that you swallow =PILL
2 a flat piece of stone that has writing cut into it

table tennis noun [U] a game in which players use BATS to hit a small light ball across a table with a low net across the middle

tabloid /ˈtæblɔɪd/ noun [C] a newspaper that has small pages and not much serious news —**tabloid** adj: *the tabloid press*

taboo /təˈbuː/ adj if something is taboo, people do not do it or talk about it because it is offensive or shocking —**taboo** noun [C]

tacit /ˈtæsɪt/ adj expressed or understood without being said directly —**tacitly** adv

taciturn /ˈtæsɪˌtɜːn/ adj someone who is taciturn does not say very much

tack¹ /tæk/ noun **1** [C] a small nail or short pin **2** [singular] a particular way of doing or achieving something: *Let's try a different tack.*

tack² /tæk/ verb [T] **1** to fix something somewhere using small nails or short pins: *There was a note tacked to the door.* **2** to sew pieces of cloth together with long loose stitches, before you sew it more carefully
PHRASAL VERB tack sth on to add something extra

tackle¹ /'tæk(ə)l/ verb [T] ★
  1 to deal with a problem: *Governments have failed to tackle the question of homelessness.*
  2 to try to take the ball from an opponent in a game such as football —*picture* → C15
  3 to talk to someone about something that they have done that you do not approve of: **tackle sb about sth** *The interviewer tackled him about his failed economic policies.*
  4 to take hold of someone and push them to the ground

tackle² /'tæk(ə)l/ noun **1** [C] an attempt to take the ball from an opponent in a game such as football **2** [U] special equipment that people use for sports: *fishing tackle* **3** [C] an attempt to take hold of someone and push them to the ground —*picture* → C15

tacky /'tæki/ adj **1** *informal* looking cheap and showing bad taste **2** slightly sticky

taco /'tækəʊ/ noun [C] a Mexican food that consists of a flat hard piece of PASTRY that is folded and filled with meat

tact /tækt/ noun [U] a careful way of speaking or behaving that avoids upsetting other people

tactful /'tæk(t)f(ə)l/ adj careful to avoid upsetting other people —**tactfully** adv

tactic /'tæktɪk/ noun [C] a method or plan for achieving something

tactical /'tæktɪk(ə)l/ adj **1** done as part of a plan for achieving something **2** involving TACTICS —**tactically** /'tæktɪkli/ adv

tactless /'tæk(t)ləs/ adj not careful about the way that you speak or behave towards other people, so that you often upset them

tad¹ /tæd/ noun *informal* **a tad** a little bit: *'How much sugar should I add?' 'Just a tad.'*

tad² /tæd/ adv *informal* **a tad** slightly: *I was a tad annoyed.*

tadpole /'tædpəʊl/ noun [C] a small animal that develops into a FROG

taffeta /'tæfɪtə/ noun [U] thick shiny cloth that is used for making women's dresses

tag¹ /tæg/ noun [C] **1 a** a name/ price tag **2** linguistics a QUESTION TAG **3** a piece of electronic equipment that is attached to a criminal or a wild animal. It shows where they are.

tag² /tæg/ verb [T] **1** to fix a label to something **2** to put an electronic tag on a criminal or a wild animal **3** to touch another player in some children's games
  PHRASAL VERB **tag a'long** *informal* to go somewhere with someone else although you are not needed

t'ai chi /ˌtaɪ 'tʃiː/ noun [U] a Chinese activity that involves doing very slow physical exercises to make your mind relax and improve your body's balance

tail¹ /teɪl/ noun ★★
  1 [C] a part that sticks out at the back of an animal's body: *When a dog is happy, it wags its tail.*
  2 [C] the part at the back of a plane
  3 [singular] **the tail of sth** the back or end of something: *at the tail of the queue*

  4 [C] *informal* someone who secretly follows someone else
  → TAILS

tail² /teɪl/ verb [T] to secretly follow someone
  PHRASAL VERB **tail 'off** to become quieter, weaker, or smaller

tailback /'teɪlbæk/ noun [C] *British* a long line of traffic that is moving very slowly

tail 'end, the noun [singular] the very last part of something

tailgate /'teɪlgeɪt/ verb [T] to drive very close to the vehicle in front of you —**tailgating** noun [U]

tail light noun [C] one of the red lights on the back of a vehicle —*picture* → C6

tailor¹ /'teɪlə/ noun [C] someone who makes clothes for men

tailor² /'teɪlə/ verb **tailor sth to/for** to make or change something for a particular person or purpose = CUSTOMIZE

tailored /'teɪləd/ adj **1** tailored clothes have the same shape as a person's body **2** made for a particular purpose or situation

tailor-'made adj **1** extremely suitable **2** designed for a particular person

tails /teɪlz/ noun **1** [U] the side of a coin that does not have a picture of a person on it **2** [plural] a man's formal jacket that is long at the back and short at the front

tainted /'teɪntɪd/ adj an event or situation that is tainted is spoilt by an unpleasant feature or quality

take¹ /teɪk/ (past tense **took** /tʊk/; past participle **taken** /'teɪkən/) verb [T] ★★★

1 move sb/sth	**12** get from opponent
2 perform action	**13** use type of transport
3 need sth	**14** use drugs
4 accept sth	**15** use milk/sugar
5 put sb in situation	**16** wear a particular size
6 win prize/election	**17** think of
7 reach out and get sth	**18** do or have sth
8 study	**19** have feeling/opinion
9 remove/steal sth	+ PHRASE
10 get picture/measure	+ PHRASAL VERBS
11 in calculation	

1 to move or carry someone or something from one place to another: *Remember to take a pen with you.* ♦ **take sb into/around sth** *What time do you take Amy to school?* ♦ *The cat had to be taken to the vet.* ♦ *Our guide took us around the cathedral.* ♦ **take sb/sth along** (=with you) *On long journeys I always take my dog along.* ♦ **take sb/sth for sth** *We took my mother for a drive in the country.* ♦ **take sb sth** *Take Debbie this cup of coffee, will you?* ♦ **take sth to sb** *Let's take the presents to them tonight.* → BRING

2 to perform an action: *Take a deep breath.* ♦ *Let's take a walk down to the river.* ♦ *The government must take action to stop this trade.* ♦ *You need to take more exercise.*

3 to need something: *Your odd behaviour is going to take a bit of explaining.* ♦ *It's going to take some doing* (=be difficult to do) *to persuade them!* ♦ **take sth to do sth** *It takes talent and dedication to become a top dancer.*

T

♦ **take sb sth** *The journey will take us about three days.*

4 to accept something: *I've decided not to take the job.* ♦ *Sorry, we don't take credit cards.* ♦ *She won't* **take** *my* **advice.** ♦ *In this job you have to be able to* **take criticism.** ♦ *That's my final price,* **take it or leave it** (=the offer will not change). ♦ *You don't have to* **take my word for it** (=believe what I am saying) – *you can ask Tom.*

5 to cause someone or something to be in a new situation: **take sb to/into sth** *Her amazing energy has taken her to the top of her profession.* ♦ *The police took the thief into custody.* ♦ *They'll take us to court if we don't pay up soon.*

6 to win a prize in a competition or a vote in an election: *Who took the silver medal?* ♦ *The Labour Party took 45 per cent of the vote.*

7 to reach out and get something with your hand: *Take as many cakes as you like.* ♦ *Let me take your coats.*

8 to study a particular subject: *I took a course in computer programming.*

9 to remove something, or to steal something: *Who's taken my pencil?* ♦ *The thieves didn't take much.* ♦ **take sth away from sb/sth** *Take the knife away from her!*

10 to get a picture or a measurement using a machine: *May I* **take a photo** *of the two of you?* ♦ *A nurse* **took his temperature** *every hour.*

11 to remove one number or quantity from another number or quantity: **take sth (away) from sth** *If you take five from ten, you're left with five.*

12 to get control of something from an opponent: *The town was finally taken after a six-week siege.*

13 to use a particular type of transport or a particular road: *Take the A14 as far as Cambridge.* ♦ *I usually* **take the bus** *to work.*

14 to put drugs or medicine into your body: ♦ *People worry that their children will start* **taking drugs.**

You **eat** food and **drink** drinks, but you **take** liquid or solid medicine: *She took a pill for her headache.* ♦ *You have to keep taking your antibiotics.*

---

15 to have milk or sugar in your tea or coffee: *Do you take milk in your coffee?*

16 to wear a particular size of clothes or shoes: *What size shoes do you take?*

17 to think about someone or something in a particular way: *He tries hard, but I just can't* **take him seriously.** ♦ *She* **took** *his remarks* **as a compliment.** ♦ **take sb/sth for sth** *She looks so young that I took her for your sister.*

18 to do, or to have something: *Please* **take a seat** (=sit down). ♦ *They're shooting at us! Quick,* **take cover!** ♦ *I did all the work, but Gill* **took all the credit.** ♦ *The rebels are* **taking control** *of the city.* ♦ *We must encourage fathers to* **take** *full* **responsibility** *for their children.*

19 to have a feeling or opinion: *I'm afraid she* **took offence** *at my remarks.* ♦ *He's never* **taken** *much* **interest** *in his kids.* ♦ *Lisa* **took pity on** *us and invited us to dinner.* ♦ *I* **take the view that** *children should be told the truth.*

PHRASE **take place** to happen: *The Olympics take place every four years.*

PHRASAL VERBS **take after sb** to look or behave like an older relative

take sth apart to separate an object into its pieces: *Ben was taking apart an old bicycle.*

take sth back 1 to take something that you have bought back to the shop because it is broken or not suitable **2** to admit that something that you said was wrong: *I'm sorry – I take it back.*

take sth down 1 to separate a large structure into its pieces **2** to write information on a piece of paper: *The police took down our addresses and phone numbers.*

take sb in 1 to allow someone to stay in your house or your country **2 be taken in** to be tricked so that you believe something that is not true

take sth in 1 to understand and remember something that you hear or read: *I'm not sure how much of his explanation she took in.* **2** to make a piece of clothing more narrow or more tight, so that it fits you

take off 1 if an aircraft takes off, it leaves the ground and starts to fly ≠ LAND **2** to become successful or popular very fast: *Her business has really taken off.* **3** *informal* to leave a place suddenly

take sth off 1 to remove a piece of clothing from your body ≠ PUT STH ON 1 **2** to spend a particular amount of time away from work: *I'm taking Monday off to go to London.*

take on sth to develop a particular character or appearance: *Our website is taking on a new look.*

take sb on 1 to start to employ someone **2** to fight or compete against someone

take sth on to accept some work or responsibility

take sb out to take someone to a place such as a cinema or a restaurant and pay for them: *She's taking her parents out for dinner.*

take sth out 1 to remove something from a place: *Henry took out his wallet.* **2** to get something officially: *When you take out insurance, read the small print.*

take sth out on sb to treat someone badly because you are angry, upset, or tired, although it is not their fault

take (sth) over to begin to do something that someone else was doing: *Jane took over as director after Richard retired.*

take sth over to take control of something, especially another company

take sb through sth to explain something to someone in detail

take to sth to start doing something as a habit: *Recently he's taken to wearing a cap.*

take to sb/sth to begin to like someone or something: *I took to John immediately.*

T

take up sth to fill a particular amount of space or time: *These files take up a lot of disk space.*

take sth up to start doing something regularly as a habit, job, or interest: *Chris has taken up jogging.* ♦ *The new teacher will take up her post in May.*

take sb up on sth to accept an offer or invitation that someone has made: *I've decided to take you up on that job offer.*

take sth up with sb to complain to someone about a problem

take² /teɪk/ noun [C] **1** a section of a film or television programme that is recorded without stopping **2** *informal* the amount of money that a business earns in a particular period of time

PHRASE **sb's take on sth** someone's opinion about something: *What's your take on the political crisis?*

takeaway /ˈteɪkəˌweɪ/ noun [C] *British* **1** a meal that you buy in a restaurant and take home to eat **2** a restaurant that sells meals that you take home to eat

taken¹ the past participle of **take¹**

taken² /ˈteɪkən/ adj **be taken with** *informal* to like someone or something very much

take-off noun [C/U] an occasion when a plane leaves the ground and starts to fly ≠ LANDING

takeover /ˈteɪkˌəʊvə/ noun [C] a situation in which one company or country takes control of another company or country → MERGER

takings /ˈteɪkɪŋz/ noun [plural] the money that a shop receives from customers

talcum powder /ˈtælkəm ˌpaʊdə/ or **talc** /tælk/ noun [U] a soft white powder that you put on your body after a bath

tale /teɪl/ noun [C] a story about imaginary events or people → OLD WIVES' TALE

talent /ˈtælənt/ noun [C/U] a natural ability for doing a particular activity well: *She had an obvious talent for music.*

talented /ˈtæləntɪd/ adj very good at something

talisman /ˈtælɪzmən/ noun [C] an object that some people believe has the power to protect you from bad things

talk¹ /tɔːk/ verb ★★★
1 [I] to speak, or to have a conversation: *Can their baby talk yet?* ♦ *Am I talking too much?* ♦ *I saw her talking to Matt.* ♦ *Everyone was busily talking with their friends.* ♦ *We were talking about you last night.* → SAY
2 [I/T] to discuss something: *You and I need to talk.* ♦ *John and Pete spent the evening talking politics* (=discussing political issues).
3 [I] to give information that should be secret: *Do you think the prisoners will talk?*

PHRASE **talk sense/nonsense/etc** *informal* to say something that is sensible/stupid/etc

PHRASAL VERBS **talk back** to reply to someone rudely: *Melanie, don't talk back to your mother!*

talk down to sb to talk to someone in a way

that shows that you think that they are less clever or important than you are =PATRONIZE

talk sb into sth to persuade someone to do something: *They talked their mother into taking a rest for a while.*

talk sb out of sth to persuade someone not to do something: *We managed to talk him out of giving up his job.*

talk sth over to discuss a problem or a plan: *You both need to talk over what happened that day.*

Other ways of saying **talk**

- **chat** to talk informally in a friendly way
- **discuss** to talk about a particular subject in detail
- **gossip** to talk about other people's private lives
- **speak** to talk to someone about something, or to be able to talk in a particular language

---

talk² /tɔːk/ noun ★★★
1 [C/U] a conversation, or conversations in general: *You need time to relax and have a talk with your children.* ♦ *There's a lot of talk in the school about the new exam system.*
2 [C] an informal lecture about a subject: *Williams gave a talk on his travels in Nepal.*
3 talks [plural] discussions between important people that are designed to solve a problem: *peace talks* ♦ *the outcome of talks between the government and the rebels* ♦ *preliminary talks on the future of the steel industry* ♦ *He visited Egypt in March for talks with the president.* ♦ *The management will be holding informal talks with union officials.*
4 [U] discussions, promises, or threats that are not worth listening to: *She says she's an expert on men, but it's all talk!*

talkative /ˈtɔːkətɪv/ adj someone who is talkative talks a lot

talker /ˈtɔːkə/ noun [C] *informal* someone who talks a lot or who talks in a particular way: *Your brother certainly is a smooth talker* (=good at persuading people by saying nice things).

tall /tɔːl/ adj ★★★
1 a tall person or object has greater height than the average person or object: *a tall thin woman* ♦ *tall buildings* → HIGH
2 used for talking about measurements of height: *He must be over six feet tall.*

PHRASE **a tall order** *informal* something very difficult that someone expects you to do

tally¹ /ˈtæli/ noun [C] a record of the number of things that someone has won or achieved

tally² /ˈtæli/ verb **1** [I] if two things such as statements or calculations tally, they match each other: *Their account doesn't tally with the facts.* **2** [T] to calculate a total

PHRASAL VERB **tally sth up** same as **tally²** 2

Talmud, the /ˈtælmʊd/ a collection of Jewish religious writings

talon /ˈtælən/ noun [C] one of the sharp nails on the feet of some birds

T

tambourine /ˌtæmbəˈriːn/ noun [C] a musical instrument that you shake or hit with your hand. It consists of a round frame with small pieces of metal around the edge.

tame¹ /teɪm/ adj **1** a tame animal has been trained not to attack people ≠ WILD **2** not exciting, powerful, or dangerous enough —**tamely** adv

tame² /teɪm/ verb [T] to train an animal not to attack people

tamper /ˈtæmpə/ PHRASAL VERB **'tamper with sth** to touch or change something that you should not touch or change, often because you want to spoil it

tampon /ˈtæmpɒn/ noun [C] an object that a woman puts inside her VAGINA to collect the blood during her PERIOD (=monthly flow of blood)

tan¹ /tæn/ noun **1** [C] a SUNTAN **2** [U] a light brown colour

tan² /tæn/ verb [I/T] if you tan, or if the sun tans your skin, the sun makes your skin darker than it was before

tan³ /tæn/ adj light brown in colour

tandem /ˈtændəm/ noun [C] a bicycle with seats for two people
PHRASE **in tandem** together and at the same time

tandoori /tænˈdʊəri/ noun [C] **1** an Indian meal that is cooked in a clay container **2** an Indian restaurant

tangent /ˈtændʒ(ə)nt/ noun [C] technical a straight line that touches the edge of a circle but does not pass through it
PHRASE **go off on/at a tangent** informal to suddenly start doing or discussing something completely different

tangerine /ˌtændʒəˈriːn/ noun [C] a fruit that is like a small orange

tangible /ˈtændʒəb(ə)l/ adj able to be seen to exist or be true ≠ INTANGIBLE: tangible evidence

tangle¹ /ˈtæŋg(ə)l/ noun [C] the untidy shape that things make when they are twisted round each other or round something else

tangle² /ˈtæŋg(ə)l/ verb [I/T] if something tangles, or if you tangle it, its parts become twisted round each other or round something else
PHRASAL VERB **'tangle with sb** informal to become involved in a fight or argument with someone

tangled /ˈtæŋg(ə)ld/ adj **1** if something is tangled, its parts are twisted round each other in an untidy way **2** very complicated and difficult to deal with
PHRASE **tangled up in sth** involved in a difficult situation

tango /ˈtæŋgəʊ/ noun [C] a dance that is done by two people who hold each other very tightly, or the music for this dance

tangy /ˈtæŋi/ adj with a taste that is strong and bitter in a pleasant way —**tang** noun [singular]

tank /tæŋk/ noun [C] ★★
1 a large metal container for liquid or gas
2 a very strong military vehicle with a large gun on the top

tankard /ˈtæŋkəd/ noun [C] a large metal cup for beer

tanker /ˈtæŋkə/ noun [C] a large ship or truck that carries petrol or oil

tanned /tænd/ adj British someone who is tanned has darker skin than before because they have spent time in the sun

Tannoy /ˈtænɔɪ/ trademark a system of LOUDSPEAKERS that is used for making announcements in public places and large buildings

tantalizing /ˈtæntəlaɪzɪŋ/ adj making you feel excited about having something that you want, especially when you cannot have it —**tantalizingly** adv

tantamount /ˈtæntəmaʊnt/ adj **be tantamount to sth** formal to have the same bad qualities or bad effect as something else

tantrum /ˈtæntrəm/ noun [C] an occasion when someone, especially a young child, suddenly behaves in a very angry way that is unreasonable or silly

tap¹ /tæp/ noun [C] ★
1 an object that is used for controlling how much water comes out of a pipe: Just turn the cold tap on for a few seconds. —picture → C2
2 the action of touching someone or something gently, or the sound that the touch makes: I felt a tap on my shoulder. ♦ We heard a tap at the window.
3 a piece of electronic equipment that is used for secretly listening to someone's telephone conversations
PHRASE **on tap** easily available: The Internet makes it possible to have all kinds of information on tap at any time.

tap² /tæp/ verb ★
1 [I/T] to touch someone or something gently: We could hear someone tapping at the door. ♦ **tap sb on sth** I tapped him on the shoulder and he jumped.
2 [T] to get something, or to use something: Several other companies were already tapping this market.
3 [T] to use electronic equipment to secretly listen to someone's telephone conversations
PHRASAL VERB **'tap into sth** same as **tap² 2**: There is a supply of skilled workers that businesses can tap into.

'tap dancing noun [U] a style of dancing in which you move your feet very quickly and make sounds with the special shoes that you wear

tape¹ /teɪp/ noun ★★
1 [C] a CASSETTE with something recorded on it or for recording something: This is a great tape – have you heard it? ♦ We need a blank tape (=one with nothing recorded on it).
2 [U] a very long thin piece of plastic that is used for recording sound, pictures, or information: We've got the concert on tape.
3 [U] a long thin band of plastic that is sticky on one side and is used for sticking things together

4 [C/U] a long thin band of cloth or plastic that is used for fastening things together or for marking the edges of an area: *Police roped off the area with yellow tape after the incident.*

tape² /teɪp/ verb **1** [I/T] to record sounds or pictures onto tape **2** [T] to stick something using sticky tape

'tape ,deck noun [C] the part of a STEREO system that is used for playing CASSETTES

'tape ,measure noun [C] a tool for measuring things that consists of a long narrow piece of cloth, soft plastic, or thin metal with numbers on it

taper /'teɪpə/ verb [I] to gradually become narrower towards one end

> PHRASAL VERB **taper 'off** to gradually become less

'tape re,corder noun [C] a piece of equipment for playing a TAPE or for recording sound on TAPE

tapestry /'tæpɪstri/ noun [C/U] a thick heavy cloth that has pictures or patterns woven into it

'tap ,water noun [U] water that comes out of a TAP in a building

tar¹ /tɑː/ noun [U] **1** a thick black liquid that is used for making the surfaces of roads **2** a sticky poisonous substance from tobacco

tar² /tɑː/ verb [T] to cover the surface of a road with tar

tarantula /təˈræntjʊlə/ noun [C] a large poisonous SPIDER

target¹ /'tɑːgɪt/ noun [C] ★★★
1 someone or something that is being attacked: *military targets such as air bases* ♦ *Foreigners have become targets for attack by terrorists.*
2 a person, organization, or idea that is being criticized or blamed: *The policy has become the target of severe criticism.*
3 something that you try to achieve: *The organization is setting a target of 2,000 new members.* ♦ *The government hasn't met its target* (=achieved it) *for reducing unemployment.* ♦ *The economy was on target to grow by more than 4 per cent.* ♦ *The film's target audience is children in the 11 to 14 age range.*
4 an object that you have to hit in a game: *Few players managed to get their shots on target.*

target² /'tɑːgɪt/ verb [T] **1** to attack or criticize someone or something: *The terrorists were targeting government buildings.* ♦ *The company had been targeted because of its bad record on pollution.* **2** to try to persuade or influence a particular group of people: *television advertising targeted at children*

tariff /'tærɪf/ noun [C] **1** a tax that a government charges on goods that enter or leave their country **2** British a list of the prices that a company charges for its goods or services

tarmac /'tɑːmæk/ noun **1** [U] British a mixture of TAR and stones that is used for making the surfaces of roads = ASPHALT **2 the tarmac**

[singular] the part of an airport where the planes stop

tarnish /'tɑːnɪʃ/ verb **1** [T] if something tarnishes your reputation or image, it makes people have a bad opinion of you **2** [I] if metal tarnishes, it loses its colour and becomes less shiny

tarot /'tærəʊ/ noun [U] a way of telling what will happen in the future by using special cards with pictures on them

tarpaulin /tɑːˈpɔːlɪn/ noun [C] a large piece of thick plastic that you use for protecting something from the rain

tart¹ /tɑːt/ noun [C] **1** a PIE that has no top and that is filled with fruit **2** *offensive* an offensive word for a woman who looks or behaves as if she wants to attract men and have sex

tart² /tɑːt/ adj with a slightly sour taste

tartan /'tɑːt(ə)n/ noun [U] a pattern of colourful lines and squares on cloth that is typical of Scotland —**tartan** adj

task /tɑːsk/ noun [C] ★★★ something that you have to do, often something that is difficult or unpleasant: *routine/daily tasks* ♦ **the task of doing sth** *Ken began the difficult task of organizing the information.*

> PHRASE **take sb to task** to severely criticize someone

taskbar /'tɑːskˌbɑː/ noun [C] *computing* a list that appears along the top or bottom of your computer screen and shows the programs that you are using or the activities that you can perform

'task ,force noun [C] a group of people who have been chosen to deal with a particular problem

tassel /'tæs(ə)l/ noun [C] a decoration on cloth that consists of a group of strings tied together at one end

taste¹ /teɪst/ noun ★★★

1 flavour	**4** short experience of sth
2 ability to judge if good	**5** sth eaten/drunk
3 types of thing you like	

1 [C/U] the flavour that something creates in your mouth when you eat or drink it: *I love the taste of chocolate.*
2 [U] the ability to judge whether something is good or bad in things such as art, fashion, and social behaviour: *She has such good taste in clothes.* ♦ *The joke was in very bad taste.*
3 [C/U] the types of thing that you like: *The meals are designed to suit all tastes.* ♦ *The girls share his taste in music.* ♦ *Even at a young age he had a taste for books.*
4 [singular] a short experience of something that you are not used to: *After 16 years in prison, it was their first taste of freedom.*
5 [singular] a small amount of food or drink

that you have in order to find out what flavour it has: *Have a taste of this wine.*

taste² /teɪst/ verb ★★

1 [linking verb] to have a particular flavour: *Although the meal was cold, it tasted delicious.* ♦ *This lemonade tastes more like water.* ♦ *These biscuits don't taste of ginger.*
2 [T] to eat or drink something and experience its flavour: *The dinner was one of the best meals I have ever tasted.* ♦ *Visitors will be able to taste different types of wines.*
3 [T] to experience something: *It is 13 years since they last tasted victory.*

'taste buds noun [plural] the areas of your tongue that recognize the flavours of food and drinks

tasteful /'teɪs(t)f(ə)l/ adj showing good judgment about what is attractive or suitable —**tastefully** adv

tasteless /'teɪs(t)ləs/ adj **1** food or drink that is tasteless has no flavour **2** showing bad judgment about what is attractive or suitable

tasty /'teɪsti/ adj tasty food has a nice flavour

tattered /'tætəd/ adj something that is tattered is torn and in very bad condition =RAGGED

tatters /'tætəz/ noun
PHRASE **in tatters 1** spoiled and likely to fail **2** torn and in very bad condition

tattoo /tæ'tuː/ noun [C] a permanent picture that is drawn on your body —**tattoo** verb [T]

tatty /'tæti/ adj *informal* old and in bad condition =SHABBY

taught the past tense and past participle of **teach**

taunt /tɔːnt/ verb [T] to shout cruel things at someone in order to make them angry or upset —**taunt** noun [C]

Taurus /'tɔːrəs/ noun [U] one of the twelve signs of the ZODIAC. A **Taurus** is someone who was born between 22 April and 21 May.

taut /tɔːt/ adj stretched tight —**tautly** adv

tawdry /'tɔːdri/ adj **1** cheap and of bad quality **2** unpleasant or immoral

tawny /'tɔːni/ adj between yellow and brown in colour

tax¹ /tæks/ noun [C/U] ★★★ an amount of money that you have to pay to the government. It is used for providing public services and for paying for government institutions: *The government has promised to lower taxes after the election.* ♦ *I was earning £1,500 a month after tax* (=after paying tax). ♦ *an increase in the tax on petrol*

tax² /tæks/ verb [T] **1** to make someone pay a tax **2** to put a tax on something **3** *formal* to cause problems or make things difficult for someone

taxable /'tæksəb(ə)l/ adj something that is taxable is something that you have to pay tax on

taxation /tæk'seɪʃ(ə)n/ noun [U] **1** the system that a government uses for collecting money in the form of taxes **2** the money that a government collects from taxes

'tax e,vasion noun [U] the use of illegal methods to avoid paying tax

,tax-'free adj something that is tax-free is something that you do not pay tax on

taxi¹ /'tæksi/ noun [C] ★★★ a car with a driver who you pay to take you somewhere =CAB: *It was late, so I took a taxi home.* ♦ *You won't have any problem getting a taxi.* ♦ *I tried to hail a taxi* (=stop one in the street) *but they all sped past.* —picture → C7

taxi² /'tæksi/ verb [I] if a plane taxies, it moves slowly along the ground

taxing /'tæksɪŋ/ adj difficult and needing a lot of physical or mental effort

'taxi ,rank noun [C] *British* a place where taxis wait for customers

taxpayer /'tæks,peɪə/ noun [C] someone who pays tax

'tax re,turn noun [C] an official document for giving details of your income so that the government can calculate the amount of tax that you have to pay

TB /,tiː 'biː/ noun [U] tuberculosis: a serious infectious disease that affects the lungs

tbsp abbrev tablespoon

tea /tiː/ noun ★★★

1 [C/U] a hot brown drink made by pouring boiling water onto the dried leaves of the tea bush, or a cup of this drink: *Do you want some more tea?* ♦ *Two teas, please.* ♦ *I'd love a cup of tea.*
2 [C/U] a hot drink made by pouring boiling water onto the dried leaves, fruit, or flowers of a particular plant, or a cup of this drink: *a cup of rosehip tea*
3 [U] the dried leaves of the tea bush, used for making tea: *a packet of tea*
4 [U] a small meal of sandwiches and cakes that is eaten in the afternoon with tea, or a cooked meal eaten in the early evening

'tea ,bag noun [C] a small paper bag with dried leaves inside that you use for making tea

teach /tiːtʃ/ (past tense and past participle **taught** /tɔːt/) verb ★★★

1 [I/T] to help students to learn something in a school, college, or university by giving lessons: *She teaches children with learning difficulties.* ♦ *How long have you been teaching here?* ♦ *I teach English at the local comprehensive.* ♦ **teach sth to sb/teach sb sth** *John teaches English to adult learners.*
2 [T] to help someone to learn a skill by showing them how to do it: **teach sb sth** *His mother had taught him some words in Spanish.* ♦ **teach sb (how) to do sth** *My uncle is going to teach me to drive this summer.*
3 [T] to change the way that someone behaves or the way that someone thinks or feels about something: **teach sb sth** *The experience taught her the importance of having good friends.* ♦ **teach sb to do sth** *These children have to be taught to share with others.*
PHRASE **teach sb a lesson** *informal* to punish someone for doing something bad so that they do not do it again

teacher /'tiːtʃə/ noun [C] ★★★ someone whose

job is to teach: *a French/maths/piano teacher*

teaching /ˈtiːtʃɪŋ/ noun ★★★
1 [U] the job of a teacher: *a career in teaching*
2 [C/U] the religious or political ideas of a particular person or group: *the teachings of Buddha* ♦ *issues that are central to traditional Christian teaching*

teacup /ˈtiːˌkʌp/ noun [C] a cup for drinking tea —*picture* → CUP

teak /tiːk/ noun [C/U] a large tree with valuable hard wood that is used for making furniture

team¹ /tiːm/ noun [C] ★★★
1 a group of people who play a sport or game against another group: *a football/ basketball team* ♦ *Are you in the hockey team this year?*
2 a group of people who work together: *a negotiating team* ♦ *a team of legal experts*

> In British English, **team** can be used with a singular or plural verb. You can say: *The team has lost three games.* OR: *The team have lost three games.*

team² /tiːm/ PHRASAL VERB ,team ˈup to work together with someone

teammate /ˈtiːmˌmeɪt/ noun [C] someone who is in the same team as you

teamwork /ˈtiːmˌwɜːk/ noun [U] work that you do together with other people

teapot /ˈtiːˌpɒt/ noun [C] a container with a handle and a SPOUT (=small tube for pouring) that you use for making and pouring tea

tear¹ /teə/ (past tense **tore** /tɔː/; past participle **torn** /tɔːn/) verb ★★
1 [I/T] to pull something so that it separates into pieces or gets a hole in it, or to become damaged in this way=RIP: *He'd torn his raincoat.* ♦ *It's very thin material that tears easily.* ♦ **tear sth to pieces/bits/shreds** *Mary tore the letter to pieces.* ♦ **tear sth open** *He tore the envelope open.*
2 [T] to remove something by pulling it away from something else with force: **tear sth out/off/away from etc** *You'll need to tear the old wallpaper off the walls.* ♦ *The storm had torn the old tree up by the roots.*
3 [I] to move somewhere very quickly, usually in an excited or uncontrolled way: *Those kids are always tearing around here on their bicycles.*

PHRASE **torn between** unable to decide which of two people or things you want most: *I was torn between my family and my career.*

PHRASAL VERBS ,tear sb aˈpart to make someone feel very sad, upset, or worried
,tear sth aˈpart to damage or destroy something completely by breaking it into pieces: *The building was torn apart by the explosion.*
,tear sb/sth aˈpart to make the people in a group or organization argue or fight so that the group or organization is destroyed
,tear sb/sth aˈway to force someone or

yourself to leave, or to stop doing something: *'Sorry,' said Douglas, tearing himself away from the conversation.*
,tear sth ˈdown to destroy or remove a structure or part of a structure
,tear sth ˈoff to remove your clothes quickly and carelessly: *The boys tore off their clothes and jumped into the water.*
,tear sth ˈup to destroy something such as a piece of paper or cloth by pulling it into pieces: *I tore up all the photos of my ex-boyfriend.*

tear² /teə/ noun [C] a hole in something where it has been torn: *There was a tear in her coat.* → WEAR²

tear³ /tɪə/ noun ★★
1 [C] a drop of liquid that comes from your eye when you cry: *Her eyes filled with tears.* ♦ *She welcomed Ian with tears of joy.*
2 **tears** [plural] the state of crying: *I was left standing there in tears* (=crying). ♦ *She slammed the phone down and burst into tears* (=suddenly started crying). ♦ *I was near to tears* (=almost crying) *when she said goodbye.* ♦ *She fought back the tears* (=tried hard not to cry) *as she told us the dreadful news.*

tearful /ˈtɪəf(ə)l/ adj crying, or feeling as if you want to cry —**tearfully** adv

tear gas /ˈtɪə ˌɡæs/ noun [U] a gas that makes your eyes sting. It is used by the police for controlling violent crowds.

tease /tiːz/ verb [I/T] to say something to someone in order to have fun by embarrassing or annoying them

teaspoon /ˈtiːˌspuːn/ noun [C] **1** a small spoon that you use for adding sugar to tea or coffee, or for measuring small amounts of liquid or powder **2** **teaspoon** or **teaspoonful** the amount of food or liquid that a teaspoon holds

tea ˌtowel noun [C] *British* a cloth that you use for drying things such as dishes and cups —*picture* → C2

techie /ˈteki/ noun [C] *informal* someone who knows a lot about technology or computers

technical /ˈteknɪk(ə)l/ adj ★★★
1 involving science or industry: *technical experts* ♦ *The job requires someone with technical knowledge.*
2 technical language is difficult to understand for people who do not know a lot about the subject: *The text is interesting and informative, without being too technical.* ♦ *a technical term in philosophy*
3 relating to the way that a machine or piece of equipment works: *delays caused by technical problems*
4 relating to the skills that are needed to perform a particular activity: *The dancers reached extremely high levels of technical skill and ability.*

technicality /ˌteknɪˈkæləti/ noun
1 **technicalities** [plural] details about a particular subject that are understood only by an expert **2** [C] a minor detail of the law that can lead to an unfair result

technically /'teknıkli/ adv **1** in a way that involves skill in doing something: *a technically accomplished player* **2** according to a strict way of understanding a rule or set of facts: *Technically the war was over, but there was still some fighting.* **3** in a way that involves the practical use of skills, processes, or equipment in science and industry: *The use of an alternative fuel is not technically feasible.*

technician /tek'nıʃ(ə)n/ noun [C] someone with technical training whose job involves working with and taking care of special equipment

technique /tek'niːk/ noun ★★
1 [C] a method of doing something using a special skill that you have developed: *surgical techniques* ♦ *a useful technique for dealing with difficult customers* ♦ *modern techniques of business management*
2 [U] the skills that are needed to perform a particular activity: *Strength, speed, and technique are what you need to be a winner.*

techno /'teknəʊ/ noun [U] a type of popular music with a fast strong beat and electronic sounds

technological /,teknə'lɒdʒık(ə)l/ adj relating to or involving technology —**technologically** /,teknə'lɒdʒıkli/ adv

technology /tek'nɒlədʒi/ noun ★★★
1 [C/U] advanced scientific knowledge that is used for practical purposes, especially in industry: *computer/military technology* ♦ *the development of new technologies*
→ INFORMATION TECHNOLOGY
2 [U] advanced machines and equipment that are developed using technology

teddy bear or **teddy** /'tedi/ noun [C] a soft toy bear

tedious /'tiːdiəs/ adj boring and continuing for too long

tee /tiː/ noun [C] in golf, a small object that you place the ball on so that you can hit it —*picture* → C15

teem /tiːm/ PHRASAL VERB **'teem with sb/sth** to contain an extremely large number of people, animals, or objects that are all moving around

teeming /'tiːmıŋ/ adj containing an extremely large number of people, animals, or objects that are all moving around: *the teeming streets of the old city*

teen /tiːn/ adj *informal* teenage

teenage /'tiːneıdʒ/ adj **1** between the ages of 13 and 19: *a teenage girl/boy* **2** relating to, or intended for, young people between the ages of 13 and 19: *teenage magazines* ♦ *teenage pregnancies*

teenaged /'tiːneıdʒd/ adj between the ages of 13 and 19

teenager /'tiːneıdʒə/ noun [C] ★ a young person between the ages of 13 and 19 —*picture* → CHILD

teens /tiːnz/ noun [plural] the years of your life between the ages of 13 and 19: *She became a tennis champion while she was still in her teens.*

teeny /'tiːni/ or **teeny weeny** /,tiːni 'wiːni/ adj *informal* very small

'tee shirt another spelling of **T-shirt**

teeter /'tiːtə/ verb [I] to stand or move in a way that is not steady, so that you seem about to fall
PHRASE **teetering on the brink/edge (of sth)** in a situation in which something bad is very likely to happen

teeth the plural of **tooth**

teethe /tiːð/ verb **be teething** if a baby is teething, it is getting its first teeth

'teething problems or **'teething troubles** noun [plural] minor problems that a new company, project, or product has in the beginning

teetotal /,tiː'təʊt(ə)l/ adj never drinking alcohol —**teetotaller** noun [C]

TEFL /'tef(ə)l/ noun [U] the Teaching of English as a Foreign Language

tel. abbrev telephone number

telecommunications /,telikə,mjuːnı'keıʃ(ə)nz/ noun [U] the science and technology of sending information by telephone, radio, or television

telecommuter /'telikə,mjuːtə/ noun [C] someone who works from home on a computer and sends work to their office using email —**telecommuting** noun [U]

teleconference /'teli,kɒnf(ə)rəns/ noun [C] a meeting that is held among people in different places using an electronic communications system

telegram /'teli,græm/ noun [C] a message that you send by telegraph

telegraph /'teli,grɑːf/ noun [U] an old-fashioned method of communicating, by sending signals through wires or by radio waves

'telegraph pole noun [C] a tall pole that supports telephone wires

telemarketing /'teli,mɑːkıtıŋ/ noun [U] TELESALES

telepathy /tə'lepəθi/ noun [U] the ability of people to communicate directly with each other's minds, without using words —**telepathic** /,teli'pæθık/ adj

telephone¹ /'teli,fəʊn/ noun ★★★
1 [C] a piece of electronic equipment that you use for speaking to someone in a different place=PHONE: *Suddenly, the telephone rang.* ♦ *Pascoe answered the telephone and said 'Hello'.* ♦ *He's been on the telephone for the past two hours.* —*picture* → C3
2 [U] the system of communicating using telephones: *a telephone line/conversation* ♦ *People are interviewed over the telephone.* ♦ *I placed my order by telephone two weeks ago.*

telephone² /'teli,fəʊn/ verb [I/T] *formal* to speak to someone using the telephone =PHONE

'telephone box noun [C] *British* a small structure that contains a telephone that you pay to use

'telephone di,rectory noun [C] a book that

contains the names, telephone numbers, and addresses of people and businesses in a particular area=PHONE BOOK

'telephone ex,change noun [C] a place with equipment that connects one telephone line to another

'telephone ,number noun [C] a series of single numbers that you use for phoning a particular person

telesales /'teli,seilz/ noun [U] *British* the activity or job of using the telephone in order to sell goods or services

telescope /'teli,skəup/ noun [C] a piece of equipment shaped like a tube that you use to make distant objects look closer and larger

Teletext /'teli,tekst/ *trademark* a system that provides news and other information for people to read on their television screens

televise /'teli,vaiz/ verb [T] to broadcast something on television

television /'teli,viʒ(ə)n/ noun ★★★

1 [C] a piece of electrical equipment with a screen that is used for watching programmes=TV: *Kelly switched on the television and stared blankly at the screen.*
2 [U] the system of broadcasting pictures and sounds by electronic signals: *a television programme/channel*
3 [U] the programmes that are shown on television: *I spent most of the evening watching television.* ♦ *I'm sure I've seen him on television.*
4 [U] the business of creating and broadcasting television programmes: *She works in television.*

Types of **television programme**

- **chat show** *British* a programme in which a well-known person interviews famous people
- **current affairs programme** a programme about politics or other subjects that are being discussed in the news
- **documentary** a programme that deals with facts or historical events
- **drama** any serious programme that tells a story
- **episode** a single programme of a series
- **game show** a programme in which people compete to win prizes
- **the news** a programme that provides the latest information about the day's events
- **series** a group of related programmes that are broadcast over a period of time
- **sitcom** a type of humorous programme in which the same characters regularly appear in funny situations
- **soap** a type of programme in which the same characters regularly appear in situations that are like ordinary life

'television ,licence noun [C] *British* an official document that you have to buy in order to use a television set in the UK

'television ,set noun [C] A TELEVISION

teleworker /'teli,wɜːkə/ noun [C] someone who works at home on a computer and communicates with their office or customers by telephone or email

—teleworking noun [U]

tell /tel/ (past tense and past participle **told** /təʊld/) verb ★★★

1 sb gives information	**6** have clear effect
2 sth gives information	**7** see difference
3 talk about story	**8** fail to keep secret
4 order/advise to do sth	**+ PHRASES**
5 know sth	**+ PHRASAL VERBS**

1 [T] to give information to someone: *If you see anything suspicious, tell the police.* ♦ **tell sb (that)** *Didn't he tell you that I wanted to see you?* ♦ **tell sb who/what/why/how etc** *Just tell me what she said.* ♦ **tell me sth** *He finally told me the reason he was so upset.* ♦ **tell sb (sth) about sth** *'Tell me about your day,' she said.* ♦ *I haven't been told anything about it.* → SAY

2 [T] if something such as a fact, event, or piece of equipment tells you something, it gives you or shows you some information: *The flashing light tells you when the battery needs recharging.* ♦ *What does this room tell you about the person who lived here?*

3 [T] if you tell a story or a joke, you give someone a spoken account of it: *Grandpa tells wonderful stories about the old days.* ♦ **tell sb sth** *Shall I tell you a joke?*

4 [T] to order or strongly advise someone to do something: *I'm not asking you – I'm telling you!* ♦ **tell sb to do sth** *I told you to be here on time this morning.* ♦ **tell sb what/how/when etc** *I told him what to do, but he wouldn't listen.*

5 [I/T] to recognize something as a result of experience or evidence: *He's lying. I can always tell.* ♦ **+whether/if** *It's never easy to tell whether he's being serious or not.* ♦ **+(that)** *Peter could tell that she was bored.*

6 [I] to have an effect that can be clearly seen, especially a bad effect: *The strain of the last few days was beginning to tell.*

7 [I/T] to recognize the difference between one person or thing and another: *Which is which? I can't tell.* ♦ *These days it's hard to tell the difference between political parties.* ♦ **tell sb/sth from sb/sth** *Can you tell butter from margarine?*

8 [I] *informal* to not keep a secret: *You promised you wouldn't tell.*

PHRASES **(I'll) tell you what** used when you are going to make a suggestion, proposal, or offer: *I'll tell you what – let's have the party here.*

I'm telling you or **I tell you** *spoken* used for emphasizing that what you are saying is true, although it may seem surprising or hard to believe: *I'm telling you – that's how it happened.*

I told you (so) used for saying that you warned someone that something bad would happen and that you have now been proved to be right

tell the time to know what time it is when you look at a clock or watch

there's no telling who/what/when/how etc

used for saying that it is impossible to be certain about something: *There was no telling how he would react.*

you never can tell used for saying that it is impossible to be certain about something: *You can never tell how long these meetings will last.*

→ TELLER, TELLING

PHRASAL VERBS **tell sb/sth apart** to recognize the difference between two people or things that are very similar: *I couldn't tell the two pictures apart.*

tell sb off *informal* to criticize someone angrily for doing something wrong: *The teacher told me off for talking again today.* ♦ *I'm going to get told off for being late.*

teller /'telə/ noun [C] someone whose job is to take your money from you or give your money to you in a bank → FORTUNE-TELLER, STORYTELLER

telling /'telɪŋ/ adj **1** very important or effective **2** showing or suggesting the truth about a situation

telltale /'tel,teɪl/ adj showing that something exists or has happened

telly /'teli/ noun [C/U] *British informal* television

temp¹ /temp/ noun [C] someone who works in an office for a limited period of time

temp² /temp/ verb [I] *informal* to work as a temp

temper¹ /'tempə/ noun **1** [C/U] a tendency to get angry very quickly: *That temper of yours is going to get you into trouble.* **2** [singular/U] a particular emotional state or mood: *Mark was in a foul temper.*

PHRASES **keep your temper (with)** to stay calm and not get angry

lose your temper (with) to become very angry

temper² /'tempə/ verb [T] *formal* to make something less strong or extreme

temperament /'temprəmənt/ noun [C/U] someone's temperament is their basic character, for example their tendency to be happy or angry, or calm or worried

temperamental /,temprə'ment(ə)l/ adj **1** someone who is temperamental gets angry easily or changes from one mood to another very quickly **2** a machine that is temperamental often does not work correctly

temperate /'temp(ə)rət/ adj never having extremely hot or extremely cold weather

temperature /'temprɪˌtʃə/ noun [C/U] ★★★ **1** a measurement of how hot or cold a place or object is: *The plants need a temperature of at least 15°C to grow well.* ♦ *Temperatures dropped below freezing last night.* ♦ *The temperature rose steadily throughout the day.* **2** the measurement of how hot your body is: *She had a very high temperature.* ♦ **take sb's temperature** (=measure it) *She took his temperature and sent him to bed.*

tempest /'tempɪst/ noun [C] *literary* a severe storm with strong winds and heavy rain

tempestuous /tem'pestʃuəs/ adj full of strong emotion

template /'templeɪt/ noun [C] something that is used as a pattern or example for something else

temple /'temp(ə)l/ noun [C] **1** a building that is used for worship in some religions **2** the flat area that is on either side of your forehead next to your eyes —*picture* → C14

tempo /'tempəʊ/ noun **1** [singular] the speed at which something happens **2** [C/U] the speed at which music is played or sung

temporary /'temp(ə)rəri/ adj ★★★ **1** existing, done, or used for only a limited period of time ≠ PERMANENT: *These measures are only temporary.* ♦ *a temporary job* **2** temporary workers do a job for a limited period of time: *a temporary lecturer* —**temporarily** /,tempə'rerəli/ adv: *Bucharest airport was closed down temporarily.*

tempt /tempt/ verb [T] to make you want to do or have something, especially something that is wrong or bad for you

temptation /temp'teɪʃ(ə)n/ noun **1** [C/U] a strong feeling of wanting to do or have something, especially something that is wrong or bad for you: *I resisted the temptation to have another piece of cake* (=stopped myself from having another piece). **2** [C] something that tempts you

tempting /'temptɪŋ/ adj something that is tempting makes you feel that you would like to do it or have it

ten /ten/ number the number 10 → NUMBER 10

tenacious /tə'neɪʃəs/ adj very determined and not willing to stop trying to do something =DOGGED —**tenaciously** adv, **tenacity** /tə'næsəti/ noun [U]

tenancy /'tenənsi/ noun [C/U] the right to use a flat, office, building, or piece of land that you rent from the person who owns it

tenant /'tenənt/ noun [C] someone who rents a flat, office, building, or piece of land from the person who owns it

tend /tend/ verb ★★★ **1** [I] to usually do a particular thing: **tend to do sth** *He tends to exaggerate.* ♦ **tend not to do sth** *I tend not to go out so much in the winter.* **2** [I/T] to take care of someone or something: *Eddie kept himself busy tending the garden.* ♦ *Doctors were tending the wounded.* ♦ *I have to tend to the children before I go out.* **3** [I] **tend towards sth** to usually have a particular quality: *Her study found that sociologists tended towards liberalism and radicalism.*

tendency /'tendənsi/ noun [C] ★ **1** an aspect of your character that you show by behaving in a particular way: *artistic/criminal/suicidal tendencies* ♦ **have a tendency to do sth** *You have a tendency to avoid arguments.* **2** a situation that is starting to develop in a particular way=TREND: *We continue to see a tendency towards globalization of brands.* ♦ **a tendency (for sb/sth) to do sth** *There is a growing tendency for students to use the Internet to do their research.*

tender¹ /ˈtendə/ adj **1** gentle in a way that shows that you care about someone or something: *Her voice was low and tender.* **2** soft, and easy to cut and eat **3** if a part of your body is tender, it is painful when you touch it

PHRASE **a tender age** a time in your life when you are still young and lack experience

—**tenderly** adv, **tenderness** noun [U]

tender² /ˈtendə/ verb [T] *formal* to formally offer something: *The Deputy Prime Minister tendered his resignation on Thursday.*

tendon /ˈtendən/ noun [C] a part of your body that connects a muscle to a bone

tenement /ˈtenəmənt/ noun [C] a large building containing flats

tenet /ˈtenɪt/ noun [C] a principle or belief

tenner /ˈtenə/ noun [C] *British informal* ten pounds

tennis /ˈtenɪs/ noun [U] a game in which two or four people hit a ball across a net using a RACKET

tenor /ˈtenə/ noun **1** [C/U] the middle and higher range of musical notes written for men to sing, or a man who sings this range **2** [singular] **the tenor of sth** the feeling, mood, or main message that you get from something

tenpin bowling noun [U] *British* BOWLING

tense¹ /tens/ adj **1** making you feel nervous and not relaxed: *a tense situation* **2** feeling nervous and not relaxed: *He was too tense to sleep.* **3** stretched tight: *tense muscles*

tense² /tens/ noun [C/U] *linguistics* a form of a verb that is used for showing when something happens. For example 'I go' is the present tense and 'I went' is the past tense of the verb 'to go'.

tense³ /tens/ or **tense (sth) up** verb [I/T] if your muscles tense, or if you tense them, they become tight

tension /ˈtenʃ(ə)n/ noun ★
1 [U] the feeling of being so nervous, worried, or excited that you cannot relax: *I tried to ease the tension* (=make it less strong) *with a joke.* ♦ *Symptoms include nervous tension, depression, and insomnia.* **2** [C/U] a situation in which there is a lack of trust between people, groups, or countries and they may attack each other: *racial tensions* ♦ *Measures are needed to reduce tension between the two states.* **3** [C/U] a situation in which opposing aims, ideas, or influences cause problems: *There is a certain tension between the freedom of individuals and the need for public safety.* **4** [U] the degree to which something such as a rope or muscle is pulled tight: *Can you feel the tension in your neck and shoulders?*

tent /tent/ noun [C] a structure made of cloth and supported with poles and ropes. You sleep in it when you are camping.

tentacle /ˈtentək(ə)l/ noun [C] one of the long thin arms that some sea creatures have

tentative /ˈtentətɪv/ adj **1** not definite, or not certain **2** not confident —**tentatively** adv

tenth /tenθ/ number **1** in the place or position that is counted as number ten **2** one of ten equal parts of something

tenuous /ˈtenjuəs/ adj weak, or not certain: *a tenuous connection*

tenure /ˈtenjə/ noun [U] **1** the period of time during which someone has an important job **2** the right of a university teacher to stay in their job permanently **3** *legal* someone's right to live on land and own it

tepid /ˈtepɪd/ adj a tepid liquid is slightly warm

tequila /tɪˈkiːlə/ noun [C/U] a strong, clear or yellow alcoholic drink from Mexico

term¹ /tɜːm/ noun ★★★

1 word/phrase	4 time sth lasts
2 aspects	5 of agreement
3 part of year	✦ PHRASES

1 [C] a word or phrase that is used for referring to or describing someone or something: *a technical/medical term*
2 terms [plural] used for saying which aspects of something you are considering or including: *In practical terms, this change is unlikely to affect many people.* ♦ *The savings, both in terms of time and money, could be considerable.*
3 [C] one of the periods of time that the year is divided into for students: *What classes are you taking this term?* ♦ *How many weeks is it till the end of term?* ♦ *He trains five times a week during term time.*
4 [C] a period of time that something lasts: *In 1988 he was re-elected for a five-year term.* ♦ *He received a prison term of six months.*
5 terms [plural] the conditions of a legal, business, or financial agreement that the people making it accept: *We have agreed the terms of the lease.* ♦ *the terms for their release from prison* ♦ *Do you accept these terms and conditions?*

PHRASES **be on good/bad/friendly etc terms** to have a good/bad/friendly etc relationship with someone: *We parted on good terms.*
come to terms with sth to learn to accept and deal with an unpleasant situation or event
in the long/short term for or after a long/short period of time: *In the long term, you'll be happier if you give up smoking.*
on speaking terms feeling friendly towards someone, and not angry with them

term² /tɜːm/ verb [T] to use a particular word or phrase for describing or referring to someone or something

terminal¹ /ˈtɜːmɪn(ə)l/ noun [C] **1** a part of an airport where passengers arrive and leave **2** a large building where train, boat, or bus services start and finish **3** a computer screen and a keyboard connected to a computer NETWORK

terminal² /ˈtɜːmɪn(ə)l/ adj a terminal illness cannot be cured and will cause someone to die —**terminally** adv

terminate /ˈtɜːmɪneɪt/ verb [I/T] *formal* to end, or to make something end —**termination** /ˌtɜːmɪˈneɪʃ(ə)n/ noun [C/U]

terminology /ˌtɜːmɪˈnɒlədʒi/ noun [U] the words and phrases that are used in a particular subject or profession

terminus /ˈtɜːmɪnəs/ noun [C] the place where a bus or train service ends

termite /ˈtɜːmaɪt/ noun [C] a small insect that eats wood and can damage buildings

terrace /ˈterəs/ noun **1** [C] British a row of houses that are joined together **2** [C] a flat area outside a building where you can sit and eat meals **3 terraces** [plural] British a series of wide low steps where you can stand in order to watch a football match

terraced house /ˈterəst ˌhaʊs/ noun [C] British a house in a row of houses that are joined together —picture → c1

terracotta /ˌterəˈkɒtə/ noun [U] a brown-red clay

terrain /təˈreɪn/ noun [U] an area of land with a particular physical feature

terrestrial /təˈrestriəl/ adj existing on the Earth, or happening on the Earth instead of in the sky or the sea

terrible /ˈterəb(ə)l/ adj ★★
1 making you feel very upset or afraid: *A few minutes later there was a terrible scream.* ♦ *Her mother's sudden death came as a terrible shock.*
2 causing or involving serious harm or damage: *She suffered terrible injuries in the attack.* ♦ *A terrible storm hit the island last night.*
3 ill, unhappy, or feeling guilty: *I feel terrible about what I said.* ♦ *What's wrong? You look terrible.*
4 very bad: *The food was terrible.* ♦ *I've always been really terrible at maths.*

terribly /ˈterəbli/ adv **1** very or extremely: *Something is terribly wrong.* **2** in a very bad way: *What's wrong? You're playing terribly today.*

terrier /ˈteriə/ noun [C] a type of small dog

terrific /təˈrɪfɪk/ adj **1** very good or interesting **2** very big or great: *We suddenly heard a terrific bang.* —**terrifically** /təˈrɪfɪkli/ adv

terrified /ˈterəfaɪd/ adj extremely frightened

terrify /ˈterəfaɪ/ verb [T] to make someone very frightened —**terrifying** adj

territorial /ˌterəˈtɔːriəl/ adj relating to the land or the part of the sea that is controlled by a particular country

territory /ˈterətri/ noun ★★
1 [C/U] an area of land that is controlled by a particular country, leader, or army: *Russian troops crossed into Austrian territory in February 1849.*
2 [C/U] an area that an animal considers to be its own, and tries to prevent others from entering: *A lion will fearlessly defend its territory.*
3 [U] an area of knowledge, study, or experience: *Social work is familiar territory to her.*
PHRASE **come/go with the territory** to be a necessary or accepted part of a situation or activity: *In professional football, serious injuries come with the territory.*

terror /ˈterə/ noun ★
1 [singular/U] a strong feeling of fear: *I remember the sheer terror of those bombing raids.* ♦ *Thousands of people fled in terror as the volcano erupted.*
2 [U] violence that is used for achieving political aims: *the war against terror* ♦ *a deliberate campaign of terror*
3 [C] something or someone that makes you very frightened: *the terrors of the night*

terrorism /ˈterərɪz(ə)m/ noun [U] ★ the use of violence in order to achieve political aims: *They were charged with conspiring to commit acts of terrorism.*

terrorist /ˈterərɪst/ noun [C] ★ someone who uses violence in order to achieve political aims: *a suspected/convicted terrorist* ♦ *a terrorist bombing*

terrorize /ˈterəraɪz/ verb [T] to frighten someone by threatening them or by using violence

terse /tɜːs/ adj a terse statement or remark is very short and shows that you are annoyed: *a terse reply* —**tersely** adv

tertiary /ˈtɜːʃəri/ adj formal relating to colleges and universities: *tertiary education*

TESOL /ˈtiːsɒl/ noun [U] Teaching English to Speakers of Other Languages

test¹ /test/ noun [C] ★★★

1 check of knowledge	4 check of object
2 check of ability	5 difficult situation
3 check of body	✦ PHRASE

1 a set of written or spoken questions that is used for finding out how much someone knows about a subject: *Did you get a good mark in your physics test?* ♦ *You're going to have to take the test again.* ♦ *I passed my English test today.* ♦ *I know I'm going to fail this test.*
2 a series of actions that someone must perform in order to show how well they can do a particular activity: *I'm still too young to take my driving test.*
3 an examination of a part of your body or of a substance that is taken from your body: *an eye test* ♦ *a test for HIV* ♦ *Your test results are fine.*
4 a process that is designed to find out whether something is satisfactory, whether something works correctly, or whether something exists somewhere: *nuclear tests in the Pacific* ♦ *Researchers conducted tests on more than 220 electric blankets.*
5 a difficult situation that shows what qualities someone or something has: *a test of strength/character*
PHRASE **put sb/sth to the test** to find out how good or effective someone or something is

test² /test/ verb [T] ★★★
1 to find out how much someone knows or how well they can do something, by giving them a set of questions to answer or an activity to perform: *The aim of the examination is to test your writing skills.* ♦ **test sb on sth** *You won't be tested on anything that you haven't already studied.*

2 to try using something such as a machine or product to find out whether it works correctly or is satisfactory: *The theory will be tested by computer simulation.* ♦ **test sth on sth** *a skin-care product that isn't tested on animals* → TRIED²

3 to examine someone's body in order to check that it is in good condition, or in order to find out whether they have a particular illness: *Debbie has to have her eyes tested.* ♦ **test sb for sth** *She was tested for hepatitis.*

4 to show how good or effective someone or something is by putting pressure on them: *They were never seriously tested by their opponents in the first half of the game.*

testament /ˈtestəmənt/ noun **(a) testament to sth** *formal* evidence that something exists or is true → NEW TESTAMENT, OLD TESTAMENT

'test ˌcase noun [C] a legal case whose result will be used as a model for similar cases in the future

testicles /ˈtestɪk(ə)lz/ noun [plural] the two round male sex organs that hang in a bag of skin behind the PENIS

testify /ˈtestɪˌfaɪ/ verb [I/T] to make a formal statement in a court of law about something that you saw, know, or experienced

testimony /ˈtestɪməni/ noun **1** [C/U] a formal statement that you make in a court of law about something that you saw, know, or experienced **2** **(a) testimony to sth** evidence that something exists or is true

'test ˌtube noun [C] a long thin glass container that is open at one end and is used in laboratories

tetanus /ˈtet(ə)nəs/ noun [U] an illness in which your jaw and neck become stiff

tether¹ /ˈteðə/ verb [T] to tie an animal to something so that it will stay in a particular area

tether² /ˈteðə/ noun [C] a rope or a chain that is used for tying an animal to something
PHRASE at the end of your tether very upset because you are no longer able to deal with a difficult situation

text¹ /tekst/ noun ★★★
1 [U] the part of a book, magazine, or computer document that consists of writing and not pictures: *There are 200 pages of text and illustrations.*
2 [C/U] a written record of the words of a speech, lecture, programme, or play: *The text of the lecture is available from the departmental office.*
3 [C] a piece of writing such as a book or play that you study: *We'll be analysing the language of literary texts.* ♦ *The play is a set text for first-year students.*
4 [C] a TEXT MESSAGE

text² /tekst/ verb [T] to send a written message to someone using a mobile phone: *Gemma didn't call or text me all day.*
—**texting** noun [U]

textbook /ˈteks(t)ˌbʊk/ noun [C] a book that contains information about a particular subject

textile /ˈtekstaɪl/ noun [C] any type of woven cloth = FABRIC

'text ˌmessage noun [C] a written message that you send or receive using a mobile phone

text messaging /ˈteks(t) ˌmesɪdʒɪŋ/ noun [U] the process of sending and receiving written messages using a mobile phone

texture /ˈtekstʃə/ noun [C/U] the way that something feels when you touch it: *a soft/rough/firm texture*

than /*weak* ðən, *strong* ðæn/ preposition, conjunction ★★★
1 used when making comparisons: *Nylon is considerably stronger than cotton.* ♦ *Is the world a safer place than it was a year ago?* ♦ *We don't want to do more than is necessary.*
2 used when you are saying that a number or amount is above or below a particular level: *a city of more than 5 million people* ♦ *I'll be back in less than a week.*
→ RATHER

thank /θæŋk/ verb [T] ★★★ to tell someone that you are grateful for something that they have done or given to you: *She didn't even thank me.* ♦ **thank sb for (doing) sth** *I just wanted to thank you for the flowers – they're beautiful.* ♦ *I'd like to thank everybody for coming along today.*
PHRASE thank God/goodness/heaven(s) used for saying that you are happy that something unpleasant has ended or has not happened: *Thank heaven nobody was injured in the crash.*

thankful /ˈθæŋkf(ə)l/ adj grateful for something, or pleased that something unpleasant is no longer happening or did not happen

thankfully /ˈθæŋkf(ə)li/ adv used for saying you are pleased that something unpleasant is no longer happening or did not happen: *Thankfully the boys are safe.*

thankless /ˈθæŋkləs/ adj a thankless activity is unpleasant, and other people are not grateful to you for doing it

thanks¹ /θæŋks/ interjection *informal* ★★★
1 used for telling someone that you are grateful for something that they have said or done: *'You're looking well.' 'Thanks.'* ♦ *Thanks for dinner – it was great.* ♦ *Thanks for reminding me.*
2 used for politely accepting something that is offered to you: *'Do you want a chocolate?' 'Thanks, I'd love one.'*
PHRASE no, thanks used for politely refusing something that is offered to you: *'Can I get you a drink?' 'No, thanks.'*

thanks² /θæŋks/ noun [plural] ★★★ things that you say or do in order to tell someone that you are grateful to them: *Please accept my heartfelt thanks for your concern and generosity.*
PHRASE thanks to because of someone or something: *Thanks to this treatment, her condition has improved.* ♦ *The railway system is in chaos, thanks to the government's incompetence.*

T

Thanksgiving /ˈθæŋksˌgɪvɪŋ/ or **Thanksgiving Day** noun [C/U] in the US and Canada, a holiday in the autumn when families have a special meal together

thank you interjection ★★★
1 used for telling someone that you are grateful for something that they have said or done: 'That's a nice jacket.' 'Thank you.' ♦ *Thank you for coming here today.*
2 used for politely accepting something that is offered to you: 'Would you like a cup of coffee?' 'Oh, thank you, that would be great.'
PHRASE **no, thank you** used for politely refusing something that is offered to you

thankyou /ˈθæŋkjuː/ noun [C] something that you say or do to tell someone that you are grateful to them

that /ðæt/ grammar word ★★★

> **That** can be:
> ■ a **determiner**: *Give me that hammer.*
> ■ a **pronoun**: *Who gave you that?*
> ■ a **conjunction**: *I didn't know that she was married.*
> ■ a **relative pronoun**: *It's a song that my mother taught me.*
> ■ an **adverb**: *Three years? I can't wait that long.*

1 (plural **those** /ðəʊz/) **the one that is known about** used for referring to someone or something that has already been mentioned or is already known about: *I know there's a problem, but I haven't got time to worry about that now.* ♦ *Why don't you ask Carmen? That's who I'd choose.* ♦ *The engine's started making that noise again.*
2 (plural **those** /ðəʊz/) **the one that you are looking at** *spoken* used for referring to someone or something that you can see or point at, although they are not very near to you: *That's Jerry's car, over there.* ♦ *Where did that stain on the carpet come from?* ♦ *Do you know who that woman in the blue dress is?* ♦ *I need these books, but you can borrow any of those.*
3 (plural **those** /ðəʊz/) **a past time or event** used for referring to a period, event, or experience in the past: *Remember that time we all went to the lake?* ♦ *There were no telephones in those days.* ♦ *That was fun. We must do it again some time.*
4 /strong ðæt, weak ðət/ **introducing a statement** used after some verbs, adjectives, and nouns in order to state an idea, fact, or reason: *Dawkins believes that his sister was murdered.* ♦ *We cannot ignore the fact that there is a shortage of qualified nurses.* ♦ *It is surprising that no one warned them of the danger.* ♦ *I'm sorry that I missed the first meeting.*

> The conjunction **that** is often left out, especially in spoken English: *I told them I was busy.*

5 /strong ðæt, weak ðət/ **used instead of 'which' or 'who'** used instead of 'which' or 'who' in order to give more information about a noun or pronoun: *We haven't met the people that live next door.* ♦ *It was the worst winter that anyone could remember.*

♦ *Is there anything else that you want to ask?*

> The relative pronoun **that** is often left out when it is the object of a relative clause: *Did you find the book you were looking for?* In formal written English **that** is not generally left out.

6 /strong ðæt, weak ðət/ **introducing a result** used after 'so' or 'such' for showing the result of something: *It was so cold that the sea froze in some places.*

> The conjunction **that** is often left out of expressions with 'so' and 'such', especially in spoken English: *I was so excited I couldn't sleep.*

7 **showing how big** *spoken* used when you use your hands for showing the size or level of something: *There was only that much left in the bottle.*
8 **very** *spoken* to a very great degree: *There's no need to get upset – it isn't that important.*
PHRASES **that is** used when explaining or correcting what you have just said: *I've always enjoyed my work – that is, I did until this new manager arrived.*
that's it or **that does it** *spoken* used when a series of situations has made you angry, so that you decide to leave or stop what you are doing
that's that *spoken* used for saying that something has been finished or finally decided
→ THIS

thatched /θætʃt/ adj with a roof made from dried plants such as STRAW

thaw¹ /θɔː/ verb **1** [I/T] if ice or snow thaws, or if something thaws it, it becomes warmer and changes into liquid **2** [I/T] if frozen food thaws, or if you thaw it, it becomes softer and ready to cook **3** [I] to become more friendly
PHRASAL VERB **thaw (sth) out 1** *same as* **thaw¹ 2** *same as* **thaw¹ 2**

thaw² /θɔː/ noun [singular] **1** a period of warmer weather that causes ice and snow to turn into water **2** an improvement in the relationship between people, countries etc

the /weak ðə, ðɪ, strong ðiː/ determiner ★★★

> **The** is used as the **definite article** before a noun.

1 **talking about sb/sth when you know who or which** used before a noun when that person or thing has already been mentioned or is known about, or when there is only one: *Have you locked the door?* ♦ *I have to look after the children.* ♦ *She brought me some cake and coffee, but the cake was stale.* ♦ *The sun was hidden behind a cloud.* ♦ *the best hotel in Paris*
2 **talking in general about one type of thing or person** used before a singular noun when making a general statement about things or people of a particular type: *People have come to depend on the car as their only means of transport.*

> DO NOT use **the** when you are referring to things or people in a general way: *Children need love and attention.*

3 with a part of an object or body used before a part of a particular thing, or a part of the body: *the sharp end of a pencil* ♦ *He had a gunshot wound in the neck.*

4 used when explaining which person or thing you are referring to: *Who was the actor who played Romeo?* ♦ *We live in the house with green shutters.*

5 in dates and times used before dates or periods of time: *the 4th of July* ♦ *popular music of the 1960s*

6 with nouns referring to actions used before a noun that refers to an action, especially when it is followed by 'of': *the destruction of a whole city* ♦ *the death of Queen Victoria*

7 with names of seas, rivers etc used before the names of seas, rivers, deserts, or groups of mountains: *the Pacific Ocean* ♦ *the Sahara* ♦ *the Alps*

> **The** is not usually used before the names of streets, towns, countries, counties, states, or continents: *My parents live in Surrey.*

8 used before an adjective in order to form a plural noun that refers to people of a particular type or people from a particular country: *a policy of taxing the rich to help the poor* ♦ *The Japanese eat a lot of seafood.*

> You should avoid using 'the' with adjectives that refer to disabilities, for example **the blind** and **the handicapped**. Many people now think that this use is offensive and prefer expressions such as **the visually impaired** and **people with disabilities**.

9 used when you are saying what type of musical instrument someone plays: *Lorna plays the violin.*

PHRASE the...the... used with 'more', 'less', and other COMPARATIVES for showing that when one thing increases or is reduced, it causes something else to increase or be reduced at the same time: *The more people who help, the better.*

theater /ˈθɪətə/ the American spelling of **theatre**

theatre /ˈθɪətə/ noun ★★
1 [C] a building or room that is used for performing plays: *We're going to the theatre tonight.*
2 [U] the activity or job of writing, performing, or organizing performances of plays: *Jenny wanted to pursue a career in the theatre.*
3 [U] plays considered as entertainment or art: *a compelling piece of theatre*
4 [C/U] *British* a room in a hospital that is used for medical operations=OPERATING THEATRE: *He's in theatre at the moment.*

theatrical /θiˈætrɪk(ə)l/ adj **1** relating to the theatre **2** theatrical behaviour is very emotional and aims to attract attention

theft /θeft/ noun [C/U] the crime of stealing something

their /ðeə/ determiner ★★★
1 belonging to, or relating to, a particular group of people or things that have already

been mentioned or when it is obvious which ones you are referring to: *chemical fertilizers and their effect on the environment* ♦ *They have children of their own.*
2 used instead of 'his or her', especially when you are referring back to a word such as 'everyone', 'someone', or 'anyone': *Everyone has their own way of doing things.*

theirs /ðeəz/ pronoun ★
1 used for referring to someone or something that belongs to or is connected with a particular group of people or animals that have already been mentioned: *Your garden is big, but I think theirs is bigger.* ♦ *They introduced us to some friends of theirs.*
2 used instead of 'his or hers', especially when you are referring back to a word such as 'everyone', 'someone', or 'anyone': *I haven't got my exam results yet, but everyone else has had theirs.*

them / *strong* ðem, *weak* ðəm/ pronoun ★★★
1 the object form of 'they', used for referring to a particular group of people or things that have already been mentioned, or when it is obvious which group you are referring to: *They've taken their families with them.* ♦ *Sykes stole the paintings and then tried to sell them.*
2 used instead of 'him or her', especially when you are referring back to a word such as 'everyone', 'someone', or 'anyone': *Someone phoned, but I told them to call back later.*

theme /θiːm/ noun [C] ★
1 the main subject of something such as a book, speech, discussion, or art exhibition: *Love and honour are the main themes of the book.*
2 theme or **theme tune** a short piece of music that is played at the beginning and end of a radio or television programme or a film: *the theme from the film* Rocky

theme park noun [C] a large park where people pay to play games and have fun and where all the entertainment is designed according to one theme

themselves /ðəmˈselvz/ pronoun ★★★
1 the REFLEXIVE form of 'they' that is used for showing that the people or things that do something are also affected by what they do: *They have no weapons to defend themselves.* ♦ *The couple had been saving up to buy themselves a house.*
2 used for emphasizing that a particular group of people are the ones that you are referring to, and not any others: *The two youths died in a fire that they themselves had started.*

PHRASES (all) by themselves 1 alone: *Why were these two small children wandering about all by themselves?* **2** without any help: *It's a brilliant idea, and they thought it up all by themselves!*
(all) to themselves not sharing something with anyone else: *Helen and Philip were able to get a table to themselves.*

then /ðen/ grammar word ★★★

> **Then** can be:
> ■ an **adverb**: *I was still at school then.*
> ■ an **adjective**: *the then prime minister, Harold Wilson*

1 at a particular time in the past or in the future: *'Did you hear him when he left the house?' 'Yes, I heard him then and when he came back.'* ♦ *I can see you next weekend. Can you wait until then?*
2 used for introducing the next thing that happens: *He glanced quickly at Sally and then looked away again.* ♦ *First Lewis will give a TV interview. Then comes the main news conference.*
3 used for saying what you think the result must be if something is true: *'Sue and I grew up together.' 'You must know her fairly well then.'* ♦ *If no one else is willing, then I'll have to do the job myself.*
4 used for referring to someone who had a particular job or position at a particular time in the past: *the then Secretary of State, Michael Forsyth*
PHRASE **now then** or **right then** or **okay then** used for getting someone's attention when you are starting to talk about something new: *Now then, I want to ask you all a serious question.*
➜ THERE

thence /ðens/ adv *literary* from a particular place or point

theology /θiˈɒlədʒi/ noun [U] the study of God and religion —**theological** /ˌθiːəˈlɒdʒɪk(ə)l/ adj

theorem /ˈθɪərəm/ noun [C] *technical* a statement that can be proved to be true

theoretical /ˌθɪəˈretɪk(ə)l/ adj **1** based on theories instead of practical experience **2** possible but not definite

theoretically /ˌθɪəˈretɪkli/ adv used for saying that something could be true or could exist: *Transmission of the virus is theoretically possible, but very unlikely.*

theorist /ˈθɪərɪst/ noun [C] someone who develops or studies theories about a particular subject

theorize /ˈθɪəˌraɪz/ verb [I/T] to develop ideas in order to explain something

theory /ˈθɪəri/ noun ★★
1 [C] an idea that explains how or why something happens: *Einstein's theory of relativity* ♦ *+that He had a theory that the germs caused disease.*
2 [U] the set of general principles that a particular subject is based on: *Marxist/literary theory*
3 [C] an idea that you believe is true, although you have no proof: *I have my own theory about why he resigned.*
PHRASE **in theory** used for saying that something is believed to be true, although it may not be true: *In theory the country is a democracy, but in practice the military holds most of the power.*

therapeutic /ˌθerəˈpjuːtɪk/ adj **1** helping to treat or cure illness **2** helping you to feel better or calmer

therapist /ˈθerəpɪst/ noun [C] someone whose job is to help people with physical, mental, or emotional problems

therapy /ˈθerəpi/ noun **1** [C/U] a form of treatment for an illness or medical condition **2** [U] treatment for someone with mental illness or emotional problems that involves talking to them

there /ðeə/ grammar word ★★★

> **There** can be:
> ■ a **pronoun**: *There's a spider in the bath.*
> ■ an **adverb**: *Wait there until I get back.*
> ■ an **interjection**: *There, that didn't hurt so much, did it?*

1 /weak ðə, strong ðeə/ **used for saying what exists** used for introducing a statement about someone or something that exists or happens: *There is plenty of time left.* ♦ *There are 24 teams competing in the tournament.* ♦ *Are there any other suggestions?*
2 **in or to that place** in or to a place that has already been mentioned, or that you are looking at or pointing to: *They're going to Hawaii, and they plan to stay there until the end of March.* ♦ *It's only a hundred miles to Oxford. You could drive there and back in a day.* ♦ *Would you like to sit over there by the window?* ♦ *There's Angela now, coming up the drive.*
3 **at a point in a process** at a particular point in a series of events, in a speech, or in a story: *I'll stop there, and answer questions.*
4 **available** available, and ready to help or to be used: *The opportunity was there, so I took it.* ♦ *If you need me, I'll be there for you.*
5 **referring to what has just happened** *spoken* used when something has just happened, for showing that you feel satisfied, sorry, annoyed etc about it: *There, everything's clean now.*
PHRASES **there and then** or **then and there** immediately at that moment and in that place: *They wanted me to make a decision there and then.*
there goes sth *spoken* used for expressing disappointment that something has failed, has been lost, or has been destroyed
there you are/go *spoken* a polite expression used when you are giving someone something
➜ AGAIN

thereabouts /ˌðeərəˈbaʊts/ adv near a particular place, amount, or time that has just been mentioned

thereafter /ˌðeərˈɑːftə/ adv *formal* after a particular time that has just been mentioned

thereby /ðeəˈbaɪ/ adv *formal* because of or by means of what has just been mentioned

therefore /ˈðeəfɔː/ adv *formal* ★★ as a result of what has just been mentioned: *The new boots are lighter and softer, and therefore more comfortable to wear.* ♦ *This is a* *binding contract. Therefore, we recommend that you review it with a lawyer.*

therein /ˌðeərˈɪn/ adv *formal* in a particular place or piece of writing that has just been mentioned

> **PHRASE** **therein lies sth** used for explaining the cause of a situation that you have just described

thermal /ˈθɜːm(ə)l/ adj **1** *science* relating to or caused by heat **2** thermal clothing is made of special material that keeps you warm

thermometer /θəˈmɒmɪtə/ noun [C] a piece of equipment that measures temperature

Thermos /ˈθɜːməs/ or **Thermos ˌflask** *trademark* a container that keeps liquids hot or cold

thermostat /ˈθɜːməʊstæt/ noun [C] a piece of equipment that controls the temperature in a building, machine, or engine

thesaurus /θɪˈsɔːrəs/ (plural **thesauruses** or **thesauri** /θɪˈsɔːraɪ/) noun [C] a book that contains lists of words that have similar meanings

these /ðiːz/ grammar word ★★★ the plural of **this**

thesis /ˈθiːsɪs/ (plural **theses** /ˈθiːsiːz/) noun [C] **1** a long piece of writing that is the final part of an advanced university degree **2** *formal* a theory that is used for explaining something

they /ðeɪ/ pronoun ★★★
1 used for referring to a group of people or things that have already been mentioned, or that are already known about: *I phoned her parents because I knew they were worried.* ♦ *It's hard to choose. They're all very nice.*
2 used instead of 'he or she': *We should give everyone a chance to say what they think.*

> ■ In spoken English and in informal written English, **they**, **them**, **their**, and **themselves** are used by many people for referring to a person without mentioning whether the person is male or female, especially when referring back to a pronoun such as 'everyone' or 'someone': *What happens if someone changes their mind?*
> ■ In more formal English, 'he or she', 'him or her', or 'himself or herself' are used instead.

3 used for referring to people in general: *They say there's going to be a war.*
4 used for referring to a government, an organization, or a group of people in authority: *They're going to ban smoking in public places.*
→ HE

they'd /ðeɪd/ short form **1** the usual way of saying or writing 'they would'. This is not often used in formal writing: *They said they'd be happy to help.* **2** the usual way of saying or writing 'they had' when 'had' is an AUXILIARY VERB. This is not often used in formal writing: *He knew they'd met somewhere before.*

they'll /ðeɪl/ short form the usual way of saying or writing 'they will'. This is not

often used in formal writing: *Hurry up! They'll be here any minute.*

they're /ðeə/ short form the usual way of saying or writing 'they are'. This is not often used in formal writing: *They believe that what they're doing is right.*

they've /ðeɪv/ short form the usual way of saying or writing 'they have' when 'have' is an AUXILIARY VERB. This is not often used in formal writing: *They've been talking about buying a new house for years.*

thick¹ /θɪk/ adj ★★★

1 long between edges	5 filling air completely
2 of measurement	6 of accent
3 not flowing easily	7 stupid
4 of plants/hair	+ PHRASES

1 a thick object or material has a long distance between two opposite sides, edges, or surfaces: *a thick woollen sweater* ♦ *a thick layer of snow*
2 used for stating the distance between the opposite surfaces or edges of a solid object: *The walls are only a few inches thick.*
3 a thick liquid is more stiff or solid than normal and does not flow easily: *a thick cream sauce*
4 growing very close together: *her thick dark hair* ♦ *a thick cluster of trees*
5 thick smoke or cloud fills the air completely, so that it is difficult to see or difficult to breathe
6 a thick ACCENT shows very clearly that the speaker comes from a particular place
7 *informal* stupid

> **PHRASES** **have a thick skin** to not be easily upset or offended by what other people say about you
> **thick with sth** full of something: *The air was thick with smoke.*

—**thickly** adv

thick² /θɪk/ adv **thick and fast** frequently and in large numbers or amounts

thick³ /θɪk/ noun

> **PHRASES** **in the thick of sth** in the most busy, active, or dangerous part of a situation, event, or activity
> **through thick and thin** in all situations, especially the most difficult ones

thicken /ˈθɪkən/ verb [I/T] to become thick, or to make something become thick

thicket /ˈθɪkɪt/ noun [C] an area with a lot of bushes and small trees growing very close together

thickness /ˈθɪknəs/ noun **1** [C/U] the measurement of how thick something is **2** [C] a layer of something

thick-skinned /ˌθɪk ˈskɪnd/ adj not easily upset or offended by what other people say about you

thief /θiːf/ (plural **thieves** /θiːvz/) noun [C] someone who steals something

thigh /θaɪ/ noun [C] the top part of your leg, above your knee

thimble /ˈθɪmb(ə)l/ noun [C] a small metal or plastic object that you wear on your finger in order to protect it when you are sewing

T

thin¹ /θɪn/ adj ★★★

1 short between edges	5 small in amount
2 with little fat on body	6 without much detail
3 of hair/fur	7 with little oxygen
4 flowing easily	+ PHRASES

1 a thin object or material has only a short distance between two opposite sides, edges, or surfaces: *a thin layer of dust* ♦ *Cut the tomatoes into* **thin slices**.
2 someone who is thin has very little fat on their body: *Charles was thin and very tall.*
3 thin hair or fur grows with spaces between the individual hairs: *a thin moustache*
4 a thin liquid contains mostly water, so that it flows easily: *a plate of meat covered with thin gravy*
5 small in number or amount: *It was a day of thin trading on the stock market.*
6 without much detail or many facts: *The evidence for his theory is rather thin.*
7 thin air has less oxygen in it than usual
PHRASES **thin air** if something appears from thin air or disappears into thin air, it appears or disappears in a sudden mysterious way
thin on the ground not available in large amounts or numbers
→ THINLY

Other ways of saying **thin**

- **emaciated** extremely thin because you have been ill, or because you do not have enough food to eat
- **lean/wiry** thin and strong
- **skinny** (*informal*) thin in a way that is not attractive
- **slender** thin in a graceful way
- **slim** thin in an attractive way
- **trim** thin because you exercise regularly

thin² /θɪn/ verb **1** [I] to become less in number, amount, or thickness: *As it grew dark, the crowd started to thin.* ♦ *Did you notice that his hair is thinning on top?* **2** [T] to make a thick liquid become less thick by adding water or another liquid to it

thin³ /θɪn/ adv in a way that produces a thin layer or piece of something: *Cut the cheese thin, so that it melts.*

thing /θɪŋ/ noun ★★★

1 object	5 aspect/quality
2 possessions	6 general situation
3 action/activity	7 idea/information
4 situation/event	+ PHRASES

1 [C] used for referring to an object that you cannot or do not want to refer to in a more specific way: *What's that thing over there on the table?* ♦ *It's one of those gadget things, isn't it?* ♦ *It's a thing used for looking inside people's ears.*
2 **things** [plural] the objects that belong to a particular person or are used for a particular purpose: *I'll pack my things for the trip tomorrow.*
3 [C] an action or activity: *I have a lot of things to do today.* ♦ *I gave back the money. Did I do the right thing?*

4 [C] a situation or event: *A funny thing happened to me today.* ♦ *I think we should just forget the whole thing.* ♦ *She doesn't find that kind of thing funny.* ♦ *Don't make a big thing out of this* (=behave as if it is more serious than it really is) – *I just said I'd be late!*
5 [C] an aspect of a situation, or a quality that someone has: *If you could change three things about your job, what would they be?* ♦ *The thing I really like about Theresa is her sense of humour.* ♦ *The funny thing is, I miss him now.* ♦ *It's a good thing that you don't need to work late.*
6 **things** [plural] used for talking about a situation in a general way: *Things have been getting better lately.* ♦ *The police soon got things under control.*
7 [C] an idea, comment, fact, or subject: *There are some interesting things in your report.* ♦ *I have a few things to say to you.* ♦ *If anyone asks you what I said, don't say a thing.*
PHRASES **among other things** used for saying that there are other details, examples etc in addition to the ones that you are mentioning: *He's a liar and a thief, among other things.*
be seeing/hearing things to think that you see or hear something that is not really there
first thing (in the morning) early in the morning
for one thing used for saying that the reason or example that you are giving is not the only one: *Well, for one thing, I'm not tall enough to play basketball.*
last thing (at night) late at night, before you go to bed
the thing is *spoken* used for introducing an answer, comment, or explanation that is related to something that was just mentioned: *'Why didn't you invite me?' 'Well, the thing is, I didn't think you would want to come.'*

thingy /ˈθɪŋi/ noun [C] *spoken* used for referring to something when you do not know or cannot remember the name of it

think¹ /θɪŋk/ (past tense and past participle **thought** /θɔːt/) verb ★★★

1 believe sth is true	6 consider sb
2 have opinion	7 have sth in your mind
3 consider facts carefully	+ PHRASES
4 remember sb/sth	+ PHRASAL VERBS
5 imagine sth	

1 [T] to believe something based on facts or ideas: *'Is Dan coming tonight?' 'I think so, but I'm not sure.'* ♦ **+(that)** *I don't think there's a bank in the village.* ♦ **be thought to do sth** *Faulty wiring is thought to have caused the fire.*
2 [I/T] to have a particular opinion about someone or something: *His colleagues* **think a lot of him** (=have a very good opinion of him). ♦ *I* **don't think much of** *Sam's new girlfriend* (=I don't like her very much). ♦ **think of sb/sth as sth** *Nobody seriously*

thought of him as a candidate for the job.
3 [I] to carefully consider facts in order to understand something, make a decision, or solve a problem: *Let's stop and think before we do anything else.* ♦ *I need to think seriously about their offer.* ♦ *I've got to think of a way to earn more money.*
4 [I] to remember someone or something: *He could never think of the woman's name.* ♦ *I often think about the time we spent in Rome.*
5 [I/T] to imagine something: *Just think of what she's suffered!* ♦ *+(that) I never thought that I'd end up working here.*
6 [I] to consider someone and their needs or situation: *It was kind of you to think of our daughter.*
7 [I/T] to have something in your mind: *I wasn't worried – I just thought, 'Why is she doing that?'* ♦ *I expect we were all thinking the same thing.*

PHRASES **come to think of it** *spoken* used for adding something to what you have said because you have just remembered something: *Come to think of it, he did mention going to the house.*

do you think...? used for asking someone politely to do something: *Do you think you could pass me my bag?*

I thought (that) *spoken* used as a polite way of suggesting something: *I thought we'd have a drink before dinner.*

think twice/again to carefully consider whether what you are planning to do is a good idea

PHRASAL VERBS **,think 'back** to think about something that happened in the past: *I've been trying to think back to that last evening.*
,think sth 'over to consider a problem or decision carefully: *Let's think over his proposal before we see him again.*
,think sth 'through to consider the facts about something in an organized and thorough way: *Have you had time to think things through?*
,think sth 'up to invent or imagine something, especially an excuse: *She'd have to think up a good reason for being late.*

think² /θɪŋk/ noun **have a think** *British* to think about something carefully

thinker /ˈθɪŋkə/ noun [C] someone who thinks about important subjects and develops new ideas

thinking /ˈθɪŋkɪŋ/ noun [U] **1** an opinion, or a set of ideas: *Can you explain the thinking behind your proposal?* **2** the way that you consider things or react to them: *What's needed here is some positive thinking.* **3** the process of considering something or reacting to something: *He had some serious thinking to do.*

'think ,tank noun [C] a group of people who work together to produce new ideas on a particular subject

thinly /ˈθɪnli/ adv **1** in a thin layer or piece: *thinly sliced tomatoes* **2** with only a few people or things that are far apart from each other: *a thinly populated area* **3** in a way that makes it easy to recognize what

the true situation really is: *a thinly disguised/veiled/concealed threat*

third¹ /θɜːd/ number **1** in the place or position counted as number 3 **2** one of 3 equal parts of something

third² /θɜːd/ noun [C] in the UK or Australia, the lowest mark for a university degree

thirdly /ˈθɜːdli/ adv used for introducing the third idea in a list

,third 'party noun [C] *formal* a person or organization that is not one of the two main people or organizations involved in something

third 'person, the noun [singular] *linguistics* the set of pronouns and verb forms that are used for referring to someone or something that is not the speaker or the person who is being spoken to

third-'rate adj of very low quality

,Third 'World, the noun [singular] countries that are poor and do not have much industrial development. People now prefer to use the expression **developing countries**.

thirst /θɜːst/ noun **1** [singular/U] the feeling or state of being thirsty **2** [singular] a strong feeling of wanting to have or do something

thirsty /ˈθɜːsti/ adj ★ feeling that you want or need to drink something: *I'm really thirsty – could I have a glass of water?*
—**thirstily** adv

thirteen /ˌθɜːˈtiːn/ number the number 13

thirteenth /ˌθɜːˈtiːnθ/ number **1** in the place or position counted as number 13 **2** one of 13 equal parts of something

thirtieth /ˈθɜːtiəθ/ number **1** in the place or position counted as number 30 **2** one of 30 equal parts of something

thirty /ˈθɜːti/ number the number 30

this /ðɪs/ grammar word ★★★

This can be:
■ a **determiner**: *He gave me this diamond ring.*
■ a **pronoun**: *This is the photograph you asked for.*
■ an **adverb**: *It's a long time since I felt this good.*

1 (plural **these** /ðiːz/) **the one that is here** used for referring to a person, thing, or place that is near you: *This is our new secretary, Veronica Taylor.* ♦ *This is my towel and that's yours.* ♦ *I bought these shoes in Italy.* ♦ *This is where I catch the bus.*
2 (plural **these** /ðiːz/) **the present one** used for referring to the present time or a present action, or to a time or action that will happen soon: *Is this your first visit to Ireland?* ♦ *I'm going to be away the whole of this week.* ♦ *Are we going to have enough fuel this winter?* ♦ *Benson was late again this morning* (=the morning of today). ♦ *I don't get much spare time these days.*
3 (plural **these** /ðiːz/) **the one that is known** used for referring to a particular fact, thing, person etc that has just been mentioned, or when it is obvious which one you are referring to: *Sometimes there's flooding, and this is why no one wants to live here.*

T

4 so *spoken* so, or to such a degree: *I haven't had this much fun since I was a kid.* ♦ *It was cold in Toronto, but it wasn't as cold as this.*

5 saying who you are used when you are saying who you are in a telephone conversation: *Hello, this is Kim Riley speaking.*

PHRASE this and that or **this, that, and the other** *spoken* various things

- **This** refers to something that you are holding or wearing, or that is nearest to you, and **that** refers to something that someone else is holding or wearing, or that is further away from you: *Do you like this shirt?* ♦ *Where did you get that hat?*
- **This** refers to things that are happening now or are just about to happen, but **that** refers to things that happened in the past, that have just ended, or that will happen in the future: *I'm enjoying this party.* ♦ *What happened at that meeting?*

thistle /ˈθɪs(ə)l/ *noun* [C] a wild plant with a thick round purple or white flower and leaves with sharp points

THNQ *abbrev* thank you: used in TEXT MESSAGES

thong /θɒŋ/ *noun* [C] **1** a long narrow piece of leather that is used for tying things **2** a piece of underwear with a very narrow piece of cloth at the back

thorn /θɔːn/ *noun* [C] a sharp point that sticks out from the stem of a plant

PHRASE a thorn in sb's side a person or thing that causes a lot of problems for someone

thorny /ˈθɔːni/ *adj* **1** difficult to deal with: *a thorny issue/question* **2** covered with thorns

thorough /ˈθʌrə/ *adj* ★
1 including everything that is possible or necessary: *a thorough investigation/examination/search* ♦ *She has a thorough understanding of the business.*
2 someone who is thorough does everything that they should and leaves nothing out: *The doctor was very thorough and asked lots of questions.*
—**thoroughness** *noun* [U]

thoroughbred /ˈθʌrəbred/ *noun* [C] a horse that belongs to a BREED (=type) that is considered of very high quality

thoroughfare /ˈθʌrəfeə/ *noun* [C] *formal* a main road through a place

thoroughly /ˈθʌrəli/ *adv* **1** very much or completely: *The children thoroughly enjoyed the show.* **2** very carefully, so that nothing is missed: *The case will be thoroughly studied before any decision is made.*

those /ðəʊz/ *grammar word* ★★★ the plural of that

though /ðəʊ/ *adv, conjunction* ★★★
1 used for introducing a statement that makes your main statement seem surprising=ALTHOUGH: *Though we are only a small country, we have a long and glorious history.* ♦ *He went on fighting even though he was wounded.*

2 but=ALTHOUGH: *I really enjoyed your lecture, though there were some parts I didn't quite understand.*
3 used when adding a statement or question that seems surprising after the previous statement: *'The Savoy's a very nice hotel.' 'Isn't it rather expensive, though?'* ♦ *The film has some interesting parts. I can't recommend it, though.*
→ AS

thought¹ /θɔːt/ *noun* ★★★
1 [C] a word, idea, or image that comes into your mind: *a comforting/sobering/chilling thought* ♦ *His mind was filled with thoughts of revenge.* ♦ *She couldn't bear the thought of seeing him again.* ♦ *The thought had crossed my mind that we were taking a big risk.* ♦ *'How about a cup of coffee?' she said, reading my thoughts* (=knowing what I was thinking).
2 [U] the mental effort that you make to understand something, make decisions, or solve problems: *Deep in thought, he did not hear the doorbell ring.* ♦ *I hope you'll give our conversation some thought* (=think about it).
3 [C] an idea or opinion about something: *Does anyone want to express their thoughts on this matter?*
4 [C/U] an intention or wish to do something: *He insists he has no thought of running for office.*

PHRASE with no thought for sth without any feeling of being worried about what might happen as a result of an action
→ FOOD

thought² the past tense and past participle of think¹

thoughtful /ˈθɔːtf(ə)l/ *adj* **1** kind and showing that you think that what other people want or need is important: *Thank you – the flowers were a very thoughtful gift.*
2 thinking seriously about something: *Beth stood there, silent and thoughtful.*
—**thoughtfully** *adv*

thoughtless /ˈθɔːtləs/ *adj* not thinking about what other people want or need
—**thoughtlessly** *adv*, **thoughtlessness** *noun* [U]

thousand /ˈθaʊz(ə)nd/ *number* ★★
1 the number 1,000
2 thousands or **a thousand** a large number or amount of people or things: *The floods have left thousands homeless.* ♦ *I still have a thousand things to do.*

thousandth /ˈθaʊz(ə)ndθ/ *number* **1** in the place or position counted as number 1,000 **2** one of 1,000 equal parts of something

thrash /θræʃ/ *verb* **1** [T] to defeat an opponent very easily in a game or competition **2** [T] to hit someone hard several times as a punishment **3** [I] to move in a violent uncontrolled way

PHRASAL VERB thrash sth out to discuss something until you find a solution or reach an agreement

thrashing /ˈθræʃɪŋ/ *noun* [C] **1** *informal* an easy victory in a game or competition **2** an act of hitting someone hard several times as a punishment

thread¹ /θred/ noun **1** [C/U] a long thin fibre used for sewing: *cotton/silk/nylon thread* ♦ *You need a longer piece of thread.* **2** [C] an idea or quality that forms a connection between things: *There is a common thread running through all the problems.* **3** [C] the raised line that curves around a screw **4** [C] *computing* a series of email messages about a particular subject

thread² /θred/ verb **1** [T] to put something long and thin through a hole or space: *Can you thread this needle for me?* **2** [I/T] to move carefully through a place, avoiding people or things that are in your way

threadbare /ˈθredˌbeə/ adj very thin because of being worn or used a lot: *a threadbare carpet/shirt*

threat /θret/ noun ★★
1 [C] someone or something that could cause harm or danger: *She is not viewed as a threat by her former employer.* ♦ *a threat to freedom* ♦ *The dispute poses a threat* (=is a threat) *to peace.*
2 [C] an occasion when someone says that they will cause you harm or problems, especially if you do not do what they tell you to do: *He would not make threats he wasn't prepared to carry out.* ♦ *After threats of legal action they stopped the building work.* ♦ *He had received several death threats.* ♦ *This isn't just an idle threat* (=a threat that is not serious).
3 [C/U] the possibility that something bad is going to happen: *Constant threat of attack makes everyday life dangerous here.* ♦ *They face the threat of terrorism every day.* ♦ *With the closure of the hospital, local jobs are under threat.*

threaten /ˈθret(ə)n/ verb ★★
1 [T] to tell someone that you will cause them harm or problems, especially in order to make them do something: *He's been threatening me for months.* ♦ **threaten to do sth** *The terrorists are threatening to kill the hostages.* ♦ **threaten sb with sth** *One man has been threatened with legal action.*
2 [T] to be likely to harm or destroy something: *Many workers feel that their jobs are threatened.* ♦ *Nearly 1,000 of the world's bird species are threatened with extinction.* ♦ **threaten to do sth** *Nuclear testing threatens to destroy our environment.*
3 [I] if something bad or unpleasant threatens, it is likely to happen or to affect you: *Rain was threatening, and it had turned cold.*
—**threatening** adj, **threateningly** adv

three /θriː/ number the number 3

three-dimensional /ˌθriː daɪˈmenʃ(ə)nəl/ adj not flat, but able to be measured in height, depth, and width

three-quarters noun [plural] three of four equal parts of something: *It took an hour and three-quarters to get home.*

threshold /ˈθreʃhəʊld/ noun [C] the point at which a limit is reached or a rule starts to apply
PHRASE **on the threshold of sth** starting a new stage in your life, or soon to discover something

threw the past tense of **throw¹**

thrifty /ˈθrɪfti/ adj careful about how you spend money so that you do not waste any

thrill¹ /θrɪl/ noun [C] **1** a sudden feeling of being very pleased and excited **2** something that makes you feel excited

thrill² /θrɪl/ verb [T] to make someone feel very pleased and excited

thrilled /θrɪld/ adj very pleased and excited: *We are thrilled that Kevin is going to join the team.*

thriller /ˈθrɪlə/ noun [C] a book, play, or film that tells an exciting story

thrilling /ˈθrɪlɪŋ/ adj extremely exciting

thrive /θraɪv/ verb [I] to become very successful, happy, or healthy —**thriving** adj: *a thriving economy*
PHRASAL VERB **ˈthrive on sth** to become successful or happy in a particular situation, especially a situation that other people would not enjoy: *Some couples thrive on conflict.*

throat /θrəʊt/ noun [C] ★★
1 the area at the back of your mouth and inside your neck: *She's in bed with a throat infection.* ♦ *Have we got any medicine for a sore throat?*
2 the front part of your neck: *The bigger man grabbed him by the throat.* —*picture* → C14

throb /θrɒb/ verb [I] **1** if a painful part of your body throbs, the pain comes and goes in a fast regular pattern **2** to make a repeated low sound: *Loud dance music throbbed in the air.* —**throb** noun [C]

throes /θrəʊz/ noun **in the throes of sth** involved in a difficult or unpleasant situation or activity

thrombosis /θrɒmˈbəʊsɪs/ noun [C/U] a serious medical condition in which your blood gets thicker and forms a CLOT that stops the blood from flowing normally

throne /θrəʊn/ noun **1** [C] a special chair that a king or queen sits on **2** **the throne** [singular] the position of being a king or queen

throng¹ /θrɒŋ/ noun [C] *literary* a large crowd of people

throng² /θrɒŋ/ verb [I/T] if people throng somewhere, a lot of them go there

throttle¹ /ˈθrɒt(ə)l/ verb [T] to hurt or kill someone by squeezing their throat so that they cannot breathe

throttle² /ˈθrɒt(ə)l/ noun [C] a piece of equipment that controls how fast a vehicle is moving by controlling the amount of fuel going into the engine

through /θruː/ grammar word ★★★

Through can be:
■ a preposition: *They were riding through a forest.*

■ an **adverb**: *There's a hole in the roof where the rain comes through.*
■ an **adjective**: *I'm through with this job.*

1 from one end or side to the other from one side of a hole, object, or area to the other: *The railway runs through a tunnel.* ♦ *The man at the gate would not let us through.* ♦ *Workers had cut through an electrical cable while they were digging.* ♦ *The path climbs steeply through the trees.*

2 during a period of time during the whole of a period of time until the end of it: *He lay awake* **all through** *the night.* ♦ *The training programme will continue* **through to** *mid-April.*

3 by means of sth by means of something, or because of something: *Most accidents occur through human error.* ♦ *skills that we can only learn through experience* ♦ *Concert tickets are being sold through the Internet.*

4 communicating by phone used for saying that you are connected to someone by phone: *I tried to phone the mayor's office, but I couldn't* **get through.** ♦ *Can you* **put** *me* **through** *to Mr Pemberton, please?*

5 affecting every part affecting every part of someone or something: *A rumour spread through the camp.* ♦ *Problems extend through the entire system.* ♦ *When she heard Bruno's voice, it sent a chill of terror through her.*

6 reading or looking at every part reading or looking at every part of something, from the beginning to the end of it: *You'd better read through the instructions carefully.* ♦ *I've been searching through all the files, but I can't find Hamilton's letter.*

7 finished finished doing or using something: *I'm not sure what time he'll be through with his meeting.*

throughout /θruːˈaʊt/ adv, preposition ★
1 in every part of a place: *The hotel has recently been redecorated throughout.* ♦ *Pollution is a serious problem in major cities throughout the world.*
2 during the whole of a period of time or an event: *House prices continued to rise throughout the 1980s.*

throw¹ /θrəʊ/ (past tense **threw** /θruː/; past participle **thrown** /θrəʊn/) verb ★★★

1 send through air	**5** look etc in direction
2 put sth somewhere	**6** put sb/sth in bad state
3 move your body	**+ PHRASES**
4 confuse sb	**+ PHRASAL VERBS**

1 [I/T] to make something leave your hand and move through the air, by moving your arm quickly: **throw sth at sb/sth** *Kids were throwing stones at the windows.* ♦ **throw sth to sb** *She threw the ball to the little boy.* ♦ **throw sb sth** *Can you throw me that rope?*
2 [T] to put something somewhere carelessly: *She hastily threw her books into the cupboard.*
3 [T] to suddenly move your body or a part of your body: *Throwing back his head, he started laughing.*

4 [T] if something throws you, it makes you confused because you were not expecting it and you did not know how to deal with it
5 [T] to suddenly look, smile etc in a particular direction: *Marco threw an angry glance at her.*
6 [T] to cause someone or something to be in a particular state or situation, especially a bad one: *A single computer problem can* **throw** *the whole office* **into chaos.**

PHRASES **throw a party** to organize a party, especially in your own home
throw a punch to hit someone with your FIST (=closed hand)
throw yourself into sth to start giving all of your attention and energy to something: *After my girlfriend left me, I threw myself into my work.*

PHRASAL VERBS **throw sth away 1** to get rid of something that you no longer want: *Have you thrown the papers away?* **2** to waste something such as an opportunity or advantage: *They lost the game after throwing away a two-goal lead.*
throw sth in to include something extra with something that you are selling, without asking for more money
throw sb out to force someone to leave a place or group: *Several people were* **thrown out of** *the party.*
throw sth out *same as* **throw sth away** 1: *I've thrown out my old boots.*
throw (sth) up *informal* if you throw up, or if you throw something up, food and drink comes back up from your stomach and out of your mouth = VOMIT
throw sth up *British* to produce something new or unexpected: *This system has thrown up a few problems.*

throw² /θrəʊ/ noun [C] **1** an action of throwing something such as a ball **2** a large piece of cloth that you put over a chair, bed etc

throwback /ˈθrəʊbæk/ noun [singular] someone or something that seems to belong to an earlier period of time

'throw-in noun [C] in football, an occasion when a player throws the ball back onto the field after it has gone out —*picture* → c15

thrown the past participle of **throw**

thru /θruː/ adv, preposition an informal way of writing 'through'

thrush /θrʌʃ/ noun [C] a brown bird with light spots on its breast

thrust¹ /θrʌst/ (past tense and past participle **thrust**) verb [T] to put something somewhere with a quick hard push: *A reporter thrust a microphone under her nose.*

thrust² /θrʌst/ noun **1** [singular] **the thrust of sth** the main idea or intention of something such as a document, speech, or policy **2** [C] a quick hard push

thud /θʌd/ noun [C] a low sound that is made by something heavy falling or hitting something —**thud** verb [I]

thug /θʌg/ noun [C] someone who behaves in an unpleasant and violent way, especially in a public place

thumb¹ /θʌm/ noun [C] ★ the part like a wide finger at the side of your hand: *She held the jewel carefully between her finger and thumb.* —*picture* → C14

PHRASE under sb's thumb completely controlled by someone else

thumb² /θʌm/ **PHRASAL VERB** 'thumb **through sth** to quickly turn the pages of a book, magazine, or newspaper

thumbnail /'θʌm,neɪl/ noun [C] **1** the nail on your thumb **2** a small picture of something shown on a computer screen, especially on a WEB PAGE

thump¹ /θʌmp/ verb **1** [T] to hit someone or something with your FIST (=closed hand) =PUNCH **2** [I] if your heart is thumping, you can feel it beating very fast, for example because you are frightened or excited

thump² /θʌmp/ noun [C] **1** a low loud sound that is made when something heavy hits something else: *He brought his hand down on the table with a thump.* **2** an action of hitting someone or something with your FIST (=closed hand)=PUNCH

thunder¹ /'θʌndə/ noun [U] the loud noise that you sometimes hear in the sky during a storm

thunder² /'θʌndə/ verb [I] **1** if it thunders, you hear thunder in the sky **2** to make a lot of noise while moving somewhere fast: *An express train thundered through the station.*

thunderous /'θʌnd(ə)rəs/ adj very loud

thunderstorm /'θʌndə,stɔːm/ noun [C] a storm with THUNDER (=loud noise) and LIGHTNING (=flashes of light) in the sky

Thurs. abbrev Thursday

Thursday /'θɜːzdeɪ/ noun [C/U] ★★★ the day after Wednesday and before Friday: *The election is being held on a Thursday.* ♦ *I had lunch with Joe on Thursday.* ♦ *Adam has his piano lesson on Thursdays* (=every Thursday).

thus /ðʌs/ adv formal ★
1 as a result of the fact that you have just mentioned=HENCE, THEREFORE: *Fewer pupils will attend the schools, and they will thus need fewer teachers.*
2 by the method that has been mentioned: *The oil producers will raise prices, thus increasing their profits.*

thwart /θwɔːt/ verb [T] formal to prevent someone from doing something that they were planning to do

thyme /taɪm/ noun [U] a small plant with very small leaves, used for adding flavour to food

tiara /ti'ɑːrə/ noun [C] a piece of jewellery that a woman wears on her head on formal occasions

tic /tɪk/ noun [C] a sudden movement of a muscle that you cannot control

tick¹ /tɪk/ verb **1** [I] if a clock or watch ticks, it makes a quiet sound every second **2** [T] British to mark something with the symbol ✓ to show that it is correct or that you have dealt with it

PHRASE what makes sb tick informal the basic

aspects of someone's personality that make them behave the way they do

PHRASAL VERBS ,tick sb 'off informal **1** British to speak angrily to someone who has done something wrong **2** American to annoy someone

,tick sth 'off British to put the symbol ✓ next to something on a list to show that you have dealt with it

,tick 'over British informal to operate steadily but not very well

tick² /tɪk/ noun [C] **1** British the symbol ✓ that you write next to an answer to show that it is correct, or next to something on a list to show that you have dealt with it **2** the quiet sound that some clocks and watches make every second **3** an insect that sucks blood

ticket /'tɪkɪt/ noun [C] ★★★
1 a piece of paper that shows that you have paid to do something such as go to a concert, visit a museum, or travel on a train, bus, plane etc: *a cinema/theatre/ match ticket* ♦ *We'll send your tickets a week before your flight.*
2 a piece of paper that says you must pay an amount of money as a punishment for breaking a traffic law: *a speeding ticket*

tickle¹ /'tɪk(ə)l/ verb **1** [T] to move your fingers gently on someone's skin in order to make them laugh **2** [I/T] if a part of your body tickles, or if something that touches your skin tickles it, you have an uncomfortable feeling on your skin

tickle² /'tɪk(ə)l/ noun [singular] a slightly sore feeling in your throat that makes you want to cough

tidal /'taɪd(ə)l/ adj connected with the regular movement of the sea towards and away from the land

'tidal ,wave noun [C] a very large wave that causes a lot of damage when it hits the land

tide¹ /taɪd/ noun [C] the regular movement of the sea towards and away from the land

tide² /taɪd/ **PHRASAL VERB ,tide sb 'over** to help someone to get to the end of a difficult period of time, especially by giving them money

tidy¹ /'taɪdi/ adj ★
1 a tidy room, desk etc has everything in the correct place or arranged properly =NEAT ≠ UNTIDY: *Try and keep your room tidy.*
2 a tidy person always puts their things away in the correct place ≠ UNTIDY —**tidily** adv, **tidiness** noun [U]

tidy² /'taɪdi/ verb [I/T] to make a place look better by putting things in the correct place
PHRASAL VERBS ,tidy sth a'way to put something back in its correct place after you have used it
,tidy yourself 'up to make yourself look better by washing your face, brushing your hair etc
,tidy (sth) 'up same as **tidy²**

tie¹ /taɪ/ (present participle **tying**) verb ★★
1 [T] to fasten two ends of a piece of string,

rope etc together with a knot, or to fasten things together with string, rope etc: *Sally bent down to tie her shoelaces.* ♦ **tie sth to sth** *They tied one end of the rope to a tree.* ♦ **tie sth together** *Tie the newspapers together before you throw them away.*

2 [T] to form a close connection between people or things: *This series **ties together** events from the past and present.* ♦ *Portugal's economy **is closely tied** to Spain's.*

3 [T] if something ties you to a particular place or situation, you cannot leave it: *Many young mothers feel **tied to** the home and children.*

4 [I/T] if two players or teams tie, they both have the same number of points at the end of a game or competition= DRAW

PHRASAL VERBS ,**tie sb** '**down** to stop someone from being free to do what they want: *I don't want a relationship that ties me down.* ,**tie** '**in with sth** if one statement, fact etc ties in with another, they both contain the same information and are therefore likely to be true

,**tie sb** '**up** to tie a rope etc tightly around someone so that they cannot move or escape

,**tie sth** '**up 1** to tie the ends of something together **2** to tie an animal to something such as a post so that it cannot get away

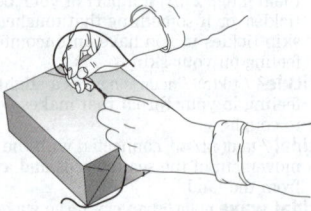

tie

tie² /taɪ/ noun [C] ★

1 a long narrow piece of coloured cloth that a man wears around his neck with a shirt: *a silk tie* ♦ *Do you have to wear a tie for work?* —*picture* → C4

2 a relationship or connection between people or things: *The treaty should **strengthen ties** between the two countries.*

3 a short piece of string or wire that is used for fastening something

4 a result of a game or competition in which each person or team has the same number of points, votes etc= DRAW: *The game finished in a tie.*

tiebreaker /'taɪˌbreɪkə/ or **tiebreak** /'taɪˌbreɪk/ noun [C] an extra part of a game or competition to decide who will win when the players have the same number of points

tied up /ˌtaɪd 'ʌp/ adj **1** very busy **2** if your money is tied up in something, it is being used for that thing and you cannot use it for anything else

'**tie-in** noun [C] *business* a product such as a toy or book that is connected with a successful film or television programme

tier /tɪə/ noun [C] **1** one of several levels in an organization or system: *the lower tiers of management* **2** one of several rows or layers of something that are all at different heights: *a wedding cake with three tiers*

tiff /tɪf/ noun [C] *informal* a minor argument

tiger /'taɪɡə/ noun [C] a large Asian wild animal that has yellowish fur with black lines. It is a member of the cat family. —*picture* → C12

tight¹ /taɪt/ adj ★★

1 close against body	**5** stretched straight/flat
2 holding sth firmly	**6** of bend on a road
3 controlled carefully	**+ PHRASE**
4 only just enough	

1 fitting closely around your body or part of your body ≠ LOOSE: *a tight shirt/dress*
2 holding someone or fastening something very firmly ≠ LOOSE: *a tight knot* ♦ *Baxter kept **a tight grip** on the prisoner's arm.*
3 controlled very carefully and strictly ≠ LAX: *Security has been very **tight** throughout the Prince's visit.*
4 if something such as time or money is tight, you have only just enough of it: *holidays for people on **a tight budget***
5 if something such as cloth or rope is tight, it is stretched so that it is completely straight or flat
6 a tight bend on a road is difficult to drive round because it curves a lot

PHRASE **keep a tight grip/hold on sth** to control something in a very strict way
—**tightly** adv: *Keep the windows tightly closed.* —**tightness** noun [U]

tight² /taɪt/ adv very firmly: *She held on tight to the handrail.*

tighten /'taɪt(ə)n/ verb **1** [T] to turn something such as a screw or lid until it is tight and you cannot turn it any more ≠ LOOSEN **2** [I/T] to become tighter, or to make something become tighter ≠ LOOSEN: *He tightened his hold on the steering wheel.*

PHRASE **tighten your belt** to spend less money

PHRASAL VERB ,**tighten (sth)** '**up** to be stricter or more serious about something such as a policy or rule: *Airport security has been tightened up since September 11.*

,**tight-** '**knit** or ,**tightly-** '**knit** adj a tight-knit community or family have very strong and close relationships with each other

tight-lipped /ˌtaɪt 'lɪpt/ adj *mainly journalism* refusing to comment on something

tightrope /'taɪtˌrəʊp/ noun [C] a piece of rope or wire high above the ground that a CIRCUS performer walks along

PHRASE **walk a tightrope** to be in a difficult situation that you have to deal with very carefully, because even a small mistake could have very bad results

tights /taɪts/ noun [plural] a piece of women's clothing that tightly covers the feet and legs up to the waist —*picture* → C5

tile¹ /taɪl/ noun [C] a flat piece of baked clay or stone that is used for covering a roof, floor, or wall —*picture* → C1

tile[2] /taɪl/ verb [T] **1** to cover a roof, floor, or wall with tiles **2** *computing* to arrange different WINDOWS on a computer screen so that you can see all of them next to each other

tiled /taɪld/ adj covered with tiles

till[1] /tɪl/ preposition, conjunction ★ until: *You'll have to wait till tomorrow.* ♦ *Just sit here till I come back.*

till[2] /tɪl/ noun [C] a piece of equipment that is used in shops for adding up the amount of money that someone has to pay and for keeping the money in=CASH REGISTER

tilt /tɪlt/ verb [I/T] to move, or to move something, so that one side is lower than the other: *The tray was tilted at an angle.* —**tilt** noun [singular]

timber /ˈtɪmbə/ noun [U] **1** trees that are used for producing wood **2** wood that is used for building houses or making furniture

time[1] /taɪm/ noun ★★★

1 hours, years etc	**6** when sth happens
2 measurement on clock	**7** time available/needed
3 period	**8** part of history/sb's life
4 occasion/experience	**9** in a race
5 moment/situation	**✦** PHRASES

1 [U] the quantity that is measured in minutes, hours, days, years etc: *Einstein tried to define the relationship between space and time.* ♦ *Time seemed to **pass** more quickly than before.*

2 [singular/U] the hours, minutes etc as shown on a clock: *Do you know what time it is?* ♦ *What time does the show start?* ♦ *Can your daughter **tell the time** yet* (=is she able to say what time is shown on a clock)*?*

3 [C/U] a particular period of minutes, hours, days, years etc: *She thought about it for a **long time**.* ♦ *She left a **short time** ago.* ♦ *How much **time** did it **take** to get here?* ♦ *I've been thinking of changing my job **for some time*** (=for a fairly long time).* ♦ *There have been improvements in the **length of time** patients have to wait for treatment.*

4 [C] an occasion on which you do something or on which something happens: *It was **the first time** we'd met.* ♦ *The next time you need financial advice, come and see me.* ♦ *Did you **have a good time** at camp?*

5 [singular/U] the moment or situation when something happens: *I was still living with my parents **at that time**.* ♦ *By the time we arrived, the other guests were already there.* ♦ *When would be **a good time** to discuss the proposal?* ♦ *It seemed like **the right time** to make the change.*

6 [U] the particular point when something should happen: *Is it closing time already?* ♦ *Come on, everyone. It's time for dinner.* ♦ *Did your plane arrive **on time**?* ♦ *it is time* **(that)** *It's time you children went to bed.*

7 [U] time that you have available for doing something in: *She will **have less time** to spend with family and friends now.* ♦ *Come and see me next week, if you get the time.* ♦ *I should be able to **find time** to phone him tomorrow.*

8 [C] a period in history or in someone's life: *The fort was built in Roman times.* ♦ *a time of political instability* ♦ *I thoroughly enjoyed my time as a teacher.*

9 [C] the amount of time that someone takes to finish a race: *She's cut two seconds off her previous best time.*

PHRASES about time 1 *spoken* used for showing that you are annoyed because something has happened later than it should: *Here they are, and about time too.* **2** used for saying that someone should do something soon: *Isn't it about time we got a new car?*

ahead of time at an earlier time than people expected

ahead of your/its etc time much more modern or advanced than most other people or things: *As an artist, he was years ahead of his time.*

all the time 1 often: *It's a very good restaurant. We go there all the time.* **2** continuously: *It rained all the time they were there.*

at a time used for saying how many things there are in each group or on each occasion: *Deal with each question separately, one at a time.*

at all times *formal* always: *Please keep your bags with you at all times.*

at one time in the past, but not now: *At one time, that kind of thing would have made me really angry.*

at times sometimes but not often: *She was fun to be with at times.*

before your time used for saying that you are too young to remember something: *These styles were a bit before my time.*

for days/weeks etc at a time continuously for a period of several days/weeks etc

for the time being at the present time, but not permanently

from time to time sometimes, but not often

have no time for to dislike someone or something

in no time (at all) or **in next to no time** very soon or very quickly

in time 1 early enough to do something: *I want to be home in time for dinner.* ♦ *We got to the airport just in time.* ♦ *in time to do sth Luckily, they got there in time to warn him about what had happened.* **2** after a fairly long period of time: *He'll forget about it in time.*

most of the time usually, or very often

of all time used for talking about people or things that are better than all others that have existed: *the greatest boxer of all time*

take your time 1 to spend too much time doing something: *They're taking their time over that report, aren't they?* **2** *spoken* used for telling someone that they do not need to hurry: *You don't have to do everything at once. Just take your time.*

time after time or **time and again** happening so often that you become annoyed

→ BEST, FOR, HARD[1]

time[2] /taɪm/ verb [T] **1** to arrange something

so that it happens at a particular time: *The exhibition has been timed to coincide with the publication of her new book.* **2** to use a clock to measure how long something takes or how often something happens: *a simple device for timing the human heartbeat*

'time ,bomb noun [C] something that is likely to have a sudden and bad effect on a situation in the future

time-consuming /'taɪm kən,sjuːmɪŋ/ adj something that is time-consuming takes a long time to do

'time ,frame noun [C] the period of time in which something happens or should be done=TIMESCALE

timeless /'taɪmləs/ adj not affected by time or changes in fashion

'time ,limit noun [C] an amount of time in which you must do something

timely /'taɪmli/ adj happening at the most suitable time ≠ UNTIMELY: *a timely reminder*

time 'off noun [U] time when you are not at work or at school

time 'out noun [U] a period of time when you stop working or stop doing what you usually do: *It's very beneficial to take time out to relax each day.*

timer /'taɪmə/ noun [C] a piece of equipment used for measuring time, or for turning a machine on or off at a particular time

times /taɪmz/ preposition *informal* multiplied by: *Two times four is eight.*

timescale /'taɪm,skeɪl/ noun [C] the period of time in which something happens or should be done=TIME FRAME

timetable /'taɪm,teɪb(ə)l/ noun [C] **1** a plan that shows the dates and times when something will take place=SCHEDULE **2** *British* a list of the times when buses, trains etc arrive and leave

'time ,zone noun [C] one of the areas that the world is divided into for measuring time

timid /'tɪmɪd/ adj shy and nervous —**timidity** /tɪ'mɪdəti/ noun [U], **timidly** adv

timing /'taɪmɪŋ/ noun **1** [C/U] the date or time when something happens or is planned to happen: *They objected to the timing of the election.* **2** [U] the ability to do or say things at the right moment

tin /tɪn/ noun ★
  1 [U] a soft light silver metal: *There used to be tin mines all around this area.*
  2 [C] *British* a closed metal container for food =CAN: *a tin of soup* ♦ *I bought three tins of beans.*
  3 [C] a metal container with a lid, used for storing things: *a cake tin*
  4 [C] *British* an open metal container in which you cook food in an oven: *a roasting/baking tin*

tinfoil /'tɪn,fɔɪl/ noun [U] a substance that looks like shiny silver paper, used for wrapping and covering food

tinge /tɪndʒ/ noun [C] a very small amount of a colour, feeling, or quality: *a tinge of sadness/nostalgia*

tinged /tɪndʒd/ adj containing a very small

amount of something: *white flowers tinged with blue*

tingle /'tɪŋɡ(ə)l/ verb [I] if a part of your body tingles, it stings slightly, for example because it is very cold or hot —**tingle** noun [C]

tinker /'tɪŋkə/ or **,tinker a'round** verb [I] to make small changes to something in order to improve or repair it

tinkle /'tɪŋk(ə)l/ verb [I] to make a high ringing sound: *Silver bells tinkled.* —**tinkle** noun [singular]

tinned /tɪnd/ adj *British* tinned food has been preserved in a metal container=CANNED

'tin ,opener noun [C] *British* an object that you use for opening TINS of food —*picture* → C2

tinsel /'tɪns(ə)l/ noun [U] long thin pieces of shiny paper that you use as a Christmas decoration

tint¹ /tɪnt/ noun [C] a small amount of a particular colour

tint² /tɪnt/ verb [T] to change the colour of your hair

tinted /'tɪntɪd/ adj slightly coloured: *a car with tinted windows*

tiny /'taɪni/ adj ★★ extremely small: *She is one of a tiny minority of female motoring journalists.* ♦ *The floor was covered in tiny bits of paper.* ♦ *a tiny little baby*

tip¹ /tɪp/ noun ★

1 narrow/pointed end	4 for rubbish
2 extra money you give	5 dirty/untidy place
3 useful suggestion	+ PHRASES

1 [C] a narrow or pointed end, especially of something long or thin: *the tip of your nose/finger* ♦ *The village is on the southern tip of the island.*
2 [C] an amount of money that you give to someone in addition to the price of a service: *Shall we leave a tip for the waiter?*
3 [C] a useful suggestion or piece of information that someone gives you: *The booklet gives some good tips on getting the most out of your software.*
4 [C] *British* a place where you take rubbish and leave it=DUMP
5 [singular] *British informal* a very dirty or untidy place

  PHRASES **on the tip of your tongue** if a word, name etc is on the tip of your tongue, you know it but cannot remember it at the time you are speaking
  the tip of the iceberg a bad situation that shows that a much more serious problem exists: *The recent riots are just the tip of the iceberg.*

tip² /tɪp/ verb **1** [T] to pour something from a container: *She tipped the sand out of her bucket.* **2** [I/T] to move into a position that is at an angle rather than upright, or to put something into a position like this: *He tipped his chair back and looked at me.* **3** [I/T] to give someone an amount of money in addition to what you owe for a service: *Don't forget to tip the driver.* **4** [T] to say who you think will get a particular job or be successful at something: *She is being tipped to take over from the managing director when he retires.*

PHRASE **tip the balance/scales** to give someone or something an advantage, so that they get or achieve something

PHRASAL VERBS **tip sb off** to give someone a warning, or to give them secret information about something

tip (sth) over if something tips over, or if someone tips it over, it falls onto its side: *Be careful that the vase doesn't tip over. ♦ He tipped his drink over.*

tip-off noun [C] *informal* a warning or secret information that you give to someone

Tipp-Ex /ˈtɪpeks/ *British trademark* a white liquid that you can use for covering mistakes in something that you are writing or typing

tipsy /ˈtɪpsi/ adj *informal* slightly drunk

tiptoe¹ /ˈtɪpˌtəʊ/ noun **on tiptoe(s)** if you stand or walk on tiptoe, you stand or walk with only the front part of your foot touching the ground

tiptoe² /ˈtɪpˌtəʊ/ verb [I] to walk very quietly with only the front part of your foot touching the ground

tirade /taɪˈreɪd/ noun [C] a long angry speech criticizing someone or something

tire¹ /ˈtaɪə/ verb [I/T] to become tired, or to make someone feel tired

PHRASE **tire of sb/sth** to become bored with someone or something

PHRASAL VERB **tire sb out** to make someone feel very tired

tire² /ˈtaɪə/ the American spelling of **tyre**

tired /ˈtaɪəd/ adj ★★★ needing to rest or sleep: *Your mother looked tired. ♦ Kids can suddenly get very tired after playing for a time.*

PHRASE **tired of (doing) sth** not wanting something, or not wanting to do something, because you are bored or annoyed with it: *I'm tired of hearing about politics.*

tireless /ˈtaɪələs/ adj *showing approval* working very hard to achieve something, with a lot of energy and determination —**tirelessly** adv

tiresome /ˈtaɪəs(ə)m/ adj making you feel bored or annoyed

tiring /ˈtaɪərɪŋ/ adj making you feel tired

tissue /ˈtɪʃuː, ˈtɪsjuː/ noun **1** [U] the substance that animal and plant cells are made of: *brain/muscle tissue* **2** [C] a piece of soft thin paper that you use for wiping your nose: *a box of tissues*

tit /tɪt/ noun [C] *impolite* a woman's breast

PHRASE **tit for tat** *informal* something that you do to harm someone because they have harmed you

titbit /ˈtɪtbɪt/ noun [C] *British* **1** a piece of interesting information **2** a small piece of food

title /ˈtaɪt(ə)l/ noun [C] ★★★
1 the name of a book, film, or other work of art: *What's the title of her new book?*
2 a word or abbreviation that is used before someone's name, for example 'Doctor', 'General', or 'Mrs'

3 a name for someone's job within a company or organization: *His new title is senior vice president.*
4 the position of a winner in a sports competition: *She's won several important singles titles this year.*

title role noun [C] the main part for someone in a film, play, or opera, that has the same name as its title

titter /ˈtɪtə/ verb [I] to laugh quietly because you are nervous or embarrassed —**titter** noun [C]

T-junction noun [C] *British* a place where one road joins another and forms the shape of the letter T

to /*weak* tə, tʊ, *strong* tuː/ grammar word ★★★

> **To can be:**
> ■ used before the basic form of a verb to form the infinitive: *I want to go home.*
> ■ a preposition: *We drove to Newport.*

1 part of an infinitive used before a verb for forming an infinitive, often when you are stating the purpose of an action, or used without the following verb instead of an infinitive: *I hope to see you next week. ♦ The system is very easy to understand. ♦ Nobody came to help me. ♦ You don't need to come if you don't want to.*

2 going somewhere used for saying the place or event where someone or something goes: *She rushed to the phone. ♦ There are daily flights to Boston. ♦ the road to the farm ♦ Robert hates going to parties.*

3 for showing who is affected by an action used for saying who or what is told, given, or shown something, or is treated or affected in a particular way: *Prizes were presented to the winners. ♦ I have already explained to everyone what the problem is. ♦ They were very kind to my mother when she was ill. ♦ Look what you've done to my new carpet! ♦ cruelty to animals*

4 in a particular direction used for saying in which direction someone or something is, is pointing, or is looking: *She pointed to a notice on the wall. ♦ Henry was standing with his back to me. ♦ There was a large bookcase to the left of the fireplace. ♦ a large township just to the south of Johannesburg*

5 in a particular relationship with sb/sth used for explaining a relationship between people or things: *a political party with ties to a terrorist group ♦ She is personal assistant to the Managing Director.*

6 when sth is connected or fastened used for stating where something is fastened or where a connection is: *The carpet had been nailed to the floor. ♦ Your computer is connected to the main network.*

7 when sth changes or develops used for saying what stage of development or change is reached: *When will all this suffering come to an end? ♦ an event that brought matters to crisis point*

8 as far as as far as a particular point or limit: *The cancer had spread to his lungs. ♦ How far is it from here to Oxford?*

T

9 until until a particular time or event: *Only another 18 days to the final exam!* ♦ *The shop stays open from 7 am to 9 pm.*

10 before the hour used when telling the time, for saying how many minutes it is before the hour: *I'll meet you at quarter to six* (=5.45).

11 for stating sb's opinion used for saying whose opinion, attitude, or knowledge is being referred to: *To most of us, work is an unpleasant necessity.* ♦ *It seems to me that there has been a lack of discipline.*

12 for showing how numbers are related used for showing the relationship between two numbers or amounts: *You get about ten of these apples to the kilo.*

13 for giving a score used for saying what the score is in a game: *Our team won by five goals to three.*

14 for showing a possible range used for showing one of the ends of a possible range: *Only about 20 to 25 per cent of the population voted for the government.* ♦ *the numbers from one to ten*

15 needed for sth used for showing that something is an important or necessary part of something else: *the answer to an important question* ♦ *the keys to my desk*

16 causing a particular reaction used for saying what your reaction is when something happens: *To her surprise, she saw that he was crying.*

PHRASES **(all) to yourself** not sharing something with anyone else: *My parents were away, so I had the house to myself.*
to and fro in one direction and then back again =BACKWARDS AND FORWARDS

toad /təʊd/ noun [C] a small animal that is similar to a FROG but has brown skin and lives mainly on land

toadstool /ˈtəʊdˌstuːl/ noun [C] a wild plant that is similar to a MUSHROOM and is often poisonous

toast¹ /təʊst/ noun **1** [U] bread that has been heated until its outside is brown and hard **2** [C] an occasion when people all drink together and say someone's name in order to express their admiration or good wishes

toast² /təʊst/ verb [T] **1** to make bread into toast **2** to drink a toast to someone

toaster /ˈtəʊstə/ noun [C] a piece of electrical equipment that you use for making toast —*picture* → C2

tobacco /təˈbækəʊ/ noun [U] a substance that people smoke in cigarettes

toboggan /təˈbɒgən/ noun [C] a small vehicle without wheels that is used for moving over snow

today¹ /təˈdeɪ/ adv ★★★
1 on this day: *I'm working today.* ♦ *Did you get any post today?*
2 at the period of time that is happening now: *Teenagers today are so sophisticated.*

today² /təˈdeɪ/ noun [U] **1** this day: *Today is Wednesday.* **2** the present period of time: *Think about today, not yesterday!* ♦ *Today's computers are so much more powerful than those of five years ago.*

toddler /ˈtɒdlə/ noun [C] a very young child who is learning how to walk —*picture* → CHILD

toe¹ /təʊ/ noun [C] ★
1 one of the five individual parts at the end of your foot: *Vera slipped off her shoes and wriggled her toes.* —*picture* → C13
2 the part of a shoe or sock that covers your toes: *shoes with pointed toes*
PHRASE **keep sb on their toes** to make someone concentrate so that they are ready to deal with any problem

toe² /təʊ/ verb **toe the line** to accept rules and obey people in authority

TOEFL /ˈtəʊf(ə)l/ trademark Test of English as a Foreign Language: an English language test for speakers of other languages that shows how well they speak English

TOEIC /ˈtəʊɪk/ trademark Test of English for International Communication: an English language test for speakers of other languages that shows how well they speak English

toenail /ˈtəʊˌneɪl/ noun [C] the hard part over the top of a toe

toffee /ˈtɒfi/ noun [C/U] a sticky brown sweet made by cooking together sugar, butter, and water

tofu /ˈtəʊfuː/ noun [U] a soft white food made from SOYA BEANS

together¹ /təˈgeðə/ adv ★★★
1 if you put or join two or more things together, you combine or connect them: *Mix together the flour, eggs, and water.* ♦ *small patches of cloth sewn together* ♦ *Now add the numbers together.*
2 near each other, or in one place: *Get all your things together.* ♦ *The book brings together essays by several different authors.*
3 with each other: *Kevin, Jack, and Dave share a house together.* ♦ *Bob and I worked together many years ago.* ♦ *Are Tanya and Pete still together* (=still in a romantic relationship)?
4 at the same time: *Everyone arrived together at around four o'clock.*

together² /təˈgeðə/ adj spoken confident, sensible, and clear about what you are doing

togetherness /təˈgeðənəs/ noun [U] a feeling of friendship and happiness in a close relationship

toggle /ˈtɒg(ə)l/ verb [I/T] computing to move from one computer operation or program to another and back again by using one key or COMMAND (=instruction)

toil /tɔɪl/ verb [I] literary to work very hard —**toil** noun [U]

toilet /ˈtɔɪlət/ noun [C] ★
1 a structure like a seat over a hole where you get rid of waste from your body
2 British a room that contains a toilet

toilet paper noun [U] soft thin paper that you use to clean yourself after using the toilet

toiletries /ˈtɔɪlətriz/ noun [plural] things such as soap and SHAMPOO that you use for keeping yourself clean

toilet roll noun [C] *British* a tube that has TOILET PAPER wrapped around it

token[1] /ˈtəʊkən/ noun [C] **1** *British* a piece of paper that you can exchange for goods of a particular value in a shop: *a book/gift token* **2** a small flat round piece of metal or plastic that you use instead of money in some machines **3** *formal* something that you do or give as a way of showing your feelings towards someone: *a token of your appreciation/gratitude/respect*

token[2] /ˈtəʊkən/ adj done in order to pretend to people that you are trying to achieve something: *a token gesture*

   PHRASE **a token woman/black/gay etc** *showing disapproval* someone who is included in a group in order to make people believe that the group is trying to include all types of people

told the past tense and past participle of **tell**

tolerable /ˈtɒl(ə)rəb(ə)l/ adj *formal* acceptable but not very good ≠ INTOLERABLE —**tolerably** adv

tolerance /ˈtɒlərəns/ noun [U] the attitude of someone who is willing to accept other people's beliefs, way of life etc without criticizing them, even if they disagree with them ≠ INTOLERANCE: *We need to show greater tolerance towards each other.*

tolerant /ˈtɒlərənt/ adj willing to accept other people's beliefs, way of life etc without criticizing them, even if you disagree with them ≠ INTOLERANT

tolerate /ˈtɒlə.reɪt/ verb [T] **1** to allow someone to do something that you do not like or approve of: *He won't tolerate anyone questioning his decisions.* **2** to accept something that is unpleasant without becoming impatient or angry: *They have tolerated poor working conditions for too long.* **3** if plants or animals tolerate particular conditions, they are able to exist in those conditions —**toleration** /ˌtɒləˈreɪʃ(ə)n/ noun [U]

toll[1] /təʊl/ noun **1** [C] an amount of money that you pay to use a bridge or road **2** [singular] the total number of people who have been killed or hurt: *The death toll from the earthquake is not yet known.*

   PHRASE **take its toll** or **take a heavy toll** to gradually harm or damage someone or something

toll[2] /təʊl/ verb [I/T] if you toll a bell, or if it tolls, it makes a slow repeated sound

tomato /təˈmɑːtəʊ/ (plural **tomatoes**) noun [C] a round red fruit that you eat raw in salads or cooked as a vegetable —*picture* → C11

tomb /tuːm/ noun [C] a place or large stone structure where a dead person is buried

tomboy /ˈtɒm.bɔɪ/ noun [C] a girl who behaves and dresses in a way that people think is more suitable for a boy

tombstone /ˈtuːm.stəʊn/ noun [C] a large stone that is put over the place where a dead person is buried

tomcat /ˈtɒm.kæt/ noun [C] a male cat

tome /təʊm/ noun [C] *literary* a large heavy book, usually about a serious subject

tomorrow[1] /təˈmɒrəʊ/ adv ★★★
1 on the day after today: *Are you going back home tomorrow?* ♦ *They're arriving tomorrow morning.*
2 in the future: *Who can say what will happen tomorrow?*

tomorrow[2] /təˈmɒrəʊ/ noun [U] **1** the day after today: *Tomorrow is Tuesday.* **2** the future: *These students are the leaders of tomorrow.*

ton /tʌn/ noun [C] **1** *British* a unit for measuring weight, containing 2,240 POUNDS and equal to 1,016 kilograms **2** *informal* a very large number or amount: *I've got tons of* (=a lot of) *things to do.* ♦ *That bag of yours weighs a ton* (=is extremely heavy)*!* **3** *American* a unit for measuring weight, containing 2,000 POUNDS and equal to 907 kilograms

tone[1] /təʊn/ noun ★

1 sound of voice	**4** phone sound
2 character of sth	**5** colour
3 quality of sound	**6** firmness of muscles

1 [C/U] the sound of someone's voice that shows what they are feeling: *His tone was angry.* ♦ *'Really?' Simone said in a disbelieving tone of voice.*
2 [singular/U] the general character of something: *The positive tone of the evening had changed completely.* ♦ *The opening remarks set the tone for the rest of the interview.*
3 [C/U] the quality of a sound: *a flute with a clear bright tone*
4 [C] a sound made by a piece of equipment such as a telephone: *I picked up the phone and just got a beeping tone.*
5 [C] a colour, or a particular SHADE (=type) of a colour: *The room is decorated in cool blue tones.*
6 [U] the firmness or healthy quality of your body, muscles, or skin: *The patient's general muscle tone is good.*

tone[2] /təʊn/

   PHRASAL VERBS **tone sth down** to make something less severe, shocking, or offensive

   tone sth up to make your body, muscles, or skin more firm and healthy

tone deaf adj unable to sing a tune correctly because you cannot hear the difference between musical notes

toner /ˈtəʊnə/ noun [U] ink in the form of a powder that you put into a printer or a PHOTOCOPIER

tongs /tɒŋz/ noun [plural] a metal or plastic object that consists of two connected arms that you push together in order to pick something up

tongue /tʌŋ/ noun [C] ★★
1 the long soft piece of flesh that is fixed to the bottom of your mouth that you use for tasting, speaking etc
2 a language: *English was clearly not his mother tongue* (=the one he first learned as a child).

→ BITE, SLIP, TIP[1]

ˌtongue-inˈcheek adj intended to be humorous and not meant seriously: *a tongue-in-cheek answer* —**ˌtongue-inˈcheek** adv

ˈtongue-ˌtied adj unable to speak because you are nervous or embarrassed

ˈtongue ˌtwister noun [C] a word or phrase that is difficult to say because it contains many similar sounds

tonic /ˈtɒnɪk/ noun **1** tonic or **tonic water** [C/U] a type of FIZZY water that has a bitter taste and is often mixed with a strong alcoholic drink **2** [singular] something that makes you feel happier or healthier

tonight¹ /təˈnaɪt/ adv ★★★ in the evening or during the night of today: *Phone me tonight when you get home.*

tonight² /təˈnaɪt/ noun [U] the evening or night of today: *tonight's performance*

tonne /tʌn/ noun [C] a unit for measuring weight, equal to 1,000 kilograms

tonsil /ˈtɒns(ə)l/ noun [C] one of the two small pieces of flesh on each side of your throat at the back of your mouth

tonsillitis /ˌtɒnsɪˈlaɪtɪs/ noun [U] an illness in which your tonsils become infected, swollen, and painful

too /tuː/ adv ★★★
1 more than is necessary or acceptable: *You're driving too fast.* ♦ *It's too cold to sit outside.* ♦ *This film is too scary for seven-year-old kids.* ♦ *You've put too much sugar in my coffee.*
2 used after mentioning an additional person, thing, or fact to show that they are also included in what you are saying = ALSO: *Helen's got a lovely voice, and she's a good dancer too.* ♦ *'I'm starting to feel hungry.' 'Me too.'*

> Do not use **too** for making additions to negative sentences. Use **not...either**: *I didn't tell my friends, and I didn't tell my wife either.*

PHRASES all/only too used for emphasizing that you wish that something did not happen so much, or that something was not true: *All too often it is the victim who gets blamed.* ♦ *I knew only too well how dangerous the operation might be.*
not too *spoken* not very: *Barbara won't be too pleased if we get there late.* ♦ *'How are you feeling?' 'Oh, not too bad.'*

took the past tense of **take¹**

tool /tuːl/ noun [C] ★★
1 a piece of equipment that you hold to do a particular type of work: *kitchen/gardening tools* ♦ *a set of tools*
2 something that you use in order to perform a job or achieve an aim: *The Internet has become an important research tool for students.*

toolbar /ˈtuːlbɑː/ noun [C] *computing* a row of ICONS (=small pictures) on a computer screen that perform particular actions when you CLICK on them

ˈtool ˌshed noun [C] a small building, often made of wood and usually in a garden, used for storing tools —*picture* → C1

toot /tuːt/ verb [I/T] if you toot a horn, or if it toots, it makes a loud high sound —**toot** noun [C]

tooth /tuːθ/ (plural **teeth** /tiːθ/) noun [C] ★★★
1 any of the hard white objects inside your mouth that you use for biting: *a loose/missing/broken tooth* ♦ *It's important to brush your teeth at least twice a day.* —*picture* → C14
2 one of a row of narrow pointed parts that form the edge of a tool or machine: *the teeth on a saw/comb* → GRIT²

toothache /ˈtuːθeɪk/ noun [singular/U] a pain in one or more of your teeth

toothbrush /ˈtuːθbrʌʃ/ noun [C] a small brush that you use for cleaning your teeth

toothpaste /ˈtuːθpeɪst/ noun [C/U] a soft thick substance that you put on a toothbrush to clean your teeth

toothpick /ˈtuːθpɪk/ noun [C] a thin pointed piece of wood that you use for removing bits of food from between your teeth

top¹ /tɒp/ noun ★★★

1 highest place/part	**4** piece of clothing
2 upper surface	**5** highest/best position
3 container lid/cover	**+** PHRASES

1 [C] the highest place, point, part, or surface of something: *We could see mountain tops in the distance.* ♦ *I left my purse at the top of the stairs.* ♦ *He sprinkled sugar on top of the cake.*
2 [C] a flat upper surface of something: *a table top*
3 [C] a lid or cover for a container or pen: *the top of the shampoo bottle*
4 [C] a piece of clothing that covers the upper part of your body: *She was wearing a red skirt and a black top.*
5 the top [singular] the highest status or most important position: *Scott has reached the top of his profession.*

PHRASES from top to bottom completely and thoroughly: *We cleaned the house from top to bottom.*
sth gets on top of you *informal* if something gets on top of you, it causes you a lot of work and worry: *Things are really getting on top of me at home.*
off the top of your head immediately and without thinking very much: *Off the top of my head, I'd say we have about 200 members.*
on top in a situation where you are in control or winning: *United stayed on top throughout most of the match.*
on top of 1 in addition to something else: *On top of all his financial problems, his wife left him.* **2** in control of what is happening: *I try to stay on top of things.* **3** very close to someone or something: *The truck was almost on top of me.*
on top of the world in a very good mood because things are going well for you
over the top more than what is considered normal or suitable

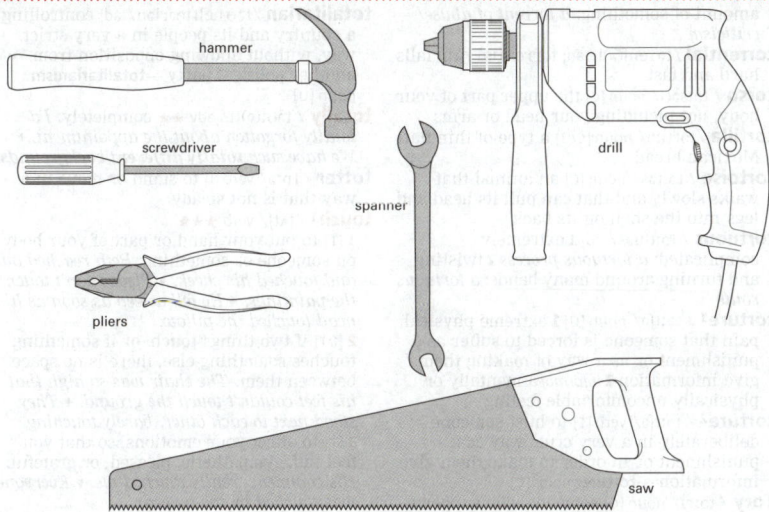

hammer

screwdriver

drill

spanner

pliers

saw

tools

top² /tɒp/ adj ★★★
1 at or on the highest part of something:
Our room is on the top floor.
2 highest in status, degree, or importance:
He's one of the top players in the league. ♦
*Our top priority now is finding shelter for
the flood victims.*

top³ /tɒp/ verb [T] **1** to be larger than a
particular amount: *The costs for the project
may top £50 million.* **2** to be in the most
important or popular position in a list of
things **3** to be better or more impressive
than something else: *I don't think I can top
your fishing story.* **4** to cover something with
a layer of something else: *pizza topped with
pepperoni*

PHRASAL VERBS **top sth 'off** to finish
something with a final activity or detail
top sth 'up 1 to completely fill a container
that is already partly full **2** to add more to
something in order to bring it up to the
level you want or need: *You can buy a card
to top up your mobile phone with £5 to £50
worth of credit.*

top-'down adj starting at a general level and
then moving to more specific things
≠ BOTTOM-UP

top 'hat noun [C] a man's tall hat that is worn
on formal occasions —*picture* → HAT

top-'heavy adj something that is top-heavy
lacks balance because it is heavier at the
top than at the bottom

topic /'tɒpɪk/ noun [C] ★★ a subject that you
write or speak about: *There has been little
research on this particular topic.* ♦ *She tried
to think of another topic of conversation.*

topical /'tɒpɪk(ə)l/ adj relating to a subject
that is of particular interest at the present
time

topless /'tɒpləs/ adj not wearing any clothes
on the upper part of your body

topmost /'tɒp,məʊst/ adj highest

topography /tə'pɒgrəfi/ noun [C/U] the
features of a particular area of land, such
as hills, rivers, and roads —**topographical**
/,tɒpə'græfɪk(ə)l/ adj

topping /'tɒpɪŋ/ noun [C] a layer of food that
you put on top of other food, for example
on ice cream or a PIZZA

topple /'tɒp(ə)l/ verb **1** [I/T] to fall, or to make
someone or something fall **2** [T] to make
someone in authority lose their power

top 'secret adj containing or involving very
important and secret information

topsy-turvy /,tɒpsi 'tɜːvi/ adj *informal*
confused and in the wrong order

Torah, the /'tɔːrə/ the first five books of the
Jewish Bible

torch¹ /tɔːtʃ/ noun [C] **1** *British* a small electric
light that you hold in your hand **2** a piece
of wood with a flame at one end that is used
as a light

torch² /tɔːtʃ/ verb [T] to set fire to something

tore the past tense of **tear¹**

torment¹ /'tɔːment/ noun [C/U] severe
physical or mental pain, or something that
causes this

torment² /tɔː'ment/ verb [T] to make someone
suffer severe physical or mental pain
—**tormentor** noun [C]

torn the past participle of **tear¹**

tornado /tɔː'neɪdəʊ/ (plural **tornadoes** or
tornados) noun [C] a very strong wind that
goes quickly round in a circle or FUNNEL

torpedo¹ /tɔː'piːdəʊ/ (plural **torpedoes**) noun
[C] a weapon that is shot under water in
order to hit a ship or a SUBMARINE

torpedo² /tɔː'piːdəʊ/ verb [T] to hit a ship or
a SUBMARINE with a torpedo

torrent /'tɒrənt/ noun **1** [C] a fast and powerful
flow of water **2** [singular] **a torrent of** a large

T

amount of something: *a torrent of abuse/ criticism*

torrential /təˈrenʃ(ə)l/ adj torrential rain falls hard and fast

torso /ˈtɔːsəʊ/ noun [C] the upper part of your body, not including your head or arms

tortilla /tɔːˈtiːə/ noun [C/U] a type of thin flat Mexican bread

tortoise /ˈtɔːtəs/ noun [C] an animal that walks slowly and that can pull its head and legs into the shell on its back

tortuous /ˈtɔːtʃuəs/ adj **1** extremely complicated: *a tortuous process* **2** twisting and turning around many bends: *a tortuous route*

torture¹ /ˈtɔːtʃə/ noun [U] **1** extreme physical pain that someone is forced to suffer as a punishment or as a way of making them give information **2** *informal* a mentally or physically uncomfortable feeling

torture² /ˈtɔːtʃə/ verb [T] to hurt someone deliberately in a very cruel way as a punishment or in order to make them give information —**torturer** noun [C]

Tory /ˈtɔːri/ noun [C] someone who supports or is a member of the Conservative Party in the UK —**Tory** adj

toss¹ /tɒs/ verb **1** [T] to throw something somewhere gently or in a careless way: *Brendon tossed the ball into the air.* **2** [I/T] to throw a coin into the air in order to make a decision based on which side the coin falls on **3** [T] to mix food with a liquid so that it becomes covered in the liquid: *Can you toss the salad for me?*

PHRASES **toss and turn** to be unable to sleep, or to sleep badly

toss your head/hair to move your head quickly upwards

toss² /tɒs/ noun [C] **1** the act of throwing something somewhere gently or in a careless way **2** the act of throwing a coin into the air in order to make a decision based on which side the coin falls on **3** the act of moving your head quickly upwards

tot /tɒt/ noun [C] **1** *informal* a small child **2** a small amount of a strong alcoholic drink

total¹ /ˈtəʊt(ə)l/ adj ★★★
1 with all the numbers or things added together: *The total cost of the project came to about £700,000.* ♦ *The total number of votes was over one million.*
2 complete=ABSOLUTE: *Why would you let a total stranger into the house?* ♦ *They sat in almost total silence the whole evening.*

total² /ˈtəʊt(ə)l/ noun [C] ★★★ the amount that you get when you add several numbers or things together: *The total for your books comes to £46.50.* ♦ *A total of 17 students signed up for the course.* ♦ *In total* (=counting everyone) *over 100 people attended.*

total³ /ˈtəʊt(ə)l/ (present participle **totalling**; past tense and past participle **totalled**) verb [T] to be a particular total as a result of everything being added together: *The company went bankrupt, with debts totalling £60 million.*

totalitarian /təʊˌtælɪˈteəriən/ adj controlling a country and its people in a very strict way, without allowing opposition from another political party —**totalitarianism** noun [U]

totally /ˈtəʊt(ə)li/ adv ★★ completely: *I'd totally forgotten about the appointment.* ♦ *We have such totally different backgrounds.*

totter /ˈtɒtə/ verb [I] to stand or move in a way that is not steady

touch¹ /tʌtʃ/ ★★★
1 [T] to put your hand or part of your body on someone or something: *Beth reached out and touched his cheek.* ♦ *Please don't touch the paintings.* ♦ *He fell asleep as soon as his head touched the pillow.*
2 [I/T] if two things touch, or if something touches something else, there is no space between them: *The chair was so high that his feet couldn't touch the ground.* ♦ *They stood next to each other, barely touching.*
3 [T] to affect your emotions, so that you feel sad, sympathetic, pleased, or grateful: *His comments really touched me.* ♦ *Everyone was touched by the tragedy.*
4 [T] to eat or drink a particular thing: *I never touch meat or dairy products.*

PHRASAL VERBS **touch 'down** if an aircraft or space vehicle touches down, it lands

'touch on sth to mention something when you are talking or writing

touch sth 'up to make a surface look better with small improvements

touch² /tʌtʃ/ noun ★★★

1 putting hand on sth	4 small feature
2 very small amount	5 ability to do sth well
3 ability to feel things	+ PHRASES

1 [singular] the action of putting your hand or part of your body on someone or something: *Bill was wakened by her touch on his shoulder.* ♦ *He shook her hand and his touch was warm and firm.*
2 [singular] a very small amount of something: *Add a touch of olive oil.*
3 [U] the SENSE that tells you what something feels like, through your skin, or when you put your fingers on it: *Children's imaginations can be stimulated through sight, touch, and smell.*
4 [C] a small feature that improves something: *The flowers in the room were a nice touch.* ♦ *The band is putting the finishing touches to their third album.*
5 [singular] your ability to do something well

PHRASES **in touch (with sb)** to see, speak to, or write to someone: *I'll be in touch next week about our trip to Paris.* ♦ *I must get in touch with the bank and arrange an overdraft.* ♦ *They moved away five years ago, but we still keep in touch.*

lose touch (with sb) to not see, speak to, or write to someone any longer: *She moved to France and we lost touch with each other.*

out of touch (with sth) 1 no longer having recent knowledge or information about something: *I haven't taught for a while so I'm a little out of touch.* **2** no longer seeing, speaking to, or writing to someone

touch-and-'go adj not certain and with a risk of death or serious failure

touchdown /'tʌtʃdaʊn/ noun [C] the moment when an aircraft or space vehicle lands on the ground

touched /tʌtʃt/ adj feeling sad, sympathetic, pleased, or grateful

touching /'tʌtʃɪŋ/ adj making you feel sad, sympathetic, pleased, or grateful

touchline /'tʌtʃlaɪn/ noun [C] one of the two lines marking the sides of a playing area in a sport, especially football

'touch ˌscreen noun [C] a computer screen that you touch in order to choose what you want to see next

touchstone /'tʌtʃˌstəʊn/ noun [C] a standard that is used for testing or judging other things

touchy /'tʌtʃi/ adj **1** tending to become angry or upset very easily **2** likely to make people angry or upset

tough /tʌf/ adj ★★

1 difficult	5 with crime/violence
2 strong	6 of meat
3 confident/determined	7 hard to break/damage
4 very strict/severe	

1 difficult: *He's having a really tough time at the moment.* ♦ *It was a tough decision to move to London.* ♦ *Many companies are facing tough competition.*

2 strong and able to deal with difficult situations or pain: *I think she'll be all right because she's tough.*

3 confident and determined to get what you want: *a tough businessman*

4 very strict and severe: *tough criticism* ♦ *We must take tough action against terrorism.* ♦ *The new mayor promises to be tough on crime.*

5 a tough place is one in which there is a lot of crime and violence: *a tough neighbourhood*

6 tough meat is very difficult to cut and CHEW

7 difficult to break or damage
—**toughness** noun [U]

toughen /'tʌf(ə)n/ verb [I/T] to become mentally or physically stronger, or to make someone become mentally or physically stronger

toupee /'tuːpeɪ/ noun [C] artificial hair that a man wears on top of his head where he has no hair

tour¹ /tʊə/ noun ★★

1 [C] a journey in which you visit several different places: *The president plans a European tour next month.* ♦ *We went on a 10-day tour of central Africa.*

2 [C/U] a journey in which a person or group visits several different places in order to perform: *The group is currently on tour in Europe.*

3 [C] a short journey around a building or place in order to see what is there: *Every weekend there are free guided tours of the castle.*

tour² /tʊə/ verb [I/T] to visit different several places for pleasure or to perform

tourism /'tʊərɪz(ə)m/ noun [U] the business of providing services for people who are travelling for their holiday

tourist /'tʊərɪst/ noun [C] ★★ someone who is visiting a place on holiday: *The islands attract more than 17,000 tourists a year.* ♦ *a tourist hotel/destination*

tournament /'tʊənəmənt/ noun [C] a series of games in which the winner of each game plays in the next game until there is only one player or team left

tourniquet /'tɔːnɪˌkeɪ/ noun [C] a piece of cloth that you tie very tight around someone's leg or arm in order to stop blood from flowing from a cut

tousled /'taʊz(ə)ld/ adj tousled hair looks untidy in an attractive way

tout¹ /taʊt/ verb **1** [T] to praise someone or something because you want other people to think that they are good or important: *The club is being touted as the best place to hear live music.* **2** [I/T] to try to persuade people to buy something by telling them about it

tout² /taʊt/ noun someone who unofficially sells tickets at high prices outside a theatre or sports ground

tow¹ /təʊ/ verb [T] to pull a vehicle or boat by fixing it to another vehicle or boat

tow² /təʊ/ noun [singular] the activity of pulling one vehicle behind another
PHRASE **in tow** *informal* if you have someone in tow, you are taking them somewhere

toward /tɔːd, təˈwɔːd/ preposition *American* TOWARDS

towards /təˈwɔːdz/ preposition ★★★

1 going, facing, or looking in a particular direction: *I saw Joanna hurrying towards me.* ♦ *Victor was standing with his back towards me.* ♦ *a path leading towards the river*

2 used when saying how you feel about someone or something, or how you treat them: *He's not feeling very friendly towards you at the moment.* ♦ *the Church's attitude towards divorce*

3 in a way that brings a process closer to a particular result: *progress towards European unity* ♦ *Not much has been done towards improving safety.*

4 near or nearer a time or place: *I'll phone you some time towards the end of the week.* ♦ *Caroline's name appeared towards the bottom of the list.*

towel /'taʊəl/ noun [C] ★ a piece of material that you use for drying your hands or body, or for drying dishes

tower¹ /'taʊə/ noun [C] ★★ a tall narrow structure, building, or part of a building: *a*

T

water tower ♦ *the Leaning Tower of Pisa* ♦ *a church tower*

PHRASE **a tower of strength** *British* someone who you can depend on for help in a difficult situation

tower² /ˈtaʊə/ verb [I] to be much taller than the people or things that are near you

ˈtower ˌblock noun [C] *British* a tall building with flats or offices on each floor

town /taʊn/ noun ★★★

1 [C] a place where people live and work that is larger than a village but smaller than a city: *a small town* ♦ *a town on the River Thames* ♦ *the northern Belgian* **town** *of Onkerzele* → CITY

2 [U] the town or city that you live in or that you are talking about: *He moved to another part of town.* ♦ *The crew was in* **town** *last week filming a new television series.* ♦ *His girlfriend flew in from out of* **town***.*

3 [U] the centre of a town where all the shops are: *We're going* **into town** *this afternoon.*

4 [singular] the people who live in a town: *Most of the town was involved with the carnival.*

PHRASE **go to town (on sth)** *informal* to do something very well, or to make something look very good by spending a lot of time or money on it

→ HOME TOWN

ˌtown ˈhall noun [C] a building that has all the offices of a town's local government

townspeople /ˈtaʊnzˌpiːp(ə)l/ noun [plural] the people who live in a town or city

toxic /ˈtɒksɪk/ adj poisonous, and harmful to humans, animals, or the environment

toxin /ˈtɒksɪn/ noun [C] a poisonous substance

toy¹ /tɔɪ/ noun [C] ★★ an object that is designed for a child to play with: *boxes full of books, toys, and games* ♦ *a toy soldier/ gun/car*

toy² /tɔɪ/ **PHRASAL VERB** **ˈtoy with sth 1** to think about an idea in a way that is not serious: *I've been toying with the idea of starting my own business.* **2** to keep touching or moving something

trace¹ /treɪs/ verb [T] ★

1 to find someone or something that you are looking for by asking questions and getting information: *Detectives have failed to trace the missing woman.*

2 to discover the origin or cause of something: *The source of the infection was traced to a farm in Yorkshire.*

3 to describe what happened in a long process or series of events: *The book traces the history of the regiment.*

4 to copy an image by putting transparent paper on top and following the lines with your pencil —*picture* → DRAW

trace² /treɪs/ noun **1** [C/U] a slight sign that someone has been present or that something has happened **2** [C] a very small amount of something

track¹ /træk/ noun ★★★

1 rough path/road	4 running/racing course
2 train line	5 recorded music
3 marks on ground	+ PHRASES

1 [C] *British* a path or road with a rough surface: *I walked along a track to the mountain village.* ♦ *There's* **a dirt track** *leading from the main road.*

2 [C/U] a railway line: *a long stretch of track* ♦ *Roads and* **railway tracks** *were flooded in southern Germany.*

3 **tracks** [plural] marks that a person, animal, or vehicle leaves on the ground: *He followed the tracks of a car to the edge of the lake.*

4 [C] a piece of ground that is used for running or racing

5 [C] a song or piece of music that is recorded on a CD: *Which is your favourite track?*

PHRASES **keep track of sth** to have information about how something is developing: *We need to keep track of how we are spending our money.*

lose track (of sth) to forget something, or to not know exactly what is happening: *I was so busy I lost all track of time.*

make tracks *spoken* to leave a place

on the right/wrong track doing or thinking the right or wrong things

on track doing things that are likely to be successful or correct: *a desperate attempt to keep the peace talks on track* ♦ **on track to do sth** *We're right on track to create two million new jobs.*

stop (dead) in your tracks to suddenly stop, for example because you are surprised

→ BEATEN, FAST TRACK

track² /træk/ verb [T] **1** to follow someone or something by looking for evidence that shows where they have gone, or by using special equipment: *The radar system tracks planes up to 50 miles from the airport.* **2** to follow the development of something: *Live television coverage allows you to track the progress of the competitors.*

PHRASAL VERB **ˌtrack sb/sth ˈdown** to find someone or something after a long search: *I finally managed to track him down in Manchester.*

trackball /ˈtrækˌbɔːl/ noun [C] *computing* a ball that is used instead of a computer MOUSE

ˈtrack ˌrecord noun [C] your reputation, based on the things that you have done or not done

tracksuit /ˈtrækˌsuːt/ noun [C] loose trousers and a loose top that you wear before or after exercising

tract /trækt/ noun [C] **1** a large area of land **2** *medical* a group of organs and tubes that work together in your body

traction /ˈtrækʃ(ə)n/ noun [U] *technical* the ability of something to move over a surface without slipping

tractor /ˈtræktə/ noun [C] a vehicle that is used on farms for pulling machines

trade¹ /treɪd/ noun ★★★

1 [U] the activity of buying and selling goods or services: *The President's tour is designed to promote investment and trade.* ♦ *Spain wants to develop its* **trade with** *the Philippines.* ♦ *the illegal* **trade in** *drugs*

2 [C] a particular area of business or industry: *the book/drug/jewellery trade*

3 [C] a job or type of work that someone is

trained to do: *He **learned his trade** in the 1960s.*

trade² /treɪd/ verb ★

1 [I/T] to buy and sell goods or services: *Investors can now **trade stocks** online.* ♦ *The group has issued threats against companies that **trade** in animal skins.* ♦ *Cuba continues to **trade with** other countries around the world.*

2 [I] to operate as a business: *The company will continue to trade under its original name.*

3 [T] to exchange something that you have for something else: **trade sth for sth** *They traded freedom for security.*

PHRASAL VERB   **trade sth in** to give something old as part of the payment for something new: *She **traded in** her old car for a new one.*

trade ,deficit noun [C] a situation in which a country is buying more things from other countries than it is selling to other countries

trade ,fair noun [C] an event at which companies show their new products

trademark /ˈtreɪdˌmɑːk/ noun [C] a name or design that belongs to a particular company and is used on its products

trade ,name noun [C] a BRAND NAME

trade-off noun [C] a situation in which you accept a disadvantage so that you can have a benefit

trader /ˈtreɪdə/ noun [C] someone who buys and sells things: *market/street traders*

tradesman /ˈtreɪdzmən/ noun [C] British old-fashioned someone who sells goods or services

trade ,union noun [C] British an organization of workers that aims to improve pay and conditions of work

tradition /trəˈdɪʃ(ə)n/ noun [C/U] ★★★ a very old custom, belief, or story: *Native American culture and traditions* ♦ *Parents bring up their children in accordance with their own traditions.* ♦ *His son **followed** the family **tradition** and entered politics.*

traditional /trəˈdɪʃ(ə)nəl/ adj ★★★

1 relating to very old customs, beliefs, or stories: *traditional Mediterranean cooking* ♦ *All the dancers and musicians wore traditional costumes.*

2 typical of the things people have usually done: *Our house was built in a traditional style.* ♦ *Many women have abandoned their traditional role as wife and mother.*
—**traditionally** adv

traditionalist /trəˈdɪʃ(ə)nəlɪst/ noun [C] someone who supports traditional ideas or methods

traffic /ˈtræfɪk/ noun [U] ★★★

1 the vehicles that are travelling in an area at a particular time: *At that time of night, there was no traffic on the roads.* ♦ *the huge volume of traffic in the city centre* ♦ *rush-hour traffic* ♦ *traffic noise/fumes/congestion*

2 aircraft, ships, and trains that travel from one place to another: *an increase in air traffic*

3 the information that passes through a communications system: *Internet traffic*

4 the process of buying and selling things such as drugs and weapons illegally: *measures to reduce the illegal **traffic in** heroin*

traffic ,jam noun [C] a line of vehicles waiting behind something that is blocking the road

trafficking /ˈtræfɪkɪŋ/ noun [U] the business of illegally buying and selling things such as drugs and weapons —**trafficker** noun [C]

traffic ,lights noun [plural] a set of red, yellow, and green lights that control traffic

traffic ,warden noun [C] British someone whose job is to check that vehicles are legally parked

tragedy /ˈtrædʒədi/ noun **1** [C/U] a very sad event that involves death or human suffering: *The trip ended in tragedy.* ♦ *We need new safety laws to prevent tragedies like this from happening again.* **2** [C] a bad situation that makes people very upset or angry: *It's a tragedy that so many young people are out of work.* **3** [C] a play in which people suffer or die, especially one in which the main character dies: *Shakespeare's tragedies*

tragic /ˈtrædʒɪk/ adj **1** causing or involving great sadness, because someone suffers or dies **2** relating to tragedy in plays or literature —**tragically** /ˈtrædʒɪkli/ adv

trail¹ /treɪl/ noun [C] ★

1 a path through the countryside, especially one designed for walking for pleasure: *The trail led down to the lake.* ♦ *We followed a winding trail into the mountains.*

2 a series of marks that shows where someone or something has been: *a trail of blood* ♦ *He **left a trail** of muddy footprints.*

3 damage or harm caused by something bad: *Hurricane Andrew left **a trail of destruction** along the coast.*

4 many pieces of connected evidence that prove someone did something wrong or illegal: *Detectives are **on the trail** of a serial killer.*

trail² /treɪl/ verb

1 move slowly	4 leave marks
2 in competition	5 pull sth behind you
3 follow sb	+ PHRASAL VERB

1 [I] to move slowly behind someone in a tired or unhappy way: *My husband usually trails behind me when I'm shopping.* **2** [I/T] to be losing in a competition or election: *A recent poll shows the Democrats trailing the Republicans.* **3** [T] to follow someone secretly in order to learn something about them: *Detectives trailed Evans for weeks.*

4 [T] to leave marks on a surface as you go through a place: *The dogs came in, trailing mud everywhere.* **5** [I/T] to pull something behind you, or to be pulled behind someone or something

PHRASAL VERB   **trail away** or **trail off** if someone's voice trails away, they gradually become silent

trailer /ˈtreɪlə/ noun [C] **1** a long container that can be fixed to a vehicle and used for moving heavy objects or large animals **2** an advertisement for a film or television programme that shows short parts of that film or programme **3** American a CARAVAN

train¹ /treɪn/ noun [C] ★★★
1 a group of railway vehicles that are connected and pulled by an engine: *a freight/passenger train* ♦ *We travelled across China by train.* ♦ *I met her on a train to Glasgow.* ♦ *More and more people got on the crowded train.* ♦ *We'll be waiting for you when you get off the train.* ♦ *If we don't leave now we'll miss the train.* ♦ *I'll meet you at the train station.* —picture → C7
2 a series of events or thoughts: *a disastrous train of events* ♦ *I'm sorry, I lost my train of thought* (=forgot what I was thinking).
3 a long part at the back of a formal dress that spreads out over the ground

train² /treɪn/ verb ★★★
1 [T] to teach someone to do a particular job or activity: *We need to recruit and train more police officers.* ♦ **train sb to do sth** *They were training him to use the new security system.*
2 [I] to learn how to do a particular job or activity: *He trained as a chef in Paris.* ♦ **train to do sth** *I have an uncle who trained to be a pilot.*
3 [I] to practise a sport regularly before a match or competition: *The players train five days a week.*
4 [T] to teach an animal to obey you or to do something: **train sth to do sth** *He had trained the dogs to attack.*

trainee /ˌtreɪˈniː/ noun [C] someone who is learning how to do a particular job or activity

trainer /ˈtreɪnə/ noun [C] **1** someone whose job is to teach people skills, or to help people to practise a sport **2** someone whose job is to train animals

trainers /ˈtreɪnəz/ noun [plural] a type of comfortable shoe that you wear in informal situations or for doing sport

training /ˈtreɪnɪŋ/ noun [U] ★★★
1 the process of teaching or learning a particular job or activity: *Counselling is a difficult job requiring skill and training.* ♦ *Employees are given training in the use of safety equipment.* ♦ *The college provides vocational training for actors.*
2 physical exercise that someone does regularly in order to practise for a sport or to stay healthy: *McColgan is currently in training for the New York marathon.*

trait /treɪt/ noun [C] a particular quality in someone's character

traitor /ˈtreɪtə/ noun [C] someone who is not loyal to their country, friends, or family

trajectory /trəˈdʒekt(ə)ri/ noun [C] technical the high curving line that is formed by the movement of an object through the air

tram /træm/ noun [C] British a long narrow vehicle for carrying passengers that travels along metal tracks in the middle of a street —picture → C7

tramlines /ˈtræmˌlaɪnz/ noun [plural] British informal the long white lines at either side of a tennis court that mark the extra playing area allowed if four people are playing —picture → C15

tramp¹ /træmp/ noun [C] **1** someone without a home or a job who moves from one place to another **2** a long tiring walk

tramp² /træmp/ verb [I/T] to walk with slow heavy steps, or to walk a long way

trample /ˈtræmp(ə)l/ verb [I/T] to put your feet down on someone or something in a heavy way that causes injury or damage

trampoline /ˈtræmpəˌliːn/ noun [C] a piece of equipment that you jump up and down on, consisting of a metal frame with a strong material stretched across it

trance /trɑːns/ noun [C] a state in which you are awake but not really conscious of where you are

tranquil /ˈtræŋkwɪl/ adj calm, still, and quiet —**tranquillity** /træŋˈkwɪləti/ noun [U]

tranquilizer /ˈtræŋkwɪˌlaɪzə/ the American spelling of **tranquillizer**

tranquillizer /ˈtræŋkwɪˌlaɪzə/ noun [C] a drug that makes people calmer when they are very worried or nervous

transaction /trænˈzækʃ(ə)n/ noun [C] formal an occasion when someone buys or sells something: *a business transaction*

transatlantic /ˌtrænzətˈlæntɪk/ adj **1** crossing the Atlantic Ocean **2** involving countries on both sides of the Atlantic Ocean

transcend /trænˈsend/ verb [T] formal to become free of things that limit what you can achieve

transcribe /trænˈskraɪb/ verb [T] to write something exactly as it was spoken

transcript /ˈtrænˌskrɪpt/ or **transcription** /trænˈskrɪpʃ(ə)n/ noun [C] a written copy of the exact words that someone said

transfer¹ /trænsˈfɜː/ verb ★★
1 [I/T] to move, or to move someone, from one job or department to another in the same company or organization: *I'm transferring to our Tokyo office next year.* ♦ **transfer sb from sth to sth** *Helen was transferred from marketing to sales.*
2 [T] to move something or someone from one place to another: **transfer sb/sth to sth** *Wait until the cakes cool before transferring them to a plate.* ♦ *The prisoner will be transferred to a maximum security unit.* ♦ *I need to transfer £500 to my daughter's account.*
3 [T] to let someone speak to another person by changing telephone lines for them: *Please hold the line while I transfer you.*
4 [T] to officially arrange for someone else to become the owner of something

transfer² /ˈtrænsfɜː/ noun [C/U] ★★ the process of moving, or being moved, from one job or place to another: *We're currently dealing with the paperwork for your transfer.* ♦ *the transfer of supplies*

transfixed /trænsˈfɪkst/ adj so surprised, shocked, or interested that you continue to look at something without moving

transform /trænsˈfɔːm/ verb [T] ★ to make someone or something completely different, especially in a positive way: *Email has transformed the way people communicate.* ♦ **transform sb/sth into sth** *They've transformed the old train station*

into a science museum. —**transformation**
/ˌtrænsfəˈmeɪʃ(ə)n/ *noun* [C/U]

transformer /trænsˈfɔːmə/ *noun* [C] *technical*
an object that changes the VOLTAGE of a
flow of electricity

transfusion /trænsˈfjuːʒ(ə)n/ *noun* [C/U] a
medical treatment in which blood from one
person is put into another person's body

transgenic /ˌtrænzˈdʒenɪk/ *adj science* a
transgenic plant or animal contains genes
from a different plant or animal

transgress /trænzˈgres/ *verb* [I/T] *formal* to do
something that is not allowed by a law,
custom, or religion —**transgression**
/trænzˈgreʃ(ə)n/ *noun* [C/U]

transient /ˈtrænziənt/ *adj* existing,
happening, or staying somewhere for a
short period of time only

transistor /trænˈzɪstə/ *noun* [C] *technical* an
object that controls the flow of electricity
inside electronic equipment

transit /ˈtrænsɪt/ *noun* [U] the movement of
people or things from one place to another:
Our suitcases were damaged in transit.

transition /trænˈzɪʃ(ə)n/ *noun* [C/U] the
process of changing from one situation,
form, or state to another: *It's not always a
smooth transition from school to
university.* —**transitional** *adj*

transitive /ˈtrænsətɪv/ *adj linguistics* a
transitive verb is always used with a DIRECT
OBJECT. Transitive verbs are marked [T] in
this dictionary. → INTRANSITIVE

transitory /ˈtrænsət(ə)ri/ *adj* temporary

translate /trænsˈleɪt/ *verb* ★
  1 [I/T] to change spoken or written words
  into a different language: *I don't speak
  Russian, so someone will have to translate.*
  ♦ **translate sth into sth** *The Bible has been
  translated into more than 100 languages.*
  2 [I] to cause a particular situation or result:
  *Will the sales increase translate into more
  jobs?*

translation /trænsˈleɪʃ(ə)n/ *noun* ★
  1 [C] a piece of work in which spoken or
  written words have been changed into a
  different language: *Some people like to make
  lists of words with translations in their own
  language.* ♦ *an English translation of
  Candide*
  2 [U] the activity of changing spoken or
  written words into a different language:
  *Most legal translation is done by lawyers
  with foreign language training.* ♦ *Try to read
  Baudelaire in the original and not in
  translation.*

translator /trænsˈleɪtə/ *noun* [C] someone
whose job is to translate spoken or written
words into a different language

translucent /trænsˈluːs(ə)nt/ *adj* clear
enough for light to pass through, but not
completely clear

transmission /trænzˈmɪʃ(ə)n/ *noun* **1** [C/U] the
process of sending electronic signals such
as radio or television signals, or a signal
that is sent in this way: *New telephone lines
allow faster data transmission by fax or
modem.* **2** [U] *formal* the process by which
something spreads from one person to
another: *the transmission of disease* **3** [C] the

part of a vehicle that takes power from the
engine to the wheels

transmit /trænzˈmɪt/ *verb* [T] **1** to send an
electronic signal such as a radio or
television signal: *The Cup Final was
transmitted via satellite to over 20 countries.*
2 *formal* to pass information, beliefs, or
attitudes to other people: *We transmit our
values to our children.* **3** *formal* to spread a
disease from one person to another: *HIV
can be transmitted by sexual contact.*

transmitter /trænzˈmɪtə/ *noun* [C] a piece of
electronic equipment that is used for
sending radio, television, or telephone
signals through the air

transparency /trænsˈpærənsi/ *noun* [C] a
photograph, drawing, or piece of writing
on plastic that you shine light through in
order to look at it on a screen

transparent /trænsˈpærənt/ *adj* **1** clear or
thin enough for you to see things through:
a transparent fabric/substance **2** not trying
to keep anything secret: *a transparent
system/process*

transpire /trænˈspaɪə/ *verb* [I] *formal* **1** to
become known: *It later transpired that the
driver of her car was drunk.* **2** to happen

transplant¹ /ˈtrænsˌplɑːnt/ *noun* [C/U] a
medical operation in which a new organ is
put into someone's body

transplant² /ˌtrænsˈplɑːnt/ *verb* [T] **1** to take a
plant out of the ground and put it in a
different place **2** to take an organ from one
person's body and put it into another
person's body

transport¹ /ˈtrænspɔːt/ *noun* [U] ★★★
  1 the system that is used for travelling or
  for moving goods from one place to another:
  road/rail transport ♦ *Auckland's **public
  transport system** is excellent.*
  2 a method of travelling or moving things
  from one place to another: *Anyone needing
  transport should ring me.* ♦ *Have you got
  your own transport?* ♦ *Flying is still the
  safest means of transport.*
  3 the action of moving goods from one place
  to another: *They have succeeded in stopping
  the transport of live animals.*

transport² /trænsˈpɔːt/ *verb* [T] ★ to move
people or things from one place to another,
usually in a vehicle: *We will need a big
truck to transport all the boxes.* ♦ *Volunteers
will be transported to the island by boat.*

transportation /ˌtrænspɔːˈteɪʃ(ə)n/ *noun* [U]
1 the action of moving goods from one place
to another **2** *American* TRANSPORT

transpose /trænsˈpəʊz/ *verb* [T] *formal* to
change the order or position of something

transvestite /trænzˈvestaɪt/ *noun* [C] someone
who wears clothing typical of the opposite
sex, especially for sexual pleasure

trap¹ /træp/ *verb* [T] ★

1 prevent from escaping	**4** catch an animal
2 of bad situation	**5** trick sb
3 catch a criminal	

1 to prevent someone from leaving a place:
*Both men were trapped inside the burning
car.* ♦ *The bomb exploded, trapping victims
in the building.*

T

2 to make someone unable to change a bad situation or way of thinking: *The two communities are trapped in a cycle of violence.* ♦ *I felt trapped by my marriage.*
3 to catch someone such as a criminal, especially by forcing them into a place that they cannot escape from: *Police officers trapped both suspects before they left the bank.*
4 to catch an animal using a trap
5 to trick someone in order to make them do or say something that they did not mean to do: **trap sb into (doing) sth** *I was trapped into admitting I had lied.*

trap² /træp/ *noun* [C] **1** a piece of equipment that is used for catching animals: *We set traps for the mice.* **2** a bad situation that is difficult to change or escape from: *He was caught in a trap of poverty.* **3** a trick that is designed to catch someone or make them do something that they did not mean to do: *We didn't know that we were walking straight into a trap.* **4** a mistake or problem that you should try to avoid: *I fell into the trap of putting work before family.* → DEATH TRAP

trapdoor /'træp,dɔː/ *noun* [C] a small door that covers an opening in a floor, ceiling, or wall

trapeze /trə'piːz/ *noun* [C] a short bar that hangs on two ropes from a high ceiling and is used by performers in a CIRCUS

trapezium /trə'piːziəm/ *noun* [C] *British technical* a shape with four straight sides, two of which are parallel —*picture* → C8

trapezoid /'træpɪ,zɔɪd/ *noun* [C] *British* a shape with four straight sides that are not parallel to each other —*picture* → C8

trappings /'træpɪŋz/ *noun* [plural] possessions that show that someone is rich, powerful, or important

trash¹ /træʃ/ *noun* [U] **1** *informal* something that is of very bad quality **2** *American* rubbish such as paper, plastic bags, used containers, etc that you get rid of=RUBBISH: *There was trash all over the fairgrounds for weeks afterwards.*

trash² /træʃ/ *verb* [T] *informal* to damage or destroy something

trash can *noun* [C] *American* a BIN for putting rubbish in

trashy /'træʃi/ *adj informal* very badly made, or of very bad quality

trauma /'trɔːmə/ *noun* [U] a feeling of being very upset, afraid, or shocked because of a bad experience, or the experience that causes this feeling

traumatic /trɔː'mætɪk/ *adj* causing you to feel very upset, afraid, or shocked

traumatized /'trɔːmə,taɪzd/ *adj* very upset, afraid, or shocked because of a bad experience —**traumatize** *verb* [T]

travel¹ /'træv(ə)l/ (present participle **travelling**, past tense and past participle **travelled**) *verb* ★★★
1 [I] to go on a journey, or visit different places: *Matt spends much of his time travelling abroad.* ♦ *We travelled around Spain for two weeks.* ♦ *Joe recently travelled to Australia on business.* ♦ *I usually travel by bus.*
2 [I/T] to move a particular distance, or at a particular speed: *We travelled 300 miles on Saturday.* ♦ *The car was travelling at about 50 miles per hour.*
3 [I] to spread from one place to another in a way that affects or influences a lot of people: *The news travelled quickly.* ♦ *Rumours travel fast.*

travel² /'træv(ə)l/ *noun* [U] ★★★ the activity of travelling: *Foreign travel never really appealed to him until he retired.* ♦ *Our agency deals mostly with business travel.* ♦ *travel arrangements/insurance*
PHRASE **sb's travels** journeys that someone makes to different places: *Her travels have taken her to many parts of the world.* ♦ *We met a lot of interesting people on our travels.*

travel agency or **travel agent's** *noun* [C] a business that helps people to plan holidays and to make travel arrangements

travel agent *noun* [C] someone whose job is to help people to plan holidays and to make travel arrangements

traveler /'træv(ə)lə/ the American spelling of **traveller**

traveller /'træv(ə)lə/ *noun* [C] ★
1 someone who is travelling, or who often travels: *Rail travellers are furious at the increase in fares.*
2 *British* someone who does not have a permanent home, and who travels from one place to another

traveller's cheque *noun* [C] a printed piece of paper that you sign and use as money when you are travelling

traverse /trə'vɜːs/ *verb* [T] *formal* to move over or across an area

travesty /'trævəsti/ *noun* [singular] something that is shocking because it is unfair or very different from what you expect

trawl /trɔːl/ *verb* [I/T] to look for someone or something by searching through a large number of things —**trawl** *noun* [C]

trawler /'trɔːlə/ *noun* [C] a boat used for fishing that pulls a large net through the water

tray /treɪ/ *noun* [C] **1** a flat piece of plastic, metal, or wood with raised edges, used for carrying food or drinks **2** a flat open container with raised edges, used for holding paper

treacherous /'tretʃərəs/ *adj* **1** very dangerous: *treacherous driving conditions* **2** someone who is treacherous cannot be trusted

treachery /'tretʃəri/ *noun* [U] the act of harming people who trusted you

treacle /'triːk(ə)l/ *noun* [U] *British* a thick sweet black liquid that is used in cooking

tread¹ /tred/ (past tense **trod** /trɒd/; past participle **trodden** /'trɒd(ə)n/) *verb* [I/T] *British* to walk, or to step on something
PHRASE **tread water 1** to not make progress **2** to stay upright in deep water by moving your legs and arms and keeping your head out of the water

tread² /tred/ *noun* [C] the pattern of lines on a tyre

treadmill /'tred,mɪl/ *noun* [C] **1** a piece of exercise equipment with a moving surface that you walk or run on —*picture* → C16 **2** a situation that is very tiring or boring because you always do the same things

treason /ˈtriːz(ə)n/ noun [U] the crime of trying to harm or destroy your country's government

treasure¹ /ˈtreʒə/ noun **1** [C] a valuable piece of art, or a valuable historical object: *the treasures of the Vatican Museum* **2** [U] a collection of valuable things, for example jewels, gold etc: *There are rumours of buried treasure in the old house.*

treasure

treasure² /ˈtreʒə/ verb [T] to think that something is very important because it gives you a lot of pleasure —**treasured** /ˈtreʒəd/ adj

treasurer /ˈtreʒərə/ noun [C] someone who is in charge of an organization's money

Treasury, the /ˈtreʒəri/ the government department that is responsible for a country's financial matters

treat¹ /triːt/ verb [T] ★★★

1 behave towards sb	4 protect sth
2 deal with sth	5 buy sb sth special
3 cure illness	

1 to behave towards someone in a particular way: *Rachel felt she had been unfairly treated.* ♦ *They treat their guests very well.* ♦ **treat sb like/as sth** *I wish you would stop treating me like a child!* ♦ **treat sb with sth** *Dean always treated my grandfather with the greatest respect.*
2 to deal with something in a particular way: **treat sth with sth** *You should treat this new evidence with caution.* ♦ **treat sth as sth** *These payments will be treated as income.*
3 to use medicine or medical methods to cure an illness: *Patients are treated using both medication and exercise.* ♦ **treat sb for sth** *She was treated for minor injuries.*
4 to put a substance on something in order to protect it or to make it stronger: **treat sth with sth** *The wood is treated with chemicals.*
5 to pay for something special for someone: **treat sb to sth** *Bob treated us to dinner at a nice restaurant.*

Words often used with treat

Adverbs often used with treat (verb, sense 1)
- TREAT + **badly, cruelly, harshly, shabbily, unfairly, unjustly**: treat someone in an unkind or unfair way
- TREAT + **equally, fairly, kindly, leniently, well**: treat someone in a kind or fair way

treat² /triːt/ noun **1** [C] a very enjoyable event or occasion: *It's a real treat to see you again.*

♦ *The band is great – you're in for a treat* (=you will enjoy it). **2** [singular] an occasion when you pay for something special for someone else: *I'd like this lunch to be my treat.* → TRICK¹

treatise /ˈtriːtɪz/ noun [C] *formal* a serious book or piece of writing about a particular subject

treatment /ˈtriːtmənt/ noun ★★★
1 [C/U] the process of providing medical care, or a particular type of medical care: *the treatment of tropical diseases* ♦ *a new treatment for heroin addiction* ♦ *She was receiving treatment for breast cancer.*
2 [U] the particular way in which you deal with someone: *the treatment of prisoners*

treaty /ˈtriːti/ noun [C] an official written agreement between countries: *a treaty on arms reduction*

treble¹ /ˈtreb(ə)l/ verb [I/T] to become three times bigger, or to make something three times bigger

treble² /ˈtreb(ə)l/ determiner something that is treble the number or amount of another thing is three times greater than it

treble³ /ˈtreb(ə)l/ noun [C/U] the highest range of musical sounds, or the part of a radio or STEREO that controls the higher sounds —**treble** adj

tree /triː/ noun [C] ★★★ a very tall plant that has branches and a thick stem made of wood: *an oak/ash/willow tree* → BARK¹, FAMILY TREE

trek /trek/ noun [C] a long tiring walk —**trek** verb [I]

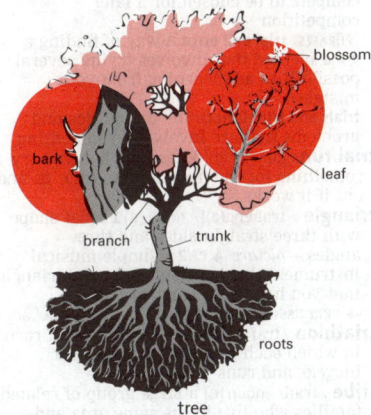

tree

trellis /ˈtrelɪs/ noun [C] an upright frame for plants to grow on

tremble /ˈtremb(ə)l/ verb [I] if you are trembling, your body is shaking, for example because you are nervous or weak: *She was trembling with anger.*

tremendous /trəˈmendəs/ adj **1** extremely great, important, or strong: *I have tremendous respect for my parents.* ♦ *We have a tremendous amount of work to do.*
2 extremely good: *We had a tremendous time on holiday.* —**tremendously** adv

tremor /ˈtremə/ noun [C] **1** a small

EARTHQUAKE **2** a slight shaking movement in your body or your voice that you cannot control

trench /trentʃ/ noun [C] a long narrow hole in the ground

trend /trend/ noun [C] ★ a gradual change or development that produces a particular result: *His designs often set the trend* (=start something that becomes popular) *for the new season.* ♦ *We've seen a trend towards more violent films this year.* ♦ *the latest trends in popular music*

> **Words often used with trend**
>
> *Adjectives often used with trend*
> ■ **current, general, growing, increasing, present, recent, rising, underlying** + TREND: used about different types of trend

trendy /ˈtrendi/ adj fashionable, but sometimes in a way that is silly or annoying

trepidation /ˌtrepɪˈdeɪʃ(ə)n/ noun [U] *formal* fear, or nervousness

trespass /ˈtrespəs/ verb [I] to go into a place without the owner's permission —**trespasser** noun [C]

trial /ˈtraɪəl/ noun ★★
1 [C/U] the process of examining a case in a court of law and deciding whether someone is guilty of a crime: *a murder/rape/fraud trial* ♦ *They're on trial for armed robbery.*
2 [C/U] the process of testing something over a period of time: *The system will operate for a six-month trial period.*
3 [C] a sports competition in which people compete to be chosen for a later competition
PHRASES **trial and error** a way of finding a good method that involves trying several possibilities and learning from your mistakes
trials and tribulations the difficulties and problems that are involved in something

trial run noun [C] an occasion when you try something for the first time in order to find out if it works

triangle /ˈtraɪæŋɡ(ə)l/ noun [C] **1** a flat shape with three straight sides and three angles —*picture* → C8 **2** a simple musical instrument that consists of a metal triangle that you hit with a bar —*picture* → PERCUSSION —**triangular** /traɪˈæŋɡjʊlə/ adj

triathlon /traɪˈæθlən/ noun [C] a type of race in which each person swims, rides a bicycle, and runs

tribe /traɪb/ noun [C] a large group of related families who live in the same area and share a common language, religion, and customs: *Native American tribes* —**tribal** adj

tribulation /ˌtrɪbjʊˈleɪʃn/ noun [C] *see* **trial**

tribunal /traɪˈbjuːn(ə)l/ noun [C] a special law court that is organized in order to judge a particular case: *a war crimes tribunal*

tributary /ˈtrɪbjʊt(ə)ri/ noun [C] a small river that flows into a larger river

tribute /ˈtrɪbjuːt/ noun [C/U] something that you do, say, or make in order to show that you respect and admire someone: *They showed the programme as a tribute to Nelson Mandela.*

PHRASES **be a tribute to** to show how good someone or something is: *This year's success is a tribute to all your hard work.*
pay tribute to to praise someone or something publicly

tribute band noun [C] a group of musicians who play the music of a famous band, and try to look and sound like them

trick¹ /trɪk/ noun [C] ★★
1 a deliberate attempt to make someone believe something that is not true, either as a joke or as a serious attempt to harm them: *At first I thought Joe was playing a trick on me.*
2 a way of entertaining people by doing something that looks like magic: *a street performer doing tricks for the crowd*
3 an effective and skilful way of doing something: *There's a trick to folding up this umbrella.* ♦ *If you want to see her, the trick is to go early.*
PHRASES **do the trick** to do what is needed in order to achieve something
trick or treat a custom in which children visit your home at HALLOWEEN and say 'Trick or treat?' as a way of asking for sweets

trick² /trɪk/ verb [T] to make someone believe something that is not true: *I suddenly realized that I'd been tricked.* ♦ **trick sb into doing sth** *He tricked me into believing that he was somebody famous.*

trickery /ˈtrɪkəri/ noun [U] the use of tricks to get what you want

trickle /ˈtrɪk(ə)l/ verb [I] **1** if a liquid trickles somewhere, a small amount of it flows there slowly: *A tear trickled down his cheek.* **2** if people or things trickle into or out of a place, a few of them arrive or leave —**trickle** noun [C]

trick question noun [C] a question that seems to have an easy answer but is really designed to trick you

tricky /ˈtrɪki/ adj difficult to do, or difficult to deal with: *a tricky problem/situation*

tried¹ the past tense and past participle of **try¹**

tried² /traɪd/ adj **tried and tested** known to be good or effective

trifle /ˈtraɪf(ə)l/ noun [C/U] a sweet food that consists of cake covered with fruit, cold CUSTARD (=yellow sauce), and cream
PHRASE **a trifle** *formal* slightly: *He felt a trifle embarrassed about the way he had behaved.*

trigger¹ /ˈtrɪɡə/ verb [T] **1** to cause something to happen: *The news of his death triggered more violence.* **2** to make a machine or piece of equipment start to work: *Someone broke a window, and this triggered the alarm.*

trigger² /ˈtrɪɡə/ noun [C] **1** the part of a gun that you pull with your finger to make the gun fire **2** something that causes something bad to happen

trillion /ˈtrɪljən/ number the number 1,000,000,000,000

trilogy /ˈtrɪlədʒi/ noun [C] a series of three books, films, or plays

trim¹ /trɪm/ verb [T] **1** to cut a small amount off something so that it looks tidy: *I just wanted her to trim my hair.* **2** to reduce the amount or number of something: *The company has trimmed £46,000 from its advertising budget.* **3** to decorate something

trim² /trɪm/ noun **1** [singular] the act of trimming something, especially hair **2** [singular/U] decoration on the edges of something: *cream leather seats with brown trim*

trim³ /trɪm/ adj healthy and thin in an attractive way

trimmings /ˈtrɪmɪŋz/ noun [plural] **1** extra parts that are added to a meal to make it traditional or more interesting **2** small objects or pieces of cloth that are used for decorating things such as clothes

trinket /ˈtrɪŋkɪt/ noun [C] a small object or decoration that is not very valuable

trio /ˈtriːəʊ/ noun [C] a group of three people or things that do something together

trip¹ /trɪp/ noun [C] ★★ an occasion when you go somewhere and come back again =JOURNEY: *a fishing/camping/sightseeing trip* ♦ *a bus/train/boat trip* ♦ *a trip to Brazil* ♦ *The whole family went on a trip to Florida.* → FIELD TRIP, ROUND TRIP

> #### Other words that mean trip
>
> ■ **crossing** a trip across water from one piece of land to another
> ■ **drive** a trip in a car
> ■ **excursion** an organized trip for a group of people
> ■ **expedition** a long and difficult trip to a place that is very far away, often made by people who are doing scientific research
> ■ **flight** a trip in a plane
> ■ **journey** a long trip from one place to another
> ■ **outing** a short trip made by a group of people who are visiting a place
> ■ **ride** a short trip in a car or bus, or on a bicycle or motorbike
> ■ **tour** a trip to a place where there are interesting things to see

trip² /trɪp/ verb **1** [I/T] to hit your foot on something and fall down, or to make someone hit their foot on something and fall down: *I'm sure she tripped me!* ♦ *I tripped over a rock.* **2** [T] to make a switch go on or off, especially by accident
PHRASAL VERB ,trip (sb) ˈup **1** to make a mistake, or to cause someone to make a mistake: *The tests are designed to trip you up.* **2** same as **trip²** 1

trip

triple¹ /ˈtrɪp(ə)l/ adj **1** involving three things of the same kind: *a triple killing* **2** three times bigger than the usual size or amount: *a triple vodka*

triple² /ˈtrɪp(ə)l/ determiner three times as much or as many: *The price they wanted was triple the amount we expected.*

triple³ /ˈtrɪp(ə)l/ verb [I/T] if something triples, or if you triple it, it increases so that it is three times bigger than before: *We had tripled our money by the end of the year.*

triplet /ˈtrɪplət/ noun [C] one of three children who were born at the same time to the same mother

tripod /ˈtraɪpɒd/ noun [C] an object with three legs, used for supporting something such as a camera

trite /traɪt/ adj a trite remark is not interesting or original because people have used it too much

triumph¹ /ˈtraɪʌmf/ noun **1** [C/U] an exciting victory or success **2** [U] the proud or excited feeling that you get when you have been successful

triumph² /ˈtraɪʌmf/ verb [I] to win a great victory, or to have a great success

triumphant /traɪˈʌmfənt/ adj showing that you are very pleased about a victory or success: *a triumphant smile/laugh/yell* —**triumphantly** adv

trivia /ˈtrɪviə/ noun [U] **1** facts about subjects such as sport, history, or television programmes that people use to answer questions in a game **2** unimportant facts or details: *The papers are just full of trivia about celebrities.*

trivial /ˈtrɪviəl/ adj not very interesting, serious, or valuable: *Why are they so upset over such a trivial matter?*

trivialize /ˈtrɪviəlaɪz/ verb [T] to make something seem less important or serious than it really is

trod the past tense of **tread¹**

trodden the past participle of **tread¹**

trolley /ˈtrɒli/ noun [C] *British* a large container with wheels that you push and use for carrying things in a supermarket or at an airport

trombone /trɒmˈbəʊn/ noun [C] a musical instrument consisting of two metal tubes. You play it by blowing into it and sliding one tube forwards and backwards. —*picture* → BRASS

troop /truːp/ verb [I] to walk somewhere in a group

troops /truːps/ noun [plural] soldiers

trophy /ˈtrəʊfi/ noun [C] a large silver cup or similar object that is given as a prize to the winner of a sports competition

tropical /ˈtrɒpɪk(ə)l/ adj in or from the hottest parts of the world

tropics, the /ˈtrɒpɪk/ the hottest parts of the world, that are near the EQUATOR (=imaginary line around the middle of the Earth)

trot¹ /trɒt/ verb [I] to walk quickly with short steps, but without running
PHRASAL VERB ,trot sth ˈout *showing disapproval* to provide an explanation, excuse, or piece of information that has been used many times before

trot² /trɒt/ noun [singular] the speed of a horse or other animal when it trots

PHRASE on the trot British informal one after the other: *We've lost five games on the trot.*

trouble¹ /ˈtrʌb(ə)l/ noun ★★★

1 problems/worries	4 when blame is likely
2 additional effort	5 violence
3 unpleasant situation	**+ PHRASES**

1 [C/U] problems, worries, or difficulties: *The company has had serious financial troubles recently.* ♦ *The plane had engine trouble and had to land in Miami.* ♦ *This old car has caused a lot of trouble for us.* ♦ *I'm having some trouble with my knee.* ♦ *He was having trouble hearing her* (=finding it difficult to hear her).

2 [U] additional or special effort that causes you problems: *I don't mind waiting – it's no trouble.* ♦ *Thank you for taking the trouble to reply.* ♦ *Growing roses is more trouble than it is worth.* ♦ **save sb the trouble of doing sth** *I'll do your shopping to save you the trouble of going out.*

3 [U] an unpleasant, difficult, or dangerous situation: *I knew we were in trouble when the lift stopped.* ♦ *The plane ran into serious trouble soon after take-off.*

4 [U] a situation for which you are likely to be blamed, criticized, or punished: *I hear she's in trouble with the police again.* ♦ *If he hears about this, you'll be in big trouble.* ♦ *I got into trouble for being late.*

5 [C/U] fighting, violence, or bad behaviour: *There's been a lot of trouble in the neighbourhood recently.* ♦ *The trouble started after a youth was arrested.*

PHRASES asking for trouble doing something that is very likely to cause you problems or difficulties: *Delaying surgery is just asking for trouble.*

the trouble with sb/sth used for talking about something that causes problems, worries, or difficulties: *The trouble with my parents is they think I'm still a child.*

trouble² /ˈtrʌb(ə)l/ verb [T] **1** to make someone worried: *I could tell that something was troubling her.* **2** spoken formal used for making a polite request: *Could I trouble you for a lift home?* ♦ *I'm sorry to trouble you, but can I borrow a pen?*

troubled /ˈtrʌb(ə)ld/ adj **1** worried about the problems that you have **2** a troubled place, time, or situation is affected by many problems

troublemaker /ˈtrʌb(ə)lˌmeɪkə/ noun [C] someone who deliberately causes a lot of problems

troubleshooting /ˈtrʌb(ə)lˌʃuːtɪŋ/ noun [U] the activity of finding out the cause of a problem and then solving it —**troubleshooter** noun [C]

troublesome /ˈtrʌb(ə)ls(ə)m/ adj causing annoying problems or difficulties

ˈtrouble ˌspot noun [C] a place where there is often fighting between groups

trough /trɒf/ noun [C] **1** a long open container that is used for holding food or water for animals **2** a period when something that rises and falls regularly is at a low level: *the peaks and troughs in demand*

trounce /traʊns/ verb [T] to easily defeat an opponent in a game, competition, election etc

troupe /truːp/ noun [C] a group of performers

trousers /ˈtraʊzəz/ noun [plural] ★★ a piece of clothing that covers your body from the waist to the feet, with separate parts for each leg: *a pair of trousers* —*picture* → C4

trout /traʊt/ (plural **trout**) noun [C/U] a fish that lives in rivers and lakes, or this fish eaten as food

trowel /ˈtraʊəl/ noun **1** a small tool with a curved blade that is used in gardens for digging **2** a small tool with a flat blade that is used for spreading substances such as CEMENT

truancy /ˈtruːənsi/ noun [U] the act or habit of staying away from school without permission

truant /ˈtruːənt/ noun [C] a child who stays away from school without permission

truce /truːs/ noun [C] a temporary agreement between two opponents to stop fighting

truck /trʌk/ noun [C] ★★ a large road vehicle that is used for carrying goods =LORRY: *a truck driver*

PHRASE have no truck with formal to not want to be involved with someone or something

trucker /ˈtrʌkə/ noun [C] someone whose job is to drive a truck

trudge /trʌdʒ/ verb [I] to walk somewhere with slow heavy steps

true /truː/ adj ★★★

1 based on facts or on things that really happened ≠ FALSE: *The film is based on a true story.* ♦ *It rains a lot in the northwest, and that is especially true of Cumbria.* ♦ **+that** *Is it true that you're looking for a new job?*

2 real or actual, especially when compared with how something seems to be: *Lara never shows her true feelings.* ♦ *The study shows that the true cost of the system is much higher than people think.*

3 having all the qualities that you expect in a particular type of person, thing, or feeling =GENUINE: *Curry was a true champion in every way.* ♦ *The country is not yet a true democracy.* ♦ *true love*

4 if you are true to someone or something, you continue to be loyal to them: *Through the years, Doug stayed true to his wife.*

PHRASES come true if a wish, dream, fear etc comes true, it really happens: *Meeting Joe was like a dream come true* (=exactly what you have always wanted).

true to life similar to what really happens in people's lives: *The characters in this novel are so true to life.*

truffle /ˈtrʌf(ə)l/ noun [C] **1** a soft chocolate sweet **2** a plant that you eat that grows under the ground and is very expensive to buy

truly /ˈtruːli/ adv **1** completely: *a truly*

wonderful job ♦ *She was someone who truly understood children.* **2** used for emphasizing that you really mean what you are saying: *I truly believe you are the right person for the job.*

trump card /'trʌmp ˌkɑːd/ noun [C] an advantage that you have that your opponent does not have

trumpet /'trʌmpɪt/ noun [C] a metal musical instrument that you play by blowing into it as you press buttons on the top —*picture* → BRASS

truncheon /'trʌntʃ(ə)n/ noun [C] a short thick stick that a police officer carries as a weapon

trundle /'trʌnd(ə)l/ verb [I/T] to roll slowly on wheels, or to make something roll slowly on wheels

trunk /trʌŋk/ noun [C]

1 main part of tree	**4** main part of body
2 large strong box	**5** boot of car
3 elephant's nose	

1 the main part of a tree that the branches grow out of —*picture* → TREE **2** a large strong box with a lid, used for storing things **3** an elephant's long nose **4** the part of your body between your waist and your head, not including your arms or head **5** *American* the BOOT of a car

trunk road noun [C] *British* a major road between large towns

trunks /trʌŋks/ noun [plural] a piece of clothing that men wear for swimming —*picture* → C5

trust¹ /trʌst/ verb [T] ★★ to believe that someone or something is good, honest, or reliable: *Both communities have to trust each other.* ♦ *Never trust cheap locks like these.* ♦ **trust sb to do sth** *Can we trust you to give John the message?* ♦ **trust sb with sth** *I trust Dana with all my secrets.*

> **Word family: trust**
>
> *Words in the same family as trust*
> - **trusting** *adj*
> - **trustworthy** *adj*
> - **distrust** *n, v*
> - **trusty** *adj*
> - **untrustworthy** *adj*
> - **mistrust** *n, v*

trust² /trʌst/ noun ★★
1 [U] a feeling that you trust someone or something: *The doctor-patient relationship has to be based on trust.* ♦ *We have to* **put our trust in** *the democratic system.*
2 [C/U] *legal* an arrangement in which a person or an organization manages someone else's money or property, or the money or property that they manage: *The land will* **be held in trust** *by the Church.*

trustee /trʌ'stiː/ noun [C] someone who is responsible for looking after money or property that belongs to someone else

trust fund noun [C] an amount of money that is invested and managed for someone, usually a child

trusting /'trʌstɪŋ/ adj willing to trust people, especially when it is not a sensible thing to do

trustworthy /'trʌs(t)ˌwɜːði/ adj someone who is trustworthy can be trusted
≠ UNTRUSTWORTHY

trusty /'trʌsti/ adj *humorous* a trusty person or possession is one that you know that you can depend on

truth /truːθ/ noun ★★★
1 [U] the actual facts about something, rather than what people think or say is true: *We finally learned* **the truth about** *Gina's past.* ♦ **Tell me the truth:** *did you take the money?* ♦ **The truth is that** *they haven't solved the problem.*
2 [U] the quality of being true: **There is some truth to his story** (=it is partly true). ♦ *Are you questioning* **the truth of** *his accusations?*
3 [C] an idea that is accepted by most people as being true: *Is it* **a universal truth** (=something that is true in all situations) *that exercise is good for you?*
PHRASE **to tell (you) the truth** used for admitting something, or for saying what you really think about something: *To tell you the truth, I don't care.*
→ HOME TRUTHS

> **Words often used with truth**
>
> *Verbs often used with truth (sense 1)*
> - **discover, establish, find out, get at, learn, uncover** + THE + TRUTH: find out the truth
> - **admit, reveal, tell** + THE + TRUTH: say what the truth is

truthful /'truːθf(ə)l/ adj **1** a truthful person says what is true, and does not lie: *He was sure she wasn't being completely truthful.* **2** a truthful statement only contains things that are true —**truthfully** adv

try¹ /traɪ/ (past tense and past participle **tried** /traɪd/) verb ★★★
1 [I/T] to attempt to do something: *Owen tried a shot at goal, but the ball went wide.* ♦ *Just try your best. I'm sure you'll be fine.* ♦ *We'll just have to* **try harder** *next time.* ♦ **try to do sth** *Just try to stay calm.* ♦ **try and do sth** *I will try and get the report to you today.*
2 [T] to do something in order to find out whether it is enjoyable, suitable, or effective: *Have you tried these biscuits? They're great!* ♦ *Let's try something different with your hair this time.* ♦ *You should try yoga if you're feeling stressed – you might like it.* ♦ **try doing sth** *She tried talking about it to Steve, but couldn't make him change his mind.*
3 [I/T] to go to a particular place in order to find something, or to go to a particular person in order to get information: *There's a hardware shop down the street – you could try there.* ♦ *Try Dina – she knows a lot about the law.*
4 [T] to judge a person or case in a court of law: *Franklin's case will be tried on 25th August.* ♦ **try sb for sth** *He was tried for murder and found guilty.*
PHRASE **try your hand at sth** to do an activity for the first time in order to find out whether you like it, or whether you are good at it

T

PHRASAL VERBS ,try sth 'on to put on a piece of clothing in order to see how it looks and whether it fits

,try sth 'out to test something in order to see what it is like or whether it is suitable or effective

try² /traɪ/ noun [C] an attempt to do something: *There are no guarantees that it will work, but it's worth a try.* ♦ *'I can't lift it.' 'Here, let me give it a try.'* ♦ *I'll have a try – I'm pretty good at fixing things.*

trying /'traɪɪŋ/ adj difficult to deal with in a way that makes you annoyed or tired: *We've all had a very trying day.*

tsar /zɑː/ noun [C] the king of Russia in the period before 1917

tsarina /zɑːˈriːnə/ noun [C] the queen of Russia in the period before 1917

T-shirt /'tiː ˌʃɜːt/ noun [C] a soft shirt that has short sleeves and no collar or buttons —*picture* → C5

tsp. abbrev teaspoon

tub /tʌb/ noun [C] **1** a small container with a lid, used for holding or storing food: *ice cream tubs* **2** a large round container with a flat bottom: *tubs of flowers and shrubs* **3** a BATHTUB

tuba /'tjuːbə/ noun [C] a large metal musical instrument that is a curved tube with a wide open end. You play it by blowing into it as you press buttons on the top. —*picture* → BRASS

tube /tjuːb/ noun ★
1 [C] a long narrow object similar to a pipe that liquid or gas can move through: *Nurses had to feed Dan through a tube.*
2 [C] a long narrow plastic or metal container that you squeeze in order to push out the soft substance inside: *a tube of toothpaste*
3 the tube [singular] *British informal* the system of underground trains in London: *a tube station/train* ♦ *She goes to work by tube.*

tuberculosis /tjuːˌbɜːkjʊˈləʊsɪs/ noun [U] a serious infectious disease that affects your lungs

tubing /'tjuːbɪŋ/ noun [U] a piece of tube, or a system of tubes

tuck /tʌk/ verb [T] to put something in a place where it looks tidy or is hidden: *She tucked her glasses into her pocket.*
PHRASAL VERBS ,tuck sth a'way to put something in a safe place
,tuck 'in *British informal* to eat food with enthusiasm: *Everybody tuck in before it gets cold!*
,tuck sb 'in to make sure that a child is warm and comfortable in bed, by covering them well: *I'll be upstairs soon to tuck you in.*
,tuck 'into sth *British informal* to eat food with enthusiasm: *The kids were tucking into a big pizza.*

Tues. or **Tue.** abbrev Tuesday

Tuesday /'tjuːzdeɪ/ noun [C/U] ★★★ the day after Monday and before Wednesday: *New Year's Day will be on a Tuesday this year.* ♦ *We are leaving on Tuesday.* ♦ *We close early on Tuesdays* (=every Tuesday).

tuft /tʌft/ noun [C] several pieces of grass, hair, feathers, or fibres that are all growing together

tug¹ /tʌg/ verb [I/T] to pull someone or something by making a short strong movement: *The little boy tugged on his mother's skirt.* → HEARTSTRINGS

tug² /tʌg/ noun [C] **1** a short strong pull **2 tug** or **tug boat** a small powerful boat that is used for pulling ships in ports

,tug-of-'war noun [C] a situation in which two people or groups try very hard to get something that they both want

tuition /tjuˈɪʃ(ə)n/ noun [U] **1** the work that a teacher does when they teach an individual person or a small group: *He's been getting private tuition in French.* **2** money that you pay to take lessons at a college, university, or private school

tulip /'tjuːlɪp/ noun [C] a colourful flower that is shaped like a cup —*picture* → C9

tumble /'tʌmb(ə)l/ verb [I] **1** if a price or value tumbles, it suddenly becomes much lower **2** to suddenly fall to the ground —**tumble** noun [C]

,tumble 'dryer noun [C] *British* a machine that you use for making clothes dry after they have been washed

tumbler /'tʌmblə/ noun [C] a drinking glass without a handle or STEM (=long thin part connected to the base)

tummy /'tʌmi/ noun [C] *informal* your stomach

tumor /'tjuːmə/ the American spelling of tumour

tumour /'tjuːmə/ noun [C] a mass of cells in your body that grow in a way that is not normal and can cause serious illness

tumultuous /tjuːˈmʌltʃʊəs/ adj noisy and excited: *tumultuous applause*

tuna /'tjuːnə/ noun [C/U] a large fish that lives in the Pacific and Atlantic Oceans, or this fish eaten as food

tune¹ /tjuːn/ noun [C] *informal* ★ a song or simple piece of music: *a Russian folk tune* ♦ *the station that plays all your favourite tunes*
PHRASES **change your tune** to change your opinion or attitude
in tune producing the right note when you sing or play music: *He can sing any song perfectly in tune.*
in tune with understanding the feelings, opinions, or needs of a group of people: *Voters felt she was in tune with their needs and problems.*
out of tune producing the wrong note when you sing or play music: *One of the guitars sounded a little out of tune.*
to the tune of used for emphasizing how large an amount of money is: *The company is in debt to the tune of £1.2 billion.*

tune² /tjuːn/ verb [T] **1** to make small changes to a musical instrument so that it will produce the correct notes **2** to make small changes to an engine or machine so that it works better

PHRASAL VERBS ,tune 'in **1** to listen to or watch a particular broadcast on the radio or television: *Millions of people tuned in to watch the election results.* **2 be tuned in (to sth)** to understand something such as a situation or other people's feelings

,tune 'up if a group of musicians tune up, they make small changes to their instruments so that they can play well together

tunic /ˈtjuːnɪk/ noun [C] **1** a long loose shirt **2** a short jacket that is part of a uniform

tunnel¹ /ˈtʌn(ə)l/ noun [C] ★ a passage through a hill or under the ground: *We watched the train enter a tunnel.*

tunnel

tunnel² /ˈtʌn(ə)l/ (present participle **tunnelling**; past tense and past participle **tunnelled**) verb [T] to dig a tunnel

,tunnel 'vision noun [U] the tendency to think only about one goal or one part of something, without thinking about anything else

turban /ˈtɜːbən/ noun [C] a long piece of cloth that is wrapped around the head like a hat. It is worn by some men in the Sikh, Hindu, and Muslim religions.

turbine /ˈtɜːbaɪn/ noun [C] a machine that produces power by using the pressure of liquid or gas on a wheel

turbulence /ˈtɜːbjʊləns/ noun [U] **1** a confusing situation in which everything is changing in an uncontrolled way: *a period of turbulence after the death of the dictator* **2** sudden violent movements of air or water

turbulent /ˈtɜːbjʊlənt/ adj **1** a turbulent situation, place, or time is one in which there is a lot of uncontrolled change: *the country's turbulent history* **2** turbulent air or water moves suddenly and violently in different directions

turf¹ /tɜːf/ noun [U] short grass and the earth that is under it

turf² /tɜːf/ *British*

PHRASAL VERB ,turf sb 'out *informal* to force someone to leave a place or an organization

turkey /ˈtɜːki/ noun [C/U] a large bird that is similar to a chicken, or the meat from this bird

turmoil /ˈtɜːmɔɪl/ noun [U] a situation in which there is a lot of excitement or uncontrolled activity: *economic/political turmoil ♦ Her life seemed to be in turmoil.*

turn¹ /tɜːn/ verb ★★★

1 change your position	**6** do/become sth else
2 change sth's position	**7** become particular age
3 change direction	**+ PHRASES**
4 move in circle	**+ PHRASAL VERBS**
5 move page	

1 [I/T] to change the position of your body or your head so that you are facing in a different direction: *She turned and smiled at me. ♦ He turned his head and looked around the room. ♦ Maria turned to the reporters and said: 'I'm innocent.' ♦ Lopez just glared at the other man and then turned away. ♦ The girls in front turned round and smiled.*

2 [T] to change the position of something so that it is pointing in a different direction: **turn sth around/round** *Turn your chairs round so you're facing me.*

3 [I/T] to change the direction in which you are moving or travelling, or to make something change direction: *We turned into our drive, glad to get home. ♦ The truck turned around and came back down the hill. ♦ Follow this road, then turn right after the school. ♦* **turn sth around/back/into etc** *They ordered the pilot to turn the plane around.*

4 [I/T] to make a circular movement, or to make something move in a circle: *I heard the key turn in the lock.*

5 [T] if you turn the page of a book or magazine, you move it in order to read a different page

6 [linking verb] to change and do something else, or to become something else: *The weather turned chilly in the afternoon. ♦ The crowd was beginning to turn violent. ♦ The lizard's skin turned green as we watched.*

7 [linking verb] to become a particular age: *He turned 40 in March.*

PHRASES **turn your back on sb/sth** to refuse to accept someone or something that you have previously accepted

turn a corner to reach a stage in which a situation improves, after a difficult period

PHRASAL VERBS ,turn (sb) a'gainst sb/sth to stop liking or supporting someone or something and start opposing them, or to make someone do this: *She's turned your whole family against you.*

,turn sth a'round to make something such as a company or team successful again after a period of being unsuccessful: *The £400 million loan will help turn the country's economy around.*

,turn sb a'way to refuse to let someone come into a place: *Reporters who visited the training ground were turned away.*

,turn 'back to return the same way that you came instead of continuing on your journey: *Bad weather forced them to turn back.*

,turn sth 'down **1** to refuse to accept an offer or request: *How could you turn down such a fantastic job?* **2** to reduce the amount of sound, heat, or light that is produced by a piece of equipment, by pressing a button or

T

by moving a switch ≠ TURN STH UP: *Can you* ***turn the music down*** *a bit?*

,turn sb 'in to tell the police about someone who has committed a crime: *His own brother turned him in.* ♦ *She turned herself in to local police.*

,turn (sth) 'into sth to change or develop into something different, or to make something change or develop into something different: *Our holiday turned into a nightmare.* ♦ *They turned her first book into a movie.*

,turn 'off to leave the road that you are travelling along in order to go along another one: *If you're coming on the M4, turn off at junction 26.*

,turn sb 'off 1 to make someone feel bored or no longer interested in something: *This sort of talk could turn a lot of voters off.* **2** to stop someone feeling sexually attracted or sexually excited ≠ TURN SB ON

,turn sth 'off to stop using a piece of equipment or a supply of gas, electricity, or water by pressing, turning, or moving something ≠ TURN STH ON: *Will you turn the television off, please?* ♦ *The emergency crew turned off the power and gas supplies.*

,turn sb 'on to make someone feel sexually attracted or sexually excited ≠ TURN SB OFF

,turn sth 'on to start using a piece of equipment or a supply of gas, electricity, or water by pressing, turning, or moving something ≠ TURN STH OFF: *Is your computer turned on?* ♦ *Let's turn the radio on and see if it works.*

,turn on sb to make a sudden and unexpected attack on someone using violence or very angry words: *The dog suddenly turned on me.*

,turn 'out 1 to develop in a particular way, or to have a particular result: *I'm sure it will all* ***turn out*** *well in the end.* ♦ *As it turned out, the storm missed Puerto Rico.* ♦ *It all turned out to be a mistake.* **2** to go somewhere in order to be present at an event or in order to take part in an activity: *Only 62% of the electorate turned out to vote.*

,turn sth 'out 1 to stop using a light by pressing a button or moving a switch ≠ TURN STH ON **2** to produce something in large numbers: *The company turns out 2,000 small planes a year.*

,turn 'over *British* to stop watching one television station and start watching another: *Let's turn over – this is really boring.*

,turn (sth) 'over to turn a page in a book or a sheet of paper so that the other side is towards you: *You may turn over your exam papers now.*

,turn sb/sth 'over to give someone or something to someone who is in a position of authority: *The local police* ***turned him over*** *to the FBI.*

,turn sth 'round *British same as* **turn sth around**
'turn to sb to go to someone for help: *There are plenty of people you can turn to for advice.*

'turn to sth to look for a particular page in a book: *Turn to page 17 for our prices.*

,turn (sth) to sth *same as* **turn (sth) into sth**: *Shock at the killings quickly turned to anger.* ♦ *Roads were turned to mud by days of rain.*

,turn 'up 1 to arrive somewhere: *She failed to turn up for work on Monday.* **2** to be found by accident after being lost or not known about: *The documents finally turned up in an office along the corridor.* **3** to happen unexpectedly: *You'll get another job: something is bound to turn up soon.*

,turn sth 'up to increase the amount of sound, heat, or light that is produced by a piece of equipment, by pressing a button or by moving a switch ≠ TURN STH DOWN: *Can you turn the volume up a bit?*

turn² /tɜːn/ noun [C] ★★★

1 time to do sth	**4** change in situation
2 in a road	**5** movement in circle
3 change of direction	**+ PHRASES**

1 the time when you can or must do something, because you are part of a group of people who are each doing the same activity, one after the other: *You've already moved your piece – it's my turn now.* ♦ *You'll just have to* ***wait your turn*** *(=be patient until it is your turn).* ♦ ***sb's turn to do sth*** *I think it's your turn to wash the dishes.*

2 a place where a road bends to the right or left: *There's* ***a very sharp turn*** *at the end of the road.*

3 a change of direction made by a person or vehicle: *He* ***made a left turn*** *into a quiet street.*

4 a change in a situation: *The weather suddenly* ***took a turn*** *for the worse (=became worse).* ♦ *We wanted to express our shock at today's tragic* ***turn of events*** *(=unexpected change in the situation).*

5 a circular movement, when something is turned around

PHRASES **in turn 1** one after the other in a particular order: *We will deal with each of these problems in turn.* **2** as a result of something that is part of a connected series of events: *Bad farming methods caused soil erosion, and this in turn made the land less productive.*

take turns or **take it in turn(s)** *British* if people take turns to do something, each of them does their share of it, one after the other: *We took turns steering the boat.*

the turn of the century/year the time around the end of one century or year and the beginning of the next one: *a mansion built at the turn of the century*

turnaround /'tɜːnəraʊnd/ noun [C] a situation in which something changes completely from a bad situation to a good one: *an economic turnaround*

turning /'tɜːnɪŋ/ noun [C] *British* a road that leads away from the road that you are travelling on

'turning ,point noun [C] a time when an important change takes place

=CROSSROADS: *1956 marked a turning point in Franco's political and personal life.*

turnip /'tɜːnɪp/ noun [C] a large round vegetable that grows under the ground

'turn-off noun [C] a road that leads off a main road or motorway

turnout /'tɜːnaʊt/ noun [singular] the number of people who come to an event: *We're expecting a good turnout at tonight's meeting.*

turnover /'tɜːnˌəʊvə/ noun [C/U] **1** the value of the goods and services that a company sells in a particular period of time **2** the rate at which people leave a business, school etc and new people arrive: *a high turnover of staff*

turnstile /'tɜːnˌstaɪl/ noun [C] a gate with metal bars that move in a circle so that only one person can go through at a time

turntable /'tɜːnˌteɪb(ə)l/ noun [C] a RECORD PLAYER, especially of the type used by DJs

turquoise /'tɜːkwɔɪz/ adj bright green-blue in colour —**turquoise** noun [U]

turret /'tʌrɪt/ noun [C] a small tower on the top of a building such as a castle

turtle /'tɜːt(ə)l/ noun [C] *British* an animal with a shell and four short legs that lives mainly in water → TORTOISE

tusk /tʌsk/ noun [C] one of the two very long pointed teeth on an animal such as an elephant

tussle /'tʌs(ə)l/ noun [C] *informal* a short fight —**tussle** verb [I]

tut /tʌt/ interjection used for representing a sound that you make with your tongue when you do not approve of something

tutor¹ /'tjuːtə/ noun [C] **1** a teacher in a college or university **2** someone who gives private lessons in a particular subject

tutor² /'tjuːtə/ verb [T] *formal* to teach one person or a small group of people

tutorial /tjuːˈtɔːriəl/ noun [C] **1** a lesson in which a small group of students discuss a subject with a tutor at a university or college **2** a book or a computer program that gives instructions on how to do something

tuxedo /tʌkˈsiːdəʊ/ or **tux** /tʌks/ noun [C] a DINNER JACKET

TV /ˌtiː ˈviː/ noun [C/U] ★★★ television: *a TV show* ♦ *What's on TV tonight?*

twang /twæŋ/ noun [singular] the sound that a tight string makes when you pull it —**twang** verb [I/T]

tweak /twiːk/ verb [T] **1** *informal* to make small changes to something in order to improve it **2** to pull or twist a part of someone's body —**tweak** noun [C]

tweed /twiːd/ noun [U] a type of thick rough cloth made from wool of different colours

tweezers /'twiːzəz/ noun [plural] a tool that you use for picking up very small objects or for pulling out hairs. It consists of two narrow pieces of metal joined at one end.

twelfth /twelfθ/ number in the place or position counted as number 12

twelve /twelv/ number the number 12

twentieth /'twentiəθ/ number in the place or position counted as number 20

twenty /'twenti/ number the number 20

twice¹ /twaɪs/ adv ★★★
1 two times: *He's phoned twice already this morning.* ♦ *I go to the gym twice a week.*
2 two times the amount or rate of something: *The United States has twice as many people as Japan.*

twice² /twaɪs/ determiner ★ two times the amount or rate of something: *Wages are rising at twice the rate of inflation.*

twiddle /'twɪd(ə)l/ verb **1** [I/T] to twist or turn something in a bored or nervous way **2** [T] to turn a control on a piece of equipment

twig /twɪg/ noun [C] a very small thin branch on a tree or bush

twilight /'twaɪˌlaɪt/ noun [U] the time in the evening when the sky is beginning to get dark=DUSK

twin¹ /twɪn/ noun [C] ★ one of two children who were born at the same time to the same mother: *my twin brother/sister*

twin² /twɪn/ adj forming a pair of two similar things: *a plane with twin engines*

twin³ /twɪn/ verb **be twinned (with sth)** if two towns in different countries are twinned, they have established a formal connection in order to encourage visits and exchange information

,twin 'beds noun [plural] two separate beds that are next to each other in the same bedroom

twinge /twɪndʒ/ noun [C] **1** a sudden unpleasant feeling: *a twinge of guilt/sadness/regret* **2** a sudden short pain

twinkle /'twɪŋk(ə)l/ verb [I] **1** if someone's eyes twinkle, they seem to shine because the person is happy **2** if lights or stars twinkle, the light from them seems to get brighter then weaker —**twinkle** noun [singular]

twirl /twɜːl/ verb [I/T] to move in circles, or to make something move in circles —**twirl** noun [C]

twist¹ /twɪst/ verb ★

1 bend out of shape	4 change meaning
2 turn sth in circle	5 have many bends
3 injure part of body	+ PHRASE

1 [I/T] to bend or turn into a different shape, or to force something out of its original shape by bending it or turning it: *The force of the explosion had twisted the metal.*
2 [T] to turn something in a circle with your hands or fingers: *Kathryn sat anxiously twisting a handkerchief in her hands.*
3 [T] to injure a part of your body by suddenly bending it too much: *I've twisted my ankle so I won't be able to play.*
4 [T] to change the intended meaning of something slightly, so that it means what you want it to mean: *You're twisting my words.*
5 [I] if a road or river twists, it has a lot of bends in it: *The path twists and turns up the mountainside.*

PHRASE **twist sb's arm** *informal* to persuade someone to do something that they do not want to do

T

twist² /twɪst/ noun [C] **1** a sudden unexpected change in a situation: *This is the final tragic twist in a long story.* **2** a bend in a road or river: *The island roads are full of twists and turns.* **3** a movement in which you turn something: *With a twist of his wrist, he untied the ropes.*

twisted /ˈtwɪstɪd/ adj **1** bent into a shape that is not normal: *All that was left of the car was a tangle of twisted metal.* **2** *informal* someone who is twisted behaves in a strange and cruel way

twitch /twɪtʃ/ verb [I] if part of your body twitches, it makes an uncontrolled movement —**twitch** noun [C]

two /tuː/ number ★★★ the number 2

   PHRASES **in two** into two pieces: *The explosion had broken the plane in two.* **put two and two together** to guess what is happening based on what you have seen or heard

two-dimensional /ˌtuː dɪˈmenʃ(ə)n(ə)l/ adj **1** a two-dimensional shape is flat **2** a two-dimensional character in a book, play, or film does not have the complicated personality of a real person

twofold /ˈtuːfəʊld/ or ˈtwo-ˌfold adj **1** twice as much, or twice as many: *a twofold increase in the amount of traffic* **2** consisting of two parts: *The aim of the campaign is twofold.* —**twofold** adv

ˈtwo-ˌtime verb [T] *informal* to be dishonest with your sexual partner by secretly having a relationship with another person

tycoon /taɪˈkuːn/ noun [C] someone rich and powerful who is involved in business or industry

tying the present participle of **tie**

type¹ /taɪp/ noun ★★★

1 [C] a group of people or things with similar qualities that make them different from other groups=KIND, SORT: *What type of dog have you got?* ♦ *It's a good price for a bike of this type.* ♦ *We provide advice to all types of businesses.*

2 [C] someone with particular interests or qualities: *The bar is popular with arty types.* ♦ *Sam isn't the romantic type.*

3 [U] letters that are printed in a book, magazine, or newspaper, or typed using a keyboard: *The book is produced in large type.*

   PHRASE **be sb's type** to have the particular qualities that someone finds attractive: *Joe's nice, but he's not really my type.*

type² /taɪp/ verb [I/T] to write something using a keyboard

typeface /ˈtaɪpfeɪs/ noun [C] a set of letters and numbers of the same design, used in printing or computing

typewriter /ˈtaɪpˌraɪtə/ noun [C] a machine with a keyboard that you use for typing words directly onto a sheet of paper

typewritten /ˈtaɪpˌrɪt(ə)n/ adj produced using a typewriter, not written by hand

typhoid /ˈtaɪfɔɪd/ noun [U] a serious disease that you can get from food or dirty water

typhoon /taɪˈfuːn/ noun [C] a tropical storm with strong winds

typical /ˈtɪpɪk(ə)l/ adj ★★★

1 like most things of the same type: *It's a typical working-class community.* ♦ *a typical reaction/response/comment* ♦ *His opinions are fairly typical of people of his generation.*

2 behaving in a way that is usual for a particular person: *She responded with typical enthusiasm.* ♦ *It was typical of him to want to help.*

3 *spoken* used for saying that you are not surprised that something bad has happened: ♦ *The show's been cancelled? Typical!* ♦ *It's typical, just when we might win, two of our players got injured.*

typically /ˈtɪpɪkli/ adv **1** usually: *The courses typically last for three days.* **2** with the typical qualities of a particular person or group of people

typify /ˈtɪpɪfaɪ/ verb [T] to be a typical example or feature of something

typing /ˈtaɪpɪŋ/ noun [U] the skill of using a TYPEWRITER or computer keyboard to write documents

typist /ˈtaɪpɪst/ noun [C] someone who types using a TYPEWRITER or a computer keyboard, especially as their job

tyranny /ˈtɪrəni/ noun [C/U] cruel and unfair treatment by someone in a position of power, especially a government —**tyrannical** /tɪˈrænɪk(ə)l/ adj

tyrant /ˈtaɪrənt/ noun [C] someone in a position of power who behaves in a cruel and unfair way

tyre /ˈtaɪə/ noun [C] ★ a thick rubber cover that fits round the wheel of a bicycle, car, or other vehicle: *a car tyre* ♦ *My bike's got a flat tyre.* —*picture* → C6

Uu

u or **U** /juː/ noun [C/U] the 21st letter of the English alphabet → U-TURN

U /juː/ pronoun *informal* a written form of 'you', used in emails and TEXT MESSAGES

ubiquitous /juːˈbɪkwɪtəs/ adj *formal* seeming to be everywhere

udder /ˈʌdə/ noun [C] the part under the body of a cow and some other female animals that produces milk

UFO /ˌjuː ef ˈəʊ/ noun [C] unidentified flying object: a mysterious object that flies through the sky, that some people think is a sign of life from other planets

ugh /ʊx, ʌg/ interjection used for writing the sound that people make when they think that something is extremely unpleasant

ugly /ˈʌgli/ adj ★

1 unpleasant to look at ≠ BEAUTIFUL

2 an ugly situation involves violent or angry behaviour: *an ugly confrontation*

uh huh /ʌ ˈhʌ/ interjection used for writing the sound that people make when they agree with something

uh-oh /ʌ ˈəʊ/ interjection used for writing the sound that people make when they realize that something has gone wrong

uh-uh /ʌ ˈʌ/ interjection used for writing the sound that people make when they disagree with something

UK, the /ˌjuː ˈkeɪ/ the United Kingdom

ulcer /ˈʌlsə/ noun [C] a sore area in your body or on your skin that sometimes BLEEDS or produces a poisonous substance: *a mouth/stomach ulcer* —**ulcerated** /ˈʌlsəreɪtɪd/ adj

Ulster /ˈʌlstə/ another name for Northern Ireland

ulterior motive /ʌlˌtɪəriə ˈməʊtɪv/ noun [C] a secret reason for doing something

ultimate¹ /ˈʌltɪmət/ adj **1** happening at the end of a process or activity = EVENTUAL: *Independence remains their ultimate political goal.* **2** if you have something such as ultimate power or responsibility, you have more power or responsibility than anyone else: *Parents must have ultimate responsibility for their children's safety.* **3** as good or as bad as possible: *The Nobel Prize is the ultimate award for any scientist.*

ultimate² /ˈʌltɪmət/ noun **the ultimate in sth** the best or most perfect example of something: *Our stylish coaches offer the ultimate in luxury travel.*

ultimately /ˈʌltɪmətli/ adv **1** after a process or activity has ended: *Technological advances could ultimately lead to even more job losses.* **2** used for emphasizing the main point that you are talking about: *What worries them, ultimately, is the cost of the scheme.*

ultimatum /ˌʌltɪˈmeɪtəm/ noun [C] a statement that orders someone to do something and threatens to punish or attack them if they do not do it

ultra- /ˈʌltrə/ prefix extremely: *an ultra-modern kitchen*

ultrasonic /ˌʌltrəˈsɒnɪk/ adj used for describing sounds that are higher than the range of sounds that humans can hear

ultrasound /ˈʌltrəsaʊnd/ noun [U] a way of producing an image of an organ or of a baby inside someone's body, using sound waves

ultraviolet /ˌʌltrəˈvaɪələt/ adj ultraviolet light is beyond the normal range of colours that humans can see —**ultraviolet** noun [U]

um /ʌm/ interjection used for writing the sound that people make when they are thinking about what to say next

umbilical cord /ʌmˈbɪlɪk(ə)l ˌkɔːd/ noun [C] a tube that connects a baby to its mother before it is born

umbrage /ˈʌmbrɪdʒ/ noun **take umbrage (at sth)** to be offended by something

umbrella¹ /ʌmˈbrelə/ noun [C] an object that you hold over your head when it is raining

umbrella

umbrella² /ʌmˈbrelə/ adj an umbrella organization consists of a lot of small groups

umpire /ˈʌmpaɪə/ noun [C] someone whose job is to make sure that players obey the rules in some sports, for example tennis, baseball, and CRICKET —*picture* → C15 —**umpire** verb [I/T]

umpteen /ˌʌmpˈtiːn/ determiner *informal* a lot of —**umpteenth** adj

UN, the /ˌjuː ˈen/ the United Nations: an international organization that encourages countries to work together in order to solve world problems

un- /ʌn/ prefix used with many adjectives, adverbs, and verbs to give the opposite meaning: *unhappy* ♦ *unhurriedly* ♦ *unzip*

unabashed /ʌnəˈbæʃt/ adj not ashamed or embarrassed

unabated /ʌnəˈbeɪtɪd/ adj *formal* without stopping

unable /ʌnˈeɪb(ə)l/ adj ★★★
PHRASE **unable to do sth** *formal* not able to do something: *Some of the children were unable to read.* ♦ *Many teenagers feel unable to talk to their parents about their problems.*

unabridged /ʌnəˈbrɪdʒd/ adj an unabridged book or article has not had any parts removed from it

unacceptable /ʌnəkˈseptəb(ə)l/ adj too bad to be allowed to continue —**unacceptably** adv

unaccompanied /ʌnəˈkʌmpənid/ adj **1** someone who is unaccompanied goes somewhere alone **2** an unaccompanied singer or musician sings or plays alone

unaccountable /ʌnəˈkaʊntəb(ə)l/ adj **1** people or organizations that are unaccountable do not have to explain their actions or decisions to anyone else **2** *formal* difficult or impossible to explain or understand —**unaccountably** adv

unaccounted /ʌnəˈkaʊntɪd/ adj **unaccounted for** if something is unaccounted for, you are unable to explain what happened to it or where it is

unaccustomed /ʌnəˈkʌstəmd/ adj unusual
PHRASE **unaccustomed to sth** not used to something

unacknowledged /ʌnəkˈnɒlɪdʒd/ adj not given the praise or admiration that you deserve

unadulterated /ʌnəˈdʌltəreɪtɪd/ adj **1** complete: used for emphasizing how good or bad a quality or feeling is **2** in a pure form with nothing added

unaffected /ˌʌnəˈfektɪd/ adj **1** not changed or influenced by something **2** sincere and natural in your behaviour

unaided /ʌnˈeɪdɪd/ adv formal without help

unaltered /ʌnˈɔːltəd/ adj not changed

unambiguous /ˌʌnæmˈbɪgjuəs/ adj clear and with only one possible meaning

unanimous /juːˈnænɪməs/ adj **1** a unanimous decision, vote, agreement etc is one that everyone agrees with **2** a group of people who are unanimous about something all agree about it —**unanimity** /ˌjuːnəˈnɪməti/ noun [U], **unanimously** adv

unannounced /ˌʌnəˈnaʊnst/ adv unexpectedly

unanswered /ʌnˈɑːnsəd/ adj **1** an unanswered question or problem has not been answered or solved **2** an unanswered letter, message, or phone call has not had a reply

unappealing /ˌʌnəˈpiːlɪŋ/ adj not attractive or enjoyable

unappetizing /ʌnˈæpɪˌtaɪzɪŋ/ adj food that is unappetizing does not look or smell good

unapproachable /ˌʌnəˈprəʊtʃəb(ə)l/ adj not friendly and not easy to talk to

unarmed /ʌnˈɑːmd/ adj not carrying a weapon

unashamedly /ˌʌnəˈʃeɪmɪdli/ adv in a way that shows that you are not embarrassed or worried about what other people think of you —**unashamed** /ˌʌnəˈʃeɪmd/ adj

unasked /ʌnˈɑːskt/ adj **1** an unasked question is a question that people have not asked **2** if you do something unasked, you do it without being asked or told to

unassailable /ˌʌnəˈseɪləb(ə)l/ adj formal impossible to defeat, criticize, or argue with

unassisted /ˌʌnəˈsɪstɪd/ adj without help

unassuming /ˌʌnəˈsjuːmɪŋ/ adj behaving in a quiet pleasant way, without wanting to attract attention=MODEST

unattached /ˌʌnəˈtætʃt/ adj not married, or not having a boyfriend or girlfriend

unattainable /ˌʌnəˈteɪnəb(ə)l/ adj impossible to achieve or obtain

unattended /ˌʌnəˈtendɪd/ adj left without being looked after or dealt with

unattractive /ˌʌnəˈtræktɪv/ adj **1** ugly **2** unpleasant or not enjoyable

unauthorized /ʌnˈɔːθəˌraɪzd/ adj done without official permission

unavailable /ˌʌnəˈveɪləb(ə)l/ adj **1** not able to go somewhere, meet someone, or do something **2** impossible to obtain

unavoidable /ˌʌnəˈvɔɪdəb(ə)l/ adj impossible to stop from happening=INEVITABLE —**unavoidably** adv

unaware /ˌʌnəˈweə/ adj not realizing that something exists or is happening

unawares /ˌʌnəˈweəz/ adv **catch/take sb unawares** to surprise someone, often making them feel confused or embarrassed

unbalanced /ʌnˈbælənst/ adj **1** mentally ill **2** giving only one view or opinion of a situation or subject=BIASED

unbearable /ʌnˈbeərəb(ə)l/ adj too unpleasant or painful to deal with —**unbearably** adv

unbeatable /ʌnˈbiːtəb(ə)l/ adj **1** impossible to defeat **2** better than anything else of the same type

unbeaten /ʌnˈbiːt(ə)n/ adj if a team, player etc is unbeaten, they have not been defeated

unbelievable /ˌʌnbɪˈliːvəb(ə)l/ adj **1** informal used for emphasizing how good, bad, impressive etc something is **2** too unlikely to be true or to be believed —**unbelievably** adv

unbending /ʌnˈbendɪŋ/ adj unwilling to change your opinions or beliefs

unbiased /ʌnˈbaɪəst/ adj fair in the way that you describe or deal with a situation

unblemished /ʌnˈblemɪʃt/ adj **1** without any faults or mistakes **2** without any marks that harm the appearance of something

unblock /ʌnˈblɒk/ verb [T] to remove something that is blocking a pipe or tube

unborn /ʌnˈbɔːn/ adj an unborn child is still inside its mother's body

unbreakable /ʌnˈbreɪkəb(ə)l/ adj impossible to break

unbroken /ʌnˈbrəʊkən/ adj **1** continuing for a long time without stopping=CONTINUOUS **2** not broken or damaged

unbutton /ʌnˈbʌt(ə)n/ verb [T] to UNDO (=open) the buttons on a piece of clothing

uncalled for /ʌnˈkɔːld fɔː/ adj insulting or offensive

uncanny /ʌnˈkæni/ adj strange and mysterious —**uncannily** adv

uncaring /ʌnˈkeərɪŋ/ adj without any sympathy for other people

unceremoniously /ˌʌnserɪˈməʊniəsli/ adv done suddenly, with no attempt to be polite

uncertain /ʌnˈsɜːt(ə)n/ adj **1** not clearly known or understood: *It is uncertain how they entered the property.* ♦ *The whole industry faces a very uncertain future.* **2** not feeling sure about something: *I left the meeting feeling uncertain about what to do next.*

PHRASE in no uncertain terms in a way that is clear and definite: *She was told in no uncertain terms that she would have to accept the deal.* —**uncertainty** noun [C/U]

unchallenged /ʌnˈtʃælɪndʒd/ adj **1** accepted as right or correct **2** not stopped from going somewhere **3** a leader or CANDIDATE who is unchallenged is not opposed by anyone

unchallenging /ʌnˈtʃælɪndʒɪŋ/ adj too easy, and therefore not very interesting

unchanged /ʌnˈtʃeɪndʒd/ adj remaining the same

unchanging /ʌnˈtʃeɪndʒɪŋ/ adj always remaining the same

uncharacteristic /ˌʌnkærɪktəˈrɪstɪk/ adj not typical of someone or something, and therefore surprising —**uncharacteristically** /ˌʌnkærɪktəˈrɪstɪkli/ adv

uncharitable /ʌnˈtʃærɪtəb(ə)l/ adj unkind in what you say or think about someone

uncharted /ʌnˈtʃɑːtɪd/ adj not shown on any map=UNEXPLORED
PHRASE **uncharted territory/waters** an activity or subject that people do not know anything about, or one that they have not experienced before

unchecked /ʌnˈtʃekt/ adj formal not controlled or prevented from happening

uncivilized /ʌnˈsɪvəˌlaɪzd/ adj behaving in a rude or offensive way

unclaimed /ʌnˈkleɪmd/ adj without a known owner

unclassified /ʌnˈklæsɪfaɪd/ adj unclassified information is available to everyone and is not secret

uncle /ˈʌŋk(ə)l/ noun [C] ★ the brother of one of your parents, or the husband of your AUNT: *The business was owned by my uncle.* ♦ *a letter from Uncle Richard* —picture → FAMILY TREE

unclear /ʌnˈklɪə/ adj not obvious, definite, or easy to understand
PHRASE **be unclear about/as to sth** to not understand something, or to not be certain about something

uncluttered /ʌnˈklʌtəd/ adj simple, tidy, and not containing any unnecessary things

uncomfortable /ʌnˈkʌmftəb(ə)l/ adj ★
1 if you are uncomfortable, you have an unpleasant or slightly painful feeling in part of your body: *You'll be uncomfortable for a few days after the surgery.* ♦ *They were sitting in a very uncomfortable position.*
2 used for describing something that makes you have an unpleasant or slightly painful feeling in part of your body: *uncomfortable clothes/shoes* ♦ *an uncomfortable-looking chair*
3 feeling embarrassed or nervous, or making you feel embarrassed or nervous =UNEASY: *A long uncomfortable silence followed.*
—**uncomfortably** adv

uncommon /ʌnˈkɒmən/ adj unusual or rare

uncommunicative /ˌʌnkəˈmjuːnɪkətɪv/ adj not willing to talk or give information

uncompetitive /ˌʌnkəmˈpetətɪv/ adj not able to compete successfully with other businesses or products

uncomplicated /ʌnˈkɒmplɪˌkeɪtɪd/ adj simple =STRAIGHTFORWARD

uncompromising /ʌnˈkɒmprəˌmaɪzɪŋ/ adj very determined, and not willing to change your opinions, plans, or actions

unconcerned /ˌʌnkənˈsɜːnd/ adj not worried about a situation or about what might happen

unconditional /ˌʌnkənˈdɪʃ(ə)nəl/ adj without limits or conditions —**unconditionally** adv

unconfirmed /ˌʌnkənˈfɜːmd/ adj with no definite proof to show that something is true: *unconfirmed reports of fighting*

unconnected /ˌʌnkəˈnektɪd/ adj not related or linked

unconscious¹ /ʌnˈkɒnʃəs/ adj **1** in a condition similar to sleep in which you do not see, feel, or think, usually because you are injured **2** an unconscious feeling or thought is one that you do not realize you have
—**unconsciously** adv, **unconsciousness** noun [U]

unconscious² /ʌnˈkɒnʃəs/ noun [singular] the part of your mind that contains unconscious feelings and thoughts that influence your behaviour=SUBCONSCIOUS

unconstitutional /ˌʌnkɒnstɪˈtjuːʃ(ə)nəl/ adj not allowed or not legal according to the rules of a particular country or organization

uncontrollable /ˌʌnkənˈtrəʊləb(ə)l/ adj **1** impossible to control or stop **2** someone who is uncontrollable behaves badly and refuses to do what other people tell them
—**uncontrollably** adv

uncontrolled /ˌʌnkənˈtrəʊld/ adj continuing without being controlled or stopped

uncontroversial /ˌʌnkɒntrəˈvɜːʃ(ə)l/ adj if an idea, statement, or situation is uncontroversial, the majority of people accept that it is right

unconventional /ˌʌnkənˈvenʃ(ə)nəl/ adj different from what most people consider to be usual or normal —**unconventionally** adv

unconvinced /ˌʌnkənˈvɪnst/ adj not certain that something is true or right

unconvincing /ˌʌnkənˈvɪnsɪŋ/ adj not likely to persuade you that something is true or right

uncooked /ʌnˈkʊkt/ adj raw, or not yet cooked

uncool /ʌnˈkuːl/ adj informal not considered popular, attractive, or fashionable

uncooperative /ˌʌnkəʊˈɒp(ə)rətɪv/ adj not willing to work with or to help another person or group

uncoordinated /ˌʌnkəʊˈɔːdɪˌneɪtɪd/ adj **1** not graceful, or not able to fully control your movements=CLUMSY **2** badly planned or organized

uncork /ʌnˈkɔːk/ verb [T] to open a bottle by taking the CORK out of it

uncountable /ʌnˈkaʊntəb(ə)l/ adj linguistics an uncountable noun has no plural form and cannot be counted in individual units. Uncountable nouns are marked [U] in this dictionary.

uncouth /ʌnˈkuːθ/ adj behaving in a way that polite people think is rude or offensive

uncover /ʌnˈkʌvə/ verb [T] **1** to find out about something that has been hidden or kept secret **2** to take the lid or cover off something

uncritical /ʌnˈkrɪtɪk(ə)l/ adj not criticizing someone or something, even when they should be criticized

uncultivated /ʌnˈkʌltɪˌveɪtɪd/ adj uncultivated land has not been used for growing crops

uncut /ʌnˈkʌt/ adj **1** allowed to grow longer without being cut: *uncut hair* **2** an uncut film or book is complete and has not had parts removed

undamaged /ʌnˈdæmɪdʒd/ adj not damaged

undaunted /ʌnˈdɔːntɪd/ adj not afraid to continue doing something, even though it might be difficult

U

undecided /ˌʌndɪˈsaɪdɪd/ adj if someone is undecided, they have not yet made a decision about something

undeclared /ˌʌndɪˈkleəd/ adj undeclared goods or profits have been illegally kept secret from the authorities, by someone who wants to avoid paying tax on them

undefeated /ˌʌndɪˈfiːtɪd/ adj not having been defeated in a particular period of time

undefended /ˌʌndɪˈfendɪd/ adj not effectively guarded or protected

undefined /ˌʌndɪˈfaɪnd/ adj **1** not clearly explained, or without clear rules or limits **2** without a clear shape or form

undemanding /ˌʌndɪˈmɑːndɪŋ/ adj **1** not expecting other people to do things for you or to pay attention to you **2** not needing much mental or physical effort

undemocratic /ˌʌndeməˈkrætɪk/ adj **1** controlled by officials or politicians who have not been elected by the people **2** not representing the wishes of the majority of people, and therefore unfair

undeniable /ˌʌndɪˈnaɪəb(ə)l/ adj certainly correct or true＝INDISPUTABLE —**undeniably** adv

under /ˈʌndə/ adv, preposition ★★★
1 below or covered by sth in or to a position directly below or covered by something: *What are you kids doing under the table?* ♦ *We drove under the bridge and came out into the High Street.* ♦ *I found the letter under a pile of books.* ♦ *Charlotte saw a light coming from under the door.*
2 below the surface below the surface of water: *The ducks kept diving under the water to catch fish.* ♦ *Jump into the water and see how long you can stay under.*
3 less than less than a particular amount, or younger than a particular age ≠ OVER: *A visa is not required for a stay of under three months.* ♦ *The nursery is open for children aged four and under.* → UNDERAGE
4 affected by sth in the process of being affected by a particular action, situation, or state: *A number of proposals are under consideration.* ♦ *I've been under a lot of stress at work lately.*
5 according to a rule according to a particular law, agreement, or system: *Under the terms of the agreement, our company will receive 40% of the profits.*
6 controlled or taught by sb with a particular person or group in control of you as your leader, manager, or teacher: *He studied under Chomsky in the 1960s.*
7 using a particular name using a particular name in some situations, often a name that is not your own: *Carson had been travelling under a false name.*
8 where sth can be found if something is under a particular title, letter etc, that is where it can be found: *Those forms are in the filing cabinet under 'Miscellaneous'.* → UNDERWAY

underage /ˌʌndərˈeɪdʒ/ adj not old enough to do something legally, for example drink alcohol or drive a car

underarm /ˈʌndərˌɑːm/ noun [C] the area of your body under your arm ＝ ARMPIT

undercarriage /ˈʌndəˌkærɪdʒ/ noun [C] the wheels of a plane and the whole structure that supports it

underclass /ˈʌndəˌklɑːs/ noun [C] the lowest social class in a society, consisting of people who are the poorest and have the least power

undercover /ˌʌndəˈkʌvə/ adj working or done secretly in order to catch criminals or get secret information —**undercover** adv

undercurrent /ˈʌndəˌkʌrənt/ noun [C] **1** a current that moves below the surface in the sea or a river **2** a feeling that exists and affects the way people behave, but is not obvious or stated directly

undercut /ˌʌndəˈkʌt/ (past tense and past participle **undercut**) verb [T] to sell something for less money than another company or shop

underdeveloped /ˌʌndədɪˈveləpt/ adj **1** an underdeveloped country or region is poor. Many people think that this word is offensive, and prefer to use the word **developing**. **2** an underdeveloped person or body has not grown as much as it should have

underdog /ˈʌndədɒɡ/ noun [C] a person or team that seems least likely to win something

underdone /ˌʌndəˈdʌn/ adj underdone food has not been cooked for long enough ≠ OVERDONE

underestimate /ˌʌndərˈestɪˌmeɪt/ verb [T] **1** to think that someone has less power or ability than they really do **2** to think or guess that something is smaller, less important etc than it really is ≠ OVERESTIMATE —**underestimate** /ˌʌndərˈestɪmət/ noun [C]

underfoot /ˌʌndəˈfʊt/ adv under your feet in the place where you are walking

underfund /ˌʌndəˈfʌnd/ verb [T] to not provide an organization, project etc with enough money to operate effectively —**underfunded** adj, **underfunding** noun [U]

undergo /ˌʌndəˈɡəʊ/ (past tense **underwent** /ˌʌndəˈwent/; past participle **undergone** /ˌʌndəˈɡɒn/) verb [T] to experience something, especially a change or medical treatment: *Thompson underwent knee surgery in April.* ♦ *The bridge has undergone repairs.*

undergraduate /ˌʌndəˈɡrædʒʊət/ noun [C] a student who is studying for a first degree at a college or university

underground /ˈʌndəɡraʊnd/ adj **1** below the surface of the ground **2** secret and usually illegal —**underground** /ˌʌndəˈɡraʊnd/ adv

Underground, the /ˈʌndəɡraʊnd/ noun [singular] a railway system that is under a city, for example in London —*picture* → C7

undergrowth /ˈʌndəɡrəʊθ/ noun [U] small thick bushes that cover the ground

underhand /ˌʌndəˈhænd/ adj *British* secret and dishonest

underlie /ˌʌndəˈlaɪ/ (present participle **underlying** /ˌʌndəˈlaɪɪŋ/; past tense **underlay** /ˌʌndəˈleɪ/; past participle **underlain** /ˌʌndəˈleɪn/) verb [T] to be the real or basic cause of or reason for something

underline /ˌʌndəˈlaɪn/ verb [T] **1** to show or emphasize that something is important or true: *The recent violence underlines the need for continuing peace talks.* **2** to draw a line under something

underlying /ˌʌndəˈlaɪɪŋ/ adj underlying causes, facts, ideas etc are the real or basic ones, although they are not obvious: *The underlying causes of the riots have been ignored.*

undermine /ˌʌndəˈmaɪn/ verb [T] to make something or someone become gradually less effective, confident, or successful

underneath /ˌʌndəˈniːθ/ adv, preposition ★★
1 in, to, or through a place directly below something, or below something that covers it: *I'll leave the key underneath the mat.* ♦ *He hid underneath the bed.* ♦ *The photographer's name was printed underneath.*
2 on the lower surface of something: *The pancakes should be golden underneath.*
3 used for describing what someone or something is really like, despite how they may seem: *Gary acts tough, but underneath he's really very kind.*

underpaid /ˌʌndəˈpeɪd/ adj not earning enough money for the work that you do
—**underpay** verb [I/T]

underpants /ˈʌndəˌpænts/ noun [plural] underwear for men worn on the lower half of the body

underpass /ˈʌndəˌpɑːs/ noun [C] part of a road or path that goes under another road or a railway

underpin /ˌʌndəˈpɪn/ verb [T] to be an important basic part of something, allowing it to succeed or continue to exist

underprivileged /ˌʌndəˈprɪvəlɪdʒd/ adj not having as many advantages or opportunities as most other people

underrated /ˌʌndəˈreɪtɪd/ adj if a person or thing is underrated, most people do not recognize how good that person or thing really is ≠ OVERRATED —**underrate** verb [T]

underscore /ˌʌndəˈskɔː/ verb [T] to emphasize something, or to show that it is important =UNDERLINE

undersea /ˌʌndəˈsiː/ adj existing or happening under the surface of the sea

undershirt /ˈʌndəʃɜːt/ noun [C] *American* a VEST

underside /ˈʌndəˌsaɪd/ noun [C] the bottom side or surface of something

understaffed /ˌʌndəˈstɑːft/ adj not having enough workers

understand /ˌʌndəˈstænd/ (past tense and past participle **understood** /ˌʌndəˈstʊd/) verb ★★★
1 [I/T] to know what someone or something means: *I didn't understand a word he was saying.* ♦ *The instructions were easy to understand.* ♦ *I'm sorry, I don't understand French.*

2 [I/T] to know how or why something happens, or what effect or influence something has: *Do they fully understand the implications of their decision?* ♦
+how/why/what etc *We are only beginning to understand how the brain functions.*
3 [I/T] to know how someone feels, or why someone does something: *I understand your concern, but the operation is completely safe.* ♦ *Does she understand why he doesn't want to see her?*
4 [T] *formal* to believe that something is true because you have heard or read it somewhere: **+(that)** *We understand that a major announcement is to be made tomorrow.*
PHRASE **make yourself understood** to know enough of another language to be able to deal with ordinary situations

---

Word family: understand

*Words in the same family as **understand***
- **understandable** *adj*
- **understandably** *adv*
- **understanding** *n*
- **misunderstand** *v*
- **misunderstood** *adj*
- **misunderstanding** *n*

---

understandable /ˌʌndəˈstændəb(ə)l/ adj
1 normal and reasonable in a particular situation **2** clear and easy to understand
—**understandably** adv

understanding¹ /ˌʌndəˈstændɪŋ/ noun ★★
1 [singular/U] knowledge about a particular subject, process, or situation: *The course will help you develop a deeper understanding of yourself.*
2 [U] sympathy that comes from knowing how other people feel and why they do things: *Suzy just needs a little understanding.*
3 [C] an agreement that is made in an informal way, or that is not expressed in words: *We have an understanding with them that we won't compete directly.* ♦ *We gave them the information on the understanding that it would not be made public.*
4 [C/U] the particular way in which you understand the meaning of something =INTERPRETATION: *My understanding was that the meeting would end at 5 o'clock.*

understanding² /ˌʌndəˈstændɪŋ/ adj willing to forgive other people or to be sympathetic, because you understand how they feel

understated /ˌʌndəˈsteɪtɪd/ adj not trying to impress people or attract their attention, and therefore attractive or effective

understatement /ˈʌndəˌsteɪtmənt/ noun [C/U] something that you say that makes something seem less important or serious than it really is

understood the past tense and past participle of **understand**

understudy /ˈʌndəˌstʌdi/ noun [C] an actor whose job is to learn someone else's part in a play, so that they can perform it if that person is ill

undertake /ˌʌndəˈteɪk/ (past tense **undertook** /ˌʌndəˈtʊk/; past participle **undertaken**

U

/ˌʌndəˈteɪkən/) verb [T] **1** to agree to be responsible for a job or project, and to do it: *The most recent survey of rare birds was undertaken in 1991.* ♦ *It is one of the largest dam projects ever undertaken.* **2** *formal* to promise to do something

undertaker /ˈʌndəˌteɪkə/ noun [C] someone whose job is to make arrangements for funerals = FUNERAL DIRECTOR

undertaking /ˈʌndəˌteɪkɪŋ/ noun [C] **1** something that you do that is difficult or complicated **2** *formal* a promise or agreement

undertone /ˈʌndəˌtəʊn/ noun [C] an idea or feeling that exists, but is not obvious

undertook the past tense of **undertake**

underused /ˌʌndəˈjuːzd/ adj not used enough

undervalue /ˌʌndəˈvæljuː/ verb [T] **1** to not recognize how important or valuable someone or something is **2** to think that something is worth less money than it really is —**undervalued** /ˌʌndəˈvæljuːd/ adj

underwater /ˌʌndəˈwɔːtə/ adj, adv existing, happening, or used under the surface of water

underway /ˌʌndəˈweɪ/ adj already started or happening: *Rescue efforts are underway.*

underwear /ˈʌndəˌweə/ noun [U] clothes that you wear next to your skin under your other clothes

underweight /ˌʌndəˈweɪt/ adj below the normal weight ≠ OVERWEIGHT

underwent the past tense of **undergo**

underworld /ˈʌndəˌwɜːld/ noun **1** [singular] the criminals in a particular community, considered as a group **2 the Underworld** in old stories, a place below the Earth's surface where people go when they die

undeserved /ˌʌndɪˈzɜːvd/ adj if something is undeserved, you get it even though you have not done anything to deserve it

undesirable /ˌʌndɪˈzaɪrəb(ə)l/ adj bad or harmful

undetected /ˌʌndɪˈtektɪd/ adj not noticed

undeterred /ˌʌndɪˈtɜːd/ adj continuing to do something, even though you are not successful or people do not support you

undeveloped /ˌʌndɪˈveləpt/ adj **1** not fully grown **2** undeveloped land has not been used for building or industry

undid the past tense of **undo**

undies /ˈʌndiz/ noun [plural] *informal* UNDERWEAR

undignified /ʌnˈdɪɡnɪˌfaɪd/ adj embarrassing or silly

undiluted /ˌʌndaɪˈluːtɪd/ adj **1** strong, with no water mixed in **2** without any attempt to make something less offensive or easier to accept

undiplomatic /ˌʌndɪpləˈmætɪk/ adj very direct, in a way that is likely to cause offence = TACTLESS —**undiplomatically** /ˌʌndɪpləˈmætɪkli/ adv

undisciplined /ʌnˈdɪsəplɪnd/ adj not well controlled

undisclosed /ˌʌndɪsˈkləʊzd/ adj not reported publicly

undiscovered /ˌʌndɪˈskʌvəd/ adj not noticed or known about

undiscriminating /ˌʌndɪˈskrɪmɪˌneɪtɪŋ/ adj deciding what you like without thinking carefully about the value or qualities of different things

undisguised /ˌʌndɪsˈɡaɪzd/ adj without any attempt to make your feelings less obvious

undisputed /ˌʌndɪˈspjuːtɪd/ adj agreed or accepted by everyone

undistinguished /ˌʌndɪˈstɪŋɡwɪʃt/ adj not very good or special

undisturbed /ˌʌndɪˈstɜːbd/ adj **1** not touched or moved **2** not interrupted by anyone

undivided /ˌʌndɪˈvaɪdɪd/ adj complete and total: *You should give this matter your undivided attention.*

undo /ʌnˈduː/ (past tense **undid** /ʌnˈdɪd/; past participle **undone** /ʌnˈdʌn/) verb **1** [T] to open or untie something so that it is no longer closed or fastened: *He undid the screws that held the cassette together.* ♦ *I can't undo my belt.* **2** [T] to have the effect of changing something back into its original, usually worse, state: *One mistake could undo all our achievements.* **3** [I/T] *computing* to give a computer an instruction to ignore the last change that you made

undone /ʌnˈdʌn/ adj **1** not closed or fastened **2** not finished

undoubtedly /ʌnˈdaʊtɪdli/ adv used for saying something is certainly true or accepted by everyone —**undoubted** adj

undress /ʌnˈdres/ verb [I/T] to remove your clothes, or to remove someone else's clothes

undressed /ʌnˈdrest/ adj not wearing any clothes

undue /ʌnˈdjuː/ adj *formal* not necessary or reasonable

undulating /ˈʌndjʊˌleɪtɪŋ/ adj having slopes and curves, or moving gently up and down in the shape of waves —**undulate** verb [I]

unduly /ʌnˈdjuːli/ adv *formal* too much

undying /ʌnˈdaɪɪŋ/ adj never-ending

unearth /ʌnˈɜːθ/ verb [T] **1** to discover someone or something that was not known before **2** to find something that is buried in the ground

uneasy /ʌnˈiːzi/ adj slightly nervous or worried about something —**unease** noun [U], **uneasily** adv

uneconomic /ˌʌniːkəˈnɒmɪk/ adj not capable of making a profit = UNPROFITABLE

uneducated /ʌnˈedjʊˌkeɪtɪd/ adj not having had much education

unemotional /ˌʌnɪˈməʊʃ(ə)nəl/ adj not showing any feelings

unemployed /ˌʌnɪmˈplɔɪd/ adj ★
1 without a job: *Have you been unemployed for a year or more?* ♦ *an unemployed actor/ engineer/teacher*
2 the unemployed people who are unemployed

unemployment /ˌʌnɪmˈplɔɪmənt/ noun [U] ★★ a situation in which people do not have jobs, or the fact that someone does not have a job: *Unemployment rose last month to its* highest level in five years. ♦ *a period of high/low unemployment*

unem'ployment ,benefit noun [U] *British* money that is provided by the government for someone who does not have a job

unending /ʌnˈendɪŋ/ adj continuing without stopping, or seeming to last for ever

unenthusiastic /ˌʌnɪnˌθjuːziˈæstɪk/ adj not excited or enthusiastic about something

unenviable /ʌnˈenviəb(ə)l/ adj difficult and not enjoyable

unequal /ʌnˈiːkwəl/ adj **1** not giving the same treatment or opportunities to everyone, and therefore unfair **2** not the same in amount, number, or size **3** involving one person, team, army etc that is much stronger than another **4** not good enough or skilful enough to do something

unequivocal /ˌʌnɪˈkwɪvək(ə)l/ adj *formal* clear and definite —**unequivocally** adv

unerring /ʌnˈɜːrɪŋ/ adj always right or accurate

unethical /ʌnˈeθɪk(ə)l/ adj morally wrong

uneven /ʌnˈiːv(ə)n/ adj **1** not smooth or level **2** not the same in size or length **3** not fairly balanced or equally shared **4** not of the same quality in all its parts=PATCHY —**unevenly** adv

uneventful /ˌʌnɪˈventf(ə)l/ adj without anything unusual or exciting happening

unexceptional /ˌʌnɪkˈsepʃ(ə)nəl/ adj not especially good or unusual

unexciting /ˌʌnɪkˈsaɪtɪŋ/ adj not interesting or exciting

unexpected /ˌʌnɪkˈspektɪd/ adj ★ surprising: *Her divorce was totally unexpected.* ♦ *Belgium's unexpected victory over France* —**unexpectedly** adv

unexplained /ˌʌnɪkˈspleɪnd/ adj an unexplained event seems to have no explanation or reason

unexplored /ˌʌnɪkˈsplɔːd/ adj **1** never visited by people **2** not thought about or considered before

unfailing /ʌnˈfeɪlɪŋ/ adj never changing or ending —**unfailingly** adv

unfair /ʌnˈfeə/ adj ★

1 not fair or reasonable=UNJUST: *It is grossly unfair* (=very unfair) *to suggest that the school was responsible for this accident.* ♦ *Two former soldiers have taken the government to court for unfair dismissal* (=the fact of being ordered to leave their job for no good reason).

2 not treating people equally: *It is unfair that not everyone got the chance to vote.* ♦ *Their very low labour costs give them an unfair advantage in the market.*
—**unfairly** adv

unfaithful /ʌnˈfeɪθf(ə)l/ adj having a sexual relationship with someone who is not your husband, wife, or usual partner

unfamiliar /ˌʌnfəˈmɪljə/ adj if you are unfamiliar with something, you have no knowledge or experience of it
—**unfamiliarity** /ˌʌnfəˌmɪliˈærəti/ noun [U]

unfashionable /ʌnˈfæʃ(ə)nəb(ə)l/ adj not popular or fashionable

unfasten /ʌnˈfɑːs(ə)n/ verb [T] to open or untie something, especially a piece of clothing or a belt=UNDO

unfathomable /ʌnˈfæðəməb(ə)l/ adj *formal* impossible to explain, or impossible to understand

unfavourable /ʌnˈfeɪv(ə)rəb(ə)l/ adj **1** not positive, or not showing approval =UNFAVOURABLE **2** an unfavourable situation is one that is not suitable for doing something in: *unfavourable weather conditions*
—**unfavourably** adv

unfazed /ʌnˈfeɪzd/ adj not worried or upset by something bad that happens

unfeasible /ʌnˈfiːzəb(ə)l/ adj not possible or practical to do or believe —**unfeasibly** adv

unfeeling /ʌnˈfiːlɪŋ/ adj not showing sympathy for other people

unfinished /ʌnˈfɪnɪʃt/ adj not finished, or not dealt with completely

unfit /ʌnˈfɪt/ adj **1** below the accepted quality or standard for a particular use or purpose: *an unfit mother* **2** not feeling healthy or strong because you do not take enough exercise

unflattering /ʌnˈflæt(ə)rɪŋ/ adj making someone seem unpleasant or not attractive

unfold /ʌnˈfəʊld/ verb **1** [T] to open something that was folded **2** [I] to happen or develop

unforeseeable /ˌʌnfɔːˈsiːəb(ə)l/ adj impossible to know about or expect

unforeseen /ˌʌnfɔːˈsiːn/ adj an unforeseen situation is one that you did not expect =UNEXPECTED

unforgettable /ˌʌnfəˈgetəb(ə)l/ adj something that is unforgettable will be remembered for a very long time=MEMORABLE
—**unforgettably** adv

unforgivable /ˌʌnfəˈgɪvəb(ə)l/ adj extremely bad and impossible to forgive =INEXCUSABLE

unforgiving /ˌʌnfəˈgɪvɪŋ/ adj not willing to forgive people

unforthcoming /ˌʌnfɔːˈθkʌmɪŋ/ adj not willing to talk or provide information

unfortunate /ʌnˈfɔːtʃ(ə)nət/ adj **1** experiencing bad luck, or caused by bad luck=UNLUCKY: *The unfortunate woman had had all her jewellery stolen.* **2** *formal* if something is unfortunate, you do not approve of it, or you wish that it had not happened: *an unfortunate accident*

unfortunately /ʌnˈfɔːtʃ(ə)nətli/ adv ★ used for saying that you wish that something had not happened, or that it was not true: *Unfortunately, Jack is leaving the company.* ♦ *Effective treatments do exist, but unfortunately they are very expensive.*

unfounded /ʌnˈfaʊndɪd/ adj not supported with facts or evidence

unfriendly /ʌnˈfren(d)li/ adj not friendly

unfulfilled /ˌʌnfʊlˈfɪld/ adj unhappy because you have not achieved what you want

unfurl /ʌnˈfɜːl/ verb [I/T] to untie or open

U

unfurnished /ʌnˈfɜːnɪʃt/ adj without any furniture

ungainly /ʌnˈɡeɪnli/ adj not moving in an attractive or graceful way

ungracious /ʌnˈɡreɪʃəs/ adj not polite or friendly —**ungraciously** adv

ungrammatical /ˌʌnɡrəˈmætɪk(ə)l/ adj not correct according to the rules of grammar

ungrateful /ʌnˈɡreɪtf(ə)l/ adj not grateful to someone who has helped you or been kind to you —**ungratefully** adv

unhappy /ʌnˈhæpi/ adj ★★
1 feeling sad or upset, or making someone feel sad or upset: *Why are you so unhappy?* ♦ *an unhappy childhood/memory*
2 not satisfied: *People are very unhappy about the high ticket prices.*
—**unhappily** adv, **unhappiness** noun [U]

unharmed /ʌnˈhɑːmd/ adj not hurt or damaged

unhealthy /ʌnˈhelθi/ adj **1** ill, or not physically fit **2** not good for you

unheard /ʌnˈhɜːd/ adj not heard by anyone, or ignored

unˈheard-ˌof adj something that is unheard-of is very unusual or has never happened before

unhelpful /ʌnˈhelpf(ə)l/ adj **1** not willing or able to help **2** not useful —**unhelpfully** adv

unhurried /ʌnˈhʌrid/ adj slow, without any worry about taking a long time —**unhurriedly** adv

unhurt /ʌnˈhɜːt/ adj not injured

unicorn /ˈjuːnɪkɔːn/ noun [C] an imaginary creature like a horse with a single long horn on its head

unidentified /ˌʌnaɪˈdentɪfaɪd/ adj not recognized or known

unification /ˌjuːnɪfɪˈkeɪʃ(ə)n/ noun [U] the process of uniting groups or countries, or the fact that they have been united

uniform¹ /ˈjuːnɪfɔːm/ noun [C] ★★ a set of clothes that you wear to show that you are part of a particular organization or school: *He was still wearing his school uniform.* ♦ *a police uniform*
PHRASE in uniform wearing a uniform: *soldiers in uniform*

uniform² /ˈjuːnɪfɔːm/ adj the same everywhere: *a uniform standard of health care* —**uniformly** adv

uniformed /ˈjuːnɪfɔːmd/ adj wearing a uniform

unify /ˈjuːnɪfaɪ/ verb [T] to unite people or countries so that they will work together —**unified** /ˈjuːnɪfaɪd/ adj

unilateral /ˌjuːnɪˈlæt(ə)rəl/ adj done or decided by one country, group, or person without the agreement of others —**unilaterally** adv

unimaginable /ˌʌnɪˈmædʒɪnəb(ə)l/ adj very difficult to imagine —**unimaginably** adv

unimaginative /ˌʌnɪˈmædʒɪnətɪv/ adj unable to think of new and interesting things

unimportant /ˌʌnɪmˈpɔːt(ə)nt/ adj not important or relevant

unimpressive /ˌʌnɪmˈpresɪv/ adj not very good

uninformative /ˌʌnɪnˈfɔːmətɪv/ adj not giving enough information and therefore unhelpful

uninformed /ˌʌnɪnˈfɔːmd/ adj not based on knowledge or correct information, and therefore wrong or unsuitable

uninhabitable /ˌʌnɪnˈhæbɪtəb(ə)l/ adj not suitable for living in

uninhabited /ˌʌnɪnˈhæbɪtɪd/ adj an uninhabited place has no people living there

uninhibited /ˌʌnɪnˈhɪbɪtɪd/ adj not embarrassed about doing or saying something that other people might be unwilling to do or say

uninspired /ˌʌnɪnˈspaɪəd/ adj not interesting or exciting

unintelligent /ˌʌnɪnˈtelɪdʒ(ə)nt/ adj not intelligent

unintelligible /ˌʌnɪnˈtelɪdʒəb(ə)l/ adj impossible to understand

unintended /ˌʌnɪnˈtendɪd/ adj not deliberate or planned

unintentional /ˌʌnɪnˈtenʃ(ə)nəl/ adj not deliberate or planned

uninterested /ʌnˈɪntrəstɪd/ adj not interested

uninterrupted /ˌʌnɪntəˈrʌptɪd/ adj continuous and not interrupted by anything

uninviting /ˌʌnɪnˈvaɪtɪŋ/ adj not attractive or pleasant

union /ˈjuːnjən/ noun ★★
1 [C] an organization that represents the workers in a particular industry=TRADE UNION: *the National Union of Teachers* ♦ *We encourage all employees to join a union.*
2 Union [C] a group of states or countries that have joined together: *the European Union*
3 [singular/U] the process of joining things together, or the state of being joined together

Union ˈJack the national flag of the UK

unique /juːˈniːk/ adj ★
1 very special, unusual, or good: *It is her use of colour that makes her work unique.* ♦ *Mark had a unique opportunity to travel with the President.*
2 not the same as anything or anyone else: *Each individual is unique.*
3 only existing or happening in one place or situation: *The problem is not unique to British students.*
—**uniquely** adv

unisex /ˈjuːnɪseks/ adj for both men and women

unison /ˈjuːnɪs(ə)n/ noun **in unison** together, or at the same time

unit /ˈjuːnɪt/ noun [C] ★★★

1 individual thing	5 small machine
2 part of institution	6 piece of furniture
3 team of people	7 part of a book
4 for measuring	

1 an individual thing that is part of a larger group: *low-cost housing units* ♦ *The sen is the smallest **unit of currency** in Malaysia.*
2 a department of an institution that has a particular purpose: *an intensive care unit*
3 a group of people who work as a team within a larger group or organization: *an army unit*
4 a standard quantity that is used for measuring something: *The gram is a unit for measuring weight.*
5 a small machine that does a particular job: *an air-conditioning unit*
6 a piece of furniture that fits together with other pieces of the same type: *kitchen units*
7 one of the parts that an educational book or course of study is divided into

unite /juːˈnaɪt/ verb [I/T] to join together, or to join people or groups together: *Our community has united to demand a safer neighbourhood.*

united /juːˈnaɪtɪd/ adj ★
1 if people are united, they agree with each other: *Local people are **united in their** opposition to the site.*
2 joined together: *a united Germany*

United Kingdom, the England, Scotland, Wales, and Northern Ireland, considered as a political unit

United Nations, the the UN

unity /ˈjuːnəti/ noun [U] a situation in which people, groups, or countries join together or agree about something

universal /ˌjuːnɪˈvɜːs(ə)l/ adj ★ involving or affecting everyone in the world, or all the members of a group or society: *universal human rights* ♦ *universal free education*
—**universally** adv

universe, the /ˈjuːnɪvɜːs/ noun [singular] space and everything that exists in it, including the Earth and all the other planets: *Are we the only form of intelligent life in the universe?*

university /ˌjuːnɪˈvɜːsəti/ noun [C/U] ★★★ an educational institution where students study for degrees and where academic research is done: *He studied at Bristol University.* ♦ *They met while they were at **university**.* ♦ *He's taking a year off before going to university.*

unjust /ʌnˈdʒʌst/ adj not fair or reasonable =UNFAIR —**unjustly** adv

unjustified /ʌnˈdʒʌstɪfaɪd/ adj not fair, or not based on any good reason

unkempt /ʌnˈkempt/ adj dirty and untidy

unkind /ʌnˈkaɪnd/ adj ★ unfriendly, insulting, or cruel: *an unkind remark* ♦ *You're being very **unkind** to your sister.*
—**unkindly** adv, **unkindness** noun [U]

unknowingly /ʌnˈnəʊɪŋli/ adv without realizing what type of situation you are involved in

unknown[1] /ʌnˈnəʊn/ adj ★
1 if something is unknown, people do not know about it or do not know what it is: *For **some unknown reason**, the plane landed at the wrong airport.*

2 not famous: *an unknown poet*

unknown[2] /ʌnˈnəʊn/ noun **1** [C] someone who is not famous **2 the unknown** [singular] things that you do not know about or have not experienced

unlawful /ʌnˈlɔːf(ə)l/ adj *legal* illegal
—**unlawfully** adv

unleaded /ʌnˈledɪd/ adj unleaded petrol does not contain LEAD

unleash /ʌnˈliːʃ/ verb [T] to do or cause something that has a very powerful or harmful effect

unless /ənˈles/ conjunction ★★★ used for saying that if something does not happen, something else will happen or will be true as a result: *I can't help you unless you tell me what's wrong.* ♦ *Unless you come now, I'm going to leave without you.* ♦ '*Are you going to stay overnight?*' '*Not unless* (=only if) *it's absolutely necessary.*'

unlicensed /ʌnˈlaɪs(ə)nst/ adj without an official LICENCE to do something

unlike /ʌnˈlaɪk/ preposition ★★
1 different from someone or something else: *The show was unlike anything we'd ever seen before.*
2 not typical of a particular person or thing: *It's so unlike Mary to go off without telling someone.*

unlikely /ʌnˈlaɪkli/ adj ★★
1 not likely to happen: *It's **highly unlikely** we'll be invited.* ♦ **unlikely to do sth** *He's unlikely ever to find a job again.* ♦ **+(that)** *It seems unlikely that she will make the same mistake next time.*
2 not typical: *He's a very unlikely romantic hero.*

unlimited /ʌnˈlɪmɪtɪd/ adj with no limits

unlit /ʌnˈlɪt/ adj dark because there are no lights

unload /ʌnˈləʊd/ verb **1** [I/T] to take goods off a vehicle **2** [T] to take the bullets out of a gun, or the film out of a camera

unlock /ʌnˈlɒk/ verb [T] to open the lock on something, usually with a key

unlucky /ʌnˈlʌki/ adj **1** having bad luck **2** happening because of bad luck **3** believed to bring bad luck —**unluckily** adv

unmanageable /ʌnˈmænɪdʒəb(ə)l/ adj extremely difficult to control or organize

unmanned /ʌnˈmænd/ adj an unmanned building, vehicle, or machine does not have anyone working in it or on it

unmarked /ʌnˈmɑːkt/ adj something that is unmarked has no words or symbols on it to show what or where it is

unmarried /ʌnˈmærid/ adj not married =SINGLE

unmistakable /ˌʌnmɪˈsteɪkəb(ə)l/ adj very easy to recognize

unmitigated /ʌnˈmɪtɪˌgeɪtɪd/ adj used for emphasizing how bad or unpleasant something is: *The whole project was an unmitigated disaster.*

unmoved /ʌnˈmuːvd/ adj *formal* feeling no sympathy or sadness

unnamed /ʌnˈneɪmd/ adj used for describing

U

a person or thing whose name is not mentioned

unnatural /ʌnˈnætʃ(ə)rəl/ adj different from what you would normally expect or experience, especially in a way that makes you feel uncomfortable: *an unnatural silence* —**unnaturally** adv

unnecessary /ʌnˈnesəs(ə)ri/ adj ★
1 used for describing something that should not have happened because it could have been avoided: *The policy had caused thousands of families unnecessary suffering.*
♦ *The delay was totally unnecessary.*
2 not needed: *Remove all unnecessary files from your computer.*
—**unnecessarily** /ʌnnesəˈserəli/ adv

unnoticed /ʌnˈnəʊtɪst/ adj, adv not seen or noticed by anyone

unobserved /ʌnəbˈzɜːvd/ adj, adv not seen by anyone

unobtrusive /ʌnəbˈtruːsɪv/ adj formal not attracting much attention —**unobtrusively** adv

unoccupied /ʌnˈɒkjʊˌpaɪd/ adj an unoccupied room, building, or seat is not being used by anyone

unofficial /ʌnəˈfɪʃ(ə)l/ adj **1** not organized or formally approved by anyone in authority **2** not having an official position or status —**unofficially** adv

unopposed /ʌnəˈpəʊzd/ adj, adv if someone does something unopposed, no one competes against them or tries to stop them

unorthodox /ʌnˈɔːθədɒks/ adj not following the usual rules or beliefs of your religion or society

unpack /ʌnˈpæk/ verb [I/T] to take things out of a suitcase, bag etc

unpaid /ʌnˈpeɪd/ adj **1** unpaid work is work that you are not paid for **2** not yet paid: *unpaid debts/bills/rent*

unpalatable /ʌnˈpælətəb(ə)l/ adj formal unpleasant to think about or accept

unparalleled /ʌnˈpærəleld/ adj formal much greater than anything else or anyone else

unpatriotic /ʌnpætrɪˈɒtɪk/ adj not proud of your country, or involved in something that harms your country

unperturbed /ʌnpəˈtɜːbd/ adj not worried or upset by something that has happened

unplanned /ʌnˈplænd/ adj not intended or expected

unpleasant /ʌnˈplez(ə)nt/ adj ★★
1 if something is unpleasant, you do not like or enjoy it: *The smell was very unpleasant.* ♦ *an unpleasant experience*
2 not friendly or kind: *She was really unpleasant on the phone.*
—**unpleasantly** adv

unplug /ʌnˈplʌg/ verb [T] to separate a piece of equipment from a power supply by taking its PLUG out of an electric SOCKET

unpopular /ʌnˈpɒpjʊlə/ adj disliked by many people —**unpopularity** /ʌnpɒpjʊˈlærəti/ noun [U]

unprecedented /ʌnˈpresɪˌdentɪd/ adj never having happened or existed before

unpredictable /ʌnprɪˈdɪktəb(ə)l/ adj changing often, in a way that is impossible to prepare for=ERRATIC —**unpredictably** adv

unprepared /ʌnprɪˈpeəd/ adj not ready for a particular situation, event, or process

unpretentious /ʌnprɪˈtenʃəs/ adj not trying to impress people with money, style, intelligence, importance etc. This word shows that you approve of this quality.

unprincipled /ʌnˈprɪnsəp(ə)ld/ adj willing to use dishonest or unfair methods in order to get what you want

unproductive /ʌnprəˈdʌktɪv/ adj not achieving any benefits or positive results

unprofessional /ʌnprəˈfeʃ(ə)nəl/ adj not behaving according to the normal standards of work or behaviour of your profession: *The rude way she treats clients is very unprofessional.* —**unprofessionally** adv

unprofitable /ʌnˈprɒfɪtəb(ə)l/ adj an unprofitable business does not make enough money=UNECONOMIC —**unprofitably** adv

unprovoked /ʌnprəˈvəʊkt/ adj an unprovoked attack is made on someone who has done nothing to deserve it

unqualified /ʌnˈkwɒlɪˌfaɪd/ adj **1** not having the education, experience, or right qualifications to do a particular job **2** complete and total, without any doubts

unquestionable /ʌnˈkwestʃ(ə)nəb(ə)l/ adj used for emphasizing how true something is, or for saying that most people believe it: *His commitment to the job is unquestionable.* —**unquestionably** adv

unreal /ʌnˈrɪəl/ adj extremely unusual and not normal —**unreality** /ʌnrɪˈæləti/ noun [U]

unrealistic /ʌnrɪəˈlɪstɪk/ adj based on hopes or wishes, and not on what is likely or possible —**unrealistically** /ʌnrɪəˈlɪstɪkli/ adv

unreasonable /ʌnˈriːz(ə)nəb(ə)l/ adj **1** not fair **2** not sensible —**unreasonably** adv

unrecognizable /ʌnˈrekəgnaɪzəb(ə)l/ adj very different from the person or place that you remember

unrelated /ʌnrɪˈleɪtɪd/ adj **1** not connected with another event, situation, subject etc: *His decision to quit was unrelated to the company's performance.* **2** not part of the same family

unrelenting /ʌnrɪˈlentɪŋ/ adj done or happening in a severe or determined way

unreliable /ʌnrɪˈlaɪəb(ə)l/ adj someone or something that is unreliable cannot be depended on

unremarkable /ʌnrɪˈmɑːkəb(ə)l/ adj very ordinary and not interesting or impressive

unremitting /ʌnrɪˈmɪtɪŋ/ adj continuing for a long time without getting better

unrepentant /ʌnrɪˈpentənt/ adj formal not sorry for something bad that you have done

unrepresentative /ʌnreprɪˈzentətɪv/ adj not typical of other people or things in the same group

unrequited /ʌnrɪˈkwaɪtɪd/ adj unrequited love is love that you feel for someone who does not love you

unreserved /ˌʌnrɪˈzɜːvd/ adj complete and sincere —**unreservedly** /ˌʌnrɪˈzɜːvɪdli/ adv

unresolved /ˌʌnrɪˈzɒlvd/ adj not dealt with or agreed on

unresponsive /ˌʌnrɪˈspɒnsɪv/ adj not reacting in the way that you want or expect

unrest /ʌnˈrest/ noun [U] angry or violent behaviour by people who are protesting against something

unrewarding /ˌʌnrɪˈwɔːdɪŋ/ adj giving you no pleasure or satisfaction

unrivalled /ʌnˈraɪv(ə)ld/ adj used for emphasizing that something is much better or more important than other similar things

unroll /ʌnˈrəʊl/ verb [T] to open out something that has been rolled up

unruffled /ʌnˈrʌf(ə)ld/ adj not nervous or upset in a difficult situation

unruly /ʌnˈruːli/ adj very difficult to control

unsafe /ʌnˈseɪf/ adj 1 dangerous 2 involving a lot of risk

unsaid /ʌnˈsed/ adj something that is unsaid is something that you think but do not say

unsatisfactory /ˌʌnsætɪsˈfækt(ə)ri/ adj not good enough

unsavoury /ʌnˈseɪvəri/ adj involving unpleasant, dishonest, or immoral things

unscathed /ʌnˈskeɪðd/ adj not harmed or damaged

unscrew /ʌnˈskruː/ verb [T] to open something by twisting its lid or top

unscrupulous /ʌnˈskruːpjʊləs/ adj willing to do things that are unfair, dishonest, or illegal

unseemly /ʌnˈsiːmli/ adj formal unseemly behaviour is not suitable and is embarrassing or upsetting

unseen¹ /ʌnˈsiːn/ adj not seen or known about by anyone

unseen² /ʌnˈsiːn/ adv without being seen by anyone

unselfish /ʌnˈselfɪʃ/ adj thinking about what other people want or need rather than what you want or need yourself —**unselfishly** adv

unsettled /ʌnˈset(ə)ld/ adj 1 nervous, confused, or upset 2 an unsettled place, situation, or period of time is one in which people feel nervous because things are changing 3 unsettled weather changes a lot and has a lot of wind and rain 4 something such as a problem or argument that is unsettled has not been dealt with successfully

unsettling /ʌnˈsetlɪŋ/ adj making you feel nervous, confused, or upset

unshaven /ʌnˈʃeɪv(ə)n/ adj a man who is unshaven has hair growing on his face because he has not SHAVED recently

unsightly /ʌnˈsaɪtli/ adj not pleasant to look at: *an unsightly scar*

unskilled /ʌnˈskɪld/ adj 1 not needing much education, training, or experience 2 not having enough education, training, or experience to do a job that needs skill

unsociable /ʌnˈsəʊʃəb(ə)l/ adj not interested in meeting people or in doing things with other people

unsolicited /ˌʌnsəˈlɪsɪtɪd/ adj unsolicited offers, advice, gifts etc are those that you get but did not ask for

unsolved /ʌnˈsɒlvd/ adj an unsolved problem or mystery is one that has not been dealt with or explained

unsophisticated /ˌʌnsəˈfɪstɪˌkeɪtɪd/ adj 1 simple and not advanced in design 2 not knowing much about things such as culture, fashion, and the modern world

unsound /ʌnˈsaʊnd/ adj 1 not safe 2 not based on sensible ideas

unspeakable /ʌnˈspiːkəb(ə)l/ adj used for emphasizing how bad something is —**unspeakably** adv

unspecified /ʌnˈspesɪˌfaɪd/ adj not mentioned or known

unspectacular /ˌʌnspekˈtækjʊlə/ adj not especially good

unspoiled /ʌnˈspɔɪld/ or **unspoilt** /ʌnˈspɔɪlt/ British adj an unspoiled place has not been changed in ways that make it less beautiful or enjoyable

unspoken /ʌnˈspəʊkən/ adj not expressed in words but understood

unstable /ʌnˈsteɪb(ə)l/ adj 1 an unstable person often becomes suddenly angry or upset 2 often affected by serious problems 3 likely to move or change and become dangerous

unsteady /ʌnˈstedi/ adj 1 not regular, calm, or normal 2 too weak or ill to walk well

unstuck /ʌnˈstʌk/ adj **come unstuck** informal to fail

unsubscribe /ˌʌnsəbˈskraɪb/ verb [I/T] computing to take your name off an Internet MAILING LIST (=list of people who receive emails)

unsubstantiated /ˌʌnsəbˈstænʃiˌeɪtɪd/ adj not proved to be true

unsuccessful /ˌʌnsəkˈsesf(ə)l/ adj 1 something that is unsuccessful does not achieve what you want: *another unsuccessful attempt to reach agreement* 2 someone who is unsuccessful does not get what they want: *Letters are sent to all unsuccessful candidates.* —**unsuccessfully** adv

unsuitable /ʌnˈsuːtəb(ə)l/ adj not suitable for a particular situation, purpose, or person: *Some of the material may be unsuitable for children.*

unsung /ʌnˈsʌŋ/ adj not famous, praised, or admired, although deserving to be

unsure /ʌnˈʃʊə/ adj not certain about something

PHRASE **unsure of yourself** not having much confidence

unsurprising /ˌʌnsəˈpraɪzɪŋ/ adj something unsurprising is what you expected

unsuspecting /ˌʌnsəˈspektɪŋ/ adj not knowing that something bad is happening or will happen

unsustainable /ˌʌnsəˈsteɪnəb(ə)l/ adj not capable of continuing at the same rate or level

U

unsympathetic /ˌʌnsɪmpəˈθetɪk/ adj **1** not kind enough to want to know about other people's problems **2** not willing to support something

untangle /ʌnˈtæŋg(ə)l/ verb [T] **1** to understand a complicated situation, or to solve a difficult problem **2** to separate things that are twisted around each other

untapped /ʌnˈtæpt/ adj not being used, but existing in large amounts that could bring profits or benefits

untenable /ʌnˈtenəb(ə)l/ adj impossible to defend as fair, suitable, or true

unthinkable /ʌnˈθɪŋkəb(ə)l/ adj impossible to imagine

untidy /ʌnˈtaɪdi/ adj **1** not arranged in a way that is tidy: *an untidy desk* **2** not keeping things tidy: *He's always criticizing me for being untidy.*

untie /ʌnˈtaɪ/ verb [T] to take the knot out of a piece of rope or string that fastens something

until /ənˈtɪl/ preposition, conjunction ★★★
1 happening or done up to a particular point in time, and then stopping: *Baker is expected to be here until the end of the week.* ♦ *You'll just have to wait until they call your name.* ♦ *Up until now, Katherine has had no major problems in her life.*
2 continuing as far as a particular place: *Stay on the bus until the big supermarket, then get off.*
PHRASE **not (...) until** used for stating the point at which something finally happens, becomes possible, or becomes true: *They didn't see each other again until the autumn.* ♦ *It was not until six o'clock that we got the first reports of trouble.*

untimely /ʌnˈtaɪmli/ adj **1** happening earlier than you expected **2** happening at a time that is not suitable, for example because it causes additional problems

untold /ʌnˈtəʊld/ adj too great to be measured

untouched /ʌnˈtʌtʃt/ adj **1** not harmed or spoiled: *Few families were untouched by the war.* **2** food or drink that is untouched has not been eaten or drunk

untoward /ˌʌntəˈwɔːd/ adj not suitable, usual, or normal

untrained /ʌnˈtreɪnd/ adj not trained to do a particular job
PHRASE **to the untrained eye** to someone with little knowledge or experience of something

untreated /ʌnˈtriːtɪd/ adj **1** receiving no medical treatment **2** in a natural state, and perhaps harmful

untried /ʌnˈtraɪd/ adj never done or used before and therefore not certain to succeed

untrue /ʌnˈtruː/ adj not based on fact

untrustworthy /ʌnˈtrʌstˌwɜːði/ adj not capable of being trusted or depended on

untruth /ʌnˈtruːθ/ noun [C] *formal* a lie

unused¹ /ʌnˈjuːzd/ adj not used

unused² /ʌnˈjuːst/ adj **be unused to (doing) sth** to not have much experience of something

unusual /ʌnˈjuːʒʊəl/ adj ★★
1 not normal, common, or ordinary: *You're in a very unusual situation.* ♦ *Local residents should contact the police if they notice anything unusual.* ♦ *There's nothing unusual about this man's appearance.* ♦ **it is unusual to do sth** *It's unusual to find so many different plants in one garden.* ♦ **it is unusual for sb to do sth** *It's most unusual for Sue to get so angry.*
2 different from other people or things in a way that is interesting, attractive, or impressive: *The designers have chosen unusual colour combinations.* ♦ *Ewing is a player of unusual talent.*

unusually /ʌnˈjuːʒʊəli/ adv **1** in a way that is not usual or typical: *Boris seemed unusually quiet.* **2** extremely: *Cambridge has several unusually good restaurants.*

unveil /ʌnˈveɪl/ verb [T] **1** to announce something officially **2** to remove the cover from something as part of an official ceremony

unwanted /ʌnˈwɒntɪd/ adj not wanted

unwarranted /ʌnˈwɒrəntɪd/ adj not fair or necessary

unwary /ʌnˈweəri/ adj not paying attention to the dangers around you

unwavering /ʌnˈweɪv(ə)rɪŋ/ adj strong and steady

unwelcome /ʌnˈwelkəm/ adj **1** unpleasant or annoying **2** an unwelcome guest or visitor is someone who you do not want to spend time with

unwell /ʌnˈwel/ adj *formal* ill

unwieldy /ʌnˈwiːldi/ adj *formal* **1** too big or complicated to work well **2** large or heavy and difficult to carry

unwilling /ʌnˈwɪlɪŋ/ adj **1** if you are unwilling to do something, you do not want to do it or you refuse to do it: *Jane was unwilling to admit she was wrong.* **2** involved in doing something that you do not want to do: *an unwilling participant* —**unwillingly** adv, **unwillingness** noun [U]

unwind /ʌnˈwaɪnd/ (past tense and past participle **unwound** /ʌnˈwaʊnd/) verb **1** [I] *informal* to begin to relax after you have been working hard or feeling nervous **2** [I/T] to become straighter or looser after being wrapped around something else, or to make something do this

unwise /ʌnˈwaɪz/ adj not sensible —**unwisely** adv

unwittingly /ʌnˈwɪtɪŋli/ adv in a way that is not conscious or deliberate —**unwitting** adj

unworkable /ʌnˈwɜːkəb(ə)l/ adj not practical, and therefore unlikely to be successful

unwound the past tense and past participle of unwind

unwrap /ʌnˈræp/ verb [T] to remove the paper or plastic that is covering something

unwritten /ʌnˈrɪt(ə)n/ adj known or understood by everyone but not official

unzip /ʌnˈzɪp/ verb [T] **1** to open a piece of clothing or a bag by pulling a ZIP (=an object with two pieces of metal that fit together to fasten something) **2** *computing* to increase the size of a file to its original size after it has been reduced

up¹ /ʌp/ *grammar word* ★★★

> **Up** can be:
> - an **adverb**: *Their voices could be heard up in our room.*
> - a **preposition**: *He climbed up the steps.*
> - an **adjective**: *the up escalator*
> - used after the verb 'to be': *He was up early the next morning.*

1 higher in or towards a higher position: *She's up in the bathroom.* ♦ *I got off my bike and walked up the hill.* ♦ *Pick your clothes up off the floor and put them away.* ♦ *The hotel is 1,500 feet up in the Black Mountains.* ♦ *We rolled on our backs and looked up at the sky.* ♦ *The kids were jumping* **up and down** *on the bed.*

2 upright, or moving towards an upright position: *He stood up and pulled a chair out for me to sit on.* ♦ *I found Hattie sitting up in bed.*

3 north in or towards the north of a region or country: *I go up to Scotland about once a month.*

4 moving near to sb/sth moving near to someone or something and then stopping: *One of the salespeople came up and asked if she could help.* ♦ *Just go* **up to** *him and say hello.*

5 further along a road etc further along a road, path etc, in a direction away from you: *He lives up the street from me.*

6 increased in amount/level at or towards an increased amount or level: *Total car sales were up £3 million over last year.* ♦ *Turn the volume up – I can't hear anything.* ♦ *Fuel prices went up by 3 per cent.*

7 not in bed awake and out of bed: *Get up! It's almost 10.00.* ♦ *I was up till midnight preparing the presentation.*

8 at an end used for stating that a period of time has ended: *Come along now, please! Time's up!*

9 in or into smaller parts divided or broken into smaller pieces or equal parts: *The prize money will be divided up among the team members.*

10 completely completely done or used so that there is nothing left: *He ate up all his dinner.* ♦ *The stream dries up in summer.*

11 fastened fastened or closed completely: *She kept Albert's letters in a bundle tied up with ribbon.* ♦ *Did you lock the house up before you left?*

12 collected collected, added, or brought together in one place: *She was busy gathering up her papers.* ♦ *Our profits are quite large when you add them all up.*

13 working a system that is up is working properly: *By ten o'clock we had the computers up again.* ♦ *The new filing system should be* **up and running** *soon.*

14 happening *spoken* used for saying or asking if something is wrong or if something is happening: *When Sara didn't come, I knew* **something was up**. ♦ *You seem rather quiet today.* **What's up?**

> **PHRASES** **up against sb/sth** competing with someone, or having a serious problem to deal with

up and down 1 backwards and forwards: *He kept walking up and down the hallway all night long.* **2** sometimes happy and well and sometimes not: *'How are you feeling?' 'Oh, up and down.'*

up for sth 1 being considered for a particular status or job: *The senator is up for re-election in 2006.* ♦ *The contract comes up for renewal soon.* **2** available for a particular purpose: *Most of the houses are up for sale.* **3** *spoken* willing to do a particular activity: *I'm planning to stay out late tonight – are you up for it?*

up to/until/till sth used for stating the latest time that something can happen, or the end of a period of time: *Laura was here up until about 5 minutes ago.* ♦ *We can make the delivery any time tomorrow up till about 10 pm.*

up to sb if something is up to you, you are responsible for deciding about it or doing it: *Do you want to stay or go? It's up to you.* ♦ *It's up to all of us to make our streets safe for children.*

up to sth 1 used for stating the most that an amount can be, or what level it can reach: *Some dinosaurs were up to twenty-seven metres long.* **2** used for stating a particular standard that something can reach: *I'm afraid the play wasn't up to our expectations.* **3** doing something wrong or secret: *When the children are quiet like this, I know they're up to something.* **4** well enough, strong enough, or good enough to do something: *She's supposed to leave hospital tomorrow, but I don't think she's up to it.* → SCRATCH²

up² /ʌp/ *verb* [T] *informal* to increase an amount, or raise something to a higher level

up³ /ʌp/ *noun* **ups and downs** *informal* a mixture of good and bad situations or experiences: *Like all couples, we've had our ups and downs.*

up-and-coming *adj* likely to become successful or popular soon

upbeat /ˈʌpbiːt/ *adj informal* happy and positive

upbringing /ˈʌpˌbrɪŋɪŋ/ *noun* [singular] the way that parents look after their children and teach them to behave

upcoming /ˈʌpˌkʌmɪŋ/ *adj* happening soon

update¹ /ʌpˈdeɪt/ *verb* **1** [I/T] to add the most recent information to something such as a book, document, or list: *The latest edition has been completely updated.* **2** [T] to tell someone the most recent news or information about something: **update sb on sth** *Dr Cooper can update us on the latest developments.* **3** [T] to make something more modern: *Our software is continually updated and improved.* → UP-TO-DATE

U

update² /ˈʌpdeɪt/ noun [C] **1** a report or broadcast that contains the most recent information **2** *computing* a piece of software that contains recent improvements to a computer program

upend /ʌpˈend/ verb [T] to turn something upside down

up ˈfront or **upfront** /ʌpˈfrʌnt/ adv **1** if you pay for something up front, you pay for it before you receive it **2** if you tell someone something up front, you are very honest from the beginning about something that might affect them —**upfront** adj

upgrade¹ /ʌpˈgreɪd/ verb **1** [I/T] to make a computer or machine more powerful or effective **2** [T] to officially give someone or something a higher status

upgrade² /ˈʌpˌgreɪd/ noun [C] a piece of equipment or software that is designed to make a computer more powerful or effective

upheaval /ʌpˈhiːv(ə)l/ noun [C/U] a sudden or violent change

uphill /ˈʌphɪl/ adj **1** towards the top of a slope or hill **2** difficult to do or achieve —**uphill** /ˌʌpˈhɪl/ adv

uphold /ʌpˈhəʊld/ (past tense and past participle **upheld** /ʌpˈheld/) verb [T] **1** if a court of law upholds something, it says that it is correct: *The Appeals Court upheld the decision of the lower court.* **2** *formal* to show that you support something: *We have an obligation to uphold the law.*

upholstery /ʌpˈhəʊlst(ə)ri/ noun [U] soft material that is used for covering chairs and other seats

upkeep /ˈʌpˌkiːp/ noun [singular/U] the process or cost of keeping property in good condition

upland /ˈʌplənd/ adj relating to an area of high land

uplands /ˈʌpləndz/ noun [plural] *British* areas of high land

uplifting /ʌpˈlɪftɪŋ/ adj making you feel happier or more hopeful

upload /ˈʌpˌləʊd/ verb [T] *computing* to send information from your computer to a larger system using the Internet

upmarket /ʌpˈmɑːkɪt/ adj very expensive, fashionable, and intended for people who have a lot of money —**upmarket** adv

upon /əˈpɒn/ preposition ★
1 *literary* on or onto something: *He believes we were put upon this earth for a purpose.*
2 *formal* used after some verbs with the same meaning as 'on': *My whole future depended upon the decision of one manager.*
3 *formal* immediately after doing something, or immediately after something happens: *Upon his release, Davis went to his mother's.*

upper /ˈʌpə/ adj ★
1 higher than something else, especially higher than one of two things that are a pair ≠ LOWER: *He had a scar on his upper lip.* ♦ *You'll be able to see more if you sit on the upper deck of the bus.*
2 near the top, or at the top of something ≠ LOWER: *There is already some snow on the*

upper slopes. ♦ *upper-body strength*
3 higher in status or rank ≠ LOWER: *the upper ranks of the army*

upper ˈcase adj upper case letters of the alphabet are CAPITAL LETTERS, for example 'A', 'F', and 'T' —**upper ˈcase** noun [U]

upper ˈclass noun **the upper class** or **the upper classes** people who have the highest social status → LOWER CLASS, MIDDLE CLASS, WORKING CLASS

upper ˈhand, the noun [singular] control or an advantage over a person or situation: *Agassi briefly got the upper hand in the second set.*

uppermost /ˈʌpəˌməʊst/ adj **1** more important than anything else **2** at or near the top

upright¹ /ˈʌpraɪt/ adv **1** sitting or standing with a straight back: *Sara was wide awake, sitting upright in her bed.* **2** in or into a straight or standing position: *Pictures were propped upright against all the walls.*

upright² /ˈʌpraɪt/ adj **1** straight and tall: *Make sure your seat is in an upright position for landing.* **2** honest: *an upright citizen*

uprising /ˈʌpˌraɪzɪŋ/ noun [C] a political situation in which a large group of people opposes and tries to defeat the government or the person who rules their country = REBELLION

upriver /ʌpˈrɪvə/ adv in the opposite direction to the way that a river flows

uproar /ˈʌprɔː/ noun [singular/U] **1** angry public criticism of something **2** a lot of noise made by people who are shouting

uproot /ʌpˈruːt/ verb [T] **1** to force someone to leave the place where they live **2** to pull a whole tree or plant from the ground

upset¹ /ʌpˈset/ adj ★
1 sad, worried, or angry about something: *Why are you so upset?* ♦ *They felt too upset to talk about the incident.* ♦ *They're all still very upset about losing the case.* ♦ *It's nothing to get upset about.* ♦ +(that) *She feels upset that we didn't tell her the truth.*
2 if your stomach is upset, you have an illness affecting your stomach, usually caused by something that you have eaten or drunk: *Phone and tell them you've got an upset stomach.*

upset² /ʌpˈset/ (present participle **upsetting**; past tense and past participle **upset**) verb [T] ★
1 to make someone feel sad, worried, or angry: *I'm sorry, I didn't mean to upset you.* ♦ *People were upset by Hansen's rude remarks.*
2 to spoil something: *I'm sorry if I've upset your plans for this evening.* ♦ *The introduction of a new species has upset the ecological balance of the lake.*
3 to knock something over accidentally = SPILL

upset³ /ˈʌpset/ noun [C] **1** an occasion when someone defeats an opponent who is considered better than them **2** an illness that affects your stomach, usually caused by something that you have eaten or drunk **3** something that makes you feel sad, worried, or angry

U

upsetting /ʌpˈsetɪŋ/ adj making you feel sad, worried, or angry

upshot /ˈʌpʃɒt/ noun **the upshot (of sth)** the result of a process or event

upside /ˈʌpsaɪd/ noun [singular] the positive aspect of a bad situation

upside 'down adv ★ with the top part at the bottom or lower than the bottom part: *The car landed upside down in a ditch.*

PHRASES **turn sb's life/world upside down** to change someone's life completely

turn sth upside down to make a place very untidy while you are searching for something

—**upside-'down** adj

upstage /ʌpˈsteɪdʒ/ verb [T] to do something so that you get more attention and admiration than someone else

upstairs /ʌpˈsteəz/ adv ★

1 on an upper level of a building with stairs ≠ DOWNSTAIRS: *The children are upstairs in bed.* ♦ *Do you know who lives in the flat upstairs?*

2 to an upper level of a building ≠ DOWNSTAIRS: *I'm going upstairs for a siesta.*

—**upstairs** /ˈʌpˌsteəz/ adj: *an upstairs window*

upstart /ˈʌpˌstɑːt/ noun [C] a new person in a group who behaves as if they are more important than the people who are already there

upstream /ʌpˈstriːm/ adv in the opposite direction to the way that a river or stream flows

upsurge /ˈʌpsɜːdʒ/ noun [singular] a sudden increase in something

uptake /ˈʌpˌteɪk/ noun **be quick/slow on the uptake** informal to take a short/long time to understand or realize something

uptight /ʌpˈtaɪt/ adj nervous and easily annoyed

up-to-'date adj **1** giving the most recent news and information: *Visit our website for the most up-to-date match reports.* ♦ *Make sure your financial records are kept up to date.* **2** modern and using the latest ideas or knowledge: *up-to-date technology*

up-to-the-'minute adj **1** containing all the most recent news and information **2** very modern

uptown /ʌpˈtaʊn/ adv American in or towards the areas of a city that are furthest away from the centre —**uptown** adj → DOWNTOWN

upturn /ˈʌpˌtɜːn/ noun [singular] an increase in something

upturned /ʌpˈtɜːnd/ adj **1** curving, pointing, or facing upwards **2** an upturned object has been moved so that its top part is at the bottom

upward /ˈʌpwəd/ adj **1** moving or turned towards a higher position **2** moving towards a higher level or amount

upwards /ˈʌpwədz/ or **upward** /ˈʌpwəd/ adv **1** towards a higher position ≠ DOWNWARDS: *She glanced upwards at the screen.* **2** towards a higher or more important level ≠ DOWNWARDS: *The initial estimate has been revised upwards.* **3** more than a particular number or amount: *Expect to spend upwards of £20 a day on food.*

uranium /juˈreɪniəm/ noun [U] a metal used for producing nuclear energy

urban /ˈɜːbən/ adj ★ relating to towns and cities ≠ RURAL: *People moved to the urban areas for jobs.* ♦ *Urban poverty is on the increase.*

urbane /ɜːˈbeɪn/ adj behaving in a pleasant, relaxed, and correct way in social situations

urge¹ /ɜːdʒ/ verb [T] ★

1 to advise someone very strongly about what action or attitude they should take: *He urged restraint in dealing with the protesters.* ♦ **urge sb to do sth** *The UN has urged them to honour the peace treaty.* ♦ **+that** *They urged that a new president be elected immediately.*

2 to make a person or animal move in a particular direction: *He urged the horse forwards.*

PHRASAL VERB **urge sb 'on** to encourage someone to keep trying to do something

urge² /ɜːdʒ/ noun [C] a strong feeling of wanting or needing to do something: *Suddenly I had an overwhelming urge to kiss him.*

urgency /ˈɜːdʒ(ə)nsi/ noun [U] the need to deal with something immediately

urgent /ˈɜːdʒ(ə)nt/ adj ★

1 urgent things are things that you need to deal with immediately: *He had some urgent business to attend to.* ♦ *The problem is becoming increasingly urgent.* ♦ *The refugees are in urgent need of food.*

2 expressing the feeling of wanting something very much or wanting it immediately: *an urgent whisper*

—**urgently** adv

urinate /ˈjʊərɪˌneɪt/ verb [I] formal to get rid of urine from your body

urine /ˈjʊərɪn/ noun [U] liquid waste from a person's or animal's body

URL /ˌjuː ɑːr ˈel/ noun [C] computing Uniform Resource Locator: an Internet address

urn /ɜːn/ noun [C] **1** a large metal container for making tea or coffee **2** a container for a dead person's ASHES (=powder that is left after the body has been burnt)

us /weak əs, strong ʌs/ pronoun ★★★ the object form of 'we', used for referring to yourself and other people with you or in your group when you are the person speaking or writing: *It wasn't our idea, so don't blame us.* ♦ *Angela came with us in our rented car.* ♦ *No one told us when we should be there.*

US, the /ˌjuː ˈes/ the United States

USA, the /ˌjuː es ˈeɪ/ the United States of America

usable /ˈjuːzəb(ə)l/ adj available or suitable to be used for a particular purpose

usage /ˈjuːsɪdʒ/ noun **1** [C/U] the way that words are used by people when they speak and write their language: *differences between British and American usage* **2** [U] the process of using something **3** [U] the amount of something that you use

use¹ /juːz/ verb ★★★

1 do sth with tool etc	5 say particular words
2 get benefit from sth	6 take illegal drugs
3 take from supply	✦ PHRASE
4 treat sb in unfair way	✦ PHRASAL VERB

1 [T] to do something using a machine, tool, skill, method etc to do a job or to achieve a result: *Using a computer is so much quicker.* ✦ *What type of soap do you use?* ✦ *Using all his charm, he managed to persuade them.* ✦ **use sth for sth** *Psychological tests are used for selection purposes.* ✦ **use sth for doing sth** *We use methane gas for heating.* ✦ **use sth as sth** *The land is being used as a car park.*

2 [T] to get a benefit for yourself from something available to you: *Only about 30 people regularly use the bus service.*

3 [T] to take an amount from a supply of something: *You've used all the hot water again.*

4 [T] to treat someone in an unfair way, for example by pretending to care about them so that they do what you want: *You know he's just using you.*

5 [T] to say or write particular words: *Don't use language like that in front of your little brother.*

6 [I/T] to take illegal drugs regularly: *In jail, he continued to use drugs.*

PHRASE **could use sth** *spoken* used for saying someone or something needs a particular thing very much: *You both look as if you could use a drink.*

PHRASAL VERB ˌuse sth ˈup to use all of a supply of something: *I've used up all my holiday entitlement, and it's only August.*

Word family: use

Words in the same family as **use**
- **usage** *n*
- **used** *adj*
- **useful** *adj*
- **useless** *adj*
- **reusable** *adj*
- **user** *n*
- **disused** *adj*
- **misuse** *n, v*
- **reuse** *v*

U

use² /juːs/ noun ★★★

1 [singular/U] the act of using something: *an unnecessary use of force* ✦ *the* **use of** *resources/technology/computers*

2 [C/U] a way of using something: *This material has a variety of manufacturing uses.* ✦ *This is not the best* **use** *of your talents.* ✦ *I kept hoping to find a* **use** *for it.*

3 [U] the right, an opportunity, or permission to use something: *We can* **have** *the* **use of** *the hall every Thursday.* ✦ *The pool was built* **for the use of** *residents* (=only for them to use).

4 [U] the ability to use a part of your body: *He* **lost the use** *of his legs in a car crash.*

PHRASES **be of use (to sb)** to be helpful or useful: *Can I be of any use?* ✦ *This information may be of use to him.*

be (of) no use (to sb) to not be helpful or useful: *This book is no use whatever.* ✦ *Get some rest or you'll be of no use to anyone.*

come into/go out of use to start or stop being used by people: *Computers first came into use in the early 1950s.*

in/out of use being used regularly, or not being used any longer: *I'll be glad to see the building in use again.*

it's no use *spoken* used for saying that something is not likely to have a successful result: *It's no use. We'll never get there on time.* ✦ **it's no use doing sth** *It's no use asking me. I don't know.*

make use of to use someone or something for a particular purpose, especially one that brings a benefit to you: *Why doesn't she make use of her singing talent?* ✦ *I hope you've* **made good use of** *your time.*

put sth to good use to use something you have for a sensible purpose that brings a benefit to you: *Do you promise to put the money to good use?*

there's no use (in) doing sth *spoken* used for saying that something that you do is not likely to have a successful result: *She realized there was no use arguing with him.*

used /juːzd/ adj ★★

1 owned by someone else before you =SECOND-HAND: *a used car*

2 no longer completely clean because of having been used: *a used towel*

used to¹ /ˈjuːst tuː/ modal verb ★★★

- **Used to** is usually followed by an infinitive: *We used to swim in the river.* But sometimes the following infinitive is left out: *I don't play golf now, but I used to.*
- **Used to** only exists as a past tense.
- Questions and negatives are usually formed with 'did' + **use to** (with no 'd'): *Did you use to work here?* ✦ *We didn't use to earn much.*

used for saying what was true or what happened regularly in the past, especially when this is not true or does not happen now: *I used to enjoy gardening, but I don't have time for it now.* ✦ *Where did you use to live before you moved here?* ✦ *I didn't use to like him, but now we're good friends.*

used to² /ˈjuːst tuː/ adj ★★ familiar with something because you have often experienced it before, so that it no longer seems difficult or strange: **used to (doing) sth** *Deborah was used to working on difficult assignments.* ✦ *I'm tired – I'm not used to these late nights.* ✦ *I haven't* **got used to** *the new system yet.*

useful /ˈjuːsf(ə)l/ adj ★★★ helpful for doing or achieving something: *a useful tool/technique/gadget* ✦ *Here's some* **useful information** *about travel in Canada.* ✦ *I was* **useful to** *them because I could speak French.* ✦ *That basket would be* **useful for** *picnics.* ✦ *Keep a record of everything that might* **prove useful.** ✦ **useful for (doing) sth** *Old pictures are useful for seeing how people used to dress.* ✦ **useful (for sb) to do sth** *Thanks. It's useful to know that.*

PHRASE **come in useful** *British* to be helpful

in a particular situation: *Your medical training might come in very useful indeed.* —**usefully** adv, **usefulness** noun [U]

useless /'juːsləs/ adj **1** useless objects have no purpose or cannot do what they were designed to do: *This technology is useless if you can't operate it.* ◆ *Why do you keep this completely useless umbrella?* **2** useless activities are not effective in achieving the purpose they were intended to achieve: *All of my efforts to persuade him were useless.* ◆ **it's useless trying to do sth** *It's useless trying to talk to her because she never listens.* **3** if someone is useless, they are not capable of achieving anything: *Don't ask Geoff – he's useless!* ◆ *I'm useless at cooking* (=very bad at it). —**uselessly** adv

user /'juːzə/ noun [C] ★
1 someone who uses something such as a service or a piece of equipment: *Software should be designed to meet the needs of users.* ◆ *Cyclists, like all **road users**, must obey traffic signs.* ◆ **users of mobile phones**
2 someone who regularly takes illegal drugs

user-friendly adj easy to use or understand

username /'juːzəˌneɪm/ noun [C] *computing* the name that is used by someone for operating a computer program

usher[1] /'ʌʃə/ verb [T] to lead someone politely somewhere
PHRASAL VERB **usher sth in** to make an activity or process begin

usher[2] /'ʌʃə/ noun [C] someone whose job is to show people where to sit

usual /'juːʒʊəl/ adj ★★★ typical of what happens in most situations, or of what people do in most situations: *She gave us her usual polite smile.* ◆ *The journey to work took longer than usual.* ◆ *It's **usual practice** to exchange business cards at the beginning of the meeting.* ◆ **it is usual (for sb) to do sth** *It's usual to ask permission before borrowing any equipment.*
PHRASE **as usual** used for saying what usually happens: *We went to bed that evening around 10.30 as usual.*

usually /'juːʒʊəli/ adv ★★★ used for saying what happens in most situations, or what people do in most situations=NORMALLY: *What time do you usually go to bed?* ◆ *We don't usually see each other at weekends.* ◆ *She's usually home by this time.*

usurp /juːˈzɜːp/ verb [T] *formal* to take a job or position that belongs to someone else

utensil /juːˈtensəl/ noun [C] something that you use for cooking or eating with

uterus /'juːt(ə)rəs/ noun [C] the organ in a woman's body where babies grow

utilities /juːˈtɪlətiz/ noun [plural] services such as gas, water, or electricity that are used by everyone

utilize /'juːtɪˌlaɪz/ verb [T] *formal* to use something —**utilization** /ˌjuːtɪlaɪˈzeɪʃ(ə)n/ noun [U]

utmost[1] /'ʌtməʊst/ adj as much as possible: *We attach the utmost importance to public safety.*

utmost[2] /'ʌtməʊst/ noun [singular] the greatest amount or degree possible
PHRASE **do/try your utmost (to do sth)** to try as hard as possible

utopia /juːˈtəʊpiə/ noun [C/U] an imaginary place or situation in which everything is perfect —**utopian** adj

utter[1] /'ʌtə/ adj complete: *It's been an utter waste of time.*

utter[2] /'ʌtə/ verb [T] *literary* **1** to say something: *They followed her without uttering a single word of protest.* **2** to make a sound: *She uttered a sharp cry of pain.*

utterance /'ʌt(ə)rəns/ noun [C] *formal* something that someone says

utterly /'ʌtəli/ adv completely: *You're being utterly unreasonable.*

U-turn /'juː ˌtɜːn/ noun [C] **1** a sudden and complete change of policy **2** a movement in which you turn a vehicle in order to travel in the opposite direction

V v

v[1] or **V** /viː/ noun [C/U] the 22nd letter of the alphabet → V-NECK

v[2] abbrev **1** verb **2** versus **3** very

V abbrev volt

vacancy /'veɪkənsi/ noun [C] **1** a job that is available: *We have several vacancies to fill in the Sales Department.* **2** a room in a hotel that is available: *We have no vacancies at all during July.*

vacant /'veɪkənt/ adj **1** a place that is vacant is available because no one else is using it **2** if a job is vacant, someone is needed to do it **3** looking as if you do not understand or are not paying attention —**vacantly** adv

vacate /vəˈkeɪt/ verb [T] *formal* to leave a place or a job so that it is available for someone else

vacation /vəˈkeɪʃ(ə)n/ noun **1** [C] a period of time when a university is closed **2** [C/U] *American* a holiday: *We're taking a vacation in Europe this summer.* —**vacation** verb [I]

vaccinate /'væksɪˌneɪt/ verb [T] to treat a person or animal with a vaccine to protect them against a disease —**vaccination** /ˌvæksɪˈneɪʃ(ə)n/ noun [C/U]

vaccine /'væksiːn/ noun [C/U] a substance that is put into your body in order to provide protection against a disease

vacuum[1] /'vækjʊəm/ noun **1** [C] an enclosed space with all the air and other gases removed from it **2** [singular] a situation in which something is missing: *the political vacuum left by his death*
PHRASE **in a vacuum** existing or happening

separately from other people or things, and not influenced by them: *Learning cannot occur in a vacuum.*

vacuum² /'vækjʊəm/ verb [I/T] to clean a room using a vacuum cleaner

vacuum ,cleaner noun [C] a piece of electrical equipment that cleans floors by sucking up dirt

vacuum ,flask noun [C] *British* a container that keeps liquids hot or cold

vagaries /'veɪgəriz/ noun [plural] *formal* unexpected changes that you cannot control

vagina /və'dʒaɪnə/ noun [C] a woman's sex organ, consisting of a tube that connects the outer sex organs to the WOMB (=place where babies grow) —**vaginal** adj

vagrant /'veɪgrənt/ noun [C] *formal* someone with no home or job who asks people for money

vague /veɪg/ adj **1** not clearly or fully explained: *Witnesses gave only a vague description of the driver.* ♦ *the vague promises of politicians* **2** a vague feeling or memory is not complete or definite: *Simon had only the vaguest idea of where she worked.* ♦ *I've got a vague memory of the hotel.* **3** someone who is vague does not clearly or fully explain something: *He was always vague when I asked about deadlines.* ♦ *She was rather vague about the details.* **4** a vague shape is not clear or not easy to see

vaguely /'veɪgli/ adv **1** in a way that is not clear: *He vaguely remembered his mother talking about it.* **2** slightly: *The interview made him look vaguely ridiculous.* **3** in a way that shows that you are not paying attention

vain /veɪn/ adj **1** unsuccessful or useless: *a vain attempt* **2** *showing disapproval* someone who is vain is very proud and thinks that they are attractive or special

PHRASE **in vain** without success
—**vainly** adv

valentine /'væləntaɪn/ noun [C] **1** a card or present that you give to someone on Valentine's Day **2** someone who you give a valentine to

Valentine's ,Day noun [C/U] 14th February, the day on which people give cards and small presents to the person who they love

valet /'vælɪt, 'væleɪ/ noun [C] a man whose job is to look after another man's clothes and cook his meals

valiant /'væliənt/ adj *formal* very brave and determined —**valiantly** adv

valid /'vælɪd/ adj ★
1 legally or officially acceptable ≠ INVALID: *a valid claim* ♦ *You will need a valid passport.* ♦ *This offer is valid for travel before the end of April.*
2 reasonable and generally accepted ≠ INVALID: *a valid argument* ♦ *These are valid reasons why we should ban tobacco advertising.*

3 accepted by a computer system ≠ INVALID: *a valid password*
—**validity** /və'lɪdəti/ noun [U]

validate /'vælɪdeɪt/ verb [T] *formal* **1** to officially prove that something is true or correct **2** to officially state that something is of a suitable standard —**validation** /,vælɪ'deɪʃ(ə)n/ noun [C/U]

valley /'væli/ noun [C] ★ a low area of land between two mountains or hills, often with a river flowing through it: *Their house has wonderful views across the valley.* ♦ *the Thames valley*

valuable /'væljʊb(ə)l/ adj ★★
1 worth a lot of money: *a valuable antique* ♦ *The necklace is not very valuable.*
2 very useful and important: *a valuable insight/lesson* ♦ *an opportunity to gain valuable experience*
3 valuable time is important because there is not much of it available

valuables /'væljʊb(ə)lz/ noun [plural] small possessions that are worth a lot of money

valuation /,væljʊ'eɪʃ(ə)n/ noun [C/U] a decision about how much money something is worth, or the process of making this decision

value¹ /'vælju/ noun ★★★
1 [C/U] the amount that something is worth, measured especially in money: *The value of the painting is not known.* ♦ *a drop/rise/fall in value* ♦ *You can't put a value on a human life.* ♦ *The ring was of little value.*
2 [U] the degree to which someone or something is useful or important: *educational/nutritional value* ♦ *documents that will be of great value to future historians*
3 [U] the amount that something is worth compared to the money that it costs: *This wine is excellent value at £4.99 a bottle.* ♦ *Customers are looking for value for their money.*

value² /'vælju/ verb [T] ★
1 to consider someone or something important: *a valued friend/colleague* ♦ *a community in which people value the knowledge of their elders*
2 to state how much something is worth: *I had the necklace valued.* ♦ *value sth at sth a contract valued at approximately £3 billion*

values /'vælju:z/ noun [plural] the principles and beliefs that influence the behaviour and way of life of a particular group or community: *Christian/Western/Islamic values*

valve /vælv/ noun [C] something that opens and closes in order to control the flow of air or liquid

vampire /'væmpaɪə/ noun [C] a character in stories who appears at night to bite people's necks and suck their blood

van /væn/ noun [C] ★ a vehicle that is used for carrying goods: *a delivery van* ♦ *We'll have to hire a van to move all this stuff.*

vandal /'vænd(ə)l/ noun [C] someone who deliberately damages or destroys things, especially public property

vandalism /'vændəlɪz(ə)m/ noun [U] the act of deliberately damaging or destroying things, especially public property

vandalize /'vændəlaɪz/ verb [T] to deliberately damage or destroy things, especially public property

vanguard, the /'vænɡɑːd/ noun [singular] the people who introduce and develop new ways of thinking, new technologies etc

vanilla /və'nɪlə/ noun [U] a flavour from the bean of a tropical plant, used in some sweet foods

vanish /'vænɪʃ/ verb [I] ★
1 to disappear in a sudden or mysterious way: *One moment she was there, the next she had vanished.* ♦ *The plane circled the airport once, then vanished.* ♦ *He vanished into the darkness.* ♦ *My calculator's vanished from my desk.*
2 to stop existing completely: *another species that has vanished* ♦ *a rapidly vanishing way of life*

vanity /'vænəti/ noun [U] the quality of being too proud of your abilities, or too interested in your appearance

vantage point /'vɑːntɪdʒ ˌpɔɪnt/ noun [C] **1** a position from which you can see things well **2** the particular ideas or beliefs that influence the way that you think about things

vapor /'veɪpə/ the American spelling of **vapour**

vapour /'veɪpə/ noun [C] very small drops of water or another liquid in the air

variable¹ /'veəriəb(ə)l/ adj capable of being changed, or changing often: *a variable rate of interest*

variable² /'veəriəb(ə)l/ noun [C] something that can change and affect a situation

variance /'veəriəns/ noun **at variance (with)** *formal* if one thing is at variance with another, they are completely different and seem to oppose each other

variant /'veəriənt/ noun [C] **1** something that is related to another thing but is not exactly the same **2** *linguistics* a different form, spelling, or pronunciation of a word

variation /ˌveəri'eɪʃ(ə)n/ noun ★
1 [C/U] differences in amount, level etc: *There was wide variation in the test scores.* ♦ *variations in temperature*
2 [C] something that is slightly different from similar things: *The dessert is a variation of a classic recipe.*

varied /'veərid/ adj including a wide range of things or people

variety /və'raɪəti/ noun ★★★
1 [singular] a number of different people or things: *Adults study for a variety of reasons.* ♦ *We've interviewed a wide variety of people.*
2 [C] a particular type of thing: *a new variety of tomato*
3 [U] the fact that something consists of different things: *Consumers are demanding more variety.*

Words often used with variety

Adjectives often used with variety (sense 1)
■ **astonishing, bewildering, enormous, great, huge, immense, infinite, large, rich, wide** + VARIETY: used about a very large number of different people or things

---

various /'veəriəs/ adj ★★★ several different: *There are various ways of solving the problem.* ♦ *vehicles of various shapes and sizes*

variously /'veəriəsli/ adv in different ways, by different people, or at different times

varnish¹ /'vɑːnɪʃ/ noun [C/U] a clear sticky liquid that is put onto wood to protect it and make it shiny

varnish² /'vɑːnɪʃ/ verb [T] to put varnish on something

vary /'veəri/ verb ★★
1 [I] to change according to the situation: *People's reactions to the drug can vary widely.* ♦ *Prices vary according to the size of the job.*
2 [I] if things vary, they are different from each other: *Rooms vary in size but all have a television and a telephone.*
3 [T] to change something: *The software allows you to vary the size of the print.*

vase /vɑːz, *American* veɪz/ noun [C] a container for cut flowers

vasectomy /və'sektəmi/ noun [C] a medical operation that makes a man unable to have children

vast /vɑːst/ adj ★ extremely large=HUGE: *I believe the vast majority of people* (=almost everyone) *will support us.* ♦ *Our dog eats a vast amount of food each day.*

vastly /'vɑːs(t)li/ adv to a great degree: *The hotel has been vastly improved.*

vat /væt/ noun [C] a large container for holding or storing liquids

VAT /ˌviː eɪ 'tiː, væt/ noun [U] value added tax: a tax on goods and services

vault¹ /vɔːlt/ verb [T] to jump over something, especially using your hands or a pole to support you

PHRASAL VERB ˌvault 'over sth *same as* **vault¹**

vault² /vɔːlt/ noun [C] **1** a strongly protected room in a bank where money, gold etc is kept **2** a curved structure that supports or forms a roof, especially in a church

VCR /ˌviː siː 'ɑː/ noun [C] video cassette recorder: a machine for recording and watching videos

VDU /ˌviː diː 'juː/ noun [C] visual display unit: a computer screen

've /əv/ short form the usual way of saying or writing 'have', added to the end of 'I', 'you', 'we', or 'they' to form the present perfect tense. This is not often used in formal writing: *We've been trying to reach you since yesterday.*

veal /viːl/ noun [U] meat from a young cow

veer /vɪə/ verb [I] to suddenly move in a different direction

veg¹ /vedʒ/ or **veg 'out** verb [I] *informal* to sit and relax without thinking about anything

veg² /vedʒ/ noun [plural] *British informal* vegetables

vegan /'viːgən/ noun [C] someone who chooses not to eat anything made from animals or fish, including eggs, milk, and cheese

vegetable /'vedʒtəb(ə)l/ noun [C] ★★★ a part of a plant used as food, for example a potato, bean, or CABBAGE: *We grow all our own vegetables.* ♦ *a vegetable garden*

vegetarian /ˌvedʒə'teəriən/ noun [C] someone who chooses not to eat meat or fish —**vegetarian** adj

vegetation /ˌvedʒə'teɪʃ(ə)n/ noun [U] *formal* plants and trees

veggie /'vedʒi/ noun [C] *British spoken* a VEGETARIAN —**veggie** adj

vehement /'viːəmənt/ adj involving extremely strong feelings or beliefs —**vehemence** noun [U], **vehemently** adv

vehicle /'viːɪk(ə)l/ noun [C] ★★★
1 a machine that you travel in or on, especially one with an engine that travels on roads, for example a car, bus, van, truck, or MOTORCYCLE
2 a way of expressing ideas or of making something happen: *He launched the newspaper as a vehicle for his campaign.*
3 a film, television show etc that is created for one actor: *The film was a vehicle for Tom Hanks.*

veil /veɪl/ noun [C] **1** a thin piece of cloth worn over a woman's head or face **2** a layer of something such as rain that prevents you from seeing very far **3** a lack of knowledge or information that prevents you from discovering the truth: *a veil of secrecy*

veiled /veɪld/ adj **1** a veiled threat, attack, or warning is not direct but is easily understood **2** covered with a veil

vein /veɪn/ noun ★
1 [C] one of the tubes in your body that carry blood to your heart
2 [C] one of the tubes that carry liquids through plants or insects
3 [C] a thin layer of a metal or other substance inside the Earth
4 [singular] a supply or amount of a particular thing: *a rich vein of talent*
PHRASE **in the same/a similar etc vein** in the same/a similar etc style or subject: *The second CD continues in the same vein as the first.*

Velcro /'velkrəʊ/ *trademark* two narrow bands of cloth with special surfaces that stick together, used for fastening clothes, shoes etc

velocity /və'lɒsəti/ noun [U] *technical* the speed that something moves at in one direction

velvet /'velvɪt/ noun [U] cloth that is very soft on one side and smooth on the other

velvety /'velvəti/ adj very soft or smooth

vendetta /ven'detə/ noun [C] a situation in which one person or group keeps trying to harm another, especially because of something that happened in the past

vending machine /'vendɪŋ məʃiːn/ noun [C] a machine that you can buy things from, for example cigarettes, sweets, or drinks

vendor /'vendə/ noun [C] someone who sells something, but not in a shop

veneer /və'nɪə/ noun **1** [C/U] a thin layer of wood or plastic that covers something and improves its appearance **2** [singular] a pleasant appearance or polite way of behaving that is not sincere

venerable /'ven(ə)rəb(ə)l/ adj very old, and wise or respected

venetian blind /vəˌniːʃ(ə)n 'blaɪnd/ noun [C] a BLIND across a window, made of flat narrow pieces joined with string

vengeance /'vendʒ(ə)ns/ noun [U] the act of harming or killing someone because they have done something bad to you=REVENGE
PHRASE **with a vengeance** used for emphasizing that something happens in an extreme way or with a lot of force

vengeful /'vendʒf(ə)l/ adj *literary* wanting or trying to harm someone because they have done something bad to you

venison /'venɪs(ə)n/ noun [U] meat from a DEER

venom /'venəm/ noun [U] **1** poison produced by some animals, especially snakes and insects **2** very strong anger or hate

venomous /'venəməs/ adj **1** capable of producing poison **2** extremely unpleasant and full of very strong anger or hate

vent¹ /vent/ verb [T] to express your feelings of anger very strongly

vent² /vent/ noun [C] a hole that allows air, gas, or smoke to escape or fresh air to enter

ventilate /'ventɪleɪt/ verb [T] to allow fresh air to enter a room or building

ventilation /ˌventɪ'leɪʃ(ə)n/ noun [U] the movement of fresh air around a room or building

venture¹ /'ventʃə/ noun [C] a new business or activity

venture² /'ventʃə/ verb **1** [I] to go somewhere unpleasant, dangerous, or exciting **2** [T] to be brave enough to say something

venture capital noun [U] money invested in a new business that may or may not be successful

venue /'venjuː/ noun [C] the place where an activity or event happens

veranda or **verandah** /və'rændə/ noun [C] a covered area along the outside of a house

verb /vɜːb/ noun [C] *linguistics* ★ a word that shows an action or a state, for example 'run' or 'remain'

verbal /'vɜːb(ə)l/ adj **1** using words, or relating to words: *verbal communication* **2** using spoken communication rather than writing: *a verbal agreement* **3** using words, not physical force: *verbal abuse* —**verbally** adv

verbal noun noun [C] *linguistics* a noun that is formed from a verb and ends in 'ing', for example 'swimming' in the sentence 'Swimming is my favourite sport'=GERUND

verbatim /vɜː'beɪtɪm/ adj, adv repeating the exact words that were used

verdict /'vɜːdɪkt/ noun [C] ★
1 an official judgment made in a court: *The jury took 16 hours to reach a verdict.* ♦ *a verdict of accidental death*
2 an opinion that you have or a decision that you make: *What's your verdict on the film?*

verge¹ /vɜːdʒ/ PHRASAL VERB **verge on sth** to almost be in a particular state: *The test was so difficult it was verging on the ridiculous.*

verge² /vɜːdʒ/ noun [C] *British* a border along the side of a road, often covered with grass PHRASE **on the verge of sth** about to do something or experience something: *The two countries were on the verge of war.*

verify /'verɪfaɪ/ verb [T] *formal* to check or prove that something is true or correct —**verification** /ˌverɪfɪ'keɪʃ(ə)n/ noun [U]

veritable /'verɪtəb(ə)l/ adj *formal* real: used for emphasizing what you saying

vermin /'vɜːmɪn/ noun [plural] small animals or insects that cause damage or disease

versa *see* vice versa

versatile /'vɜːsətaɪl/ adj **1** able to be used in many different ways: *a versatile summer jacket* **2** having a wide range of different skills and abilities: *a versatile actor* —**versatility** /ˌvɜːsə'tɪləti/ noun [U]

verse /vɜːs/ noun **1** [C] a group of words or sentences that form one section of a poem or song **2** [U] *formal* poetry **3** [C] a small group of sentences in the Bible that has a number next to it

version /'vɜːʃ(ə)n/ noun [C] ★
1 a form of something that is different from other forms or from the original: *The software comes in several different versions.* ♦ *The latest version of the film is more like the book.*
2 a description of something that happened, according to one person: *I want to hear his version of the story now.*

versus /'vɜːsəs/ preposition **1** used for showing that two people, groups, or teams are competing against each other: *A huge crowd came to watch Manchester United versus Liverpool.* **2** used for saying that two things are being compared: *the grades of male versus female students at the university*

vertebra /'vɜːtəbrə/ (plural **vertebrae** /'vɜːtəbreɪ/) noun [C] one of the small bones that form a row down the centre of your back

vertical /'vɜːtɪk(ə)l/ adj ★ standing, pointing, or moving straight up: *vertical lines* ♦ *The cliff face is almost vertical.* —*picture* → C8 —**vertically** /'vɜːtɪkli/ adv

vertigo /'vɜːtɪgəʊ/ noun [U] a loss of balance or a feeling that things around you are spinning, when you are in a very high place

verve /vɜːv/ noun [U] energy and enthusiasm

very /'veri/ grammar word ★★★

Very can be:
■ an **adverb**: *She writes very well.*
■ an **adjective**: *They went down to the very bottom of the sea.*

1 used for emphasizing that a quality exists or is true to a great degree: *The building looks very old.* ♦ *I took my music lessons very seriously.* ♦ *It was a very good film.* ♦ *Thank you very much.*
2 used for emphasizing a noun, especially a place or time that is at the top, bottom, or end of something: *Can you see that little bird right up at the very top of the tree?*
PHRASE **not very** used before adjectives and adverbs for saying that something is only slightly true, or that it is not true at all: *Victor's suggestions were not very helpful.* ♦ *She said 'hello', but not very politely.*

vessel /'ves(ə)l/ noun [C] **1** *formal* a large boat or ship **2** a tube in people, animals, or plants through which liquid flows **3** *formal* a container for liquids

vest /vest/ noun [C] **1** *British* a piece of underwear for the top half of your body —*picture* → C5 **2** *American* a WAISTCOAT

vested interest /ˌvestɪd 'ɪntrəst/ noun [singular] a special reason for wanting things to happen in a particular way, because you will benefit from this

vestige /'vestɪdʒ/ noun [C] *formal* a very small sign that remains when something has almost disappeared =TRACE

vet¹ /vet/ verb [T] to check someone's character or reputation to find out if they are suitable for a particular job =SCREEN

vet² /vet/ noun [C] **1** a doctor for animals **2** *American informal* a VETERAN

veteran /'vet(ə)rən/ noun [C] **1** someone who was in the armed forces, especially during a war **2** someone who has a lot of experience of doing a particular activity: *jazz veteran Dave Brubeck*

veterinary /'vet(ə)nri, 'vet(ə)rənəri/ adj relating to the care of animals that are ill or injured

veterinary surgeon noun [C] *British formal* a VET (=doctor for animals)

veto¹ /'viːtəʊ/ verb [T] to officially refuse to approve or allow something

veto² /'viːtəʊ/ (plural **vetoes**) noun [C/U] an official refusal to approve or allow something

vexed /vekst/ adj full of difficulties =PROBLEMATIC

VHF /ˌviː eɪtʃ 'ef/ noun [U] very high frequency: a range of radio waves that produces good sound quality

VHS /ˌviː eɪtʃ 'es/ noun [U] video home system: a system for recording television programmes at home

via /'vaɪə, 'viːə/ preposition ★
1 going through one place on the way to another place: *They flew from New York to New Delhi via Frankfurt.*
2 using a particular method or person to send or deliver something: *Blake spoke to the audience live via satellite from San Diego.*

viable /'vaɪəb(ə)l/ adj **1** able to be done, or worth doing **2** *science* able to live and grow in an independent way —**viability** /ˌvaɪə'bɪləti/ noun [U]

V

viaduct /ˈvaɪəˌdʌkt/ noun [C] a long bridge on high posts, usually across a valley

vibe /vaɪb/ noun [C] informal a general feeling that you get from a person or place: good/bad vibes

vibrant /ˈvaɪbrənt/ adj 1 lively and exciting 2 bright and colourful —**vibrancy** noun [U], **vibrantly** adv

vibrate /vaɪˈbreɪt/ verb [I] to shake very quickly with small movements —**vibration** /vaɪˈbreɪʃ(ə)n/ noun [C/U]

vicar /ˈvɪkə/ noun [C] a priest in the Church of England or the US EPISCOPAL Church

vicarage /ˈvɪk(ə)rɪdʒ/ noun [C] a vicar's house

vicarious /vɪˈkeəriəs/ adj experienced through the actions of other people —**vicariously** adv

vice /vaɪs/ noun 1 [C] a bad habit, or a bad personal quality ≠ VIRTUE 2 [U] crimes relating to sex 3 [C] a tool that holds an object firmly while you are working with it

vice-president noun [C] a politician who is next in rank to the president

vice versa /ˌvaɪsi ˈvɜːsə, ˌvaɪs ˈvɜːsə/ adv the opposite of what has been said: Should I come to your house or vice versa?

vicinity /vəˈsɪnəti/ noun [singular] the area near a particular place: a university in the vicinity of London

vicious /ˈvɪʃəs/ adj 1 extremely violent: a vicious attack 2 extremely unkind or unpleasant: He had a vicious temper. —**viciously** adv

vicious circle or **vicious cycle** noun [singular] a process in which the existence of a problem causes other problems, and this makes the original problem worse

victim /ˈvɪktɪm/ noun [C] ★★★
1 someone who has been harmed or killed as the result of a crime: a murder victim ♦ victims of violence
2 someone who has been affected by something such as an accident or illness: flood/earthquake victims ♦ She fell victim to a rare disease.
3 someone who has suffered as a result of the actions or attitudes of other people: victims of racism/discrimination

victimize /ˈvɪktɪˌmaɪz/ verb [T] to treat someone in a deliberately unfair way —**victimization** /ˌvɪktɪmaɪˈzeɪʃ(ə)n/ noun [U]

victor /ˈvɪktə/ noun [C] formal the winner of a competition or battle

Victorian[1] /vɪkˈtɔːriən/ adj relating to the period from 1837 to 1901, when Queen Victoria was queen in the UK

Victorian[2] /vɪkˈtɔːriən/ noun [C] someone who lived during the Victorian period

victorious /vɪkˈtɔːriəs/ adj having won a competition or battle

victory /ˈvɪkt(ə)ri/ noun [C/U] ★★ the fact of winning a competition or battle, or an occasion when someone wins ≠ DEFEAT: a decisive election victory for the Labour Party ♦ Spain's 3–2 victory over Russia in last night's game

video[1] /ˈvɪdiəʊ/ noun ★★★
1 [C/U] a film or television programme recorded onto VIDEOTAPE: The film will soon be available on video. ♦ We stayed in and watched a video. ♦ They made a video of the wedding.
2 [U] the activity of making films using VIDEOTAPE
3 [C] a VIDEO RECORDER

video[2] /ˈvɪdiəʊ/ verb [T] 1 to record a television programme 2 to film an event using a VIDEO CAMERA

video camera noun [C] a piece of equipment that you use for recording something onto VIDEOTAPE

video game noun [C] a game in which players use electronic controls to move images on a television or computer screen

videophone /ˈvɪdiəʊˌfəʊn/ noun [C] a telephone with a screen, on which you can see the person who you are talking to

video recorder noun [C] a piece of equipment that you use for showing videos or recording television programmes

videotape /ˈvɪdiəʊˌteɪp/ noun [C/U] a thin band of film in a plastic case, used for recording television programmes etc

vie /vaɪ/ (present participle **vying**; past tense and past participle **vied**) verb [I] formal to compete with other people for something that is difficult to get

view[1] /vjuː/ noun ★★★
1 [C] your personal opinion about something =POINT OF VIEW: What are your views on the election? ♦ He has strong views about global warming. ♦ +that It's our view that women should get paid the same as men.
2 [C/U] the things that you can see from a particular place: We had a spectacular view of the mountains from our room. ♦ The showers were in full view of (=easily seen by) everyone in the pool. ♦ The castle came into view (=became able to be seen) as we turned the corner.
3 [C] a picture or photograph of a place, especially an attractive place
PHRASES **in view of sth** because of something: In view of the shortage of time, each person may only speak for five minutes.
with a view to (doing) sth with the hope of doing something in the future

> **Words often used with view**
>
> Adjectives often used with **view** (noun, sense 2)
> ■ breathtaking, magnificent, panoramic, spectacular, splendid, superb + VIEW: used about views that are attractive and impressive

view[2] /vjuː/ verb [T] ★★
1 to have a particular opinion or attitude towards something =REGARD: **view sb/sth as** The Internet is viewed by many as a revolutionary educational tool. ♦ **view sth with sth** These results must be viewed with caution.
2 to look at or watch something: **view sth from sth** Viewed from the road, the wall looked too high to climb.

V

3 to look at information on a computer screen: *To view the next page, press 'tab'.*

viewer /ˈvjuːə/ noun [C] someone who watches television programmes

viewfinder /ˈvjuːˌfaɪndə/ noun [C] a small window in a camera, used for seeing exactly what you are photographing or RECORDING

viewing /ˈvjuːɪŋ/ noun [C/U] **1** the activity of watching a television programme or film, or an occasion when someone does this **2** the activity of looking at something, or an occasion when someone does this

viewpoint /ˈvjuːpɔɪnt/ noun [C] an opinion that you have about something

vigil /ˈvɪdʒɪl/ noun [C] a period of time when you stay quietly in a place, for example as a protest or when you are looking after someone who is ill

vigilant /ˈvɪdʒɪlənt/ adj *formal* watching a person or situation very carefully so that you will notice any problems immediately —**vigilance** noun [U]

vigilante /ˌvɪdʒɪˈlænti/ noun [C] someone who tries to catch and punish criminals by themselves, without waiting for the police

vigor /ˈvɪɡə/ the American spelling of **vigour**

vigorous /ˈvɪɡ(ə)rəs/ adj **1** full of energy, enthusiasm, and determination: *a vigorous debate/campaign* **2** strong and healthy: *a vigorous young man* —**vigorously** adv

vigour /ˈvɪɡə/ noun [U] energy, enthusiasm, and determination

vile /vaɪl/ adj extremely unpleasant =HORRIBLE

vilify /ˈvɪlɪˌfaɪ/ verb [T] *formal* to criticize someone very strongly, especially in a way that is not fair —**vilification** /ˌvɪlɪfɪˈkeɪʃ(ə)n/ noun [U]

villa /ˈvɪlə/ noun [C] a large house, especially one used for holidays

village /ˈvɪlɪdʒ/ noun [C] ★★★ a very small town in the countryside: *a Scottish fishing village* ♦ *the village shop* → CITY

village green noun [C] an area of grass in the middle of a village

villager /ˈvɪlɪdʒə/ noun [C] someone who lives in a village

villain /ˈvɪlən/ noun [C] **1** a bad character in a story, play, film etc ≠ HERO **2** an evil person or criminal

vindicate /ˈvɪndɪˌkeɪt/ verb [T] to prove that someone is right, especially when most people believed that they were wrong —**vindication** /ˌvɪndɪˈkeɪʃ(ə)n/ noun [C/U]

vindictive /vɪnˈdɪktɪv/ adj someone who is vindictive will not forgive a person who has hurt them, and tries to hurt them back —**vindictiveness** noun [U]

vine /vaɪn/ noun [C] the plant on which GRAPES grow =GRAPEVINE

vinegar /ˈvɪnɪɡə/ noun [U] a sour liquid that is used for adding flavour to food

vineyard /ˈvɪnjəd/ noun [C] a piece of land where GRAPES are grown and wine is produced

vintage¹ /ˈvɪntɪdʒ/ adj **1** vintage wine is excellent in quality and was made several

years ago **2** a vintage object or vehicle is old, but is kept in good condition **3** showing the best or most typical qualities of someone: *The record is vintage early Elvis.*

vintage² /ˈvɪntɪdʒ/ noun [C] all of the wine that is produced in a particular year, or the year that it was produced

vinyl /ˈvaɪn(ə)l/ noun [U] **1** a light strong plastic **2** records, used for listening to music before CDs were invented

viola /viˈəʊlə/ noun [C] a musical instrument that is like a large VIOLIN —*picture* → STRINGED INSTRUMENT

violate /ˈvaɪəˌleɪt/ verb [T] to break a law, agreement etc —**violator** noun [C]

violation /ˌvaɪəˈleɪʃ(ə)n/ noun [C/U] an action that breaks a law, agreement etc

violence /ˈvaɪələns/ noun [U] ★★
1 violent behaviour: *acts of violence* ♦ *Violence against women must stop.*
2 a strong force that something has, often one that causes a lot of damage: *the violence of the storm*

violent /ˈvaɪələnt/ adj ★★★

1 using physical force	**4** films etc
2 causing damage	**5** emotions/opinions
3 difficult to control	

1 using physical force to hurt people or damage property: *There were several violent incidents on the streets.* ♦ *a fall in violent crime* ♦ *He gets violent when he's been drinking.*
2 a violent wind, storm, or explosion happens with a lot of force and causes serious damage
3 painful and difficult to control: *a violent coughing fit*
4 containing a lot of violent action: *a violent film*
5 involving very strong and angry emotions or opinions: *a violent argument*
—**violently** adv

violet¹ /ˈvaɪələt/ noun **1** [C] a small plant with purple flowers and a sweet smell **2** [U] a blue-purple colour

violet² /ˈvaɪələt/ adj blue-purple in colour

violin /ˌvaɪəˈlɪn/ noun [C] a musical instrument that you hold under your chin and play by pulling a long object called a bow across its strings —*picture* → STRINGED INSTRUMENT —**violinist** noun [C]

VIP /ˌviː aɪ ˈpiː/ noun [C] very important person: used for referring to someone who receives special treatment because they are powerful or famous

viper /ˈvaɪpə/ noun [C] a type of poisonous snake

viral /ˈvaɪrəl/ adj caused by or relating to a VIRUS

virgin¹ /ˈvɜːdʒɪn/ noun [C] someone who has never had sex

virgin² /ˈvɜːdʒɪn/ adj in a natural or original state

virginity /vəˈdʒɪnəti/ noun [singular] the state of being a virgin

V

Virgo /ˈvɜːɡəʊ/ noun [C/U] one of the 12 signs of the ZODIAC. A **Virgo** is someone who was born between 22 August and 22 September.

virile /ˈvɪraɪl/ adj a man who is virile is strong, active, and full of sexual energy

virility /vəˈrɪləti/ noun [U] the strength and power that are considered typical qualities of a man

virtual /ˈvɜːtʃʊəl/ adj **1** very close to a particular condition, quality etc: *Over the years they had become virtual strangers.* ♦ *It's a virtual impossibility.* **2** computing created or shown by computers, or existing on computers or on the Internet: *a virtual community*

virtually /ˈvɜːtʃʊəli/ adv ★ used for emphasizing that a statement is almost completely true=ALMOST: *It's virtually impossible to get him to eat vegetables.*

virtual re'ality noun [U] computing images and sounds that are produced by a computer in a way that makes the user feel as if they are real

virtue /ˈvɜːtʃuː/ noun ★
1 [C] a good quality that someone has, especially a moral one ≠ VICE: *Patience is not one of my virtues.*
2 [U] formal a way of behaving in which you do what is morally good and right, and avoid doing things that are morally wrong
3 [C] an advantage or good feature that something has=MERIT: *The plan had the virtue of simplicity.*
PHRASE **by virtue of sth** because of something, or as a result of something: *I got this house by virtue of my job.*

virtuoso /ˌvɜːtʃʊˈəʊsəʊ/ noun [C] someone who is very good at a particular activity, especially playing a musical instrument

virtuous /ˈvɜːtʃʊəs/ adj behaving in a way that is morally good and right —**virtuously** adv

virulent /ˈvɪrʊlənt/ adj **1** a virulent illness is very dangerous and affects people very quickly **2** virulent feelings or actions are extremely strong and angry —**virulence** noun [U], **virulently** adv

virus /ˈvaɪrəs/ noun [C] ★
1 a very small living thing that can enter your body and make you ill, or a disease or illness caused by this: *Malaria is caused by a virus.* ♦ *The AIDS virus* ♦ *I've been in bed all week with a virus.* → BACTERIA
2 computing a program that enters your computer and damages or destroys information that you have stored: *Most viruses are spread over the Internet.*

visa /ˈviːzə/ noun [C] an official document or mark in your passport that allows you to enter or leave a country

vis-à-vis /ˌviːz ɑː ˈviː/ preposition formal compared to or relating to someone or something

viscous /ˈvɪskəs/ adj technical a viscous liquid is thick and sticky —**viscosity** /vɪsˈkɒsəti/ noun [U]

visibility /ˌvɪzəˈbɪləti/ noun [U] the distance that you can see, depending on conditions such as the weather

visible /ˈvɪzəb(ə)l/ adj **1** able to be seen: *The house is visible from the road.* **2** clear or obvious=NOTICEABLE: *There has been a visible improvement in your work.*

visibly /ˈvɪzəbli/ adv in a way that is easy to see or notice

vision /ˈvɪʒ(ə)n/ noun ★★
1 [U] the ability to think about and plan for the future, using your intelligence and imagination: *Tackling these challenges will require real vision.*
2 [C] someone's idea of how something should be done, or of how it will be in the future: *The speech gives her vision of the country's economic future.*
3 [U] the ability to see=SIGHT: *He suffers from blurred vision and headaches.*
4 [C] something that someone sees in a dream or as a religious experience
PHRASE **have visions of (doing) sth** to imagine that a particular thing is going to happen in the future: *He had visions of himself wandering the streets, homeless.*

visionary /ˈvɪʒən(ə)ri/ adj with imagination and clear, often new ideas of how things should be done: *his visionary leadership* —**visionary** noun [C]

visit¹ /ˈvɪzɪt/ verb ★★★
1 [I/T] to go and see someone and spend some time with them: *I visit my family every year at Christmas.* ♦ *We only use this room when friends come to visit.*
2 [T] to go to a place for a short period of time: *Have you visited Venezuela before?*
3 [T] to use a WEBSITE: *For more information, visit our website.*

visit² /ˈvɪzɪt/ noun [C] ★★★
1 an occasion when you visit a person or place: *I've just come over on a visit.* ♦ *What did you see on your visit to India?* ♦ *I was surprised to receive a visit from an old friend.* ♦ *It's been a long time since I've paid my Gran a visit.*
2 an occasion when an important person such as a political leader visits a place: *The president arrived in Taiwan today for a three-day visit.*

visitation /ˌvɪzɪˈteɪʃ(ə)n/ noun [C] an occasion when people think that they have seen a spirit or have received a message from God

visitor /ˈvɪzɪtə/ noun [C] ★★★ someone who visits a person or place: *Did you have any visitors today?* ♦ *Visitors to the museum will notice many improvements.*

visor /ˈvaɪzə/ noun [C] **1** a piece of clear plastic on the front of a HELMET (=hard hat) that protects your face **2** a curved piece of plastic or other material on a band that you wear on your head to protect your eyes from the sun **3** a flat object at the top of the front window of a car that you pull down to protect your eyes from the sun

vista /ˈvɪstə/ noun [C] the view that you can see from a particular place, especially a beautiful view

visual¹ /'vɪʒʊəl/ adj **1** relating to things that you can see: *the visual arts* **2** relating to sight: *a visual impairment* —**visually** adv

visual² /'vɪʒʊəl/ noun [C] something such as a drawing or photograph, especially one that helps to explain something

visual aid noun [C] a drawing, map, film etc that people can look at when they are learning about a particular subject

visualize /'vɪʒʊəlaɪz/ verb [T] to form a picture of someone or something in your mind —**visualization** /ˌvɪʒʊəlaɪˈzeɪʃ(ə)n/ noun [U]

vital /'vaɪt(ə)l/ adj ★
1 very important or necessary =ESSENTIAL: *He played a vital role in setting up the organization.* ♦ *Skilful employees are vital to the success of any company.*
2 full of energy and life: *He was young, vital, and handsome.*
3 necessary to keep you alive: *vital organs*

vitality /vaɪˈtæləti/ noun [U] **1** energy or enthusiasm **2** the quality of being exciting or successful

vitally /'vaɪt(ə)li/ adv used for emphasizing that something is very important or necessary: *It is vitally important that we find him.*

vitamin /'vɪtəmɪn/ noun [C] a natural substance in food that is necessary to keep your body healthy

vitriolic /ˌvɪtriˈɒlɪk/ adj vitriolic language or behaviour is cruel and full of hate

vivacious /vɪˈveɪʃəs/ adj lively and attractive

vivid /'vɪvɪd/ adj **1** very clear and detailed: *a vivid description/image/memory* **2** a vivid example of something shows very clearly that something exists or is true **3** a vivid colour is strong and bright —**vividly** adv, **vividness** noun [U]

vivisection /ˌvɪvɪˈsekʃ(ə)n/ verb [U] the practice of performing operations on living animals for scientific experiments

V-neck /'viː ˌnek/ noun [C] an opening for the neck in a piece of clothing, in the shape of a 'V' —**V-necked** adj —*picture* → NECKLINE

vocab /'vəʊkæb/ noun [U] *informal* vocabulary

vocabulary /vəʊˈkæbjʊləri/ noun [C/U] ★ all the words that someone knows, or all the words in a particular language, a particular book etc: *exercises designed to increase your vocabulary*

vocal /'vəʊk(ə)l/ adj **1** relating to the voice, or done with the voice **2** a vocal group of people express their opinions strongly with the result that people in authority notice them

vocal cords or **vocal chords** noun [plural] the very thin muscles inside your throat that you use for making sounds

vocalist /'vəʊkəlɪst/ noun [C] a singer, especially one who sings popular music

vocation /vəʊˈkeɪʃ(ə)n/ noun [C] a job that you do because you feel that it is your purpose in life and you have special skills for doing it

vocational /vəʊˈkeɪʃ(ə)nəl/ adj relating to the skills that you need for a particular job: *a vocational course/qualification*

vociferous /vəʊˈsɪfərəs/ adj *formal* expressing opinions loudly and with force —**vociferously** adv

vodka /'vɒdkə/ noun [C/U] a strong clear alcoholic drink, or a glass of this drink

vogue /vəʊg/ noun [singular] a fashion, or something that is fashionable

voice¹ /vɔɪs/ noun ★★★
1 [C/U] the sounds that someone makes when they speak, or the way that someone speaks: *We could hear voices in the next apartment.* ♦ *The woman at the desk greeted him in a bored voice.* ♦ *The children were very well-behaved, and I never had to raise my voice* (=speak louder or shout). ♦ *She started screaming at the top of her voice* (=very loudly).
2 [singular] the right or opportunity to express your opinions or feelings and influence what happens
3 [singular] a person, organization etc that represents a particular type of opinion or group of people: *Carter is the voice of the black minority in this area.* ♦ *the voice of reason/authority/experience*

> ### Words often used with voice
>
> *Adjectives often used with voice (noun, sense 1)*
> ■ **big, booming, loud** + VOICE: used about voices that are loud
> ■ **gentle, low, quiet, small, soft** + VOICE: used about voices that are quiet
> ■ **high-pitched, piercing, shrill** + VOICE: used about voices that are high
> ■ **deep, gruff, hoarse, husky, low** + VOICE: used about voices that are low

voice² /vɔɪs/ verb [T] *formal* to express your opinions or feelings about something: *Human rights groups have voiced their concern over the treatment of refugees.*

voice-activated /'vɔɪsˌæktɪveɪtɪd/ adj a machine or piece of equipment that is voice-activated can recognize and obey spoken instructions

voice box noun [C] the part of your throat from which you produce sounds

voicemail /'vɔɪsmeɪl/ noun [U] an electronic system that records and stores phone messages

void /vɔɪd/ noun [singular] *formal* **1** a situation in which someone or something that is important to you is no longer there **2** an extremely large empty space

volatile /'vɒlətaɪl/ adj a volatile situation can suddenly change or become more dangerous

volcanic /vɒlˈkænɪk/ adj coming from, or relating to, a volcano: *a layer of volcanic ash* ♦ *volcanic activity*

volcano /vɒlˈkeɪnəʊ/ noun [C] a mountain that forces hot gas, rocks, ASH, and LAVA (=melted rock) into the air through a hole at the top

vole /vəʊl/ noun [C] a small animal similar to a mouse but with a short tail

V

volley¹ /'vɒli/ noun [C] **1** the action of hitting or kicking a ball back to an opponent before it touches the ground **2** a lot of questions, insults etc that are all spoken or made at the same time

volley² /'vɒli/ verb [I/T] to hit or kick a ball back to an opponent before it touches the ground —*picture* → C15

volleyball /'vɒli,bɔːl/ noun [U] a sport in which two teams use their hands and arms to hit a ball to each other over a high net

volt /vəʊlt/ noun [C] a unit for measuring the power of an electric current

voltage /'vəʊltɪdʒ/ noun [C/U] the amount of power in an electric current, measured in volts

volume /'vɒljuːm/ noun ★★★
1 [C/U] an amount of something: *an increase in the volume of traffic* ♦ *Some students cannot cope with the huge volume of work.*
2 [U] the loudness of a sound, especially from something such as a television, CD player etc
3 [U] the amount of space that is contained in something or that is filled by something: *How do you calculate the volume of a cube?*
4 [C] *formal* a book

voluntary /'vɒlənt(ə)ri/ adj ★★
1 something that is voluntary is done because you choose to do it, and not because you have to ≠ COMPULSORY, MANDATORY: *Some 30,000 workers took voluntary redundancy.*
2 voluntary work is done for no pay: *My job at the hospital is purely voluntary.* —**voluntarily** /,vɒlən'teərɪli/ adv

volunteer¹ /,vɒlən'tɪə/ noun [C] **1** someone who works without expecting to be paid for what they do **2** someone who offers to do something and does not have to be made to do it **3** someone who joins the armed forces without being forced to

volunteer² /,vɒlən'tɪə/ verb **1** [I] to offer or choose to do something for someone else **2** [I/T] to work without expecting to be paid for what you do **3** [I/T] to say something or give information without being asked **4** [I] to join the armed forces without being forced to

voluptuous /və'lʌptʃʊəs/ adj a voluptuous woman has a large curved body and is sexually attractive —**voluptuously** adv

vomit¹ /'vɒmɪt/ verb [I/T] if you vomit, food comes up from your stomach and out through your mouth because you are ill

vomit² /'vɒmɪt/ noun [U] food or other substances that come up from your stomach when you vomit

voodoo /'vuːduː/ noun [U] a religion whose followers believe in magic and WITCHCRAFT

voracious /və'reɪʃəs/ adj *formal* **1** a voracious person or animal eats a lot **2** enjoying something very much and wanting to do it a lot: *a voracious reader* —**voraciously** adv

vote¹ /vəʊt/ verb [I/T] ★★★ to decide something, or to choose a representative or winner, by officially stating your choice,

for example in an election: *The Council will vote on the proposal next Friday.* ♦ *68 per cent of the union voted against striking.* ♦ *I'm going to vote for Jackson.* ♦ **vote to do sth** *The committee voted unanimously to ban alcohol from the concert.*

vote² /vəʊt/ noun ★★★
1 [C] an official choice you make between two or more issues, people etc, for example in an election: *My vote will go to the candidate who promises tax reform.* ♦ *In Britain many people cast their votes* (=make a mark to show who they are voting for) *at local schools.*
2 **the vote** [singular] the right to vote in an election

voter /'vəʊtə/ noun [C] someone who votes in an election

vouch /vaʊtʃ/

PHRASAL VERBS **'vouch for sb** to say that you believe that someone is good and will behave well in future
'vouch for sth to say that something is true, correct, or good

voucher /'vaʊtʃə/ noun [C] a piece of paper that you buy something with instead of using money

vow¹ /vaʊ/ noun **1** [C] a serious promise **2** **vows** [plural] a set of formal promises that people make to each other, for example during a wedding ceremony

vow² /vaʊ/ verb [I/T] *formal* to promise that you will do something

vowel /'vaʊəl/ noun [C] *linguistics* one of the letters a, e, i, o, or u, or the sounds that they represent

voyage /'vɔɪdʒ/ noun [C] a long journey, especially on a ship

vs abbrev versus

vulgar /'vʌlgə/ adj **1** a vulgar joke, comment, action etc has a sexual meaning that is rude or offensive **2** someone who is vulgar is rude, unpleasant, and offensive **3** showing a lack of ability to judge what is attractive, suitable etc —**vulgarly** adv

vulnerable /'vʌln(ə)rəb(ə)l/ adj weak and therefore easy to hurt, harm, or attack: *The government must help the most vulnerable groups in our society.* —**vulnerability** /,vʌln(ə)rə'bɪləti/ noun [U]

vulture /'vʌltʃə/ noun [C] a large bird that eats the bodies of dead animals

W w

w or **W** /'dʌb(ə)ljuː/ noun [C/U] the 23rd letter of the English alphabet

W abbrev **1** watt **2** West **3** Western

wacky /'wæki/ adj *informal* funny, or silly

wad /wɒd/ noun [C] **1** a thick pile of papers,

documents, or bank notes **2** a round mass of something soft

waddle /'wɒd(ə)l/ verb [I] to walk with short steps that make your body move from side to side —**waddle** noun [C]

wade /weɪd/ verb [I] to walk in water that is not very deep

PHRASAL VERB **wade through sth** to read a lot of boring information

wafer /'weɪfə/ noun [C] a very thin BISCUIT

waffle¹ /'wɒf(ə)l/ noun **1** [C] a flat cake that has deep square marks on both sides **2** [U] British informal talk or writing that uses a lot of words but does not say anything important

waffle² /'wɒf(ə)l/ or ˌwaffle 'on verb [I] British informal to talk or write using a lot of words but without saying anything important

waft /wɑːft/ verb [I] if a smell or a noise wafts, it floats through the air

wag /wæg/ verb [I/T] **1** if a dog wags its tail, it moves its tail from one side to the other several times **2** if a person wags a finger, they move it up and down, especially in order to show that they disapprove of something

wage¹ /weɪdʒ/ noun [C] ★★★ a regular amount of money that you earn for working: *a daily/hourly/weekly wage ♦ I've usually spent all my wages by Tuesday. ♦ What is the minimum wage here?*

wage² /weɪdʒ/ verb [T] to start and continue a war or fight: *The government has pledged to wage war on drugs.*

wager /'weɪdʒə/ noun [C] an agreement to win or lose an amount of money depending on the result of a competition or other event =BET —**wager** verb [T]

waggle /'wæg(ə)l/ verb [I/T] to move up and down or from side to side with short quick movements, or to make something move in this way

wagon /'wægən/ noun [C] **1** a covered vehicle with four wheels that is usually pulled by horses **2** British a large open container that is pulled by a train

waif /weɪf/ noun [C] a child who is very thin and pale

wail /weɪl/ verb **1** [I/T] to shout or cry with a long high sound because you are in pain or are very sad **2** [I] to make a long high sound: *wailing sirens* —**wail** noun [C]

waist /weɪst/ noun [C] **1** the middle part of the human body that is usually narrower than the parts above and below —*picture* → C14 **2** the part of a piece of clothing that covers your waist

waistband /'weɪs(t)bænd/ noun [C] a piece of cloth on a pair of trousers or a skirt that goes around your waist

waistcoat /'weɪs(t)kəʊt/ noun [C] British a piece of clothing without sleeves that is usually worn over a shirt and under a jacket —*picture* → C4

waistline /'weɪs(t)laɪn/ noun [C] the measurement around your waist, used especially as a way of judging how fat or thin someone is

wait¹ /weɪt/ verb [I] ★★★
1 to stay in one place until a particular thing happens or until someone arrives: *Sheryl said she'd be waiting in the lobby. ♦ He was attacked while he was waiting for a bus. ♦ They waited anxiously for news of survivors. ♦ Let's sit down and wait until Bob gets here. ♦ wait to do sth The TV showed thousands of people waiting to board buses.*
2 to delay doing something until something happens or until someone arrives: *I'm busy right now so you'll just have to wait. ♦ Should we start eating or should we wait for the others?*
3 to be hoping or expecting that something will happen: *I've been waiting for a refund cheque for several months. ♦ wait for sb/sth to do sth There's no point waiting for her to change her mind.*
4 to be ready for someone to take or use: *There's a package waiting for you in the office.*

PHRASES **sb can't wait/can hardly wait** used for saying that someone is very excited about something that is going to happen: *I can't wait for the holidays.*
keep sb waiting to make someone stay in one place or do nothing until you are ready to see them or talk to them: *We were kept waiting outside his office for over an hour.*
wait a minute/second spoken **1** used for telling someone to stop and wait for you **2** used for saying that you have just remembered or noticed something: *Wait a second, wasn't Jackie supposed to be here?* **3** used when you are slightly annoyed by something that someone has just said: *Wait a minute, that's not what I said!*

PHRASAL VERBS ˌwait a'bout British same as **wait around**
ˌwait a'round to do nothing because you are expecting something to happen, and you cannot do anything until it does: *I don't feel like waiting around for him to make up his mind.*
ˌwait 'in British to stay at home because you expect someone to come or to telephone you: *I have to wait in for a delivery this morning.*
'wait on sb to serve people in a restaurant
ˌwait 'up to not go to sleep until someone comes home

Words often used with wait

Adverbs often used with wait (verb, sense 1)
■ WAIT + **anxiously, eagerly, expectantly, impatiently, nervously, patiently, quietly**: wait in a particular mental state

---

Wait for and expect have different meanings.
■ If you **wait for** something to happen, you do not leave a place or do something else until it happens: *We waited for Alex to finish his lunch. ♦ I'm waiting for a bus.*
■ If you **expect** something to happen, you believe that it will happen: *We expected Lee to be upset. ♦ I'm expecting a phone call later.*

---

wait² /weɪt/ noun [singular] a period of time during which you wait for something: *Expect a long wait if you intend to buy tickets.* → LIE¹

waiter /'weɪtə/ noun [C] a man who brings food and drink to your table in a restaurant

W

waiting list /ˈweɪtɪŋ ˌlɪst/ noun [C] a list of people who are waiting for something to become available

waiting room /ˈweɪtɪŋ ˌruːm/ noun [C] a room where you wait for something such as a train, or for someone such as a doctor to be ready to see you

waitress /ˈweɪtrəs/ noun [C] a woman who brings food and drink to your table in a restaurant

waive /weɪv/ verb [T] to choose to officially ignore a rule, right, or claim

waiver /ˈweɪvə/ noun [C] an official statement or document that says that a right, claim, or law can be ignored

wake¹ /weɪk/ (past tense **woke** /wəʊk/; past participle **woken** /ˈwəʊkən/) verb [I/T] ★ to stop sleeping, or to make someone stop sleeping: *I woke at 5 o'clock this morning.* ♦ *Be quiet or you'll wake the baby.*

  PHRASAL VERB ˌwake (sb) ˈup *same as* **wake¹**: *Wake up! It's nearly ten o'clock!* ♦ *Don't wake me up when you come in.*

wake² /weɪk/ noun [C] **1** a meeting of friends and relations before or after a funeral in order to remember the person who died **2** the track that appears in the water behind a moving boat

  PHRASE **in the wake of sth** or **in sth's wake** happening after an event or as a result of it: *An inquiry has been set up in the wake of the crash.*

waken /ˈweɪkən/ verb [I/T] *formal* to wake up, or to wake someone up

ˈ**wake-up ˌcall** noun [C] **1** a bad experience that makes you take action in order to improve a situation: *The low test scores should serve as a loud wake-up call to teachers.* **2** a telephone call that you receive in order to wake you up

waking /ˈweɪkɪŋ/ adj relating to the time that you are awake: *I spent every waking hour working on the report.*

walk¹ /wɔːk/ verb ★★★
1 [I] to move forwards by putting one foot in front of the other: *Has your little boy learned to walk yet?* ♦ *It takes me 25 minutes to walk to work.* ♦ *Greg walked slowly towards her, smiling.* ♦ *Howard walked in with two men I'd never seen before.* ♦ *As we walked along she talked about her plans.*
2 [T] to go a particular distance by walking: *She walked three miles each day.*
3 [T] to walk somewhere with someone in order to be sure that they reach the place safely: *When Valerie worked late, Carl always walked her home.*

  PHRASES **walk all over sb** to treat someone very badly

walk the dog to walk somewhere with a dog so that it gets exercise

→ TIGHTROPE

  PHRASAL VERBS ˌwalk aˈway to leave a place, situation, or person: *Spencer turned to walk away, then stopped.*

ˌwalk aˈway with sth to win something easily: *United could walk away with the championship.*

ˌwalk ˈin on sb to walk into a room where someone is doing something that is private or secret

ˌwalk ˈoff with sth **1** to steal something: *You can't just walk off with his jacket.* **2** to win something easily

ˌwalk ˈon to continue walking in the direction that you were going in

ˌwalk ˈout **1** to suddenly leave a job or relationship: *Her husband had **walked out on** her a year before.* **2** to stop working as a way of protesting about something: *All the workers walked out on Friday night.*

Other ways of saying **walk**

- **march** to walk in a military way or with a lot of energy
- **shuffle** to walk slowly without lifting your feet off the ground
- **stagger** to walk with uneven steps, almost falling over
- **step** to move one foot forward
- **stride** to walk fast, taking big steps
- **stroll** to walk for pleasure in a relaxed way
- **tiptoe** to walk very quietly, standing on your toes
- **trudge** to walk slowly because you are very tired

---

walk² /wɔːk/ noun [C] ★★
1 a short journey that you make by walking, or the distance of this trip: *It's a five-minute walk from our house to the post office.* ♦ *It's a beautiful walk down to the beach.* ♦ *Does anyone want to go for a walk?* ♦ *Let's take a walk after we eat.*
2 the way that someone walks

  PHRASE **from all walks of life** used for saying that a group consists of all types of people with different backgrounds, jobs etc

walker /ˈwɔːkə/ noun [C] someone who walks for pleasure or for exercise

walkie-talkie /ˌwɔːki ˈtɔːki/ noun [C] a small radio that you can carry and use for communicating with someone else who also has one

walking /ˈwɔːkɪŋ/ noun [U] the activity of going for walks: *We went walking in the Malvern hills.* ♦ *a pair of strong walking boots*

ˈ**walking ˌframe** noun [C] a special frame that some people use to help them to walk, especially people who are old or disabled

ˈ**walking ˌstick** noun [C] a stick that some people use to help them to walk

Walkman /ˈwɔːkmən/ (plural **Walkmans**) trademark a type of small CASSETTE or CD player with HEADPHONES that you can carry with you

walkout /ˈwɔːkaʊt/ noun [C] a form of protest in which people stop what they are doing, and leave the place where they work or study

walkover /ˈwɔːkˌəʊvə/ noun [C] *informal* an easy victory or achievement

walkway /ˈwɔːkˌweɪ/ noun [C] a path built for people to walk along, especially one that is above ground level and that connects two buildings

wall¹ /wɔːl/ noun [C] ★★★
1 an upright side of a room or building: *The walls of the factory were covered in graffiti.* ♦ *Several paintings hung on the wall.*
2 an upright structure made of stone or brick that surrounds or divides an area of

land: *The children got into the yard by climbing over the wall.*

3 a large amount of something that forms a tall mass: *A wall of dark water approached their small boat.*

PHRASES **go to the wall** *British informal* if a business goes to the wall, it fails

go up the wall *British informal* to get very angry: *He'll go up the wall when he finds out.*

like talking to a (brick) wall used for saying that someone does not listen or react to you when you talk

run into/hit a (brick) wall to reach a point in a process where there are problems that seem impossible to solve

wall² /wɔːl/

PHRASAL VERBS **wall sth 'in** to surround something with a wall

wall sth 'off to separate a small space from a larger one by building a wall

wallaby /'wɒləbi/ noun [C] an animal like a small KANGAROO

walled /wɔːld/ adj surrounded by a wall

wallet /'wɒlɪt/ noun [C] a small flat case that you keep money, CREDIT CARDS etc in

wallop /'wɒləp/ verb [T] *informal* to hit someone or something very hard

wallow /'wɒləʊ/ verb [I] **1** *showing disapproval* to spend a lot of time feeling sad or upset: *George still seems determined to wallow in self-pity.* **2** to lie down and roll around in water, dirt, or MUD

wallpaper¹ /'wɔːlˌpeɪpə/ noun [C/U] **1** thick paper that you can stick on the walls inside a house in order to decorate them **2** the background colour or pattern that you can put on your computer screen

wallpaper² /'wɔːlˌpeɪpə/ verb [I/T] to put wallpaper onto walls

Wall Street 1 the US STOCK MARKET **2** the area in New York City where the US STOCK EXCHANGE and other major financial institutions are based

wall-to-'wall adj **1** covering the whole floor of a room: *wall-to-wall carpet* **2** *informal* filling a space or time completely: *wall-to-wall TV coverage*

wally /'wɒli/ noun [C] *British informal* a silly person

walnut /'wɔːlnʌt/ noun **1** [C] a nut you can eat that has a hard round shell **2** [C/U] the tree that this nut grows on, or the wood of a walnut tree

walrus /'wɔːlrəs/ noun [C] a large sea animal that has two very long TUSKS (=teeth)

waltz¹ /wɔːls/ noun [C] a dance in which a pair of dancers turns continuously while moving around the dance floor, or the music for this dance

waltz² /wɔːls/ verb [I] **1** to dance a waltz **2** *informal* to walk somewhere in a relaxed and confident way

wan /wɒn/ adj **1** someone who is wan looks very pale and weak because they are ill **2** a wan light is not bright

wand /wɒnd/ noun [C] a thin stick that is used for doing magic tricks

wander /'wɒndə/ verb **1** [I] to go from place to place without a particular direction or purpose: *Jim wandered into the kitchen and made some tea.* ♦ *We spent the afternoon in*

the old city, just wandering the streets. **2** [I] if your mind or thoughts wander, you stop concentrating and start thinking about other things **3** [I] if your eyes or your GAZE wanders, you stop looking at one thing and start looking at another **4** [I] *same as* **wander off** —**wanderer** noun [C]

PHRASAL VERB **wander 'off** to move away from a place where you are usually, or where people expect you to be: *It's a safe place where kids can wander off on their own.*

wane /weɪn/ verb [I] **1** to become weaker or less important **2** when the moon is waning, it looks smaller each night ≠ WAX

wangle /'wæŋg(ə)l/ verb [T] *informal* to get something that is difficult to get, especially by persuading someone in an indirect way: *I'll see if I can wangle some tickets for you.*

wanna /'wɒnə/ short form *informal* a way of writing 'want to' that shows how it sounds in informal conversation

wannabe /'wɒnəbi/ noun [C] *informal* someone who wants to be famous or successful —**wannabe** adj

want¹ /wɒnt/ verb [T] ★★★

1 to feel that you would like to have, keep, or do something: *Do you still want these old letters?* ♦ **want to do sth** *Liz wants to see the gardens.* ♦ **want sth for sth** *She wants a ticket to the concert for her birthday.*

2 to feel that you would like someone to do something, or would like something to happen: **want sb to do sth** *I want you to come with me.* ♦ **want sth from sb/sth** *I'm not sure what he wants from me.*

3 to ask for someone because you would like to see or speak to them: *Mum wants you – she's in the kitchen.* ♦ *You're wanted on the phone.*

PHRASES **all sb wants** *spoken* used for saying that someone's needs or requests are reasonable: *All I want is the truth.*

do you want sth? *spoken* used for offering something to someone, or for asking them if they would like to do something: *Do you want a cup of coffee?*

if you want *spoken* **1** used for offering to do something: *I'll make tea if you want.* **2** used for giving permission, or for agreeing with a suggestion that someone has made: *'Can I come with you?' 'If you want.'*

who wants (to do) sth? used for offering something to a group of people, or for asking if they would like to do something: *Who wants another glass of wine?*

want² /wɒnt/ noun **1** [C/U] *formal* a situation in which people do not have basic things such as food or money **2 wants** [plural] things that you want or need

PHRASE **for want of a better word/phrase/term** used for saying that you cannot think of a more exact way of describing or explaining what you mean

wanted /'wɒntɪd/ adj **1** being looked for by the police in connection with a crime **2** loved by other people

wanting /'wɒntɪŋ/ adj not as good as something should be: *UN peacekeeping forces were found wanting.*

wanton /'wɒntən/ adj *formal* causing harm or

damage for no reason: *wanton destruction*

war /wɔː/ noun ★★★

1 [C/U] fighting between two or more countries or groups, that involves the use of armed forces and usually continues for a long time: *the Vietnam War* ♦ *They have been at war for five years.* ♦ *I volunteered for the Navy when war broke out.* ♦ *The Allies declared war* (=officially said they were at war) *in 1939.*

2 [C/U] a determined effort to control or stop something, for example a disease or crime: *This is a major victory in the war against drugs.* ♦ *the war on poverty*

3 [C] a situation in which countries, organizations, or businesses compete with each other in order to gain economic advantages: *This could easily start a trade war.*

→ WARRING

war crime noun [C] the crime of killing or harming people during a war for reasons that are not allowed by international law —**war criminal** noun [C]

ward¹ /wɔːd/ noun [C] a large room in a hospital with beds for people to stay in

ward² /wɔːd/ PHRASAL VERB **ward sb/sth off** to do something in order to prevent someone or something from harming you

warden /ˈwɔːd(ə)n/ noun [C] someone whose job is to be responsible for a particular place or thing, and who checks that rules are obeyed → TRAFFIC WARDEN

warder /ˈwɔːdə/ noun [C] *British* a prison OFFICER

wardrobe /ˈwɔːdrəʊb/ noun [C] **1** a piece of furniture like a large cupboard where you can hang your clothes **2** all the clothes that someone has

warehouse /ˈweəhaʊs/ noun [C] a big building where large amounts of goods are stored

warfare /ˈwɔːfeə/ noun [U] the activity of fighting a war, or the methods that are used for fighting wars: *the rules of warfare* ♦ *germ/biological warfare*

war game noun [C] a military training exercise in which soldiers practise for a real war

warhead /ˈwɔːhed/ noun [C] the front part of a missile that explodes

warlike /ˈwɔːlaɪk/ adj likely to start wars, or always ready to go to war

warlord /ˈwɔːlɔːd/ noun [C] a military leader who controls part of a country but does not belong to the country's official armed forces

warm¹ /wɔːm/ adj ★★★

1 fairly hot in a comfortable, pleasant way ≠ COOL: *It was warm enough for us to sit outside.* ♦ *I walked fast to keep warm.*

2 warm clothes and buildings prevent you from feeling cold: *The kitchen was the warmest room in the house.* ♦ *a thick warm coat*

3 kind and friendly in a way that makes other people feel comfortable: *a warm smile* ♦ *Please give a warm welcome to tonight's special guests.*

4 warm colours have red, orange, or yellow in them —**warmly** adv

warm² /wɔːm/ verb [T] to make someone or something warm: *The morning sun warms the kitchen nicely.*

PHRASAL VERBS **warm to sb/sth** to begin to like someone or something

warm (sb/sth) up 1 to become warm, or to make someone or something become warm: *I'll warm up some soup for lunch.* ♦ *Drink this and you'll soon warm up.* **2** to prepare for a sport or activity by doing gentle exercises or practising just before it starts: *The players are already on the field warming up.*

war memorial noun [C] a structure that is built to remind people of the soldiers and other people who were killed in a war

warm-hearted /ˌwɔːm ˈhɑːtɪd/ adj friendly, kind, and generous ≠ COLD-HEARTED

warmth /wɔːmθ/ noun [U] **1** heat: *We sat near the warmth of the fire.* **2** a kind, friendly quality in someone or something

warm-up noun [C] a set of exercises that you do just before you start to play a sport, in order to prepare your body

warn /wɔːn/ verb [I/T] ★★★

1 to tell someone about a possible problem or danger, so that they can avoid it or deal with it: *Recent studies warn against drinking too much caffeine.* ♦ *Scientists warned of the threat to beaches and rivers from pollution.* ♦ **warn sb to do sth** *Police are warning all women in the area to take extra care when going out alone.* ♦ **+that** *The report warns that consumers could end up paying higher prices.* ♦ **warn sb about sth** *Travel agents are not warning tourists about the dangers of crime in holiday resorts.*

2 to tell someone that they will be punished or that something bad will happen if they do something: *Behave yourself! That's the last time I'm warning you.*

warning /ˈwɔːnɪŋ/ noun ★★

1 [C/U] an action or statement telling someone of a possible problem or danger: *By law, cigarette packets must carry a health warning.* ♦ *a warning against driving on the icy roads* ♦ *a warning of severe thunderstorms*

2 [C] a statement telling someone that they will be punished or that something bad will happen if they do something: *This is your last warning – if you're late again, you'll lose your job.*

warp /wɔːp/ verb [I/T] to become bent or curved because of damage by heat or water, or to make something do this

warpath /ˈwɔːpɑːθ/ noun **on the warpath** *informal* angry about something and looking for someone to punish for it

warped /wɔːpt/ adj **1** *informal* someone who is warped has opinions or thoughts that most people think are strange or shocking **2** bent or curved because of damage by heat or water

warrant¹ /ˈwɒrənt/ noun [C] a document written by a judge that gives the police permission to do something, for example to arrest someone or to search a house

warrant² /ˈwɒrənt/ verb [T] *formal* to make an action seem reasonable or necessary ≈ JUSTIFY

W

warranty /'wɒrənti/ noun [C] a company's written promise to repair or replace a product that you buy from them if it breaks or does not work=GUARANTEE

warren /'wɒrən/ noun [C] a place that is very difficult to find your way around because there are so many ways that you could go

warring /'wɔːrɪŋ/ adj arguing or fighting with each other

warrior /'wɒriə/ noun [C] literary a soldier

warship /'wɔːʃɪp/ noun [C] a large ship with a lot of weapons, used for fighting in wars

wart /wɔːt/ noun [C] a small hard lump that grows on your skin

wartime /'wɔːtaɪm/ noun [U] the period when a war is taking place ≠ PEACETIME —**wartime** adj

war-torn /'wɔː ˌtɔːn/ adj a war-torn country or place has been badly damaged by a war

wary /'weəri/ adj careful or nervous about someone or something, because you think that they might cause a problem —**warily** adv

was /weak wəz, strong wɒz/ see be

wash

wash¹ /wɒʃ/ verb ★★★

1 [T] to clean something with water or with soap and water: *I've got to wash the car.* ♦ *a freshly washed shirt* ♦ *You should always wash fruit before eating it.*

2 [I/T] to clean yourself or a part of your body with water or with soap and water: *He washed and dressed quickly.* ♦ ***Wash your hands*** *before you touch the food.*

3 [T] if water washes a person or object somewhere, it carries them there: *Some very strange things get washed ashore here.*

4 [I/T] to flow, or to flow to a place: *Waves were washing against the side of the boat.*

PHRASE **wash your hands of** to say or show that you do not want to be involved with something, and that you are not responsible for it: *The government had washed their hands of the affair.*

PHRASAL VERBS ˌwash sth aˈway if water washes something away, it carries it away: *Heavy rains have washed away the bridge.*

ˌwash sth ˈdown to drink a liquid in order to help you to swallow food or medicine more easily: *He had a large slice of pizza **washed down** with beer.*

ˌwash (sth) ˈoff if you wash dirt off, or if dirt washes off, you remove it by washing: *Wash all the soil off before you cook the potatoes.* ♦ *Don't worry – that'll wash off easily.*

ˌwash ˈout to be able to be removed by washing: *Permanent dyes won't wash out.*

ˌwash sth ˈout to wash something quickly, especially the inside of a container

ˌwash (sth) ˈup British to wash the plates, cups,

spoons etc after a meal: *I can help to cook and wash up.* ♦ *The breakfast things haven't been washed up yet.*

ˌwash sth ˈup if water washes something up, it carries it somewhere and leaves it there: *Two whales have been washed up on the beach.*

wash² /wɒʃ/ noun **1** [C] the process of washing someone or something: *These trousers need a wash.* ♦ *After a few washes the colour faded.* **2 the wash** [singular] clothes that are being washed, or the process of washing clothes=LAUNDRY: *Did you put my blue shirt in the wash?*

washable /'wɒʃəb(ə)l/ adj able to be washed without being damaged

washbasin /'wɒʃˌbeɪs(ə)n/ noun [C] the container in a bathroom that you use for washing your face and hands

washed-out /ˌwɒʃt 'aʊt/ adj informal very pale and ill or tired

washed-up /ˌwɒʃt 'ʌp/ adj informal someone who is washed-up will never be popular or successful again=FINISHED

washer /'wɒʃə/ noun [C] **1** a small flat ring that is used for filling the space between two metal parts, for example between a surface and the top of a screw **2** informal a WASHING MACHINE

washing /'wɒʃɪŋ/ noun [U] British clothes that need to be washed

ˈwashing ˌline noun [C] British a rope tied between poles that is used for hanging wet clothes on to dry

ˈwashing maˌchine noun [C] a machine for washing clothes

ˈwashing ˌpowder noun [U] British soap in the form of a powder that you use for washing clothes

ˌwashing-ˈup noun [U] British **1** the dishes, cups, knives, forks etc that need to be washed after a meal **2** the activity of washing the dishes and other things used for a meal

ˌwashing-ˈup ˌliquid noun [U] British liquid soap that you use for washing dishes, cups, knives, forks etc

washout /'wɒʃaʊt/ noun [C] informal a failure: *The party was a total washout.*

wasn't /'wɒz(ə)nt/ short form the usual way of saying or writing 'was not'. This is not often used in formal writing: *The food looked good, but I wasn't hungry.*

wasp /wɒsp/ noun [C] a black and yellow flying insect that can sting you —*picture* → C13

wastage /'weɪstɪdʒ/ noun [U] the amount of something that is wasted, or a situation in which something is wasted

waste¹ /weɪst/ noun ★★

1 [singular/U] the failure to use something that is valuable or useful in an effective way: *All this uneaten food – what a waste!* ♦ *It's a waste of time trying to get her to change her mind.* ♦ *The cherries will just go to waste* (=be spoiled or thrown away) *if we don't pick them soon.*

2 [C/U] the useless materials, substances, or parts that are left after you have used something: *nuclear waste*

W

waste² /weɪst/ verb [T] ★★ to use more of something than is necessary, or to use it in a way that does not produce the best results: *There were accusations that the government was wasting public money.* ♦ *A great deal of time was wasted arguing over the details of the contract.* ♦ **waste sth on sth** *Why do you waste your money on lottery tickets?*

PHRASES be wasted on sb if something is wasted on someone, they do not understand it or realize how good it is: *Don't give the smoked salmon to the children – it'd just be wasted on them.*

waste no time (in) doing sth to do something immediately

PHRASAL VERB ˌwaste aˈway to gradually become thinner and weaker over a period of time, usually because of an illness

waste³ /weɪst/ adj **1** waste substances are what is left of something after the valuable parts of it have been used **2** waste land or waste ground is land that is not being used or has not been built on

ˈwaste ˌbin noun [C] *British* a container that you put rubbish in —*picture* → C2

wasted /ˈweɪstɪd/ adj **1** not used effectively: *a wasted day* **2** extremely thin and weak **3** *informal* very drunk or strongly affected by illegal drugs

wasteful /ˈweɪs(t)f(ə)l/ adj using something carelessly, so that some of it is wasted

wasteland /ˈweɪs(t)ˌlænd/ noun [C/U] an area of land that is empty or that cannot be used

wastepaper basket /weɪs(t)ˈpeɪpə ˌbɑːskɪt/ noun [C] a small open container for rubbish such as used paper —*picture* → C3

watch¹ /wɒtʃ/ verb ★★★
1 [I/T] to look at someone or something for a period of time: *Did you watch the news last night?* ♦ *We watched helplessly as the car rolled into the river.* ♦ **watch sb/sth do sth** *Jill watched the children build sandcastles.* ♦ **watch sb/sth doing sth** *We arrived early to watch the players warming up.* → SEE
2 [T] to be careful of something: *Watch the knife! It's sharp!* ♦ **+(that)** *Watch you don't get your bag stolen.* ♦ **+how/who/what etc** *They need to watch what they spend quite carefully.*
3 [T] to look after someone or something for a short time and make sure that nothing bad happens to them: *Could you just watch the baby for a minute?*

PHRASES watch it *spoken* **1** used for telling someone to be careful **2** used for threatening someone

watch your step *spoken* **1** used for telling someone to be careful where they walk **2** used for telling someone to be careful about what they say or do, because they could get into trouble

PHRASAL VERBS ˌwatch ˈout used for telling someone to be careful: *Watch out – you're going to hit that car!*

ˌwatch ˈout for sb/sth to be careful so that you can avoid someone or something

ˌwatch ˈover sb/sth to guard, protect, or be in charge of someone or something

---

watch² /wɒtʃ/ noun [C] ★★ a small clock that you wear on your wrist

PHRASE keep (a) watch 1 to pay attention to a situation carefully so that you can deal with any changes or problems: *Scientists are keeping a close watch on pollution levels.* **2** to watch someone carefully in order to make sure that they are safe or that they do not do something bad: *Keep a watch on him in case he gets worse.*

watchdog /ˈwɒtʃˌdɒg/ noun [C] **1** a person or organization whose job is to make sure that companies that provide a particular type of service or product do not break the law or do anything harmful: *the water industry watchdog* **2** a dog that is used for guarding a building

watchful /ˈwɒtʃf(ə)l/ adj looking at something carefully, or noticing everything that is happening = VIGILANT

watchman /ˈwɒtʃmən/ noun [C] a NIGHT WATCHMAN

watchword /ˈwɒtʃˌwɜːd/ noun [C] a word or phrase that expresses the quality that someone believes is most important in a particular situation

water¹ /ˈwɔːtə/ noun ★★★
1 [U] the clear liquid that falls as rain and is used for drinking, washing, and cooking: *Wash your hands thoroughly with soap and water.*
2 [U] an area of water such as a lake or sea: *From the hotel there's a beautiful view of the water.*
3 [C/U] the surface of a lake or the sea: *I was swimming under the water near the beach.*
4 **waters** [plural] an area of water that belongs to a particular place, state, country etc: *British waters*
→ HEAD¹

water² /ˈwɔːtə/ verb **1** [T] to pour water on plants in order to keep them healthy **2** [I] if your eyes water, tears form in them because something is hurting them **3** [I] if your mouth waters when you see or smell nice food, SALIVA begins to form in your mouth

PHRASAL VERB ˌwater sth ˈdown **1** to make something such as a statement or newspaper article less offensive, powerful, or detailed **2** to add water to a drink or liquid in order to make it less strong = DILUTE

watercolour /ˈwɔːtəˌkʌlə/ noun **1** [C/U] a type of paint that is mixed with water for painting pictures **2** [C] a painting that is done with watercolour paints

ˈwater ˌcooler noun [C] a machine that makes cool water available for people to drink, especially in an office or other place where people work —*picture* → C16

watercress /ˈwɔːtəˌkres/ noun [U] a plant with leaves that are eaten in salads and sandwiches

waterfall /ˈwɔːtəˌfɔːl/ noun [C] a place where

W

water flows over the edge of a steep place onto another level below

waterfront /ˈwɔːtəfrʌnt/ noun [C] an area that is next to a river, lake, or the sea

water ˌhazard noun [C] an area of water on a GOLF COURSE designed to make it more difficult for players to get their ball onto the GREEN —*picture* → C15

waterhole /ˈwɔːtəhəʊl/ noun [C] a small area of water in a hot country where wild animals go to drink

watering can /ˈwɔːt(ə)rɪŋ ˌkæn/ noun [C] a container used for pouring water on plants. It has a handle and a long SPOUT.

waterlogged /ˈwɔːtəlɒgd/ adj waterlogged ground is too wet to walk on or play sports on

watermark /ˈwɔːtəmɑːk/ noun [C] a hidden design on a piece of paper that you can only see when you hold the paper in front of a light

watermelon /ˈwɔːtəmelən/ noun [C/U] a large round fruit that has a hard green skin and is red with small black seeds inside —*picture* → C10

water ˌpolo noun [U] a game that is played in water by two teams of seven players who get points by throwing a ball into the other team's goal

waterproof /ˈwɔːtəpruːf/ adj waterproof clothes or materials do not let water pass through them

watershed /ˈwɔːtəʃed/ noun [C] a time or event when a major change takes place =TURNING POINT

water-ˌskiing noun [U] a sport in which you stand on SKIS and ride on the surface of water while being pulled behind a boat —**water-ˌski** verb [I], **water-ˌskier** noun [C]

water ˌtable noun [C] the level below the Earth's surface where water is found

watertight /ˈwɔːtətaɪt/ adj **1** a watertight container or room is made so that water cannot enter it **2** a watertight excuse, argument, or case is so good that no one can find anything wrong with it

waterway /ˈwɔːtəweɪ/ noun [C] *formal* a river or CANAL that boats use for travelling from one place to another

watery /ˈwɔːt(ə)ri/ adj **1** containing or filled with water: *watery eyes* **2** watery food or drink contains a lot of water and has a weak taste **3** weak or pale: *watery sunlight*

watt /wɒt/ noun [C] a unit for measuring electrical power

wave¹ /weɪv/ noun [C] ★★

1 of water	4 sudden emotion
2 movement	5 lots of people
3 increase	6 of sound/light/radio etc

1 a line of water that rises up on the surface of a sea, lake, or river: *The boat was smashed by a huge wave.* ♦ *Children swam and played in the waves.*

2 a movement that you make with your hand or with an object as a way of saying hello or goodbye to someone or as a signal to them

3 a sudden increase in a particular type of behaviour or activity: *a frightening wave*

of drug-related killings ♦ *a new wave of company bankruptcies*

4 a sudden strong emotion that affects a person or group: *The invasion caused a wave of anti-American feeling.*

5 a large number of people moving or arriving somewhere at the same time: *Waves of protesters began arriving at the stadium.*

6 the way in which sound, light, a radio signal etc travels → LONG WAVE, MEDIUM WAVE, SHORT WAVE → NEW WAVE

wave² /weɪv/ verb ★★

1 [I/T] to move your hand in order to say hello or goodbye: *He smiled and waved when he saw me.* ♦ *Prince Charles waved to the crowd.* ♦ *We waved goodbye to them as the car drove off.*

2 [T] to move your hand in order to tell someone to move, to leave, or to stop annoying you: **wave sb away/off/on** *He waved me away when I offered to help.*

3 [T] to move something around in the air: *People clapped and cheered and children waved flags.*

4 [I] to move smoothly and gently from side to side: *The tall trees were waving in the wind.*

PHRASAL VERB ˌwave sth aˈside to ignore someone's ideas, feelings, or opinions because you do not think that they are important

waveband /ˈweɪvˌbænd/ noun [C] a range of radio waves that have lengths that come between particular limits

wavelength /ˈweɪvˌleŋθ/ noun [C] **1** the length of the radio wave that a radio station uses for broadcasting **2** the distance between two waves of sound or light that are next to each other

PHRASE be on the same wavelength to understand the way that another person thinks because you have the same ideas and opinions

waver /ˈweɪvə/ verb [I] **1** to not be certain about what to do =HESITATE **2** to shake and not be steady: *Her voice wavered as she said goodbye.*

wavy /ˈweɪvi/ adj a wavy line or wavy hair has a lot of waves or curls in it

wax¹ /wæks/ noun [U] **1** a solid substance that becomes liquid when it is heated. Wax is used, for example, to make CANDLES. **2** a dark yellow substance in your ears —**waxy** adj

wax² /wæks/ verb [T] **1** to make wood shiny by rubbing wax onto it **2** to remove hair by putting wax on your skin

way¹ /weɪ/ noun [C] ★★★

1 method	5 distance in space
2 manner/style	6 distance in time
3 road/path	7 aspect
4 direction/position	+ PHRASES

1 a method for doing something: +(that) *There are so many delicious ways you can prepare chicken.* ♦ **way of doing sth** *Is there any way of contacting you while you're in Africa?* ♦ **way to do sth** *The students are learning new ways to communicate in writing.* → EASY¹, HARD¹

W

2 the manner or style in which something happens or is done: **+(that)** *I love to watch the way she plays with the children.* ♦ **no way to do sth** (=not the right thing to do) *That's no way to talk to your mother.*

3 the particular road, path, or track that you use in order to go from one place to another: *I don't think this is **the right way**.* ♦ *The tourists **lost their way*** (=became lost) *and had to ask for directions.* ♦ *Is this **the way** to the Eiffel Tower?* ♦ *Does Tim **know the way** to your house from here?* ♦ *Could you please **show me the way** to the bus station?* ♦ *Don't bother picking me up. It's really **out of your way*** (=far from the road you use).* → LEAD¹

4 the direction or position where something is, or the direction in which something is standing or moving: *The bathroom is this way.* ♦ *The car was going **the wrong way**.*

5 the distance from one place to another: *The nearest shop is quite **a long way** from here.* ♦ *The children were arguing **all the way** home.*

6 a distance in time from one event to another: *The Christmas holidays were still **a long way off**.*

7 a particular aspect of something: *The evening was a great success, **in more ways than one**.* ♦ *In **a way**, I agree with you.*

PHRASES **be/get in the/sb's way** to be in the area where someone is, so that it is difficult for them to do something: *Can I move your bags? They're in my way.*

be/get/keep out of the/sb's way to be away from, or to stay away from, the area where someone is, so that you do not make it difficult for them to do something: *Make sure the kids keep out of the way while I'm working.*

be on the/its way to be about to arrive or happen: *Economists fear a recession is on the way.*

by the way used for introducing a new or extra fact or comment into a conversation: *By the way, I'll be late home tonight.*

get/have your (own) way to be allowed to do what you want, although other people want something different

get in the way of sth to prevent something from happening: *The new rules are just getting in the way of progress.*

get sth out of the way to finish doing something that is difficult or unpleasant: *I want to get this out of the way before the weekend.*

give way 1 if something gives way, it breaks because there is too much weight or pressure on it **2** to agree to something that someone else wants instead of what you want: *We will not give way to terrorism.* **3** *British* to allow another vehicle to go before you when you are driving: *Drivers must give way to cyclists.* **4** **give way to sth** to be replaced by something, especially something newer or better: *Over the next few years, the city's buses will give way to a new light rail system.*

go out of your way to do sth to make an extra effort to do something, even though it is not convenient or easy to do

have come a long way to have made a lot of progress or improvement

have a long way to go to need a lot more progress or improvement

in a big way *informal* a lot: *Investors were buying Internet stocks in a big way.*

know your way around (sth) to be very familiar with a particular place or activity

make way to move in order to allow someone to go forward or get past: *The crowd made way as police officers entered the building.*

make way for sth to provide space for something new by removing what was there before: *They plan to demolish the houses to make way for a petrol station.*

no way *spoken* **1** used for saying that something will definitely not happen: *'Are you inviting Phil to your party?' 'No way!'* **2** used for expressing surprise, or for telling someone that you do not believe them: *She said that to you? No way!*

one way or another used for saying that something will definitely happen, even though you do not know how it will happen: *One way or another, I'm going to go to Europe.*

way of life the way people normally live in a place, or the things that they normally do or experience: *Fishing has been a way of life here for centuries.* ♦ *People see this as a threat to their way of life.*

you can't have it both ways used for saying that someone cannot have all the benefits from two possible situations: *What's more important, your family or your job? You can't have it both ways.*

→ FIND¹

Other words meaning *way*

- **means** a way that makes it possible to do something
- **method** a way of doing something that involves following a detailed plan
- **procedure** a way of doing something that involves doing specific activities in a particular order
- **strategy** a way of achieving an aim that involves detailed planning
- **system** a way of doing something that involves following an organized set of rules
- **technique** a way of doing something that involves using particular skills

way² /weɪ/ *adv informal* by a large amount or distance: *Michael was way ahead of the other runners.*

PHRASE **way back** *informal* a long time ago in the past: *I graduated way back in 1982.*

waylay /ˌweɪˈleɪ/ (past tense and past participle **waylaid** /ˌweɪˈleɪd/) verb [T] to stop someone who is going somewhere, in order to talk to them or to harm them

ˌway ˈout noun [C] **1** *British* an EXIT from a place **2** a way of dealing with a problem

wayside /ˈweɪsaɪd/ noun **fall by the wayside** to not be successful or effective any longer

wayward /ˈweɪwəd/ adj difficult to control and tending to do unexpected things

WC /ˌdʌb(ə)ljuː ˈsiː/ noun [C] *British* a toilet

we /wiː/ pronoun ★★★
1 used for referring to yourself and one or more other people when you are the person speaking or writing: *We moved here soon after we were married.* ♦ *We were all glad to get back home.*

W

2 used for referring to people in general: *We live in a competitive world.*

weak /wiːk/ adj ★★

1 not physically strong	6 easily criticized
2 not strongly built	7 with a lot of water
3 not effective	8 hard to see/hear
4 easily persuaded	+ PHRASE
5 bad in quality	

1 lacking physical strength or good health ≠ STRONG: *The illness had left him too weak to speak.* ♦ *He has always had a weak heart.*
2 not strongly built and easily damaged or destroyed: *The floorboards are weak in some places.*
3 not powerful or effective, and unlikely to be successful ≠ STRONG: *We are in a weak negotiating position.* ♦ *a weak economy/ currency*
4 lacking determination and easily persuaded to do something that you should not do: *weak, indecisive leadership*
5 bad in quality or ability ≠ STRONG: *Her written work is good, but her oral skills are rather weak.*
6 a weak argument or idea is one that you can easily criticize or prove to be wrong ≠ STRONG: *The government's case is very weak.*
7 a weak liquid contains a lot of water and does not have much taste ≠ STRONG: *a cup of weak coffee*
8 a weak light, sound, or heat is one that you cannot easily see, hear, or feel ≠ STRONG

PHRASE **weak point** a fault or problem that makes something or someone less effective or attractive
—**weakly** adv

weaken /ˈwiːkən/ verb [I/T] **1** to become less strong or healthy, or to make someone or something do this **2** to become less powerful, effective, or determined, or to make someone or something do this

weakling /ˈwiːklɪŋ/ noun [C] *showing disapproval* a person or animal that is physically weak

weakness /ˈwiːknəs/ noun ★
1 [U] the state or condition of being weak: *the increasing weakness of the government*
2 [C] a fault or problem that makes someone or something less effective or attractive: *They listed the strengths and weaknesses of their product.*
3 [C] a strong liking or enjoyment of something: *You know my weakness for chocolate.*

wealth /welθ/ noun [U] ★★
1 a large amount of money and other valuable things: *a man of immense wealth*
2 the state of being rich ≠ POVERTY: *He had an obsession with power and wealth.*
3 a large amount of something that is useful or interesting: *a wealth of exciting opportunities*

wealthy /ˈwelθi/ adj rich: *a wealthy businessman*

wean /wiːn/ verb [T] to make a baby stop taking its mother's milk and start to eat solid food
PHRASAL VERB **wean sb off sth** to make someone gradually stop depending on

something that they like and have become used to

weapon /ˈwepən/ noun [C] ★★★ an object that can be used for hurting people or damaging property, for example a gun, knife, or bomb

weaponry /ˈwepənri/ noun [U] weapons

wear¹ /weə/ (past tense **wore** /wɔː/; past participle **worn** /wɔːn/) verb ★★★

1 have sth on body	5 form hole in sth
2 have hairstyle	+ PHRASES
3 have expression	+ PHRASAL VERBS
4 become thin/weak	

1 [T] to have something on your body as clothing, decoration, or protection: *He was wearing jeans and a T-shirt.* ♦ *She wasn't wearing any make-up.* ♦ *He wears glasses now.* —*picture* → DRESS
2 [T] to have a particular hairstyle: *It was fashionable for men to wear their hair long then.*
3 [T] to have a particular expression on your face: *They all wore puzzled frowns.*
4 [I] to become thinner or weaker because of being used a lot: *The carpet has worn thin in places.*
5 [T] if you wear a hole in something, you form a hole in it by using it or rubbing it a lot

PHRASES **wear thin** if something such as a feeling or explanation wears thin, it becomes gradually weaker or harder to accept
wear well to stay in good condition even after a lot of use

PHRASAL VERBS **wear (sth) away** to disappear, or to make something disappear, because it has been used or rubbed a lot: *The inscription on the ring had almost worn away.*
wear sb down to make someone gradually lose their energy or confidence
wear sth down to make something gradually disappear or become thinner by using or rubbing it: *The old stone steps had been worn down by years of use.*
wear off if a feeling wears off, it gradually disappears
wear on if time wears on, it passes
wear sb out to make someone feel very tired: *Those kids wore me out today.*
wear (sth) out to become extremely thin or damaged because of being used a lot, or to make something do this

wear² /weə/ noun [U] **1** the continuous use that something has over a period of time **2** a type of clothes for a particular activity or a particular group of people: *a menswear shop* ♦ *I didn't bring any evening wear.*
3 changes or damage that affect something when it has been used a lot
PHRASE **wear and tear** the changes or damage that normally happen to something that has been used a lot
→ WORSE³

wearing /ˈweərɪŋ/ adj making you physically or mentally tired

weary /ˈwɪəri/ adj **1** very tired **2** bored or annoyed with something that you feel has continued for too long —**wearily** adv, **weariness** noun [U]

weasel /'wiːz(ə)l/ noun [C] a small thin animal with brown fur, short legs, and a long tail

weather[1] /'weðə/ noun [U] ★★★ the conditions that exist in the atmosphere, for example, whether it is hot, cold, sunny, or wet: *The hot weather will continue through the weekend.* ♦ *We couldn't paint the outside because of the weather.*

PHRASE **under the weather** *informal* not feeling well

Words often used with weather

*Adjectives often used with **weather** (noun)*
- **beautiful, bright, fine, glorious, good, lovely, perfect, sunny** + WEATHER: used about weather that is pleasant
- **appalling, atrocious, awful, bad, foul, terrible** + WEATHER: used about weather that is unpleasant
- **cold, freezing, frosty, wintry** + WEATHER: used about weather that is cold
- **hot, muggy, warm** + WEATHER: used about weather that is hot
- **changeable, uncertain, unsettled** + WEATHER: used about weather that changes often

weather[2] /'weðə/ verb **1** [I/T] if something weathers, or if it is weathered, its appearance changes because of the effects of wind, rain etc **2** [T] to manage a difficult experience without being seriously harmed

weather-beaten adj a weather-beaten face has rough skin as a result of being outside for long periods

weather forecast noun [C] a report on what the weather will be like for a period of time in the future —**weather forecaster** noun [C]

weave /wiːv/ (past tense **wove** /wəʊv/; past participle **woven** /'wəʊv(ə)n/) verb **1** [I/T] to make cloth by crossing long THREADS over and under each other on a special machine **2** [T] to create an object by weaving or by twisting pieces of things together: *She was weaving a basket.* **3** (past tense and past participle **weaved**) [I/T] to move somewhere by going around and between things —**weaver** noun [C]

web /web/ noun [C] **1** a net of thin THREADS that a SPIDER makes in order to catch insects = COBWEB **2** a complicated set of related things: *a web of lies*

Web, the /web/ *computing* all the WEBSITES that organizations have created on their computers for people to look at using the Internet = WORLD WIDE WEB

webbed /webd/ adj if a bird or animal has webbed feet, it has skin between its toes to help it to swim

web browser noun [C] *computing* a software program that you use for finding and looking at pages on the Internet

webcam /'webkæm/ noun [C] *computing* a camera that is connected to a computer and produces images on a WEBSITE

webcast /'webkɑːst/ noun [C] *computing* a broadcast on the Internet —**webcast** verb [I/T]

webmaster /'webmɑːstə/ noun [C] *computing* someone whose job is to manage a WEBSITE

web page noun [C] *computing* a page or document that you can read on a WEBSITE

website /'websaɪt/ noun [C] *computing* a place

on the Internet where information is available about a particular subject, company, university etc

we'd /wiːd/ short form the usual way of saying or writing 'we had' or 'we would'. This is not often used in formal writing: *We'd like to hear from you.* ♦ *Although we'd only just met, I knew that I liked her.*

wed /wed/ (past tense and past participle **wed** or **wedded**) verb [I/T] *mainly journalism* to marry, or to marry someone

Wed. abbrev Wednesday

wedding /'wedɪŋ/ noun [C] ★★ a ceremony in which two people get married: *We wanted a quiet wedding.* ♦ *a wedding present/cake*

wedding anniversary noun [C] a celebration of the number of years that two people have been married

wedding ring noun [C] a ring that you wear on your left hand in order to show that you are married

wedge[1] /wedʒ/ noun [C] **1** a piece of wood, plastic, or other material that is thin at one end and wider at the other. You press it into a space to hold something in place or to force things apart. **2** a piece of something that is shaped like a wedge: *a wedge of lemon/cheese*

wedge[2] /wedʒ/ verb [T] **1** to fix something in position with a wedge **2** to push something tightly into a small space: *I wedged a piece of paper into the crack.*

Wednesday /'wenzdeɪ/ noun [C/U] ★★★ the day after Tuesday and before Thursday: *They are arriving on Wednesday.* ♦ *I go swimming on Wednesdays* (=every Wednesday). ♦ *I was born on a Wednesday.*

Weds abbrev *British* Wednesday

wee[1] /wiː/ adj *Scottish* small

wee[2] /wiː/ verb [U] *spoken* to URINATE —**wee** noun [C/U]

weed[1] /wiːd/ noun **1** [C] a wild plant that grows in places where you do not want it **2** [C/U] a plant or a mass of plants growing in water → SEAWEED

weed[2] /wiːd/ verb [I/T] to remove weeds from the ground

PHRASAL VERB **weed sb/sth out** to remove people or things from a group because they are not suitable or not good enough

weedy /'wiːdi/ adj *informal* a weedy person is thin and weak

week /wiːk/ noun [C] ★★★

1 a period of seven days, usually counted from a Sunday: *They spent two weeks in Florida.* ♦ *He works from home two days a week.* ♦ *He will meet his uncle in Geneva next week.* ♦ *We're seeing Jim a week on Tuesday* (=seven days from next Tuesday). ♦ *I'll be home Thursday week* (=the Thursday after next Thursday).
2 the five days from Monday to Friday, when most people work: *They work a 35-hour week.* ♦ *She stays in the city during the week.*

weekday /'wiːkdeɪ/ noun [C] a day that is not Saturday or Sunday

weekend /ˌwiːk'end/ noun [C] ★★★ Saturday and Sunday: *Let's go away for the weekend.* ♦ *The bus service is free at weekends.*

W

weekly[1] /ˈwiːkli/ adj happening or published once every week

weekly[2] /ˈwiːkli/ noun [C] a newspaper or magazine that is published once a week

weekly[3] /ˈwiːkli/ adv every week

weep /wiːp/ (past tense and past participle **wept** /wept/) verb [I/T] to cry

weigh /weɪ/ verb ★★

1 [linking verb] to have a particular weight: *How much do you weigh?* ♦ *The baby weighed 7 pounds at birth.* ♦ *Your suitcase weighs a ton* (=is very heavy).

2 [T] to measure how heavy someone or something is: *She weighed herself once a week.*

3 [T] to consider all the aspects of a situation carefully before making a decision: *The judge weighed all the facts before reaching a verdict.* ♦ **weigh sth against sth** *Those costs must be weighed against the environmental benefits.*

PHRASAL VERBS ,**weigh sb ˈdown 1** to be very heavy and prevent someone from moving easily **2** to cause problems for someone or something

,**weigh ˈon sb** to make someone worried

,**weigh sth ˈout** to measure an exact amount of something by weighing it

,**weigh sth ˈup** to consider the good and bad aspects of something in order to reach a decision about it

weight[1] /weɪt/ noun ★★★

1 measurement	4 sth difficult to move
2 being heavy	5 influence
3 for exercise/sport	6 sth causing trouble

1 [U] a measurement of how heavy a person or thing is: *It was about 12 pounds in weight.* ♦ *Have you lost weight* (=become thinner)*?* ♦ *Susan put on weight* (=became fatter) *after her accident.* ♦ *I am trying to watch my weight* (=control how much I eat).

2 [U] the fact or effect of being heavy: *The weight of the backpack made the child fall over.*

3 [C] a piece of heavy metal that is designed for lifting for exercise or as a sport —*picture* → C16

4 [C] a heavy object that is difficult to lift or move

5 [U] the influence or importance that someone or something has: *Simpson's opinions carry a lot of weight with* (=have a lot of influence on) *the President.* ♦ **throw your weight behind sth** *The Chief Executive is throwing his full weight behind the proposal.*

6 [singular] something that causes trouble or difficulty: *Obviously the verdict is a huge weight off my mind* (=something I no longer have to worry about).

weight[2] /weɪt/ or **ˌweight sth ˈdown** verb [T] to make something heavier by putting a weight on it in order to stop it from moving

weighted /ˈweɪtɪd/ adj designed to produce a particular effect or result by giving more importance to one thing than to another: *The tax laws are heavily weighted in favour of the wealthy.*

weightless /ˈweɪtləs/ adj having no weight, because of being outside the Earth's atmosphere —**weightlessness** noun [U]

weightlifting /ˈweɪtˌlɪftɪŋ/ noun [U] the sport of lifting heavy weights —**weightlifter** noun [C]

ˈweight ˌtraining noun [U] exercise that involves lifting weights

weighty /ˈweɪti/ adj serious and important

weir /wɪə/ noun [U] a place in a river or stream where a wall has been built across it in order to control the flow of water

weird /wɪəd/ adj strange and unusual —**weirdly** adv

weirdo /ˈwɪədəʊ/ noun [C] *informal* someone who behaves in a way that seems strange

welcome[1] /ˈwelkəm/ verb [T] ★★

1 to greet someone in a polite and friendly way when they arrive: *My aunt and uncle were waiting at the door to welcome us.*

2 to say that you approve of something that has happened, or that you are pleased about it: *They welcomed the new proposals.*

welcome[2] /ˈwelkəm/ adj ★

1 if you are welcome somewhere, people are pleased that you are there ≠ UNWELCOME: *Your friends are always welcome here.* ♦ *The neighbours made us feel very welcome.*

2 if something is welcome, people are happy about it because it is pleasant or because they need it ≠ UNWELCOME: *A cold drink would be very welcome.*

3 if someone tells you that you are welcome to do something, they mean that you are allowed to do it if you want to: *Members of the public are welcome to attend the meeting.* ♦ *You're more than welcome to stay overnight.*

4 if someone tells you that you are welcome to something, they mean that you can have it or use it, because they do not want it themselves

PHRASE **you're welcome** used as a reply to someone who has thanked you

welcome[3] /ˈwelkəm/ noun [C/U] an act of welcoming someone to a place: *He gave us a warm welcome and invited us to lunch.*

PHRASE **outstay/overstay your welcome** to stay at a place for longer than people want you to be there

welcome[4] /ˈwelkəm/ interjection used for welcoming someone to a place: *Welcome to Edinburgh.*

weld /weld/ verb [T] to join two pieces of metal by heating them and pressing them together —**welder** noun [C]

welfare /ˈwelfeə/ noun [U] **1** the health, happiness, and safety of a person or group = WELL-BEING: *Police are concerned for the welfare of the child.* **2** care that is provided by the government or another organization for people in need: *the welfare system* **3** *American* money given to people who do not have work or who are in need

ˌwelfare ˈstate noun **1 the welfare state** [singular] the system by which a country looks after its citizens by providing them with education, medical care, or money if they are unable to work **2** [C] a country that looks after its citizens by providing social and financial support

W

we'll /wiːl/ short form the usual way of saying or writing 'we shall' or 'we will'. This is not often used in formal writing: *We'll come to meet you at the airport.*

well[1] /wel/ (comparative **better** /ˈbetə/; superlative **best** /best/) adv ★★★

1 skilfully/effectively	**4** very/very much
2 in satisfactory way	**5** by large amount
3 completely	**+ PHRASES**

1 skilfully, or effectively: *She speaks Japanese really well.*
2 in a satisfactory way: *The boys were not behaving very well.*
3 completely, or thoroughly: *Shake the can well before opening.* ♦ *I don't know these people very well.*
4 very, or very much: *Rostov was well aware of the scandal he was creating.* ♦ *A trip to the new museum is well worth the effort.*
5 by a large amount of time, or by a large distance: *Pete left the party well before you got there.*

PHRASES as well (as) in addition to someone or something else: *I'd like a cup of coffee, and a glass of water as well.* ♦ *I need to go to the bookshop as well as the bank.* → ALSO
be doing well to be getting better after an illness
cannot/can't very well used for saying that it would not be wise or sensible to do something: *We can't very well tell them now.*
could/may/might well used for saying that something is likely: *The two murder cases may well be connected.*
may/might (just) as well do sth *informal* used for saying that it might be a good idea to do something, although it is not essential: *We might as well wait a little longer for them.*
well done used for giving someone praise when they do something well

well[2] /wel/ interjection ★★★

1 when replying	**4** expressing emotion
2 when asking sth	**5** for ending talk
3 after a pause	**+ PHRASES**

1 used for introducing a statement, especially one that you make as a reply: *Well, I agree with you about that.* ♦ *'So you told him what you thought of his idea, then?' 'Well, not exactly.'*
2 used for asking a question or for asking for an explanation: *Well, what did they say?* ♦ *Well, who's responsible for this mess?*
3 used after a pause, for continuing with what you were saying: *Well, as I was saying...*
4 used for expressing surprise or anger: *Well, they have a nerve!*
5 used for ending a discussion or talk: *Well thanks for calling. I'll get back to you again tomorrow.*

PHRASES oh well used for accepting a bad situation or disappointment: *Oh well, I suppose I can borrow the money from someone else.*
well, well used for expressing surprise: *Well, well, I didn't think I'd see you here.*

well[3] /wel/ (comparative **better** /ˈbetə/; superlative **best** /best/) adj ★ healthy: *'How*

are you?' 'Very well, thank you.' ♦ *I'm not feeling very well today.* ♦ *You don't look too well.* ♦ *Take care and get well soon!*

PHRASES all is well used for saying that a situation or arrangement is satisfactory: *I hope all is well back home.*
just as well helpful or convenient in the situation that exists: **+(that)** *It's just as well we have neighbours who don't mind noise.*
leave well alone to avoid trying to improve or change something that is satisfactory: *Sometimes it's better to just leave well alone.*

well[4] /wel/ noun [C] a deep hole that is dug in the ground where there is a supply of water, oil, or gas

well[5] /wel/ or **well up** verb [I] **1** if a liquid wells, it comes to the surface and begins to flow **2** if a feeling wells inside you, it becomes very strong

well-advised /ˌwel ədˈvaɪzd/ adj sensible and following good advice

well-balanced adj **1** made up of various things that form a satisfactory or healthy combination: *a well-balanced meal/diet* **2** sensible and mentally strong

well-behaved /ˌwel bɪˈheɪvd/ adj behaving in a way that is polite and quiet and does not upset people

well-being noun [U] a satisfactory state in which you are happy, healthy, and safe, and have enough money = WELFARE

well-brought-up /ˌwel brɔːt ˈʌp/ adj knowing how to behave politely because you have been taught well by your parents

well-built /ˌwel ˈbɪlt/ adj a well-built person has an attractive, strong body

well-connected adj knowing a lot of people who are important or who have influence

well-done adj well-done meat has been cooked thoroughly until all of it is brown → RARE 3

well-dressed adj wearing good, fashionable clothes

well-earned /ˌwel ˈɜːnd/ adj earned or deserved because of hard work or a difficult experience

well-established adj having existed for a long time, and having been successful or accepted for a long time

well-fed /ˌwel ˈfed/ adj getting a lot of good food to eat

well-heeled /ˌwel ˈhiːld/ adj *informal* rich

wellie /ˈweli/ noun [C] *British informal* a WELLINGTON

well-informed adj knowing a lot about a subject or a situation

wellington /ˈwelɪŋtən/ or **wellington boot** noun [C] *British* a rubber or plastic boot that does not let water in

well-intentioned /ˌwel ɪnˈtenʃ(ə)nd/ adj trying to help, but often making a situation worse = WELL-MEANING

well-kept adj a well-kept place looks good because someone looks after it carefully
PHRASE well-kept secret a fact that some people know but do not share with everyone

well-known adj known by many people, or by the people involved in a particular situation

well-mannered adj polite ≠ ILL-MANNERED, IMPOLITE

W

well-meaning adj trying to help, but often making a situation worse=WELL-INTENTIONED

well-off adj *informal* rich

well-paid adj receiving a satisfactory amount of money for the work that you do

well-preserved /,wel prɪˈzɜːvd/ adj *informal* looking younger than you really are

well-read /,wel ˈred/ adj having read many books so that you know about a lot of things

well-timed /,wel ˈtaɪmd/ adj effective because of happening at the right time=TIMELY

well-to-do adj rich and belonging to a family from a high social class

well-wisher /ˈwel ˌwɪʃə/ noun [C] someone who expresses their good wishes or sympathy to a person who they do not know

welter /ˈweltə/ noun [singular] an untidy collection of different things

went the past tense of **go**[1]

wept the past tense and past participle of **weep**

we're /wɪə/ short form the usual way of saying or writing 'we are'. This is not often used in formal writing: *We're having a party on Saturday.*

were /weak wə, strong wɜː/ see **be**

weren't /wɜːnt/ short form the usual way of saying or writing 'were not'. This is not often used in formal writing: *You weren't listening.*

werewolf /ˈweəˌwʊlf/ (plural **werewolves** /ˈweəˌwʊlvz/) noun [C] an imaginary creature who is human during the day but becomes a WOLF at night when there is a FULL MOON

west[1] /west/ noun ★★★
1 [U] the direction that is behind you when you are facing the rising sun: *We've driven from east to west.* → EAST
2 the west [singular] the part of a place that is in the west: *The country's major cities are all in the west.* ♦ *I work in the west of the city.*
3 the West [singular] the western part of the world, especially Europe and North America

west[2] /west/ adv towards the west: *You drive west to get to the lake.* ♦ *We'll camp ten miles west of town.*

west[3] /west/ adj **1** in the west, or facing towards the west: *a city on the west coast* **2** a west wind blows from the west

westbound /ˈwes(t)ˌbaʊnd/ adj going towards the west

West Coast, the the western part of the US, along the Pacific Ocean

West Country, the the south-western part of England

West End, the the part of London where there are many theatres

westerly /ˈwestəli/ adj **1** towards or in the west **2** a westerly wind blows from the west

western[1] /ˈwestən/ adj ★★
1 in the west of a place: *the western United States*
2 relating to or typical of the western part of the world, especially Europe and North America: *western attitudes* ♦ *Wages there are much lower than western levels.*

western[2] /ˈwestən/ noun [C] a film about

COWBOYS in the western United States in the 19th century

westerner /ˈwestənə/ noun [C] **1** someone who lives in or was born in the western part of a country **2** someone who is from Europe or North America

westernized /ˈwestənaɪzd/ adj influenced by American or Western European culture, technology, or values —**westernization** /,westənaɪˈzeɪʃ(ə)n/ noun [U]

westernmost /ˈwestənˌməʊst/ adj furthest towards the west

Westminster /ˈwes(t)ˌmɪnstə/ the UK parliament, based in Westminster, London

westward /ˈwestwəd/ adj towards or in the west

westwards /ˈwestwədz/ adv towards the west

wet[1] /wet/ adj ★★★
1 covered with water or another liquid: *You'd better come in or you'll get wet.* ♦ *My socks and shoes were soaking wet* (=very wet). ♦ *Her forehead was wet with sweat.* ♦ *Where have you been? You're wet through* (=completely wet)!
2 not yet dry or solid: *wet paint*
3 if the weather is wet, it is raining
4 *British showing disapproval* lacking confidence or determination

wet[2] /wet/ (past tense and past participle **wet** or **wetted**) verb [T] **1** to make something wet with water or another liquid **2** to make something such as a bed or clothes wet with URINE (=liquid waste from your body)

wet blanket noun [C] *informal* someone who spoils other people's fun by criticizing what they are doing, or by refusing to take part in it

wetsuit /ˈwetˌsuːt/ noun [C] a suit made of rubber that you wear for water sports such as DIVING and SURFING

we've /wiːv/ short form the usual way of saying or writing 'we have'. This is not often used in formal writing: *We've been waiting for a long time.*

whack /wæk/ verb [T] *informal* to hit someone or something with a lot of force —**whack** noun [C]

whacked /wækt/ adj *British informal* very tired

whale /weɪl/ noun [C] a very large sea animal that looks like a fish but breathes air through a hole on the top of its head —*picture* → C13
PHRASE **have a whale of a time** *informal* to have a lot of fun

whaling /ˈweɪlɪŋ/ noun [U] the activity of hunting WHALES

wham /wæm/ interjection used for representing the loud sound of something being hit hard

wharf /wɔːf/ (plural **wharves** /wɔːvz/) noun [C] a structure built at the edge of the land where boats can stop=DOCK

what /wɒt/ grammar word ★★★

What can be:
■ a **question pronoun**: *What do you want?*
■ a **relative pronoun**: *She showed me what she had bought.*
■ a **determiner**: *What subjects are you studying?* ♦ *What a nuisance!*
■ an **interjection**: *What! You mean I've been wasting my time?*

W

1 which thing used for asking which thing or which type of thing something is: *What's your name? ♦ What time is it? ♦ I asked her what kind of music she liked.*

2 which thing sth is used when someone knows or says which thing something is: *I told him what the problem was. ♦ We suddenly realized what was happening.*

3 a particular thing used for referring to a particular thing that is being described or explained: *You haven't given me what I asked for. ♦ What annoys me is the way he boasts about what he's done.*

4 asking sb to repeat sth *spoken* used for asking someone to repeat what they have just said because you did not hear it clearly: *'Turn the radio down, will you?' 'What?'*

> It is more polite to say 'pardon' or 'I beg your pardon'.

5 when sb calls your name *spoken* used for replying to someone when they have just called your name: *'Hey, Julie!' 'What?' 'I've got something to show you.'*

6 emphasizing a quality *spoken* used for introducing a remark in which you emphasize how big, good, bad etc someone or something is: *What awful weather we've been having! ♦ What a kind man!*

7 showing surprise *spoken* used for showing that you are surprised by something that you have just heard: *What! You mean he can't read or write?*

PHRASES so what? *spoken* used for showing someone that you think that a particular fact that they have mentioned is not important: *'But they're living together and they aren't married.' 'So what?'*

what about...? *spoken* **1** used for making a suggestion: *'When shall we meet?' 'What about Tuesday?'* **2** used for reminding someone that a particular person or thing needs to be considered: *What about Eileen? Shouldn't we invite her too?*

what for *spoken* used for asking the reason for something: *'I need to have your name and address.' 'What for?' ♦ What did you hit him for?*

what if...? **1** used for asking what would happen in a particular situation, especially an unpleasant situation: *It sounds like a good offer, but what if it's a trick?* **2** used when you are making a helpful suggestion: *What if I lend you the money?*

what's more *spoken* used for introducing an additional statement that supports what you have already said

what with *spoken* used when you are giving a number of reasons for a particular situation or problem: *The police are having a difficult time, what with all the drugs and violence on our streets.*

whatever /wɒtˈevə/ grammar word ★★★

> **Whatever** can be:
> ■ a **relative pronoun**: *You can choose whatever you like.*
> ■ a **determiner**: *We'll be ready at whatever time you get here.*
> ■ a **question pronoun**: *Whatever do you mean?*
> ■ a **conjunction**: *We must stay together whatever happens.*

> ■ an **adverb**: *There is nothing whatever to worry about.*

1 anything or everything used for referring to anything or everything that happens or is available, needed, wanted etc: *Now you are free to do whatever you want. ♦ We shall be grateful for whatever help you can give us.*

2 when sth does not matter used for saying that what happens or what is true is not important, because it makes no difference to the situation: *You know that you have our full support whatever you decide.*

3 sth you do not know used for referring to something when you do not know what it is: *He said there were 'technical difficulties', whatever that means.*

4 at all used with a noun for emphasis in a negative statement: *I have no intention whatever of leaving.*

5 emphasizing a question *spoken* used instead of 'what' in a question for showing that you are surprised, upset, or annoyed: *Whatever are you doing?*

6 used as an annoyed reply *spoken* used for showing that you are annoyed about something, or that you do not care about it, but that you will accept it: *'They say we all have to come in for the meeting on Saturday.' 'Whatever.'*

whatnot /ˈwɒtnɒt/ noun [U] *informal* other similar things: *brochures, leaflets, and whatnot*

what's /wɒts/ short form the usual way of saying or writing 'what is' or 'what has'. This is not often used in formal writing: *What's the time? ♦ What's happened?*

whatsoever /ˌwɒtsəʊˈevə/ adv used for emphasizing a negative statement =WHATEVER: *It had no effect whatsoever.*

wheat /wiːt/ noun [U] **1** tall plants that produce grain for making bread and other foods **2** wheat grains, or food made from them

wheedle /ˈwiːd(ə)l/ verb [I/T] to persuade someone using tricks, lies, or praise that is not sincere

wheel¹ /wiːl/ noun ★★★

1 [C] a circular object that turns round in order to make a car, bicycle, or other vehicle move —*picture* → C6

2 the wheel [singular] the STEERING WHEEL that is used for controlling a car or other vehicle: *Would you like me to take the wheel* (=to drive) *for a while? ♦ He had a heart attack at the wheel* (=while driving).
→ REINVENT

wheel² /wiːl/ verb **1** [T] to move something that has wheels by pushing it **2** [T] to move someone in or on an object that has wheels **3** [I/T] to move in a circle in the air, or to make something do this

PHRASE wheel and deal *informal* to use clever or slightly dishonest methods in order to get advantages in business or politics

PHRASAL VERB wheel aˈround to turn around quickly where you are standing

wheelbarrow /ˈwiːlˌbærəʊ/ noun [C] a large open container with a wheel at the front and handles at the back. You use it outside for moving things such as dirt, wood, or supplies.

wheelchair /ˈwiːltʃeə/ noun [C] a chair with large wheels that someone who cannot walk uses for moving around —*picture*
→ CHAIR

wheeler-dealer /ˌwiːlə ˈdiːlə/ noun [C] *informal* someone who uses clever or slightly dishonest methods in order to get advantages in business or politics

wheeze /wiːz/ verb [I] to breathe in a noisy way that is uncomfortable, because you are ill —**wheezy** adj

when /wen/ grammar word ★★★

> **When** can be:
> ■ a **conjunction**: *When he saw me, he waved.*
> ■ a **question adverb**: *When shall we meet?*
> ■ a **relative adverb**: *I remember the day when the war began.*

1 at what time or in what situation used for asking at what time or in what situation something happens: *When will we know our test results?* ♦ *I asked him when he was going to start work.*

2 what time sth happens used when someone knows or says at what time something happens, or in what situation it happens: *He didn't say when they would leave.*

3 at the time that sth else happens at the same time as something, or just after it has finished: *I always wear a hat when I work in the garden.* ♦ *She claims she was at a friend's house when the shooting took place.* ♦ *When it stops raining, we'll go outside.*

4 at a particular time or in a particular situation used for referring to a particular occasion or situation: *Do you remember the time when we took your mother camping?*

5 introducing surprising information used for introducing a situation that makes someone's action or behaviour seem surprising: *Why does she always drive to work when she could easily take the train?*

whenever /wenˈevə/ adv, conjunction ★
1 every time that something happens: *Whenever I hear that song, I think of you.*
2 at any time, or in any situation: *You can come and stay with us whenever you want.*
3 used for showing that you do not know when something happened or will happen: *We'll have to wait until the next committee meeting, whenever that is.*

where /weə/ grammar word ★★★

> **Where** can be:
> ■ a **question adverb**: *Where are you going?*
> ■ a **relative adverb**: *I know a place where you can hide.*
> ■ a **conjunction**: *I've hidden the money where no one will find it.*

1 used for asking what place someone or something is in, or what place they go to: *Where would you like to sit?* ♦ *I wonder where Jack's gone.* ♦ *Where did the package come from?* ♦ *Do you know where the road leads to?*

2 used when someone knows or says what place someone or something is in or what place they go to: *She didn't say where she*

works. ♦ *We can't decide where to go on holiday.*

3 used for referring to a particular place that someone or something is in or that they go to: *We were led to the dining room, where lunch was being served.*

4 used for asking about or referring to a situation or a point in a process, discussion, story etc: *Where shall I start?* ♦ *Eventually I reached the point where I was beginning to enjoy my work.*

PHRASE where does sb/sth go from here? used for asking what will happen or what will be done next in a particular situation: *The big question everyone is asking is, where does the economy go from here?*

whereabouts¹ /ˈweərəbaʊts/ noun [plural] the place where someone or something is

whereabouts² /ˈweərəbaʊts/ adv used for asking in general where someone or something is: *Whereabouts in America was he born?*

whereas /weərˈæz/ conjunction used for showing that there is an important difference between two things, people, situations etc: *Doctors' salaries have risen substantially, whereas nurses' pay has actually fallen.*

whereby /weəˈbaɪ/ adv *formal* done according to the method, arrangement, rule etc that has been referred to

whereupon /ˌweərəˈpɒn/ conjunction *formal* happening just after or because of something that has been mentioned

wherever /werˈevə/ adv, conjunction ★
1 everywhere, or anywhere: *Wherever he went, he took his dog with him.* ♦ *Garlic is a plant that grows wherever there is a warm climate.*
2 used for showing that you do not know where something is: *He said he was phoning from Landsford Park, wherever that is.*

wherewithal, the /ˈweəwɪðɔːl/ noun [singular] the money or other things that you need in order to be able to do a particular thing

whet /wet/ verb **whet your appetite (for sth)** to make you feel that you want more of something

whether /ˈweðə/ conjunction ★★★
1 used when someone does not know which of two possibilities is true: *They asked us whether we were married.* ♦ *She doesn't even know whether her daughter is dead or alive.*
2 used when someone can choose between two possibilities: *Employees are deciding whether to accept the offer.* ♦ *There was a debate over whether or not to send troops.*
3 used for saying that it does not matter which of two possibilities is true, because the situation will be the same: *Whether you like it or not, you'll have to change your lifestyle.*

> ■ Both **whether** and **if** can be used to introduce indirect questions: *She asked if/whether I liked jazz.*
> ■ Use **whether**, not **if**, before an infinitive or after a preposition: *She can't decide whether to marry him.* ♦ *I was worried about whether he would come.*

W

■ Use **whether**, not **if**, before 'or not': *I don't know whether or not we can afford it.*

whew /fju:/ interjection a way of writing the sound that you make when you are tired, hot, or surprised, or when you feel happy that something difficult or frightening has finished

which /wɪtʃ/ grammar word ★★★

Which can be:
■ a **determiner**: *Which colour do you like best?*
■ a **question pronoun**: *Which is the hottest month of the year?*
■ a **relative pronoun**: *My car, which I have owned for five years, is a Ford.*

1 used for asking for a specific choice from a limited number of possibilities: *Which would you like, tea or coffee?* ♦ *Which way did they go?* ♦ *Which of the secretaries did you talk to?*
2 used when someone knows or says who or what is chosen from a group of possibilities: *They're all so pretty – I don't know which one to choose.* ♦ *It was either whisky or vodka – I forget which.* ♦ *Did he say which hotel he was staying at?*
3 used for adding information or a comment about a thing or fact: *Bogart starred in the film* Casablanca, *which was made in 1942.* ♦ *It's a story which every child will enjoy.* ♦ *A skilled workforce is essential, which is why our training programme is so important.*

whichever /wɪtʃˈevə/ determiner, pronoun
1 used for saying that it does not matter which person or thing is involved: *I'm sure you'll have a good time whichever cruise you decide to take.* **2** used for referring to any person or thing from a group: *Whichever of us gets home first will switch the heating on.*

whiff /wɪf/ noun [singular] a slight smell of something that lasts for a very short time

while[1] /waɪl/ conjunction ★★★
1 during the time that something is happening: *Someone called while you were out.*
2 used when comparing things, situations, or people and showing how they are different: *While most children learn to read easily, some need extra help.*
3 formal despite a particular fact: *While I support you, I do not believe that you will succeed.*

W

while[2] /waɪl/ noun [singular] ★★ a period of time: *Her mother died a while ago.* ♦ *We haven't seen Barry for a while.* ♦ *Couldn't you stay just a little while longer?* ♦ *I've been waiting here quite a while.* → ONCE

while[3] /waɪl/ PHRASAL VERB **while sth away** to spend time in a relaxed way when you have nothing else to do

whilst /waɪlst/ conjunction British formal while

whim /wɪm/ noun [C] a sudden feeling that you must have or must do something that other people think is unnecessary or silly

whimper /ˈwɪmpə/ verb [I] to make small sounds of pain, fear, or sadness —**whimper** noun [C]

whimsical /ˈwɪmzɪk(ə)l/ adj slightly strange and funny

whine /waɪn/ verb [I] **1** to complain in a way

that annoys other people **2** if a dog whines, it makes a high noise, usually because it wants something —**whine** noun [C]

whinge /wɪndʒ/ (present participle **whingeing**) verb [I] British informal to complain in an annoying, unreasonable way —**whinge** noun [C]

whip[1] /wɪp/ noun [C] **1** a long thin piece of leather with a handle on one end that is used for making horses move faster **2** someone in a political party whose job is to make certain that other members are present and vote in the correct way when they are needed

whip[2] /wɪp/ verb [T] **1** to hit a person or animal with a whip **2** to remove something or move something somewhere very fast: *Sykes whipped out a gun and demanded the money.* **3** to mix a food such as cream very quickly in order to make it thicker=BEAT

PHRASE **whip sb/sth into shape** to quickly make someone or something improve or work more effectively

PHRASAL VERB **whip sth up 1** to encourage strong emotions in people **2** informal to quickly prepare something to eat

whip-round noun [C] British informal an occasion when you collect money from a group of people and give it to someone

whir /wɜ:/ another spelling of **whirr**

whirl[1] /wɜ:l/ verb **1** [I/T] to move quickly in circles, or to make something move in this way **2** [I] if your mind, thoughts, or feelings whirl, you feel very confused or upset

whirl[2] /wɜ:l/ noun [C] **1** a lot of confused activity and movement **2** a quick movement round in circles

PHRASE **give sth a whirl** informal to try a new activity

whirlpool /ˈwɜ:l.pu:l/ noun [C] an area in a river or stream where the water moves round in circles very quickly and pulls things under the surface

whirlwind /ˈwɜ:l.wɪnd/ noun [C] **1** a situation that changes very quickly, in a way that is confusing or out of control: *a whirlwind of emotions* **2** a very powerful dangerous wind that spins extremely fast

whirr /wɜ:/ verb [I] to make a fast repeated quiet sound —**whirr** noun [singular]

whisk[1] /wɪsk/ noun [C] a kitchen tool, used for mixing, that consists of several curves of wire joined to a handle

whisk[2] /wɪsk/ verb [T] **1** to mix something such as eggs or cream using a whisk or a fork=BEAT —*picture* → C2 **2** to move someone or something very quickly: *The police whisked her away in a van.*

whisker /ˈwɪskə/ noun **1** [C] one of several long stiff hairs that grow near the mouth of an animal such as a cat **2 whiskers** [plural] old-fashioned hair on a man's face

whiskey /ˈwɪski/ noun [C/U] a strong alcoholic drink from Ireland and the US that is made from grain such as BARLEY or RYE, or a glass of this drink

whisky /ˈwɪski/ noun [C/U] a strong alcoholic drink from Scotland that is made from BARLEY, or a glass of this drink

whisper[1] /ˈwɪspə/ verb ★
1 [I/T] to speak very quietly to someone, so

that other people cannot hear you: *Stop whispering, you two!* ♦ **whisper (sth) to sb** *Dad whispered a warning to us to keep quiet.*
2 [I] *literary* to make a quiet gentle sound

whisper² /ˈwɪspə/ noun [C] **1** a very quiet way of saying something to someone so that other people cannot hear you **2** *literary* a quiet gentle sound

whistle¹ /ˈwɪs(ə)l/ noun [C] **1** a small metal or plastic object that you put in your mouth and blow in order to make a high sound **2** a sound that you make by blowing through a whistle or by forcing air through your lips

whistle² /ˈwɪs(ə)l/ verb **1** [I/T] to make a high sound with a whistle or by forcing air through your lips **2** [I] to produce a high sound as a result of air passing quickly through or over something **3** [I] to move very quickly through the air

white¹ /waɪt/ adj ★★★

1 of same colour as milk	**4** ill/upset
2 of race with pale skin	**5** of tea/coffee
3 of white people	**6** of wine

1 something that is white is the same colour as milk or snow: *a white tablecloth* ♦ *The hills were white with snow.* → BLACK
2 a white person belongs to a race of people with pale skin: *The attacker was described as white, with short hair.* → BLACK
3 relating to white people, or consisting of white people: *a white neighbourhood*
4 with a very pale face because you are frightened, angry, or ill: *She suddenly turned very white and fainted.* ♦ *Luke's face was white with anger.*
5 *British* white tea or coffee has milk in it
6 white wine is a pale yellow colour
—**whiteness** noun [U]

white² /waɪt/ noun ★
1 [C/U] the colour of milk or snow: *The sign was written in white on a black background.* ♦ *We painted the walls a creamy white.* ♦ *The bride wore white* (=white clothes).
2 [C] someone who belongs to a race of people with pale skin
3 [C/U] the clear part inside an egg that surrounds the YOLK (=yellow part)
PHRASE **the whites of sb's eyes** the white parts of your eyes

whiteboard /ˈwaɪtbɔːd/ noun [C] a white plastic board in a classroom that a teacher writes on with large thick pens

white-collar adj white-collar workers work in offices

Whitehall /ˈwaɪthɔːl/ **1** a street in London where there are a lot of British government departments **2** all the officials who work in British government departments in Whitehall

White House, the 1 the official home of the President of the US, in Washington, DC
2 the people who work at the White House, including the President

white lie noun [C] a lie about something that is not important that you tell in order to avoid making someone upset

white meat noun [U] meat such as chicken or PORK that is pale after you have cooked it

whiten /ˈwaɪt(ə)n/ verb [I/T] to become pale or

white, or to make something pale or white

white paper noun [C] in some countries, a government report that gives details of policy on a particular issue

whitewash /ˈwaɪtwɒʃ/ noun **1** [singular] an attempt to stop people discovering the true facts about something **2** [U] a substance that is used for painting walls or buildings white —**whitewash** verb [T]

whitewater rafting /ˌwaɪtwɔːtər ˈrɑːftɪŋ/ noun [U] the activity of floating in a rubber boat along rivers where the current is very fast and rough

whitish /ˈwaɪtɪʃ/ adj almost white in colour

whittle /ˈwɪt(ə)l/
PHRASAL VERBS **whittle (sth) away** to gradually reduce the amount or importance of something
whittle sth down to reduce the number of people or things, or the size of something

whizz or **whiz** /wɪz/ verb [I] *informal* to move very quickly

whizzkid /ˈwɪzˌkɪd/ noun [C] *informal* a young person who is very intelligent or successful

who /huː/ pronoun ★★★
1 used for asking which person is involved in something, or what someone's name is: *Who works in that office?* ♦ *Who did you hire for the sales position?* ♦ *'Who is that?' 'It's Karen – don't you recognize her?'* ♦ *Who else did you tell the secret to?*
2 used when someone knows or says which person is involved in something or what their name is: *Curry refused to say who had organized the meeting.*
3 used for adding more information about a person: *I recently talked to Michael Hall, who lectures in music at the university.* ♦ *We only employ people who already have computer skills.*
PHRASE **who knows/cares etc** *spoken* used for saying that you do not know/care etc, and you think that no one else does: *'Won't Terry be upset?' 'Who cares? He never thinks about anyone but himself.'*

who'd /huːd/ short form the usual way of saying or writing 'who had' or 'who would'. This is not often used in formal writing: *He was the one who'd complained the loudest.* ♦ *Do you know anyone who'd be able to help us?*

whoever /huːˈevə/ pronoun ★
1 someone, or anyone: *Whoever finishes first will get a prize.* ♦ *You may choose whoever you would like to represent you.*
2 used for saying that it does not matter who is involved: *Whoever you ask, the answer is always the same.*
3 *spoken* used when you do not know who someone is or what their name is: *The film is about Celia Daniels, whoever that is.*

whole¹ /həʊl/ adj ★★★
1 all of something=ENTIRE: *My whole family came to watch me playing in the concert.* ♦ *The whole process will take months.* ♦ *Come on, let's just forget the whole thing.* ♦ *She told Tilly the whole story.*
2 not divided or broken: *Add three whole eggs plus two additional yolks.* ♦ *Some of the statues were broken, but others were still whole.*

W

3 used for emphasizing what you are saying: *We've had a whole host of problems.* ♦ *The whole point of this meeting was to discuss finances.* ♦ *They're the best ice-creams in the whole world.*

whole² /həʊl/ noun [C] ★★★ a complete thing made of several parts: *Two halves make a whole.*

> **PHRASES as a whole** considering all the parts of something as one unit: *His views are not popular with the townspeople as a whole.*
> **on the whole** used for talking about the general situation: *It was a pretty good conference on the whole.* ♦ *On the whole, she felt that the report was fair.*
> **the whole of** all of something: *I was off work for the whole of January.* ♦ *The problem will affect the whole of Europe.*

whole³ /həʊl/ adv **1** as a single piece: *The bird swallowed the fish whole.* **2** *informal* completely: *E-commerce is a whole new way of doing business.*

wholefood /ˈhəʊlˌfuːd/ noun [C/U] *British* food that does not contain artificial substances and has not been treated to make it look better or last longer

wholehearted /ˌhəʊlˈhɑːtɪd/ adj enthusiastic and complete —**wholeheartedly** adv

wholemeal /ˈhəʊlˌmiːl/ adj *British* made from flour that contains all the wheat grain, including the outer part

whole ˈnumber noun [C] *technical* a number such as 1, 32, 144 etc, rather than a number such as 0.1, 0.32, $\frac{1}{2}$, $\frac{3}{4}$ etc

wholesale /ˈhəʊlˌseɪl/ adj **1** relating to the business of selling large quantities of goods, especially to people who are going to sell them in a shop **2** affecting every part of something, or affecting every person: *the wholesale destruction of entire communities* —**wholesale** adv

wholesaler /ˈhəʊlˌseɪlə/ noun [C] a person or company that sells large quantities of goods to shops or small businesses

wholesome /ˈhəʊls(ə)m/ adj **1** wholesome food is good for you **2** thought to have a good influence on people

who'll /huːl/ short form the usual way of saying or writing 'who will'. This is not often used in formal writing: *You're the one who'll have to decide.*

W

wholly /ˈhəʊlli/ adv *formal* completely: *His behaviour is wholly unacceptable.*

whom /huːm/ pronoun *formal* ★
1 used for adding more information about a person: *This is the gentleman whom I mentioned a moment ago.*
2 used for asking or stating which person is affected by an action or is involved in something: *To whom did you speak?*

whoop /wuːp/ verb [I] to shout in a happy or excited way —**whoop** noun [C]

whooping cough /ˈhuːpɪŋ ˌkɒf/ noun [U] an infectious disease of children that causes them to cough and make a loud noise when they breathe

whoops /wʊps/ interjection used when a small accident happens, or when you make a mistake

whopping /ˈwɒpɪŋ/ adj *informal* extremely large

who's /huːz/ short form the usual way of saying or writing 'who is' or 'who has'. This is not often used in formal writing: *Who's that talking to Michael?* ♦ *Do you know anyone who's been to New Zealand?*

whose /huːz/ determiner, pronoun ★★★

> **Whose can be:**
> ■ a **determiner**: *Whose idea was it to come here?*
> ■ a **question pronoun**: *Whose is this jacket?*
> ■ a **relative pronoun**: *I asked whose it was.*

1 used for showing that someone or something belongs to or is connected with the person or thing that you have just mentioned: *Help is needed for families whose homes were destroyed in the bombing.* ♦ *a school whose reputation is excellent*
2 used for asking who someone or something belongs to or who they are connected with: *What about these glasses? Whose are they?* ♦ *Whose little girl is she?*
3 used when someone knows or says who someone or something belongs to or who they are connected with: *He wouldn't say whose names were on the list.*

who've /huːv/ short form the usual way of saying or writing 'who have'. This is not often used in formal writing: *Talk to people who've been doing the job for a while.*

why /waɪ/ adv ★★★
1 used for asking the reason for something: *Why are you so angry?* ♦ *He asked me why I was leaving early.*
2 used when someone knows or says the reason for something: *I don't know why she's always so rude.* ♦ *There are a lot of things we need to discuss, and that's why I'm here.* ♦ *I can only think of one reason why Frank should be jealous.*

> **PHRASE why not...?** *spoken* **1** used for making a suggestion: *Why not stay for lunch?* **2** used for agreeing to a suggestion or request: *'Perhaps we could all meet up at your house?' 'Yes, of course, why not?'*

wicked /ˈwɪkɪd/ adj **1** morally wrong and deliberately intending to hurt people **2** slightly cruel, but in a way that is intended to be funny: *a wicked sense of humour* **3** *informal* very good —**wickedly** adv, **wickedness** noun [U]

wicker /ˈwɪkə/ noun [U] long thin pieces of wood that are woven together to make furniture or baskets

wicket /ˈwɪkɪt/ noun [C] in the game of CRICKET, the set of three sticks that the BOWLER tries to hit with the ball

wide¹ /waɪd/ adj ★★★

1 far from side to side	4 large
2 with measurement	5 about general aspects
3 including a lot	

1 measuring a large distance from one side to the other: *Beijing's wide avenues and boulevards* ♦ *An earthquake shook a wide area of southern Italy on Saturday.*
2 measuring a particular distance from one side to the other: *The stream is about 4 feet wide.* ♦ *The roads are barely wide enough for cars.*

3 including or involving many different things or people: *Her proposal has gained* **wide support**. ♦ *his* **wide experience** *of the business world* ♦ *Workers must carry out* **a wide range** *of tasks.*
4 large: *There can be wide differences in temperature between the north and the south.* ♦ *a wide smile*
5 concerning the basic aspects of something rather than the details: *The report looks at women's employment in its* **wider** *social context.*
→ WIDTH

wide² /waɪd/ adv **1** as much as possible: *The door opened wide and people came streaming out.* ♦ *He was now wide awake and sitting up in bed.* **2** over a large area: *The news spread far and wide.*

wide-eyed /ˌwaɪd ˈaɪd/ adj with an expression that shows that you are very surprised, frightened, or impressed

widely /ˈwaɪdli/ adv ★★
1 by a lot of people, or in a lot of places: *He has travelled widely in South America.* ♦ *The drug is* **widely used** *in the treatment of cancer.*
2 by a large amount, or to a large degree: *widely different views* ♦ *Prices vary widely for products that appear to be very similar.*

widen /ˈwaɪd(ə)n/ verb [I/T] **1** to become wider, or to make something wider ≠ NARROW **2** to increase, or to make something increase ≠ NARROW

wide-ranging /ˌwaɪd ˈreɪndʒɪŋ/ adj dealing with a large variety of subjects

widescreen /ˈwaɪdˌskriːn/ adj with a screen that gives a wider view than a normal screen

widespread /ˈwaɪdˌspred/ adj happening or existing in many places, or affecting many people: *the widespread use of antibiotics* ♦ *The project has received widespread support.* ♦ *Foxes are becoming more widespread in urban areas.*

widow /ˈwɪdəʊ/ noun [C] a woman whose husband has died

widowed /ˈwɪdəʊd/ adj if someone is widowed, their husband or wife has died

widower /ˈwɪdəʊə/ noun [C] a man whose wife has died

width /wɪdθ/ noun **1** [C/U] the distance from one side of something to the other: *The path is about two metres in width.* **2** [U] the quality of being wide: *the width of his shoulders* **3** [C] the distance from one side of a swimming pool to the other

wield /wiːld/ verb [T] **1** to have, and be able to use, power or influence **2** to hold a weapon or tool and use it

wife /waɪf/ (plural **wives** /waɪvz/) noun [C] ★★★ the woman that a man is married to: *I'd better phone my wife and tell her I'll be late.* ♦ *a reception for* **the wives** *of the ambassadors* —*picture* → FAMILY TREE

wig /wɪɡ/ noun [C] a cover of artificial hair that you wear on your head

wiggle /ˈwɪɡ(ə)l/ verb [I/T] to make short quick movements from side to side, or to move something in this way —**wiggle** noun [C]

wild¹ /waɪld/ adj ★★

1 not raised by humans	**4** with no people
2 with strong emotions	**5** of weather/sea
3 not accurate	**6** exciting

1 a wild animal or plant lives or grows on its own in natural conditions and is not raised by humans: *The wild rose is a familiar sight in woods and hedges.* ♦ *This trait is common to both domestic and wild dogs.*
2 expressing or feeling strong emotions: *Hernandez entered the boxing ring to wild cheers.* ♦ *The noise drove him* **wild with** *terror.* ♦ *When Pascal scored, the fans* **went wild**.
3 not accurate, or not thought about carefully: *wild accusations/claims* ♦ *They make all sorts of wild promises.*
4 a wild area is one where people do not live or cannot live: *wild mountainous regions*
5 if the weather or the sea is wild, there is a storm with strong winds: *a wet and wild night*
6 exciting and enjoyable: *They have some pretty wild parties.*
—**wildness** noun [U]

wild² /waɪld/ adv in a natural or uncontrolled way: *I found these daisies growing wild in the meadow.*

wild³ /waɪld/ noun
PHRASES **in the wild** in a natural environment
the wilds of... an area where few or no people live

wild card noun [C] *computing* a sign or symbol used for representing any letter or number

wilderness /ˈwɪldənəs/ noun **1** [C] an area of land where people do not live or grow crops and where there are no buildings **2** [singular] a period when someone is not as successful or powerful as they were previously

wildfire /ˈwaɪldˌfaɪə/ noun **spread like wildfire** if information spreads like wildfire, a lot of people hear about it in a short period of time

wildlife /ˈwaɪldˌlaɪf/ noun [U] animals, birds, and plants that live in natural conditions

wildly /ˈwaɪldli/ adv **1** in an uncontrolled way: *Italian fans cheered wildly.* **2** extremely: used for emphasizing what you are saying: *The figures are wildly inaccurate.*

wiles /waɪlz/ noun [plural] ways of persuading or tricking someone so that they do what you want

wilful /ˈwɪlf(ə)l/ adj **1** done deliberately in order to cause damage or harm **2** determined to do what you want and not caring if you upset other people —**wilfully** adv

will¹ /wɪl/ modal verb ★★★

- **Will** is usually followed by an infinitive without 'to': *She will be angry.* Sometimes it is used without a following infinitive: *I have never borrowed money, and I never will.*
- In conversation or informal writing **will** is often shortened to **'ll**: *Do you think it'll rain?*
- **Will** has no participles and no infinitive form. **Will** does not change its form, so the third person singular form does not end in '-s': *Robert will be there.*

- Questions and negatives are formed without 'do': *Will you help me?* ♦ *They will not accept our offer.*
- The negative form **will not** is often shortened to **won't** in conversation or informal writing: *Don't worry – the dog won't bite you.*

1 talking about future actions or events used for saying what is planned or expected for the future: *The President will attend a lunch hosted by the Queen.* ♦ *Let's finish the job now – it won't take long.*

2 to be willing used for saying that you are willing to do something or that you intend to do it: *If you won't tell him the truth, I will.*

3 polite requests and offers used for asking or inviting someone to do something or for offering them something: *Will you please listen to what I'm saying! ♦ Won't you stay for lunch?*

4 showing possibility used for saying whether something is possible: *Will these gloves fit you? ♦ £30 will buy enough food for a family for a week.*

5 when sth always happens used for saying what always happens in certain situations: *Natural rubber will stretch easily when pulled.*

6 showing that you are fairly certain used for showing that you are fairly certain that something is true: *There's the doorbell. That'll be Janet.*

PHRASE sth will not work/start/open etc used for saying that you cannot make something do what it should do, although you have tried: *The engine won't start.*

will² /wɪl/ noun ★★
1 [C/U] someone's determination to do what is necessary in order to achieve what they want: *a child with a very strong will ♦ Without the will to win, the team won't go far.*
2 [singular] what someone wants to happen: *the will of the people ♦ He claims he was kept in the flat against his will.* → GOODWILL
3 [C] a legal document that explains what you want to happen to your money and possessions after you die: *Ed's father didn't leave him anything in his will.*
PHRASE at will at any time that you want or choose: *Children were allowed to enter and leave at will.*

will³ /wɪl/ verb [T] to make something happen by wishing for it very strongly

willing /ˈwɪlɪŋ/ adj ★★
1 if you are willing to do something, you do it when someone asks you ≠ UNWILLING: *They are very willing to give her the job. ♦ I wasn't willing to accept his gifts.*
2 enthusiastic about doing something ≠ UNWILLING: *a willing helper/partner/volunteer*
—**willingly** adv: *She would willingly give up her spare time to help you.* —**willingness** noun [U]

willow /ˈwɪləʊ/ noun [C] a tree with long thin branches and narrow leaves that grows near water —*picture* → C9

willpower /ˈwɪlˌpaʊə/ noun [U] the ability to control your thoughts and behaviour in order to achieve something

wilt /wɪlt/ verb [I] if a plant wilts, it gradually bends towards the ground because it needs water or is dying

wily /ˈwaɪli/ adj clever and willing to trick people in order to get what you want =CUNNING

wimp /wɪmp/ noun [C] *informal* someone who is not brave, strong, or confident

win¹ /wɪn/ (past tense and past participle **won** /wʌn/) verb ★★★
1 [I/T] to defeat everyone else by being the best, or by finishing first in a competition ≠ LOSE: *Every time we play tennis, she wins. ♦ Who won the race? ♦ The Liberals won the election. ♦ I never win at cards.*
2 [I/T] to achieve victory in a war, battle, or argument ≠ LOSE: *In an argument like that, nobody wins. ♦ No one knows who will win the war.*
3 [T] to get something as a prize for defeating other people or because you are lucky: *He won £4,000 in the lottery. ♦ Our skiing team won a gold medal at the Olympics. ♦ Raoul won first prize in a spelling contest.*
4 [T] to succeed in getting something that you want because of hard work or ability: *We've won a £3 million contract to build the new bridge. ♦ The bill is winning a lot of support from farmers.*
—**winning** adj: *the winning team/goal/ticket*
PHRASAL VERBS win sth ˈback to get back something that you have lost: *She tried hard to win back his trust.*
win sb ˈover to persuade someone to agree with you: *We've finally won him over to our point of view.*

win² /wɪn/ noun [C] an occasion when someone wins something: *This is their fourth win of the season.*

wince /wɪns/ verb [I] to make a sudden expression or movement that shows that you are embarrassed or feel pain

winch /wɪntʃ/ noun [C] a piece of equipment that uses a rope or chain for lifting or pulling things or people —**winch** verb [T]

wind¹ /wɪnd/ noun ★★★
1 [C/U] a natural current of air that moves fast enough for you to feel it: *A cold wind blew. ♦ During the night the wind picked up* (=got stronger). *♦ The helicopter can't reach them until the wind drops* (=becomes less strong). *♦ A large gust of wind swept his hat into the sea.* → HEADWIND
2 [singular] the air in your lungs: *The heavy blow knocked the wind out of him.*
3 [U] *British* gas produced in your stomach that makes you feel uncomfortable

wind² /waɪnd/ (past tense and past participle **wound** /waʊnd/) verb ★

1 wrap sth around sth	4 about car window
2 move in a curve	5 about watch/clock
3 move tape	+ PHRASAL VERBS

1 [T] to wrap or twist something around something else: *I put on my coat and wound a scarf round my neck.*
2 [I/T] to follow a course or path that curves or twists a lot: *The River Nile winds through Sudan and Egypt. ♦ The bus wound its way up the mountain.*
3 [T] to make a video or a CASSETTE TAPE

move forwards or backwards in a machine: *I've wound it back to the beginning.*
→ REWIND

4 [T] *British* to make the window of a vehicle move up or down: *Wind down the window and let some air in.*

5 [T] if you wind a watch or clock, you make it operate by turning a part of it round and round

PHRASAL VERBS **wind 'down** to relax after a period of excitement or worry =UNWIND
wind (sth) 'down to end gradually, or to finish something gradually: *The party started to wind down around 2.00 am.*
wind 'up to be in a particular place or situation that you did not plan to be in: *There were no hotels available in San Francisco, so we wound up in Oakland.*
wind sb 'up *British informal* to deliberately try to trick or annoy someone
wind sth 'up to end or close something: *I'd like to wind up the meeting soon.* ♦ *The firm was later wound up with debts of £104,000.*

wind³ /wɪnd/ verb [T] **1** to hit someone hard in the stomach, so that they have difficulty breathing **2** *British* to help a baby to get rid of the gas in its stomach by rubbing its back

windfall /'wɪn(d)fɔːl/ noun [C] an amount of money that you get unexpectedly

winding /'waɪndɪŋ/ adj with a lot of bends: *a winding lane*

wind instrument /'wɪnd ˌɪnstrʊmənt/ noun [C] a musical instrument that you play by blowing through it, such as a FLUTE or CLARINET —*picture* → WOODWIND

windmill /'wɪn(d)mɪl/ noun [C] a tall building with long pieces of wood or metal that turn in the wind, used for producing power or crushing grain

window /'wɪndəʊ/ noun [C] ★★★
1 a hole with a frame in a wall or vehicle that lets in light and air and lets you see outside, or the glass that covers this hole: *She just stood there staring out of the window.* ♦ *She was watching him from an upstairs window.* ♦ *a car with electric windows* ♦ *Do you mind if I open a window?* ♦ *Rioters set fire to cars and smashed shop windows.* —*picture* → C1
2 one of the different work areas on a computer screen: *Click on the X to close the window.*
3 a short period of time when you can do something: *I've got a window on Friday when I could see you.*

window ˌpane noun [C] a piece of glass used in a window —*picture* → C1

window-shopping noun [U] the activity of looking in shop windows but not buying anything

windowsill /'wɪndəʊˌsɪl/ noun [C] a shelf under a window —*picture* → C1

windpipe /'wɪn(d)paɪp/ noun [C] the tube that carries air into your lungs from your nose or mouth

wind power /'wɪnd ˌpaʊə/ noun [U] electricity that is created using the power of wind

windscreen /'wɪn(d)skriːn/ noun [C] *British* the large window at the front of a vehicle —*picture* → C6

windscreen ˌwiper noun [C] *British* a long thin piece of equipment that moves across a vehicle's windscreen in order to wipe and clean it —*picture* → C6

windshield /'wɪn(d)fiːld/ noun [C] *American* a WINDSCREEN

windsurfing /'wɪn(d)sɜːfɪŋ/ noun [U] a sport in which you move across water standing on a flat board with a sail that you can move —**windsurfer** noun [C]

windswept /'wɪn(d)swept/ adj **1** a windswept place has a lot of wind and not many buildings or trees to protect it **2** looking untidy because your clothes and hair have been blown around by the wind

windy /'wɪndi/ adj with a lot of wind: *a windy day*

wine¹ /waɪn/ noun [C/U] ★★★ an alcoholic drink made from grapes: *a bottle of wine* ♦ *two glasses of sweet white wine* ♦ *Spanish wines* ♦ *I'll have a red wine, please* (=a glass of red wine).

wine² /waɪn/ verb **wine and dine sb** to entertain someone by taking them out for a meal

wing /wɪŋ/ noun [C] ★★

1 part of bird/insect	**5** in sports
2 part of plane	**6** wheel cover on car
3 part of building	✦ PHRASES
4 part of organization	

1 one of the parts on a bird or insect that move up and down and allow it to fly: *a moth's delicate wings* ♦ *a blackbird flapping its wings*
2 one of the long flat parts on both sides of a plane that allow it to fly
3 a part of a building that sticks out from the main part, especially one with a particular purpose: *the east/main wing* ♦ *He works in the psychiatric wing of the hospital.*
4 a part of an organization or political party that has particular responsibilities or opinions: *the Green Party's youth wing*
5 the left or right side of a sports field, or a player who plays on the side of a sports field
6 *British* the part of a car that covers the wheel —*picture* → C6

PHRASES **under sb's wing** being looked after by someone who is older or more experienced
waiting in the wings ready to do something, or ready to be used when needed

winged /wɪŋd/ adj with wings

wing ˌmirror noun [C] *British* a small mirror on each side of a vehicle —*picture* → C6

wink /wɪŋk/ verb [I] to quickly close and open one eye as a sign to someone: *Marcus winked at me.* —**wink** noun [C]

winner /'wɪnə/ noun [C] ★★
1 someone who wins a competition, race, or prize: *The winner of the tournament gets £50,000.* ♦ *She was a gold medal winner at the last Olympics.* ♦ *The winner will be announced in October.*
2 *informal* something that is very popular or successful: *Her latest book looks like another winner.*

winnings /'wɪnɪŋz/ noun [plural] money that you win

W

winning streak noun [C] a period of time when you win a series of things

winter¹ /'wɪntə/ noun [C/U] ★★★ the season after autumn and before spring, when it is usually cold: *a cold/severe/hard winter* ♦ *a cold winter's night* ♦ *We usually go skiing in winter.* ♦ *This town is deserted in the winter.* ♦ *She wore a heavy winter coat.*

winter² /'wɪntə/ verb [I] to spend the winter in a particular place

winter solstice noun [C/U] the day of the year when the sun is above the HORIZON for the shortest amount of time

winter sports noun [plural] sports that are done on snow or ice

wintry /'wɪntri/ adj cold and typical of winter

win-win adj a win-win situation is one in which everyone benefits

wipe¹ /waɪp/ verb [T] ★
1 to clean or dry something by moving something such as a cloth over it: *Let me just wipe the table before you sit down.* ♦ *She wiped away her tears.* ♦ **wipe sth with sth** *He wiped his mouth with his serviette.*
2 to clean or dry something by moving it over a surface: *Wipe your feet before you come inside.* ♦ **wipe sth on sth** *I wish you wouldn't wipe your hands on your clothes!*
3 to remove something, or to make something disappear: *Nearly $20 billion was wiped off share prices yesterday.* ♦ *This new virus could wipe all the data from your hard drive.*

PHRASAL VERBS **wipe sth out** to destroy or get rid of something completely =ERADICATE: *We want to wipe out world hunger by the year 2010.*
wipe sth up to remove a liquid from a surface using a cloth

wipe² /waɪp/ noun [C] **1** the action of wiping something to make it clean **2** a small wet cloth for cleaning something that you use only once

wiper /'waɪpə/ noun [C] a WINDSCREEN WIPER

wire¹ /'waɪə/ noun [C/U] ★
1 a long piece of metal like a very thin piece of string: *The sticks were tied in bundles with wire.* ♦ *a wire fence/cage*
2 a long thin piece of metal that carries electricity or telephone signals: *telephone wires*

wire² /'waɪə/ verb [T] **1** to connect a piece of electrical equipment to something, or to connect the wires inside a piece of equipment **2** to send money using an electronic system

PHRASAL VERB **wire sth up** same as **wire²** 1

wireless¹ /'waɪələs/ adj not using wires: *wireless phones* ♦ *wireless data transfer*

wireless² /'waɪələs/ noun [C/U] British old-fashioned a RADIO

wiring /'waɪərɪŋ/ noun [U] the electric wires in a building, vehicle, or machine

wiry /'waɪəri/ adj **1** a wiry person is thin but looks strong **2** wiry hair is stiff and rough

wisdom /'wɪzdəm/ noun [U] the ability to make good decisions based on knowledge and experience: *The Egyptian leader was praised for his courage and wisdom.*

PHRASES **in his/her/their wisdom** humorous used for emphasizing that you do not understand why someone has done something that you think is silly
question/doubt the wisdom of (doing) sth to feel that something is probably not a sensible thing do to

wisdom tooth noun [C] one of the four large teeth that grow at the back of your mouth when you are an adult

wise /waɪz/ adj ★
1 a wise action or decision is sensible and shows that you have good judgment: *You made a wise decision when you chose to study Spanish.* ♦ *Buying those shares was a wise move.* ♦ **wise to do sth** *I don't think it's wise to teach your children at home.*
2 a wise person is able to make good choices and decisions because they have a lot of experience

PHRASE **none the wiser** spoken used for saying that you still do not know or understand something, or that someone has not found out about what you have done
—wisely adv: *They spent the money wisely.*

wish¹ /wɪʃ/ verb ★★★
1 [T] to want something to happen although it is unlikely: *I wish I was rich!* ♦ **+(that)** *Andy wished that he could think of a way of helping.* ♦ *I wish Beth would stop interfering.*
2 [T] used for saying that you feel sorry or disappointed about something that you did or did not do: *I wish I'd never come!* ♦ **+(that)** *Now he wished that he had listened more carefully.*
3 [I/T] formal to want something, or to want to do something: *You may attend the meeting if you wish.* ♦ **wish to do sth** *Please do not hesitate to contact me if you wish to discuss the matter.*
4 [T] **wish sb sth** used for saying that you hope someone enjoys something or that something good happens to them: *May I wish you all a very Merry Christmas.* ♦ *I wish you every success.* ♦ *The crowd wished them well as they left for their honeymoon.*

PHRASES **I wish** used for saying that something is not true, although you would be pleased if it were true: *'Did she give you some money?' 'I wish!'*
you wish spoken used for telling someone that the thing that they want to happen is completely impossible: *'I told Ben that Sally was my girlfriend.' 'You wish!'*

PHRASAL VERB **wish for sth** formal to want something: *What more could anyone wish for?*

wish² /wɪʃ/ noun [C] ★
1 a feeling that you want something or want to do something: *He'd expressed a wish to go there.* ♦ *I have to respect the wishes of my client.* → DEATH WISH
2 the thing that you want to have or to do: *Our one wish is to find a cure for this disease.*
3 something that you hope will happen by magic or by the power of your mind: *Make a wish and then blow out the candles.*

PHRASE **best wishes 1** used for saying that you hope that something good will happen to someone: *Please give them our best wishes for the happy day.* **2** a friendly and polite way of ending a letter or email

wishful thinking /ˌwɪʃf(ə)l ˈθɪŋkɪŋ/ noun [U] a belief that something is true, based only on the fact that you want it to be true, not on the real situation

wisp /wɪsp/ noun [C] something that has a long, thin, delicate shape: *a wisp of smoke/hair* —**wispy** adj

wistful /ˈwɪstf(ə)l/ adj slightly sad because you want to have or to do something —**wistfully** adv

wit /wɪt/ noun **1** [singular/U] the ability to use words in a clever way that makes people laugh: *a novel of great inventiveness and wit* **2 wits** [plural] the ability to think quickly and make sensible decisions: *Nurses can't afford to make mistakes. You've got to keep your wits about you.*

PHRASE **at your wits' end** so worried and tired because of your problems that you cannot think of any more ways of solving them

witch /wɪtʃ/ noun [C] a woman with magic powers

witchcraft /ˈwɪtʃkrɑːft/ noun [U] the practice of magic, especially for evil purposes

witch-hunt noun [U] *showing disapproval* an attempt to find all the people in a particular group in order to punish them unfairly

with /wɪð, wɪθ/ preposition ★★★
1 together if one person or thing is with another or does something with them, they are together or they do it together: *Hannah lives with her parents.* ♦ *chicken pie served with vegetables and mushrooms* ♦ *a problem you should discuss with your teacher*
2 having or holding sth used for saying what someone or something has or is holding: *a girl with red hair* ♦ *a room with a high ceiling* ♦ *Servants arrived with trays of tea.*
3 by means of sth used for saying what is used for doing something: *Stir the mixture with a spoon.* ♦ *Stan wiped his eyes with his hand.*
4 towards or concerning sb/sth used for saying what person or thing you have a particular feeling towards: *Why are you angry with me?* ♦ *We were disappointed with the court's decision.*
5 caused by sth used for saying what feeling causes someone or something to have a particular reaction or to be in a particular state: *She was trembling with rage.* ♦ *His face was red with embarrassment.* ♦ *The air was thick with smoke.*
6 against sb used for showing who you compete, fight, or argue against: *Don't argue with me.* ♦ *The war with France lasted for nearly 20 years.*
7 in a particular way used for describing the qualities that someone shows or the feelings that they have when they do something: *He spoke with great confidence.*
8 while doing sth used for describing the sound or expression that someone or something makes when they do something: *The bomb exploded with a loud bang.* ♦ *'Are you enjoying yourself?' he asked with a friendly smile.*
9 holding your body in a position used for describing the position of someone's body

when they do something: *Gordon was standing with his back to the window.*
10 covered or filled by sth used for saying what is in or on something: *Fill the jug with boiling water.* ♦ *The hills were covered with snow.*
11 sharing or exchanging used for saying that people share or exchange things: *She shares her food with all the family.* ♦ *Most countries had stopped trading with South Africa.*
12 relating to sth used for saying what a particular action or problem is related to: *There's nothing wrong with my eyesight.* ♦ *We're making good progress with our investigations.*

withdraw /wɪðˈdrɔː/ (past tense **withdrew** /wɪðˈdruː/; past participle **withdrawn** /wɪðˈdrɔːn/) verb ★

1 stop providing sth	4 leave a place
2 stop taking part	5 say sth is not true
3 get money from bank	

1 [T] to take something back, or to stop providing something: *The bus service in many rural areas has been withdrawn.* ♦ *Some parents have withdrawn their support from the school.*
2 [I] to no longer take part in something: *Two of the competitors threatened to withdraw.* ♦ *The injury has forced him to withdraw from the competition.*
3 [T] to take money from a bank account: *You can withdraw cash at any of our branches.*
4 [I/T] to leave a place, or to make someone leave a place: *The troops began to withdraw from the northern region.*
5 [T] to say that something that you said earlier is not in fact true: *He withdrew his remarks and apologized.*

withdrawal /wɪðˈdrɔːəl/ noun **1** [C/U] the act of stopping something or removing something: *Their withdrawal of support forced the minister to resign.* ♦ *Illness led to her withdrawal from the contest.* **2** [C/U] the process of taking an amount of money out of your bank account, or the amount of money that you take out: *You can make a withdrawal from most cash machines.* **3** [U] a period during which someone feels ill because they have stopped taking a drug that they have been taking regularly: *You may experience withdrawal symptoms.*

withdrawn[1] /wɪðˈdrɔːn/ adj very quiet and preferring not to talk to other people

withdrawn[2] the past participle of **withdraw**

withdrew the past tense of **withdraw**

wither /ˈwɪðə/ verb [I] **1** if a plant withers, it becomes dry and starts to die **2** to become weaker and then disappear

PHRASAL VERB **wither away** *same as* **wither** 2

withering /ˈwɪðərɪŋ/ adj intended to make someone feel silly or embarrassed: *a withering look/remark*

withhold /wɪðˈhəʊld/ (past tense and past participle **withheld** /wɪðˈheld/) verb [T] *formal* to deliberately not give something to someone

within /wɪðˈɪn/ adv, preposition ★★★
1 during a period of time, or before a period

W

of time ends: *Within the past few weeks, 215 people have been arrested.* ♦ *We expect an announcement within the next 24 hours.*
2 inside a place, organization, group, or person: *There were four churches within the walls of the ancient city.* ♦ *Mr Potter complained about the lack of leadership within the health service.* ♦ *She has a kind of spiritual strength that comes from within.*
3 not more than a particular distance or amount: *A bomb exploded within 50 metres of the Allied headquarters.*
4 included in the range of things that are possible, reasonable, or allowed: *Private security firms must still operate within the limits of the law.*

without /wɪðˈaʊt/ adv, preposition ★★★
1 used for saying what someone or something does not have: *I can't find the answer without a calculator.* ♦ *a dress without sleeves* ♦ *I can't afford new trainers, so I'll have to do without them* (=manage despite not having them).
2 used for saying that you do not have someone with you: *If the others don't want to come, we'll go without them.*
3 used for saying that does not happen when something else happens: *Liz closed the door without making a sound.* ♦ *an attack that came without any warning*

withstand /wɪðˈstænd/ (past tense and past participle **withstood** /wɪðˈstʊd/) verb [T] to be strong enough not to be harmed or destroyed by something

witness¹ /ˈwɪtnəs/ noun [C] ★
1 someone who sees a crime, accident, or other event happen: *Witnesses reported hearing two gunshots.* ♦ *Any witnesses to the incident are asked to contact the police.* ♦ *Detectives are appealing for witnesses.*
2 someone who tells a court what they know about a crime: *More than 20 witnesses will be called.* ♦ *a witness for the defence/prosecution*
3 someone who watches you sign an official document and then signs it to state that they have watched you

witness² /ˈwɪtnəs/ verb [T] ★
1 to see something happen, for example a crime or an accident: *Several journalists witnessed the incident.*
2 to be present when something important happens: *We are witnessing the third change of government in three years.*
3 used for saying that something happened at a particular time or in a particular place: *The 1980s witnessed enormous growth in the financial sector.*
4 to watch someone sign an official document, and then sign it yourself to state that you have watched them: *Could you witness my signature on this visa application?*

witness box noun [C] *British* the place in a court of law where witnesses stand or sit when they are answering questions

witty /ˈwɪti/ adj clever and funny

wives the plural of **wife**

wizard /ˈwɪzəd/ noun [C] **1** a man in stories who has magic powers **2** someone who is

very good at something: *a financial wizard*

wizardry /ˈwɪzədri/ noun [U] a very high level of skill at something

wizened /ˈwɪz(ə)nd/ adj old and with a lot of WRINKLES (=lines on the skin)

wobble /ˈwɒb(ə)l/ verb [I/T] to rock slightly from side to side, or to make something do this —**wobbly** adj

woe /wəʊ/ noun **1** [U] *literary* a strong feeling of sadness **2 woes** [plural] *formal* problems and worries

woefully /ˈwəʊf(ə)li/ adv used for emphasizing that something is very bad: *Medical supplies are woefully inadequate.*

wok /wɒk/ noun [C] a metal pan that is shaped like a large bowl, and is used for cooking Chinese food —*picture* → C2

woke the past tense of **wake¹**

woken the past participle of **wake¹**

wolf¹ /wʊlf/ (plural **wolves** /wʊlvz/) noun [C] a wild animal that looks like a large dog

wolf² /wʊlf/ or **wolf sth down** *informal* verb [T] *informal* to eat something very quickly

woman /ˈwʊmən/ (plural **women** /ˈwɪmɪn/) noun [C] ★★★ an adult female person: *We need more women in parliament.* ♦ *a study of women writers* → WOMEN'S

womanhood /ˈwʊmənˌhʊd/ noun [U] the state of being a woman

womanizer /ˈwʊmənaɪzə/ noun [C] *showing disapproval* a man who has sexual relationships with many women —**womanizing** noun [U]

womankind /ˈwʊmənˌkaɪnd/ noun [U] *formal* all women when they are thought of as a group

womanly /ˈwʊmənli/ adj typical of a woman, or suitable for a woman

womb /wuːm/ noun [C] the organ in a woman's body where a baby grows before it is born

women the plural of **woman**

women's /ˈwɪmɪnz/ adj relating to women: *women's magazines*

won the past tense and past participle of **win¹**

wonder¹ /ˈwʌndə/ verb ★★★
1 [I/T] to think about something because you want to know more facts, or because you are worried: *'How did they find out?' she wondered.* ♦ *I was wondering about the best place for a holiday.* ♦ *+how/what/when etc I wonder what we can do to help Sylvia.* ♦ *I wonder if they'll get married.* ♦ *I wonder whether it was wise to let her travel alone.*
2 [I] to be very impressed or surprised by something: *It's hard not to wonder at the miracle of a newborn baby.*
PHRASE **I wonder if/whether** a polite way of asking something: *I wonder if you would do me a favour?* ♦ *I was wondering whether you would like to come to the theatre with me?*

wonder² /ˈwʌndə/ noun ★
1 [U] a strong feeling of surprise or admiration: *She gazed at the ocean in wonder.* ♦ *Where is the sense of wonder we felt when we were younger?*
2 [C] something that is very impressive or surprising: *the wonders of modern technology* ♦ *Coral reefs are among the natural wonders of the world.*

W

PHRASES do/work wonders to have a very good effect on someone or something: *Fresh air and exercise do wonders for your health.* ♦ *They have worked wonders with kids that other schools had rejected.*

it's a wonder (that) used for saying that something is so bad that it is surprising that a good result can come from it: *Your writing is so small, it's a wonder anyone can read it.*

no wonder (that) used for showing that you are not surprised by something: *No wonder the children were bored – it was such a long speech.*

wonder³ /ˈwʌndə/ adj extremely good or effective: *The treatment was first regarded as a wonder cure.*

wonderful /ˈwʌndəf(ə)l/ adj ★★ extremely good: *There was a wonderful view from the window.* ♦ *Thank you so much – I had a wonderful time!* —**wonderfully** adv

wonky /ˈwɒŋki/ adj *British informal* not straight, steady, or firmly fixed in position

won't /wəʊnt/ short form the usual way of saying or writing 'will not'. This is not often used in formal writing: *I'm sorry I won't be able to come to your party.*

wont /wəʊnt/ adj **be wont to do sth** *literary* to have a habit of doing something

woo /wuː/ verb [T] **1** to try to persuade people to support you or buy something from you **2** *old-fashioned* if a man woos a woman, he tries to start a sexual or romantic relationship with her

wood /wʊd/ noun ★★★
1 [U] the substance that trees are made of, used for making furniture and other objects: *a piece of wood* ♦ *a wood floor* ♦ *tables made of wood*
2 [C] a small forest: *We walk the dog in the woods behind our house.*
PHRASE touch wood *British* used for saying that you hope for good luck, especially while you touch something that is made of wood → DEAD WOOD

wooded /ˈwʊdɪd/ adj covered with trees

wooden /ˈwʊd(ə)n/ adj ★★ made of wood: *a wooden box*

woodland /ˈwʊdlənd/ noun [C/U] an area of land that is filled with trees

woodpecker /ˈwʊdˌpekə/ noun [C] a bird that makes holes in trees using its long beak

woodwind /ˈwʊdˌwɪnd/ noun [U] musical instruments made of wood that you play by blowing into them → BRASS

woodwork /ˈwʊdˌwɜːk/ noun [U] **1** the doors, window frames, and other wooden parts of a room **2** the activity or skill of making objects from wood

woodworm /ˈwʊdˌwɜːm/ noun **1** [C] a small insect that makes holes in wood **2** [U] damage to wood that is caused by woodworms

woody /ˈwʊdi/ adj a woody plant has a strong hard stem

woof /wʊf/ noun [C] the sound that a dog makes when it BARKS

wool /wʊl/ noun [U] ★★
1 thick hair that grows on sheep and some other animals

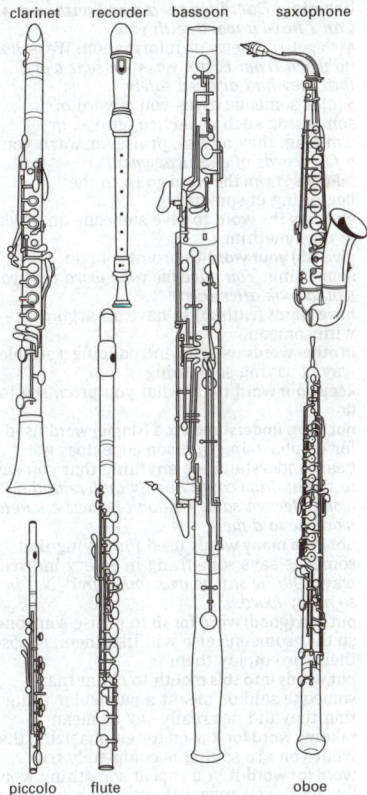

clarinet   recorder   bassoon   saxophone

piccolo   flute   oboe

woodwind instruments

2 fibre or cloth made from wool: *a ball of wool* ♦ *a wool jacket* → COTTON WOOL

woolen /ˈwʊlən/ the American spelling of **woollen**

woollen /ˈwʊlən/ adj made from wool

woolly /ˈwʊli/ adj *informal* made from wool, or similar to wool

wooly /ˈwʊli/ the American spelling of **woolly**

woozy /ˈwuːzi/ adj *informal* feeling slightly ill and unable to see or think clearly

word¹ /wɜːd/ noun ★★★

1 unit of language	4 news/information
2 things sb says	5 of advice/praise etc
3 short conversation	+ PHRASES

1 [C] a single unit of language that expresses a particular meaning by itself: *The first word that many babies say is 'Mama'.* ♦ *Can you read the words on this page?* ♦ *The Latin word for a table is 'mensa'.*
2 words [plural] someone's words are the things that they say: *The nation was facing – in the words of the Prime Minister – a choice between two evils.*
3 [singular] a short conversation or discussion, usually without other people

listening: *David* **wants a word** *with you.* ♦
Can I **have a word** *with you?*

4 [singular/U] news or information: *We've had
no* **word** *from Brian yet.* ♦ *He* **sent word**
that they had arrived safely.

5 [C] if someone gives you a word of
something such as advice, praise, or
warning, they advise, praise, or warn you:
a few **words** *of encouragement*

> **PHRASES** **from the word go** from the
> beginning of something

give/say the word to give someone an order
to do something

give (sb) your word to promise to do
something: *You gave me your* **word** *that you
would look after them.*

have words (with sb) to have an argument
with someone

in other words used for introducing a simpler
way of saying something

keep your word to do what you promised to
do

not hear/understand etc a (single) word used
for emphasizing that someone does not
hear/understand etc anything that you say
to them: *Jane could hardly understand a*
word *Mervyn said.* ♦ *I don't believe a single*
word *he told me.*

not in so many words used for saying that
someone says something in a very indirect
way: *'Did he say he was unhappy?' 'Not in
so many* **words**.*'*

put in a (good) word for sb to praise someone
so that someone else will like them, choose
them, or employ them

put words into sb's mouth to claim that
someone said or meant a particular thing
that they did not really say or mean

take my word for it used for emphasizing that
what you are saying is completely true

word for word if you repeat something word
for word, you repeat it exactly as someone
said it or wrote it

word of mouth informal conversations
between people: *Most of our customers hear
about us by* **word** *of mouth.*

words to that effect used for reporting the
general meaning of what someone has said,
rather than their exact words

→ LAST WORD

word² /wɜːd/ *verb* [T] to use words to express
something in a particular way: *You could
have* **worded** *your message a bit more clearly.*

wording /ˈwɜːdɪŋ/ *noun* [U] the words that are
used in a particular piece of writing

wordplay /ˈwɜːdpleɪ/ *noun* [U] clever or funny
use of words

word processing *noun* [U] the work or skill
of producing written documents on a
computer or word processor

word processor *noun* [C] a computer program
that you use for creating documents

wordy /ˈwɜːdi/ *adj* using too many words

wore the past tense of **wear¹**

work¹ /wɜːk/ *verb* ★★★

1 have job	**5** operate equipment
2 spend time doing sth	**6** move gradually
3 operate well	**+** PHRASAL VERBS
4 succeed/have effect	

1 [I] to have a job: *Dominic* **works** *part-time.*

♦ *She* **works** *for a big law firm in the city.*
♦ *She* **worked** *as a journalist.* ♦ *I hope to*
work *in marketing when I'm older.*

2 [I] to spend time and use effort trying to
achieve something: *I've been* **working** *in the
garden all day.* ♦ *Our thanks go to everybody
who has* **worked** *on this project.* ♦ **work** *to
do sth He worked tirelessly to improve safety
conditions in the mines.*

3 [I] to operate in a satisfactory way: *The
new telephone system seems to be* **working**
perfectly. ♦ *This pen doesn't* **work**.* ♦ *My
brain's not* **working** *very well today.*

4 [I] to succeed, or to have a particular effect:
If this plan doesn't **work**, *we'll have to think
of something else.* ♦ *The drug* **works** *by
blocking the spread of the virus.* ♦ *Criticizing
your former employer usually* **works against**
you in an interview. ♦ *The new tax system
is* **working in** *the company's favour.*

5 [T] to operate a piece of equipment: *I don't
know how to* **work** *this thing.*

6 [I/T] to move gradually, or to move
something gradually: *He managed to* **work**
one hand free of the rope.

> **PHRASAL VERBS** **work at sth** to try hard to
> develop or improve something: *Successful
> relationships don't just happen – you have
> to* **work** *at them.*

work on sth to spend time producing or
improving something: *He'll have to* **work**
on getting fit before the game.

work out 1 to have a particular cost or value:
Taking the train **works out** *more expensive
than going by car.* ♦ *The rent* **works out at**
about £360 a month. **2** to be successful, or
to end in a particular way: *If your new
arrangement doesn't* **work out**, *you can
always come back here.* ♦ *Things* **worked
out** *pretty well in the end.* **3** to do physical
exercise as a way of keeping fit

work sth out 1 to find an answer to
something by calculating it: *Use the chart
to* **work out** *how much tax you have to pay.*
2 to find a way of dealing with a problem:
We can't **work out** *how to get the Internet
connection going.*

work sb/sth out to understand someone or
something: *I can't* **work** *him out.*

work up to sth to prepare yourself for doing
something difficult: *Are you* **working up** *to
telling me that you can't pay?*

work² /wɜːk/ *noun* ★★★

1 job	**4** sth made/done in job
2 activity needing effort	**5** repairs
3 place sb does their job	**+** PHRASES

1 [U] a job that you are paid to do: *It's not
easy to* **find work** *(=get a job).* ♦ *I started*
work *(=got my first job) when I was 16.* ♦
She's been **out of work** *(=unemployed) for
over a year.*

2 [U] activity that involves physical or
mental effort: *I know you've got a lot of*
work *to do.* ♦ *Thank you for all your* **hard
work**.

3 [U] a place where someone goes to do their
job: *I walk to* **work** *and take the bus home.*

4 [C/U] something that someone makes or
does: *As a writer, she did some of her best*
work *in her late twenties.* ♦ *It's not the best*

piece of work you've ever done. ♦ *works of literature*

5 [C/U] the activity of repairing or building something: *The road has been closed for emergency repair works.*

PHRASES **at work 1** at the place where you work: *If he's not at home, he must still be at work.* **2** in the process of doing or making something: *She's currently **at work on** a new book.*

get/go/set to work (on sth) to start doing something: *Let's get to work on finding a solution to the problem.*

have your work cut out to have something difficult that you have to do

make short work of sth to deal with something quickly and easily

work of art 1 something such as a painting or SCULPTURE that an artist produces **2** something that is done in a very skilful or impressive way

→ DIRTY¹

■ You can refer to what someone does in order to get paid as their **work** or their **job**: *Do you find your work OR your job interesting?* ♦ *What kind of work OR job does he do?*

■ **Work** is uncountable with this meaning, so it never has **a** in front of it and is never plural: *He's looking for work.* ♦ *It's fascinating work.* ♦ *Has he found a job?* ♦ *She has had many different jobs.*

workable /ˈwɜːkəb(ə)l/ adj practical and likely to be effective

workaholic /ˌwɜːkəˈhɒlɪk/ noun [C] someone who spends most of their time working and is not interested in other things

workbook /ˈwɜːkbʊk/ noun [C] a book for students that contains exercises

worked up /ˌwɜːkt ˈʌp/ adj upset, angry, or excited

worker /ˈwɜːkə/ noun [C] ★★★
1 someone who works in a company or industry and is below the level of a manager =EMPLOYEE: *About 1,000 workers at the factory lost their jobs.* ♦ *farm/factory/shipyard workers*
2 used for describing how well or how quickly someone works: *He's a nice man, but quite a slow worker.* ♦ *Jan has always been **a hard worker**.*

workforce /ˈwɜːkfɔːs/ noun [singular] the total number of people who work in a particular company, industry, or country

working /ˈwɜːkɪŋ/ adj ★★★
1 a working person has a job: *working parents*
2 relating to or involving work: *After the meeting there will be **a working lunch**.* ♦ *The strikers are demanding better **working conditions**.*
3 something that is working can be operated or used: *The dining room has an attractive working fireplace.*
4 satisfactory, but not perfect or completely developed: *Applicants should have **a working knowledge** of Greek.*

PHRASE **in working order** working correctly, without any problems

working class noun **the working class** or **the working classes** the social class consisting of

people who have little money, education, or power, and who work mainly in jobs that require physical skills → LOWER CLASS, MIDDLE CLASS, UPPER CLASS

working day noun [C] **1** a day of the week when people have to work **2** the period of time that you work in one day

workings /ˈwɜːkɪŋz/ noun [plural] the parts of something such as a system, organization, or piece of equipment that control it or make it work

workload /ˈwɜːkləʊd/ noun [C] the amount of work that a person or organization has to do

workman /ˈwɜːkmən/ (plural **workmen** /ˈwɜːkmən/) noun [C] a man whose job is building or repairing things

workmanlike /ˈwɜːkmənlaɪk/ adj done or made in a professional way

workmanship /ˈwɜːkmənʃɪp/ noun [U] the standard of someone's work, or the skill that they use in making something

workout /ˈwɜːkaʊt/ noun [C] an occasion when you do physical exercise

workplace /ˈwɜːkpleɪs/ noun [C] the place where you work, or all the places where people work

worksheet /ˈwɜːkʃiːt/ noun [C] a piece of paper with exercises on it that help you to learn something

workshop /ˈwɜːkʃɒp/ noun [C] **1** an occasion when a group of people meet in order to learn about a particular subject **2** a room or building where things are made using tools and machines

workstation /ˈwɜːksteɪʃ(ə)n/ noun [C] **1** a desk with a computer for one person to work at **2** a powerful computer used in an office

worktop /ˈwɜːktɒp/ or **work surface** noun [C] *British* a flat surface in a kitchen that you use for preparing food —*picture* → C2

world¹ /wɜːld/ noun ★★★

1 all countries	4 sb's situation
2 our planet	5 being alive
3 group of countries	+ PHRASES

1 [singular] people and society in all countries: *We want to create a safer world for our children.* ♦ *They control about a quarter of the world's oil supply.* ♦ *The terrorists pose a threat to **the whole world**.* ♦ *The same problems are faced by workers **throughout the world**.*
2 the world [singular] the planet that we live on: *changes in the world's climate*
3 [C] a particular group of countries: *the economies of **the western world** (=the countries of western Europe and North America)* ♦ *It is the oldest institution in the **English-speaking world**.*
4 [C] the particular type of place or situation in which someone lives or works: *the entertainment world*
5 [singular] the state of being alive: *Thousands of babies **come into the world** (=are born) every day.*

PHRASES **do sb a/the world of good** to make someone feel very happy or healthy
in the world 1 used for emphasizing a particular quality that something has: *They produce some of the finest wines in the world.*

W

2 used for adding emphasis to a question in order to show that you are surprised or annoyed: *How in the world did they make a mistake like that?*

mean the world to sb *informal* to be very important to someone

out of this world *informal* extremely good or impressive

the outside world ordinary society, rather than places such as prisons or religious communities where people live separately from the rest of society

think the world of *informal* to like someone or something very much

→ BEST, TOP[1]

world[2] /wɜːld/ adj involving all the countries of the world: *the world championships ♦ a world war*

world-class adj at a level where you are one of the best in the world

world-famous adj known by people in all parts of the world

worldly /ˈwɜːldli/ adj a worldly person has a lot of experience and knowledge of life

PHRASE **sb's worldly goods/possessions** all the things someone owns

world music noun [U] in western Europe and North America, music from other cultures

worldwide /ˈwɜːldˈwaɪd/ adj, adv happening or existing all over the world: *a worldwide network of more than 100 organizations ♦ Our company employs 1,500 staff worldwide.*

World Wide Web, the all the WEBSITES that organizations have created on their computers for people to look at using the Internet = WEB

worm[1] /wɜːm/ noun [C] **1** a small creature with a long soft body and no bones or legs **2** *computing* a program that deliberately damages computer systems by making copies of itself

worm[2] /wɜːm/ verb **worm your way into/out of sth** to use clever methods in order to do something or in order to avoid doing something

PHRASAL VERB **worm sth out of sb** to gradually get information from someone who does not want to give it to you

worn[1] /wɔːn/ adj **1** something that is worn looks old and damaged because it has been used a lot **2** looking tired and old

worn[2] the past participle of **wear**[1]

worn out adj **1** extremely tired = EXHAUSTED **2** too old or damaged to be used any longer

worried /ˈwʌrid/ adj ★ nervous and upset because you are thinking about your problems or about bad things that could happen = ANXIOUS: *Everyone was very worried when John didn't show up. ♦ a worried look/glance/frown ♦ We are very worried about our future. ♦ Your parents are worried sick about you* (=extremely worried). *♦ +that I'm worried that he might have got lost.*

worry[1] /ˈwʌri/ verb ★★★

1 [I/T] to feel nervous and upset because you keep thinking about your problems or about bad things that could happen: *Try not to worry so much. ♦ People worry more about their health than they used to. ♦ If companies are following the rules, they've*

got *nothing to worry about. ♦ +that She worried that she might have taken on too much work.*

2 [T] to make someone feel nervous and upset: *What worries me most is the possibility of complete failure. ♦ worry yourself about sth Tell them not to worry themselves about the financial position.*

PHRASES **don't worry** used for telling someone that they do not need to do something: *Don't worry about dinner; I'll make it when I get back.*

not to worry *British spoken* used for telling someone that something is not important

worry[2] /ˈwʌri/ noun **1** [C] a problem or possibility that makes you feel worried: *financial worries ♦ My biggest worry now is how we are going to pay for it.* **2** [U] the feeling of being worried: *She was making herself ill with worry.*

worrying /ˈwʌriɪŋ/ adj making you feel worried

worse[1] /wɜːs/ adj ★★★

1 more unpleasant or bad than something else, or than before ≠ BETTER: *Our performance got worse as the game went on. ♦ The company's financial problems are getting worse and worse. ♦ The injury looked a lot worse than it really was.*

2 more ill than before ≠ BETTER: *She's feeling much worse today.*

PHRASES **make matters/things worse** to make a bad situation even worse

worse luck *British* used for saying that you wish that a situation was different

worse[2] /wɜːs/ adv **1** more badly ≠ BETTER: *They played even worse in the second half.* **2** more severely: *His leg seemed to be hurting worse than ever.*

worse[3] /wɜːs/ noun [U] something that is more unpleasant or bad: *Things were looking bad, but worse was to follow.*

PHRASES **for the worse** in a way that makes a situation worse

the worse for wear *informal* **1** ill or damaged **2** drunk

→ NONE

worsen /ˈwɜːs(ə)n/ verb [I/T] to become worse, or to make something worse ≠ IMPROVE —**worsening** adj

worse off adj **1** in a worse situation than someone else, or than before ≠ BETTER OFF **2** having less money than someone else, or than before ≠ BETTER OFF

worship[1] /ˈwɜːʃɪp/ noun [U] the activity of showing respect and love for God or a god

worship[2] /ˈwɜːʃɪp/ verb **1** [I/T] to show respect and love for God or a god **2** [T] to love and admire someone or something very much —**worshipper** noun [C]

worst[1] /wɜːst/ adj ★★★ worse than all others, or worse than at all other times: *It was the worst accident in the company's history. ♦ The noise from the airport is worst at night.*

worst[2] /wɜːst/ noun [singular] **the worst** someone or something that is worse than all others: *Even if the worst happens, you shouldn't give up hope.*

PHRASES **at worst** used for talking about the worst possibility in a situation: *At worst, we'll lose £100.*

if the worst comes to the worst *informal* used for saying what you will do if a bad situation happens

worst³ /wɜːst/ adv more badly than all others: *the areas that were worst hit by Monday's heavy rains*

worth¹ /wɜːθ/ adj ★★★

1 if you say how much something is worth, you state its value in money: *How much do you reckon the house is worth?* ♦ *a Gucci watch worth £1,000*

2 used for saying that there is a good enough reason for doing something, because it is important, enjoyable, useful etc: *The book is definitely worth reading.* ♦ *It's worth talking to your financial adviser before making your final decision.* ♦ *It was hard work, but it was worth it in the end.* ♦ *It's not worth my while to do the job for less than £150.*

3 used for saying how rich someone is: *She is now worth 20 million dollars.*

PHRASE for what it's worth *mainly spoken* used when you are telling someone something and you are not sure how useful it is

worth² /wɜːθ/ noun [U] **1** the degree to which someone or something is good, useful, or important: *The NATO alliance has proved its worth over the years.* **2** the financial value of something: *Houses are being sold at prices far below their true worth.* ♦ *millions of pounds' worth of equipment* **3** an amount measured by the time it lasts: *a week's worth of work*

worthless /ˈwɜːθləs/ adj **1** with no value, or not useful **2** a worthless person has no good qualities

worthwhile /ˌwɜːθˈwaɪl/ adj if something is worthwhile, it is worth the time, money, or effort that you spend on it: *We felt the meeting had been very worthwhile.* ♦ *It might be worthwhile to remember a few important facts.*

worthy /ˈwɜːði/ adj **1** *formal* deserving something: *He had shown himself to be worthy of their respect.* **2** a worthy person or thing has qualities that make people respect them: *a worthy winner* ♦ *The money will go to a worthy cause* (=an activity or organization that helps people).

would /wʊd/ modal verb ★★★

- **Would** is usually followed by an infinitive without 'to': *A picnic would be nice.* Sometimes it is used without a following infinitive: *They didn't do as much as they said they would.*
- In conversation and informal writing, **would** is often shortened to **'d**: *I thought you'd like a drink before dinner.*
- **Would** has no tenses, no participles, and no infinitive form. **Would** does not change its form, so the third person singular form does not end in '-s': *As a child, she would often run away from home.*
- Questions and negatives are formed without 'do': *Would you like a cup of coffee?* ♦ *He would not tell us his secret.*
- The negative form **would not** is often shortened in conversation or informal writing to **wouldn't**: *I wouldn't want to have your job.*

1 for talking about what was going to happen in the past used for showing what someone expected, intended, promised etc when they were thinking or talking about the future: *James said he would never forgive her.*

2 for talking about results of an unlikely situation used for talking about the possible results of a situation that is unlikely to happen, or that did not happen: *I'd travel first class if I could afford it.* ♦ *If I'd known you were coming, I'd have got your room ready.*

3 for giving opinions about possible situations used for saying or asking what someone thinks about a possible situation: *You wouldn't recognize the place now – it's changed so much.* ♦ *Why would anyone want to kill Jerry?*

4 for talking about past habits used for saying what someone used to do in the past: *The Campbells would sometimes invite us over for the weekend.*

5 in requests and offers used for politely asking someone for something, or for offering them something: *Would you like a cup of coffee or something?* ♦ *Would you mind waiting outside?* ♦ *Would it be all right if I used your phone?*

6 to be willing used when you think that someone is willing to do something: *Bruce would lend you the money, I'm sure.*

7 for saying what sb wants used for saying what someone wants to do, or wishes that they could do: *I wish it would stop raining.* ♦ *I think David would like to see you alone.*

PHRASE sth would not work/start/open etc used for saying that you could not make something do what it was meant to do, although you tried: *I turned the switch, but the motor wouldn't start.*

would-be adj hoping to do something: *a would-be author*

wouldn't /ˈwʊd(ə)nt/ short form the usual way of saying or writing 'would not'. This is not often used in formal writing: *I told you he wouldn't come.*

would've /ˈwʊdəv/ short form *spoken* the usual way of saying 'would have'. This is not often used in formal writing: *It would've been nice to see him again.*

wound¹ /wuːnd/ noun [C] ★ an injury in which your skin or flesh is seriously damaged: *a head wound* ♦ *a stab wound* ♦ *He had serious wounds to his stomach.*

wound² /wuːnd/ verb [T] **1** to injure someone so that their skin or flesh is seriously damaged: *Two soldiers died and three others were wounded in the attack.* **2** to hurt someone's feelings by doing or saying something unpleasant: *Her remark had deeply wounded him.*

wound³ /waʊnd/ the past tense and past participle of **wind²**

wounded /ˈwuːndɪd/ adj **1** seriously injured: *wounded soldiers* ♦ *his wounded arm* **2** feeling emotional pain: *wounded pride*

wound up /ˌwaʊnd ˈʌp/ adj *informal* nervous, worried, or angry

wove the past tense of **weave**

woven the past participle of **weave**

W

wow /waʊ/ interjection *informal* used for showing that you are very surprised or impressed by something

wrangle /ˈræŋg(ə)l/ verb [I] to argue for a long time about something complicated —**wrangle** noun [C]

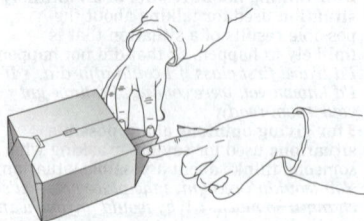

wrap

wrap /ræp/ verb [T] ★ to cover someone or something by putting paper, cloth etc round them: *Keep the cheeses fresh by wrapping each one individually.* ♦ **wrap sth in sth** *We wrapped the baby in a blanket to keep it warm.*

PHRASE **be wrapped up in sth** to spend so much time doing something that you do not notice anything else

PHRASAL VERBS **wrap sth round sth** or **wrap sth around sth** to put something around something else: *He grabbed a towel to wrap round his waist.* ♦ *We see couples with their arms wrapped round each other.*

wrap up to wear enough clothes to keep you warm

wrap sth up 1 *same as* **wrap**: *We've just finished wrapping up Susie's birthday present.* **2** *informal* to finish something: *We ought to wrap up this meeting and get back to work.*

wrapper /ˈræpə/ noun [C] a piece of paper or plastic that is wrapped around something that you buy: *sweet wrappers*

wrapping /ˈræpɪŋ/ noun [U] the paper or plastic that is wrapped around something

wrapping paper noun [U] paper that you use for wrapping presents

wrath /rɒθ/ noun [U] *formal* very great anger

wreak /riːk/ verb **wreak havoc (on)** to cause a lot of harm or damage to someone or something

wreath /riːθ/ noun [C] a circle of flowers that you put on a dead person's GRAVE

wreck¹ /rek/ verb [T] to destroy or damage something badly

wreck² /rek/ noun [C] **1** something that has been badly damaged or is in very bad condition **2** *informal* someone who looks or feels very ill or tired **3** *American* an accident that involves a vehicle

wreckage /ˈrekɪdʒ/ noun [singular/U] the parts of a vehicle or building that remain after it has been severely damaged

wrench¹ /rentʃ/ verb [T] **1** to injure a part of your body by twisting it suddenly **2** to pull and twist something strongly: *The door had been wrenched off its hinges.*

wrench² /rentʃ/ noun **1** [singular] a feeling of sadness that you get when you leave a place or a person that you love **2** [C] *American* a SPANNER

wrest /rest/ verb [T] *mainly journalism* to use force to get land, power, or possessions from someone

wrestle /ˈres(ə)l/ verb [I/T] to fight by holding someone and trying to push or throw them to the ground, especially as a sport

PHRASAL VERB **wrestle with sth** to try to deal with a difficult problem

wrestling /ˈres(ə)lɪŋ/ noun [U] a sport in which two people fight by holding each other and trying to push or throw each other to the ground —**wrestler** noun [C]

wretched /ˈretʃɪd/ adj **1** very unhappy or ill **2** *informal* used for emphasizing how much someone or something annoys you: *I eventually found the wretched letter.* **3** very unpleasant, or in very bad condition

wriggle /ˈrɪg(ə)l/ verb [I/T] to move by twisting or turning quickly, or to make something move in this way

PHRASAL VERB **wriggle out of sth** to try to avoid something

wring /rɪŋ/ (past tense and past participle **wrung** /rʌŋ/) or **wring sth out** verb [T] to twist and squeeze something in order to remove liquid from it

wrinkle /ˈrɪŋk(ə)l/ noun [C] **1** a line that appears on your skin when you get older **2** a fold in clothes that makes them look untidy —**wrinkle** verb [I/T], **wrinkled** /ˈrɪŋk(ə)ld/ adj, **wrinkly** adj

wrist /rɪst/ noun [C] the part of your body that joins your hand to your arm —*picture* → C14

wristwatch /ˈrɪs(t)wɒtʃ/ noun [C] a watch that you wear around your wrist

writ /rɪt/ noun [C] an official document that orders someone to do something

write /raɪt/ (past tense **wrote** /rəʊt/; past participle **written** /ˈrɪt(ə)n/) verb ★★★
1 [I/T] to use something such as a pen or pencil to make words, numbers, or symbols: *Emily is just learning to write.* ♦ *Write your full name in Box A.*
2 [I/T] to create something such as a book, a piece of music, or a computer program, by putting together words or symbols: *I have to write a review of my favourite film.* ♦ *Matt writes software for games machines.* ♦ *He travelled around Mexico and wrote about his experiences.* ♦ *She writes for several fashion magazines.*
3 [I/T] to create a letter or other message and send it: *I wrote to Kate last week.* ♦ **write sth to sb** *She'd written a letter to the newspaper to complain.*
4 [T] to create a formal document by writing: **write sb sth** *I'll write you a cheque for the full amount.*

PHRASAL VERBS **write back** to send a reply to someone who has sent you a letter

write sth down to write something on a piece of paper

write in to send a letter to an organization

write off to send a letter to an organization in order to ask for something: *You can write off for a free book of recipes.*

write sth off to accept that you will not receive money that someone owes you: *The US government agreed to write off debts of $170 billion.*

,write sb/sth 'off to decide that someone or something will not succeed, so that you stop giving them your attention and energy: *He thought the teachers had written him off.*

,write sth 'up to write something such as a report or research paper, using notes

'write-off noun [C] *British* a vehicle that is so badly damaged that it cannot be repaired

write-protected /ˌraɪt prəˈtektɪd/ adj *computing* containing information that cannot be changed or removed

writer /ˈraɪtə/ noun [C] ★★★ someone who writes books, stories, or articles as their job

'write-up noun [C] an article in a newspaper that gives the writer's opinion about something such as a new book or film =REVIEW

writhe /raɪð/ verb [I] to twist your body because you are feeling a lot of pain

writing /ˈraɪtɪŋ/ noun ★★★

1 act of writing	4 things that are written
2 job of creating stories	5 everything sb has written
3 written words	+ PHRASE

1 [U] the skill of producing written material by putting words together: *In the first two years, the children focus on reading and writing.*

2 [U] the job or activity of creating things such as books, poems, or newspaper articles

3 [U] words that are written or printed on something: *The label was torn and I couldn't read the writing.*

4 [U] books, poems, articles etc that have been written by a particular person or about a particular subject: *Her writing on environmental issues has been very influential.* ♦ *a course on women's writing*

5 **writings** [plural] all the books, poems, or articles that someone has written

PHRASE **in writing** in the form of a document that you can keep as proof of something: *Customers are expected to put their complaints in writing.*

written¹ /ˈrɪt(ə)n/ adj in the form of a letter or other document

written² the past participle of **write**

wrong¹ /rɒŋ/ adj ★★★

1 if there is something wrong, there is a problem: *You don't look well. Is anything wrong?* ♦ *I checked the engine, but I couldn't find anything wrong.* ♦ *There was something wrong with one of the tyres.* ♦ *She had some blood tests, but they still don't know what's wrong with her.* ♦ *What's wrong with the washing machine?*

2 not accurate, correct, or sensible =INCORRECT: *We must have gone the wrong way.* ♦ *the wrong answer* ♦ *If you think carefully, you won't make the wrong decision.*

3 not morally right=UNJUST: *Do you think it's wrong to use animals for testing new medicines?* ♦ *There's nothing wrong with living with your boyfriend in my opinion.*

4 not suitable: *It's the wrong place to build a factory.* ♦ *The colours just look wrong for a room this size.*

PHRASES **get off on the wrong foot** to start something badly, especially a relationship

the wrong way round with one part in the position where the other part should be → CORRECT²

Words often used with wrong

Adverbs often used with wrong (adj, sense 1)
■ **badly, disastrously, dreadfully, horribly, seriously, terribly** + WRONG: used for saying that there is a serious problem with something

Adverbs often used with wrong (adj, sense 2)
■ **completely, entirely, hopelessly, plainly, quite, totally** + WRONG: used for saying that something is not at all correct

wrong² /rɒŋ/ adv ★ in a way that is not correct: *Someone had tied the rope on wrong.*

PHRASES **don't get me wrong** used for explaining your comments when you think that someone has not understood them

get sth wrong to make a mistake about something: *The police got the name wrong and arrested an innocent man.*

go wrong 1 to stop working: *Then something went wrong with the engine.* **2** used when a problem happens and causes something to fail: *It's difficult to say when the relationship started to go wrong.*

wrong³ /rɒŋ/ noun [U] behaviour that is morally wrong or breaks a rule: *Small children do not know the difference between right and wrong.*

PHRASE **in the wrong** someone who is in the wrong has made a mistake and deserves the blame for it

wrong⁴ /rɒŋ/ verb [T] *formal* to treat or judge someone unfairly

wrongdoing /ˈrɒŋduːɪŋ/ noun [C/U] *formal* behaviour that is illegal or immoral

wrongful /ˈrɒŋf(ə)l/ adj unfair or illegal: *wrongful arrest/dismissal*

wrongly /ˈrɒŋli/ adv not correctly, or by mistake

wrote the past tense of **write**

wrought /rɔːt/ a past tense and past participle of **wreak**

,wrought 'iron noun [U] iron that is used for making things such as fences and gates, especially for decoration

wrung the past tense and past participle of **wring**

wry /raɪ/ adj showing that you think that something is funny but not very pleasant: *a wry smile* —**wryly** adv

wt abbrev weight

www /ˌdʌb(ə)lju: dʌb(ə)lju: ˈdʌb(ə)lju:/ abbrev the World Wide Web: used in some website addresses

W

Xx

x or **X** /eks/ noun [C/U] **1** the 24th letter of the English alphabet **2** a symbol that you use for showing that an answer is wrong **3** X used instead of saying the name of a person or place when you do not know it, or when you want to keep it secret: *Mr X* **4** *informal* a symbol that you use for writing a kiss at the end of a letter

xenophobia /ˌzenəˈfəʊbiə/ noun [U] hate of people from other countries and cultures —**xenophobic** adj

XL abbrev extra large: used on labels showing clothes sizes

Xmas /ˈkrɪsməs, ˈeksməs/ noun [C/U] *informal* CHRISTMAS

XML /ˌeks em ˈel/ noun [U] *computing* a computer language that is used for creating WEBSITES

X-ray¹ /ˈeks ˌreɪ/ noun [C] **1** a type of RADIATION that is used for looking inside things such as your body **2** a picture of the inside of someone's body that is taken using X-rays

X-ray² /ˈeks ˌreɪ/ verb [T] to take a picture of the inside of something using X-rays

xylophone /ˈzaɪləfəʊn/ noun [C] a musical instrument with a row of narrow wooden pieces that you hit with a wooden hammer —*picture* → PERCUSSION

Yy

y or **Y** /waɪ/ noun [C/U] the 25th letter of the English alphabet

yacht /jɒt/ noun [C] a boat that is used for racing or sailing

yachtsman /ˈjɒtsmən/ (plural **yachtsmen** /ˈjɒtsmən/) noun [C] someone who sails or owns a YACHT

yachtswoman /ˈjɒtsˌwʊmən/ (plural **yachtswomen** /ˈjɒtsˌwɪmɪn/) noun [C] a woman who sails or owns a YACHT

yank /jæŋk/ verb [I/T] to pull something suddenly using force=JERK

yap /jæp/ verb [I] if a dog yaps, it makes short high sounds

yard /jɑːd/ noun [C] ★★
  1 a unit for measuring length that is equal to 0.91 metres
  2 an enclosed area around a large building where people can do activities outside: *a prison yard*
  3 a large open area that is used for a particular purpose: *a builder's yard*
  4 *American* a GARDEN at the front, back, or side of a house

yardstick /ˈjɑːdˌstɪk/ noun [C] something that you compare similar things to, as a way of judging their quality or value

yarn /jɑːn/ noun **1** [U] cotton, wool, or other fibres in the form of thick THREAD (=a substance like string) **2** [C] *informal* a long story with a lot of exciting details

yawn /jɔːn/ verb [I] to open your mouth wide and take a big breath, because you are tired or bored —**yawn** noun [C]

yawn

yd abbrev yard

yeah /jeə/ adv *informal* YES

year /jɪə/ noun ★★★

1 12 months	**4** a long time
2 January to December	**5** level at school
3 period for institution	**+** PHRASE

1 [C] a period of 365 or 366 days divided into 12 months: *He lived in Paris for a few years.* ♦ *I started my job two years ago.* ♦ *He returned to China year after year* (=continuously for many years).
2 [C] a year beginning on 1 January and ending on 31 December: *We're hoping to sell the house by the end of the year.* ♦ *one of this year's best films*
3 [C] the period during which an institution operates, or the system it uses for dividing time: *the school year* ♦ *the tax year*
4 years [plural] a very long time: *It wasn't until years later that I realized how foolish I'd been.* ♦ *He hasn't been back to his country for years.*
5 *British* the level that a student is at in school: *She's in the same year as me.* ♦ *We did this subject in year 10.* ♦ *a first/second/third year* (=a student who is in the first, second etc level)

  PHRASE **five/ten etc years old** the number of years that someone has lived or that something has existed: *Their son is six years old.*

yearbook /ˈjɪəˌbʊk/ noun [C] a book containing information about what happened in a particular institution or organization during a particular year

yearly /ˈjɪəli/ adj, adv happening every year, or once every year=ANNUAL

yearn /jɜːn/ verb [I] *literary* to want something very much —**yearning** noun [C/U]

yeast /jiːst/ noun [U] a white substance that is used in making bread and beer

yell /jel/ verb [I/T] to shout loudly —**yell** noun [C]

yellow¹ /ˈjeləʊ/ adj ★★★ something that is yellow is the same colour as the sun or the middle of an egg: *yellow flowers*

yellow² /ˈjeləʊ/ noun [C/U] the colour of the sun or the middle of an egg

yellow ˈcard noun [C] in football, a small yellow card used for warning a player that they have done something wrong → RED CARD

yellowish /ˈjeləʊɪʃ/ adj similar to yellow

Yellow ˈPages *trademark* a large book that contains the telephone numbers and addresses of businesses and organizations in a particular area

yelp /jelp/ verb [I/T] to make a short loud high noise, because you are excited, angry, or in pain —**yelp** noun [C]

yep /jep/ adv *informal* YES

yes¹ /jes/ adv ★★★
1 used for saying that something is true or correct, for giving permission, or for agreeing to do something: *'Is that your car?' 'Yes, it is.'* ♦ *'Can I borrow your pen for a minute?' 'Yes, of course.'* ♦ *'Can you get it for me by this afternoon?' 'Yes, I can.'* ♦ *'Would you like me to open a window?' 'Yes, please.'*
2 used for answering someone who calls you in order to show that you have heard them: *'Erica!' 'Yes?'*
3 used for correcting someone when they make a wrong negative statement: *'She won't go.' 'Yes, she will. She just told me she would.'*
PHRASE **yes and no** *spoken* used for saying that something is only partly true: *'Were you angry?' 'Well, yes and no.'*

yes² /jes/ noun [C] an answer or a vote that expresses agreement or gives permission

yesterday¹ /ˈjestədeɪ/ adv ★★★ on the day before today: *Yesterday, we went to the zoo.* ♦ *I saw her yesterday afternoon.*

yesterday² /ˈjestədeɪ/ noun [C/U] **1** the day before today **2** *formal* a time in the past

yet /jet/ adv, conjunction ★★★
1 not before a particular time used for talking or asking about something that has not happened at a particular time, but will probably happen in the future: *She hasn't decided yet if she wants to come.* ♦ *'Are you feeling hungry?' 'Not yet.'*
2 not now, but later used for saying that something cannot or should not be done now, but will be done at a time in the future: *I can't leave the hospital yet – the doctor says maybe tomorrow.*
3 possibly now or in the future used for saying that something could still happen in the future: *The team may yet make it to the finals.*
4 ever used for saying that someone or something is the best, worst, biggest etc of their kind up to now: *This will be the Prime Minister's most important speech yet.*
5 despite sth used for introducing a statement that is surprising after what has just been mentioned: *The new computer is much more powerful; yet it costs the same.*
6 used for emphasizing a greater amount, degree, or number of times used for emphasizing that someone or something is even bigger, better, worse, more etc: *We woke to yet another grey rainy day.* ♦ *Seth*

knew that he had failed yet again.
PHRASE **as yet** *formal* used for talking about something that has not happened or been done up to now: *Police stated that there have been no arrests made as yet.*

Both **already** and **yet** are used for talking about something that happened before a particular time or before now.
■ Use **already** in positive sentences or in questions when you think it is likely that something has happened, or when you know it has happened and are surprised: *Thanks, but I've already eaten.* ♦ *Have I already given you my email address?* ♦ *Is John married already? He hardly looks old enough.*
■ Use **yet** in negative sentences and in questions, especially when you think that something should happen soon: *Kim hasn't seen the film yet, so don't tell her how it ends.* ♦ *Have you told her yet that you're leaving?*
■ Use **still** for talking about things that continue happening without changing: *Are you still working in town?* ♦ *I still love him.*
■ You can also use **still** for expressing surprise that a situation has not changed: *Why are you still here?*

yew /juː/ noun [C] a tree with dark green leaves

yield¹ /jiːld/ verb

1 produce something	**4** move or bend
2 agree to do sth	**5** let vehicle go in front
3 give sth to sb	

1 [T] to produce something: *We're hoping the farm will yield a big harvest in the autumn.* ♦ *The search for truth is beginning to yield results.* **2** [I] to finally agree to do what someone wants you to do: *The sport should not yield to every demand from the television companies.* **3** [T] to give something to someone else: *After the war, Mexico yielded a large amount of its territory to the United States.* **4** [I] *formal* if something yields when you push or pull it, it moves or bends **5** [I] *American* to allow another vehicle to go before you when you are driving

yield² /jiːld/ noun [C] the amount of something that is produced

YMCA, the /ˌwaɪ em siː ˈeɪ/ the Young Men's Christian Association: an organization that provides places for people to exercise, take courses, and sometimes rent a room for the night while travelling

yo /jəʊ/ interjection *American informal* used for getting someone's attention or for greeting someone

yob /jɒb/ noun [C] *British informal* someone who is rude, noisy, and sometimes violent =LOUT

yoga /ˈjəʊgə/ noun [U] an activity that involves exercises that are intended to make you stronger and more relaxed

yoghurt or **yogurt** /ˈjɒgət/ noun [C/U] a food made from milk that has become thick and slightly SOUR

yoke /jəʊk/ noun [C] a wooden object used for connecting animals that are pulling a vehicle
PHRASE **the yoke of sth** *formal* a situation or

Y

experience that limits your freedom

yolk /jəʊk/ noun [C/U] the yellow part of an egg

you /weak jə, weak jʊ, strong juː/ pronoun ★★★
1 used for referring to the person or people that you are talking or writing to: *Do you like oranges? ♦ I can't really trust you, can I? ♦ I'll give it to you if you want it.*
2 used for referring to people in general: *When you're with him, he makes you feel very important. ♦ You don't have to be a great cook to make pasta.*

you'd /juːd/ short form **1** the usual way of saying or writing 'you had' when 'had' is an AUXILIARY VERB. This is not often used in formal writing: *You look very tired – you'd better take a break.* **2** the usual way of saying or writing 'you would'. This is not often used in formal writing: *The doctor can see you at 3pm if you'd like to come then.*

you'll /juːl/ short form the usual way of saying or writing 'you will'. This is not often used in formal writing: *You'll get cold if you don't wear a coat.*

young¹ /jʌŋ/ adj ★★★
1 someone who is young has lived for only a short time: *a young man/woman ♦ They told him he was too young to understand. ♦ She has two **young children**.*
2 something that is young has existed for only a short time: *It's still quite a young organization.*
3 suitable for young people: *That dress is a little young for you.*
4 the young children and young adults in general
  PHRASE **young at heart** behaving or thinking in a way that is considered typical of a young person, although you are old

young² /jʌŋ/ noun [plural] a group of young animals that belong to the same family

younger /ˈjʌŋɡə/ adj not as old as you are, or not as old as someone else who you are discussing: *My younger sister, Karen, is moving to Japan.*

youngster /ˈjʌŋstə/ noun [C] a child, or a young person

your /weak jə, strong jɔː/ determiner ★★★
1 used for showing that something belongs to or is connected with the person or people who you are talking to or writing to: *You never really talk to your parents, do you? ♦ What's your address?*
2 used for showing that something belongs to or is connected with people in general: *You never forget your first kiss.*

you're /jɔː/ short form the usual way of saying or writing 'you are'. This is not often used in formal writing: *You're looking well, Peter.*

yours /jɔːz/ pronoun ★★★ used for referring to something that belongs to or is connected with the person or people who you are talking or writing to: *My pen isn't working – can I borrow yours? ♦ A friend of yours called while you were out.*
  PHRASE **Yours** or **Yours faithfully/sincerely** used at the end of a formal letter before your name

yourself /jəˈself/ (plural **yourselves** /jəˈselvz/) pronoun ★★★
1 the REFLEXIVE form of 'you', used for

showing that the person or people who you are talking to or writing to are affected by something that they do: *Did you hurt yourself? ♦ Go and get yourselves something to eat.*
2 used with 'you' for emphasizing that you mean the person or people who you are talking to or writing to, and no one else: *Think about how you yourself would like to be treated in a similar situation.*
3 *formal* used instead of 'you' in order to be formal or polite. Many people think that this use is incorrect: *Someone like yourself would be a suitable buyer for the property.*
  PHRASES **(all) by yourself 1** without help from anyone else: *Did you paint the room all by yourself?* **2** alone: *I'm sure you like to be by yourself sometimes.*
  (all) to yourself not shared with anyone else: *You have the house to yourself until five o'clock.*
  be/feel/look yourself to be, or appear to be, in your normal mental or physical state: *Take a rest – you're not quite yourself today.*

youth /juːθ/ noun ★★
1 [U] the time in your life when you are young: *In his youth, he travelled around the world. ♦ the energy of youth*
2 [C] a male teenager: *a gang of youths*
3 [U] young people in general: *the youth of the nation ♦ youth culture*

youth ˌclub noun [C] *British* a place where young people can go to meet and take part in activities

youthful /ˈjuːθf(ə)l/ adj **1** typical of young people **2** looking or behaving like a young person, although you are no longer young

youth ˌhostel noun [C] a cheap place where travellers can stay for a short period of time

you've /juːv/ short form the usual way of saying or writing 'you have' when 'have' is an AUXILIARY VERB. This is not often used in formal writing: *You've got a letter.*

yo-yo noun [C] a toy that consists of a round plastic or wooden object on the end of a string. You make it rise and fall by tying the string to your finger and moving your hand up and down.

yr abbrev year

yuck /jʌk/ interjection *informal* used for saying that you think that someone or something is dirty, ugly, or unpleasant

yucky /ˈjʌki/ adj *informal* dirty, ugly, or unpleasant

yum /jʌm/ interjection *informal* used for saying that you like the taste or smell of something

yummy /ˈjʌmi/ adj *informal* food that is yummy tastes good

yuppie /ˈjʌpi/ noun [C] *showing disapproval* someone who is young, earns a lot of money, and lives in a city in a style that is too expensive for most people

YWCA, the /ˌwaɪ dʌb(ə)ljuː siː ˈeɪ/ the Young Women's Christian Association: an organization that helps women by providing them with a place to live, giving them information etc

Y

Zz

z or **Z** /zed, *American* ziː/ noun [C/U] the 26th and last letter of the English alphabet

zany /'zeɪni/ adj *informal* strange or unusual in a funny way

zap /zæp/ verb *informal* **1** [T] to hit, harm, or destroy someone or something **2** [I/T] to quickly change the programme that you are watching on television using a REMOTE CONTROL

zeal /ziːl/ noun [U] great energy, effort, and enthusiasm

zealous /'zeləs/ adj full of energy, effort, and enthusiasm —**zealously** adv

zebra /'zebrə/ noun [C] an African animal that is similar to a horse but has black and white STRIPES on its body —*picture* → C12

zebra crossing noun [C] *British* a set of black and white lines across a road that shows where vehicles must stop when people want to cross the road

zenith /'zenɪθ/ noun [C] *literary* the time when someone or something is most successful or effective

zero¹ /'zɪərəʊ/ (plural **zeroes**) noun ★
1 [C/U] the number 0: *Add a zero to 3 and you get 30.*
2 [U] the temperature on the Celsius SCALE at which water freezes: *The temperature was 40 degrees below zero.*

zero² /'zɪərəʊ/ PHRASAL VERB **zero in on sb/sth 1** to start to give all your attention to someone or something **2** to aim at someone or something

zest /zest/ noun [U] **1** a feeling of great enthusiasm or interest **2** the skin of an orange or lemon when it is used in cooking

zigzag¹ /'zɪgzæg/ noun [C] a line or movement that makes very sharp angles, because it suddenly changes from one direction to another

zigzag² /'zɪgzæg/ verb [I] to move forwards in a line that makes very sharp angles, by suddenly changing from one direction to another

zilch /zɪltʃ/ noun [U] *informal* nothing

zillion /'zɪljən/ number *informal* a very large number

zinc /zɪŋk/ noun [U] a chemical element that is a blue-white metal

zip¹ /zɪp/ noun [C] *British* a long narrow metal or plastic object with two rows of **teeth**. It is used for opening or closing something such as a piece of clothing.

zip² /zɪp/ verb **1** [T] to close or fasten something with a zip ≠ UNZIP **2** [I] *informal* to move very quickly **3** [T] *computing* to make a computer document fill less space ≠ UNZIP

zip code noun [C] *American* a POSTCODE

zip drive noun [C] *computing* part of a computer, or a small machine that you connect to your computer, used for copying large documents onto a special DISK

zipper /'zɪpə/ noun [C] *American* a ZIP

zit /zɪt/ noun [C] *informal* a small raised infected mark on your face =PIMPLE, SPOT

zodiac, the /'zəʊdiæk/ noun [singular] 12 groups of stars that some people believe affect your character according to the positions that they are in when you are born

zombie /'zɒmbi/ noun [C] **1** *informal* someone who does not seem to know or care about what is happening around them and moves very slowly **2** a dead person who is believed to behave as though they are alive as a result of magic

zone /zəʊn/ noun [C] ★ an area where a particular thing happens: *an earthquake zone* ♦ *a traffic-free zone*

zoo /zuː/ noun [C] a place where many types of wild animals are kept so that people can see them

zoo-keeper /'zuːkiːpə/ noun [C] someone whose job is to look after the animals in a zoo

zoologist /zuˈɒlədʒɪst/ noun [C] a scientist who studies animals

zoology /zuˈɒlədʒi/ noun [U] the scientific study of animals

zoom /zuːm/ verb [I] **1** to move with a lot of speed and energy **2** if a camera zooms in or out, it makes something seem much closer or further away: *The camera zoomed in on a cat stuck in the tree.*

zoom lens noun [C] a piece of equipment that you fix to a camera so that you can take photographs of things that are very close or very far away

zzz a way of writing the sound that someone makes when they are sleeping

Z

GEOGRAPHICAL NAMES AND NATIONALITIES

The following lists show you the names and pronunciations of countries and the adjectives that are related to them. Most adjectives can be used as nouns to describe a person from a particular country (e.g. a **Belgian** is a person from **Belgium**). Where the adjective cannot be used as a noun, it is followed by an asterisk (*) and the correct term is given in the Nationalities table at the end.

Countries

NOTE: Inclusion in the following list does not imply status as a sovereign state.

Name	Adjective
Afghanistan /æfˈɡænɪstɑːn/	Afghan /ˈæfɡæn/
Albania /ælˈbeɪniə/	Albanian /ælˈbeɪniən/
Algeria /ælˈdʒɪəriə/	Algerian /ælˈdʒɪəriən/
Andorra /ænˈdɔːrə/	Andorran /ænˈdɔːrən/
Angola /æŋˈɡəʊlə/	Angolan /æŋˈɡəʊlən/
Antigua and Barbuda /ænˌtiːɡə ən bɑːˈbjuːdə/	Antiguan /ænˈtiːɡən/
Argentina /ˌɑːdʒənˈtiːnə/	Argentine* /ˈɑːdʒəntaɪn/
Armenia /ɑːˈmiːniə/	Armenian /ɑːˈmiːniən/
Australia /ɒˈstreɪliə/	Australian /ɒˈstreɪliən/
Austria /ˈɒstriə/	Austrian /ˈɒstriən/
Azerbaijan /ˌæzəbaɪˈdʒɑːn/	Azerbaijani* /ˌæzəbaɪˈdʒɑːni/
Bahamas, the /bəˈhɑːməz/	Bahamian /bəˈheɪmiən/
Bahrain /bɑːˈreɪn/	Bahraini /bɑːˈreɪni/
Bangladesh /ˌbæŋɡləˈdeʃ/	Bangladeshi /ˌbæŋɡləˈdeʃi/
Barbados /bɑːˈbeɪdɒs/	Barbadian /bɑːˈbeɪdiən/
Belarus /ˌbeləʊˈruːs/	Belorussian /ˌbeləʊˈrʌʃ(ə)n/
Belgium /ˈbeldʒəm/	Belgian /ˈbeldʒ(ə)n/
Belize /bəˈliːz/	Belizian /bəˈliːziən/
Benin /beˈniːn/	Beninese /ˌbenɪˈniːz/
Bermuda /bəˈmjuːdə/	Bermudan /bəˈmjuːdən/
Bhutan /buːˈtɑːn/	Bhutanese /ˌbuːtəˈniːz/
Bolivia /bəˈlɪviə/	Bolivian /bəˈlɪviən/
Bosnia-Herzegovina /ˈbɒzniə ˌhɜːtsəˈɡɒvɪnə/	Bosnian /ˈbɒzniən/
Botswana /bɒtˈswɑːnə/	Botswanan /bɒtˈswɑːnən/
Brazil /brəˈzɪl/	Brazilian /brəˈzɪliən/
Brunei /ˈbruːnaɪ/	Bruneian /bruːˈnaɪən/
Bulgaria /bʌlˈɡeəriə/	Bulgarian /bʌlˈɡeəriən/
Burkina Faso /bɜːˌkiːnə ˈfæsəʊ/	Burkinan /bɜːˈkiːnən/
Burundi /bʊˈrʊndi/	Burundian /bʊˈrʊndiən/
Cambodia /kæmˈbəʊdiə/	Cambodian /kæmˈbəʊdiən/
Cameroon /ˌkæməˈruːn/	Cameroonian /ˌkæməˈruːniən/
Canada /ˈkænədə/	Canadian /kəˈneɪdiən/
Cape Verde /ˌkeɪp ˈvɜːd/	Cape Verdean /ˌkeɪp ˈvɜːdiən/
Caribbean /ˌkærəˈbiːən/	Caribbean /ˌkærəˈbiːən/
Cayman Islands, the /ˈkeɪmən ˌaɪləndz/	Cayman Island* /ˈkeɪmən ˌaɪlənd/
Central African Republic, the /ˌsentr(ə)l ˌæfrɪkən rɪˈpʌblɪk/	Central African /ˌsentr(ə)l ˈæfrɪkən/
Chad /tʃæd/	Chadian /ˈtʃædiən/
Chile /ˈtʃɪli/	Chilean /ˈtʃɪliən/
China /ˈtʃaɪnə/	Chinese /ˌtʃaɪˈniːz/
Colombia /kəˈlʌmbiə/	Colombian /kəˈlʌmbiən/
Comoros /ˈkɒmərəʊz/	Comoran /kəˈmɔːrən/
Democratic Republic of the Congo, the /ˌdeməkrætɪk rɪˌpʌblɪk əv ðə ˈkɒŋɡəʊ/	Congolese /ˌkɒŋɡəˈliːz/
Republic of Congo, the /rɪˌpʌblɪk əv ˈkɒŋɡəʊ/	Congolese /ˌkɒŋɡəˈliːz/
Costa Rica /ˌkɒstə ˈriːkə/	Costa Rican /ˌkɒstə ˈriːkən/
Côte d'Ivoire /ˌkəʊt diːˈvwɑː/	Ivorian /aɪˈvɔːriən/
Croatia /krəʊˈeɪʃə/	Croatian* /krəʊˈeɪʃ(ə)n/
Cuba /ˈkjuːbə/	Cuban /ˈkjuːbən/
Cyprus /ˈsaɪprəs/	Cypriot /ˈsɪpriət/
Czech Republic, the /ˌtʃek rɪˈpʌblɪk/	Czech /tʃek/
Denmark /ˈdenmɑːk/	Danish* /ˈdeɪnɪʃ/
Djibouti /dʒɪˈbuːti/	Djiboutian /dʒɪˈbuːtiən/
Dominica /ˌdɒmɪˈniːkə/	Dominican /ˌdɒmɪˈniːkən/

Dominican Republic, the /dəˌmɪnɪkən rɪˈpʌblɪk/

Dominican /dəˈmɪnɪkən/

East Timor /ˌiːst ˈtiːmɔː/

East Timorese /ˌiːst ˌtiːmɔːˈriːz/

Ecuador /ˈekwədɔː/

Ecuadorian /ˌekwəˈdɔːriən/

Egypt /ˈiːdʒɪpt/

Egyptian /ɪˈdʒɪpʃ(ə)n/

El Salvador /el ˈsælvədɔː/

Salvadorian /ˌsælvəˈdɔːriən/

England /ˈɪŋglənd/

English* /ˈɪŋglɪʃ/

Equatorial Guinea /ˌekwətɔːriəl ˈgɪni/

Equatorial Guinean /ˌekwətɔːriəl ˈgɪniən/

Eritrea /ˌerɪˈtreɪə/

Eritrean /ˌerɪˈtreɪən/

Estonia /eˈstəuniə/

Estonian /eˈstəuniən/

Ethiopia /ˌiːθiˈəupiə/

Ethiopian /ˌiːθiˈəupiən/

Fiji /ˈfiːdʒiː/

Fijian /fiːˈdʒiːən/

Finland /ˈfɪnlənd/

Finnish* /ˈfɪnɪʃ/

France /frɑːns/

French* /frentʃ/

Gabon /ˈgæbɒn/

Gabonese /ˌgæbəˈniːz/

Gambia, the /ˈgæmbiə/

Gambian /ˈgæmbiən/

Georgia /ˈdʒɔːdʒə/

Georgian /ˈdʒɔːdʒən/

Germany /ˈdʒɜːməni/

German /ˈdʒɜːmən/

Ghana /ˈgɑːnə/

Ghanaian /gɑːˈneɪən/

Gibraltar /dʒɪˈbrɔːltə/

Gibraltarian /ˌdʒɪbrɔːlˈteəriən/

Great Britain /ˌgreɪt ˈbrɪt(ə)n/

British* /ˈbrɪtɪʃ/

Greece /griːs/

Greek /griːk/

Greenland /ˈgriːnlənd/

Greenlandic* /ˌgriːnˈlændɪk/

Grenada /grəˈneɪdə/

Grenadian /grəˈneɪdiən/

Guatemala /ˌgwɑːtəˈmɑːlə/

Guatemalan /ˌgwɑːtəˈmɑːlən/

Guinea /ˈgɪni/

Guinean /ˈgɪniən/

Guinea-Bissau /ˌgɪni bɪˈsau/

Guinea-Bissauan /ˌgɪni bɪˈsauən/

Guyana /gaɪˈænə/

Guyanese /ˌgaɪəˈniːz/

Haiti /ˈheɪti/

Haitian /ˈheɪʃ(ə)n/

Honduras /hɒnˈdjuərəs/

Honduran /hɒnˈdjuərən/

Hong Kong /ˌhɒŋ ˈkɒŋ/

Hungary /ˈhʌŋgəri/

Hungarian /hʌŋˈgeəriən/

Iceland /ˈaɪslənd/

Icelandic* /aɪsˈlændɪk/

India /ˈɪndiə/

Indian /ˈɪndiən/

Indonesia /ˌɪndəˈniːʒə/

Indonesian /ˌɪndəˈniːʒ(ə)n/

Iran /ɪˈrɑːn/

Iranian /ɪˈreɪniən/

Iraq /ɪˈrɑːk/

Iraqi /ɪˈrɑːki/

Northern Ireland /ˌnɔːð(ə)n ˈaɪələnd/

Republic of Ireland, the /rɪˈpʌblɪk əv ˌaɪələnd/

Irish* /ˈaɪrɪʃ/

Israel /ˈɪzreɪl/

Israeli /ɪzˈreɪli/

Italy /ˈɪtəli/

Italian /ɪˈtæliən/

Ivory Coast, the /ˌaɪvəri ˈkəust/

Ivorian /aɪˈvɔːriən/

Jamaica /dʒəˈmeɪkə/

Jamaican /dʒəˈmeɪkən/

Japan /dʒəˈpæn/

Japanese /ˌdʒæpəˈniːz/

Jordan /ˈdʒɔːd(ə)n/

Jordanian /dʒɔːˈdeɪniən/

Kazakhstan /ˌkæzækˈstɑːn/

Kazakh /kəˈzæk/

Kenya /ˈkenjə/

Kenyan /ˈkenjən/

Kiribati /ˌkɪrəˈbæs, ˌkɪrɪˈbɑːti/

Kiribati /ˌkɪrəˈbæs, ˌkɪrɪˈbɑːti/

North Korea /ˌnɔːθ kəˈriːə/

North Korean /ˌnɔːθ kəˈriːən/

South Korea /ˌsauθ kəˈriːə/

South Korean /ˌsauθ kəˈriːən/

Kuwait /kuˈweɪt/

Kuwaiti /kuˈweɪti/

Kyrgyzstan /ˌkɜːgɪˈstɑːn/

Kyrgyz /ˈkɜːgɪz/

Laos /laus/

Laotian /ˈlauʃ(ə)n/

Latvia /ˈlætviə/

Latvian /ˈlætviən/

Lebanon /ˈlebənən/

Lebanese /ˌlebəˈniːz/

Lesotho /ləˈsuːtuː/

Sotho* /ˈsuːtuː/

Liberia /laɪˈbɪəriə/

Liberian /laɪˈbɪəriən/

Libya /ˈlɪbiə/

Libyan /ˈlɪbiən/

Liechtenstein /ˈlɪktənstaɪn/

Liechtenstein* /ˈlɪktənstaɪn/

Lithuania /ˌlɪθjuˈeɪniə/

Lithuanian /ˌlɪθjuˈeɪniən/

Luxembourg /ˈlʌksəmbɜːg/

Luxembourg* /ˈlʌksəmbɜːg/

Madagascar /ˌmædəˈgæskə/

Malagasy /ˌmæləˈgæsi/

Malawi /məˈlɑːwi/

Malawian /məˈlɑːwiən/

Malaysia /məˈleɪziə/

Malaysian /məˈleɪziən/

Maldives, the /ˈmɔːldiːvz/

Maldivian /mɔːˈdɪviən/

Mali /ˈmɑːli/

Malian /ˈmɑːliən/

Malta /ˈmɔːltə/

Maltese /ˌmɔːlˈtiːz/

Marshall Islands, the /ˈmɑːʃ(ə)l ˌaɪləndz/

Marshallese* /ˌmɑːʃəˈliːz/

Mauritania /ˌmɒrɪˈteɪnɪə/   Mauritanian /ˌmɒrɪˈteɪnɪən/
Mauritius /məˈrɪʃəs/   Mauritian /məˈrɪʃ(ə)n/
Melanesia /ˌmeləˈniːzɪə/   Melanesian /ˌmeləˈniːzɪən/
Mexico /ˈmeksɪkəʊ/   Mexican /ˈmeksɪkən/
Micronesia /ˌmaɪkrəˈniːzɪə/   Micronesian /ˌmaɪkrəˈniːzɪən/
Moldova /mɒlˈdəʊvə/   Moldovan /mɒlˈdəʊvən/
Monaco /ˈmɒnəkəʊ/   Monegasque /ˌmɒnɪˈgæsk/
Mongolia /mɒŋˈgəʊlɪə/   Mongolian /mɒŋˈgəʊlɪən/
Montserrat /ˌmɒn(t)səˈræt/   Montserratian /ˌmɒn(t)səˈreɪʃ(ə)n/
Morocco /məˈrɒkəʊ/   Moroccan /məˈrɒkən/
Mozambique /ˌməʊzæmˈbiːk/   Mozambican /ˌməʊzæmˈbiːkən/
Myanmar /ˈmiːənmɑː/   Burmese /bɜːˈmiːz/
Namibia /nəˈmɪbɪə/   Namibian /nəˈmɪbɪən/
Nauru /nɑːˈuːruː/   Nauruan /nɑːˈuːruən/
Nepal /nəˈpɔːl/   Nepalese /ˌnepəˈliːz/
Netherlands, the /ˈneðələndz/   Dutch* /dʌtʃ/
New Zealand /ˌnjuːˈziːlənd/   New Zealand* /ˌnjuːˈziːlənd/
Nicaragua /ˌnɪkəˈrægjuə/   Nicaraguan /ˌnɪkəˈrægjuən/
Niger /ˈnaɪdʒə/   Nigerien /naɪˈdʒɪərɪən/
Nigeria /naɪˈdʒɪərɪə/   Nigerian /naɪˈdʒɪərɪən/
Norway /ˈnɔːweɪ/   Norwegian /nɔːˈwiːdʒ(ə)n/
Oman /əʊˈmɑːn/   Omani /əʊˈmɑːni/
Pakistan /ˌpɑːkɪˈstɑːn/   Pakistani /ˌpɑːkɪˈstɑːni/
Panama /ˈpænəmɑː/   Panamanian /ˌpænəˈmeɪnɪən/
Papua New Guinea /ˌpæpuə njuːˈgɪni/   Papua New Guinean /ˌpæpuə njuːˈgɪnɪən/
Paraguay /ˈpærəgwaɪ/   Paraguayan /ˌpærəˈgwaɪən/
Peru /pəˈruː/   Peruvian /pəˈruːvɪən/
Philippines, the /ˈfɪlɪpiːnz/   Philippine* /ˈfɪlɪpiːn/
Poland /ˈpəʊlənd/   Polish* /ˈpəʊlɪʃ/
Polynesia /ˌpɒlɪˈniːzɪə/   Polynesian /ˌpɒlɪˈniːzɪən/
Portugal /ˈpɔːtʃəg(ə)l/   Portuguese /ˌpɔːtʃəˈgiːz/
Puerto Rico /ˌpwɜːtəʊˈriːkəʊ/   Puerto Rican /ˌpwɜːtəʊˈriːkən/
Qatar /ˈkætɑː/   Qatari /kæˈtɑːri/
Romania /rʊˈmeɪnɪə/   Romanian /rʊˈmeɪnɪən/
Russia /ˈrʌʃə/   Russian /ˈrʌʃ(ə)n/
Russian Federation, the /ˌrʌʃ(ə)n fedəˈreɪʃ(ə)n/
Rwanda /ruˈændə/   Rwandese /ruˈændiːz/
Saint Kitts and Nevis /sənt ˌkɪts ən ˈniːvɪs/   Kittitian /kɪˈtɪʃ(ə)n/
   Nevisian /nəˈviːʃ(ə)n/
Saint Lucia /sənt ˈluːʃə/   Saint Lucian /sənt ˈluːʃ(ə)n/
Saint Vincent and the Grenadines /sənt ˌvɪns(ə)nt ən ðə ˌgrenəˈdiːnz/   Vincentian /vɪnˈsenʃ(ə)n/
Samoa /səˈməʊə/   Samoan /səˈməʊən/
San Marino /ˌsæn məˈriːnəʊ/   Sanmarinese /ˌsænmærɪˈniːz/
São Tomé and Príncipe /saʊ təˌmeɪ ən ˈprɪnsɪpeɪ/   Sao Tomean /saʊ təˈmeɪən/
Saudi Arabia /ˌsaʊdi əˈreɪbɪə/   Saudi Arabian /ˌsaʊdi əˈreɪbɪən/
   Saudi /ˈsaʊdi/
Scandinavia /ˌskændɪˈneɪvɪə/   Scandinavian /ˌskændɪˈneɪvɪən/
Scotland /ˈskɒtlənd/   Scottish* /ˈskɒtɪʃ/
Senegal /ˌsenɪˈgɔːl/   Senegalese /ˌsenɪgəˈliːz/
Seychelles, the /seɪˈʃelz/   Seychellois /seɪʃelˈwɑː/
Sierra Leone /siˌerə liˈəʊn/   Sierra Leonean /siˌerə liˈəʊnɪən/
Singapore /ˌsɪŋəˈpɔː/   Singaporean /ˌsɪŋəˈpɔːrɪən/
Slovakia /sləˈvækɪə/   Slovak /ˈsləʊvæk/
   Slovakian /sləʊˈvækɪən/
Slovenia /sləˈviːnɪə/   Slovene /ˈsləʊviːn/
   Slovenian /sləʊˈviːnɪən/
Solomon Islands, the /ˈsɒləmən ˌaɪləndz/   Solomon Island* /ˈsɒləmən ˈaɪlənd/
Somalia /səˈmɑːlɪə/   Somali /səˈmɑːli/
South Africa /ˌsaʊθ ˈæfrɪkə/   South African /ˌsaʊθ ˈæfrɪkən/
Spain /speɪn/   Spanish* /ˈspænɪʃ/
Sri Lanka /srɪ ˈlæŋkə/   Sri Lankan /srɪ ˈlæŋkən/
Sudan /suːˈdɑːn/   Sudanese /ˌsuːdəˈniːz/
Suriname /ˈsʊərɪnæm/   Surinamese /ˌsʊərɪnæˈmiːz/
Swaziland /ˈswɑːzilænd/   Swazi /ˈswɑːzi/
Sweden /ˈswiːd(ə)n/   Swedish* /ˈswiːdɪʃ/
Switzerland /ˈswɪtsələnd/   Swiss /swɪs/

Syria /'sɪriə/ | Syrian /'sɪriən/
Taiwan /ˌtaɪˈwɑːn/ | Taiwanese /ˌtaɪwəˈniːz/
Tajikistan /tɑːˌdʒiːkɪˈstɑːn/ | Tajik /tɑːˈdʒiːk/
Tanzania /ˌtænzəˈniːə/ | Tanzanian /ˌtænzəˈniːən/
Thailand /'taɪlænd/ | Thai /taɪ/
Tibet /tɪˈbet/ | Tibetan /tɪˈbet(ə)n/
Togo /'təʊgəʊ/ | Togolese /ˌtəʊgəˈliːz/
Tonga /'tɒŋə/ | Tongan /'tɒŋən/
Trinidad and Tobago /ˌtrɪnɪdæd ən təˈbeɪgəʊ/ | Trinidadian /ˌtrɪnɪˈdædiən/
| Tobagan /təˈbeɪgən/
Tunisia /tjuːˈnɪziə/ | Tunisian /tjuːˈnɪziən/
Turkey /'tɜːki/ | Turkish* /'tɜːkɪʃ/
Turkmenistan /tɜːˌkmenɪˈstɑːn/ | Turkmen /'tɜːkmen/
Tuvalu /tuˈvɑːluː/ | Tuvaluan /tuˈvɑːluːən/
Uganda /juːˈgændə/ | Ugandan /juːˈgændən/
Ukraine /juːˈkreɪn/ | Ukrainian /juːˈkreɪniən/
United Arab Emirates, the /juːˌnaɪtɪd ˌærəb ˈemɪrəts/ | Emirati /emɪˈrɑːti/
United Kingdom, the /juːˌnaɪtɪd ˈkɪŋdəm/ | British* /'brɪtɪʃ/
United States of America, the /juːˌnaɪtɪd ˌsteɪts əv əˈmerɪkə/ | American /əˈmerɪkən/
Uruguay /'jʊərəgwaɪ/ | Uruguayan /ˌjʊərəˈgwaɪən/
Uzbekistan /ʊzˌbekɪˈstɑːn/ | Uzbek /'ʊzbek/
Vanuatu /ˌvænuˈɑːtuː/ | Vanuatuan /ˌvænuɑːˈtuːən/
Vatican City /ˌvætɪkən ˈsɪti/ | Vatican /'vætɪkən/
Venezuela /ˌvenɪˈzweɪlə/ | Venezuelan /ˌvenɪˈzweɪlən/
Vietnam /ˌviːetˈnæm/ | Vietnamese /ˌviːetnəˈmiːz/
Wales /weɪlz/ | Welsh* /welʃ/
Western Sahara /ˌwestən səˈhɑːrə/ | Sahrawian /sɑːˈrɑːwiən/
Yemen /'jemən/ | Yemeni /'jeməni/
Yugoslavia /ˌjuːgəʊˈslɑːviə/ | Yugoslav /'juːgəʊslɑːv/
| Yugoslavian /ˌjuːgəʊˈslɑːviən/
Zambia /'zæmbiə/ | Zambian /'zæmbiən/
Zimbabwe /zɪmˈbɑːbweɪ/ | Zimbabwean /zɪmˈbɑːbwiən/

Nationalities

Country	Person
Argentina /ˌɑːdʒənˈtiːnə/	Argentinian /ˌɑːdʒənˈtɪniən/
Azerbaijan /ˌæzəbaɪˈdʒɑːn/	Azeri /æˈzeəri/
	Azerbaijani /ˌæzəbaɪˈdʒɑːni/
Cayman Islands, the /'keɪmən ˌaɪləndz/	Cayman Islander /ˌkeɪmən ˈaɪləndə/
Croatia /krəʊˈeɪʃə/	Croat /'krəʊæt/
Denmark /'denmɑːk/	Dane /deɪn/
England /'ɪŋglənd/	Englishman /'ɪŋglɪʃmən/
Finland /'fɪnlənd/	Finn /fɪn/
France /frɑːns/	Frenchman /'frentʃmən/
Great Britain /ˌgreɪt ˈbrɪt(ə)n/	Briton (mainly journalism) /'brɪt(ə)n/
Greenland /'griːnlənd/	Greenlander /'griːnləndə/
Iceland /'aɪslənd/	Icelander /'aɪsləndə/
Republic of Ireland, the /rɪˈpʌblɪk əv ˌaɪələnd/	Irishman /'aɪrɪʃmən/
Lesotho /ləˈsuːtuː/	Mosotho /məˈsuːtuː/
	plural Basotho /bəˈsuːtuː/
Liechtenstein /'lɪktənstaɪn/	Liechtensteiner /'lɪktənstaɪnə/
Luxembourg /'lʌksəmbɜːg/	Luxembourger /'lʌksəmbɜːgə/
Marshall Islands, the /'mɑːʃ(ə)l ˌaɪləndz/	Marshall Islander /ˌmɑːʃ(ə)l ˈaɪləndə/
Netherlands, the /'neðələndz/	Dutchman /'dʌtʃmən/
New Zealand /ˌnjuː ˈziːlənd/	New Zealander /ˌnjuː ˈziːləndə/
Philippines, the /'fɪlɪpiːnz/	Filipino /ˌfɪlɪˈpiːnəʊ/
Poland /'pəʊlənd/	Pole /pəʊl/
Scotland /'skɒtlənd/	Scot /skɒt/
Solomon Islands, the /'sɒləmən ˌaɪləndz/	Solomon Islander /ˌsɒləmən ˈaɪləndə/
Spain /speɪn/	Spaniard /'spænjəd/
Suriname /ˌsʊəriˈnæm/	Surinamer /ˌsʊəriˈnɑːmə/
Sweden /'swiːd(ə)n/	Swede /swiːd/
Turkey /'tɜːki/	Turk /tɜːk/
United Kingdom, the /juːˌnaɪtɪd ˈkɪŋdəm/	Briton (mainly journalism) /'brɪt(ə)n/
Wales /weɪlz/	Welshman /'welʃmən/

CAPITAL LETTERS AND PUNCTUATION

Capital letters

Capital letters (or upper case letters) are used:

- to begin a sentence
  You've done a fantastic job.

- for the names of people
  Jim, Helen, Andrew Walker

- for calling people by their title
  Mrs Jones, Uncle Peter, Mum

- for the personal pronoun 'I'
  Can I help?

- for the titles of films, books etc
  Notting Hill is a funny film.

  NOTE: Small words like *and, a, the*, and prepositions do not usually have capitals, unless they are the first word of the title: *The film was based on* The End of the Affair *by Graham Greene.*

- for names of organizations
  Friends of the Earth, the European Union

- for the names of places (towns, countries etc)
  Paris, Hungary

- for nationalities and languages
  English, African

- for days, months etc
  Wednesday, March, New Year's Day

Some words can be written with capitals or in lower case, depending on the meaning:

- jobs
  Sanderson was a good president. (general use)
  Paul met President Brunswick. (job title)

- compass points
  I live in the north of Scotland. (description)
  Sally works in the Far East. (place name)

Full stop (.)

Full stops are used:

- at the end of a sentence
  His sister's name is Kate.

- in abbreviations to show that letters at the end of a word are missing
  Sat. (Saturday), *pl.* (plural), *approx.* (approximately)

NOTE: In modern British English, full stops are not usually added when the abbreviation contains the last letter of the full word:
- *Mr, Dr* Mister, Doctor (used in titles)
- *Rd, Ave* Road, Avenue (used in addresses)
In American English, however, full stops are used in the above examples.

Comma (,)

Commas are used:

- in writing to represent a brief pause in a long sentence
  Everyone agrees that Anna is a very intelligent girl, but she is rather lazy.

- in lists of two or more items
  I bought some bananas, some oranges, and some potatoes.

  NOTE: This is the style used in this dictionary, but the final comma (before 'and') can be left out.

- in lists of adjectives that appear before a noun
  a large, green, wooden table

  NOTE: In the above example, commas can be left out. Commas are not used to separate adjectives in this dictionary.

- after linking words at the beginning of a sentence
  First of all, this can be dangerous.

- before and after linking words in the middle of a sentence
  Ann, on the other hand, did not agree.

- when giving additional information that can be left out
  Tony, who is usually late, turned up at 10.30.

- to introduce direct speech
  Jim said, 'I'll be late.'

  NOTE: Commas are not used after reporting verbs in reported speech:
  Jim said he would be late.

- before question tags
  You're from India, aren't you?

- in large numbers to separate digits

6,550   17,500   387,100   2,000,000

NOTE: In some languages a full point (.) is used here. In English, a full point represents a decimal point (e.g. 3.5 million = 'three and a half million' or 'three point five million').

Semicolon (;)

Semicolons are used:

- to join together two sentences with related meanings
We need better technology; better technology costs money.

- to separate long items in a list
Students are asked not to leave bicycles by the entrance; not to leave bags in the sitting room; and not to leave coats in the dining room.

Colon (:)

Colons are used:

- to introduce items in a list
You will need to provide one of the following pieces of identification: a passport, a student's card, or a driving licence.

- to introduce an explanation of the previous part of the sentence
Finally, we had to stop: we were tired and it was dark.

Quotation marks (' ')

Quotation marks (also called *speech marks* or *inverted commas*) can be single (' ') or double (" "). In modern British English, single quotation marks are used.

Quotation marks are used:

- around direct speech
'Why are we leaving so early?' Helen asked.

- around words you want to emphasize or treat in a special way:
What does 'plethora' mean?

Question mark (?)

Question marks are used:

- after a question
What's the time?

Exclamation mark (!)

Exclamation marks are used:

- to show a strong emotion such as surprise or anger

You'll never guess what! I've just got engaged!

NOTE: Exclamation marks are used in informal writing, but are not considered appropriate in formal writing.

Apostrophe (')

Apostrophes are used:

- with 's' to show who or what someone or something belongs to or is connected with
Mike is having dinner with Nicky's sister.

Did you go to yesterday's meeting?

NOTE: -'s is used when referring to a single person or thing, -s' is used when referring to more than one person or thing:

The boy's father (=the father of one boy) *demanded an explanation.*

The boys' father (=the father of more than one boy) *demanded an explanation.*

- in contractions (short forms) to show that some letters are missing
The talk wasn't (=was not) *any good.*

I'm (=I am) *only here for a week.*

That can't (cannot) *be right.*

NOTE: Do not confuse **its** (=belonging to or connected with 'it') and **it's** (=it is).

*The dog was chasing **its** tail.*

***It's** too late to do anything now.*

PHRASAL VERBS

What is a phrasal verb?

A phrasal verb is a verb with two parts: a verb (such as *go, put,* or *set*), and a 'particle' (an adverb or preposition, such as *away, out,* or *on*). The meanings of phrasal verbs are often very different from the meaning of the verb that they are based on: for example, *hold up* can mean 'to cause a delay' or 'to try to rob someone', and these meanings have no obvious connection with the idea of holding something in your hands.

How do I find phrasal verbs in the *Macmillan Essential Dictionary*?

Phrasal verbs appear at the end of the entry for the verb that they are formed from. A box saying PHRASAL VERBS makes them easy to find. Look in your dictionary at the entry for the verb *count*. You will see that *count* has five main meanings, and these are followed by some phrases that include the word *count*. After the phrases, you will see the PHRASAL VERBS box, and this is followed by several phrasal verbs, such as **count against sb** and **count on sth**.

How do phrasal verbs combine with other words?

There are several types of phrasal verb. The main ones are:

- intransitive phrasal verbs (with no object): *What time can we check in?*

  These are shown like this:

  ,check 'in 1 to arrive at a hotel and give your personal details to the person at the RECEPTION desk

- transitive phrasal verbs where the object can come in two positions – after the verb, or after the particle: *I think I'll put my jacket on.* OR *I think I'll put on my jacket.*

  These are shown like this:

  ,put sth 'on 1 to cover a part of your body with a piece of clothing or jewellery so that you are wearing it

,beat sb 'up *informal* to hurt someone by hitting or kicking them many times

The word **sb** (=someone) means that the object is a person, and the word **sth** (= something) means that the object is a thing.

- transitive phrasal verbs where the object must come after the particle: *The baby takes after his mother.*

  These are shown like this:

  'take ,after sb to look or behave like an older relative

- phrasal verbs that sometimes have an object and sometimes have no object: *Drink this and you'll soon warm up.* ♦ *The drink soon warmed her up.*

  These are shown like this:

  ,warm (sb/sth) 'up 1 to become warm, or to make someone or something become warm

- phrasal verbs with *two* objects – one after the verb, the other after the particle: *They put their success down to good planning.*

  These are shown like this:

  'put sth ,down to sth to think that something happened for a particular reason

How are phrasal verbs pronounced?

You will notice that all these phrasal verbs include symbols that show which part is 'stressed' (=spoken with more force). The symbols at **check 'in** show that you stress the word 'in'.

LABELS

Style and attitude labels

formal in current use but not used in ordinary conversation or in normal everyday writing: *augur, permissible, remuneration*

humorous used in an ironic and often friendly way: *under the influence* (=drunk)

impolite not taboo but will certainly offend some people

informal more common in speech than in writing and not used on a formal occasion: *bloke, comfy, yeah*

literary old but still used in some kinds of creative writing: *bountiful, forsake, spurn*

offensive extremely rude and likely to cause offence

old-fashioned no longer in current use but still used by some older people: *motor car, wireless*

showing approval used when it is not obvious from a definition that a word says something good about someone or something: *fearless, tireless*

showing disapproval used when it is not obvious from a definition that a word says something bad about someone or something: *babyish, smooth* (=relaxed and confident)

spoken used in speech rather than writing: *believe it or not, after you*

Subject labels

These labels show that a word is used as part of the language of a particular subject and is not used in normal everyday English:

business	*legal*	*science*
computing	*linguistics*	*technical*
journalism	*medical*	

Regional labels

British used in British English but not in American English

American used in American English but not in British English